France
a travel survival kit

Daniel Robinson
Leanne Logan

France – a travel survival kit

1st edition

Published by

Lonely Planet Publications

Head Office: PO Box 617, Hawthorn, Vic 3122, Australia
Branches: 155 Filbert St, Suite 251, Oakland, CA 94607, USA
10 Barley Mow Passage, Chiswick, London W4 4PH, UK
71 bis rue du Cardinal Lemoine, 75005 Paris, France

Printed by

Colorcraft Ltd, Hong Kong

Photographs by

Greg Alford (GA)   Adrienne Costanzo (AC)
Geert Cole (GC)   Greg Elms (GE)
Leanne Logan (LL)   Richard Nebesky (RN)
Bernie Robinson (BR)   Daniel Robinson (DR)
Simon Rowe (SR)   Paul Steel (PS)
Tony Wheeler (TW)
Comité Départemental de Tourisme (CDT)   Office de Tourisme (OT)
Parc Régional des Volcans d'Auvergne (Parc)

Front cover: *Mercure* by Antoine Coysevox, Jardin des Tuileries (Francisco Hidalgo), The Image Bank
Back cover: View from the lighthouse at Le Conquet, Brittany (GA)

Published

April 1994

Although the authors and publisher have tried to make the information as
accurate as possible, they accept no responsibility for any loss, injury or
inconvenience sustained by any person using this book.

National Library of Australia Cataloguing in Publication Data

Robinson, Daniel
France – a travel survival kit.

Includes index.
ISBN 0 86442 192 3.

1. France – Guidebooks.
I. Logan, Leanne, 1964- . II. Title.
(Series: Lonely Planet travel survival kit).

914.404839

Top: Musée des Beaux-Arts, Tours, Loire Valley (DR)
Middle: The village post office (GC)
Bottom: Flower stall in the 17e arrondissement, Paris (DR)

Top Left: Relaxing at the Saint Trophime cloister at Arles, Provence (LL)
Top Right: Statue bits stored next to the Louvre during restoration (DR)
Bottom Left: Pétanque balls in good hands (GC)
Bottom Right: Columns of the Maison Carrée, a Roman temple, Nîmes (LL)

Daniel Robinson

Daniel was raised in the USA (the San Francisco Bay Area and Glen Ellyn, IL) and Israel. He holds a BA from Princeton University in Near Eastern Studies (Arab and Islamic history and the Arabic language) and has travelled extensively in the Middle East and South, South-East and East Asia.

His previous work for Lonely Planet includes the Vietnam and Cambodia sections of our award-winning *Vietnam, Laos & Cambodia – a travel survival kit.* Daniel lives in Tel Aviv and is currently working on a PhD in history at Tel Aviv University.

Leanne Logan

First tasting Europe at the age of 12, Leanne has long been lured by travel. She completed a journalism degree at the Queensland University of Technology in Brisbane, before exploring her homeland as a reporter for several newspapers and Australian Associated Press.

In 1987 she set off through Asia and the Middle East to London where, as deputy editor of a travel magazine, her wanderlust was temporarily fed but never sated. Eventually she bought a one-way ticket to Africa. Leanne returned to Europe to write the Benelux chapters for *Western Europe on a shoestring.* While conducting research into Belgium's 350-odd beers, she met a local connoisseur, Geert Cole. The pair have been a team ever since, working on this guide as well as updating the second edition of *New Caledonia – a travel survival kit.*

Dedication from Daniel I would like to dedicate my share of this book to my parents, Rabbi Bernard & Yetta Robinson, whose support and encouragement – and logistical assistance – made this book (and an awful lot of other things) possible.

From the Authors

See page 1080 for the authors' acknowledgements.

From the Publisher

This book was edited by Adrienne Costanzo and Greg Alford, with help from Rob van Driesum. Diana Saad, Sharan Kaur and Kristin Odijk helped with the proofreading and Rowan McKinnon did the index. Chris Andrews wrote the language section and John Hajek checked the Breton vocabulary section.

Ann Jeffree coordinated the mapping, design, illustration and layout of the book, with assistance from Paul Clifton, Tamsin Wilson, Marcel Gaston, Chris Love, Jacqui

Schiff, Richard Stewart and other artists. Margaret Jung designed the front cover and Paul Clifton designed the back cover and selected the photographs. Thanks to our work-experience students Adam McCrow (mapping) and Alice Hurst (editing). Thanks also to Zahia Hafs and Isabelle Muller from our Paris office for all their help. For additional research, thanks to Michelle de Kretser, Adrienne Costanzo, Greg Alford and Rob van Driesum.

Warning & Request

Things change – prices go up, schedules change, good places go bad and bad places go bankrupt – nothing stays the same. So if you find things better or worse, recently opened or long since closed, please write and tell us and help make the next edition better.

Your letters will be used to help update future editions and, where possible, important changes will also be included in a Stop Press section in reprints.

We greatly appreciate all information that is sent to us by travellers. Back at Lonely Planet we employ a hard-working readers' letters team to sort through the many letters we receive. The best ones will be rewarded with a free copy of the next edition or another Lonely Planet guide if you prefer. We give away lots of books, but, unfortunately, not every letter/postcard receives one.

Contents

Map Legend

BOUNDARIES

.... International Boundary
................Internal Boundary
..Arrondissement Boundary

8ᵉ

SYMBOLS

⊙ NATIONAL ....National Capital
● MAJOR CITY................................Major City
● Major ....Major Town
• Minor ....Minor Town
■ ....Places to Stay
▼ ....Places to Eat
🍺 ....Places to Drink
⊠ ....Post Office
✈ .... Airport
i ....Tourist Information
◔ ....Transport
Ⓜ ....Metro Station
🅿 ....Parking
66 ....Highway Route Number
⛄☦🕌 ...... Mosque, Church, Cathedral
✡ ....Synagogue
✚ ....Hospital
☀ ....Lookout
⛺ ....Camping Area
∴ ....Place of Interest
⚑ ....Chateau
⌂ ....Hut or Chalet
▲ ....Mountain or Hill
⌒ ....Cave
⊷ ....Railway Station
...................................Bridge
⇒ ⇐ →⟩ ⟨← ....Tunnel
...................Escarpment or Cliff
⌣ ....Pass
..............Ancient or Historic Wall

ROUTES

..........................Auto Route
...............................Highway
..........................Major Road
..... Unsealed Road or Track
...................................Railway
.... TGV (Very Fast Train)
.... Cable Car or Chair Lift
..........................City Street
...................................Arcade
.... Ferry Route
.... Tram Route

HYDROGRAPHIC FEATURES

.....................River or Creek
.............Intermittent Stream
........Lake, Intermittent Lake
...........................Coast Line
...................................Swamp
...................................Canal

OTHER FEATURES

.... Salt Lake or Reef

Park, Garden or National Park

.......................Built Up Area

... Market or Pedestrian Mall

..................Areas of Interest

.... Plaza or Town Square

...........................Cemetery

Note: not all symbols displayed above appear in this book

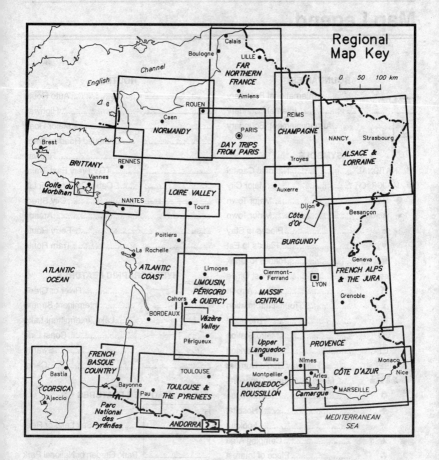

Regional Map Key

0   50   100 km

Calais
Boulogne
LILLE
FAR NORTHERN FRANCE
English Channel
Amiens
ROUEN
Caen
NORMANDY
PARIS
DAY TRIPS FROM PARIS
REIMS
CHAMPAGNE
NANCY   Strasbourg
ALSACE & LORRAINE
Troyes
Brest
BRITTANY
RENNES
Vannes
Golfe du Morbihan
NANTES
LOIRE VALLEY
Tours
Auxerre
Dijon
Côte d'Or
BURGUNDY
Besançon
Poitiers
La Rochelle
ATLANTIC OCEAN
ATLANTIC COAST
Limoges
Clermont-Ferrand
LYON
Geneva
FRENCH ALPS & THE JURA
Grenoble
LIMOUSIN, PÉRIGORD & QUERCY
Cahors
BORDEAUX
Vézère Valley
Périgueux
MASSIF CENTRAL
Upper Languedoc
Millau
PROVENCE
Nîmes
Arles
CÔTE D'AZUR
Monaco
Nice
Montpellier
LANGUEDOC-ROUSSILLON
Camargue
MARSEILLE
Bastia
CORSICA
Ajaccio
FRENCH BASQUE COUNTRY
Bayonne
Pau
TOULOUSE
TOULOUSE & THE PYRENEES
Parc National des Pyrénées
ANDORRA
MEDITERRANEAN SEA

This map shows the regional divisions of France as they are covered in this book. For more detail of each region, including a regional map, see the relevant chapter (or area within the chapter).

Introduction

For first-time and veteran visitors alike, France's most salient characteristic is its exceptional diversity. The largest country in Western Europe, France stretches from the rolling plains of the north to the jagged ridges of the Pyrenees, from the rugged coastline of Brittany to the clear, blue lakes and icy crags of the Alps, and from the limestone plains of Bordeaux – home to millions of grape vines – to the Alsatian bank of the Rhine, also ideal for cultivating grapes. There are sand dunes and glaciers, cliff-lined canyons and seemingly endless beaches, thick forests and near-desert salt marshes. And with the country's superb train system, you can – during most of the year – go skiing one day and sunbathing the next. Of course, you'll have to decide whether to go skiing in the

Alps or the Pyrenees (or in Corsica), and whether you'd like to take a dip in the English Channel, the Atlantic or the Mediterranean, but the information in this book can help solve such dilemmas.

France's cities also hold many charms. Paris's reputation as one of the world's most romantic cities can be only partly accounted for by the sheer beauty of its buildings and public spaces – beyond that you have to start adding up a myriad of intangibles. In Paris, as in many other cities, you will see people strolling along grand boulevards, picnicking in public parks and watching the world parade by from a café terrace. Museums and galleries are also a nationwide phenomenon: not only do all the major cities have exceptional museums of both art and regional culture, but so do many smaller towns. Shopping is generally best in the larger cities, but many villages make products that are famous all over the country: a cheese, perhaps, or a particularly well-regarded wine.

Over the centuries, France has received more immigrants than any other country in Europe. The groups that have made France their home range from the Celts (Gauls), Greeks and Romans – all of whom arrived in the centuries BC – to mid-20th century immigrants from France's former colonies in Indochina, sub-Saharan Africa and North Africa. In every period, elements of the culture, cuisine and artistic sense of the new arrivals were assimilated into one of the many streams of French culture. France's incredible variety of cheeses (over 400 by some accounts), sauces and other gourmet specialities reflect much more than gustatory preferences: they are part of a centuries-old legacy of cultural assimilation, fusion and metamorphosis that, in conjunction with the country's varied geographical conditions, has created out of many traditions the unique and diverse civilisation that is France.

At one time, France was on the western edge of the known world, the last stop for migrants seeking a bit of land out on the frontier. Today, as Europe moves towards unification of one sort or another, France is at the crossroads: between England and Italy, between Belgium and Spain, between North Africa and Scandinavia. Of course, this is exactly how the French have always thought of their country – at the very centre of things.

Facts about the Country

HISTORY
Gaul

The Gauls, a Celtic people, moved into what is now France between 1500 and 500 BC. By about 600 BC, they had established trading links with the Greeks, whose colonies on the Mediterranean coast included Massilia (Marseille). After several centuries of conflict between Rome and the Gauls, the Roman legions of Julius Caesar took control of Gaul around 52 BC, when a revolt led by the Gallic chief Vercingétorix was crushed at Alésia. Lugdunum (modern-day Lyon) became the administrative and economic capital of Roman Gaul in 43 BC. Christianity was introduced to Roman Gaul sometime in the early 2nd century AD, and by 250 the country had been partly Christianised.

Despite a series of civil wars and barbarian invasions, France remained under Roman rule until the 5th century AD, when the Franks (from whom the name France is derived) and other Germanic groups, including the Visigoths, Burgundians and Alemanni, took over the country. These groups adopted important parts of Gallo-Roman civilisation, including Christianity, and their eventual assimilation resulted in the fusion of Germanic culture with that of the Celts and the Romans.

Middle Ages

Two Frankish dynasties, the Merovingians and the Carolingians, ruled from 476 to 986. The Frankish tradition by which the king was succeeded by *all* of his sons, each of whom was given a piece of the kingdom, gave rise to a virtually endless series of power struggles, insurrections and invasions and led to the eventual disintegration of the kingdom into a collection of small, feudal states. In the early 8th century, the Arabs conquered Spain, which they would rule for the next seven centuries, but Charles Martel (the grandfather of Charlemagne) stopped their advance northward at Poitiers in 732, thus ensuring that France would not come under Muslim rule.

Charlemagne, who ruled from 768 to 814, significantly extended the boundaries of the kingdom and – because of France's pre-eminent political position in Europe – was crowned Holy Roman Emperor (Emperor of the West) in 800. His reign was marked by a revival of education and scholarship. During the 9th century, the Scandinavian Vikings (also known as the Normans, ie Northmen) began raiding France's western coast and later ravaged large areas of the country. They eventually settled in the lower Seine Valley and formed the Duchy of Normandy, which officially came into existence in 911.

The Capetians

The Capetian Dynasty was founded in 987, when the nobles elected Hugh Capet as their king. At the time, the domains under direct royal control were quite modest, consisting mostly of bits of land around Paris and Orléans.

Under William the Conqueror, Duke of Normandy, Norman forces conquered England in 1066, making Normandy – and later, Plantagenet-ruled England and its vast territories in France – a formidable rival of the kingdom of France. A further one-third of France came under the control of the English crown in 1154 when Eleanor of Aquitaine, whose marriage to the French king Louis VII had been annulled, married Henry of Anjou, later to become King Henry II of England. The subsequent battle between France and England for control of Aquitaine lasted for three centuries.

Between 1209 and the 1240s, the Cathar sect (an ascetic Christian sect in southern France whose followers believed the material world was evil) was suppressed by a papal inquisition and a holy war accompanied by wholesale atrocities, including mass burnings of unrepentant Cathars. The bloody work of the Albigensian Crusade (so named

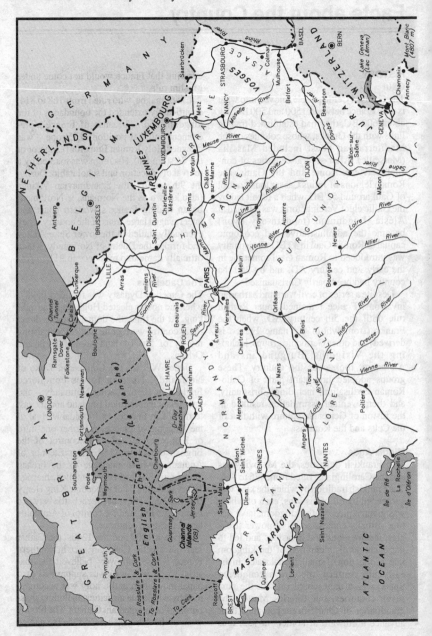

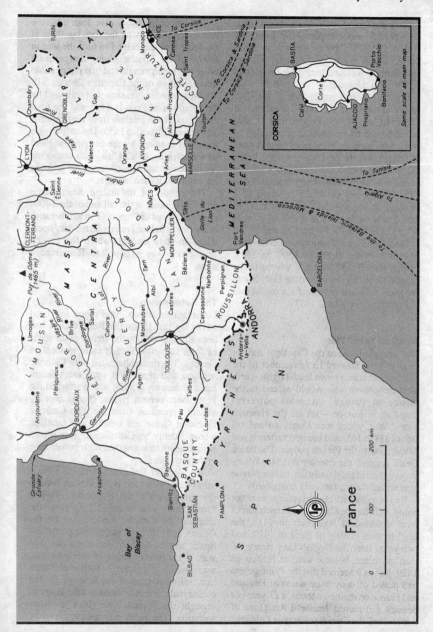

because the town of Albi was a major Cathar stronghold) was completed by Louis IX (ruled 1226-70), better known as Saint Louis, whose reputation for piety, wisdom and fairness was undimmed by his bloody activities in the south.

France played a major role in the Crusades. The First Crusade, preached at Clermont in 1095 by Pope Urban II, was accompanied by widespread persecution of Jews, who were expelled from various parts of France over the next two centuries. Louis IX is remembered for leading a Crusader expedition to the Holy Land from 1248 to 1254, four years of which he spent as a prisoner of the Muslims. He died in 1270 near Tunis on board a ship sailing to what would have been the Eighth Crusade.

Most of France's major cathedrals were erected between 1150 and 1300. In 1309, French-born Pope Clement V, who had been expelled from Rome, moved the Holy See to Avignon, where it remained – a useful tool of French policy – until 1377.

Hundred Years' War

The struggle between the Capetians and the English king Edward III (a member of the Plantagenet family) over feudal rights – and, ultimately, over who would ascend to the throne of France, the most powerful kingdom in Europe – set off the Hundred Years' War, which was fought on and off from 1337 to 1453 and brought suffering and devastation to the French people. The Black Death ravaged the country in 1348, killing about a third of the population, but the plague interrupted the warfare only temporarily.

By the early 15th century, things were not going well for the Capetians: French forces were defeated at Agincourt in 1415, the English took control of Paris in 1420, and two years later the English king Henry IV, then an infant, became king of France. In 1429, just as it seemed that the Plantagenets had pulled off a dynastic union of England and France on their own terms, a 17-year-old peasant girl named Jeanne d'Arc (Joan of Arc) rallied the French soldiery at Orléans.

The French probably give Joan a bit too much credit for saving the day, but there is no doubt that she helped to turn the war in favour of the French, giving a significant boost to French morale and making possible the coronation of the Capetian Charles VII. This momentous occasion was followed by the recapture of Paris in 1436 and the final expulsion of the English from French territory (except Calais) in 1453. The unfortunate Joan was captured by the Burgundians and turned over to the English, who convicted her of heresy and burned her at the stake in the centre of Rouen in 1431.

The culture of the Italian Renaissance arrived in France at the tail end of the 1400s during the reign of François I, in part because of a series of indecisive French military operations in Italy through which the French aristocracy was exposed to Renaissance ideas.

The Reformation

Lutheranism arrived in France in about 1519. By the 1530s the Reformation had been strengthened by the arrival of the ideas of John Calvin, a French exile resident in Geneva. Tolerance alternated with Catholic reaction and repression until the tolerant Edict of January (1562), which afforded the Protestants certain rights. It was met by violent opposition from the ultra-Catholic House of Guise and other noble families, whose fidelity to Catholicism was mixed with a desire to strengthen their power base in the provinces.

The Wars of Religion (1562-98) were a series of religious and political wars involving three parties: the Huguenots (French Protestants), who received help from the English; the Catholic League, led by the Guises and, in later stages, supported by Spain; and the Catholic-led monarchy. The war, a confusing series of persecutions, assassinations, massacres, battles and treaties, inflicted general lawlessness on the countryside, severely weakened the king and brought the French state close to disintegration. The most outrageous massacre

took place in Paris on the night of 23 to 24 August 1572, when some 3000 Huguenots, who had come to Paris to celebrate the wedding of Henry of Navarre and Margaret of Valois, were slaughtered in the notorious Saint Bartholomew's Day Massacre.

Eventually, the Huguenot Henry of Navarre, a member of the House of Bourbon, became King Henry IV, but not before he had embraced Catholicism. Regarding his conversion, he is reported to have commented that *'Paris vaut bien une messe'* ('Paris is well worth a mass'). In 1598, Henry IV promulgated the Edict of Nantes, which guaranteed the Huguenots freedom of conscience and many civil and political rights.

Henry IV, whose most important minister was the Duke of Sully, a member of a prominent Protestant family, was succeeded by Louis XIII (ruled 1610-43), whose ruthless minister, Cardinal Richelieu, is best known for his untiring efforts to establish an absolute monarchy in France and French supremacy in Europe. In 1628, Richelieu attacked the Huguenot fortress-city of La Rochelle, besieging it for 15 months, during which 23,000 of the city's 28,000 residents died of starvation.

Historical Regions of France

0   75   150 km

The regional names marked on this map appeared and reappeared at various times in France's history from around 1000 to 1789. Some short-lived or minor names have been omitted.

ATLANTIC OCEAN

MEDITERRANEAN SEA

Calais
FLANDERS
ARTOIS
PICARDY
English Channel
NORMANDY
Rouen
Reims
LORRAINE
ÎLE DE FRANCE
Paris
CHAMPAGNE
Strasbourg
PERCHE
BRITTANY
CORNOUAILLE
MAINE
ORLÉANAIS
BURGUNDY
FRANCHE-COMTÉ
ALSACE
ANJOU
TOURAINE
Tours
BLOIS
Nantes
BERRY
NIVERNAIS
Dijon
VENDÉE
POITOU
BOURBONNAIS
BRESSE
Geneva
La Rochelle
AUNIS
ANGOULÊME (ANGOUMOIS)
MARCHE
SAINTONGE
Limoges
LIMOUSIN
LYONNAIS
Lyon
SAVOY
PÉRIGORD (DORDOGNE)
Bordeaux
AUVERGNE
DAUPHINÉ
AQUITAINE (GUYENNE)
QUERCY
ROUERGUE
Orange
ALBRET
AGENAIS
Avignon
COMTAT VENAISSIN
COMTÉ DE NICE
GASCONY
ARMAGNAC
Toulouse
LANGUEDOC
PROVENCE
MONACO
NAVARRE
BÉARN
BIGORRE
FOIX
Marseille
ROUSSILLON
ANDORRA

Louis XIV

Louis XIV, the Roi Soleil (Sun King), ascended to the throne in 1643 at the age of five and ruled until 1715. For 72 years, France was dominated by the king's paternalistic and authoritarian style of government, the product of his seemingly boundless personal arrogance. Indeed, Louis XIV appears to have really believed that 'l'État c'est moi' (I am the State). Of course, you would be arrogant, too, if you had become king of the most powerful state in Europe before starting kindergarten...

In the realm of policy, Louis XIV sought to project the power of the French monarchy, bolstered by claims of divine right, both at home and abroad. In foreign affairs, he involved the country in a long series of costly wars that managed to fulfil many French territorial ambitions but terrified France's neighbours and nearly bankrupted the treasury. Towards the end of his reign, when he involved France in the disastrous War of the Spanish Succession (1701-14), Louis XIV's ambition seems to have gotten the better of his judgement.

Domestically, Louis XIV, who made few changes to the institutions of government, put huge sums of money into building his extravagant palace at Versailles, a vastly expensive architectural extension of the king's authority – and his insatiable ego. Versailles also played an important role in his domestic political strategy: by moving his court to Versailles, located 23 km south-west of Paris – by then a city of 500,000 people – he was able to sidestep the city's endless intrigues. And by turning his nobles, who posed a potential threat to royal power, into courtiers, forced to compete with each other for royal favour, he succeeded in reducing them to ineffectual sycophancy.

Louis XIV, who saw no virtue whatsoever in toleration per se, considered the very existence of the Protestant minority a threat to the unity of the state (and thus his power) and persecuted them mercilessly. After a period during which he destroyed churches, limited the professions to which they were admitted, took Protestant children away from their families and raised them as Catholics, and forcibly billeted unruly soldiers with Protestant families, he went so far as to revoke the Edict of Nantes in 1685.

End of the Ancien Régime

Louis XIV was followed by Louis XV (ruled 1715-74) who, like his great-grandfather, came to power at the age of five. He was succeeded by the incompetent – and, later in his reign, universally despised and impotent – Louis XVI.

As the 18th century progressed, new economic and social circumstances and the anti-Establishment and anticlerical ideas of the Enlightenment, whose leading lights included Voltaire, Rousseau and Montesquieu, rendered the old order dangerously out of sync with the needs of the country. But entrenched vested interests, a cumbersome power structure and royal lassitude prevented change from starting until the 1770s, by which time it was too late.

The Seven Years' War (1756-63), one of a series of ruinous wars pursued by Louis XV, was fought by Britain and Prussia against France and Austria and caused France to lose its flourishing colonies in Canada, the West Indies and India to the English. It was in part to avenge these losses that Louis XVI sided with the colonists in the American War of Independence. By and large, French military forces acquitted themselves successfully, and naturally it warmed many a French heart to see the English humiliated. The war was officially ended by the Treaty of Versailles of 1783. But the war also had two unintended results: it cost a fortune, tripling annual debt repayments at a time when enacting the necessary revenue-enhancing measures proved politically impossible; and it helped disseminate in France the radical democratic ideas which the American Revolution had thrust on the world stage.

French Revolution

By the late 1780s, Louis XVI and his Austrian-born queen, Marie-Antoinette, had managed to alienate virtually every segment of society (Remember the old joke?

Someone runs up to Marie-Antoinette and exclaims, 'The peasants are revolting', and she turns up her nose and says, 'I know'). More enlightened groups were angered by the lack of effective reforms, while conservatives were enraged that the king was making any attempt whatsoever to change the status quo.

The peasants, the urban poor, the bourgeoisie, the nobles, the upper aristocracy, reformists and reactionaries all had strong (if contradictory) reasons for being fed up with the king. When he tried to neutralise the power of the more reform-minded delegates at a meeting of the États Généraux (Estates General), convened at Versailles in May 1789 to deal with the huge national debt, the urban masses took to the streets. On 14 July a Parisian mob attacked the Invalides, where they seized weapons, and then stormed the Bastille prison, the ultimate symbol of the despotism of the *ancien régime* (France's pre-Revolutionary political and social system).

At first, the Revolution was in the hands of relative moderates. France was declared a constitutional monarchy and various enlightened changes were made, including the adoption of the Declaration of the Rights of Man. The power of the clergy was reduced, in part by confiscating Church property in order to avoid national bankruptcy.

But the landed aristocracy continued to resist any reduction in its privileges, a key demand of the rural masses, sparking a series of peasant insurrections. Both sides looked to a foreign war as the way to solve their problems. The reactionaries, supported by such powers as Austria and Prussia, thought that victory would bring about a counter-revolution. For their part, many of the Revolutionaries sought to expose and defeat the foreign-backed aristocracy once and for all and to export the Revolution to more benighted parts of the continent. Ideology aside, the business bourgeoisie was keen on the fat profits that the provisioning of armies always brings.

Neither side achieved its war aims, but as the masses armed themselves to do battle with the external threat to the Revolution posed by Austria, Prussia and the many nobles who had sought asylum there, patriotism and nationalism mixed with revolutionary fervour, popularising and radicalising the Revolution. It was not long before the moderate, bourgeois Girondins lost power in the Convention Nationale – a 749-member assembly set up after the overthrow of the monarchy in August 1792 – to the radical Jacobins, led by Maximilien Robespierre, Georges Jacques Danton and Jean-Paul Marat, who transferred effective power to the notorious Committee of Public Safety. This body virtually had dictatorial control over the country during La Terreur (the Reign of Terror – September 1793 to July 1794).

In January 1793, Louis XVI, who had tried to flee the country with his family but was recaptured near Varennes, was convicted

---

Revolutionary Calendar
During the Revolution, the Convention adopted a new, more 'rational' calendar from which all 'superstitious' associations (eg saints' days) were removed. Year I began on 22 September 1792. The months – renamed Vendémiaire, Brumaire, Frimaire, Nivôse, Pluviôse, Ventôse, Germinal, Floréal, Prairial, Messidor, Thermidor and Fructidor – were divided into three 10-day weeks *(décades).* Following the cult of nature, the poetically inspired names of the months were chosen according to the seasons: the autumn months, for instance, were Vendémiaire, derived from *vendange* (wine harvest); Brumaire from *brume* (fog); and Frimaire from *frimas* (wintry weather). The five or six remaining days of the year were used to celebrate republican festivals and were initially termed *'sans-culottides'* in honour of the *sans-culottes,* the extreme revolutionary republicans who wore pantaloons rather than the short breeches (culottes) favoured by the upper classes. The Gregorian calendar was re-established by Napoleon on 1 January 1806. ∎

of 'conspiring against the liberty of the nation' and guillotined at what is now Place de la Concorde in Paris. By autumn, the Reign of Terror was in full swing, and through the middle of 1794 some 17,000 people in every part of the country had their heads lopped off. Most of the victims were accused of being enemies of the Revolution. In the end the Revolution turned on its own, and many of its leaders, including Robespierre and Danton, followed their victims to the guillotine.

During the Reign of Terror, the country was swept by a popular movement known as de-Christianisation: churches were desecrated and closed, religious funeral processions were forbidden and Notre Dame and other cathedrals around the country were reconsecrated as Temples of Reason. During the same period, every aspect of the economy came under state control, and embryonic social welfare legislation was enacted.

Napoleon

In the chaos that reigned as the Revolution spent itself, the leaders of the French military began disregarding instructions from the increasingly corrupt and tyrannical Directoire (as the executive power in Paris was called from 1795 to 1799), pursuing instead their own ambitions on the battlefield. One dashing, daring young Corsican general by the name of Napoleon Bonaparte was particularly successful in the Italian campaign of the war against Austria, and the personal prestige brought by his victories soon turned him into an independent political force.

When the elections of 1797 looked likely to result in a much stronger monarchist contingent in the legislature, the Directoire staged a coup d'état with Napoleon's backing. But two years later, on 18 Brumaire of the year VIII (see the Revolutionary Calendar aside), when it looked like the Jacobins were again becoming a threat, Napoleon – just back from defeat in Egypt and Ottoman Palestine – overthrew the discredited Directoire and assumed power himself.

Général Napoleon Bonaparte

In the beginning, Napoleon took the title of First Consul. In 1802, a referendum declared him Consul for Life and his birthday became a national holiday. The following year, his face began to appear on coinage. By 1804, when he had himself crowned Emperor of the French by Pope Pius VII in Notre Dame in Paris, the scope and nature of his ambitions were quite obvious. But to consolidate and legitimise his authority, Napoleon needed more victories on the battlefield. So began a seemingly endless series of wars in which France came to control most of Europe.

Napoleon's victory at Austerlitz (1805), in which Austria and Russia were decisively defeated, was followed by more wars and more victories. But in 1812, in an attempt to do away with the tsar, his last major rival on the continent, Napoleon invaded Russia. This time, however, his military genius failed, and although his Grande Armée (Grand Army) captured Moscow, it was wiped out shortly thereafter by the brutal Russian winter. Prussia and Napoleon's other enemies quickly recovered from their earlier defeats, and less than two years after the fiasco in Russia, the Allied armies entered Paris. Napoleon abdicated and left

France for his tiny Mediterranean island-kingdom of Elba.

At the Congress of Vienna (1814-15), the Allies restored the Bourbons to the French throne by installing Louis XVI's brother as Louis XVIII (the second son of Louis XVI had been declared Louis XVII by monarchist exiles but died in 1795). But in March 1815, Napoleon escaped from Elba and landed in southern France. He then marched north-ward via Cannes and Grenoble, gathering a large army along the way. His 'Hundred Days' back in power ended when the English general Wellington defeated his forces at Waterloo in Belgium. Napoleon surrendered to the English, who – to make sure he never pulled a similar stunt again – exiled him to the remote South Atlantic island of Saint Helena, where he died in 1821.

Although reactionary in some ways – he re-established slavery in the colonies, for instance – Napoleon instituted a number of important reforms, including a reorgani-sation of the judicial system and the promulgation of a new legal code, the Code Civil, also known as the Napoleonic Code, which forms the basis of the French legal system to this day. More importantly, he preserved the essence of the changes wrought by the Revolution. For this, along with his many victories and the dramatic denouement to his extraordinary career, he came to be remembered by the French as a great hero.

19th Century

The 19th century was a chaotic one for France. The reign of Louis XVIII (ruled 1815-24) was dominated by the struggle between extreme monarchists, who wanted to return to the ancien régime, and people who saw the changes brought by the Revo-lution as irreversible. Charles X (ruled 1824-30) sought to restore the principle of divine right of kings, in part by re-establish-ing the power of the Church, but he handled the struggle between reactionaries and liber-als with great ineptitude and was overthrown in the July Revolution of 1830.

Louis-Philippe (ruled 1830-48), an osten-sibly constitutional monarch of upper bour-geois sympathies and tastes, was chosen by parliament to head what became known as the July Monarchy. He was overthrown in the February Revolution of 1848, in whose wake the Second Republic was established (the First Republic was set up in 1792 after Louis XVI proved unreliable as a constitu-tional monarch). In presidential elections held the same year, Napoleon's un-distinguished nephew, Louis-Napoleon Bonaparte, whose greatest, and virtually only, asset was his name (which conveyed to the masses an aura of power, law and order and the glory of empire), was overwhelm-ingly elected. Legislative deadlock led Louis-Napoleon to lead a coup d'état in 1851, after which he was proclaimed Napo-leon III, Emperor of the French.

The Second Empire (the First Empire was led by the original Napoleon) lasted from 1852 to 1870 and was characterised by a certain liberalism after 1859. During this period, France enjoyed significant economic growth. But as his uncle had done, Napoleon III – whose misleading motto was *L'Empire c'est la paix* (The empire is peace) – embroiled France in a number of conflicts, including the Crimean War (1854-56), which proved a fiasco for all involved, and a bizarre attempt to make Maximilian of Austria emperor of Mexico. But it was the Prussians who ended the Second Empire. In 1870, Bismarck (Prussia's prime minister from 1862-90) goaded Napoleon III to declare war on Prussia. Within months, the thoroughly unprepared French army had been defeated at Sedan (in north-eastern France) and, to compound the humiliation, the emperor himself was taken prisoner.

When news of the debacle reached the French capital, the Parisian masses took to the streets and demanded that a republic be declared. The Third Republic began as a provisional government of national defence – the Prussians were, at the time, advancing on Paris. But in the National Assembly elec-tions of February 1871 – required by the armistice (signed after a four-month siege of Paris so the Prussians would have someone

to negotiate a peace treaty with – the republicans, who had called on the nation to continue resistance, lost to the monarchists, who had campaigned on a peace platform.

As expected, the monarchist-controlled National Assembly ratified the Treaty of Frankfurt (1871). However, when ordinary Parisians heard of its harsh terms – France had agreed to pay a five-billion franc war indemnity and give up the provinces of Alsace and Lorraine – they revolted against the government that had accepted such a dishonourable peace. In the spring of 1871 they set up the Paris Commune to oppose the actions of the National Assembly. The Communards – as the supporters of the Commune were known – took over Paris, but were slowly pushed back in bloody street fighting in which several thousand rebels were killed by troops loyal to the National Assembly. A further 20,000 or so Communards – mostly from the working class – were summarily executed.

As the end of the Commune neared, the Communards executed a number of hostages, including the Archbishop of Paris, and burned the Hôtel de Ville (which has since been replaced by the present structure), the Tuileries Palace (the now-gone west wing of the Louvre) and other public buildings. The Communards made a final stand among the tombstones of the Cimetiere du Père Lachaise, where the last 147 of them were lined up against a wall and executed. Karl Marx interpreted the Communard insurrection as the first great proletarian uprising against the bourgeoisie, and socialists came to see its victims as martyrs of the class struggle.

The greatest moral and political crisis of the Third Republic was the infamous Dreyfus Affair, which began in 1894 when a Jewish army officer, Captain Alfred Dreyfus, was framed as a German spy, courtmartialled and sentenced to life imprisonment on Devil's Island, the notorious French penal colony off the northern coast of South America. When significant evidence of Dreyfus's innocence came to light, the intellectuals of the left and some politicians demanded that the case be reopened, but they were bitterly opposed by the army command, right-wing politicians and many Catholic groups, all of whom rallied to defend the army's honour. The issue became extremely divisive, and remained so even after Dreyfus was given a presidential pardon. A civilian court cleared him of all charges in 1906. The army and the Church hierarchy were greatly discredited by their conduct in the affair, leading to more rigourous civilian control of the military and, in 1905, the legal separation of Church and state.

The Entente Cordiale of 1904 ended colonial rivalry between France and Britain, beginning a period of cooperation that has continued to this day.

WW I

The German defeat in WW I, which regained Alsace and Lorraine for France, was achieved at an unimaginable human cost. Of the eight million French men who were called to arms, 1.3 million were killed and almost one million crippled. In other words, two of every 10 Frenchmen aged between 20 and 45 were killed in WW I. At the Battle of Verdun (1916) alone, the French (led by General Philippe Pétain) and the Germans each lost about 400,000 men. You can begin to imagine the number of French men who never returned from the trenches by looking at the long lists of *morts pour la patrie* (people who died for their country) on the war memorials found in the main square of virtually every city, town or village.

Because much of the war – including most of the static trench warfare – took place on French territory, large parts of north-eastern France were devastated. Industrial production dropped by 40%, the value of the franc was seriously undermined, and the country faced a devastating financial crisis. The Treaty of Versailles of 1919, which officially ended the war, was heavily influenced by French prime minister Georges Clemenceau, the most uncompromising of the Allied leaders, who made sure that its harsh terms included a provision that Germany pay US$33 billion in reparations.

WW II

During the 1930s, the French, like the British, did their best to appease Hitler, but two days after the German invasion of Poland (1 September 1939), the two countries reluctantly declared war on Germany. By June of the following year, France, whose generals had, as usual, been completely unprepared, had capitulated. The British expeditionary force sent to help the French barely managed to avoid capture by retreating to Dunkerque (Dunkirk) and crossing the English Channel in small boats. The hugely expensive Maginot Line (named after a French minister of war), a supposedly impregnable line of fortifications along the the Franco-German border built during the 1930s, had proved useless: the German armoured divisions had simply outflanked it by going through Belgium.

The Germans divided France into a zone under direct German occupation (in the north and along the west coast) and a puppet state based in the spa town of Vichy, which was led by General Philippe Pétain, an ageing WW I hero. Pétain's collaborationist government, whose leaders and supporters assumed that the Nazis were Europe's new masters and had to be accommodated, also believed that an ideology that had shown itself to be so successful on the battlefield shouldn't be dismissed out of hand. The 76,000 Jews deported from France (out of a total Jewish population of about 300,000) included 10,000 arrested by French authorities in the Vichy zone and handed over to the Gestapo. The vast majority were taken from Drancy (a suburb north-east of Paris) straight to Auschwitz; only 2500 survived. Thousands of Jews evaded the roundups by sheltering with French families in small villages.

After the capitulation, General Charles de Gaulle, France's undersecretary of war, fled to London and, in a famous radio broadcast on 18 June 1940, appealed to French patriots to continue resisting the Germans. He also set up a French government-in-exile and established the Forces Françaises Libres (Free French Forces), a military force dedicated to continuing the fight against

Germany. The underground movement known as the Résistance (Resistance), which never included more than perhaps 5% of the population, slowly grew to include people fleeing German conscript labour, Jewish refugees and members of the Communist Party (who joined only after Hitler attacked the USSR). The Resistance engaged in such activities as railroad sabotage (intended in part to slow the massive flow of valuable foodstuffs and raw materials to Germany), collecting intelligence for the Allies, helping Allied airmen who had been shot down and publishing anti-German leaflets.

The liberation of France began with the US, British and Canadian landings in Normandy on D-Day, 6 June 1944. On 15 August, Allied forces also landed in southern France. After a brief insurrection by the Resistance, Paris was liberated on 25 August by an Allied force spearheaded by Free French units, sent in ahead of the Americans so French forces would have the honour of liberating the French capital.

Fourth Republic

De Gaulle soon returned to Paris and set up a provisional government, but in January 1946 he resigned as provisional president, miscalculating that such a move would provoke a popular outcry for his return. A few months later, a new constitution was approved by referendum.

The Fourth Republic was a period of unstable coalition cabinets that followed one another with bewildering speed (on average, once every six months) and slow economic recovery, helped immeasurably by massive US aid. The war to reassert French colonial control of Indochina ended with the French defeat at Dien Bien Phu in 1954. France also tried to suppress an uprising by Arab nationalists in Algeria, whose population included over one million French settlers.

Fifth Republic

The Fourth Republic came to an end in 1958, when extreme right-wingers, furious at what they saw as defeatism rather than tough action in dealing with the uprising in Algeria

(one can only wonder what could be 'tougher' than the wholesale massacre of Algerian civilians carried out by French paratroops), began conspiring to overthrow the French government. De Gaulle was brought back to power to prevent a military coup d'état – and perhaps civil war. He soon drafted a new constitution that gave considerable powers to the president at the expense of the National Assembly, thus beginning the Fifth Republic, which continues to this day.

In 1961 France was rocked by an attempted coup staged in Algiers by a group of right-wing military officers. When it failed, the Organisation de l'Armée Secrète (OAS), a group of French settlers and others opposed to Algerian independence, turned to terrorism, trying several times to assassinate de Gaulle. The book and film *The Day of the Jackal* portray a fictional OAS attempt on de Gaulle's life.

In 1962 de Gaulle negotiated an end to the war in Algeria, which was granted full independence. Some 750,000 *pieds noirs* (as Algerian-born French people are known) flooded into France. In the meantime, almost all of the other French colonies and protectorates in Africa had demanded and achieved independence. Shrewdly, the French government began a programme of economic and military aid to its former colonies in order to bolster France's waning importance in international affairs by helping to create a bloc of French-speaking nations in the Third World.

The crisis of May 1968 took the government – and much of the country – by total surprise. A seemingly insignificant incident, in which police broke up yet another in a long series of protests by Paris university students, sparked a violent reaction on the streets of Paris: students occupied the Sorbonne, barricades were erected in the Latin Quarter and unrest spread to other universities. Workers joined in the protests and about nine million people participated in a general strike, virtually paralysing the country. But just as the country seemed on the brink of revolution and an overthrow of the Fifth Republic, De Gaulle defused the crisis by successfully appealing to people's fear of

General Charles de Gaulle

anarchy. When stability was restored, the government made a number of important changes, including a reform of the higher education system, which was decentralised.

In 1969 de Gaulle was succeeded as president by the Gaullist leader Georges Pompidou, who was in turn succeeded by Valéry Giscard d'Estaing in 1974. François Mitterrand, long-time head of the Parti Socialiste (Socialist Party), was elected president in 1981 and, as the business community had feared (the Paris stock market index fell by 30% on news of his victory), immediately set out to nationalise 36 privately owned banks, large industrial groups and various other parts of the economy, increasing the state-owned share of industrial production from 15% to over 30%. During the mid-1980s, however, Mitterrand followed a generally moderate economic policy and in 1988, at the age of 69, was re-elected for a second seven-year term. In the 1986 parliamentary elections, the right-wing opposition

led by Jacques Chirac received a majority in the National Assembly, and for the next two years Mitterrand was forced to work with a prime minister and cabinet from the opposition, an unprecedented arrangement known as *cohabitation*. In May 1991 Édith Cresson became France's first woman prime minister. She was replaced 10½ months later by Pierre Bérégovoy, who committed suicide after the Socialists' resounding defeat in the 1993 parliamentary elections.

In recent years, in part because of the economic situation and in part because of a resurgence of plain, old-fashioned racial prejudice, there has been increasing hostility towards the country's large minority communities, especially immigrants from North Africa and sub-Saharan Africa. These sentiments have been encouraged and taken advantage of by the racist and anti-Semitic Front National, led by Jean-Marie Le Pen, which has won 12% to 14% of the vote in recent national elections. The Front National has particularly strong support (around 25%) in southern cities such as Nice, Cannes, Toulon, Marseille and Avignon.

In the parliamentary elections of March 1993, the centre-right coalition consisting of the Rassemblement pour la République (RPR; Rally or Assembly for the Republic) and the Union pour la Démocratie Française (UDF; Union for French Democracy) won 480 seats in the 577-member Assemblée Nationale, leading to a second period of cohabitation, with Mitterrand as president and Édouard Balladur (of the RPR) as prime minister. The Front National got 12.5% of the nationwide vote but lost its only seat in the National Assembly.

GEOGRAPHY

France covers an area of 551,000 sq km and is the largest country in Europe after Russia and the Ukraine. Its outline is hexagonal, which is why the French often refer to their country as *l'hexagone*. There are natural frontiers – sea or mountains – in the north-west (the English Channel), west (the Atlantic), south (the Pyrenees, across which lies Spain), south-east (the Mediterranean)

and east (the Alps and the Jura, shared by Switzerland and Italy). France has repeatedly been invaded across its relatively flat north-east frontier, which abuts Germany, Luxembourg and Belgium.

The territory of modern-day France was assembled by centuries of conquests, treaties and carefully planned royal marriages. Despite a long tradition of highly centralised government, the country remains linguistically and culturally heterogeneous, and in some areas there is less than complete acceptance of control by Paris. In the Basque Country, Brittany and Corsica, there are even groups demanding complete independence from France.

Mountains

A significant proportion of France is covered by mountains, many of them among the most spectacular in Europe.

The Alps, Europe's greatest mountain chain, form a 1000-km arc that stretches from the Danube to the Mediterranean. The French Alps, which include Mont Blanc (4807 metres), Europe's highest peak, run along France's eastern border from Lake Geneva (Lac Léman) to the Côte d'Azur. There is permanent snow cover above about 2800 metres. Over the eons, huge glaciers have carved out great valleys. North of the Alps, the Jura Mountains, a gentle limestone range that peaks at just 1723 metres, stretch along the Swiss frontier north of Lake Geneva. The Pyrenees stretch along France's entire 450-km border with Spain, running from the Atlantic from the Mediterranean. Though the loftiest peak is only 3404 metres high, the Pyrenees can be almost as rugged as the Alps.

The Alps, the Pyrenees and the Jura, though spectacular, are young ranges in comparison with France's ancient massifs, formed between 225 and 345 million years ago. The most spectacular is the Massif Central, a huge region in the middle of France whose 91,000 sq km cover one-sixth of the entire country. It is perhaps best known for its chain of extinct volcanoes, such as the Puy de Dôme (1465 m). A number of

important rivers, including the Loire and the Dordogne, rise in the Massif Central.

France's other ancient massifs, worn down over the eons, include the Vosges, a forested upland in the country's north-east corner between Alsace and Lorraine; the Ardennes, most of which lies in Belgium and Germany and whose French part is on the northern edge of Champagne; and the Massif Armoricain, which stretches westward from Normandy and forms the backbone of Britanny and Normandy. The Massif Armoricain includes the highest point in France's western plain, 417-metre Mont des Avaloirs.

Rivers

France is drained by five major river systems:

- The 775-km-long Seine, which is widely used for navigation, passes through Paris on its way from Burgundy to the English Channel.
- The Loire, France's longest river, stretches for 1020 km from the Massif Central to the Atlantic. Its flow is eight times greater in December and January than at the end of summer.
- The Rhône, which links Lake Geneva and the Alps with the Mediterranean, is joined by the Saône at Lyon.
- The Garonne system, which includes the Tarn, Lot and Dordogne rivers, drains the Pyrenees and the

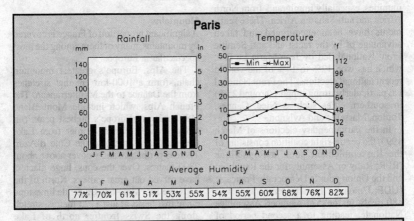

Paris

Rainfall

| | mm | in |
| J F M A M J J A S O N D | | |

Temperature

Min — Max

°c °f

Average Humidity

J	F	M	A	M	J	J	A	S	O	N	D
77%	70%	61%	51%	53%	55%	54%	55%	60%	68%	76%	82%

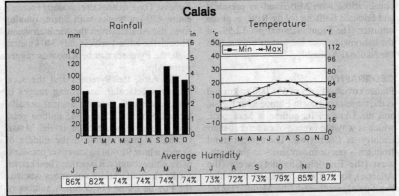

Calais

Rainfall

| | mm | in |
| J F M A M J J A S O N D | | |

Temperature

Min — Max

°c °f

Average Humidity

J	F	M	A	M	J	J	A	S	O	N	D
86%	82%	74%	74%	74%	74%	73%	72%	73%	79%	85%	87%

rest of the south-west into the Atlantic. Its long estuary begins slightly north of Bordeaux.

- The Rhine, which flows into the North Sea, forms the eastern border of Alsace for about 200 km. Its tributaries, including the Moselle and Meuse, drain much of the area north and east of Paris.

Coastline

Salt water laps – or buffets – three sides of the hexagon. France's 3200 km of coastline is remarkably diverse, ranging from the white chalk cliffs of Normandy and the treacherous promontories of Brittany to the fine-sand beaches along the Atlantic. The Mediterranean coast tends to have pebbly and even rocky beaches, though the Languedoc and some of the Roussillon beaches are sandy.

CLIMATE

Because of France's position at the western edge of the Eurasian landmass, its weather patterns are determined by oceanic, continental and Mediterranean climatic influences. In general, the country is temperate, with mild winters, except in mountain areas and Alsace.

The Atlantic has a profound impact on the north-west, particularly Brittany, whose

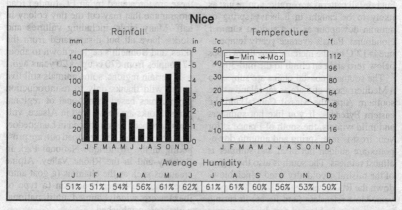

Nice

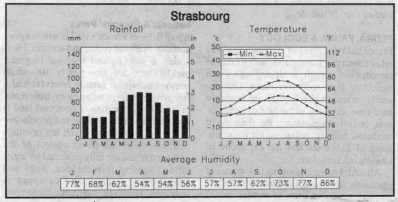

Strasbourg

weather is characterised by high humidity and lots of rain. Brittany has 200 rainy days a year compared to an average of 164 for the rest of France. The area is also subject to persistent (and sometimes violent) westerly winds.

France's north-east, especially Alsace, has a continental climate, with fairly hot summers and winters cold enough for snow to stay on the ground for weeks at a time. The wettest months in Alsace are June and July, when storms are common.

Midway between Brittany and Alsace – and affected by the climates of both – is the Paris basin. The region records the nation's lowest annual precipitation (about 575 mm) but rainfall patterns are erratic: you're just as likely to be caught in a heavy spring or autumn downpour as in a sudden summer cloudburst. Paris's average yearly temperature is 12°C but the mercury sometimes drops below zero and can climb to the mid-30s.

The southern coastal plains are subject to a Mediterranean climate as far inland as the southern Alps, the Massif Central and the eastern Pyrenees. If you like hot summers and mild winters, the south of France is for you: frost is rare, spring and autumn downpours are sudden but brief and summer is almost rainless. The south is also the region of the mistral, a cold, dry wind which blows down the Rhône valley for about 100 days a year. Most relentless (and fierce) in spring, it is sometimes blamed for driving people mad or even to suicide.

FLORA, FAUNA & ECOLOGY

France has more types of mammals than any other country in Europe and, with its mix of climates and terrains, is blessed with a rich variety of flora and other fauna. Unfortunately, many fragile species are having a hard time surviving in the face of urbanisation, intensive agriculture, the draining of wetlands, hunting, pollution, the encroachment of industries and the expansion of tourism infrastructure.

All told, France is home to 113 species of mammals, 363 species of birds, 30 kinds of amphibians, 36 varieties of reptiles and 72

kinds of fish as well as some 4200 species of plants and flowers. At least three kinds of mammals have already disappeared, and the Pyrenees ibex, Corsican deer and at least 10 species of bats are currently on the endangered list. A quarter of the fish species are also in trouble. Wolves are believed to be extinct, but some reports indicate that there may be a couple of them still roaming the Massif Central. River otters, once abundant, have fallen victim to trappers.

The once-common brown bear disappeared from the Alps in the mid-1930s, when about 300 of the animals still lived in the Pyrenees. Today, however, the Pyrenees are home to only about 15 brown bears, and even these are threatened by an EC-funded road programme that may cut the tiny colony in half. Many birds, including vultures and storks, have all but disappeared from the skies, and Bonnelli's eagle is down to about 27 couples from 670 couples 20 years ago.

In certain regions, some animals still live in the wild thanks only to re-introduction programmes based in national or regional parks. Storks are being bred in Alsace, vultures have been re-introduced in Languedoc, and beavers, once nearly wiped out, are prospering in the Armorique National Park in Brittany and in the Rhône Valley. Alpine creatures such as the chamois (a goat antelope) and the larger bouquetin (a type of ibex) were widely hunted until national parks were established.

National & Regional Parks

About 0.7% of France's land is within a *parc national* (national park), and another 7% is within a *parc naturel régional* (regional park). There are also nearly 100 small *réserves naturelles* (nature reserves) and a few private reserves set up by environmental groups. The proportion of protected land is low relative to France's size and population.

The national parks, which are uninhabited, are under the direct control of the government and are fully protected by legislation: hunting is forbidden, dogs and vehicles are banned and camping is restricted. However, the parks themselves

are relatively small (all are under 1000 sq km) and the ecosystems their establishment was supposed to protect spill over into what are called 'peripheral zones', populated areas around the parks in which tourism and and other economic activities are permitted.

France has six national parks, all of them in the mountains except for the Parc National de Port Cros, an island marine park off the Côte d'Azur. Most national park land is in the Alps, where the Vanoise, Écrins and Mercantour parks are hugely popular with summertime nature lovers and hikers. The Parc National des Pyrénées runs for 100 km along the Spanish border and is a favourite with rock climbers. The wild Parc National des Cévennes, which has a few inhabitants in its central zone, is on the border of the Massif Central and Languedoc.

The country's regional parks and nature reserves, most of which were established both to improve (or at least maintain) local ecosystems and to encourage economic development and tourism, all support human populations and are locally managed. Depending on the policies of the people in charge, regional parks and reserves may have either rigid environmental controls or policies bordering on nonchalance.

The 26 regional parks, established since 1967, are dotted all over the country, mainly in regions with diminishing populations that are facing severe economic problems. Large areas of the Massif Central and Corsica are also designated as regional parks.

Forests & Wetlands

Two millennia ago, France had about 45 million hectares of forests, but by the end of the 19th century only eight million were left. After the Industrial Revolution, some lands which had been deforested for farming were replanted with trees and today, about 14 million hectares of forests – mostly beech, oak and pine – cover roughly one-fifth of the country. The Office National des Forêts (ONF) manages most of the forest lands but they are not protected reserves and French ecologists charge that the ONF runs them less to ensure the survival of their ecosys-

tems than to bring in revenue from timber sales.

Summer forest fires are an annual dry-season hazard. Great tracts of land are burnt each year, often because of careless day-trippers or, as is sometimes the case in the Maures and Esterel ranges in the Côte d'Azur, intentionally set alight in order to get licences to build on the damaged lands. France's northern forests, particularly in the Vosges, have been affected by acid rain.

Wetlands, fantastically productive ecosystems that are essential for the survival of a great number of birds, reptiles and amphibians, are also shrinking. More than two million hectares – 3% of French territory – are considered important wetlands, but only 4% of this land is protected. Agricultural drainage systems, dykes, tourism, fishing, hunting and industrial pollution are the main causes of the wetlands' regression and degradation.

Hunting

France has some 1,700,000 hunters, many of whom head to the forests and woodlands with their dogs as soon as the five-month season opens at the end of September.

To safeguard the passage of migratory birds (the majority of Europe's species), long a target of hunters, the Directive de Brussels was introduced on 2 April 1979 to protect wild birds, their eggs, their nests and their habitats; it applies to all member states of the EC (European Community). The directive was modified on 6 March 1991 in order to include a greater number of species. The French government signed it in 1979 but didn't bother to make its provisions part of French law, so birds that can safely fly over other countries may still be shot as they cross France. Ecology activists have resorted to renting entire mountain passes on birds' flight paths in order to keep hunters away.

Ecological Issues

France may not have as many nuclear power stations as the USA, but whereas the latter ceased building new nuclear plants over a decade ago, the French progamme – the most

ambitious in the world – is still going full steam ahead. Since the late 1980s, the state-owned electric company, Electricité de France (EDF), has produced about three-quarters of the country's electricity using nuclear power. Most of France's 49 nuclear reactors are on main rivers or near the coast. France has also sought to export its nuclear technology to various Third World countries, including Iraq, whose French-built Osirak reactor was bombed by Israel in June 1981.

Because of an astute and soothing PR campaign by EDF – and the traditional French respect for people in white lab coats – antinuclear protests have been feeble, even after the Chernobyl disaster of 1986. And when protests have taken place, such as at Plogoff in Brittany in 1979 (where a decision was made to build a nuclear power station despite the locals' opposition), the technocrats – whose usual attitude is 'trust us' – completely ignored public sentiments. (In the case of Plogoff, the project was abandoned in 1981.) Nuclear waste, which is becoming an increasingly important issue, is dumped on the Cotentin peninsula in Normandy. France also accepts waste from other countries.

Many French environmentalists supported Mitterrand and the Socialists in the 1981 election, and though Mitterrand cancelled the Plogoff project, he did an about-face on the proposed scaling down of the country's nuclear programme. The Communists, junior partners in the Socialist's 1981 coalition, have always been strongly pronuclear for reasons of patriotism as well as employment.

EDF also controls France's hydroelectric programme. Rivers great and small have been dammed to produce electricity, creating huge recreational lakes but destroying the traditional habitats of many animals. Recently, an attempt to dam the Loire near Le Puy in the Massif Central was shelved after local opposition. High-voltage power lines are a blight on much of France's countryside and electrocute at least 1000 birds of prey each year. The EDF has announced that new lines will, as much as possible, run underground.

The French governement took one very positive step in mid-1992, when it finally agreed to suspend nuclear testing on the Polynesian island of Mururoa and a nearby atoll. The tests, begun in 1964, were carried out above-ground for a decade before being continued underground. The French government asserted that the underground tests posed no danger, but protestors say they have had disastrous affects on the health of the Mururoa islanders, causing increased rates of birth defects and leukaemia. In July 1985 French agents blew up the Greenpeace ship *Rainbow Warrior* in Auckland harbour, New Zealand, in an attempt to derail the organisation's protests against French nuclear tests. One person on board was killed.

At the last general election in 1993, Les Verts (The Greens), a grouping of Green parties created in the late 1960s and early '70s, were expected to receive increased support but failed to turn increased environmental concern into votes.

GOVERNMENT

France has had 11 constitutions since 1789. The present constitution, which was instituted by Charles de Gaulle in 1958, established what is known as the Fifth Republic (see History). It gives considerable power to the President of the Republic, a position held since 1981 by François Mitterrand of the Socialist Party. New presidential elections are scheduled for 1995.

The 577 members of the Assemblée Nationale (National Assembly) are directly elected in single-member constituencies for five-year terms. The 317 members of the rather powerless Sénat (Senate), who serve for nine years, are indirectly elected. The president of France, whose term lasts for seven years, has been chosen by direct election since 1962. Women were given the right to vote in 1944. The voting age was lowered from 21 to 18 in 1974.

Executive power is shared by the president and the Council of Ministers, whose members (including the prime minister) are appointed by the president but responsible to parliament. The president, who resides in the

Palais de l'Élysée (Élysée Palace) in Paris, makes all major policy decisions and serves as commander-in-chief of the armed forces. He can also dismiss the prime minister and has the power to dissolve the National Assembly.

France is one of the five permanent members of the UN Security Council. It withdrew from NATO's joint military command in 1966 and has maintained an independent arsenal of nuclear weapons since 1960. Until 1992, the French government insisted on testing such weapons in the South Pacific despite opposition from all the countries in the region.

French men are drafted into the armed forces for 10 months of service at the age of 19. Some of them opt for alternative service (eg teaching French) in developing countries.

Local Administration

France has long been a highly centralised state, as you can easily see from a glance at any road or rail map: railway lines and major highways radiate out from Paris like the spokes of a wheel. Because of the system's high degree of centralisation, local initiatives frequently get quashed by decisions made in Paris. Despite this, in 1969 the country voted against a referendum intended to approve a decentralisation plan championed by Charles de Gaulle. During the 1980s, the Socialists implemented a number of decentralisation measures.

Before the Revolution, France consisted of about two dozen major regions and a variety of smaller ones (see the map entitled Historical Regions of France). Their names (and those of their long-extinct predecessors) are still widely used, but for administrative purposes the country has, since 1790, been divided into units of about 6100 sq km called *départements* (departments). There are 96 départements in metropolitan France and a further five overseas. Most are named after geographical features, especially rivers, but are commonly known by their two-digit code, which appears as the first two digits of all postcodes in the département and as the last two

numbers on licence plates of cars registered in the département.

The government in Paris is represented in each département by a *préfet* (prefect), who is based in an imposing building in the département's capital, the *préfecture* (prefecture). The prefectures, each of which is also the seat of an elected *conseil général* (general council), were originally selected so they could be reached on horseback from anywhere in the département within one day's ride. You can tell if a town is a prefecture if the last three digits of the postcode are zeros.

Each département is subdivided into a number of *arrondissements* (for a national total of 324), each of whose main towns is known as a *sous-préfecture* (subprefecture). The arrondissements are subdivided into *cantons* (of which each département has 13 to 70), and the cantons are further divided into *communes*, the basic administrative unit of local government. Each commune – of which France has 36,400 – is presided over by a *maire* (mayor) based in a *mairie* (town hall). Over 11,000 communes have populations of less than 200.

Because of their small size, départements have proved ill-suited to the carrying out of modern regional coordination. In 1972, partly for this reason and partly as a response to growing demands for more regional autonomy, the government divided France into 22 regional divisions based roughly on the country's historical regions. Each of the new regions has an elected council and other organs, but its powers are limited and it plays no direct role in actual administration.

France's five *départements d'outre-mer* (overseas départements) are the Caribbean islands of Guadeloupe and Martinique; French Guiana, a 91,000-sq-km territory on the northern coast of South America between Brazil and Surinam; the island of Réunion, which is in the Indian Ocean east of Madagascar; and Saint Pierre et Miquelon, which is in the Atlantic just off the south coast of the Canadian province of Newfoundland. The Indian Ocean island of Mayotte, one of the Comoros Islands, has quasi-départemental status.

Regions & Départements

International Boundary
Regional Boundary
Departmental Boundary

0   75   150 km

CORSE (Corsica)

In addition, France has three *territoires d'outre-mer* (overseas territories), all of them in the South Pacific: French Polynesia, New Caledonia and the Wallis and Futuna islands. France also claims a sizeable chunk of Antarctica. These far-flung bits of French territory are often referred to collectively as DOM-TOM, the acronym of *départements d'outre-mer-territoires d'outre-mer*.

ECONOMY

The government has long played a significant *dirigiste* (interventionist) role in managing and running the French economy, which during the 1950s was one of the most tariff-protected and government-subsidised in Europe. While the EC has, in recent years, reduced protectionism, the state sector – parts of it heavily subsidised – continues to account for about one-fifth of GNP. About one-fifth of all economic activity in France takes place in the Paris region, which, thanks to the centralised bureaucracy, has 40% of the country's white-collar jobs.

Unemployment has plagued the economy since the mid-1970s, when the problem prompted the government to severely restrict

ALSACE
67 Bas-Rhin
68 Haut-Rhin

AQUITAINE
24 Dordogne
33 Gironde
40 Landes
47 Lot-et-Garonne
64 Pyrénées-Atlantiques

AUVERGNE
03 Allier
15 Cantal
43 Haute-Loire
63 Puy-de-Dôme

BASSE-NORMANDIE
14 Calvados
50 Manche
61 Orne

BRETAGNE
22 Côtes d'Armor
29 Finistère
35 Ille-et-Vilaine
56 Morbihan

BOURGOGNE
21 Côte d'Or
58 Nièvre
71 Saône-et-Loire
89 Yonne

CENTRE
18 Cher
28 Eure-et-Loire
36 Indre
37 Indre-et-Loire
41 Loir-et-Cher
45 Loiret

CHAMPAGNE
08 Ardennes
10 Aube
51 Marne
52 Haute-Marne

CORSE
2A Corse-du-Sud
2B Haute-Corse

FRANCHE-COMTÉ
25 Doubs
39 Jura
70 Haute-Saône
90 Territoire de Belfort

HAUTE-NORMANDIE
27 Eure
76 Seine-Maritime

LANGUEDOC-ROUSSILLON
11 Aude
30 Gard
34 Hérault
48 Lozère
66 Pyrénées-Orientales

LIMOUSIN
19 Corrèze
23 Creuse
87 Haute-Vienne

LORRAINE
54 Meurthe-et-Moselle
55 Meuse
57 Moselle
88 Vosges

MIDI-PYRÉNÉES
09 Ariège
12 Aveyron
31 Haute-Garonne
32 Gers
46 Lot
65 Hautes-Pyrénées
81 Tarn
82 Tarn-et-Garonne

NORD-PAS-DE-CALAIS
59 Nord
62 Pas-de-Calais

PAYS DE LA LOIRE
44 Loire-Atlantique
49 Maine-et-Loire
53 Mayenne
72 Sarthe
85 Vendée

PICARDIE
02 Aisne
60 Oise
80 Somme

POITOU-CHARENTES
16 Charente
17 Charente-Maritime
79 Deux-Sèvres
86 Vienne

PROVENCE-CÔTE D'AZUR
04 Alpes-de-Haute-Provence
05 Hautes-Alpes
06 Alpes-Maritimes
13 Bouches-du-Rhône
83 Var
84 Vaucluse

RÉGION PARISIENNE
75 Ville de Paris
77 Seine-et-Marne
78 Yvelines
91 Essonne
92 Hauts-de-Seine
93 Seine-Saint-Denis
94 Val-de-Marne
95 Val-d'Oise

RHÔNE-ALPES
01 Ain
07 Ardèche
26 Drôme
38 Isère
42 Loire
69 Rhône
73 Savoie
74 Haute-Savoie

immigration. Since that time, non-EC nationals have had a very hard time getting permission to work in France. Unemployment presently stands at 11.5%.

Although the income tax system is progressive, about two-thirds of tax revenue comes from indirect taxation, making France's tax system inequitable for French taxpayers and budget travellers alike.

Natural Resources

France's large deposits of coal, many of which are along the Belgian border, are now mostly exhausted. Iron ore is mined in Lorraine –

where two-thirds of steel production takes place – and Normandy. Bauxite (aluminium ore) was named after the Provençal village of Les Baux, near Arles, where the stuff was discovered in 1821 and first mined in 1882. Uranium is produced in the Vendée and the Massif Central.

Banking

Although a privatisation programme has recently been implemented, the government still plays a dominant role in banking and finance. State control of the Banque de France, the country's central bank, and the three largest commercial banks, Crédit Lyonnais, Société Générale and Banque Nationale de Paris, began in 1946. Most of the rest of the country's banks were nationalised by the Socialists in the early 1980s. As a result of this heavy state involvement, the banks tend to be overcautious, France's capital markets are weak and underdeveloped and the Paris stock market is much smaller than its counterparts in London or Frankfurt. Many French insurance companies are also owned by the government.

Industry

France is one of the world's most industrialised nations, with some 40% of the workforce employed in the industrial sector. About 50% of GNP comes from industrial production. However, there is poor coordination between academic research and companies that might turn good ideas into products, and the country has fewer large corporations – an important source of private capital and investment in research and development – than other industrialised nations of similar size. Many of the large firms it does have are state-owned and despite (or perhaps because of) large subsidies have difficulty competing internationally.

One of the most important components of the industrial sector is motorcar production, whose two major manufacturers employ almost 200,000 people, only one in 20 of whom are unionised. State-owned Renault, confiscated in 1945 after Louis Renault was

charged with having collaborated with the Germans, is renowned for producing economical cars with a bit of pizzazz. It almost linked up with Sweden's Volvo in 1993 but the deal fell through. Its private-sector competitor, the Peugeot-Citroën-Talbot group, makes Peugeots, which have a reputation for being sober and hardy, and Citroëns, known for their off-beat ingenuity. Together, both companies account for almost two-thirds of the cars sold in France. Production facilities are concentrated in the Paris region.

The French have seen themselves as being at the forefront of aviation technology since Louis Blériot became the first person to fly across the English Channel in 1909. The country's important aerospace industry, whose flagship is state-owned Aérospatiale, has an especially strong presence in Toulouse, where Airbuses (produced by the six-nation Airbus Industrie consortium) are assembled. France is the prime mover behind the European Space Agency's Ariane rockets, launched from French Guiana (in South America), and the strongly supported Hermès space shuttle project, until it was shelved in November 1991. The industry's most spectacular commercial flop was the Concorde, produced in the 1970s by an Anglo-French consortium. Only 14 of the supersonic jets were ever produced, and the only airlines that fly them are Air France and British Airways.

Unions

Although France's unions are quite powerful in the public sector (eg the SNCF, the SNCM and the Paris metro), which they often paralyse for a day to press their demands, they are weak in industry and commerce. Only 15% of the French workforce is unionised – the lowest proportion in the EC outside Spain and Portugal.

The huge *manifestations* (demonstrations) you often see in Paris are primarily ceremonial and belie the unions' inability to take truly effective action. The largest strike in postwar Europe took place in May 1968, when, to express support for the students' revolt, nine million French people went on strike.

France's four largest labour unions are the Communist-led Confédération Générale du Travail (CGT); the Catholic-oriented, pro-Socialist Confédération Française et Démocratique du Travail (CFDT); the moderate, pro-Socialist Force Ouvrière (FO); and the small, white-collar Confédération Générale des Cadres (CGC). The CGT and the CFDT are theoretically dedicated to the overthrow of capitalism and have tended to see cooperation with companies as a form of collaboration with the enemy.

Agriculture

France, which has a disproportionately large agricultural sector, is the largest agricultural producer and exporter in the EC. Its production of wheat, barley, maize (corn) and cheese is especially significant. The country is largely self-sufficient except for certain tropical products, like bananas and coffee. France is also an important producer of perfume, many of whose essences (eg lavender) are grown in the south-east.

Despite this, the agricultural sector is the weakest part of the economy, in large part because many of the holdings are too small and low-tech for efficient production. For instance, France has only 34 tractors per 1000 hectares, while Germany has 91. Overproduction of fruit, cheese and wine has also been a problem. French farmers consistently oppose reforming the EC's system of agricultural subsidies, and they often stage protests that involve attacking trucks bringing cheap fruit and vegetables from Spain.

France has large forestry and fishing sectors. About half of the fish caught, which include cod, halibut, herring, mackerel, sardines and tuna, are landed in Britanny.

Energy

Although France has a large petroleum refining industry, part of the country's huge chemical sector, it has to import almost all of its oil. By far the company's largest oil company is state-owned Elf-Aquitaine. The large natural gas field north of the Pyrenees at Lacq (near Pau), discovered in the 1950s, is almost exhausted.

To raise its energy self-sufficiency to the present level of almost 50% (up from 22% in 1973), France has turned from imported oil to other sources. Nuclear power accounts for three-quarters of France's electricity production, the highest rate in the world. A further one-quarter of the country's electricity is produced by hydroelectric plants, over two-thirds of them in the Alps. Brittany's Barrage de la Rance tidal power station near Saint Malo has been producing electricity from the action of the tides since 1966. There have also been experiments using the geothermal energy of France's many hot springs.

POPULATION & PEOPLE

France currently has a population of 55.8 million, one-sixth of whom reside in the Paris metropolitan area. The percentage of French people living in rural and mountain areas has been declining since the 1950s.

In the past century, internal migration has tended to increase the population of the plains at the expense of upland areas, some of which have been significantly depopulated (eg the southern Alps, the Pyrenees and the Massif Central). In rural areas, people have moved from the countryside to small towns, which have themselves been losing residents to the cities.

For much of the last two centuries, France has had a considerably lower rate of population growth than its neighbours, in part because the use of birth control for family planning began at the end of the 18th century, much earlier than anywhere else in the world.

Immigration

During the last 150 years, France has accepted more immigrants than any other European country, including significant numbers of political refugees. Despite this, most French people, regardless of their ancestry, feel that they belong to a single nation.

Between 1850 and WW I, the country received 4.3 million immigrants. A further three million immigrants arrived between the world wars, in part because the slaughter

of WW I left the country with a serious shortage of workers. From 1850 to WW II, most immigrants to France came from other parts of Europe (especially Italy, Spain, Belgium, Switzerland, Poland and Russia), but the post-WW II economic boom, also accompanied by a labour shortage, attracted several million workers – most of them unskilled – and their families from North Africa and French-speaking sub-Saharan Africa.

During the late 1950s and early '60s, as the French colonial empire collapsed, over one million French settlers returned to metropolitan France from Algeria, other parts of Africa and Indochina.

Although large-scale immigration was stopped in 1974, there has, in recent years, been a racist backlash against the country's non-white immigrant communities, especially Muslims from North Africa, who have tended to assimilate into French society and the French economy more slowly than their European predecessors. In 1993, the French government changed its immigration laws to make it harder for immigrants to get French citizenship or bring over their families.

EDUCATION

France's education system has long been highly centralised, a fact reflected in teachers' status as civil servants. Its high standards have produced great intellectuals and almost total literacy, but equal opportunities are still not available to people of all classes. Indeed, in certain areas the system is unabashedly elitist.

Private schools, most of which are Catholic (though Protestant and Jewish schools also exist), educate about 17% of students – and 23% of students planning to attend university. At almost all private schools, the state pays staff salaries and some of the operating costs on the condition that the school follow certain curriculum guidelines. As a result of the subsidies, tuition fees are very low.

Primary

One-third of children begin attending a crèche (day nursery), a jardin d'enfants (day care) or an école maternelle (nursery school) at the age of two. By age three they are joined by virtually all their peers. Until the age of 10 or 11, all children – rich or poor, gifted or slow – follow pretty much the same curriculum. Primary education became compulsory for all children between the ages of six and 13 in 1882. Education is now compulsory until the age of 16.

Secondary

Lycée (secondary school) studies are divided into two stages. The first cycle (collège), attended by children aged 11 to 15, follows a general-studies curriculum that is more or less the same in all schools. During the second cycle, which is for 15 to 18-year-olds, pupils can choose between the academic track and a less highly regarded vocational track. Some prestigious senior lycées are the almost exclusive domain of the competitive and ambitious offspring of the middle and upper classes.

Only students in the academic track can sit for the university entrance exam known as the baccalauréat and commonly referred to as le bac. At present, 73% of high school students sit for the bac, double the proportion in 1980 and considerably more than other European countries. A new vocational baccalauréat has recently been instituted.

France's secondary education has long been the target of critics who charge that the curriculum is irrelevant to modern life and that nonparticipatory teaching methods tend to foster conformism rather than creative and synthetic thinking. Reforms have been strongly resisted by the highly unionised teachers, whose generally left-wing politics have in no way moderated their resistance to change, which they fear will bring a drop in standards.

Post-Secondary

Universities Anyone who has passed the bac is entitled to a free place in one of France's 77 universities, an option taken up by about one-third of young people (again, the highest proportion in Western Europe). The catch is

that after the first year of study, students must face a gruelling examination that only 30% to 40% of them end up passing (in medicine, one in six passes). Only students who pass can continue their studies; everyone else must make do with other options, such as attending a two-year *collège universitaire*. The drop-out rate is exacerbated by the paucity of government stipends, received by only one in eight students.

French university degrees are slightly different from those granted in the English-speaking countries. A *licence*, awarded after three years, is similar to a bachelor's degree. It is followed by a *maîtrise*, roughly parallel to a master's degree, which is in turn followed in some fields by a *diplôme d'études approfondies* (DEA) or a *diplôme d'études supérieures spécialisées* (DESS), taken before completing a PhD. The prestigious *doctorat*, necessary to become a full professor, takes many years of highly specialised research. The highest-level teaching qualification is known as an *agrégation*.

The violent student protests of May 1968, which saw barricades go up on the streets of Paris, were followed by a series of wide-ranging reforms of the higher education system. In response to students' demands for a less rigid atmosphere, greater contact with teachers and more student input into university decision-making, the government decentralised the universities and gave them a certain degree of institutional autonomy. Unfortunately, many of the representative bodies established to give a greater voice to professors and students have become highly politicised. Although spending on education has risen by 40% since 1988 (from 5% to 6.6% of GDP), most universities still have far too many students for the facilities available.

In 1793, the Revolutionary government abolished the universities, some of which had been founded in the Middle Ages. They were re-established by Napoleon in 1808. The Sorbonne, established in 1257, was long the country's leading university. Now incorporated into the University of Paris system

(part of which occupies the old Sorbonne buildings in the Latin Quarter), it has for centuries helped to draw many of France's most talented and energetic people to Paris, creating a serious provincial brain drain. Today, about one-third of French students study in Paris.

Grandes Écoles Some of France's ablest and most ambitious young people do not attend the overcrowded universities. About 5% of students are enrolled in the country's 140 prestigious *grandes écoles*, elitist institutions offering training in such fields as business management, engineering and the applied sciences. Graduates of the grandes écoles have some of the best jobs in the technocracy open to them, and their careers are often helped along by extensive old-boys' networks. A high percentage of the top positions in the public sector, the traditionally less-prestigious private sector and politics are filled by grandes écoles graduates.

Students who would like to attend a grande école must take an intensely competitive nationwide exam, preparation for which involves two or three years of rigourous post-bac study.

The most prestigious grandes écoles include the École Polytechnique, the Institut d'Études Politiques (Institute of Political Studies), the École Nationale d'Administration (ENA; National School of Administration), the École des Mines (School of Mines), the École des Ponts et Chaussées (School of Civil Engineering) and the École des Hautes Études Commerciales (HEC; School of Higher Commercial Studies). The École Normale Supérieure, which trains university and lycée teachers in the humanities, has a similar status.

ARTS
Architecture
Megaliths The earliest human-made monuments to mark the French landscape were stone megaliths erected during the Neolithic period (about 4000 to 2400 BC): menhirs (single stones standing upright), dolmens

(horizontal stones supported by several vertical ones) and cromlechs (circles of stones placed upright). For details see the Megalith aside in the Brittany chapter. Although megaliths are mainly found in Brittany, particularly around Carnac, there are others in northern Languedoc (eg around the town of Mende) and on Corsica (eg Filitosa).

Gallo-Roman When the Romans arrived in France in the 1st century BC, they immediately established colonies and set about bringing the benefits of Roman civilisation to the residents of Gaul. Towards this goal, they constructed a large number of public works projects all over the country: aqueducts, fortifications, marketplaces, temples to worship Romanised Gallic deities, theatres and amphitheatres, triumphal arches and bathhouses. Whenever possible, the Romans established regular street grids.

While central and northern France is not devoid of such structures (eg Autun, Lyon and the Musée de Cluny in Paris), southern France – especially Provence and the coastal plains of Languedoc – is the place to go in search of France's Gallo-Roman legacy. Testimony to the Romans' architectural brilliance includes the Pont du Gard aqueduct between Nîmes and Avignon, the colossal amphitheatres at Nîmes and Arles, the theatre at Orange, the Maison Carrée in Nîmes and the villas, shops and public buildings in Vaison-la-Romaine.

Dark Ages Although quite a few churches were built during the Merovingian and Carolingian periods (5th to 10th centuries), many of them on sites sacred to the Romans, very little remains of them. However, traces of churches from this period can be seen at Saint Denis (north of Paris) and in Auxerre's Saint Germain abbey.

Romanesque A religious revival in the 11th century led to the construction of a large number of Romanesque (*roman*) churches, so-called because their architects adopted many architectural elements (eg vaulting) from Gallo-Roman (*gallo-romain*) buildings

still standing at the time. Romanesque buildings typically have round arches, heavy walls whose few windows let in very little light, and a lack of ornamentation that borders on the austere. What decoration there is, was inspired by the Romans.

Many of the most famous Romanesque churches -- Basilique Saint Sernin in Toulouse, for instance – were built for pilgrims en route to Santiago de Compostela in Spain (see the Background Note in the Limousin, Périgord & Quercy chapter) Others, like Caen's two famous Romanesque abbeys, were erected by prominent personalities. Chateaux built during this era reflected the political uncertainties of the Middle Ages and tended to be massive, heavily fortified structures that afforded few luxuries to their inhabitants. The Romanesque style remained popular until the mid-12th century.

Gothic The Gothic style originated in the mid-12th century in northern France, whose great wealth enabled it to attract the finest architects, engineers and artisans. Gothic structures are characterised by ribbed vaults carved with great precision, pointed (rather than rounded) arches, slender verticals, chapels along the nave and chancel (often built by rich people or guilds), refined decoration and large stained-glass windows.

The first Gothic building was the basilica in Saint Denis, which combined various late Romanesque elements to create a new kind of structural support in which each arch counteracted and complemented its neighbours. Gothic technology and the width and height it made possible subsequently spread to the rest of Europe. Cathedrals built in the early Gothic style, which lasted until about 1230, were majestic but lacked the lightness and airiness for which later works are justly famous, in part because thick stone buttresses had to be placed between the panels of stained glass (obviously, windows alone could not support the roof).

The success of early Gothic churches encouraged experimentation by architects and engineers. It was soon found that reducing the bulk of the buttresses and adding one

or two outer piers to carry the thrust created a lighter building without compromising structural integrity. This discovery gave rise to flying buttresses, which helped lift the Gothic style to its greatest achievements between 1230 and 1300. During this period, when French architecture dominated the European scene for the first time, High Gothic masterpieces such as the vastly influential cathedral at Chartres and its successors at Reims and Amiens were decorated with ornate tracery (the delicate stone ribwork on stained-glass windows) and huge, colourful rose windows.

Because of the fiasco at Beauvais cathedral, whose 48-metre-high vaults collapsed in 1272 and again in 1284, it became clear that Gothic technology had reached limits beyond which it was imprudent to go. As a result, architects became less interested in sheer size and put more energy into ornamentation.

In the 14th century, the Rayonnant (Radiant) Gothic style – named after the radiating tracery of the rose windows – developed, with interiors becoming ever lighter thanks to broader windows and more translucent stained glass. One of the most influential Rayonnant buildings was the Sainte Chapelle in Paris, whose stained glass forms a sheer curtain of glazing. Another fine monument from this period is Église Saint Urbain in Troyes.

By the 15th century, decorative extravagance rather than structural innovation dominated Gothic architecture, leading to Flamboyant Gothic, so named because its wavy stone carving was said to resemble flames. Beautifully lacy examples of Flamboyant architecture include the Clocher Neuf at Chartres, Rouen cathedral's Tour de Beurre, Église Saint Maclou in Rouen and the spire of Strasbourg cathedral. Flamboyant Gothic survived well into the 16th century despite the changes in taste brought about by the French Renaissance.

Renaissance The Renaissance, which began in Italy in the early 1400s, set out to accomplish the *renaissance* (rebirth) of classical Greek and Roman culture. It first had

an impact on France at the tail end of the 15th century, when Charles VIII began a series of invasions of Italy that would, over the next 30 years, expose the French aristocracy to Italian art and architecture. Because Milan was under French rule for the first quarter of the 16th century, much of this contact took place in Lombardy.

The French Renaissance, which saw medieval architectural techniques combined with the new ideas about proportion, symmetry and ornamentation brought from Italy, is divided into two periods: the early Renaissance and Mannerism. During the early Renaissance, a variety of classical components and decorative motifs (columns, tunnel vaults, round arches, domes, etc) were blended with the rich decoration of Flamboyant Gothic, a synthesis best exemplified by the Château de Chambord in the Loire Valley, famed for its double-helix stairway. Nearby Chenonceau and Azay-le-Rideau date from the same period. But the changeover from late Gothic to Renaissance can be seen most clearly in the Château de Blois, whose Flamboyant section was built only 15 years before its early Renaissance wing.

Mannerism began around 1530, when François I (who had been so deeply impressed by what he'd seen in Italy that he brought Leonardo da Vinci to Amboise in 1516) hired Italian architects and artists – many of them disciples of Michelangelo or Raphael – to design and decorate his new chateau at Fontainebleau. Over the following decades, French architects who had studied in Italy took over from their Italian colleagues. In 1546 Frenchman Pierre Lescot designed the richly decorated southwestern corner of the Louvre's Cour Carrée. The Petit Château at Chantilly was built about a decade later.

French Renaissance architecture was very much the province of the aristocracy, for it was they who commissioned – and lived in – the great chateaux of the Loire Valley and the Île de France, in which the feudal castle, stripped of its defensive functions, met the Italian villa. In part because so many works in the new style were designed by artists

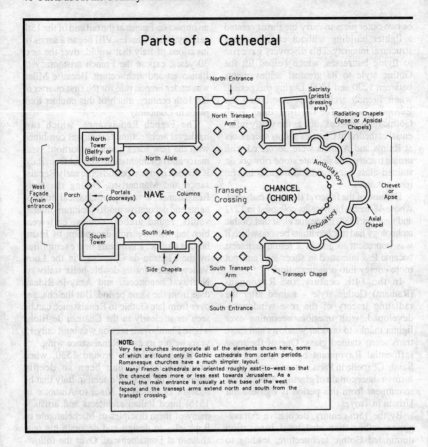

Parts of a Cathedral

North Entrance

North Transept Arm

Sacristy (priests' dressing area)

Radiating Chapels (Apse or Apsidal Chapels)

North Tower (Belfry or Belltower)

North Aisle

Ambulatory

West Façade (main entrance)

Porch

Portals (doorways)

NAVE

Columns

Transept Crossing

CHANCEL (CHOIR)

Chevet or Apse

South Tower

South Aisle

Ambulatory

Axial Chapel

Side Chapels

South Transept Arm

Transept Chapel

South Entrance

NOTE:
Very few churches incorporate all of the elements shown here, some of which are found only in Gothic cathedrals from certain periods. Romanesque churches have a much simpler layout.

Many French cathedrals are oriented roughly east-to-west so that the chancel faces more or less east towards Jerusalem. As a result, the main entrance is usually at the base of the west façade and the transept arms extend north and south from the transept crossing.

imported from Italy, the middle classes – resentful French artisans among them – remained loyal to the indigenous Gothic style, and Gothic churches continued to be built throughout the 1500s. The Mannerist style lasted until the early 1600s.

Baroque Period During the baroque era, which lasted from the end of the 1500s to the late 1700s, painting, sculpture and classical architecture were integrated to create structures and interiors of great subtlety, refinement and elegance.

The word 'baroque', which refers to a set

of varied styles, some of them brought to France from Italy, was originally a term of contempt for the baroque style's extravagant ornamentation. Indeed, the style, which thanks to Louis XIV came to be closely associated with Absolutism, remained wholly discredited until the 1950s. In part because the term is so nebulous, buildings in France are rarely called baroque. Rather, the baroque period is often subdivided into styles named after Louis XIII, Louis XIV, Louis XV and Louis XVI.

Salomon de Brosse, who designed Paris's Palais du Luxembourg (1615), set the stage

USEFUL TERMS:

Ambulatory
The ambulatory, a continuation of the aisles of the nave around the chancel, forms a processional path that allows pilgrims relatively easy access to radiating chapels, saints' relics and altars around the chancel.

Clerestory Windows
The clerestory windows, a row of tall windows above the triforium (see below), are often difficult to see because they're so high above the floor.

Cloister
The cloister (cloître), a four-sided enclosure surrounded by covered, collonnaded arcades, is often attached to a monastery church or a cathedral. In monasteries, the cloister served as the focal point of the monks' educational and recreational activities.

Narthex
The narthex is an enclosed entrance vestibule just inside the west entrance. It was once reserved for penitents and the not-yet-baptised.

Crypt
The crypt (crypte) is a chamber under the church floor in which saints, martyrs, early church figures and worthy personages are buried. In many Gothic churches, the crypt is often one of the few extant parts of earlier, pre-Gothic structures on the site. A visit to the crypt, usually reached via stairs on one or both sides of the chancel, may involve a small fee.

Rood Screen
A rood screen, also known as a jube (jubé), is an often-elaborate structure separating the chancel from the nave. Because rood screens made it difficult to see religious ceremonies taking place in the chancel, most were removed in the 17th and 18th centuries.

Rose Window
The circular stained-glass windows commonly found in Gothic cathedrals over the west entrance and at the north and south ends of the transept arms are known as rose or wheel windows. The stained-glass panels are usually separated from each other by elaborate stone bar tracery, which people inside the church see in silhouette.

Treasury
A treasury (trésor) is a secure room for storing and displaying precious liturgical objects. It may be open shorter hours than the church itself. Visiting often involves a small entry fee.

Triforium
The triforium is an arcaded or collonnaded gallery above the nave, choir or transept. Most triforia are directly above the columns that separate the aisles from the nave or the ambulatory from the chancel. From the late 13th century, larger clerestory windows often replaced the triforium.

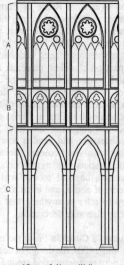

View of Nave Wall

A. Clerestory Windows
B. Triforium Gallery
C. Aisle (behind the columns)

---

for France's two most prominent early baroque architects: François Mansart, designer of the classical wing of the Château de Blois (1635), and his younger rival, Louis Le Vau, the first architect of Versailles, where Louis XIV, ever keen to associate himself with the Caesars of ancient Rome, made classicism with baroque features his official style. Baroque elements are particularly in evidence in Versailles's lavish interiors, such as the Galerie des Glaces (Hall of Mirrors). Jules Hardouin-Mansart, Le Vau's successor at Versailles, also designed the Église du Dome (1670s) at the

Invalides in Paris, considered the finest church built in France during the 17th century.

During the latter half of the 1600s, André Le Nôtre, the royal landscape architect, designed formal gardens characterised by terraces, fountains, statues and neatly clipped hedges. His works served as extensions of the chateaux to which they were attached. Le Nôtre's finest works are the Jardin des Tuileries in Paris and the gardens at Versailles.

Rococo Rococo, a derivation of baroque

that developed around the time that Paris took over from Rome as Europe's artistic centre, was popular during the Enlightenment (1700-80). In France, rococo was confined almost exclusively to the interiors of private residences and had a minimal impact on churches, chateaux and façades, which continued to follow the conventional rules of baroque classicism. Rococo interiors, such as the oval rooms of the Archives Nationales building in Paris, were lighter, smoother and airier than their 17th-century predecessors and tended towards pastels rather than vivid colours. Because of what neoclassicists saw as rococo's ornamental excesses, the word 'rococo' was long used as a term of abuse, and even today it is often used to refer to anything that suffers from overly elaborate decoration.

Vauban's Citadels From the mid-1600s to the mid-1800s, the design of defensive fortifications was dominated around the world by the work of one person, Sébastien Le Prestre de Vauban (1633-1707). Born to a relatively poor family of the petty nobility, he worked as a military engineer during almost the entire reign of Louis XIV, revolutionising both the design of fortresses and siege techniques. To defend France's frontiers, he built 33 immense citadels, many of them star-shaped and surrounded by moats, and rebuilt or refined over a hundred more.

Vauban's most famous citadel is at Lille, but his work can also be seen at Antibes, Belfort, Belle-Île, Besançon, Concarneau, Neuf-Brisach, Perpignan, Saint Jean Pied de Port and Verdun.

Neoclassicism Neoclassical architecture, which emerged in about 1780 and remained popular until the mid-19th century, had its roots in the renewed interest in classical forms sparked by the mid-18th- century flowering of archaeological enquiry. Although it was in part a reaction against rococo, it was more profoundly a search for order, reason and serenity through the adoption of the forms and conventions of Graeco-Roman antiquity: columns, simple geometric forms and traditional ornamentation.

France's greatest 18th-century neoclassical architect was Jacques-Germain Soufflot, who designed Paris's Panthéon. But neoclassicism really came into its own under Napoleon, who used it extensively for monumental architecture intended to embody the grandeur of imperial France. Well-known Paris sights designed (though not necessarily executed) during the First Empire (1804-14) include the Arc de Triomphe, La Madeleine, the façade of the Palais Bourbon, the Arc du Carrousel at the Louvre and the Paris Bourse.

Art Nouveau Art Nouveau, which emerged in Europe and the USA in the 1890s but came to be seen as outdated by around 1910, is characterised by sinuous curves and flowing, asymmetrical forms reminiscent of tendrilous vines, water lilies, the patterns on insect wings and the flowering boughs of trees. Influenced by the arrival of objets d'art from Japan, its name comes from a Paris gallery that featured works in the new style.

Art Nouveau, best known these days for its output of posters, had a profound impact on all of the applied arts, including interior design, glass-making, wrought-iron work and furniture making. All of these were expressed in Art Nouveau architecture, which combined a variety of materials – including iron, brick, glass and ceramics – in ways never before seen. France's major Art Nouveau centres were Nancy and Paris; the latter is still graced by Hector Guimard's noodle-like metro entrances. There are some fine Art Nouveau interiors in the Musée d'Orsay, an Art Nouveau glass roof over the Grand Palais and, on Rue Pavée in the Marais, a synagogue designed by Guimard.

Inner Cities & Suburbs France's inner cities are considered highly desirable places to live in, and their centuries-old buildings are eagerly sought by people of means. Conversely, many suburban districts built after the war, especially those with high-rise apartment blocks, have been all but aban-

doned by those who can afford to live elsewhere. Many of these areas, whose residents include a high percentage of poor immigrants from North Africa, suffer from crime and a variety of social problems.

Contemporary Architecture France's leaders have long sought to immortalise themselves by erecting huge, public edifices – known as *grands projets* – in Paris, but François Mitterrand has surpassed all but a handful of his predecessors.

Since the early 1980s, Paris has seen the construction of such projets as IM Pei's pyramid at the Louvre, an architectural *cause célèbre* in the late 1980s; the city's new opera house, Opéra-Bastille; the Grande Arche in the skyscraper district of La Défense; the huge science museum and park at La Villette; Parc André Citroën in the western corner of the 15e arrondissement; the new Finance Ministry offices in Bercy; and the controversy-plagued future home of the Bibliothèque Nationale (the national library) – known only half in jest as the Très Grande Bibliothèque (Very Large Library) – whose four, sun-drenched skyscrapers are supposed to house the stacks while readers peruse their books in an underground atrium.

Painting
16th Century & Earlier Sculpture and stained glass rather than paintings were the main adornments of the medieval Gothic cathedrals of northern France, in part because the many windows left little wall-space. During the 14th-century residence of the popes in Avignon, however, the Sienese, French and Spanish artists working at the papal court created an influential style of mural painting, examples of which can be seen in the city's Palais des Papes.

In the 15th century, France might have have served as a meeting ground for the rich traditions of Italy and Flanders, but the Hundred Years' War got in the way. In the 16th century, the Wars of Religion further hampered the development of French painting. Most French painters of the Renaissance copied Italian models with little verve.

17th Century Voltaire wrote that French painting began with Nicolas Poussin (1594-1665). This is certainly a biased judgement, but it is true in the sense that Poussin is the first French painter to really stand out from contemporary schools. Poussin, who continues to influence artists up to the present day, is normally considered a baroque painter, and he frequently set scenes from classical mythology and the Bible in ordered landscapes, often bathed in the golden light of late afternoon. An intense sky-blue is his colour signature.

Poussin spent most of his working life in Rome, where he was friends with Claude Gelée, better known as Claude Lorrain. His main subject was the slanting light of the Roman countryside, and in this shift of emphasis he anticipated the impressionists.

In 1648 Charles le Brun founded the Royal Academy, and, as its head, dominated French painting until the decisive intervention of Jean-Antoine Watteau. Watteau's scenes of concerts and picnics are set in gardens whose fantastic nature is emphasised by the occasional presence of characters from the Italian commedia dell'arte.

18th Century In the 18th century, Jean-Baptiste Chardin brought the humbler domesticity of the Dutch masters to French art. He was the first painter to regard still life as an essay in composition rather than a show of skill in reproduction.

In 1785 the public reacted with enthusiasm to two large paintings with clear republican messages, *The Oath of the Horatii* and *Brutus Condemning His Son* by Jacques Louis David. David became one of the leaders of the Revolution, and a virtual dictator in matters of art, where he advocated a precise, severe classicism. He nearly lost his head along with Robespierre, but was soon adopted by Napoleon as official state painter. In this capacity he produced vast pictures such as *Le Sacre de Napoléon* showing the coronation of the emperor in 1804. He is perhaps best remembered for the famous painting of Marat lying dead in his bath.

19th Century Jean Auguste Dominique Ingres, David's most gifted pupil, continued in the neoclassical line. The historical pictures to which he devoted most of his life are now generally regarded as inferior to his portraits.

The gripping *Raft of the Medusa* by Théodore Géricault is on the threshold of romanticism; if Géricault had not died young, he would probably have become a leader of the movement, along with his friend Eugène Delacroix. Delacroix searched through the histories and literatures of many countries to find subjects to suit his turbulent, dramatic style. His most famous picture, perhaps, is *La Liberté Conduisant le Peuple* (Freedom Leading the People), which commemorates the revolution of 1830.

While the romantics revamped the subject-picture, the members of the Barbizon School effected a parallel transformation of landscape painting. The school derived its name from the village of Barbizon near the forest of Fontainebleau, where Camille Corot and Jean-François Millet, among others, gathered to paint in the open air. Corot is best known for his landscapes, while Millet took many of his subjects from peasant life and had a strong influence on Van Gogh. Reproductions of his *L'Angélus* still hang over many mantelpieces in rural France.

Millet anticipated the realist programme of Gustave Courbet, a prominent member of the Paris Commune, whose paintings show the misery of manual labour and the cramped lives of the working class. Courbet was also a fine landscape painter.

Édouard Manet used realism to depict the life of the Parisian middle classes, yet he included in his pictures numerous references to the old masters. His *Déjeuner sur l'herbe* and *Olympia* were considered scandalous, largely because they broke with the traditional treatment of their subject matter.

In later years, Manet's work displayed impressionist influences, as he chose to focus on the use of colour and form, rather than the subject. Impressionism, initially a term of derision, was taken from the title of an experimental painting by Claude Monet of 1874, *Impression: soleil levant* (Impression: Sunrise). Monet was the leading figure of the school, which counted among its members Alfred Sisley, Camille Pisarro, Berthe Morisot and Pierre-Auguste Renoir. Impressionist technique obliterated sharp outlines and did away with space as a structural factor. The impressionists' main aim was to capture fleeting light effects, and light came to dominate the content of their painting. For instance, Monet painted the same subjects – cathedrals, haystacks, poplars, water-lilies – many times to show the transient effect of light at different times of day.

Edgar Degas was a fellow traveller of the impressionists, but he preferred his studio to open-air painting, and was not much interested in landscape as such. He found his favourite subjects at the racecourse and the ballet. His superb draughtmanship seized on gestures and movements ignored by earlier artists, and he invented new kinds of composition (for example, depicting subjects from an oblique angle, or letting the edge of a painting cut off a figure). Henri de Toulouse-Lautrec was a great admirer of Degas and chose similar subjects: people in the bars, brothels and music-halls of Montmartre. He is best known for his posters and lithographs in which the distortion of the figures is both caricatural and decorative.

Paul Cézanne is best known for his still lifes and landscapes depicting the south of France, while the name of Paul Gauguin immediately conjures up his studies of Tahitian women. Both he and Cézanne are usually referred to as postimpressionists, something of a catch-all term for the diverse styles which flowed from impressionism.

In the late 19th century, Gauguin worked for a time in Arles with the Dutch artist Vincent van Gogh, who spent most of his painting life in France. A brilliant, innovative painter, Van Gogh produced haunting self-portraits and landscapes in which colour assumes an expressive and emotive quality. His later technique foreshadowed pointillism, invented by Georges Seurat. Seurat

applied paint in small dots or uniform brush strokes of unmixed colour, producing fine mosaics of warm and cool tones. He combined his colour theory with a classic sense of composition.

Henri Rousseau was a contemporary of the great postimpressionists but his 'naive' art was totally unaffected by them. A customs official, he painted on Sundays, and his dreamlike pictures of the Paris suburbs, jungle and desert scenes have had a lasting influence on 20th-century art.

Gustave Moreau was a member of the Symbolist school. His treatment of mythological subjects can be seen to eerie effect in his old studio, now the Musée Moreau in Paris.

20th Century French painting in the 20th century has been characterised by a bewildering diversity of styles, two of which are particularly significant: fauvism and cubism. Fauvism took its name from the slur of a critic who compared the exhibitors at the 1906 autumn salon with wild beasts *(fauves)* because of their radical use of intensely bright colours. Among these wild painters were Henri Matisse, André Derain and Maurice de Vlaminck.

Cubism was effectively launched when, in 1907, the Spanish prodigy Pablo Picasso produced *Les Demoiselles d'Avignon*. Cubism, as developed by Picasso, Georges Braque and Juan Gris, decomposed the subject into a system of intersecting planes and presented various aspects of it simultaneously. Collages incorporating bits of cloth, wood, string, newspaper and other things that happened to be lying around were a Cubist speciality.

After WW I the School of Paris was formed by a group of expressionists, mostly foreign-born, like Amedeo Modigliani from Italy and Marc Chagall from Russia. Chagall's pictures combine fantasy and folklore.

Dada, a literary and artistic movement of revolt, started in Germany and Switzerland during WW I. It was fuelled by disgust with the war and bourgeois values, and it culti-vated scorn for commonly accepted ideas and the art of the past. In France, one of the principal dadaists was Marcel Duchamp, whose Mona Lisa adorned with moustache and goatee epitomise the spirit of the movement.

The German dadaist Max Ernst moved to Paris in 1922 and was instrumental in starting surrealism, an offshoot of dada which flourished between the wars. Drawing on the theories of Freud, surrealism attempted to reunite the conscious and unconscious realms, to permeate everyday life with fantasies and dreams. The most famous surrealist painter, the Spaniard Salvador Dali, came relatively late to the movement.

WW II ended Paris's role as the world's artistic nerve centre. Many artists left France, and though some returned after the war, the capital never regained its old magnetism.

Although the contemporary French art scene cannot compare with the brilliance of earlier periods, art is certainly not suffering from neglect in France. Many of the names mentioned in this section still appear on billboards and posters in Paris and other major cities, for we are now in the age of the 'art retrospective'. Fantastic exhibitions ensure continuing interest in the painters who made France the artistic centre of Europe. They also provide wonderful opportunities to familiarise oneself with artists or movements of particular significance.

Sculpture

At the end of the 11th century, sculptors began to decorate the portals, capitals, altars and fonts of Romanesque churches, illustrating Bible stories and the lives of saints. In Languedoc and Burgundy especially, the figures were distorted to heighten the impression of movement.

In the 13th century, when the cathedral became the centre of monumental building, sculpture spread from the central portal to the whole façade, whose brightly painted and carved surface offered a symbolic summary of Christian doctrine. Sculptors from all over Europe were trained in the ateliers which developed around the great cathedrals. In the

14th century, the Dutchman Claus Sluter, working at the court of Burgundy, introduced a vigorous realism with his sculptures for the Chartreuse de Champnol monastery in Dijon.

As well as adorning cathedrals, sculpture was increasingly commissioned for the tombs of the nobility. The royal tombs in the Basilica of St Denis, near Paris, illustrate the progress in naturalism from the 13th to the 15th centuries.

Renaissance sculpture was pre-eminently Italian, and dominated by the work of Michelangelo. In France, Pierre Bontemps decorated the beautiful tomb of Francis I at Saint Denis, and Jean Goujon created the Fontaine des Innocents in central Paris. The baroque style is exemplified by Guillaume Coustou's *Horses of Marly* at the entrance to the Champs-Élysées.

In the 19th century memorial statues in public places came to replace sculpted tombs. One of the best artists in the new mode was François Rude, who sculpted the statue of Marshall Ney outside the Closerie des Lilas in Paris and the relief on the Arc de Triomphe. Jean-Baptiste Carpeaux began as a romantic sculptor, but *The Dance* on the Opéra-Garnier in Paris and his fountain in the Luxembourg gardens look back to the warmth and gaiety of the baroque.

At the end of the 19th century Auguste Rodin overcame the conflict of neoclassicism and romanticism. His sumptuous bronze and marble figures of men and women, often intimately entwined, and often incomplete, did much to revitalise sculpture as an expressive medium. Rodin is regarded by some critics as the finest portraitist in the history of the art. His best known works include *The Kiss*, *The Thinker* and *The Burghers of Calais*.

One of Rodin's most gifted pupils was Camille Claudel. Rejected by Rodin after an affair of many years, she suffered a nervous breakdown from which she never fully recovered. Her work, along with that of Rodin, can be seen in the Musée Rodin in Paris.

One of the most important French sculp-

One of Rodin's pieces on display at the Musée Rodin in Paris

tors of the early 20th century was Aristide Maillol, whose voluptuous female nudes show his attachment to formal analysis, in direct contrast to Rodin's emotive style. Braque and Picasso experimented with sculpture, and in the spirit of dada, Marcel Duchamp exhibited 'found objects', such as a urinal, which he titled *Fountain* and signed. The Swiss-born sculptor Alberto Giacometti participated in the surrealist movement in Paris during the 1930s. After WW II he produced a disturbing series of emaciated human figures in bronze.

Literature

Middle Ages The earliest monument of French literature is the *Chanson de Roland*, an epic poem recounting the heroic death of

Charlemagne's nephew Roland, ambushed on the way back from a campaign against the Saracens (Muslims) in Spain. The events took place in 778 AD, but the poem dates from the end of the 11th century.

Medieval French literature was not only about old battles: there were also lyric poems of courtly love composed by the *troubadours*, and there was the new genre of the *roman* (literally, the romance), which often drew on Celtic stories: King Arthur and his court, the search for the Holy Grail, Tristan and Iseult. The *Roman de la Rose*, written by Guillaume de Lorris and Jean de Meung, was a new departure, manipulating allegorical figures such as Fear and Shame rather than characters. Immensely popular in the 13th century, it both resumed and put an end to the tradition of courtly love.

François Villon was condemned to death for having stabbed a lawyer in 1462, but the sentence was commuted to banishment from Paris. As well as his long police record, Villon left a body of poems charged with a highly personal lyricism, among them the *Ballade des femmes du temps jadis*, with its often-quoted refrain: *Mais où sont les neiges d'antan?* ('Where are the snows of yesteryear?').

Renaissance The great landmarks of Rennaissance literature in France are the works of Rabelais, the Pléaide and Montaigne. François Rabelais composed a farcical epic about the adventures of the giant Gargantua and his son Pantagruel. His exuberant narrative blends coarse humour with encyclopedic erudition in a vast fresco that seems to include every kind of person, occupation and jargon to be found in mid-16th-century France.

The Pléaide was a group of poets active in the 1550s and '60s, of whom the best known is Pierre de Ronsard. They are chiefly remembered for their lyric poems. Michel de Montaigne wrote a long series of short essays on all sorts of topics which constitute a fascinating self-portrait.

Classicism The 17th century is known as *le*

grand siècle because it is the century of the great French classical writers. In poetry, François de Malherbe, brought a new rigour to the treatment of rhythm. Transported by the perfection of Malherbe's verses, Jean de La Fontaine recognised his vocation and went on to write his charming *Fables* in the manner of Aesop.

Molière was an actor who became the most popular comic playwright of his time. Plays such as *Tartuffe* are staples of the classical repertoire, and are performed in translation around the world. The tragic playwrights Pierre Corneille and Jean Racine, by contrast, drew their subject matter from history and classical mythology. For instance, the subject of Racine's *Phèdre*, taken from Euripides, is a story of incest and suicide among the descendants of the Greek gods.

The mood of classical tragedy permeates *La Princesse de Clèves* by Marie de La Fayette, which is widely regarded as the first major French novel.

Enlightenment The literature of the 18th century is dominated by the Enlightenment philosophers, among them Voltaire and Jean-Jacques Rousseau. The most durable of Voltaire's works have been his 'philosophical tales', such as *Candide*, which ironically recounts the improbable adventures of a simple soul who is convinced that he is living in the best of all possible worlds, despite the many problems which befall him.

Rousseau came from Switzerland and thought of himself as an exile in France. Voltaire's political writings, in which it is argued that society is fundamentally opposed to nature, were to have a profound and lasting influence on him. Rousseau's sensitivity to landscape and its moods anticipates romanticism, and the insistence on his own singularity in *Les Confessions* makes it the first modern autobiography.

19th Century The 19th century brought Victor Hugo, widely acclaimed for his poetry as well as for his novels *Les Misérables* and *Notre-Dame de Paris*. By virtue of his enormous output, the breadth of his interests and

his technical innovations, Hugo is the key figure of French **romanticism**. He spent 20 years in exile in Belgium and on the Channel island of Guernsey after speaking out about Louis-Napoleon's dictatorial ambitions: 'Because we have had a Napoleon the Great, must we have a Napoleon the Little?' he asked. In 1885 some two million people followed his funeral procession.

Other 19th-century novelists include Stendhal, author of *Le Rouge et le noir*, the story of the rise and fall of a poor young man from the provinces who models himself on Napoleon; Honoré de Balzac, whose vast series of novels, known under the general title of *La Comédie humaine*, approaches a social history of France; Aurore Dupain, better known as George Sand, who combined the themes of romantic love and social injustice in her work; and of course Alexandre Dumas the elder, who wrote *Le Comte de Monte-Cristo* (The Count of Monte Cristo), *Les Trois Mousquetaires* (The Three Musketeers), and other swashbuckling adventures.

By the mid-19th century, romanticism was evolving into new movements, both in fiction and poetry. In 1857 two landmarks of French literature were published: *Madame Bovary* by Gustave Flaubert (1821-1880) and *Les Fleurs du mal* by Charles Baudelaire (1821-1867). Both authors were tried for the supposed immorality of their works. Flaubert won his case, and his novel about the tragic life of a provincial, middle-class woman obsessed by dreams of luxury and romance was distributed without cuts.

Émile Zola claimed Flaubert as a precursor of his school of **naturalism**. He aimed to do to the novel what Claude Bernard had done to physiology: convert it from an art to a science by the application of the experimental method. His theory may seem naive, but his practice, in the huge *Rougon-Macquart* series, was innovative and powerful. In *L'Assommoir* and *Germinal* his depiction of the misery and revolt of the proletariat has an epic grandeur.

Baudelaire was not as lucky as Flaubert with his trial. He was obliged to cut several

poems out of *Les Fleurs du mal*, and he died in poverty, practically unknown. However, his work influenced all the significant French poetry of the later 19th century.

Following on from where Baudelaire left off were the poets Paul Verlaine and Stéphane Mallarmé, who created the Symbolist movement. Arthur Rimbaud, apart from crowding an extraordinary amount of rugged, exotic travelling into his 37 years and having a tempestuous relationship with Verlaine, produced two enduring pieces of work, *Illuminations* and *Une Saison en enfer* (A Season in Hell).

20th Century Marcel Proust dominated the early 20th century with his giant novel, *A la recherche du temps perdu* (Remembrance of Things Past); it is largely autobiographical and explores in evocative detail the treasures recovered from the unconscious by 'involuntary memory'. André Gide found his voice in the celebration of homosexual sensuality; some of his later works are informed by left-wing politics, while *Les Faux Monnayeurs* brings reflections on the relation between character and author into the story.

The **surrealist movement** (see the preceding Painting section) was to be a vital force in French literature until WW II. André Breton ruled the group and wrote its Manifestos. His autobiographical narratives, such as *Nadja*, capture the spirit of the movement: the fascination with dreams, divination, and all manifestations of 'the marvellous'. As a poet Breton was overshadowed by Paul Éluard and Louis Aragon, both of whom later joined the Communist Party.

Colette enjoyed tweaking the nose of conventionally moral readers with titillating novels that detailed the amorous exploits of heroines such as the schoolgirl Claudine. A highly skilled writer, she produced several other novels and short stories which reveal a talent for acute observation and a sensuous appreciation of the world around her.

After WW II, **existentialism**, a significant literary movement, developed around Jean-Paul Sartre, Simone de Beauvoir and Albert Camus, who worked and conversed

in the cafés of Saint-Germain des Près. All three stressed the importance of the writer's political engagement. De Beauvoir, author of the ground-breaking study *The Second Sex*, has had a profound influence on feminist thinking.

In the late 1950s, some younger novelists began to look for new ways of organising a narrative. *Les Fruits d'or* by Nathalie Sarraute, for example, does away with identifiable characters and has no plot as such. Critics began to speak of the **new novel** *(nouveau roman)*, referring to the works of Sarraute, Alain Robbe-Grillet, Michel Butor, among others; however, these writers never formed a close-knit group, and their experiments have taken them in divergent directions.

In 1980 Marguerite Yourcenar, best known for memorable historical novels such as *Mémoires d'Hadrien*, became the first woman to be elected to the French Academy.

Marguerite Duras came to the notice of a large public when she won the prestigious *Prix Goncourt* with her novel *L'Amant* (The Lover) in 1984. A prolific writer and filmmaker, she is also noted for the screenplays of *India Song* and *Hiroshima mon amour*.

Philippe Sollers was one of the editors of *Tel Quel*, a highbrow, then left-wing review which was very influential in the 1960s and early '70s. His '60s novels were forbiddingly experimental, but with *Femmes* (Women) he returned to a conventional narrative style.

Another of the editors of *Tel Quel* was Julia Kristeva, best known for theoretical writings on literature and psychoanalysis. Recently she has turned her hand to fiction, and *Les Samuraï*, a fictionalised account of the heady days of *Tel Quel*, is an interesting document on the life of the Paris intelligentsia.

Daniel Pennac is widely read for his witty crime fiction *(Au bonheur des ogres, La Fée carabine)* set in Paris. A recent winner of the Goncourt was Patrick Chamoiseau, whose prize-winning novel *Texaco* recounts the social history of a shanty town in Martinique.

Cinema

The French have long had a well-deserved reputation of being intellectual film-makers and avid cinema enthusiasts. This was brought about by an industry that has been generously supported by the state and by the fact that film is regarded by the French as an important form of art and expression. French film-makers never had to struggle to make their art accepted and TV's impact was slow to be felt, never quite having the devastating effect on the number of movie-goers as it did in other Western countries. Even these days, when the cinema in France is struggling financially, there are still more movie-goers than in other countries.

France's place in the film history books was firmly noted when those cinematographic pioneers, the **Lumière brothers**, organised the world's first paying (1FF) public movie session – a series of two-minute reels – in Paris's Grand Café, Blvd des Capucines, on 28 December 1895. They went on to specialise in newsreels and documentaries, leaving Charles Pathé – often called the Napoleon of cinema – to monopolise and rapidly expand France's cinema scene prior to WW I.

The 1920s to the 1930s were unique times, as French avant-garde directors such as René Clair, Marcel Carné and the intensely productive Jean Renoir, son of the famous artist, searched for new forms and subjects. René Clair created a world of fantasy in his films in which he gave free rein to his penchant for invention. Though Carné's films were visually stunning, he presented a pessimistic world in which violence and poverty dominate. Poetic realism, strong narrative, and a strong sense of social satire mark the work of Jean Renoir.

New Wave After WW II, however, ideas and techniques gradually lost innovation, and the big names tended to go somewhat stale. The industry stagnated until the late 1950s, when a large group of new-generation directors, who had been brought up on cinema in clubs and art-houses and were full of ideas, burst onto the scene with a new genre, the *nouvelle vague* (new wave).

This group included Jean-Luc Godard,

François Truffaut, Claude Chabrol, Eric Rohmer, Jacques Rivette, Louis Malle and Alain Resnais, many of whom had written for Cahiers du Cinéma in the 1950s, a magazine of cinema critique. The one belief that united this disparate group of directors was that a film should be the conception of the film-maker rather than the product of a studio or producer, hence giving rise to the term *film d'auteur*.

With small budgets, sometimes self-financed, no glossy sets or big-name stars, they made films like *Et Dieu créa la femme* (1956; And God Created Woman), which brought sudden stardom to both Brigitte Bardot and the little fishing village of Saint Tropez, where director Roger Vadim, a young journalist, shot the film. The film, which examined the amorality of modern youth, achieved international acclaim.

A ream of films followed, among them Alain Resnais' *Hiroshima mon amour* (1959; based on the novel by Marguerite Duras) and *L'Année dernière à Marienbad* (1961; Last Year in Marienbad), which explored the problems of time and memory, and abandoned the constraints of temporal continuity. François Truffaut's *Les Quatre Cents Coups* (1959; The 400 Blows) was partly based on his own life and conformed to his idea that the director should make a personal statement with the camera. Jean-Luc Godard made such films as *À bout de souffle* (1960; Breathless), *Alphaville* (1965) and *Pierrot le fou* (1965), which showed even less concern for sequence and narrative, with frequent jump-cutting and interruptions by pop-art images and actors' comments on the film itself. The *nouvelle vague* continued until the 1970s, by which stage it had lost its experimental edge.

Other famous French directors making films at this time include Agnès Varda, Claude Chabrol and Louis Malle.

Jacques Tati Of the non-new wave directors of the 1950s and '60s, one of the most notable was Jacques Tati, who made many comic films based around the charming, bumbling figure of Monsieur Hulot and his struggles to adapt to the modern age. Tati continued to make films in the 1970s but they tended to repeat many of his earlier themes.

Contemporary Cinema In the 1980s well-regarded directors included Jean-Jacques Beineix, who created *Diva* in 1981 followed five years later by *Betty Blue* (the film's French title was the rather bizarre *37°2 le Matin*) and Luc Besson with *Subway* (1985) and *The Big Blue* (1988). Truffaut continued with such films as *Le Dernier Métro* (1980) and *La Femme d'à-côté* (1981; The Woman Next Door). In 1986 Claude Bérri came up with *Jean de Florette* followed by *Manon des Sources*, modern versions of writer/film-maker Marcel Pagnol's original works, which proved enormously popular both in France and abroad.

The state still generously subsidises the industry with advances and grants, evidenced by the 140 feature films made in France in 1991, compared to the dismal 33 made across the Channel in Britain. Despite its own healthy position, however, France is also inundated by US products, with large Gaumont cinemas in every French city screening the current US box-office titles. In 1992 US movies took 58% of the year's box office receipts, while only 35% went to French films.

Events & Stars The industry's main annual event is the **Cannes Film Festival** which, since 1946, has awarded the coveted *Palme d'Or* and other prizes to French and foreign films. French movie stars, directors, technicians etc are annually honoured with the Césars, created in 1976 as the French equivalent of Hollywood's Academy Awards.

One of the nation's earliest screen heroes was the great comic Fernandel, who was nicknamed 'Horseface' because of his inimitable grin and who triumphed in the *Don Camillo* series of the 1950s. Maurice Chevalier left for Hollywood in the 1930s, becoming the man who most epitomised Frenchmen in musicals such as *The Merry Widow*, *Gigi* and *Can Can*. Two of France's best loved actors of the 1930s and '40s were

Jean Gabin and Arletty. Gabin frequently portrayed strong-willed nonconformist characters; his most notable role was in Jean Renoir's *La Grande Illusion* (1937). Cast as the downtrodden prostitute in many films, Arletty is best remembered for her role in Marcel Carné's *Les Enfants du Paradis* (1945).

More contemporary is Philippe Noiret, a veteran of over 100 French films whose hang-dog face recently found international acclaim as the Sicilian movie-loving projectionist in *Cinema Paradiso* (1989).

However, it is Gérard Depardieu more than any other French actor who has reached worldwide audiences. Among his many films are *Le Dernier Métro* (1980), *Jean de Florette* (1986; directed by Claude Berri), *Green Card*, an American film directed by the Australian Peter Weir, and *Cyrano de Bergerac* (1990). Starring next to Depardieu in *Le Dernier Métro* was Catherine Deneuve, generally considered one of France's leading actors despite her reputation since the 1960s as one of cinema's ice maidens. Emmanuelle Béart, Isabelle Huppert and Sandrine Bonnaire are among the contemporary stars of French cinema.

CULTURE
Interacting with the French

Some visitors to Paris conclude that France would be a lovely place if it weren't for the people who live there. As in other countries, however, the more tourists a particular town or neighbourhood attracts, the less patience the locals tend to have for them.

Avoiding Offence

By following a number of simple guidelines, you can usually avoid offending anyone (except that minority of French people who consider tourists – especially those who speak English or German – inherently offensive).

A few don'ts:

- When buying fruit and vegetables anywhere except a supermarket, do not touch the items on display. Unless the shop or stallkeeper tells you to make your own selection, indicate what you want and he or she will choose the produce for you.

- In a restaurant, do *not* summon the waiter by shouting '*garçon*', which means 'boy'. Saying '*s'il vous plaît*' is the way it's done nowadays. A waiter or bar attendant is a *serveur* (masculine) or *serveuse* (feminine).

- When dining, keep your hands above the table or people will wonder what you are doing with them. When you're being served cheese (eg as the final course for dinner) and the plate of cheese slabs comes your way, remember two cardinal rules: never cut off the tip of the soft cheeses that are shaped like pieces of pie (eg Brie, Camembert); and when helping yourself to cheeses whose middle is the best part (eg blue cheese), cut them in such a way as to take your fair share of the crust.

- Money is a subject that is simply not discussed in France. Never ask how much someone makes, especially if it's a lot. Children don't even know how much their parents earn, and co-workers haven't a clue what their colleagues take home.

- French grass *(pelouse)* is meant to be looked at and praised for its greenness, *not* touched. Except in some excepted wide open areas, throwing frisbee, walking on the grass or sitting on it in preparation for a picnic is not only forbidden by some bylaw – the inspiration for the signs reading '*pelouse interdite*' – but will be looked upon by locals as hardly better than doing calisthenics on a flowerbed.

- Make sure to wear modest clothing (no shorts, short skirts or sleeveless shirts) on days when you'll be visiting churches, synagogues or mosques.

A few dos:

- The easiest way to greatly improve the quality of your casual relations with French people is to always say '*Bonjour, Monsieur/Madame/Mademoiselle*' to acknowledge the person behind the counter when you walk into a shop (boulangerie, fromagerie, etc) or café. Before you turn to leave, say '*Merci, Monsieur/Madame/Mademoiselle, au revoir*'.
  Monsieur means 'sir' and can be used with any male person who isn't a child. Addressing women is a bit trickier. *Madame* is used where 'Mrs' would apply in English, while *Mademoiselle* is supposed to be used when talking to unmarried women. When in doubt, use 'Madame'.

- It is customary for people who know each other to exchange kisses (*bises*) as a greeting. Women exchange kisses with women, men exchange kisses with women, and in many circles men also exchange kisses with men. The usual ritual is one glancing kiss on each cheek, but depending on the region (and the personalities involved), some people go for three or even four kisses.

- People who don't kiss each other will almost always shake hands. It's an important physical contact, so don't be surprised in rural areas if a farmer just in from the field offers you his wrist or even his elbow rather than his grubby hand.
- When you go out for the evening, it is highly recommended that you follow the local custom of being well-dressed and well-groomed and appearing generally respectable (if not outright fashionable). Not to do so merely invites unfriendly reactions in discos (eg from bouncers), restaurants, etc. Torn jeans may be the height of fashion in New York, but in France you're liable to be mistaken for a bum and treated accordingly.
- Many French people seem to feel that going Dutch (ie splitting the bill) at restaurants is an uncivilised custom. In general, the person who did the inviting pays for dinner, though close friends and colleagues will sometimes split the bill.
- If invited to someone's home or a party, always bring some sort of gift. Wine is fine, but *not* some 10FF *vin de table* (table wine), which everyone will know came from the discount shelf of the corner grocery. Flowers are another good stand-by, but chrysanthemums are only brought to cemeteries and will gravely offend your host.
- At the beach, stick to going starkers on recognised nudist beaches (see the Activities section). This will help maintain harmony between those French people who are not fans of nudism and visitors who are.

Spectator Sports

While soccer, rugby, golf and skiing are all enormously popular spectator sports, the French are particularly taken with tennis (especially the French Open, held in Paris's Roland Garros Stadium during May) and cycling.

The Tour de France, founded in 1903, is the world's most prestigious bicycle race. For three weeks in late June and July, some 200 or so of the world's top cyclists take on a 4000-km route, whose flat sections are interspersed with gruelling mountain passes. Changed each year, the route often strays into parts of Belgium, Switzerland, Spain and Germany. Wherever it goes, highways are blocked off hours before the colourful line of cyclists stream past in a blur, cheered on by enthusiastic spectators and followed by TV cameras mounted on motorbikes and helicopters. The race is divided into 21 daily stages, each of which is timed. At the end of the race, the rider with the lowest aggregate time is the winner. The finishing line of the final stage is always along the Champs-Élysées in Paris.

Traditional Sports

France's most popular traditional games are *pétanque* and the similar, though more formal, *boules* (similar to lawn bowls but played on a hard surface). Unlike lawn bowls, whose white-clad players throw their woods on an immaculate strip of grass, pétanque and boules (which has a 70-page rule book) are usually played by village men in work clothes on a rough gravel pitch known as a *boulodrome*, scratched out wherever a bit of flat and shady ground can be found. Especially popular in the south, the games are often played in the cool of late afternoon, sometimes with a thirst-quenching pastis near at hand. The object is to get your *boules* (biased metal balls) as close as possible to the 'jack', the small ball thrown at the start. World championships are held for both pétanque and boules.

In the Basque Country, the racquet game of *pelote*, the fastest form of which is known as *cesta punta*, is very popular. For details, see the Pelote aside in the French Basque Country chapter.

RELIGION

Church and state were separated in 1905 in the wake of the Dreyfus Affair (see History).

Catholics

Some 80% of French people say they are Catholic but, although most have been baptised, very few ever attend church. Church attendance is least unpopular among the middle classes. The French Catholic Church is generally very progressive and ecumenically minded. In Brittany many of the local saints are unrecognised by Rome.

The Holy See was based in Avignon under seven French-born popes from 1309 to 1377.

Protestants

France's Protestants (Huguenots), who were severely persecuted during much of the 16th

and 17th centuries, now number about one million. They are concentrated in Alsace, the Jura, the south-eastern part of the Massif Central and along the Atlantic coast.

John Calvin (1509-64), born in Noyon in the far north of France, was educated in Paris, Orléans and Bourges but spent much of his life in Geneva.

Muslims

Islam has at least three million adherents in France, and Muslims are now the country's second-largest religious group. The vast majority are immigrants (or the children of immigrants) who came from North Africa during the 1950s and '60s.

In recent years, France's Muslim community has been the object of racist agitation by right-wing parties and extremist groups. Many North Africans complain of discrimination by the police and employers.

Jews

There has been a Jewish community in France for most of the time since the Roman period. During the Middle Ages, the community suffered from persecution and a number of mass expulsions, but it also produced the great Biblical commentator Rashi, born in Troyes in 1040. French Jews, the first in Europe to achieve emancipation, were granted full citizenship in 1790-91. Since 1808, the French Jewish community has had an umbrella organisation known as the Consistoire, whose Paris headquarters is at 17 Rue Saint Georges (9e; metro Notre Dame de Lorette).

The country's Jewish community, which now numbers some 700,000, grew substantially during the 1960s as a result of immigration from Algeria, Tunisia and Morocco.

France has had three Jewish prime ministers: Léon Blum (1937-38), Pierre Mendès-France (1954-55), and Laurent Fabius (1984-86).

LANGUAGE

Modern French developed from the Langue d'Oïl, a group of dialects spoken north of the Loire River which grew out of the vernacular Latin used during the late Gallo-Roman period. The Langue d'Oïl eventually displaced the Langue d'Oc (from which the Mediterranean region of Languedoc got its name), the dialects spoken in the south of the country.

Standard French is taught and spoken everywhere, but its various accents and brogues are an important source of identity in certain regions. In addition, some of the peoples subjected to French rule many centuries ago have preserved their traditional languages. These include Flemish in the far north; Alsatian in Alsace; Breton (a Celtic tongue similar to Cornish and Welsh) in Brittany; Basque (a language unlike anything spoken anywhere in Western Europe) in the Basque Country; Catalan in Roussillon (Catalan is the official language of the nearby principality of Andorra); Provençal in Provence; and Corsican on the island of Corsica.

At least 200 million people worldwide speak French, which is an official language in Belgium, Switzerland, Luxembourg, Canada and over two dozen other countries, most of them former French colonies in Africa. It is also spoken in the Val d'Aosta region of north-western Italy. Various creoles are used in Haiti, French Guiana and parts of Louisiana. France has a special government ministry, the Ministère de la Francophonie, to handle the country's relations with the French-speaking world.

Unlike some countries, where when you learn ten words of the language everyone is extremely impressed, the French (particularly in Paris) tend to take it for granted that all civilised human beings should speak French. Your best bet is always to approach people in French, even if the only words you know are *'Pardon, Monsieur/Madame/ Mademoiselle, parlez-vous Anglais?'* Although the answer will often be *'non'*, especially away from the major cities, you will have broken the ice in a respectful way.

For more useful words and phrases than we have space for here, see Lonely Planet's *Western Europe Phrasebook*.

Grammar

An important distinction is made in French between *tu* and *vous* (singular), which both correspond to 'you'. *Tu* is only used when addressing people you know well or children. When addressing an adult who is not a personal friend, *vous* whould be used unless the person invites you to use *tu*. In general, younger people insist less on this distinction, and they may use *tu* from the beginning of an acquaintance.

All nouns in French are either masculine or feminine and adjectives reflect the gender of the noun they modify. The feminine form of many nouns and adjectives is indicated by a silent 'e' added to the masculine form: student, *étudiant* (m)/*étudiante* (f). The gender of a noun is often indicated by a preceding article: the/a/some, *le/un/du* (m), *la/une/de la* (f); or a possessive adjective, my/your/his/her, *mon/ton/son* (m), *ma/ta/sa* (f). In French, unlike in English, the possessive adjective agrees in number and gender with the thing possessed: his/her mother, *sa mère*.

Circumflex Accents

Letters with a circumflex accent (eg ê, ô) often indicate that an 's' has been dropped, which is why a forest is a *forêt* and a hospital is an *hôpital*. This is also why in English we have both a 'hostel' (from the Old French word) and a 'hotel' (from the modern French word *hôtel*).

Pronunciation

French has a number of sounds that Anglophones find notoriously difficult to produce. The main causes of trouble are:

- The distinction between the 'u' sound (as in *tu*) and the 'oo' sound (as in *tout*). For both sounds, the lips are rounded and projected forward, but for the 'u' the tongue is towards the front of the mouth, its tip against the lower front teeth, whereas for the 'oo' the tongue is towards the back of the mouth, its tip behind the gums of the lower front teeth.
- The nasal vowels. During the production of nasal vowels the breath escapes partly through the nose and partly through the mouth. There are no nasal vowels in English; in French there are three, all of which appear in *'bon vin blanc'* ('good white wine'). These sounds occur where a syllable ends in a single 'n' or 'm'. The 'n' or 'm' is not pronounced but indicates the nasalisation of the preceding vowel.
- The standard French 'r' is produced by moving the bulk of the tongue backwards to constrict the air flow in the pharynx while the tip of the tongue rests behind the lower front teeth. It is quite similar to the noise made by some people before spitting, but with much less friction.
- The French 'j' sound, as in the word 'je' (I), is pronounced as the 's' in 'leisure'. The letters 'zh' have been used in this book as a pronunciation guide for words that have this sound, eg 'refuge'.

Greetings & Civilities

Hello/Good morning.	*Bonjour.*
Goodbye.	*Au revoir.*
Good evening.	*Bonsoir.*
Yes.	*Oui.*
No.	*Non.*
Maybe.	*Peut-être.*
Please.	*S'il vous plaît.*
Thank you.	*Merci.*
You're welcome.	*Je vous en prie.*
Excuse me.	*Excusez-moi.*
Sorry (excuse me, forgive me).	*Pardon.*
How are you? (formal)	*Comment allez-vous?*
How are you? (informal)	*Comment va?/Ça va?*
Well, thanks.	*Bien, merci.*

Essentials

Do you speak English?	*Parlez-vous anglais?*
Does anyone speak English?	*Est-ce qu'il y a quelqu'un qui parle anglais?*
I understand.	*Je comprends.*
I don't understand.	*Je ne comprends pas.*
Just a minute.	*Attendez une minute.*
Could you please write that?	*Est-ce-que vous pouvez l'écrire?*

What country are you from?	*De quel pays êtes-vous?*	aeroplane	*avion* (m)
I am...	*Je viens...*	the boat	*bateau* (m)
from Australia	*d'Australie*	the bus (city)	*(auto)bus* (m)
from Canada	*du Canada*	the bus (intercity)	*(auto)car* (m)
from England	*d'Angleterre*	the ferry	*ferry (-boat)* (m)
from Germany	*d'Allemagne*	the tram	*tramway* (m)
from Ireland	*d'Irlande*	the train	*train* (m)
from New Zealand	*de Nouvelle Zélande*	next	*prochain/prochaine*
from Scotland	*d'Écosse*	first	*premier/première*
from Wales	*du Pays de Galle*	last	*dernier/dernière*
from the USA	*des États-Unis*		
How old are you?	*Quel âge avez-vous?*	I would like...	*Je voudrais...*
I'm...years old.	*J'ai...ans.*	a one-way ticket	*un billet aller simple*

Paperwork

Surname	*Nom de famille*	a return ticket	*un billet aller-retour*
Given name	*Prénom*	1st class	*première classe*
Date/Place of birth	*Date/Lieu de naissance*	2nd class	*deuxième classe*
Nationality	*Nationalité*	a reduced fare	*un billet à tarif réduit*
Sex	*Sexe*	How long does the trip take?	*Combien de temps durera le trajet?*
Passport	*Passeport*	The train is delayed/on time/early.	*Le train est en retard/à l'heure/en avance.*

Small Talk

What is your name?	*Comment vous appelez-vous?*	The train has been cancelled.	*Le train a été annulé.*
My name is...	*Je m'appelle...*	Do I need to change trains/platform?	*Est-ce que je dois changer de train/quai?*
I'm pleased to meet you.	*Enchanté/-ée.*	You must change trains/platform.	*Il faut changer de train/quai.*
I'm a tourist.	*Je suis un/une touriste.*		
I'm a student.	*Je suis étudiant/ étudiante.*		
Are you married?	*Êtes-vous marié/-ée?*	left-luggage locker	*consigne automatique* (f)
Do you like...?	*Aimez-vous...?*	left-luggage office	*consigne manuelle* (f)
I like...very much.	*J'aime beaucoup...*	platform	*quai* (m)
I don't like...	*Je n'aime pas...*	ticket	*billet* (m)
How do you say... in French?	*Comment dit-on... en français?*	ticket window	*guichet* (m)
		timetable	*horaire* (m)

Getting Around

I want to go to...	*Je voudrais aller à...*	I'd like to hire a...	*Je voudrais louer...*
I would like to book a seat to...	*Je voudrais réserver une place pour...*	a bicycle	*un vélo*
		a car	*une voiture*
What time does the next train leave/ arrive?	*À quelle heure part/arrive le prochain train?*	horse	*un cheval*
		Is a guide available?	*Un guide est disponible?*

Directions

Where is...?	Où est...?
How do I get to...?	Comment dois-je faire pour arriver à...?
Is it far from/near here?	Est-ce près/loin d'ici?
Where is the bus/tram stop?	Où est l'arrêt d'autobus/de tramway?
I want to go to ...	Je veux aller à ...
I am looking for...	Je cherche...
Can you show it to me (on the map)?	Est-ce que vous pouvez me le montrer (sur la carte)?
Go straight ahead.	Continuez tout droit.
Turn left ...	Tournez à gauche ...
Turn right ...	Tournez à droite ...
at the traffic lights	aux feux
at the next corner	au prochain carrefour
behind	derrière
in front of	devant
opposite	en face de
north/south	nord/sud
east/west	est/ouest

Signs

Camping Ground	Camping
Entrance	Entrée
Exit	Sortie
Full/No Vacancies	Complet
Hotel	Hôtel
Information	Renseignements
Open/Closed	Ouvert/Fermé
Police	Police
Police Station	(Commissariat de) Police
Prohibited	Interdit
Rooms Available	Chambres libres
Toilets	Toilettes, W.C.
Train Station	Gare SNCF
Youth Hostel	Auberge de Jeunesse
Ferry Terminal	Gare Maritime
Bus Station	Gare Routière
out of order	en panne
not in service	hors service

Around Town

I'm looking for...	Je cherche...
a bank	une banque
exchange office	un bureau de change
the city centre	le centre-ville
the...embassy	l'ambassade de...
my hotel	mon hôtel
the market	le marché
the police	la police
the post office	le bureau de poste/la poste
a public toilet	les toilettes
the railway station	la gare
a public telephone	une cabine téléphonique
the tourist information office	l'office de tourisme/le syndicat d'initiative

Where is (the)...?	Où est...?
beach	la plage
bridge	le pont
castle, mansion, vineyard	le château
cathedral	la cathédrale
church	l'église
hospital	l'hôpital
island	l'île
lake	le lac
main square	la place centrale
mosque	la mosquée
old city	la vieille ville
the palace	le palais
quay/bank	le quai/la rive
ruins	les ruines
sea	la mer
square	la place
tower	la tour

I'd like to make a telephone call.	Je voudrais téléphoner.
I'd like to change some...	Je voudrais changer...
money/travellers' cheques	de l'argent/des chèques de voyage

Accommodation

I'm looking for...	Je cherche...
the youth hostel	l'auberge de jeunesse
the camping ground	le camping
a hotel	un hôtel
Where can I find a cheap hotel?	Où est-ce que je peux trouver un hôtel bon marché?
What is the address?	Quelle est l'adresse?
Could you write the address, please?	Est-ce vous pouvez écrire l'adresse, s'il vous plaît?
Do you have any rooms available?	Est-ce que vous avez des chambres libres?
I would like...	Je voudrais...
a single room	une chambre pour une personne
a double room	une chambre double
a room with a shower and toilet	une chambre avec douche et W.C.
to stay in a dormitory	coucher dans un dortoir
a bed	un lit
How much is it per night/per person?	Quel est le prix par nuit/par personne?
Is breakfast included?	Est-ce que le petit déjeuner est compris?
Is there a reduction for students/ children?	Est-ce qu'il y a un tarif réduit pour les étudiants/ enfants?
Can I see the room?	Je peux voir la chambre?
Where is the bathroom/shower?	Où est la salle de bain/la douche?
Where is the toilet?	Où sont les toilettes?
Do you have a key?	Est-ce qu'il y a une clé (clef)?
Is there a lift (elevator)?	Est-ce qu'il y a un ascenseur?
I'm going to stay for...	Je resterai...
one day	un jour
two days	deux jours
a week	une semaine
I am leaving now.	Je pars maintenant.

Food

breakfast	petit déjeuner (m)
lunch	déjeuner (m)
dinner	dîner (m)
I would like the set lunch, please.	Je prends le menu.
I am a vegetarian.	Je suis végétarien/ végétarienne.
I don't eat...	Je ne mange pas de...
meat/chicken/ pork/beef/fish	viande/poulet/porc/ bœuf/poisson

See the Food section in the Facts for the Visitor chapter for more information.

Shopping

How much does it cost?	C'est combien?
I would like to buy it.	Je voudrais l'acheter.
It's too expensive for me.	C'est trop cher pour moi.
Can I look at it?	Est-ce que je peux le/la voir?
I'm just looking.	Je ne fais que regarder.
I would like to buy...	Je voudrais acheter...
clothing	des vêtements
souvenirs	des souvenirs
Do you accept credit cards?	Est-ce que je peux payer avec ma carte de crédit?
Do you take travellers' cheques?	Est-ce que je peux payer avec des chèques de voyage?
Do you have another colour/size?	Est-ce que vous avez d'autres couleurs/ tailles?
It is too...	C'est trop...
big	grand
small	petit

more/less	*plus/moins*
cheap/cheaper	*bon marché/moins cher*

Time & Dates

today	*aujourd'hui*
tonight	*ce soir*
tomorrow	*demain*
day after tomorrow	*après-demain*
yesterday	*hier*
all day/every day	*toute la journée/ tous les jours*
in the morning	*le matin*
in the afternoon	*l'après-midi*
in the evening	*le soir*
Monday	*lundi*
Tuesday	*mardi*
Wednesday	*mercredi*
Thursday	*jeudi*
Friday	*vendredi*
Saturday	*samedi*
Sunday	*dimanche*
January	*janvier*
February	*février*
March	*mars*
April	*avril*
May	*mai*
June	*juin*
July	*juillet*
August	*août*
September	*septembre*
October	*octobre*
November	*novembre*
December	*décembre*
What time is it?	*Quelle heure est-il?*
It's...o'clock.	*Il est...heures.*
in the morning	*du matin*
in the evening	*du soir*
7.00/8.00 am	*sept/huit heures du matin*
1.00 pm (13.00)	*une heure de l'après-midi (treize heures)*
2.30 pm (14.30)	*deux heures et demie (quatorze heures trente)*

9.15 pm (21.15)	*neuf heures et quart du soir (vingt-et-une heures quinze*

Numbers

0	*zéro*
1	*un*
2	*deux*
3	*trois*
4	*quatre*
5	*cinq*
6	*six*
7	*sept*
8	*huit*
9	*neuf*
10	*dix*
11	*onze*
12	*douze*
13	*treize*
14	*quatorze*
15	*quinze*
16	*seize*
17	*dix-sept*
18	*dix-huit*
19	*dix-neuf*
20	*vingt*
21	*vingt-et-un*
22	*vingt-deux*
30	*trente*
40	*quarante*
50	*cinquante*
60	*soixante*
70	*soixante-dix*
80	*quatre-vingt*
90	*quatre-vingt-dix*
100	*cent*
1000	*mille*
one million	*un million*

Health

antiseptic	*antiseptique* (m)
aspirin	*aspirine* (f)
condoms	*préservatifs* (m)
contraceptive	*contraceptif* (m)
medicine	*médicament* (m)
sunblock cream	*crème (solaire) haute protection* (f)
tampons	*tampons hygiéniques* (m)

I'm...	*Je suis...*
diabetic	*diabétique*
epileptic	*épileptique*
asthmatic	*asthmatique*
anaemic	*anémique*
I'm allergic...	*Je suis allergique...*
to antibiotics	*aux antibiotiques*
to penicillin	*à la pénicilline*
to bees	*aux abeilles*
I am constipated.	*Je suis constipé(e).*

| I have diarrhoea. | *J'ai la diarrhée.* |

Emergencies

Help!	*Au secours!*
Call a doctor!	*Appelez un médecin!*
Call the police!	*Appelez la police!*
Go away!	*Laissez-moi tranquille!*
Leave me alone!	*Fichez-moi la paix!*

Facts for the Visitor

VISAS & EMBASSIES

Embassies handle government-to-government relations. Consulates and embassies' consular sections deal with the public.

Visas

Tourist Nationals of the EC, the USA, Canada and New Zealand do not need visas to visit France as tourists for three months or less. Except for people from a handful of other European countries, everyone else must have a visa.

Among those who need visas are Australians. If you apply for a French visa in Australia (A\$54; personal cheques not accepted), the consulate will ask for a photograph, a copy of your *return* air ticket, evidence that you have travel insurance and the precise dates of your visit. The visa will be issued for a period slightly exceeding the length of stay you indicate on the application form. For longer stays (ie over a month or two), you may also have to produce a bank statement and a letter from your employer stating that you will be coming back to Australia.

If all the forms are in order, your visa will be issued on the spot. It may be worth paying A\$10 or so to have the paperwork taken care of by your travel agent. You can also apply for a visa to France after arriving in Europe – the fee is the same, but you may not have to produce a ticket all the way back to Australia. If you enter France overland, your visa may not be checked at the border, but major problems can arise if you don't have one later on (eg at the airport as you leave the country).

Long-Stay If you'd like to work or study in France or stay for over three months, apply to the French consulate nearest where you live for the appropriate sort of *long séjour* (long-stay) visa. Unless you live in the EC, it is extremely difficult to get a visa that will allow you to work in France. For any sort of long-stay visa, begin the paperwork several months before you plan to leave home (applications cannot usually be made in a third country).

Student If you'd like to study in France, you must apply for a student visa in your country of residence, as tourist visas cannot be turned into student visas after you arrive in France. People with student visas can apply for permission to work part-time (enquire at your place of study).

Au Pair For details on au pair visas, which must be arranged before you leave home (unless you're an EC resident), see Au Pair under Work.

Carte de Séjour

If you are issued a long-stay visa valid for six or more months, you'll probably have to apply for a *carte de séjour* (residence permit) within eight days of arrival in France. For details enquire at your place of study or the local *commissariat* (police station), *mairie*, *hôtel de ville* (city hall), *sous-préfecture* (subprefecture) or *préfecture* (prefecture). In Paris, students must apply to an office (metro Cambronne) at 13 Rue Miollis (15e), which is open Monday to Friday from 9 am to 4.30 pm. EC nationals should go to 93 Ave Parmentier (11e; metro Parmentier), open 9 am to 4.15 pm.

Most other people should apply to the Centre de Réception des Étrangers responsible for the arrondissement where they live. Details are available from the Préfecture de Police (☎ 1-53.71.53.71 or 1-53.73.53.73).

French Embassies & Consulates

France's diplomatic and consular representatives abroad include:

60

Algeria
    Consulate: Villa Malglaive, 1 Rue du Professeur Vincent, Alger (☎ 02-741524)
Australia
    Consulates: 492 St Kilda Rd, Melbourne, Vic 3004 (☎ 03-820 0921, 820 0944)
    31 Market Street, 20th floor, Sydney, NSW 2000 (☎ 02-261 5931, 261 5779)
    Embassy: 6 Perth Ave, Yarralumla, ACT 2600 (☎ 06-270 05111)
Belgium
    Consulate: 4 Ave des Arts, 1040 Brussels (☎ 02-2200111)
Canada
    Consulate: 130 Bloor St West, suite 400, Toronto, Ontario M5S 1N5 (☎ 416-925 8041)
    Embassy: 42 Sussex Promenade, Ottowa, Ontario K1M 2O9 (☎ 613-232 1795)
Germany
    Consulates: Kurfürstendamm 211, D1000, Berlin 15 (☎ 030-88 59 02 41/2/3)
    Johannisstrasse 2, 6600 Saarbrücken (☎ 0681-3 10 28)
    Richard Wagner Strasse 53, 7000 Stuttgart 1 (☎ 0711-23 55 66)
Hong Kong
    26th floor, Admiralty Centre, Tower Two, 18 Harcourt Road, Admiralty (☎ 5294350/2/3)
India
    2/50 Shantipath, Chanakyapuri, New Delhi 110021 (☎ 011-60 4004)
Ireland
    36 Ailesbury Road, Ballsbridge, Dublin 4 (☎ 01-2694777)
Israel
    Consulate: Migdalor Building, 1/3 Ben Yehuda St, 63801 Tel Aviv (☎ 03-510 1415/6/7)
Italy
    Consulates: Via Giulia 251, 00186 Rome (☎ 06-654 21 52)
    Corso Venezia 42, 20121 Milan (☎ 02-79 43 41/2/3)
Japan
    11-44 4-chome, Minami Azabu, Minato-ku, Tokyo 106 (☎ 03-5420 8800)
Luxembourg
    9 Blvd Prince Henri, L-1724 Luxembourg (☎ 4710911)
Morocco
    Consulates: 165 Ave Allal Ben Abdallah, Rabat (☎ 07-702316)
    2 Place de France, Tangier (☎ 09-93 2039)
New Zealand
    Robert Jones House, 1-3 Willeston St, Wellington (☎ 04-472 0200); postal address: PO Box 1695, Wellington
Netherlands
    Consulate: Vijzelgracht 2, 1017 HA Amsterdam (☎ 020-624 83 46)

South Africa
    1009 Main Tower, Cape Town Center, Heerengracht, 8001 Cape Town (☎ 021-21 5605)
    807 George Ave, Arcadia, 0083 Pretoria (☎ 012-43 5564)
Spain
    Consulates: Paseo de la Castellana 79, Edificio UAP, 28046 Madrid (☎ 91-597 3267)
    11 Paseo de Gracia, 08007 Barcelona (☎ 93-317 8150)
Switzerland
    Schosshaldenstrasse 46, 3006 Berne (☎ 031-43 24 24/5/6)
    11 Rue Imbert Galloix, 1200 Geneva (☎ 022-311 34 41)
Tunisia
    Consulate: 1 Rue de Hollande, 1000 Tunis (☎ 01-25 3866)
UK
    Consulate: 21 Cromwell Road, London SW7 2DQ (☎ 071- 838 2000). The visa section is at 6A Cromwell Place, London SW7 2EQ (☎ 071-838 2050)
    Embassy: 58 Knightsbridge, London SW1 (☎ 071-201 1000)
USA
    934 Fifth Ave, New York, NY 10021 (☎ 212-606 3688)
    540 Bush St, San Francisco, CA 94108 (☎ 415-397 4330)
    4104 Reservoir Road NW, Washington DC 20007 (☎ 202-944 6195)
    There are also consulates in Atlanta, Boston, Chicago, Honolulu, Houston, Los Angeles, Miami, New Orleans and San Juan (Puerto Rico).

Visa Extensions

Tourist visas *cannot* be extended.

If you qualified for an automatic three-month stay upon arriving in France, you'll almost certainly qualify for another three-month stay if you take the train to Geneva or Brussels and then re-enter the country. The fewer recent French entry stamps you have in your passport the easier this is likely to be. If you needed a visa, your only option is to go to a French consulate in a neighbouring country and apply for another one.

People entering France by rail or road often don't have their passports checked, much less stamped, and even at airports don't be surprised if the official just glances at your passport and hands it back without stamping the date of entry. Fear not: you're in France legally, whether or not you had to

apply for a visa before arriving (though at some point, to show your date of entry, you may be asked to produce the plane, train or ferry ticket you arrived with). If you prefer to have your passport stamped (eg you have a multiple-entry visa), you may have to run around at the border crossing to find someone with the right rubber stamp.

Foreign Embassies & Consulates in Paris

All foreign embassies are in Paris. Canada, the UK and the USA also have consulates in other major cities.

Algeria (Algérie)
    Consulate: 11 Rue d'Argentine, 16e (☎ 1-45.00.99.50; metro Argentine)

Australia (Australie)
    4 Rue Jean Rey (15e; metro Bir Hakeim); ☎ 1-40.59.33.00 (functions as an emergency number after hours). The consular section, which handles matters concerning Australian nationals, is open Monday to Friday from 9 am to noon and 2 to 5 pm (4 pm on Friday). Visas are issued on weekdays from 9.15 am to 12.15 pm.

Belgium (Belgique)
    9 Rue de Tilsitt, 17e (☎ 1-43.80.61.00; metro Charles de Gaulle-Étoile)

Canada
    35 Ave Montaigne, 8e (☎ 1-47.23.01.01; metro Alma Marceau or Franklin D Roosevelt). For Canadian citizens, the consular section is open Monday to Friday from 9 to 11.30 am and 2 to 4 pm.
    Canada also has consulates in Strasbourg and Toulouse.

Czech Republic (République Tchèque)
    Consulate: 18 Rue Bonaparte, 6e (☎ 1-44.32.02.00; metro Saint Germain des Prés).

Egypt (Égypte)
    Consulate: 58 Ave Foch, 16e (☎ 1-45.00.69.23; metro Porte Dauphine)

Germany (Allemagne)
    Consulate: 34 Ave d'Iéna, 16e (☎ 1-42.99.78.00; metro Iéna)

Hungary (Hongrie)
    Consulate: 92 Rue Bonaparte, 6e (☎ 1-43.54.66.96; metro Saint Germain des Prés)

India (Inde)
    15 Rue Alfred Dehodencq, 16e (☎ 1-45.20.39.30; metro Ave Henri Martin)

Ireland (Irlande)
    4 Rue Rude (or Rue François Rude), 16e (☎ 1-45.00.20.87; metro Argentine), between Ave de la Grande Armée and Ave Foch; open Monday to Friday from 9.15 am to noon (or by appointment).

Israel (Israël)
    3 Rue Rabelais, 8e (☎ 1-42.56.47.47; metro Franklin D Roosevelt)

Italy (Italie)
    Consulate: 5 Blvd Émile Augier, 16e (☎ 1-45.20.78.22; metro La Muette)

Japan (Japon)
    7 Ave Hoche, 8e (☎ 1-47.66.02.22; metro Courcelles)

Morocco (Maroc)
    Consulate: 12 Rue de la Saïda, 15e (☎ 1-45.33.81.41; metro Convention)

New Zealand (Nouvelle Zélande)
    7ter Rue Léonard de Vinci, 16e (☎ 1-45.00.24.11; metro Victor Hugo), one block south of Ave Foch across Place du Venezuela from 7 Rue Léonard de Vinci; open Monday to Friday from 9 am to 1 pm and 2 to 5.30 pm.

Poland (Pologne)
    Consulate: 5 Rue de Talleyrand, 7e (☎ 1-45.51.82.22; metro Varenne)
    Embassy: 1 Rue de Talleyrand, 7e (☎ 1-45.51.60.80; metro Varenne)

Russia (Russie)
    Embassy: 40-50 Blvd Lannes, 16e (☎ 1-45.04.05.50; metro Ave Henri Martin)

South Africa (Afrique du Sud)
    59 Quai d'Orsay, 7e (☎ 1-45.55.92.37; metro Invalides), near the American Church

Spain (Espagne)
    Consulate: 165 Blvd Malesherbes, 17e (☎ 1-47.66.03.32; metro Wagram)

Switzerland (Suisse)
    142 Rue de Grenelle, 7e (☎ 1-45.50.34.46; metro Varenne)

Thailand (Thaïlande)
    8 Rue Greuze, 16e (☎ 1-47.04.32.22; metro Trocadéro)

Tunisia (Tunisie)
    Consulate: 17-19 Rue de Lübeck, 16e (☎ 1-45.53.50.94; metro Iéna)

UK (Royaume-Uni or Grande Bretagne)
    Consular Section (handles matters concerning UK subjects): 9 Ave Hoche, 8e (☎ 1-42.66.38.10; metro Courcelles) near Parc de Monceau; open weekdays from 9.30 am to 12.30 pm and 2.30 to 5.30 pm.
    Embassy: 35 Rue du Faubourg Saint Honoré, 8e (☎ 1-42.66.91.42; metro Concorde or Madeleine). The UK also has consulates in Dinard, Lyon, Marseille and Nice.

USA (États-Unis)
    Consulate: 2 Rue Saint Florentin, 1er (☎ 1-42.96.12.02; metro Concorde). The American Services section is open Monday to Friday from 9 am to 4 pm. Be prepared for extremely tight security. To get information by Minitel, key in 3614 code ÉTATS-UNIS.

The USA also has consulates in Bordeaux, Lyon, Marseille, Nice, Strasbourg and Toulouse.

Vietnam
62 Rue Boileau, 16e (☎ 1-45.27.62.55; metro Exelmans)

DOCUMENTS

By law, everyone in France, including tourists, must carry some sort of ID on them at all times. For foreign visitors, this means a passport (or, for EC citizens, a national ID card or British Visitor's Passport).

All important documents should be photocopied before you leave home. Leave one copy of each at home and keep another one with you, separate from the originals.

International Driving Permit (IDP)

Many non-European drivers' licences are valid in France, but it's still a good idea to bring along an IDP, which can make life much simpler, especially when hiring cars and motorbikes. Basically a multilingual translation of the vehicle class and personal details noted on your local driver's licence, it is not valid unless accompanied by your original driver's licence.

An IDP can be obtained for a small charge from your local automobile association – bring along a passport photo and a valid licence. While you're at it, ask for a Card of Introduction, which entitles you to various free services offered by sister motoring organisations in Europe (eg touring maps and information, help with breakdowns, technical and legal advice etc).

If your driver's licence is lost, it may be very difficult to replace it without going home.

Money-Saving Documents

Because giving breaks to students but not young working people is elitist, many places give discounts based on age rather than university affiliation. However, an International Student Identity Card (ISIC), a plastic ID card with your photograph, will still pay for itself very quickly through *demi-tarif* (half-price) admission to museums and sights, discounted air and ferry tickets and cheap meals in some student restaurants. One

drawback for older students is that many places now stipulate a maximum age, usually 24 or 25. In Paris, ISIC cards are issued by AJF for 60FF (see Accommodation Services under Places to Stay in the Paris chapter).

If you're under 26 but not a student, you can apply for an International Youth Card (Carte Jeune Internationale), issued by the Federation of International Youth Travel Organisations (FIYTO), which entitles you to much the same discounts as an ISIC. Like the ISIC, it is issued by student unions or student travel agencies (AJF, Council Travel, USIT, etc). Neither card automatically entitles you to discounts, and some companies and institutions refuse to recognise them, but you won't find out until you ask.

Teachers, professional artists, museum conservators and some students (usually those studying architecture, archaeology, art history and the plastic arts) are admitted to some museums for free. In France, such people have special ID cards, but visitors from abroad who fall into any of these categories might want to bring along some proof of their affiliation.

Carte Jeunes

A Carte Jeunes (youth card; 70FF) – not to be confused with FIYTO's Carte Jeune Internationale – entitles the bearer to a wide variety of discounts in 18 European countries. Valid for one year, it is available to anyone who is under 26 on the date of purchase and who has been in France for at least six months. Details are available on Minitel – key in 3615 code CJEUNES. People with the card are also covered by 24-hour emergency service both within France (☎ 05.30.04.44) and in most other countries (☎ 33-1-47.30.04.44).

Cartes Jeunes are available at many post offices, Centres Information Jeunesse (see Useful Organisations), branches of the Caisse d'Épargne Écureuil (a savings bank) and, in small towns, local *mairies* (town halls). In Paris, you can pick one up at Accueil des Jeunes en France (AJF; ☎ 1-42.77.87.80; metro Rambuteau) at 119 Rue Saint Martin (4e).

International Youth Hostel Card

An IYHF (International Youth Hostel Federation) card is necessary only at official *auberges de jeunesse*, though it may get you small discounts at other hostels. If you don't pick one up before leaving home, it can be purchased for about 100FF at almost any French auberge de jeunesse.

Camping Carnet

A Camping Carnet is a camping ground ID that includes third-party insurance for damage you may cause. As a result, many camping grounds offer a small discount if you sign in with one. Carnets are issued by automobile associations, camping federations and, sometimes, on the spot at camping grounds.

Proving Residence

The most widely accepted way for people to prove where they live is to show an electricity and gas bill issued by EDF and GDF, France's electricity and gas companies.

CUSTOMS
VAT Refunds

If you are not a resident of the EC, you can get a refund of France's value-added tax (VAT, known as TVA in French), set at 18.6% for most goods, provided that: you're over 15; you'll be spending less than six months in France; you purchase goods worth at least 2000FF at a single shop; and the shop offers *vente en détaxe* (duty-free sales).

To arrange for a refund, you must present a passport or national ID card at the time of purchase and ask for a *bordereau* (export sales invoice), which has two pink pages and one green one. The amount of your refund is indicated on the bordereau in space B/3. Some shops may refund 14% of the purchase price rather than the full 18.6% in order to cover the time and expense involved in the refund procedure.

As you leave French territory, have all three pages of the bordereau validated by customs; if going by train, you may have to track down customs officials at the border. After checking that you are taking the goods

for which you're getting a refund out of the country, French customs will take the two pink sheets and the stamped self-addressed envelope provided by the store. The green sheet is your receipt.

French customs will then send one of the pink sheets to the shop where you made your purchase, which will then send you a *virement* (transfer of funds) in the form you request (by French franc cheque, etc).

Instant Refunds If you'll be flying out of Orly or Charles de Gaulle airports and prefer not to wait weeks and weeks to get your VAT back, certain stores can arrange for you to receive your refund as you're leaving the country. You must make such arrangements at the time of purchase.

When you arrive at the airport you have to do three things:

- Up to two hours before your flight leaves (three hours for long-haul flights), bring your bordereau, passport, air ticket and the things you purchased (don't put them in your checked luggage) to the Douane (customs) office so they can stamp all three copies of the bordereau (one of which they keep).
- Go to an Aéroports de Paris (ADP) information counter, where they will check the figures and put another stamp on the documents.
- Go to the nearest CCF Change bureau (open whenever the airport is) to pick up your refund.

MONEY
Currency

The currency of France is the franc, abbreviated in this book by the letters 'FF' following the sum. One franc is worth 100 centimes.

French coins come in denominations of 5, 10, 20 and 50 centimes and 1, 2, 5, 10 and 20FF. The 50 centimes coin is marked as ½FF. The old 10FF coins, which are made of solid copper and have *Liberté, Égalité, Fraternité* written around the edge, are no longer legal tender, so don't accept them as change. It's a good idea to keep on hand a supply of coins of various denominations for parking meters, tolls, laundrettes, etc.

Banknotes are issued in denominations of 20FF (Claude Debussy), 50FF (Maurice

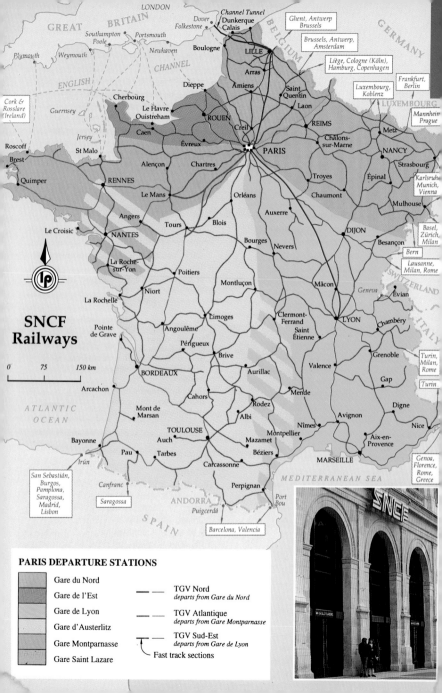

SNCF Railways

0   75   150 km

PARIS DEPARTURE STATIONS

Gare du Nord

Gare de l'Est

Gare de Lyon

Gare d'Austerlitz

Gare Montparnasse

Gare Saint Lazare

—— TGV Nord
departs from Gare du Nord

—— TGV Atlantique
departs from Gare Montparnasse

—— TGV Sud-Est
departs from Gare de Lyon
└ Fast track sections

Top: The harbour at Le Palais, Belle Île, Brittany (GA)
Middle: Pont d'Avignon (Pont San Bénézet), Avignon, Provence (GA)
Bottom: Summertime in Annecy, French Alps (CDT Haute-Savoie)
Overleaf: Lille Railway Station, Northern France (LL)

Quentin de la Tour), 100FF (Eugène Delacroix), 200FF (Montesquieu) and 500FF (Blaise Pascal). The higher the denomination, the larger the banknote. It is sometimes difficult to get change for a 500FF bill. The small type ominously warns that counterfeiters will suffer *réclusion criminelle à perpétuité* (life imprisonment).

Exchange Rates

US$1	=	5.90FF
A$1	=	3.88FF
£UK1	=	8.76FF
DM1	=	3.44FF
100 pta	=	4.24FF
ECU1	=	6.62FF
C$1	=	4.44FF
NZ$1	=	3.22FF
¥100	=	5.43FF

Exchange rates have been fluctuating wildly in recent years, so don't be surprised if France suddenly becomes 10% cheaper or 15% more expensive in your home currency. At banks and exchange bureaux, you can tell how good the rate is by checking the spread between the *achat* (buy) and *vente* (sell) rates – the greater the difference, the further each is from the interbank rate.

Cash

In general, cash is not a very good way to carry money. Not only can it be stolen, but you'll get a worse exchange rate than for travellers' cheques. The Banque de France, for instance, pays 2½% more for travellers' cheque than for cash, a sum that far exceeds the usual commission for buying travellers' cheques.

However, bringing along the equivalent of about US$100 in relatively low-denomination notes will make it easier to change a small sum of money when an inferior rate is on offer or you need just a few francs (eg at the end of your stay). Keep the equivalent of about US$50 separate from rest of your money as an emergency cache (perhaps with the emergency photocopies of your passport, plane ticket, etc). Foreign coins are nearly

useless in France unless you sell them to someone willing to carry them home.

Because of counterfeiting, it may be difficult to change US$100 notes. Most Banque de France branches – except those with with special detection equipment (eg the main one in Paris) – refuse to accept them.

Travellers' Cheques

The most important advantage of travellers' cheques is that if they are lost or stolen, you can get your money refunded. The promised 'instant' reimbursements may prove very slow indeed unless you have a record of cheque numbers, where they were purchased and which ones were cashed. Keep all such information separate from the cheques themselves.

To cover the cost of insuring travellers' cheques, most issuing companies charge a 1% commission. Except at exchange bureaux (which sometimes offer inferior rates), you also have to pay to cash them: at banks, expect a charge of 22FF to 30FF per transaction. A percentage fee may apply for very large sums. These expenses will be partly compensated by the exchange rate, which is higher for travellers' cheques than cash (though the rates offered by credit card companies are better than all but the best rates available for travellers' cheques).

The most useful travellers' cheques are those issued by American Express in US dollars or French francs or by Visa in French francs, because, unlike other types of travellers' cheques, they can be changed at a pretty good rate at many post offices. Travellers' cheques in pounds sterling, Canadian dollars, Deutschmarks and Swiss francs are widely accepted at banks, including the Banque de France. There may be a commission (usually 1%) to change French franc travellers' cheques into cash. Small-denomination travellers' cheques are not very useful – given daily expenses in France and the hassle of changing money, cheques worth the equivalent of US$100 are probably your best bet.

Among the least useful travellers' cheques are those denominated in Australian dollars.

Not even the Banque de France branch will take them, and in all but the largest cities neither will anyone else. Since it's expensive to go from Australian dollars to US dollars and then to francs – you lose money on each conversion – Aussies and other people with less-common currencies might be better off buying travellers' cheques in French francs. This also locks in the cost of your trip, preventing exchange rate fluctuations from devaluing (or appreciating) the money you've brought along.

Reimbursements If your American Express travellers' cheques are lost or stolen, call ☎ 05.90.86.00, a toll-free number (*numéro vert*) that can be dialled from public telephones without charge, and without a télécarte, from anywhere in France. It is staffed 24 hours a day. Reimbursements can be made at any American Express office.

If your Citicorp travellers' cheques are lost or stolen, call ☎ 05.46.93.69. Reimbursements are handled by a variety of French banks, not by the company's French affiliates.

Credit Cards

Overall, the cheapest way to get money in France is by using a credit (or debit) card, both to pay for things (in which case the merchant absorbs the commission) and to get cash advances. Visa (Carte Bleue) is the most widely accepted, followed by MasterCard (Access or Eurocard). American Express cards are not widely accepted except at more up-market establishments (eg three-star hotels, department stores), but they're great for getting cash at American Express offices, located in about a dozen cities. And unlike Visa or MasterCard, American Express cards can be easily replaced if lost or stolen. All three cards can be used to pay for travel by train – just present your card at any SNCF ticket window.

Credit card companies do not earn their money by shaving percentage points off their exchange rates, so by using a credit card you guarantee yourself a superior exchange rate without having to search out the nearest Banque de France. As always, the exchange rate may change – to your advantage or disadvantage – between when you use the card and the date of billing. Credit card bills go directly from French francs to your home currency, a distinct advantage for Australians, New Zealanders and other nationalities who might otherwise have to buy travellers' cheques in a third currency (eg US dollars or pounds sterling).

The only real problem with relying on plastic is that credit cards are no more reliable than the computer networks that make them possible. Even if you don't accidentally exceed your credit limit, some computer in Manhattan or Sydney could become convinced that you have, leaving you without access to cash and causing great humiliation when you try to pay for dinner and the waiter announces loudly that your card has been rejected. The point is, two different credit cards are safer than one, and it's a good idea to keep on hand a reserve of French francs in cash as well as some spare travellers' cheques. If your credit card gives you problems, try calling your issuer reverse charges (or have someone at home make enquiries for you).

Lost or Stolen Cards If your Visa is lost or stolen, call ☎ 54.42.12.12 in the provinces (staffed 24 hours a day) or in Paris ☎ 1-42.77.11.90. Report a lost MasterCard to ☎ 1-45.67.84.84. You should also report the loss to your credit card issuer back home. If your American Express card is lost or stolen, call ☎ 1-47.77.72.00 or 1-47.77.70.00, both in Paris, which are staffed 24 hours a day. In an emergency, American Express card holders from the States can call reverse charges to ☎ 202-783 7474.

Cash Advances

When you get cash advances with a credit card, you are charged a small fee for each transaction (plus, at some banks, a commission of 30FF or so), but it's usually less than what you would pay to purchase and then cash a similar sum in travellers' cheques. You can avoid paying interest (which accrues from the moment you receive the cash, not

from the end of the billing period) by depositing lots of money in your credit card account before you leave home, in effect turning it into a bank account (you may even get interest!) and transforming your credit card into a debit card. The biggest problem with credit card cash advances is that there are all sorts of limits on how much cash you can take out per week or month, regardless of your credit limit. And if you lose a Visa or MasterCard while travelling, it may be very difficult to replace, as you may have to go through the issuing bank.

It is sometimes a bit difficult to find a bank that will give cash advances, especially since some banks handle Visa but not MasterCard, or MasterCard but not Visa. Fortunately, the English term 'cash advance' seems to have made sufficient inroads in French banking circles that a request for one is likely to at least be understood. Certain post offices will also do cash advances of up to about 1800FF every seven days.

A growing number of ATMs will give you cash from your credit card, but limits are usually lower than those of banks, and there's always the remote possiblity of having your card swallowed. Even ATMs plastered with credit card emblems may reject foreign PIN codes if they're feeling Gallocentric. Overall, you may be better withdrawing cash through a live teller. Before leaving home, you might want to ask your credit card issuer for a list of ATMs in France that you can use.

Some unscrupulous exchange bureaux will advertise that they do cash advances, but instead of giving you French francs, they insist that you take your money in US dollars or some other foreign currencey, which they make you buy at their very disadvantageous 'sell' rate. If you need francs, you then have to change your dollars or pounds back again, and take a second loss on the difference between the buy and sell rates. This scheme deprives you of 20% or more of your money.

ATMs As automated teller machine (ATM) networks become more internationalised, it will become easier to take money out of your home bank account using an ATM card. Many ATMs – known in French as *distributeurs automatiques de billets* (DABs) or *guichets automatiques de banque* (GABs) – can also do credit card cash advances.

Unfortunately, some ATMs (eg those that aren't on-line) may summarily reject your request for money, and others won't accept PIN codes with more than four digits, so don't wait until you're broke in the middle of a three-day bank holiday to stock up on cash. A swallowed ATM card can be a major hassle, and worse yet, a lost Visa or MasterCard (including Access, Eurocard etc) is nearly impossible to replace without going home. However, Diners Club and American Express cards can usually be replaced at a local branch of these organisations. Check with your bank for a list of bank locations in France where your card can be used.

American Express With American Express's cash advance service, card holders can get a healthy sum of money – up to £500, US$1000, C$1000 or A$1000 every 21 days – for no charge (except the usual 1% fee to purchase travellers' cheques) by writing a personal cheque drawn on their home bank account. Gold card limits are much higher. Card holders from some countries can get money without a personal cheque by writing a cashier's cheque that includes details of their bank branch and account number.

If you have any questions about services offered by American Express, call the company's *service clientèle* (customer service office; ☎ 1-47.77.70.00) in Paris. For questions about billing in the USA, the person whose name appears on the card (but no one else) can call reverse charges to ☎ 919-668 6666.

For details on American Express offices, see Money in the sections on Paris, Andorra, Bordeaux, Cannes, Le Havre, Lyon, Marseille, Monaco, Nice, Rouen, Saint Jean de Luz, Saint Tropez and Strasbourg.

Eurocheques
Eurocheques, available if you have a European bank account, are guaranteed up to a

certain limit. When cashing them (eg at post offices), you will be asked to show your eurocheque card, marked with your signature and registration number, and perhaps a passport or ID card. Your eurocheque card should be kept separately from the cheques. Many hotels and merchants refuse to accept eurocheques because of the large commissions they involve.

Telegraphic Transfers

Telegraphic transfers are not very expensive (US$30 from the USA, A$20 from Australia), but, despite their name, can be quite slow: getting money from overseas in less than a week is a banking miracle, and waiting two weeks is not unheard of, in part because funds sent in US dollars are routed through New York. Transfers in French francs are usually the quickest since they don't have to pass through a third country. Unless relatively large sums of money are involved, credit card cash advances are a much better alternative.

The most important thing to remember when wiring money from abroad (or having someone wire it for you) is to specify with great precision the name of the bank and the branch, and which city you'd like to pick it up in. If you neglect these vital details, your funds could get sent somewhere it wouldn't even occur to you to check. If this happens, the only way to find your money may be to contact the bank from which the money was sent.

A quicker and more straightforward alternative is to have money sent via American Express, though the amount you can send is limited and the company's offices are not always conveniently located.

Another option is to send money via Citbank/Citicorp and pick it up either at Citibank Private Bank (☎ 1-44.43.45.00; metro Alma Marceau) at 17-19 Ave Montaigne (8e) in Paris (see Money in the Paris chapter) or the branch of a French bank. It usually takes two to five days for money to arrive from New York, but transactions from elsewhere in North America and other parts of the world may take up to 10 days. There's

a 1.5% commission to pick up your money in Citicorp travellers' cheques (in US dollars), a 1.25% charge (minimum US$40) for US dollars cash and a 1.25% charge (minimum 250FF) for French francs.

Changing Money

For most major *devises* (currencies), banks and exchange bureaux give a better rate for *chèques de voyage* (travellers' cheques) than for *billets* (banknotes). Using a combination of travellers' cheques and credit cards and searching out the nearest Banque de France when you have to change money are excellent ways to save a few percentage points on the total cost of your stay in France, which over the course of a month can mean enough money for an extra day or two of travel.

If you get stuck with no francs, remember that international airports, major train stations, fancy hotels and many border posts have exchange facilities that operate on weekends and at night.

Banque de France The Banque de France, France's central bank, offers *by far* the best exchange rate in the country. It does not charge any commissions (except perhaps for a 1% commission to turn French franc travellers' cheques into cash) and is therefore the best place to go if you'd like to sell your leftover pesetas or want a few Deutschmarks in your pocket when you arrive in Germany. Transactions may have a 100FF minimum. The Banque de France does not accept eurocheques or do credit card cash advances but will exchange damaged French currency and almost all out-of-circulation banknotes issued since 1945.

There are Banque de France bureaux in the prefectures of each department and about 130 other towns. If the rates posted outside seem a bit low, they may be for cash – the rates for travellers cheques are higher.

Post Offices In areas frequented by foreign tourists, many post offices perform exchange transactions for a pretty good rate, though you'll get about 3% more at the Banque de

France. The commission is 1.2% (minimum 15FF).

Post office exchange counters accept banknotes in a variety of currencies as well as travellers' cheques issued by American Express (denominated in either US dollars or French francs) or Visa (in French francs only). If you have any other kind of travellers' cheques, you're out of luck.

Banks Banks that do foreign currency transactions – many don't – usually charge somewhere between 22 and 30FF per transaction, although fees as high as 50FF are not unheard of – ask before you sign! The rates offered by banks also vary a great deal, so it pays to compare.

Depending on the local custom, commercial banks are generally open either from Monday to Friday or from Tuesday to Saturday. Hours are variable but are usually 8 or 9 am to sometime between 11.30 and 1 pm and 1.30 or 2 to 4.30 or 5 pm. Exchange services may end half an hour before closing time.

Most French banks have installed security devices intended to foil bank robbers. Many places have two sets of thick glass doors, which you open one after the other by pushing buttons attached to delay timers. The system is designed so that both doors are never open at the same time. The red light will be replaced with a green one when the door has been unlocked. Banks without such elaborate doors usually have bulletproof glass between the customers and the staff.

Exchange Bureaux In large cities, especially Paris, *bureaux de change* (exchange bureaux) are faster, easier, open longer hours and give better rates than the banks – unless you go to an exchange bureau whose business strategy is to milk clueless tourists who can't multiply or divide. Your best bet is to familiarise yourself with the rates offered by various banks, which usually charge a commission, and exchange bureaux, which are not allowed to charge commissions. On relatively small transactions, even exchange

places with less-than-optimal rates may leave you with more francs.

To be avoided if at all possible are the large chains of exchange bureaux such as Checkpoint and Exact Change. Although it is possible to bargain with them a bit on larger transactions, it's unlikely that you'll be able to get a truly competitive offer.

Some unscrupulous exchange bureaux list their *vente* (sell rates, ie the rate at which they sell foreign currency to people going abroad) in such a way that their much lower *achat* (buy rates, ie what they'll give you for foreign cash or travellers' cheques) get lost in a mass of columns and numbers. If their rates were any good they wouldn't have to resort to this kind of thing.

Costs
If you stay in hostels or bottom-end hotels and have picnics rather than dining out, it is possible to travel around France for about US$30 a day per person (US$40 in Paris). A couple staying in two-star hotels and eating one cheap restaurant meal each day should count on spending at least US$60 a day per person, not including car rental. Lots of moving from place to place, eating in restaurants, imbibing fermented liquids or treating yourself to France's many little luxuries can increase these figures dramatically.

Discounts Museums, cinemas, the SNCF, ferry companies and other institutions offer all sorts of price breaks to people under 26 or under 25; students with ISIC cards; and *le troisième age* (senior citizens), ie people over 60. Look for the words *demi-tarif* (half-price tariff) on rate charts and then ask if you qualify. See Money-Saving Documents under Documents for more information. Rail discounts are covered under Train in the Getting Around chapter. Those under 18 get an even wider range of discounts, including free entry to Musées Nationaux (museums run by the French government). Children up to about age 12 are charged lower fees at camping grounds.

If you have a rail pass, it is probably false economy to try to save money by timing your

travel so you can sleep on the train. Unless you pay extra for a couchette, a more expensive proposition than most hostels, you'll end up counting sheep from a semi-upright seat.

Ways to Save Money There are a lots of things you can do to shave francs off your daily expenditures. A few suggestions:

- Travel with someone else rather than alone – except in Andorra, singles usually cost only marginally less than doubles. Two-bed triples and quads are even cheaper per person. Bottom-end hotel rooms often cost less per person than hostel beds.
- You can get the best exchange rate and save on commissions by changing travellers' cheques at the Banque de France and using a credit card whenever possible (see Getting Money to France and Changing Money in this section).
- Avoid high-season travel to regions that raise their accommodation prices when demand goes up (eg Corsica and the Côte d'Azur during July and August, the Alps in February).
- If you stay in one place and get to know your way around, your daily costs are likely to come down.
- Avail yourself of France's plentiful free sights: bustling marketplaces, tree-lined avenues, cathedrals, churches, parks, canal towpaths, nature reserves, etc.
- Visit museums on days when entry is discounted or even free. In Paris, for instance, the Louvre is half-price for everyone on Sunday, while the Centre Pompidou is free on Sunday from 10 am to 2 pm.
- When calling home, use Home Direct services rather than IDD (see Home Direct Services under Telecommunications).
- Bring along a pocketknife and silverware so you can have picnics instead of restaurant meals. The cheapest food is sold in supermarkets and at outdoor markets (see Self-Catering under Places to Eat in each city and town listing).
- Carry a water bottle (canteen) wherever you go so you don't have to pay for a pricey cold drink each time you're thirsty (public drinking fountains are few and far between).
- In restaurants, order the *menu* (see Restaurants & Brasseries under Food) and drink tap water rather than soft drinks, mineral water or wine.
- Avoid taking trains for which you have to pay supplements and/or reservation fees. For information on reduced-rate train tickets, see Discounts in France under Train in the Getting Around chapter.

- If you'll be hiring a car, arrange for rental before you leave home or go to discount places (eg ADA) rather than the multinationals.
- Use rechargeable batteries for your radio or Walkman.

Tipping

French law requires that restaurant, café and hotel bills include the service charge (usually 10% to 15%), so a *pourboire* (tip) is neither necessary nor expected. However, most people leave the copper change or a few francs – regardless of how much the bill came to – if they liked the service, and especially if they were seated at the counter. If you've had a cup of coffee, you might leave 1FF. But if the service was bad don't feel obligated to leave a single centime. However, at truly posh restaurants a more generous gratuity may be anticipated.

In taxis, the usual tip is 2 to 3FF no matter what the fare. It is customary to give 2FF to the cinema usher who shows you to your seat.

Bargaining

People in France rarely bargain except perhaps at flea markets.

Consumer Taxes

France's VAT (value-added tax, ie national sales tax), known in French as TVA *(taxe sur le valeur ajouté)*, is 18.6% on most goods except food, medicine and books, for which it comes to 5.5%. Prices that include VAT are often marked TTC *(toutes taxes comprises)*, which means 'all taxes included'. For details on VAT refunds available to tourists, see the Customs section.

WHEN TO GO

Weather-wise, France is at its best in spring, though winter-like relapses are not unknown and the beach resorts only begin to pick up in May. Autumn is pleasant, too, but the days are fairly short and later on it gets a bit cool for sunbathing, even along the Côte d'Azur. Winter is great for snow sports in the Alps, Pyrenees and other mountain areas, but Christmas, New Year's and the February

school holidays create surges in domestic tourism that can make it very difficult to find accommodation. On the other hand, Paris has all sorts of cultural events going all winter long.

In summer, the weather is warm and even hot, especially in the south, which is one reason why the beaches, beach resorts and camping grounds are packed to the gills. Another reason is that uncounted millions of French people take their annual month-long holiday between mid-July and the end of August.

Weather Forecasts

If you understand French (or know someone who does), you can find out the *météo* (weather forecast) by calling the following numbers:

National forecast	☎ 36.68.01.01
Regional forecasts	☎ 36.68.00.00
Mountain area & snow forecasts	☎ 36.68.04.04
Marine forecast	☎ 36.68.08.08

For départemental forecasts, dial ☎ 36.68.02 plus the two digit départemental number (eg ☎ 36.68.02.75 for Paris). Dial just the eight digits whether you're in Paris or the provinces. Each call costs five télécarte units or 2.19FF per minute. By Minitel, key in 3615 code MET or 3617 code METPLUS.

Domestic Tourism

By law, French wage-earners get five weeks of paid holidays *(congés payés)* each year. Most of them take full advantage of their time off between 14 July and 31 August, when the coasts, mountains and other areas upon which France's city dwellers descend like a locust storm suffer from acute shortages of hotel rooms and campsites.

Meanwhile, in the half-deserted inland cities – only partly refilled by foreign tourists – many shops, restaurants, cinemas, cultural institutions and even hotels simply shut down so their proprietors can head out of town along with their customers. A *congé annuel* (annual closure) sign in the window usually means 'come back in September'.

Even worse, the people left behind to staff essential services tend to be more irritable and officious than usual.

The mid-winter school holidays are another period of mass domestic tourism, especially in places where you can ski. The February school holidays – staggered throughout the country but basically taken from mid-February to mid-March – bring huge numbers of people (and higher prices) to the Alps, the Pyrenees and Andorra.

WHAT TO BRING

The cardinal rule in packing is to bring the absolute minimum. Remember: whatever you have in your pack or suitcases will have to be lugged on and off trains, planes and ferries and dragged to hotels, hostels and camping grounds. When it's on your back, every 500 grams counts.

It's better to start off with too little rather than too much, as virtually anything you need is available locally. Sea-mail services have been discontinued in France, so the only way to send packages overseas is by air mail, which is very expensive, even for low-priority printed matter.

Backpacks

If you'll be doing any walking with your gear, even just from hotels to trains, a backpack is the only way to go. Unfortunately, traditional external-frame packs offer little protection for your valuables, the straps tend to get caught on things and some airlines may ask you to sign a waiver absolving them of responsibility if the pack is damaged or broken into. One of the most flexible ways to carry your belongings is in an internal-frame travelpack whose straps can be zipped inside a flap, turning it into something resembling a nylon suitcase. The most useful kind have an exterior pouch that zips off to become a daypack.

If your bag is misplaced by an airline, you have a better chance of getting it back if your name and address are marked on the inside as well as on a luggage tag, which can easily fall off or be removed.

Useful Items

Useful items to bring along include:

- a money belt with a resealable plastic bag as a liner
- photocopies of all important documents, kept separately from the originals
- large and small plastic bags to keep your gear separate, clean and – when it rains – dry
- a Swiss army knife
- a water bottle
- a portable silverware set (great for picnicking)
- thongs (flip-flops) for showers
- a medical kit (see Health)
- a sewing kit
- a padlock to lock your bag to luggage racks and to secure youth hostel lockers
- little locks for your pack zips
- a roll of emergency toilet paper (in a plastic bag)
- a sleeping sheet to keep your sleeping bag clean or for use at hostels
- a pocket short-wave radio such as a Sony ICF-1 or ICF-7600D
- rechargeable batteries (for your radio or Walkman) and a 220-volt recharger
- an adaptor or transformer for electrical appliances
- a compass
- a torch (flashlight)
- an alarm clock
- a universal bath/sink plug
- sunglasses
- one set of good clothes (including, for men, a tie)
- an elastic clothes line and a few pegs (clothes pins)

Clothes & Books

Insulation works by trapping air, so several layers of thin clothing are warmer than just one layer of something thick. Not only are multiple layers easier to dry, but they make it much simpler to shed clothes if the weather changes.

English-language books (including used books), though available, cost about twice as much in France as in the UK or North America, so voracious readers might want to bring along a supply.

TOURIST OFFICES
Local Tourist Offices

Every city, village, hamlet and one-cheese town seems to have either an *office de tourisme* (a tourist office run by some unit of local gov-

ernment) or a *syndicat d'initiative* (a tourist office run by local merchants). Both are an excellent resource and can almost always provide a local map. Some will also change foreign currency, though not for an optimal rate.

Many tourist offices will make local hotel reservations for you, usually for a fee of 1 to 15FF. Tourist offices that are part of a nationwide telex system can advance-book a room for you elsewhere in France.

Details on local tourist offices appear under Information at the beginning of each city or town listing.

Foreign Tourist Offices

French government tourist offices can provide every imaginable sort of tourist information, most of it in the form of brochures. They include:

Australia
    BNP Building (12th floor), 12 Castlereagh St, Sydney, NSW 2000 (☎ 02-231 5244); open Monday to Friday from 9 am to 2 pm.
Canada
    30 Saint Patrick St, suite 700, Toronto, Ontario M5T 3A3 (☎ 416-593 4723)
Ireland
    35 Lower Abbey St, Dublin 1 (☎ 01-703 4046)
South Africa
    PO Box 41022, Craighall 20 (☎ 011-880 8060)
UK
    178 Piccadilly, London W1V 0AL (☎ 071-629 1272)
USA
    610 Fifth Ave, New York, NY 10020 (☎ 212-257 1125)

USEFUL ORGANISATIONS
Service Culturel

The offices of the French Cultural Service, many of them attached to embassies, provide information to people who would like to study in France:

Australia
    6 Perth Ave, Yarralumla, Canberra ACT 2600 (☎ 06-270 5149 for Linguistic Services)
Canada
    175 Bloor St East, suite 606, Toronto, M4W 3R8 Ontario (☎ 416-925 8061)
Hong Kong
    Admiralty Centre, Tower Two 25/F, 18 Harcourt Road, Admiralty (☎ 529 3458/9)

India
    2 Aurangzeb Rd, 11011 New Delhi (☎ 011-301 4682)
Ireland
    1 Kildare St, Dublin 2 (☎ 01-676 2197)
Singapore
    5 Gallop Rd, Singapore 1025 (☎ 466 4866)
South Africa
    795 George Ave, Arcadia, 0083 Pretoria (☎ 012-435658, 433845)
UK
    23 Cromwell Rd, London SW7 2EL (☎ 071-838 2055)
USA
    972 Fifth Ave, New York, NY 10021 (☎ 212-439 1400)

Centres Information Jeunesse

These offices, located in many French cities and towns, have all sorts of information for young people (and anyone else, for that matter) on housing, jobs (including seasonal work), professional training and educational options. The Paris headquarters (☎ 1-45.67.35.85; metro Champ de Mars-Tour Eiffel) is near the Eiffel Tower at 101 Quai Branly (15e).

Gay & Lesbian Organisations

For information on organisations affiliated with France's homosexual community, see the Gay & Lesbian Travellers section of this chapter.

BUSINESS HOURS

Most museums are closed on either Monday or Tuesday, though in summer some are open daily, especially in the south of France. A few places (eg the Louvre) stay open until 8 pm or later one or two nights a week.

The majority of small businesses are open daily except Sunday and perhaps Monday. Hours are usually 9 or 10 am to 6.30 or 7 pm, with a midday break from noon or 1 pm to 2 or 3 pm. In the south, midday closures tend to resemble siestas and may continue until 3.30 or 4 pm.

Supermarkets are usually open Monday to Saturday, but quite a few small food shops are closed on Sunday afternoon and Monday. As a result, Sunday morning may be your last chance to stock up on provisions until Tuesday unless you find a seven-day grocery or come across a boulangerie on duty by rotational agreement. Many restaurants are closed on Sunday.

In some parts of France, including Paris, local laws require that business establishments close for one day a week. The only exceptions are family-run businesses, such as grocery stores and small restaurants. Since you can never tell what day of the week an individual merchant has chosen to take off, this book includes, where possible, details on weekly days off.

In August, lots of establishments shut down so owners and employees alike can head for the hills or the beaches.

HOLIDAYS

Most museums and shops (but not cinemas, restaurants or most boulangeries) are closed on *jours fériés* (public holidays), which are listed in the table on the following page.

Note that Shrove Tuesday (Mardi Gras; the first day of Lent), Maundy Thursday (Jeudi saint), Good Friday (Vendredi saint; the Friday before Easter) and Boxing Day (26 December) are *not* jours fériés.

When a holiday falls on a Tuesday or Thursday, the French have a custom of making a *pont* (bridge) to the nearest weekend by taking off Monday or Friday, too. The doors of banks are a good place to look for announcements of upcoming long weekends.

France's National Day, 14 July, commemorates the day in 1789 when defiant Parisians stormed the Bastille prison, thus beginning the French Revolution. Often called Bastille Day by English speakers, it is celebrated with great gusto in most of the country, and in many cities and towns it can seems as if every person and their poodle is out on the streets. In Paris and many provincial towns, National Day ends with a fireworks display.

On May Day, many people buy *muguet* (lily of the valley), said to bring good luck, to give to friends. For one day a year, French law allows anyone to sell it without a permit.

In February 1993, President Mitterrand made 16 July a national day of remembrance for the racist and anti-Semitic crimes carried out by the Vichy regime during WW II. On

16 July 1942, French police carried out the first mass arrests of French Jews, who were taken to Paris's Vélodrome d'Hiver (Vel d'Hiv) cycling arena.

CULTURAL EVENTS

Most French cities have one or more music, dance, theatre, cinema or art festivals each year. Some villages hold *foires* (fairs) and *fêtes* (festivals) to honour anything from a local saint to the year's garlic crop.

In this book, important festivals are listed under Festivals in each city and town listing, but for precise details about dates, which change from year to year, contact the local tourist office. Abroad, information is available from French government tourist offices, which can give you a copy of *Festive France*, a free 70-page booklet in English detailing festivals in every region of the country.

The one drawback of the largest festivals is that they tend to make it very difficult to find accommodation. Reserve as far in advance as possible.

January
> *Paris* Start of the Paris-Dakar motor rally; early January
> *Monte Carlo* Car rally; late January

February to March
> *Paris* The *prêt à porter* fashion shows; early February
> *Menton* Lemon Festival; late February-early March
> *Dunkerque* Pre-Lent Carnival *(Carnaval)* with Giants
> *Nice* Pre-Lent Carnival

March to May
> *Perpignan* Religious procession; Good Friday
> *Paris* Foire de Paris; end of April-May
> *Saint Tropez* Bravade – procession honouring the town; mid-May
> *Cannes* Film Festival; two weeks in mid-May
> *Bordeaux* 'Musical May' concerts
> *Saintes Maries de la Mer* Gypsy Pilgrimage; late May
> *Monaco* Grand Prix Formula One motor race; late May

May to June
> *Paris* Roland-Garros (French Open) tennis championship; May-June
> *All over the country* Fête de la Musique (music festival); 21 June
> *Le Mans* 24-hour car rally; late June
> *Strasbourg* International Music Festival; first three weeks of June

July to August
> *Avignon* Festival d'Avignon & Festival Off (fringe festival); mid-July to mid-August
> *Aix-en-Provence* International classical music, dance and theatre festival; all July
> *Antibes* Jazz Festival; all July
> *Various locations* Tour de France International

PUBLIC HOLIDAYS

New Year's Day	*jour de l'an*	1 January
Easter Sunday	*Pâques*	late March or April
Easter Monday	*lundi de Pâques*	late March or April
May Day	*fête du Travail*	1 May
Victory Day for WW II	*Victoire 1945*	8 May
Ascension Day	*Ascension*	May (40th day after Easter)
Pentecost or Whit Sunday	*Pentecôte*	mid-May to mid-June (7th Sunday after Easter)
Whit Monday	*lundi de Pentecôte*	mid-May to mid-June
Bastille Day (National Day)	*Fête Nationale*	14 July
Assumption Day	*Assomption*	15 August
All Saints' Day	*Toussaint*	1 November
Armistice Day 1918 or Remembrance Day	*onze novembre* or *Armistice 1918*	11 November
Christmas	*Noël*	25 December

cycling race; three weeks in late June-July

All over the country Bastille Day, France's National Day with fireworks displays in many cities, including the famous illumination of Carcassonne; July 14

Orange Classical Music & Opera Festival; last fortnight of July

Quimper Cornouaille Celtic Festival; late July

Corte International Folklore Festival; late July

Béziers Féria; early August

Lorient Inter-Celtic Festival; early August

Ajaccio Assumption Day and Napoleon's birthday; 15 August

September
  Lille The Braderie, a big jumble sale and fair; early September
  Deauville American cinema festival; mid-September
  Lyon Berlioz (dance) Festival; second half of September
October to November
  Paris Contemporary Art Fair; early October
  Nancy Jazz Festival; 9-24 October
  Paris Jazz Festival; October-November
  Beaune Wine Auction; third Sunday of November
December
  Marseille Santons Fair; early December

Carnival figures in Nice

POST

Postal services in France are fast, reliable and expensive. About three-quarters of letters posted in France arrive the day after they're mailed.

Each of France's 17,000 post offices has a sign reading 'La Poste'. Older branches may also be marked with the letters PTT, the abbreviation of *postes, télégraphes, téléphones*. To mail things, go to a postal window marked *toutes opérations*.

Postal Rates

Domestic letters up to 20 grams cost 2.80FF.

For international mail, there are eight different destination zones, each of which has it own tariff structure. Postcards and letters up to 20 grams cost 2.80FF within the EC and 3.70FF to most of the rest of Europe and Africa. Postcards and letters up to 20 grams cost 4.30FF to the USA, Canada and the Middle East and 5.10FF to Australasia. Aerograms (air letters) cost 5FF to all destinations. Worldwide express mail delivery is called EMS Chronopost (☎ 05.43.21.00 for information).

Sea-mail services have been discontinued in France, so sending packages overseas by regular or *économique* (discount) air mail sometimes costs almost as much as the exorbitant overweight fees charged by airlines. Packages weighing over two kg may not be accepted at branch post offices – in Paris, they're handled by the *poste principale* of each arrondissement. Post offices sell smallish boxes in four different sizes for 5.40 to 11.50FF.

Sending Mail to France

All mail to France *must* include the five-digit postcode, which begins with the two-digit number of the département. In Paris, all postcodes begin with 750 and end with the two-digit arrondissement number, eg 75004 for the 4e arrondissement (see Orientation and Post & Telecommunications in the Paris chapter for details). In each city or town listing, the local postcode is listed under Post in the Information section.

Mail to France should be addressed as follows:

John Q SMITH
48 Rue de la Poste
75021 Paris, FRANCE

The surname (family name) should be written in capital letters. As you'll notice, the French put a comma after the street number and don't capitalise 'rue'.

The notation 'CEDEX' after a city or town name simply means that mail sent to that address is collected at the post office rather than delivered to the door.

Poste Restante

To have mail sent to you via poste restante (general delivery), available at all French post offices, have it addressed as follows:

SMITH, John Q
Poste Restante Recette Principale
76000 Rouen, FRANCE

Since poste restante mail is held alphabetically by last name, it is vital that you follow the French practice of having your *nom de famille* (surname or family name) written in capital letters. In case your friends back home forget, always check under the first letter of your *prénom* (first name) as well. There's a 2.80FF charge for every piece of poste restante mail you pick up. It is usually possible to forward *(faire suivre)* mail from one poste restante address to another. When you go to pick up poste restante mail, always have your passport or national ID card handy.

Poste restante mail not addressed to a particular branch goes to the city's *recette principale* (main post office) whether or not you include the words Recette Principale in the address. If you want it sent to a specific branch post office mentioned in this book (if mentioned in the text you can be sure it is centrally located and marked on the map), write the street address mentioned in the text and omit 'Recette Principale'.

In Paris, poste restante mail not addressed

to a particular branch is sent to the city's main post office (☎ 1-40.28.20.20; metro Sentier or Les Halles) at 52 Rue du Louvre (1er). See Post & Telecommunications in the Paris chapter for details.

American Express It is also possible to receive mail (but not parcels or envelopes larger than a piece of typing paper) in care of American Express. If you don't have an American Express card or at least one American Express travellers' cheque, there's a 5FF charge each time you check to see if you've received anything. The addresses of American Express offices are listed under Money in the relevant city listings.

American Express will give mail to the addressee only, and only if you have your passport. Messages can be left for 3FF, but it's cheaper to send a domestic letter. They will hold mail for 30 days before returning it to the sender. After that, having them forward it costs 15FF for two months.

TELECOMMUNICATIONS

Thirty years ago, France had one of the worst telephone systems in Western Europe, and as recently as the mid-1970s the average wait to have a phone installed was 16 months. But thanks to massive investment in the 1970s and '80s, the country now has one of the most modern and sophisticated telecommunications systems in the world.

International Dialling to France

To call the Paris area from outside France, dial your country's international access code, then 33 (France's country code), 1 and finally the eight-digit number. To call anywhere else in France or Monaco, dial the international access code, 33 and then the eight-digit local number.

Calls from Monaco to France are like domestic calls. For information on Andorra's international phone links, see the Facts for the Visitor section of the Andorra chapter.

International Dialling from France

To call someone outside France, just dial 19, wait for the tone, and then add the country code, city code (without the initial zero) and local number. International direct dial (IDD) calls to almost anywhere in the world can be placed from public telephones, but be prepared to watch your télécarte be debited at an alarming rate.

Useful country codes include:

Australia	61
Canada	1
Hong Kong	852
Ireland	353
New Zealand	64
Singapore	65
South Africa	27
UK	44
USA	1

If you don't know the country code (*indicatif pays*) you need and it doesn't appear on the information sheet posted in most telephone cabins, consult a telephone book or dial 12 (directory enquiries). Calls to Monaco are just like domestic calls. For information on how to call Andorra from France, see the Facts for the Visitor section in the Andorra chapter.

To make a reverse-charges (collect) call (*en PCV*, pronounced 'PEI-SEI-VEI') or a person-to-person call (*avec préavis*, pronounced 'ah-VEK preh-ah-VEE'), dial 19, wait for the tone and then dial 33 plus the country code of the place you're calling. Don't be surprised if you get a recording and have to wait a while. If you're using a public phone, you must insert a télécarte (or, in the case of coin telephones, 1FF) to place operator-assisted calls through 19 (the international operator).

For directory enquiries concerning subscriber numbers outside France, dial 19, and when the tone sounds dial 3312 and finally the relevant country code (for the USA and Canada, dial 11 instead of 1). You often get put on hold for quite a while. In public phones, you can access this service without a télécarte, but from home phones the charge is 7.30FF per number.

Toll-free 1-800 numbers in the USA and Canada cannot be called from overseas.

International Rates

Phoning abroad from France is not cheap. Daytime calls to other parts of Europe cost 4.26FF a minute (to the EC and Switzerland) or 6.57FF a minute (to Scandinavia, Turkey and Eastern Europe). Reduced tariffs (3.04FF and 4.38FF, respectively) apply on weekdays from 9.30 pm to 8 am and on the weekend and public holidays from 2 pm on Saturday straight through to 8 am on Monday.

Nondiscount calls to continental USA and Canada are 6.93FF a minute. The price drops to 5.96FF Monday to Saturday from noon to 2 pm and 8 pm to 2 am; this rate also applies on Sunday and public holidays from noon to 2 am. A slightly cheaper rate – 5.23FF a minute – is in force daily from 2 am to noon. The rate to Alaska, Hawaii and the Caribbean is a whopping 18.24FF a minute.

If you're phoning Australia, New Zealand, Japan, Hong Kong or Singapore, full-price calls are a 14.22FF a minute. A rate of 11.30FF a minute applies daily from 9.30 pm to 8 am and all day on Sunday and public holidays.

Calls to Asia, non-Francophone Africa and Latin America are generally 18.24FF a minute, though to some countries a rate of 12.88FF applies daily from 9.30 pm to 8 am and all day on Sunday and public holidays.

For more information on reduced rates for direct-dial international calls, dial 19 (tone) 3312 plus the country code of the place you'd like details about. By Minitel, key in 11 and then push the Sommaire button.

Home Direct Services

It is now possible to call many parts of the globe without going through a French operator – and without paying France Telecom's exorbitant rates – by using the Home Direct *(Pays Direct)* services that have been introduced over the last few years. In many cases, you can call not only the country you're from but also a third country. For instance, people who have accounts with the US company AT&T can bill a call from France to Egypt by using AT&T's home direct service.

Home direct numbers can be dialled from public phones without inserting a télécarte. If you get disconnected in mid- conversation, tell the operator when you call back and you may be able to avoid paying the connection fee again.

The numbers listed below will connect you, free of charge, with an operator in your home country, who will verify your method of payment: by credit card, reverse charges, etc. Wait for the tone after dialling 19.

Australia	
Telecom	19-00-61
Canada	19-00-16
Hong Kong	19-00-852
Ireland	19-00-353
New Zealand	19-00-64
Singapore	19-00-65
UK	19-00-44
USA	
AT&T USA Direct	19-00-11
MCI Call USA	19-00-19
Sprint Express	19-00-87

For calls to the USA, 24-hour use of your AT&T card costs US$4.21 for the first minute (US$7.71 person to person) and US$1.06 for each additional minute. Collect calls placed via AT&T cost US$7.46 (US$7.71 person to person) for the first minute and US$1.06 thereafter. With MCI, 24-hour MCI card rates are US$3.70 for the first minute (station to station or person to person) and US$1.06 thereafter; reverse-charges calls are US$6.70 for the first minute. There's no extra charge if you ask the operator to stay on the line to make sure you don't get an answering machine. Sprint's 24-hour card rates are US$5.81 (US$9.31 person-to-person) for the first three minutes and US$1.06 thereafter. The first three minutes of a collect call cost US$8.81 (US$9.31 person-to-person).

If you call Australia via Australia Telecom (reverse charges or using a télécarte), you'll be charged A$10.17 for the first three minutes and A$2.39 for each additional minute. At the time of going to press, Optus was yet to institute Home Direct service from France. For more information, call Optus on 008-500-005 before you leave home.

A call to New Zealand billed to a Telecom card or any Visa, MasterCard, Diners' Club or American Express credit card costs NZ$4.50 (NZ$9 person-to-person) plus NZ$2.87 a minute. A reverse charges call (station-to-station or person-to-person) costs NZ$9 plus NZ$2.87 a minute.

Domestic Dialling

For telecommunications purposes, France is divided into two regions: the Paris area and the rest of France (the 'provinces').

To make calls within either region, just dial the eight-digit number. To call the provinces from Paris, dial 16, and when you hear the tone dial the local number. To call the Paris area from the provinces, dial 16, wait for the dial tone, then add 1 followed by the eight digits. A '1' written before the eight-digit subscriber number indicates that it's in the Paris area. If you come upon an old-style Paris number with seven digits, try adding a 4 to the beginning.

For France Telecom's *service des renseignements* (directory enquiries or assistance), dial 12. Don't be surprised if the operator does not speak English. The call is free from many older public phones but costs five units from newer models (eg those made by Schlumberger and Monétel) and 3.65FF from private phones. These charges are clearly a bid to encourage people to use the Minitel system (see Minitel).

There is no way to make a domestic reverse-charges call. Instead, ask the person you're calling to ring you back (see Receiving Calls at Public Phones below).

If you get a bad connection, redialling usually improves things.

Domestic Tariffs

Local calls are quite cheap: one télécarte unit lasts for six minutes. But long-distance phone calls within France are expensive, especially considering the distances involved. For destinations less than 100 km away, the regular rate is 97 centimes a minute (45 seconds per unit). To call places over 100 km away, you'll be charged 2.57FF a minute

(17 seconds per unit), a bit less than half of the cheapest rate to North America!

Like everything else in France, domestic telephone discounts are colour-coded. The regular rate for calls within France, known as the *tarif rouge* (red tariff), applies Monday to Saturday from 8 am to 12.30 pm and Monday to Friday from 1.30 to 6 pm. You get 30% off with the *tarif blanc* (white tariff), which is in force Monday to Saturday from 12.30 to 1.30 pm and Monday to Friday from 6 pm to 9.30 pm. The rest of the time, you enjoy 50% off with the *tarif bleu* (blue tariff) except between 10.30 pm and 6 am, when the *tarif bleu nuit* (blue night tariff) gives you a 65% discount. Don't worry if all this sounds complicated: coloured rate charts are generally posted in public telephone booths.

Toll-Free Numbers

Two-digit emergency numbers (see Dangers & Annoyances), Home Direct numbers and *numéros verts* (toll-free numbers – literally, green numbers – which have eight digits and begin with 05), can be dialled from public telephones without inserting a télécarte or coins.

Public Phones

Almost all public telephones in France require a phonecard known as a *télécarte*, which can be purchased at post offices, *tabacs* (tobacconists' shops), Paris metro stations and elsewhere. Cards worth 50 units (good for 50 six-minute local calls) cost 40FF, while those worth 120 units cost 96FF. Make sure your card's plastic wrapper is intact when you buy it. For overseas calls, an entire 120-unit télécarte can be eaten up in six to 7½ minutes (to Australia) or 12 to 17 minutes (to the USA or Canada). For calls down under, that's only three or four seconds per unit.

Don't be surprised if someone asks you for your used télécarte – lots of people collect them, especially the commemorative ones.

In small village post offices, you occasionally find old-style phones for which you pay at the counter after you have made your call.

Using a Télécarte All you have to do to make a domestic or international phone call with a télécarte is to follow the instructions on the LCD display.

When a public telephone's display doesn't read *hors service* (out of order), the word *décrochez* (pick up the receiver) should appear in the window. When you see the words *introduire carte ou faire numéro libre* (insert the télécarte or dial a toll-free number), insert the card into the slot chip-end first with the rectangle of electrical connectors facing upward. *Patientez SVP* means 'please wait'. On phones that have a *volet* (a shutter that you close to conceal the télécarte), you'll see the words *fermez le volet SVP* (please close the shutter).

The top line of the display will tell you your *crédit* (how many units you have left), also called a *solde* (balance), denominated in *unités* (units), while the bottom line of the LCD screen will read *numérotez* (dial). When you dial, the *numéro appelé* (number being called) will appear on the display.

After you dial, you will hear a rapid beeping followed by long beeps (it's ringing) or short beeps (it's busy). When your call is connected, the screen begins counting down your card's value. To dial again without reinserting the télécarte, depress the white receiver button very briefly and wait for the dial tone.

When the call is over, you will again be told how many *unités* you have left. After you hang up, the display will read *retirez votre carte* (remove your télécarte).

If, for any reason, something goes wrong in the dialling process, you'll be asked to *racrochez SVP* (please hang up). When the screen reads *décrochez*, start the whole process over again. *Crédit épuisé* means that your télécarte has run out of units.

Switching a Used-Up Télécarte It is possible to replace a used-up télécarte with a new one in mid-call – an especially useful feature with overseas calls – without being cut off, but only if you follow the instructions exactly. When the screen says, *crédit = 000 unités – changement de carte*, press the oval green button, insert a new télécarte in place of the old one, and when the screen reads *fermez le volet* (not before), close the shutter.

Coin Phones Most post offices still have at least a few phones that take coins (minimum 1FF) rather than télécartes. Coin phones do not give change: if you put in a 5FF or 10FF piece and there are a few francs left on the meter when you hang up, you lose them. If you need to make another call, you can take advantage of the money left on the meter by pushing the receiver button down very briefly, waiting for the tone and then dialling.

Some coin phones let you hear the dial tone before you deposit the coins, but with older models (the ones with no place for 2FF pieces) you must put in the coins before you get the tone.

Point Phone Many cafés and restaurants have privately owned, coin-operated telephones known as Point Phones, easily identifiable by their angled, plastic fronts. Point Phones usually cost 1, 1.50 or 2FF for the first unit. You cannot get the international operator or receive calls from one, but you can dial emergency numbers (no coins needed) and use home direct services. To find a Point Phone, look for blue-on-white window stickers bearing the Point Phone emblem. Since they're primarily intended for clients, it's a good idea to ask permission from the proprietor.

Receiving Calls at Public Phones All public phones except Point Phones can receive both domestic and international calls. If you want someone to call you back, just give them the eight-digit number written after the words *Ici le* or *N° d'appel* on either the tariff sheet posted next to the telephone or a little sign riveted to the wall of the phone box.

Calling from a TGV Using the public phones on TGV trains costs 15FF a minute for calls within France. Dial as if you were in the provinces, not Paris. Télécartes are sold at the snack counter.

Minitel

When it was launched in 1984, the Minitel system was a bold step into the world of on-line home access to computer data bases. Though it now appears rather primitive, the Minitel is still a very efficient way to look up telephone numbers anywhere in France; make air, rail and concert reservations; and access a wide range of data bases. The terminals, which consist of a B&W monitor and a rather clumsy keyboard, are available for no charge to anyone with a telephone. By the late 1980s there were three million of them in homes and offices.

Minitel numbers consist of four digits – either 3615 or 3616 – and a string of letters known as the *code*. Home users pay a per-minute charge but the Minitels in post offices are free for directory enquiries. For an explanation of how to use a Minitel, ask a native.

Fax, Telex & Telegraph

Virtually all French post offices can send and receive telexes, telegrams and *télécopies* (faxes, also known as *téléfaxes*), to/from anywhere in the world. Prices, however, are very high.

TIME

France uses the 24-hour clock, with the hours separated from the minutes by a lower-case letter 'h'. Thus, 15h30 is 3.30 pm, 21h50 is 9.50 pm and 00h30 is 12.30 am.

France is one hour ahead of (later than) Greenwich Mean Time (GMT/UTC). During daylight-saving time, which runs from the last Sunday in September to the last Sunday in March, France is two hours ahead of GMT/UTC.

New York is generally six hours behind Paris, so when it's 1 pm on the US East Coast it's 7 pm in France. This may fluctuate a bit depending on exactly when daylight-saving time begins and ends on both sides of the Atlantic. The time difference to Melbourne and Sydney is even more complicated because daylight-saving time takes effect during the northern hemisphere winter. The Australian east coast is between eight and ten hours ahead of France.

ELECTRICITY

France and Monaco run on 220 V at 50 Hz AC. Andorra has a combination of 220 V and 125 V, both at 50 Hz. Old-type wall sockets, often rated at 600 watts, take two round prongs. The new kinds of sockets take fatter prongs and a protruding earth (ground) prong. Adaptors to make new-type plugs fit into the old sockets are said to be illegal but are available at electricians' shops. In Paris, adaptors and transformers of all sorts are available at the BHP department store (☎ 1-42.74.90.00; metro Hôtel de Ville) at 52 Rue de Rivoli (4e).

In the USA and Canada, the 120 V electric current is at 60 Hz. While the usual travel transformers allow North American appliances to run in France without blowing up, they cannot change the Hz rate, which determines the speed of electric motors. As a result, tape recorders not equipped with built-in adaptors may function poorly.

There are two types of travel transformers; mixing them up will destroy either the transformer or your appliance. The 'heavy' kind, usually rated for 35 watts or less, is designed for use with small electric devices such as radios, tape recorders and razors. The other kind, which often weighs less even though it can handle up to 1500 watts, can be used *only* with appliances that contain heating elements, such as hair dryers and irons.

WEIGHTS & MEASURES
Metric System

France uses the metric system, which was invented after the Revolution by the French Academy of Sciences (at the request of the National Assembly) and adopted by the French government in 1795. Inspired by the same rationalist spirit in whose name churches were ransacked and turned into Temples of Reason, the metric system replaced a confusing welter of traditional units of measure, which lacked all logical basis and made conversion complicated and commerce chaotic.

For a chart of metric equivalents, see the inside back cover.

Numbers

For numbers with four or more digits, the French use full stops (periods) where Anglo-Saxons would use commas: one million thus appears as 1.000.000. For decimals, on the other hand, the French use commas, so 1.75 comes out as 1,75.

When counting on their fingers, the French start with the thumb, not the index finger. If someone holds up two fingers and a thumb, it means three, not two.

LAUNDRY

Doing laundry while travelling in France is a pretty straightforward affair. To find a *laverie libre-service* (unstaffed, self-service laundrette) near where you're staying, see Laundry under Information at the beginning of each city listing or ask at your hotel or hostel. Some places even have self-service *nettoyage à sec* (dry cleaning) for about 60FF per six kg.

French laundrettes are not cheap. Be prepared to pay 15 to 20FF per five-kg load and 2FF per six minutes of drying. Often, identical-looking machines will have different capacities (eg five kg and seven kg) and different prices.

Some machines require that you buy a *jeton* (token) from a wall-mounted dispenser, while with others you put the money directly into slots in the machine. A few require that you put coins into a central control box and push a button corresponding to the number of the unit you wish to operate. In any case, you're likely to need all sorts of peculiar coin combinations – change machines are often out of order, so come prepared. Two-franc pieces are especially handy for the *séchoirs* (dryers) and the *lessive* (laundry powder) dispenser. Don't try using hand-washing powder as most kinds make too many suds for the machines to handle.

You can choose between a number of washing cycles. *Blanc* (whites), which uses water heated to 90°C, takes the longest (sometimes up to 60 minutes, indicated by the notation *60 mn*). *Couleur* (colours) are washed at 60°C. *Synthétique* (synthetics)

uses 30 or 40°C water. *Laine* (woollens) uses cold water. You can tell what the machine is doing by consulting the dial: *prélavage* (prewash cycle), *lavage* (wash cycle), *rinçage* (rinse cycle), *essorage* (spin-dry cycle).

TOILETS & BIDETS

In older cafés and even hotels, the amenities down the hall may include a *toilette à la turque* (Turkish-style toilet), a squat toilet which many people all over Asia prefer to the sit-down type but which some Westerners seem to think is primitive. The high-pressure flushing mechanism will soak your feet if you stand too close. In hotels, the hall toilet may be in a little room all its own, with the nearest washbasin attached to the nearest shower.

Bidets

In most hotel rooms – even those without toilets or showers – you will find a bidet, a porcelain fixture that looks like a shallow toilet with a pop-up stopper in the base but is in fact a basin for washing the genitals and anal area. Originally conceived to improve the personal hygiene of aristocratic women, its uses have expanded to include everything from hand-washing laundry to soaking your feet, though it's still remarkably effective in relieving crotch chafing and related complaints. Depending on the model, hot and cold fresh water enter vertically, horizontally or from under the rim.

Public Toilets

Public toilets, signposted as *toilettes* or *w.c.* (pronounced 'VEI SEI' or 'DOO-bleh VEI SEI'), are few and far between, though small towns often have them near the mairie. In Paris, there are a number of superb public toilets from the *belle époque*, but you're more likely to come upon one of the tan, self-disinfecting toilet pods emplaced along some streets. Get your change ready: many public toilets cost 2FF.

In the absence of public amenities, you can always duck into a fast-food outlet. Except in the most tourist-filled areas, café

and restaurant owners are usually amenable to your using their toilets provided you ask politely (and with just a hint of urgency): *'Est-ce que je peux utiliser les toilettes, s'il vout plaît?'*.

BOOKS

There are so many excellent books on France that it's hard to choose just a few to recommend, though the list has been considerably shortened by limiting the selection almost exclusively to works available in paperback.

People, Society & Culture

The following books about France and its people make for fascinating reading and should be readily available.

France Today by John Ardagh – This is a good introduction to modern-day France, its politics, its people and their peculiarities.

The French by Theodore Zeldin – This book will teach you everything you wanted to know about France from making friends with farmers to being chic.

Portraits of France by Robert Daley – These easy-reading stories and accounts of various cities in France offer insights into history and contemporary life.

The Banquet Years by Roger Shattuck – This wonderful account of life and art in turn-of-the-century Paris describes one of the headiest, most innovative periods in French history.

The Second Sex by Simone de Beauvoir – A systematic examination of women's inferior status, this study was an inspiration to the feminist movement and one of the most significant books of the Existentialist era.

Feminism in France by Claire Duchen – This book charts the progress of feminism in France from 1968 to the mid-1980s.

The Food of France by Waverley Root – This excellent, region-by-region guide to French cuisine, first published in 1958 and recently reprinted in paperback, divides the country into the Domain of Butter, the Domain of Fat, the Domain of Oil and the Pyrenees, where all three are used.

A Spy in the House by Anaïs Nin (1954; Penguin) – This essay on women's psyche and sexuality is one of the five volumes of *Cities of the Interior*.

Pig Earth by John Berger – The first of three books showing the harsh life and hopes of a peasant community in France.

Down and Out in Paris and London by George Orwell (Penguin) – Orwell's excellent account of the time he spent living with tramps in London and Paris in the late 1920s.

A Book of the Basques by Rodney Gallop (hardback).

History

Citizens, a highly acclaimed and truly monumental work by Simon Schama, looks at the first few years after the storming of the Bastille in 1789. The three volumes of Alfred Cobban's *A History of Modern France* cover the period from Louis XIV to 1962. *Pétain's Crime* by Paul Webster examines the collaborationist Vichy government that ruled part of the country during WW II.

You might also take a look at any of the books by Alistair Horne, which include *The Fall of Paris* (on the Commune of 1870-71), *The Price of Glory* (on the WW I Battle of Verdun) and *To Lose a Battle* (on the French defeat in 1940). *Is Paris Burning?* is Larry Collins and Dominique Lapierre's dramatic account of the liberation of Paris in 1944.

The Age of the Cathedrals by Georges Duby is an authoritative study of the relations between art and society in medieval France.

French Literature

For suggested reading, see Literature in the Facts about the Country chapter. Most of the writers mentioned have been translated into English.

Literature by Non-French Writers

France, known for its tolerance of deviations from conventional social norms, has long attracted writers from all over the world.

A Moveable Feast by Ernest Hemingway portrays Bohemian life in Paris between the wars.

Henry Miller wrote some pretty steamy stuff set in Paris, including *Tropic of Cancer* and *Tropic of Capricorn*, both published in France in the 1930s but banned under obscenity laws in the UK and USA until the 1960s.

More recently, Peter Mayle's *A Year in Provence* and *Toujours Provence* have been bestsellers in the UK and USA. They take a witty, patronising and very English look at the French.

Other books by non-French authors include:

Flaubert's Parrot by Julian Barnes – This highly entertaining novel pays witty homage to the great French writer.
The Autobiography of Alice B Toklas by Gertrude Stein – This autobiography is an account of Stein's years in Paris, her salon on the Rue de Fleurus and her friendships with Matisse, Picasso, Braque and others.

Travel Literature

Classic works of travel literature about France include:

A Little Tour in France by Henry James – This is an account of the famous author's wanderings from Tours to Avignon.
A Sentimental Journey by Laurence Sterne – One of the classics of travel writing, this is a digressive and fanciful account of Sterne's tour by coach through France and Italy in 1765.
Travels with a Donkey by Robert Louis Stevenson – This book recounts the famous Scottish writer's journey through the remote region of the Cévennes with his donkey Modestine in 1878. The complete diary of the trip, *The Cévennes Journal*, was published in 1979.

Travel Guides

In travel guides in French, place names that begin with a definite article (eg Le Mont Saint Michel, La Rochelle, L'Île Rousse) may be listed either under Le/La/L' or under the rest of the name. For instance, La Poste (the post office) appears under L in the phone directory. Names that start with 'Saint' (abbreviated as St) are listed before names that begin with 'Sainte' (Ste), a female saint. In map and guidebook indexes, streets named after people are listed either by the last name or, as Michelin seems to prefer, by the first name or title (Général, Maréchal, etc).

Historical Michelin, a giant, family-owned rubber company, that is known as one of France's most secretive industrial corporations, has been publishing travel guides ever since the earliest days of motorcar touring, when the books were intended to promote sales of its inflatable rubber tyres.

Michelin's *guides verts* (green guides; 47 to 52FF each), which cover all of France in 24 regional volumes – 10 of which are presently available in English – are full of historical information, although the editorial approach is very conservative and regional cultures tend to be given short shrift. The green guide to all of France (about 50FF) has brief entries on the most touristed sights.

The massive *Blue Guide* (240FF) has reams of detailed information on architecture and history, but tends to emphasise historical sights at the expense of information on modern French life.

Guides to Paris Michelin's *Green Guide to Paris* (paperback), widely available in France for about 50FF, charts 27 walking itineraries all over Paris, each accompanied by excellent maps and a rather dry commentary in slightly fractured English. *Paris Step by Step* (paperback; US$9.95) by Christopher Turner, published in the UK by Pan Books, details 18 walks with maps and an eminently readable text. *Pariswalks* by Alison and Sonia Landes is another popular walking guide.

Dorling Kindersley publish a guide to *Paris* as part of their Eyewitness Travel Guides series. It is lavishly (and perhaps a trifle excessively) illustrated in colour, including '3-D' illustrations of some small sections of Paris. It also contains some upmarket hotel and restaurant recommendations.

Paris Literary Companion by Ian Littlewood, published in the USA by Perennial Library, takes you by the buildings once inhabited by famous literary personalities.

Many Parisians use *Le Petit Futé* (59FF), basically a book of useful addresses, and *Paris Pas Cher*, updated annually, which lists inexpensive shopping options. Another source of information on penny-wise living in Paris is *Paris aux Meilleurs Prix*. All three are on sale in bookshops and larger newsagencies.

Guides In French Among the French-language guides, useful only if your French is quite proficient, the best overall historical

guidebooks are those published by *Guide Bleu* (no relation to its English-language namesake), whose blue-jacketed regional and all-France guides provide accurate and balanced information on matters historical, cultural, architectural and artistic. It also mentions relevant bits of the less-glorious aspects of French history.

The *Guide du Routard* guides to France are especially popular with young French people travelling around their own country. The restaurant recommendations generally offer good value, but rock-bottom hotels rarely make an appearance, and there are very few maps. Guide du Routard's *Hôtels & Restos de France* (93FF) lists mid-range hotels and restaurants all over the country.

Hiking & Cycling Topoguides are booklets on specific long-distance trails. Usually sold for 30 or 35FF, they include trail maps and information in French on trail conditions, flora, fauna, villages en route, camp sites, *refuges*, etc. Most topoguides are published by the Fédération Française de la Randonnée Pedestre whose Paris bookshop and Centre d'Information (☎ 45.45.31.02; metro Plaisance), is at 64 Rue de Gergovie (14e). Many bookshops and local tourist offices stock a selection of titles relevant to their region. If you're coming from the UK, it might be easier and cheaper to buy the topoguides' English equivalents, published as part of the Footpaths of Europe series, before leaving home.

Walking in France by Rob Hunter (1986, Oxford Illustrated Press, £4.95) gives an overview of the GR tracks as well as general hiking information. A good guide for Alpine hiking is *Walking in the Alps* by Brian Spencer.

Mountain bike enthusiasts who can read French should look for the books of Les Guides VTT, a series of cyclists' topoguides published by Didier et Richard. Another French series to keep an eye out for is Circuits Pédestres, books of hiking and mountain bike routes published by Annecy-based Guide Franck.

Cycle Touring in France by Robin Neillands (1989; Oxford Illustrated Press; £7.95), a good companion for independent cyclists touring France, details 20 cycling tours. *Bicycle Tours of France* (US$10) by Gay & Kathlyn Hendricks, published by Plume, has details on five suggested cycling routes.

In French, the Guide du Routard publishes a paperback called *Aventures en France*, with details on hiking, mountain biking, rock climbing, boating, spelunking, skiing, horse riding, etc.

Accommodation & Restaurants Many people swear by Michelin's red-jacketed *Guide Rouge* to France (100 to 125FF), published annually, which has over 1200 pages of information on mid and upper-range hotels and restaurants in every corner of the country. Accompanied by detailed city maps and coordinated with Michelin's yellow-jacketed 1:200,000 scale road maps, it is best known for rating France's greatest restaurants with one, two or three stars. Only about 20 restaurants in the whole of France have three stars. The little symbols used instead of text are explained in English at the front of the book.

The *Guide Gault Millau France* restaurant guide (170FF), published annually, awards up to four *toques rouges* (red chefs' caps) to restaurants with exceptionally good, creative cuisine; *toques blanches* (white chefs' caps) go to places with superb modern or traditional cuisine. Each establishment is rated on a scale of one to 20. *Gault Millau* is said to be quicker at picking up-and-coming restaurants than the *Guide Rouge*. The symbols used are explained in English. An English edition is also available.

Both informative and a good read, the *Food Lover's Guide to France* (Workman, 1993) by Patricia Wells has recently been completely revised.

Vegetarian The *Annuaire Vert* (green directory; 225FF if ordered from the publisher), published annually by Éditions O.C.E.P. (☎ 1-47.00.46.46; metro Saint Amboise) at 11 Rue Saint Amboise (11e) in Paris, lists

shops that sell organic and macrobiotic foods, vegetarian restaurants, *pharmaciens-herboristes* (naturopathic pharmacies) and all sorts of organisations. The listings are by département. In Paris, the *Annuaire Vert* is available from FNAC stores.

MAPS

Road maps and city maps are available at Maisons de la Presse newsagencies, tourist offices, bookshops and even some newspaper kiosks. Where applicable, advice on maps and where to buy them is given under Information in a city or town listing.

When more than one town bears the same name, each one is given a descriptive suffix. For instance, you'll find in various parts of the country Villefranche-sur-Cher (Villefranche on the Cher River), Villefranche-sur-Mer (Villefranche by the sea) and Villefranche-du-Périgord (Villefranche in the Périgord region). Unless there's another Villefranche nearby, local people usually drop the suffix.

The best place to get Institut Géographique National (IGN) maps is at the Espace IGN (☎ 1-43.98.85.00; metro Franklin D Roosevelt) at 107 Rue La Boétie (8e), which is open Monday to Friday from 9.30 am to 7 pm and on Saturday from 10 am to 12.30 pm and 2 to 5.30 pm.

Road Maps

A variety of *cartes routières* (road maps) are available, but if you're going to be driving all around France, the best road atlas to have in the car is Michelin's *Atlas Routier France*, which covers the whole country in 1:200,000 scale (one cm = two km). It comes with either spiral or regular binding and should cost about 100FF. If you'll be concentrating on just a few regions, it might be easier and cheaper to buy Michelin's remarkably convenient yellow-jacketed 1:200,000-scale fold-out maps (8 to 12FF), identified by two-digit numeric names. The larger (and clumsier) versions, which cover the country in 17 sheets, have three-digit names and cost 23FF. Both types are available at bookshops and newsagents. Cycling with 1:200,000

scale maps is eminently possible but may sometimes require a bit of guesswork.

IGN covers France with 16 1:250,000-scale maps (24FF) and 74 1:100,000-scale maps (24FF). Both are more difficult to drive with than Michelin's maps. Michelin's redseries maps cover whole regions of Europe in 1:1,000,000 scale. They cost about 20FF each.

Intercity roads that skirt around wellknown congestion spots are indicated on a free map of France called the Bison Futé (Wily Buffalo), available at many tourist offices and 90 *points d'accueil et d'information Bison Futé* (Bison Futé welcome & information centres). Revised annually, the *itinéraires bis* (secondary itineraries) it shows are also indicated on the white-on-green highway signs that tell you how to get to various destinations – look for the word *'Bis'*, usually enclosed by a yellow square.

Hiking Maps

Didier et Richard publishes a series of 1:50,000 scale trail maps (about 67FF), perfect for hoofing it or cycling.

IGN covers all of France with about 1100 1:50,000-scale topographical maps and 2200 1:25,000-scale maps. There are two varieties in the 1:25,000 scale: the old kind (43FF), which cover the entire country; and the newer Top 25 series maps (53FF), which are availble for the Mediterranean coast, the Alps, the Pyrenees, the Basque Country and a few other areas. Map No 1748 OT (OT is short for *ouest*, ie west) covers an area slightly west of that covered by map No 1748 ET (short for *est*, ie east).

IGN's 1:1,000,000-scale grey-jacketed map No 903 shows all of France's long-distance GR trails. It is useful for stragetic planning of a cross-country hike.

City Maps

The *plans* (street maps) distributed free by most tourist offices range from superb to virtually unusable. Michelin's *Guide Rouge* (see Travel Guides) has useful little maps of most French cities and towns. Some of them

also appear, in slightly different form, in the company's *Guides Verts* (Green Guides). Michelin publishes superb 1:10,000-scale maps of Paris and Lyon. Plans-Guides Blay offers orange-jacketed street maps of 125 French cities and towns.

Abbreviations commonly used on city maps include *R* for *rue* (street), *Bd*, *Boul* or *Bould* for boulevard, *Av* for avenue, *Q* for *quai* (quay), *Cr* for *cours* (avenue), *Pl* for *place* (square), *Pte* for *porte* (gate), *Imp* for *impasse* (dead-end street), *St* for *saint* (masculine) and *Ste* for *sainte* (feminine).

Bis & Ter When a new building is put up in a location where they've run out of consecutive street numbers, a new address is formed by fusing the number of an ajacent building with the notations *bis* (twice), *ter* (thrice) or, occasionally, *quater* (four times). Thus, the street numbers 14bis or 92ter are the equivalent of 14A or 92B.

Entering Buildings In larger cities, especially Paris, the street doors of many apartment buildings can be opened only if you have the *code* (entry code), which is changed periodically. Outside intercoms (*interphones*) are rare, so if you arrive at a friend's place without the code you may have no choice but to ring them from the nearest public phone.

In some buildings, the entry code device is de-activated during the day, but to get in you still have to push a button (usually marked *porte*) to release the catch. To get *out* of doors with such devices, you usually have to push a button – also marked *porte* – mounted on the wall of the entryway somewhere near the door.

Finding the Right Apartment In most apartment buildings, the hall lights are linked to a *minuterie* (timer), which turns them on for a few minutes whenever someone pushes one of the buttons. These are usually found near the main entrance and on each floor.

If you come upon more than one *escalier* (staircase) – one on either side of the lobby,

for instance – check if the address you've been given mentions which one to take.

The doors of many French apartments are completely unmarked: not only will the occupants' names not appear, but there won't even be a number. So you'll know which door to knock on, you'll be given instructions, such as *cinquième étage, premier à gauche* (5th floor, first on the left) or *troisième étage, droite droite* (3rd floor, turn right twice). Remember that in France (and in this book), the 1st floor is the floor above the *rez-de-chaussée* (ground floor).

MEDIA
Newspapers & Magazines
English In cities and larger towns, Maisons de la Presse and railway station newspaper kiosks usually carry the informative *International Herald Tribune* (9FF), published jointly by the *New York Times* and the *Washington Post*. Edited in Paris, it comes out six times a week. Other English-language papers you can find include two British papers with European editions, the *Guardian* and the *Financial Times*; *The European*, saved from the ruins of Robert Maxwell's financial empire; and colourful *USA Today*, which packages its news in easily digestible news nuggets. *Newsweek*, *Time* and the *Economist* are widely available.

France-USA Contacts, which comes out every fortnight, consists of hundreds of ads placed by both companies and individuals (eg Anglophones about to leave the country who want to sell a few things). Distributed free at Paris's English bookshops, it can be very helpful if you're looking for cheap air tickets to the UK or USA, au pair or babysitting jobs, a short-term apartment to sublet in Paris, a used computer, a car, etc. To place an ad, contact FUSAC Centre d'Annonces (☎ 1-45.38.56.57; fax 1-45.38.98.94; metro Gaité) at 3 Rue Larochelle (14e), which is 300 metres south-east of Gare Montparnasse.

The News (7FF) is an English-language monthly published by very middle-class English people living in France. Its editorial office (☎ 53.23.84.30) is in Eymet (postcode

24500). It is available at a limited number of news kiosks, including those at Paris's railway stations.

French France's main daily newspapers are, from most widely read to least: *Le Figaro* (right; aimed at professionals, business people and the bourgeoisie); *Le Monde* (centre-left; popular with business people, professionals and intellectuals); *Le Parisien* (centre; middle class); *France Soir* (right; working and middle class); *Libération* (left; popular with students and intellectuals) and *L'Humanité* (communist; working class).

Radio & TV
AM & FM You can pick up a mixture of the BBC World Service and BBC for Europe, whose English programming is sometimes interrupted by short broadcasts in French and German, on 648 kHz AM, most easily received in north-western France. Various UK stations can be picked up near the English Channel. Along the Côte d'Azur, Riviera Radio has hourly broadcasts of BBC World Service news on 106.5 and 106.3 MHz FM. VOA Europe, the Voice of America's European service, is on 1197 kHz AM.

In the Paris area, Radio France International (RFI) broadcasts the world news in English every day from 4 to about 4.55 pm on 738 kHz AM.

In French, France Info broadcasts the news 24 hours a day. Except very late at night, there are news headlines every few minutes, which is great for learning French: if you didn't catch something last time, it will be probably be repeated again in a few minutes. In Paris, France Info is on 105.3 MHz FM. In other parts of the country, it can usually be picked up somewhere between 105.3 and 105.7 MHz FM.

Short-Wave & Long-Wave The BBC World Service can be picked up on 5975, 6195, 9410, 9760, 12095, 15070 and 15575 kHz short-wave, depending on the time of day. BBC Radio 4 broadcasts on 195 kHz long-wave;

at 1.45 am, this frequency switches over to the BBC World Service.

Although Radio Australia mainly focuses on the Asia-Pacific region, it can often be picked up on 6020, 7260, 9540, 13755, 15240, 21590 and 21725 kHz. A schedule is available from the Australian Embassy.

The VOA can usually be received on 3980, 6040, 9760, 11970 and 13205 kHz. In the late morning, VOA Europe (see AM & FM Radio) broadcasts on 11735, 15160, 15195, 21455 and 21570 kHz.

Radio Canada International, which often carries rebroadcasts of domestic CBC programming (including the World at Six), is on the air in English for 15-minute or half-hour periods in the very early morning, mid-afternoon and evening on 5995, 6050, 6150, 7235, 7295, 9670, 9750, 11905, 11935, 13650, 15305, 15315, 15325, 17795, 17820, 17875, 21545 and 21675 kHz. Schedules are available from the Canadian Embassy in Paris.

The World Service of Radio France International can be picked up in English on 6175 kHz at various times of the day, especially in the early and mid-afternoon.

TV in English Sky TV can be found in better hotels all over Europe, as can CNN and other networks. You can also pick up many cross-border TV stations, including UK stations close to the Channel. Canal+, a French subscription TV station available in many mid-range hotels, sometimes screens non-dubbed English movies.

French TV A variety of TV listings magazines costing from 2 to 10FF come out each Monday. Sold at newstands, they include *Télé K7*, *Télé Star*, *Télé 7 Jours* and *Télé Loisirs*. *Télérama* is issued on Wednesday.

Videotapes Unlike the rest of Western Europe and Australia, which use PAL (phase alternation line), French TV broadcasts are in SECAM *(système électronique couleur avec mémoire)*. North America and Japan use a third incompatible system, NTSC (National Television Systems Committee).

Non-SECAM TVs will not work in France, and French videotapes cannot be played on videocassette recorders and TVs that lack a SECAM capability.

FILM & PHOTOGRAPHY
X-Ray Machines
Be prepared to have your camera and film run through the x-ray machines at airports and the entrances to sensitive public buildings. The gadgets are ostensibly film-safe up to 1000 ASA, and laptops and computer disks are sent through without losing data, but there is always some degree of risk.

The police and gendarmes who run x-ray machines often seem to treat a request that they hand-check something as casting doubt on the power and glory of the French Republic. Arguing almost never works, and being polite is only slightly more effective unless you can do it in French. You're most likely to get an affirmative response if you are deferential and your request is moderate: just ask them to hand-check your film, not your whole camera (which could, after all, conceal a bomb). They are usually amenable to checking computer disks by hand.

Taking Photographs
Photography is rarely forbidden except in museums and art galleries. Of course, snapshots of military installations are not appreciated in any country.

When photographing people, it is basic courtesy to ask permission. If you don't know any French, smile while pointing at your camera and they'll get the picture (so, probably, will you). Brazenly snapping away at a group of old men gossiping around a village fountain could get you an earful of French expletives.

Film & Developing
Colour-print film produced by Kodak and Fuji is widely available in supermarkets, photo shops and FNAC stores. A 36-exposure roll of Kodacolor costs about 36FF for 100 ASA and 44FF for 400 ASA. Kodak B&W film rated at 400 ASA costs 26/35FF

for 24/36 exposures. One-hour developing is widely available.

For slides (*diapositives*), count on paying at least 87FF for a 36-exposure roll of Kodachrome 64, processing included. A 36-exposure roll of Ektachrome without developing costs 47/58/69FF for 100/200/400 ASA. Developing Ektachrome slides costs about 30FF for 24 exposures and 40FF for 36 exposures.

HEALTH
France is a healthy place. Your main risks are likely to be sunburn, foot blisters, insect bites, and an upset stomach from eating and drinking too much. You might experience mild stomach problems if you're not used to copious amounts of rich cream and olive oil-based sauces, but you'll get used to it after a while.

Travel health depends on your predeparture preparations and fitness, your day-to-day health care while travelling, and how you handle any medical problem or emergency that does develop. If you're reasonably fit, the only things you should organise before departure are a visit to your dentist, and travel insurance with good medical cover (see Predeparture Preparations).

Travel Health Guides
There are a number of books on travel health, most of them geared towards the tropics, where health is a major issue. Worth considering are:

Travellers' Health (Dr Richard Dawood, Oxford University Press) which is comprehensive, easy to read, authoritative and highly recommended, though it's rather large to lug around.
Travel with Children (Maureen Wheeler, Lonely Planet Publications), which includes basic advice on travel health for younger children.

Predeparture Preparations
Health Insurance Since most non-European national health plans and certain private ones in the USA won't cover you when you in France, a travel insurance policy to cover medical treatment is a must. A wide variety

of policies is available – your travel agent will have recommendations. The international student travel policies handled by STA or other student travel organisations are usually good value. Various policies offer lower and higher upper limits of coverage – when choosing one remember that medical costs can be astronomical. Make sure to check the small print:

- Some policies specifically exclude 'dangerous activities' which can include scuba diving, motorcycling, skiing, mountaineering, and even trekking. If such activities are on your agenda, you don't want that sort of policy.
- Check if the policy covers ambulances, helicopter rescue and an emergency flight home. If you have to stretch out you will need two seats and somebody has to pay for them.
- You may prefer a policy that pays doctors or hospitals directly rather than you having to pay on the spot and claim reimbursement later. If you have to claim later, make sure you get all the necessary documentation. Some policies ask you to call back (reverse charges) to a centre in your home country so a preliminary assessment of your problem can be made.

Citizens of EC countries are covered for emergency medical treatment throughout the EC on presentation of an E111 form (which confers a slightly different package of benefits than does the National Health coverage in the UK). For certain tests and procedures, you may be asked to pay a portion of the cost youself; part of this amount will then by reimbursed by your national health care system. Enquire about this at your national health service or travel agent well in advance.

The coverage provided by most private US health insurance policies continues if you travel abroad, at least for a limited period. In France, Americans usually have to pay for treatment (by cash or credit card) and then take the receipt to their insurance company for reimbursement. At present there is no special arrangement between the French national health care system and Blue Cross/Blue Shield, though the American Hospital in Paris is a Blue Cross/Blue Shield affiliate (see Medical Services under Information in the Paris chapter).

Canadians covered by the Régie de l'Assurance-Maladie du Québec and who have a valid Assurance-Maladie du Québec card can benefit from certain *prise en charge* (reimbursement) agreements with France's national health care system.

Australian Medicare provides absolutely no coverage in France, emergency or otherwise.

Medical Kit It's an excellent idea to carry a small, straightforward medical kit. A possible list includes:

- Aspirin, Paracetamol (Panadol) or Acetamenophen (Tylenol) for pain or fever
- Antihistamine (such as Benadryl) – useful as a decongestant for colds, allergies, to ease the itch from insect bites or stings or to help prevent motion sickness
- Kaolin preparation (Pepto-Bismol), Imodium or Lomotil, for possible stomach upsets
- Antiseptic and antibiotic powder or similar 'dry' spray, for cuts and grazes
- Calamine lotion to ease irritation from bites or stings
- Bandages and Band-aids for minor injuries
- Scissors, tweezers and a thermometer (note that mercury thermometers are prohibited by airlines)
- Insect repellent, sunscreen, suntan lotion, chapstick and perhaps water purification tablets

Health Preparations If you wear glasses, take a spare pair and your prescription. Losing your glasses can be a problem, but you can usually get new spectacles made quickly, competently and relatively cheaply.

If you require a particular medication, take an adequate supply, as it may be hard to find in more remote areas. The same applies for your specific oral contraceptive. If you have a prescription, it will be easier to refill it if it's made out for the generic drug rather than the brand name, which may not be distributed in France.

It's a good idea to have a prescription and a letter from your doctor to show that you legally use the medication you're bringing with you – it's surprising how often over-the-

counter drugs from one place are illegal without a prescription or even banned in another. Keep the medication in its original container. If you're carrying a syringe for some reason, have a note from your doctor to explain why you're doing so.

A Medic Alert tag is a good idea if your medical condition is not always easily recognisable (heart trouble, diabetes, asthma, allergic reactions to antibiotics, etc).

Immunisations No jabs are required to travel to France, but may be necessary to visit other European countries if you're coming from an infected area – yellow fever is the most likely requirement. If you're going to France with stopovers in Asia, Africa or Latin America, check with your travel agent or the embassies of the countries you plan to visit.

There are, however, a few routine vaccinations that are recommended whether you're travelling or not, and this Health section assumes that you've had them: polio (usually administered during childhood), tetanus and diphtheria (usually administered together during childhood, with a booster shot every 10 years), and sometimes measles. For details, see your physician or nearest health agency.

All vaccinations should be recorded on an International Health Certificate, which is available from your physician or government health department. Don't leave this till the last minute, since the vaccinations may have to be spread out over a period of time.

Basic Rules
Water Despite long-standing rumours to the contrary, tap water all over France is safe to drink. However, unlike Switzerland, the water in most French fountains is not drinkable and, like the taps in some public toilets, may have a sign reading *eau non potable* (undrinkable water). It's a good idea to take heed even if the locals tell you that 92-year-old Monsieur Bloggs down the road has been drinking from the fountain all his life.

Always beware of natural sources of water. A burbling Alpine or Pyrenean stream may look crystal clear, but it's inadvisable to drink untreated water unless you're at the spring and can see it coming out of the rock.

It's very easy not to drink enough liquids, especially on hot days or at high altitudes – don't rely on feeling thirsty to indicate when you should drink. Not needing to urinate or very dark-yellow urine is a danger sign. France suffers from a singular lack of drinking fountains, so its a good idea to carry a water bottle (canteen) with you.

Excessive sweating can lead to a loss of salt and therefore muscle cramping. Salt tablets are not a good idea as a preventative, but in places where salt is not used much, adding salt to food can help.

Water Purification This section is only relevant if you are planning extended hikes during which you'll be relying on natural water.

The simplest way of purifying water is to boil it thoroughly. Technically this means boiling for 10 minutes, something which happens very rarely. Remember that at high altitudes water boils at a lower temperature, so germs are less likely to be killed.

Simple filtering will not remove all dangerous organisms, so if you cannot boil water it should be treated chemically. Chlorine tablets (Puritabs, Steritabs or other brand names) will kill many but not all pathogens. Iodine is very effective in purifying water and is available in tablet form (such as Potable Aqua), but follow the directions carefully and remember that too much iodine can be harmful.

If you can't find tablets, tincture of iodine (2%) can be used. Two drops of tincture of iodine per litre or quart of clear water is the recommended dosage; the treated water should be left to stand for 30 minutes before drinking. Iodine loses its effectiveness if exposed to air or damp so keep it in a tightly sealed container. Flavoured powder will disguise the taste of treated water and is a good idea if you are travelling with children.

Nutrition If you're travelling hard and fast and missing meals or simply lose your appe-

tite, you can soon start to lose weight and place your health at risk.

Make sure your diet is well balanced. This is not hard to do in France where protein sources – eggs, meat, lentils and nuts – are all easy to come by. Fruit and vegetables, essential sources of vitamins, are also plentiful. Try to eat wholegrain and multicereal breads rather than just white-flour baguettes, which won't do you any harm but won't do you much good either.

If you rely on fast food, you'll get plenty of fats and carbohydrates but little else. Remember that overcooked food loses much of its nutritional value. If your diet isn't well balanced, it's a good idea to take vitamin and iron pills; women lose a lot of iron because of their periods.

Mushrooms Mushroom-picking is a favourite pastime in France as autumn approaches, but make sure you don't eat any mushrooms that haven't been positively identified as safe. If in doubt, take your finds to a pharmacy – all French pharmacists are trained to identify edible and poisonous mushrooms.

Everyday Health A normal body temperature is 37°C or 98.6°F ; more than 2°C or 3°F higher is a 'high' fever. A normal adult pulse rate is 60 to 80 beats a minute (children 80 to 100, babies 100 to 140). You should know how to take a temperature and a pulse rate. As a general rule, the pulse increases about 20 beats per minute for each 1°C rise in fever.

Respiration rate is also an indicator of illness. Count the number of breaths per minute: between 12 and 20 is normal for adults and older children (up to 30 for younger children, 40 for babies). People with a high fever or serious respiratory illness (like pneumonia) breathe more quickly than normal. More than 40 shallow breaths a minute usually means pneumonia.

Many health problems can be avoided by taking care of yourself. Maintain good hygiene and wash your hands frequently. Avoid climatic extremes: keep out of the sun when it's hot, and dress warmly when it's cold. Minimise insect bites by covering bare skin or using insect repellents when insects are around.

Medical Treatment
Emergency numbers for ambulances, the police and the fire brigade are listed in this chapter under Dangers & Annoyances.

Most major hospitals are indicated on the maps in this book, and their addresses and phone numbers are mentioned in the text. Tourist offices and hotels can put you on to a doctor or dentist, and your embassy or consulate will probably know one who speaks your language.

Public Health System France has an extensive public health care system. Anyone (including foreigners) who is sick, even mildly so, can receive treatment in the *service des urgences* (casualty ward or emergency room) of any public hospital. Hospitals try to have people who speak English in the casualty wards, but this is not done systematically. If necessary, the hospital will call in an interpreter. It's an excellent idea to ask for a copy of the diagnosis – in English, if possible – in case your doctor back home is interested.

Getting treated for illness or injury in a public hospital costs much less in France than in many other countries, especially the USA. From Monday to Saturday, being seen by a doctor (a *consultation*) costs only about 90FF (240FF from 8 pm to 8 am). On Sunday and holidays, the fee is 200FF (240FF at night). Seeing a specialist is a bit more expensive. Blood tests and other procedures, each of which has a standard fee, will increase this figure. Hospitals usually ask that visitors from abroad settle accounts right after receiving treatment, although at night and on weekends, when the payments office is likely to be closed, this may not be possible.

Dental Care For details on dental care options in Paris, see Medical Care under Information in the Paris chapter.

Pharmacies French pharmacies are almost always marked by a green cross whose neon components are lit when it's open. Pharmacists *(pharmaciens)* can often suggest treatments for minor ailments.

If you are prescribed medication, make sure you understand the dosage, how often and when you should take it. It's a good idea to ask for a copy of the prescription *(ordonnance)* so you have a record of the exact name of the medication you took, in what dosages and for how long.

French pharmacies coordinate their days and hours of closure so that a town or district won't be left without a place to buy medication. For after-hours service, consult the door of any pharmacy, which will have the name of a nearby *pharmacie de garde* (pharmacy on weekend/night duty) posted.

Climatic & Geographical Considerations

Sunburn In southern France and anywhere on water, ice, snow or sand – especially at high altitudes – you can get sunburnt surprisingly quickly, even if there's cloud cover. Use a sunscreen and take extra care to cover areas that don't normally see sun, such as your feet. A hat provides added protection, and it may be a good idea to use zinc cream or some other barrier cream for your nose and lips. Calamine lotion helps to relieve the symptoms of mild sunburn.

Remember that too much sunlight can damage your eyes, whether it's direct or reflected (glare). If your plans include water, ice, snow or sand, then good sunglasses are doubly important. Make sure they're treated to absorb ultraviolet radiation – if not, they'll actually do more harm than good by dilating your pupils and making it easier for ultraviolet light to damage the retina.

Heat Exhaustion Dehydration or salt deficiency can cause heat exhaustion. Take time to acclimatise to high temperatures and make sure you get sufficient nonalcoholic liquids. Salt deficiency is characterised by fatigue, lethargy, headaches, giddiness and muscle cramps, and in severe cases salt tablets may

help. Vomiting or diarrhoea can also deplete your liquid and salt levels.

Fungal Infections Hot-weather fungal infections are most likely to occur on the scalp, between the toes or fingers (athlete's foot), in the groin (jock itch or crotch rot) and on the body (ringworm). You get ringworm (a fungal infection, not a worm) from infected animals or by walking on damp areas, like shower floors.

To prevent fungal infections, wear loose, comfortable clothes, avoid artificial fibres, wash frequently and dry carefully. Always wear plastic sandals or thongs in showers you can't completely trust. If you do get an infection, wash the infected area daily with a disinfectant or medicated soap and water, and rinse and dry well. Apply an antifungal cream, spray or powder, available at any pharmacy. Try to expose the infected area to air or sunlight as much as possible and wash all towels and underwear in hot water as well as changing them often.

Cold Too much cold is just as dangerous as too much heat, particularly if it leads to hypothermia. Cold combined with wind and moisture (ie soaking rain) is particularly risky. If you are trekking at high altitudes or in a cool, wet environment, be prepared.

Hypothermia occurs when the body loses heat faster than it can produce it and the core temperature of the body falls. It is surprisingly easy to progress from very cold to dangerously cold through a combination of wind, wet clothing, fatigue and hunger, even if the air temperature is above freezing. It is best to dress in layers – silk, wool and some of the new artificial fibres are all good insulating materials. A hat is important, as a lot of heat is lost through the head. A strong, waterproof outer layer is essential, as keeping dry is vital. Carry basic supplies, including food that contains simple sugars to generate heat quickly, and lots of fluid to drink.

Symptoms of hypothermia are exhaustion, numb skin (particularly toes and fingers), shivering, slurred speech, irrational

or violent behaviour, lethargy, stumbling, dizzy spells, muscle cramps and violent bursts of energy. Irrationality may take the form of sufferers claiming they are warm and trying to take off their clothes.

To treat hypothermia, first get the patient out of the wind or rain, remove their clothing if it's wet and replace it with dry, warm clothing. Give them hot nonalcoholic liquids and some high-calorie (high-kilojoule), easily digestible food. This should be enough for the early stages of hypothermia, but if it has gone further, it may be necessary to place victims in a warm sleeping bag and get in with them. Do not rub patients, place them near a fire or remove their wet clothes in the wind. If possible, place a sufferer in a warm (not hot) bath.

Altitude Sickness Acute Mountain Sickness or AMS occurs at high altitude and can be fatal. There is no hard and fast rule as to how high is too high: AMS can strike at altitudes of 3000 metres, although 3500 to 4500 metres is the usual range. Very few treks or ski runs in the Alps and Pyrenees reach heights of 3000 metres or more, so it's unlikely to be a major concern.

Headaches, nausea, dizziness, a dry cough, insomnia, breathlessness and loss of appetite are all signs to heed. Mild altitude problems will generally abate after a day or so, but if the symptoms persist or become worse the only treatment is to descend – even 500 metres can help.

Motion Sickness Eating lightly before and during a trip will reduce the chances of motion sickness. If you are prone to motion sickness, try to find a place that minimises disturbance – near the wing on aircraft, close to midships on boats, near the centre on buses. Fresh air and a steady reference point like the horizon usually help, whereas reading or cigarette smoke don't. Commercial antimotion-sickness preparations, which can cause drowsiness, have to be taken before the trip commences – when you're feeling sick, it's too late. Ginger is a natural preventative and is available in capsule form.

Diseases of Insanitation

Diarrhoea A change of water, food or climate can all cause the runs; diarrhoea caused by contaminated food or water is more serious. However, a few rushed toilet trips with no other symptoms is not indicative of a serious problem.

Moderate diarrhoea, involving half a dozen loose movements in a day, is more of a nuisance. Dehydration is the main danger with any diarrhoea, particularly for children, so fluid replenishment is the number one treatment. Weak black tea with a little sugar, soda water, or soft drinks allowed to go flat and diluted 50% with water are all good.

With any diarrhoea more severe than this, go straight to the casualty ward of the nearest hospital and have yourself checked. You may need a rehydrating solution to replace minerals and salts. Stick to a bland diet as you recover.

Diseases Spread by People & Animals

Rabies Though nonexistent in Britain and rare in the rest of Europe, where it's usually dealt with swiftly and decisively by the authorities, rabies is found in many countries and is caused by a bite or scratch by an infected animal. Dogs are a noted carrier, but cats, foxes and bats can also be affected. Any bite, scratch or even lick from a mammal should be cleaned immediately and thoroughly. Scrub with soap and running water, and then clean with an alcohol solution. If there is any possibility that the animal is infected, particularly if it froths at the mouth and behaves strangely, medical help should be sought immediately. Even if it is not rabid, all bites should be treated seriously as they can become infected or result in tetanus.

Sexually Transmitted Diseases (STDs)

Sexual contact with an infected partner spreads these diseases. While abstinence is the only 100% preventative, using condoms is effective. Gonorrhoea and syphilis are the most common of these diseases: sores, blisters or rashes around the genitals, discharges, or pain when urinating are common symptoms. Symptoms may be less marked or not

observed at all in women. Syphilis symptoms eventually disappear completely but the disease continues and can cause severe problems in later years. Gonorrhoea and syphilis are treated by antibiotics. STD treatment is available in French hospitsls. Don't be shy about visiting them if you think you may have contracted something.

There are numerous other sexually transmitted diseases, for most of which effective treatment is available, though there is no cure as yet for herpes or AIDS.

AIDS Known as SIDA in French, AIDS has become a very serious problem in France. The HIV virus *(le virus VIH* in French), the human immunodeficiency virus, eventually develops into AIDS, acquired immune deficiency syndrome.

Apart from abstinence, the most effective preventative is always to practise safe sex using condoms. AIDS can also be spread through infected blood transfusions and by dirty needles – vaccinations, acupuncture and tattooing are potentially as dangerous as intravenous drug use if the equipment is not clean. It is impossible to detect the HIV-positive status of an otherwise healthy-looking person without a blood test.

France has the highest incidence of AIDS in Europe. By 1992, 12,000 to 13,000 people had died from the disease. For information on free and anonymous testing centres *(centres de dépistage)* in and around Paris, contact AIDES 24 hours a day, toll-free on ☎ 05.36.66.36 (or from, 9 am to 8 pm, on 1-44.52.00.00). AIDES' office (metro Télégraphe) at 247 Rue de Belleville (19e) in Paris is staffed Monday to Friday from 9 am to 8 pm.

In 1991-92 France was rocked by revelations that about 1500 people, many of them haemophiliacs, had been infected with HIV because as late as 1985, authorities at the National Blood Transfusion Centre had knowingly allowed contaminated blood stocks to be distributed. In 1992, a new blood agency replaced the National Blood Transfusion Centre, four of whose former officials went on trial for fraud. Three were given jail terms of two and four years, while the fourth was acquitted. Attempts by lawyers to bring to trial three former government ministers, also accused of knowing that the blood was contaminated, failed.

Condoms All pharmacies carry condoms *(préservatifs)*, and many have 24-hour automatic condom dispensers outside the door. Some brasseries and discothèques are also equipped with condom machines. The safest condoms (ie those that conform to French government standards) are marked with the letters NF *(norme française)* in black on a white oval inside a red and blue rectangle.

Cuts, Bites & Stings

Cuts & Scratches Skin punctures can easily become infected in hot climates and may be difficult to heal. Treat any cut with an antiseptic solution. Where possible, avoid bandages and Band-aids, which can keep wounds wet.

Bites & Stings Unless you're allergic to them, bee and wasp stings are usually painful rather than dangerous. Calamine lotion will give relief, and ice packs will reduce the pain and swelling. There are some spiders with dangerous bites (rare in France), but antivenins are usually available. France's small scorpions, whose stings are notoriously painful, are not considered fatal. They often shelter in shoes and clothing – when camping, always give your shoes a good shake-out before putting them on in the morning.

There are various fish and other sea creatures that can sting or bite or that are dangerous to eat. Seeking local advice is the best way of avoiding problems.

Snakes Snakes tend to keep a very low profile, but to minimise your chances of being bitten, always wear boots, socks and long trousers when walking through undergrowth where snakes may be present. Tramp heavily and they'll usually slither away before you come near. Don't put your hands

into holes and crevices, and be careful when collecting firewood.

Snake bites do not cause instantaneous death, and antivenins are usually available. Keep the victim calm and still, wrap the bitten limb tightly, as you would for a sprained ankle, and attach a splint to immobilise it. Then seek medical help, if possible with the dead snake for identification. Don't attempt to catch the snake if there is even a remote possibility of being bitten again. Tourniquets and sucking out the poison are now comprehensively discredited.

Jellyfish Local advice will help prevent you coming into contact with these sea creatures and their stinging tentacles. Stings from most jellyfish *(méduses)* are merely painful. Dousing in vinegar will de-activate any stingers which have not 'fired'. Calamine lotion, antihistamines and analgesics may reduce the reaction and relieve the pain. The Portuguese man-of-war jellyfish, which has a sail-like float and long tentacles, is very rarely fatal.

Women's Health

Some women experience irregular periods when travelling, due to the upset in routine. Don't forget to take time zones into account if you're on the pill. If you run into intestinal problems, the pill may not be absorbed. Ask your physician about these matters.

Gynaecological Problems Poor diet, lowered resistance due to the use of antibiotics for stomach upsets, and even contraceptive pills can lead to vaginal infections when travelling in hot climates. Maintaining good personal hygiene, and wearing skirts or loose-fitting trousers and cotton underwear will help to prevent infections. It's also a good idea to eat lots of yoghurt, as this helps to maintain the vagina's pH (acid/alkaline) balance.

Yeast infections (thrush), characterised by a rash, itch and discharge, can be treated with a vinegar or lemon-juice douche or with yoghurt. Nystatin suppositories are the usual

medical prescription. Trichomonas is a more serious infection; symptoms are a discharge and a burning sensation when urinating, and if a vinegar-water douche is not effective, medical attention should be sought. Flagyl is the prescribed drug. In both cases, male sexual partners must also be treated.

WOMEN TRAVELLERS

Women tend to attract more unwanted attention than men, but female travellers need not walk around France in fear: people are rarely assaulted on the street. However, the French seem to have given relatively little thought to sexual harassment *(harcèlement sexuel)*, and many men (and some women) still think that to stare suavely at a passing woman is to pay her a flattering compliment.

If you are subject to catcalls or are hassled in any way while walking down the street – and chances are high that you will be, especially if you're travelling on your own in the south – the best strategy is usually to carry on with whatever you were doing and completely ignore the macho lowlife who is disrupting your holiday. After all, all he probably wants is to elicit some sort of response that validates his existence, pathetic though it may be. Deny him that and he has failed. Trying to make a cutting retort is ineffective in English and risky in French if your slang isn't extremely proficient. You are most likely to be left alone if you have a purposeful air about you that implies you know exactly where you're going, even if you haven't a clue.

Recommended reading is the *Handbook for Women Travellers* by M & G Moss, published by Judy Piatkus Publishers (London).

Assault

Physical attack is very unlikely but, of course, it does happen. As in any country, the best way to avoid being assaulted is to be conscious of your surroundings and aware of situations that could be potentially dangerous: deserted streets, lonely beaches, large train stations (eg Paris's Gare de l'Est), etc. Using the metros until late at night is generally OK as stations are rarely deserted.

Top: Mer de Glace glacier, near Chamonix, French Alps (DR)
Middle: Port de Saint Goustan, Auray, Brittany (GA)
Bottom: Grande Plage at Biarritz, French Basque Country (DR)

Top: Strasbourg's Cathédrale Notre Dame, Alsace (CDT Bas Rhin)
Middle: Carved church doorway, Tignes, French Alps (RN); Window in an
Alpine village (RN); Fleur-de-lis on a pillar, Blois, Loire Valley (BR)
Bottom: Shop window in the old city of Autun, Burgundy (DR)

Hitching, particularly alone, is inadvisable – there are too many horror stories.

France's national rape crisis hotline (☎ 05.05.95.95) can be reached toll-free from any telephone without using a télécarte. It's staffed by volunteers Monday to Friday from 10 am to 6 pm and is run by a women's organisation called Viols Femmes Informations, whose Paris office (metro Saint Ambroise) is at 4 Square Saint Irénée (11e).

In an emergency, you can always call the police (☎ 17), who will take you to the nearest hospital, or go to the hospital yourself. In Paris, medical, psychological and legal services are available at the Service Médico-Légal (☎ 1-42.34.82.34, *poste* (ext) 8446) of the Hôtel Dieu hospital, which is right next to Notre Dame.

Women's Movement

Women were given the right to vote in 1945 by De Gaulle's short-lived post-Liberation government, but until 1964 a woman needed her husband's permission to open a bank account or get a passport. It was in such an environment that Simone de Beauvoir wrote *Le Deuxième Sexe* (The Second Sex), her treatise against the myth of the 'eternal feminine', in 1953.

France's women's liberation movement *(mouvement de la libération des femmes)* flourished along with its counterparts in other Western countries in the late 1960s and early '70s but by the mid-'80s was pretty moribund. For reasons that have more to do with French society than anything else, few women's groups function as the kind of supportive social institutions that have been formed in Australia, Britain and the USA.

In Paris, the Maison des Femmes (☎ 1-43.48.24.91; metro Charonne) at 8 Cité Prost (11e) is the main meeting place for women of all ages and nationalities. As we go to press, however, urban renewal plans threaten the old building in which it's housed and municipal bureaucrats have yet to agree on a new location. It is staffed on Monday from 6 to 7 pm, on Wednesday from 3 to 8 pm and on Friday from 6 to 8 pm. On Friday nights, a cafeteria for women opens at 8 pm.

Most large cities in France have *centres d'information sur les droits des femmes* (centres for information on women's rights), which help local women find information on employment and health services or deal with domestic violence.

GAY & LESBIAN TRAVELLERS

France is one of Europe's most liberal countries when it comes to homosexuality, in part because of the long French tradition of public tolerance towards groups of people who chose not to live by strictly conventional social codes. In addition to the large gay and lesbian communities in Paris, a thriving gay centre since the late 1970s, there are active (though somewhat more discreet) communities in cities such as Nice, Cannes, Toulouse, Lyon, Marseille, Strasbourg, Nantes, Rennes, Montpellier, Grenoble and Tours. Harassment and violence of the sort that often plague parts of London are uncommon.

In the Paris chapter, entries of particular interest to gays and lesbians are mentioned under Gay Paris in the Information section.

Organisations

Many of France's gay organisations are based in Paris. The Maison des Homosexualités (☎ 1-42.77.72.77; metro Rambuteau) at 25 Rue Michel Le Comte (3e) is open daily from 5 to 8 pm. The Maison's member organisations hold a variety of meetings and activities each week. The activist organisation Act Up Paris (☎ 1-42.01.11.47; metro Campo Formio) at 106 Blvd de l'Hôpital (13e) has meetings every Tuesday at 7.30 pm. Information on Act Up is available on Minitel – an increasingly popular way for gay and lesbian organisations to disseminate information – by keying in 3615 code ACT UP. The Paris-based hotline for both gays and lesbians, Écoute Gaie (☎ 1-48.06.19.11), is staffed on weekdays (except perhaps Wednesday) from 6 to 10 pm.

The main lesbian information service, MIEL (Mouvement d'Information et d'Expression des Lesbiennes; ☎ 1-43.79.

61.91 for a recording) is in Paris's Maison des Femmes (see Women Travellers), which also houses the Archives Lesbiennes (☎ 1-48.05.25.89 for a recording). Archives Lesbiennes' meetings are held every two weeks.

Paris-based groups set up to combat the AIDS epidemic through education include the Association des Médecins Gais (Association of Gay Medical Doctors; ☎ 1-48.05.81.71; metro Bréguet Sabin) at 45 Rue Sedaine (11e), which is staffed on Wednesday from 6 to 8 pm and on Saturday from 2 to 4 pm. For more information on AIDS and about free, anonymous AIDS tests, see AIDS in the Health section.

Gay Men

The monthly *Illico*, which has articles in French and ads from places that cater to gays, is available for free at some gay bars but costs 9FF at newsagents.

Gay guidebooks include the predominantly male *Guide Gai* (45FF) to France, Brussels and Switzerland, and the male-only *Spartacus International Gay Guide* (US$27.95 or 150FF), which lists pubs, restaurants, discothèques, saunas, sex shops and cruising areas. In Paris, both are available from Les Mots à la Bouche (see Bookshops under Information in the Paris chapter). In other countries, *Spartacus* is available from large travel bookshops or by mail order direct from the publisher: Bruno Gmünder Verlag, Mail Order, PO Box 11 07 29, D-1000 Berlin 11, Germany.

Lesbians

France's lesbian scene is much less public than its gay counterpart and is centred mainly around women's cafés and bars. The monthly national magazine, *Lesbia* (25FF) gives a rundown of what's happening around the country and is available for 25FF at some newsagents (including most of the ones at train stations) and many Parisian bookshops.

Women Going Places (£6.99 or US$14), published by UK-based Women Going Places, includes a listing on France with information on meeting places, accommo-dation and organisations. If you can't find it in a bookshop, call ☎ 071-706 2434 in the UK or 203-467 4257 in the USA. The *Annuaire des Lieux, Groupes et Activités Lesbiennes, Feministes et Homosexuelles* (35FF), issued annually, lists lesbian bars and organisations all over France. It is available from some French bookshops or can be ordered direct from the publisher, Archives Lesbiennes, whose postal address is BP 362, 75526 Paris, CEDEX 11.

DISABLED TRAVELLERS

France is not particularly well-equipped for *handicapés* (disabled people): kerb ramps are few and far between, public facilities don't necessarily have *ascenseurs* (lifts) and the Paris metro, most of it built decades ago, is virtually inaccessible. But physically disabled people who would like to travel in France can overcome these problems. The British-based Royal Association for Disability & Rehabilitation (RADAR) publishes a useful guide entitled *Holidays & Travel Abroad: A Guide for Disabled People*, which gives a good overview of facilities available to disabled travellers in Europe. Contact RADAR (☎ 071-637 5400) at 25 Mortimer St, London W1N 8AB.

In France, the Paris tourist office should be able to provide you with *Touristes Quand Même*, known in English as *Travel Just the Same: Holiday Tours in France for the Handicapped*, a two-volume set – one on Paris, the other on the rest of France – published by the Comité National Français de Liaison pour la Réadaptation des Handicapés. They list sights, public facilities and activities accessible to the physically disabled.

The SNCF publishes a pamphet called *Guide Pratique du Voyageur à Mobilité Réduite* (Practical Guide for the Traveller with Reduced Mobility), which details services available to train travellers in wheelchairs. Most of it is in French but there's one page in English. Michelin's *Guide Rouge* shows which hotels have lifts and facilities for disabled people.

DANGERS & ANNOYANCES

In general, France is a pretty safe place in which to live and travel. Though property crime is a major problem (and a favourite topic of conversation among the French), it is extremely unlikely that you will be physically assaulted while walking down the street.

Emergency Phone Numbers

The following toll-free numbers can be dialled from any public phone or Point Phone in France without inserting a télécarte or coins:

SAMU
medical treatment/ambulance		☎ 15
in Paris, also		45.67.50.50
Police		☎ 17
Fire Brigade		☎ 18

Other emergency numbers include SOS Help (English crisis hotline; ☎ 1-47.23.80.80) and the Rape Crisis Hotline (Viols Femmes Informations; ☎ 05.05.95.95) open Monday to Friday 10 am to 6 pm.

The 24-hour dispatchers of SAMU, short for Service d'Aide Médicale d'Urgence (Emergency Medical Aid Service), will take down details of your problem (there's usually someone on duty who speaks English) and then send out an ambulance with a driver (about 300FF) or, if necessary, a mobile intensive care unit. For less serious problems, SAMU can also send over a doctor for a house call. If you prefer to be taken to a particular hospital, mention this to the ambulance crew. In emergency cases (ie those requiring intensive care units), billing will be taken care of later. Otherwise, you need to pay in cash at the time that you receive assistance.

The staff of SOS Help, a Paris-based crisis hotline whose volunteers are native English speakers, are there both to talk with English-speakers who are having difficulties and to make referrals for specific problems. They are also happy to give out practical information on less-than-earth-shattering matters. SOS Help is staffed daily from 3 to 11 pm.

There are *postes d'appel d'urgence* (emergency phones) about every four km along main highways and every two km on autoroutes.

Theft

The biggest crime problem in France for tourists is theft *(vol)*. Most thieves are after cash or valuables, but they often end up with passports and other items whose loss will not only send you rushing to your nearest consulate but may destroy your holiday by putting you in a long-term bad mood.

The problems you're most likely to encounter are thefts from – and of – cars, pickpocketing and the snatching of daypacks or women's handbags, particularly in dense crowds (eg at busy train stations, on rush-hour public transport, in fast-food joints and in cinemas). A common ploy is for one person to distract you while another zips through your pockets. The south of France seems to have more crime than the north – the Côte d'Azur and Provence are notorious.

Although there's no need whatsoever to travel in fear, a few simple precautions will minimise your chances of finding yourself in a real-life American Express commercial.

Before Leaving Home Make at least one photocopy of your passport, plane ticket and other important documents, such as your address book and travellers' cheques receipts. Some people even bring along a photocopy of their birth certificate (which is useful if you have to replace a passport). Leave one copy of each document at home and keep another one with you, separate from the originals.

Write your name and address on the inside of your suitcase, backpack, daypack, address book, diary, etc. If such items are lost or stolen and later recovered, the police will have at least some chance of finding you.

Documents & Money Always keep your money, credit cards, tickets, passport, driver's licence and other important docu-

ments in a money belt worn *inside* your pants or skirt. Never carry them around in a daypack or waist pouches, which are easy for thieves to grab (or slice off) and sprint away with. The same goes for those little pouches that you wear around your neck.

Keep enough money for a day's travel separate from your money belt (eg in your daypack or suitcase). That way, you'll be penniless only if everything gets taken at once.

While theft from hotel rooms is pretty rare, it's a bad idea to leave cash or important documents in your room. Hostels are a fair bit riskier, since so many people are always passing through. If you don't want to carry your documents with you, ask the hotel or hostel's front desk to put them in the *coffre* (safe).

When on the Move Be especially careful with your passport and important documents at airports: pickpockets and professional passport thieves know that people are often careless when they first arrive in a foreign country.

The French police are very strict about security, especially at airports. Do not leave baggage unattended – they're serious when they warn that suspicious objects will be summarily blown up.

When travelling by train, especially if you'll be sleeping, the safest place for small bags is under your seat. Large bags are best off in the overhead rack right above your head, and you may want to fasten them to the rack with the straps or even a small lock. Bags left in the luggage racks at the ends of the carriage are an easy target: as the train is pulling out of a station, a thief can grab your pack and hop off. In sleeping compartments, make sure to lock the door at night.

Keep an eagle eye on your bags in train stations, airports, fast-food outlets and cinemas and at the beach. Anything you can do to make your equipment easy to watch and clumsy to carry will make it more difficult to snatch. Some people lock, zip or tie their daypack to their main pack. Affixing tiny locks to the zips will help keep out sticky

fingers. When sitting in a cinema or outdoor café, you might also wrap one strap of your daypack around your leg (or the leg of your chair).

If you leave your bags at a left-luggage office or in a luggage locker, treat your claim chit (or locker code) like cash: audacious daypack nappers have been known to take stolen chits back to the train station and thus take possession of the rest of their victims' belongings.

Parked cars and motorbikes and the contents of vehicles – especially those with out-of-town or foreign plates or car rental company stickers – are favourite targets for thieves. *Never* leave anything valuable inside your car (like other Europeans, many French people carry their removeable car radios with them whenever they park their vehicles). In fact, never leave anything at all in your car. Even a few old clothes or an umbrella left lying in the backseat may attract the attention of a passing thief, who won't think twice about breaking a window or smashing a lock to see if there's a camera hidden underneath. When you stop for lunch at autoroute rest areas, always keep the car in view.

Other Strategies The most valuable things you have with you are exposed film, your address book and your diary: if your camera gets swiped, you can buy a new one, but your photos and diary are irreplaceable, and a lost address book may mean that you'll forever lose track of some people. Except when you're travelling by aeroplane, such items are probably safer in your suitcase or main pack than in your daypack.

When going swimming, especially along the Côte d'Azur, try to leave valuables in the hotel or hostel safe. And while you're in the water, have members of your party take turns sitting with everyone's packs and clothes.

Watch out for counterfeit US banknotes, especially US$100 bills. Don't do anyone a 'favour' by changing US cash for them unless you're sure it's genuine.

Watch out for con artists: if a deal seems too good to be true, it probably is. And be

wary of sudden friendships – you never know what your 'new friends' may be after.

Drugs

Unlike countries that take a fairly benign attitude to small quantities of drugs (eg the Netherlands), France's laws – and the people who enforce them – are very strict. And when it comes to trafficking they're even stricter.

Thanks to the Napoleonic Code, the police can pretty much search anyone they want at any time, whether or not there seems to be probable cause, and they have been known to stop and search charter buses solely because they are coming from Amsterdam.

Police

France has two separate police forces. The Police Nationale, under the command of départemental prefects (and, in Paris, the Préfet de Police), includes the Police de l'Air et des Frontières (PAF), the border police. The paramilitary Gendarmerie Nationale is under the control of the Defence Minister. It handles security in small towns, along main roads, at airports, etc and includes the Garde Républicain, the president's ceremonial equestrian guard.

The dreaded Compagnies Républicaines de Sécurité (CRS), riot police heavies who always seem to travel in caravans of at least a dozen vehicles, are part of the Police Nationale. You often see hundreds of them, equipped with the latest in riot gear, at strikes or demonstrations.

Police with shoulder patches reading Police Municipale are under the control of the local mayor.

Dealing with the Police If asked a question, beat cops are likely to be correct and helpful but not more than that, though you may get a salute.

If stopped by the police for any reason, your best course of action is to be polite – even deferential – and to remain calm. It is a very bad idea to be overly assertive, and being rude or disrespectful is asking for serious trouble. The French police have wide powers of search and seizure, and if they take

a disliking to you may opt to use them. The police can, without any particular reason, decide to examine your passport, visa, etc, which is, at the very least, a hassle.

SOS Voyageurs

Many large train stations (eg Marseille) have offices of SOS Voyageurs, an organisation of volunteers (mostly retirees) who try to help travellers having some sort of difficulty. If your pack has been stolen or your ticket lost, or if you just need somewhere to change your baby, they may be able to help.

Racism

The rise in support for the extreme right-wing National Front in recent years reflects the growing racial intolerance in France, particularly against North African Muslims and, to a lesser extent, blacks from sub-Saharan Africa and France's former colonies and territories in the Caribbean.

In many parts of France, especially in the south (eg Provence and the Côte d'Azur), places of entertainment such as bars and discothèques are, for all intents and purposes, segregated: owners and their ferocious bouncers make it abundantly clear what sort of people are 'invited' to use their nominally private facilities and what sort are not. Such activities are possible in the land of *liberté*, *égalité* and *fraternité* because there is little civil rights enforcement.

Hunters

The hunting season usually runs from the end of September to the end of February. If you see signs reading *chasseurs* or *chasse gardé* strung up or tacked to trees, you might want to think twice about wandering into the area, especially if you're wearing anything that might make you look like a deer. Unless, the area is totally fenced off, it's not illegal to be there, but accidents do happen and 50 hunters die in France each year after being shot by other hunters.

Natural Dangers

There are strong undertows and currents

along the Atlantic coast, particularly in south-western Brittany.

Thunderstorms in the mountains and the hot southern plains can be extremely sudden, violent and dangerous. It's a good idea to check the weather report before you set out on a long hike.

WORK

Despite France's 11.5% unemployment rate and laws that forbid people who aren't EC nationals *(resortissants d'un pays de la CE)* from working in France, working 'in the black' (ie without documents) is still possible. People without documents probably have their best chance of finding work during fruit harvests, in Alpine ski resorts and in the Côte d'Azur's tourist industry. *Au pair* work is also very popular and can be done legally even by non-EC citizens.

The national minimum wage for non-professionals – le SMIC *(salaire minimum interprofessionel de croissance)* – is 33FF an hour. However, employers willing to hire people in contravention of France's employment laws may also be likely to ignore the minimum wage law.

For practical information on working in France, you might want to pick up *Working in France* (US$12.95) by Carol Pineau & Maureen Kelly. *Work Your Way Around the World* by Susan Griffith (paperback), published by Vacation Work, is a more general book.

Work Permits

To work legally in France you must have a residence permit known as a *carte de séjour*. Getting one is almost automatic for EC nationals and almost impossible for anyone else except full-time students.

If you're from the EC, after finding a job go to the local mairie and apply for a carte de séjour. Take three passport photos, proof of accommodation and the work contract. You'll need your passport, not a temporary visitor's passport such as that available in the UK.

Non-EC nationals cannot work legally unless they obtain a work permit *(autoris-ation de travail)* before arriving in France. This is no easy matter, as a prospective employer has to convince the authorities that there is no French person who can do the job being offered to you.

Employment Agencies

The Agence National pour l'Emploi (ANPE), France's national employment service, has offices in the cities and most large towns. It has lists of job openings, but you're not likely to find much temporary or casual work except during the grape harvest, when it makes special provisions for people interested in working in the fields. Centres Information Jeunesse (CIJ), which provide all sorts of information for young people, also sometimes have notice boards with work possibilities. Both these bodies are useless if you don't have a carte de séjour.

If you're looking for season-long agricultural work, you might contact Jeunesse et Reconstruction (☎ 1-47.70.15.88; metro Rue Montmartre) at 10 Rue de Trévise (9e) in Paris, which organises teams of grape pickers for work in Champagne, Beaujolais, Chablis and Côtes d'Or. Get in touch with them by the beginning of July. Non-EC nationals who are studying in France should send along photocopies of their student card and carte de séjour. Count on being paid 160 to 200FF a day. EC nationals might also contact SESAME (Service des Échanges et des Stages Agricoles dans le Monde; ☎ 1-40.54.07.08, fax 40.54.06.39; metro Villiers) at 9-11 Square Gabriel Fauré (17e) in Paris.

Busking

If you play an instrument or have some other talent in the performing arts, you could try busking (ie working as a street musician, actor, juggler, etc).

In Paris, amplifiers, percussion and anything you blow are technically forbidden but widely tolerated by the police so long as they're not too loud or obnoxious. Busking borders on downright legality in front of the Centre Pompidou, around Sacré Cœur and on the metro, where the RATP police are in charge. But wherever you are, your best bet

to avoid hassles is to talk to other street artists beforehand.

Hawking

Hawkers require all sorts of permits and authorisations and are not likely to last long without them.

Agricultural Work

The French government seems to tolerate undocumented workers helping out with some agricultural work, especially during harvest periods. To find a field job, ask around in areas where harvesting is taking place – trees with almost-ripe fruit on them are a sure sign that pickers will soon be needed. Many farmers prefer hiring people who know at least a bit of French. Seasonal wanted ads can be found in the magazine *Le Nouvel Agriculteur* and the weekly *La France Agricole*. The organisations listed under Employment Agencies may also be able to help.

Grape Harvest The *vendange* (grape harvest) is traditionally France's biggest taker of casual labour, requiring some 100,000 extra pairs of hands each year from mid-September to mid-October. By region, there is grape-picking work in Beaujolais and Aquitaine from 20 September to 15 October; in Pays de la Loire and the Centre from 25 September to 20 October; in Burgundy from 25 September to 10 October; and in Midi-Pyrénées and Champagne from 25 September to 30 October.

To strip grape picking of any romantic notions, it's eight to nine hours of back-breaking work, often seven days a week. The wage is about 30FF an hour but porters who carry the loads of grapes earn 6 to 7FF more than pickers. Accommodation can be anything from a rough dorm to a room in the house. Board is normally provided, but ask before you sign on. Because you're in the middle of the countryside, it's a great way to save as there's nowhere to spend your earnings.

Many wine growers have teams of experienced pickers, often from Spain, Portugal or North Africa, who arrive for the season with nearly the whole village – men, women and children – in tow. Until recently, there have also been plenty of opportunities for newcomers – individuals or small groups, but hand picking is being taken over more and more by machines (except in areas such as Champagne, where mechanical picking is forbidden).

In Burgundy, EC nationals might try contacting the Service de Vendange (Grape Harvest Service) of the Agence National pour l'Emploi (National Employment Agency) whose Burgundy office (☎ 80.24. 60.00) is at 6 Blvd Saint Jacques, 21200 Beaune. Another option is to look in *Le Bien Publique*, a Beaune daily newspaper, for employment adds. You might also try asking people who look like they're doing such work or local people connected with the wine trade for advice on growers who may need extra hands.

Other Harvests Fruits and vegies are harvested somewhere in France from mid-May to mid-October. Apples are grown nearly all over, with the harvest starting in the south (eg in Languedoc) in September and moving northward to cooler regions (eg Normandy) by October. In the département of Indre, the apple harvest is from 15 September to 31 October.

Other important harvesting regions and their crops include Brittany and Normandy for cherries and plums; the Rhône Valley and Provence for strawberries, cherries, apples, peaches, tomatoes and pears; Languedoc-Roussillon for apricots and melons; and Périgord for plums and apples. *Produits maraîchers*, a term you may come across, means market-garden crops.

Ski Resorts

The Alps are the most promising of France's ski regions for picking up hospitality work in hotels and restaurants and ski resorts with lots of British holidaymakers. The season is basically from December to April.

If you speak only English, the fashionable resort of Méribel, in the Tarentaise Valley

east of Chambéry, may be a good place to start looking, as a large number of British tour companies operate from there.

Côte d'Azur

The season on the Côte d'Azur runs from June to September. Though there's little glamour in it, selling goods on the beach is one way to make a few francs, though you've got to sell an awful lot of ice cream and chips to make a living. Expect to pocket about 3FF from each item that you sell – if you're keen, just ask one of the other sellers to put you in touch with the boss.

Possibly a smidgin more glam is working on a yacht. Cannes and Antibes are the places to start looking and March is the month, as many jobs are filled by mid-April. Yacht owners often take on newcomers for a trial period of day-crewing before hiring them for the full charter season. By late September, long-haul crews are in demand for winter voyages to the West Indies.

Archaeological Excavations

If you are interested in volunteering on an archaeological excavation in Burgundy, write (in English, if you like) to the Direction des Antiquités Historiques et Préhistoriques (☎ 80.72.53.16), 39 Rue Vannerie, 21000 Dijon, sometime between March and May and they'll send you a list of sites that will be needing volunteers for the coming summer. You can then contact the directors of the individual digs for details. Volunteers, who are provided with food and lodging (which may be very basic), are asked to stay a minimum of two or three weeks.

Au Pair

Under the au pair system, single young people aged 17 or 18 to about 30 who are studying in France live with a French family and receive lodging, full board and a bit of pocket money in exchange for taking care of the kids, babysitting, doing light housework and perhaps teaching English to the children. Most families prefer young women, but a few positions are also available for young men. Many families especially want au pairs who are native English speakers, but knowing at least some French may be a prerequisite.

For practical information, pick up *The Au Pair and Nanny's Guide to Working Abroad* by Susan Griffith & Sharon Legg, published in paperback by Vacation Work.

Working Conditions Depending on the family and the placement agency, the minimum commitment ranges from two to six months; the maximum initial stay is 12 months, extendable to 18 months. Many families prefer to hire an au pair for the entire school year (September to late June).

In general, the family provides room and board and gives the au pair 400FF a week of pocket money in exchange for up to 30 hours of work and two or three evenings of babysitting each week. By law, au pairs must have one full day off a week (usually Sunday). In Paris, some families also provide weekly or monthly metro passes. The family must also pay for French social security *(securité sociale)*, which covers about 70% of medical expenses (it's a good idea to get supplementary insurance).

All this – including pay and maximum working hours – is clearly spelled out in the standard contract *(accord)*, provided by the Direction Départemental du Travail et de l'Emploi (Départemental Office of Work & Employment), which is signed by both the family and the au pair (officially designated as a *stagiaire aide-familiale)*.

Paperwork Because the au pair system is seen by the French government as a forum in which people from other cultures can learn about France and improve their French language skills, non-EC citizens usually denied working papers can get special long-stay au pair visas. To be eligible, applicants have to arrange to study something (usually French) while in France in an officially recognised framework and must apply for their au pair visa *before* leaving their home country.

After you find a suitable family (see Placement Agencies), the family fills out a work contract *(engagement d'accueil)* and mails it to you so you can make a formal application

to the French consulate nearest your home. Sign the contract and send it to the consulate along with your passport, two copies of the application form (which the consulate can provide), an application fee, two photos, the results of a medical exam and proof that you have been admitted to a recognised programme of study. Technically, an au pair's visa lets you work only for the family that has hired you.

Non-EC nationals who decide to try to find an au pair position after getting to France cannot to do so legally and won't be covered by the protections provided for under French law.

Residents of the EC can easily arrange for an au pair job and a carte de séjour after arriving in France.

Placement Agencies Most agencies charge the au pair 500 to 700FF and collect an additional fee from the family. They usually require that applicants know at least a bit of French, enjoy working with kids, and have some experience doing so. All ask for letters of reference, either from the parents of children you've taken care of or from teachers or previous employers. Ask lots of questions, especially about living conditions and privacy – remember, there are more families looking for au pairs than there are suitable applicants.

If you are not an EC national, you must contact the placement agency from your home country at least three months in advance. Residents of the EC can apply to the agency after arriving in France. In Paris, check the bulletin boards at the American Church and Saint Joseph's Church (see Cultural Centres under Information in the Paris chapter) for details on families looking for au pairs. The Paris tourist office has a list of placement agencies. Agencies include:

Accueil Familial des Jeunes Étrangers (☎ 1-42.22.50.34; fax 1-45.44.60.48; metro Sèvres Babylone), 23 Rue du Cherche Midi (6e)
Amicale Culturelle Internationale (☎ 1-47.42.94.21; fax 1-49.24.02.67; metro Havre Caumartin), 27 Rue Godot de Mauroy (9e)

French-American Center of Provence (☎ 90.25.93.23; fax 90.25.93.24), 10 Montée de la Tour, 30400 Villeneuve-lès-Avignon

ACTIVITIES

France's varied geography and climate allow for a wide range of outdoor pursuits. If your interests are more cerebral, you can study the French language and a variety of other subjects, including French cooking.

Little of France consists of pristine wilderness. Even the remotest regions are dotted with villages and criss-crossed by roads, power lines, hydro-electric projects, etc. Not that there aren't beautiful, unspoiled places, but they're not three days' walk from the nearest road.

Hiking

France is criss-crossed by a staggering 120,000 km of *sentiers balisés* (marked walking paths) which pass through every imaginable kind of terrain in every region of the country. No permits are needed for hiking, but there are restrictions on where you can camp, especially in national parks.

Probably the best known trails are the *sentiers de grande randonnée*, long-distance footpaths whose alphanumeric names begin with the letters GR. Their markings usually consist of red and white stripes on trees, rocks, etc. Some are many hundreds of km long, such as the GR5, which goes from the Netherlands through Belgium, Luxembourg and the spectacular Alpine scenery of eastern France, before ending up in Nice. Others include the GR3, which goes through the Loire Valley; the GR4, which meanders through the Massif Central; the popular GR10, which runs along the Pyrenees from the Mediterranean to the Atlantic; and the stunning GR20, which takes you to some of Corsica's highest peaks.

The *grandes randonnées de pays* (GRP) trails, whose markings are yellow and red, usually go in some sort of loop. They are designed for intense exploration of one particular area and usually take from a few days to a week, though some are longer.

Other types of trails include *sentiers de*

promenade-randonnée (walking paths), *drailles* (paths used by cattle to get to high-altitude summer pastures) and *chemins de halage* (towpaths, built in the days when canal barges where pulled by animals walking along the shore). Shorter day-hike trails are often known as *sentiers de petites randonnées* or *sentiers de pays*; many of them are circular so that you end up where you started.

For information on hiking in France, you can contact the Fédération Française de la Randonnée Pédestre (☎ 1-47.23.62.32; metro Alma Marceau) at 9 Ave George V (8e) in Paris, publisher of most major topoguides (see Hiking & Cycling under Travel Guides in the Books section of this chapter).

The Club Alpin Français (☎ 1-42.02. 68.64, 1-42.02.75.94; metro Laumière) at 24 Ave de Laumière (19e) in Paris generally provides services (eg courses, group hikes) only to its members. Joining costs about 300FF per year (180FF for people aged 18 to 24) and includes various kinds of insurance.

For details on *refuges* and other overnight accommodation for hikers, such as *gîtes d'étape*, see the Accommodation section. The *refuges* (hiking shelters) maintained by the Club Alpin Français are open to non-members.

Mountaineering & Rock Climbing

If you're interesting in *alpinisme* (mountaineering) or *escalade* (rock climbing), you can arrange climbs with professional guides through the Club Alpin Français (see the preceding section for the address).

Cycling

The French take their cycling very seriously, and the whole country almost grinds to a halt during the annual Tour de France (see Sport under Culture in the Facts about the Country chapter).

A *vélo tout-terrain* (mountain bike or ATB), often abbreviated in French as a VTT, is a fantastic way of exploring the country-side. La Margeride in Languedoc is a particularly inviting area for mountain biking, but then again so are the Alps (see the Chamonix listing), Brittany, the Pyrenees, the Loire Valley and just about everywhere else. Some GR and GRP trials (see Hiking) are open to mountain bikes (and horses), but take care not to startle hikers. A bicycle path is called a *piste cyclable*.

Elsewhere in this chapter, information on cyclists' topoguides can be found under Travel Guides in the Books section, and there's a rundown on road maps in the Maps listing. For information on road rules, cycling organisations, transporting your bicycle to and around France and bike rental, see Bicycle in the Getting Around chapter. Details on where to rent bikes in each city or town appears at the end of each listing under Getting Around.

Horse Riding

Équitation – riding on a *cheval* (horse) – is popular around the country. For details, see Outdoor Activities in the Burgundy chapter; Horse Riding under Annecy; and the relevant sections under Bayonne (Basque Country), the Vallée d'Aspe (Pyrenees), Cahors (Quercy) and Ajaccio (Corsica), or enquire at the local tourist office.

Swimming

France has lovely beaches along all of its coasts – the English Channel, the Atlantic and the Mediterranean (including the coast of Corsica) – as well as on lakes, such as Lac d'Annecy and Lake Geneva. The fine, sandy beaches along the Atlantic coast (eg near La Rochelle) are much less crowded than their rather pebbly counterparts on the Côte d'Azur. Corsica is crowded only during July and August. Beaches on the Channel coast and southern Brittany are cooler than those further south. The public is free to use any beach not marked as private.

Topless bathing for women is pretty much the norm in France – if other people are doing it, you can assume it's OK. For information on nude bathing, see Naturism.

Surfing & Windsurfing

The finest surfing in France (and some of the

best surfing in all of Europe) is on the Atlantic coast around Biarritz. Windsurfing is popular wherever there's water and a breeze.

Naturism

France is one of Europe's most popular venues for *naturisme* (naturism or nudism). Naturist centres, most of them in the south in Languedoc-Roussillon, Provence and the Côte d'Azur, range from small rural camp sites to large chalet villages with cinemas, tennis courts and shops. Their common denominator is water – all have access to the sea, a lake, a river or, at the very least, a pool. Most are open from April to October and virtually all require that visitors have an up-to-date International Naturist Federation (INF) *licence naturiste* (naturist passport) or a *carte de vacancier* (holiday-maker's card). The latter is available at many naturist holiday centres for about 100FF but may be cheaper if purchased from the naturist organisation in your home country.

Naturist bathing is practised on all of France's coasts but is usually confined to relatively remote strips of beach because some people still find it offensive. At the naturist colony of Cap d'Agde, though, the residents are tired of *clothed* swimmers invading their stretch of sand and ruining the ambience. They have recently begun a concerted campaign to persuade such culturally insensitive interlopers to respect local sensibilities by disrobing.

For information on naturism in France, purchase a copy of *Les Nouvelles Vacances*, also known as *Naturisme Informations* and *Nat-Info*, the glossy quarterly magazine of the Fédération Française de Naturisme. It is available from most newsagents for 40FF. If you're outside France, ask the nearest French Government Tourist Office for a copy of *France – A Land for all Naturisms*.

The Fédération Française de Naturisme (☎ 1- 47.64.32.82; metro Wagram) at 65 Rue de Toqueville (17e) in Paris has a variety of brochures on *au naturel* leisure activities – many of them family-oriented – all over France. By Minitel, key in 3615 code NATURISMO.

Rafting & Canoeing

White-water rafting, canoeing and kayaking are practised on many rivers in France, particularly those that flow down from the Massif Central. The Gorges du Verdon is popular for its white-water rafting descents, while canoe and kayak companies tend to favour the Gorges du Tarn. The Fédération Française de Canoë-Kayak (☎ 1- 45.11.08.50) at 87 Quai de la Marne, 94340 Joinville-le-Pont, can supply information on canoeing and kayaking clubs around the country.

Skiing

France has more than 400 ski resorts in the Alps, the Jura, the Pyrenees, the Vosges, the Massif Central and even the mountains of Corsica. The ski season generally lasts from December to March, though it's shorter at low altitudes and longer high in the Alps. Snow conditions can vary greatly from year to year. January and February tend to have the best overall conditions, but the slopes can be very crowded during the February school holidays. Although prices differ from place to place, *ski de piste* (downhill skiing) is always quite expensive because of the cost of equipment, ski lifts, accommodation and the inevitable après-ski drinking sessions. *Ski de fond* (cross-country skiing) is much more affordable.

The Alps have some of Europe's finest – and most expensive – ski facilities. There are even a few places where you can ski on glaciers during the summer. For general information, see Skiing in the French Alps & the Jura chapter.

Smaller, low-altitude stations, which include quite a few of the resorts in the Pyrenees (see Andorra, Cauterets and Vallée d'Aspe) and the Massif Central (see Le Mont Dore), are much cheaper than their higher, classier counterparts. In the Alps, low-altitude skiing is popular on the Vercors massif (see Around Grenoble in the French Alps & the Jura chapter).

One of the cheapest ways to have a skiing holiday in France is to buy a package deal

before leaving home. Ask your travel agent for details.

French government tourist offices (see Tourist Offices) can supply you with the annual *Winter Holiday Guide*, a brochure listing about 100 French ski resorts. It is published by the Association des Mairies des Stations Françaises de Sports d'Hiver et d'Été (☎ 1-47.42.23.32; metro Havre Caumartin), better known as Ski France, based at 61 Blvd Haussmann (9e) in Paris. The Club Alpin Français office (see Hiking for the address) in Paris may also be able to provide information.

Canal Boats

For general information on canal boat rental in Burgundy, see Boating on Burgundy's Waterways at the beginning of the Burgundy chapter. Details on canal boating in the Cahors area are listed under Quercy in the Limousin, Périgord & Quercy chapter.

Crown Blue Line offers canal boat rental in Brittany (from Dinan and Messac, which is 80 km north of Nantes); Alsace & Lorraine (from Hesse, 68 km west of Strasbourg, and Boofzheim, 35 km south of Strasbourg); in the Toulouse area along the Canal du Midi (from Castelnaudary, 55 km south-east of Toulouse, and Damazan, 150 km north-west of Toulouse); and in Langudedoc and the Camargue area (from Port Cassafières, 15 km south-east of Béziers and Saint Gilles, about 20 km from both Nîmes and Arles).

In the UK, contact Crown Travel (☎ 0603-630513; fax 0603-664298) at 8 Ber Street, Norwich NR1 3EJ.

In Australia, details are available from Travellers (☎ 02-256 4444; fax 02-233 2273), Level 7, 182 George St, Sydney 2000. Prices for the smallest two-person boat are A$950 to A$1830 a week, depending on the season.

You might want to take a look at *Through the French Canals* by Philip Bristow, published by London-based Adlard Coles Nautical.

Hang-Gliding & Parapente

Deltaplane (hang-gliding) and *parapente* are the rage in many parts of France, particularly the Alps (see the Annecy and Chamonix listings), the Massif Central (see Le Mont Dore), Languedoc (see Millau) and the Pyrenees (see Bedous).

There's no accepted English term for parapente, though it's sometimes called 'parasailing' or 'parascending'. Basically, it involves running along the side of a mountain dragging a rectangular parachute behind you until it opens. The chute then fills with air and, acting like an aircraft wing, lifts you into the air. If the thermals are good you can stay up for hours, peacefully circling in the sky.

Newcomers can try out parapente with a *baptême de l'air* (tandem introductory flight) for 300 to 450FF. A five-day *stage d'initiation* (beginner's course) costs 2500 to 2900FF. See the Toulose & the Pyrenees, Alps, Massif Central and Languedoc-Roussillon chapters for more information.

Gliding

Vol à voile (gliding) is most popular in the south of France, where temperatures are warmer and thermals better. The Causse Méjean (see Florac) is a popular spot. For the addresses of gliding clubs around France, contact the Fédération Française de Vol à Voile (☎ 1-45.44.04.78; metro Sèvres Babylone) at 29 Rue de Sèvres (6e) in Paris.

Spelunking

Speleology, the scientific study of caves, was pioneered by the Frenchman Edouard-André Martel late last century, and France still has some great places for cave exploration. The Club Alpin Français (see Hiking for the address) can supply details about organised activities.

Thermalisme & Thalassothérapie

For over a century, the French have been keen fans of *thermalisme* (water cures), for which visitors with ailments ranging from rheumatism to serious internal disorders flock to hot springs resorts. Once the domain of the wealthy, thermalisme centres now offer form-and-fitness packages intended to

appeal to a broad range of people, young and old. Many of the resorts are in the Massif Central – Vichy is the oldest and most famous – but there are others along the shore of Lake Geneva and in the Pyrenees.

A salty variant of thermalisme is *thalassothérapie* (sea-water therapy), practised in sophisticated centres where physiotherapists use sea-water treatments to help both athletes and regular folk. Thalasso-thérapie centres dot the Côte d'Azur, the Atlantic Coast (eg Biarritz) and the coast of Brittany.

Language Courses

There's no better place in the world to study French than in France. A wide variety of options are available from universities, private institutes and the Alliance Française. The French Cultural Service (see Useful Organisations) has lots of information on studying in France, as do French government tourist offices and French consulates. You might also contact the Ministry of Tourism sponsored International Cultural Organisation (☎ 1-42.36.47.18; fax 40.26.34.45; metro Châtelet) at 55 Rue de Rivoli (1er), Paris.

In Paris The Accord Language School (☎ 1-42.36.24.95; fax 42.21.17.91; metro Les Halles) at 72 Rue Rambuteau (3rd floor; 1er) – between Les Halles and the Centre Pompidou – gets high marks from its students. Four-week classes on five levels (from beginning to advanced) with a maximum of 14 students (and often less) start at the beginning of each month of the year. They cost 1600FF for the *cours semi-intensif* (10 hours a week), held in the afternoon, and 2600FF for the *cours intensif* (20 hours a week), held in the morning. If you like, you can enrol for only two of the four weeks. The *cours extensif* (three hours a week for three months), which meets at night, costs 1800FF. Other options include workshops (one three-hour meeting a week for four weeks) on writing (600FF) and grammar (600FF); the remedial pronunciation workshop (450FF) meets for two hours a week for four weeks.

The school's office is open weekdays from 8.30 am to 8 pm (6 pm on Friday). If there's space, you can sign up until the first day of class.

The Alliance Française (☎ 1-45.44.38.28; metro Saint Placide), which seeks to promote French language and civilisation around the world, has its Paris headquarters at 101 Blvd Raspail (6e). Month-long French courses at all levels but of variable quality usually begin during the first week of each month; registration takes place during the five business days before the start of each session. If there's space, it's possible to enrol for just two weeks. *Intensif* courses, which meet for 3½ hours a day, cost 2360FF a month; *extensif* courses, which involve 1½ hours of class a day, cost 1180FF a month. The registration office is open Monday to Friday from 9 am to 5 pm. Bring your passport and a passport-sized photo. Payment, which must be made in advance, can be done with travellers' cheques. The mailing address of the Alliance Française is 101 Blvd Raspail, 75270 Paris CEDEX 06.

Another option is the Institut Parisien de Langue et de Civilisation Françaises (☎ /fax fax 1-40.56.09.53; metro Dupleix) at 87 Blvd de Grenelle (15e). The office is open on weekdays from 9 am to 4 pm.

Elsewhere in France Various universities, Alliance Française outposts and private schools teach French in the provinces.

In Dijon, contact the Centre International d'Études Françaises (☎ 80.30.50.20; fax 80.30.13.08) at 36 Rue Chabot Charny, 21000 Dijon.

In Provence and Languedoc, a good option is the nonprofit French-American Center of Provence (☎ 90.25.93.23; fax 90.25.93.24) at 10 Montée de la Tour, 30400 Villeneuve-lès-Avignon (near Avignon). Dedicated to cultural and educational exchanges between the USA and France, it has centres in Villeneuve-lès-Avignon, Aix-en-Provence, Marseille and Montpellier. It offers a variety of programmes for people of all nationalities who would like to learn French and expose themselves to French

culture while living with a French family. For other options in Aix-en-Provence, see Language Course in the Aix-en-Provence section.

The French-American Center's Stay-and-Study programmes place Anglophones with French families for two, three or four weeks (US$1050, US$1450 and US$1850 respectively), during which time they take French classes in the morning and go on excursions in the afternoon. On a programme known as the Language Exchange, native speakers of English aged 21 or over stay for two to six weeks with a French family. The Anglophone guest learns French and gets to know his or her hosts by teaching them English informally for 1½ hours a day in exchange for room and board. The centre charges participants US$700.

Cooking Courses

The major cooking schools are extremely expensive.

In Paris The famed Cordon Bleu cooking school (☎ 1-48.56.06.06; metro Vaugirard) at 8 Rue Léon Delhomme (15e) offers professional chef's training (nine or 15 months), three-month courses and short, themed intensive courses that last for two to five days (1780 to 4440FF). The intensive courses, which need to be paid in full at least two weeks before classes begin, consist of demonstrations in the morning and cooking by students in the afternoon.

Elsewhere in France The École de Cuisine La Varenne, whose Paris offices (☎ 1-47.05. 10.16 or 1-45.51.21.13; metro Invalides) are at 34 Rue Saint Dominique (7e), holds its courses in Burgundy at the Château du Feÿ near Joigny (☎ 86.63.18.34). From May to November, the school has themed, week-long courses that last from Sunday to Saturday. They cost about US$2000, including accommodation, food and transport to/from Paris. Five-week professional courses are also available. In the USA, call ☎ 202-337 0073.

In Provence, the French-American Center

(see Language Courses) offers one-week cooking courses.

HIGHLIGHTS

France is generally a lovely place to travel, but some aspects of the country are so outstanding that they deserve special mention.

- The streets of Paris
- Paris's Musée d'Orsay, Centre Pompidou and Musée Rodin
- The Causses region of northern Languedoc
- Arles's amphitheatre in the evening
- Mont Blanc seen from Chamonix
- Annecy's lakefront
- Tapas bars in Roussillon
- Brittany's Finistère region
- Old stone villages in Languedoc's Corbières wine country
- Hiking in the Alps, Pyrenees, Massif Central and Corsica
- Parapenting
- Carcassonne from a distance
- Île d'Ouessant off Brittany
- The Gorges du Verdon
- The École de Nancy Museum in Nancy
- Arras's central market squares
- The chateaux of Chambord, Chenonceau, Cheverny and Azay-le-Rideau (for chateau fans only)

ACCOMMODATION

France has accommodation of every sort and for every budget. For details – and, in many cases, help with reservations – contact the nearest tourist office. Information specific to Paris is listed under Places to Stay in the Paris chapter.

In many parts of France, local authorities impose a *taxe de séjour* (tourist tax) on each visitor in their jurisdiction. The prices charged at camping ground, hotels, etc may therefore be a few francs higher than the posted rates.

Camping

Camping, either in tents or in campervans, is immensely popular in France, and the country has thousands of camping grounds, many of them near streams, rivers, lakes or the ocean. The vast majority of camping

grounds close for a least a few months in winter, and some are only open in summer.

Most camping grounds have two to four stars, depending on their facilities and amenities, which, along with location and seasonal demand, determine the price. All but the most expensive camping grounds are cheaper than hostels and bottom-end hotels, but because few camp sites are near major sights, you may spend a fair bit of money and time commuting if you don't have a car. Hostels built on a large piece of land will sometimes let people pitch a tent in the backyard.

Camping à la ferme (camping on a farm) is coordinated by Gîtes de France (see Accommodation in Rural Areas), publisher of the annual guide *Gîtes d'Étape & Campings à la Ferme* (50FF). It is feasible only if you have wheels.

Camping grounds in or near cities and towns covered in this book are detailed under Places to Stay in each listing. Every effort has been made to find places open all year (or at least most of the year).

For information on camping grounds not mentioned in the text, enquire at a local tourist office. If you'll be doing lots of car camping, pick up Les 9200 *Camping Caravaning en France* (61FF), published by the Fédération Française de Camping Caravaning, which uses icons (explained in English) and comes with maps to help you find each camping ground; or Michelin's more selective *Camping Caravaning France* (57FF), which lists 3500 camping grounds. Both camping ground guides are updated annually and are available from bookshops and Maisons de la Presse.

In July and especially August, when most camping grounds are completely packed with families on their annual holiday, campers who arrive late in the day have a much better chance of getting a spot if they arrive on foot (ie without their own vehicle).

If you'll be doing overnight backpacking, remember that camping is generally permitted only in proper camp sites. Camping anywhere else (eg in a road or trailside meadow), known as *camping sauvage* in French, is usually illegal but tolerated to varying degrees. Except in Corsica, you probably won't have any problems if you're not on private land; have only a small puptent; are discreet; stay only one or two nights; take the tent down during the day; do not light a campfire; and are at least 1500 metres from a camping ground (or, in a national park, at least an hour's walk from a road). In the southern, dryer third of France, be extremely careful with fire.

If you camp out on the beach, even where the police tolerate such behaviour (eg Nice), you'll be an easy target for thieves, so plan accordingly. In areas with especially high tidal variations, (eg on the northern coast of Brittany and nearby parts of Normandy), sleeping on the beach is a good way to get drowned.

Naturist Camping Grounds For information on naturist camping, see Naturism under Activities.

Refuges & Gîtes d'Étape

A *refuge* (mountain hut or shelter; pronounced 'reh-FUZH') is a very basic dorm room established and operated by national park authorities, the Club Alpin Français or other private organisations along trails in uninhabited mountainous areas frequented by hikers and mountain climbers. Some *refuges*, which are generally marked on hiking and climbing maps, are open all year, while others are open only during the warm months.

In general, *refuges* are equipped with bunks (usually wall-to-wall), mattresses and blankets but not sheets, which you have to bring yourself. Charges average 50 or 60FF a night per person; given how much space you get, *refuges* are more expensive per square metre than most luxury hotels. Meals, prepared by the *gardien* (attendant), are sometimes available. Most *refuges* are equipped with a telephone – it's a good idea call ahead and make a reservation.

For details on *refuges*, contact a tourist office near where you'll be hiking or consult *Guide des Refuges et Gîtes des Alpes*, pub-

lished by Grenoble-based Glénat, which covers the Alps; or, for the Pyrenees, *Hébergement en Montagne*, published by Saint Girons-based Éditions Randonnées Pyrénéennes. Both should be available in bookshops or Maisons de la Presse.

Gîtes d'étape, which are usually better equipped and more comfortable than *refuges* (some even have showers), are situated in less remote areas, often in villages. They cost around 50 or 60FF per person and are listed in *Gîtes d'Étape & Campings à la Ferme* (50FF), published annually by Gîtes de France.

Staying in Rural Areas

Several types of accommodation are available for people who would like to spend time in rural areas and have a vehicle. All are represented by Gîtes de France, an organisation that acts as a liaison between *propriétaires* (owners) and renters.

A *gîte rural* is a holiday cottage (or part of a house) in either a village or on a farm. Amenities include a kitchenette and a bathroom. A gîte rural owned by a *commune* (the smallest unit of local government) is known as a *gîte communal*. In most cases, there is a minimum rental period, often one week but sometimes only a few days.

A *chambre d'hôte*, basically a B&B, is a room in a private house rented to travellers by the night. Breakfast is included.

A *gîte d'enfant* is a holiday camp for small groups of children aged three to 13. Run by a farm family, it is usually held during school holidays. Programming is often based on a theme related to everyday farm life.

Each département has a Gîtes de France *antenne* (branch) that publishes a brochure listing each gîte in its territory. Depending on agreements with individual owners, the branch may be able to handle English-language bookings through its *service de réservation*. Otherwise, you're meant to contact the owner yourself. During holiday periods, it may be necessary to reserve rural accommodation in some areas well in advance. Most owners will ask for deposits.

Gîtes de France branches are often affili-

ated with the *association départemental de tourisme rural* (departmental association for rural tourism) or the département's *maison de l'agriculture* (agriculture office) or *chambre d'agriculture* (chamber of agriculture). Details on how to find or contact the nearest Gîtes de France office are available at any local tourist office, which may also be able to supply a brochure. You can also contact the Fédération Nationale des Gîtes de France (☎ 1-47.42.25.43, 47.42.20.20; metro Havre Caumartin) at 35 Rue Godot de Mauroy (9e) in Paris. It is open Monday to Saturday from 10 am to 6.30 pm.

Staying with a French Family

Under an arrangement known as *hôtes payants* (literally, paying guests), students, young people and other visitors from abroad can stay with French families in exchange for a fee, calculated by the day, week or month.

Paris-based Amicale Culturelle Internationale (☎ 1-47.42.94.21; fax 1-49.24.02.67; metro Havre Caumartin) at 27 Rue Godot de Mauroy (9e) and Accueil France Famille (☎ 1-45.54.22.39; fax 1-45.58.43.25; metro Boucicaut) at 5 Rue François Coppée (15e) can arrange for stays both in Paris and other parts of the country. Accueil France Famille, a nonprofit organisation whose subscription fee is 285FF, charges 1200FF a week (1350FF for the first week) and 4500FF a month (minimum two months), including breakfast. Agencies that arrange hôtes payants in Paris are listed under Staying with a Family under Accommodation in the Paris chapter. For details on each agency's latest prices and conditions, call, write or fax at least six weeks in advance.

Renting an Apartment

If you don't either speak French or have a local helping you, it may be very difficult to find an *appartement* (apartment) for long-term rental. In any case, don't sign anything without having someone fluent in French legalese take a look at it.

The first hurdle is finding a landlord with a suitable apartment who's willing to entrust

it to someone who isn't French. It's not uncommon to be asked on the phone, *'Vous êtes de quelle nationalité?'* ('What nationality are you?'). People aren't usually too uptight about Americans, Canadians or Australians, but prejudice against black Africans and North Africans is rife and there are few laws to prevent owners from screening prospective tenants. After you've exhausted your personal connections, places to look for apartments to let include the *petites annonces* (classified ads) in local newspapers; *De Particulier à Particulier* (13FF), which comes out every Thursday; and, for students, the CROUS office of the nearest university. Estate agents require lots of paperwork and charge commissions of up to one month's rent.

Competition for apartments can be fierce, especially in September and October, when lots of students are searching for places. But at any time of year, finding an apartment is a matter of making your calls as soon as possible after the information you're using becomes public.

When looking at apartments, things to check include: the water pressure in the shower; whether the toilet flushes properly; that the drains are not clogged; what utensils (if any) are to be left in the kitchen; and that a high-voltage appliance won't blow the fuses (bring along a heater). Make sure everything on the *inventaire* (inventory) is there. Finally, in some buildings, only the owners can use the lift – renters have to walk.

Security will be better if the building has a front door code, especially if there's also a *concierge* or *gardien* (caretaker). Concierges, who also distribute the mail, carry out minor repairs, take out the rubbish, etc, can be either valuable allies or powerful foes. Apart from being nice to them, don't forget the expected Christmas tip.

Contracts for unfurnished places are often for one to three years. In general, tenants are required to pay one month's rent in advance in addition to a deposit equivalent to one to three months' rent. It is common for prospective tenants to have their finances checked to make sure they have the sufficient means of support (income and bank balances are what count), and in some cases an owner renting to young people may want to meet their parents.

It is common for both parties to have the right to terminate the rental agreement with two months' notice, though you can sometimes have this reduced to one month (of course, this can also work against you). If you find a landlord who prefers not to pay taxes on the rent (and thus to avoid putting anything down on paper), you may be able to reach a more flexible agreement.

Under French law, tenants are responsible for water or fire damage caused either to their own apartment or to other apartments in the building, so make sure you take out an appropriate insurance policy.

Staying at a Monastery

La Procure (☎ 1-45.48.20.25; metro Saint Sulpice) at 3 Rue de Mézières (6e) in Paris publishes *Guide Saint Christophe* (120FF), which has details (in French) on staying at monasteries all over France.

Hostels & Foyers

Official youth hostels that belong to one of France's three youth hostel associations (YHAs) are known as *auberges de jeunesse*. In university towns, you will also find *foyers* (fwa-YEI), student dormitories converted for use by travellers during the summer school holidays. Some cities and towns also have dormitories for young workers known as *foyers de jeunes travailleurs* (for men or co-ed) and *foyers de jeunes travailleuses* (for women). These places, which often take *passagères* and *passagers* (female and male short-term guests) when they have space, are relatively unknown to most travellers and thus may have room when the other kinds of hostels are full. Information on hostels and foyers is available from local tourist offices.

In Paris, expect to pay 90 to 115FF a night per person, including breakfast. In the provinces, a bunk in the single-sex dorm room generally costs somewhere from 40FF (at an out-of-the-way place with basic facilities) to 65FF. A few of the better places that aren't

official youth hostels charge up to 80FF. The simple, sometimes-optional continental breakfasts served are not a bad deal at around 15FF. Most auberges de jeunesse and some hostels and foyers have kitchen facilities of one sort or another.

Hostels and foyers generally do not accept reservations made by telephone; exceptions are mentioned in the text. In July and August, when swarms of summer backpackers descend on France, it's an excellent idea to arrive in town early enough to check in by mid-morning.

Touting is extremely un-French and is looked upon with disgust. If someone comes up to you at the train station and gives you the hard sell for a hostel, you can be sure that the establishment being promoted has made enemies of its neighbours.

Hostel Organisations Most of France's hostels belong to one of three youth hostel associations:

- Fédération Unie des Auberges de Jeunesse (FUAJ; ☎ 1-46.07.00.01; fax 1-46.07.93.10; metro La Chapelle), which has 220 youth hostels and has its headquarters at 27 Rue Pajol (18e), Paris.
- Ligue Française pour les Auberges de la Jeunesse (LFAJ; ☎ 1-45.48.69.84; metro Sèvres Babylone), which has 100 youth hostel affiliates and is based at 38 Blvd Raspail (7e), Paris.
- Union des Centres de Rencontres Internationales de France (UCRIF; ☎ 1-42.60.42.40; metro Louvre Rivoli), which runs 70 hostels and is based at 4 Rue Jean-Jacques Rousseau (1er), Paris.

FUAJ and LFAJ affiliates require IYHF or similar hostelling cards, available at any youth hostel for about 100FF (70FF at LFAJ if you're under 26). They also require that you either bring a sleeping sheet (a good-sized sheet sewn up on one long side and one short side) or rent one for 13 to 16FF per stay.

Hotels

Most French hotels have between one and four stars; the fanciest places have four stars plus an L (for 'luxury'). A hotel that has no stars (ie that has not been rated) is known as *non-homologué*, sometimes abbreviated as NH. The letters 'NN' after the rating mean the establishment conforms to the *nouvelle norme* (new standards), introduced in 1992. Hotels ratings are based on certain objective criteria (eg the size of the entry hall), not the quality of the service, the room décor or cleanliness, so some one-star places are more pleasant than nearby two or three-star establishments. Price often reflects these intangibles far more than it does the number of stars.

Most hotels offer *petit déjeuner*, which means a continental breakfast consisting of a croissant, French rolls, butter, jam and either coffee or hot chocolate. The charge is usually 16 to 40FF per person, which is a bit more than you would pay at a café. Some places in heavily touristed areas increase their high-season profits by requiring that each guest take breakfast. In one fell swoop, the effective price of a 160FF triple can jump to 235FF...Even more deplorable from the point of view of budget travellers are hotels that won't rent you a room unless you pay for *demi-pension* (breakfast and either lunch or dinner).

Bottom-End Hotels In general, hotels listed under 'bottom end' have doubles with washbasin (and, usually, a bidet) but without private bath or toilet for up to 160FF. Most of the cheaper hotels date from a time when bathing was less frequent than it is today, but they may also have more expensive rooms with shower, toilet and other amenities.

Most doubles, which generally cost only marginally more than singles, have only one double bed; triples and quads usually have two beds. Taking a shower in the hall bathroom is sometimes free but is usually *payant*, which means there's a charge of 8 to 25FF per person. Sometimes you have the option of taking a long, hot bath for the same price as a shower.

A double room in a cheap hotel often costs less than two beds in a hostel, so two people who don't mind sleeping in the same bed (or at least the same room) can save money while at the same time enjoying some privacy. Groups of three or four willing to

share two or three beds will save even more. Although it's much harder to meet your fellow travellers at a hotel than at a hostel, renting a hotel room will free you from the cumbersome hostel regulations that can make your holiday less carefree, such as night-time curfews, daytime room closures and length-of-stay limits, not to mention rambunctious school groups. And while many hostels are well out of the city centre, inexpensive hotels can almost always be found near the train station or in the centre of town.

Since 1992, when new hotel-grading regulations came into force, hotels seeking a one-star rating have had to equip each room with a telephone and stop renting rooms below a certain size. This new arrangement, intended to bring French hotel ratings into line with EC norms, will tend to help hotel chains (which have the capital to make modifications) at the expense of family-owned hotels, for whom it will, at the very least, make life difficult. Since many people shun nonstarred hotels, it also looks likely to drive many small, older hotels out of business, further shrinking the reservoir of cheap rooms.

If you're in the market for truly rock-bottom accommodation, you may come across *hôtels de passe*, hotels whose rooms are rented out for use by prostitutes. Certain parts of central Marseille and Paris's Pigalle and Rue Saint Denis areas are known to have such establishments, but so do other cities and towns. Of course, it's not that you can't get a good night's sleep in a *hôtel de passe* (if the walls are thick enough or you can keep your imagination in check, that is).

Some cheap hotels have the unpleasant habit of refusing to refund the unused part of your deposit when you decide to switch hotels or leave town earlier than planned. The moral of the story is not to prepay for nights there's any chance you won't be needing. In any case, the sooner you tell the manager you'll be departing the better your chances of being reimbursed.

If you're travelling by car, you'll be able to take advantage of the Formule 1 chain, whose hotels – usually located on the outskirts of town on a main access route – charge just 130FF for a room for one to three people.

Hôtel Meublé A *hôtel meublé* is a small hotel that rents out rooms with *cuisinettes* (kitchenettes), generally by the week and often to the same holidaying clients year after year.

Little Surprises The bottom-end hotels listed in the book are often small, family-run affairs that follow their own often idiosyncratic notions of service. Some peculiarities you should be prepared for include:

- There may be no lift to your 6th-floor room (this is especially common in Paris) and no fire escape either.
- The shower may consist of a curtainless bathtub with nowhere to hang the hand nozzle.
- The hot water taps in the shower and washbasin may be on the right rather than the left.
- Your bed may have a *traversin* (bolster), a horrible thing shaped like a large hot dog, rather than an *oreiller* (pillow).
- You many be asked to *régler* (settle your account, ie pay for your room) when you check in, not when you leave.

Mid-Range Hotels Hotels with double rooms listed under 'middle' in this book come with showers and toilets (unless otherwise noted) and usually have doubles for 160 to 300FF. Many places listed under 'bottom end' have rooms which, from the point of view of amenities and price, fall in the mid-range category.

Quite a few small, mid-range hotels belong to Logis de France, an organisation that groups hotels that meet certain standards. The Fédération Nationale des Logis de France (☎ 1-43.59.86.67; metro Franklin D Roosevelt) is based in Paris at 25 Rue Jean Mermoz (8e).

Advance Reservations Advance reservations are a good way to avoid the hassle of searching for a place to stay each time you pull into a new town. If you'll be arriving after about 11 am or noon (10 am during

periods of heavy domestic or foreign tourism, such as July and August in many areas), having a reservation can make the difference between getting a room for 120FF or paying 260FF – or even having to leave town.

At Tourist Offices Many tourist offices can help people who don't speak French make hotel reservations, usually for a small fee. In some cases, you pay a deposit that is later deducted from the first night's bill using a voucher. The staff may also have information on vacancies, but they usually refuse to make specific recommendations (if they did, the proprietors of places they didn't recommend would be sure to make a fuss). You can't take advantage of reservation services by phone – you have to stop by the office.

Some tourist offices do only same-day reservations at local hotels (or hotels within the *département*). Others are affiliated with Accueil de France, a nationwide telex system through which reservations can be made up to eight days in advance all over the country. The charge is 22 to 30FF. Tourist offices that don't provide these services can almost always supply a free list of local hotels.

By Telephone The relative cheapness of international phone calls makes it eminently feasible to call a hotel in France from anywhere in the world to find out if they have space when you'd like to come. It's easiest if you know some French, but even if you don't a little patience usually goes a long way. Double-check to make sure the hotel proprietor understands the date, day of the week and estimated hour of your arrival, and make sure you know what he or she expects in terms of a deposit or written confirmation.

When you phone some small hotels and ask if they have a room, the proprietor may respond by asking how many nights you'll be staying. This is often a sign that, obnoxious though it may seem, they are not interested in people who will be staying for just one night.

It is highly ill-regarded to make hotel reservations by telephone and then not show up. Hotel owners get really fed up, as an unrented room is lost revenue if they've had to turn people away, and some of them have simply stopped accepting telephone reservations. Sometimes, they start telling everyone who calls that they're full – other travellers will then have a slightly harder time making reservations. If you won't be able to come as planned, call the hotel and inform them as early as possible.

Deposits Many hotels, particularly bottom-end ones, accept reservations only if they are accompanied by *des arrhes* (pronounced 'dez AR'; a deposit) in French francs. Some places, especially those with two or more stars, don't ask for a deposit if you give them your credit card number or send them comfirmation of your plans by letter or fax in clear, simple English. But if you send them a fax, don't expect them to respond by fax.

Hotels usually don't like eurocheques because of the exorbitant commission (about 60FF) they have to pay to turn them into French francs. If you make a deposit by eurocheque, don't be surprised if the hotel holds it until you arrive and then returns it in exchange for cash.

To avoid bank commissions, most hotels will accept personal or cashiers' cheques only if they're in French francs.

Postal delivery within France usually takes only a couple of days, so deposits can easily be sent by postal money order. After you've made your reservations by phone, go to any post office and purchase a *mandat lettre* (money order; 13FF) in the proper amount and make it payable to the hotel. Then post it to the hotel along with written confirmation of your plans.

Same-Day Reservations Most hotels keep a few rooms unreserved, even during the peak season, so that at least some of the people who happen by looking for a place can be accommodated. As a result, a hotel that was all booked up when you called three

days ago may have space if you ring them at 9 or 10 am on the morning of the day you'll be arriving and ask them to hold a room until you arrive. Except in Paris, you can almost always find a place to stay this way, even in August, if:

- they speak English or you speak enough French;
- you sound credible;
- the hotel management hasn't had so many no-shows that they've stopped taking any telephone reservations.

Most places will hold a room only until a set hour, rarely later than 6 or 7 pm (and sometimes much earlier). If you are running late, let them know as soon as possible or they'll rent out the room at the first opportunity.

FOOD
French Cuisine

The cuisine of France is remarkably varied, with a great many regional differences based on the produce and gastronomy of each region. Culinary traditions that have been developed and perfected over the centuries have made French cooking a highly refined art. This is true of even the simplest peasant dishes, which require careful preparation and great attention to detail. Of course, the secret to success in a French kitchen is not so much elaborate techniques as the use of fresh ingredients that are locally produced and in season. Despite the many fast-food outlets that have sprung up in France in recent years, eating well is still of prime importance to most French people, who spend an amazing amount of time thinking about, talking about and consuming food.

Even if you can't afford to eat in world-class establishments, you can still enjoy France's epicurean delights by buying food at markets or speciality shops, trying the local delicacies of the particular region you're in, and avoiding the standard fare of tourist menus such as *steak-frites*, *crème renversée* and so on.

Types of Cuisine There are several different kinds of French cuisine:

- *Haute cuisine* (literally, high cuisine), which originated in the spectacular feasts of French kings, is typified by super-rich, elaborately prepared and beautifully presented multicourse meals.
- *Cuisine bourgeoise* (bourgeois cuisine) is French home cooking of the highest quality.
- *Cuisine des provinces* (provincial cuisine), also known as *cuisine campagnarde* (country cuisine), uses the finest ingredients and most refined techniques to prepare traditional rural dishes.
- *Nouvelle cuisine* (new cuisine), which made a big splash in the diet-conscious 1970s, features rather small portions served with sauces that are light rather than rich and creamy. Nouvelle cuisine is prepared and presented in such a way as to emphasise the inherent textures and colours of the ingredients.

Regional Specialities There are all sorts of reasons for the amazing variety of France's regional cuisine. Climatic and geographic factors have been particularly important: the hot south tends to favour olive oil, garlic and tomatoes, while the cooler, pastoral regions further north emphasise cream and butter. Areas near the coast specialise in mussels, oysters and saltwater fish, while those near lakes and rivers are more inclined to use freshwater fish. In Burgundy and around Bordeaux, snails plucked off the grape vines are considered culinary treasures and should not be missed.

Diverse though it is, French cuisine is seen to be typified by certain regions, most notably Burgundy, Périgord and Normandy. Burgundy and Périgord are both known for their rich, fancy food, available at equally remarkable prices. Burgundy supposedly has the greatest concentration of luxury restaurants in France and is also the breeding ground for that most prestigious variety of chicken, the *poulet de Bresse*. Périgord is renowned for its *foie gras*, its truffles and Roquefort cheese. Normandy's gastronomy is also recognised as being very French, with its cream sauces, soft, rich cheeses and the ubiquitous *tarte aux pommes*. (For more information on regional cuisine, see the Food sections in the regional chapters).

Vegetarian Vegetarians form only a small minority in France and are not very well

catered for, as specialised vegetarian restaurants are few and far between. Only the cities are likely to have vegetarian establishments, and these (listed in this book under Vegetarian in each city's Restaurants section) – may look more like laid-back cafés than an up-market restaurants. Still, their fare is *much* better than the omelettes and cheese sandwiches available from cafés.

Vegetarian restaurants, often attached to organic food shops, tend to have very limited opening hours, usually from noon to 2 pm and/or 6 to 9 pm. Some stay open later on Friday and Saturday nights, but others are closed over the weekend.

Other vegetarian options include *salad-eries*, casual restaurants that serve a long list of *salades composées* (mixed salads), though you should carefully scan the menu as many of these also include meat of some sort. Some restaurants have at least one vegetarian dish on the menu, though it may be one of the entrées (first-course dishes). Unfortunately, very few *menus* include vegetarian options. For more information on vegetarian options in France, see Vegetarian under Travel Guides in the Books section of this chapter.

Ethnic Cuisines

France has a considerable population of immigrants from its former colonies and protectorates in North and West Africa, Indochina, the Middle East, India, the Caribbean and the South Pacific, as well as refugees from every corner of the globe, so an exceptional variety of reasonably priced ethnic food is available.

North African One of the most delicious and easy-to-find North African dishes is couscous, steamed semolina usually garnished with vegetables and a spicy meat-based sauce just before it is served. It is usually eaten with lamb shish kebab, *merguez* (small, spicy North African sausages), *méchoui* (barbecued lamb on the bone), chicken or some other meat. The Moroccan, Algerian and Tunisian versions are slightly different.

East Asian France's many immigrants from the east coast of Asia, especially Vietnam and Cambodia, have brought East Asian food to every corner of the country. Chinese/Vietnamese restaurants, many of them run by ethnic Chinese who fled Vietnam, generally offer good value. In the major cities, you can also sample the cuisines of Cambodia, Japan, Korea, Tibet and Thailand.

Kosher Kosher *(cacher)* restaurants are mentioned under Places to Eat in the sections on Paris (see Marais and Opéra Area), Strasbourg and Marseille.

Meals in France

Breakfast In the continental tradition, the French start the day with a *petit déjeuner* (breakfast) usually consisting of a croissant and a light bread roll with butter and jam, followed by a *café au lait* (coffee with lots of hot milk), a small black coffee or hot chocolate. For visitors, breakfasting in a café or buying cakes or pastries from a pâtisserie is usually cheaper than eating at the hotel.

Lunch & Dinner Restaurants generally serve lunch between noon and 2 or 2.30 pm and dinner from 7 or 7.30 pm to sometime between 9.30 and 10.30 pm. Very few restaurants (except for brasseries, cafés and fast-food places) are open between 2.30 or 3 pm and 6.30 or 7 pm. In many cities and towns, the vast majority of restaurants are closed on Sunday. In cities such as Paris, where locals flee towards the beach in August, many restauranteurs padlock their establishments and leave town along with their clients.

For many French people, especially in the provinces, lunch is still the main meal of the day.

Traditional Meals As the pace of French life becomes more hectic, the three-hour midday meal is becoming increasingly rare, at least on weekdays. Dinners, however, are still turned into elaborate affairs whenever time and finances permit. For visitors, the occa-

sional splurge can be the perfect end to a day of sightseeing.

A fully fledged, traditional French meal is an awesome event, often comprising six distinct courses and sometimes more. The meal is always served with red, white or rosé wine, depending on what you are eating. The fare served at a traditional lunch *(déjeuner)*, eaten around 1 pm, is largely indistinguishable from that served at dinner *(dîner)*, usually begun around 8.30 pm.

The order in which courses are served may seem slightly odd to people from English-speaking countries:

1 an *apéritif* (a predinner liqueur plus nibblies)
2 an *entrée* (first course)
3 the *plat principal* (main course)
4 a *salade* (usually consisting of lettuce & dressing)
5 *fromage* (cheese)
6 *dessert* (dessert)
7 *fruit* (fruit)
8 *café* (coffee)
9 a *digestif* (an after-dinner liqueur)

Restaurants & Brasseries

There are lots of restaurants where you can get excellent French cuisine for around 200FF – Michelin's *Guide Rouge* is filled with them – but good, inexpensive French restaurants are in short supply. In this book, we have tried to list restaurants that offer what the French call a *bon rapport qualité-prix* (good value for money).

Some of the best French restaurants in the country are attached to hotels (or have hotels attached to them), while those on the ground floor of bottom-end hotels often have some of the best deals in town. Almost all are open to nonguests.

Routiers (truckers' restaurants), usually found on the outskirts of towns and along major roads, cater to truck drivers and can provide a quick, hearty break from cross-country driving.

Both restaurants and brasseries serve full meals, but with two principal differences:

• Restaurants usually specialise in a particular variety of food (eg regional, traditional, North African, Vietnamese, etc), whereas brasseries –

which look very much like cafés – serve more standard fare, often including *choucroute* (sauerkraut) because brasseries originated in Alsace.

Restaurants are usually open only at lunchtime (11.30 am or noon to 2 or 3 pm) and dinnertime (6 or 7 pm to 9.30 or 10.30 pm), whereas brasseries stay open from morning until night and serve meals (or at least something solid) at all times of the day.

Places to eat always have a menu *(carte)* posted outside so you can decide before going in whether the selection and prices are to your liking. It is considered extremely rude to walk out after you have sat down and received your menu.

À La Carte When ordering each dish separately (à la carte), one option is usually the *plat du jour* (dish of the day), some sort of speciality that changes from day to day. French restaurants rarely have minimum charges, so it is possible for people who aren't particularly hungry to order a main dish without the expected three or four accompanying courses. Vegetarians can assemble a meal by ordering one or more side dishes.

Menus Most restaurants offer at least one fixed-price, multicourse meal known in French as a *menu, menu à prix fixe* or *menu du jour* (menu of the day). A *menu* (not to be confused with a *carte*) almost always costs much less than ordering à la carte. In touristy places, you may also be able to order a *formule rapide* (rapid formula), a quick and cheap two or three-course meal with limited choices. In some restaurants, the *menu* is available at lunchtime only. Evening *menus* may not be served after 9 pm.

When you order a three-course *menu*, you usually get to choose an entrée, such as salad, pâté or soup; a main dish (several meat, poultry or fish dishes – including the plat du jour – are generally on offer); and one or more final courses (usually cheese or dessert).

Boissons (drinks), including wine, cost extra unless the menu says *boisson comprise* (drink included), in which case you may get

a beer or a glass of mineral water. If the *menu* says *vin compris* (wine included), you'll probably be served small *pichet* (jug) of wine. The waiter will always ask if you would like coffee to end the meal, but this will cost extra.

Menu prices vary greatly. In *routiers*, a *menu* can cost as little as 45 or 50FF, while at the most elegant establishments (ie those with one or more Michelin stars), they can start at several hundred francs. The cheapest *menu* at an average restaurant will cost between 65 and 80FF, and the most expensive *menu* may cost twice as much if not more. Many places have a *menu enfant* (children's *menu*) available for children under 12.

Restaurant meals are almost always served with bread. If your bread basket runs out, don't be afraid to ask the waiter for more (just say, *encore du pain, s'il vous plaît*).

Cafés

Cafés are an important focal point for social life in France, and sitting in a café to read, write, talk with friends or just daydream is an integral part of many French people's day-to-day existence. Many people see café-sitting – like shopping at outdoor markets – as a way of keeping in touch with their neighbourhood and maximising their chances of running into friends and acquaintances.

Only basic food is available in most cafés. Common options include a baguette sandwich filled with Camembert or pâte, a croque-monsieur or a croque-madame (see Snacks).

Three factors determine how much you'll pay in a café: where the café is situated, where you are sitting within the café and when you come.

A café located on a grand boulevard (such as Blvd du Montparnasse or the Champs Élysées in Paris) will charge considerably more than a place that fronts a semi-anonymous sidestreet. Once inside, progressively more expensive tariffs apply at the counter (*comptoir* or *zinc*), in the table area (*salle*) and on the outside terrace (*terrasse*), the best

vantage point from which to see and be seen. Some of the cheapest soft drinks may be available only at the bar. The price of drinks goes up at night (usually after 8 pm). It really comes down to this: you are not paying for your espresso or mineral water as much as for the right to occupy an attractive and visible bit of ground. Ordering a cup of coffee (or anything else) earns you the right to sit there for as long as you like. Rarely, if ever, will you feel pressured to order something else.

You usually pay the *addition* (bill) right before you leave, though if your waiter is going off duty you may be asked to pay up at the end of his or her shift.

Salons de Thé

Salons de thé (tearooms) are trendy and somewhat pricey establishments that usually offer quiches, salads, cakes, tarts, (pies) and pastries in addition to tea and coffee.

Creperies

Creperies specialise in crepes, ultrathin pancakes cooked on a flat surface and then folded or rolled over a filling. In some parts of France, the word '*crêpe*' is used to refer only to sweet crepes made with *farine de froment* (regular wheat flour), whereas savoury crepes, often made with *farine de sarrasin* (buckwheat flour) and filled with cheese, mushrooms and the like, are called *galettes*.

Fast Food

American fast-food companies, including McDonald's, have busy branches all over France, which must mean that the average French person is a lot more open to Anglo-Saxon culinary ideas than some defenders of French civilisation seem to believe.

Because of differing VAT rates, some fast-food places and ice cream shops have two sets of prices: one for takeaway food (*à emporter*), taxed at 5.5%, and the other for food you eat there (*sur place*), on which the VAT is 18.6%.

Cafeterias

Many cities have cafeteria-restaurants offering a good selection of dishes you can see before ordering, a factor that can make life easier if you're travelling with kids. Cafeteria chains include Flunch, Mélodine and Casino.

University Restaurants

All French universities have student restaurants subsidised by the Ministry of Education and operated by the Centre Régional des Œuvres Universitaires et Scolaires, better known as CROUS.

Meal tickets are sold at ticket windows, but since each university seems to have its own policy on feeding students from out-of-town, you may have to purchase a ticket from a local student. Except in Strasbourg, where an ultramodern computer-operated debit card system is in operation and can only be used by local students, people with student cards can usually get a filling cafeteria meal for 12.30FF. Ticket windows, like the cafeterias themselves, have limited opening hours, and are often closed on weekends and during school holidays (including July and August).

Self-Catering

France is justly renowned for its extraordinary chefs and restaurants, but one of the country's premier culinary delights is to stock up on delicious fresh breads, pastries, cheese, fruit, vegetables and prepared dishes and sit down for a gourmet *pique-nique* (picnic). Note that many food shops are closed on Sunday afternoon and Monday.

French food retailing is arranged so that most people buy a good part of their food from a series of small neighbourhood shops, each with its own speciality. At first, having to go to four shops and stand in four queues to fill the fridge (or assemble a picnic) may seem rather a waste of time, but the whole ritual is an important part of the way the French live their day-to-day lives.

· Since each *commerçant* (shopkeeper) specialises in purveying only one type of food, he or she can almost always provide all sorts of useful tips: which round of Camembert is ripe, which inexpensive wine will complement a certain kind of sandwich and so on.

As the whole setup is geared to people buying small quantities of fresh food each day, it's perfectly acceptable to purchase only small amounts: a few *tranches* (slices) of meat to make a sandwich, perhaps, or a *petit bout* (small chunk) of sausage. You can also request just enough for one/two people *(pour une/deux personnes)*. If you want a bit more, ask for *'encore un petit peu'*, and if you are being given too much, say *'c'est trop'*.

When you enter a shop, remember to say *'bonjour, Monsieur/Madame/Mademoiselle'* and when you leave, say *'merci, Monsieur/Madame/Mademoiselle, au revoir'*. Even small villages have a selection of food shops, and remote hamlets are usually served by mobile grocers, butchers and bakers.

Boulangerie Fresh bread is baked and sold at France's 36,000 *boulangeries*, which supply three-quarters of the country's bread.

All boulangeries have 250-gram *baguettes*, which are long (76 cm) and thin and 400-gram loaves of *pain* (bread), both of which are at their best if eaten within four hours of baking. You can store them for longer in a plastic bag, but the crust becomes soft and chewy; if you leave them out, they'll soon be inedibly hard. The *pain* is softer on the inside, has a less crispy crust than the baguette, and is slightly cheaper by weight. If you're not very hungry, ask for a *demi* (half-loaf) of baguette or *pain*. *Ficelles* are thinner, crustier versions of the baguette.

Many boulangeries also have heavier, more expensive breads made with all sorts of grain and cereals, and some of these are so scrumptious they can be eaten plain. You will also find bread flavoured with nuts, raisins or herbs. Other types of bread, which come in a wide range of sizes and shapes, vary from shop to shop and region to region, but since they are all on display, making a selection is easy.

Signs you're likely to see in boulangeries include: *pain cuit au feu de bois* (bread baked in a wood-fired oven), *pain de seigle* (rye bread), *pain complet* (wholemeal bread), *pain au son* (bread with bran), *pain de campagne* (hand-made country bread) and *pain au levain* (traditionally made yeast bread that's usually a bit chewy). The heavier breads keep much longer than the baguettes and 400-gram loaves.

To facilitate carrying it home, you can ask for your baguette or loaf of bread to be *coupé en deux* (cut in two). If you ask for the bread to be sliced, there's a small charge (50 centimes or 1FF). Many boulangeries also sell baguette sandwiches, quiche slices, bad little pizzas and various pastries.

Bread is baked at various times of day, so that fresh bread is readily available as early as 6 am and also in the afternoon. Most boulangeries close for one day a week, but the days are staggered so a town or neighbourhood is never left without a place to buy bread (except, perhaps, on Sunday afternoon). Places that sell bread but don't bake it on the premises are known as *depôts de pain*.

Pâtisserie Mouth-watering pastries are available at *pâtisseries*, which are often attached to boulangeries. Some of the most common pastries include *pain au chocolat* (similar to a croissant but filled with chocolate), *pains aux raisins* (flat, spiral pastries made with custard and sultanas) and *religieuses* (éclairs with one cream puff perched on top of another to resemble a nun's cap).

You can tell if a *croissant* (a flaky, crescent-shaped pastry often eaten for breakfast) has been made with margarine or butter by the shape: margarine croissants have their tips almost touching, while those made with butter have their tips pointing away from each other.

Confiserie Chocolate and other sweets made with the finest ingredients can be found at *confiseries*, which are sometimes combined with boulangeries and pâtisseries.

Fromagerie If you buy your cheese in a supermarket, you're likely to end up with unripe and relatively tasteless products unless you know how to select each variety. Here's where a *fromagerie*, also known as a *crémerie*, comes in: the owner, a true expert on matters cheesological, can supply you with cheese that is *fait* (ripe) to the exact degree that you request – and will usually let you taste it before you decide what to buy. Just ask, *'est-ce que je peux le goûter, s'il vous plaît'* and they will cut you a little piece from under the rind so as not to damage the cheese's appearance. Most fromageries sell both whole and half-rounds of Camembert, so you don't have to buy more than you're likely to eat in a day or two.

Most cheeses, including Camembert and Emmenthal, will last at least a couple of days without refrigeration, even in summer. Soft and blue cheeses tend to melt, however, especially if you carry them around in your daypack. In winter, you can put them (and other perishables) in a plastic bag and hang it out the window of your hostel or hotel room, though you may then be in danger of finding everything frozen in the morning.

Charcuterie A *charcuterie* is a delicatessen offering sliced meats, seafood salads, pâtés, terrines, etc. Most supermarkets have a charcuterie counter. If the word *traiteur* (trader) is written on a sign, it means that the establishment sells ready-to-eat takeaway dishes.

Fruit & Vegetables *Fruits* and *légumes* are sold by a *marchand de légumes et de fruits* and at food markets and supermarkets. Most *épiceries* have only a limited selection. You can buy whatever quantity of produce suits you, even if it's just three carrots and a peach.

The kind of produce on offer varies greatly from region to region and from season to season. Some things are available in only one small region for a limited time of the year. Many *primeurs* (the first fruits and vegetables of the season) come from Prov-. ence. *Biologique* means grown organically (ie without chemicals).

Cheese

In one of his most quoted statements, Général de Gaulle said in 1951: 'You simply cannot bring together a country that has 265 kinds of cheeses'. These days, France is said to have close to 400 cheeses, so making a selection from either a restaurant's cheese platter *(plateau de fromage)* or a cheese shop *(fromagerie)* is harder than ever.

Made from the milk of *chèvres* (goats), *vaches* (cows) or *brebis* (sheep), French cheeses may be eaten young or left to mature. Some are blue-veined, some have large holes and some are flavoured with herbs, pepper, garlic, mustard seeds or walnuts. Prices range from 30FF a kg for a soft Brie to 100FF a kg for a mouldy Roquefort, a strong-flavoured blue-veined cheese that is matured in caves.

Camembert, which originated in Normandy, should be eaten only when it's ripe and at room temperature (ie slightly soft). Though its white outer crust is eminently edible, some people prefer not to eat it. The Massif Central produces many of France's cheapest cheeses, such as the strong, blue Bleu d'Auvergne and Fourme d'Ambert. The region's red-brown Salers cows also produce Cantal, said by some to be the closest thing to English cheddar, and Tomme de Cantal, a fresh unfermented cheese. The Massif Central and Provence are also good for tasty goat cheeses (moist with a subtle taste when young, hard and powerfully flavoured when mature); you can buy them direct from small farms in the region – look out for roadside signs reading *'fromage de chèvre'*.

All cheeses are marked with the percentage of *matière grasse* (fat content as a percentage of dry weight), which sometimes reaches 60% or more. The rule is: the more fat, the better. Camembert is usually 45%.

Louis Pasteur may have been French, but many French cheeses are still made from raw, unpasteurised milk. As a result, and despite the fact that the French don't seem to be dying of cheese poisoning, bureaucrats in Brussels recently tried to end France's centuries-old production of unpasteurised cheeses, ostensibly on health grounds. Health regulations in the USA, Australia and other countries have long forbidden the importation of cheeses made from unpasteurised milk, so some of the most delicious French Camemberts and other cheeses are not available outside of France. ∎

Meat & Fish A general butcher is a *boucherie*, but for specialised poultry you have to go to a *marchand de volaille*, where *poulet fermier* (free-range chicken) will cost much more than a regular chicken. A *boucherie chevaline*, easily identifiable by the gilded horse's head out front, sells horse meat, which some people prefer to beef or mutton, in part because it is less likely to have been produced using artificial hormones. Fresh fish and seafood are available from a *poissonnerie*.

Épicerie & Alimentation A small grocery

store with little bit of everything is known as an *épicerie* (literally, a spice shop) or an *alimentation générale*. Most épiceries are considerably more expensive than supermarkets, especially in Paris, though some – such as those of the Casino and Comod chains – are more like minimarkets. Some épiceries are open on days when other food shops are closed, and many family-run operations stay open until late at night.

Supermarkets Town and city centres usually have at least one department store with a large *supermarché* (supermarket) section in the basement or on the first floor. Stores to look for include Monoprix (owned by Galeries Lafayette), Prisunic (owned by Printemps), Nouvelles Galeries and Magmod. You may also find one or more small supermarkets of the Casino chain. In Paris, the cheapest edibles are sold at the no-frills supermarkets of Ed l'Épicier. Most larger supermarkets have charcuterie and cheese counters, and many also have in-house boulangeries.

The cheapest place to buy food is a *hypermarché* (hypermarket), such as those of the Auchan, Intermarché, E Leclerc, Carrefour, Casino amd Rallye chains, where you'll pay up to 40% less for staples than at an épicerie. Unfortunatly, they're nearly always on the outskirts of town, often in an area accessible only by car.

Food Markets In most towns and cities, many of the aforementioned products are available one or more days a week at *marchés en plein air* (open-air markets), also known as *marchés découverts*, and up to six days a week at *marchés couverts* (covered marketplaces), often known as *les halles*. Markets are cheaper than food shops and supermarkets and the merchandise, especially fruit and vegetables, is fresher and of better quality.

In smaller towns and villages, markets have a vital social function. Like cafés, they are an important meeting place, especially for small-scale farmers who have their weekly chat with acquaintants while selling their wares. There is no bargaining, and weighing is often done with hand scales. Prices may even be given in old (pre-1959) francs, which were worth one modern-day centime, so don't be alarmed if you're asked to pay *quatre cent cinquante francs* (450 francs) for a 4.50FF bag of apricots.

Starters (Entrées or Hors d'Œuvres)
Assiette anglaise
    Plate of cold mixed meats and sausages
Assiette de crudités
    Plate of raw vegetables with dressings
Fromage de tête
    Pâté made with pig's head set in jelly
Soufflé
    A light, fluffy dish made with egg yolks, stiffly beaten egg whites, flour and cheese or other ingredients

Soup (Soupe)
Bourride
    fish stew
Bouillabaisse
    Mediterranean fish soup, originally from Marseille, made with several kinds of fish, including *rascasse* (spiny scorpion fish)
Bouillon
    Broth or stock
Croûtons
    Fried or roasted bread cubes, often added to soups
Potage
    Thick soup made with puréed vegetables
Soupe au pistou
    Vegetable soup made with a basil and garlic paste
Soupe de poisson
    Cream of fish soup
Soupe du jour
    Soup of the day

Meat (Viande)

Agneau	Lamb
Andouille or *Andouillette*	Tripe sausage made from pork or veal
Bifteck	Steak
Bœuf	Beef
Bœuf haché	Minced beef

Boudin Noir	Pork-blood sausage (black pudding)
Brochette	Kebab
Cervelle	Brains
Charcuterie	Cooked pork meats
Cheval, viande de	Horse meat
Chèvre	Goat
Chevreau	Kid (goat)
Chevreuil	Venison
Cuisses de grenouilles	Frogs' legs
Entrecôte	Rib steak
Faux-filet	Sirloin steak
Foie	Liver
Gibier	Game
Jambon	Ham
Langue	Tongue
Lapin	Rabbit
Lard	Bacon
Lièvre	Hare
Mouton	Mutton
Pieds de porc	Pig's trotters
Porc	Pork
Rognons	Kidneys
Sanglier	Wild boar
Saucisson	Large sausage
Saucisson fumé	Smoked sausage
Steak	Steak
Tripes	Tripe
Veau	Veal
Venaison	Venison

Chicken (Poulet) & Poultry (Volaille)

Aiguillette	Thin slice of duck fillet
Canard	Duck
Caneton	Duckling
Dinde	Turkey
Faisan	Pheasant
Foie gras de canard	Duck-liver pâté
Pigeonneau	Young pigeon
Pintade	Guinea fowl

Common Meat & Poultry Dishes

Blanquette de veau/d'agneau
Veal/lamb stew with white sauce

Bœuf bourguignon
Beef and vegetable stew cooked in red wine (usually Burgundy)

Cassoulet
Languedoc stew made with fillets of goose, duck, pork or lamb and haricot beans

Chapon
Castrated cockerel delicacy

Choucroute
Sauerkraut with sausage

Coq au vin
Chicken cooked in wine

Civet
Game stew

Fricassée
Stew with meat that has first been fried

Grillade
Grilled meats

Marcassin
Young wild boar

Quenelles
Dumplings made of a finely sieved mixture of cooked meat or fish

Steak tartare
raw ground meat (often horse meat) mixed with onion, raw egg yolk and herbs

Terms for Ordering Steak

Bleu
Nearly raw

Saignant
Very rare (literally, bleeding)

À point
Medium rare but still pretty pink

Bien cuit
literally, well cooked, but usually like medium rare

Seafood (Fruits de mer) & Fish (Poisson)

Anchois	Anchovy
Anguille	Eel
Brème	Bream
Brochet	Pike
Cabillaud	(Fresh) cod
Calmar	Squid
Carrelet	Plaice
Chaudrée	Fish stew
Colin	Hake
Coquille Saint-Jacques	Scallop
Crabe	Crab

Crevette grise	Shrimp
Crevette rose	Prawn
Écrevisse	Small, freshwater crayfish
Escargot	Snail
Gambas	King prawns
Goujon	Gudgeon (small, freshwater fish)
Hareng	Herring
Homard	Lobster
Huître	Oyster
Langouste	Crayfish
Langoustine	Very small, salt-water lobster
Maquereau	Mackerel
Merlan	Whiting
Morue	Cod
Moules	Mussels
Oursin	Sea urchin
Palourde	Clam
Raie	Ray
Raie au beurre noir	Steamed ray with melted butter
Rouget	Mullet
Sardine	Sardine
Saumon	Salmon
Sole	Sole
Thon	Tuna
Truite	Trout

Vegetables (Légumes), Herbs (Herbes) & Spices (Épices)

Ail	Garlic
Aïoli	Garlic oil
Anis	Aniseed
Artichaut	Artichoke
Asperge	Asparagus
Aubergine	Aubergine (egg-plant)
Avocat	Avocado
Basilic	Basil
Betterave	Beetroot
Cannelle	Cinnamon
Carotte	Carrot
Céleri	Celery
Cèpe	Cepe (boletus mushroom)
Champignon	Mushroom or edible fungus

Champignon de Paris	Button mushrooms
Chou	Cabbage
Chou farci	Stuffed cabbage
Citrouille	Pumpkin
Concombre	Cucumber
Cornichon	Gherkin (pickle)
Courgette	Zucchini or summer squash
Crudités	Small pieces of raw vegetables
Échalotte	Shallot
Épinards	Spinach
Estragon	Tarragon
Fenouil	Fennel
Fève	Broad bean
Frites	Potato chips or French fries
Genièvre	Juniper
Gingembre	Ginger
Haricots	Beans
Haricots Blancs	White Beans
Haricots Rouge	Kidney Beans
Haricots Verts	String or French beans
Laitue	Lettuce
Lentilles	Lentils
Maïs	Corn
Marjolaine	Sweet marjoram
Menthe	Mint
Navet	Turnip
Oignon	Onion
Olive	Olive
Origan	Wild marjoram (oregano)
Oseille	Sorrel
Panais	Parsnip
Persil	Parsley
Petit Pois	Pea
Poireau	Leek
Pomme de terre	Potato
Ratatouille	Casserole of auber-gines, tomatoes, peppers and garlic
Riz	Rice
Salade	Salad or lettuce
Sarrasin	Buckwheat
Seigle	Rye
Tomate	Tomato
Truffe	Truffle

Cooking Terms

À la broche	Spit-roasted
À la vapeur	Steamed
Au feu de bois	Cooked over a wood fire
Au four	Baked
Confit de canard	Duck preserved and cooked in its own fat
Côte	Chop of pork, lamb or mutton
Côtelette	Cutlet
En croûte	In pastry
Épaule d'agneau	Shoulder of lamb
Farci	Stuffed
Filet	Tender loin
Fumé	Smoked
Gratiné	Browned on top with cheese
Grillé	Grilled
Pané	Coated in breadcrumbs
Rôti	Roasted
Sauté	Shallow fried
Tournedos	Thick slices of fillet

Sauces & Accompaniments

Béchamel
  Basic white sauce
Mornay
  Cheese sauce
Moutarde
  Mustard
Pistou
  Pounded mix of basil, cheese, olive oil and garlic
Provençale
  Tomato, garlic, herb and olive oil dressing or sauce
Tartare
  Mayonnaise with herbs
Vinaigrette
  Salad dressing made with oil, vinegar, mustard and garlic

Fruit & Nuts

Abricot	Apricot
Amande	Almond
Ananas	Pineapple
Arachide	Peanut
Banane	Banana
Cacahuète	Peanut
Cassis	Black currant
Cerise	Cherry
Citron	Lemon
Datte	Date
Figue	Fig
Fraise	Strawberry
Framboise	Raspberry
Grenade	Pomegranate
Groseille	Red currant or gooseberry
Mangue	Mango
Marron	Chestnut
Melon	Melon
Mirabelle	Type of plum
Myrtille	Bilberries/ blueberries
Noisette	Hazelnut
Noix de cajou	Cashew
Orange	Orange
Pamplemousse	Grapefruit
Pastèque	Watermelon
Pêche	Peach
Pistache	Pistachio
Poire	Pear
Pomme	Apple
Prune	Plum
Pruneau	Prune
Raisin	Grape

Desserts & Sweets

Crème caramel
  Crème caramel
Crêpe
  Thin pancake
Crêpes suzettes
  Orange-flavoured pancakes flambéed in liqueur
Bergamotes
  Orange-flavoured confectionary
Dragée
  Sugared almond
Éclair
  Hollow pastry filled with cream
Far
  Flan with prunes (a Breton speciality)
Flan
  Egg-custard dessert

Frangipane
  Pastry filled with cream and flavoured with almonds or a cake mixture containing ground almonds
Galette
  Wholemeal or buckwheat pancake; a type of biscuit
Gâteau
  Cake
Gaufre
  Waffle
Gelée
  Jelly
Glace
  Ice cream
Glace au chocolat
  Chocolate ice cream
Île flottante
  Floating island – beaten egg white lightly cooked, floating on a creamy sauce
Macarons
  Sweet biscuit made of ground almonds, suger and egg whites
Sablé
  Shortbread biscuit
Farine de semoule
  Semolina flour
Tarte
  Tart (pie)
Tarte aux pommes
  Apple tart
Yaourt
  Yoghurt

Snacks
croque monsieur
  A grilled ham and cheese sandwich
croque-madame
  A croque-monsieur with a fried egg
frites
  chips

Food Basics
Beurre	Butter
Chocolat	Chocolate
Confiture	Jam
Crème fraîche	Cream
Farine	Flour
Huile	Oil
Lait	Milk

Miel	Honey
Œufs	Eggs
Poivre	Pepper
Quiche	Savoury egg, bacon and cream tart
Sel	Salt
Sucre	Sugar
Vinaigre	Vinegar

Utensils
Bouteille	Bottle
Carafe	Carafe
Pichet	Jug
Verre	Glass
Couteau	Knife
Cuillère	Spoon
Fourchette	Fork
Serviette	Napkin, serviette

DRINKS

Although alcohol consumption has dropped by 20% since the war – the stereotypical Frenchman no longer starts the day by 'killing the worm' *(tuer le ver)* with a shot of red wine (or something stronger) followed by a small, black coffee – the French drink more than any other national group in the world except the people of Luxembourg. On average, the French consume 15.5 litres of pure alcohol a year, compared to 8.3 litres in the USA and 8.2 litres in the UK.

In recent years, however, mineral water has made inroads against wine as the beverage of choice at meals, and though alcoholism remains a major social problem (especially in Brittany), government anti-excess campaigns – which once provoked riots in wine regions such as Languedoc – are having an impact on traditional attitudes. Less than 40% of French young people now believe that wine is essential to good health.

Nonalcoholic Drinks
Water Despite the warnings of some squeamish guidebooks, the tap water in France is safe to drink, so there is no need to buy expensive bottled water. All tap water that is not drinkable (eg at some public fountains) will have a sign reading *'eau non potable'* (undrinkable water).

If you prefer to have tap water with your meal rather than some exorbitantly priced soft drink or wine, don't be put off if the waiter scowls: French law mandates that restaurants must serve tap water to clients who so request. Make sure you ask for *de l'eau* (some water), *une carafe d'eau* (a jug of water) or *de l'eau du robinet* (tap water) or you may get pricey *eau de source* (mineral water), which comes *plate* ('flat', ie noncarbonated) or *gazeuse* (carbonated).

Eaux de source (mineral waters) such as Perrier and Vittel are very fashionable. A *Perrier tranche* is a Perrier with a slice of lemon.

Soft Drinks Soft drinks are hideously expensive in France – in a fashionable café, don't be surprised if you're charged 17FF for a little bottle of Gini or Pschitt. A demi of beer may actually be cheaper than a Coke. Even in the supermarket, soft drinks are hardly cheaper than beer, milk and even some kinds of wine.

One relatively inexpensive café drink is *sirop* (squash, ie fruit syrup), served either *à l'eau* (mixed with water), with *soda* (carbonated water) or Perrier. Basically like a strong cordial, popular sirop flavours include *cassis* (blackberry), *grenadine* (pomegranate), *menthe* (mint) and *citron* (lemon). A *citron pressé* is a glass of soda water with freshly squeezed lemon juice and sugar. A glass of freshly squeezed orange juice is an *orange pressée*. *Limonade* is lemon-lime soda (fizzy lemonade in the UK). A *panaché* is a shandy (a mixture of limonade and beer). A *diabolo* is limonade with sirop. The French are not particularly fond of drinking very cold things. If you would like your drink with ice cubes, ask for *glaçons*.

Yoghurt Drink Yop, made by Yoplait, and Dan'up, produced by Danone, are sweet yoghurt drinks somewhat similar to the sweet lassis you get on the Indian subcontinent. Both are sold in supermarkets.

Coffee A cup of coffee can take various forms, but the most ubiquitous is espresso,

made by forcing steam through ground coffee beans. A small, black espresso is called *un café noir*, *un express* or simply *un café*. You can also ask for a *grand* (large) version.

Un café crème is espresso with steamed milk or cream. *Un café au lait* is lots of hot milk with a little coffee served in a large cup (or even a bowl). A small café crème is a *petit crème*. A *noisette* (literally, hazelnut) is an espresso with just a dash of milk.

The French consider American coffee to be undrinkably weak and dishwatery (they sometimes jokingly call it *jus de chaussettes*, which means 'sock juice') but will serve it (or something similar) if you ask for *un café américain* or – because it has been 'lengthened' by adding extra hot water – *un café allongé* or *un café long*. Decaffeinated coffee is *un café décaféiné* or *un déca*.

Tea & Hot Chocolate Other hot drinks that are widely available include *thé* (tea), which is unlikely to be up to the English standard but will be served with milk if you ask for *un peu de lait frais*. Herbal tea, which is widely available (and is very popular as a treatment for minor ailments), is called a *tisane* or *infusion*. Popular herbal teas include *menthe* (mint), *camomille* (camomile) and *tilleul* (dried lime flowers).

French *chocolat chaud* (hot chocolate) is usually either excellent or undrinkable.

Wine
The French nearly always drink *vin* (wine) with their meals. A fine meal will be accompanied by an equally fine *bouteille* (bottle) of wine – *rouge* (red), *blanc* (white) or *rosé* (rosé), chosen to complement the main course. Unfortunately, wines cost several times more in restaurants than in supermarkets and the idea of Australian-style BYO (bring your own) seems distasteful to French restaurateurs.

Except for champagne, for which the following terms are used a bit differently (see the Champagne aside in the Champagne chapter for details), *brut* is very dry; *sec* is

dry; *demi-sec* is sweet; *doux* is very sweet and *mousseux* is sparkling.

In 1863, a kind of louse known as phylloxera was accidentally brought to Europe from the USA. It immediately began eating through the roots of Europe's grapevines, destroying something like 10,000 sq km of vineyards in France alone. It looked like European wine production was doomed until phylloxera-resistant root stocks were brought from California and had older varieties grafted onto them.

Quality Wine production in France is strictly supervised by the government. Under French law, wines are divided into four categories based on their quality:

- *Appellation d'Origine Contrôlée* (AOC; literally, mark of controlled place of origin) – These wines have met stringent government regulations governing where, how and under what conditions they are grown, fermented and bottled. They are almost always at least good and may be superb. A bottle of AOC wine can cost from 25FF to many hundreds of francs a bottle, depending on where it's from and which label it bears. The makers of AOC wines are the elite of the French wine industry.
- *Vins Délimité de Qualité Supérieure* (VDQS) – These are good wines from a specific place or region. Prices are similar to AOC wines.
- *Vin de Pays* Wines with this label (whose literal meaning is 'local wine') are of reasonable quality and generally drinkable. They sell for between 10 and 15FF a bottle.
- *Vin de Table* – These table wines are also known as *vins ordinaires*. You can buy litre bottles from a supermarket for under 10FF, but if you buy directly from the producer, you'll be looking at as little as 5FF a litre (bring your own container). Bad vin de table will leave you with black teeth, a sore throat and a horrible hangover. Spending an extra 5 or 10FF can often make the difference between drinkability and undrinkability.

Not even the French government can control the weather, and even within a given microclimate there are wide variations from year to year. Some outstanding *millésimes* (vintages) become legendary and are talked about for decades afterwards, whereas others are totally forgettable. Except in Alsace, wines are named after where they're grown rather than after the variety of grapes used.

Wine Tasting In wine-growing regions, *caves* (wine cellars) provide an opportunity to purchase wine straight from the *vigneron* (wine grower). Often, you'll be offered a *dégustation* (tasting), with the wine poured straight from enormous wood barrels or sparkling stainless steel vats. It's usually free, but you won't be at all popular if you sample several vintages and then leave. *Caves* often require that you buy in bulk *(en vrac)* – a five-litre minumum is common in some areas. At some *caves*, you may have to bring your own container.

Wine Bars *Bars à vins*, mostly an urban phenomenon, serve a dozen or more selected wines by the glass so you can taste and compare different varieties and vintages. Wines do not keep for very long after the bottle has been opened, but a few years back someone realised that wine in an uncorked bottle can be stabilised by replacing air inside with a nonoxidising gas.

Wine Shops Wine is sold by a *marchand de vin*, such as the shops of the Nicolas chain. The cheapest vintages often cost less than 10FF a bottle – less than a soft drink in a café – but you're usually much better off paying a bit more (at least 20FF) for something better.

In wine-making areas, you can buy wine direct from the producers at a *cave* (wine cellar), often after a free *dégustation* (tasting).

Other Alcoholic Drinks

Aperitifs Meals are often preceded by an appetite-stirring *apéritif* such as *kir* (white wine sweetened with a syrup such as cassis, ie blackcurrant syrup), *kir royale* (champagne with cassis) and *pineau* (cognac and grape juice). Port is drunk as an apéritif rather than after the meal.

All sorts of imported whiskies, commonly termed *whisky* or *scotch*, are available but are very expensive.

Pastis Pastis is a 90-proof, anise-flavoured alcoholic drink, which, as you mix it with about five parts ice water, turns cloudy. It's strong, refreshing and cheap (7FF for a two ml shot). Although it's popular all over the country, it's a particular favourite in southern France, where people sip it as an apéritif. You'll often see the brand names Pernod, Ricard and Suze painted on the walls of old stone houses – advertisements from decades past.

Digestifs A *digestif* is a drink served either at the end of or during a meal, supposedly to make room in the stomach for the next course.

France's most famous brandies are Cognac and Armagnac, both made from grapes in regions of those names. Calvados is an apple brandy made in Normandy. Poire William is a pear-based concoction. The various other sorts of brandies, many of them very strong local products, are known collectively as *eaux de vie* (literally, waters of life).

Liqueurs Produced all over France, most liqueurs are made from grapes, eau de vie, sugar and either fruit or the essences of aromatic herbs. Well-known brands include Cointreau and Bénédictine, both elaborate blends of ingredients, and orange-spiced Grand Marnier. More obscure is Salers, a bitter concoction made from the roots of the protected wild gentian plant.

Beer Beer, which is served by the *demi* (about 33 ml), is usually either Alsatian or imported from Germany or Belgium. Kronenbourg is the most common French beer. The company's Strasbourg *brasserie* (brewery) offers tours for visitors.

In pubs, beer is cheaper *à la pression* (on draught/tap) than in a *bouteille* (bottle), but prices vary widely depending on what sort of an establishment it is. At a decent but modest sort of place, count on paying about 12FF for a demi of Kronenbourg on tap. Prices often go up two or three francs as the night wears on. Strong Belgian brews such as Trappist beers are quite pricey, costing 20

and 25FF a bottle. Some of the country's least expensive beer is sold at McDonald's.

ENTERTAINMENT

Local tourist offices are generally the best source of information about what's on. In larger towns, they often have free brochures listing cultural events and entertainment taking place each week, fortnight or month.

Music

All French cities and many towns put on at least one music festival each year. For details, see the Festivals section in this chapter and specific city and town listings, or contact the local tourist office.

France's contemporary music scene is dominated by jazz and the sounds of Brazil and Africa. Celtic music, such as that featured at the Inter-Celtic Bagpipe Festival held in Lorient in Brittany, continues to gain popularity. Trashpop, a mixture of various styles ranging from heavy metal to funk, had some success internationally in the early 1990s; the zany duo, Niagara, was one of its exponents. Domestic rock music has never had wide popularity.

The songs of Édith Piaf, Georges Brassens and Belgian-born Jacques Brel continue to be popular, though you'll rarely hear them on the radio these days.

The classical music scene is very lively, with a dozen or so orchestras outside of Paris, such as Strasbourg's well-regarded Opéra du Rhin. There are innumerable classical music festivals all over France, especially during the summer. Those held in Aix-en-Provence and Orange in July are especially popular.

Cinema

If you don't want to see your favourite star slurring away in some colloquial form of French intended to approximate a Bronx, Irish or Australian outback accent, look in the film listings and on the theatre's billboard for the letters *v.o. (version originale)* or *v.o.s.t. (version originale sous-titrée)*, both of which mean that the film retains its original foreign soundtrack but has been given

French subtitles. If v.o. is nowhere to be seen, or if you notice the letters *v.f. (version française)*, it means the film has been dubbed into French. Of course, if the original version of the film was in French or some language other than English, the v.o. version will be too. Daniel once went to see a film the ads said was from the UK and in v.o. only to find during the opening scenes that the soundtrack was in Welsh!

In Paris, the film listings in *L'Officiel des Spectacles* and *Pariscope* (see Entertainment in the Paris chapter) include English-language movies' original names. However, local newspapers, cinema billboards and cinemas' answering machines generally use only the French title, which may be completely unrelated to the English one.

Cinema schedules usually list two times for each film: one for the *séance*, when the prescreening ads and previews begin; and the other, usually 10 to 25 minutes later, for the film itself. No self-respecting French *cinéphile* would dream of missing the ads, which – released from the time limits and content conventions of TV – are generally creative, entertaining and often provocative.

Film-going in France does not come cheap – count on paying 40 to 50FF for a first-run film. Most French cinemas offer reduced-price tickets (about 30 to 40FF) to students and people over 60. Everyone gets in for the reduced price on Wednesday and, at some cinemas, especially *cinémas d'art et d'essai* (art cinemas), on Monday too.

Discothèques

In French, a *discothèque* (also called a *boîte*) is any sort of establishment where music (live or recorded) leads to dancing. The music on offer ranges from jazz to rai and techno, and the guests may be gay, lesbian, straight or any combination thereof. The sign *'tenue correcte'*, which you may see displayed at various venues, means 'appropriate dress'.

Bouncers Ever wonder what happens to the French males of massive physique who

would have become football players had they been born in the USA? The answer will eye you suspiciously at the entrance to most nightclubs and discothèques. Alas, when it comes to nighttime entertainment, France is the land of the *videur* (bouncer). In some places, the bouncers are big, stupid and paid to indulge their power-hungry tendencies to keep out 'undesirables', which, depending on the place, ranges from unaccompanied men who aren't dressed right to members of certain minority groups (eg North Africans and Black Africans).

One of the jobs of a bouncer is to act as a *physionomiste* (a good judge of people's faces) and to decide, according to your overall look, if you're suitable for that particular night's entertainment. At some particularly exclusive discothèques, you have to be dressed in a manner appropriate to the night's theme, though exactly how one is supposed to know about the theme before arriving is unclear. Although locals can find their night out abruptly reconfigured by a bouncers' snap decision, tourists aren't usually held to such strict standards. All discos, however, are very careful not to admit people who are drunk.

Theatre

Long gone is French theatre's post-WW II golden age, when dramatists and directors such as Anouilh, Beckett, Camus, Genet, Ionesco and de Montherlant impressed audiences with their imaginative, innovative works. These days, the French theatre scene is dominated by the revival of old favourites and the translation of foreign hits, especially in Paris. As it has since the time of Louis XIV, Paris's Comédie-Française continues to produce French classics, staged according to time-honoured traditions.

For information on finding cheap theatre tickets in Paris, see Discount Theatre Tickets under Entertainment in the Paris chapter. One of the highlights of the theatre year is the Festival d'Avignon and the concurrent Festival Off (fringe festival), held in Avignon from mid-July to mid-August.

THINGS TO BUY

France is renowned for its *haute couture*, high-quality clothing accessories (eg Hermès scarves), lingerie, perfume, porcelain, crystal and such alcoholic beverages as wine, champagne and brandy. For information on where to find these and other items, see Things to Buy in the Paris and regional chapters.

Non-EC residents may be able to get a rebate of France's 18.6% VAT for purchases of over 2000FF at a single store – see VAT Refunds under Customs in this chapter for details.

Clothing & Shoe Sizes

Clothes and footware are sized differently in France than in the English-speaking world. For a few approximate correlations, see the tables below.

CLOTHING SIZES

Women's Tops & Dresses			Men's Shirts			Men's Suits		
UK	USA	France	UK	USA	France	UK	USA	France
8	6	36	–	14	36	30	36	38
10	8	38	14½	14½	37	32	37	40
12	10	40	15	15	38	34	38	42-44
14	12	42	15½	15½	39	–	39	44
16	14	44	–	16	40	36	40	46
18	16	46-48	16	16½	41	38	42	48
20	18	50	16½	17	42			
22	20	52						

SHOE SIZES

Women's Shoes			Men's Shoes		
UK	USA	France	UK	USA	France
3	4	35½	5½	6	39
3½	4½	36	6½	7	40
4	5	36½	7	7½	41
4½	5½	37	8	8½	42
5	6	37½	8½	9	43
5½	6½	38	9½	10	44
6	7½	39	10½	11	45

Getting There & Away

However you get to France, it's a good idea to consider taking out travel insurance, which covers you for theft or loss of luggage, cancellation of travel (you might fall seriously ill two days before departure, for example) and ticket loss (although airlines usually reissue lost or stolen tickets, legally they don't have to). Cover depends on your insurance and type of ticket, so ask your travel agent to explain where you stand. Make sure to keep a separate record of all your ticket details – or better yet, make a photocopy.

Paying for your ticket with a credit card often provides limited travel accident insurance, and you may be able to get your money back if the operator doesn't deliver. In the UK, for instance, credit card providers are required by law to reimburse consumers if a company goes into liquidation and the amount in contention is more than £100.

AIR

Air France, France's national carrier, and scores of other airlines link Paris with every part of the globe. Other French cities with direct international air links include Bordeaux, Lyon, Marseille, Nice, Strasbourg and Toulouse. 'Open jaw' returns, which let your fly into one city and out of another, may make it easier to combine a visit to France with travels elsewhere in Europe.

For details about Paris's two international airports, Orly and Charles de Gaulle, see Air under Getting There & Away in the Paris chapter. Transport between the airports and Paris is covered under To/From the Airports in the Getting Around section of the Paris chapter.

Don't forget to reconfirm your onward or return bookings by the specified time, which is usually 72 hours before departure. If you don't, there's a very real risk that you'll turn up at the airport only to find that your seat has been assigned to someone else or your flight has been rescheduled.

Travellers with Special Needs

If you have broken a leg, are travelling in a wheelchair, or require a special diet, are taking the baby, whatever, it's a good idea to compare the services offered by several airlines. Let the company you choose know of your needs as soon as possible and remind them when you reconfirm your booking and again when you check in at the airport.

Children under the age of two travel for 10% of the standard fare (or free on some airlines) as long as they don't occupy a seat. They don't get a luggage allowance either. 'Skycots', baby food, formula, nappies (diapers), etc should be provided by the airline if requested in advance. Children aged between two and 12 can usually occupy a seat for half to two-thirds of the full fare and do get a luggage allowance.

Cheap Airfares

There are two kinds of cheap tickets: official and unofficial. Official ones are advance-purchase tickets, budget fares, Apex (advance purchase excursion), super-Apex or whatever other name the airlines give to their efforts to put 'bums on seats'. Unofficial tickets are simply discounted tickets that the airlines release through selected travel agents. Don't go looking for unofficial tickets directly from the airlines: they are only available through certain travel agents. Airlines can, however, supply information on routes and timetables, and their low-season, student and senior citizens' fares can be very competitive. Some of the cheapest tickets have to be bought months in advance, and flights on popular dates usually sell out early.

Return (round-trip) tickets are usually cheaper than two one-ways, often *much* cheaper. In some cases, the return fare may be less than one-way. Also keep in mind that if you require a visa (or if upon arrival immigration officials become suspicious), you may be asked to produce either an

onward ticket or evidence of 'sufficient means of support' (ie lots of money).

Round-the-world (RTW) tickets make it easy to combine a visit to the Alps with a trek in the Himalayas and backpacking in the Rockies. If you live in Australasia, they can be no more expensive than an ordinary return fare. Prices start at about UK£850, A$1800 or US$1300. RTW tickets offered by airlines are usually put together by a combination of two companies and permit you to fly anywhere you want on their route systems so long as you don't backtrack, though there may be restrictions on how many stops you can make. You usually have to book the first sector in advance. Validity ranges from 90 days to a year. You might also look into RTW tickets put together by a travel agent using a combination of discounted tickets.

Airline tickets are nontransferable, but you sometimes find travellers trying to sell the unused portion of return tickets. Remember: when you get to the airport, officials may ask you to prove that you are the person named on the ticket. This is unlikely to happen on domestic flights, but on international routes tickets may be compared with passports. If you're flying on a transferred ticket and something goes wrong (hijack, crash) there will be no record of your presence on board.

Use the fares quoted in this book as a guide only. They are based on the rates advertised by travel agents at the time of going to press and are likely to have changed by the time you read this.

Discount Travel Agents The best way to find discount tickets is to phone around – often, only a few travel agents have access to a particular batch of discounted tickets. Find out the fare, the route, the duration of the journey, the stopovers allowed, restrictions and cancellation penalties.

You may discover that those impossibly cheap flights are 'fully booked, but we have another one that costs a bit more...' Or the flight is on an airline notorious for its poor safety record and will leave you for 14 hours in the world's least-favourite airport, where

you'll be confined to the transit lounge unless you get an expensive visa. Or the agent claims that the last two cheap seats until next autumn will be gone in two hours. Don't panic – keep ringing around.

If you are travelling from the USA or South-East Asia, you will probably find that the cheapest flights are being advertised by obscure agencies whose names have yet to reach the telephone directory. Many such firms are honest and solvent, but there are a few rogues who will take your money and disappear, to reopen elsewhere a month or two later under a new name. If you feel suspicious about a firm, don't give them all the money at once – leave a deposit of 20% or so and pay the balance when you get the ticket. If they insist on cash in advance, go somewhere else or be prepared to take a very big risk. And once you have the ticket, ring the airline to confirm that you are booked on the flight.

You may decide that it's worthwhile to pay a bit more than the rock-bottom fare in return for the safety of a better known travel agent. Firms such as STA (worldwide), Council Travel (in the USA), Travel CUTS (in Canada) and USIT (in Ireland and the UK) offer decent prices to most destinations and are unlikely to disappear overnight. Unfortunately, Council Travel is run rather chaotically, and as the summer approaches buying a ticket can be something of a headache. If you can find a travel agent who will book your Council Travel ticket for you (many will refuse), you may save yourself a lot of time on the phone.

Cheap Tickets in France Several large French chains with bureaux around the country offer relatively inexpensive air tickets. Perhaps the best known is Nouvelles Frontières (☎ 1-41.41.58.58 in Paris; Minitel: 3615 or 3616 code NF), which specialises in discounted tickets on regular and charter flights to long-haul destinations.

Other companies that publish brochures of discount flights – available at many travel agencies – include Go Voyages (Minitel: 3615 code GO VOYAGES), Forum Voyages

(Minitel: 3615 code FV) and Charters & Compagnies (Minitel: 3615 code SOS CHARTERS). The best way to find the cheapest ticket to the destination of your choice is to shop around – a travel agency with great prices to New Caledonia may not be able to get you the lowest fare to Sydney.

Since London's bucket shops tend to be cheaper than their Parisian counterparts, an option for long-haul flights is to phone Trailfinders (☎ 071-937 5400; tube High Street Kensington) at 194 Kensington High St (W8) or STA Travel (☎ 071-937 9962; tube South Kensington) at 74 Old Brompton Rd (SW7). Because travel agents across the Channel are unlikely to have many flights from Paris, you would have to get a pretty spectacular fare to make up for the cost of getting to London.

Weight Limits

Unless you're flying to/from North America across the Atlantic or the Pacific, in which case you can bring along two suitcases of fairly generous proportions, your checked luggage will be subject to a 20-kg weight limit. On most flights (with the exception of certain charters), you won't be charged if you're three to five kg over, but beyond that each kg will be assessed at 1% of the price of a full-fare 1st-class, one-way ticket. A few quick calculations will show that this can work out to be very expensive indeed (eg A$58 per kg from Australia).

To/From the UK

Flights between London and Paris on such carriers as Danair, Air UK and British Midland start at about 690FF return, but the cheapest tickets often come with all sorts of cumbersome restrictions: minimum stay, maximum stay, advance reservation requirements, mandatory Saturday night stay-over, etc. More normal fares from Paris's Charles de Gaulle Airport start at 920FF return to Heathrow. In Paris, contact Transchannel (☎ 1-40.34.71.50; metro Gare du Nord) at 24 Rue de Saint Quentin (10e).

When the Channel Tunnel opens and makes it possible to get from central London

to central Paris in 3½ hours, London-Paris flights are going to face some very stiff competition.

To/From the Channel Islands

Aurigny Air Services (☎ 0481-37426 in St Peter Port, 0534-43568 in St Helier, 33.22.91.32 in Cherbourg) has flights from Guernsey and Jersey to Cherbourg. One-way fares are £44 or 370FF.

To/From Ireland

USIT Voyages (☎ 01-679 8833 in Dublin, 1-43.29.85.00 in Paris) has one-way/ return flights to Dublin for 752/1487FF (IR£90/178), but summer charters on some dates are available for as little as 500/1000FF. Tickets to Belfast cost 800/1617FF (UK£93/185).

To/From Continental Europe

One-way discount charter fares available for flights from Paris include 550 to 700FF to Rome, 700FF (or a bit less) to Athens, 600FF to Istanbul and 600FF to Madrid. The cheapest fares are available in early spring and late autumn.

To/From the USA

The flight options across the North Atlantic, the world's busiest long-haul air corridor, are bewildering. The *New York Times*, the *LA Times*, the *Chicago Tribune* and the *San Francisco Chronicle/Examiner* all have weekly travel sections in which you'll find any number of travel agents' ads. Council Travel and STA have offices in major cities nationwide. Access International in New York offers discounts to Europe from 50 cities in the USA.

You should be able to fly New York-Paris return for US$360-450 in the low season and US$550-650 in the high season. One-way fares can work out to about half this on a stand-by basis – Airhitch (☎ 212-864 2000) specialises in this sort of thing and can get you to Europe one way for US$160/269/229 from the east coast/west coast/elsewhere in the USA. In Paris, one-way charter flights on the Paris-New York route usually cost about

1250 to 1600FF. Return fares of 2000FF are sometimes available, but a more usual fare is 2800FF.

Courier Flights Another option is a courier flight. A New York-London return ticket can be had for about US$250/500 low/high season (about US$100 more from the west coast). You can also fly one way. The drawbacks are that your stay in Europe may be limited to one or two weeks; your luggage is usually restricted to hand luggage (the courier company uses your checked luggage allowance to send its parcel), and you may have to be a local resident and apply for an interview before they'll take you on (dress conservatively, preferably in a business suit).

You can find out more about courier flights from Council Travel in New York (☎ 212-661 1450) and Los Angeles (☎ 310-208 3551); Discount Travel International in New York (☎ 212-362 3636); and Way to Go in Los Angeles (☎ 213-466 1126) and San Francisco (415-292 7801). Call two or three months in advance, at the very beginning of the calendar month.

The *Travel Unlimited* newsletter, PO Box 1058, Allston, MA 02134, publishes details of the cheapest air fares and courier possibilities for destinations all over the world from the USA and other countries, including the UK. It's a treasure trove of information. A single monthly issue costs US$5, and a year's subscription, US$25 (US$35 abroad).

To/From Canada
Travel CUTS has offices in all major cities. You might also scan the budget travel agents' ads in the *Toronto Globe & Mail*, the *Toronto Star* and the *Vancouver Province*.

For courier flights (see To/From the USA), contact FB On Board Courier Services (☎ 514-633 0740) in Montreal or Toronto (☎ 604-338 1366 in Vancouver). A return courier flight to Paris will set you back about C$350 from Toronto or Montreal, and C$425 from Vancouver.

From Paris, you may find that flights are cheaper to Montreal than to Toronto, with

one-way/return fares as low as 1100/1800FF, depending on the date.

To/From Australia
STA and Flight Centres International are major dealers in cheap air fares. The Saturday travel sections of Sydney's *Sydney Morning Herald* and Melbourne's *The Age* have many ads offering cheap fares to Europe, but don't be surprised if they happen to be 'sold out' when you call: they're usually low-season fares on obscure airlines with conditions attached.

Discounted return fares on mainstream airlines through a reputable agent like STA cost between A$1700 (October to mid-November and February) and A$2500 (June to August and mid-December). Flights to/from Perth are a couple of hundred dollars cheaper.

To/From New Zealand
As in Australia, STA and Flight Centres International are popular travel agents in New Zealand. The cheapest fares to Europe are routed through the USA. A RTW ticket may be cheaper than a return.

To/From Africa
Nairobi is probably the best place in Africa to buy tickets to Europe, thanks to the many bucket shops and the lively competition between them. Several West African countries such as Burkina Faso and The Gambia offer cheap charter flights to France. Charter fares from Morocco and Tunisia can be incredibly cheap if you're lucky enough to find a seat.

To/From the Middle East
Paris is well connected with the whole Middle East. Examples of one-way fares include Beirut (from 1300FF), Cairo (from 900FF), Istanbul (from 600FF) and Tel Aviv (from 800FF).

In Tel Aviv, some of the cheapest charters are sold by ISSTA (☎ 03-5270111), the Israeli student travel company, whose Tel Aviv office is at 109 Ben Yehuda St.

To/From East & South Asia

Hong Kong is the discount air ticket capital of Asia. Its bucket shops are at least as unreliable as those of other cities, so ask the advice of other travellers before handing over any money. Many of the cheapest fares from South-East Asia to Europe are offered by Eastern European carriers. STA has branches in Hong Kong, Tokyo, Singapore, Bangkok and Kuala Lumpur.

The cheapest flights to/from India tend to be with Eastern European carriers like LOT and Aeroflot, or with Middle Eastern airlines such as Syrian Arab Airlines and Iran Air. Bombay is the air transport hub, but tickets are slightly cheaper in Delhi. Try Delhi Student Travel Services in the Imperial Hotel, Janpath.

In Paris, Council Travel sells return flights to destinations including Bangkok (4000FF), Bombay (5230FF), Ho Chi Minh City (5870FF), Karachi (4200FF), Kathmandu (6400FF), Phnom Penh (6400FF), Singapore (5640FF) and Taipei (7000FF).

LAND

Paris, France's main rail hub, is linked with every part of Europe. Travel from northern Europe to other parts of France may involve transiting through Paris. For details on Paris's six major railway stations, see Train under Getting There & Away in the Paris chapter.

For information on discount tickets (eg BIJ tickets for international travel by people under 26), see Train in the Getting Around chapter.

Eurail Pass

If you are not a resident of Europe and expect to be really clocking up the km in France and other European countries, you might consider buying a Eurail pass. One version entitles you to unlimited rail travel for one or two months, while a Flexipass lets you take trains during any five, 10 or 15 days you select over a period of two months. Details are available from travel agents.

Contrary to popular wisdom, Eurail passes *can* be bought in Europe so long as your passport proves you've been in Europe for less than six months. In France, they are available at Orly and Charles de Gaulle airports; at two of Paris's train stations, Gare du Nord and Gare Saint Lazare; and at the railway stations in Marseille and Nice. Prices, however, may be higher than back home. If you'll be travelling only in France, you're probably better off with a France Vacances Pass (France Rail Pass) or a EuroDomino France (see Discounts Available outside France under Train in the Getting Around chapter).

Eurail passes offer reasonable value to people under 26 (people over that age can only get the pricey 1st-class versions). The Eurail Youth Flexipass costs US$220/348/474 for five/10/15 days of travel over two months. One/two months of unlimited travel costs US$508/698. In any case, a Eurail pass is only worth it if you plan to do a lot of travelling within a short space of time: Eurail itself reckons its passes only start saving money if you cover more than 2400 km within a two-week period. And while Eurail pass holders get free sitter-class passage, they must pay for all SNCF reservation fees (including those for the TGV), supplements and couchette fees (see Train in the Getting Around chapter for details).

BritFrance Railpass

The BritFrance Railpass, available to people who are not residents of the UK or France, allows unlimited rail travel within Britain and France and includes one round-trip Channel crossing. The version that is valid for five days of 2nd-class travel within a period of 15 days costs US$269 (US$229 for people under 26); 10 days of travel over the course of a month costs US$409 (US$349 for people under 26). These prices do not include reservation fees or extra charges for sleepers. Children aged four to 11 pay half the adult fare. Versions involving car rental are also available. For details, contact a travel agent or, in North America, call Rail Europe at ☎ 800-438 7245.

To/From England

When the Channel Tunnel – also known as the Eurotunnel and the Chunnel – finally opens in May 1994 after massive cost overruns, multiple delays and the deaths of seven construction workers, England and France will be linked by dry land for the first time since the last Ice Age. The three parallel, concrete-lined tunnels – two rail tunnels and a service tunnel – were bored between Folkestone and Calais through a layer of impermeable chalk marl 25 to 45 metres below the floor of the English Channel. About US$14 billion in private capital was invested in the project, the fourth attempt at tunnelling from England to France (previous efforts in 1880, 1922 and 1974 were abandoned). The consortium that built it has been awarded a concession to run the tunnel for 55 years.

For information on getting across the English Channel by ferry, see To/From England in the Sea section.

Train When the Channel Tunnel is fully operational, it will take only 3½ hours to get from London's new Waterloo Station to Paris, including 1½ hours from London to Folkestone, 30 minutes to cross the Channel and 1½ hours from Calais to Paris. If Britain ever lays a high-speed track between London and Folkestone, travel on the English side will take a mere 45 minutes.

Until the Eurotunnel's through-train operations begin, there will be three slower ways to get from London's Victoria Station (☎ 071-834 2345, 0891-888 731) to Paris by train-ferry combo:

* Via Folkestone and Boulogne to Gare du Nord (£59 or 542FF one way; 6½ hours); Channel crossing by hovercraft or SeaCat.
* Via Dover and Calais to Gare du Nord (£55 or 502FF one way; eight hours); Channel crossing by ferry.
* Via Newhaven and Dieppe to Gare Saint Lazare (£52 or 471FF for daytime passage, 351FF overnight without a sleeping berth; nine hours); day or night Channel crossing by ferry.

On all three routes, transferring from the train to the boat and then to another train involves dragging your luggage around a bit.

The tariff schedule is extremely complicated, but the cheapest way to travel is to take the night ferry from Newhaven to Dieppe. Except for the Newhaven-Dieppe night rate, a return ticket costs costs about 20% less than two one-way tickets. Children under 12 get a 50% discount, and those aged 12 to 15 get 30% off. For short trips, a special five-day excursion fare is available for only 30% more than a one-way fare.

Bus Eurolines (☎ 0582-404511 in Luton, 071-730 0202 in London, 1- 49.72.51.51 in Paris), whose London office is at 52 Grosvenor Gardens, Victoria (SW1), has bus services to various French cities, including, of course, Paris (£33 one way, £49 return; nine hours). Bookings can be made through any office of National Express, including the one at London's Victoria Coach Station on Buckingham Palace Road.

City Sprint (☎ 0304-240241 in Dover, 1-44.53.08.80 in Paris), run by Hoverspeed, has bus-hovercraft and bus-SeaCat combos from Victoria Coach Station to 3 Rue de Bellefond (9e; metro Poissonière) in Paris. The trip takes about eight hours and costs £30/49 or 290/490FF one way/return (£30/46 or 265/450FF for people under 26 or over 60). Two or three buses leave Paris every morning between 8.30 and 11 am. The office at 3 Rue de Bellefond, which is 800 metres west of Gare de l'Est along Rue Chabrol, is open weekdays from 10 am to 6 pm and on weekends from 10 to 11 am.

Car & Motorbike When the Channel Tunnel opens in the spring of 1994, high-speed shuttle trains known as Le Shuttle will whisk cars, motorbikes and coaches from Folkestone to Calais in air-conditioned, soundproofed comfort. Regular cars will travel on double-decker carriages, while vehicles over 1.85 metres high will be loaded onto single-level carriages.

Le Shuttle will run at least once an hour, 24 hours a day, every day of the year. During peak hours, there will be a train every 15

minutes. To take a car across, all you need to do is pay at the toll booth (credit cards accepted), pass through customs and passport control for both countries and then drive onto the train. During the 35-minute crossing, passengers can sit in their cars, walk around the rail carriage or use the toilets that the French argued were unnecessary. The entire process, including loading and unloading, should take about an hour.

For information on getting your car or motorbike across the English Channel by ferry, see To/From England under Sea.

To/From Continental Europe

Some of France's more obscure border posts (eg with Spain) close at 8 or 10 pm.

Train Rail services link France with every country in Europe; schedules and tickets are available from major SNCF train stations. Because of different track gauges, you often have to change trains at the border (eg to Spain and Switzerland). Most trains to the Iberian peninsula cross the Franco-Spanish border at Irún (on the Atlantic coast) and Port Bou (on the Mediterranean coast), though there are also trains via Puigcerdà (Latour de Carol).

Bus Eurolines (☎ 1-49.72.51.51 in Paris), Europe's main international carrier, has buses from Paris and other French cities to points all over Western Europe, Scandinavia, Eastern Europe and even Morocco. They are slower and less comfortable than trains but cheaper, especially if you qualify for the 10% disount available to people under 26 or over 60. Another long-haul company with more limited services is Intercars.

Eurolines has representatives across Europe, including: Eurolines/Budgetbus (☎ 020-627 51 51), Rokin 10, Amsterdam; Deutsche Touring (☎ 089-59 18 24), Arnulfstrasse 3, Munich; and Lazzi Express (☎ 06-841 74 58), Via Tagliamento 27R, Rome. For details on Eurolines offices in France, see Bus under Getting There & Away in the listings for major cities.

From Paris, Eurolines has direct overnight buses to cities including Amsterdam (240FF; eight hours), Athens (875FF; 64 hours), Istanbul (1260FF; 69 hours), Madrid (470FF; 17 hours), Oslo (860FF; 36 hours), Prague (390FF; 15 hours), Rome (570FF; 26 hours) and Warsaw (600FF; 28 hours). These fares are one way – return tickets usually cost less than two one-ways. In summer, it's not a bad idea to make a reservation a few days in advance.

Hitching For information getting to other parts of continental Europe with Allostop, see Hitching in the Getting Around chapter.

To/From East Asia

Despite the turmoil in ex-Soviet Central Asia, Iran and Afghanistan, it is still possible to get to France overland by bus and train from India, Nepal, Pakistan, China, Mongolia, Vietnam and – with a ferry trip from Yokohama to Nakhodka in Russia – Japan.

By rail, you can choose from four different routes: the trans-Siberian, the trans-Mongolian and the trans-Manchurian, which follow the same tracks across Siberia but have different eastern railheads; and the trans-Kazakhstan, which runs between Moscow and Ürümqi in north-western China. Prices can vary enormously, depending on where you buy the ticket and what is included.

SEA

Tickets and reservations for ferry travel to and from England, Ireland and North Africa and on the Corsica-Italy routes are available from most travel agencies in France and the countries served, so there's usually no need to contact the ferry companies themselves. Only a handful of ships still carry passengers across the Atlantic.

Much of the passenger traffic between mainland France and Corsica, Sardinia and North Africa is handled by the Société Nationale Maritime Corse Méditerranée (in Marseille, ☎ 91.56.30.10 for information, 91.56.30.30 for reservations), better known as SNCM. In Paris, SNCM's main office

(☎ 1-49.24.24.24; metro Madeleine) is at 12 Rue Godot de Mauroy (9e).

Food is often expensive on ferries, so it is worth bringing your own when possible. Note that if you're travelling with a vehicle, you are usually denied access to it during the voyage.

To/From England

Fares vary widely according to seasonal demand, and tickets can cost twice as much in July and August as in winter. Three or five-day excursion fares cost only marginally more than one-way tickets. Eurail passes are *not* valid for ferry travel between England and France, but some student discounts are available. Bicycles are free.

Via Far Northern France The fastest way to cross the English Channel – the trip takes only 30 to 35 minutes – is by *aéroglisseur* (hovercraft). Hoverspeed runs both SeaCats (giant Australian-built catamarans) and hovercraft from Dover (Douvres) to Calais and Folkestone to Boulogne. One-way passage on the Dover-Calais route costs £26/230FF (£16/140FF for children aged four to 16). For a small car with up to five passengers, the fee is £63/550FF to £174/1500FF, depending on the season and time of day. Hovercraft cannot operate in rough weather, so if a storm is brewing you might get there sooner by taking a car ferry or the Channel Tunnel. To contact Hoverspeed, call ☎ 0304-240241 in Dover or 05.26.03.60 in France.

Train-hovercraft/SeaCat combos start at 520FF and are sold at train stations (see Train under To/From England in the Land section). For details on City Sprint's bus-hovercraft/SeaCat services, see Bus under To/From England in the Land section.

Sealink has car ferries from Dover to Calais (1½ hours) for £24/230FF (£20/190FF on most sailings for students and senior citizens). Cars cost £70 to £170 (650FF to 1430FF) one way, including up to five passengers. Tickets for train-ferry packages are available at train stations. To contact Sealink, call ☎ 1-44.94.40.40 in Paris, 21.34.55.00 in Calais or 0304-203203 in

Dover. By Minitel, key in 3615 code SEALINK.

P&O European Ferries runs frequent car ferries from Dover to Calais (1¼ hours). One-way/return fares are £25/215FF (£15/135FF for children aged four to 13). For a one-way trip, motorbikes cost £45 to £65 (390 to 565FF), including the driver and one passenger, and motor vehicles (cars, minibuses, motorhomes) are £77 to £160 (670 to 1400FF), including up to eight passengers. P&O's Paris office (☎ 1-44.51.00.51; metro Havre Caumartin) is at 19 Rue des Mathurins (9e).

The company can also be contacted on ☎ 0304-203388 in Dover, 21.46.10.10 in Calais and 21.31.78.00 in Boulogne.

Sally Line (☎ 28.21.43.44 in Dunkerque) operates passenger ferries between Ramsgate and Dunkerque's Port Ouest, which is 10 km west of town. The trip takes 2½ hours.

Via Normandy Sealink has ferries from Newhaven to Dieppe and Southampton to Cherbourg. The four-hour Newhaven-Dieppe crossing costs £28/260FF (£24 or 210 to 240FF for students and people over 60); the regular adult return fare is £50 to £54 (450 to 500FF). For a car and up to five passengers, the tariff is £68 to £172 (650 to 1550FF) each way. The schedule of sailings varies widely according to the season, but from April to late December there are three or four round trips a day. Sealink can be reached on ☎ 0273-516699 in Newhaven, 0703-233973 in Southampton, 35.06.39.00 in Dieppe, 33.20.43.38 in Cherbourg and ☎ 1-47.42.86.87 in Paris.

Sealink's Southampton-Cherbourg run takes six hours during the day and eight hours at night. It costs £12 to £28 (120 to 280FF) for pedestrians (£10 to £26 or 100 to 240FF for students and seniors). A car costs £38 to £90 (325 to 880FF), not including passengers.

Brittany Ferries, the largest carrier in the western Channel, has ferries from Poole to Cherbourg (4½ hours) and from Portsmouth to Ouistreham (10 km north of Caen; six hours). For information, call ☎ 0202-672153

in Poole, 33.43.43.68 in Cherbourg or 31.36.36.30 in Ouistreham.

P&O European Ferries has services from Portsmouth to Le Havre (5¾ hours during the day, seven hours overnight) and Cherbourg (4¾ hours during the day, 6½ to 7½ hours overnight). On the Portsmouth-Cherbourg route, one-way fares are £18 to £31 (162 to 280FF) for adults and £9 to £15 (81 to 135FF) for children aged four to 13. The cheapest sleeping berth costs an extra £10 to £15 (90 to 135FF). For a one-way trip, motorbikes cost £9 to £15 (81 to 135FF) and cars are £81 to £189 (730 to 1700FF), including up to five passengers. P&O can be reached on ☎ 0705-827677 in Portsmouth, 35.21.36.50 in Le Havre and 33.44.20.13 in Cherbourg.

Via Brittany Saint Malo is linked by car ferry and hydrofoil with Weymouth, Poole and Portsmouth, while Roscoff has ferry links to Plymouth.

Hydroglisseurs Condor (☎ 99.56.42.29 in Saint Malo) has services from Weymouth to Saint Malo (500FF one way; 5½ hours) daily from April to September. Émeraude Lines (☎ 99.40.48.40 in Saint Malo) has car ferries from Poole to Saint Malo all year long, albeit infrequently in winter. Brittany Ferries (☎ 99.82.41.41 in Saint Malo) has Portsmouth-Saint Malo car ferries (nine hours) once or twice a day from mid-March to early November. One-way fares are 230 to 380FF per passenger and 430 to 1000FF for a car, depending on the season and time of day.

From mid-March to mid-November, Brittany Ferries (☎ 0652-674242 in Plymouth, 98.29.28.28 in Roscoff) has one to three car ferries a day from Plymouth to Roscoff (six hours). To get information on Brittany Ferries schedules by Minitel, key in 3615 code FERRYPLUS.

To/From the Channel Islands

Year-round car ferry, catamaran and hydrofoil services link Saint Malo in Brittany with the Channel Islands (the Îles Anglo-Normandes) of Jersey, Guernsey (Guernesey) and Sark (Sercq). Services are significantly reduced in winter.

From mid-March to October, Hydroglisseurs Condor (☎ 99.56.42.29 in Saint Malo, 0534-76300 in St Helier), known in English as Condor Hydrofoil, has the fastest boats to Jersey (248FF; one hour), Guernsey (285FF; 2½ hours; one to four a day) and Sark (one a day). Same-day excursion fares to the islands cost about the same as one-way fares.

Émeraude Lines (☎ 99.40.48.40 in Saint Malo, 0534-66566 in Jersey) runs catamarans and car ferries to the three islands from late March to mid-November; car ferries to Jersey run all year. Vehicle tariffs are complicated, but for the Saint Malo-Jersey run count on paying at least 513FF for a small car (not including passengers).

There may also be seasonal ferry service to the Channel Islands from Cherbourg and two towns on the west coast of Normandy's Cotentin peninsula, Carteret and Portbail.

To/From Ireland

Eurailpasses are valid for ferry crossings between Ireland and France. There is a charge to take along a bicycle.

Irish Ferries, formerly Irish Continental Ferries, has runs from Rosslare (and, from June to September, from Cork) to Le Havre and Cherbourg, both of which are in Normandy. The crossing takes 17 to 21 hours. There are only three ferries a week from September to May; sailings are daily during the rest of the year. Pedestrians pay IR£66 to IR£112 (430 to 870FFF one way); fares for students and people over 65 start at IR£49/372FF. People with a Eurailpass travel almost for free. Irish punt prices include a basic sleeping berth; if your ticket was purchased in France, the cheapest couchette will cost an extra 48FF. A car with one to four passengers costs IR£240F to IR£410 (1520 to 3280FF), depending on the season. Bicycles cost IR£14 to IR£20 (110 to 172FF).

Irish Ferries' Paris office (☎ 1-42.66. 90.90; metro Opéra) is at 32 Rue du Quatre Septembre (2e). Irish Ferries can be reached

on ☎ 01-6610714 in Dublin, 053-33158 in Rosslare, 021-504333 in Cork, 35.53.28.83 in Le Havre and 33.44.28.96 in Cherbourg.

From April to early October, Brittany Ferries (☎ 021-277801 in Cork, 98.29.28.28 in Roscoff) has weekly car ferries linking Cork with Roscoff (14 hours). From mid-June to mid-September, the company also has a weekly Cork-Saint Malo service (18 hours).

To/From Sardinia

During the warm months of the year, SNCM has car ferries from Marseille and Toulon to Porto Torres on the Italian island of Sardinia (Sardaigne in French). A one-way fare for the 18-hour trip is 385FF from late June to September and a bit less the rest of the time; the supplement for a sleeping berth stars at 100FF. Bringing a bike is 42FF extra, and small cars cost from 520 to 570FF.

For details on ferries from the Corsican port of Bonifacio to the Sardinian town of Santa Teresa, see Getting There & Away under the Bonifacio section in the Corsica chapter.

To/From Mainland Italy

A variety of ferry companies ply the waters between Corsica and Italy. For details, see the introductory Getting There & Away section of the Corsica chapter.

To/From the Balearic Islands

From late June to early September, Trasmediterranea (Balear Ferry) may link the French port of Sète with Majorca (Mallorca) and Ibiza, two of Spain's Balearic Islands. The ferries stop at Palma (15 hours) on Majorca, then Ibiza (21 hours) and finally Valencia (29 hours) on the Spanish coast. One-way tariffs start at 507FF per passenger and 914/366FF for cars/motorbikes. In Sète, ticketing is handled by SNCM, whose office (☎ 67.74.96.96) is at 4 Quai d'Alger.

To/From Algeria

Both SNCM and its Algerian counterpart, Algérie Ferries, operate ferry services linking Marseille with Algiers (Alger), Annaba, Bejaia, Oran and Skikda. Passage takes 18 to 24 hours (a bit more to Oran). Both companies charge the same prices: the one-way sitter-class fare is 860FF (970FF to Oran); sleeping berths cost an additional 100 to 130FF. Discounts of up to 30%, some limited to the off season or applicable only if you're a student or under 25 (or both), are available. A small car costs 2110FF one way and from 2960 to 3380FF return.

Algérie Ferries (☎ 91.90.64.70 in Marseille) is also known as the Entreprise Nationale de Transport Maritime de Voyageurs (ENTMV). In Algiers, Algérie Ferries' ticket office (☎ 02-64.04.20/1/2), which also handles SNCF ticketing, is at 6 Blvd Mohamed Khemisti.

To/From Tunisia

SNCM and the Compagnie Tunisienne de Navigation (CTN) operate two weekly car ferries (five in summer) between Marseille and Tunis (about 24 hours). The one-way sitter-class fare is 800FF; sleeping berths cost 100 to 140FF extra. Taking along a small car costs 1600FF one way (1730FF one way in summer); return fare (valid for six months) is 2280 to 2780FF, depending on when you travel. If you're taking along a vehicle, it is important to book ahead, especially in summer. Tickets are handled by SNCM.

In Tunis, CTN's office (☎ 01-242801) is at 122 Rue de Yougoslavie.

To/From Morocco

Car ferries run by the Compagnie Marocaine de Navigation (COMANAV) to/from Tangier (Tanger) dock at the French port of Sète, 29 km south of Montpellier. The once or twice-weekly crossing takes about 36 hours. Regular one-way/return fare is 1250/2130FF. One-way passage for students and people under 26 starts at 880FF; children pay 625FF. Groups of four or more also qualify for discounts. Motorbikes/cars start at 390/1080FF.

The company's representative in Tangier is COMANAV-Passages (☎ 09-93.26.49) at 43 Ave Abou El Alaâ El Maâri. In France,

ticketing is handled by SNCM, whose Sète office (☎ 67.74.96.96) is at 4 Quai d'Alger.

To/From the USA, Canada & Elsewhere

The days of earning your passage on a freighter to Europe have well and truly passed. Long-distance passenger ships disappeared with the advent of cheap air travel, to be replaced by a small number of luxury cruise ships.

A more adventurous (though not necessarily cheaper) alternative to liners like the *QE2* is to go as a paying passenger on a freighter. A good source of information is the *ABC Passenger Shipping Guide*, published by the Reed Travel Group (☎ 0582-60 0111), Church St, Dunstable, Bedfordshire LU5 4HB, UK. You might also contact the Freighter Travel Club of America, 3524 Harts Lake Rd, Roy, WA 98580; included in the US$18 yearly membership is a monthly bulletin, *Freighter Travel News*.

Passenger freighters typically carry six to 12 passengers. Schedules tend to be flexible and costs vary, but seem to hover around US$95 a day; vehicles can often be included for an additional fee.

One of the better known passenger freighter operators is Polish Ocean Lines. Its popular Atlantic route (weekly service) is Bremerhaven, Le Havre, Halifax, New York, Baltimore, Wilmington, New York, Le Havre, Rotterdam, Bremerhaven. It costs UK£1375 for the 28-day round trip or US$1010 for New York-Le Havre one way (prices per person in a double cabin). Contact Gdynia America Line (☎ 212-952 1280), 39 Broadway, 14th Floor, New York, NY 10006, USA.

Getting Around

Although SNCF computers will generate tickets for rail travel between any two train stations in France, and by car you are free to choose a route as circuitous as your petrol budget will allow, certain itineraries around France are inherently faster than others, in large part because of the Paris-centric nature of France's air, rail and road networks. A glance at any map of the country's TGV rail lines and *autoroutes* (expressways) will illustrate this perfectly.

If two or more widely scattered regions of France especially interest you – Alsace and the Basque Country, say, or Brittany and Corsica – you can take advantage of domestic air links, SNCF's overnight sleeper trains, SNCM ferries, the 130 km/h autoroutes or SNCF's Train + Auto service (in which both you and your car travel by rail) to minimise the time you spend getting from one region to the other.

France's domestic transport network, much of which is state-owned and subsidised, tends to be monopolistic: SNCF takes care of virtually all inter-départemental land transport; SNCM handles all ferry services to Corsica; and short-haul bus companies are either run by the département or else grouped so that each local company handles a different set of destinations. Eurolines and its privately owned competitors in the long-haul bus field are limited to international routes.

AIR

Unless you qualify for special youth, family or senior citizen fares (see Discounts), flying on France's heavily regulated domestic air network is quite expensive. Carriers with important domestic networks include Air France, Air Inter (owned by Air France), TAT (founded in 1968 as Touraine Air Transport), AOM, Air Littoral and Corsair. The government assigns routes and sets prices to avoid excessive competition.

Thanks to the high-speed TGV trains,

travel between some cities (eg Paris and Lyon) is faster and easier by rail than by air, particularly if you include the time and hassle involved in getting out to the airport and then, once you've reached your destination, to the city centre.

Any French travel agent can make bookings for domestic flights and supply details on the complicated fare system. Outside of France, Air France representatives sell tickets for many domestic flights. Information on Air Inter flights is available 24 hours a day by Minitel – just dial 3615 or 3616 code AIRINTER. Air France information is available on Minitel on 3615 or 3616 code AF. TAT's Minitel number is 3615 code TAT.

Costs

Depending on whether you qualify for reduced-price tickets (see Discounts), domestic fares cost:

Paris-Ajaccio/Bastia	505	to 1185FF
Paris-Bordeaux	205	to 775FF
Paris-Biarritz	295	to 1020FF
Paris-Grenoble	220	to 780FF
Paris-Nice	395	to 960FF
Paris-Quimper	330	to 1040FF
Lyon-Toulouse	305	to 765FF
Marseille-Strasbourg	460	to 1220FF
Nantes-Nice	570	to 1435FF

On most flights, each passenger is allowed one carry-on and 23 kg of checked baggage. Excess baggage costs only 7FF per kg. On some routes to the Alps, you can bring along your skis for no extra charge.

Discounts

Children, young people aged under 25, students under 27 and people over 60 can get discounts of 50% and more on off-peak flights designated as *blanc* (white) or *bleu* (blue). If you qualify, the most heavily discounted flights may be cheaper than long-distance rail travel (or, in the case of

Corsica, rail and ferry travel). Significant family discounts are also available to married couples travelling together and to a parent travelling with one or more children under 25 (under 27 in the case of students). For details, contact any travel agent.

To/From the Airport

For information on getting from Orly and Charles de Gaulle airports to Paris and vice versa, see To/From the Airports under Getting Around in the Paris chapter. Details on transport links to/from major provincial airports are listed under To/From the Airport in the Getting Around section of city listings.

For domestic flights, plan your travel so that you arrive at the airport no less than 20 minutes before flight time.

TRAIN

France's excellent rail network, operated by the state-owned – and heavily state-subsided – SNCF (Société Nationale des Chemins de Fer), reaches almost every part of the country. Certain uneconomical train lines have been replaced in recent years by SNCF buses, which, unlike most bus services, are free for people with rail passes. Many towns not served by train are linked with nearby railheads by intra-départemental bus.

No matter how many changes of train it takes, SNCF's information offices and ticket windows can tell you how to get from any French train station to any other and how long it will take. They'll also issue you with the proper ticket.

Remember to time-stamp your ticket before boarding (see Validating Your Ticket).

Network

France's most important train lines radiate out from Paris like the spokes of a wheel, rendering rail travel between provincial towns and cities located on different radii infrequent and rather slow. In some cases, you have to transit through Paris, which may require transferring from one of Paris's six train stations to another (see Train under

Getting There & Away in the Paris chapter for details).

Electrified track, which makes up only 26% of all SNCF track, carries three-quarters of the traffic. Many secondary and tertiary lines have rather infrequent services.

TGV

The pride and joy of the SNCF is the world-famous TGV (train à grande vitesse), whose name – pronounced 'TEI-ZHEI-VEI' – means 'high-speed train'. There are three TGV lines:

- TGV Sud-Est – links Paris's Gare Montparnasse with Lyon and the south-east, including Avignon, Marseille and Nice;
- TGV Atlantique – links Paris's Gare Montparnasse with Brittany (Rennes, Quimper, Brest, Nantes), the Loire Valley, La Rochelle, Bordeaux, the Basque Country and Toulouse;
- TGV Nord – this new line goes from Paris's Gare du Nord to Lille, Calais and, via the Channel Tunnel, London.

Although it usually travels at 300 km/h, the TGV Atlantique has, in test runs, reached 515.3 km/h, the world speed record for trains. The TGV Sud-Est goes up to 270 km/h.

Right now, the TGV Sud-Est line runs on super-fast TGV track only between Paris and Lyon; an extension to Valence is being built at a cost of almost US$10 million per km. South of there, though, political wrangling and local opposition has made choosing a route nearly impossible.

Information

Larger railway stations generally have both guichets (ticket windows) and information and reservation offices. Opening hours and phone numbers are listed under Train in the Getting There & Away section of each city or town listing.

Some people swear by the Thomas Cook European Timetable (100FF), a complete listing of Europe's train schedules, from which you can find out what domestic and international routeings are feasible without having to ask at train stations, call SNCF's often-busy information numbers or collect

lots of little time schedules. Such information makes it much easier to plan itineraries and use rail passes to their fullest. It is updated monthly and is available from Thomas Cook exchange bureaux worldwide.

Left-Luggage Services

Most larger SNCF stations have both a *consigne manuelle* (left-luggage office), where you pay 30FF per bag or 35FF per bicycle per 24 hours, and a *consigne automatique*, whose 72-hour electronic luggage lockers will issue you with a lock code in exchange for 15, 20 or 30FF, depending on the size. The old mechanical lockers cost 5 or 20FF per 24 hours. At smaller stations, you can usually check your bag with the clerk at the ticket window for 30FF. Make sure to find out when the left-luggage facilities close.

Schedules

SNCF's *horaires* (time schedules), available for free at relevant stations, can be a bit complicated to read, especially if you don't know railway French.

At the top of the schedule are two rows of numbers: the upper one lists the *numéro de train* (train number), while the lower one has space for *notes à consulter* (footnote references). The footnotes, of which there may be dozens, are explained in French at the bottom of the page.

Very often, a particular train *circule* (runs) only on Sunday or only during a certain period of the year. Alternatively, it may operate *tous les jours* (every day) *(sauf)* (except) Saturday, Sunday and/or *fêtes* (holidays). Of 20 trains listed on the schedule, only a few may be running on the day you'd like to travel. To be certain that you've understood your options, it's a good idea to ask at the information office or, in small stations, at the ticket window.

If you're making one or more transfers, you can ask the station's information office to give you a computer printout of where to change trains, the numbers of trains involved and the scheduled time of arrival and departure from each station.

Classes & Sleepers

Most French trains, including the TGV, have both 1st and 2nd-class sections. First-class carriages have the numeral 1 written near the doors.

Most overnight trains are equipped with couchettes (sleeping berths), for which you must make reservations and pay a reservation fee of 86FF. Second-class couchette compartments have six berths, while those in 1st class have only four. *Voitures-lits* (sleepers) have one, two or three real beds per compartment and cost 259 to 905FF per person. On some overnight trains, 2nd-class *sièges inclinables* (reclining seats) are available for a reservation fee of 18FF.

When you board your train, make sure you are in the right car – SNCF sometimes splits up trains in mid-journey, decoupling a few cars that are going to one destination and sending the rest of the train somewhere else.

Costs & Reservations

Train fares consist of up to four parts: the cost of passage, calculated according to the number of km you'll be travelling and whether you're going 1st or 2nd class; a reservation fee; another special fee known as a supplement; and the station surcharge. Eurail pass holders must pay both reservation fees and supplements.

Passage Not including the station surcharge, regular return (round trip) tickets cost exactly twice as much as two one-way tickets. Count on paying 50 to 66FF per 100 km of 2nd-class travel.

Reservation Fee The reservation fee (18FF except for TGVs) is optional except under three circumstances:

- If you'll be travelling by TGV, even if only for a small segment of your journey.
- If you want a bed, couchette or a siège inclinable.
- During holiday periods (eg around Easter and 14 July), when it may be necessary to make a reservation several days in advance in order to get a seat on especially popular trains).

Reservations can be made by telephone or Minitel and at any SNCF ticketing office.

Travel by super-fast TGV costs the same as going by regular train except that you must also purchase a reservation, known as a RÉSA TGV. This arrangement lets the SNCF charge more for TGV travel without abandoning its sacred egalitarian fare structure.

TGV reservations cost from 18 to 126FF, depending on expected 1st and/or 2nd-class demand. For province-to-province TGV travel (ie travel that does not begin or end in Paris), the reservation fee for 2nd-class travel is almost always 18FF. If your province-to-province trip involves passing through Paris, though (eg on the Lyon-Nantes run), it may be higher. Reservations can be changed for no charge up to one hour *after* your scheduled departure time. If you don't like your assigned seat (eg it's in a smoking car), feel free to look around for another one, though if someone who gets on at a later stop has reserved it you will have to move.

Because having a rail pass (eg Eurail) does not exempt you from paying reservation fees, and some overnight trains are equipped only with couchettes (eg most of the trains on the Paris-Nice run), the only way to avoid the reservation fee may be to take a day train with unreserved seats.

Supplements On certain non-TGV runs to/from Paris, passengers travelling during *heures de pointe* (peak periods) have to pay a *supplément* of up to 54/72FF in 2nd/1st class. Supplements do *not* apply to travel from one provincial station to another. Lines on which supplements may be charged include Paris-Strasbourg, Paris-Metz, Paris-Luxembourg and Paris-Le Havre and Paris-Cherbourg.

On the small, fold-out train schedules, a # symbol right below the train number means that supplements have to be paid on certain days of the week. On other time schedules, supplements are colour-coded: yellow means there's no supplement; grey means you have to pay the full supplement in 1st class but only a reduced supplement in 2nd;

green means the supplement is reduced in 1st class but not in 2nd; and orange means the full supplement applies in both 1st and 2nd class. On the platform, departure boards should indicate which trains require supplements.

Station Surcharge The construction of new stations and the upkeep of big, old ones is an expensive proposition for SNCF, which tries to recoup some of its costs by attaching a surcharge to tickets sold at certain stations.

Since even the tiniest SNCF bureaux can sell tickets for travel between any two train stations in France, you can avoid paying the surcharge – which on cross-country trips can amount to 20FF – by buying your ticket in advance when you happen to be at a small station with little upkeep and no mortgage. If you're beginning a day trip at a big-city station with a surcharge, you may be able to save a few francs by buying a one-way ticket and picking up another ticket back when you reach your destination.

Food Most long-distance trains have dining cars or snack bars, but you can save a a fair bit of money by bringing along your own food.

Buying a Ticket
Tickets are generally valid for up to two months after the date of purchase. At especially large stations (eg in Paris), there are separate ticket windows for travel on international, *grandes-lignes* (long-haul) and *banlieue* (suburban) lines. Tickets bought with cash can be reimbursed for cash (by you or a thief), so keep them in a safe place.

You can almost always use Visa, Master-Card or American Express credit cards issued overseas to pay for train tickets. This is an excellent way to conserve cash and pay for your travel at an optimal exchange rate. At some larger stations, one or two of the ticket windows will exchange enough foreign currency for you to buy a train ticket.

Tickets can be purchased on board the train, but unless the station where you boarded was closed, prohibitive surcharges

apply: 90FF for journeys under 74 km, 130FF for journeys of more than 74 km. TGV reservations bought on board cost an extra 50FF.

Some travel agents will issue train tickets but charge a hefty handling fee.

Discounts outside France

Eurail Pass For information on Eurail passes and the BritFrance Railpass, see Land in the Getting There & Away chapter.

Euro Domino France The new Euro Domino France, available to residents of 26 European countries (but not people who live in France), gives you three, five or 10 days of midnight-to-midnight travel during a one-month period. It is valid for travel during red, white and blue periods. On the TGV, the reservation fee is 18FF no matter where you go or when. The pass also gets you 25% off on travel from the place where it was purchased – it must be bought in your home country – to the French border.

There are three types of Euro Domino France: the youth version, with which people under 26 can travel for three/five/ten days for 115/162/241 ECU (about US$130/185/275); the adult version, which costs 142/198/293 ECU (US$160/225/335); and the children's version, good for 1st or 2nd-class travel by children under 12, which costs half the price of an adult ticket. Euro Domino France is available from major railway stations in all European countries *except* France.

France Vacances Pass Sold in North America as the France Railpass, the France Vacances Pass entitles people who are not residents of France to unlimited travel on the SNCF system for three to nine days over the course of a month. In 2nd class, the three-day version costs US$125; each additional day of travel costs US$29. These prices do not include reservation fees or couchette charges. Children aged four to 11 pay half-fare. Versions involving car rental and flights within France are also available. To validate your ticket, go to a train station ticket window before you start your first journey.

The France Vacances Pass is not sold in Europe. For details, contact a travel agent. In North America, you can also call Rail Europe on ☎ 800-438 7245.

Discounts in France

For purposes of granting discounts, SNCF divides train travel into three *périodes*: *bleue* (blue), when the largest discounts are available; *blanche* (white), when moderate discounts are available; and *rouge* (red), when there are almost no discounts. To be eligible for a given discount, each leg of your journey must begin during a period of the appropriate colour.

Except during holidays, blue periods usually apply from noon on Monday to noon on Friday and noon on Saturday to 3 pm on Sunday. There are usually white periods from noon on Friday to noon on Saturday, from 3 pm on Sunday to noon on Monday and on certain holidays. Red fares apply only on days of especially heavy traffic, such as when important holidays fall on weekends. For a complete list of red, white and blue periods for a 12-month period, ask for a *Calendrier Voyageurs* at any train station information counter.

BIJ & BSE BIJ tickets (Billets Internationals de Jeunesse, ie international youth tickets), formerly known as BIGE tickets, cost 20 to 25% less than regular tickets for international 2nd-class rail travel (one way or return) started during blue or white periods. They can be purchased by anyone aged 25 or less.

For travel within France, students aged 12 to 25 can purchase BSE tickets (Billets Scolaires et Étudiants), which also cost 20% to 25% less than regular one-way or return fares. A student card is mandatory.

To the great inconvenience of young travellers, BIJ and BSE tickets are not sold at SNCF ticket windows. Rather, you have to go to a travel agent that issues them, such as Voyages Wasteels, Frantour Tourisme, Transalpino, Council Travel or USIT. There's usually at least one such office in the vicinity of major train stations, but it may be

open only on weekdays during office hours. Such places are mentioned under Travel Agencies in city chapters.

Carrissimo The Carrissimo card, valid for travel within France only, grants the holder – who must be 12 to 25 years old – and up to three travelling companions (who must also be aged 12 to 25) a discount of 50% for 1st or 2nd-class journeys begun during blue periods and a 20% discount for travel begun during white periods. A Carrissimo card costs 190FF for four trips or 350FF for eight trips. It is available from SNCF information offices.

Billet Séjour No matter what age you are, the Billet Séjour gives you a 25% reduction for return trips within France if you meet three conditions: the total length of your trip is at least 1000 km; you'll be spending at least part of a Sunday at your destination; and you begin travel in both directions during blue periods. It is available at ticket counters and information offices.

Carte Couple With a Carte Couple – available to a man and a woman who are living together (homosexuals seem to be out of luck) – one of the two people who appear on the card pays full fare and the other gets 50% off when they travel together on trips begun during blue periods. To get a Carte Couple, which is free, bring both of your passports, proof of cohabitation and one passport-sized photo each to the information office of any major train station. 'Proof of cohabitation' means a marriage certificate, a *certificat de concubinage* (a certificate of cohabitation issued by the French government) or, for tourists, two passports with the same address on both.

Carte Kiwi A Carte Kiwi (430FF) gives the cardholder, who must be under 16 on the date of purchase, and one to four companions (either adults or children) 50% off on travel begun during blue and white periods. The discount does not apply if the child travels alone. The Carte Kiwi is sold at train station information offices.

Carte Vermeil Anyone over 60 – regardless of whether they live in France – can get a Carte Vermeil, which entitles the bearer to a 50% reduction for 1st or 2nd-class travel begun during blue periods. There are two kinds: the Carte Vermeil Plein Temps (254FF), which is good for a year and also gets you 30% off on travel undertaken in many other European countries; and the Carte Vermeil Quatre Temps (134FF), good for four journeys within France. Both are sold at the information offices and ticket windows.

Validating Your Ticket

Before boarding the train, you must validate your ticket and your reservation card by time-stamping each one separately in a *composteur*, one of those orange posts located somewhere between the ticket windows and the tracks. When you insert your ticket (with the printed side up), the machine will take a half-circle bite out of the side and print the time and date on the back. Tickets are valid for 24 hours after they've been *compostés* (validated).

Eurail and other rail passes must be time-stamped before you begin your first journey to initiate the period of validity. This must usually be done at a train station ticket window.

Always keep your ticket and reservation card with you until the end of the journey. If a *contrôleur* (inspector) catches you travelling without a ticket (or with one that hasn't been validated), you can be fined. Although an unvalidated ticket is almost like cash (it can be reused or reimbursed), tourists with unvalidated tickets are sometimes (but not always) treated more leniently than locals.

Breaking Your Journey

A train ticket is good for 24 hours after it's been validated, even if it has been punched by the conductor, so there's no problem if you want to break your journey for a few hours (or even overnight). If something out

the window looks interesting, you can simply get off at the next station and hop on a later train going in the same direction. Just make sure you arrive at your final destination within the 24 hours.

If you'd like to break your journey for more than 24 hours, buy two tickets. But if you stop somewhere and, at the last minute, decide to stay there, go to the ticket window as soon as you arrive (your ticket will be worthless after the 24 hours run out) and have them reissue you a fresh ticket for the uncompleted part of your journey.

Reimbursements

It is not at all difficult to get a *remboursement* (reimbursement) for unused SNCF rail tickets and reservation fees. Unfortunately, the rules about how much you get back are mind-bogglingly complicated. One thing is clear, though: the sooner you ask for your money back, the better. For reservations (eg for the TGV or couchettes), the cancellation fees are much lower *before* the scheduled time of departure.

SNCF tickets are generally valid for two months from the date of purchase, and you can get your money back up to two months after the period of validity ends. In other words, at least partial reimbursement is possible up to four months after the purchase date. The basic cancellation fee is 33FF.

If you paid for your ticket in cash, you can get your money back in cash if you go to an Après Vente (after sales) office at a major train station. You can also go to a regular ticket window, but they will send your reimbursement by mail in the form of a cheque in French francs. If you paid by credit card or cheque, both the Après Vente office and the ticket window will send you a cheque in the mail. Such cheques can be cashed outside of France but may be subject to handling charges.

TGV reservations can reimbursed in full (or changed) up to one hour *after* your scheduled departure. After that time, there's a 50FF cancellation fee, which means that all but the most expensive reservations become worthless.

Domestic and international couchette reservations are at least partially reimbursable up to two months after your scheduled departure. Reservations for domestic couchettes are subject to a 33FF cancellation fee per ticket (no matter how many couchettes it includes) right up until departure time. After the scheduled departure, though, there's a 40FF fee *per couchette* if you were supposed to travel in a white or blue period; no reimbursement is possible if your trip was to begin during a red period. Couchette reservations for international travel are subject to a 20FF cancellation fee per couchette before departure; after scheduled departure, there's a 50% cancellation fee.

Appealing If you get fined by a conductor for neglecting to time-stamp your ticket and feel unjustly treated, you can go to an Après Vente (After Sales) office in a major train station and try to explain what happened.

BUS

Because French transport policy is biased in favour of the state-owned rail system, the country has only extremely limited inter-regional bus services. But buses are used quite extensively for short-distance travel within départements, especially in rural areas with relatively few train lines (eg Brittany, Normandy).

For details on départemental bus services, see Getting Around at the beginning of many regional chapters and the Getting There & Away sections of major city listings.

Costs

In some areas (eg along the Côte d'Azur), you have the choice of going either by bus or train. For longer trips, buses tend to be much slower but slightly cheaper than trains, whereas on short runs they are both slower and more expensive.

TAXI

French taxis are rather expensive, especially outside the major cities, but under the right circumstances can save an awful lot of time and hassle.

Fares

For details on the taxi fares and regulations in force in major cities, see Taxi under Getting Around in the Paris chapter. In small cities and towns, where taxi drivers are unlikely to find another fare anywhere near where they let you off, there are four kinds of tariffs:

- Tariff A (3FF per km) – for return trips taken Monday to Saturday from 7 am to 7 pm
- Tariff B (4.50FF per km) – for return travel undertaken from 7 pm to 7 am and all day on Sunday and holidays
- Tariff C (6FF per km) – for one-way travel undertaken during the day from Monday to Saturday
- Tariff D (9FF per km) – for one-way travel at night and on Sundays and holidays

Since the *prise en charge* (metre fall) is 13FF, a four-km trip taken on a Sunday afternoon will cost at least 30FF. There may be a surcharge of 5 or 10FF to get picked up at a train station or airport and a fee of 5FF per bag.

CAR

Having your own wheels lets you stop at villages, lakes, secluded beaches and whatever else you happen upon, something you can't do if travelling from station to station by train. Unfortunately, this independence can be expensive, and cars are often inconvenient in city centres, where parking can be a hassle.

The French are not known for taking very good care of their cars. Some people say that Renaults and Peugeots just look better with scrapes and dented bits, while other, less charitable observers of the French automobile scene claim that the French (and especially Parisians) are simply bad drivers who don't care about their cars or anyone else's. In any case, a great game to play while driving – again, especially in Paris – is to see who can find the first car without a dent in it.

Documents

All drivers in France must carry with them at all times:

- a passport or national ID card
- a valid *permis de conduire* (driver's licence); many foreign driving licences are valid in France for up to one year
- car ownership papers, known in France as a *carte grise* (grey card)
- proof of insurance, known in France as a *carte verte* (green card)

If you're caught at a police roadblock without one or more of these documents, you may be subject to a 900FF on-the-spot fine. Photocopies of all of them should be kept in a safe place. Never leave your car ownership or insurance papers in the vehicle.

A motor vehicle entering a foreign country must display a sticker identifying its country of registration, though this rule is not always strictly enforced. Official codes for English-speaking countries include AUS (Australia), CDN (Canada), GB (Great Britain), IRL (Ireland), NZ (New Zealand), USA (United States) and ZA (South Africa).

For information on getting an International Driving Permit (IDP), see Documents in the Facts for the Visitor chapter.

Equipment

A reflective warning triangle, to be used in the event of breakdown, is compulsory. Recommended accessories – mandatory in some European countries – are a first-aid kit, a spare bulb kit, and a fire extinguisher. In the UK, contact the RAC (☎ 081-686 0088) or the AA (☎ 0345-500600) for more information.

A right-hand drive vehicle brought to France from the UK or Ireland must have deflectors affixed to the headlights to avoid blinding oncoming traffic. French cars have yellow headlights but white ones are perfectly legal.

Road Network

France, along with Belgium, has the densest highway network in Europe. Its 500,000 km of highways, many of them a legacy of the 19th century, represent about one-third of the EC total.

There are three main kinds of intercity roads: *autoroutes*, multilane divided tollways whose alphanumeric designations begin with A; *routes nationales*, main highways whose names begin with N (on older maps, RN); and *routes départementales*, secondary and tertiary local roads whose names begin with D. Autoroutes often have *aires de repos* (rest stops), some with restaurants or pricey petrol stations.

For information on roadmaps, see Maps in the Facts for the Visitor chapter.

Road Rules

In the UK, the *European Motoring Guide*, published by the RAC, gives an excellent summary of road regulations in each European country, including parking rules. Motoring organisations in other countries have similar publications.

North American drivers remember: right turns on a red light are illegal.

Speed Limits Unless otherwise posted, a speed limit of 50 km/h applies when driving in a city, town, village or hamlet, however small it may be. Though there may not be any buildings around, you must slow to 50 km/h the moment you pass a white sign on which a place name is written in black or blue letters (newer signs have a red border). The 50-km/h speed limit remains in force until you arrive at the other edge of town, where you'll pass an identical sign with a red diagonal bar across the name.

Outside built-up areas or villages, speed limits are:

- 90km/h (80 km/h if it's raining) on undivided N and D highways
- 110 km/h (90 or 100km/h in the rain) on dual carriageways (divided highways) or short sections of highway with a divider strip
- 130 km/h (110km/h in the rain) on autoroutes

Speed limits are generally not posted unless they deviate from these guidelines. If you drive at the speed limit, expect to have lots of cars coming up to within two metres of

your rear bumper, flashing their lights and then whizzing past at the first opportunity.

Priorité à Droite The most idiosyncratic – and, for tourists, the most dangerous – traffic law in France is the notorious *priorité à droite* rule, under which any car entering an intersection from a road on your right has right of way no matter how small the road it's coming from. In other words, if you're turning right from a side road onto a main road, you have priority over vehicles approaching from your left. If you're turning left, though, you have to wait for cars coming from your right.

Priorité à droite requires some getting used to, but since French drivers tend to take full advantage of their rights (which include pulling boldly into an intersection at which they have right of way), ignoring, forgetting or not fully understanding it is extremely dangerous.

At most larger *ronds-points* (roundabouts or traffic circles) – French road engineers *love* roundabouts – priorité à droite has been suspended so that the cars already in the roundabout have right of way. This circumstance is indicated by signs reading either *'vous n'avez pas la priorité'* (you do not have right of way) or *'cédez le passage'* (give way).

Priorité à droite is also suspended on *routes à caractère prioritaire* (priority roads), which are marked by a yellow diamond (actually an up-ended square) with a black diamond in the middle. Such signs appear every few km and at intersections.

Priorité à droite is reinstated if you see the same sign with a diagonal bar through it.

Alcohol France is very strict with people who drive while under the influence. To find drivers whose blood-alcohol concentration (BAC) is over 0.08% (0.80 grams per litre of blood), the police often pull cars over at random to administer breathalyser tests, carried out with gadgets called *analyseurs d'haleine*, *éthylotests* or *éthylomètres*. Fines range from 500 to 8000FF, and licences can also be suspended.

Fines *Contraventions* (fines) for serious violations (speeding, driving through a red light) range from 1300 to 3000FF. The police usually make tourists pay up immediately to prevent them from avoiding the fine by leaving the country.

Road Signs

Information on how to get to various cities, towns and intersecting highways is written in white letters on blue signs. An arrow next to the words *'toutes directions'* (literally, 'all directions') indicates the way to go unless you're going to one of the destinations specifically mentioned elsewhere on the sign. For information on Bison Futé's *itinéraires bis* (alternate routes with fewer traffic jams), see Road Maps under Maps in the Facts for the Visitor chapter.

Stop signs are red, octoganal and have the word *stop* on them. Use of the word *arrêt* seems to be limited to Quebec. *Voie unique* means 'one-lane road' (eg at a narrow bridge). *Allumez vos feux* means 'turn on your headlights'. *Sens-unique* means 'one way'.

Road signs with the word *rappel* (remember) written on or under them are telling you something that you were already supposed to know (eg the speed limit).

Road Etiquette

French drivers are assertive (though rarely downright aggressive) and expect everyone else to be, too. If you are timid or overly respectful of other drivers' possible preferences, you may increase the risk of a collision by surprising nearby drivers.

Motoring Organisations

The Paris headquarters of the Automobile Club National (☎ 1-44.51.53.99; metro Auber) is at 5 Rue Auber (9e). You might also contact the Automobile Club de l'Île de France (☎ 1-43.80.68.58; metro Argentine) at 14 Ave de la Grande Armée (17e) in Paris, which offers various insurance programmes.

Expenses

The convenience of having your own vehicle does not come cheap, but for two or more people a car may cost less than going by train (this depends in part on what rail discounts you qualify for). In addition, a car will allow you to avail yourself of less expensive campgrounds, hostels and hotels located far from the train station or city centre.

By autoroute, the drive from Paris to Nice, a distance of about 950 km (about eight hours of actual driving), costs 340FF for petrol (at 16 km a litre) and a whopping 270FF for autoroute tolls, for a total of about 610FF. This figure does not include wear and tear, depreciation, repairs, insurance or the risk of damage, theft or accident. By comparison, a regular, one-way, 2nd-class train ticket for the seven-hour Paris-Nice run costs 465FF.

Petrol *Essence* (petrol), also known as *carburant* (fuel), is incredibly expensive in France, especially if you're used to North American or Australian prices. At the time of going to press, unleaded (*sans plomb*) petrol with an IOR octane ration of 98 costs around 5.60FF a litre (US$3.70 per US gallon), while regular (leaded) fuel with an octane rating of 97 is 5.90FF a litre (US$4 per US gallon). Diesel fuel (*gazole* or *gas-oil*) is 4.20FF a litre. Filling up the tank (*faire le plein*) is most expensive at the rest stops along the autoroutes and cheapest at small rural petrol stations.

In Paris, quite a few petrol stations consist of little more than a few kerbside pumps. To find one, look for the light-blue petrol pump icons on Michelin's 1:10,000-scale map of the city (see Maps under Orientation in the Paris chapter).

Tolls Tolls are charged for travel on all auto-routes and many bridges. On autoroutes, you're essentially paying for the right to drive faster and thus save time. When you get on, a machine usually issues a little ticket that you hand over at a *péage* (toll booth) when you get off. Count on paying about 30FF per 100 km.

One way to look at autoroute tolls is as an investment in safety. Despite their higher speed limits, the autoroutes are generally much less dangerous per km travelled than the much slower highways and secondary roads, which have nonexistent shoulders (verges – *accotements*), pass through lots of little towns and wind their way around an endless succession of topographical obstacles.

Sending Your Car by Train

To save tolls, petrol costs and wear and tear on both you and the car, you can transport your vehicle across France by train. Sending a small car from Paris to Nice costs from 461FF in the off season and 1139 to 1766FF from late June to mid-August (going south) and July to early September (going north). For details, ask at a major train station information office.

Parking

In cities, finding a place to park is likely to be the single greatest hassle you'll face. In city centres, your best bet is usually to ditch the car somewhere and either walk or take public transport.

Public parking facilities are marked by signs bearing a white letter 'P' on a blue background.

Parking Techniques Most French cars are fairly small, but frequently they're not quite compact enough to fit into the only parking place in the neighbourhood. This is where the French belief that bumpers are meant to be bumped comes in handy: you back up until you tap the car behind, then you drive forward until you touch the car in front, and so on until you work your way to the kerb. Strange as it may sound, many people leave their cars in neutral so that drivers parking

nearby can gently push them backwards or forwards in the process of squeezing into a tight spot.

Parking Meters In most cities and many towns, parking near the city centre requires paying 5 to 8FF an hour and is subject to a time limit, often two hours. This lamentable circumstance is generally indicated either by the word *'payant'* written on the asphalt or by an upright sign in French.

The French love of gadgetry solutions has led to the installation of sophisticated, kerb-side *horodateurs* (parking meters), into which you feed coins according to how long you want to park. A few also ask you to punch in your *numéro d'immatriculation* (licence plate number). When you press the correct button (usually the green one – the other ones are for local residents with special permits), the machine spits out a little ticket listing the precise time after which you'll be parked illegally. Take the ticket and place it on the dashboard on the side nearest the kerb.

Most horodateurs are programmed to take into account periods when parking is free, so you can pay the night before for the first hour or two after 8 or 9 am (or whatever time metered parking begins).

Alternate Side Parking Parking on some streets is governed by an arrangement called *stationnement alterné semi-mensuel*, under which you can park on one side of the street from the 1st of the month until the evening of the 15th and on the other side from the 16th until the end of the month.

Parking Fines If you are driving a French-registered car and get a parking ticket, chances are the authorities will eventually catch up with you (or the owner). The basic fine is 75FF, but it increases exponentially if you don't pay up within the allotted period. To pay a parking fine, purchase a *timbre fiscal* (tax stamp) in the proper amount at a tabac. Affix the larger of the two sections to the ticket and, after sticking on a regular domestic postage stamp, mail it to the address indicated.

Dangers & Annoyances

Theft from and of cars is a major problem in France, especially (but by no means exclusively) in the south. Foreign and out-of-town cars (identifiable by their licence plate numbers) and rented cars are especially popular targets. *Never* leave anything in the car – in some places, thieves will break a window just to steal an umbrella lying on the seat. With hatchbacks, some people remove the panel that covers the boot (trunk) so passing criminals don't decide to find out if it's hiding anything.

When you arrive in a new city or town, it's a good idea to find a hotel and unload your belongings *before* doing any sightseeing that will require parking the car somewhere. And on your last day in town, ask the hotel manager to store your luggage until after you've done any local touring that will require leaving the car unattended.

Repairs If your car is *en panne* (breaks down), you'll have to find a *garage* that handles your *marque* (make of car). There are Peugeot, Renault and Citroën garages all over the place, but if you have a non-French car you may have trouble finding someone to service it in remote rural areas. In any case, Michelin's *Guide Rouge* lists garages at the end of each entry.

Accidents If you are involved in a minor accident with no injuries, the easiest way for the drivers to sort things out with their respective insurance companies is to fill out a Constat Aimable d'Accident Automobile (jointly agreed accident report), known in English as a European Accident Statement. In rental cars, it is usually included in the packet of documents left in the glove compartment or on the little shelf in the driver's-side door.

This form has a standardised way of recording important details about the accident: both cars' licence plate numbers, both drivers' names and addresses, information on both drivers' insurance policies, damage to the vehicles and precisely what happened. It doesn't matter which car is listed as

véhicule A and which is *véhicule B*. Both drivers sign and each gets a copy.

If your French is not fluent, find someone who can explain exactly what each word of traffic jargon means. Never sign anything you don't understand – insist on a translation and sign that only if it's acceptable. Make sure you can read the other driver's handwriting. If problems crop up, it's usually not very hard to find a police officer. To alert the police, dial 17 from any phone.

Make sure the Constat includes any information that will help you to prove that the accident was not your fault. For instance, if you were just sitting there and the other person backed into you, mention this under Observations (No 14 on the Constat). Remember, if you did cause the accident (or can't prove that you didn't), you may end up paying a hefty excess (deductible), depending on your insurance policy.

Car Rental

Given the high cost of getting a car across the English Channel or from mainland France to Corsica, and the expenses involved in driving across France, it may make sense to rent a car after you arrive in the region you'd like to explore. Airport tariffs may be higher than the rates charged in town.

The variety of special deals and terms and conditions can be confusing. The multinationals, such as Hertz, Avis, Budget Car, and Europe's largest rental agency, Europcar, are *much* more expensive than local or national companies if you walk into one of their offices and hire a car on the spot (Hertz charges 565FF a day, and Avis an astounding 960FF a day!). But if you can plan in advance, their prebooked and prepaid promotional rates can be very reasonable. They may also have fly/drive combos and other discounts that are worth looking into.

For rentals that are not arranged in advance, domestic companies such as ADA almost invariably have the best rates. Before you sign anything, make sure you understand exactly what is included in the price and what your liabilities and how many km you can drive without being charged extra. *Kilométrage*

illimité (unlimited km) gives you the most flexibility but may not be necessary for shorter jaunts. For information on insurance, see the following Insurance section.

The packet of documents you are given should include the rental contract, a photocopy of the *carte grise* (the car's registration certificate), a photocopy of the insurance policy, a Constat Aimable d'Accident Automobile (see the preceding Accidents section) and a 24-hour number to call in case of a breakdown or accident.

Rental Companies For details on car-hire companies' offices, see Car under Getting There & Away in city listings. Very few places are open on Sunday.

Some of the cheapest rental cars in France are available from ADA Location de Véhicules. At most (but not all) of ADA's 200 agencies, a very small car (eg a Peugeot 106 or an Opel Corsa) costs 359FF for one day, including 400 free km and an excess of 1000FF. The rate for a weekend (2 pm on Friday to 8 am on Monday) is 539FF, including 800 free km. For a full seven days with 1000 free km, you pay 1469FF. If you exceed the limit it costs 1FF per km. The rental fee includes 24-hour breakdown service, provided by Mondial Assistance (☎ 05.01.02.97).

Under SNCF's Train + Auto plan, you reserve an Avis car when you book your train ticket – it will be waiting for you at any of over 200 railway stations when you arrive. Tariffs, however, are very high.

Reservations It's a good idea to call and make a reservations a few days in advance, especially with the discount local companies.

Age Limits Most rental companies require that you be over 21 and have had a driver's licence for at least one year.

Insurance *Assurance* (insurance) for damage or injury you cause to other people is mandatory, but things like collision damage waivers vary greatly from company to company. The policies offered by some small, discount companies may leave you liable for up to 8000FF – when comparing rates, the most important thing to check is the *franchise* (excess or deductible). If you're in an accident that's your fault and the rental car is damaged, this is the amount for which you are liable before the collision damage policy kicks in.

Forms of Payment All the major domestic and multinational rental companies accept payment by credit card. Because you'll probably have to leave a deposit for the insurance excess and perhaps the petrol in the tank, many companies *require* that you have a credit card. Those that let you leave a deposit in cash or travellers' cheques (eg some branches of Avis, Europcar and Eurorent) may ask for evidence that you can be trusted with their vehicle (eg proof of residence or even a pay slip).

Many agencies ask you to leave a signed credit card slip without a sum written on it as a deposit. If you don't like this arrangement, ask them to make out two credit card slips: one for the sum of the rental and the other for the sum of the excess. Make sure to have the latter destroyed when you return the car.

Before You Drive Off When the person from the rental company finally hands over the keys, make sure that:

* all preexisting damage to the car is noted on your contract (inspect the car carefully)
* the *cric* (jack), *manivelle* (crank) and *clef* (wrench) are in their place
* the fuel tank is full (if it's not, note this fact on the contract or they may expect to get it back full)
* you know what all the knobs do (on many smaller cars, you have to pull out the choke to start them)

Purchase-Repurchase Plans
If you'll be needing a car in France for one to six months, it is usually cheaper to 'purchase' a brand new one from the manufacturer and then 'sell it back' than it is to rent. In reality, you only pay for the number of days you use the vehicle, but the purchase-

repurchase *(achat-rachat)* aspect of the paperwork (none of which is your responsibility) lets you save the 18.6% VAT on car rentals.

Renault's purchase-repurchase plan, known as 'Renault Eurodrive', lets you drive to 29 European countries with unlimited km. You don't need a credit card, just a passport and an international driver's licence. The minimum age is 18; there is no maxumim age. The Eurodrive plan does not involve a deposit, but payment for the period for which you would like the car must be made in advance. If you return it early, you'll be reimbursed for the unused time. Extending your contract is also possible – call the Paris office at ☎ 1-40.40.33.68 at least a week before your original return date. The car can be picked up at most of France's international airports for no charge, but it costs 500FF to drop it off anywhere except Paris.

The Special Export Sales Division of Renault's Paris office (☎ 1-40.40.32.03; fax 1-42.41.83.47; metro Porte de Pantin) at 186 Ave Jean Jaurès (19e) can arrange a car within a day or two (a week in summer). However, it is 20% to 30% cheaper to arrange your Renault purchase-repurchase car outside of France, where various discounts are available. Telephone and fax numbers of Renault Eurodrive offices abroad are listed below.

Contact them at least three or four weeks before your trip. If arranged in Paris, a 1.1-litre Renault Twingo (the cheapest model available) costs 5100FF for 23 days, 5400FF for 33 days and 68FF for each day thereafter (up to 15,396FF for six months). The price includes comprehensive insurance with no excess, unlimited km and 24-hour towing and breakdown service (☎ 05.05.15.15 in France, 33-1-47.11.13.13 in other countries). Cars with automatic transmission are also available, but right-hand drive cars are not. If you fall in love with your car, you can buy it when your purchase-repurchase agreement comes to an end.

Buying a Car

The hassle of buying a car and later selling it, the risk of losing your entire investment if something expensive goes wrong, and the cost of insurance, petrol, tolls, etc make purchasing your own vehicle worthwhile only you'll be doing a lot of driving – around France or elsewhere in Europe – for at least four months. Because of new regulations requiring that cars over 10 years old undergo regular safety tests and be repaired if they don't pass (see Contrôle Technique), dirt cheap older vehicles (ie cars costing less than US$1000) are largely a thing of the past.

Peugeots have a reputation for reliability, Renaults are known for being economical, and Citroëns are famed for combining a certain stylishness with technological innovation. But for all makes, it is said that French cars are designed to last for only seven or eight years – older models are running on borrowed time. The value of used cars up to eight years old is listed in *L'Argus* (14FF), available at news kiosks. Many kinds of non-French cars are statistically less likely to break down than French-made ones, but if they do they may be harder to fix.

RENAULT EURODRIVE OFFICES

Country	Telephone	Fax
Australia	02-299 3344 or 008-221 156	02-290 3963
Canada	514-461 1149	514-461 0207
Ireland	01-260 222	01-260 241
New Zealand	09-570 4056	09-527 7964
South Africa	011-803 3068	011-803 2815
UK	081-992 5544	081-993 2734
USA	1-800-221 1052 or 212-532 3190	212-725 5379

Finding a Car Used cars are advertised in *La Centrale de Particuliers* (13FF), which comes out on Thursday morning. Pick it up on the day it comes out – the cheaper cars sell fast, and by Tuesday you'll have reason to wonder what's wrong with the cars that are left. Since you often have to take down details in French or leave a message on an answering machine, finding a car this way is well nigh impossible if your French is not fairly proficient. In addition, you'll probably have to leave a phone number where you can be reached, a difficult proposition if you're staying at a hostel or cheap hotel without a proper front desk. In any case, when you call – 'DOM' after the number means *domicile* (home), 'BUR' means *bureau* (office) – the first thing you should find out is where the owner lives and how hard it will be for you to get out there to see it.

In Paris, many people selling their used jalopies park them along Ave de la Porte de Clignancourt (18e) near the Marché aux Puces de Saint Ouen (metro Porte de Clignancourt) from Saturday to Monday. Look for cars with *à vendre* (for sale) signs in the window.

Many repair garages sell used cars but generally restrict their offerings to expensive late-model vehicles.

Contrôle Technique In order to be sold, all passenger cars over five years old must undergo a *contrôle technique*, a thorough technical inspection which costs about 300FF at authorised garages. This procedure, whose purpose is to protect the buyer by letting them know if the car has any problems, must be carried out (and paid for) by the seller less than six months before the date of sale. Although neither party is required to repair anything, you will be asked to show the contrôle technique form when applying for registration papers and insurance, and certain kinds of problems (eg rust holes in the floorboards or body) may make it impossible to get coverage. Keep an eye out for evidence of possible expensive repairs (eg the clutch, which is easily worn down in city driving). To be extra sure that the car is in good shape (and to make sure

nothing has gone wrong since the contrôle technique was done), you might want to do your own contrôle technique before signing anything or handing over any money.

In an effort to get unsafe vehicles off the road, the French government began requiring that seven-year-old cars undergo a particularly strict contrôle technique even if they are not about to be sold. Certain categories of safety-related problems must then be fixed in order to get a special *vignette* or *macaron* (windscreen sticker) without which they can't be driven. The car must then pass the same safety test every three years. The practical result of these regulations is to make cheap, older cars requiring extensive repair work essentially worthless. Make sure you don't buy one.

Making the Purchase Every 'predriven' vehicle is being sold for a reason. If you've found a car driven by a little old lady only to the boulangerie and back, you're in luck. But since few cars have had such an idyllic existence, it's a good idea to ask the seller what has moved them to part with such a fine piece of machinery. Could the new contrôle technique tests have anything to do with it? Ask to see the owner's collection of repair receipts.

To make sure that the seller is also the car's owner, check his or her *carte nationale d'identité* (national identity card), which is also a good source of personal details, such as full name and address. Make sure to get written receipts for everything, including your deposit (if you make one).

The seller should also provide you with:

- two copies of the *certificat de cession d'un véhicule* (certificate of transfer of a vehicle)
- the car's *carte grise* (grey card), the vehicle's registration certificate, marked with the words *vendu le* or *cédé le* (sold on) and the date
- the contrôle technique form
- a *certificat de non-gage* (a certificate from the prefecture attesting that the car has not been pledged as collateral, eg for a loan)
- the *talon rouge*, a pink square of paper given as a receipt for the *vignette*, a windscreen sticker that indicates that the annual *taxe sur les automobiles*, due each November, has been paid. If the driver can't find it, don't worry – you still have the sticker.

La Centrale des Particuliers issues every seller with an optional *constat de vente d'automobile* (report on the sale of an automobile). If you found the car through La Centrale, ask the seller to fill it out and give you a copy.

Insurance The seller's liability insurance stays in force until midnight of the day you buy the car, but after that it is illegal to drive it until you have a *carte verte*, a certificate of liability insurance, part of which you insert into the sticker on the right-hand side of the windscreen. It is therefore imperative that you look into getting insurance before taking possession of the car. Insurance can be arranged before you register the car by presenting the seller's carte grise.

Three types of coverage are available:

- *garantie au tiers* (third-party liability insurance), the minimum coverage required by law, which insures you for damage you cause to other people. Count on paying at least 4000FF a year unless you have proof of a long and accident- free insurance record.
- *vol, incendie et bris de glaces* (insurance against theft, fire and broken windows).
- *tous risques* (literally, all-risk, ie comprehensive insurance that covers your car for all types of damage cased by you or anyone else).

Rates depend on how long you've had your licence and how good your driving record is. If you have a sterling insurance record, you might be eligible for a considerable discount if you can show a letter to this effect from your insurance company back home.

Most policies are valid in a variety of European countries and allow you to carry up to four passengers in addition to the driver. People other than the owner may be able to drive only if they've had a driving licence for at least three years.

Insurance is usually issued for a minimum of six months. If you sell your car earlier and show the company proof that you sold it, it should be possible to be reimbursed for the remaining time. However, you may have to wait several months to get your money, and even then it's likely to be in the form of a cheque, which cannot be cashed unless you have a bank account (either in France or abroad).

In Paris, a reliable agent with decent rates is BUSTA (☎ 1-47.05.05.04; metro Pont de l'Alma) at 9 Ave Rapp (7e).

Registration Within 15 days of purchase, you must take care of *immatriculation* (vehicle registration) and get a new carte grise. This can be done at the nearest prefecture or, in Paris, the Préfecture de Police (☎ 1-53.71.53.71; metro Cité) at 1 Rue de Lutèce (4e), open Monday to Friday from 8.30 am to 5 pm (4.30 pm on Friday).

You must bring with you:

- two copies of the *certificat de cession d'un véhicule*
- the seller's carte grise
- the contrôle technique form
- a certificat de non-gage (technically required only if the car is from a département other than the one you're registering it in)
- *attestation* (proof) of where in the département you live. As a tourist, you should be able to use as a *pièce justificative de domicile* (proof of address) an official receipt from your hotel or hostel that includes your full name and passport number.

The immatriculation charge is 142FF per *cheval* (horsepower as measured by the French system) or 71FF per cheval if the car is more than 10 years old.

If there's any chance that you'll be driving outside of France, it's a good idea to pick up a *certificat international pour automobile* (international automobile certificate; 17FF), essentially a translation of the carte grise.

Number Plates All cars are given new licence plate numbers when they change hands. When you get your carte grise, you must *immediately* drive to a garage (your best bet is one that handles the make you've bought) and ask them to punch out *plaques d'immatriculation* (number plates). The whole process, including riveting the plates to the car, should cost about 150FF and take 15 minutes.

Selling a Car

It can be very difficult to sell a car quickly, so leave enough time at the end of your trip to take care of all the formalities, such as getting a new contrôle technique. For a list of garages authorised to do contrôles techniques, stop by any prefecture, subprefecture or, in Paris, the carte grise office at the Préfecture de Police (see Registration). By Minitel, key in 3615 code ROUTE. In the back of L'Argus there are ads placed by companies that buy used cars.

When you sell your car, draw a diagonal line across the carte grise and write on it vendu le (sold on) plus the date. Take the little green insurance tag out of the sticker on the right-hand side of the windscreen (if you are owed a rebate on your insurance, the insurance company may want it). Make sure to have the buyer sign a reçu d'achat de véhicule (receipt for the purchase of a vehicle). When the deal is done, take one copy of the certificat de cession d'un véhicule to the prefecture where the car was registered. See Making the Purchase for details on what you'll have to give to the buyer. All the necessary forms are available at registration offices.

MOTORBIKE

France is made for motorcycle touring, with winding roads of good quality and stunning scenery to stimulate the senses. Just make sure your wet-weather gear is up to scratch.

Riders of any type of two-wheel vehicle with a motor must wear a helmet – if you're caught bareheaded, you can be fined 230FF and have your bike confiscated until you get one. Bikes of more than 125 cc must have their headlights on during the day. No special licence is required to ride a motorbike whose engine is smaller than 50 cc, which is why you often find places renting scooters rated at 49.9 cc.

Parking

In the cities, motorbikes are supposed to be parked in parking spots marked deux roues (two wheels), but in most places the police tolerate bikes left on the pavement so long as they don't block pedestrian traffic. In general, if other people are doing it, you'll probably be OK.

Motorbike Rental

To rent a moped, scooter, motorcycle, etc, you usually have to leave a caution (deposit) of several thousand francs, which you forfeit – up to the value of the damage to the rental bike – if you're in an accident and it's your fault. Since insurance companies won't cover theft, you'll also lose the deposit if the bike is stolen. Most places accept deposits made by credit card, travellers' cheques, eurocheques or cash.

BICYCLE

France is an eminently cyclable country, thanks in part to its extensive network of relatively lightly trafficked secondary and tertiary roads. Indeed, many people consider such backroads, a good number of which date from the 19th century, the ideal vantage point from which to view France's renowned rural landscapes. One pitfall: they rarely have proper shoulders.

More information of interest to cyclists can be found in the Facts for the Visitor chapter: general information on cycling in France is given under Activities; map options are discussed under Maps; and information on cyclists' topoguides can be found under Hiking & Cycling in the Travel Guides listing of the Books section. The Tour de France is discussed briefly under Spectator Sports in the Culture section of the Facts about the Country chapter.

Road Rules

French law mandates that bicycles must have two functioning brakes, a bell, a red reflector on the back and yellow reflectors on the pedals. After sunset and when visibility is poor, cyclists must turn on a white light in front and a red one in the rear. The name and address of the bike's owner must appear on a metal plate attached to the front of the bike. When being overtaken by a car or truck, cyclists are required to ride in single file.

Cycling Organisations

The Fédération Française de Cyclotourisme
(☎ 1-44.16.88.88; metro Corvisart) at 8 Rue
Jean-Marie Jégo (13e), just north of Rue
Bobillot, acts as a liaison between 2800
French cycling clubs. Run by volunteers, it
organises bicycle trips for members of
French and foreign cycling clubs with which
it has accords. If you write to them in
advance, they'll send you a packet of free
information in English. Touring itineraries
for one to seven-day excursions cost about
30FF each.

In the UK, the Cyclists' Touring Club
(☎ 0483-417 217) at Cotterell House, 69
Meadrow, Godalming, Surrey GU7 3HS,
can supply information to members on
cycling conditions in Europe as well as
detailed routes, itineraries and cheap insurance. Membership, which includes certain
insurance benefits, costs £24 per annum (£12
to people aged under 18, £16 for people over
65 and £40 for three or more people living at
the same address).

Transporting Your Bicycle

Air It is relatively easy to take your bicycle
with you on an aeroplane. You can either take
it to pieces and pack everything in a bike bag
or box, or simply wheel it to the check-in
desk, where it will be treated as a piece of
baggage (you may have to supply your own
box, available from bike shops). It will probably be necessary to remove the pedals and
turn the handlebars sideways so that it takes
up less space in the aircraft's hold. In either
case, so long as you bring along all the tools
you'll need for reassembly, you'll be able to
ride away from the airport terminal. Check
all this (and weight limits) with the airline
well in advance, preferably before you pay
for your ticket.

Train Within France, bicycles can be brought
along free of charge on many short-distance
trains – check at the departure station to see
if this option is available. You are responsible for loading and unloading your bicycle
from the baggage compartment. The SNCF

won't accept any responsibility for its fate,
so take off the paniers and all removable
parts (eg the pump).

On other runs, it costs 135FF to register
(enregistrer) a boxed bicycle as checked
baggage to any destination in France, regardless of distance. A bicycle box *(emballage)*,
without which the registration fee *(droit
d'enregistrement)* jumps to 180FF, is usually
available for 15FF at the station's left-
luggage office, where registration takes
place. Sending a bicycle from anywhere in
France to most other countries in Europe
costs only 50FF (plus 15FF for the box).
Special tariffs apply in Corsica.

If there's direct service to where you are
going, your bike can travel on the same train
as you do. But in France's finest bureaucratic
tradition, if a change of trains is required
your bike must be transported via Paris,
thereby ensuring that it will arrive three to
five days after you do. On the brighter side,
your bike will be automatically insured for
up to 2550FF, with supplementary insurance
(known as a *formule d'assurance*) also available. In many areas, SNCF will pick up or
deliver your bicycle for 45FF.

Bus Buses – local or intercity – almost never
take bicycles.

Sea Bicycles travel free on most trans-
Channel ferries (but not on routes to Ireland).

Bicycle Rental

Most towns have at least one shop that hires
out bicycles by the hour, day, weekend or
week. Many places offer *vélos à 10 vitesses*
(10-speeds) and low-tech one and three-
speeds for 50 to 80FF a day, but in some areas
such antiquated conveyances are fast going
the way of the penny-farthing, at least in the
rental business. In the Alps, for instance, a
growing number of shops only carry *vélos
tout-terrains* (mountain bikes or ATMs),
popularly known as VTTs. These fine
machines generally cost 70 to 120FF a day,
though prices vary according to the area,
season and quality of the bike. For details on

where to rent bicycles, see the Getting Around or Getting There & Away sections of each city or town listing.

Most rental places – especially those with expensive mountain bikes – require a 1000 or 2000FF deposit, which you forfeit if the bike is damaged or stolen. In general, deposits can be made in cash, with signed travellers' cheques or by credit card.

SNCF used to rent bicycles from lots of train station left-luggage rooms, but the company has lately decided to drop this apparently unprofitable line of business except at a limited number of stations. The success of this plan will depend in part on whether SNCF can improve the quality and maintenance of the bikes it supplies. In some stations, bicycle hire operations have been taken over by private companies.

Avoiding Theft

Never leave your bicycle locked up outside overnight or there's a good chance that come morning it will either be gone or denuded of all removable accessories. You can leave your bike in train station left-luggage offices for 35FF per 24 hours.

Repairs

Almost every good-sized town seems to have a bicycle shop, but *pièces détachées* (spare parts), for non-French bikes may be difficult or impossible to find. Overhaul your bike before setting out for France and replace parts that are likely to wear out, such as the chain, gears, brakes and tyres.

HITCHING

Hitching in France is more difficult than in Germany, Switzerland or almost anywhere else in Europe. Getting out of the big cities or travelling around the Côte d'Azur by thumb is well nigh impossible. Remote rural areas are your best bet, but few cars are likely to be going farther than the next large town.

A woman hitching on her own is taking a risk, but two women should be reasonably safe. Two men together may have a harder time getting picked up than a man travelling

alone. The best combination is probably a man and a woman travelling together. In any case, never get in the car with someone you don't trust, even if you have no idea why. Keep your belongings with you on the seat rather than in the boot.

Dedicated hitchers may wish to invest in the *Hitch-hikers Manual for Europe* by Simon Calder (paperback, published by Vacation Work, 1993).

Although many travellers hitch rides in Europe, this is not a totally safe way of getting around. Just because we explain how it works doesn't mean we recommend it.

Exploring France by Thumb

Hitching is as much a way to meet people as it is a way to get around. If you speak some French (few older people in rural areas know much English), thumbing it affords unmatched opportunities to meet French people from all walks of life.

The less like a tourist you look and feel, the better off you'll be.

On back roads you may not get long-distance rides, but you are more likely to get picked up and meet people. Drivers will often give you advice on what to see, either in the immediate vicinity or elsewhere in France.

Fishing for Rides

Hitching from city centres is pretty much hopeless: take public transport to the outskirts of town. Some people have had luck getting rides from truck drivers at truck stops, while others find that passenger cars are more likely to pick them up, either on slip roads or at petrol stations. It is illegal to hitch on autoroutes but you can stand near the entrance ramps so long as you don't block traffic. If your itinerary includes a ferry crossing, it might be worth trying to score a ride before the ferry rather than after, since vehicle tickets sometimes include a number of passengers free of charge. At dusk, give up and think about finding somewhere to stay.

To maximise your chances of being picked up, look cheerful, presentable and nonthreatening; orient your backpack so it looks as small as possible to oncoming

drivers; and make eye contact with the people driving by. It is an excellent idea to hold up a sign with your destination followed by the letters *s.v.p.* (short for *s'il vous plaît*) written on it. One traveller reports that a destination sign reading *'n'importe où'* (anywhere) works well if you aren't going to any particular place.

Preparations

Veteran hitchhikers make the following suggestions:

- Pack all your belongings in waterproof plastic bags
- Prepare a daypack so you can stash your main bag somewhere and wander around during the day
- Invest in a pair of comfortable shoes
- Bring along water purification tablets (so that in a pinch you can drink streamwater) and a basic first-aid kit
- Pack light: every kg you pack will weigh you down every time you take a step. Five kg can make the difference between being mobile and being stuck in one place
- Given how much time you'll be spending waiting around on roadsides, it's a good idea to have some sort or activity to keep you busy – writing, drawing, reading, knitting, etc

Allostop

The Allostop network helps people looking for rides get in touch with drivers going to the same destination. Travelling this way offers undeniable environmental advantages, but it requires a fair bit of advance planning (eg contacting Allostop a few days ahead) and is not that cheap, since travellers pay a portion of the drivers' petrol costs plus a standard fee (18 centimes per km) to cover administrative expenses: 30/40/50/60FF for trips under 200/300/400/500 km; 70FF for trips over 500 km. With an eight-trip *abonnement* (membership; 230FF), valid for up to two years, you just pay the per-km charge. Fees work out to 223FF from Paris to Marseille, 177FF from Paris to Geneva, 280FF from Paris to Berlin and 260FF from Marseille to Rome.

Allostop used to have bureaux (under various names) all over France but has been shrinking in recent years. It still has offices in Paris (see Hitching under Getting There & Away in the Paris chapter) and four other French cities:

Lille
    Autostop, 21 Rue Patou, 59800 Lille (☎ 20.42.08.88)
Nantes
    Voyage au Fil, CIJ de Nantes, 28 Rue du Calvaire (☎ 40.89.04.85)
Rennes
    Autostop Bretagne, CIJ Maison du Champ de Mars, 6 Cours des Alliés, 35043 Rennes (☎ 99.32.14.20)
Toulouse
    Allostop Voyages, 9 Place du Capitole (☎ 61.23.25.29)

If you're in a city without an Allostop representative, you can call their Paris office (☎ 1-42.46.00.66 or, from abroad, 1-47.70.02.01). By Minitel, dial 3615 code PROVOYA.

WALKING

Walking is the best way to get to know a new city or town. Many places in France offer superb places for strolling: parks, squares, avenues, canals, seaside promenades, etc.

BOAT

For information on renting and operating a canal boat, see Boating on Burgundy's Waterways at the beginning of the Burgundy chapter; the introductory Activities section of the Brittany chapter; and the Canal du Midi aside in the Languedoc-Roussillon chapter. Details on renting houseboats for trips along the Lot River can be found under Houseboat Rental at the beginning of the Quercy section of the Limousin, Périgord & Quercy chapter.

For a booklet listing boat rental companies around France, contact the Syndicat National des Loueurs de Bateaux de Plaisance (☎ 1-45.55.10.49) at Port de la Bourdonnais (7e) in Paris.

TOURS

Though independent travel is usually far

more rewarding than being led from bus to sight and back again, some areas are difficult to visit on your own unless you have wheels. Where relevant (eg the Loire Valley, the D-Day Beaches in Normandy), tour options are mentioned right before Places to Stay under Organised Tours.

Paris

Paris (population 2.15 million in the city, 10 million in the metropolitan area) has just about exhausted the superlatives that can reasonably be applied to cities, at least in the form of neat travel clichés. Notre Dame and the Eiffel Tower – at sunrise, at sunset, at night – have been described countless times. So have the Seine, and the subtle (and not-so-subtle) differences between the Left Bank and the Right Bank. But what writers have been unable to capture is the grandness and even magic of strolling along the city's broad avenues, which lead from impressive public buildings and exceptional museums to parks, gardens and esplanades galore. With the metro, all this and more is readily accessible – you can whizz (and screech) around under the crowds and traffic and pop up wherever you choose!

Paris probably has more landmarks familiar to people who've never been there than any other city in the world. As a result, first-time and veteran visitors alike usually arrive in the French capital with all sorts of expectations: of grand vistas, of intellectuals discussing weighty matters in cafés, of romance along the Seine, of naughty night-club revues, of rude people who won't speak English. If you look hard enough for whatever it is you expect (or hope) to discover in Paris, you can probably find it. But another approach is to set aside the preconceptions of Paris that are so much a part of English-speaking culture and to explore the city's avenues and backstreets as if the tip of the Eiffel Tower or the spire of Notre Dame weren't about to pop into view at any moment.

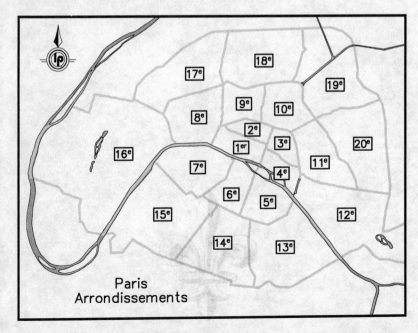

Paris
Arrondissements

ORIENTATION

In central Paris, the Rive Droite (Right Bank) – the shore to the right as you face downriver – is north of the Seine, while the Rive Gauche (Left Bank) is south of the river. Streets that are more or less parallel to the Seine are numbered from east to west, ie in the direction in which the river flows. On streets that are perpendicular to the river (or approximately so), the numbering starts at the river – building numbers get higher the further away from the Seine you go. The city covers 105 sq km, including the Bois de Boulogne and the Bois de Vincennes.

For administrative and other purposes, Paris has been divided since 1860 into 20 *arrondissements* (districts), which spiral out from the centre of the city like a clockwise snail. Paris addresses always include the arrondissement number. Arrondissements are further divided into *quartiers* (quarters).

In this book, arrondissements are listed in the heading or in parentheses immediately after the street address, using the usual French notation: *1er* for *premier* (1st), *4e* for *quatrième* (4th), 19e for *dix-neuvième* (19th), etc. On some signs or maps, you'll see the notation 4ème, 19ème, and so forth. Area subheadings under Things to See, Restaurants, etc appear in order of ascending arrondissement number.

There is virtually always a metro station within 500 metres of wherever you want to go in Paris, so all offices, museums, hotels, restaurants, etc mentioned in this text have the nearest metro stop written immediately after the telephone number (or, in a few cases, after the address). On most business cards, brochures and advertisements, the nearest metro stops are written right after the word *métro* or its abbreviation, *Mo.*

Metro stations usually have a *plan du quartier* (map of nearby streets) at some exits. They can be an invaluable aid for initial orientation in an unfamiliar area.

INFORMATION
Tourist Offices

Paris's main tourist office (☎ 49.52.53.54; fax 49.52.53.00; metro George V), also known as the Office du Tourisme et des Congrès de Paris and the Bureau d'Accueil Central, is 200 metres east of the Arc de Triomphe at 127 Ave des Champs-Élysées (8e). It is open every day of the year, except 1 January, 1 May and 25 December, from 9 am to 8 pm. This is the best source in the city for information in English on museums, concerts, expositions, theatre performances and the like. Brochures about other parts of France are available on request. For a small fee (8FF for a hostel, 20/25/40FF for a one/two/three-star hotel) and a deposit, the office can find you a place to stay in Paris, but only for the night of the day you stop by. Reservations in the provinces, available up to eight days in advance, cost 30FF.

There are tourist office annexes in all of Paris's train stations except Gare Saint Lazare. They are open daily, except Sunday and holidays, from 8 am to 9 pm (3 pm at Gare d'Austerlitz). The Gare du Nord office is also open on Sunday (but not holidays) from 1 to 8 pm. The tourist office annexe at the base of the Eiffel Tower is open from May to September daily (including holidays) from 11 am to 6 pm. All the annexes can make hotel reservations.

For details on Aéroports de Paris (ADP) information desks at the airports, see the Orly and Charles de Gaulle listings under Air in the Getting There & Away section of this chapter.

Money

Except in heavily touristed areas, many commercial banks do not exchange foreign currency (a *'no change'* sign in the window means you're out of luck). Quite a few Parisian post offices (see Post) exchange a variety of foreign banknotes, as well as American Express travellers' cheques denominated in US dollars or French francs and Visa travellers' cheques in French francs.

Unless you want to get about 10% less than a fair rate, avoid the big exchange chains like Chequepoint and Exact Change.

Airports For details on changing money at the airports, see the Orly and Charles de

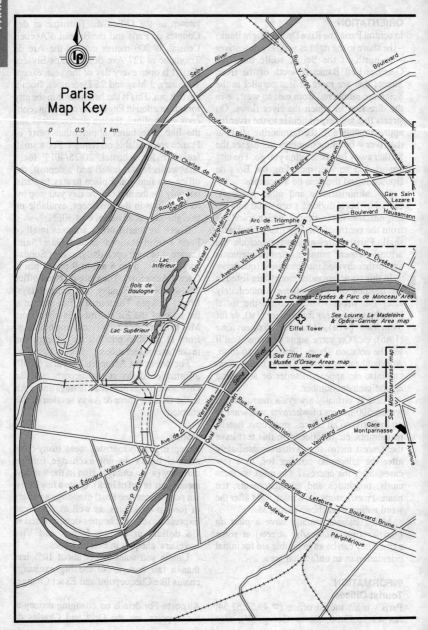

Paris
Map Key

0   0.5   1 km

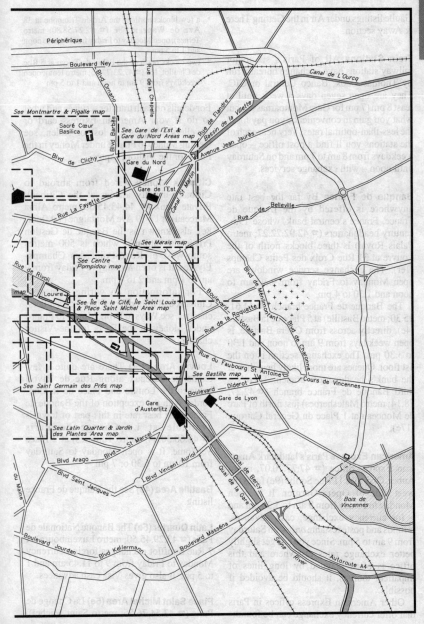

Périphérique

Boulevard Ney

Rue de la Chapelle

Canal de L'Ourcq

Rue de Flandre

Bassin de la Villette

See Montmartre & Pigalle map

Sacré Cœur Basilica

Blvd Barbès

See Gare de l'Est & Gare du Nord Areas map

Blvd de Clichy

Gare du Nord

Avenue Jean Jaurès

Gare de l'Est

Rue La Fayette

Canal St Martin

Rue de Belleville

See Marais map

Rue de Rivoli

See Centre Pompidou map

Rue de Ménilmontant

Louvre

See Île de la Cité, Île Saint Louis & Place Saint Michel Area map

Boulevard Voltaire

Rue de la Roquette

Rue de Chaonne

Rue du Faubourg St Antoine

See Bastille map

See Saint Germain des Prés map

Boulevard Diderot

Gare d'Austerlitz

Cours de Vincennes

See Latin Quarter & Jardin des Plantes Area map

Blvd St Marcel

Gare de Lyon

Blvd Arago

Blvd Saint Jacques

Quai de Bercy

Quai de la Gare

du Maine

Bois de Vincennes

Blvd Vincent Auriol

Boulevard Jourdan

Boulevard Kellermann

Boulevard Masséna

Seine River

Autoroute A4

Gaulle listings under Air in the Getting There & Away section.

Train Stations All of Paris's six major railway stations have exchange bureaux run by Thomas Cook, Banco Central or CIC. They are open seven days a week until at least 8 pm (7 pm for Gare Montparnasse), but what you gain in convenience you pay for in the less-than-optimal rates. Very near each of the stations you'll find a post office – open weekdays from 8 am to 7 pm and on Saturday until noon – with exchange services.

Banque de France By far the best rate anywhere is offered by the Banque de France, France's central bank, whose 19th-century headquarters (☎ 42.92.22.27; metro Palais Royal) is three blocks north of the Louvre at 31 Rue Croix des Petits Champs (1er). The exchange service windows are open Monday to Friday from 9.30 am to noon and 1.30 to 4 pm.

The Banque de France branch (☎ 44.61.15.30; metro Bastille) at 5 Place de la Bastille (4e), directly across from Opéra-Bastille, is open weekdays from 9 am to noon and 1.30 to 3.30 pm. The exchange section is on the 1st floor. Queues are more likely here than at the bank's headquarters branch. There's a third Banque de France branch (☎ 42.27.78.14; metro Malesherbes) just north of Parc de Monceau at 1 Place du Général Catroux (17e).

American Express Paris's landmark American Express office (☎ 47.77.70.07; metro Auber, Opéra) at 11 Rue Scribe (9e) faces the west side of Opéra-Garnier. It is open Monday to Friday from 9 am to 5.30 pm and – for currency exchange, cash advances, refunds and poste restante *only* – on Saturday from 9 am to 5 pm. Since you can get slightly better exchange rates elsewhere and this office is often plagued by long lines of impatient tourists, it should be avoided if possible.

Other American Express offices in Paris that offer currency exchange can be found:

- a few blocks north of the Arc de Triomphe at 38 Ave de Wagram, 8e (☎ 42.27.58.80; metro Ternes); open Monday to Friday from 9 am to noon and 1 to 5 pm
- two blocks north of the Palais de Tokyo at 5 Rue de Chaillot, 16e (☎ 47.23.72.15; metro Iéna); open weekdays from 9 am to noon and 1 to 5 pm

For details on cash transfer services and what to do if your American Express card or travellers' cheques are lost or stolen, see Getting Money to France under Money in the Facts for the Visitor chapter.

Citibank Money wired from abroad to Citibank usually arrives at the Citibank Private Bank (☎ 44.43.45.00; metro Alma Marceau) at 17-19 Ave Montaigne (1st floor; 8e), also known as the Banque de Gestion Privée du Citibank, which is 500 metres south-west of Rond-Point des Champs-Élysées. It is open Monday to Friday from 9 am to 1 pm and 2 to 4 pm.

For information on wiring money to Citibank and refunds for Citibank travellers' cheques, see Ways to Bring Money to France under Money in the Facts for the Visitor chapter.

Louvre Area (1er) There are quite a few exchange bureaux along Rue de Rivoli between the Louvre and Place de la Concorde. With the exception of the Banque de France, the best rate in this part of town is available at La Change de Paris (☎ 42.60.30.84; metro Tuileries) at 2 Place Vendôme. It is open Monday to Saturday from 10 am to 6.30 or 7 pm.

Bastille Area (4e) See the Banque de France listing.

Latin Quarter (5e) The Banque Nationale de Paris (☎ 43.29.45.50; metro Luxembourg) at 7 Rue Soufflot exchanges foreign currency Monday to Friday from 9 to 11.45 am and 1 to 5 pm. It also gives Visa cash advances.

Place Saint Michel Area (6e) La Change de Paris (☎ 43.54.76.55; metro Saint Michel),

at 2 Place Saint Michel has some of the best rates in all of Paris. It is open daily from 10 am to 7 pm (9 pm when there are lots of tourists around). Near the southern end of Place Saint Michel, the exchange bureau (☎ 46.34.70.46) at 1 Rue Hautefeuille also has good rates. It is open daily from 9 am to 9 pm (11 pm from June to mid-October).

Champs-Élysées (8e) Thanks to fierce competition, the Champs-Élysées is an excellent place to change foreign currency. The Bureau de Change (☎ 42.25.38.14; metro Franklin D Roosevelt) at 25 Ave des Champs-Élysées has some of the best rates in the city and is an especially good bet on weekends. It is open every day of the year from 9 am to 8 pm. There are other exchange bureaux with decent rates at Nos 71 and 73 Ave des Champs-Élysées.

Montmartre (18e) There's a bureau de change (☎ 42.52.67.19; metro Abbesses) two blocks east of Place des Abbesses at 6 Rue Yvonne Le Tac. It is open Monday to Saturday (and, from April to September, on Sunday) from 11 am to 12.15 pm and 1.15 to 7 pm.

The post office (☎ 46.06.47.83) at Place des Abbesses is equipped with a 24-hour banknote exchange machine.

Post & Telecommunications

All post offices in Paris except the two mentioned below are open Monday to Friday from 8 am to 7 pm and on Saturday from 8 am to noon.

Five blocks north of the east end of the Louvre, the main post office (☎ 40.28.20.20; metro Sentier, Les Halles) at 52 Rue du Louvre (1er) is open seven days a week, 24 hours a day, for sending mail and telegrams, picking up poste restante and making calls with télécartes. Other services, including currency exchange and Chronopost, are available only during regular post office hours. Be prepared for long lines after 7 pm. Poste restante mail not specifically addressed to a particular branch post office ends up here.

At the post office (☎ 44.13.66.00; metro George V) at 71 Ave des Champs-Élysées (8e), you can send letters and telegrams, pick up poste restante and make télécarte phone calls Monday to Saturday from 8 am to 10 pm and on Sunday and holidays from 10 am to noon and 2 to 8 pm. Exchange services are available during regular post office hours.

Postcodes Each arrondissement has its own five-digit postcode, formed by adding 750 to the arrondissement number: 75001 for the 1er (1st arrondissement), 75006 for the 6e (6th) and so forth. All mail to addresses in Paris and anywhere else in France must include the postcode.

Using the Phones For information on how to use the French phone system, see Post & Telecommunications in the Facts for the Visitor chapter.

Télécartes (phone cards) are on sale at post offices, metro ticket counters and many tabacs (tobacconists' shops).

Foreign Embassies

For information on foreign embassies and consulates in Paris, see Visas & Embassies in the Facts for the Visitor chapter.

Cultural & Religious Centres

American Center The American Center (☎ 44.73.77.77; metro Bercy), which sponsors all sorts of cultural events (eg contemporary dance, theatre and cinema, exhibitions of painting and sculpture), recently moved into its huge and striking new home at 51 Rue de Bercy (12e). The innovative, 17,000-sq-metre building, inagurated in 1993, is equipped with a 400-seat theatre, a 100-seat cinema, exhibition galleries, a restaurant, a bookstore and 23 apartments for resident artists and scholars.

British Council The British Council (☎ 49.55.73.00; metro Invalides) at 9-11 Rue de Constantine (7e), across the street from the east side of Esplanade des Invalides, has a lending library (230FF a year for membership) and a free reference library.

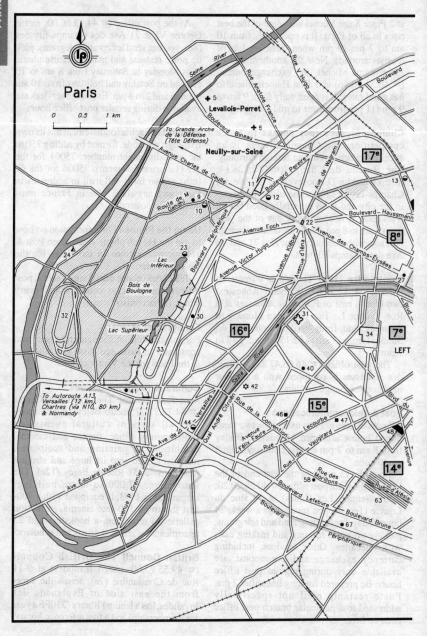

Paris

0   0.5   1 km

Seine River

Levallois-Perret

To Grande Arche
de la Défense
(Tête Défense)

Neuilly-sur-Seine

Rue V. Hugo

Boulevard

Rue Anatole France

Boulevard Bineau

Avenue Charles de Gaulle

17e

Boulevard Pereire

Ave de Wagram

Boulevard – Haussmann

8e

Route de M
Gandhi

Boulevard Périphérique

Lac
Inférieur

Bois de
Boulogne

Lac Supérieur

Avenue Foch

Avenue Victor Hugo

Avenue Kléber

Avenue d'Iéna

Avenue des Champs-Élysées

16e

Seine River

Versailles

To Autoroute A13,
Versailles (12 km),
Chartres (via N10, 80 km)
& Normandy

Quai André Citroën

Rue de la Convention

Avenue
Félix Faure

Rue de Vaugirard

Rue des
Morillons

15e

Rue Lecourbe

7e
LEFT

14e

Rue d'Alésia

Boulevard Lefebvre

Boulevard Brune

Périphérique

Ave de

Ave Édouard Vaillant

Avenue P. Grenier

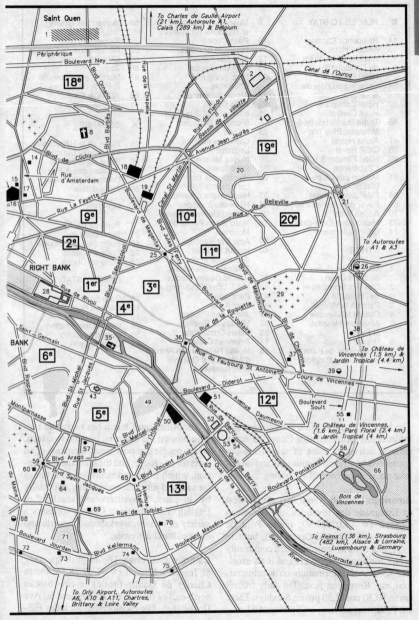

Saint Ouen

1

To Charles de Gaulle Airport
(21 km), Autoroute A1,
Calais (289 km) & Belgium

Périphérique
Boulevard Ney

Canal de l'Ourcq

18e

Rue de la Chapelle

Rue de Flandre

2

Bassin de la Villette

3

4

Rue de la Villette

Blvd Ornano

Blvd Barbès

Avenue Jean Jaurès

19e

8

14

Blvd de Clichy

Rue d'Amsterdam

18

Canal St Martin

20

15

17

16

19

Rue La Fayette

9e

21

FIAP

Rue de Belleville

20e

2e

Boulevard de Magenta

10e

Rue de

To Autoroutes
A1 & A3

25

Blvd Jules Ferry

11e

26

RIGHT BANK

1er

Blvd de Sébastopol

3e

Boulevard de Ménilmontant

29

BANK

28

Rue de Rivoli

4e

Rue de la Roquette

Boulevard Voltaire

Saint – Germain

35

38

6e

Blvd St Michel

Rue St Jacques

36

Rue du Faubourg St Antoine

37

39

To Château de
Vincennes (1.5 km) &
Jardin Tropical (4.4 km)

Blvd Raspail

43

Cours de Vincennes

Montparnasse

49

Boulevard Diderot

51

Avenue Daumesnil

12e

Boulevard
Soult

55

5e

Blvd St Marcel

50

52

To Château de Vincennes,
(1.6 km), Parc Floral (2.4 km)
& Jardin Tropical (4 km)

57

53 54

56

59

Blvd Arago

65

66

60

61

Blvd de l'Hôpital

Quai de Bercy

Bois de
Vincennes

64

Rue de Bercy

Blvd Saint Jacques

Avenue d'Italie

13e

Quai de la Gare

Boulevard Poniatowski

68

69

Rue de Tolbiac

70

71

Boulevard Masséna

To Reims (136 km), Strasbourg
(482 km), Alsace & Lorraine,
Luxembourg & Germany

72

Blvd Jourdan

73

74

Blvd Kellermann

75

Seine River

Autoroute A4

To Orly Airport, Autoroutes
A6, A10 & A11, Chartres,
Brittany & Loire Valley

du Maine

	PLACES TO STAY	9	Musée National des Arts et Traditions Populaires	58	Bureau des Objets Trouvés (Lost Property Office)
14	Résidence Cardinal	10	Paris Cycles		
15	Atlantic Hôtel	11	Palais de Congrès	62	Bibliothèque de France
17	Austin's Hôtel, Hôtel du Calvados & Hôtel Britannia	12	ADA Car Rental	63	Clothing Stores
		13	ADA Car Rental	66	Zoo
		20	Parc des Buttes Chaumont	67	Marché aux Puces de la Porte de Vanves
24	Camping du Bois de Boulogne	22	Arc de Triomphe	68	ADA Car Rental
37	Hôtel Camélia & Hôtel Central	23	Paris Cycles	71	Parc Montsouris
		26	International Bus Station (Porte de Bagnolet)	✕	SQUARES
46	Three Ducks Hostel & Mountain Bike Trip	28	Louvre		
47	Aloha Hostel	29	Cimetière du Père Lachaise	25	Place de la République
55	CISP Ravel			27	Place de la Concorde
60	Hôtel Floridor & Hôtel L'Espérance	30	Musée Marmottan	36	Place de la Bastille
		31	Eiffel Tower	59	Catacombes & Place Denfert Rochereau
61	Maison des Clubs UNESCO	32	Hippodrome de Longchamp	65	Place d'Italie
64	FIAP Jean Monnet	33	Hippodrome d'Auteuil		
69	Foyer des Jeunes Filles	34	Hôtel des Invalides		PORTES
70	Adrian Hôtel	35	Cathédrale Notre Dame		
73	Maison des États-Unis	38	Marché aux Puces de Montreuil	7	Porte de Clichy
74	CISP Kellermann			21	Porte des Lilas
		39	Acar Car Rental	45	Porte de Saint Cloud
	OTHER	40	Institut Parisien de Langue et de Civilisation Françaises	72	Porte d'Orléans
				75	Porte de Choisy
1	Marché aux Puces de Saint Ouen	41	Roland Garros Stadium		RAILWAY STATIONS
2	Cité des Sciences et de l'Industrie	42	MJLF Liberal Synagogue		
		43	Panthéon	16	Gare Saint Lazare
3	Parc de la Villette	44	Rent A Car	18	Gare du Nord
4	Cité de la Musique	49	Jardin des Plantes	19	Gare de l'Est
5	American Hospital of Paris	52	Ministry of Finance	48	Gare Montparnasse
		53	Palais Omnisports	50	Gare d'Austerlitz
6	Hôpital Franco-Britannique de Paris	54	American Center	51	Gare de Lyon
		56	Musée National des Arts d'Afrique et d'Océanie		
8	Sacré Cœur Basilica	57	SOS Dentaire		

The bulletin board outside the entrance has information on the British Council's many cultural activities, most of which are co-sponsored by French institutions and do not take place at the council's building.

American Church About 400 metres west of Esplanade des Invalides, the American Church (☎ 47.05.07.99; metro Pont de l'Alma) at 65 Quai d'Orsay (7e), built in 1931, functions as something of a community centre for English speakers and is an excellent source of information on apartments, jobs, etc. Reception is staffed daily from 9 am to 10.30 pm (7.30 pm on Sunday). There are Protestant services on Sunday at 11 am.

The American Church has two main bulletin boards: the informal board downstairs, where people can post announcements of all sorts for no charge; and the board near reception, which lists apartments for rent, things for sale and jobs that need filling, especially by au pairs, babysitters and teachers of English. The American Church sponsors a variety of classes, workshops, concerts and other cultural activities.

Catholic Churches The English-speaking St Joseph's Church (☎ 42.27.28.56; metro Charles de Gaulle-Étoile) is two blocks north-east of the Arc de Triomphe at 50 Ave Hoche (8e). The membership includes Fili-

pinos and people from the Indian subcontinent as well as Europeans and North Americans.

Mass is celebrated in English from Monday to Friday at 8.30 am; on Saturday at 11 am and 6.30 pm; and on Sunday at 9.45 am, 11 am, 12.15 pm and 6.30 pm. In July and August, there are only three Sunday masses: at 10 am, noon and 6.30 pm. Confessions in English are held on Saturday from 11.30 am to 12.30 pm and 5 to 6 pm, and on other days there is almost always an English-speaking priest on duty. Reception is staffed from 10 am to noon and 2 to 6 pm (closed Wednesday and Sunday).

Masses are celebrated in French at scores of churches around Paris, including Notre Dame.

Church of Scotland The Scots Kirk (☎ 48.78.47.94; metro Franklin D Roosevelt) at 17 Rue Bayard (8e) is half a block south of Ave Montaigne. Sunday prayers are held at 10.30 am.

Mosque For information on Paris's main *mosquée* (☎ 45.35.97.33; metro Monge), which is on Rue Georges Desplas (5e), see Mosquée de Paris under Jardin des Plantes Area in the Things to See section.

Liberal Synagogue The main synagogue (☎ 45.75.38.01; metro Charles Michels) of the Mouvement Juif Libéral de France, an affiliate of the World Union for Progressive Judaism, is at 11 Rue Gaston de Caillavet (15e), which is under the red, 30-storey Hôtel Nikko tower near the Centre Beaugrenelle shopping complex. For security reasons, the entrance is a bit hard to find – look for a small sign reading 'MJLF'. *Offices* (services) are conducted in Hebrew and French by the congregation's three rabbis *(rabbins)*, including the first woman rabbi in Continental Europe. Men are required to wear skullcaps. Services are held year round on Friday at 6.15 pm and on Saturday at 10.30 am.

There is a second, less liberal Liberal synagogue (☎ 47.04.37.27; metro Victor Hugo)

700 metres south-west of the Arc de Triomphe at 24 Rue Copernic (16e). Services are at 6 pm on Friday and 10.30 am on Saturday.

Travel Agencies
General Nouvelles Frontières (☎ 41.41.58.58), a chain which specialises in discount long-haul plane tickets, has about 15 bureaux around Paris, including those at:

* 13 Rue de l'Échelle, 1er (☎ 42.60.01.87; metro Palais Royal), which is two blocks north of the west end of the Louvre
* 66 Blvd Saint Michel, 6e (☎ 46.34.55.30; metro Luxembourg), a bit south of the Jardin du Luxembourg; open Monday to Saturday from 9 am to 7.30 pm
* 109 Rue de Rennes, 6e (☎ 45.44.01.00; metro Rennes), which is one km north-east of Gare Montparnasse; open Monday to Saturday from 9 am to 7 pm

Other travel agencies offering discount air tickets include: Selectour Voyages (☎ 43.29.64.00; metro Saint Michel) at 29 Rue de la Huchette (5e), which is open weekdays from 9.45 am to 6.30 pm; and FNAC Voyages (☎ 40.41.40.77/8/9; metro Châtelet-Les Halles) in the Forum des Halles shopping mall on Rue Pierre Lescot (1er). From the FNAC store's *billeterie* (ticket counter) on the Niveau -3 (minus three level), walk up the small staircase. It's open Monday to Saturday from 10 am to 7.30 pm.

Near the Gare du Nord, Transchannel (☎ 40.34.71.50; fax 40.34.71.52; metro Gare du Nord) at 24 Rue de Saint Quentin (10e) specialises in getting people to the other side of the English Channel. It is open Monday to Friday from 9.30 am to 7 pm and on Saturday from 10 am to 1 pm.

From June to mid-September, Anyway (☎ 40.28.00.74; fax 42.36.11.41; metro Châtelet) at 46 Rue des Lombards (1er), not far from the Centre Pompidou, offers standby flights to North America, with one-way tickets to New York for as little as 1000FF. Their other fares (with the exception of the weekly promotions) are not necessarily the cheapest around. The office is open Monday

to Friday from 10 am to 7 pm and on Saturday from 11 am to 6 pm.

Student Travel Agencies The main office of Accueil des Jeunes en France (AJF; ☎ 42.77.87.80; metro Rambuteau), right across the square from the entrance to the Centre Pompidou at 119 Rue Saint Martin (4e), does more than find travellers places to stay (see Accommodation Services under Places to Stay): it also functions as a travel agency and issues ISTC student ID cards and Cartes Jeunes. AJF's services are available to people of all ages. The office is open Monday to Saturday from 9 am to 5.30 pm (6.30 pm from June to September).

Council Travel (☎ 44.55.55.44; metro Pyramides), the US student travel company, has its main Paris office at 22 Rue des Pyramides (1er). It is open Monday to Friday from 9.30 am to 7 pm (8 pm on Tuesday) and on Saturday from 10 am to 6 pm. Council Travel has two other bureaux in Paris: at 51 Rue Dauphine (6e; metro Odéon), which is in Saint Germain des Prés; and at 16 Rue Vaugirard (6e; metro Luxembourg), which is just west of the Latin Quarter near the Palais du Luxembourg.

Holders of plane tickets issued by Council Travel in North America and elsewhere can come to these offices to get lost tickets replaced, make reservations for tickets with open returns and change flight dates (but not routes). Refunds are available from the issuing office only.

The Irish student travel outfit, USIT (☎ 43.29.85.00; fax 43.54.04.54; metro Odéon), has an office at the western edge of the Latin Quarter at 6 Rue de Vaugirard (6e). It's open Monday to Friday from 9.30 am to 6 pm and on Saturday from 1 to 4 pm. USIT has a second office (☎ 42.96.15.88; metro Bourse) a bit north of the Jardin du Palais Royal at 12 Rue Vivienne (2e). It's open Monday to Friday from 9.30 am to 6 pm (8 pm on Thursday).

BIJ Tickets BIJ and BSE discount train tickets are available at all of the student travel agencies listed here. For information

on buying a BIJ or BSE ticket near each of Paris's railway stations, see the listing for each station under Train in the Getting There & Away section of this chapter.

Left-Luggage Services
There are *consignes manuelles* (left-luggage offices) and *consignes automatiques* (luggage lockers) at all six railway stations and at both airports (but not at Aérogare des Invalides).

Books & Magazines
Guidebooks to Paris – most of them intended for people interested in self-guided walking tours – are listed under Guidebooks in the Books section of the Facts for the Visitor chapter.

Public Library
For information on the huge, free Bibliothèque Publique d'Information in the Centre Pompidou, see the Centre Pompidou listing under Things to See.

English Bookshops
Travel Guides Lonely Planet books and other travel guides are available for about double the Australian or North American cover prices from a number of stores around Place Saint Michel, including Astrolabe (☎ 46.33.80.06; metro Cluny-La Sorbonne) at 14 Rue Serpente (6e), Hachette Espace Évasion (☎ 46.34.89.51; metro Cluny-La Sorbonne) at 77 Blvd Saint Germain (6e) and Gibert Jeune (☎ 43.25.70.07; metro Saint Michel), which is on the east side of Place Saint Michel on the corner of Rue de la Huchette (5e).

But the best prices for LP titles can usually be found in the guidebook sections of the FNAC stores – there's one in the Forum des Halles shopping mall (☎ 40.41.40.00) on Rue Pierre Lescot (1er) and another one (☎ 49.54.30.00; metro Saint Placide) 500 metres north of Gare Montparnasse at 136 Rue de Rennes (6e).

General Paris's most famous English book-

shop, Shakespeare & Company (no phone; metro Saint Michel), is across the Seine from Notre Dame at 37 Rue de la Bûcherie (5e). The shop, a 1950s hang-out of Beat Generation poets, has a varied and unpredictable collection of new and used English books in English, but even the second-hand stuff doesn't come cheap. It is generally open daily from 10 am to about midnight.

Shakespeare & Co has poetry readings most Mondays at 8 pm. On many Sundays, there's a 'literary tea' in George Whitman's 3rd-floor apartment (where some of this book was written) at 4 pm. People hanging out in the store around that time may be invited (or compelled, depending on George's mood) to join the proceedings. The shop is named after Sylvia Beach's bookshop at 12 Rue de l'Odéon, closed by the Nazis in 1941, which became famous for publishing James Joyce's *Ulysses* in 1922.

The mellow Abbey Bookshop (☎ 46.33. 16.24; metro Cluny-La Sorbonne), not far from Place Saint Michel at 27 Rue de la Parcheminerie (5e), has a good selection of Canadian literature, a number of Canadian newspapers and free tea and coffee for browsers. It is also something of a gathering place for Canadian expats. The bookshop is open Monday to Saturday from 11 am to at least 10 pm and perhaps on Sunday from 3 to 10 pm.

Two blocks south of Saint Germain des Prés, the Village Voice bookshop (☎ 46. 33.36.47; metro Mabillon) at 6 Rue Princesse (6e) is open on Monday from 2 to 8 pm and Tuesday to Saturday from 11 am to 8 pm. It often sponsors poetry readings and talks.

Paris's largest English-language bookshop is W H Smith (☎ 44.77.88.99; metro Concorde) at 248 Rue de Rivoli (1er), which is one block east of Place de la Concorde. Its orientation is more English than American. From Monday to Saturday, hours are 9.30 am to 7 pm. Be prepared for very high prices.

Brentano's (☎ 42.61.52.50; metro Opéra), midway between the Louvre and Opéra-Garnier at 37 Ave de l'Opéra (2e), is open Monday to Saturday from 10 am to 6.55 pm.

Gay Bookshop Paris's pemier gay bookshop is Librairie Les Mots à la Bouche (☎ 42.78.88.30; metro Hôtel de Ville) at 6 Rue Sainte Croix de la Bretonnerie (4e), in the heart of Paris's main gay neighbourhood. It specialises in books written by homosexuals or with gay or lesbian themes, magazines (including some in English) and gay guidebooks (including the *Spartacus International Gay Guide*, the *Gay City Guide* series and the *Guide Gai* to France, Brussels and Switzerland). Most of the back wall is dedicated to books in English, including lots of novels. The shop is open Monday to Saturday from 11 am to 11 pm (midnight or 1 am on Saturday).

Maps

The most useful map of Paris is the *Paris Plan* published by Michelin, which indicates street numbers, metro exits, taxi stands, one-way streets, major public buildings, museums, petrol stations and post offices. It is in 1:10,000 scale, which means 1 cm=100 metres. It comes in both booklet form *(Paris Plan 11)* and sheet form *(Paris Plan 10/12)*; the latter is more useful if you're driving. It is available at most bookshops and some stationery stores. Make sure you get the latest edition: in the booklets, the date of publication is indicated on the last page; on the sheets it's next to the bar code.

Some people prefer the pocket-sized map books called *Paris par Arrondissement*, which have a double-page street plan of each arrondissement. The best versions have a comprehensive index of streets, a map of the metro on the inside cover and extensive lists of Parisian sights, hotels etc. Some also have a fold-out map of Paris attached to the inside back cover and street maps of nearby suburbs, such as Montreuil and Vincennes.

Lost & Found

All lost objects found anywhere in Paris – except those discovered on trains or in the railway stations – are eventually brought to the city's infamous Bureau des Objets Trouvés (Lost Property Office; ☎ 45.31. 14.80; metro Convention) at 36 Rue des

Morillons (15e), which is run by the Préfecture de Police. Since telephone enquiries are virtually impossible, you have to go there and fill out some forms to see if what you've lost has been located. The office is open from 8.30 am to 5 pm on Monday and Wednesday, to 5.30 pm on Friday, and to 8 pm on Tuesday and Thursday. In July and August, closing time is 5 pm every day.

Items found on trains or in railway stations are taken to the *objets trouvés* office of the relevant train station. Telephone enquiries (in French) are possible:

Gare d'Austerlitz	☎ 44.24.08.36
Gare de l'Est	☎ 40.18.88.73
Gare de Lyon	☎ 43.47.32.56
Gare Montparnasse	☎ 40.48.14.24
Gare du Nord	☎ 49.95.58.40
Gare Saint Lazare	☎ 40.08.95.57

Public Baths
Before WW II, a high percentage of Paris's working-class apartments lacked bathroom facilities. Even today, a fair number of poorer Parisians live in showerless flats, which is why the municipality runs 20 or so *bains-douches municipaux* (municipal bath houses), where a shower costs only 6FF – a lot less than at many cheap hotels. Facilities for both men and women are available.

Centre Pompidou Area (4e) The Bains-Douches Municipaux (☎ 42.77.71.90; metro Rambuteau) at 18 Rue du Renard – in the same building as the swimming pool – are open on Wednesday from noon to 7 pm, Thursday to Saturday from 7 or 8 am to 7 pm and on Sunday from 8 am to noon.

Île Saint Louis (4e) The Bains-Douches Municipaux (☎ 43.54.47.40; metro Pont Marie) at 8 Rue des Deux Ponts are open the same hours as their Latin Quarter counterparts.

Latin Quarter (5e) Just east of Place de la Contrescarpe, the Bains-Douches Municipaux (☎ 45.35.46.63; metro Monge) at 50 Rue Lacépède are open on Thursday from

noon to 7 pm, on Friday from 8 am to 7 pm, on Saturday from 7 am to 7 pm and on Sunday from 8 am to noon.

Gay Paris
General information for homosexual travellers is listed under Gay & Lesbian Travellers in the Facts for the Visitor chapter. In the Paris chapter, details about gay and lesbian life can be found under the following headings:

- Gay Bookshop under Bookshops in the Information section
- Gay Hotel under Marais in the Places to Stay section
- Bars under Louvre Area, Centre Pompidou and Marais in the Places to Drink listings
- French Chansons and Discothèques under Entertainment

Medical Services
There are about 50 Assistance Publique (public health service) hospitals in Paris. Each has its medical specialities, but almost all have the facilities to deal with general health problems. For information on France's public health care system, see Health in the Facts for the Visitor chapter.

Perhaps the easiest hospital to find is the Hôtel Dieu (☎ 42.34.82.34; metro Cité), founded in 651 AD, which is on the north side of Place du Parvis Notre Dame (4e), the square in front of Notre Dame. The present building was constructed from 1866 to 1878. The 24-hour emergency room (*service des urgences*) treats everything from stomach upset to serious illnesses. The payments office (*caisse centrale des consultations*), which takes cash or credit cards (but not travellers' cheques), is off the interior courtyard next to the main entrance; it's open Monday to Friday from 8 am to 5 pm. Another cashier in the Centre du Diagnostic is open on weekdays until 6.30 pm, but the rest of the time there's no way to pay without coming back during office hours.

The 187-bed American Hospital of Paris (☎ 46.41.25.25; fax 46.24.49.38), founded in 1910 and known in French as the Hôpital

Américain de Paris, is a private, nonprofit hospital offering American-style medical treatment. It is two km north-west of Porte Maillot (16e) at 63 Blvd Victor Hugo in the quiet, inner north-western suburb of Neuilly-sur-Seine. Emergency medical and dental care is available 24 hours a day. All staff members speak English, but only six of the doctors are from the USA. Care here is considerably more expensive than at public hospitals, and unless you're insured under certain policies issued by Blue Cross-Blue Shield, you may be asked to pay at least part of the projected costs when you're admitted.

For information on insurance coverage for care at the American Hospital, call ☎ 46.41.25.65. To get there by public transport, take RATP bus No 82 from in front of the Palais des Congrès (convention centre; metro Porte Maillot) at Porte Maillot (16e); Place du 18 Juin 1940 (6e & 15e; metro Montparnasse Bienvenüe); or Blvd Saint Michel (5e & 6e; metro Luxembourg) near the Jardin du Luxembourg. The postal address is 63 Blvd Victor Hugo, BP 109, 92202 Neuilly CEDEX.

A less expensive English-speaking option is the 90-bed Hôpital Franco-Britannique de Paris (☎ 46.39.22.22; metro Anatole France), which is at 3 Rue Barbès in the near north-western suburb of Levallois-Perret (postcode 92300). It is privately run but is affiliated with the French national health system, so the fees are about the same as those at Assistance Publique hospitals. Most of the staff are French, but when making an appointment you can request to see a GP from the UK. People from outside the EC are asked to pay and then later get reimbursed by their insurance companies.

The US Embassy has a list of English-speaking doctors, but private practitioners are usually quite a bit more expensive than Assistance Publique hospitals.

Dental Care Although most Assistance Publique hospitals have in-house dental clinics, La Pitié-Salpêtrière hospital (☎ 45.70.22.59; metro Gare d'Austerlitz), next to Gare d'Austerlitz at 47 Blvd de

l'Hôpital (13e), is the only one with extended hours. The regular *service de stomatologie* (dental treatment service) is open Monday to Friday from 9 am to 12.30 pm and 2.30 to 5.30 pm, and also on Saturday morning; it's a good idea to make an appointment. Emergency dental treatment, for which you don't need an appointment, is available whenever the regular dental treatment service is closed, including all night long and 24 hours a day on weekends and holidays. A consultation costs about 300FF. The billing procedure is similar to that of the Hôtel Dieu hospital.

SOS Dentaire (☎ 43.37.51.00; metro Port Royal) at 87 Blvd de Port Royal (13e) is a private dentists' office that is open when most dentists are off duty: Monday to Friday from 8 to 11.40 pm and on weekends and holidays from 9 am to noon and 2 to 11.40 pm. If you have an urgent problem, call to set up an appointment. A consultation and treatment generally costs 200 to 500FF. Payment must be made in cash.

Emergency dental care is also available at the American Hospital (see Hospitals).

Pharmacies Medications can be purchased 24 hours a day, 365 days a year at Pharmacie des Champs (☎ 45.62.02.41; fax 45.63.83.79; metro George V), which is inside the shopping arcade at 84 Ave des Champs-Élysées (8e). The staff speak English and can consult the *International Drug Directory*, which cross-references the various names under which drugs are sold around the world.

Near Notre Dame and the Hôtel Dieu hospital, Pharmacie de la Huchette (☎ 43.54.13.03; metro Saint Michel) at 16 Rue de la Huchette (5e) is open every day of the year from 9.30 am (11 am on Sunday and holidays) to 10 pm.

Vaccinations Air France's Centre de Vaccinations (☎ 43.20.13.50, 43.23.94.64; metro Invalides) in Aérogare des Invalides at 2 Rue Robert Esnault Pelterie (7e) provides immunisations against: *choléra* (80FF), *fièvre jaune* (yellow fever; 170FF), *hépatite virale B* (hepatitis B; 170FF), *méningite* (meningitis; 100FF), *tétanos et poliomyélite* (tetanus

and polio; 80FF) and other diseases. It is open Monday to Saturday from 9.45 am to 4.45 pm. You don't need an appointment.

Emergency

Emergency telephone numbers include the following:

Police	☎ 17
Fire Brigade	☎ 18
SAMU (ambulance)	☎ 15 or 45.67.50.50
Urgences Médicales (24-hour house calls)	☎ 48.28.40.04
SOS Médecin (24-hour house calls)	☎ 47.07.77.77

For more information, see the Emergency Telephone Numbers section under Dangers & Annoyances in the Facts for the Visitor chapter.

Toilets

The tan toilet pods you see on Paris's pavements are open 24 hours a day and cost 2FF. It's worth the money just to see the mechanism that automatically cleans and disinfects them after each use. Another option is to duck into a fast-food place.

Laundry

The *laveries* (laundrettes) listed here are near many of the hotels and hostels listed under Places to Stay.

Marais (4e) There's a slightly run-down (but cheap) Laverie (metro Saint Paul) at 40 Rue du Roi de Sicile. A bit to the west, the laundrette (metro Hôtel de Ville) at 35 Rue Sainte Croix de la Bretonnerie is open daily from 7.30 am to 10 pm.

The Laverie Libre Service (metro Bastille) at 4 Impasse Guéménée, which is just off Rue Saint Antoine 200 metres west of Place de la Bastille, is open daily from 7 am to 9 pm.

Bastille Area (4e & 11e) Just east of Place de la Bastille, the laundrette (metro Bastille) at 2 Rue de Lappe is open daily from 7 am to 10 pm.

Latin Quarter (5e) Thanks to the area's student population, laundrettes are plentiful in this part of Paris. Three blocks south-west of the Panthéon, the laundrette (metro Luxembourg) at 216 Rue Saint Jacques is open from 7 am to 10 pm.

Just south of the Arènes de Lutèce, the Lavomatique (metro Monge) at 63 Rue Monge is open daily from 6.30 am to 10 pm. Near Place de la Contrescarpe, Le Bateau Lavoir (metro Cardinal Lemoine) at 1 Rue Thouin is open daily from 7 am to 10 pm.

Place Saint Michel Area (6e) Just west of Place Saint Michel, there's a laundrette (metro Saint Michel) at 12 Rue Gît le Cœur.

Saint Germain des Prés (6e) There is a Lav' Club (metro Mabillon) at 56 Rue de Seine.

Gare de l'Est (10e) Two blocks north-east of the station, the laundrette (metro Château Landon) at 25 Rue du Terrage is open daily from 7 am to 10 pm.

Montmartre (18e) There are a couple of laundrettes on Rue des Trois Frères, including the Lavoir (metro Abbesses) at No 63, which is open daily from 7 am to 10 pm.

Dangers & Annoyances

Crime In general, Paris is a safe city, especially when compared to any large or medium-sized urban area in the USA, and most of it's quite well lit. You should, of course, always use common sense, and the Bois de Boulogne and Bois de Vincennes are probably best avoided after nightfall, but there is no reason not to use the metro until it stops running (around 12.45 am). As you'll notice, women *do* travel alone on the metro late at night, at least in most areas.

Nonviolent crime (such as pickpocketing and thefts from handbags or packs) is a problem wherever there are crowds, especially crowds of tourists. Places to be especially careful include Montmartre, Pigalle, the area around Forum des Halles and on the metro at rush hour.

Metro stations that are probably best avoided late at night – especially if you are alone – include Châtelet and its many seemingly endless tunnels to Les Halles and Châtelet-Les Halles stations; Blanche, Pigalle and Château Rouge in the vicinity of Montmartre and Pigalle; Gare du Nord; and Strasbourg-Saint Denis.

Remembrance of Dogs Past The Paris municipality spends vast sums of money to keep the pavements relatively passable, and the technology they employ is undeniably impressive. But evidence that a recent campaign to get people to clean up after their pooches – the latest in a long series of such noble civic efforts – has been less than a smashing success can be discerned in the form of diarrhoeal souvenirs left by recently walked poodles, often found smeared along the pavement (by daydreaming strollers, one assumes, or guidebook writers overly intent on jotting something down). Until that far-off time when Parisians – and the dog-lovers among them – modify their philosophy of life, the word on the streets is likely to remain: watch where you step.

THINGS TO SEE

Walking around is arguably Paris's most pleasant and stimulating activity. To make this chapter as useful as possible for strollers, sights are grouped by area, and areas are listed sequentially by arrondissement number, starting with the 1er and going up to the 20e. The Bois de Boulogne and the Bois de Vincennes appear at the end.

For information on Chantilly, Chartres, Compiègne, EuroDisneyland, Fontaine-bleau, La Défense, the Musée de l'Air et de l'Espace (the Aeronautics & Space Museum), Saint Denis and Versailles, see the Day Trips from Paris chapter.

Museum Information

Paris has about 70 museums of all sizes; a comprehensive list is available from the tourist office. *L'Officiel des Spectacles* magazine (see Entertainment) has brief entries in French that include up-to-the-minute opening hours.

The Musées Nationaux (museums run by the French government) in the Paris region (eg the Louvre, Musée de Cluny, Musée Picasso, Musée de l'Orangerie) are open daily except Tuesday. The only exceptions to this rule are the Musée d'Orsay, the Musée Rodin and Versailles, which are open daily except Monday. The Musées Nationaux are half-price if you're 18 to 24 or over 60, and free for people under 18.

The Musées de la Ville de Paris (☎ 42.76.67.00 for information), Paris's municipal museums, are open daily except Monday. Entry is half-price for people aged 18 to 24 and is free (half-price for special exhibitions) for people under 18 or over 60.

Museum Pass The Carte Musées et Monuments (☎ 44.78.45.81) gets you into the permanent exhibits (but not temporary exhibitions) of 65 museums and monuments in the Paris region without having to stand in the ticket queue. It costs 60/120/170FF for one/three/five consecutive days and is on sale at the museums and monuments it covers, certain metro ticket windows and the tourist office. Students, children and people over 60 may find that paying the reduced-price fee at each museum works out cheaper. In any case, the investment is worthwhile only if you've decided to do a lot of museum-hopping during a short period of time. Nothing can spoil a museum visit more thoroughly than visiting when you're all museumed out.

Louvre Area (1er & 8e)

From the enormous Palais du Louvre, you can walk in literally any direction and come upon some well-known sight, including many of Paris's most famous public spaces: the Jardin des Tuileries, the Palais Royal, Place Vendôme, Place de la Concorde, La Madeleine and, of course, the Champs-Élysées. The 1er arrondissement, like the 7e, 8e, 16e and the southern 17e, has long been a chic residential area for people of means.

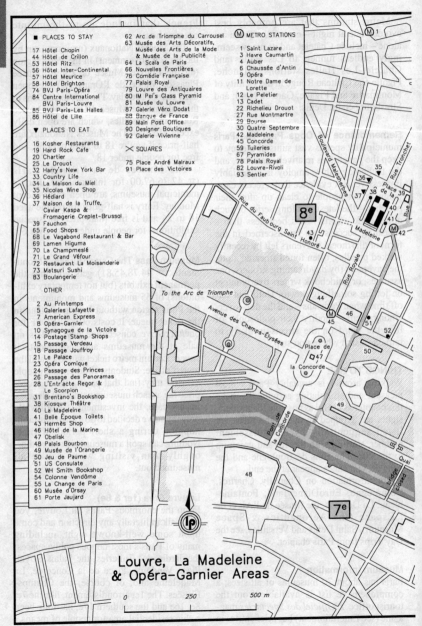

■ PLACES TO STAY
17 Hôtel Chopin
44 Hôtel de Crillon
53 Hôtel Ritz
56 Hôtel Inter-Continental
57 Hôtel Meurice
58 Hôtel Brighton
74 BVJ Paris-Opéra
84 Centre International
   BVJ Paris-Louvre
85 BVJ Paris-Les Halles
86 Hôtel de Lille

▼ PLACES TO EAT
16 Kosher Restaurants
19 Hard Rock Cafe
20 Chartier
25 Le Drouot
32 Harry's New York Bar
33 Country Life
34 La Maison du Miel
35 Nicolas Wine Shop
36 Hédiard
37 Maison de la Truffe,
   Caviar Kaspa &
   Fromagerie Creplet-Brussol
39 Fauchon
65 Food Shops
68 Le Vagabond Restaurant & Bar
69 Lamen Higuma
70 La Champmeslé
71 Le Grand Véfour
72 Restaurant La Moisanderie
73 Matsuri Sushi
83 Boulangerie

   OTHER
2 Au Printemps
5 Galeries Lafayette
7 American Express
8 Opéra-Garnier
10 Synagogue de la Victoire
12 Postage Stamp Shops
15 Passage Verdeau
18 Passage Jouffroy
21 Le Palace
23 Opéra Comique
24 Passage des Princes
26 Passage des Panoramas
28 L'Entracte Regor &
   Le Scorpion
31 Brentano's Bookshop
38 Kiosque Théâtre
40 La Madeleine
41 Belle Époque Toilets
43 Hermès Shop
46 Hôtel de la Marine
47 Obelisk
48 Palais Bourbon
49 Musée de l'Orangerie
50 Jeu de Paume
51 US Consulate
52 WH Smith Bookshop
54 Colonne Vendôme
55 La Change de Paris
60 Musée d'Orsay
61 Porte Jaujard

62 Arc de Triomphe du Carrousel
63 Musée des Arts Décoratifs,
   Musée des Arts de la Mode
   & Musée de la Publicité
64 La Scala de Paris
66 Nouvelles Frontières
76 Comédie Française
77 Palais Royal
79 Louvre des Antiquaires
80 IM Pei's Glass Pyramid
81 Musée du Louvre
87 Galerie Véro Dodat
88 Banque de France
89 Main Post Office
90 Designer Boutiques
92 Galerie Vivienne

✕ SQUARES
75 Place André Malraux
91 Place des Victoires

Ⓜ METRO STATIONS
1 Saint Lazare
3 Havre Caumartin
4 Auber
6 Chaussée d'Antin
9 Opéra
11 Notre Dame de
   Lorette
12 Le Peletier
13 Cadet
22 Richelieu Drouot
27 Rue Montmartre
29 Bourse
30 Quatre Septembre
42 Madeleine
45 Concorde
59 Tuileries
78 Palais Royal
82 Louvre-Rivoli
93 Sentier

8ᵉ

7ᵉ

Louvre, La Madeleine
& Opéra-Garnier Areas

0   250   500 m

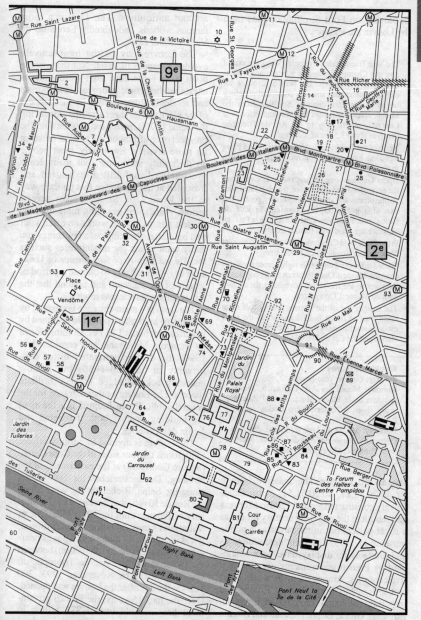

Exploring on Foot Strolling options from the Louvre are legion:

- The Voie Triomphale (Triumphal Way), the axis of Ave des Champs-Élysées as it heads north-west-ward from the Louvre, has been a favourite for elegant promenades since its construction, which began in the 16th century. Strolling from the Louvre across Jardin des Tuileries and Place de la Concorde all the way to the Arc de Triomphe involves about 3.5 km of walking.

- North of the Tuileries, Rue Saint Honoré and Place Vendôme have some of the most expensive stores in Paris.

- Opéra-Garnier is one km north of the Louvre along the prestigious Ave de l'Opéra, which is lined with airline offices and shops selling luxury goods. You can also get to Opéra-Garnier via Rue de Castiglione, Place Vendôme and Rue de la Paix, all of which are lined with famous luxury boutiques.

- From Place de la Concorde, it's a short and elegant walk up Rue Royale to La Madeleine.

- Since Jardin des Tuileries is right across the Seine from the Musée d'Orsay, you can easily pop across the river to see the sights covered in the section entitled Musée d'Orsay Area.

- The eastern end of the Louvre is only half a km north-west of Île de la Cité and about the same distance south-west of the lively streets around Les Halles and the Centre Pompidou.

Weekly Closures

Sunday: Galerie Véro-Dodat

Monday: Musée des Arts Décoratifs, Musée des Arts de la Mode, Musée de la Publicité, many shops in Galerie Véro Dodat, Jeu de Paume

Tuesday: Musée du Louvre, Musée des Arts Décoratifs, Musée des Arts de la Mode, Musée de la Publicité, Musée de l'Orangerie

---

Musée du Louvre The massive Louvre (☎ 40.20.53.17, 40.20.51.51; metro Palais Royal), constructed around 1200 as a fortress and rebuilt in the mid-16th century for use as a royal palace, began its career as a public museum in 1793. The paintings, sculptures and artefacts on display have been assembled by French governments over the past five centuries. Among them are works of art and artisanship from all over Europe and important collections of Assyrian, Egyptian, Etruscan, Greek, Coptic, Roman and Islamic art and antiquities. The Louvre's most famous work is undoubtedly Leonardo da Vinci's *Mona Lisa*.

The Louvre may be the most actively avoided museum in Paris. Not that people don't come – the huge high-season queues attest that they come in droves – but tourists and residents alike, daunted by the richness of the place and its sheer size (the side facing the Seine is 700 metres long) often find the prospect of an afternoon at a smaller museum far more inviting. Eventually, most people do their duty and come, but many leave overwhelmed, unfulfilled, exhausted and frustrated at having gotten lost on their way to the *Mona Lisa*. Since it takes several serious visits to get anything more than the briefest glimpse of the works on offer, your best bet – after checking out a few things you really want to see (eg masterpieces such as the *Winged Victory of Samothrace* or *Venus de Milo*) – is probably to choose a period or section of the museum and pretend that the rest is somewhere across town.

The Louvre's main entrance is covered by a 21-metre-high **glass pyramid** designed by American architect I M Pei. Commissioned by François Mitterrand and completed in 1990, the design generated bitter controversy in the mid-1980s but is now generally acknowledged to be a brilliant success. The Louvre's other entrance for the general public, **Porte Jaujard**, is at the tip of the building nearest both the Seine and Jardin des Tuileries.

The Louvre is divided into four sections. Sully forms the four sides of the Cour Carrée (Square Courtyard) at the eastern end of the building. Denon stretches for 500 metres along the Seine. Richelieu, the wing along the Rue de Rivoli, was occupied by the Ministry of Finance until the late 1980s. One of Mitterrand's most ambitious *grands projets*, it was inaugurated – along with a huge underground complex (the fourth section) between the pyramid and the Arc de Triomphe du Carrousel – on 18 November 1993, 200 years to the day after the Louvre was opened. Over the past 15 years, the French government has invested over US$1 billion in

restoring, renovating and enlarging the Louvre.

From Thursday to Sunday, the Louvre is open from 9 am to 5.30 pm. On Monday and Wednesday, it's open from 9 am to 9.30 pm, but on Monday only the Richelieu wing is open after 5.30 pm. Ticket sales end 30 minutes before closing time. The entrance fee is 35FF (20FF if you're 18 to 25 or over 60), but on Sunday everyone gets in for 20FF. The Louvre is most crowded on weekends, especially – for obvious reasons – on Sunday. In summer, be prepared for long queues. The best times to come if you want to avoid the crowds are early in the morning or on Wednesday night.

Hall Napoléon, the split-level public area under the pyramid, includes an exhibit on the history of the Louvre, a bookshop, a restaurant, a café and auditoriums for concerts, lectures and films. It is open from 9 am to 10 pm (closed Tuesday). Daypacks and other small items must be left at the free *vestiaire* (cloakroom), which is on the Accueil level under the escalators to the Denon wing. The *bagagerie* next door handles larger bags.

English-language **guided tours** (☎ 40. 20.52.09) lasting 1½ hours are held four times a day (seven times a day in summer) except on Sunday – when the museum is too crowded – and Tuesday. They leave from the Accueil des Groupes desk under the pyramid. Tickets cost 32FF (free for children under 13) on top of the museum entry fee. Groups are limited to 20, so it's a good idea to sign up half an hour or 45 minutes before departure time.

Free brochures with rudimentary maps of the museum are available at the information desk in Hall Napoléon. One-and-a-half-hour **cassette tours** (*acoustiguides*) in six languages, available until 4 pm, can be rented for 28FF under the pyramid. Detailed explanations in a variety of languages, printed on heavy, plastic-coated *feuillets* (sheets), are stored on racks in each display room.

Musée des Arts Décoratifs The Museum of Decorative Arts (☎ 42.60.32.14; metro Tuileries) at 107 Rue de Rivoli occupies the western tip of the northern wing of the Louvre. It displays a fine collection of furniture, ceramics, jewellery, glass and other objets d'art from the Middle Ages, the Renaissance, the Louis XIV and Louis XV periods, the 19th century and the Art Nouveau and Art Deco periods. It also has contemporary works. It's open from 12.30 pm (noon on Sunday) to 6 pm. Entrance costs 25FF (16FF reduced price).

In the same part of the Louvre you'll find the **Musée des Arts de la Mode** (Museum of Costume & Fashion), which displays fabrics and clothing from the 18th century to the present and the affiliated **Musée de la Publicité** (Museum of Advertising). Both are presently closed for renovation.

Palais Royal This complex, which briefly housed young Louis XIV in the 1640s, is across Place du Palais Royal from the north side of the Louvre. Construction was begun in the 17th century by Cardinal Richelieu, though most of the present neoclassical complex dates from the latter part of the 18th century. Today, it houses a number of important government bodies, including the Conseil d'État (Council of State), the Conseil Constitutionnel (Constitutional Council, which rules on the constitutionality of laws) and the Ministry of Culture. The interior is closed to the public. The colonnaded building facing Place André Malraux is the **Comédie Française** (founded in 1680), the world's oldest national theatre.

Just north of the main part of the palace is the **Jardin du Palais Royal**, an enclosed park with lots of trees and iron benches. During the late 1700s, there was something of a permanent carnival here, and all sorts of things hard to find elsewhere in Paris (eg incendiary political tracts) were openly available; since this was the private domain of the Duc d'Orléans, the police were unable to interfere. On 12 July 1789, Camille Desmoulins came to the gardens and made a fiery speech that helped push Paris towards open revolt.

The east side of the Jardin du Palais Royal is lined with arcades sheltering antique and

antiquarian book shops, while on the other side there are art galleries, jewellery shops and even a place that specialises in toy soldiers (at No 34). Le Grand Véfour, one of Paris's oldest and most illustrious restaurants, is at the north end (see Louvre Area under Restaurants). At the south end you'll come across a controversial **sculpture** of black-and-white striped columns by Daniel Buren, installed in 1986.

There are entrances to the Jardin via the Palais Royal and from Rue de Beaujolais, which is linked to Rue des Petits Champs by a number of narrow passageways. The park is open daily from 7 am (7.30 am from October to March) to sometime between 8.30 pm (in winter) and 11 pm (in summer).

Galerie Véro Dodat For a quick taste of 19th-century Paris, it's hard to beat this shopping arcade between 19 Rue Jean-Jacques Rousseau and 2 Rue du Bouloi, which opened in 1826 and retains its 19th-century skylights, ceiling murals and store fronts. The shops specialise in antiques, objets d'art (including some new and startling items), art books (at No 15) and fashion accessories (such as the scarves on sale at No 16).

Jardin des Tuileries The formal Tuileries Gardens, which begin just west of the Louvre, were laid out in their present form (more or less) in the mid-1600s by André Le Nôtre, who also did the gardens at Versailles. The Tuileries soon became the most fashionable spot in Paris for parading about in one's finery. On 10 August 1792, after Louis XVI and his family had fled from the Louvre via the Tuileries, enraged revolutionaries attacked the Swiss Guards (responsible for palace security) and butchered 600 of them in the gardens. In recent decades, the Jardin des Tuileries and its trees and flowers have fallen into a state of neglect; a programme to revamp them is set to be completed in 1995.

The **Voie Triomphale**, the western continuation of the Tuileries' east-west axis, follows the Champs-Élysées to the Arc de Triomphe and, eventually, to the Grande Arche in the new skyscraper district of La Défense.

Place Vendôme Eight-sided Place Vendôme and the arcaded and colonnaded buildings around it were built of hard limestone from 1687 to 1721. In March 1796, Napoleon married Josephine in the building at No 3 (formerly the city hall of the 2e arrondissement). The Ministry of Justice has been at Nos 11-13 since 1815. Today, the buildings around the *place* house the Hôtel Ritz and some of Paris's most fashionable and expensive jewellery shops, including Cartier at Nos 7 and 23. **Rue de Castiglione**, which goes south to Jardin des Tuileries, and **Rue de la Paix**, which leads north to Opéra-Garnier, are also lined with fine jewellery shops.

Originally, Place Vendôme was built to showcase a giant statue of Louis XIV, which was destroyed during the Revolution. The 43.5-metre column now in the centre of the square, **Colonne Vendôme**, consists of a stone core wrapped in a 160-metre-long bronze spiral made from 1250 Austrian and Russian cannon captured by Napoleon at the Battle of Austerlitz (1805). The bas-reliefs on the spiral depict Napoleon's victories of 1805-07. The statue on top, placed there in 1873 after its predecessors had been replaced or toppled in 1815, 1833, 1863 and 1871, depicts Napoleon as a Roman emperor.

Musée de l'Orangerie The Musée de l'Orangerie (☎ 42.97.48.16; metro Concorde), which is in the south-west corner of the Jardin des Tuileries at Place de la Concorde (1er), displays important impressionist works, including a series of Monet's *Nymphéas* (Water Lilies) and paintings by Cézanne, Matisse, Picasso, Renoir and Soutine.

It is open from 9.45 am to 5.15 pm. Entrance costs 33FF (24FF for people aged 18 to 25 or over 60); everyone pays 24FF on Sunday.

Jeu de Paume The Galerie Nationale du Jeu de Paume (☎ 47.03.12.50; metro Concorde),

housed in a one-time *jeu de paume* (real tennis court) built in 1861 during the reign of Napoleon III, is in the north-west corner of the Jardin des Tuileries. Once the home of a good part of France's national collection of impressionist works (now in the Musée d'Orsay), it reopened in 1992 as a gallery for innovative, two-month exhibitions of contemporary art (ie art from the last 20 or 30 years).

It is open Tuesday to Friday from noon to 7 pm (9.30 pm on Tuesday) and on Saturday and Sunday from 10 am to 7 pm. Entrance costs 35FF (25FF for young people aged 13 to 18, students under 26 and people over 60).

Place de la Concorde Vast, cobbled Place de la Concorde, situated between Jardin des Tuileries and the eastern end of Ave des Champs-Élysées, was laid out between 1755 and 1775. The 3300-year-old, pink granite **obelisk** in the middle was given to France in 1831 by Muhammad Ali, viceroy and pasha of Egypt. It is 23 metres high, weighs 230 tonnes and is from the Temple of Ramses at Thebes in upper Egypt. The eight statues of feminine forms adorning the four corners of the square represent France's largest cities.

In 1793, Louis XVI's head was chopped off by a guillotine set up in the north-west corner of the *place* near the statue representing the city of Brest. During the next two years, a guillotine – this one near the entrance to the Jardin des Tuileries – was used to behead another 1343 people, including Marie-Antoinette and, six months later, the Revolutionary leader Danton. Robespierre lost his head three months after Danton. The square was given its present name after the Reign of Terror in the hope that it would be a place of peace and harmony.

The two imposing buildings on the north side of Place de la Concorde are the **Hôtel de la Marine**, headquarters of the French navy, and the **Hôtel de Crillon**, now a luxury hotel. In 1778, the treaty by which France recognised the independence of the USA was signed in the Hôtel Crillon by Louis XVI and Benjamin Franklin, among others.

Rue Royale Rue Royale is home to some of the most elegant boutiques in Paris.

La Madeleine The neoclassical Church of St Mary Magdalen (☎ 42.65.52.17; metro Madeleine), universally known as La Madeleine, is 350 metres north of Place de la Concorde along Rue Royale (8e). Built in the style of a Greek temple, it was consecrated in 1842 after almost a century of design changes and construction delays. It is surrounded, Parthenon-like, by 52 twenty-metre-high Corinthian columns. The interior is open Monday to Saturday from 7.30 am to 7 pm and on Sunday from 7.30 am to 1.30 pm and 3 to 7 pm.

The **monumental staircase** out the front affords one of Paris's most quintessential panoramas: down Rue Royale to the obelisk in the middle of Place de la Concorde and on across the Seine to the 18th-century **Palais Bourbon**, now home of France's Assemblée Nationale (National Assembly). The gold dome of the Invalides is a bit to the right of the Palais Bourbon.

Place de la Madeleine The cheapest *belle époque* attraction in Paris is the **public toilets** on the east side of La Madeleine, which date from 1905. Entry costs 2.20FF (2FF for urinals). There has been a **flower market** on the east side of the church since 1832. It is open Monday to Saturday.

For information on **Fauchon** and other famous luxury food stores around Place de la Madeleine, see Around La Madeleine under Self-Catering in the Places to Eat section.

Centre Pompidou Area (1er & 4e)
A few blocks west of the Centre Pompidou, the huge pedestrian zone around Les Halles is always filled with people, just as it was for the 850 years when the area served as Paris's main marketplace. During the day, the main attractions are museums, art galleries, shops and places to eat, while at night – and into the wee hours of the morning – restaurants, theatres and discos draw Parisians out for a night on the town.

PARIS

The maze of subterranean passageways that link the interconnected Châtelet, Châtelet-Les Halles and Les Halles metro stations are considered a bit risky late at night.

Exploring on Foot The streets around Forum des Halles are lined with restaurants. The grassy area on top of the shopping mall is perfect for lounging and people-watching.

The Centre Pompidou is one km east of the Louvre and 800 metres north of Notre Dame. The Marais, with its many museums,

is only a few blocks east of the Centre Pompidou and the Hôtel de Ville. Place de l'Hôtel de Ville, a vast, fountain-lined square paved with bright stone, is the perfect place to lick ice cream on a sunny day.

The part of Rue Saint Denis north of the Centre Pompidou is lined with sex shops and prostitutes.

Weekly Closures
Tuesday: Centre Pompidou

Centre Pompidou The Centre Georges Pompidou (☎ 44.78.49.68 for information,

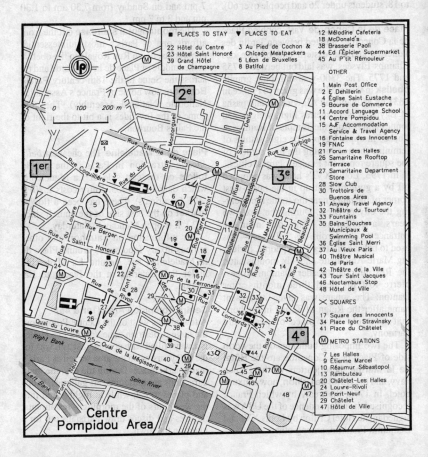

■ PLACES TO STAY	▼ PLACES TO EAT
22 Hôtel du Centre	3 Au Pied de Cochon &
23 Hôtel Saint Honoré	Chicago Meatpackers
39 Grand Hôtel	6 Léon de Bruxelles
de Champagne	8 Batifol

12 Mélodine Cafeteria
18 McDonald's
38 Brasserie Paoli
44 Ed l'Épicier Supermarket
45 Au P'tit Rémouleur

OTHER
1 Main Post Office
2 E Dehillerin
4 Église Saint Eustache
5 Bourse de Commerce
11 Accord Language School
14 Centre Pompidou
15 AJF Accommodation Service & Travel Agency
16 Fontaine des Innocents
19 FNAC
21 Forum des Halles
26 Samaritaine Rooftop Terrace
27 Samaritaine Department Store
28 Slow Club
30 Trottoirs de Buenos Aires
31 Anyway Travel Agency
32 Théâtre du Tourtour
33 Fountains
35 Bains-Douches Municipaux & Swimming Pool
36 Église Saint Merri
37 Au Vieux Paris
40 Théâtre Musical de Paris
42 Théâtre de la Ville
43 Tour Saint Jacques
47 Noctambus Stop
48 Hôtel de Ville

✕ SQUARES
17 Square des Innocents
34 Place Igor Stravinsky
41 Place du Châtelet

Ⓜ METRO STATIONS
7 Les Halles
9 Étienne Marcel
10 Réaumur Sébastopol
13 Rambuteau
20 Châtelet-Les Halles
24 Louvre-Rivoli
25 Pont-Neuf
29 Châtelet
47 Hôtel de Ville

Centre Pompidou Area

44.78.12.33 for the switchboard; metro Rambuteau), also known as the Centre Beaubourg, is dedicated to displaying and promoting modern and contemporary art. Thanks in part to its vigourous schedule of outstanding temporary exhibitions, it is by far the most visited sight in Paris. The **square** on the Centre's west side attracts buskers, street artists, musicians, jugglers, mimes and, Parisians complain, pickpockets and drug dealers. The fanciful, colourful **fountains** at Place Igor Stravinsky, on the Centre's south side, were created by Jean Tinguely and Niki de Saint-Phalle.

The design of the Centre Pompidou has not ceased to draw wide-eyed gazes and critical comment since its construction between 1972 and 1977. In order to keep the

One of the fanciful fountain sculptures near Centre Pompidou

exhibition halls as spacious and uncluttered as possible, the architects – one Italian, the other British – put the building's 'insides' on the outside. The purpose of each of the ducts, pipes and vents that enclose the centre's glass walls can be divined from the paint job: escalators and lifts are red, electrical circuitry is yellow, the plumbing is green and the air-conditioning system is blue.

The Centre Pompidou consists of several distinct parts, each of which has its own entrance fees; tickets for all sections are sold at the ticket windows on the ground floor. The **Musée National d'Art Moderne** (MNAM), which displays France's national collection of modern and contemporary (ie 20th century) art, is open from noon (10 am on weekends and public holidays) to 10 pm. Entrance costs 30FF (20FF for people aged 18 to 24 or over 60), but everyone gets in for free on Sunday from 10 am to 2 pm. The **Galeries Contemporaines**, which form part of the MNAM, host temporary shows with separate admission fees. The 5th-floor **Grande Galerie**, which is used for major expositions last three or four months (with a one to 1½-month break between shows), also has its own, usually steep admission fees.

The free, three-storey **Bibliothèque Publique d'Information** (BPI; ☎ 42.77.12.33) is a huge, noncirculating library equipped with the latest high-tech information retrieval systems. Among the 2300 periodicals are quite a few English- language newspapers and magazines from around the world. The BPI is open from noon (10 am on weekends and holidays) to 10 pm. The BPI is so popular that, from 2 to 4 pm, you sometimes have to wait in line to get in. The entrance is on the 2nd floor.

If you'll be visiting several parts of the complex on the same day, the Forfait 1 Jour (One-Day Pass), which costs 57FF (40FF if you're aged 13 to 24), is a good deal, especially if you take a guided tour. **English-language tours** (1½ hours), which cost 30FF (20FF reduced price, free with the One-Day Pass), are available during summer and school holiday periods.

Forum des Halles Les Halles, Paris's main wholesale food market, occupied the area just south of Église Saint Eustache from around 1110 until 1969, when it was moved out to the suburb of Rungis. In its place, Forum des Halles, a huge (and, many charge, horribly ugly) underground shopping mall, was constructed in the high-tech, glass-and-chrome style briefly in vogue in the 1970s. The complex's four levels of shops, built around an open courtyard, have proved highly popular with Parisian shoppers, especially those in search of reasonable prices.

On top of Forum des Halles is a popular park area where people sit, picnic and sunbathe on the lawn while gazing at the flying buttresses of Église Saint Eustache. During the warm months, street musicians and other performers display their talents all around Forum des Halles, especially at **Square des Innocents**, whose centre is adorned by a multitiered Renaissance fountain, **Fontaine des Innocents** (1549). The square and the fountain are named after Cimetière des Innocents, a cemetery on this site from which two million skeletons were transferred to the Catacombes in the 1780s. One block south of the fountain is **Rue de la Ferronnerie**, where in 1610 Henri IV was assassinated by Ravaillac while passing No 11 in his carriage.

Église Saint Eustache This majestic church (metro Les Halles), one of the most attractive in Paris, is just north of the grassy area on top of the Forum des Halles. Constructed between 1532 and 1637, its general design is Gothic. The classical west façade was added in the mid-18th century.

Inside, there's some exceptional Flamboyant archwork holding up the ceiling of the chancel, though most of the interior ornamentation is Renaissance and classical, as you can see from the cornices and Corinthian columns. The gargantuan, 101-stop, 8000-pipe organ above the west entrance is used for concerts, a long tradition here. The nave and choir are lined with chapels, some containing tombs, including that of Louis XIV's finance minister, Jean-Baptiste Colbert (1619-83). Except during services, the

church is open Monday to Saturday from 8.30 am to 7 pm and on Sunday from 8.15 am to 12.30 pm and 3 to 7 pm.

Hôtel de Ville Paris's city hall (☎ 42.76. 40.40; metro Hôtel de Ville) was rebuilt in the neo-Renaissance style between 1874 and 1882 after having been gutted during the Paris Commune of 1871. The ornate façade is decorated with 108 statues of noteworthy Parisians. Free guided tours (☎ 42.76. 59.27/46) of the interior are held in French every Monday at 10.30 am except on public holidays and during official functions. The visitors' entrance is at 29 Rue de Rivoli (4e), where there's also a hall used for temporary exhibitions of all sorts.

The Hôtel de Ville faces majestic, fountain and lamp-adorned **Place de l'Hôtel de Ville**, known as Place de Grève until 1830. For centuries, Paris held many of its celebrations, rebellions and public executions on this site. A strike is called a *grève* in French because the unemployed used to congregate here in centuries past.

To protect the Hôtel de Ville from the destructive effects of pigeon guano, all the ledges and horizontal surfaces are covered with thin metal spikes intended to prevent the birds from making a successful landing. This system is used all over France.

La Samaritaine Rooftop Terrace There's an amazing 360° panoramic view of Paris from the roof of Building 2 of La Samaritaine department store (☎ 40.41.20.20; metro Pont Neuf), which is on Rue de la Monnaie (1er) just north of Pont Neuf. The 11th-floor lookout has a huge *table d'orientation* (viewpoint indicator) that shows you what you're looking at. You can have something to drink at the outdoor café on the 10th floor, reached by taking the lift to the 9th floor. La Samaritaine is open Monday to Saturday from 9.30 am to 7 pm (10 on Thursday).

Marais (3e & 4e)
The Marais (literally, the Marsh), the area of the 4e arrondissement directly north of Île Saint Louis, was in fact a swamp until the

13th century, when it was converted to agricultural use. In the early 1600s, Henri IV built Place des Vosges, turning the area into the Paris's most fashionable residential district and attracting weathy aristocrats, who erected luxurious but discreet **hôtels particuliers** (private mansions). When the aristocracy moved to Versailles and Faubourg Saint Germain during the late 17th and 18th centuries, the Marais and its mansions passed into the hands of ordinary Parisians.

Today, the Marais is one of the few neighbourhoods of Paris that still has almost all of its pre-Revolutionary architecture. In recent years the area has become trendy, but it's still home to a long-established Jewish community and is a major centre of Paris's gay life. On Friday and Saturday nights, the Marais is crowded with people out dining or bar-hopping with friends.

A number of the 16th and 17th-century hôtels particuliers, many built around enclosed garden courtyards, have been turned into museums.

Exploring on Foot Some of the most interesting places for a stroll include Rue des Rosiers, Rue des Francs Bourgeois and Place des Vosges.

The Marais is within easy walking distance of much of central Paris:

- The Centre Pompidou is a few blocks north-west of Rue des Rosiers.
- Place de la Bastille is only a few hundred metres south-east of Place des Vosges.
- Tranquil Île Saint Louis is right across Pont Louis-Philippe from the southern Marais. Notre Dame is a few hundred metres further south-west.
- The Louvre is a bit over one km west of the Hôtel de Ville along Rue de Rivoli.

Some of Paris's most interesting shops for cute little decorative items – the kind of expensive things with which a trendy young Parisian might enliven a classy apartment – are in the Marais, especially along Rue du Bourg Tibourg, Rue Sainte Croix de la Bretonnerie, Rue Saint Merri, Rue du Roi de

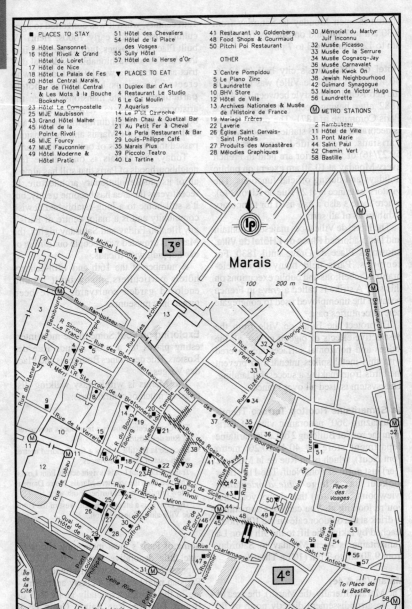

Sicile and Rue François Miron (all metro Saint Paul or Hôtel de Ville).

Jewish Neighbourhood When renovation was begun in the 1960s, the Marais was a poor but lively Jewish neighbourhood centred around **Rue des Rosiers**. In the 1980s, the area underwent a process of gentrification and today is one of Paris's most fashionable neighbourhoods, especially favoured by young professionals. Trendy and expensive boutiques – and the rising rents and property values they have brought – now threaten to push out the remaining Jewish bookshops and *cacher* (kosher) groceries, butcher shops and restaurants. See Marais under Restaurants for details. The area is very quiet on Saturday.

On Rue Pavée between Rue des Rosiers and Rue de Rivoli is the so-called **Guimard synagogue**, built in 1913, which is renowned for both its Art Nouveau architecture (the work of Hector Guimard, who designed the famous noodle-like metro entrances) and the extreme Orthodoxy of its members, who refuse to have anything to do with the organised Orthodox Jewish community, the Consistoire. The interior is closed to the public.

Mémorial du Martyr Juif Inconnu The Memorial to the Unknown Jewish Martyr (☎ 42.77.44.72; metro Pont Marie or Saint Paul) at 17 Rue Geoffroy l'Asnier (4e), established in 1956 and reopened in 1992 after two years of renovations, includes a memorial to the victims of the Holocaust, various temporary exhibits and small permanent exhibits on the 1st, 2nd and 3rd

floors. The memorial is open from 10 am to 1 pm and 2 to 5.30 pm (5 pm on Friday). There is no entry charge.

The building also houses a research centre and a library (open in the afternoon by appointment only).

Place des Vosges In 1605, King Henri IV decided to turn the Marais into Paris's most sought-after residential district. The result of this initiative was Place des Vosges (4e; metro Bastille or Chemin Vert), inaugurated in 1612 as Place Royale, a square ensemble of 36 symmetrical houses with ground-floor arcades, steep slate roofs and large dormer windows. Only the earliest houses were built of brick: to save time, the rest were given timber frames and faced with plaster, later painted to resemble brick. Duels were once fought in the elegant park in the middle. The *place* received its present name in 1800 to honour the Vosges *département*, the first in France to pay its taxes. Today, the arcades around Place des Vosges are occupied by up-market art galleries, pricey antique shops and elegant places to sip tea.

Victor Hugo lived at 6 Place des Vosges from 1832 to 1848. His house, the **Maison de Victor Hugo** (☎ 42.72.10.16), is now a municipal museum and can be visited from 10 am to 5.40 pm. The entry fee is 17FF (9FF for students, free for people over 60).

Gay Marais For more information about gay life in the neighbourhood, see Marais under Restaurants, Cafés and Places to Drink; and, in the Information section, Gay Bookshop under Bookshops.

Musée Carnavalet Also known as the Musée de l'Histoire de Paris (☎ 42.72.21.13; metro Saint Paul or Chemin Vert) at 23 Rue de Sévigné (3e), this museum of Paris's history is housed in two hôtels particuliers: the mid-16th-century, Renaissance-style Hôtel Carnavalet, once home to the late 17th-century writer Madame de Sévigné; and the late 17th-century Hôtel Le Peletier de Saint Fargeau. The artefacts on display chart the history of Paris from the Gallo-Roman

period to the 20th century. The museum has the most important collection anywhere of documents, paintings, books and other objects from the French Revolution.

The Musée Carnavalet is open (except on public holidays) from 10 am to 5.40 pm; ticket sales stop at 5.15 pm. Entrance costs 26FF (14FF reduced price) unless there's a temporary exhibition, in which case the price goes up a bit.

Musée Picasso The Picasso Museum (☎ 42.71.25.21; metro Saint Paul or Chemin Vert) at 5 Rue de Thorigny (3e), housed in the mid-17th century Hôtel Salé, is one of Paris's best loved art museums. Displays include engravings, paintings, ceramic works, drawings and an unparalleled collection of sculptures that the heirs of Pablo Picasso (1881-1973) donated to the French government in lieu of inheritance taxes. You can also see part of Picasso's personal art collection, which includes works by Braque, Cézanne, Matisse and Dégas.

The Musée Picasso, which was inaugurated in 1985, is open from 9.30 am to 6 pm. The entry fee is 26FF (17FF reduced price).

Musée de la Serrure This museum (☎ 42.77.79.62; metro Saint Paul or Chemin Vert) at 1 Rue de la Perle (3e), also known as the Musée Bricard, showcases a collection of locks, keys and door knockers assembled since 1830 by the Bricard family, owners of Société Bricard, a French lock-making company. Part of the collection, which is arranged chronologically from the Roman period to the present, consists of locks made by Bricard's competitors and purchased for the purpose of industrial espionage. One lock, made around 1780, traps your hand in the jaws of a bronze lion if you try to use the wrong key. Another lock, this one from the 19th century, shoots anyone who trys to use the incorrect key!

The Musée de la Serrure is open from 2 to 5 pm. Entrance costs 20FF (10FF for people over 60, free for children under 18).

Musée Cognacq-Jay The Musée Cognacq-Jay (☎ 40.27.07.21; metro Saint Paul) at 8 Rue Elzévir (3e) brings together oil paintings, pastels, sculpture, objets d'art, jewellery, porcelain and furniture from the 18th century. The objects on display, assembled by the founders of La Samaritaine department store, give a pretty good idea of upper-class tastes during the Age of Enlightenment. It is open from 10 am to 12.30 pm and 1.45 to 5.40 pm. Entry costs 17FF (9FF for students).

Musée Kwok On The small Musée Kwok On (☎ 42.72.99.42; metro Saint Paul), which occupies an informal, warehouse-like structure at the far side of the courtyard at 41 Rue des Francs Bourgeois (4e), has colourful exhibits of costumes, masks, marionettes and shadow puppets used in theatre performances and festivals in East and South-East Asia. It is open (except on public holidays) from 10 am to 5.30 pm. Entrance costs 15FF (10FF for children, students and people over 60).

Archives Nationales France's national archives are housed in the impressive, early 18th-century Hôtel de Soubise (metro Rambuteau) at 60 Rue des Francs Bourgeois (3e). The complex also contains the **Musée de l'Histoire de France** (☎ 40.27.60.96), where you can see some of the most important documents in French history, including a Merovingian document on papyrus from around 630 AD, the Edict of Nantes (1598), the revocation of the Edict of Nantes (1685), Louis XIV's will (1715) and the Assemblée Nationale's text of the Déclaration des Droits de l'Homme (Declaration of the Rights of Man), prepared on 20 August 1789. The ceiling and walls of the early 18th-century interior are extravagantly painted and gilded in the rococo style.

The Musée de l'Histoire de France is open (except on holidays) from 2 to 5.45 pm. Entrance costs 15FF (10FF for teachers and people under 25 or over 60).

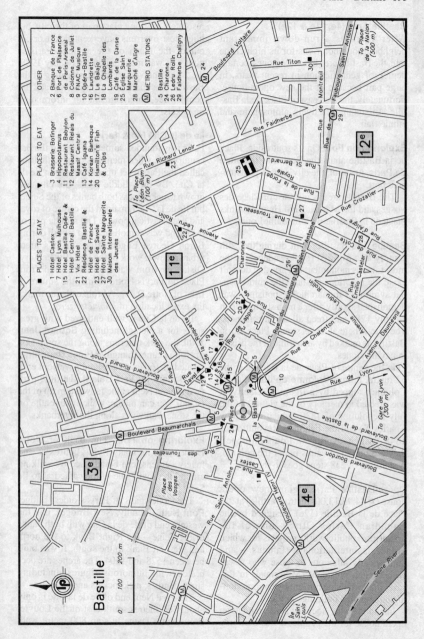

Bastille

0   100   200 m

PLACES TO STAY

- 1 Hôtel Castex
- 7 Hôtel Lyon Mulhouse
- 15 Hôtel Bastille Opéra &
  Hôtel Central Bastille
- 21 Vix Hôtel
- 22 Residence Bastille &
  Hôtel de France
- 23 Hôtel de Savoie
- 27 Hôtel Sainte Marguerite
- 30 Maison Internationale
  des Jeunes

▼ PLACES TO EAT

- 3 Brasserie Bofinger
- 4 Hippopotamus
- 11 Restaurant Babylon
- 12 Restaurant Relais du
  Massif Central
- 13 Café Iguana
- 14 Korean Barbeque
- 20 Hamilton's Fish
  & Chips

OTHER

- 2 Banque de France
- 6 Port de Plaisance
  de Paris-Arsenal
- 8 Colonne de Juillet
- 9 FNAC Musique
- 10 Opéra-Bastille
- 16 Laundrette
- 17 Le Balajo
- 18 La Chapelle des
  Lombards
- 19 Café de la Danse
- 25 Église Saint
  Marguerite
- 28 Marché d'Aligre

(M) METRO STATIONS

- 5 Bastille
- 24 Charonne
- 26 Ledru Rollin
- 29 Faidherbe Chaligny

Bastille Area (4e, 11e & 12e)

After years as a run-down immigrant neighbourhood notorious for its high crime rate, the Bastille area has undergone a certain degree of gentrification in recent years, in large part because of the new opera house. Fortunately, the area east of Place de la Bastille still retains its lively atmosphere and ethnic flair.

Exploring on Foot On its south side, Place de la Bastille abuts the **Port de Plaisance de Paris-Arsenal**, the city's main pleasure-boat port.

The Bastille area is just east of Place des Vosges and the Marais. Blvd Henri IV links Place de la Bastille with Île Saint Louis.

Bastille The Bastille, built during the 14th century as a fortified royal residence, is the most famous monument in Paris that doesn't exist: the notorious prison – the quintessential symbol of monarchic despotism – was demolished shortly after a mob stormed it on 14 July 1789 and freed all seven prisoners. The site where it once stood, Place de la Bastille, is marked by an outline of the prison in paving stones.

In the centre of Place de la Bastille is the 52-metre, bronze **Colonne de Juillet** (July Column), topped by a figure of Liberty. It was erected in memory of the victims of the July Revolution of 1830 (which overthrew Charles X) and the February Revolution of 1848 (which overthrew Louis-Philippe); they are buried in vaults under the column. A staircase of 238 steps goes to the top.

Opéra-Bastille Paris's giant new opera house (☎ 44.73.13.00; metro Bastille) at 2-6 Place de la Bastille (12e), designed by the Canadian Carlos Ott, is one of the grand(iose) public-works projects for which France is internationally famous – and domestically infamous to those who resent each French president (Mitterrand, in this case) immortalising himself by commissioning huge public buildings in Paris.

Intended by the Socialist Mitterrand as an opera house for the people, it was built in a resolutely working class part of the city, but huge cost overruns have kept ticket prices out of the reach of the average Parisian punter. It was inaugurated on 14 July 1989, the 200th anniversary of the storming of the Bastille. The main auditorium can seat 2700 people. See Entertainment for information on tickets.

Île de la Cité (4e & 1er)

Paris was founded sometime during the 3rd century BC, when members of a Celtic tribe called the Parisii set up a few huts on Île de la Cité. By the Middle Ages, the city had grown to encompass both banks of the Seine, but Île de la Cité remained the centre of royal and ecclesiastical power. The middle part of the island was demolished and rebuilt during Baron George Eugène Haussmann's great urban renewal work of the late 19th century. Distances from Paris are measured from Place du Parvis Notre Dame, the square in front of Notre Dame. A bronze plaque marks the exact location of *kilomètre zéro*.

Île de la Cité is well-endowed with great spots for a picnic, including **Square Jean XXIII**, the park that runs along the south side of Notre Dame; triangular **Place Dauphine**, created in 1607, at the island's western end; and **Square du Vert Galant**, the little park next to Pont Neuf at the far western tip of the island. You can picnic, walk or sunbathe on the stone walkways along the riverbanks.

Exploring on Foot The back of Notre Dame, with its many flying buttresses and lovely gardens, can be admired by walking around the south side of the cathedral to Île Saint Louis.

The stone spans of Paris's oldest bridge, **Pont Neuf** (literally, New Bridge), link the western end of Île de la Cité with both banks of the Seine – the Right Bank to the north and the Left Bank to the south. It was built between 1578 and 1604. The arches are decorated with humorous figures, including street dentists, pickpockets and loiterers.

The Pont Neuf end of Île de la Cité is only about 500 metres south-east of the Louvre. From Notre Dame, it's an 800-metre walk

north to the Centre Pompidou and a short stroll south to the Latin Quarter.

From Notre Dame, if you walk south-eastward along the south bank of the Seine you come to the Musée de la Sculpture en Plein Air and other riverside delights covered under Jardin des Plantes Area.

> **Weekly Closures**
> Most sights on Île de la Cité are open seven days a week.
> **Sunday:** Trésor (treasury) of Notre Dame

Notre Dame Notre Dame (☎ 43.26.07.39; metro Cité or the RER exits of metro Saint Michel), Paris's cathedral, is one of the most magnificent achievements of Gothic architecture. Built on a site occupied by earlier churches – and, some two millennia ago, a Gallo-Roman temple – Notre Dame was begun in 1163 and completed around 1345. The interior is 130 metres long, 48 metres wide and 35 metres high and can accommodate over 6000 worshippers. Some 12 million people visit each year.

Notre Dame is known for its sublime balance, although if you look closely you'll see all sorts of minor dissymmetries introduced, in accordance with Gothic practice, to avoid monotony. These include the slightly different shapes of each of the three main entrances, whose statues were once brightly coloured to make them more effective as Bible lessons for the illiterate masses. Inside, exceptional features include three spectacular **rose windows**, the most renowned of which are the window over the west façade, which is a full 10 metres across, and the window on the north side of the transept, which has remained virtually unchanged since the 13th century. The 7800-pipe organ was restored in 1990-92 at a cost of US\$2 million. One of the best views of Notre Dame is from Square Jean XXIII, the lovely little park behind the cathedral, where you can see the mass of ornate **flying buttresses** that encircle the chancel and hold up its walls and roof.

Notre Dame is open daily from 8 am to 7 pm, though on Saturday it may be closed for upkeep from 12.30 to 2 pm. There is no charge to go inside. The **Trésor** at the back of the cathedral, which contains precious liturgical objects, is open from 9.30 am to 5.30 pm; admission is 15FF (10FF for students).

There are **guided tours** of the cathedral in English on Wednesday at noon; tours are held daily in July and August. **Free concerts** are held every Sunday at 5 or 5.30 pm. From Monday to Saturday, there are **masses** in the Chapelle du Saint Sacrément at 8 am, 9 am and noon and in the choir at 6.15 pm. On Sunday, masses are held in the nave at 8, 8.45, 10 and 11.30 am, and 12.30 and 6.30 pm.

The **north tower** (☎ 43.29.50.40) is to the right and around the corner as you walk out of the main entrance. From the base, a long, spiral climb up 238 steps gets you to the top of the **west façade**, from where you can view many of the cathedral's most ferocious gargoyles, not to mention a good part of Paris. Tickets are on sale daily from 9.30 am (10 am from November to March) to 4.30 pm (November to March), 5.30 pm (April to mid-June and mid-September to October) or 6.30 pm (mid-June to mid-September). The tower closes half an hour after ticket sales end. The entrance fee is 26FF (20FF for people aged 18 to 24 or over 60, 6FF for children).

Notre Dame gargoyles

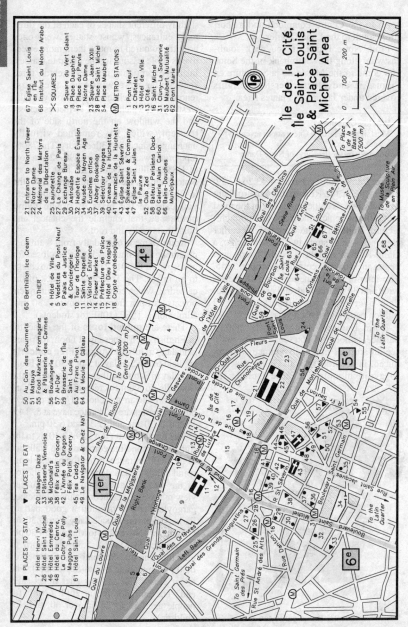

Île de la Cité,
Île Saint Louis
& Place Saint
Michel Area

0   100   200 m

- ■ PLACES TO STAY
  - 7   Hôtel Henri IV
  - 26 Hôtel Saint Michel
  - 46 Hôtel Esmeralda
  - 48 Hôtel du Centre,
        Le Cloître & Polly
        Maggoo Pubs
  - 61 Hôtel Saint Louis

- ▼ PLACES TO EAT
  - 20 Häagen Dazs
  - 33 Pâtisserie Viennoise
  - 36 McDonald's
  - 38 Félix Potin Grocery
  - 42 L'Année du Dragon &
        Félix Potin Grocery
  - 45 Tea Caddy
  - 49 Le Navigator & Chez Maï

  - 50 Au Coin des Gourmets
  - 51 Matsuya
  - 55 Nicolas Market, Fromagerie
        & Pâtisserie des Carmes
  - 56 Boulangerie
  - 57 Al-Dar
  - 59 Brasserie de l'Île
        Saint Louis
  - 63 Au Franc Pinot
  - 64 Le Moule à Gâteau
  - 65 Berthillon Ice Cream

OTHER
  - 4   Hôtel de Ville
  - 5   Vedettes du Pont Neuf
  - 9   Palais de Justice
        & Conciergerie
  - 10 Tour de l'Horloge
  - 11 Sainte Chapelle
  - 12 Visitors Entrance
  - 14 Flower Market
  - 15 Préfecture de Police
  - 17 Hôtel Dieu Hôpital
  - 18 Crypte Archéologique

  - 21 Entrance to North Tower
  - 22 Notre Dame
  - 24 Memorial des Martyrs
        de la Déportation
  - 25 Laundrette
  - 27 La Change de Paris
  - 29 Exchange Bureau
  - 30 Astrolabe
  - 32 Hachette Espace Evasion
  - 34 Musée du Moyen Age
  - 35 Eurolines office
  - 37 Abbey Bookshop
  - 39 Selectour Voyages
  - 40 Bateau Ivre Café
  - 41 Pharmacie de la Huchette
  - 43 Église Saint Séverin
  - 44 Shakespeare & Company
  - 47 Église Saint Julien
        le Pauvre
  - 52 Club Zed
  - 58 Bateux Parisiens Dock
  - 60 Galerie Alain Carion
  - 66 Bains-Douches
        Municipaux
  - 67 Église Saint Louis
        en l'Île
  - 68 Institut du Monde Arabe

  ✕ SQUARES
  - 6   Square du Vert Galant
  - 8   Place Dauphine
  - 19 Place du Parvis
        Notre Dame
  - 23 Square Jean XXIII
  - 28 Place Saint Michel
  - 54 Place Maubert

  Ⓜ METRO STATIONS
  - 1   Pont Neuf
  - 2   Châtelet
  - 3   Hôtel de Ville
  - 13 Cité
  - 16 Saint Michel
  - 31 Cluny–La Sorbonne
  - 53 Maubert Mutualité
  - 62 Pont Marie

Crypte Archéologique Under the square in front of Notre Dame, the Archaeological Crypt (☎ 43.29.83.51), also known as the Crypte du Parvis, displays *in situ* the remains of structures from the Gallo-Roman and later periods. It is open daily from 10 am to 4.30 pm (5.30 pm from April to September). Entrance costs 26FF (17FF for people 18 to 24 or over 60). If you'll also be climbing up the north tower of Notre Dame, you can purchase a *billet jumelé* (combination ticket) valid for both for 45FF.

Sainte Chapelle The gem-like Sainte Chapelle (☎ 43.54.30.09; metro Cité), whose upper chapel is illuminated by a veritable curtain of luminous 13th-century **stained glass** (the oldest and perhaps finest in Paris), is inside the **Palais de Justice** (law courts), which is on the west side of Blvd du Palais (1er). Consecrated in 1248, the Sainte Chapelle was built in only 33 months to house what was believed to be Jesus' crown of thorns and other relics purchased by King Louis IX (Saint Louis) earlier in the 13th century.

From October to March, it is open daily from 10 am to 4.30 pm. The rest of the year, hours are 9.30 am to 6 pm. Tickets cost 26FF (17FF for you're 18 to 24 or over 60). A ticket valid for both the Sainte Chapelle and the nearby Conciergerie costs 40FF. The main entrance to the Palais de Justice is enclosed by a fine, 18th-century gate, but visitors have to use the entrance directly opposite 7 Blvd du Palais. Be prepared to pass through airport-type security.

Except under special circumstances, French **trials and sentencings** are open to the public, so you're more than welcome to wander around the long hallways of the Palais de Justice and, if you can find a court in session, to observe the proceedings. The law courts operate Monday to Friday from 9 am to noon and 1.30 to 6 pm, but in general, civil cases are heard in the morning, while criminal trials – which are more interesting – begin after lunch. After a couple of hours of arguments, the judges usually switch to sentencing previously tried defendants before returning to trial proceedings. To find

a trial in progress, your best bet is to find a *tribunal correctionelle* (criminal court) that's in session. The men and women in black robes are magistrates, barristers or officers of the court and may be able to point you in the right direction.

Conciergerie The Conciergerie (☎ 43.54.30.06; metro Cité) was a luxurious royal palace when it was built in the 14th century but later lost favour with the kings of France and was turned into a prison and place of torture. During the Terror (1793-94), the Conciergerie was used to incarcerate presumed enemies of the Revolution before they were brought before the Revolutionary Tribunal, which met next door. Among the 2600 prisoners held here before being sent in tumbrils to the guillotine were Queen Marie-Antoinette, the Revolutionary radicals Danton and Robespierre and, finally, the judges of the tribunal themselves.

The huge Gothic **Salle des Gens d'Armes** (Hall of the Men of Arms) dates from the 14th century and is the largest surviving medieval hall in Europe. The clock tower on the corner of Quai de l'Horloge and Blvd du Palais, **Tour de l'Horloge**, has held aloft a public clock – Paris's first – since 1370.

The Conciergerie, whose entrance is at 1 Quai de l'Horloge, is open daily from 10 am to 5 pm. From April to September hours are 9.30 am to 6 pm. The entry fee is 26FF (17FF if you're 18 to 24 or over 60). A billet jumelé that also gets you into the Sainte Chapelle costs 40FF. An excellent guidebook, *The Conciergerie*, is available for 26FF at the entrance.

Flower Market Île de la Cité's famous *marché aux fleurs* (metro Cité), Paris's oldest, has been at Place Louis Lépine (4e) – the area just north of the Préfecture de Police – since 1808. It is open Monday to Saturday (and when holidays fall on Sunday) from 8 or 9 am to about 7 pm.

On Sunday, the marché aux fleurs is transformed into a *marché aux oiseaux* (bird market). Small house pets are also on sale.

Mémorial des Martyrs de la Déportation At the south-eastern tip of Île de la Cité, behind Notre Dame, is the Deportation Memorial (1962), a stark, haunting monument to the 200,000 citizens and residents of France – including 76,000 Jews, all but a handful of whom were killed – deported by the Nazis. The 200,000 bits of backlit glass represent each of the deportees. It is open daily from 10 am to noon and 2 to 5 pm.

Île Saint Louis (4e)

The smaller of Paris's two islands, Île Saint Louis, is just upstream from Île de la Cité. It consisted of two uninhabited islands – sometimes used for duels – until the early 1600s, when three enterprising men (a building contractor and two financiers) worked out a deal with Louis XIII: they would create one island out of the two and build two stone bridges to link it to the mainland and in exchange would receive the right to subdivide and sell the newly created real estate. This they did with great success, and between 1613 and 1664 the entire island was covered with fine new houses. Little has changed since then except that many of the buildings are now marked with plaques detailing when some person of note lived there.

Exploring on Foot On warm days and clear nights, the area around **Pont Saint Louis** (the bridge linking the two islands) and **Pont Louis-Philippe** (the bridge to the Marais) is one of the most romantic spots in all of Paris. On Pont Saint Louis and the nearby quays, which afford wonderful views of Notre Dame's flying buttresses, lovestruck couples mingle with buskers playing classical or ethnic music and teenage skateboarding virtuosos. After nightfall, the Seine dances with the watery reflections of streetlights, car headlights, stop signals and the dim glow escaping from the curtained windows of bourgeois apartments. Occasionally, tourist boats with superbright floodlamps cruise by, casting ever-changing shadows of the trees and bridges. This area makes a lovely stop

on a walk from the Latin Quarter to the Marais.

The island's 17th-century houses of grey stone and the small-town shops that line the streets and quays impart a village-like provincial calm. **Eglise Saint Louis en l'Île** (metro Pont Marie) at 19bis Rue Saint Louis en l'Île, a French Baroque-style church built from 1656 to 1725, often has concerts of classical music. It may be closed to visitors from noon to 2 pm.

If circumambulating the island makes you hungry, you might want to join the line at one of the shops selling Berthillon ice cream, reputedly Paris's best. Berthillon's original shop is at 31 Rue Saint Louis en l'Île. (See Île Saint Louis under Restaurants & Cafés for details.)

Latin Quarter (5e & 6e)

Known as the Latin Quarter because all communication between students and professors took place in Latin until the Revolution, this area has been the centre of Parisian higher education since the Middle Ages. It has become increasingly touristy in recent years, and its near monopoly on the city's academic life has waned as students have moved to other campuses, especially since 1968. But the Latin Quarter still has a large population of students and academics affiliated with the Sorbonne (now part of the University of Paris system), the Collège de France, the École Normale Supérieure and various other institutions of higher learning.

Exploring on Foot Almost every street in the area bordered by the Jardin du Luxembourg, Blvd Saint Germain, Rue Monge and Rue Claude Bernard has something unique to offer. Among the liveliest is **Rue Mouffetard** (see Latin Quarter under Restaurants and Self-Catering), one of the oldest streets in the city. The intense urbanness of the Latin Quarter is softened by the green expanses and pools of the Jardin du Luxembourg.

Shop-lined **Blvd Saint Michel**, popularly known as the 'Boul Mich' ('bool mish'), runs along the border between the 5e and the 6e arrondissements. Bustling **Blvd Saint**

Germain stretches over three km from Île Saint Louis westward past Saint Germain des Prés all the way to the Palais Bourbon (the Assemblée Nationale building).

The Latin Quarter is across the Seine from Île de la Cité and Notre Dame. The area east of the Latin Quarter is covered in the section entitled Jardin des Plantes Area.

> **Weekly Closures**
> **Tuesday:** Musée National du Moyen Age

Musée National du Moyen Age The Museum of the Middle Ages (☎ 43.25. 62.00; metro Cluny-La Sorbonne), Paris's premier museum of the Middle Ages, displays tapestries, statuary, illuminated manuscripts, arms, furnishings and objects of gold, ivory and enamel. Perhaps the museum's greatest masterpiece is a series of six late 15th-century tapestries from the southern Netherlands known as **La Dame à la Licorne** (the Lady and the Unicorn), hung in a round room on the 1st floor. The museum is housed in two structures: the frigidarium and other remains of **Gallo-Roman baths** from around the year 200 AD; and the late 15th-century **Hôtel de Cluny**, once the residence of the abbots of Cluny, the finest example of medieval civil architecture in Paris.

The museum, whose entrance is opposite the park next to 31 Rue du Sommerard (5e), is open from 9.30 am to 5.05 pm. The entrance fee is 26FF (17FF if you're 18 to 24 or over 60). On Sunday, everyone pays 17FF.

Sorbonne Paris's most famous university, the Sorbonne, was founded in 1253 by Robert de Sorbon, confessor of Louis IX (Saint Louis), as a college for 16 poor theology students. After centuries as France's major theological centre, it was closed in 1792 by the Revolutionary government but was reopened under Napoleon. Today, the Sorbonne's main complex (bounded by Rue de la Sorbonne, Rue des Écoles, Rue Saint Jacques and Rue Cujas) and other buildings in the vicinity house several of the 13 autonomous universities created when the Université de Paris was reorganised following the violent student protests of 1968.

Place de la Sorbonne links Blvd Saint Michel with **Chapelle de la Sorbonne**, the university's domed church, which was built between 1635 and 1642. It is closed except when there are special exhibitions.

Panthéon The domed landmark now known as the Panthéon (☎ 43.54.34.51; metro Luxembourg or Cardinal Lemoine), at the eastern end of Rue Soufflot (5e), was commissioned around 1750 as an abbey church, but because of financial problems the massive structure wasn't completed until 1789. Two years later, the Constituent Assembly converted it into a secular mausoleum for the *grands hommes de l'époque de la liberté française* (great men of the era of French liberty), removing all Christian symbols and references. After a further stint as a church, the Panthéon once again became a secular necropolis. Permanent guests of the Panthéon include Voltaire, Jean-Jacques Rousseau, Louis Braille, Émile Zola, Jean Moulin and René Cassin. Personages removed for reburial elsewhere after a reevaluation of their greatness include Mirabeau and Marat.

The Panthéon's ornate marble interior is gloomy in the extreme, but you do get a great view of the city from around the colonnaded dome, which is visible from all over Paris. From October to March, the Panthéon is open daily from 10 am to 5.30 pm. The rest of the year, hours are 10 am to 6 pm. Ticket sales end 45 minutes before closing time. Entry costs 26FF (17FF for people aged 18 to 25 or over 60).

Église Saint Étienne du Mont This lovely church (metro Cardinal Lemoine), at the back of the Panthéon at Place de l'Abbé Basset (5e), was built between 1492 and 1626. The most exceptional feature of the Gothic interior is its graceful **roodscreen** (*jubé*), the bridge-like structure that separates the chancel from the nave and from which sermons were delivered. It dates from 1535. During the 15th and 16th centuries,

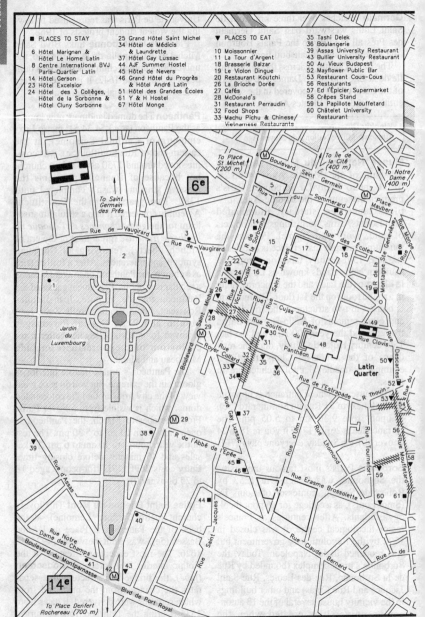

■ PLACES TO STAY
- 6 Hôtel Marignan &
     Hôtel Le Home Latin
- 8 Centre International BVJ
     Paris–Quartier Latin
- 14 Hôtel Gerson
- 23 Hôtel Excelsior
- 24 Hôtel des 3 Collèges,
     Hôtel de la Sorbonne &
     Hôtel Cluny Sorbonne
- 25 Grand Hôtel Saint Michel
- 34 Hôtel de Médicis
     & Laundrette
- 37 Hôtel Gay Lussac
- 44 AJF Summer Hostel
- 45 Hôtel de Nevers
- 46 Grand Hôtel du Progrès
     & Hôtel André Latin
- 51 Hôtel des Grandes Écoles
- 61 Y & H Hostel
- 67 Hôtel Monge

▼ PLACES TO EAT
- 10 Moissonnier
- 11 La Tour d'Argent
- 18 Brasserie Balzar
- 19 Le Violon Dingue
- 20 Restaurant Koutchi
- 26 La Brioche Dorée
- 27 Cafés
- 28 McDonald's
- 31 Restaurant Perraudin
- 32 Food Shops
- 33 Machu Pichu & Chinese/
     Vietnamese Restaurants

- 35 Tashi Delek
- 36 Boulangerie
- 39 Assas University Restaurant
- 43 Bullier University Restaurant
- 50 Au Vieux Budapest
- 52 Mayflower Public Bar
- 53 Restaurant Cous-Cous
- 56 Restaurants
- 57 Ed l'Épicier Supermarket
- 58 Crêpes Stand
- 59 La Papillote Mouffetard
- 60 Châtelet University
     Restaurant

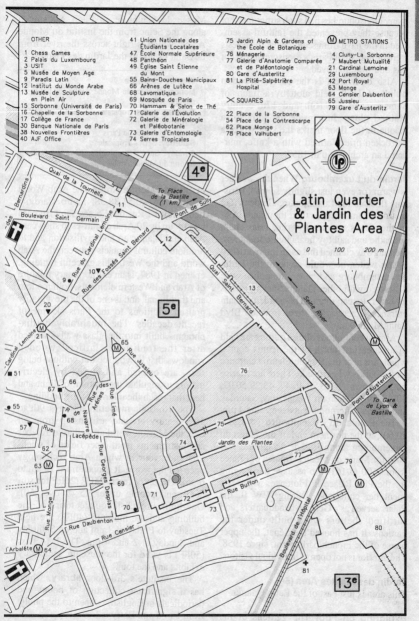

OTHER
1 Chess Games
2 Palais du Luxembourg
3 USIT
5 Musée de Moyen Age
9 Paradis Latin
12 Institut du Monde Arabe
13 Musée de Sculpture
   en Plein Air
15 Sorbonne (Université de Paris)
16 Chapelle de la Sorbonne
17 Collège de France
30 Banque Nationale de Paris
38 Nouvelles Frontières
40 AJF Office

41 Union Nationale des
   Étudiants Locataires
47 École Normale Supérieure
48 Panthéon
49 Église Saint Étienne
   du Mont
55 Bains-Douches Municipaux
66 Arènes de Lutèce
68 Lavomatique
69 Mosquée de Paris
70 Hammam & Salon de Thé
71 Galerie de l'Évolution
72 Galerie de Minéralogie
   et Paléobotanie
73 Galerie d'Entomologie
74 Serres Tropicales

75 Jardin Alpin & Gardens of
   the École de Botanique
76 Ménagerie
77 Galerie d'Anatomie Comparée
   et de Paléontologie
80 Gare d'Austerlitz
81 La Pitié-Salpêtrière
   Hospital

✕ SQUARES

22 Place de la Sorbonne
54 Place de la Contrescarpe
62 Place Monge
78 Place Valhubert

Ⓜ METRO STATIONS

4 Cluny-La Sorbonne
7 Maubert Mutualité
21 Cardinal Lemoine
29 Luxembourg
42 Port Royal
63 Monge
64 Censier Daubenton
65 Jussieu
79 Gare d'Austerlitz

Quai de la Tournelle

4ᵉ

To Place
de la Bastille
(1 km)

Pont de Sully

Boulevard Saint Germain

des Bernardins

Rue du Cardinal Lemoine

Rue des Fossés Saint Bernard

Quai Saint Bernard

Latin Quarter
& Jardin des
Plantes Area

0   100   200 m

Seine River

5ᵉ

Cardinal Lemoine

Rue Jussieu

Rue des Arènes

Rue Linné

76

Pont d'Austerlitz

To Gare
de Lyon &
Bastille

R de Navarre

Lacépède

75

78

Jardin des Plantes

77

Rue Monge

Rue Georges Desplas

69

71

72

73

Rue Buffon

79

Rue Daubenton

Rue Censier

l'Arbalète

64

Boulevard de l'Hôpital

80

81

13ᵉ

many large churches had such structures, but because they prevented the faithful assembled in the nave from seeing what the priests were doing, all of Paris's roodscreens except this one were removed.

Also of interest is the carved **wooden pulpit** of 1650, held aloft by a figure of Samson, and the 16th and 17th-century **stained glass**. Just inside the entrance, a plaque in the floor marks the spot where a defrocked priest, armed with a knife, murdered an archbishop in 1857.

Jardin du Luxembourg When the weather is warm (or even just slightly sunny), Parisians flock to the Luxembourg Gardens (6e; metro Luxembourg) in their thousands to sit in the chairs and read, write, relax, talk, sunbathe and sail toy boats in the fountains. Hemingway claimed that as an impoverished young writer, he would come to the Jardin du Luxembourg and, when the police were distracted with other matters, catch pigeons in order to eat them. The gardens' main entrance is across the street from 65 Blvd Saint Michel.

Almost continuous **chess games** are held in an area just north of the tennis courts, which are near the Rue de Fleurus entrance on the park's western side. There are **marionette shows** (☎ 43.26.46.47, 43.29.50.97; 20FF) for children on Wednesday, Saturday and Sunday afternoons between 2 and 4 pm.

The **Palais du Luxembourg** (☎ 42.34. 20.60), at the northern end of the Jardin du Luxembourg along Rue de Vaugirard, was built for Marie de Médicis (queen of France from 1600 to 1610) to assuage her longing for the Pitti Palace in Florence, where she spent her childhood. During WW II, the Palais served as a German headquarters, and fortified shelters were built under the gardens. It has housed the Sénat, the upper house of the French parliament, since 1958. The interior is not open to individual visitors.

Jardin des Plantes Area (5e)
This area is just east of the Latin Quarter.

Exploring on Foot The gardens of the

Musée de Sculpture en Plein Air stretch along the Seine from the Institut du Monde Arabe, which is right across the river from Île Saint Louis, to the Jardin des Plantes.

Weekly Closures
Monday: Institut du Monde Arabe (including the library)
Tuesday: Serres Tropicales, Muséum National d'Histoire Naturelle
Friday: Mosquée de Paris
Saturday: Serres Tropicales
Sunday: Serres Tropicales, library of the Institut du Monde Arabe

Institut du Monde Arabe The Arab World Institute (☎ 40.51.38.38; metro Cardinal Lemoine) at 1 Rue des Fossés Saint Bernard was set up by 20 Arab countries to showcase Arab and Islamic art and civilisation and to promote cultural contacts between the Arab world and the West. This graceful building, opened in 1987, is an extraordinary mixture of Arab and Western elements, both modern and traditional, and is one of the most highly praised additions to the Paris skyline of recent decades. The **mushrabiyah** (diaphragms built into the glass walls), named after the traditional latticed wooden windows that let you see out without being seen, are opened and closed by electric motors to regulate the amount of light and heat that reach the interior of the building.

The 7th-floor **museum** displays 9th to 19th-century art and artisanship from all over the Muslim world as well as astrolabes and instruments from other fields of scientific endeavour in which Arab technology once led the world. It is open from 10 am to 6 pm. The entry fee is 25FF (20FF for students and people under 25 or over 60). One-hour French-language tours of the building and the museum (40FF) are held Tuesday to Friday at 3 pm and on Saturday and Sunday at 2 and 4 pm. The IMA pass (50FF) is valid for the museum, temporary exhibits and the tour.

The institute's 3rd-floor **library**, which has a significant collection of books and periodicals in English, is open to the public from 1 to 8 pm. Entry is free.

The **Lebanese restaurant** (☎ 46.33. 47.70) on the 9th floor, a superb place for a mint tea, affords great views of the Seine, the east end of Notre Dame, Île Saint Louis and the Right Bank. It's open from noon to midnight or 1 am (closed Monday).

Musée de Sculpture en Plein Air The Open-Air Sculpture Museum, a lovely spot for a stroll or a picnic, is an imaginatively landscaped riverside promenade that stretches along the Seine for about 600 metres from the Institut du Monde Arabe to the Jardin des Plantes. Colourful riverboats are often moored along the pedestrian quay.

Jardin des Plantes Paris's botanical gardens (metro Gare d'Austerlitz or Jussieu), founded by Louis XIII in 1626, are endearingly informal and even decrepit, as if a group of dedicated but conservative, underfunded and slightly absent-minded professors had been running the place for a couple of centuries. The first greenhouse was added in 1714. The gardens are open daily from 8 am (7.15 am in summer) until sometime between 5.30 pm (in the dead of winter) and 7.45 pm (in summer).

The **Serres Tropicales** (greenhouses), also known as the Jardin d'Hiver (Winter Garden), are open from 1 to 5 pm (ticket sales end at 4.30 pm). Admission costs 12FF (8FF reduced price). The **Jardin Alpin** (Alpine Garden) and the **gardens of the École de Botanique** (Botanical School), both of which are free, are open from April to September on Monday, Wednesday, Thursday and Friday from 8 to 11 am and 1.30 to 5 pm.

The northern section of the Jardin des Plantes is taken up by the **Ménagerie** (☎ 40.79.37.94; metro Jussieu), a medium-sized zoo founded in 1794. During the Prussian siege of Paris in 1870, most of the animals were eaten. It is open daily from 9 am to 5 or 5.30 pm. From April to September, it stays open until 6 pm (6.30 pm on Sunday and holidays). Ticket sales end half an hour before closing time. Entrance costs 25FF (13FF for children, students aged 16 to 25 and people over 60). There's a children's

playground near the Ménagerie's western entrance.

The **Muséum National d'Histoire Naturelle** (☎ 40.79.30.00, 43.6.54.26; metro Censier Daubenton or Gare d'Austerlitz), created by a decree of the Convention in 1793, was the site of important scientific research in the 19th century. It is housed in four different buildings along the southern edge of the Jardin des Plantes.

The **Galerie de Minéralogie et Paléobotanie**, which covers mineralogy and paleobotany (ie fossilised plants) and costs 25FF (15FF for children aged 6 to 17, students and people over 60), has an amazing exhibit of giant natural crystals and a basement display of precious objects made from minerals.

The **Galerie d'Anatomie Comparée et de Paléontologie** has displays on comparative anatomy and paleontology and costs 18FF (12FF reduced price). Both are open (except on public holidays) from 10 am to 5 pm (11 am to 6 pm on weekends from April to September). Ticket sales end half an hour before closing time.

The **Galerie d'Entomologie**, whose speciality is the study of bugs, is open from 2 to 5 pm (closed holidays). Entry costs 12FF (8FF reduced price). The soon-to-open **Galerie de l'Évolution** is dedicated to the history of evolution and its implications for humankind.

Mosquée de Paris Paris's central mosque (☎ 45.35.97.33; metro Monge), whose entrance is on the building's west side next to the square minaret at Place du Puits de l'Ermite, was built between 1922 and 1926 in an ornate Hispano-Moorish style. In the Islamic tradition – Islam forbids images of people or animals – the two serene courtyards are elaborately decorated with verses from the Koran and coloured tiles in geometrical designs. Shoes must be removed at the entrance to the prayer hall. There are guided tours (15FF, 10FF for students) from 9 am to noon and 2 to 6 pm. Visitors must be modestly and respectfully dressed (women should not wear shorts or sleeveless blouses).

The mosque complex includes a North African-style salon de thé and a *hammam* (bathhouse; ☎ 43.31.18.14), both of whose entrances are opposite the southern corner of the Jardin des Plantes at 39 Rue Geoffroy Saint Hilaire. The hammam is open from 10 or 11 am to 8 or 9 pm: Monday, Wednesday, Thursday and Saturday are women's days, while Friday and Sunday are reserved for men. It costs 65FF; a massage is an extra 50FF.

Arènes de Lutèce This heavily reconstructed, 2nd-century Roman amphitheatre (metro Monge), discovered in 1869, could once seat around 10,000 people for gladiatorial combats and other events. Today, it is used by neighbourhood young people to play football and *boules* (bowls). There are entrances at 49 Rue Monge and opposite 7 Rue de Navarre. Entry is free.

Saint Germain des Prés (6e)

Centuries ago, Église Saint Germain des Prés and its affiliated abbey, founded by King Childebert in 542 AD, owned most of the 6e and 7e arrondissements. The neighbourhood around the church was built starting in the late 1600s, and these days is famous for its 19th-century charm and its cafés, like Les Deux Magots, Café de Flore and Brasserie Lipp (see Saint Germain des Prés under Restaurants), in which existentialism was born and legendary Left Bank intellectuals once argued over coffee.

These days, though, only wealthy intellectuals can afford the housing prices. There is a cluster of lively bars, cafés and restaurants around Carrefour de l'Odéon (metro Odéon).

Exploring on Foot A stroll through the area between Église Saint Germain des Prés and the Institut de France is a good way to get a feel for the area. **Rue Bonaparte, Rue des Beaux-Arts** and **Rue de Seine** are lined with galleries of Western and African art, antique dealers and antiquarian bookshops. **Place de Furstemberg**, a lovely, shaded square, is named after an ex-bishop of Strasbourg who laid out the area in 1699.

Saint Germain des Prés is one km west of Notre Dame. The most direct route to Place Saint Michel is along Rue Saint André des Arts.

The most enjoyable way to cover the distance between Saint Germain des Prés and the Latin Quarter is to visit Église Saint Sulpice on your way to Jardin du Luxembourg.

If you walk to the northern end of Rue Bonaparte, you'll find yourself at the Seine, whence it's a short trans-riverine stroll to the Louvre. If you go east, you'll soon reach Pont Neuf and the western tip of Île de la Cité, while a turn westward will take you along Quai Malaquais and Quai Voltaire to the Musée d'Orsay.

Weekly Closures
Monday: Many of the art galleries, Musée de la Monnaie
Tuesday: Musée Eugène Delacroix
Saturday: Bibliothèque Mazarine at the Institut de France
Sunday: Many of the art galleries, Bibliothèque Mazarine

Église Saint Germain des Prés The Romanesque-style Église Saint Germain des Prés (☎ 43.25.41.71), the oldest (though hardly the most interesting) church in Paris, was built in the 11th century on the site of a 6th-century abbey. It has since been altered many times, but the bell tower over the west entrance has changed little since 1000 apart from a spire that was added in the 19th century.

France's Merovingian kings were buried here during the 6th and 7th centuries, but their tombs disappeared during the Revolution. The interior is disfigured by truly appalling polychrome paintings and frescoes from the 19th century. The church, which is often used for concerts, is open daily from 8 am to 7 or 7.30 pm.

In early September 1792, a group of priests was hacked to death by a Revolutionary mob in what is now **Square Félix Desruelles**, the park between the church and

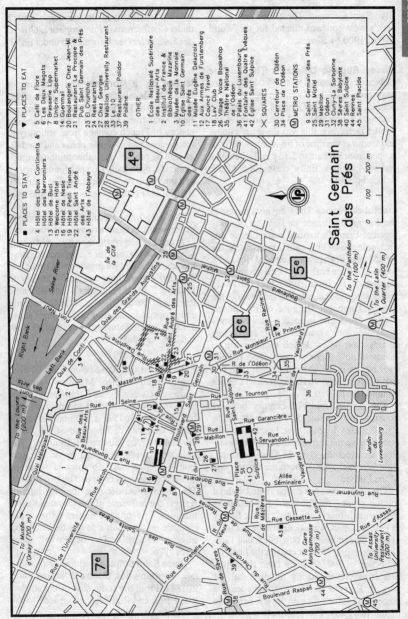

PLACES TO STAY
4 Hôtel des Deux Continents &
   Hôtel des Marronniers
13 Hôtel de Buci
15 Welcome Hôtel
16 Hôtel de Nesle
19 Hôtel Petit Trianon
22 Hôtel Saint André
   des Arts
43 Hôtel de l'Abbaye

▼ PLACES TO EAT
5 Café de Flore
6 Les Deux Magots
7 Brasserie Lipp
8 Uniprix Supermarket
14 Guenmaï
20 Boulangerie Chez Jean-Mi
21 Restaurant Le Procope &
   Pub Saint Germain des Prés
23 El Cruncho
24 Restaurants
27 Chez Georges
28 Tour University Restaurant
33 Le 10
37 Restaurant Polidor
39 Poilâne

OTHER
1 École Nationale Supérieure
   des Beaux-Arts
2 Institut de France &
   Bibliothèque Mazarine
3 Musée de la Monnaie
10 Église Saint Germain
   des Prés
11 Musée Eugène Delacroix
12 Aux Armes de Furstemberg
17 Council Travel
18 Lav' Club
26 Village Voice Bookshop
35 Théâtre National
   de l'Odéon
36 Palais du Luxembourg
41 Fontaine des Quatre Évêques
42 Église Saint Sulpice

✕ SQUARES
30 Carrefour de l'Odéon
34 Place de l'Odéon

Ⓜ METRO STATIONS
9 Saint Germain des Prés
25 Saint Michel
29 Mabillon
31 Odéon
32 Cluny–La Sorbonne
38 Sèvres Babylone
40 Saint Sulpice
44 Rennes
45 Saint Placide

Saint Germain
des Prés

Blvd Saint Germain. The glazed arch at the park's west end was created for the World Fair of 1900 by Sèvres.

Musée Eugène Delacroix The Eugène Delacroix Museum (☎ 43.54.04.87; metro Mabillon or Saint Germain des Prés) is behind Église Saint Germain des Prés at 6 Place de Furstemberg. Also known as the Atelier Delacroix, this was the artist's home and studio at the time of his death in 1863. It is open from 9.45 am to 5.15 pm. Ticket sales end at 4.45 pm. Entry costs 19FF (15FF reduced price).

Institut de France The Convention created the Institut de France in 1795 by bringing together France's various academies of arts and sciences. The most famous is the **Académie Française**, founded in 1635, whose 40 members (known as the *Immortels*, ie Immortals) are officially responsible for safeguarding the purity of the French language. Because of its conservatism – endemic in such august bodies – many of France's greatest writers and philosophers have been denied membership in favour of now-forgotten personages fawned over by the Establishment of their day. The first woman (Marguerite Yourcenar) was not admitted until 1980.

The domed, mid-17th-century building housing the Institut de France (☎ 43.29.55.10; metro Mabillon or Louvre-Rivoli), considered a masterpiece of French neoclassical architecture, is at 23 Quai de Conti, right across the Seine from the eastern end of the Louvre.

The only part which can be visited without joining a tour is the **Bibliothèque Mazarine** (Mazarine Library), the oldest public library in France, which was opened to the public in 1689. You can visit the bust-lined, late 17th-century reading room or consult the library's collection of 500,000 items from 10 am to 6 pm. It is closed during the first half of August. Entry is free but you must leave a piece of ID at the office on the left-hand side of the entryway. For information on tours

(40FF), usually held on weekends, check under Conférences in *Pariscope* or *L'Officiel des Spectacles* (see Information under Entertainment).

Musée de la Monnaie The Museum of Coins & Medals (☎ 40.46.55.33/35; metro Pont Neuf) at 11 Quai de Conti – just across Pont Neuf from Île de la Cité – traces the history of French coinage from antiquity to the present and includes coins and medals, as well as presses and other minting equipment. It is open daily except Monday from 1 to 6 pm (9 pm on Wednesday). The entry fee is 20FF (15FF for students and people over 60).

The Hôtel des Monnaies, which houses the museum, became a royal mint during the 18th century and is still used by the Ministry of Finance to produce commemorative medals. Except in August, tours in French of the mint's workshops are held Tuesday to Friday at 2.15 pm. The mint's shop is around the side of the building at 2 Rue Guénégaud and is open Monday to Friday from 9 am to 5.45 pm and on Saturday from 10 am to 1 pm and 2 to 5.30 pm.

Église Saint Sulpice St Sulpicius' Church (metro Saint Sulpice, Mabillon), situated midway between Église Saint Germain des Prés and the Jardin du Luxembourg, was built between 1645 and 1745 on the site of earlier churches dedicated to St Sulpicius, 6th-century Archbishop of Bourges. The Italianate façade, designed by an architect from Florence, has two rows of superimposed columns and is topped by two towers. The neoclassical décor of the vast interior reflects the influence of the Counter-Reformation. The **chapel** nearest the main entrance on the south side was decorated by Eugène Delacroix. The **organ loft** dates from 1776.

Place Saint Sulpice is adorned by a fountain, **Fontaine des Quatre Évêques**, built in 1844. From the south side of the square, Rue Férou and Rue Servandoni lead to the Jardin du Luxembourg.

Montparnasse (6e, 14e & 15e)

Around WW I, writers, poets and artists of the avant-garde abandoned Montmartre and moved to Montparnasse, shifting the centre of Paris's artistic ferment to the area around Blvd du Montparnasse. Chagall, Modigliani, Léger, Soutine, Miró, Kandinsky, Picasso, Stravinsky, Hemingway, Henry Miller and Cocteau as well as political exiles such as Lenin and Trotsky all used to hang out here at various times, talking endlessly in the cafés and restaurants for which the quarter is still famous. Montparnasse remained a creative centre until the mid-1930s.

Today, especially since the construction of the new Gare Montparnasse complex, there is very little to remind visitors of the area's bohemian past. Blvd du Montparnasse and its many fashionable cafés and cinemas attract large numbers of Parisians after dark.

Exploring on Foot The eastern end of Blvd du Montparnasse is just a few blocks south of the Jardin du Luxembourg (see Latin Quarter).

Weekly Closures
Sunday: Musée de la Poste

Blvd du Montparnasse Blvd du Montparnasse and nearby streets, which are lined with cinemas, restaurants and fashionable cafés, make up one of Paris's most important nightlife districts. For details about such historic cafés as La Coupole and Le Dôme, see Montparnasse under Restaurants & Cafés.

Tour Montparnasse If you consider the 209-metre-high Montparnasse Tower (☎ 45.38.52.56; metro Montparnasse Bienvenüe) at 33 Ave du Maine (15e) one of the most egregious examples of architectural arrogance to blot the Paris skyline, then a visit to the top of the tower – about the only place in the city where the tower itself can't be seen – may be worth considering. The view is most spectacular around sunset, when, if you stay long enough (the sun sets pretty slowly at this latitude), you can also see the city at night.

Admission to the observatory on the 56th floor costs 33FF (39FF including a visit to the open-air terrace on the 59th floor); students pay 22 and 30FF respectively. From Easter to September, the tower is open daily from 9.30 am to 11 pm. The rest of the year, it is open from 10 am to 10 pm (11 pm on Friday, Saturday and holidays). A guidebook (15FF) is available in six languages. To get to the ticket window, follow the signs to the *'visite panoramique – 56e et 59e étages'*.

Musée de la Poste The Postal Museum (☎ 42.79.24.24 or, for a recording, 43.79.23.45; metro Montparnasse Bienvenüe, Gare Montparnasse exit), which is a few hundred metres south-west of Tour Montparnasse at 34 Blvd de Vaugirard (5th floor; 15e), illustrates the history of postal service – a matter of particular importance in a

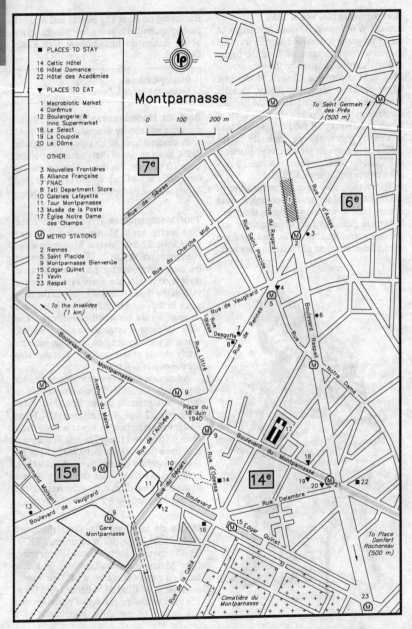

Montparnasse

0   100   200 m

■ PLACES TO STAY
14 Celtic Hôtel
16 Hôtel Domance
22 Hôtel des Académies

▼ PLACES TO EAT
1 Macrobiotic Market
4 Dorémus
12 Boulangerie &
   Inno Supermarket
18 Le Select
19 La Coupole
20 Le Dôme

OTHER
3 Nouvelles Frontières
6 Alliance Française
7 FNAC
8 Tati Department Store
10 Galeries Lafayette
11 Tour Montparnasse
13 Musée de la Poste
17 Église Notre Dame
   des Champs

Ⓜ METRO STATIONS
2 Rennes
5 Saint Placide
9 Montparnasse Bienvenüe
15 Edgar Quinet
21 Vavin
23 Raspail

7ᵉ

6ᵉ

15ᵉ

14ᵉ

To Saint Germain
des Prés
(500 m)

To the Invalides
(1 km)

Rue de Sèvres

Rue du Cherche Midi

Rue Saint Placide

Rue du Regard

Rue d'Assas

Boulevard Raspail

Rue de Rennes

Rue de Vaugirard

Rue L'Blaise

Rue Desgoffe

Rue Littré

Boulevard du Montparnasse

Avenue du Maine

Rue de l'Arrivée

Place du
18 Juin
1940

Boulevard du Montparnasse

Notre Dame

Rue Armand Moisant

Boulevard de Vaugirard

Rue du Départ

Rue d'Odessa

Boulevard

Rue Delambre

Gare
Montparnasse

Boulevard

15 Edgar Quinet

Rue de la Gaîté

Cimetière du
Montparnasse

To Place
Denfert
Rochereau
(500 m)

highly centralised state like France – from Roman times to the present. The 15 rooms showcase the original designs of French stamps, antique postal and telecommunications equipment, models of postal conveyances and all sorts of other items.

The museum is open from 10 am to 6 pm (closed holidays). Entrance costs 18FF (9FF for students, teachers, children and senior citizens). Special exhibitions (☎ 42.79.23.28), staged in an area next to the ground-floor lobby, are usually open Monday to Saturday from 10 am to 6 pm. They generally cost 25FF (12.50FF reduced price). There's a philatelic sales counter in the ground-floor lobby.

Cimetière du Montparnasse Montparnasse Cemetery (☎ 43.20.68.52; metro Edgar Quinet or Raspail) at 3 Blvd Edgar Quinet (14e) is a few blocks east of the Montparnasse Tower. It contains the graves of such notables as Charles Baudelaire, Guy de Maupassant, François Rude, Chaim Soutine, Constantin Brancusi, Camille Saint-Saëns, André Citroën, Simone de Beauvoir and Jean-Paul Sartre. It is open daily from 8 am to 5.30 pm (7.30 am to 6 pm from mid-March to mid- November).

Musée d'Orsay Area (7e)

The area of the Left Bank between the Musée d'Orsay and Rue de Babylone is known as the Faubourg Saint Germain. The city's most fashionable neighbourhood in the 1700s, its sumptuous walled homes were built by aristocrats and financiers, many of whom were later beheaded or exiled during the Revolution. Quite a few of these mansions have been turned into embassies or government ministries.

The Second Empire-style Ministère des Affaires Étrangères (Foreign Ministry), built from 1845 to 1855 and popularly referred to as the **Quai d'Orsay**, is at 37 Quai d'Orsay. It is just west of the **Palais Bourbon** at 33 Quai d'Orsay, which now houses France's Assemblée Nationale.

Exploring on Foot Some of the 7e arrondissement's most interesting 18th-century mansions are along three east-west oriented streets: **Rue de Lille**, **Rue de Grenelle** and **Rue de Varenne**. Without an official invitation, the mansions can only be glimpsed through the gates.

The Musée d'Orsay is only a few hundred metres south-west of the western end of the Louvre, but don't even *think* of visiting them both in the same day. The grassy expanse north of the Invalides, Esplanade des Invalides, is directly across the river from the Grand Palais and the Petit Palais.

Weekly Closures
Monday: Musée d'Orsay, Musée Rodin
Thursday: Égouts de Paris
Friday: Égouts de Paris

Musée d'Orsay The Musée d'Orsay (☎ 40.49.48.84 for information, 45.49.11.11 for a recording in French; metro Musée d'Orsay), along the Seine at 1 Rue de Bellechasse, displays France's national collection of paintings, sculptures, objets d'art and other works produced between 1848 and 1914, including the fruits of the impressionist, postimpressionist and Art Nouveau movements. It thus fills the chronological gap between the Louvre and the Musée National d'Art Moderne at the Centre Pompidou. The Musée d'Orsay is spectacularly housed in a former railway station built in 1900 and reinaugurated in its present form in 1986.

Many visitors take the lifts next to the ticket windows or the escalators at the far end of the building straight to the famous **impressionists** (Monet, Renoir, Pissarro, Sisley, Degas, Manet, Van Gogh, Cézanne) and **neoimpressionists** (Seurat, Matisse) on the skylight-lit upper level. But there's also a great deal to see on the ground floor, including some early works by Manet, Monet, Renoir and Pissarro. The middle level has some magnificent **Art Nouveau rooms**.

The Musée d'Orsay is open from 10 am (from 9 am on Sunday and from mid-June to

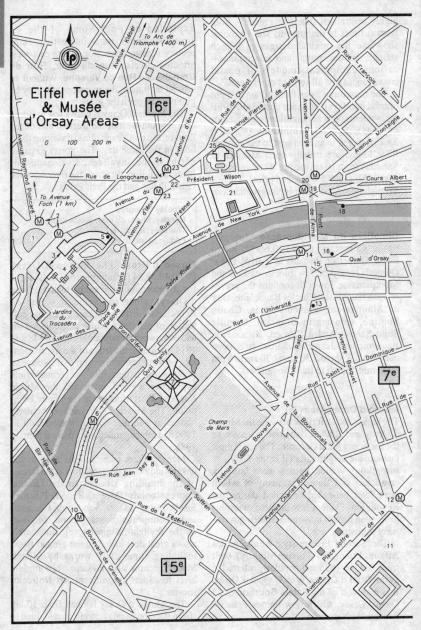

Eiffel Tower
& Musée
d'Orsay Areas

0   100   200 m

To Arc de
Triomphe (400 m)

To Avenue
Foch (1 km)

Avenue Raymond Poincaré

Avenue Kléber

Avenue Foch (1 km)

Avenue d'Iéna

Rue de Chaillot

Avenue Pierre 1er de Serbie

Avenue George V

Rue François 1er

Avenue Montaigne

16e

Rue de Longchamp

Président   Wilson

Cours   Albert

Avenue du

Avenue d'Iéna

Rue Fresnel

Avenue de New York

Pont de l'Alma

Place de Varsovie

Seine River

Quai d'Orsay

Rue de l'Université

Nations Unies

Jardins
du
Trocadéro

Avenue des

Pont d'Iéna

Quai Branly

Champ
de Mars

Avenue de la Bourdonnais

Avenue Rapp

Rue Saint-

Avenue Bosquet

Dominique

Rue de

7e

Pont de
Bir Hakeim

Rue Jean

Avenue de Suffren

Rue de la Fédération

Avenue J Bouvard

Avenue Charles Risler

Place Joffre

Avenue de la

15e

Boulevard de Grenelle

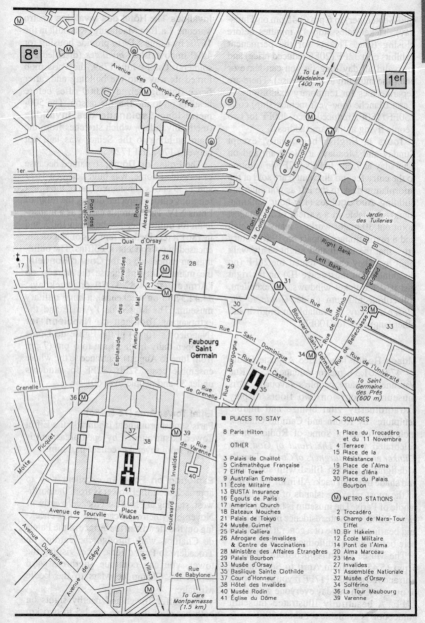

8e

1er

Avenue des Champs-Élysées

To La Madeleine (400 m)

Place de la Concorde

Jardin des Tuileries

Pont des Invalides

Pont Alexandre III

Pont de la Concorde

Quai d'Orsay

Right Bank

Left Bank

bridge closed

17

26

28

29

27

31

30

32

33

Rue de Solférino

Rue de Lille

Invalides

Avenue du Mar Gallieni

Esplanade des Invalides

Rue Saint Dominique

Faubourg Saint Germain

34

Rue de Bellechasse

Rue de l'Université

Boulevard Saint Germain

Rue de Bourgogne

Rue Las Cases

35

To Saint Germaine des Prés (600 m)

Grenelle

36

Rue de Grenelle

39

Rue de Varenne

Motte Picquet

37

38

41

40

Avenue de Tourville

Place Vauban

Boulevard des Invalides

Avenue Duquesne

Avenue de Ségur

Ave de la Mor...

Rue de Babylone

To Gare Montparnasse (1.5 km)

■ **PLACES TO STAY**

8 Paris Hilton

OTHER

3 Palais de Chaillot
5 Cinémathèque Française
7 Eiffel Tower
9 Australian Embassy
11 École Militaire
13 BUSTA Insurance
16 Égouts de Paris
17 American Church
18 Bateaux Mouches
21 Palais de Tokyo
24 Musée Guimet
25 Palais Galliera
26 Aérogare des Invalides
   & Centre de Vaccinations
28 Ministère des Affaires Étrangères
29 Palais Bourbon
33 Musée d'Orsay
35 Basilique Sainte Clothilde
37 Cour d'Honneur
38 Hôtel des Invalides
40 Musée Rodin
41 Église du Dôme

✕ **SQUARES**

1 Place du Trocadéro
   et du 11 Novembre
4 Terrace
15 Place de la
   Résistance
19 Place de l'Alma
22 Place d'Iéna
30 Place du Palais
   Bourbon

Ⓜ **METRO STATIONS**

2 Trocadéro
6 Champ de Mars-Tour
   Eiffel
10 Bir Hakeim
12 École Militaire
14 Pont de l'Alma
20 Alma Marceau
23 Iéna
27 Invalides
31 Assemblée Nationale
32 Musée d'Orsay
34 Solférino
36 La Tour Maubourg
39 Varenne

mid-September) to 6 pm (9.45 pm on Thursday). Ticket sales stop 45 minutes before closing time. Tickets for the permanent exhibits cost 32FF (20FF reduced price) and are valid all day long (ie you can leave or enter the museum as you please). There are separate fees for temporary exhibitions. A Carte Blanche (one-year membership) costs 250FF (180FF reduced price, 400FF for two people living at the same address).

Tours in English begin daily, except Sunday and Monday, at 11.30 am and on Thursday at 7 pm; tickets (32FF in addition to the entry fee; no discounts) are sold at the information desk to the left as you enter the building. **Audioguides** (1½-hour Walkman tours), available in a variety of languages, point out 30 major works – many of which had a revolutionary impact on 19th-century art – that the uninitiated might easily walk right by. They can be rented for 28FF (no discounts; you must leave ID) on the right just past the ticket windows. An excellent, full-colour museum guide, *Guide to the Musée d'Orsay*, is available in English and other languages for 100FF.

Musée Rodin The Musée Auguste Rodin (☎ 47.05.01.34; metro Varenne) at 77 Rue Varenne is many people's favourite Paris museum. Rooms on two floors display extraordinarily vital bronze and marble sculptures by Rodin and Camille Claudel, including casts of some of Rodin's most celebrated works: *The Hand of God*, *The Thinker* and *The Burghers of Calais*. There's a delightful **garden** filled with sculptures and shade trees out back. All in all, this is one of the most relaxing islands of calm in the whole of Paris. The museum is housed in the Hôtel Biron, a private residence built in 1728 and bearing the name of a general who lived here before being guillotined in 1793.

The Musée Rodin is open from 10 am to 5 pm (5.45 pm from April to September). Entrance costs 26FF (17FF if you're 18 to 25 or over 60). On Sunday everyone gets in for 17FF. A beautifully illustrated museum guidebook is available for about 50FF.

Invalides The **Hôtel des Invalides** (metro Varenne, La Tour Maubourg) was built in the 1670s by Louis XIV to provide housing for 4000 impoverished *invalides* (disabled ex-soldiers). On 14 July 1789, the Paris mob forced its way into the building and, after fierce fighting, seized 28,000 rifles before heading on to the Bastille prison. The 500-metre-long **Esplanade des Invalides** (metro Invalides), which stretches from the main building to the Seine, was laid out between 1704 and 1720.

The **Église du Dôme**, so named because of its gilded dome, was built between 1677 and 1735 and is considered one of the finest religious edifices erected during the reign of Louis XIV. The church's career as a mausoleum for military leaders began in 1800, and in 1861 it received the remains of Napoleon, encased in six concentric coffins. The buildings on either side of the **Cour d'Honneur**, the main courtyard, house the **Musée de l'Armée** (☎ 44.42.37.70 on weekdays, 44.42.37.68 on weekends), a huge military museum. The Musée de l'Armée and the extravagant **Tombeau de Napoléon 1er** (Napoleon's Tomb) in the Église du Dôme are open daily from 10 am to 6 pm (7 pm from June to August). Entrance to the whole ensemble costs 32FF (22FF for students under 30 and people over 60).

Eiffel Tower Area (7e & 16e)

Paris's most prominent landmark, the Eiffel Tower, is surrounded by open areas and is not far from several excellent museums.

Exploring on Foot An excellent way to approach the Eiffel Tower is from the north-west, starting at Place du Trocadéro et du 11 Novembre (metro Trocadéro). After checking out the view from the terrace of the Palais de Chaillot, walk through the Jardins du Trocadéro to Pont d'Iéna. After visiting the tower, you can continue south-eastward across the Champ de Mars to the École Militaire.

The Eiffel Tower and nearby sights on both banks of the Seine are 1.5 to two km

south of the Arc de Triomphe. Ave Kléber cuts through the fashionable 16e.

Weekly Closures
Monday: Musée d'Art Moderne de la Ville de Paris
Tuesday: Palais de Chaillot (Musée de l'Homme, Musée de la Marine, Musée du Cinéma, Musée des Monuments Français), Musée Guimet
Thursday & Friday: Égouts de Paris

Eiffel Tower The Tour Eiffel (☎ 45.50. 34.56; metro Champ de Mars-Tour Eiffel) faced massive opposition from Paris's artistic and literary elite when it was built for the Exposition Universelle (World Fair) of 1889, held to commemorate the centenary of the French Revolution. It was almost torn down in 1909 but was spared for purely practical reasons – it proved an ideal platform for the transmitting antennas needed for the new science of radiotelegraphy. It was the world's tallest structure until 1930.

The Eiffel Tower, named after its designer, Gustave Eiffel, is 320 metres high, including the television antenna at the very tip. This figure can vary by as much as 15 cm, as the tower's 7000 tonnes of steel, held together by 2.5 million rivets, expand in warm weather and contract when it's cold. When you're done peering upwards through the girders, you can choose to visit any of the three levels open to the public. The lift, which follows a curved trajectory, costs 18FF for the first platform (57 metres above the ground), 35FF for the second (115 metres) and 52FF for the third (276 metres). Children aged four to 12 pay 8/17/24FF respectively; there are no youth or student rates. Walking up the *escalier* (stairs) in the *pilier sud* (south pillar) to the first or second platforms costs 10FF.

The tower is open every day from 9.30 am (9 am from late March to early September) to 11 pm (midnight from early July to early September). The stairs are open from 9 am to 6.30 pm; they stay open until 11 pm from early July to early September and on Friday, Saturday and the eve of holidays from late May to early July. If you can, try to visit on a day when visibility isn't obscured by haze.

Champ de Mars The grassy area south-east of the Eiffel Tower, whose name means Field of Mars (Mars was the Roman god of war), was originally a parade ground for the **École Militaire** (Military Academy), the huge, classical building at the south-eastern end of the lawns whose graduates include Napoleon (Class of 1785). It was built from 1751 to 1769.

In 1783 the Champ de Mars (metro École Militaire or Champ de Mars-Tour Eiffel) was the site of one of the world's first balloon flights. During the Revolutionary period, two important mass ceremonies were held here: the Fête de la Fédération (Festival of Federation), held on 14 July 1790 to celebrate the first anniversary of the storming of the Bastille; and the Fête de l'Être Suprême (Festival of the Supreme Being) of 1794, at which Robespierre presided over a ceremony that established a Revolutionary state religion.

When the weather is good, young Parisians flock to the Champ de Mars to engage in such activities as skateboarding and rollerskating. There are **marionette shows** (☎ 48.56.01.44; metro École Militaire; 14FF) most days at 3.15 and 4.15 pm (closed Thursday and Friday).

Jardins du Trocadéro The Trocadéro Gardens (metro Trocadéro), whose fountains and statue garden are grandly illuminated at night, are across Pont d'Iéna from the Eiffel Tower. They are named after the Trocadéro, a Spanish stronghold near Cadiz captured by the French in 1823.

Palais de Chaillot The two curved, colonnaded wings of the Palais de Chaillot – built for the World Exhibition of 1937 – and the terrace between them afford an exceptional panorama of the Jardins du Trocadéro, the Seine and the Eiffel Tower.

The vast complex houses four museums, all of whose entrances are at Place du Trocadéro et du 11 Novembre (16e). The

Musée de l'Homme (Museum of Human-kind; ☎ 44.05.72.72), has anthropological and ethnographic exhibits from Africa, Asia, Europe, the Arctic, the South Pacific and the Americas. The **Musée de la Marine** (Maritime Museum; ☎ 45.53.31.70) is noted for its ship models. The film memorabilia at the **Musée du Cinéma Henri Langlois** (Cinema Museum; ☎ 45.53.74.39) illustrates the history of the seventh art. The **Musée des Monuments Français** (French Monuments Museum; ☎ 47.27.35.74), a rather unlikely institution, traces the history of French monumental art using plaster casts and reproductions.

The far eastern tip of the Palais de Chaillot contains the **Cinémathèque Française** (☎ 47.04.24.24), which screens several non-dubbed (v.o.) films almost every day. See Cinema under Entertainment for details.

Musée Guimet The Guimet Museum (☎ 47.23.61.65; metro Iéna) at 6 Place d'Iéna (16e), which is about midway between the Eiffel Tower and the Arc de Triomphe, displays antiquities and works of art from South Asia (Afghanistan, India, Nepal, Pakistan and Tibet), South-East Asia (Cambodia) and East Asia (China, Japan and Korea). It is open from 9.45 am to 6 pm. Entrance costs 26FF (14FF reduced price).

Palais de Tokyo The Palais de Tokyo at 11 Ave du Président Wilson (16e), built – like the Palais de Chaillot – for the World Exhibition of 1937, houses the **Musée d'Art Moderne de la Ville de Paris** (Modern Art Museum of the City of Paris; ☎ 47.23.61.27; metro Iéna). Its collections include representatives of just about every major artistic movement of the 20th century (fauvism, cubism, the School of Paris, surrealism and expressionism) as well as the fruits of other less classifiable approaches. The more famous artists with works on display include Matisse, Picasso, Braque, Soutine, Modigliani, Chagall and Dufy.

The museum is open (except holidays) from 10 am to 5.30 pm (8.30 pm on Wednesday). Tickets cost 14 to 35FF, depending on what sort of temporary exhibition is on.

Égouts de Paris A city cannot grow, prosper and become truly great unless some way is found to deal with the important question of...sewerage. In Paris, you can learn all about this aspect of Paris's greatness by visiting the Musée des Égouts de Paris (Paris Sewers Museum; ☎ 47.05.10.29; metro Pont de l'Alma), a unique working museum whose entrance – a rectangular maintenance hole – is across the street from 93 Quai d'Orsay (7e). As raw sewage with all sorts of vaguely familiar objects floating in it flows beneath your feet, you walk through 480 metres of sewerage tunnels, breathing the odoriferous air and passing artefacts illustrating the development of Paris's wastewater disposal system. Unlike most museums in France, the Égouts have excellent explanatory signs in English, German and Spanish. At the end of the walk, visitors are treated to a 20-minute slide show on wastewater management.

The Égouts are open (except when rain threatens to flood the tunnels) from 11 am to 4 or 5 pm (6 pm in summer). The entry fee is 24FF (19FF for students and seniors).

Champs-Élysées Area (8e & 16e)

This grand avenue, whose name means Elysian Fields (Elysium was where Greek and Roman mythology held that happy souls dwelt after death), links Place de la Concorde with the Arc de Triomphe. Since the Second Empire (1852-70), it has come to symbolise the style and *joie de vivre* of life in Paris.

The triangular area whose corners are at Place de la Concorde, the Arc de Triomphe and Place de l'Alma is known as the **Triangle d'Or** (golden triangle). This is where you'll find some of Paris's richest residents, finest hotels and most fashionable couture houses (see Fashion under Things to Buy).

Exploring on Foot For details on the Voie Triomphale, see Exploring on Foot under Louvre Area.

The most attractive part of Ave des

Champs-Élysées is the shady, grass-covered stretch between Place de la Concorde and Rond-Point des Champs-Élysées. Ave Montaigne, home of haute couture, makes a good place to start exploring the Triangle d'Or.

The Petit Palais and Grand Palais are just one km north of the Invalides and the nearby Musée Rodin. The Eiffel Tower is separated from the Arc de Triomphe by about two km of the fashionable 16e arrondissement.

Weekly Closures
Monday: Musée du Petit Palais, Palais de la Découverte

Ave des Champs-Élysées Popular with the mid-19th-century aristocracy as a stage on which to parade their wealth, the two-km-long Ave des Champs-Élysées has, in recent decades, been largely taken over by airline offices, cinemas and car showrooms – well as fast-food restaurants, overpriced cafés and other establishments well-suited to separating enthralled but hungry tourists from their money. The wealthy denizens of the Triangle d'Or consider the Champs-Élysées to be completely – but not quite inexorably – degraded and popularised, by which they mean the same thing. The even-numbered side of Ave des Champs-Élysées between Rond-Point des Champs-Élysées and Rue de Berrie is perforated by a series of **shopping arcades**.

In recent years, the municipality has been investing lots of money to give the Champs-Élysées some of its sparkle back, in part by adding trees and toning down the fast-food joints.

Rue du Faubourg Saint Honoré The eastern section of Rue du Faubourg Saint Honoré (1er & 8e) has some of Paris's most renowned couture houses as well as the famous Hermès shop. Other luxury items available here include jewellery and fine antiques.

The most noteworthy of the 18th-century mansions along Rue du Faubourg Saint Honoré is **Palais de l'Élysée**, official residence of the French president and symbol of his extensive powers, which is at the intersection of Ave de Marigny (8e) and Rue du Faubourg Saint Honoré. Built in 1718, it has housed 19 French presidents since 1873. The interior is closed to the public.

Musée du Petit Palais The Petit Palais (☎ 42.66.96.24, 42.65.12.73; metro Champs Élysées-Clemenceau), built for the Exposition Universelle of 1900, is on Ave Winston Churchill (8e). The Musée des Beaux-Arts (Fine Arts Museum) that it houses specialises in medieval and Renaissance porcelain, clocks, tapestries, drawings, etc and 19th-century French painting and sculpture, all from the collections of the City of Paris. It is open from 10 am to 5.40 pm. The entry fee is 26FF (14FF reduced price). Temporary exhibitions usually cost 35FF (25FF reduced price).

Grand Palais The Grand Palais (☎ 44.13. 17.30; metro Champs-Élysées), which is across Ave Winston Churchill (8e) from the Petit Palais and was also built for the Exposition Universelle of 1900, is used to stage special exhibitions. It has an iron frame and an Art Nouveau-style glass roof. The main entrance faces Ave des Champs-Élysées.

Palais de la Découverte This fascinating science musem (☎ 40.74.80.00 for the switchboard, 43.59.18.21 for a recording in French; metro Champs-Élysées Clemenceau) on Ave Franklin D Roosevelt (8e) has interactive exhibits on astronomy, biology and medicine, chemistry, mathematics and computer science, physics and earth sciences. Although the signs, explanations and excellent public demonstrations are in French, much of the material is self-explanatory if you still remember a bit of high school physics and biology. The two **Euréka rooms** have exhibits for young children.

Palais de la Découverte is open from 9.30 am to 6 pm (7 pm on Sunday and holidays). Entrance costs 22FF (11FF for students and people under 18 or over 60). The **planetarium**, which has five shows a day (in French), costs 15FF (10FF reduced price).

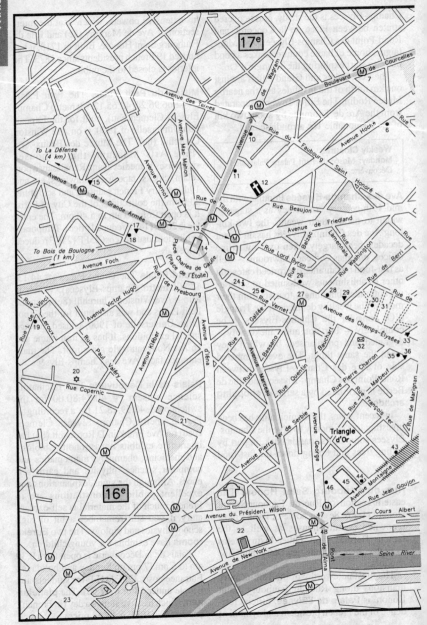

17^e

16^e

To La Défense
(4 km)

To Bois de Boulogne
(1 km)

Boulevard de Courcelles

Avenue des Ternes

Avenue de Wagram

Rue du Faubourg Saint Honoré

Avenue Hoche

Avenue Mac Mahon

Avenue Carnot

Avenue de la Grande Armée

Rue de Tilsitt

Rue Beaujon

Avenue de Friedland

Rue Lord Byron

Rue Balzac

Rue Lamennais

Rue Washington

Rue de Berri

Place Charles de Gaulle
(Place de l'Étoile)

Avenue Foch

Rue de Presbourg

Avenue Victor Hugo

Rue de Vinci

Rue L. de Leroux

Rue Paul Valéry

Avenue Kléber

Avenue d'Iéna

Rue Copernic

Rue Vernet

Rue Galilée

Rue de Bassano

Avenue Marceau

Rue Quentin

Avenue des Champs-Élysées

Rue de Ponthieu

Rue Bauchart

Rue Pierre Charron

Rue Marbeuf

Rue François 1er

Rue de Marignan

Triangle
d'Or

Avenue Pierre 1er de Serbie

Avenue George V

Avenue Montaigne

Rue Jean Goujon

Avenue du Président Wilson

Cours Albert

Pont de l'Alma

Seine River

Avenue de New York

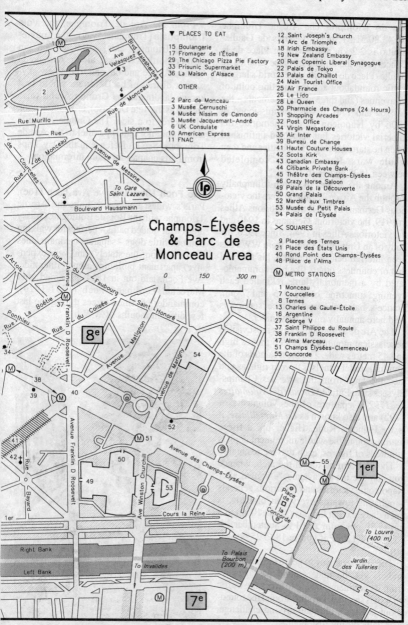

▼ PLACES TO EAT
15 Boulangerie
17 Fromager de l'Étoile
29 The Chicago Pizza Pie Factory
33 Prisunic Supermarket
36 La Maison d'Alsace

OTHER
2 Parc de Monceau
3 Musée Cernuschi
4 Musée Nissim de Camondo
5 Musée Jacquemart-André
6 UK Consulate
10 American Express
11 FNAC

12 Saint Joseph's Church
14 Arc de Triomphe
18 Irish Embassy
19 New Zealand Embassy
20 Rue Copernic Liberal Synagogue
22 Palais de Tokyo
23 Palais de Chaillot
24 Main Tourist Office
25 Air France
26 Le Lido
28 Le Queen
30 Pharmacie des Champs (24 Hours)
31 Shopping Arcades
32 Post Office
34 Virgin Megastore
35 Air Inter
39 Bureau de Change
41 Haute Couture Houses
42 Scots Kirk
43 Canadian Embassy
44 Citibank Private Bank
45 Théâtre des Champs-Élysées
46 Crazy Horse Saloon
49 Palais de la Découverte
50 Grand Palais
52 Marché aux Timbres
53 Musée du Petit Palais
54 Palais de l'Élysée

✕ SQUARES
9 Places des Ternes
21 Place des États Unis
40 Rond Point des Champs-Élysées
48 Place de l'Alma

Ⓜ METRO STATIONS
1 Monceau
7 Courcelles
8 Ternes
13 Charles de Gaulle-Étoile
16 Argentine
27 George V
37 Saint Philippe du Roule
38 Franklin D Roosevelt
47 Alma Marceau
51 Champs Élysées-Clemenceau
55 Concorde

Champs-Élysées
& Parc de
Monceau Area

0   150   300 m

Arc de Triomphe The Arc de Triomphe (☎ 43.80.31.31; metro Charles de Gaulle-Étoile) is 2.2 km north-west of Place de la Concorde in the middle of Place Charles de Gaulle (Place de l'Étoile), the world's largest traffic roundabout and the meeting point of 12 avenues (and three arrondissements – the 8e, 16e and 17e). It was commissioned in 1806 by Napoleon to commemorate his imperial victories but remained unfinished when he started losing – first battles and then whole wars. It was finally completed between 1832 and 1836.

Among the armies to march triumphally through the Arc de Triomphe were the victorious Germans in 1871, the victorious Allies in 1919, the victorious Germans in 1940 and the victorious Allies in 1944. Since 1920, the body of an Unknown Soldier from WW I has been interred beneath the arch, his fate and that of countless others like him commemorated by a memorial flame rekindled each evening sometime between 5 and 7 pm. France's national remembrance service is held here annually on 11 November.

The Arc de Triomphe, Paris's most visible neoclassical monument, is 49.5 metres high and 45 metres wide. The most famous of the four high-relief panels is to your right as you face the arch from the Ave des Champs-Élysées side. Entitled *Départ des Volontaires de 1792* (Departure of the Volunteers of 1792) and also known as *La Marseillaise*, it is by François Rude. Higher up, a frieze running round the whole monument depicts hundreds of figures, each two metres high.

The platform on top of the arch, whence you can see the 12 avenues – named after Napoleonic victories and illustrious generals – radiating towards every part of Paris, is open daily, except holidays, from 10 am to 5 pm (5.30 pm from April to September). It costs 31FF (20FF if you're 18 to 25 or over 60).

The only sane way to get to the base of the arch is via the underground passageways from its perimeter: trying to cross the traffic on foot is suicidal. Driving around the roundabout is Paris's ultimate driving challenge, especially during rush hour.

From the Arc de Triomphe, the **Voie Triomphale** (Triumphal Way) – the Louvre-Arc de Triomphe axis – stretches 4.5 km further north-westward along Ave de la Grande Armée and beyond to the new skyscraper district of **La Défense**, whose best known landmark, the **Grande Arche** (also known as the Tête Défense), is a hollow cube 112 metres to a side. The Grande Arche is almost (but not quite) parallel to the Arc de Triomphe. See La Défense in the Day Trips from Paris chapter for more information.

Ave Foch Ultraexclusive Ave Foch (16e), Paris's widest boulevard, links the Arc de Triomphe with the Bois de Boulogne. Grassy areas with shaded paths – perfect for walking neurotic little dogs – separate the main lanes of traffic from the stately (and *very* expensive) apartment buildings along either side. Ave Foch, laid out in 1854, is named after Maréchal Ferdinand Foch (1851-1929), commander of Allied forces during the last few difficult months of WW I.

Parc de Monceau Area (8e)

The Parc de Monceau is at the northern edge of the plush 8e arrondissement, one of Paris's most elegant and expensive residential districts.

Exploring on Foot In the immediate vicinity of the park, you can explore the luxury apartment-lined streets of the 8e and 17e arrondissements.

Parc de Monceau is one km north-east of the Arc de Triomphe (along Ave Hoche) and a bit over one km north of Rond-Point des Champs-Élysées.

Weekly Closures
Monday: Musée Cernuschi, Musée Nissim de Camondo, Musée Jacquemart-André
Tuesday: Musée Nissim de Camondo, Musée Jacquemart-André

Parc de Monceau Pass though one of the gates in the elaborate wrought-iron fence around the Parc de Monceau (metro Monceau) and you're surrounded by classical statues and Paris's most immaculately tended lawns, flowerbeds and trees. From the many benches, you can watch the city's most impeccably dressed children out with their nannies or on their way home from expensive private schools. Nearby streets are lined with opulent mansions and grand apartment buildings from the mid-19th century. The world's first parachute jump was made here from a balloon in 1797. The park is open daily until 7.45 pm (9.45 pm from April to October).

Musée Cernuschi The Cernuschi Museum (☎ 45.63.50.75; metro Monceau) at 7 Ave Velasquez displays a collection of ancient Chinese art (funerary statues, bronzes, ceramics) and works from Japan assembled during the 19th century by the banker Henri Cernuschi. It is open from 10 am to 5.40 pm. Entry costs 17FF (9FF reduced price).

Musée Nissim de Camondo The Nissim de Camondo Museum (☎ 45.63.26.32; metro Monceau, Villiers) at 63 Rue de Monceau displays 18th-century furniture, wood panelling, tapestries, porcelain and other objets d'art collected by Count Moïse de Camondo, who had this museum established in memory of his son Nissim, who died in WW I. It is open from 10 am to noon and 2 to 5 pm (closed holidays). Tickets cost 20FF (14FF reduced price).

Musée Jacquemart-André The Jacquemart-André Museum (☎ 42.89.04.91; metro Saint Philippe du Roule) at 158 Blvd Haussmann, which is 400 metres south of the Parc de Monceau, is housed in an opulent residence built during the mid-19th century. The collection includes paintings by Rembrandt and Van Dyck and works from the Italian Renaissance by Bernini, Botticelli, Carpaccio, Donatello, Mantegna, Tintoretto, Titian and Uccello. The museum also has furniture, tapestries and enamels. It is open Wednesday to Sunday. Entry costs 35FF (20FF reduced price).

Opéra-Garnier Area (8e & 9e)

Opéra-Garnier, Paris's famous opera house, is surrounded by the Grands Boulevards, great 19th-century avenues whose *belle époque* elegance – enhanced by Haussmann's construction of Place de l'Opéra – has largely given way to the traffic and pedestrian tumult of modern commerce.

Exploring on Foot The Grands Boulevards and nearby streets make for a stimulating stroll. Places you might explore include:

- Department store-lined Blvd Haussmann
- Rue de la Chaussée d'Antin, which was enormously fashionable in the late 1700s
- Blvd des Capucines and Blvd de la Madeleine, which take you the 600 metres to La Madeleine
- Rue de la Paix, known for its jewellery shops, which leads to Place Vendôme
- One-km-long Ave de l'Opéra, which goes straight to the Louvre

---

Weekly Closures
Sunday: Opéra-Garnier, department stores on Blvd Haussmann

Opéra-Garnier Paris's renowned opera house (☎ 40.01.24.93; metro Opéra) at Place de l'Opéra (9e), designed in 1860 by Charles Garnier to showcase the splendour of Napoleon III's France, is one of the most impressive monuments erected during the Second Empire. The extravagant **entrance hall**, with its **Grand Escalier** (great staircase), is decorated with multicoloured, imported marble and a gigantic chandelier. The **ceiling** of the auditorium was painted by Marc Chagall in 1964.

Opéra-Garnier is open to visitors daily from 10 am to 5.30 pm. The entrance fee is 28FF (15FF for children aged 10 to 16). Opera performances now take place at the new Opéra-Bastille at Place de la Bastille, but Opéra-Garnier is still used for concerts and ballets. See Entertainment for details on ticket sales.

Blvd Haussmann Right behind Opéra-Garnier is Blvd Haussmann (8e & 9e), the heart of a commercial and banking district where you'll find some of Paris's most famous department stores, including **Galeries Lafayette** at 40 Blvd Haussmann and **Au Printemps** at 64 Blvd Haussmann. For more information, see the Things to Buy section.

The thoroughfares around Blvd Haussmann are lined with the kind of elegant, 19th-century buildings for which Paris is famous.

19th-Century Arcades Stepping into the covered shopping arcades off Blvd Montmartre is the easiest way to visit early 19th-century Paris. **Passage des Panoramas** (metro Rue Montmartre) at 11 Blvd Montmartre (2e), which was opened in 1800 and received Paris's first gas lighting in 1817, was expanded in 1834 with the addition of four other *passages*: Feydeau, Montmartre, Saint Marc and Des Variétés.

Directly across Blvd Montmartre between Nos 10 and 12 Blvd Montmartre is **Passage Jouffroy** (metro Rue Montmartre), which leads across Rue de la Grange Batelière (9e) to **Passage Verdeau**. Both shelter shops selling antiques, old postcards, antiquarian books, doggie toys, imports from Asia and the like. A bit to the east at 97 Rue de Richelieu (2e) is **Passages des Princes** (metro Richelieu Drouot), where many of Paris's pipe-makers are concentrated.

Gare de l'Est Area (10e)

There's a lively, working-class area (metro Château d'Eau, Gare de l'Est) with an ethnically mixed population – including many Indians, Pakistanis, Turks and Kurds – around Blvd de Strasbourg and Rue du Faubourg Saint Denis, especially south of Blvd de Magenta.

Porte Saint Denis (metro Strasbourg Saint Denis), the 24-metre-high triumphal arch at the intersection of Rue du Faubourg Saint Denis and Blvd Saint Denis, was built in 1672 to commemorate Louis XIV's campaign along the Rhine. On the north side, carvings represent the fall of Maastricht (in 1673, not 1993). Two blocks to the east, at the intersection of Rue du Faubourg Saint Martin and Blvd Saint Denis, is another triumphal arch, 17-metre-high **Porte Saint Martin**, erected in 1674 to commemorate the capture of Besançon and the Franche-Comté region by Louis XIV's armies.

Canal Saint Martin (10e & 19e)

The little-touristed Saint Martin Canal (metro République, Gare de l'Est, Jaurès and others) is one of Paris's hidden delights. The 4½-km-long waterway, parts of which are higher than the surrounding land, was built in 1806 to link the Seine with the 108-km Canal de l'Ourcq, which goes from La Villette north-eastward to La Ferté Milon. Its partly shaded towpaths are a wonderful place for a romantic stroll or bike ride past **locks** (nine of them), metal bridges and ordinary Parisian neighbourhoods.

Between Porte de Plaisance de Paris-Arsenal (the pleasure-boat marina next to Place de la Bastille; metro Bastille) and Square Frédéric Lemaître (10e; metro République), the Canal Saint Martin disappears under reinforced concrete vaults for over two km. The northern half of the canal, which links Square Frédéric Lemaître with

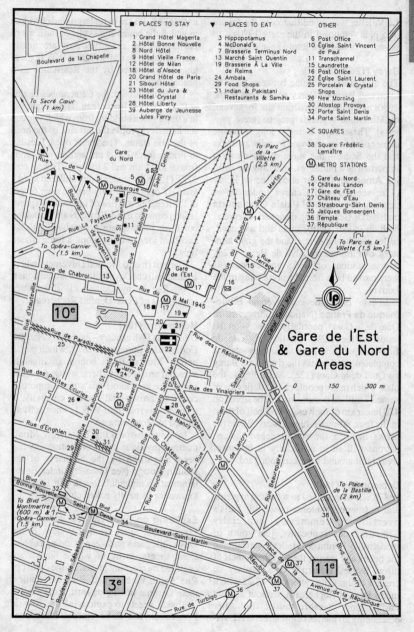

■ PLACES TO STAY

1 Grand Hôtel Magenta
2 Hôtel Bonne Nouvelle
8 Nord Hôtel
9 Hôtel Vieille France
12 Hôtel de Milan
18 Hôtel d'Alsace
20 Grand Hôtel de Paris
21 Sibour Hôtel
23 Hôtel du Jura & Hôtel Crystal
28 Hôtel Liberty
39 Auberge de Jeunesse Jules Ferry

▼ PLACES TO EAT

3 Hippopotamus
4 McDonald's
7 Brasserie Terminus Nord
13 Marché Saint Quentin
19 Brasserie À La Ville de Reims
24 Ambala
29 Food Shops
31 Indian & Pakistani Restaurants & Samiha

OTHER

6 Post Office
10 Église Saint Vincent de Paul
11 Transchannel
15 Laundrette
16 Post Office
22 Église Saint Laurent
25 Porcelain & Crystal Shops
26 New Morning
30 Allostop Provoya
32 Porte Saint Denis
34 Porte Saint Martin

✕ SQUARES

38 Square Frédéric Lemaître

Ⓜ METRO STATIONS

5 Gare du Nord
14 Château Landon
17 Gare de l'Est
27 Château d'Eau
33 Strasbourg-Saint Denis
35 Jacques Bonsergent
36 Temple
37 République

Gare de l'Est
& Gare du Nord
Areas

0   150   300 m

La Villette, was saved thanks to the failure of a plan – mooted in the early 1970s – to pave it over and turn it into an autoroute.

Bercy (12e & 13e)

The area along the Seine between Gare de Lyon and Porte de Bercy spent most of the 1980s as a huge construction site for several of Mitterrand's grands projets (great projects). These days, Bercy – long a remote corner of the city enclosed by railway tracks and the Seine – has some of Paris's most important new buildings, including the striking **American Center** at 51 Rue de Bercy (12e; see Cultural Centres under Information); the octagonal **Palais Omnisports** on Blvd de Bercy (12e), designed to serve as both an indoor sports arena and a concert, ballet and theatre venue; and the giant **Ministry of Finance** on Blvd de Bercy (12e), whose minions of clerks and economists were moved here from the north wing of the Louvre.

In late 1996, the controversial **Bibliothèque de France** (National Library; metro Quai de la Gare), popularly known – on the model of the TGV – as the Très Grande Bibliothèque (very large library), is set to be completed right across the river from Bercy on Quai de la Gare (13e). According to the plan, which many people charge defies logic, some 17 million documents will be stored on 420 linear km of shelves, almost half of them in the four, 80-metre-high towers. While the books bake in the sun-drenched towers, patrons will sit in artificially lit basement areas built around a sunken courtyard.

Catacombes (14e)

In 1785, it was decided to solve the hygienic and aesthetic problems posed by Paris's overflowing cemeteries (especially Cimetière des Innocents, just south of modern-day Forum des Halles) by exhuming the bones and storing them in the tunnels of three disused quarries. One ossuary so created is the Catacombes (☎ 43.22.47.63; metro Denfert Rochereau), without a doubt Paris's most macabre tourist site. After descending 20 metres below street level, vis-

itors follow 1.6 km of underground corridors in which the bones and skulls of millions of Parisians from centuries past are neatly stacked along the walls. During WW II, these tunnels were used by the Résistance as a headquarters.

The route through the Catacombes begins at Place Denfert Rochereau. The entrance is in a small green building from which you can see in perfect profile the left side of the head of the lion statue. The site is open Tuesday to Friday from 2 to 4 pm and on weekends from 9 to 11 am and 2 to 4 pm. Tickets cost 27FF (15FF for students and children aged 7 to 16). I'm not sure why people over 60 get in for free, but a series of unpleasant speculations come to mind...Tripods are forbidden but flash pictures are no problem. It's an excellent idea to bring along a torch (flashlight).

The exit (metro Mouton Duvernet), where a guard will check your bag for stolen bones, is on Rue Remy Dumoncel, 700 metres south-west of Place Denfert Rochereau.

Montmartre (18e)

During the 19th century – especially after the Communard uprising of 1871, which began here – Montmartre's bohemian lifestyle attracted artists and writers, whose presence turned the area into Paris's most important centre of artistic and literary creativity. It retained this role until WW I, when activity shifted to Montparnasse.

In English-speaking countries, Montmartre's mystique of unconventionality has been magnified by the notoriety of the **Moulin Rouge** (see Cabarets under Entertainment), a nightclub founded in 1889 and known for its nearly naked chorus girls.

Exploring on Foot The real attraction of Montmartre, apart from the view, is the area's little parks and steep, winding cobblestone streets, many of whose houses are engulfed by creeping plants. At the corner of Rue Saint Vincent and Rue des Saules, there's even a small **vineyard**, Paris's last.

Lovely streets to explore include Rue de l'Abreuvoir, Rue Saint Vincent, Place Con-

Top Left: View of Latin Quarter from Notre Dame, Paris (GA)
Top Right: Parc du Champ de Mars, from the Eiffel Tower, Paris (GA)
Bottom Left: Looking down the Champs-Élysées, Paris (GA)
Bottom Right: View of the Seine River from Notre Dame, Paris (GA)

Top: Restaurant adorned with Christmas decorations, Paris (RN)
Middle: Cinema hoarding, Paris (GA); French-style advertising, Paris (DR);
Gargoyles guard Notre Dame, Paris (GA)
Bottom: Arc de Triomphe at night, Paris (PS)

stantin Pecqueur and **Place Émile Goudeau**, where Kees Van Dongen, Max Jacob, Amedeo Modigliani and Pablo Picasso once lived in great poverty in a building Jacob dubbed the **Bateau Lavoir** (floating laundry shed).

From Place des Abbesses, walking 200 metres south along Rue Houdon will take you to Place Pigalle and Blvd de Clichy, the lively heart of the seedy Pigalle district.

The RATP's sleek, ultramodern *funiculaire* (funicular railway) – really a glorified, slightly horizontal lift – up Montmartre's south slope whisks visitors from Square Willette (metro Anvers) to a point just below the main entrance to Sacré Cœur. It runs until 12.45 am and costs one metro/bus ticket each way. Weekly and monthly Carte Orange coupons and Paris Visite and Formule 1 metro/bus passes (none of which is on sale here) are also valid.

Weekly Closures
Monday: Musée du Vieux Montmartre, Musée d'Art Naïf
Friday: Musée d'Art Juif
Saturday: Musée d'Art Juif

Sacré Cœur The Basilique du Sacré Cœur (Sacred Heart Basilica; ☎ 42.51.17.02; metro Lamarck Caulaincourt), perched at the very top of Butte de Montmartre (Montmartre Hill), was built from contributions to fulfil a vow of contrition taken by Parisian Catholics after the humiliating Franco-Prussian war of 1870-71. Construction of the structure began in 1873, but it wasn't consecrated until 1919.

On warm evenings, people congregate on the steps below the church to play guitars, sing and contemplate the stunning view of Paris and beyond (visibility can reach 50 km when it's clear). While the basilica's domes are a well-loved part of the Parisian skyline, the Romano-Byzantine architecture of the rest of the building – typical of the exceptionally garish taste of the late 19th century – is, how shall we say...somewhat lacking in grace. But although the building has been described as 'hideous', behind the purists'

contempt and vehemence there's usually more than a little affection.

The basilica is open daily from 6.45 am to 11 pm or midnight. The **dome** and the **crypt**, which cost 15FF (8FF for students) and 10FF (4FF for students) respectively, are open daily from 9 am to 6 pm (7 pm from about April to September). A combined ticket for both costs 25FF (13FF for students).

Place du Tertre A bit west of **Église Saint Pierre**, the only building left from the great abbey of Montmartre, is Place du Tertre, once the main square of the village of Montmartre. It is now filled with cafés, restaurant tables, excited tourists and starving artists selling their works (you can tell they're starving because they spend most of their time painting tourists' heads...on paper, of course). The whole scene is as animated as an amusement park, but hardly more authentic.

Musée du Vieux Montmartre The Museum of Old Montmartre (☎ 46.06.61.11; metro Lamarck Caulaincourt) at 12 Rue Cortot, also known as the Musée de Montmartre, displays paintings, lithographs and documents relating to the area's politically rebellious and bohemian-artistic past. It's hard to appreciate what the big deal is (and to justify the admission fee) unless you know something about Montmartre's mythology – and can read French. There's a lush and wild little garden out the back. The museum is open from 11 am to 5.30 pm. Entry costs 25FF (15FF for students).

Musée d'Art Naïf Max Fourny The Museum of Naive Art, founded in 1986, is housed in **Halle Saint Pierre** (☎ 42.58. 72.89; metro Anvers) at 2 Rue Ronsard, across Square Willette from the base of the funicular railway. The colourful, vivid paintings – gathered from around the world – are immediately appealing, thanks in part to their whimsical and generally optimistic perspective on life. The museum, each of whose exhibitions has a theme, is open from 10 am

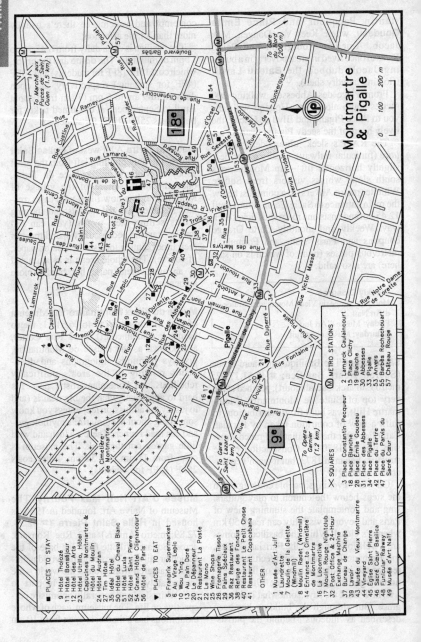

Montmartre & Pigalle

0   100   200 m

PLACES TO STAY
- 9 Hôtel Tholozé
- 11 Hôtel Bonséjour
- 12 Hôtel des Arts
- 23 Hôtel Utrillo, Hôtel Capucines Montmartre & Hôtel du Moulin
- 24 Hôtel Audran
- 27 Tim Hôtel
- 35 Idéal Hôtel
- 50 Hôtel du Cheval Blanc
- 51 Hôtel Luxia
- 52 Hôtel Saint Pierre
- 54 Grand Hôtel Clignancourt
- 56 Hôtel de Paris

▼ PLACES TO EAT
- 5 Franprix Supermarket
- 6 Au Virage Lepic
- 10 Wou Ying
- 13 Au Pain Doré
- 20 Le Dépanneur
- 21 Restaurant La Poste
- 22 Le Mono
- 25 Wine Shops
- 26 Fromagerie Tissot
- 36 Refuge des Fondus
- 38 Raz Restaurant
- 40 Restaurant Le Petit Chose
- 41 Restaurant Copacabana

OTHER
- 1 Musée d'Art Juif
- 4 Laundrette
- 7 Moulin de la Galette
- 8 Moulin Radet (Windmill)
- 14 Entrance to Cimetière de Montmartre
- 16 La Locomotive
- 17 Moulin Rouge Nightclub
- 32 Post Office & 24-Hour Exchange Machine
- 37 Bureau de Change
- 39 Lavoir
- 43 Musée du Vieux Montmartre
- 44 Vineyard
- 45 Église Saint Pierre
- 46 Sacré Cœur Basilica
- 48 Funicular Railway
- 49 Musée d'Art Naïf

× SQUARES
- 3 Place Constantin Pecqueur
- 18 Place Blanche
- 28 Place Émile Goudeau
- 31 Place des Abbesses
- 34 Place Pigalle
- 42 Place du Tertre
- 47 Place du Parvis du Sacré Cœur

Ⓜ METRO STATIONS
- 2 Lamarck Caulaincourt
- 15 Place Clichy
- 19 Blanche
- 30 Abbesses
- 33 Pigalle
- 53 Anvers
- 55 Barbès Rochechouart
- 57 Château Rouge

most famous in Paris after Père Lachaise. It contains the graves of such well-known personages as the writers Émile Zola, Alexandre Dumas the younger, Stendahl and Heinrich Heine, the composers Jacques Offenbach and Hector Berlioz, the painter Edgar Degas, the filmmaker François Truffaut and the dancer Nijinsky.

The entrance nearest the Butte de Montmartre is at 20 Rue Rachel, down the stairs from 10 Rue Caulaincourt. From mid-March to early November, it is open daily from 8 am (8.30 am on Saturday, 9 am on Sunday and holidays) to 6 pm (last entry at 5.45 pm). The rest of the year, it's open from 8 am to 5.30 pm.

Pigalle Only a few blocks south-west of the tranquil, residential streets of Montmartre is lively Pigalle (9e and 18e), one of Paris's two major sex districts (the other, near Forum des Halles, is along Rue Saint Denis). But Pigalle is more than simply a sleazy red-light district: though the area around Blvd de Clichy between the Pigalle and Blanche metro stops is lined with neon-lit porn shops and striptease parlours, there are also plenty of trendy nightspots, including several all-night cafés and La Locomotive disco. The Moulin Rouge cabaret restaurant is nearby. For details, see Entertainment.

Despite the prostitutes, peep shows and general seediness, Pigalle is so filled with people of all sorts (including whole buses of tourists) that even late at night it's not unsafe, especially if you're with other people. However, after nightfall the Abbesses metro stop is considered safer than the Blanche, Pigalle and Château Rouge metro stops.

La Villette (19e)
Parc de la Villette (metro Porte de la Villette or Porte de Pantin), one of the city's most ambitious green-space projects of recent decades, stretches along both sides of the Canal de l'Ourcq (the continuation of Canal Saint Martin) in Paris's far north-eastern corner. This 30-hectare expanse of grass, trees, themed gardens, whimsical monumental sculpture (known as *folies*, ie follies),

to 6 pm. Tickets cost 22FF (16FF for students under 26, teachers and residents of the 18e).

The **Musée en Herbe** on the ground floor puts on temporary exhibitions for children.

Musée d'Art Juif The small Museum of Jewish Art (☎ 42.57.84.15; metro Lamarck Caulaincourt), on the 3rd floor of the Jewish community centre at 42 Rue des Saules, has a modest, haphazardly displayed collection of ritual objects, synagogue models and paintings. It is open from 3 to 6 pm (closed Jewish holidays). It is closed during August. Entrance costs 30FF (20FF for students, 10FF for children). There has been a plan to move the Musée d'Art Juif to 71 Rue du Temple, which is near the Centre Pompidou, since the late 1970s.

Cimetière de Montmartre Montmartre Cemetery (☎ 43.87.64.24; metro Place Clichy) was established in 1798 and is the

walkways, bridges and modern buildings, was designed by the Swiss Bernard Tschumi and completed in 1993. It stretches 600 metres from the Cité des Sciences et de l'Industrie southward to the Cité de la Musique.

Cité des Sciences et de l'Industrie

The enormous City of Science & Industry (☎ 36.68.29.30; metro Porte de la Villette) at the northern end of Parc de la Villette has all sorts of super hi-tech exhibits on matters scientific. The dazzle-'em-with-gadgets presentation reflects France's traditionally deferential approach to technology and white lab-coated scientists, whom the public seems to think know best (as they once did in the English-speaking world) and who can still get away with creating patronising museums. This attitude may help explain why there has been so little popular opposition in France to nuclear power. All in all, the older Palais de la Découverte science museum (on the Champs-Élysées) is more engaging.

The Cité des Sciences and its affiliated components make for a pricey visit. The Cité Pass, which costs 45FF (35FF reduced price), gets you into the museum – open daily, except Monday, from 10 am to 6 pm (7 pm on weekends) – and the French navy submarine Argonaute (commissioned in 1957), which is 150 metres south-east of the main building. A visit to the submarine alone costs 25FF (no discounts). A free, English-language map-brochure and the detailed Guide to the Permanent Exhibitions (20FF) are available at the main entrance to the Cité, near which guided **headset tours** in English and other languages are available for 15FF.

Géode

In the Géode (☎ 42.05.50.50), the giant, gleaming, stainless-steel ball at the back of the main building, you can see films projected on a wraparound screen every hour from 10 am to 9 pm daily except Monday (daily during school holiday periods). A ticket costs 55FF (40FF reduced price). A combo ticket for the Géode and the Cité des Sciences – available only at the Géode –

costs 90FF (75FF reduced price). During peak visiting hours, it's a good idea to buy a ticket as far in advance as possible.

Cinaxe

The Cinaxe (☎ 42.09.34.00), a 60-person cinema that moves with the action on the screen, is a bit south-west of the Cité des Sciences buiding. It is open from 11 am to 7 pm daily except Monday and costs 32FF (27FF reduced price).

Cité de la Musique

The Cité de la Musique complex (metro Porte de Pantin), which is at the southern edge of Parc de La Villette at 209 Ave Jean Jaurès, houses the Conservatoire Nationale Supérieure de Musique (National Higher Conservatory of Music of Paris; ☎ 42.06.28.79). Beginning in late 1994, it will also include a **music museum** (☎ 40.03.77.30).

Cimetière du Père Lachaise (20e)

The most visited cemetery in the world is Cimetière du Père Lachaise (☎ 43.70.70.33; metro Philippe Auguste, Père Lachaise or Gambetta), founded in 1805, whose ornate tombs of famous people form a sort of open-air sculpture garden. Among the one million people buried here are the composer Chopin; the writers Molière, Apollinaire, Oscar Wilde, Balzac, Marcel Proust, Gertrude Stein and Colette; the artists David, Delacroix, Pissarro, Seurat and Modigliani; the actress Sarah Bernhardt; the singer Édith Piaf; the dancer Isadora Duncan; and even those immortal 12th-century lovers, Abélard and Héloïse. The only thing most younger visitors come to see is the tomb (in Division 6) of 1960s rock star **Jim Morrison**, lead singer for the Doors, who died of a drug overdose in 1971.

On 27 May 1871, the last of the Communard insurgents, cornered by government forces, fought a hopeless, all-night battle among the tombstones. In the morning, the 147 survivors were lined up against the **Mur des Fédérés** (wall of the Federalists) and shot. They were buried where they fell in a mass grave.

Maps indicating the location of the graves

of famous people are posted around the cemetery, but you can pick up free photocopied maps at the Conservation office (signposted as 'Bureau'), which is in the three-storey building up the hill and to the right from the entrance (metro Philippe Auguste) opposite 23 Blvd de Ménilmontant. It's open Monday to Friday from 8 am to 5.30 or 6 pm and on Saturday from 8.30 am to noon.

The cemetery itself, which has five entrances, is open daily from 8 am to 5.30 pm. From mid-March to early November, hours are 7.30 am to 6 pm. On Saturday, it opens at 8.30 am; on Sunday and holidays opening time is 9 am.

Bois de Boulogne (16e)

The 8.65-sq-km Boulogne Wood, located on the western edge of the city (see the general Paris map), is endowed with gardens, forested areas, lawns, meandering paths, cycling trails and *belle époque* cafés. The park owes its informal layout to its mid-19th-century designer, Baron Haussmann, who took his inspiration from London's Hyde Park rather than the more formal French tradition.

Weekly Closures
Monday: Musée Marmottan
Tuesday: Musée National des Arts et Traditions Populaires

Gardens The enclosed **Parc de Bagatelle**, in the Bois' north-western corner, is renowned for its beautiful gardens. They surround the **Château de Bagatelle**, built in 1775. There are areas dedicated to roses (which bloom from June to October), irises (May) and water lilies (August).

The **Pré Catelan park** includes a garden in which you can see the plants, flowers and trees mentioned in Shakespeare's plays.

Musée National des Arts et Traditions Populaires The National Museum of Popular Arts & Traditions (☎ 44.17.60.00; metro Les Sablons), near the Jardin d'Acclimatation at 6 Route du Mahatma Gandhi, has displays on French folk arts and crafts and life in rural France before and during the Industrial Revolution. It is open from 10 am to 5.15 pm. Tickets cost 17FF (11FF reduced price). Everyone gets in for 11FF on Sunday.

Jardin d'Acclimatation The Jardin d'Acclimatation (☎ 40.67.90.80/82; metro Les Sablons), a children-oriented amusement park on Route du Mahatma Gandhi (at the northern edge of the Bois), is open every day, all year long from 10 am to 6 pm (7 pm on Sunday). Entrance costs 10FF.

Inside the Porte Madrid entrance to the Jardin d'Acclimatation is the **Bowling de Paris** (☎ 40.67.94.00), a bowling alley that is open daily from 11 am (10 am on weekends) to 2 am. Games cost 20 to 30FF per person, with higher tariffs after 8 pm and on weekends. Shoe rental is 10FF. This place also has French and American billiards and snooker.

Musée Marmottan A few blocks east of the Bois de Boulogne, between Porte de la Muette and Porte de Passy, the Marmottan Museum (☎ 42.24.07.02; metro La Muette) at 2 Rue Louis Boilly has the largest collection anywhere of works by the impressionist painter Claude Monet. It is open from 10 am to 5.30 pm. Entrance costs 35FF (15FF reduced price).

Activities Rowboats can be rented at the **Lac Inférieur** (metro Ave Henri Martin), the largest of the park's lakes and ponds. In the southern part of the Bois are two *hippodromes* (horse- racing tracks), **Longchamp** (for flat races) and **Auteuil** (for steeplechases). For more information, see Horse Racing under Entertainment.

Paris Cycles (☎ 47.47.76.50 for a recorded message) rents one-speed bicycles at two locations: on Route du Mahatma Gandhi (metro Les Sablons) across from the Porte Sablons entrance to the Jardin d'Acclimatation amusement park; and near the Pavillon Royal (metro Avenue Foch) at the northern end of the Lac Inférieur. Charges are 26/80FF an hour/day. From mid-

April to mid-October, bicycles are available daily (unless it rains) from 10 am to sundown. During the rest of the year, there are rentals daily during school holidays and on Wednesday, Saturday and Sunday.

Nocturnal Goings-On Each night after about 10 pm, especially on weekends, little sections of the Bois de Boulogne are taken over by prostitutes of all sorts (the great majority of whom have AIDS, according to a recent study). They are joined by professionals and amateurs with exceptional sexual preferences and interests.

At the western end of Ave Foch are the *échangistes* (people interested in partnerswapping). Male exhibitionists flash at cars travelling through the park along the lanes that go from Porte Dauphine to Porte d'Auteuil. Voyeurs congregate south-west of Porte Dauphine behind Université Paris IX. There are also gathering places for transvestites, transsexuals and people who arrange orgies. Locals advise both men and women not to walk alone at night, but if you're with at least one other person, the park's nocturnal habitués are unlikely to assault you.

Bois de Vincennes (12e)
Paris's other large English-style park, the 9.29-sq-km Bois de Vincennes, is in the far south-eastern corner of the city (see the general Paris map). The **Parc Floral** (Floral Garden; metro Château de Vincennes, just south of the Château de Vincennes (see below), is on Route de la Pyramide. The **Jardin Tropical** (tropical garden; RER stop Nogent-sur-Marne) is at the park's eastern edge on Ave de la Belle Gabrielle.

Every year from the end of March to early May, the Bois de Vincennes hosts a huge amusement park known as the **Foire du Trône**.

> **Weekly Closures**
> **Tuesday:** Musée National des Arts d'Afrique et d'Océanie

Musée National des Arts d'Afrique et d'Océanie The National Museum of African & Oceanian Art (☎ 44.74.84.80; metro Porte Dorée) at 293 Ave Daumesnil has sections on the art of the South Pacific (including Australia), North Africa and western and central Africa. The residents of the **tropical aquarium** include Nile crocodiles.

It is open weekdays from 10 am to 5.20 pm and on weekends from 12.30 to 6 pm. The entry fee is 27FF (20FF if you're 18 to 24 or over 60).

Zoo The Parc Zoologique de Paris (☎ 44.75. 20.10 for a recording; metro Porte Dorée), founded in 1934, is on Ave Daumesnil 250 metres east of the Blvd Périphérique (the ring road around Paris). Like the Ménagerie in the Jardin des Plantes, it is run by the Muséum National d'Histoire Naturelle. From April to September, it is open daily from 9 am to 5.30 pm (6 pm on Sunday and holidays). The rest of the year, hours are 9 am to 5 pm (5.30 pm on Sunday). The entrance fee is 35FF (20FF for students under 26 and people over 60).

Château de Vincennes The Château de Vincennes (☎ 43.28.15.48; metro Château de Vincennes), situated at the northern edge of the Bois de Vincennes, is a bona fide royal chateau complete with massive fortifications and a moat. Louis XIV spent his honeymoon in the mid-17th century **Pavillon du Roi**, the westernmost of the two royal pavilions flanking the **Cour Royale** (Royal Courtyard). The 52-metre-high **Donjon** (Keep), completed in 1369, was used as a prison during the 17th and 18th centuries.

You can walk around the grounds for free, but the only way to see the more interesting sights – the Gothic **Chapelle Royale**, built between the 14th and 16th centuries, and the Donjon, which contains a small historical museum – is to take a guided tour (in French, with an information booklet in English). Tickets cost 26FF (13FF if you are 18 to 24 or over 60) and are on sale in the Donjon. Tours begin daily between 10 am and 4.15 pm (6 pm from April to September). The main entrance, which is opposite 18 Ave de Paris in the inner suburb of Vincennes, is

right next to the Château de Vincennes metro stop, the eastern terminus of line No 1.

ACTIVITIES

Paris's weekly entertainment pamphlets, *Pariscope* and *L'Officiel des Spectacles* (see Information under Entertainment), list up-to-date information in French on every imaginable sort of activity. The entries entitled Activités Sportives or Sports et Loisirs provide details on: group hikes *(randonnées pédestres)*, cycling (including group rides; *cyclisme)*, rock-climbing excursions *(escalade)*, parachuting *(parachutisme)*, ultralight aircraft flights *(aviation ultralégère)*, swimming pools *(piscines)*, ice-skating rinks *(patinoires)*, bowling alleys *(bowlings)*, canoeing *(canoë-kayak)*, squash, tennis, golf, etc.

Excursions and outings by boat, helicopter and hot-air balloon *(montgolfière)* appear under Promenades. Lectures and guided tours (almost all in French) are under Conférences. Not all of these activities are listed in both *Pariscope* and *L'Officiel des Spectacles.*

Language Courses

For information on studying French in Paris, see Language Courses under Activities in the Facts for the Visitor chapter.

Sports

The brochure *Paris Sportif*, published by the Mairie de Paris (the Paris municipality), lists the addresses of the city's 36 swimming pools, 38 stadiums, 114 gymnasiums and 170 tennis courts. For information in French on opening hours and other matters concerning sporting activities and facilities in Paris, call Allo Sports on ☎ 42.76.54.54. It is staffed on weekdays from 10.30 am to 5 pm (4.30 pm on Friday).

ORGANISED TOURS

Bus

From late April to September, RATP's Balabus follows a 50-minute route that passes by many of Paris's most famous sights. Heading west, it begins at Gare de Lyon (Rue de Bercy) and then goes to Place Saint Michel, the Louvre, the Musée d'Orsay, Place de la Concorde, the Champs-Élysées, the Arc de Triomphe and out to the bus station at La Défense. It runs every 10 to 20 minutes from noon to 9 pm and costs one to three bus/metro tickets, depending on how far you go. For details, enquire at a metro station.

PariBus (☎ 42.88.92.88) runs red London-style double-decker buses in a 2¼-hour circuit that takes in the Palais de Chaillot, the Eiffel Tower, the Champ de Mars, the Louvre, Notre Dame, the Musée d'Orsay, Opéra-Garnier, the Arc de Triomphe and the Grand Palais. For 100FF (50FF for children aged four to 12), you can get on and off the bus (whose progress through the city is accompanied by commentary in English and French) at whatever sights you like over a period of two days. You can begin your journey at any of the nine stops. Tickets are sold on board. Brochures showing the exact locations of PariBus's stops are available at many hotels. This is basically a more elaborate (and pricier) version of the Balabus service.

Two other companies run two-hour, 145FF tours of the city accompanied by taped commentary in a variety of languages. Cityrama (☎ 44.55.61.00) picks up people near the western end of the Louvre at 4 Place des Pyramides (1er; metro Tuileries), while Paris Vision (☎ 42.60.30.01) has departures not far away at 214 Rue de Rivoli.

Bicycle

Mountain Bike Trip (☎ 48.42.57.87; metro Félix Faure), based in the Three Ducks Hostel (☎ 48.42.04.05) at 6 Place Étienne Pernet (15e), runs well-reviewed mountain bike tours of Paris (in English) that were thoroughly enjoyed by people I (Daniel) talked to. The tours, which last from 11 am until sometime between 5 and 6.30 pm, are held, weather permitting, every day all year round, though they are most likely to be cancelled in January and February. The cost, including rental, is 118FF. It's best to phone between 8 am and 9 pm the day before you'd

like to go to reserve a place. Mountain Bike Trip also runs five-day bike tours of the Loire Valley.

Boat

During summer, the Batobus river shuttle stops at various places in the centre of Paris: the Eiffel Tower, the Musée d'Orsay, the quay opposite the Louvre and near the Hôtel de Ville. The boats come by every 45 minutes and cost 12FF per journey. Unlimited travel for the whole day costs 60FF.

The Bateaux Mouches company (☎ 40. 76.99.99 for an English recording, 42.25.96.10; metro Alma Marceau), which is based on the north bank of the Seine just east of Pont de l'Alma (8e), runs the biggest tour boats on the Seine. From November to March, there are sailings at 11 am, 2.30 pm, 4 pm and 9 pm and, depending on demand, at other times as well. The rest of the year, boats depart every half-hour from 10 am to noon and 1.30 to 11 pm. A 1¼-hour cruise costs 40FF (20FF for those under 16).

Vedettes du Pont Neuf (☎ 46.33.98.38; metro Pont Neuf), whose home port is at the far western tip of Île de la Cité (1er), operates one-hour boat circuits between Île Saint Louis and the Eiffel Tower. Boats generally leave every half-hour between 10 am and noon and 1.30 to 6.30 pm. From April to October and on Friday, Saturday and Sunday from November to March, there are night cruises from 9 to 10.30 pm. A ticket costs 40FF (20FF for children under 10).

Les Bateaux Parisiens (☎ 44.11.33.44), based just north of the Eiffel Tower at Port de la Bourdonnais (7e), also runs river circuits and lunch and dinner cruises. This company has another dock (☎ 43.26.92.55; metro Maubert Mutualité) across from Notre Dame on Quai de Montebello (5e).

FESTIVALS
Bastille Day (14 July)

Paris is *the* place to be on France's National Day (Bastille Day). In the morning, there's a military parade along the Champs-Élysées, accompanied by a flyover of military aircraft, for which that august avenue is lined with reviewing stands for every sort of dignitary imaginable. Mere tourists may have trouble getting a good view unless they arrive early. Much of the city centre, which is closed to cars, fills with pedestrians out to celebrate *liberté*, *égalité* and *fraternité* among France's omnipresent riot police.

On the night of the 14th, a huge display of *feux d'artifice* (fireworks) is held near the Eiffel Tower around 11 pm. The best views are from the Left Bank and the bridges over the Seine (large parts of the Right Bank are sealed off by police).

On the 13th and 14th at night, about a dozen *bals des sapeurs-pompiers* (dances sponsored by Paris's fire brigades and paramedics) are held at fire stations around the city. For details, check the newspapers (eg the local *Le Parisien*, available at news kiosks).

PLACES TO STAY

To figure out where a hostel or hotel is located, turn to the map in this book with the same name as the heading under which it is listed. For instance, places to stay mentioned under Gare de l'Est Area are marked on the map entitled Gare de l'Est & Gare du Nord Areas.

Exceptions: hostels listed under 12e Arrondissement, 13e & 14e Arrondissement and 15e Arrondissement and hotels that appear under Place de la République Area, Place de la Nation Area, Gare Saint Lazare Area and Place Denfert Rochereau are marked on the general Paris map.

Accommodation Services

AJF No matter what age you are, Accueil des Jeunes en France (AJF) can *always* find you accommodation, even in summer. It works like this: you come in on the day you need a place to stay and pay the AJF for the accommodation (plus a 10FF fee) and they give you a voucher to take to the hostel or hotel. Prices range from 240 to 400FF a night and, thanks to special AJF discounts, are often less than the price you'd pay if you contacted the hotel yourself. The earlier in the day you come, the better: the convenient and cheap places

always go first. To keep up with demand, AJF runs a number of its own hostels, which in summer are augmented by seconded student dormitories.

AJF's main office (☎ 42.77.87.80; metro Rambuteau) is at 119 Rue Saint Martin (4e), right across the square from the entrance to the Centre Pompidou. It is open Monday to Saturday from 9 am to 5.30 pm (6 pm from June to September). Be prepared for long queues during summer.

At Gare du Nord, the AJF office (☎ 42.85. 86.19; metro Gare du Nord; 10e) is open daily from June to mid or late-September from 7.30 am to 9.30 pm. It is on the other side of the SNCF information office from platform 19 – just look for the long queue.

In the Latin Quarter, the AJF office (☎ 43.54.95.86; metro Port Royal) at 139 Blvd Saint Michel (5e) is open in summer Tuesday to Saturday from 10 am to 6 pm.

Tourist Office The Paris tourist office (☎ 49.52.53.54; metro George V) at 127 Ave des Champs-Élysées (8e) and its six annexes can find you a place to stay for the evening of the day you stop by. Double rooms at participating hotels start at about 170FF. There is a fee of 8FF for a hostel bed and 20/25/40FF for a room at a one/two/three-star hotel. For further details, see Tourist Offices under Information at the start of this chapter.

Camping

Camping du Bois de Boulogne (☎ 45.24. 30.00) on Allée du Bord de l'Eau (16e), the only camping ground within the Paris city limits, is along the Seine at the far western edge of the Bois de Boulogne. For two people with a tent, it costs 40 to 70FF a night depending on the season. Reception is open 24 hours a day, all year long. This place is especially crowded in summer, but they always have space for a small tent (though not necessarily for a car). Despite the fearsome reputation of the Bois de Boulogne (see Bois de Boulogne under Things to See), the area around the camp ground is not dangerous, even at night, and theft is a minor

problem, almost always involving valuables and money, rather than camping equipment or packs.

From April to September, the Porte Maillot metro station, 4.5 km east of the camping ground, is linked to Camping du Bois de Boulogne by privately operated shuttle buses (10FF each way, 30FF for a two-day pass). They run daily from 8.30 am to 1 pm and 5 pm to sometime between 11 pm and 1 am. During July and August, they run every half-hour from 8.30 am to 1 am. Year round from 6 am to about 8 pm, you can take either bus No 244 from the Porte Maillot metro stop or bus No 244C from the Port d'Auteuil metro stop.

The Paris tourist office has a sheet listing dozens of other camp grounds in the départements surrounding Paris.

B&Bs

If you'd like to meet local people during your stay in Paris, *Bed & Breakfast 1* (☎ 43.35. 11.26; fax 40.47.69.20; metro Port Royal) at 7 Rue Campagne Première (14e) can arrange for one to four (and in some cases up to six) people to stay in any of 400 private homes in Paris and its inner suburbs. They try to match guests with hosts of similar age and professional background. All the homes are near metro or RER stations.

One/two people pay 250/290FF to 360/460FF a night, depending on the location (a key factor) and level of comfort (eg private or shared bathroom). The minimum stay is two nights; discounts of 30 to 50% are available if you stay more than a month. The reservation fee is 50FF per person though they often give reductions for two or more people. You can either make a reservation in advance, in which case you'll be asked for payment in full, or give Bed & Breakfast 1 a ring after your arrival in Paris. Except during September, they can always find you something on short notice, even for the same night. The office is open on weekdays from 9 am to 1 pm and 2 to 7 pm; from December to February, hours are 10 am to 1 pm and 2 to 6 pm.

Pensions de famille, which are similar to

B&Bs, cost upwards of 140FF per person a day. For details, ask the Paris tourist office for its list of such places entitled *Liste Non-Limitative des Pensions de Famille*.

Staying with a Family

Under an arrangement known as *hôtes payants* (paying guests), students and young people from abroad can stay with French families, especially those interested in cultural exchange of one degree or another. In general you rent a room from them and enjoy access (sometimes limited) to the family's kitchen, bathroom and telephone.

Accueil Familial des Jeunes Étrangers (☎ 45.49.15.57; metro Sèvres Babylone) at 23 Rue du Cherche Midi (6e) can find you a room with a family for 3000 to 3500FF a month, including breakfast. It's also possible to take dinner with the family. For stays of less than a month, expect to pay about 130FF a day. There's a 500FF subscription fee (1000FF for stays of over three months).

Amicale Culturelle Internationale (☎ 47.42.94.21; fax 49.24.02.67; metro Havre Caumartin) at 27 Rue Godot de Mauroy (9e) can arrange for family stays for about 215FF a day, including breakfast and dinner. The minimum stay is two weeks. The office is open Monday to Friday from 10 am to 12.30 pm and 2 to 6 pm.

The Paris tourist office has a list of organisations that arrange hôtes payants. It is entitled *Associations Plaçant les Jeunes en Hôtes Payants*.

Short-Term Apartments

Bed & Breakfast 1 has fully furnished apartments starting at 350FF a day. The minimum stay is two weeks. See the B&Bs listing for contact details.

Allô Logement Temporaire (☎ 42.09.00.07; fax 46.07.14.41; metro La Chapelle) at 4 Place de la Chapelle (18e) – 400 metres north of Gare du Nord – is a nonprofit organisation that acts as a liaison between apartment owners and foreigners looking for furnished apartments for periods of one week to one year. Small studios of about 20 sq metres cost 700 to 1000FF a week.

For information on what's available, call, write or fax with details on what part of the city or suburbs you prefer and how many rooms you need. October is the hardest month to find a place, but over the summer so many places are available that it is usually possible to find something within a matter of days. Before any deals are signed, the company will arrange for you to talk to the owner by phone, assisted by an interpreter if necessary. There is a 250FF annual membership fee and, in addition to the rent (paid directly to the owner), a charge of 100FF for each month you rent for. The office is open Tuesday to Saturday from noon to 8 pm.

Serviced Apartments

Flatotel (☎ 05.34.53.45 or 45.75.62.20; metro Charles Michels) at 14 Rue du Théâtre (15e) has 20-sq-metre studios (550FF a day), larger studios (from 750FF a day) and two to five-room apartments. All are equipped with kitchen facilities. The minimum stay is one day. The office is open weekdays from 9 am to 6 pm.

Renting an Apartment

For general information on renting an apartment in France, see Rental under Accommodation in the Facts for the Visitor chapter. The hardest time to find a place in Paris is October, when everyone is back from their summer holidays and students are searching for academic-year digs.

About 2000FF a month will get you a tiny garret room (nine sq metres minimum) with a washbasin but with no telephone, no proper place to cook and no private toilet. There may not even be a communal shower, so to bathe you'll have to go to a friend's place or a public bathhouse. These rooms, often occupied by students, are frequently converted *chambres de bonne* (maids' quarters) on the 6th or 7th floor of old, lift-less apartment buildings in good neighbourhoods.

Small, unfurnished/furnished studios start at about 3000/3600FF a month, though

prices vary widely depending on the area: in less desirable areas, studios may be as cheap as 2000F a month, and apartments for 2600FF are not unheard of.

If you've exhausted your word-of-mouth sources (expats, students, EC nationals living temporarily in Paris), it's a good idea to check out the bulletin boards at the American Church (see Cultural Centres under Information). People who advertise there are unlikely to fear renting to foreigners, may speak some English and might be willing to sign a relatively short-term contract. *France USA Contacts*, a free periodical issued every two weeks and available at most English-language bookshops, and the bulletin board at Shakespeare & Co (see Bookshops under Information) might also have a few leads.

If you know a bit of French (or know someone who does), you'll be able to consult several periodicals available from newsagents: *De Particulier à Particulier* (13FF) and *La Centrale de Particuliers* (13FF), both issued each Thursday; *La Semaine Immobilière* (10FF); and the new *A Vendre A Louer* (7FF). You might also try the daily *Le Figaro*. You'll have to do your calling in French. If you have access to a telephone, you could place an apartment-wanted ad in *De Particulier à Particulier* and have people call you.

The *Union Nationale des Étudiants Locataires* (National Union of Student Tenants; ☎ 46.33.30.78; metro Port Royal) at 120 Rue Notre Dame des Champs (6e) will let anyone with a student card who pays the 100FF annual fee (photo required) consult its lists of available apartments and chambres de bonne. The usual rental period is the academic year or 12 months; it's harder to find places for just one semester. The office is open on weekdays from 10 am to noon and 2 to 6 pm; Wednesday hours are 10 am to 1.30 pm and 2 to 8 pm.

The Paris tourist office's sheet entitled *Logements pour Étudiants* lists other organisations that can help find accommodation for students who'll be in Paris for at least a semester.

On the Water

If you've arrived by pleasure boat, you can anchor it quite cheaply at the *Port de Plaisance de Paris-Arsenal* (metro Bastille or Quai de la Rapée), which stretches for 500 metres from the Seine to Place de la Bastille. About 200 moorings for vessels up to 25 metres long are available by the day, month or year. The daily rates for a six to eight-metre boat up to 2.5 metres wide are between 42FF (October to March) and 82FF (June to August); monthly rates are quite a bit cheaper. Electricity, fresh water and telephone link-ups are available, as are showers, mail service, fuel and washing machines. About 70% of the people staying here are foreigners.

The Capitainerie (harbour master's office; ☎ 43.41.39.32; metro Quai de la Rapée) at 11 Blvd de la Bastille (12e) has details on fees and regulations. It is open daily from 9 am to 6 pm. From April to June and during September, hours are 9 am to 7 pm (8 pm on weekends); July and August hours are 8 am to 8 pm. There's a laundrette on the ground floor of the Capitainerie.

Hostels & Foyers

Paris's hostels and *foyers* (student residence halls) are much more expensive than their provincial counterparts. Beds under 100FF a night are hard to find, so two people who don't mind sleeping in the same bed may find basic rooms in bottom-end hotels a less expensive proposition. Groups of three or four willing to share two or three beds will save even more.

Many hostels allow guests to stay for a maximum of three nights, especially in summer, though places that have age limits (eg up to 30) tend not to enforce them. Only official auberges de jeunesse (youth hostels) require that guests present IYHF cards. Curfews at Paris hostels are generally at 1 or 2 am. Few hostels accept telephone reservations from individuals, but those that do are noted in the text.

Louvre Area (1er) The modern, 204-bed *Centre International BVJ Paris-Louvre*

(☎ 42.36.88.18; metro Louvre-Rivoli) at 20 Rue Jean-Jacques Rousseau, which was completely redone in 1991, is only a few blocks north-east of the Louvre. A bunk in a single-sex room for two to 10 people costs 110FF, including breakfast. Guests do not need IYHF cards but should be under 35. On the day you arrive, you can't get into your room until 2.30 pm, but after that rooms are accessible all day long. Curfew is at 2 am. No kitchen facilities are available. There is almost always space if you come by in the morning, even in July and August. Reservations are not accepted, but if you're on your way over you can call and request that they hold a spot for two hours.

The two other BVJ *centres internationaux* in the 1er arrondissement have the same tariffs and rules as BVJ Paris-Louvre. The 55-bed *Centre International BVJ Paris-Les Halles* (☎ 40.26.92.45; metro Louvre-Rivoli) is around the corner from BVJ Paris-Louvre at 5 Rue du Pélican. The 68-bed *Centre International BVJ Paris-Opéra* (☎ 42.60.77.23; fax 42.33.40.53; metro Pyramides) is at 11 Rue Thérèse.

Place de la République Area (3e, 10e & 11e) The *Auberge de Jeunesse Jules Ferry* (☎ 43.57.55.60; metro République or Oberkampf) is a few blocks east of Place de la République at 8 Blvd Jules Ferry (11e; see the Gare du Nord & Gare de l'Est map). It's a bit institutional but the atmosphere is fairly relaxed and – an added bonus – they don't accept groups.

A bed in a two, four or six-person room costs 100FF, including breakfast. The rooms are closed from 10 am to 2 pm; curfew is from 1 to 6 am. If the beds are all taken, the staff will try to help you find somewhere else to stay. There is a Franprix supermarket down the block at 28 Blvd Jules Ferry.

Marais (4e) The *Maison Internationale de la Jeunesse et des Étudiants* (☎ 42.74.23.45 for the switchboard), better known as MIJE, runs three *hôtels de jeunes* (young people's hostels) in attractively renovated 17th and 18th-century residences in the Marais. A bed

in a single-sex dorm room with shower costs 115FF, including breakfast. Rooms are closed from noon to 4 pm; curfew is from 1 to 6 am. Individuals can make reservations up to five days in advance by coming to the hostel in person before 10 pm and paying in full. The maximum stay is seven nights. During summer and other busy periods, you probably won't find a place after about mid-morning.

The largest of the three, *MIJE Fourcy* (fax 42.74.08.93; metro Saint Paul; 230 beds), is at 6 Rue de Fourcy. *MIJE Fauconnier* (fax 42.71.61.02; metro Saint Paul or Pont Marie; 110 beds) is two blocks away at 11 Rue du Fauconnier. *MIJE Maubisson* (metro Hôtel de Ville; 90 beds) is half a block south of the Mairie (town hall) du 4e Arrondissement at 12 Rue des Barres.

Latin Quarter (5e) The *Centre International BVJ Paris-Quartier Latin* (☎ 43.29.34.80; fax 42.33.40.53; metro Maubert Mutualité) at 44 Rue des Bernardins has the same tariffs and rules as the other BVJ hostels (see Louvre Area).

The clean, friendly *Y & H Hostel* (☎ 45.35.09.53; metro Monge), whose name is short for 'young & happy', is at 80 Rue Mouffetard, a hopping, happening street known for its food market and many restaurants and pubs. A bed in a cramped room with a washbasin costs 95FF. A hostelling card is not necessary, but priority is given to young people. It is closed from 11 am to 5 pm. The 1 am curfew is strictly enforced. Don't plan on sticking around for very long, as you usually cannot stay for more than a few days. Reservations can be made if you make a deposit for the first night. In summer, the best way to get a place is to stop by at about 9 am.

From July to September, AJF transforms the École des Mines (School of Mines) dorm at 270 Rue Saint Jacques into a *summer hostel* (metro Port Royal, Luxembourg). The telephone number changes from year to year, so your best bet is to call or visit one of the AJF reservation offices (see Accommodation Services). Guests are supposed to be

between 18 and 35, but enforcement is rather laid-back. A nonbunk bed in a spartan triple costs 105FF, including breakfast; there are also a few doubles and singles. Kitchen facilities are not available. You can check in anytime from 7 am to 9 pm, but the rooms are closed from 10 am to 2 pm. There is no curfew.

Bastille Area (11e & 12e) The *Auberge Internationale des Jeunes* (☎ 47.00.62.00; fax 47.00.33.16; metro Ledru Rollin), at 10 Rue Trousseau (11e), 700 metres east of Place de la Bastille is a friendly hostel that attracts a young, international crowd and is very full in summer. Beds cost just 81FF in clean, utilitarian rooms with bunks for four or six and 91FF in doubles, including breakfast. They'll hold a bed for you if you call from the train station.

The *Maison Internationale des Jeunes* (MIJPC; ☎ 43.71.99.21; fax 43.71.78.58; metro Faidherbe Chaligny) at 4 Rue Titon (11e) is 1.3 km east of Place de la Bastille. A bed in a spartan dorm room for two, three, five or eight people costs 105FF, including breakfast. Curfew is at 2 am. The upper age limit of 30 is not strictly enforced. Telephone reservations are accepted only on the day you arrive; your chance of finding a place is greatest if you call between 8 and 10 am. The maximum stay is theoretically three days, but they usually let people stay up to a week.

AJF's newly renovated *Résidence Bastille* (☎ 43.79.53.86; metro Voltaire) at 151 Ave Ledru Rollin (11e) is about 900 metres northeast of Place de la Bastille. Beds cost 105FF. Reception is open from 7 am to 12.30 pm and 2 pm to 1 am.

12e Arrondissement The *Centre International de Séjour de Paris Ravel* (☎ 44.75.60.00; metro Porte de Vincennes), better known as CISP Ravel, is on the southwestern edge of the city at 4-6 Ave Maurice Ravel. A bed in a 12-person dormitory is 97FF; staying in a two to five-person room costs 122FF. Singles are 143FF. All prices include breakfast. Stays are usually limited

to three nights, but there are no age restrictions. Reception is open from 6.30 am to 1.30 am. Reservations are accepted from individuals up to two days before they arrive. People staying here get a discount at the swimming pool next door.

To get to CISP Ravel from the Porte de Vincennes metro station, walk south on Blvd Soult, turn left onto Rue Jules Lemaître and then go right onto Rue Maurice Ravel.

13e & 14e Arrondissements The *Foyer International d'Accueil de Paris Jean Monnet* (☎ 45.89.89.15; metro Glacière), known as FIAP Jean Monnet for short, is at 30 Rue Cabanis (14e), which is a few blocks south-east of Place Denfert Rochereau. The modern, carpeted rooms are pretty luxurious by hostelling standards. A bed in a room for eight/four/two people is 115/140/160FF; singles are 240FF. Rooms specially outfitted for disabled people *(handicapés)* are available. There's usually a maximum stay of a few days. Telephone reservations are accepted only on the day you'll be arriving. Curfew is at 2 am.

The *Centre International de Séjour de Paris Kellermann* (☎ 45.16.37.38; metro Porte d'Italie), usually referred to as CISP Kellermann, is at 17 Blvd Kellermann (13e), which is 1.3 km south of Place d'Italie. There are no age limits, and the maximum stay is six nights. A bed in an attractive room for eight, furnished with industrial-strength furniture, costs 97FF; a double or quad is 122FF per person. Singles are 143FF. All prices include sheets and breakfast. Facilities for disabled people are available. Curfew is at 1.30 am. There are no kitchen facilities. Telephone reservations are accepted if you call the day you'll be arriving.

The rather institutional *Maison des Clubs UNESCO* (☎ 43.36.00.63; metro Glacière) is up the ramp at 43 Rue de la Glacière (13e), which is about midway between Place Denfert Rochereau and Place d'Italie. A bed in a large, unsurprising room for three or four people is 90FF; singles/doubles cost 115/100FF per person. Theoretically, the hostel accepts only 18 to 25-year-olds, but they're

not strict about this, and if you're in your 30s you've definitely got a shot. Individuals cannot make reservations (priority is given to groups), so your best bet is to ring up at about 10 am on the day you need a place. Curfew is at 1.30 am.

The *Maison des États-Unis* (☎ 45.89. 35.79; metro Cité Universitaire) at 15 Blvd Jourdan (14e), a university dorm during the academic year, accepts travellers from July to late September (and perhaps part of June as well). It is usually full in July. Singles (all they have) cost 135FF a night or 2850FF a month. The minimum stay is three nights. There is a toilet, shower and kitchen on each floor. Reception is open Monday to Friday from 10 to 11.30 am and 4 to 6 pm. The nearby *Collège Franco-Brittanique* (44.16. 24.00) at 9 Blvd Jourdan (14e), which accepts travellers during the same period, is a bit cheaper. Although they're at the southern edge of the 14e, these places are a quick metro ride from the city centre thanks to the RER stop right across the street.

The friendly, Protestant-run *Foyer des Jeunes Filles* (☎ 45.89.06.42; fax 45. 65.46.20; metro Glacière) at 234 Rue de Tolbiac (13e), also known as the Foyer Tolbiac, houses women trainees *(stagiaires)* and workers *(travailleuses)* – but not students – of all religions who are between the ages of 18 and 25. The minimum stay is usually one month, but from mid-June to early September (and, if there's space, during the rest of the year), it accepts *women* travellers with no minimum or maximum stay and no upper age limit. There may be space here when other places around Paris are full. A single room costs 100FF (including breakfast from Monday to Saturday) plus a one-time annual fee of 30FF. There are kitchens on each floor. Reservations can be made by phone or fax, and reception is open 24 hours a day. There's no curfew. The hostel is about 600 metres south of the nearest metro stop, Glacière, so you might want to take bus No 21 or 62.

15e Arrondissement The friendly, down-to-earth *Three Ducks Hostel* (☎ 48.42.04.05;

metro Félix Faure) is at 6 Place Étienne Pernet, which is at the southern end of Rue du Commerce. Also known as Hostal Trois Canards, it's a favourite with young back-packers, whose more exuberant exponents may get a bit noisy at night. A bunk bed costs 85FF. Telephone reservations are accepted. The hostel has kitchen facilities, especially useful after a trip to the Super Franprix supermarket at 63 Rue de la Croix Nivert. For information on the mountain bike tours run from here, see Bicycle under Organised Tours. By the way, this place was named after three ducks who used to live in the courtyard.

The *Aloha Hostel* (☎ 42.73.03.03; metro Volontaires) at 1 Rue Borromée is about a km west of Gare Montparnasse. It is run by the same people as the Three Ducks Hostel. Beds cost 75FF. Curfew is 1 am.

Hotels

A veritable plague of renovations, redecorations and other improvements has turned many of Paris's finest fleabag hotels into bright, spotless two-star places where the sheets are changed daily and the reception-ists aren't rude. The guests – not backpackers or students, as in the old days, for such people can't afford the new rates – no longer meet each other on the landing while waiting, towel-clad, for the shower. Another little bit of Paris romance, lost forever...

But not all is lost. Quite a few bottom-end hotels (ie places whose showerless, toiletless doubles costs less than 180FF) have so far been spared the onslaught of investment and repairs. There are clusters of such places in the Marais (4e), the Bastille area (4e, 11e and 12e), the Gare de l'Est area (10e) and Montmartre (18e).

Most cheap hotels – especially the better ones in desirable neighbourhoods – fill up quickly, even in winter, and in July and August almost all of them are completely booked up. If you know in advance the dates you'll be in Paris, it's a good idea to make reservations as many weeks ahead as possible. A three-minute international phone call to reserve a room (followed, if necessary, by

written confirmation or a deposit) is a lot cheaper than wasting your first day in Paris looking for a place to stay. For details on making reservations, see Hotels under Accommodation in the Facts for the Visitor chapter.

If you'll be getting to Paris without hotel reservations and plan to look for something cheap, your best bet is to arrange to arrive early in the morning and then to phone or drop by the hotels that interest you. The best time to show up is when yesterday's guests are likely to be checking out (ie around 9 or 10 am). One tip: hotels that cater to domestic businesspeople, often located in less-touristed arrondissements such as the 11e, 13e and 14e, tend to have space on weekends and during August (when everyone goes on holiday) but are often filled during September and October (Paris's convention season). Be prepared for the possibility that nothing will pan out and you'll have to compromise on location, pay more money or settle for a hotel far from the city centre. Trying to make a reservation on short notice is rather difficult, especially during summer and around Christmas and Easter, even if you call a few days ahead and offer to pay in advance.

Many cheap hotels have two or three rooms that are true bargains – 100FF a night or even less – and mention this fact on the rate boards posted (by law) near reception. Unfortunately, these rooms are almost always taken by long-term residents (eg students in Paris for the semester). In the following pages, rooms whose prices are so attractive that, for all intents and purposes, they don't exist, have generally not been listed.

Louvre Area (1er) You can't get much more central than the 1er arrondissement, but don't expect to find bucolic tranquillity.

Bottom End The 13-room *Hôtel de Lille* (☎ 42.33.33.42; metro Palais Royal) at 8 Rue du Pélican has clean singles/doubles with washbasin and cheap, tasteless ceiling tiles for 170/200FF. Doubles with shower are 250FF. A token for the shower costs an appalling 30FF.

Top End The three-star, 70-room *Hôtel Brighton* (☎ 42.60.30.03; fax 42.60.41.78; metro Tuileries) at 218 Rue de Rivoli has lovely singles/doubles/triples starting at 390/490/850FF. The rooms that overlook the Jardin des Tuileries are the most popular, especially those on the 4th and 5th floors, from which you can see over the trees. The staff are helpful and professional.

Luxury The 142-room, 45-suite *Ritz* (☎ 42. 60.38.30; fax 42.86.00.91; metro Opéra) at 15 Place Vendôme, one of the world's most legendary – and expensive – hotels, has singles/doubles for 2450/3350FF to 3200/4150FF. Junior suites begin at 5600FF; regular suites are 6900FF and up. Prices are lower for most of the period from November to February and during July and August. An extra bed is 600FF. If you'd like something heartier than a continental breakfast (170FF), you can order an American breakfast (230FF). The hotel restaurant, L'Espadon, has two Michelin stars. Facilities include a health club, a swimming pool and squash courts.

The colonnaded *Hôtel de Crillon* (☎ 44. 71.15.00; fax 47.42.72.10; metro Concorde) at 10 Place de la Concorde (8e) is the epitome of classic French luxury. The sumptuous public areas inside this two-centuries-old building are decorated with sparkling chandeliers, original sculptures, gilt mouldings, tapestries and inlaid furniture. Large singles/doubles with traditional furnishings and pink marble bathrooms cost 2400/3300FF; suites start at 6300FF.

The *Hôtel Meurice* (☎ 44.58.10.10; fax 44.58.10.15; metro Tuileries) at 228 Rue de Rivoli, built in 1907, positively oozes elegance. The stunning public spaces, modelled on those of Versailles, are decorated with gilded furniture, chandeliers and trompe l'œil paintings. Singles/doubles start at 2200/2500FF; suites are 5000 to 15,000FF. An extra bed is 350FF. Continental/American breakfasts are 130/190FF. The restaurant

has one Michelin star. At the end of WW II, Suite 108 – later used by Salvador Dalí – served as the office of the German commander of Paris, General Dietrich von Choltitz, who ignored orders from Berlin to destroy Paris before the Allies captured it.

The 450-room *Hôtel Inter-Continental* (☎ 44.77.11.11; fax 44.77.14.60; metro Tuileries) at 3 Rue de Castiglione, built around a white marble courtyard, has singles/doubles from 1750/2000FF. Suites cost 2800 to 20,000FF. An extra bed is 400FF. Three kinds of breakfast are available: continental (95FF), American (140FF) and Japanese (170FF). The *belle époque* building is an historic monument.

Centre Pompidou Area (1er & 4e)

This hopping part of town, midway between the Louvre and the Marais, has excellent metro links to most of the city, though few major sights are more than a 15-minute walk away. The Châtelet-Les Halles metro station is linked to Charles de Gaulle Airport by Roissyrail and to Orly by Orlyval.

The one-star *Hôtel Saint Honoré* (☎ 42.36.20.38, 42.21.46.96; fax 42.21.44.08; metro Châtelet) at 85 Rue Saint Honoré (1er) is only one block south-west of Forum des Halles. Singles and doubles cost 170FF (with washbasin), 280FF (with shower) and 420FF (with two beds, shower and toilet). Hall showers are 15FF.

The one-star, 16-room *Hôtel du Centre* (☎ 42.33.05.18; fax 42.33.74.02; metro Châtelet), just south of Forum des Halles at 20 Rue du Roule (1er), has small, characterless doubles with shower and toilet for 320FF. A somewhat more expensive option is the *Grand Hôtel de Champagne* (☎ 42.36.60.00; fax 45.08.43.33; metro Châtelet) at 17 Rue Jean Lantier (1er), whose doubles cost 640FF.

Marais (4e)

The Marais is only a short walk from some of Paris's most interesting neighbourhoods: the Centre Pompidou area, Île Saint Louis, Île de la Cité, the Bastille area and the Latin Quarter.

Bottom End The basic and slightly noisy *Hôtel Rivoli* (☎ 42.72.08.41; metro Hôtel de Ville) at 44 Rue de Rivoli is one of the best deals in town. Room rates range from 110FF (for a single with running water) to 200FF (for a double with bath and toilet). The front door is locked from 1 to 6 am. Parts of this book were written in tiny, 6th-floor room No 25. Two buildings away, the *Grand Hôtel du Loiret* (☎ 48.87.77.00) at 8 Rue des Mauvais Garçons has doubles starting at 160FF. Rooms with shower are 210FF. Hall showers cost 15FF. If you call ahead, they'll hold a room for up to two hours.

The *Hôtel Moderne* (☎ 48.87.97.05; metro Saint Paul) at 3 Rue Caron has basic doubles for 160FF (with washbasin), 190FF (with shower) and 220FF (with shower and toilet). There's a toilet and shower (15FF) a half-flight of stairs up or down from each floor. Telephone reservations are not accepted, but if you call in the morning they'll usually hold a room for a few hours.

The *Hôtel Pratic* (☎ 48.87.80.47) is right around the corner at 9 Rue d'Ormesson. Singles/doubles cost 150/220FF with washbasin, 240/260FF with shower and 280/320FF with a bath and toilet. If you call ahead, they'll hold a room until noon.

You might also try the *Hôtel de la Pointe Rivoli* (☎ 42.72.14.23) at 125 Rue Saint Antoine, opposite the exit of the Saint Paul metro station. Singles/doubles with washbasin start at 85/100FF; doubles with shower and toilet are 200FF.

A block south of Place des Vosges you'll find the one-star *Sully Hôtel* (☎ 42.78.49.32; metro Bastille) at 48 Rue Saint Antoine. Doubles start at 180FF with washbasin, 240FF with shower and 260FF with shower and toilet. A two-bed quad with washbasin costs 300FF. The hall shower costs 10FF. A block further east, the *Hôtel de la Herse d'Or* (☎ 48.87.84.09; metro Bastille) at 20 Rue Saint Antoine has singles/doubles with washbasin from 150/190FF; rooms for one or two people with shower and toilet are 250FF. Showers are 10FF.

Mid-Range The family-run *Hôtel de Nice*

(☎ 42.78.55.29; fax 42.78.36.07; metro Hôtel de Ville), an especially friendly and homy place at 42bis Rue de Rivoli, has comfortable doubles/triples/quads with shower and toilet for 340/420/500FF. Many of the rooms have balconies on which guests have been known to sunbathe. Hall showers are free; breakfast is 30FF.

The *Hôtel Sansonnet* (☎ 48.87.96.14; fax 48.87.30.46 metro Hôtel de Ville) at 48 Rue de la Verrerie has singles/doubles with shower and toilet for 350/390FF, including breakfast.

The 16-room *Hôtel de la Place des Vosges* (☎ 42.72.60.46; fax 42.72.02.64; metro Bastille) at 12 Rue de Birague is superbly situated right next to Place des Vosges. The rooms, though they have nice bathrooms, are rather plain and of average size. Singles/doubles start at 290/395FF. There's a tiny lift from the 1st floor.

The *Hôtel Le Palais de Fes* (☎ 42.72. 03.68; metro Hôtel de Ville) at 41 Rue du Roi de Sicile has fairly large, modern doubles for 200FF (with washbasin) and 250FF (with shower and toilet). There are toilets on each floor. Hall showers are 20FF. Reception is either inside the ground-floor Moroccan restaurant or on the 1st floor.

Top End The family-run, three-star *Grand Hôtel Malher* (☎ 42.72.60.92; metro Saint Paul) at 5 Rue Malher has singles/doubles from 470/570FF.

The three-star, 27-room *Hôtel Le Compostelle* (☎ 42.78.59.99; fax 40.29.05.18; metro Hôtel de Ville) at 31 Rue du Roi de Sicile has carpeted singles/doubles with TV from 300/400FF. The rooms are tasteful but not fancy. There are no triples or quads. This place is closed during August.

One block north-west of Place des Vosges, the three-star *Hôtel des Chevaliers* (☎ 42.72. 73.47; fax 42.72.54.10; metro Chemin Vert) at 30 Rue de Turenne (3e) has singles and doubles for 560FF. Two-bed doubles are 610FF, triples go for 760FF.

Gay Hotel The only all-gay hotel in Paris is the *Hôtel Central Marais* (☎ 48.87.56.08;

fax 42.77.06.27; metro Hôtel de Ville) at 33 Rue Vieille du Temple. Most of the clients are male, but women are also welcome. Singles/doubles with one bathroom for every two rooms are 380/460FF. Reception is open from noon to at least 8 pm, but guests cannot leave their bags, much less check in, before noon. This place is almost always full, so make reservations well in advance. The management speak English and will hold a room for you if you give them your credit card number over the phone.

Bastille Area (4e, 11e & 12e) The Bastille quarter, formerly a poor, immigrant neighbourhood, has become one of Paris's trendiest nightlife areas since the construction of the new opera house.

A number of hotels just west of Place de la Bastille on Rue Saint Antoine are listed in the Marais section.

Bottom End The older, 20-room *Hôtel Bastille Opéra* (☎ 43.55.16.06; metro Bastille) is just off Place de la Bastille at 6 Rue de la Roquette (11e). Singles/doubles with washbasin start at 120/160FF. Showers are free. Reception is on the 1st floor – to get in, push the button on the intercom to the left of the door on the ground floor. New guests can check in 24 hours a day. Telephone reservations are not accepted, but if you call from the train station they'll hold a room for you for an hour or two.

If you're desperate, you might try the rundown *Hôtel Central Bastille* (☎ 47.00.31.51; metro Bastille) at 16 Rue de la Roquette (11e), whose less-than-spotless singles/doubles costs 130/160FF (with washbasin) and 200FF (with shower). Reception is open 24 hours a day.

The *Vix Hôtel* (☎ 48.05.12.58; metro Bastille or Ledru Rollin) is 400 metres east of Place de la Bastille at 19 Rue de Charonne (11e). It's a bit dreary and is not the cleanest hotel I've ever seen, but there are plenty of singles/doubles without shower for 90/110FF. Doubles with shower range from 135 to 145FF. Hall showers cost 15FF. They do not usually accept telephone reservations.

The *Hôtel de France* (☎ 43.79.53.22; metro Voltaire) at 159 Ave Ledru Rollin (11e), 250 metres south of Place Léon Blum, is a hotel with decent, well-maintained rooms. Singles/doubles with shower and telephones cost 150/200FF.

In the same area, you might try the *Hôtel de Savoie* (☎ 43.72.96.47; metro Voltaire) at 27 Rue Richard Lenoir (11e), 200 metres south of Place Léon Blum. Singles/doubles start at 130/150FF; showers are 20FF. If you call on the day you're coming, they'll hold a room until the late afternoon.

Mid-Range The cheery, 24-room *Hôtel Castex* (☎ 42.72.31.52; fax 42.72.57.91; metro Bastille), 200 metres south-west of Place de la Bastille at 5 Rue Castex (4e), has been run by the same family since 1919. Quiet, old-fashioned (but immaculate) singles/doubles cost 210/270FF with shower and 260/290FF with shower and toilet. Adding a child's bed costs 70FF. Reception is open daily from 7 am to midnight, but you can get in late at night with the door code. This is an excellent bet but usually requires making reservations at least three weeks ahead.

Half a block north of Place de la Bastille you come to the two-star, 41-room *Hôtel Lyon Mulhouse* (☎ 47.00.91.50; fax 47.00.06.31; metro Bastille) at 8 Blvd Beaumarchais (11e). Doubles/triples/quads start at 320/450/500FF.

Île de la Cité (1er & 4e) The island has only one hotel, the exceptional *Hôtel Henri IV* (☎ 43.54.44.53; metro Cité, Saint Michel) at 25 Place Dauphine (1er), a quiet, triangular square at the western end of the island. It has perfectly adequate singles for 130FF; doubles cost 160 to 190FF. Showers (14FF) and toilets are in the hall. Reception is open until 8 pm. This place is usually booked up several months in advance, but the odd cancellation makes it worth giving them a call.

Île Saint Louis (4e) This quiet island is one of the most expensive neighbourhoods in Paris to live – or rent a hotel room.

The three-star, 21-room *Hôtel Saint Louis* (☎ 46.34.04.80; fax 46.34.02.13; metro Pont Marie) at 75 Rue Saint Louis en l'Île has appealing but unspectacular singles and doubles for 665FF (765FF wth two beds). The basement breakfast room dates from the early 1600s.

Place Saint Michel Area (5e) The Latin Quarter, Saint Germain des Prés, the islands and the Marais are all within a ten-minute stroll of this somewhat touristy corner of Paris. The Saint Michel metro station is linked to both airports by Orlyrail, Orlyval and Roissyrail.

The run-down *Hôtel du Centre* (☎ 43.26.13.07; metro Saint Michel) at 5 Rue Saint Jacques has very basic doubles starting at 110FF and doubles with shower for 150FF. Hall showers are 20FF. Reservations are not accepted. Reception is open until midnight.

The *Hôtel Esmerelda* (☎ 43.54.19.20; metro Saint Michel) is at 4 Rue Saint Julien le Pauvre, right across the Seine from Notre Dame. The three 150FF singles are almost always booked up months in advance – singles/doubles with shower and toilet cost 310FF.

The *Hôtel Saint Michel* (☎ 43.26.98.70; metro Saint Michel) is a block west of Place Saint Michel at 17 Rue Gît le Cœur (6e). Singles/doubles with running water are 195/220FF, including breakfast. A double with shower and toilet is 350FF, including breakfast.

Latin Quarter (5e) The Quartier Latin's mid-range hotels are very convenient for professors participating in scholarly colloquia, so rooms are hardest to find when such events are usually scheduled: October and March to July. The Luxembourg metro station is linked to both airports by Roissyrail and Orlyval.

Bottom End The *Hôtel de Médicis* (☎ 43.54.14.66 for reception, 43.29.53.64 for the public phone in the hall; metro Luxembourg), a few blocks south-west of the Panthéon at 214 Rue Saint Jacques, is

exactly what a cockroach-infested, dilapidated Latin Quarter dive for impoverished students should be like. Very basic singles start at 75FF, but the cheapest rooms are usually occupied. Basic doubles/triples are 140/225FF. Reservations are not accepted and, if you need a refund, getting your money back may prove a bit difficult.

Mid-Range The older, 36-room *Grand Hôtel du Progrès* (☎ 43.54.53.18; metro Luxembourg) at 50 Rue Gay Lussac, run by an English-born Australian woman and her French husband, is one of the best deals in the area. Singles with washbasin start at 148FF. Large, old-fashioned singles/doubles with a view and morning sunlight are 220/240FF (with washbasin and bidet) and 310/330FF (with shower and toilet). All prices include breakfast. Hall showers cost 15FF. The minimum stay is three days and rooms should be paid for upon arrival. Credit cards are not accepted. This place *may* be closed in August.

Around the corner, the clean *Hôtel de Nevers* (☎ 43.26.81.83) at 3 Rue de l'Abbé de l'Épée has singles/doubles/triples with washbasin for 150/250/350FF, including breakfast. Rooms with shower, toilet and breakfast are 250/300/400FF. Reception closes at 10.30 or 11 pm.

Another one-star place with a bit of character is the family-run *Hôtel Gay Lussac* (☎ 43.54.23.96; metro Luxembourg) at 29 Rue Gay Lussac. Small singles/doubles with washbasin start at 250/280FF. Doubles/three-bed quads with shower and toilet are 350/500FF. All prices include breakfast. Reception closes at 10 pm.

In the northern part of the Latin Quarter, the friendly, one-star *Hôtel Marignan* (☎ 43.25.31.03; metro Maubert Mutualité), an older place at 13 Rue du Sommerard, has pleasantly old-fashioned singles/doubles/triples/quads with washbasin for 160/270/360/440FF, including breakfast. None of the 30 rooms has a shower or toilet, but hall showers are free. Hand-washed clothes can be dried next to the basement furnace. You must check in before 10.30 pm.

Nearby, the two-star, 63-room *Hôtel Le Home Latin* (☎ 43.26.95.15; fax 43.29.87.04) at 15-17 Rue du Sommerard, completely reoutfitted in 1992, has serviceable, soundproofed singles/doubles/triples with shower, toilet, TV and annoying neon lights for 340/395/550FF. A two-room suite for four people is 700FF.

The two-star *Hôtel André Latin* (☎ 43.54.76.60; fax 40.51.77.10; metro Luxembourg) at 52 Rue Gay Lussac has nondescript and somewhat charmless singles and doubles with TV for 470FF.

There is a cluster of two and three-star hotels along Rue Victor Cousin and nearby Rue Cujas. The *Grand Hôtel Saint Michel* (☎ 46.33.33.02/65.03; metro Luxembourg) at 19 Rue Cujas is an excellent deal: simple but serviceable singles/doubles/triples/quads with shower and toilet start at 250/300/450/500FF. Some rooms have attached balconies. Reception is open 24 hours a day. Reserve as far in advance as possible.

Across the street, you might try the 80-room *Hôtel Excelsior* (☎ 46.34.79.50; fax 43.54.87.10) at 20 Rue Cujas. Singles/doubles/triples cost 210/300/365FF with washbasin and 345/400/465FF with shower and toilet. Hall showers are free.

The two-star *Hôtel des 3 Collèges* (☎ 43.54.67.30; fax 46.34.02.99) at 16 Rue Cujas has modern, tasteful singles/doubles with TV from 350/420FF.

The two-star *Hôtel de la Sorbonne* (☎ 43.54.58.08; fax 40.51.05.18; metro Luxembourg) at 6 Rue Victor Cousin has pleasant though smallish singles and doubles with TV for 380/420FF with one/two beds. Next door, the two-star *Hôtel Cluny Sorbonne* (☎ 43.54.66.66; fax 43.29.68.07) at 8 Rue Victor Cousin has pleasant, well-kept singles and doubles from 370FF. The lift is the size of a telephone booth. If you'll be checking in before 1 pm, you can usually reserve a room by telephone without sending a deposit.

You might also try the *Hôtel Gerson* (☎ 43.54.28.40; metro Cluny-La Sorbonne) at 14 Rue de la Sorbonne, which has

singles/doubles/triples for 280/300/400FF; singles/doubles with washbasin and bidet are 200/280FF.

Top End The 48-room *Hôtel des Grandes Écoles* (☎ 43.26.79.23; fax 43.25.28.15; metro Cardinal Lemoine), which is set around a lovely, geranium-filled courtyard, is at the end of the cobblestone alley at 75 Rue du Cardinal Lemoine. Slightly quaint singles and doubles start at 350FF with washbasin and 500FF with shower and toilet. A bed for a third person is 100FF. Make reservations at least a month ahead (two months in summer).

The *Hôtel Monge* (☎ 43.26.87.90; fax 43.54.47.25; metro Monge) at 55 Rue Monge has modern but less-than-heartwarming singles/doubles/triples with TV from 350/400/550FF. Reception is open 24 hours.

Saint Germain des Prés (6e) Most of the hotels in this delightful Left Bank neighbourhood are on the pricey side. The two and three-star places are most full in September and October, a traditional season for trade fairs and conventions.

Bottom End The unique and somewhat eccentric *Hôtel de Nesle* (☎ 43.54.62.41; metro Odéon, Mabillon) at 7 Rue de Nesle, a favourite with students and young people from all over the world, is a good place to meet other travellers. Singles cost 200FF; a bed in a double is 130FF, including breakfast and use of the hall showers. If you come alone, they'll find you a roommate. Since reservations are not accepted, the only way to get a place here is to stop by in the morning (10 or 11 am at the latest, especially in summer).

Mid-Range The *Hôtel Petit Trianon* (☎ 43.54.94.64; metro Odéon) at 2 Rue de l'Ancienne Comédie has singles from 170FF and doubles with shower from 320FF. Doubles/triples with shower and toilet are 370/450FF.

The *Hôtel Saint André des Arts* (☎ 43.26.96.16; fax 43.29.73.34; metro Odéon) at No 66 on restaurant-lined Rue Saint André des Arts has singles/doubles with shower and toilet for 310/400FF, including breakfast. This place also has a few singles with washbasin for 210FF.

The *Hôtel de Buci* (☎ 43.26.89.22; fax 46.33.80.31; metro Mabillon) at 22 Rue de Buci – *not* Debussy or WC! – has singles/doubles for 290/320FF (with shower) and 390/420FF (with shower and toilet). All prices include breakfast.

The *Welcome Hôtel* (☎ 46.34.24.80; fax 40.46.81.59; metro Mabillon) at 66 Rue de Seine – which is a few metres from 148 Blvd Saint Germain – is nothing special, but it's right on one of Paris's liveliest market streets. Nondescript singles/doubles with lots of windows, shower, toilet and TV are 340/495 to 395/515FF. The prices drop by about 40FF during slow periods. Credit cards are not accepted. The lift is so small there's no room to turn around. Telephone reservations cannot be made after 8 pm.

Top End The two-star, 40-room *Hôtel des Deux Continents* (☎ 43.26.72.46; fax 43.25.67.80; metro Saint Germain des Prés) at 25 Rue Jacob has spacious and flowery doubles/triples from 550/810FF.

The *Hôtel des Marronniers* (☎ 43.25.30.60; fax 40.46.83.56; metro Saint Germain des Prés), a three-star, 37-room place at 21 Rue Jacob, has less-than-huge singles/doubles from 450/640FF. There is a garden out the back.

A truly luxurious option south of Blvd Saint Germain is the charming *Hôtel de l'Abbaye* (☎ 45.44.38.11; fax 45.48.07.86; metro Saint Sulpice) at 10 Rue Cassette. Doubles cost 840 to 1350FF.

Montparnasse (6e & 14e) Gare Montparnasse is served by Air France buses from both airports.

Your best bet in this area is the *Hôtel des Académies* (☎ 43.26.66.44; metro Vavin) at 15 Rue de la Grande Chaumière (6e), which has been run by the same friendly family since 1920. Singles with running water cost 150FF; doubles are 200FF (with shower) and

240 to 255FF (with shower and toilet). The proprietors decided against installing lifts because they like having contact with their guests – if there were lifts, everyone would hurry straight to their rooms...

The *Celtic Hôtel* (☎ 43.20.93.53, 43.20. 83.91; metro Edgar Quinet) is two blocks east of Montparnasse Tower at 15 Rue d'Odessa (14e). Simple singles/doubles start at 170/200FF. Doubles with shower cost 240FF (260FF with toilet as well). Rooms with two beds are 230 to 290FF. Hall showers cost 15FF.

The less-than-friendly *Hôtel Domance* (☎ 43.20.63.15; metro Edgar Quinet) at 17 Blvd Edgar Quinet (14e) has singles/doubles with shower starting at 200/250FF.

Eiffel Tower Area (7e & 15e) This rather affluent part of Paris is linked to Orly Airport by Orlyrail, which stops at the Champ de Mars-Tour Eiffel metro station.

The 455-room *Paris Hilton* (☎ 42.73.92. 00 or 05.31.80.40; fax 47.83.62.66; metro Champ de Mars-Tour Eiffel) is one block south of the Eiffel Tower at 18 Rue Jean Rey (15e). Singles are 1600 to 1850FF, doubles go for 1800 to 2300FF.

Gare Saint Lazare Area (8e & 9e) This part of town is only a few blocks north of Opéra-Garnier and the famous department stores of Blvd Haussmann.

Bottom End The homy, 12-room *Résidence Cardinal* (☎ 48.74.16.16; metro Liège – closed after 8.30 pm and on Sunday and holidays – or metro Place Clichy) is a *pension en famille* (family-style guesthouse) in a typical Parisian apartment building at 4 Rue du Cardinal Mercier (2nd floor; 9e). The spotless, old-fashioned rooms, some of which have balconies, haven't changed since the 1920s. Singles/doubles cost 140/180FF with washbasin and toilet and 160/220FF with shower. All prices include breakfast. The minimum stay is three days. Kitchen facilities are not available. To get in the street door, push the silver button at the top of the gold keyboard to the right of the door; after

10 pm you need the code. From the entry hall, take the stairs on the right.

The one-star *Austin's Hôtel* (☎ 48.74. 48.71; fax 48.74.39.79; metro Saint Lazare) at 26 Rue d'Amsterdam (9e) has ordinary singles/doubles/triples from 144/195/229FF with washbasin and 223/240/274FF with shower; all prices include breakfast. There are no rooms with private toilet. Hall showers cost 14FF. You can check in 24 hours a day.

If you're in a bind, you might try the ineptly managed *Hôtel du Calvados* (☎ 48.74.39.31; metro Saint Lazare) at 20 Rue d'Amsterdam (9e). Singles/doubles with washbasin and bidet go for 180/220FF, but hall showers cost an outrageous 30FF! Doubles/triples with bath and toilet are 300/380FF.

Mid-Range There are quite a few two and three-star hotels along Rue d'Amsterdam (9e), which runs along the eastern side of Gare Saint Lazare. The *Hôtel Britannia* (☎ 42.85.36.36; fax 42.85.16.93; metro Saint Lazare) at 24 Rue d'Amsterdam (9e) has doubles/triples for 380/430FF. The hallways are narrow and the rooms, though pleasant and clean, are on the small side.

Top End The three-star, 93-room *Atlantic Hôtel* (☎ 43.87.45.40; fax 42.93.06.26; metro Liège or Europe) at 44 Rue de Londres (8e), right behind Gare Saint Lazare, is affiliated with Best Western. The large, airy and immaculate singles/doubles/triples with TV and minibar start at 500/680/920FF, including breakfast.

Opéra-Garnier Area (9e & 2e) The streets around Blvd Montmartre, which is 700 metres east of Opéra-Bastille, are a major nightlife area. Place de l'Opéra is linked to Charles de Gaulle Airport by Roissybus.

The two-star, 36-room *Hôtel Chopin* (☎ 47.70.58.10; fax 42.47.00.70; metro Rue Montmartre) is at 46 Passage Jouffroy (9e), which is down one of Paris's delightful, 19th-century shopping arcades from 10-12 Blvd Montmartre. Singles/doubles/triples

with TV cost 400/440/590FF. The arcades close at 10.30 pm, but hotel guests can get in by ringing the lighted *sonnette de nuit* (doorbell).

Gare du Nord Area (10e) Gare du Nord, one of Paris's most important stations for international trains, is linked to Charles de Gaulle Airport by Roissyrail and RATP bus No 350 and to Orly Airport by Orlyval. This may not be one of the city's most attractive districts, but it is not dangerous. If you spend the night in the train station, though, watch out for thieves.

Bottom End The friendly, old-fashioned *Hôtel de Milan* (☎ 40.37.88.50; metro Gare du Nord) at 17 Rue de Saint Quentin is about midway between Gare du Nord and Gare de l'Est. Clean, quiet singles/doubles cost 140/170FF with washbasin and bidet, 160/190FF with toilet and TV and 250FF with shower, toilet and TV. All three categories are an excellent deal. Triples/quads with toilet start at 300/400FF. Hall showers cost 18FF. Reception is open 24 hours. There's always space in the morning.

The modest *Hôtel Bonne Nouvelle* (☎ 48.74.99.90; metro Gare du Nord) at 125 Blvd de Magenta has shower-equipped singles for 160FF and doubles with shower for 160 to 210FF. A bed for a third person raises the room rate by 30%. Reception is open until 1 am.

The nearby *Grand Hôtel Magenta* (☎ 48.78.03.65; metro Gare du Nord) at 129 Blvd de Magenta has clean, spacious singles and doubles for 140FF with washbasin and bidet, 180FF with shower and 220FF with shower and toilet. Rooms for three to five people start at 300FF. Hall showers are a steep 25FF. Reception is open until 2 am.

A number of the cheap hotels around Montmartre are only about 750 metres northwest of Gare du Nord.

Mid-Range There are lots of two-star hotels around Gare du Nord. The two-star, 50-room *Hôtel Vieille France* (☎ 45.26.42.37; fax 45.26.99.07; metro Gare du Nord) at 151

Rue La Fayette has singles and doubles for 190FF with washbasin and bidet and 280FF with shower and toilet. The rooms are spacious, pleasant and soundproofed. Hall showers are free. Reception is staffed 24 hours.

The rather expensive *Nord Hôtel* (☎ 45. 26.43.40; fax 42.82.90.23), which is right across from Gare du Nord at 37 Rue de Saint Quentin, has clean, quiet singles/ doubles/triples with TV for 295/400/515FF, including breakfast.

Gare de l'Est Area (10e) This lively, working-class part of Paris has its attractions even if your train doesn't pull into Gare de l'Est. RATP bus No 350 to/from Charles de Gaulle Airport stops right in front of the station.

Bottom End The friendly, one-star *Sibour Hôtel* (☎ 46.07.20.74; fax 46.07.37.17; metro Gare de l'Est) at 4 Rue Sibour, formerly the Hôtel du Centre, is an excellent deal. The whole, 45-room place was recently renovated. Old-fashioned doubles with high ceilings cost 185FF with washbasin and bidet and 275FF with shower, toilet and TV. Hall showers cost 15FF. Reception is open 24 hours.

The old but well-maintained *Hôtel d'Alsace* (☎ 40.37.75.41; metro Gare de l'Est) at 85 Blvd de Strasbourg has bright, clean singles/doubles/two-bed triples/quads for 130/185/225/250FF with washbasin. Doubles with shower are 225FF. The fireplaces give the rooms a bit of old-time charm. Hall showers cost 10FF. The entrance is on the left-hand side of the driveway. Reception is open 24 hours.

The *Hôtel Liberty* (☎ 42.08.60.58; fax 42.40.12.59; metro Château d'Eau) at 16 Rue de Nancy (1st floor) is a step up from the rock-bottom places listed in the following paragraph. Clean, plain singles/doubles start at 125/170FF with washbasin, 170/ 195FF with shower and a very reasonable 190/230FF with shower and toilet. Triples are also available. Hall showers cost 10FF.

After 1 am, when reception closes, ring the bell.

The one-star *Hôtel du Jura* (☎ 47.70. 06.66; metro Château d'Eau) at 6 Rue Jarry is in an ethnically mixed, working-class area a few blocks south of Gare de l'Est. Singles/doubles/triples cost 140/185/225FF with washbasin and bidet and 170/210/ 250FF with shower. Hall showers are 20FF. This place often has space during August.

Down the block, the no-star *Hôtel Crystal* (☎ 47.70.07.40) at 8 Rue Jarry has basic and slightly dilapidated singles/doubles for 100/120FF with washbasin and bidet. Doubles with shower are 150FF. There are no triples. Hall showers are free. Reception closes at 1 am.

There's a cluster of hotels on Rue du Château d'Eau between Blvd de Strasbourg and Rue du Faubourg Saint Denis.

Mid-Range The extravagantly named *Grand Hôtel de Paris* (☎ 46.07.40.56; fax 42.05.99.18; metro Gare de l'Est) at 72 Blvd de Strasbourg has pleasant, soundproofed singles/doubles/triples/quads for 300/350/ 450/500FF. This well-run place has 49 rooms and a tiny lift. If you stay at least three or four days, they may throw in breakfast (30FF) for free.

Place de la Nation Area (11e & 12e) This little-touristed part of Paris is on the Château de Vincennes-La Défense metro line, which serves most of the Right Bank. It is linked to Charles de Gaulle Airport by RATP bus No 351.

The one-star, family-run *Hôtel Camélia* (☎ 43.73.67.50; metro Nation) is a half-block north of Place de la Nation at 6 Ave Philippe Auguste (11e). Pleasant, well-kept rooms for one or two people cost 160FF with washbasin, 200FF with shower and 240FF with shower and toilet. Hall showers cost 20FF. This place, most of whose clients are French businesspeople, closes during August and around Christmas and New Year.

Just up the block, you might try the modest *Hôtel Central* (☎ 43.73.73.53; metro Nation) at 16 Ave Philippe Auguste (11e),

which is quiet and clean but whose proprietor is somewhat picky about clients. She's been known to tell people who call up that the place is full even when it's not, and she especially dislikes loud families that eat in the room. In any case, doubles/quads with washbasin and bidet are 150/240FF. None of the rooms has a shower, and the hall version costs a steep 30FF (less if you stay for a few days).

13e Arrondissement Paris's Chinatown is south of Place d'Italie along Ave d'Ivry and Ave de Choisy. The Porte de Choisy metro station is linked to Orly Airport by RATP bus No 183.

The *Adrian Hôtel* (☎ 45.70.76.00; metro Tolbiac) at 102 Ave de Choisy has small, motelish doubles/triples from 220/270FF. It is closed during July.

Place Denfert Rochereau (14e) Place Denfert Rochereau is linked to both airports by Orlybus, Orlyval and Roissyrail.

The *Hôtel Floridor* (☎ 43.21.35.53; fax 43.25.65.81; metro Denfert Rochereau) at 28 Place Denfert Rochereau has singles/ doubles for 256/281FF (with shower) and 274/299FF (with shower and toilet). All prices include breakfast served in your room.

The *Hôtel L'Espérance* (☎ 43.21.41.04; metro Denfert Rochereau) is right around the corner at 1 Rue de Grancey. Doubles cost 180FF (with washbasin and bidet) and 255FF (with shower).

Montmartre (18e) Montmartre is one of the most charming, leafy neighbourhoods of Paris. Most of the bottom-end hotels are around the base of the hill.

Bottom End The *Hôtel Tholozé* (☎ 46.06. 74.83; metro Abbesses) is half-a-block down the hill from Moulin de la Galette (one of the two windmills between Ave Junot and Rue Lepic) at 24 Rue Tholozé. Doubles cost 150FF with washbasin and 200FF with shower and toilet. Triples with shower and toilet are 300FF. Breakfast (optional) is served from 8.30 to 11 am and costs 20FF.

The friendly, family-run *Hôtel Saint Pierre* (☎ 46.06.20.73; metro Anvers) is only two blocks from the stairs up to Sacré Cœur in an old building at 3 Rue Seveste. The 36 rooms are musty and a bit run down but are eminently serviceable. Singles/doubles with washbasin cost 120/140FF; a double with shower and toilet is 180FF. There are no hall showers. Reception closes at 12.30 am.

The 38-room *Hôtel du Cheval Blanc* (☎ 46.06.38.77; metro Anvers) at 20 Rue d'Orsel has singles/doubles/triples for 130/150/200FF with washbasin and 200/240/280FF with shower. Hall showers cost 20FF. Reception is open 24 hours. This place almost always has space in the morning, even in summer.

The *Hôtel Bonséjour* (☎ 42.54.22.53; metro Abbesses), a block north of Rue des Abbesses at 11 Rue Burcq, has basic but pleasant singles from 110 to 130FF and doubles for 170FF. A token good for six minutes of water in the ground-floor shower costs 10FF. If you'll be coming back after 10 pm, make sure to get a front-door key.

The *Hôtel Audran* (☎ 42.58.79.59; metro Abbesses) is on the other side of Rue des Abbesses at 7 Rue Audran. Singles/doubles start at 100/140FF. There is a toilet on each floor and a shower (10FF) on the 1st floor. The front door is locked at 1 am; they may only give the code to long-term residents.

The *Idéal Hôtel* (☎ 46.06.63.63; metro Abbesses) at 3 Rue des Trois Frères has simple but adequate singles/doubles starting at 120/160FF. A shower is 20FF. If you ring up from the station, they'll hold a room for a few hours. Reception, which is on the 1st floor, is open 24 hours a day.

If you're hard up for a place to stay, you might try the run-down, 48-room *Grand Hôtel Clignancourt* (☎ 46.06.29.98; metro Barbès Rochechouart) at 4 Rue de Clignancourt, which is opposite McDonald's. Basic singles/doubles/triples with washbasin and bidet cost 110/130/170FF. Hall showers cost 20FF. Reception is open until 2 am. There are always rooms available in the morning.

Another hotel-of-last-resort is the *Hôtel de Paris* (☎ 46.06.27.03; metro Chateau Rouge) at 10 Rue Poulet, which is about 500 metres east of Sacré Cœur in a lively, ethnically mixed area. Singles cost 100 to 110FF, doubles start at 140FF. Hall showers cost 20FF. After nightfall, locals report that it's prudent to avoid the Château Rouge metro stop.

Mid-Range The friendly *Hôtel des Arts* (☎ 46.06.30.52; metro Abbesses), which was completely rebuilt in 1991, is at 5 Rue Tholozé. This two-star place, which is equipped with a lift, has doubles with one/two beds, shower and toilet from 410/440FF.

The 64-room *Tim Hôtel* (☎ 42.55.74.79; fax 42.55.71.01; metro Abbesses) at shady, cobbled Place Émile Goudeau – the street address is 11 Rue Ravignan – has neat, modern singles/doubles for 325/410FF; a third bed for a child under 12 is 110FF. This is a good choice if you place more value on location than room size. Some of the rooms on the 4th and 5th floors have stunning views of Paris.

The three decent two-star places on Rue Aristide Bruant are generally less full in July and August than in spring and autumn. The 30-room *Hôtel Utrillo* (☎ 42.58.13.44; fax 42.23.93.88; metro Abbesses) at No 7 has singles/doubles/triples from 290/360/490FF. Some rooms can take an additional bed for 60FF. The 30-room *Hôtel Capucines Montmartre* (☎ 42.52.89.80; fax 42.52.29.57) at No 5 has singles/doubles with TV and minibar for 325/420FF, including breakfast. A bed for a third person is 70FF. The 27-room *Hôtel du Moulin* (☎ 42.64.33.33; fax 46.06.42.66) at No 3 has singles from 340FF and doubles from 400FF. All rooms have TV and minibar. An additional bed costs 80FF.

The 45-room *Hôtel Luxia* (☎ 46.06.84.24; fax 46.06.10.14; metro Anvers) at 8 Rue Seveste, a block from the stairs up to Sacré Cœur, takes mainly groups, but at least a few rooms are almost always left for independent travellers. Plain, clean singles/doubles/triples with shower, toilet and TV are 280/300/390FF. Reception is open 24 hours.

Airports At Charles de Gaulle, the two-star, 575-room *Hôtel Arcade* (☎ 48.62.49.49) at 10 Rue du Verseau, 95701 Roissy, is right next to the Roissy-Aéroport Charles de Gaulle RER station (and under the highway from terminal T9). It is linked to all three terminals by the free Navette Aéroport (airport shuttle bus). Singles and doubles cost 410FF. Day use (8.30 am to 7 pm) costs 300FF.

At Orly, the 300-room *Hôtel Arcade* (☎ 46.87.33.50; fax 46.87.29.92), linked to both terminals by the interterminal navette (shuttle bus), has doubles for 375 to 450FF, depending on the season. Day use costs 350FF.

PLACES TO EAT
Restaurants & Cafés

Most of Paris's thousands of restaurants – including some 2000 Chinese and Vietnamese places – offer excellent value, by Parisian standards at least. Well-to-do locals are willing to pay dearly for a well-placed table in a famous café along a prestigious boulevard, so prices for a spot along Blvd du Montparnasse or around Saint Germain des Prés don't come cheap. But the intense competition tends to quickly rid the city of places with bad food or prices that Parisians feel are out of line.

The major exception to this free market paradise is comprised of certain unscrupulous or enterprising tourist restaurants, where the staff can safely assume that the evenings diners will never be seen again even if the food is superb. Areas where you should be especially careful – and to avoid for your big Paris splurge – include the immediate vicinity of Notre Dame, the streets in the 5e just east of Place Saint Michel, the immediate vicinity of the Louvre (1er), Blvd des Champs-Élysées (8e) and Place du Tertre in Montmartre (18e).

Many restaurants are closed on Sunday, and very few stay open between 2.30 or 3 pm and 6.30 or 7 pm. Places open 24 hours a day (or nearly) include Au Pied du Cochon and Brasserie Paoli in the Centre Pompidou area; La Maison d'Alsace on the Champs-Élysées;

Le Dépanneur in Pigalle; and (under Places to Drink) Pub Saint Germain des Prés.

Louvre Area (1er) This part of the 1er arrondissement has lots of establishments catering to tourists – locals tend to gravitate towards Les Halles – but a few places are worth mentioning. A number of mid-range restaurants are located along Rue de Montpensier (metro Palais Royal), which runs along the west side of Jardin du Palais Royal. There's a cluster of authentic Japanese places a few blocks north of the Louvre.

French Le Grand Véfour (☎ 42.96.56.27; fax 42.86.80.71; metro Pyramides), at the northern edge of the Jardin du Palais Royal at 17 Rue de Beaujolais, has been serving the French elite since 1784. Its traditional French and Savoyard cuisine and 18th-century elegance have earned it two Michelin stars. Count on spending 600 to 800FF per person for dinner. A lunch *menu* is available for 305FF, not including wine. Le Grand Véfour is closed on Saturday and Sunday and during August. Reservations for dinner should be made about 10 days ahead; for lunch, two or three days should suffice.

Restaurant La Moisanderie (☎ 42.96. 92.93; metro Palais Royal) has two addresses: 52 Rue de Richelieu and 47 Rue de Montpensier. A *menu* of French cuisine costs 110FF; wine starts at 60FF a bottle. It is open Monday to Saturday from 11.30 am to 3.30 pm and 7 to 10 pm.

Japanese Businesspeople from Japan in search of real Japanese food flock to Rue Sainte Anne and other streets of Paris's 'Japantown', which is just west of the Jardin du Palais Royal. Many of the restaurants offer surprisingly good value.

Stepping into *Lamen Higuma* (☎ 47.03. 38.59; metro Pyramides) at 32bis Rue Sainte Anne is like ducking into a corner noodle shop in Tokyo. To the delight of the almost exclusively Japanese clientele (the only French people we saw there were chatting in Japanese), the high-temperature woks are forever filled with furiously bubbling soups

or flaming vegetables. A meal-sized bowl of noodles in broth costs only 36 to 44FF. Food is served daily from 11.30 am straight through to 10 pm. The lunch and dinner *menus* (about 60FF) are not served from 2.30 to 5 pm.

At *Matsuri Sushi* (☎ 42.61.05.73; metro Pyramides), a sushi bar at 36 Rue de Richelieu, plates of sushi (20FF at lunch, 22 to 30FF in the evening) make their way around the restaurant on a little conveyor belt. It is open Monday to Friday from noon to 2.30 pm and 7 to 10.30 pm (11.30 pm on Friday) and on Saturday from 7 to 11.30 pm.

Other Down the block from the BVJ Paris-Louvre hostel, *Pizza Rico* (☎ 42.36.11.57; metro Louvre-Rivoli) at 16 Rue Jean-Jacques Rousseau (1er) has various Italian specialities and a *menu* for 59FF. It is open Monday to Saturday from noon to 2.45 pm and 6.30 to 11 pm. There are a number of other reasonably priced restaurants along Rue Jean-Jacques Rousseau.

The *Vietnamese/Chinese place* (☎ 42.33.38.32; metro Louvre-Rivoli) near the BVJ Paris-Louvre hostel at 19 Rue Jean-Jacques Rousseau has a 69FF *menu*. It is open daily from noon to 2.30 pm and 7 to 11 pm. The *grill* at 14 Rue Jean-Jacques Rousseau has a 61FF *menu*.

Centre Pompidou Area (1er & 4e) There are scores of restaurants offering good value in all directions from Forum des Halles, but few of them (except the fast-food joints) are particularly inexpensive. Streets lined with places to eat include Rue des Lombards, up-market bar and bistro-lined Rue Montorgueil, and the narrow streets north and east of Forum des Halles.

French A favourite with young, *branchés* (plugged-in, ie 'with-it') Parisians is *Batifol* (☎ 42.36.85.50; metro Les Halles, Étienne Marcel), an attractive bistro at 14 Rue Mondétour (1er) that serves meals nonstop every day from 11 am to 1 am. Specialities include pot au feu (stewed beef and vegetables; 58FF) and moelle (beef marrow

spread on bread; 30FF). Generous plats du jour cost 50 to 60FF. This building has been a bistro (under various names) since 1938.

Au P'tit Rémouleur (☎ 48.04.79.24; metro Châtelet) at 2 Rue de la Coutellerie (4e) is a small, typically French restaurant offering fish, bouillabaisse (50FF), mussels and various main dishes (40 to 64FF). The *menu* is 63FF. It's open Monday to Saturday from noon to 3 pm and 7 to 11 pm.

Perhaps the most famous restaurant in this part of town is *Au Pied de Cochon* (☎ 42.36.11.75; metro Les Halles) at 6 Rue Coquillière (1er), whose pieds de cochon (pigs' trotters; 80 to 120FF) and other pork dishes (eg tripe; 75FF) long fed both bourgeois·theatre-goers and porters from the nearby market. The clientele has become more uniformly up-market since 1969, but as in the days of Les Halles, Au Pied de Cochon is still open 24 hours a day, seven days a week. In summer, they always have a pet pig hanging out at the counter or on the pavement.

Léon de Bruxelles (☎ 42.36.18.50; metro Les Halles) at 120 Rue Rambuteau (1er), which is on the northern side of Forum des Halles, is dedicated to only one thing: the preparation of mussels (moules). Meal-size bowls of mussels, served with chips and bread, start at 59FF. This place is open daily from 11.45 am to midnight (1 am on Friday and Saturday nights).

Brasserie Paoli (☎ 42.33.98.53; metro Châtelet) at 104 Rue de Rivoli (1er), which is decorated with brass, mirrors and grape-bunch lamps, is one of the few places in Paris open 365 days a year, 22 hours a day (it closes from 6 to 8 am). The food here has received good reviews, and meals – including the two-course 69FF *menu* – are available from noon to 5 am. Salads are 54 to 60FF. Beer is 19FF per demi (26FF at night); coffee is 9FF (15FF after 11 pm).

Other *Chicago Meatpackers* (☎ 40.28.02.33; metro Les Halles), a huge, well-appointed place at 8 Rue Coquillière (1er), specialises in home-made American hamburgers (62 to 75FF), ribs and Häagen Dazs

desserts. The restaurant section is open every day of the year from 11.30 am to 1 am. The bar at the back charges 29FF for a pint of beer. The décor and ambience are as American as any place with English bartenders can be. Check out the model train that rides around on a track suspended from the ceiling.

This part of Paris is a fast-food lovers' paradise. *KFC* (☎ 40.26.61.14; metro Châtelet-Les Halles) at 31-35 Blvd de Sébastopol (1er) is open daily from 11 am to midnight (1 am on Friday and Saturday nights).

Pizza Hut (☎ 42.33.71.43; metro Châtelet-Les Halles) at 1 Square des Innocents (1er) is open daily from 11 am to 11 pm (midnight on Friday and Saturday nights). It's open until midnight every day from May to September. A pizza for three or four people costs 87 to 151FF.

For hamburger fans, there's a *Burger King* across from 25 Rue Aubry Le Boucher (4e) and a *McDonald's* at Square des Innocents (1er).

Kids with a preference for the conventional may enjoy *Mélodine cafeteria* (☎ 40.29.09.78; metro Rambuteau; 3e), whose entrances – which are across from the north side of the Centre Pompidou – are at 42 Rue Rambuteau and 21 Rue Beaubourg. Most main dishes cost 25 to 40FF. Salads are available. Food is served daily from 11 am to 10 pm.

Marais (4e) The Marais is filled with small eateries of every imaginable sort, including many Jewish places. Streets to browse for a restaurant include Rue Sainte Croix de la Bretonnerie, Rue Vieille du Temple (the gay heart of the Marais) and Place du Marché Sainte Catherine.

French *Le P'tit Gavroche* (☎ 48.87.74.26; metro Hôtel de Ville) at 15 Rue Sainte Croix de la Brettonerie, also known as Bistro du Marais, attracts tablefuls of raucous working-class regulars, so this is not the place to come for a quiet date. Meals are served Monday to Saturday from noon to

2.30 pm and 7 pm to midnight. Drinks are available from 8 am to 2 am. The daily *menu*, available until about 10 pm (or whenever they run out), costs 45FF. Main dishes are also about 45FF. A little carafe of wine is 10FF.

The *Louis-Philippe Café* (☎ 42.72.29.42; metro Pont Marie) at 66 Quai de l'Hôtel de Ville has two sections: a ground-floor café, open daily from 9 am to 2 am, where coffee is 5/10FF at the bar/seated and beer is 10/14FF (2FF more after 10 pm); and a 1st-floor restaurant, reached via a 19th-century spiral staircase, where food (including an 82FF *menu)* is served from noon to 3 pm and 7 to 11 pm. The background music is mellow.

Le Gai Moulin (☎ 42.77.60.60; metro Rambuteau), a small, modern place at 4 Rue Saint Merri, serves traditional French cuisine from noon to 2 pm and 7.30 to 11.30 pm (closed Tuesday). From May to September, it's open seven days a week but just for dinner (7 pm to 12.30 am). A *menu* is available for 94FF. The clientele are mostly gay men.

Jewish The heart of the old Jewish neighbourhood, Rue des Rosiers, has quite a few kosher and kosher-style restaurants, most of which are closed on Friday evening, Saturday and Jewish holidays.

Société Rosiers Alimentation (☎ 48.87.63.60; metro Saint Paul) at 34 Rue des Rosiers has kosher foodstuffs and Israeli takeaway food, including shwarma (chawarma) and falafel. It is open Sunday to Thursday from 10 am (noon for falafel) to 11 pm and on Friday from 10 am until one hour before sunset (it's the last kosher place to close on Friday). Pay at the cash register before picking up your order.

Yahalom Traiteur (☎ 42.77.12.35) at 22 Rue des Rosiers, a kosher deli, is open daily, except Friday, after about 3 pm and Saturday from 11.30 am to 10.30 pm. Couscous is 70FF. For Israeli dishes, a good choice is *Chez Rami et Hanna* (☎ 42.78.23.09) at 54 Rue des Rosiers, which is open weekdays from 11 am to 3.30 pm and 6 pm to 1.30 am. On Saturday and Sunday, hours are 11.30 am to 2 am.

The best known Jewish restaurant in Paris is *Restaurant Jo Goldenberg* (☎ 48.87. 20.16) at 7 Rue des Rosiers, founded in 1920. The food is kosher-style but not actually kosher according to Jewish law. The starters (25FF) and apple strudel are excellent, though the main dishes (70FF) aren't as good as what you can find in New York. Jo Goldenberg is open every day (including Saturday) except Yom Kippur from 8.30 am until about midnight. The bullet holes in the window date from 1982, when Palestinian terrorists attacked this place, killing six people, including the son of the proprietor.

Fresh breads and Jewish-style Central European pastries, including apple strudel and cakes made with poppy seeds, are available at the two Finkelsztajn bakeries on Rue des Rosiers. *Florence Finkelsztajn* (☎ 48.87. 92.85), which is also a deli, is in a blue-tiled building across from 32 Rue des Rosiers. It's open daily except Tuesday and Wednesday. *Sacha Finkelsztajn bakery* (☎ 42.72.78.91), down the block at 27 Rue des Rosiers, is open Wednesday to Sunday from 9.30 am to 1.30 pm and 3 to 7.30 pm.

A few blocks east, Polish-Jewish cuisine is on offer at the homy *Restaurant Pitchi Poi* (☎ 42.77.46.15; metro Saint Paul) at 7 Rue Caron, which is at Place du Marché Sainte Catherine. Family photos have been accumulating on the walls since it was founded in 1981. A *menu* is available for 145FF (70FF for children).

Vegetarian *Piccolo Teatro* (☎ 42.72.17.79; metro Saint Paul) at 6 Rue des Écouffes is an intimate place with stone walls, a beam ceiling and cosy little tables. The *menus* cost 53 and 74FF for lunch and 85 and 110FF for dinner; the attractive and tasty assiette végétarienne (vegetarian plate) is 60FF. Most of the ingredients are macrobiotic. This place is open from noon to 3 pm and 7 to 11 pm (closed Monday and Tuesday). It is often busy in the evening.

If you're in the mood for something light, you might try *Aquarius* (☎ 48.87.48.71; metro Rambuteau) at 54 Rue Sainte Croix de la Bretonnerie, which has a calming, airy atmosphere that makes you think of fresh bean sprouts. It is open Monday to Saturday from noon to 9.45 pm but the plat du jour is available only from noon to 2 pm and 7 to 9.45 pm. They have a two-course *menu* for 52FF.

Other The very popular and trendy Tex-Mex *Restaurant Le Studio* (☎ 42.74.10.38; metro Rambuteau), which is in the courtyard at 41 Rue du Temple, has tacos, enchiladas and chimichangas for 65 to 78FF. This is Texas as only the French could imagine it! While dining, you may be able to watch people learning the flamenco at the Centre de Danse du Marais (Marais Dance Centre), which is across the courtyard. Le Studio is open weekdays from 7.30 pm to midnight and on weekends from 12.30 to 3.30 pm and 7.30 pm to 12.30 am.

La Perla Restaurant & Bar (☎ 42.77. 59.40; metro Saint Paul) at 26 Rue François Miron, which is popular with younger, *branchés* (with-it) Parisians, specialises in light, California-style Mexican dishes such as guacamole (27FF), nachos (27FF) and burritos (42FF). Meals are served Monday to Friday from noon to 3 pm and 7 to 11 pm and on weekends nonstop from noon to 11 pm.

Marais Plus (☎ 48.87.01.40; metro Saint Paul) at 20 Rue des Francs Bourgeois is a mellow salon de thé that specialises in quiches (50FF) and tarts (pies; 35FF). It is open daily from 10 am to 7.30 pm.

Inexpensive *Minh Chau* (☎ 42.71.13.30; metro Hôtel de Ville) is a tiny Vietnamese place at 10 Rue de la Verrerie with tasty main dishes for only 26 to 32FF. It's open Monday to Saturday from 11.30 am to 3 pm and 5.30 to 11pm.

Île de la Cité & Île Saint Louis (4e) Île Saint Louis is generally known as an expensive place to eat, but there are a few mid-range options. The food shops (see Self-Catering), though pricey, offer outstanding quality.

French *Brasserie de l'Île Saint Louis* (☎ 43.54.02.59; metro Pont Marie) at 55 Quai de Bourbon, founded in 1870, occupies

a superb spot next to Pont Saint Louis. The Alsatian-style choucroute garnie (sauerkraut with meat; 80FF) is reputed to be excellent, but you can enjoy the location by ordering just a coffee (5FF at the bar, 10FF at a table and 12FF on the terrace) or a beer (10FF at the bar, 15FF inside and 18FF on the terrace). This place is open from 11.45 am (6 pm on Thursday) to 1 or 2 am (closed Wednesday).

Ice Cream Berthillon (☎ 43.54.31.61; metro Pont Marie) at 31 Rue Saint Louis en l'Île is reputed have the most delicious ice cream in Paris. While the fruit flavours are justifiably renowned, the chocolate, coffee and Agenaise (Armagnac & prunes) flavours are incomparably richer. The takeaway counter is open Wednesday to Sunday from 10 am to 8 pm. One/two/three tiny scoops cost 8/14/18FF. The salon dégustation (sit-down area) is open the same days from 2 to 8 pm.

In a forceful demonstration of Gallic non-commercialism, Berthillon closes during school breaks so the staff can take family holidays: in February, at Easter, around All Saints' Day (1 November) and during summer (from early July to early September). Fortunately, other shops in the vicinity continue to sell Berthillon products, albeit at a slight premium. Just look for lines of people smacking their lips or go to 88 Rue Saint Louis en l'Île or No 17, 25 or 27 on Rue des Deux Ponts.

The Häagen Dazs shop (☎ 40.51.08.51; metro Hôtel de Ville) at 1 Rue d'Arcole on Île Saint Louis is open daily from noon to 8, 9 or 10 pm (midnight in summer).

Place Saint Michel Area (5e) Paris's largest concentration of tourist restaurants is squeezed into a maze of narrow streets across the Seine from Notre Dame and bound by the river, Rue Saint Jacques, Blvd Saint Germain and Blvd Saint Michel. This area's Greek, North African and Middle Eastern restaurants attract mainly foreigners, most of whom are unaware that some people refer to Rue de la Huchette (and nearby streets such as Rue Saint Séverin and Rue de la Harpe) as 'bacteria alley' because of the high inci-

dence of food poisoning among those who yield to the blandishments of the door attendants. There are persistent rumours that to keep costs down, some of these places recycle undrunk wine from patrons' glasses. To add insult to injury, many of the poor souls who eat here are under the impression that this is the famous Latin Quarter...

Although you'll probably be better off if you give a miss to the establishments that ripen their meat and seafood in the front window, it is still possible to get a cheap, decent meal around Place Saint Michel.

French Le Navigator (☎ 43.54.35.86; metro Maubert Mutualité) at 63 Rue Galande serves traditional French cuisine from 11.45 am to 2.30 pm and 6.45 to 11 pm (closed Monday). It is closed during February. Menus are available for 85FF (before 8 pm), 120, 140 and 180FF.

Asian East of Rue Saint Jacques, Au Coin des Gourmets (☎ 43.26.12.92; metro Maubert Mutualité) at 5 Rue Dante serves superb Cambodian food, much of it gently seasoned with lemongrass (citronelle) and coconut milk (lait de coco). This place is open from noon to 2.30 pm and 7 to 10.30 pm (closed Tuesday). Reservations are recommended.

Matsuya (☎ 43.54.58.84; metro Maubert Mutualité), a Japanese place at 39 Rue Galande, has lunch menus for 38 to 55FF, dinner menus for 54 to 148FF and sashimi for 35 to 45FF. It is open daily from noon to 2.30 pm and 7 to 11 pm.

Tiny Chez Maï (☎ 43.54.05.33; metro Maubert Mutualité), a hole-in-the-wall Vietnamese place at 65 Rue Galande, is open daily from noon to 2 pm and 7 to 11 pm. Main dishes cost only 25 to 30FF; soup is 20FF.

L'Année du Dragon (☎ 46.34.23.46; metro Saint Michel) at 10 Rue Saint Séverin, which serves slightly greasy Chinese and Vietnamese food, has menus for as little as 35FF. It is open daily from noon to 2.30 pm and 6.30 to 11 pm.

Other For Lebanese food, try Al-Dar (☎ 43. 25.17.15) at 8-10 Rue Frédéric Sauton. The

snack-traiteur (deli) section on the corner, open daily from 7 am to midnight, has quite a selection of dishes from the Levant, including sweet Lebanese pastries and kebab sandwiches (17FF). The restaurant is open daily from 12 to 3 pm and 7 pm to midnight.

For a delightful selection of scrumptious apple-cinnamon strudel, Sacher tortes, tourtes (quiche-like pies; 23FF) and the like, drop by *Pâtisserie Viennoise* (☎ 43.26. 60.48; metro Cluny-La Sorbonne) at 8 Rue de l'École de Médicine (6e), which is on the other side of Blvd Saint Michel from the Musée de Cluny. It is open Monday to Friday from 9 am to 7.15 pm but is closed from mid-July to the end of August.

In the 'bacteria alley' area, quite a few *sandwich shops* sell baguette halves or thirds with various fillings for around 17FF. There's a *McDonald's* (metro Cluny-La Sorbonne) at the corner of Blvd Saint Germain and Rue de la Harpe.

The *Häagen Dazs* ice-cream place (☎ 40.51.73.72; metro Saint Michel) at 30 Rue de la Huchette is open Wednesday to Sunday from 12.30 to 8 pm (10 am to 11 pm in summer). One scoop costs 13FF.

The *Tea Caddy* (☎ 43.54.15.56; metro Saint Michel) at 14 Rue Saint Julien le Pauvre is a fine place to sip English tea. It is open from noon to 7 pm (closed Tuesday and Wednesday).

Latin Quarter (5e) The area around Rue Mouffetard is filled with scores of places to eat and is especially popular with students. It is ever-so-slightly seedy and attracts lots of tourists but is still a much better bet than Rue de la Huchette.

French Reasonably priced *Restaurant Perraudin* (☎ 46.33.15.75; metro Luxembourg) at 157 Rue Saint Jacques hasn't changed much since about 1907. Specialities include bœuf Bourguignon (54FF), gigot d'agneau (leg of lamb; 54FF) and confit de canard (conserve of duck; 56FF). At lunchtime, there's a *menu* for 60FF. It is open Tuesday to Saturday from noon to 2.15 pm and 7.30

to 10.15 pm, and Monday from 7.30 to 10.15 pm; it's closed on Sunday.

La Papillote Mouffetard (☎ 43.31.75.66, 43.36.66.46; metro Monge) at 13 Rue du Pot de Fer, which has *menus* for 65 (lunch only), 98 and 138FF, is a bit less touristy than some of its neighbours. French and international dishes are served daily from noon to 2.30 pm and 7 pm to midnight.

For croissants, pastries, little pizzas and the like, try *La Brioche Dorée* (metro Luxembourg) at 65 Blvd Saint Michel, opposite the entrance to Jardin du Luxembourg. It is open Monday to Saturday from 7 am to 8 pm.

A long-time Left Bank favourite is *Brasserie Balzar* (☎ 43.54.13.67; metro Cluny-La Sorbonne) at 49 Rue des Écoles, whose walls are decorated with a mix of mirrors and smoke-stained prints and paintings. Tea is 20FF, café au lait is 15FF and beer on tap is 16FF. The plat du jour costs about 90FF. Le Balzar is open daily from 8 am to 2 am; it is closed in August.

Some of the best discount crepes in Paris are sold in a *stand* at 61 Rue Mouffetard (metro Monge), which is open daily from 11 am to 2 am. Savoury crepes (eg with cheese) are only 11 to 23FF; sweet crepes are 7 to 22FF.

Rue Soufflot (metro Luxembourg) is lined with cafés.

Other For Tibetan food, a good choice is *Tashi Delek* (☎ 43.26.55.55; metro Luxembourg) at 4 Rue des Fossés Saint Jacques, which is open Tuesday to Saturday from noon to 2.30 pm and 7 to 10 pm, and Monday from 7 to 10 pm; it's closed on Sunday. Lunch *menus* are 58 to 65FF; the 105FF dinner *menu* includes wine.

Machu Pichu (☎ 43.26.13.13; metro Luxembourg) at 9 Rue Royer Collard has Peruvian main dishes for 60 to 80FF. It is open from noon to 2 pm and 7.30 to 11 pm daily except Saturday lunchtime and Sunday.

Hungarian specialities at *Au Vieux Budapest* (☎ 46.33.09.51; metro Cardinal Lemoine) at 40 Rue Descartes include paprikash (beef goulash; 75FF), poulet au

paprika (paprika chicken; 75FF) and goulash soup (40FF). The *menu* is 95FF, including wine. There is often live music. This place is open daily from 8.30 pm to 2 am; you can order dinner up to midnight. It may also open up for lunch.

The informal Afghan *Restaurant Koutchi* (☎ 44.07.20.56; metro Cardinal Lemoine) at 40 Rue Cardinal Lemoine, whose name means 'nomad' in Pashto, has lunch *menus* for 58 and 78FF. Most main dishes are 60 to 85FF. It is open Monday to Saturday from noon to 2.30 pm and 7 to 11 pm.

There are a number of Chinese and Vietnamese restaurants along Rue Royer Collard (metro Luxembourg) and several more along Rue Descartes (metro Cardinal Lemoine).

Restaurant Cous-Cous (☎ 43.26.66.43; metro Monge) at 6 Rue Mouffetard, also known as La Rose Mouffetard, serves some of the cheapest sit-down food in town, including generous portions of unspectacular couscous starting at only 29FF. A thin steak with chips is 25FF. This place is open daily from 11 am to midnight.

The *Häagen Dazs* (☎ 40.51.03.51; metro Monge) at 3 Place de la Contrescarpe is open daily from 11.30 am to about 10 pm (midnight from May to September).

Like its clones around town, the *McDonald's* (metro Luxembourg) on the corner of Rue Soufflot and Blvd Saint Michel has what may be Paris's cheapest coffee. It is open daily from 10 or 11 am to midnight or 1 am.

Jardin des Plantes Area (5e) The quiet streets east of the Latin Quarter have a few excellent options.

French *La Tour d'Argent* (☎ 43.54.23.31/ 43.54.10.08; metro Cardinal Lemoine, Pont Marie), on the 6th floor at 15 Quai de la Tournelle, is one of the few restaurants in Paris with three Michelin stars. Its most famous delicacy is canard. The lunch *menu*, not available on Sunday and holidays, costs 375FF. First courses are 210 to 530FF, main dishes cost 310 to 520FF and desserts go for 110 to 150FF. La Tour d'Argent is open daily except Monday. Lunch reservations should be made 10 days in advance; for dinner, reserve three weeks ahead.

Moissonnier (☎ 43.29.87.65; metro Cardinal Lemoine) at 28 Rue des Fossés Saint Bernard is renowned for its excellent Lyon-influenced cuisine. Count on a full meal costing about 220FF. It's open daily, except Sunday night and Monday, from noon to 2 pm and 7 pm to 9.15 pm. It is closed from the end of July to early September.

Other You can sip mint tea from tiny glasses (9FF) or sample sweet North African pastries at the Paris Mosque's *salon de thé* (☎ 43.41. 18.14; metro Monge) at 39 Rue Geoffroy Saint Hilaire. It is open daily from 10 am to 10 pm.

On the top floor of the Institut du Monde Arabe, *Restaurant Fakhr el-Dine* (☎ 46.33. 47.70; metro Cardinal Lemoine) at 1 Rue des Fossés Saint Bernard serves tea and Lebanese cuisine.

Saint Germain des Prés (6e) There are lots of restaurants all along Rue Saint André des Arts (metro Saint Michel, Odéon), including a few down the covered passage between Nos 59 and 61. There's a cluster of lively bars, cafés and restaurants a bit further east around Carrefour de l'Odéon.

French At 41 Rue Monsieur le Prince, *Restaurant Polidor* (☎ 43.26.95.34; metro Odéon) and its décor date from 1845, so a meal here is like a quick trip back to Victor Hugo's Paris. *Menus* of traditional, family-style French cuisine are available for 55FF (lunch only) and 100FF. Specialities include bœuf Bourguignon (44FF) and blanquette de veau (veal in white sauce; 60FF). All the guests are seated together at tables of six, 10 or 16. Polidor is open daily from noon to 2.30 pm and 7 to 12.30 pm (11 pm on Sunday). Reservations are not accepted.

Restaurant Le Procope (☎ 43.26.99.20; metro Odéon) at 13 Rue de l'Ancienne Comédie, Paris's oldest café, was popular with literary and artistic figures during the

late 17th century, philosophers (including Voltaire and Rousseau) during the 18th century, and revolutionary leaders (Marat, Danton and Robespierre among them) during the Revolution. Traditional French specialities, served amidst a décor of crimson walls, gilded mouldings and marble floors, include seafood and coq au vin. *Menus* are available for 99FF (11 am to 8 pm only), 119FF (after 11 pm) and 289FF. Meals are served daily from 11 am to 1 am.

There are three famous eating and sipping establishments near Église Saint Germain des Prés. *Les Deux Magots* (☎ 45.48.55.25; metro Saint Germain des Prés) at 170 Blvd Saint Germain was once a favourite haunt of Jean-Paul Sartre and André Breton. The name derives from the café's two wooden statues of Chinese dignitaries, left over from a store that once occupied this site and known as the two *magots* (figurines). In good weather (roughly April to mid-October), the huge terrace is full of people enjoying the view of the belfry of Église Saint Germain des Prés. The famous home-made hot chocolate (28FF) is served in steaming porcelain pitchers by waiters clad in long white aprons. Coffee is 20FF; beer on tap is 25FF. Food includes sandwiches (32 to 38FF), salads, quiches and cold plates of roast beef (75FF), smoked salmon (135FF) and foie gras with toast (125FF). A continental breakfast costs 75FF. Les Deux Magots is open daily from 7.30 am to 1.30 am.

The Art Deco-style *Café de Flore* (☎ 45.48.55.26) at 172 Blvd Saint Germain still looks very much as it did in the days of Jean-Paul Sartre, Simone de Beauvoir, Albert Camus and Picasso, with red-upholstered booths, a mosaic floor and walls covered with marble and mirrors. These days, it's still popular with Left Bank intellectuals. The outdoor terrace is a sought-after place to sip beer (40FF) during summer. Sandwiches are 32 to 60FF. Food is served daily from 7 am to 1.30 am.

The tuxedoed waiters at *Brasserie Lipp* (☎ 45.48.53.91) at 151 Blvd Saint Germain, where politicians rub shoulders with editors,

serve expensive food daily from 8.30 am to 2 am. Many people make a big fuss about sitting downstairs rather than upstairs, which is considered nowheresville. You might do better simply finding a table across the street.

Vegetarian *Guenmaï* (☎ 43.26.03.24; metro Saint Germain des Prés, Mabillon), a macrobiotic food shop at 2bis Rue de l'Abbaye, serves meals Monday to Saturday from 11.45 am to 3.30 pm.

Other *El Chuncho* (☎ 46.33.29.64; metro Odéon) at 59 Rue Saint André des Arts, also known as Saint André Crêperie, serves unspectacular but relatively inexpensive Mexican food daily from noon to 3 pm and 7 to 11 pm. Salads cost 40FF, steaks are 50 to 70FF. The owner is Mexican, but the burritos (50FF) look suspiciously like small crepes. In Mexico, the crepes probably resemble burritos...

Montparnasse (6e, 14e & 15e) Blvd du Montparnasse, one of Paris's premier avenues for café sitting, is lined with fashionable and pricey cafés, restaurants and hamburger joints, especially between Rue de Rennes and Blvd Raspail.

La Coupole (☎ 43.20.14.20; metro Vavin), a vast café-restaurant at 102 Blvd de Montparnasse (14e), has been popular with artists (including Soutine, Man Ray, Chagall and Josephine Baker) since its founding in 1927. Count on about 200FF per person for a meal. It is open daily from 7.30 am to 2 am.

Nearby, *Le Dôme* (☎ 43.35.25.81; metro Vavin) at 108 Blvd de Montparnasse (14e) has been a great place for sipping coffee since the turn of the century. It is open Tuesday to Sunday from 8 am to 2 am.

Champs-Élysées (8e) Most of the places to eat along Ave des Champs-Élysées are not particularly good value, in large part because the clientele consists of just-off-the-bus tourists. For a good dinner, you're better off in the Marais, the Latin Quarter or Montmartre, but a few restaurants offer good (if not particularly cheap) fare.

Top: Notre Dame on the Seine River, Paris (PS)
Left: Sacre Cœur at Montmartre, Paris (GA)
Right: Modern architecture of the Georges Pompidou Centre, Paris (GA)

Top: Place de la Concorde, Paris (PS)
Left: A flea market in the 4e arrondissement, Paris (DR)
Right: Interior of the Musée d'Orsay, Paris (GA)

La Maison d'Alsace (☎ 43.59.44.24; metro Franklin D Roosevelt) at 39 Ave des Champs-Élysées serves food 24 hours a day, 365 days a year. Specialities include seafood (oysters are 102 to 156FF a dozen), choucroute Strasbourgeoise (Strasbourg-style sauerkraut; 82FF) and meat dishes (79 to 146FF). Beer, served only on the terrace, is 23/38/68FF for 25/50/100 cl.

The Chicago Pizza Pie Factory (☎ 45.62. 50.23; metro George V) is just off Ave des Champs-Élysées at 5 Rue de Berri. Chicago-style pizzas for two people cost 76 to 170FF, chilli is 63FF and desserts are 34 to 46FF. For lunch on weekdays, you can order a 64FF *menu*. It is open daily from 11.45 am to 1 am. At the bar, happy hour is Monday to Friday from noon to 3 pm and daily from 6 to 7.30 pm.

Opéra Garnier Area (9e & 2e) Neon-lit Blvd Montmartre (metro Rue Montmartre, Richelieu Drouot) and nearby bits of Rue du Faubourg Montmartre – neither of which are anywhere near the neighbourhood of Montmartre – are crowded with all sorts of restaurants.

French The décor and ambience at *Le Drouot* (☎ 42.96.68.23; metro Richelieu Drouot) at 103 Rue de Richelieu (1st floor; 2e) haven't changed since the late 1930s, so it's not at all difficult to imagine that you're back in prewar Paris. The prices are very reasonable: main courses are 35 to 45FF, cider or beer is 10FF and a three-course traditional French meal with wine involves expenditure of only about 70FF. Le Drouot is open daily from 11.45 am to 3 pm and 6.30 to 10 pm.

Chartier (☎ 47.70.86.29; metro Rue Montmartre) at 7 Rue du Faubourg Mont-martre (9e), another Paris gem run by the same management as Le Drouot, is famous for its large dining room, virtually unaltered since 1896. The crowds of jovial diners, seated around and between the columns running down the middle, create the same sort of busy atmosphere the place must have had during the *belle époque*. The prices and

fare are similar to those at Le Drouot. Clients are seated daily from 11 am to 3 pm and 6 to 9.30 pm. Reservations are not accepted, so you may have a bit of a wait during more popular hours.

Vegetarian *Country Life* (☎ 42.97.48.51; metro Opéra) at 6 Rue Daunou (2e) serves an all-you-can-eat buffet lunch (58FF) on weekdays from 11.30 am to 2.30 pm. The attached food shop is open Monday to Friday from 10 am to 6.30 pm (3 pm on Friday).

Other Paris's hopping *Hard Rock Cafe* (☎ 42.46.10.00; metro Rue Montmartre) at 14 Blvd Montmartre (9e), housed in the former theatre where Maurice Chevalier made his debut, attracts businesspeople for lunch and young, trendy Parisians at night. Salads are 68 to 80FF, meat dishes are mostly 65 to 95FF, and sandwiches are 55 to 75FF. A vegetarian burger (65FF) is also available. Draft beer is 22FF per demi. Food is served every day of the year except Christmas from 11.30 am to 1 or 2 am. The boutique (open daily from 10 am to 12.30 am) does a roaring business selling T-shirts (100FF) and jackets.

Just south of the Cadet metro stop, there are a number of cacher restaurants along Rue Richer, Rue Cadet and Rue Geoffrey Marie.

Around La Madeleine (8e & 9e) For information on Fauchon and other gourmet food shops near La Madeleine, see Self-Catering.

Gare du Nord (10e) Many of the places around Gare du Nord serve food all day long and are open until the wee hours of the morning.

French *Brasserie Terminus Nord* (☎ 42.85. 05.15; metro Gare du Nord) at 23 Rue de Dunkerque, also known as Brasserie 1925, looks much as it did between the wars. The copper bar, white tablecloths and brass and wood fixtures are reflected brightly by the mirrored walls, making this a fine spot for a last, nostalgically Parisian meal before catching a train. A 109FF *menu* is available

for lunch and after 11 pm. Full meals are served daily from 6.30 am to 12.30 am.

Solid beef meals are the speciality of *Hippopotamus* (☎ 48.78.29.26; metro Gare du Nord) at 27 Rue de Dunkerque. *Menus* cost 64, 98 and 135FF. Food is served daily from 11.30 am to 4 pm and 6 pm to 1 am; there is no afternoon closure on Friday, Saturday and Sunday.

Other McDonald's has an outlet at 25 Rue de Dunkerque.

Gare de l'Est (10e) The tiny restaurants off Blvd de Strasbourg serve some of Paris's best Indian and Pakistani food. At many places, food is available throughout the afternoon.

French The *Brasserie À La Ville de Reims* (☎ 46.07.88.34; metro Gare de l'Est) at 129 Rue du Faubourg Saint Martin has *menus* – served daily from 11 am to 3 pm and 6.30 to 11 pm – for 50 and 68FF. Light meals are available from 6.30 am straight through to 2 am.

Indian & Pakistani *Ambala* (☎ 48.01.06.98; metro Château d'Eau) at 11 Rue Jarry does a roaring takeaway business, but there's also counter space if you want to eat in. The clientele is almost exclusively from the subcontinent. Dhal costs 18FF, a piece of tandoori chicken is 18FF and a chapati is 3FF. Meals are served Monday to Saturday from 9 am to 9 pm.

There are several inexpensive Indian and Pakistani places in Passage Brady, a covered shopping arcade two blocks south of the Château d'Eau metro station. *Samiha* (☎ 47.70.16.57) at Nos 71-73 has what may be the cheapest *menu* in Paris: meat curry, rice and salad for 25FF. Food is served Monday to Saturday from noon to 11 pm.

Bastille Area (4e, 11e & 12e) Narrow, scruffy Rue de Lappe may not look the part, but it's one of the trendiest café streets in Paris, attracting a young, alternative crowd. Things start to pick up only very late at night.

Ethnic restaurants can be found throughout the area, including nearby Rue de la Roquette.

French *Brasserie Bofinger* (☎ 42.72.87.82; metro Bastille) at 5-7 Rue de la Bastille (4e), founded in 1864, is the oldest brasserie in Paris. The décor of brass, wood, glass partitions and mirrors dates from the early 20th century (the floor is from 1931). Specialities include choucroute and seafood. First courses cost 40 to 108FF, mains are 100 to 120FF. The 166FF *menu* includes half a bottle of wine. Bofinger is open daily from noon to 3 pm and 7.30 pm to 1 am, with no afternoon closure on Saturday and Sunday. Reservations are necessary in the evening, especially on the weekend, and for Sunday lunch.

Family-run *Restaurant Relais du Massif Central* (☎ 47.00.46.55; metro Bastille), a small, unpretentious place at 16 Rue Daval (11e), serves French food inspired by the cuisine of the Massif Central. *Menus* are available for 60FF (lunch only), 79, 89 and 99FF. It is open Monday to Saturday from noon to 3 pm and 7.30 to midnight.

Hippopotamus (☎ 42.72.98.37; metro Bastille) at 1 Blvd Beaumarchais (4e), part of a well-regarded national chain, has solid, steak-based *menus* for 64, 98 and 135FF. Meals are served daily from 11.30 am to 1 am.

Other Among the pizza places and restaurants from distant continents you'll find Paris's only fish-and-chips shop, *Hamilton's Fish & Chips* (☎ 48.06.77.92; metro Ledru Rollin) at 51 Rue de Lappe (11e), which gets good reviews from homesick English expats. A small/large battered cod is 21/29FF; chips cost 9/18FF. The shop is open Monday to Saturday from noon to 2.30 pm and 6.30 pm to midnight (1 am on Friday and Saturday).

The small *Restaurant Babylon* (☎ 47.00. 55.02; metro Bastille) at 21 Rue Daval (11e) serves truly excellent shwarma (20FF takeaway, 25FF eat in) as well as falafel. The tables are round and tiny. It is open Monday to Saturday from 11 am to 1 am.

At the fashionably pink-and-grey *Korean barbecue* (☎ 48.07.80.98; metro Bastille) at 5 Rue de la Roquette (11e), the food is cooked on gas grills installed in the middle of each table. *Menus* cost 68, 88, 113 and 143FF. It is open daily from noon to 2.30 pm and 6.30 to 12.30 pm.

Montmartre & Pigalle (18e) There are dozens of cafés and restaurants around Place du Tertre but they are touristy and overpriced. A much better bet are the places along Rue des Trois Frères, which is at the bottom of the south-west side of the hill. Many are open every day of the week (including Sunday), but only for dinner.

French Traditional French cuisine, including some regional dishes, is served in an ambience of semiformal elegance at *Restaurant Le Petit Chose* (☎ 42.64.49.15; metro Abbesses) at 41 Rue des Trois Frères. The *menus* cost 95 and 160FF. It is open daily from 7 to 11 pm.

A more down-to-earth option for French cuisine is the small, mellow *Au Virage Lepic* (☎ 42.52.46.79; metro Lamarck Caulaincourt) at 61 Rue Lepic, which has a loyal following among locals. The atmosphere is set by the red-and-white checked plastic tablecloths and the assorted memorabilia decorating the walls. Specialities include boudin noir (black pudding) for 49FF. Red wine is 8FF a glass. This place is open from 7.30 pm to 2 am daily except Tuesday. It is closed during August.

An old Montmartre favourite is *Refuge des Fondus* (☎ 42.55.22.65; metro Abbesses) at 17 Rue des Trois Frères, whose speciality is fondues. For 80FF, you get wine (in a *biberon*, ie baby bottle) and a good quantity of either fondue Savoyarde (cheese) or fondue Bourguignonne (meat). This place is open daily from 7 pm to 2 am (last seating around midnight). It's usually necessary to make reservations a couple of days ahead.

The exclusive *Restaurant La Poste* (☎ 42.80.66.16; metro Blanche or Pigalle) at 34 Rue Duperré (9e), a favourite haunt of *branchés* actors, serves a mix of French and

Moroccan dishes daily from 8 pm to midnight. Meat dishes are 90 to 130FF. Reservations are recommended. Dress fashionably.

Other For delicious, authentic Togolese (West African) cuisine, you can't beat *Le Mono* (☎ 46.06.99.20; metro Abbesses, Blanche) at 40 Rue Véron, which has been run by a friendly Togolese woman and her family for almost 20 years. Specialities – made with special imported ingredients – include lélé (flat, steamed cakes made from white beans and shrimp and served with tomato sauce; 24FF), mafé (beef or chicken served with peanut sauce; 48FF) and gbekui (a sort of goulash made with spinach, onions, beef, fish and shrimp; 52FF). Vegetarian dishes are prepared upon request. Le Mono is open from 7 pm to midnight (or later) daily except Wednesday.

Raz (☎ 42.59.88.80; metro Abbesses), a South Indian restaurant at 11 Rue des Trois Frères, is open daily from 11.30 am to 3 pm and 5.30 pm to midnight or 1 am. *Menus*, available until 10 or 10.30 pm, are 59 and 75FF.

Restaurant Copacabana (☎ 42.62.24.96; metro Abbesses) at 32bis Rue des Trois Frères serves dishes such as feijoada (black beans and meat prepared with green cabbage and manioc flour; 85FF) and xinxim de galinha (chicken cooked in a sauce of dried prawns, crushed peanuts, cashews and palm oil; 70FF). It is open daily except Monday from 7 pm until the people who order at midnight finish eating.

If you're in the mood for cheap Cantonese food, try *Wou Ying* (☎ 42.51.24.44; metro Abbesses) at 24 Rue Durantin, on the corner of Rue Tholozé. It is open daily from noon to 2.30 pm and 7 to 11.30 pm. On weekday evenings before 9.30 pm, they offer a *menu* for 50FF.

Places to Drink
Louvre Area (1er) While the Marais is the main centre of gay life in Paris, there are some pleasant bars a bit further west.

Lesbian Bar The relaxed, dimly lit *La Champmeslé* (☎ 42.96.85.20; metro Pyramides) at 4 Rue Chabanais (2e) plays mellow music for its patrons, about 75% of whom are lesbians (the rest are mostly gay men). The only lesbian bar in Paris, it was founded in 1979. The back room is reserved for women, the rest is mixed. Each month, art by a different woman artist is displayed. Beer on tap or fruit juice is 25FF (30FF late at night). La Champmeslé is open daily from 6 pm to 2 am. French *chansons* (songs) are performed live every Thursday at 10 pm.

Gay Bar *Le Vagabond Restaurant & Bar* (☎ 42.96.27.23; metro Pyramides) at 14 Rue Thérèse is popular with older gay men, some of whom began coming here when it was founded in 1957. The bar is open from 6 pm to 3 am (closed Monday). French cuisine is served from 8 pm to 12.30 am; the *menu* is 140FF. To get in, push the white button to the left of the door and they'll buzz you in. This place is for gay men only.

Centre Pompidou Area (1er & 4e) *Le Bar*, a new place at 5 Rue de la Ferronerie (1er) is a gay bar one block south of Square des Innocents. It is always crowded.

Marais (4e) *La Tartine* (☎ 42.72.76.85; metro Saint Paul) at 24 Rue de Rivoli offers 60 selected reds, whites and rosés for 7.50 to 15FF a glass. There's not much to eat except sandwiches and, of course, tartines beurrées (buttered bread) for 5FF. Little has changed here since the days when the gas lighting fixtures were still in use. La Tartine is open Thursday to Monday from 8 am to 10 pm and also on Wednesday afternoon.

The slightly offbeat *Au Petit Fer à Cheval* (☎ 42.72.47.47; metro Hôtel de Ville) at 30 Rue Vieille du Temple, so named because of its horseshoe-shaped bar, is often filled to overflowing with friendly, mostly straight young regulars, many of whom hail from overseas. Beer is 12FF at the bar and 15FF if you sit down (4FF more after 10 pm). The plat du jour, which changes each day, is 58 to 75FF. The all stainless-steel bathroom

looks like it came out of a Flash Gordon flick or a Jules Verne novel. This place is open daily from 9 am (11 am on weekends) to 2 am. Food is available nonstop from noon.

Gay & Lesbian Bars The Marais – especially the area around the intersection of Rue Vieille du Temple and Rue Sainte Croix de la Bretonnerie – has been Paris's main centre of gay social life since the early 1980s.

Bar de l'Hôtel Central (☎ 48.87.99.33; metro Hotel de Ville) at 33 Rue Vieille du Temple, founded in 1980, is one of the best known gay bars in the city. The clientele is mostly male. It is open daily from 4 pm to 2 am. A demi is 11FF (14FF after 10 pm).

Other bars in the same area include the 1950s-style *Amnesia Café* (☎ 42.72.16.94) at 42 Rue Vieille du Temple, open daily from noon (2 pm on Sunday) to 2 am, where cocktails start at 50FF; and *Subway* (☎ 42.77.41.10) at 53 Rue Sainte Croix de la Bretonnerie, open from 3 pm to 2 am. *Coffee Shop* (☎ 42.74.71.52), a small café at 3 Rue Sainte Croix de la Bretonnerie, is open daily from noon to midnight.

Quetzal Bar (☎ 48.87.99.07; metro Hôtel de Ville) at the corner of Rue de la Verrerie and Rue des Mauvais Garçons (literally, Street of the Bad Boys) is so popular with young Parisian gay men that the clientele often spills over onto the pavement. A demi on tap is 13FF. It is open Monday to Friday from noon to 2 am (3 am on Friday night) and on weekends from 4 pm to 2 am (3 am on Saturday). Happy hour is from 6 to 8 pm.

Duplex Bar d'Art (☎ 42.72.80.86; metro Rambuteau) at 25 Rue Michel Lecomte (3e), one of the oldest gay bars in Paris (it was established in 1980), also acts as something of an art gallery, exhibiting different paintings each month. A gay and lesbian students' group meets here every Wednesday from 8 to 11 pm. Beer on tap is 15FF (20FF after 10 pm). This place is open daily from 8 pm to 2 am.

Île Saint Louis (4e) *Au Franc Pinot* (☎ 43.29.46.98; metro Pont Marie), a small unimposing wine bar at 1 Quai de Bourbon,

specialises in the wines of Burgundy but also has bottles from Bordeaux and other regions. About 20 different wines are sold by the glass (from 20FF) at any given time. Meat and cheese plates are available for 40 to 60FF. Au Franc Pinot is open Tuesday to Saturday from 11 am to 1 am. In the 17th-century basement, there's a restaurant with *menus* for 150FF (lunch) and 190FF (dinner). Food is served from noon to 2 pm and 7 pm to midnight.

Place Saint Michel Area (5e) *Le Cloître* (☎ 43.25.19.92; metro Saint Michel) at 19 Rue Saint Jacques is an unpretentious, relaxed place whose mellow background music seems to please the young Parisians who congregate here. It is open daily from 3 pm to 2 am. A demi of beer on tap costs 12FF at night; Guinness is 17FF. In the back, you can play chess for 10FF any time, except after 10 pm on Friday, Saturday and holidays, when it gets too crowded.

The informal, friendly *Polly Maggoo* (☎ 46.33.33.64), up the street at 11 Rue Saint Jacques, was founded in 1967 and still plays music from that era. This place, which attracts quite a few English speakers resident in Paris, is open daily from 1 pm to 4 or 5 am (it's one of the few nightspots with a police licence to stay open after 2 am). Chess and backgammon are available from noon to 8 pm and are free. Beer starts at 15.50FF for a demi.

Latin Quarter (5e) Lots of English speakers gather at *Le Violon Dingue* (☎ 43.25.79.93; Maubert Mutualité), a rather loud and dirty American-style bar at 46 Rue de la Montagne Sainte Geneviève. It is open daily from 6 pm to 1.30 or 2 am. A pint of beer costs 10FF during happy hour (6 to 9 pm) – when everything is half-price – and 20FF the rest of the time.

Mayflower public bar (☎ 43.54.56.47; metro Cardinal Lemoine) is 300 metres to the south at 49 Rue Descartes, which is right where Rue Mouffetard begins. This place, decorated with American licence plates, attracts an up-market, pubby clientele. A

demi of beer is 20FF during the day and 30FF after 9 pm. It's open daily from 9 am to 4 am.

Saint Germain des Prés (6e) The friendly *Chez Georges* (☎ 43.26.79.15; metro Mabillon) at 11 Rue des Canettes, whose smoke-darkened walls are decorated with photos of musicians who once played here, is popular with young people, and you'll often find a few native English speakers here. It is said that the red linoleum bar replaced a zinc one recycled into war material by the Germans during WW II. Chez Georges is open Tuesday to Saturday from noon to 2 am, but is closed from 14 July to 15 August. The dank cellar, suffused with mellow music, opens at 10 pm. There may be live music after 10.30 pm. Beer in bottles starts at 13FF (15FF at night), and coffee is 4.50 to 12FF.

Le 10 (☎ 43.26.66.83; metro Odéon) at 10 Rue de l'Odéon attracts local and foreign university students and au pairs, many in their late teens or early 20s. The taped music ranges from jazz to the Doors and Joe Cocker to Yves Montand. The orange lighting adds a warm glow to the smoke-darkened posters on the walls. The house speciality, sangria, is 20FF a glass. Beer in bottles is 20 to 30FF. Le 10 is open daily from 5.30 pm to 2 am.

Pub Saint Germain des Prés (☎ 43.29. 38.70; metro Odéon) at 17 Rue de l'Ancienne Comédie is open every day of the year, 24 hours a day. About 450 different kinds of beer are available in bottles, and two dozen more on tap. A demi on tap is 26FF in the section out the back with the mosaic floor called Taverne Le Parrot and 35FF (39FF after 8 pm) in the 1st and 2nd-floor *belle époque*-style Bistro Rive Gauche. When there's live music in the downstairs piano bar (10 pm to 4 am), beer is 74FF. There's a 24-hour restaurant on the 1st floor.

Opéra Garnier Area (9e & 2e) Back in the prewar years, when there were several dozen American-style bars in Paris, *Harry's New York Bar* (☎ 42.61.71.14; metro Opéra) at 5 Rue Daunou (2e) was one of the most

popular, with clients including Ernest Hemingway and F Scott Fitzgerald. The collection of North American university pennants on the wood-panelled walls – brought in by guests – began during that era. The Cuban mahogany interior dates from the mid-19th century and was brought over lock, stock and barrel from Manhattan's 3rd Ave in 1911. In 1923, the bar was purchased and renamed by a Scottish-born American bartender named Harry MacElhone, whose grandson Duncan is the present proprietor.

Harry's New York Bar is open every day of the year except 24 and 25 December from 10.30 am to 4 am. There's live piano music (usually soft jazz) in the basement nightly from 10 pm to 2 or 3 am. Beer costs 28FF (35FF after 10 pm), but in the basement the only thing available is scotch (50FF) or cocktails (from 36FF). Prices are 5 to 10FF higher during concerts.

Bastille Area (11e) *Café Iguana* (☎ 40.21. 39.99; metro Bastille) at 15 Rue de la Roquette, a round, split-level place, is very *branché* and draws socially with-it people in their 20s and early 30s. Cocktails (42 to 50FF) are the speciality; beer on tap is 18 to 24FF (20 to 24FF after 10 pm). It is open daily from 9 am to 5 am.

Montmartre (18e) *Le Dépanneur* (☎ 40.16. 40.20; metro Blanche) at 27 Rue Fontaine (9e), whose modern décor has a Mexican theme, is one block south-east of Place Blanche. The house speciality is tequila (25FF). Beer is 15FF (30FF from 10 pm to 7 am). Happy hour is from 6 to 8 pm. The limited selection of food, served all the time, includes chilli con carne for 60FF (70FF after 10 pm), salads and sandwiches. Brunch (75FF) is served from 7 am to 7 pm. Le Dépanneur is open 24 hours a day, every day of the year. With one drink, you can stay all night.

University Restaurants

The Centre Régional des Œuvres Universitaires et Scolaires, better known as CROUS (☎ 40.51.37.10), runs 17 *restaurants universitaires* (student cafeterias) in Paris, about half of them in the 5e and 6e arrondissements. Tickets for institutional but filling three-course meals cost 12.30FF for students with ID, 19.20FF if you have a Carte Jeune or an ISTC card and 24FF for nonstudent guests of students. Some of the restaurants also have à la carte 'brasseries'. In general, CROUS restaurants have rather confusing opening times that change according to weekend rotational agreements among the restaurants and school holiday schedules. Only one university restaurant stays open during July; a different one is on duty during August.

There are several university restaurants in the Latin Quarter. The *Châtelet* (☎ 43.31. 51.66; metro Censier Daubenton) at 8 Rue Jean Calvin (5e) – just off Rue Mouffetard – is open during the academic year on weekdays from 11.30 am to 1.45 pm and 6.30 to 8 pm; it's open on Friday night from October to March only. *Bullier* (☎ 43.54.93.38; metro Port Royal) is in the Centre Jean Sarrailh at 39 Rue Bernanos (2nd floor; 5e). Lunch and dinner are served Monday to Friday and, during some months, on weekends as well (days and times are posted). The ticket window, which is up one flight of stairs, is open from 11.30 am to 2 pm and 6 to 8 pm.

In the 6e arrondissement, *Mabillon university restaurant* (☎ 43.25.66.23; metro Mabillon) is at 3 Rue Mabillon. One of the most pleasant CROUS restaurants in town is *Assas* (☎ 46.33.61.25; metro Port Royal, Notre Dame des Champs) on the 7th floor of the Faculté de Droit et des Sciences Économiques (Law & Economics Faculty; metro Vavin), which is south of the Jardin du Luxembourg at 92 Rue Assas. After climbing all those flights of stairs – there's no lift – you will have earned both the great view and perhaps a little something extra for dessert...The ticket window is on the 6th floor.

Self-Catering

Buying your own food is one of the best ways to keep travel costs down. For details

on how French food shops work, see Self-Catering under Food in the Facts for the Visitor chapter. Supermarkets, which are few and far between, are much cheaper than *épiceries* (grocery stores), such as those of the Félix Potin chain. Many food shops are closed on Sunday and/or Monday and take a siesta between 12.30 or 1 pm and 3 or 4 pm.

Paris has an exceptional number of places perfect for picnicking: parks, the courtyards of public buildings, quays along the Seine and so forth. If it's cold and rainy, you can always take refuge in a metro station...

Paris is underequipped when it comes to drinking fountains – café owners are said to prefer that you buy your liquid refreshment from them – but thanks to a certain 19th-century Englishman named Wallace, potable water is available at various places around town from dark-green fountains topped with spiked domes held aloft by four maidens. Each one used to be equipped with a tin cup, but modern hygienic concerns have left the water, which squirts straight down, hard to get at without a cup or water bottle.

Food Markets The very freshest and best quality fruits, vegetables, cheeses, prepared salads, etc at the lowest prices in town are on offer at Paris's neighbourhood food markets. The *marchés découverts* (open-air markets) – 60 of which pop up in public squares around the city two or three times a week – are open from 7 am to 1 pm. There are also a dozen *marchés couverts* (covered market-places), open daily, except Sunday afternoon and Monday, from 8 am to sometime between 12.30 and 1.30 pm and from 3.30 or 4 to 7.30 pm. To find out which days there's a market near your hotel and at what time, ask anyone who lives in the neighbourhood.

Biologique (organically grown) fruit and vegetables are available at the *Marché Biologique* (metro Rennes), which is on Blvd Raspail (6e) between Rue du Cherche Midi and Rue de Rennes. It is open every Sunday from 7 am to 1.30 pm (and perhaps later).

The little *fruit and vegetable stands* you

sometimes see in metro stations often have ripe produce at excellent prices.

Louvre Area (1er) There are several food shops one block north of the western end of the Louvre. The *Félix Potin grocery* (metro Tuileries) at 205 Rue Saint Honoré is open Monday to Friday from 8 am to 8 pm and on Saturday from 8.30 am to 7.30 pm. The *boulangerie* (metro Tuileries) at 302 Rue Saint Honoré is open from 7 am to 8 pm (closed Tuesday).

Wine costing anywhere from 9FF to 4500FF a bottle is available at the *Nicolas wine shop* (metro Tuileries) at 189 Rue Saint Honoré, which is open on Monday from 3.30 to 7.30 pm, Tuesday to Friday from 9 am to 7.30 pm and on Saturday from 10 am to 7.30 pm.

Near the eastern end of the Louvre, there is a small *boulangerie* (metro Louvre-Rivoli) at 6 Rue Jean-Jacques Rousseau. Sandwiches are made on request. It is open Monday to Saturday from 7 am to 8 pm.

Centre Pompidou Area (1er & 4e) The *Ed l'Épicier supermarket* (metro Hôtel de Ville), which is through the anonymous wooden doorway at 80 Rue de Rivoli (4e), is by far the cheapest place to buy food in this part of Paris, though you'll have to look elsewhere for fruit and vegetables. It is open Monday to Saturday from 10 am to 8 pm.

Marais (4e) For information on where to find Jewish-style Central European pastries, see Jewish under Marais in the Restaurants & Cafés section.

You'll find quite a few food stores on Rue de Rivoli and Rue Saint Antoine around the Saint Paul metro stop. There's a *boulangerie* (closed Sunday) at 109 Rue Saint Antoine, a *fruit and vegetable shop* (closed Monday) and a *fromagerie* (closed Sunday afternoon and Monday) at 97-99 Rue Saint Antoine and a *wine shop* (closed Monday) at 95 Rue Saint Antoine.

Gourmaud at 91 Rue Saint Antoine is one of the few gourmet shops in Paris where you can assemble an entire picnic in one stop. In

addition to scrumptious prepared dishes, including quiches and roasted chickens, you can pick up stuffed escargots (snails; 5.40FF each), cheese, chocolate, pastry, bread and wine. It is open daily (except perhaps Monday) from 9 am to 10 pm.

The *supermarket* at 119 Rue Saint Antoine has a small in-house *boulangerie*. It is open Monday to Saturday from 8 am to 8 pm. The smaller *Franprix supermarket* at 135 Rue Saint Antoine is open Monday to Saturday from 8 am to 8 pm and on Sunday from 9 am to 1 pm.

Bastille (4e, 11e & 12e) There are lots of *food shops* along Rue de la Roquette towards Place Léon Blum.

Île Saint Louis (4e) There are *boulangeries* and *fruit and vegetable shops* on Rue Saint Louis en l'Île and Rue des Deux Ponts. *Fromageries* can be found at Nos 38 and 76 Rue Saint Louis en l'Île.

Le Moule à Gâteau (metro Pont Marie) at 47 Rue Saint Louis en l'Île has superb fancy breads. The small, round poppy-seed roll (4.80FF) is so tasty it's practically a meal in and of itself. Le Moule is open from 8.30 am to 8 pm (closed Monday).

Place Saint Michel Area (5e) Fresh breads and superb pastries are available two blocks south of Notre Dame at the *boulangerie* (metro Maubert Mutualité) at 10 Rue Lagrange, which has superb pain aux raisins (raisin-custard swirls). It is open Tuesday to Sunday from 7.15 am to 8 pm.

There is a cluster of *food shops* in the vicinity of Place Maubert (metro Maubert Mutualité) and nearby Rue Lagrange, both of which are 300 metres south of Notre Dame. Barbecued publishers are no longer available here (Place Maubert is where Rabelais's publisher, Étienne Dolet, was burnt at the stake in 1546), but on Tuesday, Thursday and Saturday from 7 am to 1 pm, the *place* is transformed into a *food market*.

The excellent *fromagerie* (metro Maubert Mutualité) at 47 Blvd Saint Germain is open from 7 am to 1 pm and 3.30 to 7.30 pm daily except Sunday afternoon and Monday. The boulangerie next door, *Pâtisserie des Carmes*, is open from 7 am to 8 pm (closed Wednesday).

In the restaurant cluster around Rue de la Huchette (metro Saint Michel), there are *Félix Potin groceries* at 18 Rue Saint Séverin (open Monday to Saturday from 8 am to 1 pm and 4 to 8.15 pm) and 16 Rue de la Harpe (open Monday to Saturday from 8 am to 1 pm and 3.45 to 8 pm).

Latin Quarter (5e) One of Paris's oldest and liveliest outdoor *food markets* is along Rue Mouffetard (metro Monge). It is open daily except Sunday afternoon and Monday.

There's a bunch of *food shops* of all sorts along Rue Saint Jacques (metro Luxembourg) between Nos 172 and 218 (ie the area just south of Rue Soufflot). At 198 Rue Saint Jacques, there's a *fromagerie* and a *Nicolas wine shop*. You'll find a *boulangerie* nearby at 16 Rue des Fossés Saint Jacques.

Further east, the super-cheap *Ed l'Épicier supermarket* (metro Monge) at 37 Rue Lacépède is open Monday to Saturday from 9 am to 7.30 pm.

Saint Germain des Prés (6e) The largest cluster of *food shops* in the neighbourhood is one block north of Blvd Saint Germain around 18 Rue de Buci and 77 Rue de Seine. Most are closed on Sunday afternoon and Monday, though the *Champion supermarket* at 79 Rue de Seine is open Monday to Saturday from 8.40 am to 9 pm.

Boulangerie Chez Jean-Mi (metro Odéon) at 10 Rue de l'Ancienne Comédie, is open 24 hours a day Monday to Saturday from 6 am to 9 pm. The *Nicolas wine shop* at 4 Rue de l'Ancienne Comédie is open Monday to Saturday from 9 am to 1 pm and 3.30 to 9 pm.

The *Uniprix* (☎ 45.48.18.08; metro Saint Germain des Prés) at 50-52 Rue de Rennes has a supermarket at the back of the basement level. It's open Monday to Saturday from 9 am to 7.55 pm.

The most famous boulangerie in all of France is *Poilâne* at 8 Rue du Cherche Midi

(metro Saint Sulpice). This is where Lionel Poilâne bakes his renowned sourdough, known as *pain Poilâne* – sold in hundreds of shops around Paris – in wood-fired ovens. The shop is open Monday to Saturday from 7.15 am to 8 pm.

For organically grown foodstuffs, you might try *Guenmaï* (metro Saint Germain des Prés, Mabillon) at 2bis Rue de l'Abbaye, right behind Église Saint Germain des Prés. The store is open Monday to Saturday from 9 am to 8.30 pm.

Montparnasse Area (6e & 14e) The *boulangerie* (metro Montparnasse Bienvenüe, Edgar Quinet) across from the south-east side of the Montparnasse Tower at 27 Rue du Départ (14e) is open Monday to Friday from 6.45 am to 8 pm. The *Inno* supermarket (metro Montparnasse Bienvenüe, Edgar Quinet), 50 metres south along Rue du Départ, is open Monday to Saturday from 9 am to 7.50 pm (8.50 pm on Friday). The food section is in the basement.

North of Montparnasse Tower, *Dorémus* (metro Saint Placide), which is next to 125 Rue de Rennes (6e), has superb prepared main dishes, salads, terrines, cheeses and fresh foie gras. It is open from 8.30 am to 7.30 pm (closed Sunday and Monday). There are other *food stores* nearby.

Champs-Élysées Area (8e, 16e & 17e) The *Prisunic* (metro Franklin D Roosevelt) at 62 Blvd des Champs-Élysées (8e) has a supermarket section in the basement. It is open Monday to Saturday from 9.45 am to midnight.

One block west of the Arc de Triomphe, *Fromager de l'Étoile* (metro Charles de Gaulle Étoile, Grande Armée exit) at 11 Ave de la Grande Armée (16e) has cheese, a limited selection of wines and Häagen Dazs ice cream. It is open Tuesday to Saturday from 9 am to 1 pm and 4 to 7.30 pm. The *boulangerie* (metro Argentine) a couple of blocks further west at 36 Ave de la Grande Armée (17e) is open from 6.30 am to 8 pm (closed Friday).

La Madeleine Area (8e & 9e) Place de la Madeleine (metro Madeleine), where you'll find Paris's finest food shops (including the legendary Fauchon), is the luxury food centre of the luxury food capital of the world. The delicacies on offer don't come cheap, but even travellers on a modest budget can turn a walk around La Madeleine into a gastronomic odyssey. Most places are open Monday to Saturday.

Fauchon The windows of *Fauchon*, which takes up a whole corner of Place de la Madeleine around No 26, are filled with incredibly beautiful and mouth-watering delicacies, on sale in about 10 different departments. Items available at the *gastronomie* counter include foie gras of goose for 1230FF per 800 grams and fancy chickens with their most beautiful feathers left on. The fruits et légumes section has the most perfect fruit and vegetables you've ever seen, including peaches for 65FF a kg and exotic items from South-East Asia. Fauchon is open Monday to Saturday from 9.40 am to 7 pm (9.30 pm for the fromagerie and gastronomie departments).

The payment procedure at Fauchon, which was founded in 1886, is a peculiar combination of the 19th and 21st centuries. At the first counter you visit, the sales person will give you a magnetic card on which details of your selections have been encoded. When you've finished ordering goods in other departments – each of which will add information to the card – you take the card to any cash register, where you'll be given a receipt that will allow you to go back and pick up your purchases, which by this time will have been properly wrapped.

The *cafeteria* in the basement (under the épicerie) sells hot drinks, sandwiches, cold dishes, exquisite pastries and other items at five separate counters. It is open Monday to Friday from 9.40 am to 7 pm. There is a restaurant, *Trattoria*, on the first floor.

Some Fauchon products are sold by selected shops around the world, but if you can't find exactly what you're looking for

you can place an international order by calling or faxing Fauchon's *service export.*

Other Another famous luxury foods shop is *Hédiard* at 21 Place de la Madeleine, which consists of two adjacent sections selling prepared dishes, tea, coffee, jams, wine, pastries, fruit and vegetables, etc. It is open Monday to Saturday from 9 am to 9 pm.

If you've always wanted to taste fine truffles, *Maison de la Truffe* at 19 Place de la Madeleine may be your chance. Not only does this place sell fresh truffles – black French ones from late October to March, white Italian ones from mid-October to December – but it also has a small sit-down area (open noon to 7 pm) where you can sample dishes made with the prized fungus for 95 to 165FF. Foie gras costs 120 to 225FF. Maison de la Truffe is open Monday to Saturday from 9 am to 8 pm.

Caviar Kaspa at 17 Place de la Madeleine specialises in caviar and smoked salmon. Caviar from the ex-Soviet side of the Caspian Sea sells for 282FF per 100 grams. A stuffed sturgeon (the fish that produces caviar) is mounted on the wall over the right-hand counter. Caviar Kaspa is open Monday to Saturday from 9 am to midnight. The *restaurant section* is open from 11.30 am to midnight.

You'll find about 250 kinds of cheese at *Fromagerie Creplet-Brussol* at 17 Place de la Madeleine, which is open on Monday from 2 to 7.30 pm and Tuesday to Saturday from 9 am to 7.30 pm. A *dégustation de fromages* (cheese tasting) plate with eight kinds of cheese, bread and 25 cl of wine costs 70FF.

The large *Nicolas wine shop* at 31 Place de la Madeleine has bottles of wine for up to 35,000FF. It is open Monday to Saturday from 9 am to 8 pm.

La Maison du Miel, a block north of Place de la Madeleine at 24 Rue Vignon (9e), has a huge selection of honey made from the pollen of different kinds of flowers. It is open Monday to Saturday from 9.30 am to 7 pm (6 pm on Monday).

Gare de l'Est & Gare du Nord Areas (10e) *Marché Saint Quentin* (metro Gare de l'Est, Gare du Nord), a covered market at 90 Blvd de Magenta, is open from 8 am to 1 pm and 3.30 to 7.30 pm daily except Sunday afternoon and Monday.

The stretch of Rue du Faubourg Saint Denis (metro Strasbourg Saint Denis) north of Blvd Saint Denis is one of the cheapest places in Paris to buy food. The area has a distinctively Middle Eastern air, and quite a few of the groceries offer Turkish and North African specialities. Many of the food shops are closed on Sunday afternoon and Monday.

Montmartre (18e) Most of the food stores in this area are along Rue des Abbesses (metro Abbesses), which is about 500 metres south-west of Sacré Cœur.

Pains Spéciaux, a boulangerie at 24 Rue des Abbesses (100 metres north-west of Place des Abbesses), is open from 7 am to 8 pm (closed Monday). *Fromagerie Tissot* at 32 Rue des Abbesses is open from 8.30 am to 1 pm and 4 to 8 pm (closed Monday afternoon and Sunday).

The *Nicolas wine shop* at 31 Rue des Abbesses and *Caves des Abbesses wine shop* at 43 Rue des Abbesses are both open from 9 or 9.30 am to 1 pm and 4 to 8 pm (closed Sunday afternoon and Monday).

There is a *Franprix supermarket* (metro Lamarck Caulaincourt) at 44 Rue Caulaincourt. It is open Monday to Saturday from 8.30 am to 7.25 pm (7.45 pm on Friday and Saturday). *Au Pain Doré*, a boulangerie down the block at 22 Rue Caulaincourt, is open Monday to Saturday from 7.30 am to 9 pm.

ENTERTAINMENT
Information
Exhaustive information in French on films, concerts (classical, jazz, rock, pop, etc), operas, theatre performances, dance, cabarets and so on is listed in two competing publications that come out each Wednesday: *L'Officiel des Spectacles* (2FF) and *Pariscope* (3FF). Both are available at any newspaper kiosk.

You can hear recorded suggestions in English on cultural and other events taking place in Paris by calling ☎ 47.20.88.98. This line operates 24 hours a day.

Tickets Reservations and ticketing for most cultural events (concerts, operas, theatre productions, jazz performances, etc) are handled by a number of large ticket outlets, among them FNAC (pronounced 'f'nuck') and Virgin Megastore.

Virgin Megastore (☎ 40.74.06.48, ask for *réservations des spectacles*; metro Franklin D Roosevelt) at 60 Ave des Champs-Élysées (8e) has its billeterie (ticket office) in the basement. It is open Monday to Saturday from 10 am to 11.45 pm (12.45 am on Friday and Saturday nights) and on Sunday and holidays from noon to 11.45 pm. You can make reservations by telephone on weekdays from 11 am to 2 pm and 3 to 6 pm. Payment must be made within a week by personal cheque (in French francs), eurocheque or *mandat postal* (postal money order) in French francs. Tickets will be sent to you by post.

FNAC has billeteries, also known as the *service des spectacles*, at a number of its stores around town, including:

- 1-7 Rue Pierre Lescot (1er), on the -3 level of the Forum des Halles shopping mall (☎ 40.41.40.00; metro Châtelet-Les Halles); open Monday to Saturday from 10 am to 7.30 pm
- 136 Rue de Rennes (6e; ☎ 49.54.30.00; metro Saint Placide), about 600 metres north of Gare Montparnasse
- 28 Ave de Wagram (8e; ☎ 47.66.52.50; metro Ternes), three blocks north of the Arc de Triomphe

The commission is 10 to 20FF a ticket. Reservations can't be made over the phone but they can be made by Minitel (key in 3615 FNAC): just type in your credit card number and the tickets will be sent to you by mail. People with a FNAC *carte d'adhérent* (membership card; 150FF for three years) get discounts of 10 to 40% on certain tickets. Tickets cannot be returned or exchanged unless a performance is cancelled.

Other ticket outlets include SOS Théâtre (☎ 44.77.88.55; metro Madeleine) at 6 Place de la Madeleine (8e); Agence Perossier (☎ 42.60.58.31, 42.60.26.87; metro Madeleine), also at 6 Place de la Madeleine (8e); and Cityrama (☎ 44.55.60.00; metro Louvre Rivoli) at 147 Rue Saint Honoré (1er).

Discount Theatre Tickets On the day of a performance, the Kiosque Théâtre (no phone; metro Madeleine), which is across from 15 Place de la Madeleine (8e), sells theatre tickets for 50% off the usual price (plus a commission of 15FF). Tickets to concerts, operas and ballets may also be on sale. The seats available are often the most desirable.

The Kiosque Théâtre is open Tuesday to Saturday from 12.30 to 8 pm and on Sunday from 12.30 to 4 pm. By contract, every Paris theatre – even if it has the most popular show in town – has to supply the Kiosque with at least four tickets, so bargain-hunting fans often arrive an hour or more before it opens. The earlier you come by the better the chance of finding a ticket to the performance you want; your chances are also better during the week than on Saturday or Sunday.

Starting at about 8 or 8.30 pm on the night before a performance, coloured lights are lit next to the names of Paris's theatres posted on the kiosk's exterior walls. A green light means tickets to the theatre's next performance are still available, a red light means they're sold out. Many theatres close in July and August.

Kiosque Théâtre has a second location, known as Ticket Kiosque Théâtre (no phone), in Forum des Halles on the level below Niveau -3 (the minus three level). More precisely, it's in the shop area *inside* the Châtelet-Les Halles RER station, so you have to pass through the turnstiles to get there. It's open from 12.30 to 7.30 pm daily except Sunday, Monday and holidays. On Saturday, tickets for afternoon performances go on sale at 12.30 pm, while those for evening shows are available from 2 pm.

Cinemas
Over 250 different films are screened in Paris

PARIS

each week. Not only are a fair number of them in English, but most are subtitled rather than dubbed! The offerings are listed alphabetically by their French title as well as by arrondissement in *Pariscope* (under Toutes les Salles) and *L'Officiel des Spectacles* (under Programmes des Cinémas). Both mention the English titles. For an explanation of movie-going in France, see Cinema under Entertainment in the Facts for the Visitor chapter.

Parisian movie-going does not come cheap. Expect to pay around 45FF for a ticket. Students and people under 18 and over 60 usually get discounts of about 25% except on Friday, Saturday and Sunday nights. On Wednesday (and sometimes Monday), most cinemas give discounts to everyone. Cinemas usually change their offerings on Wednesday, but during the Cannes Film Festival (mid-May) some showings may begin on Friday. Be careful with your bags inside the cinema – thieves have been known to strike while moviegoers are distracted by the on-screen action. One recommended precaution: wrap the strap of your pack or bag around your leg.

There's a cluster of cinemas along Blvd Saint Germain in the 6e arrondissement near Carrefour de l'Odéon (metro Odéon) and lots more along Ave des Champs-Élysées (8e; metro George V, Franklin D Roosevelt). The fashionable cinemas on Blvd du Montparnasse (6e & 14e; metro Montparnasse Bienvenüe, Vavin) and nearby streets show mostly dubbed (v.f.) feature films.

The *Cinémathèque Française* (☎ 47.04. 24.24; metro Trocadéro), a government-supported institution dedicated to showing films of all sorts – many of them seldom-screened classics – almost always leaves its foreign offerings undubbed (in v.o.). Several screenings take place almost every day at two locations: in the far eastern tip of the Palais de Chaillot (in the part nearest Ave Albert de Mun (16e); metro Trocadéro or Iéna) and at 18 Rue du Faubourg du Temple (11e; metro République). Tickets cost 22FF (15FF reduced price). See *Pariscope* or *L'Officiel des Spectacles* to find out what's playing.

Classical Music, Ballet & Opera

Paris is always filled with all sorts of orchestral, organ and chamber music concerts. Some are even free, such as those held at *Notre Dame* (4e) each Sunday afternoon at 5 or 5.30 pm. From April to October, concerts are also held in the *Sainte Chapelle* (4e); the cheapest seats are 95FF (75FF for students under 25). Other noted church venues are *Église Saint Sulpice* in the 6e and *Église Saint Eustache* near Forum des Halles (1e).

Museums with concert series include the *Musée du Louvre* (☎ 40.20.50.50), which has a series of midday and evening chamber music concerts from September to June; the *Musée d'Orsay* (☎ 40.49.48.84), whose daytime performances are sometimes free for museum visitors; and the *Centre Pompidou* (☎ 42.61.56.75), where contemporary and avant-garde music is performed at the Institut de Recherche et de Coordination Acoustique/Musique (IRCAM).

Opéra-Bastille *Opéra-Bastille* (☎ 44.73. 13.00 for reservations, 43.43.96.96 for a recording in French; metro Bastille) at 2-6 Place de la Bastille (12e) has been Paris's main opera house since its opening in 1989. It's also used as a venue for concerts and ballets.

The opera season lasts from late September to mid-July. Tickets, on sale at the usual ticket outlets, cost 125 to 570FF. To get the worst seats in the house (50FF), you have to stop by the ticket office, which is to the right of the black granite staircase and is open Monday to Saturday from 11 am to 6.30 pm (5 pm in summer). If there are unsold tickets, students and people over 60 can get good seats for about 100FF 10 or 15 minutes before the curtain goes up. It is possible to make reservations by phone – just make sure you pay for them at least one hour before the show begins. Tickets go on sale 14 days before the performance date.

Opéra-Garnier Paris's glorious old opera house, *Opéra-Garnier* (☎ 40.17.35.35 for recorded information, 47.42.53.71 for reservations; metro Opéra) at Place de l'Opéra

(9e) is now used only for concerts and ballet. The cheapest regular tickets, which get you a seat high above the stage (or with an obstructed view), cost as little as 15 to 30FF. Subject to availability, people under 25 and over 65 may be able to purchase decent seats quarter of an hour before the curtain rises for 60FF; ask for the *tarif spécial*. The box office is open Monday to Saturday from 11 am to 6.30 pm. Regular ticket sales begin 14 days before the performance date.

Théâtre de la Ville The municipal *Théâtre de la Ville* (☎ 48.87.54.42; metro Châtelet), which is on the eastern side of Place du Châtelet (4e), plays host to theatre, dance and music performances. Tickets cost 75 to 150FF. Depending on availability, people under 26 may be able to get discounts on Wednesday, Thursday and Sunday. The ticket office is open daily from 11 am to 9 pm (6 pm on Sunday and Monday). In July and August, when there are no performances, it's open only on weekdays.

Théâtre Musical de Paris On the western side of Place du Châtelet (1er) is the *Théâtre Musical de Paris* (☎ 40.28.28.40; metro Châtelet), marked on the front as the Théâtre Municipal du Châtelet. It has mostly opera but also hosts musical comedy, ballet and various kinds of concerts. The ticket office is open daily from 11 am to 7 pm; in July and August, when the place practically shuts down, it's open only on weekdays. Tickets cost 55 to 70FF for the worst seats and 190 to 465FF for the best ones. Students under 25 can get unsold tickets for about 50FF starting 15 minutes before performance time.

Théâtre des Champs-Élysées This theatre (☎ 47.20.08.24; metro Champs Élysées-Clemenceau) at 15 Ave Montaigne (8e) is famed for its Sunday morning concerts.

Theatre
Almost all of Paris's theatre productions, including those written in other languages,

are performed in French. There are a few English-French troupes around, though – look for ads on metro poster boards and in English-language periodicals.

The *Comédie Française* (☎ 40.15.00.15; metro Palais Royal), whose impressive home is next to the Palais Royal at Place André Malraux (1er), is the world's oldest national theatre group. Founded in 1680 under Louis XIV, its repertoire is based on the works of such French theatrical luminaries as Corneille, Molière, Racine, Beaumarchais, Marivaux, and Musset, though in recent years contemporary and even non-French works have been performed.

Music
Small Concert & Theatre Venues *New Morning* (☎ 45.23.51.41 for a recording; metro Château d'Eau), which is across the street from 10 Rue des Petites Écuries (10e), has concerts of jazz, funk, salsa, Brazilian music, world music, etc. There are shows three to seven nights a week at 9 or 9.30 pm, with the second set ending at about 1 am. Tickets usually cost 110 to 130FF and can be purchased at major ticket outlets, though they are usually available at the door. This place is very informal: there are no dress rules and everyone is welcome.

Café de la Danse (☎ 48.05.65.23, 47.00. 57.59; metro Bastille), whose informal 400-place auditorium was saved from the wreckers' ball in 1992, is just off Rue de Lappe at 5 Passage Louis-Philippe (11e). In addition to rock concerts, this place has dance performances, musical theatre and poetry readings. The entrance is through the unmarked grey doors. Tickets are available from FNAC.

The intimate, 123-seat *Théâtre du Tourtour* (☎ 48.87.82.48; metro Châtelet) at 20 Rue Quincampoix (4e) has something on every night from Tuesday to Saturday: theatre productions (80FF), often from the classical French repertoire (eg Voltaire, Balzac), at 7 pm; modern theatre (100FF) at 8.30 pm; and music (90FF) in styles ranging from rock to French chansons at 10.30 pm. There's a 20FF discount for students and

people under 25 or over 60. Performances take place in a 15th-century cellar classified as an historic monument. Reservations can be made by phone, usually on the day of the performance, and you can pick up your tickets 20 minutes before show time. Tickets are also available at FNAC or the kiosk at Place de la Madeleine.

French Chansons For information on afternoon accordion concerts, see Le Balajo under Discothèques.

Informal *Le Piano Zinc* (☎ 42.74.32.42; metro Rambuteau) at 49 Rue des Blancs Manteaux (4e) has three levels: a ground-floor bar; a basement room where a pianist accompanies people from the audience overcome by the desire to sing Piaf and Brel favourites; and, one floor below, a vaulted cellar with a TV-equipped bar. The guests are mostly gay but everyone is welcome. Le Piano Zinc is open from 6 pm to 2 am (closed Monday). The pianist begins playing at 10 pm. There is no cover charge except on Friday, Saturday and the eve of public holidays, when you have to buy a drink (35FF without alcohol, 45FF with) at the entrance. Beer is 13FF (19FF after 10 pm). Happy hour is from 6 to 8 pm.

At *Au Vieux Paris* (no phone; metro Hôtel de Ville) at Rue de la Verrerie (4e), the patrons – mostly young Parisians – are given sheets with the words of French chansons and everyone sings along to the accompaniment of an accordion and Madame Françoise, the feisty and idiosyncratic proprietor. On Friday and Saturday nights singing begins at around midnight but it's a good idea to come by around 11 pm to get a place.

One of the highlights of a visit to the Marché aux Puces de Saint Ouen (see Flea Markets under Things to Buy) is *Chez Louisette* (☎ 40.12.10.14; metro Porte de Clignancourt), where market-goers crowd around little tables to eat lunch and hear an old-time *chanteuse* (female singer) belt out Edith Piaf numbers to the accompaniment of an accordion. Chez Louisette is inside the maze of Marché Vernaison not far from 130

Ave Michelet, the boulevard on the other side of the highway from the metro stop and Ave de la Porte de Clignancourt (18e). It is open at lunchtime on Saturday, Sunday and Monday only. Main dishes are 65 to 135FF.

Jazz Paris has been a great centre of jazz performance since the interwar period. For the latest on jazz happenings around town, check the listings in *L'Officiel des Spectacles* or *Pariscope*.

Caveau de la Huchette (☎ 43.26.65.05; metro Saint Michel) at 5 Rue de la Huchette (5e), where virtually all the jazz greats have played since 1946, holds live jazz concerts in a medieval *caveau* (cellar) used as a courtroom and torture chamber during the Revolution. It is open every night from 9.30 pm to 2.30 am (3 am on Friday, 4 am on Saturday and the night before public holidays); concerts start at 10.15 pm.

Entrance costs 55FF (50FF for female students) from Sunday to Thursday, 65FF on Friday and 70FF on Saturday and the night before holidays. Beer (optional) starts at 18FF a bottle. Everyone is welcome and dress is casual, but you should be properly dressed for a night out (ie no short pants). Details on coming attractions are posted on the door. The bands, which hail from all over the world (including the USA, Eastern Europe and Russia), change every four to six days.

For information on performances at New Morning, see Small Concert & Theatre Venues.

Discothèques

A *discothèque*, as distinct from a 'disco' in English, is just about any sort of place where music leads to dancing. The truly *branché* crowd considers showing up before 1 am an egregious breach of good taste.

The discothèques favoured by the Parisian 'in' crowd change frequently, and many are officially private, which means that they can refuse entry to whomever the often thug-like *videurs* (bouncers) – especially numerous and zealous around Pigalle – don't like the look of. Tourists are often spared the worst

of it, but single men may not be admitted simply because they're single men, even if their clothes are subculture-appropriate. Women, on the other hand, get in for free on some nights. Get the picture? Don't go out on the town in search of *liberté*, *égalité* and *fraternité*...None of this comes cheap: expect to pay an absolute minimum of 50FF on weekdays and 60FF on weekends.

Le Balajo *Le Balajo* (☎ 47.00.07.87; metro Bastille), a mainstay of the Parisian dance hall scene since the time of Edith Piaf, is two blocks north-east of Place de la Bastille at 9 Rue de Lappe (11e). It is open to the public for dancing on Monday and from Thursday to Saturday nights from 11 pm to 5 am, but dancing begins in earnest at 2 or 3 am. Sometimes the DJs concentrate on a particular genre (jazz, pop, techno, funk, etc), while on other nights they run through the last half-century of music decade by decade.

Traditional *musette* (accordion music) – great for *rétro* (pre-1940s style) dancing – is played on Saturday and Sunday afternoons from 3 to 6.30 pm. At night, admission costs 100FF and includes one drink; in the afternoon, entry is 50/25FF with a beer/nonalcoholic drink. Women can wear pretty much whatever they want, but men have to be a bit dressed up. Tennis shoes are verboten. Men unaccompanied by women may not be admitted. Tourists may have an easier time getting past the bouncers than locals.

La Chapelle des Lombards You can dance to music from all over the Caribbean at *La Chapelle des Lombards* (☎ 43.57.24.24; metro Bastille) at 19 Rue de Lappe (11e), whose DJs spin the LPs and CDs Tuesday to Saturday from 11.30 pm to about 6 am. On Tuesday and Wednesday, there's a concert of Caribbean music from 8 to 10.30 pm. Entry (including one drink) costs 100FF from Tuesday to Thursday and 120FF on Friday and Saturday. Jeans and running shoes are not permitted.

La Locomotive *La Locomotive* (☎ 42.57. 37.37; metro Blanche) at 90 Blvd de Clichy

(18e), which is in Pigalle next to the Moulin Rouge nightclub, has three floors, each offering a different ambience and a different kind of music (though the emphasis throughout is on rock). It is open nightly, except Monday, from 11 pm until 6 am (7 am on weekends). Entrance costs 60FF from Tuesday to Thursday and 100FF on Friday and Saturday, including one drink. On Sunday night, men pay 60FF and women get in for free.

Le Palace The DJs at *Le Palace* (☎ 42.46. 10.87; metro Rue Montmartre) at 8 Rue du Faubourg Montmartre (9e) play all sorts of danceable music – retro, 70s, techno, rock, soul, etc – for the mostly young clientele. The main discothèque on the ground floor is mixed gay and straight; the 1st-floor bar is mostly gay. The separate section in the basement is reserved for women and attracts lots of lesbians.

There are no dress rules except that you can't wear *baskets* (sneakers or running shoes) or jeans with holes in them. Entrance (including one drink) costs 100FF from Monday to Thursday and 130FF from Friday to Sunday. Le Palace is open nightly from 11 pm to 4 or 5 am, but things really pick up after 1 am.

Le Palace's enduringly popular Gay Tea Dance (60FF, including a drink), held on Sunday from 5 to 10.30 or 11 pm, takes up all three floors. It is for gay men only.

L'Entr'acte & Le Scorpion This disco (☎ 40.26.01.93; metro Rue Montmartre) at 25 Blvd Poissonière (2e), one km east of Opéra-Garnier, consists of two separate sections. On the ground floor, *L'Entr'acte*, which is for lesbians only, is open Monday to Saturday from 10 pm (midnight on Saturday night) to 5 am (7 am on Saturday and Sunday mornings). Thursday is a '70s night. There's no cover charge except on Saturday night, when there's a 50FF entry fee.

In the cellar, *Le Scorpion*, which is reserved for gay men, is open daily from midnight to 6 am. There's no entry fee except on Friday and Saturday nights, when the

cover charge is 65FF. Music in both sections includes disco, techno and new wave. To get in, you have to have the right look, which even the bouncers couldn't quite define.

Le Queen This new and very popular disco at 102 Ave des Champs-Élysées (8e) attracts gay men as well as a few lesbians. Techno music rules. There's no entry fee except on weekends, when the 70FF charge gets you a drink.

Slow Club The unpretentious *Slow Club* (☎ 42.33.84.30; metro Châtelet) at 130 Rue de Rivoli (1er), which occupies a dark cellar two floors below street level used decades ago to ripen Caribbean bananas for nearby Les Halles, is a place for people who really want to dance the night away. The live bands attract both students and couples in their 30s, 40s and 50s. The music varies from night to night but includes jazz, rock'n'roll and, on Sunday, rockabilly, which is popular with teenagers.

The Slow Club, whose name dates from 1957, is open Tuesday to Saturday from 10 pm to 3 am (4 am on Friday and Saturday nights). Entry costs 55FF (50FF for women students) from Tuesday to Thursday, 70FF on Friday and Saturday. Bottled beer (optional) is 27FF. Everyone is welcome, but though men don't need a tie, they do need to look respectable (ie don't come in shorts, ripped jeans or running shoes). It often gets crowded after 1.30 am, especially on weekends.

Trottoirs de Buenos Aires *The* place in Paris for watching and dancing the tango is *Trottoirs de Buenos Aires* (☎ 40.26.29.30; metro Châtelet) at 37 Rue des Lombards (1er), three blocks south of Forum des Halles. A three-person band, perhaps brought all the way from Argentina, provides the authentic accompaniment. From Wednesday to Saturday, shows take place at 8.30 and 10.30 pm; on Sunday there's a ball in the afternoon and evening. The 8.30 pm performances may be cancelled in July and August.

On Friday and Saturday nights, Trottoirs turns itself into a *tangothèque* (the tango equivalent of a disco) at 12.30 am. Entry costs 50FF on Tuesday and Wednesday, 100FF from Thursday to Saturday and the price of a drink (40 to 50FF) on Sunday evening. No cover charge applies on Sunday afternoon. A tango class (90FF) is held every Saturday at 2.30 pm.

La Scala de Paris The three dance floors and five bars at *La Scala* (☎ 42.61.64.00; metro Palais Royal) at 188 Rue de Rivoli (1er) are lit by thousands of little flashing lights and pulsate to the sound of funk, rap and sometimes even '80s disco. The patrons are mostly in the 18-to-30 age group and include people from all over Europe.

La Scala is open every night from 10.30 pm to dawn, though things only start to pick up sometime after midnight. Entry costs 80FF (90FF on Saturday night), including one drink. Women get in for free from Sunday to Thursday except on the eve of public holidays. Jeans and running shoes are OK so long as they're clean and expensive.

Club Zed The DJs at *Club Zed* (☎ 43.54. 93.78; metro Maubert Mutualité) at 2 Rue des Anglais (5e) – one block north of 70 Blvd Saint Germain – play a combination of 1950s and '60s rock'n'roll, jazz and java. The arched stone basement is perfect for dancing, but the volume doesn't preclude having a conversation.

Zed is open Wednesday to Saturday from 10.30 pm to 4 am (5 am on Friday and Saturday nights). On Wednesday and Thursday, entrance costs 50FF, including a beer. On Friday and Saturday, when it costs 100FF, you have a wider selection of drinks. Don't come sloppily dressed.

Cabaret

Paris's risqué cancan revues, dazzling pseudo-Bohemian productions featuring hundreds of performers – including female dancers both with and without elaborate costumes – are about as representative of 1990s Paris as crocodile wrestling is of 1990s Aus-

tralia. The guests are mostly foreign businessmen – about the only people who can afford the stiff ticket prices.

The legendary *Moulin Rouge* (☎ 46.06. 00.19; metro Blanche) at 82 Blvd de Clichy (18e), whose name means Red Windmill, is in the heart of Pigalle. Tickets don't come cheap: if you stand at the bar, it costs 220FF, but if you prefer to sit down the price jumps to 465FF (including half a bottle of champagne). Dinner (at 8 pm) costs 670FF, including champagne. There are shows every night at 10 pm and midnight.

The *Paradis Latin* (☎ 43.25.28.28; metro Cardinal Lemoine) at 28 Rue du Cardinal Lemoine (5e) is known for its extravagant, nonstop performances of songs, dances and nightclub numbers. The whole staff, including the waiters, often participate. The show begins at 10 pm every night except Tuesday and costs 465FF, including half a bottle of champagne or two drinks. Dinner begins at 8 pm and costs 670FF, including the 10 pm show. Reservations can be made by telephone.

Other cabarets include the *Crazy Horse Saloon* (☎ 47.23.32.32; metro Alma Marceau) at 12 Ave George V (8e), and *Le Lido* (☎ 40.76.56.10; metro George V) at 116 Ave des Champs-Élysées (8e). The *Folies Bergères* closed at the end of 1992 after losing lots of money.

Spectator Sports

Football Although rugby league has a stronger following in the south of France, it has some support in the capital. Rugby union is more popular still, as the enduring success of the powerful Paris-St Germain club testifies. The French national teams in both codes have always been notoriously difficult to beat at home – in the rugby union Test series of 1993, world champions Australia defeated France in Paris for the first time ever.

In soccer, French national teams have traditionally been famous for their flair and imaginative attacking play. France has never won the World Cup, however. Many major national and international matches are played at the Palais Omnisports, Bercy. For details of forthcoming games, check newspapers or sports magazines.

Cycling Virtually the whole city comes to a standstill for the concluding leg of the Tour de France. Although the other routes vary every year, the race always concludes with a final dash along the Champs-Élysées.

Horse Racing One of the cheapest ways to spend a relaxing, outdoor afternoon in the company of Parisians of all ages, ethnic groups and walks of life is to go to the horse races. Of the six *hippodromes* (racecourses) in the Paris area, *Hippodrome d'Auteuil* (☎ 45.27.12.25, 49.10.20.26; metro Porte d'Auteuil) in the south-east corner of the Bois de Boulogne (16e) is one of the most accessible. Its speciality is steeplechases. The entrance fee is just 5FF for a place on the *pelouse* (grassy area) in the middle of the track and 22FF (37FF on Sunday and holidays) for a seat in the *tribune* (stands).

Each type of horse racing – of which *plat* (flat racing) is the most basic – has its season. Steeplechases generally take place from about February to April, though the Auteuil track is active in summer and autumn as well. Races are often held on Sunday afternoons, with half a dozen or so heats scheduled between 2 and 5.30 pm. To find out when the next race day will be, consult almost any French newspaper. If you can read a bit of French (and don't mind being mistaken for a regular punter), you might ask your neighbourhood newsagent for a copy of *Paris Turf*, the horse-racing weekly that comes out each Sunday.

Part of the fun of a day at the races is to buy yourself a stake in the proceedings by placing a bet. The minimum bet is only 10FF. Information on the horses and their owners, trainers and jockeys is available from the free programmes. Additional statistics on each horse's record are printed in *Paris Turf*. The odds are displayed on TV screens near the betting windows. You can bet that your horse will come in *gagnant* (in first place), *placé* (in first or second place) or *placé jumelé* (in first, second or third place). If your horse

wins, take your ticket back to any betting window to collect your windfall, which, if you're lucky, will be enough for a beer or two.

On race days, there are food stalls just outside the racecourse entrance. Inside the grounds, beer is on sale from 15FF a bottle.

Getting There & Away To get back to the city by metro on weekends and holidays, you have change trains at the Boulogne-Jean Jaurès stop, which is one stop in the wrong direction.

THINGS TO BUY

Paris has shopping options to suit all tastes and all budgets. Garments, for instance, can be selected at the ultrachic couture houses along Ave Montaigne or plucked from *shmatte*-strewn flea-market tables. Average Parisians, though, are more likely to head to Forum des Halles or Rue d'Alésia.

Department Stores

Depending on what you're looking for, Paris's world-renowned department stores may make up for their generally high prices with selection and convenience. In certain sections (eg perfume), you'll find lots of little kiosks, each exhibiting a particular brand name and staffed by *démonstratrices* (demonstrators) brought in by the company that makes the products.

Two of Paris's 'big three' department stores have their flagship stores just north of Opéra-Garnier. Au Printemps (☎ 42.82. 57.87; metro Havre Caumartin) at 64 Blvd Haussmann (9e) has one of the world's largest perfume departments and holds weekly fashion shows. It is open Monday to Saturday from 9.35 am to 7 pm (10 pm on Thursday).

Galeries Lafayette (☎ 42.82.36.40; metro Auber, Chaussée d'Antin) at 40 Blvd Haussmann (9e), housed in two adjacent buildings linked by a pedestrian bridge, features over 75,000 brand-name items, including a wide selection of fashion accessories. It is open Monday to Saturday from 9.30 am to 6.45 pm. Galeries Lafayette has another store (☎ 45.38.52.87; metro Mont-

parnasse Bienvenüe), open Monday to Saturday from 9.15 am to 7.15 pm, on Rue du Départ (15e) at the base of Tour Montparnasse.

The third of the 'big three', La Samaritaine (☎ 40.41.20.20; metro Pont Neuf), consists of four buildings between Pont Neuf (1er) and Rue de Rivoli, one of which – triangular Building 1 between Rue de la Monnaie and Rue du Pont Neuf – is devoted solely to toys and candy. A colour-coded brochure in English, available at store entrances, explains where to find different kinds of items. La Samaritaine is open Monday to Saturday from 9.30 am to 7 pm (10 on Thursday). For details on the view from the roof, see La Samaritaine Rooftop Terrace under Centre Pompidou Area in the Things to See section.

The enormous Bazar de l'Hôtel de Ville (☎ 42.74.90.00; metro Hôtel de Ville), usually known simply as BHV ('bei-ahsh-vei'), is known for its houseware, hardware and do-it-yourself supplies, including a wide selection of electrical adapters. It is across the street from the Hôtel de Ville at 52 Rue de Rivoli (4e) and is open Monday to Saturday from 9.30 am to 7 pm (10 pm on Wednesday).

Forum des Halles

The huge Forum des Halles shopping mall (1er; metro Châtelet-Les Halles), an unattractive and poorly conceived underground shopping complex, is a smashing success with Parisian shoppers, especially those in search of fashionable items that aren't overpriced.

La Défense

A bit west of Paris proper in the skyscraper district of La Défense, the massive Quatre Temps (or 4 Temps) shopping mall (metro La Défense), one of Europe's largest, has 250 shops known for their generally reasonable prices. Most stay open Monday to Saturday from 10 am to 7.30 or 8 pm. There is direct access to Quatre Temps from the metro station. For more information on the area, see La Défense in the Day Trips from Paris chapter.

Fashion

Some of the fanciest clothes in Paris (and thus the whole world) are sold by the *haute couture* houses of Ave Montaigne (1er; metro Franklin D Roosevelt or Alma Marceau). In this area just south of Ave des Champs-Élysées you'll find the shops of:

Inès de la Fressange at No 14	☎ 47.23.08.94
Christian Lacroix at No 26	☎ 47.20.68.95
Christian Dior at No 30	☎ 40.73.54.44
Celine at No 38	☎ 49.52.08.79
Chanel at No 42	☎ 40.70.12.33
Valentino at No 17	☎ 47.23.64.61
Guy Laroche at No 29	☎ 40.69.69.50
Nina Ricci at No 39	☎ 47.23.78.88
Thierry Mugler at No 49	☎ 47.23.37.62
Givenchy, 8 Ave George V	☎ 47.20.81.31

Most are open Monday to Saturday. The clients, including (as you'd expect) elegantly dressed women accompanied by immaculately trimmed poodles, are at least as interesting as the garments. New collections are released twice a year – for spring/summer and autumn/winter – with great fanfare: famous models parade around exclusive hotels and get written about all over the world.

There is another cluster of couture houses and exclusive clothing stores just north of Place de la Concorde along Rue du Faubourg Saint Honoré (8e; metro Concorde) and Rue Saint Honoré (1er; metro Tuileries, Concorde). Hermès (40.17.47.17; metro Madeleine) is at 24 Rue du Faubourg Saint Honoré (8e).

Quite a few younger and more innovative designers have boutiques in the area south of Saint Germain des Prés (6e & 7e). Places to look – all near metro Saint Sulpice – include Blvd Saint Germain, which has the ultra-Parisian Sonia Rykiel (☎ 49.54.60.60) at Nos 175 and 194; Rue des Saints Pères, where you'll find Inès de la Fressange at No 81; Rue de Grenelle; Rue du Cherche Midi; Rue de Rennes, which has Kenzo Studio at No 60-62; and Place Saint Sulpice, where you can pop into Yves Saint Laurent Rive Gauche at No 6.

Paris's trendiest designer boutiques are 500 metres north of the Louvre around Place des Victoires (1er & 2e; metro Bourse, Sentier), where you'll find Kenzo at No 3. Along nearby Rue Étienne Marcel (1er & 2e; metro Les Halles), exclusive boutiques include Comme des Garçons at No 42, Yohji Yamamoto at No 47 and Dorothée Bis at No 46.

The postmodern designs of Jean-Paul Gaultier are on sale a few blocks to the west at 6 Rue Vivienne (2e; metro Bourse). Towards Forum des Halles – and near Église Saint Eustache – on Rue du Jour (1er; metro Les Halles), the modern, casual styles of Agnès B are available in the shops at No 3 (for men; ☎ 42.33.04.13) and No 6 (for women; ☎ 45.08.56.56); Junior Gaultier (☎ 40.28.01.91), which carries Jean-Paul Gaultier's more affordable line, is at 7 Rue du Jour (1er).

In recent years, the Marais (3e & 4e; metro Saint Paul) has attracted a growing number of fashionable clothing shops. You'll find the practical jackets and jeans of Chevignon, which aren't quite as popular as they were a few years back, at the Chevignon Trading Post (☎ 42.72.42.40) at 4 Rue des Rosiers. Lolita Lempicka is not far away at 13bis Rue Pavée. Under the exclusive arcades of Place des Vosges, Issey Miyake is tucked away at No 3. There are other interesting shops along Rue des Francs Bourgeois.

For more everyday clothing, there are lots of shops along Rue de Rivoli, which gets less expensive as you move east from the 1er arrondissement into the 4e (metro Hôtel de Ville).

Clothing and shoe shops are legion along Rue de Rennes (6e; metro Rennes or Saint Placide), where you'll find inexpensive wearables at Paris's great working-class department store, Tati (☎ 45.48.68.31) at No 140.

In the 14e arrondissement, the part of Rue d'Alésia between Ave du Maine (metro Alésia) and Rue Raymond Losserand (metro Plaisance) is lined with places that sell clothes and accessories, including designer seconds and samples.

There are big *soldes* (sales) of clothing

and footwear each year from the end of June until sometime in July.

Leather Goods

Quality leather goods are sold along Rue du Cherche Midi (6e; metro Saint Sulpice, Sèvres Babylone) and the eastern end of Rue de Grenelle (6e & 7e; metro Saint Sulpice).

Jewellery

The place to go window-shopping for fantastically expensive jewellery is the area around Place Vendôme (1er; metro Tuileries, Opéra). You'll find Cartier shops at Nos 7 and 23 Place Vendôme, and similar offerings along nearby streets: Rue de Castiglione (1er); Rue de la Paix (2e), which has Cartier outlets at Nos 11-13; and Rue du Faubourg Saint Honoré (8e).

Less expensive jewellery is sold at various places around the city. Funky items, many of them imported, can be found in the Marais, including Rue des Francs Bourgeois (3e & 4e).

Costume jewellery is available at the flea markets.

Art Galleries

In Saint Germain des Prés (6e; metro Saint Germain des Prés), there are quite a few art galleries in the area around the École Nationale Supérieure des Beaux-Arts (National Fine Arts Academy), especially Rue Bonaparte, Rue des Beaux-Arts and Rue Jacob. Many specialise in antiquities or ethnic art from Africa.

There are art galleries of all sorts in the vicinity of the Centre Pompidou. Places to look include Rue Sainte Croix de la Bretonnerie (4e; metro Hôtel de Ville or Rambuteau) in the western Marais and, two blocks west of the Centre Pompidou, Rue Quincampoix (3e & 4e; metro Rambuteau or Châtelet-Les Halles).

Antiques

Just north of the Louvre at Place du Palais Royal (1er), Louvre des Antiquaires (metro Palais Royal) houses about 250 antique shops. There are also quite a few antique

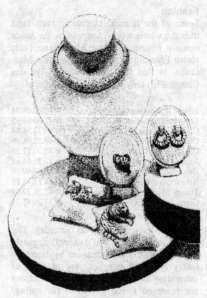

shops along Rue du Faubourg Saint Honoré (1er & 8e; metro Champs Élysées-Clemenceau).

Near Opéra-Garnier, Passage Jouffroy (metro Rue Montmartre), a 19th-century shopping arcade opposite 11 Blvd Montmartre (9e), and the contiguous Passage Verdeau contain shops selling antiques, old postcards, antiquarian books and the like. Galerie Véro Dodat (1er; metro Palais Royal), between 19 Rue Jean-Jacques Rousseau and 2 Rue du Bouloi, also has a number of antique shops. It is open Tuesday to Saturday.

Near Saint Germain des Prés (6e), there are a number of shops selling antiques and antiquarian maps and books around Rue Bonaparte (metro Saint Germain des Prés) and Rue Jacob. Aux Armes de Furstemberg (☎ 43.29.79.51; metro Mabillon) at 1 Rue de Furstemburg, which specialises in nautical antiques and old globes, is open Monday to Saturday from 10.30 am to 12.30 pm and 2 to 7 pm.

For information on Paris's flea markets, see Flea Markets in this section.

Fancy Paper

All sorts of items made from exquisite Florentine *papier à cuve* (paper hand-decorated with marbled designs) – created using a complicated process invented in the 17th century – are on sale at Mélodies Graphiques (☎ 42.74.57.68; metro Pont Marie) at 10 Rue du Pont Louis-Philippe (4e). It is open from 11 am to 7 pm (closed Monday). There are several other fancy paper shops along the same street.

Bouquinistes

Along the Seine, the southern quays near Notre Dame (Quai de Montebello, Quai de la Tournelle) and the northern quays around the Hôtel de Ville (Quai de Gesvres, Quai de l'Hôtel de Ville) are lined with *bouquinistes*, booksellers whose used and antiquarian books, magazines and prints are stored, when they're closed, in lockers attached to the wall overlooking the river.

Pots, Pans & Cutlery

The most incredible selection of professional-quality cookware, much of it specially designed for the preparation of French cuisine, is displayed from floor to ceiling at E Dehillerin (☎ 42.36.53.13; fax 45.08.86.83; metro Les Halles) at 18-20 Rue Coquillière (1er). You're sure to find something that even the best equipped kitchen is lacking, since you can choose from pots and pans in every imaginable size and shape (including many in solid copper), dozens of kinds of knives, a whole range of spatulas (the largest could double as an oar), ladles that can scoop up up to two litres, and 40 different types of *fouets* (whisks)! VAT-free purchases and shipping home can be arranged. E Dehillerin also has a repair service for copper pots and pans.

The shop, which was founded in 1820 and has been run by the same family for four generations, is open on Monday from 8 am to 12.30 pm and 2 to 6 pm, and Tuesday to Saturday from 8 am to 6 pm; in August, there's a lunch break from 12.30 to 2 pm.

Porcelain & Crystal

The shops along glamourless Rue de Paradis (metro Château d'Eau), which is in the 10e arrondissement near Gare de l'Est, specialise in beautiful porcelain and crystal made by France's most renowned producers.

Electronics, Cameras & Film

Stereos, car radios, videocassette recorders, cameras, computers and the like are *much* more expensive in France than in the USA, Singapore, Hong Kong or Andorra, but if you must make a purchase in the land of the TVA the stores of the FNAC chain are an excellent bet. They carry a wide selection of photographic supplies (film, paper) and can process film (including Kodachrome slides purchased without prepaid processing) relatively quickly. FNAC stores also sell tickets to cultural events (see Tickets under Entertainment).

The FNAC (☎ 49.54.30.00; metro Saint Placide) at 136 Rue de Rennes (6e) is open Tuesday to Saturday from 10 am to 7 pm and on Monday from 1 to 7 pm. The FNAC store in the Forum des Halles shopping mall (metro Châtelet-Les Halles) at 1-7 Rue Pierre Lescot (1er) is open Monday to Saturday from 10 am to 7 pm.

Music Recordings

CDs are generally more expensive in France than they are in North America. Count on paying a minimum of 110FF.

The four levels of the Virgin Megastore (☎ 40.74.06.48; metro Franklin D Roosevelt) at 60 Ave des Champs-Élysées (8e) display a vast selection of CDs and cassette tapes. The videocassettes are mostly SECAM, though a few PAL and NTSC tapes are also available. It is open Monday to Saturday from 10 am to midnight (1 am on Friday and Saturday) and on Sunday and holidays from noon to midnight. Tickets to all kinds of performances are sold at the billeterie in the basement.

FNAC Musique (☎ 43.42.04.04; metro Bastille) at 4 Place de la Bastille (12e), which is next to Opéra-Bastille, specialises in CDs, cassettes and LPs. It is open Monday to

Saturday from 10 am to 8 pm (10 pm on Wednesday and Friday). The other FNAC stores (see Electronics, Cameras & Film) also carry a large selection of CDs and tapes.

Tea
Mariage Frères (☎ 42.72.28.11; fax 42.74.51.68; metro Hôtel de Ville) at 30-32 Rue du Bourg Tibourg (4e) specialises in tea and tea-drinking accessories. The 450 kinds of tea in stock come from 30 countries; the most expensive is a variety of Japanese *thé vert* (green tea) that costs 490FF for 100 grams. The shop is open from 10.30 am to 7.30 pm (closed Monday).

The 19th-century-style salon de thé, where you can order a cup of any of the teas sold in the store, is open from noon to 7 pm. Scones (40FF), pastries and dishes made with tea (eg fish in tea sauce) are also available. In the summer you can cool off with five kinds of tea-flavoured ice cream. There's a display of 19th-century tea boxes and teapots on the 1st floor.

Mariage Frères, founded in 1854, has another shop (☎ 40.51.82.50; metro Odéon) at 13 Rue des Grands Augustins (6e). It is closed on Tuesday.

Monastery-Made Products
Produits des Monastères (☎ 48.04.39.05; metro Hôtel de Ville or Pont Marie) at 10 Rue des Barres (4e) sells jams, biscuits, cakes, muesli (granola), honey, herbal teas and sweets made in Benedictine and Trappist monasteries. It is open Tuesday to Saturday from 10 am to 12.20 pm, 2 to 5.30 pm and 7.30 to 8 pm. On Sunday, it's open before and after mass at nearby Église Saint Gervais: from 10 to 10.30 am and 12.30 to 1 pm. The shop is closed in August. Next door, the section selling ritual objects and religious books is open slightly longer hours.

Postage Stamps
Paris's Marché aux Timbres (stamp market; metro Champs Élysées-Clemenceau), just off Ave des Champs-Élysées at the intersection of Ave de Marigny and Ave Gabriel (8e),

is open on Thursday, Saturday, Sunday and holidays from 10 am to 5 pm.

The largest concentration of stores selling items of philatelic interest is on and around Rue Drouot (9e), which is between metro Le Peletier and metro Richelieu Drouot.

For information on the Musée de la Poste and its philatelic window, see Montparnasse under Things to See.

Minerals & Fossils
On Île Saint Louis, Galerie Alain Carion (☎ 43.26.01.16; metro Pont Marie) at 92 Rue Saint Louis en l'Île (4e) has an exceptionally fine collection of museum-quality minerals, meteorites, fossils and crystals from 40 different countries, some of them in the form of earrings, broaches and pendants. Prices range from 15FF to 15,000FF. The store, open Tuesday to Saturday from 10.30 am to 1 pm and 2 to 7.30 pm, is worth a visit just to see the extraordinary specimens on display.

Flowers
Paris's most famous flower markets are at Place Louis Lepine (4e; metro Cité) on Île de la Cité; on the east side of La Madeleine (8e; metro Madeleine); and at Place des Ternes (8e & 17e; metro Ternes).

Flea Markets
Paris's *marchés aux puces*, easily accessible by metro, can be great fun if you're in the mood to browse for unexpected treasures among the *brocante* (second-hand goods) and bric-a-brac on display. Some new goods are also available. A bit of bargaining is expected.

Marché aux Puces de Saint Ouen This vast flea market (metro Porte de Clignancourt), founded in the late 19th century and said to be Europe's largest, is at the northern border of the 18e arrondissement. If you arrive by metro, walk north along Ave de la Porte de Clignancourt, where the stalls begin, and cross under the Blvd Périphérique (the ring road) to the inner suburb of Saint Ouen. The market is centred around Rue des

Rosiers and nearby Ave Michelet, Rue Voltaire, Rue Paul Bert and Rue Jean-Henri Fabre. It is open to the public on Saturday, Sunday and Monday from 8 am to 7 pm (later during summer). Don't come expecting bargains – if there were any, the antique dealers who come to make their purchases on Friday probably snapped them up.

The stalls – of which there are over 2000 – are grouped into eight *marchés* (market areas), each with its own specialities. For instance, there's a dense concentration of antique shops along the narrow pedestrian streets of Marché Vernaison, which is the area north of Rue des Rosiers and west of Ave Michelet. You'll find a further 350 antique sellers in Marché Dauphiné at 138-140 Rue des Rosiers. Along Ave de la Porte de Clignancourt, Ave Michelet and Rue Jean-Henri Fabre, many of the places sell cheap, new clothing, shoes, leather goods, costume jewellery, etc.

Information on the Marché aux Puces de Saint Ouen is available from the Centre d'Information (☎ 40.10.13.92) at 154 Rue des Rosiers, which is open Saturday, Sunday and Monday from 9.30 am to 6 pm. The annual *Guide Officiel & Pratique des 'Puces'*, which bills itself in English as the *Complete Guide to the Greatest 'Fleamarket' in the World* (50FF), has details on where to find various categories of items. While shopping, watch out for pickpockets.

Marché aux Puces de Montreuil Perhaps the best bet for second-hand clothes – some of very good quality – is Marché aux Puces de Montreuil (metro Porte de Montreuil), which is in the south-eastern corner of the 20e arrondissement on Ave de la Porte de Montreuil, between the Porte de Montreuil metro stop and the ring road. It was established in the 19th century. The 500 stalls also sell *dégriffé* clothes (designer seconds), engravings, jewellery and linen. It is open on Saturday, Sunday and Monday from 7 am to about 7 pm.

Marché aux Puces de la Porte de Vanves This market (metro Porte de Vanves), which

dates from 1920 and is known for its fine selection of junk (records, fans, lamps, etc), is in the far south-western corner of the 14e arrondissement along Ave de la Porte de Vanves, Ave Georges Lafenestre and Rue Marc Sangnier. It is open on Saturday and Sunday from 7 am to 7.30 pm. On Sunday mornings from March to October, painters show their works along Ave Georges Lafenestre.

Marché d'Aligre Smaller and more central than the other three, this market (metro Ledru Rollin) at Place d'Aligre (12e) – a bit east of Place de la Bastille – is open until about 1 pm (closed Monday). This is one of the best places in Paris to rummage through cardboard boxes filled with old clothes and one-of-a-kind accessories worn decades ago by fashionable (and not-so-fashionable) Parisians.

GETTING THERE & AWAY
Air
Paris has two major international airports, both run by the city's airport authority, Aéroports de Paris (ADP). For information on transport options between the city and the airports, see To/From the Airports under Getting Around in this chapter. For information on air links to Paris, see Air in the Getting There & Away chapter.

Orly Aéroport d'Orly is 16 km south of central Paris. International flights use Orly-Sud (the south terminal). Orly-Ouest (the west terminal) handles domestic flights by Air France, Air Inter, Air Liberté, Air Littoral, Corsair, TAT and other carriers.

Information For flight and other information call ☎ 49.75.15.15 or 49.75.12.12 via the switchboard) from 6 am to 11.45 pm. By Minitel, you can get flight information on 3615 code HORAV.

At Orly Sud, the ADP information desk is on the Rez-de-Chaussée (ground floor) near Porte H. ADP's information desk at Orly-Ouest is on the Niveau Arrivée (arrival level). Both are open daily from 6 am to

11.45 pm and both can help with hotel reservations (room prices start at 250 or 300FF).

Money At Orly-Sud, the CCF Change near Porte F is open daily from 6.30 am to 11 pm, but the rate is inferior. There is no exchange bureau at Orly-Ouest. The post offices in both terminals can change banknotes in most major currencies, American Express travellers' cheques in US dollars or French francs and Visa cheques in French francs. Usually, they can also do Visa cash advances.

Post & Telephone At Orly-Sud, the post office (☎ 46.87.11.88) in the Sous Sol (basement) is open Monday to Friday from 8 am to 7 pm and on Saturday until noon. The Orly-Ouest post office (☎ 46.87.15.40), which is on the Niveau Arrivée, is open Monday to Saturday from 6.30 am to 7 pm, and on Sunday from 8.30 am to 6 pm.

Télécartes (telephone debit cards) can be purchased at the post offices or from the blue vending machine at Orly-Sud's Porte H.

Left-Luggage Office There are *consignes* (left-luggage offices) on Orly-Sud's Rez-de-Chaussée and Orly-Ouest's Niveau Arrivée. The charge is 20FF a bag (40FF for oversize items, eg a bike) for 24 hours.

Train Reservations & Ticketing The SNCF has a reservations and ticketing office (☎ 48.84.26.74) in the Orly-Sud terminal next to Porte H. It is open Monday to Friday from 8 am to 8 pm and on weekends from 10 am to 1 pm and 2.45 to 6 .30 pm. This is one of the few places in France where you can buy a Eurail pass.

Getting Around A free *navette* (shuttle bus) links Orly-Sud, Orly-Ouest, certain parking lots and the Hôtel Arcade (see Airports under the Places to Stay section).

Charles de Gaulle Aéroport Charles de Gaulle, also known as Roissy-Charles de Gaulle because it's in the Paris suburb of Roissy, is 27 km north of the city centre.

Charles de Gaulle Aiport consists of three terminal complexes. Aérogare 2, whose four semicircular terminals (2A, 2B, 2C and 2D) face each other in pairs, handles mainly Air France traffic, though a few companies that have agreements with Air France (eg Canadian Airlines, Sabena) also dock here. Long-haul flights use terminal 2A, while intra-European flights (including a few by other airlines) use 2B and 2D. Most other foreign carriers use the cylindrical Aérogare 1. Aérogare T9 is used exclusively by charter companies and operates only from April to September.

The airport terminals close after the last flight leaves (usually around 11.15 pm) and reopen to take passengers for the first flight of the morning (at 5 or 5.30 am). People who have early morning flights can stay all night in Aérogare 2 in the Boutiquaire area. In Aérogare 1, ticketed early-morning passengers can spend the night inside the building, although all the entrances except Porte 24 on both the Niveau Arrivée (arrival level) and Niveau Départ (departure level) levels are locked.

Information Flight and other information is available in English or French 24 hours a day on ☎ 48.62.22.80. By Minitel, you can get flight information on 3615 code HORAV.

There are Information ADP desks on all four levels of Aérogare 1 (at Porte 36), in all four terminals of Aérogare 2 and, whenever there are flights, at Aérogare T9. You can make hotel reservations at the ADP bureaux, but the cheapest rooms available cost 250 or 300FF.

Money CCF Change (☎ 48.62.73.71) has seven bureaux at Aérogare 1 and Aérogare 2. In summer, there's another one at Aérogare T9. Their rates are dismal. Most are open daily from 6.30 am to 11.30 pm.

If you have banknotes in most major currencies, American Express travellers' cheques in US dollars or French francs, or Visa travellers' cheques in French francs, you'll get a much better rate at the airport's post offices.

The ATM machines in Aérogare 1 (on the Niveau Boutiquaire, ie boutique level) and Aérogare 2 (in the Boutiquaire area) should be able to give credit card cash advances.

Customs If you have a VAT refund to arrange, there are a number of *douane* (customs) offices around the airport, including one in Aérogare 1 (on the Niveau Départ near Porte 12) and another one (☎ 40.24.99.00) in terminal 2A of Aérogare 2 (between Sorties 5 and 6). They are open whenever flights are leaving.

Post & Telecommunications The post offices (☎ 48.62.54.24) in Aérogare 1 and in Aérogare 2's Boutiquaire area (☎ 48.62.54.24) are open Monday to Friday from 8 am to 7 pm and on Saturday until noon. The bureau at Aérogare 2 has an extensive collection of French telephone books and offers post-paid international phone calls.

Télécartes (telephone debit cards) are available at the post offices and at a number of tabacs (tobacconists' shops) around the airport.

Left-Luggage Office There are consignes in Aérogare 1's Niveau Boutiquaire and Aérogare 2's Boutiquaire area (under Porte 14). The charge is 20FF a bag (40FF for oversize items) for 24 hours.

Places to Eat In Aérogare 1, there are a number of restaurants on the Niveau Boutiquaire, including a very expensive Burger King that's open daily from 10 am to 11 pm.

Train Reservations & Ticketing The SNCF has two online offices at Charles de Gaulle:

* in Aérogare 1 (☎ 48.62.22.18) on the Niveau Arrivée near Porte 22
* in Aérogare 2 (☎ 48.62.73.28) in the Boutiquaire area

Both are open daily from 7.30 am to 8.30 pm. The Aérogare 1 office can issue Eurail passes to people who are not residents of Europe.

Getting Around Every eight minutes, the free Navette Aéroport (airport shuttle bus) links all three aérogares with each other and with Roissy-Aéroport Charles de Gaulle RER (commuter rail) station. They also stop at the Hôtel Arcade (see Airports under Places to Stay).

Airline Offices See Travel Agencies under Information for details on where to find cheap air tickets. Travel agents frequently offer tickets for less than the 'official' tariffs charged by airline reps, but the airline offices handle reconfirmations, which should be done by telephone 72 hours before your scheduled departure.

The airline offices listed here do not appear on the maps, but most are either along Ave de l'Opéra (1er & 2e), between Place de l'Opéra and La Madeleine (2e, 8e & 9e), or along Ave des Champs-Élysées (8e). Those not listed can be found, arranged by arrondissement, in the Paris yellow pages under *transports aériens*.

Aer Lingus
    47 Ave de l'Opéra, 2e (☎ 47.42.12.50; metro Opéra)
Aeroflot
    33 Ave des Champs-Élysées, 8e (☎ 42.25.43.81; metro Franklin D Roosevelt)
Air Afrique
    29 Rue du Colisée, 8e (☎ 44.21.32.32; metro Saint Philippe du Roule)
Air Algérie
    28 Ave de l'Opéra, 2e (☎ 47.03.74.00 for reservations; metro Pyramides)
Air France
    For information: ☎ 44.08.24.24
    For reservations: 44.08.22.22
    By Minitel, key in 3615 code AF
    For recorded flight information in French: ☎ 43.20.12.55 (arrivals), 43.20.13.55 (departures)
    Offices (open Monday to Saturday from 9 am to 6 pm):
    119-121 Ave des Champs-Élysées, 8e (☎ 42.99.23.64; metro George V)
    Aérogare des Invalides, 2 Rue Robert Esnault Pelterie, 7e (metro Invalides)
    4 Place Edmond Rostand, 6e (☎ 43.25.73.95; metro Luxembourg)
Air Guadeloupe
    See Air Martinique
Air India
    1 Rue Auber, 9e (☎ 42.66.90.60; metro Opéra)

Air Inter
For information: ☎ 45.46.90.00
For flight information: ☎ 46.75.11.11
Offices:
49 Ave des Champs-Élysées, 8e (☎ 47.23.59.58;
metro Franklin D Roosevelt). Open daily from 9
am (noon on Sunday and holidays) to midnight.
Air France and other domestic and international
tickets are sold here.
Aérogare des Invalides, 2 Rue Robert Esnault
Pelterie, 7e (☎ 45.55.07.72; metro Invalides)

Air Liberté
131 Blvd Sebastopol, 2e (☎ 40.28.43.31,
49.79.09.09; metro Réaumur Sébastopol)

Air Littoral
☎ 47.35.70.71

Air Martinique
57 Rue Pierre Charron, 8e (☎ 42.56.21.00; metro
Franklin D Roosevelt)

Air UK
3 Rue de Choiseul, 2e (☎ 49.27.98.01; metro
Quatre Septembre)

Alitalia
69 Blvd Haussmann, 8e (☎ 44.94.44.00; metro
Havre Caumartin)

All Nippon Airways
91 Ave des Champs-Élysées, 8e (☎ 44.31.44.31;
metro George V)

American Airlines
109 Rue du Faubourg Saint Honoré, 8e
(☎ 42.89.05.22 or 05.23.00.35 toll free; metro
Saint Philippe du Roule)

Austrian Airlines
9 Blvd Malesherbes, 8e (☎ 42.66.34.66; metro
Madeleine)

Bangkok Airways
90 Ave des Champs-Élysées, 8e (☎ 42.89.55.45;
metro George V)

Bangladesh Biman
90 Ave des Champs-Élysées, 8e (☎ 42.89.11.47;
metro George V)

British Airways
12 Rue de Castiglione, 1er (☎ 47.78.14.14; metro
Tuileries)

British Midland
3 Rue Meyerbeer, 9e (☎ 47.42.30.62; metro
Chaussée d'Antin)

Canadian Airlines
24 Ave Hoche, 8e (☎ 49.53.07.07; metro Ternes)

Cathay Pacific
267 Blvd Pereire, 17e (☎ 40.68.98.99; metro
Neuilly-Porte Maillot)

China Airlines
90 Ave des Champs-Élysées, 8e (☎ 42.25.63.60;
metro George V)

Continental
92 Ave des Champs-Élysées, 8e (☎ 42.99.09.09,
05.25.31.81 (toll free); metro George V)

Corsair
☎ 49.79.49.79, 42.73.10.64

Egypt Air
1bis Rue Auber, 9e (☎ 44.94.85.00; metro Opéra)

El Al
24 Blvd des Capucines, 9e (☎ 47.42.41.29,
47.42.45.19; metro Madeleine)

Garuda Indonesian
75 Ave des Champs-Élysées , 8e (☎ 44.95.15.50;
metro George V)

Iberia
11 Place des Cinq Martyrs du Lycée Buffon, 14e
(☎ 40.47.80.90; metro Gaîté)

Japan Air Lines
75 Ave des Champs-Élysées, 8e (☎ 44.35.55.00;
metro George V)

Kenya Airways
38 Ave de l'Opéra, 2e (☎ 47.42.33.11; metro
Opéra)

KLM
36 Ave de l'Opéra, 2e (☎ 44.56.19.00 or, for
reservations, 44.65.18.18; metro Opéra)

LOT Polish Airlines
18 Rue Louis Le Grand, 2e (☎ 47.42.05.60;
metro Opéra)

Lufthansa
21-23 Rue Royale, 8e (☎ 42.65.37.35; metro
Madeleine)

MAS (Malaysian Airline System)
12 Blvd des Capucines, 9e (☎ 47.42.26.00; metro
Opéra)

Malév Hungarian Airlines
7 Rue de la Paix, 2e (☎ 42.61.57.90; metro
Opéra)

Middle East Airlines (MEA)
6 Rue Scribe, 9e (☎ 42.66.93.93; metro Auber)

Northwest Airlines
16 Rue Chauveau Lagarde, 8e (☎ 42.66.90.00;
metro Madeleine)

Pakistan International (PIA)
90 Ave des Champs- Élysées, 8e (☎ 45.62.92.41;
metro George V)

Philippine Airlines
1 Place André Malraux, 1er (☎ 42.96.01.40;
metro Palais Royal)

Qantas
7 Rue Scribe, 9e (☎ 44.94.52.00; metro Auber)

Royal Air Maroc
38 Ave de l'Opéra, 2e (☎ 44.94.13.10; metro
Opéra)

Royal Jordanian
12 Rue de la Paix, 2e (☎ 42.61.57.45; metro
Opéra)

Royal Nepal
2 Rue Saint Victor, 5e (☎ 40.46.95.21; metro
Cardinal Lemoine)

Sabena
19 Rue de la Paix, 2e (☎ 44.94.19.19/31; metro
Opéra)

SAS
30 Blvd des Capucines, 9e (☎ 47.42.06.14; metro Madeleine)

Singapore Airlines
43 Rue Boissière, 16e (☎ 45.53.90.90; metro Boissière)

South African Airways (SAA)
350 Rue Saint Honoré, 8e (☎ 49.27.05.50; metro Opéra)

Swissair
4 Rue Ferrus, 14e (☎ 45.81.11.01; metro Glacière)

TAP (Air Portugal)
9 Blvd de la Madeleine, 1er (☎ 44.86.89.50 or, for reservations, 44.86.89.89; metro Madeleine)

TAT
17 Rue de la Paix, 2e (☎ 42.61.82.10, 42.79.05.05; metro Opéra)

Thai
23 Ave des Champs-Élysées, 8e (☎ 44.20.70.80; metro Franklin D Roosevelt)

Tower Air
4 Rue de La Michodière, 2e (☎ 44.51.56.56; metro Quatre Septembre)

Tunis Air
17 Rue Daunou, 2e (☎ 42.12.31.31; metro Opéra)

TWA
6 Rue Christophe Colomb, 8e (☎ 40.69.70.00; metro George V)

United
34 Ave de l'Opéra, 2e (☎ 47.42.25.14/44; metro Opéra)

UTA
3 Blvd Malesherbes, 8e (☎ 40.17.46.46, 40.17.44.44; metro Madeleine)

Train

Stations Paris has six major railway stations (*gares*), each of which handles passenger traffic to different parts of France and Europe. The easiest way to figure out which station you need is to consult the coloured SNCF Railways map in the Getting Around chapter.

Getting to, from or between train stations is fairly straightforward since the metro (or metro/RER) station attached to each one bears the same name as the train station (for details on how to use the metro, see the Getting Around section of this chapter).

The Paris tourist office has annexes in all of Paris's train stations except Gare Saint Lazare. They are open from 8 am to 9 pm (3 pm at Gare d'Austerlitz) daily except Sunday and holidays; the Gare du Nord office is also open on Sunday (but not holidays) from 1 to 8 pm. All of them handle hotel reservations.

There are Thomas Cook, Banco Central or CIC exchange bureaux in all of the stations, but better rates are offered by nearby post offices (open weekdays from 8 am to 7 pm and on Saturday from 8 am to noon) and, in most cases, commercial banks on surrounding streets.

All six stations have both left-luggage offices and luggage lockers (*consignes automatiques*) of various sizes.

For details on train-ferry services to London, see To/From England under Sea in the Getting There & Away chapter.

Gare d'Austerlitz Gare d'Austerlitz (metro Gare d'Austerlitz), which is on Blvd de l'Hôpital (13e), is responsible for trains to the Loire Valley, Spain and Portugal and non-TGV trains to south-western France (Bordeaux, the Basque Country, etc).

The information office, which is at the far end of the hall behind track 11, is open Monday to Saturday from 7 am to 9 pm and on Sunday from 9 am to 8 pm. BIJ tickets are sold at the Wasteels office on the Cour Départ, which is outside the door to the right as you approach the Information Réservation Vente office. It's open Monday to Saturday from 6 to 11.30 am and 1.45 to 7 pm and on Sunday from 6 to 9 am.

The only place to change money is the Banco Central (☎ 45.84.91.40) behind track 11, open daily from 7 am to 9 pm. The rates are truly dismal, but they do credit card cash advances. When the tourist office is closed, the nearby Bureau de Remboursement can help with hotel reservations; the fees are the same as at the tourist office. You can take a *douche* (shower; 20FF) or *bain* (bath; 29FF) at the Cour Arrivée (behind track 21) from 6 am to 7.30 pm.

Gare de l'Est Gare de l'Est (☎ 40.18.88.85; metro Gare de l'Est), which is at the northern end of Blvd de Strasbourg (10e), handles traffic to parts of France east of Paris (such as Champagne, Alsace and Lorraine), Lux-

embourg, parts of Switzerland (Basel, Lucerne, Zürich), southern Germany (Frankfurt, Munich) and points further east.

The SNCF information office is open Monday to Saturday from 7 am to 9 pm and on Sunday and holidays from 8 am to 8 pm. The tourist office annexe (☎ 46.07.17.73) is behind Voie 27 (platform 27). BIJ tickets are available from Frantour Tourisme (☎ 46.07.38.37), which is one level below the tracks in the area of shops at the metro station entrance. It is open Monday to Friday from 9 am to 12.45 pm and 2 to 6 pm.

There is a post office with exchange services at 160 Rue du Faubourg Saint Martin (10e), opposite the exit next to Voie 28.

Gare de Lyon Gare de Lyon (metro Gare de Lyon), which is off Blvd Diderot (12e), is responsible for both regular and TGV Sud-Est trains to places south-east of Paris, including Dijon, Lyon, Provence, the Côte d'Azur, the Alps, parts of Switzerland (Bern, Geneva, Lausanne), Italy and points beyond.

The CIC bank (☎ 43.41.52.70) is open daily from 6.30 am to 11 pm; the commission is 22FF. There is an American Express cash machine nearby.

Gare Montparnasse Gare Montparnasse (metro Montparnasse Bienvenüe), which is at the intersection of Ave du Maine and Blvd de Vaugirard (15e; next to the Montparnasse Tower), handles trains to Brittany and places between Paris and Brittany (Chartres, Angers, Nantes). It is also the Paris terminus of the TGV-Atlantique, which serves Tours, Bordeaux, Nantes and other destinations in south-western France.

Long-distance *(grande ligne)* tickets are on sale on the same level as the tracks. There is an American Express cash machine behind track 13.

Gare du Nord Gare du Nord (metro Gare du Nord), which is on Rue de Dunkerque (10e), is responsible for trains to the northern suburbs of Paris, northern France (Lille, Calais), the UK, Belgium, northern Germany, Scandinavia, Moscow, etc. It handles the new TGV Nord, which serves Calais and, via the Channel Tunnel, London. Be especially vigilant here for pickpockets, con artists and thieves, all of whom are attracted by the crowds of travellers and the penniless backpackers who spend the night in the station.

The SNCF information office is open daily from 8 am to 8 pm (7 am to 9 pm from June to mid-September). BIJ tickets are on sale at Voyages Wasteels, which is open Monday to Friday from 9.30 am to 12.30 pm and 1.30 to 6.30 pm and on Saturday from 8.30 am to 2.30 pm.

To change money, you can go to the BNP bank across from the station's main entrance at 23 Rue de Dunkerque (10e), which is open Monday to Friday from 9 am to 5 pm. There's a post office with exchange services on the side of the station facing Rue du Faubourg Saint Denis. (See the Gare de l'Est & Gare du Nord Area map.)

Gare Saint Lazare Gare Saint Lazare (metro Saint Lazare), at 13 Rue d'Amsterdam (8e), handles traffic to Normandy and, in coordination with Dieppe-Newhaven ferries, to England.

The SNCF information office, which is 50 metres behind Voie 2 (platform 2), tries to help tourists with nontrain matters in the absence of a tourist office annexe. It is open Monday to Saturday (except holidays) from 7 am to 8 pm. For tickets and information on international travel, go to the Service International office in the middle of the hall, which is open daily from 7.15 am to 8 pm (and from 8.30 to 10.15 pm for night trains to England).

The Thomas Cook exchange bureau (☎ 43.87.72.51) near the Service International office is open daily from 7 or 8 am to 8 pm (9 pm in summer). The post office at 15 Rue d'Amsterdam, which can change money, is through the side exit next to Voie 27. BIJ tickets are sold in the Frantour Tourisme agency (☎ 43.87.61.89) through the passage behind Voie 12. It's open Monday to Friday from 9 am to 5.30 pm.

Train Information For information in French on trains departing from any of the stations, call ☎ 45.82.50.50 daily from 7 am to 11 pm. By Minitel, key in 3615 SNCF.

For details on tourist office annexes and exchange bureaux at the railway stations, see the preceding paragraphs on each station.

Fares Fares to destinations around France and abroad include:

Destination	Fare (FF)	Duration (hours)
Amsterdam	356	7
Berlin	775	12½
Copenhagen	1036	15¾
Geneva	366	3½
Lille	150	1*
Madrid	869	12
Marseille	383	4¾*
Nantes	216	2*
Nice	465	7*
Rome	617	15
Toulouse	326	5½*
Strasbourg	247	4

* by TGV

Buying a Ticket In general, stations have separate ticket windows *(guichets)* and platforms *(voies* or *quais)* for suburban *(banlieue)* trains and long-haul trains *(grandes lignes)*. There may also be special ticket counters for international travel *(services internationaux)*.

Getting Your Money Back *Remboursement* (reimbursement) for train tickets purchased anywhere in France is often available from ticket windows. When the problem is complicated, you can go to Gare du Nord's Service Clientèle office (☎ 49.95.58.12), which is off the balcony overlooking the tracks through the door marked 'Porte 12'.

The office is open daily from 7 am to 10.45 pm. At Gare d'Austerlitz, the Bureau de Remboursement (☎ 48.84.14.18 via the switchboard) is next to the tourist office, which is behind track 21 off the Cour Arrivée. It's open daily from 6 am to midnight.

Bus
Domestic Because the French government prefers to avoid competition with the state-owned rail system and the heavily regulated domestic airlines, there is no domestic, inter-city bus service to or from Paris.

International For information on bus-ferry services to London, see To/From England under Sea in the Getting There & Away chapter.

Eurolines runs buses from Paris to cities all over Europe, including London (see Bus under Land in the Getting There & Away chapter for details). The company's new Gare Routière Internationale (international bus terminal; ☎ 49.72.51.51; metro Galieni), is at Porte de Bagnolet (on the eastern edge of Paris) between Ave Ibsen (20e) and Ave du Général de Gaulle in the inner suburb of Bagnolet. The Eurolines counter will change money for a ridiculously low rate. Luggage lockers are available.

Eurolines's ticket office (☎ 43.54.11.99; metro Cluny-La Sorbonne) at 55 Rue Saint Jacques (5e) is open Tuesday to Saturday from 9.30 am to 1 pm and 2.30 to 7 pm. In summer, it's not a bad idea to make a reservation a few days in advance.

Allostop Provoya (☎ 42.46.00.66; metro Château d'Eau) at 84 Passage Brady (10e), best known for liaising between drivers and travellers going to the same destination, sells bus tickets for Eurolines, Weri and Der Bus.

Hitching
Getting out of Paris by standing near highway entrance ramps or in petrol stations doesn't usually work very well. Your best bet is probably to take an RER train out to the suburbs and try from there. Remember to exercise care when hitching.

Allostop Provoya (☎ 42.46.00.66 or, from abroad, 1-47.70.02.01; metro Château d'Eau) at 84 Passage Brady (10e) links up travellers and drivers going to the same destination. The office is open Monday to Friday from 9 am to 7.30 pm and on Saturday from 9 am to 1 pm and 2 to 6 pm. See Hitching in the Getting Around chapter for more information.

GETTING AROUND

Paris's public transit system, most of which is operated by RATP (short for Régie Autonome des Transports Parisiens), is one of the most efficient in the world. It's also one of the Western world's great urban travel bargains. Free metro/RER/bus maps are available at the ticket windows of metro/RER stations and at tourist offices.

Strikes, a time-honoured way for French organised labour get its demands taken seriously, are an accepted part of French life, though they often create utter chaos with little notice. Since everyone knows what a complete strike of the metro would do to Paris, the metro workers need only hint at such a possibility by shutting down one line here and another there to get their point across. Especially in May, be prepared for sudden disruptions.

To/From the Airports

At both Orly and Charles de Gaulle, a selection of bus, metro and RER (suburban commuter rail) options allows you to choose the mode of transport into the city that will get you nearest your final destination. If you're not sure exactly where in Paris you need to get to, ask at one of the Aéroports de Paris (ADP) information counters or consult the maps in this chapter. If you know what arrondissement you need, you can easily figure out which of the stations mentioned in the text is closest. And if you know what metro station you need, you might try to choose a transport option that will require the fewest transfers once you get into the city. Metro maps are available from airport information desks.

Air France buses (☎ 48.64.30.20) link Orly and Charles de Gaulle airports every 20 minutes from 6 am to 11 pm. When traffic is not heavy, the ride takes 50 minutes. The trip costs 64FF but is free for Air France passengers with connecting flights. Taking a combination of Roissyrail and Orlyval costs 76FF and takes about an hour. Taking a taxi should cost around 275FF.

For details on the SNCF's train ticketing facilities at the airports, see Air in the Getting There & Away section of this chapter.

Orly All six public transport options linking Orly with the city run daily every 15 minutes or so (less frequently late at night) from sometime between 5.30 and 6.30 am to 11 or 11.30 pm. At Orly-Sud, buses can be boarded at Porte H; at Orly-Ouest, the bus stops are on the Niveau Arrivée around Porte C, Porte D and Porte E. Information on ground transport is posted on large, backlit, yellow signs emplaced around the arrival areas.

- *Orlyrail* (27FF), which runs until a bit past 11 pm, is the quickest way to get to the Left Bank and the 16e arrondissement. Take the free shuttle bus to the Pont de Rungis-Aéroport d'Orly RER (commuter rail) station, which is on the C2 line, and get on a train heading into the city.
  Stops in Paris include Gare d'Austerlitz (13e; 35 minutes) and the Saint Michel (5e), Invalides (7e) and Champ de Mars-Tour Eiffel (15e & 7e) RER stations. The tickets, which are valid for onward travel by metro, are available from vending machines marked Orlyrail SNCF-RATP (exact change may be necessary) or from the ticket window of the RER station.
  If heading from Paris to Orly (last train around 10.40 pm), take a C2 train codenamed ROMI or MONA towards Massy-Palaiseau.
- *Orlyval*, a completely automated (ie driverless) shuttle train, links both Orly terminals with the Antony RER station, whence RER Line B whisks you to Paris metro/RER stations, including Saint Michel (5e), Châtelet-Les Halles (1er) and Gare du Nord (10e). The trip, which takes about 30 minutes, costs 45FF, including 1st-class passage on the RER and metro travel within the city. Taking Orlyval and then Roissyrail to Charles de Gaulle Airport costs 76FF and takes about an hour. When heading from Paris to Orly, take RER line B4 towards Saint Rémy-lès-Chevreuse; make sure the train you get on stops at Antony.
- *Orlybus*, which costs 25FF or six bus/metro tickets, takes you to the Denfert Rochereau metro station (25 minutes), which is in the heart of the 14e arrondissement. Buy a ticket from the driver or at the *caisse* (cashier) next to the ADP information desk near Porte H.
- *Air France buses* (☎ 43.23.97.10) charge 32FF (83/103FF for three/four people travelling together) to take you to two Left Bank metro hubs, Gare Montparnasse (15e; metro Montparnasse Bienvenüe) and Aérogare des Invalides (7e; metro Invalides; 30 to 50 minutes), which is near the

Seine next to Esplanade des Invalides.

On your way into the city, you can request to get off at the Porte d'Orléans or Duroc metro stops. Tickets are sold on the bus.

- *Jetbus* (☎ 60.48.00.98), which costs 20FF, takes you to the Villejuif-Louis Aragon metro stop, which is a bit south of the 13e arrondissement on the city's southern fringe. You'll have to buy a metro ticket to get into the city. Tickets for Jetbus are sold on board.
- *RATP bus No 183*, which costs four bus/metro tickets, goes to Porte de Choisy (metro Porte de Choisy), which is at the southern edge of the 13e arrondissement. It can be rather slow. Tickets are available at the ADP desk or from the driver.

A daytime taxi ride into Paris costs about 110FF (plus 6FF per piece of luggage over five kg). At night, the per-km tariff is higher but traffic is lighter, so the fare comes out about the same.

Charles de Gaulle There are five public tranport options for travel between Aéroport Charles de Gaulle and Paris. Unless otherwise indicated, they run from sometime between 5 and 6.30 am until 11 or 11.30 pm.

- The fastest way to get to/from the city is by *Roissyrail* (35FF), whose last train in both directions is sometime around midnight. Every eight minutes, a free Navette Aéroport takes you from the aérogares to the Roissy-Aéroport Charles de Gaulle RER (commuter rail) station, whence RER line B whisks you to the Gare du Nord (10e), Châtelet-Les Halles (1er; 35 minutes), Saint Michel (5e), Luxembourg (5e) or Denfert Rochereau (14e) RER stations. Tickets – good for onward metro travel in Paris – are available at the Roissy-Aéroport Charles de Gaulle RER station.

  If heading from Paris to the airport, take line B3; make sure you get a train that stops at Roissy-Aéroport Charles de Gaulle (check the destination boards over the platform or look for any train whose four-letter destination code begins with E). Regular metro ticket windows can't sell tickets, so you'll have to buy one at Gare du Nord (in the underground Banlieue section) or at the RER station where you board.

  Nothing will physically prevent you from boarding the train with a regular metro ticket, but if an inspector catches you *in flagrante delicto* (or while you're on the train outside of Zone 1), you may be fined.

  Eurail passes are valid for travel from Charles de Gaulle to Gare du Nord (but not beyond).

- *Roissybus* (30FF), run by RATP, links Charles de Gaulle with Place de l'Opéra (9e). To be precise, the stop is on the corner of Rue Scribe and Rue Auber not far from American Express. The trip takes about 45 minutes.
- *Air France buses* (Cars Air France; ☎ 42.99.20.18) link the airport with the Arc de Triomphe (metro Charles de Gaulle-Étoile; the stop is at the end of Ave Carnot nearest the traffic circle around the Arc) and the Palais des Congrès at Porte Maillot (metro Porte Maillot), which is at the western edge of the city on the border between the 16e and 17e arrondissements.

  The ride costs 48FF (112/140FF for three/four people travelling together) and takes around 40 minutes. Buses leave about every 15 minutes from 5.40 am (6 am from the airport) to 11 pm. At Aérogare 1, the bus stops on the Niveau Arrivée near Porte 34; at Aérogare 2, you can catch it at terminal 2A (Sortie 5), terminal 2B (Porte 6), terminal 2C and terminal 2D (Porte 6).

  A second Air France bus (☎ 43.23.82.20) with different airport stops links Charles de Gaulle with Gare Montparnasse (metro Montparnasse Bienvenüe), which is on the Left Bank on the border of the 14e and 15e arrondissements. The ride costs 64FF (144/170FF for three/four people) and takes about 60 minutes. From the airport to the city, the buses run every hour on the half-hour from 7.30 am to 7.30 pm; from the city to the airport, they leave Gare Montparnasse every hour on the hour from 7 am to 9 pm.

- RATP has two public buses linking Charles de Gaulle with the eastern half of the Right Bank and some of the city's northern suburbs. Both stop at Aérogare 1 (on the Niveau Boutiquaire 50 metres outside Porte 36) and Aérogare 2 (terminal 2A, Porte 10; terminal 2B, Porte 1; terminal 2D, Porte 12) and cost six bus/metro tickets or 36FF (five tickets or 30FF if you have a two-zone Carte Orange). Buy your ticket on board.

  RATP Bus No 350 goes to Porte de la Chapelle (18e) on the city's northern edge and two of Paris's major train stations, Gare du Nord (10e) and Gare de l'Est (10e). From the airport to the city, it runs daily from 6.30 am to 11.50 pm; from the city to the airport, it runs from 5.30 am to 10.50 pm. There are departures every 15 minutes or so (every 25 minutes at night and on Sunday and holiday mornings). The trip takes 50 minutes (60 or 70 minutes during rush hour).

  RATP Bus No 351 goes to Ave du Trône (11e and 12e), which is on the eastern side of Place de la Nation (metro Nation). From the airport to the city, it runs daily every half-hour or so from about 6 am to 9.15 pm; from the city to the airport, it runs from 5.50 am to 8.20 pm.

By taxi, a ride to the city centre should cost 170 or 180FF in the daytime (seven days a week) and 220 to 240FF at night (7 pm to 7 am). If traffic is bad, count on paying a bit more. Luggage costs 6FF per bag over five kg.

Metro & RER

Paris's underground (subway) network consists of two separate but linked systems: the Métropolitain, known as the *métro*, which has 13 lines and over 300 stations, many marked by Hector Guimard's famous noodle-like Art Nouveau entrances; and the suburban commuter rail network, the RER (pronounced 'ehr-er-ehr', short for Réseau Express Régional), which, along with certain SNCF lines, is divided into eight concentric suburban zones. For convenience' sake, the term metro is used in this chapter to refer to the Métropolitain as well as any part of the RER system within Paris proper.

A free metro map with a station index (known as the *Petit Plan de Paris*), is available at metro ticket windows. A less useful ADP version is available from airport information desks. Michelin's *Paris Plan 11* has an excellent coloured metro map at the back (the *Plan 10/12* map also has a coloured metro map).

The whole metro system, whose construction began at the turn of the century, has been designed so that no point in Paris is more than 500 metres from a metro stop. Some places in the city centre are within a few hundred metres of up to three stations. The station nearest each hotel, museum, etc mentioned in the text is listed immediately after the telephone number, but you may be able to reduce the number of transfers you'll have to make (and thus get there faster) by selecting a station slightly further from the beginning and/or end point of your journey.

For metro stations many Parisians try to avoid late at night, see Dangers & Annoyances under Information.

How it Works – Métropolitain Each Métropolitain train is known by the name of its end-of-the-line stop, which means that trains on the same line have different names depending on which direction they are travelling in. For instance, trains on the line that links Porte de Clignancourt with Porte d'Orléans are known as *direction* (towards) *Porte de Clignancourt* when heading that way and *direction Porte d'Orléans* when going in the opposite direction. In stations served by more than one line, blue-on-white *direction* signs show you how to get to the platform for trains going to the terminal station mentioned on the sign. On metro lines that split into several branches and thus have more than one end-of-the-line station, the final destination of each train is indicated on the front, sides and interior of the train cars, usually by illuminating a backlit panel.

Each line is also officially known by a number from one to 13, but the numbers' only function is to appear on signs – Parisians not only don't use them, they don't even know them. And don't remember metro lines by the colours in which they appear on your map: each official and privately printed

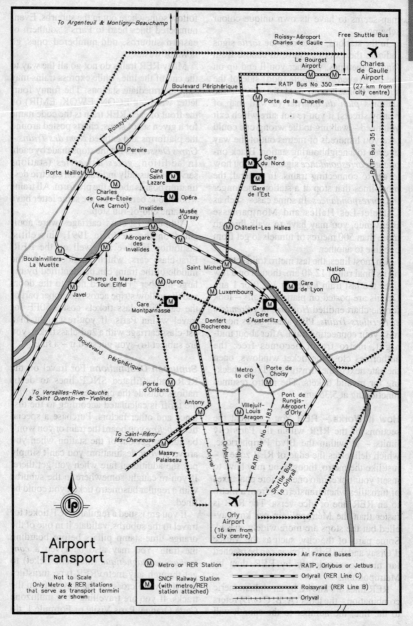

To Argenteuil & Montigny-Beauchamp

To Versailles-Rive Gauche & Saint Quentin-en-Yvelines

To Saint-Rémy-lès-Chevreuse

Roissy-Aéroport Charles de Gaulle

Free Shuttle Bus

Charles de Gaulle Airport (27 km from city centre)

Le Bourget Airport

RATP Bus No 350

Boulevard Périphérique

Porte de la Chapelle

RATP Bus 351

Roissybus

Pereire

Gare du Nord

Gare de l'Est

Porte Maillot

Charles de Gaulle-Étoile (Ave Carnot)

Gare Saint Lazare

Opéra

Invalides

Musée d'Orsay

Châtelet-Les Halles

Aérogare des Invalides

Boulainvilliers-La Muette

Champ de Mars-Tour Eiffel

Duroc

Saint Michel

Nation

Javel

Gare Montparnasse

Luxembourg

Gare de Lyon

Gare d'Austerlitz

Denfert Rochereau

Boulevard Périphérique

Metro to city

Porte de Choisy

Porte d'Orléans

Antony

Villejuif-Louis Aragon

Pont de Rungis-Aéroport d'Orly

RATP Bus No 183

Massy-Palaiseau

Orlyval

Orlybus

Jetbus

Shuttle Bus to Orlyrail

Orly Airport (16 km from city centre)

LP

Airport Transport

Not to Scale
Only Metro & RER stations that serve as transport termini are shown

M Metro or RER Station

■ SNCF Railway Station (with metro/RER station attached)

▶▶▶▶▶ Air France Buses
·········· RATP, Orlybus or Jetbus
–·–·–·– Orlyrail (RER Line C)
✗✗✗✗✗✗ Roissyrail (RER Line B)
┼┼┼┼┼┼ Orlyval

PARIS

map seems to have its own unique colour scheme.

In the stations, white-on-blue *sortie* signs indicate the exits you have to choose from (and, sometimes, whether you'll end up on the *pair* (even) or *impair* (odd) side of the street). Consult a map of the city or the station's *plan du quartier* (a wall map of nearby streets) if you're not sure which exit you need – walking to the wrong one could take you hundreds of metres out of the way or even to a neighbouring station. Black-on-orange *correspondance* signs show you how to get to connecting trains. In general, the more lines that stop at a station, the longer the *correspondances*. In some cases, such as Châtelet-Les Halles and Montparnasse Bienvenüe, you may have to walk through more than 500 metres of tunnels to get from one line to another.

On most lines, the last metro train sets out on its final run at 12.40 am, though on a few lines the last train leaves at 12.20 or 1 am. Details are posted on platform walls – look for the chart entitled *Horaires des Premiers et Derniers Trains*. Plan ahead so as not to miss your connecting train. After about midnight, metro travel becomes free: the authorities close the ticket windows, open the gate next to the turnstiles and stop checking for invalid tickets. The metro resumes functioning at 5.35 am.

How it Works – RER You can treat the sections of the RER within the Paris city limits – ie within the Blvd Péripherique, which delineates the edge of RER zone 1 – just like the metro, though you may have to insert your ticket into one or more phalanxes of turnstiles when transferring from a metro to an RER line or vice versa. The RER is faster than the Métropolitain per km travelled but the stops are more widely spaced. Some parts of the city, such as the Musée d'Orsay and the Eiffel Tower, can be reached far more conveniently by RER than by Métropolitain.

RER lines are known by an alphanumeric combination – the letter (A, B, C or D) refers to the line, the number to the spur it will follow somewhere out in the suburbs. Even-numbered lines head to Paris's southern or eastern suburbs, odd-numbered ones go north or west.

Many RER trains do not go all the way to the end of the line, while express trains may skip intermediate stations. The funny four-letter word (eg EGON, EWOK, EMIR) on the front of each RER train is the code name for a given set of stops; charts posted around the platforms and entitled *Nom des Trains – Gares Desservies* list the stops made by each. In addition, *gares desservies* (stations served) are usually indicated on electric destination boards above the platform. All trains whose code begins with the same letter have the same end-of-run stop.

Although 1st-class carriages were abolished on the metro in 1991, this elitist institution is alive and well on the RER. First-class cars, which are located in the middle of the train, can be identified by the large number '1' painted next to the doors and the yellow stripe across the upper part of the car. First-class tickets cost 9.50FF for travel within Paris. If you're caught in a 1st-class carriage with a 2nd-class ticket, you are subject to – you guessed it – a fine.

Suburban Destinations For travel on the RER and affiliated SNCF lines to destinations outside the city (ie in zones 2 to 8), the tariff is calculated according to the distance and other factors. Purchase a special ticket *before* you board the train or you won't be able to get out of the station when you arrive at your destination: you can't simply pay the additional fare when you get there. If you're caught somewhere in the suburbs with a regular bus/metro ticket, you could be fined.

If you are issued a regular SNCF ticket for travel to the suburbs, validate it in one of the orange time-stamp pillars before boarding the train. You may also be given a *contremarque magnétique* (magnetic ticket) to get through any metro/RER-type turnstiles you'll have to cross on the way to/from the tracks. If you are travelling on a multizone Carte Orange, Paris Visite or Formule 1, do

not punch the magnetic *coupon* in SNCF's orange time-stamp machines. By the way, some RER/SNCF tickets to Paris purchased in the suburbs allow you to transfer to the metro while others do not – if in doubt, ask the person selling you the ticket.

If you are trying to save every franc and have a Carte Orange, Paris Visite or Formule 1, you can get off at the last permitted station and purchase a ticket for just that segment of your journey not covered by your pass.

Unfortunately, buying tickets for suburban RER lines is a bit complicated because some are run by the RATP and others by the SNCF. You're best bet is to explain where you're going to the person at the ticket counter of the metro or RER station you're starting out from. For some destinations, you'll be able to buy a ticket on the spot. For others, however, you'll have to purchase a ticket at the station where you actually board the RER train to the suburbs.

Information For information on metros, RER trains and buses, call ☎ 43.46.14.14 between 6 am and 9 pm. By Minitel, key in 3615 RATP at any time of the day or night.

Information on SNCF's suburban services is available on ☎ 45.65.60.00. By Minitel, key in 3615 SNCF.

Bus/Metro Tickets The same 2nd-class tickets are valid on buses, trams, the Montmartre funiculaire, the metro and – for travel within the Paris city limits – the RER. They cost 6.50FF if bought individually and 39FF for a *carnet* of 10. Children under four travel free; tickets for children aged four to nine cost 18FF for a carnet of ten. Children over 10 pay full fare. Tickets are sold at every metro station, though not always at each and every entrance. Ticket prices usually go up on 1 August, when half the city is away on holiday.

Groups of 10 or more children under 16 and accompanied by an adult can get half-price tickets on the metro (but not the bus) – ask for a *demande de transport* form at any metro ticket counter.

One ticket lets you travel between any two metro stations no matter how many transfers are required. You can also use it on the RER commuter rail system for travel within Paris (that is, within zone 1). However, it cannot be used to transfer from the metro to a bus, from a bus to the metro or between buses. Always keep your ticket until you arrive at your destination and exit the station – if an RATP inspector catches you without a ticket, or with an invalid one, you may be assessed an on-the-spot fine.

Weekly & Monthly Tickets The cheapest way to avoid metro ticket queues and fumbling with piles of expensive single-ride tickets is to do as the Parisians do and get a Carte Orange, a bus/metro/RER pass whose accompanying *coupon* (magnetic ticket) comes in weekly and monthly versions. You can get tickets for travel in two to eight urban and suburban zones, but unless you'll be using the suburban commuter lines an awful lot, the basic ticket – valid for zones 1 and 2 – is probably enough.

The *coupon hébdomadaire* (weekly ticket), which costs 59FF for zones 1 and 2, is valid from Monday to Sunday. Even if you'll be in Paris for only three or four days, it may very well work out cheaper than purchasing single-ride tickets, and it will certainly cost less than buying three days' travel on a Formule 1 or Paris Visite tourist pass. The validity of the *coupon mensuel* (monthly ticket; 208FF for zones 1 and 2) begins on the first day of each calendar month. Both are on sale in metro & RER stations from 6.30 am to 10 pm and at certain bus terminals. Weekly *coupons* for the following week are available starting each Friday. The monthly ticket is on sale from the 20th of the month before it becomes valid.

To get a Carte Orange, bring a small photograph of yourself – available for 20FF (for four) from automatic photo booths emplaced in some metro stations – to any metro or RER ticket counter. Request a Carte Orange (which is free) and the kind of *coupon* you'd like. To prevent tickets from being used by more than one person, you

must write your surname and given name *(nom* and *prénom)* on the Carte Orange, and the number of your Carte Orange on each weekly or monthly *coupon* you buy (next to the words *Carte No)*. If you don't and the inspectors catch you, you're not much better off than a turnstile jumper. And each time you come to a battery of turnstiles, slip your magnetic ticket into the ticket slot – hopping over and then producing a valid Carte Orange ticket is unlikely to save you from a fine.

Tourist Passes The rather pricey Formule 1 and Paris Visite passes, intended for use by tourists, allow unlimited travel on the metro, the RER, buses, the Noctambus system, trams and the Montmartre funicular railway. Unlike the Carte Orange, they do not require a passport photo, though you should write your card number on the ticket.

The Formule 1 card and its attendant *coupon* allow unlimited travel for one day in two, three or four zones. The version valid for zones 1 and 2 costs 27FF. The four-zone version, which lets you go all the way out to Versailles and to Orly Airport (but not by Orlyval), costs 55FF. The Formule 1 Aéroports (80FF) will get you to Orly Airport (on Orlyrail or Orlybus), Charles de Gaulle Airport (on Roissyrail, Roissybus or RATP bus No 350 or 351), and EuroDisneyland. Formule 1 passes are on sale at all metro and RER ticket windows as well as SNCF stations in the Paris region.

Paris Visite passes are valid for three or five consecutive days of 1st-class travel in either three or four zones. The one-to-three zone version costs 90/145FF for three/five days. The one-to-five zone type, which is valid for travel to both airports (but not by Orlyval) as well as EuroDisneyland, costs 200/275FF for three/five days. Paris Visite is a lot more expensive than a weekly two-zone Carte Orange ticket and is a waste of money unless you'll be travelling a great deal on the RER's suburban lines. Paris Visite can be purchased at larger metro and RER stations and SNCF bureaux in Paris and at the airports.

Fines If you can't produce a valid ticket for the transit police inspectors (eg your weekly *coupon* doesn't have your Carte Orange number on it) or if you jump the turnstiles/exit barriers and are caught, you'll be assessed a hefty on-the-spot fine *(indemnité forfaitaire)*. They'll also check your identity documents and may have a glance at your visa...You might try speaking English and looking confused, but don't count on charming the inspectors out of doing their jobs.

Bus

Paris's extensive bus network tends to get overlooked by visitors, in part because the metro is so quick, efficient and easy to use. But if you can handle the bus map on RATP's *Grand Plan de Paris*, available free at many metro and RER stations, you may find that despite the traffic jams and fumes, travelling above ground in the sunlight is a welcome change from the lightless metro tunnels. Buses are also a good way to get to know the city – if you travel by metro, it's pretty hard to get a sense of what there is to see between where you get on and where you get off.

Unless you have a Carte Orange or one of the tourist passes, short bus rides within the city (ie rides in one or two bus zones) cost one bus/metro ticket; longer rides require two. Transfers to other buses or the metro are not allowed. Coloured strips along the edge of the route maps posted at bus stops indicate how far your *1er billet* (1st ticket) will get you and at what point you'll need a *2e billet* (2nd ticket). Travel to the suburbs costs two to six tickets, depending on the distance (for instance, the trip to either airport costs six tickets). Special tickets valid only on the bus can be purchased from the driver.

Whatever kind of single-journey ticket you have, you must cancel *(oblitérer)* it in the *composteur* (cancelling machine) next to the driver. People without tickets or whose tickets aren't cancelled are seldom caught, but when they are the on-the-spot fines are hefty. If you have a Carte Orange, Formule 1 or Paris Visite pass, just flash it at the driver when you board. Do *not* cancel your magnetic *coupon*.

When waiting at a bus stop, keep an eye out for the bus you want to take and signal the driver as it approaches. Some lines still employ buses with open-air sections in the back where you can get high on carbon monoxide and watch the city roll by without the sensory insulation imposed by smudged safety glass.

Buses with two-digit numbers remain within Paris proper, while those with three-digit numbers also serve suburban areas. Bus lines whose numbers are indicated at bus stops by white numerals on a black circle run daily except Sunday and holidays. Buses indicated by black numerals on a white circle operate every day. Hours of operation vary from line to line. At rush hours, buses on some lines cover only part of their usual route, an arrangement indicated by a slash through the number on the front of the bus. Some lines only run until 8.30 pm.

Noctambus After the metro shuts down at around 12.45 am, the Noctambus network, whose symbol is a black owl silhouetted against a yellow circle, links the Châtelet-Hôtel de Ville area (4e) with lots of places on the Right Bank (served by lines A to H) and a few destinations on the Left Bank (served by lines J and R).

Noctambus buses begin their runs 350 metres south of the Centre Pompidou from the even side of Ave Victoria (4e), between the Hôtel de Ville and Tour Saint Jacques; look for the little night owl symbol on the stops. All 10 lines depart every hour on the half-hour from 1.30 to 5.30 am; line R also leaves at 1, 2, 3, 4 and 5 am. You can get off at any point along the route (not just at the usual bus stops) – just signal to the driver.

If you don't have a Carte Orange or a Paris Visite or Formule 1 pass, a ride costs three bus/metro tickets or 16.50FF (four tickets or 22FF if your journey involves a transfer).

Tram
The Paris area's only tram line, which began operation in 1992, links the northern inner suburbs of Saint Denis and Bobigny.

Taxi
The drivers of Paris's 15,000 taxis have acquired a reputation for paying little heed to riders' convenience – or the official taxi regulations. People often report being refused a ride because the driver didn't feel like going to the destination they requested. Another common complaint: it can be difficult to find a taxi late at night (after 11 pm) or in the rain. Some run-ins with cabbies, though, are at least in part a result of visitors' unfamiliarity with Paris's arcane taxi regulations. A brief exploration of how the city's taxi system works may therefore save aggravation.

Fares Taxi fares are based on distance if you're travelling faster than 29 km/h and on how long it takes if you're going slower. The metre begins at 12FF; this is known as the *prise en charge*. Within the city (ie within the Blvd Périphérique), it costs 3.01FF per km for travel undertaken Monday to Saturday from 7 am to 7 pm, when tariff A is in force. At night and on Sundays and holidays, when tariff B applies, it's 4.68FF per km. It costs 120FF an hour to have a taxi sit and wait for you (or when the taxi is doing less than 29 km/h).

Tariff A may look a lot cheaper than tariff B, but because traffic is generally heavier during the day, the same trip might actually end up being cheaper at night. During the day, count on paying 40 to 50FF for a ride from Notre Dame to the Arc de Triomphe. A ride from Notre Dame to Sacré Cœur will set you back about 65 or 80FF.

For trips to the suburbs (including the airports), tariff B applies during the day (seven days a week) and tariff C (6.33FF per km) applies from 7 pm to 7 am.

By law, Paris taxis charge all sorts of peculiar surcharges: 5FF for picking you up at a train station, Aérogare des Invalides or the Avenue Carnot airport bus terminal; 5FF for a fourth adult passenger (though the driver has the right to refuse); 6FF for each piece of luggage over five kg; 3FF extra for an animal (but the driver can refuse to take people with pets). There is a full list of

surcharges on the side window behind the driver. The same sticker also lists the licence plate number of the taxi.

The driver is supposed to take the shortest route to your destination, but you can request that he or she take any route you choose. You can have people you know join you in the taxi or get out of it anywhere along your route for no extra charge. Passengers *always* ride in the back seat (unless there are four of you).

Tipping Tips are not obligatory, but no matter what the fare is, most Parisians tip from 2FF (the minimum) to 5FF.

Hailing a Taxi It is possible to try flagging down a taxi anywhere, but the easiest way to find one is to walk to the nearest *tête de station* (taxi stand), which you can find by consulting Michelin's 1:10,000 Paris map. It is uncool (but not uncommon) for people in a hurry to flag down a taxi half a block from a *tête de station* to avoid standing in the queue. One of the most difficult times of the week to find a taxi is between 1 and 2 am on a Saturday night, when many restaurants and bars close. When the metro (or part of it) is on strike, count on having a very hard time finding an unoccupied taxi.

You can tell if a taxi is free if the white 'Taxi Parisien' sign on the roof is illuminated *and* none of the three coloured tariff lights right under it is on. When one of the tariff lights is lit, it means the taxi either has a passenger inside or has been dispatched to pick someone up. The lights also tell anyone watching the taxi drive by what tariff is being used by the meter *(compteur)* inside the cab: the tariff A light is white; the tariff B light is orange; and the tariff C light is blue. When the Taxi Parisien sign is turned off or is covered, it means the cabbie is off duty.

By law, a taxi driver cannot refuse to take a passenger (including a handicapped person or a blind person with a guide dog) to anywhere in Paris or the three surrounding départements *except* during the last half-hour of their shift, when they are allowed to accept only fares to destinations near where

they live. You can tell what time a driver is supposed to end his or her shift by checking the white-on-black numerals in the box facing out the back window, which indicate the hour according to the 24-hour clock.

By Phone If you order a cab by telephone, the meter is switched on the moment the driver gets word of your call, wherever that may be (though it's rarely very far from where you're being picked up). The meter will keep running while the driver is waiting for you to say goodbye to your hosts or get your luggage ready. The point is, don't be surprised (or feel cheated) if the meter reads a bit more than 12FF when you start your journey.

Radio-dispatched taxi companies include:

Taxis Bleus	☎ 49.36.10.10
Artaxi	☎ 42.41.50.50
G7 Radio	☎ 47.39.47.39
Alpha Taxis	☎ 45.85.85.85
Taxis-Radio Étoile	☎ 42.70.41.41

Complaints At the end of your ride, you are legally entitled to receive a *bulletin de voiture* (receipt) that includes the taxi's *numéro d'immatriculation* (licence plate number). To register a complaint, send the taxi's licence plate number and the time and date you had a problem (or better yet, a copy of your receipt, which should have all this information) to: Service des Taxis, 36 Rue des Morillons, 75732 Paris CEDEX 15.

Car & Motorbike

Driving in Paris is nerve-wracking but not impossible by any means except for the insecure, fainthearted or indecisive. Most side streets are one way *(sens unique)*, and without a good map (such as Michelin's *Paris Plan* number 10, 11 or 12), trying to get around town by car will make you feel like a rat in a maze crowded with other rats. In general, the best way to get across the city is via one of the major boulevards, unless, of course, it's rush hour and traffic has come to a standstill. Then all you can do is find a parking place and take the metro, except that

if you're in one of the central arrondissements of the city it won't be easy to find a parking place – and even if you do, you'll have to come back within two hours to plug the parking meter...

The ultimate test of Parisian driving is the 10-lane roundabout that swirls around the Arc de Triomphe in utter anarchy, especially at rush hour. Don't forget to give priority to cars approaching from the right *(priorité à droite)*...And remember that the further in towards the Arc you go, the more difficult it will be to get back to the outer lanes again.

Except when it's clogged by rush hour traffic, the fastest way to get all the way across Paris is usually the Blvd Périphérique, the ring road (beltway) that encircles the city, following more or less the city walls built in the 1840s and rendered obsolete not long thereafter. The entrances/exits all have names beginning with the words 'Porte de' (Gate of).

Some of Paris's worst traffic jams take place at 1 am on a Saturday night.

Parking In many parts of Paris, almost all the legal parking places are marked *payant*, which means that: you have to pay 5 to 8FF an hour to park your car there; and you can't leave your car for more than a limited period of time, usually two hours.

Feed coins into the *horodateur* (parking ticket machine) according to how long you plan to park there, and place the time-stamped ticket on the passenger side of the dashboard where it's visible from the pavement. In most areas, parking is free on weekdays before 9 am and after 7 pm, on weekends and during August (the parking inspectors are on holiday, too). On streets with one-side-only parking, you can park on one side for the first two weeks of the month and on the other side from the 15th to the end of the month.

Large municipal parking garages, many of which are underground, usually charge about 10FF an hour or, for periods of 12 to 24 hours, 80FF (almost the same price as the cheapest parking ticket!). Many municipal parking garages close relatively early (11 pm) and some may not be open on Sunday.

It is forbidden to park caravans (campers) and mobile homes in certain parts of the city, and even where permitted, such vehicles cannot be left in the same place for more than 24 hours. For details, contact the police.

It is technically illegal to park a motorbike on the pavement, but it is generally tolerated on wide pavements so long at the bike doesn't get in the way of people walking by. When in doubt, look around to see if other people are doing it.

Rental The easiest (if not cheapest) way to turn a stay in Paris into an uninterrupted series of hassles is to take upon yourself responsibility for a rented car. If driving the car doesn't destroy your holiday-induced sense of carefree spontaneity, parking the damn thing (or trying to) just may.

But for travel outside of the city (day trips or excursions to Burgundy, the Loire Valley, etc), Paris is not a bad place to hire a car. Some of your options include the following.

Small, Inexpensive Companies ADA, one of France's cheapest car rental companies, has several offices in Paris. The bureau (☎ 45.72.36.36; metro Porte Maillot) at 271 Blvd Pereire (17e) is linked to Charles de Gaulle Airport by one of the Air France bus lines, which stops across the street at the Palais des Congrès at Place de la Porte Maillot. ADA's other offices are at 98 Rue du Général Leclerc (14e; ☎ 40.92.55.23; metro Alésia) and, near Gare Saint Lazare, at 74 Rue de Rome (8e; ☎ 42.93.65.13; metro Rome).

Acar (☎ 43.79.76.48; metro Porte de Vincennes) at 77 Rue de Lagny (20e) has Fiat Pandas with 100 free km for 218FF a day (with a 3500FF excess, or deductible) or 253FF a day (with a 500FF excess), including insurance. Weekly rates are 1523FF with 700 free km (including 35FF a day to reduce the excess to 500FF). Additional km cost 1.15FF each. Acar's office is open Monday to Saturday from 8 am to 7 pm. It's a good

idea to reserve in advance, especially for holiday weekends and during summer.

Rent A Car (☎ 43.45.98.99) has offices near the new American Center at 79 Rue de Bercy (12e; metro Bercy) and at 84 Ave de Versailles (16e; metro Mirabeau). Fiat Pandas with unlimited km cost 268FF a day (including insurance and a 69FF-a-day charge to bring the excess down to 1200FF). The weekly rate is 1495FF. The Rue de Bercy office is open Monday to Friday from 8 am to 7 pm and on Saturday from 9 am to 1 pm and 2 to 7 pm.

Large, Expensive Companies Avis (☎ 45. 50.32.31) has offices at all six train stations and a dozen other locations around Paris. Europcar (☎ 30.43.82.82) has about 20 bureaux around the city, including Aérogare des Invalides (7e; metro Invalides). Hertz (☎ 47.88.51.51) also has lots of offices around Paris, including one at Aérogare des Invalides (7e; metro Invalides). To reserve a Budget car, call their reservation centre (☎ 46.86.65.65).

Various major car rental companies (Avis, Citer, Hertz, Budget and Europcar) have offices at Orly Airport (in the Orly-Sud terminal next to Porte C) and Charles de Gaulle Airport (in Aérogare 1 on the Niveau Arrivée

and in Aérogare 2 in the Boutiquaire area). Several are open daily from 6 am to midnight. Higher rates may apply for airport rental, and you may have to return the car to the airport.

For information on purchase/repurchase plans, see the Car and Motorbike sections in the Getting Around chapter.

Bicycle

Paris, with its heavy traffic and impatient drivers, is not particularly well suited to cycling. However, you can cycle in the parks, such as the Bois de Boulogne (16e) and the Bois de Vincennes (12e). You can also ride along the Canal Saint Martin (10e & 19e) and then along the south bank of the Canal de l'Ourcq (19e), which continues for over 60 km westward to La Ferté-Milon. Note that bicycles left locked up outside overnight may have parts stolen.

For information on bicycle tours, see the Organised Tours section of this chapter.

Rental Remarkably few places in Paris rent bicycles. Mountain Bike Trip (see Organised Tours) charges 90FF a day for mountain bikes. For details on bike rental in the Bois de Boulogne, see Activities under Bois de Boulogne.

At a number of RER/SNCF stations in the Paris region, including those at Fontainebleau-Avon and the Forêt de Rambouillet (☎ 30.41.84.32), you can rent bikes on weekends during the warm months (daily in July and August at Fontainbleau-Avon). Three-speeds/mountain bikes cost 100/150FF a day. For more information, pick up a brochure at an SNCF information office or try calling Bicyclub on ☎ 47.66.55.92.

Train Travel with Bikes It is relatively easy to take your bicycle out to the Paris suburbs and beyond, where parks, forests, chateaux and untrafficked backroads beckon. Bikes can be carried along for no charge in the *fourgons* (baggage cars) or *compartiment fourgons* (baggage compartments) of most SNCF trains (except RER line A) serving the Paris region. This service is available daily except during weekday rush hours (6.30 to 9.30 am and 4.30 to 7 pm). For details, enquire at an SNCF information office.

River Taxi
For information on touring the city centre by boat, see the Organised Tours section.

Day Trips from Paris

The region surrounding Paris is known as the Île de France (Island of France) because of its position between four rivers: the Aube, the Marne, the Oise and the Seine. It was from this relatively small area that, starting around 1100, the kingdom of France began to expand.

Today, the region's exceptional sights, including Saint Denis, Versailles, Fontainebleau and Chartres, and its excellent rail and road links with the French capital make it an especially popular day-trip destination for Parisians and Paris-based visitors alike. The many woodland areas around the city, which include the Forêt de Fontainebleau, the Forêt de Chantilly and the Forêt de Compiègne, offer opportunities for outdoor activities such as rambling, cycling, horse riding and – at Fontainebleau – rock climbing. The GR1 is only one of several GR trails that pass through the forest areas of the Île de France.

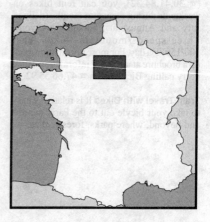

INFORMATION

> **Weekly Closures**
> **Sunday morning:** Basilique de Saint Denis, the Clocher Neuf and the Trésor at Cathédrale de Chartres
> **All day Sunday:** shops in Les Quatre Temps at La Défense
> **Monday:** Musée de l'Air et de l'Espace, Château de Versailles, Musée Lambinet at Versailles
> **Tuesday:** Château de Fontainebleau, Château de Chantilly, Musée Vivant du Cheval at Chantilly, Château de Compiègne, Clairière de l'Armistice (near Compiègne)

Telephone

All phone numbers in this chapter *except* those in Chantilly, Chartres and Compiègne are in the Paris dialling area. To call Chartres, Chantilly or Compiègne from Paris, dial 16 and wait for the tone before dialling the eight-digit local number. To call Paris from these towns, dial 16, wait for the tone, and then dial 1 followed by the eight-digit number.

For more information on how to use the French telephone system, see Telecommunications in the Facts for the Visitor chapter.

Books

Michelin's green guide *Île de France – The Region around Paris* has lots of historical and architectural information.

GETTING THERE & AWAY

From Paris, all of the places covered in this chapter can be reached by RER or SNCF train in an hour or less. For details, see Getting There & Away under each listing.

You can call the SNCF on ☎ 45.65.60.00 and the RATP on ☎ 43.46.14.14. By Minitel, key in 3615 code RATP.

GETTING AROUND

Bicycles can be brought along on many (but not all) suburban trains on weekends, holidays, and, except during rush hour (6.30 to 9.30 am and 4.30 to 7 pm), on Wednesday. Contact the RATP or SNCF (see the preceding paragraph) for details.

AROUND PARIS

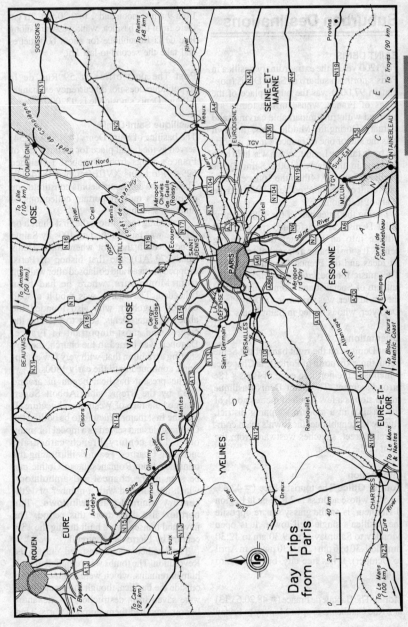

Day Trips
from Paris

0   20   40 km

Suburban Destinations

SAINT DENIS

For 1200 years, the extraordinary basilica in Paris's northern suburb of Saint Denis (population 97,000) was the burial place of the kings of France, whose ornate tombs are adorned with truly remarkable carvings and statuary. During the Middle Ages, the town was the site of one of France's most important trade fair, the Lendit, which was held here starting in the early 1100s. Saint Denis declined from the 14th to the 16th centuries as a result of the Hundred Years' War and the Wars of Religion.

During the latter half of the 19th century, Saint Denis was transformed from a small village into an important manufacturing centre. It soon became a stronghold of socialist ideas and the French Communist party. The music for the *Internationale*, once the anthem of Socialist and Communist parties the world over, was written in 1888 by Pierre Degeyter, who is buried in Saint Denis.

Orientation

Saint Denis is on the right bank of the Seine about three km north of Porte de la Chapelle, which is at the northern edge of Paris's 18e arrondissement. The Saint Denis-Basilique metro stop is a few hundred metres north of the basilica in a modern shopping district. Rue de la République, the town's main commercial street, stretches westward from the front of the basilica.

Information

Tourist Office The tourist office (☎ 42.43. 33.55), whose address is 2 Rue de la Légion d'Honneur, is on the grassy square opposite the basilica's single bell tower. It is open Monday to Saturday from 9.30 am to 12.30 pm and 1.30 to 6 pm (2 to 6.30 pm from April to October). It has free city, bus and metro maps.

Money The Banque de France (☎ 48.20.63.13) at 2 Rue Catulienne is open Monday to Friday

from 9 am to noon and 1 to 3.30 pm. To get there from the basilica, walk westward along Rue de la République for about 600 metres and take the second-to-last left.

Post The post office at 59 Rue de la République does not do currency exchange.

Saint Denis's postcode is 93200.

Basilique Saint Denis

The basilica of Saint Denis (☎ 48.09.83.54) served as the burial place for all but a few of France's kings from Dagobert I (reigned 629-39) to Louis XVIII (reigned 1814-24). Their tombs and mausoleums constitute one of Europe's most important collections of funerary sculpture.

According to tradition, the first church on this site was built in the late 400s by Sainte Geneviève on the spot where Saint Denis (died 273 AD), the first bishop of Paris, dropped his head and collapsed after walking from Montmartre, where he had been beheaded. The church was rebuilt around 630 by Dagobert, who also founded the abbey of Saint Denis, soon to become the richest and most important in France. Dagobert was buried in the church, thereby starting a tradition that, with very few exceptions, continued until the early 1800s.

The present basilica, begun in around 1135 by the irrepressible Abbott Suger, changed the face of Western architecture. It was the first major structure to be built in the Gothic style, and served as a model for many other 12th-century French cathedrals, including Chartres. Features illustrating the transition from Romanesque to Gothic can be seen in the **chancel** and **ambulatory**, which are adorned with a number of 12th-century **stained-glass windows**. The **narthex** also dates from this period. The nave and transept were built during the 13th century by Pierre de Montreuil.

The basilica was devastated during the Revolution. The tombs were emptied of their human remains, which were dumped in pits outside the basilica, though the mausoleums were saved from destruction by Alexandre Lenoir, who had them stored in Paris. They

were brought back in 1816; the royal bones were reburied in the crypt a year later. Restoration of the structure was begun under Napoleon, but most of the work was done by Viollet-le-Duc from 1858 until his death in 1879. Saint Denis has been a cathedral since 1966.

The basilica is open from 10 am to 5 pm (7 pm from April to September). The ticket counters close 30 minutes earlier. You can visit the nave for no charge, but to get to the interesting bits in the transept and chancel you have to pay 26FF (17FF for people aged 18 to 25 or over 60, 6FF for children aged 7 to 17).

Tombs The 800 people buried at Saint Denis include France's kings and queens, their children and close relatives, and a few outstanding servants of the throne. In many cases, the monarchs' bodies were buried here without their hearts and entrails, which were interred at other locations.

The tombs – all of which are now empty – are decorated with life-size figures of the deceased. Those built before the Renaissance are adorned with *gisants* (recumbent figures), which were carved after 1285 from death masks and are thus fairly realistic. Louis IX (Saint Louis; 1214-70) decided that all his royal predecessors should have elaborate tombs of their own, so though he had little idea what they looked like, he commissioned recumbent figures for each of them. The oldest tombs are those of Clovis I (died 511) and his son Childebert I (died 558), brought to Saint Denis during the early 19th century.

During the Renaissance, the tombs became elaborate, two-storey affairs: on top, the king and queen are shown kneeling piously, dressed in their finest clothes, while below, they appear as naked, emaciated corpses. The finest Renaissance tombs include those of **Louis XII** (1462-1515) and **Anne of Brittany** (1476-1514); **François I** (1494-1547) and **Claude de France** (1499-1524), whose mausoleum is in the form of a Roman triumphal arch; and **Henri II** (1519-59) and **Catherine de Médicis** (1519-89).

Archaeological excavations in the 12th-century **crypt** have uncovered extensive tombs from the Merovingian era (5th and 6th centuries) and the Carolingian period (late 8th century). The oldest of the tombs dates from around 570 AD.

Sarcophagus, Basilique St Denis

Guided Tours The best way to get a sense of the historical, cultural and artistic importance of the tombs (and the people they were built to honour) is to pick up a *casque audioguide*, a headset that picks up infrared signals in French, English or German, at the ticket booth. They are available for no extra charge. Count on the full tour taking about 1¼ hours.

Musée d'Art et d'Histoire

Saint Denis's excellent Museum of Art & History (☎ 42.43.05.10) at 22bis Rue Gabriel Péri occupies a restored Carmelite convent founded in 1625 and later presided over by Louise de France, the youngest daughter of Louis XV. It was abandoned in 1792. Displays include reconstructions of the Carmelites' cells, an 18th-century **Apothicairerie** (apothecary's shop) and, in the archaeology section, items found during excavations around Saint Denis, including a 12th-century backgammon game, a knitted cap from the 14th century and the remains of an early 16th-century button and bead-making factory. There's also a section of modern art. The walls are decorated with 174 pious sayings, just as they were in the 1700s.

On the 2nd floor, there's an extensive col-

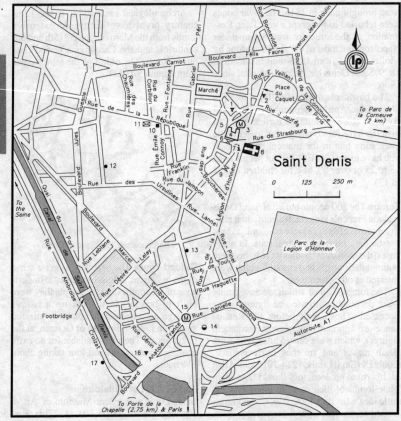

Saint Denis

0   125   250 m

lection of politically charged posters, cartoons, lithographs and paintings from the 1871 **Paris Commune**. The items were amassed beginning in the 1930s by the Communist-led local government, whose members – like Marx – saw the Commune as a workers' revolution. By the way, the words of the *Internationale* were written during the last week of the Commune by Eugène Pottier.

The Musée d'Art et d'Histoire is open daily except Tuesday and holidays; hours are 10 am to 5.30 pm (2 to 6.30 pm on Sunday). Entry costs 15FF (10FF for students, teach-

ers and people over 60, free for children under 16).

Musée Christofle

Christofle, the world-famous gold and silverware company that pioneered electroplating, has a museum (☎ 49.22.40.00) a bit over one km south of the basilica at 112 Rue Ambroise Croizat. Housed on the premises of their factory, whose plant-covered brick buildings date from 1878, it displays works in gold and silver in the styles of various periods. The pre-18th-century pieces are reproductions, many of them made during

■ PLACES TO STAY		OTHER		ⓜ METRO STATIONS
10	Hôtel de la Poste	4	Hôtel de Ville	3 Saint Denis-Basilique
		7	Tourist Office	15 Porte de Paris
▼ PLACES TO EAT		8	Basilique Saint Denis	
		11	Post Office	✕ SQUARES
1	Paul Boulangerie et	12	Banque de France	
	Pâtisserie	13	Musée d'Art et	5 Place Jean Jaurès
2	Carrefour supermarket		d'Histoire	6 Place Victor Hugo
16	Supermarché Casino	14	Bus Depot	9 Place de la Légion
		17	Musée Christofle	d'Honneur

the late 1800s, when the company did a roaring trade with Napoleon III. The museum is open Monday to Friday from 8.30 am to 1 pm and 2 to 5 pm. Entry is free. Christofle's products are not on sale here.

Parc de la Corneuve

This 4.4-sq-km park, whose green expanses surround a lake on which you can rent boats, is about two km east of the basilica out on Rue de Strasbourg and its continuation, Ave Romain Rolland. Facilities include bike paths and children's playgrounds.

Festivals

Saint Denis's summer classical music festival, the Festival de Saint Denis (☎ 42.43. 77.72), takes place each year during June and early July. Concerts are held in the basilica and other venues around town. Tickets are available in Paris from FNAC and Virgin Megastore.

Places to Stay

The one-star *Hôtel de la Poste* (☎ 48.20. 04.69) at 21 Rue Émile Connoy (next to 51 Rue de la République) has simple but serviceable singles/doubles with washbasin for 130/150FF. Doubles with shower and toilet are 180FF. The hall shower is 20FF. This place is closed in August but usually has room during periods when the bottom-end hotels in Paris are full up (eg in July and around Christmas). If the hotel looks closed, go to the Café Ginestet, the bar at 55 Rue de la République.

Places to Eat

Restaurants There are a number of restaurants in the modern shopping area around the metro stop.

Self-Catering There's a *food market* on Tuesday, Friday and Sunday from 7 am to 1 pm at Place Jean Jaurès.

The *Carrefour supermarket* at 4 Place du Caquet, two blocks to the right as you exit the metro station, is open Monday to Saturday from 8.30 am to 9 pm (10 pm on Friday). *Paul Boulangerie et Pâtisserie* at 3 Rue Jean Jaurès is open Monday to Saturday from 5 am to 8 pm (7.30 pm on Saturday).

Towards the Musée Christofle, the giant *Supermarché Casino* on Blvd Anatole France near Canal de Saint Denis is open Monday to Saturday from 9 am to 9 pm. It has an in-house boulangerie.

Getting There & Away

Metro From the Saint Lazare, Champs Élysées-Clemenceau, Invalides, Montparnasse Bienvenüe and other Paris metro stations on line No 13, take a train to the end-of-the-line station, Saint Denis-Basilique. Make sure you get on one going to Saint Denis, *not* Asnières-Gennevilliers – check the sign on the front of the train or the backlit panels on the outside and inside of each car. Saint Denis signs are blue rather than yellow.

The trip takes 20 minutes from Champs Élysées-Clemenceau and costs one regular metro ticket. You can also use the cheapest

kind of Carte Orange coupon, valid for zones 1 and 2. To get to the basilica from the metro station, follow the white-on-brown signs to the 'Basilique'.

Bus Various buses link Saint Denis with other Parisian suburbs. For details, pick up a *Grand Plan Nord Parisien* at a metro ticket window.

LA DÉFENSE

La Défense, Paris's skyscraper district, is three km west of the 17e arrondissement. Set on the sloping west bank of the Seine, its ultramodern architecture and 40-storey office buildings are radically different from centuries-old Paris – but no less French. This mini-Manhattan is well worth a visit if you think you'll enjoy strolling around vast public spaces adorned with giant works of contemporary art and lined with towering buildings, among them some superb examples of modern architecture at its best.

La Défense, one of the world's most ambitious urban construction projects, was begun in the late 1950s. Its first major structure was the Centre des Nouvelles Industries et Technologies (Centre for New Industries & Technologies), better known as **CNIT**, inaugurated in 1958 and renovated in 1989. During the mid-1970s, when skyscrapers fell out of favour, office space in La Défense became hard to sell or lease: whole buildings stood empty and the entire project appeared in jeopardy. But things picked up in the 1980s, and today, La Défense's has about 50 buildings, the highest of which is the 45-storey, 178-metre **Fiat tower**. Over 100,000 people work at La Défense for some 900 companies, including many of Europe's largest industrial concerns. Most of the district's 35,000 residents live in high-rise apartment blocks.

La Défense was built under the direction of EPAD, the Établissement Public pour l'Aménagement de La Défense (Public Establishment for the Development of La Défense). Its acronym makes frequent, Big Brotherish appearances on brochures and signs proclaiming EPAD's wondrous deeds.

Orientation

The La Défense-Grande Arche metro/RER station is underneath the huge Les Quatre Temps shopping mall.

If you stand on the steps of the Grande Arche, the world's largest hollow cube, and face eastward towards Paris, Les Quatre Temps shopping mall is to your right; the CNIT complex, a triangular building whose arched, concrete roof is supported at only three points, is to your left; and Ya'akov Agam's colourful tile fountain – a convenient landmark – is 400 metres straight ahead across the Parvis (square), a multilevel pedestrian mall. The 700-metre-long, sloping Esplanade du Général de Gaulle links the fountain with the Seine.

La Défense is divided into 11 semi-randomly numbered *quartiers* (quarters).

Information

Tourist Office Info Défense (☎ 47.74. 84.24), which is in front of the CNIT building, is open daily from 10 am to 7 pm. The free, easy-to-use colour maps of La Défense (English version available) come with information on some of the more noteworthy skyscrapers. Details on cultural activities are also available.

Post There are post offices in Les Quatre Temps and the CNIT building.

La Défense's postcode is 92400 Courbevoie.

Grande Arche

The remarkable Grande Arche (☎ 49.07. 27.57), designed by Danish architect Otto von Spreckelsen, is a hollowed-out cube of glass and white marble over 100 metres to a side. It represents a window open to the world.

Inaugurated on 14 July 1989, the Grande Arche forms the western terminus of the eight-km-long **Grande Axe** (great axis), which stretches from the Louvre pyramid through the Jardin des Tuileries and along the Champs-Élysées to the Arc de Triomphe, Porte Maillot and finally the Esplanade of La

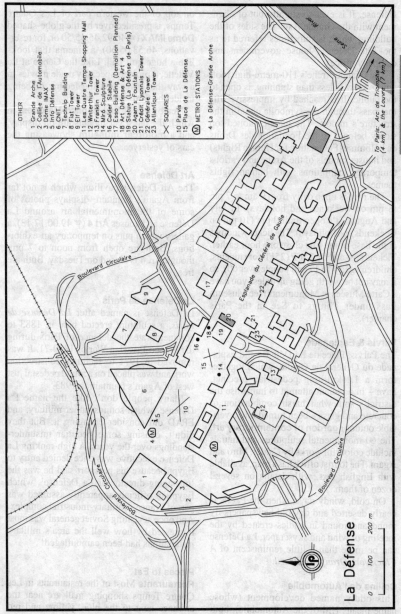

OTHER

1 Grande Arche
2 Colline de l'Automobile
3 Dôme IMAX
5 Info Défense
6 CNIT
7 Tête Défense Building
8 Fiat Tower
9 Elf Tower
11 Les Quatre Temps Shopping Mall
12 Winterthur Tower
13 Franklin Tower
14 Miró Sculpture
16 Calder Stabile
17 Esso Building (Demolition Planned)
18 Art Défense & Art 4
19 Statue (La Défense de Paris)
20 Agam's Fountain
21 Crédit Lyonnais Tower
22 Générale Tower
23 Atlantique Tower

SQUARES

10 Parvis
15 Place de la Défense

Ⓜ METRO STATIONS

4 La Défense–Grande Arche

To Paris: Arc de Triomphe
(4 km) & the Louvre (7 km)

Boulevard Circulaire

Esplanade du Général de Gaulle

Boulevard Circulaire

0   100   200 m

La Défense

LP

Défense. It is ever-so-slightly out of alignment with the Grande Axe. The sides of the building, which is sometimes referred to as the Tête Défense, house government and company offices.

The Grande Arche's 110-metre-high roof, whose view is less than stunning, is open to the public. It is reached by impressive lifts that pass through the symbolic cloud in the structure's middle. The underexploited top storey belongs to the Fondation des Droits de l'Homme (Foundation for Human Rights) and houses models of the Arche and various temporary exhibitions with human rights themes.

The roof is open daily from 9 am to 7 pm (8 pm on weekends and holidays). In July and August, it's open until 9 pm (10 pm on weekends and holidays). The ticket windows at the base of the lifts close one hour earlier. Tickets cost a hefty 35FF (25FF for students, children aged 4 to 17 and people over 60), so it may not be worth going up unless you have a Carte Musées et Monuments (see Museum Pass under Things to See in the Paris chapter).

Parvis & Esplanade

The Parvis, Place de La Défense and Esplanade du Général de Gaulle, which together form a 1.1-km-long pedestrian precinct, have – in a valiant attempt to humanise the district's somewhat harsh combination of concrete and glass – been turned into a veritable outdoor **garden of contemporary art**. The 60 monumental sculptures and murals include colourful works by Calder, Miró and Agam. The tourist office has a map, available with English text, with details on several dozen of them.

On cold, windy days, when the Parvis is nearly deserted and day-old newspapers fly round and round in eddies created by the meeting of wind and skyscraper, La Défense can be more than a little reminiscent of *A Clockwork Orange* or *Brazil*.

Colline de l'Automobile

This oddly named development (whose name means Hill of the Automobile), built on top of the western part of Les Quatre Temps, is presided over by the globe-shaped **Dôme IMAX** (☎ 46.92.45.45/50 or, for reservations, 46.53.05.60), a cinema that looks like a huge golf ball. Like the Géode at La Villette, it projects specially made movies in a way that gives you the feeling of being inside the film.

Nearby you'll find **Espace Marques**, in which the latest car models are on display, and a **motorcar museum** showcasing the cars of yesteryear.

Art Défense

The Art Défense pavilion, which is not far from Agam's fountain, displays photos of some of the monumental art around La Défense and houses **Art 4** (☎ 49.00.17.13), a gallery which puts on temporary art exhibitions. Both are open from noon to 7 pm, though Art 4 is closed on Tuesday. Both are free.

La Défense de Paris

La Défense is named after *La Défense de Paris*, a sculpture erected here in 1883 to commemorate the defence of Paris during the Franco-Prussian War of 1870-71. It was removed in 1971 to facilitate construction work and was placed on a round pedestal just west of Agam's fountain in 1983.

Many people don't like the name La Défense, which sounds rather military, and EPAD did consider changing it. But they didn't, causing some peculiar misunderstandings over the years. A high-ranking La Défense executive was once denied entry to Egypt because his passport said he was the 'managing director of La Défense', which Egyptian officials apparently assumed was part of France's military-industrial complex. And once, a visiting Soviet general was most impressed by how well the area's military installations had been camouflaged!

Places to Eat

Restaurants Most of the restaurants in Les Quatre Temps shopping mall are near the entrance next to the blue, yellow and red

blob-like statue by Miró. *La Pizza* is on Niveau 2 (level 2) at Place de la Patinoire.

Inside CNIT, cheap meals can be had at *Pomme de Pain* (☎ 46.92.11.62), a sandwich shop, and *Suculus* (☎ 46.92.12.16). Both are open Monday to Saturday from 10.30 or 11 am to 7 pm.

Self-Catering On Niveau 1 (level 1) of Les Quatre Temps, the 32-cash-register *Auchan Hypermarché* is open from 9 am (8.30 am on Saturday, 9.45 am on Monday) to 9.45 pm daily except Sunday and holidays.

Things to Buy
The three-storey Les Quatre Temps (Les 4 Temps), one of Europe's largest shopping malls, opened in 1981. The 250 shops, 140 of which sell clothing, have a reputation for reasonable prices. Most are open Monday to Saturday from 10 am to 7.30 or 8 pm.

There's a FNAC store with a ticket outlet in the CNIT complex.

Getting There & Away
Under the Parvis and the Esplanade, a tangle of roads, highways, train lines, bus stops, parking lots and pedestrian passages allow easy access to La Défense.

Train The SNCF has an information and reservation office underneath Les Quatre Temps. It is diagonally across the hall from the entrance to the La Défense-Grande Arche metro station and is open from 7.30 am to 8 pm daily except Sunday and holidays.

Metro The La Défense-Grande Arche metro station, also known as Grande Arche de la Défense, is the western terminus of metro line No 1, whose other end-of-the-line station is Château de Vincennes. The ride from the Louvre takes about 15 minutes.

MUSÉE DE L'AIR ET DE L'ESPACE
The Aeronautics & Space Museum (☎ 49. 92.71.71) in Paris's northern suburb of Le Bourget has over 100 aircraft, dozens of rockets and spacecraft and other displays charting the history of flight and space ex-

ploration. It is open from 10 am to 5 pm (6 pm from May to October). Entry costs 25FF (20FF for children under 16 and students).

Nearby Le Bourget Airport, which is used mostly by private aircraft, hosts the famous Paris Air Show in June of odd-numbered years.

Getting There & Away
The museum is served by RATP bus No 350, which you can pick up near Gare du Nord (metro Gare du Nord) on Rue du Faubourg Saint Denis (to the left as you walk out the station's main façade) and next to Gare de l'Est (metro Gare de l'Est) on Rue du 8 Mai 1945. You can also catch bus No 152 at Porte de la Villette (19e; metro Porte de la Villette).

EURODISNEY
It took US$4.4 billion and five years of work to turn the beet fields 32 km east of Paris – chosen from among 200 prospective sites – into EuroDisney Resort, which opened in April 1992 amidst much fanfare. Although Disney stockholders have been less than thrilled with the bottom line so far, the many visitors – mostly families with young children – seem to be having a great time exploring the gleaming new facilities and carefully tended gardens.

Unsurprisingly, EuroDisney opened amidst much moaning from France's intellectuals, who expended countless hours of mental effort tying to outdo each other's denunciations of Disney's 'cultural colonialism'. One overwrought critic called the park 'a construction of hardened chewing gum and idiotic folklore taken straight out of comic books written for obese Americans', while another went so far as to declare it 'a cultural Chernobyl'.

Disney's front-line PR staff responded by emphasising that EuroDisney was bringing native European fairy tales – Snow White, Sleeping Beauty, Peter Pan, Pinocchio, etc – back to their home continent. They also let it be known that not only did Walt Disney serve in France as an ambulance driver for the American Red Cross during WW I, but his name can be traced back to the Norman port

of Isigny-sur-Mer, whence his d'Isigny ancestors set forth in 1066 to participate in the Norman invasion of England. Meanwhile, some French intellectuals mused that if Mickey Mouse posed such a grave threat to French civilisation, France must be in a pretty sorry state.

But while Disney's PR whiz-kids seem to have proven to be the equals of the Left Bank intellectuals, they have been unable to fill EuroDisney's six huge hotels or sell enough souvenirs and food to turn a profit (ticket sales account for only a small part of the complex's projected revenues). Analysts disagree on the source of the malaise, but aside from citing Europeans' leisure habits – which are apparently very different from those of the visitors to the Disney theme parks in California, Florida and Japan – they generally agree that part of the problem seems to be meteorological: for about half the year, Paris – like the rest of northern Europe – is pretty chilly, and architectural compensations such as heated walkways can only accomplish so much. But at least one sore point has finally been cleared up: after initially refusing to sell alcohol inside the theme park, Disney's wholesome executives finally relented in August 1993.

EuroDisney has a staff of about 12,000, which goes up to 17,000 or 18,000 during summer. Officially known as 'cast members', they have been selected and trained to be unfailingly cheery and helpful. This has been achieved in part by some Brave New World-style regulations, attacked as repressive by French labour unions: not only are visible tattoos, beards, moustaches, long fingernails and oversized earrings forbidden, but cast members – who cannot be fat – are specifically required to wear both deodorant and 'appropriate undergarments'! More importantly, they all must speak English.

In winter EuroDisneyland is open daily from 10 am to 6 pm (9 pm on Saturday night). In summer it's open daily from 9 am to 11 pm.

Orientation

EuroDisney Resort occupies 19.43 sq km, an area one-fifth the size of Paris. It presently consists of lots of open fields and four built-up areas. **EuroDisneyland**, the 55-hectare theme park, is 250 metres north-west of the Marne-la-Vallée-Chessy train station. Tickets are sold under the pink, Victorian-style Hôtel Disneyland. The **Resort Complex**, which begins just south of the train station, includes the 18,000-sq-metre Festival Disney entertainment centre, five hotels and Lac Buena Vista, an arm of which is known as the Rio Grande. The **golf course** is three km south-east of EuroDisneyland. The entrance to **Camp Davey Crockett**, the forested camping ground, is seven km south-west of EuroDisneyland.

A second theme park, **Disney MGM Studios-Europe**, was supposed to be added by 1995, but EuroDisney's present financial woes make it unlikely that the company will be spending an additional US$3 billion anytime soon.

Information

Disney Information The park is totally bilingual and all signs are written in both French and English. Maps are provided at the entrance.

Details about entertainment, special events and facilities for disabled visitors are available from a number of information booths scattered around EuroDisneyland, including one in City Hall, which is on Town Square right inside the entrance. You can also call Guest Relations on ☎ 64.74.30.00.

If you'd like information about Euro-Disney before you arrive, call ☎ 49.41.49.10 or, in the UK, 071-753-2900. Both numbers are staffed by English-speaking personnel.

Regional Tourist Office In Festival Disney, the high-tech Maison du Tourisme (☎ 60.43. 33.33), run in part by the Conseil Régional de l'Île de France, has information (including lots of brochures) on the eight departments that make up the Île de France. It is open daily from 10 am until sometime in the evening (midnight from May to early September). For a small fee, the staff will help with hotel reservations.

Believe it or not, you can actually take a tour of the tourist office! The free commentary, provided by infrared headsets, will introduce you to the delights of the Île de France region.

Money At the park's main entrance, the bureau de change on the ground floor of the Hôtel Disneyland stays open until one hour before the park closes. Inside the park, you can change money at a number of information booths. BNP has two ATM machines along Main Street. Most shops and restaurants accept major credit cards, French franc travellers' cheques and eurocheques.

In Festival Disney, the post office can change foreign cash, eurocheques and travellers' cheques (American Express in US dollars and French francs and Visa in French francs) whenever it's open. If you have a MasterCard or Visa credit card, it can also give cash advances, furnishing your money in the form of American Express travellers' cheques if you so desire.

People staying at any of the EuroDisney hotels can change money at the front desk.

Post The post office in Festival Disney is open seven days a week from 11 am to 1.30 pm and 3 to 7 pm. Summer hours are longer. The philatelic desk sells stamps and related items from France, Andorra, Monaco and French overseas territories such as Saint Pierre et Miquelon.

Stamps for domestic and international postage can be purchased at some of the Eurodisneyland shops that sell postcards. Letter boxes are scattered around the park.

EuroDisney's postcode is 77705 Marne-la-Vallée.

Guidebooks & Maps All guests are presented with a Guest Guide, which details what there is to see and do, and a Programme des Spectacles/Entertainment Program listing the week's shows, parades, etc.

Not only has Hachette published a EuroDisney guide (60FF), but Michelin has issued a special green guide (55FF) that includes a Who's Who of Disney characters.

The latter work also has information on selected sights in Paris and the Île de France.

Michelin's *plan-guide* (map) of the park costs 20FF.

Left-Luggage EuroDisneyland's Consigne/ Guest Storage is right next to the entrance gate in a building called Relations Visiteurs/ Guest Relations. It is open daily from 9 am to 7 pm (9 pm on weekends). A compartment large enough for a suitcase or several day packs costs 10FF.

There are small, coin-operated storage lockers (10FF) underneath Main Street Station, which is just inside the park entrance.

Lost & Found Lost items can be reported or claimed at City Hall (☎ 64.74.25.00).

Stroller & Wheelchair Rental Strollers (pushchairs) and wheelchairs can be rented for 30FF a day (plus a 20FF deposit) at Town Square, which is just inside the main entrance.

Lost Children Lost children are taken to the Baby Care Centre, which is on the Main Street side of the Central Plaza near Victoria's Home-Style Cooking.

Babies Babies can be changed or nursed and their bottles warmed at the Baby Care Centre, which is on the Central Plaza near Victoria's Home-Style Cooking. Many rest rooms also have baby change tables.

Babysitting is not available.

Pets Dogs and cats (except seeing-eye dogs) are not allowed into EuroDisneyland, but there's a *chenil* (kennel) – officially known as the Accueil Animaux/Animal Care Centre – between the visitors' parking lot and the train station. Generally, only dogs and cats are accepted, so leave your iguana at home. The cost is 45FF per animal a day. People staying in the hotels, Camp Davey Crockett or camper vans parked in the parking lot can board their pets all day long and until noon the next day for 65FF. The animals, which

stay in spacious, stainless-steel cages, are fed with products made by Friskies, the kennel's 'partner' (ie corporate sponsor).

Medical Services The first-aid station (☎ 64.74.23.00) is on the Central Plaza next to Plaza Gardens Restaurant.

Laundry There's a laundrette at the Hôtel Cheyenne and two more at Camp Davey Crockett, one at the camping ground and the other at the bungalows.

EuroDisneyland

EuroDisneyland, isolated from the outside world by a clever layout and grassy embankments, is divided into five *pays* (lands). **Main Street, USA**, just inside the main entrance, is a spotless avenue reminiscent of a small American town, circa 1900. The adjacent **Frontierland** is a re-creation of the 'rugged, untamed American West'. **Adventureland**, intended to evoke the Arabian Nights and the wilds of Africa, is home to that old Disneyland favourite, Pirates of the Caribbean. **Fantasyland** brings fairy-tale characters such as Sleeping Beauty, Snow White and Pinocchio to life. And in **Discoveryland**, the high-tech rides and futuristic movies pay homage to Leonardo da Vinci, H G Wells, George Lucas and – to assuage French sensitivities – Jules Verne.

Disney engineers have tried to make the 'pre-entertainment areas' – Disney parlance for queues – as pleasant as possible, but be prepared to spend a lot of time being pre-entertained.

Tickets Credit-card-like *passeports*, which afford unlimited, all-day access to all rides and activities (except the shooting gallery), cost 225/425/565FF for one/two/three not necessarily consecutive days; children aged three to 11 pay 150/285/375FF. There are no student discounts. One-year passeports cost 1350/900FF for adults/children.

Passeports are sold underneath the Hôtel Disneyland and, for people staying at EuroDisney hotels, at hotel front desks. Payment can be made by major credit card,

French franc travellers' cheques or eurocheque. The ticket windows close one hour before the park closes.

The main entrance to EuroDisneyland is to the right as you approach the Hôtel Disneyland. The exit, where you can have your hand stamped if you'll be re-entering later in the day (make sure to hang onto your entry ticket), is on the other side of the hotel.

Guided Tours

If you'd like to get a general overview of EuroDisneyland and, after buying your passeport, still have 45FF to burn (30FF for children aged three to 11), you can take a guided tour. Tickets are on sale at the main entrance and City Hall.

Boat Rental

During the warm months, Toobies (round rubber boats with motors) can be rented for 50FF a half-hour at the Marina del Ray, which is on Lac Buena Vista in Festival Disney.

Swimming

Each of the hotels except the Hôtel Cheyenne and the Hôtel Santa Fe has at least one themed swimming pool, open to hotel guests only. There's a swimming pool at Camp Davey Crockett, too.

Tennis

There are tennis courts at Camp Davey Crockett (50FF an hour) and the Hôtel New York (100FF an hour).

Golf

The 18-hole golf course, which is three km south-east of EuroDisneyland, is open to the public. It is linked to other parts of Euro-Disney Resort by shuttle bus.

Ice Skating

In winter, the fountain in front of the Hôtel New York becomes an ice-skating rink that's supposed to evoke Christmas at the Rockefeller Center. Two hours of skating costs 50FF (30FF for children), including skate rental.

AROUND PARIS

Places to Stay

Camping *Camp Davey Crockett* (☎ 49.41. 49.10 or fax 49.30.71.00/70 for the Central Reservations Office, 60.45.69.00 for the camping ground operator), a lovely, forested area whose entrance is seven km south-west of the theme park, is open all year. It costs 300FF to park a caravan or pitch a tent at the 181 camping sites, which come equipped with water taps, electrical link-ups and barbecues. It's a good idea to reserve in advance.

Camp Davey Crockett is linked to the other parts of EuroDisney Resort by a free shuttle bus. If you opt to drive to Euro-Disneyland, you'll have to pay for parking. At the main cluster of buildings, you can rent bicycles (35FF for 24 hours) and electric golf carts (150FF for 24 hours) for use within the camping ground only.

The food store (☎ 60.45.68.85) in the Alamo Trading Post, part of the main cluster of buildings, is open daily from 7.30 am to 11 pm. It also sells English-language newspapers.

Camper Van Until more places are available at Camp Davey Crockett, people who've arrived by camper van can stay overnight in a special part of the visitors' parking lot, dubbed *Camp Pinocchio*. There aren't any shower facilities, but toilets are available. Overnight tickets (150FF), valid for the whole next day, go on sale at the toll booth from 4 pm.

Bungalows The 414 bungalows at *Camp Davey Crockett*, which cost 890/1090FF a night (500/550FF from November to 15 April), can sleep up to four/six people. Each has two double beds (plus two bunk beds in six-person bungalows) and a little kitchen with fridge, dishwasher, microwave, stove and electric burners. Outside, there's a picnic table and barbecue grill. The bungalows are not equipped with air-con.

Hotels EuroDisney has six enormous hotels (☎ 49.41.49.10 or fax 49.30.71.00/70 for the Central Reservations Office), five of them in the Resort Complex and a sixth, the Hôtel

Disneyland, at the entrance to EuroDisney-land. Each one has its own all-American theme, reflected in the architecture, the landscaping, the décor, the food on offer in the restaurants and even the costumes of the staff. Given the problems EuroDisney has had in filling the existing 5200 rooms, it seems doubtful whether 13,000 additional rooms, slated to be built by 2017, will be constructed on schedule.

All of the hotel rooms have two double beds (or, in the case of the Hôtel Cheyenne, one double bed and two bunk beds) and can sleep four people. Certain rooms can be linked up to form suites. Rooms specially equipped for disabled guests are also available.

Rooms are most expensive during the peak season, which lasts from mid-April to sometime between mid-September and late October. Peak season prices are also in force from about 18 December to 2 January. Prices are lowest during what EuroDisney calls the 'value season', which lasts from November to mid-April except on weekends and around Christmas. Room prices do not include tickets to the park.

Mid-Range EuroDisney's least expensive hotels are the Hôtel Santa Fe and the Hôtel Cheyenne, between which you'll find a children's playground with teepees and a wooden stockade, Fort Apache, and a silvery flying saucer, half-buried after a less-than-perfect landing. The rooms come with TV and minibar but lack air-con or room service. Heating is provided by separate units in each room.

The 1000-room *Hôtel Santa Fe* (☎ 60.45. 78.00), the least expensive of EuroDisney's hotels, is just south of the Rio Grande. The New Mexico-style architecture, painted in earth tones and landscaped with desert plants, comes complete with a drive-in movie screen on which an enormous Clint Eastwood looks permanently macho. Rooms cost 490 to 690FF all year.

On the north bank of the Rio Grande, the 14 buildings of the 1000-room *Hôtel Cheyenne* (☎ 60.45.62.00) – each with its own

hokey name – are arranged to resemble a Hollywood version of a Wild West frontier town. Large rooms cost 550 to 750FF, depending on the season. Breakfast (55FF, 35FF for children under 12) is available at the Western-style Chuck Wagon Cafe from 7 to 11 am. From 11 am to 12.30 pm, you can brunch at the Red Garter Saloon. Lunch is served from 12.30 to 3 pm (4 pm on Saturday and Sunday); dinner hours are 6 pm to midnight.

Top End EuroDisney's four pricier hotels come with air-con, central heating, room service and swimming pools.

The 1011-room, wood-and-stone *Sequoia Lodge* (☎ 60.45.51.00), which is supposed to evoke the USA's national parks, costs 750 to 900FF. The 1098-room, New England-style *Newport Bay Club* (☎ 60.45.55.00) charges 750FF to 1100FF.

In the luxury category, the 574-room *Hôtel New York* (☎ 60.45.73.00), vaguely reminiscent of Rockefeller Center, Gramercy Park and Manhattan brownstones, charges 1100 to 1600FF. At the park entrance, the 500-room *Hôtel Disneyland* (☎ 60.45.65.00), costs 1300 to 1950FF. The pink pavilions, intended to evoke a turn-of-the-century beach resort in Florida or California, were designed by Disney's brainstorming 'imagineers' rather than its architects.

Places to Eat
For information on low-fat, salt-free or other special meals, enquire at City Hall.

Restaurants You'll find six American-style restaurants in Festival Disney and lots of other places to eat inside the theme park, among them restaurants, self-service cafeterias and food carts selling ice cream, bagels, pretzels, potatoes and the like. The prices are not cheap, but neither are they completely outrageous, at least by French standards.

Each of the hotels has at least one restaurant. As you would expect, the décor and cuisine are coordinated with the overall theme.

Self-Catering You're not supposed to bring food or drink into EuroDisneyland, and picnicking within the theme park is forbidden, but you can safely munch on a home-made sandwich without hiding it in your jacket between bites. EuroDisneyland is one of the only places in France with an adequate supply of drinking fountains.

There's an Air de Pique-Nique/Picnic Area on the south side of the train station next to the *tapis roulant* (moving walkway).

The only *food shop* within EuroDisney Resort is at Camp Davey Crockett (see Camping).

Entertainment
EuroDisneyland Every day at 3 pm (4 pm from April to early September), La Parade Disney – a procession of marching bands, Disney characters and floats – winds its way from It's a Small World to the Central Plaza and then on to Town Square.

Live performances take place throughout the day all around the park: there's jazz, Dixieland and ragtime music along Main Street, brass bands in Discoveryland, jugglers and acrobats in Fantasyland and Wild West scenes (bank robberies, shoot-outs and so on) in Frontierland. For details, check the Programme des Spectacles/Entertainment Program handed out at the park entrance.

During the summer, there are **fireworks** each night at 9.55 and 10.30 pm

Festival Disney Each evening at 6 and 9 pm (9 pm only from mid-November to March), dozens of horses, longhorn cattle and even buffaloes (bisons) participate in **Buffalo Bill's Wild West Dinner Show** (☎ 60.45. 71.00 for reservations), loosely based on Buffalo Bill's European tour of the 1890s. Tickets cost 300FF (200FF for children), including a dinner of baby back ribs, corn-on-the-cob and apple pie.

Live **country music** is performed every night at Billy Bob's Country Western

Saloon, which is in Festival Disney. It is open from 5 pm to 2 am.

Things to Buy

EuroDisneyland's numerous shops sell the usual blown glass, paper cut-outs and toffee – made while you watch – as well as souvenir clothing and Disney books and tapes.

Getting There & Away

To/From the Airports Buses known as Navettes VEA link EuroDisney's bus terminal and hotels with both Orly and Charles de Gaulle airports for 75FF (free for children under 12). They run about every 45 minutes from 7.30 am to at least 8.30 pm. Tickets are sold on board. At Charles de Gaulle, the Navettes VEA stop at Aérogare 1 (Porte 30 on the Niveau Arrivée) and Aérogare 2 (terminal 2D and terminal 2A near Sortie 11).

Taxis to/from either airport cost about 350FF (500FF from 7 pm to 8 am and on Sunday and holidays).

Train To get from Paris's Right Bank to EuroDisney, take RER line A4 to its terminus, Marne-la-Vallée-Chessy, which is only 250 metres from the park's main entrance. You can catch A4 trains, which run every 15 minutes or so, at Nation, Gare de Lyon, Châtelet-Les Halles, Auber, Charles de Gaulle-Étoile and La Défense. All the trains going to Marne-la-Vallée have four-letter codes beginning with the letter Q. The trip costs 35FF (31FF from Gare de Lyon or Nation) each way and takes 35 to 40 minutes. The last train back to Paris leaves EuroDisney at around midnight.

The Marne-la-Vallée TGV station, which is in the same building as the RER station, is on the new stretch of track linking the TGV Nord with the TGV Sud-Est.

Taxi There's a taxi rank next to the bus station, which is on the south side of the train station. A taxi to/from the centre of Paris costs about 350FF (500FF from 7 pm to 8 am and on Sunday and holidays).

Car & Motorbike To get to EuroDisney from Paris, take Autoroute A4, which begins at Porte de Bercy (in the city's south-eastern corner) and runs along the north bank of the Seine. Get off at the Parc EuroDisneyland exit.

If you're staying in one of the EuroDisney hotels, you can park for free next to your hotel. Guests who have difficulties walking can park in Special Services Parking, next to the Hôtel Disneyland.

Day-trippers can park in the 11,386-space visitors' parking lot. All-day parking costs 40FF for a car, 25FF for a motorbike and 60FF for a camper van. You can leave and re-enter throughout the day so long as you keep your original parking ticket. During school holiday periods, it's a good idea to arrive early in the day, as there are often long queues at the toll plaza from 9 to 11 am.

The toll plaza opens one hour before the theme park. The parking lot exit closes one hour after the last event at Festival Disney ends (ie at 2 or 3 am). In the morning, it opens at the same time as the toll plaza.

Getting Around

Train The Old West-style EuroDisneyland Railroad, whose open-air cars are pulled by a steam engine, goes all the way around EuroDisneyland and passes by a mock-up of the Grand Canyon. It has three stations, one just inside the main entrance, a second in Frontierland and the third on the far side of the park in Fantasyland (behind the Fantasy Festival Stage).

Shuttle Bus Free, yellow shuttle buses link the bus terminal (next to the train station) with various parts of EuroDisney Resort, including the hotels and Camp Davey Crockett.

Chateaux

VERSAILLES

Versailles, site of the grandest and most famous chateau in all of France, served as France's political capital and the seat of the royal court for almost the entire period from

1682 to 1789, when Revolutionary mobs massacred the palace guard and dragged Louis XVI and Marie-Antoinette off to Paris, where they were later guillotined.

In its heyday, the thousands of aristocrats who resided at Versailles were frequently joined by delegations from distant lands, including Siam (1686) and Persia (1715). In 1787, one of the last such missions came from Vietnam to lobby for military aid.

In 1783, England, France and Spain formally recognised the independence of the USA by the Treaty of Versailles. After the Franco-Prussian War of 1870-71, the victorious Prussians proclaimed the establishment of the German Empire from the chateau's Galerie des Glaces (Hall of Mirrors), the same room where, in 1919, another Treaty of Versailles officially ended WW I and imposed harsh conditions on a defeated Germany.

Because so many people consider Versailles one of those must-see destinations, the chateau attracts over three million visitors a year. Unfortunately, this state of affairs seems to bring out the worst in some of the people who work at the chateau. During July and August, the most crowded months of the year, the best way to avoid the lines is to arrive first thing in the morning. Don't come on Monday, when the chateau is closed.

By the way, they won't let you into the chateau if you are improperly dressed or if you've brought along a large, bulky item such as a backpack or pram (baby carriage). Such objects should be checked at a train station left-luggage office.

Orientation

The Château de Versailles faces Place d'Armes, from which three grand avenues radiate: Ave de Paris, Ave de Saint Cloud and Ave de Sceaux. A vast formal garden stretches westward from the palace.

Versailles has three train stations. Versailles-Rive Gauche is 700 metres south-east of the Château de Versailles on Ave du Général de Gaulle. Versailles-Chantiers is 1.3 km south-east of the chateau on Ave de

Sceaux. And Versailles-Rive Droite is 1.2 km north-east of the chateau on Rue du Maréchal Foch.

Information

Tourist Office The tourist office (☎ 39.50.36.22) is at 7 Rue des Réservoirs, just north of the north end of the chateau. From October to April, it is open daily from 9 am to 12.30 pm and 2 to 6.15 pm. During the rest of the year, it is open daily from 9 am to 7 pm. Its brochure of *promenades historiques* (historic walks) indicates the location of over two dozen noteworthy sites around town.

From May to October, the tourist office has a *stand d'information* (☎ 30.84.76.61) in a tent pitched near the chateau gates on Place d'Armes. It is staffed from 9 am to 7 pm (6 pm in October).

Château de Versailles

The enormous Château de Versailles (☎ 30.84.74.00) was built in the mid-1600s during the reign of Louis XIV – the Roi Soleil (Sun King) – to project both at home and abroad the absolute power of the French monarchy, then at the height of its autocratic splendour. Its size and décor also reflect Louis's boundless appetite for self-glorification. The structure, on which some 30,000 workers and soldiers toiled, proved so vastly expensive that it impoverished the entire kingdom of France.

Among Versailles's assets was its distance from the political intrigues of Paris: out here, away from the city, it was much easier for the king to keep an eye on his scheming nobles. Louis XIV's plan to rein in the aristocracy worked brilliantly, all the more so because court life transformed the nobles into sycophantic courtiers, who ended up expending most of their energy vying for royal favour.

The chateau complex consists of four parts: the main palace building, a classical structure with innumerable wings, grand halls and sumptuous bedchambers; the vast gardens, laid out in the 17th century in the formal French style; and two out-palaces, the late 17th-century Grand Trianon and the

mid-18th-century Petit Trianon. The ensemble has undergone relatively few alterations since its construction.

The main palace, whose eastern side is 580 metres long, is built around three successive courtyards. The **Cour des Ministres** (Ministers' Courtyard), separated from Place d'Armes by a wrought-iron fence, is flanked by the two Ailes des Ministres (Ministers' Buildings). The **Cour Royale** (Royal Courtyard) is divided from the Cour des Ministres by an equestrian statue of Louis XIV. The **Cour de Marbre** (Marble Courtyard), paved with black and white marble squares, is surrounded on three sides by the **Château Vieux**, Louis XIII's old hunting lodge.

History About two decades into his 72-year reign (1643-1715), Louis XIV decided to enlarge the hunting lodge his father had built at Versailles and turn it into a palace big enough for the entire court, which numbered some 6000 people. To accomplish this task he hired four supremely talented people: the architect Louis Le Vau; his successor Jules Hardouin-Mansart, who took over in the mid-1670s; the painter and interior designer Charles Le Brun; and the landscape artist André Le Nôtre, whose workers flattened hills, drained marshes and relocated forests as they laid out the seemingly endless gardens, ponds and fountains.

Le Brun and his hundreds of artisans decorated every moulding, cornice, ceiling and door of the interior with the most luxurious and ostentatious of appointments: frescoes, marble, gilt woodcarvings and the like. Many of the themes and symbols used by Le Brun are drawn from Greek and Roman mythology. The **Grand Appartement du Roi** (King's Suite), for example, includes rooms dedicated to Hercules, Venus, Diana, Mars and Mercury. It is no coincidence that the **Salle du Trône** (Throne Room) is also known as the Salon d'Apollon (Apollo's Chamber), as Apollo (the Graeco-Roman god of light, music, poetry and healing) represented the Greek ideal of beauty. The conspicuously consumptive ornateness reaches its apotheosis in the **Galerie des Glaces** (Hall of Mirrors), a 75-metre-long ballroom with 17 huge mirrors on one side and, on the other, an equal number of windows looking out on the gardens and the setting sun. The former were designed to reflect the ceiling frescoes (which relate the history of Louis XIV's early life) and allowed the splendidly arrayed guests to watch themselves – and each other – while dancing.

Opening Hours & Tickets The main building is open from 9 am to 5.30 pm (6.30 pm from May to September). It closes for only four holidays: 1 January, 1 May, 8 May and 25 December.

Entrance to the **Grands Appartements** (State Apartments), which include the Galerie des Glaces and the **Appartement de la Reine** (Queen's Suite), costs 40FF (26FF for people aged 18 to 25 or over 60). On Sunday, everyone gets in for 26F, so the crowds are even worse than usual. Tickets are on sale at Entrée A (entrance A; also known as Porte A), which, as you approach the building, is off to the right from the equestrian statue of Louis XIV. Many parts of the main palace cannot be visited unless you take a tour (see Guided Tours). Entrée H has facilities for the disabled, including a lift.

The Grand Trianon, which costs 20FF (13FF reduced price), is open Tuesday to Sunday from 10 am to 12.30 pm and 2 to 5.30 pm (6.30 pm in summer); there's no midday closure on weekends. The Petit Trianon, open the same days and hours, costs 12FF (8FF reduced price).

The gardens are open every day of the week (unless it's snowing) from 7 am to nightfall (ie sometime between 5.00 and 9.30 pm, depending on the season). They are free *except* on Sunday from May to September, when the fountains are in operation and entrance costs 19FF.

It may be worthwhile purchasing a Carte Musées et Monuments (60/120/170FF for one/three/five consecutive days), which gets you into the main palace and the Trianons as well as more than 60 other museums and monuments in Paris and the Île de France.

AROUND PARIS

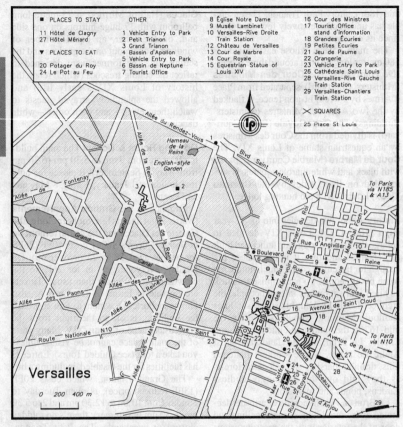

PLACES TO STAY	OTHER	8 Église Notre Dame	16 Cour des Ministres
11 Hôtel de Clagny	1 Vehicle Entry to Park	9 Musée Lambinet	17 Tourist Office stand d'information
27 Hôtel Ménard	2 Petit Trianon	10 Versailles-Rive Droite Train Station	18 Grandes Écuries
▼ PLACES TO EAT	3 Grand Trianon	12 Château de Versailles	19 Petites Écuries
	4 Bassin d'Apollon	13 Cour de Marbre	21 Jeu de Paume
20 Potager du Roy	5 Vehicle Entry to Park	14 Cour Royale	22 Orangerie
24 Le Pot au Feu	6 Bassin de Neptune	15 Equestrian Statue of Louis XIV	23 Vehicle Entry to Park
	7 Tourist Office		26 Cathédrale Saint Louis
			28 Versailles-Rive Gauche Train Station
			29 Versailles-Chantiers Train Station
			✕ SQUARES
			25 Place St Louis

Versailles

0   200   400 m

Guidebooks Unless you have some sense of the historical and aesthetic context of what you're seeing, Versailles can seem like little more than a series of gaudy, gilded rooms. If you opt not to take a tour (see Guided Tours), a chateau guidebook is an excellent investment, especially if a number of people will be using it.

Several excellent books in English are on sale near the ticket counters at Entrée A. These include *Versailles: Tour of the Château* by Daniel Meyer, the chateau's curator, and *Versailles* (50FF), which contains half a dozen articles on various aspects

of the chateau and its gardens. The Michelin green guide to the Île de France has a detailed entry on Versailles.

Guided Tours Eight different *visites guidées* (guided tours; 22FF in addition to the entry price) are available in English from 10 am to 4 pm (4.45 pm from May to September). The six that leave from Entrée D are led by guides. At Entrée A and Entrée C, you can rent *audioguides* (cassette tours).

Gardens The vast gardens, laid out between 1661 and 1700 in the formal French style, are

famed for their geometrically aligned terraces, flowerbeds, tree-lined paths, ponds and fountains. The many statues of marble, bronze and lead were made by the finest sculptors of the period. The English-style garden out near the Trianons is more pastoral and has meandering (rather than angular) paths.

The 1.6-km-long, 62-metre-wide **Grand Canal**, oriented to reflect the setting sun, is intersected by the one-km **Petit Canal**, creating a cross-shaped body of water with a perimeter of over 5.5 km.

The **Orangerie**, situated 200 metres south of the main building, was intended for the wintertime storage of 3000 sensitive trees, including 2000 orange trees, planted in moveable tubs.

Fountains The largest fountains are the **Bassin de Neptune** (Neptune Fountain), which is 300 metres north of the northern tip of the main palace building, and the **Bassin d'Apollon** (chariot of Apollo), which is at the eastern end of the Grand Canal.

On Sundays from May to September, the fountains are turned on at 11.15 am for the 20-minute **Grande Perspective** and from 3.30 pm to 5 pm for the longer and more elaborate **Grands Eaux**. On days when the fountain shows take place, there is a 19FF fee to get into the gardens.

The Trianons Across the gardens, about 1.5 km north-west of the main building, are Versailles's two out-palaces. The larger one, the **Grand Trianon**, was built in 1687 for Louis XIV and his family, who used it as a place of escape from the rigid etiquette of court life. Napoleon I had it redone in the Empire style. The **Petit Trianon**, built in the 1760s, was redecorated in 1867 by the Empress Eugénie, who added Louis XVI-style appointments.

A bit further north is the **Hameau de la Reine** (Queen's Hamlet), a mock rural village of thatch or slate-roofed cottages constructed from 1775 to 1784 for the amusement of Marie-Antoinette.

Getting Around If you prefer not to walk from the main building to the Grand Canal and the Trianons, you can take a *petit train* (little motorised train; ☎ 39.50.55.12) from the back terrace of the palace's north wing. The petits trains operate Tuesday to Sunday from December to February. A round trip costs 28FF (16FF for children aged 3 to 12).

Another way to get to the Grand Trianon is to sail along the Grand Canal and Petit Canal in a bateau mouche (☎ 39.49.02.78). The dock is not far from the Bassin d'Apollon fountain.

For 13FF you can drive your car to the Trianons via the gates on Blvd de la Reine, Blvd Saint Antoine and Rue Saint Cyr.

Boat Rental From March to mid-October, guests can paddle around the Grand Canal in four-person rowboats for 53FF an hour. They can be hired near the Bassin d'Apollon fountain every day from 10 am to 6 pm.

Other Sights

The attractive town of Versailles is – like the chateau – a creation of Louis XIV. However, most of the buildings around today date from the 18th and 19th centuries.

Jeu de Paume In May 1789, in an effort to deal with the huge national debt and to moderate dissent by reforming the tax system, Louis XVI convened at Versailles the États-Généraux (States General), a body made up of over a thousand deputies representing the three estates: the nobility and the clergy, most of whom were exempted from paying taxes; and the third estate, representing the middle classes. When the third estate, whose members constituted a majority of the delegates, was denied entry to the États-Généraux's usual meeting place, they met separately in the Salle de Jeu de Paume (Royal Tennis Court), where they constituted themselves as a National Assembly on 17 June. Three days later they took the famous Tennis Court Oath, swearing not to dissolve the assembly until Louis XVI had accepted a new constitution. This act of defiance sparked protests of support and, a short while

later, open rebellion. Less than a month after the Tennis Court Oath, a Parisian mob stormed the Bastille.

The Jeu de Paume, built around 1686, is 350 metres south-east of the chateau on Rue du Jeu de Paume. It is closed to the public except during July and August, when it can be visited either on Saturday afternoon or Sunday morning. Contact the tourist office for details.

Musée Lambinet Housed in a lovely 18th-century residence, the Musée Lambinet (☎ 39.50.30.32) at 54 Blvd de la Reine displays antique furniture, carved wood panelling, paintings, medieval religious art and objects from the period of the Revolution. It is open from 2 to 6 pm.

Grandes & Petites Écuries Ave de Paris, Ave de Saint Cloud and Ave de Sceaux, the three wide thoroughfares that fan out eastward from Place d'Armes, are separated by two large, late 17th-century stables, the Grandes Écuries and the Petites Écuries. During July and August, the Grandes Écuries, which house a **museum of carriages**, can be visited on Sunday from 2 to 4 pm.

Cathédrale Saint Louis Built between 1743 and 1754, this graceful though austere cathedral is known for its 3131-pipe organ. It faces Place Saint Louis.

Église Notre Dame This church on Rue de la Paroisse, built by Mansart in the late 1600s, served as the parish church of the king and his courtiers. It has a fine sculpted pulpit.

Places to Stay
The cheapest hotel in town is the *Hôtel Ménard* (☎ 39.50.47.99) at 8 Rue Ménard, whose doubles begin at 120FF with washbasin and bidet and 190FF with shower and toilet. Not far from the Versailles-Rive Droite station, a good bet is the two-star *Hôtel de Clagny* (☎ 39.50.18.09) at 6 Impasse de Clagny. Singles with washbasin and bidet are 180FF; doubles with shower and toilet are 250FF.

Places to Eat
Restaurants *Le Pot au Feu* (☎ 39.50.57.43) at 22 Rue Satory, whose *menu* costs 115FF, is a good bet for a splurge. It is closed on Saturday at midday and Sunday. *Potager du Roy* (☎ 39.50.35.34) at 1 Rue du Maréchal Joffre, open Tuesday to Saturday, has *menus* for 120 and 169FF.

Self-Catering Picnicking is not allowed in the chateau gardens.

Entertainment
During the warm months, the chateau and its gardens play host to a varity of audiovisual extravaganzas, including the Grands Eaux fountain displays (see Fountains) and the Fêtes de Nuit, a sound, light, fountains and fireworks show of Versaillian proportions. The Fêtes de Nuit, which are held around the Bassin de Neptune on a couple of Saturday nights in July, cost 50 to 160FF. For details on these and other programmes, contact the tourist office.

From April to November, classical music is featured in afternoon concerts known as Samedis Musicaux (musical Saturdays). Tickets cost about 50FF (35FF if you're under 26 or over 60). In winter, performances generally take place on Tuesdays. For more information, call the Centre de Musique Baroque de Versailles (☎ 39.49.48.24) at 16 Rue Sainte Victoire or contact any FNAC ticket outlet in Paris.

Getting There & Away
Versailles is 23 km south-west of central Paris.

Train Versailles has three railway stations: Versailles-Rive Gauche, Versailles-Chantiers and Versailles-Rive Droite. Each is served by trains that stop at a different set of Paris's RER and SNCF stations. Eurail pass holders can travel for free on the SNCF trains but not on those operated by the RER.

RER line C5 takes you from Gare d'Austerlitz and other Left Bank RER stations, including Saint Michel and Champ de Mars-Tour Eiffel, to Versailles-Rive Gauche

(13.50FF), which is only 700 metres from the chateau. Check the electronic destination lists on the platform to make sure you take a train that goes all the way to Versailles.

The SNCF has trains from Gare Montparnasse to Versailles-Chantiers (13.50FF), a 1.3-km walk from the chateau. Many trains on this line continue on to Chartres, making it possible to visit Versailles before spending the night in Chartres. From Paris's Gare Saint Lazare, there are SNCF trains to Versailles-Rive Droite (16FF), which is 1.2 km from the chateau.

Bus RATP bus No 171 takes you from the Pont de Sèvres metro stop in Paris all the way to Place d'Armes, which is right in front of the chateau.

FONTAINEBLEAU

The town of Fontainebleau (population 19,500), 65 km south-east of Paris, is renowned for its elegant Renaissance chateau, one of France's largest royal residences, whose exceptionally rich furnishings make it particularly worth a visit. The town is surrounded by the beautiful Forêt de Fontainebleau, favourite hunting ground of a long line of French kings, including Louis IX, Charles V, François I and Louis XIV.

The chateau, which is much less crowded and pressured than Versailles, is closed on Tuesday.

Orientation

The Château de Fontainebleau is about three km south-west of the train station along (from east to west) Ave Franklin Roosevelt, Blvd du Général Leclerc, Rue Aristide Briand, Rue Grande (the town's main commercial street) and Rue Dénecourt.

Information

Tourist Office The tourist office (☎ 64.22. 25.68) at 31 Place Napoléon Bonaparte is open from 9 am to 12.30 pm and 2 to 6 pm daily except Sunday afternoon and Tuesday. From June to September, it's open from 9 am to 7 pm daily except Sunday and holidays.

The summer annexe in front of the chateau is open seven days a week. The tourist office can provide information on hotels, chambres d'hôte and gîtes ruraux. Hotel reservations cost 2FF.

Money Most banks are open Tuesday to Saturday, but the Banque de France (☎ 64.22.21.66) at 192 Rue Grande is open Monday to Friday from 8.30 to noon and 1.30 to 3.30 pm.

Post There is a post office across Place Napoléon Bonaparte from the tourist office.

Fontainebleau's postcode is 77300.

Cultural Centre The Écoles d'Art Américaines (American Art Schools; ☎ 47.35.92.50), created in 1921, are housed in the chateau buildings around the Cour des Cuisines (Kitchen Court), also known as the Cour Henri IV. From late June to mid-August, when they host American university students of art, architecture, design and music, there are art exhibitions and free recitals three times a week. Information is available in the building to the right as you enter the courtyard throught the wrought-iron gate.

Maps The Fontainebleau area is covered by IGN's 1:25,000-scale map No 2417 OT, entitled *Forêt de Fontainebleau* (53FF).

Château de Fontainebleau

The enormous Château de Fontainebleau (☎ 64.22.34.39), whose list of former tenants reads like a Who's Who of French royal history, is one of the most beautifully ornamented and furnished chateaux in all of France. Every centimetre of the walls and ceilings is richly adorned with wood panelling, gilded carvings, frescoes, tapestries and paintings. The parquet floors are of the finest wood, the fireplaces are ornamented with exceptional carvings and much of the furniture consists of Renaissance-era originals.

History The first chateau on this site was built sometime in the early 1100s and

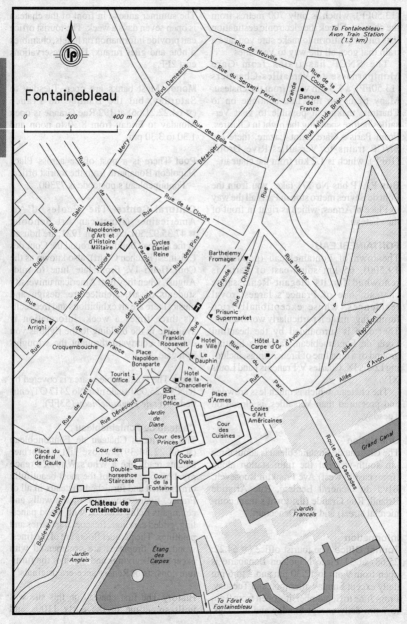

Fontainebleau

0   200   400 m

enlarged by Louis IX in the 1200s. Only a single medieval tower survived the energetic Renaissance-style reconstruction undertaken by François I (reigned 1515-47), whose superb artisans, many of them brought from Italy, blended Italian and French styles to create what is known as the First School of Fontainebleau. During this period, the *Mona Lisa* hung here amidst other fine works of art in the king's collection.

During the latter half of the 16th century, the chateau was further enlarged by Henri II, Catherine de Médicis and Henri IV, whose Flemish and French artists created the Second School of Fontainebleau. Even Louis XIV, builder of Versailles, got in on the act: it was he who hired Le Nôtre to redesign the gardens. But his most (in)famous act at Fontainebleau was the revocation in 1685 of the Edict of Nantes, which since 1598 had guaranteed freedom of conscience to France's Protestants.

Fontainebleau, which was not damaged during the Revolution (though its furniture was lost), was especially beloved by Napoleon, who did a fair bit of restoration work. Napoleon III also came here frequently.

During WW II, the chateau was turned into a German headquarters. Liberated in 1944 by US General George Patton, part of the complex served as an Allied and then a NATO headquarters from 1945 to 1965.

Hours & Tickets The interior of the chateau is open from 9.30 am to 12.30 pm and 2 to 5 pm; in the future it may be open all day. The last visitors are admitted 45 minutes before closing time. Tickets for the Grands Appartements and the Musée Napoléonien cost 26FF (14FF for people 18 to 24 or over 60, free for those under 18 and people in wheelchairs) and are good for the whole day. The Musée Chinois, which has a separate entry fee of 12FF (7FF reduced price), sells tickets until 30 minutes before closing time.

The gardens (free), are open seven days a week from early morning until sundown (sometime between 5 and 9 pm, depending on the season). In winter, parts of the garden may be closed if personnel are in short supply.

Guidebook The best way to get a sense of what you're looking at, as well as who created it and when, is to walk around the chateau with some sort of guidebook. *The Château de Fontainebleau*, an excellent English-language pamphlet written by Colombe Samoyault-Verlet, the chateau's conservator, is avalailable for 15FF.

Guided Tours Tours in English of the Grands Appartements depart several times a day from the staircase near the ticket windows.

Chateau As successive monarchs added their own wings to the chateau, five irregularly shaped courtyards were created. The oldest and most interesting is the **Cour Ovale** (Oval Courtyard), no longer oval thanks to construction work by Henri IV. It incorporates the sole remnant of the medieval castle, its keep. The largest is the **Cour des Adieux** (Farewell Courtyard), also known as the Cour du Cheval Blanc (Courtyard of the White Horse). The more dramatic name dates from 1814 when Napoleon, about to be exiled to Elba, bid farewell to his guards from the bottom of the famous **double-horseshoe staircase**, built under Louis XIII in 1634.

The **Grands Appartements** (State Apartments) include a number of outstanding rooms. The spectacular **Chapelle de la Trinité** (Chapel of the Trinity), whose ornamentation dates from the first half of the 1600s, is where Louis XV married Marie Leczinska in 1725 and where the future Napoleon III was christened in 1810. **Galerie François 1er**, a gem of Renaissance architecture, was decorated from 1533 to 1540 by Il Rosso, a Florentine follower of Michaelangelo. In the wood panelling, François I's monogram, a letter 'F', appears repeatedly along with his emblem, a dragonlike salamander.

The mid-16th-century **Salle de Bal**, a 30-metre-long ballroom also used for receptions

and banquets, is renowned for its mythological frescoes, marquetry floor and Italian-inspired coffered ceiling. The large windows afford views of the Cour Ovale and the gardens. The gilded bed in the 17th and 18th-century **Chambre de l'Impératrice** was never used by Marie-Antoinette, for whom it was made in 1787. The gilding in the **Salle du Trône**, the royal bedroom before the Napoleonic period, is in three shades: golden, greenish and yellowish.

The **Petits Appartements** (Private Apartments of the emperor and empress) can only be visited with a guide.

Musée Napoléon 1er This museum of Napoleonia, also known as the Musée Napoléonien, has a collection of personal effects (uniforms, hats, coats, ornamented swords) and decorative knicknacks that belonged to Napoleon and his relatives. Many of the items are gilded, enamelled or bejewelled. The entrance is on the 1st floor opposite the Grands Appartements.

Musée Chinois The four rooms of the Chinese Museum, which is on the ground floor next to the *vestiaire* (cloakroom), are filled with beautiful ceramics and other objects brought to France from East Asia during the 19th century. Some of the items, which are from the personal collection of Empress Eugénie, wife of Napoleon III, were gifts of a delegation from Siam (Thailand) in 1861, while others were stolen by a Franco-British expeditionary force sent to China in 1860. The last room is decorated with 18th-century Chinese lacquer panels and huge silk ceiling tapestries.

Gardens On the north side of the chateau, the **Jardin de Diane**, a formal garden created by Catherine de Médicis, is home to a flock of male (multicoloured) and female (brown) peacocks *(paons)*. When the birds get too numerous, a few are sold for 1000 to 1500FF each. The marble fountain in the middle of the garden, decorated with a statue of Diana, Goddess of the Hunt, and four urinating dogs, dates from 1603.

Le Nôtre's formal, mid-17th-century **Jardin Français** (French Garden), also known as the Grand Parterre, is to the west of the **Cour de la Fontaine** (Courtyard of the Fountain) and the **Étang des Carpes** (Carp Pond). The **Grand Canal** was excavated in 1609 during the reign of Henri IV and predates the canals at Versailles by over half a century. The informal **Jardin Anglais** (English Garden), laid out in 1812, is west of the Étang des Carpes. The **Forêt de Fontainebleau**, crisscrossed by paths, begins 500 metres south of the chateau.

Boats From late May to August (and on weekends in September), rowboats can be rented at the Étang des Carpes for 35/55FF per half/whole hour.

Musée Napoléonien d'Art et d'Historie Militaire
Fontainebleau's second Napoleonic museum, housed in a late 19th-century mansion at 88 Rue Saint Honoré, has exhibits of military uniforms and weapons. It is open Tuesday to Saturday from 2 to 5 pm.

Forêt de Fontainebleau
This 250-sq-km forest surrounding the town of Fontainebleau is one of the loveliest wooded tracts in the Paris region. Its forest cover is provided by oaks, beeches, birches and more recently planted pines. The many trails – including parts of the **GR1** and **GR11** – are great for jogging, hiking, cycling and horse riding. Parisian rock-climbing enthusiasts have long been coming to the many sandstone ridges, rich in cliffs and overhangs, to hone their skills before setting off for the Alps. Two gorges especially worth visiting are the **Gorges d'Apremont**, about seven km north-west of Fontainebleau near Barbizon, and, a few km south of Apremont, the **Gorges de Franchard**.

Michelin's green guide entitled *Île de France* has several detailed hiking itineraries. The tourist office sells a small topoguide, *Guide des Sentiers de Promenades dans le Massif Forestier de Fontainebleau* (30FF),

Day Trips from [...]

324 Day Trips from [...]

Bicycle O[...]
and Fo[...]
brin[...]

[...]UND PARIS

whose maps and text (in French) cover almost 20 walks in the forest.

Places to Stay

The two-star *Hôtel de la Chancellerie* (☎ 64.22.21.70) at 1 Rue de la Chancellerie has old-fashioned doubles/triples with shower and toilet for 220/280FF. Reception is open daily, year round. You might also try the *Hôtel La Carpe d'Or* (☎ 64.22.28.64) at 21bis Rue du Parc, where doubles cost 194FF with washbasin and bidet and 224FF with shower and toilet.

Places to Eat

Restaurants There are a number of good French restaurants at Place Franklin Roosevelt and the streets leading off it, including *Le Dauphin* (☎ 64.22.27.04) at 24 Rue Grande, which is closed on Tuesday night and Wednesday. On Rue de France, two good choices are *Chez Arrighi* (☎ 64.22.29.43) at No 53 and *Croquembouche* (☎ 64.22.01.57) at No 43.

Self-Catering The *Prisunic* at 58 Rue Grande is open Monday to Saturday from 8.45 am to 7.30 pm. The food section is on the 1st floor. *Barthelemy Fromager* is not far away at 92 Rue Grande.

Entertainment

Cultural Events One weekend a month, from May to September the Relève de la Garde (changing of the guards at the chateau) is re-enacted as it was performed during the time of Napoleon I.

Getting There & Away

Train Between 22 to 25 daily commuter trains link Paris's Gare de Lyon with Fontainebleau-Avon (39FF; 45 to 60 minutes). Since the service is intended primarily for commuters, trains *to* Paris are plentiful in the morning and those heading out of Paris are most frequent in the evening. In off-peak periods, there's about one train an hour. The last train back to Paris leaves Fontainebleau a bit before 10 pm.

At the Gare de Lyon, tickets are on sale at

the Banlieue (sub[...]
Grandes Lignes (lon[...]
and 48. Eurail passes [...]
taineleau-Avon is a s[...]
means all) of the tra[...]
Veneux, Montereau, [...]
Laroche-Migennes and [...]

Because the tracks [...] south-east from Paris keep crisscrossing each other, figuring out where to go at Gare de Lyon to catch your train can be rather confusing. Fontainebleau-Avon may appear on the schedule boards, but then again it may not. And whereas most trains – specifically, those indicated on the schedule boards by alphanumeric codes – depart from the TGV-Grandes Lignes section of Gare de Lyon, a few leave from the Gare de Banlieue (Suburban Station), also known as the Gare Souterraine (Underground Station), which is three levels below the Grandes Lignes tracks. To find out when the next train to Fontainebleau leaves and how to find it, your best bet is to enquire at one of the station's information booths.

At Fontainebleau-Avon train station, the information office (☎ 64.22.38.57, 64.22.39.82) is open from 9 am to 8 pm daily except Sunday and holidays. For information and reservations, you can also call ☎ 64.30.50.50. Upon arrival, it's a good idea to pick up a free schedule so you know when trains to Paris will be leaving.

Getting Around

Bus The train station is linked to the chateau (7.80FF each way; 12 minutes) by Les Cars Verts' line A (☎ 64.23.71.11, 64.45.55.55), which runs from 5.30 am to 9 pm about every 20 minutes (every 30 minutes early in the morning and late at night). The schedule is arranged so each incoming train is met by a bus. The last bus from the chateau to the train station leaves a bit after 9 pm (11 pm on Sunday).

Taxi To order a taxi, call ☎ 64.22.00.06 (radio-dispatched), 64.22.38.53 (at the train station) or 64.22.26.03 (in town).

two or three Paris-Fontainebleau
tainebleau-Paris trains a day, you can
g along your bicycle for no charge. For
details, call the Fontainebleau-Avon train
station (see Train under Getting There &
Away).

RATP and SNCF-run Bicyclub (☎ 47.66.
55.92), whose office is in the Fontainebleau-
Avon train station, rents bikes on weekends
and holidays from mid-March to late
November. It's open daily during July and
August. Hours are 9 am to 7 pm (6 pm in
March, October and November). Tariffs for
children's bikes/three-speeds/mountain
bikes are 20/25/40FF an hour and
80/100/150FF a day (plus a 30FF annual
membership, reduced to 15FF for people
under 16 and foreign tourists).

Cycles Daniel Reine (☎ 64.22.72.41) at
14 Rue de la Paroisse rents mountain bikes
all year round for 50/80FF a half/whole day.
Weekend and holiday rates are 80/100FF. A
2000FF deposit is required. The shop is open
Tuesday to Saturday from 9 am to 12.30 pm
and 2 to 7 pm and on Sunday from 9 am to
6 pm.

CHANTILLY

The elegant town of Chantilly (population
11,300), 48 km north of Paris, is best known
for its heavily restored but imposing chateau,
which is surrounded by lakes, gardens and a
vast forest. The town has been an important
horse-racing venue since the 1830s, when
equestrian dandies first began congregating
here. These days, its racetrack hosts a
number of prestigious events each June, and
the Chantilly region – home to some 3000
racehorses – is one of France's most important training centres for thoroughbreds.

The Château de Chantilly is best known
for its gardens, stables and paintings, all but
a handful of which are rather ordinary. If
you're primarily interested in furnished interiors, you're much better off at Versailles
or Fontainebleau. Don't come on Tuesday,
when the major sights are closed.

The name Chantilly is derived from Can-
tilius, a Gallo-Roman who built the first
fortification here; it is also used to refer to a

kind of whipped cream. In the 18th century,
the town was known for its production of
lace and porcelain.

Orientation

The chateau is slightly over two km east of
the train station. The most direct route is to
walk through the Forêt de Chantilly along
Route de l'Aigle, but you'll get a better sense
of the town by taking Ave du Maréchal Joffre
and Rue de Paris to Rue du Connétable,
Chantilly's main street.

Information

Tourist Office The tourist office (☎ 44.57.
08.58) at 23 Ave du Maréchal Joffre is open
from 9 am to 12.30 pm and 2 to 6 pm (closed
Sunday and Tuesday). From May to September, it's also open on Sunday from 9 am to
noon.

Post & Telephone Chantilly's postcode is
60500.

Chantilly is *not* in the Paris dialling area.
For more information, see Telephone under
Information at the beginning of this chapter.

Maps IGN's 1:25,000-scale map No 2412
OT (53FF), entitled *Forêts de Chantilly*,
covers the Chantilly area.

*Carte de Découverte des Milieux Naturels
et du Patrimoine Bâti* (36FF), a 1:100,000-
scale map available at the tourist office,
shows sites in the area of historic and touristic interest, such as churches, chateaux,
museums and ruins.

Château de Chantilly

Chantilly's chateau (☎ 44.57.08.00), left in
shambles after the Revolution, is of interest
mainly because of the gardens and a number
of superb paintings. It consists of two
attached buildings entered through the same
vestibule. The **Petit Château** was built
around 1560 for Connétable Anne de
Montmorency (1492-1567), who served six
French kings as a diplomat and warrior and
died in battle against the Protestants. The
attached Renaissance-style **Grand Château**,
completely demolished during the Revolu-

AROUND PARIS

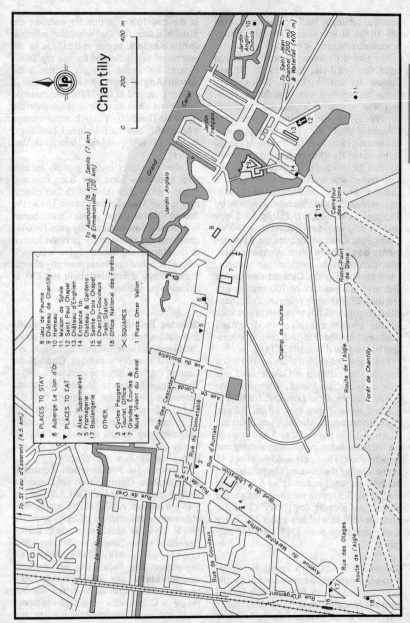

Chantilly

0   200   400 m

To Aumont (6 km), Senlis (7 km)
& Ermenonville (20 km)

To Saint Jean Channel (200 m)
& Waterfall (400 m)

Jardin Anglo-Chinois

Jardin Français

Jardin Anglais

Grand Canal

Champ de Course

Forêt de Chantilly

Carrefour des Lions

Rond-Point de Diane

Route de l'Aigle

Rue des Otages

Route de l'Aigle

La Nonette

To St Leu d'Esserent (4.5 km)

Rue de Crell

Rue de Paris

Rue d'Aumale

Rue de la Libération

Blvd de la Libération

Avenue du Maréchal Joffre

Rue de Gouvieux

Rue d'Orgemont

Ave du Bouteille

Rue du Connétable

Rue des Cascades

Avenue du Maréchal Joffre

PLACES TO STAY
■ Auberge Le Lion d'Or

PLACES TO EAT
▼ Atac Supermarket
5   Fromagerie
17 Boulangerie

OTHER
3   Cycles Peugeot
4   Tourist Office
7   Grandes Ecuries &
    Musée Vivant du Cheval

8   Jeu de Paume
9   Château de Chantilly
10 Hameau
11 Maison de Sylvie
12 Saint Paul Chapel
13 Château d'Enghien
14 Entrance & Gardens
15 Sainte Croix Chapel
16 Chantilly-Gouvieux
    Train Station
18 Office National des Forêts

× SQUARES
1   Place Omer Vallon

tion, was rebuilt by the Duc d'Aumale in the late 1870s. It served as a French military headquarters during WW I.

The Grand Château, to the right as you enter the vestibule, contains the **Musée Condé**. Its unremarkable, 19th-century rooms are adorned with furnishings, paintings and sculptures haphazardly arranged according to the whims of the Duc d'Aumale, son of King Louis-Philippe, who donated the chateau to the Institut de France at the end of the 19th century on the condition that the exhibits not be reorganised. The most remarkable works are hidden away in a small room called the **Sanctuaire** (Sanctuary), whose contents include paintings by Raphael (1483-1520), Filippino Lippi (1457-1504) and Jean Fouquet (late 1400s).

The Petit Château contains the **Appartements des Princes** (Princes' Apartments), which are straight on from the entrance. Their highlight is the **Cabinet des Livres** (Library), a repository of 700 manuscripts and over 12,000 other volumes. The **Chapelle** (Chapel), which is to the left as you walk into the vestibule, consists of woodwork and windows from the mid-16th century assembled by the Duc d'Aumale in 1882.

The signs and guided tours are in French only, but the giftshop in Galerie des Cerfs sells a decent guidebook, *Chantilly: The Condé Museum & the Domaine*, for 40FF.

The chateau is open from 10 am to 6 pm. From November to March, when hours are 10 am to 12.30 pm and 2 to 5 pm, you can use the same ticket in both the morning and the afternoon. The ticket window closes 45 minutes before the chateau. The park is open from 10 am until sunset (5 or 5.30 pm in winter, 7 or 7.30 pm in summer). Entry to the chateau and its park costs 35FF (25FF for students, 9FF for children under 12). Entry to the park alone costs 15FF (9FF for children).

Gardens The chateau's lovely but long-neglected gardens were once among the most spectacular in France. The formal **Jardin Français**, whose flowerbeds, lakes and Grand Canal were laid out by Le Nôtre in the mid-1600s, is directly north of the main building. To the west, the informal **Jardin Anglais**, begun in 1817, is in the process of being cleaned up and replanted. East of the Jardin Français, is the rustic **Jardin Anglo-Chinois** (Anglo-Chinese Garden), created in the 1770s. Its semiwild foliage and silted-up waterways surround the **Hameau** (hamlet), a mock rural village whose mill and half-timbered buildings, built in 1774, inspired the Hameau at Versailles.

Other structures in the gardens include three **chapels** – Saint Jean, Saint Paul and Sainte Croix – built (along with four others) by Anne de Montmorency in the 1530s; the **Jeu de Paume** (Royal Tennis Court), begun in 1756 and now occasionally used for concerts; and the 18th-century pavilion known as the **Maison de Sylvie** (Sylvie's House), whose furnished interior is presently closed. The **Château d'Enghien**, built in 1770, is closed to the public.

Grandes Écuries The chateau's magnificent stables, built from 1719 to 1740 to house 240 horses and over 400 hunting hounds, are next to Chantilly's famous **Champ de Course** (racecourse), inaugurated in 1834. The stables house the **Musée Vivant du Cheval** (Living Horse Museum; ☎ 44.57. 13.13), a horse-lover's dream museum. The 31 rooms display everything from riding equipment (eg dozens of kinds of bits) to horsey toys and even paintings of famous horses. All signs are in English.

A 30-minute **Présentation Équestre Pédagogique** (Introduction to Dressage Riding) takes place at 11.30 am, 3.30 pm and 5.15 pm daily except Tuesday. Longer, more elaborate demonstrations of dressage riding (80FF, 70FF for children) are held during December and on Sunday and holiday afternoons during May, June, July and September. The horses live in luxurious **wooden stalls** built, like the whole structure, by Louis-Henri de Bourbon, the 7th Prince de Condé, who – it is said – believed he would be reincarnated as a horse and

wanted to make sure stables befitting his rank would be waiting for him.

The museum, founded in 1982, is open from 10.30 am to 5.30 pm (6 pm on weekends). From May to August, it doesn't close until 6 pm (7 pm on weekends and holidays) and may be open on Tuesday. Entry to the museum and dressage show costs 44FF (34FF for students and people over 60).

Forêt de Chantilly

The Forêt de Chantilly, once a royal hunting estate, covers 63 sq km. Its tree cover, patchy in places because of poor soil and overgrazing by deer, includes beeches, oaks, chestnuts, limes and pines. A massive reafforestation programme adds over 100,000 young saplings each year.

The forest is crisscrossed by a variety of walking and riding trails. In some areas, straight paths laid out centuries ago meet at multiangled *carrefours* (crossroads). Long-distance trails that pass through the Forêt de Chantilly include the **GR11**, which links the chateau with the town of Senlis; the **GR1**, which goes from Luzarches to Erme-nonville; and the **GR12**, which goes north-eastward from four lakes known as the **Étangs de Commelles** (Four Lakes) to the Forêt d'Hallate.

Hikes *Randonnées autour de Chantilly et Senlis* (20FF), an unbound topoguide available at the tourist office, has details in French on 10 hikes in the vicinity of Chantilly and Senlis.

For information on *promenades commentées* (guided walks) in the Forêt de Chantilly, led by a forest ranger and held from June to September on Saturday and Sunday at 3 pm, contact the Chantilly bureau of the Office National des Forêts (☎ 44.57.03.88). The walks begin at the Carrefour de la Table de Montgrésin and cost 15FF (10FF for children aged 10 to 16).

Places to Stay

Camping There are camping grounds in the vicinity of Chantilly in Aumont (☎ 44.60.00.42), Ermenonville (☎ 44.54.00.08) and

Saint Leu d'Esserent (☎ 44.56.07.18, 44.56.60.48).

Hotels Only 100 metres from the Grandes Écuries, the seven-room *Auberge Le Lion d'Or* (☎ 44.57.03.19) at 44 Rue du Connétable has large and cheery singles with washbasin for 110FF, one-bed doubles with shower for 180FF, and shower-equipped rooms for three/four/five people for 230/280/330FF. New guests cannot check in on Wednesday, when reception – which is in the restaurant – is closed. The hotel shuts down from 20 December to 20 January.

Places to Eat

Restaurants There are a number of restaurants along Rue du Connétable.

Self-Catering Midway between the train station and the chateau, the *Atac supermarket* at Place Omer Vallon is open Monday to Friday from 9 am (8.30 am on Wednesday) to 12.30 pm (1 pm on Wednesday) and 2.30 to 7.30 pm. Saturday hours are 8.30 am to 7.30 pm.

Near the train station, you'll find a *boulangerie* at 4 Rue des Otages. There's a *fromagerie* not far from the Grandes Écuries at 68 Rue du Connétable.

Entertainment

Horse Racing During the first half of June, the French Jockey Club holds six horse races at Chantilly's Champ de Course (☎ 44.62.41.00), including the Prix du Jockey Club on the first Sunday in June and the Prix de Diane on the second Sunday. Both races are for three-year-olds. For details on dates and times, call the tourist office.

Fireworks Chantilly's annual international fireworks competition, Nuits de Feu, is held on the Friday and Saturday nights of the third weekend in June. Tickets, available in Paris from FNAC, cost 60FF for one night or 80FF for both.

Getting There & Away

Train Paris is linked to Chantilly-Gouvieux

train station (35FF one way; 30 to 45 minutes) by a mixture of RER and regular SNCF trains. There are 36 trains a day (26 on Sunday and holidays), but they are timed for the convenience of commuters (ie there are lots of trains *to* Paris from 8 to 10 am and *from* Paris from 4 to 6.30 pm). In the morning, there are departures from Gare du Nord at least once or twice an hour. In the evening, there are trains back to Paris every hour or so until at least 11 pm.

The dozen weekday RER trains that are code-named CODA, CECI and CADE begin their runs at Châtelet-Les Halles metro station before stopping at Gare du Nord. The other 24 weekday trains – signposted for a variety of destinations, including Creil, Amiens, Compiègne and Saint Quentin – start at Gare du Nord, where Chantilly-bound trains use both the Grandes Lignes and Banlieue platforms. Eurail passes are valid for travel on all trains to Chantilly but *not* for the segment between Châtelet-Les Halles and Gare du Nord.

Car To get to Chantilly from Paris by car, take the N16 or the A1.

Getting Around
Bus There are no buses from the train station to the chateau.

Taxi There's a taxi stand in front of the train station. To order a cab, call ☎ 44.57.10.03 or 44.57.01.20.

Bicycle Cycles Peugeot (☎ 44.57.09.24) at 9 Ave du Maréchal Joffre rents out bikes.

Towns & Cities

CHARTRES
The magnificent 13th-century cathedral of Chartres, crowned by two soaring spires – one Gothic, the other Romanesque – rises from the rich farmland 90 km south-west of Paris, dominating the medieval town around its base.

Thanks to its relics and statues of the Virgin Mary, the cathedral was a major pilgrimage centre during the Middle Ages. Indeed, the town of Chartres (population 40,000, double that including the suburbs), present-day prefecture of the *département* of Eure-et-Loir, has been attracting pilgrims for over two millennia: the Gallic Druids may have had a sanctuary here, and the Romans apparently built themselves a temple dedicated to the Dea Mater (mother-goddess), who was later interpreted by Christian missionaries as prefiguring the Virgin Mary. The earliest church on the site, the first in France dedicated to the Virgin Mary, dates from the 4th century.

The vast majority of Chartres's many visitors pop in by tour bus and zip off after an hour or two, leaving most of this pleasant provincial town – which is dotted with carefully tended flower gardens – relatively untouristed.

When to Visit
Come on a bright, sunny day if you want to get a really good look at the cathedral's exquisite stained-glass windows, many of which appear rather dim because of an exterior patina left by centuries of weathering. Local weather information in French is available from the Station Météo on ☎ 37.68.02.37.

In the late afternoon, the windows in the cathedral's northern wall – which actually faces north-west – are lit up by the setting sun.

What to Bring
If you're serious about seeing the detail of the stained-glass windows, bring along a pair of binoculars.

Orientation
The medieval sections of Chartres are situated along the Eure River and on the hillside that rises from its west bank. The cathedral, which is visible from almost everywhere in town, is about 500 metres east of the train station. The main commercial streets are Rue Noël Ballay, Place du Cygne and Place

Marceau. The modern town is south of the train station and the cathedral around Place des Épars.

Information
Tourist Office The tourist office (☎ 37.21. 50.00) is across Place de la Cathédrale from the cathedral's main entrance. It is open Monday to Friday from 9.30 am to 6, 6.30 or 6.45 pm, depending on the season. Saturday hours are 9.30 am to 5 pm (6 pm from March to October).

From May to September, the office is also open on Sunday from 10 am to noon and 3 to 6 pm. Hotel reservations in the département of Eure-et-Loir cost 20FF (plus a 50FF deposit). The brochure entitled *Chartres: Ville d'Art* provides lots of information on the town.

Money Most banks are open Tuesday to Saturday.

The Banque de France (☎ 37.91.59.03) at 32 Rue du Docteur Maunoury is open Tuesday to Saturday from 8.45 am to 12.30 pm and 1.45 to 3.30 pm.

Post & Telephone The main post office at Place des Épars is open Monday to Friday from 8.30 am to 7 pm and on Saturday from 8.30 am to noon.

Chartres's postcode is 28000.

Chartres is *not* in the Paris dialling area. For more information, see Telephone under Information at the beginning of this chapter.

Laundry The Lav' Club at 68 Rue du Grand Faubourg is open daily from 7 am to 9 pm.

Walking Tour
Self-guided cassette tours of the old city for one or two people can be rented at the tourist office for 35FF.

One of the best views of town can be had from the **Jardin Public de la Route d'Ablis**, a public park on the main road from Paris.

Cathédrale Notre Dame
Chartres cathedral (☎ 37.21.56.33), one of the crowning architectural achievements of Western civilisation, was built in the Gothic style during the first quarter of the 13th century to replace an earlier Romanesque cathedral that had been devastated – along with much of the town – by fire on the night between 10 and 11 June 1194. Because of effective fundraising among the aristocracy and donations of labour by the common folk, construction took only 25 years, conferring on the structure a high degree of architectural unity. Unlike so many other Gothic cathedrals, Chartres has been spared both postmedieval modifications and the ravages of war and revolution. It is open daily from 7.30 am to 7 pm (7.30 pm from April to September).

Chartres's statues and ornamentation survived the Revolution for the same reason that everyday life in this country can seem so complicated: the vaunted French bureaucratic approach to almost everything. As antireligious fervour was nearing fever pitch in 1791, the Revolutionaries decided that the cathedral deserved something more radical than mere desecration: demolition. The question was, how should such a massive structure be demolished? To find an answer, they appointed a committee, whose admirably thorough members deliberated for four or five years, by which time the Revolution's fury had been spent and the plan was shelved.

Notre Dame is truly immense. It is 130 metres long and 64 metres from side to side at the transept. The nave, which is 16.4 metres across, is the widest in France; its vault is 36 metres above the floor. The nave has only one aisle on each side, but the chancel, where ceremonies attended by thousands of pilgrims were once held, has a double ambulatory.

The above-ground portion of the cathedral incorporates three Romanesque features that survived the 1194 fire: the Portail Royal, the Clocher Vieux and the lower part of the Clocher Neuf.

Portail Royal All three of the cathedral's entrances have richly ornamented triple portals, but the west entrance, known as the

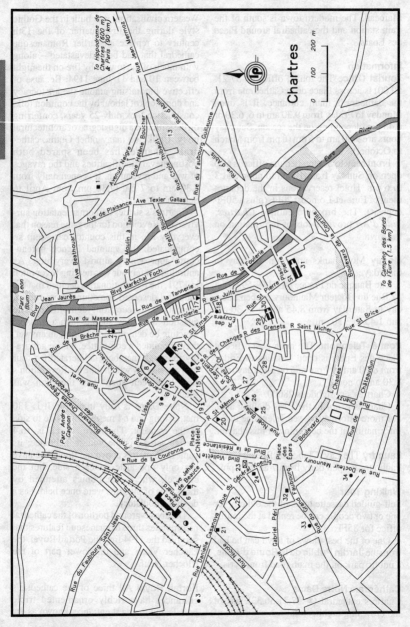

Chartres

0   100   200 m

To Hippodrome de
Chartres (600 m)
& Paris (90 km)

To Camping des Bords
de l'Eure (1.5 km)

■ PLACES TO STAY

1   Auberge de Jeunesse
6   Hôtel de l'Ouest
7   Hôtel Jehan de Beauce
21 Hôtel Le Goût Royal
24 Hôtel de la Poste
32 Hôtel de l'Écu

▼ PLACES TO EAT

16 Le Café Serpente & La Reine de
    Saba
17 Boulangerie & Le Cours des Halles
20 Boulangerie
25 Monoprix Supermarket
26 Boulangerie

    OTHER

2   Collégiale Saint André
3   Le Compa
4   Bus Station
5   Railway Station
8   Musée des Beaux-Arts
9   Centre International du Vitrail
10 La Galerie du Vitrail
11 Cathédrale Notre Dame
12 La Crypte
13 Jardin Public de la Route d'Ablis
14 Portail Royal
18 Prow-Shaped House
19 Tourist Office
22 Prefecture Building
23 Main Post Office
30 Église Saint Aignan
31 Église Saint Pierre
33 Lav' Club
34 Banque de France

✕ SQUARES

15 Place de la Cathédrale
27 Place du Cygne
28 Place Marceau
29 Place Saint Aignan

Vieux (Old Bell Tower), also known as the Tour Sud (South Tower), was begun in the 1140s. It is the tallest Romanesque steeple still standing.

Clocher Neuf A visit to the 115-metre-high Clocher Neuf (New Bell Tower), also known as the Tour Nord (North Tower), the Tour Gothique (Gothic Tower) and the Clocher Jehan de Beauce (Belfry of Jehan de Beauce), is well worth the ticket price and the long, spiral climb. A 70-metre-high platform on the lacy, Flamboyant Gothic spire, built from 1507 to 1513 by Jehan de Beauce after an earlier wooden spire burned down, affords superb views of the three-tiered flying buttresses; the mid-19th-century copper roof, made green by a patina of verdigris; the Clocher Vieux; a number of gargoyles; the entire town of Chartres; and much of the surrounding countryside.

The tower entrance is in the north transept arm just inside the late 13th-century, Gothic **Porche Nord** (North Porch), whose statues represent such Old Testamant figures as Joseph, Solomon, the Queen of Sheba, Isaiah and Jeremiah. Like its southern counterpart, the **Porche Sud** (South Porch), which portrays the Last Judgement, it is decorated with hundreds of figures that were originally painted in bright colours. Both porches are surmounted by rose windows.

From April to September, the Clocher Neuf can be visited from 9.30 to 11.30 am and 2 to 5.30 pm (5.15 pm on Saturday). The rest of the year, hours are 10 to 11.30 am and 2 to 4 pm (November to February) or 4.30 pm (October and March). The fee is 20FF (12FF if you're 18 to 25 or over 60). Children under 18 must be accompanied by an adult.

Stained Glass The cathedral's extraordinary stained-glass windows, almost all of which are 13th-century originals, form one of the most important ensembles of medieval stained glass anywhere in the world. Many of the panes were donated by guilds and incorporate elements relating to their donors. During both world wars, the windows – of which there are over 160,

Royal Portal, is the only one that predates the fire. Carved from 1145 to 1155, its superb statues, whose features are elongated in the Romanesque style, represent the glory of Christ.

Clocher Vieux The 105-metre Clocher

including three 13-metre rose windows – were taken down and stored for safe-keeping.

The three most important non-13th-century windows are in the wall above the west entrance between the three entryways and the rose window. Survivors of the fire of 1194, they were made around 1150. The depth and intensity of their blue tones, known as Chartres blue, are renowned.

The floor of the cathedral is decorated with a 12.8-metre-wide **labyrinth** set in dark and light stone. If it were untangled, it would be 261 metres long. No one seems to know why it's there.

The **choir screen** was begun by Jehan de Beauce in 1514.

Trésor Chapelle Saint Piat, at the far end of the chancel from the west entrance, houses the cathedral's treasury, where you can see beautiful ritual objects and the **Voile de Notre Dame** (Veil of Our Lady), also known as the Sainte Chemise (Holy Chemise) and the Chemise de la Vierge (Chemise of the Virgin), a piece of cloth said to have been worn by the Virgin Mary when she gave birth to Jesus. It was given to the cathedral by Charles the Bald in 876 and was of great importance during the medieval period, when people believed that saints interceded on earth through their relics. In the 12th and 13th centuries, when Mary became an extremely important figure in Western Christianity, this relic – which priests brought out from the crypt three days after the great fire of 1194 – helped to make Chartres an extremely popular pilgrimage destination.

From Easter to 1 November, the treasury is open from 10 am to noon and 2 to 5 pm. The rest of the year (except January), it's open in the afternoon (2 to 4.30 or 5 pm). There is no charge to visit. Photography is forbidden.

Crypte The 110-metre-long, tombless Romanesque crypt underneath the cathedral was built from 1020 to 1024. The largest crypt in France, it can be visited only if you join a 30-minute guided tour (☎ 37.21. 56.33) in French. A written English translation is available. Tours begin at the cathedral's souvenir shop, La Crypte, which is outside the south entrance at 18 Rue du Cloître Notre Dame. There are four or five departures a day between 11 am and 5 pm. Tickets cost 10FF (7FF for students).

English-Language Tours It's well worth timing your visit to coincide with the fascinating tours led by Chartres expert Malcolm Miller, an Englishman who's been lecturing to groups of visitors about the cathedral's history and architecture since 1958. His tours, which make the cathedral and its ornamentation come alive, usually include an explanation of how to read some of the stained-glass windows, intended – like the portals – to edify the illiterate medieval masses by relating stories from the Old and New Testaments.

Tours are held Monday to Saturday from Easter to sometime in November (and, perhaps, during winter as well). Unless there is a wedding or funeral, there are two *different* tours each day: at noon and 2.45 pm. The cost is 30FF (20FF for students).

Books Malcolm Miller's books, including *Chartres Cathedral* (100FF in large format paperback), are on sale in the gift shop.

Musée des Beaux-Arts

Chartres's fine arts museum (☎ 37.36.41.39) at 29 Rue du Cloître Notre Dame, whose entrance is through the gate next to the cathedral's north portal, is housed in the former **Palais Épiscopal** (Bishop's Palace), most of which was built in the 17th and 18th centuries. Its collections include 12 mid-16th-century enamels made by Léonard Limosin for François I, paintings from the 1500s to 1800s, wooden sculptures from the Middle Ages, 17th and 18th-century harpsichords and, oddly enough, some artefacts from New Caledonia.

The museum, which hosts a harpsichord festival each May, is open from 10 am to noon and 2 to 5 pm (closed Tuesday). From April to October, hours are 10 am to 6 pm. Entrance costs 10FF (5FF for students and people over 60).

Centre International du Vitrail

The International Centre of Stained-Glass Art (☎ 37.21.65.72), which has exhibits on stained-glass production, history and restoration, is housed in a half-timbered former granary built over the **Enclos de Loëns**, an extraordinary 13th-century cellar whose three aisles are covered by Gothic vaulting. The Enclos is not usually open to the public.

The centre has three exhibitions a year of medieval, Renaissance and contemporary stained glass. The centre, which is down the hill from the cathedral's north portal at 5 Rue du Cardinal Pie, is open daily from 9.30 am to 12.30 pm and 1.30 to 6 pm. From April to September, hours are 9.30 am to 7 pm. It is closed for about two weeks between exhibitions. The entry fee is 15FF (12FF for students and people over 60).

Old City

Chartres's carefully preserved old city is north-east and east of the cathedral along the banks of the Eure, which is spanned by a number of footbridges. From Rue du Cardinal Pie, the stairs known as **Tertre Saint Nicolas** and **Rue Chantault** – the latter lined with old houses – lead down to the empty shell of the mid-12th-century **Collégiale Saint André**, a Romanesque collegiate church closed in 1791 and severely damaged in the early 1800s and 1944.

Rue de la Tannerie and its continuation along the river's east bank, **Rue de la Foulerie**, are lined with flower gardens, millraces and the restored remnants of riverside trades: washhouses, tanneries and the like. **Rue aux Juifs** (street of the Jews) has been extensively renovated, but parallel **Rue des Écuyers** has a number of houses from around the 16th century, including the prow-shaped, half-timbered structure at No 26. **Rue du Bourg** also has some old houses.

From Place Saint Pierre, you get a good view of the flying buttresses holding up the 12th and 13th-century **Église Saint Pierre**. Once part of a Benedictine monastery founded in the 7th century, it was outside the city walls and was thus vulnerable to attack: that's why the entrance is through the base of a fortress-like, pre-Romanesque **bell tower**, which dates from around 1000. The fine, brightly coloured **clerestory windows** in the nave, choir and apse are from the late 13th and early 14th-centuries.

Église Saint Aignan at Place Saint Aignan, built in the 16th century, is interesting for its wooden barrel-vault roof, added in 1625, and its brightly painted interior, which dates from about 1870.

Le Compa

The Conservatoire du Machinisme et des Pratiques Agricoles (☎ 37.36.11.30) at 1 Rue de la République, better known as Le Compa, has imaginative exhibits of agricultural implements and machinery illustrating the mechanisation of agriculture. Founded in 1990, it is housed in a *rotonde* (steam locomotive repair shed) used from 1905 to 1968.

Le Compa is open from 9 am (10 am on Sunday) to 12.30 pm and 1.30 to 6 pm (7 pm on Sunday; closed Saturday). Entrance costs 20FF (15FF for students and people over 60). The ticket counter has free brochures in English and sells a great selection of toy farm vehicles. Guided tours (25FF, 20FF reduced price) may be available in English.

Activities

The tourist office has handouts in French with maps of walking trails in the vicinity of Chartres.

Places to Stay

Chartres has a number of two-star hotels offering good value. They are pretty full from June to September, but if you arrive by 11 am you should be able to find a room.

Camping *Camping des Bords de l'Eure* (☎ 37.28.79.43) is on Rue de Launay about 2.5 km south-east of the train station. It is open from Easter to the second week of September. Two adults with a tent and vehicle pay 41FF. To get there from the train station or Place des Épars, take bus No 8 to the Vignes stop.

Hostel The pleasant and calm *Auberge de Jeunesse* (☎ 37.34.27.64; fax 37.35.75.85) at 23 Ave Neigre is about 1.5 km east of the train station via the ring road (Blvd Charles Péguy and Blvd Jean Jaurès). By bus, take

line No 3 from the train station and get off at the Rouliers stop.

Reception is open daily from the early morning until 10 am and from 6 to 10 pm (11 pm in summer). If you arrive before 12.30 pm, a member of staff may be around to let you drop off your bags. A bed costs 59FF, including breakfast. Guests must have a hostelling card. Curfew is 10.30 pm in winter and 11.30 pm in summer. The hostel is closed from the Monday before Christmas to the first Monday in February.

Hotels – Train Station Area The *Hôtel de l'Ouest* (☎ 37.21.43.27), a two-star place across the street from the train station at 3 Place Pierre Sémard, has clean, carpeted doubles/triples from 120/170FF (with washbasin and bidet), 170/210FF (with shower) and 210/280FF (with shower and toilet). Singles are slightly cheaper. The hall shower costs 10FF.

Almost next door, the *Hôtel Jehan de Beauce* (☎ 37.21.01.41; fax 37.21.59.10) at 19 Ave Jehan de Beauce (1st floor) has clean, decent doubles from 110FF, 170FF (with shower) and 200FF (with shower and toilet). Triples and quads are also available.

The *Hôtel Le Goût Royal* (☎ 37.36.57.45) at 17 Rue Nicole is 200 metres to the right as you exit the train station. Simple doubles with washbasin and bidet are 130FF. Hall showers cost 10FF. Reception, which is at the bar, is closed on Sunday morning.

Hotels – Around Place des Épars The *Hôtel de l'Écu* (☎ 37.21.34.59) at 28 Rue du Grand Faubourg has singles/doubles with washbasin for 100/110FF. Doubles with shower and perhaps toilet cost 160 to 200FF. The rooms, some of which are quite large, are unsurprising. The hall shower costs 22FF. On Sunday and holidays, reception closes at 3 pm.

The two-star *Hôtel de la Poste* (☎ 37.21.04.27; fax 37.36.42.17) at 3 Rue du Général Koenig (Place des Épars) has singles/doubles from 200FF with shower and 250FF with shower and toilet. Triples/quads/quints cost 315/370/390FF.

Places to Eat

Restaurants *Le Café Serpente* (☎ 37.21. 68.81), a brasserie and salon de thé opposite the south porch of the cathedral at 2 Rue du Cloître Notre Dame, has main dishes for 50 to 60FF and large salads for 40 to 60FF. It is open daily from 10 am to 1 am.

La Reine de Saba (☎ 37.21.89.16), down the block at 8 Rue du Cloître Notre Dame, is a casual restaurant specialising in traditional French food. *Menus* cost 70 and 90FF. It is open daily from 9.30 am to 6 or 7 pm (8.30 am to 11 pm from April to September). Salads and croque-monsieurs are available all day long; meals are served from 12.15 to 3 pm and 7 to 9.30 pm. It is closed during January.

Cafés There are a number of *cafés* around Place Marceau.

Self-Catering About 200 metres south-west of the cathedral, the *boulangerie* at 19 Rue Sainte Même is open from 7.30 am to 12.30 pm and 3 to 7 pm (closed Sunday and Wednesday). It is closed in either July or August.

There's another *boulangerie* next to 5 Rue Noël Ballay. The *Monoprix supermarket* at 21 Rue Noël Ballay is open Monday to Saturday from 9 am to 7 pm.

In the old city, the *boulangerie* at 5 Rue du Bourg, at the northern end of Rue aux Juifs, is open from 7 am to 1 pm and 3 pm (5 pm on Sunday) to 7.45 pm (closed Wednesday). Nearby, *Le Cours des Halles* at 19 Rue du Bourg has vegetables, fruit, cheese and, when the boulangerie is closed, bread. It is open from 8 am to 8 pm daily except Sunday afternoon.

Entertainment

For information on concerts, the summertime Festival d'Orgue (Organ Festival) and other cultural events, contact the tourist office.

The Hippodrome de Chartres (☎ 37.34. 93.73) on Rue Jean Mermoz (Route d'Ablis) has horse races on many weekends (especially Sunday) from mid-March to May.

Things to Buy

Quite a few Chartres-based artisans work either restoring medieval stained glass or creating their own works. La Galerie du Vitrail (stained-glass gallery; ☎ 37.36. 10.03), which is opposite the cathedral's north portal at 17 Rue du Cloître Notre Dame, sells contemporary stained glass alongside items from the late 19th and early 20th centuries. It's interesting to look around even if you don't have 10,000FF to spare. The gallery is open Tuesday to Saturday, and from Easter to October on Sunday too.

There's a flower market at Place du Cygne on Tuesday, Thursday and Saturday.

Getting There & Away

Train The railway station (☎ 37.28.50.50 for information) at Place Pierre Sémard is 500 metres west of the cathedral. The information office is open Monday to Saturday from 8.30 am to 7.30 pm and on Sunday from 9.30 am to noon and 2.30 to 7 pm. The station has both luggage lockers and a left-luggage office.

There are about 18 round trips a day from Paris's Gare Montparnasse (61FF one way), where tickets are sold at the Banlieue counters. However, the train won't necessarily leave from the Banlieue enclosure. Express trains take 50 minutes; other trains take 60 to 70 minutes. Chartres is outside the eight RER zones.

On the way to Chartres, many of the trains stop in Versailles at the Versailles-Chantiers station, so you could spend the day in Versailles and then sleep in Chartres or stop off in Versailles on your way from Chartres to Paris. The last train back to Paris leaves Chartres at around 9 pm on weekdays and an hour or so later on weekends. There is also direct rail service to/from Nantes, Quimper and Brest.

Bus The bus station (☎ 37.21.30.35), which is at Place Pierre Sémard, is the first building to the right as you exit the train station. It is open on weekdays from 6.55 am to 6.30 pm and on Saturday from 7.30 am to 1 pm and 3.30 to 5.40 pm. There is bus service to

Orléans and various towns in the départe-ment of Eure-et-Loir, including Auneau, Châteaudun, Châteauneuf-en-Thymerais, Dreux, Gallardon, Senonches and Toury.

Car & Motorbike Chartres is on the way from Paris to Brittany, the Loire Valley, Nantes and the Atlantic coast. From Paris, you can take either the N10 or the A10 and then the A11.

Getting Around

Bus Local bus maps are available at the tourist office.

Taxi There is a taxi stand at the train station. To order a taxi 24 hours a day, call ☎ 37.36. 00.00.

COMPIÈGNE

Favoured by the rulers of France as a country retreat since Merovingian times, Compiègne (population 45,000) reached the height of its popularity in the mid-19th century under Napoleon III (ruled 1852-70). Today, the city is a favourite day trip for well-to-do Pari-sians, particularly on Sunday afternoons. The chateau is closed on Tuesday.

On 23 May 1430, Joan of Arc was cap-tured at Compiègne by the Burgundians. They sold her to their allies, the English, who – with the help of pro-English French clerics – convicted her of heresy and then burned her at the stake at Rouen. During WW II, thousands of people, including many Jews, were loaded onto trains and sent to Nazi concentration camps from the Compiègne suburb of Royallieu, site of one of the largest transit camps established in occupied France.

Information

Telephone Compiègne is *not* in the Paris dialling area. For more information, see Telephone under Information at the begin-ning of this chapter.

Things to See

Compiègne's principal drawing card is the old royal palace on Place du Général de Gaulle, known officially as the **Musée National du Château de Compiègne** (☎ 44.40.04.37). Set on the edge of a large forest (see the Around Compiègne listing), a favoured hunting ground for generations of French kings, it was given its present form under Louis XV, who commissioned the flamboyant architect Ange-Jacques Gabriel to rebuild the dilapidated palace left by his great-grandfather, Louis XIV. The work con-tinued from 1752 to 1786. After the Revolution, the structure was used by Napo-leon I, who did some renovation work of his own. Later, it was an especial favourite of Napoleon III, who used to throw big hunting parties here.

In addition to the royal apartments, fur-nished in the styles of the 18th century and the mid-19th-century Second Empire, the palace houses the **Musée de la Voiture**, which displays early motorcars as well as vehicles that predate the age of the internal combustion engine.

The chateau is open from 9.15 am to 4.30 pm (6 pm in summer). The last tours – the only way to see the palace – leave 45 minutes before closing time. Admission, including the tour, is 30FF (19FF for 18 to 25-year-olds). On Sunday, entrance is only 19FF for everyone.

Getting There & Away

Compiègne is 82 km north-east of Paris. There are frequent trains from Paris's Gare du Nord (60FF; one hour) to Compiègne's train station. The centre of town is south-east of the train station across the Oise River.

AROUND COMPIÈGNE
Forêt de Compiègne

The 220-sq-km Forêt de Compiègne, one of the most attractive forest areas in the Île de France, begins on the southern and western outskirts of Compiègne.

Clairière de l'Armistice

Clairière de l'Armistice (Armistice Clear-ing; ☎ 44.40.09.27), where WW I was officially brought to an end, is seven km east of Compiègne (towards Soissons). Early on

the morning of 11 November 1918 – a date still commemorated annually in many countries – in the railway carriage of the Allied supreme commander, Maréchal Ferdinand Foch, Foch and German representatives signed an armistice set to come into force on 'the 11th hour of the 11th day of the 11th month'.

On 22 June 1940 – shortly after German bombing had destoyed much of Compiègne – in the same railway car, the French were forced to sign the armistice that recognised the German conquest of France. The carriage was later taken for exhibition to Berlin, where it was destroyed by Allied bombing in 1943.

A replica of the original carriage has been placed at Clairière de l'Armistice to commemorate the first signing ceremony (most French guidebooks prefer to forget about the second one). It is open from 9 am to noon and 2 to 5.15 pm (6.15 pm in summer); it is closed on Tuesday. Admission costs 10FF.

ROUEN & GIVERNY

For information on visiting Rouen, which is 70 minutes by express train from Paris's Gare Saint Lazare, and Monet's home of Giverny, see the Normandy chapter.

Far Northern France

Many travellers coming from England and Belgium first set foot on French territory in far northern France (Nord de France), a name which conveniently groups the three regions at the far northern tip of the hexagon: Flanders (Flandre), Artois and Picardy (Picardie). As in most of France's outlying regions, life here has its own, distinctive character, especially along the Belgian border in the Nord département, where the culture and people's identity include many identifiably Flemish elements.

Travellers' reactions to far northern France usually depend to a large extent on how they arrive, how long they stay and whether the sky is blue or grey. Let's face it: far northern France – densely populated, highly industrialised and intensively farmed – is not one of France's more fabled or beloved regions. It is best known for the conical slag heaps left over from the mining industry and the sobering battlefields and memorials from the two world wars. In recent decades the region has been in a prolonged economic decline: the last coal pit closed in December 1990, and the metallurgical industry is having troubles of its own.

But if you've got the time and the inclination to do a bit of exploring, there's a lot more to discover here than tourist lore (or the lack of it) would suggest. Imposing cathedrals soar above ancient cities like Amiens, while castles and monuments dot the forests and gentle hills to the south of the Flanders plain. Lille, the region's largest and most important city, is 51 km north of Arras, whose picturesque 17th and 18th-century squares have no equal in France.

Before Western Europe was subdivided into its current complement of nation-states, the part of far northern France nearest the Belgian border, together with much of Belgium and a bit of Holland, made up a medieval principality known as 'Flanders'. The traditional language, Flemish, which is nearly identical to Dutch, is still spoken at

home in villages near the border. Unlike anywhere else in France, the people of Flanders drink more beer than wine, especially during the carnivals or annual fairs known as *braderies*, when Giants (see the Giants aside) come out of hiding to join the whole village in celebrating.

When your bike is pushed backwards or your umbrella rendered useless by a raging storm, you can take refuge in the area's cosy pubs, a great place to sip mulled wine or nurse a strong Belgian beer while waiting for the sun to return.

Geography

Far northern France is bordered by Belgium in the north-east, Champagne in the east, the Paris basin in the south and Normandy in the south-west. The region is separated from the UK by the Straits of Dover (Pas de Calais), the narrowest bit of the English Channel (La Manche). From much of the coast you can see the white cliffs of south-eastern England.

The coastline nearest England is dominated by a cluster of busy commercial and passenger ports: Calais, Dunkerque (Dunkirk) and Boulogne-sur-Mer (commonly

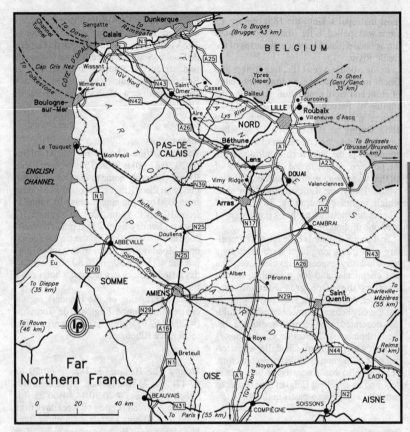

known as Boulogne). The Channel Tunnel, also known as the Chunnel or Eurotunnel, surfaces just south of Calais.

Getting There & Away

Whereas some people across the Channel may fear that the Channel Tunnel will deposit hordes of rabid rats on England's peaceful shores, on the French side the project is seen as the opening of a new frontier and a herald of better times. For more information on the Channel Tunnel, see To/From England under Land in the introductory Getting There & Away chapter.

In addition to the Channel Tunnel, options for crossing the Channel include: car ferries, SeaCats and hovercraft (aéroglisseurs) from Dover to Calais; ferries and SeaCats from Folkestone to Boulogne; and ferries from Ramsgate to Dunkerque. For details, see To/From England under Sea in the introductory Getting There & Away chapter. Calais, Boulogne and Dunkerque are all about 300 km north-west of Paris.

LILLE

Lille (population 172,000), only 15 km from the Belgian frontier, is France's northern-

most metropolis. Until the 18th century, its name was spelled 'L'Île' (the island) because it was once situated between two arms of the Deûle River.

In the Middle Ages Lille, like Bruges and Ghent in Belgium, was an important centre of cloth and wool production. It became the capital of French Flanders following its capture in a nine-day siege by Louis XIV in 1667. During the 19th century, the wretched working and living conditions of the people employed in the huge textile industry made the polluted, overcrowded city a symbol of all that was wrong with the Industrial Revolution. Today, the Lille metropolitan area, which includes Tourcoing, Roubaix and other industrial suburbs, has a population of over one million.

By French standards Lille is not a compelling city: it has long been surrounded by a sea of industry (especially textiles, steel, coal and chemicals) and has a sombre air that matches the often-grey Flemish sky. However, its old quarter is attractive enough, and the city boasts a number of ornate buildings decorated in the Flemish tradition. Lille, the birthplace of Charles de Gaulle, boasts Vauban's extraordinary Citadelle, a masterpiece of 17th-century military architecture. The city also has some lively bars where downing an excellent Belgian beer comes as naturally as sipping a pastis in the Midi.

Orientation

Lille is centred around three public squares:

Place du Général de Gaulle, Place du Théâtre and Place Rihour, where the tourist office is. The Vieille Ville is north of Place du Général de Gaulle. South of Place Rihour is a small, pedestrianised quarter around Rue de Béthune. The train station is about 500 metres south-east of Place du Général de Gaulle.

Information

Tourist Office The main tourist office (☎ 20.30.81.00) is in the 15th-century Palais Rihour (formerly home to the Dukes of Burgundy) at Place Rihour. It is open on Monday from 1.30 to 6 pm and Tuesday to Saturday from 10 am to 6 pm. During summer it's open on Sunday from 2 to 6 pm. The small annexe (☎ 20.06.40.65) at the train station is open Monday to Saturday from 9 am to 12.45 pm and 4.15 to 8.30 pm (6.30 pm on Saturday). Both offices can reserve a hotel room for you.

For information on the Flanders region, contact the Comité Régional de Tourisme (☎ 20.60.69.62), near the main tourist office at 26 Place Rihour.

Money The Banque de France (☎ 20.40.47.47) is at 75 Rue Royale. More central is Crédit Lyonnais (☎ 20.30.44.44) at 28 Rue Nationale, which is open on weekdays from 8 am to 4.30 pm. There's a Barclays Bank two blocks west. Both the main tourist office and the annexe have exchange services.

The Giants

In far northern France, as in a number of other parts of Western Europe, *Géants* (Giants) – huge wickerwork statues up to 8½ metres tall animated by a person standing inside – emerge to run about, dance and add to the merriment of local carnivals and feast days. Each has a name and a personality, usually based either on characters from legends or on remarkable personages from local history. The Giants marry each other and have children, creating, over the years, complicated family relationships. When old and tatty they die, providing an occasion for all the locals to turn out for the final blaze.

A tradition in this region (though nowhere else in France) since the 16th century, nearly 200 Giants now live in towns around the Far North, including Dunkerque, Douai, Bailleul, Aire-sur-la-Lys and Cassel. Your best chance to see them is at pre-Lent carnivals and during Easter (eg Easter Monday) and summer festivities. ∎

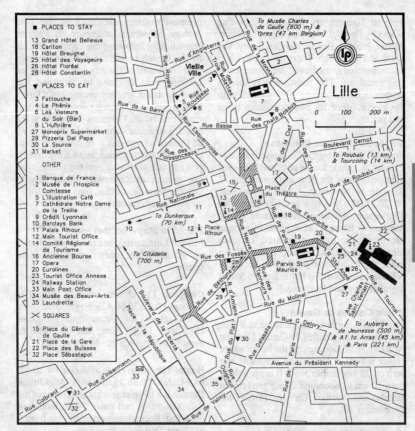

FAR NORTH

PLACES TO STAY

13 Grand Hôtel Bellevue
18 Cariton
19 Hôtel Breughel
25 Hôtel des Voyageurs
26 Hôtel Floréal
28 Hôtel Constantin

PLACES TO EAT

3 Fattouche
4 Le Phénix
6 Les Visteurs
   du Soir (Bar)
8 L'Huftrière
27 Monoprix Supermarket
29 Pizzeria Del Papa
30 La Source
31 Market

OTHER

1 Banque de France
2 Musée de l'Hospice
   Comtesse
3 L'Illustration Café
7 Cathédrale Notre Dame
   de la Treille
9 Crédit Lyonnais
10 Barclays Bank
11 Palais Rihour
12 Main Tourist Office
14 Comité Régional
   de Tourisme
16 Ancienne Bourse
17 Opera
20 Eurolines
23 Tourist Office Annexe
24 Railway Station
33 Main Post Office
34 Musée des Beaux-Arts
35 Laundrette

SQUARES

15 Place du Général
   de Gaulle
21 Place de la Gare
22 Place des Buisses
32 Place Sébastapol

To Musée Charles
de Gaulle (600 m) &
Ypres (47 km Belgium)

Lille

0   100   200 m

To Roubaix (13 km)
& Tourcoing (14 km)

To Dunkerque
(70 km)

To Citadelle
(700 m)

To Auberge
de Jeunesse (500 m)
& A1 to Arras (45 km)
& Paris (221 km)

Post The main post office (☎ 20.54.70.13) at 7 Place de la République is open on weekdays from 8 am to 5 pm and on Saturday from 8 am to noon.

Lille's postcode is 59000.

Laundry The Lavorama on Rue Ovigneur is open daily from 7 am to 8 pm.

Emergency For 24-hour medical emergencies, contact the Médecins de Garde de Lille (☎ 20.98.25.25) at 13 Blvd de la Liberté. The Cité Hospitalière (☎ 20.44.59.62) is at 2 Ave Oscar Lambret.

Ancienne Bourse

From Place Rihour, cobblestone streets lead east to Place du Théâtre and the ornate old Stock Exchange, a Flemish Renaissance structure built in 1652 that incorporates elements of the Louis XIII style.

North of the Ancienne Bourse is Lille's most inviting quarter for idle wandering – the **Vieille Ville**.

Musée des Beaux-Arts

The outstanding Fine Arts Museum (☎ 20.57.01.84) at the southern end of Place de la République has a superb collection of

15th to 20th-century paintings, including works by David, Delacroix, Goya, El Greco, Monet, Picasso, Renoir, Rubens, Sisley, Van Dyck and Van Gogh. There are also exhibits of archaeology, medieval sculpture, coins and ceramics. The museum was due to reopen in the autumn of 1993 – check with the tourist office for new admission times and prices.

Musée de l'Hospice Comtesse

Founded in 1236 by the Comtesse Jeanne de Flandre as a home for the poor and later used as an orphanage, the Hospice Comtesse at 32 Rue de la Monnaie – now a museum (☎ 20.51.02.62) – is a lovely example of 17th-century sandstone architecture. Inside this former hospital are exhibits of antique furniture, the decorative arts, Flemish tilework and the like. It is open from 10 am to 12.30 pm and 2 to 6 pm (closed Tuesday). Admission costs 10FF but is free on Saturday afternoon and Wednesday.

Musée Charles de Gaulle

Five blocks north of the Hospice at 9 Rue Princesse is the Charles de Gaulle Museum (☎ 20.31.96.03), occupying the house where France's WW II leader and president was born on 22 November 1890. It is open daily from 10 am to noon and 2 to 5 pm (closed Monday and Tuesday). Entry is 7FF (2FF for those under 16).

Musée d'Art Moderne du Nord

This well-regarded museum, eight km east of Lille in the new city of Villeneuve-d'Ascq, has hundreds of works of modern art, many from the period between 1900 and 1940. Artists represented include Braque, Modigliani, Léger and Picasso. It is open daily, except Monday and Tuesday, from 10 am (2 pm on Wednesday) to 6.30 pm. To get there, take metro line No 1 (in the direction of 4 Cantons) to Pont de Bois. From there take bus No 41 to Parc Urbain.

Citadelle

Known as the Queen of Citadels, this pentagonal, star-shaped fortress was built by the greatest military architect of the 17th century, Sébastien Le Prestre de Vauban, immediately following the capture of Lille by the French in 1667. Situated on marshland north-west of the city centre, its angled bastions were designed to withstand hits from the latest artillery projectiles. During both world wars, many people were executed here by the Germans. These days, the massive structure – the best preserved of all of Vauban's fortresses – continues to function, as Vauban intended, as an army base. If you can talk your way past the guards, you can wander in. Otherwise, from May to October the tourist office runs tours (30FF) on Sunday afternoon.

Places to Stay – bottom end

Most of Lille's many one and two-star hotels are in the slightly seedy area near the train station.

Camping The closest camping ground is *L'Image* (☎ 20.35.69.42), 10 km north-west of Lille at 140 Rue Brune in the suburb of Houplines. To get there, take the metro to Saint Philibert, then bus No 77 or 79.

Hostel The *Auberge de Jeunesse* (☎ 20.52.98.94; fax 20.88.29.09) at 1 Ave Julien Destrée is a 10-minute walk south-east of the train station. A bed costs 54FF, including breakfast. Reception is open all year from 5 to 11 pm. Parking is available.

Hotels Facing the station, one of the cheapest options is the *Hôtel des Voyageurs* (☎ 20.06.43.14) at 10 Place de la Gare, where singles/doubles start at 70/80FF. The beds are a bit lumpy but the rooms are clean. Another good choice is the quiet *Floréal* (☎ 20.06.36.21) at 21 Rue Sainte Anne with singles/doubles from 90/110FF.

Towards the centre, the *Breughel* (☎ 20.06.06.69; fax 20.63.25.27) at 35 Parvis Saint Maurice has a range of decent rooms starting at 130FF. In the pedestrianised part of the city centre, the *Constantin* (☎ 20.54.32.26) at 5 Rue des Fossés is probably your best bet,

with singles (just two of them) for 80FF and doubles from 130FF.

Places to Stay – top end

The *Grand Hôtel Bellevue* (☎ 20.57.45.64; fax 20.40.07.93) at 5 Rue Jean Roisin is centrally located and has very comfortable rooms and friendly staff. Singles/doubles are in the range of 375/760FF. Also central is the plush *Carlton* (☎ 20.55.24.11; fax 20.51.48.17) at 3 Rue de Paris, close to the Ancienne Bourse. Elegant singles/doubles cost 690/790FF.

Places to Eat

Rue de Béthune is lined with rather unexciting restaurants. The haunts on Rue Royale in the Vieille Ville have more character.

Restaurants *Pizzeria Del Papa* (☎ 20.54.20.21) at 8 Rue d'Amiens attracts a young crowd by offering cheap pizzas from only 25FF. A block away, *La Source* (☎ 20.57.53.07) at 13 Rue du Plat is a macrobiotic food shop with a relaxing vegetarian restaurant at the back. It's open Monday to Saturday until 7 pm (9 pm on Friday).

On Rue Royale, you might try *Le Phénix* (☎ 20.55.75.10), an Indian restaurant at No 19. It is closed on Sunday and at lunchtime on Saturday and Monday. For Lebanese food, *Fattouche* (☎ 20.06.69.82) at 25 Rue des Trois Molettes serves a lunchtime *menu* (entrée plus plat du jour) for 38FF. Prices are higher in the evening.

Le Hochepot (☎ 20.20.54.17.59) at 6 Rue Nouveau Siècle offers delicious regional specialities at reasonable prices. *Menus* cost between 130 and 180FF. Try the coq à la bière or the carbonade, a Flemish beef stew that is also cooked in beer.

For fabulous seafood and traditional French cuisine, try *L'Huîtrière* (☎ 20.55.43.41) at No 3 of the curiously named Rue des Chats Bossus (street of the Hunchback Cats). Decorated with mosaics both inside and out, this appealing restaurant doubles as a fish shop and delicatessen. Inside you will find impressive displays of crustaceans in large glass tanks. Fresh game birds, such as

pheasants, are also on offer. À la carte meals will cost around 280 to 500FF. The restaurant is closed on Sunday evenings and from the last week of July to the end of August.

Self-Catering The *Monoprix supermarket* on Rue du Molinel is open Monday to Saturday from 8.30 am to 7.15 pm (8 pm on Friday). A *food market* is set up on Place Sébastopol on Wednesday and Saturday mornings. The Vieille Ville harbours some great delicatessens with all sorts of irresistible delicacies. One of the best is *Cnockaert* at 37 Rue Grande Chaussée, with a goose in the window.

Entertainment

Bars In the Vieille Ville, *L'Illustration* at 18 Rue Royale is a dark cosy café with a good selection of Belgian brews selling for double what they cost across the border. Round the corner on Rue Jean-Jacques Rousseau, you can play chess under purple fluorescent lights in *Les Visiteurs du Soir*. Near the station you will find cheaper pubs along Ave Charles Saint Venant.

Getting There & Away

Train The train station is on Place de la Gare, about 500 metres south-east of Place du Général de Gaulle. The information office (☎ 20.78.50.50) is open Monday to Saturday from 8.30 am to 7 pm.

Lille, an important rail junction, has frequent trains to – among other places – Paris's Gare du Nord (150FF; 2¼ hours; one hour by TGV), Calais (70FF; 1¼ hours), Dunkerque (64FF; two hours), Boulogne (91FF; 2½ hours) and Arras (46FF; four hours). Internationally, there are trains to Brussels (Bruxelles in French; 71FF; 1¾ hours) and Antwerp (Anvers in French; 85FF; 1¾ hours).

Bus The Eurolines office (☎ 20.78.18.88) at 23 Parvis Saint Maurice is open Tuesday to Saturday from 9 am to noon and 2 to 7 pm.

Hitching Autostop (☎ 20.42.08.88) has an office in the Centre de Jeunesse at 21 Rue

Patou. For more information about Hitching see the Getting Around chapter.

Getting Around

Lille's fully automatic metro, inaugurated in 1983, was the first of its kind in the world. Both the metro and local buses are run by TCC (☎ 20.98.50.50), which has an information kiosk under the train station. A number of local buses stop at Place des Buisses, which is next to the train station. A single ride costs 7FF on either the bus or metro.

DUNKERQUE

It's hard to think of a more uninspiring introduction to France than Dunkerque (population 70,000), France's northernmost town. Its economy is based on heavy industry and the huge commercial harbour, the third-largest in France. Swept by regular storms and with clouds of pollution shading its beaches, Dunkerque is not somewhere you're likely to be tempted to spend much time, especially since it's much less important as a passenger port than either Calais or Boulogne. If you're passing through, do it quickly or during the pre-Lent period, when the people of Dunkerque forget their town's usual greyness and put on one of the most colourful carnivals in far northern France.

History

Dunkerque, whose name means Church of the Dunes in Flemish, was contested by France, England, Holland and Spain in the 16th and 17th centuries because of its strategic position on Europe's north coast. It was captured once and for all by France in 1662. Under Louis XIV, it served as a base for French privateers, including the daring Jean Bart (1650-1702), who preyed on English and Dutch ships.

In May and June 1940, Dunkerque earned a place in the history books when 350,000 men of the British Expeditionary Force and other Allied troops, sent to defend France against German aggression, were surrounded by the advancing German armies. Hundreds of small fishing craft and pleasure boats braved heavy artillery and air attacks to ferry almost all of the troops from the beaches of Dunkerque to the safety of England. Conducted in the difficult early part of WW II, this unplanned and chaotic retreat was considered an important demonstration of British resourcefulness and determination. By the end of WW II, over three-quarters of Dunkerque had been turned into ruins.

Orientation

The town centre, set well back from the sea, is around Place du Général de Gaulle and Place Jean Bart. The harbour lies to the west and north-west. The beach, with its waterfront esplanade, Digue de Mer, is north-east of the centre.

Information

The tourist office (☎ 28.26.27.28) is in the base of the belfry (originally part of the church of Saint Éloi) on Rue de l'Amiral Ronarc'h. It is open Tuesday to Friday from 9 am to 12.30 pm and 1.30 to 6.30 pm and on Saturday from 9 am to 6.30 pm. The tourist office annexe (☎ 28.26.28.88), on the waterfront at 46 Digue de Mer, is only open from Easter to 30 September daily from 9 am to 7 pm. When the banks are closed, both the main office and the annexe will exchange money.

Post The main post office is on Place du Général de Gaulle.

Dunkerque's postcode is 59140.

Musée des Beaux-Arts

The Fine Arts Museum (☎ 28.66.21.57) at Place du Général de Gaulle has an unspectacular collection of Flemish, Dutch, Italian and French works, many from the 17th century. Over 100 boat models are on display on the ground floor. The museum is open from 10 am to noon and 2 to 6 pm (closed Tuesday). Admission is 6FF.

Musée d'Art Contemporain

Of more interest is the Contemporary Art Museum (☎ 28.59.21.65) on Ave des Bains,

next to the channel known as Exutoire des Wateringues. It is housed in a striking modern building surrounded by a sculpture garden. Works on display date from 1950 to the present. It is open from 10 am to 7 pm (6 pm in winter) daily except Tuesday. Admission is 6FF. This place is 1.25 km north of the centre towards the beach – to get there, take bus No 3.

Festivals

Dunkerque's carnival, held before Lent, originated with the town's cod fishermen, for whom it constituted a final fling before setting off for months of fishing in the waters off Iceland. Today, each part of the city has its 'gang' of costumed revellers who consummate the festivities (held in the pre-Lent period) by gathering at the Hôtel de Ville and pelting everyone with kippers.

Places to Stay

Camping The three-star *Camping Municipal* (☎ 28.69.26.68), on the beach four km east of the train station on Blvd de l'Europe, is open from 1 March to 30 November. It costs 5FF to pitch a tent and 12FF per person. To get there, take bus No 3 to the end of the line.

Hostel Thanks to its location on the beach two km north-east of the train station, the *Auberge de Jeunesse* (☎ 28.63.36.34) at Place Paul Asseman is an excellent choice. A bed costs 43FF. Reception is open from 5.30 to 11 pm. To get there from the train station, take bus No 3 (the last one is at 9 pm) ـo the Piscine stop and follow the signs.

Hotels There's a cluster of hotels in front of the train station. One of the cheapest is the *Hôtel à la Gare du Nord* (☎ 28.66.88.34) at 7 Place de la Gare, which has basic singles/ doubles from 95/110FF. More welcoming is the *Hôtel de Bretagne* (☎ 28.59.02.20) at 4 Place de la Gare, which has reasonable singles/doubles for 110/120FF.

For something more stylish, the *Hôtel XIXe Siècle* (☎ 28.66.79.28), at 1 Place de la Gare, on the corner to the left as you leave

the train station, has comfortable singles/ doubles from 160FF/200FF. There are plenty of better options on the seafront along Digue de Mer – bus No 3 will take you there. The *Hôtel Familial* (☎ 28.63.23.90), half a block from the sea at 3 Rue de la Digue, has rooms from 100FF.

Places to Eat

Dunkerque is a good place to gorge yourself with *moules* (mussels).

Restaurants Around the train station, the place offering the best value is *Le Pénélope* at 9 Place de la Gare, where two local women serve three-course lunch *menus* for 47FF. This place is closed on weekends. In the town centre, *Aux Halles* (☎ 28.66.64.39), a brasserie up the street from the tourist office at 35 Rue de l'Amiral Ronarc'h, has a basic *menu* for 38FF.

At the beach, the *Auberge de Jeunesse* (☎ 28.63.36.34) at Place Paul Asseman offers a copious lunch for 40FF. *Produits de la Mer* (☎ 28.63.38.92) at 12 Place Paul Asseman has a range of reasonably priced seafood *menus*. Attached to the *Hôtel Familial* (☎ 28.63.23.90) at 3 Rue de la Digue is a cheap, traditional restaurant offering discounts for students. They have a *menu* for 49FF.

Self-Catering A number of *food shops* are located near the tourist office, and a *food market* is held on Place du Général de Gaulle on Wednesday and Saturday mornings.

Getting There & Away

Train The train station (☎ 20.78.50.50) is about 800 metres south-west of the town centre. Among the destinations served are Paris's Gare du Nord (172FF; three hours; six a day), Arras (75FF; 1¼ hours) and Lille (61FF; 1⅓ hours). The last train to Lille is at 7.30 pm.

Boat Sally Line, the only passenger ferry company operating from Dunkerque, links the Port Ouest (western port), which is about about 10 km west of town, with Ramsgate,

England. Sally Line's main office (☎ 28.21.43.44) at Port Ouest is open on weekdays from 9 am to 5.30 pm; for later sailings, it opens an hour before departure. In town, the company has an information kiosk midway between the tourist office and the train station on Rue des Fusiliers Marins. It is open Monday to Saturday from 12.30 pm to 7.30 pm.

There are two ways to get from Dunkerque to the Port Ouest: you can take one of Sally Line's shuttle buses from the company's information kiosk (free); or you can take local bus No 7 (12FF), which runs until 5.30 pm, from the train station.

For details on trans-Channel ferry schedules and tariffs, see the Sea section in the introductory Getting There & Away chapter.

Getting Around

Dunkerque's local buses stop at Place de la Gare, where the local public transport company, STDE (☎ 28.60.08.00), has an information office.

CALAIS

'I hate it so much yet I'm always so glad to see it ...'
Charles Dickens (1861)

Calais (population 80,000), only 34 km from the English town of Dover (Douvres in French), has long been the principal passenger port for travel between the UK and mainland Europe. Richard I (nicknamed Cœur de Lion, or the Lion-Heart), king of England, helped to launch the town's popularity with trans-Channel travellers when he passed through the city on his way to the Third Crusade in 1190. His compatriots liked the town so much that in 1346 King Edward III of England returned to besiege and then capture the town; thus began over 200 years of English rule. The French retook Calais in 1558 but lost it to the Spaniards for two years in the mid-1590s. In mid-1944, during the three months before its liberation, the Germans used Calais as a base to launch flying bombs against Britain.

Each year, modern-day Calais – often referred to in the UK as the Gateway to Europe – serves as a transit point for more than 10 million people crossing the Strait of Dover. Most continue quickly onwards to more alluring destinations, for, apart from a couple of museums and Rodin's famous sculpture, *The Burghers of Calais*, there's little to see in town except a horde of shops, restaurants and hypermarkets, all ablaze with English signs designed to attract money-laden day-trippers.

The much-heralded Channel Tunnel ducks under the Channel 12 km south-west of Calais near the village of Sangatte. The land between Sangatte and Coquelles, another once-quiet village on the outskirts of Calais, has been turned into a maze of new road and rail lines. Blown way over budget and plagued by delays, the tunnel is expected to open in May 1994.

Orientation

The centre of Calais, whose main square is Place d'Armes, is encircled by canals and harbour basins. The Gare Centrale, Calais's main train station, is 650 metres south of Place d'Armes – follow Rue Royale, which is lined with restaurants and shops. Further south still, around the main post office, is the centre of the nontouristic part of town.

The ferry terminal and the other train station, Gare Calais-Maritime, are about 1.2 km north of Place d'Armes. Further north still, about three km from Place d'Armes, is the Hoverport (the hovercraft port).

Information

Tourist Office The tourist office (☎ 21.96.62.40) at 12 Blvd Georges Clemenceau is open Monday to Saturday from 9 am to 12.30 pm and 2.30 to 6.30 pm. From July to mid-September it's open daily from 9 am to 7.30 pm. Hotel reservations cost 10FF.

Money In the town centre, Crédit Maritime Mutuel (☎ 21.97.81.00) at 20 Place d'Armes is open on weekdays from 9.15 am to noon and 1.30 to 4.45 pm. It charges a 15FF commission. The Royal Change (☎ 21.97.79.29) at 4 Rue Royale, an exchange bureau with

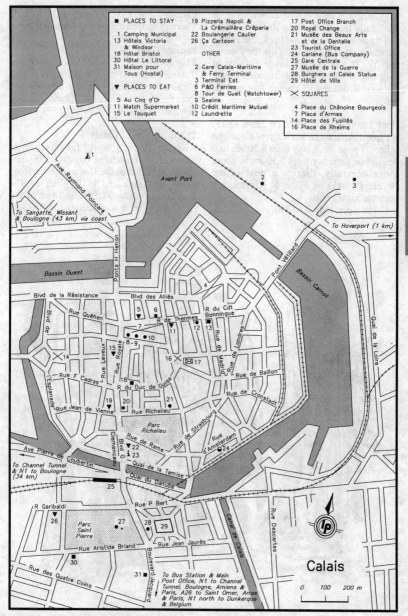

FAR NORTH

PLACES TO STAY
1 Camping Municipal
13 Hôtels Victoria & Windsor
18 Hôtel Bristol
30 Hôtel Le Littoral
31 Maison pour Tous (Hostel)

PLACES TO EAT
5 Au Coq d'Or
11 Match Supermarket
15 Le Touquet

19 Pizzeria Napoli & La Crémaillère Crêperie
22 Boulangerie Caulier
26 Ça Cartoon

OTHER
2 Gare Calais-Maritime & Ferry Terminal
3 Terminal Est
6 P&O Ferries
8 Tour de Guet (Watchtower)
9 Sealink
10 Crédit Maritime Mutuel
12 Laundrette

17 Post Office Branch
20 Royal Change
21 Musée des Beaux Arts et de la Dentelle
23 Tourist Office
24 Cariane (Bus Company)
25 Gare Centrale
27 Musée de la Guerre
28 Burghers of Calais Statue
29 Hôtel de Ville

SQUARES
4 Place du Chanoine Bourgeois
7 Place d'Armes
14 Place des Fusillés
16 Place de Rheims

Calais

0   100   200 m

slightly lower rates but no commission, is open daily from 9.30 am to 10 pm.

There's round-the-clock currency exchange (☎ 21.97.33.38) at the ferry terminal. You'll aiso find exchange bureaux at both train stations. Outside banking hours, the tourist office will change foreign currency.

Post The main post office (☎ 21.36.43.13) at Place d'Alsace, one km south of the tourist office, is open weekdays from 8.30 am to 6 pm and on Saturday from 8.30 am to noon. More centrally, there's a post office (☎ 21.34.49.45) on Place de Rheims; it's open the same hours.

Calais's postcode is 61200.

Laundry The Lavomatique at 34 Rue de Thermes is open daily from 7 am to 8 pm.

Tour de Guet

The 13th-century watchtower at Place d'Armes is one of the few remnants of pre-20th-century Calais – the city was bombed from the air at the end of WW I and virtually demolished in WW II.

The Burghers of Calais

Auguste Rodin's world-famous bronze statue of six emaciated but proud figures, known in French as the *Monument des Bourgeois de Calais* and in English as *The Burghers of Calais*, stands in front of the Hôtel de Ville. It was sculpted in 1895 to

The Burghers of Calais

honour the six citizens of Calais who, in 1347, after eight months of obstinate defiance of the besieging English forces, surrendered themselves and the keys to the starving city to Edward III in an effort to prevent the town's population from being massacred. In the end, Edward spared both the people of Calais and their six brave leaders. There are other castings of *The Burghers of Calais* in Paris (in the garden of the Musée Rodin), London, Washington, DC, and Los Angeles.

Musée des Beaux-Arts et de la Dentelle
The Museum of Fine Arts & Lace (☎ 21.46.62.00) at 25 Rue Richelieu has a large collection of lace samples in addition to exhibits on local history and displays of 19th and 20th-century art. It is open from 10 am to noon and 2 to 5.30 pm (closed Tuesday). Admission is 10FF (5FF for children). Entrance is free on Wednesday.

Musée de la Guerre
The War Museum (☎ 21.34.21.57), which occupies a bunker built as a German naval headquarters, is opposite the Hôtel de Ville in Parc Saint Pierre. Displays trace local events during WW II. From March to December it is open daily from 10 am to 5 pm. Entrance costs 13/8FF for adults/children.

Places to Stay
Camping The nearest camping ground is the two-star *Camping Municipal* (☎ 21.97.89.79), at the entry to the harbour just off Ave Raymond Poincaré. Open all year, it charges 36FF for two people, including a tent and parking. To get there from the Gare Centrale, take bus No 3 and get off at the Pluviose stop.

Hostel As its name implies, the *Maison pour Tous* (☎ 21.34.69.53) at 41 Blvd Jacquard welcomes everyone, including young travellers, but only from June to September. A bed in a very basic dorm room costs 35FF.

Hotels The *Hôtel Le Littoral* (☎ 21.34.47.28) at 71 Rue Aristide Briand, across the

park from the Gare Centrale, has spacious if somewhat sparingly decorated singles/doubles/triples/quads starting at 100/120/140/160FF. The central and friendly *Hôtel Bristol* (☎ 21.34.53.24) at 15 Rue du Duc de Guise has cosy attic rooms from 130/140FF for singles/doubles. The *Hôtel Victoria* (☎ 21.34.38.32) at 8 Rue du Commandant Bonningue is a homy, two-star hotel with one-star prices. Singles/doubles start at 105/120FF. A few doors up the road at 2 Rue du Commandant Bonningue is the plusher and more expensive *Hôtel Windsor* (☎ 21.34.59.40; fax 21.97.68.59).

Places to Eat
Calais does not lack places to eat – a good place to look is on Rue Royale and along nearby side streets.

Restaurants On Place d'Armes, *Au Coq d'Or* (☎ 21.34.79.05) at No 31 offers grilled dishes and seafood; *menus* start at 50FF. This place is closed on Wednesday. *Le Touquet* (☎ 21.34.64.18), nearby on Rue Royale, is nothing special but it has a good 60FF *menu* which includes a glass of wine.

Pizzeria Napoli (☎ 21.34.49.39) at 2 Rue Jean de Vienne has *menus* from 40FF. It is closed on Monday. *La Crémaillère Crêperie* (☎ 21.96.20.55), just up the street at 12 Rue Jean de Vienne, has a huge choice of Breton crepes. *Menus* start at 36FF.

Behind the Gare Centrale, *Ça Cartoon* (☎ 21.34.99.34) at 7 Rue Garibaldi has a 70FF *menu* which includes wine and coffee. The nearby *Le Littoral* (☎ 21.34.47.28) at 71 Rue Aristide Briand, attached to the hotel of the same name, serves a three-course *menu* on its leafy patio for 60FF.

Self-Catering The *Match supermarket* on Place d'Armes is open weekdays from 9 am to 12.30 pm and 2.30 to 7.30 pm and Saturday from 9 am to 5.30 pm. In July and August it's also open on Sunday from 9 am to noon. Towards the main post office, the *Prisunic supermarket* at 17 Blvd Jacquard is open Monday to Saturday from 8.30 am to 7.30

pm. From May to December it's also open on Sunday.

Next to the tourist office, *Boulangerie Caulier* at 18 Blvd Georges Clemenceau is open on Monday and Wednesday to Saturday from 7 am to 7.30 pm; Sunday hours are 7 am to 1 pm.

Things to Buy

Calais has long been famous for its mechanically produced lace, but as far as popularity with the masses goes, dainty doilies are far less in demand than ordinary French wines and cheeses, which are snatched up by eager day-trippers from across the Channel. Billboards emblazoned with the names of the nearest suburban hypermarkets – and precise directions on how to get there – assault your eyeballs as soon as your feet hit dry land. If you're without a car, you can get from the Gare Centrale to the *Mammouth hypermarket* on Ave Roger Salengro by taking bus No 5. To get to the *Continent hypermarket*, which is on Rue Vervant Toumaniantz about three km east of the town centre, hop on bus No 4 at the Gare Centrale.

Getting There & Away

Train Calais has two train stations: the Gare Centrale (Gare Calais-Ville), 650 metres south of Place d'Armes; and the smaller Gare Calais-Maritime, near the ferry terminal. In 1993, Calais was connected to Paris's Gare du Nord by TGV.

At the Gare Centrale, the information office (π 21.80.50.50) is open on weekdays from 9.30 am to 12.30 pm and 1.30 to 7 pm and on Saturday from 9 am to 12.30 pm and 1.30 to 6 pm. The ticket office at the Gare Calais- Maritime is open from 8 am to 9 pm.

Most trains to Paris's Gare du Nord (176FF; 3½ hours by regular train; one hour 50 minutes by TGV) leave from the Gare Centrale and go via Boulogne and Amiens (Lille in the case of the TGV). There are also three daily trains to Paris from the Gare Calais-Maritime, timed to meet up with incoming Sealink ferries; the last train leaves at about 7.45 pm (8.15 pm on Sunday). Cities with direct trains from Calais include Boulogne (36FF; 40 minutes; 17 a day) and Lille (92FF; 1¾ hours; 10 a day). From Lille there are connecting trains northward to Brussels and Amsterdam.

Bus The bus station is one km south of the tourist office on Blvd Léon Gambetta. Buses serving the Calais area are run by Cariane (π 21.34.74.40), whose office is at 10 Rue d'Amsterdam but whose buses also stop in front of the train station. Cariane has three buses a day to Boulogne (32FF; 40 minutes) and Dunkerque (35FF; 50 minutes).

Car Car rental firms in Calais include ABAS (π 21.34.67.67) at 14 Rue des Thermes, Avis (π 21.34.66.50) at 36 Place d'Armes and Budget (π 21.96.42.20) at 44 Place d'Armes. Europcar has offices at 22 Place d'Armes (π 21.97.31.72; fax 21.97.92.79), the ferry terminal (π 21.96.73.40) and the Hoverport (π 21.96.47.16). Citer (π 21.96. 44.44), near the train station at 17 Rue du Commandant Bonnigue, is probably among the cheapest in town.

For information on the Channel Tunnel, see To/From England under Land in the introductory Getting There & Away chapter. A new highway connecting Calais with Rouen is expected to be finished by 1994.

Ferry Boats to/from Dover dock at the ferry terminal, which is slightly over one km north of Place d'Armes. If you have a vehicle, go to the Terminal Est (East Terminal). For details on tariffs and schedules, see To/From England under Sea in the introductory Getting There & Away chapter.

P&O Ferries has two offices in Calais. The one in the centre of town (π 21.46.04.40) at 41 Place d'Armes is open on weekdays from 8.30 am to 6 pm and on Saturday until noon. The other one (π 21.46.10.10), which is at the Terminal Est, is open 24 hours a day. Sealink's office (π 21.34.55.00) at 2 Place d'Armes is open on weekdays from 9 am to 12.30 pm and 1.30 to 6 pm. Sealink can also be reached on π 21.46.80.00. at its ferry terminal office, which is open 24 hours a day throughout the year.

Hovercraft SeaCats and hovercraft to Dover, operated by Hoverspeed (☎ 05.26.03.60), depart from the Hoverport, which is three km north-east of the town. Hoverspeed's office is at the Hoverport.

Getting Around

Bus Local buses, run by STCE (☎ 21.36.45.65), operate from a hub at the theatre, which is about 700 metres south of the Gare Centrale, near the junction of Blvd Jacquard and Blvd Gambetta. Many lines also stop at the Gare Centrale.

Taxi There's a taxi rank outside the Gare Centrale. To order a taxi, call SDF Taxi (☎ 21.97.05.22) or Union (☎ 21.96.29.29). A taxi from the Gare Centrale to the Hoverport should cost about 45FF day or night (50FF on Sunday).

Bicycle During summer, bikes can be hired at the Gare Centrale for 50FF for the first day and 40FF for each additional day.

To/From the Ports All the ferry companies serving Calais operate free shuttle buses from the centre of town to the relevant port of embarkation. The buses leave about 45 minutes before the ship is scheduled to set sail. Hoverspeed and Sealink buses (last one at 6 pm) leave from the Gare Centrale; P&O's buses (last one at 8.15 pm) depart from the company's office at Place d'Armes.

AROUND CALAIS

The shoreline between Calais and Boulogne, the **Côte d'Opale** (Opal Coast), is characterised by chalky cliffs, sand dunes and vast beaches that are often buffeted by gale force winds. Marking the halfway point is **Cap Gris Nez** (Cape Grey Nose), which affords excellent views across the Channel to the coast of England.

BOULOGNE

Although Boulogne-sur-Mer (population 44,000) is the most important fishing port in France, a fact that won't be lost on your nostrils, the city is also the most inviting of France's three main Channel ports. Here, unlike Calais, you are unmistakably in France. The rectangular Ville Haute (Upper City), whose ramparts date from the 13th century, is perched on a hill overlooking the modern Basse Ville (Lower City) and the Channel.

North of town along the Côte d'Opale (see the Around Calais section), there are white chalk cliffs, beaches and scattered remains from the world wars. The Colonne de la Grande Armée (Column of the Grand Army), three km north of Boulogne, commemorates the troops and naval vessels that Napoleon assembled here from 1803 for his projected invasion of England, an operation put on indefinite hold by the Battle of Trafalgar (1805).

Orientation

Boulogne is a pleasant town for wandering around, especially if it's your first day in France. Central Boulogne consists of three distinct parts: the walled, hilltop Ville Haute; the modern Basse Ville, which is sandwiched between the Ville Haute and the Liane River; and the ferry port area on the west bank of the Liane. The streets leading from Quai de la Poste through Place Dalton up to the Ville Haute are the liveliest part of town.

From the Gare Maritime, foot passengers reach the town by a covered flyover that ends at Pont Marguet, the bridge next to the tourist office. There are two train stations: the main Gare Centrale, 800 metres south of the Ville Haute, and the small Gare Maritime rail terminal at the ferry dock.

Information

Tourist Office The tourist office (☎ 21.31.68.38) is on Quai de la Poste. Most of the year it's open Monday to Saturday from 9 am to 7 pm and Sunday from 10 am to 1 pm and 2 to 5 pm. In July and August it's open daily from 9 am to 8 pm or later. The staff will make reservations for local hotels for no charge.

Money The Banque de France (☎ 21.30.01.12) at 1 Place Angleterre is open on week-

FAR NORTH

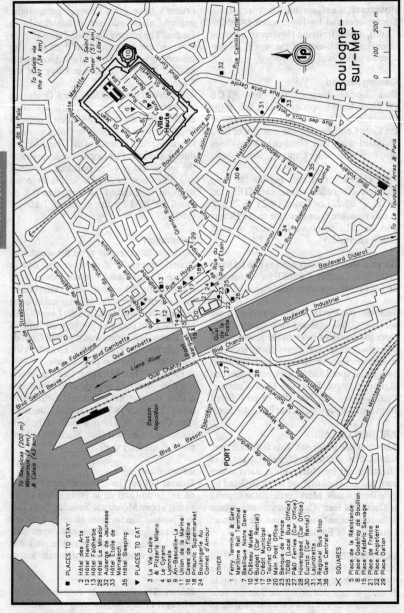

Boulogne-
sur-Mer

0   100   200 m

PLACES TO STAY

- 2   Hôtel des Arts
- 12 Hôtel Hamiot
- 13 Hôtel Faidherbe
- 32 Hôtel Le Dorado
- 33 Auberge de Jeunesse
- 35 Hôtel Étoile de Marrakech
- Hôtel Sleeping

PLACES TO EAT

- 3   La Vie Claire
- 4   Le Cyrano
- 9   An-Bascaille–La Lyonnais
- 11 Union de la Marine
- 16 Caves de Fidéline
- 18 Prisunic Supermarket
- 24 Boulangerie Au Cornet d'Amour
- 3   La Vie Claire
      & Pizzeria Milano

OTHER

- 1   Ferry Terminal & Gare Maritime Rail Terminal
- 7   Basilique Notre Dame
- 10 Château Musée
- 14 Budget (Car Rental)
- 17 Crédit Municipal
- 19 Tourist Office
- 20 Main Post Office
- 23 Banque de France
- 25 TCRB (Local Bus Office)
- 27 P&O Ferries (Car Office)
- 28 Hoverspeed (Car Office)
- 30 Euroto (Car Rental)
- 31 Laundrette
- 34 Regional Bus Stop
- 36 Gare Centrale

✕ **SQUARES**

- 5   Place de la Resistance
- 8   Place Godefroy de Bouillon
- 15 Place Frédéric Sauvage
- 21 Place de France
- 22 Place Angleterre
- 29 Place Dalton

days from 8.45 to 11.55 am and 1.20 to 3.55 pm. Crédit Municipal (☎ 21.91.07.46) at 10 Rue du Pot d'Étain is open on weekdays from 8.45 am to noon and 1.30 to 5.15 pm. You can also change money at the exchange bureau in the Gare Maritime, which is open from 9.45 am to noon and 1.15 to 6.15 pm and whenever a boat arrives.

Post The main post office (☎ 21.31.65.40) at Place Frédéric Sauvage is open on weekdays from 8.30 am to 6.30 pm and on Saturday from 8.30 am to noon. Foreign currency can be exchanged here.

Boulogne's postcode is 62200.

Laundry The Lavomatique at 51 Rue Nationale is open daily from 5.30 am to 9 pm.

Ville Haute

The rectangular Ville Haute, which is about 800 metres east of the tourist office along Grande Rue, is a medieval island set in the middle of the bustle of the Basse Ville, which was completely rebuilt after WW II. The dominant feature of the Ville Haute is the domed **Basilique Notre Dame** (1827-66), built on the site of a cathedral destroyed during the Revolution. Its architecture was influenced by a number of famous cathedrals, including St Peter's in Rome and St Paul's in London.

Château-Musée

Near the Basilique at the north-eastern end of Rue de Bernet is the Château-Musée (☎ 21.80.56.78), a 13th-century castle housing everything from Egyptian sarcophagi to 19th-century Inuit (Eskimo) masks. It's open from 10 am to 6 pm (closed Tuesday). Admission is 20FF for adults and 13FF for students and children. If you plan to see both this museum and Nausicaa, the discount combination ticket costs 55/35FF for adults/children.

Nausicaa

France's largest marine aquarium, Nausicaa (☎ 21.30.98.98), is on Blvd Sainte Beuve right next to the beach and the Liane River

about one km north of the tourist office. Opened in 1990, this ultramodern complex is open daily from 10 am to 8 pm (6 pm in winter). Admission for adults/students/children is 48/43/33FF.

Places to Stay

Unlike Calais, Boulogne has lots of cheap one and two-star hotels.

Camping The three-star *Camp du Phare* (☎ 21.31.69.20) is three km south-west of town on Quai de la Violette in Le Portel. It is open from 1 April to 30 September. To get there, take bus No 3.

Four km north of Boulogne in the seaside village of Wimereux, the two-star *Olympic* (☎ 21.32.45.63) at 49 Rue de la Libération is open from 15 March to 31 October. It charges 20FF per person. To get there, take bus No 1 or 2 (last one at 8 pm) from Place de France.

Hostel The *Auberge de Jeunesse* (☎ 21.31. 48.22; fax 21.80.94.23), near the Ville Haute at 36 Rue Porte Gayole, charges 57FF per person, including breakfast. Reception is open daily from 5 to 11 pm. This hostel is closed during the three weeks after Christmas.

Hotels You can't get any more central than the *Hôtel Hamiot* (☎ 21.31.44.20), which is above a busy brasserie at 1 Rue Faidherbe. Decent singles/doubles start at 100/110FF. Up the road at 12 Rue Faidherbe, the *Hôtel Faidherbe* (☎ 21.31.60.93; fax 21.87.01.14) has plush rooms starting at 150FF. *Le Mirador* (☎ 21.31.38.08), on the corner of Rue de la Lampe and Blvd Daunou, has basic but pleasant doubles from 120FF. Overlooking the port, the *Hôtel des Arts* (☎ 21.31. 53.31) at 102 Blvd Gambetta has ordinary singles/doubles from 97/119FF. Parking is available.

Near the Gare Centrale, the *Étoile de Marrakech* (☎ 21.31.38.42) at 226 Rue Nationale has really cheap rooms from 82FF. The friendly *Hôtel Sleeping* (☎ 21.80.62.79)

at 18 Blvd Daunou has average rooms from 90/110FF. It also has a bar.

Places to Eat

Boulogne's many seafood restaurants are somewhat scattered around town. Quai Gambetta and Place Dalton are good places to look for both *fruits des mer* (seafood) and traditional French cuisine. Prices in the Ville Haute tend to be higher than in the Basse Ville.

Restaurants *Caves de Fidèline* at 22 Rue du Pot d'Étain has a seafood *menu* for 87FF. The slightly drab *Union de la Marine* (☎ 21.31.38.83), on the waterfront at 18 Quai Gambetta, has three-course meals from 75FF.

Le Cyrano (☎ 21.31.66.57) at 6 Rue Coquelin has a basic but solid three-course *menu* for 48FF. On the same street, *Café de l'Aquarium* (at No 1) and *Pizzeria Milano* (☎ 21.30.01.88) have similar prices. *La Vie Claire* at 15 Rue Coquelin is a health-food shop with a corner for dine-in customers.

In the Ville Haute, the pedestrianised Rue de Lille offers several choices, including *Lyonnais* at No 11, which has standard *menus* from 75FF. *An-Bascaille-La* (☎ 21.80.57.30), opposite the Hôtel de Ville on Place Godefroy de Bouillon, specialises in Caribbean food. Their *menus* start at 59FF.

Near the Gare Centrale, the brasserie of the *Hôtel Étoile de Marrakech* (☎ 21.31.38.42) at 226 Rue Nationale specialises in couscous. It is closed on Wednesday.

Self-Catering There's a *food market* at Place Dalton on Wednesday and Saturday mornings. The *Prisunic supermarket* on Rue de la Lampe is open Monday to Thursday from 9 am to noon and 2 to 7 pm, on Friday from 9 am to 8 pm and on Saturday from 8.45 am to 7 pm. Down the same road at No 9, *Boulangerie Au Cornet d'Amour* is open daily from 7 am to 7 pm.

Getting There & Away

Train Boulogne has two train stations: the main Gare Centrale (Gare Boulogne-Ville) on Blvd Voltaire, which is about one km south-east of the tourist office, and the Gare Maritime rail terminal at the port. There are only two trains a day from the latter – both go to Paris's Gare du Nord via the Gare Centrale. One leaves daily at 4 pm, while the other runs Monday to Saturday at 7.40 pm.

The information office at the Gare Centrale (☎ 21.80.50.50) is open Monday to Saturday from 9.10 am to noon and 2 to 6.45 pm. There are direct trains to Paris's Gare du Nord (140FF; three hours; seven a day), Lille (91FF; 2½ hours), Amiens (80FF; 1½ hours; 10 a day), Arras (83FF; 1¾ hours; five a day) and Calais (36FF; 40 minutes; 17 a day). If you're heading straight for the Côte d'Azur, the overnight train via Avignon and Nice leaves nightly at 8.15 pm.

Bus There's no bus station as such – instead buses leave from a stop on Blvd Daunou. Buses to Calais are operated by Cars Cariane (☎ 21.34.74.40 in Calais), while services south to Le Touquet are run by Voyages Dumont. Check with the tourist office for details.

Car Car hire companies with local offices include Budget (☎ 21.87.50.60) at 4 Rue Faidherbe, Euroto (☎ 21.30.32.23) at 96 Rue Nationale and Hertz (☎ 21.31.53.14) at 85 Rue Victor Hugo. Europcar (☎ 21.80.95.62) has an agency at the ferry terminal. To contact ADA, probably the cheapest bet around, call ☎ 21.80.97.34.

Hitching To go to Paris via Abbeville, take bus No 17 to the last stop, which is one block from the N1 motorway.

Boat Regular ferry services between Boulogne – which is 45 km from Folkestone – and the English coast began in Roman times shortly after Emperor Claudius launched his conquest of England from Boulogne in 43 AD. These days, passenger ferries and SeaCats dock at the ferry terminal, which is westward across the river from the town centre. For details on tariffs and schedules, see To/From England under Sea in the introductory Getting There & Away

chapter. SeaCats operated by Hoverspeed (☎ 21.30.27.26) link Boulogne with Folkestone. Hoverspeed has two booking offices, one on Rue de Solferino for those with vehicles and the other at the ferry terminal for pedestrians. The office on Rue de Solferino is open daily from 9.15 am to 7.45 pm.

Getting Around

Bus Local buses are run by TCRB, better known as Le Bus, which has an information office (☎ 21.83.51.51) at 14 Rue de la Lampe. The main bus hub is on Place de France. A ticket for a single ride costs 6FF.

Taxis Taxis wait at both the Gare Maritime ferry dock and the Gare Centrale. To order a taxi, call ☎ 21.91.25.00.

AMIENS

Amiens (population 132,000), midway between the Channel ports of far northern France and Paris, is a convenient first (or last) stop in the 'real' France for trans-Channel travellers keen to steer clear of day-tripping shoppers. Although the city, once the capital of Picardy, suffered serious damage in both world wars, it proudly boasts France's largest cathedral (in terms of area) and has several interesting museums. The city, built along a marshy stretch of the Somme River, is also the city nearest the site of one of the bloodiest engagements of WW I, the First Battle of the Somme. The peaceful farmland near the site of the battle is marked by numerous war cemeteries.

Amiens was the birthplace of Pierre Choderlos de Laclos (1741-1803), author of *Les Liaisons Dangereuses* (Dangerous Liaisons), and was the adopted home of science fiction writer Jules Verne.

Orientation

Cathédrale Notre Dame and its spire provide the most obvious landmark in central Amiens. The main square is Place Gambetta. The train station, which is about a km east of Place Gambetta, has its own very obvious landmark, a 26-storey concrete tower known

as the Tour Perret. The Centre Commercial shopping complex is next to the train station.

Information

Tourist Office The main tourist office (☎ 22.91.79.28) is at 12 Rue du Chapeau de Violette near the 12th-century belfry, which was originally the town hall but served as a prison in the 16th century. It is open Monday to Saturday from 10 am to noon and 2 to 7 pm. The hotel reservation service is free.

The tourist office annexe (☎ 22.92.65.04) at the train station is open daily from 8 am (9.30 am on Sunday) to 7 pm (8 pm in summer). From May to mid-October, the tourist office has a kiosk (☎ 22.91.61.74) in front of the cathedral on Place Notre Dame; it's open daily from 9 am to 10 pm.

Money The Banque de France is south of the town centre on Rue de la République. Near the train station, the Banque Populaire in the basement of the Centre Commercial is open Tuesday to Saturday from 9.15 am to 12.30 pm and 1.45 to 5.45 pm. There are more banks on Place René Goblet.

Post The main post office (☎ 22.33.44.44) at 7 Rue des Vergeaux is open on weekdays from 8 am to 7 pm and on Saturday from 8 am to noon. There's a branch post office near the train station at 35 Place Alphonse Fiquet.

Amiens's postcode is 80000.

Laundry The laundrette just off Place Vogel at 43 Port d'Aval is open daily from 8 am to 8 pm.

Saint Leu Quarter

The medieval Saint Leu quarter north of the cathedral is the best place in town for a stroll, although overenthusiastic postwar renovations have rendered it reminiscent of a Hollywood movie set.

Cathédrale Notre Dame

The largest cathedral in France, Notre Dame Cathedral was begun in 1220 and finished (except for the lateral chapels and a few other bits) only 50 years later. Its unity of style, achieved thanks to the quick construction

(quick for cathedrals, that is), and the immenseness of the interior – the structure is 145 metres long, 70 metres wide at the transepts and 43 metres high in the middle of the nave – make this a truly superb example of Gothic architecture. The main doorway, sculpted in the 1230s, is famous for the finely executed figure of Jesus known as *Le Beau Dieu* (Christ in Serenity). The slender, 112-metre-high steeple, which was added in the 16th century, can be seen from wide and far. The cathedral is open daily from 7.30 am to 5 pm (7 pm from April to September).

Musée de Picardie

This museum (☎ 22.91.36.44), installed in an impressive building at 48 Rue de la République, has displays of local prehistory, Gallo-Roman and Mediterranean archaeology, medieval art, paintings from the 15th and later centuries and Revolutionary-era ceramics. It's open from 10 am to 12.30 pm and 2 to 6 pm (closed Monday). Admission is 15/5FF for adults/students but is free on Sunday.

Musée d'Art Local et d'Histoire Régionale

The Local Art & Regional History Museum (☎ 22.91.81.12) at 36 Rue Victor Hugo displays furniture and art from the time of Louis XV. Opening hours and admission prices are the same as for the Musée de Picardie.

Centre de Documentation Jules Verne

Jules Verne (1828-1905), the science fiction author whose novels (*Around the World in 80 Days*, *Journey to the Centre of the Earth* and *20,000 Leagues under the Sea*) foresaw some of the 20th century's most important scientific discoveries (eg space travel, the submarine, scuba diving gear, TV), wrote some of his most famous works in the turreted house at 2 Rue Charles Dubois. Now known as the Jules Verne Information Centre (☎ 22.45.37.84), it contains exhibits on his life, and is open Tuesday to Saturday from 9.30 am to noon and 2 to 6 pm. Entry costs 10/5FF for adults/children.

Les Hortillonnages

This cluster of market gardens, set among 300 hectares of waterways just 700 metres north-west of the city, has supplied the city with vegetables since the Middle Ages. From the entrance, a small kiosk (☎ 22.92.12.18) at 56 Blvd Beauvillé, punts take you around the peaceful canals. A one-hour tour costs 25/20FF for adults/children (no student discount). It is closed from 1 November to 1 April. The rest of the year it's open daily from 2 to 6 or 7 pm (4 or 5 pm in autumn).

Places to Stay

Hostel The startlingly red *Auberge de Jeunesse* (☎ 22.89.69.10; fax 22.45.13.04) at 6 Rue Saint Fuscien charges 60FF for a bed in a double or quad. Breakfast costs another 15FF. Reception closes at about 6.30 pm – if you'll be arriving later just telephone in advance. To get there from the train station, head south along Blvd de Belfort to the Jules Verne monument, turn left and cross the square. The hostel is just up on the right.

Hotels Around the train station, the best of the cheap hotels is probably the *Central Anzac* (☎ 22.91.57.91) at 17 Rue Alexandre Fatton. Started as a pub run by an Australian ex-serviceman, it has clean, comfortable singles/doubles from 120/155FF. The *Hôtel à l'Habitude* (☎ 22.91.69.78) at 7 Place Alphonse Fiquet has rooms from 135FF.

In the centre, the cosy *Le Goblet* (☎ 22.91.62.58) at Place René Goblet, on the corner of Rue Allart, has a few comfortable doubles from 100FF but the street noise can be annoying. *Les Touristes* (☎ 22.91.33.45) at 22 Place Notre Dame, which affords excellent straight-on views of the cathedral, has singles/doubles starting at 90/130FF. Nearby, *La Renaissance* (☎ 22.91.70.23) at 8bis Rue André is in the same price bracket. The lovely *Hôtel Victor Hugo* (☎ 22.91.57.91) at 2 Rue de l'Oratoire has stylish singles/doubles from 95/160FF.

Places to Eat

Up-market restaurants are plentiful in the Saint Leu area, especially on Rue des Majots

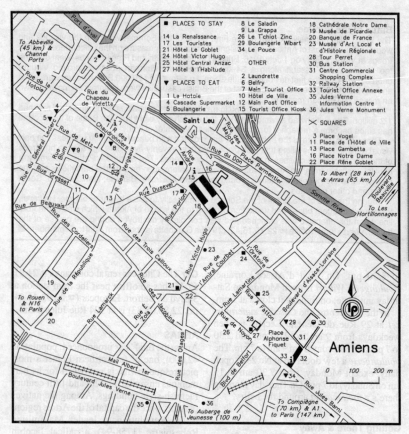

Map legend:

■ PLACES TO STAY
14 La Renaissance
17 Les Touristes
21 Hôtel Le Goblet
24 Hôtel Victor Hugo
25 Hôtel Central Anzac
27 Hôtel à l'Habitude

▼ PLACES TO EAT
1 La Hotoie
4 Cascade Supermarket
5 Boulangerie
8 Le Saladin
9 La Grappa
26 Le T'chiot Zinc
29 Boulangerie Wibart
34 Le Pouce

OTHER
2 Laundrette
6 Belfry
7 Main Tourist Office
10 Hôtel de Ville
12 Main Post Office
15 Tourist Office Kiosk
18 Cathédrale Notre Dame
19 Musée de Picardie
20 Banque de France
23 Musée d'Art Local et d'Histoire Régionale
28 Tour Perret
30 Bus Station
31 Centre Commercial Shopping Complex
32 Railway Station
33 Tourist Office Annexe
35 Jules Verne Information Centre
36 Jules Verne Monument

✕ SQUARES
3 Place Vogel
11 Place de l'Hôtel de Ville
13 Place Gambetta
16 Place Notre Dame
22 Place Rêne Goblet

and Rue du Don. For cheaper fare, you're better off in the city centre.

Restaurants The appealing *Le Pouce* at 16 Place Alphonse Fiquet (next to the train station) serves reasonable *menus* from 55FF and plats du jour from 38FF. It is closed on Monday. The small and inviting *Le T'chiot Zinc* (☎ 22.91.43.79) at 18 Rue de Noyon has a plat du jour for 42FF and offers a free apéritif to guests of the Central Anzac hotel. This place is closed on Sunday and Monday. *Le Saladin* (☎ 22.92.05.15) at 4 Rue des Chaudronniers has a range of cold and warm

salads from 45 to 70FF. Near the belfry, *La Grappa* (☎ 22.91.65.77) at 14 Rue Léon Blum is a popular pizzeria with pizzas from 32FF.

For a very cheap meal, you might try *La Hotoie*, a university restaurant on Rue de la Hotoie. It's open daily from 11.40 am to 13.15 pm and 6.40 to 8.15 pm but unless you've got an international student card you'll have to buy a ticket (12.30FF) from a student or pay full price (25FF).

Self-Catering Next to the train station, the *Match supermarket* in the Centre Commercial is open Monday to Saturday from 9 am

---

Battle of the Somme

The WW I Allied offensive known as the First Battle of the Somme, waged in the villages and woodlands north-east of Amiens, was designed to relieve the pressure on the beleaguered French troops at Verdun. Early on 1 July 1916, British, Commonwealth and French troops 'went over the top' in a massive assault along a 34-km front. But the German positions proved virtually unbreachable. On the first day of the battle alone, an astounding 20,000 British troops were killed and another 40,000 were wounded. Most of the British casualties were infantrymen mowed down en masse by German machine guns.

By the time the offensive was called off in mid-November, casualties on all sides had reached 1.2 million. The British had advanced 12 km, the French only eight km. The Battle of the Somme has since become a metaphor for the meaningless slaughter of war.

These days, the site of the battle is once again dotted with peaceful farming villages. The only visual reminders of the killing that took place here over seventy-five years ago are the hundreds of thousands of white crosses in the area's 200 cemeteries. *The Somme – Paths of Memory*, a booklet available from the Amiens tourist office, has information on both the battlefields and the memorials to the offensive's victims, young men from Australia, Canada, New Zealand, South Africa and other countries.

Touring the area of the Battle of the Somme is only really feasible by car or bicycle. However, there are infrequent buses and trains from Amiens to the village of Albert, which was at the front line when the offensive was launched and was completely destroyed during the course of the battle. Albert's tourist office (☎ 22.75.16.42) at 9 Rue Gambetta is open from April to September. ∎

---

to 8.30 pm. On Blvd d'Alsace-Lorraine, *Boulangerie Wibart* is open Monday to Saturday until late; on Sunday it closes at 1 pm.

In the city centre, the *Cascade supermarket* at 29 Rue du Général Leclerc is open weekdays from 9 am to 12.30 pm and 2.30 to 7 pm and Saturday from 9 am to 7 pm. The *boulangerie* a few doors up at No 23 is open daily, except Monday, from 7.30 am (8.15 am on Sunday) to 7 pm. On Thursday morning there's a *food market* around the belfry.

Getting There & Away

Train Amiens's main train station, Gare du Nord (☎ 22.92.50.50 for information), is on Place Alphonse Fiquet. The information office is open Monday to Saturday from 8 am to 7 pm.

Destinations served include Paris's Gare du Nord (94FF; 1¼ hours), Lille (87FF; 1½ hours; 11 a day), Calais (110FF; 2½ hours), Rouen (84FF; 1½ hours) and Dieppe (84FF). More locally, there are trains to Arras (51FF; 1¼ hours; five a day) via Albert (30FF; 40 minutes).

Bus The bus station (☎ 22.92.27.03) is in the basement of the Centre Commercial. Buses to Albert cost 27FF.

Car The Citer car rental company (☎ 21.91. 57.45) has an office near the train station at 3 Blvd de Belfort. Europcar (☎ 22.92.41.64; fax 22.80.08.83) is at 104 Rue Jules Barni.

ARRAS

Arras (the final 's' is pronounced; population 42,000), one of far northern France's most picturesque towns, is renowned for its harmonious ensemble of 17th and 18th-century Flemish-style buildings. Among the natives of Arras, once the capital of the Artois region, is the Revolutionary leader Maximilien Robespierre (1758-94), a radical Jacobin who dominated the Committee of Public Safety during some of the bloodiest months of the Reign of Terror. After losing his political support, he lost his head – upon the guillotine – as well.

Arras makes a good base for visiting Vimy Ridge (see the Around Arras section), a windswept plateau captured by Canadian troops in 1917. It is topped by a memorial to the tens of thousands of Canadians who died in France in WW I.

Orientation

Place des Héros – where the tourist office is – and the adjoining Grand'Place are the heart

and soul of Arras. The train station is 600 metres south-east of Place des Héros at the south-eastern end of Rue Gambetta, Arras's main commercial thoroughfare. To get from the train station to the town centre, head north-west on Rue Gambetta and turn right at the second street, Rue Ronville.

Information

The tourist office (☎ 21.51.26.95) is at Place des Héros in the Hôtel de Ville. It is open Monday to Saturday from 9 am to noon and 2 to 6 pm.

Money There is a Banque de France (☎ 21.23.90.00) at 1 Rue Ernestale, the north-west continuation of Rue Gambetta. It's open Tuesday to Saturday from 8.30 am to noon and 1.30 to 3.30 pm. There are several other banks on Rue Gambetta.

Post The post office (☎ 21.22.94.94) is on Rue Gambetta.

Arras's postcode is 62000.

Flemish Houses

Two market squares which date from the 11th century, Place des Héros and Grand' Place, are surrounded by the pride of Arras: 155 Flemish-baroque houses from the 17th and 18th centuries. The structures, built of brick and stone and sharing common colonnaded arcades, vary in details (eg the rounded gables are of different sizes) but have a basic stylistic unity. The area was heavily damaged in WW II, and the process of restoring the houses was only recently completed.

Hôtel de Ville

The Flemish Gothic-style Hôtel de Ville at Place des Héros dates from the 16th century but was restored after WW I. For 11FF (5FF if you're under 16), you can hop on the lift to the top of the 75-metre **belfry**, from which there's a fine panorama over the city. You can get a different view of the city by taking a tour of the ancient **souterrains** (tunnels) – also known as *boves* (cellars) – under Place des Héros. These were used during times of war as a refuge from the violent events happening above-ground. Thirty-five minute tours, which begin in the basement, cost 11FF (6FF for people under 16); 50-minute tours are 17FF (10FF for under 16s). The **Historama**, a dull narration of the town's history, costs 9FF (6FF for those under 16).

If you'd like to take in Arras from all the proffered perspectives – aerial, subterranean and historical – a discount ticket to all three costs 25FF (13FF for people under 16). From 15 April to 15 October, the Hôtel de Ville, the belfry and the souterrains are open Monday to Saturday from 10 am to noon and 2 to 6 pm and Sunday from 10 am to noon and 3 to 6.30 pm. The rest of the year, they're open Tuesday to Saturday from 2 to 6 pm and Sunday from 10 am to noon and 3 to 6 pm.

Musée des Beaux-Arts

Arras's Fine Arts Museum (☎ 21.71.26.43) at 22 Rue Paul Doumer, housed in the central section of the mid-18th-century Abbaye Saint Vaast, has exhibits of Gallo-Roman artefacts found around here, medieval sculpture, 15th-century arras (tapestries) and French, Flemish and other paintings from the 16th to 19th centuries. It is open daily, except Tuesday, from 10 am to noon and 2 to 6 pm (5 pm from October to March); Sunday hours are 10 am to noon and 3 to 6 pm. Admission is 16/8FF for adults/children.

Places to Stay

Camping The nearest camp site is the *Camping Municipal* (☎ 21.71.55.06) at 166 Rue du Temple, a 10-minute walk east of the train station.

Hostel The *Auberge de Jeunesse* (☎ 21.23. 54.53), open from 1 March to 31 October, is in the centre of town at 59 Grand'Place; a bed costs 40FF. Reception opens at 5 pm.

Hotels Cheap hotels are in short supply. To the right as you exit the train station is *Le Passe Temps* (☎ 21.71.58.38) at 1 Place Foch, with good doubles from 130FF. Street parking is available. Nearer the centre of town, *Le Commerce* (☎ 21.71.10.07) at 28 Rue Gambetta is slightly more expensive.

Les Trois Luppars (☎ 21.07.41.41) at 49 Grand'Place has comfortable rooms from 180FF. *Hôtel Diamant* (☎ 21.71.23.23) at 5 Place des Héros affords close-ups of the belfry. Rooms start at 220FF.

Places to Eat

Restaurants The panelled *Les Grandes Arcades* (☎ 21.23.30.89) at 10 Grand'Place has *menus* from 72FF and reasonably priced plats du jour. *La Rapière* (☎ 21.55.09.92) at 44 Grand'Place has a 65FF *menu*. *La Cave*, a few doors away, has *menus* starting at 68FF. For cheaper fare, the unpretentious *Café-Brasserie Georget* at 42 Place des Héros offers a plat du jour for 30FF.

Self-Catering A *food market* is set up on Place des Héros every Saturday morning. There are supermarkets and boulangeries along Rue Gambetta.

Getting There & Away

Train The information desk at the train station (☎ 21.73.50.50) is open from 7.30 am to 7.30 pm.

Arras is on the Lille-Paris line, so there are lots of trains to Paris's Gare du Nord (127FF; 1¾ hours; hourly) and Lille (46FF; hourly). There are also direct services to Boulogne (83FF; 1¼ hours; five a day), Calais (92FF; two hours; 12 a day) and Dunkerque (75FF; 1¼ hours; six a day).

Bus The bus station (☎ 21.51.34.64) is two blocks south-west of the train station at Rue Abbé Bergen. The information office is open on weekdays from 7 am to 7 pm and until noon on Saturday. To get there from the train station, head west on Blvd Carnot (on the left as you exit the train station) and turn left onto Ave du Maréchal Leclerc.

Car Europcar (☎ 21.71.08.46; fax 21.43.80.41) is near the train station at 3 Rue de Douai. Citer has an office (☎ 21.55.39.10) at 2 Rue des Rosati. ADA, usually the cheapest, can be reached on ☎ 21.24.04.33.

Taxi Allo Taxi (☎ 21.58.18.17) can take you around town as well as to nearby battlefield sites, including the Canadian Memorial at Vimy Ridge.

Battle of Vimy Ridge

At dawn on a cold morning on 9 April 1917, soldiers of the Canadian Corps began an assault against the heavily fortified German trenches dug into Vimy Ridge. After several days of bitter fighting, the German positions – which had repulsed a French attack in 1915 – were captured with heavy losses. Given to Canada by the French government in 1922, the site of the battle has been turned into a memorial to the 60,000 Canadians who lost their lives in France in WW I.

The former battlefield has been left pretty much unaltered since WW I. The landscape, cratered by mines and artillery, is still lined with trenches, and red danger signs warn visitors not to stray off the paths because of unexploded shells and unrecovered bodies. One major change since 1917 has been the replacement of the prewar forest – destroyed in the fighting – by trees brought over from Canada.

The towering, limestone **Mémorial Canadien**, a striking monument built in 1936, is inscribed with the names of the 11,000 Canadians killed in France during WW I whose bodies were never found. On clear days, you can see for miles over the sombre, coal hill-studded landscape. The site is open all year; between April and September, Canadian students conduct free, half-hour tours. At other times of the year, the guard in the security kiosk (open 10 am to 6 pm) can supply you with an information pamphlet.

There are dozens of military cemeteries in and between the villages around Arras.

Vimy Ridge is about 10 km north of Arras on the N17. If you don't mind walking a bit, you can take Westeel bus No 105 (towards Lille) from Arras's bus station; ask the driver to stop at the Vimy Ridge turn-off, which is three km from the memorial. Another option, especially for several people travelling together, is to take a taxi from Arras. ■

Normandy

Often compared to the countryside of southern England, Normandy (Normandie) is the land of the *bocage* (farmland subdivided by hedges and trees). Since the war, there has been a trend to cut down the hedgerows *(haies)* – one of the reasons why the WW II fighting in Normandy was so difficult – but in many areas they still break up the landscape into a patchwork of enclosed fields. Winding their way among the hedgerows are sunken lanes, whose grassy sides are coated with yellow primroses in spring. At some points, the lanes are so deep that they hide the houses from view, many of which have stone or half-timbered walls and thatched roofs.

Set among this peaceful, pastoral landscape are Normandy's cities and towns. Rouen is well endowed with medieval architecture, including a spectacular cathedral; Caen boasts some fine Norman Romanesque abbeys; and Bayeux, home to the 11th-century Bayeux Tapestry, is only a dozen km from the D-Day landing beaches. Between Rouen and Paris is Giverny, the garden home of Claude Monet. At Normandy's southwestern corner, on the border with Brittany, is the world-famous island abbey of Mont Saint Michel. Normandy's two most important port cities are Le Havre and, at the tip of the Cotentin Peninsula, Cherbourg.

Along the Côte d'Albâtre (Alabaster Coast), the area south-west of Dieppe, dramatic chalk cliffs rise above rough pebble beaches. Further west, the coastline is padded by sand. Because it has the closest beaches to Paris (only a couple of hours by train), much of the Normandy coast is lined with seaside resorts, including Fécamp, Honfleur and the up-market twin towns of Deauville and Trouville, still fashionable watering holes for Parisians and English visitors alike. During the late 19th century, the Norman coast attracted a number of Impressionist painters.

The Battle of Normandy (1944) left its mark on the region, most tangibly when you

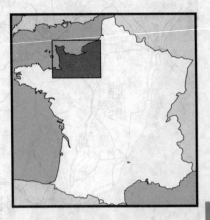

see the postwar architecture of cities like Caen, intangibly in the still-vivid memories of the people. In 1994, Normandy will commemorate the 50th anniversary of the D-Day landings and the ensuing battles.

History
The decisive event that led to Normandy becoming an historical entity was the invasion by the Vikings in the 9th century. Originally consisting of bands of plundering freebooters, many of these raiding groups from Scandinavia eventually established settlements in present-day Normandy and adopted Christianity. In 911 the French king Charles the Simple and the Viking chief Hrölfr agreed to make the Rouen region home to the Norsemen (or Normans), from whom the region derived its name.

In 1066 the duke of Normandy crossed the English Channel with 6,000 soldiers. His forces crushed the English (Saxons) in the Battle of Hastings, and the duke – known to history as William the Conqueror – eventually became king of England. These events ultimately led to the establishment of the Plantagenet dynasty. The Channel Islands,

NORMANDY

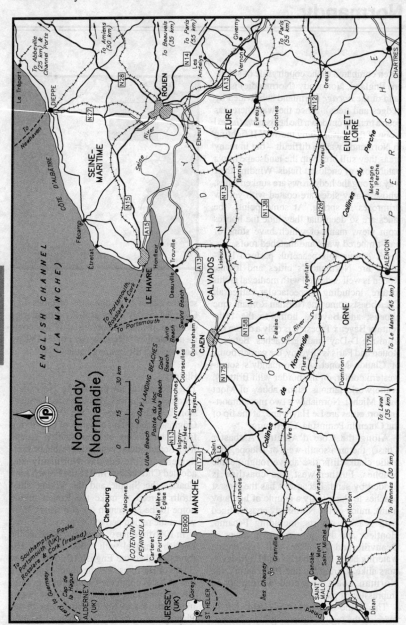

Food & Drink

Known as the land of cream and butter, Normandy is famous for the incredible richness and superior quality of its local produce, particularly its dairy products. Each Norman cow produces an annual average of five tonnes of milk, which is why the region supplies something like half of France's milk, butter, cream and cheese, all omnipresent in the local cuisine. Among the cheeses, Camembert (known in Normandy since the time of William the Conqueror) is king, but there are a great many others, including Neufchâtel, Pont l'Évêque and Livarot. Cream and butter go into the creation of the many rich, thick sauces that accompany fish, meat and vegetable dishes.

Apples are another staple of Norman cuisine, and cider is used extensively in cooking, particularly in meat and poultry dishes, a tradition that sets the region apart from the rest of France.

Charcuteries abound in Normandy, their windows displaying terrines, pâtés and tripe. Also common are galantines, a cold dish of boned, stuffed, pressed meat (especially pork) that is presented in its own jelly, often with truffles and pistachio nuts. One Norman dish that may not be to everyone's taste is *tripes à la mode de Caen*, made with ox feet, cider, Calvados, carrots, leeks, onions and herbs. The tripe is cooked for about twelve hours in a *tripière*, a special earthenware pot with a small opening that ensures minimum evaporation.

Certain pork dishes are peculiar to the region, and include *andouille de Vire*, a lightly smoked chitterling sausage with black skin that is sold in slices and eaten cold; *andouillettes*, small tripe sausages that are usually grilled and served with hot mustard; and *rillettes*, potted belly of pork.

Rouen is famous for its duck dishes. The ducks are strangled in order to retain the blood, which is then used to make the accompanying sauces. The most typical dish is *canard à la rouennaise*, but there are countless other duck dishes, and recipes vary from one town to another.

Trouville and Honfleur are the places to go for fish and seafood. The markets there are crammed with goodies: lobsters, crayfish, langoustines, prawns, tiny scallops, plump oysters, delicious small mussels and an endless variety of fish. Specialities include mussel soup, made with stock, white wine and cream, and *sole à la normande*.

Cidre (cider), made from apple juice, is bubbly, lightly alcoholic and refreshing. There are two kinds: *doux* (sweet) and *brut* (dry).

Calvados is to the apple what Cognac is to the grape. This strong apple brandy (whose most reputed variety comes from the Vallée d'Auge) is sometimes lengthened by adding cider to make *pommeau*, which is drunk as a strong (18% alcohol) apéritif. Calvados is used in the preparation of sauces and also in desserts – try apple tart flambéed in Calvados and served with Normandy's inimitable cream, or Calvados-filled chocolates. A *trou Normand* (literally, Norman hole) is a glass of Calvados drunk in the middle of a meal to make room for the next course.

Bénédictine, a liqueur made in Fécamp, also features in desserts, such as in delicious flambéed *crêpes Bénédictine*. ■

---

just off the Norman coast, were attached to England in 1066 (they are still British crown dependencies). During the 11th and 12th centuries, many abbeys and churches were built in both Normandy and England in the region's version of Romanesque architecture, known as the Norman style.

During the Hundred Years' War, the duchy switched back and forth between French and English rule. England ruled the region (except for Mont Saint Michel) for about 30 years until France achieved permanent control in 1450.

In the 16th century Normandy, a Protestant stronghold, was the scene of much fighting between the Catholics and Huguenots. King Henry IV of France did not gain control of Rouen until 1594.

During WW II, a force of 7000 mainly Canadian troops participated in a disastrous landing near Dieppe in 1942. On 6 June 1944 – better known as D-Day – 45,000 Allied troops landed on the beaches near Bayeux. The Battle of Normandy followed, and after several months and 100,000 deaths, German resistance was finally broken.

Geography

Normandy stretches from the English Channel and north-eastern Brittany in the west to the Paris basin and Picardy (covered in the Far Northern France chapter) in the

east. The region is often divided into Haute Normandie (Upper Normandy) and Basse Normandie (Lower Normandy). The two are separated by the Seine River, which flows from Paris through Rouen before emptying into the Channel near Le Havre at the Baie de la Seine.

The Cotentin Peninsula, at whose northern tip lies Cherbourg, divides the Baie de la Seine from the Golfe de Saint Malo, which is famed for its extraordinary tides. The Channel Islands (the Îles Anglo-Normandes to the French) are a few tens of km west of the Cotentin Peninsula.

Getting There & Away

Ferries to and from England dock at the Channel ports of Cherbourg, Dieppe, Le Havre and Ouistreham (near Caen). Ireland is connected by ferry with Cherbourg and Le Havre. The Channel Islands are accessible from the Breton port of Saint Malo and, in the warm season, from Cherbourg, Carteret and Portbail. For details on ferry schedules and tariffs, see Sea in the Getting There & Away chapter.

By train, Paris is only a couple of hours from the coast.

Getting Around

The major towns are all adequately connected by train, but the buses serving smaller towns and villages are somewhat infrequent, suited more to getting children to and from school than to transporting travellers.

Hitching is no problem on major roads, but off the main tracks, it may be slow going. Visitors who would like to spend some time exploring Normandy's rural areas might consider renting a car – see Getting There & Away under Bayeux, Cherbourg and Rouen for information on rental companies.

Rouen & Côte d'Albâtre

ROUEN

The city of Rouen (population 105,000) is known for the many spires and church towers that dominate its skyline. The old city is graced with over 700 half-timbered houses, quite a few of which have rough-hewn beams and posts that were probably off kilter when they were set in place and have become eye-poppingly more so over the centuries. Rouen also has a renowned Gothic cathedral and a number of excellent museums. The city – for centuries the farthest downriver the Seine had been bridged – was occupied by the English during the Hundred Years' War, during which the young French heroine Jeanne d'Arc (Joan of Arc) was tried here for heresy and burnt at the stake.

Rouen can be visited as an overnight trip (or even a day trip) from Paris. Like Paris, Rouen makes an excellent base for a day trip to Monet's home at Giverny (see the Giverny section).

Orientation

The passenger train station, Gare Rouen-Rive Droite, is at the northern terminus of Rue Jeanne d'Arc, the major thoroughfare in the city centre. The old city is centred around Rue du Gros Horloge, which links Place du Vieux Marché with the cathedral.

Information

Tourist Office The tourist office (☎ 35.71. 41.77) is in a wonderfully ornate, early 16th-century building at 25 Place de la Cathédrale (opposite the façade of Cathédrale Notre Dame). It is open Monday to Saturday from 9 am to 12.30 pm and 2 to 6.30 pm. From May to September, it's open Monday to Saturday from 9 am to 7 pm and on Sunday from 9.30 am to 12.30 pm and 2.30 to 6 pm. For a fee, the staff will make hotel reservations anywhere in France.

Money The Banque de France (☎ 35.52. 78.08) at 32 Rue Thiers is open weekdays from 8.45 am to 12.30 pm and 1.30 to 3.30 pm.

The Bureau de Change (☎ 35.88.00.65) at 9 Rue des Bonnetiers has good rates. It's open Monday to Saturday from 10 am to 7 pm. There are half a dozen banks along Rue

Jeanne d'Arc between the Théâtre des Arts and the Palais de Justice.

American Express (☎ 35.98.19.80) is at 1-3 Place Jacques Lelieur.

Post The main post office (☎ 35.08.73.83) at 45bis Rue Jeanne d'Arc is open weekdays from 8 am to 7 pm and on Saturday until noon. Exchange services are available.

Rouen's postcode is 76000.

Travel Agencies Voyages Wasteels (☎ 35. 71.92.56), 70 metres south of the train station at 111bis Rue Jeanne d'Arc, sells discount air tickets and BIJ train tickets. It's open Monday to Saturday from 9 am to 12.30 pm and 1.30 to 7 pm (6 pm on Saturday).

Bookshops For English-language books, the bookshop (☎ 35.70.57.42) on 5 Rue de Basnage is open Tuesday to Saturday from 9.30 am to 12.30 pm and 1.30 to 7 pm and Monday from 9.30 am to 12.30 pm.

Laundry North of the centre, there's a laundrette at 73 Rue Beauvoisine. The laundrette diagonally opposite 44 Rue d'Amiens is open daily from 7 am to 9 pm. There are two other laundrettes nearby, one next to 53 Rue d'Amiens, the other across the street from 18 Rue d'Amiens.

Old City

Like the rest of Rouen, the old city suffered enormous damage during WW II, but it has since been painstakingly restored. The main street is **Rue du Gros Horloge**, which runs from Cathédrale Notre Dame to **Place du Vieux Marché**, where 19-year-old Jeanne d'Arc was burned at the stake in 1431. **Église Jeanne d'Arc**, the striking church marking the site, was completed in 1979. It's open daily, except Friday and Sunday mornings, from 10 am to 12.30 pm and 2 to 6 pm. There is a covered food market (see Places to Eat) next to the church.

Rue du Gros Horloge is spanned by an early 16th-century gatehouse holding aloft the **Gros Horloge**, a large medieval clock with only one hand. The late 14th-century belfry of the Gros Horloge is open from late March or early April to September daily except Tuesday, Wednesday morning and holidays. Hours are 10 am to noon and 2 to 6 pm.

The incredibly ornate **Palais de Justice** (law courts), which was left a shell at the end of WW II, has been restored to its early 16th-century Gothic glory, though the 19th-century façade along Rue Jeanne d'Arc still shows extensive bullet and shell damage. The extraordinary Flamboyant Gothic courtyard, entered through a gate on Rue aux Juifs, is well worth a look. Under the courtyard is the Monument Juif, a structure used by Rouen's Jewish community in the early 12th century (see the Monument Juif listing).

Cathédrale Notre Dame

Rouen's cathedral, which was painted repeatedly by Monet, is one of the masterpieces of French Gothic architecture. Built between 1201 and 1514, it suffered extensive damage during WW II and has been undergoing restoration for decades. It is open daily from 8 am to noon and 2 to 7 pm (6.30 pm on Saturday, 6 pm on Sunday). From March to November, there is no midday closure on Sunday. Sunday morning, when masses are held, is a bad time to visit.

Romanesque sections include the lower part of the north tower (to the left as you face the west front) and the **crypt**, both of which are remnants of an earlier cathedral completed in 1062 and destroyed by fire in 1200. There are guided visits (10FF) to **Chapelle de la Vierge**, final resting place of many important church officials, every Saturday and Sunday afternoon. During July and August, there are tours every day in both the morning and afternoon.

Musée Le Secq des Tournelles

This fascinating museum of the blacksmith's craft (☎ 35.71.28.40 at the Musée des Beaux Arts) showcases locks, keys, scissors, tongs, pocketknives and other utensils made of wrought iron. Crafted between the 3rd and 19th centuries, they demonstrate how exquisite artisanship can turn the necessary and

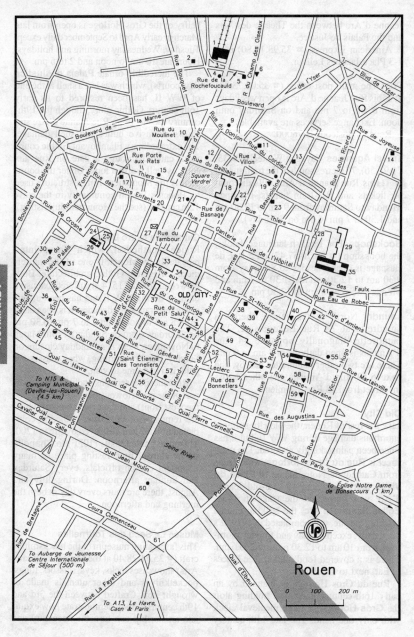

NORMANDY

Rouen

0   100   200 m

To N15 &
Camping Municipal
(Deville-les-Rouen)
(4.5 km)

To Auberge de Jeunesse/
Centre Internationale
de Séjour (500 m)

To Église Notre Dame
de Bonsecours (3 km)

To A13, Le Havre,
Caen & Paris

NORMANDY

mundane – a door lock, for instance – into something quite beautiful.

The museum, housed in a desanctified 16th-century church (given to secular uses since the Revolution), is on Rue Jacques Villon across the street from 27 Rue Thiers. It is open from 10 am to noon and 2 to 6 pm Thursday to Monday and 2 to 6 pm on Wednesday. It's closed on Tuesday. The entry fee is 11FF (free for students, 5.50FF for people over 65).

Other Museums

The **Musée des Beaux-Arts** (Fine Arts Museum; ☎ 35.71.28.40) at 35 Rue Thiers features paintings from the 16th to the 20th centuries. Some parts of the building may be closed until renovations are completed in 1994 or 1995.

The **Musée de la Céramique** (☎ 35.07.31.74), whose speciality is 16th to 19th-century faïence (decorated earth-

enware), most notably that produced in Rouen, is behind Square Verdrel park on Rue du Bailliage. The building it occupies dates from 1657. Ticket prices and opening hours at both museums are the same as at the Musée Le Secq des Tournelles.

Église Saint Maclou

Although this Flamboyant Gothic church, whose entrance is next to 56 Rue de la République, was built between 1437 and 1521, much of the decoration dates from the Renaissance. It is open daily from 10 am to noon and 2 pm (3 pm on Sunday) to 6 pm.

Aître Saint Maclou

This curious (and almost unique) ensemble of half-timbered buildings, built between 1526 and 1533, is decorated with macabre, 16th-century woodcarvings of skulls, cross-bones, grave-diggers' tools, and the like. As late as 1780, the courtyard was used as a

burial ground for victims of the plague. It is now the municipal École des Beaux-Arts (School of Fine Arts; ☎ 35.71.38.49). The courtyard, whose entrance is behind Église Saint Maclou at 186 Rue Martainville, can be visited for free every day from 8 am to 8 pm.

Église Saint Ouen

Église Saint Ouen, a 14th-century abbey church, is an especially refined example of the High Gothic style. The entrance is through the garden along Rue des Faulx. It is open from 10 am to 12.30 pm and 2.30 to 6 pm (closed Tuesday).

Monument Juif

In 1976, in the course of restoration work on the Palais de Justice, an exceptionally rare building used by the Rouen Jewish community around 1100 was uncovered beneath the courtyard. The Romanesque structure, located in the centre of what was then Rouen's Jewish quarter, is believed by archaeologists to have been either a synagogue, a house of study or a private home. It still has bits of Hebrew graffiti carved into the stone walls. The street running past the monument is known to this day as Rue aux Juifs (Street of the Jews).

Guided tours of the underground site (in French and, if there's demand, partly in English) leave from the tourist office at either 2 pm on Saturday (from October to April) or 11 am on Sunday (from May to September). The cost is 25FF (21FF if you're under 25 or over 60). You can usually just show up, though to be on the safe side you might want to make reservations at the tourist office a day or two in advance.

Église Notre Dame de Bonsecours

It's a pleasant, three-km walk south-eastward from central Rouen to the hilltop church of Notre Dame de Bonsecours, which overlooks the Seine. Next to the church, there is an Allied cemetery from WW I – in 1914, part of the British Expeditionary Force disembarked at Rouen, and the city was later the site of a number of Allied military hospitals.

For a pleasant stroll, walk eastward along the Seine on the Quai de Paris and then take Ave Aristide Briand, Route de Bonsecours and finally Route de Paris. By bus, take bus No 21 from the Théâtre des Arts and get off at the Mairie de Bonsecours stop. This line runs until 9.30 pm on weekdays and about 8.30 pm on weekends.

Places to Stay – bottom end

Rouen has heaps of very cheap hotels. Most of them are north of the city centre, though there are also a few good options in the old city.

Camping The *Camping Municipal* (☎ 35. 74.07.59) on Rue Jules Ferry in the suburb of Deville-lès-Rouen is five km north-west of the train station. It is open year round except in February. Two people with a tent pay 46FF. To get there from the train station, take bus No 2 and get off at the Mairie of Deville-lès-Rouen. The bus runs until around 10 pm.

Hostel Rouen's *Auberge de Jeunesse/Centre Internationale de Séjour* (☎ 35.72.06.45) is at 17 Rue Diderot, 2.5 km south of the train station. It is served by bus No 5 (from Rue Jeanne d'Arc) and bus No 12 (from the train station), both of which run until about 11 pm. Get off at the Diderot stop. Beds (two or six to a room) cost 53.50FF, including breakfast and sheets.

Gîtes d'Étape The tourist office has information on gîtes d'étape in the Rouen area.

Hotels – North of the Centre The spotless *Hôtel Normandya* (☎ 35.71.46.15), a pleasant, family-run place at 32 Rue du Cordier, has singles/doubles – some with shower – for 90/100 to 130/140FF. A bath or shower is 15FF. The quiet, pleasant *Hôtel du Square* (☎ 35.71.56.07) at 9 Rue du Moulinet has singles/doubles from 90/115FF. Rooms with shower and toilet start at 165FF.

The family-run *Sphinx* (☎ 35.71.35.86) at

130 Rue Beauvoisine has doubles from 80 to 90FF. The *Napoléon* (☎ 35.71.43.59), a small, comfortable place at 58 Rue Beauvoisine, has singles from 85 to 130FF; doubles are 10FF more.

Near the train station, the *Hôtel de la Rochefoucauld* (☎ 35.71.86.58) at 1 Rue de la Rochefoucauld – a rather busy corner – has singles/doubles/triples from 90/120/165FF. Showers are 15FF (20FF for two).

The very French *Hostellerie du Vieux Logis* (☎ 35.71.55.30) at 5 Rue de Joyeuse has a relaxed and pleasantly derelict atmosphere. There's parking next to the beautiful garden out the back. Singles and doubles start at 110FF, triples cost 140FF.

Hotels – City Centre You can't get much more central than the *Hôtel du Palais* (☎ 35.71.41.40), between the Palais de Justice and the Gros Horloge at 12 Rue du Tambour. Singles or doubles without shower start at 100FF; two-bed triples with shower are 150FF. The two-star *Hôtel La Cache Richard* (☎ 35.71.04.82), next door at 10 Rue du Tambour, has singles/doubles from 115/130FF, though most rooms are a bit more.

The pleasant *Hôtel Saint Ouen* (☎ 35.71.46.44) is opposite the garden of Église Saint Ouen at 43 Rue des Faulx. Simple rooms begin at 80/90FF for one/two people. The *Modern' Hôtel* (☎ 35.71.14.42) at 59 Rue Saint Nicolas is only one block from the cathedral. The cheapest singles and doubles cost 75 to 90FF.

The basic *Hôtel Jacqueline* (☎ 35.89.26.09), at 16 Rue Porte aux Rats, has some of the cheapest rooms in the city – singles and doubles are only 55 to 90FF. This place is often filled with long-term guests. No reservations are accepted. The *Hôtel des Flandres* (☎ 35.71.56.88), nearby at 12 Rue des Bons Enfants, has doubles for 100FF (with washbasin and bidet), 140FF (with shower) and 160FF (with shower and toilet).

Places to Stay – middle
Near the train station, the friendly, well-appointed *Hôtel des Familles* (☎ 35.71.

69.61) at 4 Rue Pouchet has singles for 120 to 160FF; one-bed doubles with are 145 to 205FF. All rooms have telephones and most are equipped with cable TV.

A good mid-range option in the shadow of the cathedral is the *Hôtel de la Cathédrale* (☎ 35.71.57.95) at 12 Rue Saint Romain. It's built around the leafy courtyard of a 17th-century half-timbered house and has singles/doubles from 205/250FF.

Near the river, the *Hôtel Au Coin Fleuri* (☎ 35.70.68.88) at 8-10 Rue de Québec has singles/doubles starting at 120/140FF.

Places to Eat
Restaurants Near Place du Vieux Marché, there are several decently priced places on Rue du Vieux Palais. *La Galetteria* (☎ 35.88.98.98), opposite 17 Rue du Vieux Palais, has crepes for around 30FF. It's closed on Sunday. *Pizzeria Pépé* (☎ 35.07.44.94) at 19 Rue du Vieux Palais, which has two-person pizzas from 48FF, is open from noon to 2.30 pm and 7 to 10.30 pm Monday to Friday and 7 to 10.30 pm Saturday. Across the street, there's Lebanese food at *La Phenicia* (☎ 35.88.46.22), open from noon to 2.15 pm and 7 to 11 pm Tuesday to Saturday, 7 to 11 pm Sunday and noon to 2.15 pm on Monday.

There are a number of unexciting but cheap restaurants on Rue d'Amiens and Rue de la République. The *Hôtel des Flandres* (see Places to Stay) has a decent three-course *menu* for 57FF.

The intimate *La Vieille Auberge* (☎ 35.70.56.65) at 37 Rue Saint Étienne des Tonneliers has an enticing 69FF *menu* including local specialities such as canard (duck) flambé au Calvados. It is closed on Monday. Although the name gives no clue, *Au Temps des Cerises* (☎ 35.89.98.00) at 51 Rue Saint Nicolas specialises in cheese cuisine. A three-course lunch *menu* costs 49FF (75FF for dinner). You can taste-test cheeses for 10FF each. This place is closed on Sunday and Monday.

Vegetarians might try *Natural* (☎ 35.98.15.74), which is behind the tourist office at 3 Rue du Petit Salut. This snack bar-

equipped health food shop serves a 65FF *menu* – two courses plus a cold drink and coffee – at lunchtime.

Pub *Bar Charles* (☎ 35.70.73.39), a relaxed pub at 6 Rue du Général Giraud, is open daily until 1 am. Beers start at 12FF (15FF after 10 pm). Sandwiches and meals are also available.

Self-Catering The covered *food market* at Place du Vieux Marché operates from 7 am to 7 pm (closed Monday).

Near the train station, the *boulangerie* at 24 Rue du Champ des Oiseaux, 150 metres to the left as you exit the terminal, is open Monday to Saturday from 7 am to 8 pm. North of the centre, there are a number of food shops between Nos 63 and 73 Rue Beauvoisine.

Near Église Saint Maclou, the *Alimentation Générale* at 78 Rue de la République is open daily from 8 am to 10.30 pm. There are also some food shops on Rue Alsace-Lorraine.

Entertainment
Music From April or May to September, there are often concerts in Rouen's various churches. Enquire at the tourist office for details.

Cinema The Cinéma Melville (☎ 35.98.79.79) at 12 Rue Saint Étienne des Tonneliers sometimes has nondubbed films, though French and dubbed movies predominate. The tourist office can provide you with monthly listings.

Things to Buy
Colourful faïence ceramics – an important Rouen product during the 16th to 19th centuries – can be purchased at several shops on the streets around the perimeter of the cathedral. There are antique shops nearby on Rue Saint Romain and, further east, on Rue Eau de Robec.

Getting There & Away
Train The attractive Gare Rouen-Rive Droite

(☎ 35.98.50.50 for information), built in 1912-28, sits at the northern end of Rue Jeanne d'Arc on Place Bernard Tissot. The information office is open Monday to Saturday from 8 am to 6.30 pm. The ticket counter and the luggage room are open daily from 6 am to 9.30 pm. Luggage lockers are available from 5 am to midnight.

Rouen is only 70 minutes by express train from Paris's Gare Saint Lazare (95FF). There are two dozen trains a day in each direction, the latest at about 10 pm (towards Rouen) and 9 pm (towards Paris). There are also trains to Amiens (84FF; 1½ hours; three a day), Caen (107FF; two hours; 10 a day), Dieppe (49FF; 45 minutes; 12 a day), Le Havre (64FF; one hour; 12 a day) and – by TGV – to Lyon (325FF).

Bus The grim bus station (☎ 35.71.23.29 or 35.71.81.71) on Rue des Charrettes has hardly changed since about 1960. The information office, on the bottom level next to the *quais*, is open weekdays from 8 am to noon and 1.50 to 5.45 pm (5 pm on Friday) and on Saturday from 8 to 11 am.

Four different companies, all represented by SATAR, serve Dieppe (55FF; 1¾ hours; three a day) and towns along the coast west of Dieppe, including Fécamp (two a day) and Le Havre (70FF; 2½ hours; a dozen a day). Destinations around Rouen include Elbeuf (via Les Essarts, the car racetrack), Évreux (52FF; six a day), Jumièges and Louviers. The buses to Dieppe and Le Havre are *much* slower than the train and are no bargain. Most lines stop running sometime around 7 pm.

Car For car rental, you might try the following companies:

ADA
    65 Quai Cavalier de la Salle (☎ 35.72.25.88)
Hertz
    main office, 38 Quai Gaston (☎ 35.98.16.57);
    train station bureau 15 Place Bernard Tissot
    (☎ 35.70.70.71)
Avis
    in the train station (☎ 35.53.17.20)

Claude Monet

One of the most important figures in modern art, Claude Monet, born in Paris in 1840, was the undisputed leader of the impressionists. He grew up near Le Havre, where in his late teens he started painting nature in the open air, a practice that was to affect his work throughout the rest of his career.

By the time he was 17, Monet was studying in Paris at the Académie Suisse with artists such as Pissarro. Influenced by the intensity of the light and colours of Algeria, where he spent some time during his military service, Monet concentrated on painting landscapes, developing an individual style which aimed to capture on canvas the immediate impression of the scene before him, rather than precise details.

During the Franco-Prussian war of 1870-71, Monet travelled to London, where he discovered the works of Turner and Constable. Consequently, painting from his houseboat on the Seine at Argenteuil, he focused on the effects of light and air and in particular on the play of light on the water's surface. He also began using the undisguised, broken brush strokes that best characterise the impressionist style.

It was in the late 1870s that Monet first began painting pictures in series, in order to study the effects of the changing conditions of light and the atmosphere. The most well known of these paintings include the Rouen cathedral series, which were painted in the 1890s. In 1883, four years after the death of his first wife, Camille, he moved to Giverny with Alice Hoschedé, with whom he had begun a liaison in 1876, her five children from a former marriage, and his sons, Jean and Michel. Here he set about creating an environment where he could study and paint the subtle effects and changes of colour that varying tones of sunlight had on nature.

Alice died in 1911, followed three years later by Monet's eldest son, Jean. Soon after the portly, white-bearded artist built a new studio and started painting the *Nymphéas* (Water Lilies) series. The huge dimensions of some of these works, together with the fact that the pond's surface takes up the entire canvas, meant the abandonment of composition in the traditional sense and the virtual disintegration of form. A huge job that took twenty years, the series was completed just before Monet died, in his bed, in 1926. ∎

Getting Around

Bus The local bus network is operated by TCAR, whose information office (☎ 35.52.52.65) at 70 Rue de Fontenelle (around the corner from 79 Rue Thiers) is open weekdays from 8 am to 6 pm (in July and August, 8 am to noon and 1.30 to 5.30 pm). Tickets cost 4.50FF if bought on board. Carnets of 10 are available for 31.80FF at Le Bus outlets in the train station (at ticket counters Nos 9 and 10) and at the bus hub next to the Théâtre des Arts.

Rides to the suburbs cost one to three tickets depending on the distance. A *carte tourisme*, valid for unlimited travel for one/two/three days, is available at the tourist office for 19/29/39FF.

Bicycle Rouen Cycles (☎ 35.71.34.30) at 45 Rue Saint Éloi rents mountain bikes and 10-speeds for 120/320FF a day/week. It's open Tuesday to Saturday from 8.30 am to 12.15 pm and 2 to 7.15 pm.

GIVERNY

Situated between Paris and Rouen and ideal as a day trip from either, the Musée Claude Monet, or Giverny as it's more commonly known, was the home and flower-filled garden of one of France's leading impressionist artists, Claude Monet. Here he painted some of his most famous series of works, including the *Décorations des Nymphéas* (the Water-Lilies).

Opened to the public in 1980, Giverny attracts about 380,000 visitors a year. That figure is likely to increase thanks to the new American Impressionist Museum, which opened nearby in 1992.

Musée Claude Monet

Monet's home (☎ 32.51.28.21) is open from 1 April to 31 October (closed Monday). The gardens are open from 10 am to 6 pm, but the house is closed from noon to 2 pm. Admission to the house and gardens costs 30FF (20FF for students and children).

The seasons have an enormous effect on Giverny, and if you like a particular variety of flower you might want to plan your visit around the time it blooms. From early to late spring, daffodils, tulips, rhododendrons, wisteria and irises progressively appear, followed by poppies and lilies. By June nasturtiums, rose trees and sweet peas are out; around September there are dahlias, sunflowers and hollyhocks.

The hectare of land that Monet owned became two distinct areas, cut by the Chemin du Roy, a small railway line which unfortunately was converted into what is now the busy D5 road.

The area to the north is the **Clos Normand**, home to Monet's famous pastel pink-and-green house and the Water Lily studio. These days this studio is the entrance hall, adorned with precise reproductions of his works and ringing with cash register bells from busy souvenir stands. Outside are the symmetrically laid-out gardens.

From the Clos Normand's far corner, a tunnel leads under the D5 to the **Water Garden**. Having bought this section of land in 1895 after he had started to become known, Monet dug a pool (fed by the Epte, a tributary of the nearby Seine), nurtured water lilies and constructed the Japanese bridge, which has since been rebuilt. Draped with purple wisteria, the bridge blends into the asymmetrical foreground and background, creating the intimate atmosphere for which the 'Painter of Light', as he was called by a close friend, was famous.

American Impressionist Museum

The American Impressionist Museum (☎ 32.51.94.65) is 100 metres down the road from Giverny at 99 Rue Claude Monet. It's open from 10 am to 6 pm (closed Monday). Entry costs 30FF (20FF for students, 15FF for children aged seven to 12).

Getting There & Away

Giverny is about 76 km north-west of Paris and 66 km south-east of Rouen. The nearest town is Vernon (☎ 32.38.50.50 for train information), nearly seven km to the northwest on the Paris-Rouen train line.

From Paris's Gare Saint Lazare (58FF; 50 minutes), there are four trains before midday to Vernon. For the return trip there's roughly one train an hour between 5 and 9 pm. From Rouen (49FF; 40 minutes), four trains leave before noon; to get back, there's about one train every hour between 5 and 10 pm.

Once in Vernon it's still a hike to Giverny. There are only two local buses a day, leaving Vernon at 9.15 am or 3.25 pm. Bikes are a good alternative and can be hired from the railway station for 44/55FF a half/full day. A hefty 1000FF deposit is required. The other common option is to walk or hitch.

DIEPPE

Dieppe (population 35,000) is a venerable but rather run-down seaside resort long favoured by British weekend trippers. It looks like the town's fortunes will continue to slump as Calais increases in importance as a trans-Channel transit point, but even after the Channel Tunnel begins operation, Dieppe will retain certain geographical advantages: it's the Channel port nearest Paris (165 km); and Newhaven, with which Dieppe is connected by ferry, is the closest Channel port to London (130 km).

There's not much to see or do in Dieppe, but the town makes a convenient stopover on your way to or from the UK. The nearby countryside is pleasingly pastoral.

History

Privateers based in Dieppe pillaged Southampton in 1338 and blockaded Lisbon two centuries later. The first European settlers in Canada included many natives of Dieppe. The town was one of France's most important ports during the 16th century, when Dieppois ships regularly sailed to West Africa and Brazil.

At dawn on 19 August 1942, some 7000 Allied troops – mostly Canadians – stormed ashore at eight points along the coast around Dieppe. This raid, the first post-Dunkerque action on French soil by Allied forces,

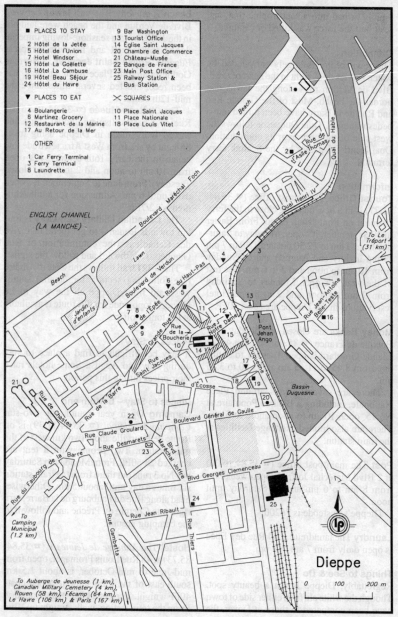

NORMANDY

PLACES TO STAY
2 Hôtel de la Jetée
5 Hôtel de l'Union
7 Hotel Windsor
15 Hôtel La Goëlette
16 Hôtel La Cambuse
19 Hôtel Beau Séjour
24 Hôtel du Havre

PLACES TO EAT
4 Boulangerie
6 Martinez Grocery
12 Restaurant de la Marine
17 Au Retour de la Mer

OTHER
1 Car Ferry Terminal
3 Ferry Terminal
8 Laundrette

9 Bar Washington
13 Tourist Office
14 Église Saint Jacques
20 Chambre de Commerce
21 Château-Musée
22 Banque de France
23 Main Post Office
25 Railway Station &
   Bus Station

SQUARES
10 Place Saint Jacques
11 Place Nationale
18 Place Louis Vitet

ENGLISH CHANNEL
(LA MANCHE)

Beach

Boulevard Maréchal Foch

Quai Henri IV

Quai du Hâble

Rue de l'Asile Thomas

To Le
Tréport
(31 km)

Lawn

Boulevard de Verdun

Beach

Jardin
d'enfants

Rue du Haut-Pas

Rue de l'Épée

Grande Rue

Rue de la Boucherie

Rue Notre Dame

Rue Duquesne

Pont
Jehan
Ango

Rue Jean-Antoine
Belle-Teste

Rue Saint Jacques

Rue d'Écosse

Bassin
Duquesne

Rue de Chastes

Rue de la Barre

Boulevard Général de Gaulle

Rue Claude Groulard

Rue Desmarets

Blvd Maréchal Joffre

Blvd Georges Clemenceau

Rue du Faubourg de la Barre

To Camping
Municipal
(1.2 km)

Rue Jean Ribault

Rue Gambetta

Rue Thiers

To Auberge de Jeunesse (1 km),
Canadian Military Cemetery (4 km),
Rouen (58 km), Fécamp (64 km),
Le Havre (106 km) & Paris (167 km)

Dieppe

0   100   200 m

rapidly turned into a catastrophic rout, and over half the force was killed or captured.

Orientation

The town centre is largely surrounded by water. Ferries dock right in the heart of town. Blvd de Verdun runs along the lawns that border the beach. Most of the Grande Rue and Rue de la Barre have been turned into a pedestrian mall. Quai Duquesne follows the west side of the port area; its continuation, Quai Henri IV, passes by the Sealink ferry terminal.

Information

Tourist Office The tourist office (☎ 35.84. 11.77) is in a new building close to the ferry terminal on Pont Jehan Ango. From Easter to 30 September, it's open Monday to Saturday from 9 am to 12.30 pm and 1.30 to 7 pm (8 pm in July and August) and on Sunday from 10 am to noon and 2 to 6 pm. The rest of the year, it's open Monday to Saturday from 9 am to noon and 2 to 8 pm. Hotel reservations in the Dieppe area cost 20FF.

Money Banks are closed on Monday. The Banque de France (☎ 35.06.97.00) at 4 Rue Claude Groulard is open Tuesday to Saturday from 8.45 to 11.55 am and 1.30 to 3.45 pm.

There are several banks around Place Nationale, including a Banque Populaire at No 15, open 10 am to noon and 2 to 5 pm. There are also limited exchange facilities at the train station.

Post The main post office (☎ 35.84.16.00) at 2 Blvd Maréchal Joffre is open weekdays from 8 am to 6 pm and on Saturday until noon.

Dieppe's postcode is 76200.

Laundry The laundrette at 44 Rue de l'Épée is open daily from 7 am to 9 pm.

Things to See & Do

Regrettably, Dieppe is not a beauty spot. Though the white cliffs on either side of town have been compared to those at Dover, the beach is gravelly. The vast **lawns** between Blvd de Verdun and the beach were laid out in the 1860s by that seashore-loving imperial duo, Napoleon III and his wife, Empress Eugénie. **Église Saint Jacques**, a Norman Gothic church at Place Saint Jacques, has been reconstructed several times since the mid-12th century.

The **Château-Musée** (☎ 35.84.19.76) on Rue de Chastes displays model ships and carved ivory made in Dieppe using tusks brought by sea from West Africa, a trade that began in the early 16th century. It's open from 10 am to noon and 2 to 5 pm (closed Tuesday). From June to September, it's open daily until 6 pm. Admission for adults/children is 12/7FF.

The **Canadian Military Cemetery** is four km towards Rouen – to get there, take Ave des Canadiens (the continuation of Rue Gambetta) southward and follow the signs.

The **GR21 trail** follows the Côte d'Albâtre (see following section for details) southwestward from Dieppe all the way to Le Havre. A topoguide for this route is available at the tourist office.

Places to Stay

It may be difficult to find a place to stay during July and August. Some hotels raise their prices during this period.

Places to Stay – bottom end

Camping Open year round, the two-star *Camping Municipal* (☎ 35.84.11.39) is on Route de Pourville about two km west of the train station. Two people with a tent are charged 28.50FF. From Monday to Saturday bus No 3 runs out there from the train station six times a day until about 5 pm. Otherwise, head along Rue du Faubourg de la Barre, turn right into Chemin du Prêche and follow it to the camping ground.

Hostel The *Auberge de Jeunesse* (☎ 35.84.85.73) at 48 Rue Louis Fromager, open from mid-June to mid-October, is about 1.5 km south-east of the train station. A bed costs 40FF a night. There's a kitchen and laundry. From the train station, walk straight up Blvd

Bérigny to the Chambre de Commerce from where you take bus No 2 to the Château Michel stop. The last bus is at 8 pm (8.25 pm on Sunday).

Hotels The *Hôtel du Havre* (☎ 35.84.15.02) at 13 Rue Thiers has ordinary but decent singles from 85FF. Doubles with shower start at 105FF, while two-bed rooms for two or three people go for 150FF.

The *Hôtel de la Jetée* (☎ 35.84.89.98) at 5 Rue de l'Asile Thomas has plain but serviceable singles and doubles/triples/quads from 115/200/220FF.

The *Beau Séjour* (☎ 35.84.13.90) at 4 Place Louis Vitet has ordinary rooms for one/two people from 98/110FF. You might also try the recently renovated *La Goëlette* (☎ 35.82.00.72) at 6 Rue Notre Dame, which has singles/doubles from 85/95FF.

There are a number of small hotels along Rue du Haut Pas and its continuation, Rue de l'Épée, including the *Hôtel de l'Union* (☎ 35.84.35.52) at 47 Rue du Haut Pas. Very basic singles/doubles cost 85/100FF.

Places to Stay – middle
The *Hôtel La Cambuse* (☎ 35.84.19.46) at 42 Rue Jean Antoine Belle-Teste has clean, recently redone doubles with shower for 120FF or 160FF. An extra bed is 25FF.

The *Hotel Windsor* (☎ 35.84.15.23), on the seafront (though a long way from the water) at 18 Blvd de Verdun, has small, garishly coloured doubles with full amenities from 250FF.

Places to Eat
There are quite a number of tourist restaurants – some with 60FF *menus* – along Quai Henri IV. The peninsula across Pont Jehan Ango from Quai Duquesne sports a number of cafés.

Restaurants One of the cheapest and least touristy restaurants in town is at the *Hôtel de l'Union*, whose 52FF *menu* is available daily, except Wednesday, at lunchtime. In summer it's also available for dinner. Even

cheaper is the *Buffet de la Gare* in the train station, which has an ordinary 50FF *menu*.

On Place Louis Vitet, *Au Retour de la Mer* (☎ 35.84.04.81) has a standard *menu* for 62FF. Two blocks up, *Restaurant de la Marine* (☎ 35.84.17.54), on the corner of Rue Notre Dame and Arcades de la Bourse, has a seafood *menu* for 65FF.

Self-Catering On Tuesday, Thursday and Saturday, the *food market* between Place Saint Jacques and Place Nationale is open from 6 am to 1 pm (5 pm on Saturday).

Near the ferry terminal, the *boulangerie* at 15 Quai Henri IV is open from 8 am to 8.30 pm (closed Monday). There are other *boulangeries* along the Grande Rue, Rue Saint Jacques and Rue de la Boucherie. You'll find *grocery stores* on Rue de la Barre, Rue de l'Épée and Rue du Haut Pas. *Martinez grocery* at 44 Rue du Haut Pas is open from 7.30 am to 8.30 pm (closed Monday).

Entertainment
Bar Washington (☎ 35.40.23.85) at 41 Rue de l'Épée, a small unpretentious place, is open daily from 2 pm to 2 am. A demi of beer costs 8FF (9FF after 10 pm).

Getting There & Away
Train The train station (☎ 35.98.50.50 for information, in Rouen) is on Blvd Georges Clemenceau. The information office is open weekdays from 9 am to 7 pm and on Saturday from 9 am to noon and 2 to 6.15 pm.

The paucity of direct trains to Paris's Gare Saint Lazare (108FF; 2¼ hours) is partly made up for by frequent services to Rouen (47FF), which is 45 to 60 minutes from Dieppe and only 70 minutes from Paris's Gare Saint Lazare. The last train from Dieppe via Rouen to Paris leaves at 6.30 pm Monday to Saturday; on Sunday and holidays, there is service to Paris (via Rouen) at 8.45 pm.

Bus The bus station (☎ 35.84.21.97), in the same building as the train station, is open from 9 am to 6.30 pm daily except Sunday

NORMANDY

and holidays, when there are no buses. There are services to Fécamp (61.50FF; one a day, two or three a day in July and August), Tréport (32.50FF; five a day) and Rouen (58FF; 1¾ hours; three a day).

Boat The first ferry service from Dieppe to England (Brighton, to be exact) was established in 1790. These days, Sealink (☎ 35.06.39.00) runs car ferries between Dieppe and Newhaven. The ferry terminal (for pedestrians) on Quai Henri IV is open daily from 9 am to 6 am. Cars must follow Quai du Hable round to the vehicle terminal on the waterfront. For details on prices and schedules, see the Sea section in the introductory Getting There & Away chapter.

Getting Around

Bus The local bus network, Stradibus, is operated by STUD (☎ 35.84.49.49). There are 11 lines, varying considerably in frequency of services. Some run on Sunday, others don't, some until 6 pm, others until 8 pm. All buses stop at either the train station or the nearby Chambre de Commerce. The tourist office has a list of the lines and timetables. A single ticket costs 5.70FF, a 10-ticket carnet 36FF.

Taxi Taxis can be ordered by calling ☎ 35.84.20.05.

CÔTE D'ALBÂTRE

Stretching for 100 km from Dieppe south to Étretat, the tall, white cliffs and stony beaches of the Côte d'Albâtre (Alabaster Coast) are reminiscent of the coast of southern England. Small villages and a few resorts nestle in the dry valleys leading down from the Caux, a chalky inland plateau.

Without a car, the Côte d'Albâtre is rather inaccessible. However, hikers can follow the coastal GR21 from Dieppe to Le Havre. The Côte d'Albâtre's two main destinations are Fécamp and Étretat, both of which are towards the coast's southern end.

Fécamp

Fécamp was little more than a fishing village until the 7th century when it became the base for an order of Benedictine monks. The 'medicinal elixir' that one of them concocted a thousand years later and which is marketed these days as Bénédictine, is now one of the most famous after-dinner liqueurs in the world.

Information Opposite the Palais Bénédictine on Rue Alexandre Le Grand is the tourist office (☎ 35.28.51.01), open Monday to Saturday from 9 am to 12.15 pm and 1.45 to 6 pm; in summer it's open daily from 9.30 am to 6.30 pm.

Palais Bénédictine An ornate, Renaissance-style building, the Bénédictine Distillery (☎ 35.28.00.06) at 110 Rue Alexandre Le Grand is geared up to tell you everything about the history and making of this golden liqueur – except the exact recipe. Tours start in a sacred art museum and continue through the forgery room, where some 800 or so bottles of illegal Bénédictine imitations are proudly showcased. In the fragrant plant room you can smell a handful of some of the 27 herbs and spices used to make the potent elixir, such as saffron, myrrh and cinnamon, which are blended in copper vats in the nearby distillery.

Opening hours for the Palais vary. From Easter to 3 July and mid-September to mid-November, it's open from 10 am to noon and 2 to 5.30 pm; from 4 July to mid-September it's open from 10 am to 6 pm. From mid-November to Easter there are only two visits a day – at 10.30 am and 3.30 pm. Admission is 24/20/12FF for adults/students/children and includes a free shot at the end – before you leave via the gift shop.

Getting There & Away See the Le Havre and Dieppe sections for train and bus information.

Étretat

Marking the southern point of the Côte d'Albâtre the small village of Étretat, which is about 20 km south-west of Fécamp, has long been renowned for its cliffs. Featuring

the most unusually shaped rock formations in the area, you'll see them long before you arrive, plastered on all the region's tourist brochures, usually silhouetted against a rosy sunset and appearing somewhat deceivingly to be one rock.

They are in fact made up of two parts, the Manneport Arch and the 70-metre-high Aiguille (needle), which pierces the surface of the water behind the Arch. From the western end of Étretat's stony beach, a path leads to the clifftop from where there's a fine view of the rocks. On the opposite cliff, a memorial marks the place where two pilots were last seen in their attempt to cross the Atlantic in 1927.

Getting There & Away Located about 28 km north of Le Havre, Étretat is not served by any public transport. The inland D940 road is not what you could call ideal hitching ground.

LE HAVRE

Le Havre (population 200,000), France's second most important port, is also a much-used gateway for ferries to Britain and Ireland. Sadly, there's not too much more you can say in favour of this coastal city, sitting on an overhanging lip of land west of where the Seine River meets the sea. Obliterated in WW II by bombing raids which killed 4000 of its residents, the city was rebuilt around its historic remains by Auguste Perret, one of the leading modern architects of the time. The result is a regimented grid of wide, ruler-straight central streets lined with row upon row of three-storey, reinforced concrete buildings. West of the city, the area north of the Seine is lined with shipyards, chemical plants and other industries.

Orientation

With such a rigid layout of streets, it's hard to get lost. Centrally, the only landmark you'll need is the huge public square – unquestionably one of Europe's largest – named after the equally voluminous Hôtel de Ville which is located there. Ave Foch runs

westward to the sea and the Port de Plaisance. To the east, Blvd de Strasbourg heads to the train station. Rue de Paris cuts southward straight down to the P&O ferry terminal on Blvd Kennedy and its extension, Quai de Southampton.

Information

Tourist Office The main tourist office (☎ 35.21.22.88) is in the foyer of the Hôtel de Ville. It's open Monday to Saturday from 8.45 am to 12.15 pm and 1.30 to 6 pm.

In summer only (1 June to 30 September) there's also a tourist office bureau (☎ 35.21.50.26) at the P&O ferry terminal and smaller kiosks at the Irish Ferries terminal and the train station.

Money Outside of banking hours, an exchange bureau (☎ 35.21.53.98) opposite the P&O terminal at 41 Blvd Kennedy is open daily all year. Its hours vary with the season – in July and August it's open Monday to Saturday from 7 am to 8 pm and on Sunday from 9 am to noon and 2 to 6 pm; in June and September the hours are the same except that there's an hour's break from 12.30 pm and a 10 am start on Sunday. From October to May it closes at 7 pm (5 pm on Sunday).

American Express (☎ 35.42.59.11) is at 57 Quai Georges V.

Post The main post office (☎ 35.42.45.67) at Rue Jules Siegfried is open weekdays from 8 am to 7 pm and Saturday until noon.

Le Havre's postcode is 76600.

Musée des Beaux-Arts

There's only one sight worth raving about and that's the Musée des Beaux-Arts (☎ 35.42.33.97) on Blvd Kennedy, about 200 metres west of the P&O ferry terminal. Noted for its fine collection of impressionist paintings, including some by Monet, it also has a good selection of works by Raoul Dufy, a native of Le Havre. It's open Wednesday to Sunday from 10 am to noon and 2 to 6 pm. Admission is free.

NORMANDY

Places to Stay

Though there is not a surfeit of cheap places, some budget accommodation can be found.

Places to Stay – bottom end & middle

Camping The closest camping ground to the centre is *Camping de la Forêt de Montgeon* (☎ 35.46.52.39), nearly three km north of town in a 250-hectare forest. It's open from 1 April to 30 September and charges 38FF for one or two people with a tent. From the station, take bus No 11 until it has gone past the Jenner Tunnel, then walk straight up through the park for another 1.5 km.

Hostel Although there's no official youth hostel, the large *YMCA* (☎ 35.42.47.86) at 153 Blvd de Strasbourg, about 400 metres west of the train station, will take in travellers with youth hostel cards. It charges 38/45FF for a dorm/single room and 13FF for breakfast.

Hotels A line of nondescript, neon-lit hotels faces the train station. However, hidden down an alley also opposite the station (to the right of the Hertz office) is the *Hôtel d'Yport* (☎ 35.25.21.08) at 27 Cours de la République. It's friendly with a range of rooms including basic singles/doubles/triples from 85/150/195FF. A hall bath costs 20FF extra. Doubles and triples with shower start at 190/210FF. It has a private garage (30FF).

Also very close to the station is *Hôtel Parisien* (☎ 35.25.23.83) at 1 Cours de la République, on the corner of Blvd de Strasbourg. It's a clean and pleasant place with singles/doubles from 190/220FF.

Near the P&O ferry terminal, there are a couple of decent places. The *Hôtel Le Monaco* (☎ 35.42.21.01) at 16 Rue de Paris – turn right as you leave the ferry terminal and take the first left – has shipshape singles/doubles/triples/quads from 110/150/230/385FF. It's closed for a fortnight from mid-February. Nearby, the tiny *Le Ferry Boat* (☎ 35.42.29.55) at 11 Quai de Southampton has a few rooms from 120FF but it's often full.

Places to Stay – top end

The *Hôtel Le Mercure* (☎ 35.19.50.50) is on Chaussée d'Angoulême, across from the Bassin du Commerce. It's one of the top hotels in town and charges from 600/690FF for singles/doubles.

Near the opposite end of the Bassin du Commerce is the *Hôtel Le Bordeaux* (☎ 35.22.69.44) at 147 Rue Louis Brindeau. It costs 360/490FF for singles/doubles.

Places to Eat

Restaurants The best hunting ground for a decent-priced meal is one of the many hotel/restaurants in front of the train station. *Le Pie Assiet* (☎ 35.25.40.67) at 25 Cours de la République is probably the cheapest, with a 56FF *menu*. It is closed on Sunday.

Another budget option is the restaurant at the *YMCA* (see the previous Hostel section), open for lunch only, which serves a decent 28FF plat du jour.

The restaurant at the *Hôtel Le Monaco* has excellent seafood *menus* from 130FF.

Getting There & Away

Train Le Havre's train station (☎ 35.43. 50.50 for information) on Cours de la République is about one km east of the city centre. The information office is open Monday to Saturday from 8.30 am to 6.30 pm. The main rail destinations are Rouen (63FF; one hour; 15 a day) and Paris's Gare Saint Lazare (139FF; 2¼ hours; 11 a day). A secondary line goes north to Fécamp (39FF; 1¼ hours; five a day) but you must change at Bréauté-Beuzeville.

Bus The bus station (☎ 35.26.67.23) is to the left as you leave the train station. Two companies – the Caen-based Bus Verts du Calvados and Rouen's Transports Joffet – run regional services from here to Caen, Honfleur, Rouen and other destinations.

Boat P&O European Ferries (☎ 35.21. 36.50), which links Le Havre with Portsmouth, uses the P&O terminal on Blvd Kennedy, which is about 800 metres from the main tourist office. The information desk is

open weekdays from 8.30 am to 6 pm and weekends from 9 am to 3 pm and 5 to 8 pm. Bus No 3 runs between the ferry terminal and the train station.

Irish Ferries (☎ 35.53.28.83) has services to both Rosslare and Cork. Its terminal is on Route du Môle Central about three km south of the centre. The office is open from 9 am to noon and 2 to 6 pm. There's an exchange service at the terminal. A special bus takes passengers from the ferry terminal to the train station and vice versa.

For information on schedules and prices for both companies see the Sea section in the Getting There & Away chapter.

Calvados

The *département* of Calvados – named after a reef near Arromanches whose name derives from the *Salvador*, a ship of the Spanish Armada wrecked there in 1588 – stretches from Honfleur in the east to Isigny-sur-Mer in the west. It is famed for its rich pastures and production of butter, cheese and a cider brandy known as Calvados. The D-Day beaches stretch along almost the entire coast of Calvados.

HONFLEUR

The picturesque seaside town of Honfleur (population 8400) sits opposite Le Havre at the mouth of the Seine. Because it's only about 200 km north-west of Paris – closer to the capital than almost any other point on the coast – multitudes of Parisian day-trippers flock to the town. There are no beaches in Honfleur itself, but not far away there are some fine stretches of sand for summer bathing. Just 15 km south-west along the coast are the luxury resorts of Deauville and Trouville.

During the 19th century, Honfleur attracted a steady stream of artists, among them noted impressionists. The town escaped damage during WW II and retains much of its traditional architecture. Because of extensive siltation, centuries-old wooden

houses that once lined the seafront quay are now hundreds of metres inland. In recent years, Honfleur has gone up-market, becoming charming and even quaint.

History
Honfleur's seafaring tradition dates back over a thousand years. After the Norman Invasion of England in 1066, goods bound for England were shipped across the Channel through Honfleur. The town played an important role in the early European exploration and settling of the Americas, and within 25 years of Columbus's first voyage, ships from Honfleur had visited Brazil, Newfoundland and the mouth of the Saint Lawrence River in Canada.

In 1608, Samuel de Champlain set sail from here on his way to found Quebec City. In 1681, Cavelier de la Salle started out from Honfleur to explore what is now the USA. He reached the mouth of the Mississippi and named the area Louisiana in honour of King Louis XIV, ruler of France at the time. During the 17th and 18th centuries, Honfleur achieved a certain degree of prosperity thanks to trade with the West Indies, the Azores and the west coast of Africa.

Orientation
Honfleur is centred around the Vieux Bassin (old harbour). To the east is the heart of the old city, known as the Enclos (enclosure) because it was once enclosed by fortifications. To the north is the Avant Port (outer harbour), home of the fishing fleet. Quai Sainte Catherine fronts the Vieux Bassin on the west. Rue de la République begins on the south side of the Vieux Bassin and runs southward. The Plateau de Grâce, with Chapelle Notre Dame de Grâce on top, is west of town.

Information
Tourist Office The tourist office (☎ 31.89. 23.30) is in the Enclos at Place Arthur Boudin, north along Rue de la Ville from the bus terminal. Between Easter and September it is open Monday to Saturday from 9 am to 12.30 pm and 2 to 6.30 pm. During the rest

of the year, hours are 9 am to noon and 2 to 5.30 pm. From Easter to October the office is also open on Sunday from 10 am to noon and 3 to 5 pm.

Honfleur's postcode is 14600.

Église Sainte Catherine

This wooden church, whose stone predecessor was destroyed during the Hundred Years' War, was built by the people of Honfleur during the second half of the 15th and early 16th centuries. It is believed that they chose to use wood, which could be worked by local shipwrights, in an effort to save money. The structure the town's ship carpenters created, which was intended to be temporary, has a vaulted roof that looks suspiciously like an upturned ship's hull. The church is also remarkable for its twin naves. The juxtaposition of wood beams and stained glass creates a certain warmth that is in contrast to the colder ambience of stone churches. Église Sainte Catherine is open to visitors daily from 9 am to noon and 2 to 6 or 6.30 pm except during prayers.

Clocher Sainte Catherine

The church's freestanding wooden bell tower, Clocher Sainte Catherine (☎ 31.89. 54.00), was constructed during the second half of the 15th century. It was built apart from the church for both structural reasons (so the church roof would not be subject to the bells' weight and vibrations) and reasons of safety (a high tower was more likely to be hit by lightning). The former bell-ringer's residence at the base of the tower houses a small museum of liturgical objects, but of more interest are the huge, rough-hewn beams.

From mid-March to September the Clocher is open from 10 am to noon and 2 to 6 pm (closed Tuesday). The rest of the year, it's open weekdays, except Tuesday, from 2.30 to 5 pm and on weekends from 10 am to noon and 2.30 to 5 pm. Tickets cost 17FF (13FF for students) and also get you into the Musée Eugène Boudin.

Musée Eugène Boudin

This museum (☎ 31.89.54.00) on Rue de l'Homme de Bois at Place Eric Satie has a large collection of Norman impressionist works such as those of Boudin, Dubourg and Monet. It has the same opening hours and entry fees as the Clocher Sainte Catherine.

Harbours

The Vieux Bassin, whence great expeditions to the New World once set forth, now shelters mainly pleasure boats. The nearby quais and streets, especially **Quai Sainte Catherine**, are lined with tall, narrow houses – many fronted with bluish-grey slate shingles – dating from the 16th to 18th centuries. The **Lieutenance**, once the residence of the town's royal governor, is at the mouth of the old harbour.

The **Avant Port**, on the other side of the Lieutenance from the Vieux Bassin, is home to Honfleur's 50 or so inshore fishing vessels. Further north, **dykes** line both sides of the entrance to the port. Either harbour makes a pleasant route for a walk to the seashore.

Musée de la Marine

Honfleur's small Nautical Museum is just east of the Vieux Bassin in Église Saint Étienne (Saint Stephen's Church), which was begun in 1369 and enlarged during the English occupation (1415-50). Displays include assorted model ships and ship's carpenters' tools.

From mid-June to mid-September, it's open daily from 10.30 am to noon and 2.30 to 6 pm. During the rest of the year, it is open on Saturday afternoon, Sunday and holidays and during school holidays *only*; the hours are the same. The museum is closed during January and the first half of February. Entrance costs 11FF (6FF for students). If you'll also be visiting the Musée d'Art Populaire, you can buy a ticket for both museums (20FF, or 11FF for students).

Musée d'Art Populaire

Next to the Musée de la Marine on Rue de la Prison, the Museum of Popular Art (☎ 31.89.

14.12) occupies a former prison and houses dating from the 16th and 17th centuries. It contains 12 furnished rooms of the sort you would have found in the shops and wealthier homes of Honfleur between the 16th and 19th centuries.

It can be visited only if you join one of the guided tours (in French), which leave about once an hour. Opening hours are the same as those of the Musée de la Marine. Entrance to both museums costs 20FF (11FF for students).

Greniers à Sel

The two huge Salt Stores (☎ 31.89.02.30) on Rue de la Ville, down the block from the tourist office, were built in the late 17th century of stone and oak timber in order to store the salt – subject to a special tax, the *gabelle* – needed by the fishing fleet to cure its catch of herring and cod. For most of the year, the only way to see the Greniers is to take a guided tour (enquire at the tourist office). During July and August the halls host art exhibitions (15FF, or 10FF for students) and concerts.

Chapelle Notre Dame de Grâce

This chapel, built between 1600 and 1613, is at the top of the Plateau de Grâce, a forested, hundred-metre-high hill about a km west of the Vieux Bassin. There's a great view.

Beach

The beach nearest Honfleur is a bit under a km west of the Vieux Bassin.

Places to Stay

Honfleur is not a cheap place to sleep.

Camping *Camping Le Phare* (☎ 31.89. 10.26), about 500 metres north-west of the Vieux Bassin along Blvd Charles V, is open from April to September. It costs 20/30/12FF per person/tent site/car.

Hotels The *Bar de la Salle des Fêtes* (☎ 31.89.19.69) at 8 Place Albert Sorel, 400 metres south-west of the Vieux Bassin (follow Rue de la République), charges

150FF (including breakfast) for each of its four double rooms. The *Auberge de la Claire* (☎ 31.89.05.95) at 77 Cours Albert Manuel, 700 metres further south-west, has doubles from 170FF.

The *Hôtel Le Hamelin* (☎ 31.89.16.25) at 16 Place Hamelin has rooms plus breakfast for 230FF. The very central *Hôtel des Cascades* (☎ 31.89.05.83) at 17 Place Thiers has rooms from 225FF. *Hôtel Le Moderne* (☎ 31.89.44.11) at 20 Quai Lepaulmier has rooms from 210FF.

Places to Eat

Restaurants Places to dine are abundant, but they don't come cheap – *menus* start at about 80FF. The *Hôtel Le Moderne* (see Hotels) is one of the less expensive places, with *menus* from 71FF. Otherwise you'll just have to splurge along with everyone else. One highly recommended spot is the cosy *La Tortue* (The Turtle; ☎ 31.89.04.93) at 36 Rue de l'Homme de Bois, whose succulent seafood *menus* start at 95FF.

Self-Catering The Saturday *food market* at Place Sainte Catherine runs from 8 am to 1 pm. There's a *Champion supermarket* just west of Rue de la République near Place Albert Sorel. It's open Monday to Saturday from 8.30 am to 12.30 pm and 2.30 to 7.30 pm; there's no midday closure on Saturday.

Things to Buy

There are quite a few art galleries and crafts shops along the streets east and north of Église Sainte Catherine. On Saturday mornings, local artisans sell their creations at Place Arthur Boudin and along Rue de la Ville.

Getting There & Away

Bus The bus station (☎ 31.89.28.41) is east of the Vieux Bassin on Cours des Fossés. The information window is open Monday to Saturday from 9 am to 12.15 pm and 2.45 to 6 pm (4 pm on Saturday) and on Sunday from 9 am to 12.15 pm and 2 to 4 pm.

Inter-Normandie, operated by Bus Verts (☎ 31.44.77.44), has service via Deauville

(19FF; 30 minutes; line No 20) to Caen (61FF; two hours). In the other direction, the same line goes northward to Le Havre (52FF; 1½ hours). Line No 50 goes to Lisieux. There's a 12% discount for people under 26 and, on Sunday, for everyone.

CAEN

Caen (population 113,000), the capital of Basse Normandie (Lower Normandy), was one of the many Norman cities to suffer heavily in WW II. Bombed on D-Day, the city burned for over a week before eventually being liberated by the Canadians, only to be then shelled by the Germans. Three-quarters of the city was flattened, the only vestiges of the past to survive being the ramparts around the chateau and the two great abbeys, all built by William the Conqueror when he founded the city in the 11th century. Much of the medieval city was built using 'Caen stone', a creamy local limestone similar to that used in the construction of London's Westminster Abbey.

Linked to the sea by a canal running parallel to the Orne River, Caen has seen rapid expansion in recent years and these days is a bustling university city. It acts also as a transport terminal for Ouistreham, a minor passenger port for ferries to England (see the Getting There & Away section for Caen).

Orientation

Caen's modern heart is characterised by a few pedestrianised shopping streets and a few busy boulevards. The largest, Ave du 6 Juin, links the centre, which is based around the southern end of the chateau, with the train station to the south-east.

Information

Tourist Office The main tourist office (☎ 31.86.27.65) on Place Saint Pierre is open Monday to Saturday from 9 am (10 am on Monday) to noon and 2 to 7 pm. From June to mid-September it doesn't close at midday and is also open on Sunday from 10 am to 12.30 pm and 3 to 6 pm. Hotel reservations cost 11FF for places in Caen and 22FF for places elsewhere in France.

From June to August the tourist office booth in the train station is open Monday to Saturday from 9 am to 12.30 pm and 1.30 to 6 pm.

Money The Banque de France (☎ 31.86. 19.10) at 14 Ave de Verdun is open weekdays from 9 am to 12.15 pm and 2 to 3.30 pm.

Crédit Agricole (☎ 31.86.15.15) at 1 Blvd du Maréchal Leclerc is open weekdays from 9 am to 12.15 pm and 2 to 5.45 pm and on Saturday from 9 am to 12.25 pm and 1.30 to 5 pm. From May to September the tourist office has exchange services on Sunday and bank holidays.

Post The main post office (☎ 31.39.35.78) at Place Gambetta is open weekdays from 8 am to 7 pm and on Saturday until noon.

Caen's postcode is 14000.

Laundry The laundrette at 15 Rue de l'Équipe d'Urgence is open daily from 7 am to 8 pm.

Mémorial – Un Musée pour la Paix

Caen's best known museum is the Memorial – A Museum for Peace (☎ 31.06.06.44), which has two somewhat contradictory aims: to memorialise the years of WW II and at the same time to promote world peace. The exhibits may help visitors to 'reflect on the scourge of war', as one brochure put it, but you're probably better off thinking of it as a thoughtful war museum rather than a peace museum. All signs are in French, English and German.

A visit consists of three distinct parts:

- A history of Europe's descent into a total war, tracing events from the end of WW I through the rise of Fascism to the 1944 Battle of Normandy.

- Three segments of unnarrated film footage (50 minutes in total) taken from the archives of both sides. This documentary material is enlivened by re-enacted scenes from *The Longest Day* (a film about the D-Day landings) and a movie about railway sabotage. The last film of the day begins at 6 pm (8 pm from June to August).

- An exhibit on winners of the Nobel Peace prize, housed in a former German command post underneath the main building.

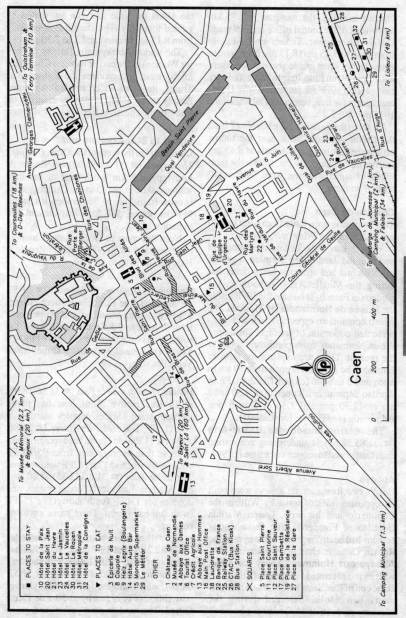

PLACES TO STAY
10 Hôtel de la Paix
20 Hôtel Saint Jean
21 Hôtel du Havre
23 Hôtel Le Jasmin
24 Hôtel Le Vaucelles
30 Hôtel Le Rouen
31 Hôtel Métropole
32 Hôtel de la Consigne

▼ **PLACES TO EAT**
3 Épicerie de Nuit
8 Coupole
9 Héla Légrix (Boulangerie)
14 Hôtel Auto Bar
15 Monoprix Supermarket
29 Le Météor

OTHER
1 Château de Caen
4 Musée de Normandie
2 Abbaye aux Dames
6 Tourist Office
7 Crédit Agricole
13 Abbaye aux Hommes
16 Main Post Office
18 Laundrette
22 Banque de France
25 Railway Station
26 CTAC (Bus Kiosk)
28 Bus Station

✕ **SQUARES**
5 Place Saint Pierre
11 Place Courtonne
12 Place Saint Sauveur
17 Place Gambetta
19 Place de la Résistance
27 Place de la Gare

NORMANDY

Opened in 1988, the museum is 2.75 km north-west of the tourist office on Esplanade Dwight Eisenhower. Tickets are sold daily from 9 am to 5.45 pm (8.15 pm from June to August), but once inside you can stay there until 7 pm (9 pm from June to August). Entry costs 45FF (19FF for students). WW II veterans get in for free; veterans of all wars since 1945 pay 20FF.

To get to the museum, take bus No 17 from the Crédit Agricole bank near the tourist office; the last bus back departs at 8.45 pm (earlier on Sunday). By car, follow the multitude of signs with the word 'Mémorial' written on them.

Château de Caen

This fortress is open daily from 6 am to 7.30 pm (9.30 pm from May to September).

Visitors can walk around the **ramparts** and visit the **Jardin des Simples**, a garden of medicinal and aromatic herbs cultivated during the Middle Ages. A book on the garden (in French) is on sale for 30FF inside the **Musée de Normandie** (☎ 31.86.06.24), which contains an especially rich and well-presented collection of artefacts illustrating life in Normandy from prehistoric times to the present. There are explanatory signs in English. The museum is open from 10 am to noon and 2 to 6 pm (closed Tuesday). From April to September it's open from 9.30 or 10 am to 12.30 pm and 1.30 or 2 to 6 pm. Admission is 6FF (3FF for students).

The nearby **Musée des Beaux-Arts** (☎ 31.85.28.63) is undergoing renovation and is supposed to reopen sometime in 1994.

Abbeys

Caen's two Romanesque abbeys were built on opposite sides of town by William the Conqueror and his wife, Queen Matilda (Matilda of Flanders), after these distant cousins had been 'forgiven' in the eyes of the Roman Catholic church for marrying. The **Abbaye aux Hommes** (Abbey for Men), with its multiturreted Église Saint Étienne, is at the end of Rue Saint Pierre. It was here that many townsfolk sheltered during the bombing raids in 1944. Today it's home to the Hôtel de Ville and can be visited by guided tour only. The church is open daily from 8.15 am to noon and 2 to 7.30 pm.

The starker **Abbaye aux Dames** (Abbey for Women) at the end of Rue des Chanoines to the west, incorporates the Église de la Trinité, inside of which is Matilda's tomb. Access to the abbey is also by guided tour. Entry to the church is free.

Places to Stay – bottom end

Camping On the bank of the Orne, *Camping Municipal* (☎ 31.73.60.92) on Route de Louvigny, 2.5 km south-west of the train station (take bus No 13 to the Camping stop) is open from May to September. It charges 9FF per person, 5FF for a tent site and 5FF to park.

Near the coast at Ouistreham, *Camping des Pommiers* (☎ 31.97.12.66) on Rue de la Haie Breton is open all year.

Hostels The *Auberge de Jeunesse* (☎ 31.52.19.96) at 68 Rue Eustache Restout charges 55FF (including breakfast) but is open only from 1 June to 30 September. It's 1.5 km south-west of the train station – take bus Nos 5 or 17 (last one at 9 pm) to the Cimetière de Vaucelles stop.

Hotels The *Hôtel de la Paix* (☎ 31.86.18.99) at 14 Rue Neuve Saint Jean has plain, medium-sized singles/doubles starting at 100/110FF. The *Hôtel du Havre* (☎ 31.86.19.80) at 11 Rue du Havre has average rooms of more than average size from 95/102FF without shower and 121/142FF with shower. The *Saint Jean* (☎ 31.86.23.35) at 20 Rue des Martyrs has nicely done singles and doubles for 130FF (with shower) or 150FF (with full bathroom). There's free enclosed parking.

Near the train station, *Le Vaucelles* (☎ 31.82.23.14) at 13 Rue de Vaucelles has rooms starting at 95FF (120FF with shower). Hall showers are free. *Le Jasmin* (☎ 31.52.08.16), where singles/doubles with shower cost 100/120FF, is nearby at 39 Rue Pierre Girard. The hard-to-miss yellow-and-green

Hôtel de la Consigne (☎ 31.82.23.59) at 40 Place de la Gare has doubles from 95FF.

Places to Stay – middle

Two-star hotels vary considerably, with double rooms from 110 to 275FF. A couple of cheaper ones in this bracket face the train station at Place de la Gare.

The *Hôtel Le Rouen* (☎ 31.34.06.03) at No 8 has decent rooms from 140FF. A few doors along is the modern but rather characterless *Métropole* (☎ 31.82.26.76; fax 31.82.30.89) at No 16. Basic rooms start at 130FF, with shower and other mod cons from 170FF.

Places to Eat

Summer night life centres on the brasseries along the Bassin Saint Pierre.

Restaurants The tiny pedestrianised quarter around Rue du Vaugueux, to the south-east of the chateau, is one of Caen's most popular dining spots. Lots of little, mid-priced restaurants compete here for the custom of tourists and locals alike.

Nearby, *Coupole* (☎ 31.86.37.75) at 6 Blvd des Alliés has a good-value *menu* for 47FF, salads from 32FF and a selection of local dishes. Another central option is *Hôtel Auto Bar* (☎ 31.86.12.48) at 40 Rue de Bras, a locals' hang-out with a string of different *menus*, the cheapest costing 50FF for a three-course feast including a glass of wine.

Down near the train station is the similar *Le Météor* (☎ 31.82.31.35) at 55 Rue d'Auge. This tiny haunt charges only 42FF for a three-course *menu*, including a glass of wine.

Self-Catering In the city centre, the *Monoprix* at 45 Blvd Maréchal Leclerc has a downstairs supermarket that's open Monday to Saturday from 9 am to 8 pm. Late-night purchases can be made at *Épicerie de Nuit* at 23 Rue Porte au Berger, open from 8 pm to 2 am (closed Monday). Exquisite gâteaux and 250 sorts of bread are available at *Heiz Legrix* at 8 Blvd des Alliés, open daily from 7 am to 8 pm.

For *food markets* head to Place Saint Sauveur on Friday, Blvd Leroy (behind the train station) on Saturday and Place Courtonne on Sunday.

Getting There & Away

Train The train station (☎ 31.83.50.50 for information) is 1.5 km south-east of the tourist office. The information office is open Monday to Saturday from 7.30 am to 7.30 pm. The ticket windows are open daily from 5 am to 8.30 pm.

Caen is on the Paris-Cherbourg line. There are connections to Paris's Gare Saint Lazare (148FF; 2½ hours; 13 a day), Bayeux (30FF; 20 minutes), Cherbourg (90FF; 1½ hours; four a day), Rennes (160FF; three hours; two a day), Rouen (107FF; two hours; 10 a day) and, via Le Mans, Tours (162FF; 3¾ hours, five a day).

Bus The new bus station (☎ 31.44.77.44) is next to the train station at Place de la Gare. Bus Verts serves the entire Calvados département, including Bayeux (bus No 30; 50 minutes), the eastern D-Day beaches, Honfleur (61FF), the ferry port at Ouistreham (25FF; 35 minutes), Falaise, Lisieux and Vire. The office is open weekdays from 7.30 am (6.30 am on Monday) to 7 pm and Saturday from 9 am to 6 pm. In July and August it's also open on Sunday from 9 am to 1 pm.

Most buses stop both at the bus station and in the centre of town at Place Courtonne, where there's a Bus Verts information kiosk. During the summer school holidays (July and August, more or less), the Ligne Côte du Nacre goes to Bayeux (two hours) twice a day via Ouistreham and the eastern D-Day beaches.

If you arrive in Caen by bus, your ticket is valid on city CTAC buses for one hour. If you purchase your intercity ticket in advance, your ride *to* the bus station to catch your bus is free.

Boat Brittany Ferries (☎ 31.96.80.80 at Ouistreham) has sailings from Ouistreham, 10 km north of Caen, to Portsmouth,

NORMANDY

England. For more information, see the Sea section in the introductory Getting There & Away chapter. For details on getting to Ouistreham, see the previous entry.

Getting Around

Bus CTAC city bus Nos 7 and 15 run between the train station, where the company has an information kiosk, to the tourist office. A single ride costs 5.50FF. Services generally stop between 8 and 9 pm.

BAYEUX

Bayeux (population 13,000) was made famous by two trans-Channel invasions: the conquest of England by the Normans under William the Conqueror in 1066, an event graphically depicted on the world-famous Bayeux Tapestry; and the Allied D-Day landings of 6 June 1944, which began the liberation of Nazi-occupied France. On the day after D-Day, Bayeux became the first French town to be freed. Incredibly, though it's only 10 km from the coast, Bayeux survived the war virtually unscathed.

These days, Bayeux is an attractive town with several worthwhile museums. It is an excellent base for visits to sights associated with the Allied landings. For information on the landing beaches, see the following D-Day Beaches section.

Orientation

Cathédrale Notre Dame, one km north-west of the train station, is the major landmark in the centre of town.

Information

A *billet jumelé* (combination ticket), valid for all four museums detailed here and available at each, costs 50FF (26FF for students, 29FF if you're over 65).

Tourist Office The tourist office (☎ 31.92. 16.26), in a half-timbered 14th-century building at 1 Rue des Cuisiniers, is open Monday to Saturday from 9 am to 12.30 pm and 2 to 6.30 pm. During July and August it's also open on Sunday from 10 am to 12.30 pm and 3 to 6.30 pm.

Money Banks are open Tuesday to Saturday, but the tourist office will change money when the banks are closed. The Société Générale at 30 Rue Saint Malo is open 8.30 am to 12.30 pm and 1.45 to 5 pm.

Post The main post office (☎ 31.92.04.35) on Rue Larcher is open weekdays from 8 am to 7 pm and on Saturday until noon. Foreign currency exchange services are available.

Bayeux's postcode is 14400.

Maps The Maison de la Presse (☎ 31.92. 05.36) at 53 Rue Saint Martin, 30 metres from the Bayeux tourist office, has a number of maps of the D-Day beaches. It is open Monday to Saturday from 7.45 am to 12.30 pm and 2 to 7 pm.

Laundry The Lavomatique at 13 Rue du Maréchal Foch is open daily from 8 am to 8 pm.

Bayeux Tapestry

The Bayeux Tapestry, a 68.5-metre-long strip of coarse linen decorated with woollen embroidery, was commissioned by Odo, Bishop of Bayeux and half-brother of William the Conqueror, sometime between 1066 and 1082 (when Odo was disgraced for raising troops without William's permission).

The tapestry, probably made in England, recounts the dramatic story of the Norman Invasion and the events that led up to it – from the Norman perspective, of course – in a sequence of 58 panels presented like a modern comic strip, with action-packed scenes following each other in quick succession. The events are accompanied by written commentary in rather bad Latin – even if you've never studied Latin, you might have a go at reading the captions. The scenes themselves are filled with depictions of 11th-century Norman dress, food, tools, cooking and weapons. Halley's Comet, which passed through our part of the solar system in 1066, also makes an appearance.

In 1792, local volunteers, heeding a call from the National Assembly to defend the

William the Conquerer & the Norman Invasion of England

From an unpromising beginning, William the Conqueror became one of the most powerful men of the medieval period and ruler of two kingdoms. The son of Robert I of Normandy and his concubine Arlette (he was commonly referred to during his lifetime as 'William the Bastard'), William ascended the throne of Normandy at the age of five. In spite of several attempts by rivals – not least within his own family – to kill him and his advisors, he managed to survive and properly take over the running of Normandy at the age of 15. For a period of about five years, from when he was about 20, he set about regaining his lost territory and feudal rights; he also put down several rebellions. By 1047, he had begun to think of expanding Norman influence.

In England, King Ethelred II (a relative of William's) apparently promised that upon his death, the throne would pass to William. In addition, when the most powerful Saxon lord in England, Harold Godwinson of Wessex, was shipwrecked on the Norman coast, he was made to promise William that the English crown would pass to Normandy.

In January 1066 Ethelred died without an heir. The great nobles of England (and very likely the majority of the Saxon populace) supported Harold's claim to the throne, and he was crowned on January 5. He immediately faced several rivals to his throne, William being the most obvious one. But while William was preparing to send an invasion fleet across the Channel, a rival army consisting of an alliance between Harold's estranged brother Tostig and Harold Hardrada of Norway landed in the north of England. Harold marched north and engaged them in battle at Stamford Bridge, near York, on 25 September. He won an overwhelming victory, and both Harold Hardrada and Tostig were killed.

Meanwhile, William had crossed the Channel unopposed with an army of about 6000 men, including a large cavalry force, landing at Pevensey before marching to Hastings. Making remarkably quick time southwards from York, Harold faced William with about 7000 men from a strong defensive position on 13 October. William put his army into an offensive position, and the battle commenced on 14 October.

Although William's archers scored many hits among the densely packed and ill-trained Saxon peasants, the latter's ferocious defence terminated a charge by the Norman cavalry and drove them back in disarray. For a while, William faced the real possibility of losing the battle. However, using all the knowledge and tactical ability he had gained in numerous campaigns against his rivals in Normandy, he used the cavalry's rout to draw the Saxon infantry out from their defensive positions, whereupon the Norman infantry turned and caused heavy casualties on the undisciplined Saxon troops. The battle started to turn against Harold – his other two brothers were slain, and he himself was killed (by an arrow through the eye, according to the Bayeux Tapestry) late in the afternoon. The embattled Saxons fought on until sunset, and then fled, leaving the Normans effectively in charge of England. William immediately marched to London, ruthlessly quelled the opposition, and on Christmas day, 1066, was crowned king of England.

Thus, William became king of two realms and entrenched the feudal system of government under the control of Norman nobles. Continuing Saxon peasant unrest soured his opinion of the country, however, and he spent most of the rest of his life after 1072 in Normandy, only going to England when compelled to do so. He left most of the governance of the country to the bishops.

In Normandy he continued to expand his influence by military campaigns or by stategic marriages; in 1077, he took control of Maine, but then fought Philip I of France over several towns on their mutual border. In 1087 he was injured during an attack on Mantes, and died at Rouen a few weeks later. ■

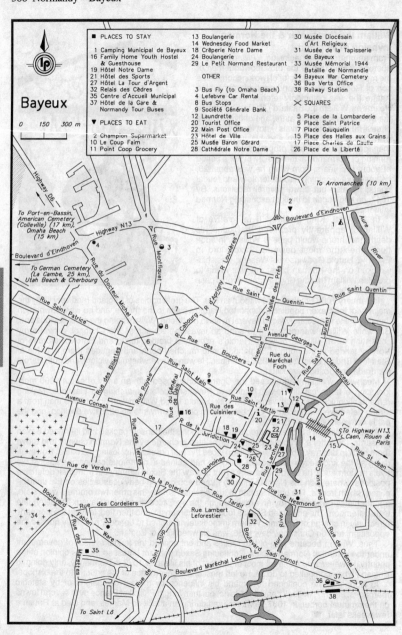

Bayeux

0   150   300 m

■ PLACES TO STAY

1 Camping Municipal de Bayeux
16 Family Home Youth Hostel & Guesthouse
19 Hôtel Notre Dame
21 Hôtel des Sports
27 Hôtel La Tour d'Argent
32 Relais des Cèdres
35 Centre d'Accueil Municipal
37 Hôtel de la Gare & Normandy Tour Buses

▼ PLACES TO EAT

2 Champion Supermarket
10 Le Coup Faim
11 Point Coop Grocery
13 Boulangerie
14 Wednesday Food Market
18 Crêperie Notre Dame
24 Boulangerie
29 Le Petit Normand Restaurant

OTHER

3 Bus Fly (to Omaha Beach)
4 Lefebvre Car Rental
8 Bus Stops
9 Société Générale Bank
12 Laundrette
20 Tourist Office
22 Main Post Office
23 Hôtel de Ville
25 Musée Baron Gérard
28 Cathédrale Notre Dame
30 Musée Diocésain d'Art Religieux
31 Musée de la Tapisserie de Bayeux
33 Musée Mémorial 1944 Bataille de Normandie
34 Bayeux War Cemetery
36 Bus Verts Office
38 Railway Station

✕ SQUARES

5 Place de la Lombarderie
6 Place Saint Patrice
7 Place Gauquelin
15 Place des Halles aux Grains
17 Place Charles de Gaulle
26 Place de la Liberté

To Arromanches (10 km)

Boulevard d'Eindhoven

Aure River

Highway D6

To Port-en-Bessin, American Cemetery (Colleville) (17 km), Omaha Beach (15 km)

Highway N13

Boulevard d'Eindhoven

To German Cemetery (La Cambe, 25 km), Utah Beach & Cherbourg

Rue du Docteur Michel

Rue Montfiquet

Rue Saint Patrice

Rue Saint Quentin

Rue d'Aprigny

Rue Louvières

Rue Saint Quentin

Rue de la Vallée des Prés

Avenue Georges

Rue Saint Laurent

Rue des Billettes

Rue Cabourg

Rue des Bouchers

Avenue

Rue du Maréchal Foch

Rue Saint Clemenceau

Rue Saint Malo

Rue Royale

Rue du Général de Dais

Avenue Conseil

Rue des Terres

Rue Saint Martin

Rue des Cuisiniers

R de la Juridiction

Rue Larcher

To Highway N13, Caen, Rouen & Paris

Rue St Jean

Rue de Verdun

R de la Poterie

Chanoines

Rue aux Coqs

Boulevard

Rue des Cordeliers

Rue Fabien Ware

Rue Tardif

Rue Lambert Leforestier

Rue de Nesmond

Rue de Crémel

Rue de Saint-Loup

Rue des Marettes

Boulevard Maréchal Leclerc

Aure River

Boulevard Sadi Carnot

To Saint Lô

1
2
3
4
5
6
7
8
10
11
12
13
14
15
16
17
18 19
20
21
22
23
24 25
26
27
28
29
30
31
32
33
34
35
36 37
38

NORMANDY

Revolution against its enemies, appropriated the tapestry for use as a cover for one of their wagons. At the last minute, as the wagon train was already heading out of town, a local official managed to convince the revolutionaries to use something more solid. Two years later, the tapestry – seen as a vestige of the *ancien régime* – was almost cut up into strips and used to decorate a float dedicated to the Goddess of Reason. Napoleon had the tapestry exhibited around France to drum up support for his projected invasion of England.

The tapestry is housed in the **Musée de la Tapisserie de Bayeux** (☎ 31.92.05.48), part of the Centre Guillaume le Conquérant on Rue de Nesmond. It is open daily from 9 or 9.30 am to 12.30 pm and 2 to 6 or 6.30 pm. From mid-May to mid-September the museum does not close at midday and may stay open until 7 pm. The entry fee is 25FF (13FF for students and people over 65).

For once, all the explanatory plaques are in both French and English. The excellent taped commentary (available in six languages; 5FF) which visitors listen to while viewing the tapestry renders the roomful of explanations upstairs somewhat unnecessary. Remember that the English are depicted with moustaches and the backs of the Norman soldiers' heads are shaved. A 14-minute long film in English, screened on the 2nd floor in the Salle de Cinéma, is shown every 40 minutes. The last showing is at 5.15 pm (5.55 pm from July to mid-September).

Cathédrale Notre Dame

Considered an exceptional example of Norman Gothic architecture, most of this rather austere building dates from the 13th century. Romanesque sections from the late 11th century include the crypt, the arches of the nave and the lower portions of the towers on both sides of the main entrance. The tower over the transept was added in the 15th century; its copper dome dates from the 1860s.

The cathedral is open Monday to Saturday from 8 am to noon and 2 to 7 pm, and on Sunday from 9 am to 12.15 pm and 2.30 to 7 pm.

Musée Diocésain d'Art Religieux

Also known as the Musée d'Art Sacré (☎ 31.92.14.21), this museum of religious art is just south of the cathedral on Rue Lambert Leforestier. It is not especially interesting unless you're a fan of altar implements and clerical garb.

It is open daily from 10 am to 12.30 pm and 2 to 6 pm (7 pm from July to mid-September). The entry fee is 10FF (5FF for students, 6FF for people over 65).

Conservatoire de la Dentelle

The Lace Conservatory (☎ 31.92.73.80), on the other side of the ticket counter from the Musée Diocesain d'Art Religieux, is dedicated to the preservation of the techniques traditionally used to make lace *(dentelle)*. This is the only place in France where you can watch some of France's most celebrated lacemakers painstakingly creating intricate designs using dozens of bobbins and hundreds of pins.

Lace is meant to be looked through, and its quality is judged by the contrast between areas with different knot densities. In the mid-19th century, the Bayeux region had some 60,000 lacemakers. Sections of lace were made by 'subcontractors' in the countryside and assembled into seamless, larger pieces in Bayeux's one great manufactory, Lefébère. Much of the production was destined for the South American market.

Exceptional examples of the lacemaker's art on display at the Conservatoire include a fan-shaped piece of black lace (hung in a frame on the wall) which took 1200 hours to make and won a gold medal in a national competition in 1989. About 900 bobbins (separated into groups by layers of cloth) and thousands of pins (a different pin is necessary for almost every knot) were used in its production.

The Conservatoire also gives lacemaking classes and sells lacemaking materials. Small lace objects, the product of something like 50 hours of work, are on sale for around 700FF. The museum is open the same hours as the Musée Diocesain d'Art Religieux.

Musée Baron Gérard

This museum (☎ 31.92.14.21) at Place de la Liberté specialises in porcelain (including local products), lace and 15th to 19th-century painting. The huge plane tree out the front, the Arbre de la Liberté (Tree of Liberty), was planted in 1797.

The museum is open daily from 9.30 or 10 am to 12.30 pm and 2 to 6 or 6.30 pm. From June to September, it is open from 9 am to 7 pm. The entry fee is 15FF (8FF for students, 10FF for people over 65).

Musée Mémorial 1944 Bataille de Normandie

This municipal war museum (☎ 31.92.93.41) on Blvd Fabian Ware rather haphazardly displays thousands of photos, uniforms, weapons, newspaper clippings, etc associated with D-Day and the Battle of Normandy. It is open daily from 9.30 or 10 am to 12.30 pm and 2 to 6 or 6.30 pm. From June to August, the hours are 9 am to 7 pm. Entrance costs 20FF (10FF for students). A 30-minute film in English is screened two to five times a day. There are always showings in the late morning (10.30 or 11 am) and in the afternoon (sometime between 3.15 and 4 pm).

Bayeux War Cemetery

This peaceful cemetery, located on Blvd Fabien Ware a few hundred metres west of the Musée Mémorial 1944 Bataille de Normandie, is the largest of the 18 Commonwealth military cemeteries in Normandy. It contains 4648 tombs of soldiers from the UK and 10 other countries. Many of the 466 Germans buried here were never identified, and the headstones are simply marked 'Ein Deutscher Soldat' (A German Soldier). There is an explanatory plaque in the small chapel to the right as you enter the grounds. The structure across Blvd Fabian Ware commemorates 1807 Commonwealth MIAs with no known grave.

Places to Stay

Camping The *Camping Municipal* (☎ 31.92.08.43) on Blvd d'Eindhoven, 1.5 km north of the centre, is open from mid-March to mid-November. A tent site costs 6.20FF; guests pay 11.50FF each. If you arrive when the office is closed, set yourself up and stop by later. The Champion supermarket across the road is open Monday to Saturday from 9 am to 8 pm.

A limited number of tents can be pitched in the back garden of the *Family Home* youth hostel (see Hostels). The charge is 50FF per person, including breakfast.

Hostels The *Family Home* youth hostel and guesthouse (☎ 31.92.15.22) at 39 Rue du Général de Dais is an excellent place to meet other travellers and exchange information. A bed in a dorm costs 81FF (73FF with a youth hostel card), including breakfast. Single rooms are 125FF. Telephone reservations are accepted. Multicourse French dinners prepared by Madame LeFèvre herself – 'incredible feasts' according to travellers – cost only 55FF, including wine. Vegetarian dishes are available on request. Guests can use the kitchen when Madame LeFèvre is not busy in there.

The *Centre d'Accueil Municipal* (☎ 31.92.08.19) at 21 Rue des Marettes, one km south-west of the cathedral, is a large, modern place that nevertheless manages to be both efficient and friendly, but don't count on meeting other travellers. Groups predominate. Antiseptic but comfortable singles (all they have) are a great deal at 75FF (including breakfast at 8 am). They usually accept reservations by telephone. A hostelling card is not necessary.

Chambres d'Hôte The tourist office has information on chambres d'hôte (rural B&Bs) in the Bayeux area. The cheapest cost about 100FF for two.

Hotels Near the train station, the old but well-maintained *Hôtel de la Gare* (☎ 31.92.10.70) at 26 Place de la Gare has singles/doubles from 85/100FF. Two bed triples/quads are 160FF and showers are free. There are no late trains so it's usually pretty quiet at night.

Near the cathedral, the *Notre Dame*

(☎ 31.92.87.24) at 44 Rue des Cuisiniers is a two-star hotel with half a dozen cheaper rooms, including serviceable doubles from 130FF. Hall showers cost 20FF. Doubles with shower and toilet are 210FF. This is an excellent deal given the location and amenities.

The *Hôtel des Sports* (☎ 31.92.28.53) at 19 Rue Saint Martin has tastefully appointed singles/doubles with shower from 140/170FF. *La Tour d'Argent* (☎ 31.92.30.08) at 31 Rue Larcher has large, quiet singles and doubles starting at 110FF. An extra bed is 45FF. This place does not accept telephone reservations. From October to May reception is closed on Monday.

The attractive *Relais des Cèdres* (☎ 31.21.98.07), in an early 20th-century mansion at 1 Blvd Sadi Carnot, has doubles from 120 to 260FF; the more expensive rooms have a shower and toilet.

Places to Eat

Restaurants For traditional Norman food prepared with apple cider, you might try *Le Petit Normand* (☎ 31.22.88.66) at 35 Rue Larcher. *Menus* start at 49FF. This place is open from noon to 2 pm and 7 to 10 pm daily except Sunday and Thursday evenings (daily in July and August).

Crêperie Notre Dame (☎ 31.21.88.70), half a block from the cathedral at 8 Rue de la Juridiction, is open from noon to 2 pm and 7 to 9 pm (and often later). It is closed in December.

Le Coup Faim (☎ 31.92.86.43), a sandwich shop at 42 Rue Saint Martin, is open Monday to Saturday from 8.30 am to 7 pm (7.30 pm in summer).

Self-Catering An *open-air market* is held along Rue Saint Jean on Wednesday morning and at Place Saint Patrice on Saturday morning. Teurgoule, a sweet cinnamon-flavoured rice pudding typical of the Bayeux region, is usually available at the market. There are a number of *food shops* along Rue Saint Martin and Rue Saint Jean between the tourist office and Place des Halles aux Grains.

Boulangerie Desdevises at 32bis Rue Saint Martin (opposite the tourist office) is open daily, except Thursday, from 6.45 am to 8 pm (6 pm on Sunday). *Boulangerie La Cathédrale* at 37 Rue Bienvenu has excellent chocolate-and-custard pastries. It is open from 7 am to 8 pm (closed Wednesday).

The *Point Coop* grocery (☎ 31.21.39.06) at 23 Rue du Maréchal Foch is open Tuesday to Saturday from 8.30 am to 12.15 pm and 2.30 to 7.15 pm and on Sunday from 9 am to noon.

Things to Buy
The Conservatoire de la Dentelle sells handmade lace items.

Getting There & Away
Train To the south-east, the train station (☎ 31.92.80.50, 31.83.50.50 for information) at Place de la Gare is open daily from 6 am to 9 pm (10.30 pm on Friday) and on Sunday from 7.30 am to 8 pm. Trains from here serve Paris's Gare Saint Lazare (via Caen), Caen (28FF; 20 minutes; 10 a day) and Cherbourg (69FF; one hour; eight a day). There's service to Quimper via Rennes.

Bus Bus Verts (☎ 31.92.02.92, 31.44.77.44 in Caen) offers rather infrequent service from the train station and Place Saint Patrice to Caen, the D-Day beaches, Vire and elsewhere in the département of Calvados. The schedules are arranged for the convenience of pupils coming into Bayeux for school in the morning and going home in the afternoon. The Bus Verts office, across the parking lot from the train station, is open weekdays from 9 am to noon and 2 to 5 pm. It is closed during most of July. There are timetables posted in the train station and at Place Saint Patrice.

Bus No 70 goes westward from Bayeux to the American cemetery at Colleville, Omaha Beach, Pointe du Hoc and Isigny. Line No 74 serves Arromanches, Gold Beach, Juno Beach and Courseulles. During July and August *only*, the Ligne Côte de Nacre goes to Caen via Arromanches, Gold, Juno and Sword beaches, and the town of Ouistreham.

NORMANDY

THE BATTLE OF NORMANDY, 1944

By early 1944 it was obvious to all observers that an Allied invasion of the continent was inevitable sometime in either spring or summer of that year. For months, Allied forces had been building up to an extraordinary degree in Great Britain. A total of 2,000,000 troops were crowded into the island, along with huge quantities of weapons, supplies and equipment.

The final plans for Operation Overlord – as the Allied invasion of occupied France was code-named – entailed an assault by three paratroop divisions and five seaborne divisions, along with 1000 planes, 300 gliders and countless ships and boats. The total invasion force was 45,000, and 15 divisions were to follow once successful beachheads were established. The Royal and US navies supplied over 1500 ships to escort and protect the invasion armies.

Allied intelligence successfully managed to convince the Germans that invasion across the narrow Channel crossing to Calais was more likely, and so fortifications were much stronger in this region than in Normandy. This was in spite of both Hitler's and Rommel's intuition that Normandy was the more likely invasion site.

Because of the action of tides and weather patterns, Allied planners only had a few days available each month to launch the invasion. On 4 June, very bad weather set in, so the operation was delayed for a day. On 5 June, the weather was only a little improved, but General Dwight D Eisenhower, Allied commander-in-chief, decided that 6 June was to be the day.

D-Day, 6 June 1944

The first actions were undertaken by the parachute divisions, who were dropped behind enemy lines in the very early morning of 6 June. Although their actual tactical victories were few, they caused enormous confusion in German ranks; suddenly groups of Allied soldiers seemed to be all around the base of the Cotentin Peninsula and in pockets east of Caen. More importantly, because of the paratroops' relatively small numbers, the German high command didn't at first believe that the real invasion had begun.

Sword, Juno & Gold Beaches These beaches, stretching for about 35 km from Ouistreham to Arromanches, were attacked by the British 2nd Army, which included sizable detachments of Canadians and smaller groups of Commonwealth, Free French and Polish forces.

At Sword, initial German resistance was quickly overcome, and the beach was secured after about two hours. Infantry pushed inland from Ouistreham to link up with paratroops around Ranville, but soon suffered heavy casualties as their supporting armour fell behind, trapped in a huge traffic jam on the narrow coastal roads. Nevertheless, they were within five km of Caen by 4 pm, but a heavy German armoured counterattack forced them to dig in. Thus, in spite of all their successes, Caen, one of the prime D-Day objectives, was not taken on the first day as envisaged.

At Juno, Canadian brigades cleared the beach in 15 minutes and headed inland. Obstacles and mines took a heavy toll of the infantry, but by noon they had pushed south and east of Creuilly. Late in the afternoon, the German armoured divisions that had halted the British from Sword were deflected towards the coast and held Douvres, thus threatening to drive a wedge between the Sword and Juno forces. However, the threat of encirclement caused them to withdraw by the next day.

At Gold Beach, the attack by the main body of British forces was at first chaotic; the initial ferocious bombardment of German positions by air and sea apparently hadn't silenced enough of the defenders' big guns. By 9 am, though, Allied armoured divisions were on the beach and several brigades pushed inland. By afternoon, they had joined up with the Juno forces and were a mere three km from Bayeux.

On all three beaches Hobart's odd-looking 'Funnies' – specially designed armoured amphibious vehicles designed to clear minefields, breach walls and wire entanglements and provide support and protection for infantry – proved their worth. Their construction and successful deployment was due to the ingenuity and foresight of the British Major-General Hobart.

Omaha & Utah Beaches For some reason, US General Omar Bradley decided that his US 1st Army didn't need the Funnies – a mistake that was to cost his men dearly at Omaha. It was compounded by the loss of 27 tanks which had been launched from landing craft too far out from the beach. Thus, the US 5th Corps had to land on a well-defended beach with virtually no armoured cover at all. The landing itself was close to a shambles; troops had to struggle though deep water to the beach, where they collected in exhausted little groups, facing devastating fire from enemy positions and with little prospect of support. Eventually, a precarious toehold was gained; the Germans, lacking reserves, were forced to fall back a little way. Nevertheless, 1000 Allied soldiers were killed at Omaha on D-Day, out of an overall total of 2500.

At Utah, US forces faced little resistance, and got off the beach after two hours. By noon, the beach had been cleared with the loss of only 12 men. Pockets of troops held large tracts of territory to the west of the landing site, and the town of Sainte Mère Église was captured; some units managed to link up with the US paratroops in the area.

The Beginning of the End

Four days later, the Allied forces held a coastal strip about 100 km long and 10 km deep. After having landed in such force, the Allies couldn't be dislodged. Nevertheless, fierce fighting for Caen reduced most of the city to rubble; numerous small towns and villages in the area suffered the same fate. Montgomery's plan successfully drew the weight of German armour towards Caen, thus leaving the US army further west to consolidate and push northwards up the Cotentin Peninsula.

The port of Cherbourg was a major prize; after a series of fierce battles, it fell on June 29. However, its valuable facilities were blown up by the Germans, so it remained out of service until autumn. To overcome the likely logistical problems, the Allies had devised the remarkable 'Mulberry harbours'. These were enormous floating harbours which were towed from England, and set up off the Norman coast. They were indispensable in allowing large amounts of supplies to be taken quickly off ships and onto the roads leading to the front. A big storm from 19 to 22 June, however, destroyed the harbour stationed at Omaha Beach and damaged the Gold Beach installation.

The fierce Battle of the Hedgerows was fought mainly by the Americans up and down the Cotentin Peninsula. The land of the bocage, divided into countless fields bordered by walled roads and hedgerows, made ideal territory for the German defenders. Nevertheless, unlike their glory days of 1940, the Germans were now forced into static defensive tactics, and once the Allies broke out from the beachheads and engaged superior numbers of tanks and artillery, the end was nigh for the Germans in Normandy.

By the end of July, US army units had smashed through to the border of Brittany; by mid-August, two German armies had been surrounded and destroyed near Falaise and Argentan; and on August 20, US forces crossed the Seine at several points about 40 km north and south of Paris. ■

During summer, Bus Verts lines generally run until 5.30 or 6 pm.

Car For three or more people, renting a car is cheaper than a tour. Lefèbvre car rental (☎ 31.92.05.96), on Blvd d'Eindhoven at the Esso petrol station, charges 370FF for one day with unlimited km and 500FF for two days with 300 free km. You lose the 2000FF excess (deductible) if you're in an accident that's your fault. The office is open from 8 am to 8 pm daily except Sunday afternoon (daily from July to mid-September).

Getting Around

Bus The buses that link Bayeux with its suburbs are operated by ByBus (☎ 31.92.02.92), which is based at Place de la Gare. All four lines stop at Place Saint Patrice.

Taxi Taxis can be ordered 24 hours a day by calling ☎ 31.92.92.40.

Bicycle Some of the D-Day sites along the coast can be easily reached by bicycle.

Ten-speeds can be rented at the train station for 50FF a day. One-speeds are available for the same price from the Family Home youth hostel (see Hostels under Places to Stay).

D-DAY BEACHES

The D-Day landings, code-named Operation Overlord, were the largest military operation in history. Early on the morning of 6 June 1944, swarms of landing craft – part of a huge fleet of boats and ships of all sorts – hit the beaches and tens of thousands of soldiers began pouring onto French soil. Aircraft dropped 23,490 men by parachute.

Most of the 135,000 Allied troops who were transported to France that day stormed ashore or disembarked along 80 km of beaches code-named (from west to east) Utah, Omaha, Gold, Juno and Sword. The landings on D-Day (*Jour J* in French) were followed by the 76-day Battle of Normandy, during which the Allies suffered 210,000 casualties, including 37,000 troops killed. German casualties were around 200,000; another 200,000 German soldiers were taken prisoner.

The best introduction to what happened here and why is Caen's Musée Mémorial (see the Caen section). Once on the coast, a well-marked circuit links the battle sites, near which holiday-makers sunbathe. Cows use the bombed-out bunkers to shield themselves from the wind. Many of the villages near the D-Day beaches have small museums which display war memorabilia collected by local people after the fighting.

Information

Maps A number of maps of the D-Day beaches – the area is also known as the Côte du Nacre (Mother-of-Pearl Coast) – are available at tabacs, newsagents and bookshops in Bayeux and elsewhere. The best, newest and most expensive map is called *D-Day 6.6.44 Jour J* and sells for about 40FF.

Arromanches

To make it possible to unload the vast quantities of cargo necessary to prosecute the war, the Allies established two prefabricated ports code-named (and known to this day) as **Mulberry Harbours**. The harbour established at Omaha Beach was completely destroyed by a ferocious gale two weeks after D-Day, but the other one, Port Winston, can still be seen at Arromanches, a seaside town 10 km north-east of Bayeux.

The harbour consists of 146 massive cement caissons towed over from England and sunk to form a semicircular breakwater inside which floating quays were moored. In the three months after D-Day, 2.5 million men, four million tonnes of equipment and 500,000 vehicles where unloaded here. At low tide you can walk out to many of the caissons. The best view of Port Winston is from the hill east of town.

The well-regarded **Musée du Débarquement** (☎ 31.22.34.31) in Arromanches explains the logistics and importance of Port Winston and makes a good first stop before visiting the beaches. It is open every day from 9 to 11.30 am and 2 to 5.30 pm. From

May to August, museum hours are 9 am to 6.30 pm. People already in the museum can stay there until half an hour after closing time. The last guided tour (in French, with a written text in English) leaves 45 minutes before closing time (both at midday and in the evening). Admission is 25FF (12FF for students and those under 16).

Longues-sur-Mer

The massive 152-mm German guns on the coast near Longues-sur-Mer, six km west of Arromanches, were designed to hit targets some 20 km away, which in June 1944 included both Gold Beach (to the east) and Omaha Beach (to the west). Half a century later, the mammoth artillery pieces are still sitting in their colossal concrete emplacements, which in wartime were covered with camouflage nets and tufts of grass.

Parts of *The Longest Day*, a movie about D-Day, were filmed both here and at Pointe du Hoc. On clear days, the Bayeux cathedral, eight km away, is visible to the south.

Omaha Beach

The most brutal fighting of 6 June took place a dozen km north-west of Bayeux along seven km of coastline known as Omaha Beach. As you stand on the gently sloping sand, try to imagine how the American soldiers must have felt running inland towards the German positions along the nearby ridge...A memorial marks the site of the first American military cemetery on French soil, where soldiers killed right on the beach were buried. Their remains were later reinterred at Colleville or in the USA.

These days, Omaha Beach is lined with holiday cottages and is popular with swimmers and sunbathers. Little evidence of the war remains apart from a single concrete boat used to carry tanks ashore.

Juno Beach

Dune-lined Juno Beach, 12 km east of Arromanches, was stormed by Canadian troops. A Cross of Lorraine marks the spot where General Charles de Gaulle came ashore shortly after the landings. These days,

young people come to the fishing port of **Graye-sur-Mer** to find the nightlife that is lacking in Bayeux.

Military Cemeteries

The bodies of the Americans who lost their lives during the Battle of Normandy were either sent back to the USA (if their families so requested) or buried in the **American Military Cemetery** (☎ 31.22.40.62) at Colleville, 17 km north-west of Bayeux, which contains the graves of 9386 American soldiers and a memorial to 1557 others whose remains were never found. The huge, immaculately tended expanse of white crosses and Stars of David, set on a hill overlooking Omaha Beach, testifies to the extent of the killing which took place around here in 1944. The cemetery is open from 8 am to 5 pm; from about mid-April to September, hours are 9 am to 6 pm. From Bayeux, the cemetery can be reached by Bus Vert's line No 70, but service is infrequent.

By tradition, soldiers from the Commonwealth killed in the war were buried near where they fell. As a result, the 18 **Commonwealth military cemeteries** in Normandy follow the line of advance of British and Canadian troops. Many of the gravestones are adorned with personal inscriptions composed by the families of the dead. The Commonwealth cemeteries are always open. There is a Canadian military cemetery at **Bény-sur-Mer**, which is a few km south of Juno Beach and 18 km east of Bayeux. See the Bayeux section for information on the mostly British Bayeux War Cemetery.

Some 21,000 German soldiers are buried in the **German military cemetery** near the village of La Cambe, 25 km west of Bayeux. Hundreds of other German dead were buried in the Commonwealth cemeteries, including the Bayeux War Cemetery.

Pointe du Hoc Ranger Memorial

At 7.10 am on 6 June, 225 US Army Rangers scaled the 30-metre cliffs at Pointe du Hoc, where the Germans had emplaced a battery of huge artillery guns whose range of up to 20 km made them a serious threat to Allied

ships and beachheads. The guns, as it turns out, had been transferred elsewhere, but the American commandos captured the gun emplacements (huge circular cement structures) and the German command post (next to the two flag poles) and then fought off German counterattacks for two days. By the time they were relieved on 8 June, 77 of the rangers had been killed and 58 more had been wounded.

Today, the site, which France turned over in perpetuity to the US government in 1979, looks much as it did half a century ago. The ground is pockmarked with huge bomb craters, and visitors can walk among and inside the German fortifications, some of which were blown apart by Allied aerial bombing and naval artillery. In the German command post, you can still see where the wooden ceilings were charred by American flame-throwers. As you face the sea, Utah Beach, which runs roughly perpendicular to the cliffs here, is 14 km to the left.

Pointe du Hoc is 12 km west of the American cemetery. The site is open all the time. From April to September the command post is open daily from 8 or 9 am to 5.30 pm (4.30 pm on Friday). During the rest of the year, it is open from 8 am to 4.30 pm every day (except on weekends from January to March).

Sainte Mère Église

As he neared the earth, one luckless US paratrooper got snagged on the church steeple of Sainte Mère Église, a village 10 km west of Utah Beach. To avoid being shot by German troops, he played dead for several hours until the village was captured by US forces.

Organised Tours

Given the limitations posed by other forms of transport (see Getting There & Away in the Bayeux section), a bus tour may be a good way to see the D-Day beaches.

Normandy Tour (☎ 31.92.10.70 – after 7 pm is best) is run by the enthusiastic, English-speaking son of the proprietors of the Hôtel de la Gare at 26 Place de la Gare

in Bayeux, where the operation is based. Times and itineraries are very flexible – basically whatever you and the other people coming along are interested in. Tours that stop at Juno Beach, Arromanches, Omaha Beach, the American cemetery and Pointe du Hoc cost 100FF per person (90FF for students). Excursions to see Norman country life (cheesemakers, etc) are also possible.

Bus Fly (☎ 31.22.00.08) has offices at 24 Rue Montfiquet in Bayeux but reservations are most easily made through the Family Home youth hostel (☎ 31.92.15.22) at 39 Rue du Général de Dais. A half-day guided tour to major sites associated with the landings costs 120FF (100FF for students, 60FF for children), including museum entrance fees. For about 25FF, Bus Fly will transport you to Omaha beach so you can make your own way back. Trips to Mont Saint Michel cost 150FF.

Getting There & Away

See Getting There & Away in the Bayeux section for information on buses.

Manche

The département of Manche, surrounded on three sides by La Manche (the English Channel), includes the entire Cotentin Peninsula. Its 320 km of coastline stretches from Utah Beach (see the previous D-Day beaches section) north-westward to the port city of Cherbourg and then south to magnificent Mont Saint Michel. The fertile inland areas are crisscrossed with hedgerows. The economy is based on dairy products, cattle raising and apple growing.

The Cotentin Peninsula's north-west corner is especially lovely, with its unspoilt stretches of rocky coastline sheltering tranquil bays and stone villages lost in time and isolation. Due west lie the Channel Islands of Jersey (25 km from the coast) and Guernsey, accessible by ferry from Saint Malo in Brittany and, during the warm months, from the Norman towns of Carteret and Portbail.

For the last two decades, the Manche region has become known as 'Europe's nuclear dump'. On the peninsula's western tip at La Hague is France's first uranium waste treatment plant, which is well hidden until you're right at its heavily fortified perimeter. Further south at Flamanville is a sprawling power plant. The Cherbourg shipyards build the latest nuclear submarines.

Getting Around

There are trains to and from Cherbourg, but the rest of the Manche region is not all that well serviced by public transport (ie local buses).

CHERBOURG

Sheltered between the breakwater and the *bocage* is Cherbourg (population 30,000), the biggest but hardly the most appealing town in this part of Normandy. A port city and naval base, it's busy with transatlantic cargo ships and passenger ferries crossing to England and Ireland.

The city sits at the tip of the Cotentin Peninsula, guarded against the Channel's changing moods by a huge breakwater built about 1.5 km out to sea in the mid-1800s.

In WW II Cherbourg was liberated three weeks after D-Day. After clearing the harbour, which had been laced with mines and whose facilities had been largely destroyed, it became a vital Allied supply base, relieving the load on the artificial harbour at Arromanches (see the D-Day Beaches section).

Orientation

The Bassin du Commerce, a wide central waterway, divides inner Cherbourg, separating the 'living' half of the city to the west from the deserted streets around the ferry terminal to the east.

Information

Tourist Office The tourist office (☎ 33.93.52.02) at 2 Quai Alexandre III is open weekdays from 9 am to noon and 2 to 6 pm and on Saturday morning. From June to September it's also open on Sunday. The staff will make hotel reservations for no charge.

Money The Banque de France (☎ 33.43.01.93) at 22 Quai Alexandre III is open weekdays from 9 am to noon and 1.30 to 3.30 pm.

Crédit Lyonnais (☎ 33.93.19.11) at 16 Rue Maréchal Foch is open weekdays from 8.30 am to noon and 1.30 to 5.30 pm. Money can also be changed at the post office. When-

NORMANDY

Jean-François Millet

Jean-François Millet (1814-75) was born to a peasant family near Cherbourg. He spent his early years working the land but moved to Paris in 1837 to make his living as a portrait painter. However, he continued to spend quite a bit of time in Cherbourg. His interest turned to religious and mythological themes until the Revolution of 1848, which affected him profoundly. Thereafter, he made peasant life the focus of his art. His paintings of men and women toiling in the fields were potent social commentaries, and it is for these scenes that he is best remembered. Many of his works show people's struggle for existence during a time of enormous social upheaval, when rural populations were deserting agricultural areas and heading for France's burgeoning industrial cities. His interest in the peasantry resulted in repeated charges of being a socialist.

By the 1860s, Millet – along with Theodore Rousseau – was one of the chief figures of the Barbizon School, named after a hamlet in the forest of Fontainebleau where he had settled. After 1868 Millet gained a degree of official recognition. In his later years, he concentrated on landscapes rather than portraits.

Millet's subtle and powerful works had a profound effect on many painters who came after him, including Seurat, Redon and Van Gogh. Many people associate Millet with his contemporary Gustave Courbet because both artists challenged established classical and romantic conventions. ■

NORMANDY

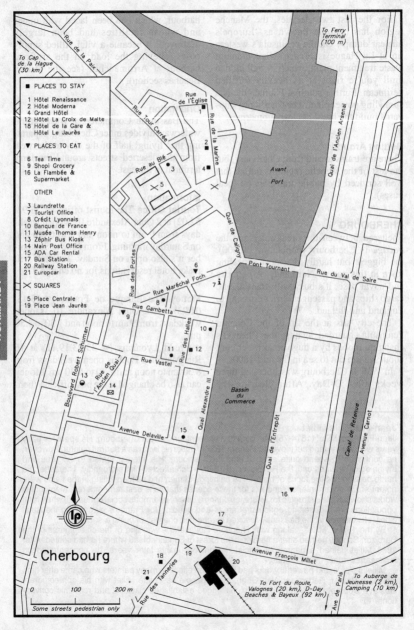

PLACES TO STAY
1 Hôtel Renaissance
2 Hôtel Moderna
4 Grand Hôtel
12 Hôtel La Croix de Malte
18 Hôtel de la Gare &
   Hôtel Le Jaurès

▼ PLACES TO EAT
6 Tea Time
9 Shopi Grocery
16 La Flambée &
   Supermarket

OTHER
3 Laundrette
7 Tourist Office
8 Crédit Lyonnais
10 Banque de France
11 Musée Thomas Henry
13 Zéphir Bus Kiosk
14 Main Post Office
15 ADA Car Rental
17 Bus Station
20 Railway Station
21 Europcar

✕ SQUARES
5 Place Centrale
19 Place Jean Jaurès

Cherbourg

0   100   200 m

Some streets pedestrian only

ever a ferry arrives, the exchange desk at the ferry terminal is open but their rates are lower than those of the banks.

Post The main post office (☎ 33.08.87.00) at 1 Rue de l'Ancien Quai is open weekdays from 8 am to 7 pm and on Saturday until noon.

Cherbourg's postcode is 50100.

Laundry The Laverie at 62 Rue au Blé is open daily from 7 am to 10 pm.

Viewpoint

Even from the port-front tourist office, the breakwater wall is hard to see. A good vantage point is from **Fort du Roule**, which watches over the city from the south. A road weaves up from Ave Étienne Lecarpentier, off Ave de Paris south-east of the train station.

Musée Thomas Henry

This museum (☎ 33.44.41.11), upstairs in the cultural centre on Rue Vastel, has 200 works by French, Flemish, Italian and other artists, but it's the 30 paintings by Millet (see the aside on Millet) which make it worth the visit. It's open from 10 am to noon and 2 to 6 pm (closed Tuesday). Entry costs 5FF.

Places to Stay

As staying overnight in Cherbourg is not high on most travellers' itineraries, finding somewhere to stay tends to be easy.

Camping The nearest camping ground is *Camping du Fort* (☎ 33.22.27.60), 10 km to the east of town at Bretteville-en-Saire. It's open all year and charges 6/3FF per person/tent. To get there, take one of the two daily buses to Bretteville.

Hostel About two km from town, the *Auberge de Jeunesse* (☎ 33.44.26.31) at Ave Louis Lumière is open from 1 April to 30 October and charges 56FF, breakfast included. Reception is closed between 10 am and 5 pm. Take the Zéphir bus No 5 (the stop is to the right as you exit the train station; last

bus at 8 pm) to the Cité Deslandes stop, backtrack 100 metres to the intersection, turn right and it's on the next corner.

Hotels Quai de Caligny has plenty of mid-range options. There are cheaper spots in the backstreets north of the tourist office.

The *Hôtel Moderna* (☎ 33.43.05.30) at 28 Rue de la Marine has decent, basic rooms from 120FF (150FF with shower). The cheaper and less appealing *Grand Hôtel* (☎ 33.43.04.02) at 42 Rue de la Marine has singles/doubles from 100/120FF.

At the end of the street, the *Renaissance* (☎ 33.43.23.90) at 4 Rue de l'Église has port-front views with comfortable rooms starting at 148/158FF.

La Croix de Malte (☎ 33.43.19.16) at 5 Rue des Halles has well-equipped doubles from 150FF.

Facing the train station, the *Hôtel de la Gare* (☎ 33.43.06.81) at 10 Place Jean Jaurès has adequate rooms from 95/115FF. A couple of doors along at 4 Place Jean Jaurès, the *Hôtel Le Jaurès* (☎ 33.43.06.35) has rooms from 120FF but it's closed on Sunday. The brasserie below can get pretty lively.

Places to Eat

Restaurants Quai Caligny is lined with restaurants but the view of the fishing boats bobbing nearby tends to push up prices. In the streets behind here – Rue Tour Carrée and Rue de la Paix – you'll find a wider choice of both cuisine and price.

Just round the corner from the tourist office, a place called *Tea Time* (☎ 33.94. 46.47) at 39 Rue Maréchal Foch has salads from 44FF as well as grilled dishes and coffee. If you can forgo atmosphere, *La Flambée* (☎ 33.44.49.03) on the 1st floor of the Centre Continent, across Ave François Millet from the train station, has a reasonable 54FF three-course *menu*.

Self-Catering Market days are Tuesday and Thursday until about 5 pm at Place de Gaulle and Place Centrale. The latter also operates on Saturday morning.

Opposite the train station is a huge *super-*

NORMANDY

market in the Centre Continent at Quai de l'Entrepôt, open Monday to Saturday from 8.30 am to 9.30 pm. The little *Shopi grocery* at 57 Rue Gambetta is open weekdays from 8.30 am to 12.30 pm and 2.30 to 7.30 pm, and on Saturday from 8.30 am to 12.30 pm and 3 to 7 pm.

Getting There & Away

Train The train station (☎ 33.57.50.50 for information) is at the southern end of Bassin du Commerce, about 600 metres from the tourist office. The information desk is open Monday to Saturday from 9 am to 12.30 pm and 2 to 6.30 pm and on Sunday from 9.30 to 11.30 am and 3 to 5 pm.

Destinations served include Paris's Gare Saint Lazare (200FF; 3½ hours; six a day) via Caen (86FF; 1½ hours), Pontorson (near Mont Saint Michel; 124FF; 2½ hours; five a day) and Rennes (161FF; 3½ hours; two a day).

Bus Buses operate from the Autogare (☎ 33.44.32.22) on Ave Jean François Millet, which is to the right directly across the road from the train station. The information desk is open weekdays from 8 am to noon and 2 to 6 pm. The main regional bus line that operates from here is STN (☎ 33.43.24.42), which has services to Bretteville (for campers).

Car All the big-name rental companies are present. Europcar and Hertz have free customer service telephones at the ferry terminal.

ADA
   2 Ave Delaville (☎ 33.20.65.65)
Europcar
   4 Rue des Tanneries (☎ 33.44.53.85)
Hertz
   43 Rue du Val de Saire (☎ 33.20.48.11)

Boat The four companies with services to either England or Ireland have offices in the reception hall of the ferry terminal, which is 1.5 km north of the train station at the end of Quai de l'Ancien Arsenal. Generally the companies make sure their information and booking desks are open two hours before departure and 30 minutes after the arrival of each ferry. The hall itself is open from 5.30 am to 11.30 pm.

Brittany Ferries (☎ 33.43.43.68) operates to Poole, England; Irish Ferries (☎ 33.44. 28.96) sails to Rosslare, Ireland; P&O European Ferries (☎ 33.44.20.13) handles the link to Portsmouth, England; and Sealink (☎ 33.20.43.38) has ferries to Southampton. For details on prices and schedules see the Sea section of the introductory Getting There & Away chapter.

Getting Around

Bus City buses are run by Zéphir (☎ 33.22. 40.58), which has an information kiosk on Blvd Robert Schuman. Buses leave from either outside the kiosk or at various points around Place Jean Jaurès (near the train station). Single tickets cost 5.20FF.

Taxi Taxis can be called on ☎ 33.53.17.04. The 1.5-km trip between the train station and ferry terminal costs about 30FF.

MONT SAINT MICHEL

No matter how many pictures you've seen, it is difficult not to be at least slightly overwhelmed by your first glimpse of Mont Saint Michel. Around the base are the ancient ramparts and a jumble of houses inhabited by the 120 people who live here. Covering the summit is the massive abbey, a soaring ensemble of buildings in a hodgepodge of architectural styles. The abbey is topped by a slender spire at whose tip – 152 metres above the sea – is a gilded statue of Saint Michel (the Archangel Michael) and the dragon. At night, the whole thing is brilliantly illuminated.

Mont Saint Michel's fame derives in part from the area's extraordinary tides, which are in many ways even more amazing than the abbey itself. Depending on the orbits of the moon and, to a lesser extent, the sun, the difference in the level of the sea between low tide and high tide can reach 15 metres. At low tide, the Mont looks out on to bare sand

stretching many km into the distance. At high tide – only six hours or so later – this huge expanse of tideland will be under water. It is said that when the tide comes in, seawater races across the sand 'at the clip of a galloping horse'. Because of progressive siltation, the Mont and causeway (constructed in 1879 for a railway line) are completely surrounded by the sea only during the highest of tides (those given a grade of 90 or more).

To stop the siltation, proposals have been raised to break down the last km of the causeway and replace it with a bridge or tunnel, which would allow the natural current to flow again. However, local opposition and high-level bureaucrats have yet to be won over. Meanwhile, the flow of tourists – two million a year – continues and on peak days, when *trop, c'est trop*, the gates are closed (temporarily) to stop the stream.

Note that some guidebooks list Mont Saint Michel under 'L' (for Le Mont Saint Michel) in the index.

History

According to Celtic mythology, Mont Saint Michel was one of the sea-tombs to which the souls of the dead were conveyed. In 708 AD, Saint Michael appeared to Aubert, Bishop of Avranches, and told him to build a devotional chapel on the summit of the Mont. In 966 Richard I, Duke of Normandy, transferred Mont Saint Michel to the Benedictines, who turned it into an important centre of learning and, later, something of an ecclesiastical fortress, with a military garrison at the disposal of the abbot – and the king.

In the early 15th century, during the Hundred Years' War, the English blockaded and besieged Mont Saint Michel three times and, for a while, even occupied Tombelaine, the tiny island two km north of the Mont. But the fortified abbey withstood these assaults and managed to remain the only place in all of western and northern France not to fall into English hands. However, all this martial activity turned the abbey into a base for powerful and ambitious churchmen rather than a place of reflection and scholarship.

During the Revolution, Mont Saint Michel was used to incarcerate political prisoners. Later, the abbey served as a prison for ordinary criminals. Conservation and restoration was begun in 1874. Monks and nuns renewed their presence on the Mont in 1969.

Orientation

There is only one opening in the ramparts: Porte de l'Avancée. The only street, the Grande Rue, is lined with touristy shops. Pontorson, the nearest town, is nine km south along the D976. There are parking lots (10FF) not far from the Mont.

Information

Tourist Office The tourist office (☎ 33.60. 14.30) is up the stairs to the left as you enter Porte de l'Avancée. It is open Monday to Saturday from 9 am to noon and 2 to 6 pm. From Easter until sometime in autumn, it's also open on Sunday from 9.30 am to noon and 1 to 6.30 pm. During July and August it's open daily from 9 am to 7 pm. If you are interested in what the tide will be doing during your visit, ask for a copy of the *horaire des marées* (tide timetable).

Books *The Mont Saint Michel*, a pamphlet written by Lucien Bély and published by Éditions Ouest-France, is a surprisingly readable history of the abbey and its inhabitants. Souvenir shops along the Grande Rue sell it for 26FF.

Dangers & Annoyances Straying away from the Mont can be risky: you could get stuck in quicksand (from which Norman soldiers are depicted being rescued in one scene of the Bayeux Tapestry) just as the tide comes rushing in...

Walking Tour

When the tide is out, it's possible to walk all the way around Mont Saint Michel, a distance of about a km. A favourite activity of youthful visitors – especially lovers with something to tell the world – is to inscribe giant messages in the sand.

NORMANDY

Abbaye du Mont Saint Michel

The Mont's major attraction is the renowned abbey (☎ 33.60.04.52), which is all the way at the top of the Grande Rue. It is open daily, except holidays, from 9.30 to 11.45 am and 1.45 to 5 pm (4.15 pm during January and the first half of February). From mid-May to mid-September it's open from 9.30 am to 6 pm.

A few rooms of the abbey can be visited without a guide, but given the Mont's rich history and the remarkable diversity of its architecture, it's well worth taking a guided tour (the only option in the busy months). One-hour tours in English and other languages, available year round (except perhaps in winter), cost 32FF (21FF if you're aged 18 to 24). From June to September, there are eight English tours a day; the rest of the year, there are three or four. The last tour in English leaves at least half an hour before closing time.

The abbey's **Église** was built on the rocky tip of the mountain. To be more precise, the transept rests on solid rock while the nave, choir and transept arms are supported by the massively built rooms below. The church is famous for its mixture of different architectural styles: the nave (11th and 12th centuries) is Romanesque while the choir (late 15th century) is Flamboyant Gothic.

The buildings on the north side of the Mont are known as the **Merveille** (Marvel). The famous **cloister** is surrounded by a double row of delicately carved arches resting on granite pillars. The early 13th-century **Réfectoire** (Dining Hall) is illuminated by a wall of recessed windows, a remarkable arrangement given that the sheer drop-off precluded the use of flying buttresses. The High Gothic **Salle des Hôtes** (Guest Hall), which dates from 1213, has two giant fireplaces. Imagine the king and his entourage seated at huge tables, dining sumptuously with some of the most powerful monks in all of France...

The stones used to build the abbey were brought to the Mont by boat and then pulled up the hillside using ropes. What looks like a treadmill for gargantuan gerbils was in fact powered by half a dozen 19th-century prisoners, who, by turning the wheel, hoisted a sledge up the side of the abbey.

Museums

The Grande Rue at times resembles a fair – people try to talk you into the sensational, 16-minute **Archéoscope** spectacle or the **Musée Grévin**, a wax museum with a mishmash of pseudo-historical exhibits. The **Musée Maritime** is a bit more serious with some explanations about the bay. A combined ticket for the three costs 66/35FF for adults/children; individually they're 40/30FF.

Places to Stay

Camping *Camping du Mont Saint Michel* (☎ 33.60.09.33) is on the D976 (the road to Pontorson) only two km from the Mont. This grassy, shaded camping ground is open from February to mid-November and charges 12FF per person, 11FF for a tent site and 11FF for parking. There are several other camping grounds a couple of km further towards Pontorson.

Hostel The *Centre Duguesclin* (☎ 33.60. 18.65) in Pontorson operates as a youth hostel from June to September. A bed in a three-bunk room costs 45FF a night; you must bring your own sheets. Reception is open from 10 am to noon and 5 to 10 pm, but if you arrive when reception is closed you can leave luggage in the common room. Guests don't need a youth hostel card.

The hostel is about one km from the train station. To get there, turn right at the Courriers Bretons office onto Rue du Docteur Tizon, go left onto Rue du Couësnon and then right onto Rue du Général Patton. The hostel is on the left in a three-storey stone building.

Hotels – Mont Saint Michel About the best deal on the Mont is the *Hôtel de la Croix Blanche* (☎ 33.60.14.04) on the Grande Rue. Its rooms are relatively inexpensive at around 200FF for singles and doubles, more with shower.

The restaurant *La Mère Poulard* (☎ 33.60. 14.01) also rents some very expensive rooms for around 750FF per person.

Hotels – Pontorson There are a number of cheap hotels across Place de la Gare from the Pontorson train station.

The *Hôtel de France* (☎ 33.60.29.17) at 2 Rue de Rennes has singles/doubles from 75/110FF and triples/quads from 140/150FF. Showers are free except in summer. Telephone reservations are not accepted during July and August. Next door, the *Hôtel Le Rénové* (☎ 33.60.00.21) at 4 Rue de Rennes has simple doubles with do-it-yourself interior design for 130 to 170FF (140 to 180FF in July and August). Triples or quads cost 230FF.

The *Hôtel de l'Arrivée* (☎ 33.60.01.57) at 14 Rue du Docteur Tizon has simple doubles/triples/quads with washbasin for 80/145/160FF. Doubles with shower cost 145FF. Hall showers cost 15FF.

Places to Eat
The tourist restaurants around the base of the Mont are not bargains. A few places along the Grande Rue sell sandwiches. One place that is worth trying is the restaurant in the *Hôtel de la Croix Blanche*, which has good *menus* from 70 to 100FF.

If you wish to taste omelettes said to be made according to Annette Poulard's 'secret' recipe from last century, try *La Mère Poulard* on the Grande Rue. It's not exactly cheap, however: *menus* range from 200 to 480FF.

Self-Catering The supermarket nearest the Mont is the *Supermarché* (☎ 33.60.09.33) next to Camping du Mont Saint Michel, two km south of the Mont. It's open from February to October from 8 am to 8 pm (10 pm in July and August).

In Pontorson, there's a *boulangerie* (closed Monday) half a block from the train station at 12 Rue du Docteur Tizon. There's a *Champion supermarket* near the Centre Duguesclin youth hostel.

Entertainment
During the summer, there are *son et lumière* (sound-and-light) shows at the Mont every night except Sunday.

Getting There & Away
Train There are trains to the tiny Pontorson-Mont Saint Michel railway station (☎ 33.57. 50.50 for information) from Caen (via Folligny; 72FF; 2¼ hours; six a day) and Rennes (via Dol; 58FF; 50 minutes; three a day). Train schedules are posted at the station. To get here from Paris, catch a train to either Caen (from Gare Saint Lazare) or Rennes (from Gare Montparnasse).

Bus STN (☎ 33.58.03.57 in Avranches) bus No 15 runs from the Pontorson train station to Mont Saint Michel all year (20FF return). There are nine buses a day in July and August (half a dozen on weekends and holidays) but fewer during the rest of the year. Most of the buses are synchronised with trains to/from Paris, Rennes and Caen.

For information on buses and tours from Saint Malo, which is 52 km west of the Mont, see Getting There & Away in the Saint Malo section of the Brittany chapter. The Pontorson office of Courriers Bretons (☎ 33.60. 11.43, 99.56.79.09 in Saint Malo) is 60 metres to the left as you exit the train station. It's open weekdays from 10 am to noon and 5.30 to 7 pm. Courriers Bretons buses on their way *to* Mont Saint Michel do not pick up passengers in Pontorson.

Bicycle Bikes can be rented at the Pontorson train station. E Videloup (☎ 33.60.11.40) at 1bis Rue du Couësnon, halfway between the train station and the Centre Duguesclin youth hostel (see Hostel for directions), has three and 10-speeds for 30FF a day; mountain bikes are 50FF a day. This place is open Tuesday to Saturday from 8.30 am to 12.30 pm and 2 to 7 pm and on Monday from 8.30 am to 12.30 pm.

NORMANDY

Brittany

Brittany (Breizh in Breton, Bretagne in French) commands the rugged western tip of France. Centuries of independence followed by relative isolation from the rest of France have forged a distinctive culture, language and way of life. The all-dominating sea is never more than 60 km away from even the remotest parts of the interior.

Many people say that there are two Brittanys: the 1100-km-long coast, known as L'Armor (Land of the Sea), and the secretive interior, L'Argoat (Land of the Woods). The coastline, swept by the rough Atlantic Ocean and the somewhat calmer waters of the English Channel, is dotted with lighthouses and is characterised by rocky coves that shelter tiny port villages and *abers* (tidal inlets), which extend far inland. Unfortunately, much of the coastline is lined with houses. The offshore islands, some of which are protected havens for sea birds, can get overcrowded by tourists during summer.

Inland, paths lead to ruined castles, legendary forests and farms built in pink, grey and black local stone. Though many of the villages are lovely, L'Argoat is a relatively little-visited part of Brittany. On the whole, tourists tend to stick to the main cities like Quimper and Saint Malo, and towns like Vannes or Dinan, all proud of their rich historical and architectural heritage. Much older are the mysterious megaliths that dot the land, especially around Carnac.

History & Identity

Brittany was first inhabited by Neolithic tribes, whose menhirs and dolmens are still scattered throughout the region. Around the 6th century BC, they were joined by the region's first wave of Celtic immigrants. Julius Caesar conquered the region in 56 BC, and it remained in Roman hands until the 5th century AD.

Following the departure of the Romans, a second wave of Celts – driven from what is

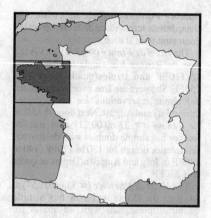

now Britain and Ireland by the Anglo-Saxon invasions – crossed the Channel and settled in Brittany. In the 5th and 6th centuries, the region was gradually Christianised by Celtic missionaries, after whom many Breton towns (eg Saint Malo and Saint Brieuc) are named.

In the 9th century, Brittany's national hero, Nominoë, revolted against French rule, taking control of both Rennes and Nantes (see the Atlantic Coast chapter). Shortly thereafter, his successors managed to repulse the Normans (Vikings). Because of its location, the Duchy of Brittany spent the Middle Ages being contested by the kings of both France and England. After a series of royal weddings, the region became part of France in 1532.

Over the centuries, Brittany has retained a separate regional identity and has become far less assimilated into the French linguistic and cultural mainstream than most areas of the mainland. Recently, there has been a drive for cultural and linguistic renewal, and ties have been established with the Celtic cultures of Ireland, Wales, Cornwall and Galicia in Spain.

To this day, some Bretons have not aban-

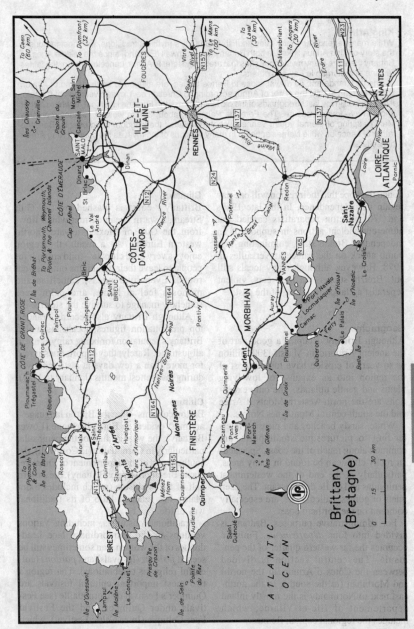

Brittany (Bretagne)

0   15   30 km

ATLANTIC OCEAN

King Arthur

While many legends and fairy tales flourish in Brittany's mythical traditions, the most famous is the story of King Arthur, linked to both Brittany and Cornwall (England) since the Middle Ages. In Brittany there are many mysterious sites that are said to refer to Arthur, Lancelot, Merlin, the fairies Viviane and Morgan le Fay and others.

The Île Grande and Île d'Aval, close to Perros Guirec, are alleged to be the island of Avalon where Morgan le Fay, the sister of Arthur according to Chrétien de Troyes's versions of the tale, lived. Hidden in the last strongholds of the old inland forest, the Forêt de Huelgoat, is where Arthur should have found treasure. The Forêt de Paimpont, about 30 km west of Rennes, contains Merlin's spring of eternal youth. Vannes was the capital of the kingdom ruled over by Ban, the father of Lancelot, while Nantes appears in many versions of the myth as the court of King Arthur himself. ■

doned the hope that their region will one day regain its independence. In the late 1960s and '70s, Breton separatists carried out numerous violent actions in support of an independent Breton state, culminating in a bomb attack on the palace at Versailles in 1978. However, although many locals still put 'Breizh' stickers on their cars, violent separatist agitation is a thing of the past.

Geography

Although Brittany occupies a good part of the ancient Armoricain Massif, 300 million or so years of erosion have turned most of the region into an expanse of low-lying plains and gentle uplands. The only exceptions are the north-western Monts d'Arrée and the south-central Montagnes Noires.

White, sandy beaches and pleasant inlets leading to picturesque small ports, are common along much of the coast. Spectacular rocky cliffs can be found in many areas, particularly at the end of the westernmost peninsulas and on Île de Ouessant. The deep inlets or gorges, called abers, are especially common on the northern coast.

For administrative purposes, Brittany is divided into four *départements*. Finistère occupies the far western quarter of the peninsula. The central section is divided between the Côtes d'Armor (to the north) and Morbihan (to the south). In the northeast next to Normandy is the mostly inland département of Ille-et-Vilaine, which includes the regional capital, Rennes.

Climate

Brittany's coast is washed by the Gulf Stream, a warm ocean current which flows from the Gulf of Mexico towards northwestern Europe. As a result, the region enjoys a very mild climate – mild enough for people to leave their geraniums outside year round. Even hydrangeas, camellias and mimosas feel at home, and palm trees somehow manage to survive the storms.

Although Brittany also records France's top precipitation figures, locals insist that Brittany's reputation for being rainy is not at all justified. Rarely, they report, does it rain for more than a few days at a stretch, even during the wettest months (January to May).

Culture

Breton customs – like the Breton language – are most evident in Basse Bretagne (Lower Brittany), the western half of the peninsula, particularly in Cornouaille (ie Cornwall), the southern part of the département of Finistère. Haute Bretagne (Upper Brittany), the eastern half of the peninsula (which includes Saint Malo), has retained little of its traditional way of life.

Traditional costumes, including various versions of the extraordinary lace headdresses of the women, can sometimes still be seen at *fest-noz* (festivals) and *pardons* (colourful religious celebrations). The region's two most important cultural festivals are Quimper's Festival de Cornouaille (see Festivals under Quimper) and the Festival Inter-Celtique (Inter-Celtic Festival), which

takes place in Lorient in early August (see Festivals under Lorient).

Religious Art

The stone *calvaires* (calvaries) at Lampaul-Guimiliau, Saint Thégonnec and Sizun, with their sculpted stories of saints and other local types, speak eloquently of the strong Celtic influence in Breton religious life. Brittany has a long list of saints unrecognised by Rome.

Also typically Breton is the *enclos paroissial* (enclosed parish), which consists of a walled enclosure, entered through a monumental gate, within which are contained the church, an ossuary and a calvary. Good examples are at Lampaul-Guimiliau, Plougastel-Daoulas and St Thégonnec. Everywhere chapels and wayside crosses mark nearly every 'cross' road.

Language

The indigenous language of Brittany, Breton (Breiz), is a Celtic language closely related to Cornish and Welsh and, more distantly, to Irish and Scottish Gaelic. These days, it's still spoken by about 600,000 mostly older people, about half of whom speak it at home. Although the number of Breton speakers – many of whom live in Finistère – is diminishing, there has recently been a linguistic renaissance among younger people, accompanied by a revival of Breton literature and theatre.

After the Revolution, the French government made a concerted effort to suppress Breton and replace it with French (the same thing was done to France's other regional languages). Even 20 years ago, if a school-child spoke in the classroom in Breton – their mother tongue! – they were punished by having to hold a stick (intended to symbolise their shameful deed) which was only passed on when another child uttered something in Breton. Recently, things have changed, and about 20 privately subsidised schools now teach in Breton. Eventually, the goal is to expand Breton-medium schooling through high school.

A few helpful Breton expressions are:

Breton	French	English
demad, demat	bonjour	hello
d'ur wech all	à une autre fois	see you again
kenavo	au revoir	goodbye
trugarez	merci	thank you
yehed mad,		
yec'hed mat	à votre santé	cheers

The following are some Breton words you may come across, especially in place names. Note that the spelling may vary.

aber	embouchure	mouth
ar	le, la	the
aven	rivière	river
bae	baie	bay
bed	monde	world
bihan	petit	little
kromm, crom	courbé	curved
deiz	jour	day
douar	terre	earth
dour	eau	water
enez	île	island

The Breton Flag & Emblems

The flag of Brittany consists of nine horizontal black and white stripes, representing each of Brittany's nine ancient *pays* (regions). In the upper left-hand corner is a field of ermine, a stoat often used in a stylised version in emblematic art. It is considered *the* symbol of Brittany. You'll come across it on many cities' flags and logos in the region.

A symbol also often seen is the Triskell (from the Greek *triskelês* – on three legs), a decorative motif used by the Celts since 450 BC. It is still very representative of Celtic countries, evoking images of the sun or the eternal wheel of life and death. ■

fao, faou	hêtre	beech tree
fest-noz	fête de nuit	night festival
gall	français	French
koad, goat	forêt	forest
gwenn	blanc	white
whel	haut	high
...ig, ic	–	diminutive suffix = little
izel	bas	low
kember, kemper	confluent	confluence
ker	cher	dear
loc'h	lagune	lagoon
mên/mein	pierre	stone
menez	montagne	mountain
mor	mer	sea
nant	vallée	valley
penn	tête, bout	head, end
plou, plo, ple...	paroisse	parish (used only as a prefix in place names)
poull	mare	pond
raz	détroit	strait
roz, ros	tertre	hillock, mound
ster, stêr, steir	rivière	river
stif, stivell	source	well
tann	chêne	oak tree
telenn	harpe	Celtic harp
ti	maison	house
trev, tre, treo	trève	parish division
trêz	sable	sand
uhel	haut	high

Activities

Sailing and windsurfing are very popular. The region's scuba diving – around the rocky archipelagos and gardens of algae – is probably the best in France.

A slow but interesting way to cross the region is by canal boat along the canals and waterways from Brest or Dinan to Nantes. See Canal Boats under Activities in the Facts for the Visitor chapter and Boating on Burgundy's waterways in the Burgundy chapter for details. For information on canal boats, moorings and locks contact the Service de la Navigation (☎ 99.59.20.60 in Rennes; ☎ 97.64.11.36 in Lorient).

Food

Brittany is known for its *crêpes*, especially the buckwheat *(sarrasin)* variety called *galettes* (in other parts of France a galette is also a shortbread type of biscuit). Crepes are usually washed down with *cidre* (cider).

Brittany is also a paradise for lovers of the fruits of the sea: fish, oysters, mussels and clams are abundant. In some ports, the catch is sold straight away in the local fish market.

Getting There & Away

Ferries of various sorts link Saint Malo with the Channel Islands and the English ports of Weymouth, Poole and Portsmouth. From Roscoff, there are ferries to Plymouth, England, and Cork, Ireland. For more information, see To/From England and To/From Ireland under Sea in the Getting There & Away chapter and the Getting There & Away listings under Saint Malo and Roscoff.

Getting Around

All of Brittany's major towns and cities are linked by rail, but the tracks basically follow the coast; there are no services to or across the interior. This is where the bus network takes over – it is extensive but services are often infrequent.

Given the appeal of exploring more out-of-the-way destinations and the limits posed by rail and bus transport, you may want to consider renting a car or motorbike. The autoroutes in Brittany are toll free.

Cycling is a popular pastime, and Brittany has produced some of France's best cyclists, whose status as local heroes is bolstered by their supposed typically stubborn Breton character and their distinctive way of handling the French cycling establishment.

Like everywhere in France, hitching can be fun and informative, particularly if you get a ride in a farmer's rusty Citroën down a slow back road. But as always, take the usual precautions.

Finistère

Brittany's most western region, Finistère (meaning 'Land's End'), is also the most Breton in character. It is known for its numerous calvaries and *pardons*, especially in Cornouaille, the area of southern Finistère whose name commemorates the early Celts

who sailed from Cornwall and other parts of Britain to settle here. This is where you're most likely to hear people speaking Breton. The area's major city, Quimper, stages an annual festival celebrating Celtic culture.

Brest, Finistère's other main city, is at the far western tip of the peninsula. Along the southern coast there are numerous fishing ports, including the engaging towns of Concarneau and Douarnenez. At Pont Aven, near Quimperlé, painters including Gauguin and Bernard founded the School of Pont Aven.

Finistère is surrounded by the sea, which pounds the rocky cliffs and deep abers that make up much of the rugged coastline. The sea breeze sweeps as far inland as the Monts d'Arrée, the eastern frontier of the Parc Naturel Régional d'Armorique. Off the coast, islands including Île d'Ouessant, Île Molène and Île de Sein are buffeted by strong currents. Some 350 lighthouses, buoys and radar installations help render the area's busy and treacherous sea routes more secure.

QUIMPER

Situated at the confluence (kemper in Breton) of two rivers, the Odet and the Steïr, Quimper (pronounced 'kam-PAIR'; population 60,000) has successfully preserved its Breton architecture and atmosphere. It is considered by many to be the cultural and artistic capital of Brittany, and some even refer to the city – once the capital of Cornouaille and now the prefecture of Finistère – as the 'soul of Brittany'. For the traveller, Quimper is an especially relaxing city to wander around and explore.

Orientation

The old city is centred around Cathédrale Saint Corentin, which is 700 metres west of the train and bus stations. Mont Frugy overlooks Quimper from the south bank of the Odet River.

Information

Tourist Office The tourist office (☎ 98.53. 04.05) at Place de la Résistance is open Monday to Saturday from 9 am to noon and 2 to 6 pm. During May, June and the first half

of September, afternoon hours are 1.30 to 6.30 pm (7 pm in June). During July and August, it's open from 8.30 am to 8 pm. The office is open on Sunday and holidays from May to mid-September; hours are 10.30 am to 12.30 pm. The staff will make hotel reservations in Finistère for the cost of a phone call.

Money The Banque de France (☎ 98.90. 70.00), near the train station at 29 Ave de la Gare, is open Tuesday to Saturday from 8.45 am to noon and 1.30 to 3.30 pm. The Crédit Lyonnais at 33 Ave de la Gare is open Tuesday to Saturday from 8 am to noon and 1.45 to 5.15 pm.

There are a number of banks on Rue Amiral Ronarc'h and few more at Place Saint Corentin. Most are closed on Monday, but the Crédit Agricole (☎ 98.95.46.33) at 14 Place Saint Corentin is open Monday to Saturday from 8.30 or 9 am to 12.30 pm and 2 to 5.40 pm (4.40 pm on Monday and Saturday).

Post The main post office (☎ 98.95.65.85) at 17 Blvd de Kerguélen is open weekdays from 8 am to 7 pm and on Saturday until noon.

Quimper's postcode is 29000.

Travel Agencies Bretagne Voyages (☎ 98. 95.61.24) at 20 Rue du Parc sells air, boat and BIJ train tickets. It is open Monday to Saturday from 9 am to noon and 1.30 to 6 pm (5 pm on Saturday).

Laundry The Lav' Seul laundrette at 9 Rue de Locronan, two blocks north of Église Saint Mathieu, is open daily from 7 am to 10 pm. Le Raton Laveur, next to the bus station parking lot at 2 Rue Jacques Cartier, is open from 8 am to 10 pm.

Walking Tour

Strolling along the quays that run along both banks of the Odet River is a fine way to get a feel for the city. The old city is known for its many centuries-old houses, which are

BRITTANY

■ PLACES TO STAY

4 Hôtel Celtic
36 Hôtel de l'Ouest
37 Hotels

▼ PLACES TO EAT

5 Euzen Traiteur
   (Prepared Foods)
6 Boulangerie Louis Tandé
12 Monoprix Supermarket
13 Covered Market
25 Aux Jardins du Midi
   Supermarket

32 Crêperie du Frugy
33 Crêperies
34 Le Pacha
35 Le Lotus d'Or

OTHER

1 Torch' VTT
   (Bicycle Rental)
7 Église Saint Mathieu
10 Musée des Beaux-Arts
   & Hôtel de Ville
14 Crédit Agricole Bank
16 Ar Bed Keltiek &
   François le Villec Shops

17 Cathédrale Saint
   Corentin
18 Musée Départemental
   Breton
19 Cathedral Garden
20 Main Post Office
21 Prefecture Building
22 Police Station
23 Theatre
24 Laundrette
26 Crédit Lyonnais Bank
27 Banque de France
28 Bus Station & Biciclub
   (Bicycle Rental)
29 Railway Station

31 Tourist Office
38 Faïenceries HB Henriot

✕ SQUARES

2 Place de la Tourbie
3 Place de Locronan
8 Place de la Tour
   d'Auvergne
9 Place Au Beurre
11 Place Laennec
15 Place Saint Corentin
30 Place de la
   Résistance

Quimper

0   250   500 m

To Auberge
de Jeunesse
(600 m) &
Camping
Municipal
(700 m)

To Concarneau (24 km)
& Lorient

To Highway D34,
Benodet (17 km) &
Concarneau (24 km)

especially in evidence on **Rue Kéréon**. For a view over Quimper, take the path near the tourist office up 70-metre-high **Mont Frugy**.

Cathédrale Saint Corentin

Quimper's cathedral, built between 1239 and 1515 (with spires added in the 1850s), incorporates many Breton elements, including – on the west façade between the spires – an equestrian statue of King Gradlon, the mythical 5th-century founder of Quimper. The early 15th-century nave is out of line with the choir, built two centuries earlier. The cathedral's patron saint is Saint Corentin, the town's first bishop, who, according to legend, ate half of a miraculous fish each morning and threw the rest back in the river. Each day, the same fish would reappear whole and offer itself to the saint.

Inside the cathedral, there's a 17th-century statue of Santig Du (Saint Jean Discalcéat; 1279 to 1349) in the right-hand arm of the transept. People who've asked for the intervention of the saint and had their petition answered often leave a loaf of bread on the table in front of the statue, the only one in the cathedral not destroyed during the Revolution. The bread is then available for any poor person who comes by.

Museums

The **Musée Départemental Breton** (☎ 98. 95.21.60), next to the cathedral in the former bishop's palace, houses exhibits on the history, traditional furniture, costumes, crafts and archaeology of Finistère. It is open daily, except Monday and Sunday morning, from 9 am to noon and 2 to 5 pm. From June to September, it's open daily from 10 am to 6 pm. The entry fee is 20FF (10FF for students and children); it may be slightly higher from June to September.

The **Musée des Beaux-Arts** (☎ 98.95. 87.50), which is near the cathedral in the Hôtel de Ville at 40 Place Saint Corentin, has French, Breton, Flemish, Dutch, Spanish and Italian paintings from the 16th to early 20th centuries. It reopened in 1993 after extensive renovations.

Faïencerie Tour

Faïenceries HB Henriot (☎ 98.90.09.36) on Rue Haute, founded in 1690, produces Quimper ware, a kind of brightly coloured faïence (glazed earthenware) for which the town is famous. There are frequent factory tours on weekdays from 9 or 9.30 to 11.30 am and 1.30 or 2 pm to 4.30 pm (3 pm on Friday); the cost is 12FF (7/5FF for students/children).

Hiking

The topoguide *Balades en Pays de Quimper*, on sale at the tourist office for 40FF, has details on 21 one to five-hour hikes in the vicinity of Quimper. It includes excellent maps, an explanatory text (in French) and estimates of the hikes' *longueur* (length) and *durée* (duration).

Festivals

The Festival de Cornouaille, a showcase for the traditional music, costumes and culture of Brittany, is held every year between the third and fourth Sundays of July. After the traditional festival, concerts of classical music are held at different venues around town.

Places to Stay

It is extremely difficult to find a place to stay during the Festival de Cornouaille.

Camping The *Camping Municipal* (☎ 98. 55.61.09), open all year, is about one km west of the old city. To get there, take Rue de Pont l'Abbé north-west from Quai de l'Odet and keep walking straight when Rue de Pont l'Abbé veers left. At the youth hostel, which is at 6 Ave des Oiseaux, turn left.

From the train station, take bus No 1 (which runs Monday to Saturday only) and get off at the Chaptal stop. Tariffs are very reasonable: 7FF per person, 5FF for a shower, 2FF for a site and 4FF to park. The office is staffed from 11 am to noon and 7 to 8 pm (closed Wednesday and Sunday).

Hostel The *Auberge de Jeunesse* (☎ 98.55. 41.67), which is open from April to October,

is near the Camping Municipal at 6 Ave des Oiseaux. A bed costs 43FF and breakfast is 17FF. For details on how to get there, see Camping.

Gîtes The tourist office has information on gîtes (private houses where travellers can stay, rather like B&Bs) and can help make reservations. For information on gîtes ruraux (B&Bs on farms), contact the Chambre d'Agriculture (☎ 98.52.48.00) on Allée Sully.

Hotels The friendly Hôtel de l'Ouest (☎ 98.90.28.35) at 63 Rue Le Déan, up Rue Jean-Pierre Calloch from the train station, has large, pleasant singles/doubles/triples/quads from 95/140/170/210FF. Doubles with shower and toilet are 180FF. Hall showers cost 15FF.

There's a string of hotels opposite the station, including the Hôtel Pascal (☎ 98.90.00.81) at 17bis Ave de la Gare, which has a few ordinary doubles for 100 or 120FF. Singles/doubles/quads with shower and toilet are 140/160/270FF. Hall showers are free. The Hôtel Le Derby (☎ 98.52.06.91) at 13 Ave de la Gare has good-sized singles/doubles with shower, toilet and TV from 150/200FF.

The Hôtel Celtic (☎ 98.55.59.35), 100 metres north of Église Saint Mathieu at 13 Rue Douarnenez, has doubles without/with shower starting at 90/140FF. Doubles with shower and toilet are 200FF. Hall showers are free.

Places to Eat

Restaurants Across the river from the cathedral, there's a string of creperies on Rue Sainte Catherine at Nos 11, 15 and 16. Crêperie du Frugy (☎ 98.90.32.49) at 9 Rue Sainte Thérèse is open Tuesday to Saturday from noon to 2.30 pm and 6.30 to 10.30 pm and Sunday from 6.30 to 10.30 pm only. It's closed on Monday. Crepes cost 6 to 38.50FF.

Near the train station, there are a number of restaurants on Rue Le Déan and Rue Jean Jaurès, including a Vietnamese place called Le Lotus d'Or at 53 Rue Le Déan and Le Pacha (☎ 98.53.04.13), a Moroccan restaurant at 37 Rue Le Déan.

Self-Catering Boulangerie Louis Tandé at 15 Rue du Chapeau Rouge has outstanding whole-grain and multicereal breads. It is open Tuesday to Saturday and one Monday in three (in rotation with nearby boulangeries) from 7 am to 7.30 pm. Except in summer, it's closed for half an hour or so from 1.30 pm. Euzen Traiteur, which has meats, prepared dishes and especially tasty gnocchi (dumplings), is down the block at 10 Rue du Chapeau Rouge. It is open Monday to Saturday from 8 am to 7.30 pm.

The Monoprix supermarket on Quai du Port au Vin (near the covered market) is open Monday to Saturday from 9 am to 12.30 pm and 2 to 7 pm.

Near the train station, the Aux Jardins du Midi supermarket at 41 Ave de la Gare is open daily from 8 am (7.30 am on Saturday, 8.30 am on Sunday) to 8 pm. There's a boulangerie at 47 Ave de la Gare.

Entertainment

From late June to the first week in September, traditional Breton music is performed every Thursday evening at 9 pm in the Jardin de l'Évêché (the garden at the back of the cathedral). The entrance fee is about 30FF.

Things to Buy

Almost all the shops in Quimper are closed on Sunday, and many places stay closed on Monday as well.

Ar Bed Keltiek (☎ 98.95.42.82) at 2 Rue du Roi Gradlon has a wide selection of Celtic music, pottery, jewellery and books. It is open Tuesday to Saturday from 10 am to noon and 2 to 7 pm. During July and August, it's open Monday to Saturday from 8.30 or 9 am to about 7.30 pm, and on Sunday from 10 am to 1 pm and 2.30 to 6 pm. François le Villec (☎ 98.95.31.54), which is next door at 4 Rue du Roi Gradlon, specialises in faïence and high- quality textiles, decorated with traditionally inspired original designs. It is open Monday to Saturday from 9 am to noon

and 2 to 7 pm. From June to August it's open daily from 9 am to 7 pm.

Quimper is famous for its brightly coloured faïence, which is known round the world as Quimper ware. Watch out for the touristy souvenir shops, though – much of their Quimper ware should be labelled 'Taiwan ware' or 'Portugal ware'. For information on factory tours, see the previous Faïencerie Tour entry.

Getting There & Away

Train The train station (☎ 98.90.50.50 for information) is east of the centre of town on Ave de la Gare. The information office is open daily from 8.30 am (9.30 am on Sunday) to 6.30 or 7 pm. During July and August, hours are 8 am to 7 pm. The ticket counters are open from 5 am to 11 pm.

To get to Paris's Gare Montparnasse (243FF; five hours), you can pick up a TGV in Rennes. Destinations within Brittany include Brest (72FF; 1¼ hours; eight a day), Vannes (77FF; 1½ hours; seven a day) and Morlaix (97FF, 1¾ hours), from where there are trains to Roscoff and Saint Malo (173FF).

Bus The bus station is to the right as you exit the train station. Schedules are posted on the station building and on the uprights around the parking lot. The office (☎ 98.90.17.83) serves two bus companies, Castric (☎ 98.56.33.03) and Le Cœur (☎ 98.54.40.15 in Pouldreuzic). It is open daily, except Saturday afternoon and Sunday, from 9 am to noon and 2.30 to 6.30 pm (9.30 am to noon and 2 to 6.30 pm in July and August). Destinations include Audierne, Pont l'Abbé and Saint Guénolé. There's reduced service on Sunday and in the off season.

CAT (☎ 98.44.46.73 in Brest), whose office is at 5 Blvd de Kerguélen, has buses to Brest, Douarnenez, Pointe du Raz and Roscoff.

Caoudal (☎ 98.56.96.72 in La Forêt-Fouesnant) has service to Concarneau (18.50FF; 30 minutes), Pont Aven (one hour) and Quimperlé. Its buses stop at Place Saint Corentin (near the cathedral) and opposite

the bus station at Café Nantaïs (23 Ave de la Gare).

For information on SNCF buses to Concarneau (19FF) and Quiberon, enquire at the train station.

Car To contact ADA, call ☎ 98.52.25.25. Europcar (☎ 98.90.00.68) is near the train station at 12 Rue de Concarneau.

Getting Around

Bus The QUB information booth at Place de la Résistance (near the tourist office) is open Monday to Saturday from 8 am to noon and 2 to 6 pm. Buses stop running around 7 pm and do not operate on Sunday. Single tickets cost 5.30FF.

Bicycle Possible destinations for a cycling trip include Bénodet (17 km), Concarneau (24 km) and even Pointe du Raz (50 km).

Torch' VTT (☎ 98.53.84.41) at 58 Rue de la Providence rents mountain bikes for 69/100FF a half/whole day (49/69FF from October to April). The shop is open Monday to Saturday from 9.30 am to 8 pm and has lots of information on cycling routes.

Biciclub (no phone), across the parking lot from the train station, has three-speeds for 60FF a day, 10-speeds for 80FF and mountain bikes for 100FF. During the summer *only*, it's open daily from 9 am to 7 pm.

CONCARNEAU

Concarneau (Konk-Kerne in Breton; population 18,000), France's third most important trawler port, is 24 km south of Quimper. Much of the tuna brought ashore here was caught in the Indian Ocean and off the coast of Africa. The town is slightly scruffy and at the same time a bit touristy, but it's refreshingly unpretentious and is near several decent beaches.

Orientation

Concarneau curls around the busy Port de Pêche (fishing port). Quai d'Aiguillon, home to the tourist office, runs north-to-south along the harbour, turning into Quai Peneroff before passing the Ville Close (walled city).

BRITTANY

It continues southward to the Port de Plaisance (pleasure-craft port) and Place de la Croix.

Information

Tourist Office The tourist office (☎ 98.97. 01.44), a bit north of the Ville Close on Quai d'Aiguillon, is open Monday to Saturday from 9 am to 6 pm. From mid-May to June, it's also open on Sunday from 9 am to 12.30 pm. During July and August, it's open Monday to Saturday from 9 am to 8 pm and on Sunday from 9 am to 1 pm and 5 to 8 pm.

Money The Société Générale at 10 Rue Général Morvan, half a block west of the tourist office, is open weekdays from 8.10 am to noon and 1.35 to 5.10 pm. There are several other banks in the vicinity.

Post There is a post office with exchange services 150 metres north-east of the tourist office on Quai Carnot.

Concarneau's postcode is 29900.

Ville Close

The Ville Close, built on a 350-metre-long island fortified between the 14th and 17th centuries, is reached from Quai Peneroff by a bridge to the west gate. It is jam-packed with touristy shops and restaurants, but there are good views from the **ramparts**, which are open for strolling every day from Easter to September from 10 am to noon or 12.30 pm and 2 to sometime between 6 and 7.30 pm. There is no midday closure during July and August. The entrance fee is 4/2FF for adults/children. The ticket office is to the left, just inside the west gate.

Musée de la Pêche

This museum (☎ 98.97.10.20), on Rue Vauban not far from the west gate, has interesting exhibits and dioramas on everything you didn't know you wanted to know about the fishing industry over the centuries. The aquariums contain mostly edible varieties of marine life.

The museum is open daily from 10 am to 12.30 pm and 2 or 2.30 pm to 6 pm. During

July and August, hours are 9.15 am to 8.30 pm. The entry fee for adults/children is 35/25FF (no student discount).

Beaches

To get to **Plage des Sables Blancs**, which is 1.5 km north-west of the tourist office on Baie de la Forêt, take bus No 1 and get off at Les Sables Blancs stop. To get to **Plage du Cabellou**, which is several km south of town, take bus No 2 and get off at Le Cabellou stop.

Places to Stay

Many of Concarneau's hotels and camp grounds close for several months over winter. At the height of the summer season, accommodation can be hard to find, and some of the two and three-star hotels increase their prices by 20 or 30FF a room.

Camping Concarneau's half a dozen camp grounds include *Camping Moulin* (☎ 98.50.53.08, 98.97.09.37) at 49 Rue de Tregunc, which is 600 metres south-east of the Ville Close. It is open from Easter to September and charges 15/8FF for adults/children and 15FF for a site and parking. You can get there by taking either bus No 2 or the ferry from the Ville Close (see Getting Around); in the latter case, continue down Rue Mauduit.

Camping Lanadan (☎ 98.97.17.78), about 100 metres north of Plage des Sables Blancs on Route de la Forêt, is open from mid-June to mid-September. It is served by bus No 1 and costs 9.50/6.50FF for adults/children plus 11/5F for a site/parking.

Hostel The *Auberge de Jeunesse* (☎ 98.97. 03.47) is superbly situated on the waterfront at Place de la Croix (next to the small granite church). A bed costs 40FF; breakfast is 16FF. Reception is open daily from 9 to noon and 6 to 8 pm, but the dining room, where you can leave luggage, is open all day.

Hotels The *Hôtel Les Voyageurs* (☎ 98.97. 08.06) at 9 Place Jean Jaurès has doubles from 125FF (160FF with shower). Hall

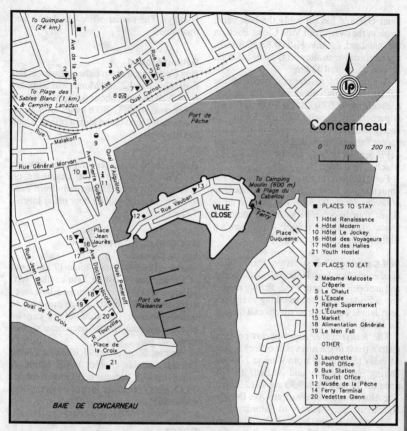

Concarneau

0   100   200 m

To Quimper
(24 km)

Ave de la Gare

Rue Alain Le Lay

Rue du Lin

To Plage des
Sables Blanc (1 km)
& Camping Lanadan

Ave Alain Le Lay

Quai Carnot

Port de
Pêche

Rue
Malakoff

Rue Général Morvan

Quai d'Aiguillon

Ave Pierre Guéguin

To Camping
Moulin (600 m)
& Plage du
Cabellou

Rue Vauban

VILLE
CLOSE

Ferry

Place
Duquesne

Place
Jean
Jaurès

Ave Docteur Nicolas

Quai Peneroff

Port de
Plaisance

Rue Jean Bart

Quai de la Croix

R. Tourville

Place de
la Croix

BAIE DE CONCARNEAU

■ PLACES TO STAY
1 Hôtel Renaissance
4 Hôtel Modern
10 Hôtel Le Jockey
16 Hôtel des Voyageurs
17 Hôtel des Halles
21 Youth Hostel

▼ PLACES TO EAT
2 Madame Malcoste
Crêperie
5 Le Chalut
6 L'Escale
7 Rallye Supermarket
13 L'Écume
15 Market
18 Alimentation Générale
19 Le Men Fall

OTHER
3 Laundrette
8 Post Office
9 Bus Station
11 Tourist Office
12 Musée de la Pêche
14 Ferry Terminal
20 Vedettes Glenn

BRITTANY

showers are free. The downstairs bar is frequented on Fridays by a jovial crowd from the market. Around the corner, the more refined *Hôtel des Halles* (☎ 98.97.11.41) on the Enclos de Servigny has rooms with shower and TV from 175FF. There's street parking nearby.

Opposite the tourist office, the *Hôtel Le Jockey* (☎ 98.97.31.52) at 11 Ave Pierre Guéguin has singles/doubles with shower from 120/160FF. On Rue du Lin, a quiet lane north of the port, the *Hôtel Modern* (☎ 98.97.03.36) at No 5 is run by a talkative old Breton lady and her daughter. It has large

singles/doubles from 150/180FF and a private garage. The cheapest joint in town is the *Hôtel Renaissance* (☎ 98.97.04.23), which is at the northern end of town at 56 Ave de la Gare. A basic room here starts at 100FF.

At Plage des Sables Blancs, the *Hôtel des Sables Blancs* (☎ 98.97.01.39) has beachfront rooms from 170FF. It's open from April to October.

Places to Eat
Restaurants Designed like an old sea dogs' haunt, *L'Écume* (☎ 98.97.33.27) at 3 Place

Saint Guénolé has probably the best value *menu* in the overpriced Ville Close. Back on the mainland, *Le Men Fall* (☎ 98.50.80.80), a pizzeria down an alley off Quai de la Croix, is open daily until 11 pm.

A number of restaurants north of the fishing port offer good value for money. *L'Escale* (☎ 98.97.03.31) at 19 Quai Carnot is particularly popular with the locals – a hearty lunch or dinner *menu* (available daily except Saturday night and Sunday) costs just 41FF. Similar is *Le Chalut* (☎ 98.97.02.12), which is next door.

For excellent, home-style crepes try the unpretentious little creperie called *Madame Malcoste* (☎ 98.97.36.57) at 17 Ave de la Gare. Your basic crêpe au beurre (buttered pancake) costs only 6.50FF – and there's a slight discount if you order two.

Self-Catering The stalls in the *covered market* on Place Jean Jaurès sell all the basics and are open daily until 1 pm. The big market day is Friday, with traders taking over Place Jean Jaurès until their stomachs call them in for lunch.

The *Rallye Super supermarket* on Quai Carnot (next to the main post office) is open Monday to Saturday from 9 am to 7.30 pm. During most of July and August, it's also open on Sunday from 9.30 am to 12.30 pm. The *Alimentation Générale* at 8 Ave Docteur Nicolas is open Monday to Saturday from 7.30 am to 9.30 pm (8 pm on Saturday) and on Sunday from 7.30 am to 1 pm and 6 to 8.30 pm.

Getting There & Away
Bus The bus terminal is next to the tourist office. Local bus companies include Caoudal (☎ 98.97.35.31), which runs five buses a day (less on Sunday) to Quimper (18.60FF; 30 minutes), Pont Aven and Quimperlé. Caoudal's office, across the parking lot from the bus terminal, is open weekdays from 8.45 am to 1.15 pm and 3 to 6 pm. In July and August, it's also open on Saturday.

Autocars Castilla-Le Naour (☎ 98.06. 82.18) sends buses eastward along the coast to Port Manech daily except Sunday and holidays. The tourist office has details and timetables.

Getting Around
Bus Concarneau's two rather infrequent bus lines, Nos 1 and 2, run Monday to Saturday from 7.20 am until about 6.30 pm. A single ticket costs 4.60FF. Both buses stop at the bus terminal next to the tourist office, which has timetables.

Boat A small passenger ferry plies between the Ville Close and Place Duquesne on Concarneau's eastern shore daily from 7 am to 8 pm (usually with an hour off at lunch). Tickets cost 2.50FF.

AROUND CONCARNEAU
Îles de Glénan
The nine Îles de Glénan, about 17 km south of Concarneau, boast an 18th-century fort, sailing and skin diving schools, a bird sanctuary and a few houses. From mid-June to mid-September the archipelago can be reached by boat from Concarneau's pleasure-craft port.

Vedettes Glenn (☎ 98.97.10.31) at 17 Ave Docteur Nicolas charges 80FF return. A round trip with Vedettes de l'Odet (☎ 98.50. 72.12, 98.57.00.58 for their Bénodet office) costs 85FF.

BREST
Sheltered by a wide natural harbour known as the Rade, Brest (population 160,000) is one of France's major naval ports. Destroyed by continual bombardments during WW II, it was rebuilt on the foundations of its long naval past. Today, the starched white uniforms of the French Navy are still very much in evidence.

But it is not a particularly attractive city, lacking the atmosphere of tradition and history that prevails in nearby places such as Quimper. But from here (as well as from the village of Le Conquet further west) boats sail to the windswept isles of Ouessant and Molène.

Top: Village of Sauzon on Belle Île, Brittany (GA)
Middle: Sunset at Le Conquet, Brittany (GA); Painted doorway, Rochefort-sur-
Terre, Brittany (GA); Stone cross, Saint Gildas de Rhuys, Brittany (GA)
Bottom: Frozen lake near Belz, Brittany (GA)

Top: Young musicians, Place du Parvis, Notre Dame, Paris (DR)
Middle: Woman in folk costume, Alsace (CDT Bas-Rhin); Relaxing in the moat of a chateau, Nantes, Brittany (DR); *Feria* time in Languedoc (LL)
Bottom: Dancing the *Sardane,* Perpignan, Roussillon (LL)

Information

The tourist office (☎ 98.44.24.96) at 8 Ave Georges Clemenceau is open Monday to Saturday from 9.30 am to 12.30 pm and 2 to 6 pm. Summer hours are 9 am to 7 pm.

Oceanopolis

The ultramodern Oceanopolis (☎ 98.34. 40.40) at the Port de Plaisance (take bus No 72 from the centre) has lovely aquariums with algae forests, seals, crabs and anemones. From 1 May to 30 September it's open daily from 9.30 am to 6 pm. During the rest of the year it's open Tuesday to Sunday from 9.30 am to 5 pm (6 pm on weekends) and on Monday from 2 to 5 pm. Admission is 45 (35FF for those under 25).

Musée de la Marine

Housed in the much rebuilt, fortified Château de Brest, the Musée de la Marine (☎ 98.22.12.39) is a portside Maritime Museum with rather under-equipped displays. But you can walk around the nine-to-12-metre-thick chateau walls, which offer magnificent views over the Rade and the naval harbour. It's open from 9.15 to 11.30 am and 2 to 5.30 pm (closed Tuesday). Entry is 20/10FF for adults/children.

Places to Stay

Brest is not somewhere many people would choose to stop overnight. But if you're stuck, the best place is probably the *Auberge de Jeunesse* (☎ 98.41.90.41), located three km east of the grey city centre at the Port de Plaisance (behind the Oceanopolis). It charges 40FF a night. To get there, take bus No 72.

Near the train station, the *Hôtel de la Gare* (☎ 98.44.47.01) on Blvd Gambetta has cheapish rooms. The *Hôtel l'Avenir* (☎ 98. 44.21.86) is on Ave Georges Clemenceau near the tourist office.

Getting There & Away

Brest's train station (☎ 98.80.50.50) is to the west of the centre on Blvd Gambetta. Trains from here run south-east to Quimper (72FF; 1¼ hours) or north-east to Morlaix (61FF;

1½ hours), from where there are connections to Roscoff.

Ferries to Île d'Ouessant, operated by the Service Maritime Départemental (☎ 98.80. 24.68), leave from the Port de Commerce east of the chateau. For details, see Getting There & Away in the following Île d'Ouessant section.

PARC NATUREL RÉGIONAL D'ARMORIQUE

Of France's 33 regional parks, the Armorique Regional Park (Park An Arvorig) is a special one. Taking in the Monts d'Arrée, it stretches west along the Presqu'île de Crozon (Crozon peninsula) and includes the reserves of Île d'Ouessant and the Molène archipelago.

By joining land and sea in a 1100-sq-km protected area, the park aims to protect the various landscapes, ecosystems and human environments that coexist here. A number of little museums showcasing local customs are scattered around the park. They include the Écomusée on Île d'Ouessant.

For more information, contact the park's head office (☎ 98.21.90.69) in Hanvec, 50 km north of Quimper on the D18, four km north-east of the N165 (the main road to Brest). Tourist offices in the vicinity also have general information.

ÎLE D'OUESSANT

Île d'Ouessant (Enez Eussa – The Highest – in Breton, Ushant in English), a wild but hauntingly beautiful island 20 km from the mainland, probably best epitomises the ruggedness of the Breton coast. An old local saying, '*Qui voit Ouessant voit son sang*' ('He who sees Ouessant sees his blood'), dramatically expresses its untamed nature and the fear inspired by the area's powerful currents and treacherous rocks. Eight km long, the crab-claw-shaped island serves as a beacon for over 50,000 ships entering the Channel each year.

Traditionally, the sea provided islanders with both a livelihood and a way of life; from the age of 11, boys sailed off. The interiors of the houses, partitioned by little more than

wooden panels, very much resembled the insides of a boat and were decorated with furniture made from wood found washed ashore. Outside, the houses were painted in symbolic colours: blue and white for the Virgin Mary, green and white to symbolise hope.

While the locals' long isolation from the rest of the world is to an extent over, some old customs remain. Old women still make lace crosses to represent the souls of their husbands who never returned from the sea; the little black Ushant sheep are free to roam around; and *ragoût de mouton*, lamb baked for five hours under a layer of roots and herbs, retains its popularity. In summer, the 1062 regular inhabitants are outnumbered by about 2000 seasonal residents and another 1000 day-trippers. But even with the extra crowds, Ouessant retains its untamed air.

Orientation & Information

The only village of reasonable size is Lampaul, three km from where the ferries dock. It has a handful of hotels and shops.

In the heart of the village is the tiny tourist office (☎ 98.48.85.83), open Monday to Saturday from 10.30 am to noon and 2 to 4.30 pm. In summer it's open from 10 am to 1 pm and 2 to 7 pm (10 am to 1 pm on Sunday). It sells brochures (10FF) with maps outlining four walks of between 10 and 17 km in length; the text is in French.

Lighthouses & Walks

About eight km separate Ouessant's western and eastern extremities, each boldly marked by a powerful lighthouse. Standing tall before the setting sun is the black-and-white striped **Phare de Créac'h**, the world's most powerful lighthouse. Just north of the ferry dock is the **Phare du Stiff**.

The entire island is ideal for (very windy) walks. A 45-km path follows the craggy, rocky coastline, passing through some grand scenery.

Museums

Heading west from Lampaul, the **Écomusée** (☎ 98.48.86.37), also known as the Maison du Niou, has simple but moving displays on local life arranged in two typically colourful houses furnished in the traditional style. It's open daily, except Monday, from October to May from 2 to 4 pm (later in some months); from June to September it's open daily from 10.30 am to 6.30 pm.

The **Musée des Phares et des Balises** (☎ 98.48.80.70), a lighthouse museum appropriately positioned under the Phare de Créac'h, tells the intriguing story of these vital installations. A 30-minute walk west of Lampaul, the museum is open daily, except Monday, from 10.30 am to 6.30 pm; winter hours are from 2 to 4 pm. Admission is 20/10FF for adults/children.

Places to Stay & Eat

The *Camping Municipal* (☎ 98.48.84.65) in Lampaul looks more like a football field than a camping ground. It's open from March to November.

Although Lampaul has four hotels, only the *Hôtel l'Océan* (☎ 98.48.80.03) is open all year. It has bay-view rooms and a lively bar underneath.

A less touristy, more serious place is the *Centre Ornithologique* (☎ 98.48.82.65), a km out of Lampaul towards Phare de Créac'h. Basically a centre for bird watchers and nature lovers, this modern functional place has rooms for 40FF per person, including use of the kitchen and common room.

The hotels have decent restaurants specialising in lamb and sting ray. There is a small *supermarket* in Lampaul as well as a *boulangerie* or two.

Getting There & Away

Ferries to Ouessant are run by the Penn Ar Bed (End of the World) line which sails either from Brest's Port de Commerce or from Le Conquet, 24 km west of Brest. The voyage from Brest takes 2½ hours, from Le Conquet it's 1½ hours. There are four boats a day – the first at 8.30 am, the last at 4.30 pm.

In summer, daily boats leave from Brest at 8.30 am and from Le Conquet at 8.30, 9.30 and 11 am and at 5.30 pm. Returning from

Ouessant, there are boats bound for Le Conquet at 9.45 am and 4.30, 5 and 7 pm – the 5 pm boat continues to Brest. In winter, there is a daily boat leaving from Brest at 8.30 am and from Le Conquet at 9.30 am. From Ouessant, boats leave for Le Conquet at 4.30 and 5 pm, the latter one continuing to Brest.

A return adult ticket costs 160FF/130FF from Brest/Le Conquet; children up to 10 years pay half-price. In summer, advance bookings are highly advised. Tourists cannot bring their cars over and bikes can only be taken if you board at Brest.

For more ferry information, contact the Service Maritime Départemental (☎ 98.80. 24.68) at the Port de Commerce in Brest.

Getting Around
A shuttle bus covers the three km from the ferry terminal to Lampaul (10FF).

Cycling around Ouessant often involves fighting strong headwinds. Ouessancycles (☎ 98.48.83.44), which has a kiosk at the ferry terminal (☎ 98.48.80.13) on Ouessant's eastern side, rents bikes for 35FF a day.

ROSCOFF
Protected from the furious seas by the nearby island of Batz, the small town of Roscoff (Rosko; population 3700), whose old granite houses surround a small bay, is the southernmost – and probably the most attractive – Channel port for entering France by ferry from Britain or Ireland. Nearby areas of the English Channel are home to a wide variety of kinds of algae, some of which are used in *thalassothérapie* (a health treatment using sea water). Roscoff's hinterland is known for its *primeurs* (early fruits and vegies), such as cauliflowers, tomatoes and artichokes, which flourish here thanks to the area's gentle microclimate.

Many people associate Roscoff with Brittany Ferries, a controversial and dynamic company whose success story started here in 1973. Prompted by the need of Breton vegetable farmers to find new markets abroad, Alexis Gourvennec, a tough, vocal native, lobbied the French government to construct a deep-water port in Roscoff. When it was built, the local farmers' cooperative braved the scorn of the established companies to launch a ferry service to Plymouth. Brittany Ferries is now the largest carrier in the western Channel.

Orientation
Roscoff is arrayed around the fishing and pleasure port, which is sheltered by several cement piers. Place de la République, on the waterfront, is the town's focal point.

Information
Tourist Office The tourist office (☎ 98.61. 12.13) at 46 Rue Gambetta, which heads north from Place de la République, is open Monday to Saturday from 9 am to noon and 2 to 6 pm. In July and August, it's open Monday to Saturday from 9 am to 7 pm and on Sunday from 9.30 am to 12.30 pm.

Money There's a 24-hour banknote exchange machine in the ferry terminal. In town, the Caisse d'Épargne (☎ 98.69.72.69) at 9 Rue Gambetta, near the tourist office, is open Tuesday to Saturday from 8.30 am to noon and 1.30 to 5.30 pm (4 pm on Saturday).

Things to See
Unless you're into thalassothérapie or water sports such as scuba diving, there's little to keep you occupied in Roscoff besides the town's **museum** and **aquarium**.

Places to Stay
Camping There's a camping ground 500 metres from the beach at *Manoir de Kerestat* (☎ 98.69.71.92), 2.5 km south of Roscoff in Kerestat. No buses pass nearby. Fees are 9/6FF per adult/child and 6FF for a tent site.

Hotels Facing the train station, the *Hôtel de la Gare* (☎ 98.61.21.42) at 2 Rue Ropartz Morvan has basic singles/doubles/triples for 115/125/150FF. The *Hôtel Le Centre* (☎ 98.69.72.03), at 5 Rue Gambetta near the

BRITTANY

tourist office, has doubles from 160FF and triples for 350FF.

For a great location on the headland across the port from the tourist office, the *Hôtel Bellevue* (☎ 98.61.23.38) at Blvd Sainte Barbe has rooms starting at 230FF. It's closed from mid-November to mid-March.

Getting There & Away

Train & Bus The tiny train station (☎ 98.69.70.20) is on Rue Ropartz Morvan about 500 metres from the tourist office. To get to the tourist office, turn right into Rue Vloche as you leave the station, then right onto Rue Brizeux. Follow it until it curves around to the left into Rue Jules Ferry, which leads to Place de la République. The ticket office at the station is open from 6.20 am to 1 pm and 1.30 to 7 pm (9.20 am to 5 pm on Sunday).

From the train station, there are trains or buses (about five daily) to Morlaix (24FF; 30 minutes), from where there are connections west to Brest (61FF; 1½ hours), south to Quimper (97FF; 1¾ hours) and east to Lannion (58FF; three hours; five daily) and Saint Brieuc (81FF; 1¾ hours; five daily).

Car There are several car rental counters inside the ferry terminal.

Boat Brittany Ferries (☎ 98.29.26.00) sail to Plymouth in England and Cork in Ireland. Boats leave from the modern Gare Maritime de Bloscon, open daily from 9 am to midnight. It's about 1.5 km east of the tourist office – to get to town, head straight up the hill as you leave the ferry terminal, turn right and then take the first left into Rue de Plymouth. This leads down to the pleasure port, which you follow around to the left to Place de la République.

AROUND ROSCOFF
Île de Batz

Just a couple of km offshore, the four-sq-km Île de Batz (Enez Vaz; population 750) is a charming island with some good beaches. The *Auberge de Jeunesse* (☎ 98.61.77.69) is open from April to September.

Boats to the island take 15 minutes and are run by *Vedettes Blanches* (☎ 98.61.78.87). They leave from the old port in Roscoff at high tide and at the end of the long pier when the tide's out. Return tickets cost 26/13FF for adults/children. During July and August they leave hourly between 8 am and 8 pm; during the rest of the year, services are less frequent.

Morbihan Coast

Morbihan, the département covering Brittany's south-central section, stretches from Redon in the east to Lorient near the Finistère frontier. Although its inland areas are largely unspoilt, it is the coast – particularly around the regional capital, Vannes – that attracts most visitors. The Golfe du Morbihan (Morbihan Gulf), enclosed by arms of land which leave only a narrow outlet to the Atlantic, is virtually an inland sea – (*Mor-bihan* means Little Sea in Breton). About 40 of its islands are inhabited. Oysters are actively cultivated around the gulf, which is also something of a paradise for birds.

West of the gulf, the Presqu'Île de Quiberon, a narrow, claw-shaped peninsula, makes it about halfway to Belle Île, an island separated from the town of Quiberon by 12 km of open sea. The whole Morbihan region is a showcase of the architectural achievements of the Neolithic period – at nearly every crossroad, you'll see signs pointing to megalithic sites, of which Carnac is the most famous.

VANNES

Gateway to the Golfe du Morbihan, Vannes (Gwenned; population 48,000) is a lovely town – small enough to feel intimate, close enough to the sea to taste the salt air and old enough to have a long and interesting history. The medieval heart of town is almost as lively as it was centuries ago.

In pre-Roman times Vannes was the capital of the Veneti, a Gallic tribe of intrepid sailors who fortified their town with a sturdy wall (part of which remains) and built a

formidable fleet of sailing ships. The Veneti were conquered by Julius Caesar after a Roman fleet defeated them in a battle off Brittany's south-eastern coast. Under the 9th-century Breton hero Nominoë, the town became the centre of Breton unity. In 1532 the union of the Duchy of Brittany with France – achieved through a series of royal marriages – was proclaimed in Vannes.

These days, Vannes is the best starting point for exploring the Golfe du Morbihan. The old town's narrow, winding streets, lined with half-timbered houses, shops and creperies, lead down to the tiny port, from which boats set sail to the islands that dot the Golfe du Morbihan. From Vannes, you can also pick up buses to Carnac and Quiberon.

Orientation

Except for the salty breeze, you'd hardly know Vannes was on the coast. Its small yacht-filled port sits at the end of a canal-like waterway 1.5 km from the gulf's entrance. Île de Conleau, about 3.5 km south of the town, is an island connected to the mainland by a causeway.

Information

Tourist Office The tourist office (☎ 97.47. 24.34) at 1 Rue Thiers is open Monday to Saturday from 9 am to noon and 2 to 8 pm. In the peak season (roughly June to September) it's open nonstop from 9 am to 7 pm and on Sunday from 10 am to 1 pm. It can exchange foreign currency, but only on Sunday when the banks are closed.

Money Near the train station, the Banque de France (☎ 97.54.28.31) at 55 Ave Victor Hugo is open weekdays from 8.45 am to 12.15 pm and 1.30 to 3.30 pm.

Centrally, there are banks along Rue Thiers. The Banque Crédit Industriel de l'Ouest (☎ 97.42.59.70) at 2 Place du Maréchal Joffre is open Tuesday to Friday from 8.30 am to 12.25 pm and 2 to 5.45 pm and on Saturday from 8.30 am to 12.25 pm and 2 to 4 pm.

Post The main post office (☎ 97.01.33.33) at 2 Place de la République is open weekdays from 8 am to 7 pm and on Saturday until noon.

Vannes's postcode is 56000.

Bookshops The Maison de la Presse (☎ 97.47.18.79) at 1 Rue Joseph le Brix has a small range of English novels as well as a good selection of maps. It's open Monday to Saturday from 8.15 am to 12.15 pm and 1.45 to 7 pm.

Laundry The small Le Bras laundrette at 5 Ave Victor Hugo is open daily from 7 am to 9 pm.

Walking Tour

The tourist office has a free walking-tour pamphlet in English that takes you past the major sights of the **old town**. A small section of the **ramparts** is accessible for wandering (the stairs up are tucked away in Rue des Vierges). The ramparts afford fine views over the manicured gardens set in the former moat. You can also see the black tops of the **Vieux Lavoirs** (old laundry houses), though they are better seen from Rue Porte Poterne.

Museums

Opposite Cathédrale Saint Pierre, Vannes's premier museum is the **Musée de la Cohue** (☎ 97.47.35.86). Named after the 14th-century building in which it is housed, it has been, over the centuries, a produce market, law courts and seat of the *parlement* of Brittany. Today La Cohue is home to both the **Musée des Beaux-Arts** and the **Musée du Golfe et de la Mer**. The latter has displays on various aspects of human, marine and bird life in the gulf.

La Cohue is open daily from 10 am to noon and 2 to 6 pm (closed Sunday and Tuesday between 15 September and 15 June); admission for adults/children is 15/8FF.

Festivals

During the film festival held in April, a few nondubbed (v.o.) films are screened in

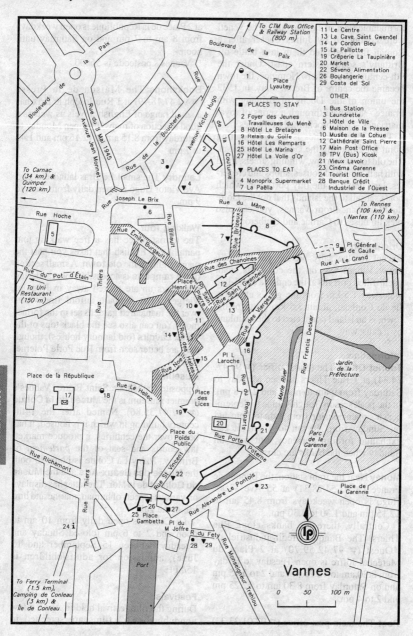

To CTM Bus Office
& Railway Station
(800 m)

11 Le Centre
13 La Cave Saint Gwenöel
14 Le Cordon Bleu
15 La Paillotte
19 Crêperie La Taupinière
20 Market
22 Séveno Alimentation
26 Boulangerie
29 Costa del Sol

OTHER

1 Bus Station
3 Laundrette
5 Hôtel de Ville
6 Maison de la Presse
10 Musée de la Cohue
12 Cathédrale Saint Pierre
17 Main Post Office
18 TPV (Bus) Kiosk
21 Vieux Lavoir
23 Cinéma Garenne
24 Tourist Office
28 Banque Crédit
Industriel de l'Ouest

■ PLACES TO STAY

2 Foyer des Jeunes
Travailleuses du Menè
8 Hôtel Le Bretagne
9 Relais du Golfe
16 Hôtel Les Remparts
25 Hôtel Le Marina
27 Hôtel La Voile d'Or

▼ PLACES TO EAT

4 Monoprix Supermarket
7 La Paëlla

Boulevard de la Paix
Boulevard de la Paix

Place
Lyautey

Rue de la Paix
Rue de la Boucherie
Avenue du 8 Mai 1945
Avenue Jean Monnet
Avenue Victor Hugo
Rue de la Coulume

To Carnac
(34 km) &
Quimper
(120 km)

Rue Joseph Le Brix

Rue du Mène

To Rennes
(106 km) &
Nantes (110 km)

Rue Hoche

Rue Émile Burgault
Rue Billault
Rue Brizeux

Pl Général
de Gaulle

Rue 5

Rue du Pot d'Étain

Rue des Chanoines

Rue A Le Grand

To Uni
Restaurant
(150 m)

Rue Thiers

Place
Henri IV

Rue Saint Gwenöel
Rue des Vierges

Jardin
de la
Préfecture

Rue Francis Decker

Marle River

Rue des Halles
Rue Noë

Pl L
Laroche

Rue du Rempart

Place de la République

Rue Le Helec

Place
des Lices

Parc
de la
Garenne

17

18

19

20

21

Rue Porte Poterne

Place du
Poids Public

Rue Richemont

Rue Thiers

Rue St Vincent

22

Rue Alexandre Le Pontois

23

Place
de la
Garenne

24 i

25 Place
Gambetta

26

27

Pl du
M Joffre

28 29

R du Fety

Rue Monseigneur Tréhiou

To Ferry Terminal
(1.5 km),
Camping de Conleau
(3 km) & île de Conleau

Port

Vannes

0   50   100 m

BRITTANY

Cinéma Garenne on Rue Alexandre le Pontois.

Places to Stay

Camping About three km south of the tourist office, the three-star *De Conleau* camping ground (☎ 97.63.13.88) on Ave du Maréchal Juin has views over the calm waters of the gulf. It's open from 1 April to 30 September and charges 14/7FF for adults/children plus 11FF for a tent site. Bus No 2 (last one at 7.30 pm) from Place de la République stops at the gate.

Hostel While the official youth hostel seems to be perpetually 'under construction', there are two *foyers* open to travellers. *Foyer des Jeunes Travailleuses du Menè* (☎ 97.54. 33.13) at 14 Ave Victor Hugo has single rooms for 65FF (60FF for people under 26). Breakfast is 10FF extra. It's open from 7 am to 11 pm.

There's also the women-only *Foyer Madame Molé* (☎ 97.47.29.60) at 10 Place Théodore Decker, along the port a block south of the tourist office. A bed costs 60FF (50FF for those under 25).

Hotels – Train Station Area Facing the station, *Le Richemont* (☎ 97.47.12.95) at 26 Place de la Gare has good basic rooms from 110FF (177FF with shower). The friendly *Hôtel Anne de Bretagne* (☎ 97.54.22.19) at 42 Rue Olivier de Clisson – go right as you exit the station and then take the first left – has singles/doubles with TV and shower from 135/165FF.

Hotels – Old Town Place Gambetta has two of the best choices in town. The *Hôtel La Marina* (☎ 97.47.22.81) at No 4 has relaxing, modern rooms which receive the morning sun and have views over the marina and the crowded brasseries below. Prices start at 160FF. If you prefer your sun after lunch, the *Hôtel La Voile d'Or* (☎ 97.42. 71.81) opposite at No 1 has doubles for 120FF to 160FF.

Just outside the old town walls, the *Hôtel La Bretagne* (☎ 97.47.22.81) at No 36 on busy Rue du Mène has ordinary rooms from 100FF, and 145FF with toilet and shower. A block away, the *Relais du Golfe* (☎ 97.47. 14.74; fax 97.47.15.21) on Place du Général de Gaulle has singles/doubles from 130FF, triples from 250FF. Just inside the walls, the intimate *Les Remparts* (☎ 97.54.11.90) at 4 Rue des Vierges has rooms from 200FF.

If you have an unrestricted budget, you might consider the prestigious *Hôtel Roof* (☎ 97.63.47.47) at the tip of Île de Conleau. Waterfront rooms with serene views over the sheltered bay go for 450FF.

Places to Eat

The streets in and around the old town are the best area for dining.

Restaurants Hidden under the turret on Place des Lices, the popular *Crêperie la Taupinière* (☎ 97.42.57.82) at No 9 has a three-crepe *menu* that includes a quarter-litre of cider for 42.50FF. It is closed on Thursday. *Costa del Sol* (☎ 97.42.47.93) at 7 Place du Maréchal Joffre is a Spanish creperie with a Breton *menu* – a butter galette, a galette complète (wholemeal galette), a crêpe fraise (strawberry crepe) and a quart of cider, all for 45FF. The warm atmosphere and the crepes of *La Cave Saint Gwenöel* (☎ 97.47.47.94) at 23 Rue Saint Gwenöel come highly recommended. It is closed on Monday.

La Paëlla on Rue Brizeux serves plates of its namesake for 39FF and jugs of sangria for 29FF. It's closed Sunday and Monday. *Le Centre* (☎ 97.54.25.14), at 7 Place Saint Pierre opposite the cathedral, has a standard three-course *menu* from 48FF. *La Paillotte* (☎ 97.47.21.94), upstairs at 8 Rue des Halles, has pizzas from 30FF, while just up the road, tropical *Le Cordon Bleu* serves a fine assortment of salads from 23FF. It also has a 58FF *menu*.

For snacks until midnight, *Croiserie Express* (☎ 97.47.82.08) beside *Hôtel La Marina* on Place Gambetta has foot-long sandwiches for 10 to 15FF.

University Restaurant There's a small *University Restaurant* (☎ 97.47.81.01) on Rue

de la Loi. Strictly speaking, you have to be a student to eat there. Meal tickets cost 17FF and must be bought in advance.

Self-Catering On Wednesday and Saturday mornings, a fruit and vegie *market* takes over Place du Poids Public. Fresh meat is sold in the covered market round the corner.

The *Monoprix supermarket* at 1 Place Joseph Le Brix has a boulangerie as well as an upstairs grocery section. It is open Monday to Saturday from 8.45 am to 7.30 pm. *Boulangerie Jean Degrez* at 1 Rue Saint Vincent is open from 7 am to 8.30 pm (closed Tuesday).

Just through the 18th-century gate, Porte Saint Vincent, *Séveno Alimentation* at 12 Rue Saint Vincent is open Monday to Saturday from 8.30 am to 12.30 pm and 3 to 7.30 pm and on Sunday from 10 am to noon.

Getting There & Away

Train Vannes's train station (☎ 97.42.50.50 for information) on Place de la Gare is about 1.5 km north of the tourist office to the right at the end of Ave Victor Hugo. The information office is open Monday to Saturday from 9 am to 6.50 pm and on Sunday from 9 am to noon and 2 to 6.50 pm.

There are trains via Rennes (87FF; one hour) to Paris's Gare Montparnasse (248FF plus TGV fee; 3½ hours; three a day), Auray (18FF; 15 minutes), Quimper (77FF; 1½ hours; seven a day) and Nantes (86FF; 1½ hours; six a day). For details on trains to Quiberon via Plouharnel (near Carnac), see Getting There & Away in the following Quiberon section.

Bus Regional buses are run by two companies – CTM and TTO. The CTM office (☎ 97.01.22.10), which is opposite the train station, is open weekdays from 9 am to noon and 2 to 6.30 pm and on Saturday from 9 am to 12.30 pm. Its buses cover destinations in Morbihan including Port Navalo (32FF), Pontivy (43FF) and Ploërmel (43FF) as well as Rennes (85FF) and Nantes (86FF).

The TTO office (☎ 97.47.29.64) at 4 Rue du 116ème (at the intersection of Ave Victor Hugo and Blvd de la Paix) is open weekdays from 8 am to 12.30 pm and 1 to 6.30 pm, and on Saturday from 6.30 am to 12.30 pm and 2 to 6 pm. Its Cariane bus (line Nos 23 and 24) goes via Auray to Carnac (38FF; 1¼ hours; eight a day) and on to Plouharnel and Quiberon (50FF; 1¾ hours).

Car To contact ADA, call ☎ 97.42.59.10. Europcar (☎ 97.42.43.43) is at 48 Ave Victor Hugo.

Getting Around

Bus The local TPV line has an information kiosk (☎ 97.47.41.78) at the main bus hub on Place de la République. It's open weekdays from 9 am to 12.15 pm and 3 to 6 pm. A single ticket costs 5.70FF. You can get information on TPV's routes from the CTM regional bus office at the train station.

Bicycle Bikes can be hired from the train station luggage office for about 50FF a day (more in summer) plus a 500FF deposit. The office is open weekdays from 8 to 11.50 am and 2 to 5.30 pm and on weekends from 9 to 11.50 am and 2 to 6 pm. Hours are longer in summer.

AROUND VANNES
Golfe du Morbihan Islands

There are about 40 'habitable' islands in the Golfe du Morbihan, 36 of them privately owned by artists, actors and the like. One of these private domains is **Île de Gavrinis**, home to Morbihan's best decorated dolmens (see the aside on The Megaliths of Carnac in this chapter). It can be visited by appointment only – ask at the tourist office for details.

The two largest islands, **Île d'Arz** and the larger **Île aux Moines**, are both publicly owned and are home to several small villages. Though there's little of note on them apart from palm trees, palm groves and beaches, they're popular day trips from Vannes. Boats (130FF return; two boats a day), run by Navix (☎ 97.46.60.00), leave from the ferry terminal at the end of Ave Maréchal de Lattre de Tassigny in Vannes,

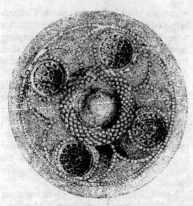

Celtic openwork disk

which is 1½ km from the tourist office. Out of season, the notice board in the tourist office can tell you when the next boat excursion around the Golfe du Morbihan will be leaving. Count on paying about 105/60FF for adults/children for a four-hour trip.

The islands are also accessible by regular ferries. To Île d'Arz, boats leave from Île de Conleau; to Île aux Moines, boats leave from Port Blanc, 13 km south-west of Vannes.

CARNAC

Carnac (Garnag; population 4000) sits on the doorstep of some of the world's most renowned megalithic sites. Located about 32 km west of Vannes, the town is made up of the old village, Carnac Ville, and a more modern, rather boring seaside resort, Carnac Plage, whose long, sandy Grande Plage on the sheltered Baie de Quiberon is a popular bathing beach.

Orientation

Carnac Ville and Carnac Plage are 1.5 km apart. They're joined by Ave de Salines, which heads south from just past the *gendarmerie*

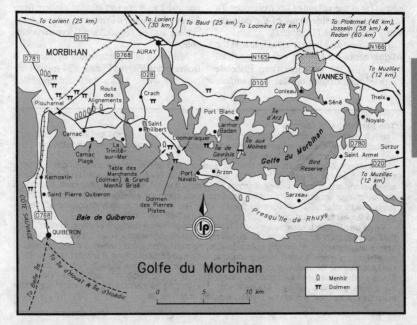

BRITTANY

on Route de Plouharnel, the road from Plouharnel (the nearest rail junction).

Information

Tourist Offices The main tourist office (☎ 97.52.13.52) is in Carnac Plage at 74 Ave des Druides, two blocks back from the beach. It's open Monday to Saturday from 9 am to noon and 2 to 6 pm. In July and August it's open from 9 am to 7 pm and on Sunday from 10 am to 1 pm and 2 to 6 pm.

The small tourist office annexe in Carnac Ville is behind the cathedral on the central Place de l'Église. From Easter to September it's open from 9 am to 12.30 pm and 2.30 to 6 pm, and in July and August from 10 am to 5 pm.

Post Carnac's postcode is 56340.

Megaliths

Carnac's megalithic sites start north of Carnac Ville and stretch for 13 km north and east as far as the village of Locmariaquer. To see the details inside many of the dolmens you'll need a torch (flashlight).

The closest and largest menhir line is the **Alignements du Ménec**, one km north of Carnac Ville; to get there from Place de l'Église, head straight up Rue de Courdiec,

which is a block before the church. The area is fenced off to protect the 1170 menhirs that were being damaged by people trampling around and on themn But they're easily seen from the road or the roof of the nearby Archéoscope.

From here, Route des Alignements heads east to the more impressive **Alignements de Kermario** (1000 menhirs in ten lines), also a protected site but with a specially built viewing platform. Further still is the **Alignements de Kerlescan**, a much smaller grouping (600 menhirs in 13 lines) but the only one where you're free to wander around.

Near Locmariaquer, the big monuments are the **Table des Marchands**, a 30-metre-long dolmen, and the **Grand Menhir Brisé**, the region's largest menhir, which once stood 20 metres high but is now lying horizontally and, sadly, in several pieces. These two are off the D781 just before the village. The site is open all year, but from 30 March to 31 October an office is open from 10 am to 1 pm and 2 to 5 pm (no midday closure from June to September). During this period, tours costing 10/5FF for adults/children are available.

Just south of Locmariaquer by the sea is **Dolmen des Pierres Plates**, a 24-metre-long chamber whose rocky walls are decorated

---

The Megaliths of Carnac

The culture of the megalithic rose during the Neolithic period between 4500 and 2000 BC, created by people whose lives were based on agriculture and herding, a radical change from the hunters and gatherers in the earlier Palaeolithic era.

The most noticeable features of Neolithic culture are: *menhirs*, stones between one and 20 metres high, weighing between two and 200 tons and planted upright in the ground (in Breton, *men* means stone and *hir* means long); *dolmens* (*dol* meaning table), stone burial chambers, standing on their own or accessed by a narrow passage, often engraved with symmetrical designs; and *tumuli*, earth mounds which covered the dolmens. The most spectacularly decorated dolmens and the largest tumuli are on Gavrinis, an island in the Golfe de Morbihan.

While menhirs and dolmens are found in other parts of France (and elsewhere in Europe), it's their concentration around Carnac which has made this region famous. There's a wealth of sites, from solitary menhirs protruding from a field to the most impressive feature, the *alignements*, parallel lines of menhirs running for several kms and capped by a *cromlech*, a semicircle of stones. Unlike dolmens, the meaning of menhirs has not been deciphered, though theories abound. Solitary rocks have been explained as everything from phallic symbols to sign posts indicating that a burial ground is nearby. It has been suggested that the *alignements* have astronomical and religious significance, though the mystery remains unsolved. ■

Asterix the Gaul

Galling (Gaul-ing?) though it may be for present-day Bretons, Brittany is probably best known for being the home of Asterix, or Astérix as he is known to the French. Goscinny and Uderzo's brilliant comic creation has been an enduring favourite of both children and adults for over a generation.

For those unfamiliar with the exploits of this plucky little Gaul, all is explained at the start of each book: the year is 50 BC and all of Gaul has been conquered by the Romans – except for one small village. The eccentric and freedom-loving inhabitants cannot be defeated because a magic potion brewed by their druid makes them invincible in battle. In each book Asterix and his somewhat dim but loyal and good-natured friend Obelix somehow end up having all kinds of adventures, including voyages to various parts of the known and unknown world. The humour of the series is characterised by outrageous puns and word plays (which the English translators manage to transfer admirably from the original French), slapstick routines and fine visual jokes. For example, when the Goth tribes from Germania speak, their speech balloons contain Gothic script. The books also have great fun with supposed national characteristics; in *Astérix chez les Bretons* (Asterix in Britain), the Britons cease fighting with the Romans halfway through a battle in order to have a tea break!

In some books, invention flags a little and the formula wears a bit thin – the Gauls have an adventure, sink the pirate ship again, beat up yet another Roman patrol. At their best, however, the stories are hilarious and witty. In addition, the satire can be biting, as in *Obelix and Co*, which contains a superb send-up of modern advertising and capitalist marketing theory. Overall, though, the series is simply meant to be fun, for kids aged nine to 90. ∎

with impressive, multishaped engravings. Unfortunately, no buses run to Locqmariaquer from Carnac (there's a very infrequent service from Auray) but it's cyclable and not an impossible hitch along the D781.

Musée de Préhistoire

Established in 1882, this Prehistory Museum (☎ 97.52.22.04) at 10 Place de la Chapelle in Carnac Ville, a block up from Place de l'Église, is an excellent introduction to the megalithic sites. It chronicles life in and around Carnac from the Palaeolithic era to the Middle Ages, featuring, of course, the Neolithic era. Free English booklets will guide you adequately through the two floors.

The museum is open from 10 am to noon and 2 to 5 pm daily except Tuesday (daily in July and August). From June to 30 September it's open until 6 or 6.30 pm. Entrance costs 30FF for adults (11FF for students and children).

Archéoscope

Sitting partially hidden next to the Alignements du Ménec is the new Archéoscope (☎ 97.52.07.49) on Route des Alignements. The 25-minute show uses light, sound and special movement effects to take you back to Neolithic times.

From mid-February to mid-November, it's open daily from 10 am to noon and 2 to 6.30 pm. From May to October *only*, there are three English-language shows a day. Admission for adults/students/children is 40/30/20FF. A viewing stand (no charge) on top of the building gives a good view of the *alignements*.

Places to Stay

Camping There's a cluster of camping grounds about two km north of Carnac Ville – head straight up Rue de Courdiec past the menhirs until you see the signs. The three-star *Les Pins* (☎ 97.52.18.90) is open from April to November and charges 12/8FF for adults/children plus 25FF for the tent site and parking. Prices are dearer in July and August.

In Carnac Plage, three-star *Camping Nicolas* (☎ 97.52.95.42) on Blvd de Légenèse, west of the tourist office one block from the sea, is open from April to October. It has a laundry.

Hotels In Carnac Ville, *Le Râtelier* (☎ 97.52.05.04) on quiet Chemin du Douet, a block south-west of Place de l'Église, has

rustic charm, low ceilings and timber furnishings. Rooms with a shower start at 210FF. This place is closed in January. The new *Hôtel d'Arvor* (☎ 97.52.96.90; fax 97.52.81.73), at No 5 on busy Rue Saint Cornély, is open all year. Singles/doubles start at 190/220FF.

La Licorne (☎ 97.52.10.59), at 5 Ave de l'Atlantique, overlooks a small saltwater lake and has comfortable rooms from 160FF (220FF with shower). It is open all year.

The newly renovated *Hoty Hôtel* (☎ 97.52.11.12) at 15 Ave de Kermario, two blocks east of the tourist office, is open from Easter to mid-November. Rooms start at 150FF. Another cheapie is *La Frégate* (☎ 97.52.97.90) at 14 Allée des Alignements (next to the tourist office), open from April to September.

Places to Eat

Restaurants In Carnac Ville, *Le Râtelier* (see Hotels) has a gourmet *menu*, served in a setting illuminated by firelight and stained-glass windows, for 90FF. *La Caliorne* (☎ 97.52.92.05) at 8 Rue de Colary has snacks and standard *menus* from 59FF, while just down from Place de l'Église, *Chez Yannick* (☎ 97.52.08.67) on 8 Rue du Tumulus is a lush garden creperie serving galettes from 13FF.

In summer, Ave des Druides and the small streets around the tourist office in Carnac Plage are packed with creperies and restaurants.

Self-Catering On Wednesday and Sunday there's a market just off Place de l'Église in Carnac Ville.

There are several *supermarkets* along Route de Plouharnel as you enter Carnac Ville. The *Intermarché* is open Monday to Saturday from 8.30 am to 12.30 pm and 3 to 7 pm. In summer, it's open Monday to Saturday from 8.30 am to 8 pm and on Sunday from 9.30 am to 12.30 pm.

In Carnac Plage, the *Super U supermarket* at 188 Ave des Druides, about one km east of the tourist office, is open Monday to Saturday from 9 am to 12.30 pm and 3 to 7 pm

(there's no midday closure on Saturday). In summer it's also open Sunday mornings.

Getting There & Away

Train The nearest train station is in Plouharnel, four km north-west of Carnac Ville. Plouharnel is on the seasonal Auray-Quiberon line (see Getting There & Away under Quiberon for details).

Bus TTO's Cariane buses between Vannes and Quiberon stop in Carnac Ville outside the gendarmerie on Route de Plouharnel (from the stop, continue straight on to get to Place de l'Église). In Carnac Plage the stop is at the tourist office. For more information on buses, see Getting There & Away in the Vannes section.

Getting Around

Bicycle In summer, bicycles can be hired in Carnac Ville from Lorcy (☎ 97.52.09.73) at 6 Rue de Courdiec, which is on the road to the Alignements du Ménec. In Carnac Plage, a few blocks from the tourist office, you can hire bikes at Le Randonneur (☎ 97.52.02.55) at 20 Ave des Druides or Cycl'Up (☎ 97.52.91.76) at No 40 on the same street.

QUIBERON

At the end of the narrow, 15-km-long peninsula south-west of Carnac lies Quiberon (Kiberen; population 4800), a popular seaside town surrounded by sandy beaches and a wild coastline swept at times by enormous seas. It's also the port for ferries to Belle Île. Monsieur Hulot took his unforgettable holiday at Quiberon.

Orientation

One main road, the D768, leads into Quiberon. At the end of it is the train station, from where the town winds down to a sheltered bay lined by the town's main beach, the Grande Plage.

Information

Tourist Office The tourist office (☎ 97.50. 07.84) is on the main road between the train station and the Grande Plage at 7 Rue de

Verdun. It is open Monday to Saturday from 9 am to 12.30 pm and 2 to 6.30 pm. In July and August it's open from 9 am to 8 pm and on Sunday from 10 am to noon and 5 to 8 pm.

Post Quiberon's postcode is 56170.

Beaches

The beach is *the* attraction in and around Quiberon. The Grande Plage attracts families while further towards the peninsula's tip are larger, less crowded spots. The peninsula's western side is known as the Côte Sauvage (Wild Coast). It's great for a windy cycle but too rough for swimming.

Places to Stay

Camping All the camping grounds round Quiberon are very close to the beach. *Camping Municipal le Conguel* (☎ 97.50.19.11) at Blvd de la Teignouse, close to the expensive Sofitel Hôtel, is open all year and costs 8.40/4FF per adult/child and 4.60/5FF for a tent site/parking.

Hostel Quiberon's *Auberge de Jeunesse* (☎ 97.50.15.54) at 45 Rue du Roc'h Priol, a few blocks south-east of the train station, is a basic place open only from May to 30 September.

Hotels About the cheapest place in town is the *Hôtel Bon Accueil* (☎ 97.50.07.92) at 6 Quai de l'Houat, along the waterfront to the right as you face the port. It has good value rooms from 105FF. In front of the port, the *Hôtel Le Corsaire* (☎ 97.50.15.05) at 24 Quai de Belle Île has rooms starting at 130FF, or 145FF with shower.

The *Hôtel l'Idéal* (☎ 97.50.12.72) at 43 Rue de Port Haliguen, two blocks east of the train station, has singles/doubles from 200/240FF.

Places to Eat

Restaurants Like the hotels, Quiberon's restaurants tend to be expensive. The restaurants in the *Bon Accueil* and *Le Corsaire* hotels have reasonably priced *menus*. Other-

wise, if you have the means to get there, try *La Chaloupe*, a *routier* (truckers' restaurant) six km north of Quiberon at Kerhostin – heading towards Quiberon, turn left at the traffic lights. It's unpretentious and has a hearty lunch *menu* for 45FF, served Monday to Saturday.

Self-Catering There's a *Stoc supermarket* on Rue de Verdun downhill from the tourist office.

Getting There & Away

Train Trains only run to Quiberon during the peak months of July to early September. The station (☎ 97.42.50.50) is on Rue de la Gare, basically at the end of the main road into Quiberon.

To get to the tourist office from the train station, turn left as you exit the station and follow the main road as it curves right to Rue de Verdun.

The nearest major train station is Auray (☎ 97.42.50.50 for information), 23 km north-east on the Lorient-Paris rail line. Quiberon-Auray trains all stop at Plouharnel, the closest station to Carnac.

Bus TTO's Cariane line (see Getting There & Away in the Vannes section) connects Quiberon with Carnac, Auray (24FF) and Vannes (50FF; 1¾ hours). Buses stop at the train station in Quiberon.

Boat Ferries from Quiberon to Belle Île and the smaller islands of Houat and Hoëdic are run by the Compagnie Morbihannaise (☎ 97.31.80.01). In Quiberon the ferry terminal is at Port Maria, at the western end of the Grande Plage. On Belle Île, ferries dock at Le Palais. The voyage to Belle Île takes 45 minutes. Ferries run all year, with at least five services a day, though in summer and on weekends there are many more.

Return fares are 78FF (51FF for children under nine). A bike is 34FF; cars, depending on size, cost from 364 to 422FF. Passenger prices are the same to car-free Houat and Hoëdic, but services to these islands are

BRITTANY

much less frequent (sometimes only one a day).

Getting Around
Bicycle Cycles Loisirs (☎ 97.50.10.69) at 3 Rue Victor Golvan, up the hill from the tourist office and the first left, has bikes for 47/220FF a day/week and scooters for 80FF an hour.

BELLE ÎLE
As its name implies, Belle Île, which is about 15 km south of Quiberon, is a beautiful island. Vauban built one of his citadels here, but it is far less impressive than the natural rock formations.

Twenty km long and nine km wide, Belle Île is bound by relatively calm waters to the north and by the crashing force of the Atlantic to the south. Home to 4300 winter inhabitants, the population rises to 35,000 in summer. Fortunately, the island is large enough to accommodate so many visitors without feeling crowded.

Information
Tourist Office The tourist office (☎ 97.31.81.93) is in the main town, Le Palais, on the wharf to the left when you get off the ferry. From July to mid-September it's open Monday to Saturday from 9 am to 12.30 pm and 2 to 7.30 pm. During the rest of the year it's open from 9 am to noon and 2 to 5.30 pm. It's open on Sunday morning all year from 10 am to noon.

Things to See & Do
The main village is **Le Palais**, a cosy port dominated by the citadel which Vauban strengthened in 1682, following centuries of Anglo-French disputes over control of the area. There are three other smaller villages – Sauzon, Bangor and Locmaria – each located at one of the island's extremities. The English occupied the island for two years from 1761.

Belle Île's wild southern side has spectacular rock formations, a few small, natural ports and a number of *grottes* (caves). The most famous, **Grotte de l'Apothicairerie** (Cave of the Apothecary's Shop), is an awesome cavern into which the waves roll from two sides. It used to be regularly visited but because of 'frequent deadly accidents', as the warning signs point out, it's now officially closed. There's nothing to stop you from making your way carefully down the slippery rocks, but you should only attempt it on a very calm day at low tide.

A pedestrian-only track follows the island's entire coastline. If you're going by bike, ask at the tourist office for its brochure of *sentiers côtiers* (coastal paths), which shows the best cycling routes.

Places to Stay
Camping There are 10 camping grounds dotted round Belle Île; most are two-star places open only from May to October. The municipal *Les Glacis* (☎ 97.31.41.76) in Le Palais, at the base of the citadel, is the closest to the port.

Hostels On Belle Île, the *Auberge de Jeunesse* (☎ 97.31.81.33) in Le Palais is open all year and charges 43FF a night (58FF with breakfast). For hikers, there are a couple of *gîte d'étapes* on the island – one along the coast a km south of Le Palais (☎ 97.31.55.88) and another in Locmaria (☎ 97.31.73.75).

Hotels & B&Bs The hotels on Belle Île are pricey. The cheapest is the *Hôtel La Belle Isloise* (☎ 97.31.84.86) in Le Palais. Better are the *chambres chez l'habitant* (B&Bs) – ask at the tourist office for a list.

Places to Eat
On Belle Île seafood deservedly rules. For a sumptuous splurge, try the highly recommended *La Saline* (☎ 97.31.84.70) on Route du Phare heading out of Le Palais.

There are small *supermarkets* in the villages.

Getting There & Away
In Le Palais, Les Car Verts (☎ 97.31.82.50) on Quai de l'Acadie rents *décapotables* – open-topped deux chevaux (2CV) Citroëns

– for 270FF a day. It's a rare chance to try one of these great, typically French cars whose era has sadly ended.

There's a handful of bike and scooter rental places near Le Palais's port.

LORIENT
In the 17th century the Compagnie des Indes (the French East India Company) founded the Port de l'Orient; the name was later abbreviated to Lorient. Ever since, it has been one of the most important ports in France. In WW II, it held U-boat pens; during fierce fighting in 1945 the city was almost entirely destroyed.

Thus, although Lorient is one of France's largest cities, there is very little of interest to travellers. However, fans of Celtic culture will enjoy the large Festival Inter-Celtique, and Lorient's variety of accommodation makes it a useful base for exploring nearby areas in Morbihan and Finistère.

Orientation
Lorient is set on a large natural harbour. The centre of town is about one km south-east from the train station and the bus station.

Information
Tourist Office The tourist office (syndicat d'initiative; ☎ 97.21.07.84) is on the Quai de Rohan, in the Musée de la Mer. In July and August it's open on weekdays from 9 am to 7 pm, the same hours with a two-hour lunch break from noon on Saturday, and on Sunday from 2 to 6 pm. The rest of the year it has shorter opening hours and is closed on Sunday.

Post The main post office is in the centre of town on the Quai des Indes.

Lorient's postcode is 56100.

Festival Inter-Celtique
For 10 days in early August, Lorient is given over to a celebration of Celtic culture, especially music, literature and dance. People from Ireland, Scotland, Wales, Cornwall and certain parts of Spain join the Bretons for a triumphant celebration of their common Celtic heritage.

Accommodation is hard to find at this time so it's best to book in advance. Likewise, some of the festival events require booking; enquire at the tourist office in Lorient.

Places to Stay
Hostel The Auberge de Jeunesse (☎ 97.37. 11.65) is three km out of town at 41 Rue Victor Schoelcher. Dorm beds cost 65FF, with breakfast included. The hostel is closed from 22 December to the end of January. To get there from the station take Bus C and get off at the Auberge de Jeunesse stop.

Hotels Lorient has a large number of hotels in all price ranges, so except for the duration of the Festival Inter-Celtique it shouldn't be difficult to find a place to stay.

The one-star Hôtel d'Arvor (☎ 97.21. 07.55) at 104 Rue Lazare Carnot is a small, pleasant place located about 600 metres south-west of Quai de Rohan. Rooms cost from 110 to 170FF a double.

The two-star Hôtel-Restaurant Gabriel (☎ 97.37.60.76) is located on the other side of the fishing port at 45 Ave de la Perrière. Rooms cost 150FF a double, including shower and toilet.

Moving more up-market, the two-star Hôtel Victor Hugo (☎ 97.21.16.24) is well situated at 36 Rue Lazare Carnot, close to the port. Comfortable rooms with TV cost 215/250FF for singles/doubles.

The top-end Hôtel Mercure (☎ 97.21. 35.73; fax 97.64.48.62) is right in the centre of things at 31 Place Jules Ferry. Rooms with TV, shower and toilet cost 400/500FF for singles/doubles.

Places to Eat
There are numerous restaurants in town. A good bet for fish is Le Poisson d'Or (☎ 97.21.57.06) at 1 Rue Maître Esvelin. Restaurant Le Saint Louis (☎ 97.21.50.45) has a good menu.

The Hôtel d'Arvor has a good, cheap restaurant, with menus for 75FF and 120FF. The restaurant is closed around Christmas and

BRITTANY

New Year. The *Hotel/Restaurant Gabriel* has a range of *menus* costing from 50 to 120FF.

Getting There & Away
Train Lorient is served by TGVs from Paris's Gare de Montparnasse (270FF). Other trains go to Brest, Quimper, Vannes (45FF), Rennes (115FF) and places in between.

Getting Around
Boat Ferries depart frequently in summer for Île de Groix and Belle Île from the ferry docks in town.

Rennes

While plenty of French cities claim to sit at some important crossroad, Rennes (population 203,000) really does. Capital of Brittany since its incorporation into France in the 16th century, the city developed at the junction of the highways linking the northern and far western ports of Saint Malo and Brest with the former capital, Nantes (see the Atlantic Coast chapter), and the inland city of Le Mans.

Until the 1950s Rennes was known for its dignified buildings and dull character – or as one local saying put it: 'Nothing ever catches on here except fire', referring to the blaze which swept through the town in the 18th century. But the appointment of a lively mayor, Henri Fréville, put an end to such civic pessimism. He encouraged commercial development and expanded the universities (the city now has 40,000 students). Rennes's population has doubled in the past half-century. Despite all this, Rennes's refined atmosphere has little in common with the rest of Brittany, and unless you're using it as a transit point, it's probably not worth a detour.

Orientation
The city centre is divided into northern and southern sectors by La Vilaine, a river channelled into a cement-lined canal which disappears underground just before the central square, Place de la République. The northern area, which includes the pedestrianised old town, is the most appealing. To the south, the city is garishly modern, with ugly shopping complexes such as the Centre Colombier.

Information
Tourist Office The main tourist office (☎ 99.79.01.98) is on Pont de Nemours on Place de la République. Most of the year it's open Monday to Saturday from 10 am to 12.30 pm and 2 to 6.30 pm. Between mid-June and mid-September it's open from 9 am to 7 pm and on Sunday from 10 am to 1 pm and 3 to 5 pm. The tourist office annexe at the train station is open weekdays from 8 am to 8 pm and weekends from 9 am to 1 pm and 2 to 6 pm.

Money The Banque de France (☎ 99.38.76.76) at 25 Rue de la Visitation is open weekdays from 8.45 am to noon and 1.30 to 3.30 pm. Inside the train station, the Crédit Agricole is open Tuesday to Saturday from 9.30 am to 1 pm and 2.15 to 6.45 pm (4 pm on Saturday).

Post The main post office (☎ 99.31.42.72), near the train station at 27 Blvd du Colombier, is open weekdays from 8 am to 7 pm and on Saturday from 8 am to noon. On Place de la République there's another bureau (☎ 99.79.50.71) open the same hours. Both hold onto poste restante mail and have foreign exchange services.

Rennes's postcode is 35000.

Laundry The laundrette at 23 Rue de Penhoët is open daily from 7 or 7.30 am to 10 pm. Near the train station, Clean Fil on Place du Colombier in the Centre Colombier is open the same hours.

Old Town
Much of medieval Rennes was gutted by *le grand incendie*, the great fire of 1720, which engulfed 900 homes in an eight-day conflagration. The half-timbered houses that survived now make up the old city, Rennes's most picturesque quarter, which is bordered

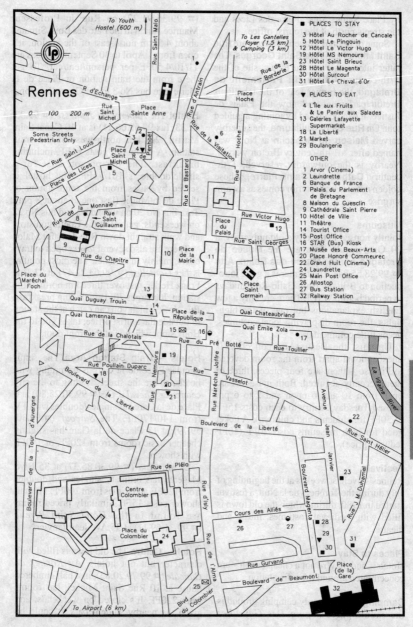

Rennes

0   100   200 m

Some Streets
Pedestrian Only

BRITTANY

■ PLACES TO STAY
3   Hôtel Au Rocher de Cancale
5   Hôtel Le Pingouin
12 Hôtel Le Victor Hugo
19 Hôtel MS Nemours
23 Hôtel Saint Brieuc
28 Hôtel Le Magenta
30 Hôtel Surcouf
31 Hôtel Le Cheval d'Or

▼ PLACES TO EAT
4   L'Île aux Fruits
    & Le Panier aux Salades
13 Galeries Lafayette
    Supermarket
18 La Liberté
21 Market
29 Boulangerie

OTHER
1   Arvor (Cinema)
2   Laundrette
6   Banque de France
7   Palais du Parlement
    de Bretagne
8   Maison du Guesclin
9   Cathédrale Saint Pierre
10 Hôtel de Ville
11 Théâtre
14 Tourist Office
15 Post Office
16 STAR (Bus) Kiosk
17 Musée des Beaux-Arts
20 Place Honoré Commeurec
22 Grand Huit (Cinema)
24 Laundrette
25 Main Post Office
26 Allostop
27 Bus Station
32 Railway Station

by Place Sainte Anne, Place des Lices and the streets north of the tourist office.

Some of Rennes's loveliest streets are **Rue Saint Michel** and **Rue Saint Georges**. The latter intersects Place du Palais, site of the 17th-century **Palais du Parlement de Bretagne**, the former seat of the rebellious Breton parlement and now the Palais de Justice. It can be visited by joining a guided tour. On **Rue Saint Guillaume**, the superbly carved **Maison du Guesclin** at No 3 was named after a 14th-century Breton warrior. Nearby is the outwardly reserved, 17th-century **Cathédrale Saint Pierre**, whose golden neoclassical interior comes as a warm surprise.

Museums
Jointly housed in the city's old university at 20 Quai Émile Zola are the **Musée de Bretagne** and the **Musée des Beaux-Arts** (☎ 99.28.55.84). The former is a good introduction to Brittany from Gallo-Roman days to period before WW I. There are only a few English explanations but one of the highlights, the room displaying local costumes, needs little commentary.

Upstairs, the Beaux-Arts collection is unexceptional apart from the room devoted to Picasso – there are four pieces, three of them recently acquired. Both museums are open from 10 am to noon and 2 to 6 pm (closed Tuesday). Entry to each costs 15FF (7.50FF for students and children). A ticket good for both museums costs 20FF (10FF reduced price).

Festivals
Rennes's liveliest week is at the beginning of July during the Tombées de la Nuit, a festival started in 1980, during which the old town is filled with medieval costumes, music and theatre.

Places to Stay
Hotels – and they're not a cheap bunch – are concentrated around the train station.

Camping Rennes's only camping ground is the municipal *Camping Des Gayeulles*

(☎ 99.36.91.22) on Rue du Professeur Maurice Audin in the Parc des Bois. Situated about 4.5 km north-east of the station, it's open from 1 April to 30 September. Fees are 11/10/4.50FF per person/tent/car. To get there from the train station or Place de la Marie take bus No 3 to the Gayeulles stop.

Hostel The *Auberge de Jeunesse* (☎ 99.33.22.33; fax 99.59.06.21) is at 10 Canal Saint Martin, 2.5 km north-west of the train station. A dorm bed costs 61FF, including breakfast. The per-person cost for a single/double is 101/71FF. The hostel is served by buses from the train station or Place de la Mairie (last one at about 8 pm). Take bus No 20 on weekdays and bus No 22 on weekends; get off at the Coétlogon stop, and walk straight down Rue de Saint Malo.

There are also several *foyers* open to travellers, mainly in summer. The most popular is *Les Gantelles* (☎ 99.63.22.47) at 21 Rue Franz Heller, just over three km north of the station. It charges 70FF, including breakfast. Bus No 7, which you can catch at the station or outside the tourist office, takes you to the Houx stop, which is at the front door.

Hotels – Train Station Area The semicircular Place de la Gare is brimming with hotels, as are the streets leading to the city centre. *Le Cheval d'Or* (☎ 99.30.25.80) at 6 Place de la Gare has singles/doubles with TV from 140/170FF. The *Surcouf* (☎ 99.30.59.79) at 13 Place de la Gare has slightly cheaper basic rooms from 120FF, or 140FF with shower.

Le Magenta (☎ 99.30.85.37) at 35 Blvd Magenta has ordinary singles and doubles from 120FF, and triples from 200FF. The hall shower costs 15FF. Similarly priced rooms are found in the *Hôtel Saint Brieuc* (☎ 99.31.69.11) at 35 Ave Jean Janvier.

Hotels – Centre The old town is filled with character but not hotels. *Au Rocher de Cancale* (☎ 99.79.20.83), in a half-timbered house at 10 Rue Saint Michel, has rooms from 220FF. It's closed on weekends, and given the nearby student bars, it could be

noisy. *Le Pingouin* (☎ 99.79.14.81) at 7 Place du Haut des Lices has singles/doubles/quads from 200/220/300FF.

Just out of the centre, *Le Victor Hugo* (☎ 99.38.85.33) at 14 Rue Victor Hugo has a good location and ordinary rooms from 110/140FF. South of the tourist office, the shipshape *MS Nemours* (☎ 99.78.26.26; fax 99.78.25.40) at No 5 on the bus-only Rue de Nemours has spotless singles/doubles with shower and TV from 240/260FF.

Places to Eat

Despite having such a large population of students, Rennes has few cheap restaurants. Rue Saint Georges is *the* street for indulging in crepes.

Restaurants In the old town, *L'Île aux Fruits* (☎ 99.79.01.06) on Rue de Penhoët has a lunch-only *menu* for 62FF. *Le Panier aux Salades* (☎ 99.79.20.97), next door at No 15, has salads from 35FF. It is closed on Sunday and Wednesday evenings.

South of the tourist office is *La Liberté* (☎ 99.78.30.23) at 48 Blvd de la Liberté, also closed on Sunday and Wednesday evenings. It has a decent 52FF three-course *menu*.

Many of the hotels facing the station have *menus* from about 60FF and serve snacks until late.

University Restaurant There's a *University restaurant* at 46 Rue Jean Guéhenno, about 10 minutes' walk north-east of the centre (just continue along Rue Guillaudot). You will need to buy a ticket from a student. It's open weekdays from 11.45 am to 1.15 pm and 6.45 to 8 pm. A small cheap pizzeria is attached.

Self-Catering There's a covered *market hall* on Place Honoré Commeurec. Stalls are open Monday to Saturday from 7 am to 6.30 pm, though some take a couple of hours off for lunch. A *market* is held at Place des Lices on Saturday morning.

The *Galeries Lafayette* department store on Quai Duguay Trouin has a grocery section open Monday to Saturday from 9 am to 7 pm.

If you'd like fresh bread on Sunday, the *boulangerie* in the old town on Rue Saint Michel is open from 7 am to 1 pm and 2 to 8 pm. There's another Sunday *boulangerie* at the train station on Blvd Magenta; it's open from 7 am to 1.30 pm and 3 to 8.30 pm.

Entertainment

Cinemas Two cinemas screen nondubbed films: *Arvor* (☎ 99.38.72.40) at 29 Rue d'Antrain and *Grand Huit* (☎ 99.30.88.88) in the Maison de la Culture at 1 Rue Saint Hélier. Ask at the tourist office for *Contact*, a free guide which lists their programmes.

Bars For a drink, the terrace cafés and pubs along Rue Saint Michel attract a lively student crowd.

Gay Disco There's a very popular gay disco called *Le Batchi* (☎ 99.79.62.27) at 34 Rue Vasselot. It is open Tuesday to Saturday.

Getting There & Away

Air Rennes's Saint Jacques Airport (☎ 99.29. 60.00) is six km south-west of town.

Train The modern train station (☎ 99.65. 50.50 for information) on Place de la Gare is equipped with banks, shops and a large train information office which is open daily from 8 am to 7.30 pm. Major destinations include Paris's Gare Montparnasse (207FF plus TGV fee; two hours; hourly trains until 8 pm), Saint Malo (61FF; one hour; seven a day), Vannes (87FF; one hour; 10 a day) and Nantes (101FF; 1½ hours; six a day).

Bus The bus station on Blvd Magenta (the other entrance is on Cours des Alliès) has an information office (☎ 99.30.87.80) that is open weekdays from 7 or 8 am to 6.30 pm and on Saturday from 9 am to 1.45 pm. Several companies operate from here, including Cariane Atlantique, which offers service to Nantes (86FF; two hours); TAE, which goes to Dinan (58FF; 1¼ hours) and Dinard (1¾ hours); and TIV, which serves Fougères (42FF; one hour).

BRITTANY

Car ADA can be contacted on ☎ 99.38. 59.88. Europcar (☎ 99.51.60.61; fax 99.54.21.16) has a bureau at the train station in the Centre Commerical de la Gare.

Hitching Allostop (☎ 99.30.98.87) is in Maison du Champ de Mars on Cours des Alliés. It is open weekdays from 10 am to 5.30 pm and on Saturday morning.

Getting Around
To/From the Airport Saint Jacques Airport is connected to the city by bus No 57, which stops at Place de la République.

Bus Though there are plans for a metro, buses are it for a few years yet. They are run by STAR (☎ 99.79.37.37) whose information kiosk is on Place de la République. Single tickets cost 5.50FF. Most buses leave from or pass by one of two major hubs – Place de la République and Place de la Mairie. Some also leave from the train station.

Taxi Taxis (☎ 99.30.66.45) line up outside the train station.

North Coast

The central part of Brittany's north coast belongs to the Côtes-d'Armor département, which changed its name from Côtes-du-Nord (North Coast) in 1990 so people would stop confusing it with the highly industrialised Nord département around Dunkerque. Côtes-d'Armor stretches from Perros Guirec, near the north-east corner of Finistère, to Saint Briac, which is just west of the up-market beach resort of Dinard. Dinard, ever-popular Saint Malo, the oyster-growing town of Cancale and other points along the Baie du Mont Saint Michel are in the département of Ille-et-Vilaine. Mont Saint Michel itself is in Normandy.

The rugged stretch of coast between Le Val André in the west and Pointe du Grouin in the east is known as the Côte d'Émeraude (Emerald Coast). The area, which includes Dinard, Saint Malo and the Rance estuary, is famous for its numerous peninsulas and promontories, many of which afford spectacular sea views. The best way to explore the Côte d'Émeraude is to walk along part of the GR34 trail, which runs along the entire coast of both départements. The largest offshore islands are Île de Bréhat, eight km north of the port town of Paimpol, and Les Sept Îles, 18 km west of Perros Guirec. The medieval town of Dinan, which is about 20 km from the coast, is on the Rance River south of Saint Malo.

SAINT MALO
The Channel port of Saint Malo (population 47,000) is one of the most popular tourist destinations in Brittany, and with good reason. Situated at the mouth of the Rance River, it is famed for its walled city and nearby beaches. The area has some of the highest tidal variations in the world – depending on the lunar and solar cycles, the high-water mark is often 13 metres or more above the low-water mark. As you'll soon notice, the tide comes in and goes out twice every 24 hours.

Saint Malo is an excellent base from which to explore the Côte d'Émeraude. Mont Saint Michel – technically part of Normandy (and included in that chapter in this book) – can be visited as a day trip from Saint Malo.

History
Saint Malo is named after a certain Maclou, a Welsh monk who moved here in the 6th century and became one of the first bishops of Aleth (present-day Saint Servan).

During the 17th and 18th centuries, Saint Malo was one of France's most important ports, serving both merchant ships and government-sanctioned pirates, known more politely as privateers. Although fortification of the city was begun in the 12th century, the most imposing military architecture dates from the 17th and 18th centuries, when the English – the favourite victims of Malouin privateers – posed an ever-present threat.

Orientation

The commune of Saint Malo consists of the contiguous resort towns of Saint Servan, Saint Malo, Paramé and Rothéneuf. The old city, signposted as 'Intra-Muros' (between the walls) and also called the Ville Close (Walled City), is connected to Paramé by the Sillon isthmus, which leads to a three-km-long beach, La Grande Plage.

Esplanade Saint Vincent, where the tourist office and bus station are located, is a giant parking lot just outside the old city's Porte Saint Vincent. The train station is 1.25 km south-east of Esplanade Saint Vincent.

Information

Tourist Office The efficient tourist office (☎ 99.56.64.48), near the old city on Esplanade Saint Vincent, is open Monday to Saturday from 9 am to noon and 2 to 6 or 6.30 pm. From Easter to September, it's open on Sunday from 10 am to noon and 2 to 5 or 5.30 pm. During July and August, it is open Monday to Saturday from 8.30 am to 8 pm and on Sunday from 10 am to 6.30 pm. There is a hotel reservation service (2FF fee).

Money Near the train station, there are banks along Blvd de la République and at Place de Rocabey. All are open weekdays from about 8.30 am to 12.15 pm and 1.30 to 5 pm.

In the old city, the Caisse d'Épargne at 14 Rue de Dinan (three blocks up from Porte de Dinan) is open weekdays from 8.45 am to noon and 1.30 to 5.30 pm (5 pm on Friday). The Bureau de Change (☎ 99.40.21.10) at 2 Rue Saint Vincent gives a miserable rate. It is open from mid-March to mid-November daily from 10 am to 7 pm (9 am to 10 pm from June to September).

Post The main post office (☎ 99.20.51.78), near Place de Rocabey at 1 Blvd de la Tour d'Auvergne, is open weekdays from 8 am to 7 pm and on Saturday until noon. In the old city, the branch post office at Place des Frères Lamennais is open weekdays from 8.30 am to 12.30 pm and 1.30 to 6.30 pm and on Saturday mornings. During July and August it stays open at midday. Both offices offer exchange services.

The Saint Servan post office (☎ 99.81.55.07) at 36 Rue Ville Pépin is open weekdays from 8 am to noon and 1.45 to 6.45 pm and on Saturday from 8 am to noon. Currency exchange services are available.

The postcode of Saint Malo (including Saint Servan, Paramé and Rothéneuf) is 35400.

Laundry The laundrette at 25 Blvd de la Tour d'Auvergne (on the north side of Place de Rocabey) is open daily from 7 am to 9 pm.

Old City

In August 1944, in the course of the battle that drove the Germans from Saint Malo, 80% of the old city was destroyed. After the war, the principal historical monuments were faithfully reconstructed, but the rest of the area was rebuilt in the style of the 17th and 18th centuries, with allowances made for the needs of a modern city.

Cathédrale Saint Vincent, begun in the 11th century, is noted for its medieval and modern stained-glass windows.

The **ramparts** *(remparts)*, built between the 12th and 18th centuries, survived the war and are largely original. They afford superb views in all directions: the freight port, the interior of the old city, the Channel. There is free access to the **ramparts walk** at Porte de Dinan, the Grande Porte, Porte Saint Vincent and elsewhere. Photos mounted along the ramparts show what the city looked like after the fighting in 1944.

Museums

The **Musée de la Ville** (☎ 99.40.71.11), next to Porte Saint Vincent in the Château de Saint Malo, specialises in the history of the city and the Pays Malouin (the area around Saint Malo). From April to October, the museum is open daily from 9.30 am to noon and 2 to 6.30 pm. The rest of the year it's open from 10 am to noon and 2 to 5.30 pm (closed Tuesday). Admission is 16FF (8FF for students).

BRITTANY

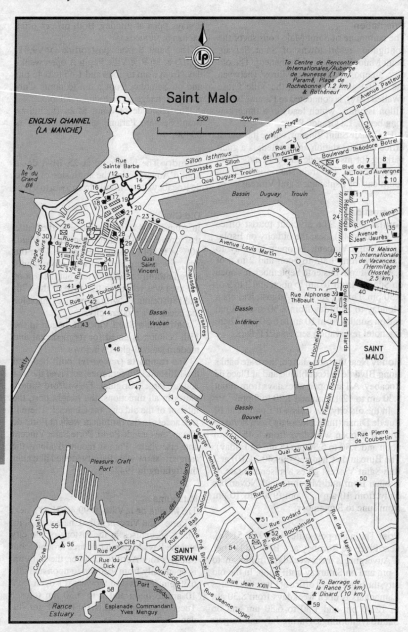

Saint Malo

ENGLISH CHANNEL
(LA MANCHE)

To Centre de Rencontres
Internationales/Auberge
de Jeunesse (1 km),
Paramé, Plage de
Rochebonne (1.2 km)
& Rothéneuf

0   250   500 m

To
Île du
Grand Bé

Rue
Sainte Barbe

Sillon Isthmus

Grande Plage

Chaussée du Sillon

Quai Duguay Trouin

Rue
de l'Industrie

Boulevard Théodore Botrel

Blvd de
la Tour d'Auvergne

Bassin Duguay Trouin

Avenue Pasteur

Rue Ernest Renan

Avenue Jean Jaurès

To Maison
Internationale
de Vacances,
l'Hermitage
(Hostel;
2.5 km)

Rue
du Boyer

Rue Broussais

Plage de Bon
Secours

Quai
Saint Vincent

Quai Saint Louis

Avenue Louis Martin

Rue Alphonse
Thébault

Rue de Toulouse

Chaussée des Corsaires

Bassin
Vauban

Bassin
Intérieur

Boulevard de la République

Boulevard des Talards

Rue Hochelage

SAINT
MALO

Jetty

Bassin
Bouvet

Rue George Clémenceau

Quai de Trichet

Avenue Franklin Roosevelt

Rue Pierre
de Coubertin

Pleasure Craft
Port

Plage des Bas Sablons

Quai du Val

Rue du Val

Rue George

Rue Godard

Rue Bougainville

Rue de la Marne

Corniche
d'Aleth

Rue de la Cité

Rue du
Dick

Rue des Bas Sablons

Rue Pré Brécel

Rue Ville Pépin

SAINT
SERVAN

Quai Solidor

Port Solidor

To Barrage de
la Rance (5 km)
& Dinard (10 km)

Rance
Estuary

Esplanade Commandant
Yves Menguy

Rue Jean XXIII

Rue Jeanne Jugan

BRITTANY

■ PLACES TO STAY		51	Codec Supermarket	41	Caisse d'Épargne

■ PLACES TO STAY

3	Hôtel Le Neptune
5	Hôtel de l'Embarcadère
8	Hôtel de l'Avenir
11	Hôtel Le Vauban
17	Hôtel Port Malo
18	Hôtel du Commerce
28	Hôtel Le Victoria
31	Hôtel Armoricaine
33	Hôtel Au Gai Bec
35	Hôtel de Moka
36	Hôtel de l'Europe & Hôtel de la Petite Vitesse
39	Hôtel Suffren
48	Hôtel de la Mer
49	Hôtel Ferry Émeraude
56	Camping Municipal Cité d'Aleth
59	Hôtel de l'Arrivée

▼ PLACES TO EAT

2	Intermarché Supermarket
22	Tourist Restaurants
34	Food Shops
37	Boulangerie
45	Boulangerie

| 51 | Codec Supermarket |
| 52 | Boulangerie Heurtebise |

OTHER

1	Fort National
4	Diazo Vélocation (Bicycle Rental)
6	Main Post Office
7	Laundrette
10	Église de Rocabey
12	Aquarium
13	Musée de Cire
14	Château de Saint Malo
15	Exotarium Malouin
16	Musée de la Ville
19	Porte Saint Vincent
20	Esplanade Saint Vincent
21	Bureau de Change
23	Tourist Office & Bus Station
24	Banks
26	Post Office Annexe
27	Cathédrale Saint Vincent
29	Grande Porte
30	Porte des Bés
32	Porte Sainte Pierre
40	Railway Station

41	Caisse d'Épargne
42	Porte de Dinan
43	Émeraude Lines Ferries to Dinard
44	Esplanade de la Bourse
46	Gare Maritime de la Bourse (Ferry Terminal)
47	Gare Maritime du Naye (Car Ferry Terminal)
50	Hospital
53	Post Office
54	Parc de Bel Air
55	Fort de la Cité
58	Musée International du Long Cours Cap-Hornier & Château de Solidor

✕ SQUARES

9	Place de Rocabey
25	Place des Frères Lamennais
38	Place de la Grande Hermine
57	Place Saint Pierre

Across the courtyard in Tour Quic-en-Groigne, the **Musée de Cire** (Wax Museum; ☎ 99.40.80.26) has taped commentaries to guide you through eight famous moments in Saint Malo's history. The same text takes 35 minutes in English, 40 minutes in French and 55 minutes in German!

The **Musée de Poupées et de Jouets** (☎ 99.40.15.51) at 13 Rue de Toulouse exhibits dolls, doll houses and toys from the past. It is open from July to mid-September *only*. Daily hours are 10 am to 1 pm and 2 to 7 pm.

Aquarium

Built into the old city walls, the Aquarium (☎ 99.40.91.86), next to Place Vauban, has about a hundred tanks filled with some of the world's most colourful and extraordinary fish. Across the street, the smaller and less impressive **Exotarium Malouin** displays

various sorts of live reptiles (crocodiles, turtles, snakes) and some huge spiders.

Both are open daily from 9 am to noon and 2 to 6 or 7 pm. From July to mid-August, they are open from 9 am to 10 or 11 pm. The entry fee for each is 19FF (14FF for students); entry to both is 33FF (28FF for students).

Île du Grand Bé

The Île du Grand Bé, where the writer and statesman Chateaubriand is buried, can be reached at low tide from Plage de Bon Secours, which is at the base of the city walls next to Porte des Bés. When the tide comes in, the submersible causeway remains impassable for about six hours.

Saint Servan

Across Anse des Sablons from Saint Malo, Saint Servan's **Fort de la Cité** was built in

BRITTANY

the mid-18th century and served as a German stronghold during WW II. The thick steel pillboxes flanking the fortress's walls were heavily scarred by Allied shells in 1944. The interior of the fort, now used by caravanners, is theoretically closed to visitors, but no one will stop you if you walk into the Camping Municipal via the main entrance (see map).

The **Musée International du Long Cours Cap-Hornier** (☎ 99.40.71.56) is in the **Château de Solidor** (built 1382), which is on Esplanade Commandant Yves Menguy. The museum has nautical instruments, ship models and other exhibits on the sailors who, between the early 17th and early 20th centuries, sailed around Cape Horn (the southern tip of South America). There is a great view from the top of the tower. The museum is open from 10 am to noon and 2 to 5.30 pm (closed Tuesday). From May to September, it is open daily from 9.30 am to noon and 2 to 6.30 pm. Tickets cost 16FF (8FF for students).

Port Solidor The picturesque little bay of Port Solidor slightly east of the Château de Solidor is an excellent place to get a sense of just what Saint Malo's incredible tidal variations mean. At high tide, the moored boats bob up and down in the waters of the English Channel. At low tide – a mere six or seven hours later – the boats will be sitting on dry land a hundred metres from the water's edge.

Barrage de la Rance

The D168 to Dinard passes over the Rance Tidal Power Station (☎ 99.46.21.89), a hydroelectric dam across the estuary of the Rance River about seven km from Saint Malo. It uses Saint Malo's extraordinarily high tides to generate 8% of the electricity consumed in Brittany. The 750-metre-long dam, built between 1963 and 1967, has 24 turbines that are turned at high tide by sea water flowing into the estuary and at low tide by water draining into the sea. Unfortunately, it has played havoc with the estuary's delicate ecosystem and the idea has not been tried elsewhere.

Near the lock on the Dinard side of the

dam is a small, subterranean visitors' centre (*circuit de visite*), open daily from 8.30 am to 8 pm, which has recorded explanations in French, English and German on how the power station (*usine marémotrice*) works. Buses to Dinard go over the dam – for details see Bus in the Getting There & Away section.

Beaches

The **Grande Plage**, which stretches north-eastward from the Sillon isthmus, is lined with vertical tree trunks stuck there to serve as breakwaters. **Plage de Rochebonne** is further along the coast to the north-east.

In Saint Servan, **Plage des Bas Sablons** is popular with older sunbathers. It has a cement wall that keeps the sea from receding all the way to the yacht harbour at low tide.

Walks

Suggested routes for strolling include the following:

- In the old city, walk around the ramparts (see the Old City section).
- From Porte de Dinan on the south side of the old city, walk southward via Plage des Bas Sablons (see Beaches) to Fort de la Cité and the Corniche d'Aleth, a footpath which circumnavigates the Aleth peninsula.
- From the old city, head north-eastward along the Sillon isthmus and the Grande Plage to Plage de Rochebonne (see Beaches) and the thriving beach resort of Paramé, a distance of three km. Rothéneuf is 1.5 km further north.
- From Saint Malo or the Château de Solidor (Saint Servan), walk (or cycle) via the Barrage de la Rance to Dinard, a distance of about 10 km.

Organised Tours

Bus For information on bus tours of the Saint Malo area (including Mont Saint Michel), see Bus under Getting There & Away.

Boat From May to September, Émeraude Lines (☎ 99.40.48.40) runs small ferries from its dock just outside the old city's Porte de Dinan to the Îles Chausey (80/110FF one way/return; 90 minutes each way), the Île de Cézembre (46FF return; 20 minutes each

way) and Dinan (2½ hours each way). For details on boats to Dinard, see Getting There & Away in the Dinard section.

Places to Stay

Camping Camping on the beach is a sure way to get wet, if not drowned.

The *Camping Municipal Cité d'Aleth* (☎ 99.81.60.91) in Saint Servan, which offers exceptional views, is open all year and always has room for yet another small tent. It charges 14.50FF per person, 8FF for a tent site and 6FF to park. In summer it is served by bus No 1. During the rest of the year, your best bet is bus No 6.

Hostels Saint Malo has two good youth hostel options. The *Centre de Rencontres Internationales/Auberge de Jeunesse* (☎ 99.40.29.80) is in Paramé at 37 Ave du Père Umbricht, just over two km north-east of the train station. A bed in a four or six-person room is 59FF, doubles cost 70FF per person, and singles with shower and toilet are 100FF, all including breakfast. There are volleyball and tennis courts at the front; equipment is available from reception. For food, there's a Stoc supermarket 150 metres west of the hostel. You can check in at any time. From the train station, take bus No 5.

The *Maison Internationale de Vacances l'Hermitage* (☎ 99.56.22.00), also in Paramé at 13 Rue des Écoles, is very laid-back as hostels go (eg they accept telephone reservations). A dorm bed costs only 44FF (57FF with breakfast); sheets are 21FF. In the summer, you can stay in a large tent they set up in the yard for 34FF (46FF with breakfast). Four-person bungalows with kitchenette cost 250FF. This place is 2.5 km east of the train station – to get there, take bus Nos 2 or No 4.

Hotels It is often difficult to find a room during July and August. Among the cheaper hotels, the noisy and charmless places near the train station are the first to fill up. If you're looking for something inexpensive, the hotels around Place de Rocabey are prob-

ably your best bet, though there are also a few good deals in the old city.

Place de Rocabey The *Hôtel Le Vauban* (☎ 99.56.09.39) at 7 Blvd de la République is one of the cheapest places in town, with very basic singles/doubles for 80/100FF (100/120FF from April to September). Hall showers are free. Be prepared for traffic noise and the bells of the nearby church. The small *Hôtel de l'Avenir* (☎ 99.56.13.33) at 31 Blvd de la Tour d'Auvergne has rooms for 100FF (130FF with shower). Hall showers cost 15FF.

The *Hôtel l'Embarcadère* (☎ 99.56.39.58) at 53 Quai Duguay Trouin is on the Sillon isthmus a few hundred metres west of Place de Rocabey. Ordinary singles and doubles with one bed start at 105FF, while a two-bed double is 140FF. Showers cost 10FF.

The *Hôtel Le Neptune* (☎ 99.56.82.15), an older, family-run place at 21 Rue de l'Industrie, has adequate doubles from 115FF. Hall showers are free. Doubles with shower and toilet cost 160FF.

Train Station Area The *Hôtel de Moka* (☎ 99.56.29.86) at 49 Ave Jean Jaurès has rooms with high ceilings, large windows and old-fashioned furniture. Singles/doubles are 100/110FF; triples and quads go for 130FF. Showers are free. They might not accept telephone reservations in July and August.

The somewhat noisy *Hôtel de l'Europe* (☎ 99.56.13.42) at 44 Blvd de la République offers modern, nondescript doubles from 110FF (130FF from mid-April to August). Shower-equipped rooms without/with toilet are 170/195FF (195/220FF in summer). There are no hall showers. The *Hôtel de la Petite Vitesse* (☎ 99.56.31.76), next door at 42 Blvd de la République, has good-sized but noisy doubles from 90FF (130FF with shower) and two-bed quads for 160FF. Hall showers cost 20FF. Telephone reservations are not accepted in summer.

The *Hôtel Suffren* (☎ 99.56.31.71) at 4 Blvd des Talards has unsurprising doubles with/without use of a shower from 110/

BRITTANY

130FF. A two-bed quad costs 180FF, including use of the shower.

Old City The friendly, family-run *Hôtel Au Gai Bec* (☎ 99.40.82.16) is in the hopping heart of the old city at 4 Rue des Lauriers or 9 Rue Thévenard, depending on how you look at it. Singles/doubles start at 100FF (160FF with shower). Hall showers are free. They won't accept telephone reservations unless you're at the train station and are about to head over. The hotel is closed from mid-November to mid-December.

The *Hôtel Le Victoria* (☎ 99.56.34.01) at 4 Rue des Orbettes has doubles from 130FF. Showers are free. The *Hôtel Armoricaine* (☎ 99.40.89.13) at 6 Rue du Boyer (near the post office) has decent doubles from 130FF (220FF with shower and toilet). Showers are 12FF.

The recently renovated *Hôtel Port Malo* (☎ 99.20.52.99) at 15 Rue Sainte Barbe is a medium-sized place 150 metres from Porte Saint Vincent. Singles/doubles with shower and toilet are 180/240FF (200/260FF from May to September).

Saint Servan The *Hôtel de la Mer* (☎ 99.81.61.05) at 3 Rue Dauphine is right next to Plage des Bas Sablons and less than a km from the old city. Singles/doubles start at 95/130FF. Showers cost 15FF. If you call after arriving in Saint Malo, they'll hold a room for an hour or so. This place is closed in February. To get there, take bus No 2 or 5 and get off at Rue George V.

The *Hôtel de l'Arrivée* (☎ 99.81.99.57) at 83 Rue Ville Pépin has nondescript doubles from 120FF. Telephone reservations are not accepted between June and September.

The *Hôtel Ferry Émeraude* (☎ 99.81.66.76), just over a km south-east of the old city at 2 Rue Le Pomellec, has doubles with shower, toilet, telephone and TV from 245FF.

Places to Eat
Restaurants In the old city, there are lots of tourist restaurants and pizzerias in the area between Porte Saint Vincent, the Grande Porte and the cathedral. Other places line the streets nearest the Plage de Bon Secours. Creperies can be found just inside Porte de Dinan.

Restaurant Au Gai Bec (☎ 90.40.82.16) at 4 Rue des Lauriers, part of the hotel of the same name, specialises in French cuisine. *Menus* start at 79FF. This place is open from noon to 2 pm and 7 to 9.30 pm daily except Sunday afternoon and Monday. In July and August it's open daily except for midday on Monday.

Near the train station, the *Hotel de Moka* has a good-value lunch *menu*, intended primarily for local workers. A four-course meal plus wine costs only 45FF.

Self-Catering During July and August many places stay open on their weekly day of closure.

The cheapest place to buy food is the *Intermarché supermarket*, two blocks from Place de Rocaby on Blvd Théodore Botrel. It's open Monday to Saturday from 9 am to 12.15 pm and 3 to 7.15 pm; there's no midday closure on Saturday. In July and August, it's also open on Sunday morning.

In the old city, there are a number of *food stores* along Rue de l'Orme, including a cheese shop (closed Sunday and Monday) at No 9, a fruit and vegie store (closed Sunday) at No 8 and two *boulangeries*. There is a small *boulangerie* (closed Sunday) just inside the Grande Porte at 1 Grande Rue.

Near the train station, there is a *boulangerie* (closed Thursday) at 6 Ave Jean Jaurès and another *boulangerie* (closed Wednesday) at 26 Blvd des Talards.

In Saint Servan, there is a *Codec supermarket* at 15 Rue Ville Pépin. *Boulangerie Heurtebise* at 23 Rue Ville Pépin, which has a tearoom, is open daily except Monday.

Entertainment
During July and August, concerts of classical music are held in Cathédrale Saint Vincent and elsewhere in the city. Call or drop by the tourist office for details.

Getting There & Away

Train At the train station, the information office (☎ 99.65.50.50) is open daily from 9 am to 12.30 pm and 1.30 to 6.30 pm (9 am to 7 pm in July and August). The left-luggage room closes at 1 pm, reopens at 2 pm and stays open until 7.30 pm (7 pm on Sunday, 9.30 pm on Friday).

There is direct service to Paris's Gare Montparnasse (230FF one way; 4¼ hours) in summer only. During the rest of the year, you have to change trains at Rennes (61FF; one hour), but the trip takes as little as three hours. More locally, there are services to Dinan (43FF; one hour; six a day) and to Lannion (116FF; four hours; six a day). You can also get to Quimper.

Bus The bus station, where all the companies mentioned here have offices, is at Esplanade Saint Vincent. Many buses also stop at the train station.

Tourisme Verney (☎ 99.40.82.67) handles the regular services run by TIV (Transports d'Ille-et-Vilaine; ☎ 99.82.26.26) to Cancale, Dinan, Dinard (via the Barrage de la Rance) and Rennes. TIV buses to Dinard, which run a bit less than once an hour until 7 pm or so, stop at both Esplanade Saint Vincent and the Saint Malo train station.

During July and August, Tourisme Verney runs excursions (with English-speaking guides) to various destinations, including Mont Saint Michel (120FF). The office is open weekdays and Saturday morning from 8.30 am to noon and 1.45 to 6.15 pm. In July and August, it is open Monday to Saturday from 8.30 am to 7 pm.

Les Courriers Bretons (☎ 99.56.79.09) has regular services to Cancale (34FF return; nine a day) and Mont Saint Michel (89FF return; 1¼ hours each way). The daily bus to Mont Saint Michel leaves in the late morning, returning at about 7 pm. During July and August there are four round trips a day. The office is open from 8.30 am to 12.15 pm and 2 to 6.15 pm daily except Saturday afternoon and Sunday (daily except Sunday in summer).

Car To contact ADA, call ☎ 99.56.06.15. Citer (☎ 99.81.66.69) has a bureau at the ferry terminal. Europcar (☎ 99.56.75.17; fax 99.56.86.74) is near the train station at 16 Blvd des Talards.

Boat Ferries link Saint Malo with the Channel Islands (Îles Anglo-Normandes) and Weymouth, Portsmouth and Poole in England. Services are significantly reduced in winter. For information on schedules and tariffs, see the Sea section in the Getting There & Away chapter.

In Saint Malo, hydrofoils, catamarans and the like depart from Gare Maritime de la Bourse, while car ferries use Gare Maritime du Naye (also known as the Terminal Ferries). Both are south of the old city. Émeraude Lines' shuttles to Dinard depart from just outside the old city's Porte de Dinan (see Getting There & Away in the Dinard section).

Hydroglisseurs Condor (☎ 99.56.42.29) serves Jersey, Guernsey and Sark (all mid-March to October) and Weymouth, England (April to September). From mid-March to September, their office in Gare Maritime de la Bourse is open daily from 7 am to 8.30 pm. The rest of the year, it's open Monday to Saturday from 9 am to noon and 2 to 6 pm.

Émeraude Lines (☎ 99.40.48.40) runs ferries to Jersey, Guernsey and Sark as well as Poole, England. Service is most regular from late March to mid-November. Car ferries to Jersey and Poole run all year, albeit infrequently in the winter. Émeraude's prices are marginally cheaper than Condor's. Émeraude's office in Gare Maritime de la Bourse is open daily (weekdays only from mid-November to mid-March) from 7 or 8.30 am to noon and 2 to 6 pm. During July and August, it is open Monday to Saturday from 7 am to 7 pm and on Sunday from 9 am to 6.30 pm.

Brittany Ferries (☎ 99.82.41.41) has car ferries to Portsmouth, England, once or twice a day (Monday to Saturday during some months) from early March to December. Its office in Gare Maritime du Naye is open Monday to Saturday from 8 am to 12.30

pm and 2 to 6.30 pm. In summer it's open daily from 8 am to 9 pm.

Getting Around

Bus Saint Malo Bus operates seven lines, one of which – line No 1 – operates only during summer. Tickets cost 6.80FF and are valid on Courriers Bretons buses for travel within Saint Malo. They can be used for transfers up to one hour after having been time-stamped.

Buses usually run until about 7.15 pm, but in summer certain lines keep running until about midnight (a bit before midnight on Sunday and holidays). The company's information office at Esplanade Saint Vincent (☎ 99.56.06.06) is open from 8.30 or 9 am to noon and 2 to 6.15 or 6.30 pm daily except Saturday afternoon and Sunday (daily except Sunday in summer).

Esplanade Saint Vincent, where the tourist office and bus station are located, is linked with the train station by bus Nos 1, 2, 3 and 4.

Taxi Taxis can be ordered from Taxis Malouin (☎ 99.81.30.30) and Taxi Ameline (☎ 99.82.92.57).

Bicycle Diazo Vélocation (☎ 99.40.31.63), on the Sillon isthmus at 47 Quai Duguay Trouin, is open Monday to Saturday from 9 am to noon and 2 to 6 pm. Bikes cost 50/80FF for one/two days. Bicycles can also be hired from Bicyclub, which is near the train station exit (follow the *sortie* signs). Three- speed/10-speed/mountain bikes cost 60/80/100FF a day.

DINARD

While Saint Malo's old city and beaches are oriented towards middle-class family tourism, Dinard (population 10,000) sets out to attract the sort of well-heeled clientele – especially from the UK and the USA – who have been coming here since the town became popular with the English aristocracy in the mid-19th century. Indeed, Dinard retains something of the air of a turn-of-the-century English beach resort, especially in

summer, when the atmosphere is vivified by striped bathing tents, spiked *belle époque* mansions (perched above the turquoise waters) and sea-view promenades with elderly English couples adorning each bench. Dinard is living proof of how well wealthy French and English people at play get along.

Staying in Dinard can be a bit hard on the budget, but since the town and its many delights are just across the Rance Estuary from Saint Malo, it makes a splendid day trip by foot, bus or boat.

Orientation

Plage de l'Écluse (also known as the Grande Plage), down the hill from the tourist office, runs along the northern edge of town between Pointe du Moulinet and Pointe de la Malouine.

To get there from the Embarcadère (where boats from Saint Malo dock), walk 200 metres north-westward along Rue Georges Clemenceau. Place de la Gare, where the disused train station stands, is one km southwest of the tourist office.

Information

Tourist Office The tourist office (☎ 99.46.94.12) is in a round, colonnaded building at 2 Blvd Féart. It is open Monday to Saturday from 9 am to noon and 2 to 6 pm. During July and August it's open daily from 9.30 am to 7.30 pm.

Post The main post office is just south of Ave Édouard VII at Place Rochaid.

Dinard's postcode is 35800.

Foreign Consulate Her Majesty's government is represented in this far-flung outpost of British settlement by the UK Consulate (☎ 99.46.26.64) at 8 Blvd de la Libération.

St Bartholomew's British-American Church

This Anglican church, built in 1871 from contributions, is on Rue Faber 50 metres up the hill from 25 Ave George V. Like other such bits of England overseas, this structure

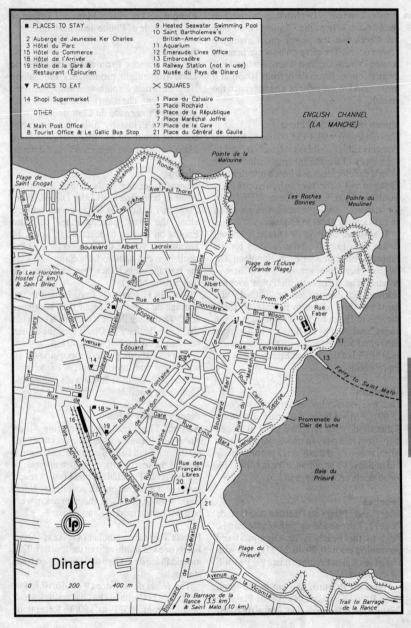

PLACES TO STAY
2 Auberge de Jeunesse Ker Charles
3 Hôtel du Parc
15 Hôtel du Commerce
18 Hôtel de l'Arrivée
19 Hôtel de la Gare & Restaurant l'Épicurien

PLACES TO EAT
14 Shopi Supermarket

OTHER
4 Main Post Office
8 Tourist Office & Le Gallic Bus Stop

9 Heated Seawater Swimming Pool
10 Saint Bartholemew's British-American Church
11 Aquarium
12 Émeraude Lines Office
13 Embarcadère
16 Railway Station (not in use)
20 Musée du Pays de Dinard

SQUARES
1 Place du Calvaire
5 Place Rochaid
6 Place de la République
7 Place Maréchal Joffre
17 Place de la Gare
21 Place du Général de Gaulle

ENGLISH CHANNEL (LA MANCHE)

Dinard

BRITTANY

is more impossibly English than anything on the London side of the Channel could ever be. Check out the pigeon-proof swinging screen doors. The clergy who serve here are rotated in from England. There is a library of English books (open daily from 10 am to 6 pm) around to the right as you approach the church.

Musée du Pays de Dinard

This museum (☎ 99.46.81.05), at 12 Rue des Français Libres, displays artefacts related to the history of the Dinard area, including the town's development as a beach resort. From Easter to mid-November *only*, it's open daily from 2 to 6 pm. Entrance costs 15FF (10FF for students). Anglophone visitors are given an explanatory sheet in English.

The Musée du Pays de Dinard is housed in the Villa Eugénie, built in 1868 for the Empress Eugénie, wife of Napoleon III. Eugénie herself never spent time here – because of an argument with 'Polee' over her beloved pet dog (which he loathed), she spent the 1868 season in Biarritz. In 1869, she was in Egypt for the inauguration of the Suez Canal. And by the time the 1870 season had rolled around, war with the Prussians – and the end of the Second Empire – was fast approaching...

Aquarium

The unspectacular aquarium (☎ 99.46. 13.90) of the Musée Nationale d'Histoire Naturelle is at 17 Ave George V. It's open daily from mid-May to mid-September from 10 am to noon and 2 to 6 pm (7 pm on Sunday and holidays). The entrance fee is 10FF (5FF for students up to the age of 25).

Beaches

Wide, sandy **Plage de l'Écluse** (the Grande Plage) is surrounded by fashionable hotels. Next to the beach is an Olympic-sized **swimming pool** (☎ 99.46.22.77) filled with heated sea water. Entrance costs 19FF (10FF for students).

Plage du Prieuré, one km to the south along Blvd Féart, isn't as smart as Plage de l'Écluse but is less crowded. **Plage de Saint**

Énogat is a km west of Plage de l'Écluse on the other side of Pointe de la Malouine.

Walks

Dinard's famous **Promenade du Clair de Lune** (moonlight promenade) runs along Baie du Prieuré south-westward from the Embarcadère. The town's most civilised walk links the Promenade du Clair de Lune with Plage de l'Écluse by following the rocky coast of Pointe du Moulinet, whence Saint Malo's old city can be seen across the water.

Hiking

Beautiful seaside trails extend along the water in both directions from Dinard. From Plage de l'Écluse, the GR34 goes westward along the coast, passing Plage de Saint Énogat on its way to Saint Briac, some 14 km away. If you are in the mood for a 10-km stroll, you can walk to/from Saint Malo via the Barrage de la Rance (see Things to See under Saint Malo).

The GR34 trail runs from Dinard to the Barrage de la Rance; a spur then continues southward along the west coast (left bank) of the Rance Estuary to Dinan (see the Dinan section), a distance of about 40 km.

The tourist office sells a topoguide (5FF) with maps and information (in French) on coastal trails entitled *Sentiers du Littoral du Canton du Dinard*.

Places to Stay & Eat

Hostels The small but attractive stone *Auberge de Jeunesse Ker Charles* (☎ 99.46. 40.02) at 8 Blvd l'Hôtelier, about 600 metres west of the tourist office, is open all year. A bed costs 60FF, including breakfast. A much larger and more expensive hostel, *Les Horizons* (☎ 99.46.05.05), is about three km west of town on the road to Saint Briac.

Hotels There are a number of less expensive hotels one km south-west of the tourist office around Place de la Gare and the disused train station.

The *Hôtel de la Gare* (☎ 99.46.10.84) at 28 Rue de la Corbinais has basic singles and doubles from 105FF to 150FF. Reception,

which is closed on Sunday after 3 or 3.30 pm, is inside Restaurant l'Épicurien, which has a three-course *menu* for 45FF. The *Hôtel de l'Arrivée* (☎ 99.46.13.05) at 5 Place de la Gare has singles/doubles for 130/180FF; showers are 25FF. The *Hôtel du Commerce* (☎ 99.46.11.19) at 52 Rue de la Gare has basic singles/doubles from 100/120FF. It is closed on Sunday. The restaurant has a *menu* for 55FF, including coffee and wine.

The *Hôtel du Parc* (☎ 99.46.11.39), a bit closer to the centre at 20 Ave Édouard VII, has a couple of cheap rooms for one/two people starting at 95/130FF. Doubles with shower and toilet start at 230FF.

Self-Catering There is a *Shopi supermarket* at 45 Rue Gardiner, which is one block north of Place de la Gare and one block south of Ave Édouard VII. There are a couple of *boulangeries* one block south-west of the tourist office at Place de la République.

Getting There & Away
Train Train services to Dinard have been discontinued, but during part of June and all of July and August, a few SNCF buses a day link up with trains arriving in Saint Malo, thus adding Dinard to SNCF's official destination list. These buses take train passengers *only*. On Friday nights, Dinard is served by TIV buses synchronised to meet the late trains to Saint Malo, which arrive at about 10 and 11 pm.

Bus For details on buses from Saint Malo, see Tourisme Verney under Getting There & Away in the Saint Malo section. In Dinard, buses stop at both Place de la Gare (the old train station) and near the tourist office (at Le Gallic stop).

Boat From April to mid-October, the Bus de Mer (literally, sea bus, ie ferry) run by Émeraude Lines (☎ 99.40.48.40 in Saint Malo, 96.46.10.45 in Dinard; see Organised Tours under Saint Malo) links Saint Malo's Porte de Dinan with Dinard's Embarcadère, which is at 27 Ave George V. The trip costs 20/30FF one way/return (12/20FF for chil-

dren) and takes 10 minutes. There are eight to 14 runs a day between 9 or 10 am and sometime around 6 pm.

POINTE DU GROUIN DOMAINE NATUREL DÉPARTEMENTAL
This nature reserve is on the wild, beautiful coast between Saint Malo and Cancale. An effort is being made to protect and restore the vegetation here. Île des Landes, just off the coast, is home to great numbers of giant cormorants. These black, fish-eating birds, which are 90 cm long and have a 170-cm wingspan, are among the largest sea birds in Europe.

Getting There & Away
Via the coastal trail (the GR34), Pointe du Grouin is seven km from Cancale and 18 km from Saint Malo. By road (the D201), it's four km from Cancale and 18 km from Saint Malo.

There is bus service from Saint Malo and Cancale during the summer school holidays (roughly July and August). From Monday to Saturday, four of the nine Courriers Bretons buses on the Saint Malo-Cancale run stop at the reserve. On Sunday, all three of the company's Saint Malo-Cancale buses stop here.

CANCALE
Cancale (population 5000) is a relaxed fishing port famed for its oyster beds *(parc à huîtres)*. The town even has a museum dedicated to oyster farming *(ostréiculture)*, the **Musée de l'Huître** (☎ 99.89.69.99), which is open from March to October (closed Monday).

The port area occupies one side of a small bay. Cancale's fleet of small fishing boats moors just off the sandy bathing beach.

Information
Tourist Office The tourist office (☎ 99.89. 63.72) is near Place de l'Église at 44 Rue du Port. It is open Tuesday to Saturday (and possibly Monday) from 8.30 am to 12.30 pm and 2 to 6 pm. In July and August it's open daily from 9 am to 8 pm.

Money There are several banks around Place de l'Église, at least one of which offers currency exchange services every day of the week except Sunday. When all the banks are closed (in the evening and on Sunday), the tourist office will change money.

Places to Stay & Eat
The *Hôtel de l'Arrivée* (☎ 99.89.80.46) at 28 Rue Victor Hugo, one block inland from the port and only 100 metres from the Port de la Houle bus stop, has doubles/triples for 110/160FF. Theoretically, this place is open from Easter to mid-October and during school holidays, but if you call a day or two in advance the proprietor will open up at any time of the year.

You might also try the small *Hôtel de la Mairie* (☎ 99.89.60.10) at 39 Rue du Port, which has doubles from 120FF. Showers are free.

Many of the restaurants along the port feature oysters (huîtres).

Self-Catering The *Comod supermarket* at Place de l'Église is open Monday to Saturday from 8.30 am to noon and 2.45 to 7 pm. From mid-June to mid-September, it is open Monday to Saturday from 8.30 am to 1 pm and 2.30 to 7.30 pm, and on Sunday from 9 am to 12.30 pm.

Across the square, *Pâtissier-Traiteur Chevalier* is open from 8 am to 12.30 pm and 2.30 to 7 pm (closed Wednesday). During July and August, it is open every day of the week from 7.30 am to 7.30 pm.

Getting There & Away
Cancale is 14 km east of Saint Malo.

Bus Cancale has two bus stops, one at Place de l'Église and another a few hundred metres down the hill at Port de la Houle. Les Courriers Bretons (☎ 99.56.79.09) and TIV (☎ 99.82.26.26) have year-round services to/from Saint Malo. See Bus under Getting There & Away in the Saint Malo section.

Hiking Expect it to take about five hours to cover the Cancale-Saint Malo leg of the GR34 trail, which follows the coast and passes by Pointe du Grouin nature reserve.

Getting Around
Le Cycle Gondange (☎ 99.89.60.87) at 4 Rue Général Leclerc, 100 metres west of Place de l'Église, rents three-speeds/mountain bikes for 40/90FF a day. It is open Tuesday to Saturday (and also on Monday in July and August) from 9 am to noon and 2 to 7 pm.

DINAN
Perched above the Rance River valley about 34 km south of Saint Malo, the medieval town of Dinan (population 12,800) has been attracting visitors for centuries. Once totally surrounded by ramparts, 14 stone towers and a good part of the walls are still standing, as are some beautiful 15th-century half-timbered houses. The town's historic air is most palpable at the end of September, when locals dressed in medieval garb are joined by some 40,000 visitors for a rollicking two-day festival in Dinan's tiny old town.

Orientation
Naturally enough nearly everything of interest, except the picturesque port area, is within the tight confines of the old town, which is centred around Place de Merciers. Place Duclos is the centre of the modern town.

Information
Tourist Office Located in one of the overhanging houses, the tourist office (☎ 96.39. 75.40) at 6 Rue de l'Horloge is open Monday to Saturday from 9 am to noon and 2 to 5.45 pm. From 1 June to 30 September it's open from 9 am to 7 pm.

Money The Banque de France (☎ 96.39. 45.35) on Rue Thiers is open on weekdays from 9 am to noon and 1.30 to 3.30 pm.

Post The main post office (☎ 96.85.12.07) on Place Duclos is open on weekdays from 8.30 am to 6.45 pm, and on Saturday until noon.

Dinan's postcode is 22100.

Laundry The laundrette opposite Église Saint Malo at 33 Grande Rue is open Monday to Saturday from 8.30 am to 8 pm.

Old Town

Wandering the recently recobbled streets of the old town is Dinan's main attraction. The tourist office has a pamphlet (6FF) that devotes a page to doing just this.

Two streets not to miss – particularly if you're heading down to the port – are **Rue du Jerzual** and its continuation, **Rue du Petit Fort**. They have oodles of art shops and some restaurants, and end at a neck-craning view of the viaduct.

Back up in the old town, the most attractive half-timbered houses hang over the central **Place des Merciers**. Near by, the feminine form of the **Tour de l'Horloge** (clock tower), whose tinny chimes rattle over the rooftops every quarter hour, rises from Rue de l'Horloge. In summer you can climb up to its tiny balcony (10FF).

To the east, there's an excellent view over the Rance Valley from **Tour Sainte Catherine**.

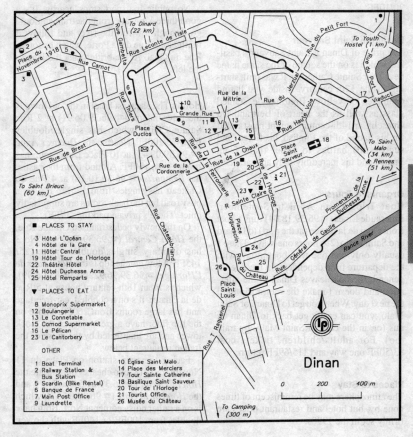

PLACES TO STAY
3 Hôtel L'Océan
4 Hôtel de la Gare
11 Hôtel Central
19 Hôtel Tour de l'Horloge
22 Théâtre Hôtel
24 Hôtel Duchesse Anne
25 Hôtel Remparts

PLACES TO EAT
8 Monoprix Supermarket
12 Boulangerie
13 Le Connetable
15 Comod Supermarket
16 Le Pélican
23 Le Cantorbery

OTHER
1 Boat Terminal
2 Railway Station & Bus Station
5 Scardin (Bike Rental)
6 Banque de France
7 Main Post Office
9 Laundrette
10 Église Saint Malo
14 Place des Merciers
17 Tour Sainte Catherine
18 Basilique Saint Sauveur
20 Tour de l'Horloge
21 Tourist Office
26 Musée du Château

Dinan

0   200   400 m

To Camping (300 m)

BRITTANY

Musée du Château

Housed in the keep of the ruins of the 14th-century castle on Rue du Château, this museum (☎ 96.39.45.20) tells Dinan's history and includes displays of colourful wooden religious statues from the 16th century. The museum's opening hours vary depending on the season. From 1 June to 15 October, it's open daily from 10 am to 6.30 pm; from mid-March to 31 May and mid-October to mid-November it's open from 10 am to 12 noon and 2 to 6 pm (closed Tuesday); and from February to mid-March it's open from 1.30 to 5.30 pm (closed Tuesday). Admission for adults/children is 20/10FF.

Basilique Saint Sauveur

The pride of Dinan is Saint Sauveur's basilica, which is on the square of the same name near Tour Sainte Catherine. It was built starting in the 12th century. Inside you'll find examples of yellow, Breton-style stained glass as well as the heart of Bertrand Du Guesclin, a 14th-century knight most noted for his hatred of the English, his fierce (and successful) battles to expel them from France and his incredibly ugly appearance.

Organised Tours

Boat Trips From April to September, Émeraude Lines (☎ 96.39.18.04) runs a boat from Quai de la Rance (at the port) to Dinard and Saint Malo (2½ hours one-way). There's usually only one one-way boat a day, with the departure time dependent on the tide. In general, the boat leaves Dinan in the afternoon and doesn't make the return trip until the next day. When you get to Dinard or Saint Malo, you can easily get back to Dinan by bus (or, in the case of Saint Malo, by train too). For adults/children, tickets cost 83/50FF one way and 115/69FF return.

Places to Stay

The atmosphere may be reminiscent of times gone by, but hotel and restaurant prices are firmly set in the 1990s.

Camping The nearest camping ground is the two-star *Camping Municipal* (☎ 96.39.11.96) at 103 Rue Chateaubriand, 500 metres south of the centre. It's open from March to November and charges 21/32FF for one/two people with a tent.

Hostel The *Auberge de Jeunesse* (☎ 96.39.10.83; fax 96.39.10.62) at Vallée de la Fontaine des Eaux sits by a stream in a green valley. A bed costs 43FF; breakfast is 16FF. Double rooms are available but you should book them in advance, especially in summer. Reception is closed from 11 am to 5 pm.

No public transport stops nearby. It's a good three-km walk from the train station – go through town to the river and follow it north along Rue de la Porte, which becomes Rue du Quai. At the bridge take the lane to the left.

Hotels The cheapest hotel in the old town is the tiny *Théâtre* (☎ 96.39.06.91) at 2 Rue Sainte Claire, which has singles/doubles from 75/100FF. Nearby, the *Duchess Anne* (☎ 96.39.09.43) at 10 Place Duguesclin has rooms from 160FF. Around from the castle, the *Remparts* (☎ 96.39.10.16) at 4 Rue du Château has singles from 125FF. It's on a busy road but the back rooms are supposedly quiet. There's private parking (17FF).

On the newly pedestrianised Grande Rue, the *Hôtel Central* (☎ 96.39.56.95) at No 3 has ordinary singles/doubles from 125/145FF. A few notches up is the *Hôtel Tour de l'Horloge* (☎ 96.39.96.92; fax 96.83.06.99), which is in an 18th-century house at 5 Rue de la Chaux. It's on a cobbled, car-free lane and has large rooms from 260FF. Those on the top floor have a great view of the clock tower and are unaffected by the noise of the Italian restaurant below.

Facing the train station on Place du 11 Novembre 1918, two cheaper options are the *Hôtel l'Océan* (☎ 96.39.21.51) at No 9 and the *Hôtel de la Gare* (☎ 96.39.04.57), which is on a rather noisy corner at No 1. Both have doubles from 100FF, or 140FF with shower.

Places to Eat

Pleasant restaurants are scattered along the port and through the old town. Those in search of a drink need go no further than Rue de la Cordonnerie, a small alley packed with pubs.

Restaurants In one of the houses hanging over Place des Merciers is the average-priced creperie *Le Connétable* (☎ 96.39.06.74). Round the corner, *Le Pélican* (☎ 96.39.47.05) at 3 Rue Haute Voie has good-priced *menus* but is closed on Wednesday evening and Sunday. Elegant *Le Cantorbery* (☎ 96.39.02.52) at 6 Rue Sainte Claire serves a tasty, three-course *menu* from 62FF.

If you have a car or don't mind a hike out of town, *La Marmite* (☎ 96.39.04.42) at 91 Rue de Brest is a routier hotel/restaurant with hearty *menus* that offer excellent value. It's closed on Saturday night and Sunday.

Self-Catering Market mornings are Thursday at Place Duguesclin and Saturday on Rue Carnot.

There's an upstairs supermarket in the *Monoprix* on Rue de la Ferronerie. It's open on Monday from 9 am to 12.30 pm and 2.30 to 7 pm and Tuesday to Saturday from 9 am to 7 pm. The little *Comod grocery* on Rue de l'Apport is also open on Sunday from 8.30 am to 12.30 pm.

The *boulangerie* at 20 Rue de la Mittrie is open Tuesday to Saturday from 7 am to 1 pm and 2.30 to 7.30 pm, and on Sunday from 8 am to 1 pm and 4 to 7 pm.

Getting There & Away

Train The train station (☎ 96.39.22.39) is outside the old town on Place du 11 Novembre 1918, about one km north-west of the tourist office. The ticket office is open Monday to Saturday from 6 am to 7 pm and on Sunday from 8.15 am to 8 pm. Trains to Paris's Gare Montparnasse go via Rennes (61FF; 1¼ hours). More locally, there are services to Saint Malo (43FF; one hour; six a day) and west via Pont à Vendin to Lannion (92FF; 2½ hours; seven a day).

Bus Buses leave from the bus station, which is to the right as you come out of the train station, and in the centre of town at Place Duclos. Services to Dinard and Saint Malo are run by CAT (☎ 96.39.21.05), which has an office at the station. Buses to Rennes are run by TAE (for details see Getting There & Away in the Rennes section).

Getting Around

Bikes can be hired from the train station. For a better selection, try Scardin (☎ 96.39.21.94), which is just up the road at 30 Rue Carnot. It charges 45/80FF for a city bike/mountain bike.

PAIMPOL

Paimpol (Pempoull; population 8300) is a small port on the Côte du Goëlo, the border region between the 'real' Brittany and the rest of the country (see the aside on Le Goëlo – The Real Brittany). Until early this century, many of the fishermen who set sail from here would fish in the waters of Iceland for seven months at a stretch. Many never returned, the victims of storms and disease.

These days, Paimpol's port is harbours more pleasure craft than fishing vessels. The town's sea-dog atmosphere comes to life every two years, when a marine song festival, held at the end of August, attracts a gathering of old wooden sailing boats. Paimpol is the closest port to the Île de Bréhat (Enez Vriad), the tiny island eight km north of town whose local population of 300 is nearly overwhelmed by beach-seeking tourists in summer.

Information

The tourist office (☎ 96.20.83.16), in the Mairie on Rue Bertho, is open Tuesday to Saturday from 9 am to noon and 2 to 5 pm. From June to mid-September it's open from 9 am to 12.30 and 2 to 7.30 as well as on Sunday morning.

Places to Stay

The quiet two-star *Camping Municipal de Cruckin* (☎ 96.20.78.47) on Rue de Cruckin

---

Le Goëlo – The Real Brittany

Le Goëlo is the region marking the northern end of an imaginary line, running from north to south, that separates 'Breton Brittany' to the west from what the locals call 'Gallic Brittany' to the east. Someone from Paimpol, for example, is a real Breton, whereas a neighbour from Binic, only 25 km east, is a 'Gallo' Breton (*gal* in Breton, meaning 'abroad'). Gallic Brittany (also known as High Brittany, or Haute Bretagne) is predominantly French-speaking, while in Breton (Basse or Lower) Brittany many people still speak the regional tongue, heard these days mainly in Finistère. The demarcation line runs from Plouha (between Paimpol and Binic) south to Vannes in Morbihan. ■

---

is on the beautiful Baie de Kérity, two km south-east of town off the road to Plouha. You can also camp on the grounds of the *Auberge de Jeunesse* (☎ 96.20.83.60) in the Château de Kerraoul, 1.5 km north-west of the town centre.

There are a few cheap port-front hotels. The *Hôtel des Chalutiers* (☎ 96.20.82.15) at 5 Quai Morand has singles/doubles for 100/120FF, while the *Hôtel Le Goëlo* (☎ 96.20.82.74) on Quai Duguay Trouin has rooms from 100/150FF.

Getting There & Away

Train & Bus The train station (☎ 96.20.81.22) is on Ave Général de Gaulle. It's a few minutes' walk to the tourist office – to get there head straight up Rue du 18 Juin, turn left into Rue de l'Église, take the first right and then turn left.

The closest major rail junction is Guingamp (32FF; 40 minutes; seven a day) from where there are frequent trains west to Brest and east to Dinan.

Buses to Saint Brieuc cost 35FF and take 1½ hours.

Boat Ferries to Île de Bréhat, run by Vedettes de Bréhat (☎ 96.20.03.47), leave from the port at Pointe de l'Arcouest, six km north of town. The trip takes 10 minutes and costs 31FF for a return ticket. Taking a bicycle costs another 31FF, but no bikes are allowed on board when the boat is full. Boat schedules vary depending on the season but it's more or less hourly in summer and five times a day in winter.

Getting Around

Buses run by CAT leave four times a day from Paimpol's train station (11FF one way) to connect with ferries to Île de Bréhat.

Bikes can be hired at the port in Paimpol for 35FF a day.

PERROS GUIREC & LANNION

One of the older resorts along the Côte de Granit Rose, Perros Guirec (Perroz Gerec; population 8000) sits at the northern end of Brittany's northernmost peninsula. It's a rather exclusive resort town, flanked by two harbours – the new sheltered marina to the south-east and the old fishing port of Ploumanac'h about two km to the west. Between the two harbours winds a wild coastline of rose-coloured granite, sculpted and smoothed by the elements into the strangest shapes imaginable. These are interrupted by a few half-moon beaches and coves where sea otters feel at home. To the north lie the protected Sept Îles, a paradise for sea birds.

While Perros can be pricey for overnight halts, the town of Lannion (Lannuon), 12 km inland, has a decent youth hostel. Lannion is the nearest railhead.

Orientation

Perros has two distinct parts: the main upper town on the hill and the marina area at its base. They're about one km apart if you wind your way up along the small roads, or double that distance if you follow the coastal Blvd de la Mer around Pointe du Château, the ritzy peninsula that extends eastward from town.

Information

The tourist office (☎ 96.23.21.15) is in the upper town at 21 Place de la Mairie. It is open Monday to Saturday from 9 am to noon and 2 to 6.30 pm, in summer from 9 am to 1 pm and 2 to 7.30 pm.

Beaches

There are several beaches close to Perros. The main one is **Plage de Trestraou**, to the north about one km downhill from the tourist office. The others are much smaller and isolated, located on either side of Pointe du Château to the east.

Walks

For a fantastic walk along the coast, you can follow the GR34 from Plage de Trestraou through the pink rock world to Ploumanac'h. All up, it's about three km each way.

Places to Stay

Camping Four camping grounds are dotted around the area. Four-star *Camping Le Ranolien* (☎ 96.91.43.58) has the best location: it's close to the sea, between the rocks off the road to Ploumanac'h. It is open from February to mid-November.

The cheaper two-star *West Camping* (☎ 96.91.43.82), just 500 metres further towards Ploumanac'h, is open from September to May. CAT's bus No 15 (see Getting Around) will drop you off close to both.

Hostels There are two year-round youth hostels located about 10 km from Perros. Inland at Lannion, *Les Korrigans* (☎ 96.37.91.28) at 6 Rue du 73 Territorial is a three-minute walk from the train station – go to the right as you leave, then follow the signs. It charges 43FF a night plus 15FF for breakfast. Reception is open weekdays from 9 am to 7 pm (8 pm in summer) and weekends from 10 am to noon and 6 to 8 pm.

The other hostel, *Le Toëno* (☎ 96.23.52.22), is on the coast 10 km west of Perros near the town of Trébeurden on Route de la Corniche. To get there take CAT bus No 15 from the train station in Lannion or from

Perros's Mairie and ask the driver to stop at the Auberge de Jeunesse.

Hotels In Perros's upper town, the *Hôtel de Bretagne* (☎ 96.37.00.33) at 32 Ave Général de Gaulle is a block south-west of the tourist office, just off the road to Ploumanac'h. It has singles/doubles for 170/200FF. Keep going for another block and you'll come to the *Hôtel les Violettes* (☎ 96.23.21.33) at 19 Rue du Calvaire, a Victorian-style house with rooms starting at 105/125FF.

In the marina area, on the main road overlooking the port, is the *Hôtel le Suroit* (☎ 96.23.23.83) at 81 Rue Ernest Renan, which has rooms from 110FF.

Places to Eat

All three hotels listed here have decent *menus* from 50FF (the Hôtel les Violettes) to 68FF (the Hôtel le Suroit).

Self-caterers will find a *Comod supermarket* just south-west of the tourist office on Blvd Aristide Briand. It's open Monday to Saturday from 8.30 am to 12.30 pm and 3 to 7.30 pm. In summer, it's also open on Sunday morning.

Getting There & Away

Buses operated by CAT (☎ 96.37.02.40) shuttle between Perros and Lannion's train station. In Perros they stop at both the marina and the tourist office. A single ticket costs 13FF.

From the Lannion train station (☎ 96.37.03.01) there are rail connections via Plouaret Trégor eastward to Guingamp and on to Saint Brieuc (52FF; 65 minutes); and westward via Morlaix to Roscoff (58FF; three hours; five a day) and Brest (75FF; 2½ hours; six a day).

Getting Around

Bus CAT bus No 15 runs from Lannion's train station to Perros, west to Ploumanac'h and Trégastel and on to Trébeurden. There are about five buses a day (except on Sunday). In each town, the bus stops at the either the tourist office or the main square in each town.

BRITTANY

Bicycle In Lannion, bikes can be hired from the youth hostel for 60/80FF for a half/full day. Ask at reception for a map of the region's best cycling tracks. Bikes can also be rented at the train station for 55FF the first day; tariffs get progressively cheaper the longer you hire for.

AROUND PERROS GUIREC
Les Sept Îles

Situated about five km offshore, the Seven Islands are home to an important gannet colony and are also the breeding ground for many other sea birds, including puffins, cormorants, storm petrels and oyster catchers.

Between mid-March and the end of September, Les Vedettes Blanches (☎ 96.23. 22.47) organises morning boat trips around the islands. You can get off at Île aux Moines but the others are protected and strictly off limits. The 1¼-hour trip costs 60/45FF for adults/children; the 2½-hour version is 80/50FF. Boats leave from the western end of Plage de Trestraou.

Alsace & Lorraine

Though often spoken of as if they were one, Alsace and Lorraine, neighbouring regions in France's north-eastern corner, are linked by what is little more than an accident of history: Alsace and part of Lorraine were annexed by Germany in 1871, and in the decades before WW I they became a major focus of French nationalism. But that's about where the connection ends.

Alsace, popularly thought of as a land of colourful, half-timbered houses sprouting red and pink geraniums and topped by storks' nests, is nestled between the Vosges Mountains and the Rhine River, final resting place of the long-disputed Franco-German border. It is perhaps France's most 'un-French' region, in the sense that it is distinct from the rest of the country in language, cuisine, domestic architecture, traditional dress and all the little details that give a place its atmosphere and ambience. Particularly after overhearing Alsatians conversing in the local language, tourists often comment that 'it's more German than French'. But while Alsace is unlike any other region in France, it is also quite distinct in culture and identity from anything across the Rhine in Germany. Throughout France, the people of Alsace have a reputation for being hard-working, well-organised and tax-paying.

To foreigners, Lorraine is probably associated more with quiche than the medieval kingdom of Lotharingia from which its name derives. One of France's chief industrial regions, it has little of Alsace's picturesque quaintness. Instead, its population centres tend to be sturdy towns based on heavy industries such as coal, iron and salt mining and steel production. This is particularly true of areas near the border with Luxembourg and Germany. Agriculture also plays an important role in the economy, especially in the central Lorraine plateau and areas further south. Historically, Lorraine has had two capitals: Metz in the north and, further south, Nancy.

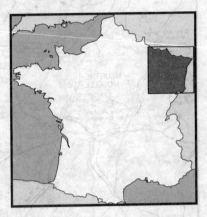

Alsace

The Vosges Mountains form the border between Alsace and Lorraine. Alsace, which is only about 200 km long and no more than 50 km wide, occupies the plains that stretch eastward from the Vosges to the Rhine.

Alsace is made up of two *départements*: Bas Rhin (Lower Rhine), which is based around the regional capital, Strasbourg; and Haut Rhin (Upper Rhine), which covers the region's more southerly reaches, including the département's picturesque capital of Colmar. Germany is just across the busy, barge-laden Rhine River, whose western bank is in Alsace as far south as Basel, Switzerland. The northern edge of Alsace touches Germany, while the region's southern border is coincident with the Franco- Swiss frontier.

Alsace's major towns tend to be a few km west of the Rhine along the much smaller Ill River, which runs parallel to the Rhine. Indeed, the name Alsace – *Illsass* in Alsatian – means Country of the Ill. Alsace's Route du Vin (Wine Route), which begins near Strasbourg and continues southward to

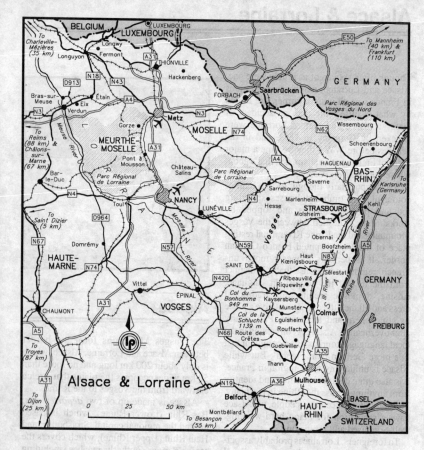

Colmar and Thann, wends its way through the vineyards and picture-postcard villages along the eastern foothills of the Vosges.

The Vosges Mountains are an ancient but gentle range, thickly forested with pine and, in places, oak and beech trees. The area is popular with families on holiday and unpretentious cross-country skiers. The Route des Crêtes (Route of the Crest), a road established during WW I to assure north-south communications for the French military, is famous for its ruined castles and the views it affords from up near the crest of the mountains. The northern section of the Vosges is a

park, the Parc Naturel Régional des Vosges du Nord, beloved by hikers and mushroom gatherers.

History

Alsace was inhabited by the Celts as far back as 1000 BC. Following its conquest by Julius Caesar in the 1st century BC, the area came under significant Roman cultural influence. The region, which was Christianised under the Merovingians, constituted a part of the Holy Roman Empire from the 800s until – at least nominally – the mid-17th century. During the Reformation, Protestantism made significant inroads in Alsace, particularly in Strasbourg.

French influence in Alsace began at the end of the 1500s during the Wars of Religion (1562-98) and increased during the Thirty Years' War (1618-48), when Alsatian cities, caught between opposing Catholic and Protestant factions, turned to France for assistance. The region was attached to France in 1648, when Louis XIV enshrined his territorial claims in the Treaty of Westphalia.

By the time of the French Revolution, after over a century of considerable autonomy, the Alsatians felt far more connected to France than to Germany. Indeed, the upper classes had already begun to adopt the French language. But over two centuries of French rule did little to dampen 19th-century German enthusiasm for a foothold on the west bank of the southern Rhine. The Franco-Prussian War of 1870-71, a supremely humiliating episode in French history, ended with the Treaty of Frankfurt (1871). France ceded Alsace and part of Lorraine to the German Reich and had to pay the unprecedented sum of five billion francs in indemnities.

Faced with the radical Germanisation of the two regions (German replaced French at university and in schools), people had to choose whether they wanted to retain their French nationality and move to France, or keep living in their homes and become Germans. According to some estimates, one-tenth of the regions' inhabitants left. Among those who remained, the German annexation was very unpopular.

During WW I, Alsatian men were conscripted into the German army and ended up fighting their former French compatriots. Meanwhile, anyone from Alsace who was on French territory when war broke out was regarded by France as an 'enemy alien' and interned. The Nobel Peace Prize laureate Dr Albert Schweitzer, who was born in Alsace in 1875 but was living at the time in French Equatorial Africa, was among those detained. Following Germany's defeat in WW I, Alsace and Lorraine were returned to France, but the French government's programme to reassimilate the area (eg by replacing church schools with state-run ones and banning German-language newspapers) gave rise to a strong home-rule movement.

Germany's second annexation of Alsace and Lorraine in 1940 – and indeed the occupation of all of France – was supposed to have been made impossible by the state-of-the-art Maginot Line (see the Maginot Line aside). Immediately after Germany annexed the area, about half a million people fled Alsace. This time, the Germanisation campaign was particularly harsh: anyone caught speaking French was imprisoned, and even the Alsatian language was banned.

After the war, Alsace was once again returned to France. Intra-Alsatian tensions ran high, however, as those who had left came back and confronted former neighbours whom they suspected of having collaborated with the Germans. To make Alsace into a symbol of hope for future Franco-German (and pan-European) cooperation, Strasbourg was made the seat of the Council of Europe (Conseil de l'Europe) in 1949 and was later chosen as the headquarters of the European Parliament.

Language

The language of Alsace, Alsatian, is an Alemmanic dialect of High German similar to dialects spoken in nearby parts of Germany and Switzerland. It has no official written form, and pronunciation varies slightly from one area to another. Despite a series of heavy-handed attempts by both the French and the Germans to 'Frenchify' or 'Germanify' the region, in part by restricting (or even banning) the use of the Alsatian language, it is still spoken by many Alsatians, especially older people in rural areas.

Alsatian is known for its sing-songy intonations, which also characterise the way some Alsatians speak French. It is said that the better someone from Alsace speaks standard German, the less likely they are to have a marked Alsatian accent in French.

Food

Even travellers adept at coping with French menus may at first draw a blank when confronted with the selection of dishes in traditional Alsatian restaurants. On the savoury side, dishes you're likely to find include *baeckeoffe* (also spelled *baekeoffe* and *backehofe)*, which means 'baker's oven'. This stew, made of several kinds of meat (often pork, mutton and beef) which have been marinated for two days before being cooked with potatoes and onions, is traditionally prepared at home before being taken to the oven of a nearby bakery to be cooked. *Choucroute* is sauerkraut (chopped and pickled cabbage) served with sausage, pork or ham; it is often accompanied by cold, frothy beer or a local wine. *Flammeküeche*, a thin layer of pastry topped with cream, onion, bacon and sometimes cheese or mushrooms and cooked in a wood-fired oven, is translated into French (with less than stellar precision) as *tarte flambée*. A *ziwelküeche* (or *tarte à l'oignon*) is an onion tart. Alsace produces some excellent *charcuterie*, including bacon, Strasbourg sausages, smoked ham and smoked pork chops.

Alsace's pâtisseries are particularly well-stocked with scrumptious pastries, including *kougelhopf*, a sultana-and-almond cake easily identifiable by its ribbed, dome-like shape (except at Christmas, when it may be moulded to look like Santa Claus or some other character likely to appeal to children). *Tarte alsacienne* is a custard tart made with local fruits. Many pâtisseries also have the most irresistible chocolate pralines, which sell for around 25FF per 100 grams (about 2FF each).

Alsace also has it's own kinds of eating establisments. *Winstubs* ('VEEN-shtub') serve both wine (by the glass or carafe) and many hearty, traditional Alsatian dishes, many of them prepared with...wine! *Bierstubs* ('BEER-shtub') primarily serve beer – often dozens, scores or even hundreds of different kinds. Although most do offer light snacks (eg tarte flambée), they don't usually serve multicourse meals.

Alsatians tend to eat a bit earlier than elsewhere in France. Restaurants usually begin serving lunch pretty close to noon and open for dinner at 6 or 6.30 pm (rather than 7 or 7.30).

The Maginot Line

The famed Maginot Line, named after André Maginot (1877-1932), French minister of war from 1929 to 1931, was one of the most spectacular blunders of WW II. This elaborate, mostly subterranean defensive network, built between 1930 and 1940, was the pride of 1930s France. It included everything France's finest military architects thought would be needed to defend France in a 'modern war' of poison gas, tanks and aeroplanes: reinforced concrete blockhouses, infantry bunkers (some housing 600 soldiers), subterranean lines of supply and communication, minefields, antitank canals, floodable basins and even artillery emplacements that popped out of the ground to fire and then disappeared. The only things visible above ground were firing posts and lookout towers. The line stretched along the Franco-German frontier from the Swiss border all the way round to Belgium where, for political and budgetary reasons, it stopped.

The Maginot Line even had a slogan: *Ils ne passeront pas* (They won't get through).

'They' – the Germans – never did. Rather than attack the Maginot Line straight-on, Hitler's armoured divisions simply circled around through Belgium and invaded France across its unprotected northern frontier. They then attacked the Maginot Line from the rear. Against all the odds – and with most of northern France already in German hands – some of the fortifications held out for a few weeks. When resistance became hopeless, thousands of French troops managed to escape to Switzerland, where the Swiss promptly interned them until the following year.

In both Lorraine and Alsace, parts of the Maginot Line are open for visits, but without your own wheels they're a bit hard to get to. One of the largest underground forts in Lorraine is **Fermont** (see the Verdun section). In Alsace, it is possible to visit **Schoenenbourg**, which is about 45 km north of Strasbourg near the village of Betschdorf. ■

ALSACE

Wine

Alsace, France's third most important wine-making region (after Bordeaux and Burgundy), has been producing wine uninterruptedly since about the year 300 AD. These days, the region makes almost exclusively white wines – most of them produced nowhere else in France – that are known for their clean-tasting freshness and lightening effect on the often heavy local cuisine. Some Alsatian whites even go with red meat.

Unlike other French wines, those made in Alsace bear varietal names. That is, the name on the bottle derives from the variety of grape used (ie Riesling) rather than from the name of the place where the grapes were grown. The four most important grape varieties are Riesling, known for its subtlety; the more pungent Gewürztraminer; the robust, high-alcohol Tokay-Pinot Gris; and Muscat, which is not as sweet here as the muscat grapes produced further south. Edelzwicker is premium wine made from a blend of different grapes.

Eaux de vie (brandies), are made and flavoured with locally grown fruit and nuts. Of the many varieties, kirsch, a cherry concoction, is the most famous. Alsace also brews about half of France's beer.

STRASBOURG

Cosmopolitan and prosperous Strasbourg (population 450,000, including the suburbs) is France's great north-eastern metropolis and the intellectual and cultural capital of Alsace. The city, whose name means City of the Roads' in German, is aptly titled, for it is situated on the vital transport arteries – road, water and rail – that since Roman times have linked northern and central Europe with the Mediterranean. Located only a few km west of the Rhine, Strasbourg has also been a lively cultural and intellectual crossroads, a tradition that continues thanks to the city's international student population of 45,000.

Towering above the restaurants, pubs and *bars à musique* of the lively old city – an excellent place to explore on foot – is the cathedral, a medieval marvel in pink sandstone near which you'll find one of the finest ensembles of museums in all of France. Strasbourg's distinctive architecture, including the centuries-old, half-timbered merchants' houses, and its exemplary orderliness impart on the city an unmistakably Alsatian ambience.

Before being attached to France in 1681, Strasbourg was effectively ruled for several centuries by a guild of citizens whose tenure imparted a certain democratic character on the city. During this period, a university was founded (in 1566) and several leaders of the Reformation took up residence here. Johannes Gutenberg worked in Strasbourg from about 1434 to 1444 perfecting his printing press and the moveable metal type that made it so revolutionary. Three centuries later, the German poet, playwright, novelist and philosopher Johann Wolfgang von Goethe (1749-1832), studied law (and fell in love) here.

The religious struggles that followed the Reformation hit Strasbourg with particularly divisive ferocity. To this day, a number of pairs of churches – one Catholic, the other Protestant – bear the same name (eg Église Saint Pierre-le-Jeune). In one case, Église Saint Pierre-le-Vieux, the same structure houses two churches, with separate entrances for Protestant and Catholic worshippers.

When it was founded in 1949, the Council of Europe decided to base itself in Strasbourg, hoping that the city, so long bitterly contested between France and Germany, would become a symbol of European cooperation and friendship. The organisation's huge headquarters, Palais de l'Europe, is used for one week each month (except during July and August) by the European Parliament, the legislative branch of the EC (now officially known as the European Union).

Orientation

The city centre is about 3.5 km west of Pont de l'Europe, a bridge that links the French bank of the Rhine River with the German city of Kehl. The Strasbourg train station is 400 metres west of the Grande Île (literally, Large

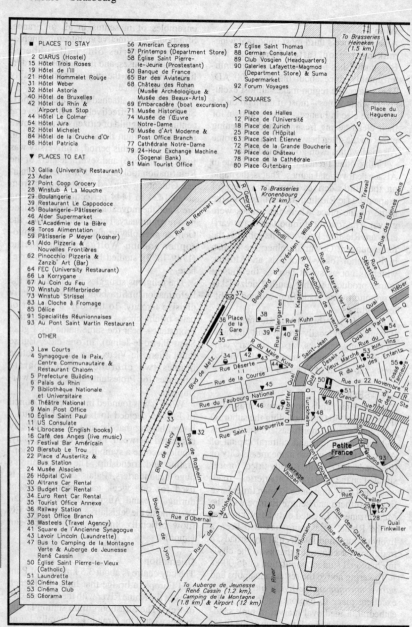

■ PLACES TO STAY

2 CIARUS (Hostel)
15 Hôtel Trois Roses
19 Hôtel de l'Ill
21 Hôtel Hommelet Rouge
31 Hôtel Weber
32 Hôtel Astoria
40 Hôtel de Bruxelles
42 Hôtel du Rhin &
   Airport Bus Stop
44 Hôtel Le Colmar
54 Hôtel Jura
82 Hôtel Michelet
84 Hôtel de la Cruche d'Or
86 Hôtel Patricia

▼ PLACES TO EAT

13 Gallia (University Restaurant)
23 Adan
27 Point Coop Grocery
28 Winstub À La Mouche
29 Boulangerie
39 Restaurant Le Cappodoce
45 Boulangerie-Pâtisserie
46 Alder Supermarket
48 L'Académie de la Bière
49 Toros Alimentation
59 Pâtisserie P Meyer (kosher)
61 Aldo Pizzeria &
   Nouvelles Frontières
62 Pinocchio Pizzeria &
   Zanzib' Art (Bar)
64 FEC (University Restaurant)
66 La Korrygane
67 Au Coin du Feu
70 Winstub Pfifferbrieder
73 Winstub Strissel
83 La Cloche à Fromage
85 Délice
91 Specialités Réunionnaises
93 Au Pont Saint Martin Restaurant

OTHER

3 Law Courts
4 Synagogue de la Paix,
   Centre Communautaire &
   Restaurant Chalom
5 Prefecture Building
6 Palais du Rhin
7 Bibliothèque Nationale
   et Universitaire
8 Théâtre National
9 Main Post Office
10 Église Saint Paul
11 US Consulate
14 Librocase (English books)
16 Café des Anges (live music)
17 Festival Bar Américain
20 Bierstub Le Trou
22 Place d'Austerlitz &
   Bus Station
24 Musée Alsacien
26 Hôpital Civil
30 Altrans Car Rental
32 Budget Car Rental
35 Euro Rent Car Rental
35 Tourist Office Annexe
36 Railway Station
37 Post Office Branch
38 Wasteels (Travel Agency)
41 Square de l'Ancienne Synagogue
43 Lavoir Lincoln (Laundrette)
47 Bus to Camping de la Montagne
   Verte & Auberge de Jeunesse
   René Cassin
50 Église Saint Pierre-le-Vieux
   (Catholic)
51 Laundrette
52 Cinéma Star
53 Cinéma Club
55 Géorama

56 American Express
57 Printemps (Department Store)
58 Église Saint Pierre-
   le-Jeune (Prostestant)
60 Banque de France
65 Bar des Aviateurs
68 Château des Rohan
   (Musée Archéologique &
   Musée des Beaux-Arts)
69 Embarcadère (boat excursions)
71 Musée Historique
74 Musée de l'Œuvre
   Notre-Dame
75 Musée d'Art Moderne &
   Post Office Branch
77 Cathédrale Notre-Dame
79 24-Hour Exchange Machine
   (Sogenal Bank)
81 Main Tourist Office

87 Église Saint Thomas
88 German Consulate
89 Club Vosgien (Headquarters)
90 Galeries Lafayette-Magmod
   (Department Store) & Suma
   Supermarket
92 Forum Voyages

✕ SQUARES

1 Place des Halles
12 Place de l'Université
18 Place de Zurich
25 Place de l'Hôpital
63 Place Saint Étienne
72 Place de la Grande Boucherie
76 Place du Château
78 Place de la Cathédrale
80 Place Gutenberg

Strasbourg

0   100   200 m

To Parc de l'Orangerie,
Swiss Consulate
(750 m) & Parc de
l'Europe (1.2 km)

To Pont de l'Europe
(3 km), Centre International
de Recontres du Parc du Rhin
(3.5 km) & Kehl, Germany
(5 km)

To Pont de l'Europe (4 km), Centre
International de Recontres du Parc du
Rhin (4.5 km) & Kehl, Germany (5 km)

ALSACE

Island), the core of ancient and modern-day Strasbourg, which is delimited by the Ill River on the south and the Fossé du Faux Rempart, a branch of the Ill, on the north. It is linked to the rest of the city by 20 bridges. About a third of the Grande Île is pedestrianised, and work is underway to increase this percentage by 1994.

The main public square on the Grande Île is Place Kléber. Other main squares include Place Broglie and Place Gutenberg. Strasbourg's museums are clustered around the cathedral, whose spire is visible from all over town. The quaint Petite France area in the Grande Île's south-western corner is subdivided by canals. The Palais de l'Europe is about three km north-east of the cathedral.

Information

Tourist Office The main tourist office (☎ 88.32.57.07) is at 10 Place Gutenberg. From November to Easter it is open Monday to Saturday from 9 am to 12.30 pm and 1.45 to 6 pm and on Sunday from 9 am to 12.30 pm and 2 to 5 pm. From Easter to May and during October, it's open daily from 9 am to 6 pm; from June to September the hours are 8 am to 7 pm. The tourist office can make hotel reservations all over Alsace (10FF) and, during working hours, elsewhere in France, too. They also sell carnets of bus tickets and have free bus maps. *Strasbourg Actualités*, a French-language monthly listing everything from cultural activities (opera, theatre, orchestra concerts, dance, jazz, etc) to the hours of the local *patinoire* (ice-skating rink), is also available free of charge.

There's a tourist office annexe (☎ 88.32. 51.49) outside the train station on Place de la Gare. It's due to move to a new, underground home when the tramway construction at Place de la Gare is finished in 1994 or 1995. The office is open daily from 9 am to 12.30 pm and 1.45 to 6 pm; from November to March it may be closed on weekends. June to September hours are 8 am to 7 pm. There's a second annexe (☎ 88.61.39.23) with similar hours just west of Pont de l'Europe.

For information on the Alsace region, try the Office Départemental de Tourisme (☎ 88.22.01.02), south of Place Broglie at 9 Rue du Dôme.

Money The Banque de France (☎ 88.32. 30.14), whose public entrance is on Impasse de Birschheim, the alley next to 9 Place Broglie, is open weekdays from 9 am to 12.30 pm and 1.30 to 3.30 pm. The first-ever performance of the French national anthem, *La Marseillaise* (see the La Marseillaise aside), was held in this building in 1792. The event is commemorated by a plaque. American Express (☎ 88.75.78.75) at 31 Place Kléber is open on weekdays from 8.45 am to noon and 1.30 to 6 pm.

Several 24-hour cash exchange machines are scattered around town. There's one at the Sogenal bank on Place Gutenberg and another outside the tourist office annexe next to the train station.

The Banque CIAL bureau (☎ 88.23. 35.99) in the train station is open Monday to Friday from 9 am to 1 pm and 2 to 7.30 pm and on Saturday, Sunday and holidays from 9 am to 8 pm. The commission is 15FF and the rate is not too bad. The exchange bureau near the Pont de l'Europe tourist office is open daily until at least 5 pm.

Post The main post office (☎ 88.23.37.23), which is opposite 8 Ave de la Marseillaise, is open weekdays from 8 am to 7 pm and on Saturday until noon. The branch post office next to the train station (to the left as you exit) is open the same hours. The branch at Place de la Cathédrale is also open the same hours except that it closes at 6.30 pm on weekdays. All three have exchange services.

Strasbourg's postcode is 67000.

Foreign Consulates The US Consulate (☎ 88.35.31.04) is at 15 Ave d'Alsace, 500 metres east of Place de la République. It is open Monday to Friday from 9.30 am to noon and 2 to 5 pm. If there's an emergency when the consulate is closed, you can leave a message on the answering machine. The nearest cities where you can replace a US passport are Paris and Stuttgart.

Canadians with passport difficulties can contact the honorary Canadian Consulate (☎ 88.96.25.00), which is located in the offices of a German-owned petro-chemical company that used to be a Canadian-owned petro-chemical company.

The German Consulate (☎ 88.32.61.86) is at 15 Rue des Francs Bourgeois. Switzerland has a consulate (☎ 88.35.00.70) at 11 Blvd du Président Edwards, close to the Palais de l'Europe.

Travel Agencies Nouvelles Frontières (88.25.68.50) at 4 Rue du Faisan is open Monday and Saturday from 9 am to noon and 2 to 5.30 pm and Tuesday to Friday from 9 am to 6 pm. Inexpensive air tickets are also available from Forum Voyages (☎ 88.32.42.00) at 49 Rue du 22 Novembre, which is open weekdays from 9.30 am to 7 pm and Saturday from 10 am to 12.30 pm and 1.30 to 6 pm.

Near the train station, BIJ tickets can be purchased at Wasteels (☎ 88.32.40.82), 13 Place de la Gare, which is open Monday to Saturday from 9 am to 7 pm (6 pm on Saturday).

Books & Maps Géorama (☎ 88.75.01.95) at 20-22 Rue du Fossé des Tanneurs has an excellent range of local and national maps. The headquarters of the hiking organisation Club Vosgien (☎ 88.32.57.96) at 16 Rue Sainte Hélène has a wide selection of hiking maps and topoguides. It is open Monday to Saturday from 8 am (9 am on Saturday) to noon and 2 to 6 pm.

Librocase (☎ 88.25.50.31), a bookshop with second-hand books at 2 Quai des Pêcheurs, has a whole shelf of English-language novels for 10 to 25FF, which is very cheap for France. It is open Monday to Friday from 9 am to 7 pm. During the school holidays in February, at Easter and during July and August hours are 1 to 7 pm.

Le Strassbuch: Le Guide de Strasbourg, put out each year by local students, lists virtually every sort of establishment where a local person might be tempted to spend their money, including places to eat and shops. It is available around town for 20FF.

Laundry The most central laundrette on the Grande Île is at 29 Grand' Rue. It's open daily from 7 am to 8 pm. Near the train station, Lavoir Lincoln at 4 Rue Déserte is open daily from 8 am to 8 pm.

Medical Services The Hôpital Civil (☎ 88.16.17.18) is at 1 Place de l'Hôpital.

Walking Tour

With its up-market shopping streets, bustling public squares and a large (and increasing) number of pedestrian malls, Strasbourg's centre is a great place for an aimless stroll. The streets of the **old city**, particularly around the cathedral, are especially enchanting at night. There are watery views from the paths along the **Ill River** and the canal of the **Fossé du Faux Rempart**. From the Terrasse Panoramique on top of **Barrage Vauban**, which was built to prevent riverborne attacks on the city, you look out on the Ill River and Petite France; it is open daily from 7.30 am to 5 pm (8 pm from May to mid-October).

La Petite France, with its half-timbered houses lining the quaint lanes and canals, is another good area for a walk. The city's parks (see Parc de l'Orangerie and Other Parks) provide a welcome respite from the traffic and congestion of the Grande Île.

Cathédrale Notre Dame

Strasbourg's impossibly lacy Gothic cathedral, built of rose-coloured sandstone, was begun in 1176 after an earlier cathedral had burned down in 1145. The west façade – which can be viewed to best advantage from Rue Mercière – was completed in 1284, but the 142-metre spire, the tallest of its time, was not in place until 1439; its southern companion was never built. Following the Reformation and a long period of bitter stuggle, the cathedral came under Protestant control and was not returned to the Catholic Church until Louis XIV took over the city in 1681. During the Revolution, hundreds of the cathedral's statues were smashed, but fortunately a plan to get rid of the spire was never carried out. The structure was damaged by Prussian artillery in 1870 and by Allied bombing in 1944. Some of the many statues decorating the cathedral are copies – the originals can be seen in the superb Musée de l'Œuvre Notre-Dame (see the Museums listing).

The cathedral (☎ 88.37.33.12) is open daily except during mass from 7 to 11.40 am and 12.45 to 6.30 pm. The 12th to 14th-century **stained-glass windows** shine like jewels on bright days. The colourful **organ case** dates from the 14th and 15th centuries. The three-storey high, mixed Gothic and Renaissance-style contraption just inside the south entrance is the **horloge astronomique** (astronomical clock), a late 16th-century clock (the mechanism dates from 1842) that strikes noon every day at precisely 12.30 pm. To pay for the clock's upkeep, there is a 4FF charge to see the carved wooden figures do their thing, which is why only the cathedral's south entrance is open between 11.40 am and the end of the show.

The 66-metre-high platform above the façade – from which the **tower** and its Gothic openwork **spire** soar another 76 metres – affords a stork's-eye view of Strasbourg. If you don't mind climbing up over 300 spiral steps, it can be visited daily from 9 am (8.30 am in July and August) to 4.30 pm (November to February), 5.30 pm (March and October), 6.30 pm (April to June and September) or 7 pm (July and August). The entrance (☎ 88.32.59.00) is at the base of the bell tower that was never built. Tickets cost 10FF (7FF for students). The two giant gerbil wheels were used to hoist stones. There's some late 18th and early 19th-century graffiti on the tower.

From April to September a *son et lumière* show is held inside the cathedral at 9 pm (enter by the southern entrance).

Église Saint Thomas

This Protestant church on Rue Martin Luther, built in the late 12th century and turned into a Lutheran cathedral in 1529, is best known for the evocative mausoleum of Marshal Maurice of Saxony, considered a masterpiece of 18th-century French sculpture. Erected on the order of Louis XV, it depicts Maurice – in full dress uniform – stepping boldly into a coffin held open by a shrouded figure of Death while a grieving, bare-breasted France tries to hold Death at bay. To the Marshal's right lie the defeated heraldic animals of Austria (the eagle), England (the leopard) and Holland (the lion). Note that the church is configured so that all of the members of the congregation sit facing the altar, placed in what was once the transept crossing.

Museums

Strasbourg's most important museums are located in the immediate vicinity of the cathedral. All are open daily, except Tuesday, with the exception of the Musée d'Art Moderne and the Musée de l'Oeuvre Notre Dame, which are open daily. Hours are 10 am to noon and 2 to 6 pm (10 am to 6 pm on Sunday from April to October). Each museum charges 15FF (8FF for students who are under 26). Entrance is free if you're under 18, over 65 or a teacher (ID required). The museum authorities (☎ 88.32.48.95 for any queries) are working on a combination ticket as well as experimenting with free admission until 2 pm on Sundays. Ask at the tourist office for details on the current situation.

The **Musée de l'Œuvre Notre-Dame** (☎ 88.32.88.17), housed in a group of 14th and 15th-century buildings at 3 Place du Château, is Strasbourg's single most outstanding museum. It displays one of France's finest collections of Romanesque, Gothic and Renaissance sculpture (in both stone and wood), including many of the cathedral's original statues, brought here for preservation and display. The *Tête du Christ* (Head of Christ), part of a stained-glass window from the mid-1000s – the oldest work of its kind in France – is in Room II. The celebrated figures of a downcast and blindfolded *Synagoga* (representing Judaism) and a victorious *Église* (the Church triumphant), which date from around 1230 and once

The Diamond Necklace Affair

The notorious affair of the diamond necklace took place at the court of Louis XVI in 1785. The main character behind the scandal was an adventuress named Jeanne de la Motte, who claimed to be a descendant of the Valois line. Wanting to acquire an ostentatious diamond necklace made by the court jewellers, Böhmer and Basenge, and worth 1.6 million livres, she played upon Cardinal Louis de Rohan's wish to ingratiate himself with the queen, Marie Antoinette. De la Motte convinced de Rohan that the queen sought to acquire the necklace secretly and that he could help her to do so. In fact, though the jewellers had made repeated attempts to sell the necklace to Marie-Antoinette, she had consistently refused to buy it.

It was agreed with the jewellers that the necklace would be paid for in instalments, with de Rohan acting as guarantor.

Far from being delivered to the queen, as de Rohan believed it would be, the necklace was quickly taken to Paris and then London, where it was broken up and sold.

When the first instalment wasn't paid, the jewellers went directly to the queen, whereupon the plot was quickly uncovered. De Rohan was sent to the Bastille; Jeanne de la Motte was sentenced to life imprisonment but managed to escape to London two years later. In 1786 the cardinal was acquitted but was stripped of all his offices. Most of the other people who had conspired in the intrigue were also acquitted. Ironically, the person who suffered the most as a result of the scandal was Marie-Antoinette, as the public was confirmed in its belief that she was both a spendthrift and a person of little moral character. ■

---

flanked the south entrance to the cathedral (now replaced by copies), are in Room VI. Synagoga is shown holding a broken lance in her right hand while the tablets of the law slip from her left.

The **Château des Rohan**, also known as the Palais Rohan (☎ 88.32.48.95), at 2 Place du Château was built between 1732 and 1742 as a residence for the city's prince-bishops, one of whom, Cardinal Louis de Rohan, later become famous for his role in the notorious Affair of the Diamond Necklace of 1785 (see the Diamond Necklace Affair aside).The chateau houses three museums, each with its own 15FF entrance fee.

The **Musée Archéologique** in the basement was reopened in 1992 after extensive renovation. It covers the period from one million BC to 800 AD. The **Musée des Arts Décoratifs** on the ground floor includes a series of lavish rooms that illustrate the life-style of the rich during the 18th century. Louis XV and Marie-Antoinette once slept here (in 1744 and 1770 respectively). There are also rooms dedicated to 18th century faïence from Strasbourg and Hagenau and oversize public clocks (and their inner workings). The **Musée des Beaux-Arts**, which has a rather staid collection of French,

Spanish, Italian, Dutch and Flemish painters from the 14th to the 19th centuries, is on the 1st floor.

The **Musée d'Art Moderne** (☎ 88.32. 48.95) at 5 Place du Château (2nd floor) has a fine collection of modern painting and sculpture from the impressionists (circa 1870) to the present. Its collection – only a tiny part of which is on display at any one time – includes works by Monet, Manet, Chagall, Klimt and lots of other big names. If all goes according to plan, much more of the collection will be on view when the museum moves to new, much-expanded quarters at Place Sainte Marguerite in 1996.

The **Musée Alsacien** (☎ 88.35.55.36) at 23 Quai Saint Nicolas, housed in three 16th and 17th-century houses, affords a fascinating glimpse into Alsatian life over the centuries. Displays in the two dozen rooms include kitchen equipment (stoves, ceramics, biscuit cutters), colourful furniture, children's toys and even a tiny, 18th-century synagogue.

The **Musée Historique** (☎ 88.32.25.63) at 3 Place de la Grande Boucherie illustrates the history of Strasbourg. It is housed in the late 16th-century Grande Boucherie, once the city slaughterhouse.

ALSACE

La Petite France

Crisscrossed by narrow streets, canals and locks, this small quarter in the south-west corner of the Île is picture-postcard material and everyone knows it. The half-timbered houses, meticulously maintained and sprouting veritable thickets of geraniums, attract multitudes of tourists, but its Alsatian atmosphere is indeed charming, especially early in the morning or late in the evening.

Jewish Sites

There seems to have been a Jewish community in Strasbourg during Roman times. The city had a sizeable Jewish population in the Middle Ages, but despite protection from the bishop it suffered a number of massacres and expulsions. From 1399 to 1791, Jews were forbidden to live in Strasbourg or even stay there after nightfall – all Jews had to leave the city before the sounding of a special horn. During this period, many Jews took up residence in the villages around Strasbourg. Today, there are about 15,000 Jews in Strasbourg. The Jewish community radio station, Radio Judaica, broadcasts on 102.9 MHz FM.

Strasbourg's main synagogue, **Synagogue de la Paix** (Synagogue of Peace), which was built in 1958 along with the Centre Communautaire (Jewish community centre) situated in the same complex, is 300 metres north-east of Place de la République at 16 Ave de la Paix. It is on the south-western edge of the grassy, tree-shaded Contades park in a neighbourhood with a sizeable Jewish population. Part of the complex was desecrated by neo-Nazi thugs in late 1992.

The city's main prewar synagogue, which was inaugurated in 1898, was burned and then razed by the Germans in 1940 in an effort to obliterate all traces of the Strasbourgeois Jewish community, whose members had, by the time of the fire, either fled the city (along with a good part of the population) or been loaded onto trucks and expelled. At the site on Quai Kléber where the synagogue once stood, in a little park called **Square de l'Ancienne Synagogue**, is a monument recalling the structure.

Parc de l'Orangerie

The shaded paths, flowerbeds, children's playgrounds and swan-dotted lake of Parc de l'Orangerie are a favourite with local families, especially on sunny Sunday afternoons. From April to mid-October (except when it's raining), you can rent **rowing boats** (☎ 88.61.07.89) on Lac de l'Orangerie for 25FF per half-hour. The **bowling alley** (☎ 88.61.36.24), which overlooks the lake, is open on Monday from 2 pm to midnight, Tuesday to Friday from 11 am to 1 am and weekends from 10 am to midnight (2 am on Saturday night). Games cost between 10FF (before 3 pm on weekdays) and 27FF (after 8 pm and on weekends); bowling shoes are 7FF. This place also has billiard tables.

The Orangerie is across Ave de l'Europe from Palais de l'Europe, two km north-east of the cathedral. To get there from Rue du Vieux Marché aux Vins or Place Broglie, take bus No 3, 13 or 23 to the Orangerie stop. To get to the park's eastern end, you can also take bus No 15 from the train station or Place Broglie to the Quartier des XV stop; then, on foot, walk in the direction the bus was going for a few hundred metres along Rue du Conseil des Quinze. As you can see from the architecture, many of the grand apartment buildings between the Orangerie and the Grande Île were built when Strasbourg was part of Imperial Germany.

Other Parks

Just across the Fossé du Faux Rempart from Place Broglie is **Place de la République**, a round, flower-filled formal garden encircled by impressive public buildings: the Prefecture, the Palais du Rhin (the former imperial palace), the Théâtre National and the Bibliothèque Nationale et Universitaire (National & University Library). The war memorial in the middle conveys the tragedy of war rather than its ostensible glory.

The **Contades**, a shaded, grassy park with a children's playground, is two blocks north of Place de la République. The large building on the park's western edge is the city's main synagogue (see Jewish Sites).

Palais de l'Europe

There are free tours of Palais de l'Europe – headquarters of the Council of Europe and meeting-place of the European Parliament – from Monday to Friday at 2.30 pm *except* when the parliament is in session. The tours are open to both individuals and groups, but the nationality of the latter determines the language used, which is rarely English. Individuals should call ☎ 88.17.50.07 a day in advance to make reservations (and find out what language the next day's tour will be conducted in). Tours begin at the Centre de Presse on Allée Spach.

Hiking

The Strasbourg section (☎ 88.35.30.76) of the Club Vosgien, a regional hiking organisation, has hikes (or ski trips in winter) in which travellers are invited to participate. Reservations for their trips, which are usually held on Sundays and Wednesdays, should be made a couple of days ahead at the club's office at 71 Ave des Vosges. It is staffed Monday to Friday from 5 to 7 pm and Saturday from 10 am to noon. The price is usually 45 to 60FF for nonmembers. The office also sells maps and topoguides and can provide hiking information.

Organised Tours

City Tours For information on guided tours of Strasbourg and nearby areas, contact the tourist office or call ☎ 88.37.67.37. CTS, the local public transport company, runs tours of the city by *mini-train* (motorised train) from Place du Château (just south of the cathedral).

Boat Tours Boat excursions around Strasbourg (☎ 88.84.13.13 for information, 88.32.75.25 for the dock) leave from the *embarcadère* (dock) behind the Château des Rohans. From mid-February to March and in November and December, there are three departures a day; from April to October there are a lot more, including – from May to early October – night cruises. The 1¼-hour excursions cost 33FF (17.50FF for students and children under 17) during the day and slightly more at night.

Brewery Tours Alsace brews something like half of France's domestically made beer. Two of Strasbourg's largest *brasseries* (breweries) offer guided tours of their production facilities to people who like beer enough to call ahead for reservations.

Brasseries Heineken (☎ 88.62.90.80) is 2.5 km north of the Grande Île at 4 Rue Saint Charles (near the corner of Route de Bischwiller) in Strasbourg's inner suburb of Schiltigheim (postcode 67300). There are free, two-hour tours in French, German or English (depending on group bookings) at various times on weekdays between 8 am and 4 pm. Reservations are mandatory. To get there, take bus No 4, 14 or 24 (northbound) from Place Kléber and get off at the Schiltigheim-Mairie stop.

La Marseillaise

Though you'd never guess from the name, France's stirring national anthem, *La Marseillaise*, was written in Strasbourg. In April 1792, at the beginning of the war with Austria, the mayor of Strasbourg – in whose city a garrison was getting ready for battle – suggested that the Revolutionary army should have a catchy and patriotic tune to sing while marching off to bring the blessings of liberty to the rest of Europe. He approached Claude Rouget de Lisle, a young army engineer with a minor reputation as a composer, who after a furious all-night effort came up with a marching song entitled *Chant de guerre de l'armée du Rhin* (War Song of the Army of the Rhine). It was first performed in the mayor's house (now Strasbourg's Banque de France building) by the mayor himself. The soul-stirring tune (and its bloody lyrics) achieved rapid popularity, and by August it was on the lips of volunteer troops from Marseille as they marched northward to defend the Revolution. ∎

Brasseries Kronenbourg (☎ 88.27.41.59) is 2.5 km north-west of the Grande Île at 68 Route d'Oberhausbergen. Free French-language tours are conducted four or five times a day Monday to Friday except on holidays. When you call to make reservations, ask when there will be tour in English. To get to the brewery, take bus No 7 (towards Hautepierre Maillon) from Rue du Vieux Marché aux Vins or Place Broglie and get off at the Jacob stop.

Festivals

Christmas is celebrated with great festivity in Alsace. One of the region's biggest fairs is Strasbourg's Christmas market, held on Place Broglie from early December until Christmas Eve.

The Festival International de Musique is held in June or July. Various other cultural events are also held in summer. Musica, a festival of contemporary music, is held in September or October.

Places to Stay – bottom end

Many of the city's hotel rooms are reserved up to a year in advance from Monday to Thursday during the one week each month from September to June when the European Parliament is in session. However, unplanned cancellations do sometimes free up rooms at the last minute. To find out exactly when the parliament will be meeting, call the tourist office before you arrive in Strasbourg.

Camping The municipal *Camping de la Montagne Verte* (☎ 88.30.25.46) at 2 Rue Robert Forrer, open from March to October, is a wide expanse of grass partly shaded by young trees. It costs 10.50FF to park and pitch a tent; each adult is charged 10.50FF. There is excellent bus service (see Auberge de Jeunesse René Cassin under Hostels) – get off at the Nid de Cigognes stop, which is one stop past the Auberge de Jeunesse stop. Walk northward along Rue du Schnokeloch, which passes under the train tracks, and take the first right onto Rue Robert Forrer.

The *Auberge de Jeunesse René Cassin*

(see the next section) has room to pitch tents at the back. The charge, including breakfast, is 38FF per person.

Hostels Strasbourg has three decent hostels to choose from. The shiny, modern *Centre International d'Accueil et de Rencontre Unioniste de Strasbourg* (CIARUS; ☎ 88.32.12.12; fax 88.32.17.37), a 200-bed Protestant-run hostel at 7 Rue Finkmatt, is about one km north-east of the train station. People of all ages and faiths are welcome, and no hostelling card is necessary. Per-person tariffs (including breakfast) range from 75FF in a room with six or eight beds to 105FF in a double, probably outfitted with a bunk bed. Singles are 170FF. Rooms are single-sex and equipped with shower and toilet. CIARUS also has rooms and facilities for the handicapped. Curfew is at 1 am.

No reservations are accepted from individuals, but even during busy periods (eg European Parliament sessions – yes, at least one parliamentarian does stay here) they usually have space in the morning. To get to CIARUS from the train station, take bus No 10 or 20 (northbound) and get off at the Place de Pierre stop.

The *Auberge de Jeunesse René Cassin* (☎ 88.30.26.46; fax 88.30.35.16) is at 9 Rue de l'Auberge de Jeunesse, about two km south-west of the station. A bed costs 62FF in a room for four to six people and 88/136FF in a double/single, including breakfast. Reception is open daily from 7 am to noon, 1 to 7 pm and 8 to 11.30 pm. Curfew is at midnight (1 am from March to October). A hostelling card is mandatory.

The hostel is linked with the city centre (Rue du Vieux Marché aux Vins) and the train station area (Quai Altorffer) by bus Nos 3, 13 and 23, which run every 10 to 15 minutes (less frequently on weekends) from 6 am to 11.30 pm. Get off at the Auberge de Jeunesse stop, walk a few metres in the direction the bus was going to Rue de l'Auberge de Jeunesse and turn right.

The *Centre International de Rencontres du Parc du Rhin* (☎ 88.60.10.20; fax 88.61.33.37), near the Rhine on Rue des

Cavaliers, is six km east of the train station near Pont de l'Europe (the bridge over the Rhine). This place is relatively expensive: singles/doubles/triples cost 171/106/91FF per person, including breakfast. To get there from in front of the train station or Place Kléber, take bus No 11 or 21 to the Parc du Rhin stop and walk south for about 800 metres. The last bus is at 11.20 pm. From Kehl (Germany) take CTS bus No 21.

Hotels Thanks to Strasbourg's many expense-account visitors, the vast majority of the city's hotels have been upgraded to at least two stars, leaving relatively few one-star places for budget travellers.

Hotels – Train Station Area The one-star *Hôtel Le Colmar* (☎ 88.32.16.89) at 1 Rue du Maire Kuss (1st floor) may have linoleum floors and sound-tiled ceilings, but it's cheap and convenient and the rooms are clean and serviceable. Singles/doubles/triples start at 105/125/150FF with washbasin and bidet and cost 145/160/190FF with shower. Rooms for one/two people with shower and toilet cost 160/175FF. Hall showers cost 17FF. Breakfast is 19FF.

The *Hôtel Weber* (☎ 88.32.36.47; fax 88.32.19.08) at 22 Blvd de Nancy, the continuation of Blvd de Metz, is 400 metres south of the train station. This is hardly the most attractive or exciting part of Strasbourg, but it's convenient if you arrive by train. Nondescript singles/doubles cost 95 to 105FF (with washbasin) or 180/220FF (with shower and toilet). Triples and quads with shower and toilet are 270FF. Hall showers are 12FF and breakfast is 21FF.

Nearby, the *Hôtel Astoria* (☎ 88.32.17.22) at 7a Rue de Rosheim has plain singles/doubles from 100/120FF and an assortment of rooms for three to five persons from 180FF. Showers are free.

Hotels – Grande Île A good bet is the *Hôtel Patricia* (☎ 88.32.14.60; fax 88.32.19.08) at 1a Rue du Puits, a quiet backstreet near Rue des Serruriers. Its generally dark, rustic interior fits in well with the local ambience.

Ordinary singles/doubles with washbasin cost 105/130FF; doubles with shower are 170FF (180FF with shower and toilet). There's a 12FF charge to use the hall shower. Breakfast costs 21FF. Reception is open from 8 am to 8 pm.

The *Hôtel Michelet* (☎ 88.32.47.38) is a small, family-run establishement with one star at 48 Rue du Vieux Marché aux Poissons, a busy street whose name means Street of the Old Fish Market. Double rooms cost 105FF with washbasin, 150FF with shower and 175FF with shower and toilet. Hall showers cost 12FF. An extra bed is only 20 or 25FF. Breakfast in your room costs a mere 15FF. From the train station, take bus No 1 or 11 and get off at Place Gutenberg.

The friendly, one-star *Hôtel Jura* (☎ 88.32.12.72) at 5 Rue du Marché is about equidistant from the train station and the cathedral. Old-fashioned but cosy doubles cost 130FF (with washbasin and bidet) and 180FF (with shower). Triples with shower are 200FF. Room 7 has a sexy red neon 'hôtel' sign right outside the window, but it's equipped with two twin beds! Hall showers are free and breakfast is 20FF. The hotel is closed between noon and 2 pm.

Places to Stay – middle
The city is amply provided with tourist-class hotels.

Train Station Area Place de la Gare and nearby Rue du Maire Kuss are lined with neon-lit two and three-star hotels. The *Hôtel du Rhin* (☎ 88.32.35.00; fax 88.23.51.92) at 7-8 Place de la Gare has rooms starting from 170FF.

The older *Hôtel de Bruxelles* (☎ 88.32.45.31; fax 88.32.06.22), a two-star place at 13 Rue Kuhn, has clean and fairly large singles/doubles/triples/quads with shower, toilet and TV for 215/235/300/340FF. They also have a few rooms for one, two and three people for 130 to 180FF. This place offers very good value.

Cathedral Area The *Hôtel de la Cruche d'Or* (☎ 88.32.11.23) at 6 Rue des Tonneliers was upgraded to two stars in late 1992. Despite its proximity to the cathedral, this place is remarkably peaceful at night, as cars are only allowed on the street below between 6 and 10 am.

Across the river, the superbly situated but somewhat flimsily built *Hôtel Hommelet Rouge* (☎ 88.35.48.92; fax 88.24.08.92) at 2 Quai des Bateliers has singles/doubles for 220/250FF. An extra bed is 70FF. Breakfast costs 25FF.

Also on the south bank of the Ill, the two-star *Hôtel de l'Ill* (☎ 88.36.20.01; fax 88.20.94.94) at 8 Rue des Bateliers has singles/doubles for 145/170FF (with wash-basin), 180/210FF (with shower) and 215/250FF (with shower and toilet). Hall showers are free. Breakfast costs 25FF.

The *Hôtel Trois Roses* (☎ 88.36.56.95; fax 88.35.06.14) at 7 Rue de Zurich has comfort-able but pretty small singles/doubles with TV and minibar for 270/370FF. The largest doubles, which cost 445FF, can take a third bed for 60FF extra. Several rooms are outfit-ted for handicapped guests. A continental/buffet breakfast costs 42/52FF. There's no charge to use the sauna. Free parking is available behind the hotel.

Places to Eat
Strasbourg has a lot more Turkish restaurants than most other French cities. In winter, a bag of roasted chestnuts, sold by street vendors for 20FF, is a good way to warm up.

Restaurants – Cathedral Area
The immediate vicinity of the cathedral has lots of touristy restaurants, but they can't be described as cheap. For details on winstubs in this area, see the Winstubs listing.

In the area north-east of the cathedral are a number of places popular with students and other locals. *Pinocchio* (☎ 88.36.56.50) at 4 Place Saint Étienne is a small place with good pizzas from 35FF. The relaxed and immensely popular *Aldo Pizzeria* (☎ 88.36.00.49) at 8 Rue du Faisan has design-it-your-self pizzas with a choice of 29 toppings (40FF), huge salads with 36 possible in-gredients (39FF), tartes flambées, pasta

dishes and ice-cream desserts. It is open daily from 11.30 am to 2 pm and 6.30 to 11.30 pm. Home (or hotel) delivery (☎ 88.37.95.15) is available daily from 10.30 am to 2 pm and 5.30 to 11.30 pm.

For Breton crepes in a relaxing environ-ment, try *La Korrygane* (☎ 88.37.07.34) on discreet Place du Marché Gayot, off Rue des Frères. Local specialities can be sampled at *Au Coin du Feu* (☎ 88.35.44.85) at 10 Rue de la Râpe, which has decent *menus* starting at 59FF, though à la carte dishes are consid-erably pricier.

What is said to be the world's largest cheese platter is prepared at *La Cloche à Fromage* (☎ 88.23.13.19) at 27 Rue des Tonneliers. Unfortunately, the prices are no more modest than the platter's dimensions. *Délice* at 17 Rue de la Division Leclerc has dine-in or takeaway doner kebabs from 16FF.

If you're in the mood for something exotic, you might try *Spécialités Réunion-naises* at 11 Rue Sainte Hélène, about 500 metres west of the cathedral. This place serves the cuisine of the French Indian Ocean island of Réunion. Main dishes cost 49 to 62FF.

Slightly south of Place d'Austerlitz try the popular *Adan* (☎ 88.35.70.84) at 6 Rue Sédillot, which is more like a coffee shop than a restaurant. *Menus* start at 45FF. It is open Monday to Saturday from noon to 2 pm only.

Restaurants – Petite France
Petite France's many restaurants include *Au Pont Saint Martin* (☎ 88.32.45.13) at 15 Rue des Moulins, which specialises in Alsatian dishes, including choucroute (62FF) and baeckeoffe (available daily for 78FF). Vege-tarians can order the fricassée de champignons (mushroom fricassee; 42FF). The lunch *menu* costs 52FF. Au Pont Saint Martin is open every day from noon to 2.30 pm and 6 to 11 pm.

Restaurants – Train Station Area
Res-taurant Le Cappodoce (☎ 88.23.00.25, 88.32.88.95) at 15 Rue Kuhn serves excel-

lent, freshly prepared Turkish food in an informal dining room. Main meat or chicken dishes cost 45 to 70FF, and salads cost 15 to 25FF. Meals are served from noon to 2.30 pm and 6 pm to midnight daily except Sunday at midday.

Restaurants – Kosher The *cafeteria* of the ORT-Laure Weil school (☎ 88.36.17.71) at 11 Rue Sellénick serves *cacher* (kosher) lunch (noon to 1 pm) and dinner (7 to 8 pm) every day of the week except during school holidays (eg at Passover, during July and August and at the end of December). Local students can use their magnetic CROUS card; nonstudents can buy a meal ticket for 26FF except on the Sabbath. You must have reservations for Friday dinner and Saturday lunch – drop by on Thursday.

Restaurant Chalom (☎ 88.36.56.30) in the Centre Communautaire, which is in same complex as Synagogue de la Paix at 16 Ave de la Paix, serves lunch daily, except Saturday, from noon to 2 pm. It is closed from mid-July to mid-August.

Pâtisserie P Meyer, a kosher (dairy) pâtisserie and salon de thé at 9 Rue de la Nuée Bleue, is open Monday to Thursday from 7.30 am to 7 pm, on Friday from 7.30 am until sometime between 2 pm (in winter) and 5 pm (in summer) and – when they don't have a wedding to cater for – on Sunday from 7.30 am to 1 pm.

Winstubs *Winstub Strissel* (☎ 88.32.14.73), which is near the cathedral at 5 Place de la Grande Boucherie, has a typical winstub ambience, with wooden floors, benches and panelling and colourful stained-glass windows. A quarter-litre of wine will cost 14 to 26FF. *Menus* are available for 53 and 66FF. This place is open Tuesday to Saturday from 10 am to 11 pm, though their hearty Alsatian meals are served only from 11.45 am to 2 pm and 6.30 to 9.30 pm.

Winstub Pfifferbrieder (☎ 88.32.15.43) at 9 Place du Marché aux Cochons de Lait is open Monday to Saturday from 11 am to 11 pm.

In the Petite France area, try *À La Mouche* (☎ 88.36.04.18) at 43 Rue Finkwiller, which is open daily from noon to 2 pm and 6.30 to 11 pm. Baeckeoffe (63FF) is available on Friday and Saturday nights.

Bierstubs *Le Trou* (☎ 88.36.91.04), in a vaulted brick cellar at 5 Rue des Couples, serves the usual bierstub munchies (tarte flambée for 25FF, pretzels for 5FF each) as well as 100 to 150 kinds of beer. Prices for a demi on tap start at 14FF; most bottles are in the 25 to 33FF range. Le Trou is open daily from 9 pm (8 pm from mid-September to March) to 4 am.

At *L'Académie de la Bière* (☎ 88.32.61.08, 88.23.21.83) at 17 Rue Adolphe Seyboth, you can sit at rough-hewn wooden tables and sip your 10FF beer (15FF after 8 pm) every day from 8 pm (11 am on weekends) to 4 am. Breakfast costs 18FF.

Student Restaurants Unfortunately for student travellers, to get into most of Strasbourg's university restaurants, you need a *carte à memoire*, an ultramodern magnetic debit card which costs a minimum of 200FF (including a 50FF deposit). It is on sale at the CROUS offices (☎ 88.36.16.91) at 1 Quai du Maire Diétrich. This is the kind of 'technological progress' that can turn usually reasonable student backpackers into sworn Luddites...

There are three small consolations: it is possible to get reimbursed for the unused portion of your magnetic card; some CROUS-affiliated restaurants let you buy a meal ticket at the door for about 25FF; and if you know a card-carrying local student with whom you'd like to dine, they can get you in on their magnetic card.

The student restaurants with good local reputations include *FEC* at 3 Place Saint Étienne and *Gallia* (☎ 88.35.22.32) at 1 Quai du Maire Dietrich. The latter is strong on substance if not on selection, but for vegetarians the choice is limited. Both are open weekdays (and alternate weekends) from around 11.30 am to 1 pm and 6.30 to 8 pm. At Gallia (but not FEC) you can pay in cash, but come early to beat the queue.

Self-Catering Great places for picnicking include the *quais* along the Ill and the Fossé du Faux Rempart, Place de la République, the Contades park and Parc de l'Orangerie. If a more purely urban environment doesn't bother you, there are benches at Place Kléber, Place Gutenberg and Place Broglie.

If you're around Place Kléber, there's a *Suma supermarket* on the 3rd floor of the Galeries Lafayette-Magmod store at 34 Rue du 22 Novembre. It has an in-house boulangerie, a large selection of cheese, fruit, vegetables of excellent quality and lots of wine. It is open Monday to Saturday from 9 am to 7 pm.

In the Petite France area, the *Point Coop* grocery at 18 Rue Finkwiller is open daily, except Wednesday afternoon and Sunday, from 8.30 am to 12.15 pm and 3 to 7 pm (2.30 to 5 pm on Saturday). The *boulangerie* at 14 Rue Finkwiller, which has multicereal breads, is open Monday to Friday from 5.30 am to 7 pm and Saturday from 5.30 am to 1 pm.

Near the train station, there is an *Alder supermarket* across the street from 42 Rue du Faubourg National. It is open Monday to Friday from 8 am to 12.30 pm and 2.30 to 7 pm and on Saturday from 8 am to 1 pm and 2.30 to 6 pm. There's a *boulangerie-pâtisserie* with extraordinary chocolates (about 2FF each) down the block at 30 Rue du Faubourg National. It is open Monday to Saturday from 7 am to 7 pm and Sunday from 8 am to 6 pm.

Entertainment

On summer nights, the lively pedestrianised streets of the Grande Île ring with the sounds of street musicians and local folk bands.

Live Music The *Café des Anges* (☎ 88.37. 12.67) at 5 Rue Sainte Catherine, whose extreme informality positively oozes mellowness, is a *bar à musique* that puts on live concerts almost every night at around 9.30 or 10 pm. Sunday night is dedicated to rock, while on other nights the programme may be anything from salsa to North African rai. Tickets generally cost 30 to 40FF, but the entrance fee to the *bœufs* (jam sessions) on Monday (blues) and Tuesday (jazz) is just 10FF. No reservations are necessary (or even possible). Beers are 9FF (15FF after 10 pm). The café is open Monday to Friday from 11 am until very, very late; on Saturday from 3 pm to 1 am (or later); and on alternating Sundays from 7 pm to 11 pm or midnight. This place may be closed during August.

The friendly *Zanzib' Art bar* (☎ 88.37. 91.81) at 1 Place Saint Étienne has live music performances in the *caveau* (cellar). There is a fee for some of the concerts, which usually begin at about 10 pm. Beers start at 8FF (12FF to 15FF after 9 pm) but Belgian beers are pricier. Coffee is 6FF (10FF after 9 pm).

Cinemas Strasbourg has two movie houses that screen nondubbed (v.o.) flicks. The five-screen *Cinéma Club* (☎ 88.32.01.48) at 32 Rue du Vieux Marché aux Vins charges 42FF (31FF for students and people over 60, except on weekends).

The four-screen *Cinéma Star* (☎ 88.22. 66.42), which is nearby at 27 Rue du Jeu des Enfants, charges 40FF (30FF for people under 18, students and people over 60 except on Saturday evening and Sunday). At both places, everyone gets in for the reduced price on Wednesday.

Bars *Festival Bar Américain* (☎ 88.36. 31.28), a fashionable and rather up-market American-style bar at 4 Rue Sainte Catherine, is open daily from 6 pm (9 pm from October to March) to 4 am. A demi of beer costs 20FF. Check out the ceiling fans, which are all run by what can only be described as a very long fan belt.

Bar des Aviateurs (☎ 88.36.52.69) at 12 Rue des Sœurs, whose poster and photo-covered walls and long wooden counter give the place a forties-ish sort of feel, is open every day from 6 pm to 3 am (4 am on Friday and Saturday nights). Beers are always 20FF.

Things to Buy

Strasbourg's many shopping streets include S-shaped Rue du 22 Novembre and Rue des Francs Bourgeois. The city's most fashionable clothing shops are on Rue des

Hallebardes. Close to Place Kléber are the city's two largest department stores: Galeries Lafayette-Magmod at 34 Rue du 22 Novembre and Printemps at 1-5 Rue de la Haute Montée, the continuation of Rue du Vieux Marché aux Vins.

Getting There & Away

Air Aéroport Strasbourg International (☎ 88.64.67.67, 88.78.40.99) is 12 km south-west of the city centre (towards Molsheim) near the village of Entzheim.

Train The train station information office (☎ 88.22.50.50) is open Monday to Friday from 8 am to 8 pm and on weekends and holidays from 9 am to 7 pm. The terminal building is open 24 hours a day. Tickets bought here carry a station tax of up to 6FF.

Certain especially popular trains to/from Paris (247FF; four hours; at least nine a day) – but not to/from other destinations – require payment of a supplement of up to 54FF in 2nd class. Overnight sleeper service to Paris is available.

Strasbourg is well-connected by rail with Colmar (51FF; 30 to 50 minutes; 15 to 22 a day), Nancy (90FF; 1½ hours; 10 a day), Metz (104FF; about 1½ hours; seven a day) and Lyon (five hours; five a day). There are also connections to Chamonix (307FF; nine to 12 hours; two or three a day in winter) and Nice (435FF; 11 hours; three a day), among other places.

Internationally, there are regular trains to Basel (Bâle; 95FF; 1¼ hours; 11 to 17 a day), Geneva (325FF; 4½ or five hours; 10 a day), Amsterdam (406FF; 10 hours; four a day), Frankfurt (188FF; three hours), Munich (München in German; 332FF; at least five hours; six a day), Hamburg (604FF) and Vienna (631FF; 10 hours; three a day). Service is most frequent on Sunday and least frequent on Saturday.

Bus The information office (☎ 88.28.20.30) of the bus station, which is on Place d'Austerlitz, is open Monday to Saturday from 7.30 am to 6.30 pm. Eurolines (☎ 88.22.57.90) has an office north-east of

the cathedral at 5 Rue des Frères but its coaches arrive and depart from the bus station.

Strasbourg city bus No 21 links the train station and Place Kléber with Pont de l'Europe (the bridge over the Rhine) and Marktplatz in Kehl, Germany. CTS line No O runs from Strasbourg's Place des Halles to the town of Obernai about once every one or 1½ hours. The last bus back leaves Obernai at 5.30 pm (6.10 pm on Sunday and holidays).

Car Near the train station, Euro Rent (☎ 88.75.07.75) at 14 Rue Déserte rents small cars with unlimited km for 400FF a day, 500FF for a two-day weekend and 650FF for a three-day weekend. Their office is open from 8 am to noon and 2 to 6 pm daily except Saturday afternoon and Sunday. There's another Euro Rent office at the airport.

A few blocks south, Altrans (☎ 88.75.51.51) at 4 Rue d'Obernai has cars for 430FF a day, including insurance and 200 free km but with 2300FF excess. It is open from 8 am to noon and 2 to 6.30 pm daily except Saturday afternoon, Sunday and holidays. Budget (☎ 88.75.68.29) is at 31 Ave de Nancy.

Getting Around

To/From the Airport The Navette Aéroport (shuttle bus) to the airport (31FF) operates daily from 5.30 am to 8 pm. On weekdays it runs every half-hour, and on weekends there's a bus once every 1½ to three hours. There are stops near the train station (in front of the Hôtel du Rhin at 7-8 Place de la Gare) and at Place Kléber (in front of the American Express office). Timetable information is available from the tourist office.

Bus & Tram Strasbourg's excellent public transport network, CTS, combines good geographical coverage with frequent service. By the mid-1990s the company's buses will be joined by electric trams.

Tickets cost 7FF each if bought on board, but for 24FF (19FF for 4 to 11 year olds) you can get a Multipass (a carnet of five tickets)

ALSACE

from the tourist office, CTS information bureaux, post offices and some tabacs. The tourist office and CTS bureaux also sell the Tourpass (20FF), which is valid for 24 hours of travel from the moment you time-stamp it. The weekly Hebdopass (57FF) is good from Monday to Sunday. Students under 27 can get a Campuspass, which is valid for one calendar month and costs only 105FF.

In the city centre area, bus No 1 is identical to bus Nos 11 and 21 – it's only in the suburbs that their routes diverge. The same goes for Nos 3, 13 and 23 and Nos 4, 14 and 24. Buses from Strasbourg's city centre run until about 11.30 pm.

CTS has Autobus Billets Information offices in the train station (open Monday to Friday from 6.15 am to 6.30 pm except during July and August, when hours are reduced) and next to the American Express office at 31 Place Kléber (open Monday to Friday from 7.30 am to 6.30 pm and on Saturday from 9.30 am to noon and 1.30 to 6 pm). For bus information, call Allobus at ☎ 88.28.20.30.

Taxi Novotaxi (☎ 88.75.19.19) and Taxi (☎ 88.36.13.13) both operate round the clock. There are taxi ranks in front of the train station and at Place Kléber.

Car There are large parking garages at Place Kléber and Place Gutenberg.

Bicycle Rickety bikes can be hired for 40/55FF per half/full day from the train station's left-luggage office (☎ 88.75.41.63), which is signposted as 'Consigne Manuel' and 'Bagages'. It is open daily from 6.30 am to 9 pm. The Grande Île will soon have a number of *pistes cyclables* (bicycle lanes).

AROUND STRASBOURG

For information on Alsace's **Route du Vin** (Wine Route), which runs the length of the region from near Strasbourg southward via Colmar to Thann, see the Route du Vin section following.

COLMAR

The colourful town of Colmar (population 65,000), capital of the département that produces Alsace's fruity, dry wines, sits on the plain between the Vosges Mountains and the Rhine; it is almost exactly midway between Strasbourg and Basel, Switzerland (about 70 km from each). The picturesque town centre is a maze of cobbled pedestrian malls and restored, Alsatian-style buildings from the late Middle Ages and the Renaissance. Many streets are enlivened by half-timbered houses painted in bold tones of blue, orange, red or green. The world-famous Musée d'Unterlinden is home to the spectacular *Issenheim Altarpiece*.

Colmar is at its liveliest during ten days in the first half of August, when the town throws its annual Foire des Vins (see Festivals). Many villages along the Route du Vin (see the Route du Vin listing), which can be explored by car or bus using Colmar as a base, have similar celebrations that continue to the end of summer. Colmar can easily be visited on a day trip from Strasbourg.

Orientation

Avenue de la République links the charmless area around the train station and bus terminal with the Musée d'Unterlinden and the nearby tourist office, a distance of about one km. The old city is south-east of the Musée d'Unterlinden. Petite Venise runs along the Lauch River at the southern edge of the old city. The town centre, which is largely pedestrianised, can be easily explored on foot.

Information

Tourist Office The efficient tourist office (☎ 89.20.68.92) is opposite the Musée d'Unterlinden at 4 Rue d'Unterlinden. The friendly staff are on duty from 9 am to noon and 2 to 6 pm (7 pm in July and August) daily except Saturday afternoon and Sunday. From Easter to mid-November the tourist office is also open on Saturday afternoon from 2 to 5 pm and Sunday from 9.30 am to 12.30 pm. The tourist office can make reservations for both hotels and rental cars. It is also a good place to pick up a copy of *Actualités Colmar*, a monthly booklet which details what's happening around town.

Money The Banque de France (☎ 89.41.25.78) is roughly midway between the train station and the Musée d'Unterlinden at 46 Ave de la République. It is open on weekdays from 8.45 am to 12.10 pm and 1.50 to 3.30 pm. The tourist office will change money whenever it's open, but the rate is not very good. In addition, there might be a 24-hour banknote exchange machine outside the tourist office. At other times it may be possible to exchange money at the train station's information office.

Post The main post office (☎ 89.41.19.19), near the Banque de France at 36 Ave de la République, is open Monday to Friday from 8 am to 6.30 pm and Saturday from 8 am to noon. Exchange services are available.

Colmar's postcode is 68000.

Laundry Near the tourist office, there's a laundrette in the Centre Golbéry at 59 Cours Sainte Anne; it's open from 7 am to 9 pm daily. South of the old city, the laundrette at 8 Rue Turenne is open daily from 8 am to 9 pm.

Medical Services Hôpital Pasteur (☎ 89.80.40.00 for emergencies) at 39 Ave de la Liberté is 700 metres west of the train station. It is served by bus Nos 1 and 3.

Musée d'Unterlinden

The Unterlinden Museum (☎ 89.20.15.58), housed in a 13th-century former Dominican monastery that was once a stronghold of Rhenish mysticism, is famous around the world for the *Issenheim Altarpiece* (Rétable d'Issenheim), which has been acclaimed as one of the most dramatic and pathos-filled works of art ever created. The carved and gilded wooden figures were made by Nicolas of Hagenau in the late 15th century, while the wooden wings – which originally closed over each other to form a three-layered illustration of events from the New Testa-

ment – were painted by Grünewald between 1511 and 1516.

The Musée d'Unterlinden also displays several other medieval altarpieces, an Alsatian wine cellar (including a 17th-century press), armour and weapons from the 15th and 16th centuries, pewterware, Strasbourg faïence and objects from the Revolutionary period. The basement houses nonpermanent exhibitions of modern art and the museum's archaeological collection.

From November to March the Musée d'Unterlinden is open from 9 am to noon and 2 to 5 pm (closed Tuesday). During the rest of the year, it's open seven days a week from 9 am to noon and 2 to 6 pm (and perhaps between noon and 2 pm as well). Ticket sales end half an hour before closing time in both the morning and the afternoon. Tickets cost 25FF (15FF for students under 30, 20FF for people over 65). For information on guided tours during July and August, contact the tourist office.

Old City

The medieval streets of the old city, including the **Grand' Rue** and **Rue des Marchands,** are lined with half-timbered houses. **Maison Pfister**, which is opposite 36 Rue des Marchands, was built in 1537 and is remarkable for its exterior decoration: delicately painted panels, an elaborate oriel window and a carved, wooden balcony. The house next door at 9 Rue des Marchands, which dates from 1609, has a wooden sculpture of an uptight-looking *marchand* (merchant) on the corner. The **Maison des Têtes** (House of the Heads) at 19 Rue des Têtes, also built in 1609, has a fantastic façade crowded with all manner of carved stone faces and heads. It is now home to the Bourse aux Vins de Colmar, a wine store run by a local vintners' cooperative.

Colmar has a number of small **quartiers** (quarters) – not much more than single streets, really – which, thanks to careful restoration, preserve some of the ambience that existed back when each was home to a specific guild. At the south-eastern end of Rue des Marchands near the **Quartier des Tan-**

ALSACE

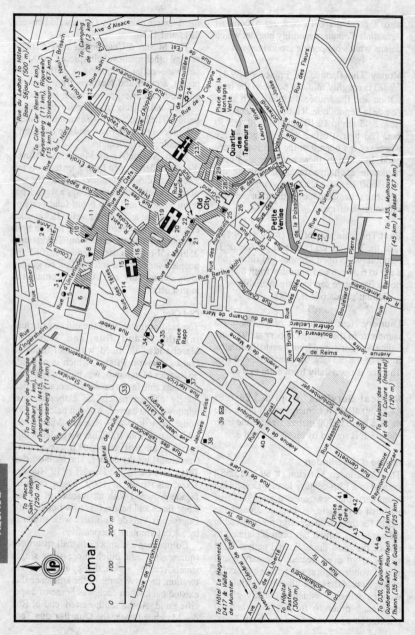

Colmar

neurs (Tanners' Quarter) is the **Ancienne Douane** (Old Customs House), built in 1480. Now used for temporary exhibitions and concerts, it is the town's most interesting example of late medieval civil architecture.

Rue des Tanneurs, with its tall houses and rooftop verandas for drying hides, intersects the colourful **Quai de la Poissonnerie**, the former fishers' quarter, which runs along the River Lauch. This quiet waterway was once used by farmers bringing their goods to market, but these days its main contribution to Colmar's commercial life is to provide the water that has given the pretty **Petite Venise** (Little Venice) area – also known as Quartier de la Krutenau – its rather fanciful name.

Musée Bartholdi

Dedicated to the life and work of the 19th-century Colmar native who gave New York (and the world) the Statue of Liberty, Frédéric Auguste Bartholdi (1834-1904), the Musée Bartholdi (☎ 89.41.90.60) at 30 Rue des Marchands displays some of the sculptor's work and personal memorabilia in the house where he grew up.

From April to October the museum is open daily from 10 am to noon and 2 to 6 pm; it may also stay open at midday. During the rest of the year, it is open on weekends *only* from 10 am to noon and 2 to 5 pm. Admission is 15FF (5F for students).

Churches

The 13th and 14th-century **Collégiale Saint Martin** is an unusually intimate Gothic church on Place de la Cathédrale. Commonly referred to as a cathedral (though Colmar is not the seat of a bishop), this structure of pink sandstone is known for the sober ambulatory around the octagonal choir and, outside, the peculiar, Chinese-style copper spire, erected in 1572. The colourful tile roof is reminiscent of the roofs usually associated with Burgundy. It's open daily from 8 am to 6 pm (7 pm from Easter to September).

Église des Dominicains, a desanctified Gothic church at Place des Dominicains, is known for its 14th and 15th-century stained glass and Martin Schongauer's celebrated painting, *La Vierge au Buisson de Roses* (The Virgin in a Rose Arbour), which dates from 1473. The church is open daily from

ALSACE

mid-March to November only, from 10 am to 6 pm. Entrance costs 8FF (5FF for students under 30).

Hiking

A free mini-topoguide entitled *Proposals of Walking Tours in the Region of Colmar* is available at the tourist office. The information on trail markers and route options is meant to be used with the relevant hiking maps, such as those published by the Club Vosgien (a regional hiking organisation), which cost 52FF each. You might also plan your own route using the network of *sentiers viticoles* (vineyard trails), which take walkers through small villages and among the colourful, fragrant fields of grapevines.

There are buses from Colmar (see Bus under Getting There & Away) to the starting points of a number of interesting trails on the eastern slopes of the Vosges, including those at the Col de la Schlucht in the Vallée de Munster (the whole circuit, including the Sentier des Roches, takes about five hours) and the Col de Bonhomme in the Kaysersberg valley. Both are about 20 km west of Colmar.

Organised Tours

During July and August the tourist office *may* run 1½-hour guided visits in English of the Musée d'Unterlinden (at 10 am) and the town (at 11.30 am). The charge is 20FF for each or 30FF for both.

Festivals

At the Foire Régionale des Vins d'Alsace (Regional Wine Fair of Alsace), which attracts large numbers of visitors to Colmar for 10 days during the first half of August, Alsatian wine producers present their vintages for tasting and sale. The fair is also a good place to sample local food specialities.

From July to mid-September, Colmar plays host to a number of music festivals, including the Festival International de Colmar, held during the first half of July. Details are available from the tourist office.

Places to Stay – bottom end

Colmar is not a cheap overnight halt. During parts of spring and summer, most hotel rooms are booked up in advance, especially around Easter and from mid-July to mid-August. The period of the Foire des Vins (the first half of August) is especially busy. Since many of the hotels in Strasbourg cater primarily to business travellers and therefore tend to have space during holiday periods, you might consider staying in Strasbourg and visiting Colmar on a day trip.

Camping The three-star *Camping de l'Ill* (☎ 89.41.15.94) on Route de Neuf-Brisach in Horbourg-Wihr is just over three km east of the train station. It is open from 1 February to 30 November and costs 12FF for a tent or van plus 14/8FF per adult/child. To get there, take bus No 1 from the train station to the Port du Canal stop – the camping ground is 800 metres on the right.

Hostels Probably your best bet in Colmar is the *Maison des Jeunes et de la Culture* (MJC; ☎ 89.41.26.87), also known as the Centre International de Séjour (CIS), near the station at 17 Rue Camille Schlumberger. It's friendly and more flexible than the official youth hostel and has longer opening hours. A bed costs 39FF per person (not including breakfast) in rooms for two or more people. Reception is open Monday to Saturday from 7 am to noon and 2 to 11 pm and on Sunday from 8 am to noon and 5 to 11 pm.

The *Auberge de Jeunesse Mittelhart* (☎ 89.80.57.39) at 2 Rue Pasteur charges 56FF per person, including breakfast; there's a 20FF supplement if you're in a double. Meals are available for 38 to 60FF. Reception is open from 8 to 10 am and 5 pm to midnight, and curfew is at midnight. From the train station, the hostel is just over two km north along the railway tracks and then west on Route d'Ingersheim. From the train station or the Unterlinden stop, take bus No 4 and get off near the Lycée Technique (technical high school) at the Pont Rouge stop.

Hotels The cosy and convenient *Hôtel La Chaumière* (☎ 89.41.08.99) at 74 Ave de la République, diagonally opposite the train station, has simple and rather small rooms with washbasin and bidet for 150FF. Singles/doubles with shower, toilet and TV are 200/220FF. Hall showers cost 15FF. Reception is closed on Sunday from 2 to 5 pm.

About 700 metres west of the train station, the *Hôtel Le Hagueneck* (☎ 89.80.68.98) at 83 Ave du Général de Gaulle compensates for its distance from the town centre with rooms that start at 120FF.

In the centre of town, the *Hôtel Kempf* (☎ 89.41.21.72) at 1 Ave de la République – a rather noisy street corner – is the cheapest option, with singles/doubles for 110/120FF.

Places to Stay – middle
Near the post office, the *Hôtel Majestic* (☎ 89.41.45.19; fax 89.24.08.62) at 1 Rue de la Gare has singles/doubles from 170/225FF. Private parking is available. The *Hôtel Rhin et Danube* (☎ 89.41.31.44; fax 89.24.54.37), a two-star place at 26 Ave de la République, is about midway between the train station and the Musée d'Unterlinden. It has old-fashioned doubles with high ceilings for 200FF (with shower) or 250FF (with shower and toilet). A triple/quad with bath and toilet is 330/390FF.

In the centre of town, the *Hôtel Ville de Nancy* (☎ 89.41.23.14), which is at No 48 on pedestrianised Rue Vauban, has decent singles/doubles from 150/180FF. A short walk north-east of the centre, the venerable *Hôtel Beau Séjour* (☎ 89.41.37.16; fax 89.41.43.07) at 25 Rue du Ladhof, which has been around since 1913, was recently renovated. Single/doubles with all the amenities start at 230/260FF.

The *Hôtel Primo* (☎ 89.24.22.24; fax 89.24.55.96) at 5 Rue des Ancêtres is two blocks north of the Musée d'Unterlinden. The rooms for one or two people, accessible by lift, are modern in a tacky sort of way and cost 175FF (with a washbasin and TV) or 250FF (with a shower, toilet and TV). Hall showers are free.

Places to Stay – top end
The luxurious *Hôtel Terminus-Bristol* (☎ 89.23.59.59; fax 89.23.92.26), founded in 1925, is right across the street from the train station at 7 Place de la Gare. Singles/doubles start at 350/500FF.

Places to Eat
Colmar's gastronomical options are great for the tastebuds but not for the beltline – or the wallet.

Restaurants In terms of both cuisine and décor, one of Colmar's most enjoyable splurges can be had at *Le Petit Bouchon* (☎ 89.23.45.57) at 11 Rue d'Alspach. Set in an old Alsatian house, this place has *menus* from 78FF. It is closed on Wednesday and Thursday at midday as well as during the last week of July and first week of August.

La Maison Rouge (☎ 89.23.53.22) at 9 Rue des Écoles specialises in Alsatian cuisine, including spit-roasted ham (53FF). The four-course *menu* costs 73FF. It is open from noon to 2.30 pm and 6.30 to 9.30 pm daily except Sunday evening and Monday at midday. *Unterlinden* (☎ 89.41.18.73), at 2 Rue d'Unterlinden next to the tourist office, has average-priced local cuisine. It's closed Sunday night and Tuesday.

In the heart of the old city, *Le Bec Fin* (☎ 89.41.73.76) at 8 Place du Marché aux Fruits is a cosy tearoom known for its winter sun and year-round ice creams. Light dishes such as quiche cost 38FF. It is open Tuesday to Sunday from 10 am to 10 pm. *Au Forum* (☎ 89.23.55.66) at 6 Place de la Mairie (next to one of the entrances to the Monoprix supermarket) is a tearoom with a good selection of salads. *Menus* start at 48FF. It is open Monday to Saturday from 8 am to 6.30 pm.

Cafeterias For the truly budget conscious, the *Cafétéria Monoprix* (☎ 89.41.22.57), upstairs at 4 Quai de la Sinn (across the square from the Musée d'Unterlinden), has *menus* for 25 to 50FF. It's open Monday to Saturday from 7.30 am to 9.30 pm.

The inexpensive *Flunch cafeteria* (☎ 89.23.56.56) at 8 Ave de la République is

ALSACE

open daily from 11.30 am to 2.30 pm and 5.30 to 9.30 pm.

Self-Catering There is a *Monoprix super-market* with an in-house boulangerie directly across the square from the entrance to the Musée d'Unterlinden. It is open Monday to Saturday from 8.30 am to 7.30 pm (8 pm on Friday). Slightly out of the centre, one block west of Hôtel Ville de Nancy on Route de Neuf-Brisach, is a large *Suma supermarket*; it is open the same hours as the Monoprix. Plenty of parking is available.

Colmar has two weekly *food markets*: one on Thursday morning at Place de l'Ancienne Douane and the other on Saturday morning at Place Saint Joseph, which is 800 metres west of the old city and 600 metres south-east of the Auberge de Jeunesse Mittelhart.

In the old city, *Fromagerie Saint Nicolas* at 18 Rue Saint Nicolas, which sells only the finest traditionally made cheeses, is open Monday afternoon to Saturday from 9 am to 12.30 pm and 2 to 7 pm. For exotic fish and seafood – including fresh, ready-to-eat crevettes (prawns) and various seafood salads – try *Poissonnerie Colmarée*, in Petite Venise at 13 Quai de la Poisonnerie. It is open Tuesday to Saturday from 7 am to 12.15 pm and 2.15 to 7.15 pm (5 pm on Saturday).

Getting There & Away

Train The train station is about one km south-west of the tourist office and the quaint part of town. The information office (☎ 89.24.50.50) is open Monday to Saturday from 8 am to 7.30 pm and on Sunday from 9.10 am to 8 pm. There is frequent service to Strasbourg (51FF; 29 to 43 minutes; 12 a day), Mulhouse (38FF; 20 minutes; 16 a day) and Besançon (121FF; two hours; eight a day). To get to Paris's Gare de l'Est, you have to change trains at Strasbourg.

Bus The bus terminal – a parking lot, really – is to the right as you exit the train station. Several companies have buses to neighbouring villages; most follow either the Route du Vin or major highways. Service is severely reduced on Sunday and holidays. Hours are posted at the bus terminal, which is where most buses begin their runs (or at least pick up passengers). The *Actualités Colmar* booklet, available at the tourist office, lists the various companies, their destinations and timetables.

For the car-less, public bus is an excellent way to visit many parts of Alsace's Route du Vin (see the Route du Vin section). Two companies offer service to Riquewihr (11FF; 30 minutes): Pauli (☎ 89.78.25.13), which has six runs a day Monday to Saturday, and Martinken (☎ 89.73.36.07, 89.48.12.22), whose three buses all run in the afternoon (Monday to Friday). Martinken also stops in nearby Ribeauvillé (13FF; 40 minutes). STAHV (☎ 29.34.20.34 in Épinal, 89.41. 40.27 in Colmar) has buses to Kaysersberg (10FF; 30 minutes; 16 a day), which is 12 km north of Colmar. Two other companies, Kunegal (☎ 89.24.65.65, 89.24.65.50) and Sodag, share regular service to points south of Colmar, including Eguisheim (five minutes), Gueberschwihr (15 minutes), Rouffach (30 minutes) and Guebwiller (45 minutes).

Car Citer (☎ 89.24.09.09; fax 89.24.46.26), whose office is two km north of the old city at 4 Rue Timken, has an arrangement whereby you can reserve a vehicle at the tourist office and have it delivered there. Europcar (☎ 89.24.11.80; fax 89.24.46.26) is at Place Rapp, opposite 8 Ave de la République.

Getting Around

Bus Colmar's buses are operated by the local public transit company, TRACE (☎ 89.41. 65.41). All nine lines – which run from Monday to Saturday until 7.30 or 8 pm – stop at the Unterlinden (Point Central) hub, which is next to the tourist office and the Musée d'Unterlinden. Service is drastically reduced on Sunday and holidays, when line Nos 1 to 9 are replaced by line Nos A and B, which run about once an hour between 1 and 6.30 or 7 pm. Unterlinden (Point Central) is linked to the train station by bus Nos 1, 2, 3, 4, 5, A and B; from Monday to Saturday, there's at least one bus every 10 minutes. A

Storks

Cigognes (storks), long a feature of Alsatian folklore, have become something of a regional symbol. The birds traditionally spend the winter in Africa and then migrate to Europe for the warm months, feeding from marshes and building the twig platforms that serve as nests on church steeples, rooftops and tall trees. However, the draining of the marshes along the Rhine and hunting in Africa reduced their numbers catastrophically, and by the early 1980s there were only a couple of pairs left in Alsace.

Centres have now been set up in Alsace to hatch and raise storks in order to establish a permanent Alsatian stork population. Their wings are clipped at an early age in the hope that if the birds' migratory instinct can be bred out of them, they will stay in Alsace throughout the year, delighting the locals and avoiding the dangers posed by lax enforcement of hunting laws along their migratory routes. ■

single ride costs 4.50FF and a carnet of eight tickets is 27FF.

Taxi There's a taxi rank at the station. You can order a taxi 24 hours a day by calling ☎ 89.41.40.19.

Bicycle Cycles Meyer (☎ 89.79.12.47) at 6 Rue du Pont Rouge, which is across Route d'Ingersheim from the Auberge de Jeunesse Mittelhart, rents regular bicycles for 70FF a day and mountain bikes for 90FF. The store is closed on Sunday and Monday. The bikes available from the train station are cheaper: 50FF a day (plus a 500FF deposit). The rental office is open daily from 5 am to 9 pm.

ROUTE DU VIN

Meandering for 120 km along the eastern foothills of the Vosges, the **Route du Vin d'Alsace** (Wine Route of Alsace) wends its way through villages brightened by colourful half-timbered houses, surrounded by vine-clad slopes and guarded by hilltop castles. Combine this with numerous roadside *caves*, where you can sample (*déguster*) Alsace's wines (mostly dry whites), and you have one of the region's busiest tourist tracks. Local tourist offices can supply you with a brochure, *The Wine Route of Alsace*, which details the Route du Vin and gives a bit of information on each village it passes.

The Route du Vin stretches from Marlenheim, about 20 km west of Strasbourg, southward via Colmar to Thann, 35 km futher south-west. En route are some of Alsace's most colourful villages – many extensively rebuilt after being flattened in WW II – such as **Riquewihr**, 15 km north of Colmar. Though often twee and touristy, the area is still a working centre of wine-making, its economy based on 13,000 hectares of vines and the 'liquid gold' they produce.

You're more likely to see storks' nests, perched like flamboyant hats on top of spires, towers or high trees (see the Storks aside), along the Route du Vin than anywhere else in the region.

Getting There & Away

The Route du Vin can be easily visited by car, but it's also possible to explore the area on bicycle or by hopping on and off local buses. For details on these transport options, see Bus under Getting There & Away and Bicycle under Getting Around in the Colmar section. The Colmar tourist office has bus

ALSACE

schedules and can offer suggestions for possible excursions.

ÉCOMUSÉE

The Écomusée (☎ 89.48.23.44), located about 30 km south of Colmar off the A35 to Mulhouse, is a reconstituted Alsatian village modelled on the still-plentiful real thing. Fifty houses were taken from where they originally stood and rebuilt here to create a showcase for the skills of bakers, blacksmiths and other traditional artisans from centuries past. The Écomusée is open all year and costs 48/26FF for adults/children.

MULHOUSE

The modern, industrial city of Mulhouse (population 114,000; pronounced 'Mu-LOOZE'), 45 km south of Colmar, has none of the quaint Alsatian charm that typifies its northern neighbours. But it does have several prestigious museums which are worth a detour if you're an enthusiast of the specialised fields they cover.

The **Musée National de l'Automobile** (☎ 89.42.29.17) at 192 Ave de Colmar displays early motorcars, including Bugattis, Rolls Royces and a host of other aristocratic makes. It is open daily from 10 am to 6 pm except from October to April, when it's closed on Tuesday. The entrance fee is as up-market as the cars on display: 50FF (20FF for students and children).

For steam-train buffs, there's the **Musée Français du Chemin de Fer** (☎ 89.42. 25.67), housed in a disused railway station west of the city centre off the A36 at 2 Rue Alfred de Glehn. It's open daily from 9 am to 5 or 6 pm. Entry is 35FF (15FF for students and children).

The **Musée de l'Impression sur Étoffes** (Museum of Textile Printing; ☎ 89.45. 51.20) at 3 Rue des Bonnes-Gens, next to the post office, has a collection of eight million fabric samples from all over the world. From October to May it is open Wednesday to Monday from 10 am to noon and 2 to 6 pm; from June to mid-September it's open daily from 9 am to 12.30 pm and 2 to 6 pm. Admission for adults/students/children is 24/15/7FF.

Lorraine

The plateau of Lorraine lies west of the Vosges. The region, which is much larger than Alsace, occupies the sprawling Lorraine plateau and nearby areas. The region is bordered by Belgium, Luxembourg and Germany in the north, the plains of Champagne in the west and the Jura region in the south. At its heart is Nancy, one of Lorraine's two main metropolises and among the most refined and beautiful cities in France. It boasts a central square of unequalled beauty and some of the finest examples of Art Nouveau architecture you'll find outside of Brussels or Paris.

The region's other main city is Metz, which in Roman times was on an important north-south trade route. These days it's better known for the stunning stained-glass windows that illuminate its massive cathedral. To the west lies the town of Verdun, its name forever linked to the unimaginable horror of WW I.

History

Lorraine made its first major appearance on the pages of history in 843 with the signing of the Treaty of Verdun, which divided the Frankish territories of the Carolingian emperor Louis I between his three sons. Lothair I got Francia Media, a swathe of territory that stretched from the Netherlands to Italy. Upon the death of Lothair I, his second son, also named Lothair, inherited the northern area, which stretched from the North Sea to the Alps and became known as the kingdom of Lotharingia. In German, Lorraine is still known as Lothringen.

Lorraine was the birthplace of a peasant girl named Jeanne d'Arc (Joan of Arc), who became France's national heroine during the Hundred Years' War by stirring the French royalist army to resist the English and their allies. Born in 1412 in the village of Domrémy, south-west of Nancy, she left home at the tender age of 16, believing that divine voices directed her to support the dauphin Charles, who, thanks to her support (and stubbornness), was crowned Charles VII in Reims (Champagne) in 1429. Lorraine became part of France in 1766 upon the death of Stanislaw I, the former king of Poland and father-in-law of Louis XV, who had been given Lorraine in 1738 by the treaties that ended the War of the Polish Succession (1733-38).

During the 17th century, Lorraine was fortified by the construction of a number of massive fortresses designed by the foremost military architect of the period, Vauban. Along with the Maginot Line, these fortifications are a major port of call for enthusiasts of what is known as 'military tourism'.

Despite the political and social turbulence that accompanied the annexation of part of Lorraine to Germany in 1871, the region's important coal and iron industries continued to develop. Around the turn of the century, the Art Nouveau movement had become established in Nancy, and its legacy can still be enjoyed. Verdun, site of wholesale slaughter in 1916-17, bears silent testimony to the destruction and insanity of WW I.

More recently, Lorraine has had to deal with the decline of its heavy industries, which failed to modernise during the postwar period and were severely hit by the steel slump of the late 1970s. The region's economic plight has been partly alleviated by the introduction of new industries: Renault and Citroën have both set up new factories, as have German plastic manufacturers.

Food

In Lorraine, many a restaurant menu offers *quiche lorraine*, a savoury dish which consists of a pastry shell filled with a mixture of cream, eggs and bacon. Another regional speciality is yellow *mirabelle* plums, sweet in season but at other times best ingested in the form of a local plum brandy of the same name.

NANCY

Nancy (population 330,000) has an air of refinement found nowhere else in industrial Lorraine. With a much-vaunted gilded central square, sumptuous, cream-coloured buildings and shop windows filled with fine chocolates and fragile works of glass, the former capital of the dukes of Lorraine seems as opulent today as it did during the 16th to 18th centuries, when much of the city centre was built.

Nancy thrives on a combination of innovation and sophistication. These characteristics are accentuated by the presence of the École de Nancy, the city's premier museum, home to many sinuous works of the Art Nouveau movement, which flourished here thanks to the rebellious spirit of local artists. Further examples of their work can be found on the street: look for the stained-glass windows that grace the entrances to a number of banks and private homes.

Orientation

In the heart of Nancy is the beautifully proportioned 18th-century Place Stanislas and adjoining Place de la Carrière, both designed to connect the narrow, twisting streets of the 11th-century Vieille Ville, which is to the north, with the rigid right angles of the 16th-century Ville Neuve to the south. Place Stanislas is about 800 metres north-east of the train station at the bottom (north-east end) of busy, one-way Rue Stanislas. The western end of Rue Stanislas is graced by a large gate, Porte Stanislas.

Nancy's sights and hotels are scattered around both the new and old cities. Most things (except the École de Nancy and the cheapest hotels) are within walking distance of Place Stanislas.

Information

Tourist Office The tourist office (☎ 83.35. 22.41) at 14 Place Stanislas is open Monday to Saturday from 9 am to 7 pm (6 pm from December to February) and Sunday from 10 am to 1 pm. The hotel reservation service is free.

Money The Banque de France (☎ 83.34. 37.00) is three blocks west of the train station at 2 Rue Chanzy. It is open weekdays from

Nancy

0   100   200 m

To Metz
via A31
(51 km)

To Metz
via N57
(57 km)

Parc de la
Pépinière

To Toul (23 km)
& Verdun
(108 km)

To Lunéville (30 km),
Colmar (127 km) &
Strasbourg (150 km)

To Auberge de
Jeunesse Rémicourt
(4 km), Camping
de Brabois (5 km)
& Neufchâteau
(59 km)

Parc Sainte
Marie

■ PLACES TO STAY

15 Hôtel de la Poste
20 Hôtel Choley
22 Hôtel Académie
25 Hôtel Piroux
39 Hôtel Poincaré
41 Hôtel Moderne
42 Hôtel Crois
   de Bourgogne
44 Hôtel Pasteur

▼ PLACES TO EAT

3 Le Caveau de la
   Grand' Rue
7 Crêp Show
8 Boulangerie Massin
9 Le Panier Gourmand
23 Cours Léopold
   (Uni Restaurant)
29 Excelsior Flo
32 La Cigogne
33 Covered Market
34 Match Supermarket
35 L'Alsacien
36 Le Grill d'Attila

OTHER

2 Porte de la Craffe
4 Musée Historique Lorrain
6 Arc de Triomphe
10 Musée des Beaux-Arts
11 Tourist Office
12 Hôtel de Ville
13 Main Post Office
16 Bus Station
17 Cathédrale
18 Caveau des Dom's
19 Le Pub Stanislas
21 Le Blueberry (Bar)
24 Porte Stanislas
26 Bus to Auberge de Jeunesse
27 Railway Station
30 Banque de France
31 Nouvelles Frontières
37 Laundrette
38 Laundrette
40 Cameo Cinéma
45 Musée de l'École de Nancy

✕ SQUARES

1 Place du Luxembourg
5 Place de la Carrière
14 Place Monseigneur Ruch
28 Place Thiers
43 Place Paul Painlevé

LORRAINE

9 am to 12.15 pm and 1.30 to 3.30 pm. There is also a string of banks along Rue Saint Jean.

Post The main post office (☎ 83.39.27.10) at 8 Rue Pierre Fourier is open weekdays from 8 am to 7 pm and on Saturday until noon.

Nancy's postcode is 54000.

Travel Agencies Nouvelles Frontières (☎ 83.36.76.27) at 4 Rue des Ponts is open Tuesday to Friday from 9 am to 6.30 pm and Monday and Saturday from 9 am to noon and 2 to 6 pm.

Laundry Le Bateau Lavoir (☎ 83.35.47.47) at 124 Rue Saint Dizier is open daily from 7 am to 9 pm. Closer to the train station, the Lavomatique on Rue de l'Armée Patton is open the same hours.

Medical Services For medical emergencies, call the central hospital (☎ 83.37.24.24), which is on the corner of Rue Albert Lebrun and Ave Maréchal de Lattre de Tassigny, about one km south-east of Place Stanislas.

Walking Tour
The tourist office has two good pamphlets, both free and in English, which take you to many of the city's most interesting – and often hidden – sights. *Itinéraire 1900* focuses on **Art Nouveau** works, whereas *Nancy Historique*, which starts at **Place Stanislas**, moves from the 18th century back in time to the medieval charm of the old town. *Nancy Historique* takes you right up to 14th-century **Porte de la Craffe**, the city's oldest stone gateway, which sits imposingly at the northern end of the old city's main thoroughfare, the Grande Rue.

Place Stanislas
Often filled with tourists doing pirouettes as they take in the 360° of magnificence, this square is named after Stanislaw Leszczynski, the dethroned king of Poland (ruled 1704-9 and 1733) who, thanks to his son-in-law Louis XV, ruled Lorraine in the mid-1700s. In an effort to unite the old and

new cities, he tore down the walls that separated them and commissioned this square.

The buildings that surround the square – including the Hôtel de Ville, which takes up the entire southern edge – are considered one of the finest ensembles of 18th-century architecture in France. Opposite the Hôtel de Ville, the squat tourist office sits in front of the Arc de Triomphe (Triumphal Arch). Place Stanislas was added to UNESCO's World Heritage list in 1986.

Museums
In and around Nancy, there are 11 museums whose specialities range from traditional arts to zoology and motorcars. Many are closed on Tuesday. If you'd like to visit both the Musée des Beaux-Arts and the École de Nancy, a discount ticket is available for 16FF.

Musée de l'École de Nancy Housed in a villa about two km south-west of the city centre, the School of Nancy Museum (☎ 83.40.14.86) at 36 Rue du Sergent Blandan brings together a heady collection of curvaceous pieces produced by the turn-of-the-century Art Nouveau movement. Reacting against the bland artistic temperament and imitative historicism of the time, its exponents – including Nancy glass manufacturer Émile Gallé – used, among other media, locally produced iron and glass to create a new, sinuous aesthetic in the arts, design and architecture.

The museum is open daily, except Tuesday, from 10 am to noon and 2 to 6 pm (5 pm from October to March). Entry costs 13FF (9FF for students and children). From the train station, take bus No 6 or 26 to the Painlevé stop.

Musée des Beaux-Arts On Place Stanislas, the Fine Arts Museum (☎ 83.37.65.01) is housed in an 18th-century mansion that is arguably more outstanding than the exhibition of French and Italian baroque, rococo and contemporary works inside. Glass fans may like to see the crystal gallery. This museum is open from 10.30 am to 12.30 pm and 1.30 to 5.45 pm daily except Monday

LORRAINE

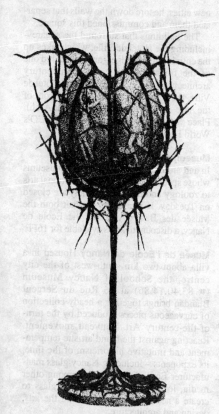

Art Nouveau chalice in the Musée de l'École de Nancy

morning and Tuesday. Admission costs the same as the École de Nancy but is free for students and children on Wednesday.

Musée Historique Lorrain Located in the heart of old Nancy, this museum (☎ 83.32. 18.74) at 64 Grande Rue, housed in the mostly 16th-century Ducal Palace, traces the region's history from Gallo-Roman days to the 17th century and includes exhibits of regional art and folklore. From 1 May to 29 September, it is open daily, except Tuesday, from 10 am to 6 pm; during the rest of the

year, hours are 10 am to noon and 2 to 5 pm. Admission is 15FF.

Musée de Zoologie et Aquarium Tropical The Zoology Museum & Tropical Aquarium (☎ 83.32.99.97), situated at the entrance to the botanical gardens at 30 Rue Sainte Catherine, has an interesting collection of tropical fish.

Musée de l'Histoire du Fer South-east of Nancy, at 1 Ave du Général de Gaulle in Jarville, is the Museum of Ironwork (☎ 83.56.01.42), which looks at the history of iron since prehistoric times and the stages of production from extraction to the finished product. From October to June it is open daily from 2 to 5 pm (6 pm from July to September) except Tuesday. Morning visits are possible in summer if arranged beforehand.

Musée de l'Automobile Vintage cars are the focus of this museum (☎ 83.40.22.81), which is located in the Forêt de Haye, 10 km west of Nancy on the N4. It is only open on Wednesday and weekends from 2 to 5 pm, but visits can be arranged at other times if you call beforehand.

Places to Stay
Nancy's budget hotels are scattered haphazardly around the old and new cities and the area west of the train station.

Camping *Camping de Brabois* (☎ 83.27. 18.28) at Ave Paul Muller, open from 1 April to 31 October, is on a hill about a km south of the Auberge de Jeunesse. It costs 12FF per person and 6FF for a tent and car. To get there by bus, take line No 26 to the Camping stop (see Auberge de Jeunesse in the next section for transport details).

Hostels The *Auberge de Jeunesse Rémicourt* (☎ 83.27.73.67), in an old chateau surrounded by a peaceful park, is four km south of the centre at 149 Rue de Vandœuvre. A bed costs 41.50FF and breakfast is 11FF.

LORRAINE

The hostel is open weekdays from 8 am to 10 pm and weekends from 5.30 to 10 pm. Bus Nos 4, 6 and 26 head out this way and can be picked up on Rue Stanislas, to the left as you exit the train station. From Monday to Saturday, take the convenient bus No 26 (the last one is at 8 pm) to the Saint Fiace stop and then follow the signs for 400 metres. On Sunday, when line No 26 doesn't run, the other two buses will drop you off in the vicinity of the hostel.

Several university dorms around Nancy are open to travellers during school holiday periods. For details, contact CROUS (☎ 83.91.88.00).

Hotels – Train Station Area If you've arrived by rail, the most convenient cheap hotel is the *Hôtel Piroux* (☎ 83.32.01.10) at 12 Rue Raymond Poincaré, whose rooms start at 130FF. Reception is open daily until 11 pm. Four blocks west on the same busy street, the two-star *Hôtel Poincaré* (☎ 83.40.25.99) at No 81 has pleasant doubles with TV from 140FF and private parking for an extra 20FF.

The friendly *Hôtel Crois de Bourgogne* (☎ 83.40.01.86) at 68bis Rue Jeanne d'Arc, one km from the train station, has rooms from 120FF; showers are 15FF extra. To get there, take bus No 8. Plenty of parking is available around the nearby square. Across the street at 73 Rue Jeanne d'Arc, the *Hôtel Moderne* (☎ 83.40.14.26) in no way lives up to its name but probably has the cheapest beds in town: singles from 44FF and doubles/triples starting at 90FF.

Round the corner from the École de Nancy, but close to nothing else, is the *Hôtel Pasteur* (☎ 83.40.29.85) at 47 Rue Pasteur. Clean and homey rooms start at 90FF, and showers cost 10FF. To get there, take bus No 6 or 26.

Hotels – Old & New Towns The cheapest option in the city centre is the *Hôtel de la Poste* (☎ 83.32.11.52), squeezed into a corner at 56 Place Monseigneur Ruch, next to the bus station and the cathedral. The entrance is grand, the rooms less so, but reasonable singles/doubles start at 95/105FF.

The *Hôtel Académie* (☎ 83.35.52.31) at 7bis Rue des Michottes, halfway between the train station and Place Stanislas, has rooms from 95/122FF. It also has a garage. Around the corner, the *Choley* (☎ 83.32.31.98) at 28 Rue Gustave Simon, which has been around since 1875, is ideal for a splurge. It is quaint and rustic and has low, beamed roofs. Basic doubles start at 185FF; rooms with very small baths cost 220FF. Advance reservations are usually necessary.

Places to Eat

Unlike Nancy's hotels, many of the city's restaurants are clustered together.

Restaurants – Old Town *Le Panier Gourmand* at 37 Rue des Maréchaux, open daily, has *menus* of local cuisine starting at 55FF. At the opposite end of the street, the *Crêp Show* (☎ 83.30.48.18) at 4 Grande Rue is an unpretentious little creperie/omeletterie/saladerie with decent prices. Vegetarian salads are available from 35FF. This place is open daily until 1 am. At the northern end of this old road, *Le Caveau de la Grand'Rue* (☎ 83.37.81.98) at No 92 has *menus* from 45FF. It is closed on Saturday at midday and Sunday.

The most convenient university restaurant is *Cours Léopold* at 16 Cours Léopold.

Restaurants – New Town At No 33 Rue des Ponts, *L'Alsacien* (☎ 83.37.33.99) has lunch *menus* from 49FF; prices are higher in the evening. The house speciality is tarte flambée (see Food in the introduction to Alsace). This place is closed on Sunday and Tuesday evenings. Next door at *Le Grill d'Attila* (☎ 83.30.30.07), reasonably priced carnivorous feasts are available daily except Saturday at midday and Sunday. Closer to the centre, *La Cigogne* (☎ 83.32.11.13) at 4 Rue des Ponts has lunch and dinner *menus* for 51FF.

For a seafood splurge amid turn-of-the-century elegance, try *Excelsior Flo* (☎ 83. 35.24.57) at 50 Rue Henri Poincaré. The coffee here may be expensive, but it's worth it for the fun of sitting in this Parisian-style brasserie which dates from 1904. It's open daily for lunch and from 7 pm to 12.30 am.

Self-Catering The *Match supermarket* on Rue du Grand Rabbin Haguenauer is open Monday to Saturday from 6 am to 1 am (midnight on Saturday). The *covered market* on Place Henri Mangin is open Tuesday to Saturday from 6 am to 6 pm. *Boulangerie Massin*, close to Place Stanislas at 10 Rue des Maréchaux, is open 24 hours a day.

Entertainment

Much of Nancy's nightlife is centred around Rue Saint Jean and nearby streets in the new town.

Live Music For jazz, *Le Blueberry* bar at 20bis Rue Gustave Simon is open Monday to Saturday night from 7 pm to 2 am. Two popular live music venues are *Terminal Export* at 2 Rue Sébastien Leclerc (one block west of Parc de la Pépinière) and, more centrally, *Caveau des Dom's* at 21 bis Rue Saint Dizier. The tourist office can provide programmes of their scheduled gigs.

Cinema There's a good selection of non-dubbed films at *Cameo* (☎ 83.28.83.28), which is at 16 Rue de la Commanderie.

Getting There & Away

Train The train station, open from 5 am to midnight, is on Place Thiers. The information office (☎ 83.56.50.50) is open daily from 9 am to 7.30 pm (6.30 pm on Saturday). The left-luggage counter is open Monday to Saturday from 6.45 am to 9.30 pm and on Sunday from 1.30 to 8.30 pm. Lockers are also available.

Major destinations include Paris's Gare de l'Est (189FF; three hours; four daily), Besançon (168FF; four hours; nine a day), Metz (46FF; 35 minutes; hourly) and Strasbourg (90FF; 1½ hours; 10 daily).

Bus The bus station is next to the cathedral at Place Monseigneur Ruch, close to Rue Saint Georges. Among the destinations served is Verdun (82FF; 2¾ hours; six a day).

Car Europcar (☎ 83.37.57.24; fax 83.37.81.18) is near the train station at 18 Rue de Serre. For ADA Location de Véhicules, call ☎ 83.35.28.39.

Getting Around

Bus The local bus company CGFTE (☎ 83.35.54.54) has an office at 3 Rue du Docteur Schmitt. Most lines stop around the train station. A single ticket costs 5.80FF, and a 10-ticket carnet is 35FF.

Taxi There's a taxi rank outside the train station. To order a taxi, call ☎ 83.37.65.37.

METZ

Like Strasbourg on the other side of the Vosges, Metz (pronounced 'Mess'; population 200,000), the present-day capital of Lorraine, serves as a junction for many international rail lines. As the locals like to put it, their city is 'at the crossroads of Europe', a claim whose foundations go back to Roman times, when Metz was a junction on the highways linking the English Channel with the Rhine and south-western Germany with Italy.

The city was capital of the East Merovingian kingdom and during the Carolingian era was an important intellectual centre. Metz was later an autonomous town within the Holy Roman Empire, to which it belonged from 923 to the 14th century. Although Metz became Protestant during the Reformation, a siege by the Holy Roman Empire in 1552 was successfully resisted with the help of the Catholic king of France, Henry II. The city was ceded to France in 1648 by the Treaty of Westphalia.

When Metz was occupied and annexed by Germany in 1870-71, a quarter of the population, given the choice of either accepting German nationality or leaving their homes, fled to French territory. Many of the city's major public buildings date from the period when Metz was part of the German Empire.

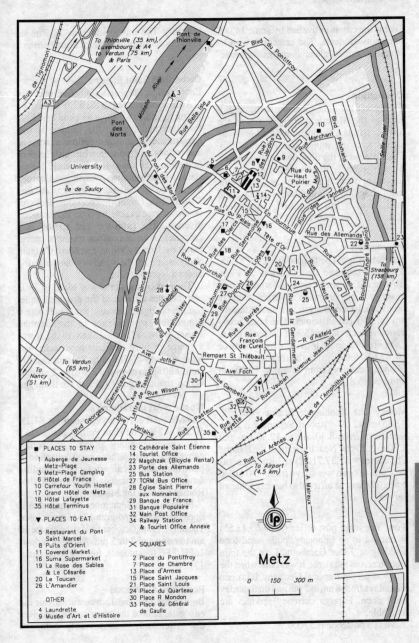

PLACES TO STAY
- 1 Auberge de Jeunesse Metz-Plage
- 3 Metz-Plage Camping
- 6 Hôtel de France
- 10 Carrefour Youth Hostel
- 17 Grand Hôtel de Metz
- 18 Hôtel Lafayette
- 35 Hôtel Terminus

▼ PLACES TO EAT
- 5 Restaurant du Pont Saint Marcel
- 8 Puits d'Orient
- 11 Covered Market
- 16 Suma Supermarket
- 19 La Rose des Sables & Le Césarée
- 20 Le Toucan
- 26 L'Amandier

OTHER
- 4 Laundrette
- 9 Musée d'Art et d'Histoire
- 12 Cathédrale Saint Étienne
- 14 Tourist Office
- 22 Magchzak (Bicycle Rental)
- 23 Porte des Allemands
- 25 Bus Station
- 27 TCRM Bus Office
- 28 Église Saint Pierre aux Nonnains
- 29 Banque de France
- 31 Banque Populaire
- 32 Main Post Office
- 34 Railway Station & Tourist Office Annexe

✕ SQUARES
- 2 Place du Pontiffroy
- 7 Place de Chambre
- 13 Place d'Armes
- 15 Place Saint Jacques
- 21 Place Saint Louis
- 24 Place du Quarteau
- 30 Place R Mondon
- 33 Place du Général de Gaulle

Metz

0   150   300 m

LORRAINE

Today, the city is enlivened by some 14,000 university students. The cathedral, with its stunning stained glass, is the major attraction.

Orientation

Sitting on a natural incline above the confluence of the Moselle and Seille rivers, the town centre is a chaotic nework of one-way streets weaving round, and eventually to, Place d'Armes, the dignified central square. To the south is Rue Serpenoise, once an important Roman highway and today the main shopping thoroughfare. Further south still, over a km downhill from Place d'Armes, is the train station.

Information

Tourist Office The tourist office (☎ 87.55. 53.76) is opposite the cathedral on Place d'Armes. It's open Monday to Saturday from 9 am to 6 pm (9 pm in summer). Sunday hours are 10 am to 5 pm in summer and 10 am to 1.30 pm in winter. The hotel reservation service charges 5% of the room price.

There's also a tourist office annexe (☎ 87.65.76.69) inside the train station that is open weekdays from 11 am to 12.30 pm and 1.30 to 8 pm.

Money The Banque de France (☎ 87.74. 43.86) at 12 Ave Robert Schuman is open weekdays from 8.30 am to 12.30 pm and 1.30 to 3.30 pm. Near the station, the Banque Populaire (☎ 87.37.71.22) at 3 Rue François de Curel is open weekdays from 8.30 am to 6 pm. The tourist office also has an exchange service.

Post The main post office (☎ 87.63.13.55) is housed in an imposing, pink- sandstone building at 9 Rue Gambetta. Like the train station across the street, it was built when the city was part of Imperial Germany. It is open weekdays from 8 am to 7 pm and on Saturday until noon. Foreign currency services are available.

Metz's postcode is 57000.

Laundry The Lavomatique at 22 Rue du Pont des Morts is open daily from 7 am to 7 pm.

Cathédrale Saint Étienne

Enormous St Stephen's Cathedral on Place d'Armes was created in the 13th century by fusing together two separate churches. Like the other buildings in the vicinity, it was constructed of mustard-yellow sandstone and is now covered with a blackish layer of pollution. The cathedral is famed for its stained-glass windows, which have earned the edifice the nickname *Lanterne du Bon Dieu* (God's Lantern). The three decks of windows, remarkable for their richness and diversity, date from the 13th to the 20th centuries, with a number of more recent panes by Jacques Villon and Marc Chagall. Sadly, some of the windows are suffering under a layer of grime.

The neo-Gothic portal was added in 1903 and includes a statue of the prophet Daniel (on the far right). Because the statue bore a remarkable resemblance to the German Kaiser Wilhelm II (ruled 1888-1918), it was a source of mirth until its moustache was removed in 1940. The cathedral is open daily from 7.30 am to noon and 2 to 6 pm. Entrance is free, though it costs 12FF to see the crypt.

Musée d'Art et d'Histoire

The Metz Art & History Museum (☎ 87.75. 10.18) at 2 Rue du Haut Poirier, housed in a 15th-century granary and a 17th-century convent, brings together a good collection of paintings and local artefacts, including funerary urns and statues dating from Gallo-Roman times to the Middle Ages.

From June to September the museum is open from 9 am to noon and 2 to 6 pm (closed Tuesday). From October to May hours are 10 am to noon and 2 to 5 pm. Admission costs 16FF (8FF for students, free for those under 15).

Porte des Allemands

Built in the 13th and 15th centuries, this old city gate, east of the town centre near Rue des Allemands, was severely damaged during WW II. Its name derives from a hospital of the Knights Hospitallers of Our Lady of the Germans, which was once nearby.

Place Saint Louis

Known under various names in the past, Place Saint Louis acquired its current name in the 18th century. All around this attractive square are medieval arcades and merchants' houses dating from the Renaissance.

Église Saint Pierre aux Nonnains

Metz boasts one of the oldest churches in France: Église Saint Pierre aux Nonnains on Rue de la Citadelle. Parts of the structure were built during the 4th century as a Roman basilica (ie as a court of justice and a place of assembly). It became a chapel in the early 7th century.

Promenade de l'Esplanade

One of the pleasant promenades along the Moselle River, the Promenade de l'Esplanade, near the Palais de Justice, affords great views of the islands of Saint Symphorien and Saulcy.

Places to Stay

Metz offers relatively few inexpensive places to spend the night. Near the train station, there's a handful of hotels along Rue Lafayette but, surprisingly, they're pricier than the hotels in the city centre.

Camping The very basic *Metz-Plage Camping* (☎ 87.32.05.58), on the bank of the Moselle about 500 metres north-west of the centre, is just south of the Auberge de Jeunesse. Open from May to September, it charges 16/28FF for one/two adults. To get there from the train station, take bus No 3. The entry gate is on Rue du Pont des Morts, just before Pont des Morts.

Hostel There are two youth hostels in Metz. The *Auberge de Jeunesse Metz-Plage* (☎ 87.30.44.02; fax 87.36.60.79) is close to Place du Pontiffroy, which is beside the river on the opposite side of town from the train station. It has dorm beds for 55FF and triples

for 150FF, including breakfast. There's no curfew. In summer, it's a good idea to book a few days ahead. Bus Nos 3 and 11 from the train station stop at the front door; the last one is at 8.30 pm.

The other hostel, *Auberge de Jeunesse Carrefour* (☎ 87.75.07.26; fax 87.36.71.44), is on 6 Rue Marchant just behind the Musée d'Art et d'Histoire. It costs 57FF including breakfast. The rooms are open all day.

Hotels One of the most central options is the *Hôtel de France* (☎ 87.75.00.02) at 25 Place de Chambre, just below (west of) the cathedral. The rooms are ordinary, with patchwork wallpaper and the odd dripping tap, but it's probably the cheapest place around. Singles/doubles start at 80/90FF; showers are 15FF extra. There's parking at the front except on Saturday mornings, when the square is taken over by a market.

On the pedestrianised Rue des Clercs, the *Lafayette* (☎ 87.75.21.09) at No 24 has doubles from 100FF, triples (three beds) for 200FF and quads (two beds) for 170FF; a shower is 15FF. On the other side of the street, the newly renovated *Grand Hôtel de Metz* (☎ 87.36.16.33) at 3 Rue des Clercs has plusher doubles from 125FF and an expensive private garage (40FF).

Near the train station, the best bet is the two-star *Hôtel Terminus* (☎ 87.66.81.18) at 13 Rue La Fayette, which has decent singles/doubles from 120/130FF.

Places to Eat

A good place to start looking for restaurants is Place Saint Louis and nearby streets.

Restaurants The totally un-French *Le Toucan* (☎ 87.76.18.08) at 46 Place Saint Louis has fiery Mexican cuisine and décor. Main courses start at 50FF. This place is open daily for lunch from 11.30 am and for dinner from 6.30 pm. Two streets away, *Le Césarée* (☎ 87.74.15.47) at 2bis Rue Dupont des Loges is an elegant but cosy pizzeria with pizzas from 35FF. Cheaper, more varied fare can be had next door at *La Rose des Sables*.

L'Amandier (☎ 87.36.55.11) at 32 Rue du

Coëtlosquet, whose regional cuisine is served in an atmosphere of country charm, is a good place for a splurge. *Menus* start at 72FF. L'Amandier is open daily.

Another elegant option is *Restaurant du Pont Saint Marcel* (☎ 87.30.12.29) at 1 Rue du Pont Saint Marcel. Here, everything is typical of Lorraine, from the succulent dishes to the costumes worn by the waiters. It has *menus* from 93FF. The restaurant is closed on Sunday evening and Monday.

North of the cathedral, *Puits d'Orient* (☎ 87.36.66.05) at 20b Rue des Jardins has an Algerian *menu* for 65FF. This place is closed on Sunday evening and Monday.

Self-Catering The *covered market* in front of the cathedral is open daily except Monday. There's a small *food market* on Monday, Thursday and Saturday mornings at Place Saint Jacques. *Supermarché Suma* in the basement of the modern commercial centre at Place Saint Jacques is open Monday to Saturday from 8.30 am to 7.30 pm.

Getting There & Away

Air Aéroport de Metz-Frescaty (☎ 87.38.31.32) is six km south-west of the city centre.

Train Metz is the largest station in north-eastern France. The train station is about one km south of the city centre on Place de Gaulle. It stays open all night. The information office (☎ 87.63.50.50) is open Monday to Saturday from 8.30 am to 7.30 pm (6 pm on Saturday).

Direct trains link Metz with many destinations, including Paris (184FF; three hours; eight a day), Nancy (46FF; 35 minutes; hourly), Strasbourg (93FF; 1½ hours; six a day) and Verdun (55FF; 1¾ hours; five a day). Internationally, there are services to Germany (including Bonn and Cologne), Luxembourg and Belgium.

Bus Two regional bus companies have offices at the bus station, which is at Place Coislin, just east of Place du Quarteau. Les Courriers Mosellans (☎ 87.34.60.00) has buses to Gorze (26FF; 45 minutes; buses

leave at 11.15 am and 6.15 pm). The other company, Les Rapides de Lorraine (☎ 87.63.65.65), links Metz with Veckring. There are also buses to Verdun (70FF; 1¾ hours; eight a day).

Car Europcar (☎ 87.66.21.80) is near the train station at 11 Rue La Fayette. Citer (☎ 87.65.51.33) is at 71-73 Ave André Malraux.

Getting Around

Bus Local buses are run by TCRM (☎ 87.76.31.11), which has an information and ticket office on Place de la République. Tickets cost 5FF.

Bicycle Bikes can be hired from Magihzak (☎ 87.74.13.14) at 65 Rue des Allemands. Mountain bikes cost 70FF a day.

AROUND METZ
Parc Naturel Régional de Lorraine

The Lorraine Regional Park is split into two sections: the larger part is south-west of Metz and west and north-west of Nancy, while the smaller part is south-east of Metz and north-east of Nancy. Both areas are forested and speckled with lakes that attract fishers and families on holiday. They also contain some of Lorraine's most picturesque villages, including **Gorze** (population 1200), site of a Benedictine abbey founded in the 8th century. Gorze is 20 km south-west of Metz and can be reached by bus or bike (see Bus under Getting There & Away in the Metz section).

For more information about the park, contact the park headquarters (☎ 83.81.11.91) at Pont à Mousson (postcode 54700), which is 32 km south of Metz and 31 km north of Nancy. It is linked to both cities by the A31.

Maginot Line

The Metz area was heavily fortified by the Germans before WW I and, as part of the Maginot Line (see the Maginot Line aside), by the French between the wars. The largest single Maginot Line bastion in the area was

Hackenberg, situated 15 km east of Thionville and 30 km north-north-east of Metz near the village of Veckring. This massive fortress has 10 km of underground tunnels, four km of which can be visited by an electric trolley which takes you past such subterranean installations as a kitchen, a hospital, a generating plant and ammunition stores.

Hackenberg is open to visitors from April to October on weekends from 2 to 3 pm. For more information, call ☎ 82.91.30.08. Buses from Metz to Veckring are run by Les Rapides de Lorraine (see Bus under Getting There & Away in the Metz section).

VERDUN

From the moment you arrive in Verdun (population 24,500), you are reminded of the horrific events that took place in and around the town during the Battle of Verdun (1916-17). During the 18 months of savage fighting that has come to be known as *l'enfer de Verdun* (the hell of Verdun), nearly 800,000 soldiers – 400,000 Frenchmen and almost as many Germans – were killed; Churchill referred to the town as 'the anvil upon which French manhood was...hammered to death'.

Although Verdun itself, one of France's most heavily fortified strongholds, was never taken by the Germans (the closest they got was five km away), the town – once its inhabitants had been evacuated – was almost totally destroyed by artillery bombardments. In the hills to the north and east of Verdun, where most of the fighting took place, the brutal combat, carried out with artillery, flame-throwers and poison gas, completely wiped nine villages off the map.

In 1920, the Unknown Soldier chosen for re-interment under the Arc de Triomphe in Paris was taken from the countless unidentified corpses collected from the battlefield at Verdun. More recently, the town has adopted the title of 'World Capital of Peace', an action which, though little more than declarative, expresses the locals' fervent wish that the slaughter of 1916 never be repeated.

The subdivision of the Carolingian empire in western and central Europe among Charlemagne's three grandsons, which began the process of subdividing Europe into distinct countries and set the stage for over a thousand years of Franco-German rivalry and warfare, began in Verdun in 843 with the signing of the Treaty of Verdun. Over the centuries, Verdun has suffered repeatedly from the wars between Germany and France: it was besieged and briefly occupied by Prussian forces in 1792, and again came under siege by the Prussians in 1870. This time, the town was under German occupation for three years, prompting the French to construct the fortifications that would later be contested in the Battle of Verdun. In September 1944, after it had been liberated by American forces, Verdun was heavily bombed by the Germans.

Orientation

Central Verdun straddles the Meuse River, but the livelier part of town, the Ville Haute (Upper Town), is on the river's left (western) bank, which rises up to the cathedral. The train station is 700 metres north of the cathedral. The tourist office is on the right bank about 900 metres south-east of the train station. Verdun's wide streets were laid out in the years following WW I.

Information

Tourist Office Verdun's modern tourist office (☎ 29.86.14.18) is on the right bank at Place de la Nation – from the left bank, go through the fortified Porte Chaussée and then cross the bridge of the same name. From mid-September to April, it is open Monday to Saturday from 9 am to noon and 2 or 2.30 pm to 5.30 or 6 pm; Sunday hours are 10 am to 1 pm. From May to mid-September, it is open Monday to Saturday from 8 or 8.30 am to 7 or 8 pm; Sunday hours are 9 am to 5 pm. Hotel bookings are free.

Money The Banque de France (☎ 29.86.23.96) at 10 Quai de la République is open weekdays from 8.15 am to noon and 1.35 to 3.30 pm. The tourist office can exchange foreign currency.

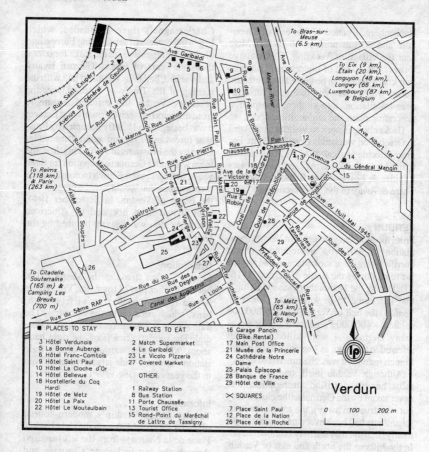

Verdun

0   100   200 m

PLACES TO STAY
3 Hôtel Verdunois
5 La Bonne Auberge
6 Hôtel Franc-Comtois
9 Hôtel Saint Paul
10 Hôtel La Cloche d'Or
14 Hôtel Bellevue
18 Hostellerie du Coq
   Hardi
19 Hôtel de Metz
20 Hôtel La Paix
22 Hôtel Le Moutaulbain

PLACES TO EAT
2 Match Supermarket
4 Le Garibaldi
23 Le Vicolo Pizzeria
27 Covered Market

OTHER
1 Railway Station
8 Bus Station
11 Porte Chaussée
13 Tourist Office
15 Rond-Point du Maréchal
   de Lattre de Tassigny

16 Garage Poncin
   (Bike Rental)
17 Main Post Office
21 Musée de la Princerie
24 Cathédrale Notre
   Dame
25 Palais Épiscopal
28 Banque de France
29 Hôtel de Ville

SQUARES
7 Place Saint Paul
12 Place de la Nation
26 Place de la Roche

Post The main post office, on the corner of Quai de Londres and Ave de la Victoire, is open weekdays from 8 am to 7 pm and on Saturday until noon.

Verdun's postcode is 55100.

Things to See

There are a number of war monuments around town, with motifs ranging from troops lined up in soldierly comradeship to a Winged Victory screaming in horror.

Citadelle Souterraine This huge fortress (☎ 29.86.62.02), just over one km west of

the tourist office on Rue du 5ème RAP, was designed by Vauban. In 1916, its seven km of underground galleries, with facilities including a bakery, a hospital and a petrol station, became a veritable city for 10,000 civilians and soldiers. The Citadelle is open from mid-April to 31 December daily from 9.30 am to noon and 2 to 5.30 pm. In July and August hours are 9.30 am to 8 pm. Admission is 17/13/8FF for adults/students/children. To get to the Citadelle from the bus station, take bus No 2 to the Groupe Scolaire stop and walk down the hill to the left.

For information on memorials and battlefield sites near Verdun, see the following Verdun Battlefields listing.

Cathédrale & Palais Épiscopal At the top of the Ville Haute is the magnificent cathedral, built between the 11th and 16th centuries in a mixture of Romanesque and Gothic styles. Also worth visiting is the 14th-century cloister, built in the Flamboyant Gothic style.

The elegant Bishop's Palace was designed in the 18th century by Robert de Cotte, Louis XV's main architect, who also designed the Palais de Rohan in Strasbourg.

Musée de la Princerie Formerly a private residence, this 16th-century building on Rue de la Belle Vierge now serves as the municipal museum. Its 14 rooms are full of interesting exhibits. Particularly worthwhile seeing are the Romanesque and Gothic sculptures, a typical Lorraine dining room, and souvenirs of Verdun dating back to the Middle Ages. From April to October the museum is open from 9.30 am to 12.30 pm and 2 to 6 pm (closed Tuesday).

Porte Chaussée Built in the 16th century, the imposing Porte Chaussée, next to the Pont Chaussée, is one of the gates of the original town walls.

Places to Stay

Verdun has an excellent selection of hotels in all price brackets. There's no youth hostel.

Camping The three-star *Camping Les Breuils* (☎ 29.86.15.31), open from 1 April to mid-October, is on Allée des Breuils about two km south-west of the train station. It costs 14FF per person and 10FF to pitch a tent. To get there from the bus station, take bus No 2 to the Groupe Scolaire stop and then walk down towards the river.

Hotels – Train Station Area Your best option is probably the *Hôtel Verdunois* (☎ 29.86.17.45) at 13bis Ave Garibaldi, which has singles/doubles from 100/120FF.

There's private parking at the back. *La Bonne Auberge* (☎ 29.86.05.16), which is next door, has the cheapest rooms in town. Singles/doubles start at 60/78FF but you get what you pay for. Alternatively, the *Hôtel Franc-Comtois* (☎ 29.86.05.46) at 9 Ave Garibaldi has basic but comfortable rooms starting at 90FF. Hall showers cost 10FF.

Hotels – Centre Two-star comfort for one-star prices can be had at the *Hôtel Saint Paul* (☎ 29.86.02.16) at 12 Place Saint Paul, which has rooms from 95/110FF. The rustic *La Cloche d'Or* (☎ 29.86.03.60), next door at No 10, is marginally dearer.

Two blocks south (up the hill) is *Hôtel La Paix* (☎ 29.86.02.94) at No 40 on busy Rue Mazel. It has adequate rooms from 100FF. Those on the top floor almost look down the barrels of the Victory Monument cannons across the road. Around the corner, the *Hôtel de Metz* (☎ 29.86.00.15) at 8 Rue Edmond Robin has basic rooms from 60/80FF and two-bed quads – excellent value – from 110FF. Unfortunately, there's no hall shower.

Another quiet, backstreet choice is the *Le Montaulbain* (☎ 29.86.00.47) at 4 Rue de la Vieille Prison, with rooms from 115FF. This place is open round the clock. Parking is available nearby.

For something more up-market, try *Hôtel Bellevue* (☎ 29.84.39.41; fax 29.86.09.21), at 1 Rond-Point du Maréchal de Lattre de Tassigny. It has a relaxing ambience and comfortable singles/doubles for 160/350FF. The hotel also has a restaurant. The three-star *Hostellerie du Coq Hardi* (☎ 29.86.36.36; fax 29.86.09.21) at 8 Ave de la Victoire offers elegant rooms in a refined setting. Singles/doubles cost 320/650FF.

Places to Eat

Verdun has no shortage of reasonably priced restaurants, including several which are attached to the hotels listed under Places to Stay. There are also brasseries and bars in abundance – just head down any of the small streets leading to the river from Rue Mazel or walk along Quai de Londres.

Restaurants With a four-course *menu* for 50FF, the humble *routière* (truckers' restaurant) in La Bonne Auberge (☎ 29.86.05.16), next door to Hôtel Verdunois at 11 Ave Garibaldi, is an obvious choice for the budget conscious. Next door, *Le Garibaldi* (☎ 29.86.10.21) is slightly more pretentious but offers seafood *menus* from only 52FF. This place is closed on Tuesday.

In the town centre, *Le Vicolo Pizzeria* (☎ 29.86.43.14) on Rue des Gros Degrés has decent pizzas for 35 to 45FF.

The restaurant of the *Hostellerie du Coq Hardi* has high-quality cuisine and an excellent wine cellar. There are *menus* from 195 to 440FF and à la carte meals cost between 300 and 450FF.

Self-Catering If you're in town on Tuesday or Friday morning, you can pick up the basics in the old *covered market* on the corner of Rue du Rû and Rue Victor Schleiter. Otherwise, you can buy provisions at the *Match supermarket* on Ave du Général de Gaulle, which is just to the right as you leave the train station. It is open Monday to Saturday from 9 am to 12.15 pm and 3 to 7.15 pm.

Getting There & Away
Train Verdun is on a secondary rail line so connections are not particularly frequent. The modern little train station (☎ 29.86.25.05) is on the north-western side of town at the northern end of Rue Saint Exupéry. There's no information office, but the ticket windows are open daily from 6.30 am to noon and 1 to 7 pm.

There are trains to Châlons-sur-Marne (five daily) with connections to Paris's Gare de l'Est (161FF; 3¼ hours), Épernay (92FF), Reims (103FF; 2½ hours), Metz (55FF; 1¾ hours; five a day) and Nancy (78FF; 1¾ hours; only one train at 10 am). For travel to both Metz and Nancy, buses are more frequent than the trains.

Bus The bus station is on Rue des Frères Boulhaut about 500 metres east of the train station. Les Rapides de la Meuse (☎ 29.86.02.71) has an information desk that is open weekdays from 8.30 am to noon and 2 to 6.15 pm. Regional services include buses to Metz (70FF; 1¾ hours; eight a day) and Nancy (82FF; 2¾ hours; six a day).

Car Euro Rent (☎ 29.86.50.49) is at 22 Rue Victor Schleiter.

Getting Around
Bus Buses that serve Verdun and the immediate vicinity are run by SIVOM (☎ 29.86.70.71) and leave from either Porte Chaussée or the bus station.

Bicycle Garage Poncin (☎ 29.84.14.12) on Ave de Douaumont (a block south-east of the tourist office) rents mountain bikes from 120/180FF for one/two days. It is open Tuesday to Saturday from 9 am to noon and 2 to 6.45 pm.

AROUND VERDUN
Fermont
Fermont (☎ 82.39.35.34 for the secretariat), one of the larger underground fortresses of the Maginot Line (see the Maginot Line aside), is about 56 km north of Verdun. Thirty metres deep, it withstood three days of heavy bombardment when the Germans attacked on 21 June 1940 but surrendered a few days later. It was retaken by the French in September 1944. These days, you can take a two-hour tour (25/15FF for adults/children) in which a small electric trolley transports you from one subterranean army block to another. Fermont is open for visits by individuals from 1 May to 30 August *only*; tours leave daily at 1.45 pm.

Fermont is in the forest 13 km south-west of Longwy and about six km east (along the D17A) of Longuyon. Unfortunately, Longuyon is not linked to Verdun by public transport.

VERDUN BATTLEFIELDS
On the Western Front, the outbreak of WW I in August 1914 was followed by a long period of trench warfare in which neither side made any significant gains. To break the stalemate, the Germans decided to change

tactics, attacking a target so vital for military and symbolic reasons that the French would throw every man they had into its defence. These troops would then be slaughtered, 'bleeding France white' and causing the French people to lose their will to resist. Germany, so the German general staff believed, would then win the war. The target selected for this bloody plan was the heavily fortified city of Verdun.

The Battle of Verdun began on the morning of 21 February 1916. After the heaviest shelling of the war to that date, German forces went on the attack and advanced with little opposition for four days, capturing, among other unprepared French positions, the Fort de Douaumont. French forces were resupplied, regrouped and rallied by General Philippe Pétain (later leader of the collaborationist Vichy government during WW II), who slowed the German advance by launching several French counterattacks. During March and April, the ridges and hills north and north-west of Verdun – including what came to be known as *Le Mort-Homme* (Dead Man's Hill) – were taken and retaken by both sides with incredible casualties. Fort de Vaux fell to the Germans on 7 June.

By July, German advance units were only five km from Verdun at Fort de Souville, but their offensive had ground to a halt. From October 1916 to October 1917, French forces recaptured most of the territory they had lost at the beginning of the battle, but the Germans were not pushed back beyond the positions they held in February 1916 until American troops and French forces launched a coordinated offensive in September 1918.

Bras to Eix

The sites detailed in this section are all located between the villages of Bras-sur-Meuse (6½ km north of Verdun on the D964) and Eix (nine km east of Verdun on the N18 to Étain). Most of the places of interest in this area are either on or very near the D913. The sites are listed from north to south (ie from those nearest Bras-sur-Meuse to those nearest Eix).

Tranchée des Baïonnettes On 10 June 1916, two companies of the 137th Infantry Regiment of the French Army were buried alive here while waiting in the *tranchées* (trenches) with fixed *baïonnettes* (bayonets) for a ferocious artillery bombardment to end. The memorial consists of a line of plain wooden crosses standing on top of a long mound of dirt and protected by a heavy cement roof.

Ossuaire de Douaumont Standing on top of a ridge overlooking reafforested land, the huge Douaumont Ossuary (☎ 29.84.54.81), France's most important WW I memorial, houses the remains of 130,000 unidentified French and German soldiers. Inside, the glow from the orange windows tries in vain to warm the chilling row of sarcophagi.

Outside, the 15,000 white crosses of the **Cimetière National** (National Cemetery) lead away from a black stone plaque signed by Mitterrand and Kohl and engraved with the words: 'We have forgiven, we have understood, we have become friends'. From the top of the 46-metre-high projectile-shaped **bell tower**, you can look out on the nearby battlefields.

The ossuary is open from 1 March to 30 November from 9 am to noon and 2 to 5.00 pm. From 1 May to early September it's open from 9 am to 6.30 pm.

Fort de Douaumont About one km northeast of the ossuary and the D913 lies Douaumont (☎ 29.84.18.85), the strongest of the 38 forts built to protect Verdun. Because the French high command disregarded warnings of an impending German offensive, it had only a skeleton crew when the Battle of Verdun began. By the fourth day it had been easily captured by a small contingent of Germans. Douaumont was not recaptured by the French until October 1916 in an assault led by colonial regiments from Morocco, Somaliland and Senegal, who suffered heavy casualties. Nowadays, a single soldier stands guard.

From mid-February to mid-December the fort is open daily except Monday. Hours vary depending on the month, but it's basically open from 9 or 10 am to noon and 2 to 5 or 6 pm. From 1 April to 31 October there's no midday closure. Entry costs 15/8FF for adults/children.

Musée Mémorial de Fleury This memorial museum (☎ 29.84.35.34) is situated near the former site of the village of Fleury, annihilated during savage fighting in which it changed hands 16 times. In an attempt to ensure that the world does not forget what happened around here, the exhibits tell the story of the Battle of Verdun using newsreel footage, photos, documents and military equipment.

The museum is open all year except from mid-December to mid-January daily from 9 am to noon and 2 to 5.30 pm. Between mid-March and mid-September, the hours are 9 am to 6 pm. Entrance costs 18/9FF per adult/child.

Fort de Vaux About three km from the D913, Vaux (☎ 29.84.18.85) was taken by the Germans in early June 1916 after the French defenders, who had run out of everything including breathable air, were forced to surrender. It was recaptured five months later.

The entry fees and opening hours are the same as those of Fort de Douaumont except that Vaux is closed on Wednesday.

Military Cemeteries

The **Cimetière Américain de Romagne-sous-Montfaucon**, where 14,000 American soldiers are buried, is 37 north-west of Verdun near the village of Romagne-sous-Montfaucon. Scattered among the commemorative sites and memorials, in the area north, north-west and west of Verdun, are **French and German military cemeteries**.

Organised Tours

From May to mid-September the Verdun tourist office runs a four-hour **guided tour** of the main memorials and forts. The tour begins at 2.15 pm and costs 135FF for adults.

Getting Around

To visit the battlefields on your own, you'll need a car (see Car under Getting There & Away in the Verdun, Metz or Nancy sections), a bicycle (and good leg muscles; see Getting Around in the Verdun section) or a very patient thumb. The Verdun tourist office has a free map whose route, if followed religiously, takes in every site.

By SIVOM bus (see Getting Around in the Verdun listing), the closest you can get to the battlefields is Bras-sur-Meuse (10FF; 10 minutes; five a day).

Champagne

The Champagne region has become famous around the world thanks to its most famous product: the prestigious sparkling wines that have been made here since the days of Dom Pérignon. Only bubbly from this region – grown, aged and bottled according to the strictest standards – can, according to French law, be labelled as champagne.

Champagne, which came under the French throne in 1314, is a sparsely populated region in the middle of northern France, midway between Calais and Alsace. It is bordered on the west by the Île de France, on the east by Lorraine and on the south by Burgundy. Northern Champagne runs into the French Ardennes, part of a massif which continues up through south-eastern Belgium and into Germany. The Ardennes region, once part of the pre-Revolutionary province of Champagne, is today once again united with Champagne – bureaucratically, at least – in the same administrative region.

The production of champagne takes place primarily in two *départements*, the Marne and the Aube. Over the years, intense rivalry between the two – and, for far longer, between their largest cities – has led to the creation of two regional capitals: Reims, which governs the north, and the ancient, picturesque city of Troyes, which looks after the south. Between the two sits the town of Épernay, the self-proclaimed capital of champagne (the drink) and probably the best place to head to if you're in the area primarily to indulge in *dégustation* (tasting). Two Routes du Champagne (champagne routes) wind through the region: one between Épernay and Reims (see the Around Reims section), the other in the area east of Troyes (see Around Troyes).

The main attractions of the Ardennes are its outdoor activities, though these are pretty much limited to the forests north of the main town, Charleville-Mézières, where the Meuse River flows through a deep valley steeped in folklore and legends. Stout *sanglier* (wild

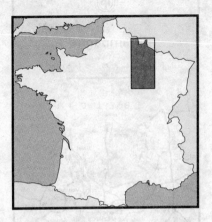

boar) and deer roam the forests around here, as do hunters. Seven signposted tourist routes crisscross the region, but without wheels they're hard to explore, as is most of the area once you get away from Charleville-Mézières.

REIMS

Continually in competition with Troyes for dominance of the Champagne region, Reims (anglicised as Rheims, and pronounced 'rance' with a French 'r'; population 185,000) has long played an important role in French history. More than two dozen French kings, including Charles VII, were crowned in the 'Coronation City', as Reims has become known.

More recently, Reims came under German occupation three times: in 1870, during WW I and again during WW II. Though under German occupation for only 11 days in 1914, the city spent the rest of WW I in the middle of the fighting, and 85% of the city's houses were destroyed by artillery shells fired from German positions on nearby hills. Until they were evacuated, city residents took refuge in the honeycomb of champagne cellars underneath the city's streets. Reims was again

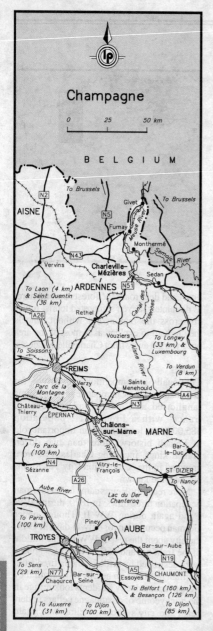

Champagne

0   25   50 km

BELGIUM

To Brussels
To Brussels
Givet
N2
N5
Fumay
AISNE
Meuse River
Monthermé
N43
Semois River
Vervins
Charleville-Mézières
Sedan
To Laon (4 km) & Saint Quentin (36 km)
ARDENNES
N51
A26
Canal des Ardennes
Rethel
Vouziers
To Longwy (33 km) & Luxembourg
To Soissons
Aisne River
To Verdun (8 km)
REIMS
Sainte Menehould
Parc de la Montagne
Verzy
A4
N3
Château-Thierry
ÉPERNAY
Châlons-sur-Marne
MARNE
Marne River
To Paris (100 km)
N4
Vitry-le-François
Bar-le-Duc
Sézanne
ST DIZIER
A26
To Nancy
Aube River
Lac du Der Chanteroq
To Paris (100 km)
Piney
AUBE
TROYES
Bar-sur-Aube
To Sens (29 km)
N77
N19
A5
CHAUMONT
Chaource
Bar-sur-Seine
Essoyes
To Belfort (160 km) & Besançon (126 km)
To Auxerre (31 km)
To Dijon (100 km)
To Dijon (85 km)

severely damaged during WW II. On 7 May 1945, Germany's unconditional surrender was signed here, effectively bringing an end to WW II in Europe.

These days, many visitors come to Reims eagerly anticipating the popping of champagne corks and the delicate fizz of tiny bubbles...But if you're expecting a free champagne tasting, brace yourself for an unpleasant surprise – or better still, head south to the champagne *maisons* in Épernay.

Orientation

The labyrinth of one-way streets – known to have collapsed occasionally under the weight of passing vehicles – makes walking the best way to get around the centre of Reims. There are a number of pedestrianised streets in the heart of the city near Place Drouet d'Erlon and Rue de Talleyrand. The A4 autoroute to Paris cuts through the city one km south-west of the centre.

Information

Tourist Office The tourist office (☎ 26.47. 25.69) is through the stone archways to the left (north-west) of the cathedral at 2 Rue Guillaume de Machaulthas. Hotel reservations cost 7FF. They also have a foreign exchange service. From October to Easter, the office is open Monday to Saturday from 9 am to 6.30 pm and on Sunday from 9.30 am to 5.30 pm. The rest of the year, it's open Monday to Saturday from 9 am to 7.30 pm and on Sunday from 9.30 am to 6.30 pm.

Money The Banque de France (☎ 26.40. 00.30) at 1 Place de l'Hôtel de Ville is open weekdays from 8.45 am to 12.20 pm and 1.40 to 3.45 pm.

There are plenty of banks in the city centre, including the Crédit du Nord (☎ 26.40. 07.88) at 16 Rue de Talleyrand, which is open on weekdays from 8 am to 12.10 pm and 1.45 to 5.15 pm.

Post The main post office (☎ 26.88.44.22) is near the train station at Place du Boulingrin. It is open weekdays from 8 am to 7 pm and Saturday from 8 am to noon. The branch at

CHAMPAGNE

1 Rue Cérès, through the archway from Place Royale, is open weekdays from 8.30 am to 6 pm and Saturday from 8 am to noon.

Reims's postcode is 51100.

Laundry The Lav-o-Clair at 29 Rue Chanzy is open daily from 7 am to 9 pm.

Squares
Despite the enormous damage Reims suffered during WW I and WW II, much of the city has been meticulously restored. Reims is graced by a number of elegant public squares, including **Place Royale** and **Place du Forum**.

Cathédrale Notre Dame
Reims's world-famous cathedral, begun in 1211 and completed over 300 years later, was for centuries the traditional site of royal coronations. It was badly damaged during WW I but was painstakingly restored, only to have its statue-covered, 13th-century façade face a new enemy: pollution. Many of the statues and tapestries that were removed for restoration were never put back – you can see them in the Palais du Tau. The interior, one of the most brilliant accomplishments of Gothic architecture, is brightened by two beautiful rose windows.

The cathedral, which is at the north-eastern end of Rue Libergier, is open daily from 7.30 am to 7.30 pm.

Basilique Saint Remi
This basilica, which is about 1.5 km south-east of the tourist office at Place Saint Remi, is Reims's most revered church. It is also northern France's largest Romanesque church, though repeated restorations have not left intact much of the original 11th-century structure, which was begun in 1007. The interior is remarkably long and narrow: 122 by 26 metres.

The basilica is open from 8 am (9 am on Thursday and Saturday) to sunset. To get there, take bus No A from the train station or the Théâtre stop and get off at the the Saint Remi stop.

Museums
The **Palais du Tau** (Tau Palace Museum; ☎ 26.47.74.39), which is at Place du Cardinal Luçon, was built in 1690. Its spacious rooms house tapestries, sculptures and other stunning artefacts that once graced the cathedral. It is open daily from 9.30 am to 12.30 pm and 2 to 6 pm, except in July and August, when the hours are 9.30 am to 6.30 pm. Admission is 23FF.

US General Dwight D Eisenhower's war room, where Germany officially captitulated on 7 May 1945, is known as the **Salle de Reddition** (Surrender Room). It is now a museum (☎ 26.47.84.19); the original battle maps are still affixed to the walls. Located at 12 Rue Franklin Roosevelt (behind the train station), the museum is open from 10 am to 12 and 2 to 6 pm (closed Tuesday). Admission costs 8FF.

Champagne Cellars
At least a dozen *caves* in and around Reims are open for tours. At some places you can just turn up, but at others you must ring ahead. Some have free tours, while others charge a fee, but in either case, you'll be hard-pressed to get a taste.

A couple of the cellars are relatively central. **Mumm** (☎ 26.49.59.70) at 34 Rue du Champ de Mars is the largest producer in Reims, with an output of 10 million bottles a year. From 1 March to 31 October, Mumm is open daily from 9 to 11 am and 2 to 5 pm. The rest of the year, it's closed on weekends. Tours are free. **Lanson** (☎ 26.78.50.50), nearby at 12 Blvd Lundy, has been around since 1760. Visits – possible only on weekdays – are by appointment.

Another option is to head 1.5 km southeast of the city centre to the green belt around Place des Droits de l'Homme. **Taittinger** (☎ 26.85.45.35), an old-style cellar at 9 Place Saint Nicaise, is open weekdays from 9.30 am to 1 pm and 2 to 5.30 pm. From 1 March to 30 November, it is also open on weekends from 9 am to noon and 2 to 6 pm. The tours, which include a video, cost 15FF. To get there from the train station or the city

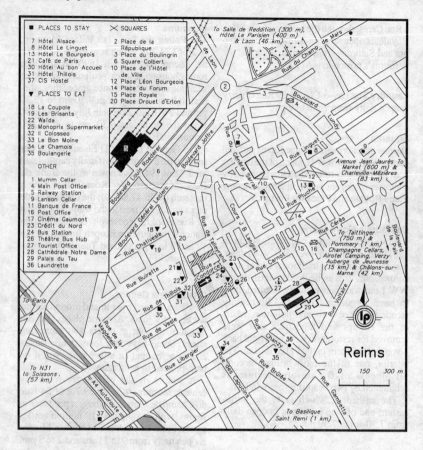

■ PLACES TO STAY		✕ SQUARES
7	Hôtel Alsace	2 Place de la
8	Hôtel Le Linguet	République
13	Hôtel Le Bourgeois	3 Place du Boulingrin
21	Café de Paris	6 Square Colbert
30	Hôtel Au bon Accueil	10 Place de l'Hôtel
31	Hôtel Thillois	de Ville
37	CIS Hostel	12 Place Léon Bourgeois
		14 Place du Forum
▼ PLACES TO EAT		15 Place Royale
		20 Place Drouet d'Erlon
18	La Coupole	
19	Les Brisants	
22	Waïda	
25	Monoprix Supermarket	
32	Il Colosseo	
33	Le Bon Moine	
34	Le Chamois	
35	Boulangerie	
OTHER		
1	Mumm Cellar	
4	Main Post Office	
5	Railway Station	
9	Lanson Cellar	
11	Banque de France	
16	Post Office	
17	Cinéma Gaumont	
23	Crédit du Nord	
24	Bus Station	
26	Théâtre Bus Hub	
27	Tourist Office	
28	Cathédrale Notre Dame	
29	Palais du Tau	
36	Laundrette	

centre, take bus No A to the Saint Timothée stop.

On the nearby hill sits **Pommery** (☎ 26. 61.62.55), whose street address is 5 Place du Général Gouraud. Its sizeable cellar is housed in an old Roman quarry. From mid-March to early November, this place is open on weekdays from 2 to 5 pm and on weekends from 9.20 to 11.20 am and 2 to 5 pm. In July and August, it is open daily from 9.20 am to 5 pm. Tours are free. Bus No A will take you to the Saint Timothée stop, whence you can take either bus No R to the Gouraud stop or walk (it's about 600 metres).

Festivals

In mid-June, two festivals run back to back to form one huge, five-day extravaganza. The three-day Les Sacres du Folklore, one of northern France's most celebrated folk festivals, is followed by Les Fêtes Johanniques, a medieval celebration that pays tribute to Joan of Arc, who brought Charles VII to Reims for his coronation in 1429.

Places to Stay

Inexpensive accommodation is not usually hard to come by, though in July and August it's a good idea to book ahead.

Benevolent angels; sculpture detail, Cathédrale Notre Dame, Reims

Camping The camping ground nearest Reims is the three-star *Airotel de Champagne* (☎ 26.85.41.22), which is on Ave Hoche about five km south-east of the train station. It costs 16FF for a tent and 19/8.50FF for each adult/child. This place is open from Easter to September. From the station, take bus No F to the Parc des Expos stop.

Hostels The *Centre International de Séjour* (CIS; ☎ 26.40.52.60) at Parc Léo Lagrange has singles/doubles for 73/122FF; breakfast is 9FF. Reception is open until 11 pm. This place is about 1.5 km south-west of the train station. To get there, take bus No H from the Théâtre stop and get off at the Pont de Gaulle stop.

The nearest official youth hostel is the *Auberge de Jeunesse* (☎ 26.97.90.10) at Rue du Bassin in the village of Verzy, about 15 km south-east of the city. It costs 55FF per person, including breakfast. Unfortunately, Verzy is not served by public transport.

Hotels – Train Station Area Located about 900 metres north of the station, the quiet *Hôtel Le Parisien* (☎ 26.47.32.89) at 3 Rue Périn has basic singles/doubles for 80/85FF; showers are 15FF extra. To get there from the station, you can either walk (head north along Blvd Joffre, then turn left onto Ave de Laon) or take bus No A to the Saint Thomas stop.

The *Hôtel Alsace* (☎ 26.47.44.08; fax 26.47.44.52) at 5 Rue du Général Sarrail, which is 500 metres from the station, has ordinary singles/doubles from 105/120FF and triples for 150FF; showers cost 12FF extra.

Hotels – City Centre There are plenty of affordable places to stay scattered throughout the city centre. To the north is the pleasant and cheap little *Hôtel Le Bourgeois* (☎ 26.47.42.72) at 5 Place Léon Bourgeois, on the corner of Rue Pluche. Rooms start at 85/115FF for a single/double without shower. There are no hall showers. Two blocks away, the airy and sunny *Hôtel Le Linguet* (☎ 26.47.31.89) at 14 Rue Linguet has rooms from 75/90FF.

On Place Drouet d'Erlon, a local nightlife centre, the *Café de Paris* (☎ 26.47.48.89) at No 33 has singles/doubles from 90/100FF. It may be noisy until late at night. Two blocks away along the slightly quieter Rue de Thillois, the *Hôtel Thillois* (☎ 26.40.65.65) at No 17 has rooms from 80/100FF. Even cheaper is *Au Bon Accueil* (☎ 26.88.55.74), down the road at No 31.

Places to Eat
There are lots of options for eating and drinking at Place Drouet d'Erlon, but you'll find places with less inflated prices on nearby side streets.

Restaurants Just off Place Drouet d'Erlon, *Les Brisants* (☎ 26.40.60.41) at 13 Rue de Chativesle has a 71FF, four-course *menu*. It can be enjoyed on the little back terrace. Across the road is the self-service *La Coupole* (☎ 26.47.86.28), with main courses from 34FF. Two blocks south, *Il Colosseo* (☎ 26.47.68.50) at 9 Rue de Thillois is a modern, average-priced pizzeria in the shell of the dilapidated opera house.

Just south of the centre, *Le Bon Moine* (The Good Monk; ☎ 26.47.33.64) at 14 Rue des Capucins is a two-star hotel with an affordable restaurant. The four-course *menu* costs 72FF. One block away, *Le Chamois* (☎ 26.88.69.75) at 45 Rue des Capucins has a good-value, three-course lunch *menu* for 45FF.

Self-Catering The *Monoprix* at 1 Rue de Talleyrand is open Monday to Saturday from 8.30 am to 7.30 pm. On any day except Wednesday, you might try the *boulangerie* at 48 Rue Chanzy, which is open from 7 am to 8.30 pm.

Waïda at 3 Place Drouet d'Erlon is a tea room-cum-boulangerie. It's open Monday to Saturday from 7 am to 8 pm and on Sunday from 7 am to 1 pm and 2.30 to 8 pm. *Street markets* take over Place du Boulingrin on

Wednesday and Saturday mornings (until 2 pm) and Ave Jean Jaurès on Sunday morning (until 1 pm).

Entertainment
Brasseries and cafés with terraces line Place Drouet d'Erlon, the focal point of Reims's nightlife. *Cinéma Gaumont* (☎ 26.47.54.54) at No 72 screens nondubbed movies. For details on local happenings, pick up a copy of the pamphlet entitled *Rendez-vous* at the tourist office.

Getting There & Away
Train The train station (☎ 26.88.50.50 for information) is behind Square Colbert, which is 900 metres north-west of the tourist office. The station is linked to the tourist office by bus Nos A, C and F. The information office is open weekdays from 8.30 am to 7 pm and on Saturday from 9 am to 6.15 pm. The station building is open from 5 am to 11 pm.

Destinations served by direct trains include Paris's Gare de l'Est (100FF; 45 minutes; seven a day), Charleville-Mézières (61FF; 50 minutes; seven a day), Épernay (28FF; 30 minutes; 15 a day) and Châlons-sur-Marne (35FF; 40 minutes; 10 a day). There are also trains to Strasbourg, Dijon, Lyon, Avignon, Marseille and Nice. The best way to get to Troyes is by bus.

Bus The bus station is on the corner of Rue Talleyrand and Rue Condourcet. Transchampagne buses (STDM; ☎ 26.65.17.07) to Châlons-sur-Marne and Troyes (90FF; two hours) pick up passengers both here and at the train station. This line operates three times a day on weekdays and twice on Saturday.

Car Eurorent (☎ 26.47.15.80) is at 4 Rue Duquenelle. Citer (☎ 26.04.68.56) has an agency at 38 Ave P Vaillant-Couturier in the Reims suburb of Tinqueux.

Getting Around
Bus TUR (☎ 26.88.25.38), which runs the local buses, has an information kiosk near

Champagne

Champagne appeared on the French wine scene in the late 17th century thanks to Dom Pierre Pérignon, the innovative cellar master of the Benedictine Abbey at Hautvillers (near Reims), who perfected a technique for making sparkling wine of consistent quality (earlier bubbly had proved remarkably – even explosively – unpredictable). He then proceeded to put his product in strong, English-made bottles (the local bottles couldn't take the enormous pressure) and capped them, thereby sealing in the bubbles, with a new kind of bottle stopper – mushroom-shaped corks brought from Spain. The 'king of wine and wine of kings' is still favoured by kings and other people who can afford to pay handsomely for the pleasure of having their palates tickled by millions of tiny bubbles.

Champagne is made using only three varieties of grapes: Chardonnay, Pinot Noir and Pinot Meunier. Each vine is vigorously pruned and trained to produce a small quantity of high-quality grapes. Indeed, to maintain exclusiveness (and prices), the amount of champagne that can be produced each year is limited to between 160 and 220 million bottles. The majority of this is consumed in France.

The process of making champagne – carried out by innumerable *maisons* (houses), large and small – is a long one. There are two fermentations, the first in casks, the second after the wine has been bottled and had sugar and yeast added. In years of a less-than-excellent vintage, wines from other years are blended together to create what is known as 'nonvintage champagne'.

During the two months that the bottles are aged – stacked horizontally – in cellars kept at 12˚C, the wine they contain becomes effervescent. The sediment that forms in the bottle is removed by *remuage*, a painstakingly slow process in which each bottle is turned a fraction of a rotation every day for weeks until the sludge works its way down to the cork. Next comes *dégorgement*: the neck of the bottle is frozen, creating a blob of solidified champagne and sediment which is then removed.

At this stage, the champagne's sweetness is determined by adding varying amounts of syrup dissolved in old champagne. If the final product is labelled *brut*, it is very dry. *Extra-dry* mean it's dry, *sec* is slightly sweet and *demi-sec* is sweet. There's also *rosé* (pink champagne), a gentle blend of red and white wines that has long been snubbed by connoisseurs. Lastly, the bottles of young champagne are laid horizontally in a cellar. Ageing lasts for between two and five years (and sometimes longer), depending on the *cuvée* (vintage). ■

the cathedral at 6 Rue Chanzy. Most buses can be picked up either at the Théâtre stop on Rue de Vesle or nearby.

Taxi For taxis call ☎ 26.47.05.05 or 26.02.15.02.

AROUND REIMS
Route Touristique du Champagne
This 75-km Champagne route meanders from Reims to Épernay and passes through three important wine-growing areas: the Montagne de Reims, the Côte des Blancs and the Vallée de la Marne. It goes through and around the **Parc Naturel Régional de la Montagne**, a regional park that encompasses the strange forest of Faux de Verzy, near Verzy, where beech trees live in total disorder, gnarled and often with two or more trunks.

From Épernay, the Route du Champagne continues southward to Sézanne. En route, you pass through numerous villages where private maisons welcome those in search of a taste of bubbly. Ask local tourist offices for information on the Route Touristique and an official maison list, which has useful tips on each place: whether it's free, if you must telephone before stopping by and in what languages the *vigneron* (wine grower) can communicate.

ÉPERNAY
Épernay (population 27,700), an ordinary-looking provincial town set amidst the vineyards that cover the gentle slopes of the Marne River valley, is home to some of the world's most famous champagne houses. Their headquarters are situated in a long row along Épernay's main street, Ave de Cham-

pagne, considered by some the richest street in the world. Indeed, tens of millions of bottles of champagne – just waiting to be popped open for some sparkling celebration – are being aged in Épernay's many km of subterranean galleries (one of which hosted a car rally in 1950 without the loss of a single bottle). By train, Épernay can be visited as a day trip from Reims.

Orientation & Information

Épernay's main street, Ave de Champagne, is the focus of most of the town's activities.

Tourist Office The modest tourist office (☎ 26.55.33.00) at 7 Ave de Champagne is open Monday to Saturday from 9.30 am to 12.30 pm and 1.30 to 7 pm, and on Sunday from 11 am to 4 pm. From mid-October until Easter, it's closed on Sunday, and during the rest of the week stays open only until 5 pm. The staff will reserve a hotel room for a stiff 25FF fee. There's no exchange service.

Money The Banque de France (☎ 26.55. 59.00) at Place de la République is open weekdays from 8.45 am to noon and 1.45 to 4 pm.

Post The main post office (☎ 26.55.59.31) on Place Hugues Plomb is open weekdays from 8 am to 7 pm and on Saturday from 8 am to noon.

Épernay's postcode is 51200.

Laundry The laundrette on Ave Jean Jaurès is open daily from 7 am to 9 pm.

Champagne Houses

Épernay has 10 well-known champagne maisons, most of them along Ave de Champagne and thus easily accessible both on foot and by car. At some of them, your visit alone will be reason enough to open a bottle, while at others – as in Reims – there's a fee to get in but nothing to taste.

Heading down Ave de Champagne, the first *maison* you come to is **Moët & Chandon** (☎ 26.54.71.11) at No 20, which is only a few metres from the tourist office. The free tours at this prestigious house end with a tasting. Moët is open on weekdays from 9.30 am to noon and 2 to 5 pm. From 1 April to 31 October, it's also open on weekends. For the next 700 metres or so of the avenue, every building is a champagne

The cellar of Moët & Chandon

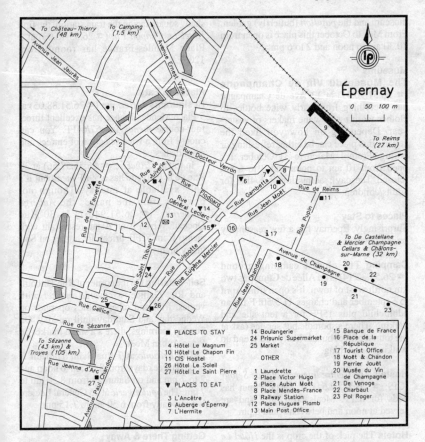

Épernay

0   50   100 m

To Château-Thierry (48 km)
To Camping (1.5 km)
Avenue Jean Jaurès
Avenue Ernest Vallé
To Reims (27 km)
Rue Docteur Verron
Rue de la Juiverie
Rue Gambetta
Rue de Reims
Rue Godard
Rue Général Leclerc
Rue Jean Moët
Rue Pupin
Rue de la Fauvette
Rue Saint Thibault
Rue Cuissotte
Rue Eugène Mercier
To De Castellane & Mercier Champagne Cellars & Châlons-sur-Marne (32 km)
Avenue de Champagne
Rue Jean Chandon
Rue Gallice
Rue de Sézanne
To Sézanne (43 km) & Troyes (105 km)
Rue Jeanne d'Arc
Avenue Paul Chandon

■ PLACES TO STAY	14 Boulangerie	15 Banque de France
	24 Prisunic Supermarket	16 Place de la République
4 Hôtel Le Magnum	25 Market	17 Tourist Office
10 Hôtel Le Chapon Fin		18 Moët & Chandon
11 CIS Hostel	OTHER	19 Perrier Jouët
26 Hôtel Le Soleil	1 Laundrette	20 Musée du Vin de Champagne
27 Hôtel Le Saint Pierre	2 Place Victor Hugo	21 De Venoge
	5 Place Auban Moët	22 Charbaut
▼ PLACES TO EAT	8 Place Mendès-France	23 Pol Roger
	9 Railway Station	
3 L'Ancêtre	12 Place Hugues Plomb	
6 Auberge d'Épernay	13 Main Post Office	
7 L'Hermite		

maison: Perrier Jouët, De Venoge, Charbaut, Pol Roger. Most require that you call ahead for an appointment.

At the far end of Ave de Champagne, nearly 1.5 km south-east of the tourist office on the edge of the vineyards, is **Mercier** (☎ 26.54.75.26) at No 73, which claims to be France's 'most well known brand'. Tours of its Espace Mercier are free and highly entertaining, providing a taste of the flair and glitter which – supposedly – spice life's celebrations as soon as a champagne cork is popped. Everything here is on a grand scale, from the entrance guarded by the second-

biggest barrel in the world (it can hold the equivalent of 200,000 bottles) to the elevator that transports you 30 metres underground to the laser-conducted train. In summer, Mercier is open Monday to Saturday from 9.30 to 11.30 am and 2 to 5 pm, and on Sunday from 9 am to 7 pm. In winter, it opens only on weekends; the hours are the same as in summer.

Between Moët and Mercier is **De Castellane** (☎ 26.55.15.33), which is just off the Avenue at 57 Rue de Verdun. The 15FF cellar tours do not include a wine tasting. There's an additional fee to visit the champagne museum and the *papillon* (butterfly) garden. From May to October this place is open from 10.30 am to noon and 2 to 6 pm.

Museums
The **Musée du Vin de Champagne** (☎ 26.51.90.31) at 13 Ave de Champagne has everything from early wine bottles to clothes worn by the wine makers of yester-year. Depending on how you liked the cellars, this place can be either refreshing or boring. From 1 March to 31 October, it's open from 10 am to noon and 2 to 6 pm (closed Tuesday); admission is 8/4FF for adults/children.

Places to Stay
Surprisingly, Épernay has a few reasonably priced hotels.

Camping The closest camping ground (☎ 26.55.32.14) is on Allée de Cumières two km north-west of town. It's open from April to September and charges 11/5.50FF for an adult/child plus 15FF for a tent site and parking. There's sporadic bus service (ask at the tourist office) but it's likely you'll end up walking or hitching.

Hostels The *Centre International de Séjour* (CIS; ☎ 26.51.62.51) at 2 Rue Pupin has beds for 62FF. Meals cost 39FF and are served at noon and between 7 and 8 pm.

Hotels The pick of the crop is the *Hôtel Le Saint Pierre* (☎ 26.54.40.80) a little way out of the centre at 1 Rue Jeanne d'Arc. Occupying an elegant mansion built early in the century, this place has rooms that aren't as characterful as the building but are an excellent deal at 93/105FF for a single/double. Private parking is available.

A few streets closer to the centre, the *Hôtel Le Soleil* (☎ 26.54.51.80) at 44 Rue Eugène Mercier has only four rooms, all for 110FF. There's a popular bar below.

Right in the centre, the *Hôtel Le Magnum* (☎ 26.55.65.69) at 18 Rue de la Juiverie has decent but more expensive rooms starting at 90/130FF for a single/double. On the cool, shady square facing the train station, the fine *Hôtel Le Chapon Fin* (☎ 26.55.40.03) at 2 Place Mendès-France has rooms from 120FF.

Places to Eat
Restaurants *L'Hermite* (☎ 26.51.88.05) at 5 Place Mendès-France has excellent three/four-course *menus* for 57/64FF. You can choose from a wide selection of entrées and main dishes.

In town, *L'Ancêtre* (☎ 26.55.57.56) at 20 Rue de la Fauvette has a 59FF *menu* but it's only available at midday. Though not obvious from the name, the *Auberge d'Épernay* (☎ 26.51.94.67) at 30 Rue Docteur Verron is an Asian restaurant with *menus* from 52FF; prices are higher on Saturday nights.

Self-Catering On the corner of Rue Thibault and Rue Gallice, a *covered market* with vegies, fruit and other edibles operates on Wednesday and Saturday until midday. On Sunday mornings, there's a small market on Place Auban Moët.

The *Prisunic* at 7 Rue Saint Thibault is open on weekdays from 8.30 am to noon and 2 to 7 pm and on Saturday from 8.30 am to 7 pm. The *boulangerie* at 25 Général Leclerc is open daily from 6.30 am to 7.15 pm.

Getting There & Away
Train Épernay's train station is at Place Mendès-France, just a few minutes' walk from the centre. The information office is open Monday to Saturday from 9 am to noon and 2 to 6 pm. At other times of the day, information is available at the ticket windows; you might also call the SNCF information office in Reims (☎ 26.88.50.50).

There is rail service to Paris's Gare de l'Est (95FF; 1¼ hours; eight a day), Reims (28FF; 30 minutes; 15 a day), Châlons-sur-Marne (30FF; 15 minutes), Saint Dizier, Metz, Verdun (via Châlons-sur-Marne) and Strasbourg.

TROYES

Though not quaint, Troyes (population 65,000) – like Reims, one of the historic capitals of Champagne – is a pleasant enough city, with lots of medieval and Renaissance houses, a number of interesting churches and some unique and very worthwhile museums. Effective town planning has, in recent years, added a few well-conceived new features, such as the Marché des Halles (covered market). Unlike Reims and Épernay, Troyes does not have any champagne cellars.

History

In the 12th and 13th centuries, Troyes, which is on the Seine River, grew exceptionally prosperous as a consequence of its trade fairs, three-month-long affairs which attracted artisans and merchants from all over Western Europe. It is thanks to these fairs that gold, silver and other precious metals are, to this day, measured in troy ounces. In 1524, a huge conflagration turned much of Troyes, including 1000 of its houses, into ashes.

In the early 16th century, Troyes began to produce *bonneterie* (hosiery). Later, especially after the mid-1700s, when mechanical looms based on English designs were introduced, production expanded to include socks, stockings, hats and bonnets. Hosiery's hold over life in Troyes continued to grow until even the destitute children living in the local charity hospital had to earn their keep by working the looms. Before long, the town had become the knitwear capital of France, a title it has retained to this day.

Orientation

Tourist brochures never tire of pointing out that the city centre, which is bounded by Blvd Gambetta, Blvd Victor Hugo, Blvd du 14 Juillet and the Seine, is shaped like a champagne cork. The train station and the tourist office are at the cork's westernmost extremity. Most of the city's sights and activities are in the square part of the cork 'below' (south-west of) the cork's bulbous head.

However, the cathedral and the Musée d'Art Moderne are in the 'head' in a district known as Quartier de la Cité. The old town is centred around the 17th-century Hôtel de Ville (on Place Alexandre Israël) and nearby Église Saint Jean.

Information

Tourist Office The main tourist office (☎ 25.73.00.36) is a block from the train station at 16 Blvd Carnot. From mid-September to June, it is open Monday to Saturday from 9 am to 12.30 pm and 2 to 6.30 pm; it *might* also be open on Sunday and major holidays. From 1 July to 15 September, it's open Monday to Saturday from 9 am to 8.30 pm (7.30 pm in September) and on Sunday and holidays from 10 am to noon and 2.30 to 5.30 pm.

The tourist office will make hotel reservation in Troyes for 15FF; there's a 22FF fee for bookings in the rest of France. It will exchange money when the banks are closed, but the rate is not very good. The booklet *Flânerie dans le Vieux Troyes* (A Stroll in Old Troyes) is available for 17FF.

From July to mid-September the tourist

Rashi

During the 11th and 12th centuries, a small Jewish community was established in Troyes under the protection of the counts of Champagne. Its most illustrious member was Rabbi Shlomo Yitzhaki (1040-1105), who is better known by his acronym, Rashi (Rachi in French). His commentaries on the Bible and the Talmud, which are still vastly important to Jews and have had an impact on Christian Bible interpretation, combine literal and nonliteral methods of interpretation, making extensive use of allegory, symbolism and parable. In 1475 his Bible commentary became the first book to be printed in Hebrew. Rashi's habit of explaining difficult words and passages in the vernacular (written in Hebrew characters) has made his writings an important source for scholars of Old French. ■

office's main annexe (☎ 25.73.36.88) at 24 Quai Dampierre is open Monday to Saturday from 10.30 am to 12.30 pm and 2 to 6.30 pm. In summer, the tourist office also has nine *points d'acceuil* (information tables) at various spots around town, including at six of the churches.

Money The Banque de France (☎ 25.42.44.46/47), 250 metres from the train station at 6 Blvd Victor Hugo, is open weekdays from 9 am to 12.30 pm and 1.30 to 4 pm.

Some commercial banks are open Monday to Friday, while others are open from Tuesday to Saturday. The BNP on Rue Émile Zola is open weekdays from 8.35 am to 12.05 pm and 1.40 to 5.25 pm. There are other banks around the Hôtel de Ville.

Post The main post office (☎ 25.42.32.32) at 38 Rue Louis Ulbach is open weekdays from 8 am to 7 pm and on Saturday from 8 am to noon. Near the train station, the branch (☎ 25.73.09.69) at Place Général Patton, which does not exchange foreign currency, is open Monday to Friday from 8 am to 6.30 pm and on Saturday from 8 am to noon.

Troyes's postcode is 10000.

Bookshop The Maison de la Presse at 27 Rue Émile Zola has a decent selection of English novels. It's open Monday to Saturday from 7.30 am to noon and 2 to 7 pm.

Laundry The Salon Lavoir GTI at 15 Rue de Turenne is open daily from 7 am to 9 pm.

Old Town

Unlike the half-timbered houses elsewhere in France, whose vertical beams are held in place by timbers set either at an angle or in the form of an 'X', those in Champagne use horizontal beams to stabilise their vertical timbers. Many such houses can be seen in Troyes's old town, which was rebuilt after the devastating fire of 1524 and has recently been renovated, especially along Rue Paillot de Montabert, Rue Champeaux and Rue de Vauluisant.

Off Rue Champeaux, a stroll along tiny

Ruelle des Chats (literally, Alley of the Cats), which is as dark and narrow as it was four centuries ago, is like stepping back into the Middle Ages.

Cathédrale Saint Pierre et Saint Paul

Troyes's cathedral (☎ 25.80.09.60), which is at the north-eastern end of Rue de la Cité, was begun in 1208 but wasn't finished until well into the 16th century. As a result, it incorporates elements from every period of Champenois Gothic architecture. The Flamboyant Gothic **west façade**, for instance, is from the mid-16th century, whereas the chancel and transepts are over 250 years older. The interior is illuminated by a spectacular series of about 180 **stained-glass windows** from the 13th to the 17th centuries.

The cathedral is open daily from 9 am to noon and 3 to 5 or 6 pm. In the summer months, it's open from 8.30 am to 7.30 pm. The tiny **treasury**, which costs 8FF (5FF for students, 3FF for children under 12), is open on weekends and holidays from 2.30 to 6 pm; from July to the end of September, it is open the same hours every day except Monday.

Église Sainte Madeleine

Troyes's oldest (and most interesting) church, named in honour of St Mary Magdalen, is on the corner of Rue Général de Gaulle and Rue de la Madeleine. The early Gothic nave and transept date from the mid-12th century, but the choir and tower weren't built until the Renaissance.

The main attraction is the arched, Flamboyant Gothic **roodscreen** *(jubé)*, the intricately carved, unsupported stone canopy at the transept end of the choir. It is one of a handful of France's once-numerous roodscreens – which served to separate the congregation from the clergy – that were not removed. The statue of a deadly serious **Saint Martha**, which is around the pillar from the wooden pulpit in the nave, is considered a masterpiece of the 15th-century Troyes School.

From July to mid-September this church is open daily from 10.30 am to 7 pm. In June and from mid-September to the end of

Troyes

LP

0   100   200 m

CHAMPAGNE

To Camping (2.5 km), Parc Naturel
Régional de la Forêt d'Orient (25 km),
Bar-sur-Aube (53 km), Châlons-sur-Marne
(80 km), Epernay & Reims (via N77)

To N19 Sézanne (62 km),
Epernay (81 km) & Reims
(108 km)

Ave de Chomedey de Miasonneuve

Ave Major Général G Vanier

To Notre Dame
en l'Ile (Hostel)
(150 m)

Quartier
de la
Cité

Seine River

Rue Kléber

Rue Jacquin

Cours

Rue Mitantier

Rue Graszon

Rue Hennequin

Rue Boucherat

Rue de la Cité

Quai des Comtes de Champagne

Quai Dampierre

Rue Urbain

Rue de la République

Rue Pithou

Rue Gambetta

Rue Général

Boulevard Gambetta

Rue Camille

Old
Town

Rue Champeaux

Rue Émile

Rue Turenne

Rue Louis Ulbach

Rue Raymond

Poincaré

Rue Jaillant

Rue Général

Rue Roger Salengro

Rue Paul Dubois

Boulevard Carnot

Rue Voltaire

Rue Courtalon

Avenue
Maréchal
Joffre

To Sens
(65 km)

Boulevard Victor Hugo

Rue Jeanne d'Arc

Boulevard du 14 Juillet

Ave Pierre Brossolette
(to Auberge de Jeunesse
(4 km), Lusigny-sur-Barse (13 km),
Bar-sur-Aube (53 km),
& Essoyes (43 km)

PLACES TO STAY	
16	Hôtel Le Trianon
21	Hôtel du Théâtre
23	Hôtel Thiers
27	Hôtel Le Marigny
29	Hôtel de Paris
32	Hôtel de la Gare
37	Patriotel
38	Royal Hôtel
40	Hôtel Splendid & ADA Car Rental
47	Select Hôtel
48	Hôtel Butat

PLACES TO EAT	
1	Casino Supermarket
3	Café du Musée
9	L'Arcisen
13	La Boîte à Fromage
15	Marché des Halles
17	Santa Fé American Restaurant
18	Boulangerie
19	De l'Étoile
24	Resto Station Istanbul
35	Le Self du Centre
37	Restaurant du Royal Hôtel
46	Les Quatre Saisons
49	Fromagerie
52	Restaurant de l'Alhambra
54	Au Bon Bec
55	Aux Délices de l'Escargot
56	De Provence
58	Prisunic Supermarket

OTHER	
2	Abbaye Saint Loup
5	Cathédrale Saint Pierre et Saint Paul
6	Musée d'Art Moderne
7	Musée de la Pharmacie de l'Hôtel Dieu
8	Tourist Office Annexe
11	Théâtre de Champagne
12	Monument to Rashi
14	Église Saint Rémy
20	Basilique Saint Urbain
22	Église Sainte Madeleine
26	Hôtel de Ville
28	Synagogue
34	Railway Station
35	Bus Station
36	Main Tourist Office
38	Post Office
39	Europcar Car Rental
42	Banque de France
43	Maison de l'Agriculture
44	Hôtel de Vauluisant
45	Église Saint Pantaléon
50	Salon Lavoir GTI
51	Maison de l'Outil et de la Pensée Ouvrière
53	Cinéma Le Paris
57	Église Saint Jean
59	BNP (Bank)
60	Maison de la Presse
62	Main Post Office

✕ SQUARES	
4	Place Saint Pierre
10	Place de la Libération
33	Place de la Gare
41	Place Général Patton
61	Place Langevin

October, it may be open a couple of hours a day, but during the rest of the year it's closed except during services.

Other Churches

Troyes's other seven old churches include the Renaissance-style **Église Saint Pantaléon**, built from 1508 to 1672 on the erstwhile site of a synagogue. The interior is decorated with dozens of 16th-century statues, most of them made by local artisans. In July and August (and perhaps during the first half of September), it is open daily. During the rest of the year, is is closed except during mass.

The Gothic **Basilique Saint Urbain** at Place Vernier was begun in 1262 by Troyes-born Pope Urban IV, whose father's shoemaking shop once stood on this spot. The west porch was added in the late 19th century. While the choir is being reinforced – a multiyear project – the fine 13th-century stained-glass windows will remain in storage. The church's best known statue is that of **La Vierge au Raisin**, a graceful, early 15th-century stone carving of the Virgin, which is in the choir.

Jewish Sites

There is a striking **monument to Rashi** (Rachi) across from 5 Rue Louis Mony (next to the Théâtre de Champagne). The writing around the base is not in standard 'square' Hebrew characters but rather in what is known as 'Rashi script', a Hebrew alphabet used by Jewish scholars during the Middle Ages.

The present-day Jewish community numbers only about 120 families, most of them of North African origin. The **Synagogue** (☎ 25.73.53.01) at 5 Rue Brunneval, built partly in a mock 16th-century style, was inaugurated in 1987. It is open only during prayers. The **Institut Universitaire Rachi**, which offers courses on Jewish thought to both Jews and non-Jews, is across the street. It is run by a former chief rabbi of France, Rabbi Sirat.

Museums

A combined ticket *(billet groupé)* valid for entrance to the four municipal museums – the Hôtel de Vauluisant, the Musée d'Art Moderne, the Musée de la Pharmacie de l'Hôtel Dieu and the Abbaye Saint Loup – costs 20FF (10FF if you're under 18). All four are free on Wednesday.

Hôtel de Vauluisant Troyes's most interesting museum is the unique **Musée de la Bonneterie** (Hosiery & Knitwear Museum; ☎ 25.42.33.33, ext 3592), which is hidden away in the 16th-century, Renaissance-style Hôtel de Vauluisant at 4 Rue de Vauluisant (just behind Église Saint Pantaléon). The knitwear industry's rise to fame and fortune is traced with displays of old nightcaps, slippers and other such objects. On the lower level, there are some very impressive gadgets, all invented for the purpose of knitting things.

The Hôtel de Valuisant also contains the **Musée Historique de Troyes et de la Champagne**, which has exhibits on the history of Troyes as well as exhibits of religious statuary, paintings (especially 16th-century) and coins. Both museums are open from 10 am to noon and 2 to 6 pm (closed Tuesday). Admission is 15FF (5FF for those under 18) but is free on Wednesday.

Maison de l'Outil et de la Pensée Ouvrière No less specialised than the hosiery museum is the Museum of Tools & Crafts (☎ 25.73.28.26), located in the 16th-century Hôtel de Mauroy at 7 Rue de la Trinité. Exhibits include thousands of lovingly displayed hand tools – many from the 18th century – used by artisans of all sorts; many have obviously been worn down over several decades by workers' hands and the materials they were shaping.

This museum is open daily from 9 am to noon and 2 to 6 pm; admission is 20FF for adults.

Musée d'Art Moderne Back in this century, the very worthwhile Museum of Modern Art (☎ 25.80.57.30), housed in the former episcopal palace (16th, 17th and 19th centuries), is next to the cathedral at Place Saint Pierre. Its exhibits are made up primarily of an amazing collection of art dating from 1850 to 1950 that was donated to the State by local hosiery magnates Pierre and Denise Lévy. The catalogue reads like a who's who of modern art: Cézanne, Matisse, Picasso and Modigliani, to name just a few. Also included is a collection of African and South Pacific art and some delightful turn-of-the-century works by local artist Maurice Marinot.

The museum is open from 11 am to 6 pm (closed Tuesday and holidays). Entry costs 15FF (10FF for people over 65, 5FF for people under 18).

Musée de la Pharmacie de l'Hôtel Dieu This former hospital (☎ 25.76.13.78), founded in the 12th century, is on Quai des Comtes de Champagne opposite the tourist office's main annexe. The two *cadrans solaires* (sundials) – one above the other – that face the street on an angled wall date from 1764.

The fully outfitted, wood-panelled **pharmacy** (☎ 25.80.98.97), which looks just as it did when it was built in the early 1700s, is known for the wooden boxes on which the names and pictures of the medicinal plants

they contained are painted. The hundreds of jugs and jars on display were used for storing medicines, salves, balms and the like.

This place is open from 10 am to noon and 2 to 6 pm (closed Tuesday). Entrance costs 10FF (5FF for people under 18). The 18th-century **chapelle** and the **crypte**, which are free, are open from 3 to 7 pm (closed Tuesday).

Abbaye Saint Loup This former abbey (☎ 25.42.33.33, ext 3592) at 1 Rue Chrestien de Troyes has been turned into a museum with four sections:

- natural history (to the right of the entrance): mostly a collection of skeletons and stuffed animals;
- the regional archaeology museum (in the cellar), which covers everything from prehistory to the Roman period and the Merovingian era;
- the *beaux-arts* (fine arts) section (on the 1st floor), whence you can gaze into a vast (50-metre-long), 17th-to-19th-century library, whose 18 rows of shelving hold 46,000 rare books from the 16th to 18th centuries;
- a room of somewhat eroded bits of medieval churches (capitals, gargoyles, etc).

The Abbaye is open from 10 am to noon and 2 to 6 pm (closed Tuesday and holidays). Entrance costs 15FF (10FF if you're over 65, 5FF if you're under 18).

Festivals
The Nuits de Champagne is a two-week festival of rock, jazz, French songs and the like held each year sometime in October. The Semaine Chantante, a week of choral concerts (especially by childrens' choruses), takes place on even-numbered years in the middle of July.

Places to Stay – bottom end
Troyes has quite a good selection of inexpensive hotels. Most of them have at least some rooms with both shower and toilet.

Camping The *Camping Municipal* (☎ 25. 81.02.64) at 7 Rue Roger Salengro in Pont Sainte Marie is about 3.5 km north-east of the train station. It is open from April to 15

October and charges 11.80FF for a tent site and parking plus 7.60FF per adult. There's a supermarket nearby. To get there take bus No 1 (last one at 7 pm) from Place Langevin and get off at the J Guesde stop.

You can camp at the Auberge de Jeunesse (see Hostels) for 22FF per person.

Down on the Farm For information on places to stay in the countryside (gîtes ruraux, fermes auberges, gîtes d'étape and camping à la ferme), contact the Maison de l'Agriculture (☎ 25.73.25.36) at 2bis Rue Jeanne d'Arc, which is 600 metres south of the train station.

Hostels *Notre Dame en l'Île* (☎ 25.80. 54.96) at 10 Rue de l'Île, a church-affiliated hostel run by nuns and lay volunteers, accepts travellers of all backgrounds for short stays. Beds, most of them in simple but large, clean doubles, are 45FF each (plus 15FF for sheets). Showers and toilets are in the hall. Unmarried couples might want to stay elsewhere.

Reception is open Monday to Saturday from 9 to 11.30 am and 2 to 6 pm; if you'll be arriving after 6 pm or on Sunday, call ahead and they'll leave the key in the kitchen. Reservations can be made by telephone. There's no curfew, but you need to pick up a key if you'll be coming back after 10.30 pm. To get to the hostel from the train station, take bus No 1 (towards Pont Sainte Marie) and get off at Rue Kleber. This line runs until about 9 pm.

The *Auberge de Jeunesse* (☎ 25.82.00.65; fax 25.72.93.78), at 2 Rue Jules Ferry in the Troyes suburb of Rosières (postcode 10430), is about 5.5 km south of the train station. They charge 43FF for a bed, 15FF for sheets, 16FF for breakfast and 45FF for a meal. A hostelling card is not mandatory. Reception is open daily, year round from 8 am to noon and 2 to 10 pm. To get out there, take bus No 6 from the train station or Place Langevin to the Thénard terminus. Then take bus No 11 to the Liberté stop. The last No 6 leaves at 8.45 pm. Unfortunately, there are very few No 11 buses on weekdays, even fewer on Saturday and none at all on Sunday. On weekdays, the last No 11 starts its run at 5.55 pm.

For information about staying in *foyers* during the summer school holidays, ask at the tourist office.

Hotels – Train Station Area The two-star *Hôtel de la Gare* (☎ 25.78.22.84; fax 25.74.16.26), a bar-hotel at 8 Blvd Carnot, has rooms with washbasin and bidet for 130FF. Rooms with shower cost 185FF (215FF with shower and toilet). There's plenty of street parking out the front. Up the road, the cheaper but rather prim *Hôtel Splendid* (☎ 25.73.08.52) at No 44 has decent singles/doubles from 105/140FF. It's on a busy intersection.

Hotels – City Centre The choice here is ample. The friendly *Hôtel du Théâtre* (☎ 25.73.18.47) at 35 Rue Jules Lebocey has singles/doubles for 90/100FF (with washbasin and bidet), 103/113FF (with shower) and 125/135FF (with bath). None of the rooms has private toilets. Hall showers cost 19FF. Breakfast is 15FF. Reception is closed on Sunday after 4 pm and on Monday; if you'll be arriving during these periods, call ahead.

Another old classic is the 27-room *Hôtel de Paris* (☎ 25.73.11.70) at 56 Rue Roger Salengro. Fairly large singles/doubles are 95/105FF (with washbasin and bidet) and 145/170FF (with bath and toilet). The inside rooms are quieter. Hall showers cost 15FF extra. Breakfast is 23FF.

The *Hôtel Le Trianon* (☎ 25.73.18.52) at 2 Rue Pithou (across from the Marché des Halles) has singles/doubles with washbasin and toilet from 90/120FF. Rooms for three or four people are 200FF. Hall showers are free. Reception is closed on Sunday after 2 pm. If you like to sleep in, beware – the loudspeakers on the street are designed to get you up and out into the shops.

The bright orange, modern exterior of the *Select Hôtel* (☎ 25.73.36.16) at 1 Rue de Vauluisant hides a slightly run-down but cheap enough place. Basic but serviceable rooms with washbasin start at 75/100FF. A two-bed quad with washbasin and bidet is 150FF. Hall showers are free. Breakfast is 19FF. It has linoleum floors and tacky wallpaper, but the rooms have high ceilings and the location is great. Reception is closed on Tuesday from noon to 6 pm.

Nearby, at 50 Rue de Turenne, the two-star *Hôtel Butat* (☎ 25.73.77.39) has singles/doubles for 140/160FF (with shower) and 150/170FF (with shower and toilet). Triples with bath and toilet go for 240FF. There are no hall showers. Reception, whose staff cannot be described as gushingly personable, is closed on Sunday from 1 to 5 pm.

If you're stuck, you might try the *Hôtel Le Marigny* (☎ 23.73.10.67), which is in an old house at 3 Rue Charbonnet. Singles/doubles cost 100 to 135FF without shower *or* toilet, 145/175FF with shower and 165/195FF with shower and toilet. Hall showers are 15FF extra. The rooms are decent enough but the hotel as a whole is run down, musty and even a bit dirty.

Places to Stay – middle

The two-star *Hôtel Thiers* (☎ 25.73.40.66; fax 25.73.74.33) at 59 Rue Général de Gaulle has rather plain singles and doubles with TV for 150/190FF (with washbasin and bidet), 170/200FF (with shower) and 190/240FF (with shower and toilet). Triples with shower and toilet are 300FF. The hall shower is free – ask for the key at reception.

At Place de la Gare (opposite the train station), the *Patiotel* (☎ 25.79.90.90; fax 25.78.48.93) has rooms for one or two people for 215FF.

Places to Stay – top end

Near the train station, the three-star *Royal Hôtel* (☎ 25.73.19.99; fax 25.73.47.85) at 22 Blvd Carnot is run by a friendly and welcoming couple. Large, soundproofed and tasteful singles/doubles/triples with TV are 280/380/435FF. Breakfast is 40FF. There's an excellent restaurant on the ground floor. Overall, this place offers very good value. It is closed from 20 December to 10 January.

Places to Eat

Troyes has a good choice of affordable eateries in the city centre.

French – up-market *Les Quatre Saisons* (☎ 25.73.66.15) at 14 Rue de Turenne uses lots of fresh, local products for its Champagne-style French cuisine. It has *menus* for 90FF (lunch only), 115FF and 160FF. This place is open from noon to 2 pm and 7.45 to 10 pm (closed Sunday and holidays). It's a good idea to make reservations on Saturday night.

The well-regarded *Restaurant du Royal Hôtel* (☎ 25.73.19.99) at 22 Blvd Carnot on the ground floor of the Royal Hôtel, offers traditional French cuisine in an elegant dining room. It is open Tuesday to Saturday from noon to 2.30 pm and 7.30 to 9.30 pm, on Sunday for lunch only, and on Monday for dinner. There are *menus* for 89FF (not available on Saturday night or for Sunday lunch) and 128FF. Their regional specialities include andouillette (chitterling sausage) and Chaource cheese.

French – inexpensive *Del'Étoile* (☎ 25.73.12.65), a lively local restaurant at 11 Rue Pithou, has *menus* from 55/60FF. The more humble *Le Provençal* (☎ 25.73.24.64) at 18 Rue Général Saussier has various *menus* starting at 45FF, wine included. *L'Arcisien* (☎ 25.73.99.49) at 6 Place de la Libération has a stylish 55FF *menu*. *Le Théâtre* (☎ 25.73.18.47) at 35 Rue Jules Lebocey – affiliated with the hotel of the same name at the same address – has decent *menus* from 55FF.

For a good range of salads or a 52FF *menu*, you might try the tropically decorated *Aux Délices de l'Escargot* (☎ 25.73.02.27) at 90 Rue Urbain IV. Not far away at 82 Rue Urbain IV is *Au Bon Bec* (☎ 25.73.09.53). Their 55FF, three-course *menu*, which includes a little pitcher of wine, is available at midday from Tuesday to Saturday.

Near the cathedral, *Café du Musée* (☎ 25.80.58.64) away from the tourist throng at 59 Rue de la Cité, has a relaxed creperie on the 1st-floor. Near the station, *Le Self du*

Jardin (☎ 25.73.06.68) at 9 Rue Paul Dubois has cheap fare; main dishes are about 30FF.

Middle Eastern If you're in the mood to dine on Algerian couscous (55 to 75FF) amidst Moorish-style décor, try *Restaurant de l'Alhambra* (☎ 25.73.18.41) at 31 Rue Champeaux. This place is open daily from noon to 2 pm and 7 to 11 pm (or later).

Resto Station Istanbul (☎ 25.73.00.74) at 3 Rue Paillot de Montabert, which is open daily from noon to 2 pm and 7 to 10 pm, has Turkish food, including wood-grilled shish kebab. There are *menus* for 68 and 98FF.

Tex-Mex *Santa Fé American Restaurant* (☎ 25.73.99.02) at 12 Rue Pithou, half a block from the Marché des Halles, serves what passes in France for Tex-Mex food. Salads are 35 to 41FF, steak starts at 56FF and chilli con carne is 49FF. It is closed on Sunday and Monday.

Self-Catering There are benches, which are ideal for picnicking, in the park along Blvd Carnot (near the train station) and at the flowery Place de la Libération.

The lively and popular *Marché des Halles*, a newly renovated, 19th-century market-place situated between Rue Général de Gaulle and Rue Claude Heuz, is the best place in town to shop for food. It is open Monday to Saturday until 7 pm and on Sunday from 9 am to 12.30 pm; from Monday to Thursday, it closes between 12.45 and 3.30 pm.

La Boite à Fromage, a cheese shop at 18 Rue Général de Gaulle, is open Tuesday to Friday from 8.30 am to 12.30 pm and 3 to 7.30 pm, Saturday from 8.30 am to 1 pm and 3 to 7.30 pm, and Sunday 10 am to 12.30 pm. There are lots of other food stores (including a couple of East Asian groceries) along the same block.

The city's most outstanding boulangerie is *Le Fournil d'Hervé* at 6bis Rue de la République. The *boulangerie* at 5 Rue Pithou is open on Sunday as are others, depending on their roster, which are scattered throughout town.

The *Prisunic supermarket* at 71 Rue Émile Zola is open Monday to Saturday from 8.30 am to 7.15 pm. The *Casino supermarket* at 30 Blvd Danton is open until about 11 pm. The *fromagerie* at 63 Rue de Turenne is open on Monday and Wednesday to Saturday from 9 am to 12.30 pm and 3.30 to 7.30 pm, and on Sunday from 9.30 am to 12.30 pm.

Entertainment
The pedestrianised areas are best for hunting down bars and pubs. *Café du Musée* (☎ 25.80.58.64) at 59 Rue de la Cité, which is also listed under Places to Eat, is a good spot for a drink.

For nondubbed films, check what's on at *Cinéma Le Paris* (☎ 25.73.18.53) at 107 Rue Émile Zola.

Getting There & Away
Train The train station (☎ 25.73.50.50 for information) is at the western end of Ave Maréchal Joffre, the western continuation of Rue Général de Gaulle. The information office is open, from 8.30 am to noon and 2 to 7 pm (closed Sunday and holidays); the station itself is open from 4.30 am (6 am on weekends) to 10.15 pm (9 pm on Saturday).

Major destinations include: Paris's Gare de l'Est (105FF; 1½ to two hours; nine a day), Chaumont (66FF; 50 minutes; nine a day), Mulhouse (180FF; 3½ hours; three or four a day) and Basel (Bâle in French; 192FF; 3¾ hours; three to five a day).

To travel north to Reims, Châlons-sur-Marne and other points north of Troyes, you're best bet is to take a bus – by train, you have to go via either Paris (!) or Chaumont.

To get to Dijon (131FF; 2¾ hours; two a day), Lyon, Avignon and Nice (412FF; nine hours), you have to change trains at Chaumont or Culmont-Chalidrey.

Bus Coach services fill in some of the gaping holes left by Troyes's rather pathetic rail links to northern Champagne and Burgundy. The bus station (☎ 25.73.59.89) is just across Place de la Gare as you exit the train station. The bus office, which is in a corner of the train station building, is open Monday to Friday from 9.30 am to 12.30 pm and 3.30 to 6.30 pm. Bus schedules are posted on the big square sign next to the toilet pod. Some bus schedules are also available at the tourist office.

Transchampagne (STDM; ☎ 26.65. 17.07) serves Reims (90FF; two hours) and Châlons-sur-Marne three times a day on weekdays and twice on Saturday. Les Courriers de l'Aube (☎ 25.82.23.43) operates regional services, including lines to Sens (66FF; three a day, one a day in summer) and Châtillon-sur-Seine (three times a day except on Sunday), whence there are buses to Dijon. Rapides de Bourgogne (☎ 86.46. 90.90) has two buses a day (at 6.55 am and 6.20 pm) to Laroche-Migennes (two hours), which is on the Paris-Dijon train line and is very near Auxerre and Avallon, both in Burgundy.

Car ADA Location de Véhicules (☎ 25.73. 41.68; fax 25.73.41.71) is not far from the train station at 36 Blvd Carnot. It is open Monday to Saturday from 8 am to noon and 2 to 7 pm. If you call ahead, you can pick up a car during the midday break or on Sunday morning.

Europcar (☎ 25.73.27.66; fax 64.22. 26.85) at 2 Rue Voltaire is open daily except Sunday and holidays.

Getting Around
Bus Local buses are run by TCAT (☎ 25.81. 09.10, 25.81.39.38). As we go to press, the company is in the process of moving its main terminal to Place des Halles and restructuring the city's bus network. The local transport information in this listing is from *before* the reorganisation and may therefore be somewhat out of date.

Travel within the city centre (*zone centrale*), which is indicated by the colour green on bus maps and at bus stops, costs half as much as does travel out to the suburbs; in the latter case, you need a *zone entière* ticket. Schedules are posted at each stop. Most bus lines do not run much past 7.30 or 8 pm and are less frequent on Sunday (when they start at around 11 am) than during the rest of the week..

Car There is a 500-place subterranean parking lot under the Marché des Halles.

Taxi To order a taxi 24 hours a day, call ☎ 25.78.30.30. There's a taxi rank near the train station next to the Grand Hôtel.

AROUND TROYES
Parc de la Forêt d'Orient & Chaource
The Parc Naturel Régional de la Forêt d'Orient, 70,000 hectares of forests, fields, villages and three large lakes, is about 25 km east of Troyes. In the warm season, you can swim, sail, windsurf, waterski and engage in other such watery activities. The Maison du Parc (park headquarters; ☎ 25.41.35.57) is in Piney (postcode 10220).

The village of **Chaource**, 29 km to the south, makes the region's most distinctive cheese, an eponymous product which is simultaneously flaky and gluey.

Route du Champagne
Depending on whom you talk to in this part of Champagne, a discussion about champagne will produce either good-humoured banter or bitter recriminations. For while the Aube department, of which Troyes is the capital, is a major producer of champagne (about 20 million bottles annually), it gets none of the recognition accorded the Marne département and its big maisons around Reims and Épernay. Much of the acrimony dates back to 1909, when the Aube growers were excluded from Champagne's Appellation d'Origine Contrôlée (AOC) growing area. Two years later, they were also forbidden to sell their grapes to producers up north, resulting in months of strikes and chaos; eventually, the army was called in. It was another 16 years before the Aube wine growers could again display the prestigious (and lucrative) AOC tag on their labels, but by then the northern producers had firmly established themselves and had come to dominate the market.

Today, champagne production in the Troyes area takes place on a modest scale compared to what goes on up north. However, the Aube does have its own Route du Champagne. It loops from Bar-sur-Seine (about 33 km south-east of Troyes) to Bar-sur-Aube (about 35 km north-east of Bar-sur-Seine) and back again. Private cellars en route are open for visits. For details on the Route du Champagne, ask at the local tourist offices or stop by the tourist office in Troyes.

Loire Valley

From the 15th to the 18th century, the Loire Valley was the playground of kings, princes, dukes and nobles who expended the wealth of the nation and family fortunes to turn it into a vast neighbourhood of lavish (and not-so-lavish) chateaux. Today, the region is a favourite destination of tourists seeking architectural testimony to the glories of the Middle Ages and the Renaissance.

The earliest chateaux in the Loire Valley were medieval fortresses (châteaux forts), some constructed hastily in the 9th century as a defence against the marauding Vikings (Normans). These structures were built on high ground and, from the 11th century – when stone came into wide use – were often outfitted with massive walls topped with battlements, fortified keeps, loopholes (arrow slits) and moats spanned by drawbridges.

As the threat of invasion lessened – and cannon (mid-15th century) rendered castles almost useless for defence – the architecture of new chateaux (and the new wings added to older ones) began to reflect a different set of priorities, including aesthetics and comfort. Under the influence of the Italian Renaissance, whose many innovations were introduced to France at the end of the 15th century, the defensive structures so prominent in the early chateaux metamorphosed into whimsical, decorative features, prominent at Azay-le-Rideau, Chambord and Chenonceau. Instead of being built on isolated hilltops, the Renaissance chateaux were placed near a body of water or in a valley and proportioned to harmonise with their surroundings. Most chateaux from the 17th and 18th centuries are grand country houses, built in the neoclassical style and set amidst formal gardens.

Orientation

This chapter covers the area along and near the Loire River between Blois and Chinon and includes many of France's most

renowned chateaux. For information on Nantes, see the Atlantic Coast chapter.

Information

If one of your goals in chateau-hopping is historical and architectural edification, you might want to pick up an English version of Michelin's green guide to the area, *Châteaux of the Loire*. The tourist offices in Blois and Tours sell it for 45FF.

Organised Tours

Half-day and full-day organised trips to two or three chateaux in a row may prove less expensive per visit (and a lot less hassle) than taking public transport. For details, see Bus Excursions under Organised Tours in the sections entitled Blois Area Chateaux and Tours Area Chateaux.

Getting There & Away

The Loire Valley is only an hour or two by train from Paris's Gare d'Austerlitz (for non-TGV trains) and Gare Montparnasse (for TGV trains). If you're in Paris, the area can easily be visited as a short excursion or as a stopover on the way to Brittany, the Atlantic

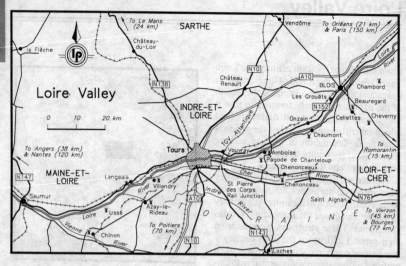

Loire Valley

0   10   20 km

To Le Mans (24 km)
SARTHE
la Flèche
Château-du-Loir
Vendôme
To Orléans (21 km) & Paris (150 km)
N138
Château Renault
N10
A10
BLOIS
Chambord
Les Grouëts
Beauregard
INDRE-ET-LOIRE
N152
Onzain
Cellettes
Cheverny
TGV Atlantique
Chaumont
To Angers (38 km) & Nantes (120 km)
To Romorantin (15 km)
MAINE-ET-LOIRE
Tours
Vouvray
Amboise
Pagode de Chanteloup
LOIR-ET-CHER
N147
Langeais
River   Villandry
Cher
River
Chenonceaux
Saumur
A10
St Pierre des Corps Rail Junction
Chenonceau
Ussé
Azay-le-Rideau
Indre
River
Saint Aignan
N76
To Vierzon (45 km) & Bourges (77 km)
Vienne
River
Chinon
To Poitiers (70 km)
N10
N143
Loches
T O U R A I N E

coast, Bordeaux, the Basque Country or even Spain.

Getting Around

Train & Bus Public transport from Blois, Amboise, Tours and Chinon (where there are places to stay) to the chateaux is limited and, at times, pretty inconvenient. From Tours, you can get to a number of chateaux by train and SNCF bus, both of which accept Eurail passes. From Blois, local TLC buses are more useful. Transport details are listed under Getting There & Away in the sections entitled Blois Area Chateaux and Tours Area Chateaux and under Getting There & Away at the end of each chateau listing.

Car For three or four people, car rental may be cheaper than buses, trains or tours, especially if you can take advantage of reduced weekend rates. For rental information, see Car under Getting There & Away in the Blois, Tours and Chinon sections.

Bicycle Cycling across the beautiful (and flat!) countryside is an excellent way to get around, though count on really clocking up the km if you schedule more than one

chateau per outing. A 1:200,000-scale Michelin road map or a 1:50,000-scale IGN map is indispensable to find your way around the rural backroads.

BLOIS

The medieval town of Blois (population 50,000; pronounced 'Blwah', with the accent at the end of the word), was once the seat of the powerful counts of Blois, from whom France's Capetian kings were descended. From the 15th to 17th centuries, the town was a major centre of court intrigue, and during the 16th century it served as something of a second capital of France. A number of truly dramatic events – involving some of the most important personages in French history, kings Louis XII, François I and Henri III among them – took place inside the city's outstanding attraction, the Château de Blois, which is right in the middle of town.

The old city, seriously damaged by German attacks in 1940, retains its steep, twisting medieval streets. Blois is quiet at night, but if you're not exhausted after a day of touring you can check out the bowling alley...

Several of the most rewarding chateaux in

the Loire Valley, including Chambord and Cheverny, are within a 20-km radius of the town. See the sections entitled Blois Area Chateaux, Amboise and Tours Area Chateaux for details.

Orientation

The compact town of Blois – almost everything is within 10 minutes' walk from the train station – is on the north bank of the Loire River. The old city is the area south and east of the Château de Blois, which towers over Place Victor Hugo. Blois's modern commercial centre is around Rue du Commerce and Rue Denis Papin; the latter is connected to Rue du Palais by a monumental staircase. Pont Jacques Gabriel is linked to Rue Denis Papin by riverside Place de la Résistance.

Information

Tourist Office The tourist office (☎ 54.74. 06.49) at 3 Ave Jean Laigret is housed in the early 16th-century Pavillon Anne de Bretagne, an outbuilding of the Château de Blois. From October to March, it is open Monday to Saturday from 9 am to noon and 2 to 6 pm. From April to September, it's open Monday to Saturday from 9 am to 7 pm and on Sunday and holidays from 10 am to 1 pm and 4 to 7 pm.

For no charge, the staff will call around to find you a hotel room; making an actual reservation (using the voucher system) costs only 5FF within the *département* of Loir-et-Cher.

Money The Banque de France is down the block from the railway station at 4 Ave Jean Laigret. It is open Tuesday to Saturday from 8.45 am to 12.15 pm and 1.45 to 3.45 pm.

There are a number of banks facing the river along Quai de la Saussaye, which is near Place de la Résistance. The tourist office changes money whenever it's open – the rate's OK but the commission is 22FF.

Post The post office (☎ 54.78.08.01), which has a currency exchange service, is near Place Victor Hugo on Rue Gallois. It is open weekdays from 8 am to 7 pm and on Saturday from 8 am to noon.

Blois's postcode is 41000.

Medical Services The Centre Hospitalier de Blois (☎ 54.78.00.82) is two km north-east of the town centre on Mail Pierre Charlot. To get there, take bus No 1 from the railway station or bus No 4 from Place de la République.

Laundry The laundrette at 1 Rue Jeanne d'Arc is open daily from 7.30 am (9 am on Sunday) to 8.30 pm. There's another laundrette at 2 Rue de la Garenne.

Château de Blois

The Château de Blois (☎ 54.78.06.62, 54.74. 16.06) is not the most impressive in the area, but it has a compellingly bloody history, and its mixture of architectural styles is extraordinary. The chateau's four distinct sections are: medieval (13th century); Flamboyant Gothic (1498-1503), from the reign of Louis XII; very early Renaissance (1515-24), from the reign of François I; and classical (17th century).

During the Middle Ages, the counts of Blois received homage and meted out justice in the huge **Salle des États Généraux** (States General Hall), a part of the feudal castle that somehow survived wars, rebuilding and – most dangerous of all – changes in taste. The brick-and-stone **Louis XII section**, which includes the hall where entrance tickets are sold, is ornamented with porcupines, Louis XII's symbol. The Italianate **François I wing**, begun only 14 years after the Louis XII wing was completed, includes the famous **spiral staircase**, a magnificent structure decorated with repetitions of François I's insignia, the royal 'F' and the salamander. The ornate exterior of the François I wing can be seen from Place Victor Hugo. By the way, François I's retinue included about 15,000 people; when the court moved, some 12,000 horses were required. The chateau was damaged during the Revolution and served as a barracks from

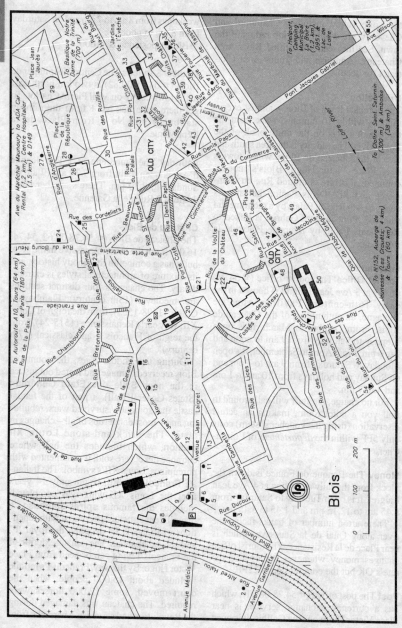

Blois

PLACES TO STAY			
3	Hôtel Saint Jacques		
4	Hôtel Le Savoie		
6	Grand Hôtel de la Gare et Terminus		
12	Hôtel François 1er		
16	Hôtel Arcade		
23	Hôtel du Bellay		
24	Hôtel L'Étoile d'Or		
25	Hôtel Le Lys		
35	Hôtel/Restaurant Les Trois Marches		
53	Hôtel Saint Nicolas		
55	Hôtel Le Pavillon		

PLACES TO EAT			
1	Intermarché Supermarket		
5	Boulangerie		
36	Les Glycines		
37	Le Relais des Gardes		
38	La Mesa		
42	Packman		

43	La Tocade	
46	Au Bouchon Lyonnais	
47	Boulangerie-Pâtisserie Blond	
48	Restaurant Le Maïdi	
49	Marché Couvert Halle Louis XII	
51	Boulangerie	
52	Boulangerie	
54	Au Rendez-Vous des Pêcheurs	

OTHER		
2	Bowling de Blois	
7	Railway Station	
8	Bus Station	
10	Taxi Booth	
11	Banque de France	
14	Laundrette	
15	Avis Car Rental	
17	Tourist Office	
18	Post Office	
19	Église Saint Vincent	
21	Point Bus Office	

22	Château de Blois	
26	Palais de Justice	
27	Prefecture Building	
28	Bus Stops	
29	Palais de la Culture et de Congrès	
32	Maison des Acrobates	
33	Cathédrale Saint Louis	
34	Hôtel de Ville	
39	Discothèque Avenue Foch	
40	Bar du Puits Châtel	
41	Laundrette	
44	Sports Motos Cycles	
50	Église Saint Nicolas	

SQUARES		
9	Place de la Gare	
13	Square Pasteur	
20	Place Victor Hugo	
30	Place Guerry	
31	Place Saint Louis	
45	Place de la Résistance	

1788 to 1841 before being restored in the mid-19th century.

The most infamous episode in the history of the Château de Blois occurred during the chaotic 16th century, a period of violence between Protestants (Huguenots) and Catholics. On 23 December 1588 at about 8 am, King Henri III summoned the duke of Guise, a leader of the Catholic League (which threatened the authority of the king, himself a Catholic), to his Salle du Conseil (Study). When the duke reached the Chambre du Roi (King's Chamber, marked on the brochures as room No 12), he was set upon by 20 royal bodyguards, some armed with daggers, others with swords. When the violence was over, the king, who had been hiding behind a tapestry, stepped into the room to survey the duke's perforated body. Henri, overjoyed by the success of the assassination, informed his mother, Catherine de Médicis (who died a few days later) and went merrily to mass. Henri III was himself assassinated eight months later.

The chateau houses a small **archaeological museum**, a **Musée des Beaux-Arts** and the **Musée Robert-Houdin**, which displays clocks and other objects invented by the great Blois-born magician Jean-Eugène Robert-Houdin (1805-71), after whom the great Houdini named himself. All three museums have the same opening hours as the chateau but close between noon and 2 pm.

From November to mid-March, the Château de Blois is open daily from 9 am to noon and 2 to 5 pm; from mid-March to October, hours are 9 am to 6 pm. It is closed on 25 December and 1 January. The entrance fee is 30FF (15FF if you are aged seven to 25 or over 60). A free guided tour in English can often be arranged – ask one of the staff members at the entrance. There's a **sound-and-light show** (60FF) every night from June to mid-September; the English version takes place after the French one.

Your entry ticket also gets you into the **Musée d'Art Religieux**, which is across the Loire in Cloître Saint Saturnin on Rue Munier. It is open daily from June to September and on weekends during the last half of

May and in October; hours are 10 am to 12.30 pm and 2 to 6.30 pm.

Old City

The brown explanatory signs tacked up around the old city are both informative and in English. Part of the area has been turned into a pedestrian mall. As you'll notice, many of the buildings have white façades, red brick chimneys and roofs of blue slate.

Cathédrale Saint Louis is named after Louis XIV, who assisted in rebuilding the structure after the devastating hurricane of 1678. The crypt dates from the 10th century. The cathedral *may* be closed between noon and 3 pm and after 6 pm. The **Hôtel de Ville** (city hall) is right behind the cathedral; note the **sundial** across the courtyard on the Ecclesiastical Tribunal building. There is a great view of Blois and both banks of the Loire from the **Jardins de l'Évêché** (Gardens of the Bishop's Palace), which are at the back of the cathedral.

The **Maison des Acrobates** (House of the Acrobats) at 3 Place Saint Louis, across the square from the west façade of the cathedral, is one of the few medieval houses in Blois not destroyed during WW II. The building, which dates from the late 15th century, is so-named because its timbers are decorated with characters taken from medieval farces, including acrobats.

Basilique Notre Dame de la Trinité

This modern, concrete church, finished in 1939 and consecrated 10 years later, is about 800 metres north-east of the cathedral.

Activities

At the **Lac de Loire** (☎ 54.78.82.05 in Vineuil), a lake north-east of town towards Orléans (take the D951, which follows the river's south bank), you can try your hand at sailing, water skiing, canoeing, rowing, bopping around on pedal boats and other water sports. From mid-June to mid-September, it's linked to Blois (5.30FF one way) by the TLC shuttle bus to Chambord and Cheverny (see Organised Tours in the Blois Area Chateaux section).

Places to Stay

Blois's hotels are most heavily booked in July and August.

Places to Stay – bottom end

Camping The three-star *Camping Municipal La Boire* (☎ 54.74.22.78) is 2.5 km east of the train station on the south bank of the Loire. More precisely, it is on Blvd du Docteur Alexis Carrel near Pont Charles de Gaulle (a highway bridge over the river) and the *hélistation* (heliport). It is open from March to November. Two people with a tent are charged 33FF (37FF with a car). There is no bus service from town.

Hostels The *Auberge de Jeunesse* (☎ 54.78. 27.21), at 18 Rue de l'Hôtel Pasquier in the village of Les Grouëts, is 4.5 km south-west of the Blois train station. It is open from March to mid-November, but call before coming – it's often full. Beds in the two large, single-sex dorm rooms cost 39FF; the optional breakfast is 16FF. Kitchen facilities are available. Rooms are locked from 10 am to 6 pm.

To get to the hostel from Blois, take local TUB bus No 4 from Place de la République (linked to the train station by TUB bus Nos 1, 2, 3 and 6) or Place Valin de la Vaissière (along the river); it runs until 7 or 7.30 pm. If hitching, head south-westward along the northern quai of the Loire, which becomes the N152. At Les Grouëts, walk along Rue Basse des Grouëts to No 32 and turn onto Rue de l'Hôtel Pasquier. Follow it under the tracks and then up the hill for a few hundred metres.

Hotels Near the train station, your best bet is the one-star *Hôtel Saint Jacques* (☎ 54.78. 04.15) at 7 Rue Ducoux. The rooms are ordinary but the staff go out of their way to be friendly. Doubles start at 100 or 115FF. Doubles with shower, toilet and TV are 175FF; similar triples or quads are 240FF. A bath or shower is 15FF.

The *Grand Hôtel de la Gare et Terminus* (☎ 54.74.24.57) at 6-8 Ave Jean Laigret has singles/doubles with shower and toilet for

120/150FF; quads with bath and toilet are 261FF. The rooms are spacious but, like the whole place, are slightly run-down. Reception is generally open daily until 11 pm. The *Hôtel François 1er* (☎ 54.78.97.86) is at 39 Ave Jean Laigret, 120 metres east of the station. Their cheaper doubles start at 120F; hall showers are free.

In the old city, the *Hôtel Saint Nicolas* (☎ 54.78.05.85, 54.78.41.09) at 33 Rue des Trois Marchands is open all year except from mid-December to mid-January. Simple, old-fashioned singles/doubles start at 90/125FF; showers are 12FF.

North of the old city, the *Hôtel du Bellay* (☎ 54.78.23.62) at 12 Rue des Minimes is open from mid-March to mid-November. This place has a few very pleasant doubles for 115FF; hall showers are free. Double rooms with bath and toilet are 180FF. Nearby, the *Hôtel L'Étoile d'Or* (☎ 54.78.46.93) at 7 Rue du Bourg Neuf has doubles from 140FF (240FF with shower and toilet). Showers cost 10FF.

Across the river from the old city, the *Hôtel Le Pavillon* (☎ 54.74.23.27) at 2 Ave Wilson has ordinary doubles with high ceilings from 95FF. Doubles/triples/quads with shower and toilet are 200/240/320FF. Hall showers cost 15FF.

Places to Stay – middle

Near the train station, the family-run, two-star *Hôtel Le Savoie* (☎ 54.74.32.21; fax 54.74.29.58) at 6 Rue Ducoux has neat, well-kept singles/doubles with shower, toilet and TV for 190/210FF.

In the old city, an excellent bet is the friendly, family-run *Hôtel Les Trois Marches* (☎ 54.74.48.86) at 58 Rue Foulerie, just down the hill from the cathedral. The 12 eminently serviceable singles and doubles cost 180FF with shower and TV and 250FF with bath, toilet and TV. From November to March, reception is open on Sunday from noon to 5 pm only.

You might also try the *Hôtel Le Lys* (☎ 54.74.66.08) at 3 Rue des Cordeliers, whose doubles with shower and toilet go for 210 to 250FF.

The modern *Hôtel Arcade* (☎ 54.78.24.14; fax 54.78.83.88) at 4 Rue Jean Moulin, part of a large chain, has singles/doubles/triples for 295/320/380FF.

Places to Eat

There's a cluster of popular restaurants along Rue Foulerie. Most of Blois's eateries are closed for Sunday lunch.

Restaurants – French Crowds of people out for a splurge make *Au Bouchon Lyonnais* (☎ 54.74.12.87) at 25 Rue des Violettes (above Rue Saint Lubin) a busy place. Main dishes of traditional French cuisine cost 70 to 120FF; *menus* are 96 and 165FF. It is open Tuesday to Saturday from noon to 2 pm and 7 to 10 pm. In July and August, it opens up on Sunday night.

Another fine spot for an excellent meal is *Au Rendez-Vous des Pêcheurs* (☎ 54.74.67.48) at 27 Rue du Foix, which – as its name indicates – specialises in fish (84 to 140FF), brought fresh each morning from the Loire and the sea and cooked in the French tradition. The *menu* costs 130FF. It is closed Sunday and on Monday at lunchtime.

Restaurant Les Trois Marches (☎ 54.74.48.86) at 58 Rue Foulerie, in the hotel of the same name, specialises in traditional French cuisine, especially fish dishes. *Menus*, served on spotless white tablecloths, are available for 68 and 93FF; a children's *menu* is 35FF. This place is open daily, except Saturday at midday and Sunday; from April to October, it's open on Sunday evening.

La Tocade (☎ 54.78.07.78) at 9-11 Rue du Chant des Oiseaux offers inexpensive French food from 11.30 am to 3 pm and 6.30 to 10.30 or 11 pm daily except Sunday night and Monday (daily from Easter to September). *Menus* cost 63, 90 and 135FF.

For crepes, galettes and cider, you might try *Le Relais des Gardes* (☎ 54.74.36.56) at 52 Rue Foulerie, a stone, stucco and wood-beam place that's closed at midday Sunday and on Monday. A 60FF *menu* is available. There are a number of *brasseries* at Place de la Résistance.

Restaurants – Italian *La Mesa* (☎ 54.78.70.70), a very popular Franco-Italian joint, is at 11 Rue Vauvert, which is up the alleyway from 44 Rue Foulerie. *Menus* are 70 and 120FF; a good selection of salads is also on offer. La Mesa, whose large courtyard is perfect for dining alfresco, is open daily from noon to 2 pm and 7 to 11 pm, though from December to February it may be closed on Sunday.

Les Glycines (☎ 54.74.17.95) at 54 Rue Foulerie has spaghetti (26 to 50FF), pizza (36 to 48FF), lasagne and other Italian fare. It's closed at midday Saturday and on Sunday; from Easter to September, it's open on Sunday evening.

Restaurants – North African *Restaurant Le Maïdi* (☎ 54.74.38.58), in the old city at 42 Rue Saint Lubin, has couscous from 50FF. It's open from noon to 2 pm and 6.30 to 10 or 11 pm daily except Thursday (daily in July and August). In July and August, it is also open on Thursday evening.

Fast Food Central Blois's one fast-food joint is *Packman* (☎ 54.74.11.88) at 25 Rue Denis Papin, purveyor of some of the world's worst hamburgers. Fortunately, this place also has less inedible pastries, pizzas, quiches and sandwiches. It is open daily until 11 pm (later on weekends and during July and August).

Self-Catering Most food stores are closed on Sunday and/or Monday.

The *Intermarché supermarket*, which is west of the train station on Ave Gambetta, has an in-house boulangerie. It is open Monday to Saturday from 9 am to 12.15 pm and 2.30 or 3 to 7.15 pm.

In the old city, the *Marché Couvert Halle Louis XII* (covered market) near Quai de l'Abbé Grégoire is, for the most part, open Tuesday to Saturday from 7 am to 12.30 pm and 3 to 7 pm. *Boulangerie-Pâtisserie Blond* at 11 Rue Anne de Bretagne has a good variety of breads. It is open Monday to Saturday from 6.45 am to 2 pm and 3.30 to 8 pm. There is a *boulangerie* opposite 23 Rue des Trois Marchands and another at No 29 on the same street (closed Monday).

Across the street from the railway station, the *boulangerie* at 10 Ave Jean Laigret is open Monday to Saturday from 6 am to 8.30 pm.

Entertainment

Towns don't come much quieter than Blois, at least in the off season. The pedestrian zone in the old city (around Rue du Commerce) is almost dead after nightfall, though things are a bit livelier east of Rue Denis Papin and around Place Louis XII. *Discothèque Avenue Foch* (☎ 54.74.47.03) at 3 Rue du Puits Châtel is open nightly, except Monday, from 10 pm.

On weekends from mid-June to August, *Bar du Puits Châtel* (☎ 54.78.04.36) at 1 Rue du Puits Châtel has live music starting at 9 pm on Friday and 6 pm on Saturday. There's a surcharge of 3FF a drink during the performances.

One of the town's few nightspots is a bowling alley, *Bowling de Blois* (☎ 54.42.42.27), which is right across the tracks from the train station at 6 Rue Alfred Halou. It is open daily from 3 pm to 2 am; in August, it opens at 8 pm on weekdays. Games cost 17 to 30FF per person, depending on when you come (nights and weekends are the most expensive). Shoe rental is 7FF. Billiards costs 10FF a game.

Things to Buy

The Marché Régional de la Brocante (Regional Flea Market; ☎ 54.78.45.76) is held on the second Sunday of each month around Rue Jeanne d'Arc (just north-east of Place de la Résistance).

Getting There & Away

Train The train station (☎ 47.20.50.50 in Tours) is at the western terminus of Ave Jean Laigret. The information office is open Monday to Saturday from 9 am to 7 pm. Ticket windows stay open Monday to Saturday from 5.30 am to 9.30 pm and on Sunday from 6 am to 10.50 pm. The left-luggage office is open daily from 6.30 am to 7.30 pm;

the luggage lockers are accessible 24 hours a day.

Service from Blois to Paris's Gare d'Austerlitz (111FF; at least 10 a day via Orléans) takes at least 1¾ hours by direct train but only one hour via Orléans. The nearest stop of the TGV-Atlantique, whose Paris station is Gare Montparnasse, is near Tours at Saint Pierre des Corps. Bordeaux (211FF; eight a day) is five hours by direct train but only 3¼ hours if you change to a TGV at Saint Pierre des Corps. To get to La Rochelle (172FF), you can either take the daily direct train or change at either Saint Pierre des Corps or Poitiers (97FF; nine a day). Nantes (153FF) can be reached via Tours or Saint Pierre des Corps.

About two-thirds of the trains to Tours (44FF; 40 minutes; 14 to 17 a day) stop at Amboise (30FF; 20 minutes).

Bus For information on transport to and from nearby chateaux, see Getting There & Away and Organised Tours at the beginning of the Blois Area Chateaux section.

Car ADA (☎ 54.74.02.47) at 108 Ave du Maréchal Maunoury (the D149) is three km north-east of the train station. It is open Monday to Saturday from 8 am to noon and 2 to 7 pm. To get there, take bus No 1 from the train station or bus No 4 from Place de la République to the Cornillettes stop.

Avis (☎ 54.74.48.15) at 6 Rue Jean Moulin is open Monday to Saturday from 8 am to noon and 2 to 7 pm.

Getting Around
Bus Buses within Blois, run by TUB, operate from Monday to Saturday until 7 or 7.30 pm (10.30 or 11 pm on Saturday night). On Sunday and holidays, service is greatly reduced. Route maps are posted in most bus shelters – as you'll see, all the lines except No 4 stop at the train station. Tickets cost 5.30FF if bought singly or 31FF for a carnet of 10. For information, enquire at the Point Bus office (☎ 54.78.15.66) at 2 Place Victor Hugo.

Taxi To order a taxi, call the taxi booth (☎ 54.78.07.65) in front of the train station.

Bicycle Near the train station, the Hôtel Saint Jacques (☎ 54.78.04.15) at 7 Rue Ducoux rents three-speeds for 60FF a day (50FF in winter). Sports Motos Cycles (☎ 54.78.02.64) at 6 Rue Henri Drussy, which rents 10-speeds for 35FF a day, is open Tuesday to Saturday from 9 am to noon and 2 to 6.30 pm.

BLOIS AREA CHATEAUX
The Blois area is endowed with some of the finest Loire Valley chateaux, including spectacular Chambord, magnificently furnished Cheverny, castle-like Chaumont (also accessible from Tours) and more modest Beauregard. The town of Amboise is also easily accessible from Blois.

The Blois tourist office has information on *spectacles* (sound-and-light shows, etc) held at many of the chateaux during the summer.

Organised Tours
Bus Excursions Given the state of public transport, car-less travellers staying in Blois who'd like to see more than one chateau in a single day may want to avail themselves of the commentary-free excursions run by Blois-based TLC (☎ 54.78.15.66), the area's public bus company. They run from mid-June to mid-September, on weekends between late May and mid-June, and on the days around Easter, Pentecost and Ascension Day.

TLC offers two route options, both of which start at the Blois train station:

- a *navette* (shuttle bus) to Lac de Loire, Chambord and Cheverny (60FF return, 45FF for students and people over 60), which does the circuit twice daily in each direction;
- an all-day excursion (*circuit journée*) to Chaumont, Chenonceau and Amboise (100FF, 80FF reduced price), which leaves at about 9 am on Tuesday, Thursday, weekends and holidays. For this tour, it is possible to arrange to be picked up at the youth hostel in Les Grouëts.

Prices do not include admission fees, but tour participants are eligible for special tariffs.

Helicopter For information on helicopter tours, call 54.74.35.52. The hélistation is near Pont Charles de Gaulle, which is two km north-east of Blois. A 10-minute flight costs 270FF per person; 17 minutes in the air costs 440FF per person.

Getting There & Away

Bus The TLC bus system of the département is set up to transport school kids into Blois in the morning and to get them home after school. As a result, afternoon service from the countryside to Blois is limited on some lines. There is reduced service during the summer school holidays and on Sunday. All times quoted in this chapter are approximate and should be verified with the company before you make plans.

Your best source of bus information is the Point Bus office in Blois. It is open weekdays, except Monday morning, from 8 am to 12.10 pm and 1.30 to 6 pm and on Saturday from 9 am to 12.10 pm and 1.30 to 4.30 pm. In July and August, it's open weekdays, except Monday morning, from 8.30 am to 12.10 pm and 1.30 to 5.30 pm and on Saturday from 9 am to noon.

TLC buses to destinations in the vicinity of Blois depart from Blois's Place Victor Hugo (in front of the Point Bus office) and the bus station – little more than a bus stop –

which is next to the brasserie next to Blois's train station.

Taxi At the taxi booth (☎ 54.78.07.65) in front of the Blois train station, it is possible to hire a taxi for travel to one or more chateaux. A round trip (including a one-hour stop at each destination) costs 200FF to Cheverny, 220FF to Chambord and 365FF to Chenonceau; Sunday and holiday rates are 290, 310 and 545FF respectively. Various chateau combinations are possible.

Bicycle The countryside around Blois, with its many quiet country backroads, is perfect for cycling. Unfortunately, Chambord, Cheverny and Chaumont are each 16 to 20 km from Blois. An excursion to both Chambord and Cheverny, which are 20 km from each other, is therefore a 60-km proposition, quite a bit for one day if you're not an active cyclist.

See Getting Around in the Blois section for details on bike rental. For much of the year, bicycles can also be rented at the Château de Chambord.

Château de Chambord

The Château de Chambord (☎ 54.20.31.32), whose construction was begun in 1519 by King François I (reigned 1515-47), is the largest and most spectacular chateau in the entire Loire Valley. Its Renaissance architecture and decoration, grafted onto a feudal

Château de Chambord

ground plan, may have been inspired by Leonardo da Vinci, who, at the invitation of François I, lived in Amboise (45 km southwest of here) from 1516 until his death three years later. If you're going to see more than one chateau, leave 440-room Chambord for last or the rest may seem unlivably small by comparison.

Chambord is the creation of François I, whose emblems – the royal monogram (a letter 'F') and salamanders of a particularly fierce disposition – adorn many parts of the building. Though forced by liquidity problems to leave his two sons unransomed in Spain and to help himself to both the wealth of his churches and his subjects' silver, the king kept 1800 construction workers and artisans busy for 15 years. At one point, he even suggested that the Loire be rerouted so it would pass by Chambord! Eventually, a smaller river, the Cosson, was diverted instead. François I died before the building's completion, a task left to his royal successors, Henri II and Louis XIV, who came here quite often. Molière first staged two of his most famous plays at Chambord to audiences that included Louis XIV.

The chateau's famed **double-helix staircase**, attributed by some to Leonardo himself, consists of two spiral staircases that wind around the same central axis but never meet. The rich ornamentation is in the style of the early French Renaissance. It's easy to imagine mistresses and lovers chasing each other up and down the staircases, with their sweating consorts and assorted servants not far behind...

The royal court used to assemble on the Italianate **rooftop terrace**, reached via the double helix staircase, to watch military exercises, tournaments and the hounds and hunters returning from a day of stalking deer. As you stand on the terrace (once described as resembling an overcrowded chessboard), all around you are the towers, cupolas, domes, chimneys, dormers, mosaic slate roofs and lightning rods that form the chateau's imposing skyline.

Tickets to the chateau are on sale daily from 9.30 to 11.45 am and 2 to 4.45 pm

Anne de Pisselou, a lady-in-waiting at Chambord, one of the many women who captured the heart of François I

(October to March), 5.45 pm (April to June and September) or 6.45 pm (July and August). Guests already in the chateau can stay there for half an hour after ticket sales end. Chambord does *not* close at midday from mid-June to the second week of September and during certain holiday periods. The entrance fee is 31FF (20FF for people aged 18 to 24 and over 60). A brochure in half a dozen languages is available for 3FF behind the ticket counters. The maps are its most useful feature, since the chateau is blessed with excellent explanatory signs in French, English, German, Spanish and Italian.

Information Tourist information is available at the entrance to the chateau and at the Centre d'Information Touristique (☎ 54.20. 34.86) at Place Saint Michel (the parking lot surrounded by tourist shops), which is open daily from early April to mid-October; hours are 10 am to 7 pm.

Domaine de Chambord The chateau is in the middle of the Domaine de Chambord , a 54-sq-km hunting preserve reserved for the use of the president of the Republic. The public is allowed to stroll around 12 sq km of the property, which is surrounded by a 33-km-long wall, the longest such wall in Europe. Trail maps and bicycles are available at the Centre d'Information Touristique.

Entertainment During the summer months, the **Spectacle d'Art Équestre** (equestrian show; ☎ 54.20.31.01) is held at the stables (écuries) near the chateau. There are performances at 11.45 am and 5 pm. The cost is 40FF. There is a **sound-and-light show** every night from about mid-April to mid-October, but the English version is staged on Friday and Saturday nights only.

Getting There & Away Chambord is 16 km east of Blois and 20 km north-east of Cheverny.

During the school year, TLC line No 2 averages three daily round trips from Blois to Chambord (17.20FF one way). The first bus out to Chambord leaves Blois a bit after noon on Wednesday and Saturday and around 2 pm on other days. The last bus back to Blois leaves Chambord at 5.30 pm on weekdays and 4.30 pm on weekends and holidays. During July and August, your only bus option is TLC's shuttle bus (see Bus Excursions at the beginning of the Blois Area Chateaux section).

Getting Around Bicycles (great for exploring the grounds) are available from the Centre d'Information Touristique for 25FF an hour, 40FF for two hours and 80FF a day.

Château de Cheverny

The Château de Cheverny (☎ 54.79.96.29), the region's most magnificently furnished chateau, was built between 1604 and 1634. After entering the building through its finely proportioned neoclassical façade, visitors are treated to room after sumptuous room outfitted with the finest of period appointments: furniture, canopied beds, tapestries

(note the amazing *Abduction of Helen* in the Salle d'Armes, the former armoury), paintings, chimneypieces, parquet floors, painted ceilings and walls covered with embossed Córdoba leather. The most richly furnished rooms are the Chambre du Roi (in which no king ever slept because no king ever stayed at Cheverny) and the Grand Salon (Great Drawing Room).

As was the custom among the nobility of centuries past, Viscount Arnaud de Sigalas, whose family has owned Cheverny since it was built, maintains an active interest in hunting with hounds. His 80 dogs, which are a cross between English fox terriers and French Poitevins, are quite beautiful no matter what you think of using them to kill deer. The **soupe des chiens** (feeding of the dogs) takes place at the kennels (a small cement enclosure not far from the entrance to the grounds) at 5 pm daily except Sunday and holidays (from mid-September to March, daily except Tuesday, weekends and holidays). Next to the kennels is the trophy room, a macabre chamber whose walls, pillars and ceiling are covered with the antlers of almost 2000 stags hunted since the 1850s.

Cheverny is open daily from 9.15 or 9.30 am to noon and 2.15 to 5 pm (November to February), to 5.30 pm (October and March), 6 pm (the last half of September) or 6.30 pm (April and May). From June to mid-September, the chateau stays open every day from 9.15 am to 6.45 pm. The entry fee is 28FF (20FF for students). Visitors are given an information sheet in one of nine languages. The park around the chateau is closed to visitors.

Entertainment During July and August, the chateau plays host to a *spectacle historique* (historical re-enactment).

Getting There & Away Cheverny is 16 km south-east of Blois and 20 km south-west of Chambord.

TLC bus No 4 from Blois to Romorantin stops at Cheverny (14.40FF one way). All year long, buses leave Blois Monday to Saturday at 6 or 6.30 am and noon. Coming back to Blois, the last bus leaves Cheverny at 7.40 pm; on Sunday and holidays, the last bus is at 8.15 pm (6.30 pm during July and August).

Château de Chaumont

The Château de Chaumont (☎ 54.20.98.03), set on a bluff overlooking the Loire, looks as much like a feudal castle as any chateau in the area. Its most famous feature is the luxurious **Écuries**, where it's not difficult to imagine four horses being led away to pull the ornate coach of some duke or prince...Present your entrance ticket from the main building to get in.

In 1560, Catherine de Médicis (France's powerful queen-mother) took revenge on Diane de Poitiers (the mistress of her late husband, King Henry II) by forcing her to accept Chaumont in exchange for her favourite residence, the Château de Chenonceau (see the Tours Area Chateaux section). During the years after the USA won independence, Benjamin Franklin, then serving as US ambassador to France, was a frequent guest at Chaumont.

Tickets to this state-owned chateau are on sale daily from 9.15 to 11.35 am and 1.45 to 3.45 pm (5.35 pm from April to September). There is no midday closure in July and August. The chateau stays open for half an hour after ticket sales end. The entrance fee is 25FF (14FF for people aged 18 to 24 and over 60). Some of the rooms have explanatory plaques in English and several other languages. The **park** around the chateau, with its many cedars, is free and is open daily from 9 am to 5 pm (7 pm from April to September).

Wine Tasting From Easter to September, there is free wine tasting in the small building 50 metres up Rue du Village Neuf from the bottom of the path up to the chateau. A dozen wine producers from the Touraine area take turns displaying and selling their products, especially premium AOC (*appellation d'origine contrôlée*) wines, the quality of which is controlled by strict laws. Opening hours depend on the preferences of each vineyard's representative.

Place to Eat There is a *boulangerie* (☎ 54. 20.98.47) at 5 Rue Maréchal Leclerc, which is half a block from the path to the chateau. It is open from 7.30 am to 7.30 pm daily except Sunday afternoon and Monday (every day of the week during July and August).

Getting There & Away The Château de Chaumont is 20 km south-west of Blois and 20 km north-east of Amboise in the village of Chaumont-sur-Loire, which is on the south bank of the Loire. The path leading up to the park and chateau begins at the intersection of Rue du Village Neuf and the D751, known in town as Rue Maréchal Leclerc.

By rail, take a local train on the Blois-Tours line and get off at Onzain, which is two km from the chateau. The station is across the Loire from the chateau. If you're coming by bicycle, you're best off taking the quiet backroads on the south bank of the river.

Château de Beauregard

Beauregard (☎ 54.70.40.05, 54.70.46.64), only six km south of Blois, is relatively modest in size, demonstrating the limitations of being a fabulously wealthy noble rather than a prince or the king. Built in the mid-16th century and enlarged a hundred years later, it is set in the middle of a large, forested park. The count and countess who own the place still live in one wing, which is why only half a dozen rooms are open to the public.

Beauregard's most noteworthy feature is the **Portrait Gallery**, which contains 327 portraits of famous people who lived between the 14th and 17th centuries; most were painted from other paintings. The portrait of each French king is surrounded by paintings of VIPs who lived during his reign. The floor is overlaid with 17th-century Delft tiles decorated with figures of soldiers on the march: cavalry, lancers, infantry, artillery and so forth.

From April to September, Beauregard is

open daily from 9.30 am to noon and 2 to 6.30 pm; there is no closure at midday during July and August. During the rest of the year (except mid-January to mid-February, when it's closed), the chateau is open from 9.30 am to noon and 2 to 5.00 pm (closed Wednesday). Tariffs are 20FF (15FF for students under 25 and people over 65). A free information handout in a number of languages is available at reception.

Getting There & Away The Château de Beauregard makes a good destination for a short bike ride from Blois (it's a 12-km round trip). It can also be visited on the way to Cheverny. There is road access to the chateau from both the D765 (the Blois-Cheverny road) and the D956 (turn left at the village of Cellettes).

TLC Bus No 5B from Blois towards Saint Aignan stops at the village of Cellettes (11.20FF), which is one km south-west of the chateau. The first bus from Blois to Cellettes leaves weekdays and Saturday at noon. Unfortunately, there's no afternoon bus back except one operated by Transports Boutet (☎ 54.34.43.95), which passes through Cellettes around 6.30 pm from Monday to Saturday and – except during August – at about 6 pm on Sunday.

AMBOISE

The picturesque town of Amboise (population 11,400), nestled under its fortified chateau on the south bank of the Loire, reached the pinnacle of its importance during the decades around 1500, when luxury-loving King Charles VIII enlarged the chateau and King François I held raucous parties there. These days, the town makes the most of its association with Leonardo da Vinci, who lived out his last years here under the patronage of François I.

Amboise makes an easy day trip from Blois or Tours. It is 34 km downstream (south-west) of Blois, 23 km upstream (east) of Tours, and only 10 km north-west of the Château de Chenonceau (see Tours Area Chateaux for details).

Orientation

The railway station, which is across the river from the centre of town (follow the signs to 'Centre Ville'), is about 800 metres from the chateau. Le Clos Lucé (Leonardo da Vinci's house) is 500 metres south-east of the chateau entrance along Rue Victor Hugo. Amboise's main commercial (and tourist) street is Rue Nationale, which runs roughly parallel to the river.

Information

Tourist Office The tourist office (Accueil d'Amboise; ☎ 47.57.01.37) is in a little round pavilion along the river opposite 7 Quai Général de Gaulle. They have a free guide to walking around Amboise entitled *Pedestrian Circuits in Town*. Hotel reservations within a 10-km radius are free. A map of the Amboise area, entitled *Val de Cisse*, is on sale for 18FF.

The office is open the following hours:

November to mid-March
    9 am-12.30 pm, 3-6 pm Mon-Sat
    Closed Sunday
Mid-March to mid-June & October
    9.30 am-12.30 pm, 1.30-6.30 pm Mon-Sat
    10 am-noon Sunday
Mid-June to September
    9 am-12.30 pm, 1.30-8.30 pm Mon-Sat
    10 am-noon, 4-7 pm Sunday

Money Opposite the chateau entrance, the Banque Populaire at 12 Place Leclerc is open Monday to Friday from 8.30 am (9.30 am on Monday) to 12.15 pm and 2 to 5.15 pm. The Crédit Mutuel at 8 Quai Général de Gaulle is open Tuesday to Saturday from 9 am to 12.30 pm and 2 to 5.30 pm (4.30 pm on Saturday).

The Crédit Agricole at 51 Rue Nationale has an ATM that is supposed to give cash advances to holders of Visa, MasterCard (Eurocard). There are other banks on Rue Nationale at No 34 and across from No 26.

Post The post office at 20 Quai Général de Gaulle is open on weekdays from 8.30 am to 12.15 pm and 1.30 to 6.15 pm and on Saturday until noon. Exchange services are available.

Amboise's postcode is 37400.

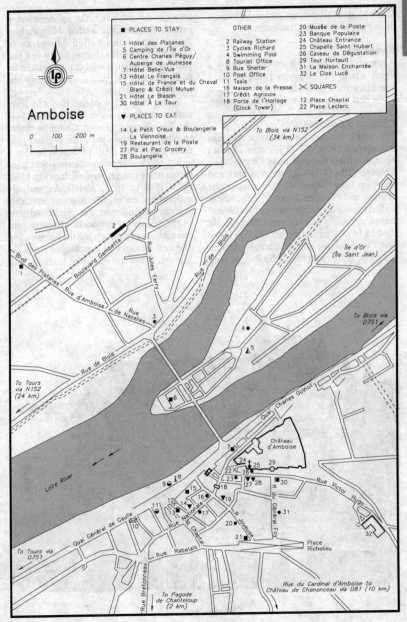

Amboise

0   100   200 m

■ PLACES TO STAY

1 Hôtel des Platanes
5 Camping de l'Île d'Or
6 Centre Charles Péguy/
   Auberge de Jeunesse
7 Hôtel Belle-Vue
13 Hôtel Le Français
15 Hôtel de France et du Cheval
   Blanc & Crédit Mutuel
21 Hôtel Le Blason
30 Hôtel À La Tour

▼ PLACES TO EAT

14 Le Petit Creux & Boulangerie
   La Viennoise
19 Restaurant de la Poste
27 Pic et Pac Grocery
28 Boulangerie

OTHER

2 Railway Station
3 Cycles Richard
4 Swimming Pool
8 Tourist Office
9 Bus Shelter
10 Post Office
11 Taxis
16 Maison de la Presse
17 Crédit Agricole
18 Porte de l'Horloge
   (Clock Tower)

20 Musée de la Poste
23 Banque Populaire
24 Château Entrance
25 Chapelle Saint Hubert
26 Caveau de Dégustation
29 Tour Hurtault
31 La Maison Enchantée
32 Le Clos Lucé

✕ SQUARES

12 Place Chaptal
22 Place Leclerc

Maps Maps of all sorts are sold at the Maison de la Presse at 24 Rue Nationale.

River View

Amboise is protected from the river by a dyke, whose flower-covered heights are a fine place for a riverside promenade. Some of the best views of town are from the bridge.

Château d'Amboise

The rocky outcrop on which the Château d'Amboise (☎ 47.57.00.98) now sits has been fortified since Roman times. King Charles VIII (1470-98), who was born and grew up here, began work to enlarge the chateau in 1492 after a visit to Italy, where he had been deeply impressed by the Italians' artistic creativity and luxurious lifestyle. He died in 1498 after hitting his head on a low lintel while on his way to a tennis game in the moat. King François I, who also grew up here (as did his sister, the reform-minded French Renaissance author Margaret of Angoulême, also called Margaret of Navarre), lived in the chateau for the first few years of his reign, a wild period marked by balls, masquerade parties, tournaments and festivities of all sorts.

Today, only a few of the 15th and 16th-century structures are extant. These include the Flamboyant Gothic **Chapelle Saint Hubert** and, inside the main building, the **Salle des États** (Hall of States), where a group of Protestant conspirators was tried before being hung from the balcony in 1560. From 1848 to 1852, Abdelkader, military and political leader of the Algerian resistance to French colonisation, was imprisoned here.

The chateau's **ramparts** afford a panoramic view of the town and the Loire Valley. The best way to exit the chateau is via the souvenir shop: the side door leads to **Tour**

Château d'Amboise

Hurtault (begun in 1495), whose interior consists of a circular ramp decorated with sculptured faces.

The entrance to the chateau is a block east of Quai Général de Gaulle (walk along Rue François 1er). It is open daily from 9 am to noon and 2 pm until sometime between 5 and 6.30 pm, depending on the season. During July and August, it's open nonstop from 9 am to 6.30 pm. The entrance fee is 28FF (18FF for students aged 24 or younger).

Le Clos Lucé

Leonardo da Vinci came to Amboise in 1516 at the invitation of François I. Until his death three years later (at the age of 67), Leonardo lived and worked in Le Clos Lucé (☎ 47.57.62.88) at 2 Rue du Clos Lucé, a brick manor house 500 metres up Rue Victor Hugo from the chateau.

The interior, decorated with faded tapestries and less-than-thrilling period furniture, is unimpressive. About the only thing to see that's connected with Leonardo are 40 modern scale models of some of his multifarious inventions, built using his notes. The park around the building is lovely.

Except during January, Le Clos Lucé is open daily from 9 am to 7 pm (6 pm during November, December and February). The entry fee is a steep 31FF (25FF for students, 16FF for children aged 7 to 16). A free brochure in English is available at the turnstile. The road to Le Clos Lucé passes troglodytic dwellings – caves in the limestone hillside in which local people still live.

La Maison Enchantée

This privately run museum (☎ 47.23.24.50) at 7 Rue du Général Foy displays over 250 *automates* (automaton dolls), cleverly and comically arranged in miniature scenes. They were created over 12 years by the man and woman who run the museum, which is open daily, except Monday (daily from April to September), from 10 am to noon and 2 to 6 pm (7 pm from April to September). Entrance costs 20FF (12FF for kids up to age 14).

Musée de la Poste

The municipal postal museum (☎ 47.56. 00.11) at 6 Rue Joyeuse has an interesting collection of stagecoach and ship models, mail carriers' bags and uniforms, lithographs and the like. It is housed in the 16th-century Hôtel Joyeuse, built by architects brought over from Italy. There's a lovely Renaissance garden off the courtyard.

From October to March, it is open from 10 am to noon and 2 to 5 pm daily except Monday; the rest of the year, hours are 9.30 am to noon and 2 to 6.30 pm. Tickets cost 15FF (7FF for children and students, free for students of fine arts and the history of art).

Wine Tasting

The Caveau de Dégustation (☎ 47.57.23.69) opposite 14 Rue Victor Hugo (at the base of the south side of the chateau), run by local *viticulteurs* (winegrowers), is open from the Sunday before Easter to sometime in September daily from 10 am to 7 pm. The tasting is free but you have to pay 1FF to use the toilets next door!

Places to Stay

Accommodation is hardest to find in July and August.

Places to Stay – bottom end

Camping The attractive *Camping de l'Île d'Or* (☎ 47.57.23.37), on Île d'Or (the island in the middle of the Loire, also known as Île Saint Jean), is open from Easter to the first weekend in October. There's a charge of 13.20FF a tent (19.80FF including parking) and 11FF per adult. The swimming pool next door costs 6.50FF.

Hostel The lively *Centre Charles Péguy/ Auberge de Jeunesse* (☎ 47.57.06.36) is about midway between the train station and the chateau on Île d'Or. Beds cost 46FF; breakfast is 14FF. If you arrive when reception is closed, ring the bell around the back. In general, you can't check in on Monday.

Hotels The older *Hôtel de France et du Cheval Blanc* (☎ 47.57.02.44; fax 47.57.69.54) at 6-7 Quai Général de Gaulle is nothing fancy, but large doubles cost only 130FF with washbasin and bidet and 185FF with shower and toilet. Unfortunately, there is no hall shower. This place is closed in December and January.

The eight-room *Hôtel À La Tour* (☎ 47.57.25.04) at 32 Rue Victor Hugo has singles/doubles/triples with washbasin and bidet for 90/135/200FF; showers are free. Reception (at the bar) is closed on Thursday except from June to 15 September. The hotel is closed during November.

Near the train station, you might try the 18-room *Hôtel des Platanes* (☎ 47.57.08.60), which is about 600 metres west of the train station at 7 Blvd des Platanes. Large doubles with washbasin start at 120FF; doubles/triples/quads with shower and toilet start at 160/210/240FF. Hall showers are free. From November to March, reception is closed on Saturday and Sunday unless you have a reservation.

Places to Stay – middle

The small, two-star *Hôtel Le Français* (☎ 47.57.11.38) at 1 Place Chaptal (diagonally across from the tourist office) has comfortable, sound-proofed doubles from 230FF with shower and toilet. They also have a couple of cheaper shower-equipped rooms without toilet.

The two-star *Hôtel Le Blason* (☎ 47.23.22.41; fax 47.57.56.18) at 11 Place Richelieu is housed in a restored 15th-century building. The rooms mix the modern (cheap walls and prefabricated bathrooms) with the medieval (beam ceilings) and cost 290/320/380/440FF for one/two/three/four people.

There are a number of hotels at the south end of the bridge over the Loire, including the three-star *Hôtel Belle-Vue* (☎ 47.57.02.26) at 12 Quai Charles Guinot, where singles/doubles start at 230/300FF, including breakfast. It is closed from 15 November to Easter.

Places to Eat

Restaurants The informal *Restaurant de la Poste* (☎ 47.57.68.02) at 5 Rue d'Orange has *menus* of French food for 49, 81, 109 and 151FF. It is open daily from May to October and six days a week the rest of the year.

There are a number of touristy fast-food joints along Rue Nationale, Quai Général de Galle and Rue Victor Hugo.

Salads (35 to 55FF), steak and fries (50FF) and similar fare are available at *Le Petit Creux* (☎ 47.23.11.99) at 48bis Rue Nationale, which from April to September is open daily from noon to midnight; the rest of the year, it's open Tuesday to Saturday from noon to 3 pm only.

Self-Catering Below the chateau entrance, the small *boulangerie* at 10 Rue Victor Hugo is open from 7.15 am to 8 pm daily except Monday (daily from June to September). Nearby at 2 Rue Victor Hugo, the *Pic et Pac* grocery is open Monday to Saturday from 8.30 or 9 am to 12.30 pm and 3 to 7.15 pm.

On Rue Nationale, *Boulangerie La Viennoise* at No 42 is open from 7.30 am to 1 pm and 3.30 to 7.30 pm (closed Monday). In July and August, it's open daily from 7.30 am to 7.30 pm.

Getting There & Away

Train The train station is across the river from the centre of town on Blvd Gambetta. About two-thirds of the trains on the Blois-Tours line (14 to 17 a day) stop at Amboise. Fares are 30FF to Blois (20 minutes) and 23FF to Tours (20 minutes). The last train back to Tours departs a bit after 7 pm; to Blois, the last train may be earlier, but check at the station – on certain days, there are later trains.

There are luggage lockers (5FF) at the station.

Bus Buses to and from Amboise (including the TLC summertime shuttle from Blois) stop at the bus shelter across the parking lot from the tourist office, a much more convenient place to begin a visit than the train station (on the down side, the buses are much slower). Hours are posted.

Les Rapides de Touraine's Line 10B, which links the town with Tours's bus station (21.40FF one way, 36.50FF return) Monday to Saturday, runs seven or eight times a day (four times a day during the summer school holidays).

From Monday to Saturday, two or three daily round trips link Amboise with the Château de Chenonceau; there are buses to the chateau at 10 am (and, during July and August, at 2.30 pm) and buses back to Amboise at 12.30 (and, during July and August, at around 4.40 pm).

Getting Around

Taxi At the railway station, you can call for a cab from the structure out front that looks like a bus shelter. In town, taxis (☎ 47.57. 30.39) are available near the tourist office at 10 Rue Descartes.

Bicycle Cycles Richard (☎ 47.57.01.79) at 21 Rue de Blois is at the train-station end of the bridge. Street/mountain bikes are 50/90FF a day. The shop is open from 9 am to noon and 2.30 to 7 pm (closed Sunday and Monday).

AROUND AMBOISE
Pagode de Chanteloup

This seven-storey Chinese-style pagoda, 44 metres in height, is one of the more pleasing follies left to us from 18th-century France. Built between 1775 and 1778, it combines contemporary French architectural fashions with elements from China, a subject of great fascination at the time. From the top of the pagoda, visitors are rewarded with an impressive view of the Loire Valley. Also visible are the overgrown outlines of the once-splendid pools, gardens and forest paths that surrounded the estate's 18th-century chateau, torn down in 1823.

From late March to September the Pagode de Chanteloup (☎ 47.57.20.97) is open daily from 10 am to 7 pm. From October to 11 November, it's open on weekends and bank holidays from 2 to 6 pm. It is closed the rest of the year. Admission costs 20FF (15FF for students under 25).

Getting There & Away The pagoda is about 2.5 km south of Amboise. Go south on Rue Bretonneau and follow the signs to 'La Pagode'.

TOURS

Whereas Blois remains essentially medieval in layout and small-townish in atmosphere, lively Tours (population 136,000; 270,000 in the metropolitan area) has the cosmopolitan and bourgeois air of a miniature Paris, with wide 18th-century avenues, formal public gardens, café-lined boulevards and a major university. There are also a number of worthwhile museums. Tours is the only town in the Loire Valley with much nightlife, and the restaurants are among the best in the region. Locals believe that the French spoken here is the purest in all of France.

Tours, founded under the Romans, has twice served as France's capital, at least briefly. In 1870, during the Franco-Prussian War, the provisional government of national defence fled Paris – Interior Minister Gambetta got out of the besieged city by balloon – and established itself at Tours for several months. The city later fell to the Prussians. Seventy years later, as French resistance to the German invasion collapsed in mid-June 1940, the French government briefly relocated to the city before moving on to Vichy. Shortly thereafter, Tours was badly damaged by German bombardments, which were accompanied by a devastating fire. The city's historic quarters were meticulously restored after the war.

Tours makes an excellent base for forays out to nearby chateaux, especially if your preference is for inexpensive accommodation. See Tours Area Chateaux, Blois Area Chateaux and Amboise for details.

Orientation

Thanks to the spirit of the 18th century, Tours is very efficiently laid out. Its focal point is Place Jean Jaurès, where the city's major thoroughfares – Rue Nationale, Blvd

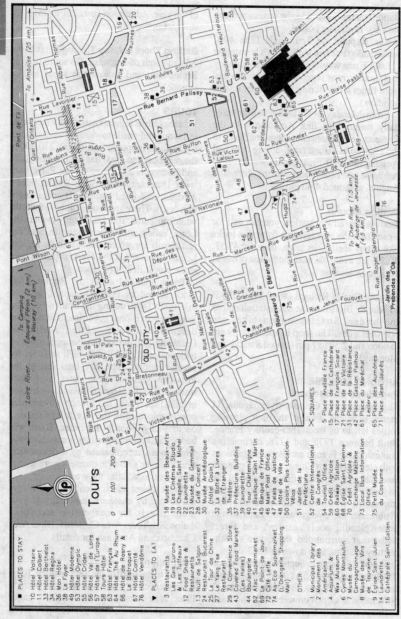

Tours

0   100   200 m

To Amboise (25 km)

To Camping
Edouard Péron (2 km)
& Vouvray (10 km)

Loire River

Pont Wilson

Pont de Fil

To Cher River (1.5 km)
& Auberge de Jeunesse
(4.5 km)

OLD CITY

PLACES TO STAY
- 10 Hôtel Voltaire
- 11 Hôtel Colbert
- 33 Hôtel Berthelot
- 34 Hôtel Regina
- 36 Hôtel
- 38 Le Foyer
- 49 Hôtel Moderne
- 53 Hôtel Olympic
- 55 Hôtel Criden
- 56 Hôtel Val de Loire
- 57 Hôtel de l'Europe
- 58 Tours Hôtel
- 63 Hôtel Français
- 64 Hôtel Thé Au Rhum
- 66 Hôtel de Rosny &
       Restaurant
- 67 Hôtel Comté
- 76 Hôtel Vendôme

PLACES TO EAT
- 3   Restaurants
       Les Gais Lurons
       & Les Tuffeaux
- 12 Food Shops &
       Restaurants
- 13 Nuit de Saigon
- 24 Restaurant Bucarest
- 25 La Tour de Chine
- 27 Le Yang Tse
       Restaurant
- 29 7J Convenience Store
- 43 Covered Food Market
       (Les Halles)
- 44 Boulangerie
- 52 Atac Supermarket
- 72 Le Point du Jour
- 74 Clé Gaffe
- 74 As-Eco Supermarket
       (L'Orangerie Shopping
       Mall)

OTHER
- 1   Municipal Library
- 2   Monument des
       Américains
- 4   Aquarium &
       Wax Museum
- 6   Cycles Montaubin
- 7   Musée du
       Campagnonnage
- 8   Musée des Vins
       de Touraine
- 9   Église Saint Julien
- 14 Laundrette
- 16 Cathédrale Saint Gatien
- 18 Musée des Beaux-Arts
- 19 Les Cinémas Studio
- 20 Chapelle Saint Michel
- 22 Laundrette
- 23 Musée du
- 28 Café Concert
- 30 Musée Archéologique
       (Hôtel Goüin)
- 32 La Boîte à Livres
       de l'Étranger
- 35 Théâtre
- 37 Préfecture Building
- 39 Laundrette
- 40 Tour Charlemagne
- 41 Basilique Saint Martin
- 45 Banque de France
- 46 Main Post Office
- 47 Palais de Justice
- 48 Hôtel de Ville
- 50 Loisirs Plus Location
       Vélos
- 51 Jardin de la
       Préfecture
- 52 Centre International
       de Congrès
- 54 Crédit Agricole
- 59 Crédit Agricole
- 60 Railway Station
- 68 Église Saint Étienne
- 70 Crédit Agricole &
       Exchange Machine
- 73 Local Bus Information
       Office
- 75 Petit Musée
       du Costume

✕ SQUARES
- 5   Place Anatole France
- 15 Place de la Cathédrale
- 17 Place François Sicard
- 21 Place de la Victoire
- 31 Place de la Résistance
- 42 Place Gaston Pailhou
- 61 Place du Maréchal
       Leclerc
- 65 Place des Aumônes
- 71 Place Jean Jaurès

Heurteloup, Ave de Grammont and Blvd Béranger – meet. The railway station is 300 metres east of Place Jean Jaurès. The old city, centred around Place Plumereau, is 400 metres west of Rue Nationale.

The northern boundary of the city is demarcated by the Loire River, which flows roughly parallel to the Cher River, three km to the south. The Loire and the Cher run side-by-side until they join 15 km west of the city.

Information

Tourist Office The tourist office (☎ 47.05.58.08) is across Rue Bernard Palissy from the new Centre International de Congrès, which faces the train station. It is open Monday to Saturday from 9 am to 12.30 pm and 1.30 to 6 pm. From June to August, it's open Monday to Saturday from 8.30 am to 7 pm and on Sunday from 10 am to 12.30 pm and 3 to 6 pm. Hotel reservations (made using vouchers) cost 6FF in the département of Indre-et-Loire and 30FF elsewhere in France. *Tours – The Loire Valley*, an excellent little English-language booklet with a multicoloured map, costs only 2FF.

The tourist office also sells the Carte Multi-Visites (50FF), which gets you into most of the city's museums and is also valid for a *visite guidée thématique* (thematic guided tour) of the city.

The tourist office runs 2½-hour walking tours of the city daily at 10 am from late April to October. They cost 35FF (22FF for children); narration is in French and, if you so request, in English. From June to September, thematic guided tours, also on foot, begin at 2.30 pm daily except Sunday and Monday.

Money Most banks in Tours are closed on Sunday and Monday.

The Banque de France (☎ 47.20.73.41) at 2 Rue Chanoineau is open Tuesday to Saturday from 8.45 am to noon and 1.30 to 3.30 pm. Cross the veranda and go through the doors under the sign reading 'Bureaux'.

Next to the train station, the Crédit Agricole (☎ 47.20.84.85) at 10 Rue Édouard Vaillant is open Monday to Friday from 9 am to 12.30 pm and 1.30 to 5.15 pm (4.15 pm on Friday). Inside the train station, Help Hotels (☎ 47.20.00.26) – the name reflects its sideline of making hotel reservations – gives a terrible rate but is open seven days a week from 8 am to 7.30 pm.

There are a number of banks around Place Jean Jaurès, including a Crédit Agricole (open Tuesday to Saturday) with a 24-hour banknote exchange machine at the south-eastern edge of the *place*.

Post The main post office (☎ 47.60.34.00) is 200 metres west of Place Jean Jaurès at 1 Blvd Béranger. It is open weekdays from 8 am to 7 pm and on Saturday from 8 am to noon. Currency exchange is available.

Tours's postcode is 37000.

Bookshops La Boîte à Livres de l'Étranger (☎ 47.05.67.29) at 2 Rue du Commerce has an excellent selection of English-language fiction (Penguins, etc) and nonfiction. It is open from 9.15 am to noon and 2 to 7 pm Tuesday to Friday and 9.30 am to noon on Saturday.

Laundry Near the train station, the laundrette at 20 Rue Bernard Palissy is open every day from 7 am to 9 pm. In the old city, the laundrette at 56 Rue du Grand Marché is open daily from 7.30 am to 9 pm. And near the cathedral, the laundrette at 149 Rue Colbert is open daily from 7 am to 9 pm.

Walking Tour

Tours is an especially pleasant city for strolling. The **old city**, a neighbourhood of restored, half-timbered houses, is centred around **Place Plumereau**, which has served as the area's main square since the Middle Ages. The wood-and-brick houses on the south side of Place Plumereau date from the 1400s. There are a number of interesting Romanesque, Gothic, Renaissance and neo-classical houses along **Rue Briçonnet** at Nos 16, 21, 25, 29 and 31.

Rue Nationale, which links Place Jean Jaurès with the river (spanned by 18th-century Pont Wilson, rebuilt after it collapsed in 1978), was laid out beginning in

1763. The whole area was largely destroyed in 1940. Also of interest is the area around the Musée des Beaux-Arts, which includes Cathédrale Saint Gatien. For information on the cathedral and the museums you'll come upon in these areas, see the following paragraphs and consult the map.

Musée des Beaux-Arts

Tours's Fine Arts Museum (☎ 47.05.68.73), housed in the 17th and 18th-century Palais de l'Ancien Archevêché (Former Archbishops' Palace) at 18 Place François Sicard, has an excellent collection of paintings, furniture and objets d'art from the 14th to 20th centuries. It is especially proud of two 15th-century altar paintings by Mantegna, *Christ au Jardin des Olivers* (Christ in the Olive Garden) and *La Résurrection*. Both were taken from Italy by Napoleon.

The museum is open from 9 am to 12.45 pm and 2 to 6 pm (closed Tuesday). Entrance costs 30FF (15FF for students, free if you're over 60). In the courtyard there's a truly magnificent **cedar of Lebanon** that was planted when Napoleon was emperor of the French (ie sometime between 1804 and 1815). There's a charming **flower garden** behind the cedar.

Cathédrale Saint Gatien

St Gatien Cathedral, the fourth church constructed on this site, was built from the 13th to 16th centuries in a succession of Gothic and Renaissance styles. Various parts represent the 13th century (the choir), the 14th century (the transept), the 14th and 15th centuries (the nave) and the 15th and 16th centuries (the façade). The tops of the two 70-metre-high **towers** (presently closed to the public) date from the Renaissance. There's a fine view of the **flying buttresses** from behind the cathedral. The interior is renowned for its stained-glass windows, many of which date from the 13th to 15th centuries.

Volunteers at the Accueil table give free guided tours daily, except on Sunday and between noon and 3 pm, but only some of them speak English. Brochures in English are available for 1FF from a self-service

table. The Renaissance-era **cloître** (cloister) can be visited with a guide (12FF) daily, except Sunday morning, from 9 am to noon and 2 to 5 pm (6 pm from April to September). You can get a glimpse of the cloister – including the spiral staircase, the extra buttresses for the north transept and the remains of the city's Roman walls (look for two layers of bricks in the foreground) – through the wrought-iron fence to the right as you exit through the west façade.

Musée du Campagnonnage

Tours's unique Museum of Craftmen's Societies (☎ 47.61.07.93) at 8 Rue Nationale displays the products of crafts rendered obsolete by the Industrial Revolution. The three associations of artisans which founded it have existed since at least the 16th century. The museum is open from 9 am to noon and 2 to 5 pm (6 pm from April to mid- June) daily except Tuesday. From mid-June to mid-September, it's open daily from 9 am to 6.30 pm. Tickets cost 20FF (10FF for students).

Musée des Vins de Touraine

The Touraine Wine Museum (☎ 47.61. 07.93), which is a few metres away at 16 Rue Nationale, occupies the vaulted, 13th-century wine cellars of Saint Julien Abbey, whose former abbey church, the Gothic **Église Saint Julien**, is next door. The museum does not give out wine samples but it does have a roomful of displays on the significance of wine and the traditions associated with it. Hours are the same as those of the Musée du Campagnonnage. Entrance costs 10FF (5FF for students).

Musée du Gemmail

This museum (☎ 47.61.01.19) at 7 Rue Murier specialises in *gemmail* (pronounced 'zheh-MAI'), an artistic medium that consists of superimposed pieces of coloured glass embedded in a colourless enamel and lit from behind. Gemmail was conceived in 1935, perfected in 1950 and popular in the 1950s and 1960s. The museum is open daily, except Monday, from mid-March to mid-

October only. Hours are 10 am to noon and 2 to 6.30 pm. Tickets cost 25FF (15FF for students).

Musée Archéologique de Touraine

The Touraine Archaeological Museum (☎ 47.66.22.32) is at 25 Rue du Commerce in the Hôtel Goüin, a splendid Renaissance residence built around 1510 for a wealthy merchant. Its Italian-style façade – all that was left after the conflagration of June 1940 – is worth seeing even if the eclectic assemblage of prehistoric, Gallo-Roman, medieval, Renaissance and 18th-century artefacts doesn't interest you.

Except during December and January, the museum is open daily from 10 am to 12.30 pm and 2 to 6.30 pm (5.30 pm from February to mid-March and during October and November). From mid-May to September, it's open daily from 10 am to 7 pm. The entrance fee is 16FF (11FF for students, 13FF for people over 60).

Basilique Saint Martin

Fans of late 19th-century ecclesiastical architecture may want to drop by this extravagant, pseudo-Byzantine church on Rue Descartes, erected between 1886 and 1924. In winter, it may be closed from noon to 2 pm. **Tour Charlemagne** (Charlemagne Tower), one of the few remains of a 12th-century basilica replaced by Rue des Halles in 1802, is across the street from the northern end of Basilique Saint Martin.

Petit Musée du Costume

About 600 costumed dolls, many of them quite old, are on display at this small museum (☎ 47.61.59.17) at 54 Blvd Béranger. It is open from 9.30 am to 11 am and 2 to 5 pm (closed Monday). Entrance costs 25FF (20FF for students).

Aquarium & Wax Museum

The unimpressive buildings of the **Château de Tours** at 25 Quai d'Orléans – across from the Pont de Fil pedestrian suspension bridge – house a nicely done **Aquarium Tropical** (☎ 47.64.29.52), open daily except Sunday

morning (daily in July and August). Entrance costs 22FF (17FF for students, 12FF for children under 12).

Nearby, the 31 scenes in the **Historial de Touraine wax museum** (☎ 47.61.02.95) give a pretty good idea of the way key events in the region's history may have appeared. Entry costs 29FF (21FF for students, 19FF for children aged 7 to 16). An English-language brochure costs 3FF. It is open daily.

Organised Tours

For information on tours of Tours, see Tourist Office under Information. For details on visiting nearby chateaux by bus or minibus, see Organised Tours under Transport in the Tours Area Chateaux section.

Places to Stay– bottom end

Camping Camping Édouard Péron (☎ 47. 54.11.11) at Place Édouard Péron, 2.5 km north-east of the train station on the north bank of the Loire, is open from mid-May to about mid-September. To get there from Place Jean Jaurès, take bus No 7 towards Sainte Radegonde Ermitage; you can also take bus Nos 60 or 61.

Hostels Le Foyer (☎ 47.05.38.81) at 16 Rue Bernard Palissy, 400 metres north of the train station, is a dormitory for workers of both sexes aged 16 to 25. If they have space (which is most of the time, though availability is best in July and August), they accept travellers of all ages. Doubles cost 65FF per person per night. Breakfast is 7.50FF. Cooking facilities are not available. Reception is open for check-in weekdays from 8 am to 7 pm and on Saturday from 8 am to 2.30 pm. It is not possible to check in on Sunday.

Tours's Auberge de Jeunesse (☎ 47.25. 14.45) is five km south of the train station (and two km south of the Cher River) in Parc de Grandmont. A bed costs 55FF, including breakfast. Rooms are locked from 10 am to 5 pm. Until 8 pm, you can take bus No 1 or No 6 from Place Jean Jaurès. Between 10 pm and about midnight, take Semitrat's Bleu de

Nuit Sud line (look for the yellow crescent moon symbol) and get off at the Monge stop.

Hotels – Train Station Area Tours is a gold mine of inexpensive and decent hotels. Most of Tours's cheapies are within walking distance of the train station.

The grand old *Hôtel Val de Loire* (☎ 47. 05.37.86) is around the corner from the train station at 33 Blvd Heurteloup. This place looks just like it did when it was a turn-of-the-century bourgeois home, with hardwood floors, high ceilings and some of the gas lighting fixtures still in place. Singles/doubles start at 80/130FF with washbasin and bidet, 130/160FF with shower and 170/210FF with bath and toilet. Hall showers cost 15FF.

The cheapest hotel in town is the *Tours Hôtel* (☎ 47.05.59.35), which is next to the train station at 10 Rue Édouard Vaillant. Very basic singles start at about 60FF, while doubles go for 70 to 85FF; a two-bed quad is 110FF. Showers cost 10FF. On the other side of the station, the *Hôtel Français* (☎ 47.05.59.12) at 11 Rue de Nantes has singles and doubles without/with shower from 100/120FF. Hall showers cost 20FF. Neither of these places accepts telephone reservations.

The *Hôtel Thé Au Rhum* (☎ 47.05.06.99) at 4-6 Place des Aumônes has simple, clean singles for 60 to 80FF and doubles from 75 to 95FF. A large triple is 130FF. Showers are free. New guests cannot check in on Sunday and holidays, when reception is closed. Another good bet is the *Hôtel Comté* (☎ 47.05.53.16), 150 metres further south at 51 Rue Auguste Comte. Singles cost 66 to 99FF, doubles start at 83FF, and two-bed triples are 115 to 132FF. The rooms are nothing fancy but given the price are a very good deal. This place closes for two weeks in February.

The *Hôtel Olympic* (☎ 47.05.10.17), 200 metres north of the train station at 74 Rue Bernard Palissy, has singles and doubles from 100FF with washbasin and bidet and 135FF with shower. Shower-equipped, two-bed rooms for two to four people are 200FF.

Reception is at the bar until 10 pm, when it moves to the 1st floor. *Mon Hôtel* (yes, the name means 'my hotel'; ☎ 47.05.67.53) is 500 metres north of the train station at 40 Rue de la Préfecture. Singles/doubles with a oversize bed start at 85/95FF. Showers are 15FF. The reception area is a bit dank and dark but the rooms were recently redone.

An excellent choice a bit further from the station is the *Hôtel Vendôme* (☎ 47.64. 33.54) at 24 Rue Roger Salengro. This cheerful place, run by a friendly couple, has simple but decent singles/doubles starting at 85/95FF with washbasin and bidet and 140/160 with shower and toilet. A triple with shower is 200FF. Hall showers cost 15FF.

Hotels – Near the River The *Hôtel Voltaire* (☎ 47.05.77.51) is 900 metres north of the train station at 13 Rue Voltaire. Basic but pleasant singles and doubles with shower start at 115FF; a two-bed triple with shower costs 175FF. Hall showers are 12FF. Overall, it's a good deal. Down the block, the *Hôtel Regina* (☎ 47.05.25.36) at 2 Rue Pimbert has neat, well-maintained singles/doubles from 93/115FF without shower and 165/210FF with shower and toilet. Hall showers cost 15FF. There's a TV room on the ground floor. Both these places are open all year except for two weeks around Christmas and New Year.

The *Hôtel Berthelot* (☎ 47.05.71.95), a block away at 8 Rue Berthelot, has clean, simple doubles of decent size for 100/120FF without/with shower; two-bed triples are 150/170FF. Showers are 10FF. The rooms in back are quietest.

Places to Stay – middle
Tours's two-star hotels generally offer good value.

Train Station Area To the right as you exit the railway station, the two-star *Hôtel de l'Europe* (☎ 47.05.42.07; fax 47.20.13.89) at 12 Place du Maréchal Leclerc has high ceilings and strip-carpeted hallways that give it an early 20th-century ambience. The huge rooms, equipped with old-fashioned furnishings, cost 230/280/320FF for a single/double/triple with shower and toilet. An extra bed is 40FF.

The warm, family-run *Hôtel Moderne* (☎ 47.05.32.81; fax 47.05.71.50) at 1-3 Rue Victor Laloux has decent one/two-bed doubles with high ceilings, showers and toilets from 248/275FF; similar rooms without toilet are 190FF. The *Hôtel Criden* (☎ 47.20.81.14; fax 47.38.03.84) at 65 Blvd Heurteloup has spacious public areas and comfortable but unsurprising rooms with bath, toilet and TV from 273/305FF for a single/double. A regular-sized bed can be added for 63FF. Locked parking is 18FF. Having your cat or dog stay with you costs 42FF.

A slightly less expensive option is the two-star *Hôtel de Rosny* (☎ 47.05.23.54) at 19-21 Rue Blaise Pascal, where singles/doubles/triples cost 150/200/310FF with shower, toilet and TV.

Near the River The pleasant, two-star *Hôtel Colbert* (☎ 47.66.61.56) at 78 Rue Colbert has rooms that range in size from large to enormous. Singles/doubles with shower, toilet and TV start at 205/235FF; an additional bed is 65FF.

Places to Eat

The old city has quite a few restaurants, pizza places, cafés, creperies and boulangeries at Place Plumereau and along nearby streets, especially Rue du Grand Marché. There's another cluster of food shops and restaurants along Rue Colbert. For café-restaurants, you can't beat Place Jean Jaurès and nearby bits of Ave de Grammont.

French – up-market Tours has a number of fine options for a splurge. *Restaurant Les Gais Lurons* (☎ 47.64.75.50) at 15 Rue Lavoisier specialises in traditional but sophisticated French cuisine. Absolutely everything is made fresh on-site. *Menus* are available for 98, 135 and 190FF. This place is open Monday to Friday from noon to 2.15

pm and 7.30 to 10 pm and on Saturday from 7.30 to 10 pm.

Nearby, *Restaurant Les Tuffeaux* (☎ 47.47.19.89) at 19-21 Rue Lavoisier is another excellent choice. The innovative *cuisine gastronomique* is made with lots of fresh local products. *Menus* are 110, 150 and 200FF. It is open Tuesday to Saturday from noon to 1.30 pm and 7.30 to 9.30 pm and Monday from 7.30 to 9.30 pm. At both these places, reservations are a good idea for dinner, especially on Friday and Saturday.

French – inexpensive *Café Leffe* (☎ 47.61.48.54) at 15 Place Jean Jaurès is named after a beer from Belgium called Abbaye de Leffe – Belgian beers (13.50FF) are a speciality. It is open daily from 7 am to 2 am; full meals are served from 11.30 am to 2.30 pm and 6.30 to 11.15 pm. Moules marinières (mussels cooked with onions) and frites (chips) cost 52FF, including a demi of beer.

The hugely popular *La Villa Médicis* (☎ 47.66.80.26) at 19 Place Jean Jaurès has a wide variety of steaks (58 to 88FF) as well as salads (24 to 55FF) and pizzas (32 to 55FF). The two-course lunch *menu* is about 50FF. It is open daily from 11.45 am to 2.30 pm and 7 pm to midnight.

Near the railway station, the simple but attractive *Le Bistroquet* (☎ 47.05.12.76) at 17 Rue Blaise Pascal has *menus* of solid French food from 49FF (weekday lunches), 59, 75 and 120FF. Their speciality is paella, a Spanish rice dish made with seafood, chicken and pork. It is open from noon to 1.30 pm and 7.30 to 9.30 pm daily except Friday evening and Sunday. *Thé Au Rhum* (☎ 47.05.06.99) at 4-6 Place des Aumônes has simple French fare, including crepes (14 to 30FF) and meat dishes (25 to 50FF). There are *menus* for 45 and 65FF.

Other The *Restaurant Indien Surya* (☎ 47.64.34.04), located at 65 Rue Colbert, has a selection of North Indian dishes including curries, tandoori items and all sorts of rice biryani. It is open from noon to 2.30 pm and 7 to 11 pm daily, except Monday when it's open in the evening only. The lunch *menu* costs 49FF.

The *Nuit de Saïgon* (☎ 47.66.67.70), a Chinese/Vietnamese place at 121 Rue Colbert, has *menus* from 65FF.

In the old city, *La Tour de Chine* (☎ 47.66. 49.10) opposite 18 Rue du Grand Marché has *menus* for 38FF (lunch only) and 50FF.

The hole-in-the-wall *Le Yang Tse* (☎ 47. 61.47.59) at 83bis Rue du Commerce, whose main dishes cost only 20 to 35FF, is open daily from noon to 2.30 pm and 5.30 to 11.30 pm or midnight.

Resonably priced Romanian food is available at the *Restaurant Bucarest* (☎ 47.20. 04.20) at 15 Rue du Grand Marché. The lunch *menu* is 35FF; on weekdays, there's also a 50FF *menu*.

Vegetarian South of Place Jean Jaurès, *Le Point du Jour* (☎ 47.05.34.00) at 38bis Ave de Grammont has vegetarian *menus* for 55FF (lunch) and 69FF (dinner). It is open from noon to 3 pm (2 pm on Sunday) and 7 to 10 pm (closed Sunday evening). Fish is served in the evening and on Friday.

Self-Catering Lovely places for a picnic include Place François Sicard (near the Musée des Beaux-Arts), the garden of the Musée des Beaux-Arts (behind the cedar) and the Jardin de la Préfecture.

Les Halles, Tours's covered market, is 500 metres west of Rue Nationale at Place Gaston Pailhou. It is open Monday to Saturday from 6 am to 7 pm and on Sunday from 6 am to 1 pm. The *boulangerie* at 30 Place Gaston Pailhou is open from 7 am to 7.30 pm (closed Monday).

In front of the train station at 5 Place du Maréchal Leclerc, the *Atac supermarket* – which has an in-house boulangerie – is open Monday to Saturday from 8.30 am to 8 pm and on Sunday from 9.30 am to 12.30 pm. *Boulangerie La Liegeoise*, whose specialities include multicereal breads, is nearby at 8 Place du Maréchal Leclerc. It is open Monday to Saturday (including holidays) from 6.15 am to 8.30 pm.

At Place Jean Jaurès, there is an *As-Eco*

supermarket at No 19bis (inside the L'Orangerie shopping mall). It has an in-house bakery and a nice selection of prepared salads and is open Monday to Saturday from 9 am to 8 pm and on Sunday from 9 am to 12.30 pm.

In the old city, there are several *boulangeries* along Rue du Grand Marché. To cure a late-night attack of the munchies, the place to go is the *7J convenience store* at 14 Rue de Constantine, which is open every day from 7 am to 11 pm.

East of Rue Nationale, there are lots of food shops along Rue Colbert. The *boulangerie* at 62 Rue Colbert, which offers a good selection of multi-grain breads, is open Tuesday to Saturday from 6.30 am to 2 pm and 3 to 8 pm and on Sunday from 6.30 am to 3 pm. Other boulangeries on the same street stay open on Monday.

Entertainment

Music *Café-Concert Les Trois Orfevres* (☎ 47.64.02.73) at 6 Rue des Orfèvres (off Rue du Commerce) has live music (rhythm-and-blues, blues, rock, soul, jazz) nightly from Wednesday to Saturday from 10 pm to 4 am (unless the hall has been rented out for a private party). Entry costs 35 to 50FF; students usually get a reduction. A demi of beer costs 20FF on tap.

Cinema Les Cinémas Studio (☎ 47.05.22.80 for a recorded message), whose entrance is opposite 17 Rue des Ursulines, shows subtitled (rather than dubbed) films. The day's dozen or so screenings begin at 1.30 pm (5 pm in July and August). Titles, which always include several films in English, are changed every Wednesday. Tickets cost 33FF (24FF if you're over 60).

Getting There & Away

Train The train station (☎ 47.20.50.50 for information) is off Blvd Heurteloup at Place du Maréchal Leclerc. The information office is open from 8.30 am to 6.30 pm daily except Sunday and holidays. Tickets are on sale from 5.15 am to 10.15 pm (11.45 pm Friday to Sunday). Tours is linked to Saint Pierre des Corps by shuttle trains synchronised to meet the mainline trains.

To get from Paris to Tours by rail (149FF), you can either take a TGV from Gare Montparnasse (149FF plus the reservation fee; 70 minutes), which sometimes requires a change of trains at Saint Pierre des Corps. Or you can take a direct non-TGV train from Paris's Gare d'Austerlitz (149FF; two to 2½ hours). There are TGV and non-TGV services to Bordeaux (196FF; 2½ hours by TGV) and Poitiers (72FF; about one hour; a dozen a day) and non-TGVs to Nantes (127FF; 1¾ hours) and La Rochelle (154FF; three hours).

Quite a few of the chateaux around Tours can be reached by train or SNCF bus. For details, see the Organised Tours and Getting There & Away listings under Tours Area Chateaux, Blois Area Chateaux and Chinon. About two-thirds of the trains to Blois (44FF; 40 minutes; 14 to 17 a day) stop at Amboise (23FF; 20 minutes).

Bus Les Rapides de Touraine (☎ 47.46. 06.60) handles services within the département of Indre-et-Loire. Schedules are posted at the bus terminal (*halte routière*; ☎ 47.05.30.49), which is in front of the train station at Place du Maréchal Leclerc.

Long-haul international carrier Eurolines (☎ 47.66.45.56) has a ticket office at 76 Rue Bernard Palissy. It's open Monday to Saturday from 9 am to noon and 1.30 to 6.30 pm.

For details on bus transport to nearby chateaux, see the Getting There & Away listings in the Tours Area Chateaux section.

Car ADA (☎ 47.64.94.94) is a bit south of the centre of town at 49 Blvd Thiers, which is 250 metres west of the huge Hôtel Altea at Place Thiers (the intersection of Ave de Grammont and Blvd Thiers). It's open Monday to Saturday from 8 am to noon and 2 to 7 pm (6.30 pm on Saturday). To get there by bus, take bus No 3 or 6 from the train station or bus No 1, 2, 3, 5 or 9 (southbound) from Place Jean Jaurès; get off at the Thiers stop.

Europcar (☎ 47.64.47.76), near the rail-

way station at 76 Blvd Bernard Palissy, is open from 8 am to noon and 2 to 6.30 pm daily except Sunday and holidays.

Getting Around
Bus The bus network serving Tours and its suburbs is known by its acronym, Semitrat. Almost all lines stop at Place Jean Jaurès. Three Bleu de Nuit lines operate nightly from about 9.30 pm to a bit past midnight.

Tickets, which cost 6.20FF if bought singly, are valid for one hour after being time-stamped. A carnet of 10 tickets costs 48FF. An announcement board at the front of the bus informs passengers of the name of the *station suivante* (next stop).

Semitrat has an information office (☎ 47.66.70.70), known as Espace Bus, at Place Jean Jaurès next to Café Leffe. It is open daily, except Sunday, from 7.30 am to 7 pm (6.30 pm on Saturday). During July and August, it opens at 8.30 am.

Taxi Call Taxi Radio (☎ 47.20.30.40) to order a cab.

Bicycle Cycles Montaubin (☎ 47.05.62.27), which is near the river at 2 Rue Nationale, rents 10-speeds/mountain bikes for 70/100FF a day and 100/200FF per three-day weekend (Saturday to Monday). A 1000FF deposit is required. The shop is open Tuesday to Saturday from 9.15 am to noon and 2 to 7 pm.

From July to mid-September, Loisirs Plus Location Vélos (☎ 47.46.28.38) has an office near the railway station at 20 Blvd Heurteloup. It's open daily from 8 am to noon and 1.30 to 7 pm. Three-speeds and mountain bikes cost 60/100FF a half/whole day and 500FF a week. The company's other office (☎ 47.46.28.38), further east at 214 Rue Jolivet, is open all year.

AROUND TOURS
Wine Tasting in Vouvray
The village of Vouvray (population 2500), 10 km north-east of Tours (on the N152) on the north bank of the Loire, is not an attractive place no matter how much wine you've

sampled. But the town has about 50 *caves* producing fine white wines, and many of them are open for tasting and sales, especially during the warm months. To find them, look for signs reading 'dégustation' or '*cave*' or contact the tourist office.

Information The tourist office (☎ 47.52. 68.73) is on the corner of the N152 and the D46 (Ave Brulé), while the syndicat d'initiative (☎ 47.52.70.48) is at the intersection of Rue de la République and Rue Gambetta. One of these is scheduled to be done away with, but whichever one survives will be able to provide information on wine tasting in the vicinity and will probably be open from at least May to September, though not on Sunday afternoon.

Places to Eat On Friday and Tuesday morning, there's a *food market* on Ave André Maginot, which is near the *Unico supermarket* (closed Sunday) at 12 Rue Rabelais.

Getting There & Away Semitrat's bus No 61, which links Tours with Vernou, will take you from Place Jean Jaurès in Tours (in front of the Palais de Justice) to Vouvray (20 minutes; 10 a day, three on Sunday afternoon). The last bus back to Tours leaves at around 7 pm (approximately 6.30 pm on Sunday).

TOURS AREA CHATEAUX

Tours, with its many cheap hotels and decent train and bus links, makes a good base for visits to some of the most interesting of the Loire chateaux, including Chenonceau, Villandry, Azay-le-Rideau, Langeais, Amboise (see the Amboise section) and Chaumont (see Blois Area Chateaux). If you have a Eurail pass, it will get you to more chateaux from Tours than from any other railhead in the region.

Organised Tours

Several companies offer English-language tours of the major Loire Valley chateaux, with different itineraries available each day of the week. Reservations can be made at the Tours tourist office (where you can arrange to be picked up); you can also phone the company yourself. Prices include entrance fees (organisers pay group rates), a major expense if you go on your own.

Marques Dos Santos (☎ 47.37.15.60) at 16 Rue de l'Hospitalité charges 95 to 180FF for personalised minibus tours. Touraine Évasion (☎ 47.66.52.32 on weekdays; 47.66.63.81 on Sunday morning and Saturday), which also uses minibuses (for eight passengers), has daily trips from Easter to September. Prices are similar. With both these companies, groups of five to seven people can hire a minibus and a driver and create their own itineraries.

Services Touristiques de Touraine (☎ 47. 05.46.09), a larger company based in the train station, has half-day tours (120FF to 140FF) and all-day tours (200FF) by full-sized bus daily from April to September. Buses depart from in front of the train station.

Entertainment

The tourist office in Tours has information on sound-and-light shows, medieval re-enactments, and other *spectacles* performed at the chateaux during the summer.

Getting There & Away

More train and bus details are listed under Getting There & Away at the end of each chateau listing.

Train Many of the chateaux of the Loire Valley – including Amboise (23FF), Azay-le-Rideau (25FF), Blois (44FF), Chenonceau (32FF), Chaumont, Chinon (41FF), Langeais (22FF) and Saumur and, somewhat less conveniently, Villandry (14FF to Savonnières) – can be reached from Tours by train or SNCF bus, both of which accept Eurail passes. If you'd like an up-to-date timetable for the most convenient trains to the chateaux, ask at a train station for the brochure *Les Châteaux de la Loire en Train*, a new edition of which comes out each summer. The *Guide Régional TER*, also available at many train stations, has a more complete schedule.

Bus Les Rapides de Touraine (☎ 47.46.06.60), based in Tours at 1 Rue de Lorraine (1.5 km south of the the train station), has limited bus service to the area around Tours. The company's buses, which stop at the bus station – and, in some cases, Place Jean Jaurès as well – do *not* run on Sunday. Getting out to the chateaux by bus is fairly expensive, and an organised tour might actually work out not only faster and simpler but also cheaper. All times quoted here are approximate, so verify them before making plans.

From Tours, you can make an all-day bus circuit (57FF) to Chenonceau and Amboise by taking Les Rapides de Touraine bus No 10B for the hour-long ride to Chenonceau at 10 am (9.30 am in July and August); catching the bus from Chenonceau to Amboise (35 minutes) at 12.30 pm (during July and August, there's another bus at 4.40 pm); and then taking either the bus (at 5.20 pm) or a train (the last one's a bit after 7 pm) back to Tours.

Car For car rental information, see Getting There & Away at the end of the Tours section.

Bicycle For bicycle rental information, see Getting Around at the end of the Tours section. Equip yourself with a decent roadmap (available at bookshops and larger newsagents) before heading out of the city. On certain trains, you can take along a bicycle free of charge, allowing you to cycle either there or back. Details are available from train station information offices.

Château de Chenonceau

Castles don't get much more fairytale-like than 16th-century Chenonceau (☎ 47.23.90.07), which comes complete with stylised (rather than defensive) moat, drawbridge, towers and turrets. The interior is filled with period furniture, tourists, paintings, tourists, tapestries, tourists and tourists, all of only moderate interest. In all fairness to the chateau's owners, the huge numbers of visitors are handled very well.

The nicest thing about Chenonceau is its gardens and forests and the vistas they afford of the castle's exterior. One of the series of remarkable women who created Chenonceau, Diane de Poitiers, mistress of King Henri II, planted the garden to the left (east) as you approach the chateau down the avenue of plane trees. After the death of Henri II in 1559, she was forced to give up her beloved Chenonceau by the vengeful Catherine de Médicis, Henri II's wife, who then applied her own formidable energies to the chateau and, among other works, laid out the garden to the right (west) as you approach the castle. In the 18th century, Madame Dupin, the owner at the time, brought Jean-Jacques Rousseau to Chenonceau as a tutor for her son. During the Revolution, the affection with which the peasantry regarded Madame Dupin saved the chateau from the violent fate of many of its neighbours.

The 60-metre-long **Galerie** over the Cher River, built by Catherine de Médicis, was converted into a hospital during WW I. Between 1940 and 1942, the demarcation line between Vichy-ruled France and the German-occupied zone ran down the middle of the Cher: the castle itself was under direct German occupation, but the Galerie's southern entrance was in the area controlled by Marshal Pétain. For many people trying to escape to the Vichy zone, this room served as a crucial crossing point.

Chenonceau is open all year from 9 am until sometime between 4.30 pm (mid-November to mid-February) and 7 pm (mid-March to mid-September. The entrance fee is 35FF (25FF for students). During July and August, you can paddle around the moat and the Cher River in rowboats for 10FF per half-hour.

Getting There & Away The Château de Chenonceau, situated in the town of Chenonceaux, is 34 km east of Tours, 10 km south-east of Amboise and 40 km south-west of Blois.

Milk-run local trains *(omnibus)* on the Tours-Vierzon line stop at Chisseaux, two km east of Chenonceaux. There are also two or three trains a day from Tours to

Chenonceaux station (32FF), which is only 500 metres from the chateau.

From Monday to Saturday during July and August, certain runs (two a day) of Les Rapides de Touraine's bus No 10 from Tours stop at Chenonceaux (33.50FF one way, 57FF return); buses back to Tours depart around 12.15 pm and 4.30 pm. During the school year, line No 10 has one round trip to Chenonceaux daily except Sunday.

For travel between Chenonceau and Amboise, there are two or three round trips daily except Sunday. Throughout the year, buses leave Amboise at 10 am (and, during July and August, at 2.30 pm); buses back to Amboise depart Chenonceau at 12.30 (and, during July and August, at around 4.40 pm).

Château de Villandry

The Château de Villandry (☎ 47.50.02.09) has some of the most spectacular formal gardens anywhere in France. The **Jardin d'Ornement** (Ornamental Garden) is made up of intricate, geometrically pruned hedges and flower beds loaded with abstract, romantic symbolism (explained in the free English-language brochure you can pick up at the entrance).

Between the chateau and the nearby village church, the **Potager** (Kitchen Garden) is a cross between the vegetable plots in which medieval monks grew their food and the formal gardens so beloved in 16th-century France. Vegetables of various hues as well as pear trees, roses and other flowers are used to form nine squares, each different than its neighbours. Between the Kitchen Garden and the church, there's a plot of **herbs** and **medicinal plants**.

All told, Villandry's gardens occupy five hectares and include over 1150 lime trees, hundreds of grape trellises and some 52 km of landscaped plant rows. Villandry is at its most colourful from May to mid-June and August to October but is well worth a visit at other times of the year as well.

The chateau itself was completed in 1536, making it the last of the major Renaissance-style chateaux to be built in this area. The

interior, whose sparsely furnished, 18th-century rooms and hallways are adorned with mediocre paintings, is eminently skipable, though the 13th-century Moorish **mosque ceiling** from Spain is of moderate interest. The magnificent view from the tower – whence the intricate gardens can be seen in their entirety, as can the parallel Loire and Cher rivers – is only slightly better than the one that can be had for no extra cost from the terraced hill east of the chateau.

Villandry's gardens are open daily from 9 am (8.45 am from June to August) to 5 pm (November to February), 6 pm (March, April and October), 7.30 pm (May and September) or 8 pm (June to August). The chateau itself – which, unlike the gardens, is closed from 11 November to mid-February – can be visited until sometime between 5.30 and 6.30 pm. Entry to the gardens costs 24FF (22FF for children and students aged 18 to 25); it's an additional 13FF to see the chateau interior either with or without a French-speaking guide.

Getting There & Away The Château de Villandry is in the village of Villandry, which is 17 km south-west of Tours, 31 km north-east of Chinon and 11 km north-east of Azay-le-Rideau. By road, the shortest route from Tours is the D7, but cyclists will find less traffic on the D88 (which runs along the south bank of the Loire) and the D288 (which links the D88 with Savonnières). If heading south-westward from Villandry towards Langeais and/or Ussé, the best bike route is the D16, which has no shoulders but is lightly trafficked.

The only public transport from Tours to Villandry is the train to Savonnières (14FF; 10 to 20 minutes; two or three a day), which is about four km east of Villandry. The first train from Tours is at around noon; the last train back to Tours is at 1.30 pm (5.30 pm on Saturday, 7.30 pm on Sunday). It may be possible to bring your bicycle on the train with you. The tour companies listed under Organised Tours all have at least two trips a week that include a stop at Villandry.

Château d'Azay-le-Rideau

Azay-le-Rideau (☎ 47.45.42.04), built on an island in the Indre River and surrounded by a quiet pool dotted with lily pads, is one of the most harmonious and elegant of the Loire chateaux. It is adorned with stylised fortifications and turrets intended both as decoration and to indicate the rank of the owners. All around the building are lawns and stands of rare trees.

The bloodiest incident in the chateau's history – a subject of invariable fascination for modern-day chateau-goers – occurred in 1418. During a visit to Azay, then a fortified castle, the crown prince (later King Charles VII) was insulted by the Burgundian guard. Enraged, he had the town burned and executed some 350 soldiers and officers. The present chateau was begun exactly a century later by Giles Berthelot, one the the king's less-than-selfless financiers. When the prospect of being audited and hanged drew near, he fled abroad and never completed the structure. The finishing touches weren't put on until the 19th century.

From October to March, the chateau can be visited daily from 10 am to 12.30 pm and 2 to 4.30 pm. From April to June and in September, it is open from 9.30 am to 5.30 pm. During July and August, hours are from 9 am to 6.30 pm. The park stays open half an hour later than the interior of the chateau. Tickets cost 25FF (14FF if you're aged 18 to 24 or over 60). You can either walk around on your own (a free explanatory sheet in English is available) or join a guided tour (in French) at no extra cost.

Getting There & Away Azay-le-Rideau, which is in a town of the same name, is 26 km south-west of Tours. SNCF has year-round service from Tours to Azay by either train or bus for 25FF (two or three a day); the station is 2.5 km from the chateau. The last train/bus to Tours leaves Azay at about 6 pm (9 pm on Sunday).

Langeais

The main attraction in the flowery little town of Langeais (population 4000) is the massive Château de Langeais at Place Pierre de Brosse.

Information The town's tourist office (☎ 47.96.58.22), which is near the chateau at 15 Place Pierre de Brosse, has information on hotels, chambres d'hôtes, gîtes, restaurants, wine cellars and walks in the area. It is open Monday to Saturday from 3 to 6 pm. From Easter to May, it's open Monday to Saturday from 9 am to noon and 3 to 6 pm. From June to September, it's open daily from 9 am (10 am on Sunday) to 12.30 pm and 3 to 7 pm (6 pm on Sunday). There are also extended hours during the Easter and Christmas school holidays.

Château de Langeais Built in the late 1460s to cut the most likely invasion route from Brittany, the Château de Langeais (☎ 47.96.72.60) presents two faces to the world. The side facing the town is still very much a 15th-century fortified castle, with almost windowless, machicolated walls (ie walls from which missiles and boiling liquids could be dropped on attackers) rising forbiddingly from the drawbridge. The sections facing the courtyard, however, are outfitted with the large windows, dormers and decorative stonework that are characteristic of later chateaux designed for more refined living. The **ruined donjon** across the garden from the castle dates from around 944 and is the oldest such structure in France.

Langeais has what may be the Loire Valley's most interesting interior, after 17th-century Cheverny. The unmodernised configuration of the rooms and the authentic **period furnishings** (chests, beds, stools, tables, chairs, etc) give you a pretty good idea of what the place looked like during the 15th and 16th centuries (ie before and during the early Renaissance period). The walls are decorated with fine but somewhat faded Flemish and Aubusson **tapestries**, many of which are in the millefleurs (thousand flowers) style. In one room, wax figures re-enact the marriage of King Charles VIII and Duchess Anne of Brittany, which took place right here on 6 December 1491 and which brought about the final union of France and Brittany. The event also put an end to the chateau's strategic importance.

The Château de Langeais, which is owned by the Institut de France, is open from 9 am to noon and 2 to 5 pm (closed Monday). From 15 March to 2 November, it's open daily from 9 am to 6.30 pm (10 pm in July and August). Entrance costs 30FF (23FF for people over 60, 17FF for students 25 and under). Guided tours are conducted in French only, but there are explanatory signs in English and several other languages.

Wine Tasting The Cave de la Château, which is in the castle wall at Place Pierre de Brosse (where the round rampart meets a square bit of the wall), has free tasting and sales of wines from the immediate vicinity of Langeais. Each day a different wine is featured. It is open from July to 15 September daily from 9.30 am to 7.30 pm.

Places to Eat There are a number of restaurants and food shops along the streets around the walls of the chateau.

Getting There & Away Langeais is 24 km south-west of Tours and 14 km west of Villandry.

The Langeais railway station (☎ 47.96.82.19), 400 metres from the Château de Langeais, is on the Tours-Savonnières-Saumur line. The trip from Tours (22FF; four a day) takes 20 to 30 minutes. The last train back to Tours is at 6.30 pm (7.20 or 8.10 pm on Sunday and holidays). By train, it's 10FF to Savonnières (four km from Villandry) and 34FF to Saumur.

Château d'Ussé

The privately owned 16th and 17th-century Château d'Ussé (☎ 47.95.54.05), perched on the edge of the Forêt de Chinon, looks like a turreted fairytale castle, but there's nothing really outstanding about it except the entry fee, which is the highest in the area. The ornate exterior, built of tufa (a soft, whitish, local stone), is crumbling, and the façades

around the **Renaissance-style courtyard** are in pretty bad shape.

Inside, a number of the furnished rooms are enlivened by mannequins dressed in **historical costumes**; the themed exhibits are changed annually. The gardens were laid out be André Le Nôtre, who also did the Jardin des Tuileries in Paris. Among the outbuildings is a Renaissance-style **chapel** (1528).

Ussé is open daily from 9 am to noon and 2 to 6 pm (7 pm from Easter to 14 July and during September). From 15 July to August, hours are 9 am to 6.30 pm; from October to 11 November, it's open daily from 10 am to noon and 2 to 5.30 pm. The chateau is closed from 11 November to 14 March. The entry fee is a steep 49FF for everyone except children aged nine to 16, who pay 19FF. The frequent 45-minute guided tours – you must join one to see certain parts of the chateau – are in French, but a written text in English is distributed to Anglophones at the start of the tour.

Getting There & Away Ussé is 38 km southwest of Tours (along the D7) and 13 km north of Chinon.

The nearest the railway line gets to Ussé is Rivarennes, 6.5 km east of the chateau, so for all intents and purposes there is no public transport unless you hitch the last bit. A few of the tours (see Organised Tours earlier) stop at Ussé.

CHINON

Chinon's massive, 400-metre-long castle towers over the town's medieval quarter, whose uneven, cobblestone streets are lined with ancient houses, some built of decaying tufa stone, others of half-timbers and brick. The triangular, black slate roofs and the white tufa give the town a distinctive appearance.

Villandry, Azay-le-Rideay, Langeais and Ussé can easily be visited from Chinon if you have your own transport.

Orientation

The main street in the medieval quarter is Rue Haute Saint Maurice, which becomes Rue Voltaire as you move east. The railway

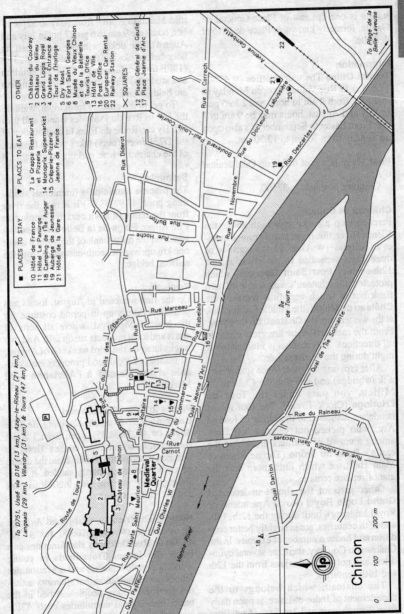

Chinon

To D751, Ussé via D16 (13 km), Azay-le-Rideau (21 km), Villandry (29 km), Langeais (31 km) & Tours (47 km)

PLACES TO STAY
10 Hôtel de France
11 Hôtel La Panurge
18 Camping de l'Île Auger
19 Auberge de Jeunesse
21 Hôtel de la Gare

PLACES TO EAT
7 La Grappa Restaurant et Pizzeria
14 Monoprix Supermarket
15 Crêperie-Pizzeria Jeanne de France

OTHER
1 Château du Coudray
2 Château du Milieu
3 Grand Logis Royal
4 Château Entrance & Tour de l'Horloge
5 Dry Moat
6 Fort Saint Georges
8 Musée du Vieux Chinon et de la Batellerie
9 Tourist Office
13 Hôtel de Ville
16 Post Office
20 Europcar Car Rental
22 Railway Station

SQUARES
12 Place Général de Gaulle
17 Place Jeanne d'Arc

Route de Tours
Château de Chinon
Medieval Quarter
Rue Haute Saint Maurice
Rue Voltaire
Rue Jeanne d'Arc
Rue du Commerce
Rue Carnot
Rue du Puits des Bancs
Rue Rabelais
Rue Marceau
Rue Hoche
Rue Buffon
Rue de 11 Novembre
Rue Diderot
Boulevard Paul-Louis Courier
Rue du Docteur P Labussière
Rue Descartes
Rue A Correch
Avenue Gambetta
Quai Charles VII
Quai Pasteur
Quai Jeanne d'Arc
Quai du Raineau
Rue du Faubourg Saint Jacques
Quai Danton
Quai de l'Île Sonnante

Vienne River
Île de Tours

To Plage de la Belle Laveuse

0   100   200 m

station is one km east of Place Général de Gaulle, formerly known as Place de l'Hôtel de Ville.

Information

Tourist Office The tourist office (☎ 47.93. 17.85) at 12 Rue Voltaire is open Monday to Saturday from 9 am to noon and 2 to 6 pm. In July and August, hours may be 9 am to 7 pm. From Easter to September, it's also open on Sunday from 10 am to 12.30 pm.

Post There is a post office on Quai Jeanne d'Arc.

Chinon's postcode is 37500.

Château de Chinon

Perched atop a rocky spur high above the Vienne River, this huge, mostly ruined medieval fortress (☎ 47.93.13.45) consists of three parts separated by waterless moats: 12th-century **Fort Saint Georges**, which protected the chateau's vulnerable eastern flank but of which very little remains; the **Château du Milieu** (the Middle Castle) and, at the western tip, the **Château du Coudray**. From the ramparts, there are great views in all directions. The chateau is illuminated at night during the tourist season.

After crossing the moat (once spanned by a drawbridge) and entering the Château du Milieu, you pass under the **Tour de l'Horloge** (Clock Tower). The four rooms inside are dedicated to the career of Joan of Arc, who picked out Charles VII from among a crowd of courtiers in 1429 in the castle's **Salle du Trône** (Throne Room or Main Hall), of which little more than the giant fireplace remains.

Other parts of the almost undecorated **Grand Logis Royal** (Royal Apartments or Royal Lodging), built during the 12th, 14th and 15th centuries, are in slightly better condition and house a number of exhibits. In the Château du Coudray, there are several cylindrical and polygonal donjons from the 12th and 13th centuries.

The chateau, which belongs to the département of Indre-et-Loire, is open daily from 9 am to noon and 2 to 5 pm (6 pm from mid-March to April); from May to September, hours are 9 am to 6 pm (7 pm in July and August). The ticket window closes half an hour before closing time. Entry costs 23FF (19FF for people over 60, 17FF for children and students). Free guided visits in English are held seven times a day all year long.

To get to the chateau from town, walk up the hill to Rue du Puits des Bancs and turn left. By car, Route de Tours (a continuation of the D751 from Tours) takes you to the back of the chateau, where parking is available.

Swimming

The **piscine municipale** (municipal swimming pool; 47.93.08.45) is across the river from the centre of town next to Camping de l'Île Auger. **Plage de la Belle Laveuse** is a beach on the north bank of the Vienne about one km upriver (ie south-eastward) from the railroad bridge.

Festivals

On the first weekend in August, locals and performers dress up in period costume for the Marché Médiéval, where all sorts of crafts and local products are on sale. And two weeks later, on the third weekend of August, all manner of local food products are available at the **Marché à l'Ancienne** (Old Market).

Places to Stay – bottom end

Camping The riverside *Camping de l'Île Auger* (☎ 47.93.08.35), open from 1 April (or Easter, whichever comes first) to October, is across the Vienne from the centre of town. The site is partly shaded. It costs about 9.20FF per tent site, 9.20FF to park and 10.50FF per adult.

Hostels The friendly, year-round *Auberge de Jeunesse* (☎ 47.93.10.48; fax 47.98. 44.98) on Rue Descartes also functions as a Foyer des Jeunes Travailleurs (a young working people's hostel) and a Maison des Jeunes (an organisation that sponsors activities for local young people). A bed in the basic, institutional dormitories costs 42FF. You can reserve a place and leave your bags all day long, but check-in is from 6 to 10.30 pm. If you'll be returning after the 10.30 pm curfew, ask for a key. Guests can use the laundry facilites, the large kitchen and the TV room. You don't need a hostelling card to stay here.

Hotels The *Hôtel Le Panurge* (☎ 47.93. 09.84) at Place Général de Gaulle has quite ordinary singles and doubles from 135FF (with washbasin) and 160FF (with shower). A triple or quad with shower is 190FF. Hall showers are 20FF.

Places to Stay – middle
The comfortable *Hôtel de France* (☎ 47.93. 33.91) at 47-49 Place Général de Gaulle has pleasant singles and doubles for 230 to 320FF. Some rooms can take an extra bed (60FF). Enclosed parking is 35FF a night. From October to March, reception closes at noon on Sunday. The hotel is closed during December and January.

Across the street from the train station, the *Hôtel de la Gare* (☎ 47.93.00.86) at 14 Ave Gambetta, also known as the Gar' Hôtel, has large but plain doubles/quads with shower and toilet for 230/320FF. Reception may be closed on Sunday from 2 to 4 pm. The hotel closes during the last half of December.

Places to Eat
Restaurants For pizzas (29 to 48FF), salads (27 to 43FF) and savoury crepes (galettes; 23 to 29FF), a good choice is *Crêperie-Pizzeria Jeanne de France* (☎ 47.93.20.12) at 12

Place Général de Gaulle, which is open daily from noon to 2.30 pm and 7 to 11 pm. It is closed in January.

On Rue Haute Saint Maurice, *La Grappa Restaurant et Pizzeria* (☎ 47.93.19.29) at No 50 has a *menu* for 68FF. It is open daily, except Monday, from noon to 2 pm and 7 to 10 pm (later in summer).

Self-Catering The *Monoprix* at 22 Place Général de Gaulle is open Monday to Saturday from 9 am to 12.30 pm and 2.15 to 7.15 pm. In summertime, it does not close at midday. The food section is at the back.

Getting There & Away
Train The train station, which is one km east of the medieval quarter, is served by both *autorails* (railcars) and SNCF buses; the latter, marked 'car' or 'autocar' on schedules, cannot take bicycles. From Tours (41FF; one hour; four to six a day, two on Sunday and holidays), Chinon is on the same rail line as Azay-le-Rideau. The last train/bus from Chinon to Tours is at 5.40 pm (7.40 pm on Sunday and holidays).

Car Europcar (☎ 47.93.03.67) has an office on Rue Gambetta opposite the train station.

Getting Around
Bicycle Ten-speeds can be rented at the Auberge de Jeunesse (see Hostel under Places to Stay) on Rue Descartes for 30/50FF a half/whole day. Mountain bikes are also available.

Atlantic Coast

France's Atlantic coast stretches from the English Channel all the way to the Spanish frontier. Its major cities and sights include Nantes, which is near the mouth of the Loire River; La Rochelle, once an important Huguenot stronghold; the nearby Île de Ré; Bordeaux, capital of the Bordeaux wine-growing region; and the coastal resort of Arcachon, known for its huge dune.

The northern part of the Atlantic seaboard is covered in the Brittany chapter; details on the far south are in the French Basque Country chapter.

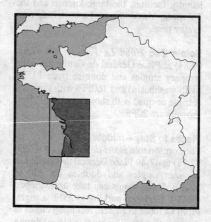

History

The south-western quarter of France, named Aquitania by the Romans, was later known as Aquitaine and Guyenne (or Guienne). The Duchy of Aquitaine was united with France in 1137, when Eleanor of Aquitaine married Louis VII. But after Louis VII divorced Eleanor, she married Henry Plantagenet, soon to be crowned Henry II, King of England. The entire territory became an English crown possession upon Eleanor's death, precipitating centuries of warfare between France and England. The last English presence in the area ended in 1453.

NANTES

Nantes (population 245,000), the country's seventh-largest city, is the most important commercial and industrial centre in west-central France. It is also a particularly well-managed city, something visitors will notice in the new tram system, the efficient tourist office, the fine museums and the carefully tended parks and gardens. Highlights include the chateau and the Jardin des Plantes.

Nantes, which is on the north bank of the Loire River 56 km from the Atlantic, was historically part of Brittany but is today in the Pays de la Loire administrative region. The Edict of Nantes, a landmark royal charter guaranteeing civil rights and freedom of conscience and worship to France's Protestants, was signed here by Henri IV in 1598. During the Reign of Terror, the guillotine was deemed too slow by the local representative of the Committee of Public Safety. Instead, suspected counter-Revolutionaries were stripped, tied together in pairs and loaded onto barges that were then sunk in mid-river.

Orientation

The city centre's two main arteries are north-south Cours des 50 Otages – named in memory of 50 people taken hostage and shot by the Germans in 1941 – and an east-west boulevard that connects Cours John Kennedy (to the east) to Quai de la Fosse (to the west). They intersect at the Gare Centrale bus/metro hub at Place du Commerce, at whose western edge is the tourist office. Two short blocks north of Place du Commerce, Place Royale is linked to Cours des 50 Otages by Rue d'Orléans. The old city is between the chateau and Cours des 50 Otages.

The small streets that run along the sides of many major thoroughfares are known as

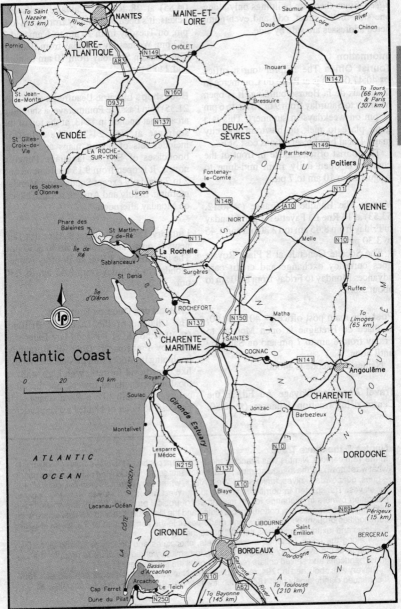

ATLANTIC COAST

Atlantic Coast

0   20   40 km

allées. Since there are buildings only along one side of the street, odd and even-numbered addresses are side by side.

Information
Tourist Office The helpful tourist office (☎ 40.47.04.51) is at Place du Commerce in the Palais de la Bourse building. It is open Monday to Saturday from 9 or 10 am to 6 pm (7 pm on weekdays in summer). This is a good place to pick up bus/tram and city maps. Local hotel reservations cost 5FF.

The tourist office annexe in front of the chateau is open daily from mid-June to August from 10 am to 7 pm.

Money The Banque de France (☎ 40.12.53.53) at 14 Rue La Fayette is open Monday to Friday from 8.45 am to 12.30 pm and 1.45 to 3.30 pm.

The Société Générale at 8 Place Royale does currency exchange and credit card advances Monday to Friday from 8.30 am to about 5 pm.

Post The main post office (☎ 40.12.60.00) at Place de Bretagne is open Monday to Friday from 8 am to 7 pm and on Saturday until noon.

Nantes's postcode is 44000.

Travel Agencies Voyage Au Fil, in the Centre d'Information Jeunesse (☎ 40.89.04.85) at 28 Rue du Calvaire, sells BIJ tickets. It's open on Monday from noon to 6 pm, on Tuesday from 10 am to 1 pm and 2 to 7 pm, Wednesday to Friday from 10 am to 7 pm and on Saturday from 10 am to noon and 2 to 5 pm.

Bookshops Librairie Beaufreton (☎ 40.48.21.35) is in Passage Pommeraye, a shopping arcade that opened in 1843, at the top of the staircase at Nos 24-30. The selection includes lots of hiking maps and several bookcases of English-language Penguin novels. It is open from 9.15 am to noon and 2 to 7 pm daily except Sunday and Monday morning. In July and August, it's also closed on Monday afternoon.

Laundry The laundrette at 8 Allée des Tanneurs is open daily from 7 am to 8.30 pm. The laundrette at 3 Rue du Bouffay is open Monday to Saturday from 8.45 am to 7.30 pm.

Château des Ducs de Bretagne
The Château of the Dukes of Brittany (☎ 40.41.56.56) at 1 Place Marc Elder was built by François II, Duke of Burgundy, beginning in 1466. From the outside, it looks like a medieval fortress, with high walls, a moat and crenellated towers, but the inner courtyard is built like a Renaissance-style palace. The Edict of Nantes was considered

---

Nantes & the Slave Trave
In the 18th century, Nantes was France's most important centre of the slave trading industry. In what was known as 'the triangular trade', local merchants sent ships carrying manufactured goods – guns, gunpowder, knives, trinkets – to West Africa, where they were bartered to local warlords for slaves. Transported in horrific conditions to the West Indies, the slaves were then sold to plantation owners in exchange for an assortment of tropical products. Finally, the ships, laden with sugar, tobacco, coffee, cotton, cocoa, indigo and the like, sailed back to Nantes, where such commodities brought huge profits – and made possible the construction of the splendid public buildings and luxurious mansions that still grace the city.

All along the Loire, factories making sweets, chocolates and preserves sprang up to take advantage of the availability of sugar. Nearby, ironsmiths worked overtime to produce the leg-irons, handcuffs and spiked collars required to outfit the slave ships.

Slavery was abolished in 1794, re-established by Napoleon in 1794 and suppressed after 1827. It continued clandestinely until 1848, when it was finally abolished in France's colonies. ■

(though not actually signed) here by Henry IV in 1598.

The **Musée d'Art Populaire Régional**, reached via a semicircular staircase, displays Breton costumes, *coiffes* (women's headdresses), ceramics, furniture and ironwork, including a scale once used to weigh cannon produced at the Indret armaments works. Across the courtyard, the **Musée des Salorges** has exhibits on the maritime, colonial and commercial history of Nantes and the Nantes area, including lots of neat ship models and a 1:500-scale model of the city in 1905. Part of one wall is dedicated to the city's role in the 18th-century slave trade between Africa and the West Indies.

The museums are open daily, except Tuesday and holidays (daily in July and August), from 10 am to noon and 2 to 6 pm. The courtyard and ramparts are open the same hours daily except holidays; in July and August, they are open daily from 10 am to 7 pm.

Entry to the courtyard is free; walking around the ramparts involves a nominal fee. The museums cost 20FF (10FF for students and people over 65) but are free for everyone on Sunday. A ticket good for four municipal museums is available for 30FF. A free English-language brochure on the chateau is available at the entrance.

Guided tours (20FF; 15FF for students and people over 60), held once a day from mid-June to mid-September, are available in English.

Cathédrale Saint Pierre et Saint Paul

The Gothic cathedral at Place Saint Pierre was built over a period of more than four centuries. The west front and the towers are from the latter half of the 15th century; the three naves are from the 16th century; and the transept and choir were begun in the mid-17th century, though the latter wasn't finished until the late 1800s.

The **tomb** of François II (ruled 1458-88), Duke of Brittany, and his second wife, Marguerite de Foix, is considered a masterpiece of Renaissance art. The statue facing the nave, which represents **Prudence**, has a

female body and face on one side and a bearded male face on the other! Entry to the 11th-century **crypt** is free. The cathedral is open from 8.45 am to nightfall or 7 pm, whichever comes first.

Musée des Beaux-Arts

The renowned Fine Arts Museum (☎ 40.41. 65.65) at 10 Rue Georges Clemenceau displays mainly paintings, including three famous works by Georges de La Tour. The monumental building, constructed in the 1890s, provides superb spaces for viewing the canvasses, especially the larger ones. It is open from 10 am to noon and 1 to 5.45 pm on Monday and from Wednesday to Saturday; Sunday hours are 11 am to 5 pm. Entry costs 20FF (10FF for students and people over 65).

Île Feydeau

The channels of the Loire that once surrounded Feydeau Island, the area south of the Gare Centrale, were filled in after WW II, but the area's 18th-century mansions, built by rich merchants from profits made in the slave trade, are still standing. Some of them are adorned with the stone carvings of African slaves.

Jardin des Plantes

Nantes's Jardin des Plantes, right across Blvd de Stalingrad from the train station's northern entrance, is one of the most exquisite botanical gardens in France, with ponds, fountains, beautifully tended flower beds, putting-green lawns and even a few California redwoods (sequoias). There are hothouses and a children's playground at the northern end.

Muséum d'Histoire Naturelle

The old-fashioned but excellent Natural History Museum (☎ 40.41.67.67) at 12 Rue Voltaire, founded in 1799, has displays of fossils, minerals, hundreds of kinds of wood and stuffed mammal, bird and fish specimens. There's also a **vivarium** with live pythons, crocodiles and even a green iguana. It is open from 10 am to noon and 2 to 6 pm

ATLANTIC COAST

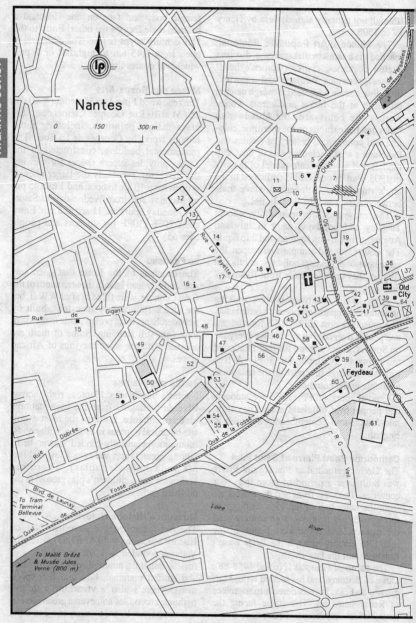

Nantes

0   150   300 m

1

2

5

6

11

10

9

8

12

13

14

19

18

16 i

17

38

37

Old
City

42

43

39

64

41

40

44

45

48

46

58

47

56

57 i

59

Île
Feydeau

49

52

53

60

51

50

54

55

61

Rue La Fayette

Gigant

Rue   de

Rue

Dobrée

Blvd de Launay

To Tram
Terminal
Bellevue

Qual   de

Quai de la Fossé

Fossé

Otages

des   50

Cours   des

R G   Veil

Loire

River

To Maillé Brézé
& Musée Jules
Verne (800 m)

Q de Versailles

ATLANTIC COAST

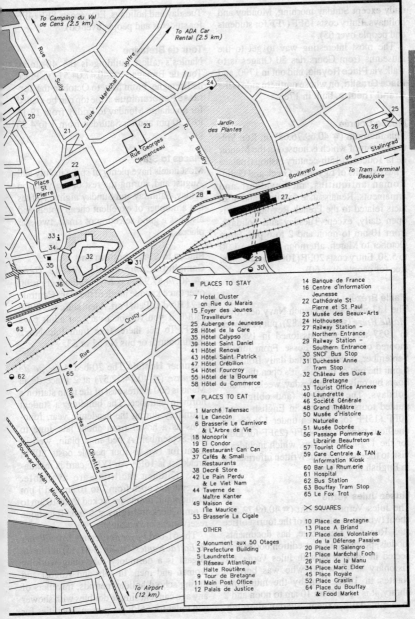

To Camping du Val
de Cens (2.5 km)

To ADA Car
Rental (2.5 km)

Rue Maréchal Joffre

Rue Sully

Jardin
des Plantes

Rue Georges
Clemenceau

R. S. Baudry

Boulevard de Stalingrad

To Tram Terminal
Beaujoire

Place
St
Pierre

Rue Crucy

Rue des Olivettes

Boulevard Jean Monnet

To Airport
(12 km)

PLACES TO STAY

7 Hotel Cluster
   on Rue du Marais
15 Foyer des Jeunes
   Travailleurs
25 Auberge de Jeunesse
28 Hôtel de la Gare
35 Hôtel Calypso
39 Hôtel Saint Daniel
41 Hôtel Renova
43 Hôtel Saint Patrick
47 Hôtel Crébillon
54 Hôtel Fourcroy
55 Hôtel de la Bourse
58 Hôtel du Commerce

PLACES TO EAT

1 Marché Talensac
4 Le Cancún
6 Brasserie Le Carnivore
   & L'Arbre de Vie
18 Monoprix
19 El Condor
36 Restaurant Can Can
37 Cafés & Small
   Restaurants
38 Decré Store
42 Le Pain Perdu
   & Le Viet Nam
44 Taverne de
   Maître Kanter
49 Maison de
   l'Île Maurice
53 Brasserie La Cigale

OTHER

2 Monument aux 50 Otages
3 Prefecture Building
5 Laundrette
8 Réseau Atlantique
   Halte Routière
9 Tour de Bretagne
11 Main Post Office
12 Palais de Justice

14 Banque de France
16 Centre d'information
   Jeunesse
22 Cathédrale St
   Pierre et St Paul
23 Musée des Beaux-Arts
24 Hothouses
27 Railway Station –
   Northern Entrance
29 Railway Station –
   Southern Entrance
30 SNCF Bus Stop
31 Duchesse Anne
   Tram Stop
32 Château des Ducs
   de Bretagne
33 Tourist Office Annexe
40 Laundrette
46 Société Générale
48 Grand Théâtre
50 Musée d'Histoire
   Naturelle
51 Musée Dobrée
56 Passage Pommeraye &
   Librairie Beaufreton
57 Tourist Office
59 Gare Centrale & TAN
   Information Kiosk
60 Bar La Rhumerie
61 Hospital
62 Bus Station
63 Bouffay Tram Stop
65 Le Fox Trot

✕ SQUARES

10 Place de Bretagne
13 Place A Briand
17 Place des Volontaires
   de la Défense Passive
20 Place R Salengro
21 Place Maréchal Foch
26 Place de la Manu
34 Place Marc Elder
45 Place Royale
52 Place Graslin
64 Place du Bouffay
   & Food Market

daily except Sunday morning, Monday and holidays. Entry costs 15FF (7FF for students and people over 65).

The most interesting way to get to the museums from Cours des 50 Otages is to walk via **Place Royale**, laid out in 1790, and **Place Graslin**, on whose northern side is the **Grand Théâtre**, built in 1788.

Musée Dobrée

This museum (☎ 40.69.76.08) on Rue Voltaire – part of which is housed in the Manoir de la Touche, a 15th-century bishops' palace – has exhibits of Egyptian, Greek and Gallo-Roman antiquities, medieval art and armaments, Renaissance furniture and artefacts related to the French Revolution. It is open daily, except Tuesday and holidays, from 10 am to noon and 2 to 6 pm. From October to March, afternoon hours are 1.30 to 5.30. Entry costs 20FF (10FF for students, free for people over 60).

Maillé Brézé

The 133-metre-long French Navy destroyer *Maillé Brézé* (☎ 40.69.56.82), put in service in 1957 and decommissioned in 1988, is moored on Quai de la Fosse. From June to September, it can be visited daily from 2 to 6 pm; the rest of the year, it's open the same hours but only on Wednesday, weekends and holidays. The excellent (and obligatory) guided tours – available in English – cost 30FF (15FF for children under 12) for the one-hour version and 45FF (25FF for kids) for the 1½-hour version, which includes a visit to the engine room. Written information in English is available.

Musée Jules Verne

The Jules Verne Museum (☎ 40.69.72.52), about two km south-west of the tourist office at 3 Rue de l'Hermitage, has documents, models, posters and first-edition books connected in some way with Jules Verne, the visionary sci-fi writer who was born in Nantes in 1828. Run by the municipal library, it is open from 10 am to noon and 2 to 5 pm daily except Sunday morning,

Tuesday and holidays. Entry costs 8FF (4FF for students and people over 60).

Tour de Bretagne

Nantes's tallest building is the 40-storey Tour de Bretagne (☎ 40.47.04.51) at Place de Bretagne. From May to October, the **Terrasse Panoramique** at the top can be visited for no charge Monday to Friday from 12.15 to 1.30 pm and on Saturday from 1 to 4.30 pm.

Places to Stay

Most hotels have plenty of space in July and August and, during the rest of the year, on Friday, Saturday and Sunday nights. Nantes has a number of excellent cheap hotels and also has a good selection of small, two-star places.

Places to Stay – bottom end

Camping *Camping du Val de Cens* (☎ 40.74.47.94), open year round, is a bit over three km due north of the Gare Centrale at 21 Blvd du Petit Port. A tent site costs 20FF (30FF if you've got a car); an adult pays 15FF. To get there, take tram line No 2 (northbound) or bus No 51 or 53.

Summer Hostels The 70-bed *Auberge de Jeunesse* (☎ 40.14.32.57) at 2 Place de la Manu is 600 metres east of the train station's northern entrance. The building, a student dormitory during the academic year, functions as a hostel from about late June to mid-September. A bed in a plain, well-lit room for two to four people costs 50FF; breakfast is 16FF. An IYHF card is mandatory. Kitchen facilities are available. Reception is open from 7 to 10 am and 1 pm to midnight; rooms are locked from 10 am to 5 pm. Check-in begins at 5 pm. Telephone reservations are possible.

The 61-bed *Foyer des Jeunes Travailleurs 'L'Édit de Nantes'* (☎ 40.73.41.46) at Rue de Gigant is a dormitory for young working women and men. In July and August and during school holiday periods, travellers of any age can rent simple doubles with shower and toilet for 56FF per person. Facilities for the handicapped are available. Reception is open weekdays from 9 am to 6 pm; if you'll be arriving on the weekend, call ahead so they can leave a key with the guard. To get there, take bus No 24 from the Gare Centrale and get off at the Édit de Nantes stop.

Hotels – Old City The *Hôtel Renova* (☎ 40.47.57.03; fax 51.82.06.39) at 11 Rue Beauregard, run by the same family since 1966, has doubles for 100FF (with washbasin and bidet), 120FF (with shower) and 130FF (with shower and toilet). There are no hall showers. In July and August, reception is closed on Sunday from 2 to 6 pm.

Near the chateau, the *Hôtel Calypso* (☎ 40.47.54.47) at 16 Rue de Strasbourg (1st floor) has quiet, pleasant singles/doubles for 98/108FF (with washbasin), 125/140FF (with shower) and 148/163FF (with shower, toilet and TV). The pricier rooms are quite spacious, though the prefab showers are tiny. Hall showers cost 12FF.

The *Hôtel Saint Daniel* (☎ 40.47.41.25) at 4 Rue du Bouffay has big, ordinary doubles for 110FF (with washbasin), 120FF (with shower) and 145FF (with shower and toilet). Hall showers are 15FF. A TV is 20FF extra. Reception is closed on Sunday from noon to 9 pm.

Hotels – West of Cours des 50 Otages The family-run *Hôtel de la Bourse* (☎ 40.69.51.55) at 19 Quai de la Fosse (next to the Médiathèque tram stop) is one of the best deals in town. It has tidy doubles for 90FF (with washbasin and bidet), 105FF (with shower) and 135FF (with shower and toilet). Hall showers are 16FF. Reception is closed on Sunday from 2 to 7 pm.

Around the corner, the *Hôtel Fourcroy* (☎ 40.44.68.00) at 11 Rue Fourcroy is another excellent bet. Run by the same family since 1978, it has pleasant and exceptionally well-kept doubles for 132FF (with shower) and 148FF (with shower and toilet). Hall showers are free.

The *Hôtel Saint Patrick* (☎ 40.48.48.80) at 7 Rue Saint Nicolas (3rd floor; no lift) was founded many years ago by an Irish couple,

who gave the place its name. Old and slightly musty doubles cost 100FF (with washbasin) and 130FF (with shower). Hall showers are 12FF. On Sunday, reception is closed from 11 am to 6 pm.

Places to Stay – middle
Train Station Area There are a number of hotels in the charmless area right across from the train station's northern entrance, including the 28-room *Hôtel de la Gare* (☎ 40.74.37.25; fax 40.93.33.71) at 5 Allée du Commandant Charcot. Small doubles with shower and toilet start at 185FF.

West of Cours des 50 Otages The venerable *Hôtel de France* (☎ 40.73.57.91; fax 40.69.75.75), a three-star place at 24 Rue Crébillon, occupies a converted 18th-century mansion. Sound-proofed singles/doubles with high ceilings start at 325/349FF. The rooms that cost 430/460FF are huge.

The 16-room *Hôtel du Commerce* (☎ 40.47.02.13) at 1 Place du Commerce (across the square from the tourist office) has big, sparsely furnished singles/doubles with shower, toilet and TV for 225/235FF.

East of Cours des 50 Otages There's a cluster of hotels on Rue du Marais, which is on tram line No 2. They include the one-star *Hôtel d'Orleans* (☎ 40.47.69.32) at No 12 and the one-star *Armoric Hôtel* (☎ 40.47.49.08) at No 10.

Places to Eat
Nantes has an exceptionally varied selection of ethnic restaurants. Quite a few eateries have lunch *menus* that offer excellent value.

In the old city, there is a cluster of cafés and small restaurants in the lively area around Rue de la Juiverie and Rue des Petites Écuries.

French *Le Pain Perdu* (☎ 40.47.74.21) at 12 Rue Beauregard has tasty, family-style French cuisine and specialities from the Landes region, including foie gras, confit de canard and magret de canard. All the ingredients are fresh. The *menus* are 69 and

89FF. It is open Tuesday to Sunday from noon to 2 pm and 7 to 11 pm.

Grand, old *Brasserie La Cigale* (☎ 40.69.76.41) at 4 Place Graslin is still graced by original 1890s tilework walls and painted ceilings, both of which mix baroque with Art Nouveau. Breakfast is served daily from 8 to 11 am, lunch from 11.45 am to 2.30 pm and dinner from 6.45 pm to 12.30 am. The *menus* cost 69 and 125FF.

Brasserie Le Carnivore (☎ 40.87.47.00) at 7 Allée des Tanneurs has diverse offerings including a variety of meat dishes, smoked salmon and paella. The *menus* cost 50FF (weekday lunches only) and 85FF. It is open daily from noon to midnight, with a slightly reduced selection from 3 to 6 pm.

Popular *Taverne de Maître Kanter* (☎ 40.48.55.28), a brasserie at 1 Place Royale, serves Alsatian-style sauerkraut, oysters and other seafood. *Menus* cost 56FF. Meals are served daily nonstop from noon to 2 am.

Across from the entrance to the chateau, reasonably priced *Restaurant Can Can* (☎ 40.47.02.50) a 7 Rue des États has a 39FF *menu* and a variety of main dishes for around 50FF. Mixed salads are 42 to 48FF. It is open from 11.30 am to 1.30 pm and 7.30 to 10 pm daily except Saturday at midday, Sunday and holidays.

Vegetarian *L'Arbre de Vie* (☎ 40.08.06.10) at 8 Allée des Tanneurs offers a vegetarian and macrobiotic alternative to Le Carnivore next door. Lunch *menus* cost 55 and 65FF; at night the only *menu* costs 125FF. Except in August and on holidays, it is open Tuesday to Saturday from noon to 1.45 pm and 7.30 to 10 pm.

Other *Maison de l'Île Maurice* (☎ 40.73.94.71) at 4 Rue Kléber specialises in the spicy curries of the Indian Ocean island of Mauritius. The *menus* cost 50FF (lunch only), 72 and 96FF. It is open Monday to Saturday from noon to 1.30 pm and 7.30 to 10.30 pm.

El Condor (☎ 40.12.09.67) at 4 Rue Armand Brossard, Nantes's only Chilean restaurant, has *menus* for 47FF (lunch only), 68 and 85FF. It is open from noon to 2.30 and 7.30 to 11 pm daily except Wednesday and Sunday. A few blocks to the north, *Le Cancün* (☎ 40.35.61.16) at 8 Allée de l'Erdre serves Mexican dishes daily, except Sunday, from 7.30 to 11 pm. The two-course *menus* cost 62 to 89FF.

Le Viet Nam (☎ 40.20.06.26) at 14 Rue Beauregard has a tasty Vietnamese lunch *menu* for only 38FF (weekdays only). Other *menus* are 60 and 85FF. It is open from noon to 2 pm and 7 to 10.30 pm daily except Sunday and at midday on holidays.

Self-Catering The *food market* at Place du Bouffay is open from 7 am to 12.30 or 1 pm daily except Monday. *Marché Talensac*, a covered market on Rue Talensac, is open daily from 8 am to 12.30 pm.

The *Monoprix* at 2 Rue du Calvaire is open Monday to Saturday from 9 am to 8 pm. The food section is at the back of the ground floor on the side facing Rue Pré. In the old city area, the huge *Decré store*, across the street from 5 Rue du Moulin, has a food section that is open Monday to Saturday from 9 am to 7 or 7.30 pm.

Entertainment
Tickets for many events are available at the tourist office.

Bar *Bar La Rhumerie* (☎ 40.35.48.75), a trendy, up-market place at 17 Rue Kervégan, is open Monday to Saturday from 5 pm (7 pm on Saturday) to 2 am (4 am on Friday and Saturday nights). A beer on tap is 20FF.

Discothèques The DJs at *Le Fox Trot* (☎ 40.89.17.29) at 32 Rue Crucy play a mix of tango, waltz, zouk, passo, '50s rock and top-50 hits. The dancing area has cushioned seats around the periphery and lots of tiny coloured lights on the walls. It is open daily, except Sunday and Monday nights, from 10 pm to 5 am. The cover charge, which includes one drink, is 70FF (80FF on Friday and Saturday). Casual clothing is fine but you need to look decent.

Things to Buy

There are a number of department stores around Place des Volontaires de la Défense Passive and Rue du Calvaire. More shops can be found east of Cours des 50 Otages along Rue de la Marne.

Getting There & Away

Air Aéroport Nantes-Atlantique (☎ 40.84. 80.00) is about 12 km south-east of the centre of town.

Train The train station (☎ 40.08.50.50 for information) has two entrances: the Accès Nord at 27 Blvd de Stalingrad and the new Accès Sud across the tracks on Rue de Lourmel. The information offices at both are open from 9 am to 7 pm daily except Sunday and holidays.

Destinations served include Bordeaux (207FF; four hours; four a day), La Rochelle (118FF; 1¾ hours; four a day) and Quimper (160FF). The trip to/from Paris (216FF) takes two hours by TGV. In summer, there are non-TGVs to Paris (3½ hours).

Bus The bus station (☎ 40.47.62.70), across from 13 Allée de la Maison Rouge, is used by buses serving the parts of the Loire-Atlantique département that are south of the Loire, including the seaside towns of Pornic (50FF; 1¼ hours) and Saint Brévin-les-Pins.

The Réseau Atlantique *halte routière* (bus stop; ☎ 40.20.46.99) at 5 Allée Duquesne handles buses to places in the département of Loire-Atlantique that are north of the Loire. There is talk of moving it to another location.

SNCF's buses to Pornic, Saint Gilles Croix de Vie and Poitiers stop across the street from the train station's southern entrance. For details, ask in the station.

Car Thrifty, Budget and Hertz have offices right outside the train station's southern entrance.

ADA (☎ 40.49.33.49) is at 170 Blvd Jules Verne, about three km north-east of the city centre and about half a km south-west of the Haluchère stop on tram line No 1. It is open

Monday to Saturday from 8 am to noon and 2 to 7 pm.

Getting Around

Transport in and around Nantes is extremely well organised and efficient.

To/From the Airport Nantes's airport bus, Tan-Air, links the airport with the Gare Centrale and the train station's northern entrance. The ride takes 20 minutes. On weekdays, there are 14 buses a day from 6 am to 8 pm; the last bus heading towards the city leaves the airport around 11 pm. Service is considerably reduced on weekends. The special one-way ticket (32FF) is valid on the whole TAN system for one hour after time-stamping.

Bus & Tram Nantes's urban mass transit system is run by TAN (☎ 40.29.39.39). The city's new tram system, which replaces an earlier tram network phased out in 1958, has two lines which intersect at the Gare Centrale at Place du Commerce, the city centre's main bus and tram transfer point. Line No 1, whose termini are Jeaujoire and Bellevue, runs more or less east-to-west as it passes through the city centre, linking the train station with points west. Line No 2 runs north-to-south along Cours des 50 Otages.

Most bus lines run until 8 or 9 pm. From 9.15 pm to 12.15 am, TAN has 10 circular lines known as the Service de Nuit; all pass by the Gare Centrale.

Bus/tram tickets, sold singly (7FF) by bus (but not tram) drivers and in carnets of five/10 (25/45FF), are valid for one hour after time-stamping for travel in any direction. A *ticket journalier*, valid all day long, costs 16FF; time-stamp it only the first time you board a bus. A *billet hébdomadaire*, valid from Monday to Sunday, costs 50FF. Most of these tickets can be purchased from the ticket machines at tram stops and from many tabacs.

TAN's Informations Vente (information and ticket sales) kiosk at the Gare Centrale is open Monday to Friday from 7.15 am to 7 pm. The ticket window is also open on

Sunday from 10 am to 12.15 pm and 1.15 to 5.45 pm.

Taxi At the train station, taxis are easiest to catch outside the southern entrance. To order a taxi day or night, call 40.69.22.22 or 40.69.25.25.

LA ROCHELLE

La Rochelle (population 78,000) is a laid-back but lively city midway down France's Atlantic seaboard. There are lots of tourists here, especially in July and August, but most of them are of the domestic, middle-class variety: unpretentious families or young people out to have fun. A major university is being built here and promises to attract even more young people.

Although the city centre is beachless, the nearby Ile de Ré is encircled by tens of km of fine sand beaches.

History

La Rochelle, former capital of the province of Aunis, was one France's foremost seaports from the 14th to 17th centuries, and local shipowners were among the first to establish trade links with the New World. Many of the early French settlers in Canada – including the founders of Montreal – set sail from here in the 1600s.

During the 16th century, La Rochelle, whose spirit of mercantile independence made it fertile ground for Protestant ideas, incurred the wrath of Catholic loyalists, especially during the Wars of Religion. After the notorious St Bartholomew's Day massacre of 1572, many of the Huguenots who survived took refuge here.

In 1627, La Rochelle – by that time an established Huguenot stronghold – was besieged by Louis XIII's forces under the personal command of Cardinal Richelieu. By the time they surrendered after 15 months of resistance, all but 5000 of the city's 28,000 residents had died of starvation. The city recovered, albeit slowly, but was dealt further blows by the revocation of the Edict of Nantes in 1685 and the loss of French

Canada – and the right to trade with North America – to the English in 1763.

During WW II, the German submarine base here was repeatedly attacked by Allied aircraft, whose bombs devastated the town. The 'La Rochelle pocket' did not surrender to the Allies until 8 May 1945.

Orientation

La Rochelle is centred around the Vieux Port (old port), to the north of which lies the old city. The tourist office is on the south side of the Vieux Port in an area known as Le Gabut. The train station is linked to the Vieux Port by 500-metre-long Ave du Général de Gaulle.

Place du Marché is one km north of the train station and 250 metres north of the old city. Place de Verdun, 250 metres west of Place du Marché, is linked to Tour du Grosse Horloge by Rue du Palais and Rue Chaudrier.

The seaside neighbourhood of Les Minimes is three km south-west of the city centre. The city's commercial port is 5.5 km west of town at La Pallice, which is not far from the bridge to the Île de Ré.

Information

Tourist Office The tourist office (☎ 46.41. 14.68) in Le Gabut is open Monday to Saturday from 9 am to 12.30 pm and 2 to 6 pm. From June to September, hours are Monday to Saturday from 9 am to 7 pm (8 pm during July and August) and Sunday from 11 am to 5 pm. Local hotel reservations cost 10FF (25FF elsewhere in France).

Money The Banque de France (☎ 46.51. 48.00) at 22 Rue Réaumur is open Monday to Friday from 8.30 am to noon and 1.30 to 3.30 pm.

In the old city, the Crédit Lyonnais (☎ 46.27.67.05) at 19 Rue du Palais is open on weekdays from 8.20 am to 12.10 pm and 1.35 to 5 pm. The ATM is open daily from 6.30 am to 9.30 pm. There are a number of other banks in the immediate vicinity.

From June to September, the tourist office will change money daily, except Thursday,

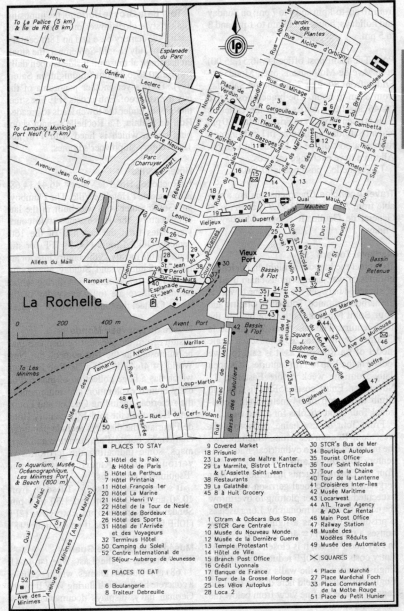

La Rochelle

■ PLACES TO STAY	9 Covered Market	30 STCR's Bus de Mer
3 Hôtel de la Paix	18 Prisunic	34 Boutique Autoplus
& Hôtel de Paris	23 La Taverne de Maître Kanter	35 Tourist Office
5 Hôtel Le Perthus	29 La Marmite, Bistrot L'Entracte	36 Tour Saint Nicolas
7 Hôtel Printania	& L'Assiette Saint Jean	37 Tour de la Chaine
11 Hôtel François 1er	38 Restaurants	40 Tour de la Lanterne
20 Hôtel La Marine	39 La Galathée	41 Croisières Inter-îles
21 Hôtel Henri IV	45 8 à Huit Grocery	42 Musée Maritime
22 Hôtel de la Tour de Nesle		43 Locarwest
24 Hôtel de Bordeaux	OTHER	44 ATL Travel Agency
26 Hôtel des Sports	1 Citram & Océcars Bus Stop	& ADA Car Rental
31 Hôtel de l'Arrivée	2 STCR Gare Centrale	46 Main Post Office
et des Voyageurs	10 Musée du Nouveau Monde	47 Railway Station
32 Terminus Hôtel	12 Musée de la Dernière Guerre	48 Musée des
50 Camping du Soleil	13 Temple Protestant	Modèles Réduits
52 Centre International de	14 Hôtel de Ville	49 Musée des Automates
Séjour-Auberge de Jeunesse	15 Branch Post Office	
	16 Crédit Lyonnais	✗ SQUARES
▼ PLACES TO EAT	17 Banque de France	
	19 Tour de la Grosse Horloge	4 Place du Marché
6 Boulangerie	25 Les Vélos Autoplus	27 Place Maréchal Foch
8 Traiteur Debreuille	28 Loca 2	33 Place Commandant
		de la Motte Rouge
		51 Place du Petit Hunier

from 10 am to 1 pm and 4 to 7 pm; on Sunday and holidays, hours are 11 am to 1 pm and 3 to 5 pm.

Post The main post office (☎ 46.51.25.00) at 52 Ave de Mulhouse is open Monday to Friday from 8 am to 7 pm and on Saturday from 8 am to noon. The branch post office (☎ 46.30.41.35) across from the Hôtel de Ville is open Monday to Friday until 6.30 pm and on Saturday until noon. In Les Minimes, there is a post office at 15 Rue du Lazaret. All three have exchange services.

La Rochelle's postcode is 17000.

Travel Agencies Cheap charters are available from ATL (☎ 46.41.71.77) at 1 Ave du Général de Gaulle. It is open Monday to Friday.

Medieval Towers

To protect the harbour at night and defend it in times of war, an enormous chain used to be stretched between the two stone towers at the harbour entrance, **Tour de la Chaîne** and **Tour Saint Nicolas**; both were built in the 14th century. The basement of Tour de la Chaîne (☎ 46.50.52.36) houses a scale model of La Rochelle as it is said to have looked in the 13th to 17th centuries. It is open daily from the week before Easter to 11 November. Entry costs 15FF. Visitors can climb to the top of the 34-metre-high, pentagonal Tour Saint Nicolas for a fine view.

From Tour de la Chaîne, you can walk west along Rue-sur-les-Murs, which follows the medieval walls, to cylindrical, mid-15th-century **Tour de la Lanterne**, also known as Tour des Quatre Sergents in memory of four sergeants from the local garrison who were executed in 1822 for plotting to overthrow the newly reinstated monarchy. Long used as a prison and later as a lighthouse, it now houses a **museum** (☎ 46.41.56.04). Except in July and August, it is closed on Tuesday. Entry costs 18FF (10FF reduced price). The English graffiti on the walls was carved by English privateers held here during the 18th century. There's a fine view from below the octagonal spire.

Tour de la Grosse Horloge, the imposing Gothic-style clock tower on Quai Duperré, has a 14th-century base and an 18th-century top. From July to mid-September, the small archaeological museum inside is open daily from 2.30 to 6.30 pm (midnight on Saturday). There's yet another panorama of the city from the roof. Entry costs 5FF. The street that passes under the tower leads to arcaded **Rue du Palais**, La Rochelle's main shopping street, which is lined with 17th and 18th-century shipowner's homes.

Hôtel de Ville

La Rochelle's Hôtel de Ville (☎ 46.41.14.68) is at Place de l'Hôtel de Ville. The Flamboyant Gothic outer wall was built in the late 15th century; the Renaissance-style courtyard dates from the last half of the 16th century. Guided tours (14FF; 7FF for students) of the mostly 19th-century interior are held on Saturday and Sunday afternoons. From June to September and during school holidays, there are tours every day of the week. Contact the tourist office for details.

Musée du Nouveau Monde

Visitors from the Western hemisphere may be interested in the Museum of the New World (☎ 46.41.46.50) at 10 Rue Fleuriau, which has a large collection of material on early French exploration and settlement of the Americas, including Quebec and Louisiana. Housed in the mid-18th-century Hôtel de Fleuriau, the displays include paintings, engravings, objets d'art, furniture and early maps, some indicating the territories of various Native American tribes and 'Esquimaux' (Eskimos).

It's open daily, except Tuesday, from 10.30 am to 12.30 pm and 1.30 to 6 pm; Sunday hours are 3 to 6 pm. Entry costs 12FF (10FF for students, free if you're under 18).

Musée de la Dernière Guerre

The Museum of the Last War (☎ 46.41. 14.68) at 8 Rue des Dames, which occupies a concrete bunker built during WW II by the German navy, displays documents, newspapers, propaganda posters, etc illustrating everyday life during the German occupation. The walls retain their original German paintings (the bunker was used for parties). In July and August, it is open from 10 am to 6 pm Tuesday to Saturday. Entry costs 22FF (17FF for students and children).

Temple Protestant

The sober, even austere Protestant church at 2 Rue Saint Michel is remarkable for its contrast to most of France's Catholic churches. An earlier building on this site served La Rochelle's Protestant community from 1563 until the siege of 1628. The current building, which dates from the late 17th century, became a Protestant church after the Revolution. The interior took on its present form during the last 75 years of the 19th century.

Tour de la Lanterne, La Rochelle

Musée Maritime

At the Musée Maritime (☎ 46.50.58.88) at Bassin des Chalutiers, you can visit a tugboat, a fishing boat and the frigate *France I*, outfitted for meteorological research. Tickets, which cost 36FF for adults and 18FF for children, are sold daily from 10 am to 6.30 pm.

Les Minimes

The modern neighbourhood of Les Minimes, three km south-west of the city centre, has the largest pleasure craft port on Europe's Atlantic seaboard as well as a small beach. See Getting Around for details on getting there.

About midway between the Vieux Port and Les Minimes is the **Musée des Automates** (☎ 46.41.68.08) on Rue La Désirée, which displays some 300 automated dolls from centuries past. Almost next door is the **Musée des Modèles Réduits** (☎ 46.41. 64.51), where you can see miniature cars, trains, ships and a variety of model buildings. Both are open daily (except during January) from 10 am to noon and 2 to 6.30 pm; from June to August, hours are 9.30 am to 6.30 pm. Entry to each museum costs 30FF; a 50FF *billet jumelé*, good for both, is also available.

The innovative **Aquarium** (☎ 46.44. 00.00) on Ave du Lazeret, inaugurated in 1988, has shark tanks as well as aquariums for smaller fish. It is open every day of the year; the entry fee is 37FF (no discounts). Next to the beach, the less-than-thrilling **Musée Océanographique** (☎ 46.45.17.87) has lots of stuffed marine mammals as well as skeletons of the same creatures. It is open daily, except Sunday morning and Monday. Entry costs 15FF.

Beaches

La Rochelle's only beach is a short strip of often-crowded sand in Les Minimes. See Getting Around for bus and ferry information.

Festivals

The **Francofolies**, a five-day festival held

each year in mid-July, brings together musicians and other artists from La Francophonie (the French-speaking world), including Quebec. The official festival is accompanied by a *festival 'off'* (fringe festival). Both events attract lots of young people.

La Rochelle's 10-day **Festival International du Film** runs from the end of June to early July.

Places to Stay

La Rochelle has a shortage of cheap hotels. Most hotels charge high-season rates from sometime in the spring until September or October, so warm-season bargains are pretty hard to find. During July and August, virtually all the hotels are full by noon.

Places to Stay – bottom end

Camping During the warm season, dozens of camping grounds open up around La Rochelle and on Île de Ré. Many of them are so full in July and August that even hikers with pup tents are turned away.

The camping ground nearest the city centre is *Camping du Soleil* (☎ 46.44.42.53), also known as Camping Municipal Les Minimes, which is on Ave des Minimes (Ave de Marillac on some maps) about a km southwest of the centre of town. It is open from May to September and is often completely full. Two persons with a tent are charged 40FF. To get there, take bus No 10.

Camping Municipal Port Neuf (☎ 46.43.81.20) on Blvd Aristide Rondeau is in the Port Neuf area, three km west of the city centre along Ave Jean Guiton. It's open year round. Prices are similar to those at Camping du Soleil. To get there, take bus No 6 from the train station or Quai Vavin.

Hostel The *Centre International de Séjour-Auberge de Jeunesse* (☎ 46.44.43.11) is two km south-west of the train station on Ave des Minimes in Les Minimes. A bed costs 62FF; a double room is 154FF. Curfew is midnight (1 am in summer). To get there, take bus No 10 and get off at the Lycée Hotelier stop (next to the bowling alley). This line runs until about 7.15 pm.

Hotels – City Centre The *Hôtel Henri IV* (☎ 46.41.25.79) is in the middle of the old city at Place de la Caille; the official address is 31 Rue des Gentilshommes. Doubles start at 120FF. You can get a room for two with shower, toilet and TV for 170FF.

The *Hôtel de Bordeaux* (☎ 46.41.31.22, 46.41.24.43) is at 43-45 Rue Saint Nicolas, which runs parallel to Quai Valin. Doubles cost 125FF (140FF from May or June to September). During the summer, breakfast (25FF) is pretty much obligatory. It is closed during December and January.

Hotels – Place du Marché Area The 18-room *Hôtel de la Paix* (☎ 46.41.33.44; fax 46.50.51.28), in an 18th-century building at 14 Rue Gargoulleau, has a few doubles with washbasin for 130FF. Doubles with shower and toilet are 170FF (200FF from Easter to September). Huge, old-fashioned rooms with fireplace are 280/300FF (300/340FF during the warm season) for four/five people. Hall showers are free.

The *Hôtel Le Perthus* (☎ 46.41.10.16), next to the covered market at 17 Rue Gambetta, has singles and doubles from 95FF. Doubles with shower and toilet are 135FF; quads with shower cost 180FF. Hall showers are free. During July and August, *demi-pension* (half-board) is obligatory. If you'll be arriving on Sunday afternoon or evening, when reception is closed, call ahead and they'll leave you a key at the nearby pizza place.

The slightly dilapidated and inefficient *Hôtel Printania* (☎ 46.41.22.86) at 9 Rue du Brave Rondeau has singles and doubles from 120FF. Doubles with shower and toilet are 200FF; triples and quads with shower are 170FF. Hall showers cost 6FF. The miserly croissant-less breakfasts (20FF) are obligatory from June to August. This place may have room when everywhere else is full.

Places to Stay – middle

Because they're farther from the centre of town, the places listed under Place du Marché Area are cheaper for what you get than the hotels around the Vieux Port.

Near the Vieux Port The *Hôtel La Marine* (☎ 46.50.51.63), a family-run, one-star place at 30 Quai Duperré (2nd floor), has nondescript but clean doubles with shower from 160FF. Doubles/triples/quads with with shower and toilet are 190/230/330FF. Reception is closed on Sunday afternoon.

The *Hôtel de l'Arrivée et des Voyageurs* (☎ 46.41.40.68; fax 46.67.38.92) at 5 Rue de la Fabrique, a one-star place with a two-star level of comfort, has doubles/quads with shower, toilet, TV and hair dryer from 211/301FF. Prices are lower in winter. Breakfast (28FF) is obligatory from July to mid-September. In the winter, reception may be closed on Sunday afternoon.

The nearby *Terminus Hôtel* (☎ 46.50. 69.69; fax 46.41.73.12) at 7 Rue de la Fabrique has unsurprising singles/doubles with shower and toilet for 220/250FF; off-season prices are about 15% less.

The 28-room *Hôtel de la Tour de Nesle* (☎ 46.41.05.86; fax 46.41.95.17) at 2 Quai Louis Durand has ordinary doubles with shower, toilet and TV for 230FF (260FF from June to September).

You might also try the one-star *Hôtel des Sports* (☎ 46.41.15.75) at 18 Place Maréchal Foch, whose shower and toilet-equipped rooms cost 160 to 265FF.

Place du Marché Area The pleasant *Hôtel de Paris* (☎ 46.41.03.59; fax 46.41.03.24) at 18 Rue Gargoulleau has clean, tidy doubles/triples/quads with shower, toilet and TV for 180/230/260FF (230/280/320FF from April to September).

The 38-room *Hôtel François 1er* (☎ 46.41.28.46; fax 46.41.35.01) at 15 Rue Bazoges has doubles for 278 to 375FF (less in the winter). A number of French kings stayed in this building in the 15th and 16th centuries.

Places to Eat
Restaurants There are lots of touristy restaurants along Quai Duperré and along Rue de la Chaîne, which is just west of Tour de la Chaîne. The Place du Marché area has a number of inexpensive restaurants and pizzerias.

A local speciality you might want to try is mouclade Rochelaise (mussels in a cream and curry sauce).

La Marmite (☎ 46.41.17.03) at 14 Rue Saint Jean du Pérot, whose beautiful wood panelling and bannisters give it a nautical air, has high-quality seafood, fish and cuisine du marché (food based on what's available in the marketplace). The *menus* cost 170, 280 and 360FF. It is open daily, except Wednesday (daily from July to September), from noon to 2 pm and 7 to 10 pm. Reservations are recommended for dinner, especially on Saturday and holidays, and for Sunday lunch. Another candidate for a splurge is *Bistrot L'Entracte* (☎ 46.50.62.60) at 22 Rue Saint Jean du Pérot. It is closed on Sunday.

Classical French cuisine is available at elegantly rural *La Galathée* (☎ 46.41.17.06) at 45 Rue Saint Jean du Pérot, whose *menus* cost 70, 99 and 135FF. It is open daily except Tuesday evening and Wednesday (open daily in July and August). *L'Assiette Saint Jean* (☎ 46.41.75.75), a small, rustic place at 18 Rue Saint Jean du Pérot, specialises in fish and seafood prepared according to local recipes. The *menu* costs 85FF.

La Taverne de Maître Kanter (☎ 46.41. 42.88), a brasserie at 15 Quai Valin, is open daily from noon to midnight. A meat dish plus either mussels, oysters or fish soup costs 79FF.

Self-Catering In the old city, the *Prisunic* (☎ 46.41.69.11) across from 55 Rue du Palais is open Monday to Saturday from 8.30 am to 7.30 pm (9 pm from mid-June to mid-September). The food section is in the basement; there's a *boulangerie* on the ground floor. Almost across the street, the *boulangerie-pâtisserie* at 41 Rue du Palais is open daily, except Sunday (daily in July and August), from 7.30 am to 8 pm.

Near the train station, the *8 à Huit* grocery at 9 Ave du Général de Gaulle is open daily except Sunday from 8 am to 12.45 pm and 3 to 7.30 pm. It may be open on Sunday morning in July and August.

The large *covered market* at Place du Marché is open daily from 6 am to 1 or 1.30 pm. The *boulangerie* at 29 Rue Gambetta is open daily except Thursday from 6 am to 8.30 pm. *Traiteur Debreuille* at 4 Rue Gambetta, which has all sorts of prepared dishes, is open daily from 8 am to 1.30 pm (2 pm on Sunday) and 3 pm (4 pm on Sunday) to 8.15 pm.

Entertainment

In July and August, there are free organ concerts at the *Protestant church* every Friday at 6 pm.

Getting There & Away

Train The train station (☎ 46.41.50.50 for information) is at the southern end of Ave du Général de Gaulle. The information office is open from 9 am to 6.45 pm daily except Sunday and holidays.

Destinations served by at least a few direct trains include Bordeaux (122FF; two hours), Nantes (113FF; two hours), Marseille (nine hours) and Toulouse (230FF). Getting to most other places, including Bayonne (207FF), Lourdes (four hours), Nice (453FF) and Tours, involves a change of trains. If you're coming from Paris (237FF), you can take either a TGV from Gare Montparnasse (four hours) or a non-TGV train from Gare d'Austerlitz (five hours). Only two non-TGVs are direct – the rest of the time you have to change at Poitiers.

Bus Citram (☎ 46.99.01.36 in Rochefort) and Océcars (☎ 46.41.20.40) buses, which serve destinations in the département of Charente-Maritime, stop in the north-west corner of Place de Verdun.

For information on buses to the Île de Ré see the Getting There & Away section in the Île de Ré listing.

Car ADA, near the train station at 1 Rue du Général de Gaulle (☎ 46.41.02.17), is open Monday to Saturday from 8 am to noon and 2 to 7 pm. Budget, Europcar, Eurorent and Hertz have offices along the same block.

Boat Croisières Inter-Îles (☎ 46.50.51.88) at 14 Cours des Dames, about 200 metres south-west of Tour de la Chaîne, has ferries to destinations including the Île de Ré (38FF one way to Sablanceaux), the Île d'Aix (90/130FF one way/return), Fort Boyard and the Île d'Oléron (100FF one way, 130/140FF return to Saint Denis/Boyardville). The services run from May to September; during April, boats operate only on weekends.

Getting Around

Bus The local bus network is known as STCR Autoplus (☎ 46.34.02.22). The *gare centrale* (central terminal), where all of STCR's lines stop, is at Place de Verdun. The company's main information office, the Boutique Autoplus, is in Le Gabut at 5 Rue de l'Aimable Nanette, which is across the street from the tourist office. Most lines run until sometime between 7.15 and 8 pm.

A single-ride ticket, valid for 45 minutes after it's time-stamped, costs 7FF; a seven-ride ticket is 34.30FF. A bus pass valid for 24 hours after it's time-stamped costs 24FF; a three-day pass is 58FF.

Bus No 10 links Place de Verdun, the Vieux Port (Quai Valin) and Ave de Colmar (one block north of the train station) with Les Minimes.

Taxi Another of STCR's innovative transport ideas is Taxi Autoplus, a 24-hour system whereby you pay the driver a flat rate of 28FF for travel for up to four people between the two city-centre *bornes d'appel* (terminal posts) – round, white posts marked 'Autoplus' – and any of 46 *bornes* around town. The bornes in the city centre are on Cours des Dames (near Tour de la Chaîne) and at Place de Verdun. The catch (for visitors) is that the *carte d'appel*, the card you use to activate the borne's telephone, costs 35FF. It is available at STCR's Place de Verdun kiosk and the Boutique Autoplus.

Conventional taxis can be ordered 24 hours a day by calling ☎ 46.41.55.55 or 46.41.22.22.

Car The city centre, an impossible maze of one-way streets, turns into a giant traffic jam in summer. The area has a severe shortage of parking places.

Bicycle In 1976, in an effort to encourage people to leave their cars at home, the La Rochelle municipality bought 250 yellow one-speed bikes for the free use of both local people and visitors. The scheme, inspired by a similar programme in Amsterdam, has since been modified to prevent theft, but its '90s incarnation, Les Vélos Autoplus, is alive and well across the street from 11 Quai Valin. From May to September, bikes are available daily from 9 am to 12.30 pm and 1.30 to 7 pm. An adult's or child's bike (lock included) is free for the first two hours; after that the charge is 6FF per hour. Keeping the bike overnight or for an extra day costs 60FF. You must leave some sort of ID as a deposit. Child seats are available for no charge.

Near the tourist office, Locarwest (☎ 46.41.10.60) at 14 Quai de la Georgette has one-speeds/mountain bikes/tandems for 40/60/90FF per 24 hours.

Loca 2 (☎ 46.41.84.32) at 48 Rue Saint Jean du Pérot, open year round except during January and February, has high-quality city bikes for 60FF, mountain bikes for 105FF and tandems for 150FF a day. People under 25 get a 25% discount. The shop is open from 8.30 am to 8 pm (10 pm in July and August) daily except Wednesday (daily in July and August).

The Auberge de Jeunesse in Les Minimes rents out bikes during July and August.

Boat STCR's Bus de Mer (Sea Bus) links the Vieux Port (Tour de la Chaîne) with Les Minimes. From April to September, boats from the Vieux Port depart every hour on the hour from 9 am to 7 pm (except at 1 pm). In July and August, frequency is upped to twice an hour and service continues until 11 or 11.30 pm. The rest of the year, the Bus de Mer runs only on Sunday and holidays and during school vacation periods. A single journey costs 10FF.

AROUND LA ROCHELLE

The crescent-shaped **Île d'Aix** (pronounced 'Ai'), a 1.33-sq-km, car-less island 16 km due south of La Rochelle, was fortifed by Vauban and later used as a prison. It has some nice beaches.

Fort Boyard, built during the first half of the 1800s, is a curious, oval-shaped island/ fortress between the Île d'Aix and the nearby **Île d'Oléron**. For information on boat trips to all three islands, see Boat under Getting There & Away for La Rochelle.

ÎLE DE RÉ

The Ile de Ré (year-round population 11,000), whose eastern tip is nine km west of the centre of La Rochelle, is connected to the mainland by a graceful, three-km toll bridge completed in 1988. The island gets more hours of sunlight than anywhere in France except for the Mediterranean coast.

In summer, the island's many beaches and seasonal camp grounds are a favourite destination for families with young children, in part because the water is shallow and safe and the sun is bright and warming but less harsh than along the Mediterranean. Young people also flock here, helping to increase the island's population 20-fold in August. Much of the island can be visited as a day trip from La Rochelle.

Île de Ré's main town is the fishing port of Saint Martin-de-Ré (also known as Saint Martin-en-Ré), which is on the north coast about 12 km from the bridge. The island's interior is covered with low pine forests, fields of wild grasses and areas where grapes, asparagus, potatoes, hay and other crops are cultivated when the tourists aren't around. In most villages, the houses are traditional in design: one or two-storey whitewashed buildings with green shutters and red Spanish-tile roofs

The island boasts 70 km of coastline, including 20 or 30 km of fine sand beaches. Most of the north coast is taken up by mudflats and oyster beds. The island's western half curves around a bay known as the Fier d'Ars, which is lined with *marais salants* (salt evaporation pools), saltwater marshes and a nature reserve for birds, **Lilleau des Niges**. Sea walls have been built along some exposed parts of the coast to protect villages from violent storms.

Orientation

The Île de Ré is about 30 km long and from 100 metres to five km wide. The D735 runs from Sablanceaux, at the western end of the bridge from the mainland, along the northern coast to Saint Martin-de-Ré; on to La Couarde-sur-Mer on the south coast; and finally past the salt pools to Phare des Baleines, the lighthouse at the island's far western tip.

Information

Tourist Office In summer, almost every village has its own syndicat d'initiative. Saint Martin has the island's largest tourist office (☎ 46.09.20.06), which is on Ave Victor Bouthillier across the street from the Rébus office. From November to Easter, it's open Monday to Saturday from 10 am to noon and 3 to 6 pm. From June to mid-September, it's open daily from 10 am to 7 pm (noon on Sunday). The rest of the year, hours are variable. This is a good place to pick up maps of the island and its villages. The staff have details on places to stay and can phone around to find you a room.

Money In Saint Martin de Ré, the Crédit Agricole along the south side of the port is open Tuesday to Saturday from 9 am to 12.15 pm and 1.30 to 5 pm (4 pm on Saturday). The nearby Crédit Industriel de l'Ouest is open Monday to Friday from 8.20 am to 12.25 pm and 1.35 to 4.45 pm.

Post Saint Martin de Ré's postcode is 17410.

Saint Martin de Ré

The picturesque fishing village of Saint Martin de Ré (population 2500), entirely surrounded by Vauban's 17th-century fortifications, is especially attractive when the bright coastal sun reflects off the white houses and sailboats. In summer, it is full of tourists walking around eating ice cream and pizza. You can walk along most of the ramparts, but the **Citadelle** (1681), which has been a prison for over two centuries, is closed to the public.

The fortified Gothic **Église**, three blocks south of the port, was damaged in 1692 in artillery attacks launched by an Anglo-Dutch fleet, but it still functions with an incongruous wood-and-tile roof. There's a great view from the **bell & clock tower**.

The **Musée Naval et Ernest Cognacq** (☎ 46.09.21.22), located in a 15th to 17th-century building across the street from the Rébus office, has an eclectic collection of furniture, ceramics, coins, etc. It is open from Wednesday to Sunday.

Phare des Baleines

At the western tip of the island is 57-metre Phare des Baleines (Lighthouse of the Whales), built of stone in 1854 and still operating. You can climb up the 257 steps to the top daily from 10 am to noon and 2 to 6 pm (a bit later in summer). Behind it is an old lighthouse, built in 1679, a shady garden and tidal pools. The pines and cypresses of the **Forêt du Lizay** stretch along the coast northwest of here.

Activities

Beaches The best beaches on the Île de Ré are along the southern edge of the main part of the island (ie east and west of La Couarde) and around the island's western tip (ie northeast and south-east of Phare des Baleine). Near Sablanceaux, there are sandy beaches along the south coast towards Sainte Marie. Many of the beaches are bound by dunes that have been fenced off to protect the vegetation.

The **Plage de la Conche des Baleines** is on the north-west coast between Phare des Baleines and the town of Les Portes. Scenes from *The Longest Day*, a film about the D-Day landings, were shot here. There's an unofficial **naturist beach** near the outskirts of Les Portes; access is via the Forêt du Lizay.

Other Activities Tourist offices have details

on horse riding, water sports, bike rental, etc. La Maison des Marais (☎ 46.29.45.11) at 18 Rue de l'École in Saint Clément-des-Baleines sponsors nature walks from late June to early September.

Places to Stay

There are no cheap hotels on the Île de Ré. Every hotel room and camping site on the island is totally full from 14 July to 25 August. During the summer, many hotels are booked up two or more months in advance.

Camping All but a handful of the island's many dozens of camping grounds are seasonal, but *Les Chardons Bleus* (☎ 46.30. 23.75) on Route de La Flotte in Sainte Marie-La Noue is open year round.

Pitching your tent anywhere but in a camping ground is forbidden.

Hotels In Saint Martin de Ré, the one-star *Hôtel de Sully* (☎ 46.09.26.94) on Rue Jean Jaurès is open from April to September, around the Christmas and February school holidays and on all weekends. Singles/ doubles with shower are 140/170FF; doubles with shower and toilet start at 210FF.

The two-star, 30-room *Hôtel des Colonnes* (☎ 46.09.21.58), on the south side of the port at 19 Quai Job-Foran, is open year round except from mid-December to the end of January. One-bed doubles start at 330FF.

The two-star *Hôtel du Port* (☎ 46.09. 21.21; fax 46.09.06.85) at Quai de la Poitevinière, open year round, has doubles with shower, toilet and TV from 290FF (320FF from July to September).

Places to Eat

In Saint Martin de Ré, the port is lined with tourist restaurants.

It's a lot cheaper to buy picnic food in La Rochelle than on the island. In Saint Martin de Ré, the *marché* on the south side of the port at Rue Jean Jaurès is open daily except Monday (daily in summer) from 6.30 am to 1 pm. There is a cluster of *food shops* nearby.

Getting There & Getting Around

The bridge from the mainland begins about six km west of the centre of La Rochelle.

Bus To get from La Rochelle to Sablanceaux (25 minutes), the narrow neck of land at the island's eastern tip, you can pick up STCR bus No 1a from La Rochelle's train station, Quai Valin or Place de Verdun. There's a 2FF surcharge, payable to the driver, for riding across the bridge (see Getting Around in the La Rochelle listing for details on tickets). The same route is also covered by the Rébus system (☎ 46.09.20.15 in Saint Martin de Ré), whose La Rochelle stops are at the train station parking lot, the Vieux Port (next to Tour de la Grosse Horloge) and Place de Verdun.

Rébus provides the only public transport from La Rochelle to island destinations other than Sablanceaux; it also covers intra-island routes. From La Rochelle, there are excruciatingly slow buses to destinations including Saint Martin de Ré (23FF; 55 minutes; eight a day) and La Flotte (18.50FF; 45 minutes; eight a day). The Ré 1 line goes along the south coast and to the island's western tip; the Ré 2 line covers the north coast of the main part of the island.

During the school year, the schedule is arranged so that commuters and students can travel to La Rochelle in the morning and get back to the island in the afternoon. Except in the summer, there is very limited service on Sunday and holidays.

Car For automobiles, the bridge toll is a whopping 110FF return (payable on your way *to* the island); a car with a camping trailer costs 220FF. By the way, the locals pay an annual bridge fee of 1000FF.

Bicycle Cycling is an extremely popular way to get around the island, which is flat and has a pretty good network of *pistes cyclables* (bicycle paths). A biking map with a few paragraphs of English text, *Guide des Itinéraires Cyclables*, is available at tourist offices. If you'll be bringing a bike from the mainland, your first expense will be crossing the bridge: cyclists have to pay a 10FF toll!

At Sablanceaux, bicycles can be rented from Cycland (☎ 46.09.65.27 in La Flotte), whose kiosk is to the left as you come off the bridge. It is staffed from mid-March or early April to late November and is usually open Monday to Friday from 9.30 am to noon and 2.30 to 6.30 pm. From June to mid-September it's open daily. City/mountain bikes are 45/75FF a day.

In summer, practically every hamlet has somewhere to rent bikes, and Cycland opens five more offices. In Saint Martin de Ré, Île de Ré Vélos (no phone), three short blocks south of the port at Place de l'Église, is open daily from June to September and during the Christmas, February and Easter school holidays.

Hitching To hitch to the island, the best place to stand is just past the bridge's toll plaza.

Boat In the warm season, Croisières Inter-Îles (☎ 46.09.87.27) has ferries from Sablanceaux and Saint Martin de Ré to the Île d'Aix (130FF return) and the Île d'Oléron.

BORDEAUX

Bordeaux (population 211,000) is known for its neoclassical architecture, wide avenues and well-tended public squares and parks, all of which give the city a certain 18th-century grandeur. The general state of the buildings may give the impression that Bordeaux has seen better (or at least more prosperous) times, but its excellent museums, ethnic diversity, lively university community (the city has some 60,000 students) and untouristed atmosphere make it much more than just a convenient stop on the way from Paris to Spain.

Bordeaux, which is about 100 km from the Atlantic at the lowest bridging point on the Garonne River, was founded by the Romans in the 3rd century BC. From 1154 to 1453, it prospered under the rule of the English, whose fondness for the region's red wines – known across the Channel as claret – gave

impetus to the local wine industry. Even today, the city's single most important economic activity is the marketing and export of Bordeaux wines.

Bordeaux has briefly served as the capital of France three times: during the Franco-Prussian war of 1870-71; at the beginning of WW I (1914); and for the two weeks in 1940 before the Vichy government was proclaimed.

Orientation

The city centre lies between Place Gambetta and the 350 to 500-metre-wide Garonne River, which is usually a muddy brown. From Place Gambetta, Place de Tourny is 500 metres to the north-east and the tourist office is 500 metres to the east. The bus station is two blocks north-west of Place de Tourny.

The train station, known as Gare Saint Jean, is about three km south-east of the city centre. Cours de la Marne stretches from the train station to Place de la Victoire, which is linked to Place de la Comédie by the 1.1-km Rue Sainte Catherine pedestrian mall.

Information

Tourist Office The tourist office (☎ 56.44. 28.41) at 12 Cours du 30 Juillet is open daily from 9 am to 7 pm (8 pm from June to September). The free city map suggests an itinerary for a walking tour. Hotel reservations in the Bordeaux area cost 5FF; the charge is 22FF for reservations elsewhere in the country.

The tourist office annexe at the train station is open daily from 9 am (10 am on Sunday from October to May) to 7 pm. The tourist office at the airport is open daily from 8 am (10 am on Sunday) to 7 pm.

Information on the Gironde département is available from the Maison du Tourisme de la Gironde (☎ 56.52.61.40) at 21 Cours de l'Intendance. It is open Monday to Saturday from 9 am to 7 pm.

For information on visiting the Bordeaux vineyards and chateaux, see the Bordeaux Wine-growing Region listing.

Money The Banque de France (☎ 56.00. 14.95), around the corner from the tourist office at 15 Rue Esprit des Lois, is open weekdays from 9 am to noon and 1 to 3.30 pm.

Most commercial banks are open Monday to Friday, though a few are also open on Saturday morning. There are lots of commercial banks near the tourist office on Cours de l'Intendance, Rue Esprit des Lois and Cours du Chapeau Rouge.

American Express (☎ 56.52.40.52) at 14 Cours de l'Intendance is open Monday to Friday from 8.45 am to noon and 1.30 to 6 pm. Cash advances are available.

The Thomas Cook bureau (☎ 56.91. 58.80) at the train station is open seven days a week from 8 am to 8 pm. During July and August, it usually stays open until 9.30 pm.

Post The main post office (☎ 56.96.62.30), which is west of the city centre at 36 Rue du Château d'Eau, is open Monday to Friday from 8 am to 7 pm and on Saturday from 8 am to noon.

Central Bordeaux's postal code is 33000. The postcode of the area around the train station is 33800.

Foreign Consulates Bordeaux has some 40 consulates, including:

UK
    353 Blvd du Président Wilson (two km northwest of the tourist office; ☎ 56.42.34.13); open Monday to Friday from 9 am to 1 pm and 2.30 to 5.30 pm.
USA
    22 Cours du Maréchal Foch (☎ 56.52.65.95); the American Services section is open weekdays from 9 am to noon and, by appointment, from 2 to 4 pm.

Travel Agencies Near Place de Tourny, there is a cluster of travel agencies along Allées de Tourny, including Nouvelles Frontières (☎ 56.44.60.38) at No 31. It is open Monday to Saturday from 9 am to 7 pm (6 pm on Saturday).

Across from the train station, Wasteels (☎ 56.91.97.17) at Place Casablanca sells BIJ tickets. It is open Monday to Saturday from 9 am to noon and 2 to 6.45 pm.

Bookshops Bradley's Bookshop (☎ 56.52. 10.57) at 32 Place Gambetta has a wide selection of English-language books, including lots of fiction and some Lonely Planet guides. It is open on Monday from 2 to 7 pm and Tuesday to Saturday from 9.30 am to 12.30 pm and 2 to 7 pm. Lonely Planet guides are also available across the square at the Virgin Megastore.

Maps Most maps of Bordeaux have west at the top – the locals have apparently gotten used to seeing the Garonne at the bottom of the map.

Laundry Near Place de Tourny, the laundrette at 5 Rue de Fondaudège is open daily from 7 am to 8 pm. South of Place Gambetta, the Lavomatique at 27 Rue de la Boëtie is open daily from 7 am to 9 pm; as of this writing, there's no change machine and no soap dispenser.

Medical Services Hôpital Saint André (☎ 56.79.56.79) at 1 Rue Jean Burguet is 400 metres south of Cathédrale Saint André.

Dangers & Annoyances Some locals are convinced that certain neighbourhoods – those inhabited by lots of immigrants, to be precise – are a risky proposition after nightfall. This perception probably has more to do with prejudice than reality, but late at night it's probably best for women not to walk around alone in the seedy area near the train station and around Place de la Victoire and Église Saint Michel.

Museums
Bordeaux has some truly superb museums. The Musée d'Art Contemporain and the Musée d'Aquitaine are open daily except Monday; most of the rest are open daily except Tuesday. On Wednesday, most museums are free.

The outstanding **Musée d'Aquitaine** (☎ 56.10.17.10), located at 20 Cours

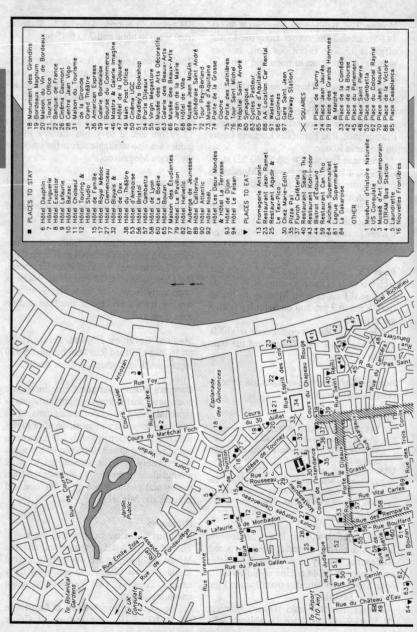

■ PLACES TO STAY

6 Hôtel Dauphin
7 Hôtel Huguerie
8 Hôtel Excelsior
9 Hôtel Lafaurie
10 Hôtel Balzac
11 Hôtel Choiseul
12 Hôtel Touring &
     Hôtel Studio
15 Hôtel de Famille
17 Hôtel Royal Médoc
27 Hôtel Clemenceau
32 Hôtel Blayais &
     Hôtel Dijeaux
38 Hôtel du Théâtre
53 Hôtel d'Amboise
56 Hôtel Bristol
57 Hôtel Gambetta
58 Hôtel de Lyon
60 Hôtel La Boëtie
65 Hôtel Boulan
77 Maison des Etudiants
79 Hôtel Le Pavillon
87 Auberge de Jeunesse
89 Hôtel California
90 Hôtel Atlantic
92 Hôtel Noël,
     Hôtel Les Deux Mondes
     & Hôtel La Terrasse
93 Hôtel de Dijon
94 Hôtel Le Faisan

▼ PLACES TO EAT

13 Fromagerie Antonin
23 Restaurant Jean Ramet
25 Restaurant Agadir &
     Le Tex-Pico
30 Chez Marie-Edith
35 Pizza Paï
37 Flunch Cafétéria
40 Restaurant Seang Tha
43 Restaurant Sobhi-noor
     & Restaurant Cabou
59 Restaurant Can Tho
64 Auchan Supermarket
81 Lagrue Supermarket
84 La Dakaroise

OTHER

1 Muséum d'histoire Naturelle
2 US Consulate
3 Musée d'Art Contemporain
4 CITRAM Bus Station
5 Laundrette
16 Nouvelles Frontières

18 Monument des Girondins
19 Maison du Vin de Bordeaux
20 Bordeaux Magnum
21 Tourist Office
22 Banque de France
26 Cinéma Gaumont
28 Centre Jean Vigo
31 Maison du Tourisme
     de la Gironde
34 Grand Théâtre
36 American Express
39 Galerie Bordelaise
41 Bourse du Commerce
42 Galerie de l'Imagine
47 Hôtel de la Douane
49 Main Post Office
50 Cinéma UGC
51 Bradley's Bookshop
54 Porte Dijeaux
55 Virgin Megastore
61 Musée des Arts Décoratifs
63 Galerie des Beaux-Arts
66 Musée des Beaux-Arts
68 Jardin de la Mairie
69 Hôtel de Ville
69 Musée Jean Moulin
71 Cathédrale Saint André
72 Tour Pey-Berland
73 Musée d'Aquitaine
74 Porte de la Grosse
     Cloche
75 Porte des Salinières
76 Tour Saint Michel
78 Hôpital Saint André
82 Synagogue
83 Cycles Pasteur
85 Porte d'Aquitaine
88 AA Location Car Rental
91 Wasteels
96 Eurolines
97 Gare Saint Jean
     (Railway Station)

✕ SQUARES

14 Place de Tourny
24 Place Jean Jaurès
29 Place des Grands Hommes
     & Marché
33 Place de la Comédie
42 Place de la Bourse
45 Place du Parlement
48 Place Saint Pierre
52 Place Gambetta
62 Place du Colonel Raynal
86 Place de la Victoire
95 Place Casablanca

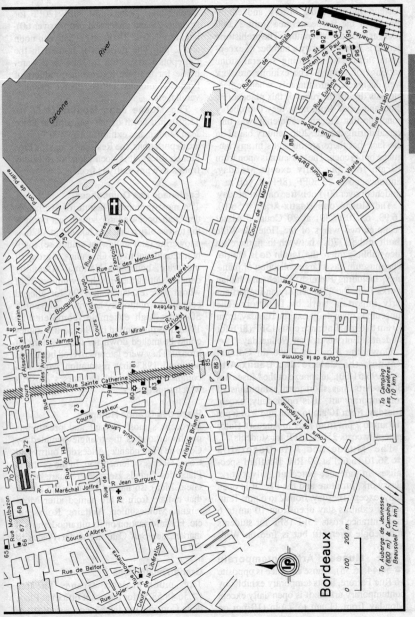

Pasteur, illustrates the history and ethnography of the Bordeaux area from 25,000 years ago to the 19th century. The prehistoric period is represented by a number of exceptional artefacts, including several stone carvings of women. The exhibits are very well designed. Unfortunately, when archaeologists dig up the ruins of this place a few thousand years from now, they'll probably conclude that French proficiency was universal during the late 20th century based on the fact that there are no signs in any language but French. The museum is open from 10 am to 6 pm daily except Monday. Entrance costs 13.50FF (8FF if you're a student or over 60) but is free on Wednesday.

The **Musée des Beaux-Arts** (☎ 56.10. 16.93, 65.10.17.49) at 20 Cours d'Albret occupies two wings of the Hôtel de Ville (built in the 1770s); between them there's a nice public garden, the **Jardin de la Mairie**. The museum has a large collection of paintings, including Flemish, Dutch and Italian works from the 17th century and a particularly important work by Delacroix. The museum is open daily, except Tuesday, from 10 am to 6 pm. Entrance costs 15FF (8FF for students). Entry is free on Wednesday.

Down the block at Place du Colonel Raynal, the **Galerie des Beaux-Arts** (☎ 56.96.51.60), an annexe of the Musée des Beaux-Arts, has short-term exhibitions of contemporary art. It is open daily, except Tuesday, from 10 am to noon and 2 to 6 pm (10 am to 7 pm from May to August). Entry generally costs 25FF (15FF for students).

The **Musée des Arts Décoratifs** (☎ 56.10.15.62) at 39 Rue Bouffard specialises in faïence, porcelain, silverwork, glasswork, furniture and the like. It is open daily, except Tuesday, from 2 to 6 pm. Temporary exhibits stay open from 10 am to 6 pm. Entrance costs 15FF (8FF for students and people over 60) but is free on Wednesday.

The **Musée d'Art Contemporain** (☎ 56.44.16.35), whose entrance is opposite 16 Rue Ferrère, hosts temporary exhibits by contemporary artists. It is open daily except Monday from 11 am to 7 pm (10 pm on

Wednesday). Tickets cost 30FF (20FF for students 25 and under and people over 60), but entry is free if you arrive between noon and 2 pm. The museum is housed in the Entrepôts Lainé, built in 1824 as a warehouse for the rare and exotic products of France's colonies: coffee, cocoa, peanuts, vanilla, etc.

The **Musée Jean Moulin** (☎ 56.10. 15.80), just north of the cathedral at Place Jean Moulin, has exhibits on WW II France: the deportations, the Resistance and the Free French forces. It is open Monday to Friday from 2 to 6 pm. Entry is free.

Esplanade des Quinconces

The most prominent feature of Esplanade des Quinconces, a large square just north of the tourist office that was laid out in 1820, is a towering (and somewhat grandiose) fountain-monument to the Girondins, a group of moderate, bourgeois National Assembly deputies during the French Revolution, 22 of whom were executed in 1793 for alleged counter-Revolutionary activities. The entire 50-metre-high ensemble, completed in 1902, was dismantled in 1943 so the statues could be melted down for their 52 tons of bronze. They were later recovered but it was not until 1983 that restoration work was completed. Check out the horses' nostrils which squirt water.

Place des Grands Hommes

Bordeaux's most elegant and prestigious neighbourhood is the triangle bounded by Cours de l'Intendance, Allées de Tourny and Cours Georges Clemenceau. In the centre is Place des Grands Hommes (Square of the Great Men), so named because the streets that radiate from it are named after Montaigne, Montesquieu, Voltaire, Rousseau, etc. For information on its ultramodern food market, see Self-Catering under Places to Eat.

Grand Théâtre Area

The much-praised Grand Théâtre (☎ 56.48.58.54 for the ticket office) at Place de la Comédie is a huge, neoclassical structure surrounded by a Corinthian colonnade decorated with 12 huge figures of the Muses and Graces. It was built in the 1770s and restored in 1992. Tours of the interior (25FF, 20FF for students and people over 60) are held when the performance schedule permits – the nearby tourist office has details.

A bit to the east along the river, **Place de la Bourse**, built between 1731 and 1755, is flanked by the old Hôtel de la Douane (Customs House) and the Bourse du Commerce (Stock Exchange). The nearby riverside area is a fairly lifeless string of parking lots.

Place Gambetta Area

Porte Dijeaux, a former city gate built in 1748, leads from pedestrianised Rue Porte Dijeaux to Place Gambetta and its beautiful garden. Nowadays, it's an island of calm and flowers in the midst of the city centre's hustle and bustle, but during the Reign of Terror that followed the Revolution, a guillotine emplaced here severed the heads of 300 alleged counter-Revolutionaries.

The city's main shopping area is east of Place Gambetta along Rue Porte Dijeaux, boutique-lined **Cours de l'Intendance** and **Rue Saint Catherine**, where you'll find several major department stores. **Galerie Bordelaise**, a 19th-century shopping arcade, is at the intersection of Rue Porte Dijeaux and Rue Sainte Catherine.

Cathédrale Saint André

In 1137, the future King Louis VII married Eleanor of Aquitaine in St André Cathedral, whose entrance faces Place Jean Moulin. The cathedral's 15th-century belfry, **Tour Pey-Berland**, stands behind the choir, whose chapels are nestled among the flying buttresses. The cathedral can be visited Monday to Saturday from 7.30 to 11.30 am and 2 to 6.30 pm and on Sunday from 8 am to 12.30 pm and 2.30 to 5.30 pm.

Porte de la Grosse Cloche

This 15th-century clock tower, once the city hall belfry, spans Rue Saint James. Like so many other medieval structures in France, it was restored in the 19th century.

Synagogue

Bordeaux's impressive Synagogue (☎ 56. 91.79.39), inaugurated in 1882, is between Nos 6 and 18 on Rue du Grand Rabbin Joseph Cohen. Its architecture is a mixture of Sephardi and Byzantine styles. During WW II, the interior was ripped apart by the Nazis, who turned the complex into a prison. After the war, it was painstakingly rebuilt according to the original plans. Visits are possible Monday to Thursday from 3 to 5 pm. Just ring the bell of the side entrance, which is around the corner at 213 Rue Sainte Catherine.

Jardin Public

Laid out in the English style, these 19th-century public gardens include Bordeaux's **Muséum d'Histoire Naturelle** and its **Jardin Botanique** (☎ 56.52.18.77) at 5 Place Bardineau. The latter can be visited on weekdays from 9 am to noon and 2 to 5pm.

Festivals

Each May, Mai Musical brings three weeks of classical music to Bordeaux. The city also has various concerts around 21 June to celebrate the national Fête de la Musique.

Places to Stay

There is a rather seedy neighbourhood of sex shops, x-rated movie theatres, all-night restaurants and legitimate hotels in the immediate vicinity of the train station. Unless you're just passing through town, you'll be much better off – in terms of both price and value – if you hop on a bus to Place Gambetta, Place de la Victoire, the tourist office or Place de Tourny.

Most hotels have plenty of space in the summer and cheap hotels are plentiful.

Places to Stay – bottom end

Camping *Camping Beausoleil* (☎ 56.89. 17.66), open all year, is about 10 km southwest of the city centre at 371 Cours du

Général de Gaulle (the N10) in Gradignan (postcode: 33170). Two people with their own tent pay 50FF. To get there, take bus G from Place de la Victoire towards Gradignan Beausoleil and get off at the last stop.

Camping Les Gravières (☎ 56.87.00.36), also open all year, is 10 km south-east of downtown Bordeaux at Place de Courréjean in Villenave d'Ornon (postcode: 33140). Tariffs are 16FF for a tent site and 17FF per adult. To get there, take bus B from Place de la Victoire towards either Corréjean (get off at the end of the line) or La Hontan (whence it's a 15-minute walk). From the train station, it's quickest – if the timing works out – to take an SNCF train towards Langon or Agen (three to seven a day) and get off at Villenave d'Ornon; the station is a 15-minute walk from the camping ground.

Hostels The *Maison des Etudiantes* (☎ 56. 96.48.30) at 50 Rue Ligier, a dorm for women students during the academic year, accepts female and male student travellers (student ID required) from July to September. If there's space, you can check in at any time of the day or night. A bed costs 47FF, including sheets and use of the showers and kitchen. The rooms are simple and a bit run-down but the general atmosphere is friendly. To get there from the train station, take bus No 7 or 8 to the Bourse du Travail stop and walk 400 metres west on Cours de la Libération.

The charmless *Auberge de Jeunesse* (☎ 56.91.59.51) at 22 Cours Barbey is 650 metres west of the train station. A spot in a utilitarian, eight-bed room is only 39FF (44FF if you don't have an IYHF card). The 1st-floor women's section and the 2nd-floor men's section are reached by separate staircases! Rooms are theoretically closed from 9.30 am to 6 pm, but they'll usually let you sleep in. More of a problem is the draconian curfew at 11 pm. Talk to the manager in advance if you'll be staying out late for a concert, etc. On the brighter side, they accept reservations made by telephone. Reception is open daily from 8 to 9.30 am and 6 to 11 pm.

Hotels – Place Gambetta Area To get to this area from the train station, take bus No 7 or 8 and get off at Place du Colonel Raynal (for the Hôtel Boulan and the Hôtel La Boëtie) or Place Gambetta.

There are a couple of excellent deals in the area between Place Gambetta and the Musée des Beaux Arts. The quiet *Hôtel Boulan* (☎ 56.52.23.62) at 28 Rue Boulan has modest singles/doubles with high ceilings for 90/95FF (100/120FF with shower). The charge for hall showers is 15FF. The *Hôtel La Boëtie* (pronounced 'bo-eh-SEE'; ☎ 56.81.76.68; fax 56.81.24.72) at 4 Rue de La Boëtie has modern singles/doubles with TV, toilet, telephone and shower starting at about 120/135FF. Triples and quads are 180FF.

The *Hôtel d'Amboise* (☎ 56.81.62.67) at 22 Rue de la Vieille Tour is through Porte Dijeaux from Place Gambetta. The rooms are small, dark and have carpeted walls, but the location is excellent and the price is right: 65 to 100FF for a single, 90 to 110FF for a double. Singles/doubles with shower and toilet are 110/120FF. Hall showers cost 10FF for 10 minutes. There is free locked parking for two-wheeled vehicles. This place is closed from mid-December to mid-January.

The friendly *Hôtel de Lyon* (☎ 56.81. 34.38; fax 56.81.24.72) at 31 Rue des Remparts has singles/doubles with shower, toilet and TV for 120/135FF. Try not to get one of the small rooms on the 3rd floor.

Hotels – Place de la Victoire Area To get to this area from the train station, take bus No 7 or 8 and get off at Place de la Victoire.

The family-run *Hôtel Le Pavillon* (☎ 56.91.75.35) at 6 Rue Honoré Tessier, a block from the Musée d'Aquitaine, is one of the best deals in town. Large, slightly dilapidated singles/doubles without shower start at 85/90FF; two-bed doubles are 95FF.

Another good bet is the *Hôtel Helvetic* (☎ 56.91.54.61) at 1 Rue André Dumercq. Huge, plain singles/doubles cost 80/90FF. Two-bed doubles and rooms for three or four persons cost 125FF. Showers are 10FF.

Hotels – Tourist Office Area To get to this part of town from the train station, take bus No 7 or 8 and get off at the Grand Théâtre.

The charmingly old-fashioned *Hôtel Blayais* (☎ 56.48.17.87) at 17 Rue Mautrec has fairly large doubles for 110FF (with washbasin and bidet) and 135FF (with shower). They haven't made a bathroom in that shade of green in decades! Reception may be closed on Sunday afternoon. Showers (up to one a day) are free.

Another nice place with vintage furnishings is the *Hôtel de Dax* (☎ 56.48.28.42), at 7 Rue Mautrec, where large, simple, clean doubles/triples with washbasin and bidet cost 110/130FF. Showers are free.

Hotels – Place de Tourny Area To get to Place de Tourny from the train station, take bus No 7 or No 8 and get off at Place Gambetta (these lines stop at Place de Tourny only when heading *towards* the train station).

The best cheap choice in this part of town is the two-star *Hôtel Touring* (☎ 56.81.56.73) at 16 Rue Huguerie, which has gigantic, spotless singles/doubles for 110/130FF (with washbasin and bidet), 160/180FF (with shower) and 180/200FF (with shower and toilet). Some of the rooms have fireplaces. The 29-room *Hôtel de Famille* (☎ 56.52.11.28; fax 56.51.94.43) at 76 Cours Georges Clemenceau has ordinary but homy singles/doubles with washbasin and bidet from 110/120FF; rooms with shower and toilet are 180/195FF. Hall showers are free.

The *Hôtel Studio* (☎ 56.48.00.14; fax 56.81.25.71) at 26 Rue Huguerie has charmless but eminently serviceable singles from 98 to 135FF, doubles from 120 to 135FF, triples from 160 to 180FF and quads for 180FF – the price depends on the size of the room. All rooms are equipped with a flimsy shower, a toilet and a TV with cable.

The same family-run company, based in the Hôtel Studio, operates three other one-star places with identical prices in the same area: the *Hôtel Huguerie* (☎ 56.81.23.69) at 67 Rue Huguerie; the *Hôtel Excelcior* at 58 Rue Huguerie, whose courtyard is perfect for parking bicycles; and the *Hôtel Lafaurie* (☎ 56.48.16.33) at 35 Rue Lafaurie de Monbadon.

The *Hôtel Choiseul* (☎ 56.52.71.24) at 13 Rue Huguerie has simply furnished singles with washbasin for 90FF and doubles with shower and toilet for 140FF.

Hotels – Train Station Area The popular *Hôtel La Terrasse* (☎ 56.91.42.87) at 20 Rue Saint Vincent de Paul has clean singles and doubles from 95FF. Doubles with shower cost 140FF. Hall showers are 15FF. The *Hôtel Les Deux Mondes* (☎ 56.91.63.09), nearby at 10 Rue Saint Vincent de Paul, is a decent sort of place with lots of foreign guests during the summer. Rates are 105/126FF for singles/doubles with showers and 189FF for two-bed triples. The *Hôtel Noël* (☎ 56.91.62.48) at 8 Rue Saint Vincent de Paul has doubles/triples with shower starting at 98/120FF.

One of the last places to fill up (for good reason) is the musty, run-down *Hôtel de Dijon* (☎ 56.91.76.65), which is right across from the station at 22 Rue Charles Domercq. Singles/doubles start at 85/95FF, while showers cost 10FF. Telephone reservations are not accepted.

Places to Stay – middle
For information on getting from the train station to the hotel clusters in the city centre, see each heading under Places to Stay – bottom end.

Place Gambetta Area The *Hôtel Bristol* (☎ 56.81.85.01; fax 56.51.24.06) at 2 Rue Bouffard has pleasant doubles/triples with four-metre-high ceilings, bathroom, toilet and TV for 240/270FF. The *Hôtel Gambetta* (☎ 56.51.21.83; fax 56.81.00.40) at 66 Rue Porte Dijeaux has small, sound-proofed doubles with shower, toilet, TV and minibar for 270FF.

The 45-room *Hôtel Clemenceau* (☎ 56.52.98.98; fax 56.81.24.91) at 4 Cours Georges Clemenceau has somewhat cramped singles/doubles/triples with shower, toilet and TV for 235/275/305FF.

Place de Tourny/Tourist Office Area Near Esplanade des Quinconces, the three-star 45-room *Hôtel Royal Médoc* (☎ 56.81.72.42; fax 56.51.74.98) at 3 Rue de Sèze has comfortable, sound-proofed singles/doubles/triples for 330/360/390FF.

The *Hôtel du Théâtre* (☎ 56.79.05.26; fax 56.81.15.64) at 10 Rue de la Maison Daurade has utilitarian singles/doubles/quads with shower, toilet and TV from 190/270/300FF. Some rooms are much larger than others. It may be possible to add an extra bed for 30FF.

The old-fashioned, 13-room *Hôtel Balzac* (☎ 56.81.85.12) at 14 Rue Lafaurie de Monbadon has large singles/doubles/triples with shower and toilet for 180/200/220FF. The *Hôtel des Quatre Sœurs* (☎ 56.48.16.00; fax 56.01.04.28) at 6 Cours du 30 Juillet, right next to the tourist office, has unspectacular singles with carpeted walls for 100 to 270FF and doubles for 250 to 370FF. The more expensive rooms are larger and more pleasant than the cheaper ones.

Train Station Area There are lots of two-star places around here, including the 62-room *Hôtel Le Faisan* (☎ 56.91.54.52), which is directly across from the station at 28 Rue Charles Domercq. It has pleasant singles/doubles/triples with shower, toilet and TV for 200/250/300FF. Rooms for people in wheelchairs are available.

The 36-room *Hôtel Atlantic* (☎ 56.92.95.22; fax 56.94.21.42) at 69 Rue Eugène Leroy has singles/doubles with shower, toilet and TV from 230/250FF. Two short blocks west, the 17-room *Hôtel California* (☎ 56.91.58.97; fax 56.91.61.90) at Rue Eugène Leroy has pleasant, well-maintained singles/doubles with bath, toilet and TV from 250/270FF.

Places to Eat

The cafés, ethnic restaurants and sandwich shops across from the train station stay open until late at night (or even 24 hours, as in the case of the place at 45 Rue Charles Domercq).

There are a number of restaurants at 18th-century Place du Parlement. West of Place Gambetta, quite a few inexpensive restaurants, many of them offering North African food, can be found on and around Rue du Palais Gallien.

French *Restaurant Jean Ramet* (☎ 56.44.12.51) at 7-8 Place Jean Jaurès serves traditional French cuisine amidst mirrors, white tablecloths and sparkling tableware. Lunch *menus* cost 150 and 200FF; dinner is à la carte only. This place is open Monday to Friday. It is closed for two weeks in mid-August.

Restaurant Baud et Millet (☎ 56.79.05.77) at 19 Rue Huguerie, next to the Hôtel Choiseul, serves cheese-based cuisine – most (but not all) dishes are vegetarian. An all-you-can-eat meal of raclette and fondue Savoyarde costs 90FF; the *menus* cost 110 to 170FF. In the basement, there's a buffet with 200 kinds of cheeses! The wine list is extensive. Food is served Monday to Saturday from 9 am to midnight.

Chez Marie-Edith (☎ 56.51.75.90) at 27 Cours de l'Intendance serves reasonably priced French cuisine in an elegant, modern dining room. *Menus* cost 49FF (Monday to Saturday lunch only), 59FF and 89FF. Meals are served daily from noon to 2.30 pm and 7 to 11.30 pm. This place serves as a salon de thé from noon to 11.30 pm or midnight.

French bistro-style meat and fish dishes are available at *Bistrot d'Édouard* (☎ 56.81.48.87) at 15 Place du Parlement, whose *menus* cost 59FF (for lunch and dinner until 8.30 pm), 97FF and 125FF. It is open Tuesday to Saturday (daily from May to October) from noon to 2.15 pm and 7 to 11 pm.

African *La Dakaroise* (☎ 56.92.77.32), at 9 Rue Gratiolet, specialises in dishes from Senegal and other parts of West Africa. It is open daily from 7 to 11.30 pm.

Restaurant Agadir (☎ 56.52.28.04) at 14 Rue du Palais Gallien specialises in couscous. It is open daily. There are several Middle Eastern and North African sandwich and pastry shops nearby.

Asian *Restaurant Seang Thaï* (☎ 56.44.29.78) at 33 Rue Saint Remi serves cuisine typical of the Chinese community in Thailand. *Menus* cost 43FF (not available on Saturday night), 54FF and 63FF. It is open Monday to Saturday from 11 am to 2.30 pm and 6 to 11 pm. There are about a half-dozen other Chinese-Vietnamese and Chinese-Cambodian restaurants in the immediate vicinity.

South of Place Gambetta, *Restaurant Can Tho* (☎ 56.81.40.38) at 16 Rue Villeneuve serves Chinese and Vietnamese food. The *menu* costs only 40FF, but be prepared for abrupt service. It is open daily, except Sunday at midday, from noon to 2 pm and 7 to 10.30 pm.

Restaurant Koh-i-noor (☎ 56.51.17.55) at 3 Rue du Puits des Cujols serves North Indian and Pakistani cuisine, including tandoori and biryani dishes, to the accompaniment of Urdu music. *Menus* cost 63FF (lunch only), 99, 119 and 149FF. It is open daily from noon to 2.30 pm and 7.45 to 11.30 pm.

Other *Le Tex Pico* (☎ 56.48.58.11) at 10 Rue du Palais Gallien has tacos (30FF), enchiladas (34FF) and rouleaux Mexicains (Mexican spring rolls; 30FF). This isn't the sort of Mexican food you're likely to find in North America, but it's inexpensive and tasty. This place is open daily from 6.30 pm to 1 am.

Pizza Paï (☎ 56.81.35.80) at 26 Cours de l'Intendance has pizza (38 to 54FF) and a 40-item all-you-can-eat salad bar (39FF). The *menus* cost 60FF (weekday lunch only) and 75FF; both include wine. Food is served daily from 11.30 am to 10 pm.

The *Flunch Cafétéria* (☎ 56.48.28.38) at 4-6 Cours de l'Intendance (1st floor) has a wide selection of cheap, self-service cafeteria food. Main dishes are 19 to 45FF. Meals are served daily from 11 am to 2.30 pm and 6 to 10 pm; drinks and some food are available during the afternoon.

Self-Catering In the basement of the modern, mirror-plated *Marché des Grands Hommes* at Place des Grands Hommes, there are up-market stalls offering fruit, vegetables, cheeses, bread, sandwiches and pastries. The market is open Monday to Saturday from 7 am to 7.30 pm.

There is a huge, cheap *Auchan supermarket* (☎ 56.93.81.60) in the Centre Commercial Mériadeck, whose eastern entrance is opposite 58 Rue du Château d'Eau. Opening hours are Monday to Saturday from 8.30 am to 10 pm. The *Lagrue supermarket* (☎ 56.91.66.70) at 190 Rue Sainte Catherine is open daily except Sunday from 8.30 am to 8 pm.

Near the bus station, *Fromagerie Antonin* (☎ 56.81.61.74) at 6 Rue Fondaudège is open Monday to Saturday from 8 am to 12.30 pm and 3.30 to 7.30 pm. The *boulangerie* across the street at 9 Rue Fondaudège is open daily.

In the neighbourhoods around Église Saint Michel, the aroma of bulk spices emanates from the scattered *food stores* that cater to the North Africans, sub-Saharan Africans, Spanish, Portuguese, Vietnamese and other immigrant groups who live here.

Entertainment

At night, lively areas include the streets west of Place Gambetta, Place du Parlement and the area just north of Place de la Victoire.

Tickets for concerts, sporting events, bullfights, etc in Bordeaux, Paris, Toulouse, Marseille and other cities are available from the *billeterie* (☎ 56.56.05.55) in the Virgin Megastore at 15-19 Place Gambetta.

Cinema Nondubbed films are shown at several local movie houses. The *Centre Jean Vigo* (☎ 56.44.35.17), an art cinema at 6 Rue Franklin that's also known as Cinéma Trianon, has five daily screenings (three on Sunday). Tickets costs 33FF (26FF for students). Everyone pays the reduced price on Wednesday.

The 10-screen *Cinéma Gaumont* (☎ 56.48.13.38 for a recording; 56.52.03.54 for the office), located at 9 Cours Georges Clemenceau, charges 40 to 43FF (30 to 33FF for students from 8 pm Sunday until Friday night).

Cinéma UGC (☎ 56.44.31.17 for a recording; 56.44.34.94 for the office) at 7 Rue Castelnau d'Auros, which is down the alley from 20 Rue Judaïque, usually has at least one v.o. film. Tickets cost 40 to 45FF; 34FF discount tickets for students and people over 60 are available from Monday to Friday.

Gay Disco *Le 18* (☎ 56.52.82.98) at 18 Rue Louis de Foix is a few blocks south-west of Place Gambetta.

Things to Buy

Bordeaux wine in all price ranges is on sale at three speciality shops near the tourist office. Bordeaux Magnum (☎ 56.48.00.06) at 3 Rue Gobineau, open Monday to Saturday from 8 am to 7.30 pm, can supply you with a Château Latour 1949 (4800FF) or a bottle of Armagnac from 1865 (16,200FF) as well as cheaper vintages – some for as little as 18FF. Vinothèque is next to the tourist office at 8 Cours du 30 Juillet, and L'Intendant is across the street at 2 Allées de Tourny.

Mostra (☎ 56.51.01.03) at 4 Rue du Parlement Sainte Catherine sells useful household items whose innovative styling elevates some of them into the realm of art. It is open from 10.30 am to 1 pm and 2 to 7.30 pm daily except Sunday and Monday. Galerie Imagine (☎ 56.51.18.22) at 16 Rue du Parlement Sainte Catherine has some interesting ceramics, sculptures and paintings. It is open Monday to Saturday from 10.30 am to 7.30 pm; during July and August, hours are 2 to 7.30 pm and on Friday and Saturday nights from 10 pm to midnight.

The Virgin Megastore (☎ 56.56.05.56) at 15-19 Place Gambetta, which carries a huge selection of CDs, tapes and books, is open Monday to Friday from 10 am to midnight. There's a very popular café on the 4th floor and another on the roof.

Near the Musée des Beaux-Arts, there are antique shops along Rue Bouffard.

Getting There & Away

Air Aéroport International de Bordeaux (☎ 56.34.50.50) is 10 km west of the city centre.

Train Bordeaux's train station, Gare Saint Jean (☎ 56.92.50.50 for information), is about three km from the city centre at the southern terminus of Cours de la Marne. The information office is open Monday to Saturday from 9 am to 7 pm (6.30 pm on Saturday) and on Sunday and holidays from 10 am to 12.30 pm and 2 to 6.30 pm. The showers (14FF) next to Quai 1 at Gate 41 are open daily from 5 am to 11 pm. The arrival hall is open 24 hours a day but some of the luggage lockers may not be accessible from 11 pm to 5 am. Be extra careful with your bags here.

Bordeaux is one of France's major rail transit points – there are trains from here to almost everywhere. Destinations served include Bayonne (130FF; two hours), Geneva (364FF; change at Lyon), Nice (398FF) and Toulouse (163FF; two hours; 10 a day). For information on getting to Saint Émilion and Arcachon, see Getting There & Away under those listings.

From Paris (290FF), you can take either the TGV Atlantique (three hours) from Gare Montparnasse or one of the few non-TGVs (five hours) which use Paris's Gare d'Austerlitz.

Bus Buses to places all over the Gironde (and parts of nearby départements) leave from the Citram bus station (☎ 56.43.04.04), whose two entrances are at 14 Rue de Fondaudège and opposite 69 Rue Lafaurie de Monbadon. The information office is open Monday to Friday from 9 am to noon and 2 to 6 pm (5 pm on Friday). When it's closed, you can call ☎ 56.44.93.59 (staffed 5.30 am to 9 or 10 pm).

Destinations include Blaye (on the north bank of the Gironde estuary), Cap Ferret (south-west of Bordeaux near the Bassin d'Arachon), Soulac-sur-Mer (on the coast just south of the mouth of the Gironde estuary), Montalivet (on the coast 40 km north-west of Bordeaux) and Libourne (30 km east of Bordeaux). For details on buses to Saint Émilion, see Getting There & Away in the Saint Émilion listing.

Eurolines (☎ 56.92.50.42), across from the train station at 32 Rue Charles Domercq, handles buses to the Iberian Peninsula, Morocco, England, Italy, etc. The office is open Monday to Saturday from 9 am to 7 pm.

Car Budget (☎ 56.91.41.70) is near the train station at 12 Rue Charles Domercq. Europcar (☎ 56.31.20.30) is nearby at 35 Rue Charles Domercq.

Cheaper deals are available at AA Location (☎ 56.92.84.78), whose office is 500 metres west of the train station at 185 Cours de la Marne. A small car costs 299/500FF a day/weekend with 200 free km and a 2000FF excess (deductible).

Getting Around
The city centre is fairly large but can easily be explored on foot.

To/From the Airport The Navette Aéroport (Airport Shuttle) links the train station, the tourist office and the bus No 17 stop at Place Gambetta with the airport (32FF; 35 to 45 minutes). It runs once or twice an hour every day from 6 am to sometime between 9.45 and 11 pm.

If you arrive by air, another option is to take CGFTE bus No 73 from the airport to Mérignac-Cité des Pins and then bus M to Place Gambetta or Place de la Comédie (the tourist office). If you're going *to* the airport, bus M to Mérignac can be picked up at Place Jean Jaurès or Allées de Tourny. Unless you have a bus ticket from a carnet (see the following paragraph), the cost is 14FF (two 7FF single tickets).

Bus Bordeaux's urban bus network is known as CGFTE (☎ 57.57.88.88). Single tickets, sold on board, cost 7FF and are *not* valid for transfers. Ten-ticket carnets (44FF) come with two *talons* (coupons) bearing the same serial number as the tickets – you may be asked to show one of them when transferring. You can transfer up to three times after

your initial ride but don't forget to time-stamp your ticket each time you board. The last time-stamping must be done less than 60 minutes after the first.

CGFTE has *espaces accueil* (information bureaux) at the train station, Place Gambetta (4 Rue Georges Bonnac), Place de Tourny (10 Cours de Verdun) and Place Jean Jaurès. They can supply you with an easy-to-use *Plan Poche* (route map). The cheap Carte Bordeaux Découverte, which allows unlimited bus travel for one day (19FF) or three days (45FF), can be purchased at the tourist office or a CGFTE information bureau, though you probably won't need it unless you're staying near the train station or at one of the camping grounds.

As you exit the train station, the bus stops are to the left. To get to the city centre, take bus No 7 or 8, whose stops include Place de la Victoire, Place Gambetta, Cours de l'Intendance and Cours du 30 Juillet. In the other direction, they take a slightly different route, stopping at Place de Tourny, Cours Georges Clemenceau, Place Gambetta and Place de la Victoire. Both lines run until around 11.40 pm.

Taxi To order a cab in central Bordeaux, call ☎ 56.48.03.25 (Place de Tourny) or 56.91.47.05 (Place de la Victoire). For a taxi to the airport, call ☎ 56.97.11.27.

Car There is an underground parking garage under Place Gambetta.

Bicycle Cycles Pasteur (☎ 56.92.68.20) at 42 Cours Pasteur (near Place de la Victoire) has 10-speeds and mountain bikes for 50FF a day. It is open Monday to Friday from 9 am to noon and 2 to 6.30 pm. A 1600FF deposit is required.

BORDEAUX WINE-GROWING REGION
The 1000-sq-km wine-growing area around the city of Bordeaux, part of which is also known as the Bordelais, is – along with Burgundy – France's most important producer of top-quality wines.

Bordeaux is subdivided into 53 *appellations* (production areas whose climate and soil impart distinctive characteristics upon the wine produced there) that are grouped into six *familles*. The majority of the region's diverse wines (reds, rosés, sweet and dry whites, sparkling wines, etc) have earned the right to include the abbreviation AOC *(Appellation d'Origine Contrôlée)* on their labels, indicating that the contents have been grown, fermented and aged according to strict regulations governing such matters as the number of vines permitted per hectare. The region's production averages 660 million bottles of wine per year.

Bordeaux has many thousands of chateaux, a term that in this context refers not to palatial residences but rather to the properties where grapes are raised, fermented and then matured. The smaller chateaux often accept walk-in visitors, but for many of the larger and better known ones (eg Château Mouton-Rothschild) you'll have to make an appointment. Most of the chateaux are closed in August. Each vineyard has different rules about tasting *(dégustation)* – at some it's free, others make you pay, while yet others don't serve wine at all.

Information

In Bordeaux, the Maison du Vin de Bordeaux (☎ 56.00.22.66) at 3 Cours du 30 Juillet (across the street from the tourist office) has lots of information on chateau visits.

First you have to decide which growing area you'd like to visit. When you've made your decision – perhaps with the help of the Maison's colour-coded map of *appellations* – the staff will give you the address of the local *maison du vin* (a sort of tourist office for wine-growing areas), which will have details on which chateaux are open and when.

The Maison du Vin de Bordeaux is open weekdays from 8.30 am to 6 pm. From June to mid-October, it is open on Saturday from 9 am to 12.30 pm and 1.30 to 5 pm. There is free wine tasting at 10.30 am, 11.30 am, 2.30 pm and 4.30 pm.

Organised Tours

From mid-June to mid-October, Bordeaux-based travellers can visit a variety of chateaux by bus tour. Afternoon excursions, held daily from mid-June to mid-September, cost 130FF (110FF for students). All-day trips, available a couple of days a week, cost 240FF (230FF for students). Commentary is in French and English. There is a different itinerary each day. Reservations can be made at the Bordeaux tourist office – stop by at least a day in advance.

For information on tours of the Bordeaux wine country from Saint Émilion, see the Saint Émilion listing.

Getting There & Away

For details on bus services from Bordeaux to the winegrowing areas, see Bus under Getting There & Away in the Bordeaux listing.

SAINT ÉMILION

The village of Saint Émilion (population 2800), 39 km east of Bordeaux, sits on two limestone hills that look out over the Dordogne River valley. The Saint Émilion area has ideal soil and climate conditions for growing wine grapes and is renowned for its full-bodied, deeply coloured reds. Wines have been produced here since Gallo-Roman times.

In the 8th century, a Benedictine monk from Brittany named Émilion moved into a local cave with its own spring. A monastery later grew around the site of his hermitage. During the Middle Ages, Saint Émilion was a stop on one of the routes to Santiago de Compostella. The modern-day town, still surrounded by medieval ramparts (begun in the 13th century), is characterised by steep, narrow cobblestone streets and stone houses with red tile roofs. As the sun sets, the whole town turns a golden hue.

Orientation

Rue Guadet (as the D122 is known as it passes through town) is Saint Émilion's main commercial street. Place du Marché is in the centre of town next to the Église Monolithe.

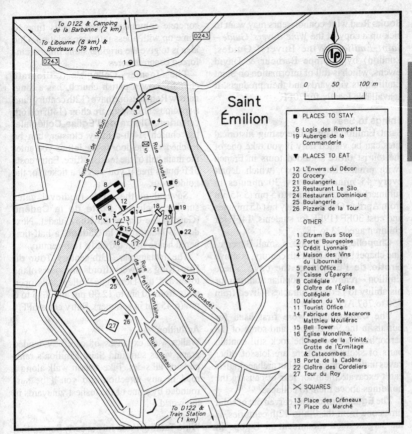

Saint Émilion

■ PLACES TO STAY
6   Logis des Remparts
19 Auberge de la
    Commanderie

▼ PLACES TO EAT
12 L'Envers du Décor
20 Grocery
21 Boulangerie
23 Restaurant Le Silo
24 Restaurant Dominique
25 Boulangerie
26 Pizzeria de la Tour

    OTHER
1   Citram Bus Stop
2   Porte Bourgeoise
3   Crédit Lyonnais
4   Maison des Vins
    du Libournais
5   Post Office
7   Caisse d'Épargne
8   Collégiale
9   Cloître de l'Église
    Collégiale
10 Maison du Vin
11 Tourist Office
14 Fabrique des Macarons
    Matthieu Mouliérac
15 Bell Tower
16 Église Monolithe,
    Chapelle de la Trinité,
    Grotte de l'Ermitage
    & Catacombes
18 Porte de la Cadène
22 Cloître des Cordeliers
27 Tour du Roy

✕ SQUARES
13 Place des Créneaux
17 Place du Marché

Information

Tourist Office The tourist office (☎ 57.24.
72.03) at Place des Créneaux is open daily
from 9.30 am to 12.30 pm and 1.45 to 6 pm.
From June to early September, hours are 9.30
am to 7 pm (9.30 am to 12.30 pm and 1.45
to 7 pm on weekends).

It has quite a few brochures in English and
a list of Saint Émilion-area chateaux that can
be visited; those that have tours in English
are indicated. Before visiting a chateau, it's
a good idea to phone ahead – someone at the
tourist office may be able take care of this for
you.

Money The Crédit Lyonnais near Porte
Bourgeoise will exchange foreign currency
Monday to Friday from 8.30 am to noon and
2 to 4 pm. The Caisse d'Épargne on Rue
Gaudet is open from 8.30 am to 12.30 pm
and 1.30 to 5 pm (6 pm on Friday) daily
except Saturday afternoon, Sunday and
Monday.

Post The post office on Rue Gaudet, open
Monday to Friday from 8.30 am to noon and
3 to 6 pm and on Saturday until noon, will
change foreign currency.

Saint Émilion's postcode is 33330.

Books Real wine connoisseurs may want to pick up a copy of the *Wine Buyers' Guide – Saint Émilion* (Wine Buyers' Guides, London) by Philippe Barbour & David Ewens, which is full of information on Saint Émilion, its vineyards and their products. It is available locally for 70FF.

Things to See

Saint Émilion's most interesting historical sites can be visited only if you take one of the tourist office's guided tours in French (with printed English text), which depart every 45 minutes (every 30 minutes in summer) daily from 10 am to 5 pm (5.45 pm from April to October). They last 45 minutes and cost 30FF (19FF for students, 14FF for children aged 13 to 18).

Chapelle de la Trinité, a small Benedictine chapel built in the 13th century, is above **Grotte de l'Ermitage**, the cave where Émilion – renowned in popular tradition for his ability to perform miracles – lived from 750 to 767 AD.

The **Catacombes** were first used for burials in the 9th century, and some of the sarcophagi carved in the rock still contain parts of skeletons. There are lots of other caves under Saint Émilion but archaeologists can't excavate them for fear of causing the buildings above them to collapse.

The **Église Monolithe**, carved out of solid limestone from the 9th to 12th centuries, is the largest such monument in Europe in terms of the volume of stone that was quarried (the interior is 20 by 38 metres and has an 11-metre-high ceiling). The **bell tower** directly above the church, which has a Romanesque base and a Gothic spire, was built from the 12th to the 15th centuries. You can climb to the top of the tower, from where there's a great view. In summer, it's open the same hours as the tourist office; the rest of the year, enquire in the tourist office. The fee is 6FF.

Architects were surprised to discover a few years back that the bell tower, which weighs 3500 tonnes, was supported by only two pillars. To prevent collapse, the interior of the Église Monolithe was filled with 28 concrete columns to give experts time to come up with a less intrusive solution. One idea is to give the original stone pillars reinforced concrete cores.

The former **Collégiale** (collegiate church), now a parish church, has a long, narrow Romanesque nave (12th century) and a spacious, almost square choir (14th to 16th centuries). **Cloître de l'Église Collégiale**, the church' 14th-century cloister, can be reached via the door to the left as you enter the main hall of the tourist office. Entry costs 5FF but is free if you've got a ticket for the guided tour.

Several of the city's medieval gates survive, including **Porte de la Cadène** (Gate of the Chain) on Rue Guadet. Next door is **Maison de la Cadène**, a half-timbered house from the early 16th century.

The rectangular, 13th-century **Tour du Roy** (King's Tower) affords fine views of the town and the Dordogne Valley. It is open daily from 10 am to 12.30 pm and 2.15 to 6 pm (6.45 pm in summer). Entry costs 6FF.

Activities

Walks Vast expanses of carefully tended grape vines surround Saint Émilion's ramparts on all sides. Take a short walk along a road in any direction and you'll be surrounded by some of the lushest vineyards in the world.

Wine Tasting From July to early September, the Maison du Vin (see Things to Buy) offers *initiations à la dégustation* (introductory winetasting classes) twice a day. The one-hour sessions (100FF) are conducted in French but the guide may speak a bit of English.

Organised Tours

The Bordeaux tourist office and Citram run bus excursions to Saint Émilion – ask at the Bordeaux tourist office for details.

On weekdays from June to early September, Saint Émilion's tourist office organises two-hour afternoon chateau visits in French and English. The cost is 51FF (31FF for children aged 12 to 18).

ATLANTIC COAST

Places to Stay

The tourist office has a list of chambres d'hôte in the vicinity of Saint Émilion.

Camping Camping de la Barbanne (☎ 57. 24.75.80), on the D122 about two km north of Saint Émilion, is open from April to mid-October. A tent site costs 21FF; adults pay 17FF each.

Hotels The Auberge de la Commanderie (☎ 57.24.70.19) on Rue des Cordeliers has big, nicely furnished doubles with dark wallpaper for 170FF (with washbasin and bidet) and 300FF (with shower and toilet). Demi-pension (breakfast and dinner) is obligatory in July and August. Hall showers are free.

The three-star Logis des Remparts (☎ 57.24.70.43; fax 57.74.47.44) on Rue Guadet has pleasant doubles for 290FF to 350FF.

Places to Eat

Saint Émilion is not a cheap place to dine – expect to pay at least 75 to 85FF for a menu.

Restaurants Restaurant Dominique (☎ 57. 24.71.00) on Rue de la Petite Fontaine serves a variety of local specialities. It offers a formule rapide for 60FF and menus for 85 and 130FF. It's open from noon to 2 pm and 7 to 9.30 or 10 pm daily except Monday (daily from June to September) but is closed from Christmas to mid-February. You might also try Restaurant Le Silo (☎ 57.74.45.44) on Rue Gaudet, which has menus for 85 and 120FF.

Crepes (14 to 30FF) and pizza (43 to 49FF) are on offer at Pizzeria de la Tour (☎ 57.24.68.91), right below the Tour du Roy on Rue de la Grande Fontaine. From Easter to October, food is served daily from 10.30 am to midnight. The rest of the year (except November), it's open on Friday night, Saturday and Sunday.

Bar à Vins Saint Émilion's only wine bar is L'Envers du Décor (☎ 57.74.48.31) on Rue du Clocher, which is open Monday to Saturday from noon to 7.30 pm. Local wines cost 20 to 50FF per glass. You can also eat here – the plat du jour is 65FF.

Self-Catering If you'll be picnicking, it's a good idea to buy the food (or at least everything but the bread) before arriving in town.

The boulangerie (☎ 57.51.73.88) on Rue Gaudet is open daily from 7.30 am to 12.30 pm and 3.30 pm (earlier in summer, 4 pm in winter) to 7 pm.

The boulangerie (☎ 57.24.72.11) on Rue de la Grande Fontaine is open daily (except Monday from October to June) from 7.30 am to 7 pm (7.30 pm in summer). There's a grocery on Rue Guadet at Rue des Girondins; it's closed on Monday.

Things to Buy

Wine Saint Émilion, whose streets are lined with shops selling wine, is the perfect place to sample and purchase Bordeaux wine. Most places offer free tasting to serious buyers.

Around the corner from the tourist office, the Maison du Vin (☎ 57.74.42.42) at Place Pierre Meyrat sells wines for the same price you'd pay at the chateaux. It is open Monday to Saturday from 9.30 am to 12.30 pm and 2 to 6 or 6.30 pm and on Sunday from 10 am to 12.30 pm and 2.30 to 6.30 or 7 pm. From late July to early September, it's open daily until 7 pm.

About 500 different wines are available at the Maison des Vins du Libournais (☎ 57.24.65.60), which is at the northern edge of town on Rue Guadet. It is open daily from 9 am to 7 pm (8 pm from June to October).

Macaroons Three local bakeries make macarons, soft cookies made from almond flour, egg whites and sugar. They are baked on sheets of paper for about 12 minutes at 180°C to 200°C. The recipe was brought to Saint Émilion in the 17th century by Ursuline nuns.

Fabrique de Macarons Matthieu Moulierac (☎ 57.74.41.84) on Tertre de la Tente bakes macaroons on the premises and sells them for 30FF per two dozen. It is open daily from 2 to 6 pm (10 am to 7 pm from May to October). There's another *macaroon bakery* next to the post office.

Getting There & Away
For a day trip from Bordeaux, taking the bus to Saint Émilion and the train back may be your best bet.

Train Saint Émilion is on SNCF's tertiary Bordeaux-Bergerac line. Bordeaux's Gare Saint Jean is linked to Saint Émilion (41FF; 35 to 45 minutes) by two daily round trips (one or two on Sunday and holidays). The last autorail back to Bordeaux leaves Saint Émilion's train station, which is a bit over one km south of town, daily at about 6.30 pm. Buy your ticket on the train.

Libourne, a stop on the TGV Atlantique line, is linked to Saint Émilion (8FF; 10 minutes) by four buses a day. The bus station is next to the train station. For bus details, contact Citram in Bordeaux.

Bus Citram has five round trips a day (two during the summer) from Bordeaux to the northern edge of Saint Émilion (34.50FF each way; one hour). There may be a change of buses at Libourne.

During the summer, the most convenient bus leaves Bordeaux at 10.15 am (9.45 or 11.30 am on Sunday and holidays); the last bus back to Bordeaux leaves Saint Émilion at 5 pm (6.30 pm on Sunday and holidays). During July and August, buses to Saint Émilion can be boarded at the Bordeaux tourist office.

ARCACHON
The beach resort of Arcachon (population 11,800), known for its fine weather and oyster farming, became popular with bourgeois residents of Bordeaux at the end of the 19th century. Its major attraction is the extraordinary Dune du Pilat, Europe's highest sand dune, which is about eight km south-west of town. Arcachon, a very quiet place except in summer, is well served by trains and makes an uncomplicated day trip from Bordeaux.

Orientation
Arcachon is on the south side of the triangular Bassin d'Arcachon (Arcachon Bay), which is linked to the Atlantic by a three-km-wide channel just west of town. The narrow peninsula of Cap Ferret is on the other side of the outlet. The Dune du Pilat is eight km south of Arcachon.

Arcachon's main street is Blvd de la Plage, which is one block inland from the beach. The train station, 500 metres south of the beach, is linked to Blvd de la Plage and Jetée Thiers (a pier) by Ave Gambetta.

Information
Tourist Office The tourist office (☎ 56.83. 01.69) is 200 metres to the left as you exit the train station at Place Roosevelt. It is open Monday to Saturday from 9 am to 12.30 pm and 2 to 6 pm. In July and August, it's open daily from 9 am to 7 pm (12.30 pm on Sunday). The staff don't make hotel reservations but can provide information on where rooms are available.

From June to September, the tourist office has an annexe (*point d'information*; ☎ 56.83. 38.15) next to the casino, whose address is 163 Blvd de la Plage. In June and September, it's open Friday to Sunday from 10 am to noon and 4 pm to 7 pm (10 pm on Saturday). In July and August, it's open daily from 10 am to noon and 4 to 10 pm (9 pm on Sunday).

Money The Banque de France, across the street from the tourist office at 55 Blvd Général Leclerc, is open Monday to Friday from 8.45 am to noon and 1.15 to 3.30 pm.

There are a couple of banks at Place Lucien de Gracia, including a Caisse d'Épargne that's open Monday to Friday from 9 am to 12.30 pm and 2 to 5.30 pm (4.30 pm on Friday). The Crédit Agricole next to 250 Blvd de la Plage changes money Monday to Friday from 8.30 am to 12.10 pm and 1.50 to 4.30 pm.

Post The main post office, across from the tourist office at Place Président Roosevelt is open Monday to Friday from 8 am to 7 pm and on Saturday until noon.

Arcachon's postcode is 33120. Pyla Plage's postcode is 33115.

Central Arcachon

The flat area bordering the **Plage d'Arcachon**, the town's beach, is known as the **Ville d'Été** (Summer Quarter). The liveliest section is around **Jetée Thiers**, a pier that affords nice views of the Bassin d'Arcachon and the town.

The **Aquarium et Musée** (☎ 56.83.10.22) at 2 Rue du Professeur Jolyet, which has a collection of local sea creatures, is not particularly exciting. From the week before Easter to mid-October, it's open daily from 10 am tó 12.30 pm and 2 to 7 pm; summer hours are longer. Entrance costs 17FF (12FF for children aged three to 10).

The **Ville d'Hiver** (Winter Quarter), on the tree-covered hillside south of the Ville d'Été, dates from the turn of the century. In decades past, rich people used to come here either to recover from tuberculosis or to amuse themselves with other rich people.

A lovely pedestrian promenade lined with trees, playgrounds and bits of grass runs westward from the Plage d'Arcachon to **Plage Péreire**, **Plage des Abatilles** and Pyla-sur-Mer.

Dune du Pilat

The main attraction in the Arcachon area is the remarkable Dune du Pilat, also known as the Dune de Pyla, a 114-metre-high sand dune that stretches along the mouth of the Bassin d'Arcachon for almost three km. For information on getting there, see Bus under Getting Around.

The dune's eastern (inland) side is as steep as an Olympic ski jump. At the bottom, the tops of dead trees, smothered by the dune as it moves relentlessly eastward, poke out of the sand. The slope facing the Atlantic, dotted with tufts of grass, is much gentler.

The view from the top is magnificent. To the west you can see the sandy shoals at the mouth of the Bassin d'Arcachon, including the Banc d'Arguin bird reserve, and Cap Ferret. In the other direction, dense pine forests stretch from the base of the dune eastward almost as far as the eye can see.

Parts of the beach are watched by lifeguards from mid-June to mid-September. Elsewhere, caution is advised: sections of the coast are subject to a powerful current known as a *baïne*. Don't count on being able to buy anything to eat around the dune.

The road from Arcachon to the Dune du Pilat – Blvd de la Côte d'Argent and its continuation in Pyla-sur-Mer, Blvd de l'Océan – passes by the old villas of the Ville d'Hiver and the lovely summer cottages of Pyla-sur-Mer, nestled among the pine trees.

Parc Ornithologique

The **Bassin d'Arcachon** is a shallow, 250-sq-km tidal bay. Only 20% of its area is under water at low tide, providing the ideal habitat for both migrating and non-migrating birds. Information and displays on the 260 species of birds that visit the area each year are available at the Parc Ornithologique (bird reserve; ☎ 56.22.68.43) in Le Teich, in the south-east corner of the bay. Situated 15 km east of Arcachon on the D650, it is open daily during school holiday periods and from June to September and on weekends the rest of the year. Summer hours are 10 am to 6 pm. Entry costs 23FF (15FF for children).

Organised Tours

Boat Excursions UBA (see Boat under Getting There & Away), runs boat excursions to the Banc d'Arguin (a sand bank off the coast of the Dune du Pilat), around the Bassin d'Arcachon and up the Eyre River. In July and August, it also has fishing trips.

Places to Stay

During July and August, it is extremely difficult to find accommodation. During this period, many hotels require that you take demi-pension.

Places to Stay – bottom end

Camping The steep, inland side of the Dune du Pilat is lined with five large and rather pricey camping grounds, most of them half hidden in a forest of pine trees. During July and August, most have spaces until about noon if you have a small tent. For information on getting there by bus, see under Getting Around.

Three-star, 580-place *Camping de la Forêt* (☎ 56.22.73.28) on Route de Biscarosse (the D218) is the first camping ground you come to when heading south. It is wall-to-wall tents and campervans but has a great location and attracts lots of young people (some of whom are a bit rowdy). A flight of wooden stairs leads up the dune to its highest point. Amenities include a grocery, a snack bar and a pool. Two people with a tent and car are charged 82FF.

Farther south, three-star *Pyla Camping* (☎ 56.22.74.56), also a bit crowded, is open from early May to September. Amenities include a restaurant, a swimming pool and a grocery. A tent site costs 38FF, including parking; adults/children under seven pay 22/20FF. Prices are 20% less in May, June and September. Three-star, 300-site *Camping de la Dune* (☎ 56.22.72.17), open from May to the beginning of October, is slightly nicer. Tariffs are about the same.

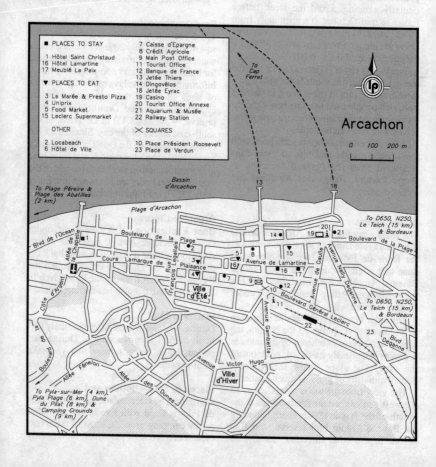

PLACES TO STAY
1 Hôtel Saint Christaud
16 Hôtel Lamartine
17 Meublé La Paix

PLACES TO EAT
3 La Marée & Presto Pizza
4 Uniprix
5 Food Market
15 Leclerc Supermarket

OTHER
2 Locabeach
6 Hôtel de Ville

7 Caisse d'Epargne
8 Crédit Agricole
9 Main Post Office
11 Tourist Office
12 Banque de France
13 Jetée Thiers
14 Dingovélos
18 Jetée Eyrac
19 Casino
20 Tourist Office Annexe
21 Aquarium & Musée
22 Railway Station

SQUARES
10 Place Président Roosevelt
23 Place de Verdun

Arcachon

0   100   200 m

Hostel The nearest *Auberge de Jeunesse* (☎ 56.60.64.62) is at 87 Ave de Bordeaux in Cap Ferret (postcode 33970), which is on the other side of the mouth of the Bassin d'Arcachon. For transport information, see Bus under Getting There & Away and Ferry under Getting Around.

Hotels The friendly *Hôtel Saint Christaud* (☎ 56.83.38.53) at 8 Allée de la Chapelle, open from early April to late October, has doubles for 150FF (with washbasin and bidet) and 220FF (with shower). Hall showers are free. Demi-pension (178FF per person) is obligatory in July and August. Except in July and August, this place usually has places in the morning.

The 26-room *Meublé La Paix* (☎ 56.83. 05.65) at 8 Ave de Lamartine, also known as Location Chambres La Paix, is open from May to October. Doubles with breakfast cost 167FF (with washbasin and bidet), 197FF (with toilet) and 218FF (with shower and toilet); prices are a bit lower in the off season. Triples and quads with washbasin and bidet are 223/276FF. Hall showers are free.

Places to Stay – middle
Prices rise precipitously in summer.

Arcachon The 31-room *Hôtel Lamartine* (☎ 56.83.95.77; fax 57.52.20.75) at 28 Ave de Lamartine is open from about March to December. The price of a double ranges from 250FF (in winter) to 380FF (June to mid-September).

Pyla Plage The grand old *Hôtel Haïtza* (☎ 56.22.74.64; fax 56.22.10.23), a three-star place at 1 Ave Louis Gaume, is one block from the beach. It is open from early April to September. Doubles with shower and toilet start at 400FF, but from mid-July to the end of August demi-pension (165FF per person extra) is obligatory.

The *Hôtel Oyana* (☎ 56.22.72.59) at 52 Ave Louis Gaume, open from April to September, is 500 metres down the hill from the bus stop near the Ttiki Etchea restaurant. In April and May, doubles with shower and

toilet cost 250 to 300FF. The rest of the time, demi-pension (288FF per person) is obligatory.

Places to Eat
Arcachon is known for its seafood, especially oysters.

Restaurants *La Marée* (☎ 56.83.24.05), a popular seafood place at 21 Rue de Lattre de Tassigny, is open from Easter to October. Fish soup and mussels cost 22FF each; grilled salmon is 55FF. For 25FF, you get six small oysters, a glass of white wine, bread and paté. It is open daily from noon to 2.30 pm and 7 to 10.30 pm.

From June to September, *Restaurant La Paix*, the restaurant of the Meublé La Paix hotel, has French *menus* for 54, 70 and 110FF. It's open daily from noon to 2 pm and 7.30 to 10 pm.

Presto Pizza (☎ 56.83.59.24), a take-out pizza place at 49 Cours Lamarque de Plaisance, is open daily from 5 to 9.30 pm. On weekends (daily from July to mid-September), it's also open from 10.30 am to 1 pm.

In summer, the beachfront promenade between the two piers is lined with touristy restaurants and places offering pizza and crepes.

Self-Catering The lively *food market* on Rue Expert (just north of the Hôtel de Ville) is open daily except Monday (daily from about June to September) from 8 am to 1 pm.

Near the beach, the *Leclerc supermarket* at 224 Blvd de la Plage is open Monday to Thursday from 9 am to 12.30 pm and 2.30 to 7.30 pm and on Friday and Saturday from 9 am to 7.30 pm. Summer hours are longer. The *Uniprix* at 46 Cours Lamarque de Plaisance, whose food section is on the 1st floor, has similar hours but closes at 7 pm.

Getting There & Away
Train Some of the trains from Bordeaux to Arcachon (47FF; 45 minutes; at least 15 a day) are coordinated with Paris-Bordeaux TGVs. In summer, the last train back to

Bordeaux leaves Arcachon at about 9 pm (a bit later on Sunday and holidays).

Bus There are no buses from Bordeaux to Arcachon, but Citram has rather slow service from Bordeaux to Cap Ferret (65FF; 1¾ hours; seven to nine a day).

Motorbike Locabeach (see Bicycle under Getting Around) has 50 cc Vespa Ciaos from 80/145FF per half/whole day. Mopeds are 140/225FF, 125 cc motorcycles are 280/410FF. Deposits range from 2500 to 8000FF.

Boat From June to September, UBA (☎ 56.54.60.32) has ferries about once an hour from Jetée Thiers and Jetée Eyrac to Cap Ferret (27/40FF one-way/return). The rest of the year, there is at least one run a day on Monday, Wednesday and Friday.

Getting Around

Bus From June to September, Autobus d'Arcachon (☎ 56.83.07.60), based at 47 Blvd du Général Leclerc, has daily buses from the train station to the Dune du Pilat parking lot (8FF plus 3.20FF per backpack; 30 minutes) and the five camping grounds along the dune's eastern side (16FF). Buses generally run every 45 minutes or so from about 8 am to a bit after 7 pm. The rest of the year, when the buses go only as far south as Pyla Plage (Haïtza), they run about eight times a day except on Sunday and holidays. A schedule is available at the tourist office.

Taxi To order a cab, call 56.83.30.03.

Bicycle From mid-June to mid-September, Dingovélos (☎ 56.83.44.09) on Rue Grenier rents tandems, triplos, quatros and quintuplos (bikes with places for two to five riders). The charge is 18FF per person per half-hour. Conventional one-person bikes are 40 to 50FF a day. This place is open daily from 9.30 am to 1 am.

Locabeach (☎ 56.83.39.64) at 326 Blvd de la Plage rents three and 10-speeds for 30/45FF per half/whole day and mountain bikes for 45/70FF. It's open from 9 am to 12.30 pm and 2 to 7.30 pm Tuesday to Saturday. From June to September, it's open daily from 9 am to 8 pm (11 pm during July and August).

French Basque Country

The département of Pyrénées-Atlantiques in France's far south-western corner is the only part of the Basque Country (Euzkadi in Basque) located north of the Pyrenees. Known in French as the Pays Basque, the region is a good base for day trips to the verdant western Pyrenees and the Spanish Basque Country, both of which begin less than 25 km south of the two main cities, the cultural capital of Bayonne and the glitzy beach resort of Biarritz.

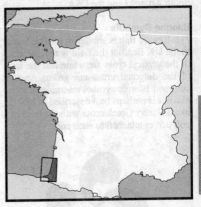

History

The early history of the Basques, who live in a region on the Bay of Biscay that straddles the French-Spanish border, is largely unknown. Roman sources mention a tribe called the Vascones living in the area. The Basques took over what is now south-

western France in the 6th century. They were converted to Christianity in the 10th century and are now known for their devotion to Catholicism.

After resisting invasions by the Visigoths, Franks, Normans and Moors, the Basques on both sides of the Pyrenees emerged from the turbulent Middle Ages with a fair degree of local autonomy, which they lost in France during the Revolution. The French Basque Country, part of the duchy of Aquitaine, was under English rule from the mid-12th century – when Eleanor of Aquitaine, divorced by French King Louis VII, remarried Henry of Anjou, later King Henry II of England – until the mid-15th century.

Basque nationalism flourished before and during the Spanish Civil War (1936-39), when German aircraft flying for Francisco Franco's fascists ravaged the Spanish city of Guernica (1937), symbol of the Basque nation and a centre of Basque nationalist activities. Until Franco's death in 1975, many Spanish Basque nationalists and anti-Franco guerrillas sheltered in France. Some Basques still dream of carving an Euzkadi state out of the Basque areas of Spain and

France, and a few support the terrorist organisation ETA (Euzkadi ta Askatsuna, which means Basque Homeland & Liberty). Hundreds of thousands of Basques live in South America and the USA.

Basque Symbols

The Basque flag is similar in general layout to the UK flag but the field is red, the arms of the vertical cross are white and the arms of the diagonal cross are green. Another common Basque symbol resembles a swastika but is perhaps best described as looking like a skinny Greek cross with the head of a golf driver attached to each end.

Basque symbol

Language

The Basque Language (Euskara in Basque) is the only language in south-western Europe to have withstood the onslaught of Latin and its derivatives. It's origins are shrouded in mystery. Theories tying it to the Hamito-Semitic language group and languages spoken in the Caucasus region of the former USSR have been discredited, and it is thought that similarities with long-dead Iberian may have resulted from contact between the Basques and the Iberians rather than from a common origin.

Basque was an unwritten language in the Middle Ages, making it difficult to resist the encroachment of the Romance languages. The first book in Basque was printed in 1545 and marked the beginning of Basque literature. Basque is now spoken by about a million people in Spain and France, almost all of whom are bilingual. In the French Basque Country, the language is widely spoken in Bayonne but is even more common farther inland.

Sport

Bullfighting Corrida, Spanish-style bull-fighting in which the bull is killed, has devotees all over the south of France, including Bayonne. Tournaments are held about half a dozen times each summer. Tickets cost 80 to 400FF. Advance reservations are usually necessary – information is available at tourist offices. The matadors are either French or Spanish.

Food

One of the most essential ingredients in Basque cooking are the deep-red chillies you will see hanging out to dry in summer, brightening up houses and adding that dynamite touch to many of the region's dishes. Equally characteristic is the goose fat that is used to cook almost everything from eggs to *garbure*, a filling cabbage and bean soup. The pâté de foie gras (goose liver pâté) and the confit d'oie (see Perigord in the Limousin, Périgord & Quercy chapter) are also excellent. Fish dishes abound on the coast, with tuna and sardines being the particular speciality of Saint Jean de Luz. Other local delicacies include baby eels, trout and *salmis de palombe*, wood pigeon stew with a rich brown sauce.

The locally cured, salty *jambon de Bayonne*, Bayonne ham, is another staple of Basque cuisine.

Things to Buy

For information on Basque linen and Basque sweets, see Things to Buy in the Saint Jean de Luz section.

Getting There & Away

Train to Spain For rail travel to Spain, you have to switch trains at Irún because the track gauge changes at the border. The best way to get to the Spanish Basque city of San Sebastián is to catch an SNCF train to Hendaye, whence you can take El Topo, a privately operated shuttle train that runs

Pelote Basque

Pelote Basque, known in Basque and English as *pelota*, is the name given to a group of games native to the Basque Country that are played with a *pelote* (a hard ball with a rubber core) and either *mains nues* (bare hands) or some sort of a scoop-like racquet made of wicker, leather or wood.

In the Basque Country, *cesta punta*, also known as *jaï alaï*, the world's fastest game played with a ball, is the most popular variety of pelota. Developed from a type of handball, it became quicker and quicker after the introduction of rubber – brought to Europe from South America – made it possible to produce balls with more bounce. In the 1920s and '30s, cesta punta was a big hit in Chicago and New Orleans but lost popularity when betting was outlawed. Introduced to Cuba in 1900, the game was banned after the Revolution of 1959.

Cesta punta is played with a *chistera*, a curved wicker scoop worn strapped to the wrist, with which players catch the ball and hurl it back with great force. Matches take place in a jaï alaï, also known as a *cancha*, a court with three walls (the fourth side is open) that is usually about 53 metres long. The walls and floor are made of special materials that can withstand repeated impacts of the ball, whose speed can reach 300 km/h. A cancha and its tiers of balconies for spectators constitute a *fronton*. Other types of pelota (eg joko-garbi, main nue, pala, paleta, pasaka, rebot and xare) are played in outdoor, one-wall courts, also known as frontons, and in enclosed structures called *trinquets*.

For information on pelota tournaments, see Entertainment in the sections on Bayonne, Biarritz, Saint Jean de Luz and Saint Jean Pied de Port. For information on introductory cesta punta lessons, see Pelote Basque in the Biarritz section. ■

every half-hour. ATCRB (see Bus under Getting There & Away in the Bayonne, Biarritz and Saint Jean de Luz sections) has buses to San Sebastián.

BAYONNE

Bayonne (Baiona in Basque; population 43,000) is the cultural and economic capital of the French Basque Country. Unlike the up-market beach resort of Biarritz, a short bus ride away, Bayonne retains much of its Basqueness: the architecture, for instance, is typical of the region, and you're quite likely to hear locals speaking Basque among themselves. Most of the Basque-language graffiti you see around town is the work of nationalist groups seeking an independent Basque state, though some of it calls for a halt to *korrida* (bullfighting).

The city, founded as Lapurdum by the Romans, is known for its smoked ham, chocolate and marzipan. The latter two products were introduced in the late 15th century by Jews fleeing the Spanish Inquisition. According to tradition, the *baïonnette* (bayonet) was developed here in the early 1600s. Bayonne reached the height of its commercial prosperity in the 18th century, when Basque corsaires landed cargoes even more valuable than the cod caught by the fishing fleet off the coast of Newfoundland, which Basque mariners claim to have 'discovered' in 1372.

Orientation

The Adour and Nive rivers, which meet at Bayonne, split the town into three areas. Saint Esprit, where the train station is located, is north of the Adour River. Grand Bayonne, the oldest part of town, is on the west bank of the Nive River. Petit Bayonne, east of the Nive, is an old residential area with a number of arcaded streets.

Pont Saint Esprit, the bridge over the Adour River, links Place de la République with Place du Réduit and the contiguous Place de la Liberté, which abuts the Hôtel de Ville. Nearby Rue Port-Neuf, Rue Lormand and Rue Victor Hugo are lively, shop-lined pedestrian malls.

The nondescript suburban sprawl of Anglet (the final 't' is pronounced) fills in the area between Bayonne and the beach resort of Biarritz, eight km to the west. The urban area made up of Bayonne, Anglet and Biarritz (population 127,000) is sometimes abbreviated as BAB. The best map of the conurbation is STAB's local bus map.

BASQUE COUNTRY

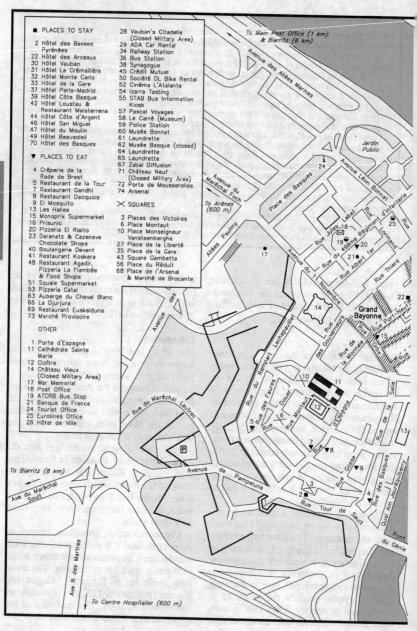

■ PLACES TO STAY
2   Hôtel des Basses
    Pyrénées
22 Hôtel des Arceaux
30 Hôtel Vauban
31 Hôtel La Crémaillère
32 Hôtel Monte Carlo
33 Hôtel de la Gare
37 Hôtel Paris-Madrid
39 Hôtel Côte Basque
42 Hôtel Loustau &
    Restaurant Maisterrena
44 Hôtel Côte d'Argent
46 Hôtel San Miguel
47 Hôtel du Moulin
49 Hôtel Beausoleil
70 Hôtel des Basques

▼ PLACES TO EAT
4   Crêperie de la
    Rade de Brest
5   Restaurant de la Tour
7   Restaurant Gandhi
8   Restaurant Dacquois
9   El Mosquito
15 Monoprix Supermarket
20 Prisunic
20 Pizzeria El Rialto
23 Daranatz & Cazenave
    Chocolate Shops
40 Boulangerie Devant
41 Restaurant Koskera
48 Restaurant Agadir,
    Pizzeria La Flambée
    & Food Shops
51 Squale Supermarket
53 Pizzeria Catal
63 Auberge du Cheval Blanc
66 La Djurjura
69 Restaurant Euskalduna
73 Marché Provisoire

    OTHER
1   Porte d'Espagne
11 Cathédrale Sainte
    Marie
12 Cloître
14 Château Vieux
    (Closed Military Area)
17 War Memorial
18 Post Office
19 ATCRB Bus Stop
21 Banque de France
24 Tourist Office
25 Eurolines Office
26 Hôtel de Ville

28 Vauban's Citadelle
    (Closed Military Area)
29 ADA Car Rental
34 Railway Station
36 Bus Station
38 Synagogue
45 Crédit Mutuel
50 Société DL Bike Rental
52 Cinéma L'Atalante
54 Izarra Tasting
55 STAB Bus Information
    Kiosk
57 Pascal Voyages
58 Le Carré (Museum)
59 Police Station
60 Musée Bonnat
61 Laundrette
62 Musée Basque (closed)
64 Laundrette
65 Laundrette
67 Zabal Diffusion
71 Château Neuf
    (Closed Military Area)
72 Porte de Mousserolles
74 Arsenal

✕ SQUARES
3   Places des Victoires
6   Place Montaut
10 Place Monseigneur
    Vansteenberghe
27 Place de la Liberté
35 Place de la Gare
43 Square Gambetta
56 Place du Réduit
68 Place de l'Arsenal
    & Marché de Brocante

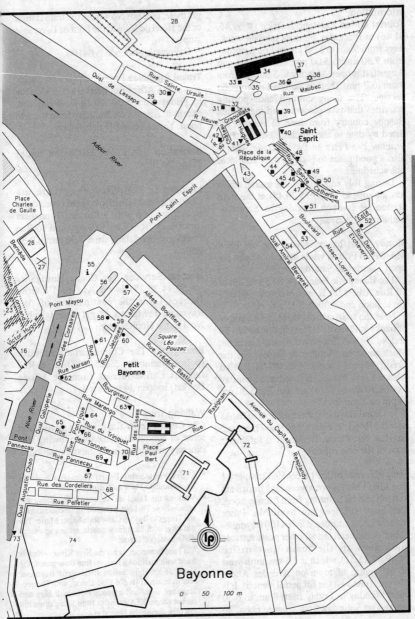

28

Quai de Lesseps

Rue Sainte Ursule

33
34
37
38
35
36
Rue Maubec

29
30

31
32
39

R Neuve
Graouillats
40

Saint
Esprit

Le Château Vieux
R Hugues

42
41

Place de la
République

48

Rue Sainte Catherine

44
49
50

43
45
46
47

51

Adour River

Boulevard

52

53

Rue de l'Esté

Rue Denis

Alsace-Lorraine

Quai Amiral Bergeret

54

Pont Saint Esprit

Place
Charles
de Gaulle

Bernède

26
27

55

i

56

57

Allées Boufflers

Pont Mayou

Rue Laffitte

Quai des Corsaires

58
59

Square
Léo
Pouzac

Rue Jacques

61
60

Rue Frédéric Bastiat

Rue Bernède

Rue Command

23

Victor Hugo

16

Petit
Bayonne

Rue Marsan

62

Quai Galuperie

Nive River

Bourgneuf

63

Rue Marengo

64

Rue Pontrique

65
66

Rue du Trinquet

Rue des Lisses

Avenue du Capitaine Resplandy

Rue Ravignan

Rue

Pont
Pannecau

Rue des Tonneliers

69
70

Place
Paul Bert

Rue Pannecau

67

71

72

Quai Augustin Chao

Rue des Cordeliers

68

Rue Pelletier

73

74

Bayonne

0   50   100 m

Information

Tourist Office The tourist office (☎ 59.46. 01.46) at Place des Basques is open weekdays from 9 am to 5.30 pm and on Saturday from 9.30 am to 5.00 pm. During July and August, it is open Monday to Saturday from 9 am to 7 pm. There is no hotel reservation service. The many cultural and sporting activities that take place around the French Basque country from June to August are listed by date in the brochure entitled *Programme des Fêtes en Pays Basque*. This is also a good place to pick up train and local bus schedules.

During July and August, the tourist office has an annexe (☎ 59.55.20.45) at the train station. It is open Monday to Saturday, including holidays.

Money Most banks in Bayonne are open Monday to Friday, while those in Anglet are open Tuesday to Saturday.

The Banque de France (☎ 59.59.02.29) at 18 Rue Albert 1er is open weekdays from 9 am to noon and 1.30 to 3.35 pm.

Near the train station, there are a number of banks at Place de la République (at No 20 and No 26) and along Blvd Alsace-Lorraine. Most are open Monday to Friday, but the Crédit Mutuel (☎ 59.55.06.08) at 7 Blvd Alsace-Lorraine is open Tuesday to Saturday from 8.30 am to 12.30 pm and 2 to 5.30 pm (4 pm on Saturday).

In Grand Bayonne, there are lots of banks near the Hôtel de Ville, along Rue Thiers and on Rue du 49ème Régiment d'Infanterie (east of the post office).

Post The post office (☎ 59.59.32.00) at 11 Rue Jules Labat is open weekdays from 8 am to 6 pm and on Saturday from 8 am to noon. Exchange services are available. Poste restante items addressed to '64100 Bayonne-Labat' come later, but all other poste restante mail goes to the main post office (☎ 59.52.15.51), which is 1.5 km north-west of the centre of town on Ave des Allées Marines (just past the Elf petrol station). It is open Monday to Friday from 8 am to 6.30 pm and on Saturday from 8 am to noon. To

get there, take bus No 4 from the train station or the Hôtel de Ville to the Pont de l'Aveugle stop.

Bayonne's postcode is 64100.

Travel Agencies Pascal Voyages (☎ 59.25. 48.48) at 8 Allées Boufflers is open Monday to Friday from 8.30 am to 6.30 pm and, except in August, on Saturday from 9 am to noon. You can buy BIJ tickets here.

Bookshop See Zabal Diffusion under Things to Buy.

Laundry In Petit Bayonne, there are laundrettes at 25 Rue Bourgneuf (open daily from 7 am to 8 pm), 9 Rue des Tonneliers (open daily from 7 am to 9 pm) and 16 Rue Pontrique (open daily from 7.30 am to 9.30 pm).

Medical Services The Centre Hospitalier (☎ 59.44.35.35) is on Ave de l'Interne Jacques Loeb, the continuation of Ave Raymond de Martres. To get there, take bus No 3 to the Hôpital stop.

Emergency The Commisariat de Police (police station; ☎ 59.25.77.00) at 6 Rue Jacques Lafitte (across from the Musée Bonnat) is open 24 hours a day.

Walking Tour

City Centre Loop You can get a pretty good sense of central Bayonne by following this itinerary, which begins at the train station:

- Cross Pont Saint Esprit from Place de la République to Place du Réduit.
- Walk to the Hôtel de Ville and then along the arcaded Rue Port-Neuf (famed for its chocolates – see Things to Buy) to Cathédrale Sainte Marie. The **old city**, with its narrow streets, retains an essentially medieval layout.
- Via Pont Pannecau, cross the Nive River, which is lined with traditional houses. **Rue Bourgneuf**, the heart of strongly nationalistic Petit Bayonne, retains much of its old-time charm, with Basque-language signs and a number of small bars and barber shops. ETA guerillas from Spain often hid out here during the Franco era.

- Circle back to Pont Saint Esprit via Place Paul Bert (next to the fortified **Château Neuf**, which dates from 1489) the Musée Basque and the Musée Bonnat.

Ramparts Walk

Thanks to Vauban's 17th-century fortifications, now covered with grass and dotted with trees, the city centre is surrounded by a green belt. You can walk along the old ramparts by following **Rue du Rempart Lachepaillet**, lined with stately, Basque-style apartment buildings, and **Rue Tour de Sault**.

Adour River

Each time the tide comes in, the Adour changes directions, flowing vigorously inland (south-eastward) rather than towards the sea (north-westward). Bayonne is eight km south-east of the mouth of the Adour.

Cathédrale Sainte Marie

Bayonne's Radiant Gothic cathedral is at the southern end of Rue Port-Neuf and its continuation, Rue de la Monnaie, in the heart of the old city. Begun in 1258, when Bayonne was ruled by the English, it was completed after the area came under French control in 1451. These political changes are reflected in the cathedral's ornamentation, which includes the English coat-of-arms, three leopards, and that most French of symbols, the fleur-de-lis (look at the keystones in the ceiling arches).

The choir and ambulatory incorporate elements typical of the Gothic churches of Champagne. Some of the stained glass dates from the Renaissance. Many of the statues that once graced the church's crumbly exterior were smashed during the Revolution. The 64-metre spires were built in the 1870s.

The cathedral is closed from noon to 2.30 pm (3 pm on Sunday).

Cloître From about May to September, the 14th-century cloisters of Cathédrale Sainte Marie are open from 10 am to noon and 2.30 to 6 pm daily except Sunday and on Monday morning. Tickets cost 12FF (6FF for stu-

dents, children and people over 60). The entrance is through the little door next to the bar at 83 Rue d'Espagne. During the rest of the year, the entrance is across the street from 1 Place Monseigneur Vansteenberghe and there is no fee, but the hours are reduced to weekday afternoons from 2 to 6 pm.

Musée Bonnat

The Musée Bonnat (☎ 59.59.08.52) at 5 Rue Jacques Laffitte in Petit Bayonne displays a diverse assortment of 13th to early 20th-century works collected by the painter and art collector Léon Bonnat (1833-1922), a native of Bayonne, including a whole room of paintings by Peter Paul Rubens (1577-1640). It is open from 10 am to 11.30 am and either 2.30 or 3 to 6.30 pm (8.30 pm on Friday) daily except Tuesday and holidays. From mid-September to mid-June it is closed on Friday mornings. The entry fee is 15FF (5FF for students).

Le Carré

Le Carré (literally, The Square) at 12 Rue Frédéric Bastiat, an annexe of the Musée Bonnat, puts on free exhibitions of contemporary art. It is open daily, except Tuesday and holidays, from 10 to 11.30 am and 2.30 to 6 pm (8 pm on Friday). In summer, afternoon hours are 3 to 6.30 pm (8.30 pm on Friday).

Musée Basque

The Basque Museum (☎ 59.59.08.98), a highly regarded ethnographic museum on Rue Marengo in Petit Bayonne, has been closed since the late 1980s because the beams holding up the floors of its 16th-century building are in danger of collapsing. If funding comes through – and no one seems to know when it will – the museum, which belongs to the Bayonne municipality, may reopen sometime in the mid-1990s.

Izarra Tasting

Izarra, a local liqueur made with dozens of exotic herbs according to a secret recipe invented in 1835, is produced at the Distillerie de la Côte Basque (☎ 59.55.09.45), which is in Saint Esprit at 9 Quai Amiral Bergeret. Free 45-minute tours (English text available) with tasting and sales at the end are conducted Monday to Friday from 9 to 11.15 am and 2 to 4.30 pm. From mid-July to August tours are held Monday to Saturday from 9 to 11.15 am and 2 to 6.15 pm.

Beaches
For information on bathing in Biarritz and Anglet, see the Biarritz section.

Sports Courses
The Auberge de Jeunesse d'Anglet (see Hostel under Places to Stay) offers very popular one-week *stages* (courses) in such sports as golf, surfing, *voile* (sailing), *Morey Boogie* (body-boarding), *plongée sous-marine* (scuba diving) and *équitation* (horse riding).

The courses, which last from Sunday evening to Saturday afternoon and are in French (though the instructors usually speak at least some English), cost 1800 to 2130FF (1990 to 2360FF in the middle of summer), including accommodation, meals and equipment. For details, call, fax or write to the hostel and they'll send you documentation. You will need to make reservations at least a month in advance.

Festivals
Bayonne's most important annual festival is the five-day Fête de Bayonne, which begins on the first Wednesday in August. The Fête includes a *course des vaches* (running of the cows), a parody of Pamplona's 'running of the bulls' in which it's the people – dressed in white with red scarves around their necks – who chase the cattle rather than the other way around. The festival also includes Basque music, corrida-type bullfighting, a *cavalcade de chars* (parade of floats) and rugby matches (rugby is a favourite sport in this area).

Places to Stay – bottom end
Accommodation is most difficult to find from mid-July to mid-August, especially during the five-day Fête de Bayonne.

Camping Despite their mediocre facilities, northern Anglet's three camping grounds remain popular because they're within 10 minutes' walk of the beach. All are accessible by bus from Bayonne and Biarritz. You can pitch a tent in the yard of the *Auberge de Jeunesse d'Anglet* (see Hostel) for 39FF per person, including breakfast.

The chaotically run *Camping du Fontaine Laborde* (☎ 59.03.48.16), open from June to September, is on Allée de Fontaine Laborde, not far from the Auberge de Jeunesse. It may have mangy grass and scraggly trees, but *lots* of young backpackers camp here. Charges are 15.50FF per adult, 14FF for a camp site and 8FF to park. It often fills up in July and August. To get there, take the bus to the Auberge de Jeunesse but get off at the Fontaine Laborde stop.

Camping de la Chambre d'Amour (☎ 59.03.71.66) on Rue Julien Castanier, an unspectacular place open from late April to mid-September, is also popular with young people. It charges 17FF for a camp site, 17FF per adult (25% less from late April to June) and 10FF to park. It's a bit of a hike from the Chapelle stop on bus line No 6.

Camping Municipal de l'Adour (☎ 59.63. 16.16) at 130 Ave de l'Adour is on the south bank of the Adour River, 500 metres from the beach. It is open from early June to mid-September and charges 11FF per person, 12.80FF for a rather exposed camp site and 4.20FF to park. Necessary improvements have not been made because this place may be replaced by a pleasure-boat port. To get there, take bus No 4 to the second-last stop.

In southern Anglet, on the south side of Aérodrome de Parme (the airport), the three-star *Camping de Parme* (☎ 59.23.03.00) on Route de l'Aviation is open all year. Charges are 18FF per adult and 30FF per tent site, including parking. The nearest bus stop (called Parme) is a bit over one km to the north-west – it's near the airport end of line No 6. The Biarritz-La Négresse train station is 1.5 km south-west of the camping ground.

Hostel The *Auberge de Jeunesse d'Anglet*

(☎ 59.63.86.49; fax 59.63.38.92) at 19 Route des Vignes in Anglet (postcode 64600) is one of the liveliest youth hostels in France. It is open from February to November; reception hours are 8.30 to 10 am and 6 to 10 pm (8.30 am to 10 pm in July and August). A bed in a seven-person dorm costs 60FF, including breakfast. There are no kitchen facilities, but lunch and dinner are available. In summer, come by between 8.30 and 10 am to get one of the few spots that open up each morning. For information on sports courses, see Activities. Guests can rent bicycles for 50FF a day, surfboards for 30FF an hour and body boards and flippers for 25FF an hour.

To get there from the Bayonne train station, take bus No 4 to La Barre and then catch bus No 6 (or, during summer, the Navette des Plages) to the Auberge de Jeunesse stop. You can also take bus No 1 or 2 to Biarritz and change to a northbound bus No 6 (or the Navette des Plages). From the Biarritz-La Négresse train station, take bus No 6.

Hotels Bayonne is well-supplied with cheap hotels. In summer, they fill up by noon.

Hotels – Saint Esprit The *Hôtel Paris-Madrid* (☎ 59.55.13.98) is to the left as you exit the train station. Run by a friendly English-speaking couple who have lived in Canada and England, the hotel is popular with young travellers. The cheapest singles cost 80FF, and big, pleasant doubles without/with shower cost 110/130FF. Doubles/triples/quads with shower and toilet are 150/180/210FF, and hall showers are 10FF. Reception is open 24 hours a day.

The *Hôtel de la Gare* (☎ 59.55.06.63), which is in the train station building under the clock tower, has singles/doubles with shower from 90/120FF. Triples and quads cost 200FF. Reception is at the bar in the restaurant.

The *Hôtel du Moulin* (☎ 59.55.13.29) at 12 Rue Sainte Catherine, run by a welcoming older couple who lived in California for a number of years, may be the best deal in town. Singles cost 75 to 90FF, doubles are 90 or 105FF, and triples/quads cost anywhere from 115 to 180FF. Showers are 10FF. The ground-floor restaurant serves excellent meals.

The *Hôtel Beausoleil* (☎ 59.55.00.10), up the block at 23 Rue Sainte Catherine, has doubles starting at 130FF; showers are free. The more pleasant *Hôtel San Miguel* (☎ 59.55.17.82) at 8 Rue Sainte Catherine is slightly more expensive. Spacious doubles with big beds cost 140/170FF without/with shower; doubles with shower and toilet are 190FF with one bed and 240FF with two beds. Hall showers are 15FF.

The *Hôtel Côte d'Argent* (☎ 59.55.17.68) at 5 Blvd Alsace-Lorraine has singles/doubles/triples from 100/120/150FF. Reception is closed on Sunday except from mid-July to August. The entire hotel is closed in October.

The *Hôtel Monte Carlo* (☎ 59.55.02.68), owned by the same people as the Hôtel de la Gare, is opposite the train station at 1 Rue Sainte Ursule. Singles and doubles start at 80FF (130FF with a shower); hall showers are free. Telephone reservations are not accepted.

The *Hôtel Vauban* (☎ 59.55.11.31) at 13 Rue Sainte Ursule has average singles/doubles with shower for 140/180FF. A two-bed quad with shower is 180FF.

You might also try the less-than-spotless and chaotically managed *Hôtel La Crémaillère* (☎ 59.55.12.35) at 3 Rue Sainte Ursule, which has run-down doubles starting at 72FF (97FF with shower). Hall showers are 10FF. Reception is open daily until at least midnight.

Hotels – Grand Bayonne The one-star *Hôtel des Arceaux* (☎ 59.59.15.53) is right in the middle of Grand Bayonne at 26 Rue Port-Neuf. Large but rather bare doubles/triples with washbasin and bidet cost 120/155FF; doubles/triples with shower, toilet and TV are 175/215FF.

Hotels – Petit Bayonne The least expensive hotel in Petit Bayonne is the *Hôtel des*

Basques (☎ 59.59.08.02), next to 3 Rue des Lisses (on Place Paul Bert). Large, nonde-script singles and doubles with washbasin and bidet start at 80FF (135FF with two beds). Singles and doubles with shower and toilet are 125FF (170FF with two beds). Showers cost 10FF. This place is closed for three weeks in October.

Places to Stay – middle
Saint Esprit The two-star, 46-room *Hôtel Côte Basque* (☎ 59.55.10.21) at 2 Rue Maubec has unsurprising doubles with fairly spacious bathrooms for 170FF (with wash-basin) or 290FF (with shower, toilet and TV). Two-bed doubles/quads with shower, toilet and TV are 310/350FF.

Grand Bayonne The two-star, 41-room *Hôtel des Basses Pyrénées* (☎ 59.59.00.29; fax 59.59.42.02) has entrances at Place des Victoires and 12 Rue Tour de Sault. Doubles/triples/quads with shower and toilet start at 280/350/400FF. There are also a few rooms with washbasin for 150 to 190FF.

Places to Stay – top end
Saint Esprit The three-star *Hôtel Loustau* (☎ 59.55.16.74; fax 59.55.69.36) at 1 Place de la République occupies a recently reno-vated building that dates from 1785. Sparsely adorned doubles/triples with shower cost 310/450FF, and doubles with shower and toilet are 450FF. From October to May prices are 3% to 5% less. There are good views of the river from the upper floors. Reception is open 24 hours a day.

Places to Eat
Bayonne offers a wide variety of moderately priced dining options. Many of the restau-rants in Saint Esprit are along Rue Sainte Catherine.

Restaurants – French One of Bayonne's best restaurants is elegant *Auberge du Cheval Blanc* (☎ 59.59.01.33) at 68 Rue Bourgneuf, whose offerings include unique dishes invented by the young chef. *Menus* cost 130, 178, 228 and 350FF. It is open

Tuesday to Sunday from noon to 3 pm and 8 to 10.30 pm (daily from July to September). Reservations are necessary on holidays.

Restaurant de la Tour (☎ 59.59.05.67) at 5 Rue des Faures has *menus* of regional cuisine for 70FF (lunch only; not available on Sunday), 98FF and 170FF. Is is open from noon to 2.30 pm and 7.30 to 10.30 pm (closed Tuesday).

Restaurant Au Clos Saint Esprit (☎ 59.55. 16.74), in the Hôtel Loustau at 1 Place de la République, has traditional French cuisine and regional specialities. *Menus* cost 80, 100 and 160FF (50FF for children). Meat dishes are 55 to 90FF and fish dishes are 77 to 89FF. It is open daily (Monday to Friday from November to Easter).

Restaurants – Basque Bayonne is an excellent place to sample Basque cuisine.

In Saint Esprit, *Restaurant Koskera* (☎ 59.55.20.79) at 3 Rue Hugues has *plats du jour* of hearty Basque fare for 35FF, *menus* from 59FF and a selection of salads. It is open Monday to Saturday from noon to 2 pm only. From mid-June to September it's also open in the evening from 8 to 10.30 pm.

Restaurant Maisterrena (☎ 59.55.15.13) at 3 Place de la République (next to the Hôtel Loustau on Rue Neuve), is marked by a sign reading 'Hôtel, Restaurant, Bar'. Four-course *menus* of cafeteria-quality food cost 40FF and, though the plates and glasses are chipped, the food seems to be a real hit with the almost-exclusively local clientele. This place is open for meals from noon to 2 or 2.30 pm and 7 to 8.30 pm daily except Sunday evening.

The restaurant of the *Hôtel du Moulin* (☎ 59.55.13.29) at 12 Rue Sainte Catherine is a real centre of neighbourhood social life. Great five-course *menus* cost about 60FF. In general, meals are served only to people staying at the hotel, but if you ask Madame Idiart she might make an exception.

In Petit Bayonne, *Restaurant Euskalduna* (☎ 59.59.28.02) at 61 Rue Pannecau has a *menu* for 100FF and main dishes for 70 to 90FF. Most of the clients are locals. It is open

Tuesday to Saturday from noon to 2 pm and 7.30 to 9.30 pm.

In Grand Bayonne, a good bet is the unpretentious *Restaurant Dacquois* (☎ 59.59.29.61) at 48 Rue d'Espagne. It is open Monday to Saturday from 8 am to 8.30 pm and serves breakfast, lunch and dinner. *Menus* with a choice of various main dishes and hors d'œuvres costs 52FF.

Crêperie de la Rade de Brest (☎ 59.59.13.62) at 7 Rue des Basques uses traditional Breton recipes brought all the way from Brittany by its Brest-born owner. Both crepes and galettes cost 10 to 34FF. It is open Tuesday to Saturday from noon to 2 pm and 7 to 10 pm (11 pm on Friday and Saturday). During July and August it is also open on Monday evening.

Pizzerias *Restaurant/Pizzeria La Flambée* (☎ 59.55.08.45) at 11 Rue Sainte Catherine has a medieval, agricultural and maritime décor and serves pizza, fish and grilled-meat dishes. The *menu* costs 75FF. It is open daily except Sunday at midday and Wednesday (daily except for Sunday lunch in July and August).

The small *Pizzeria Catal* (☎ 59.55.18.29) at 14 Blvd Alsace-Lorraine has pizzas from 33 to 40FF and spaghetti for 25 to 40FF. It is open Monday to Saturday.

In Grand Bayonne, *Pizzeria El Rialto* (☎ 59.59.02.30) at 7 Rue du 49ème Régiment d'Infanterie is open from noon to 2.15 pm and 7 to 10 pm (10.30 pm in summer) daily except Sunday and holidays. Pizzas and pasta dishes cost 34 to 59FF.

Other *La Djurjura* (☎ 59.25.56.63) at 8 Rue Pontrique serves the cuisine of the Kabyles, a Berber people most of whom live in Algeria. It is open daily. *Restaurant Agadir* (☎ 59.55.66.56) at 3 Rue Sainte Catherine has southern Moroccan-style couscous for 50 to 70FF and *menus* for 45, 65 and 75FF. It is open Tuesday to Sunday from noon to 2 pm and 7 to 11 pm.

Restaurant Gandhi (☎ 59.25.55.25) at 29 Rue d'Espagne, run by immigrants from Darjeeling, is Bayonne's only Indian restaurant. Offerings include tandoori specialities, various dishes fried in butter and lassis (15 to 19FF). The four vegetarian dishes cost about 37FF. A 60FF *menu* is available for lunch except on Sunday and holidays. It is open Tuesday to Sunday (daily except Monday at midday in August and September).

El Mosquito (☎ 59.25.78.05) at 12 Rue Gosse has dishes from all over Central and South America. The 70FF *menus* – one vegetarian, the other with meat – are available nightly (until 8.30 pm on Friday and Saturday). The restaurant, owned by a Spaniard who has travelled widely in Latin America, is open for dinner only from Monday to Saturday (daily from July to September).

Self-Catering Most food stores are closed on Sunday and, often, all or part of Saturday or Monday as well.

Near the train station, *Boulangerie Devant* at 36 Place de la République is open from 7 am to 1 pm and 3 to 7.30 pm daily except Sunday afternoon. Along nearby Rue Sainte Catherine, there are *fruit & vegetable shops* at Nos 10 and 29 (both closed Sunday and on Monday afternoon), a *grocery* at No 39 (closed Saturday afternoon and Sunday) and a *boulangerie* at No 43. The *Squale supermarket* at 17 Blvd Alsace-Lorraine is open Monday to Saturday from 8.30 am to 12.30 pm and 3 to 7.20 pm (no midday closure on Saturday).

Grand Bayonne's central market, *Les Halles*, is on the west quai of the Nive, but until a new building goes up where the old one used to be, the stalls have moved to a *marché provisoire* (temporary market) on the east side of the Nive just north of Pont du Génie. Les Halles are usually open Tuesday to Saturday from 6 am to 1 pm and Thursday to Saturday from 3.30 to 6.30 or 7 pm (6 pm in winter), but the temporary market may be open only in the morning.

In Grand Bayonne the *Prisunic*, with entrances at 27 Rue Victor Hugo and 1-3 Quai Amiral Dubourdieu, is open Monday to Saturday from 8.30 am to 7 pm. The food section is on the 1st floor. The *Monoprix supermarket* at 8 Rue Orbe, open the same days and hours, has a small food section at the back. There are a number of food stores along Rue Port-Neuf and Rue d'Espagne.

Entertainment
Cinema *Cinéma L'Atalante* (☎ 59.55.76.63) at 7 Rue Denis Etcheverry in Saint Esprit screens nondubbed films. A ticket costs 33FF.

Bars There are lots of small bars scattered around Petit Bayonne, especially along Rue Bourgneuf.

Pelote Basque From October to May or June, *Trinquet Saint André* (☎ 59.59.18.69), in Petit Bayonne at 18 Rue du Trinquet, has professional main nue matches every Thursday at 4 pm. Entry costs 35FF or 45FF, depending on where you sit.

Bullfighting In summer corridas are held at the *Arènes* (Arena), which is 800 metres west of Grand Bayonne along Ave du Maréchal Foch.

Things to Buy
Bayonne has long been known for its fine chocolate, which can be purchased at several shops along partly arcaded Rue Port-Neuf, including Daranatz at No 15 and Cazenave at No 19.

Zabal Diffusion (☎ 59.25.43.90) at 52 Rue Pannecau has a large selection of cassettes (55 to 90FF) and CDs of Basque music. It also carries lots of books (including a few in English) on Basque history and culture and hiking in the Basque country. It is open from 9.15 am to 12.30 pm and 2.30 to 7.30 pm daily except Monday morning and Sunday.

There's a *marché de brocante* (flea market) every Friday morning from 8 am to noon at Place de l'Arsenal.

Getting There & Away
Air The airport serving Bayonne, Biarritz and Anglet, Aérodrome de Parme, is five km

south-west of central Bayonne and 2½ km south-east of the centre of Biarritz.

Train The train station (☎ 59.55.50.50 for information) is in Saint Esprit at Place de la Gare. The information office is open Monday to Saturday from 9 am to noon and 2 to 6.30 pm. In July and August, it's open daily from 9 am to 7.30 pm. There are luggage lockers with a 72-hour maximum time limit on platform 1.

TGVs to/from Paris's Gare Montparnasse (341FF plus TGV reservation fee) take five hours. The three daily non-TGV trains to Paris's Gare d'Austerlitz take about eight hours. Within the Basque Country, there are fairly frequent trains to Saint Jean de Luz (21FF; 25 minutes) and Saint Jean Pied de Port (41FF) and the Franco-Spanish border towns of Hendaye (33FF; 40 minutes) and Irún. There are also trains to Bordeaux (122FF; 1½ hours by TGV; about a dozen a day), Lourdes (91FF; six a day), Nice (405FF; one overnight train, one all-day train), Pau (72FF; 1⅓ to two hours; eight a day) and Toulouse (180FF; four hours).

Bus ATCRB's rather slow buses (☎ 59.26.06.99 in Saint Jean de Luz) follow the coast from Bidart (9.90FF) to Saint Jean de Luz (17.80FF; 40 minutes) and also serve Hendaye (29.80FF; 1½ hours). There are 12 runs a day (eight on Sunday and holidays) between 8 am and 8 pm. From Monday to Saturday, there are two to four buses a day to the Spanish city of San Sebastián (40.50FF; 1¾ hours). Both lines leave from the ATCRB bus stop at 9 Rue du 49ème Régiment d'Infanterie. Because of summer-season traffic, the trips sometimes take twice as long as scheduled.

Bayonne's tiny bus station (☎ 59.55.17.59) is next to the train station at Place de la Gare. It is open weekdays from 9 am to noon and 2 to 6 pm. Tickets are sold on the buses. RDTL serves destinations in Landes, the département north of Pyrénées-Atlantiques (the département in which Bayonne is located), including Capbreton, Dax (38FF), Léon, Seignosse and Vieux

Boucau-les-Bains. To get to the beaches along the coast north of Bayonne (eg Mimizan and Moliets), take the line to Vieux Boucau (33.50FF; 1¼ hours). TPR has buses to Pau.

The Eurolines office (☎ 59.59.19.33) at 3 Place De Gaulle has buses to London (20 hours), Tangier (Morocco; 23 hours), Madrid and other places all over Spain and Portugal. It is open on weekdays from 9 am to noon and 2 to 6 pm. In July and August it's open Tuesday to Saturday from 10 am to noon and 2 to 6 pm.

Car ADA (☎ 59.55.71.96) has an office two blocks from the train station at 10 Quai de Lesseps. It is open Monday to Saturday from 8 am to 7 pm.

Getting Around
To/From the Airport Bus No 6 links BAB's airport, Aérodrome de Parme, with Biarritz and Anglet.

Bus The bus network linking Bayonne, Biarritz and Anglet is known as STAB. Tickets cost 7FF if bought on board or 5.40FF each if purchased in carnets of five or ten (4.20FF for children aged four to 10), available at STAB kiosks and some tabacs. Tickets remain valid for an hour after they have been time-stamped. The times that buses leave their end-of-the-line stations are posted at bus stops (plastic posts that look like the handle of a giant, cheap dinner knife with the blade plunged into the pavement).

In Grand Bayonne, STAB's information and ticket kiosk (☎ 59.59.04.61) at Place du Réduit is open Monday to Saturday from 7.30 am to 6.30 pm.

Line No 1 links the Bayonne train station with the centre of Biarritz. On weekdays, the last buses in both directions leave at about 8.40 pm. On Saturday and Sunday nights and every day during the summer school holidays (approximately July and August), the last Bayonne-Biarritz bus departs at 11.20 pm and the last Biarritz-Bayonne bus begins its run at about midnight.

Line No 2 starts at the Bayonne train station and passes through the centre of Biarritz before continuing on to the Biarritz-La Négresse train station. The last bus in both directions begins its run every evening at 8 pm (about 7.30 pm on Sunday and holidays).

Bus No 6 links the centre of Biarritz with the Anglet coast (to the north) and the airport (to the south-east). It runs 12 or 13 times a day from 7 am (8 am on Sunday and holidays) to about about 7.15 pm.

From July to mid-September *only*, STAB's Navette des Plages (beach shuttle) connects central Biarritz with the beach-lined Anglet coast (to the north) and Plage de la Côte des Basques (to the south). It runs at least once an hour from 9.40 am to 7 pm (10.20 am to 6.20 pm on Sunday and holidays).

Taxi There's a taxi rank in front of the train station. The trip from Bayonne to Biarritz costs 70 to 80FF, depending on the traffic (100FF at night). To order a taxi, call ☎ 59.59.48.48.

Bicycle In July and August, Société DL (☎ 59.55.71.67) at 27 Rue Sainte Catherine rents mountain bikes for 25/70/100FF per hour/half-day/day. It is open Monday to Saturday from 9 am to 1 pm and 2 to 9 pm.

BIARRITZ
The classy coastal town of Biarritz (population 26,000 in winter, about 100,000 in mid-summer), eight km west of Bayonne, got its start as a beach resort for Europe's aristocracy in 1854, when Spanish-born Empress Eugénie and her husband, Emperor Napoleon III, began coming here. In later decades, Biarritz became popular with wealthy Britons and was visited by Queen Victoria and King Edward VII, both of whom have streets named in their honour. These days, the Biarritz area still draws an international crowd thanks to its fine beaches, casinos and some of the best surfing in Europe; though it once billed itself as the 'queen of resorts and the resort of kings', it's now more commonly referred to as *la Californie de l'Europe* (the California of Europe). The 'season' lasts from June to September.

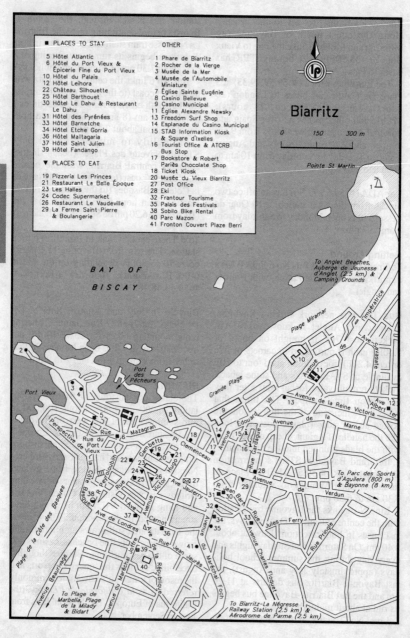

■ PLACES TO STAY

5 Hôtel Atlantic
6 Hôtel du Port Vieux &
  Épicerie Fine du Port Vieux
10 Hôtel du Palais
12 Hôtel Leihora
22 Château Silhouette
25 Hôtel Berthouet
30 Hôtel Le Dahu & Restaurant
  Le Dahu
31 Hôtel des Pyrénées
33 Hôtel Barnetche
34 Hôtel Etche Gorria
36 Hôtel Maïtagaria
37 Hôtel Saint Julien
39 Hôtel Fandango

▼ PLACES TO EAT

19 Pizzeria Les Princes
21 Restaurant La Belle Époque
23 Les Halles
24 Codec Supermarket
26 Restaurant Le Vaudeville
29 La Ferme Saint Pierre
  & Boulangerie

OTHER

1 Phare de Biarritz
2 Rocher de la Vierge
3 Musée de la Mer
4 Musée de l'Automobile
  Miniature
7 Église Sainte Eugénie
8 Casino Bellevue
9 Casino Municipal
11 Église Alexandre Newsky
13 Freedom Surf Shop
14 Esplanade du Casino Municipal
15 STAB Information Kiosk
  & Square d'Ixelles
16 Tourist Office & ATCRB
  Bus Stop
17 Bookstore & Robert
  Pariès Chocolate Shop
18 Ticket Kiosk
20 Musée du Vieux Biarritz
27 Post Office
28 Eki
32 Frantour Tourisme
35 Palais des Festivals
38 Sobilo Bike Rental
40 Parc Mazon
41 Fronton Couvert Plaze Berri

Biarritz

0   150   300 m

Pointe St Martin

BAY OF BISCAY

To Anglet Beaches,
Auberge de Jeunesse
d'Anglet (2.5 km) &
Camping Grounds

Plage Miramar

Port
des
Pêcheurs

Port Vieux

Grande Plage

Avenue de la Reine Victoria

To Parc des Sports
d'Aguilera (800 m)
& Bayonne (8 km)

Plage de la Côte des Basques

To Plage de
Marbella, Plage
de la Milady
& Bidart

To Biarritz-La Négresse
Railway Station (2.5 km) &
Aérodrome de Parme (2.5 km)

Top: Vieux Port & Tour de la Grosse Horloge, La Rochelle (DR)
Left: Old city gate, Bordeaux (GA)
Right: Farm scene in the Landes département (GC)

Top: Stained-glass angel, Musee des Beaux-Arts, Dijon (GE)
Middle: Ceiling by Marc Chagall, old Paris Opera House, Paris (GE)
Bottom: Paintings in the Louvre, Paris (PS)

The wealth assembled in Biarritz is given a cosmopolitan aspect by assorted incongruous imports: Southern California-style surf shops, a blue-domed Russian Orthodox church, and feet shod in boating shoes à la New England. But even more than the town itself, it's the summer visitors who exude prosperity, and the sense of entitlement that comes with it.

Orientation

The centre of Biarritz is Place Clemenceau, which is 200 metres south of the southern end of the main beach, the Grande Plage. Lighthouse-topped Pointe Saint Martin is at the northern end of Plage Miramar, the northern continuation of the Grande Plage.

The hilltop Port Vieux area is 400 metres west of Place Clemenceau around the Port Vieux (Old Port), the little inlet just south of the statue-topped rock known as Rocher de la Vierge.

Information

Tourist Office The tourist office (☎ 59.24. 20.24), one block east of Ave Édouard VII at Square d'Ixelles, is open daily from 9 am to 12.30 pm and 2 to 6.15 pm (3 to 6 pm on weekends). From June to September opening hours are 8 am to 8 pm. Maps of the town cost 1FF. The city's monthly guide to sporting events, concerts and other cultural activities is called *Biarritzcope*.

From June to August you can also pick up the *Programme des Fêtes en Pays Basque*, a listing of cultural activities around the French Basque Country. The tourist office does not handle local hotel reservations, but you can book a room in other parts of France for 22FF.

Money There are lots of commercial banks around Place Clemenceau.

Post The post office is one block south of Places Clemenceau on Rue de la Poste. It's open weekdays from 8.30 am to 7 pm and on Saturday from 8.30 am to noon.

Biarritz's postcode is 64200.

Travel Agencies For information on Frantour Tourisme, see Train under Getting There & Away.

Bookshops Bookstore (☎ 59.24.48.00) at 27 Place Georges Clemenceau has a small selection of English books.

Walking Tour

The most imposing landmark along the **Grande Plage** (see Beaches) is the stately **Hôtel du Palais**, a palace-sized villa built for the Empress Eugénie (wife of Napoleon III and empress of France from 1853-71) in 1854 and now used as a luxury hotel. King Edward VII stayed here in 1906 and 1910. Across Ave de l'Impératrice is **Église Alexandre Newsky**, a Russian Orthodox church built to serve the spiritual needs of the Russian aristocrats who used to come here before the Russian Revolution of 1917.

To the north, on vegetation-covered Pointe Saint Martin, you can see the **Phare de Biarritz** (Biarritz Lighthouse), whose tip is 73 metres above sea level. From mid-June to mid-September the small **rocky islets** at the south end of the Grande Plage are illuminated on Wednesday and Saturday nights from about 10.30 to 11.30 pm.

From below the Casino Bellevue, which is at the south end of the Grande Plage, a **promenade** follows the rocky coast above the old **Port des Pêcheurs** (fishing port), these days filled with bobbing pleasure boats. The Byzantine and Moorish-style **Église Sainte Eugénie** at Place Sainte Eugénie was built in 1864 for – who else? – Empress Eugénie.

The mauve cliffs continue westward to **Rocher de la Vierge** (Rock of the Virgin), a stone island reached by a bridge that gets splashed in stormy weather. It is named after the white statue of the Virgin and baby Jesus on top, protected by some nasty steel spikes. From the rock, you can see the coast of the Landes département stretching northward and, far to the south, the mountains of the Spanish Basque Country.

Just west of Rocher de la Vierge there are two interesting museums: the Musée de la

Mer and the Musée de l'Automobile Miniature. The narrow streets of the **Port Vieux area**, which overlooks a small beach, are a few hundred metres to the south-east.

Along the south side of the promontory is a hillside road aptly named **Perspective de la Côte Basque**. It affords views of Plage de la Côte des Basques and the coastal cliffs that run southward.

Musée de la Mer

Biarritz's Museum of the Sea (☎ 59.24. 02.59), completely redone in 1992, is on Esplanade des Anciens Combattants next to the footbridge to Rocher de la Vierge. The ground-floor **aquarium** has 24 tanks of underwater beasties from the Bay of Biscay (Golfe de Gascogne), the area of the Atlantic bound by the south-west coast of France and the north coast of Spain. The 1st floor has exhibits on commercial fishing and whaling, as Biarritz was once a whaling port. The four *phoques* (seals), one of which is blind, are fed in their seawater pool daily at 10.30 am and 5 pm. A nearby pool holds *requins* (sharks), fed on Tuesday and Friday at 11 am and on Wednesday and Sunday at 4.30 pm.

The museum is open daily from 9.30 am to 12.30 pm and 2 to 6 pm. Opening hours in July and August are 9 am to midnight. Entry is 40FF (30FF for students, 20FF for children aged 5 to 12).

Musée de l'Automobile Miniature

This museum of miniature motorcars (☎ 59.24.56.88), situated right behind the Musée de la Mer at the top of the hill, is a veritable paradise for kids who like tiny toy cars. Even adults could easily spend several hours examining the 7000 palm-sized vehicles from around the world, arranged by make and use. The construction equipment is almost all yellow, while the fire engines are nearly all painted red.

The Musée de l'Automobile Miniature is open daily from 2 to 6 pm and, on weekends and during school holiday periods, from 10 am to noon. From mid-June to mid-September it's open daily from 10 am to 7 pm. Entry is 20FF (15FF for children aged six to 17).

Musée du Vieux Biarritz

The Museum of Old Biarritz (☎ 59.24. 86.28), in a desanctified Anglican church on Rue Broquedis, has exhibits on the history of Biarritz. It is open from 3 to 6 pm daily except Thursday and Sunday.

Beaches

Biarritz's fashionable beaches are wall-to-wall with people on sunny summer days. They are especially crowded at high tide, when row after row of bathers get chased up the beach to the dwindling strip of dry sand.

In season, the **Grande Plage** is lined with brightly coloured striped bathing tents. North of the Hôtel du Palais is **Plage Miramar**, bound on the north by Pointe Saint Martin. At low tide (ie when not all the sand is below the water line, there is **nude bathing** at the northern end of Plage Miramar (beyond the boulders).

North of Pointe Saint Martin, the fine beaches of **Anglet** stretch northward for four km. They are served by bus No 6 and the Navette des Plages.

South of Rocher de la Vierge, there is a small, protected beach at the **Port Vieux**. The long, exposed **Plage de la Côte des Basques**, which completely disappears at high tide, begins a few hundred metres farther down the coast. The cliff above the Plage de la Côte des Basques has been stabilised at great expense.

At the southern end of Plage de la Côte des Basques are two more beaches: **Plage de Marbella** and **Plage de la Milady**. By bus, take line No 6 or the Navette des Plages to the Marbella stop.

Surfing

For information on surfing courses, contact the tourist office or Freedom Surf Shop (☎ 59.24.38.40, 59.23.34.13) at 2 Ave de la Reine Victoria. Count on paying about 300FF for a day's instruction.

Ice Skating

After baking by the seaside, you can slide around on the icy expanses of the Patinoire d'Anglet (☎ 59.63.17.30), also known as

Patinoire de la Barre, which is on the beach near where the northern end of Blvd des Plages meets the western end of Ave de l'Adour. To get there, take bus No 4 or 6 or the Navette des Plages to their northern termini.

The rink is open every afternoon from 2 to 5 pm (6 pm on Sunday), Tuesday to Saturday night from 9 to 11 pm and Sunday morning from 9 to 11 am. July and August hours are slightly different. Entry costs 18FF (12FF on Wednesday and Thursday nights and Sunday morning except in July and August). Skate rental is 13FF.

Pelote Basque

Introductory 1½-hour cesta punta lessons are available in Biarritz for 100FF per person (including equipment) for a minimum of four people. For information, contact the Biarritz Athlétique Club (☎ 59.23.91.09), whose office is two km east of the centre of Biarritz in the Parc des Sports d'Aguilera on Ave Henri Haget. You will need to book a few days in advance.

Golf

There are a number of golf courses in Anglet. For details, contact the tourist office.

Places to Stay – bottom end

Cheap hotels are a fast-disappearing species in Biarritz, but the town has quite a selection of decent, two-star hotels in the 250FF a night range, some of them housed in converted 19th-century villas.

From September to June it is relatively easy to find rooms in Biarritz. In July and August, however, when all the hotels are packed to the gills, it may be worthwhile staying in Bayonne and commuting to Biarritz by bus, especially if you're on a tight budget.

Camping & Hostel For details on Anglet's camping options and the Auberge de Jeunesse d'Anglet, see Places to Stay in the Bayonne section. The *Hôtel Barnetche* (☎ 59.24.22.25) at 5 Rue Charles Floquet has dorm beds for 80FF per person.

Hotels The friendly *Hôtel Berthouet* (☎ 59. 24.63.36), near Les Halles at 29 Rue Gambetta, has clean singles/doubles with hardwood floors and slightly outdated furnishings for 110/130FF with washbasin, 160/190FF with washbasin and bidet and 180/210FF with shower. Prices are a bit lower in winter. Hall showers are 20FF. It is open all year and is an excellent deal. Reception is staffed daily until 10 pm.

Nearby, the *Château Silhouette* (☎ 59.24. 20.83) at 30 Rue Gambetta, built in 1730, is a gem of an old-fashioned hotel. By decision of the feisty proprietor, it is open from June to October *only*. Large, simply furnished singles and doubles cost 125 to 150FF. There may be a one-week minimum stay. Hall showers are 15FF.

The friendly *Hôtel Fandango* (☎ 59.24. 23.42) at 13 Ave Maréchal Joffre is open from May to September *only*. Simple singles/doubles of good size start at 160/190FF with washbasin and bidet and 190/250 with shower. Hall showers are free.

The one-star *Hôtel des Pyrénées* (☎ 59. 24.20.22) at 3 Rue de Gascogne has singles/doubles/triples from 140/160/170FF.

You might also try the *Hôtel Leihora* (☎ 59.24.28.31) at 8 Rue Albert 1er, which has singles and doubles, some with kitchenettes, for 120 to 160FF in the off season and 220FF in summer. All rooms have showers.

Places to Stay – middle

The two-star, 11-room *Hôtel Etche Gorria* (☎ 59.24.00.74) at 21 Ave du Maréchal Foch (next to the Palais des Festivals) occupies a converted villa with a lovely terrace and has a park across the street. Doubles with washbasin and bidet start at 150FF, and doubles with shower and toilet are 240FF. Hall showers are free. An extra bed costs 70FF. It is open all year.

The *Hôtel Maïtagaria* (☎ 59.24.26.65) at 34 Ave Carnot, under the same management since 1968, has large, comfortable and spotless singles/doubles/triples/quads with shower, toilet and TV for 180/230/ 275/290FF. The common sitting room has a fireplace. The hotel is open all year long.

BASQUE COUNTRY

The *Hôtel Saint Julien* (☎ 59.24.20.39) at 20 Ave Carnot is open from mid-March to November. Doubles with shower and toilet cost 220FF (300FF in July and August).

The one-star, seven-room *Hôtel Le Dahu* (☎ 59.24.26.38) at 6 Rue Jean Bart is open all year. Large but ordinary and somewhat shabby singles/doubles/triples/quads with shower and toilet cost 170/190/250/270FF. Singles with shower are 160FF. Reception, which is in the restaurant, is closed from 3 to 6 pm, and from October to mid-June on Monday also.

In the Port Vieux area, the *Hôtel du Port Vieux* (☎ 59.24.02.84) at 43 Rue Mazagran has large, eminently serviceable singles/doubles for 161/182FF with washbasin, 203/226FF with shower and 209/242FF with shower and toilet, including breakfast. Hall showers are 15FF. Telephone reservations are not generally accepted. Reception is open daily until 11 pm. This place is open from Easter to mid-November.

Nearby, the two-star *Hôtel Atlantic* (☎ 59.24.34.08) at 10 Rue du Port Vieux has singles/doubles with washbasin for 140/150FF and singles/doubles/triples/quads with shower and toilet for 160/210/250/260FF (a bit less in winter). Hall showers are 10FF per person. The Hôtel Atlantic is open all year, but it's a good idea to call ahead from November to February, when reception may not be staffed.

Places to Eat

Restaurants There are quite a few decent little restaurants scattered around Les Halles.

Restaurant Le Vaudeville (☎ 59.24.34.66) at 5 Rue du Centre serves high-quality regional cuisine in an elegant maroon dining room. Specialities include Basque cuisine from both sides of the Franco-Spanish border. Expect to pay about 150FF for an à la carte meal, including wine. Main dishes are 60 to 100FF. Le Vaudeville is closed Monday and on Tuesday at midday (but open on Monday evenings from June to September).

Not far away, *Restaurant La Belle Époque* (☎ 59.24.66.06) at 10 Rue Victor Hugo has a variety of French regional dishes as well as a few items from Spain and the Antilles. The décor was inspired by the *belle époque*, but the background music is 1930s-style jazz. Fish costs 75 to 110FF, meat dishes are 65 to 118FF. It is open from 12.15 to 2.30 pm and 7.15 to 10.30 pm (11 pm in summer) Tuesday to Sunday (daily in July and August).

Restaurant Le Dahu (☎ 59.24.26.38) at 6 Rue Jean Bart, attached to the hotel of the same name, serves traditional French cuisine daily except Monday (daily from 15 June to September) in a rustic dining room. Lunch and dinner *menus* cost 70, 105 and 150FF; the weekday plat du jour is 40FF.

Pizzeria Les Princes (☎ 59.24.21.78) at 13 Rue Gambetta has pizzas for 35 to 45FF and spaghetti for about 40FF. It is open from noon to 2 pm and 7 to 11 pm daily except Wednesday and on Thursday at midday. It is open daily in July and August but is closed from mid-December to mid-January. Takeaway food is available.

Self-Catering Biarritz's covered market, *Les Halles*, is two blocks south of Place Clemenceau. It is open daily from 5 am to 1.30 pm. There are lots of *food shops* in the immediate vicinity, including a *Codec supermarket* at 2 Rue du Centre.

A bit east of Place Clemenceau, *La Ferme Saint Pierre* at 14 Ave de Verdun sells cheese, wine and some ready-to-eat dishes. It is open Monday to Saturday from 8 am to 1 pm and 4 to 8 pm. There's a *boulangerie* almost next door at 16 Ave de Verdun.

In the Port Vieux area, *Épicerie Fine du Port Vieux* at 41 Rue Mazagran has cheese, wine, fruit, vegies and prepared foods, including foie gras and gâteau Basque (Basque-style cake). A convenient if pricey place to assemble a gourmet picnic, it is open daily from 7 am to 1 pm and 3 to 8.30 pm (7 am to 9 pm from June to October).

Entertainment

Reservations for many cultural and sporting events can be made at the ticket kiosk (☎ 59.24.69.20) at Place Clemenceau.

Pelote Basque From July to early September, *Fronton Couvert Plaze Berri* (☎ 59.22.15.72) at 42 Ave du Maréchal Foch has tournament play every Tuesday and Friday night at 9 pm. Tickets cost 35FF. During the rest of the year, various tournaments – including the Basque and French championships of *paleta cuir* and *pala corta* (kinds of pelota played with wooden racquets) – are held here, often on Sunday afternoons. Entry is free except for the semifinals and finals. When no matches are being played, you can visit the ball-scarred court – overlooked by three tiers of narrow balconies – by walking through the bar.

In July and August, the outdoor fronton (no tel) at *Parc Mazon*, which is off Ave du Maréchal Joffre, has chistera matches on Saturday afternoon, Monday night and sometimes on other nights.

Parc des Sports d'Aguilera (☎ 59.23.91.09), two km east of central Biarritz on Ave Henri Haget, has professional cesta punta matches from mid-June to mid-September every Wednesday and Saturday evening at 9 pm. Tickets cost 40 to 50FF, depending on the level of competition. Reservations can be made at the ticket kiosk at Place Clemenceau. The Parc des Sports is linked to Biarritz and Bayonne by bus No 1.

Cultural Events From mid-June to mid-September, the Gala Sportif et Folklorique (Sports & Folklore Gala) is held every Monday at 9 pm at Parc Mazon, off Ave du Maréchal Joffre. The show, which includes Basque dancing and a pelota exhibition, costs about 45FF.

During the same period, there are free concerts three nights a week at Place Clemenceau, the Port Vieux, in front of Église Sainte Eugénie and other venues around town. There's usually a folklore performance at Esplanade du Casino Municipal on Sunday nights. For details, contact the tourist office.

Things to Buy
Basque music and crafts and guidebooks to the Basque Country are available at Eki

(☎ 59.24.79.64), 21 Ave de Verdun, open from 9 am to noon and 3 to 7 pm daily except Sunday and Monday morning.

Delicious chocolates and Basque sweets (see Things to Buy in the Saint Jean de Luz section) can be purchased at Robert Pariès (☎ 59.22.07.52) at 27 Place Clemenceau.

Getting There & Away
Air See Air under Getting There & Away in the Bayonne section.

Train The Biarritz-La Négresse train station is three km south of the centre of Biarritz at the southern terminus of Ave du Président John F Kennedy (the southern continuation of Ave du Maréchal Foch). To get there from the centre of Biarritz or the Bayonne train station, take bus No 2.

Near the centre of Biarritz, SNCF information and tickets are available at Frantour Tourisme (☎ 59.24.00.94), a travel agency at 13 Ave du Maréchal Foch. It is open Monday to Friday from 9 am to noon and 1.30 or 2 to 6.30 pm and on Saturday morning. From April to September it is also open on Saturday afternoon from 2 to 5 pm.

Bus The rather slow buses run by ATCRB (☎ 59.26.06.99 in Saint Jean de Luz), which stop right outside the tourist office, follow the coast southward to Bidart, Saint Jean de Luz and Hendaye. From Monday to Saturday there are also buses to San Sebastián, Spain (33.50FF). Tickets are sold on board. See Bus under Getting There & Away in the Bayonne and Saint Jean de Luz sections for more information on ATCRB.

Hitching Don't bother trying to hitch between Bayonne and Biarritz – people don't stop.

Getting Around
To/From the Airport Aérodrome de Parme is linked to Biarritz by STAB bus No 6.

Bus For a rundown on the STAB bus system, which serves Bayonne, Anglet and Biarritz, see Getting Around in the Bayonne section.

Biarritz has a STAB information kiosk (☎ 59.24.26.53) on Ave Louis Barthou, which is across Square d'Ixelles from the tourist office. It is open Monday to Saturday from 8 am to noon and 1.30 to 6 pm.

Taxi To order a radio-dispatched taxi, call ☎ 59.23.62.62.

Motorbike & Bicycle Sobilo (☎ 59.24.94.47) at 24 Rue Peyroloubilh rents three speeds/mountain bikes for 45/90FF a day (plus a 500/1000FF deposit); 50 cc mopeds/scooters are 100/185FF (plus a 2000/3000FF deposit), including a helmet. The shop is open March to November from 9 am to noon and 3 to 7 pm daily, except Wednesday and Sunday. In July and August it's open daily from 9 am to 1 pm and 3 to 8 pm.

SAINT JEAN DE LUZ

The attractive seaside town of Saint Jean de Luz (Donibane Lohitzun in Basque; population 13,000), 20 km south-west of Bayonne at the mouth of the Nivelle River, is the most Basque of the region's beach resorts. Built along one side of a sheltered bay, it has a colourful history of whaling (begun in the 11th century) and privateering (17th to 19th centuries). Saint Jean de Luz and its sister-town of Ciboure make a perfect day trip from Bayonne or Biarritz.

Saint Jean de Luz is still an active fishing port and is known for its large catches of sardines (from the waters off Portugal and Morocco), tuna (from the Bay of Biscay and West Africa) and anchovies (from the Bay of Biscay).

Orientation

The train station is 500 metres south-east of the beach at the southern end of Ave de Verdun. The tourist office is 200 metres away at Place du Maréchal Foch, which is at the northern end of Ave de Verdun. The main streets in the town centre are pedestrianised Rue de la République and Rue Gambetta, which links Place Louis XIV with Blvd Thiers. The beach, divided from the centre of town by a dyke, is on the south-east side of an oval bay (Baie de Saint Jean de Luz) protected from the open ocean by three mid-19th-century *digues* (breakwaters).

Ciboure, Saint Jean's sister town, is on the left bank of the Nivelle River, which is spanned by Pont Charles de Gaulle.

Information

Tourist Office The tourist office (☎ 59.26.03.16) at Place du Maréchal Foch is open Monday to Saturday from 9 am to 12.30 pm and 2 to 7 pm. During July and August it's open Monday to Saturday from 9 am to 7.30 pm and on Sunday and holidays from 10 am to 12.30 pm. The staff do not usually make hotel reservations but will help foreigners who don't speak French. This is a good place to pick up train and ATCRB bus schedules.

Money The Société Générale (☎ 59.26.04.31) at 7 Blvd Victor Hugo is open Tuesday to Saturday from 8.30 am to 12.15 pm and 2.15 to 5 pm. Change Plus (☎ 59.51.03.43), an exchange bureau at 9 Rue du 14 Juillet (across from 27 Rue Gambetta), is open Monday to Saturday from 9.30 am to 12.30 pm and 2.30 to 7.30 pm. From June to September it's open Monday to Saturday from 8 am to 8 pm and on Sunday from 10 am to 1 pm and 4 to 7 pm.

Socoa Voyages (☎ 59.26.06.27; fax 59.51.09.27) at 31 Blvd Thiers, the only American Express office between Bordeaux and the Spanish border, can exchange American Express and other travellers' cheques, give cash advances, replace lost or stolen travellers' cheques (but not credit cards) and receive poste restante mail. It is open from 9 am to 12.30 pm and 2.30 to 6.30 pm daily except Sunday and holidays.

Post The post office at 44 Blvd Victor Hugo is open Monday to Friday from 9 am to 12.15 pm and 1.45 to 5.30 pm (8.30 am to 6 pm in July and August) and on Saturday from 8.30 am to noon.

In Ciboure, the post office at 3 Quai Maurice Ravel is open Monday to Friday from 9 am to noon and 2 to 5 pm and on Saturday from 9 am to noon.

BASQUE COUNTRY

Saint Jean de Luz

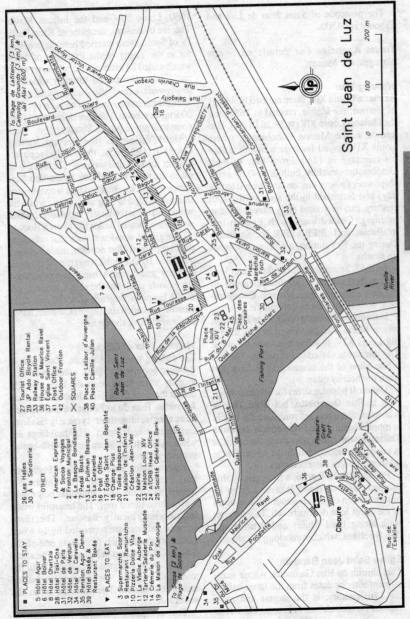

PLACES TO STAY
5 Hôtel Agur
6 Hôtel Bolívar
8 Hôtel Ohartzia
28 Hôtel Toki-Ona
31 Hôtel de Paris
32 Hôtel de Verdun
34 Hôtel La Caravelle
35 Pension Agur Deneri
39 Hôtel Bakéa &
   Restaurant Bakéa

PLACES TO EAT
3 Supermarché Score
9 Restaurant Ramuntcho
10 Pizzeria Dolce Vita
11 La Vieille Auberge
12 Tarterie-Saladerie Muscade
14 Crèmerie du Pin
19 La Maison de Kanouga

OTHER
1 American Express
   & Socoa Voyages
2 Fronton Municipal
4 Le Basque Bondissant
7 Pedal Boats
13 Le Pullman Basque
15 La Cave salée
16 Post Office
17 Église Saint Jean Baptiste
18 Change Plus
20 Toiles Basques Larre
21 Maison de l'Infante &
   Création Jean-Vier
22 Mairie
23 Maison Louis XIV
24 ATCRB Head Office
25 Société Générale Bank
26 Les Halles
30 À la Sardinerie
27 Tourist Office
29 JP Ado Bicycle Rental
33 Railway Station
36 House of Maurice Ravel
37 Église Saint Vincent
41 Post Office
42 Outdoor Fronton

× SQUARES
38 Place de Latour d'Auvergne
40 Place Camille Julian

The postcode of Saint Jean de Luz and Ciboure is 64500.

Travel Agencies For details on Socoa Voyages, see Money.

Walking Tour

At **Place Louis XIV**, there are two buildings of interest: the **Mairie**, erected in 1657, and the **Maison Louis XIV** (☎ 59.26.01.56), also known as the Maison Lohobiague, where Louis XIV stayed for over a month before his marriage in 1660. From May to mid-October, the structure, built in 1643 by a rich shipowner (whose descendants own it to this day) and furnished in the style of the 17th century, can be visited daily except Sunday morning. Guided tours, with English text available, cost 20FF (15FF for students). During the Revolution, a guillotine was set up nearby.

In 1558, Spanish troops sacked Saint Jean de Luz and started a fire that destroyed all but one stone building, **Maison Esquerrenea**, now on Rue de la République.

Maison de l'Infante on Quai de l'Infante, where Marie-Thérèse stayed before marrying Louis XIV, is a few blocks to the west. The interior is closed to the public. There is a fine **view** of the commercial fishing port from the nearby quay.

The most popular street for window shopping is **Rue Gambetta**, but **Blvd Thiers**, whose northern reaches run along the beach, is more elegant. Like **Promenade Jacques Thibaud**, which also runs along the beach, it is lined with modern buildings, most of them white or in light pastel colours.

Pointe Sainte Barbe, a promontory that juts into Baie de Saint Jean de Luz in its north-eastern corner, is about one km north of the Saint Jean de Luz beach. To get there, walk along Blvd Thiers and **Promenade des Rochers**, which runs along the shore.

Église Saint Jean Baptiste

This church on Rue Gambetta, whose magnificent interior dates from the latter half of the 17th century, is the largest and most famous Basque church in France. On 9 June

1660, Louis XIV and the infanta Marie-Thérèse of Austria, daughter of King Philip IV of Spain, were married here, as provided for in the Treaty of the Pyrenees of 1659, which ended 24 years of war between France and Spain. The **portal** through which the newlyweds exited the church was sealed after the ceremony and can be seen opposite 20 Rue Gambetta. The church is closed from noon to 2 pm (3 pm on Sunday).

Until Vatican II (the Second Vatican Council; 1962-65), there was separate seating for men and women. The men, who sat in the three tiers of **oak balconies** (five tiers at the back) – reached by a wrought-iron stairway – used to sing as a chorus while the women sat near the family sepulchres, which were once located under the church floor.

The gilded wooden statues that ornament the exceptional **altar screen**, made between 1665 and 1670, exhibit a mixture of classical severity and Spanish baroque exuberance. An *ex-voto* model of the ship *L'Aigle*, a gift of the Empress Eugénie after the real thing narrowly escaped sinking off Ciboure, hangs in the middle of the church.

Walking Tour of Ciboure

The fishing town of Ciboure (Zubiburu in Basque; population 5800), quieter and less touristy than Saint Jean de Luz, is right across the river from Saint Jean de Luz. **Rue Agorette, Rue de la Fontaine** and **Rue de l'Escalier** retain their typically Basque architecture and aspect. The buildings are white with either green or reddish-brown shutters and balconies.

Église Saint Vincent on Rue Pocalette, built during the 16th and 17th centuries, is topped by an unusual octagonal bell tower with a three-tiered roof. The beautiful wood interior is typically Basque. The three wooden galleries are supported by 14 wood pillars, each of which represents one of the Stations of the Cross in Jerusalem. The altars are beautifully sculpted and gilded. Until the mid-19th century, the dead were buried inside the church. The entrance is on the south side.

The composer **Maurice Ravel** (1875-

1937), whose mother was Basque (his father was Swiss), was born in the Dutch-style house at 27 Quai Maurice Ravel (No 12 by the old numbering).

The village of **Socoa** is 2.5 km north-west of Ciboure along Quai Maurice Ravel and its beachside continuation, Blvd Pierre Benoit. The **fort** was built in 1627 and was later improved by Vauban. You can walk out to the **Digue de Socoa**, the breakwater at the western tip of Baie de Saint Jean de Luz. Socoa is served by ATCRB buses.

Beaches

Saint Jean de Luz's sandy beach, popular with families, is fairly wide at low tide but gets progressively narrower as the tide comes in. In 1749 a tidal wave devastated much of the town.

Bathing tents, set up from June to September, cost 35FF a day. Parasols are 25FF a day. The daily rate for a *transat* (deck chair) is 15FF. You can also rent by the week, fortnight and month.

The **Plage de Socoa** is several km west of Ciboure along Blvd Pierre Benoit. It is served by ATCRB buses (see Bus under Getting There & Away).

Pedal Boats

From July to the first week in September, you can rent *pédalos* (catamaran pedal-boats; ☎ 59.26.97.41) on the beach between Rue Garet and Rue Tourasse for 30/50FF per half/whole hour.

Surfing

The sheltered Baie de Saint Jean de Luz is much too calm for surfing, but locals do manage to catch a few waves at **Plage de Lafitenia**, which is almost four km north-east of the centre of town near the camping grounds. It is served by ATCRB buses going to Bayonne and Biarritz.

Deep-Sea Fishing

In July and August, Le Basque Bondissant (☎ 59.26.25.87) at 100 Rue Gambetta runs daily deep-sea fishing trips (120FF) on the *Marie Rose* from 8 am to noon. From 2 to 4

pm, they have pleasure cruises down the coast to Spain.

Bullfighting

Saint Jean de Luz does not have its own bullfighting arena, but tickets for corridas in other parts of the French Basque Country are on sale during July and August at Le Pullman Basque (☎ 59.26.03.37), 33 Rue Gambetta.

Organised Tours

From June to September Le Pullman Basque (see previous paragraph) has half/full-day excursions for 75/110FF to San Sebastián, Pamplona, Guernica and other destinations in Spain. Buses leave from in front of the tourist office. The company's office is open from 9 am to noon and 2.30 to 6.30 pm daily except Saturday afternoon and Sunday.

From July to mid-September it's open daily from 9.30 am to 1 pm and 2.30 (3.30 pm on Sunday) to 8 pm.

Festivals

The *fête patronale* (saint's day) of Saint Jean Baptiste (St John the Baptist) is celebrated on the weekend before 24 June. The festivities begin on Friday night with a concert by local choral groups at Église Saint Jean Baptiste. On Saturday, bonfires are lit in front of the church and the Mairie. On Sunday, there are outdoor music and dance performances around town.

La Nuit de la Sardine (Night of the Sardine) is not a horror 'movie but rather an evening of music, folklore and dancing held twice each summer: on the Saturday that falls on or before 14 August and on the second Saturday in August. Staged outdoors next to the jaï alaï on Ave André Ithurralde, each of the 2000 places costs 40FF. Sardines, tuna, cakes, cheese, sandwiches, etc are on sale. The festivities begin at 9 pm.

La Nuit du Thon (Night of the Tuna), which falls on the first Saturday after 1 July, brings wandering musicians to Place du Maréchal Foch, Place des Corsaires, Quai Maréchal Leclerc and Ciboure. Local sports organisations set up stands and sell tuna-based dishes. There are also two balls: at

Place Foch, a local orchestra plays traditional Basque music and rock, while in a more formal venue, a larger orchestra plays music broadcast live by France Inter radio. Around midnight, there is a fireworks display at the port.

Places to Stay – bottom end

Many hotels get the same summer clients year after year, so it is extremely difficult to find a room in July and August, when in any case prices rise by 50% or more. During the same period, some hotels require that you take half-pension.

Camping About three km north of the centre of Saint Jean de Luz, eight camping grounds are located in an area not too far from the coast. *Camping Luz Europ* (☎ 59.26.51.90) in Quartier Acotz, open from mid-March to October, charges 17.50FF per adult and 25FF for a tent site, including parking.

Camping Elgar (☎ 59.26.85.85) in Quartier Erromardie is open from mid-April to September. Two people with a tent are charged 41FF (49FF with a car). To get there, you can take any of the ATCRB buses linking Saint Jean de Luz with Biarritz and Bayonne (see Bus under Getting There & Away).

Hotels Near the train station, a good non-summer option is the 14-room *Hôtel de Verdun* (☎ 59.26.02.55) at 13 Ave de Verdun. Ordinary but large doubles cost 130FF with washbasin and bidet, 145FF with shower and 180FF with bath and toilet (170, 220 and 255FF respectively from July to September). Hall showers are free. Some of the doubles have two large beds and can sleep up to four people. In July and August half-pension (120FF per person extra) is obligatory. This place is closed in December.

The 17-room *Hôtel Toki-Ona* (☎ 59.26.11.54) at 10 Rue Marion Garay, open from Easter to September, has singles/doubles/triples with washbasin and bidet for 120/145/170FF. Breakfast (24FF) is usually obligatory. Hall showers are 8FF.

Two blocks from the beach, the two-star *Hôtel Bolivar* (☎ 59.26.02.00) at 18 Rue

Sopite is open from June to September. Singles and doubles cost 160FF with washbasin, 230FF with shower and 250FF with bath and toilet. Prices are slightly lower in June and September.

Places to Stay – middle

There are a number of mid-range hotels in Ciboure.

Saint Jean de Luz Opposite the train station, the two-star, 29-room *Hôtel de Paris* (☎ 59.26.00.62) at 1 Blvd du Commandant Passicot has nondescript, medium-sized singles/doubles/triples/quads with shower, toilet and TV for 180/200/240/260FF (260/295/340/360FF in July and August). It is closed in January. Reception is staffed until 11 pm.

The friendly *Hôtel Agur* (☎ 59.26.21.55) at 96 Rue Gambetta, whose English proprietor has been here since 1976, is open from 15 March to 15 November. Modern, functional singles/doubles/triples/quads with shower, toilet and TV start at 240/275/340/430FF (285/310/380/510FF from July to mid-September). Reception is open daily from 7 am to 11 pm.

Ciboure In the centre of Ciboure, friendly, one-star *Hôtel Bakéa* (☎ 59.47.34.40) at 9 Place Camille Julian has doubles and triples with shower and toilet for 200 to 250FF. It is open all year.

The 20-room *Hôtel La Caravelle* (☎ 59.47.18.05), open all year, is at the western end of Blvd Pierre Benoit, next to the mouth of the harbour and a small beach. Doubles/two-bed quads with shower and toilet are 260/320FF. ATCRB buses to Socoa pass by here.

Two blocks inland, *Pension Agur Deneri* (☎ 59.47.15.18) at 14 Impasse Muskoa (or up the long flight of stairs at 22 Rue du Docteur Micé) has a lovely garden and great views of Saint Jean and its bay. Owned by the same family since 1946, it is open from sometime in April to September and requires that you take at least half-pension, which costs 170FF per person (180FF in July and

August). The rooms have private showers but toilet facilities are communal.

Places to Stay – top end

The two-star, 15-room *Hôtel Ohartzia* (☎ 59.26.00.06; fax 59.47.26.08), half a block from the beach at 28 Rue Garat, is open all year. The pleasant rooms, all of which are doubles with bath, toilet and TV, cost 390FF (410 to 460FF in summer), including breakfast. If you'll be arriving after 8 pm, call ahead.

Places to Eat

Considering its size, Saint Jean has quite a few excellent dining options. A number of rather pricey establishments are to be found along Rue de la République. There are a number of cafés at Place Louis XIV.

Restaurants – Saint Jean de Luz *La Vieille Auberge* (☎ 59.26.19.61) at 22 Rue Tourasse, run by the same family since 1954, serves traditional French and Basque cuisine, including ttorro (Basque bouillabaisse). Moules marinières (mussels cooked in their own juice with onions) are 39FF. The *menus* cost 69, 99 and 119FF. It is open daily, except Tuesday evening and Wednesday (in July and August, daily except Tuesday at midday).

Rustic *Restaurant Ramuntcho* (☎ 59.26. 03.89) at 24 Rue Garat has a mix of French regional and south-western French dishes you're unlikely to find elsewhere. The cook's husband is from Normandy, so the sauces are made with lots of fresh cream. Specialities include duck and fish. The *menus* cost 85, 115 and 160FF.

Tarterie-Saladerie Muscade (☎ 59.26. 96.73) at 20 Rue Garat specialises in two things: *tartes* (tarts or pies; 20 to 45FF), both savoury ones made with cheese, mushrooms, fish, vegetables, etc and sweet ones for dessert; and *salades composées* (mixed salads; 35 to 60FF). Vegetarian options are available. The restaurant is open daily from noon to 2.30 pm and 7 to 9 or 10 pm (slightly longer hours in July and August); it is closed in January.

For a truly unique dining experience, it's hard to beat the informal and enormously popular *À la Sardinerie* (☎ 59.51.18.29), located between Place du Maréchal Foch and the fishing port. Open from mid-June to mid-September, it serves only freshly cooked sardines (26FF for a plate of about five) and *thon* (tuna; 43 to 47FF) and one kind of omelette (15FF). The whole setup is designed to maximise the number of sardines eaten by each client, and the one giant dining room is continually abuzz with young waiters rushing about with plates of fish and bread. It is open daily from 11.30 am to 2.30 pm and 6 to 10 pm. There is often a queue in the evening.

Pizzeria Dolce Vita (☎ 59.26.12.16) at 39 Rue Tourasse has pizzas and pasta for 35 to 55FF. Children's plates are 25FF. It is open from noon to 2 pm and 7 to 10.30 pm (later in summer) daily except Tuesday night and Wednesday (daily from 15 June to 15 September).

Restaurants – Ciboure *Restaurant Bakéa* (☎ 59.47.34.40) at 9 Place Camille Julian, on the ground floor of a hotel of the same name, is a superb choice for a splurge. Their spectacularly good seafood dishes include chipirones à l'encre (cuttlefish; 70FF), ttorro (210FF for two), merlu koskera (hake; 190FF for two) and a plateau de fruits de mer (seafood platter; 150FF) with over a dozen kinds of edible sea creatures. It is open daily, except Tuesday night and Wednesday (daily in July and August).

Self-Catering A food market is held every Tuesday and Friday morning (every morning in July and August) around the *marché couvert* (les Halles).

Crémerie du Pin at 41 Rue Gambetta sells a fine selection of cheeses from 7 am to 12.30 pm and 3 to 7.30 pm Monday to Saturday (open Sunday morning in summer). There are a number of other *food shops* along nearby parts of Rue Gambetta.

The *Supermarché Score* at 87 Rue Gambetta is open Monday to Saturday from 8.30 am to 12.30 pm and 3 to 7 pm (7.30 pm in July and August).

Entertainment

Pelote Basque Cesta punta matches take place at the *jaï alaï* (☎ 59.26.61.30) across the street from 43 Ave André Ithurralde (also known as the Route de Bayonne and the N10), which is one km north-east of the train station. From late June to early September tournaments are held every Tuesday and Friday from about 9 pm to midnight. Music or dance performances liven up the half-time. Tickets cost 60 to 80FF.

In Ciboure, there is an outdoor *fronton* on Rue des Écoles.

Rugby Saint Jean de Luz's Fête du Rugby (Rugby Festival) is held each year around 15 August.

Things to Buy

Sweets Saint Jean de Luz is an excellent place to try Basque pastries and sweets such as *mouchous* (almond biscuits), *gochuak* (biscuits made with hazelnuts), *kanougas* (cubes of rich, chewy chocolate or coffee candy, wrapped in metallic paper, *macarons* (macaroons) and gâteau Basque.

La Maison du Kanouga (☎ 59.26.01.46), a somewhat pricey pâtisserie and chocolate shop at at 9 Rue Gambetta, has scrumptious biscuits for about 3FF each and gâteau Basque from 28FF. It is open daily from 7 am to 12.30 pm and 2 to 7 pm (7 am to 10 pm in July and August and around Christmas and Easter).

Basque Linen Saint Jean de Luz is one of the best places in the Basque Country to purchase tea towels, tablecloths, serviettes (napkins), oven gloves, pot holders and aprons made of colourful *linge Basque* (Basque linen).

A good selection of such items is available at La Caravelle (☎ 59.26.28.61), 64 Rue Gambetta. It is open Tuesday to Saturday from 10 am to 12.15 pm and 3 to 7 pm. From April to September it's open Monday to Saturday from 9.30 am to 12.30 pm and 3 to 7.30 pm. Toiles Basques Larre (☎ 59.26.02.13) at 4 Rue de la République (Place Louis XIV) also carries Pyrenean wool items. It's open from 9.30 am to 12.30 pm and 2.30 to 7 pm daily except Sunday and Monday morning. From July to September it's open daily from 9 am to 1 pm and 2.30 to 8 pm.

Basque linen with more of a designer flair is available at Création Jean-Vier (☎ 59.26.66. 26), on the ground floor of Maison de l'Infante on Rue de l'Infante. It is open from 15 April to 15 November daily from 9.30 am to 7.30 pm (midnight from July to mid-September).

Getting There & Away

Saint Jean de Luz is 54 km south-west of Bayonne and about 10 km north-east of the Spanish border town of Irún. It is a quick, easy train trip from Bayonne or Biarritz.

Train The Saint Jean de Luz-Ciboure train station (☎ 59.55.50.50 in Bayonne for information) sells tickets from 5.40 am to 9.30 pm. The luggage lockers are open from 6 am to 11 pm.

There are at least 20 trains a day to Bayonne (22FF; 25 minutes), Biarritz (13FF; 13 minutes) and the border town of Hendaye (13FF; 12 minutes), whence there are shuttle trains to San Sebastián in Spain. For details on trains serving Saint Jean de Luz, pick up the time schedule entitled 'Dax-Hendaye'.

Bus The head office of ATCRB (☎ 59.26. 06.99) at 5 Place du Maréchal Foch, 20 metres from the tourist office, is open from 9 am to noon and 2 to 6.30 pm daily except Saturday afternoon and Sunday. About a dozen buses a day (eight on Sunday and holidays) follow the coast to Bidart, Biarritz (13.80FF) and Bayonne (17.80FF; 40 minutes). Some of the company's 20 runs to Hendaye (13.80FF) go along the coast, while others pass through inland villages. The short run to Socoa (5.20FF), which goes through Ciboure, runs seven to nine times a day except on Sunday and holidays. Tickets are sold on the bus. Because of traffic, ATCRB buses are slow and often late, especially in summer.

ATCRB also has buses to the Spanish Basque city of San Sebastián (23FF; one hour) at 9 am and 2.30 pm on Tuesday, Thursday and Saturday (Monday to Saturday from June to 14 October). Pesa, a Spanish bus company that shares its bus stops with ATCRB, has year-round, Monday to Saturday service to San Sebastián at 9.15 am and 12.45 pm.

Getting Around

Taxi There is a taxi rank to the left as you exit the train station. To order a taxi, call ☎ 59.26.10.11.

Motorbike & Bicycle JP Ado (☎ 59.26. 14.95) at 5-7 Ave Labrouche rents five and ten-speed bicycles for 50/265FF a day/week and 50 cc motorbikes for 410 to 485FF a week. The shop is open Tuesday to Saturday from 8 am to noon and 2 to 7 pm (daily in July and August).

LA RHUNE

La Rhune, a 900-metre-high, antenna-topped mountain 10 km south-east of Saint Jean de Luz that is half in France and half in Spain, is something of a symbol of the French Basque Country. There are spectacular views of the whole region from the summit, which can be reached from Col de Saint Ignace on foot or by a 4.2-km *crémaillère* (cog-wheel railway; ☎ 59.54. 20.26; 34FF return), built in 1924. The train runs around Easter and from May to September.

From June to September, Le Basque Bondissant (☎ 59.26.25.87) at 100 Rue Gambetta in Saint Jean de Luz has buses from Blvd du Commandant Passicot (near the train station) to Col de Saint Ignace (7.50FF each way; 30 minutes). There are three round trips daily except on weekends and holidays (daily except Sunday and holidays in July and August). The first two leave Saint Jean de Luz at 11 am and 2.30 pm. The company's office, whose hours are 9 am to noon and 2 to 6 pm, is closed on Saturday afternoon and Sunday.

SAINT JEAN PIED DE PORT

The walled Pyrenean town of Saint Jean Pied de Port (Donibane Garazi in Basque; population 1700), 55 km south-east of Bayonne and eight km from the Spanish border, was once the last stop in France for pilgrims heading south to Santiago de Compostela. Today, the town, set in a river valley surrounded by hills, retains much of its rural Basque character despite its popularity with visitors.

Saint Jean Pied de Port makes a superb day trip from Bayonne. Half the reason for coming up here is the scenic trip from Bayonne – both the rail line and the main road, the D918, pass through rocky hills, forests and lush meadows dotted with white farmhouses. If you really want to get away from it all, you can rent a bike and head off into the hills.

Orientation

The centre of town, Place du Général de Gaulle and the contiguous Place du Trinquet, is 600 metres south of the train station along Ave Renaud. Place Floquet is on the south side of the Nive River. Rue de la Citadelle, up the hill from Place du Trinquet, is linked to Rue d'Espagne by the Vieux Pont. The Citadelle is at the top of the hill that borders the east side of town.

Information

Tourist Office The tourist office (☎ 59.37. 03.57) at 14 Place du Général de Gaulle is open from 9 am to noon and 2 to 7 pm daily except Sunday and holidays. From mid-June to mid-September it's also open on Sunday and holidays from 10.30 am to 12.30 pm and 3.30 to 6.30 pm.

Money The Crédit Agricole just up the hill from the post office will exchange foreign currency. It is open Monday to Friday from 9 am to 12.15 pm and 1.45 to 5 pm. This is the only bank in town with an ATM.

Post The post office at 1 Rue de la Poste is open Monday to Friday from 9 am to noon and 2 to 5 pm and on Saturday from 9 am to noon.

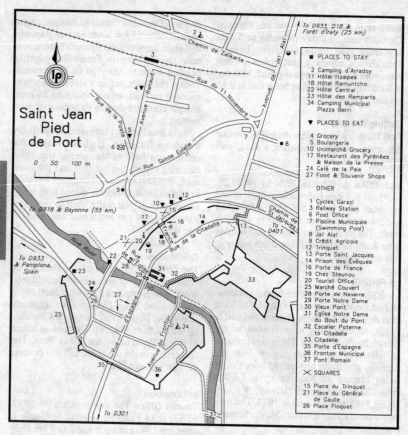

Saint Jean
Pied
de Port

0   50   100 m

To D918 & Bayonne (55 km)

Nive River

To D933
& Pamplona,
Spain

To D301

To D933, D18 &
Forêt d'Iraty (25 km)

PLACES TO STAY

2 Camping d'Arradoy
11 Hôtel Itzalpea
18 Hôtel Ramuntcho
22 Hôtel Central
23 Hôtel des Remparts
34 Camping Municipal
   Plazza Berri

PLACES TO EAT

4 Grocery
5 Boulangerie
10 Unimarché Grocery
17 Restaurant des Pyrénées
   & Maison de la Presse
24 Café de la Paix
27 Food & Souvenir Shops

OTHER

1 Cycles Garazi
3 Railway Station
6 Post Office
7 Piscine Municipale
   (Swimming Pool)
8 Jaï Alaï
9 Crédit Agricole
12 Trinquet
13 Porte Saint Jacques
14 Prison des Évêques
16 Porte de France
19 Chez Steunou
20 Tourist Office
25 Marché Couvert
28 Porte de Navarre
29 Porte Notre Dame
30 Vieux Pont
31 Église Notre Dame
   du Bout du Pont
32 Escalier Poterne
   to Citadelle
33 Citadelle
35 Porte d'Espagne
36 Fronton Municipal
37 Pont Romain

SQUARES

15 Place du Trinquet
21 Place du Général
   de Gaulle
26 Place Floquet

Saint Jean Pied de Port's postcode is
64220.

Maps The Maison de la Presse (☎ 59.37.
07.13) at 23 Place du Général de Gaulle
carries hiking maps of the area. It is open
Monday to Saturday from 7 am to 12.30 pm
and 2.30 to 7.30 pm and on Sunday from 8
am to 12.30 pm.

Walking Tour

From Place du Trinquet, walk through **Porte
de France**, one of the gates in the town's
15th-century ramparts, which were built by

the Navarrese. Rue de France leads up the
slope to **Rue de la Citadelle** in the heart of
the old town, many of whose 16th and 17th-
century houses have the date of construction
carved into the lintel. **Église Notre Dame du
Bout du Pont**, the church at the bottom of
Rue de la Citadelle at **Porte Notre Dame**,
was built in the 17th century. **Rue de
l'Église**, the town's main thoroughfare in the
1600s, leads to **Porte de Navarre**.

From the **Vieux Pont**, you can often see
40-cm-long trout swimming away happily in
the crystal-clear water. One observer
counted over three dozen fish waiting in the

shallows for food to happen by! As the Nive River passes through town, fishing is forbidden – and the fish know it. **Rue d'Espagne** (see Things to Buy) heads southward from the bridge.

The **Pont Romain**, a stone bridge 500 metres upriver from the Vieux Pont on the pastoral outskirts of town, is a perfect place for a picnic.

From the right bank of the Nive, right behind the church, a narrow *escalier poterne* (back staircase) leads through a gate and along the lichen, moss and creeper-covered stone ramparts to the **Citadelle**, built in 1628 and reoutfitted by military engineers of the Vauban school around 1680. It is now a school. The Citadelle, which affords a wonderful view of the town, the Nive River valley and the surrounding hills, can also be reached by walking up a rough cobblestone street that heads up the hill from Rue de la Citadelle.

Prison des Évêques, opposite 48 Rue de la Citadelle, served as a prison from the 1500s until WW II, when the Germans used it to intern people caught while trying to flee to Spain. The vaulted, Gothic-style 13th-century **dungeon** has all the characteristics that make dungeons dungeonlike: moist stone walls, a single tiny barred window and general gloominess. The ground floor, built in the 16th century, houses a few less-than-thrilling displays. It is open daily from Easter to mid-November. Entry costs 7FF (2FF for children aged two to 12).

Hiking & Cycling

The GR10 and the GR65 pass right through Saint Jean Pied de Port. See Maps under Information for details on where to buy hiking maps.

Saint Jean Pied de Port is a great place to begin a day ride into the Pyrenean foothills, where the only sounds you'll hear are cowbells and sheep munching grass. Just take any of the secondary or tertiary roads leading out of town. You can bring along bicycles free of charge on certain SNCF trains (eg the 9.20 am train) and then cycle back down to the coast.

5 Itinéraires Balisés (20FF), sold by the tourist office, is a packet of rudimentary maps for five circular backroad walks from Saint Jean Pied de Port. The routes are perfect for mountain biking. The tourist office also has a brochure on six beautiful hikes in the **Forêt d'Iraty**, 25 km south-east of here on the Spanish border. The only way to get there is by car.

Swimming

The Piscine Municipale (Municipal Swimming Pool; ☎ 59.37.05.56) on Rue du 11 Novembre is open from May to mid-October. Entry is 10FF (7.50FF for children aged six to 14).

Places to Stay – bottom end

Camping The *Camping Municipal Plazza Berri* (☎ 59.37.11.19) on Ave du Fronton occupies a lovely, riverside site with lush grass and thick tree cover. It is open from mid-April to September. Tariffs are 10FF per adult, 5FF for a camp site and 3FF to park.

Near the train station, *Camping d'Arradoy* (☎ 59.37.11.75) at 4 Chemin de Zalikarte is open from the first Sunday in March to the end of October. Adults pay 6.50FF, a tent site is 5FF and parking is 3FF.

Chambres d'Hôte Ask the tourist office for information on accommodation with families in the vicinity.

Hotels The cheapest hotel in town is at the *Hôtel des Remparts* (☎ 59.37.13.79) at 16 Place Floquet, open all year except on Saturday and Sunday nights from November to March. Rustic, unadorned singles/doubles cost 120/135FF with washbasin and bidet and 150/160FF with shower and toilet.

Places to Stay – middle

The classy *Hôtel Central* (☎ 59.37.00.22; fax 59.37.27.79) at 1 Place du Général de Gaulle, built in the 19th century, is open from 10 February to 22 December. Large, comfortable doubles with shower and toilet cost 290 to 380FF (10% less in the off season).

The back rooms look out on to a small waterfall.

The *Hôtel Ramuntcho* (☎ 59.37.03.91) at 1 Rue de France (up the hill from the Porte de France) is open from January to mid-November. Doubles with shower and toilet cost from 240 to 260FF, depending on the season.

The *Hôtel Itzalpea* (☎ 59.37.03.66; fax 59.37.33.18) at 5 Place du Trinquet has doubles with shower and toilet from 180FF. It is open all year.

Places to Eat

There are a number of restaurants around Place du Trinquet, Place du Général de Gaulle and Place Floquet. Many places offer trout dishes – this area is known for its trout fishing – and *poulet Basquaise* (Basque-style chicken).

Restaurants The impeccably elegant *Restaurant des Pyrénées* (☎ 59.37.01.01) at 19 Place du Général de Gaulle, in the luxurious Hôtel des Pyrénées, has two Michelin stars. *Menus* of classical French and Basque cuisine cost 200FF (not available on Sunday or holidays), 280, 360 and 450FF. The restaurant is closed on Tuesday (except from July to mid-September), from 20 November to 20 December and during most of January.

The restaurant in the *Hôtel Itzalpea* (see Places to Stay – middle), which serves family-style regional cuisine all year long, is open daily except Saturday (daily in July and August). *Menus* cost 68, 80 and 140FF. The restaurant in the *Hôtel Ramuntcho* (see Places to Stay – middle) is open daily except Wednesday (daily in July and August). *Menus* cost 72, 85 and 95FF.

Café de la Paix (☎ 59.37.00.99) at 4 Place Floquet, open from July to mid-September, has pizzas and paella. The *menus* cost 59, 85 and 125FF.

Self-Catering There's an all-day *food market* every Monday at Place du Général de Gaulle.

Near the train station, the *grocery* at 35 Ave Renaud is open Monday to Saturday from 7.30 am to 12.30 pm and 2.30 to 7.30 or 8 pm and on Sunday from 7.30 am to 12.30 pm. The small *boulangerie* at 2 Rue de la Poste (across from the post office) has gâteau Basque. It is open Monday to Saturday from 8 am to 8 pm and on Sunday from 8 am to 1 pm.

Near the tourist office, there's a *Unimarché grocery* at 3 Place du Trinquet.

On Rue d'Espagne, the grocery shop at No 12 is open Monday to Saturday and, during July and August, on Sunday morning also. There are other food shops nearby, including a *dépôt de pain* (bread shop; closed Wednesday except in July and August) at No 9 and a *boulangerie* at No 38.

Entertainment

Pelote Basque All year long, the *trinquet* at 7 Place du Trinquet has professional main nue and pala matches every Monday at 5 pm. Tickets cost 50FF. For information, call Bar du Trinquet, also known as Bar de la Terrasse, on ☎ 59.37.09.34.

The huge, new *jaï alaï* on Ave de Jaï Alaï plays host to cesta punta championships in July and August on Saturday nights at 9 pm.

In July and August the open-air Fronton Municipal on Ave du Fronton has pelota matches on Friday at 5 pm.

Things to Buy

On Monday morning from 8 to 11 am, farmers sell lambs, sheep, pigs, calves and cows at the Marché Couvert.

Along Rue d'Espagne, a number of stores sell Basque linen, berets and other useful souvenirs.

Getting There & Away

Train Saint Jean Pied de Port (☎ 59.37.02.00) is the terminus of a rail line that begins in Bayonne (41FF; one hour). There are three or four trains a day (five a day in July and August). Bags can be stored with the station staff for 30FF each.

For a day trip from Bayonne, your best bet is the train that leaves Bayonne at around 9.20 am. The last train back to Bayonne leaves Saint Jean Pied de Port at 4.45 pm (6.50 pm in July and August).

Getting Around

Taxi To order a taxi, call ☎ 59.37.05.00, 59.37.02.92 or 59.37.05.70.

Bicycle From late June to early September, bikes can be rented daily at Chez Steunou (☎ 59.37.25.45) at 12 Place du Général de Gaulle, right next to the tourist office. Three and five-speeds are 35/50FF per half/whole day. A 200FF deposit is required.

Near the train station, Cycles Garazi (☎ 59.37.21.79) at 1 Place Saint Laurent rents bikes from mid-May to early September. Mountain bikes cost 70/100FF per half/whole day. The shop is open from 9 am to noon and 2 to 6 or 7 pm.

Toulouse & the Pyrenees

The Pyrenees mountains stretch for 430 km from the Atlantic (the Bay of Biscay) in the west to the Mediterranean in the east, forming a natural boundary between France and Spain. Some of the most spectacular peaks and mountain valleys are in and around the Parc National des Pyrénées, which is about 150 km south-west of the region's largest city, Toulouse. Pau is the transport gateway to the Vallée d'Aspe, while the pilgrimage city of Lourdes has SNCF bus links to the mountain town of Cauterets.

For information on the far western section of the Pyrenees, see the Basque Country chapter. The eastern end of the chain is in Roussillon. There's more information on the Pyrenees in the Andorra chapter.

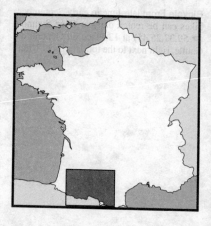

Regional Information

If you're in Paris, information on the Pyrenees region is available at the Maison des Pyrénées (☎ 1-42.61.58.18; metro Quatre Septembre) at 15 Rue Saint Augustin (2e).

TOULOUSE

Toulouse (population 359,000), whose metropolitan area has a population of 650,000, is France's fourth-largest city (after Paris, Lyon and Marseille). It is renowned for its high-tech industries, including some of the most advanced aerospace facilities in Europe. It is also a major centre of higher education: the city's universities, founded to combat Catharism in 1229, and its *grandes écoles* (of which there are 14) and other institutes have more students (83,000) than any other French provincial city. Despite these assets, Toulouse is not a particularly attractive or interesting place, though it does have a number of fine museums and several exceptional churches, including the Romanesque Basilica of Saint Sernin.

Because there are no stone quarries anywhere near Toulouse, all the older buildings in the city centre are made of rose-red brick;

most also have tile roofs. Unfortunately, some bricks weather faster than others, so many of the façades are pockmarked by chipped, cracked and crumbled bricks, imparting on the city an undeserved look of dereliction. Toulouse is known as *la ville rose* (the pink city) both because of the colour of its buildings and because of the long Socialist tenure in city hall.

Toulouse is best avoided in August, when a large percentage of the population heads for the beach and many shops, restaurants and businesses close.

History

Toulouse, known as Tolosa during the Roman period, served as the Visigoth capital from 419 to 507 AD. It was unsuccessfully besieged by the Muslims in 721. In the 12th and 13th centuries, the counts of Toulouse supported the Cathars; however, three centuries later, during the Wars of Religion, the city sided with the Catholic League. Many Toulouse merchants grew rich in the 16th and 17th centuries from the woad (pastel) dye trade, which collapsed when the Portuguese began importing indigo from India.

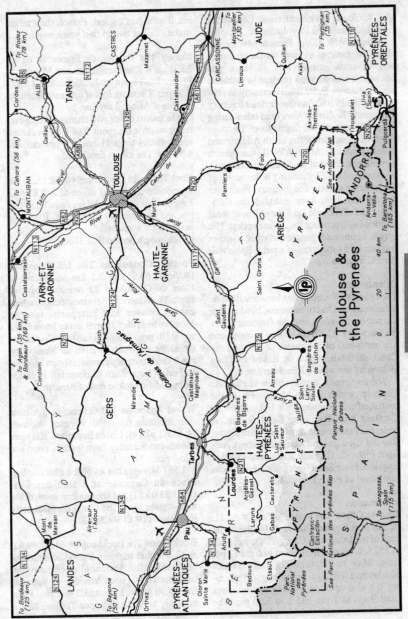

Toulouse &
the Pyrenees

TOULOUSE

The Toulouse Parlement ruled Languedoc from 1420 until the Revolution.

Around WW I, the French government chose Toulouse as a centre for the manufacture of arms and aircraft, in large part because it was deemed prudent to establish such industries as far from Germany as possible. In the 1920s, Antoine de Saint Exupéry (author of *The Little Prince*) and other daring pilots pioneered mail flights from Toulouse to north-west Africa, the south Atlantic and South America. After WW II, the French govenment decided to build on the city's aeronautical base by making it the centre of the country's aerospace industry. Passenger planes built here have included the Caravelle, the Concorde and the Airbus; local factories also produce the Ariane rocket. The city's economic prospects were further brightened by the entry of nearby Spain into the EC in 1986.

Orientation

The centre of Toulouse lies between Blvd de Strasbourg and its continuation, Blvd Lazare Carnot (to the east), and the Garonne River (to the west). The train station is about one km north-east of the centre of town on the Canal du Midi, which is linked to Place Wilson by the wide Allées Jean Jaurès.

The city centre's main square is Place du Capitole, which is one block west of the tourist office. Rue du Taur links Place du Capitole with Basilique Saint Sernin. A pedestrian mall made up of Rue Saint Rome, Rue des Changes and Rue des Filatiers goes from Place du Capitole southward to Place Esquirol. Place Saint Georges is a few blocks north-east of Place Esquirol.

Information

Tourist Office The tourist office (☎ 61.11. 02.22) is at Square Charles de Gaulle in the base of the Donjon du Capitole, a tower built in 1525. It is open from 9 am to 6 pm (7 pm from May to September) daily except Sunday and holidays. From May to September it's also open on Sunday and holidays from 9 am to 1 pm and 2 to 5.30 pm. The staff do not usually make hotel reservations, but if you don't speak French they might make a call or two to find you a room.

Money The Banque de France (☎ 61.61. 35.35) at 4 Rue Deville is open Monday to Friday from 9 am to 12.20 pm and 1.20 to 3.30 pm. There are lots of commercial banks on Rue d'Alsace-Lorraine.

The tourist office will change foreign currency worth up to about 500FF on weekends and holidays from 11 am to 1 pm and 2 to 4.30 pm. The rate is pretty bad.

Post The main post office (☎ 62.15.30.00) is opposite the tourist office at 7-9 Rue La Fayette. It is open weekdays from 8 am to 7 pm and on Saturday until noon. Exchange services are available.

Toulouse's postcode is 31000.

Foreign Consulates The US Consulate (☎ 56.52.65.95) is 2.5 km south-east of Place du Capitole at 22 Ave du Maréchal Foch. The American Services section, which cannot reissue lost passports, is open Monday to Friday from 9 am to noon and 2 to 5.30 pm. The Canadian Consulate (☎ 61.99.30.16) at 30 Blvd de Strasbourg, run by an honourary consul, is open Monday to Friday from 9 am to noon but is closed from mid-July to the end of August.

Travel Agencies BIJ tickets are available near the train station at Voyages Wasteels (☎ 61.62.67.14), 1 Blvd Bonrepos. It is open Monday to Saturday from 9 am to noon and 2 to 7 pm.

USIT Voyages has an office a bit north of Place du Capitole at 5 Rue des Lois (☎ 61.23.03.61) and another one south of the train station along the Canal du Midi at 16 Rue Riquet (☎ 61.99.38.47).

Bookshops The Bookshop (☎ 61.22.99.92) at 17 Rue Lakanal has a good selection of books in English. You can also sell them your used books. It's open Monday to Saturday from 9.30 am to 1 pm and 2 to 7 pm. From mid-July to August it's open Tuesday to Saturday from 10 am to noon and 3 to 7 pm.

Laundry South of Allées Jean Jaurès, the laundrette at 37 Rue des 7 Troubadours is open daily. The laundrette at 5 Rue Maury is open until 9 pm.

Medical Services CHR de Rangueil (☎ 61.32.25.33, 61.53.11.33), a hospital on Chemin du Vallon, is 5.5 km south of Place du Capitole near Université Paul Sabatier. To get there by bus, take No 2 from the train station or Rue d'Alsace-Lorraine.

Dangers & Annoyances Toulouse's red-light district – Rue Bertrand de Born, Rue Lafon, Place de Belfort, Rue Denfert Rochereau and Rue Héliot – is between the train station and the centre of town. The prostitutes and sex shops aren't likely to cause any problems for passers-by, but the area attracts lots of idle and vaguely menacing men, so single women should probably avoid the area after nightfall.

Walking Tour
The best way to get a feel for the city centre is to wander around. The most interesting sights in Toulouse are listed here in a walkable order. If you'll be visiting several museums, you might want to pick up a museum pass known as a Passeport – ask about it at the tourist office or the first museum you come upon.

Place du Capitole
Place du Capitole, one block west of the tourist office, is the city's main square. On its east side is the 128-metre-long façade of Toulouse's city hall, the **Capitole** (☎ 61.22.29.22, ext 3412), so named because the municipal magistrates who once ran the city were known as *capitouls*. Built in the early 1750s, the structure has become an important focus of civic pride. Next door is the **Théâtre du Capitole**, which puts on operas and operettas.

The interior of the Capitole, whose **Salle des Illustres** (Hall of the Illustrious) was decorated at the end of the 19th century, can be visited daily except on weekends and holidays. Henri II, Duke of Montmorency,

who had the audacity to rebel against Cardinal Richelieu, was executed in the interior courtyard – built in 1606 – in 1632.

The **Vieux Quartier** (Old Quarter), which has hardly changed since the 18th century, is south of Place du Capitole around Rue Saint Rome and Rue des Changes, both of which are reserved for pedestrians.

Basilique Saint Sernin
The chancel of this 115-metre-long basilica (☎ 61.21.80.45), the largest and most complete Romanesque structure in France, was built of brick from 1080 to 1096; the nave was added in the 12th century. No significant architectural changes have been made since 1271. This former Benedictine abbey church was an important stop on the way to Santiago de Compostela in Spain (see the Santiago de Compostela aside in the Limousin, Périgord & Quercy chapter), whose cathedral, begun about the same time, is almost identical in design.

The basilica is topped by a magnificent, eight-sided **tower** whose lower three storeys – those with rounded arches – date from the early 13th century; the upper two storeys date from the mid-13th century. The spire is from the 15th century.

Inside, the **ambulatory** is lined with chapels and gilded, 17th-century reliquaries. The two-level **crypt**, rebuilt in the 13th and 14th centuries, contains a number of medieval reliquaries. Directly above the crypt is the sculpted, mid-18th-century **tomb of Saint Sernin**, topped by a baldachin (canopy). The north transept arm is decorated with a 12th-century fresco of the Resurrection of Christ.

The basilica is open Monday to Saturday from 8 am to noon and 2 to 6 pm and Sunday from 9 am to 12.30 pm and 2 to 7 pm. During July and August it's open from 8 am (9 am on Sunday) to 6.30 pm (7.30 pm on Sunday). The ambulatory and crypt, which cost 8FF to enter, are open from 10 to 11.30 am and 2.30 to 5 pm daily except Sunday morning; in July and August opening hours are 10 am (12.30 pm on Sunday) to 6 pm.

TOULOUSE

TOULOUSE

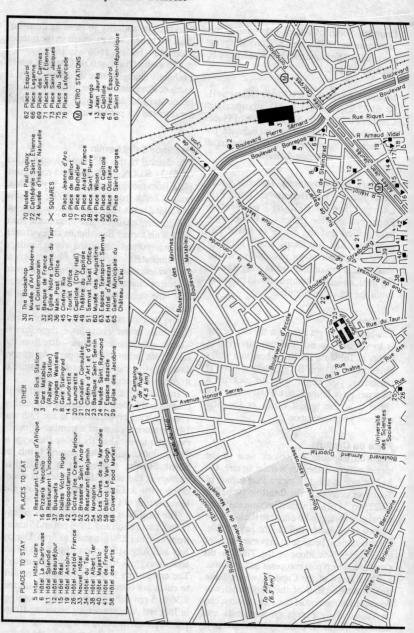

■ PLACES TO STAY

5   Inter Hôtel Icare
6   Hôtel La Chartreuse
11 Hôtel Splendid
12 Hôtel Beauséjour
15 Hôtel Réal
26 Hôtel Antoine
28 Hôtel Anatole France
33 Nouvel Hôtel
34 Hôtel du Taur
38 Hôtel Albert 1er
40 Hôtel Majestic
41 Hôtel de France
58 Hôtel des Arts

▼ PLACES TO EAT

1   Restaurant L'Image d'Afrique
16 Pizzeria Vecchio
18 Restaurant L'Indochine
37 Busquets
39 Halles Victor Hugo
42 Hippopotamus
43 Octave Ice Cream Parlour
53 Restaurant Saint André
54 Monoprix
55 Les Caves de la Maréchale
59 Bistrot Le Van Gogh
68 Covered Food Market

OTHER

3   Main Bus Station
4   Gare Matabiau
    (Railway Station)
7   Voyages Wasteels
8   Gare Stalingrad
14 Laundrette
20 Laundrette
21 Canadian Consulate
22 Cinéma Utopia et d'Essai
23 Basilique Saint Sernin
24 Musée Saint Raymond
27 Espace Bazacle
29 Église des Jacobins
30 The Bookshop
31 Musée d'Art Moderne
    et Contemporain
32 Banque de France
35 Église Notre Dame du Taur
36 Main Post Office
45 Cinéma Rio
47 Tourist Office
48 Capitole (City Hall)
49 Théâtre du Capitole
51 Semvat Ticket Office
60 Musée des Augustins
63 Semvat Transport Servat.
64 Hôtel d'Assézat
65 Galerie Municipale du
    Château d'Eau

70 Musée Paul Dupuy
72 Cathédrale Saint Étienne
74 Musée d'histoire Naturelle

✕ SQUARES

9   Place Jeanne d'Arc
10 Place de Belfort
17 Place Bachelier
25 Place Anatole France
28 Place Saint Pierre
44 Place Wilson
50 Place du Capitole
57 Place Saint Georges

62 Place Esquirol
66 Place Laganne
69 Place des Carmes
73 Place Saint Étienne
75 Place Saint Jacques
76 Place du Salin
76 Place Lafourcade

Ⓜ METRO STATIONS

2   Marengo
13 Jean Jaurès
46 Capitole
61 Place Esquirol
67 Saint Cyprien-République

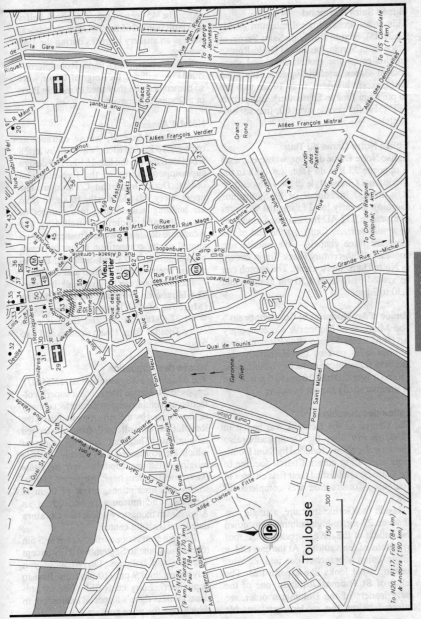

TOULOUSE

Toulouse

To N124, Colomiers (9 km), Lourdes (170 km) & Pau (184 km)

To N20, N117, Foix (84 km) & Andorra (190 km)

To Étienne Billières

To US Consulate (1 km)

To Auberge de Jeunesse (1 km)

To CHR de Rangueil (hospital; 4 km)

0   150   300 m

Garonne River

Musée Saint Raymond

This small archaeological museum (☎ 61. 22.21.85), next to Basilique Saint Sernin at Place Saint Sernin, has lots of Gallo-Roman antiquities on the ground floor and some ancient Greek artefacts upstairs. It's open daily, except holidays, from 10 am to 5 pm (6 pm from June to September). Entry costs 8FF (5FF for people over 60, free for students).

Église Notre Dame du Taur

Église Notre Dame du Taur, whose entrance is opposite 23 Rue du Taur, was built in the Meridional Gothic style in the 14th century. It is named in honour of St Saturninus (Sernin), an early local evangelist who was martyred in 257 AD by being tied to the tail of a wild *taureau* (bull). At the end of the nave are three chapels – the middle one contains a 16th-century Black Virgin known as Notre Dame du Rempart. The church can be visited daily from 8.30 am to noon and 2.30 to 7 pm.

Musée d'Art Moderne et Contemporain

The Museum of Modern & Contemporary Art (☎ 61.21.34.50) at 69 Rue Pargaminières is housed in part of the Réfectoire des Jacobins (Dominican Refectory), built in the 1300s. It is open from 10 am to 5 pm (6 pm in summer) daily except Tuesday.

Église des Jacobins

The Church of the Jacobins was begun in 1230, shortly after the Dominicans (also known as Jacobins), founded by Saint Dominique in 1215 to preach Church doctrine to the Cathars, established their first chapter in Toulouse. Construction was completed in 1385.

Inside the Gothic structure, a single row of seven 22-metre-high columns runs down the middle of the nave, supporting the roof by means of fan vaulting. At the east end, a single column branches out into 22 ribs, forming what looks like a palm tree. The relics of **St Thomas Aquinas**, one of the early leaders of the Dominican order, are interred below the modern, grey-marble

altar. The 45-metre-high, octagonal belfry was built from 1265 to 1298. The church was used as an artillery barracks during the 19th century.

The Jacobins, who – under Robespierre – ruled France during the Reign of Terror, were so named because they used to meet in Paris in a Dominican convent.

Hôtel d'Assézat

The Hôtel d'Assézat, whose entrance is opposite 18 Rue de Metz, was built by a rich woad merchant in the late 1550s. The design superimposes three of the five classical orders: Doric, Ionic and Corinthian. The upper storey was added in the 1600s. In 1896 the building was donated to a number of local learned societies, including the Académie des Jeux Floraux, named after an annual poetry competition begun by seven troubadours in 1323 and dedicated to promoting poetry in both French and Occitan.

The courtyard can be visited all day long. The **Musée de l'Histoire de la Médecine** (Museum of the History of Medecine; ☎ 61.31.89.06) on the 2nd floor is open every Tuesday from 10 am to noon and 2 to 6 pm.

Musée des Augustins

The Musée des Augustins (☎ 61.23.55.07), opposite 34 Rue de Metz, has a superb collection of paintings and stone artefacts, many of them seized by the government during the Revolution or collected from destroyed monuments. The stone carvings, most of which are Romanesque or Gothic, include religious statuary, capitals, *clefs de voûte* (keystones), sarcophagi, gargoyles, tombstones and inscriptions, a few of them in Hebrew. The museum is housed in an Augustinian monastery whose two **cloisters** date from the 14th century.

The museum is open from 10 am to 5 pm (6 pm from June to September) daily except Tuesday and holidays. On Wednesday it stays open until 9 pm (10 pm from June to September). Entry costs 8FF (free for students) unless there's a special exhibition, in which case the price goes up.

Cathédrale Saint Étienne

St Stephen's Cathedral, whose entrance is behind (south of) 62 Rue de Metz, has a rather peculiar layout. The vast nave, begun around 1100 and modified in 1211, is out of line with the choir, built in the northern French Gothic style as part of an ambitious (and unfinished) late 13th-century plan to rebuild the cathedral along a different axis. Especially interesting is the improvised Gothic vaulting that links the two sections. The rose window dates from 1230 and the organ case from four centuries later. Both the west and north entrances are worth a look – the former was added in the 15th century, the latter in 1929. The cathedral is open daily from 7.30 am to 7 pm.

Musée Paul Dupuy

The Paul Dupuy Museum (☎ 61.22.21.83) at 13 Rue de la Pleau, which occupies the 17th and 18th-century Hôtel de Besson, has a fine collection of objets d'art, glasswork, medieval religious art, faïence, armaments and rare clocks and watches. The mid-17th-century **pharmacy** is from Toulouse's Jesuit college. This museum is open from 10 am to 5 pm (6 pm from June to September) daily except Tuesday and holidays. Entry costs 8FF (free for students), or more if there's a special exhibition on.

Gardens

The **Grand Rond**, a huge roundabout-cum-park, and the **Jardin des Plantes** (Botanical Gardens), two of the greenest parts of central Toulouse, are a few blocks south-west of Musée Paul Dupuy. The city's **Musée d'Histoire Naturelle** (Natural History Museum; ☎ 61.52.00.14) is on the north side of the Jardin des Plantes at 35 Allées Jules Guesde.

Galerie Municipale du Château d'Eau

Housed in a *château d'eau* (water-pumping station) built in 1822, this municipal photography museum (☎ 61.42.61.72) at Place Laganne (at the western end of Pont Neuf) puts on superb temporary exhibitions of works by some of the world's finest photographers. There is at least one new exhibition

each month. Founded in 1974, it has ... Toulouse's most visited museum.

The Château d'Eau is open from 1 to 7 pm daily except Tuesday and holidays. Entry costs 10FF (5FF for students, free if you're under 12 or over 60). Everyone gets in for 5FF on Sunday.

Espace Bazacle

Espace Bazacle (☎ 61.21.23.81 for a recording, 61.23.23.81) at 11 Quai Saint Pierre, owned by Electricité de France (France's electricity company), hosts all sorts of temporary exhibitions. It is housed in a 12th-century mill and is part of a working, 19th-century hydroelectric plant (☎ 61.21.63.83) which you may be able to visit. Except from July to mid-September, it is open from 10 am to noon and 2 to 6 pm daily except on weekends and holiday mornings.

Organised Tours

Aérospatiale Tours From Monday to Saturday, the aerospace company Aérospatiale has 1½-hour tours (50FF; 45FF for students) of its huge Clément Ader aircraft factory (where Airbus's A330 and A340s are assembled) in Colomiers, which is about 10 km west of the city centre. For information and reservations, call ☎ 61.15.44.00 a few days in advance. In August you can make reservations at the tourist office and, on Monday and Friday afternoons, take advantage of free buses from Place du Capitole.

Walking Tours From July to September, the tourist office runs two-hour walking tours of the city in French (42FF).

Places to Stay – bottom end

Most of Toulouse's hotels cater to business people, so rooms are easiest to find when there's little business to conduct: on Friday, Saturday and Sunday nights and during July and August.

Camping *Camping de Rupé* (☎ 61.70.07.35), also known as Camping de Sesquières, is six km north-west of the train station. From Ave des États-Unis, go west for

300 metres along Chemin du Pont de Rupé. This is not the most appealing camping ground you'll come across, and the 300 sites are often full, but Camping de Rupé is easily accessible by bus: from Place Jeanne d'Arc, which is linked to the train station by bus Nos 2 and 5, take bus line P. A tent site costs 6.50FF and adults pay 14FF each.

Hostels The 59-place *Auberge de Jeunesse* (☎ 61.80.49.93) at 125 Ave Jean Rieux is a bit over two km south-east of the train station. A bed in a large dormitory costs 39FF; breakfast is 15FF. Curfew is at 11 pm unless you pay a 50FF deposit for a key. Rooms are locked from 10 am to 5.30 pm. Reception is open daily from 8 to 10 am and 5 to 11 pm. This place is most full in July and August, when the cheap hotels are most empty.

To get there by bus from the train station, take the No 14 (towards Purpan) to Place Dupuy and then cross the *place* to take the No 22 (towards La Terrasse) to the Leygues stop. Both lines run daily until about 8.45 pm.

Hotels Almost all of the cheap hotels around the train station and the nearby red-light district, centred around brightly lit Place de Belfort (see Dangers & Annoyances), are dirty, noisy and run by unpleasant people. Few, if any, offer good value. If you arrive by rail, your best bet is to walk to Allées Jean Jaures or take bus No 2 or 5 to the centre of town.

Hotels – Allées Jean Jaurès The *Hôtel Antoine* (☎ 61.62.70.27) at 21 Rue Arnaud Vidal, a pleasant, older place on a quiet street, has singles/doubles from 90/120FF; doubles/quads with shower and toilet are 160/215FF. Hall showers are 10FF. You might also try the *Hôtel Réal* (☎ 61.62.94.34) at 30 Allées Jean Jaurès, whose plain doubles cost 120FF with washbasin, 150FF with shower and 165FF with shower and toilet. There are no hall showers. Reception is open 24 hours a day – after 1 am, ring the bell.

Your best option north of Allées Jean Jaurès is probably the *Hôtel Beauséjour* (☎ 61.62.77.59) at 4 Rue Caffarelli. Singles/doubles start at 65/80FF; doubles with shower and toilet are 150FF. An extra bed is 40FF. The shower costs 10FF. At the risk of being treated uncivilly, you might try the *Hôtel Splendid* (☎ 61.62.43.02) at 13 Rue Caffarelli, whose basic, run-down singles/doubles start at 80/95FF. Hall showers are 15FF. It is closed during most of August.

Hotels – City Centre You can't beat the location of the *Hôtel des Arts* (☎ 61.23.36.21) at 1bis Rue Cantegril, which is just off Place Saint Georges. Adequate doubles, some of which are a bit noisy, cost 125FF with washbasin and 155FF with shower and toilet. Showers cost 10FF per person or 15FF per room.

Just south of Halles Victor Hugo, the *Hôtel Majestic* (☎ 61.23.04.29) at 9bis Rue du Rempart Villeneuve has large but slightly run-down singles/doubles with shower and toilet for 120/140FF; rooms with washbasin are slightly cheaper. Hall showers are free.

The *Hôtel Anatole France* (☎ 61.23.19.96) at 46 Place Anatole France has hotel-chain-style doubles for 100FF (with washbasin) and 140FF (with shower and toilet).

Places to Stay – middle
Most of Toulouse's mid-range hotels offer much better value for money than the bottom-end ones.

Train Station Area Blvd Bonrepos, across the Canal du Midi from the train station, is lined with two and three-star hotels, some of them in an alarming state of dilapidation. This area is isolated from the centre of the city by the Place de Belfort red-light district, so unless you're just passing through you're probably better off staying in the city centre.

The two-star, 34-room *Inter Hôtel Icare* (☎ 61.62.89.79; fax 61.62.85.95) at 11 Blvd Bonrepos has spacious, soundproofed singles/doubles with shower and toilet for 210/250FF. The family-run *Hôtel La Char-*

treuse (☎ 61.62.93.39) at 4bis Blvd Bonrepos has small, clean singles/doubles with shower, toilet and TV for 160/195FF.

City Centre Just east of Halles Victor Hugo, Rue d'Austerlitz is lined with two-star hotels. The well-run, 64-room *Hôtel de France* (☎ 61.21.88.24, 61.21.54.19; fax 61.21.99.77), whose entrances are at 5 Rue d'Austerlitz and 4 Rue Victor Hugo, has spotless, comfortable doubles/quads with shower and toilet from 195/275FF (175/255FF on Friday, Saturday and Sunday nights). The staff speak English.

Two blocks west of Halles Victor Hugo, the pleasant *Hôtel Albert 1er* (☎ 61.21.17.91; fax 61.26.09.64) at 8 Rue Rivals has comfortable singles/doubles/quads with shower, toilet, TV and minibar for 225/235/350FF. Prices are about 30FF less on weekends, during school holidays and in July and August.

Just north of Place du Capitole, the 56-room *Hôtel du Taur* (☎ 61.21.17.54) at 2 Rue du Taur has quiet, fairly spacious singles/doubles with shower, toilet and TV for 195/210FF. Antoine de Saint Exupéry used to stay here in the late 1920s. Across the street, the 17-room *Nouvel Hôtel* (☎ 61.21.13.93) at 13 Rue du Taur (1st floor) has plain doubles for 135FF with washbasin and 145FF with shower; two-bed doubles and triples with shower and toilet are 210FF. Hall showers are 8FF.

Places to Eat

When the weather is good, Place Saint Georges is almost entirely taken over by café tables; at night, it's one of the liveliest spots in town. Both Blvd de Strasbourg and the perimeter of Place du Capitole are lined with restaurants and cafés. Lots of places around town have lunch *menus* for 50 to 60FF.

Near the train station, there are a number of unexciting but inexpensive places to eat along Rue de Bayard.

French *Les Caves de la Maréchale* (☎ 61.23.89.88), through the arch at 3 Rue Jules Chalande (east of Rue Saint Rome),

specialises in both regional cuisine and dishes invented by the convivial chef. Housed in the magnificently vaulted brick cellar of a pre-Revolutionary convent, it is open from noon to 2 pm and 8 to 11 pm daily except Sunday and Monday at midday. *Menus* cost 70FF (lunch) and 129FF (dinner). It's a good idea to make reservations for dinner.

Restaurant Benjamin (☎ 61.22.92.66) at 7 Rue des Gestes (west of Rue Saint Rome), in a setting that is a mixture of classical columns and modern décor, serves nouvelle cuisine, including saumon (salmon), foie gras, terrines and duck cutlets. The chef likes to combine all sorts of elements to create original and adventuresome dishes. *Menus* start at 57FF (lunch) and 74FF (dinner). It's open Monday to Saturday from noon to 2 pm and 7.45 to 11 pm.

Bistrot Le Van Gogh (☎ 61.21.03.15) at 21 Place Saint Georges has regional specialities such as cassoulet (85FF), parillade (eight different kinds of fish; 130FF) and home-smoked salmon (85FF). The *menus* cost 65FF (lunch) and 135FF (dinner). Beer is 13FF. Le Van Gogh is open daily from 7 am to 2 am. The huge terrace is open whenever the weather permits.

The mellow *Brasserie Saint André* (☎ 61.22.56.37) at 39 Rue Saint Rome is two floors below street level in a cellar with a round ceiling that makes you feel like you're in the upper half of a brick submarine. The *menus* (75 and 95FF), soups, omelettes, crepes, cider on tap (18FF per half-litre) and main courses (35 to 78FF) attract a varied clientele that includes lots of young people. Meals are served all night long, Monday to Saturday from 7.45 pm to 7 am (7.30 am on Saturday and Sunday mornings).

Hippopotamus (☎ 61.23.27.34) at 1 Blvd de Strasbourg serves solid beef meals daily from 11.30 am to 3 pm and 6.30 pm to 1 am. The *menus* cost 64 and 92FF. Steaks, the house speciality, are 72 to 106FF.

Other The *Restaurant L'Image d'Afrique* (☎ 61.58.48.10) at 7 Ave de Lyon, run by an immigrant from Senegal, is one long block north of the train station. The lunch *menu* costs 55FF; dinner *menus* cost 70 and 80FF. It is open from noon to 2 pm and 7 to 11 pm daily except midday on Wednesday and Sunday.

Restaurant L'Indochine (☎ 61.62.17.46) at 46 Place Bachelier served Chinese and Vietnamese cuisine from noon to 2 pm and 7 to 11 pm daily (except sometimes at midday on Sunday). The *menus* cost 42 and 59FF. The portions are large but some of the sauces are a bit bizarre.

Pizzeria Vecchio (☎ 61.63.85.92) at 22 Allées Jean Jaurès, a thriving place with a large warm-weather terrace, is open daily from 12.15 to 2 pm (2.30 pm on Sunday) and 7.15 to 11.30 pm.

Near Place Saint Georges, *Pizzeria Le Vesuvio* (☎ 61.21.39.95) at 8 Rue Alexandre Fourtanier is open Monday to Saturday from noon to 2.30 pm and 7.30 to 11.30 pm (7 to 11 pm from late September to sometime in May). Near Place du Capitole, *Pizzeria Peppino* (☎ 61.23.13.84), a small pizzeria at 20 Rue des Gestes, is open Monday to Saturday from noon to 2 pm and daily, except Sunday and Tuesday, from 6.30 to 10 pm. *Menus* cost 50FF (lunch) and 75FF (dinner).

There are *McDonald's* restaurants at 10 Allées du Président Roosevelt and on the northern side of Place du Capitole.

Octave ice cream parlour (☎ 62.27.05.21) at 11 Allées du Président Roosevelt serves incredibly rich ice cream daily from 10 am (2 pm on Monday) to about 2 am. Cones with one to five scoops cost 10 to 26FF. Avoid breathalyser tests after eating the Armagnac or Grand Marnier flavours.

Self-Catering *Halles Victor Hugo*, a large food market at Place Victor Hugo, is on the ground floor of a multilevel parking garage. It is open Tuesday to Sunday from 6 am to 1 pm. At Place des Carmes, which is at the southern end of the Rue Saint Rome-Rue des Filatiers pedestrian mall, you'll find a large, round *covered food market*. There's a small *market* selling organically grown food at Place du Capitole on Tuesday and Saturday until about 1 pm.

The *Monoprix* at 39 Rue d'Alsace-Lorraine, whose supermarket section is on the 1st floor, is open Monday to Saturday from 8.30 am to 7.30 pm.

Busquets at 10 Rue de Rémusat has a wide selection of wines (11 to 3000FF) and luxury food items, quite a few of them from this part of France. This is a good place to pick up an edible gift. It is open Monday to Saturday from 9 am to 12.30 pm and 2.30 to 7.30 pm.

Entertainment
The tourist office has all sorts of up-to-date information on Toulouse's lively cultural life. From late June to August it sells tickets (50 to 70FF) for a series of concerts known as Musique d'Été (Summer Music).

Diurnal and nocturnal café activity is centred around Place Saint Georges, Blvd de Strasbourg and Blvd Lazare Carnot.

Jazz From October to May or June, *Le Bacchus* jazz cellar, which is at Place Saint Georges next to No 21 (Bistrot Le Van Gogh), has live jazz on Tuesday to Saturday nights from 6 to 8 pm and 10 pm to 2 am.

Cinemas Two cinemas have nondubbed foreign films; details on the offerings appear in the regional daily *La Depêche du Midi*, which you can consult at the tourist office.

Cinéma Rio (☎ 61.23.66.20) at 24 Rue Montardy (one block south of Place Wilson) has screenings in its three halls every day at about 2.30 pm and in the evening. Tickets cost 40FF (30FF for students and people under 18 or over 60). The *Cinéma d'Art et d'Essai* (☎ 61.29.81.00) at 13 Rue Saint Bernard, also known as Cinéma ABC, changes films every Wednesday. It is closed for most of August.

Things to Buy
Toulouse's main shopping district, filled with department stores and expensive boutiques, is around Rue du Taur, Rue d'Alsace-Lorraine, Rue de la Pomme, Rue des Arts and nearby streets. Place Saint Georges is surrounded by fashionable shops.

On Wednesday, Place du Capitole hosts a flea market.

Getting There & Away

Air Aéroport International de Toulouse-Blagnac (☎ 61.42.44.00) is about eight km north-west of the city centre in the suburb of Blagnac.

Train Toulouse's train station, Gare Matabiau (☎ 61.62.50.50 for information), is on Blvd Pierre Sémard about a km north-east of the city centre. The information office is open from 7.30 am to 7.50 pm daily except Sunday and holidays. The station is closed from 1.30 to 3 am. Ticket window Nos 17 to 19 will change enough foreign currency to cover the cost of your ticket.

Destinations served by direct trains include Albi (57FF; up to a dozen a day), Bayonne (186FF; four hours; six a day), Bordeaux (158FF; two hours; 10 a day), Cahors (78FF; eight a day; 1¼ hours), Marseille (226FF; three to four hours; nine a day), Montpellier (153FF) and Nice (305FF; at least six hours; five a day). The route to Paris (326FF) is covered by TGVs via Bordeaux to Gare Montparnasse (5¼ hours) and non-TGVs via Cahors to Gare d'Austerlitz (6½ to seven hours).

In the city centre, SNCF has an information and ticketing office in Espace Transport Semvat (see Bus & Metro under Getting Around) at 7 Place Esquirol. It is open on weekdays from 2 to 6 pm.

Bus The poorly run main bus station (☎ 61.48.71.84) at 68-70 Blvd Pierre Sémard, to the right as you exit the train station, is best avoided if possible. Buses from here go to destinations including Agen, Albi, Auch, Carcassonne, Castelnaudary, Montauban and two gateways to Andorra, Ax-les-Thermes and Pas de la Casa (south of l'Hospitalet).

Semvat's intercity Arc-en-Ciel buses, which serve destinations in Haute Garonne and nearby départements, use Gare Stalingrad (☎ 61.62.87.12), which is two blocks south-west of the train station at 20 Rue Stalingrad. It is open daily from 6 a.. 8 pm. There are plans to transfer Arc-en-Cie. buses to the main bus station.

The Intercars office (☎ 61.58.14.53) in the main bus station handles buses to Andorra (135FF one way), Portugal, Morocco and parts of Spain. It's open Monday to Saturday from 9 am to noon and 2 to 7 pm (6 pm on Saturday). Other parts of Spain and Morocco are handled by Eurocars (☎ 61.26.40.04), whose office in the bus station is staffed on weekdays from 9 am to 1 pm (noon on Monday) and 2 to 6.30 pm (6 pm on Monday). Saturday hours are 9 to 11.30 am and 12.30 to 5 pm.

Getting Around

To/From the Airport The Navette Airport (airport shuttle; 20FF), operated by TRG (☎ 61.30.04.89, 61.71.31.99), links Toulouse with Aéroport International de Toulouse-Blagnac. Buses *to* the airport run every 20 minutes (every 40 to 60 minutes on weekends) from about 6 am to 9 pm (8 pm on weekends); they can be picked up at the bus station (from the platform nearest the train station) and at a stop next to 19 Allées Jean Jaurès (near the Jean Jaurès metro station).

Bus & Metro The local public transport company is called Semvat (☎ 61.41.70.70 for information). A single-ride ticket, available from bus drivers, costs 6.50FF (9FF to the suburbs). A carnet of 10 tickets costs 47FF (70FF to the suburbs). Tickets are valid for 45 minutes (one hour on suburban routes) after they've been time-stamped and can be used for up to three transfers. Most bus lines run daily until 8 or 9 pm. Bus du Nuit (night bus) lines, all of which start at the train station, run from 9 pm to midnight. The new metro began operation in 1993.

The Semvat ticket kiosk across the parking lot from the train station (near the Hôtel Altea Matabiau) can supply you with a route map. It is open Monday to Saturday from 6.30 am to 7.30 pm. To get from the train station to the city centre, take bus No 2 or 5. Some buses stop near the ticket kiosk,

TOULOUSE

while for others you have to walk around the corner to Allée Georges Pompidou.

In the city centre, Semvat has an information and ticket office, known as Espace Transport Semvat, at 7 Place Esquirol. It is open Monday to Friday from 8.30 am to 6.30 pm and on Saturday until 12.30 pm. There's a Semvat ticket window at 9 Place du Capitole.

Taxi There are 24-hour taxi stands at the train station (☎ 61.62.37.34), Place Wilson (☎ 61.21.55.46) and Place Esquirol (☎ 61. 21.56.42).

Car In the city centre, there's a parking garage under Place du Capitole. Except on Sunday, you can park for free at Place Saint Sernin. Near Blvd de Strasbourg, there's a multistorey parking garage above the Halles Victor Hugo market.

ALBI

Almost all of central Albi (population 48,000), including the huge, fortress-like Gothic cathedral begun in the late 13th century, is built from bricks of reddish clay dug from the nearby Tarn River. Albi is best known as the namesake of the Albigensian heresy of the 12th and 13th centuries and the cruel crusade that crushed it (see the Cathars aside in the Languedoc-Roussillon chapter).

Displaying both Toulousain and Languedoc influences, the town has a very southern feel. It is laid-back and not overrun with tourists, though English holidaymakers are slowly migrating here from Périgord to the north. One of Albi's most famous natives was Henri Toulouse-Lautrec (1864-1901), whose paintings are perhaps best known for portraying brothel life in Paris in the late 1800s. A vast number of his works are shown in the Musée Toulouse-Lautrec.

Orientation

Though the town straddles the Tarn River, there's little reason to cross to the northern bank except for a great view of the town centre and the stone arches of Pont Vieux.

Central Albi has an unusually chaotic layout. The cathedral dominates the western side of town; from it a number of pedestrianised streets radiate, leading to Place du Vigan, Albi's commercial and nightlife centre, in the eastern side of town. The lonely train station area lies about a km to the southwest.

Information

Tourist Office In the shade of the cathedral, the tourist office (☎ 63.54.22.30) on Place Sainte Cécile is open Monday to Saturday from 9 am to noon and 2 to 6 pm. Between June and September it's open from 9 am to 7.30 pm and on Sunday from 10.30 am to 12.30 pm and 4.30 to 6.30 pm. Hotel bookings cost 10FF. On Monday, when the banks are closed, there's a foreign exchange service.

Money The Banque de France (☎ 63.54. 17.39) at 17 Rue Dominique de Florenceis open Tuesday to Saturday from 8.30 am to noon and 1.30 to 3.40 pm.

Post The main post office on Place du Vigan is open weekdays from 8 am to 7 pm and Saturday until noon.

Albi's postcode is 81000.

Laundry The Lavomatique on Rue Émile Grand is open daily from 7 am to 9 pm.

Walking Tour

For a good overall picture of the town head down to **Pont 22 Août 1944**, the main bridge over the Tarn. Named after the date of Albi's liberation at the end of WW II, the view is especially fine on cool mornings as the sun starts to warm up the town's red tones and highlights the arched bridges. A plaque on the wall of the **Maison Natale de Toulouse-Lautrec** in the street named after the artist marks the house where he was born. However, you can only visit the house in August.

Cathédrale Sainte Cécile

As much a fortress as a church, this mighty

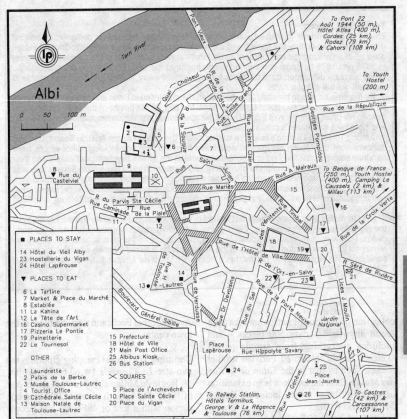

Albi

PLACES TO STAY
14 Hôtel du Vieil Alby
23 Hostellerie du Vigan
24 Hôtel Lapérouse

PLACES TO EAT
6 La Tartine
7 Market & Place du Marché
8 Establé
11 La Kahina
12 La Tête de l'Art
16 Casino Supermarket
17 Pizzeria Le Pontie
19 Painetterie
22 Le Tournesol

OTHER
1 Laundrette
2 Palais de la Berbie
3 Musée Toulouse-Lautrec
4 Tourist Office
9 Cathédrale Sainte Cécile
5 Maison Natale de
   Toulouse-Lautrec

15 Prefecture
18 Hôtel de Ville
21 Main Post Office
25 Albibus Kiosk
26 Bus Station

SQUARES
5 Place de l'Archevêché
10 Place Sainte Cécile
20 Place du Vigan

cathedral on Place Sainte Cécile was begun in 1282, less than four decades after the crusade against the Cathars. Built entirely of red brick in the Meridional Gothic style, it was finished (mostly) in 1392 and consecrated in 1480. It is certainly not what you would call attractive – indeed, it's most impressive feature is its sheer bulk. The **tower** is 78 metres high.

In contrast with the plain, sunburnt exterior, the interior is elaborately decorated. Indeed, not a single patch of wall or ceiling was left untouched by the Italian artists who painted it in the early 1500s. An intricately carved **rood screen** from around 1500, which lost many of its statues in 1794, spans the 18-metre-wide sanctuary. The **stained-glass windows** in the apse and choir date from the 14th to the 16th centuries. The cathedral is closed from noon to 2 pm except from July to September.

Musée Toulouse-Lautrec

Next to the cathedral, the Toulouse-Lautrec Museum is housed in the **Palais de la Berbie**, a fortress-like archbishop's palace built between the 13th and 15th centuries.

This museum houses the most extensive

Toulouse-Lautrec
The work of Henri de Toulouse-Lautrec, painter, lithographer and poster designer, influenced many artists, particularly the fauves and expressionists. Born in Albi in 1864, Toulouse-Lautrec grew up in an aristocratic environment as his family were descendants of the counts of Toulouse. In 1878 and 1879 he broke one thighbone and fractured the other in two horse riding accidents. While his body developed quite normally, his legs wasted away, leaving him short and unable to walk without the aid of a cane.

By the time he was in his early 20s, he was studying painting in Paris and had met such artists as Van Gogh and the symbolist Émile Bernard. In 1890, at the height of the *belle époque* and despite his great admiration of Edgar Degas, he abandoned impressionism and took to observing and sketching gay Paree's colourful nightlife.

Among Toulouse-Lautrec's favourite subjects were the cabaret singer Aristide Bruant, can-can dancers from the Moulin Rouge and prostitutes from the Rue des Moulins, all of whom were carefully studied and sketched in a style that revealed the artist's psychological insight into their character and his ability to capture movement and expressions in a few simple strokes. He was an avid draughtsman, with a sure line and fast strokes; his sketches were made on anything from a scrap of paper to a tablecloth, while tracing paper or buff-coloured cardboard were his preferred painting surfaces. His paintings and posters are characterised by large areas of colours, simplified forms and free-flowing lines.

His life at this time was certainly not limited to observation and work. He thoroughly enjoyed the nightlife scene, the gossip, and the drinking, overindulgence in which was to lead to his early death. Following a mental breakdown in 1899, he was committed to a sanatorium, where he remained for a few months. In August of the same year he suffered a stroke which left him partly paralysed. He was taken to his mother's home, Château de Malromé, where he died on 9 September 1901. ■

collection of Toulouse-Lautrec's works to be found anywhere – over 500 pieces – and includes everything from simple pencil sketches to his celebrated Parisian brothel scenes, such as that in the *Salon de la Rue des Moulins*. On the top floor is an exhibition of works by other artists, including Degas, Matisse and Rodin.

From 1 April to 30 September the museum is open daily from 10 am (9 am in July and August) to noon and 2 to 6 pm (5 pm the rest of the year, when it's also closed on Tuesday). Entry costs 18FF (9FF for students).

Festivals
The biggest events on the calendar are the theatre festival, held at the end of June and beginning of July, and a classical music festival in the last two weeks of July.

Places to Stay
Albi is not overflowing with budget hotels. There are a few near the train station along Ave Maréchal Foch, and a couple more in the town centre.

Camping The closest camping ground is the two-star *Le Caussels* (☎ 63.60.37.06) just off Route de Millau about two km north-east of Place du Vigan. It charges 24FF for one person with a tent or 48FF for two people with a tent and car. It's open from 1 April to 30 October. There's a small on-site grocery store. Bus No 2 or 5 from Place Jean Jaurès stops nearby. From the train station, you'll either have to walk to Place Jean Jaurès or take bus No 1.

Hostel The *Maison des Jeunes et de la Culture* (MJC; ☎ 63.54.53.65) at 13 Rue de la République, also known as the Auberge de Jeunesse, is about 400 metres north-east of Place du Vigan. It has dorm beds for as little as 24FF and breakfast for 12FF but may be closed during some weekends in winter. To get there from the train station, take bus No 1 to the République stop and head straight down Rue de la République.

Top: Parking problems in the wilderness, near Lac de Bious Artigues,
in the Pyrenees (DR)
Bottom: Early morning over Albi, on the Tarn River, near Toulouse (LL)

Top: Field of sunflowers in the Champagne region (LL)
Middle: Gannets with their young, Brittany (OT Perros Guirec); Buzzard,
Auverge (Parc); Black woodpecker, Auvergne (Parc)
Bottom: Cow grazing in a country lane, Golfe du Morbihan, Brittany (GA)

Hotels – Train Station Area The cheapest rooms in town are in the *Hôtel Terminus* (☎ 63.54.00.99) opposite the station at 33 Ave Maréchal Foch. This place looks a bit rough and the bar below may get noisy, but the rooms are decent enough. Basic attic singles/doubles start at 75/80FF and doubles with shower at 130FF. There's a hall shower, which is free or *payant* depending on whom you ask.

Continue along the tree-lined avenue for 100 metres or so and you'll come to two neighbouring hotels, both pleasant and with little to tell them apart except for the price. The *Hôtel George V* (☎ 63.54.24.16) at No 29 has doubles with shower from 120FF while the *Hôtel La Régence* (☎ 63.54.01.42) at No 27 has basic rooms from 110FF or 150FF with shower. A hall shower costs 10FF.

Hotels – Centre Ideally located at the beginning of the pedestrianised area, the *Hôtel du Vieil Alby* (☎ 63.54.14.69) at 25 Rue Toulouse-Lautrec has good, basic doubles from 130FF (150FF with shower). The hall shower is 15FF and parking costs 35/5FF for a car/bike. On the edge of the town centre, the mustard-toned *Hôtel Lapérouse* (☎ 63.54.69.22) at 21 Place Lapérouse has cosy rooms, all with showers, from 130/170FF for a single/double. There's also a pool at the back.

For something more up-market, the three-star *Hostellerie du Vigan* (☎ 63.54.01.23) at 16 Place du Vigan is centrally located and has spacious modern rooms and a popular restaurant. You might find the hotel a bit noisy on Friday and Saturday nights when Place du Vigan's terraces come alive. Singles/doubles start at 200/350FF. For a more serene option, head to *Hôtel Atlea* (☎ 63.47.66.66) at 41 Rue Porta, just across Pont 22 Août 1944 from the centre. Built along the Tarn River, this three-star hotel has elegant singles/doubles for 310/480FF with simply superb views of the city.

Places to Eat & Drink
Albi's restaurant scene is somewhat limited – the streets around the cathedral are the best hunting ground. Place du Vigan is the nightlife arena, and many brasseries here stay open until late.

Restaurants Down the atmospheric little Rue de la Piale, *La Tête de l'Art* (☎ 63.38.44.75) at No 7 has a 70FF four-course *menu*. Further along, past where the street changes name to Rue Caminade, you'll find *La Kahina*, a laid-back little place. It is basic but popular, with *menus* from 51FF.

Behind (west of) the cathedral, *Establée* (☎ 63.38.99.79) on Rue du Castelviel is a quaint half-timbered house with a small terrace. Lunchtime *menus* start at 65FF but at dinner they jump to 98FF. Opposite the tourist office, locals and foreigners alike are attracted to the large terrace of *La Tartine* on Place de l'Archevêché. It offers a 65FF *menu* but the traffic noise – not to mention the fumes – can be unpleasant.

The *Buffet de la Gare* (☎ 63.54.28.30) on Place Stalingrad at the train station, has an unpretentious 70FF four-course *menu* that includes a glass of wine. *Le Tournesol* (☎ 63.38.38.14) a small vegetarian restaurant on Rue de l'Ort-en-Salvy. It serves a plat du jour for 40FF, and is open Tuesday to Saturday from noon to 2 pm and on Friday and Saturday from 7.15 to 9.30 pm.

On Place du Vigan, *Pizzeria Le Pontie* (☎ 63.54.16.34) has pizzas from 40FF. It is open until 1 am.

Self-Catering Fresh fare can be picked up daily (except Monday) from the *halles*, a lovely covered market on Place du Marché. The *Casino* supermarket on Lices Georges Pompidou is open Monday to Saturday from 8.30 am to 12.30 pm and 2.30 to 7.30 pm (nonstop on Friday and Saturday). *Painetterie* on Place du Vigan sells bread and a few other edibles and is open daily from 7 am to 8 pm.

Getting There & Away
Train The train station (☎ 63.54.50.50 for information) at Place Stalingrad is about one km south-west of the tourist office in an

TOULOUSE

isolated part of town. There's no information office as such but the ticket windows are open from 5.30 am to 9.30 pm. To get into town, you can take bus No 1 (last one at 7 pm), which goes to Place du Vigan. If you're walking, head up the tree-lined Ave Maréchal Joffre (to the left as you leave the station), and then turn left into Ave du Général de Gaulle which leads onto Place Lapérouse. From here Rue de Verdusse leads straight to the cathedral.

There are major train connections via Rodez (58FF; one hour) to Millau (100FF; two hours) or Toulouse (55FF; one hour; hourly).

Bus The bus station is on Place Jean Jaurès but there's no real office. If you're after information or timetables, ask in the little café (☎ 63.54.58.61) on the square. There are limited services to Cordes (25FF; 30 minutes; one bus at 7.45 am) and Castres (37FF; 50 minutes; six a day).

Getting Around

Bus Local buses are run by Albibus (☎ 63. 38.43.43) which has an information kiosk at the northern end of Place Jean Jaurès, the main bus hub. Single tickets cost 4FF. Buses don't run on Sundays.

PAU

The pleasant and laid-back city of Pau (population 140,000, including the suburbs), former capital of the Béarn region, is famed for its mild climate, flower-filled public parks and magnificent views of the Pyrenees. In the mid-19th century, it was a favourite wintering spot for wealthy English people, who introduced steeplechases, golf and fox hunting. These days, the city owes its prosperity to a high-tech industrial base and the huge natural gas field at Lacq, 20 km to the north-west, discovered in 1951. The university was founded in 1970.

If you have a car, Pau – plentifully supplied with cheap hotels – makes a good base for forays into the Pyrenees. It is pretty dead in August.

Orientation

The train station is separated from Blvd des Pyrénées, Place Clemenceau and the centre of town by a steep hill, outfitted with a tiny funicular railway. The chateau and the Vieille Ville are at the western end of Blvd des Pyrénées; Parc Beaumont is at its eastern end. Semipedestrianised Rue des Cordeliers, in the heart of the shopping district, connects Rue Maréchal Joffre with Place de la Libération. Centre Bosquet is a huge, modern commercial and residential complex on Cours Bosquet.

Information

Tourist Office The Office Municipal du Tourisme (☎ 59.27.27.08) at Place Royale is across the square from the upper end of the funicular railway. It is open Monday to Saturday from 9 am to noon and 2 to 6 pm. In July and August it's open daily from 9 am to 7 pm (6 pm on Sunday). Hotel reservations in the Pau area are free. The brochure entitled *Pau – Ville Authentique*, available in English, includes a walking tour of the old part of town.

Money The Banque de France at 7 Rue Louis Barthou is open Monday to Friday from 8.30 am to noon and 2.30 to 3.30 pm.

There are a number of commercial banks along Rue Maréchal Foch. If you have a cash crunch on a Sunday or holiday, try the front desk of the Hôtel Continental (☎ 59.27. 69.31) at 2 Rue Maréchal Foch.

Post The main post office (☎ 59.98.98.62) at 1 Cours Bosquet is open Monday to Friday from 8 am to 6.30 pm and on Saturday until noon. Exchange services are available.

Pau's postcode is 64000.

Books & Maps Hiking maps, topoguides (including *Walking in the Pyrenees*), a variety of books on the region and some Lonely Planet titles are available at Librairie des Pyrénées (☎ 59.27.78.75) at 14 Rue Saint Louis, half a block from the tourist office. It's open Monday to Saturday from 9 am (10 am on Monday) to noon and 2 to 7 pm.

Laundry The Laverie Automatique at 66 Rue Émile Garet is open daily from 7 am to 10 pm.

Medical Services The Centre Hospitalier (☎ 59.92.48.48) at 4 Blvd Hauterive (ie the northern end of Ave Pouguet) is the last stop on bus line Nos 3 and 6.

Walking Tour

Majestic **Blvd des Pyrénées**, laid out at the beginning of the 1800s, runs along the crest of the hill overlooking the train station. If it's clear, you can see a variety of Pyrenean peaks – the small *table d'orientation* (viewpoint indicator) opposite 20 Blvd des Pyrénées explains what you're looking at. At the eastern end of Blvd des Pyrénées is the 12-hectare **Parc Beaumont**, a lovely English-style park. The lawn, flowers and park are shaded by trees representing a wide variety of species.

The western end of Blvd des Pyrénées leads to the chateau and the narrow streets of the picturesque **Vieille Ville**.

Château

The Château (☎ 59.82.38.00) at 2 Rue du Château, former home of the kings of Navarre, was built as a fortress in the 13th and 14th centuries and transformed into a Renaissance palace by Margaret of Angoulême (Margaret of Navarre) in the 16th century. Neglected in the 18th century and turned into a barracks after the Revolution, it was in terrible condition by 1838, when Louis-Philippe and, later, Napoleon III had the interior completely redone. Most of the ornamentation and furniture, including the oak dining room table that seats 100, date from the 19th century. The chateau's most outstanding feature is its superb collection of 16th to 18th-century **Gobelins tapestries**, considered one of the finest in Europe.

The collection of Sèvres porcelain includes a number of *bourdalous*, decorated chamber pots from the 17th and 18th centuries. During the long sermons delivered by Jesuit preachers known as bourdalous, the aristocratic women in the audience could relieve themselves without having to leave the hall by placing the pots under their skirts. In the room where Henri IV was born in 1553, you can see what is said to be his **cradle**, an upturned tortoise shell that, it was hoped, would bring the future king longevity and strength.

The interesting **Musée Béarnais** (☎ 59.27.07.36), reached by taking the spiral staircase at the far end of the courtyard to the 3rd floor, has displays on the architecture, furniture, costumes, etc of the Béarn region. The natural history section has some ghastly stuffed animals. One display case shows how Béarn berets – worn by armies around the world as well as by the Basques – are made. It is open daily from 9.30 am to noon and 2 to 5 pm (6 pm from mid-April to mid-October). Entry costs 6FF (free for children under 18 accompanied by an adult).

THE PYRÉNÉES

Bernadotte

Jean-Baptiste Bernadotte, born in 1763 in the building now occupied by Pau's Musée Bernadotte, enlisted in the French army at the age of 17. An enthusiastic supporter of the Revolution, he spent the 1790s as a distinguished general and diplomat, serving both the Revolutionary government and Napoleon and acquiring a reputation as a talented and humane administrator.

Meanwhile, in Stockholm, the Swedish Riksdag concluded that the only way out of the country's dynastic and political crisis was to bring in an outsider. Full of respect for French military prowess, they turned to Bernadotte, electing him crown prince in 1810. Despite Napoleon's expectations, he did not follow a pro-French foreign policy. Indeed, in the 1813 Battle of Leipzig, Swedish troops under his command helped the Allies deal Napoleon his first major defeat. In 1818, after several years as regent, Bernadotte became King Charles XIV John; he died in office in 1844. The present king of Sweden is the seventh ruler in the Bernadotte dynasty. ■

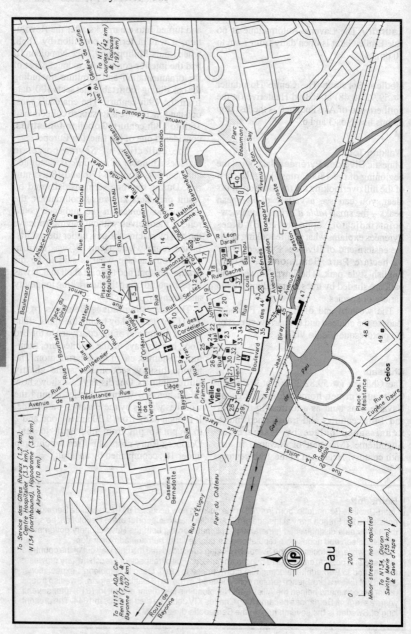

To Service des Gîtes Ruraux (1.2 km),
Hôspital (1.3 km),
N134 (northbound), Hipodrome (3.6 km)
& Airport (10 km)

To N117, ADA Car
Rental (7 km) &
Bayonne (107 km)

Route de Bayonne

To N134, Oloron
Sainte Marie (35 km),
& Cave d'Aspe

Pau

Minor streets not depicted

0   200   400 m

To N117,
Lourdes (42 km)
& Toulouse
(197 km)

■ PLACES TO STAY	24	Fromagerie	28	Château
	25	Le Marilyn Bar	29	Tour de la Monnaie
2 Logis des Jeunes	26	La Zarzuela	34	Office Municipal
Michel Hounau	27	Au Fruit Défondu &		du Tourisme
6 Hôtel Supervie		Pizzeria La Tour	36	Palais des Pyrénées
7 Hôtel Carnot		du Parlement	37	STAP Bus Information
13 Hôtel Continental	33	Restaurant Le Clocher		& Citram Pyrénées
17 Hôtel de la Pomme d'Or	41	La Cité d'Angkor	38	TPR Bus Office
18 Hôtel Le Bourbon			40	Casino Municipal
20 Hôtel Le Béarn		OTHER	42	Banque de France
30 Hôtel d'Albret			44	Table d'Orientation
32 Mon Auberge	1	Cinéma Le Méliès		(Viewpoint Indicator)
39 Hôtel Central	3	Romano Sport	46	Funicular Railway
45 Hôtel du Funiculaire		(Bike Rental)	47	Railway Station
48 Camping Base de	4	Laverie Automatique		
Plein Air	9	Musée Bernadotte	✕	SQUARES
49 Foyer des Jeunes	11	Prefecture		
Travailleurs	14	Centre Bosquet	8	Place de la Libération
	15	Musée des	19	Place Clemenceau
▼ PLACES TO EAT		Beaux-Arts	31	Place Reine Marguerite
	16	Main Post Office	35	Place Royale
5 Les Halles	21	Librairie des Pyrénées	43	Square George V
10 West Side Bar & Grill	22	Compagnie du Sud		
12 Prisunic Supermarket	23	Romano Sport		

On the side of the chateau overlooking the river are two square, 14th-century towers: 33-metre **Tour Gaston Phoébus**, made of brick; and brick-and-stone **Tour de la Monnaie**, which has a lift inside. Nearby are some of the flower gardens for which Pau is famous. West of the chateau is the shady **Parc du Château**.

The chateau is open daily from 9.30 to 11.45 am and 2 to 4.45 pm (5.45 pm from mid-April to mid-October). Entrance, including the obligatory one-hour guided tour, costs 26FF (14FF if you're under 26). An information sheet in English is available.

Musée Bernadotte

The Bernadotte Museum (☎ 59.27.48.42) at 6 Rue Tran has exhibits illustrating the peculiar story of how a Pau-born French general became the king of Sweden and Norway (see the Bernadotte aside). Displays include letters, documents, engravings, paintings and memorabilia. The museum is open Tuesday to Sunday from 10 am to noon and 2 to 6 pm. Entry costs 10FF (5FF for children and students).

Musée des Beaux-Arts

Pau's Fine Arts Museum (☎ 59.27.33.02), whose entrance is opposite 15 Rue Mathieu Lalanne, is quite a decent provincial museum. Among the works on exhibit is a variety of 17th to 20th-century European paintings, including some by Rubens, El Greco and Degas. It is open from 10 am to noon and 2 to 6 pm (closed Tuesday). Entry costs 10FF (5FF for students).

Activities

Romano Sport (☎ 59.27.30.54) at 27 Rue Maréchal Joffre sells equipment for hiking, mountain climbing, skiing and spelunking. For details on the other Romano Sport shop, see Bicycle under Getting Around.

Places to Stay – bottom end

Pau's hotels, which offer some of the best value for money anywhere in France, are busiest during April, May, June, September and October, when both tourists and business people are in town. But even during these months, you can always find a room in the morning.

Camping Although it's directly across the Gave de Pau (the river) from the train station, *Camping Base de Plein Air* (☎ 59.06.57.37), near the Mairie in the suburb of Gelos (postcode 64110), is 2.5 km from the railway station by road. To get there by bus, take the No 1 from Place Clemenceau or Rue Marca. It's open from mid-May to mid-September. Tariffs are 22FF for a tent site (including parking) and 13FF per adult.

Rural Accommodation The tourist office has a list of chambres d'hôtes, gîtes d'étape and campings à la ferme in the Pau area. For more information on rural accommodation and help with reservations, contact the Service des Gîtes Ruraux (☎ 59.80.19.13) in the Maison d'Agriculture at 124 Blvd Tourasse, north of the city centre. It is open Monday to Friday from 9 am to 12.30 pm and 2 to 5 pm.

Hostels From mid-June to mid-September the friendly *Logis des Jeunes Michel Hounau* (☎ 59.30.45.77) at 30ter Rue Michel Hounau has a plentiful supply of single rooms for travellers. Even during the school year, when it functions as a *foyer* for young people working or studying in Pau, there are always at least five rooms available for people passing through. Singles (all they have) with washbasin cost 80FF (61FF if you're under 26 or have a hostelling card). You can check in 24 hours a day – if the door is locked, just ring the bell. Kitchen facilities are available on the 3rd and 4th floors.

In the suburb of Gelos near Camping Base de Plein Air (see Camping), the *Foyer des Jeunes Travailleurs* (☎ 59.06.53.02) has a year-round youth hostel section. Beds cost 67FF (48FF with a hostelling card).

Hotels The friendly, family-run *Hôtel d'Albret* (☎ 59.27.81.58), an older, 12-room place at 11 Rue d'Albret (near Place Reine Marguerite), is an exellent deal: large, clean doubles with washbasin and bidet cost only 80FF; the two rooms with shower and toilet are 120FF. Hall showers are 10FF. Except in

summer, reception may be closed on Sunday from noon to 7 pm.

The family-run, 17-room *Hôtel Le Béarn* (☎ 59.27.52.50) at 5 Rue Maréchal Joffre (1st floor) is another fine choice. Large, old-fashioned doubles cost only 85FF with washbasin and bidet and 130FF with huge, toilet-equipped bathrooms. Hall showers cost 10FF. *Mon Auberge* (☎ 59.82.80.99) at 9 Rue de Foix (also near Place Reine Marguerite) has doubles from 100FF. It is closed during August.

The 20-room *Hôtel de la Pomme d'Or* (☎ 59.27.78.48), which occupies a former *relais de chevaux* (coaching inn) at 11 Rue Maréchal Foch (1st floor), has singles/doubles/triples with washbasin and bidet for 85/95/140FF. Hall showers are 10FF. To get in or out of the ground floor entrance, push the button on the doorpost. If you arrive after midnight, ring the bell to wake up the night clerk.

Somewhat further from the train station, the 13-room *Hôtel Supervie* (☎ 59.27.90.54 during the day, 59.87.83.32 after 8.30 pm) at 1 Rue Nogué (1st floor) has large, decent doubles/two-bed quads with shower and toilet for 110/195FF. It also has doubles/quads with washbasin and bidet for 70/130FF, but there are no hall showers. There's a TV room for guests. Reception is closed on Sunday except in August.

Around the corner, you might try the no-star, eight-room *Hôtel Carnot* (☎ 59.27.88.70) at 13 Rue Carnot (2nd floor), whose large, simple singles/doubles/triples with washbasin, bidet and linoleum floors cost 65/85/100FF. Hall showers are 11FF. Reception is closed on Sunday after noon.

Places to Stay – middle

Pau's mid-range hotels generally offer very good value.

Train Station Area The only hotel right near the railway station is the eight-room *Hôtel du Funiculaire* (☎ 59.27.01.40) at 2 Ave Jean Biray, which is next to the lower end of the funicular railway. Decent rooms with shower, toilet, TV and soundproofed windows cost 200 to 250FF for one to three people.

City Centre The central *Hôtel Le Bourbon* (☎ 59.27.53.12; fax 59.82.90.99) at 12 Place Clemenceau has very comfortable singles/doubles/triples with shower, toilet and TV starting at 200/250/330FF. Some of the rooms have air-con.

Another excellent bet is the 28-room *Hôtel Central* (☎ 59.27.72.75; fax 59.27. 33.28) at 15 Rue Léon Daran. Large rooms with spacious bathrooms and soundproofed windows cost 220/240/280FF for one/two/ four people; the largest rooms are Nos 2, 15, 16, 19, 21 and 28. There's a French billiard table in the ground-floor public area.

Places to Eat

There's a cluster of restaurants near the chateau on Rue Sully, Rue Henri IV, Rue du Moulin and Rue du Château. You'll find a number of *brasseries* along Blvd des Pyrénées around Square George V.

Restaurants – French The *Restaurant Le Clocher* (☎ 59.27.72.83) at 8 Rue de Foix has *menus* of cuisine from Béarn and the Landes regions for 72, 90 and 140FF. Mixed salads are 35 to 60FF. It is open Monday to Saturday from noon to 2 pm and 7 to 10 pm.

Au Fruit Défondu (☎ 59.27.26.05) at 3 Rue Sully has 10 types of cheese, fish, meat and chocolate fondues, as well as pierrades (meats that you grill yourself) and raclette (melted cheese with cold cuts). Food is served from 7 pm to 1.30 am (closed Tuesday).

Restaurants – Other *Pizzeria La Tour du Parlement* (☎ 59.27.38.29) at 36 Rue du Moulin, popular with locals as well as visitors, is open from noon to 2.30 pm and 7 pm to 1 am daily except Tuesday (daily from May to October).

West Side Bar & Grill (☎ 59.82.90.78) at 3 Rue Saint Jacques (near Place de la Libération) has a wood plank floor, 1950s American memorabilia on the walls and a miniature train that runs on a track suspended from the ceiling. The all-American menu, like the décor, was influenced by the 15 years spent by one of the owners in California and Hawaii. Steak and other meat dishes are 55 to 85FF. *Menus* are available from 62FF. Food is served from noon to 2 pm and 8 to 10.30 pm daily except Saturday at midday and Sunday.

La Cité d'Angkor at 4 Rue Navarrot is open Tuesday to Saturday. *Menus* cost 60 and 79FF.

Self-Catering Bench-equipped public spaces where you might want to picnic include Blvd des Pyrénées, Place Royale, Parc Beaumont, Parc du Château and Place de la Libération.

Les Halles, a large food market at Place de la République, is open Monday to Saturday; except on Saturday, it's closed from 1 to 3.30 pm. On Wednesday and Saturday mornings, there's a *food market* at Place du Foirail.

The *Prisunic* at 22 Rue Maréchal Foch, whose supermarket section is in the back, is open Monday to Saturday from 8.30 am to 7 pm. The Centre Bosquet on Cours Bosquet includes a *Champion supermarket*.

Near the Vieille Ville, there's a cluster of *food shops* around Place Reine Marguerite. *La Zarzuela* at 28 Rue Maréchal Joffre, where you can choose from a selection of freshly prepared foods, including paella, is open Monday to Friday from 8 am to 2 pm and 4 to 8 pm and on Saturday until 1 pm. The *fromagerie* at 24 Rue Maréchal Joffre is open Monday to Saturday from 9 am to 12.30 pm and 3.15 to 7.30 pm. There are several *boulangeries* nearby.

Entertainment

Cinema The only cinema in Pau with non-dubbed English films is *Cinéma Le Méliès* (☎ 59.83.73.33 for the answering machine, 59.27.60.52 for the office) at 6 Rue Bargoin, off Rue Pasteur. It is closed from late July to late August.

Bar *Le Marilyn Bar* at 6 Rue René Fournets (at Place Reine Marguerite) has photos of Marilyn Monroe on the walls above the red, American diner-style couches. The intimate little corners are perfect for sipping a beer (20FF) or a cocktail (35 to 50FF) to the accompaniment of mellow jazz or music from the 1950s. Le Marilyn is open Monday to Saturday from 6 pm to 2 am.

The bar of the *West Side Bar & Grill* (see Restaurants) is open Monday to Saturday from 11 am (2 pm on Saturday) to 2 am.

Horse Racing The renowned *Hippodrome du Pont Long* (☎ 59.32.07.93 for information), north of the centre, has seasonal steeplechases, especially in the spring and autumn.

Getting There & Away

Air The Aéroport de Pau-Pyrénées (☎ 59.33.21.29) is about 10 km north-west of central Pau.

Train The train station (☎ 59.55.50.50) is at the eastern end of Ave Jean Biray. The information office is open from 9 am to 6 pm daily except Sunday and holidays.

Pau is linked to destinations in the Pyrenees including Bedous (in the Vallée d'Aspe; 47FF; one hour; four a day), the Spanish railhead of Canfranc (63FF; 2¼ hours; three a day), Laruns (in the Vallée d'Ossau; 34FF) and Lourdes (34FF; 30 minutes; nine a day).

Long-haul destinations served by direct trains include Bayonne (72FF; 1¼ hours; five a day), Bordeaux (143FF; 2½ to 3½ hours; eight a day), Marseille (291FF; seven to eight hours; two direct trains a day), Nice (368FF; 10 to 11 hours; two a day) and Toulouse (131FF; 2¾ hours; six a day). There are six daily trains to Paris: three TGVs to Gare Montparnasse (five hours) and three non-TGVs (including two overnight trains) to Gare d'Austerlitz.

Bus TPR (☎ 59.27.45.98) at 2 Place Clemenceau (actually a bit south of the *place* on Rue Gachet) has three runs a day (one a day on Sunday and holidays in July and August) to Bayonne (2¼ hours) and Biarritz (2½ hours). It also has buses to Lourdes (30FF;

1¼ hours; four to six times a day), Mauléon, Orthez, Monein and other towns in the area.

Citram Pyrénées (☎ 59.27.22.22), whose office is on Rue Gachet in the Palais des Pyrénées complex, has regular buses to Agen and offers various excursions.

Car The ADA office (☎ 59.81.21.70) at 9 Rue Bernard Palissy in the Pau suburb of Lescar (postcode 64230) is seven km north-west of town (towards Bayonne) on the N117. To get there, turn off the N117 just past the giant Casino supermarket. If you call ahead, they'll deliver the car to you in town. The office is open Monday to Saturday from 8 am to noon and 2 to 7 pm (4 pm on Saturday).

Getting Around

To/From the Airport The Navette Aéroport (airport shuttle; 25FF; ☎ 59.02.45.45) meets most incoming flights. There are four runs a day to the airport; pick-up points are at the train station and 5 Place Clemenceau (opposite the florist).

Funiculaire The railway station is linked to Blvd des Pyrénées by a funicular railway, a hilarious little contraption that saves you over five minutes of uphill walking. It was built in 1908 by the hotels along Blvd des Pyrénées to save their guests from cardiovascular fitness, which was terribly unfashionable at the time, at least among the rich. Monday to Saturday, cars leave every three to four minutes from 7 am to 9.30 pm; Sunday hours are 1.30 to 9 pm. Travel is free.

Bus STAP Aubobus Urbains (☎ 59.27.69.78), the local bus company, has a Bureau d'Information on Rue Gachet in the Palais des Pyrénées complex. Bus maps are also available at the tourist office. Bus No 7 goes links the train station with Place Clemenceau, but most people walk.

All nine local bus lines stop at Place Clemenceau. Route maps are posted at stops. Buses run daily except Sunday and holidays from about 6.30 am to 7 or 7.30 pm. Single tickets, sold on board, cost 6FF. A carnet of four tickets good for eight rides costs 23FF and is available at some tabacs. The Carte Rubis, good for unlimited travel for a week (Monday to Saturday), costs 35FF. Tickets are valid for one hour after they've been time-stamped but can't be used for round trips.

Taxi There's a taxi stand at Place Clemenceau.

Bicycle Romano Sport (☎ 59.80.21.31) at 42 Ave du Général de Gaulle rents mountain bikes for 50/100FF a half/whole day. It's open Monday to Saturday (daily from December to March) from 9 am to noon and 2 to 7 pm.

LOURDES

Lourdes (year-round population 18,000) was just a sleepy market town in 1858 when Bernadette Soubirous (1844-79), an illiterate, 14-year-old peasant girl, saw the Virgin Mary, dressed in white, in a series of 18 visions that took place in a cave near town. The girl's account of the apparition was investigated by the diocese and, later, the Vatican and confirmed as a bona fide miracle. Bernadette, who lived out her short life as a nun, was beatified in 1925 and canonised eight years later, thus becoming St Bernadette.

These events set Lourdes on the path to becoming the world's most visited pilgrimage site. Each year, the town receives some five million pilgrims from all over the world, more than Jerusalem, Rome or Mecca and almost 300 for every permanent resident. Among the faithful, whose numbers are growing each year, are many sick people seeking a miraculous cure to their afflictions. But whatever their reasons for being in Lourdes, the pilgrims tend to be remarkably good-natured – after all, they may be on a religious mission, but they're also on holiday in France! On summer nights, groups of pilgrims wander in and out of the brightly lit souvenir shops and restaurants, making the whole town centre seem like a giant carnival. The pilgrimage season lasts from March to October, with peaks around Catholic holidays.

Accompanying the fervent, almost medieval piety of the pilgrims is an astounding display of commercial exuberance that is reminiscent of the bazaars of the Middle East. If your sense of propriety and good taste is governed by the Anglo-Protestant preference for understatement, it can all seem unspeakably tacky. Granted, the souvenir wall thermometers on sale all over town are undignified by any standard. But the choice of souvenirs – affordable and flashy things made of cast plastic and blinking Christmas lights – makes it too easy to discount the significance of the experience these knick-knacks are supposed to commemorate to the people who spend their life savings to come here.

Lourdes is a sister-city of – where else? – Czestochowa in Poland.

Orientation

Lourdes's two main east-west streets, both of which are lined with souvenir shops, are Blvd de la Grotte and, 300 metres south, Rue de la Grotte. Both lead to the Sanctuaires Notre Dame de Lourdes, but Blvd de la Grotte takes you to the main entrance and the Esplanade.

The principal north-south thoroughfare, known as Chaussée Maransin where it passes over Blvd de la Grotte, runs between Ave de la Gare (which runs by the train station) and Place du Champ Commun, where the tourist office is.

Information

Tourist Office Lourdes's tourist office (☎ 62. 94.15.64) at Place du Champ Commun is open Monday to Saturday from 9 am to noon and 2 to 6 pm (7 pm from Easter to mid-October). From Easter to mid-October it is also open on Sunday and holidays from 10 am to noon. From July to September it is open daily and there's no midday closure except on Sunday and holidays, when hours are 10 am to 12.30 pm and 1.30 to 6 pm.

For information on the Sanctuaires Notre

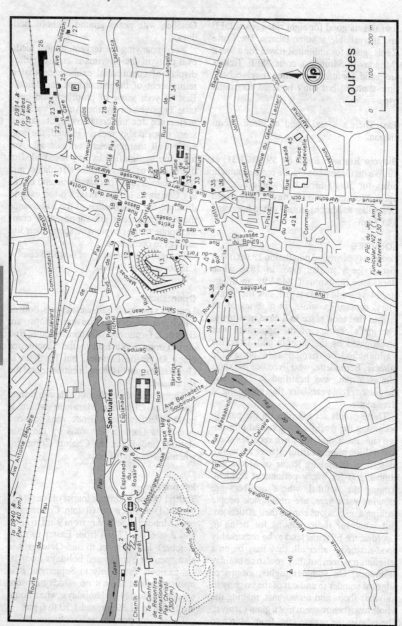

Lourdes

THE PYRENEES

■ PLACES TO STAY	OTHER		25	Buses to Grotte de Massabielle
15 Hôtel Saint Sylve	1	Pools	26	Railway Station
16 Hôtel Chrystal	2	Grotte de Massabielle	28	Piscine de la Coustète
18 Hôtel Duchesse Anne	3	Entreé des Lacets	29	Main Post Office
	4	Basilique Supérieure	30	Lav' Net
20 Hôtel de l'Annonciation	5	Crypt	31	Librairie L Carret
	6	Basilique du Rosaire	32	BNP (Bank)
22 Hôtel d'Annecy	7	Statue of Crowned Virgin	33	Crédit Lyonnais
23 Hôtel Lutetia	8	Forum Information	36	Caisse d'Épargne
24 Hôtel Terminus	10	Basilique Souterraine	38	Musée du Gemmail
27 Hôtel du Viscos		Saint Pie X	39	Musée Grévin
34 Camping de la Poste	11	Maison Paternelle de Sainte Bernadette	40	Cinéma Pax
46 Camp des Jeunes	12	Entrance to Chateau	42	Tourist Office
	13	Chateau Fort & Musée Pyrénéen	45	Bus Station
▼ PLACES TO EAT	14	Entrance to Chateau (with lift)	✕	SQUARES
35 McDonald's	19	Laverie Libre Service	9	Place de la Merlasse
41 Halles et Marchés	21	Centre Hospitalier Général & Bernadette's School	17	Place Jeanne d'Arc
43 Boulangerie			37	Place du Marcadal
44 Prisunic Supermarket				

THE PYRENEES

Dame de Lourdes, including brochures in a variety of languages, drop by the Forum Information (☎ 62.42.78.78), on the Esplanade next to the statue of the Crowned Virgin. It is open daily from 9 am to noon and 2 to 6 pm. Summer hours are 8.30 am to 6.30 pm.

Visitors to the Sanctuaires should be dressed modestly – at the very least, don't wear short shorts or skirts or sleeveless shirts, whatever some of the pilgrims may be wearing.

The grounds can be entered 24 hours a day via the Entrée des Lacets, which is on Rue Monseigneur Theas, the continuation of Blvd de la Grotte. For information on buses from the train station, see Getting Around.

Money The Caisse d'Épargne (☎ 62.94.12.14) at 17 Place du Marcadal (at the eastern end of Rue de la Grotte) is open weekdays from 8.45 am to noon and 1.15 to 5 pm. There are several other banks nearby.

The BNP at 2 Place de l'Église is open Monday to Friday from 8.35 to 11.55 pm and 1.35 to 5 pm. The Crédit Lyonnais at 13 Rue

Saint Pierre has an ATM that gives cash advances for some foreign credit cards.

Post & Telephone The main post office (☎ 62.94.00.00) at 1 Rue de Langelle is open Monday to Friday from 8.30 am to 7 pm and on Saturday until noon. It has foreign currency services and a 24-hour banknote exchange machine. Two telephone cabins are set aside for post-paid domestic and international calls.

Lourdes's postcode is 65100.

Bookshops Hiking maps and a few English-language pulp novels are available at Librairie L Carret (☎ 62.94.00.29) at 7 Rue Saint Pierre. It is open Monday to Saturday from 8.30 am to noon and 2 to 7 pm.

Laundry The Lav' Net in the arcade at 4 Rue de Langelle (opposite the main post office) is open daily from 8 am to 8 pm. Each washing machine load costs 25FF. There's a Laverie Libre Service on the ground floor of the building at 10 Chaussée Maransin (across from the Hôtel Ibis).

Medical Services The Centre Hospitalier Général (☎ 62.42.42.42) at 2 Ave Alexandre Marqui is about 300 metres west of the train station.

Sanctuaires Notre Dame de Lourdes

The Sanctuaries of Our Lady of Lourdes, the huge religious complex that has grown up around the cave where Bernadette's visions took place, are west across the Gave de Pau from the town centre. Development of this area began within a decade of the events of 1858, and the expansion has gone on ever since. You won't be alone if you find it difficult to understand how the gaudy late 19th-century architecture, more reminiscent of Disneyland than the majesty of a Gothic cathedral, inspires awe and devotion. But clearly it does.

The most revered site in the complex, the cavern where Bernadette had her visions, is variably known as the **Grotte de Massabielle** (Massabielle Cave), the Grotte Miraculeuse (Miraculous Cave) or the Grotte des Apparitions (Cave of the Appearances). It is hung with the crutches of generations of cured cripples. Nearby are 17 **pools** – six for men, 11 for women – in which 400,000 people seeking to be healed immerse themselves each year. Miraculous cures are becoming rarer and rarer – the last medically certifiable case took place in 1976.

The main 19th-century section of the Sanctuaires has three parts. On the west side of Esplanade du Rosaire between the two ramps is the neo-Byzantine **Basilique du Rosaire** (Basilica of the Rosary), inaugurated in 1889. One level up is the **crypt**, opened in 1866 and reserved for silent worship. On top is the spire-topped, neo-Gothic **Basilique Supérieure** (Upper Basilica), completed in 1876. All are open until 6 or 7 pm.

From the Sunday before Easter to at least mid-October, there are **processions aux flambeaux** (torch-light processions) nightly at 8.45 pm. The **Procession Eucaristique**, also known as the Procession du Saint Sacrement (Blessed Sacrament Procession), in which groups of pilgrims carrying banners march along the Esplanade, takes place daily during the same period at 4.30 pm. In case of rain, it is held inside the the bunker-like **Basilique Souterraine Saint Pie X**, described by some as a cross between a football stadium and an underground parking garage. It was built in 1959 in the Fallout Shelter style then at the height of its popularity. It is 200 metres long, 80 metres wide and can hold 20,000 people. Instead of stained-glass windows, it has back-lit works of gemmail (for details, see Musée du Gemmail in the Tours listing).

Chemin de la Croix Also known as the Chemin du Calvaire, the 1.5-km Chemin de la Croix (Way of the Cross) leads up the forested hillside from near the Basilique Supérieure. Inaugurated in 1912, it is lined with 14 life-size statues representing the events leading up to Jesus' crucifixion. Notice how the various participants in the drama are portrayed. The devout mount the stairs to the first station on their knees. The path is open from 7 am to 7 pm (8 am to 5.30 pm in the winter).

Musée Grévin

The town's wax museum, (☎ 62.94.33.74) at 87 Rue de la Grotte, also known as the Musée de Cire de Lourdes, has life-size dioramas of important events in the lives of both Jesus Christ and Bernadette Soubirous. It is open from April to October daily from 9 to 11.30 am and 1.30 to 6.30 pm. During July and August it's also open in the evening from 8.30 to 10 pm. Entry costs 27FF (15FF for students).

Musée du Gemmail

There's a small gemmail museum in the basement at 74 Rue de la Grotte. A display of documents related to Bernadette Soubirous and her life occupies the ground floor.

Maison Paternelle de Sainte Bernadette

Moulin de Boly, the mill where Bernadette was born, is down the alley next to 55 Blvd de la Grotte. The free, self-guided tour of the furnished rooms – protected from memento-hungry pilgrims by steel fencing and chicken wire – ends up at St Bernadette's bedroom, whose only exit leads into a souvenir shop.

Château Fort

The medieval Château Fort des Comtes de Bigorre (Fortified Castle of the Counts of Bigorre), most of whose buildings date from the 17th and 18th centuries, houses the **Musée Pyrénéen** (☎ 62.94.02.04), whose less-than-thrilling displays include furnished rooms, stuffed wild animals, traditional games and agricultural implements typical of the region. The gardens, which contain a group of 1:10-scale models of Pyrenean houses, afford fine views of the Sanctuaires. The top of the **donjon**, reached by climbing 104 steps, holds aloft a French tricolour.

If you want to take a lift up to the Château Fort, go to the entrance opposite 42 Rue du Fort; otherwise, you can walk up the ramp at the north end of Rue du Bourg. Both entrances are open daily, except Tuesday and holidays (daily from April to September), from 9 to 11 am and 2 to 5 pm (6 pm from April to September). The museum and chateau close an hour later – at noon and 6 pm (7 pm from April to September). The entry fee is 26FF (13FF for children aged six to 12; no discount for students).

Bernadette's School

The school where Bernadette studied and lived from 1860 to 1866, run by the Sœurs de Nevers (Sisters of Nevers), is now part of the town's Centre Hospitalier Général. Inside the grey, collonnaded building near the entrance to the complex, you can visit the small chapel where she first took communion and have a look at a display of some of her personal effects, including a spoon and one of her socks. You can view the exhibits for no charge daily from 2 to 4 pm; from Easter to October hours are 9 am to noon and 2 to 7 pm.

Pic du Jer

The Pic du Jer, whose 948-metre summit affords a panorama of Lourdes and the central Pyrenees, can be reached by a funiculaire (☎ 62.94.00.41) whose lower station is on Blvd d'Espagne 1½ km due south of the tourist office. It operates from Easter to 11 November. The first ascent is at 9.30 am; the last descent of the morning is at 11.50 am. In the afternoon, the first trip up is at 2 pm and the last trip down is usually at 6.20 pm. A return ticket costs 32FF (16FF for children aged six to 12). The funicular is linked with the Sanctuaires by local bus.

Activities

Swimming Piscine de la Coustète (☎ 62.94. 02.06), the municipal swimming pool on Blvd du Lapacca, is open daily from July to mid-September from 10 am to 6.30 pm. Entry costs 12.30FF (7.30FF for children under 14).

Places to Stay

Lourdes has over 350 hotels, more than any city in France except Paris. Indeed, there are probably more hotels per sq km here than anywhere else on the face of the earth.

The busiest periods are around Easter, Pentecost and Ascension Day and during May, August, the first half of September and the first week of October. Rooms are most difficult to find from about 12 to 17 August, when France's Pèlerinage Nationale (national pilgrimage) is held. In winter, the town is very, very quiet and most of the hotels shut down.

Streets in the town centre which have lots of hotels include Blvd de la Grotte, Rue Basse, Rue de la Fontaine, Rue du Bourg, Rue Baron Duprat and Chaussée du Bourg. Near the train station, there are hotels along Ave de la Gare, Ave Helios, Chaussée Maransin and Cité Pax.

Places to Stay – bottom end

Camping The camping ground nearest the centre of town, *Camping de la Poste* (☎ 62.94.40.35) at 26 and 26bis Rue de Langelle, is open from the Sunday before Easter to October. The tiny plot of land, surrounded by buildings, has only about two dozen spots, so during August it's a good idea to arrive in the morning. Tariffs are 9FF per person, 13FF for a tent site and 6FF per shower. There are several larger, more pleasant camping grounds around the town of Argelès-Gazost, 12 km south-west of Lourdes along the N21.

From June to September pilgrims can pitch a tent at the Camp des Jeunes (see Hostels) for 18FF per person.

Hostels The small *Centre de Rencontres Internationales Pax Christi* (☎ 62.94.00.66), 500 metres west of the Grotte de Massabielle at 4 Chemin de la Forêt, is open during July and August. It gives priority to young pilgrims (especially groups) but accepts other travellers if there's room. Bed and breakfast costs only 38FF (10FF more if you don't have a hostelling card). Sheets are 18FF. The volunteer staff prefer that people staying here take their meals (36FF) with other guests and participate in community life.

From June to September young pilgrims (but not curious tourists) can stay at the *Camp des Jeunes* (☎ 62.42.79.95), one km south-west of the Santuaires off Rue Monseigneur Rodhain. Run by the Oblates of Mary Immaculate, it resembles a summer camp, with all sorts of group religious activities for young people. Space in a dorm room costs 25FF. Bring your own sheets or sleeping bag. Reception is staffed 24 hours a day.

Hotels Lourdes has a wide selection of cheap hotel rooms. Those listed under Town Centre offer the best value.

Hotels – Train Station Area The family-run *Hôtel du Viscos* (☎ 62.94.08.06; fax 62.94.26.74) at 6 Ave Saint Joseph, to the left as you exit the train station, is open from 1 February to mid-December. Unadorned singles/doubles cost 85/135FF with washbasin and bidet and 110/170FF with prefab bathrooms. Hall showers are free.

The two-star, 50-room *Hôtel Lutetia* (☎ 62.94.22.85; fax 62.94.11.10) at 19 Ave de la Gare is open all year except from early

January to early February. Ordinary singles/doubles cost from 106/130FF (with washbasin) to 195/212FF (with shower and toilet). Hall showers are 18FF.

Nearby, the *Hôtel d'Annecy* (☎ 62.94.13.75) at 13 Ave de la Gare is open from the week before Easter to late October. Very plain singles/doubles/triples/quads cost 90/135/160/180FF with washbasin and 130/170/190/200FF with shower and toilet. Hall showers are 10FF. There's an 11 pm curfew.

Hotels – Centre The family-run *Hôtel de l'Annonciation* (☎ 62.94.22.78) at 23 Blvd de la Grotte, open all year, has clean, serviceable singles/doubles/quads with shower and toilet from about 100/120/220FF. Rooms with five beds cost 350FF.

The *Hôtel Saint Sylve* (☎ 62.94.63.48) at 9 Rue de la Fontaine, another family-run place, is also open all year. Its large, ordinary singles/doubles cost 65/120FF with washbasin, 80/140FF with shower and 90/150FF with shower and toilet. Rooms with shower and toilet for three to eight people cost 210 to 320FF. Hall showers are free.

Hotels – Elsewhere *Camping de la Poste* rents doubles/quads with washbasin and bidet for 110/150FF. Showers are 6FF. Kitchen facilities are available.

Places to Stay – middle
Almost all the mid-range hotels have a selection of rooms with shower and toilet.

Train Station Area The two-star *Hôtel Terminus* (☎ 62.94.68.00, 62.94.39.33) at 31 Ave de la Gare is open from Easter to mid-November. Singles/doubles cost 138/170FF with washbasin and bidet and 180/280FF with shower and toilet. There are also a few simple singles for 95FF.

Centre On bustling Blvd de la Grotte, the older, one-star *Hôtel Duchesse Anne* (☎ 62.94.06.45; fax 62.94.60.48) at No 16 is open from early February to 2 November. Simple singles/doubles/triples/quads, many of them with balconies, cost 90/130/145/165FF with washbasin and bidet and 135/180/200/240FF with shower and toilet. Hall showers are free.

The *Hôtel Chrystal* (☎ 62.94.00.36) at 16 Rue Basse has cheap, modern singles/doubles for 110/135FF (with washbasin and bidet) and 150/180FF (with shower and toilet). It is open from February to October.

Places to Eat

Restaurants Most pilgrims eat at their hotels, but there are quite a few undistinguished restaurants scattered around town, especially along streets lined with hotels. The town's *McDonald's* is at Place du Marcadal.

Self-Catering The *Halles et Marchés*, the huge covered market opposite the tourist office, is open Monday to Saturday (daily from Easter to mid-October) from 7 am to 1 pm.

The *Prisunic supermarket* across the street from the Halles et Marchés has a food section at the back. It's open Monday to Saturday from 9 am to 12.30 pm and 2.30 to 7 pm. Nearby, the *boulangerie* at 1 Place du Champ Commun is open from 7 am to 1 pm and 2.30 to 7.15 pm (closed Monday). From July to mid-September it's open daily from 7 am to 7.30 pm.

Near the train station, there are *grocery/souvenir shops* on Ave de la Gare at Nos 14 and 25.

Entertainment

Cinema From April to mid-October the same two films about St Bernadette are always playing at *Cinéma Pax* (☎ 62.94.52.01), down the small street opposite 64 Rue de la Grotte. During the rest of the year, it functions as a regular cinema.

Nightlife During the pilgrimage season, Lourdes's most interesting night-time activity is to wander around Blvd de la Grotte.

Getting There & Away

Train The railway station (☎ 62.94.10.47) is one km east of the Sanctuaires on Ave de la Gare.

Since so many pilgrims arrive by rail, Lourdes is well-connected by direct train to cities all over France, including Bayonne (five a day; 1¾ hours), Bordeaux (161FF; 2½ hours), Dijon (399FF), Geneva (530FF; 12 hours; two a day), Lyon (331FF), Marseille (281FF), Nice (nine to 11 hours; three a day), Pau (34FF; 30 minutes; nine a day) and Toulouse (111FF; two hours; seven a day). Options to Paris (365FF) include three non-TGV trains to Gare d'Austerlitz, two of which are overnight sleepers; TGVs use Gare Montparnasse.

Bus The bus station (☎ 62.94.31.15), down Rue Anselme Lacadé from the tourist office, has services to Pau (30FF; 1¼ hours; four to six times a day), Argelès-Gazost, Bagnères de Bigorre, Bétharram (west of Lourdes), Pierrefitte (south of Argelès-Gazost; 30 minutes) and Tarbes (30 minutes; four to six a day). The ticket windows are open from 8.30 or 9 am to noon and 2 to 6.45 pm daily except Saturday afternoon and Sunday. All the buses also stop at the train station, where tickets are sold on board.

SNCF buses to the Pyrenean towns of Cauterets (34FF; 50 to 60 minutes; four to six a day) and Luz Saint Sauveur (34FF; 1¼ hours; three to five a day) leave from the train station parking lot; they also stop near the bus station, but only if you flag them down. Transports Claude Dubié (☎ 62.94.48.60/51) has two buses a day from Luz Saint Sauveur to Gavarnie (40 minutes).

Getting Around

Bus From the Sunday before Easter to mid-October, local buses link the train station (the stop is next to the Hôtel Terminus) with the Grotte de Massabielle. A ride costs 9FF (5FF from the station to the centre of town). Buses run every 15 minutes from 7.45 to 11.45 am and 1.45 to 6.15 pm.

Taxi There's a taxi stand (☎ 62.94.31.30) in the parking lot of the train station.

Car Lourdes is one big traffic jam in summer – if you have a vehicle, your best bet is to park it somewhere (there are plenty of places near the train and bus stations) and walk.

PARC NATIONAL DES PYRÉNÉES

The Pyrenees National Park, one of France's six national parks, stretches for about 100 km along the French-Spanish border from the Vallée d'Aspe in the west to the Vallée d'Aure in the east. Its width varies from 1.5 to 15 km. Created in 1967, it covers an area of 457 sq km that includes 230 high-altitude lakes and the highest point in the French Pyrenees, the 3298-metre Sommet du Vignemale.

About 12% of the park is forested. The many rivers and cascades are fed both by springs and by some 2000 mm of annual precipitation, much of which falls as snow – the park is usually covered with snow from November to May. The French side of the range, especially the western section, is much rainier and greener than the Spanish side.

Pyrenees National Park border symbol ·

To the north, the park is bordered by 2060 sq km of populated land which is managed by the national park but is not fully protected. The area has a population of about 34,000. To the south, on the other side of the border, is a Spanish national park, 150-sq-km Parque Nacional de Ordesa, and 1000 sq km of game reserves.

Fauna

Protected fauna found in the national park and nearby areas include the 100 to 200-kg *ours brun* (brown bear), of which there are only about 15 left (the bear's prime habitat was not included in the park because of local opposition); the *lynx* (lynx), another animal whose prime habitat is outside the park's boundaries; the *isard* (izard or chamois), a goat antelope; the *marmotte* (marmot), reintroduced about four decades ago and now resident in about 200 colonies; the *lagopède* (ptarmigan), a kind of grouse; and such endangered birds of prey as the *gypaète barbu* (bearded vulture), *vautour fauve* (light-brown vulture) and *aigle royal* (golden eagle).

Information

Park Offices National park offices with visitors centres are located at Arrens, Arudy, Cauterets, Etsaut, Gabas, Gavarnie, Luz Saint Sauveur and Saint Lary-Soulon. Most – though not the one at Cauterets – are closed during the cold half of the year.

Weather For weather information, call the météo (weather bureau) on ☎ 36.68.02.65 (for the département of Hautes-Pyrénées) or 36.68.02.64 (for the département of Pyrénées-Atlantiques).

Maps Each of the six valleys of the national park is covered by a *pochette* (folder) of hiking itineraries in French entitled *Promenades dans le Parc National des Pyrénées*. Intended for use with hiking maps, they are on sale at national park offices and local tourist offices.

The topoguides covering some 700 km of Pyrenean trails (including the GR10) have

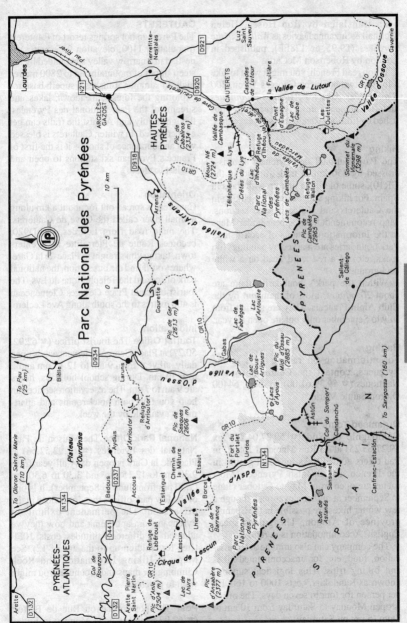

THE PYRENEES

been translated by Bob Hosea, Helen McPhail & Suzanne Davies as *Walking in the Pyrenees* (£9.95 or 128FF), published in London by Robertson McCarta.

If you read French, you might want to take a look at two books by Georges Véron, *100 Randonnées dans les Pyrénées-Atlantiques* and *100 Sommets des Pyrénées*, both published by Éditions Randonnées Pyrénéennes.

Hiking

The Parc National des Pyrénées is crisscrossed by 350 km of trails (including the GR10), some of which link up with trails in Spain. For hiking suggestions, see Hiking in the Cauterets and Vallée d'Aspe sections. Map recommendations appear under Maps in the Information sections of each listing. Park boundaries are marked by paintings (on rocks, etc) of a red izard head on a white background.

Within the park's boundaries there are about 20 *refuges*, most of them run by the Club Alpin Français. They are staffed from July to September only but are open all year.

Rafting

For information on rafting trips in the Pyrenees, contact the Centre de Sports Nautiques (☎ 59.39.61.00) at Soeix, 64400 Oloron Sainte Marie.

Organised Tours

Compagnie du Sud (☎ 59.27.04.24; fax 59.27.63.25) at 23 Rue Maréchal Joffre in Pau offers guided treks for small groups in the French and Spanish Pyrenees. Most routes are open from May to October (June to September at higher elevations), though a few winter hikes are possible in the Spanish province of Aragon. The guides speak English. Accommodation is in *refuges*.

The company can also arrange accommodation, food, etc, for unaccompanied hikes and biking trips. This logistical support, known as Randokits, costs 1000 to 1600FF per person for four to seven days. The office is open Monday to Saturday from 10 am to 7 pm (5 pm on Saturday).

CAUTERETS

The Pyrenean hot springs resort of Cauterets (population 1100; elevation 935 metres) is nestled in a narrow valley surrounded by the steep slopes of mountains up to 2800 metres high. In summer, it makes a superb base for exploring the forests, meadows, lakes and streams of the Parc National des Pyrénées, though in July and August the trails can get a bit crowded. In winter, Cauterets is blessed with an abundance of snow – it is the first of France's Pyrenean ski stations to open and the last to close.

Orientation

Cauterets is spread out for about a km along a small river called the Gave de Cauterets. The main road from Lourdes, the D920, becomes Route de Pierrefitte as it enters town, taking you straight to Place de la Gare, where you'll find the bus station, the national park office and the Téléphérique du Lys. The tourist office at Place Georges Clemenceau is 400 metres to the south along Ave Leclerc.

Information

Tourist Office The tourist office (☎ 62.92.50.27) at Place Georges Clemenceau is open daily, all year from 9 am to 12.15 pm and 2 to 6.30 pm. During school holidays, hours are 9 am to 7 pm. The reservation service can help you find both hotel rooms and apartments available by the week.

National Park Office The Maison du Parc National des Pyrénées (☎ 62.92.52.56) at Place de la Gare is open daily all year from 9.30 am to 12.15 pm and 3.30 to 6.30 pm (7.30 pm from June to September). It is one of the few park offices that don't close in the off season. The permanent exhibit on Pyrenean flora and fauna and how they've adapted to different altitudes costs 10FF (free for children up to the age of 12). See Maps & Hiking Information and Rock Climbing for maps and brochures you might want to purchase.

Post The post office on Rue de Belfort (☎ 62.92.53.93) is open Monday to Friday

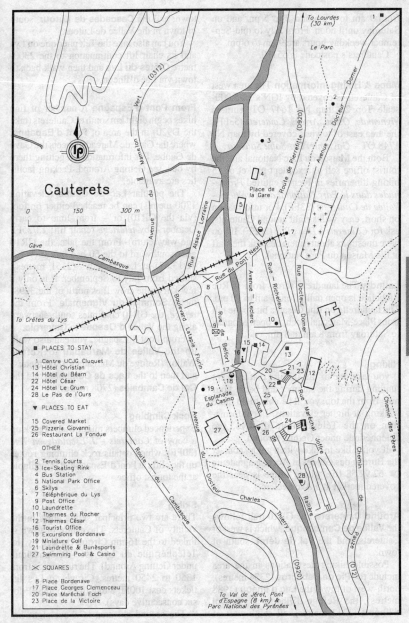

Cauterets

0   150   300 m

■ PLACES TO STAY
1 Centre UCJG Cluquet
13 Hôtel Christian
14 Hôtel du Béarn
22 Hôtel César
24 Hôtel Le Grum
28 Le Pas de l'Ours

▼ PLACES TO EAT
15 Covered Market
25 Pizzeria Giovanni
26 Restaurant La Fondue

OTHER
2 Tennis Courts
3 Ice-Skating Rink
4 Bus Station
5 National Park Office
6 Skilys
7 Téléphérique du Lys
9 Post Office
10 Laundrette
11 Thermes du Rocher
12 Thermes César
16 Tourist Office
18 Excursions Bordenave
19 Miniature Golf
21 Laundrette & Bunèsports
27 Swimming Pool & Casino

✕ SQUARES
8 Place Bordenave
17 Place Georges Clemenceau
20 Place Maréchal Foch
23 Place de la Victoire

from 9 am to noon and 2 to 5 pm and on Saturday until noon. From July to mid-September weekday hours are 9 am to 6 pm.

Cauterets's postcode is 65110.

Maps & Hiking Information The area west of Cauterets is covered by IGN's 1:25,000-scale Top 25 map No 1647 OT, entitled *Vignemale, Ossau, Arrens, Cauterets* (53FF); the area east of town is covered by map No 1748 OT – *Gavarnie, Luz Saint Sauveur*.

Both the Maison du Parc National and the tourist office sell an excellent packet of 15 hiking itineraries in French entitled *Promenades dans le Parc National des Pyrénées – Vallée de Cauterets* (33FF). For information on short, easy walks right around Cauterets, ask for *Cauterets à Deux Pas* (30FF). If you have questions about itineraries, ask the staff at the Maison du Parc National.

Laundry The laundrette across from 16 Rue Richelieu is open daily from 7 am to 10 pm. The laundrette on Rue César, a bit up the hill from Place Maréchal Foch, is open Monday to Saturday from 8 am to 8 pm.

Hiking

If you take one of the ski lifts that are kept running during the summer and begin your hike from the top, you'll be able to do more walking at higher elevations. For information on the Téléphérique du Lys, see Téléphérique under Getting Around.

If you'd like to hike with a guide, contact the Bureau des Guides et Accompagnateurs (☎ 62.92.58.16), whose office is near the covered market at 5 Ave Leclerc.

Around Cauterets The GR10 trail follows the **Vallée de Cambasque**, which is west of Cauterets, and the **Val de Jéret**, south of town.

Possible hiking destinations in the area include the **Pic de Cabaliros** (2334 metres), north-west of town; the **Lac d'Ilhéou** (1988 metres), the Refuge d'Ilhéou at the **Col d'Ilhéou** (2242 metres), all south-west of

town; and the **Cascades de Lutour**, south of town in the Vallée de Lutour.

You can also take the Téléphérique du Lys and its chair lift continuation to the 2300-metre **Crêtes du Lys** and then walk back to town via Lac d'Ilheou.

From Pont d'Espagne A number of fine hikes begin eight km south of Cauterets (take the D920) in the area of **Pont d'Espagne**, where the Gave de Marcadau meets the Gave de Gaube. For information on getting there by bus, see Getting Around. Parking facilities are available.

The popular **Lac de Gaube** (elevation 1700 metres) can be reached either on foot (via the GR10) or – from June to early October – by *télésiège* (chair lift; 13/25FF one way/return). From the lake, the GR10 goes southward to the 60-bed *refuge* (☎ 62. 42.13.67) at Les Oulettes (2151 metres), staffed from July to September. It is only a few km as the crow flies north of the 3298-metre **Sommet du Vignemale**. From the *refuge*, the GR10 continues south-eastward along the **Vallée d'Ossoue** to **Gavarnie**.

From Pont d'Espagne, you can also walk up the **Vallée de Marcadau** to Refuge Wallon (Refuge du Marcadau; 1866 metres) and then to the **Lacs de Cambalès** and the **Col de Cambalès** (2708 metres).

Rock Climbing

Experienced climbers might want to pick up a copy of *Cauterets – L'Escalade en Tête* (30FF), which details rock climbing routes up the cliffs at Pont d'Espagne. It is available at the tourist office.

Skiing

There are two principal skiing areas in the vicinity of Cauterets. The centre of town is linked to the 16-run **Cirque du Lys** by the Téléphérique du Lys (see Téléphérique under Getting Around). The runs range from 1350 to 2450 metres. Cirque du Lys lift tickets cost 100FF a day (475 to 588FF for six consecutive days).

The second ski area is about eight km

south of Cauterets at **Pont d'Espagne** (see Hiking). In addition to downhill runs, reached via the Télésiège de Gaube, there are five long cross-country trails. An afternoon/all-day lift ticket costs 38/51FF. For information on bus links with Cauterets, see Bus under Getting Around.

The École de Ski Français (☎ 62.92.55.06 at Cirque du Lys) offers group/individual ski lessons from 60/150FF per person.

Skis can be hired for about 75FF a day, including boots, from a number of shops around town. Skilys (☎ 62.92.58.30), across Place de la Gare from the bus station, is open daily from 8 am to 7 pm (8 am to 8 pm during the Christmas, February and Easter school holidays).

Taking the Waters

Cauterets's hot springs, which emerge from the earth at 36 to 53°C, have attracted *curistes* since the 19th century. Thermes César (☎ 62.92.51.60) at 3 Place de la Victoire is open almost all year round.

Other Activities

About 200 metres south-west of the tourist office is Esplanade du Casino, also known as Esplanade des Œufs, where you'll find cafés, an indoor swimming pool (☎ 62.92.61.30), a bowling alley (☎ 62.92.52.14), a miniature golf course and the town's large casino. There's an ice-skating rink (*patinoire*; ☎ 62.92.58.48) at Place de la Gare.

Places to Stay

Cheap beds are nearly impossible to find in July and August. Many hotels – though none of the ones listed here – require that you take at least demi-pension.

Camping There are a number of camping grounds slightly north of town along Ave du Mamelon Vert. You can pitch a tent at the Centre UCJG Cluquet (see Tents & Bungalows) for 18FF per person.

Refuges For details on getting to the *refuges Wallon*, *Les Oulettes*, and *d'Ilhéou*, see Hiking.

Gîte d'Étape *Le Pas de l'Ours* (☎ 62.92.58.07) at 21 Rue de la Raillère is open from 15 May to 15 October and 20 December to 25 April. A bed in one of the two 10-person dorm rooms costs 48FF, including use of the kitchen. Doubles with shower and toilet cost 200FF.

Tents & Bungalows The friendly *Centre UCJG Cluquet* (☎ 62.92.52.95) is on Ave Docteur Domer 300 metres north of the tennis courts. From June to mid-September, a bed in one of the five tents, each of which sleeps about a dozen people, costs 35FF, including use of the shower and the fully equipped kitchen. Space is almost always available. This place also has nine extremely basic wood and cement bungalows, each with two or three beds, that are available all year despite the lack of heating. Rental by the day, weekend or week costs 45FF per person.

To make reservations from mid-September to mid-June contact M Scripiec (☎ 62.93.10.98) at 5 Rue Jeanne d'Albret, 65000 Tarbes.

Hotels Around the corner from the tourist office, the *Hôtel du Béarn* (☎ 62.92.53.54) at 4 Ave Leclerc is open from Christmas to September. Plain but large and well-lit doubles with washbasin and bidet cost 100 to 130FF. Hall showers are 6FF.

The friendly, 21-room *Hôtel Le Grum* (☎ 62.92.53.01) at 4 Rue de l'Église is open all year except from 25 October to 10 December. Rooms for one/two/three/four people cost 80/110/140/170FF with washbasin and bidet and 120/150/180/210FF with shower and toilet. Hall showers are free. The *Hôtel Christian* (☎ 62.92.50.04) at 10 Rue Richelieu, open from mid-April to mid-October, has big doubles with high ceilings for 110FF (with washbasin and bidet) and 180FF (with shower and toilet). Triples and quads are also available. Hall showers are free.

The two-star *Hôtel César* (☎ 62.92.52.57) at 3 Rue César, half a block down the hill from Thermes César, is open all year except

THE PYRENEES

from 20 April to 20 May, during October and from 5 to 15 December. Attractive singles/doubles cost 100/140FF with washbasin and bidet; doubles/triples are 210/230FF with shower and toilet.

Places to Eat

The best places for restaurant hunting are Rue de la Raillère, Place Maréchal Foch and Rue Richelieu.

Restaurants *Restaurant La Fondue* (☎ 62.92.62.60) at 7 Ave de l'Esplanade, right across the river from the casino, is open daily from mid-June to September and from December to late April or early May. Hours are noon to 2 pm and 7 to 11 pm. The house speciality is fondue: Bourguignonne (75FF), fish (85FF) and magret de canard (duck cutlet; 95FF). Prices include chips and a salad.

Pizzeria Giovanni (☎ 62.92.57.80) at 5 Rue de la Raillère is open from mid-June to early November and mid-December to mid-May. Except during school holidays, it may be open only in the evening.

Self-Catering Around the corner from the tourist office, the *covered market* at 5 Ave Leclerc is open from 7 am to 12.30 pm and 4 pm (3.30 pm in summer) to 7.30 pm (closed Sunday afternoon). During February, July and August, a few stalls stay open on Sunday afternoon. There are two grocery stores – a *Codec* at No 7 and a *Casino* at No 2 – on the same block.

Getting There & Away

All public transport to Cauterets passes through Lourdes, 30 km to the north.

Train Cauterets is not served by train, but the SNCF office in the bus station (see Bus) handles ticketing and reservations to any destination.

Bus The wooden bus station (☎ 62.92.53.70) at Place de la Gare looks like a cross between the set of a western and a giant cuckoo clock. It is open from 9 am to noon

and 3 to 6.30 pm (7 pm from June to October) daily except Saturday afternoon and Sunday (daily from June to September).

SNCF buses link the Lourdes train station with Cauterets's bus station (34FF; 50 to 60 minutes; four to six a day). The last bus to Lourdes leaves at about 7.30 pm.

Getting Around

Bus Excursions Bordenave (☎ 62.92.53.68) has buses to Pont d'Espagne (15FF) daily during July and August and three times a week in June and September – unless it rains or no one shows up, that is. Buses leave Cauterets at 9.30 am and 2 pm; the last bus back to Cauterets leaves Pont d'Espagne at about 5.15 pm. From 20 December to approximately the end of March, the company has daily buses to the Télésiège de Gaube at Pont d'Espagne. Hours are about the same as during the summer.

Bordenave's buses leave from the bus station. Tickets are sold at the company's office at 8 Place Georges Clemenceau (opposite the tourist office), which is closed from 12.30 to 4 pm, and right before departure at the bus station.

Taxi To order a taxi, call Excursions Bordenave on ☎ 62.92.53.68 or, after hours, on ☎ 62.92.52.74.

Bicycle Skilys (☎ 62.92.58.30), which is across Place de la Gare from the bus station, rents mountain bikes for 60/100FF a half/whole day. An ID is required as a deposit. For mountain bike hire, you might also try Bunèsports on Rue César.

Téléphérique The Téléphérique du Lys (☎ 62.92.51.58) at 1 Ave Docteur Domer operates from June to mid or late September and from December to the end of the ski season (usually around late April). It goes to 1850-metre Cirque du Lys, where you can catch the Télésiège du Grum up to Crêtes du Lys (2300 metres). The one-way/return trip costs 24/40FF to Cirque du Lys and a further 15/26FF to Crêtes du Lys. The lifts usually run until about 5.30 pm.

VALLÉE D'ASPE

The Aspe Valley, which is in the Béarn region at the western edge of the Parc National des Pyrénées, is drained by the Gave d'Aspe, which flows north from the 2000-metre peaks around the Col du Somport to the town of Oloron Sainte Marie, 40 km away. The valley gets a lot of vehicle traffic, but nearby hills, mountains and valleys, accessible only on foot, remain relatively untouched by the 20th century. The whole area is remarkably green, even in summer.

Bedous (population 1100), the largest village in the area, is set in a wide, fairly flat part of the Vallée d'Aspe. The starting point for several lower-elevation hikes, it is also a good place to stock up on food. Accous (population 200), about three km south by road, has a couple of places offering parapente and hang-gliding courses.

In the narrow upper valley, Etsaut and nearby Borce, surrounded by the steep slopes of nearby mountain peaks, are a good base for higher-elevation hikes. About three km south of Etsaut is **Fort du Portalet**, an early 19th-century fortress that overlooks a particularly narrow and defensible bit of the valley. From 1941 to 1945 it was used as a prison by the Germans.

Orientation

The N134 runs along the length of the Vallée d'Aspe from Oloron Sainte Marie to the Col du Somport, which is on the French-Spanish border.

Bedous is about 22 km south of Oloron Sainte Marie; the N134 is known as Rue Gambetta as it passes through Bedous. About 2½ km to the south is the turn-off to Accous, whose centre (in so far as there is one) is about 800 metres east of the N134.

Etsaut is a further nine km south. Tiny Borce is a bit up the western side of the valley from Etsaut. Lescun is three km south-west of the N134 at a point midway between Bedous and Etsaut.

Information

Informal sources of information on the area (eg hiking itineraries, outdoor activities, equipment rental) include Le Choucas Blanc in Bedous and the Maison de l'Ours in Etsaut, both detailed under Gîtes d'Étape, and the Maison des Jeunes et de la Culture in Etsaut.

Tourist Offices Bedous's syndicat d'initiative (☎ 59.34.53.14) is at Place François Sarrail in the arcaded Mairie building, opposite the church. To get there, turn off Rue Gambetta (the N134) at No 17. From June to September it's open Monday to Saturday from 9 am to noon and 2 to 6 pm. The rest of the year, it may be open only in the morning.

National Park Offices The best place to get hiking information is at the Maison du Parc National (☎ 59.34.88.30) in Etsaut, housed in the former train station. It is open from May to September and around Easter, All Saints' Day (1 November) and Christmas. Entry to the small visitors' centre, which has exhibits on the rare brown bear, costs 10FF (free for children up to age 16).

Post The Bedous post office, on Rue Gambetta between Nos 28 and 30, is open Monday to Friday from 9 am to noon and 1.45 to 4.45 pm and on Saturday until noon.

In Etsaut, the post office is in the centre of the village next to the church. Foreign currency services are available. It is open Monday to Friday from 9 am to noon and 1.30 to 4.30 pm and on Saturday until 11.30 am.

The postcode of Bedous, Accous and Etsaut is 64490.

Money In Bedous, money can be changed at the Caisse d'Épargne, located on the side of the Mairie building that faces Rue Pierre Portes. It is open Tuesday to Saturday from 8.30 am to noon and 1.30 to 5 pm (4.30 pm on Saturday).

Maps & Hiking Information The best hiking map of the area is 1:50,000-scale *Pyrénées Carte No 3*, published by Édition Randonnées Pyrénées. Another option is IGN's 1:25,000-scale blue series map No 1547 OT (53FF).

THE PYRENEES

Promenades dans le Parc National des Pyrénées – Vallée d'Aspe (33FF) is a useful packet of information sheets in French on 12 hikes in and around the Vallée d'Aspe.

If you'd like to trek with a guide, call the Bureau des Guides et Accompagnateurs on ☎ 59.34.71.48.

Laundry The Maison des Jeunes et de la Culture in Etsaut (see Hostel) has a washing machine and dryer.

Hiking

Hikers starting in Bedous have a number of options. To the east, you can walk via the viewpoint indicator to the Plateau d'Ourdinse and then to **Aydius**. Aydius can also be reached by taking the D237; but however you get there, you can return to Bedous via Accous, the **Col d'Arrioutort** or even Etsaut. East of Aydius there are two *refuges*, the Refuge d'Ilbech and the Refuge d'Arrioutort.

Another option from Bedous is to head westward to the **Col de Bouezou**. The trail later links up with the GR10, which you can take back to the Vallée d'Aspe via Lescun or even Etsaut. The Refuge de Labérouat is a few km north-west of Lescun.

From Lescun (950 metres; population 200), whose slate roofs once sheltered a leper colony, you get a good view of the **Cirque de Lescun**, the jagged mountains that overlook the town to the west. Another trail leads south-westward to the **Lac de Lhurs** (1691 metres). Another possible destination in this area is the **Cabane d'Ansabère**.

From Etsaut, you can walk south and then east along a part of the GR10 known as the **Chemin de la Mâture**, used in the 18th century to harvest timber for the Bayonne shipyards. A difficult segment of the trail continues south-eastward to the **Lacs d'Ayous**. West of Etsaut, the GR10 goes via the village of Borce to the **Col de Barrancq**, whence there are trails back to the valley via Lhers and Lescun.

From Sansanet, a parking lot at a hairpin curve in the N134 a few km towards Etsaut from the border, a trail leads to the **Ibón de Astanés** (also spelled Ibon de Estanès and

Lac d'Estaens), the largest lake in the area. The walk up and back, an international event given that the lake is in Spain, takes about five hours. The GR11 passes by the Ibón de Astanés.

About 15 km west of Bedous, a number of fine hikes begin at Arette Pierre Saint Martin (see Skiing).

Cycling

For information on renting mountain bikes, see Getting Around.

Parapente

In Accous near the Maison Despourrins (see Gîtes d'Étape), the École de Parapente Ascendance (☎ 59.34.52.07; fax 59.34. 53.33) offers accompanied *baptêmes de l'air* (introductory flights) for 250FF. Six-day intro courses, held from April to September, cost 2000FF plus board and lodging; more advanced courses are also available. Flights begin from mountainsides 800 metres above the valley floor. From October to March, Parapente Ascendance is open only on weekends.

Hang-Gliding

Virvolta (☎ 59.34.50.30), also based in Accous near the Gîte d'Étape Maison Despourrins, has half-day, accompanied baptêmes de l'air for 330FF. Its week-long *deltaplane* (hang-gliding) courses (1800FF, not including board and lodging), held from June to September, are practicable only if you speak French.

Skiing

There is cross-country skiing at **Col du Somport** (1632 metres), but the area's major ski stations are just across the border in the Spanish province of Aragon: **Candanchú** (☎ 974-37 31 92/4), a favourite of King Juan Carlos, which has 23 lifts and 22 runs from 1560 to 2400 metres; and **Astún** (☎ 974-37 30 34), whose 13 lifts and 35 runs are at 1700 to 2200 metres. Both are rather expensive. For transport information, see Getting There & Away.

About 15 km (and a half-hour drive) due

west of Bedous is the ski station of **Arette Pierre Saint Martin** (☎ 59.66.20.09, 59.34.61.07), known for its abundance of snow. To get there, take the D442 and the D441 (if these are snowbound you have to take the D918 and the D132, which take twice as long).

The Maison des Jeunes et de la Culture (see Hostel) rents downhill and cross-country skis for about 40FF a day, including boots, and snowboards and monoskis for 75FF a day.

Horse Riding

From May to December, you can hire horses at the Auberge Cavalière (see Hotels), three km south of Etsaut. The charge is 200/300FF for afternoon/all-day rides; longer excursions are also possible. Advance reservations are necessary.

Places to Stay

The Vallée d'Aspe is filled with cheap but very basic accommodation.

Camping In Bedous, the pleasant *Camping Municipal* (☎ 59.34.70.45 at the village hall) is 400 metres down the hill along the street that intersects Rue Gambetta between Nos 26 and 28. It is open from early March to November. Tent sites cost 5FF and adults pay 11FF.

At the intersection of the N134 and the turn-off to Accous nearest Bedous, you'll find the grassy, 35-site *Camping Despourrins* (☎ 59.34.71.16). It is open almost all year long but there's hot water only from May to October. In summer, charges are 13FF for a tent site and 11FF per adult.

About 1.3 km up the hill from Borce along the D739, *Camping de Borce* (☎ 59.34.87.29 from July to August, 59.34.86.15 the rest of the year) is open from about mid-June to mid-September, but you can stay there at other times of the year if you call ahead. Fees are 11FF for a tent site and 13FF per adult. Camping de Borce is on the GR10.

Refuges For mention of some of the *refuges* in the mountains around the Vallée d'Aspe, see Hiking.

Gîtes d'Étape In Bedous, the friendly, 47-bed *Le Choucas Blanc* (☎ 59.34.53.71) at 4 Rue Gambetta (the N134) is open all year. Basic dorm beds cost 40FF from about May to mid- November and 45FF the rest of the year. Breakfast/dinner, both of which are optional, cost 12/50FF. Kitchen facilities are available. The owner can supply tips on hiking itineraries and can even drop you off at the trailhead.

In Accous, the 18-place *Maison Despourrins* (☎ 59.34.53.50 from May to early October, 59.39.97.23 from October to April; fax 59.34.53.33) has beds for 48FF. Lunch/dinner, which may not be available from October to April, costs 43/68FF, including wine and coffee. It is open all year.

In Etsaut, the 20-bed *La Maison de l'Ours* (☎ 59.34.86.38), also known as the Centre d'Hébergement Leo Lagrange, is next to the parking lot in the centre of the village. A bed in a room for two to four people costs 65FF (a bit less for kids under 12). It's open all year. People staying here can participate in all sorts of outdoor activities, including mountain biking (50/100FF a half/whole day) and *tir à l'arc* (archery).

In Borce, *Camping de Borce* (see Camping) also has a very basic gîte d'étape with space for 18 people. Individuals can stay here from mid-June to mid-September for 42FF. The triple-decker bunks are reminiscent of the 3rd-class sleeping arrangements on Chinese river ferries.

Hostel In Etsaut, the 60-bed *Maison des Jeunes et de la Culture* (☎ 59.34.88.98; fax 59.34.86.91), also known as the Auberge de Jeunesse and the Centre International de Séjour, has beds in barracks-like dorms for 42FF (40FF with a hostelling card, 34FF with a Carte Jeunes). To get there from the centre of the village, take the alleyway next to the church. There's no curfew and rooms are accessible all day. Kitchen facilities are available. Showers are free to guests but cost 6FF to people just passing through (eg hikers).

Hotels In Bedous, the eight-room *Hôtel Chez Handaye* (☎ 59.34.70.31) at 12 Rue

Gambetta, open all year, charges 70/80FF for big, basic doubles with washbasin and one/two beds. Showers are free. Reception is closed on Tuesday except from July to mid-September.

In Etsaut, the two-star *Hôtel des Pyrénées* (☎ 59.34.88.62; fax 59.34.86.96), the only hotel in the village, has doubles for 140FF (with washbasin and bidet) and 200FF (with shower and toilet). It is open all year.

Three km south of Etsaut on the N134, the 12-room *Auberge Cavalière* (☎ 59.34.72.30) is open all year. Doubles cost 150FF; a third (or fourth) bed costs 50FF.

Places to Eat
Restaurants Three km south of Etsaut, the popular *Auberge Cavalière* (see Hotels) has all sorts of tasty Pyrenean specialities cooked on a wood fire, including *garbure* (a thick soup made with fresh vegetables, beans, cabbage and ham) and *poule au pot* (chicken stuffed with vegetables and prepared with tomato sauce). The *menus* cost 70 to 165FF. This place is open daily throughout the year from noon to 2 pm and 8 to 9.30 pm.

In Etsaut, the restaurant of the *Hôtel des Pyrénées* (see Hotels) has *menus* for 68 to 150FF.

Self-Catering In Bedous, there is a *food market* next to the Mairie on Thursday morning. The *Casino grocery* at 5 Rue Gambetta is open daily except Sunday afternoon and Monday (daily except Sunday afternoon from June to early September); hours are 7.30 am to 12.30 pm and 3 to 7.30 pm. There's another *grocery* at 9 Rue Gambetta.

Entertainment
Bar The most popular hang-out in Bedous is the *Bar Chez Handaye* at 12 Rue Gambetta.

Things to Buy
Lots of places sell the valley's excellent cheeses – look for hand-lettered signs advertising *fromages*.

Getting There & Away
The Vallée d'Aspe has been a trans-Pyrenean transport route since long before the time of Julius Caesar, whose legionnaires marched through the area. It has also served as a crossing point to Spain for medieval pilgrims on their way to Santiago de Compostela and the armies of Napoleon.

These days, as part of an EC initiative to improve road links between France and Spain, there are plans to widen the N134 and build a road tunnel under the Col du Somport. The project faces a great deal of local opposition – not only will the increased traffic devastate the area's pastoral calm, which is already under threat, but the narrow southern reaches of the valley will end up being almost completely buried under asphalt.

The 1632-metre Col du Somport is the only pass in the central Pyrenees that is open throughout the winter.

Train & Bus All public transport to the Vallée d'Aspe goes through Pau. SNCF has services from Pau to the Spanish railhead of Canfranc-Estación, an enormous railway station whence there are trains to Saragossa and other parts of Spain. Traffic is handled by trains only as far south as Oloron Sainte Marie – the rest of the route is covered by four or five daily SNCF buses, which take the N134 all the way up the Vallée d'Aspe to the Col du Somport, Candanchú and finally Canfranc. The bus route up the valley parallels the derelict railway tracks, built from 1908 to 1928 and abandoned in 1970 when the bridge at l'Estanguet collapsed under the weight of an overloaded train.

From Oloron Sainte Marie's train station (☎ 59.39.00.61), destinations served include Bedous (30 minutes; 22FF) and Canfranc (1¾ hours; 44FF). In Bedous, there are stops at the parking lot near Le Choucas Blanc and in front of the Gendarmerie (police station). To get to Accous, you'll have to walk or hitch about 800 metres from the N134. The bus stop in Etsaut is at the main square, which doubles as a parking lot.

Getting Around

Given the relative infrequence of SNCF buses on the Oloron Sainte Marie-Canfranc run, getting around the valley is very difficult unless you have a car or hitch.

Bicycle In Bedous, VTT Nature (☎ 59.34. 75.25), on the N134, 300 metres south of the post office (right before the Total station), has mountain bikes for 60/110FF a half/whole day. A 2000FF deposit is required. The staff can provide free maps of suggested cycling routes in the area. Guided rides, with the option of driving to a high spot so you end up going mostly downhill, cost 120/220FF per person for a half/whole day.

In Etsaut, mountain bikes can be hired at the Maison des Jeunes et de la Culture (see Hostel under Places to Stay) for 55/95FF a half/whole day.

Andorra

The Catalan-speaking Principality of Andorra (population 60,000), one of Europe's smallest countries, is nestled between France and Spain in the middle of the Pyrenees Mountains. Except for the novelty of visiting such a tiny political anomaly, it's hard to think of a compelling reason to come to Andorra unless you need to do some duty-free shopping.

More remote parts of the principality are quite spectacular and remain relatively unspoiled by the overdevelopment and motor traffic that plagues the towns. There's relatively little to see of cultural or historical interest other than a number of Romanesque parish churches and a few simple but elegant stone bridges.

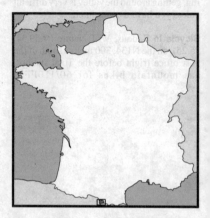

Facts about the Country

HISTORY

By tradition, Andorra's independence is credited to Charlemagne, who captured the region from the Muslims in 803 AD, and his son Louis I (Louis the Pious), from whom the area's inhabitants are said to have received a charter of liberties. This tradition is enshrined in the national anthem, adopted in 1921, which includes the line: 'The Great Charlemagne, my father, freed us from the Arabs...'

The earliest known written record of Andorra (Andorre in French) is an order from Charlemagne's grandson Charles II (Charles the Bald) which granted the Valleys of Andorra to Sunifred, Count of the Earldom of Urgell, in 843. The Act of Consecration for the cathedral in the nearby town of La Seu d'Urgell, which dates from around 860 (not 839 as many sources claim), mentions Andorra's parishes as part of the territory of the Count of Urgell.

The country's first constitutional documents, the Pareatges (Paréages in French; Acts of Joint Overlordship) of 1278 and 1288, were drawn up to settle conflicting claims of seigniorial rights made by the Catholic Bishop of Urgell (now in Spain) and the Count of Foix (now in France). These feudal agreements, under which the bishop and the count agreed to share sovereignty, form the basis of Andorra's government to this day and are thus among the oldest such documents still in force. The Pareatges ended up creating a peculiar political equilibrium that has saved Andorra from being swallowed up by its powerful neighbours and thus sharing the fate of all but a handful of Europe's medieval principalities, earldoms and duchies.

Over the centuries, there have been numerous periods of tension between the co-princes as well as conflicts of interest between the powers they represent. After the Revolution, France, inheritor of the lands and prerogatives of the Count of Foix, abolished all feudal rights, including the role of the French head-of-state in Andorran affairs. But in 1806, at the request of the Andorrans, it was reinstated by Napoleon. Andorra remained neutral during WW I, the Spanish Civil War and WW II.

GEOGRAPHY

Andorra, which has a territory of only 468 sq km, is situated on the southern slopes of the Pyrenees. At its maximum, it measures 25 km from north to south and 29 km from east to west. Most of its forty or so towns and hamlets – some with just a few dozen people – are situated in a group of mountain valleys whose streams join to form the country's main river, the Gran Valira, created near Andorra-la-Vella by the confluence of the Valira del Orient and the Valira del Nord.

Pic de Coma Pedrosa (2942 metres) in the west of the country is the principality's highest mountain. The lowest point, which is on the Spanish frontier at La Farga de Moles, is 838 metres above sea level. The road from France passes over 2408-metre-high Port d'Envalira, the highest pass in the Pyrenees. Andorra's mountain peaks remain snow-capped until early summer.

GOVERNMENT

For the seven centuries preceding 1993, Andorra had a unique form of government known as a co-principality because its sovereignty was vested in the persons of two co-princes: the president of the French Republic and the Catholic bishop of the Spanish town of La Seu d'Urgell (Seo de Urgel). The French head-of-state inherited the job from France's pre-Revolutionary kings, to whom the position passed in 1607 from the successors to the counts of Foix. The Bishop of Urgell is the last Catholic bishop – other than the Pope – who retains temporal powers (during the Middle Ages, many bishops had all sorts of feudal prerogatives and a great deal of political authority).

In March 1993, about 75% of the 9123 native Andorrans who are eligible to vote (less than one-sixth of the population) cast ballots in a constitutional referendum that established Andorra as an independent, democratic 'parliamentary co-principality'. Under the new constitution, which placed full sovereignty in the hands of the Andorran people, the French and Spanish co-princes will continue to function as joint heads-of-state but will have reduced powers. The new constitution also provides for separate legislative, executive and judicial branches; gives the government the power to raise revenue through income tax; and permits Andorran citizens to form trade unions and political parties.

The country's elected parliament is known as the Consell General (Council General); its forerunner, the Consell de la Terra (Council of the Land), was established in 1419. Its 28 members – four from each of the seven parishes – are elected for four-year terms. The Consell General meets three or four times a year and is chaired by a *síndic* (president) and a deputy síndic. Under a system adopted in 1981, Andorra also has an executive branch, known as the Conseil Exécutif (Executive Council). It is presided over by the *cap del govern* (head-of-government), who is elected by the Consell General. The Conseil Exécutif consists of four to six *consellers de govern* (government councillors) who are appointed by the cap del govern. Women were given the right to vote in 1970. Andorra is not a member of the EC.

For administrative purposes, Andorra is divided into seven parishes (*parròquies* in Catalan, *paroisses* in French). Six of the parishes have existed since at least the 9th century. A seventh, Les Escaldes-Engordany, was created in 1978 by lopping off part of the parish of Andorra-la-Vella; the exact border between the two has yet to be settled. A small area near the French border is claimed by two parishes but unfortunately, the historical documents necessary to settle the dispute have disappeared. As a compromise, the area is considered to be part of both parishes.

ECONOMY

The Andorran economy is based on duty-free shopping, tourism (10 million people visit the country every year) and banking. The most important component of the agricultural sector, which makes up only 1.2% of total economic activity, is the production of tobacco. The government has a very considerable operating deficit.

ANDORRA

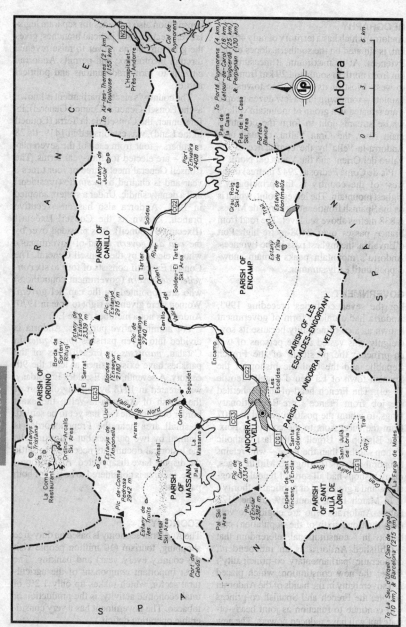

POPULATION & PEOPLE

Only about a quarter of Andorra's 60,000 inhabitants, almost two-thirds of whom live in Andorra-la-Vella and its suburbs, are Andorran nationals. The rest are Spaniards (27,000), Portuguese (4000), French (4000) and assorted other nationalities. All Andorran citizens over 18 can vote.

LANGUAGE

Andorra's official language is Catalan, the language of Catalonia. It is closely related to Castellano (Castilian Spanish) and, to a lesser extent, French. Local lore has it that everyone in Andorra speaks all three languages, but there are plenty of people (Iberian immigrants, perhaps) who can't understand more than 10 words of French. Trilingual restaurant menus provide a good opportunity to compare Catalan with Spanish and French. Few people understand much English.

Some useful words you're likely to need:

yes	*sí*
no	*no*
goodbye	*adéu*
good evening	*bona tarda*
good morning	*bon dia*
good night	*bona nit*
today	*avui*
tomorrow	*demà*
yesterday	*ahir*
avenue	*avinguda*
lake	*estany*
mountain peak	*pic*
parish	*parròquia*
public square	*plaça*
river	*riu*
street	*carrer* (abbrev. 'C/')

Facts for the Visitor

VISAS & EMBASSIES

Visas are not necessary to visit Andorra: the authorities figure that if Spain or France let you in, that's good enough for them. It is very unlikely that you will have your documents checked when entering or leaving the principality (though French and Spanish customs officials may take an interest in what you're bringing back with you), but you are required by law to carry a passport or national identity card and to present it when checking into a hotel so the management can register you with the police.

Andorra does not have any diplomatic legations abroad, nor are there any embassies in the capital, Andorra-la-Vella.

MONEY

Andorra, which has no currency of its own, uses the Spanish peseta (abbreviated 'pta') and the French franc. Except in Pas de la Casa (on the French frontier), prices are usually marked in pesetas (the currency in which taxes are collected), but you can pay in either currency almost everywhere except the post offices. If you opt to pay in francs, the exchange rate selected by the merchant may not be the most favourable.

Exchange Rates

US$1	5.35FF	100 pta
UK£1	9.80FF	183 pta
A$1	4.04FF	76 pta
1FF	–	18.6 pta
100 pta	5.35FF	–

Tipping

Service is not included in restaurant prices.

TOURIST OFFICES

For information on tourist offices in Andorra-la-Vella, see the Andorra-la-Vella listing. Each parish has its own *unió proturisme* (tourism promotion office).

Andorra's tourist offices abroad include the following:

Belgium
    10 Rue de la Montagne, 1000 Brussels (☎ 2-5021211; fax 2-5133934)
France
    26 Ave de l'Opéra, 75001 Paris (☎ 1-42.61.50.55; fax 1-42.61.41.91)
Spain
    Carrer Marià Cubí 159, 08021 Barcelona (☎ 93-200-0655; 93-200-0787, fax 93-414-1863)

ANDORRA

UK
> 63 Westover Road, London SW18 (☎ 81-874-4806)

USA
> 73-27 193 St, Fresh Meadows, NY 11366 (☎ 718-486-3060; fax 212-688-8683)

USEFUL ORGANISATIONS

For weather information, call 24035 (in French), 24247 (Spanish) or 23933 (Catalan).

BUSINESS HOURS

Small stores and banks take a short siesta between 1 pm and 3, 3.30 or 4 pm.

POST & TELECOMMUNICATIONS
Post

Domestic and international postal services are provided by two separate networks of post offices, one operated by France since 1931, the other by Spain since 1928. Andorran stamps denominated in francs are printed, issued and sold by the French post office, which then delivers the letters they've been affixed to. Stamps in pesetas are printed, issued, sold and delivered by the Spanish system. Andorran stamps of both types are valid only for items posted within Andorra. Regular French and Spanish stamps cannot be used to mail things from the principality. Letters mailed in Andorra to destinations within the country are free and do not need stamps.

International postal rates are the same as those in force in the issuing country; the French tariffs tend to be slightly cheaper. Locals advise that it's faster to route your international mail (except to Spain) via France, something you can easily accomplish by using stamps denominated in francs. By the way, there are two kinds of postboxes, one for each postal system, but if you use the 'wrong' one your letter will be transferred to the other system for processing.

Letters to Andorra-la-Vella marked 'poste restante' – a phrase taken from French, of course – are quite logically sent to the town's French post office (see Post under Information in the Andorra-la-Vella listing).

There's a 2.80FF charge for each letter you pick up. You can also receive poste restante mail via the American Express office in Andorra-la-Vella (see Money under Information in the Andorra-la-Vella listing). The best way to get a letter to Andorra is to address it to 'Principauté d'Andorre via FRANCE'. If writing from France, the postcode is 99000.

Telephone

Until 1967, Andorra had virtually no telephone system. To call directory assistance, dial 11; operators speak Catalan, Spanish and French.

International To call Andorra from France, dial 628 (16-628 in the Paris area) before the five-digit local number. From Spain, dial 9738 before the five-digit number. To call Andorra from other countries, you have two options: you can either dial the international access code and then 34 (Spain's country code), 738 (Andorra's Spanish regional prefix) and the five-digit number; or you can dial the international access code followed by 33 (France's country code), 628 and then the local number.

To call France from Andorra, dial 7 (71 for the Paris area) and then the eight-digit local number. To call Spain, dial 9 followed by the regional prefix and the local number. To call other countries, dial 0 and then the country code, area code and local number. The international operator can be reached by dialling 19. It does not seem to be possible to access French home-direct services from Andorran public telephones. To France and Spain, telephone rates are 50% cheaper between 10 pm and 8 am and all day on Sunday and holidays.

Public Telephones Except for a few older phones that take pesetas (or francs at Pas de la Casa), public telephones use Andorran *tele-tarjas* (telephone cards), which operate on the same principle as the *télécartes* used in France (see Post & Telecommunications in the Facts for the Visitor chapter). They are not valid outside of Andorra. Tele-tarjas worth 50 units (one unit is good for one local call of about three minutes) can be purchased for 500 pta at post offices, tobacconists and some tourist offices; 100-unit cards cost 900 pta.

Reverse-charge (collect) calling is not available except to Spain, and then only from the STA calling offices in Andorra-la-Vella (see Information in the Andorra-la-Vella listing) and Sant Julià de Lòria (at Place de la Germandat).

TIME

Andorra, like France and Spain, is one hour ahead of GMT/UTC. During summer time (daylight savings time), which runs from the last Sunday in September to the last Sunday in March, it is two hours ahead of GMT/UTC.

ELECTRICITY

The electric current is either 220V or 125V, both at 50 Hz.

RADIO

Radio Valira (☎ 63777) is a private, Andorra-la-Vella-based radio station that broadcasts on 93.3 MHz and 98.1 MHz in the FM band. It has a half-hour news programme in English on weekdays at 2.30 pm.

DANGERS & ANNOYANCES

The attitude of the Andorran government towards pretty much everything can be described as laissez-faire, which makes for cheap shopping but lots of minor hassles. Unlike France, the country's minimal legislation to protect the consumer often remains unenforced, so that hotels (unclassified by any starring system) and petrol stations sometimes neglect to post their prices and restaurants are free to refuse to serve tap water with meals. The road system is underdeveloped and inadequate, leading to traffic chaos amidst the unsightly buildings erected – until recently, at least – with very little regard for aesthetics.

Emergency telephone numbers (which are free) include:

Police	☎ 10
Ambulance (SAMU)	☎ 16
Fire or Ambulance	☎ 18

ACTIVITIES
Hiking

The tranquillity of Andorra's beautiful and relatively unspoiled back country begins only a few hundred metres from the bazaar-like bustle of the towns. The country's north-west (see the Parish of Ordino section) has some especially nice areas for hiking. All told, Andorra has over 50 lakes hidden among the soaring mountains.

The GR7 trail, which traverses the Pyrenees from the Mediterranean to the Atlantic, passes through the southern part of Andorra and has a number of variations. The GR11 also passes through the principality. Hikers can sleep for free in the numerous *refuges* (see the following Accommodation listing). A 1:50,000 scale *mapa topogràfic* of the country costs 475 pta in bookshops. Maps in 1:10,000 scale (!) are also available.

French-speakers might want to pick up *L'Andorre Par A. Kill*, an excellent hiking guide that includes maps. It is easier to find in France than in Andorra. Tourist offices sell a French-language booklet of hiking itineraries entitled *Guide des Itinéraires* (1100 pta); the Catalan version is called *Guia de Camins*.

Skiing

Andorra has five downhill ski areas (*estació d'esquí*). For information on Ordino-Arcalís, see the Parish of Ordino section. Pas de la Casa-Grau Roig (☎ 20391/9 for information; fax 23036), which has about 30 lifts (mostly towlines), is on the Franco-Andorran border a bit south of Port d'Envalira.

Sector Pas de la Casa (☎ 55977, 55116) is on the eastern slopes of the col, while *sector* Grau Roig (☎ 51218/9) is on the western side. Soldeu-El Tarter (☎ 21197, 51151; fax 61982, 51567) is midway between Port d'Envalira and Canillo. Arinsal (☎ 35077; fax 36242) and Pal (☎ 36236; fax 35904) are in the west of the country.

Ski passes cost somewhere between 2600 and 3100 pta a day at Pas de la Casa-Grau Roig and Soldeu-El Tarter; Ordino-Arcalís and Arinsal are somewhat cheaper. In the winter, the ski stations are linked to Andorra-la-Vella by bus.

ANDORRA

ACCOMMODATION

Almost all of Andorra's hotels stay open all year. They are fullest in July and August and from December to March, but since the turnover is high (except in winter, most people stay just long enough to do a bit of shopping), rooms are almost always available in midmorning. Singles are generally much cheaper than doubles. The use of hall showers is included in the price of the room. Many smaller hotels have no one on the staff who speaks English or even French, so it may prove difficult to make reservations by telephone if you don't know Catalan or Spanish.

There are no youth hostels in Andorra. The 26 unstaffed *refuges* (*refugi* in Catalan) – mountain huts for the use of shepherds and hikers (one room for each) – are free and do not require reservations. Most have bunks, fireplaces and sources of potable water. Tourist offices have brochures and maps indicating the location of the *refuges*.

Tourist offices can provide information on apartments available for short-term rental.

THINGS TO BUY

Because customs duties and excise taxes are very low and – at least for now – there's no value-added tax (VAT), Andorra has become famous as a duty-free bazaar for electronics, photographic equipment, alcohol, cigarettes, perfumes, leather goods, designer clothing, luxury foods, running shoes, toys, etc. If you know exactly what you're looking for, you can probably find it (or something similar from among last year's models). But if you don't know what you want, Andorra is not such a great place to shop around: since most places sell a little bit of everything (a few car radios, some watches, etc), salespeople know very little about the merchandise on offer and usually can't produce more than a few roughly similar models for comparison.

If you search out the best price (pricing varies widely from shop to shop) and bargain a bit, the prices for most electronics goods are about 40% less than those in France and 25% below what you'll find at the duty-free shops at Paris's airports. However, the same goods are available for much less in the USA, Singapore and Hong Kong.

It is not uncommon to come across goods that are not from the latest model year. Some shops add a surcharge of 4% if you opt to pay by credit card, much more than the cost of a cash advance. If you're buying something that comes with a warranty, make sure to have the store fill in the warranty card and rubber-stamp it. Some warranties are valid only in the country of purchase, so it's a good idea to read the fine print! Beware of confusion – unintentional or otherwise – that may result from going back and forth between pesetas, francs, US dollars and your home currency.

Since 1991, Andorra has had commercial accords with the EC that allow people entering the Community to bring with them duty-free goods worth three times the value permitted travellers coming from other non-member countries. Certain goods, such as alcohol, tobacco, perfume, coffee and tea, are subject to quantitative limits.

Getting There & Away

AIR

The major airports nearest Andorra are those in Toulouse, France (180 km to the north), Perpignan, France (130 km to the east), and Barcelona, Spain (200 km to the south).

LAND

Train

There is no railway service within Andorra, but a number of train stations not far away in France and Spain are linked to the principality by bus.

To/From France There are buses to Andorra from three train stations along SNCF's line from Toulouse to Latour de Carol: L'Hospitalet-Près-l'Andorre (☎ 61.05.20.78; 91FF from Toulouse), which has daily bus links all year long; Ax-les-Thermes (☎ 61.64.20.72; 80FF from Toulouse), whence there are one or two buses a day from May to October; and Latour de Carol (☎ 68.04. 80.69 from 7 am to 8 pm), served by one or two buses a day. Latour de Carol is linked to Perpignan (110FF; 3½ hours; six a day) by SNCF and to Barcelona (57FF; 3 to 3½ hours) by rather slow Spanish trains.

For information on getting from these railheads to Andorra, see the Short-Haul Bus listing. If you speak French, Catalan or Spanish (or can find someone who can), you might want to call either the relevant railway station or the bus company concerned so you can take one of the trains synchronised with the bus schedule.

To/From Spain The Spanish train station nearest Andorra is at Puigcerdà, which is five km (by rail) from the French railhead of Latour de Carol. Puigcerdà – whence there are trains to Barcelona and, via Latour de Carol, to Toulouse and Perpignan – is one hour by Alsina Graells bus from La Seu d'Urgell; for details, see the Long-Haul Bus listing. For information on getting to Andorra from Latour de Carol and La Seu d'Urgell, see the Short-Haul Bus listing.

Short-Haul Bus

Societat Franco-Andorrana de Transports and its sister company, La Hispano Andorrana (☎ 21372 for both), link Andorra-la-Vella and other Andorran towns to destinations just over the border in France and Spain. The company's main office is in Andorra-la-Vella at Carrer la Llacuna 14, which is around the corner from Plaça Guillemó. It is open Monday to Saturday from 9.30 am to 1.30 pm and 3 to 7 pm and on Sunday from 9.30 am to 2 pm. It can provide bus schedules (these can also be consulted at the municipal tourist office). The left-luggage room, open the same hours as the office, charges just 50 pta a day to store a backpack or suitcase.

Both companies' buses stop at Plaça Guillemó in Andorra-la-Vella. Tickets are sold on board. When Col d'Envalira is closed because of snow, buses are rerouted via Latour de Carol. The hours given here have remained unchanged for several years but could, of course, be modified. A quick call to

the company or the relevant French train station (see Train) by someone who speaks French, Catalan or Spanish could prevent you from getting stranded or having to thumb it.

To/From France Buses from Andorra-la-Vella to L'Hospitalet-Près-l'Andorre (630 pta or 34FF; two to three hours), the train station nearest Andorra, via 2408-metre Port d'Envalira leave Andorra-la-Vella daily, all year long at 5.45 am and 3.30 or 4 pm. Buses from L'Hospitalet to Andorra depart at 7.40 am and 6.30 pm.

From 1 May to 31 October, there is a daily service to/from Ax-les-Thermes (780 pta or 42FF; 2¼ to 3¼ hours), another SNCF railhead. Buses to Ax-les-Thermes leave Andorra-la-Vella at 8.15 am (and 11 am from mid-July to mid-September); departures from Ax-les-Thermes are at 4.15 pm (and noon in summer).

Autos Pujol Huguet (☎ 41019), which is based in Sant Julià de Lòria, runs a bus once a day (twice a day from July to September) from Sant Julià de Lòria via Plaça Guillemó in Andorra-la-Vella to Pas de la Casa (on the French border), Porté Puymorens and Latour de Carol (55 pta; 2½ hours), which is served by trains from Toulouse, Perpignan and Barcelona. Latour de Carol, just across the border from the Spanish town of Puigcerdà, is only about eight km from Llivia, a Spanish enclave surrounded by French territory.

To/From Spain There are seven daily runs (five on Sunday) from Andorra-la-Vella to La Seu d'Urgell (230 pta; 45 minutes), which is about 10 km south of the Andorran frontier. Buses leave Andorra-la-Vella daily at 9 and 11.30 am, 1.30, 4 and 8 pm; from Monday to Saturday, there are also buses at 8 am and 6 pm. From La Seu d'Urgell, buses depart daily at 8 and 9.30 am, 12.15, 2 and 8 pm; from Monday to Saturday, there are additional departures at 3.20 and 6 pm.

For details on buses from La Seu d'Urgell to the Spanish railhead of Puigcerdà, see the following section.

ANDORRA

Long-Haul Bus

Alsina Graells (☎ 27379, 26567) at Carrer Prat de la Creu 24 links Andorra-la-Vella with Barcelona. The company also has buses from Puigcerdà (see To/From Spain under Train) to La Seu d'Urgell, whence it's a short bus ride to Andorra (see the Short-Haul Bus listing). The office is open daily, except Sunday afternoon and holiday afternoons, from 9.30 am to 2.30 pm and 5 to 7 pm. The company's Barcelona office (☎ 93-302-4086, 93-302-6545) is at Ronda Universitat 4. They also have a bureau in La Seu d'Urgell (☎ 973-354422).

Alsina Graells buses to Barcelona (1965 pta) leave Andorra-la-Vella daily at 7 am and 2.30 pm; from Monday to Saturday, there's also a bus at 6 am. The trip takes 3¾ hours if you go via the Cadí Tunnel and 4½ hours if you don't. Buses from Puigcerdà to La Seu d'Urgell (one hour) leave daily at 7.30 am, 2.30 and 5.30 pm; buses from La Seu d'Urgell to Puigcerdà depart at 9.30 am, 12.30 and 7 pm.

A number of other companies that handle long-distance transport to Spain, France and beyond share a ticket office (☎ 26289) at Carrer Prat de la Creu 24. It is open on Monday and Wednesday from 9 am to 1 pm and 4 to 7 pm; on Tuesday from 9 am to 1 pm and 4 to 7, 8 or 9 pm; on Thursday from 9 am to 3 pm and 5 to 7 pm; on Saturday from 7 am to 1 pm and 4 to 6 pm; and on Sunday from 7 to 11 am. It is closed on Friday.

Samar (☎ 26289) has a fortnightly bus from Andorra southward to Lerida (Lleida; 1050 pta), Zaragoza (☎ 976-434304; six hours), Madrid (4100 pta; 11 hours), Granada, Malaga and other places on the way to Algeciras. The company's Madrid office (☎ 91-468-4236) is at Estación Sur de Autobuses, Canarias 17. In the direction of France (where ticketing is handled by Intercars), the same line serves various destinations between Toulouse (☎ 61. 58.14.53) and Nice (☎ 93.80.08.70).

Airbus has a weekly bus from Andorra down the east coast of Spain to Murcia (☎ 968-291911) and Cartagena (☎ 968-501419; 13 hours) via Valencia. Nortbus, also known as Andor-Inter, operates a biweekly line that goes all the way across northern Spain to Tuy (18 or 19 hours), which is on the Spanish-Portuguese border near the Atlantic. The Nortbus office in Tuy (☎ 968-630375) is at Avenida de Portugal 60.

For information on other bus services to Spain, consult the schedules posted at the municipal tourist office. For information on buses from Toulouse, see the Getting There & Away section for that city in the Toulouse & the Pyrenees chapter.

Car

By road, Andorra is 858 km from Paris, 464 km from Nice, 225 km from Barcelona and 853 km from Madrid. The drive into the principality from France over 2408-metre Port d'Envalira is long, tortuous and exhausting but not lacking in mountain panoramas.

A tunnel from L'Hospitalet-Près-l'Andorre to Spain, which will allow vehicle traffic to bypass Andorra, is under construction. A proposed tunnel from France to Andorra under Port d'Envalira is still on the drawing board.

Petrol is about 15% cheaper in Andorra than in Francen There are a number of petrol stations between Port d'Envalira and Pas de la Casa so you can (re)enter France with a full tank.

Getting Around

BUS

The Cooperativa Interurbana (☎ 20412) is responsible for bus transport within Andorra. The front window of each of the company's red-and-white buses displays a sign listing the names of both the town where the bus started its run and the town where it will end up. Locals may know that a bus on the south side of Avinguda Príncep Benlloch couldn't possibly be going to Sant Julià de Lòria, but visitors may not. When you buy your ticket from the driver, its a good idea to confirm that the bus is indeed heading to where you'd like to go.

Buses from Les Escaldes to Sant Julià de Lòria (80 pta) stop in Andorra-la-Vella near the Pyrénées department store (which is at Avinguda Meritxell 21) and at Plaça Guillemó. Buses to La Massana and Ordino (100 pta) leave from the Plaça Príncep Benlloch stop, which is opposite 6 Avinguda Príncep Benlloch. Buses to Encamp (80 pta) also leave from the Plaça Príncep Benlloch stop. All three lines operate daily every 15 to 30 minutes from 7 am (7.30 am on Sunday) to 9.30 pm (8.30 pm to Ordino).

Buses link Andorra-la-Vella with the neighbouring parish of Les Escaldes-Engordany (60 pta) every 15 minutes from 8.45 am to 8.15 pm. There are buses to Canillo (170 pta) and Soldeu (255 pta), both in the Parish of Canillo, once an hour from 8 or 9 am to 7 or 8 pm. From Andorra-la-Vella, there is one bus a day to Pas de la Casa, two a day to El Serrat (Parish of Ordino) and three a day to Arinsal (Parish of Massana; 135 pta). In winter, there are buses from Andorra-la-Vella to the ski stations.

CAR

Andorra's road system consists of three main highways. The CG1 (CG stands for Carretera General) links Andorra-la-Vella with Sant Julià de Lòria and the Spanish border, whence it's a further 10 km to La Seu d'Urgell. The CG2, which has a lot in common with the road from Srinagar to Leh in Indian Kashmir, goes from Andorra-la-Vella via Les Escaldes, Encamp, Canillo, Soldeu and Pas de la Casa to France. CG3 begins in the capital and passes through La Massana, Ordino and Llorts on its way to the Ordino-Arcalís ski area.

The speed limit in populated areas is 40 km/h. Because of road conditions (lots of hairpin curves) and the constant traffic jams, it is rare for a vehicle to approach the inter-hamlet speed limit of 90 km/h. Andorra-la-Vella suffers from semi-permanent near-gridlock for much of the year. Using a seat belt is not mandatory but motorcycle helmets are.

The parking police seems to be a major source of service-sector employment. Foreign-registered cars may safely ignore the first few parking tickets, but after that your vehicle may get towed away and held hostage until you pay up. You could try ignoring the wheel clamps attached to egregiously misparked vehicles but this approach often produces less-than-satisfactory results. Fines for moving violations have to be paid on the spot.

Andorra-la-Vella

Andorra-la-Vella (Vella is pronounced 'VEY-yah'; population 20,500 in the parish), the capital of the principality and its largest town, is given over almost wholly to the retailing of tax-free electronics and luxury goods. Unless you love to shop, there isn't all that much to do in this overgrown, duty-free bazaar. If they put a roof over the area, added a few fountains and spruced things up a bit, they could call it a shopping mall...Andorra la Malla, perhaps!

Andorra-la-Vella is along the Gran Valira River at an elevation of 1000 metres. It is surrounded by mountains up to 2400 metres high. There is good transport by public bus from here to most parts of the principality. Andorra-la-Vella means Andorra the Old in Catalan and is rendered Andorre la Vieille in French and Andorra la Vieja in Spanish.

Orientation

Andorra-la-Vella is strung out along one main street, the name of which changes from Avinguda Meritxell to Avinguda Príncep Benlloch at Plaça Rebés. The Historic Quarter (Barri Antic) stretches from the Església Parroquial de Sant Esteve to Plaçeta del Puial. Many intercity buses stop at Plaça Guillemó, also known as Place des Arcades.

The suburb of Santa Coloma is south-west of Andorra-la-Vella along Avinguda Príncep Benlloch, which becomes Avinguda de Santa Coloma and then the CG1 (the highway to Spain). The spa town of Les

ANDORRA

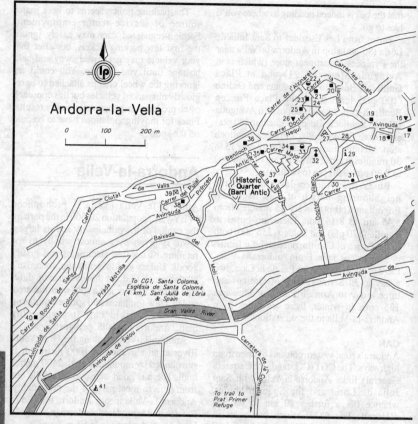

Andorra-la-Vella

0   100   200 m

Historic Quarter (Barri Antic)

To CG1, Santa Coloma,
Església de Santa Coloma
(4 km), Sant Julià de Lòria
& Spain

Gran Valira River

To trail to
Prat Primer
Refuge

ANDORRA

Escaldes is along the eastern extension of Avinguda Meritxell, Avinguda Carlemany, which turns into the CG2 (the highway to France).

Information

Tourist Offices The helpful municipal tourist office *(caseta d'informació i turisme;* ☎ 27117), which is across the street from Avinguda Meritxell 44, is open daily from 9 am to 1 pm and 4 to 8 pm (7 pm on Sunday). During July and August, it's open daily from 9 am to 9 pm (7 pm on Sunday). The office has maps, all sorts of brochures, postage stamps and tele-tarjas. Domestic and international bus schedules are posted. An excellent booklet entitled *The Parish of Andorra-la-Vella* (50 pta) gives lots of background on the capital and includes a number of suggestions for day hikes.

The national tourist office *(sindicat d'initiativa-oficina de turisme;* ☎ 20214) is at the top of Carrer Doctor Vilanova between Plaça del Poble and Plaça Rebés. It's open Monday to Saturday from 10 am (9 am in July and August) to 1 pm and 3 to 7 pm and on Sunday from 10 am to 1 pm.

In Les Escaldes, there's a tourist office

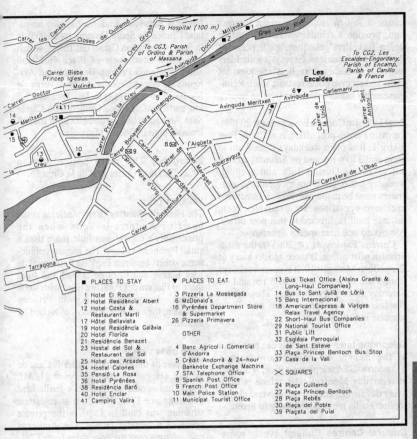

■ PLACES TO STAY

1 Hotel El Roure
2 Hotel Residència Albert
12 Hotel Costa &
   Restaurant Marti
17 Hôtel Bellavista
19 Hotel Residència Galàxia
20 Hotel Florida
21 Residència Benazet
23 Hostal del Sol &
   Restaurant del Sol
25 Hotel des Arcades
34 Hostal Calones
35 Pensió La Rosa
36 Hotel Pyrénées
38 Residència Baró
40 Hotel Enclar
41 Camping Valira

▼ PLACES TO EAT

3 Pizzeria La Mossegada
6 McDonald's
16 Pyrénées Department Store
  & Supermarket
26 Pizzeria Primavera

OTHER

4 Banc Agricol i Comercial
  d'Andorra
5 Crèdit Andorrà & 24-hour
  Banknote Exchange Machine
7 STA Telephone Office
8 Spanish Post Office
9 French Post Office
10 Main Police Station
11 Municipal Tourist Office

13 Bus Ticket Office (Alsina Graells &
   Long-Haul Companies)
14 Bus to Sant Julià de Lòria
15 Banc Internacional
18 American Express & Viatges
   Relax Travel Agency
22 Short-Haul Bus Companies
29 National Tourist Office
31 Public Lift
32 Església Parroquial
   de Sant Esteve
33 Plaça Príncep Benlloch Bus Stop
37 Casa de la Vall

✕ SQUARES

24 Plaça Guillemó
27 Plaça Príncep Benlloch
28 Plaça Rebés
30 Plaça del Poble
39 Plaçeta del Puial

ANDORRA

(☎ 20963) at Plaça dels Coprínceps, which is about one km east of the STA telephone office.

Money Banks are open Monday to Friday from 9 am to 1 pm and 3 to 5 pm and on Saturday from 9 am to noon. There are banks every hundred metres or so along Avinguda Meritxell (at Nos 32, 40, 61, 73, 80 and 96), at Plaça Príncep Benlloch (next to No 2) and on Avinguda Príncep Benlloch (No 25). The Banc Internacional (☎ 20043) at Avinguda Meritxell 32 and the Banc Agricol i Comercial d'Andorra at Avinguda Meritxell 73

have 24-hour automatic teller machines that process Visa and MasterCard cash advances. Crèdit Andorrà, next to the river at Avinguda Meritxell 80, has a 24-hour banknote exchange machine.

American Express (☎ 22044; fax 27055) is represented in Andorra-la-Vella by Viatges Relax travel agency, whose office is in the Historic Quarter at Carrer Roc dels Escolls 12. It is open from 9 am to 1 pm and 3.30 to 7 pm Monday to Friday and from 9 am to 1 pm on Saturday. It's closed on Sunday and holidays. The office cannot change money (you have to go to a bank for that), but it can reissue a lost or stolen American Express card, provide a reimbursement for lost or stolen travellers' cheques, cash personal cheques for American Express cardholders (payment is made in travellers' cheques, not cash) and receive poste restante mail. Reimbursements usually take less than an hour.

Post La Poste Correus Francesos (☎ 20408), the main French post office, is at Carrer Pere d'Urg 1. It is open weekdays from 9 am to noon and 3 to 6 pm and on Saturday from 9 am to noon. During July and August, weekday hours are 9 am to 7 pm. All purchases must be made with French francs. No exchange operations are available. Poste restante mail is directed to this post office. Almost no-one here speaks Spanish.

Correus Espanyols (☎ 20657), the main Spanish post office, is three blocks away at Carrer Joan Maragall 10. It is open weekdays from 9 am to 1 pm and 3 to 5 pm and on Saturday from 9 am to 1 pm. They accept pesetas only. Speaking French here is an exercise in futility.

Telephone International calls can be placed at the Servei de Telecomunicacions d'Andorra (STA telephone office; ☎ 21021) at Avinguda Meritxell 110, which is open every day from 9 am to 9 pm. Reverse charge (collect) calls are available only to Spain.

Cultural Centres Cultural events sometimes take place at Plaça del Poble, around whose perimeter one finds Andorra-la-Vella's theatre and its music academy. Contact the tourist office for details on festivals, dance performances, etc.

Travel Agencies Viatges Relax (☎ 22044, fax 27055) at Carrer Roc dels Escolls 12, which doubles as the local representative of American Express, is also a full-service travel agency. It can issue French and Spanish rail tickets, book SNCM and Channel ferries and issue air tickets. See American Express under Money for opening times.

Medical Services Andorra has two hospitals. Clínica de Santa Coloma (☎ 21905) is in Santa Coloma on Carrer Gil Torres, which is 1.5 km south-west of Plaça Guillemó along Avinguda Príncep Benlloch and Avinguda de Santa Coloma. Clínica Verge de Meritxell (☎ 21521) is in Les Escaldes 1.5 km north-east of Plaça Guillemó on Carrer Sant Andreu, which is one block up the hill from Avinguda Doctor Mitjavila.

Emergency The main police station (☎ 21222) is at Carrer Prat de la Creu 16.

Walking Tour

The **Historic Quarter** (Barri Antic) was the heart of Andorra-la-Vella when the principality's capital was little more than a small Pyrenean village. The narrow cobblestone streets between Església Parroquial de Sant Esteve and Casa de la Vall and from there to Plaçeta del Puial are lined with stone houses. Away from Avinguda Príncep Benlloch, the area is relatively untouched by tourism.

Casa de la Vall

The pride of the Historic Quarter is Casa de la Vall (House of the Valley; ☎ 21234), which has served as Andorra's parliament building since 1702. This three-storey stone structure was built in 1580 as the private home of a wealthy family. The Andorran coat-of-arms over the door dates from 1761.

Downstairs is **Sala de la Justicia**, the only courtroom in the whole country. Upstairs, in the **Sala del Consell** (Council General Chamber), the 28 members of the Andorran parliament sit in the red chairs along the walls. The consellers de govern sit in the blue chairs, while the three red chairs at the far end of the room are for the síndic, the deputy síndic and the parliamentary secretary. The **Chest of the Seven Locks** (Set Panys) once held Andorra's most important official documents. It could not be opened unless a key-bearing representative from each of the parishes was present. For more information on how Andorra is governed, see Government under Facts about the Country at the beginning of this chapter.

There are free, 20-minute guided tours of Casa de la Vall in Catalan, French, Spanish and sometimes English on weekdays and alternating Saturday mornings (every Saturday in July and August). They leave about once an hour from 9.30 or 10 am to noon and 3 or 4 pm to 6 pm. The easiest way to find Casa de la Vall is to walk up Carrer de la Vall from Avinguda Príncep Benlloch.

National Philatelic Museum

The Museu Filatèlic (☎ 29129) exhibits Andorran coins and paper currency as well as postage stamps. Formerly on the 2nd floor of Casa de la Vall, it is being moved to an as-yet-undetermined location.

Església Parroquial de Sant Esteve

Andorra-la-Vella's parish church is at the edge of the Historic Quarter across the street from Plaça Príncep Benlloch. The mostly modern interior is of little interest, though the decorated Romanesque apse has remained relatively unmodified. The paintings date from as far back as the 13th century.

Plaça del Poble

This large public square occupies the roof of the Edifici Administratiu, a modern government office building that also houses a number of Andorra-la-Vella's cultural institutions, such as the convention centre, the theatre and the music academy. It is a popular gathering place for locals, especially in the evenings. Various cultural events are held here. The lift in the south-east corner of Plaça del Poble whisks you down to Carrer Prat de la Creu.

Organised Tours

Excursions Nadal (☎ 21138; fax 20642) at Avinguda del Pessebre 94 in Les Escaledes-Engordany offers half and full-day bus excursions around the principality.

Places to Stay – bottom end

Camping Càmping Valira (☎ 22384), which is at the southern edge of town off Avinguda de Salou, charges 400 pta for each person, 400 pta for a tent and 400 pta for a car. There's a small indoor swimming pool and a food store on the site. It is open all year and always has space in the morning. Telephone reservations are accepted; during July and August, they are accepted a maximum of 24 hours in advance.

Hotels There are a number of relatively cheap hotels around Plaça Guillemó, but inexpensive places can also be found elsewhere in town.

Hotels – Plaça Guillemó Area The helpful, 15-room Residència Benazet (☎ 20698) at Carrer la Llacuna 21 (1st floor) has large, serviceable singles/doubles/triples/quads for 1200/2400/3600/4000 pta.

The Hostal del Sol (☎ 23701) at Plaça Guillemó 3 has tiny, utilitarian doubles with shower for 2500 to 3500 pta; triples are 3800 to 5200 pta. Quads cost 4500 to 6000 pta depending on the time of year. Reception is either on the 1st floor or in the ground-floor Restaurant del Sol. Telephone reservations are not accepted on weekends or in August.

Nearby at Plaça Guillemó 5, the Hotel des Arcades (☎ 26693, 21355) has doubles with shower and toilet for 3200 to 5100 pta, including breakfast. Adding a third person costs an extra 1100 pta.

Hotels – East of Plaça Guillemó The Hotel Costa (☎ 21439) at Avinguda Meritxell 44 has basic but clean singles, doubles, triples and quads for 1200 pta per person. Reception is on the 3rd floor; take the stairs on the left of the ground-floor shopping arcade. The 45-room Hôtel Bellavista (☎ 21288) at Avinguda Meritxell 26 (across from the Pyrénées department store) is a bit run down and isn't exactly spotless, but it's central and fairly inexpensive: doubles without/with shower and toilet cost 2000/4500 pta.

The Hotel El Roure (☎ 25483) at Avinguda Doctor Mitjavila 24 has doubles for 3100 pta, including breakfast. The Hotel Residència Albert (☎ 20156), down the block at Avinguda Doctor Mitjavila 16, has singles/doubles for 1500/3000 pta. This place does not accept telephone reservations.

Hotels – West of Plaça Guillemó In the Historic Quarter, the *Pensió La Rosa* (☎ 21810) at Antic Carrer Major 18 has nondescript singles/doubles for 1600/2800 pta and triples/quads for 3300/4400 pta.

The *Residència Baró* (☎ 21484), also known as the Habitacions Baró, is at Carrer del Puial 21, which is at the top of the stairs opposite Avinguda Príncep Benlloch 53. This place, one of the cheapest in town, *may* have rooms for 1350 to 1600 pta.

At the southern end of town, the *Hotel Enclar* (☎ 20310) at Carrer Roureda de Sansa 18 has doubles without/with shower and toilet for 2700/3200 pta; quads are 4400/5850 pta.

Places to Stay – middle
The *Hotel Residència Galàxia* (☎ 26975) is at Avinguda Meritxell 9 on the 3rd floor. As you walk into the arcade, take the lift or stairs on the right. Large, plain singles and doubles with shower, toilet, TV and video are 3500 pta; a room with a view costs 500 pta more. Reception is open daily from 9.30 am to 9 pm. This place does not accept reservations.

In the heart of the Historic Quarter, the quiet *Hostal Calones* (☎ 21312) at Antic Carrer Major 8 has unadorned and slightly dilapidated singles/doubles with large bathrooms for 2800/4150 pta. Huge rooms for three/four people cost 6200/7600 pta.

Places to Stay – top end
The 74-room *Hotel Pyrénées* (☎ 60006; fax 20265) at Avinguda Príncep Benlloch 20, a classy place built in 1940, is only one block from Casa de la Vall. It has a tennis court and a swimming pool. Singles/doubles/triples cost 4400/6400/8350 pta, including breakfast. At certain times of the year *demi-pension* (half-board) is mandatory. Parking costs 700 pta per 24 hours.

The *Hotel Florida* (☎ 20105; fax 61925) at Carrer la Llacuna 15 (one block from Plaça Guillemó) is the equivalent of a three-star hotel. Modern, lift-accessed doubles including breakfast cost 6500 pta in the low season. The price jumps to 7800 pta on weekends, around Christmas and Easter, in August and at the height of the ski season.

Places to Eat
It seems to be something of a local custom for restaurants to try to manoeuvre clients into drinking mineral water (100 pta) instead of tap water. The lines used by waiters vary – one fellow told me they'd run out of water pitchers!

Restaurants At Plaça Guillemó 3, *Restaurant del Sol* (☎ 23701) has French-style *menus* for 850 pta and 1200 pta. It is open daily, except Tuesday and during the month of November, from 12.30 to 3.30 pm and 7.30 to at least 10 pm.

Restaurant Marti (☎ 20946), which is hidden at the back of the 1st floor of the building at Avinguda Meritxell 44, has *menus* for 730 and 1000 pta. It is open daily from noon to 3.30 pm (4 pm on weekends) and 8 to 10 pm (10.30 pm on weekends).

The restaurant of the *Hôtel Pyrénées* (☎ 60006) at Avinguda Príncep Benlloch 20 serves Catalan, French and Spanish dishes in an ambience of sparkling chandeliers and two-tone tablecloths. Though most diners are people staying at the hotel, nonguests are also welcome. The *menu* costs 2100 pta; meat and fish dishes cost 1100 to 2000 pta. This place is open from 1 to 3 pm and 8 to 10 pm.

Other The modern *Pizzeria La Mossegada* (☎ 23131) has two entrances, one along the river at Avinguda Meritxell 73 and the other across the street from the Fiat dealership at Avinguda Doctor Mitjavila 2. Pizzas cost 600 to 775 pta; grilled meat dishes are 1100 to 1400 pta. This place, which has a riverside dining terrace in summer, is open from noon to 4 pm and 8 to 11 pm daily except Wednesday (daily from June to September).

Near Plaça Guillemó, *Pizzeria Primavera* (☎ 21903) at Carrer Doctor Nequi 4 has pizzas for 350 to 600 pta and a *menu* for 800 pta. Meat dishes are also available. It is open daily from noon to 4 pm and 8 pm to midnight.

McDonald's at Avinguda Meritxell 105 is open Monday to Thursday from 11 am to 11 pm and Friday to Sunday from 10 am to 1 am. During July and August, it's open daily from 10 am to 1 am.

Self-Catering Most of the places that call themselves supermarkets (*supermercat* or *supermarché*) specialise in luxury edibles and imbibables heavily taxed in France and Spain. Check out the cheese rounds the size of truck tyres!

The *supermarket* on the 2nd floor of the Pyrénées department store at Avinguda Meritxell 21 has lots of imported luxury goods but also carries bread, pastries, vegetables, fruits, cheese and the like. It is open Monday to Saturday from 9.30 am to 8 pm and on Sunday from 9 am to 7 pm. There's a Godiva chocolate shop near the checkout counters – expect to pay at least 4500 pta a kg!

In the Historic Quarter, there are a number of small grocery shops between Església Parroquial de Sant Esteve and Casa de la Vall.

Things to Buy
Most of Andorra-la-Vella's duty-free shops are along Avinguda Príncep Benlloch (the eastern part), Avinguda Meritxell and Avinguda Carlemany (technically in Les Escaldes).

Getting There & Away
Buses to France and Spain and domestic buses to Sant Julià de Lòria leave from in front of the Hostal del Sol at Plaça Guillemó. Buses to Ordino, Encamp and elsewhere depart from the Plaça Príncep Benlloch stop, which is opposite Avinguda Príncep Benlloch 6. For details, see the Getting There & Away and Getting Around listings in this chapter's introductory section. Bus schedules are posted at the municipal tourist office.

Getting Around
Most of the capital's streets were completely renumbered in 1990. Addresses from before that date (eg in brochures) will direct you to the wrong end of town.

AROUND ANDORRA-LA-VELLA
Església de Santa Coloma
Santa Coloma's church, mentioned in documents from the 9th century, is Andorra's oldest, but it's pre-Romanesque form has been modified over the centuries. The four-storey, almost-round **campanile** was built in the 12th century, apparently in two stages. All the church's 12th-century Romanesque murals except one Agnus Dei (an image of a lamb) were taken to a Berlin museum for conservation in the 1930s and are still there. The church is five km south-west of Plaça Guillemó; to get there, take Avinguda Príncep Benlloch and then Avinguda de Santa Coloma.

National Automobile Museum
The Museu Nacional de l'Automòbil (☎ 32266) is in Encamp at Avinguda Príncep Episcopal 64. It has about 70 motorcars from 1898 to 1950 as well as 50 motorcycles and 50 bicycles. It is generally open Monday to Saturday and can be reached from Andorra-la-Vella by public bus.

Hiking
From Santa Coloma, a path leads northward up the hill to **Capella de Sant Vincenç d'Enclar** (20 minutes), which before the Pareatges of 1288 was the site of an important castle. These days, one can see – in addition to the view – a recently reconstructed church, a cemetery, several silos and some ruins. The trail continues up to **Pic d'Enclar** (2382 metres), which is on the Spanish border. A path can then be followed eastward along the ridge to **Pic de Carroi** (2334 metres), which overlooks Santa Coloma from the north.

The **Rec del Solà** (elevation: about 1100 metres) is an almost-flat, 2.5-km path that follows a small irrigation canal that runs along the hillside a bit north of Andorra-la-

Vella. Another option is to hike southeastward from Andorra-la-Vella's Carretera de la Comella up to the *refuge* of **Prat Primer**, where it's possible to stay overnight. The walk up takes about two hours.

For information on these and other hikes, contact the municipal tourist office.

Parish of Ordino

The mountainous Parish of Ordino (population 1400) encompasses Andorra's northernmost territory.

ORDINO-ARCALÍS SKI AREA
The Ordino-Arcalís ski area (☎ 64500, 36320; fax 37300) is in the parish's far northwestern corner. During the winter, there are 11 lifts (mostly tow lines) and 16 ski runs of all levels of difficulty. In summer, this beautiful mountainous area – a number of the rugged peaks reach 2800 metres – has some of Andorra's most rewarding hiking trails.

Orientation
Restaurant La Coma, which is at the end of the paved road, is at the upper extreme of the ski area at an altitude of 2200 metres.

Hiking
The trail behind Restaurant La Coma leads eastward across the hill and over the ridge to a group of beautiful mountain lakes, **Estanys de Tristaina**. The walk to the first lake takes about 30 minutes.

In the warm season, walks can also be started from the 2700-metre-high upper terminus of Telecadira La Coma (La Coma Chairlift), which is across the road from the restaurant. It operates daily during July and August from 10 am to 5 pm. Summer fees are 350/500 pta one way/return.

Skiing
In winter, Ordino-Arcalís has lots of snow and a decent selection of runs but can be rather cold and is often windy. Telecadira La Coma (see Hiking) operates for skiers from

December to mid-May. A lift ticket costs 1650 to 2000 pta a day, depending on whether high-season rates apply.

Places to Eat
Restaurant La Coma (no telephone), which serves mostly snacks, is open from December to early May. From the end of June to early September, it's open from 10 am to 6 pm daily except Monday (daily in August and September).

Getting There & Away
The only way up here is to drive or hitchhike. Public buses serve Ordino and El Serrat (see Bus under Getting Around in this chapter's introductory section).

Getting Around
Bicycle Restaurant La Coma rents mountain bikes from the end of June to early September. During this period, it's open from 10 am to 6 pm daily except Monday (daily in August and September). Charges are 525 pta for one hour, 1200 pta for four hours and 1800 pta a day.

LLORTS
The tiny mountain village of Llorts (pronounced 'Yorts'; population 99), which is at an altitude of 1413 metres, has retained its traditional architecture, near-pristine mountain setting and tobacco fields. This is one of the most unadulterated spots in the whole country.

Hiking
A trail leads up the valley west of town (along Riu de l'Angonella) to a group of lakes, **Estanys de l'Angonella**. Count on spending 3½ hours to get up there.

From a bit north of the village of El Serrat (population 53; 1600 metres), which is four km up the valley from Llorts, a secondary road leads to the **Borda de Sorteny** *refuge*. From there, a trail continues on to a lake called **Estany de l'Estanyó** (2339 metres) and a mountain known as **Pic de l'Estanyó** (2915 metres).

From Arans (population 72; 1360 metres),

a village a couple of km south of Llorts, a trail goes north-eastward to **Bordes de l'Ensegur** (2180 metres), where there's an old shepherds' hut.

Places to Stay

Camping A couple of hundred metres north of Llorts is *Càmping Els Pradassos* (☎ 37142, proprietor's home ☎ 22550), perhaps the most attractive camping ground in all of Andorra, which is open from the end of June to early September. This place, named after the cow pasture in which it is situated (every field in Andorra has a proper name), is surrounded by forested mountains. It even has its very own spring. This place is also very inexpensive: 175 pta per person, 175 pta per tent and 175 pta per vehicle. Bring your own food.

Hotel The *Hotel Vilaró* (☎ 35225), 200 metres south of the village limits, has doubles with washbasin and bidet for 2800 pta. It is open all year except from mid-November to Christmas.

Getting There & Away

There are usually two buses a day from Andorra-la-Vella to El Serrat. Buses leave Llorts at 7.45 am and 2.45 pm; departures from Andorra-la-Vella are at 1 and 8.30 pm. Ordino, which is five km down the valley, is served by fairly frequent buses.

ORDINO

Ordino (population 743; 1298 metres) is much larger than Llorts but, despite recent development, has also kept its Andorran character.

Information

The tourist office kiosk (*ofici de turisme*; ☎ 36963) is on highway CG3. There are a number of banks at the Plaça, which is 50 metres up the hill from the tourist office.

Casa d'Areny de Plandolit

The ancestral home (☎ 36908) of the d'Areny de Plandolit family, built in the 17th century and modified in the mid-19th century, is now a museum. The family's most illustrious member was Don Guillem, síndic and leader of the political reform movement that got the Nova Reforma passed in 1866. The house, which has furnished rooms and is of typically Andorran design, is open from 10 am to 3 pm and 3 to 6 pm Tuesday to Saturday and 10 am to 3 pm on Sunday. It's closed on Monday.

Hiking

There is a trail from Ordino via the village of Segudet northward up the mountainside towards Pic de Casamanya (2740 metres). It does not go all the way to the summit. The round trip takes around four hours.

Places to Stay & Eat

Just off the Plaça, in the alley behind the Crèdit Andorrà bank, is the *Hotel Quim* (☎ 35013), which is run by a friendly older woman. Doubles/triples with shower cost 3000/3500 pta.

There is a food shop with bread, *Commerç Fleca Font* (☎ 35141), at the Plaça near the Banc Internacional. It is open daily, except Sunday afternoon, from 7 am to 2 pm and 4 to 8 pm. Spring water flows from two spouts right outside the door.

Getting There & Away

The bus from Andorra-la-Vella (100 pta), which stops opposite Avinguda Príncep Benlloch 6, runs daily from 7 am (7.30 am on Sunday) to 8.30 pm about every 30 minutes. However, there are no departures from Andorra-la-Vella at 1.30 and 2.30 pm and none from Ordino at 2 pm.

ANDORRA

Parish of La Massana

The Parish of La Massana (population 4400) is north-west of Andorra-la-Vella along the Spanish frontier.

LA MASSANA

The town of La Massana (population 2164) is less attractive than its smaller neighbours further north in the Parish of Ordino but has a number of fairly inexpensive places to stay.

Orientation & Information

The tourist office kiosk (*informació turisme*; ☎ 35693) is at Plaça del Quart, which is along La Massana's main street, the Carretera General (the CG3).

Hiking

From Arinsal, which is about seven km north-west of La Massana and served by three buses a day from Andorra-la-Vella, a trail leads north-westward to a 2260-metre-high lake called **Estany de les Truits**. The walk up takes around 2½ hours. From the lake, there's a trail all the way up to the highest point in Andorra, 2942-metre **Pic de Coma Pedrosa**.

Places to Stay

Camping *Càmping Santa Catarina* (☎ 35065 at the proprietors' home), which is just outside the La Massana town limits along the road to Ordino (the CG3), is open from the end of June to the end of September. The camping ground, situated in a grassy field next to a rushing stream, charges 220 pta per person and 200 pta for a tent or car. The bus stops a bit down the hill from the camping ground opposite the Hotel Xalet Costes de Giberga.

Hotels The *Hotel Naudi* (☎ 35095, 35444), in the centre of town on the Carretera General, has singles/doubles/triples from 2600/2700/4000 pta including breakfast. It is closed during October. The *Hostal Marsà* (☎ 35165) is up the street across from the La Caixa bank. Doubles/triples are 2400/3200 pta. The *Hotel Palanques* (☎ 35007) on the Carretera General near the Banca Mora (a bank) has doubles and triples for 2200 pta per person, including demi-pension.

Places to Eat

The pizzeria/restaurant on the ground floor of the *Hotel Naudi*, which has pizzas for 600 to 700 pta, is open daily from 12.30 to 3 pm and 7.30 to 10.30 pm (or later). It is closed on Wednesdays during November, January, May and June.

Establiments Molnè (☎ 35020), a food shop on the Carretera General two buildings from Banca Mora, is open from 9 am to 1.30 pm and 4 to 8 pm daily, except Sunday afternoon.

Getting There & Away

The bus from Plaça Príncep Benlloch in Andorra-la-Vella runs daily about twice an hour from 7 am (7.30 am on Sunday) to 9.30 pm.

Limousin, Périgord & Quercy

Limousin, Périgord and Quercy are tucked away in south-central and south-western France between the Massif Central and the coastal Aquitaine basin. Though these three regions are contiguous, share similar histories and are firmly steeped in rural life, they are noticeably different.

Périgord and Quercy no longer exist as administrative regions, but they are important historical and cultural regions and are therefore considered more representative of this part of France than the current administrative divisions. (Périgord belongs to the region of Aquitaine, and Quercy to the Midi Pyrénées.) The current region of Limousin has virtually the same boundaries as the former province of Limousin.

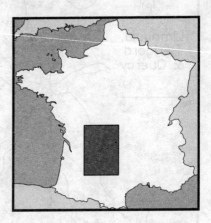

Limousin

The tranquil, green region of Limousin, dotted with old churches and castles, is the northernmost of the three regions covered in this chapter and presents the quintessential image of rural France. It forms the western part of the Massif Central, a mountainous plateau region. The region's economy is based on agriculture, and in particular on cattle and sheep farming. Long overlooked by tourists, it is only in recent years, as off-the-beaten-track holidays have become popular, that Limousin has been considered a worthy destination. With its many rivers, springs and lakes, it is a great destination if you want to go fishing, sailing, canoeing or kayaking.

Limousin is made up of three *départements*. In the west is Haute-Vienne, whose capital, Limoges, is also the capital of the Limousin region. On Limoges's eastern flank spread the rural Creuse and Corrèze départements, with the large towns of Tulle and Brive-la-Gaillarde close to each other in the south, and nearby, the picturesque village of Uzerche.

In the local dialect, *'limousine'* is a heavy cloak worn by shepherds; by extension the word has come to mean a large luxury car.

History

Although Limousin's history is not as well known as that of Périgord, it also goes back to prehistoric times. Traces of Neanderthal people have been found south of Brive-la-Gaillarde in southern Limousin. Limousin took its name from the Gallic tribe of the Lemovices, but the area was taken over by the Romans around 49 BC and in 27 BC became part of the province of Aquitania, later to be known as Aquitaine. In 1152 Aquitaine came under English control after the marriage of Eleanor of Aquitaine to Henry Plantagenet, who was to become Henry II of England two years later. Limousin was won back by the French in the early 1200s, but during the Hundred Years' War, Aquitaine, together with Calais, was surrendered to the English by the Treaty of Calais (1360). The French reconquered Limousin in 1370 and 1374 and, though the

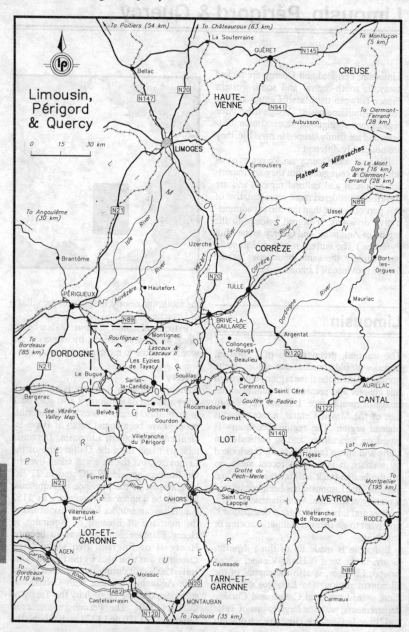

Limousin,
Périgord
& Quercy

0   15   30 km

LIMOUSIN

The Pilgrimages to Santiago de Compostela

While Lourdes may be one of the most visited Christian pilgrimage destinations of the 20th century, in the Middle Ages this role was reserved (after Jerusalem and Rome) for Santiago (Spanish for St James) de Compostela, the historic capital of Galicia in the north-western corner of Spain. Beginning in the 11th century, more than half a million pilgrims would come each year from all over Europe to express devotion, thanks or penance to the apostle St James, who was martyred in Jerusalem in 44 AD and whose tomb was miraculously discovered in the village of Padrón, near present-day Santiago de Compostela, in 813 AD. In the 9th century a basilica was built to house the saint's relics, and the town of Santiago de Compostela soon grew up around it, eventually becoming a focus of faith for Christians in Spain and various other European countries. Santiago de Compostela (Saint Jacques de Compostelle in French) assumed particular importance for the French because of the affinity they felt for the Spaniards in their struggle against the Muslim Moors, who had ruled much of the Iberian Peninsula since the 8th century.

The pilgrims followed four main paths to cross France: one started in Paris and continued to Bordeaux; a second one went through Burgundy (via Vézelay and Limoges); the third went through the region of Auvergne (via Clermont-Ferrand); and the fourth went through the Midi (via Arles). The thousands of pilgrims brought wealth and commerce to every town and village they passed by. Pilgrims would often visit abbeys, famous churches, chapels and shrines containing the relics of saints (some of which became pilgrimage destinations in themselves). Hospices were also established along the paths to house the pilgrims. The four routes merged as they crossed the Pyrenees, forming the Asturian path and the Camino Francés (French Way), both of which led directly to Santiago de Compostela.

Cairns topped with a cross showed that the pilgrims were on the right path. Dressed in wide capes and bearing staffs, the pilgrims wore felt hats on which were sewn badges of the scallop shell, a symbol that came to be known as the badge of St James. The symbol can still be seen in many places along the way. ■

disputes continued, it remained under French control. In 1607 the region was united with the French crown by Henry of Navarre (Henry IV).

In the Middle Ages, Limousin lay on the route of the pilgrimage to Santiago de Compostela (see the Santiago de Compostela aside). Many churches were built along the the pilgrims' routes.

During this century the population of Limousin has plummeted dramatically, as it has in much of France's rural heartland; some 25% of Limousin's inhabitants, many of them young people, have left for the cities. Only 735,800 people now live in Limousin (compared to around one million in the mid-1890s), making it the least densely populated area of France.

LIMOGES

Neither compelling nor uninviting, Limoges (population 160,000) is an amiable city which was founded in Roman times at the point where the Vienne River could be

forded. By the 11th century it had become one of the main stops on the pilgrimage route to Santiago de Compostela in Spain but except for the odd relic, traces of these past eras are hard to find.

For the last few centuries Limoges has been acclaimed for its production of fine porcelain and enamel. And though more prestige is attributed to the former, the latter attracts enthusiasts from around the world, particularly during the Biennial of Contemporary Enamel, which shows new and inventive applications of this ancient art form.

Orientation

Place Jourdan sits smack in the middle of central Limoges, separating three distinct areas. The train station area is to the northeast, crisscrossed by large boulevards. The widest of these, Ave du Général de Gaulle, leads to the station, Gare des Bénédictins, the only remarkable feature of this characterless quarter. To the south-east is the smaller and

LIMOUSIN

older of the two rival town centres, the Cité quarter, built on a hill along the Vienne River and dominated by Cathédrale Saint Étienne. The Château quarter, which acquired its name from a fortress built here in the 12th century, grew around the abbey of St Martial, the site of which is now occupied by Place de la République. This is today's commercial centre, redeemed by a few pedestrianised streets and half-timbered houses.

Information

Tourist Office The tourist office (☎ 55.34. 46.87) on Blvd de Fleurus is open Monday to Saturday from 9 am to noon and 1.30 to 6.30 pm. In July and August it's open from 9 am to 8 pm and on Sunday from 10 am to 2 pm. The staff will make hotel reservations for free.

For information on the Haute-Vienne département, head to the welcoming Maison du Tourisme (☎ 55.79.04.04) on Place Denis Dussoubs. It's open weekdays from 9 am to noon and 1.30 to 5.30 pm. From mid-June to mid-September it is also open on Saturday (from 10 am).

Money The Banque de France (☎ 55.77. 13.72) at 8 Blvd Carnot is open weekdays from 8.45 am to 12.15 pm and 1.30 to 3.30 pm. There are several banks are on Place Jourdan. You can also change money at the tourist office or the train station information office.

Post The main post office (☎ 55.44.44.44) is on Rue de la Préfecture near Place Stalingrad. It is open weekdays from 8 am to 7 pm and Saturday from 8 am to noon.

Limoges's postcode is 87000.

Laundry The small laundrette at 28 Rue Delescluze is open daily throughout the year from 7 am to 9 pm.

La Cité

Cathédrale Saint Étienne Begun in 1273, construction of the cathedral continued until the 19th century. Mainly Gothic in style, it has an elegant, partly Romanesque bell tower and an early 16th-century portal in the Flamboyant Gothic style. The main doors, the Portail Saint Jean, have beautiful carvings depicting the lives of SS Martial and Stephen. Inside, highlights include a highly ornate Italian Renaissance rood screen (a partition separating the chancel from the main part of the church), some interesting tombs and some notable 15th and 16th-century stained-glass windows.

Museums In the former 18th-century bishop's palace, next to Cathédrale Saint Étienne, is the **Musée Municipal du Palais de l'Évêché**, which contains a modest but well-presented display of local Gallo-Roman lapidary, pieces of enamel work from the 12th to the 20th centuries, Egyptian artefacts, and a handful of lesser known paintings by Auguste Renoir, born in Limoges in 1841. The upstairs section is devoted to displays showing what Limoges looked like in Roman days, though all that's left of the Roman city are a few amphitheatre stones in the **Jardin d'Orsay** on Rue Couraud. The museum is open from 10 to 11.45 am and 2 to 4.45 pm (closed Tuesday). From June to 30 September it's open until 5.45 pm and from July to September it's also open on Tuesday; admission is free.

Next to the municipal museum in the Jardin de l'Évêché is the new **Musée de la Résistance**, dedicated to the local Resistance fighters of WW II; it has the same opening hours and is also free.

Le Château

On summer nights the town's historic buildings are lit up, and if you have two spare hours you can wander through the old quarters following the *Parcours de Lumière* (literally, Path of Light) signs. Don't miss the pedestrianised **Rue de la Boucherie**, off Place Saint Aurélien, so named because of the butchers' shops that lined the street in the Middle Ages. In this and nearby streets you will find many half-timbered houses.

One building you won't find in the Château quarter is **St Martial's Abbey**, the pilgrim's resting place, now reduced to an outline on Place de la République. St Martial came to Limoges in the 3rd century and, having converted the town's residents to Christianity, became Limoges's bishop. He died here and in 848 the abbey was founded over his tomb. The crypt containing the saint's tomb is in Place de la République and can be visited from July to September.

Église Saint Pierre du Queyroix Just south-east of Place de la République, this church was rebuilt shortly after being destroyed by fire in 1213, making it the oldest of Limoges's churches. It has an impressive tower dating from the 13th century.

Église Saint Michel des Lions Two granite lions standing on either side of the tower door give this church its name. Perched on the spire of the church's 65-metre-high tower is a huge copper ball. Built between the 14th and 16th centuries, the church contains the relics of St Martial's head as well as a number of beautiful 15th-century stained-glass windows and some 17th and 18th-century statuary. It is just north of Place de la Motte on Rue Adrien Dubouché.

Enamel
Limoges has been an important centre for *émail* (enamel) since the 12th century. To see some examples of this fine art, your best bet is to visit the little street-front ateliers around Rue Raspail, which leads to the Cité. Some of these, such as **Émaux Actuels** (☎ 55.32. 51.97) at 11 Rue des Tanneries, are best described as small galleries. It's tiny and the two artists don't speak English, but as long as you're not with a large group you'll be welcomed to the workroom at the back of the shop. In general it's open daily from 7.30 am to 7 pm. There is also a collection of enamel at the Musée Municipal.

Porcelain
The name Limoges has been synonymous with porcelain since the 1770s, when European artists were trying to copy what the Chinese had already perfected in the 13th century. Three factors distinguish porcelain from other baked-clay pottery: it is very white, hard and translucent. Made from kaolin (a fine white clay) and feldspar (a hard rock-forming mineral), hard-paste porcelain became popular in Limoges after an exceptionally pure form of kaolin was found in the nearby village of Saint Yrieix. Porcelain is fired twice: once at about 1450°C prior to being painted, and then again at a much lower temperature after enamel (also called overglaze) has been applied.

For lovers of this art, the place to head to is the **Musée National Adrien Dubouché** (☎ 55.77.45.58) at 8bis Place Winston Churchill. One of France's two most prestigious ceramic collections (the other is in Sèvres, south-east of Paris), it has 12,000 pieces,

---

The Art of Enamel
The basic enamel-making process involves fixing powdered lead glass coloured with metallic oxides to a base made of gold, silver, bronze, copper or some other metal. It acquires its translucent quality by being fired several times at about 800°C. Deposits of rare metallic oxides near Limoges enable the town's enamel-makers to create the rich, deep colours for which the town's enamelware is renowned.

The best time to see this enamel in Limoges is during the Biénnale d'Émail Contemporain, an innovative international exhibition held every two years from July to December. The next one is to be held in 1994. Each Biénnale consists of two sections: the main one, made up of works from 40 artists selected by an international panel, is displayed in the old Chapelle du Lycée Gay Lussac on Rue du Collège; the other part is dedicated to enamel from a particular period (eg Art Deco). ■

including local works and pieces from countries such as China and Iran. It is open from 10 am to noon and 1.30 to 5.15 pm (closed Tuesday); it is also open on public holidays except for 1 May. Entry is 17FF for adults, 9FF for students and those between 18 and 25 years, and free for those under 18.

The only place you can watch porcelain being made is at **Le Pavillon de la Porcelaine** (☎ 55.30.21.86), located about three km from the centre on the RN20 to Toulouse. Geared for mass tourism, it's mainly a salesroom for factory-priced pieces. In summer, however, there are also hourly demonstrations. It's open Monday to Saturday from 8.30 am to 7 pm. Between Easter and 31 October it is also open on Sunday. Admission is free. If you don't have a car, take bus No 15 from the Hôtel de Ville, which stops at the door.

A Limoges Ewer

Other Attractions

Every second Sunday of the month, an antique market bustles around Place Saint Étienne. From the end of September to the first week of October the **Festival International des Francophonies** showcases art and music from Quebec and French-speaking countries in Africa.

Places to Stay – bottom end

The majority of Limoges's hotels have two, one or no stars, so there's no need to worry about blowing your budget.

Camping The closest camping ground is the three-star *Vallée de l'Aurence* (☎ 55.38. 49.43) on Ave d'Uzurat, which is on the edge of the Bastide forest about 3.5 km north of the train station. Open all year, it charges 12FF per person and 5FF per tent or car. To get there take bus No 20 from Place Jourdan to the Louis Armand stop and then walk beside the lake for about 500 metres.

Hostel Serving as a youth hostel, the *Foyer des Jeunes Travailleuses* (☎ 55.77.63.97) at 20 Rue d'Encombe Vineuse is a dismal place with not a scrap of atmosphere. It's open all year. There's someone at reception until late. It has single rooms only and charges 60FF a night and 15FF for breakfast.

Hotels Plenty of cheap hotels are located around the train station, including two quiet options in Rue du Général du Bessol. The *Hôtel Familia* (☎ 55.77.51.40) at No 18 is calm and friendly, with two sections separated by a courtyard. Basic singles/doubles at the back start at 80/85FF; the more pleasant front rooms with shower start at 105/120FF. Next door, the *Hôtel Mon Logis* (☎ 55.77. 41.43) at No 16 has a similar ambience. Rooms, all including shower, start at 120FF.

Overlooking the Champ de Juillet gardens is the welcoming *Hôtel de France* (☎ 55.77.78.92) at 23 Cours Bugeaud, with pastel-toned rooms from 85/100FF or 160FF for doubles with shower.

In the Château district, try the *Hôtel des Beaux-Arts* (☎ 55.79.42.20; fax 55.79.

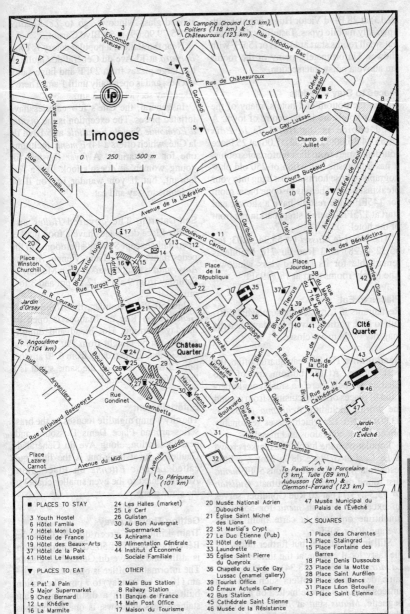

Limoges

0   250   500 m

To Camping Ground (3.5 km),
Poitiers (118 km) &
Châteauroux (123 km)

Château Quarter

Cité Quarter

Jardin
d'Orsay

To Angoulême
(104 km)

Jardin
de
l'Évêché

Place
Winston
Churchill

Place
Lazare
Carnot

To Périgueux
(101 km)

To Pavillon de la Porcelaine
(3 km), Tulle (89 km),
Aubusson (86 km) &
Clermont-Ferrand (123 km)

Champ de
Juillet

Place
Jourdan

■ PLACES TO STAY
3 Youth Hostel
6 Hôtel Familia
7 Hôtel Mon Logis
10 Hôtel de France
19 Hôtel des Beaux-Arts
37 Hôtel de la Paix
41 Hôtel Le Musset

▼ PLACES TO EAT
4 Pat' à Pain
5 Major Supermarket
9 Chez Bernard
12 Le Khédive
16 La Marmite

24 Les Halles (market)
25 Le Cerf
26 Gulistan
30 Au Bon Auvergnat
   Supermarket
34 Achirama
38 Alimentation Générale
44 Institut d'Économie
   Sociale Familiale

OTHER
2 Main Bus Station
8 Railway Station
11 Banque de France
14 Main Post Office
17 Maison du Tourisme

20 Musée National Adrien
   Dubouché
21 Église Saint Michel
   des Lions
22 St Martial's Crypt
27 Le Duc Étienne (Pub)
33 Laundrette
35 Église Saint Pierre
   du Queyroix
36 Chapelle du Lycée Gay
   Lussac (enamel gallery)
39 Tourist Office
40 Émaux Actuels Gallery
42 Bus Station
45 Cathédrale Saint Étienne
46 Musée de la Résistance

47 Musée Municipal du
   Palais de l'Évêché

✕ SQUARES
1 Place des Charentes
13 Place Stalingrad
15 Place Fontaine des
   Barres
18 Place Denis Dussoubs
23 Place de la Motte
28 Place Saint Aurélien
29 Place des Bancs
31 Place Léon Betoulle
43 Place Saint Étienne

LIMOUSIN

29.13) at 28 Blvd Victor Hugo, popular with upwardly mobile types. Tastefully decorated but small rooms start at 110FF, or155FF with shower. Unfortunately, many of the rooms are above a noisy intersection.

Places to Stay – middle
Unlike the bottom-end hotels, many of the two-star hotels are in the centre of town. A good choice is the *Hôtel de la Paix* (☎ 55.34.36.00; fax 55.32.37.06) at 25 Place Jourdan. Apart from the comfortable rooms, it has a fantastic collection of 250 old phonographs whose horns almost hang into your breakfast plate. There is just one basic room for 145FF – the rest all have a shower and start at 175FF. There's street parking in front of the hotel.

The *Hôtel le Musset* (☎ 55.34.34.03; fax 55.32.45.28) at 3 Rue du 71e Mobile is remarkable for its stained-glass windows. The lovely rooms start at 180/195FF.

Places to Eat
Restaurants in Limoges are somewhat difficult to find, particularly on Sunday when the majority of them are closed.

Restaurants The Château quarter offers the best choice. At the bottom end of Rue Charles Michels there's a small conglomeration of places offering cuisines from around the world, including *Achirama* (☎ 55.34.33.00) at No 12, which serves reasonably priced Indian vindaloos and masalas.

Popular with the lunchtime market crowd is *Le Cerf* at 5 Place de la Motte, a little restaurant with an unpretentious 50FF *menu*. Just round the corner, the intimate *Gulistan* (☎ 55.34.73.71) at 20 Rue Gondinet, serves an excellent Kurdish *menu* for 55FF (at lunchtime only). À la carte main dishes average 40 or 50FF.

Still in this quarter but further north, try the tasty local cuisine at the timber-framed *La Marmite* (☎ 55.33.38.34) at 1 Place Fontaine des Barres. It offers such delicious entrées as goat's cheese melted on a toasted baguette. *Menus* start at 78FF. For a good choice of salads, served behind stunning

stained-glass windows, go to *Le Khédive* (☎ 55.79.96.69) at 39 Blvd Carnot.

Near the station, a popular eatery is *Chez Bernard* at 13 Ave du Général de Gaulle. It has large pizzas from 29FF and huge sandwiches, and is open daily until 1 am. There's takeaway service until 3 am.

In general, the Cité's few eateries have inflated prices. The exception is the *Institut d'Économie Sociale Familiale* at 5 Blvd de la Cité, which offers a 44FF *menu*, including one for vegetarians. A *foyer* (hostel) for young women, it doesn't look like a restaurant, but if you wander in you'll be welcome to stay and eat.

Self-Catering The covered *Halles* and nearby Place des Bancs have a food market open daily except Sunday afternoon. On the pedestrianised Rue Haute Vienne, *Au Bon Auvergnat* is a supermarket open Monday to Saturday from 9 am to 12.15 pm and 3 to 7 pm.

Just off Place Jourdan, the *Alimentation Générale* on Rue du Maupas is open on Sunday morning. Hot bread and doughy snacks can be bought from *Pat' à Pain* on Ave Garibaldi, open daily from 6.30 am to 9 pm. Closer to town on the same street is a large *Major supermarket*.

Entertainment
The city's limp nightlife focuses on the brasseries around Place Denis Dussoubs and, near the station, along Ave du Général de Gaulle. A local hang-out is the little pub called *Le Duc Étienne* on Place Saint Aurélien, next to the even smaller chapel of the same name.

Getting There & Away
Train Limoges's green-domed Gare des Bénédictins (☎ 55.01.50.50 for information) is at the end of Ave du Général de Gaulle. The information office is open daily from 9 am (10 am on Sunday) to 7 pm. The station, built in 1929 with a distinct tower and stained-glass windows, is one of the most striking in France. It's open 24 hours a day.

There are major connections to Paris's Gare d'Austerlitz (220FF; 3¾ hours; nine a day), Bordeaux (143FF; 3½ hours; eight a day), Clermont-Ferrand (164FF; five hours; two a day), Périgueux (69FF; 1¼ hours; 12 a day) and Toulouse (184FF; 3½ hours; eight a day).

Bus There are two bus stations – a semi-deserted *place* on Rue Charles Gide and the main one on Place des Charentes near the youth hostel. Regional transport is organised by the Régie Départementale des Transports (☎ 55.77.39.04), which has an office at Place des Charentes. It is open on weekdays from 7.30 to 11.30 am and 1.30 to 5 pm.

Car Near the train station, the car rental company Citer (☎ 55.79.40.05) has an office at 27 Ave du Général de Gaulle.

Getting Around
TCL buses serve the city and suburbs but as there isn't a central station, buses leave from various points around town, including Place Jourdan, the Hôtel de Ville and Gare des Bénédictins. The tourist office sells local bus route maps for 5FF. Single tickets cost 6FF.

AUBUSSON & USSEL
On the main road to the Massif Central, 86 km east of Limoges, is Aubusson (population 5100), where the traditional crafts of tapestry and woodwork (the latter using the region's abundant chestnut trees) are still practised. The town has been acclaimed for its tapestries and carpets since the 16th century, and Beauvais and Gobelins tapestries are still made here on hand looms.

Don't miss the **Musée Départemental de la Tapisserie** in the Centre Culturel Jean Lurçat, offering comprehensive information about the art of tapestry making (closed Tuesday mornings). It is also possible to visit the **École Nationale d'Art Décoratif** (National School of Decorative Art), open from July to September. If you tire of tapestries, wander up to the remains of the **chateau** of the counts of Aubusson. The syndicat d'initiative (☎ 55.66.32.12) is in

Rue Vieille. The hilltop town of Ussel, south-east of Limoges, is also on one of the main roads to the Massif Central. It is worth visiting for its turreted houses from the 15th and 16th centuries. Of particular note is the **Hôtel de Ventadour**, built in the late 15th century. The tourist office (☎ 55.72.11.50) is at Place Voltaire.

PLATEAU DE MILLEVACHES
Aubusson and Ussel are separated by the Plateau de Millevaches in eastern Limousin. Its name, of Celtic origin, refers to the many springs in the area (and not to a thousand cows!). This rocky region, which reaches 978 metres at its highest point, is sparsely populated, has a harsh climate and is at its best in autumn, when everything is covered in purple heather. The countryside is speckled with patches of reddish brown, the colour of Limousin cattle, whose highly valued beef naturally dominates the local gastronomy. From this plateau, the Vézère River starts its course south-westward eventually running through the famous prehistoric Vézère Valley in Périgord.

BRIVE-LA-GAILLARDE
Located on the left bank of the Corrèze River close to its confluence with the Vézère River, Brive-la-Gaillarde (population 50,000) is 93 km south of Limoges in the Corrèze département. Having fought off various assailants over the centuries, Brive earned the name 'la gaillarde' (the bold one).

The town is centred around **Église Saint Martin**, at Place Charles de Gaulle, which has retained very few of its original Romanesque features. Opposite the church is the Hôtel de Ville.

The most outstanding of Brive's beautiful old houses is the **Hôtel de Labenche** (built in 1450) on Blvd Jules Ferry. Nearby, the **Musée Ernest Rupin** displays a motley collection of exhibits in a fine house in Louis XIII style. The **Musée Édmond Michelet**, 4 Rue Champanatier, focuses on the French Resistance of WW II.

The tourist office (☎ 55.24.08.80) is at Place 14 Juillet. Brive's postcode is 19100.

LIMOUSIN

Brive is a convenient base for exploring much of Limousin, Périgord and Quercy. The town has good transport connections as it is at the crossing of the Paris-Toulouse and Bordeaux-Geneva road and rail routes.

AROUND BRIVE

If you do base yourself in Brive, there are several nearby villages which are worth visiting. Set on a promontory on the Vézère River, **Uzerche** (34 km north of Brive) is one of the most picturesque towns in Limousin. Among its many attractions, which include turreted houses, is the Romanesque Église Saint Pierre. Fortified in the 14th century, it has a notable bell tower and an 11th-century crypt. One of the entrances to the town is Porte Bécharie, a 14th-century town gate which was once part of the old town walls.

The tourist office (☎ 55.73.15.71), open from April to October only, is at Place Lunade.

Another appealing village is **Collonges-la-Rouge**, 21 km south-east of Brive, whose main claim to fame lies in its red-sandstone houses. It still has its 15th-century town gates and many fine old mansions. **Beaulieu-sur-Dordogne**, 44 km south-east of Brive, features the Romanesque Église Saints Pierre et Paul, formerly a Benedictine abbey and one of the major stopping places for pilgrims en route to Santiago de Compostela. Wander through the town to see Beaulieu's picturesque old houses, built in the 14th and 15th centuries.

Périgord

Although the name Périgord dates back to pre-Roman times, the region is better known in English-speaking countries as the 'Dordogne', the name of the département that covers most of the area and of one of Périgord's seven rivers.

Périgord was one of the cradles of human civilisation. A number of local caves, such as the world-famous Lascaux, are adorned with extraordinary prehistoric paintings, and there have been major finds here of the remains of Neanderthal and Cro-Magnon people.

However, prehistoric sites are not the only reason to visit Périgord. To make other attractions more widely known to visitors, the local tourism authority has created four colour-coded regions. Périgord Vert (green) takes in the fields and forests to the north; Périgord Blanc (white) is the central area surrounding the capital, Périgueux; Périgord Pourpre (purple) lies to the south around the vineyards of Bergerac; and Périgord Noir (black) takes in the Dordogne River valley, with its many chateaux and characteristic dark oak and pine forests, and the Vézère Valley. Between these two valleys is the attractive medieval town of Sarlat-la-Canéda. This area attracts a great many tourists, particularly from the UK and the Netherlands.

History

Périgord's history begins in Palaeolithic times (see the following Vézère Valley section). A Gallic tribe known as the Petrocorii settled here, making Périgueux their capital, but were succeeded by the Romans. During the reign of Emperor Augustus (ruled 27 BC to 14 AD), both Périgord and Quercy belonged to the province of Aquitania, which took in western France south of the Loire River. Périgueux, named Vesuna by the Romans, served as one of the provincial capitals.

As part of Aquitaine, Périgord also came under English rule and was subsequently fiercely disputed by the French and English. It became part of France in 1398 and, together with Limousin, was formally integrated into the royal domain in 1607.

Périgord's architecture, mostly made up of chateaux and defensive *bastides* (fortified towns built in the 14th and 15th centuries), testifies to the bloody battles waged here during the Middle Ages and the Hundred Years' War.

Food

Périgord is reputed to be one of France's

gourmet capitals and is especially renowned for the fresh, locally grown products that form the essence of its cuisine. Specialities include such expensive delicacies as *truffes* (truffles), edible subterranean fungi of varying colours, sizes and shapes that grow on the roots of certain oak and hazelnut trees. The truffles of Périgord, which are black and rough in texture, are the most valued in French cuisine because of their distinctive aroma. They are at their best when eaten fresh as they only keep for a week and lose some of their savour when preserved. These highly prized black truffles, traditionally hunted out by specially trained pigs between November and March, are usually added to other dishes and sauces but are also delicious in omelettes.

The love-it or hate-it *pâté de foie gras* is made from the bursting liver of force-fed geese, and is sometimes flavoured with cognac and truffles. *Confit de canard* or *confit d'oie* are duck or goose joints cooked very slowly in their own fat. The preserved duck or goose is left to stand for three months before being eaten and keeps for many months. Other choice delicacies include *cou d'oie farci* (goose's neck stuffed with pork and veal mince) and *faisan au Verjus* (pheasant cooked in verjuice, the juice of unripe grapes).

Wine is produced mainly around Bergerac in Périgord's south, with equal harvests of red and white wines, both dry and sweet. The best known red wine is called the Côtes de Bergerac. An excellent sweet vintage is Monbazillac, usually drunk with dessert.

PÉRIGUEUX

Built over 2000 years ago around a curve in the gentle Isle River, Périgueux (population 35,300), capital of Périgord and prefecture of the Dordogne département, rests these days on two laurels: its proximity to the Vézère Valley's prehistoric sites and its status as the capital of one of France's true gourmet regions. Neither is really reason enough to make a big detour to get here, especially if you're without a car, as the valley is still quite a long way off (though

there are guided tours) and local specialities are an acquired taste and quite expensive. On the other hand, Périgueux boasts one of the country's best prehistoric museums and is full of life during the week-long Mime Festival at the beginning of August.

Orientation

The town is divided into three sections. The main one is the medieval and Renaissance old town (known as Puy Saint Front), which was built on a hill and whose mainly pedestrianised streets sweep down from Blvd Michel Montaigne to the Isle River. South-west of the old town is the even older, but less clearly defined, Gallo-Roman quarter (the Cité), whose centre is the ruined amphitheatre. About one km north-west of the old town is the train station area, rich in cheap hotels.

Information

Tourist Office The main tourist office (☎ 53.53.10.63) is at 26 Place Francheville next to the 15th-century Tour Mataguerre. The office is open Monday to Saturday from 9 am to noon and 2 to 6 pm. From 15 June to 15 September it's open daily from 9 am to 7 pm (to 5 pm Sunday). In summer there are three additional information kiosks (with varying hours) around town – one in front of Cathédrale Saint Front, another on Place André Maurois and a third at the northern end of Blvd Montaigne.

For regional information, the Maison du Tourisme (☎ 53.53.44.35) at 16 Rue du Président Wilson is open weekdays from 9.30 am to noon and 2 to 4.30 pm.

Money The Banque de France (☎ 53.03.30.30) is on Place Franklin Roosevelt and is open weekdays from 8.45 am to 12.15 pm and 1.35 to 3.35 pm. Other banks are spread out along Blvd Montaigne.

Post The main post office (☎ 53.53.60.82), at Rue du 4 Septembre, is open weekdays from 8 am to 7 pm and Saturday from 8 am to noon.

Périgueux's postcode is 24000.

Laundry Near the train station La Lavandière on Rue Gambetta is open daily from 6 am to 10 pm. It outshines its seedy counterpart on Rue des Mobiles de Coulm, which is open daily from 8 am to 9.30 pm.

Puy Saint Front

The most appealing part of Périgueux is the old town quarter around the cathedral, which has a marked circuit (follow the 'Vieille Ville' signs) tracing such quaint streets as Rue du Plantier. It is now a classified historical area – many of the buildings have been renovated and preserved – and is closed to traffic.

Puy Saint Front was established around the abbey of Saint Front in the 5th century. In 1356, during the Hundred Years' War, France lost the town to the English but managed to regain it in 1360. Wander along Rue Limogeanne and nearby streets, including Rue Éguillerie and Rue de la Miséricorde, to see some of the town's impressive Renaissance houses. Walk down to the Pont des Barris for the best view of the town; there are also many interesting old houses along the riverbank; in Renaissance times they belonged to the town's merchants.

Musée du Périgord

France's second most important prehistoric museum after that at Les Eyzies (see that section), the Musée du Périgord (☎ 53.53.16.42) on Cours Tourny has prehistoric tools and implements from some of the world's earliest human inhabitants as well as a large Gallo-Roman collection. It is open daily, except Tuesday, from 10 am to noon and 2 to 5 pm (6 pm in summer); admission for adults/students is 10/5FF, free for those under 18.

Cathédrale Saint Front

When seen against the evening sky, this five-domed cathedral next to Place de la Clautre looks like something you would find in old Constantinople. Originally Romanesque, it was almost totally rebuilt in a pseudo-Oriental style in the mid-19th century. One of the great stopping places for pilgrims en route to

Santiago de Compostela, who came to worship the relics of Saint Front, the cathedral is most impressive from the outside. The interior is devoid of distinctive characteristics, and the attached cloister, originally in the Romanesque style, is a now a strange mixture of styles.

Église Saint Étienne de la Cité

This 12th-century church on Place de la Cité served as Périgueux's cathedral until it was supplanted by Cathédrale Saint Front in 1669. Only two cupolas and two bays remain of the original structure because the church was much damaged by Huguenots in 1577 during the Wars of Religion (1562-98).

Amphitheatre & Tour de Vésone

Built in the 3rd century AD, only a few arches remain of this Roman amphitheatre, as the rest was dissasembled and carried off to construct other buildings. Once able to hold 20,000 spectators, these days all that is left apart from a few broken, detached arches is a fountain in the grassy centre, now a free swimming pool well patronised by locals under the age of five.

The round tower of Vésone is the only trace of a Gallo-Roman temple thought to have been dedicated to the goddess Vesuna, the protector of the town. It is in a garden south of the amphitheatre at the end of Rue Romaine, on the other side of the railway tracks.

Tour Mataguerre

Reconstructed in the 15th century, this tower on Place Francheville once formed part of the ramparts of Puy Saint Front along with numerous other towers, which have now disappeared.

Organised Tours

Taxi Delmotte (☎ 53.53.70.47) offers regional circuits, including trips to Lascaux II (see Prehistoric Sites under the Vézère Valley) and the Dordogne and Vézère valleys. Destinations vary according to the day of the week – the Tuesday and Thursday trips (from 140FF) are to Les Eyzies and

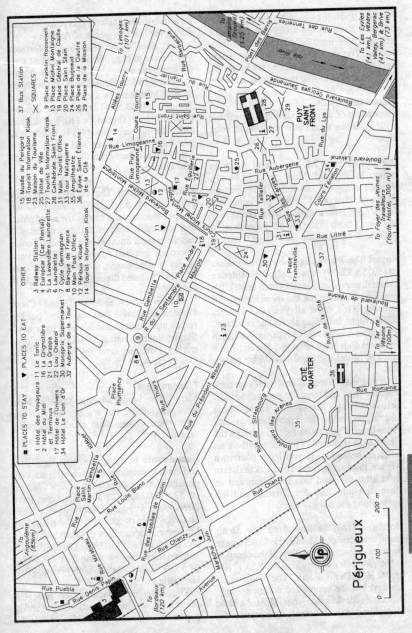

Périgueux

PÉRIGORD

PLACES TO STAY
1 Hôtel des Voyageurs
2 Hôtel du Midi
et Terminus
17 Hôtel de l'Univers
34 Hôtel Le Lion d'Or

▼ PLACES TO EAT
11 Le Tonic
16 La Grignotière
21 La Grappa
22 Lou Chabrol
30 Monoprix Supermarket
32 Auberge de la Tour

OTHER
3 Railway Station
4 Europcar (Car Rental)
5 La Lavandière Laundrette
6 Laundrette
7 Cycle Camagnan
8 Banque de France
10 Main Post Office
12 Péribus Kiosk
14 Tourist Information Kiosk

15 Musée du Périgord
18 Tourist Information Kiosk
23 Maison du Tourisme
25 Hôtel de Ville
26 Tourist Information Kiosk
28 Cathédrale Saint Front
31 Main Tourist Office
33 Tour Mataguerre
35 Amphitheatre
36 Église Saint Étienne
de la Cité

37 Bus Station
✕ SQUARES
9 Place Franklin Roosevelt
13 Place Michel Montaigne
19 Place Général de Gaulle
20 Place Saint Silain
24 Place Bugeaud
27 Place de la Cloutre
29 Place de la Mission

Lascaux II, while those on Monday, Wednesday and Saturday go along the Dordogne Valley. There must be a minimum of three people. The guy who runs the tour speaks only a little English. Bookings are by phone; it's a good idea to ring two days in advance.

Places to Stay

The choice of accommodation is ample but with the summer crowds you should book ahead.

Camping About 2.5 km east of the train station is *Barnabé Plage* (☎ 53.53.41.45), situated along the Isle River. It is open all year and charges 12.50FF per adult and 11.50/7.50FF for a tent/car. To get there take bus No D from Place Michel Montaigne to the Rue des Bains stop (last bus at 6 pm).

Hostel The *Foyer des Jeunes Travailleurs* (☎ 53.53.52.05), also called Résidence Lakanal, serves as a small youth hostel. It's a welcoming place but has room for only 16 travellers. It's open all year and charges 60FF a night, including sheets and breakfast. Reception is open weekdays from 4 to 8 pm and weekends from noon to 1 pm and 7 to 8 pm. The hostel also has a good-value restaurant.

Its address is Blvd Lakanal but it's set back from the road and there are no signs to indicate the way. Bus No G from Place Montaigne goes to the nearby Lakanal stop. From here, if you're on foot go through the Club Lakanal grounds – the hostel is the long building behind it. If you have your own wheels, head south down Blvd Lakanal, turn right after the pool into Blvd Bertrand de Born, left into Rue des Thermes and left again along the railway track.

Hotels – Train Station Area Rue Denis Papin and Rue des Mobiles de Coulm have heaps of one-star places. One of the cheapest is the *Hôtel des Voyageurs* (☎ 53.53.17.44) at 26 Rue Denis Papin. The linoleum is cracked but the rooms are decent enough, especially for the price – 68/75FF for a basic single/double (hall showers are free) or 93FF

for a double with shower. This place is closed during the last two weeks of August.

Next door at the *Hôtel de la Terrasse* you'll have to beg, borrow and almost steal the key to see a room before taking it. Across the road at 18 Rue Denis Papin, on the corner of Rue Mirabeau, is the *Hôtel du Midi et Terminus* (☎ 53.53.41.06), a huge, amiable place with basic singles for 110FF or doubles (all with shower) from 140FF. Quads with two beds plus shower and toilet go for 170FF. It's closed from late September to mid-October.

Hotels – Centre The two-star *Hôtel de l'Univers* (☎ 53.53.34.79) at 18 Cours Michel Montaigne is one of the most pleasant, affordable options in the city centre. It has three small attic doubles without shower (there's a free hall shower) for 130FF and plenty of other rooms, all with shower, from 150FF. It's closed during the last fortnight in January.

Le Lion d'Or (☎ 53.53.49.03) at 17 Cours Fénelon also has a two-star rating but the rooms are ordinary and it's on a busy road. Singles/doubles start at 85/140FF. It's closed during February and on Monday from October to April.

Places to Eat

Many places loudly advertise that they have local specialities, but it's best to scan the menu first to see what exactly is being served.

Restaurants In the centre, Rue Éguillerie and the side streets that branch off it are very popular. A few places, such as *Lou Chabrol* (☎ 53.53.10.84) at 22 Rue Éguillerie, have three-course *formule rapide menus* for 50FF. *La Grignotière* (☎ 53.53.86.91) at 6 Rue Puy Limogeanne specialises in salads and offers a vegetarian *menu* for 75FF. Cheaper salads and snacks can be found at *Le Tonic* (☎ 53.09.51.94), a health club/gym at 4 Rue Gambetta.

The *Hôtel de l'Univers* (see Hotels – centre) has a vine-covered terrace and a popular lunch *menu* from 75FF, while *La*

Grappa (☎ 53.09.74.88) on Place Saint Silain is a popular pizzeria with outdoor tables in a pleasant, shady area.

Along Rue des Farges is *Auberge de la Tour* (☎ 53.54.38.11), which dishes up a reasonable *menu* for 50FF (lunchtime only). The four-course dinner *menu* costs 80FF. A few hotels at the train station have standard *menus* for about 65FF – the *Hôtel du Midi et Terminus* (see Hotels – Train Station Area) is a favourite with the locals.

Self-Catering A *food market* is held in Place de la Clautre on Wednesday until about 1 pm. The *Monoprix* on Place Bugeaud has a large grocery section upstairs. It's open Monday to Saturday from 8.30 am to 7.30 pm.

Getting There & Away

Train Périgueux's train station is on Rue Denis Papin, about one km north-west of the main tourist office. It is connected to Place Montaigne by bus No A. The information office (☎ 53.09.50.50) is open daily from 9 am to 7 pm (from 10.30 am on Sunday), and the terminal is open from 4.30 am to midnight.

There are major connections from here to Bordeaux (87FF; 1¼ hours; 13 a day) and Limoges (69FF; one hour; 11 a day). There are several ways to get to Toulouse, but the cheapest, which costs 168FF and takes four hours, is via Agen.

Services on short-distance routes are infrequent. To Bergerac (66FF; 1½ hours) there's just one direct train at midday. To Brive-la-Gaillarde (55FF; 1¼ hours) there are five a day, and to Sarlat (66FF; 1½ hours) trains leave at 7 am and 7 pm. To Les Eyzies (37FF; 40 minutes), on the Agen line, there are four trains a day.

Bus The bus station is on Place Francheville between Blvd de Vésone and Rue Littré. There's no information office, though on weekdays you might find someone in the baggage office (☎ 53.08.91.06) between 9 and 10 am, 11.30 and noon, 2 and 3 pm and 4.30 to 6 pm. Services to most local destinations are as infrequent as the trains, if not

more so. CFTA runs three buses a day to Bergerac (38FF) and Sarlat (39FF). There's an evening bus to Hautefort and a weekly bus to Brantôme. For Montignac there is a bus on weekdays at 6.15 pm (31FF; one hour).

Car Europcar (☎ 53.08.15.72) is near the train station at 7 Rue Denis Papin.

Getting Around

Bus Péribus has buses and minibuses running to and from the main hub at Place Montaigne. For information, go to the Péribus kiosk (☎ 53.53.30.37), where you can buy single tickets for 6FF and 10-ticket carnets for 35FF.

Bicycle Cycles Germagnan (☎ 53.53.41.91) at 96 Ave Maréchal Juin hires bicycles for 55FF a day or 330FF a week. A deposit of 500FF is required.

AROUND PÉRIGUEUX

Bergerac

A Protestant stronghold in the 16th century, Bergerac (pop 27,000; 47 km south-west of Périgueux) is now an important agricultural market for all of south-west Périgord. Much of the town was reconstructed to repair damage sustained during the Wars of Religion.

Worth visiting are the old town and the old harbour quarter, which have retained some of the town's old-time character. Situated close to the Monbazillac vineyards, Bergerac has long been known for its wine-production and its role in the wine trade. Also an important tobacco-growing centre, Bergerac has an interesting **Musée du Tabac** (Tobacco Museum), housed in the 17th-century Maison Peyrarède on Rue de l'Ancien Port.

The tourist office (☎ 53.57.03.11), at 97 Rue Neuve d'Argenson near the old town, is open daily, except Sunday and on Monday morning.

Domme

Set on a steep promontory on the Dordogne River, the village of Domme (pop 1000) is one of the few bastides to have retained most

PÉRIGORD

of its 13th-century ramparts, including the Porte des Tours and Porte Dalbos. Underneath the village is a stalactite-filled cave. The entrance to the cave is opposite the syndicat d'initiative (☎ 53.28.37.09), which is on Place de la Halle.

There are spectacular views from the Promenade des Falaises. Domme is best seen on a day trip from Sarlat-la-Canéda (12 km to the north); however, if you have your own transport, it is also possible to do so from Périgueux, which is 75 km north-west.

SARLAT-LA-CANÉDA

Usually known simply as Sarlat, this beautiful, well-restored Renaissance town (population 10,000), capital of Périgord Noir, lies north of the Dordogne River between Les Eyzies and Souillac. The town grew up around a Benedictine abbey founded in the 9th century. By the Middle Ages it had become prosperous and owned 85 churches and a great deal of the surrounding land.

Caught between French and English territory, Sarlat was severely damaged during the Hundred Years' War and, later, during the Wars of Religion. Despite this, Sarlat managed to retain its medieval air, and the town's sandstone buildings, mostly dating from the 16th and 17th centuries, were spared modernisation thanks to decisions taken by André Malraux, de Gaulle's Minister of Culture from 1958-68. The Loi Malraux, passed in 1962, bestowed considerable government funding on the town to enable it to maintain its historic, ochre-coloured buildings. It's no secret, however, that Sarlat is an architectural treasure, and in high summer the town is overrun with tourists.

Orientation

Modern-day Sarlat stretches for 2.5 km from the hospital in the north to the train station in the south. Encircled by boulevards, the heart-shaped old town is the centre of town life. It is cut in half by the ruler-straight Rue de la République (known as La Traverse), carved out during the last century to distance the western quarter from the more refined east. The restored eastern half of the town

attracts most of the visitors. The western half, which has not been restored, tends to be much less popular but is still worth exploring.

At the centre of town is Place de la Liberté, featuring the town hall and lots of old houses now occupied by exclusive shops. Rue de la Liberté leads south to Place de Peyrou and the cathedral. The one-way Rue de Cahors runs south from the old town to the roundabout at Place du Maréchal de Lattre de Tassigny (commonly called 'Le Pontet'), which is in front of the viaduct near the train station. From the station, Ave Aristide Briand – which becomes Ave Thiers – runs north to the old town.

Information

Tourist Office The main tourist office (☎ 53.59.27.67) is in the beautiful Hôtel de Maleville, made up of three Gothic houses, on Place de la Liberté. It's open Monday to Saturday from 9 am to noon and 2 to 6 pm. From June to September it's also open on Sunday from 10 am to noon and 3 to 6 pm.

During July and August there's an annexe (☎ 53.59.18.87) north of the old town on Ave du Général de Gaulle. It is open Monday to Saturday from 9 am to noon and 2 to 6 pm. Both offices make free accommodation bookings.

Post The main post office (☎ 53.59.12.81) is on Place du 14 Juillet just south of the old town.

Sarlat's postcode is 24200.

Old Town

The tourist office has a brochure with information on the enticing streets around **Place du Marché aux Oies**, in particular **Rue des Consuls**. Near Place André Malraux is the notable façade of the Renaissance **Maison de la Boétie**, birthplace of the writer Étienne de la Boétie (1530-63), a close friend of the writer Montaigne.

Cathédrale Saint Sacerdos

Originally part of a Benedictine abbey built in the mid-9th century, the cathedral is a

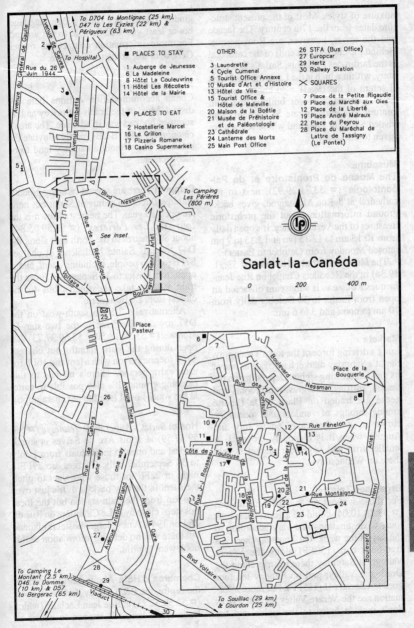

PLACES TO STAY

1 Auberge de Jeunesse
6 La Madeleine
8 Hôtel La Couleuvrine
11 Hôtel Les Récollets
14 Hôtel de la Mairie

PLACES TO EAT

2 Hostellerie Marcel
16 Le Grillon
17 Pizzeria Romane
18 Casino Supermarket

OTHER

3 Laundrette
4 Cycle Cumenal
5 Tourist Office Annexe
10 Musée d'Art et d'Histoire
13 Hôtel de Ville
15 Tourist Office &
   Hôtel de Maleville
20 Maison de la Boétie
21 Musée de Préhistoire
   et de Paléontologie
23 Cathédrale
24 Lanterne des Morts
25 Main Post Office

26 STFA (Bus Office)
27 Europcar
29 Hertz
30 Railway Station

SQUARES

7 Place de la Petite Rigaudie
9 Place du Marché aux Oies
12 Place de la Liberté
19 Place André Malraux
22 Place du Peyrou
28 Place du Maréchal de
   Lattre de Tassigny
   (Le Pontet)

Sarlat-la-Canéda

0   200   400 m

To D704 to Montignac (25 km),
D47 to Les Eyzies (22 km) &
Périgueux (63 km)

To Hospital

To Camping
Les Périères
(800 m)

See Inset

Place
Pasteur

To Camping Le
Montant (2.5 km),
D46 to Domme
(10 km) & D57
to Bergerac (65 km)

To Souillac (29 km)
& Gourdon (25 km)

Boulevard Nessman

Rue des Consuls

Rue Fénelon

Rue Montaigne

Rue de la République

Rue J-J Rousseau

Côte de Toulouse

Place de la Bouquerie

Boulevard Voltaire

Boulevard Henri Arlet

Rue de Cahors

Avenue Thiers

Avenue Aristide Briand

Ave de la Gare

Viaduct

one way

one way

Avenue du Général de Gaulle

Avenue de Selves

Rue du 26 Juin 1944

Avenue Gambetta

Blvd Nessman

Rue de la République

Bld Henri Arlet

Boulevard Voltaire

PÉRIGORD

mixture of styles. Most of the present structure dates from the 17th century. The façade and the tower, however, are Romanesque. Behind the chevet (east end) of the cathedral is the Jardin des Pénitents, Sarlat's first cemetery, within which is the Lanterne des Morts (Lantern of the Dead), also known as Tour Saint Bernard, a tower built in the 12th century to commemorate St Bernard, who visited Sarlat in 1147 and whose relics were given to the abbey.

Museums

The **Musée de Préhistoire et de Paléontologie** (☎ 53.31.29.92), next to the cathedral at 3 Rue Montaigne, gives background information about the prehistoric treasures of the Vézère Valley. It's open daily from 10.15 am to 12.15 pm and 2.15 to 7 pm (closed Monday from October to Easter).

The **Musée d'Art et d'Histoire** (☎ 53.31.19.34) in the Récollets Chapel on Rue Jean-Jacques Rousseau is a museum of sacred art open from Easter to 30 October daily from 10 am to noon and 3 to 6 pm.

Markets

Long a driving force of the town's economy, Sarlat's Saturday market has to rate as one of its most interesting sights. Depending on the season, truffles, foie gras, mushrooms and geese are traded on Place de la Liberté among throngs of vendors and spectators. However, it is best avoided in July and August, when it is hideously crowded. A smaller fruit and vegetable market is held there on Wednesday.

Organised Tours

For those without a car, HEP! Excursions (☎ 53.28.10.04) could be a godsend. It runs tours to destinations that vary according to the day of the week. On Thursday there is a five-hour trip (130FF) along the Vézère Valley; on Saturday there's a trip along the Dordogne Valley; and on Sunday the tour goes to Lascaux II (115FF). For more information see the Vézère Valley section. Prices don't include entry to the sights and the

guides' English is basically sign language, but at least you will be able to get around. For more information contact the owner, Gérard, or ask at the tourist office.

Places to Stay

Cheap accommodation options here are dismal. Most of the hotels are pricey and, in summer, booked way in advance. The area's *chambres d'hôte* (B&Bs) partly alleviate the situation, but without a car they tend to be inconvenient.

Camping There are several camping grounds within a three-km radius of Sarlat but none are open all year. The nearest to town is the four-star *Les Périères* (☎ 53.59.05.84), about 800 metres to the north-east along the D47 towards Sainte Nathalène. It charges 87FF for two people, including a tent, and is open from Easter to 30 September. From the train station, take the town's bus to the closest stop, La Bouquerie.

Alternatively, 2.5 km south-west on the D57 towards Bergerac is the two-star *Le Montant* (☎ 53.59.18.50 or 53.59.37.73). It's open during the same months but charges 37FF for one person with a tent and 16FF for each extra person. There's no bus to this camping ground. It's also possible to camp at the youth hostel (see the next paragraph).

Hostel Sarlat's *Auberge de Jeunesse* (☎ 53.59.47.59) at 15bis Ave de Selves is small, modest and open to individuals from 1 July to 30 September only. Charges are 39FF a night or 22FF for those who want to pitch their tent in the tiny backyard. It's just over two km from the train station but the local bus stops close by at Le Cimetière on Rue du 26 Juin 1944. A new, larger hostel is planned but there was no definite information as this book went to print.

Chambres d'Hôte About 1.5 km north of the centre, the B&B run by *Josette Bouynet* (☎ 53.59.32.73) at Rue Jean Leclaire (which leads to the hospital) is open to guests all year. There are five rooms with private shower and toilet for 135FF, plus 15FF for breakfast.

For a great view over the valley, try the chambre d'hôte belonging to *Françoise Forget* (☎ 53.59.06.49) high up on Route des Pechs, which has seven rooms from 80FF for one person and 95 to 130FF for two; breakfast is 22FF extra. To get there, turn right as you exit the train station onto Rue du Stade, the continuation of Ave de la Gare, and then turn left onto Route des Pechs. The tourist office has a complete list of chambres d'hôte.

Hotels The large, chateau-like *La Couleuvrine* (☎ 53.59.27.80; fax 53.31.26.83) at 1 Place de la Bouquerie has beautifully furnished rooms, all with shower and toilet, from 200FF. Some rooms also come with TV, and there's one small basic room for 140FF. The hotel is usually closed during the last three weeks of January and the last fortnight of November. There's parking at the front and the local bus stops at the doorstep.

In a quieter location is the friendly *Hôtel Les Récollets* (☎ 53.59.00.49) at 4 Rue Jean-Jacques Rousseau. The hotel, open all year, has decent rooms from 155FF. The hall shower is free. Near the tourist office is the *Hôtel de la Mairie* (☎ 53.59.05.71), 13 Place de la Liberté, with basic doubles from 160FF; it is closed from mid-November to 20 December.

For three-star comfort, try *La Madeleine* (☎ 53.59.10.41; fax 53.31.03.62) at 1 Place de la Petite Rigaudie, which has singles/doubles from 320/400FF. The spacious rooms have air-conditioning, TV and telephone. The hotel is closed from January to mid-March, and the hotel's restaurant, which offers excellent regional dishes, is closed from mid-November to mid-March.

Another very pleasant hotel is the three-star *Hostellerie de Meysset* (☎ 53.59.08.29; fax 53.28.47.61), three km west of town on the road to Les Eyzies. Set in a lovely park, it has attractive rooms from 375/440FF and a very good restaurant. It is closed from early October to mid-April.

Places to Eat

Budget-conscious travellers were not in mind when Sarlat's restaurateurs created their menus.

Restaurants Three-course *menus* generally start at 75FF. There are two reasonably priced places facing each other on Côte de Toulouse, off Rue de la République. *Pizzeria Romane* (☎ 53.59.23.88) at No 3 has a pleasant ambience and good fare. Pizzas start at 32FF and there's a Périgord *menu* for 79FF, including confit de canard. Across the street at No 2, *Le Grillon* (☎ 53.28.35.52) has several *menus* from 55FF.

More up-market is *Hostellerie Marcel* (☎ 53.59.21.98) at 8 Avenue de Selves, which specialises in the cuisine of the region. *Menus* range from 80 to 220FF. The restaurant is closed from mid-November to mid-February and on Monday. During July and August it is open daily.

Self-Catering Quite a few shops sell such delicacies as foie gras (200-gram tins cost 75FF). Better value is the *Casino supermarket* on Rue de la République, open Tuesday to Saturday from 8 am to 12.30 pm and 2.30 to 7.30 pm and Sunday from 8 am to noon. In July and August it's open daily from 8 am to 7.30 pm.

For details on *food markets*, see the preceding Markets section.

Getting There & Away

Train Sarlat's tiny train station (☎ 53.59.00.21) is 1.25 km south of the old town at the end of Ave de la Gare. The ticket windows are open from 6 am to 7 pm daily.

Rail connections are not particularly frequent. For Périgueux (66FF; 1½ hours) and Les Eyzies de Tayac (41FF; 50 minutes), which are on the same line, there are three trains a day leaving at 7.39 am, 3.28 pm and 7.28 pm. There are four trains a day to Bordeaux (105FF; 2½ hours) and two (8.30 am and 1.30 pm) to Toulouse (105FF; three hours).

Bus Bus services are even worse than the trains. As there is no bus station, buses leave from the train station, Place Pasteur or Place de la Petite Rigaudie, depending on the destination. The STFA busto Périgueux via Montignac (19FF; 25 minutes), the closest town to Lascaux II, leaves from Place de la Petite Rigaudie at 6 am. STFA's office (☎ 53.59.01.58) on Rue de Cahors is open weekdays from 9 am to noon and 2 to 5 pm.

Car & Motorbike Europcar (☎ 53.31.18.25), 12 Ave Aristide Briand, and Hertz (☎ 53.59. 05.94), Le Pontet, are both close to the train station.

Périgord Moto is two km south-east of the train station (☎ 53.59.42.95) on Route de Souillac. It has a variety of cycles, ranging from mopeds for 50/80/195FF for half/one/ three days to scooters for 130/180/510FF. Deposits start at 2000FF. It's advisable to ring before you head out there.

Getting Around

Bus Sarlat's one bus route, serviced by minibuses, runs the length of the modern-day town. The stop nearest the train station is Le Pontet. To get there turn left out of the station and go down the hill; the stop is on your left before the viaduct. Buses run from about 8.30 am to 4.45 pm.

Bicycle There are about six bike rental outlets but in peak times you should book ahead. Close to the youth hostel is Cycles Cumenal (☎ 53.31.28.40) at 8 Ave Gambetta with city/mountain bikes for 50/80FF a day.

VÉZÈRE VALLEY

There are nearly 200 prehistoric sites in Périgord. The most famous ones, including the world-renowned cave paintings in Lascaux, are located in the Vézère Valley. Stretching from Le Bugue, near where the Vézère and Dordogne rivers merge, north to Montignac, the valley's centre is Les Eyzies, a small village that is clearly reaping all the benefits of mass tourism. About 20 km

south-east is Sarlat-la-Canéda, also touristy but with a more human face. With a car, Sarlat is the most pleasant base from which to explore the valley. Périgueux, however, is just 40 km north-west and offers a greater choice of budget accommodation.

If you don't have your own transport, limited day tours are run from both Sarlat and Périgueux (see the Organised Tours section in the listing for each town). There are also sporadic buses and trains from both towns (for details see the relevant Getting There & Away sections).

Les Eyzies de Tayac

At every crossroad in Les Eyzies there are signs telling you how to get to the other sites. This section describes a few of the more accessible or famous prehistoric sites, starting at Les Eyzies and then following the valley 24 km north-east to Montignac. The prehistoric sites of Les Eyzies and the surrounding area constitute one of the major centres of the Upper Palaeolithic period. The main sites are the caves of Moustier, Font de Gaume, Combarelles, La Madeleine, Laugerie-Basse and the Cro-Magnon shelter.

As one of the world's major prehistoric centres, the village of Les Eyzies (population 850), at the confluence of the Vézère and Beune rivers, attracts a great many tourists. There is a tourist office (☎ 53.06.97.05) at Place de la Mairie which is open from mid-March to October.

Musée National de la Préhistoire This pre-history museum (☎ 53.06.97.03) has some of the oldest art works in the world and an excellent collection of artefacts, including 37,000-year-old carved limestone blocks. It also provides very good background information about the area's prehistoric sites.

From December to March it is open daily, except Tuesday, from 9.30 am to noon and 2 to 5 pm (6 pm from April to June and September to November); in July and August it is open from 9.30 am to 6 pm. Admission is 17FF (9FF for students, free for those under 18).

Musée de l'Abri Pataud In the heart of Les Eyzies, the Abri Pataud Museum (☎ 53.02. 92.46) was once a rock shelter for Cro-Magnon people, whose lifestyle is the focus of the displays. It is open Tuesday to Sunday from 10 am to noon and 2 to 5.30 pm. In July and August it's open daily from 9.30 am to 7 pm. It is closed in January. Entry costs 22/10FF for adults/children.

Around Les Eyzies de Tayac

Grotte de Font de Gaume Just over one km north-east of Les Eyzies on the D47 is Font de Gaume, a cave with a narrow main gallery and several side passages. On the walls are over 200 remarkably sophisticated paintings of bison, reindeer, horses, mammoths and woolly rhinoceroses. It is believed that they were painted over 10,000 years ago during the Upper Palaeolithic period, but some may be over 15,000 years old. Some paintings are in one colour only, whereas others show a variety of colour, mostly red, brown and black. The figures are quite realistic and lively, showing lots of movement and an attempt at three-dimensionality. Some have images superimposed upon them, revealing the development of the artists' technique. Another important feature of the paintings is that they show the use of engraving, as some of the animals have a black, engraved outline.

Stone Age Humans

Prehistory, the study of the past of a particular region before the appearance of written records, relies solely on archaeological evidence. The Palaeolithic Age, also known as the Old Stone Age, covers the period from 2,000,000 to 10,000 years ago, when primitive people who used unpolished chipped stone tools first emerged.

Sometime between 1,500,000 and 300,000 years ago, *Homo erectus* appeared in Europe. These hominids had a fully erect posture, used stone tools, hunted and were omnivorous (ie ate meat, snakes, birds, eggs, vegetables and fruit). Having mastered the use of fire, they were able to cook their food and live in caves and in colder areas, making possible their migration to the colder (and even glaciated) areas of Europe.

About 90,000 to 40,000 years ago, during the Middle Palaeolithic age, Neanderthal people (thought to be early representatives of *Homo sapiens*) inhabited Europe. They made crude flake-stone tools, hunted animals, lived in caves and buried their dead. Several of their skeletons have been found in the cave of Le Moustier near Les Eyzies and at Le Bugue. Mousterian people, who are associated with Neanderthals, have left the earliest evidence in Western Europe of the use of fire and the practice of burying the dead.

During a dramatic change of climate about 35,000 years ago, the Neanderthal people disappeared. They were followed by Cro-Magnon people, a later variety of *Homo sapiens*. Much taller than their predecessors (over 170 cm, or five feet seven inches tall), these Cro-Magnon people had nimble hands, larger brains, long, narrow skulls and short, wide faces. They were skilful hunters, and with their improved tools and hunting techniques were able to kill reindeer, bison, horses and mammoths.

Prehistoric art began with Cro-Magnon people. They started drawing, painting and sculpting, using a variety of different techniques. Their initial simplistic drawings and engravings of animals gradually became far more detailed and realistic, as in the Lascaux caves (see that section). They also decorated tools, played music, danced, performed assorted ceremonies (for instance, magical rituals to enhance fertility) and had fairly complex social patterns.

In the Mesolithic period, which began about 10,000 years ago (after the last glaciation), hunting and fishing became very efficient and wild grains were harvested. The Neolithic period (about 6000 to 4500 years ago), also known as the New Stone Age, saw the advent of polished-stone tools. Warmer weather caused great changes in flora and fauna, ushering in the practice of farming and stock rearing. Cereals were grown, as were peas, beans and lentils. Communities were therefore more settled and villages were built. Pottery decorated with geometric patterns became common, as did woven fabric. This was also the time in which the first megalithic monuments were erected. ■

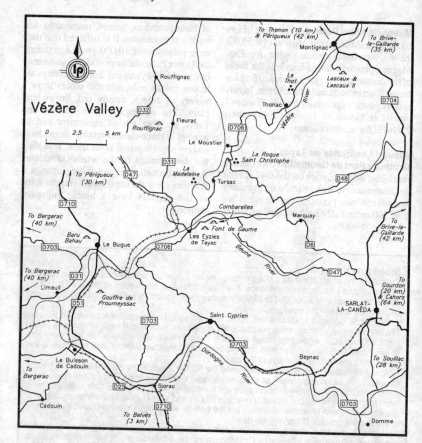

Vézère Valley

0   2.5   5 km

Try to reserve tickets to see the cave as they are often sold out very early in the day if not days before. Only 20 people are allowed in at a time. From October to March the cave is open daily, except Tuesday, from 10 am to noon and 2 to 4 pm; from April to September it is open from 9 am to noon and 2 to 6 pm. Admission is 31/17/7FF for adults/students/children. To book tickets or for information ring ☎ 53.06.97.48.

Grotte des Combarelles A couple of km north of Font de Gaume is the cave of Combarelles, renowned for the thousands of

superimposed engravings found there. They were discovered early this century and are believed to have been painted over 15,000 years ago, possibly by a hunting cult. Most of the engravings depict animals, in particular reindeer and bison, but there are also some half-human, half-animal figures.

Visiting hours are the same as for Font de Gaume. Again, it is difficult to get tickets; ring ☎ 53.06.97.72 to book tickets or for information.

La Roque Saint Christophe This limestone cliff measuring about 800 metres in length is nine km north-east of Les Eyzies and about eight km south of Montignac on the D706. The 100 or so caves in the cliff were home to Neanderthal people about 50,000 years ago. During the Middle Ages, a village was established here around a feudal chateau. Later it served as a natural bastion against the English.

You can visit La Roque Saint Christophe daily from 15 March to 11 November from 10 am to 6 pm (in July and August from 9.30 am to 7 pm). Entry is 24/18/13FF for adults/students/children. For information ring ☎ 53.50.70.45.

Montignac

The town of Montignac (population 2900), on the Vézère River, achieved sudden fame after the discovery of the nearby Grotte de Lascaux. The tourist office (☎ 53.51.82.60) is on Place Léo Magne. It is a relaxing place with picturesque riverside houses and a good base from which to explore the Lascaux caves.

Getting Around

To get to Montignac by car take the D706 from Les Eyzies, or the D704 from Sarlat-la-Canéda. From Les Eyzies or Montignac, there's no public transport to get you further along the valley. Hitching is feasible along the main D706, but if you're aiming for sites off it, the wait could be long.

Around Montignac

Le Thot A museum and animal park, Le Thot (☎ 53.53.44.35) attempts to recreate prehistoric life and art. It's 1.5 km off the D706 from a point five km south of Montignac and is open Tuesday to Sunday from 10 am to noon and 2 to 5.30 pm. In July and August it's open daily from 9.30 am to 7 pm. It is closed in January. Admission costs 35FF per adult (18FF for students and children) but in the high season you must buy your tickets in Montignac near the tourist office before heading out there.

Lascaux & Lascaux II The Lascaux Cave, located about 2.5 km south of Montignac at the end of a sealed road off the D704, was discovered in 1940, some say by four teenage boys searching for their dog, which had fallen down a hole. The hole led to one of the most outstanding examples of prehistoric cave art in the world. By 1948 the cave, made up of a large cavern and several galleries, had been opened to the general public; however, it was closed 15 years later after it was realised that human breath and the resulting carbon dioxide and condensation were making a green fungus grow over the paintings and causing the colours to fade. The drawings and paintings, which are around 15,000 years old, are thought to have been the site of a hunting cult where magical rites were performed.

These days all you can see is **Lascaux II** (☎ 53.53.44.35), a precise cement replica of the most famous section of the painted original, which is just a few hundred metres away. It is a stunning reproduction of the vivid portrayal of bulls, horses and reindeer found in the original cave.

Only 2000 visitors are allowed into Lascaux II daily. Tours take 40 people and in the high season leave 10 minutes apart.

Lascaux II is open Tuesday to Sunday from 10 am to noon and 2 to 5.30 pm. In July and August it's open daily from 9.30 am to 7 pm. It is closed in January. Most of the year, tickets cost 45/20FF for adults/children, can be bought on site and are also valid for entry to Le Thot. In July and August, however, tickets *must* be purchased from the tourist office at Montignac (see that section) and it is best to get there early as queues are long. Guided visits in English are run hourly from 10 am to 4 pm.

There are also other painted caves in the area, but they are not as spectacular. About eight km north of Les Eyzies, there is a 11-km-long cave at **Rouffignac**, commonly known as the 'mammoth' cave because, apart from its other rock carvings, it has over 100 carvings of mammoths. The 40-metre long Lascaux II, however, is far more evocative and is much more successful at conjuring up the world of the prehistoric artist.

Quercy

Quercy lies south of Limousin and east of Périgord. It comprises two areas: Haut Quercy, a limestone plateau covered with oak forests and cut by impressive canyons; and Bas Quercy, a hilly region in the Garonne Valley. Its capital, Cahors, is surrounded by some of the region's finest vineyards.

Flowing through the region is the Lot River, which springs up near Mont Lozère in the Cévennes. The scenic but largely untouristed Vallée du Lot, overlooked by picturesque villages and cutting through dramatic limestone plateaux, is a great area to explore, offering many opportunities for hikers, cyclists and kayak enthusiasts.

History

Originally occupied by a Celtic people known as the Cadurci, Quercy was taken over by the Visigoths in the 5th century and the Franks in the 6th century. The Plantagenets gained some rights over Quercy by the Treaty of Xaintes (1259), which eventually led to fierce fighting between France and England. The French ceded Quercy to England in 1360 by the Treaty of Brétigny, but in 1443 France regained control of the region. War commenced again in the 16th century as Catholics and Huguenots contested the area during the Wars of Religion. Montauban became a Huguenot stronghold, sustaining severe losses as a result of Catholic persecution. Cahors and Rodez, on the other hand, supported the Catholic cause.

Houseboat Rental

One of the most relaxing ways to see the countryside and vineyards around Cahors and visit the towns and villages along the Lot (eg Luzech, Saint Cirq Lapopie) is to rent a houseboat. For details, contact the Centrale de Réservation Loisirs Accueil (see the next paragraph); you might also call the two Cahors-based rental companies, Baboumarine (☎ 65.30.08.99) and Lot Plaisance

(☎ 65.35.36.87). For details on Crown Blue Line, which has a base at Douelle (15 km west of Cahors), see Canal Boats under Activities in the Facts for the Visitor chapter. For general information on boating in France, see Boating on Burgundy's Waterways at the beginning of the Burgundy chapter.

CAHORS

Cahors (population 21,000), former capital of the Quercy region, is a quiet town whose relaxed atmosphere makes it a fine place to get a taste of the Midi. Surrounded by a bend in the Lot River and a ring of scrub-covered hills, it is endowed with a couple of minor Roman sites and a large (if unspectacular) medieval quarter. The weather is mild in winter, hot and dry in summer and generally delightful in the spring and autumn, which may be why the town, and the surrounding département of Lot, seem especially popular with visitors from the UK.

During Roman times, when it was known as Divona Cadurcorum, Cahors was renowned for its production of linen cloth. It was later occupied by the Visigoths (471) and the Muslims (mid-700s). By the 13th century, the town had become a prosperous commercial and financial centre, thanks in part to its merchants and moneylenders (ie bankers). Pope John XXII, a native of Cahors and the second of the Avignon popes, established a university here in 1331, which was closed in 1751.

Orientation

Cahors occupies a rocky, limestone peninsula formed by one of the Lot River's many hairpin curves. The river's outer bank follows a ring of low, vegetation-dotted cliffs, the highest of which is Mont Saint Cyr (264 metres).

The town is just the right size to be explored on foot. The main commercial thoroughfare, the north-south oriented Blvd Léon Gambetta, is named after Cahors-born Léon Gambetta (1838-82), one of the founders of the Third Republic and briefly premier

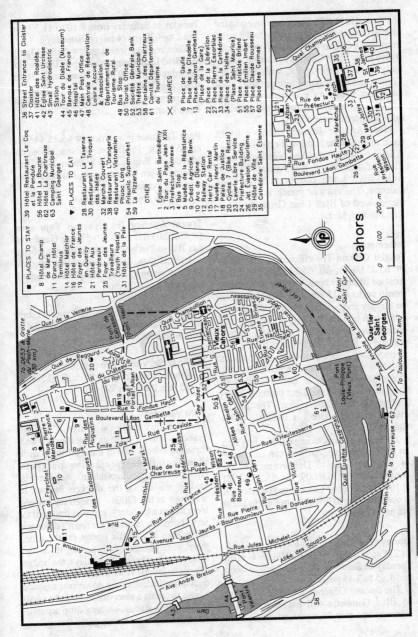

Cahors

PLACES TO STAY
- ■ Hôtel Champ
  de Mars
- 8 Grand Hôtel
  Terminus
- 14 Hôtel Melchior
- 16 Hôtel de France
- 19 Foyer des Jeunes
  en Quercy
- 21 Hôtel Aux
  Perdreaux
- 25 Foyer des Jeunes
  Travailleurs
  (Youth Hostel)
- 31 Hôtel de la Paix
- 39 Hôtel Restaurant Le Coq
- 53 Hôtel Terminus
- 56 Hôtel La Bourse
- 62 Hôtel La Chartreuse
- 63 Camping Municipal
  Saint Georges

▼ PLACES TO EAT
- 28 Restaurant La Taverne
- 30 Restaurant Le Troquet
  des Halles
- 32 Marché Couvert
- 38 Restaurant L'Orangerie
- 40 Restaurant Vietnamien
  Phuoc Long
- 54 Prisunic Supermarket
- 59 La Pizzeria

OTHER
- 1 Église Saint Barthélémy
- 2 Tour du Pape Jean XXII
- 3 Préfecture Annexe
- 4 Bus Stop
- 5 Musée de la Résistance
- 9 Crédit Agricole Bank
- 10 Arc de Diane
- 12 Railway Station
- 15 Hertz Car Rental
- 17 Musée Henri Martin
- 18 Palais de Justice
- 20 Cycles Libre Service
- 24 Prefecture Building
- 26 Jet Evasion Cycles
- 29 Hôtel de Ville
- 35 Cathédrale Saint Étienne
- 36 Street Entrance to Cloister
- 37 Cloister
- 41 Hôtel des Roaldès
- 42 Église Saint Urcisse
- 43 Small Hydroelectric
  Station
- 44 Tour du Diable (Museum)
- 45 Banque de France
- 46 Hospital
- 47 Main Post Office
- 48 Centrale de Réservation
  Loisirs Accueil
  & Association
  Départementale de
  Tourisme Rural
- 49 Bus Stop
- 50 Tourist Office
- 52 Société Générale Bank
- 55 Théâtre Municipal
- 58 Fontaine des Chartreux
- 61 Comité Départemental
  du Tourisme

✕ SQUARES
- 6 Place de Gaulle
- 7 Place de la Citadelle
- 13 Place Jounot Gambetta
  (Place de la Gare)
- 22 Place de la Libération
- 23 Place Pierre Escorbiac
- 33 Place de la Cathédrale
- 34 Place des Halles
  (Place Saint Maurice)
- 51 Place Aristide Briand
- 55 Place Émilien Imbert
- 57 Place Claude Rousseau
- 60 Place des Carmes

of France (1881-82). This plane-tree-shaded avenue divides the new quarters (to the west) from Vieux Cahors (Old Cahors; to the east). It also links Place Charles de Gaulle, essentially a large parking lot, with Place des Carmes and Pont Louis-Philippe (also called the Vieux Pont). An even-numbered street address is often blocks away from a similar odd-numbered street address.

Place Aristide Briand, Cahors's lively main square, is the home of the tourist office; Allées Fénelon stretches westward from Place Aristide Briand. Rue Président Wilson links Blvd Léon Gambetta with Pont Valentré. The railway station is about 600 metres west of Blvd Léon Gambetta along Rue Joachim Murat.

Information

Tourist Offices The efficient tourist office (☎ 65.35.09.56; fax 65.23.98.66) at Place Aristide Briand is open Monday to Saturday from 9 am to 12.15 pm and 2 to 6.30 pm, and on Sunday and holidays from 10 am to noon and 3 to 6 pm. During July and August it's open from 9 am to 12.30 pm and 1.30 to 7 pm, and on Sunday and holidays from 10 am to noon and 3 to 6 pm. Hotel reservations cost 5FF within the département. The brochure *Sésame pour le Lot*, available in English, has lots of excellent practical information on the Cahors area. The tourist office's mailing address is BP 207, 46004 Cahors CEDEX.

For brochures (including some in English) on the Lot département, you can call, write or fax the Comité Départemental du Tourisme (☎ 65.35.07.09; fax 65.23.92.76) at 107 Quai Eugène Cavaignac (1st floor). It is open Monday to Friday from 8 am to 12.30 pm and 1.30 to 6 pm.

Money The Banque de France (☎ 65.23.24.25) at 318 Rue Président Wilson is open Tuesday to Saturday from 8.45 am to noon and 1.45 to 3.45 pm.

The Société Générale (☎ 65.35.17.02) at 85 Blvd Gambetta will exchange foreign currency and give Visa cash advances from

Tuesday to Saturday from 8.10 to 11.30 am and 2 to 4.30 pm (4 pm on Saturday).

The Crédit Agricole bank (☎ 65.30.13.40) at 2 Blvd Léon Gambetta is open Tuesday to Saturday from 8.30 to 11.30 am and 1.30 to 4.30 pm. There is a 30FF commission. Several other banks are found along Blvd Léon Gambetta.

Post The main post office (☎ 65.35.44.93), at 257 Rue Président Wilson, is open Monday to Friday from 8 am to 7 pm and Saturday from 8 am to noon. Exchange services are available.

Cahors's postcode is 46000.

Travel Agency Jet Évasion Tourisme (☎ 65.22.05.05) at 24 Blvd Léon Gambetta has BIJ rail tickets and can arrange cheap charter flights. It is open daily (except Monday morning and Sunday) from 9 am to noon and 2 to 6.30 pm.

Laundry In Vieux Cahors, the Laverie Libre Service at Place de la Libération is open daily from 8 am to 8 pm.

Medical Services The hospital, Centre Hospitalier Jean Rougier (☎ 65.20.50.50), is at 335 Rue Président Wilson.

Pont Valentré

This fortified medieval bridge – one of France's finest – consists of six arches and three tall towers, two of them outfitted with machicolations (projecting parapets equipped with openings taht allow defenders to drop missiles on the attackers below). It was built in the 1300s – though the towers were added a bit later – and was intended to serve primarily as part of the town's defences rather than as a traffic bridge (at the time, there wasn't much worth getting to on the river's western bank). These days, the bridge affords a lovely view of the river in both directions, including the downriver cascade – built to create a reservoir to power a small hydroelectric station – whose drop accentuates the water's brownish-green tint.

The middle tower, **Tour du Diable** (Devil's Tower), houses a small museum with displays on the bridge and the town. All the labels are in French. It is open during July and August only – daily hours are 9.30 am to 12.30 pm and 2 to 6.30 pm. Entrance costs 12FF (6FF for students and children over 12).

Fontaine des Chartreux

In Gallo-Roman times, this pool on the left bank of the Lot, opposite Allées des Soupirs, was used in the worship of Divona, after whom the Roman city was named. Archaeologists have recently discovered a large number of coins minted between 27 BC and 54 AD that were apparently thrown into the water as offerings. Under the pool is a flooded cavern which divers have explored to a vertical depth of 137 metres. Cahors has pumped its drinking water from the Fontaine des Chartreux since 1880.

Cathédrale Saint Étienne

The Romanesque-style St Stephen's Cathedral, the first church in France to be crowned with cupolas (an obvious import from the East), was consecrated in 1119 and partly rebuilt between 1285 and 1500. Each of the 18-metre-wide cupolas is 32 metres above ground. The early Gothic chapels lining the nave date from the 13th century and the massive belfry and fortified west façade date from the 14th century.

The cloister (cloître), which can be reached from the choir (or through the entrance opposite 59 Rue de la Chantrerie), is in the Flamboyant Gothic style of the early 16th century. Most of the decoration was mutilated during the Wars of Religion and the Revolution. One of the rooms off the cloister, **Chapelle Saint Gausbert**, named after a late 9th-century bishop of Cahors, houses a small collection of precious liturgical objects; the frescoes of the Last Judgement date from 1497 to 1502. From July to mid-September the cathedral is open from 10 am to noon and 2 to 6 pm (closed Monday).

Vieux Cahors

Until the 19th century, the town was confined to the area east of what is now Blvd Léon Gambetta; the western half of the peninsula was taken up by a number of convents and their gardens. Now known as Vieux Cahors, the medieval area is densely packed with old, though not necessarily picturesque, four-storey houses linked by streets and alleyways so narrow you can almost touch both sides at once. The area around the Marché Couvert and Place de la Cathédrale are enlivened by an outdoor market on Wednesday and Saturday (see Self-Catering under Places to Eat).

It is possible to walk around the three sides of Cahors by following the quays along the town's riverside perimeter.

Hôtel des Roaldès

Also known as the Maison Henri IV (☎ 65.35.04.35), this private residence at 271 Quai Champollion has been owned by the same family since its construction in the 15th century. Built of brick, stone and timber, it consists of two separate buildings linked by a spiral staircase. The interior is furnished with 16th to 18th-century Louis XIII-style furniture. In 1580, during the Wars of Religion, the Protestant Henri of Navarre (who later became the Catholic King Henri IV of France) captured the Catholic stronghold of Cahors and stayed in this house for one night.

The Hôtel des Roaldès is open to the public on major holidays and, from 15 June to September, daily from 10 am to 6.30 pm (4.30 pm on Saturday). Entrance is 20FF (5FF for children under 10) and the informal guided tour is in French. To call the owner, who will show you around, ring the cowbell.

Musée Henri Martin

Also known as the Musée Municipal (☎ 65.23.14.00), this museum at 792 Rue Émile Zola has some archaeological artefacts and a collection of works by the Cahors-born pointillist painter Henri Martin (1893-1972). From July to mid-September only it is open from about 10 am to noon and

3 to 6 pm (closed Tuesday). Unless there's a special exhibition, entrance is free.

Tour du Pape Jean XXII

This square, 34-metre-high tower at 1-3 Blvd Léon Gambetta – the tallest structure in town – was built in the 14th century as part of the **Palais Duèze**, home of Jacques Duèse, who later became Pope John XXII (1316-34). The interior is closed to the public. The adjacent Rue de la Tour leads to the entrance of the 14th-century **Église Saint Barthélémy**, with its massive brick and stone belfry.

Musée de la Résistance

This small Resistance Museum at 96 Rue Pierre Mendès-France (on the north side of Place Charles de Gaulle) is open daily from 2.30 to 6.30 pm. Entry is free.

Arc de Diane

Die-hard fans of Roman architecture might want to visit the Arch of Diana, a stone archway with red-brick stripes that once formed part of a Gallo-Roman bathhouse. It is opposite 24 Rue Charles de Freycinet.

Caves

The most famous of the many caves in the vicinity of Cahors is the **Grotte du Pech-Merle** (☎ 65.31.27.05), about 30 km east of Cahors near the village of Cabrerets. Seven chambers along the cave's 1200-metre length are decorated with some of the finest Palaeolithic drawings (of animals, human figures, etc) that are still open to the public.

The cave is open daily from the Sunday before Easter to October from 9.30 am to noon and 1.30 to 5.30 pm (4.45 pm during October). The bus from Cahors's railway station to Capdenac, which stops a few km south of the cave at the village of Bouziès, runs at least three times a day. It is operated by the SNCF, Transports Belmon et Fils (☎ 65.35.11.64 in Cahors) and SARL Laurens et Fils (☎ 65.34.18.99 in Capdenac-le-Haut). On most days, the last bus back leaves Bouziès at around 3 pm.

Hiking

In addition to the GR36 and the GR65, both of which pass through Cahors, the département of Lot has numerous marked trails for day hikes (*sentiers de promenade or sentiers de petites randonnées*). Other Grande Randonnée trails that cross the département include the GR6, GR46, GR64 and GR652. French-language topoguides for the GR36 cost about 70FF.

Mont Saint Cyr, the 264-metre-high, antenna-topped hill across the river from Vieux Cahors, affords fine views of the town and the surrounding countryside. It can be easily climbed on foot – the trail begins near the south end of Pont Louis-Philippe (built in 1838).

For details (in French) on other day hikes from Cahors, you might want to check the topoguides in the *Promenades et Randonnées* series published by the Comité Départemental du Tourisme du Lot. They are available at the tourist office for 35FF.

Cycling

The Cahors area offers all sorts of backroads and off-road options for cyclists. Many of them are detailed in the French-language topoguide *Cyclotourisme en Quercy* (40FF) and in the topoguides of the *Promenades et Randonnées* series (see Hiking). For information on bicycle rental, see Bicycle under Getting Around.

Organised Tours

The Centrale de Réservation Loisirs Accueil (☎ 65.22.19.20; fax 65.30.06.11), in the Chambre d'Agriculture du Lot at 53 Rue Bourseul, can arrange canoe, bicycle and horse-riding **trips**, food preparation courses and **boat rental** on the Lot River. If you'd like to take a hassle-free **hike**, they can provide an itinerary and arrange for accommodation, meals and even the transport of your bags. Such activities can often be booked at short notice. The office is open Monday to Friday from 8 am to noon and 2 to 6 pm. The postal address is BP 162, 46003 Cahors CEDEX.

Festivals

For information on the various cultural activities that take place during July and August, ask for the relevant brochure at the tourist office. The four-day Festival de Blues, held sometime in July, brings big-name stars to Cahors.

Places to Stay – bottom end

Rooms are hardest to come by in July and August. Cahors's least expensive hotels do not register new guests on Sunday unless you call ahead.

Camping The two-star *Camping Municipal Saint Georges* (☎ 65.35.04.64) on Ave Anatole de Monzie is right across the river from the south end of town. Its riverside site is hemmed in by heavily trafficked roads but there are shaded, grassy sites to pitch your tent. This place is open from mid-April to mid-November and charges 10FF for a tent site, 11FF per adult and 5FF per child aged three to seven. The office is generally closed from noon to 4.30 pm.

Hostels The *Foyer des Jeunes Travailleurs* (☎ 65.35.64.71) at 20 Rue Frédéric Suisse, also known as Résidence Frédéric Suisse, serves as a youth hostel throughout the year, though during the school year most of the rooms are occupied by students and trainee workers. Beds costs 43FF (47FF for people without an IYHF card); breakfast is 13FF, meals are 43FF. The office is open from 9 am to noon and 2 to 7 pm daily except Saturday afternoon and Sunday. A concierge is on duty the rest of the time. Reservations can be made by telephone.

The old and very basic *Foyer des Jeunes en Quercy* (☎ 65.35.29.32) at 129 Rue Fondue Haute, which is run by nuns, provides accommodation for students during the academic year but welcomes travellers of all religions, sexes and ages during the summer school holidays (approximately July and August). A simple bed in a single or triple with washbasin and crucifix costs 65FF, including breakfast. Dinner is 28FF. There's no curfew. You can cook using the burners next to the

dining room. Reservations can be made by telephone, but there's always space in summer.

Gîtes For hikers, there are 30 gîtes d'étape around the Lot département. Details are available from tourist offices or in the brochure *Sésame pour le Lot*.

For information on staying out in the countryside (gîtes ruraux, chambres d'hôte, fermes auberges, camping à la ferme and gîtes d'enfants), visit, call or write to the Association Départementale de Tourisme Rural (☎ 65.22.32.83) at 53 Rue Bourseul (mailing address: BP 162, 46003 Cahors CEDEX). The office is open Monday to Friday from 8 am to noon and 2 to 5.30 pm (5 pm on Friday).

On the ground floor, the Centrale de Réservation Loisirs Accueil (☎ 65.22.19.20; fax 65.30.06.11), which has the same opening hours but closes at 6 pm, can help make reservations. Most gîtes need to be reserved in advance and require a stay of at least one week.

Hotels In Vieux Cahors next to the Marché Couvert, the 22-room *Hôtel de la Paix* (☎ 65.35.03.40) at Place des Halles (Place Saint Maurice) has basic but clean singles and doubles for 110FF (with washbasin and bidet), 120FF (with shower) and 130FF (with shower and toilet). The hall shower costs 10FF. Reception is closed on Sunday and holidays, so call ahead if you'll be arriving then.

A block to the east, the seven-room *Hôtel Le Coq et La Pendule* (☎ 65.35.28.84) at 10 Rue Saint James has very basic doubles with shower for 135FF. Reception (at the bar) is closed on Sunday – again, phone ahead if you'd like to check in on Sunday.

The friendly *Hôtel La Bourse* (☎ 65.35.17.78), a decent sort of place at 7 Place Claude Rousseau, has singles and doubles with washbasin and bidet for 90FF, and two-bed doubles for 135FF. A shower costs 10FF. Reception (at the bar) is closed on Sunday.

Opposite the train station, the two-star *Hôtel Melchior* (☎ 65.35.03.38, 65.35.04.71; fax 65.23.92.75) has adequate, but hardly attractive, singles/doubles with shower and toilet for 145 to 165FF; two-bed doubles are 195FF. Singles and doubles with washbasin, situated in the annexe, are 110FF. Reception (at the bar) is closed on Sunday except during July and August. This place is closed for two weeks in January.

You might also try the *Hôtel Aux Perdreaux* (☎ 65.35.03.50) at 137 Rue du Portail Alban (ie Place de la Libération), which has two rooms for about 120FF and 10 more rooms with shower and toilet from 180FF.

Places to Stay – middle

Near the train station, the three-star *Hôtel de France* (☎ 65.35.16.76; fax 65.22.01.08) at 252 Ave Jean Jaurès has 80 nondescript but comfortable singles/doubles with shower, toilet, TV and minibar for 195/200FF; two-bed doubles are 210FF. Reception is open 24 hours a day. The buffet breakfast is 40FF. This place is closed for two weeks around Christmas and New Year.

Across the Lot from the south end of town, the three-star, riverside *Hôtel La Chartreuse* (☎ 65.35.17.37; fax 65.22.30.03) is on Chemin de la Chartreuse in a neighbourhood known as Quartier Saint Georges. Singles/doubles with shower and toilet cost 180/210FF. Many have balconies overlooking the river.

North of Vieux Cahors, you might try the tiny (four-room) *Hôtel Le Champ de Mars* (☎ 65.23.93.01) at 17 Blvd Léon Gambetta, whose shower-and-toilet-equipped doubles start at 165FF. Reception (at the bar) is closed on Sunday.

Places to Stay – top end

The *Grand Hôtel Terminus* (☎ 65.35.24.50; fax 65.22.06.40) at 5 Ave Charles de Freycinet (one block uphill to the left as you exit the train station) was built around 1920, but unfortunately the rooms do not live up to the promise of the stained-glass-adorned lobby. Rooms for one to four people with shower, toilet and TV cost 240 to 275FF. Reception is open 24 hours a day. Enclosed parking costs 25FF a night.

Places to Eat

Most restaurants are closed on Sunday.

Restaurants – expensive The rustically elegant *Restaurant La Taverne* (☎ 65.35. 28.66) at Place Pierre Escorbiac (next to the Hôtel de Ville) specialises in French and regional cuisine and has *menus* for 125, 185 and 250FF, and main dishes for 65 to 95FF. It is open from noon to 2.30 pm and 8 to 10.30 pm daily except Tuesday evening and Wednesday (daily in July and August). Reservations are necessary on weekends.

Restaurants – inexpensive The friendly and utterly unpretentious *Restaurant Le Troquet des Halles* (☎ 65.22.15.81) on Rue Saint Maurice, near Place des Halles, offers the best value for money in town. The lunch and dinner *menu*, popular with the people who make their living in Vieux Cahors, costs only 40FF, including wine; the plat du jour is 32FF. If you order a bowl of soup (10FF), it comes with a glass of wine. You can also buy a steak at the nearby Marché Couvert and the chef will cook it for you for 6FF. This place is open Monday to Saturday from 6.45 am (6 am on Wednesday and Saturday) to sometime between 10 pm and 2 am (it closes latest in summer).

A block to the east is the modest *Le Coq et la Pendule* (☎ 65.35.28.84) at 10 Rue Saint James, a restaurant/bar in a hotel of the same name serving coq au vin and other dishes to a friendly, local clientele. It is open Monday to Saturday from noon to 4 pm and 7 to 11 pm.

Popular *La Pizzeria* (☎ 65.35.12.18) at 58 Blvd Léon Gambetta has pizzas (28 to 52FF), pasta (24 to 52FF) and large salads (34 to 44FF). It is open Monday to Saturday from noon to 2 pm and 7.15 to 10 pm.

Restaurant Vietnamien Phuoc Loc (☎ 65. 35.43.53, 65.23.95.89) is at 68 Rue Saint James. The plat du jour costs 33FF.

Vegetarian The totally vegetarian *Restaurant L'Orangerie* (☎ 65.22.59.06) at 41 Rue Saint James has *menus* for 68 and 92FF; salads cost 20 to 26FF, main dishes are 30 to

42FF. The décor is fashionable but not trendy. It is open Tuesday to Saturday from noon to 2 pm and 7 to 9 pm.

Self-Catering The *Marché Couvert*, also known as Les Halles, at Place des Halles is open Tuesday to Saturday from 7.30 am to 12.30 pm and 3 to 7 pm and Sunday and holidays from 9 am to noon. There's an *open-air market* around the Marché Couvert and at Place de la Cathédrale on Wednesday and Saturday. If Wednesday or Saturday turns out to be a holiday, the market shifts to Tuesday or Friday. There are *food shops* nearby along Rue de la Préfecture and at Place de la Libération.

On the other side of the fountain from the tourist office, the *Prisunic supermarket* at Place Aristide Briand (go down the stairs to the right at you approach the Théâtre Municipal) is open Monday to Friday from 9.15 am to 12.15 pm and 3 to 7 pm and Saturday from 9.15 am to 12.30 pm and 2.30 to 7 pm. There's another entrance at Place Émilien Imbert.

Entertainment
From October to April *Restaurant Le Troquet des Halles* (see Places to Eat) has live concerts (jazz, rock, blues) every other Friday or Saturday night. Concerts are held here every Saturday night at 9 pm during July and August.

Things to Buy
Regional specialities, available at tourist-oriented shops as well as food markets and local shops, include deep-red Cahors wine (governed by Appellation d'Origine Contrôlée rules), foie gras, truffles and *cabécou* (a small, round goat's cheese).

Getting There & Away
Train The railway station (☎ 65.22.50.50 for information) is at Place Jouinot Gambetta (Place de la Gare). The information office is open daily, except weekends and holidays, from 8 am to noon and 2 to 6 pm.

Cahors is on the Toulouse-Paris train line. Destinations served include Paris's Gare d'Austerlitz (289FF; seven a day; about 5½ hours during the day), Toulouse (78FF; eight a day; 70 minutes), Montauban (49FF; eight a day; 45 minutes), Limoges (130FF; six a day; two hours 10 minutes), Bordeaux (via Montauban; 174FF), Marseille (via Toulouse; 265FF) and Nice (via Toulouse).

Bus The bus services linking Cahors with destinations around the Lot département, designed primarily to get children to and from school, are poorly organised. A variety of companies, including the SNCF, operate buses to Capdenac, Castelnau-Montratier, Duravel, Figeac, Gourdon, Labastide-Murat, Marminiac, Monsempron, Montcuq, Rodez, Saint Céré, Saux and Varaire (and points between Cahors and these places), but some services operate only a few times a week. Exploring the area by bus without the *horaire* (timetable) published by the Conseil Général du Lot, usually available at tourist offices, could prove frustrating.

In Cahors, buses stop at one or more of the following three locations: in front of the railway station (hours for some lines are posted); along Rue Saint Géry just west of Allées Fénelon; and in the parking lot next to the prefecture annexe at Place Charles de Gaulle (hours are not posted).

Car Europcar (☎ 65.22.35.55) is at 68 Blvd Léon Gambetta. Hertz (☎ 65.35.34.69) is opposite the train station at 385 Rue Anatole France.

Getting Around
Bicycle Cycles 7 (☎ 65.22.66.60), a full-service bicycle shop at 417 Quai de Regourd, rents bicycles all year long. Ten-speeds/mountain bikes cost 50/80FF a day, while better mountain bikes are 120FF a day. Half-day rates are also available. A helmet costs 10FF a day. In general, a deposit of 2000FF is required. This place is open Tuesday to Saturday from 9 am to noon and 2 to 7 pm. From late May to September it's open Monday to Saturday from 9 am to 7 pm.

QUERCY

AROUND CAHORS
Rocamadour

Rocamadour (population 650) makes a good day trip from Cahors (59 km south-west). The town has a spectacular setting, carved as it is into the rock face of the **Causse de Gramat**, a great limestone plateau in the north of Quercy. (The word 'causse' is a derivation of 'cau', the local word for *chaux*, or lime.) Commanding the town is a 12th-century castle, which you can reach either by a lift or by the steep stairway lined with the Stations of the Cross. Having negotiated the stairs (or taken the lift) you will come to Place Saint Amadour with its seven churches. This is where you will find **Chapelle Notre Dame**, with its statue of the Black Madonna, renowned for the miracles she is believed to have performed.

Rocamadour derives its name from Saint Amadour, a local hermit who is said to have established the town as a place of pilgrimage. By the Middle Ages it had become one of the main stopping places for pilgrims on their way to Santiago de Compostela (see that aside).

Although the town still attracts pilgrims, it is now tourists who come in droves. Avoid the town in July and August as this is when it is at its most crowded.

Gouffre de Padirac

The area around Rocamadour abounds with caves, the most famous of which is the Gouffre de Padirac, 11.5 km north-east of Rocamadour. This huge 75-metre-deep pothole in the Causse de Gramat leads to an extensive underground cave system that has been open to the public since 1898. You can visit the stalactite and stalagmite-filled galleries by foot and go on a boat trip on the underground river, which is over six km long.

From the train station at Rocamadour-Padirac, you have to walk or hitch the 10 km to the cave. In summer there is a bus to the cave.

Figeac

The small town of Figeac on the Célé River (68 km north-east of Cahors) is worth visiting for its picturesque **old town**, which still has many of its medieval houses. It was founded by Benedictine monks and became an important stopping place for pilgrims travelling from Conques (east of Figeac) to Santiago de Compostela. It was later to become a Protestant stronghold.

The tourist office (☎ 65.34.06.25) is in Hôtel de la Monnaie (the former mint) on Place Vival. Near Place Champollion is a fascinating **museum** tracing the work of the brilliant linguist and historian Jean-François Champollion, who in the 1820s used the Rosetta Stone (found by Napoleon's expeditionary force to Egypt in 1799) to lay down much of the groundwork for the deciphering of Egyptian hieroglyphics.

There are trains from Rocamadour southeast to Figeac. From Cahors the D13 will get you to Figeac, but a far more interesting route is the D662, which follows the meandering course of the Lot River.

Saint Cirq Lapopie

The village of Saint Cirq Lapopie (population 200) looks down on the Lot River from its clifftop position 25 km east of Cahors. It features many old houses which have been perfectly restored. Climb up to the chateau ruins for an awe-inspiring view of the village and the Lot Valley.

Buses from Cahors's bus station run to Saint Cirq Lapopie daily.

MONTAUBAN

Situated on the right bank of the Tarn River, Montauban (population 53,000) is the capital of the département of Tarn-et-Garonne. The town was founded in 1144 by Alphonse Jourdain, Count of Toulouse. It is the second-oldest bastide in southern France after Mont de Marsan in the Aquitaine region. Although the town sustained significant damage during the Inquisition in the 13th century, in 1317 it became the head of a diocese.

It was ceded to the English by the Treaty of Brétigny (1360), but was regained by the French in 1369. Montauban became a Huguenot stronghold around 1570, and was chosen as was one of the four cities where the Huguenots were free to worship publicly. The Edict of Nantes (1598), promulgated by Henry IV, brought further royal concessions to the Huguenots, allowing freedom of conscience to all and granting Protestants the same civil rights as Catholics, including the right to worship publicly in certain towns and eligibility for all offices.

Protestant rights were soon curtailed by Richelieu, Louis XIII's principal minister, who was determined to secure absolute power for the monarchy. In 1629 Montauban surrendered and Richelieu had the town's fortifications destroyed. Following the repeal of the Edict of Nantes by Louis XIV, the town's Protestants again suffered persecution.

Orientation
Place Nationale is in the heart of town. This attractive square is surrounded by arcaded buildings and houses dating from the 17th century. The train station is west of the centre on Ave Mayenne, on the other side of the Tarn River. There is a good view of the town from the early 14th-century Pont Vieux.

Information
Tourist Office The tourist office (☎ 63.63.60.60) is in the Ancien Collège at 2 Rue du Collège. It is open Monday to Saturday from 9 am to noon and 2 to 7 pm. During July and August it is also open on Sunday from 10 am to noon and 3 to 6 pm.

Post The post office is at 6 Blvd Midi-Pyrénées.

Montauban's postcode is 82000.

Musée Ingres
The neoclassical painter Jean Auguste Dominique Ingres was born in Montauban in 1780. Many of his works are exhibited in the Musée Ingres (☎ 63.63.18.04) at 19 Rue de la Mairie, in a former bishop's palace, on the site of a castle of the counts of Toulouse. The museum is open from 10 am to noon and 2 to 6 pm Tuesday to Saturday, and on Sunday afternoon; in July and August it is open daily. Admission is 15FF (free for children and students).

Cathédrale Notre Dame
The cathedral (17th and 18th centuries), in Place Franklin-Roosevelt, contains the *Vow of Louis XIII*, one of Ingres's masterpieces.

Église Saint Jacques
The 14th and 15th-century brick church of St James, built in the Gothic style typical of the south of France, overlooks the town.

Places to Stay & Eat
Montauban can be visited on a day trip from Toulouse, but there are a couple of good hotels if you decide to stay overnight. *The Hôtel Orsay* (☎ 63.66.06.66) opposite the train station offers reasonably priced rooms. Singles/doubles cost 180/310FF, and breakfast is 28FF. This hotel also has a very good restaurant.

For something more up-market, try the three-star *Hôtel Ingres* (☎ 63.63.36.01), 10 Ave Mayenne, which has pleasant singles/doubles with private bath for 310/420FF. There is parking available.

Getting There & Away
Train & Bus The train station (☎ 63.62.22.11 for information) is at the southern end of Avenue Mayenne. There are trains to Paris, Toulouse, Bordeaux, Agen and Moissac.

Buses to Albi, Moissac and Toulouse leave from the bus station (☎ 63.63.88.88) on Avenue Mayenne.

Burgundy

The Dukedom of Burgundy (Bourgogne), situated on the great trade route between the Mediterranean and northern Europe, waxed wealthier and more powerful than the Kingdom of France during the 14th and 15th centuries. It was also larger, and at its height counted Holland, Flanders, Luxembourg and much of the rest of what is now Belgium and far northern France (Picardy, Artois) among its noncontiguous territories. Some of the finest musicians, artists and architects from these lands were brought to the Burgundian capital, Dijon, where they initiated a period of exceptional artistic activity whose legacy still graces the city. Although in the early 1400s it was not beyond the realm of the possible that the Kingdom of France might eventually be absorbed into Burgundy (after all, it was the Burgundians who captured Joan of Arc, later selling her to the English), in the end history unfolded the other way around, and Burgundy became part of France in 1477.

These days, Burgundy is famous for its superb wines (along with Bordeaux, the region produces France's greatest wines), great gastronomy and architectural heritage. Buildings of note include a large number of medieval and Renaissance-era private residences in addition to churches – many of which are topped by the region's distinctive, multicoloured tile roofs – and monasteries. Many of the latter belonged to either the ascetic Cistercian order or its bitter rival, the less severe but powerful and very rich Benedictine order. The Benedictines, who in the 1100s controlled some 1450 monasteries across Europe, had their headquarters at the enormous abbey of Cluny (about 75 km south of Dijon), which was virtually destroyed during and after the Revolution.

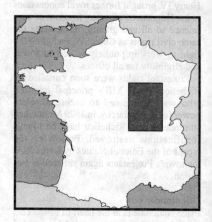

FOOD & DRINK
Cuisine
Burgundian cuisine is solid, substantial and served in generous portions. The region's best known dish, *bœuf bourguignon* is beef cooked in a red wine sauce made with mushrooms, onions and bacon bits. Any dish described as *à la bourguignonne* will be prepared with a similar wine sauce (known as a *meurette* in these parts). Many other Burgundian dishes are made with cream. Burgundy is renowned for its excellent restaurants, whose talented chefs are able to avail themselves of the region's high-quality vegetables, meats and wines. By the way, *fondue bourguignonne*, which is almost unknown in these parts, is named not after Burgundy but after the Percée de Bourgogne, a pass near Neuchâtel, Switzerland.

The region's most famous condiment is mustard, which, like the grape vine, was introduced to Gaul by the Romans. Indeed, Dijon is the mustard-making capital of the world. Its multitude of speciality mustards are made with everything from tarragon to honey and range in taste from delicate to fiery. See Things to Buy in the Dijon section for details on where to purchase real Dijonnais mustards.

Other traditional Burgundian products

Burgundy (Bourgogne)

0   15   30 km

Map labels:

To Paris (100 km)
SENS
AUBE
To Troyes (10 km)
To Nancy (80 km)
CHAUMONT
HAUTE-MARNE
N77
TGV Sud-Est
N6
Chaource
Bar-sur-Seine
A5
Joigny
St Florentin
Chateauvillain
D65
Migennes
To Paris (150 km)
AUXERRE
Tonnerre
Château de Tanlay
Chatillon-sur-Seine
Langres
N74
Chablis
Château d'Ancy-le-Franc
A6
Area
N151
YONNE
Montbard
Former Abbey of Fontenay
Vermenton
D6
CÔTE-D'OR
A31
Vézelay-Sermizelles Railway Station
Semur-en-Auxois
N71
Asquins
Avallon
Vitteaux
A38
DIJON
Clamecy
Vézelay
Menades
Canal de Bourgogne
St Père
A6
See Côte d'Or Map
N5
Varzy
St Jean de Losne
Dun-les-Places
Saulieu
Pouilly-en-Auxois
DÔLE
Corbigny
St Brisson
N81
To Besançon (40 km)
NIÈVRE
Parc Naturel Régional du Morvan
N6
Saône River
To Nevers (20 km)
D978
Château Chinon
Château de Sully
BEAUNE
A36
Doubs River
Mt Beuvray
AUTUN
Chagny
N73
Decize
Étang-sur-Arroux
CHALON-SUR-SAÔNE
To Geneva
N81
LE CREUSOT
Luzy
N80
MONTCEAU
SAÔNE-ET-LOIRE
Seille River
Louhans
N78
MOULINS
N79
N70
Canal du Centre
Tournus
A6
TGV Sud-Est
Digoin
Butte de Suin
N83
Paray-le-Monial
Charolles
Cluny
MÂCON
Canal de Roanne à Digoin
Chaufailles
N79
BOURG-EN-BRESSE
To Geneva (88 km)
To Lyon (20 km)
A40
A42
To Chambéry (85 km)
Roanne

NIVERNAIS
Yonne
Canal du Nivernais
Canal Latéral à la Loire
Loire River
Arroux
B R E S S E

include gingerbread (which traditionally takes six to eight weeks to prepare), black *escargots* (snails) raised on grape leaves – reputed to be the tastiest in all of France – and blackcurrants. The latter are used to make both jams and *crème de cassis*, a sweet blackcurrant liqueur that is combined with white wine (traditionally Aligoté) to make the apéritif known as kir.

Wine

For information on Burgundian wines, see the Côte d'Or listing.

MEDIA
Radio

From July to early September, information in English on festivals, exhibitions and other cultural events being held in Burgundy is broadcast daily at 6 pm on 103.7 MHz (in the Dijon and Beaune areas) and 87.8 MHz (in the Châtillon-sur-Seine and Montbard areas) on the FM band. There are also broadcasts in German (9 am), French (10.30 am) and Dutch (11 am).

WORK

For information on getting a job on the *vendange* (grape harvest), which takes place in late September and early October, or summertime archaeological excavations, see Work in the Facts for the Visitor chapter.

OUTDOOR ACTIVITIES

Burgundy is endowed with vast open spaces given over to both forests and various kinds of agriculture. The 173,000-hectare Parc Naturel Régional du Morvan (Morvan Regional Park), which was created in 1970 and takes up virtually the whole hilly, village-dotted area between Autun, Avallon and Vézelay, offers hiking (along the GR 13, for instance), horse riding, cycling, fishing, river canoeing and, on the lakes, water sports.

The Maison du Parc (☎ 86.78.70.16; fax 86.78.74.22), the park's headquarters, is in Saint Brisson (postcode 58230), which is about 90 km west of Dijon. The southern part of the park can be reached by bus from Autun; the northern section is accessible by bus from Avallon.

The département of Côte d'Or, of which Dijon and Beaune are part, has many hundreds of km of trails (including parts of the GR2 and the GR7), a number of which take you through some of France's most beautiful wine-growing areas. *Hiking Tours – La Côte d'Or*, a brochure published by the Comité Départemental de la Randonnée Pédestre de la Côte d'Or, provides a brief summary of hiking itineraries, the maps you'll need and accommodation (gîtes, camping grounds, etc). It is available at tourist offices.

GETTING AROUND
Train

If you'll be doing a lot of travelling by train around Burgundy, ask at a train station for a copy of the free booklet of schedules entitled *Guide Régional des Transports*, which covers all the region's train routes.

Boating on Burgundy's Waterways

One of the most relaxing ways to see Burgundy is to rent a boat for a leisurely cruise along one of the region's 1200 km of canals and navigable rivers, whose slow-moving, tree-lined channels pass through some of the most beautiful countryside in France. Travel upriver is accomplished through the use of locks *(écluses)*, where you can hop ashore and meet the lock-keeper, who may, as a sideline, sell local produce, such as fruit or cheese. It is good form to help open the sluice gates. There is no charge to pass through a lock, though some people leave a tip with the lock-keeper.

Generally, the boats available for hire can accommodate from four to 12 passengers and are outfitted with sleeping berths, sheets, blankets, pillows, a fridge, a hotplate, an oven, silverware, plates, a shower and a toilet. Anyone over 18 can pilot a river boat without a special licence (though you do need a licence to fish). Before departure, first-time skippers are given instructions on relevant laws and conventions and how to operate the boat. The speed limit is 6 km/h on the canals and 10 km/h on the rivers.

Since most of the canals are 38.5 metres wide, there's plenty of space to stop your craft or moor for the night wherever you like: at an interesting historical site, at a village or in the middle of nowhere. Figure on covering about 20 to 25 km a day. Personal equipment you might want to bring along includes binoculars, tennis shoes and wet-weather gear.

Burgundy's navigable inland waterways include the rivers Yonne, Saône and Seille and a network of canals excavated between the 17th and 19th centuries to link three of France's most important rivers: the Saône, the Loire and the Rhône. Among these works of prerail engineering are the Canal de Bourgogne (which has 189 locks and one 3.3-km-long tunnel along its 242 km), the Canal du Nivernais, the Canal du Centre (known for its lively traffic of commercial barges), the Canal du Loing, the Canal de Briare (built between 1604 and 1642), the Canal Latéral à la Loire and the Canal de Roanne à Digoin. Navigational charts and guidebooks for the area are published by Éditions Cartographiques Maritimes and Vagnon and are available either where you pick up your boat or at well-stocked bookshops. With a few exceptions, the locks are open for passage every day of the year except 1 January, Easter Sunday, 1 May, Pentecost (ie Whit Sunday), 14 July, 1 November, 11 November and 25 December.

The Comité Régional de Tourisme de Bourgogne (☎ 80.50.10.20; fax 80.30.59.45), whose mailing address is Boîte Postale 1602, 21035 Dijon CEDEX, publishes an excellent information brochure entitled *Boating Holidays in Burgundy*.

Rental Canal boats can be rented for a weekend (late Friday afternoon to Monday morning), a short week (from Monday afternoon to Friday morning), a week (Saturday afternoon to Saturday morning or Monday afternoon to Monday morning) or a number of weeks. However, from late June to early September, when demand is at its most intense, the minimum rental period is generally one week.

For a four-person craft, the rates for a weekend or short week range from 1500FF

(10 October to 10 April) to 2100FF (in late spring or the latter half of September). Weekly rates are 2500FF from 10 October to 10 April and rise to a peak of 4800FF in July and August. These prices do not include fuel, for which you should figure on paying 400 to 500FF a week, depending on how far you travel.

Although for much of the year rental can be arranged with only a day or two's advance notice, it's a good idea to reserve in advance, especially if you're not familiar with the exact dates of France's school holidays. If you want to have any chance of getting a boat in July and August, reservations must be made several months in advance.

Among the places where you can arrange boat rental is Bateaux de Bourgogne (☎ 86.52.18.99, 86.51.12.05; fax 86.51.68.47) at 1-2 Quai de la République, 89000 Auxerre, a grouping of about a dozen companies that hire out boats from a number of places in Burgundy, including Auxerre itself. The office is open Monday to Friday (and, from mid-March to mid-October, on Saturday, too) from 8.30 am to noon and 2 to 6.30 pm (5.30 pm on Friday).

To get a copy of Bateaux de Bourgogne's excellent and detailed brochure and a booking form, visit their office or contact them by letter, fax or phone. The company requires a 30% deposit when the booking is made and full payment four weeks before your scheduled holiday. Before sailing away, you have to leave a deposit equal to the boat's insurance excess (deductible), which is somewhere between 2000 and 5000FF. Except in cases of illness or death in the family, reimbursement may not be possible if you cancel your reservation less than four weeks before your rental date.

Other rental companies you might contact include:

Aquarelle
Port de Plaisance, Quai Saint Martin, 89000 Auxerre (☎ 86.46.96.77; fax 86.52.55.31). It is one of the member companies of Bateaux de Bourgogne. The office is open Monday to Friday (and, from April to October, on weekends too) from 9 am to noon and 2 to 6 pm (7 pm from April to October).

Burgundy Cruisers

8 Route Nationale, 89460 Cravant-Accolay (☎ 86.81.54.55). Its boats depart from Vermenton, 23 km south-east of Auxerre.

Navigation Fluviale du Charolais

Boîte Postale 4, 71160 Digoin (☎ 85.85.29.19, 85.88.92.31). Digoin is 67 km south of Autun.

Locaboat Plaisance

Port au Bois, 89300 Joigny (☎ 86.91.72.72; fax 86.62.42.41). It has boats leaving from Dijon, Joigny (27 km north-west of Auxerre) and Corre (110 km north-east of Dijon).

Crown Blue Line

See Canal Boats under Activities in the Facts for the Visitor chapter for details on Crown Blue Line, which has bases at Saint Jean de Losne (35 km south-east of Dijon) and Pouilly-en-Auxois (45 km west of Dijon).

Balloon

Air Adventures (☎ 80.90.74.23; fax 80.90. 72.86), based in Pouilly-en-Auxois (43 km west of Dijon), offers hot-air balloon (*montgolfière*) rides over Burgundy whenever that weather conditions permit. For details, call, fax or write to them. Their mailing address is Ave du Général de Gaulle, 21320 Pouilly-en-Auxois. You might also contact Air Escargot (☎ 85.87.12.30) at Remigny, 71150 Chagny (16 km south of Beaune). Many travel agents in France can make bookings.

DIJON

The prosperous city of Dijon (population 146,000), capital of the dukes of Burgundy for almost 500 years (from the early 11th century until the late 1400s), reached the height of its brilliance during the 14th and 15th centuries under Philippe le Hardi (Philip the Bold), Jean sans Peur (John the Fearless) and Philippe le Bon (Philip the Good). During their reigns, the Burgundian court was among the continent's most illustrious, and Dijon was turned into one of the great centres of European art.

Modern Dijon, mustard capital of the world, is one of the most appealing of France's provincial cities, with an inviting city centre graced by elegant residences built during the Middle Ages and the Renaissance. Despite its long history, the city has a distinctly youthful air, in part because of the major university situated here.

Dijon is just north of the renowned vineyards of the Côte d'Or, one of the world's foremost wine-growing regions.

Orientation

Dijon's main thoroughfare runs from the train station to Église Saint Michel. Ave Maréchal Foch links the train station with the tourist office; Rue de la Liberté, a semi-pedestrian mall that serves as the main shopping street, runs between Porte Guillaume (a triumphal arch erected in 1788) and the Palais des Ducs (Ducal Palace). The social centre of old Dijon is Place François Rude, a popular hang-out when the weather is nice. Place Grangier, with its many bus stops and the main post office, is a block north of Rue de la Liberté. The main university campus is a couple of km east of the centre of town.

Information

The Carte d'Accès aux Musées, a combo ticket that gets you into Dijon's seven major museums, costs only 14FF (7FF for students and people over 60). It can by purchased at museum ticket counters. All Dijon's museums are closed on Tuesday, except the Musée Magnin, which is closed on Monday. Several museums are free on Sunday.

Tourist Office The main tourist office (☎ 80.43.42.12) is at Place Darcy, which is 300 metres east of the train station along Ave Maréchal Foch. From mid-November to mid-April, it is is open every day from 9 am to noon and 2 pm to 7 pm. During the rest of the year, hours are 9 am to 8 pm (9 pm from June to mid-September) daily. It is closed on 25 December and 1 January. Hotel reservations cost 15FF for places in Burgundy and 30FF for places elsewhere in France.

Their free English (or part-English) brochures include a hotel and restaurant guide for Dijon and its environs, a tourist map of the city centre and a list of the city's museums. A 1:250,000 scale road map of the Dijon area costs 23FF. For information on tours offered by the tourist office, see the Organised Tours section.

The tourist office annexe (☎ 80.30.35.39) at 34 Rue des Forges, which is opposite the north side of the Palais des Ducs, is housed in the magnificent Hôtel Chambellan (see the Medieval & Renaissance Houses section). It is open Monday to Friday from 9 am to noon and 2 to 6 pm (5 pm on Friday from mid-November to mid-April).

Money The Banque de France (☎ 80.40.41.50), at 2 Place de la Banque (just north of the Halles du Marché, the city's covered market), is open Monday to Friday from 8.45 am to noon and 1.15 to 3.30 pm.

Rue de la Liberté is home to a number of banks, among them the Crédit Lyonnais at 6 Rue de la Liberté. The banks at Place du Théâtre (near the Musée des Beaux-Arts) include a Caisse d'Épargne (☎ 80.63.10.60) at 1 Rue Philippe Pot, where currency can be exchanged Monday to Friday from 9 am to 5 pm (4.30 pm on Friday). There are a couple of exchange bureaux at Place Grangier (next to the main post office).

The tourist office will change money – at disadvantageous rates – whenever it's open. The Caixa Bank at 23 Place Darcy (opposite the tourist office) has a 24-hour banknote exchange machine.

Post The main post office (☎ 80.50.62.14, 80.50.61.11) is at Place Grangier. It's open weekdays from 8 am to 7 pm and on Saturday from 8 am to noon. Exchange services are available.

Dijon's postcode is 21000.

Travel Agencies BIJ tickets can be purchased at the Frantour Tourisme office (☎ 80.43.32.01; open Monday to Friday) in the train station building and at the Wasteels office (open Monday to Saturday) at 20 Ave Maréchal Foch.

Reasonably priced, long-haul air tickets are available from Nouvelles Frontières (☎ 80.31.89.30) at 7 Place des Cordeliers, which is open Monday to Friday from 9 am

to 1 pm and 2 to 7 pm, and on Saturday from 9 am to noon and 2 to 6 pm.

Maps Dijon's best source of maps is the Institut Géographique National (IGN) store (☎ 80.30.33.67) at 2 Rue Michelet. It's open Monday to Thursday from 9 am to noon and 2 to 5 pm and on Friday from 9 am to 4 pm.

Laundry Two blocks north of the train station, the Lavomatique at 36 Rue Guillaume Tell, which also has self-service dry cleaning, is open daily from 6 am to 9 pm. The laundrette at 41 Rue Auguste Comte, midway between the Palais des Ducs and Place de la République, charges 20FF for 8 kg. The self-service laundries at 17 Rue Pasteur and 28 Rue Berbisey are open daily from 7 am to 9 pm.

Medical Services The Hôpital Général (☎ 80.41.81.41) is at 3 Rue Faubourg Raines.

Walking Tours

The most interesting area for a walk is along Rue de la Liberté and the streets around Église Notre Dame (see Medieval & Renaissance Houses).

Palais des Ducs

The Palais des Ducs et des États de Bourgogne (Palace of the Dukes & States-General of Burgundy) served as the palace of the dukes of Burgundy. Its classical appearance is the result of 17th and 18th-century remodelling and additions carried out at the behest of the States-General of Burgundy, whose three estates (the Nobility, the Clergy and the Third Estate) used to meet here every three years beginning in 1688.

Dijon's Hôtel de Ville occupies most of the western part of the palace. The Salle des États is closed to the public, but you can visit the **Escalier Gabriel**, a monumental marble staircase off the passageway in the south side of the Cour (courtyard) de Flore. It was built between 1733 and 1738 and is named after the architect who designed it. The room at the top is used for art and photography exhibitions.

Dijon

0   125   250 m

Many streets are one-way
or pedestrian only

Avenue Victor Hugo

Rue Guillaume Tell

Avenue Montmartre

Rue Jacques Cellerier

Rue des Fleurs

Rue Audra

Rue Devosge

Rue du Château

Rue des Godrans

15

Rue des Perrières

R. du Rosoir

Ave de la 1ère Armée

Place
Darcy

Boulevard de Brosses

6

1

3

5

Ave Maréchal Foch

7   8

9

10

Place
Darcy

12

Rue de
la Poste

Place
Grangier

Temple

13

14

Rue
du Château

Rue
Musette

Rue
Liberté

Rue
du Bourg

33   34

Boulevard de Sévigné

11

Rue Dr Chaussier

Rue du Maret

28

29

Rue du Chapeau
Rouge

30

32

53

Rue Bossuet

Avenue Albert 1er

To Chartreuse de
Champmol (1 km),
Camping du Lac
(1.3 km) &
Paris (313 km)

Jardin de
l'Arquebuse
(Botanical
Gardens)

Rue de l'Arquebuse

Rue Mariotte

23

24

25

Place
Saint
Bénigne

26

27

Rue Michelet

31

Rue Danton

Pl. Bossuet

50   51

52

Rue Piron

Rue Charrue

Rue du
Faubourg Raines

Rue du Fbg Raines

Ouche River

Rue Condorcet

Rue Monge

48   49

Rue

Berbisey

66

Rue Sainte Anne

65

64

Quai Nicolas Rolin

Rue de l'Hôpital

63

R. de la Manutention

Rue de Tivoli

Rue Turgot

Canal de Bourgogne

Place du
1er Mai

Port du
Canal

Ave Jean Jaurès

To ADA
Car Rental
(1 km)

Rue du Transvaal

Rue du Petit Cîteaux

Rue Daubenton

Misericorde

Rempart

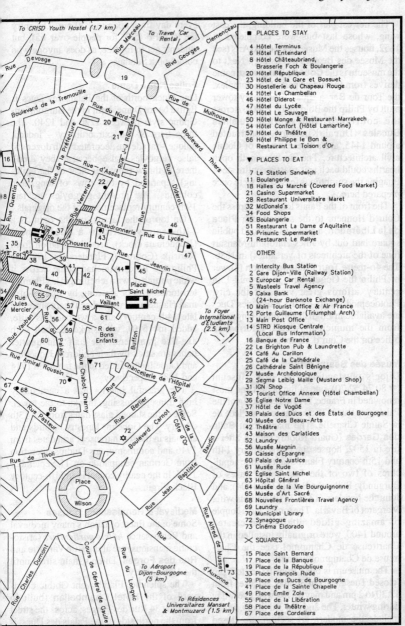

■ PLACES TO STAY

4 Hôtel Terminus
6 Hôtel l'Entendard
8 Hôtel Châteaubriand,
   Brasserie Foch & Boulangerie
20 Hôtel République
23 Hôtel de la Gare et Bossuet
30 Hostellerie du Chapeau Rouge
44 Hôtel Le Chambellan
46 Hôtel Diderot
47 Hôtel du Lycée
48 Hôtel Le Sauvage
50 Hôtel Monge & Restaurant Marrakech
54 Hôtel Confort (Hôtel Lamartine)
57 Hôtel du Théâtre
66 Hôtel Philippe le Bon &
   Restaurant La Toison d'Or

▼ PLACES TO EAT

7 Le Station Sandwich
11 Boulangerie
18 Halles du Marché (Covered Food Market)
21 Casino Supermarket
28 Restaurant Universitaire Maret
32 McDonald's
34 Food Shops
40 Boulangerie
51 Restaurant La Dame d'Aquitaine
53 Prisunic Supermarket
71 Restaurant Le Rallye

OTHER

1 Intercity Bus Station
2 Gare Dijon-Ville (Railway Station)
3 Europcar Car Rental
5 Wasteels Travel Agency
9 Caixa Bank
   (24-hour Banknote Exchange)
10 Main Tourist Office & Air France
12 Porte Guillaume (Triumphal Arch)
13 Main Post Office
14 STRD Kiosque Centrale
   (Local Bus Information)
16 Banque de France
22 Le Brighton Pub & Laundrette
24 Café Au Carillon
25 Café de la Cathédrale
26 Cathédrale Saint Bénigne
27 Musée Archéologique
31 IGN Shop
33 Segma Leibig Maille (Mustard Shop)
35 Tourist Office Annexe (Hôtel Chambellan)
36 Église Notre Dame
37 Hôtel de Vogüé
38 Palais des Ducs et des États de Bourgogne
40 Musée des Beaux-Arts
42 Théâtre
49 Maison des Cariatides
52 Laundry
56 Musée Magnin
59 Caisse d'Epargne
60 Palais de Justice
61 Musée Rude
62 Église Saint Michel
63 Hôpital Général
64 Musée de la Vie Bourguignonne
65 Musée d'Art Sacré
68 Nouvelles Frontières Travel Agency
69 Laundry
70 Municipal Library
72 Synagogue
73 Cinéma Eldorado

✕ SQUARES

15 Place Saint Bernard
17 Place de la Banque
19 Place de la République
39 Place François Rude
41 Place de la Sainte Chapelle
49 Place Émile Zola
55 Place de la Libération
58 Place du Théâtre
67 Place des Cordeliers

BURGUNDY

The newest part of the building, the east wing, whose last bits were completed in 1852, houses the Musée des Beaux-Arts (see the Musée des Beaux-Arts listing). Next to the museum is the **Cour de Bar**, whose name derives from the oldest part of the complex, the Tour de Bar, a squat, four-storey tower built by Philip the Bold in the 1360s. Across the courtyard, the vaulted **Cuisines Ducales** (Ducal Kitchens), constructed around 1445, are a fine example of Gothic civil architecture. The six mammoth open hearths could each spit-roast an entire steer. Imagine the sumptuous feasts that were once prepared here...

The front of the Palais looks out across the Cour d'Honneur to the semicircular **Place de la Libération**, a gracious, arcaded public square laid out by Jules Hardouin-Mansart (one of the architects of Versailles) in 1686. The 46-metre **Tour Philippe le Bon** (Tower of Philip the Good), built in the mid-15th century, affords great views of the city. Photocopied sheets on the Palais des Ducs are available in English and other languages from the municipal Accueil-Information office on the Cour d'Honneur.

Musée des Beaux-Arts
Dijon's outstanding Fine Arts Museum (☎ 80.74.52.70), one of the richest and most renowned in France, is in the east wing of the Palais des Ducs. The entrance is at Place de la Sainte Chapelle. The magnificent **Salle des Gardes** (Guard Room), rebuilt after a fire in 1502, houses the extraordinary 14th and 15th-century Flamboyant Gothic sepulchres of two of the first Valois dukes of Burgundy: Philip the Bold (1342-1404); and John the Fearless (1371-1419) and his wife, Margaret of Bavaria. The tombs and a couple of amazing gilded altarpieces, created around 1400, were originally installed in the Chartreuse de Champmol (see the Chartreuse de Champmol listing).

The museum is open from 10 am to 6 pm (closed Tuesday). On Sunday, it closes from 12.30 to 2 pm and may do likewise every day during winter. The 2nd and 3rd floors, which include the modern art section, are closed every day from noon to 2.20 pm. The entry fee is 10FF (5FF for people over 65), but students get in for free, as does anyone who comes on a Sunday.

Église Notre Dame
One block north of the Palais des Ducs is Église Notre Dame, built in the Burgundian-Gothic style between 1220 and 1240. The three tiers of the extraordinary – indeed, unique – façade are decorated with dozens of false gargoyles (false because they aren't there to throw rainwater clear of the building) separated by two rows of long, thin columns. The present gargoyles are late 19th-century replacements of the originals.

On top of the façade, on the right, is a 14th-century **Horloge à Jacquemart** (Jacquemart clock), brought to Dijon from Kortrijk (Courtrai), Flanders, in 1382 by Philip the Bold, who had come across it while putting down a rebellion in his Flemish territories. Hours are rung by figures of a man (Jaquemart, who's been there since the late 14th century) and a woman (his wife, added in 1610), who strike the bell with axe-like hammers. The half and quarter hours are stuck by their children, Jaquelinet and Jaquelinette, added to the family in 1714 and 1881 respectively.

The graceful interior has a particularly high transept crossing, thanks to the tower. Some of the stained glass dates from the 13th century. The Gobelins tapestry of birds and animals in the south transept arm dates from 1946 and commemorates Dijon's liberation from German occupation on 11 September 1944. In the nearby chapel is an 11th-century Black Virgin.

Medieval & Renaissance Houses
Some of the finest of Dijon's many medieval and Renaissance *hôtels particuliers* (aristocratic mansions) are along **Rue Verrerie** and **Rue des Forges**, Dijon's main street until the 18th century.

The splendid, Flamboyant Gothic courtyard of the **Hôtel Chambellan** (built in 1490) at 34 Rue des Forges, across the street from the north side of the Palais des Ducs, is now home to a branch of the tourist office. At the top of the spiral stone staircase, there's a remarkable bit of vaulting – a sort of male caryatid holding a basket supports the roof.

Rue de la Chouette, where there are more old residences, runs along the north side of Église Notre Dame. It is named for the small, stone owl *(chouette)* carved into the exterior corner of one of the chapels on the north side of the church, which people pet to gain happiness and wisdom. The **Hôtel de Vogüé** at 8 Rue de la Chouette, erected around 1614, is known for its ornate Renaissance-style courtyard. It is now occupied by municipal offices. The courtyard, reached via an arched entryway built in the early 18th century, is open to visitors all day every day.

A couple of blocks further east at 28 Rue Chaudronnerie, the **Maison des Cariatides** (House of the Caryatids), built in the early 17th century by a rich family of copper merchants, has a façade decorated with stone caryatids and faces.

Église Saint Michel

Construction of Église Saint Michel, which is a few hundred metres east of the Musée des Beaux-Arts, was begun in the 15th century in the Flamboyant Gothic style. By the 16th century, when it came time to build the west front, architectural tastes had changed, and the church was given an impressive, richly ornamented Renaissance façade, considered among the most beautiful in France. The two cupola-topped towers date from 1667.

Musée Rude

The small Musée Rude (☎ 80.66.87.95), housed in a desanctified church on Rue Vaillant (opposite the façade of Église Saint Michel), has quite a few works (and copies of works) by the sculptor François Rude (1784-1855), who was born in Dijon. From June to September *only*, the museum is open from 10 am to noon and 2 to 5.45 pm (closed Tuesday). Entrance is free.

Musée National Magnin

The collection of 2000 assorted works of art assembled by the sister-and-brother team of Jeanne and Maurice Magnin around the turn of the century are today housed in the Magnin family's ancestral home, a mid-17th-century residence at 4 Rue des Bons Enfants.

The Musée Magnin (☎ 80.67.11.10) is open from 10 am to noon and 2 to 6 pm (closed Monday). From June to September, it does not close at midday. The entrance fee is 12FF (7FF for students under 25).

Palais de Justice

The law courts, which are one block southeast of Place de la Libération on Rue du Palais, were built as the Palais du Parlement du Bourgogne (Palace of the Burgundian Parliament) in the 16th and 17th centuries. Although modified in the 19th century, it retains its Renaissance-style façade of 1572. The wooden door is a copy (the original is in the Musée des Beaux-Arts).

Inside, the **Chambre Dorée**, which dates from 1522, retains much of its original decoration; when the court is not in session, it's open at no charge to visitors. When the court *is* in session, it may be possible to sit in on a trial.

Cathédrale Saint Bénigne

Situated on top of what may be the tomb of St Benignus (who by tradition is held to have brought Christianity to Burgundy in the 2nd century), Cathédrale Saint Bénigne was built in the Burgundian Gothic style as an abbey church between 1280 and the early 14th century. The spire was added in 1894. Many of the great figures of Burgundy's history are buried inside.

The cathedral is open daily from 8.45 am to 7 pm. From around Easter to October *only*, the Romanesque crypt (3FF) – all that remains of a large Romanesque abbey church constructed between 1001 and 1026 – is open daily from 9 am to 6 pm.

Musée Archéologique

The Archaeological Museum (☎ 80.30. 88.54), whose collections include a number of rare Celtic and Gallo-Roman artefacts, is next to the cathedral at 5 Rue du Docteur Maret. It is open from 9 am (9.30 am from June to August) to noon and 2 to 6 pm (closed Tuesday). There is no midday closure during June, July and August. Entry costs 9FF but is free on Sunday and holidays.

The Romanesque chamber on the lowest level, part of a Benedictine abbey founded in the 9th century, is from the early 11th century. The huge, vaulted hall upstairs is the abbey's dormitory, an early Gothic structure built in the 12th and 13th centuries. The museum has on display a number of extremely rare Celtic (Gallic and Gallo-Roman) artefacts made of wood, stone and metal, including jewellery from 950 BC, votive figures from the 1st century AD and a bronze representation of the goddess Sequana standing on a boat, also from the 1st century.

Musée d'Art Sacré

This museum (☎ 80.30.06.44) at 15 Rue Sainte Anne displays ecclesiastical objects from the 12th to 19th centuries. It is housed in the rotunda and chapels of a neoclassical church completed in 1709. Look for the radiant sun emblems of the Sun King, Louis XIV, during whose reign it was built. This place is worth a visit just for the building, though if you like ritual objects the ones here are of more interest than those in most cathedral treasuries. The museum is open from 9 am to noon and 2 to 6 pm (closed Tuesday). Entrance costs 8FF (4FF reduced price).

Musée de la Vie Bourguignonne

Almost next door at 17 Rue Sainte Anne is the Musée de la Vie Bourguignonne (☎ 80.30.65.91), whose period rooms – housed in a 17th-century Cistercian convent – illustrate how the rural people of Burgundy lived, cooked, dressed, etc in centuries past. The museum also hosts frequent temporary exhibitions of a high calibre. Regrettably, all the signs are in French. This place is open the same hours as the Musée d'Art Sacré. The entry charge is 9FF (4.50FF for people aged 18 to 24 or over 65); students and teachers get in for free.

Synagogue

Dijon's domed and turreted main synagogue was inaugurated in 1879. The structure, built in the Romano-Byzantine style, is 500 metres south of the Musée des Beaux-Arts on Rue de la Synagogue.

Chartreuse de Champmol

This charterhouse (chartreuse, ie Carthusian monastery), founded in 1383 by Philip the Bold, Duke of Burgundy, as a burial place for himself and his Valois successors, was decorated by the most illustrious artists of the period. It was almost completely destroyed during the Revolution (1793), but a number of medieval masterpieces survived, including the magnificent tombs and retables now on display in the Salle des Gardes in Dijon's Musée des Beaux-Arts. At the charterhouse site, you can still see the Puits de Moïse (Well of Moses) and the Portail de la Chapelle (Doorway to the Chapel).

Although the spacious, parklike campus now serves as a psychiatric hospital, these works are open to the public without charge every day from 8 am to 6 pm (unofficially until 8 pm). The main entrance (☎ 80.42.48.48 for the gatehouse) is 1.5 km west of the train station at 1 Rue Chanoine Kir, but there are plans to open up the 15th-century gate on Ave Albert 1er, which is only 700 metres from the train station. To get to the main entrance, take bus No 12 (towards Fontaine d'Ouche) from the train station or Rue de la Liberté and get off at the Hôpital des Chartreux stop. To get there on foot, walk westward from the train station along Blvd Albert 1er.

The **Puits de Moïse**, a hexagonal grouping of six Old Testament figures created between 1395 and 1405 by Haarlem-born Claus Sluter, is a truly exceptional work of sculpture. It takes its name from the bearded figure of Moses (who, as was usual in Church art of the Middle Ages and Renaissance, is portrayed as having horns because the Hebrew word 'karnayim', which means both 'horns' and 'rays of light' but in the context of the Moses story has the latter meaning, was misunderstood by translators).

All six figures (the other five are of Daniel, David, Isaiah, Jeramiah and Zachariah), whose medieval garb was once brightly painted, are endowed with realistic postures and facial expressions that evoke with great power the difficulties they suffered as leaders. To get to the Puits de Moïse from the entrance, follow the signs and the grey line for about 400 metres.

Sluter fans may also want to visit the **Portail de la Chapelle**, created from 1389 to 1394 and now inside the chapel's antechamber. Philip the Bold and Margaret of Flanders are portrayed kneeling on either side of the Virgin, who is holding the infant Jesus. Their expressions and postures are remarkable for their vigour and realism. The couple is watched over by St John the Baptist (his patron saint) and St Catherine (her patron saint). The chapel itself dates from 1840.

Organised Tours
The tourist office runs (or acts as ticket agent for) a number of guided tours. The most flexible option is their two-hour Visite Autoguidée (Self-Guided City Tour). The 35FF fee gets you a Walkman, a commentary (in English, French, German or Italian) on cassette tape and a map. During July, August and September, walking tours of Dijon in French (though the guide may know some English) leave every day from the main tourist office at 3 pm – and, during July and August, at 10 pm from the Place de la Libération entrance to the Palais des Ducs. The cost is 35FF (20FF for students).

Half and full-day coach trips (175 to 310FF) to various parts of Burgundy (eg vineyards and chateaux in the Beaune area), conducted in English and French, are available several times a week from mid-April until late October.

Festivals
Dance and music troupes come from five continents to participate in the city's Folkloriades Internationales et Fêtes de la Vigne, a folklore festival held each year in late August or early September. Information is available from the Dijon tourist office or the Festival de Musiques et Danses Populaires (☎ 80.30.37.95; fax 80.30.23.44), 27 Blvd de la Trémouille, 21025 Dijon CEDEX.

Places to Stay – bottom end
For two or more people, the simplest rooms at one of Dijon's many inexpensive one and two-star hotels will be less expensive, and a lot more convenient, than staying at one of the hostels. Many of the smaller hotels are closed on Sunday afternoon from noon to 5 pm.

Camping The two-star *Camping du Lac* (☎ 80.43.54.72) at 3 Blvd Chanoine Kir (named after the Dijon mayor who invented the apéritif that bears his name) is 1.5 km west of the train station behind the psychiatric hospital. It is open from April to mid-November. Guests pay 8FF each, a tent emplacement is 4FF and parking costs 4FF. If you arrive on foot, there's almost always room for a small tent.

To get here from the train station, take bus No 12 (towards Fontaine d'Ouche) and get off at Hôpital des Chartreux stop. Service stops around 8 pm. On foot, go out the train station exit next to the stairs leading up to track *(voie)* J and turn right (westward) onto Blvd Albert 1er. Turn left onto Blvd Chanoine Kir and then take an almost immediate left.

Hostels The *Foyer International d'étudiants* (☎ 80.71.51.01) at 6 Rue Maréchal Leclerc, 2.5 km east of the centre of town, accepts travellers all year round if there's space (which is most of the time, even in summer). Single rooms are 55FF a night. The cafeteria serves light food every day from 7.30 am (9 am on weekends) to 10 pm. To get there, catch bus No 4 (towards Apollinaire) along Ave Victor Hugo or on Rue de la Liberté and get off at the Billardon stop. This line runs until about 8 pm.

The *Centre de Rencontres Internationales et de Séjour de Dijon* (CRISD; ☎ 80.71.32. 12), Dijon's large (320-bed) and institutional youth hostel, is 2.5 km north-east of the centre of town at 1 Blvd Champollion. Prices range from 62FF (for a bed in a dorm room for up to eight people) to 130FF (for a single). Guests who are not members of a hostelling association pay 8FF extra for the first three nights. Rooms are locked from 10 am to 4 or 5 pm but there's no curfew. Amenities include washing machines and, next door, a municipal swimming pool. Self-service meals cost 37.50 to 44FF. To get to CRISD, take bus No 5 (towards Épirey) from Place Grangier – the last one leaves the city centre every day at about 8.15 pm.

From late May until sometime in September (and during the rest of the year if there's space), travellers can stay at the *Résidence Universitaire Mansart* (☎ 80.66.18.22), a university dorm 2.5 km south-east of the centre of town on the main university campus. The address is 94 Rue Mansart (also spelled 'Mansard'). Reception (the *secrétariat)*, which is in a building made of green glass, is open weekdays from 10 am to noon and 1.15 to 4.45 pm (they may close a bit earlier in July and August). When it's closed, a sign on the door will direct you to the *concierge* or, after 9 pm, the *veilleur de nuit* (night watchperson). New guests can register any time of the day or night. If you have an international student ID card, the charge is 57FF per person. Otherwise, it costs 75FF. To get out here, catch bus No 9 (towards Facultés) at either the train station or along Rue de la Liberté and get off at the Mansart stop.

If Mansart is full, you might try the *Résidence Universitaire Montmuzard* (☎ 80.39.68.22), which is a five-minute walk north at 8 Ave Alain Savary, behind the Faculté de Droit (Law Faculty). The office is open Monday to Friday from 9.30 am to noon and 1.30 to 4.30 pm. Like Mansart, outside of normal business hours there's either a *concierge* or a night watchperson on duty. Prices and conditions are the same as at Mansart.

Hotels – Near the Train Station The two-star *Hôtel Châteaubriand* (☎ 80.41.42.18; fax 80.67.64.51) at 3 Ave Maréchal Foch (1st floor) has singles and doubles for 130 to 165FF (with washbasin and bidet), 140 to 180FF (with shower) and 170 to 190FF (with shower and toilet). Some of the doubles have two twin beds. The rooms are not exactly cheery, but they are spacious and retain a certain old-fashioned charm. Overall, it's a good deal. Breakfast costs 24FF. The hall showers are free.

The *Hôtel l'Entendard* (☎ 80.41.51.32) at 4 Rue des Perrières, half a block from the main tourist office, has serviceable singles and doubles with shower for 130FF (150FF with two beds) and quads with shower and toilet for 250FF. Breakfast is 20FF. Private parking is available. Reception is closed after 9 pm and all-day Saturday. This place closes for two weeks in mid-July and another two weeks around Christmas and New Year.

The *Hôtel de la Gare et Bossuet* (☎ 80.30.46.61), also known as the Hôtel Bossuet et de la Gare, is 250 metres from the train station at 16 Rue Mariotte. On a charm scale from one to 10, this place would score a minus three. Indeed, it has less ambience and warmth than any other hotel we have seen anywhere in France. However, if what you're looking for is an inexpensive place near the train station to store yourself for the night and you don't mind abiding by a few petty and rather annoying rules (ie after 8 pm, when the reception desk closes, you can't check in, pick up the shower key or – without the code, which is changed every single day – even get in the front door), this place is eminently serviceable. Small, nondescript singles/doubles/triples start at 113/131/174FF with washbasin and 143/161/199FF with toilet and shower, including breakfast. On Sunday, reception is closed from noon to 5 pm. Rooms are almost always available in the morning.

Hotels – City Centre The two-star *Hôtel Le Sauvage* (☎ 80.41.31.21; fax 80.42.06.07) at 64 Rue Monge, also signposted as the Hostellerie du Sauvage and the Hôtel du Sauvage, occupies a *relais de poste* (post-house) dating from the 15th century. The large, quiet singles and doubles, many of which overlook the grapevine-shaded courtyard, cost from 130FF (with washbasin and bidet) to 180FF (with shower and toilet). Breakfast is 25FF, while use of the hall showers is free.

Down the block, the friendly and accommodating *Hôtel Monge* (☎ 80.30.55.41) at 20 Rue Monge has singles/doubles starting at 115/125FF with washbasin and 150/160FF with shower. Singles/doubles/two-bed triples with shower, toilet and TV cost 190/200/250. Watch out for super-soft, concave mattresses. Hall showers are 15FF.

The *Hôtel du Théâtre* (☎ 80.67.15.41) at 3 Rue des Bons Enfants is an old place only a block from the Palais des Ducs. Large, simple rooms, some with lots of light, start at 85FF. Singles and doubles with shower are 95 to 112FF; quads with shower cost 200FF. There are no hall showers. This place is often full.

The small *Hôtel Confort* (☎ 80.30.37.47), also known as the Hôtel Lamartine, is at 12 Rue Jules Mercier, an alley off Rue de la Liberté. Decent singles and doubles start at 115FF with washbasin, 145FF with shower and 165FF with shower and toilet. There is a 23FF charge to use the hall shower. On Sunday, reception is closed from noon to 5 pm.

The two-star *Hôtel Le Chambellan* (☎ 80.67.12.67), half a block north of Église Saint Michel at 92 Rue Vannerie, has singles/doubles/two-bed triples with washbasin and bidet for 110/110/140FF. Singles/doubles cost 120/150FF with shower and 160/190FF with shower, toilet and TV. Breakfast (25FF) can be taken in the 17th-century courtyard. Reception closes at 11 pm. From the train station, the Hôtel du Théâtre, Hôtel Confort and Hôtel Le Chambellan can be reached by bus No 12 (towards Quetigny), which can be caught along Blvd de Sévigné.

Hotels – East of the City Centre The *Hôtel Diderot* (☎ 80.67.10.85) at 7 Rue du Lycée has singles, doubles and two-bed triples with washbasin and bidet for 100 to 180FF. The large rooms have high ceilings and are furnished in the prewar style. Showers cost 15FF. Reception may be closed on Sunday afternoon.

The *Hôtel du Lycée* (☎ 80.67.12.35) at 28 Rue du Lycée has ordinary but adequate rooms for 100 or 110FF (with washbasin and bidet) or 130 to 150FF (with shower). For 230FF you can get a room with shower and toilet for up to five people. Hall showers are free. Reception is closed on Sunday from noon and 5 pm. If you arrive late at night, use the buzzer by the door.

To get to either hotel from the train station, take bus No 12 (towards Quetigny) from Blvd de Sévigné and get off at the Théâtre Vaillant stop, which is near Église Saint Michel. You can also take bus No 4 (towards Saint Apollinaire) or bus No 14 (towards Chevigny) from Place Darcy and get off at the Berlier stop, which is on Rue Paul Cabet.

Places to Stay – middle
Near the Train Station There are a number of two and three-star hotels along Ave Maréchal Foch. The rather impersonal, 30-room *Hôtel Terminus* (☎ 80.43.53.78; fax 80.42.84.17) at 22 Ave Maréchal Foch has huge but rather tacky singles/doubles/two-bed doubles with shower, toilet and TV for 200/250/300FF. An extra bed costs 100FF. Breakfast costs 28FF. This place has a lift. Reception is open 24 hours a day.

North of the City Centre The *Hôtel République* (☎ 80.73.36.76; fax 80.72.46.04) is half a block from Place de la République at 3 Rue du Nord. Large, unpretentious singles and doubles cost 157FF with shower and 172FF with shower and toilet. Two-bed triples and quads with shower and toilet are 230FF. If you arrive late at night, ring the bell. To get there from the train station, take bus No 6 (towards La Fleuriée) or bus No 7 (towards Cité du Soleil) and get off at the République Rousseau stop.

Places to Stay – top end
City Centre The four-star, 31-room *Hostellerie du Chapeau Rouge* (☎ 80.30.28.10; fax 80.30.33.89) at 5 Rue Michelet, which is part of the Best Western Hotels group, has

been at this site since 1847. Most of the elegant, air-conditioned singles and doubles cost between 435 and 575FF, though they also have a few rooms for 320FF. The hotel is equipped with a lift and cable-connected TVs. Breakfast costs 55FF. Parking is 16FF. For information on the renowned Hostellerie du Chapeau Rouge restaurant, see the French restaurant section under Places to Eat.

The 27-room *Hôtel Philippe le Bon* (☎ 80.30.73.52; fax 80.30.95.51), a three-star place at 18 Rue Sainte Anne that opened in 1992, has fairly luxurious, comtemporary singles/doubles with cable TV for 300/350 to 350/380FF. Private parking is available at no extra cost. For information on Restaurant La Toison d'Or, which is at the same address and is under the same management, see Places to Eat.

Places to Eat

French For superb traditional Burgundian cuisine, the elegant restaurant of the *Hostellerie du Chapeau Rouge* (☎ 80.30. 28.10; fax 80.30.33.89) at 5 Rue Michelet – long the proud possessor of one Michelin star – is an excellent choice. In addition to à la carte meals, they offer a lunch *menu* for 210FF (including wine) and a dinner *menu* for 190FF (not including wine). The restaurant is open daily from noon to 1.45 pm and 7.30 to 9.45 pm. Reservations are recommended for dinner, especially on weekends.

Restaurant La Toison d'Or (☎ 80.30. 73.52; fax 80.30.95.51) at 18 Rue Sainte Anne, which is also known as the Restaurant Compagnie Bourguignonne des Œnophiles, serves French gastronomic cuisine in a rustic medieval setting. If ordered à la carte, the main dishes cost 90 to 170FF; *menus* are available for 130 and 240FF. This place is open for lunch and dinner daily except Sunday evening.

Restaurant La Dame d'Aquitaine (☎ 80. 30.36.23, 80.30.45.65; fax 80.49.90.41) at 23 Place Bossuet, which is also called Restaurant Le Vinarium, serves south-western French cuisine in a 13th-century crypt. *Menus* for 168, 180 and 225FF are on offer. It is closed all-day Sunday and on Monday

at midday. Another option for quality French cuisine is *Restaurant Le Rallye* (☎ 80.67. 11.55) at 39 Rue Chabot Charny, which has *menus* for 90, 150 and 220FF as well as an à la carte selection. It is open from noon to 2.30 pm and 7.30 to 9.30 pm daily except Sunday and holidays.

Brasseries & Sandwiches You'll find a number of reasonably priced brasseries and cafés along Ave Maréchal Foch, including the café-style *Brasserie Foch* (☎ 80.41. 27.93) at 1bis Ave Maréchal Foch. From Monday to Saturday, it serves meals continuously from 11 am to 10 pm (and sometimes later). The plat du jour is 38FF, and *menus* start at 48FF.

Le Station Sandwich (☎ 80.41.25.25) at 5 Ave Maréchal Foch, purveyor of baguette sandwiches (10 to 20FF) to hungry train travellers and locals, is open daily from 9.30 am to 2 am.

North African *Restaurant Marrakech* (☎ 80. 30.82.69) at 20 Rue Monge offers huge portions of excellent couscous starting at 35FF (without meat) and 46FF (with chicken). Meals are served every evening from 5.30 pm to midnight, and Thursday to Sunday from 10.30 am to 2.30 or 3 pm.

Student Cafeterias The *Restaurant Universitaire Maret* (☎ 80.40.40.34) at 3 Rue du Docteur Maret, next to the Musée Archéologique, has cheap cafeteria food. Except during July and August, it is open on weekdays and one weekend a month. Lunch is served from 11.45 pm to 1.15 pm, dinner is from 6.45 to 7.45 pm. Tickets, on sale on the ground floor whenever the restaurant is open, cost 11.50FF for students.

Both Résidence Universitaire Mansart and Résidence Universitaire Montmuzard (see Hostels under Places to Stay) have university restaurants, at least one of which is open virtually every day.

Bars The *Café Au Carillon* (☎ 80.30.63.71), opposite the cathedral at 2 Rue Mariotte, is extremely popular with young locals. A demi of beer starts at 11FF. Except during August, it is open Monday to Saturday from 6.30 am to 12.30 or 1 am (2 am in summer). Another favourite with students is the informal *Café de la Cathédrale* (☎ 80.30.42.10), across the street at 4 Place Saint Bénigne. A demi of basic draught beer costs 10FF whether you sit inside or on what is said to be the largest *terrasse* in Dijon. It is open daily from 6.30 am to 2 am.

Le Brighton Pub (☎ 80.73.59.32), an English-style pub at 33 Rue Auguste Comte, is open daily from 3 pm (5 pm in winter) until 3 am (4 am on Friday and Saturday nights). In addition to 60 kinds of bottled beer (which regulars sip from their personal mugs, kept in locked cubby holes on the wall) and 60 kinds of whisky, they offer 10 sorts of beer on tap for 13 to 15FF (20FF after 8 pm). From September to May, there is live music (rock, jazz, Irish folk, etc) on Thursday, Friday and Saturday nights starting at about 10.30 pm.

Self-Catering Among the city parks that are perfect for picnics are Square Darcy (next to the tourist office), which was laid out in 1881; Place des Ducs de Bourgogne (just north of the Musée des Beaux-Arts); Place Saint Michel (next to Église Saint Michel); and Jardin de l'Arquebuse, the spacious green area across Ave Albert 1er from the train station.

Dijon has a wide variety of food stores conveniently located in the city centre. The cheapest place to purchase edibles is the *Halles du Marché*, a 19th-century covered market 150 metres north of Rue de la Liberté. It is open Tuesday, Friday and Saturday from 6 am to 1 pm. There are a number of food shops in the immediate vicinity, including a *Nicolas wine shop* (☎ 80.49.94.04) at 6 Rue François Rude (closed all-day Sunday and Monday morning) and several *boulangeries*. There is a *Prisunic supermarket* south of Rue de la Liberté at 11-13 Rue Piron; the food section is upstairs. It is open Monday to Saturday from 8.45 am to 8 pm.

There's a *Casino supermarket* at 16 Rue Jean-Jacques Rousseau, which is half a block south of Place de la République. It is open from 8 am to 12.30 pm and 3 to 7.30 pm daily, except Sunday afternoon and Monday morning. There are five *boulangeries* and a number of *food shops* along the same block.

Near the main tourist office, there is a *boulangerie* at 1 Blvd de Sévigné. It is open Monday to Saturday from 7 am to 7 pm (6.30 pm on Saturday). During July and August, it's closed on Saturday afternoon. The *boulangerie* at 1 Ave Maréchal Foch, which sells ready-made sandwiches, is open daily from 6 am to 8 pm. Near Église Saint Michel, there are *boulangeries* at 81 Rue Vannerie (closed Sunday afternoon and Saturday) and 57 Rue Vannerie.

Entertainment

Cinema The *Cinéma Eldorado* (☎ 80.66.51.89; 80.66.12.34 for a recording in French) at 21 Rue Alfred de Musset specialises in foreign movies that are subtitled rather than dubbed. There are screenings seven days a week starting at about 2 pm. Regular tickets cost 38FF. The 29FF student rate is not available on Saturday or Sunday before 8 pm. The cinema is closed from mid-July to mid-August.

Theatre Dijon's *Théâtre* (☎ 80.67.20.21 for information, 80.67.23.23 for reservations) is at Place du Théâtre, next to the Musée des Beaux-Arts. Operas and operettas are staged from mid-October to late May. The ticket office is open on Monday from 4 to 7 pm and Tuesday to Saturday from 10 am to 7 pm. During July and August, it's open Tuesday to Saturday from 2 to 7 pm. Year-round telephone reservations can be made from Tuesday to Saturday between 2 and 7 pm. Information on performances is available at the tourist office.

Things to Buy

Segma Leibig Maille (☎ 80.30.41.02) at 28 Rue de la Liberté (two shops away from McDonald's) sells nothing but that Dijon speciality, fancy mustard. This is the factory store of the company that makes Grey Poupon and other, more powerful, mustards.

It is open weekdays from 9 am to noon and 2.15 to 7 pm. Saturday hours are almost the same.

Getting There & Away

Air Aéroport Dijon-Bourgogne (☎ 80.67.67.67), Dijon's airport, is six km south-east of the city. There are direct flights to Bordeaux, Clermont-Ferrand, Lille, Toulouse and London's Stanstead Airport.

The Dijon office of Air France (☎ 80.42.89.90) is at Place Darcy in the same little building as the main tourist office.

Train The train station (☎ 80.41.50.50 for information), Gare Dijon-Ville, replaced an earlier structure destroyed in 1944. The information office is open from 8.30 am to 7.15 pm (6.45 pm on Saturday); it's closed on Sunday and holidays.

By TGV, getting to/from Paris's Gare de Lyon (184FF plus the reservation fee; 28 trains a day on weekdays, 23 on weekends) takes only one hour 40 minutes. Non-TGV trains, also to/from Gare de Lyon, take two hours 20 minutes or more. Trains to Lyon's Gare de Perrache or Gare de la Part-Dieu (127FF; about two hours; 18 trains a day on weekdays, 11 to 14 on weekends) are all non-TGV.

There are direct, non-TGV trains to Nice (353FF; seven a day; 7½ hours) and Strasbourg (196FF; eight a day; four hours). For details on train service to Beaune, Autun, Auxerre, Avalon and Vézelay, see the Getting There & Away section under each town's listing.

Bus The intercity bus station (gare routière); ☎ 80.42.11.00) is next to the train station. The Transco information counter is open from 7.30 am to 12.30 pm and 1.45 to 6.30 pm daily except Saturday afternoon and Sunday. There is excellent service from here to destinations all over the département of Côte d'Or. Transco bus No 44 to Beaune (32.80FF; one hour 10 minutes) stops at lots of wine-making villages along the way. See Bus under Getting There & Away in the Beaune section for details.

There's one round trip a day to Autun (68.80FF; 2½ hours); departure from Dijon is around noon. From Monday to Saturday, there are three daily buses to Avallon (two hours 10 minutes); on Sunday, there's only one or two. See Getting There & Away under Avallon for details. To get to Troyes (in Champagne), change buses at Châtillon-sur-Seine.

Car ADA Location de Véhicules (☎ 80.51.90.90) is at 109 Ave Jean Jaurès, 2.5 km south of the train station. To get there, catch bus No 16 (towards Chenove Post) from Place Grangier and get off at the Bourroches Jaurès stop. The office is open Monday to Saturday from 8 am to noon and 2 to 7 pm.

Another inexpensive car rental place you might try is Travel 'Car (☎ 80.72.31.00) at 28 Blvd de la Marne, which is 400 metres north-east of Place de la République.

Getting Around

To/From the Airport From the train station or Rue de la Liberté, take local bus No 5 (towards Longvic) and get off at the Longvic Mairie stop, whence it's a 10-minute walk to the airport.

Bus Dijon's extensive urban bus network is run by STRD (☎ 80.30.60.90). Individual rides cost 4.90FF, a carnet of five tickets is 15.50FF. Seven different bus lines stop along Rue de la Liberté and five more stop at Place Grangier. Bus lines are known by their number and the name of the terminus station. Most STRD buses run Monday to Saturday from 6 am to 8 pm. Sunday service lasts from 1 to 8 pm.

STRD's Kiosque Centrale (information office) at Place Grangier, which has schedules and an excellent route map, is open Tuesday to Friday from 7.15 am to 12.15 pm and 1.15 to 7.15 pm and on Monday and Saturday from 7.15 am to noon and 2 to 7.15 pm.

Taxi There is a taxi rank in the parking lot of the train station. To order a cab by telephone, call ☎ 80.41.41.12.

Top: View of the Cure River valley from Vézelay's old cemetery, Burgundy (DR)
Bottom: View of Auxerre across the Yonne River, Burgundy (DR)

Top: Sun-soaked vineyard in the Corbières, Languedoc (GC)
Middle: Bringing down the wine harvest, Languedoc (GC); Wooden wine barrel
façade, Épernay, Champagne (LL); Wine labels of France (LL)
Bottom: Waiting for the ice to arrive (LL)

CÔTE D'OR

Burgundy's finest vintages come from the vine-covered Côte d'Or (Golden Hillside), the eastern, limestoney slopes of the escarpment that runs south from Dijon for about 60 km. The northern section, the Côte de Nuits, stretches from the village of Fixin south to Corgoloin and produces reds known for being full-bodied and very robust. The southern section, the Côte de Beaune, lies between Aloxe-Corton and Santenay and produces both great reds and great whites. The Côte d'Or's red wines are made from Pinot Noir grapes, while for the whites both Pinot Blanc and Chardonnay are used. All Burgundy's vines are grafted onto a kind of rootstock native to the USA and brought here because it is resistant to the phylloxera beetle, which devastated the region's vines during the late 19th century.

Wine-making villages you might want to stop by include, from north to south (more or less), Marsannay-la-Côte, Fixin, Brochon, Gevrey-Chambertin, Vougeot, Vosne-Romanée, Nuits Saint Georges, Aloxe-Corton and Savigny-lès-Beaune, all north of Beaune; and, south of Beaune, Pommard, Volnay, Saint Romain, Rochepot, Auxey-Duresses, Meursault, Puligny-Montrachet and Santenay.

The Beaune-area villages with cellars offering wine-tasting (dégustation) include:

Aloxe-Corton
    Château Corton-André (☎ 80.26.44.25, fax 80.26. .43.57)
    Clos des Langres (☎ 80.62.98.73)
Savigny-lès-Beaune
    Metairie de Villamont (☎ 80.26.82.06, 80.21. 52.13)
Pommard
    Château de Pommard (☎ 80.22.12.59, 80.22. 07.99)
Meursault
    Domaine Delagrange (☎ 80.21.22.72)
    Château de Meursault (☎ 80.21.22.98)
    Ropeteau Frères (☎ 80.21.24.73)

Wine Tasting

The villages of the Côte d'Or offer innumerable opportunities to sample and purchase excellent wines at or near where they have

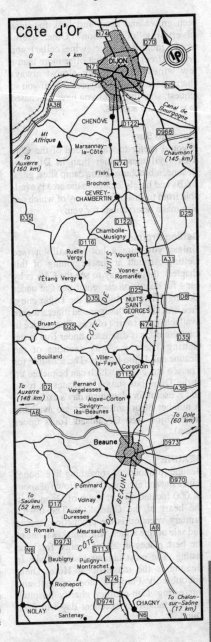

Côte d'Or

been grown and aged. Just look for signs advertising 'dégustation'. Other useful words include a *cave* (wine cellar) and *gratuit* (free). Places that offer more than a few wines for sampling almost always charge a fee. Many vineyards will, if you so request, ship the wines you have purchased to your home address.

Places to Stay

If you'd prefer to stay in one of the Côte d'Or's villages rather than in Dijon or Beaune, a brochure listing camp sites, gîtes, B&Bs and hotels located in the area is available from tourist offices, many of which can also make reservations for you.

Getting Around

Unless you hire a hot-air balloon (see Getting Around at the beginning of this chapter), the best way to see the Côte is by car – for details on car rental, see Car under Getting There & Away in the Dijon entry. Free brochures with suggested itineraries are available from tourist offices. Bus service to the Côte d'Or is discussed under Bus in the Getting There & Away sections of the Beaune and Dijon listings. The schedule for Transco bus No 44, which can be picked up at the Dijon bus station, indicates its route and is useful for planning a day's excursion. A number of organised tours are available from Dijon (see Organised Tours under Dijon).

BEAUNE

Beaune (pronounced something like 'bone' with a flat and elongated 'o'), a town of about 21,000 located 44 km south of Dijon, is in the heart of the Côte d'Or. The town's primary vocation is the production, ageing and sale of fine wines, which makes it one of the best places in all of France for wine tasting. The most famous historical site in Beaune is the magnificent Hôtel Dieu, undoubtedly France's most opulent and interesting 15th-century charity hospital. Beaune makes an excellent day trip from Dijon.

Orientation

The tourist office, which is one km west of the train station, is only a few hundred metres from the Hôtel-Dieu, the basilica, a number of cellars where you can taste the local wines and the pedestrian mall (Rue Monge and Rue Carnot). The blob-shaped old city is delineated by a boulevard with seven names that goes around the exterior of the old ramparts.

Information

Tourist Office Beaune's tourist office (☎ 80.22.24.51; fax 80.24.06.85) is on Rue de l'Hôtel-Dieu opposite the entrance to the Hôtel-Dieu. It is open every day from 9 am to 7.15 pm; from Easter to November it stays open until 11 pm or midnight. It is closed on 25 December and 1 January. The tourist office has a free map of the town and lists (in French) of cellars in Beaune and its environs that offer wine tasting. Hotel reservations in Beaune and nearby areas cost 1FF.

During July, August and the first half of September, there are free guided tours of the town (in French) at 3 pm daily except Sunday and holidays.

Money The Banque de France at 26 Place Monge is open Monday to Friday from 8.30 am to noon and 1.45 to 3.45 pm.

Some of Beaune's commercial banks are open Monday to Friday, while others are open Tuesday to Saturday. There are several banks with exchange services around Place Monge. The tourist office will change money on Saturday afternoon, Sunday and holidays until 7 pm.

Post The post office (☎ 80.24.34.04) at 7 Blvd Saint Jacques is open Monday to Friday from 8 am to 7 pm and on Saturday from 8 am to noon. Currency exchange is available.

Beaune's postcode is 21200.

Bookshops The book section of Athenaeum de la Vigne et du Vin (☎ 80.22.12.00) at 7 Rue de l'Hôtel-Dieu (next to the tourist office) sells books, including some in English, connected in various ways with wine. They also have wine maps of France

A Bastion des Filles
B Bastion Notre Dame
C Tour Blondeau
D Bastion Saint Jean
E Bastion Sainte Anne
F Grosse Tour
G Bastion de l'Hôtel Dieu
H Bastion des Dames

Beaune

To Église Saint Nicolas (400 m),
Camping Ground (700 m),
Highway N74 & Côte de Nuits

To N74, D973 &
Côte de Beaune

0   150   300 m

PLACES TO STAY

16 Hôtel de France
22 Hôtel des Remparts
32 Hôtel de la Poste
34 Cluster of Two &
    Three-Star Hotels
38 Hôtel Rousseau
40 Hôtel Au Grand
    Saint Jean

PLACES TO EAT

20 Casino Grocery
21 Le Tast' Fromage
23 Restaurant Bernard
    Morillon
24 Le Bistrot de l'Huître
26 Covered Market
29 Restaurant le
    Gourmandin
33 Au P'tit Creux Pizza
    Restaurant

39 Restaurant Maxime
43 Casino Supermarket

OTHER

1   Porte Saint Nicolas
2   Caves de la Reine
    Pédauque
3   Théâtre
4   Patriarche Père et Fils
5   Musée des Beaux-Arts
    & Musée
    Étienne-Jules Marey
6   Hôtel de Ville
7   Butterfield & Robinson
    (Bicycle Rental)
8   Belfry
10 Cave Abbaye
    de Mazières
11 Basilique Collégiale
    Notre Dame
12 Banque de France
13 Hertz

14 Budget Car Rental
17 Train Station
18 Transco Bus Stop
19 Musée du Vin
    de Bourgogne
25 Tourist Office
27 Hôtel Dieu
28 Athenaeum de la
    Vigne et du Vin
    (Bookshop)
30 Marché aux Vins
31 Transco Bus Stop
35 Cave du Couvent
    des Cordeliers
36 Caves J de la Roseray
37 Caves Calvet
42 Post Office

SQUARES

9   Place Monge
15 Place de la Gare
41 Place Madeleine

and 1:25,000 scale IGN maps of Burgundy. Athenaeum is open daily from 10 am to 1 pm and 2 to 7 pm.

Hôtel-Dieu

One of Burgundy's architectural highlights is Beaune's Flemish-Burgundian Gothic charity hospital, the celebrated Hôtel-Dieu des Hospices de Beaune (☎ 80.24.45.00), founded in 1443 by Nicolas Rolin, chancellor to Duke Philip the Good, and his wife, Guigone de Salins. After the building ceased to function as a hospital in 1971 (when its medical functions were transferred to more modern premises), many of the wards and other rooms were restored to their 15th-century glory. Part of the complex is still used as an old-folks' home. The hospital's incredibly valuable endowment, 58 hectares of prime vineyards bequeathed by Nicolas Rolin, produces wine that is auctioned each year (on the third Sunday in November) to raise money for medical care and research.

The Hôtel-Dieu's halls, wards, pharmacy, kitchen, and various exhibits (eg of medical utensils) provide a fascinating look at late medival life. The famous multicoloured roof of geometrically arranged glazed tiles can be viewed from the **Cour d'Honneur** (the courtyard), above which is a double row of dormer windows, each decorated with weather vanes and other delicate leadwork.

The darkened room off the hall lined with tapestries contains the brilliant *Polyptych of the Last Judgement*, a multipanel masterpiece commissioned by Nicolas Rolin in 1443 from the Flemish artist Roger van der Weyden. At the bottom of this very literal interpretation of the Last Judgement, naked dead people are depicted climbing out of their graves: those on the left are welcomed into heaven (a golden cathedral), while on the right, the terror-stricken damned tumble into the fires of hell. The walls of this room are hung with several outstanding tapestries.

From mid-November to the end of March, the Hôtel-Dieu is open daily from 9 to 11.30 am and 2 to 5.30 pm. From April to mid-November, it's open every day from 9 am to 6.30 pm. Entrance costs 25FF (20FF for

students). Make sure you pick up the excellent English-language brochure at the ticket window. The really cash-strapped can get a free glimpse of the courtyard from the arch at the entrance.

Basilique Collégiale Notre Dame

Construction of this collegiate church, which was affiliated with the Benedictine monastery of Cluny, was begun in 1120. Although the nave, ambulatory and apsidal chapels are Burgundian-style Romanesque, other elements are Gothic: the choir was redone in the 13th century; the large west porch, the bell tower and the flying buttresses date from the 14th century; and the lateral chapels were built in the 15th century. The upper part of the tower over the transept crossing was added during the Renaissance (16th century). Inside, the five wool and silk panels of the *Tapisseries de la Vie de la Vierge Marie* (Tapestries of the Life of the Virgin Mary) date from the late 15th century.

The church is open daily from 8 am to 6 or 7 pm. The basilica is surrounded by a neighbourhood of quaint, narrow streets.

Musée du Vin de Bourgogne

Housed in a one-time palace of the dukes of Burgundy (built between the 14th and 18th centuries) on Rue d'Enfer, the Museum of the Wines of Burgundy (☎ 80.22.08.19) has exhibits on how vines are planted and tended, grapes are picked and wines are aged, barrelled and bottled. It is open from 9.30 am to 6 pm every day, except from December to March, when it's closed on Tuesday. Entry costs 25FF (17FF for students and people over 60). A room-by-room tour booklet is available at the ticket counter for 3FF.

Ramparts

The fortifications around the old city, surrounded by a wild, overgrown area given over in part to growing cherries and vegetables, shelter within their thick stone walls privately owned cellars containing countless bottles of wine. The ramparts can be circumnavigated by walking along Blvd Jules

Ferry, Blvd Maréchal Joffre and the rest of the boulevards that encircle the old city.

Museums

The south wing of the Hôtel de Ville, housed in a 17th-century Ursuline convent, contains two museums (☎ 80.24.56.78/92): the **Musée des Beaux-Arts**, which has a collection of assorted paintings and sculptures from the 15th to 19th centuries, including works by Beaune native Félix Ziem (1821-1911); and the **Musée Étienne-Jules Marey**, dedicated to the work of one of the pioneers of motion-picture photography. The entrance to both museums is across the street from 9 Rue de l'Hôtel de Ville. An entry ticket – also good for the Musée du Vin de Bourgogne – costs 20FF (7FF for students and people over 60). The museums are open daily from April to November *only* from 2 to 6 pm. From June to September, they are also open from 9.30 am to 1 pm.

Wine Tasting

Under Beaune's buildings, streets and ramparts, millions of dusty bottles of wine are, at this very moment, being aged to perfection in cool, dark cobweb-lined cellars permeated by the wonderful odour of grapes and fermentation. A number of them can be visited on informative guided tours. Others are given over primarily to tasting – and, of course, selling – wines. The latter offer a superb opportunity to sample and compare a dozen or so premium wines. Some of the visits are free, but the ones that charge a fee (usually 25 to 40FF) include either a more elaborate tour or a much better selection of things to taste. The tourist office has a complete list of cellars that can be visited.

The **Marché aux Vins** (☎ 80.22.27.69) is on Rue Nicolas Rolin, 30 metres south of the tourist office. For 40FF, you get a *taste-vin* (a small metal cup which costs 10FF if you want to keep it) with which you can sample about 40 wines (half a dozen whites, the rest reds) displayed on upturned wine barrels in the candle-lit, barrel-lined Église des Cordeliers (a desanctified church built from the 13th to 15th centuries) and the cellars

beneath it. The best wines are located near the exit. The Marché aux Vins is open daily from 9.30 am to noon and 2.30 to 6 pm (6.30 pm during the warmer half of the year). It is closed from 15 December until the end of January.

The **Cave du Couvent des Cordeliers** (☎ 80.22.14.25) at 6 Rue de l'Hôtel-Dieu offers free samples of three or four wines extracted from barrels with a giant eye-dropper *(a pipette)* during the guided tour (conducted mostly in French) of the 13th-century cellars. From Monday to Saturday, opening hours are 9 am to noon and 2 to 6 pm (6.30 pm during April, May, June and September, 7 pm during July and August). On Sunday and holidays, it's open all year round from 9.30 am to noon and 2.30 to 6.30 pm.

Virtually across the street, the **Caves J de la Roseray** (☎ 80.22.25.68) at 15 Rue de l'Hôtel-Dieu, part of whose cellar is from the 17th century but the rest of which is modern, lets you taste 17 different wines (one-third of them white) for 40FF (plus 10FF if you want to keep the taste-vin). With the list available at the entrance, you can taste the wines on offer at your own pace and in whatever order you like. This place is open daily from 9.30 am to noon and 2 to 6 pm (6.30 pm in summer).

Whereas the main activity in most cellars you can visit is tasting wines rather than ageing them, the **Caves Calvet** (☎ 80.22.06.32) at 6 Blvd Perpreuil are used primarily to age the oak casks and bottles of wine purchased by Calvet from growers three or four months after harvest. Although the usual ageing period is two to five years, the oldest bottle stored in these 14th, 15th and 19th-century cellars, whose temperature is a constant 13°C to 15°C, dates from 1865. Given the thick cobwebs on the ceilings, you most certainly would not want to be in here if gravity reversed itself...

The Caves Calvet are open from 9 to 11.30 am and 2 to 5 pm (closed Monday). During December, January and February, they are also closed on Saturday and Sunday. The guided tours (conducted in French or English), which begin every half-hour, are the most interesting and informative in

Beaune. The 25FF charge for visitors aged over 16 includes the sampling of five wines.

Patriarche Père et Fils (☎ 80.24.53.01; fax 80.24.53.03) at 6 Rue du Collège, which has the largest *caves* in Burgundy, offers samples of 11 wines for 40FF (30FF for students, free for accompanied young people under 18). It is open daily from 9.30 to 11.30 am and 2.30 to 5.30 pm but is closed from mid-December to late January.

Caves de la Reine Pédauque (☎ 80.22. 23.11; fax 80.26.42.00), at the intersection of Blvd Maréchal Joffre and Rue de Lorraine, has free wine tasting. It is open daily from 9 am (10 am on Sunday from October to May) to 11.30 am and 2 to 5.30 pm (6 pm from June to September).

Festivals
The Rencontres Musicales de Beaune, a series of classical music concerts, takes place every year at the end of June and in early July. During the first week of September, the Fête de la Vigne brings folklore groups from around the world to the town. On the third Sunday in November, the Hospices de Beaune (see the Hôtel-Dieu listing) auctions the premium wines grown in its vineyards.

Places to Stay
Beaune's hotels are most full in September and October, when people come for the grape harvest and to enjoy the autumn weather.

Places to Stay – bottom end
Camping The four-star *camping ground* (☎ 80.22.03.91) at 10 Rue Auguste Dubois is open from mid-March to October. To get there from the tourist office, go north on Rue du Faubourg Saint Nicolas for one km and turn left at Église Saint Nicolas. A tent site costs 17FF, including parking; each adult pays 11.50FF. If you want to be sure of getting a place, come before noon.

Hotels The *Hôtel Rousseau* (☎ 80.22.13.59) at 11 Place Madeleine, which is 600 metres from the train station and only one block from the old city, is run by a friendly older woman. Large, old-fashioned singles with washbasin and bidet are 100FF, doubles are 140 to 170FF, two or three-bed triples are 220FF and three-bed quads/quints are 270/350FF, including breakfast. There are no rooms with interior showers or toilets. Reception is open daily until 11.30 pm.

Places to Stay – middle
The quiet two-star *Hôtel de France* (☎ 80.24. 10.34; fax 80.24.96.78) is directly opposite the train station at 35 Ave du 8 Septembre. Large, spotless singles/doubles/ two-bed doubles with shower and toilet cost 200/240/260FF. Three-bed quads are 280 to 310FF. An additional bed, available in some rooms, is only 30FF. Breakfast costs 28FF. Overall, it's a good deal.

The 106-room *Hôtel Au Grand Saint Jean* (☎ 80.24.12.22; fax 80.24.15.43), a two-star place at 20 Rue du Faubourg Madeleine, has doubles with shower and toilet from 203FF. There are several other two and three-star hotels around Place Madeleine. There's also a cluster of two and three-star hotels on the south-west side of town along Rue du Faubourg Bretonnière.

Places to Stay – top end
The *Hôtel des Remparts* (☎ 80.24.94.94, 80.24.06.34; fax 80.24.97.08), a three-star place in a 17th-century mansion at 48 Rue Thiers, has huge doubles, some with beam ceilings, for 290 to 360FF and quads for 490FF. Breakfast costs 35FF. This hotel is closed during the last week in January and the first half of February.

The luxurious, four-star *Hôtel de la Poste* (☎ 80.22.08.11; fax 80.24.19.71) at 5 Blvd Georges Clemenceau has rooms in the annexe without air-con or lift access for 350FF (500FF from April to June and September to October). In the main building, doubles start at 500FF (750FF in the high season); suites cost up to 1500FF.

Places to Eat
French One of Beaune's best options for traditional French cuisine is *Restaurant Bernard Morillon* (☎ 80.24.12.06; fax

80.22.66.22) at 31 Rue Maufoux, which was recently awarded one Michelin star. Meals are served in an elegant dining room or the nearby courtyard, both of which date from around the 16th century. *Menus* are available for 160, 290, 380 and 420FF. If ordered à la carte, main dishes (including lots of fish dishes) cost from 140 to 185FF. This restaurant is closed Monday, Tuesday at midday and during February. Hours are noon to 2 pm and 7.30 to 10 pm. Reservations are a good idea for dinner, especially in September and October.

Restaurant Maxime (☎ 80.22.17.82; fax 80.24.90.81) at 3 Place Madeleine offers reasonably priced Burgundian cuisine in an attractive dining room whose blue walls set off the white tablecloths. There are *menus* for 70, 88 and 160FF; à la carte, bœuf bourguignon costs 51FF. This place is open from noon to 2 pm and 7 to 9.30 pm daily except Monday. It is closed during February. There are a number of other restaurants nearby.

Restaurant Le Gourmandin (☎ 80.24.07.88) at 8 Place Carnot, whose specialities include coq au vin (chicken cooked in wine sauce) and bœuf bourguignon, is open daily from noon to 2 pm and 7 to 11 pm (or later); it's closed Tuesday and Sunday evening. The *menu* costs 85FF.

Quick Meals *Le Bistrot de l'Huître* (☎ 80.24.71.28) at 47 Rue Maufoux specialises in oysters, which cost 39/61FF for half a dozen for small/large ones. *Au P'tit Creux Pizza Restaurant* (☎ 80.22.78.08) is not far away at 9 Rue du Faubourg Bretonnière. It has pizzas (46 to 65FF), salads (15 to 33FF) and pasta dishes and is open from noon to 2 pm and 7 to 11 pm (midnight in summer) daily except Wednesday.

Self-Catering In the centre of the old city, a *food market* is held at Place Carnot and in the covered market building next to the tourist office every Saturday morning until about 1 pm.

The *Casino grocery* at 14 Rue Monge is open Monday to Saturday from 6.30 am to 1 pm and 3 to 7.30 pm. From June to Septem-

ber it's also open on Sunday from 9 am to 1 pm. Cheese is available at *Le Tast' Fromage*, a fromagerie on the Rue Carnot pedestrian mall at Rue Monge.

The huge *Casino supermarket* 400 metres south-east of Place Carnot has entrances at 28 Rue du Faubourg Madeleine and on Rue du Faubourg Perpreuil. It is open Monday to Saturday from 8.30 am to 7.30 pm.

Things to Buy
See Wine Tasting earlier for information on where to taste and purchase wine.

Getting There & Away
Train Beaune's train station (☎ 80.22.13.13), whose ticket windows are open daily from 6 am to 11 pm, is served by local trains on the Dijon-Lyon and Dijon-Nevers lines. Service to Dijon (33FF; 15 to 20 a day) takes 20 to 25 minutes; the last train from Beaune to Dijon leaves at about 10.40 pm every night. The trip to Lyon's Gare de la Part-Dieu or Gare de Perrache (102FF; eight to 10 a day) takes 1½ to two hours.

There are five to eight trains a day to Nevers (2½ to three hours). Beaune is served twice a day by TGVs from Paris's Gare de Lyon. To get to Autun (61FF), change at Étang-sur-Arroux.

Bus Transco bus No 44 from Dijon to Beaune (35FF) is a good bet if you want to stop along the way (there are vineyards at virtually every stop) and aren't in a hurry (the trip takes a bit over an hour, three times as long as the train). It runs eight times a day except on Sunday and holidays, when there are only two buses in each direction, both in the afternoon. The first two buses leave Dijon at 6.45 and 7.45 am; the next one is at 11 am, the last at about 7 pm. In the other direction, the last bus departs from Beaune around 6.15 pm. Bus No 44 also serves wine-making villages *south* of Beaune, including Meursault, Auxey-Duresses and La Rochepot. Transco has one bus to/from Autun every day of the week.

In Beaune, Transco buses stop at several places, including across the street from the train station and opposite 7 Blvd Georges Clemenceau (across the street from the Hôtel de la Poste).

Car Budget can be contacted on ☎ 80.22.29.92.

Getting Around

Taxi There is a taxi stand at the train station. To order a taxi 24 hours a day, call ☎ 80.24.19.55.

Bicycle Butterfield & Robinson, a Toronto-based tour operator that runs walking, hiking and cycling tours, has an office (☎ 80.24.19.99) at 5 Rue de Citeaux, which is behind (across the tracks from) the train station. From April to August (and, if the bikes aren't booked for groups, in September and October as well), they rent out 18-speed road/mountain bikes for 60FF per half-day and 100FF a day. The per-day charge goes down the longer you rent for (eg to 420FF a week).

The office is open Monday to Friday from 8 am to noon and 1.30 to 6 pm and weekends from 9 am to noon and 2 to 6 pm.

AUTUN

Autun, a tidy, attractive town of 17,000 people situated 85 km south-west of Dijon, is set on a low rise nestled between tree-covered hills (to the south-east) and farmland (to the north). Today, it is a quiet subprefecture, but in the 1st centuries AD it was one of the most important cities in Roman Gaul. Known then as Augustodunum (in honour of the Roman Emperor Augustus, who founded the city around 10 BC), its six km of ramparts were topped by 54 towers and pierced by four gates. The city also had all the other accoutrements of a Roman metropolis: two theatres, an amphitheatre, a system of aqueducts, a circus, etc. Autun was repeatedly sacked by Barbarian tribes beginning in 269 AD, but its fortunes revived in the Middle Ages, when an impressive cathedral was erected. Many of the buildings in the city centre date from the 17th and 18th centuries.

Autun is a good base for exploring the southern part of the Parc Naturel Régional du Morvan (Morvan Regional Park; see Outdoor Activities at the beginning of this chapter).

Orientation

The train station, which is on Ave de la République, is linked to Autun's commons-turned-parking lot, the Champ de Mars, by the town's main drag, 500-metre-long Ave Charles de Gaulle. The Hôtel de Ville is at the north-east corner of the Champ de Mars. The hilly area around the cathedral, reached via narrow, twisting cobblestone streets, is known as the old city. The main shopping areas are around the Champ de Mars and along Rue aux Cordeliers and Rue Saint Saulge, both of which are closed to vehicular traffic. The Arroux River, a tributary of the Loire, flows past Autun's northern outskirts.

Information

Tourist Office The tourist office (☎ 85.52.20.34; fax 85.86.10.17) is 600 metres south-east of the train station at 3 Ave Charles de Gaulle. From Easter to September it is open Monday to Saturday from 9 am to noon and 2 to 7 pm. The rest of the year, it is open Monday to Friday from 9 am to noon and 2 to 6 pm, and on Saturday from 9 am to noon only.

The tourist office annexe (☎ 85.52.56.03) at 5 Place du Terreau (next to the cathedral), commonly known as the 'Point I' (short for *point d'information*), is open from June to September every day from 9 am to 7 pm.

Money The Banque de France (☎ 85.52.23.24) at 38 Ave Charles de Gaulle is open Monday to Friday from 8.40 am to 12.10 pm and 1.30 to 3.40 pm.

The Crédit Mutuel at 6 Rue du Général A Demetz (on the south side of the Champ de Mars) is open Tuesday to Friday from 8.30 am to 12.15 pm and 1.35 to 5.50 pm, and on Saturday from 8.30 am to 12.15 pm. The Crédit Agricole at 8 Rue J & B de Lattre de Tassigny (on the east side of the Champ de

Mars) is open Monday to Friday from 8.15 am to noon and 1.45 to 5.30 pm.

Post The post office opposite 11 Rue Pernette is open Monday to Friday from 8.30 am to 6.30 pm and on Saturday from 8.30 am to noon. Currency exchange is possible.

Autun's postcode is 71400.

Bookshops IGN and other maps as well as some guidebooks can be purchased at Librairie Chandelon (☎ 85.52.24.72) at 17bis Ave Charles de Gaulle. It is open Tuesday to Saturday from 9 am to noon and 2 to 7 pm.

Emergency There is a police station (☎ 85.52.14.22) right in the centre of town at 29ter Ave Charles de Gaulle.

Cathédrale Saint Lazare

This Burgundian-style Romanesque cathedral was built of locally quarried sandstone in the 12th century with the express purpose of housing the sacred relics of St Lazarus. The architects took some of their inspiration from local and other monuments left by the Romans, which is why the style is called Romanesque. Significant additions (eg the bell tower, the upper section of the choir, the chapels on both sides of the nave) were made in the 15th and 16th centuries. The square towers over the entrance date from the 19th century. Visits should not be made during mass.

The **tympanum** over the main entrance, which illustrates the Last Judgement, is considered an outstanding example of Romanesque sculpture. It was carved in the 1130s by Gislebertus, whose name is written below Jesus' right foot. Across the bottom, the saved are on the left while the damned, including a woman whose breasts are being eaten by snakes, are on the right. Hell is on the far right of the main panel; heaven is immediately to the left and right of Jesus' head. The outermost of the three arches enclosing the tympanum is decorated with the representations of the signs of the Zodiac and the labours of the months (the agricultural work necessary during each month of the year).

The cathedral is renowned for the vivid 12th-century capitals that adorn many of its pillars. However, a good number of those in situ are in fact 19th-century copies, the originals having been removed for structural reasons to the **Salle Capitulaire**. To get there, walk through the door on the right side of the choir and up two flights of the circular staircase.

The 80-metre-high **belfry**, whose 230 steps begin in a corner of the left transept, affords a fine view of the town and its environs. It was erected in 1462. The serve-yourself tickets cost 3FF each. The Renaissance-style fountain next to the cathedral, **Fontaine Saint Lazare**, dates from the 16th century.

Musée Rollin

The Rollin Museum (☎ 85.52.09.76) at 5 Rue des Bancs occupies the 19th-century Hôtel Lacomme and, across the courtyard, the 15th-century Hôtel Rolin, home of Nicolas Rolin, chancellor to the duke of Burgundy, who founded the Hôtel-Dieu in Beaune.

The Gallo-Roman collection, most of which was discovered in or around Autun, is displayed on the ground floor of the Hôtel Lacomme. It includes a ceremonial helmet *(casque de parade)* in the third room, a three-horned bronze bull on an altar *(autel avec statuette de taureau tricornu)* in the fifth room and lots of fine bronze figurines and mosaics.

The ground floor of the Hôtel Rolin houses a collection of 12th-century Romanesque sculpture, including a lintel known as *La Tentation d'Ève* (the Temptation of Eve) thought to have been carved by Gislebertus around 1130. The 1st floor contains a well-known collection of 15th and 16th-century French and Flemish works, many of them created here in Autun. Nicolas Rolin's son Jean, bishop of Autun, makes an appearance in the oil-on-wood painting known as *La Nativité avec le Cardinal Jean Rolin en Donateur* (Nativity with the donor Cardinal Jean Rolin), created by Le Maître de Moulins around 1480.

The museum is open daily except Tuesday. From April to September, hours are 9.30

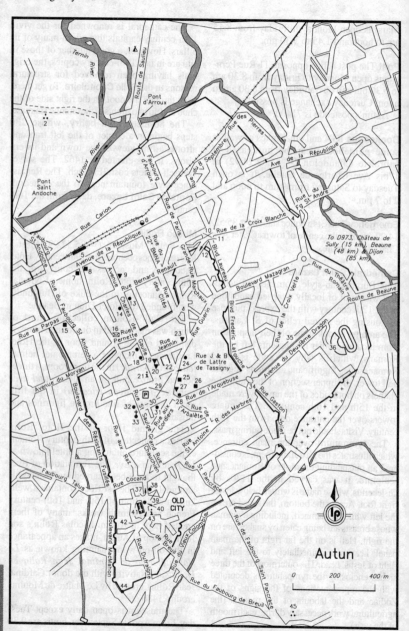

Autun

0   200   400 m

To D973, Château de
Sully (15 km), Beaune
(48 km) & Dijon
(85 km)

OLD
CITY

PLACES TO STAY

1 Camping Municipal du Pont d'Arroux
7 Hôtel de France
8 Hôtel Commerce et Touring
15 Hôtel le Petit Paris
25 Hôtel Le Grand Café
26 Hôtel de la Tête Noire

▼ PLACES TO EAT

9 Boulangerie
19 Casino Grocery
20 Caveau Eden (Wine Shop)
23 Le Château Bleu
27 Prisunic Supermarket

OTHER

2 Temple de Janus
3 Porte d'Arroux (Roman Gate)
4 Porte Saint André (Roman Gate)
5 Railway Station
6 RSL Bus Information Bureau
11 Rue Saint Nicholas
12 Musée Lapidaire
13 Banque de France
14 Police Station

16 Post Office
17 Lyonnaise de Banque
18 Librairie Chandelon
21 Tourist Office
22 Hôtel de Ville & Municipal Library
24 Crédit Agricole
28 Cycles Tacnet
29 Champ de Mars
30 Rue du Général Demetz
31 Crédit Mutuel
32 Gate to Lycée Bonaparte
33 Église Notre Dame
35 Promenade des Marbres
36 Roman Theatre
37 Rue des Bancs
38 Musée Rollin
40 Fontaine Saint Lazare
41 Cathédrale Saint Lazare
43 Tourist Office Annexe
44 Tour des Ursulines
45 Pierre de Couhard

✕ SQUARES

10 Place Pierre Saint Yves
34 Place de Charmasse
39 Place Saint-Louis
42 Place de Terreau

am to noon and 1.30 to 6 pm. The rest of the year, it is open from 10 am to noon and 2 (2.30 on Sunday) to 4 pm (5 pm on Sunday). Entry costs 12FF (6FF for students).

Porte d'Arroux

Built during the reign of Constantine, this mortarless Roman gate – one of four that pierced Augustodunum's city walls – is particularly well preserved. It has four arches, two large ones for vehicular traffic and two smaller ones for pedestrians, all of which are still used for their original purposes. From the river side of the gate, you can see, above the arches, fluted pilasters topped with delicate Corinthian capitals. The two pyramid-shaped hills visible to the north of town are mine tailings.

Musée Lapidaire

At the Lapidary Museum (☎ 85.52.35.71), which is at 10 Rue Saint Nicolas, Gallo-

Roman statuary is displayed around a delightful flower garden and inside a 12th-century Romanesque chapel. The tombstones, mosaics and capitals from the 1st to 4th centuries are joined by some objects from the 14th and 15th centuries. This museum is open daily, except Tuesday, from 10 am to noon and 2 to 4 pm (4.30 pm on Sunday from October to mid-April). From mid-April to September, it stays open until 6 pm. The museum is closed throughout February.

Porte Saint André

Another of Roman Augustodunum's gates, the 1st-century Porte Saint André is similar in design to Porte d'Arroux.

Promenade des Marbres

This long, tree-lined promenade is perfect for strolling, picnicking or playing *boules* (bowls). Across Ave du Deuxième Dragon, the main building of the 17th-century École

Militaire (Military Preparatory School) has an especially colourful Burgundian-style tile roof.

Roman Theatre

Autun's Théâtre Romain, which could once hold some 16,000 people, was the largest theatre in all of Roman Gaul. It was severely damaged in the Middle Ages, when much of its stone was hauled off for re-use. Though much of what's left is was heavily restored in the 19th century, visitors can try to imagine how the theatre must have looked when filled with cheering spectators watching some gory Roman entertainment. Today, it is used for less bloody events, such as concerts.

From the top of the theatre, you get a splendid view of the verdant outskirts of town. The blob-like pointy thing you see on the forested hillside to the south-east is the **Pierre de Couhard** (Rock of Couhard), the 27-metre-high remains of a pyramid from the Gallo-Roman period that was probably either a tomb or a cenotaph. The hedges across the road from the theatre shield two boules grounds, a favourite gathering place for locals.

Municipal Library

At the back of the public lending library (bibliothèque; ☎ 85.52.28.79) on the 2nd floor of the Hôtel de Ville is a room stacked to the ceiling with books confiscated by the state from monasteries and other religious institutions during the Revolution. Selected works from among the 60,000 books brought here – including some beautifully illuminated bound manuscripts from the 9th to 15th centuries and a number of priceless incunabula (books printed before Easter 1500) – are on display from July to September.

The library is open Monday to Saturday from 10 am to noon and 2 to 6 pm (5 pm on Saturday).

Temple de Janus

Long associated – incorrectly – with the Roman god Janus, this massive, 24-metre-high square tower (only two of whose walls are extant) seems to have been built in the 1st century AD for worship according to the Celtic tradition of the Gauls. The enterior was once painted in vermilion. To get to the temple, which is in the middle of farmland 800 metres due north of the train station, you can either take the path along the north bank of the L'Arroux River from the bridge just north of the Porte d'Arroux; or walk or drive from Pont Saint Andoche (the bridge at the north end of Rue du Faubourg Saint Andoche). The temple is not fenced and can be visited any time.

Three Short Walks

Pleasant walks *extra-muros* (outside the city walls) include the following:

- For a lovely stroll along the exterior of the tower-topped and crenellated city walls, parts of which date from Roman times but most of whose upper sections are late medieval, walk from Ave du Morvan south along Blvd des Résistants Fusillés and Blvd MacMahon. After passing the 12th-century **Tour des Ursulines** (the statue-topped tower at the city's southern tip), walk north-east on Rue du Faubourg Saint Blaise, Rue Raquette and Rue du Vieux Colombier. To get to the old city, turn left (north-westward) on Rue Saint Pancrace.

- From Rue Saint Pancrace, you can also take Rue du Faubourg Saint Pancrace and head into the countryside and out to the Pierre de Couhard (see the Roman Theatre listing).

- North of town, the Temple de Janus (see the Temple de Janus listing) makes a good excuse to venture into the farmland a bit. It can be visited as part of a loop from Pont Saint Andoche to Porte d'Arroux.

Organised Tours

From 1 July to 15 September, there are guided walking tours in French (and, if the guide is an Anglophone, in English too) of the old city and the cathedral. They depart from Place du Terreau (next to the cathedral) daily at 10 am and 3 pm and last about two hours. The charge is 18FF. For details, ask at the tourist office or the tourist office annexe.

Festivals

The Musique en Morvan festival (☎ 85.52.

45.43), which brings concerts (especially choral ones) to Autun and other places in the Morvan area, is held for 10 days in mid-July. Autun's Gallo-Roman past is re-enacted by hundreds of local residents on three weekends (Friday and Saturday nights) between late June and early September in a performance known as Il Était une Fois Augustodunum (Once upon a Time in Augustodunum). Tickets cost 65FF (35FF for children aged six to 12). Information on both events is available from the tourist office.

Places to Stay

Autun has several inexpensive accommodation options.

Camping Camping Municipal du Pont d'Arroux (☎ 85.52.10.82), which occupies a shady and beautiful (though densely packed) spot on the Ternin River, is 700 metres north of the Porte d'Arroux at 1 Route de Lucenay l'Évêque. It is open from a week before Easter to October. The restaurant and small grocery store are open from mid-June until the end of August. Two people with a vehicle and a tent are charged 37FF (49FF in July and August, when there's a night watchperson). There is always space in the morning.

Hotels The Hôtel de France (☎ 85.52. 14.00) at 18 Ave de la République (opposite the train station) has pleasant, soundproofed doubles with shower and toilet for around 200FF. The tidy Hôtel Commerce et Touring (☎ 85.52.17.90) at 20 Ave de la République has unsurprising singles and doubles with TV for 125FF (with washbasin), 165FF (with shower) and 175FF (with shower and toilet). Triples with shower and toilet are 200FF. There are almost always places available in the morning. It's closed in October.

You might also try the nine-room Hôtel Le Grand Café (☎ 85.52.27.66), which is on the Champ de Mars at 19 Rue J & B de Lattre de Tassigny. Rooms with shower cost 150FF with one bed and 180FF with two beds. A room with bath and toilet is 215FF. Reception, which is at the bar, is closed on Sunday.

The hotel is also closed during the last half of October.

Hôtel de la Tête Noire (☎ 85.52.25.39; fax 85.86.33.90), a two-star place at 1-3 Rue de l'Arquebuse (one block east of the Champ de Mars) has four rooms with washbasin and bidet for 110 to 125FF and rooms with shower and toilet for 170 to 262FF. It is closed in March. From April to September, reception is closed on Saturday from noon to 4.30 pm. The rest of the year, reception is closed after 3 pm on Friday and all-day Saturday.

Places to Eat

There are a number of restaurants around the Champ de Mars and a few more near the cathedral.

French For creative French cuisine, the well-regarded Le Château Bleu (☎ 85.86. 27.30) at 3 Rue Jeannin is an excellent choice. It is open daily except Monday evening and Tuesday. There are menus for 80FF (not available on weekends or holidays), 115, 145 and 185FF. Reservations are a good idea on weekends.

Self-Catering There is a Prisunic supermarket with a boulangerie at the back at 21 Rue J & B de Lattre de Tassigny (on the Champ de Mars). It is open Monday to Saturday from 8.30 am to 7.30 pm. The Casino grocery at 6 Ave Charles de Gaulle is open Tuesday to Saturday from 7.15 am to 12.30 pm and 2.15 to 7.30 pm, and from 7.15 am to 12.30 pm on Sunday. It's closed on Monday except from mid-July to mid-August.

Near the train station, the boulangerie at 50 Ave Charles de Gaulle is open from 6 am to 7 pm daily except Monday and perhaps Sunday afternoon.

Things to Buy

There are a number of antique shops on Grande Rue Chauchien between the Champ de Mars and the Cathédrale Saint Lazare.

The Caveau Eden wine shop at 2 Ave

Charles de Gaulle (across the street from the tourist office) is closed on Monday.

Getting There & Away

Train The train station (☎ 85.93.50.50) is on Ave de la République. The ticket windows are open Monday to Saturday from 8.30 am to 7.15 pm and on Sunday from noon to 7.30 pm.

Autun is on a slow, secondary rail line that requires changing trains to get almost anywhere except Avallon (61FF; 1¾ hours), Auxerre (91FF; three hours) and Laroche-Migennes (three hours 20 minutes), a stop on the main Paris-Dijon line. This line, whose extension to Autun has only four trains a day (two on Sunday and holidays), also serves Sermizelles-Vézelay (two hours), which is 10 km north of Vézelay (see Getting There & Away under Vézelay).

The best way to get to Dijon (83FF; nine a day on weekdays, five or six on weekends and holidays), Beaune (61FF) and Nevers is to change at Étang-sur-Arroux (18 minutes; five to nine a day), which is a bit south-west of Autun. The trip to Paris's Gare de Lyon (176FF; three or four a day) requires a change of train at Avallon, Auxerre or Laroche-Migennes; you can also take an RSL bus (see the next section) to Le Creusot, where you can pick up a TGV (1½ hours; six or seven a day, fewer on Saturday) to Paris's Gare de Lyon. Lyon (131FF) can be reached via Chagny or Chalon-sur-Saône.

On certain runs, the SNCF uses buses (which leave from the train station parking lot) rather than trains or autorails. There are two or three buses a day to both Chagny (39FF) and Chalon-sur Saône (47FF), both of which have onward rail connections to Lyon and Dijon.

Bus RSL (☎ 85.52.30.02) has limited bus service linking the Autun train station with Dijon (to Dijon daily at 5 pm, from Dijon daily at noon), Chalon-sur-Saône, Le Creusot (four to six on weekdays, one or two on weekends) and Château Chinon, which is west of Autun in the Parc Naturel Régional du Morvan.

RSL's information bureau at 13 Ave de la République has schedules posted in the window. It is open Monday to Friday from 8 am to noon and 2 to 6 pm. Bus schedules are also available at the tourist office. See the Train listing for information on SNCF buses.

Getting Around

Car There are hundreds of parking places at the Champ de Mars.

Bicycle Cycles Tacnet (☎ 85.86.37.83) at 1 Rue de l'Arquebuse (just east of the Champ de Mars) has mountain bikes for 60/110FF per half/full-day. The weekly rate is 600FF. It is open Tuesday to Saturday from 9 am to noon and 2 to 7 pm, and 9 am to noon on Monday. It's closed on Sunday. One possible destination for a day-long ride from Autun is the Château de Sully.

AROUND AUTUN
Château de Sully

The Château de Sully (☎ 85.82.01.08), the 16th-century Renaissance-style residence in which Marshal Mac-Mahon (President of France from 1873-79) was born in 1808, is sometimes called the 'Fontainebleau of Burgundy'. The north façade was rebuilt in the 18th century. The interior is not open to the public, but the huge gardens can be visited daily from the Saturday before Easter until the end of October from 8 am to 7 pm. The charge is 10FF. Wine produced on the estate can be purchased from the concierge.

The chateau is 15 km east of Autun (towards Beaune) on the outskirts of the quiet village of Sully. It makes a good cycling destination, especially if you'd like to see a bit of the Burgundian countryside. From Autun, take the D973 eastward (towards Beaune) and then the D326 heading north-east. RSL bus 625 to Épinac links Autun with Sully every Friday morning and on the first and third Wednesday mornings of the month.

AUXERRE

Auxerre (pronounced 'Oh-Sair', with the accent on the second syllable) is a pretty

Château de Sully

average French provincial town of 42,000 people situated midway between Paris and Dijon (166 km south-east of Paris, 149 km north-west of Dijon). It is not overrun with tourists but has a number of noteworthy religious buildings, including a well-known cathedral and a unique 9th-century Carolingian crypt. The hilly old city, on the left bank of the Yonne River (a tributary of the Seine), is graced by a number of belfries and spires and lots of steep-roofed, half-timbered houses. It is surrounded by nondescript 19th-century and postwar neighbourhoods.

Auxerre is good base for exploring northern Burgundy, including the Auxerrois, the wine-growing area just east of the city. The most famous wine of the Auxerrois is Chablis, a delicate, dry white wine made with Chardonnay grapes in and around the village of Chablis. If you have a car, Vézelay is only a short drive away from Auxerre. The city's pleasure-boat port makes this an excellent place to rent canal boats for excursions on the region's canals and rivers (see Boating on Burgundy's Waterways at the beginning of this chapter).

Orientation

Auxerre is bisected by the Yonne River. The train station is 700 metres east of the river. The old city rises from the slopes along the river's west (left) bank. Rue de l'Horloge is part of a pedestrian precinct in the middle of the old city.

Information

Tourist Office The efficient and helpful tourist office (☎ 86.52.06.19; fax 86.51.23.27) is on the ground floor of the Maison du Tourisme at 1-2 Quai de la République. It is open Monday to Saturday from 9 am to 12.30 pm and 2 to 6.30 pm. From July to mid-September, it is open Monday to Saturday from 9 am to 7 pm and on Sunday from 9.30 am to 12.30 pm and 2 to 7 pm. Hotel reservations cost 10FF in town and 15FF elsewhere in the département of Yonne. The office has a number of informative brochures in English.

The tourist office annexe (☎ 86.51.10.27) at 16 Place des Cordeliers is open from mid-June to mid-September.

Money The Banque de France at 1 Rue de la Banque (next to the Palais de Justice) is open Monday to Friday from 8.30 am to 12.15 pm and 1.45 to 3.30 pm.

Auxerre's banks, a number of which are located between Place Charles Surugue and Place Charles Lepère, are open either Monday to Friday or Tuesday to Saturday. The tourist office will change money on Sunday and on other days between the time the banks close and the time the tourist office closes.

Post The main post office, which is at Place Charles Surugue, is open Monday to Friday from 8 am to 7 pm and on Saturday from 8 am to noon. Currency exchange is available.

Auxerre's postcode is 89000.

Laundry The laundrette at 138 Rue de Paris is open daily from 7 am to 9 pm. There is another laundrette at 105 Rue du Pont, near Pont Paul Bert.

Pont Paul Bert

Some of the best views of the old city are from Pont Paul Bert, the bridge that links Ave Jean Jaurès with Quai de la République. A bridge has stood on this site for much of the period since Roman times, but most of the present structure dates from 1857.

Cathédrale Saint Étienne

This impressive if relatively small Gothic cathedral (☎ 86.52.31.68), consecrated to St Stephen, was constructed between the 13th and 16th centuries on the site of an earlier Romanesque cathedral and three even earlier churches, including a Christian sanctuary built in the early 5th century by Saint Amatre (Amator).

The Flamboyant Gothic west front was built from the 14th to the 16th centuries. Its weathered limestone portals, which were damaged in the Wars of Religion, date from the 13th and early 14th centuries. The façade's northern corner is topped by a 68-metre-high **bell tower** (presently closed for repairs), completed in the mid-1500s. The Auxerrois never quite got around to building its southern counterpart.

The nave and the transept are from the 14th and 15th centuries, while the rose windows in the transept arms date from the mid-1500s. The choir and ambulatory are the product of the 1200s, as are the stained-glass windows around the ambulatory, which relate stories from the Old Testament in vivid reds and blues. The cathedral is open daily from 8 am to 7 pm. During July and August, there are free organ concerts every Sunday at 5 pm.

The **crypt**, which was built around 1030 and is the only part of the Romanesque cathedral that is extant, is open daily, except Sunday mornings, from 9 am to noon and 2 to 6 pm (5 pm on Sunday during July and August). From November or December to February or March, it is closed on Sunday. Entrance costs 5FF. The 11th to 13th-century frescoes include a scene of Jesus on horseback that is unlike any other known in Western art. The **trésor** (treasury) is open the same hours as the crypt and also costs 5FF.

Abbaye Saint Germain

Founded in the 6th century by Queen Clotilde, (Clovis's wife) on the site where St Germanus (bishop of Auxerre in the 5th century) was buried in 448 AD, this former Benedictine abbey (☎ 86.51.09.74) rose to great prominence in the Middle Ages, when it attracted students from all over Europe. In

1567, during the Wars of Religion, it was pillaged by the Huguenots. Now a museum, it can be visited from 9 am to noon and 2 to 6 pm (closed Tuesday). From mid-June to mid-September, hours are 9 am to 12.30 pm and 2 to 6.30 pm except on Friday, when it's open continuously from 9 am to 8 pm. Entrance costs 16FF but is free for students and people with a Carte Jeunes; the same ticket is valid for the Musée Leblanc-Duvernoy. An information sheet in English is available for no charge at the ticket counter.

The mostly Gothic **abbey church** was built between the 13th and 15th centuries. The 51-metre-high belfry ended up detached from the church when several bays at its west end were razed in 1811. Under the church is the abbey's best known feature: its extensive Carolingian **crypts**, whose famous frescoes, which date from around 850 AD, are among the oldest yet found in France. They were discovered in 1927 beneath some 17th-century paintings. The crypts themselves, the most important Carolingian monument in Burgundy, form a veritable subterranean church. They must be visited with a guide; tours begin every hour (every half-hour in summer).

The monastery buildings around the cloister, which date from the 14th to 17th centuries, house Auxerre's **Musée d'Art et d'Histoire**. Gallo-Roman antiquities are displayed on the 1st floor, while the 2nd floor houses a collection of prehistoric and protohistoric stone implements. Sections dedicated to fine arts (painting, sculpture, etc) and contemporary art are being added.

Tour de l'Horloge

The spire-topped clock tower over Rue de l'Horloge was built in 1483 as part of the city's fortifications on the site of the city's main gate during Gallo-Roman times. The spire was destroyed by fire in 1825 and rebuilt in 1891. On the 17th-century clock, the hand with a sun on one end indicates the time of day. The other hand, which has an orb on one side, shows what day of the lunar month it is; it makes a complete rotation every 29½ days.

Musée Leblanc-Durvernoy

This museum (☎ 86.52.44.63) at 9 Rue d'Égleny displays early 18th-century tapestries from Beauvais (four of which have Chinese themes), faïence from Burgundy and elsewhere, paintings, etc. It occupies a private residence built during the 18th century. The museum is open from 2 to 6 pm (closed Tuesday and holidays). From mid-June to mid-September, it stays open until 6.30 pm (8 pm on Friday). Entrance costs 10FF but is free for students, for everyone who comes on a Wednesday and for people with entry tickets from the Abbaye Saint Germain.

Boat Rental

Bateaux de Bourgogne (☎ 86.52.18.99, 86.51.12.05; fax 86.51.68.47), an organisation representing a dozen companies that rent boats for trips along Burgundy's canals and rivers, is based on the 1st floor of the tourist office building at 1-2 Quai de la République. For general information on boat rental in Burgundy, see Boating on Burgundy's Waterways at the beginning of this chapter.

Organised Tours

From mid-June to mid-September you can join a group (maximum six people) and travel in little trucks that look an awful lot like Bangkok-style tuk-tuks for a half-hour tape-recorded tour of Auxerre in English, French, German or Dutch. The fee is 30FF (25FF each if you're in a group of four or more, 15FF for children aged 5 to 15). The tuk-tuks, which begin their run from outside the tourist office, operate from 10 am to 7 pm and depart when full.

Festivals

The Festival de Jazz takes place during the last week of June.

Places to Stay – bottom end

The tourist office has documentation on gîtes ruraux, gîtes d'étape, camping à la ferme (camping sites on farms) and chambres d'hôte (B&Bs) in the Auxerre area.

Auxerre

To N77 & Troyes (82 km)

To the Auxerrois, Chablis (18 km), Avallon (50 km), Vézelay (52 km), & Autun (112 km) & Dijon (140 km)

To Camping Ground (800 m)

Avenue du Maréchal Juin

Avenue de la Résistance

Footbridge

Rue des Mignottes

Rue Paul Doumer

Rue Jules Ferry

Rue Kruger

Avenue Gambetta

Rue des Prés Coulons

Rue Desmoulins

Avenue Jean Jaurès

Avenue de la Tournelle

Rue Camille

Rue de Brazza

Avenue Bourbotte

Rue Jules Guignier

Rue St-Martin les St-Martins

Yonne River

Port de Plaisance

Quai de la Marine

Quai du Batardeau

Quai de la République

Rue A. Charles

Rue de Preuilly

Rue de la Fraternité

Boulevard Vauban

Rue des Migraines

Rue Faubert

Rue Marceau

Boulevard de la Chaînette

Avenue Charles de Gaulle to Autoroute A6, Sens (57 km) & Paris (166 km)

Rue du Lycée J Amyot

Rue de Paris

Rue Michelet

Grand Caire

Rue du Pont

Rue de la Banque

Rue Française

Rue Paul Armandot

Rue du 24 Août

Rue d'Eckmühl

Rue de l'Égalité

Boulevard du 11 Novembre

Rue du Temple

Rue Germain Bernard

Boulevard Vaulabelle

Rue Marie Noël

Rue du Puits des Dames

Rue Saint Pèlerin

Rue Milliaux

Rue Joubert

Rue Paul Bert

Rue Fécauderie

Rue des Bouchéries

Rue des Sous Murs

Rue Lombards

Rue Fourier

Rue Dampierre

LA MARINE QUARTER

OLD CITY

PLACES TO STAY		34	Inno Store	19	Europcar (Car Rental)
		39	Restaurant Le	21	Pont Paul Bert
2	Hôtel Normandie		Trou Poinchy	23	Tourist Office Annexe
14	Hôtel Saint Sébastien	42	Food Market	24	Focepy (Bike Rental)
17	Hôtel Aquarius			27	Tour de l'Horloge
18	Foyer des Jeunes		OTHER	28	Musée Leblanc-
	Travailleurs				Duvernoy
20	Hôtel Morin &	1	Intercity Bus Station	29	Église Saint Eusèbe
	Restaurant La	3	Laundrette	30	Rue René Schaeffer
	Vie en Rose	4	Abbaye Saint	31	Main Post Office
33	Hôtel Le Commerce		Germain & Musée	37	Église Saint Pierre
36	Hôtel de Seignelay		d'Art et d'Histoire	38	Laundrette
	& Restaurant de	8	Palais de Justice	40	Police Station
	Seignelay	9	Banque de France		
41	Foyer des Jeunes	11	Cathédrale Saint	✕	SQUARES
	Travailleuses		Etienne		
		12	Tourist Office &	5	Place Saint Germain
▼	PLACES TO EAT		Bateaux de	7	Place Saint Nicolas
			Bourgogne	10	Place Saint Étienne
6	Restaurant Le Quai	15	Gare Auxerre-Saint	25	Place des Cordeliers
13	E Leclerc Supermarket		Gervais (Railway	26	Place Charles Lepère
	& Happy Man Pizzeria		Station)	32	Place Charles Surugue
22	Restaurant Jean-Luc	16	Eco Location	35	Place des Véens
	Barnabet		(Car Rental)	43	Place de l'Arquebuse

Camping The *camping ground* (☎ 86.52.11.15) at 8 Route de Vaux, 1.5 km south of the train station and a similar distance southeast of the old city, is open from April to September. The fees are 11FF per person, 5.50FF for place to pitch a tent and 6.50FF for a car. From the old city (Place Robillard or Blvd du 11 Novembre), take bus No 3 towards the Normandie terminus (Les Piedalloues).

Hostels From May to August, the 152-room *Foyer des Jeunes Travailleurs* (☎ 86.46.95.11) at 16 Ave de la Résistance – almost two km from the old city but only 400 metres from the train station – functions as a youth hostel. Basic, dorm-like singles cost 62FF (75FF if you don't have a hostelling card), including breakfast. Doubles are 130FF. Both men and women are welcome. Reception is open daily from 9 am to 10 pm. There's no curfew and rooms are open all day long. Reservations can be made by telephone. You might want to call to make sure they have room before walking out here.

There *may* be rooms available between September and April.

The *Foyer des Jeunes Traivailleuses* (☎ 86.52.45.38), slightly south of the old city at 16 Blvd Vaulabelle, is run by the same organisation as the Foyer des Jeunes Travailleurs. Both men and women are accepted. The charge is 75FF per person. To get there from the train station, take bus No 1 or 6 and get off at the Vaulabelle stop.

Hotels – Train Station Area The *Hôtel Saint Sébastien* (☎ 86.46.90.21), opposite the train station at 9 Rue Paul Doumer, has simple but large singles and doubles with shower and toilet for only 120FF. There's free parking around the back. Reception is closed after 8 pm and on Sunday.

Near the river, the *Hôtel Morin* (☎ 86.46.90.26) at 4 Ave Gambetta has singles/doubles for 80/130FF (with washbasin and bidet), 110/160FF (with shower) and 150/210FF (with bath and toilet). Triples/quads with shower are 210/260FF. Reception is open daily until 11 pm.

BURGUNDY

Places to Stay – middle

Train Station Area The two-star *Hôtel Aquarius* (☎ 86.46.95.02) at 33 Ave Gambetta has small but soundproofed and recently renovated singles/doubles/triples with shower, toilet and TV for 215/255/295FF. The price is a bit high for what you get. Reception is closed daily from 3 to 5.30 pm and on Sunday after 3 pm.

Old City The pleasant *Hôtel de Seignelay* (☎ 86.52.03.48; fax 86.52.32.39) at 2 Rue du Pont is centered around a quiet courtyard. Part of the hotel dates from the 17th century. Spacious doubles with shower, toilet and TV cost 270FF and rooms for three or four people with the same amenities are 300FF. If you have one of the singles with washbasin for 120FF, it costs 20FF to use the shower in the hall. Breakfast costs 30FF. Parking in the locked garage is 20FF. In summer it's a good idea to make reservations. The hotel is closed from mid-February to mid-March and on Monday from October to June.

The *Hôtel Le Commerce* (☎ 86.52.03.16; fax 86.52.42.37) is at 5 Rue René Schaeffer, a very central location across from the main post office. Attractive doubles with shower, toilet and TV are 200 to 260FF; rooms for three or four persons go for 320 to 380FF. The buffet breakfast is 36FF. The private garage costs 30FF.

Bus Station Area The two-star *Hôtel Normandie* (☎ 86.52.57.80; fax 86.51.54.33) at 41 Blvd Vauban has rooms for 220 to 280FF.

Places to Eat

French – expensive An excellent choice for a splurge is *Restaurant Jean-Luc Barnabet* (☎ 86.51.68.88) at 14 Quai de la République, which specialises in innovative versions of traditional French dishes and has been awarded one star by Michelin. *Menus* are available for 160 and 230FF (300FF including wine). There's also a children's *menu* for 95FF. Breton lobster (homard) is available from July to September. You can eat either in the spacious, modern dining room or on the geranium-bedecked terrace. A row of windows lets you watch the chefs at work.

The restaurant is open Tuesday to Saturday from noon to 2.30 pm and 7 to 9.30 pm and noon to 2.30 pm on Sunday. It's closed on Monday. Reservations are recommended for dinner on Friday and Saturday and lunch on Sunday.

French – middle *Restaurant de Seignelay* (☎ 86.52.03.48) at 2 Rue du Pont (in the Hôtel de Seignelay) specialises in classic French and Burgundian cuisine. The rustic dining room has been much upgraded since it served as a stable in the 17th century. *Menus* are available for 63, 98, 125 and 190FF. Except from July to September, this restaurant is closed on Monday. It may also be closed on Sunday evening.

Restaurant Le Quai (☎ 86.51.66.67) is at 4 Place Saint Nicolas, a picturesque public square in La Marine quarter, once the heart of Auxerre's commercial activity. Meals, including a *menu* for 70FF and a plat du jour for 60FF, are served daily from noon to 2 pm and 7.30 to 11.30 pm (midnight on Saturday). Between 11 am and 1 am, this place turns into a café.

Restaurant Le Trou Poinchy (☎ 86.52.04.48) at 34-36 Blvd Vaulabelle is a pretty good deal for the price. First courses cost 40 to 60FF and main dishes are 42 to 95FF. *Menus* are available for 75, 90, 115, 130 and 185FF. From April to September, it is open daily from noon to 2.30 pm and 7 to 10.30 pm. The rest of the year, it's closed on Wednesday and Sunday evening.

Italian The inexpensive *Restaurant La Vie en Rose* (☎ 86.46.90.26) is at 4 Ave Gambetta, a few blocks from the train station. The lunch *menus* cost 56 and 62FF; for dinner there's a 79FF *menu*. This place is open every day at midday and in the evening (until 11 pm). In July and August food is served uninterruptedly from 11 am to 11 pm.

Takeaway pizza is available Monday to Saturday from 11 am to 11 pm at *Happy Man Pizzeria* (☎ 86.52.62.82), which is on Ave Jean Jaurès next to the E Leclerc supermarket.

Self-Catering The *food market* at Place de l'Arquebuse, which is off Rue du Temple from the centre of the old city, is open on Tuesday and Friday mornings.

Near the train station, the *E Leclerc supermarket* between Rue des Prés Coulons and Ave Jean Jaurès is open Monday to Thursday from 9 am to 12.30 pm and 2.30 to 7.30 pm, and on Friday and Saturday from 9 am to 7.30 pm (8 pm on Friday). In the old city, the *Inno store* at 2 Rue du Temple has a food section at the back. It is open Monday to Saturday from 8.30 am to 7.30 pm (8 pm on Friday).

Getting There & Away

Train Gare Auxerre-Saint Gervais (☎ 86.46.93.94; call 86.46.50.50 for SNCF's information service) is on Rue Paul Doumer. The information office is open Monday to Saturday from 8.30 to 11.50 am and 12.15 to 7.30 pm.

Auxerre is on a secondary rail line whose relatively infrequent trains link Laroche-Migennes, a rail junction 15 to 25 minutes north of town on the main Paris-Dijon line, with Avallon (61FF; 1¼ hours) and Autun (93FF; three hours). The trip to Paris's Gare de Lyon (113FF; 1¾ to 2½ hours; eight a day) may require a change of trains at Laroche-Migennes. The last train to Paris leaves Auxerre at 7.30 pm. To get to Dijon (113FF; two to 2½ hours; six or seven a day), you also have to change at Laroche.

Bus The intercity bus station (☎ 86.46.90.66) is on Rue des Migraines. From Monday to Saturday, Les Rapides de Bourgogne (☎ 86.46.90.90) has buses to destinations all over the département of Yonne (including Avallon, Tonnerre and Sens) as well as Nevers and Troyes (in Champagne). Société Rouillard has a round trip from Vézelay to Auxerre (one hour 20 minutes) each Wednesday. The bus leaves Vézelay at 12.30 pm; it departs from Auxerre for the trip back at 5 pm.

Car For car rental, you might try Eco Location (☎ 86.46.61.87) at 13 Rue Jules Ferry, which is right across from the train station. A small car with 100/500 free km costs 220/460FF for one day. The weekend rate (including 500 km) is 560FF. It costs 40FF a day extra to cancel the 4000FF excess.

Getting Around

Bus Le Bus (☎ 86.46.90.90) operates six bus lines, known by their number and the name of the terminal station, which run until sometime between 6.30 and 7.30 pm. Some lines (eg Nos 4 and 5) run only once an hour or less. Schedules are posted at bus stops. Line Nos 1, 2 and 6 link the train station with the city centre, though line No 2 takes the long way around.

Taxi When trains arrive, taxis congregate at the train station. To order a cab 24 hours a day, call ☎ 86.52.51.52 or 86.48.77.96.

Bicycle Focepy (☎ 86.51.86.00), a non-profit organisation with offices at 9 Rue Dampierre, rents mountain bikes all year, except during July and August, for about 60FF a day. It is open Monday to Friday from 9 am to noon and 1.30 to 6.15 pm.

AVALLON

The once-strategic walled town of Avallon (population 9500) is set on a picturesque hilltop overlooking the valley of the Cousin River. The urban charms of the old city's medieval and Renaissance buildings are only a few hundred metres from the tree-covered slopes along the river and its tributaries.

If you don't have a car, Avallon's bus links make it the most convenient place from which to mount a day trip to Vézelay. The town is also a good base for visits to the northern section of the Parc Naturel Régional du Morvan (see Outdoor Activities at the beginning of this chapter). From November to Easter, Avallon is very quiet, at least as far as tourism is concerned.

Orientation

The train station is 900 metres north of Place Vauban, which along with Promenade des Terreaux and Place des Odebert forms Avallon's main square. The walled old city, which begins just south of Place Vauban, is

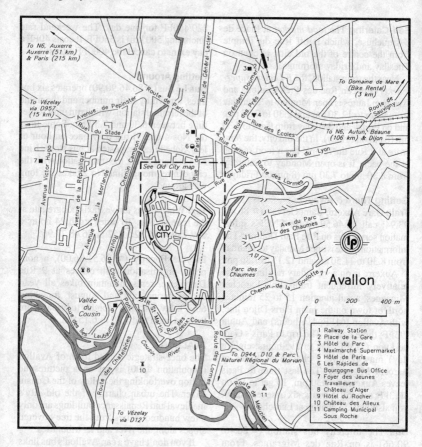

Avallon

1	Railway Station
2	Place de la Gare
3	Hôtel du Parc
4	Maximarché Supermarket
5	Hôtel de Paris
6	Les Rapides de Bourgogne Bus Office
7	Foyer des Jeunes Travailleurs
8	Château d'Alger
9	Hôtel du Rocher
10	Château des Alleux
11	Camping Municipal Sous Roche

built on a roughly triangular granite hilltop with ravines to the east and west. The old city's main commercial street is Grande Rue Aristide Briand.

Information

Tourist Office The tourist office (☎ 86.34. 14.19), which is in a 15th-century house at 4 Rue Bocquillot, is open Tuesday to Saturday (and, from Easter to October, on Sunday and Monday as well) from 9 am to 12.30 pm and 2 to 6.30 pm. During July and August, it's open daily from 9.30 am to 7.30 pm. There's no hotel reservation service, but if you're looking for a place in Avallon they'll call around for you to see where there's space. Ask for a copy of their brochure *Visitor's Guide to Old Avallon*, which provides historical notes for a self-guided tour of the old city.

Money Avallon's banks are closed on Sunday and Monday. The Caisse d'Épargne on Rue Tour du Magasin (off Place Vauban) is open Tuesday to Saturday from 8.30 am to noon and 1.30 to 5.45 pm.

Post Avallon's postcode is 89200.

Travel Agencies Yonne Voyages (☎ 86.34. 04.43) at 51 Grande Rue Aristide Briand sells BIJ tickets. It is open from 9 am to noon and 2.30 to 6.30 pm Monday to Thursday, 9 am to noon on Friday, and 9.30 am to noon on Saturday. It's closed on Sunday.

Walking Tour

Construction of Avallon's fortifications was begun in the 9th century following devastating attacks on the town by Muslim armies from Moorish Spain (731) and the Normans (843). The walls, with their many 15th to 18th-century towers and bastions, can be circumambulated by walking along Rue Tour du Magasin, Ruelle sous les Remparts and Rue de la Fontaine Neuve from either Place Vauban/Promenade de Terreaux or the **Petite Porte**, the gate at the old city's southern tip. The main street *intra muros* (within the walls), Grande Rue Aristide Briand and its continuation, Rue Bocquillot, pass by most of the city's most interesting sights, including **Tour de l'Horloge**, a clock tower built in the middle of the 15th century. Many of the old city's side streets are graced by houses dating from the Middle Ages and the Renaissance.

Promenade de la Petite Porte, the lime tree-shaded area just outside the Petite Porte, affords views across the valley to the **Château d'Alger** and, on the other side of the Cousin River, the **Château des Alleux**.

Église Saint Lazare

A sanctuary dedicated to St Mary was erected on this site in the 4th century; its crypt, the only part of the structure still extant, is under the choir. The present collegiate church was built around 1100, but the masses of pilgrims who came here to visit a piece of the skull of St Lazarus – the relic was believed to provide protection from leprosy – soon rendered the structure inadequate, and in the mid-12th

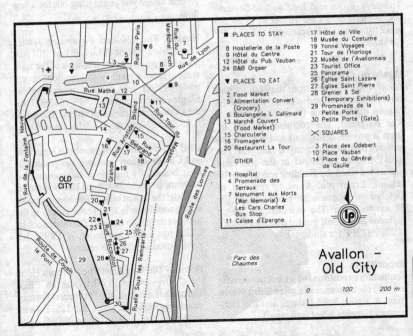

PLACES TO STAY
- 8 Hostellerie de la Poste
- 9 Hôtel du Centre
- 12 Hôtel du Pub Vauban
- 24 B&B Orgaer

PLACES TO EAT
- 2 Food Market
- 5 Alimentation Convert (Grocery)
- 6 Boulangerie L. Gallimard
- 13 Marché Couvert (Food Market)
- 15 Charcuterie
- 16 Fromagerie
- 20 Restaurant La Tour

OTHER
- 1 Hospital
- 4 Promenade des Terraux
- 7 Monument aux Morts (War Memorial) & Les Cars Charles Bus Stop
- 11 Caisse d'Epargne
- 17 Hôtel de Ville
- 18 Musée du Costume
- 19 Yonne Voyages
- 21 Tour de l'Horloge
- 23 Tourist Office
- 25 Panorama
- 26 Église Saint Lazare
- 27 Église Saint Pierre
- 28 Grenier à Sel (Temporary Exhibitions)
- 29 Promenade de la Petite Porte
- 30 Petite Porte (Gate)

SQUARES
- 3 Place des Odebert
- 10 Place Vauban
- 14 Place du Général de Gaulle

Avallon – Old City

Parc des Chaumes

0   100   200 m

century the nave was made larger (though somewhat crooked) by moving the west front 20 metres further west.

The church has two Burgundian-style Romanesque doorways (the third was crushed when the north belfry collapsed in 1633). The portal of the left-hand one is enclosed by five concentric stone arches bearing sculptures of cherubs, the signs of the zodiac, the labours of the months, etc. The remarkable decoration over the other doorway is vegetable and floral.

Musée de l'Avallonnais

This museum (☎ 86.34.03.19) at Place de la Collégiale (behind the tourist office), which was founded in 1862, has a little bit of everything: minerals, fossils, armaments, popular religious art, 20th-century silverwork and paintings, including 58 expressionist sketches by Georges Rouault (1871-1958). It is open from mid-April to 31 October *only*; hours are 10 am to noon and 2 to 6 pm (closed Tuesday). From mid-June to mid-September, opening hours are 10 am to 12.30 pm and 2 to 6.30 pm. A ticket costs 15FF (7.50FF for students).

Musée du Costume

About 100 costumes from the 18th to 20th centuries are displayed in period rooms at the **Musée du Costume** (☎ 86.34.19.95) at 6 Rue Belgrand. The costumes (which are from a private collection) and the accompanying tableaux are changed each year. The mid-19th-century chapel in the basement was added when this building was a Catholic school. From mid-April to the end of October *only*, the museum is open daily from 11 am to 5 pm. The entrance fee, which includes an optional guided tour (in French), is 20FF (12FF for students).

Expositions

Temporary expositions of art and handicrafts are held each summer in **Église Saint Pierre** (next to Église Saint Lazare) and the 18th-century **Grenier à Sel** (salt store).

Hikes

The tourist office has a free map of the route to take for an eight-km, two-hour circuit around the old city walls and through the surrounding countryside. It is entitled *Avallon Découverte*.

Organised Tours

From July to about mid-September, the tourist office sponsors guided tours of the city (in French) every Tuesday and Saturday at 3 pm. The charge is 25FF.

Places to Stay – bottom end

Camping The attractive *Camping Municipal sous Roche* (☎ 86.34.10.39), which is a couple of km south-east of the old city and three km south of the train station, is set in the middle of a forest on the banks of the shallow Cousin River. It is open from 15 March to 15 October. The charges are 15FF per adult, 10FF for a place to pitch a tent and 10FF for parking. This is the kind of camping ground where you could hang out for a few days.

Hostels The 150-bed *Foyer des Jeunes Travailleurs* (☎ 86.34.01.88) at 10 Ave Victor Hugo, two km south-west of the train station, is not a youth hostel but does accept travellers all year long if there's space. Singles/doubles cost 68/100FF (63/90FF for the second and subsequent nights). Breakfast is 13.50FF. Meals are available for 40FF.

B&B From Easter to September, Geneviève and Claude Orgaer rent out two rooms in their beautifully furnished, three-centuries-old home (☎ 86.34.28.85) at 5 Rue Bocquillot, opposite the tourist office. The lovely double with a washbasin is 160FF; the toilet's in the hall, but there's no shower. The other double, which has a bath and toilet, is 250FF. It's possible to call ahead to reserve.

Hotels – Old City Area The 14-room *Hôtel du Centre* (☎ 86.34.40.10) at 16 Place Vauban has old-fashioned but recently renovated singles and doubles for 125FF (with washbasin and bidet), 140 to 190FF (with shower and toilet) and 170 to 250FF (with bath and toilet). Triples and quads with shower and toilet are 190FF. Adding an additional bed costs 35FF. There are no hall showers. Reception is closed on Wednesday.

The *Hôtel de Paris* (☎ 86.34.10.05) at 45-47 Rue de Paris has utterly nondescript doubles for 80FF (with washbasin) and 120FF (with shower). Triples and quads with shower are 160FF. Rooms for two to four people with bath and toilet cost only 170FF. Reception is closed on Thursday and also on Sunday from 3 to 7 pm.

Hotels – Train Station Area The *Hôtel du Parc* (☎ 86.34.17.00), across the street from the train station, has ordinary but eminently serviceable singles/doubles with washbasin for 125/145FF. Rooms for one or two people cost 145FF with shower and 200FF with shower and toilet. Use of the hall shower costs 15FF. If you'll be coming back after 11 pm, ask for a key. The hotel is closed from 15 December to 15 January.

Hotels – Outskirts The 14-room *Hôtel du Rocher* (☎ 86.34.19.03) at 11 Rue des Îles Labaume in the Vallée du Cousin (the Cousin River valley) is the best deal in town if you don't mind rooms without showers or toilets. Plain, old-fashioned, wood-panelled doubles/two-bed quads are just 85/125FF. A 15-minute shower costs 2FF. Unfortunately, this place is inconvenient to get to (it's about 2.5 km south-east of the train station) unless you have a car. Reception is closed on Monday unless it's a holiday. The hotel shuts down from mid-December to mid-January.

Places to Stay – middle
The *Hôtel du Pub Vauban* (☎ 86.34.02.20) at 3 Rue Mathé (Place Vauban) has nondescript but comfortable doubles with shower, toilet and TV for 190 to 220FF.

Places to Stay – top end
The three-star *Hostellerie de la Poste* (☎ 86.34.06.12; fax 86.34.47.11) at 13 Place Vauban is a former mail coach stop (thus the courtyard) that dates from 1707. Over the

centuries it has hosted distinguished guests, including Napoleon (on his way back from exile on the island of Elba) and American presidents Eisenhower and Kennedy. The antique-style décor is comfortable but not conspicuously luxurious. There's a lovely flower garden out the back. Quiet singles cost 250 to 400FF, while doubles are 450 to 750FF. The suites are 1100FF. Free parking is available. The hotel is usually closed from mid-November to early April.

Places to Eat
Restaurants *Restaurant La Tour* (☎ 86.34. 24.84) at 84 Grande Rue Aristide Briand (at the base of Tour de l'Horloge) has pizzas (30 to 47FF) and crepes (12 to 25FF). It is open from noon to 2 pm and 7 to 10.30 pm Tuesday to Saturday, and 7 to 10.30 pm on Sunday. It's closed on Monday.

Self-Catering Good places in town for a picnic include the garden behind Abbatiale Saint Lazare and Promenade de la Petite Porte, which is just outside the Petite Porte.

The cheapest supermarket in Avallon is the *Maximarché* on Rue des Prés, midway between the train station and the old city. It is open Monday to Saturday from 9 am to 7 pm (8 pm on Friday).

The *food market* at Place des Odebert is open on Thursday and Saturday mornings. The *marché couvert* next to Place du Général de Gaulle is open on Saturday morning.

To assemble a meal on other days of the week, *Alimentation Convert*, a small grocery at 4 Place des Odebert, is open daily from 8.30 am to 12.30 pm and 2 to 7.30 or 8 pm. Almost across the street at 12 Rue de Paris, *Boulangerie L Gallimard* is open from 6 am to 8 pm (closed Monday).

There are a number of boulangeries and food shops around Place Vauban and along Grande Rue Aristide Briand, including the *charcuterie* at 17 Grande Rue Aristide Briand, which has meats, cheeses and prepared salads. It is open from 8.30 am to 12.30 pm and 2.30 to 7.30 pm daily except Sunday afternoon and Monday. The *fromagerie* at 3 Place du Général de Gaulle is open from 9 am to 12.30 pm and 3.30 to 7.30 pm daily except Sunday afternoon and Monday.

Getting There & Away
Train Avallon's train station (☎ 86.34. 01.01), which is at Place de la Gare, is linked to Paris's Gare de Lyon (143FF; three hours), usually with a change at Laroche-Migennes; to Dijon (three or more hours; five to eight a day) via both Laroche-Migennes and Autun; to Autun (61FF; about 1¾ hours; four to six a day) and to Auxerre (61FF; 1¼ hours; four to six a day). There are connections to all sorts of other destinations via Laroche-Migennes. For information on getting to Vézelay by train and bus, see Getting There & Away under the Vézelay listing.

Bus From Monday to Friday, it is possible to take a day trip to Vézelay on buses operated by Les Cars de la Madeleine (☎ 86.33. 25.67), whose stop in Avallon is at Café de l'Europe (☎ 86.34.04.45) at 7 Place Vauban. For details, see Getting There & Away in the Vézelay listing.

From Monday to Saturday, Transco (☎ 80.42.11.00 in Dijon) bus No 49 links Dijon with Avallon's train station three times a day. Buses leave Avallon at around 6.15 am, noon and 5 pm; departures from Dijon are at about 7 am, 12.20 pm and 6 pm. On Sunday, there is a bus from Avallon at 5 pm and buses from Dijon at 12.20 and 6 pm. The trip takes 2¼ hours and is, in most cases, faster, cheaper and more convenient than the train. Schedules are available at the tourist office.

A good way to get into the Parc Naturel Régional du Morvan is to take the bus run by Les Cars Charles (☎ 86.84.61.67) from Avallon's Monument aux Morts (the war memorial at the intersection of Rue de Lyon and Rue du Maréchal Foch) to Dun-les-Places (1½ hours), a village 25 km south of Avallon. This line has five round trips each week: on Tuesday (once in the morning, once in the afternoon), Thursday (same hours as Tuesday) and on Saturday morning.

Les Rapides de Bourgogne (☎ 86.34. 00.00), which operates buses to destinations

all over the département of Yonne (including Auxerre), has an office at 35 Rue de Paris. It is open from 8.30 am to noon and 3 to 5 pm daily except Saturday afternoon and Sunday.

Getting Around
Car There's parking in front of Église Saint Lazare and at Promenade des Terreaux.

Bicycle Bicycles can be rented at the train station every day from 9 am to 9 pm. The cost is 55FF a day (44FF a half-day).

Domaine de Mare (☎ 86.34.55.30) in Sauvigny-le-Bois, which is four km north of town along D957, has mountain bikes for 90FF a day (65FF for a half-day) and 450FF a week. Reservations can be made by telephone. It is open daily from June to September. During the rest of the year, you can get in touch by phone; the best times to call are early in the morning or at night.

VÉZELAY
The tiny village of Vézelay (population 550) is one of the architectural and historical gems of France. Perched on a hilltop for defence purposes, this medieval walled town is surrounded by some of the most beautiful countryside in Burgundy – a patchwork of vineyards, sunflower fields, hay and grazing sheep.

Vézelay is 15 km from Avallon and 51 km from Auxerre and lies within the Parc Naturel Régional du Morvan (see Outdoor Activities at the beginning of this chapter). With or without a car, it makes a delightful day trip from Avallon. In the warm months, Vézelay is often crowded with visitors, but in winter there are very few tourists, especially in January.

History
A Benedictine monastery was established on this hilltop in the 9th century after an earlier monastery at what is now the village of Saint Père had been ravaged by the Normans (Vikings). Thanks to the relics of St Mary Magdalene, to which great miracles were attributed, Vézelay became an important site of pilgrimage in the 1000s and 1100s. It also

served as the starting point of one of the four pilgrimage routes to Saint Jacques de Compostelle (Santiago de Compostela) in Spain (see the aside on Santiago de Compostela in the Limousin, Périgord & Quercy chapter).

Vézelay reached the height of its renown and power in the 12th century. St Bernard, leader of the Cistercian order, preached the Second Crusade here in 1146 in the presence of French king Louis VII; and in 1190, France's King Philip Augustus and England's King Richard the Lion-Heart met up here before setting out on the Third Crusade. Louis IX (Saint Louis) visited the town several times in the 13th century.

Orientation

Place du Champ-de-Foire, the parking lot that doubles as a bus terminal, is linked to the basilica (which is at the summit of the hill) by Rue Saint Étienne and its continuation, Rue Saint Pierre.

Information

Tourist Office The syndicat d'initiative (☎ 86.33.23.69; fax 86.33.34.00) is on Rue Saint Pierre. From April to October *only*, it's open from 10 am to 1 pm and 2 to 6 pm daily except Wednesday and Sunday (daily in July and August). Hotel reservations in Vézelay cost 10FF. During the months when the office is closed, the telephone number for tourist information is (☎ 86.33.24.62. The postal address (valid all year) is Boîte Postale 13, 89450 Vézelay.

Money There are no banks. It *may* be possible to change money at the tourist office, but don't count on it.

Post There's a post office on Rue Saint Étienne.

Vézelay's postcode is 89450.

Walking Tour

Starting from the Place du Champ-de-Foire, it is possible to walk around Vézelay's medieval ramparts along what is known as the **Promenade des Fossés**. Within the walls, all of the streets (of which there are only about half a dozen) are lined with picturesque old houses.

Basilique Sainte Madeleine

This former abbey church (☎ 86.33.24.36) was founded in the 9th century under Charlemagne and completely rebuilt between the 11th and 13th centuries. In 1569 (during the Wars of Religion), it was trashed by the Huguenots. Further damage was inflicted during the Revolution, when parts were demolished, and by lightning strikes. By the 19th century, it was – like many medieval churches in France – on the point of collapse. In 1840, the restoration architect Viollet-le-Duc undertook the daunting task of rescuing the structure. The massive restoration project he led, during which significant parts of the building were completely rebuilt (eg the west front and its doorways) continued for 20 years.

As its name implies, Basilique Sainte Madeleine houses what, during the Middle Ages, were believed to be the relics of St Mary Magdelene. During the 11th and 12th centuries, when this was an abbey church affiliated with Cluny, huge numbers of pilgrims came to Vézelay to celebrate her saint's day, 22 July. In 1120, during the annual pilgrimage, the nave caught fire and over a thousand pilgrims, trapped inside the blazing structure, perished. The tradition of celebrating 22 July continues, and every year celebrations – including a procession in which the relics are paraded around town – are held.

The early 13th-century **tympanum** between the mid-12th-century narthex (prenave, ie entry hall) and the nave is considered a masterpiece of Burgundian-style Romanesque sculpture. The carvings, mercifully untouched by vandals or restorers, illustrate the Pentecost. Jesus, seated on a throne on the almond-shaped panel in the middle, is pictured with the Apostles on either side. His hands are outstretched to welcome all the known peoples of the earth – the Arabs, the Armenians, the Byzantines, the Cappadocians (the Turks), the Ethiopians, the Jews, etc – represented by the figures on the

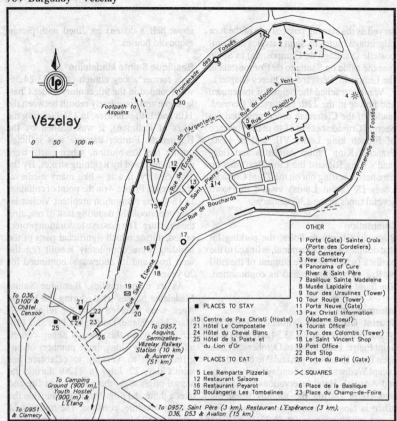

Vézelay

Footpath to Asquins

0   50   100 m

To D36, D100 & Châtel Censoir

To D957, Asquins, Sermizelles-Vézelay Railway Station (10 km) & Auxerre (51 km)

To Camping Ground (900 m), Youth Hostel (900 m) & L'Étang

To D951 & Clamecy

To D957, Saint Père (3 km), Restaurant L'Espérance (3 km), D36, D53 & Avallon (15 km)

OTHER

1 Porte (Gate) Sainte Croix (Porte des Cordeliers)
2 Old Cemetery
3 New Cemetery
4 Panorama of Cure River & Saint Père
5 Basilique Sainte Madeleine
8 Musée Lapidaire
9 Tour des Ursulines (Tower)
10 Tour Rouge (Tower)
11 Tour Neuve (Gate)
13 Pax Christi Information (Madame Boeuf)
14 Tourist Office
17 Tour des Colombs (Tower)
18 Le Saint Vincent Shop
19 Post Office
22 Bus Stop
26 Porte du Barle (Gate)

■ PLACES TO STAY

15 Centre de Pax Christi (Hostel)
21 Hôtel Le Compostelle
24 Hôtel du Cheval Blanc
25 Hôtel de la Poste et du Lion d'Or

▼ PLACES TO EAT

5 Les Remparts Pizzeria
12 Restaurant Saisons
16 Restaurant Peyrot
20 Boulangerie Les Tombelines

✕ SQUARES

6 Place de la Basilique
23 Place du Champ-de-Foire

eight panels above the Apostles. The lintels are decorated with fantastical figures representing pagan peoples marching towards Jesus and the True Faith. They are endowed with all sorts of bizarre features – grotesquely large ears, the heads of dogs, etc – that illustrate how foreignness was seen by the unworldly artists of the period. On the recessed arch enclosing the whole scene, the signs of the zodiac alternate with medallions depicting the labours of the months.

The interior is a study in comparative architecture. The enormous **nave** (which is 62 metres long, 12 metres wide and 18 metres high), rebuilt using stone of various shades in the decade and a half following the great fire of 1120, is in the Romanesque style; it is endowed with round arches and small windows, features typical of Romanesque churches. The transept and choir, on the other hand, date from around 1215 and have ogival arches and much larger windows, two of the hallmarks of Gothic architecture. The **sculpted capitals** adorning the two rows of colums in the nave are quite famous. There is a mid-12th-century **crypt** under the transept crossing.

The basilica is open from sun-up to sundown (7 am to 7 pm in summer). In July and August, it is also open on Tuesday and

Friday nights from 9 to 10.30 pm. The entrance is through a small door on the building's south side. An English-language guide booklet is available for 25FF. In July and August, the basilica is staffed by friendly volunteer guides who may speak English. **Tour Saint Michel**, the bell tower on the south side of the west front, is presently closed to visitors because of safety concerns. Its counterpart on the façade's north side was never built. The basilica's exterior is illuminated at night during the warm part of the year.

Musée Lapidaire

This small museum is next to the basilica in the chapter house and its cloisters, which were extensively restored by Viollet-le-Duc in the 19th century. There are entrances from the parking lot and via the basilica's south transept.

Panorama

The park behind the basilica affords wonderful views of the Cure River valley and nearby villages, including Saint Père and other parts of the northern Morvan. This is a great spot for a picnic.

Old Cemetery

From the north side of the basilica, a dirt road leads northward down to the old cemetery (on the left) and the new cemetery (on the right). There are lovely views from here northward along the Cure River valley.

Hikes

You can walk from Vézelay in almost any direction and find yourself within minutes in the midst of the gorgeous countryside of the Morvan. From the village of Asquins, which is at the foot of the hill, there are footpaths along the Cure River. There's a footpath to Asquins from the Promenade des Fossés.

Organised Tours

During July and August there are guided tours (in French) on Saturday at 3 pm. Enquire at the tourist office.

Places to Stay

Most of the places to stay in Vézelay close for at least part of the winter. There are quite a number of hotels in the villages around Vézelay, perfect if you have a car. Details are available from local tourist offices.

Places to Stay – bottom end

Camping The *camping ground* (☎ 86.33. 24.18 in the summer, 86.33.25.57 in the off season) is on a grassy hillside 900 metres south-west of Place du Champ-de-Foire along the road towards L'Étang. It costs 10FF per person, 3FF for a tent and 3FF for parking. There's a youth hostel here as well. This is an excellent spot for a few days of lounging around in the countryside.

There are also *camping grounds* in the villages of Saint Père (☎ 86.33.26.62) and Asquins (☎ 86.33.20.14, 86.33.30.80).

Hostels Vézelay has two very cheap hostelling options. The small, unassuming *youth hostel* (☎ 86.33.24.18 in the summer, 86.33.25.57 in the off season) is located at the camping ground. It *may* be open only from May to September. The charge is 40FF per person and 15FF for sheets. You must have a hostelling card. Kitchen facilities are available. The rooms are closed from 10 am to 5 pm.

The dilapidated, informal *Centre de Pax Christi* (☎ 86.33.26.73) on Rue de l'École, which is affiliated with a Catholic youth organisation but accepts travellers of all backgrounds, is open from Easter to mid-November. A dorm bed costs only 36FF for the first night and 26FF for subsequent nights. There is a 16FF charge to use the kitchen. To find out if they have room (and, if there is, to pick up the key), go *before* 8 pm to the home of Madame Bœuf (☎ 86.33.21.69), a woman who runs the centre on a voluntary basis, at 85 Rue Saint Pierre. It's the grey house with geraniums in the windows across the street from 70 Rue Saint Pierre.

Hotels The *Hôtel du Cheval Blanc* (☎ 86.33. 22.12; fax 86.33.34.29) at Place du Champ-de-Foire has only eight rooms, ranging in price from 80FF (with washbasin) to 180FF (with shower but without toilet). The hotel stays open all year, but reception is closed for 1½ days a week (the schedule changes from week to week). In July and August, though, it's open every day.

Places to Stay – middle

The two-star *Hôtel Le Compostelle* (☎ 86. 33.28.63; fax 86.33.34.34) at 1 Place du Champ-de-Foire has modern, spotless and soundproofed doubles in tan, pink and grey for 240 to 300FF; the more expensive rooms have a better view. Triples are 350FF, while quads (with four single beds, two of which are in a loft) cost 420FF. Breakfasts are available for 30 and 47FF. Reservations are necessary on holiday weekends. This place is closed in January.

Places to Stay – top end

The three-star *Hôtel de la Poste et du Lion d'Or* (☎ 86.33.21.23; 86.32.30.92) at Place du Champ-de-Foire has doubles for 340 to 580FF. Breakfast is 41FF. It is open from early April to early November.

Restaurant L'Espérance (☎ 86.33.20.45; fax 86.33.26.15), which is three km from Vézelay (see Places to Eat), also has a luxury hotel. Rooms cost 640 to 1200FF; breakfast is 100FF. It's advisable to reserve two months ahead.

Places to Eat

French – expensive *Restaurant L'Espérance* (☎ 86.33.20.45; fax 86.33.26.15) in Saint Père-sous-Vézelay (three km towards Avallon from Vézelay along the D957) is one of only about 20 restaurants in all of France that have been awarded three stars by Michelin. It is owned by the chef, Marc Meneau. To be sure of getting a place, reservations should be made a week in advance, though sometimes there's space the day before. *Menus* range from 560 to 750FF. L'Esperance is closed on Tuesday, on Wednesday at midday and from early January to early February.

French – inexpensive The informal, rustic *Restaurant Peyarot* (☎ 86.33.27.34) at 39 Rue Saint Étienne specialises in such regional dishes as escargots and coq au vin. They have a *menu* for 56FF. From early to mid-March to the end of November, this place is open from noon to 3 pm and 7 to 10 pm (closed Wednesday). In July and August, the weekly closure is either Wednesday evening or Thursday evening.

Vegetarian *Restaurant Saisons* (☎ 86.33. 31.66) on Rue de l'École specialises in home-grown, macrobiotic vegetarian dishes, including delicious quiche (28FF). It is open for lunch (noon to 2.30 pm) daily, except Thursday, in the summer *only*. This place is run by the daugher of Max-Pol Fouchet (1913-80), a writer who lived in this house.

Pizza *Les Remparts Pizzeria* (☎ 86.33. 34.15) at Place de la Basilique has pizzas (36 to 45FF) and several local dishes. Lunch is served daily except Tuesday; it's also open in the evening on weekends. From July to September and during school holidays, it is open daily from noon to 3 pm and 7 to 10 pm.

Self-Catering The *Casino grocery* on Rue Saint Étienne is open Monday to Saturday from 8.30 am to 12.30 pm and 3 to 7 pm and from 8.30 am to noon on Sunday; it's closed on Wednesday. In July and August, the store is open every day from 8.30 am to 7.30 pm; September hours are the same except that it closes from 1 to 2.30 pm and is open on Sunday from 9 am to 7 pm.

Boulangerie Les Tombelines at 12 Rue Saint Étienne doubles as a tea room. It is open from 7.30 am to 8 pm daily except Wednesday (daily from July to September).

Entertainment

During summer there are all sorts of concerts and cultural events here. Details are available at the tourist office.

Things to Buy

Locally made jams, honey cake, *pains d'épices* (gingerbread), mustard, sweets, wines and other alcoholic beverages are on sale at *Le Saint Vincent* (☎ 86.33.27.79), which is opposite 31 Rue Saint Étienne. It is open daily from the week before Easter until 11 November. Hours are 9.30 am to 1 pm and 2.30 to 7 pm. Other stores nearby carry similar local products.

Getting There & Away

Train & Bus Without a car, getting to Vézelay is a bit complicated but not dauntingly so. Transport is easiest from Avallon, but with a train-bus combo is also possible from Auxerre, Autun, Dijon, Paris and elsewhere. It's not a bad idea to give Les Cars de la Madeleine a call before setting out, especially if the cancellation of a particular bus will leave you totally stranded. All the tourist office personnel I (Daniel) talked to (including those in Vézelay itself) were poorly informed about the finer points of bus service to/from Vézelay.

Les Cars de la Madeleine (☎ 86.33.25.67) operates buses linking Place du Champ-de-Foire in Vézelay with Avallon's Café de l'Europe (☎ 86.34.04.45), which is at 7 Place Vauban. From Monday to Friday during the school year, the first bus *to* Vézelay (15FF; 20 minutes on most runs) leaves Avallon at 8.15 am; the last bus back departs from Vézelay at 4.30 pm (1 pm on Wednesday). During the summer school holidays, there's an Avallon-Vézelay bus from Monday to Friday at 8.15 am; the last Vézelay-Avallon bus departs at 6.30 pm. There's also an Avallon-Vézelay bus on Saturday at 11.30 am but there's no way to get back in the afternoon unless you hitch, take a taxi or walk.

Société Rouillard links Vézelay with Auxerre (1 hour 20 minutes) every Wednesday. The bus leaves Vézelay at about 12.30 pm; it departs from the Auxerre bus station for the trip back at 5 pm.

The Sermizelles-Vézelay train station (☎ 86.33.41.78), which is about 10 km north of Vézelay, is on the rail line linking Laroche-Migennes with Auxerre (50 minutes to Sermizelles; five or six a day), Avallon (15 minutes; five or six a day) and Autun (two hours; three to five a day). There are also trains (via Laroche-Migennes) from Paris and Dijon to Sermizelles-Vézelay.

During the summer school holidays, there are buses from the Sermizelles-Vézelay train station to the village of Vézelay (10.50FF; 20 minutes) at 10 am Monday to Saturday and 3.20 pm Monday to Friday; Vézelay-Sermizelles buses depart at 9.30 am Monday to Saturday and 2.55 pm Monday to Friday. During the school year, there is only one round trip a day from Monday to Saturday: Sermizelles to Vézelay at 10 am, Vézelay to Sermizelles at 9.30 am.

Taxi To order a taxi for travel in the vicinity of Vézelay (eg to/from Sermizelles-Vézelay train station), call ☎ 86.33.25.67 or 86.33.24.45.

Hitching It is said to be fairly easy to hitch around these parts – given the lack of public transport, the locals tend to be sympathetic.

Bicycle The D957 is the shortest way to get from Avallon to Vézelay (15 km), but this route is heavily trafficked, doesn't have shoulders and isn't particularly attractive. The less direct tertiary roads known as the D53 and the D36 (via Island and Menades) are much quieter and more scenic, in part because they'll take you through (and over) quite a few hills.

Lyon

The grand city of Lyon (Lyons; population 418,000) is the focal point of a prosperous urban area of almost two million people, the second-largest conurbation in France. Founded by the Romans over 2000 years ago, it has spent the last 500 years as a commercial, industrial and banking power-house. Despite its reputation for being a bit staid, bourgeois and even austere, present-day Lyon is endowed with outstanding museums, a dynamic cultural life, an important university, classy big-city shopping and lively pedestrian malls that are great for strolling. Lyon is also renowned for its cuisine – it is, after all, one of the gastronomic capitals of France and the world, even for people on a budget.

History

Lyon, founded in 43 BC as a military colony under the name of Lugdunum, served under Augustus as the capital of the Roman territories known as the Three Gauls. Christianity was introduced in the 2nd century AD, when the city was at the height of its Roman glory.

Lyon's extraordinary prosperity began in the 16th century, when banks were established and great commercial fairs – begun in the early 1400s – were held, giving an impetus to trade. Printing with moveable type arrived in 1473, a mere two decades after its invention, and within 50 years Lyon was one of Europe's foremost publishing centres, with several hundred resident printers.

Silk-weaving had been introduced in the 15th century, but it was not until the mid-1700s that the city became the silk-weaving capital of Europe. Industrial relations during the 19th century were dominated by a number of bitter silk-weavers' strikes (the result of inhumane working conditions and extremely low pay) in which hundreds of people were killed. The famous *traboules*, a network of covered passageways in Croix Rousse and Vieux Lyon originally built to facilitate the transport of silk during inclem-

ent weather, proved very useful to the Resistance during WW II.

From 1942 to 1944, the local Gestapo chief, Claus Barbie ('the Butcher of Lyon'), was responsible for killing some 4000 people and deporting 7500 others to concentration camps. In 1983, after being extradited from Bolivia (where he had settled after working for US counterintelligence in the late 1940s), he was tried for crimes against humanity and sentenced to life imprisonment. In 1944, as the Germans retreated, they blew up all but one of the city's two dozen bridges.

Lyon has been an important centre of scientific enquiry since the 18th century and has produced such eminent inventors as the physicist André-Marie Ampère (1775-1836), after whom the basic unit of electric current was named, and the Lumière brothers, pioneers in the field of motion picture photography. The novelist and aviator Antoine de Saint Exupéry (1900-44), author of *The Little Prince*, was also born here. Lyon is the site of the world headquarters of the International Criminal Police Organisation, better known as Interpol.

Top: Autumn in the village of Venosc, French Alps (OT Les Deux Alpes)
Left: Winter in the village of Tignes, French Alps (RN)
Right: Summer-only residences, Haute Maurienne Valley, French Alps (GC)

Top: Interior of the Musée des Beaux-Arts, Strasbourg, Alsace (GA)
Middle: Stained-glass window, Cathédrale Saint Jean, Perpignan (LL);
The *cardabelle*, a natural barometer (GC); Old café doorway (LL)
Bottom: Evening at a French café (LL)

Orientation

Lyon's bustling city centre is on the Presqu'île, a long 500-to-800-metre-wide peninsula bounded by the Rhône and Saône rivers. At the northern end, the elevated area 500 metres north of Place des Terreaux is known as Croix Rousse. Enormous Place Bellecour is 1.2 km south of Place des Terreaux and one km north of Place Carnot. Place Carnot is just north of Gare de Perrache, one of Lyon's two train stations. Place de la République is about midway between Place des Terreaux and Place Bellecour;

Place Ampère is halfway between Place Bellecour and Gare de Perrache. Vieux Lyon, situated on the west bank of the Saône, is sandwiched between the river and the hilltop area known as Fourvière.

The other train station, Gare de la Part-Dieu, is two km east of the Presqu'île in a modernistic commercial district known as La Part-Dieu. It is dominated by the Crédit Lyonnais building, a reddish cylindrical tower topped with a pyramid. The Lyon suburb of Villeurbanne begins 2.5 km east of the northern Presqu'île.

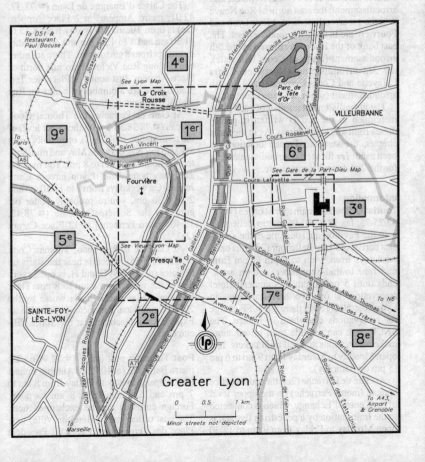

Greater Lyon

In this chapter, the city's highlights are divided into four listings entitled Vieux Lyon, Fourvière, the Presqu'île and Elsewhere in Lyon. Accommodation and places to eat are listed according to their proximity to Place des Terreaux, Place de la République, Place Bellecour, Place Ampère, Gare de Perrache, Vieux Lyon and La Part-Dieu areas.

Arrondissements Lyon proper is divided into nine arrondissements. The area of the Presqu'île south of Rue Neuve (one block north of the Banque de France) forms the 2nd arrondissement; the area north of Rue Neuve is in the 1st arrondissement. Vieux Lyon and Fourvière are in the 5th arrondissement. The east bank of the Rhône is covered by the 6th arrondissement (north of Cours Lafayette), the 3rd arrondissement (between Cours Lafayette and Cours Gambetta) and the 7th arrondissement (south of Cours Gambetta).

The arrondissement number of each place mentioned in the text is written in parentheses right after the address. As in the Paris chapter, the standard French notation has been used: *1er* for the 1st arrondissement, *2e* for the 2nd arrondissement, etc.

Information

Tourist Office The main tourist office (☎ 78. 42.25.75; fax 78.37.02.06; metro Bellecour) is in the Pavillon du Tourisme in the southeast corner of Place Bellecour (2e). It is open weekdays from 9 am to 6 pm (7 pm from mid-June to mid-September) and on weekends until 5 pm (6 pm in summer). Hotel reservations at one/two/three-star hotels in Lyon cost 5/10/15FF; there's a 30FF charge for reservations elsewhere in France. The SNCF desk can provide train information, make reservations and sell train tickets. It is open Monday to Saturday from 9 am to 6 pm (5 pm on Saturday).

At Gare de Perrache (2e), the tourist office annexe (metro Perrache) on the upper level of the Centre d'Échange, which is connected to the train station by a pedestrian flyover, is open Monday to Friday from 9 am to 12.30 pm and 2 to 6 pm and on Saturday from 9 am to 5 pm.

Money The Banque de France (☎ 72.41. 25.10/25; metro Cordeliers) is at 14 Rue de la République (2e) next to Place de la Bourse. It is open Monday to Friday from 8.45 am to 12.15 pm and 1.30 to 3.30 pm. American Express (☎ 78.37.40.69; metro Bellecour) is near Place de la République at 6 Rue Childebert (2e). It's open Monday to Friday from 9 am to noon and 2 to 6 pm; from May to September it's also open on Saturday morning.

The Caisse d'Épargne de Lyon (☎ 78.37. 42.01; metro Ampère) at 2 Place Ampère (2e) is open Tuesday to Friday from 8.15 to 11.30 am and 1 to 4.30 pm and on Saturday mornings from 8 am to noon. There are other banks along Rue Victor Hugo just north of Place Ampère. Just south of Place des Terreaux, there are a number of banks on Rue du Bât d'Argent.

At Gare de Perrache, the Thomas Cook bureau (☎ 78.38.38.84) on the upper level of the train station building is open daily from 8.30 am to 7 pm. Between May and mid-September hours are 8 am to 8 pm. You may get a slightly better rate if you have a Carte Jeunes. On weekdays from 9 to 11.30 am and 2 to 4.30 pm, you're probably better off going to the Société Générale (☎ 78.42. 15.46; metro Perrache) at 12 Place Carnot (2e).

At Gare de la Part-Dieu, Thomas Cook (☎ 72.33.48.55), which is near the stairs up to Voies (platforms) G and H, is open every day of the week from 8 am to 8 pm. Their less-than-stellar rate is made worse by the 20FF commission. American Express has an Express Cash machine near the Sortie Villette exit.

Post The main post office (☎ 72.40.65.22; metro Bellecour) at 10 Place Antonin Poncet (2e) is open Monday to Friday from 8 am to 7 pm and Saturday from 8 am to noon. Foreign currency can be exchanged here. The post office (metro Hôtel de Ville) near Place des Terreaux at 3 Rue du Président

Édouard Herriot (1er) also has a currency exchange service; it is open Monday to Friday from 8 am to 7 pm and on Saturday from 8.30 am to noon. The branch post office (metro Ampère) at 8 Place Ampère (2e) is open weekdays from 8.30 am to 6.30 pm and on Saturday from 8 am to noon.

Lyon's five-digit postcode consists of the digits '6900' followed by the number of the arrondissement (one to nine), which is listed in parenthesis after each address mentioned in the text.

Foreign Consulates The UK consulate (☎ 78.37.59.67; metro Bellecour) on the 4th floor at 24 Rue Childebert (2e) is open on weekdays from 10 am to 12.30 pm and 2.30 to 5 pm. The US consulate (☎ 78.24.68.49; metro Foch) is across the Rhône from Place des Terreaux on the 4th floor at 7 Quai du Général Sarrail (6e). The American services section is open weekdays from 9 am to noon and 2 to 5 pm (4 pm on Friday).

Travel Agencies Council Travel (☎ 78.37.09.56; metro Ampère), the US-based student travel agency, has an office at 36 Quai du Docteur Gailleton (2e). This is a good place to pick up cheap air tickets, especially if you're a student. BIJ rail tickets are also sold here. The office is open from 9.30 am to 12.30 pm and 1.30 to 6.30 pm daily except Saturday afternoon and Sunday. It may also be open on Saturday afternoon from 1.30 to 5 pm.

BIJ tickets are also available at the Voyages Wasteels office (☎ 78.37.80.17; metro Perrache) on the upper level of the Centre d'Échange, the building connected by flyover to Gare de Perrache. It's open Monday to Saturday from 9 am to 7 pm (6 pm on Saturday). The other Voyages Wasteels office (☎ 78.42.65.37; metro Ampère) at 5 Place Ampère (2e) is open Monday to Saturday from 9 am to noon and 2 to 6.30 pm (5.30 pm on Saturday).

USIT Voyages (☎ 78.24.15.70) is at 28 Blvd des Brotteaux (6e), 700 metres north of La Part-Dieu train station.

Books & Maps By far the best street plan of Lyon is Michelin's 1:10,000 scale map, known as publication No 30 (or, with a street index, No 31). *Le Petit Paume* is a guide (in French) to Lyon's restaurants, night life, etc written by local university students.

The Eton English Bookshop (☎ 78.92.92.36; metro Bellecour) at 1 Rue du Plat (2e) has lots of new paperbacks as well as some Lonely Planet titles. It is open on Monday from 2 to 7 pm and Tuesday to Saturday from 10 am to 12.30 pm and 1.30 to 7 pm. Students receive a 5% discount.

There is a huge public library *(bibliothèque municipale*; ☎ 78.62.85.20; metro Part-Dieu) in La Part-Dieu at 30 Blvd Vivier Merle (3e), directly opposite the Part-Dieu train station. Nonlending services are available to residents and nonresidents alike Monday to Saturday from 10 am to 7.30 pm (6.30 pm on Saturday). English-language newspapers, books and periodicals are housed on the ground floor (in the Salle d'Information Générale) and on the 2nd floor (in the Salle de Lettres et de Sciences). This is great place to catch up on the news while waiting for a train. The UK consulate reference library is on the 3rd floor at 24 Rue Childebert (2e), one floor below the consulate itself. It is open on weekdays from 10 am to noon and 2.30 to 5 pm.

Laundry Lav Plus (metro Perrache or Ampère) at 28 Rue de Condé (2e) is open daily from 6.30 am to 7.30 pm. Self-service dry-cleaning *(dégraissage à sec)* is available. The Lavadou laundrette (metro Ampère) at 19 Rue Sainte Hélène (2e) is open daily from 7 am to 8 pm. Self-service dry-cleaning costs 50FF for four kg.

Medical Services Hôpital Hôtel-Dieu (☎ 78.92.20.00; metro Bellecour) is at 1 Place de l'Hôpital (2e), one block south-east of the American Express office.

Vieux Lyon

Old Lyon, whose narrow streets are lined with over 300 medieval and Renaissance (15th to 17th-century) houses, lies at the base of Fourvière hill. It consists of three districts: Saint Paul at the northern end, Saint Jean in the middle and Saint Georges in the south. The area underwent urban renewal two decades ago and has since become a trendy area in which to live and socialise.

Many of the most interesting **old buildings** are along Rue du Bœuf, Rue Juiverie, Rue des Trois Maries and Rue Saint Jean. There are a number of pleasant cafés around **Place Saint Jean** (5e; metro Vieux Lyon), which is next to the cathedral.

Cathédrale Saint Jean Begun in the late 12th century, the cathedral (☎ 78.92.82.29) has a notable 14th-century astronomical clock in the north transept. The west façade was damaged by the Huguenots and again during the French Revolution. The cathedral, also known as Primatiale Saint Jean, can be visited from 8 am to noon and 2 to 7.30 pm (5 pm on weekends and holidays). The **trésor** (treasury) is open daily, except Tuesday, from 2 to 5.45 pm (5 pm on weekends). The entrance fee is 18FF (10FF if you're under 25 or over 60).

Musée Gadagne This museum (☎ 78.42. 03.61; metro Vieux Lyon), housed in a 16th-century building at 12 Rue de Gadagne (5e), has two sections: the **Musée de la Marionette** (puppet museum), which was founded by Laurent Mourguet (1769-1844), creator of the Punch-and-Judy-type puppet Guignol, now one of the symbols of Lyon; and the **Musée Historique**, which illustrates the history of Lyon and some of its products. Both are open daily, except Tuesday and some bank holidays, from 10.45 am to 6 pm (8.30 pm on Friday). The entry fee is 20FF (10FF for students). An English-language guidebook is on sale for 15FF.

Fourvière
Two millennia ago, the Romans built the city of Lugdunum on the slopes of Fourvière. Today, the hill – topped by the Tour Métallique, a grey, Eiffel Tower-like structure erected in 1893 and now used as a TV transmitter – affords spectacular views of Lyon and its two rivers.

There are several footpaths up the slope, but the easiest way to the top is to take the *funiculaire* (funicular railway) from next to the Vieux Lyon metro stop, which is at Place Saint Jean in Vieux Lyon. The Fourvière line, whose upper terminus is right behind the basilica, operates daily until 8.30 pm; trains run every 10 minutes. You can either use a bus/metro ticket, a one-way ticket (7FF) or a special return ticket (valid all day, 9.50FF). Tickets must be time-stamped before boarding.

Musée Gallo-Romain The truly exceptional Museum of Gallo-Roman Civilisation (☎ 78.25.94.68; Fourvière funicular station) at 17 Rue Cléberg (5e) is well worth seeing even if you don't consider yourself a fan of Roman history. Among the museum's extraordinary artefacts – almost all found in the Rhône Valley – are the remains of a four-wheeled vehicle from around 700 BC, several sumptuous mosaics and lots of Latin inscriptions, including the bronze text of a speech made by Lyon-born Roman emperor Claudius in 48 AD. The two rebuilt **Roman theatres** next to the museum, the larger of which is the oldest such structure in France, are still used for concerts of all sorts.

The museum, inaugurated in 1975, is open Wednesday to Sunday (closed bank holidays), from 9.30 am to noon and 2 to 6 pm. Admission is 20FF (10FF for students). Guidebooks to the museum in French, English and German are on sale for 35FF.

Basilique Notre Dame de Fourvière Like Sacré Cœur in Paris, this basilica (☎ 78.25. 51.82 for the sacristy; Fourvière funicular station), completed in 1896, was built by subscription to fulfil a vow taken by local Catholics during the disastrous Franco-Prussian War of 1870. The august *Blue Guide* declares it 'hideous...in a depraved taste which should be seen to be believed', and indeed, its ornamentation is a superb example of the exaggerated enthusiasm for embellishment that dominated French

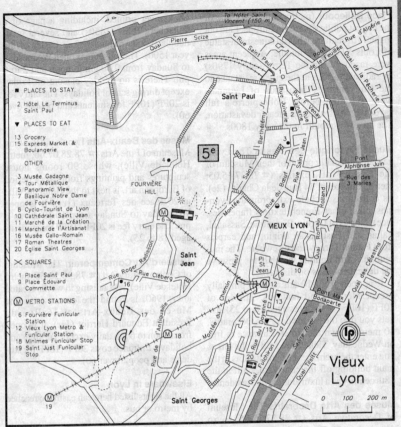

PLACES TO STAY
2 Hôtel Le Terminus
   Saint Paul

PLACES TO EAT
13 Grocery
15 Express Market &
    Boulangerie

OTHER
3 Musée Gadagne
4 Tour Métallique
5 Panoramic View
7 Basilique Notre Dame
   de Fourvière
8 Cyclo-Tourist de Lyon
10 Cathédrale Saint Jean
14 Marché de la Création
14 Marché de l'Artisanat
16 Musée Gallo-Romain
17 Roman Theatres
20 Église Saint Georges

SQUARES
1 Place Saint Paul
9 Place Édouard
   Commette

METRO STATIONS
6 Fourvière Funicular
   Station
12 Vieux Lyon Metro &
    Funicular Station
18 Minimes Funicular Stop
19 Saint Just Funicular
    Stop

Saint Paul

5ᵉ

FOURVIÈRE
HILL

Saint
Jean

VIEUX LYON

Pl
St
Jean

Saint Georges

Vieux
Lyon

0   100   200 m

church architecture during the late 19th
century. If overwrought marble and mosaics
are not your cup of tea, the panoramic view
from the nearby terrace stills merits a visit.
The basilica is open daily from 7 am to 7 pm;
from October to March it may be closed from
noon to 2 pm.

Tour de l'Observatoire Next to the basilica
is the Departement of the Observatory Tower, open from April to
October and during school holidays every
day from 10 am to noon and 2 to 6.30 pm.
During the rest of the year, it's open (weather
permitting) on weekends only. Tickets cost

6FF for adults and 3FF for children. It's a
260-step climb to the top.

Presqu'île
The four horses of the fountain at **Place des
Terreaux** (metro Hôtel de Ville) symbolise
rivers galloping seaward. Fronting the
square is the **Hôtel de Ville**, built in 1655 but
given its present façade in 1702. There are
up-market shops along and around **Rue de
la République**, known for its 19th-century
buildings. The southern half of Rue de la
République is a pedestrian mall, as is **Rue
Victor Hugo**, which runs southward from

Place Bellecour (metro Bellecour), one of the largest public squares in Europe. Laid out in the 17th century, it has an equestrian statue of Louis XIV in the middle. Adjacent areas were razed during the Terror (early 1790s) by radicals furious at the city's resistance to the Convention. Thousands of Lyonnais were executed before Robespierre's fall saved the city from even greater devastation. The area was rebuilt in the early 1800s.

Musée Historique des Tissus The Lyonnais are especially proud of their Museum of the History of Textiles (☎ 78.37.15.05; metro Ampère) at 34 Rue de la Charité (2e). Its collections include extraordinary Lyonnais silks; other French textiles (tapestries, lace); fabrics of Coptic, Byzantine, Sassanid, Italian and East Asian origin; and carpets from Persia, Turkey and elsewhere. The museum has dim lighting which helps preserve the delicate objects on display.

It is open from 10 am to 5.30 pm daily except Monday and holidays. The fee of 20FF (10FF for students aged 18 to 25) also gets you into the Musée des Arts Décoratifs, 40 metres down the street. Entrance is free on Wednesday. Tickets are sold to the left as you enter the arch; the museum itself is in the main building off the courtyard, built in the 18th century as a luxurious private residence.

Musée des Arts Décoratifs The Museum of Decorative Arts (☎ 78.37.15.05; metro Ampère) at 30 Rue de la Charité (2e) has three storeys of period rooms filled with furniture, tapestries, wallpapers, ceramics, silver and so forth, much of it from the 18th century. The same entry ticket is valid for the Musée Historique des Tissus. The two institutions are open the same hours but the Musée des Arts Décoratifs closes between noon and 2 pm.

Musée de l'Imprimerie The history of printing, a technology that had firmly established itself in Lyon by the 1480s, is illustrated by the Museum of Printing (☎ 78.37.65.98; metro Cordeliers) at 37 Rue de la Poulaillerie (2e). Among the exhibits are some of the first

books ever printed, including a page of a Gutenberg Bible (1450s) and several incunabula (books printed before Easter of the year 1500). The museum is open Wednesday to Sunday from 9.30 am to noon and 2 to 6 pm. There is no midday closure on Friday except during school holidays. The entry fee is 20FF (10FF for students and people over 60).

Musée des Beaux-Arts Lyon's outstanding Museum of Fine Arts (☎ 78.28.07.66; metro Hôtel de Ville), whose 90 rooms house sculptures and paintings from every period of European art, is next to the Hôtel de Ville at 20 Place des Terreaux (1er). It is open Wednesday to Sunday from 10.30 am to 6 pm. The entry fee is 20FF (10FF for students aged 18 to 25).

Musée d'Art Contemporain The Museum of Contemporary Art (☎ 78.30.50.66; metro Hôtel de Ville), specialising in works created after 1960, is round the corner from the Musée des Beaux-Arts at 16 Rue du Président Édouard Herriot (1er). It is open from noon to 6 pm daily except Tuesday and holidays. Entrance costs 20FF (10FF for students and people over 60).

Elsewhere in Lyon
All the sights listed here can easily be reached by metro or bus.

Centre d'Histoire de la Résistance et de la Déportation The WW II headquarters of Lyon's notorious Gestapo chief, Claus Barbie, at 14 Ave Berthelot (7e) has been turned into a museum (☎ 78.72.23.11; metro Perrache or Jean Macé) commemorating French resistance to German occupation and the fate of thousands of French people – including 76,000 Jews – deported to Nazi concentration camps. This museum, which opened in late 1992 and supersedes the old Musée de la Résistance, is 600 metres east across the Rhône from Gare de Perrache. It is open Wednesday to Sunday. Entrance costs 20FF (10FF for students and people over 60).

Maison des Canuts Set up by the Guild of Silk Workers, who are known as *canuts* in French, this museum (☎ 78.28.62.04; metro Croix Rousse) traces the history of Lyon's silk-weaving industry. Weavers are usually on hand to demonstrate the art of operating traditional silk looms. It is open daily, except Sunday and holidays, from 8.30 am (9 am on Saturday) to noon and 2 to 6.30 pm (6 pm on Saturday). Entry costs 6FF. The Maison des Canuts is at 10-12 Rue d'Ivry (4e), 300 metres north of the Croix Rousse metro stop (walk along Rue du Mail). On foot, it is one km north of (up the hill from) Place des Terreaux.

Institut Lumière The Institut Lumière (☎ 78.00.86.68; metro Monplaisir Lumière) at 25 Rue du Premier Film (8e), three km south-east of Place Bellecour along Cours Gambetta, has a permanent exhibition on the work of motion-picture pioneers Auguste and Louis Lumière, who are credited with shooting the world's first movie in 1895. **La Fondation de la Photographie**, housed in the same building, puts on temporary photographic exhibitions. The institute is open from 2 to 6 pm (closed Monday). The entrance fee for adults is 10 to 25FF, depending on what sort of temporary exhibition is on. A programme of films being screened here is available at the tourist office.

Parc de la Tête d'Or This 105-hectare public park (☎ 78.89.53.52), laid out in the 1860s in the English style, is graced by a lake, a botanical garden, a zoo and a renowned *roseraie* (rose garden) whose tens of thousands of rose bushes represent over 350 varieties. When the weather's good, visitors can rent boats, play miniature golf and engage in other outdoor activities. The park's western gate, which is at Place du Général Leclerc (6e), is 1.8 km north-east of Place des Terreaux. From Ave du Maréchal de Saxe (6e and 3e; metro Saxe Gambetta or Foch), take bus No 4 northbound.

The park itself is open daily from 6 am to 9 pm (11 pm from April to September). The open-air section of the **Jardin Botanique** (☎ 78.89.16.02; metro Masséna), in the park's south-eastern corner, is open daily from 8 to 11.30 am and 1 to 5 pm; the greenhouses, including one with carnivorous plants, are open from 8.30 to 11.30 am and 1.30 to 4.45 pm. The **Jardin Alpin** (Alpine Garden) is only open from March to October daily from 8 to 11.30 am.

Guignol puppet shows (☎ 78.93.71.75, 78.28.60.41), held at Place de l'Observatoire, take place throughout the year (weather permitting) on Wednesday, Saturday, Sunday and holiday afternoons. During school holidays, they are held every day. The cost is 13FF for adults and 10FF for children.

Guignol

Musée de l'Automobile Henri Malartre This fine museum (☎ 78.22.18.80) of vintage automobiles, motorcycles and bicycles, many of them made in France in the earliest days of motor transport, is in the Lyon suburb of Rochetaillée-sur-Saône, 11 km north of Lyon. It's open every day of the year except 25 December and 1 January from 9 am to 6 pm; the ticket windows close at 5 pm. Entrance costs 20FF (10FF for students and people over 60, free for those under 18). The museum is served by bus No 40 from Quai de la Pêcherie (1er), which is 200 metres west of Place des Terreaux (metro Hôtel de Ville), and bus No 70 from Gare de la Part-Dieu (metro Part-Dieu). By car, take the D433, which follows the east bank of the Saône.

Hiking
Sentiers Pédestres du Rhône (50FF), a topoguide with 1:50,000 scale maps published by the Comité Départemental du Tourisme Pédestre du Rhône, covers over 50 hikes you can take in the Lyon area. It is on sale at the tourist office.

Boat Rides
Navig-Inter (☎ 78.42.96.81; metro Bellecour or Vieux Lyon) operates river excursions from the dock opposite 3 Quai des Célestins (2e).

Organised Tours
For information on bus and walking tours (including some in English) of Lyon and nearby areas, contact the tourist office or its Bureau des Guides (☎ 78.42.25.75, ext 59; fax 78.37.02.06; metro Vieux Lyon) at 5 Place Saint Jean (5e) in Vieux Lyon.

Festivals
On the second weekend in June, during the Fête des Pennons a tale of life in medieval Lyon is acted out by hundreds of volunteers at Place Bellecour. Tickets cost 90FF (72FF for Carte Jeunes holders and people over 60, 45FF for children under 12).

On even-numbered years from about mid-September to early October, Lyon plays host to a dance festival called the Biennale de la Danse. On odd-numbered years during the same period, a festival of classical music known as the Biennale de la Musique takes place.

The Festival de Musique Sacrée (Festival of Sacred Music) is held in Vieux Lyon from mid-November to early December.

On 8 December, the city celebrates the Festival of the Immaculate Conception with its own Fête des Lumières (Festival of Lights). At 8 pm, a procession of people carrying candles wends its way from Place Saint Jean (5e) to Basilique Notre Dame de Fourvière. People not out marching place candles in the windows of their homes.

Places to Stay
Because many Lyon hotels, including the cheapest ones, cater to businesspeople, between September and June they are much more likely to be full Monday to Thursday than on weekends.

Places to Stay – bottom end
Camping The *Camping Municipal Porte de Lyon* (☎ 78.35.64.55) is about 10 km east of Lyon in Dardilly. This attractive and well-equipped camping ground is open from March to October and charges 45FF to pitch a tent (including parking). To get there by car, take highway N6, the eastern continuation of Cours Gambetta. By bus, take No 19 (towards Ecully-Dardilly) from the Hôtel de Ville.

Hostels The *Auberge de Jeunesse* (☎ 78.76.39.23) is 5.5 km south-east of Gare de Perrache at 51 Rue Roger Salengro in Vénissieux (postcode 69200). Beds are 43FF and breakfast costs 16FF. Kitchenette facilities are available. Rooms are closed from 10 am to 5 pm; curfew is at 11.30 pm. To get to the hostel from Gare de Perrache, take the metro to Place Bellecour and then catch bus No 35 (towards Corbas), from in front of the main post office; use the same ticket you did for the metro. Get off at the Georges Levy stop, which is 100 metres from the hostel. If you don't mind walking a bit (or after 9 pm, when bus No 35 stops running), you can take bus No 53 (towards Saint Priest) direct from Gare de Perrache. Get off at the États-Unis-Viviani stop, which is 300 metres from the hostel. From Gare de la Part-Dieu, take bus No 36 (towards Minguettes) and get off at the Viviani-Joliot-Curie stop.

The *Centre International de Séjour* (☎ 78.01.23.45, 78.76.14.22) is 4.3 km south-east of Gare de Perrache at 46 Rue du Commandant Pégoud (8e), behind 101 Blvd des Etats-Unis. People of all ages are welcome. Students/non-students pay 70/77FF for a bed in a quad,

89/95FF per person in a double and 113/121FF for a single, including breakfast and sheets. Kitchenettes are available. Reception is open from 7.30 am to 8.30 pm. On the day you arrive, you can get into your room from 2 pm. The front door is locked each night at 2 am. From the train stations, take the same buses as for the Auberge de Jeunesse. If you're on bus No 36 or 53, get off at the États-Unis-Beauvisage stop.

The *Résidence Benjamin Delessert* (☎ 78.61.41.41; metro Jean Macé), two km south-east of Gare de Perrache at 145 Ave Jean Jaurès (7e), is a university dorm during the academic year but accepts travellers between June and September. Singles (almost all they have) cost 70FF a night or 450FF a week, including sheets. New guests can check in 24 hours a day. From Gare de la Part-Dieu, take the metro to the Jean Macé stop, which is on Place Jean Macé. From Gare de Perrache, which by metro is two transfers away from Jean Macé, take bus No 39 (towards the Bron Parilly stop) to Place Jean Macé. From there, walk under the railroad tracks and continue south on Ave Jean Jaurès for a few hundred metres.

Hotels – Near Place des Terreaux The recently renovated *Hôtel Le Terme* (☎ 78.28.30.45; metro Hôtel de Ville) on the 1st floor at 7 Rue Sainte Catherine (1er), one block north of Place des Terreaux, has simply furnished singles/doubles with washbasin for 110/165FF; doubles are 190FF with shower and 240FF with shower and toilet. The pricier rooms come with TV. Hall showers are free. The *Hôtel Croix Paquet* (☎ 78.28.51.49; metro Croix Paquet) is 300 metres north-east of Place des Terreaux at 11 Place Croix Paquet (1er). This friendly, family-run place is old and run down on the outside but clean and cheery on the inside. Take lift B to the 3rd floor. Singles/doubles start at 100/110FF and two-bed doubles with shower are 180FF. Hall showers cost 15FF.

Hotels – Near Place Bellecour The homy and even quaint *Hôtel des Célestins* (☎ 78.37.63.32; metro Bellecour) on the 2nd floor

at 4 Rue des Archers (2e) is right in the city's commercial centre. It has singles and doubles for 140FF (with washbasin and bidet) and 160FF (with shower). Triples with shower start at 220FF. There is no charge to use the hall showers. There are no rooms with private toilets. Reception is open all the time except from 5 to 7 am.

On the 2nd floor of the old building at 5 Rue des Marronniers (2e) is the *Hôtel des Marronniers* (☎ 78.37.04.82; metro Bellecour). Serviceable singles/doubles with washbasin and bidet start at about 100/130FF. The hall shower costs 9FF.

Hotels – Near Place Ampère There are a number of reasonably priced hotels in the vicinity of central and lively Place Ampère, which is 500 metres north of Gare de Perrache. The clean, newly renovated *Hôtel Vaubecour* (☎ 78.37.44.91; metro Ampère) on the 2nd floor at 28 Rue Vaubecour (2e) has singles with washbasin and bidet for 95 and 106FF. Doubles without/with shower start at 117/165FF. Two-bed doubles are 170FF. Showers cost 12FF. The *Hôtel d'Ainay* (☎ 78.42.43.42; metro Ampère) on the 2nd floor at 14 Rue des Remparts d'Ainay (2e) is just off Place Ampère. Simply furnished singles/doubles cost 120/127FF without shower, 162/168FF with shower and 178/185FF with shower and toilet. Hall showers are 18FF. Breakfast is not available.

The *Hôtel Le Saint Étienne* (☎ 78.37.01.92; metro Ampère) is a clean, efficient place at 22 Rue Jarente (2e), next to 39 Rue Victor Hugo. Small singles/doubles are 95/120FF. Rooms with showers cost 160/175FF without/with a toilet. Breakfast (15FF per person) may be obligatory.

Hotels – Near Gare de Perrache You pay a premium to stay within a couple of blocks of Gare de Perrache. However, there are a number of inexpensive places slightly north of Gare de Perrache in the slightly seedy area around Place Carnot.

The cheapest place in town is the very basic *Hôtel Le Beaujolais* (☎ 78.37.39.15; metro Perrache) at 22 Rue d'Enghien (2e).

LYON

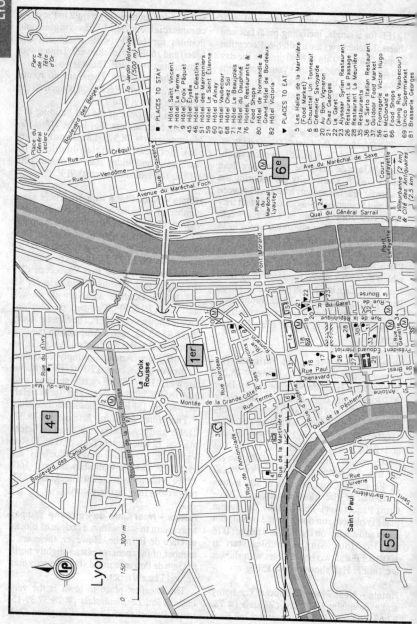

PLACES TO STAY
- 4 Hôtel Saint Vincent
- 7 Hôtel Le Terme
- 9 Hôtel Croix Pâquet
- 45 Hôtel Élysée
- 46 Hôtel des Célestins
- 51 Hôtel des Marronniers
- 59 Hôtel Le Saint Étienne
- 60 Hôtel d'Ainay
- 67 Hôtel Vaucouleur
- 68 Hôtel Chez Soi
- 71 Hôtel Le Beaujolais
- 74 Hôtel du Dauphiné
- 76 Hotels, Restaurants & Food Shops
- 80 Hôtel de Normandie & Grand Hôtel de Bordeaux
- 82 Hôtel Victoria

▼ PLACES TO EAT
- 5 Les Halles de la Martinière (Food Market)
- 6 Chouette! Un Tonneau!
- 8 Crémerie Savoyarde
- 20 Au Bon Vigneron
- 21 Chez Georges
- 22 Le Garet
- 25 Alyssaar Syrian Restaurant
- 26 Restaurant Le Passage
- 28 Restaurant La Meunière
- 35 Restaurants
- 36 Le Sarto Italian Restaurant
- 37 Outdoor Food Market
- 56 Fromagerie Victor Hugo
- 61 McDonald's
- 66 Food Shops (along Rue Vaubecour)
- 69 Unica Supermarket
- 81 Brasserie Georges

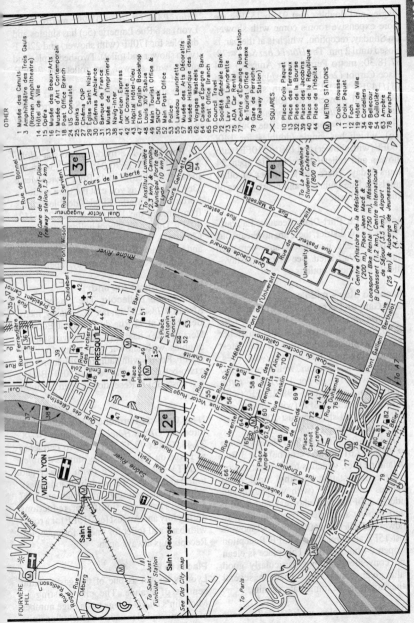

OTHER

1 Musée des Canuts
3 Amphithéâtre des Trois Gauls (Roman Amphitheatre)
14 Hôtel de Ville
15 Opéra
16 Musée des Beaux-Arts
17 Musée d'Art Contemporain
18 Post Office Branch
24 US Consulate
25 Banks
28 Cinéma CNP
29 Eglise Saint Nizier
30 Cinémas Ambiance
31 Banque de France
33 Musée de l'Imprimerie
38 Navig-Inter
41 American Express
42 UK Consulate
43 Flon English Bookshop
48 Louis XIV Statue
49 Main Tourist Office & SNCF Desk
50 SNCF Desk
52 Main Post Office
53 Police
55 Lavadou Laundrette
57 Musée des Arts Décoratifs
58 Musée Historique des Tissus
62 Voyages Wasteels
65 Caisse d'Epargne Bank
65 Post Office Branch
70 Council Travel
72 Société Générale Bank
73 Lav Plus Laundrette
75 ADA Car Rental
77 Centre d'Echange Bus Station & Tourist Office Annexe
79 Gare de Perrache (Railway Station)

✕ SQUARES

10 Place Croix Paquet
13 Place des Terreaux
32 Place de la Bourse
39 Place des Jacobins
40 Place de la République
44 Place Carnot

Ⓜ METRO STATIONS

2 Croix Rousse
11 Croix Paquet
12 Foch
19 Hôtel de Ville
34 Bellecour
54 Guillotière
63 Ampère
78 Perrache

Singles and doubles cost 91 to 152FF; the more expensive rooms come with shower. On Sunday, reception, which is at the bar, is closed until 2 pm. The *Hôtel Chez Soi* (☎ 78. 37.18.30; metro Perrache or Ampère) at 4 Place Carnot (2e) has singles/doubles from 131/142FF (161/171FF with shower and toilet). Hall showers cost 10FF. You might also try the *Hôtel du Dauphiné* (☎ 78.37. 24.19; metro Perrache) at 3 Rue Duhamel (2e), which has singles/doubles for 140/160FF (with shower) and 190 to 210FF (with shower and toilet). Reception is open 24 hours a day. There are a number of other hotels on Rue Duhamel and nearby parts of Rue de la Charité.

Hotels – La Part-Dieu Because La Part-Dieu is a new district, there are no cheap, old hotels (or cheap, new hotels) anywhere near Gare de la Part-Dieu. See Places to Stay – middle for pricier options.

Places to Stay – middle
Near Gare de Perrache The two-star *Hôtel de Normandie* (☎ 78.37.31.36; fax 72.40. 98.56; metro Perrache) at 3 Rue du Bélier (2e) is a pleasant mixture of the latest remodelling and half-century-old tiles, mouldings, etc. Spacious, well-kept singles/doubles with TV go for 152/172FF (with washbasin and bidet), 198/229FF (with shower) and 238/278FF (with shower and toilet). The hall showers cost 20FF. Reception is open day and night.

The two-star, lift-equipped *Hôtel Victoria* (☎ 78.37.57.61; metro Perrache) is at 3 Rue Delandine (2e), which is to the right as you exit the train station building. Singles and doubles cost 160FF (with washbasin and bidet), 200FF (with shower) and 220FF (with shower and toilet). Triples/quads with shower and toilet are 260/300FF. Hall showers cost 15FF and breakfast is 23FF. Reception is open 24 hours a day. This place is clean and convenient but not particularly good value given what you get. There are several other hotels in the immediate vicinity.

Vieux Lyon The pleasant *Hôtel Le Terminus*

Saint Paul (☎ 78.28.13.29; metro Vieux Lyon) at 6 Rue Lainerie (5e) has singles and doubles for 170FF (with shower) and 220FF (with shower and toilet). Two-bed triples and quads with shower and toilet are 240FF. Breakfast is 40FF.

The attractive *Hôtel Saint Vincent* (☎ 78. 28.67.97) is just across the Saône from the old city at 9 Rue Pareille (1er). Singles/doubles with shower cost 170/200FF.

La Part-Dieu The modern, two-star *Hôtel Athéna* (☎ 72.33.70.04; fax 72.34.56.89; metro Part-Dieu) is at 45 Blvd Vivier Merle (3e), to the left as you exit the train station's Sortie Vivier Merle. Singles/doubles/triples from among the 122 rooms cost 235/312/405FF. During all school holidays (summer, Christmas, February and Easter), doubles and triples are available for 248FF. Breakfast costs 35FF. Reception is always open.

Places to Stay – top end
Near Place Bellecour The classy *Hôtel Élysée* (☎ 78.42.03.15; fax 78.37.76.49; metro Bellecour) at 92 Rue du Président Édouard Herriot (2e) has very attractive singles/doubles with shower and toilet for 300/320FF. Rooms with bath are 20FF more, and a two-bed double with bath is 350FF. Breakfast costs 35FF. Reception is open 24 hours a day.

Near Gare de Perrache The comfortable, three-star *Grand Hôtel de Bordeaux* (☎ 78. 37.48.02; fax 78.37.58.73; metro Perrache) at 1 Rue du Bélier (2e) has singles/doubles with TV for 340/390FF (with shower and toilet) and 380/435FF (with bath and toilet). Triples/quads with bath and toilet are 505/575FF. There are significant reductions during July and August (eg 315FF for a room with bath and toilet for one to four people). Reception is always open.

Places to Eat
Lyon is known as one of the gastronomic centres of France. The city's listing in Michelin's *Guide Rouge* has a huge number of recommended restaurants, including quite

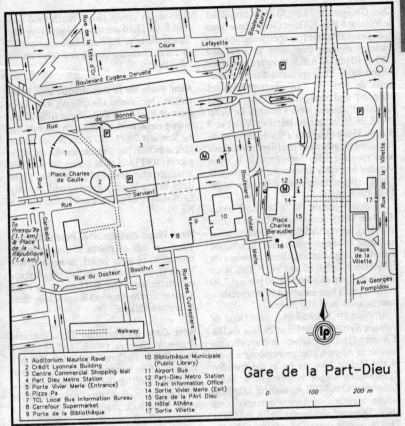

Gare de la Part-Dieu

1 Auditorium Maurice Ravel
2 Crédit Lyonnais Building
3 Centre Commercial Shopping Mall
4 Part Dieu Metro Station
5 Porte Vivier Merle (Entrance)
6 Pizza Pa
7 TCL Local Bus Information Bureau
8 Carrefour Supermarket
9 Porte de la Bibliothèque
10 Bibliothèque Municipale (Public Library)
11 Airport Bus
12 Part-Dieu Metro Station
13 Train Information Office
14 Sortie Vivier Merle (Exit)
15 Gare de la Part Dieu
16 Hôtel Athéna
17 Sortie Villette

0   100   200 m

a few that have been honoured with one or more of Michelin's coveted stars.

France's most famous chef, Paul Bocuse, runs a three-star restaurant (☎ 78.22.01.40; fax 72.27.85.87) in Collonges-au-Mont-d'Or, 12 km north of the city. Lunch/dinner *menus* are 390/710FF.

Near Place des Terreaux *Restaurant Le Passage* (☎ 78.28.11.16; metro Hôtel de Ville), which has one Michelin star, is down the passageway at 8 Rue du Plâtre (1er). The décor of modern art, mirrors, white table cloths and preserved foliage is eclectic but elegant. Specialities include fish, homard aux lentilles (lobster prepared with lentils) and escalope de foie gras poêlée (fried escalope of goose liver). There are *menus* of French gastronomic cuisine for 175FF (lunch only), 275 and 340FF. Le Passage is open daily except Saturday at midday and Sunday. Reservations are a good idea on weekends during the school year.

There are two *bouchons* – small, friendly, unpretentious restaurants that serve traditional, often pork-based Lyonnais cooking – near Place des Terreaux. (In French, a bouchon is also a bottle stopper and a traffic jam.) Homy

LYON

Chez Georges (☎ 78.28.30.46; metro Hôtel de Ville) at 8 Rue du Garet (1er), whose main dishes cost 33 to 69FF, is open weekdays and Saturday evening from noon to 2 pm and 7.30 to 10 pm. At lunch, there are *menus* for 76 and 99FF. Their specialities include quenelle de brochet (boiled dumplings of chopped and seasoned pike), tripe and cervelle d'agneau (lamb's brains). *Le Garet* (☎ 78.28.16.94; metro Hôtel de Ville) at 7 Rue du Garet (1er) has a warm atmosphere enhanced by groups of old friends who have been meeting here for years. It is open Monday to Friday from noon to 2 pm and 7.30 to 10 pm. Most main dishes are in the 35 to 80FF range.

Au Bon Vigneron (☎ 78.28.92.87; metro Hôtel de Ville), nearby at 21 Rue de l'Arbre Sec (1er), serves traditional French cuisine, including Lyonnais specialities. In addition to the à la carte selection, there are *menus* for 59FF (lunch only), 85 and 98FF. This place is open daily from noon to 2.30 pm and 7.30 to 10.30 pm. There are about 10 other restaurants in a radius of 100 metres.

Alyssaar (☎ 78.29.57.66; metro Hôtel de Ville), a Syrian restaurant at 29 Rue du Bât d'Argent (1er), specialises in the delicious cuisine of Aleppo, 'the gastronomic capital of the Middle East' as far as the friendly, Syrian-born owner is concerned. Main dishes cost 42 to 58FF. An assiette du khalife (seven varieties of hors d'œuvres) costs 56FF. There are also *menus* for 78 and 98FF. This restaurant is open Monday to Saturday for dinner only (7.30 pm to midnight).

The friendly *Restaurant La Meunière* (☎ 78. 28.62.91; metro Cordeliers), a bouchon at 11 Rue Neuve (1er), is unpretentious but elegant in a cosy sort of way. Lyonnaiseries (Lyon specialities) on the menu include andouillettes (chitterling sausages), tripe and boudin (blood sausage). There are *menus* for 80, 95 and 140FF. If you make a meal of the salad bar, it costs 90FF. This restaurant is open Tuesday to Saturday from noon to 2 pm and 7.45 to 10 pm. There are all sorts of ethnic restaurants in the immediate vicinity.

Chouette! Un Tonneau! (☎ 78.27.42.42; metro Hôtel de Ville) at 17 Rue d'Algérie (1er) serves cheap, tasty French food nonstop from 11.30 am to midnight every day. Salads are 11 to 26FF and omelettes cost 17 to 26FF. There are quite a few other restaurants nearby.

Near Place de la République Rue Palais Grillet (1er; metro Cordeliers), one block west of Rue de la République (though not quite parallel to it), is lined with places to eat. *Le Sarto* (☎ 78.42.05.79), an Italian restaurant at No 22, has a reputation for excellent pizzas (40FF) and pasta dishes (40 to 42FF). It is open from noon to 2 pm and 7 to 11 pm daily except Sunday evening and Monday. *Le Nabab* is a Pakistani and Indian place at No 30.

Near Place Bellecour & Place Ampère There are lots of places to eat, including several hamburger joints, along the Rue Victor Hugo pedestrian mall (metro Ampère and Bellecour). The *McDonald's* at Place Ampère (metro Ampère) is open daily from 10 am to midnight.

Near Gare de Perrache The venerable *Brasserie Georges* (☎ 78.37.15.78; metro Perrache) at 30 Cours de Verdun (2e) is a huge, old-time brasserie that can accommodate over 500 diners. The decorations – ceiling murals, floor tiles, upholstered red seats – haven't changed in over half a century. The brasserie-style fare includes several choucroutes (sauerkraut dishes). The plat du jour costs 60FF, and *menus* are 82, 105 and 120FF. Beer starts at 13FF. This place is open every day of the year from 7 am to midnight. From mid-September to April live music is played on Saturday nights from 9 pm to midnight.

Rue de Condé, two blocks north of Gare de Perrache, is home to a number of Chinese restaurants, including *La Chine* (☎ 78.37. 45.05; metro Perrache or Ampère) at 21 Rue de Condé (2e). It is open Tuesday to Sunday from noon to 2 pm and 7 to 11 pm. Lunch/dinner *menus* start at 42/58FF. Nearby, there are several restaurants along Rue Duhamel and Rue de la Charité.

La Part-Dieu *Pizza Paï* (☎ 78.95.13.93; metro Part-Dieu) is in the Centre Commercial (3e) – the huge shopping mall opposite Gare de la Part-Dieu – at Porte Vivier Merle, the entrance nearest the train station. Pizzas cost 38 to 56FF, ard there are also pasta and meat dishes. This place is open seven days a week from 11 am to 10 pm. There are a number of other informal restaurants in the Centre Commercial.

University Restaurants For students, the cheapest meals in town are at the *restaurants universitaires* run by CROUS. These include *La Madeleine* (☎ 78.72.80.62; metro Garibaldi) at 360 Rue Garibaldi (7e), two km east of Place Ampère. In general, the restaurant and brasserie are open weekdays from 11.30 am to 1 pm and 6.30 to 7.45 pm. On Saturday, the hours are the same but only the à la carte brasserie is open. Meal tickets valid at the restaurant (but not the brasserie) cost 12.30FF for students and 25FF for nonstudents. Tickets are sold on weekdays from 11.30 am to 1 pm; if you come at dinner, ask around to find someone who'll sell you one.

Self-Catering Lyon's many picnic spots include Place Bellecour, Place des Terreaux, the quays along the Rhône and the Saône, and the terrace behind Basilique Notre Dame de Fourvière.

Near Place des Terreaux *Les Halles de la Martinière* (metro Hôtel de Ville), a covered marketplace at 24 Rue de la Martinière (1er), is open from 6.30 am to 12.30 pm and 4 to 7.30 pm daily except Sunday afternoon and Monday.

North of Place des Terreaux, there is a superb fromagerie, *Crémerie Savoyarde*, (metro Croix Paquet) at 26 Rue des Capucins (1er). It is open from 6 am to 1 pm and 3 to 7.30 pm daily except Saturday afternoon and Sunday. Their Saint Marcellin is fantastic. For bread, try the *Boulangerie Parisienne* (metro Hôtel de Ville; closed Sunday) nearby at 3 Rue Romarin (1er). This place also has great pain aux raisins (spiral raisin-and-custard pastries).

Near Place Bellecour The outdoor *food market* (metro Bellecour or Cordeliers) along Quai Saint Antoine and Quai des Célestins (2e), which border the Saône, is open from 7 am to 12.30 pm (closed Monday).

Near Place Ampère There are lots of food shops along Rue Vaubecour (2e; metro Ampère), including a *boulangerie* at No 26 that is open Monday to Friday from 6.30 am to 2 pm and 3.30 to 7.30 pm, and Saturday from 6.30 am to 1 pm. The *boulangerie* at No 8 is open Tuesday to Saturday from 6.40 am to 1.30 pm and 3 to 7.30 pm, and Sunday from 6.40 am to 12.30 pm. The *Casino grocery* (☎ 78.37.17.09) at No 5 is open Tuesday to Saturday from 7.30 am to 12.30 pm and 3.30 to 7.30 pm, and Sunday from 7.30 am to noon. The *UGA grocery* (☎ 78.37.21.91) at No 28 is open Monday to Saturday from 6.45 am to 9 pm.

Fromagerie Victor Hugo (metro Ampère) at 26 Rue Sainte Hélène (2e) is a particularly fine cheese shop. It is open Tuesday to Saturday from 8.30 am to 1 pm and 3.30 to 8 pm.

Near Gare de Perrache There are a number of food stores on Rue Duhamel (2e; metro Perrache), including a *boulangerie* at No 10 (closed Saturday afternoon and Sunday) and a *grocery* at No 12 (open daily from 7 am to 10 pm).

The *Unico supermarket* (metro Perrache or Ampère) at 60 Rue de la Charité (2e) is open Monday to Saturday from 8.30 am to 12.30 pm and 3.30 to 7.15 pm (7.30 pm on Friday and Saturday).

Vieux Lyon In the old city, there are a number of food shops on Rue du Doyenné (5e; metro Vieux Lyon), including a North African *boulangerie* at No 11 that is open Tuesday to Sunday from 7 am to 1 pm and 3 to 9 pm. The *Express Market* in the same building is open Tuesday to Saturday from 7.30 am to 12.30 pm and 3.30 to 7.30 pm, and Sunday from 9 am to noon. There's another *grocery* (metro Vieux Lyon) at 1 Ave du Doyenné (5e), next to Place Édouard Commette. It's open Monday to Saturday from 6.30 am to 10 pm.

La Part-Dieu There is a *Carrefour supermarket* (metro Part-Dieu) inside the Centre Commercial on Niveau 3 (the upper level) near the Porte de la Bibliothèque entrance. It is open Monday to Saturday from 9 am to 10 pm.

Entertainment

For up-to-date information on Lyon's lively cultural life, which includes theatre, opera, dance, classical music, jazz, variety shows and sporting events, enquire at the tourist office or consult their brochure *Spectacles Événements*, published several times a year. *Lyon Poche* (6FF), a listing in French of local cultural events, including films, comes out every Tuesday. It is available at newsagents.

Discothèques The tourist office's pamphlet *Guide de Lyon* includes a list of discos (*rétro*, Antillean, gay, etc).

Cinemas Nondubbed, foreign-language films are shown at two cinemas on the Presqu'île. *Cinémas Ambiance* (☎ 78.28.14.84 for the answering machine or 78.28.07.52 for the ticket office; metro Cordeliers) at 12 Rue de la République (2e), next to the Banque de France, has three projection halls. Tickets cost 43FF; the reduced price of 33FF is valid for students and people over 60 daily except – from September to June – on Saturday night, Sunday afternoon and holidays. Everyone gets in for 33FF on Wednesday.

Cinéma CNP (☎ 78.42.33.22; metro Hôtel de Ville or Cordeliers) is a block away at 40 Rue du Président Édouard Herriot (1er). It has four auditoriums. Tickets cost 40FF; students and people over 60 pay 30FF (35FF on weekends and holidays). Everyone gets in for 30FF on Wednesday.

Things to Buy

Every Sunday morning until noon or 1 pm, Vieux Lyon (5e; metro Vieux Lyon) plays host to two outdoor markets: the Marché de l'Artisanat on Quai Fulchiron, which has items produced by local artisans (jewellery, pottery, etc); and the Marché de la Création along Quai Romain Rolland, where artists sell paintings, sculptures, photographs, etc. A postage stamp market is held in Place Bellecour on Sunday and holidays from 7 am to noon.

La Cité des Antiquaires (☎ 72.44.91.98) at 117 Blvd Stalingrad in the Lyon suburb of Villeurbanne is the third-largest antique market in Europe. It is open Thursday to Sunday from 10 am to 12.30 pm and 2.30 to 7 pm. In summer it's closed on Sunday afternoon.

The huge Centre Commercial (3e; metro Part-Dieu) at La Part-Dieu, opposite Gare de la Part-Dieu, has many dozens of shops.

Getting There & Away

Air Lyon's airport, Aéroport International Lyon-Satolas (☎ 72.22.75.05) is 25 km east of the city. There are direct flights to dozens of cities in Europe, North Africa, North America, etc.

Train Lyon has two railway stations: Gare de Perrache and Gare de la Part-Dieu. There are lots of exceptions, but in general, trains that begin or end their runs in Lyon use Perrache, whereas trains passing through the city stop at Part-Dieu. Some trains, including most of the Lyon-Paris TGVs, stop at both stations. There are a lot more hotels near Perrache than there are in the vicinity of Part-Dieu.

For travel between the stations, you can go by metro (change at Charpennes), but if there happens to be a non-TGV train going from one station to the other you can take it without buying a special ticket. If you do not have a reservation and will be taking a train that stops at both stations, you'll have a better chance of finding a *non-réservé* (unreserved) seat if you get on at whichever station the train stops at first.

If you travel to/from Paris (258FF) by TGV (two to 2½ hours; 22 to 30 a day), you'll be assessed a TGV reservation fee of 18 to 126FF, depending on when you travel. There are also a few non-TGV trains on this route; they take four hours during the day and five hours on the overnight runs. As you would expect, trains between Lyon and Paris use the capital's Gare de Lyon. Except for travel to Nantes (359FF; five to seven hours; eight a day), Rennes and Lille, the reservation fee from Lyon for province-to-province travel by TGV is always 18FF.

Lyon has direct rail links to all parts of France and Europe, including Strasbourg (245FF; five hours; five a day), Geneva (109FF; two hours; six a day), Grenoble (86FF; 1¼ hours; nine a day on weekdays), Chamonix (166FF; 4½ hours; four a day), Dijon (126FF; 1¾ to 2¼ hours; 14 to 18 a day), Marseille (198FF; three to 3½ hours; 13 to 15 a day), Nice (279FF; five hours during the day, six hours overnight; 14 a day) and Bordeaux (300FF; 7½ to nine hours; four a day).

Gare de Perrache The complex that includes Gare de Perrache (☎ 78.92.50.50 for information; 2e; metro Perrache) consists of two main buildings: the Centre d'Échange, whose bowels serve as a bus terminal and metro station; and, southward over the pedestrian bridge, the railway station itself. In the station, the information office on the lower level is open Monday to Saturday from 8 am to 7.30 pm. For information on trains about to depart, enquire at the Accueil office. There are luggage lockers on the lower level. SOS Voyageurs (☎ 78.37.03.31), the travellers' aid organisation, has an office near the Sortie Nord (north exit). Télécartes are on sale at the tabac in the Centre d'Échange.

Gare de la Part-Dieu The Part-Dieu train station (☎ 78.92.50.50 for information; 3e; metro Part-Dieu), part of a huge complex of modern office blocks and shopping areas, is two km east of Place de la République. The information office, is to the right as you go out the Sortie Vivier Merle exit; it's open Monday to Saturday from 9 am to 7.30 pm. There are luggage lockers near the stairs up to platforms G and H. The *consigne manuelle* (left-luggage office), which is to

the right when you exit Sortie Vivier Merle, is open Monday to Friday from 8.30 am to 7.30 pm.

The Part-Dieu branch of SOS Voyageurs (☎ 72.34.12.16), open daily from 8 am to 10 pm, is especially friendly and helpful. Not only do the volunteers try to assist people with problems of any sort (sickness, theft, lost luggage, etc) but they'll also help travellers find a hotel, hostel, etc. Télécartes are available at the Thomas Cook office.

Bus Intercity buses, of which there are relatively few, depart from the bus terminal under the Centre d'Échange, next to Gare de Perrache. Out-of-town buses use the east side of the platform, while local buses use the west side. Timetables and other information are available from the information office of Lyon's mass transit authority, TCL (☎ 78.71.70.00 for intercity bus information), which is on the lower level of the Centre d'Échange. Tickets for travel on buses run by private companies are sold by the driver.

Getting Around

To/From the Airport Buses from the city to Aéroport Lyon-Satolas cost 42FF and take 40 minutes from Gare de Perrache and 30 minutes from Gare de la Part-Dieu. At Part-Dieu, the stop is across the plaza from the Sortie Vivier Merle exit. Buses going to the airport run every 20 minutes (every 30 minutes on weekends and holidays) from 5 am to 9 pm. There are runs from the airport to Lyon between 5 am and 11 pm. Aéroport Lyon-Satolas is also served by buses from Grenoble, Chambéry and Valence.

Metro & Bus Lyon's metro is run by the city's rapid transit company, TCL (☎ 78.71.80.80), which also operates the city's bus network. The four fast, quiet metro lines are known as A, B, C and D; on some route maps, the two funicular railway lines that link Vieux Lyon with Fourvière and Saint Just are listed as line F. When places mentioned in the text are within 600 metres of a metro station, the name of the stop is listed right after the phone number.

Tickets, which cost 7FF if bought individually, are valid for one-way travel on buses, trolley buses, the metro and the funiculaires. They can be used for an hour after being time-stamped for the first time; restamp the ticket each time you transfer. Up to three transfers are permitted but round trips are not. A carnet of six tickets, available at metro stations, costs 38FF (30.50FF for students under 26). Carnets of 20 tickets (116FF; 93FF for students) are sold at TCL agencies and many tabacs. The Ticket Liberté (20FF), good for unlimited travel during one calendar day, is an excellent deal. It can be bought on or before the day you use it at TCL information offices and some tabacs. Time-stamp the Ticket Liberté only once, the first time you use it.

The metro starts operating at 5 am and the last metro begin its final run at about midnight. Tickets must be time-stamped before you enter the platforms, which – miracle of miracles! – have no turnstiles. The Navette Presqu'île, a bus that links Saint Paul (the northern district of Vieux Lyon) and Place des Terreaux with Gare de Perrache, costs only 3.50FF a ride (32FF for a carnet of 10). It operates daily, except on Sunday and holiday afternoons, from 7 am to 8.30 pm. It travels north along Rue Vaubecour and Rue du Président Édouard Herriot and south along Rue de Brest, Quai Tilsitt and Rue de la Charité.

Near Gare de la Part-Dieu, TCL has an Information-Vente bureau (☎ 78.71.70.00; metro Part-Dieu) at 19 Blvd Vivier Merle (3e). It is open Monday to Friday from 8 am to 6.30 pm and Saturday from 9 am to 5 pm. At Gare de Perrache, there's an information

office on the lower level of the Centre d'Échange, the building linked to Gare de Perrache by a pedestrian flyover. It's open Monday to Saturday from 6.30 am to 7.30 pm. There are also TCL offices in the Bellecour and Vieux Lyon metro stations, at 43 Rue de la République (2e; metro Cordeliers) and at Place de la Croix Rousse (4e; metro Croix Rousse).

Taxi To order a taxi 24 hours a day, call Taxis Lyonnais (☎ 78.26.81.81) or Allô Taxi (☎ 78.28.23.23). For travel to the airport, try AAA Taxi Aéroport (☎ 72.22.70.90) or Taxi Aéroport Lyon-Satolas (☎ 78.54.69.88).

Car ADA Location Véhicules (☎ 78.37.93.93; metro Perrache) at 42 Quai du Docteur Gailleton (2e) is open Monday to Saturday from 8 am to 12.30 pm and 1.30 to 7 pm.

Bicycle Except in winter, mountain bikes can be rented for 120FF a day (or 430FF a week) from Locasport (☎ 78.61.11.01; metro Jean Macé), which is at 62 Rue du Colombier (7e), one block east of Place Jean Macé. The store is open on Monday afternoon and Tuesday to Saturday from 9 am to noon and 2 to 7 pm. To get there, take the metro to the Jean Macé stop. On foot, it's 1.3 km east of Gare de Perrache across the Rhône and along Ave Berthelot.

Cycling aficionados who are visiting Lyon are invited to participate in the group rides of Cyclo-Tourist de Lyon (☎ 78.42.44.08; metro Vieux Lyon), a cycling club based at 19 Rue du Bœuf (5e) in Vieux Lyon. There is usually someone there on weekdays from 3 to 7 pm. The club's regular meetings are held on the second Tuesday of the month at 7 pm.

French Alps & the Jura

'Lances des glaciers fiers, rois blancs' (Lances of proud glaciers, white kings)
— **Arthur Rimbaud**

The French Alps, where fertile, green valleys meet soaring peaks topped with craggy, snowbound summits, are one of the most awe-inspiring mountainscapes in the world. In summer, visitors can take advantage of hundreds of km of magnificent hiking trails and engage in all sorts of warm-weather sporting activities. In winter, the area's fine ski resorts attract snow-sport enthusiasts from around the world. Facilities were further upgraded in preparation for the 1992 Winter Olympics held in Albertville and nearby towns.

The first half of this chapter covers mountainous areas where you can hike and ski, including the mountains and valleys around Mont Blanc (see the Chamonix section). During the warm months, Annecy, Thonon and Chambéry offer the best of the French Alps' lowland delights: swimming, hiking, parapente and the like. Grenoble, former capital of Dauphiné, provides big-city amenities and hiking opportunities, while nearby there are less expensive low-altitude ski stations. North of Lake Geneva, Besançon and the Jura Mountains' town of Métabief offer a taste of the Franche-Comté region.

Orientation

The Alps stretch from Lake Geneva (Lac Léman) 370 km south almost to the Côte d'Azur. France's border with Italy follows the Alps' highest ridges and peaks.

The Alps' two major historic regions are Savoy and Dauphiné. Savoy covers the northern portion of the Alps and culminates in Europe's highest mountain, Mont Blanc, at whose base sits the town of Chamonix. To the west, Annecy acts as the gateway to much of Savoy, while further south sits the region's historic capital, Chambéry. Dauphiné, which is south of Savoy, is home to the capital of the Alps, Grenoble. Dauphiné stretches eastward all the way to Briançon and the Italian border.

North of Lake Geneva, the Jura Mountains form an that extends arc northward towards the Rhône River and Alsace.

Geography

The Alps – whose name is derived from the Ligurian word *alp*, which means 'pasture' – have served as a barrier between Europe's peoples and countries since ancient times. Formed about 44 million years ago, the peaks and valleys have been sculpted by erosion and, especially over the past 1.6 million years, massive glaciation. Both these factors have endowed the Alpine river valleys, which are up to four km lower than nearby peaks, with mild climates and rich soils, making them eminently suitable for human settlement.

The Alps' dense road network handles a significant proportion of Western Europe's motor vehicle and goods traffic, creating enormous air pollution problems. Other factors that contribute to the degradation of the Alpine environment include the high

FRENCH ALPS

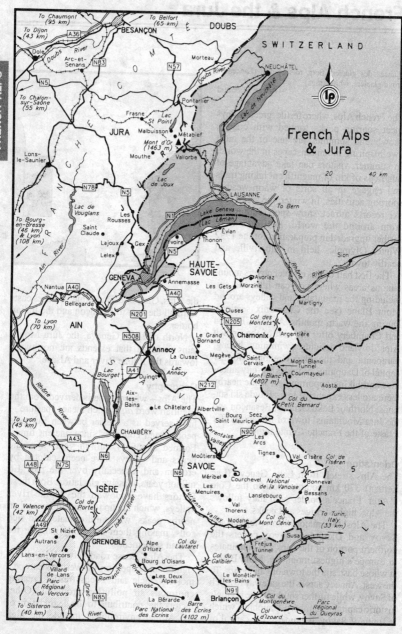

To Chaumont (95 km)
To Belfort (65 km)
To Dijon (43 km)
DOUBS
SWITZERLAND
BESANÇON
A36
Dole
Doubs River
Morteau
N83
Arc-et-Senans
Doubs River
NEUCHÂTEL
N5
Pontarlier
Lac de Neuchâtel
lp
To Chalon-sur-Saône (55 km)
Frasne
Lac St Point
Métabief
French Alps & Jura
JURA
Mont d'Or (1463 m)
0   20   40 km
Lons-le-Saunier
Mouthe
Vallorbe
N78
N5
Lac de Joux
LAUSANNE
Lac de Vouglans
Les Rousses
N1
Lake Geneva (Lac Léman)
To Bern
To Bourg-en-Bresse (46 km) & Lyon (108 km)
Saint Claude
Lajoux
Gex
voire
Évian
Thonon
Sion
Lelex
HAUTE-SAVOIE
Rhône River
Ain River
Nantua
A40
GENEVA
Annemasse
Avoriaz
Les Gets
Morzine
Martigny
Bellegarde
N201
A40
Cluses
Col des Montets
To Lyon (70 km)
AIN
N508
N205
Argentière
Le Grand Bornand
Chamonix
Annecy
La Clusaz
Mont Blanc Tunnel
Lac Bourget
A41
Lac Annecy
Megève
Saint Gervais
Courmayeur
Duingt
N212
Mont Blanc (4807 m)
Aix-les-Bains
Le Châtelard
Albertville
Aosta
To Lyon (45 km)
Rhône River
Bourg
Col du Petit Bernard
A43
CHAMBÉRY
N6
Saint Maurice
Seez
Tarentaise Valley
N90
Les Arcs
A48   N75
Moûtiers
Tignes
Val d'Isère
Col de l'Iseran
SAVOIE
Méribel
Courchevel
N6
Parc National de la Vanoise
Bonneval
To Valence (42 km)
ISÈRE
Les Menuires
Lanslebourg
Bessans
Col de Porte
Val Thorens
A49
St Nizier
Maurienne Valley
Modane
Col du Mont Cénis
To Turin, Italy (33 km)
Autrans
GRENOBLE
Alpe d'Huez
Col du Lautaret
Susa
Lans-en-Vercors
Fréjus Tunnel
Villard de Lans
Bourg d'Oisans
Col du Galibier
Parc Régional du Vercors
N85
Les Deux Alpes
Le Monêtier-les-Bains
N91
Venosc
To Sisteron (40 km)
La Bérarde
Briançon
Col du Montgenèvre
Romanche River
Drac River
Isère River
Barre des Écrins (4102 m)
Parc National des Écrins
Col d'Izoard
Parc Régional du Queyras

concentration of heavy industries (chemicals and metallurgy) and mass tourism, which has grown exponentially since 1960 and continues to expand despite the relative shortness (and unpredictability) of the annual snow season.

Climate

The Alps are characterised by extreme climatic diversity because the temperature and precipitation patterns of any given place are primarily a function of elevation and exposure – factors that vary widely from locale to locale. As you would expect, the southern slopes are warmer than areas with northern exposure.

In most years, from December to April there's enough snow for skiing even at lower altitude stations. In spring (late spring and summer at higher elevations), carpets of flowers unfold next to and among the magnificent forests. Throughout the year, the weather is changeable but is generally better in the morning than in the late afternoon, when cloud cover and thunderstorms are common.

For weather information, call the météo on ☎ 36.68.00.00 (for the regional report) or 36.68.04.04 (for the snow and mountain report). For the departmental report, dial ☎ 36.68.02 plus the two-digit departmental number.

Dangers & Annoyances

In areas with lots of snow, avalanches pose a very real danger. On glaciers, be careful of crevasses. A fall or accident in an isolated area can be fatal if no one finds you, so never ski, hike or climb alone.

At high altitudes, where the sun's ultraviolet radiation is much stronger than at sea level (and is intensified by reflections off the snow), it's a good idea to wear sunglasses and put sunscreen on exposed skin.

The air is often very dry – take along a water bottle when hiking and drink more liquids than you might elsewhere. Also, be aware of the possibility of hypothermia after a sweaty climb or a sudden drenching storm, as you'll cool off quickly while enjoying the cold, windy panorama.

Parks

The Alps – unlike the mountain ranges of western North America – are not a pristine wilderness with huge tracts of land virtually

Mont Blanc

FRENCH ALPS

untouched by human activities. Rather, the habitable parts of the French Alps support a relatively dense population, and the region's many villages, towns and ski resorts are linked by an extensive network of roads and highways.

Fortunately, parts of the Alps are within the boundaries of three national and two regional parks, in which wildlife is protected. The national parks – Vanoise (in Savoy), Écrins (in Dauphiné) and Mercantour (along the Italian border just north of the Côte d'Azur) – are surrounded by much larger peripheral zones where human habitation and many economic activities are permitted.

Together with the regional parks of Queyras (on the Italian border south of Briançon) and the Vercors (south-west of Grenoble), the Alps are endowed with the greatest concentration of parks in France.

Warm-Weather Activities

Fantastic hiking trails wend their way up and around the mountains near Mont Blanc and criss-cross the national parks, and the GR5 traverses the entire Alps. Rafting, canoeing, mountain biking and hang-gliding (delta-plane) are also popular, as is parapente, the sport of floating down from somewhere high – the top of an aerial tramway line, for instance – suspended from a wing-shaped, steerable parachute that allows you (if you're both lucky and skilled) to catch updrafts and fly around for quite a while. An initiation flight (baptême de l'air) with an instructor (moniteur) costs 300 to 450FF. A five-day beginners' course (stage d'initiation) costs 2500 to 2900FF. A second five-day course, which prepares you to pursue the sport on your own, costs the same.

Skiing

Snow sports, once reserved for the truly wealthy, have become more and more accessible to middle-class people over the last few decades. Each winter – especially during the school holidays in February and March – millions of holiday-makers head to the Alps for downhill skiing, cross-country treks, snowboarding and the colour and spectacle

that accompanies them. Unfortunately, the huge numbers of visitors and the facilities they require are having a negative impact on the region's ecology.

For information on individual ski stations, consult the sections of this chapter on Chamonix, Annecy, Morzine, Bourg Saint Maurice, Méribel, Around Grenoble and Métabief.

Cross-Country Skiing Known in French as ski de fond, cross-country skiing is practised in various parts of the Alps (eg in the Vercors range near Grenoble), but is most popular further north in the Jura Mountains. Both these regions have moderate downhill pistes too. The atmosphere at cross-country stations is more relaxed and casual than in the higher ski resorts, and the prices reflect the lower altitudes, simpler equipment and lack of lift fees.

The Season The ski season starts in earnest a few days before Christmas and ends towards the end of April, but in years of heavy snowfall it's possible to ski from as early as November until as late as mid-May. At the beginning and end of the season, as well as in January, accommodation and lift tickets are available at considerable discounts, and many resorts offer promotional deals. It's advisable to give the slopes a wide berth during the February and March school holidays, when prices are at their peak and most accommodation needs to be booked well in advance. Summer skiing on high-altitued glaciers is available in a few areas.

Information Each ski station and nearby Alpine town has a tourist office that can provide information on skiing and other activities as well as weather bulletins and public transport details. Often, the local accommodation service (which can help with reservations for hotels, chalets, etc) and the ski school are located in the same building.

Ski Equipment & Schools All the essential items – skis, boots and stocks – can be hired in the ski shops found in every resort. The

FRENCH ALPS

more prestigious the station, the higher the rental prices. It's a good idea to equip yourself with sunglasses and gloves and stock up on sunscreen.

The École de Ski Français (ESF; French Skiing School), which has branches at practically every station, and the smaller ski schools you find at some resorts offer private and group lessons to both adults and children. For a series of six group lessons, count on paying around 300FF at low-altitude resorts and up to 400FF in high-altitude places. One-on-one private lessons can cost as much as 500FF for an afternoon. Smaller ski schools exist in some resorts. A week of snowboarding classes costs about 1500FF.

Lifts & Passes A daunting range of contraptions cover the slopes to spare skiers from having to walk up the hill each time they want to ski down. Gadgets you're likely to come across include *téléskis* (ski tows, also known as drag lifts), *télésièges* (chair lifts), *télécabines* or *gondolas* (lots of enclosed bubbles that can hold two or four people), *téléphériques* (cable cars capable of holding up to 50 people) and *funiculaires* (funicular railways).

Ski passes are the best way to use all of the above. Every resort has it's own system, but in general passes (lift tickets) – usually available for one, two or three days, a week, a fortnight or even a whole season – give access to: a group of lifts; the lifts in one sector of the resort; or the station's whole skiable domain, plus that of the neighbouring resort. For advanced skiers, the passes covering a larger area are generally the best deal. Beginners and moderately experienced skiers may not want to pay for access to the most perilous runs.

Pistes Most resorts have a combination of both alpine and cross-country pistes. Downhill runs, ranging in length from a few hundred metres to tens of km, are colour-coded to indicate the level of difficulty: green (the easiest), blue (for average skiers), red (difficult) and black (only for very experienced skiers).

Package Deals Most resorts offer excellent-value discount packages, especially during quiet periods. They usually include a week's accommodation (in a hotel, studio or apartment), a lift pass and perhaps also ski hire and lessons.

The packages offered by the FUAJ youth hostel association cost 2600FF per person and include a week's hostel accommodation, full board, lessons, ski hire and a ski pass. Less expensive versions may also be available. The organisation's annual *Montagne* (mountain) brochure and provides details.

Insurance At some resorts you'll get a discount on lift tickets and lessons if you have a *Carte Neige*, an insurance plan sold at all resorts which costs about 150FF for 10 days or 180FF for the season. The fee for cross-country skiers is 40FF.

Activities off the Slopes

There are plenty of things to do in the Alps in winter besides putting on skis – highlights include parapente and hang-gliding (see Warm-Weather Activities). Dog-sledge excursions can be organised as can motorised outings on snow scooters (snowmobiles), though the latter are considered a menace by skiers and a blight by environmentalists. Helicopter flights, ice skating on lakes or rinks, saunas, watching curling or ice hockey matches...the list goes on.

Of course, there's also *après ski* – everything that takes place after a hard day on the slopes. Local tourist offices can supply you with details on entertainment and organised social activities.

Places to Stay & Eat

Each resort has a central reservation service which books accommodation in hotels, studios (for up to four people), apartments and chalets. The latter range from one to four rooms and are capable of accommodating up to 16 people. Prices depend on the number of stars a place has and the time of year. During 'the season', most hotels prefer to work on the basis of full pension (three meals a day) or *demi-pension* (breakfast and either lunch or dinner) though you'll find a few offering just bed and breakfast.

Most of the restaurants in ski resorts make life hard on low-budget travellers. One way to reduce dining costs is to rent a studio or apartment equipped with a kitchen.

On the slopes, you'll ski past plenty of 'altitude' restaurants, whose prices are generally directly proportional to the altitude. A small, black coffee taken above 3000 metres, for example, will cost about 15FF.

Getting There & Away

The major international airports nearest the Alps are Aéroport de Genève-Cointrin near Geneva, Switzerland, and Satolas Airport near Lyon. On a clear day and with the right flight path, the view through the aeroplane window is the best introduction to the Alps you can get.

Rail service to many parts of the Alps is excellent and is continually being improved. Train service reaches deep into many valleys and, where the tracks end, regional buses take over. Each winter, the SNCF puts out a booklet entitled *La neige en direct*, which details train services from Paris to ski resorts all over France.

Roads, like railway lines, follow the valleys as far as possible, finally either tunnelling through the mountains or going over a high pass *(col)*. The Mont Blanc and Fréjus tunnels connect the French Alps with Italy as do a number of major cols – Petit Saint Bernard (2188 metres) near Bourg Saint Maurice, Mont Cénis (2083 metres) in the Haute Maurienne Valley and Montgenèvre (1850 metres) near Briançon. Roads signs indicate whether the passes are open or blocked. To get to many ski resorts by car you'll need snow chains *(chaînes)*, which are available from any hypermarket. Road signs will warn if they're necessary.

Getting Around

Train and regional bus services are efficient and plentiful, especially in the ski season, when buses shuttle between major rail hubs and the resorts. Certain mountain passes, such as the Col du Galibier (2558 metres)

and the Col de l'Iséran (2770 metres), are generally closed between November and June, depending on snowfall. Tourist offices can tell you if they're open.

Savoy

Bordered by Switzerland and Italy, Savoy (Savoie – pronounced 'sav-WA') rises from the southern shores of Lake Geneva and keeps rising until it reaches the massive Mont Blanc, which dominates Chamonix. Further south, long U-shaped valleys are obvious relics of ancient glaciers which created lakes such as Lake Annecy as well as France's largest natural lake, Lake Bourget, which is near Aix-les-Bains.

Although Savoy is divided into two *départements*, Haute-Savoie and the Savoie, the people of the whole region are known as Savoyards. Despite centuries of French cultural influence, they have somehow managed to keep their identity, and often speak their own dialect, which reveals Provençal influences. In the remote valleys, such as in the Haute Maurienne (close to the Parc National de Vanoise), rural life goes on as it has for centuries, and the people continue to struggle with the harsh climate and the ever-present threat of avalanches.

History

Savoy was long ruled by the House of Savoy, which was founded by Humbert I (or the Whitehanded, as he was known), in the mid-11th century. During the Middle Ages, the dukes of Savoy extended their territory eastward to other areas of the western Alps, including the Piedmont region of what is now Italy.

In the 16th century the dukes of Savoy began to shift their interest from Savoy to their Italian territories; in 1563 they moved their capital from Chambéry to Turin. However, they continued to rule Savoy and managed to resist repeated French attempts to take over the mostly French-speaking region. Savoy was annexed by France in 1792 but was returned 23 years later.

In 1720, Victor Amadeus II, Duke of Savoy, became king of Sardinia, and over the next century important territories in northern Italy, including Genoa, came under Savoy control. In the mid-1800s, the House of Savoy worked to bring about the unification of Italy under Piedmontese leadership, a goal which they achieved in 1861 with the formation of the Kingdom of Italy under King Victor Emmanuel II of the House of Savoy. However, in exchange for Napoleon III's acceptance of the new arrangement and the international agreements that led up to it, Savoy – along with the area around Nice – was ceded to France in 1860.

CHAMONIX

The town of Chamonix (population 10,000; altitude 1035 metres), site of the 1924 Winter Olympiad, sits in a valley surrounded by far and away the most spectacular scenery in the French Alps. The area is almost Himalayan in its awesomeness: the tongues of deeply crevassed glaciers many km long ooze valleyward in the gullies between the icy spikes and needles around Mont Blanc, which soars 3.8 vertical km above the valley floor.

In late spring and summer, the glaciers and high-altitude snow and ice – whose year-round presence has given Mont Blanc (White Mountain) its name – serve as a glistening backdrop for meadows and hillsides carpeted with flowering plants, bushes and trees. There are some 310 km of hiking trails in the Chamonix area.

In winter, the superb skiing on 200 km of downhill and cross-country ski runs is made both convenient and varied by four dozen ski lifts.

Orientation

The mountain range to the east of the valley, the Aiguilles de Chamonix, is characterised by lots of glaciers and includes the mind-boggling mass of Mont Blanc (4807 metres). The almost-glacierless Aiguilles Rouges range, whose highest peak is Le Brévent

(2525 metres), runs along the western side of the valley.

Argentière, a fine base for hiking and skiing, is a quiet valley village nine km north-east of Chamonix and nine km from the Swiss border.

Information

Tourist Office The tourist office (☎ 50.53. 00.24) at Place de l'Église is open daily from 8 or 8.30 am to 12.30 pm and 2 to 7 pm. During July and August, it's open from 8.30 am to 7.30 pm. It can provide you with all sorts of useful brochures on ski-lift hours and costs, *refuges*, camping grounds, parapente schools, etc. Upstairs, the Centrale de Réservations Hôtelières (☎ 50.53.23.33) will reserve accommodation for stays of at least three nights.

Maison de la Montagne The Maison de la Montagne is near the tourist office at 109 Place de l'Église. On the ground floor is the Bureau des Guides, where mountain guides can be hired.

The Office de Haute Montagne (2nd floor; ☎ 50.53.22.08), which serves walkers, hikers and mountain climbers, has maps and information on trails, hiking conditions, the weather, *refuges* (they can help non-French speakers make reservations) and more. It is open Monday to Friday from 8.30 am to 12.30 pm and 2 or 2.30 to 6 or 6.30 pm, and in the afternoon on Saturday. From the end of June to the end of September, it's open daily until 6.30 pm.

Weather Any time of the year, the success of a visit to Chamonix depends in part on the vagaries of the weather. Clouds, for instance, can turn a spectacular vista (eg from the Aiguille du Midi) into something resembling what you see through the aeroplane window when flying inside a cloud. Bulletins from the meteorological service are posted in the window of the tourist office and at the Maison de la Montagne; the latter may have English translations.

It's a good idea to come equipped with

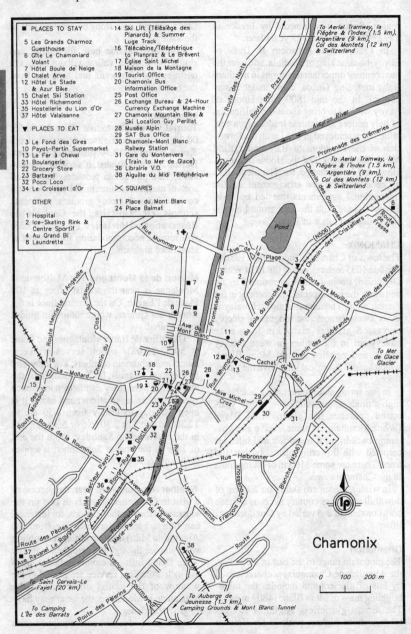

FRENCH ALPS

■ PLACES TO STAY

5 Les Grands Charmoz Guesthouse
6 Gîte Le Chamoniard Volant
7 Hôtel Boule de Neige
9 Chalet Arve
12 Hôtel Le Stade & Azur Bike
15 Chalet Ski Station
33 Hôtel Richemond
35 Hostellerie du Lion d'Or
37 Hôtel Valaisanne

▼ PLACES TO EAT

3 Le Fond des Gires
10 Payot-Pertin Supermarket
13 Le Fer à Cheval
22 Grocery Store
32 Bartavel
32 Poco Loco
34 Le Croissant d'Or

OTHER

1 Hospital
2 Ice-Skating Rink & Centre Sportif
4 Au Grand Bi
8 Laundrette

14 Ski Lift (Télésiège des Planards) & Summer Luge Track
16 Télécabine/Téléphérique to Planpraz & Le Brévent
17 Église Saint Michel
18 Maison de la Montagne
19 Tourist Office
20 Chamonix Bus Information Office
25 Post Office
26 Exchange Bureau & 24-Hour Currency Exchange Machine
27 Chamonix Mountain Bike & Ski Location Guy Perillat
28 Musée Alpin
29 SAT Bus Office
30 Chamonix-Mont Blanc Railway Station
31 Gare du Montenvers (Train to Mer de Glace)
36 Librairie V.O.
38 Aiguille du Midi Téléphérique

✕ SQUARES

11 Place du Mont Blanc
21 Place Balmat

Chamonix

0   100   200 m

warm clothing, as it can get pretty cool at night even in summer.

Money Between the tourist office and the post office, there are several places to change money. The Change (☎ 50.55.88.40) at 21 Place Balmat offers a decent rate and is open daily from 9 am to 1 pm and 3 to 7 pm (8 am to 8 pm from July to early September and around Christmas). Outside is a 24-hour exchange machine that accepts banknotes in any of 15 flavours. The exchange service at the tourist office is open on weekends and bank holidays (and, during July and August, on weekdays as well).

Post The post office (☎ 50.53.15.90) at Place Balmat is open weekdays from 8 am to noon and 2 to 6 pm and on Saturday until noon. During July and August, weekday hours are 8 am to 7 pm.

Chamonix's postcode is 74400.

Bookshops English books are on sale at Librairie V.O. (☎ 50.53.50.70) at 24 Ave Ravanel Le Rouge, which is open from 9 am to noon and 2 to 7.30 pm.

Maps The *Carte des Sentiers de Montagne en Eté* (Summer Trails Map; 20FF), which is adequate for straightforward day hikes (and also indicates the locations of *refuges*), is on sale along with other maps at the Maison de la Montagne and the tourist office. The best map of the area is the 1:25,000 scale IGN map entitled *Massif du Mont Blanc*.

Emergency The Centre Hospitalier (☎ 50. 53.04.74) is at 543 Rue Joseph Vallot.

Laundry The Lav' Matic at 223 Rue Joseph Vallot (on the ground floor of a building called The Mummery) charges an exorbitant 25FF per load. It's open daily (except sometimes on Thursday) from 8 am to 8.30 pm.

Aiguille du Midi

The Aiguille (pronounced 'ay-G'WEE') du Midi (3842 metres), a lone spire of rock eight km across glaciers, snow fields and rocky

crags from the summit of Mont Blanc, is unique in its accessibility to people with limited interest in scaling sheer cliffs. The views in all directions are truly breathtaking and should not be missed just to save a few francs...In general, visibility is best and rain least likely early in the morning.

The téléphérique (☎ 50.53.30.80) from Chamonix to the Aiguille du Midi is the highest aerial tramway in the world. From July to September, you can take the transglacial ride to **Pointe Helbronner** (3466 metres) on the Italian border, where there's some summer skiing, and then to the Italian resort town of **Courmayeur**. Return tickets from Chamonix to the Aiguille du Midi cost 150FF; it's an extra 70FF return to Pointe Helbronner. One-way prices are only 20% to 25% less than the return trip. A ride to the

One of the many needle-shaped peaks in the French Alps

tramway's halfway point, Plan de l'Aiguille (2308 metres) – an excellent place to start hikes during summer – costs 47FF one way. No student discounts are available.

The téléphérique, which runs all year (except during maintenance work), begins operating at 8 am (6 am in July and August). The last ride up is at 4.45 pm. It takes 40 minutes to get to Italy. Be prepared for long queues – the earlier in the morning you get there, the better. You can make advance reservations 24 hours a day by calling ☎ 50.53.40.00.

Le Brévent

Le Brévent (2525 metres), the highest peak on the west side of the valley, is known for its great views of Mont Blanc and the rest of the east side of the valley. It can be reached by a combination of télécabine and téléphérique (☎ 50.53.13.18), which costs 48/68FF one way/return. Service begins at 8 am (9 am in winter); the last trips up/down are at 5 pm/5.45 pm in summer and an hour or so earlier in winter. Quite a few hiking trails (including various routes back to the valley) can be picked up at either Le Brévent or at the tramway's midway station, Planpraz (1999 metres; 40FF one way).

Mer de Glace

The heavily crevassed Mer de Glace (Sea of Ice), the second-largest glacier in the Alps, is 14 km long, 1800 metres wide and up to 400 metres deep. It moves 45 metres a year at the edges and up to 90 metres a year in the middle. It has become a popular tourist destination thanks to a cog-wheel rail line built between 1897 and 1908. In the 17th century, the Mer de Glace – like other glaciers in the area – reached the bottom of the valley, destroying houses and burying cultivated land.

The **Grotte de la Mer de Glace** (12FF), an ice cave that lets you get a look at the glacier from the inside, is open from the end of May to the end of September. The interior temperature is 2°C to 5°C below zero. Since 1946, the cave has been carved anew each spring – the work is begun in February and

takes about 3⅓ months. Look down the slope for last year's cave to see how far the glacier has moved.

With new avalanche-proofing over parts of the railway tracks, the train – which leaves from Gare du Montenvers (☎ 50.53.12.54) in Chamonix and takes you to an altitude of 1913 metres – is suppsed to run throughout the year. The last train up departs at 5.30 or 6 pm (earlier after mid-September) and comes down half an hour later. The 20-minute trip costs 40/53FF one way/return. A combined ticket valid for the train, the cable car to the ice cave (11FF return) and the ice cave itself costs 71FF. There are often long queues during July and August.

The Mer de Glace can also be reached on foot via the Grand Balcon Nord trail from Plan de l'Aiguille, the midway point on the Aiguille du Midi téléphérique. The uphill trail from Chamonix (two hours) begins near the summer luge track. Traversing the glacier and its many crevasses is dangerous without proper equipment and a guide.

Réserve des Aiguilles Rouges

This nature reserve (3300 hectares), 12 km north of Chamonix at Col des Montets, is known for its particularly beautiful and diverse Alpine vegetation. The visitors' centre (☎ 50.54.02.24, 50.54.12.26) is open from June to September from 8.30 am to 12.30 pm and 1.30 to 7.30 pm. Nearby is a two-km botanical trail lined with scores of Alpine plants. Transport to the Col des Montets is infrequent (see Bus under Getting Around for details).

Musée Alpin

The Musée Alpin (☎ 50.53.25.93) on Ave Michel Croz in Chamonix displays artefacts, lithographs and photos illustrating the history of mountain climbing and other Alpine sports. From June to mid-October, it's open daily from 2 to 7 pm; between Christmas and Easter, hours are 3 to 7 pm. It's closed during the rest of the year. Entrance costs 15FF.

Warm-Weather Activities

Hiking In late spring and summer (mid-June

to October, more or less), the Chamonix area has some of the most spectacular hiking trails anywhere in the Alps. In general, the more rewarding trails and the more dramatic views are to be found at higher elevations, which can be reached in minutes by aerial tramway. The téléphériques shut down in the late afternoon, but in June and July there is enough light to hike until 9 pm or even later.

The fairly flat **Grand Balcon Sud** trail along the Aiguilles Rouges (western) side of the valley stays up around 2000 metres and affords great views of Mont Blanc and nearby glaciers. On foot, it can be reached from behind Le Brévent télécabine station. If you prefer to avoid a vertical km of uphill walking, take either the Planpraz (40FF) or La Flégère (32FF) lifts.

From Plan de l'Aiguille (47FF), the **Grand Balcon Nord** takes you to the Mer de Glace (see the Mer de Glace listing), whence you can hike or take the cog-wheel train down to Chamonix. There are a number of other trails from Plan de l'Aiguille.

There are trails to **Lac Blanc** (2350 metres), a turquoise lake surrounded by mountains, from either the top of Les Praz-L'Index aerial tramway (44FF one way) or La Flégère (30FF one way), the line's midway transfer point.

From the southern end of the Réserve des Aiguilles Rouges' botanical walk at Col de Montets (1461 metres), 12 km north of Chamonix, a trail on the east side of the road leads up to L'Aiguillette des Posettes (2201 metres). Count on taking 2½ hours to go up and 1½ hours to come down. For more information, see the Réserve des Aiguilles Rouges.

Cycling Many of the trails around the bottom of the valley (eg the Petit Balcon Sud) are perfect for mountain biking. See the Getting Around section for information on bike rental.

In season, Chamonix's Club de Cyclotourisme has a group ride every Sunday. It begins sometime between 7 and 8 am at Au Grand Bi at 240 Ave du Bois du Bouchet.

Parapente The sky above Chamonix is often dotted with colourful parapentes floating slowly down from the snowy heights. Initiation flights with an instructor cost 450FF; a five-day course costs 2500 to 2900FF.

For details, contact the École de Parapente (☎ 50.53.50.14) at 79 Ave Whymper or Chamonix Parapente (☎ 50.55.99.22) at 278 Rue Paccard.

Espace Sensation (☎ 50.55.99.49), another parasailing school, is at 132 Place de Chamonix Sud. For more information, contact the tourist office.

Ice-Skating The indoor ice-skating rink (*patinoire*; ☎ 50.53.12.36) at 165 Route de la Patinoire (in the Centre Sportif) operates almost all year. It is open daily from 3 to 6 pm and every Wednesday from 9 to 11 pm. In summer, it is also open daily from 10 am to noon. The entry fee is 24FF; skate rental is 15FF.

Summer Luge The summer luge track (☎ 50.53.08.97) is open from May to the end of September every day (unless it's raining) from 10 am to noon and 1.30 to 6 pm. During July and August, opening hours are 10 am to 7.30 pm.

Other Activities For more information on sports in the valley, enquire at the Club des Sports (☎ 50.53.11.57) of the Centre Sportif (☎ 50.53.12.36). The Pass' Sport is a carnet of 10/15/20 vouchers (300/450/600FF) which let you participate in a wide range of activities.

Winter Activities
Skiing The Chamonix area has 160 km of marked ski runs, 40 km of cross-country trails and 62 ski lifts – some with upper stations as high as 3500 metres – divided into several groups. The Grands Montets and Aiguille du Midi areas are like entering a different world, where you ski under a clear blue sky beside glaciers and amazing spires of rock. The Brévent area is on the other side of the valley.

The famous 20-km-long Vallée Blanche

descent, which takes four hours, leads from the top of the Aiguille du Midi over the Mer de Glace and through the forests back to Chamonix.

During summer, there is limited (and expensive) skiing from Pointe Helbronner on the Italian frontier, which is accessible by aerial tramway (see Aiguille du Midi). The runs, which are down a glacier, are only about 800 metres long and are served by four tow lines.

Equipment Dozens of sports stores around Chamonix rent out ski equipment. Count on paying 35FF a day (235FF a week) for regular skis and 30FF a day (200FF a week) for shoes. Ski Location Guy Perillat (☎ 50. 53.54.76) at 138 Rue des Moulins rents skis daily from 9 am to noon and 2 to 7 pm. Cross-country skis are available from Au Grand Bi (☎ 50.53.14.16) at 240 Ave du Bois du Bouchet.

Lessons The ESF (☎ 50.53.22.57) at the Maison de la Montagne is open from 8.30 am to noon and 2 to 7 pm. A two-hour group lesson costs 70FF; 12 lessons over six days cost 570FF.

Lifts The tourist office sells a ski pass – valid for all the ski lifts in the valley (except Les Grands Montets) and unlimited bus transport – for 310/930FF for two/seven days (280/840FF during discount periods). Each lift system also has single tickets or day passes. The Téléphérique de l'Aiguille du Midi costs 120/150FF one way/return. The Le Brévent day pass is 112FF.

Other Activities Two guide organisations, the Compagnie des Guides (☎ 50.53.00.88) at 190 Place de l'Église and the Association Indépendante des Guides offer adventure programmes such as Héliski, in which a helicopter drops you on a glacier or a mountain peak so you can ski down.

Places to Stay
During July, August and the ski season,

hotels are heavily booked. Many strongly prefer guests who take full board.

Hiking areas and ski lifts in the northern Chamonix Valley are as easily accessible from Argentière, which is on the rail line nine km north-east of Chamonix. For transport information, see Getting Around.

Places to Stay – bottom end
Camping – Chamonix In general, camping costs 30/50FF for one/two people and 7 to 15FF for a site. Because of the altitude, it's often chilly at night.

L'Île des Barrats (☎ 50.53.51.44), near the base of the Aiguille du Midi cable car, is open from June to September. The three-star Les Deux Glaciers (☎ 50.53.15.84) on Route des Tissières in Les Bossons, three km south of Chamonix, is closed from mid-November to mid-December. To get there, take either the train to Les Bossons or Chamonix Bus (see Getting Around) to the Tremplin-le-Mont stop.

There are a number of camping grounds a couple of km south-west of town in the village of Les Pèlerins. These include Le Mazot (☎ 50.53.41.02) at 1400 Route des Pèlerins (on the other side of Route Blanche from the youth hostel), which is open from late May to September; and Les Arolles (☎ 50.53.14.30) at 281 Chemin du Cry. The latter is open from late June to September. Take Les Houches bus to Les Tissourds stop.

Camping – Argentière Glacier d'Argentière (☎ 50.54.17.36) at 58 Chemin des Moilettes, open from June to mid-September, is 700 metres towards Switzerland from the Argentière train station. Campers pay 16FF each and 7FF for a tent site.

Refuges Most mountain refuges, which cost 40 to 50FF a night, are accessible to hikers, though a few can be reached only by mountain climbers. Breakfast and dinner, prepared by the warden, are often available. It's advisable to call ahead to reserve a place. For information on refuges, contact the Maison de la Montagne or the tourist office.

Among the easier-to-reach refuges are one

at Plan de l'Aiguille (2308 metres; ☎ 50. 53.55.60), the intermediate stop on the Aiguille du Midi cable car, and another at La Flégère (1877 metres; ☎ 50.53.06.13), the midway station on Les Praz-L'Index aerial tramway.

Hostels The *Auberge de Jeunesse* (☎ 50.53. 14.52) is a couple of km south-west of Chamonix at 103 Montée Jacques Balmat in Les Pèlerins. By bus, take the Chamonix-Les Houches line and get off at the Pèlerins École stop. Beds in rooms of four or six cost 66FF; doubles are 80FF per person. There's no kitchen and meals cost 44FF. You can't check-in until after 5 pm. The hostel is closed from October to mid-December.

The *Hôtel Montenvers* (☎ 50.53.00.33) overlooks the Mer de Glace glacier from the top of the Mer de Glace cog-wheel railway line. To get there, you can either walk (see Hiking under Warm-Weather Activities) or take the train (see Mer de Glace). Rooms here cost hundreds of francs but dorm beds are only 90FF. Bring your own food. It's open from mid-June to mid-September *only*.

Gîtes d'Étape – Chamonix The *Chalet Ski Station* (☎ 50.53.20.25) is at 6 Route des Moussoux, next to the Planpraz/Le Brévent télécabine station. Beds cost 45FF a night, there's a 15FF charge for sheets, and showers are 5FF. This place is closed from mid-May to late June and mid-September to mid-December.

The semirustic *Gîte Le Chamoniard Volant* (☎ 50.53.14.09) is on the north-eastern outskirts of town at 45 Route de la Frasse. A bunk in a cramped, functional room for four, six or eight costs 60FF; sheets are 15FF. Use of the kitchen is free. Reception is open from 10 am to 10 pm and the staff speak English. This place is most crowded in July. The nearest bus stop is called La Frasse.

Gîte La Montagne (☎ 50.53.11.60), by far the most attractive of Chamonix's three gîtes, is on a beautiful, forested site at 789 Promenade des Crémeries, 1.5 km north of the train station (if arriving by bus, get off at La Frasse stop). Unfortunately, the non-English speaking management is very strict about all sorts of things, creating an atmosphere that is far from mellow. Telephone reservations are accepted only on the day you're arriving, rooms are locked from 10 am to 5 pm, and curfew is at 11 pm. A bunk in a jam-packed room costs 60FF (including use of the kitchen). This place is closed from 11 November to 20 December.

Gîtes d'Étape – Argentière Argentière has several great gîtes. The relaxed and exceptionally friendly *Gîte d'Étape Le Belvédère* (☎ 50.54.02.59) at 501 Route du Plagnolet is 250 metres down the hill from the Argentière train station and near the Argentière Sud bus stop. In summer, a dorm bed costs 37FF (40FF per person in a quad). Spartan rooms for two, three and four people are 116FF, 159FF and 184FF respectively. In winter, prices are slightly higher. The kitchen costs 6FF a day. Dinner (54FF) and breakfast (18FF) are available.

The *Gîte du Moulin* (☎ 50.54.05.37) is one km north of Argentière at 32 Chemin du Moulin. The closest train station is Montroc, 200 metres away. If coming by bus, ask the driver to stop near the gîte. A dorm bed costs 45FF and you must bring your own sheets. This place is closed from the end of September to 20 December.

Another decent gîte in the area is the *Chalet Refuge La Boerne* (☎ 50.54.05.14), which is in Tréléchamps, two km towards Vallorcine and the Swiss border from Argentière. A bed costs 42FF in summer and 60FF in winter, including use of the kitchen. A sleeping sheet is 10FF. During summer, they strongly prefer that you also take dinner and breakfast (135FF). From the Montroc train station, follow the signs (it's a 700-metre walk). By bus, get off at Montroc. It's a good idea to telephone before dropping by.

Hotels *Les Grands Charmoz Guesthouse* (☎ 50.53.45.57) at 468 Chemin des Cristalliers, next to the railway tracks 600 metres north of the train station, is run by a friendly, laid-back American couple. Doubles cost

154FF, including use of the shower and sheets (but not towels). Dorm beds are 57FF. For stays of more than a week, ask about the three apartments upstairs.

The *Hôtel Valaisanne* (☎ 50.53.17.98) is a small, family-owned place at 454 Ave Ravanel Le Rouge, 900 metres south of the town centre. It has doubles from 155FF (more in the high season). At the *Hostellerie du Lion d'Or* (☎ 50.53.15.09) at 255 Rue du Docteur Paccard, doubles start at 185FF. Reception is in the ground floor restaurant or the bar next door.

Places to Stay – middle
Hotels – Chamonix The centrally located *Hôtel Le Stade* (☎ 50.53.05.44) at 79 Rue Whymper (the entrance is round the back on the 1st floor) has simple but pleasant singles/doubles from 132/204FF; triples are 291FF.

Off a quiet lane further north, the pleasant, local-style *Chalet Arve* (☎ 50.53.02.31) at 60 Impasse des Anémones has singles/doubles/triples from 125/160/345FF in the low season, 155/200/435FF in the high. There's parking nearby.

The little *Boule de Neige* (☎ 50.53.04.48) at 362 Rue Joseph Vallot has a lively bar and singles/doubles from 150/200FF; showers are 10FF extra. The enormous *Richemond* (☎ 50.53.08.85) at 228 Rue du Docteur Paccard has rooms for one/two people from 190/300FF.

Hotels – Argentière The small *Hôtel Marti* (☎ 50.54.11.01) at 182 Route du Village charges 147FF for a double. Showers are free. To get there from the train station, walk up the hill for 200 metres, turn right at the tourist office and continue on past the church. Another place to try is the *Hôtel Carrier* (☎ 50.54.02.16) at 242 Rue Charlet Stratton, 150 metres up the hill from the train station.

Places to Eat
Restaurants *Le Fer à Cheval* (☎ 50.53.13.22) at 118 Rue Whymper is reputed to have the best fondue Savoyarde in town.

Cheese/meat fondues cost 57/80FF per person.

A favourite with people staying at the nearby gîtes is the self-service *Le Fonds des Gires* (☎ 50.55.85.76) at 350 Ave du Bois du Bouchet. It's open for lunch (noon to 2 pm) daily all year (except during January) and for dinner (7 to 9 pm) only in July and August. The three plats du jour cost 35 to 45FF.

The *Boule de Neige* (see Places to Stay – middle) has a standard 60FF *menu*. There are lots of restaurants offering pizza, fondue, etc in the streets leading off from Place Balmat. On the square itself, *Bartavel* (☎ 50.53.26.51) has pizzas from 35FF. Nearby on Rue du Docteur Paccard, *Poco Loco* has cheaper pizzas and *menus* from 59FF.

Self-Catering The *Payot-Pertin supermarket* at 117 Rue Joseph Vallon is open Monday to Saturday from 8.15 am to 12.30 pm and 2.30 to 7.30 pm, and on Sunday from 8.30 am to 12.15 pm. The *boulangerie* at 31 Place de l'Église is open daily from 6.30 am to 12.30 pm and 2.30 to 7.30 pm.

The *grocery store* at 23 Place de l'Église is open Monday to Saturday from 8.15 am to 12.15 pm and 2 to 7 pm. Bread and pastries can also be bought from *Le Croissant d'Or* at 294 Rue du Docteur Paccard.

Getting There & Away
Train The narrow-gauge train line from Saint Gervais-Le Fayet (20 km west of Chamonix) to Martigny, Switzerland (42 km north of Chamonix), stops at 11 towns in the valley, including Argentière. There are nine to 12 round trips a day. To go into Switzerland, you have to switch trains at the border (at Châtelard or Vallorcine) because the track gauge changes. From Saint Gervais-Le Fayet, there are trains to all parts of France.

The Chamonix-Mont Blanc train station is in the middle of town. Information counters (☎ 50.53.00.44) are open Monday to Saturday from 9 am to noon and 2 to 6.30 pm. From June to September and December to April, they're open on Sunday, too. Ticket counters are staffed daily from 6 am to 8 pm. Major destinations include Paris's Gare de

Lyon (324FF plus TGV reservation fee; six to seven hours; five a day), Lyon (165FF; four to 4½ hours; four to five a day) and Geneva, Switzerland (75FF; two to 2½ hours via Saint Gervais, longer via Martigny). There's an overnight train to Paris every night of the year.

Bus The bus station is in part of the train station building. The office of SAT Autocar (☎ 50.53.01.15) has opening hours posted on the door, but in general it's open Monday to Friday (six days a week from December to April, daily during July and August). Buses run to Annecy (78FF), Grenoble and Geneva (135FF; 1½ to two hours). Italian destinations include Courmayeur (46FF; 40 minutes) and Turin (130FF; three hours).

Getting Around
Bus Bus transport in the valley is handled by Chamonix Bus, which has an information office (☎ 50.53.05.55) near the tourist office at Place de l'Église. In winter, it's open daily from 8 am to 7 pm. The rest of the year, hours are 8 am to noon and 2 to 6.30 pm (7 pm from June to August).

Bus stops are marked by black-on-yellow roadside signs. From mid-December to mid-May, there are 13 lines to all the ski lifts in the area. The rest of the year, there are only two lines, both of which leave from Place de l'Église and pass by the Chamonix Sud stop. One line goes south to Les Houches via either Les Moussoux (nine a day) or Les Pèlerins (eight a day). The other goes north via Argentière to Col des Montets. Buses do not run after 7 pm (6 or 6.30 pm in June and September).

Buses to the Réserve des Aiguilles Rouges go via Les Nants to Col des Montets (six a day in July and August, one a day during June and the first half of September).

Taxi There's a taxi stand (☎ 50.53.13.94) outside the train station.

Bicycle Between April and October, Au Grand Bi (☎ 50.53.14.16) at 240 Ave du Bois du Bouchet has three and 10-speeds for 65FF

a day, mountain bikes for 100FF and tandems for 150FF. It's open Monday to Saturday from 8.30 am to noon and 2 to 7 pm.

Chamonix Mountain Bike (☎ 50.53.54.76) at 138 Rue des Moulins, run by an Aussie and an Englishman, is open daily from 9 am to noon and 2 to 7 pm. The tariff is 50FF for two hours or 120FF for a full day. Prices are similar at Azur Bike (☎ 50.53.50.14) at 79 Rue Whymper, open daily from 9 am to 7 pm.

ANNECY
Annecy (population 50,000; altitude 448 metres), the rather chic and expensive capital of Haute-Savoie, is the perfect place to spend an extremely relaxing holiday. Visitors in a sedentary mood can sit along the lakefront and feed the swans or mosey around the geranium-lined canals of the old city. For once, there's no pressure to see yet another art museum or chateau – mercifully, there's only one of each in Annecy.

The town – located at the northern tip of the incredibly blue, 14.6-km-long Lake Annecy (Lac d'Annecy) – is an excellent base for water sports of all sorts as well as hiking and cycling. In winter there is bus transport to low-altitude ski stations only a few tens of km away.

Orientation
The train and bus stations are 500 metres north of the Vieille Ville, which is centred around the canalised Thiou River (Canal du Thiou). The modern town centre is between the main post office and the Centre Bonlieu, home of the tourist office.

The lakefront town of Annecy-le-Vieux is just east of Annecy. Sévrier, also on the lake, is five km south of Annecy on Rue des Marquisats, which becomes the N508.

Information
Tourist Office The tourist office (☎ 50.45.00.33), which is between Rue Président Favre and Rue Jean Jaurès in the Centre Bonlieu, is open Monday to Saturday from 9 am to noon and 1.45 to 6.30 pm; there's no midday closure during July and August. It's

open on Sunday from 9 am to noon and 1.45 to 6 pm except from mid-October to mid-May, when Sunday hours are 3 to 6 pm.

The tourist office doesn't make hotel reservations but can supply information on where rooms are available. They have local bus maps (free), a trail map for the Forêt du Crêt du Maure (20FF) and a 1:25,000-scale IGN map of Lake Annecy (55FF). The latter is highly recommended if you'll be doing any real hiking.

Money The Banque de France (☎ 50.51.40. 69) at 9 bis Ave Chambéry is open weekdays from 8.45 am to 12.15 pm and 1.45 to 3.45 pm.

The Banque de Savoie (☎ 50.52.80.05) at 2 Rue du Pâquier is open weekdays from 9 am to 12.25 pm and 1.30 to 5.30 pm. From mid-July to mid-September, it's also open on Saturday from 9 am to 4 pm. There's a 24-hour currency exchange machine in the Crédit Lyonnais in the Centre Bonlieu.

Opposite the main post office, the Banque de Savoie (☎ 50.51.43.19) at 4 Rue Saint François de Sales is open Tuesday to Saturday from 8.45 am to 12.15 pm and 1.30 to 5.45 pm (4.30 pm on Saturday).

Post The main post office (☎ 50.33.68.20) at 4bis Rue des Glières is open weekdays from 8 am to 7 pm and Saturday until noon. Foreign currency can be exchanged.

Annecy's postcode is 74000.

Emergency There's a hospital (☎ 50.88. 33.33) at 1 Ave de Trésun. The Hôtel de Police (police headquarters; ☎ 50.45.21.61) is at 15 Rue des Marquisats.

Laundry The Lav' Plus at 10 Ave de Chambéry is open daily from 8 am to 7.30 pm.

Walking Tour

Just walking around and taking in the water, flowers, grass and quaint buildings is the essence of a visit to Annecy. The Vieille Ville can be viewed to best advantage from both sides of the restaurant-lined Canal du Thiou.

Just east of the old city, behind the Hôtel de Ville, are the flowery **Jardins de**

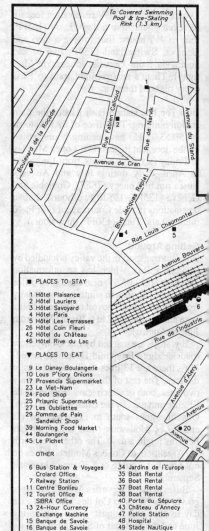

To Covered Swimming Pool & Ice-Skating Rink (1.3 km)

■ PLACES TO STAY
1 Hôtel Plaisance
2 Hôtel Lauriers
3 Hôtel Savoyard
4 Hôtel Paris
5 Hôtel Les Terrasses
26 Hôtel Coin Fleuri
42 Hôtel du Château
46 Hôtel Rive du Lac

▼ PLACES TO EAT
9 Le Danay Boulangerie
10 Lous P'tiory Onions
17 Provencia Supermarket
23 Le Viet-Nam
24 Food Shop
25 Prisunic Supermarket
27 Les Oubliettes
29 Pomme de Pain Sandwich Shop
39 Morning Food Market
44 Boulangerie
45 Le Pichet

OTHER
6 Bus Station & Voyages Crolard Office
7 Railway Station
11 Centre Bonlieu
12 Tourist Office & SIBRA Office
13 24-Hour Currency Exchange Machine
15 Banque de Savoie
16 Banque de Savoie
18 Main Post Office
19 Laundrette
20 Banque de France
21 Église Notre Dame de Liesse
22 Cathédrale Saint Pierre
28 Musée d'Histoire d'Annecy
30 Église Saint Maurice
32 Église Saint François
33 Hôtel de Ville
34 Jardins de l'Europe
35 Boat Rental
36 Boat Rental
37 Boat Rental
38 Boat Rental
40 Porte du Sépulcre
43 Château d'Annecy
47 Police Station
48 Hospital
49 Stade Nautique des Marquisats
50 Sports Évasion (Bike & Ski Rental)

✕ SQUARES
8 Place de la Gare
14 Place de la Libération
31 Place de l'Hôtel de Ville
41 Place du Château

l'Europe, shaded by giant redwoods brought all the way from California. The grassy expanse of the **Champ de Mars**, across the Canal du Vasse from the redwoods, is perfect for playing Frisbee.

A truly fine stroll can be had by walking from the Jardins de l'Europe along Quai de Bayreuth and Quai de la Tournette to the Base Nautique des Marquisats (see More Serious Boats) and beyond. Another fine promenade begins at the Champ de Mars and goes eastward around the lake towards **Annecy-le-Vieux**.

Vieille Ville

The Vieille Ville, an area of narrow streets on either side of the Canal du Thiou, retains much of its 17th-century appearance despite recent quaintification and touristification. On the island in the middle, the Palais de l'Isle (a former prison) houses the **Musée d'Histoire d'Annecy et de la Haute-Savoie** (☎ 50.51.02.33), which outlines the region's history and culture. It's open from 10 am to noon and 2 to 6 pm daily except Sunday and holidays (daily from July to September). Entrance is free.

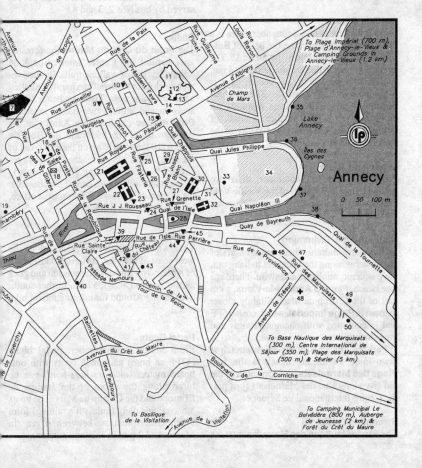

Château d'Annecy

The **Musée d'Annecy** (☎ 50.45.29.66), housed in the 13th-to-16th-century chateau overlooking the town, has a varied permanent collection that includes examples of local artisanship and miscellaneous objects about the region's natural history. It also puts on innovative temporary exhibitions. It's open from 10 am to noon and 2 to 6 pm daily except Tuesday (daily in July and August). Admission is 20/10FF for adults/students but is free on Wednesday (except during school holidays). The climb up to the chateau is worth it just for the view.

Carillon Concert

From mid-June to mid-September, there is a carillon concert, played on the bells of **Basilique de la Visitation** (☎ 50.66.17.37), every Saturday in the late afternoon. At 4 pm, immediately preceding the concert, there is a guided visit (15FF) of the 37-bell chromatic carillon and various displays on carillon playing. The basilica is south of (straight up the hill from) the old city at the top of Ave de la Visitation.

Organised Tours

From mid-June to September, there are guided tours (in English) of the Vieille Ville on Tuesday at 2.30 pm. The tourist office has details.

Sunbathing & Swimming

In the warm months, there are all sorts of grassy areas along the lakefront to hang out, have a picnic, sunbathe and swim. There is a free beach, **Plage d'Annecy-le-Vieux**, a km east of the Champ de Mars. Slightly closer to town is **Plage Impérial**, which costs 15FF and is equipped with changing rooms and other amenities.

Perhaps Annecy's most pleasant stretch of lawn-lined swimming beach is the free **Plage des Marquisats**, one km south of the old city along Rue des Marquisats (just past the Centre International de Séjour).

Swimming Pools

The **Stade Nautique des Marquisats** (☎ 50. 45.39.18) at 29 Rue des Marquisats has three outdoor swimming pools and lots of lawn. From mid-May to early September, the complex is open from 9 am (10 am on Sunday and holidays) to 7 pm (8 pm from mid-June to mid-August). The entrance fee is 16FF, but if you leave you have to pay again to get back in. There are showers, changing rooms, a free place to check your stuff and a snack bar.

The **covered pool** (*piscine*; ☎ 50.57.56. 02) at 90 Chemin de Fins (on the corner of Blvd du Fier) is open from mid-August to June. The entrance fee is 16FF. The pool is served by bus Nos 2, 3 and 8.

Hiking

The **Forêt du Crêt du Maure**, the forested area behind the Centre International de Séjour, has lots of walking trails. It is conveniently close to town but can hardly be called a pristine wilderness. There are better hiking areas in and around two nature reserves: **Bout du Lac** (20 km from Annecy at the southern tip of the lake) and the **Roc de Chère** (10 km from town on the east coast of the lake). Both can be reached by Voyages Crolard buses (see Getting There & Away).

Maps and topoguides can be purchased at the Maison de la Presse and the tourist office, both in the Centre Bonlieu.

Cycling

There's a bike path (*piste cyclable*) along the west coast of the lake. It starts 1.5 km south of Annecy (on Rue des Marquisats) and goes all the way to Duingt, 12 km further south. See Getting Around for information on bike rental.

Pedal Boats

From March to November, pedal boats (47FF an hour) and small boats with outboard motors (*moteurs hors-bord*) can be hired along the shore of the Jardins de l'Europe and the Champ de Mars. The boats are available daily (unless it's raining) from 9 am until sometime between 6 pm (in March) and 9 pm (in July and August).

More Serious Boats

The Base Nautique des Marquisats, across from the CIS, is a centre for all sorts of aquatic activities. **Kayaks** and **canoes** can be rented from the Canoë-Kayak Club d'Annecy (☎ 50.45.03.98) for 50FF per person for two hours (84FF per person with an instructor). From June to September, there is usually someone in the office from 9 am to noon and 1 to 5 pm. They also offer kayaking and canoeing courses.

Between June and mid-September, the Société des Regattes à Voile d'Annecy (SRVA; ☎ 50.45.48.39) rents all sorts of sailing boats (Laser X4s, catamarans, etc) and sailboards (*planches à voile*). The latter cost 80/120FF for one/two hours. The Société also has sailing courses. The office is generally open weekdays from 9 am to noon and 2 to 5 pm (and often later).

In the same complex, the Club Nautique d'Aviron rents **rowing hulls**. The equipment storage facility is staffed for two hours in the morning and two hours in the evening daily except Monday and Friday. Precise hours are posted outside.

Skin Diving

The Club Subaquatique Alpin in the Base Nautique des Marquisats rents out equipment for skin diving (*plongée sous-marine*).

Ice Skating

There is an ice-skating rink (*patinoire*; ☎ 50.57.56.02) at 90 Chemin de Fins in the same complex as the covered swimming pool. The entrance fee is 16FF; skate rental is 10FF. See Swimming Pools for transport information.

Miniature Golf

Near the Plage Impérial in Annecy-le-Vieux, there is a miniature golf course (☎ 50.66.04.99) at 2 Ave du Petit Port, which is 500 metres east along Ave d'Albigny from the Champ de Mars. From April to October, it's open daily from 1 to 10 pm (10 am to 11 pm in July and August). The charge is 19FF per person.

Bowling

If bowling is your cup of tea (so to speak), the Bowling International d'Annecy-Sévrier (☎ 50.52.43.49) is five km south of Annecy at the southern end of the town of Sévrier. It is open every day from 7 pm to 2 am. It opens at 2.30 pm on weekends and on rainy days in summer; on Wednesday, Saturday and Sunday during the rest of the year; and daily during the Christmas and Easter school holidays.

To get to the bowling alley, take the N508 (the continuation of Rue des Marquisats). You can get there by Crolard buses (see Getting There & Away).

Horse Riding

The Centre Équestre de Sévrier-Semnoz (☎ 50.52.48.23) on Route de la Planche in Sévrier (near the bowling alley), is open all year. It is open from 9 am to noon and 2 to 7 pm (closed Thursday). Groups of four or more can go on accompanied rides for 80FF an hour per person. A full day of horse riding (équitation) costs 330FF, while a half-day (from 9 am to noon) is 170FF. Reservations must be made in advance.

Parapente

Col de la Forclaz, the huge ridge overlooking Lake Annecy from the east, is a perfect spot from which to descend by parapente, a wing-shaped, steerable parachute. For details on parapente courses (2200FF for five days) and initiation flights (450FF), as well as hang-gliding, ring ☎ 50.52.89.85.

Winter Sports

Annecy itself doesn't usually get much snow, but there's lots of cross-country skiing at Le Semnoz (about 15 km south-east of town) and both downhill and cross-country skiing at La Clusaz (tourist office ☎ 50.02.60.92) and Le Grand Bornand (tourist office ☎ 50.02.20.33), both of which are 32 km east of Annecy. Count on paying 110FF a day for a lift ticket. All three can be reached by Crolard buses (see Getting There & Away for details).

In Annecy, skis can be rented from Sports Évasion (☎ 50.51.21.81) at 30 Rue des Marquisats, which is open Monday to Saturday from 9 am to noon and 2 to 7 pm. Snowboards *(surf de neige)* are available from Regate Service (☎ 50.45.74.75) at 34 Rue des Marquisats, which is closed on Sunday and perhaps Monday.

Places to Stay – bottom end

Camping *Camping Municipal Le Belvédère* (☎ 50.45.48.30), open from 1 April to 15 October, is 2.5 km south of the train station in the Forêt du Crêt du Maure. To get there, turn off Rue des Marquisats onto Ave de Trésun, take the first left and follow Blvd de la Corniche. From mid-June to early September, you can take bus No 91 from the train station (see Auberge de Jeunesse in the Hostels section for details). The camping ground charges 15/13FF per person/tent.

Near the lake in Annecy-le-Vieux, *Le Pré d'Avril* (☎ 50.23.64.46) at 56 Rue du Pré d'Avril is open all year. It usually charges 21FF to pitch a tent (including parking) and 15FF per person. In summer, two people with a tent and a car pay 67FF.

Hostels The modern *Centre International de Séjour* (☎ 50.45.08.80), on a superb lakeside site at 52 Rue des Marquisats, has beds in antiseptic singles/doubles/quads (all with shower, toilet and sheets) for 113/78/57FF respectively. Rooms are open all day and there is no curfew. Places usually become available each morning. Reservations can be made by telephone between 8 am and 5 pm.

The *Auberge de Jeunesse* (☎ 50.45.33.19) is four km from town at 16 Route du Semnoz in the Forêt du Semnoz. A bed costs 41FF; breakfast (obligatory from July to September) is 16FF. Rooms are locked from 11 am to 5 pm. There's a small kitchen. From mid-June to early September *only*, bus No 91 (the Ligne des Vacances) runs from the train station and the Hôtel de Ville to the hostel (seven a day) between 9 am and 7 pm. During the rest of the year, you have to hoof it or hitch – from Camping Le Belvédère (see Camping) follow Route du Semnoz. In 1994,

the hostel is supposed to move to a new location at the Annecy end of Route du Semnoz.

Hotels Cheap hotels are in short supply in Annecy. It's most difficult to find accommodation from mid-July to mid-August.

The small *Rive du Lac* (☎ 50.51.32.85), superbly located near the Vieille Ville and the lake at 6 Rue des Marquisats, has modestly furnished rooms with one or two beds for 130/170FF with shower.

North of the train station, the *Hôtel Savoyard* (☎ 50.57.08.08), a sterile, dorm-like (and, some say, spooky) place at 41 Ave de Cran, has singles/doubles starting at 110FF (180FF with shower and toilet). Hall showers are 10FF. The *Plaisance* (☎ 50.57.30.42) at 17 Rue de Narvik has simple but neat and well-lit rooms from 110/130FF. Doubles with toilet and shower are 180FF.

The pleasant *Les Terrasses* (☎ 50.57.08.98) at 15 Rue Louis Chaumontel has singles/doubles from 140/160FFF. From June to September, guests who stay more than a night or two must take their meals here, which gets expensive. This place is closed from November to January.

Places to Stay – middle

Town Centre For a serene view over Annecy's lantern-lit lanes it's hard to go past the *Hôtel du Château* (☎ 50.45.27.66) at 16 Rue du Château, just below one of the towers of its namesake. Cosy singles/doubles start at 150/170FF. There's a large terrace and private parking. It's closed from mid-October to mid-December.

The *Coin Fleuri* (☎ 50.45.27.30) at 3 Rue Filaterie has slightly more expensive rooms in a rustic, old stone tower. Prices start at 160FF.

North of the Train Station This quiet suburban area offers two good options. The *Hôtel Paris* (☎ 50.57.35.98) at 15 Blvd Jacques Replat has a sun terrace and reasonably priced singles/doubles/triples from 120/150/190FF.

Even more pleasant is *Lauriers* (☎ 50.57.25.46) in a free-standing house at 10 Rue Fabien Calloud. It has lovely rooms from

150FF for a single or double, 300FF (with shower and toilet) for a triple or quad. There's plenty of shady private parking and a garden. This place is open only from April to mid-October.

Places to Eat

Restaurants In the Vieille Ville, the streets on both sides of the Canal du Thiou are lined with touristy restaurants, most of which are remarkably similar to each other.

Les Oubliettes (☎ 50.45.39.78) at 10 Quai de l'Isle is one of the more reasonably priced places, with pizzas from 40FF and a wide choice of other main courses. Just across the canal *Le Pichet* (☎ 50.45.32.41) at 13 Rue Perrière has a big terrace and three-course *menus* starting at 60FF. *Le Viet-Nam* (☎ 50. 45.35.43) at 5 Rue Jean-Jacques Rousseau has a 58FF lunchtime *menu*.

Rue Perrière and Rue de l'Isle have several cheap, hole-in-the-wall *sandwich shops. Pomme de Pain* on Rue Joseph Blanc has decent sandwiches for 15 to 21FF. It's open daily from 11 am to 8.30 pm (11 pm in summer).

In the town centre, there are good pizzas (from 32FF) and large salads at *Lous P'tiory Onions* (☎ 50.51.34.41) in Le Grand Passage at 36 Rue Sommeiller. The lunch *menu* costs 49FF.

Self-Catering In the Vieille Ville, there's a *food market* along Rue Sainte Claire on Sunday, Tuesday and Friday from 6 am to 12.30 pm. The *boulangerie* at 16 Rue Perrière has excellent pain campagnard (country loaf). It's open from 7 am to 1 pm and 2.30 to 8 pm daily except Thursday (daily in summer).

The *food shop* at 7 Rue Jean-Jacques Rousseau is open daily from 8 am to 8 pm. For cheaper fare, the *Prisunic* on the corner of Rue du Lac and Rue Notre Dame has an upstairs grocery section which is open Monday to Saturday from 8.30 am to 12.15 pm and 2.15 to 7 pm.

In the town centre, the *boulangerie* at 27 Rue Carnot (closed Monday) has a good selection of nonwhite breads. The small *Pro-vencia supermarket* across from the main post office is open Monday to Saturday from 8.15 am to 12.15 pm and 2.45 to 7.15 pm. North of the train station, there are several food stores along Ave de Cran.

Getting There & Away

Train The modernistic train station (☎ 50.66. 50.50 for information) is on Place de la Gare. The information counters are open daily from 8.30 am (9 am on Sunday) to 7 pm. The ticket windows stay open from 5 am to 10.30 pm.

There are frequent trains – not all of them direct – to Paris's Gare de Lyon (287FF plus TGV reservation fee; 3¾ hours), Nice (224FF via Lyon, 308FF via Grenoble; eight to nine hours, faster with a change of train), Lyon (102FF; two hours), Chamonix (80FF; 2½ to three hours) and – via Aix-les-Bains – to Chambéry (43FF; 50 minutes).

The night train to Paris (eight hours), which is often full on Friday and Saturday nights, leaves at 10.30 or 11.20 pm. Sleepers cost 86FF extra.

Bus The bus station, Gare Routière Sud, is next to the train station on Rue de l'Industrie. Voyages Crolard (☎ 50.45.08.12), open Monday to Saturday from 6.15 am to 12.30 pm and 1.15 to 7.30 pm, has regular service to points around Lake Annecy (including Roc de Chère on the eastern shore and Bout du Lac at the southern tip) and places east of Annecy (including ski stations such as La Clusaz and Le Grand Bornand and the towns of Albertville and Chamonix). Service on shorter runs ceases around 7 pm (earlier on Sunday and holidays).

Autocars Frossard (☎ 50.45.73.90), open Monday to Saturday except holidays from 7.45 am to 12.30 pm and 1.45 to 7 pm, sells tickets to Annemasse, Chambéry, Évian, Geneva, Grenoble, Nice and Thonon. Autocars Francony (☎ 50.45.02.43) has buses to destinations including Chamonix, Chambéry and Megève. Most do not run on Sunday or holidays. The office at the bus station is open weekdays from 7.15 to 11 am and 2.15 to 6.15 pm.

Car Europcar (☎ 50.51.40.05; fax 50.45. 66.18) is near the train station at 3quater Ave de Chevènes.

Getting Around

Bus The muncipal bus company, SIBRA (☎ 50.51.72.72), has an information bureau (☎ 50.51.70.33) across the covered courtyard from the tourist office. It's open Monday to Saturday from 8.30 am to 7 pm.

Buses run Monday to Saturday from 6 am to 8 pm. On Sundays, 20-seat minibuses – identified by letters rather than numbers – provide limited service. Bus No 91 (the Ligne des Vacances), which serves the youth hostel, runs only from mid-June to early September. Bus tickets cost 5.70FF; a carnet good for eight rides is 27.50FF. Weekly coupons cost 38FF.

Taxi For taxis based at the bus station call ☎ 50.45.05.67.

Bicycle Bicycles can be rented from Sports Évasion (☎ 50.51.21.81) at 30 Rue des Marquisats, open Monday to Saturday from 9 am to noon and 2 to 7 pm. Mountain bikes cost 50/80FF for a half/full day.

CHAMBÉRY

Chambéry (population 55,000), which lies in a wide valley between Annecy and Grenoble, has long served as one of the principal gateways between France and Italy. Occupying the entrance to the valleys that lead to the main Alpine passes, the town was the capital of Savoy from the 13th century until 1563. Its old quarter was built around the castle of one of the dukes of Savoy.

Orientation

Busy dual carriageways along a narrow canal separate the town's northern sprawl, which starts near the train station, from the city's compact old section. The Fontaine des Éléphants, the old city's focal point, is at the north-east end of Rue de Boigne, which runs south-westward to the Château des Ducs.

Information

Tourist Office The tourist office (☎ 79.33. 42.47) in the Maison du Tourisme at 24 Blvd de la Colonne is open Monday to Saturday from 9 am to noon and 2 to 6.30 pm. It has no foreign exchange service but will reserve accommodation for free.

The same building is home to the Association Départementale de Tourisme (☎ 79. 85.12.45), where you can get information on the Savoy region. The same building also contains the Gîtes de France office (☎ 79.33.22.56).

Park Office The headquarters (☎ 79.62.30. 54) of the Parc National de la Vanoise is at 135 Rue Docteur Julliand.

Money Most banks, including the following two, are closed on Sunday and Monday. The small Banque de Savoie branch in the Mercure Hôtel at Place de la Gare is open from 9 am to 1 pm and 3 to 7 pm. Next to the tourist office, the Crédit Lyonnais is open from 8.15 to 11.45 am and 1.40 to 4.45 pm (4.15 pm on Saturday).

Post The main post office (☎ 79.96.69.01) at Square Paul Vidal is open weekdays from 8 am to 7 pm and on Saturday until noon.

Chambéry's postcode is 73000.

Laundry The laundrette at 1 Rue Doffet is open daily from 7.30 am to 8 pm.

Château des Ducs de Savoie

The chateau around which the town was built, an opulent 14th-century castle on Place du Château, houses the region's Conseil Général (regional council). It can be visited only from March to December on a guided tour (20FF, sometimes in English) organised by the tourist office. Tours take in the adjoining **Sainte Chapelle**, built in the 15th century to house the Holy Shroud (the cloth believed to have been used to wrap the crucified Christ), which was taken to Turin in 1860 when Savoy became part of France.

FRENCH ALPS

Fontaine des Éléphants

Splendidly dominating the intersection of Blvd de la Colonne and Rue de Boigne, this fountain with its four great behemoths was sculpted in 1838 in honour of Général de Boigne, a local who made a fortune in the East Indies. When he returned home, he bestowed some of his wealth on the town and was honoured posthumously with this monument. The arcaded street that leads from the fountain to the Château des Ducs and bears his name was one of his most important local projects.

Museums

If you'd like to see all three of the museums detailed here, you might want to buy a 20FF combination ticket. Otherwise each museum costs 10FF (5FF for students and children).

A block from the fountain is the **Musée Savoisien** (☎ 79.33.44.48) on Blvd du Théâtre. Occupying a 13th-century monastery, it showcases local archaeological finds, including a gallery of 13th-century wall paintings which had been hidden by a false roof inside a local mansion. Exhibits of traditional Savoyard mountain life are displayed on the 2nd floor.

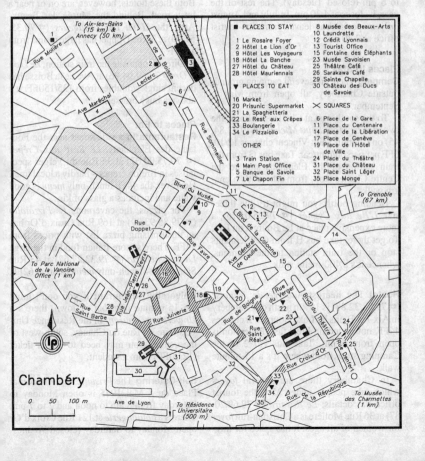

PLACES TO STAY
1 Le Rosaire Foyer
2 Hôtel Le Lion d'Or
9 Hôtel Les Voyageurs
18 Hôtel La Banche
27 Hôtel du Château
28 Hôtel Mauriennais

PLACES TO EAT
16 Market
20 Prisunic Supermarket
21 La Spaghetteria
22 Le Rest' aux Crêpes
33 Boulangerie
34 Le Pizzaiollo

OTHER
3 Train Station
4 Main Post Office
5 Banque de Savoie
7 Le Chapon Fin
8 Musée des Beaux-Arts
10 Laundrette
12 Crédit Lyonnais
13 Tourist Office
15 Fontaine des Éléphants
23 Musée Savoisien
25 Théâtre Café
26 Sarakawa Café
29 Sainte Chapelle
30 Château des Ducs de Savoie

SQUARES
6 Place de la Gare
11 Place du Centenaire
14 Place de la Libération
17 Place de Genève
19 Place de l'Hôtel de Ville
24 Place du Théâtre
31 Place du Château
32 Place Saint Léger
35 Place Monge

To Aix-les-Bains (15 km) & Annecy (50 km)

To Grenoble (67 km)

To Parc National de la Vanoise Office (1 km)

To Résidence Universitaire (500 m)

To Musée des Charmettes (1 km)

Chambéry

0   50   100 m

It's open from 10 am to noon and 2 to 6 pm (closed Tuesday).

The **Musée des Beaux-Arts** (☎ 79.33. 75.03) at Place du Palais de Justice houses a rich collection of 14th to 18th-century Italian works. It's open the same hours as the Musée Savoisien.

The **Musée des Charmettes** (☎ 79.33. 39.44), about 1.5 km south-east of the town, occupies the country house of French philosopher and writer Jean-Jacques Rousseau, and his lover, Baronne de Warens, lived in bliss for several years. From April to September, it's open from 10 am to noon and 2 to 6 pm (closed Tuesday). The rest of the year, it closes at 4.30 pm. In July and August *only* a special bus leaves from the tourist office at 2.30 pm.

Places to Stay

Camping There are several camping grounds outside Chambéry, all open from May to September.

To the south-east at Challes-les-Eaux, the two-star *Le Mont Saint Michel* (☎ 79.72.84. 45) on Chemin Saint Vincent charges 12/10/6FF per person/tent/car. Take bus G from the train station or the Éléphants stop to the Centre Challes stop, from where it's a one-km walk.

Heading north, you might try the three-star *L'Île aux Cygnes* (☎ 79.25.01.76), a more expensive place at Le Bourget du Lac. To get there, take bus H from the Éléphants stop or the train station to the terminus, whence it's a 400-metre walk.

Hostel The nearest *Auberge de Jeunesse* (☎ 79.88.32.88) is 15 km north of Chambéry in Aix-les-Bains by Lake Bourget. It charges 44FF, not including breakfast. Reception is open from 6 pm. Take bus No 2 to the Camping stop, from where it's a 15-minute walk.

In Chambéry there are several *foyers* which take people under 25 – the tourist office has details. *Le Rosaire* (☎ 79.69.20. 87) at 36 Rue Molière is a Christian-run *foyer* for women of all ages. It has space for trav-

ellers in summer only. A room plus breakfast costs 100FF.

Hotels In the old town, the *Hôtel La Banche* (☎ 79.33.15.62) at 10 Place de l'Hôtel de Ville is quiet and has average singles and doubles from 110FF and triples for 130 to 200FF.

Just outside the old town, the *Mauriennais* (☎ 79.69.42.78) at 2 Rue Sainte Barbe offers a view up to the chateau and no-frills singles/doubles from 70/90FF. The *Hôtel du Château* (☎ 79.69.48.78) at 37 Rue Jean-Pierre Veyrat has similar rooms for slightly more. Both these hotels, however, are on or near a busy road. Behind the Musée des Beaux-Arts, the *Hôtel Les Voyageurs* (☎ 79.33. 57.00) at 3 Rue Doppet has large rooms from 130FF.

Directly opposite the train station, *Le Lion d'Or* (☎ 79.69.04.96) at Ave de la Boisse has decent singles/doubles from 135/150FF. It's above a busy brasserie.

Places to Eat

Restaurants In a side street near the Fontaine des Éléphants, *Le Rest' aux Crêpes* (☎ 79.75.00.07) at 35 Rue du Verger specialises in Breton crepes – hardly a local treat. However, the 44FF lunch-only *menu* is good value and includes a glass of kir.

For pizzas, the cavernous *Le Pizzaiollo* (☎ 79.85.93.29) at 169 Rue Croix d'Or has an unsurprising pizza list with prices from 34FF. There's more Italian food in the large *La Spaghetteria* (☎ 79.33.27.62) at 43 Rue Saint Réal – lunch-only *menus* start at 62FF.

University Restaurant If you don't mind the 15-minute hike out of town, there's a *University restaurant* in the Résidence Universitaire on Rue du Chaney, south-west of the centre. You may need to buy a ticket (12.30FF) from a student.

Self-Catering The *Prisunic supermarket* at Place du 8 Mai 1945 is open Monday to Saturday from 8 am to noon and 2 to 7 pm. There's a *boulangerie* at 121 Rue Croix d'Or open Monday to Saturday (closed Wednesday) from 7 am to 1 pm and 2.30 to 8 pm and on Sunday from 7.30 am to 1 pm and 4.30 to 7.30 pm. On Saturday a *food market* is held at Place de Genève until midday.

Entertainment
Pubs & Cafés *Le Chapon Fin* at 4 Rue Doppet, next to the Musée des Beaux-Arts, is a favourite student haunt – smoky and dark inside but with plenty of airy terrace tables. *Sarakawa Café* on Rue Jean-Pierre Veyrat has a little terrace which backs onto the market place. The *Théâtre Café* on Place du Théâtre has a popular terrace which is lively until very late on summer nights.

Getting There & Away
Train Chambéry's railway station (☎ 79.85. 50.50) is 400 metres north-west of the tourist office at Place de la Gare. The information office is open Monday to Saturday from 8 am to 12.20 pm and 1.30 to 6.20 pm. The station itself is open from 5 am to 1 am.

There are major rail connections to Paris's Gare de Lyon (289FF plus TGV fee; 3¼ hours; six a day), Annecy (43FF; 50 minutes; 10 a day) and Grenoble (49FF; 1¼ hours; eight a day). There are also trains up the Maurienne Valley to Modane (66FF; 1¼ hours; five a day) and on to Turin in Italy.

Bus The bus station (☎ 79.69.11.88) is on Place de la Gare to the left as you exit the train station.

Getting Around
The main hub for local buses run by STAC (☎ 79.69.61.12) is along Blvd de la Colonne just before the Fontaine des Éléphants. Many buses also stop at the train station. In general, they run Monday to Saturday until about 8 pm.

MÉRIBEL
Most of the events of the 1992 Winter Olympics took place in the Tarentaise area west of Albertville, in the Isère Valley as far upriver as Tignes and in a number of smaller valleys whose streams feed the Isère. Many of the side-valley venues were situated in Les Trois Vallées (the Three Valleys), the largest skiable area in the world, at the heart of which lies Méribel (1400 metres). Established in 1939, this wealthy ski station, 46 km south-east of Albertville, consists of a cluster of hamlets. It has retained the atmosphere of an Alpine village thanks to a decision in the mid-1940s to employ only traditional Savoyard architectural styles. In the early 1990s, Méribel's facilities were upgraded to stage many of the women's Olympic events.

Méribel is the most central of four resorts hidden away in the Three Valleys. Over the hills to the east of town lies the large resort of Courchevel (1850 metres), while to the west, the Belleville Valley is home to Les Menuires (1800 metres) and crowned by Val Thorens (2300 metres). The four are connected by 200 ski lifts and 600 km of marked runs, including two Olympic runs. There are 110 km of cross-country runs.

Information
Tourist Office The central Maison du Tourisme houses the tourist office (☎ 79.08. 60.01), a hotel reservation service (☎ 79.00. 50.00), an American Express bureau (☎ 79. 08.60.01) and a transport information counter. The Maison du Tourisme is open from 9 am to 7 pm.

Lift Tickets Méribel Valley alone has 73 alpine ski runs (for a total of 120 km) and 47 ski lifts. Many of these start or pass through Mottaret, a transit point 300 metres above the town, from where the valley's highest lift (2910 metres) climbs Mont Vallon. The Méribel Valley pass, which is good for beginners, costs 156/304/844FF for one/ two/seven days. Intermediate and advanced skiers can purchase the Three Valleys pass, which allows use of all area lifts and costs 186/363/1006FF for one/two/seven days.

Lessons The ESF (☎ 79.08.60.31), whose office is in the Maison du Tourisme, offers group lessons for 145/580FF for one/five days. A second school called Ski Cocktail (☎ 79.08.54.51), based in the Galerie des

Cimes, offers six-day skiing courses (two hours a day) for 695FF as well as snowboard and monoski courses.

Places to Stay
Of the seven hotels built for the Olympics, all but two display three or four stars – one-star hotels became extinct in Méribel long ago. Consequently, accommodation prices are exorbitant. A cheaper alternative is to base yourself in Courchevel (☎ 79.08.00.29 for the central reservations office), where there is twice the number of hotels.

If you're intent on staying in Méribel, the new *Hôtel du Moulin* (☎ 79.00.53.67) has doubles from 300FF a night. *Le Doron* (☎ 79.08.60.02) in the heart of the village has bed and breakfast from 500FF. Up the slope from the village, the *Neige et Soleil* (☎ 79.08.62.39) has rooms on a demi-pension basis from 380FF.

Getting There & Away
Vehicle access to Méribel was made easier thanks to the four-lane A430 built for the Olympics. It links Chambéry (90 km north-west) with the nearest town, Moûtiers, 17 km north of Méribel.

Geneva and Lyon-Satolas airports are connected to Méribel by shuttle bus services. There's an SNCF information bureau (☎ 79.00.53.28) at the tourist office. The closest train station is in Moûtiers (☎ 79.24.01.11), from where there are connections to Paris (four hours) and Chambéry (55FF; 1⅓ hours).

Regional buses are operated by Transavoie (☎ 79.08.54.90) and run between Méribel and Moûtiers (52FF; five on weekdays, more on weekends).

BOURG SAINT MAURICE
Deeper in the Tarentaise Valley, Bourg Saint Maurice (810 metres) is an old market town surrounded by mountains. Known locally as 'Bourg', it sits at the gateway to some of Savoy's best known ski resorts. Tignes (2100 metres) with its older neighbour, Val d'Isère (1850 metres), are about 25 km to the south. Les Arcs (1600 to 2000 metres) is straight up the hill from Bourg. A modern new *funiculaire* zips skiers up to Les Arcs in seven minutes (14 km by road), making it eminently feasible to stay in Bourg or one of the two nearby youth hostels.

Information
Tourist Office Bourg's tourist office (☎ 79.07.04.92), on Ave Maréchal Leclerc opposite the train station, is open Monday to Saturday from 8.30 am to noon and 2 to 6.30 pm (Sunday from 10 am to noon). For ski information, contact the Société des Montagnes de l'Arc (☎ 79.41.55.55) at Les Arcs 1800. For accommodation, contact the reservation service (☎ 79.07.04.92).

Lift Tickets Les Arcs is divided into three sections – Arc 1600, Arc 1800 and Arc 2000. Together they form 150 km of downhill pistes with 72 lifts. Passes cost 175/935FF for one/seven days. The funiculaire (☎ 79.07.29.03) from Bourg to Arc 1600 is free if you have a lift ticket.

Lessons The ESF (☎ 79.06.43.07) offers a week-long course for 550FF.

Places to Stay
There are two hostels in the village of Seez, four km east of Bourg. *La Verdache* (☎ 79.41.01.93) is open from 20 December to mid-September and charges 38FF for a bed. The other hostel, *Maison de l'Edelweiss* (☎ 79.41.06.11) on Rue de la Libération, costs 55FF. It is open from 1 December to mid-May and mid-July to mid-September. To get there, take the Val d'Isère bus (see Getting There & Away for details).

As for hotels, there's a handful of reasonable options, two of which offer packages that include room (with a shower), demi-pension and a ski pass. The *Hostellerie du Petit Saint Bernard* (☎ 79.07.04.32) on Ave du Stade has a six-day deal for 2590FF, while *Le Concorde* (☎ 79.07.08.90) on Ave Maréchal Leclerc charges 3280FF.

La Vallée de l'Arc (☎ 79.07.04.12) at 49 Grande Rue has basic doubles from 160FF.

On the same street the *Hôtel du Centre* (☎ 79.07.05.13) has rooms from 140FF.

Getting There & Away

Major train connections to and from Bourg's modern railway station (☎ 79.85.50.50) include Paris's Gare de Lyon (326FF plus TGV fee; six hours), Chambéry (67FF; two hours; seven a day) and Lyon (124FF; three hours; five a day). There's a direct night train to Paris.

Regional buses, operated by Martin (☎ 79.07.04.49), leave from next to the train station. There are two buses a day to Les Arcs, seven to Seez (21FF) and Val d'Isère (56FF) and six to Tignes (56FF).

PARC NATIONAL DE LA VANOISE

A wild mix of high mountains, steep valleys and glaciers, the Parc National de la Vanoise became France's first national park in 1963. It covers 530 sq km – basically the eastern part of the massif located between the Tarentaise Valley to the north and the Maurienne Valley to the south. It's a hiker's heaven, with nearly 500 km of marked trails and 42 *refuges* dotted around the rugged terrain. The scenery is simply spectacular – snow-capped peaks mirrored in ice-laced lakes are just a start. Marmots and chamois, as well as France's largest colony of Alpine ibex *(bouquetin)*, graze free and undisturbed among the larch trees and over it all reigns the eagle.

Though on foot you can get to the park from many of the famous ski resorts, such as Méribel and Tignes, sitting just outside the park's northern border, the easiest route to the park is through the somewhat forgotten and isolated Haute Maurienne Valley, the part of the Maurienne Valley above the town of Modane. From here a chain of rough-hewn, shaggy stone villages stretches up to the hamlet of Bonneval, behind which rises the Col d'Iséran (2770 metres). Halfway along, the village of Lanslebourg (1400 metres) makes a good base from which to explore the park. It is home to the Maison du Parc (park office) and has some fantastic baroque art and the odd hotel.

Orientation & Information

Sitting at the base of the Col du Mont Cénis (2083 metres; open June to November) to Italy, Lanslebourg has been especially quiet since the opening in 1980 of the 12-km-long Fréjus Tunnel, which runs from near Modane to Italy.

The Maison du Parc (☎ 79.05.91.57), near the *gendarmerie* (police station), has information on the park and a list of *refuges*. You can also get park information at the Maison du Val Cénis (☎ 79.05.23.66), which is nearby on the main road. The best map of the region is 1:50,000 scale IGN map No 11, *Parc de la Vanoise*.

Baroque Chapels & Museum

A particular curiosity of the Haute Maurienne Valley are the many local chapels, whose humble, unattractive exteriors hide rich interiors of superb baroque art. Some also have murals from the 15th century.

Much of the decoration was done by artists from Turin, one of the centres of baroque art during the 17th century, who came to the valley by crossing over the Col du Mont Cénis.

Unfortunately, in recent years most of the chapels have had to be locked to prevent vandalism. But if you enquire at the Maison du Parc or the Espace Baroque they'll be able to arrange a key for you. Up the valley from Lanslebourg, **Lanslevillard** (two km) and **Bessans** (12 km) have chapels with exceptional walls, ceilings, statues and ornamentation.

The **Espace Baroque** (☎ 79.05.90.42), a new museum in an old church in Lanslebourg, is a good place to get acquainted with the valley's baroque tradition. Its contemporary displays and explanations are exceptionally good. Large English-language information cards are available at the entry. From late June to mid-September the museum is open from 10 am to noon and 3.30 to 7.30 pm. Admission is 25/15FF for adults/children.

Hiking

Hikers have a fine network of small trails to choose from – the Maison de Val Cénis has a *Randonnées* booklet, which details, with maps, a dozen half-day or all-day treks.

The trail from Lanslebourg up to the Turra Fort (2500 metres), from where there are great views over the Lac du Mont Cénis, generally takes about three hours. To really take in the region, you can follow all or part of Le Grand Tour de Haute Maurienne – a hike of five days or more around the upper reaches of the valley. There are 15 *refuges* or gîtes d'étape en route.

The GR5 and GR55 pass through the park and there are also paths linked to the Écrins National Park to the south and the Gran Paradiso National Park in Italy. Tracks are usually passable from June to the end of October – the Maison du Parc has full information.

Summer Skiing
In summer it's possible to ski on the Grand Pissaillas glacier at Col d'Iséran, 23 km north-east of Lanslebourg.

Places to Stay
In Lanslebourg there's a small *camping ground* (☎ 79.05.82.83) as well as a hostel-type *Centre International de Séjour* (CIS; ☎ 79.05.92.30), which takes individuals in summer.

There is an *Auberge de Jeunesse* (☎ 79.05.90.96) in the hamlet of Les Champs, which is on the east side of Lanslevillard. It's open from mid-December to 30 September.

There are five hotels in Lanslebourg but the only one open all year is the warm, welcoming, two-star *Hôtel La Vieille Poste* (☎ 79.05.93.47) on the main road through town. It's sometimes closed on weekends.

Getting There & Away
The trains serving the valley leave from Chambéry and run as far as the Modane railway station (☎ 79.05.10.09), which is about 25 km south-west of Lanslebourg. A ticket from Chambéry to Modane (2⅓ hours) costs 66FF.

From Modane, Transavoie buses go to Lanslebourg (one hour). Once a day (in the evening) they go further into the valley to Bessans and Bonneval.

MORZINE
Morzine (1000 metres) is one of 15 villages along the Swiss border in the northern Chablais area, which is more commonly called the Portes du Soleil (Gates of the Sun). The slopes, at altitudes ranging from 1000 to 2300 metres, are crisscrossed by a network of 650 km of runs connected by 220 lifts. The area also has 80 km of cross-country tracks.

With its wooden chalets topped by snow, Morzine has kept something of its traditional atmosphere of an Alpine village. The car-free resort of Avoriaz (1800 metres) hangs above Morzine. From Les Gets (1172 metres), south-west in the next valley towards Cluses, you can ski back to Morzine.

Information
Tourist Office The Maison du Tourisme (☎ 50.79.03.45) in the village centre has an accommodation service (☎ 50.79.11.57) and an exchange bureau and can supply transport and lift information. Ski information is also available at the Ski Club Morzine (☎ 50.79.07.10) at Place du Téléphérique du Pléney, 300 metres from the Maison du Tourisme. The ESF is also located there.

Ski Equipment For six days, you'll be looking at about 280/140FF to hire skis/boots. Cross-country skis cost 270FF. Those with good equilibrium can test it on a mono-ski, which costs 90FF a day.

Lift Tickets Portes du Soleil lift passes cost 160/306/848FF for one/two/six days.

Lessons The ESF (☎ 50.79.13.13) charges 95FF for one group lesson. Six half/full-day lessons cost 435/680FF.

Packages The Forfait Sportif (1220FF) includes a six-day lift pass, 10 days of Carte Neige insurance and six half-day ski lessons. The Portes du Soleil Hôtel Pass includes seven days in a hotel with demi-pension (or a week in a studio with kitchenette) plus a ski pass for between 2000 to 3000FF per person, depending on the dates.

Places to Stay

There are two *Auberges de Jeunesse* in the area. One, in the heart of Morzine (☎ 50. 79.14.86), is open from 1 November to mid-April and mid-June to mid-September. The other is in Les Gets (☎ 50.79.14.86) and is open from late December to mid-April and 1 July to mid-September. They are both heavily booked by groups and people on week-long holiday packages.

Morzine's less expensive hotels include *Le Panorama* (☎ 50.79.13.95) on the road to Thonon and *L'Hermine Blanche* (☎ 50.79. 14.13) heading up to Avoriaz.

Getting There & Away

The Genève-Cointrin Airport, 50 km north of Morzine, is linked to Morzine during the ski season by bus (150FF; five a day).

The closest train stations are Thonon, 34 km north, and Cluses, 31 km south. For train information, call ☎ 50.66.50.50.

SAT (☎ 50.79.15.69) operates regional buses with connections to Thonon (five a day) and Cluses (55FF; 45 minutes). It also operates regular services between Morzine, Les Gets and Avoriaz.

THONON

Thonon-les-Bains (population 30,000) is the main town on the French (ie southern) side of Lake Geneva. The city, behind which rise the Chablais peaks, is across the water from the Swiss city of Lausanne.

A residence of the dukes of Savoy in the Middle Ages, Thonon is renowned for its thermal waters, as is the smaller but better known resort of Évian-les-Bains, nine km to the east.

Thonon is a peaceful overnight stop in summer, with serene lake cruises to keep you occupied during the day. In winter it's deadly quiet.

Orientation

The centre of town, which is built up above the lake, is between Place de l'Hôtel de Ville

and the train station, just south of the main square, Place des Arts. Ave du Général Leclerc is the main road down to the lake and the boat dock at Port des Rives. From the port, Quai de Ripaille follows the lake around to the duke's chateau.

Information

Tourist Office The tourist office (☎ 50.71. 55.55) on Place du Marché is open Monday to Saturday from 9 am to 1 pm and 2 to 7 pm. To get there from the train station, head straight up Ave de la Gare to Blvd du Canal. Turn right and follow it past the next big intersection into Ave Jules Ferry. The first street to the left leads onto Place du Marché.

From June to September there's a lakeside tourist office annexe (☎ 50.26.19.94) at Port des Rives. It's open daily from 9 am to 7 pm.

Swimming

There is a series of swimming pools – or *plage municipal* (municipal beach) as it's wishfully called – by the lake at the end of Quai de Ripaille. Admission costs 14/7FF for adults/children. In season, the pools are open from 9 am to 8 pm.

Boats

Small outboard motorboats (120FF an hour) and pedal boats (80FF an hour) can be hired from Bateaux Locations (☎ 50.71.69.84) at Port des Rives.

One-week Catamaran/windsurfing courses run by the Club de Voile (☎ 50.71.07.29) cost about 580/520FF respectively.

Places to Stay

Camping *Camping Saint Disdille* (☎ 50.71. 14.11), three km north-east of town near Port Ripaille, charges 18FF per person and 18FF for a tent site. To get there from the station, take bus No 4 to the terminus.

Hostel The *Centre International de Séjour* (☎ 50.71.00.91) at La Grangette, 1.5 km south-west of town off the N5 to Geneva, has rooms plus breakfast for 76FF. To get there you can either walk or take La Grangette bus to its terminus, from where it's a 50-metre walk.

Hotels The *Hôtel Les Trois Vallées* (☎ 50.71. 12.15) at 1 Ave des Vallées has ordinary singles/doubles from 80/110FF and two-bed quads from 140FF. To get there on foot, turn right out of the train station into Rue J Blanchard and then right again. After crossing the footbridge over the railway line, turn left and keep going till you reach the large intersection – the hotel is on your right.

The centrally located *Hôtel de Lausanne* (☎ 50.71.07.13) on Place du Château near the funicular terminal has rooms from 140FF.

Places to Eat

The *Hôtel Les Trois Vallées* has a cheap restaurant (closed Sunday) with basic fare as well as snacks (a croque-monsieur is 15FF and pizza is 16FF).

Self-caterers have a *supermarket* at the start of Ave du Général de Gaulle, the main road leading out of town towards Geneva. The weekly *food market* is held each Thursday on and around Place du Marché.

Getting There & Away

Train The train station is a block south-west of Place des Arts at the end of Ave de la Gare. The information office (☎ 50.71.31.98) is open daily from 9 am to noon and 2 to 6.15 pm; the ticket windows are staffed from 5 am to 10 pm. Trains go south-west to Geneva (72FF; two hours; seven a day) and Bellegarde, where you can pick up the TGV connection to Paris's Gare de Lyon, and east to Évian (8FF; 10 minutes).

Bus The SAT bus company (☎ 50.71.08.54) has regular lines into the Chablais Mountains. Destinations include Morzine (55FF), and Évian (46FF). Buses that leave from the train station are connected with train arrivals.

Boat The Swiss CGN company (☎ 50.71. 14.71) serves the main cities and towns around the lake, hopping from one port to another. In Thonon, boats leave from Port des Rives, stopping in Yvoire (31FF; 35 minutes) before continuing via several Swiss villages to Geneva (80FF; two hours). Boats heading in the other direction go to Évian (30FF; 35 minutes) and across to Lausanne (55FF; 1¼ hours) or eastward to Montreux (near the lake's eastern end). Return tickets are cheaper than buying two one-ways. For 155FF you can get a pass for one full day of unlimited sun-deck basking.

Getting Around

Local buses are run by BUT (☎ 50.26.50.74) and depart from Place des Arts. Bus No 8 goes down to Port des Rives. A funiculaire links Place du Château, near the Hôtel de Ville, with Port des Rives for 6FF.

AROUND THONON

The village of **Yvoire**, situated at the northern tip of a blunt peninsula 16 km west of Thonon, is a picturesque medieval stone village with a small port, pebbled coves and plenty of geraniums. In the other direction, **Évian** is a more luxurious and exclusive

---

Lake Geneva

The crescent-shaped Lake Geneva (elevation 372 metres) – known as Lac Léman in French – is Europe's largest Alpine lake. It's almost an inland sea, complete with cities (Geneva and Lausanne are the largest), fishing ports and stony beaches. Measuring 72 km in length, it is on average eight km wide (13 km at its maximum) and 80 metres deep (310 metres at its deepest point).

Forming a natural border between Switzerland and France, the lake is fed and drained mainly by the Rhône River. It has very clear and unpolluted waters despite the many activities that take place upon and around it. Its appearance changes constantly: the surrounding mountains may disappear in fog or clouds and sudden winds can make the surface swell as on any sea.

The north side (the *adret*), which lies along the Swiss Riviera and is bordered by vineyards, offers visitors an almost Mediterranean climate and a great view of the Alps. From the south shore (the *avers*), the horizon is limited to the quasi-straight line of the Jura Mountains. ■

version of Thonon, whose spring waters are available around the world in those familiar plastic bottles. Both places make ideal day trips from Thonon, as do destinations in Switzerland – Geneva is 33 km to the south-east and Lausanne is just across the lake. For information on boat services, see Getting There & Away under Thonon.

Dauphiné

Dauphiné, which encompasses the territories south and south-west of Savoy, stretches from the Rhône River in the west to the Italian border in the east. It takes in the city of Grenoble and, a bit further east, the mountainous Écrins National Park. The gentler terrain of the western part of Dauphiné is typified by the Vercors Regional Park, much loved by cross-country skiing fans. In the east, the town of Briancon stands guard at the Italian frontier.

History
The area now known as Dauphiné was inhabited by the Celts and then the Romans. By the 11th century it was under the rule of Guigues I, the Count of Albon, whose great-grandson Guigues IV (ruled 1133-42) was the first local count to bear the name of Dauphin. By the end of the 1200s, the name 'Dauphin' had been transformed into a title and the fiefs held by the region's ruling house, La Tour du Pin, were known collectively as Dauphiné. The rulers of Dauphiné continued to expand their territories, which gave them control of all the passes through the southern Alps.

In 1339 Humbert II established Grenoble university. Ten years later, however, lacking both money and a successor, he sold Dauphiné to the French king, Charles V, who started the tradition whereby the eldest son of the king of France (ie the crown prince) ruled Dauphiné and bore the title 'dauphin'. The region was annexed to France by Charles VII in 1457.

GRENOBLE
Grenoble (population 160,000), host of the 1968 Winter Olympics, is the undisputed intellectual and economic capital of the French Alps. It's also the focus of the Dauphiné region, sitting in a broad valley surrounded by mountains – the Chartreuse to the north, the Vercors to the south-west and Alpine peaks stretching east to Italy.

Grenoble is a spotlessly clean city with something of a Swiss feel, perhaps because of the ultramodern tram system. It gained its reputation as a progressive, dynamic city in the 1960s, when the Socialist Hubert Dubedout served as mayor. People from all over France flocked here, attracted by social, artistic and technological innovations, and eventually came to outnumber the native Grenoblois. The large university serves a student body of 36,000. Grenoble also has important facilities for nuclear and micro-electronic research.

Orientation
The old city is centred around Place Grenette and Place Notre Dame, both of which are about one km east of the train and bus stations. There are lots of inexpensive hotels in the vicinity of Place Condorcet. The main university campus is a couple of km east of the centre on the south side of the Isère River.

Information
Tourist Office The Maison du Tourisme at 14 Rue de la République houses the tourist office (☎ 76.54.34.36), an SNCF train information and ticketing counter, and a local bus information counter. All three are open Monday to Saturday from 9 am to 6 pm. During summer, the tourist office, which can make hotel reservations, stays open until 6.30 pm (from about mid-May to mid-June) or 7 pm (mid-June to mid-September). The Maison du Tourisme is served by both tram lines (see Getting Around).

Hiking Information La Maison de la Randonnée (☎ 76.51.76.00) at 7 Rue Voltaire is *the* place to go for hiking information. It has maps (40 to 67FF), topoguides, day-hike guides and detailed information on gîtes d'étape, *refuges*, itineraries etc...It's open weekdays from 9 am to 6 pm and on Saturday from 10 am to noon and 2 to 6 pm.

The Club Alpin Français (CAF) (☎ 76.87. 03.73) at 32 Ave Félix Viallet can provide information on its *refuges*.

Money The Banque de France (☎ 76.87.53. 61), on the corner of Blvd Édouard Rey and Ave Félix Viallet, is open weekdays from 8.45 am to 12.15 pm and 1.30 to 3.30 pm.

There are several banks along Blvd Édouard Rey, including the Lyonnaise de Banque (☎ 76.28.79.76) at No 11, which gives Visa cash advances. It's open weekdays from 8 am to noon and 1.15 to 5 pm. The Banque de la Région Dauphinoise at Place Notre Dame is open Tuesday to Friday from 8 am to noon and 1.30 to 5.30 pm, and on Saturday from 8 am to noon and 1 to 4 pm.

Post The main post office (☎ 76.43.53.31) at 7 Blvd Maréchal Lyautey is open weekdays from 8 am to 6.45 pm and on Saturday morning. More central is the post office next to the tourist office, open weekdays from 8 am to 6 pm and on Saturday until noon. Across the tram tracks from the train station there's a branch post office open weekdays and Saturday morning from 10 am to noon and 1.30 to 5 pm.

Grenoble's postcode is 38000.

Travel Agencies Voyages Wasteels (☎ 76. 46.36.39) at 20 Ave Félix Viallet has air and BIJ tickets. It's open Monday to Saturday from 9 am to noon and 2 to 7 pm (6 pm on Saturday). BIJ tickets are also available at the Centre Information Jeunesse (☎ 76.54. 70.38) at 8 Rue Voltaire, open weekdays from 1 to 6 pm.

Bookshop English books are available at Just Books (☎ 76.44.78.81) on 1 Rue de la Paix, which is open Tuesday to Saturday from 9.30 am to noon and 2 to 7 pm. From September to February, it's also open on Monday.

Emergency The police headquarters (☎ 76. 60.40.40) is on Blvd Maréchal Leclerc.

Laundry The Lav' Club at 3 Rue Alphand is open daily from 7 am to 10 pm, as is the laundrette at 14 Rue Thiers.

Fort de la Bastille

Fort de la Bastille, built in the 16th century (and expanded in the 19th) to control the approaches to the city, sits on the north side of the Isère River 263 metres above the old city. It affords spectacular views, including, on clear days, Mont Blanc. Three viewpoint indicators *(tables d'orientation)* – one just west of the téléphérique station, the other two on the roof of the building just east of it – explain what you're looking at. A sign near the disused Mont Jalla chair lift (300 metres beyond the arch next to the bathrooms) indicates the hiking trails that pass by here.

To get to the fort, a téléphérique (cable car; ☎ 76.44.33.65) leaves from Quai Stéphane Jay. One-way/return travel costs 18.50/29FF (10/15.50FF for students). From November to March, the téléphérique runs until 6 pm; during the rest of the year it runs until midnight – except on Sunday and Monday from April to mid-June and mid-September to October, when the last run is at 7.30 pm. A variety of trails and a road lead up the hillside to the fort.

Musée Dauphinois

Occupying a beautiful 17th-century convent, this museum (☎ 76.87.66.77) at 30 Rue Maurice Gignoux is near the bottom of the hill on top of which sits Fort de la Bastille. From the city centre, it is most easily reached by the Pont Saint Laurent footbridge. The museum has good displays on the crafts and history of the Dauphiné region, with a particular focus on the mountain people's traditional way of life.

It's open from 9 am to noon and 2 to 6 pm (closed Tuesday). Admission is 15FF (10FF for students and people over 60).

Musée des Beaux-Arts

Grenoble's Musée des Beaux-Arts, known

for its outstanding collection of paintings and sculpture (considered one of the best in the provinces), moved to new quarters at Place de Lavalette (in the old city) in late 1993. Exhibits include an enormous work by the Flemish artist Peter Paul Rubens as well as a renowned modern collection that features pieces by Chagall, Léger, Matisse, Modigliani, Picasso and many others. It's open daily except Tuesday.

Hiking

A number of beautiful trails can be picked up in Grenoble or very nearby (eg from Fort de la Bastille). The Parc Naturel Régional du Vercors (☎ 76.95.40.33) is just west of the city.

See Hiking Information under Information for details on where to buy maps and find out about trail options.

Skiing

For information on skiing near Grenoble, see the Around Grenoble section. Buses and trains link Grenoble with many Alpine ski stations.

Places to Stay – bottom end

Camping *Camping Les Trois Pucelles* (☎ 76.96.45.73), open all year, is at 58 Rue des Allobroges (one block west of the Drac River) in Grenoble's western suburb of Seyssins. To get there from the train station, take the tramway towards Fontaine and get off at the Maisonnat stop. Then take bus No 51 (last one around 9 pm) to Mas des Îles and walk east on Rue du Dauphiné. A place to camp and park costs 30/43FF for one/two people.

Hostels The *Auberge de Jeunesse* (☎ 76.09.33.52) is at 10 Ave du Grésivaudan in Echirolles (postcode 38130), 5.5 km south of the train station. It charges 60FF per person including breakfast; reception is open from 7.30 am to 11 pm. To get there from Cours Jean Jaurès, take bus No 8 (last one about 9 pm) to the Quinzaine stop (look for the Casino supermarket).

The *Foyer de l'Étudiante* (☎ 76.42.00.84) at 4 Rue Sainte Ursule accepts travellers from the end of June to the end of September for a minimum stay of one week. Singles/doubles/triples cost 260/220/165FF a week per person.

The *Association pour le Logement des Étudiants et Jeunes Travailleurs* (ALEJT; ☎ 76.54.24.81) on Rue de l'Université in the university campus *may* accept travellers for a maximum of three nights from June to September. It costs 60FF a night – take bus No 41 from Place Docteur Martin to the Champ Roman stop.

Hotels Around the train station, the *Hôtel Alize* (☎ 76.43.12.91) at 2 Rue Amiral Courbet has recently redecorated, modern singles/doubles from 100/150FF.

In the Place Condorcet area, one km south-east of the station, the *Hôtel Lakanal* (☎ 76.46.03.42) at 26 Rue des Bergers attracts a young, friendly crowd. Singles/doubles start at 96/122FF (150/180FF with shower and toilet). Hall showers are 14FF.

A block away, the *Hôtel Condorcet* (☎ 76.46.20.64) at 8 Rue Condorcet has doubles from 120FF. The *Hôtel des Doges* (☎ 76.46.13.19) at 29 Cours Jean Jaurès has basic singles/doubles from 100/120FF; showers cost 15FF.

The quiet, comfortable *Hôtel Victoria* (☎ 76.46.06.36) at 17 Rue Thiers has doubles for 116FF; hall showers are 20FF. It's closed in August. You can park in the courtyard for 15FF. The relaxed *Hôtel Beau Soleil* (☎ 76.46.29.40) at 9 Rue des Bons Enfants has rooms from 105/125FF (10FF more with a TV). Hall showers are 15FF. The *Hôtel Colbert* (☎ 76.46.46.65) at 1 Rue Colbert (2nd floor) has singles/doubles with high ceilings from 95/125FF; showers are 15FF. Doubles with shower and toilet are 175FF.

In the city centre, the *Hôtel du Mouch-erotte* (☎ 76.54.61.40) at 1 Rue Auguste Gaché has huge, clean rooms in a great location. With showers, singles/doubles start at 114/154FF, triples/quads cost 208/256FF and basic single/doubles cost 100/134FF; the hall

FRENCH ALPS

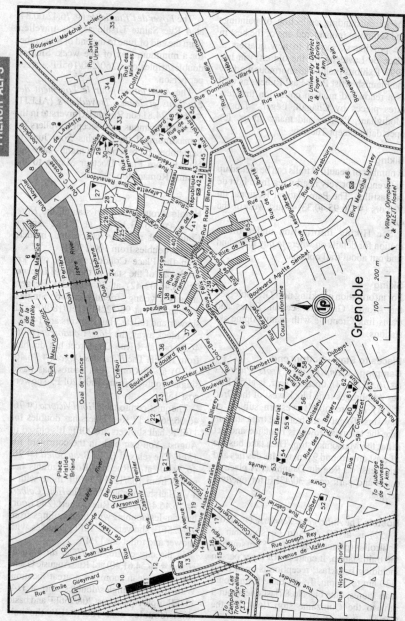

Grenoble

PLACES TO STAY

14 Hôtel Alpazur
15 Hôtel Alize
16 Lux Hôtel
18 Hôtel Arcade
34 Foyer de l'Étudiante (Summer Hostel)
38 Hôtel Beaulieu
47 Hôtel du Moucherotte
51 Hôtel Saint Bruno
52 Hôtel Colbert
54 Hôtel des Doges
56 Hôtel Victoria
58 Hôtel Beau Soleil
60 Hôtel Condorcet
62 Hôtel Lakanal
65 Hôtel de la Poste

▼ PLACES TO EAT

17 Grocery Store
19 Boulangerie
20 University Restaurant
22 La Chandelle Pizzeria
27 Namastay Indian Restaurant
29 Le Tunis Restaurant
30 Le Tonneau de Diogène

31 Los Tacos
41 Prisunic Supermarket
44 Les Halles & Place Sainte Claire Market
49 La Panse Restaurant
53 Boulangerie
57 Produce Shop
61 Food Shops

OTHER

1 Jardin des Dauphins
2 Pont de la Porte de France
4 Mountain Bike Grenoble
5 Pont Marius Gontard
6 Musée Dauphinois
7 Pont St Laurent
8 Pont de la Citadelle
9 Musée des Beaux-Arts
10 Bus Station
11 Railway Station
13 Post Office & Gare Europole Tram Station
21 Club Alpin Français
23 Voyages Wasteels
24 Téléphérique to Fort de la Bastille
33 Cathédrale Notre Dame
35 Police Headquarters

36 Banque de France
37 Lyonnaise de Banque
39 Église Saint Louis
42 Post Office
43 Tourist Office (Maison du Tourisme)
45 Laundrette
46 Centre Information Jeunesse
48 Just Books
50 Maison de la Randonnée
55 Laundrette
66 Main Post Office

✕ SQUARES

3 Place Hubert Dubedout
12 Place de la Gare
25 Place d'Agier
26 Place St André
28 Place Aux Herbes
32 Place Notre Dame
40 Place Grenette
59 Place Condorcet
63 Place Championnet
64 Place Victor Hugo

shower is 20FF. The pleasant and friendly *Hôtel de la Poste* (☎ 76.46.67.25) at No 25 on pedestrianised Rue de la Poste has singles/doubles/triples for 80/130/180FF; showers are free. Overall, this is an excellent deal. The *Hôtel Beaulieu* (☎ 76.46.30.90) at 14 Rue Saint François is a clean, modern place with rooms for one/two people from 90/100FF; showers cost 15FF for two.

Places to Stay – middle

If you'd like to stay near the train station and are looking for something very quiet, try the *Hôtel Saint Bruno* (☎ 76.96.32.49), which is down the alley from 6 Rue Michelet. Airy, newly renovated doubles/triples/quads start at 100/170/200FF. The *Lux Hôtel* (☎ 76.46.41.89) at 6 Rue Crépu, a quiet backstreet south of the station, is tidy and friendly. Rooms with shower start at 160/170FF. There's plenty of street parking around.

Round the corner, the *Hôtel Alpazur* (☎ 76.46.42.80) at No 59 on the pedestrianised Ave Alsace-Lorraine has a colourful assortment of rooms from 140FF, or 160FF with shower. Those at the front have balconies whence you can watch the trams swish past. Across the road at 52 Ave Alsace-Lorraine, the *Hôtel Arcade* (☎ 76.46.00.20) offers an all-you-can-eat breakfast for 32FF. The rooms are sterile but functional – doubles with all the usual amenities cost 250FF.

Places to Eat

Restaurants For excellent food at reasonable prices, try *Le Tonneau de Diogène* (☎ 76.42.38.40) at 6 Place Notre Dame, which attracts a young, lively crowd. The plat du jour is 42FF and salads are 10 to 28FF. It's open daily from 7 am to midnight. Their other Grenoble location, *Chouette! Un Tonneau!* (☎ 76.46.92.36), is a few blocks east of Place Condorcet at 5 Rue Aubert Dubayet. It is open Monday to Saturday from 10.30 am to 10.30 pm.

Also on Place Notre Dame, *Los Tacos* (☎ 76.42.25.96) has tacos (14FF) that look more like crepes than the North American version. It's open on Monday from 7 pm to midnight and Tuesday to Saturday from noon to 10.30 or 11 pm. *La Panse* (☎ 76.54.09.54) at 7 Rue de la Paix, which specialises in traditional French cuisine, offers a 65FF lunch *menu* that is especially good value. It is open Monday to Saturday from noon to 1.30 pm and 7.15 pm to 10 pm.

Namastay Indian Restaurant (☎ 76.54.29.89) at 2 Rue Renauldon has vegetarian and non-vegetarian main dishes for 30 to 55FF. It is open Tuesday to Saturday from noon to 1.15 pm and 7.15 to 11.15 pm and also on Monday evening.

Le Tunis (☎ 76.42.47.13) at 5 Rue Chenoise has excellent Tunisian couscous from 38FF. It is open daily from noon to 2 pm and 6 to 10.30 pm. There are more North African places along and around Rue Renauldon and Rue Chenoise. The area around Place Condorcet has lots of places to eat, including several Chinese restaurants.

Pizzeria *La Chandelle* (☎ 76.87.87.46) at 24 Ave Félix Viallet has good-sized pizzas for 37FF.

University Restaurant From mid-September to mid-June, the *Restaurant Universitaire* at 5 Rue d'Arsonval is open weekdays from 11.20 am to 1.15 pm and 6.20 to 7.50 pm. Tickets (12.30/25FF for students/nonstudents) are sold at lunchtime only.

Self-Catering Near the tourist office, *Les Halles* are open from 6 am to 1 pm (closed Monday). There's a *food market* at Place Sainte Claire on Wednesday until noon.

The *boulangerie* nearest Les Halles is at 4 Rue Auguste Gaché; it's closed on Sunday afternoon and Monday. The particularly well-stocked *fromagerie* a block away at 17 Rue Bayard is open Tuesday to Saturday from 6 am to 12.30 pm and 3 to 7.30 pm.

The *Prisunic* at 22 Rue Lafayette, which

has a basement grocery section and an in-house boulangerie, is open Monday to Saturday from 8.30 am to 7 pm.

In the Place Condorcet area, there's a *boulangerie* at 31bis Cours Berriat (closed Monday) and a *produce shop* with high-quality produce at 15 Cours Berriat. It's open Tuesday to Saturday from 6 am to 12.30 pm and 3.30 to 7.30 pm. There are a number of *food shops* (closed on Sunday) around 2 Rue Turenne.

Entertainment

The pamphlet *Lumières sur la Ville*, issued every three months by the tourist office, lists cultural events. *DAHU*, which is published each September by local students, is a guide (in French) to Grenoble's cinemas, discos, restaurants, etc. It's available for 12FF at many tabacs.

Getting There & Away

Air The Aéroport de Grenoble-Saint Geoirs, which handles domestic flights, is 45 km north of the city. There are international flights to Aéroport Lyon-Satolas (☎ 72.22.75.05), which is 95 km north-west of the city off the A43 to Lyon.

Train The train station (☎ 76.47.50.50 for information) on Rue Émile Gueymard is right next to the Gares Europole tram stop, which is served by both tram lines. The information offce is open daily from 8.30 am to 7.15 pm. The station and at least one ticket window are open straight through from 4 am to 2 am. SNCF has an information and ticketing counter in the tourist office building (see Tourist Office under Information).

Destinations served include Paris's Gare de Lyon (303FF; 3⅓ hours by TGV), Chambéry (46FF; 70 minutes; 14 a day), Chamonix (153FF), Lyon (94FF; 1½ hours; five a day) and Nice (273FF). There are three daily trains to Turin (125FF) and Milan (173FF) in Italy. You can also easily get to Geneva (102FF; four daily).

Bus The bus station is next to the train station. VFD (☎ 76.47.77.77), whose window is open daily from 6.45 am to 7 pm, has services to Geneva (130FF; 2½ hours) and Nice (267FF; five hours; via Castellane, which is near the Gorges du Verdon) as well as Alpine destinations such as Albertville, Annecy (85FF; one hour 40 minutes), Bourg d'Oisans, Chamonix (138FF; three hours), Gap and the ski stations on the Vercors range.

Unicar (☎ 76.87.90.31) handles tickets to Marseille (134FF), Gap, Valence and other destinations. Its ticket windows are open Monday to Saturday from 6.30 am to 6.30 pm and on Sunday from 7.30 am to noon and 1.30 pm to 6.30 pm.

Intercars (☎ 76.46.19.77) handles long-haul destinations – Italy, Spain, Portugal and London.

Car Europcar (☎ 76.96.92.72; fax 76.48.14.70) is near the train station at 94 Cours Jean Jaurès.

Getting Around

To/From the Airport The bus to Aéroport Lyon-Satolas (Lyon's international airport; 120FF; 65 minutes), operated by Valencin-based Cars Faure (☎ 78.96.11.44), stops at the bus station. Ticketing is handled by Unicar (see Bus under Getting There & Away).

Bus & Tram The local mass transit company, TAG, has two ultramodern tram lines, A and B. Both stop at the tourist office and the train station. Bus and tram tickets cost 6.50FF and are available from ticket machines at tram stops and from bus drivers. They must be time-stamped either in the little blue machines located at each tram stop or on board the bus. Tickets are valid for transfers – but not round trips – within one hour of being time-stamped.

A carnet of 10 tickets, sold at many tabacs and newsagents' around town, costs 40FF. A weekly pass, Carte Avantag, is available for 61FF at the TAG information desk (☎ 76.09.36.36) situated inside the tourist office. This is also a good place to pick up an easy-to-use route map. Most buses cease functioning rather early, sometime between 7 and 9 pm.

Taxi Radio-dispatched taxis can be ordered by calling ☎ 76.54.42.54.

Bicycle Mountain Bike Grenoble (☎ 76.87.44.45) at 6 Quai de France has mountain bikes for 130FF for the first day, 100FF for the second day and 80FF a day thereafter. A 2000FF deposit is required. It's open Tuesday to Saturday from 9 am to noon and 2 to 7 pm.

AROUND GRENOBLE
Skiing

Most of the low-altitude ski areas around Grenoble are pretty relaxed, attracting people after a reasonably cheap ski holiday rather than the fluoro flashy crowds drawn to the high-altitude, high-visibility resorts further north. Stations in the area include Col de Porte and Le Sappey, both north of Grenoble; and westward on the Vercors range, Saint Nizier du Moucherotte, Lans-en-Vercors and Villard de Lans. Buses link all five resorts with Grenoble's bus station.

Summer skiing, which is quite expensive, is possible during June and July (and even into August) at several high-altitude ski stations east of Grenoble, including the Alpe d'Huez (see the Parc des Écrins section) and Les Deux Alpes (see Les Deux Alpes section).

Information The Grenoble Université Club (GUC Ski; ☎ 76.57.47.72) at 25 Rue Casimir Brenier in Grenoble, open daily from 2 to 4.35 pm (Wednesday and Friday till 7 pm), offers inexpensive skiing for students and nonstudents of all ages. There's a 200FF membership fee that includes insurance (150FF if you show a Carte Neige insurance card). You might also contact Ski-Pop Grenoble at the Auberge de Jeunesse (see Hostels under Places to Stay in the Grenoble section).

Lans-en-Vercors

Situated about 25 km south-west of Grenoble, Lans-en-Vercors (1020 metres) is one of the most relaxed ski villages on the Vercors plateau. There's none of the adrenalin of high-Alpine descents here, and nor is there a bustling night life. Instead, families and kids abound and, outside school holidays, the hotels often have *non-complet* (vacancy) signs up.

From Lans-en-Vercors, hourly shuttle buses run to the Stade de Neige (snow stadium), an area of moderate, wooded slopes crowned by Le Grand Cheval (1807 metres), about four km east. On the village's southern doorstep you'll find 90 km of cross-country tracks, most of them over gentle undulating fields.

Information The tourist office (☎ 76.95.42.62), which is on the main road through town, is open Monday to Saturday from 9 am to noon and 2 to 6.30 pm and on Sunday morning.

Ski Equipment Three sports shops hire ski equipment. Alpine skis cost 60/300FF for one/six days; cross-country skis are 45/210FF.

Lift Tickets Ski passes costs 65/120FF for a day/weekend or 350FF for six days. There is also a six-day Ski Pass Vercors (610FF), which gives access to the 190 km of slopes in all the surrounding ski stations. Use of the cross-country tracks costs 28/140FF for a day/week.

Lessons The ESF (☎ 76.95.43.19) is at the Stade de Neige. One lesson costs 60FF, six cost 305FF.

Places to Stay For 610FF per person, the Formule Plus – available through the tourist office – will get you a week's accommodation in a four-person studio plus a lift ticket. If you prefer to stay in a hotel, the cost is 1750FF, including demi-pension.

The *Hôtel au Bon Acceuil* (☎ 76.95.42.02) at the low end of the village has pleasant doubles for 185FF. *Le Val Fleuri* (☎ 76.95.41.09) on the main road behind the church has a sunny back terrace and rooms from 144FF. A few km out of the village on the road to Autrans, the *Auberge de la Croix Perrin* (☎ 76.95.40.02) is on a high pass,

which is convenient for starting a cross-country slide. Rooms start at 140FF.

Getting There & Away VFD (☎ 76.47.77.77 in Grenoble) has five buses a day (less on weekends) from Grenoble. Stops include Lans-en-Vercors (30FF; 50 minutes) and Villard de Lans (40FF; one hour).

LES DEUX ALPES
Les Deux Alpes (1600 metres) is the largest summer skiing area in Europe. From mid-June to early September, you can ski on two glaciers which peak at 3425 metres. Les Deux Alpes is also a popular winter resort, especially with the English.

The main skiing domain lies below La Meije (3983 metres), one of the highest peaks in the Parc National des Écrins. There are almost 200 km of marked pistes and 65 lifts. The town itself, stretched out for 1.5 km along a busy main street, looks a bit messy.

Information
Tourist Office Everything revolves around the Maison des Deux Alpes in the village centre. It houses the tourist office (☎ 76.79.22.00), the Club des Sports (for sporting activities; ☎ 76.80.51.29) and the Reservation Centre (☎ 76.79.28.50), which can help with accommodation.

Ski Equipment Equipment hire costs about 120/250FF for one/six days, everything included.

Lift Tickets There are four kinds of ski passes, priced according to what slopes you can handle and what lifts you'll need. The one-day blue pass for beginners, gives you access to 20 lifts for 70FF. The all-lifts-included red pass costs 158/300/670FF for one/two/five days. A six-day Galaxie Pass (780FF) entitles you to a day's skiing both here and at other resorts, including the Alpe d'Huez and Le Grand Serre near Briançon.

Lessons Les Deux Alpes has two ski schools: the ESF (☎ 76.79.21.21) in the

Maison des Deux Alpes and the International Ski School (☎ 76.79.04.21).

Places to Stay

In January, the Reservation Centre can organise a week's accommodation in a studio plus a ski pass for 1150FF per person (minimum two people). In a two-star hotel with demi-pension, the cost is 2250FF, including – except in the high-season – a ski pass.

Apart from this, the cheapest hotels are *Les Gentianes* (☎ 76.80.50.27), with rooms from 210FF a night, and the *Bel Alpe* (☎ 76.80.52.11), with rooms from 230FF.

Getting There & Away

Les Deux Alpes is about 75 km south-east of Grenoble. VFD (☎ 76.47.77.77) runs buses from Grenoble (84FF; 1½ hours; five a day) and Briançon. From the latter, buses go via Bourg d'Oisans (104FF; 1¾ hours; two a day).

BRIANÇON

One of Europe's highest towns, Briançon (population 13,000; altitude 1300 metres) sits on a rocky outcrop at the meeting of five valleys. Long a frontier post, Briançon's fortified old town guards the road to the Col de Montgenèvre (1850 metres), a pass to Italy (20 km north-east) that has been used since Roman times. In the late 17th century, Vauban was called in to make the town impregnable after it was razed during a regional war. Since then, the population has expanded and the town has crept down the slopes to encompass the Durance River valley.

Briançon is sandwiched between the awesome terrain of the Parc National des Écrins to the west and the regional Parc du Queyras to the south.

Orientation

The town is split into two sections. The Vieille Ville (or *ville haute*), with its quaint pedestrianised streets, sits high above its counterpart, the lower town (*ville basse*). The train station is to the south in the suburb of Sainte Catherine. The upper and lower towns are connected by Ave de la République. Entry to the Vieille Ville is either from the Champ de Mars (on the old town's northern side) or, if you're hoofing it up from the low town, through Porte d'Embrun.

Information

Tourist Office The tourist office (☎ 92.21.08.50) in the Porte de Pignerol in the Vieille Ville is open daily from 9 am to noon and 1.30 to 6.30 pm (5 pm on Sunday).

For information on the Parc National des Écrins, stop by the Maison du Parc (☎ 92.21.08.49) at 35 Ave du Lautaret.

Money The bank nearest the train station is the Crédit Agricole (92.25.49.00) on Ave du Général de Gaulle. It's open Monday to Saturday from 8 am to noon and 2 to 5 pm (4.30 pm on Saturday). In the Vieille Ville there's another branch at 10 Grande Rue.

Post The main post office (☎ 92.21.13.41) at Champ de Mars is open weekdays from 8.30 am to 6 pm and on Saturday until noon.

Briançon's postcode is 05102.

Laundry The LavPlus in Central Parc is open daily from 7 am to 9 pm.

Vieille Ville

While the Vieille Ville's narrow streets are an ambler's delight, there's not all that much to see. The main street, the Grande Rue, is also known as the Grande Gargouille (great gargoyle) because of the drain that gushes down the middle of it. There are fountains spurting everywhere in the old part of town. Ave Vauban affords some fine views of the snow-capped peaks of the Écrins park.

Collégiale Built by Vauban in the early 18th century, the Church of Our Lady & St Nicholas is characteristically heavy and fortified, its twin towers dominating the Vieille Ville's skyline. The church is open daily.

Fort du Château The 18th-century Castle Fort sits imposingly above the Vieille Ville. You can visit it from mid-July to mid-September but only on a guided tour organised by the tourist office.

Téléphérique

The téléphérique from Ave René Froger goes up to Le Prorel, one of the highest points of Le Grand Serre Chevalier mountain range. In summer it runs in July and August only, from 9 am to 4.30 pm. A return ticket costs 55/30FF for adults/children.

Activities

In winter, there's plenty of skiing down the slopes of Le Grand Serre Chevalier, the range that stretches from Briançon to Le Monêtier-les-Bains, 15 km north-west. In summer, parapente, rafting, cycling and canyoning are all organised through H2O (☎ 92. 20.38.98) in Central Parc. For organised treks ask next door at the Bureau des Guides (☎ 92.20.15.73).

Places to Stay

Many hotels close for one or more months (usually May, October and November). During the peak season they often demand that guests take demi-pension at least.

Camping The two-star municipal *Camping de la Schappe* (☎ 92.21.04.32) sits at the base of the fort, halfway between the train station and the Vieille Ville. It's open from mid-June to mid-September only.

Hostel The nearest youth hostel is *Serre Chevalier* (☎ 92.24.74.54), about eight km north-west at Serre Chevalier-le-Bez near Villeneuve-la-Salle. It charges 43FF a night. In winter it's a popular skiing base. To get there from the train station or the Champ de Mars, take the Rignon bus (every two hours; last one at 6.45 pm) in the direction of Le Monêtier-les-Bains to Villeneuve-la-Salle, whence it's a 500-metre walk.

Hotels The hotels in the Vieille Ville are the best in town. The cheapest up here is the *Hôtel des Remparts* (☎ 92.21.08.73) at 14 Ave Vauban (closed November and December and for two weeks from mid-May). The rooms at the front bask in the afternoon sun and have a good view of the mountains. Prices start at 120FF and parking is avail-

able. The *Hôtel de la Paix* (☎ 92.21.37.43) at 3 Rue Porte Méane, open all year, has comfortable rooms with modern furnishings from 150FF.

Less expensive options in the lower town and Sainte Catherine include the *Hôtel de la Gare* (☎ 92.21.00.49) at Ave du Général de Gaulle, which has large, blandly furnished rooms from 110FF. It's on a noisy corner. One block away, *L'Univers* (☎ 92.21.01.31) at 19 Rue Pasteur (closed May and October) has rooms from 85/120FF.

Le Glacier (☎ 92.21.00.03) at 22 Rue Centrale is the cheapest place in town, with basic doubles from 95FF. It's closed in June and October. Up the road at No 4, the *Hôtel de la Chaussée* (☎ 92.21.10.37) has up-market singles/doubles from 140/170FF; showers cost 10FF extra.

Places to Eat

As with hotels, the higher up the hill you are, the more you pay to eat. Nightlife revolves around the few bars along Rue Centrale.

Restaurants The *Hôtel des Remparts* (see Hotels) has some of the least expensive *menus* around – 55FF for three courses or 63FF for four. Good Savoyard fondues for 62FF per person simmer at *Le Bistrot du Temple* (☎ 92.20.23.57) on Place du Temple.

For a pricier fondue – and a variety of other local dishes – in a nonsmoking atmosphere, try the cavernous *Le Rustique* (☎ 92.21.00.10) at 36 Rue Pont d'Asfeld. Snacks and pizzas costing 33/48FF for one/two people are available at *La Boule d'Or* (☎ 92.21.16.47) at 27 Grande Rue.

In the lower town, the *Hôtel de la Gare* (see Hotels) has a 58FF *menu* that includes a quarter *pichet* of wine and a coffee. On Rue Centrale, *L'Origan* (☎ 92.20.10.09) at No 25 has excellent pizzas from 28FF.

Self-Catering On Ave Maurice Petsche there's a *Brio supermarket* open weekdays from 8.30 am to 12.15 pm and 2.15 to 7.30 pm, and Saturday from 8.30 am to 7.30 pm. On Wednesday there's a *food market* in the car park just off Rue Centrale.

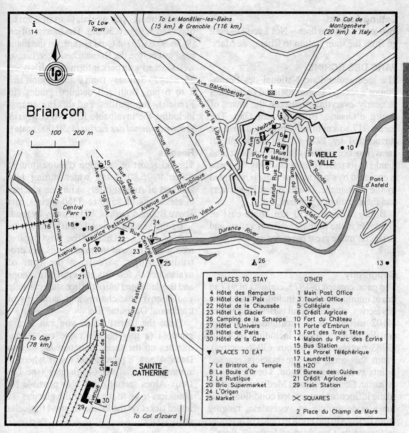

Briançon

0   100   200 m

PLACES TO STAY

- 4 Hôtel des Remparts
- 9 Hôtel de la Paix
- 22 Hôtel de le Chaussée
- 23 Hôtel Le Glacier
- 26 Camping de la Schappe
- 27 Hôtel L'Univers
- 28 Hôtel de Paris
- 30 Hôtel de la Gare

▼ PLACES TO EAT

- 7 Le Bistrot du Temple
- 8 La Boule d'Or
- 12 Le Rustique
- 20 Brio Supermarket
- 24 L'Origan
- 25 Market

OTHER

- 1 Main Post Office
- 3 Tourist Office
- 5 Collégiale
- 6 Crédit Agricole
- 10 Fort du Château
- 11 Porte d'Embrun
- 13 Fort des Trois Têtes
- 14 Maison du Parc des Écrins
- 15 Bus Station
- 16 Le Prorel Téléphérique
- 17 Laundrette
- 18 H2O
- 19 Bureau des Guides
- 21 Crédit Agricole
- 29 Train Station

✕ SQUARES

- 2 Place du Champ de Mars

FRENCH ALPS

Getting There & Away

Train Briançon's station (☎ 92.51.50.50 for information), which is at the end of the line from Gap, is at the southern end of Ave du Général de Gaulle, about 1.5 km from the Vieille Ville. The ticket windows are open from 5.30 am to 8 pm and when there's a train due to depart.

To Paris's Gare de Lyon (374FF; 10½ hours) there's a direct overnight train leaving at 8 pm. Two quicker daytime services (seven hours) go via Grenoble, where they connect with the TGV. Other major destinations include Gap (61FF; 1½ hours; five a day),

Grenoble (137FF; four hours; four a day) and Marseille (182FF; four hours; three a day).

Bus The bus station is at the intersection of Ave du 159 RIA and Rue Général Colaud. SCAL (☎ 92.21.12.00) has an office here and runs a daily bus to Gap (45FF; two hours), Digne (100FF; 3¼ hours; except Sunday) and Marseille (5¾ hours). VFD buses (☎ 76.47.77.77 in Grenoble) go via Bourg d'Oisans (104FF; 1¾ hours) to Grenoble (127FF; 2¼ hours; two a day). To Turin in Italy (65FF; three hours), a bus leaves from the train station daily at 3.35 pm.

Getting Around

Two local TUB bus lines – Nos 1 and D – both go from the train station to Champ de Mars.

PARC DES ÉCRINS

The spectacular Parc National des Écrins, France's second-largest national park, takes in nearly everything between the towns of Bourg d'Oisans, Briançon and Gap. The park's 917 sq km of fully protected land are surrounded by 1770 sq km of peripheral areas, most of which is largely unspoilt land thanks to its relative inaccessibility. The area is enclosed by steep narrow valleys, sculpted by the Romanche, Durance and Drac rivers and their erstwhile glaciers.

Bourg d'Oisans, 50 km south-east of Grenoble in the Romanche River valley, and Briançon make great bases for exploring the park.

Geography

The park, created in 1973, consists of 917 sq km of uninhabited land, including the Massif des Écrins, whose summit is Barre des Écrins (4102 metres). It is surrounded by other equally majestic peaks, including La Meije (3983 metres) and Pelvoux (3946 metres). From this area, Ice age glaciers reached points as far away as Lyon. The meeting of Atlantic, Continental and Mediterranean climatic influences has created conditions ideal for a wide variety of vegetation, ranging from fir trees in the north to fields of lavender in the south. One-third of France's flora – some 2000 species – grows in the park, which is known for its toendra (reindeer moss) and desert plants. Animals that inhabit the park include hares, marmots, foxes, chamois and golden eagles. Ibex were reintroduced in the late 1970s.

Information

Several Maisons du Parc, open all year, can provide detailed information on the park. The park headquarters is in Gap (☎ 92.51. 40.71) at 7 Rue Colonel Roux, 05000 Gap. There's also a large office in Briançon.

In Bourg d'Oisans, the Maison du Parc (☎ 76.80.00.51), on Rue Gambetta in the

town centre, is open weekdays from 8 am to noon and 1.30 to 6.30 pm. The tourist office (☎ 76.80.03.25) at Quai Girard, on the main road just before the Romanche River, is also well stocked with park information. It's open Monday to Saturday from 9 am to noon and 2 to 6 pm. Both sell detailed guides (in French), topoguides and hiking maps, including the invaluable IGN No 6, *Massif et Parc National des Écrins* (1:50,000 scale).

Resorts

The ski resort of the **Alpe d'Huez** (tourist office ☎ 76.80.35.41), which during July and part of August offers skiing on glaciers at elevations of 2530 to 3350 metres, sits above Bourg d'Oisans, 10 km away by road.

Up the Vénéon Valley, 12 km to the south-east of Bourg d'Oisans, the tinyl typical mountain village of **Venosc** clings to a protruding slope, safe from the roar of avalanches. A few arts and craft workshops and the dedicated tourist office staff can help you discover the charms and hardships of traditional Dauphiné life.

From the tourist office you can take a gondola (a tiny bubble cable car) eight-minutes up the sheer mountainside to **Les Deux Alpes,** a popular ski resort where in summer you can ski on glaciers (see Les Deux Alpes section). It's also possible for nonskiers to go to the top of the glaciers – a return ticket on the Dôme Express funicular costs 100FF.

Musée des Minéraux et de la Faune des Alpes

This museum (☎ 76.80.27.54), off Rue du Docteur Daday behind the church in Bourg d'Oisans, is an introduction to what you can (or once could) see in the park. It houses displays of current or vanishing Alpine fauna and rare minerals. It's open from 2 to 6 pm daily except Tuesday; it's closed from 15 November to 15 December. Admission is 17FF (5FF for children).

Hiking

There are plenty of zigzagging paths used for centuries by shepherds and smugglers from points all along the Romanche Valley. From Bourg d'Oisans there is a path to Villard Notre Dame (1525 metres; two hours), and from Venosc there's one to Les Deux Alpes (1660 metres; 1½ hours). The national park publication *Dix Itinéraires* (Ten Itineraries; in French only) is a good companion for treks and climbs of up to seven hours.

Experienced hikers can take the GR54, known also as the 'Tour de l'Oisans' (215 km), which follows the contours of the land at altitudes ranging between 700 to 2800 metres. It's a difficult 10 to 20-day trek. Places to stock up on provisions can be four or five days apart and avalanches are possible.

There's a Hiking Guide Office (☎ 76.79. 54.83) in the tiny village of La Bérarde, 31 km south-east of Bourg d'Oisans at the end of the Vénéon Valley (at the base of Barre des Écrins). The Club Alpin Français (CAF; ☎ 76.74.53.83) also has an office here.

Other Activities

Rock climbers can visit the park accompanied by the guides of the Compagnie des Guides Oisans (☎ 76.80.18.69) in Bourg d'Oisans. At Venosc, Vénon Eaux Vives (☎ 76.80.23.99) organises trips by raft (130 to 180FF for a half-day) or kayak (100 to 140FF). It also hires out mountain bikes for 90FF a day.

Places to Stay & Eat

Within the park's central zone there are about 32 *refuges*, most of them run by the CAF. The charge is 25 to 50FF a night.

A handful of gîtes d'étape are located on the outskirts of the park. Some are open all year but most are not. Expect to pay about 50FF a night. The *Gîte d'Étape Les Amis de la Montagne* (☎ 76.80.06.94) in Venosc has dorms for 42FF. A full list of accommodation is available from the Maison du Parc and the tourist office.

In Bourg d'Oisans there are plenty of camping grounds, including a cluster down the road from the tourist office, on the road to the Alpe d'Huez. The four-star *La Cascade* (☎ 76.80.02.42) is open from February to 30 September. Many of the cheaper grounds are open in summer only.

Bourg d'Oisans has about 10 hotels, most of which are open all year, including the very comfortable *Hôtel Beau Rivage* (☎ 76.80. 03.19) at Rue des Maquis de l'Oisans, the road running behind the tourist office. It has rooms from 125/140FF and an excellent restaurant. *Le Réghaia* (☎ 76.80.03.37), on Ave Aristide Briand just past the tourist office, has rooms from 140/150FF.

For supplies, there's a *Timy supermarket* on the main road through town.

Getting There & Away

VFD buses (☎ 76.80.00.90 in Bourg d'Oisans, 76.47.77.77 in Grenoble) serve the Romanche Valley and Briançon. They operate from the bus station on Ave de la Gare, the main road into Bourg d'Oisans.

From Grenoble, VFD bus No 300 runs to Bourg d'Oisans (45FF; 1⅓ hours; eight a day). From Briançon, VFD's bus No 306 stops in Bourg d'Oisans (104FF; 1¾ hours; two a day).

From Bourg d'Oisans, there are a few buses a day to the Alpe d'Huez (15 minutes) and Les Deux Alpes (40 minutes). To Venosc, La Bérarde and most other smaller places in the valley you'll have to rely on your thumb.

The Jura

The Jura Mountains, a range of rounded, dark, wooded hills and verdant, undulating plateaux, stretch for 360 km along the Franco-Swiss border from the Rhine to the Rhône (ie from just north of Geneva to near Basel). Part of the Franche-Comté region, the French Jura has not been affected very much by tourism and is consequently a fine retreat for people in search of tranquillity. The historic capital of Franche-Comté is Besançon. The region's most famous cheese is Comté.

Known as France's premier cross-country skiing area, the Jura – whose name comes from a Gaulish word meaning 'forest' – seem far away from the touristic craziness of the Alps. The range is dotted with ski stations from north of Pontarlier all the way south to Bellegarde. Les Rousses, situated somewhere in the middle, is the most renowned, but there are many smaller, more intimate stations, such as Métabief, Lamoura and Lelex. Franche-Comté is also known for its superb hiking trails.

BESANÇON

Besançon (population 160,000) is the ancient and modern capital of Franche-Comté. Sitting tightly surrounded by hills on the northern reaches of the Jura range, it was first settled in Gallo-Roman times. It later became an important stop on the early trade routes between Italy, the Alps and the Rhine. Since the 18th century, it has been a noted clock-making centre.

The town is pleasant enough and deservedly proud of its title as the 'greenest town in France', but it has little of special interest to detain visitors. If you have a car or a tent, it will be the forests, mountains and nature trails throughout Franche-Comté that you're more likely to remember.

Orientation

Besançon's old town is neatly encased by a horseshoe-shaped curve of the Doubs River. The tourist office and train station are both just outside this loop. The main street, pedestrianised Grande Rue, a former Roman highway, slices right through the old centre.

Information

Tourist Office Sitting serenely by the river, the tourist office (☎ 81.80.92.55) at 2 Place de la 1er Armée Française is open Monday to Saturday from 9 am (10 am on Monday) to noon and 1.30 to 6 pm (5 pm on Saturday). In July and August it's also open on Sunday from 9 am to noon. It has an exchange service, will book accommodation and sells a range of local hiking maps.

For all sorts of information on the Franche Comté region, on subjects ranging from the best fishing spots to mountain bike trails, head to the Conseil Régional de Franche-Comté (☎ 81.83.50.47) at 9 Rue de Pontarlier. It keeps regular business hours.

Centre d'Information Jeunesse This youth information centre (☎ 81.83.20.40) at 27 Rue de la République sells BIJ train tickets and has a travel/accommodation notice board. It's also the home of the Autostop office. The centre is open Tuesday to Friday from 10 am to noon and 1.30 to 6 pm, and Saturday and Monday from 1.30 to 6 pm.

Money The Banque de France (☎ 81.83.12.22) at 19 Rue de la Préfecture is open weekdays from 9 am to 12.15 pm and 1.15 to 3.30 pm. Money can also be changed at the tourist office and the train station information office.

Post The main post office (☎ 81.53.81.12), which handles poste restante, is a fair way out of the centre at 4 Rue Demangel. It's open weekdays from 8 am to 7 pm and on Saturday until noon. The more convenient branch at 23 Rue Proudhon is open the same hours.

Besançon's postcode is 25000.

Laundry The laundrette at 54 Rue Bersot is open daily from 7 am to 8 pm. The laundrette at 14 Rue de la Madeleine is open from 6.30 am to 8.30 pm.

Musée des Beaux-Arts et d'Archéologie

Thought to be France's oldest museum, the Musée des Beaux-Arts (☎ 81.81.44.47) at 1 Place de la Révolution houses an impressive collection of paintings, including primitive and Renaissance works. Franche-Comté's long history of clock-making is also showcased here, but the displays will soon move to the **Musée du Temps** in the Granvelle Palace at 96 Grande Rue. The Musée des Beaux-Arts is open from 9.30 am to noon and 2 to 5.50 pm (closed Monday). Entry costs 16FF but is free for students, children – and, on Wednesday and Sunday, everyone.

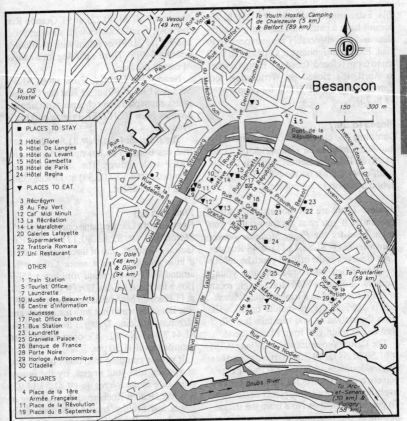

Besançon

0   150   300 m

■ PLACES TO STAY
2 Hôtel Florel
6 Hôtel De Langres
9 Hôtel du Levant
15 Hôtel Gambetta
18 Hôtel de Paris
24 Hôtel Regina

▼ PLACES TO EAT
3 Récrégym
8 Au Feu Vert
12 Caf' Midi Minuit
13 La Récréation
14 Le Maraîcher
20 Galeries Lafayette
   Supermarket
22 Trattoria Romana
27 Uni Restaurant

OTHER
1 Train Station
5 Tourist Office
7 Laundrette
10 Musée des Beaux-Arts
16 Centre d'information
   Jeunesse
17 Post Office branch
21 Bus Station
23 Laundrette
25 Granvelle Palace
26 Banque de France
28 Porte Noire
29 Horloge Astronomique
30 Citadelle

✕ SQUARES
4 Place de la 1ère
   Armée Française
11 Place de la Révolution
19 Place du 8 Septembre

To Vesoul (49 km)
To Youth Hostel, Camping de Chalezeule (5 km) & Belfort (89 km)
To CIS Hostel
To Dole (46 km) & Dijon (94 km)
To Pontarlier (59 km)
To Arc-et-Senans (30 km) & Poligny (58 km)
Doubs River

Citadelle

Built by Vauban in the late 1600s, Besançon's Citadelle (☎ 81.82.16.22) sits at the top of Rue des Fusillés de la Résistance. You can get a sense of the strength of the citadelle by walking along the ramparts. In winter they afford good views of the red (or white) roofs below.

Within the walls there are three museums focusing on local culture, natural history and, more soberingly, the rise of Nazism and fascism and the French resistance movement. Displays on the latter subject are found in the **Musée de la Résistance et de la Déportation**. The Citadelle is open daily from 9.15 am to 6.15 pm; from October to March, hours are 9.45 am to 4.45 pm. Entry costs 22/15FF for adults/children and includes admission to the museums, which are closed on Tuesday.

The Citadelle is a steep 15-minute walk from the **Porte Noire** (Black Gate), one of the few visible remains of Besançon's Roman days.

Horloge Astronomique

Housed in Cathédrale Saint Jean, which is just below the Citadelle on Rue du Chapitre, this astronomical clock (☎ 81.81.12.76) doesn't have a patch on Strasbourg's equivalent and is considerably more expensive to visit. Except in January, it's open from 9.30 am to 6 pm (closed Tuesday). From October to April, it's closed on Wednesday, too. Entrance costs 18FF (10FF for people aged 18 to 25).

Places to Stay

Camping The closest camping ground is the four-star *Camping de Chalezeule* (☎ 81.88.04.26) on Route de Belfort, which is five km north-east of town on the N83. There is no public transport to get out there.

Hostels There are two hostels, both out of the centre. If you're at the train station you might head for the *Foyer Mixte de Jeunes Travailleurs* (☎ 81.88.43.11) at 48 Rue des Cras. It serves as the official youth hostel but is often filled with students and young workers. It charges 80FF for a single room or 60FF for a bed in a triple or quad; breakfast is 10FF. It's a 20-minute uphill walk from the station or you can take bus No 7 (last one at midnight) from Place Liberté.

The *Centre International de Séjour* (CIS; ☎ 81.50.07.54) at 19 Rue Martin du Gard has singles/doubles/quads for 84/56/48FF per person; breakfast costs 16FF extra. There's a lively bar and, once again, plenty of students. To get there, take bus No 8 from the station, get off at the Intermarché supermarket on Blvd Winston Churchill and cut between the apartment blocks – the hostel's on the hill.

Hotels – Outside the Old Town If you're looking for good value for money, the *Hôtel Florel* (☎ 81.80.41.08) at 6 Rue de la Viotte is the pick of Besançon's hotels. It has basic singles/doubles from 95/110FF; showers are 15FF extra. There's space for a few cars out the front. The *Hôtel De Langres* (☎ 81.82.08.14) at 4 Rue Richebourg has rooms from 80/120FF but it's at the top of a very steep hill and is often full.

Hotels – Old Town Down a quiet alley in the heart of the old town, the recently renovated *Regina* (☎ 81.81.50.22) at 91 Grande Rue has cosy, floral doubles with shower, toilet and TV for 218FF or rooms with two double beds for 249FF. There's parking for a couple of cars in the lane.

Nearby, the *Hôtel de Paris* (☎ 81.81.36.56; fax 81.61.94.90) at 33 Rue des Granges is less atmospheric but cheaper, with singles/doubles from 105/173FF. Private parking is available.

The *Hôtel du Levant* (☎ 81.81.07.88) at 9 Rue des Boucheries has musty doubles for 150FF with shower. The similarly priced *Gambetta* (☎ 81.82.02.33) at 13 Rue Gambetta is a better bet.

Places to Eat

Restaurants Local cuisine can be tried in *Le Maraîcher* (☎ 81.81.80.13) at 10 Rue Gustave Courbet, one of three restaurants in a little arcade. It has a *menu Comtois* for around 70FF and a *menu rapide* for 55FF. Down the road, *Au Feu Vert* (☎ 81.82.17.20) at 11 Place du Marché has *menus* from 40FF. Rue Bersot is brimming with restaurants and pizzerias, including *Trattoria Romana* (☎ 81.81.44.77) at No 52. It's open Monday to Saturday until 11.30 pm.

If people pumping iron don't bother you as you dig into your vegies, try the downstairs café in the *Récrégym* (☎ 81.53.14.92) at 6 Ave Denfert Rochereau. Specialising in salads and healthy snacks, it's open daily from 9 am to 9 pm (from noon on Tuesday and Thursday).

La Récréation (☎ 81.83.00.03) at 12 Rue Luc Breton (at the back of the parking lot) is a *salon de thé* that serves salads (around 35FF) and other edibles. For late-night snacks, try *Caf' Midi Minuit* (☎ 81.81.12.89) at 13 Grande Rue, which serves until midnight.

University Restaurant There's a *University restaurant* at 36 Rue Mégevand opposite the theatre. On the ground floor you can pay cash; it's cheaper upstairs (12.30FF for three courses), but you'll need to buy a ticket from a student. In general, it's open Monday to Saturday from 11.30 am to 1 pm and 6.30 to 7.45 pm, and on Sunday for lunch only.

Self-Catering The centrally located *Galeries Lafayette*, entered from either Grande Rue or Rue des Granges, has a grocery section in the basement. It's open Monday to Saturday from 9 am to 7 pm.

Getting There & Away

Train The train station (☎ 81.53.50.50 for information) is 800 metres up the hill from the city centre at the north-western end of Ave Maréchal Foch. The information office is open daily from 8.30 am to 6.15 pm.

There are major connections to Paris's Gare de Lyon (209FF plus TGV fee; 2½ hours; five a day), Dijon (62FF; one hour; 14 a day), Lyon (127FF; 2½ hours; five a day) and Belfort (64FF; one hour; four a day). To get to Frasne (near the Métabief ski resort in the Jura Mountains), you'll have to change trains in Mouchard.

Bus Buses to Métabief (53FF; two hours) and other Jura ski resorts are operated by Monts Jura from the bus station (☎ 81.83.06.11), which is at 9 Rue Proudhon.

Getting Around

Bus Bus No 24 links the train station with the centre (5FF).

Bicycle If you have good leg muscles, you might want to tackle Besançon's hilly terrain with bikes hired from the Service Bagages (☎ 81.80.39.15) at the station. Bikes cost 30/40FF for a half/full day and are available from 5.30 am to 11.30 pm.

AROUND BESANÇON

Envisaged by its designer as the 'ideal city', the late 18th-century **Saline Royale** (Royal Salt Works; ☎ 81.54.45.00) at Arc-et-Senans, 30 km south of town off the N83 to Arbois, is a showpiece of early Industrial Age town planning. Although his dream was never realised, Claude-Nicolas Ledoux's semicircular saltworks is listed as a World Heritage sight and is a must for anyone interested in the layout of towns.

Opening hours and prices vary depending on the month, but it's usually open daily from 9 or 10 am to noon and 2 to 5 or 6 pm. From June to September, hours are 9 am to 6 pm. Peak season admission for adults/students/children under 16 is 22/15/9FF. There are three trains a day from Besançon (31FF; 35 minutes).

MÉTABIEF

Métabief (altitude 1000 metres) is living proof that the Jura is not overdeveloped. Located 18 km south of Pontarlier on the main road to Lausanne, the resort groups six traditional villages that offer access to a remarkable skiing area comprising 250 km of cross-country trails and 45 km of alpine pistes. Lifts take you almost to the top of Mont d'Or (1463 metres), the area's highest peak, from where a fantastic 180° panorama stretches over the foggy Swiss plain to Lake Geneva and from the Matterhorn to Mont Blanc.

Les Hôpitaux Neufs, three km from the Centre d'Accueil at the main lift station is the main village. For skiers, there's a free shuttle bus between the two.

Information

Tourist Office The main tourist office (☎ 81.49.13.81) at Ave Les Hôpitaux Neufs is open from 9 am to noon and 2 to 6 pm. The branch (☎ 81.49.16.79) at the Centre d'Accueil, which keeps the same hours, is open from Christmas until Easter and in July and August.

Ski Equipment All the sports shops hire equipment – it costs around 65 to 75FF a day for everything.

Lift Tickets Lift passes cost 85/160/460FF for one/two/seven days. For cross-country skiers, it costs 25FF a day (15FF reduced price) or 100/40FF a week to use the pistes.

Lessons The ESF (☎ 81.49.04.21) at the Centre d'Accueil has two-hour lessons for 60FF; it costs 270FF for six sessions.

Activities

Ice skating is possible on the six-km-long Lake Saint Point, about six km east of town, or the even longer Lake Joux, located further south. A day of snow-shoe walking through the forest with guide and a meal costs 100FF. For a faster pace there are half-day or full-day dog-sledge trips.

Places to Stay

The tourist office can organise a week's stay in a hotel, (including full board), six skiing lessons, a ski pass and a 20% reduction on skis and boot hire for 1800FF. In a four-person studio, the same deal (minus meals) is 840FF per person. The same package for cross-country fans is 1600FF in a hostel and 630FF in a studio.

In Les Hôpitaux Neufs, the *Hôtel Robbe* (☎ 81.49.11.05) has doubles from 120FF a night. *Les Deux Saisons* (☎ 81.49.00.04) has reasonable singles/doubles for 115/135FF. More appealing is *Les Sapins* (☎ 81.49.90. 90) in the quiet village of Longevilles, four km south of Métabief on the route of the Grande Traversée du Jura (see the aside below). It has rooms from 110FF and a typical local *menu* for 60FF.

Getting There & Away

The closest railway station is in Frasne (☎ 81. 49.81.54), 25 km west on the rail line between Dijon and Vallorbe (the latter is just over the Swiss border). From Frasne, there are five buses a day which pass through both Métabief and Les Hôpitaux Neufs.

Grande Traversée du Jura

The Grande Traversée du Jura (GTJ) – the Grand Jura Crossing – is a 210-km cross-country skiing track from Villers-le-Lac (north of Pontarlier) to Hauteville-Lompnes (south-west of Bellegarde). The path peaks at 1500 metres near the town of Mouthe (south of Métabief) and follows one of the coldest valleys in France. After the first 20 km, the route briefly crosses into Switzerland, but most of the time it runs close to the border on the French side. Well maintained and very popular, the crossing takes 10 full days of skiing to cover – a feat for the ultrafit and dedicated.

Part of the GTJ – the 76 km from Lamoura to Mouthe – is followed each year during the world's second-largest cross-country skiing competition, the Transjurassienne. Held in late February, the challenge is taken up by more than 4000 skiers, who charge off in an incredible blaze of colour.

For information on the GTJ and accommodation possibilities along the route, contact Relais de Randonnée Étapes Jura (☎ 84.41.20.34) in Lajoux (postcode 39310). The best map of the area is the IGN 1:50,000 scale map entitled *Ski de Fond – Massif du Jura*. ∎

Massif Central

The Massif Central is one of those regions that not only the tourists ignore. This mountainous core of France's enormous heartland has long been looked upon by the French as a rural backwater where isolated communities continue to do battle against a harsh climate without the support of the younger generation, who leave in droves in search of a higher standard of living in the cities.

For centuries, the wild Massif Central was penetrated only by conquerors or those with a mission, such as pilgrims on their way to Spain or crusaders on their way to the Holy Land (the First Crusade was launched from Clermont-Ferrand). Its landscape is unique in France, dimpled with the cones of ancient volcanoes, such as the Puy de Dôme, and in parts laced with tongues of solidified lava. The hot mineral springs that bubble forth from the mountains, have given rise to one of the country's most dense concentrations of spa towns, among them Vichy and Le Mont Dore. Mineral water from this area is bottled, marketed and drunk all over the world.

Except in the few large cities, such as the regional capital, Clermont-Ferrand, life is primarily rural. The rich volcanic soil sustains maize, tobacco and vineyards, while at higher elevations, the green pastures are grazed by cows and sheep whose milk produces some of the country's cheapest cheeses – you'll come across the powerful Bleu d'Auvergne and slightly sour-tasting Cantal everywhere in France. Industry, like tourism, has made few inroads except in Clermont-Ferrand, where France's rubber industry has an unshakable grip.

Religion too has long had a tight hold on the people of the Massif Central, known for their devout lifestyles. Modest statues of the Madonna and Christ can be found in many of the region's fine Romanesque churches, while more spectacular versions dominate the skylines of Murat in the Cantal and Le Puy-en-Velay to the east.

Tourism in the region reflects the agrarian scene, and back-to-nature-style holidays are now very much in vogue. Two large regional parks, the dramatic Parc Naturel Régional des Volcans d'Auvergne and its tamer eastern neighbour, the Livradois-Forez, together make up France's largest protected environment. They offer a wide range of outdoor pursuits, including cross-country skiing, hang-gliding, canoeing and, of course, hiking. Even during July and August, when almost everybody is on holiday, the Massif Central is a part of the country where there's room to breathe.

Geography

The Massif Central region is hard to define, because it refers to the very large mountainous region in south-central France and everybody seems to have different ideas about where it begins and ends. Roughly speaking, it is bordered by Berry and Burgundy to the north, and by the wide Rhône Valley to the east. The Grands Causses and Cévennes separate it from the steamy Languedoc plain in the south, and Périgord and Limousin lie to the west.

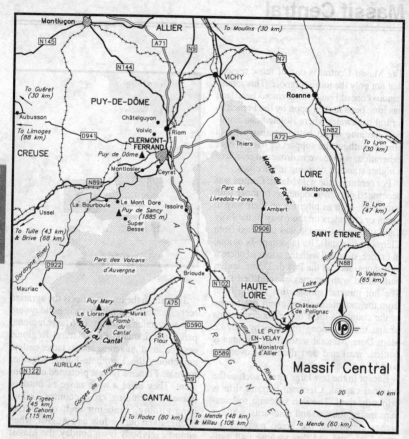

The heart of the Massif Central is the Auvergne, one of France's former provinces and now an administrative region comprising the four *départements* of Allier, Puy de Dôme, Cantal and Haute Loire. Parts of eastern Limousin can also be included in the Massif Central region, along with the *départements* of Creuse and Lozère.

Formed millions of years before the Alps or Pyrenees, the volcanic landscape of the Massif Central is best known for its *puys*, or volcanic cones. The Puy de Dôme west of Clermont-Ferrand is one of the most spectacular, but there are many more throughout the region, most notably in the Parc des Volcans d'Auvergne to the south. Sometimes the puys are merely the lava 'plugs' that remained when the surrounding cones eroded away, as is the case with the steep crag topped by the Saint Michel d'Aiguilhe chapel in Le Puy-en-Velay. The word 'puy' comes from the Latin word '*podium*', meaning 'platform', and these days the puys are often used as take-off platforms for hang-glider and parapente flights – perhaps the best way to view this strange landscape. The highest peak in the Massif Central is the Puy de Sancy (1885 metres).

Another fundamental characteristic of the region is water. Lakes have filled the volcanic craters or have built up behind ancient lava flows. The area also gives rise to some of France's great rivers, including the Dordogne, Allier, Lot and Loire. The latter starts its mighty journey to the Atlantic from south of Le Puy-en-Velay. Many of these rivers have been tamed by hydroelectric schemes, though a recent plan to dam the Loire near Le Puy-en-Velay was abandoned after much public protest.

Activities

The Massif Central is a virtual paradise for outdoors enthusiasts. Local tourist offices are generally the best source of information – look for the free regional *Sports & Loisirs* booklet, an annual listing of where you can do what. One of the best maps for the region is IGN's No 2432, entitled *Massif du Sancy* (scale 1:25,000).

Hiking & Cycling Hiking is probably the most popular activity throughout the Massif Central. The forested or shorn mountain slopes aren't as steep or arduous as the Alps but still pose a challenge for most. Thirteen GR tracks, including the GR4, as well as hundreds of smaller footpaths and circular trails wind through the region, which is dotted with gîtes d'étape for overnight halts. Cyclists, especially mountain-bike enthusiasts, also make use of these tracks. Mountain bikes as well as city bikes can be rented in many towns.

Skiing In winter the undulating terrain favours cross-country skiing. For information, contact Auvergne Ski de Fond (☎ 73.90.23.14) at 23 Place Delille, 63000 Clermont-Ferrand. However, several ski resorts, particularly Le Mont Dore and neighbouring Super Besse, as well as Super Lioran near Murat in the south, also have downhill runs and full alpine facilities.

Hang-Gliding The topography and thermals of the Massif Central make it ideal for hang-gliding and parapente. Introductory courses are offered by private organisations; local tourist offices will have details. The FUAJ youth hostel organisation also offers courses – for more details, see Skiing and Parapente under Le Mont Dore.

Getting Around

Getting to the major towns in the Massif Central is no longer the difficult task it was a couple of decades ago. Clermont-Ferrand and Vichy are on one of the main rail links between Paris and the south. Services to Le Mont Dore, Le Puy-en-Velay and Murat, however, can be a bit tedious as they are all on secondary lines.

Once in these places, exploring the immediate vicinity will pose considerable challenges if you don't have your own transport. Trains are backed up by very limited regional bus networks. These are reasonably numerous in the area around Clermont-Ferrand, but become fewer and sparser as you head deeper into the Massif Central.

Clermont-Ferrand

Clermont-Ferrand (population 136,000; altitude 430 metres), the bustling capital of the département of Puy-de-Dôme, is by far the largest city in the Massif Central. It sits to the east of a series of puys known as the Monts Dômes, the highest of which is the Puy de Dôme (1465 metres), which looks down on the city from just 10 km away.

Clermont-Ferrand, originally called Nemessos, was known in Roman times as Augustonemetum and Castrum Claremunte. Christianised in the 3rd century, it was the meeting place for the synod at which Pope Urban II proclaimed the First Crusade in 1095. It was also the birthplace of Blaise Pascal (1623-62), the mathematician, physicist and all-round genius who contributed so much to our knowledge of hydraulics, atmospheric pressure and the theory of probability.

Widely referred to as just 'Clermont', the city's hyphenated name came about in 1731

MASSIF CENTRAL

when Clermont joined with its neighbour and former rival, Montferrand, now little more than a north-eastern suburb. Today the city has a thriving university and is the hub of France's rubber industry – better known to the rest of the world as the Michelin tyre empire, which has its headquarters here.

The old town centre is built on a long-extinct volcano, resulting in dramatic black buildings made of lava which are not, as the tourist office takes great pains to emphasise, that colour from modern-day pollution. There's a wide range of accommodation, and the city is considerably enlivened by the local student population, making it a good base for excursions into the northern parts of the Massif Central.

Orientation

Although the old town is the heart of present-day Clermont, the city has several distinct focal points. The commercial centre is the large, uninspiring Place de Jaude, dominated by a statue of Vercingétorix, the chief of the Arverni who in 52 BC almost turned back the Roman conquest of Gaul.

North-east of this square lies the largely pedestrianised old town. Its many narrow streets, including the main thoroughfare, Rue des Gras, slope gently up the volcanic hill crowned by Cathédrale Notre Dame on Place de la Victoire. As if a separate entity, the train station lies to the city's east, one km from the cathedral and 1.5 km from Place de Jaude (connected by bus No 14).

Information

Tourist Office The main tourist office (☎ 73. 93.30.20) is at 69 Blvd Gergovia, about five minutes' walk south of Place de Jaude, next to the bus station. It's open weekdays from 8.45 am to 6.30 pm, Saturday from 9 am to noon and 2 to 6 pm. From 1 June to 30 September the hours are longer: Monday to Saturday from 8.30 am to 7 pm, Sunday from 9 am to noon and 2 to 6 pm. The office is also home to a train information and reservation kiosk.

Just to the left as you exit the train station is a tourist office annexe (☎ 73.91.87.89), open weekdays from 9.15 to 11.30 am and 12.15 to 5 pm; in summer it is also open on

---

The Celtic Hero

Vercingétorix, chief of the Celtic Arverni tribe, almost foiled Julius Caesar's conquest of Gaul, which had stunned even the Romans by its ruthless efficiency. After overrunnnig most of Gaul in 57-56 BC, Caesar spent the years 55-52 BC trying to consolidate his achievements by playing one tribe off against the other. Meanwhile, Vercingétorix had been busy uniting the tribes between the Loire and Garonne rivers and raising an army that could match the Roman legions in its discipline.

In the summer of 52 BC, Vercingétorix's forces thrashed Caesar's troops at Gergovia near Clermont-Ferrand, the heart of Arvernian territory. The event was the signal for all but five of the tribes in Gaul to rise against Rome and join forces with Vercingétorix, who became the closest symbol they had to a national leader.

Over the following months, the Gauls hounded the Romans with guerrilla warfare and engaged them in several pitched battles that proved inconclusive. In one such battle near Dijon, Vercingétorix was forced to retreat. He headed for the hill town of Alésia (present-day Alise) to regroup his troops, hoping to draw the enemy into the surrounding valley arms where they could be attacked from behind by a Gallic relief force. This strategy proved to be a big mistake.

The Romans, grand masters in the art of siege warfare which Caesar had perfected, surrounded the town with an intricate system of earthworks. They beat off the relief force in a hard-fought battle, and it was only a matter of time before Alésia was starved into surrender. Gallic resistance collapsed and by 50 BC Roman rule in Gaul was no longer being challenged.

Vercingétorix was taken to Rome where he was paraded in chains in Caesar's triumphal procession. As a final insult, he was left languishing in prison for six years before being put to death by strangulation. ■

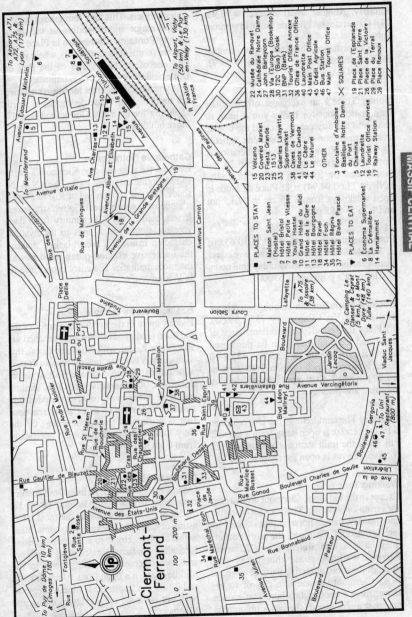

MASSIF CENTRAL

PLACES TO STAY

1 Maison Saint Jean (Hostel)
2 Hôtel Bristol
4 Hôtel de Vitesse
9 Youth Hostel
10 Grand Hôtel du Midi
11 Hôtel de la Gare
13 Hôtel Bourgogne
18 Hôtel Ravel
34 Hôtel Foch
35 Hôtel Régina
37 Hôtel Blaise Pascal

PLACES TO EAT

6 Économa Supermarket
8 La Crémaillère
14 Hammamet
15 Volcano
20 Covered Market
23 Tresta Grande
25 Galeries Lafayette Supermarket
33 Caves de Vermont
38 Caves de Vermont
41 Roots Canada
42 Le Cèdre
44 Le Naturel

OTHER

3 Fontaine d'Amboise
4 Basilique Notre Dame du Port
5 Laundrette
12 Chamina
16 Tourist Office Annexe
17 Railway Station
22 Musée du Ranquet
24 Cathédrale Notre Dame
27 John Barleycorn
28 Via l'Europe (Bookshop)
30 T2C (Bus) Kiosk
31 BNP (Bank)
32 Tourist Office Annexe
36 Gîtes de France Office
40 Laundrette
43 Main Post Office
45 Crédit Agricole
46 Bus Station
47 Main Tourist Office

✕ SQUARES

19 Place de l'Esplanade
21 Place Saint Pierre
26 Place de la Victoire
29 Place du Terrail
39 Place Renoux

Clermont-Ferrand

MASSIF CENTRAL

Saturday. Another small annexe (☎ 73.93.24.44) operates on Place de Jaude in summer only.

For information about the region, contact the Comité Régional de Tourisme (☎ 73.93.04.03) at 43 Ave Julien.

Money There's an exchange office at the train station, but for banks you'll have to head into the city centre. Round the corner from the main tourist office, the Crédit Agricole (☎ 73.30.58.30) at 3 Ave de la Libération is open weekdays from 8.15 am to 6.30 pm (until noon on Saturday). More centrally, BNP (☎ 73.60.94.94) at 11 Place de Jaude is open weekdays from 8.25 am to 12.15 pm and 1.25 to 4.55 pm.

Post The main post office (☎ 73.30.63.00) at Rue Maurice Busset is open weekdays from 8 am to 7 pm and on Saturday until noon.

Clermont's postcode is 63000.

Books & Maps English-language novels are available at Via l'Europe (☎ 73.92.39.60), 15 Place du Terrail. An excellent range of local and national maps can be purchased from La Cartographie (☎ 73.91.67.75) at 10 Place Renoux, which is open from 9 am to 12.30 pm and 1.30 to 5 pm (closed Monday morning and Sunday).

Laundry The laundrette in the city centre at 6 Place Renoux is open daily from 7 am to 8 pm. Near the train station, the laundrette at 62 Ave Charras is open the same hours.

Walking Tour

Except in the old town, Clermont is not a city for serious wandering. There's a lot of traffic and, frankly, there's not a lot that is likely to interest visitors. That said, the tourist office does have a free *Welcome to Clermont-Ferrand* walking guide that takes you through the more attractive parts of town.

As Clermont-Ferrand is a city of **fountains**, there's another brochure that guides you past every one of the city's ubiquitous water gurglers. This long tour takes you past all the major sights, ending at the 16th-century **Fontaine d'Amboise** in Place de la Poterne (north of the cathedral), where you'll find one of the best views of the Puy de Dôme and its neighbouring summits.

If you have time, quiet **Montferrand**, two km north-east of Place de Jaude, is worth exploring for its many Gothic and Renaissance buildings.

Cathédrale Notre Dame

Even on the sunniest day, Clermont's twin-spired Gothic cathedral looks like it's in the shade. Gracing the top end of Rue des Gras, it's one of France's great Gothic structures. It was built in the 13th century from dark volcanic stone, which adds to its mystical character. Inside it's even blacker, making the impressive **stained-glass windows** all the more dramatic. The entry is on Place de la Victoire.

Basilique Notre Dame du Port

Hidden away in the north-east corner of the old town (and most interestingly reached via Rue Blaise Pascal, with its lava edifices), this 12th-century basilica, just off Rue du Port, is a beautiful example of the soft style of Auvergne Romanesque art. The sunken entrance gives way to sculptured stone columns and, at the far end, the discreet apse that is warmly lit (in the morning) by the fiery stained-glass windows. It's open daily from 8 am to 7 pm.

Musée du Ranquet

Occupying one of the city's finest 16th-century mansions, the Ranquet Museum (☎ 73.37.38.63) at 34 Rue des Gras is the most interesting of Clermont's several museums, all of which are free. Home to a Pascal exhibition (including his famous calculating machine) and local mementoes dating back to the Middle Ages, it's open from 10 am to noon and 2 to 5 pm (6 pm from June to September), but is closed on Sunday morning and Monday.

Hiking

Chamina (☎ 73.90.94.82) at 24 Ave Édouard Michelin (open weekdays from 2 to 6 pm) can supply information on hiking and gîtes d'étape, as well as detailed maps and anything else you need to know about the mountains.

Places to Stay

There's no shortage of decent accommodation. The hostels and most of the hotels are quite evenly divided between the train station area and the city centre.

Camping There are a couple of camping grounds around Clermont but nothing really close to town. The three-star *Le Chanset* (☎ 73.61.30.73) at Ave Jean Baptiste, about five km south-west in Ceyrat on the N89 to Tulle, is open all year and charges 10/5FF per adult/child plus 5FF for a car. Take bus No 4 from Place de Jaude or the train station to the Préguille stop.

Hostels Conveniently located just metres to the right as you leave the train station is the IYHF youth hostel, the *Auberge du Cheval Blanc* (☎ 73.92.26.39) at 55 Ave de l'Union Soviétique. It's open from 2 March to 31 October only and charges 41FF for a bed. In the city centre, the *Maison Saint Jean* (☎ 73.37.14.31) at 17 Rue Gaultier de Biauzat is open all year and charges 80FF including breakfast. Bus No 2 will get you there from the station, but it's wise to phone ahead to check on vacancies.

Gîtes Ruraux Information and booking of gîtes ruraux can be made through the Relais Départemental des Gîtes de France at 26 Rue Saint Esprit.

Hotels – Train Station Area There are several hotels lining busy Ave de l'Union Soviétique, which runs by the train station. The cheapest is the friendly and totally unpretentious *Petite Vitesse* (☎ 73.91.36.41) at No 63, four doors up from the youth hostel. Rooms go for 75FF, or 120FF with a shower. More up-market, the *Grand Hôtel*

du Midi (☎ 39.92.29.41) at No 39, directly opposite the station entrance, has good singles/doubles from 145/155FF.

For something a bit quieter, try the hotels along Ave Charras. The *Bourgogne* (☎ 73.91.68.92) at No 31 has comfortable singles/doubles from 95/120FF, or 135/170FF with shower. Closer to the station is the similarly priced *Hôtel de la Gare* (☎ 73.92.07.82) at No 76.

If you're still searching, *Hôtel Ravel* (☎ 73.91.51.33) at 8 Rue de Maringues, next to the defunct covered market, has rooms from 100/120FF. It's a two-star place, and while the foyer's somewhat grim, there are many decent rooms upstairs.

Hotels – City Centre The cheapest option in the heart of the old town is the *Blaise Pascal* (☎ 73.91.31.82), near the cathedral at 6 Rue Massillon. Clean and adequate but noisy singles/doubles start at 70/82FF. The pick of Clermont's bottom-end hotels, however, is the two-star *Régina* (☎ 73.93.44.76) at 14 Rue Bonnabaud. Tidy rooms start at 110/130FF. There's a private garage opposite (25FF for 24 hours).

Just round the corner, the *Hôtel Foch* (☎ 73.93.48.40) at 22 Rue Maréchal Foch has cheaper rooms from 100/110FF. At the northern end of town, near the Saint Pierre market, a good choice is the *Hôtel Bristol* (☎ 73.37.25.65) at 6 Rue Sainte Rose. Spacious rooms start at 115/135FF, and there's private parking for 24FF.

Places to Eat

Clermont-Ferrand is not known as a gourmet heaven, but you can still eat well and for a reasonable price in many of the city's hotels and restaurants.

Restaurants – Train Station Area Just past the youth hostel on Blvd de l'Union Soviétique, *La Crémaillère* (☎ 73.90.89.25) has a *menu* for only 40FF. At the other end of the street, *Volcano* (☎ 73.91.54.26) at 23 Blvd de l'Union Soviétique has pizzas from 36FF, and a lunchtime *menu* for 45FF. This place is open every day until midnight. *Hammammet* (☎ 73.92.08.93) at 48 Ave Albert et

Elisabeth has Tunisian specialities and a *menu* for 49FF. The *Bourgogne* (see Places to Stay) has a standard 45FF *menu*.

Restaurants – City Centre One particularly bountiful area of the old town is the top end of cobbled Rue des Chaussetiers. Down a small cobblestone alley at No 3 you'll find *1513* (☎ 73.92.37.46), a cosy creperie open daily until 1 or 2 am. At No 28, *Fiesta Grande* (☎ 73.31.39.70) has Mexican dishes from 40FF and live music on Wednesday nights. *Caves de Vermont* (☎ 73.90.92.67) at 16 Rue Massillon is a dark and enticing bar-restaurant with *menus* from 59FF. À la carte dishes are more expensive.

Canadians won't be able to miss the moose in the window of *Roots Canada* (☎ 73. 90.73.74) at 16 Rue Ballainvilliers. The décor is tacky and artificial but the steaks (from 59FF) are real. A few doors along at No 30, a little Lebanese place called *Le Cèdre* (☎ 73.92.72.50) has a great-value *menu* – 38FF including wine. The laid-back *Le Naturel* (☎ 73.35.41.21) at 8 Blvd Léon Malfreyt specialises in healthy salads from 16FF and macrobiotic plats du jour from 45FF. It's open for lunch only (closed Sunday).

University Restaurant There's a dirt-cheap *university restaurant* at 25 Rue Étienne Dolet, but to eat there you may have to buy a ticket from a student. On foot, it's about 800 metres south of the tourist office, or you can take bus No 12 to the Dolet stop.

Self-Catering The blue and yellow contraption on Place Saint Pierre could well be the most modern *covered market* in France. All the basics are sold here Monday to Saturday from 6 am to 7 pm. The adjoining Rue de la Boucherie, one of the city's oldest streets, is lined with *food shops*.

The *Galeries Lafayette* department store on Place de Jaude has a basement supermarket open Monday to Saturday from 8.30 am to 7 pm. Near the train station, the little *Économa supermarket* on Ave Édouard Michelin is open Monday to Saturday

(except Wednesday) from 7 am to 12.30 pm and 2.30 to 7.30 pm, Sunday from 8 am to noon.

Entertainment
Clermont's most enticing nightlife is tucked away along the paved streets of the old town. There are plenty of sleazy bars lining Place de Jaude. Near the cathedral, *Caves de Vermont* (see Places to Eat) is a cosy, inviting pub. The large, green *John Barleycorn* is an Irish stronghold a block away on Rue de Terrail.

Getting There & Away
Air Clermont's Aulnat Airport (☎ 73.62.71. 00) is seven km east of the city. It handles domestic flights only.

Train The train station (☎ 73.92.50.50 for information) is on Ave de l'Union Soviétique, about 1.5 km east of Place de Jaude. Bus No 14 runs between the two. The train information office is open daily (except Sunday) from 8 am to 7.30 pm. The ticket windows are staffed from 5 am to 2 am.

Major train connections include to Paris's Gare de Lyon (211FF; 3½ hours; nine a day), Lyon (129FF; three hours; six a day) and Limoges (164FF; five hours; two a day). The scenic train journey known as *Le Cévenol* winds its way through the mountains southward to Nîmes (165FF; 4½ hours) and on to Marseille (215FF; six hours).

There are local trains to Vichy (41FF; 35 minutes), Le Mont Dore (52FF; 1½ hours), Le Puy-en-Velay (98FF; 2¼ hours) and Murat (80FF; two hours).

Bus The bus station is next to the main tourist office on Blvd Gergovia. The information and ticket kiosk (☎ 73.93.13.61) is open Monday to Saturday from 8.30 am to 6.30 pm. Short-haul buses serve destinations including Riom (16.90FF; 30 minutes), Vichy (46FF; two hours) and Super Besse (45FF; 1¼ hours). In July and August, there's a bus on Monday and Thursday to the top of the Puy de Dôme (54FF return; 30

minutes). The bus that leaves at 1.30 pm returns at 7 pm.

Car Citer car rental (☎ 73.27.20.00) is at 111 Blvd Gustave Flaubert in the east of the city.

Getting Around

Bus An extensive network of local buses is operated by T2C, which has an information kiosk on Place de Jaude, the central bus hub. It is open on weekdays from 8 am to 6.30 pm. Timetables can also be picked up from the main tourist office.

The city is divided into two zones, but zone one tickets (valid for an hour) will get you almost everywhere. These cost 6FF for a single ticket or 42.50FF for a 10-ticket carnet. There's also a *Carte de Jour* (Day Card) for 19FF.

Taxi Taxis wait outside the train station. To order a taxi, call Allo Taxi (☎ 73.90.75.75) or Taxi Radio (☎ 73.92.57.58).

Bicycle From April to October you can hire bikes for 70FF a day from the train station luggage office, which is open from 5.30 am to 10.30 pm. You have to pay a 1000FF deposit.

AROUND CLERMONT-FERRAND
Puy de Dôme

Covered in snow in winter and outdoor adventurers in summer, the Puy de Dôme often serves as one of the more gruelling stages in the prestigious annual Tour de France cycling race. The Celts and later the Romans worshipped gods from the summit (there are remains of a Roman temple dedicated to Mercury), but nowadays the summit is dominated by a big TV transmitter.

From the top there's a fantastic panorama over the surrounding puys, Clermont-Ferrand, and the Monts Dores to the south. Parapente and hang-gliding enthusiasts use the summit as a launching platform. Introductory flights with an instructor cost about 350FF; five-day courses cost 2000FF. Several companies organise flights – the main tourist office in Clermont-Ferrand has details.

The summit can be reached either by the 'mule track' – an hour's climb starting at the Col de Ceyssat, which is three km off the D941 – or by the six-km road which spirals steeply up to the summit. There's a bus from Clermont-Ferrand to the summit in July and August only (see the Clermont-Ferrand Getting There & Away section).

See the Parc des Volcans section for more information.

Riom

Riom, the medieval capital of Auvergne and still an important judiciary centre, is 15 km north of Clermont-Ferrand. The old town, with its many magistrates' mansions built of dark volcanic stone from the quarries in Volvic, is a living museum. It's well worth a visit, but you can see everything on an easy day trip from Clermont-Ferrand. The place is very quiet at night.

South of the old town in Rue du Commerce, the 15th-century **Église Notre Dame du Marthuret** is famous for its beautiful 14th-century sculpture, *Virgin with Bird*. The original is in a chapel on the south side of the church (the one in the entrance is a copy). The **Musée Mandet** on Rue de l'Hôtel de Ville has a reasonable collection of paintings and Roman objects, but of more interest is the **Musée d'Auvergne** on Rue Delille, with a fascinating display of Auvergne folk art and other local objects.

Beyond the western outskirts of Riom is the former Benedictine abbey of **Mozac**, with a 12th-century church in Auvergnat Romanesque style that is known for its capitals. Seven km south-west of Riom is the town of **Volvic**, famous for its spring water and its quarries, which provided the lightweight but strong volcanic stone used in so many buildings in the area, including Cathédrale Notre Dame in Clermont-Ferrand; the ruins of the nearby **Château de Tournoël** dominate the countryside and are worth visiting for the stunning view.

Frequent buses and trains connect Riom with Clermont-Ferrand and Vichy.

Parc des Volcans

One of France's largest regional parks, the Parc Naturel Régional des Volcans d'Auvergne – usually called the Parc des Volcans – stretches for 120 km from the smooth, cone-shaped volcanoes known as the Monts Dômes (or simply the Puys) in the north, past the spectacular Monts Dores to the older, more rugged Monts du Cantal in the south of the park. The volcanic activity in this region started about 20 million years ago, with the last eruptions, in the Monts Dômes, petering out about 6000 years ago.

Many of the 150 towns and villages in the park are built of sombre volcanic stone. It's a wild and beautiful country, ideal for hiking.

Information

The park's head office is in Montlosier (☎ 73.65.67.19), about 20 km south-west of Clermont-Ferrand on the D5, a small road off the main N89 from Clermont-Ferrand to Tulle. It's open weekdays from 8.30 am to 12.30 pm and 1.30 to 5.30 pm.

From March to October there's a bureau on the summit of the Puy de Dôme. If you're coming from the south-west, there's another office in Aurillac (☎ 71.48.68.68) at 10 Rue du Président Delzons (postcode 15000), which is open all year.

THE VOLCANOES
Monts Dômes

This northern range, west of Clermont-Ferrand, consists of a chain of 80 'recent' volcanoes, the best known of which is the **Puy de Dôme** – the highest (1465 metres) and oldest of the group. See Puy de Dôme in the Around Clermont-Ferrand section for more information.

Monts Dores

Three million years older than their northern neighbours, the Monts Dores culminate in the **Puy de Sancy** (1885 metres), the Massif Central's highest point. In winter it's a popular downhill ski station. The spa town of Le Mont Dore lies at its base, making it an ideal summer and winter centre for exploring much of this region. See also Puy de Sancy in the following section on Le Mont Dore.

Monts du Cantal

The south of the park is dominated by the bald slopes of the Monts du Cantal, the remains of a super-volcano worn down over the millennia and one of the Massif Central's wildest areas. The summit is the **Plomb du Cantal** (1858 metres), a lonely, desolate peak, often shrouded in heavy, swirling cloud even in summer. The town of Murat (see the following Murat section) is the best place to base yourself if you want to explore this area.

LE MONT DORE

The little spa town of Le Mont Dore (population 2000; altitude 1000 metres) lies in a narrow valley along the Dordogne River, not far from its source. A road runs south to the base of the Puy de Sancy, the mountain to which Le Mont Dore owes much of its living.

Although it's an architecturally sombre town, built from dark, volcanic stone quarried locally, it is very lively. In winter it attracts skiers, and *curistes* heading for the medicinal spas; in summer it lures hikers and hang-gliders to the heights of the nearby puys. Le Mont Dore is well worth a visit.

Orientation

About 50 km south-west of Clermont-Ferrand, Le Mont Dore measures no more than one km from one end to the other. From the train station, at the north-western end of town, it's a gentle uphill walk to the town centre.

Information

Tourist Office The tourist office (☎ 73.65. 05.71) at Ave de la Libération, in the central park attached to the ice-skating rink, will make free hotel reservations. There is an SNCF information office in the same building. The tourist office is open Monday to Saturday from 9 am to 12.30 pm and 2 to 6.30 pm, Sunday from 10 am to noon and 4 to 6 pm; in winter, Sunday hours are from 9 am to noon and 2 to 5 pm.

Money The Chalus Bank (☎ 73.65.20.78) at Rue Ramond is open weekdays from 8.20 to 11.55 am and 1.35 to 5.25 pm, as is the BNP (☎ 73.65.20.64) at Rue Meynadier.

Post The main post office (☎ 73.65.05.48) at Place Charles de Gaulle is open weekdays from 8 am to noon and 2 to 5 pm, Saturday until noon. From mid-June to mid-September it's open nonstop from 8 am to 7 pm.

Laundry The laundrette (☎ 73.65.52.36) beside the church at 31 Square André is open daily from 10 am to noon and 5 to 7 pm.

Établissement Thermal

The Établissement Thermal (☎ 73.65.05.10) on Place du Panthéon retains some of the columns of the huge hot-springs complex that existed here in Roman times. The waters are known for their curative properties in healing respiratory ailments, particularly asthma. You can purify your system during a session of multiple water, gas and heat

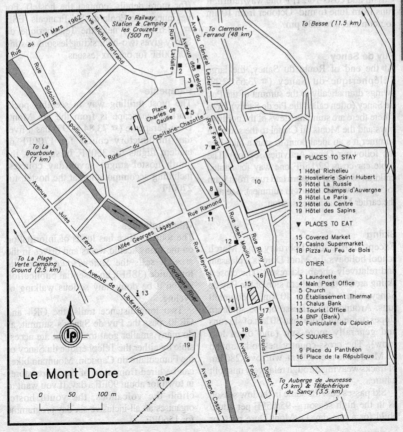

Le Mont Dore

To Railway Station & Camping les Crouzets (500 m)

To Clermont-Ferrand (48 km)

To Besse (11.5 km)

Place Charles de Gaulle

To La Bourboule (7 km)

To La Plage Verte Camping Ground (2.5 km)

Dordogne River

To Auberge de Jeunesse (3 km) & Téléphérique du Sancy (3.5 km)

0   50   100 m

■ PLACES TO STAY

1 Hôtel Richelieu
2 Hostellerie Saint Hubert
6 Hôtel La Russie
7 Hôtel Champs d'Auvergne
8 Hôtel Le Paris
12 Hôtel du Centre
19 Hôtel des Sapins

▼ PLACES TO EAT

15 Covered Market
17 Casino Supermarket
18 Pizza Au Feu de Bois

OTHER

3 Laundrette
4 Main Post Office
5 Church
10 Établissement Thermal
11 Chalus Bank
13 Tourist Office
14 BNP (Bank)
20 Funiculaire du Capucin

✕ SQUARES

9 Place du Panthéon
16 Place de la République

MASSIF CENTRAL

treatments costing from 16FF, depending on what you order. If you'd rather view than participate, guided half-hour tours (5FF) are given on weekdays.

Funiculaire du Capucin

Built in 1898, this funicular railway (☎ 73.65.01.25) tows you in *belle-époque* style to the Pic du Capucin, the 1270-metre-high wooded plateau above the town, which offers great views. From here, you can join up with the GR30, which winds its way south to the Puy de Sancy. The funicular leaves from behind Hôtel des Sapins off Ave René Cassin and costs 16/21FF one way/return. It runs from June to mid-October from 10 am to noon and 2 to 6.30 pm.

Puy de Sancy

At the end of Route du Sancy, the large Téléphérique du Sancy (☎ 73.65.92.23) swings dramatically to the summit of the Puy de Sancy (often called the Pic de Sancy), from where there are stunning views of the northern puys and the Monts du Cantal to the south. In summer it's an ideal point to start a hike (see the following Other Activities section). The cable car costs 22/15FF one way for adults/children or 28/22FF return and runs from 9 am to 5 pm in winter (6 pm in summer). See also the earlier Monts Dores section.

Skiing

Except during the February and March school holidays, Le Mont Dore is a pleasant and relatively cheap ski resort. The closest skiing area is the northern side of the Puy de Sancy, where there are 40 km of downhill runs. Around Super Besse on the southern slopes, there are more than 80 km of ski runs and generally more sun (and often less snow). The cross-country network around Le Mont Dore is excellent, with over 280 km of tracks weaving through relatively unspoilt nature.

Ski passes cost the same in the low season as in the high season – 95/65FF per adult/child for a one-day Le Mont Dore pass, or 105FF for a combined Le Mont Dore-Super Besse pass. There's also a two-day Le Mont Dore pass for 170/115FF; for three or more days, you can get a combined pass, which costs 225/170FF. A free skiers' shuttle bus runs between Le Mont Dore and the Téléphérique du Sancy.

For ski hire, boot-plus-ski prices range from 40 to 100FF depending on the quality. Cross-country skis range from 30 to 42FF. Equipment can be hired from about 15 sport shops in the town.

FUAJ, the youth hostel association, offers a week-long skiing package for 1420FF, including bed, all meals, ski hire and lift pass (for more details, contact the hostel). For beginners, the École du Ski Français (ESF, ☎ 73.65.07.43) near the Téléphérique du Sancy gives two-hour skiing lessons costing 60/300FF for one/six lessons.

Parapente

The most thrilling way to see this pockmarked landscape is from the air. Monts Dore Parapente (☎ 73.84.57.97) has a five-day introductory course for 1700FF or tandem flights for 350FF. In summer, the youth hostel stages seven-day courses, including accommodation at the hostel, for 2700FF.

Other Activities

The tourist office has loads of information on the many scenic walks and drives in the area. It sells the *Sancy/Haute Dordogne* topoguide (38FF), an essential publication if you'll be doing any serious walking or cycling.

Two long-distance trails, the GR4 and GR30, pass the Puy de Sancy's summit, as do many smaller goat tracks that are accessible by either the Téléphérique du Sancy or the Funiculaire du Capucin. Mountain bikes can be hired from most of the sports stores in town for about 90FF a day. If you want to climb the volcanoes, the youth hostel organises an all-inclusive six-day programme for 1560FF.

Places to Stay – bottom end

Accommodation in Le Mont Dore is abundant, but in July and August it's advisable to book ahead.

Camping There are four camping grounds in the vicinity, but the most convenient is the two-star *Les Crouzets* (☎ 73.65.21.60) on Ave des Crouzets just across the river as you exit the train station. It's open all year and charges 9.70/5.40FF per adult/child, plus 5.40FF for a tent site and 3.80FF for a car. *La Plage Verte* (☎ 73.65.04.30) on Route de la Tour d'Auvergne is up on the plateau 2.5 km west of town (there's no public transport). It's open from 15 May to 30 September and charges 10/6/4FF per person/tent/car.

Hostel Ideally situated for summer and winter mountain activities, the *Auberge de Jeunesse* (☎ 73.65.03.53; fax 73.65.26.39) sits in the shadow of the Puy de Sancy, about 3.5 km uphill from the town on Route du Sancy. There's an assortment of rooms, including some with sky-high bunks for the adventurous. Claustrophobic doubles cost twice the single bunk rate. It's open all year (and all day) and charges 43/12/16FF per person for a bed/sheets/breakfast. Book ahead, especially in winter. There's a bus from the train station and the tourist office right to the doorstep. Tickets cost 8.50/12.80FF for a one-way/return trip, with the last bus leaving the station at 5.25 pm.

Hotels The *Hôtel du Centre* (☎ 73.65.03.28) at 8 Rue Jean Moulin, above the lively Café de Paris, is the budget choice, with singles/doubles/triples going for 65/70/85FF. The hall shower is free and the atmosphere swings. For something more sedate, try the *Hostellerie Saint Hubert* (☎ 73.65.01.92) down a quiet, hidden lane at 4 Rue Lavialle. Basic rooms for one or two start at 85FF (125FF with shower), and triples at 140FF. The nearby *Hôtel Richelieu* (☎ 73.65.00.38) on 14 Ave des Belges is similarly priced but musty.

Heading back into the town centre, the friendly *Hôtel La Russie* (☎ 73.65.05.97) on

8 Rue Favart has comfortable singles/doubles from 100FF and triples from 140FF. Across the road, the *Hôtel Champs d'Auvergne* (☎ 73.65.00.37) at No 18 has basic doubles from 99FF, with shower from 145FF.

Opposite the train station, the garishly bright and modern *Hôtel Terminus* (☎ 73.65.00.23) on Ave Guyot Dessaigne has singles/doubles starting at 88FF.

Places to Stay – middle

If you want to hop from your hotel into hot spring water, the *Hôtel Le Paris* (☎ 73.65.01.79; fax 73.65.20.98) at 11 Place du Panthéon is the place to book into. Directly opposite the Établissement Thermal, it has singles/doubles with shower from 260/290FF. Equally grand but for half the price, *Hôtel des Sapins* (☎ 73.65.05.05) at 5 Ave de la Libération has singles/doubles from 130/145FF, or 160/170FF with bath.

Places to Eat

Since many of Le Mont Dore's visitors are here on pension or *demi-pension* packages, you'll find that most of the hotels have restaurants offering good-value *menus*.

Restaurants The restaurant in the *Hôtel Champs d'Auvergne* offers probably the cheapest (48FF) three-course *menu* in town. The *Hostellerie Saint Hubert* has a toasty fireplace and good *menus* from 65FF. The *Hôtel du Centre* serves hearty snacks, including a croque-monsieur for 18FF and omelettes for 25FF. *Pizza au Feu de Bois* (☎ 73.65.25.90) on Ave Foch is as huge and hot as its pizzas, which start at 36FF.

Self-Catering The *Casino supermarket* at Place de la République is open Monday to Saturday from 8 am to 12.30 pm and 3 to 7.30 pm, and Sunday from 8 am to 12.30 pm and 4 to 7 pm. Opposite is a small *covered market* that comes to life in summer only.

Getting There & Away

The train station (☎ 73.92.50.50), at the north-western end of Ave Michel Bertrand, is open Monday to Saturday from 5.30 am to 9 pm, Sunday from 8 am to 10 pm. Connections include Paris's Gare de Lyon (237FF; six hours), for which you have to change trains in Clermont-Ferrand (52FF; 1½ hours; four a day).

LA BOURBOULE

La Bourboule, on the Dordogne River seven km west of Le Mont Dore, is another spa town dating back to Roman times. Its facilities cater for children with allergies and asthma. Although it doesn't have as many star attractions in the immediate vicinity as Le Mont Dore, its setting is equally beautiful and it is an altogether quieter alternative. The tourist office (☎ 73.81.07.99) is on Place de l'Hôtel de Ville.

MURAT

The southern reaches of the Parc des Volcans are best explored from Murat, a small town hidden in a natural amphitheatre dominated by the Bonnevie, a huge basaltic crag from which a white Madonna keeps guard. About 50 km north-east of Aurillac, Murat is conveniently close to the Plomb du Cantal and the neighbouring Puy Mary (1787 metres), as well as the Super Lioran ski station. The GR400, which winds around both these peaks, also passes the town.

Orientation & Information

Murat's little train station sits at the base of the town on Place du 19 Mars 1962. As you leave the station, Ave de la République runs straight up the hill into the town centre.

The tourist office (☎ 71.20.09.47) on Place de l'Hôtel de Ville is open daily during July and August from 10 am to noon and 3 to 7 pm (on Sunday until noon). The rest of the year it is open from 10 am to noon and 2 to 5 pm but is closed on Thursday and Sunday. Regional hiking maps can be bought from the nearby Maison de la Presse.

Things to See

The town's steep streets offer some interesting photo opportunities, or you can take in the whole panorama from the **Bonnevie**, a

strenuous half-hour climb. Good views can also be had from another crag, the **Bredons**, 2.5 km south of town, which is crowned by a 15th-century chapel.

Across the road from the tourist office, the **Maison de la Faune** (☎ 71.20.03.80) has a well-presented display of mainly local fauna, giving a good idea of what to expect if you cross the path of a wild boar.

Places to Stay

The *Camping Municipal* (☎ 71.20.01.83), way to the south of town on Rue de la Stade, charges 8FF per person.

As for hotels, choice is limited to five places, which are often overloaded in July and August. They're all reasonably priced and close to the train station. The cheapest is the *Hôtel du Stade* (☎ 71.20.04.73) at 35 Rue du Faubourg Notre Dame, which has singles/doubles from 95/100FF. The two-star *Les Messageries* (☎ 71.20.04.04) at 18 Ave du Docteur Mallet is plusher, with rooms starting at 210FF.

Getting There & Away

For train information, ring the station on ☎ 71.20.07.20. There are six trains a day both to Clermont-Ferrand (80FF; two hours) and Aurillac (40FF; 1¼ hours). Regional buses are nonexistent. On weekdays there is one bus a day from Murat to Saint Flour (22FF; 30 minutes) leaving at 6.30 pm. From Murat to Aurillac (33FF; 1½ hours) there is also one bus a day – at 6.25 am (during school terms) and at 8.45 am (during school holidays).

Vichy

Vichy (population 27,700) has two very different claims to fame. During the latter half of the 19th century, especially during the *belle époque*, Vichy was a fashionable spa where the rich and famous flocked to revel in concerts, culture and curing waters. During WW II, the puppet government of Marshal Pétain, which ruled what became known as 'Vichy France', was established in the town.

Given France's tendency to forget wartime collaboration, it is hardly surprising that only the earlier of these two periods is in evidence in modern-day Vichy. Leftovers from the town's turn-of-the-century heyday, which began when Napoleon III dipped his toe in Vichy's waters in 1861, are everywhere and range from the Grand Casino and the plush Opera House to the souvenir shops plastered with posters recalling the town's days of elegance and glamour.

Almost all reminders of the period between July 1940 and August 1944, when WW I hero Marshal Philippe Pétain and his collaborationist government helped the German army and the Gestapo rule France, have long since been blotted out. Pétain set up his government here in this so-called 'unoccupied zone' because it was a wealthy town with an excellent telephone network and an abundance of empty hotels for government officials to occupy.

After the war, Vichy never regained its prewar status as a resort. The waters, however, which have been drawing people since Roman times, have retained their reputation as a cure for a multitude of ailments, and still attract primarily elderly curistes in search of relief from their rheumatism, arthritis and digestive and intestinal ailments. In summer they come to take the waters by drinking, nasal inhalations, spraying and wallowing, under the supervision of more than 100 doctors. But the curistes are a dying breed, and these days Vichy is looking more and more to younger members of the fitness-and-beauty set to keep the town bubbling, especially in winter when not much happens.

There's not much to draw non-curistes to Vichy – even in summer – except for its belle-époque charm. Of the nine springs, six are drinkable; the other three are for external use only.

Orientation

Life in Vichy revolves around the stately, triangular Parc des Sources, created in the mid-1800s to impress Napoleon III. On the park's western side is the tourist office, and in pavilions at either end of the park the town's waters bubble forth. Nearby, Rue Georges Clemenceau is the main dining and shopping thoroughfare in the newly pedestrianised city centre.

Sitting on the dammed Allier River, the town's western and southern sides are graced by the Parcs de l'Allier – over two km of wooded parks, once again a legacy of Napoleon III. Across the river is the suburb of Bellerive, where you'll find the youth hostel and camping grounds.

Information

Tourist Office The tourist office (☎ 70.98.71.94) at 19 Rue du Parc is housed in the former Hôtel du Parc, the building from which the Vichy government ruled. It's open from 9 am to noon and 2 to 6.30 pm, but is closed on Saturday afternoon and Sunday. From 1 May to 30 September, it's open daily from 9 am to 12.30 pm and 1.30 to 7 pm, Sunday from 9.30 am to 12.30 pm and 3 to 7 pm. Hotel rooms can be booked free of charge in the office next door (same telephone), which is open similar hours.

Money The Banque de France (☎ 70.98.64.11) at 7 Rue de Paris is open weekdays from 8.40 am to 12.10 pm and 1.30 to 3.30 pm. The Crédit Agricole (☎ 70.32.31.04) at 8 Place d'Allier is open Tuesday to Saturday from 9 am to 12.30 pm and 2.30 to 6 pm. Foreign currency can also be exchanged at the tourist office.

Post The main post office (☎ 70.59.90.90) at Place Charles de Gaulle is open weekdays from 8 am to 7 pm and Saturday until noon.

Vichy's postcode is 03200.

Laundry The little Lavomatique at 37 Rue d'Alsace is open daily from 7 am to 9 pm.

Hall des Sources

The glass Hall des Sources, looking rather run down at the northern end of Parc des Sources, is where four of Vichy's springs

MASSIF CENTRAL

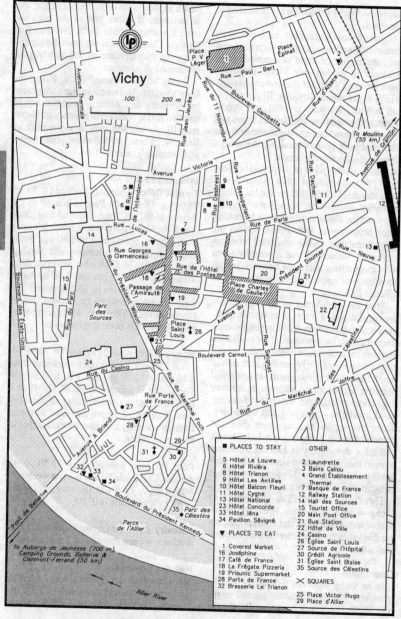

Vichy

■ PLACES TO STAY

5 Hôtel Le Louvre
6 Hôtel Riviéra
8 Hôtel Trianon
9 Hôtel Les Antilles
10 Hôtel Balcon Fleuri
11 Hôtel Cygne
13 Hôtel National
23 Hôtel Concorde
33 Hôtel Iéna
34 Pavillon Sévigné

▼ PLACES TO EAT

1 Covered Market
16 Joséphine
17 Café de France
18 La Frégate Pizzeria
19 Prisunic Supermarket
28 Porte de France
32 Brasserie Le Trianon

OTHER

2 Laundrette
3 Bains Callou
4 Grand Établissement
   Thermal
7 Banque de France
12 Railway Station
14 Hall des Sources
15 Tourist Office
20 Main Post Office
21 Bus Station
22 Hôtel de Ville
24 Casino
26 Église Saint Louis
27 Source de l'Hôpital
30 Crédit Agricole
31 Église Saint Blaise
35 Source des Célestins

✕ SQUARES

25 Place Victor Hugo
29 Place d'Allier

bubble forth. They range in temperature from 18°C to 42°C and in taste from drinkable to disgusting. During the season this place is lined with curistes, cups in hand, comparing ailments and drinking to their health. You can wander in for free but you'll have to pay 8FF to taste any of the waters out of a 1FF plastic cup.

There are two other main springs in the town: the **Source de l'Hôpital** at the southern end of the park; and the **Source des Célestins**, in the park of the same name on Blvd Kennedy.

Thermal Baths

Vichy has two thermal-bath establishments: the blue-domed **Grand Établissement Thermal** and, behind it, the US$20 million **Bains Callou**, Europe's most modern thermal health centre, opened in 1990. Both are on Ave Thermale at the northern end of Parc des Sources.

Although the baths are frequented mainly by long-term clients, it's possible to undergo a single session of any one of an incredible range of processes, ranging from a standard sauna (40FF) to intestinal showers (86FF), dry or wet massages (119 to 172FF), or hand and foot *pulvérisation* (spraying; 234FF).

The baths are generally open Monday to Saturday from 10 am to noon and 4.30 to 8.30 pm.

Other Sights & Activities

The old town south of the Parc des Sources is worth a wander. The old **Église Saint Blaise**, wedded to a new church built in 1935, contains a Black Madonna, patron saint for the sick who visit Vichy in search of a cure.

If you're looking for something to do, the beautiful, English-style **Parcs de l'Allier** are ideal for a picnic. You could catch an organ concert in **Église Saint Louis** on Place Saint Louis (details from the tourist office), or cross the river and engage in many kinds of sport in the huge **Parc Omnisports Pierre Coulon** north-west of town.

Places to Stay

With over 200 hotels to choose from – the majority of them in the one or two-star category – finding somewhere to stay won't be at all difficult. In winter, however, many hotels close for several months.

Camping Nearby camping grounds are numerous but none is open all year. The closest are in a cluster across the river in Bellerive – see the next section for details on how to get there. The one-star *Camping Municipal* (☎ 70.32.30.11), next door to the Auberge de Jeunesse at 17 Rue du Stade, charges 11/18FF for one/two people with a tent and is open from 1 April to 31 October. Nearby, along Rue Claude Décloître, there are another three camping grounds; the two-star *Nouvelle Europe* (☎ 70.32.26.63) charges 34/54FF for one/two persons with a tent and is open from 1 May to 15 September.

Hostel Just over two km south-west of the train station in Bellerive, the *Auberge de Jeunesse* (☎ 70.32.25.14) at 19 Rue du Stade charges 41FF for a bed and 19FF for sheets. It's open from 1 April to 31 October. To get there from the station, take bus No 4 to the Pont de Bellerive stop just across the river. The hostel is behind the Centre Commercial (shopping centre).

Hotels – Train Station Area There are several hotels facing the station, one of the most reasonable being *Hôtel National* (☎ 70.98.28.59) at 105 Ave des Célestins. Singles/doubles start at 80/100FF. Private parking is available. West along Rue de Paris is the similarly priced *Cygne* (☎ 70.98.21.03) at 4 Rue Dacher.

Hotels – City Centre The quiet Rue Desbrest has a cluster of good options. The *Balcon Fleuri* (☎ 70.98.52.38) at No 10 has singles/doubles from 84/110FF, or 100/130FF with shower. The *Trianon* (☎ 70.97.95.96), across the road at No 7, charges 100/110FF. It is closed for three weeks from mid-December. *Les Antilles* (☎ 70.98.27.01) at No 16 has rooms from 100FF.

Overlooking the Parc des Sources, the *Hôtel Concorde* (☎ 70.98.32.63) at 4 Rue du Président Wilson charges 75/120FF. It also has studios for one or two people, available by the week starting at 1000FF. Near the thermal baths, the three-star *Le Louvre* (☎ 70.98.27.71) at 15 Rue de l'Intendance has excellent-value rooms from 150FF and a superb restaurant. Down the road at No 5, *Hôtel Riviéra* (☎ 70.98.22.32) has basic but decent rooms from 100/120FF.

Hotels – Riverfront *Hôtel Iéna* (☎ 70.32. 01.20) at 56 Blvd du Président Kennedy has rooms from 75/100FF, with sunny balconies (at the front only) overlooking the Parcs de l'Allier. Next door at No 50 is Vichy's four-star *Pavillon Sévigné* (☎ 70.32.16.22), the former home of the 17th-century writer Madame de Sévigné, who claimed that Vichy's waters cured her paralysed hand, enabling her to continue writing and thus bring further fame to the town. Don't even think of staying here unless you can afford to pay upwards of 700FF.

Places to Eat

As with hotels, many restaurants are tightly shuttered from October to May.

Restaurants For the best four-course feast in town, head for the *Hôtel Le Louvre* (see Places to Stay), where the 54FF *menu* includes a carafe of wine; you choose the hors d'œuvres and dessert from an extensive buffet. It's available at this price for lunch and dinner except on Saturday night and Sunday.

Nearby, *Joséphine* (☎ 70.98.08.14) at 30 Rue Lucas is a popular creperie/restaurant with salads from 25FF and crepes from 20FF. It is closed on Monday. Around the corner on Rue Georges Clemenceau, *Café de France* (☎ 70.98.20.16) has *menus* from 65FF. There's live jazz on Friday nights. This place is open until 1 am. Across the road in the covered Passage de l'Amirauté you can dine on pizzas at *La Frégate* (☎ 70.97.77.85) at No 26.

Overlooking Parc des Sources, the pretty, pink *Porte de France* (☎ 70.32.14.41) at 7 Rue Porte de France has elegant *menus* from 60FF. For the same price you can wine and dine down by the river in the popular, sunny *Brasserie Le Trianon* (☎ 70.32.14.40) at 60 Blvd Kennedy (closed Tuesday night and Wednesday).

Self-Catering The *covered market* on Place P V Léger is open Monday to Saturday. A large *food market* is held nearby on Place Épinat on Wednesday morning. The *Prisunic* at 16 Rue Georges Clemenceau has an upstairs supermarket that is open Monday to Saturday from 8.30 am to 7.30 pm.

Getting There & Away

Train Vichy's train station (☎ 70.46.50.50 for information) is about one km from the tourist office at the eastern end of Rue de Paris. The information office is open Monday to Saturday from 8.30 am to 12.30 pm and 1.30 to 6 pm.

There are major connections from here to Paris's Gare de Lyon (203FF; three hours; nine a day), Bourges (104FF; two hours; seven a day), Clermont-Ferrand (41FF; 35 minutes; nine a day) and Lyon (113FF; 2¼ hours; six a day).

Bus The bus station is on Place Charles de Gaulle. The information/ticket office (☎ 70. 98.41.33) is open weekdays from 8.30 am to noon and 2 to 6 pm.

Car ADA (☎ 70.98.49.49) is at 44 Ave du Président Doumer.

Getting Around

Vichy's bus system, known as 'Le Bus', operates from the bus station, which is next to the post office on Place Charles de Gaulle. All four lines stop here and at the train station. A single ticket costs 5.20FF; a carnet of 10 is 39FF. Buses stop running at about 7 pm.

Le Puy-en-Velay

Officially known as Le Puy-en-Velay but commonly referred to as Le Puy, this beautiful little town, capital of the département of Haute-Loire, has long attracted travellers to its striking volcanic location – a notable feat considering it's a small place (population 21,000) pretty far from anywhere. Sitting in a fertile valley fed by the Loire, it is surrounded by a landscape of undulating farmland formed long ago by volcanic activity.

During the Middle Ages, Le Puy was an important stop on the pilgrimage trail to Santiago de Compostela (see that aside in the Limousin, Périgord & Quercy chapter) in Spain, and even today the people here are still devoutly Catholic. The pre-Lent carnival is popularly celebrated, and religious statues adorn many house fronts and street corners. The town's top two sights are an enormous red statue of the Madonna and a little chapel perched high up on a volcanic plug.

Because geographical isolation dictated Le Puy's need for self-reliance, local industry flourished from the Middle Ages. By the 17th century the town had become an important centre for the production of fine-quality *dentelle* (lace). Today there's little evidence of the town's lace-making legacy except in the museum and the old town's lace shops, which are struggling to keep the craft alive for touristic purposes.

Le Puy's sights involve a fair bit of climbing, but the effort is worth it.

Orientation

The town centre is surrounded by a circle of boulevards, inside of which is a ring of smaller roads around the heart of the old town. The central hub is Place du Breuil, north of which lies the pedestrianised old town, its narrow streets rising gradually to the cathedral. The train and bus stations are a short hike out of the centre to the east. If you arrive by car, there's shady parking on the western side of Place du Breuil.

Information

Tourist Office The main tourist office (☎ 71. 09.38.41) on Place du Breuil hands out a brochure (in English) with three walking tours to guide you past every conceivable sight. It is open daily from 8.30 am to noon and 1.30 to 6 pm; the exceptions are July and August, when it's open nonstop from 8.30 am to 7.30 pm, and from 1 October to 10 April, when it's closed on Sunday.

On the way to the cathedral there's a tourist office annexe (☎ 71.05.99.02) at 23 Rue des Tables. From June to September it is open Monday to Saturday from 9 am to noon and 2 to 7 pm.

For the sights that charge an entry fee, you might want to buy the 28FF discount combination ticket (possibly available from April to September only), which is sold at both tourist offices or at the sights themselves.

Money The Banque de France (☎ 71.02.18. 66) is to the west of the Musée Crozatier at 30 Blvd Alexandre Clair. It is open weekdays from 8.15 am to noon and 1.30 to 4 pm. There's a cluster of banks around Place du Breuil.

Post The main post office (☎ 71.07.02.00), at 8 Ave de la Dentelle, is open weekdays from 8 am to 7 pm, Saturday to noon.

Le Puy's postcode is 43000.

Laundry The Lavo Self on Rue Chèvrerie is open Monday to Saturday from 7.30 am to noon and 1 to 8 pm.

Old Town

It's well worth spending a few hours exploring the old town. The commercial centre is around Place du Plot and along Rue Pannessac. The latter features many old buildings. Sculptured faces look down from the house of the Michel brothers, situated between Rue du Consulat and Rue Chamarlenc.

Cathédrale Notre Dame

Visible from afar, this unusual cathedral sits at the top of the steep, cobbled Rue des Tables. Originally the site of a Roman temple, it was started in the 11th century and

MASSIF CENTRAL

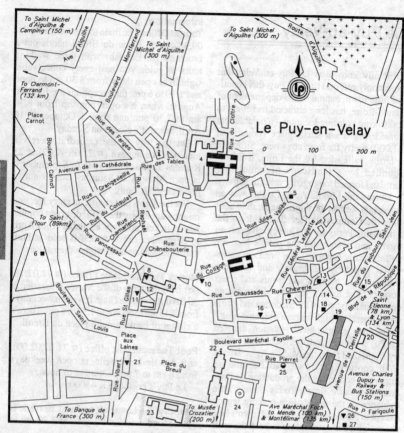

Le Puy-en-Velay

0   100   200 m

PLACES TO STAY	21	Pepino	20	Main Post Office
	26	Casino Supermarket	22	Main Tourist Office
5 Auberge de Jeunesse			23	Jardin Henri Vinay
6 Hostellerie de la Poste		OTHER	25	TUDIP (Local Bus
13 Hôtel Le Veau d'Or				Information)
18 Hôtel Les Cordeliers	1	Rocher Corneille &		
19 Hôtel Le Régional		Statue Notre	✕	SQUARES
27 Hôtel Bristol		Dame de France		
	2	Tourist Office Annexe	7	Place du Plot
▼ PLACES TO EAT	3	Cloisters	12	Plac de la Halle
	4	Cathédrale Notre	14	Place Cadelade
8 Maison Terrasse		Dame	24	Place Michelet
10 La Mamounia	9	Hôtel de Ville		
11 Chantal Paul	15	Verveine Distillery		
16 Boulangerie	17	Laundrette		

added to and renovated in subsequent eras. The result is a Romanesque-style structure adorned with Byzantine features and a colourful striped and patterned porch and façade. The venerated Black Madonna has pride of place on the baroque high altar.

Just to the left through the porch is the entry to the **cloister**, built in the 11th and 12th centuries and adorned with Romanesque friezes. The reliquary chapel has a famous Renaissance fresco entitled *Arts Libéraux*.

Opening hours for the cloister vary with the season. From 1 April to 30 June they're open daily from 9.30 am to 12.30 pm and 4 to 6 pm; from 1 July to 30 September they're open nonstop from 9.30 am to 7.30 pm; from 1 October to 31 March they're open from 9.30 am to noon and 2 to 4.30 pm (without midday closure on Sunday). Admission costs 20FF (12FF for those 18 to 25, 6FF for those under 18).

Rocher Corneille & Statue Notre Dame de France

Topped by the bright-red statue of Notre Dame de France, the massive Corneille Rock rises from the northern end of the old town above the cathedral. Once part of a volcano, it was crowned in 1860 by a 16-metre-high statue of the Madonna (22 metres if you include the bulbous base) made from melted-down cannons captured in the Crimean War. The walk up, which starts behind the cathedral on Rue du Cloître, is well worth it for the superb view of the town and the surrounding Velay countryside.

Opening hours are a bit complicated: from 1 May to 30 September the site is open from 9 am to 7 pm; from mid-March to 30 April it closes at 6 pm; and from 1 October to 15 March it's open from 10 am to 5 pm. Then there are the following exceptions: closed Tuesday from 1 November to 15 March, and closed completely (except Sunday afternoons) all through December and January. Entry costs 9/4.50FF for adults/children.

Saint Michel d'Aiguilhe

Depending on which way you enter Le Puy, this little 10th-century chapel, built high upon what was the vent of an ancient volcano, will be the first or last thing you see. Sitting 80 metres up on a lava pinnacle at the northern end of town (just off Ave d'Aiguilhe), it is reached by 268 steep steps which wind up to the 12th-century bell tower and the beautiful mosaic façade that adorns the chapel doorway.

As for opening hours, the monthly variations could fill a book, but basically it's open daily from 15 March until 31 May from 10 am to noon and 2 to 6 pm; from 1 June to 15 September from 9 am to 7 pm; and from mid-September to mid-November from 9.30 am to noon and 2 to 5.30 pm. The rest of the year it's open only during school holidays, but is closed when there's too much snow or ice for a safe ascent. Entry costs 8/5FF for adults/children. It's about 1.25 km from the main tourist office or slightly less if you cut through the old town. You can also take bus No 6 from Place Michelet, which stops right out the front.

Musée Crozatier

At the southern end of the Jardin Henri Vinay behind the tourist office, the interesting Crozatier Museum (☎ 71.09.38.90) brings together archaeological finds and the works of early regional artisans. There's an impressive collection of lace on the 2nd floor, including an incredible, 500-bobbin *carreau* (the square on which lace was made) complete with the unfinished work.

From 1 May to 30 September the museum is open from 10 am to noon and 2 to 6 pm (closed Tuesday). The rest of the year, it's open until 4 pm and is closed on Sunday morning; it is closed during February. The admission for adults/children is 11/5.50FF, except between October and April when it's free on Sunday afternoons.

Festivals

Le Puy's pre-Lent carnival is celebrated with fervour. The Festival Folklorique International, celebrating music from around the world, is held for a week from mid-July. The Fêtes Renaissance du Roi de l'Oiseau, a frolicking revival of 17th-century Le Puy, takes place in the second week of September.

Places to Stay

Despite its touristic appeal, Le Puy has only a few budget hotels.

Camping Le Puy's only camping ground, *Camping Bouthezard* (☎ 71.09.55.09) just off Ave d'Aiguilhe, couldn't be more impressively located. Dominated by Chapelle Saint Michel d'Aiguilhe, it's spread along the Borne River about 1.25 km from the main tourist office (bus No 6 stops out the front). One person with a tent and car is charged 40.50FF; each extra person costs just 1FF. One/two backpackers with a tent pay 20/29FF. It's open from one week prior to Easter until mid-October.

Hostel High up in the old town, the *Auberge de Jeunesse* (☎ 71.05.52.40; fax 71.02.62.08) at 9 Rue Jules Vallès is part of the Pierre Cardinal cultural centre. It's a welcoming place, with a kitchen and a car park out the back. Reception is generally open from 8 am to 11 pm (11.30 pm in summer). In winter the weekend hours are slightly different: 8 am to noon and 8 to 10 pm. A bed costs 33FF a night. The hostel, which is open all year, is about 600 metres from the train and bus stations, but it's a steep, uphill walk most of the way.

Hotels If you're looking for accommodation with character, there's one obvious choice: *Les Cordeliers* (☎ 71.09.01.12; fax 71.09.30.38) at 17 Rue des Cordelières. Probably the best piece of advice about this place is to see it for yourself. The guy who runs it is full of life and humour, as you'll see from the zany collection of rooms, with décor ranging from Japanese Imperial to full-on mirrors. The more nondescript doubles start from 100FF. There are also huge rooms with full amenities and two double beds for 165 or 215FF, depending on whether you use one or both beds. The hotel's restaurant is equally worthwhile.

Totally opposite is the unpretentious *Hôtel Le Veau d'Or* (☎ 71.09.07.74) above the little café at 7 Place Cadelade. It's friendly enough but dark and austere, with spiral stairs designed to make you dizzy. There are only four rooms, all at 85FF, but not a shower to be found. This place is closed in September.

A block away, the *Hôtel Le Régional* (☎ 71.09.37.74) at 36 Blvd Maréchal Fayolle is larger, with adequate, basic rooms from 90FF; a shower is 15FF extra. It's pleasant but on a noisy intersection. On the other side of town is the more appealing *Hostellerie de la Poste* (☎ 71.09.33.50; fax 71.02.26.13) at 53 Blvd Saint Louis. Singles and doubles with toilet start at 120FF (160FF with a shower in the room). Unfortunately, it too is on a main road much favoured by riders of mopeds with no mufflers.

The *Hôtel Bristol* (☎ 71.09.13.38; fax 71.09.51.70) at 7 Ave Foch is a two-star Logis de France establishment in 1930s style. It's a pleasant place with a quiet garden, and the restaurant isn't bad either. Doubles range from 195 to 280FF.

Places to Eat

Despite the many tourists and relatively expensive accomodation, you'll have no trouble finding meals that are good value.

Restaurants With 16 entrées to choose from and even more desserts, the 69FF four-course *menu* served by *Les Cordeliers* (see Places to Stay) is hard to beat. So is the delicious home-made pineapple sorbet. Needless to say it's an immensely popular place, but there's a large terrace and an even bigger interior where you can generally find a spot. It is closed on Monday in winter.

The *Hostellerie de la Poste* (see Hotels) has an equally enormous choice of dishes, many of them local. There's an exceptionally cheap 45FF *menu* (not available on Sunday), though for a better selection you'll have to order the 60FF one. For the atmosphere of a local diner, try little *Chantal Paul* on Place de la Halle. The five-course lunchtime *menu* starts with salad and ends with a 45FF bill.

La Mamounia (☎ 71.09.11.81) at 4 Rue du Collège is a Moroccan restaurant with couscous for 68FF. *Pepino* at 9 Rue Vibert (closed Tuesday and Sunday) has pizzas cooked in a wood-fired oven starting at 28FF.

Self-Catering A *street market* springs up around the town's oldest fountain on Place du Plot every Saturday morning.

The large *Casino supermarket* on the corner of Rue Farigoule and Ave Maréchal Foch is open Monday to Saturday from 8.30 am to 8 pm. Throughout town are plenty of little corner Casino groceries.

Maison Terrasse at 3 Place du Plot has fine-quality, expensive edibles such as chickens from Bresse as well as fruit and vegetables. It is open on Sunday mornings. Just off Place du Plot, there are a couple of *boulangeries* along Rue Chènebouterie. On Sunday, the *boulangerie* at 45 Blvd Maréchal Fayolle is open until 1 pm.

Things to Buy

If you're after lace, the steep, cobbled Rue des Tables is full of shops where young assistants demonstrate the old craft, which has been all but lost to machines. Liqueur-lovers might want to try the local green or yellow nectar, the Verveine du Velay, a sweet blend of 33 regional plants made in the Verveine distillery on the corner of Rue du Faubourg Saint Jean and Blvd de la République. Though the distillery is not usually open for visits, the shop at the entrance, Pagès, sells the liqueur as well as every other local product, down to gift-wrapped packets of green lentils. Pagès is generally open Monday to Saturday from 10.30 am to noon and 3 to 7 pm; in summer it's also open on Sunday.

Getting There & Away

Train Le Puy's train station (☎ 71.02.50.50 for information) is at the eastern end of Ave Charles Dupuy, about 500 metres from the main tourist office. The information office is open Monday to Saturday from 9 am to 1 pm and 2.30 to 6 pm. The station itself is staffed from 5 am to 11.30 pm.

Trains are not frequent, with just three a day to Clermont-Ferrand (98FF; 2¼ hours), and seven to Saint Étienne (64FF; 1½ hours)

and Lyon's Gare de Perrache (98FF; three hours). South-west to Mende (124FF; 3¾ hours) there are only two trains. You may be better off going by bus because it's both cheaper and quicker.

Bus The bus station (☎ 71.09.25.60) is on Place Maréchal Leclerc, just to the right as you exit the train station. The information office is open Monday to Saturday from 8.30 am to 12.30 pm and 2.30 to 7 pm. Several companies operate regional services from here, including Autocars Hugon Tourisme, which has one or two buses a day to Mende (70FF; two hours).

Getting Around

Local buses are run by TUDIP, which has an information office (☎ 71.05.41.11) at 6 Rue Pierret, which is just past the main local bus hub on Place Michelet. Single tickets cost 5FF, or there are four/10-ticket carnets for 16/35FF. The office is open weekdays from 8.30 am to noon and 1.30 to 6.30 pm (closed Monday morning).

AROUND LE PUY-EN-VELAY

On the outskirts of Le Puy, about five km north-west of the town centre, the remains of the 14th-century **Château de Polignac** sit on a volcanic plateau formed as the surrounding countryside eroded away. The place was once home to the powerful Polignac family, who virtually ruled over Velay from the 11th to the 14th centuries. It can be visited in summer.

The wild **Allier River** west of Le Puy has cut some pretty impressive gorges that are home to small villages lost in time. Head north from Monistrol d'Allier to admire the local churches.

Hikers can explore the highlights of the varied **Velay countryside** by following the GR40. The tourist office in Le Puy can supply the necessary information. The roads around Le Puy offer plenty of scenic drives if you have your own transport.

Provence

Provence spends the vast majority of the year bathed in the most glorious southern sunlight. Along the coast, the Mediterranean reflects and refracts the sun's rays, making for sharp, distinct colours. Inland, the hues are subtler and more subdued: the red-tile roofs and blue skies are softened by an infinite variety of greens (olive green, fruit orchard green, vegetable-leaf green) and by the looming presence of limestone hills, often wrapped in a gentle haze.

Provence's natural charms combine with over two millennia of human enterprise to create a delightful and harmonious whole. Many cities and towns date from at least Roman times and offer a wonderful array of cultural treasures, ranging from Roman theatres (still used for music festivals) and medieval fortifications to outstanding art museums. The region's population centres are furnished with generous public spaces – just as they were under Augustus – and the locals spend a good part of their lives out-of-doors, sipping pastis in a café, perhaps, or playing *pétanque* (bowls).

History

Provence was settled over the centuries by the Ligurians, the Celts and the Greeks, but it was only after its conquest by Julius Caesar in the mid-1st century BC and its integration into the Roman Empire that the region really began to flourish. Many exceptionally well-preserved Roman theatres, aqueducts (particularly the Pont du Gard) and other ancient buildings can still be seen in such towns as Arles, Nîmes and Orange. All these towns played an important role in spreading Roman commerce and civilisation up the Rhône River. After the collapse of the Roman Empire in the late 5th century, Provence suffered invasions by the Visigoths, Burgundians and the Ostrogoths. The Arabs – who for some time held the Iberian Peninsula and parts of France – were eventually defeated in the 8th century.

During the 14th century, the Catholic Church – under a series of French-born popes – moved its headquarters from feud-riven Rome to Avignon, thus beginning the most resplendent period in that city's history. Provence became part of France in 1481-86, but Avignon and the nearby Comtat Venaissin remained under papal control until the Revolution.

Geography

Provence stretches along both sides of the Rhône River from a bit north of Orange down to the Mediterranean, and along France's southern coast from the Camargue salt marshes in the west to Marseille and beyond in the east. East of Marseille is the Côte d'Azur, which though historically part of Provence is covered in this book in a separate chapter.

The spectacular Gorges d'Ardèche, created by the often-torrential Ardèche River, are west of the Rhône. South of Arles, the Camargue marshlands – actually the delta of the Rhône River – are within a triangle formed by the Grand Rhône to the east and the Petit Rhône to the west.

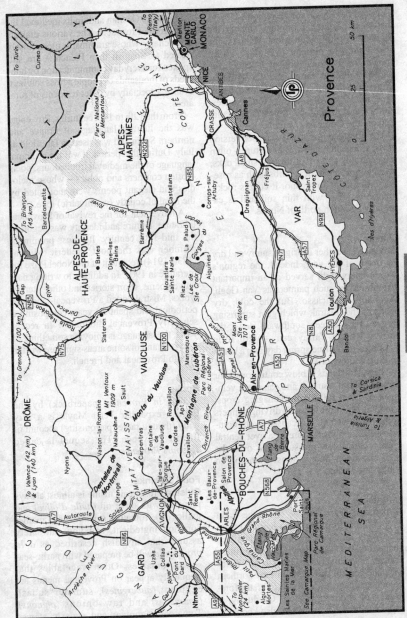

East of the Rhône are the region's famous east-west oriented mountain chains: the Baronnies, 1909-metre Mont Ventoux, the arid Vaucluse plateau (Vaucluse hills), known for its production of lavender, the rugged Lubéron range and the Alpilles. Clinging to the hillsides are picturesque villages made up of sturdy, stone houses. Further east is Europe's most spectacular canyon, the Gorges du Verdon.

The *garrigue* (garigue), a sparser version of the Corsican maquis, is a mixture – often impenetrably spiky – of thistles, small oaks, lavender and Provençal herbs such as rosemary, thyme and oregano. It covers rocky, limestone areas with thin soil and is especially common north of Nîmes.

Climate

Provence's weather is bright, sunny and dry for much of the year. Indeed, the region's extraordinary light served as an important inspiration for such painters as Van Gogh, Cézanne and Picasso. But the cold, dry winds of the mistral, which gain surprising fury as they careen southward down the narrow Rhône Valley can – with little warning – turn a fine spring day into a bone-chilling wintery one.

The mistral tends to blow continuously for several days at a stretch and can reach velocities of over 100 km/h, damaging crops, whipping up forest fires and driving tempers to the fraying point. It is caused by the coincidence of a high-pressure area over central France and a low-pressure area over the Mediterranean and is most common in winter and spring.

Language

A thousand years ago, *oc* (from the Latin *hoc*) and *oïl* (from the Latin *hoc ille*) were the words for 'yes' in the Romance languages of what is now southern and northern France, respectively. As Paris-based influence and control spread, so did the northern French language, the *Langue d'Oïl*, the forerunner of modern French. Gradually, it supplanted the *Langue d'Oc*, also known as Languedoc, Occitan and, in its medieval literary form, Provençal. The various dialects of Occitan – whose grammar is more closely related to Spanish than French – are still spoken for everyday communication by hundreds of thousands of people across southern France, especially by older residents of rural areas.

From the 12th to 14th centuries, Provençal was the literary language of France and northern Spain and was used as far afield as Italy. During that period, it was the principal language of the medieval troubadours, poets – often courtiers and nobles – whose melodies and elegant poems were motivated by the ideal of courtly (or chivalric) love.

A movement for the revival of Provençal literature, culture and identity was begun in the mid-19th century. Its most prominent member was the poet Frédéric Mistral (1830-1914), recipient of the Nobel Prize for literature in 1904. In addition to writing narrative poems, short stories and other literary works, Mistral edited a Provençal-language periodical and spent 20 years composing a scholarly Provençal dictionary. In recent years, the language is enjoying something of a revival, and in some areas signs are written in both Provençal and French.

Books

A Year in Provence (paperback) by the English expatriate Peter Mayle is a very witty (though rather patronising) account of life in Provence. The sequel is called *Toujours Provence*.

Food & Drinks

Cuisine Provençal cuisine is almost always prepared with olive oil (*huile d'olive*) and garlic (*ail*). Tomatoes (*tomates*) are another common ingredient, and you can safely assume that any dish described as *à la provençale* will be prepared with garlic-seasoned tomatoes. Other vegetables that frequently appear on Provençal menus are eggplant (*aubergines*), summer squash (*courgettes*) and raw onions (*oignons*). Tomatoes, eggplant and squash, stewed together along with green peppers, garlic and various aromatic herbs, produce that perennial Provençal favourite, *ratatouille*. But perhaps the vegetable most typical of the region is the artichoke *(artichaut)*.

Aïoli is a sauce prepared by mixing mayonnaise (made with olive oil, of course) with lots of freshly crushed garlic. It is spread generously on hot or cold vegetables, such as asparagus *(asperges)*, eggs, fish, etc.

Provence's most famous soup is *bouillabaisse*, which is made with at least three kinds of fresh fish cooked for 10 minutes or so in broth with onions, tomatoes, saffron and various herbs, including laurel (bay leaves), sage and thyme. It is sometimes prepared with seafood as well. Bouillabaisse, which is eaten as a main course, is usually served with toast and *rouille*, a spicy sauce that some people mix into the soup but which others spread on the toast. The most renowned bouillabaisse is made in Marseille.

Provence is sometimes called 'the garden of France' because of its superb spices, fruits and vegetables, which include garlic, almonds, olives, grapes, cherries, strawberries, fresh figs (both little green ones and large purple ones), apricots, plums, peaches, pears, quince, Cavaillon melons and asparagus. The region is also famous for its locally milled olive oil, honey and fresh goat cheese. Truffles *(truffes)* are harvested from November to April. Depending on the season, all these delicacies are available fresh at local food markets.

Wines Provence's finest (and most renowned) vintage is Châteauneuf-du-Pape, a full-bodied red wine grown 10 km south of Orange which has an alcohol content of up to 15%. The diverse wines known under the name Côtes du Rhône grow at various places along 200 km of the Rhône River, some of them as far north as Vienne (just south of Lyon). The area from Aix-en-Provence eastward to the Var River valley produces *vins ordinaires* – reds, rosés and whites – known as Côtes de Provence.

Pastis, a licorice-flavoured apéritif, can be wonderfully refreshing on a hot day, especially if sipped on a shaded terrace.

Getting There & Away
Boat For information on ferry services from Marseille to Sardinia, Algeria and Tunisia, see Sea in the Getting There & Away chapter. For details on ferries from Marseille to Corsica, see Getting There & Away in the Corsica chapter.

Marseille Region

MARSEILLE
The cosmopolitan and much-maligned port of Marseille (Marseilles), France's second city (population 880,000) and its third most populous urban area (population 1.1 million), is not in the least bit cutsified, spiffified or quaintified for the benefit of tourists. Its urban geography and atmosphere – utterly atypical of Provence, by the way – are a function of the diversity of its inhabitants, the majority of whom are immigrants (or the descendants of immigrants) from Greece, Italy, Armenia, Spain, North Africa (Muslims, Jews, pieds-noirs), West Africa and Indochina. Although Marseille is notorious for organised crime and racial tensions (the extreme right polls about 25% citywide), visitors who like exploring on foot will be rewarded with more sights, sounds, smells and big-city commotion than almost anywhere else in France.

History
Around 600 BC, a trading post known as Massalia (or Massilia) was founded at what is now the city's old port by Greek mariners from Phocaea, a city in Asia Minor. In the 1st century BC, Marseille backed Pompey rather than Caesar, whose forces captured the city in 49 BC and exacted commercial revenge by confiscating the fleet and directing Roman trade elsewhere. Massalia retained its status as a free port and was, for a while, the last Western centre of Greek learning, but the city soon declined and

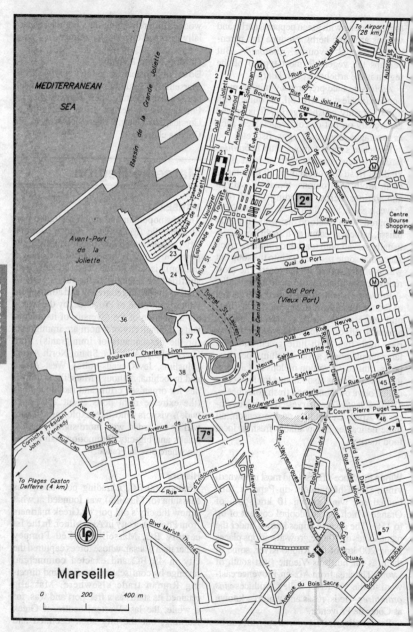

MEDITERRANEAN
SEA

Bassin de la Grande Joliette

Avant-Port
de la
Joliette

PROVENCE

To Airport
(28 km)

Rue Fauchier

Rue de la Joliette

Rue de la République

Centre
Bourse
Shopping
Mall

2e

Grand' Rue

Quai du Port

Old' Port
(Vieux Port)

Quai de Rive Neuve

Boulevard de la Corderie

Cours Pierre Puget

7e

Boulevard Charles Livon

Boulevard André Aune

Corniche Président John F Kennedy

Avenue Pasteur

Avenue de la Corse

Rue Cap Dessemond

To Plages Gaston
Defferre (4 km)

Rue d'Endoume

Blvd Marius Thomas

Avenue du Bois Sacré

Marseille

0   200   400 m

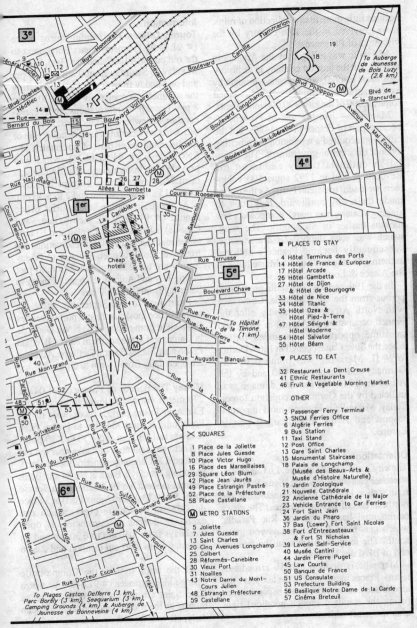

3e

1er

4e

5e

6e

To Auberge
de Jeunesse
de Bois Luzy
(2.6 km)

Blvd de
la Blancarde

To Hôpital
de la Timone
(1 km)

To Plages Gaston Defferre (3 km),
Parc Borély (3 km), Seaquarium (3 km),
Camping Grounds (4 km) & Auberge de
Jeunesse de Bonneveine (4 km)

PROVENCE

■ PLACES TO STAY

4   Hôtel Terminus des Ports
14 Hôtel de France & Europcar
17 Hôtel Arcade
26 Hôtel Gambetta
27 Hôtel de Dijon
    & Hôtel de Bourgogne
33 Hôtel de Nice
34 Hôtel Titanic
35 Hôtel Ozea &
    Hôtel Pied-à-Terre
47 Hôtel Sévigné &
    Hôtel Moderne
54 Hôtel Salvator
55 Hôtel Béarn

▼ PLACES TO EAT

32 Restaurant La Dent Creuse
41 Ethnic Restaurants
46 Fruit & Vegetable Morning Market

OTHER

2   Passenger Ferry Terminal
3   SNCM Ferries Office
6   Algérie Ferries
9   Bus Station
11 Taxi Stand
12 Post Office
13 Gare Saint Charles
15 Monumental Staircase
18 Palais de Longchamp
    (Musée des Beaux-Arts &
    Musée d'Histoire Naturelle)
19 Jardin Zoologique
21 Nouvelle Cathédrale
22 Ancienne Cathédrale de la Major
23 Vehicle Entrance to Car Ferries
24 Fort Saint Jean
36 Jardin du Pharo
37 Bas (Lower) Fort Saint Nicolas
38 Fort d'Entrecasteaux
    & Fort St Nicholas
39 Laverie Self-Service
40 Musée Cantini
45 Jardin Pierre Puget
45 Law Courts
50 Banque de France
51 US Consulate
53 Préfecture Building
56 Basilique Notre Dame de la Garde
57 Cinéma Breteuil

✕ SQUARES

1   Place de la Joliette
8   Place Jules Guesde
10 Place Victor Hugo
16 Place des Marseillaises
29 Square Léon Blum
42 Place Jean Jaurès
49 Place Estrangin Pastré
52 Place de la Préfecture
58 Place Castellane

Ⓜ METRO STATIONS

5   Joliette
7   Jules Guesde
13 Saint Charles
25 Cinq Avenues Longchamp
25 Colbert
28 Réformés-Canebière
30 Vieux Port
31 Noailles
43 Notre Dame du Mont-
    Cours Julien
48 Estrangin Préfecture
59 Castellane

became little more than a collection of ruins. It was revived in the 10th century by the viscounts of Provence.

Marseille was pillaged by the Aragonese in 1423, but the greatest calamity in its history took place in 1720, when plague – brought by a merchant vessel coming from Syria – killed some 50,000 of the city's 90,000 inhabitants.

Marseille – like the rest of Provence – became part of France in the 1480s, but the city soon acquired a reputation for rebelling against the central government. The population enthusiastically embraced the Revolution, and in 1792 some 500 volunteers were sent to defend Paris. As the troops made their way northward, they took to singing a catchy new march composed a few months earlier in Strasbourg. The song, which was soon dubbed *La Marseillaise*, subsequently became France's national anthem. (See the aside on La Marseillaise in the Alsace & Lorraine chapter.)

In the 19th century, Marseille grew prosperous from the colonial trade. Commerce with North Africa grew rapidly after the French occupation of Algeria in 1830, and maritime opportunities expanded further when the Suez Canal opened in 1869. During WW II, Marseille was bombed by the Germans and Italians in 1940 and by the Allies in 1943-44. Further damage was inflicted by the German occupation forces. Today, Marseille is France's most important seaport and is the second-largest port in Europe.

Orientation

The city's main thoroughfare, La Canebière, stretches eastward from the Vieux Port. The train station is north of La Canebière at the northern end of Blvd d'Athènes. The city's commercial heart is around Rue Paradis, which gets more fashionable as you move south. The ferry terminal is at the western end of Blvd des Dames.

Marseille is divided into 16 arrondissements. Places mentioned in the text have the arrondissement number listed in parentheses (using the standard French notation) right after the street address.

Information

Tourist Offices The helpful tourist office (☎ 91.54.91.11; metro Vieux Port), next to the old port at 4 La Canebière (1er), is open Monday to Saturday from 9 am to 7.30 pm and on Sunday from 10 am to 5 pm. During the summer, it is open daily from 8.30 am to 8 pm. Local hotel reservations are free; reservations elsewhere in France cost 22FF. The office has on hand an extensive collection of free brochures on all parts of the country. The SNCF desk (☎ 91.95.14.31), which can provide train information and sell tickets, is open Monday to Friday (except holidays) from 9.15 am to 12.30 pm and 2 to 5.30 pm.

At the train station, the tourist office annexe (☎ 91.50.59.18; metro Gare Saint Charles) is behind Voie E (platform E) next to the main entrance. Hotel reservations are free here, too. It is open Monday to Friday from 9 am to 12.30 pm and 2 to 6.30 pm; during July and August, it's open Monday to Saturday from 9 am to 7 pm.

From June to mid-September, there are tourist office kiosks at the old port (Quai des Belges); in front of Basilique Notre Dame de la Garde; and at the southern end of Blvd du Prado near Plages Gaston Defferre. All three are open daily from 10 am to 6 pm.

Money The Banque de France (☎ 91.04.10.27; metro Estrangin Préfecture) at Place Estrangin Pastré (6e), a block west of the Prefecture, is open Monday to Friday from 8.45 am to 12.30 pm and 1.30 to 3.30 pm.

There are a number of banks near the old port on La Canebière (metro Vieux Port), including Barclay's Bank at No 34 and Bank Leumi France at No 29. Change de la Bourse (☎ 91.54.10.13; metro Vieux Port) at 3 Place du Général de Gaulle (1er), which can exchange dozens of currencies, is open weekdays from 8.30 am to 6.30 pm and on Saturday from 8.30 am to noon and 2 to 6 pm.

At the train station, the Comptoir de Change Méditerranéen (☎ 91.84.68.88; metro Gare Saint Charles) – the only exchange bureau in town open on Sunday – is open daily, all year from 8 am to 6 pm. Unfortunately, the rates are quite dismal. The banknote exchange machine at the tourist office operates whenever the office is open.

American Express (☎ 91.91.41.72; metro Vieux Port or Noailles) at 39 La Canebière (1er) can change money, issue cash advances and take care of lost or stolen travellers' cheques and American Express cards. It is open weekdays from 8 am to 6 pm and on Saturday from 8 am to noon and 2 to 5 pm.

Post The main post office (☎ 91.95.47.32; metro Colbert) at 1 Place de l'Hôtel des Postes (1er) is open weekdays from 8 am to 7 pm and on Saturday from 8 am to noon. Exchange services are available.

Near the train station, the post office (☎ 91. 50.89.25; metro Gare Saint Charles) at 11 Rue Honnorat (3e) – which does not change currency – is open weekdays from 8.30 am to 6.30 pm and on Saturday from 8.30 am to noon.

Postcode Marseille's postcode consists of the digits 130 plus the arrondissement number (01 through 16). As in the Paris listing, '1er' means '1st arrondissement' (postcode 13001) and '6e' means '6th arrondissement' (postcode 13006).

Foreign Consulates The UK Consulate (☎ 91. 53.43.32; metro Castellane) is near Place Castellane at 24 Ave du Prado (6e). It's open Monday to Friday from 9 am to noon and 2 to 5 pm.

The US Consulate (☎ 91.54.92.00; metro Estrangin Préfecture) is at 12 Blvd Paul Peytral (6e) near the Prefecture building. The American services section is open weekdays from 8.30 am to noon and 1 to 5.30 pm.

Travel Agencies Voyages Wasteels (☎ 91. 95.90.12; metro Noailles) at 87 La Canebière (1er) sells BIJ tickets and offers the usual services of a travel agent. It is open Monday to Saturday from 9 am to 12.30 pm and 2 to 6.30 pm (5.30 pm on Saturday).

Bookshops Librairie Feuri Lamy (☎ 91.33. 57.91; metro Vieux Port) at 21 Rue Paradis

(1er) has a collection of English-language novels. It is open Tuesday to Saturday from 9 am to noon and 2 to 7 pm and on Monday from 2 to 7 pm. Lonely Planet guides are available from FNAC on the 2nd floor of the Centre Bourse shopping centre (metro Vieux Port), which is off Cours Belsunce (1er).

Laundry The Laverie Self-Service (metro Vieux Port) at 5 Rue Breteuil (1er) is open daily from 7 am to 8 pm.

Medical Services Hôpital de la Timone (☎ 91. 38.60.00; metro La Timone) is at 264 Rue Saint Pierre (5e).

Dangers & Annoyances Despite the city's fearsome reputation for underworld criminality, the streets of Marseille are probably no more dangerous than those of other French cities. Unfortunately, a number of popular English-language guidebooks seem to have collected their information on street crime in Marseille at a convention of the racist Front National, whose propaganda often blames crime (and the rest of France's problems) on immigrants from North Africa.

As elsewhere, street crime (bag-snatching, pickpocketing) is best avoided by keeping your wits about you and your valuables hard to get at. Guard your luggage very carefully, especially at the train station, and *never* leave anything inside a parked motor vehicle. As usual, problems can be minimised with a money belt.

It is probably a good idea for lone visitors – especially women and, as one policeman I talked to put it, men who are not 'muscle-men-gorillas' – to avoid at night the Belsunce area, a poor, immigrant neighbourhood southwest of the train station bounded by La Canebière, Blvd d'Athènes, Rue Bernard du Bois, Cours Belsunce and Rue d'Aix. In general, you are best off arriving in Marseille during the day.

Walking Tours
Old Port Area Marseille grew up around the old port (metro Vieux Port), where ships have docked for at least 26 centuries. The

PROVENCE

main commercial docks were transferred to the coast north of here in the 1840s, but the old port is still active as a harbour for fishing craft, pleasure yachts and ferries to the Château d'If. The harbour entrance is guarded by **Fort Saint Nicolas** (on the south side) and, across the water, **Fort Saint Jean**, founded in the 13th century by the Knights Hospitaller of St John of Jerusalem. Most of the present structure dates from the 17th century.

In 1943, the neighbourhood on the north side of the Quai du Port – at the time a seedy area with a strong Résistance presence – was systematically dynamited by the Germans. It was rebuilt after the war. There are two museums near the 17th-century **Hôtel de Ville**: the Musée des Docks Romains and the Musée du Vieux Marseille. The **Panier Quarter**, most of whose residents are North African immigrants, is a bit further north. The Centre de la Vieille Charité museum sits at the top of the hill.

On the south side of the old port, the lively **Place Thiars** pedestrian zone (1er; metro Vieux Port), with its many late-night restaurants and cafés, stretches southward from Quai de Rive Neuve.

To get from one side of the harbour entrance to the other, you can walk through the Tunnel Saint Laurent, which surfaces in front of the cathedral (near Fort Saint Jean) and, on the south side, just east of Fort Saint Nicolas. It replaced a *pont à transbordeur* (transporter bridge) – a high framework from which a platform that moved from shore to shore was suspended – which was destroyed in August 1944 when German forces wrecked the harbour before attempting to withdraw (they were instead surrounded and captured).

The most lively part of Marseille – always crowded with people of all races and ethnic groups – is around the intersection of La Canebière and Cours Belsunce (metro Vieux Port or Noailles). The Musée de la Marine is inside the imposing Chambre de Commerce building, while the nearby **Centre Bourse** shopping centre houses the Musée d'Histoire de Marseille. The area north of La Canebière

and east of Cours Belsunce, known as the **Belsunce area** (metro Noailles), is a poor immigrant neighbourhood. A walk around (not recommended at night) is like a quick trip to Algiers.

Also worth a stroll is the more fashionable **6th arrondissement**, especially the area between La Canebière and the **Prefecture building** (metro Estrangin Préfecture). Rue Saint Ferréol, half a block east of the Musée Cantini, is a pedestrian shopping street.

Along the Coast Another fine place for a stroll during the day (and, in the summer, at night) is along **Corniche Président John F Kennedy** (7e), which runs along the coast for 4.5 km. It begins 200 metres west of the **Jardin du Pharo**, a park with nice views of the port, and continues southward to Plages Gaston Defferre and **Parc Borély**, a large park that encompasses the **Jardin Botanique** and 18th-century **Château Borély** (☎ 91.73.21.60), now a museum. The **Seaquarium** (☎ 91.71.00.46) is a large aquarium at Place Amiral Muselier (8e), near Plages Gaston Defferre.

Along almost its entire length, Corniche Président John F Kennedy is served by bus No 83, which goes to both the old port (Quai des Belges) and the Rond-Point du Prado metro stop.

Museums
Except where noted, the museums listed below are open from 10 am to 5 pm daily except Monday; from June to September, hours are 11 am to 6 pm. All admit teachers with some sort of identifying document and students for half the price indicated. People over 65 get in free.

Centre de la Vieille Charité The Old Charity Cultural Centre (☎ 91.56.28.38; metro Joliette) is at 2 Rue de la Charité (2e) in the mostly North African Panier Quarter. The superb permanent exhibits and imaginative temporary exhibitions are housed in a workhouse and hospice built between 1671 and 1745 and recently restored after serving as a barracks (1905), a rest home for soldiers (during WW I) and low-cost housing for people who lost their homes in WW II. Three levels of arcades surround the courtyard, in whose centre is a chapel topped with an egg-shaped dome.

The regular entrance fee is 10FF for the museum of Mediterranean archaeology, 10FF for the museum of African art, 20FF for the special exhibitions and 25FF for everything. Concerts and other cultural event are held here in the summer.

Musée du Vieux Marseille The Museum of Old Marseille (☎ 91.55.28.72; metro Vieux Port), which is behind the 17th-century Hôtel de Ville at 2 Rue de La Prison (2e), occupies the mid-16th-century Maison Diamantée, so named because of the diamond-shaped stone lozenges on its façade. Displays include antique Provençal household items, playing cards (for which Marseille has been known since the 17th century) and the equipment to make them, and photos of the city under German occupation. Entrance costs 10FF.

Musée Cantini Musée Cantini (☎ 91.54.77.75; metro Estrangin Préfecture), off Rue Paradis at 19 Rue Grignan (6e), has a permanent exhibit of 17th and 18th-century Provençal ceramics and rotating exhibitions of modern and contemporary art. The entrance fee is 10FF (15FF during exhibitions).

Musée d'Histoire de Marseille Roman history buffs might want to check out the Marseille Historical Museum (☎ 91.90.42.22; metro Colbert), which is just north of La Canebière on the ground floor of the Centre Bourse shopping mall (1er). Exhibits include the freeze-dried remains of a merchant vessel – discovered by accident in 1974 – that plied the waters of the Mediterranean in the late 2nd century AD. The 19-metre-long timbers, which include five different kinds of wood, show evidence of having been repaired repeatedly. To preserve the soaked and decaying wood, the whole thing was freeze-dried right where it now sits. Year round, the museum is open Monday to Saturday from noon to 7 pm. The entrance fee is 10FF.

Roman buildings, uncovered during construction of the shopping centre, can be seen just outside the museum in the **Jardin des Vestiges** (Garden of Ruins), which fronts Rue Henri Barbusse (1er).

Musée des Docks Romains The Museum of Roman Warehouses (☎ 91.91.24.62; metro Vieux Port), on the north side of the old port at Place Vivaux (2e), displays *in situ* part of the 1st-century AD Roman warehouses and docks discovered in 1947 during the archaeological excavations that preceded the rebuilding of this area. The huge jars could store 800 to 2000 litres. Entrance costs 10FF.

Chambre de Commerce The colonnaded Chamber of Commerce building on La Canebière, built from 1854 to 1860, houses the **Musée de la Marine** (Naval Museum; (☎ 91.39.33.33; metro Vieux Port), which costs 10FF (5FF for students and people over 60). For about half the year, the ship models and engravings are replaced by an art exhibition (35FF; no reduction for students). Both are open daily (with the possible exception of Tuesday) from 9 or 10.30 am to 6 or 6.30 pm. King Alexander I of Yugoslavia was assassinated by a Croatian separatist agent right outside the Chambre de Commerce building in 1934.

Palais de Longchamp Colonnaded Longchamp Palace (metro Cinq Avenues Longchamp), constructed in the 1860s, is at the eastern end of Blvd Longchamp on Blvd Philippon (4e). It was designed in part to disguise a *château d'eau* (water tower) – an apparatus that delivers water at the desired pressure – built at the terminus of an aqueduct from the Durance River. The two wings house the **Musée des Beaux-Arts** (☎ 91.62.21.17), whose speciality is 15th to 19th-century paintings, and the **Musée d'Histoire Naturelle** (☎ 91.62.30.78).

PROVENCE

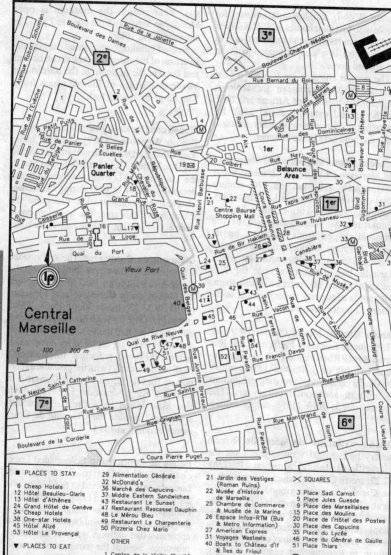

Central Marseille

0   100   200 m

Basilique Notre Dame de la Garde

If you like great panoramic views or over-wrought 19th-century architecture, consider a walk up to Basilique Notre Dame de la Garde, an enormous Romano-Byzantine basilica one km south of the old port. It stands on the highest point in the city, a hilltop 162 metres above sea level.

The site had long served as a look-out when the first chapel here was built by a hermit in 1241. In the 16th century, the chapel became a place of pilgrimage, especially for sailors who started a tradition of bringing the votive offerings (ex-votos) that decorate the structure's interior. The present domed basilica, ornamented with all manner of coloured marble, intricate mosaics, murals and gilded objects, was erected between 1853 and 1864. The bell tower is topped by a nine-metre-high gilded statue of the Virgin Mary.

The basilica and the crypt are open daily from 7.30 am to 5.30 pm (7 am to 7.30 pm in the summer). Bus No 60 links the old port (Cours Jean Ballard) with the basilica.

Nouvelle Cathédrale

Marseille's Romano-Byzantine cathedral (☎ 91.90.53.57; metro Joliette), just off Quai de la Tourette (2e), is topped with cupolas, towers and turrets of all shapes and sizes. The structure, built from 1852 to 1893 – a period not known for decorative understatement – is enormous: 140 metres long and 60 metres high (from the ground to the top of the cross). It dwarfs the nearby **Ancienne Cathédrale de la Major**, a mid-11th-century Provençal-Romanesque structure that stands on the site of what was once a temple of Diana. It is presently closed to the public because pieces of the ceiling keep falling in.

The Nouvelle Cathédrale is open from 9 am to noon and 2.30 to 6 pm (closed Monday). From mid-June to mid-September, it is open every day and does not close at midday except on Sunday and Monday.

Château d'If

The Château d'If (☎ 91.59.02.30), the 16th-century fortress-turned-prison made infamous by Alexandre Dumas's classic work of fiction, *The Count of Monte Cristo*, is on a three-hectare island 3.5 km west of the entrance to the old port. Among the people incarcerated here were all sorts of political prisoners, hundreds of Protestants (many of whom perished in the dungeons), the Revolutionary hero and legendary seducer Mirabeau (brought here for six months at the request of his father), the rebels of 1848 and the Communards of 1871. The Île d'If is not particularly interesting unless you've read the book or love either prisons or islands.

The chateau can be visited daily from 9 am to 6 pm (or whenever the last boat of the day returns to Marseille). The entrance fee is 25FF (14FF for people aged 18 to 24 and over 60).

Boats (☎ 91.55.50.09; metro Vieux Port) to the Château d'If leave from the old port (Quai des Belges) about once an hour from 9 am to noon and 2 to 5 pm. The 20-minute trip costs 35FF return. In summer, the last boat to the island departs at 6 or 6.30 pm.

Îles du Frioul

The islands of Ratonneau and Pomègues, each of which is about 2.5 km long, are few hundred metres from the Château d'If. They were linked by a dyke in the 1820s. For over two centuries starting in the 1600s, the islands were used as a place of quarantine for people suspected of carrying plague or cholera, diseases which could bring catastrophe if brought ashore. Today, the rather barren islands – whose total area is about 200 hectares – shelter seabirds, rare plants and bathers and are dotted with fortifications (used by German troops during WW II) and the ruins of the old quarantine hospital, **l'Hôpital Caroline**. A number of cultural events are held here in the summer.

The boats to the Château d'If also serve the Îles du Frioul. The trip out here from Marseille costs 35FF return; the charge is 55FF return if you also want to stop off at the Château d'If.

Beach

Marseille's main beach, one-km-long

Plages Gaston Defferre (formerly Plage du Prado), is four km south of the city centre. To get there, take bus No 19, 72 or 83 from the Rond-Point du Prado metro stop or bus No 83 from the old port (Quai des Belges). On foot, you can follow Corniche Président John F Kennedy, which runs along the coast.

Places to Stay

The hotels around the train station are convenient if you arrive by rail, but places elsewhere around town offer much better value.

The good news is that Marseille has some of France's cheapest hotels – you can still find rooms for 50FF a night! The bad news is that many of these establishments are filthy dives in unsafe areas whose sideline is renting out rooms by the hour. Some of them don't even have any showers! I've mentioned where such 'bargains' can be found, but all of the places listed by name in this section are reputable and relatively clean.

Places to Stay – bottom end

Camping Tents can be set up on the grounds of the *Auberge de Jeunesse de Bois Luzy* (☎ 91.49.06.18) for 22FF per person. See Hostels for more information.

Camping Municipal Les Vagues at 52 Ave de Bonneveine (8e) and *Camping de Bonneveine* at 187 Ave Clot Bey (8e), both of which are 4.5 km south of the city centre near Plages Gaston Defferre, are presently closed. Rumour has it that one of them (probably Bonneveine) *may* be reopened – contact the tourist office for an update. To get out there, take bus No 44 from the Rond-Point du Prado metro stop.

Hostels The *Auberge de Jeunesse de Bonneveine* (☎ 91.73.21.81) is about 4.5 km south of the city centre at 47 Ave Joseph Vidal (8e). A bed in a six-person room costs 71FF for the first night and 56FF for subsequent nights, including breakfast. A place in a two or four-person room is 79FF a night. There's no curfew from April to December. Valuables should be kept in the automatic lockers (5FF each time you open them). To

get to the youth hostel, take bus No 44 from the Rond-Point du Prado metro stop and get off at the Place Bonnefon stop. You can also take bus No 19 from the Castellane metro stop or bus No 47 from the Sainte Marguerite Dromel metro stop.

There's another youth hostel, the *Auberge de Jeunesse de Bois Luzy* (☎ 91.49.06.18), at 76 Ave de Bois Luzy (12e), which is 4.5 km east of the city centre in the Montolivet neighbourhood. Beds cost 40FF; breakfast is 16FF. A hostelling card is mandatory. To get out there, take bus No 6 from near the Réformés Canebière metro stop or bus No 8 from La Canebière.

Hotels – Train Station Area The one-star *Hôtel Beaulieu-Glaris* (☎ 91.90.70.59; fax 91.56.14.04; metro Gare Saint Charles) is down the grand staircase from the train station at 1-3 Place des Marseillaises (1er; see the Central Marseille map). Plain and poorly maintained singles with washbasin are 110 to 120FF; similar doubles/triples cost 130/180FF. Singles/doubles/triples with shower and toilet are 180/190/230FF. Hall showers are 15FF. Breakfast is 25FF (don't let them put it on your bill if you don't want it). The rooms overlooking the street are noisy.

The old-fashioned and rather run-down but friendly *Hôtel de France* (☎ 91.90.18.82; metro Gare Saint Charles) at 1 Blvd Maurice Bourdet (1er; see the Marseille map) has basic singles/doubles/triples with washbasin and bidet for 95/180/200FF, including breakfast. Doubles/triples with shower are 200/220FF. Hall showers cost 15FF. The rooms overlooking the street are noisy.

There's a cluster of small, extremely cheap hotels of less-than-pristine reputation along Rue des Petites Maries (1er).

Hotels – North of La Canebière All the hotels in this section can be found on the Marseille map.

Allées Léon Gambetta (1er) is home to several quite decent establishments. The *Hôtel Gambetta* (☎ 91.62.07.88; metro

Réformés Canebière) at No 49 has singles without shower for 90FF and singles/doubles with shower from 120/150FF. Hall showers are 15FF, but if you stay a few days the friendly proprietor may throw one in for free.

The *Hôtel de Dijon* (☎ 91.62.62.22; metro Réformés Canebière) at No 33 has fairly large, pleasant singles and doubles for 92 or 104FF and doubles/triples with shower from 140/180FF. Hall showers are 20FF.

The *Hôtel de Bourgogne* (☎ 91.62.19.49; metro Réformés Canebière) at No 31 has singles and doubles with washbasin from 100FF; triples cost 160FF. Rooms with a shower for one or two people are 180FF. None of the rooms have private toilets. Hall showers are free. If there's space, an extra bed costs 30FF.

The *Hôtel Ozea* (☎ 91.47.91.84; metro Réformés Canebière) is at 12 Rue Barbaroux (1er), which is across Square Léon Blum from the eastern end of Allées Léon Gambetta. This place, which welcomes new guests 24 hours a day (late at night just ring the bell three times to wake up the night clerk), has clean, old-fashioned doubles without/with shower for 100/130FF. There are no hall showers.

The *Hôtel Pied-à-Terre* (☎ 91.92.00.95; metro Réformés Canebière) is down the street at 18 Rue Barbaroux (1er). The well-kept singles and doubles, which cost 100/130FF without/with shower, are a bit on the small side. Hall showers cost 20FF. Reception is open until 1 am.

Hotels – South of La Canebière There are lots of rock-bottom hotels – most run by North African immigrants – along Rue Sénac de Meilhan, Rue Mazagran and Rue du Théâtre Français and around Place du Lycée (all metro Réformés Canebière). A bit to the west, Rue des Feuillants (metro Noailles) also has a number of one-star hotels.

The downmarket *Hôtel Titanic* (☎ 91.48.01.56) at 27 Rue Sénac de Meilhan (1er), which is considerably less luxurious than its namesake (and *much* less likely to strike an iceberg), has singles/doubles with wash-basin and bidet from 50/70FF. Hall showers cost 15FF. The rooms are dilapidated and not the cleanest but you can certainly sleep in them, whatever the neighbours may be doing.

The *Hôtel de Nice* (☎ 91.48.73.07), down the block at 11 Rue Sénac de Meilhan, is a step up from most other places in the area. Doubles without/with shower are 120/140FF; hall showers cost 20FF per person. Both these places accept new guests 24 hours a day. See the Marseille map for their location.

The *Hôtel Le Provençal* (☎ 91.33.11.15; metro Vieux Port), a few blocks from the old port at 32 Rue Paradis (1er; see the Central Marseille map), has singles and doubles from 90FF and doubles/triples with shower for 120/180FF. Hall showers are 15FF; breakfast is 21FF.

Hotels – Prefecture Area All the hotels in this section are on the Marseille map.

The *Hôtel Salvator* (☎ 91.48.78.25; metro Estrangin Préfecture) at 6 Rue Salvator (6e) is in a decent area half a block east of the Prefecture building. Doubles with high ceilings and almost-antique furniture cost 90/120FF without/with shower. Hall showers are 20FF.

The two-star *Hôtel Sévigné* (☎ 91.81.29.20; metro Estrangin Préfecture) at 28 Rue Breteuil (6e) has singles and doubles with shower, toilet, tile floors and exceptionally high ceilings for 120 to 150FF. Triples are 220 to 240FF. There's a public parking lot nearby at 22 Rue Breteuil. Overall, it's an excellent deal. You might also try the *Hôtel Moderne* (☎ 91.53.29.93; metro Estrangin Préfecture), which is next door at 30 Rue Breteuil (1er). Rooms start at 85FF with washbasin and bidet, 100FF with shower and 150FF with shower and toilet.

The 18-room *Hôtel Béarn* (☎ 91.37.75.83; metro Estrangin Préfecture) at 63 Rue Sylvabelle (6e) has quiet, colourfully decorated singles/doubles for 85/100FF (with shower) and 140/140FF (with shower and toilet). Two-bed doubles and triples with shower and toilet are 180FF. Guests can

PROVENCE

watch TV in the common room. Breakfast is 20FF. Reception closes at 11 pm or midnight.

Hotels – Ferry Terminal Area

The *Hôtel Terminus des Ports* (☎ 91.90.22.47; metro Joliette) at 59 Blvd des Dames (2e; see the Marseille map) is only one block from the ferry terminal. Singles/doubles cost 100/150FF with shower and 62/100FF without; use of the hall shower costs 15FF. Reception is open from 7 am to 1 am. There are a couple of other hotels nearby on Rue Mazenod.

Places to Stay – middle

Down the grand staircase from the train station, the two-star *Hôtel d'Athènes* (☎ 91. 90.03.83, 91.90.12.93; metro Gare Saint Charles) at 37-39 Blvd d'Athènes (1er; see the Central Marseille map) has average but well-kept singles and doubles with shower and toilet for 190FF. The hotel's one-star section, known as the Hôtel Little Palace, offers somewhat cheaper rooms, including quads for 220FF.

Places to Stay – top end

At the old port, the elegant *Hôtel Alizé* (☎ 91.33.66.97; 91.54.80.06; metro Vieux Port) at 35 Quai des Belges (1er; see the Central Marseille map) has pleasant, fairly spacious singles/doubles with air-con and soundproofed windows for 275/295FF (335/355FF with a view of the old port). Breakfast is 35FF.

The friendly, venerable *Grand Hôtel de Genève* (☎ 91.90.51.42; fax 91.90.76.24; metro Vieux Port) at 3bis Rue Reine Elisabeth (1er; see the Central Marseille map) is a three-star place that, though rather tastelessly modernised (there's pine panelling in the stairwell!), hasn't lost all of the old-time charm promised by the façade. Large rooms with TV for one, two or three people cost 290FF; even bigger rooms with air-con are 380FF. Air-con suites with a view of the port are 450FF. The buffet breakfast costs 40FF.

Near the train station, the clean, safe and predictable *Hôtel Arcade* (☎ 91.95.62.09; fax 91.50.68.42; metro Gare Saint Charles) is at 1 Square Narvik (1er; see the Marseille map), which is on the south side of the terminal building on the same level as the tracks. The 172 singles/doubles/triples/quads cost 285/310/360/360FF. Breakfast is 35FF.

Places to Eat

Marseille's restaurants offer an incredible variety of cuisines. Unless otherwise noted, all of the places listed below are on the Central Marseille map.

Restaurants – French & Regional

Along the Quai de Rive Neuve (1er), there are quite a few touristy places offering bouillabaisse. One place you might try is *Restaurant Rascasse Dauphin* (☎ 91.33.17.25; metro Vieux Port) at No 6, which has *menus* for 59 and 75FF and bouillabaisse for 75FF (110FF with prawns). It is open from 11.30 am to 2.30 pm and 6.30 to 11 pm daily except Thursday (daily from June to September). The bouillabaisse restaurants along Quai du Port are somewhat more expensive.

The pedestrian streets around Place Thiars are crowded with cafés and restaurants, especially in the summer. The up-market *La Charpenterie* (☎ 91.54.22.89; metro Vieux Port) at 22 Rue de la Paix (1er) specialises in regional cuisine, including bouillabaisse (140FF per person; call ahead half a day in advance), crab soup (35FF), hot oysters (six for 48FF), mussels (38FF) and various kinds of fish. There are *menus* for 98 and 160FF. This place is open Monday to Saturday from noon to 2.30 pm and 7.30 to 10.30 pm.

Another popular seafood place is *Le Mérou Bleu* (☎ 91.54.23.25, 91.54.21.00; metro Vieux Port) at 32-34 Rue Saint Saëns (1er), which has seafood dishes (62 to 95FF), hot first courses (40 to 80FF), pasta, etc. The *menu* costs around 100FF. *Pizzeria Chez Mario* (☎ 91.54.48.54; metro Vieux Port) at 8 Rue Euthymènes (1er) has pizzas (32 to 40FF), pasta (50FF), fish and grilled meats (85 to 110FF). It is open daily from noon to 2.30 pm and 7.30 pm (8 pm from June to September) to 11.30 pm

Restaurant La Dent Creuse (☎ 91.42.05.67;

metro Noailles) is just south of La Canebière at 14 Rue Sénac de Meilhan (1er; see the Marseille map). Main dishes start at 38FF; lunch/dinner *menus* cost 50/79FF. This place is open Tuesday to Friday from noon to 2 or 2.15 pm and 7.30 pm to midnight, Saturday and Sunday from 7.30 pm to midnight, and Monday from noon to 2.15 pm.

Restaurants – North African The *Roi du Couscous* (☎ 91.91.45.46; metro Colbert or Jules Guesde) at 63 Rue de la République (2e) serves couscous for 40 to 60FF. It is open from noon to 2.30 or 3 pm and 7.30 to 10.30 pm (closed Monday).

Restaurants – Ethnic Cours Julien (metro Notre Dame du Mont-Cours Julien; 6e), which is a few blocks south of La Canebière, offers an incredible variety of cuisines: Antillean, Pakistani, Thai, Lebanese, Tunisian, Italian and so forth. See the Marseille map for its location.

On the north side of the old port, *Restaurant Hoan Kim* (☎ 91.91.01.32) at 7 Rue Bonneterie (2e) is open Monday to Saturday from noon to 2.30 pm and 7 to 11.30 pm. This place has Vietnamese and Chinese *menus* for 50 to 60FF but they're not available in the evening on Friday or Saturday. There are several other Vietnamese/Chinese places in the immediate vicinity.

Restaurant Le Sunset (☎ 91.33.27.77; metro Vieux Port) at 24 Rue Pavillon (1er) has kosher Israeli food, including falafel (25FF), tehina (20FF), hummus (20FF) and eggplant salad (20FF). At midday, there's a 50FF *menu*. It is open Sunday to Thursday from noon to 2 pm and 7 to 11 pm and Friday from noon to 2 pm. In winter, when the Sabbath ends early, it is also open on Saturday night after sundown.

Restaurants – Vegetarian The *Auberge 'In'* (☎ 91.90.51.59; metro Colbert) is a vegetarian restaurant a few hundred metres north of the old port at 25 Rue du Chevalier Roze (2e). Giant salads cost 40 to 44FF. Meals are served Monday to Saturday from noon to 2 pm and 7 to 10 pm. The food store

and salon de thé (closed at mealtimes) are open from 9 am to 11 pm.

Fast Food There's a bunch of cheap *take-aways* (metro Noailles) selling pizza, Middle Eastern sandwiches of various sorts and other such edibles on Rue des Feuillants (1er), which intersects La Canebière just east of Cours Saint Louis. Cours Belsunce and the section of Cours Saint Louis nearest La Canebière are lined with inexpensive *sandwich kiosks* (metro Vieux Port or Noailles). *McDonald's* (metro Noailles) is at the intersection of La Canebière and Blvd Ougommier.

Self-Catering There's an up-market supermarket (metro Vieux Port) with an in-house bakery, lots of ready-to-eat salads and cartons of imported Häagen Dazs ice cream in the *Galeries Lafayette*, a department store a block north of La Canebière in the Centre Bourse shopping mall complex. It is open Monday to Saturday from 9 am to 7 pm. The most convenient entrance is at 28 Rue de Bir Hakeim (1er).

At the *Marché des Capucins* (metro Noailles), one block south of La Canebière on Rue Longue des Capucins (1er), you can purchase fruit and vegetables from 7 am to 7 pm daily except Sunday and holidays. South of the old port, there is a high-quality *fruit and vegetable market* (metro Estrangin Préfecture) near the Palais de Justice on Cours Pierre Puget (6e; see the Marseille map). It is open Monday to Saturday from 7.30 am to 1 pm.

A few blocks south of the train station, the *alimentation générale* grocery (metro Noailles) at 3 Blvd d'Athènes (1er) is open Monday to Saturday from 6 am to midnight.

Entertainment
Information on cultural events, concerts, films, etc is printed in *L'Officiel des Loisirs* (5FF at newspaper kiosks) and *7 Jours, 7 Nuits*, a free brochure issued each Wednesday and available from the tourist office, cinemas, etc.

Tickets to concerts and other performances can be purchased from the *billeterie*

PROVENCE

(ticket counter; ☎ 91.39.94.00 for the switchboard) of the FNAC store in the Centre Bourse shopping mall (metro Vieux Port).

Cinema *Cinéma Paris* (☎ 91.33.41.54 for the office; 91.33.15.59 for the answering machine; metro Vieux Port) at 31 Rue Pavillon shows nondubbed (v.o.) films in three halls. Screenings take place daily, all year, between 2 and 10 pm. Tickets cost 42FF (32FF for students). Everyone gets the cheaper price on Wednesday.

You might also try *Cinéma Breteuil* (☎ 91. 37.88.18 for a recording) at 120 Blvd Notre Dame.

Bars & Clubs Note the earlier warning under Dangers & Annoyances about going out in certain areas at night, especially if you're on your own.

For a good and varied selection of rock, reggae, country and other kinds of live music, try *La Maison Hantée* (☎ 91.92.09. 40) at 10 Rue Vian (6e). Nearby at 63 Cours Julien, *Il Caffe* is a pleasant watering hole; it's open Monday to Saturday until 10 pm.

Le Stendhal is a popular bar at 92 Rue St Jean de Bernady (1er). It has a good selection of foreign beers and occasional live music. ·

Getting There & Away

Air Aéroport International Marseille-Provence (☎ 42.78.21.00), also known as Aéroport Marseille-Marignane, is 28 km north-west of the city.

Train Marseille's passenger train station, which is served by both metro lines, is called Gare Saint Charles (☎ 91.08.50.50 for information; metro Gare Saint Charles).

All the trains to Paris's Gare de Lyon (383FF) are TGVs (4¾ hours; 10 a day) except one daytime run (7¾ hours) and at least two overnight sleepers. There are direct trains to Aix-en-Provence (33FF; 35 minutes; at least 18 a day), Arles (64FF; 45 minutes), Avignon (one hour), Barcelona (8½ hours), Bayonne (eight or nine hours; two a day), Bordeaux (321FF; 5¼ to six hours; five a day), Colmar (8½ hours),

Geneva (257FF; six hours), Lourdes (6½ hours; two a day), Lyon (200FF; three to 3½ hours; 13 to 15 a day), Montpellier, Nantes (10¾ to 11¾ hours; at least two a day), Nice (143FF; 1½ to two hours; over two dozen a day), Nîmes (85FF; 1¼ hours; 12 a day), Orange (one hour 20 minutes; 10 a day), Pau (six hours; two a day), Strasbourg (nine to 11 hours; two or more a day), Toulouse (228FF; four hours; nine a day) and many other destinations. There's even a night train to Calais (486FF), Lille and Brussels.

The information and reservation office, which is one level below the tracks, is open from 9 am to 8 pm daily except Sunday and holidays. The Après Vente office, which handles ticket reimbursements, is open Monday to Friday from 8 am to noon and 2 to 5.15 pm. The station itself is open from 4 am to 1 or 1.30 am. The luggage lockers *(consigne automatique)* behind Voie L (platform L) are open from 6.30 am to 1 am.

If you have any sort of problem (especially if you've had documents or money stolen), the volunteer retirees in the SOS Voyageurs office (☎ 91.62.12.80), across the corridor from the police post, will try to help. They're open Monday to Saturday from 9 am to noon and 1 to 7 pm, though they may have reduced hours in July and August.

The SNCF desk (☎ 91.95.14.31; metro Vieux Port) in the tourist office at 4 La Canebière (1er) can supply train information and issue tickets. It is open Monday to Friday (except holidays) from 9.15 am to 12.30 pm and 2 to 5.30 pm.

Bus The bus station *(gare des autocars;* ☎ 91.08.16.40; metro Gare Saint Charles) is at Place Victor Hugo (3e), 150 metres to the right as you exit the train station. The remarkably efficient Accueil Renseignements (information) counter is open Monday to Saturday from 7.45 am to 6.30 pm and on Sunday from 9 am to noon and 2 to 6 pm. It doubles as a left-luggage office and charges only 6FF per bag a day – much less than the SNCF. Tickets are sold either at company ticket counters (which are closed most of the time) or on the bus. Schedules are posted.

PROVENCE

There are frequent buses to Aix-en-Provence (20FF; 35 minutes via the autoroute, one hour or more via the N8) as well as Arles (76FF; two hours 20 minutes; two a day), Avignon (35 minutes by direct bus; seven a day), Cannes (110FF; two hours), Carpentras, Cassis, Cavaillon, Digne-les-Bains (70FF; 2½ hours; four a day), Nice (direct or via the coast; 124FF for adults; 2¾ hours), Nice airport, Orange, Salon and other destinations. The buses are slower than the train but cost about the same. On some routes, students under 26 and people over 60 qualify for significant discounts (eg 80FF to Cannes or Nice). There is infrequent service to Castellane (see Getting There & Away in the Gorges du Verdon listing).

Eurolines has buses to Spain (eight hours to Barcelona), Belgium, the Netherlands, Morocco and other countries. Their counter (☎ 91.50.57.55) in the bus station is staffed Monday to Saturday from 8 am to 5.30 pm.

Intercars (☎ 91.50.08.66; fax 91.08.72.34; metro Gare Saint Charles), which is down the monumental staircase from the train station at 14 Place des Marseillaises (1er), has buses to England, Spain, Portugal and Morocco. Each week, there are two buses to London (700FF; 20 hours), two to Madrid (370FF; 20 hours) and one to Algeciras (550FF; 32 hours). People under 26 or over 60 get 10% or 15% off. Buses stop in front of the office, which is open Monday to Friday from 8.30 am to noon and 2 to 6.30 pm and on Saturday from 6.30 am to noon and 5 to 5.30 pm.

Car Thrifty (☎ 91.05.92.18; metro Gare Saint Charles), near the train station at 6 Blvd Voltaire (1er), is one of the best deals in town. It is open Monday to Saturday from 8 am to noon and 2 to 7 pm. Europcar (☎ 91.90.11.00; fax 91.25.71.26; metro Gare Saint Charles), which is nearby at 7 Blvd Maurice Bourdet (1er), is open Monday to Friday from 7.30 am to 7.30 pm and on Saturday from 8 am to noon and 2 to 7 pm. Because they cater mostly to businesspeople, their weekend rates are quite attractive.

Boat Marseille's passenger ferry terminal (gare maritime; metro Joliette), one of the most active on France's Mediterranean coast, is on Quai de la Joliette (2e) at the foot of Blvd des Dames. The vehicle entrance is at the south end of Quai de la Tourette.

The Société Nationale Maritime Corse Méditerranée (SNCM; ☎ 91.56.30.10 for information, 91.56.30.30 for reservations) links Marseille with Corsica (see Getting There & Away in the Corsica chapter), Sardinia, Tunisia and the Algerian ports of Algiers, Annaba, Bejaia, Oran and Skikda. SNCM's office (metro Joliette) at 61 Blvd des Dames (2e) is open weekdays from 8 am to 5.30 or 6 pm and on Saturday from 8.30 am to noon and 2 to 5.30 pm.

Algérie Ferries (☎ 91.90.64.70; metro Joliette) at 29 Blvd des Dames (2e), SNCM's Algerian counterpart, charges the same fares as SNCM to/from the same Algerian ports. The office is open weekdays from 8 am to 6 pm (5 pm on Friday) and on Saturday from 8 am to noon. Ticketing and reservations for the Tunisian and Moroccan ferry companies, Compagnie Tunisienne de Navigation (CTN) and Compagnie Marocaine de Navigation (COMANAV; departures from Sète), are handled by SNCM.

For more information on ferry services to/from North Africa and Sardinia, see Sea in the Getting There & Away chapter.

Getting Around

To/From the Airport Every day of the year, TRPA (☎ 91.50.59.34 in Marseille, 42.89.03.65 at the airport) links Aéroport International Marseille-Provence (38FF; one hour) with Marseille's train station. Buses to the airport leave from just outside the train station's main entrance every 20 minutes from 5.30 am to 9.50 pm; buses from the airport depart from 6.20 am to 10.50 pm.

Bus & Metro Marseille has two fast, well-kept metro lines (known as Métro 1 and Métro 2), an extensive bus network and one tram line. Metro stations are marked by white-on-brown signs bearing an angular letter M.

PROVENCE

The metro (which began operation in 1977), the tram line and most buses run from 5 am to 9 pm. From 9 pm to 12.30 am, metro and tram routes are covered every 15 minutes by surface buses M1, M2 and 68; stops are marked with fluorescent green signs reading 'métro en bus' ('metro-by-bus'). Thirteen *autobus de nuit* (night buses) – all but two of which are identified by letters rather than numbers – run from 9.30 pm to 12.45 am; most begin their runs in front of the Espace Infos-RTM office (metro Vieux Port or Noailles) at 6-8 Rue des Fabres (1er). When there is an important football match or a major concert late at night, the metro may keep operating until 12.30 am.

Bus/metro tickets (8FF) can be used on any combination of metro, bus and tram for 70 minutes after they've been time-stamped so long as you keep moving in the same general direction. When you buy a carnet of six tickets – available for 36F at metro stations and many tabacs and stationery shops *(librairies-papeteries)* – you get two coupons *(talons)* marked with the same serial number as your tickets; to use a ticket as a transfer you must show one of the coupons. Tram stops have modern blue ticket distributors that should be used to time-stamp your ticket before you board.

For information on Marseille's public transport system (or to buy a carnet), you can drop by Espace Infos-RTM (☎ 91.91.92.10). It is open weekdays from 8.30 am to 5.30 pm. During July and August, it's closed from 12.30 to 2 pm.

Taxi There's a taxi stand to the right as you exit the train station through the main entrance. Marseille Taxi (☎ 91.02.20.20) and the Maison du Taxi (☎ 91.95.92.50) will dispatch a taxi 24 hours a day.

AIX-EN-PROVENCE

Aix-en-Provence (population 130,000), Aix (pronounced like the letter 'X') for short, is one of France's most graceful cities. It owes its atmosphere of sophisticated if slightly snobbish civility to the harmonious fusion of majestic public squares, shaded avenues and gurgling, mossy fountains. Some 200 elegant *hôtels particuliers* (large, private residences), many exhibiting the unmistakable influence of Italian baroque, date from the 17th and 18th centuries. The city is enlivened by a student population of about 30,000 – including a good many Americans – attracted by the Universities of Aix-Marseille, whose forerunner was established in 1409.

History

Aix was founded as a military camp under the name of Aquae Sextiae (the Waters of Sextius) in 123 BC on the site of thermal springs, which are still flowing to this day. It was established after Roman forces under the proconsul Sextius Calvinus had destroyed the Ligurian Celtic stronghold of Entremont, three km to the north, and enslaved its inhabitants. In the 12th century, the counts of Provence made Aix their capital. The city reached the height of its glory as a centre of art and learning under the enlightened King René (1409-80), a brilliant polyglot who brought to his court painters from around Europe (especially Flanders) and instituted administrative reforms for the benefit of his subjects.

One of the most prominent orators and politicians during the early phases of the Revolution, the notorious seducer Mirabeau (1749-91), was a native of Aix. So was the great postimpressionist painter Paul Cézanne, born here in 1839, whose art was scorned by the public and even his family until shortly before his death in 1906. Cézanne often set up his easel a bit east of Aix near Mont Sainte Victoire, which he painted again and again.

Orientation

Cours Mirabeau, Aix's main boulevard, stretches from La Rotonde, a huge round-about also known as Place du Général de Gaulle, eastward to Place Forbin. The oldest part of the city, Vieil Aix, is north of Cours Mirabeau; most of the streets, alleys and public squares in this part of town are closed to vehicular traffic. South of Cours Mirabeau is the Quartier Mazarin, whose regular street grid was laid out in the 17th century. The

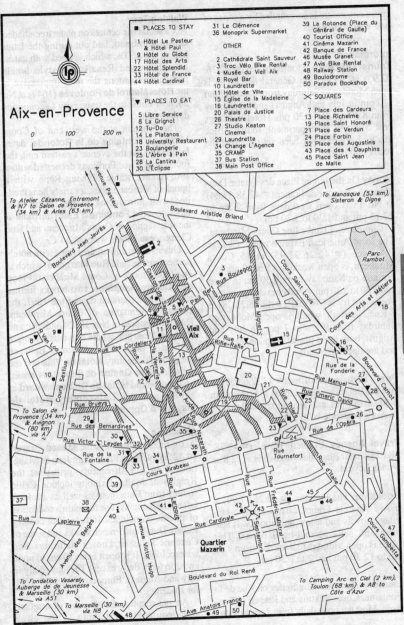

Aix-en-Provence

0   100   200 m

■ PLACES TO STAY

1 Hôtel Le Pasteur
  & Hôtel Paul
9 Hôtel du Globe
17 Hôtel des Arts
22 Hôtel Splendid
33 Hôtel de France
44 Hôtel Cardinal

▼ PLACES TO EAT

5 Libre Service
8 La Grignot
12 Tu-Do
14 Le Platanos
18 University Restaurant
23 Boulangerie
25 L'Arbre à Pain
28 La Cantina
30 L'Éclipse

31 Le Clémence
36 Monoprix Supermarket

OTHER

2 Cathédrale Saint Sauveur
3 Troc Vélo Bike Rental
4 Musée du Vieil Aix
6 Royal Bar
10 Laundrette
11 Hôtel de Ville
15 Église de la Madeleine
16 Laundrette
20 Palais de Justice
26 Theatre
27 Studio Keaton
   Cinema
29 Laundrette
34 Change L'Agence
35 CRAMP
37 Bus Station
38 Main Post Office

39 La Rotonde (Place du
   Général de Gaulle)
40 Tourist Office
41 Cinéma Mazarin
42 Banque de France
46 Musée Granet
47 Avis Bike Rental
48 Railway Station
49 Boulodrome
50 Paradox Bookshop

✕ SQUARES

7 Place des Cardeurs
13 Place Richelme
19 Place Saint Honoré
21 Place de Verdun
24 Place Forbin
32 Place des Augustins
43 Place des 4 Dauphins
45 Place Saint Jean
   de Malte

To Atelier Cézanne, Entremont
& N7 to Salon de Provence
(34 km) & Arles (63 km)

To Manosque (53 km),
Sisteron & Digne

Boulevard Aristide Briand

Parc Rambot

Boulevard Jean Jaurès

Vieil Aix

To Salon de
Provence (34 km)
& Avignon
(80 km)
via A7

To Fondation Vasarely,
Auberge de de Jeunesse
& Marseille (30 km)
via A51

To Marseille (30 km)
via N8

Quartier
Mazarin

Boulevard du Roi René

To Camping Arc en Ciel (2 km),
Toulon (68 km) & A8 to
Côte d'Azur

Ave Anatole France

PROVENCE

entire city centre is surrounded by a series of one-way boulevards.

Information

Tourist Office Aix's tourist office (☎ 42.26.02.93) at 2 Place du Général de Gaulle is open Monday to Saturday from 8 am to 7 pm (10 pm in July and August) and on Sunday from 8.30 am to 12.30 pm. Hotel bookings cost 5FF. As an experiment, tourist office kiosks have recently been set up along the roads into town.

Money On the serene Place des Quatre Dauphins, the Banque de France (☎ 42.38.57.64) at No 18 is open weekdays from 9 am to 12.15 pm and 1.30 to 3.30 pm.

Commercial banks line Cours Mirabeau. The local American Express agent, Change l'Agence (☎ 42.26.93.93) at 15 Cours Mirabeau, is open weekdays from 9 am to 7 pm and on Saturday from 9.30 am to noon and 2.30 to 5.30 pm. Another exchange bureau you might try is CRAMP (☎ 42.38.28.28) at 7 Rue Nazareth, which is open Monday to Saturday from 9 am to 7 pm. In July and August, both these places keep longer hours and are open on Sunday.

Post The main post office (☎ 42.27.68.00) on Ave des Belges is open Monday to Friday from 8.30 am to 7 pm and on Saturday until noon.

Aix's postcode is 13100.

Travel Agency Council Travel (☎ 42.38.58.82) is near Place des Augustins at 12 Rue Victor Leydet.

Bookshop The Paradox (☎ 42.26.47.99) at 6 Ave Anatole France carries English-language novels and a few guidebooks. It also buys and sells second-hand books. This place is open Monday to Saturday from 9.30 am to 12.30 pm and 2 to 6.30 pm.

Laundry There are laundrettes on Rue de la Fontaine, Cours Sextius and Rue de la Fonderie. Most are open daily from 7 am to 8 pm.

Walking Tour

Aix's social life centres on plane tree-shaded **Cours Mirabeau**, laid out during the latter half of the 1600s, which is lined with cafés, bookshops and Renaissance-style hôtels particuliers. Among the most impressive is the **Hôtel Maurel de Pontevès** (1647) at No 38, now home to the university's economics department.

The fountain at the west end of Cours Mirabeau, **Fontaine de la Rotonde**, dates from 1860. At the avenue's eastern end, the fountain at Place Forbin is decorated with a 19th-century statue of King René with a bunch of Muscat grapes, a variety he is credited with introducing to the region. The moss-covered **Fontaine d'Eau Thermale** at the intersection of Cours Mirabeau and Rue Clemenceau spouts water at 34°C.

Other streets and squares lined with hôtels particuliers include **Rue Mazarine**, which is one block south of Cours Mirabeau; **Place des Quatre Dauphins**, two blocks further south, whose fountain dates from 1667; the eastern continuation of Cours Mirabeau, **Rue de l'Opéra** (at Nos 18, 24 and 26); and **Place d'Albertas**, where live music is often performed on summer evenings. Between the mid-17th-century **Hôtel de Ville** and the cathedral, **Rue Gaston de Saporta** is graced by the splendid **Hôtel de Châteaurenard** at No 19 and the 18th-century **Hôtel de Maynier d'Oppede** at No 23.

Museums

Aix's finest museum is the **Musée Granet** (☎ 42.38.14.70) at Place Saint Jean de Malte, housed in a 17th-century priory of the Knights of Malta. Exhibits include Celtic statues from Entremont as well as artefacts left by the Romans. The museum's collection of paintings includes 16th to 19th-century Italian, Dutch and French works and some of Cézanne's lesser known paintings and watercolours. It is open from 10 am to noon and 2 to 6 pm daily except Tuesday (daily in July and August). Entry costs 13.50FF (7FF for students).

An unexceptional collection of artefacts and documents pertaining to the city's history is housed in the **Musée du Vieil Aix** (☎ 42.21.43.55) at 17 Rue Gaston de Saporta, near the cathedral. It's open the same hours as the Musée Granet but is closed on Monday. Admission is 10FF (5FF for students). The **Musée des Tapisseries** (Tapestry Museum; ☎ 42.21.05.78) is at 28 Place des Martyrs de la Résistance. The **Musée Paul Arbaud** at 2a Rue du Quatre Septembre displays books and manuscripts and has a collection of Provençal faïence.

Cathédrale Saint Sauveur

Aix's cathedral incorporates architectural features representing every period from the 5th to 18th centuries. The main Gothic structure, built between 1285 and 1350, includes as part of its south aisle the 12th-century Romanesque nave of an earlier church. The chapels were added in the 14th and 15th centuries. There is a 5th-century sarcophagus in the apse. The *Triptyque du Buisson Ardent* (Triptych of the Burning Bush; circa 1470) in the nave is by Nicolas Froment.

Paul Cézanne Trail

Cézanne, Aix's most celebrated artist (at least after his death), did much of his painting in and around the city. If you're interested in the minute details of his day-to-day life – where he ate, drank, prayed and worked – just follow the **Chemin de Cézanne**, marked by round, bronze markers in the pavement that begin at the tourist office. The markers are coordinated with a guide, *In the footsteps of Paul Cézanne*, which you can pick up before setting off. This booklet also takes in sites in the vicinity of Aix which inspired Cézanne's art, including Mont Sainte Victoire.

Over the years, Cézanne worked in a number of studios around town, including one on the ground floor of what is now the Musée Granet. His last studio, now opened to the public as the **Atelier Paul Cézanne** (☎ 42.21.06.53), is on a hill about 1.5 km north of the tourist office at 9 Ave Paul Cézanne. It has been left exactly as it was when he died in 1906 and though none of his works are here, his tools are. It's open from

10 am to noon and 2 to 5 pm (6 pm from June to September) daily except Tuesday. Entrance costs 12.50FF (6FF for students). To get there, take bus No 1 to the Cézanne stop.

Fondation Vasarely

The Vasarely Foundation (☎ 42.20.01.09) at 1 Ave Marcel Pagnol, which is about four km west of town near the youth hostel, is the creation of Hungarian-born artist Victor Vasarely, who sought to brighten up grey urban areas with huge, colourful works that integrated art with architecture. Vasarely's works are displayed here in several six-sided spaces recognisable from afar by their black-and-white, geometrical designs. Two of Vasarely's most famous works are the roof of the Palais de Congrès in Monaco and the entrance hall of Paris's Gare Montparnasse.

The foundation is open from 9.30 am to 12.30 pm and 2 to 5.30 pm daily except Tuesday (daily in July and August). Tickets cost 35FF (20FF for children). To get there, take bus No 10 or 12 to the Vasarely stop.

Markets

Aix is the premier market town in Provence. A mass of fruit and vegetable stands are set up each morning on **Place Richelme**, just as they have been for centuries. Depending on the season, you can buy olives, goat cheese, garlic, lavender, peaches – the list goes on and on. There's another market at **Place des Prêcheurs** on Tuesday, Thursday and Saturday mornings.

A **flower market** enlivens the square in front of Église de la Madeleine on Sunday mornings; on Tuesday, Thursday and Saturday mornings, it moves to the square next to the Hôtel de Ville. Also on Tuesday, Thursday and Saturday mornings, a *marché aux puces* (flea market) occupies Place de Verdun, which is in front of the Palais de Justice.

Language Courses

Aix is a popular place for people from English-speaking countries to study French. The American Center for Language & Culture (☎ 42.38.42.38) at 409 Ave Jean-Paul Coste has courses of varying length and intensity. It charges 1370FF for 20 hours of instruction and 2230FF for 36 hours spread over nine days.

The Université de Provence organises cheaper summer courses and can provide accommodation. For more information, contact the Université de Provence (☎ 42.59. 22.71) at 29 Ave Robert Schuman.

Festivals

Each July, the Festival d'Art Lyrique et de Musique brings the most refined classical music, opera and ballet to such settings such as Cathédrale Saint Sauveur and the old Théâtre on Rue de l'Opéra. Tickets cost at least 200FF per performance. Fortunately, practitioners of more laid-back musical expression (ie buskers of all sorts) bring the festival spirit to Cours Mirabeau.

Places to Stay

Although Aix is a student town, it is not a cheap overnight stop. In July and August, when hotel prices rise precipitously, it may be possible to stay in the university dorms – the tourist office has details.

Places to Stay – bottom end

Camping Camping Arc en Ciel (☎ 42.26. 14.28), open from April to 30 September, is at Pont des Trois Sautets, which is about two km south-east of town on the road to Nice. Two people with a tent pay 60FF; additional people are charged 23FF each. To get there, take bus No 3 to Les Trois Sautets stop.

Hostel The Auberge de Jeunesse (☎ 42.20. 15.99) is at 3 Ave Marcel Pagnol, which is nearly two km west of the centre. The first night costs 74FF, including breakfast; subsequent nights are 63FF. Meals are available for 43FF. Rooms are locked between 10 am and 5.30 pm. There are laundry facilities and a bar. To get to the hostel, take bus No 10 or 12 from La Rotonde to the Vasarely stop.

Hotels Just north of Blvd Jean Jaurès, the Hôtel Le Pasteur (☎ 42.21.11.76) at 14 Ave Pasteur offers rooms with a shower and toilet – but, in some cases, without a window – for

120FF. The Hôtel Paul (☎ 42.23.23.89), next door at No 10, has similar singles/doubles from 110/170FF. Both these places are a 10-minute walk from the tourist office. You can also take minibus No 2 from La Rotonde or the bus station.

On the eastern fringe of the city centre, the laid-back Hôtel des Arts (☎ 42.38.11.77) at 69 Blvd Carnot has decent rooms with shower and toilet from 175FF. Another option is the Splendid (☎ 42.38.19.53) on Rue Thiers, but though it's central it's often full – and doesn't come close to living up to its name. Singles/doubles start at 155/180FF.

Places to Stay – middle

The Hôtel Cardinal (☎ 42.38.32.30; fax 42.21.52.48) at 22 Rue Cardinale has large rooms with shower, toilet and a mix of modern and period furniture. In the off season, prices start at 200/250FF for a single/double; high-season prices begin at 220/260FF. The similar Hôtel de France (☎ 42.27.90.15) at 63 Rue Espariat has serviceable singles/doubles from 190/210FF.

Just out of the pedestrianised area, the Hôtel du Globe (☎ 42.26.03.58) at 74 Cours Sextius has pleasant singles with toilet from 160FF and doubles with shower and toilet from 220FF. Though it's on a main street, this place isn't particularly noisy at night.

Places to Stay – top end

Aix is very well endowed with three and four-star hotels though many are on the outskirts of town. Close to the centre, the elegant Hôtel Pullman (☎ 42.37.61.00) at 24 Blvd du Roi René has all the creature comforts, including a large outdoor pool and solarium. Modern rooms start at 500/600FF for a single/double.

Places to Eat

Aix has lots of lovely places to dine, but the prices do little to moderate the town's up-market gastronomic image. Fortunately, cuisines brought from overseas are both plentiful and of high quality.

Aix's pastry speciality is the calisson, a small confection made with almond paste.

Restaurants Aix's cheapest – and possibly its only unpretentious – dining street is Rue Van Loo, which is lined with tiny restaurants offering Asian, Italian and carnivorous cuisines. Prices are pretty standard – around 50FF for a three-course *menu*. *La Grignot* (☎ 42.26.64.33) at No 20 has a *menu* of pizza, salad and a drink for 40FF.

Rue de la Verrerie and Rue Félibre Gaut offer various options if you'd like to eat both well and conspicuously. Vietnamese food is the area's forte, and *Tu-Do* on Rue Félibre Gaut is one of its least expensive purveyors.

A block north of La Rotonde, you might check out Place des Augustins, a small square lined with restaurants. As long as you don't mind elbowing the diner next to you, *Le Clémence* (☎ 42.27.99.77) at 1 Rue Victor Leydet is the most reasonable. Just off Place des Augustins, *L'Éclipse* on Rue Victor Leydet is a late-night sandwich joint open until 1 am.

For Greek food, *Le Platanos* (☎ 42.21.33.19) at 13 Rue Rifle-Rafle offers a 59FF *menu* at lunchtime and an 89FF *menu* for dinner. Mexican food can be enjoyed at *La Cantina* (☎ 42.27.82.94) at 45 Rue Manuel, a rooftop restaurant with chilli con carne for 49FF.

Vegetarian *L'Arbre à Pain* (☎ 42.26.08.88) at 4 Rue Emeric David is closed on Sunday and in the evening from Monday to Wednesday. When it's open, salads start at 30FF; main dishes are available from 35FF.

University Restaurants For a very cheap meal, there's a *Uni restaurant* (☎ 42.38.03.68) at 2 Cours des Arts et Métiers. You may have to buy a ticket from a student. It is generally open from 11.15 am to 1.15 pm and 6.30 to 7.30 pm.

Self-Catering For information on Aix's *food markets*, see Markets earlier. The *Monoprix* on Cours Mirabeau has a grocery section in the basement, which is open Monday to Saturday from 8.45 am to 7.30 pm.

For late night supplies, *Libre Service de l'Hôtel de Ville* at 4 Rue Paul Bert is open from 9 am to 1 am. The *boulangerie* on Rue Tournefort never closes.

Entertainment

Cinema The people of Aix are particularly fond of *le septième art* (the seventh art), and two cinemas are dedicated solely to screening nondubbed films. *Cinéma Mazarin* (☎ 42.26.99.85) at 6 Rue Laroque, which has three *salles*, charges 34FF (29FF for students and, on Wednesday, everyone). The small *Studio Keaton* (☎ 42.26.86.11) at 45 Rue Manuel is slightly cheaper.

Pubs Aix's cafés and brasseries, particularly those with terraces on Cours Mirabeau, are designed for the sort of people-watching that is not entirely free of pretension. The most famous hang-out for intellectuals is *Café des Deux Garçons* at 53 Cours Mirabeau.

For something a little less conspicuous, head into the backstreets. A popular student hang-out is the *Royal Bar* on Place des Cardeurs, which has an enormous terrace and a jumble of tables.

Bullfighting

In *mise à mort* bullfighting *(corrida)*, which is popular in Spain, Latin America and parts of southern France, a bull bred to be aggressive is killed in a colourful and bloody ceremony involving picadors, toreadors and horses. But not all bullfighting ends with a dead bull. In a *course Camarguaise* (Camargue-style bullfight), white-clad *razeteurs* try to remove ribbons tied to the bull's horns with hooks held between their fingers.

In Arles, the bullfighting season begins around Easter with a bullfighting festival known as the Feria and runs until September. The Feria includes both courses Camarguaises and corridas. Depending on where you sit in the arena and the importance of the event, expect to pay 80FF to 200FF for a course Camarguaise and 90 to 350FF for a corrida. ■

Pétanque If you'd like to watch a game of pétanque, head to the *boulodrome* in Parc Jourdon, which is on Ave Anatole France. In the late afternoon, over 100 old-timers gather here either to play or to watch their friends play.

Gay Disco *La Chimère* (☎ 42.23.36.28) is a popular gay disco at Montée d'Avignon.

Getting There & Away
Train Aix's tiny train station, which is at the south end of Ave Victor Hugo, is open from 5.45 am to 10 pm. The information office is open Monday to Saturday from 8.45 am to 7 pm. To get information by phone, ring the SNCF in Marseille on ☎ 91.08.50.50. There are frequent services to Marseille (33FF; 35 minutes; at least 18 a day), whence there are connections to everywhere.

Bus The busy, run-down bus station, served by quite a few different companies, is at the western end of Rue Lapierre. The information office (☎ 42.27.17.91) is open Monday to Saturday from 6 am to 7 pm. In July and August, it's also open on Sunday from 8 am to 4 pm. There's no left-luggage room or lockers.

There are buses from here to Marseille (20FF; 35 minutes via the autoroute, one hour or more via the N8; quay No 28 or 29), Arles (60FF; 1¾ hours; two a day); Avignon via the highway (78FF; one hour; six a day), Avignon via secondary roads (64FF; 1½ hours; four a day) and Toulon (75FF; one hour; four a day).

SAA buses to Apt (1½ hours; two a day) leave at 7.50 am and 6.05 pm. Autocars Sumian has service to the Gorges du Verdon (see the Gorges du Verdon section).

Car Citer (☎ 42.63.06.79) is at 45 Blvd Aristide Briand. To contact ADA, call ☎ 42.38.92.92.

Getting Around
Bus Public buses and minibuses are operated by Autobus Aixois (☎ 42.27.86.22), whose information desk at the tourist office

is open on weekdays from 2.30 to 6.30 pm. La Rotonde is the main bus hub. Most services run until 8 pm. Single tickets cost 6FF; a carnet of 10 is 30FF.

Taxi Taxis can be found outside the bus station. To order a cab, call ☎ 42.27.71.11.

Bicycle The rental place nearest the train and bus stations is Avis (☎ 42.21.64.16) at 11 Cours Gambetta, which charges 100FF a day. Troc Vélo (☎ 42.21.37.40) at 62 Rue Boulegon has around-the-town bikes for 30/50FF a half/full day; a deposit of 1000FF is required. Mountain bikes cost 50/100FF and require a 2000FF deposit. The shop is open Monday to Saturday from 9 am to noon and 2 to 5 pm.

The Vaucluse

The Vaucluse is Provence at its most picturesque. Many of the area's towns date from Roman times and still boast impressive Gallo-Roman arches, theatres and other structures. The villages, which spring to life on market days, are surrounded by some of France's most alluring countryside, brightened by the rich hues of wild herbs, lavender and grape vines. The whole area is watched over by Mont Ventoux, the highest peak in Provence.

Geography
The Vaucluse is shaped like a Chinese fan with Avignon, the region's capital, as the hinge. Orange, famed for its ancient theatre, and the smaller Roman town of Vaison-la-Romaine are north of Avignon and west of Mont Ventoux. Carpentras, near the centre of the Vaucluse, also dates from Roman times but is better known for its ancient Jewish community. A bit to the south is the Fontaine de Vaucluse, to the east of which are Gordes and Roussillon, enticing Provençal villages overlooking a fertile valley. A bit further east is Apt, one of the best bases for exploring the Lubéron range which lies to the south.

Getting Around
If you don't have access to a car, it is possible to get from town to town by local bus, but the frequency and pace of bus services are very much in keeping with the relaxed tempo of Provençal life.

AVIGNON
Avignon (population 91,000) acquired its ramparts and its reputation as a city of art and culture during the 14th century, when Pope Clement V and his court, fleeing political turmoil in Rome, established themselves near Avignon. From 1309 to 1377, the Holy See was based in Avignon under seven French-born popes, and huge sums of money were invested in building and decorating the papal palace and other important Church edifices. Under the popes' tolerant rule, the city became a place of asylum for Jews and political dissidents.

Opponents of the move to Avignon – many of them, like poet Petrarch, Italians – called Avignon 'the second Babylonian captivity' and charged that the city had become a den of criminals and brothel-goers and was unfit for papal habitation. Pope Gregory XI left Avignon in 1376, but his death two years later led to the Great Western Schism (1378-1417), during which rival popes – up to three at one time, each with his own College of Cardinals – resided at Rome and Avignon and spent most of their energies denouncing and excommunicating each other. They also expended great efforts to gain control of church revenues, among whose sources was the sale of indulgences.

Even after the Schism was settled and a pope acceptable to all factions established himself in Rome, Avignon remained under papal rule and continued to serve as an important cultural centre. The city and the nearby Comtat Venaissin (now the département of Vaucluse) were ruled by papal legates until 1791, when they were annexed to France.

Today, Avignon continues its traditional role as a patron of the arts, most notably through its annual performing arts festival. Avignon's other attractions include a bus-tling (if slightly touristy) walled city and a number of interesting museums, including several across the Rhône in Villeneuve-lès-Avignon. The newer postwar neighbourhoods outside the walls are singularly lacking in charm. Avignon is a good base for day trips to other parts of Provence and the Vaucluse area, including Orange, Carpentras, Mont Ventoux, Fontaine de Vaucluse and Vaison-la-Romaine. The people of Avignon spend August recovering from the festival, often by going on holiday.

Orientation
The main avenue within the walled city (intra-muros) runs northward from the train station all the way to Place de l'Horloge – it's called Cours Jean Jaurès south of the tourist office and Rue de la République north of the tourist office. Place de l'Horloge is 200 metres south of Place du Palais, which abuts the Palais des Papes. The city gate nearest the train station is Porte de la République; the city gate next to Pont Édouard Daladier is Porte de l'Oulle.

Villeneuve-lès-Avignon, the Avignon suburb on the right (north-west) bank of the Rhône River, is reached by crossing the two branches of the river and Île de la Barthelasse, the island that divides them. Villeneuve-lès-Avignon's main street is called Rue de la République.

Information
Tourist Offices The tourist office (☎ 90.82.65.11) is 300 metres north of the train station at 41 Cours Jean Jaurès. It's open Monday to Saturday from 9 am to 1 pm and 2 to 6 pm (5 pm on Saturday). It has a free English-language brochure of the city's sights.

The ticket counter at Pont Saint Bénézet functions as a tourist office annexe (☎ 90.85.60.16). It is open from 9 am to 1 pm and 2 to 5 pm (closed Monday). From April to September, it's open every day from 9 am to 6.30 pm.

In Villeneuve-lès-Avignon, the municipal tourist office (☎ 90.25.61.33; fax 90.25.91.55) is at Place Charles David (Place du Marché).

PROVENCE

See Places to Stay for information on Vaucluse Tourisme Hébergement, the departmental hotel reservation service.

Money The Banque de France (☎ 90.86.56.64) is at the northern end of Place de l'Horloge. It is open Monday to Friday from 8.35 am to 12.05 pm and 1.55 to 3.35 pm.

Many of the banks – a number of which are located near the tourist office – and exchange bureaux offer rates considerably lower than those available at the Banque de France. There are 24-hour banknote exchange machines at the Lyonnais de Banque, across the street from 8 Rue de la République, and at the Caixa bank, opposite 67 Rue Joseph Vernet.

Post The main post office (☎ 90.86.78.00) is on Cours Président Kennedy, which is through Porte de la République from the train station. It is open Monday to Friday from 8 am to 6 pm and on Saturday from 8 am to noon. Currency exchange stops at 5 pm on weekdays and 11 am on Saturday.

The postcode of Avignon (including Île de la Barthelasse) is 84000. The postcode of Villeneuve-lès-Avignon, which is in a different département, is 30400.

Cultural Centres For more information on the French-American Center of Provence (☎ 90.25.93.23; fax 90.25.93.24) at 10 Montée de la Tour in Villeneuve-lès-Avignon, see Language Courses under Activities and the Au Pair section under Work in the Facts for the Visitor chapter.

Travel Agencies Frantour Tourisme (☎ 90.86.52.73), which sells BIJ, air and ferry tickets, is in the train station building, to the right as you exit the arrival hall. It is open Monday to Friday from 8.30 am to noon and 2 to 5.45 pm.

Bookshops The Maison de la Presse (☎ 90.82.00.99) is across from the tourist office at 34 Cours Jean Jaurès.

Medical Services The Centre Hospitalier (☎ 90.89.91.31) is 2.5 km south of the train station on Rue Raoul Follereau. Known as Hôpital Sud on bus maps, it is the southern terminus of bus line Nos 1 and 3.

Laundry Both the Salon Lavoir at 19 Rue des Lices and the Lavomatique at 27 Rue du Portail Magnanen are open daily from 7 am to 8 pm. La Fontaine Salon Lavoir is at 66 Place des Corps Saint and is open daily from 7 am to 9 pm.

Dangers & Annoyances Avignon has the third-highest per-capita crime rate in France and is notorious for thefts, especially from cars. Be doubly careful during the festival.

Walled City
Avignon's most interesting bits are within the roughly oval walled city, which is surrounded by 4.3 km of ramparts built between 1359 and 1370. They were restored during the 19th century but the original moats were not re-excavated, leaving the crenellated fortifications looking rather less imposing than they once did. But even in the 14th century this defence system was hardly state-of-the-art: the towers were left open on the side facing the city and machicolations (openings in the parapets to drop things on or shoot at attackers) are lacking in many sections.

The city's classiest shopping streets, Rue Saint Agricol and the northern part of Rue Joseph Vernet, are just west of Place de l'Horloge.

Palais des Papes Avignon's leading tourist attraction is the Palace of the Popes (☎ 90.27.50.71/3) at Place du Palais, a huge Gothic structure built during the 14th century as a fortified palace for the pontifical court. It is of interest in large part because of the dramatic events that took place here, since the undecorated stone halls, though impressive, are nearly empty. The best view of the Palais des Papes complex is from across the river in Villeneuve-lès-Avignon.

Six centuries ago, the seemingly endless halls, chapels, corridors and staircases – now nearly bare except for a few damaged frescoes – were sumptuously decorated with tapestries, paintings and the richest of furnishings. If you know a bit about medieval Catholic history, you might try to imagine what the rooms were like when cardinals and royal emissaries in ceremonial raiment paraded purposefully about, attended by armies of servants, clerks and factotums...During the 17th and 18th centuries, the building served as the residence of the papal legates who ruled Avignon. It was ransacked during the Revolution and later used as a prison and a barracks.

The Palais des Papes is open daily from 9 am to 12.45 pm and 2 to 6 pm. From April to October, it is open uninterruptedly from 9 am to 6, 7 or 8 pm. When the palace closes at midday, morning ticket sales end at 11.45 am; in the evening, the ticket window closes 45 minutes to an hour before the palace does. You can have a look at the main courtyard for free, but visiting the palace's interior costs 27FF (19FF for students and people over 60). One-hour guided tours (35FF, 27FF if you qualify for the discount) are available in English from April to October, usually at 10 am and 3 pm. Occasionally – especially in summertime – special exhibits may raise the entrance fees by 10FF or so.

Musée du Petit Palais This museum (☎ 90.86.44.58), which served as a bishops' and archbishops' palace during the 14th and 15th centuries, is at the far northern end of Place du Palais. It houses an outstanding collection of 13th to 16th-century Italian religious paintings. This museum is open from 9.30 to 11.50 am and 2 to 6 pm (closed Tuesday). Ticket sales end 30 minutes before closing time in both the morning and the afternoon. Tickets cost 16FF (8FF for students and people over 60). A free brochure in English is available at the ticket window.

Cathédrale Notre Dame des Doms This unexciting Romanesque cathedral is on the north side of the Popes' Palace. Built in the mid-12th century, it was repeatedly redecorated – the baroque-style galleries, for instance, were added in the 17th century. Like Avignon's other church buildings, it was sacked during the Revolution.

Rocher des Doms Just up the hill from the cathedral is Rocher des Doms, a delightful bluff-top park that affords great views of the Rhône, Pont Saint Bénézet, Villeneuve-lès-Avignon, the Alpilles, etc. A semicircular viewpoint indicator tells you what you're looking at. There's also a playground for children and a duck pond. This is a perfect spot for a picnic in a city singularly lacking in public benches.

Conservatoire de Musique Avignon's Conservatory of Music, which is across Place du Palais from the Palais des Papes, occupies the former Hôtel des Monnaies (Mint), which was built in 1619 to house a papal legation led by Cardinal Scipione Borghese. His coat-of-arms decorates the ornate, baroque-style façade.

Musée Calvet The Musée Calvet (☎ 90.86. 33.84) at 65 Rue Joseph Vernet, housed in the elegant Hôtel de Villeneuve-Martignan (1754), is closed for repairs until about 1995.

Musée Lapidaire The Statuary Museum (no tel) at 27 Rue de la République, housed in the baroque-style, 17th-century former chapel of a Jesuit college, is the archaeological annexe of the Musée Calvet. Displays include stone carvings from the Gallo-Roman, Romanesque and Gothic periods. It is open from 10 am to noon and 2 to 6 pm (closed Tuesday). Entrance is free.

Musée Louis Vouland This small but interesting museum (☎ 90.86.03.79) at 17 Rue Victor Hugo displays a fine collection of 17th and 18th-century decorative arts, including faïence and some superb French furniture. It is open from Tuesday to Saturday from 2 to 6 pm; from June to September, it's open from 10 am to noon as well. Entrance costs 20FF (10FF for students and people over 65).

PROVENCE

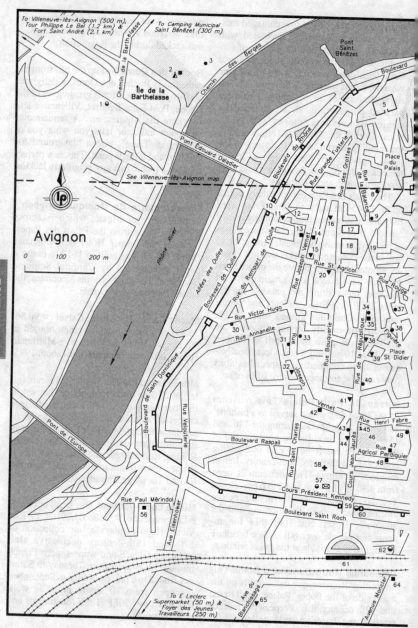

To Villeneuve-lès-Avignon (500 m),
Tour Philippe Le Bel (1.2 km) &
Fort Saint André (2.1 km)

To Camping Municipal
Saint Bénézet (300 m)

Pont
Saint
Bénézet

Île de la
Barthelasse

Chemin de la Barthelasse

Chemin des Berges

Boulevard

Place
du Palais

Pont Édouard Daladier

Boulevard du Rhône

Rue Grande Fusterie

Rue des Grottes

Rue de la Balance

See Villeneuve-lès-Avignon map

Avignon

0   100   200 m

Rhône River

Allées des Oulles

Boulevard de l'Oulle

Rue du Rempart de l'Oulle

Rue Joseph Vernet

Rue St Agricol

Rue Rouge

Rue de la République

Rue Victor Hugo

Rue Annanelle

Rue Bouquerie

Place
St Didier

Boulevard de Saint Dominique

Rue Velouterie

Rue Joseph Vernet

Rue Vernet

Rue Henri Fabre

Pont de l'Europe

Boulevard Raspail

Rue Saint Charles

Cours Jean Jaurès

Rue Agricol Perdiguier

Rue Paul Mérindol

Cours Président Kennedy

Ave Eisenhower

Boulevard Saint Roch

To E Leclerc
Supermarket (50 m) &
Foyer des Jeunes
Travailleurs (250 m)

Ave du Blanchissage

Avenue Monclar

■ PLACES TO STAY

2   Camping Bagatelle
    & Auberge Bagatelle
13 Hôtel Mignon
14 Hôtel Le Provençal
28 Avignon Squash Club
    (Hostel)
35 Hôtel Danieli
42 Hôtel Innova
47 Hôtel du Parc
48 Hôtel Pacific &
    Hôtel Splendid
54 Hôtel des Arts
56 Hôtel Saint Roch
64 Hôtel Monclar &
    Location Vélos
    Minibus

▼ PLACES TO EAT

11 Restaurant Café
    des Artistes
15 Casino Grocery
16 Simple Simon
    Tea Lunch
20 Boulangerie Salel
22 Indian Moon &
    Le Pain Bis
23 Restaurant Song Long
27 Supermarché Casino
32 Le Petit Bedon
36 Shopi Supermarket
39 Nani Restaurant
41 Snack Sandwich Shop
44 Brasserie Le Palais

52 Au Bain Marie
65 University Restaurant

OTHER

1   La Barthelasse Bus
    Stop
3   Municipal Swimming
    Pool
4   Entrance to Pont Saint
    Bénézet & Tourist
    Office Annexe
5   Musée du Petit Palais
6   Cathédrale Notre
    Dame des Doms
7   Palais des Papes
8   Conservatoire de
    Musique
9   Banque de France
10 Porte de l'Oulle
17 Opéra d'Avignon
18 Hôtel de Ville
25 Synagogue
26 Porte Saint Lazare
29 Caserne Chabran
    Army Barracks
30 Musée Louis Voland
31 Caixa Bank (24-Hour
    Banknote Exchange)
33 Musée Calvet
34 Lyonnais de Banque
    (24-Hour Banknote
    Exchange Machine)
37 Cinéma Utopia
    (two screens)

38 Cinéma Utopia (one
    screen) & Institute
    for American
    Universities
40 Musée Lapidaire
43 Maison de la Presse
45 Tourist Office
49 Koala Bar
51 Salon Lavoir
    (Laundrette)
53 Lavomatique
    (Laundrette)
55 Cycles Peugeot 84
57 Main Post Office &
    Bus No 10 (to
    Villeneuve-lès-
    Avignon)
58 Hospice Saint Louis
59 Porte de la République
60 Local Bus
    Information Office
61 Railway Station
62 Locarplus & Other
    Car Rental Places
63 Bus Station

✕ SQUARES

12 Place Crillon
19 Place de l'Horloge
21 Place Carnot
24 Place Jérusalem
46 Square Agricol
    Perdiguer
50 Place des Corps Saints

Synagogue The first synagogue (☎ 90.85.
21.24) at what is now 2 Place Jérusalem was
built in 1221. A 13th-century oven used to
bake unleavened bread for Passover can still
be seen, but the rest of the present round,
domed, neoclassical structure dates from
1846. The prayers here follow the North
African rite.

The synagogue can be visited Monday to
Friday from 10 am to noon and 3 to 5 pm. To
call someone from the management, push the
button on the intercom. Visitors should be
modestly dressed (no short pants or sleeveless shirts) and men will be asked to cover
their heads. If you're interested in other
Jewish sights in south-central France, ask for

an English copy of the free brochure entitled
Route du Patrimoine Juif du Midi de la France.

Pont Saint Bénézet

St Bénézet's Bridge (☎ 90.85.60.16) was
built from 1177 to 1185 to link Avignon with
what later became Villeneuve-lès-Avignon.
The 900-metre-long structure was repaired
and rebuilt several times before all but four
of its 22 spans – over both channels of the
Rhône and the island in the middle, Île de la
Barthelasse – were washed away once and
for all in the mid-1600s. Yes, this is the **pont
d'Avignon** mentioned in the French nursery
rhyme.

If you want to stand *on* the bridge (rather

than look at it from a distance from Rocher des Doms or Pont Édouard Daladier), you can do so – in exchange for 10FF (5FF for students and seniors) – every day, except Monday, from 9 am to 1 pm and 2 to 5 pm. From April to September, it's open daily from 9 am to 6.30 pm. The ticket window doubles as an annexe of the tourist office. A short section of the ramparts is open free of charge to visitors.

Villeneuve-lès-Avignon

Villeneuve-lès-Avignon (also spelled Villeneuve-lez-Avignon; population 9500), which is across the Rhône from Avignon, was founded in the late 13th century. It became known as the City of Cardinals because many cardinals affiliated with the papal court built large residences (known as *livrées*) in the town despite the fact that it was in territory ruled by the French crown rather than the pope. Villeneuve has a number of sights as interesting as those offered by Avignon.

The multisite ticket known as the Passeport pour Villeneuve (35FF) gets you into Chartreuse du Val de Bénédiction, Fort Saint André, Musée Pierre de Luxembourg, the Cloître of the Collégiale and Tour Philippe le Bel. The latter three sights are all open from 10 am to noon and 2 to 5 pm daily except Tuesday (daily from mid-June to mid-September). From April to September, hours are 10 am to 12.30 pm and 3 to 7.30 pm. All three are closed during February.

For information on bus transport from Avignon to Villeneuve-lès-Avignon, see under Getting Around later in this section.

Chartreuse du Val de Bénédiction The Val de Bénédiction Charterhouse (☎ 90.25. 05.46) at 60 Rue de la République, founded in 1356 by Pope Innocent VI, was once the largest and most important Carthusian monastery in France. Today, the silence of its stone cells, halls, chapels and cloisters – ransacked during the Revolution and thereafter abandoned – reproduces the contemplative quiet that must have pervaded the

place centuries ago when it was inhabited by the hermit-like monks of the Carthusian order.

The marble plaques next to the street entrance show how high the floodwaters of the Rhône reached in 1840 and 1856. The largest cloister, **Cloître Saint Jean**, which gives you an idea of the architecture and layout of the charterhouse, can be visited without paying the entrance fee – just walk past the ticket counter to the end of the corridor and open the wooden door. In the 14th-century church, the delicately carved **mausoleum of Pope Innocent VI** (died 1362) – removed during the Revolution and returned here in 1963 – is an extraordinary example of Gothic artisanship.

The Chartreuse is open daily from 9.30 am to 5.30 pm (9 am to 6.30 pm from April to September). Entrance costs 25FF (14FF for students aged 18 to 25 and people over 60). A billet jumelé good for both the Chartreuse and Fort Saint André costs 30FF. An explanatory sheet in English is available at the ticket counter.

Playwrights, film scriptwriters and composers are invited to stay and work at the Chartreuse du Val de Bénédiction under a programme funded by the French Ministry of Culture.

Musée Pierre de Luxembourg The Pierre de Luxembourg Museum (☎ 90.27.49.66) on Rue de la République near Place Jean Jaurès has a fine collection of religious art taken from the Chartreuse during the Revolution, including quite a few paintings from the 15th, 16th and 17th centuries. The museum's most exceptional objects include the *Vierge en Ivoire* (Ivory Virgin), a superb 14th-century Virgin carved out of an elephant's tusk, which is in the room opposite the ticket counter; the nearby 15th-century *Vierge Double Face*, a marble Virgin whose two faces point in opposite directions; and *Couronnement de la Vierge* (Coronation of the Virgin), painted by Enguerrand Quarton in 1453, which is displayed on the 1st floor. Entrance costs 12FF (6.30FF reduced price).

Église Collégiale The former collegiate church (no tel) on Rue Montolivet (just off Rue de la République), now a regular parish church, was established in 1333. To visit the rather empty, late 14th-century **cloître**, part of which has been privately owned since Church property was sold off during the Revolution, ring the bell of the sacristy, which is to the left of the 18th-century altar. A visit to the cloister costs 7FF (4.50FF reduced price).

Tour de Philippe le Bel This 32-metre-high defensive tower (☎ 90.27.49.68) was built in the 14th century at what was, at the time, the western end of Pont Saint Bénézet. The platform on top, reached after a long, circular climb, affords a superb panorama of Avignon's walled city, the river and the surrounding countryside, especially in the late afternoon. Entrance costs 7FF (4.50FF reduced price).

Fort Saint André This 14th-century fortress, built on Mont Andaon by the king of France to keep an eye on events across the river in the papal domains, also affords lovely views. The **fortified gate** is a fine example of medieval military architecture.

Swimming

The municipal *piscine olympique* (olympic swimming pool) on Île de la Barthelasse (next to Camping Bagatelle and the Auberge Bagatelle) is open from mid-May to mid-September. To get there by bus, see Camping Bagatelle under Camping.

Festivals

The world-famous Festival d'Avignon, founded in the late 1940s, is held every year from mid-July to mid-August. It attracts many hundreds of performance artists (actors, dancers, musicians, etc) who put on some 300 *spectacles* of all sorts each day in every imaginable venue. There are, in fact, two simultaneous events: the prestigious, expensive and government-subsidised official festival; and the Festival Off, which consists of performers who, on their own initiative (and at their own expense), just decide to show up and perform. Needless to say, the festival attracts incredible numbers of people, creating major accommodation and transportation headaches.

Information on the official festival can be obtained by contacting the Bureau du Festival (☎ 90.82.67.08; fax 90.85.09.32) at 8bis Rue de Mons, 84000 Avignon.

Places to Stay

During the festival, it is nearly impossible to find a hotel room in Avignon unless you've made reservations many months in advance. The tourist office has information on special Festival-period dormitory accommodation. If you opt to stay elsewhere in the region and commute, be prepared for traffic jams and crowded trains. Sleeping outside is illegal and could be dangerous – thefts are a problem and assaults not unknown.

On the brighter side, hotel rooms are readily available in August, when places in the rest of the Vaucluse département are at a premium.

Hotel reservations anywhere in the département of Vaucluse can be made through Vaucluse Tourisme Hébergement (☎ 90.82.05.81; fax 90.86.54.77), whose bureau in the train station is next to the information and reservation office. The charge for a booking in a one/two-star hotel is about 15/25FF. The office, which also has information on chambres d'hôte, can always find you a room, but not necessarily in the locality of your preference. It is open Monday to Friday from 9 am to 6 pm and, from Easter to September, on Saturday from 10 am to 5 pm. Holiday hours are 10 am to 5 pm. During the festival, it's open every day from 9 am to 8 pm.

Places to Stay – bottom end

Camping *Camping Bagatelle* (☎ 90.86.30.39, 90.85.78.45; fax 90.27.16.23), open year round, is an attractive, shaded camping ground a bit north of Pont Édouard Daladier on Île de la Barthelasse. It is 850 metres from the walled city. Charges are 15FF per adult, 6.50FF to pitch a tent and 6.50FF for parking. Reception is open from 8 am to 9 pm, but you can arrive 24 hours a day. On-site amenities include a minimarket, a cafeteria and a place to do laundry. To get there by public transport, take bus No 10 from in front of the main post office and get off at La Barthelasse stop.

Camping Municipal Saint Bénézet (☎ 90. 82.63.50), also on Île de la Barthelasse, is a bit further north on Chemin de la Barthelasse. It is open from the first Monday in March until October. Charges are 16FF per person and 12.50FF for a camp site and parking.

Hostels – Avignon The new, 210-bed *Auberge Bagatelle* (☎ 90.86.30.39, 90.85. 78.45; fax 90.27.16.23) is part of a large, parklike area on Île de la Barthelasse that includes Camping Bagatelle. A bed in a room for two, four, six or eight people costs 49FF. Rooms are locked from 1 to 5 pm, but there's no curfew.

The friendly *Avignon Squash Club* (☎ 90.85.27.78) at 32 Blvd Limbert (near the Supermarché Casino) is both a place for people to play squash and a travellers' hostel. A bunk in a converted squash court costs 45FF; renting an entire squash court without beds in it costs 40FF for 40 minutes (if you don't travel with your squash racquet you can borrow one from the management). There are no kitchen facilities. A safe is available for valuables.

From November to May, travellers can check in Monday to Saturday from 9 am to 10 pm; you cannot arrive on Sunday. From June to October, reception is open seven days a week from 8 to 11 am and 5 to 11 pm. Reservations can be made by telephone except during the festival, when a deposit is necessary. To get to the hostel by public transport, take bus No 2 from the main post office and get off at the Thiers stop – it's in front of the Caserne Chabran army barracks, which provide long-term accommodation to French nationals only.

During the summer school holidays, the *Foyer des Jeunes Travailleurs* (☎ 90.85. 35.02) at 33 Ave Eisenhower, also known as the Foyer Hameau de Champfleury, rents out dorm rooms to travellers.

Hostels – Villeneuve-lès-Avignon Clean, well-managed *Résidence Pierre Louis Loisil* (☎ 90.25.07.92) on Ave Pierre Sémard next to Place de la Croix theoretically accepts only groups but welcomes individual travellers if there's room (there usually is). Telephone reservations are accepted. A bed in a three or four-person room costs 55FF; breakfast is 14FF. Facilities for the handicapped are available. There's no curfew and rooms are open all day long. To get there from the Avignon train station, take bus No 10 to the Frédéric Mistral stop (see Bus under Getting Around for transport details).

You might also try the *Foyer YMCA* (☎ 90.25.46.20), also known as the Foyer International de Pont d'Avignon-UCJG/YMCA, which is at 7bis Rue de la Justice. From March to October, individuals are welcome for up to three nights. A bed in a very basic room for two to four people costs 90FF, including breakfast. To get there, take bus No 10 to the Pont d'Avignon stop.

Hotels – Within the Walls Hotels not within walking distance of the train station can easily be reached by bus. Many of the bottom-end hotels have decent rooms with shower and toilet.

The *Hôtel Pacific* (☎ 90.82.43.36) is only 300 metres from the train station at 7 Rue Agricol Perdiguier. Small but clean singles/doubles with high ceilings cost 100/130FF; doubles/triples/quads with shower are 150/180/200FF. Toilets are in the hall. Hall showers are free. Breakfast is a good deal at 20FF. This place is closed in January.

Down the block, the *Hôtel du Parc* (☎ 90. 82.71.55) at 18 Rue Agricol Perdiguier has rather ordinary singles and doubles for 110FF (without shower) and 140FF (with shower). A quad with shower costs 200FF. Hall showers are 10FF; toilets are in the hallway. When preparing your bill, they may assume you're taking the optional breakfast (18FF).

The *Hôtel Splendid* (☎ 90.86.14.46) at 17 Rue Agricol Perdiguier offers singles/doubles with shower for 120/170FF; singles/doubles with shower and toilet start at

PROVENCE

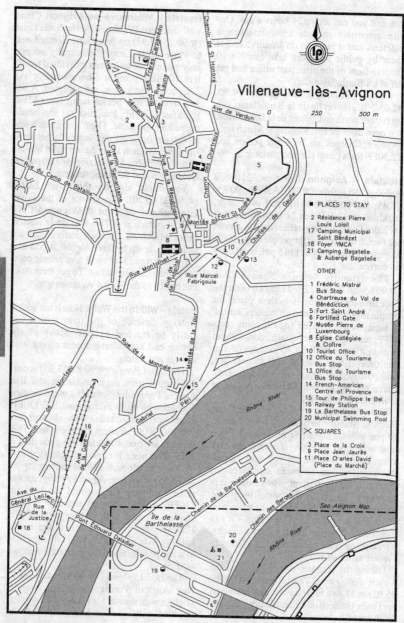

Villeneuve-lès-Avignon

0   250   500 m

■ PLACES TO STAY
2 Résidence Pierre
  Louis Loisil
17 Camping Municipal
  Saint Bénézet
18 Foyer YMCA
21 Camping Bagatelle
  & Auberge Bagatelle

OTHER
1 Frédéric Mistral
  Bus Stop
4 Chartreuse du Val de
  Bénédiction
6 Fort Saint André
7 Fortified Gate
7 Musée Pierre de
  Luxembourg
8 Église Collégiale
  & Cloître
10 Tourist Office
12 Office du Tourisme
  Bus Stop
13 Office du Tourisme
  Bus Stop
14 French-American
  Centre of Provence
15 Tour de Philippe le Bel
16 Railway Station
19 La Barthelasse Bus Stop
20 Municipal Swimming Pool

✕ SQUARES
3 Place de la Croix
9 Place Jean Jaurès
11 Place Charles David
  (Place du Marché)

Rhône River

See Avignon Map

Île de la
Barthelasse

Rhône River

150/200FF. Rooms for three or four people are 220 to 250FF. Hall showers cost 10FF. Breakfast is 20FF.

The friendly *Hôtel Innova* (☎ 90.82. 54.10; fax 90.82.54.39) at 100 Rue Joseph Vernet has comfortable, soundproofed doubles without/with shower for 130/150FF; rooms for two/three/four people with shower and toilet cost 180/200/240FF. Prices are slightly higher in summer. Hall showers are free. Breakfast costs 22FF.

The one-star *Hôtel Mignon* (☎ 90.82. 17.30; fax 90.85.78.46), three blocks west of Place de l'Horloge at 12 Rue Joseph Vernet, has spotless, well-kept and soundproofed singles/doubles with shower for 130/165FF and doubles/triples/quads with shower and toilet for 195/220/280FF. To get there by bus, take No 10 from in front of the main post office and get off at the Porte de l'Oulle stop.

The *Hôtel des Arts* (☎ 90.86.63.87) at 7-9 Rue de l'Aigarden has dim and even grim singles/doubles for 120/150FF. Doubles/ triples with shower are 180/230FF. Breakfast may be included. An extra bed is 50FF.

Hotels – Outside the Walls The family-run *Hôtel Monclar* (☎ 90.86.20.14) at 13 Ave Monclar is in an 18th-century building just across the tracks from the train station. Eminently serviceable doubles cost 150FF with sink and bidet, 170FF with shower and 200FF with shower and toilet. Two-bed triples and quads cost 210 to 250FF. This place has its own parking lot and a nice little garden out the back.

Places to Stay – middle
The two-star *Hôtel Le Provençal* (☎ 90.85. 25.24; fax 90.82.75.81) at 13 Rue Joseph Vernet has doubles with shower, toilet and TV for 200 to 220FF. To get there by bus, take No 10 from in front of the main post office and get off at Porte de l'Oulle.

Outside the walls, the *Hôtel Saint Roch* (☎ 90.82.18.63; fax 90.82.78.30) at 9 Rue Paul Mérindol has large, airy doubles with shower, toilet and TV for 180 to 195FF; triples and quads are 350FF. Breakfast costs 25FF. There's an attractive garden in the back.

Places to Stay – top end
You can't get any more central than the classy, 30-room *Hôtel Danieli* (☎ 90.86. 46.82; fax 90.27.09.24) at 17 Rue de la République. Singles/doubles with all the amenities cost 350/390FF.

Places to Eat
From Easter until mid-November, half of Place de l'Horloge gets taken up by touristy restaurants and cafés. *Menus* start at 65FF.

French – expensive If you're in the mood to splurge on French and Provençal cuisine, a good bet is *Le Petit Bedon* (☎ 90.82.33.98) at 70 Rue Joseph Vernet, whose specialities include frogs' legs and escargots. The *menus* (there's no à la carte service) cost 95FF (lunch only) and 145FF. This place is open Tuesday to Saturday from noon to 1.45 pm and 7.30 to 10 pm and on Monday from noon to 1.45 pm.

Au Bain-Marie (☎ 90.85.21.37) at 5 Rue Petramale, whose elegant dining rooms wrap around the courtyard, has a *menu* for 128FF (153FF for fish). It is open Monday to Friday from noon to 1.30 pm and 8 to 10 pm and Saturdy from 8 to 10 pm.

Restaurant Café des Artistes (☎ 90.82.63. 16) at Place Crillon offers a *menu* (150FF) as well as salads, grilled meats and a plat du jour (100 to 160FF). It is open Monday to Saturday (daily during the festival) from noon to 2 pm and 8 to 11 pm.

French – inexpensive *Brasserie Le Palais* (☎ 90.82.53.42) at 36 Cours Jean Jaurès (across the street from the tourist office) has a wide selection of dishes. *Menus* start at 55FF. Meals are served every day of the year from noon to 3 pm and 7 pm to midnight. Breakfast is available from 6 to 11 am.

Nani Restaurant (☎ 90.82.60.90) at the intersection of Rue de la République and Rue Théodore Aubanel has large salads for 48 to 55FF and grilled meat dishes for 55 to 60FF.

Asian *Restaurant Song Long* (☎ 90.86. 35.00) at 1 Rue Carnot (next to Place Carnot) offers a wide variety of excellent Vietnamese cuisine, including 16 *plats végétariens* (various vegetarian soups, salads, first courses and main dishes). Most main dishes cost 35 to 40FF. Portions are small but delicious. Lunch/dinner *menus* start at 42/60FF. Song Long is open daily from 11 am to 2.15 pm and 7 to 11.30 pm.

Indian Moon, which specialises in cuisine from the Indian subcontinent, is just through the arch opposite 6 Rue Armand de Pontmartin. It has *menus* for 68 to 95FF; the vegetarian *menu* costs 69FF.

Vegetarian *Le Pain Bis* (☎ 90.86.46.77) at 6 Rue Armand de Pontmartin is open Tuesday to Saturday from noon to 2 pm and 7.30 to 10 pm and Monday from noon to 2 pm. *Menus* cost 54 and 67FF. Restaurant Song Long and Indian Moon (see under Asian restaurants) also offer vegetarian dishes.

Other *Snack* (☎ 90.82.48.92), the signless sandwich shop at 26 Rue de la République, has remarkably cheap crepes (6 to 10FF) and sandwiches (10 to 16FF). It is open daily from 7 am to 1 am.

Simple Simon Tea Lunch (☎ 90.86.62.70) at 26 Rue Petite Fusterie is a delightful place for an afternoon cuppa (20FF) with cake, pie, scones or cheesecake (24FF). Meals (50 to 55FF for the plat du jour) are available all afternoon long. This place, which is closed in August, has rather strange hours: it's open Tuesday to Saturday from noon to 7 pm.

University Restaurant The *Restaurant Universitaire* of the Faculté de Droit (Law Faculty), which is opposite 9 Ave du Blanchissage, is open from October to June except during university holidays. Meals are served from 11.30 am to 1.30 pm and 6.30 to 7.30 pm daily except Saturday evening and Sunday. People with student cards can buy tickets (12.30FF or 28FF, depending on whether they make you pay the guest price) at the CROUS office (☎ 90.82.42.18) next to the restaurant, which is open on Monday, Tuesday, Wednesday and Friday from 10 am to 12.30 pm.

Self-Catering There is a food market every morning except Monday in the *Halles* at Place Pie.

Near Place de l'Horloge, *Boulangerie Salel* at 17 Rue Saint Agricol is open Monday to Saturday from 7.45 am to 7.30 pm. The *Casino grocery* at 22 Rue Saint Agricol is open Monday to Saturday from 7.30 am to 12.30 pm and 3.30 to 7.30 pm; in July and August, it's also open on Sunday morning. Avignon's fanciest food shops are along Rue Joseph Vernet and Rue Saint Agricol.

There is a *Shopi supermarket* with its own boulangerie across from 16 Rue de la République. A bit south of the railway tracks, the huge *E Leclerc supermarket* at 10 Ave Eisenhower is open Monday to Saturday from 9 am to 7.15 pm (7 pm on Saturday, 8 pm on Friday). It has an in-house boulangerie.

Entertainment
Cultural Events For information on the Festival d'Avignon, see the listing under Festivals. Tickets for many cultural events and performances are sold at the tourist office.

Concerts From October to June, the *Opéra d'Avignon* (☎ 90.82.42.42 for information) at Place de l'Horloge, housed in an imposing structure built in 1847, stages operas, operettas, plays, symphonic concerts, chamber music concerts and ballet. Depending on what's playing, ticket prices range from 30 to 90FF in the 4th gallery and from 120 to 360FF in the orchestra. Students of all ages can get tickets for half-price – if you'd like to reserve by post, send along a photocopy of your student card. The ticket office is open Monday to Saturday from 11 am to 6 pm; it is closed during August.

Cinemas The only movie theatre in town with nondubbed movies is *Cinéma Utopia* (☎ 90.82.65.36), which has one screening hall at 5 Rue Galante and two others at 15 Rue Galante (the Rue Galante hall may be moving in 1994). Tickets for the six daily screenings, which go on sale about 15 minutes before each performance (get there early to join the queue), cost 29FF. *La Gazette Utopia*, their free booklet of screening schedules and film reviews, is available at the tourist office, bookshops and other places around town.

During the French-American Film Workshop (Rencontres Cinématographiques Franco-Américaines), which is held during the week before the Festival d'Avignon (ie in early July), tickets for screenings of films by independent filmmakers from the USA and France are available at 4 Rue Figuière for about 30FF a film. A six-day subscription is available through the French-American Center of Provence (see Cultural Centres).

Bar The *Koala Bar* (☎ 90.86.80.87), founded and run by Australian ex-rugby player Rod Bussing, is an extremely popular hangout for English-speakers, including American university students and Aussie rugby league professionals brought in to play for Avignon. It's at No 2 on Place des Corps Saints, whose name – which means Square of the Holy Bodies – was not originally intended as a reference to the prostitutes who work around here.

A demi on tap usually costs 9 to 11FF, but the price drops to an incredible 5FF during happy hour (9 to 10 pm on Wednesday, Friday and Saturday). A full litre of beer is 36FF (20FF during happy hour). The Koala Bar is open daily until 1 am (1.30 am in summer, 3 am during the festival).

Getting There & Away
Air Aéroport d'Avignon-Caumont (☎ 90.81.51.15) is eight km south-east of Avignon.

Train The train station (☎ 90.82.50.50 for information) is across Blvd Saint Roch from Porte de la République. The information counters are open from 9 am to 6.30 pm daily except Sunday and holidays. The small SNCF station at Villeneuve-lès-Avignon, which handles only goods trains, sells passenger tickets without a station surcharge – for passage to Paris, for instance, you can save 20FF by buying your ticket in Villeneuve-lès-Avignon rather than Avignon.

There are frequent trains to Arles (33FF; 20 to 25 minutes; 14 to 18 a day), Marseille (one hour), Nice (196FF), Nîmes (41FF; 30 minutes; 15 a day), Orange (26FF; 15 minutes; 17 a day) and Paris's Gare de Lyon (342FF).

Bus The bus station (halte routière; ☎ 90.82.07.35) is in the basement of the building down the ramp to the right as you exit the train station. The information windows are open Monday to Friday from 8 am to noon and 2 to 6 pm (5 pm on Friday), but don't count on getting much information. Tickets are sold on the buses, which are run by 19 different companies.

Places you can get to by bus include Aix-en-Provence (78FF for the one-hour trip via the highway, 64FF for the 1½ hour trip along secondary roads; about a dozen a day), Apt (1¼ hours), Arles (two hours; four direct a day), Carpentras (16.60FF; 45 minutes; about 15 a day), Cavaillon (35 minutes), Fontaine de Vaucluse (one hour; two or three a day), Marseille (35 minutes by direct bus; seven a day), Montelimar (two hours), Nice (one a day), Nîmes (1¼ hours; five a day), Orange (40 minutes; about 20 a day), Pertuis (two hours), Pont du Gard, Uzès (38FF; one hour; five a day) and Vaison-la-Romaine (30FF; 1¼ hours). Most lines operate on Sunday at reduced frequency. A schedule is posted in the waiting room.

Two bus companies offering long-haul services have offices at the far end of the bus platforms. Iberbus (☎ 90.85.30.48), which has buses to Spain, Italy, Portugal and England (16½ hours to London), is open Monday to Friday from 8 am to noon and 2 to 6 pm (5 pm on Friday). Eurolines (☎ 90.85.27.60) can get you all over Europe.

Car Location Vélos Minibus (☎ 90.85.56.63) at 11 Ave Monclar offers Renault R5s with unlimited kilometrage for 380FF a day and 600FF for the weekend, including insurance. The office is open Monday to Friday from 9.30 am to noon and 3 to 6.30 pm and on Saturday from 9.30 am to noon.

PROVENCE

Locarplus (☎ 90.85.81.61; on Sunday ☎ 90.94.80.67 at the owner's home), which is in the Chambre Syndicale de l'Automobile at 2a Ave Monclar, has similar prices. A number of companies, including Europcar, Citer, Budget and Hertz, also have offices at 2a Ave Monclar.

Getting Around

Bus Local bus tickets cost 6FF each if bought from the driver; a carnet of five tickets good for 10 rides costs 36FF at TCRA offices and certain tabacs, newsagents and boulangeries. A monthly ticket costs 135FF. From Monday to Saturday, buses run from 7 am to about 7.40 pm; on Sunday, buses are much less frequent and most lines run only between 8 am to 6 pm. The two most important bus transfer points are the Poste stop (the main post office) and the Place Pie stop.

Carnets and free bus maps are available at Bus Urbains Accueil-Vente (☎ 90.82.68.19), in the wall of the old city across Blvd Saint Roch from the train station. It is open Monday to Friday from 8.15 am to noon and 1.45 to 6.30 pm and on Saturday from 8.45 am to noon. The bus kiosk at Place Pie (☎ 90.85.44.93) is also open on Saturday afternoon.

Villeneuve-lès-Avignon is linked with Avignon by bus No 10, which stops in front of the main post office and on the west side of the walled city near Porte de l'Oulle. Unless you want to take the grand tour of the Avignon suburb of Les Angles, take a bus marked 'Villeneuve puis Les Angles' (rather than 'Les Angles puis Villeneuve'). For the major sights, get off at the Office du Tourisme or Frédéric Mistral stops.

From Monday to Saturday, bus No 10 runs two or three times an hour from 7.30 am to 7.30 pm. On Sunday and holidays, there are only five Villeneuve-puis-Les Angles buses a day and not all of them stop at the Poste and/or Porte de l'Oulle; the last one's at 6.15 pm.

Taxi There's a taxi stand (☎ 90.82.20.20) in front of the train station arrival area.

Bicycle Cycles Peugeot 84 (☎ 90.86.32.49), which is named after the Vaucluse's two-digit department number, is at 80 Rue Guillaume Puy. Three-speeds and 10-speeds cost 50FF for one day, 110FF for three days and 270/600FF for 10/30 days. The deposit in case of theft is 1200FF. The shop is open Tuesday to Saturday from 8 am to noon and 2 to 7 pm (6 pm on Saturday).

Location Vélos Minibus (☎ 90.85.56.63) at 11 Ave Monclar is open from 9.30 am to noon and 3 to 6.30 pm daily except Saturday afternoon and Sunday. It rents three-speeds/10-speeds/mountain bikes for 50/60/70FF a day. The deposit is 1300FF.

ORANGE

Orange (population 28,000), a small, instantly likeable market town 31 km north of Avignon, is the northernmost of Provence's attractive Rhône Valley towns. It is best known for the Théâtre Antique, the best preserved Roman theatre in the world, built when Orange was an important Roman colony. Each summer, the Théâtre hosts a prestigious international opera festival known as Les Chorégies.

Through a 16th-century marriage with the German House of Nassau, the House of Orange – the princely dynasty that had ruled Orange since the 12th century – became active in the history of the Netherlands and later, through William III (William of Orange), Great Britain. The town, which had earlier been a stronghold of the Reformation, was ceded to France in 1713 by the Treaty of Utrecht, but to this day many members of the royal house of the Netherlands are known as the 'princes/princesses of Orange-Nassau'.

Through the House of Orange, the town has namesakes around the world: in South Africa (the Orange Free State), Ireland (the Orange Order), New South Wales (the city of Orange) and several US states, including New Jersey and Connecticut. However, Orange County, California, and the American college football game known as the Orange Bowl commemorate the fruit, whose name is of Sanskrit origin and came to English via Persian and Arabic.

Top Left: A courtyard in Gordes, Provence (GC)
Top Right: A painted tenement in the Panier Quarter, Marseille, Provence (DR)
Bottom Left: Green waters of the Gorges du Verdon, Provence (GC)
Bottom Right: The striking scenery of Moustiers Sainte Marie, Provence (LL)

Top: Food market on Cours Pierre Puget, Marseille (DR)
Middle: Scrumptious spread in a delicatessan (AC); Window of a luxury
food shop, Paris (DR); Cheeses of Normandy (CDT Calvados)
Bottom: A boulangerie/pâtisserie, the French corner shop (LL)

Orientation

The train station is a bit over one km east of the centre of town (Place de la République) along Ave Frédéric Mistral and Rue de la République. Rue Saint Martin links Place de la République and nearby Place Clemenceau with the tourist office, which is 250 metres to the west. The Théâtre Antique is two blocks south of Place de la République.

Information

Tourist Office The main tourist office (☎ 90.34.70.88) is on Cours Aristide Briand, on the western side of town. From 1 April to 30 September, it is open Monday to Saturday from 9 am to 7 pm and on Sunday from 10 am to 6 pm. The rest of the year, it's open Monday to Saturday from 9 am to 6 pm.

In front of the Théâtre Antique, the small tourist office annexe on Place des Frères Mounets is open from April to September from 10 am to 6 pm.

Théâtre Antique

Orange's magnificent Roman theatre, designed to seat about 10,000 spectators, was probably built during the time of Augustus Caesar (ruled 27 BC to 14 AD). Its **stage wall** *(mur de scène)*, the only such Roman structure still standing in its entirety (except for a few mosaics and the roof), is 103 metres wide and almost 37 metres high. Its plain exterior can be viewed from Place des Frères Mounets.

From 1 April to early October, the Théâtre is open daily from 9 am to 6.30 pm. The rest of the year, hours are 9 am to noon and 1.30 to 5 pm. Tickets cost 23FF (17FF for students and children) and also get you into the unexciting **Musée de la Ville** (Municipal Museum) across the road, known for its Roman *cadastres* (land survey registers).

Arc de Triomphe

Orange's Roman triumphal arch, one of the most remarkable of its kind in France, is at the northern end of plane tree-lined Ave de l'Arc de Triomphe. Probably built around 20 BC, it is 19 metres high and eight metres deep. The exceptional friezes commemorate Julius Caesar's victories over the Gauls in 49 BC, triumphs of which the Romans wished to remind every traveller approaching the city. The arch has been restored several times since 1825.

Festivals

In June, the Théâtre Antique comes alive with all-night jazz concerts, cinema screenings and various musical events.

During the last fortnight in July, the Théâtre Antique plays host to Les Chorégies, a series of weekend operas. Your only chance of getting a seat is to reserve months beforehand, but it's possible to catch a glimpse of the action from the lookout atop Colline Saint Eutrope, the unattractive hillside park behind the Théâtre.

Places to Stay

Rooms may be hard to come by during the summer.

Camping The three-star *Le Jonquier* (☎ 90.34.19.83), which is near the Arc de Triomphe on Rue Alexis Carrel, is open from mid-March to the end of October. It charges 25FF per adult plus 28FF per tent. To get there, take bus No 1 from the République stop (on Ave Frédéric Mistral 600 metres from the train station) to the Arc de Triomphe. From there, walk 100 metres back, hang a right onto Rue des Phocéens and then turn right again into Rue des Étudiants – the camping ground is across the football field.

Hotels Your best bet is to find something central. Though a little worn out, the *Hôtel Fréau* (☎ 90.34.06.26) at 3 Rue Ancien Collège has reasonable singles/doubles starting at 90/120FF. It closes in August, when things get too busy. To get there from the tourist office, head towards the town centre and take the third street on the left.

A block north of the Théâtre Antique, the *Arcotel* (☎ 90.34.09.23) at 8 Place aux Herbes is a homy place whose helpful owner enjoys talking about travel. Singles/doubles/triples start at 95/125/140FF. Around the corner, the slightly more chic

Saint Florent (☎ 90.34.18.53) at 4 Rue du Mazeau has nice, clean singles/doubles from 120/140FF.

Near the north-east corner of Place Clemenceau, the *Lou Cigalou* (☎ 90.34. 10.07) at 4 Rue Caristide has comfortable rooms from 140FF.

Places to Eat
Restaurants East of Place Clemenceau, there are a number of moderately priced restaurants on Rue du Pont Neuf, including *Perle d'Oran*, which has good couscous for 45FF and a lunch *menu* for 60FF. *La Sangria* (☎ 90.34.31.96) at 3 Place de la République has filling *menus* for 60FF.

For a cooling treat, you might try *Naranja* on Place de Langes (a block east of Place Clemenceau), which serves freshly squeezed fruit juices from 12FF.

Self-Catering On Thursday, there's a *food market* on Cours Pourtoules, two blocks south-east of the Théâtre Antique.

Getting There & Away
Train Orange's tiny train station, at the eastern end of Ave Frédéric Mistral, is nearly 1.5 km east of the main tourist office. For schedule information, ask at the ticket window or ring the SNCF in Avignon (☎ 90.82.50.50). There are a few luggage lockers inside the station.

Trains from here go in two directions – northward to destinations such as Lyon (132FF; 2¼ hours; 13 a day) and southward to Avignon (26FF; 15 minutes; 17 a day), Marseille (one hour 20 minutes; 10 a day) and beyond.

Bus The bus station (☎ 90.34.15.59) is a bit south-east of the centre of town on Cours Pourtoules. There is service to Avignon (40 minutes; about 20 a day), Carpentras (40 minutes; five a day), Marseille and Vaison-la-Romaine (22.50FF; 45 minutes; three a day).

Getting Around
Bus To get from the train station to the centre

of town, take bus No 2 from Rue Jean Reboul (walk straight on as you exit the station and take the first left) to either the Théâtre stop or – for the main tourist office – the Gasparin stop.

VAISON-LA-ROMAINE
Vaison-la-Romaine (population 5800), 28 km north of Carpentras and 47 km north-east of Avignon, is endowed with extensive Roman ruins as well as a picturesque medieval neighbourhood.

In the 2nd century BC, the Romans conquered an important Celtic city on this site and renamed it Vasio Vocontiorum. The Roman city flourished, in part because it was granted considerable autonomy, but around the 6th century the Barbarian invasions forced the population to move to the hill across the river, which was easier to defend. The counts of Toulouse built a castle on top of the hill in the 12th century. The resettlement of the original site began in the 17th century, covering the Gallo-Roman ruins with buildings that would later make life difficult for 20th-century archaeologists.

The Roman remains discovered at Vaison include villas decorated with mosaics, colonnaded streets, public baths, a theatre and an aqueduct; the latter brought water from Mont Ventoux. Some of these finds have yet to be opened to the public, though there are plans to do so in the mid-1990s.

Vaison, like Carpentras, is a good base to explore the Mont Ventoux region.

Orientation
Vaison is bisected by the Ouvèze River. The Roman city centre, on top of which the modern city centre has been built, is on the river's right (north) bank; the medieval Haute Ville is on the left (south) bank. In the Roman/modern city, Grande Rue heads north-westward from the Pont Romain bridge, changing its name near the Roman ruins to Ave du Général de Gaulle.

To get from the bus station to the tourist office, turn left as you leave the station and take the first left into Rue Colonel Parazols, which leads past the Puymin site to the tourist office.

Information

The tourist office (☎ 90.36.02.11) is just off Ave du Général de Gaulle at Place du Chânoine Sautel. It's open daily from 9.30 am (10 am on weekends) to noon and 2 to 5.45 pm.

Gallo-Roman Ruins

Those of Vaison's Gallo-Roman ruins that have been excavated can be visited at two sites: **Quartier de Puymin**, which is on the east side of Ave du Général de Gaulle, and **Quartier de la Villasse**, which is west of Ave du Général de Gaulle.

Quartier de Puymin, whose entrance is next to the tourist office, is the more interesting of the pair. It includes houses, mosaics and a theatre, designed to accommodate some 6000 people, built around 20 AD (during the reign of Tiberius). The **Musée Archéologique** displays artefacts unearthed at Vaison. Its collection of statues includes the silver bust of a 3rd-century patrician and likenesses of Hadrian and his wife Sabina. At Villasse, you can visit the mosaic and fresco-decorated house in which the silver patrician's bust was discovered.

Both sites are open daily from 10 am to 4 pm. From June to August, hours are 9 am to 12.30 pm and 2 to 6.45 pm. In November and December, it's open from 10 am to 12.30 pm and 2 to 5.45 pm. Admission to both sites costs 30FF (15FF for students and people aged 18 to 25, 10FF for children). From March to October, there are guided tours every day; English-language tours are held at 11 am on Mondays.

Notre Dame de Nazareth

This former cathedral, which is a bit west along Ave Jules Ferry from Quartier de la Villasse, was built in the Provençal Romanesque style from the 11th to the early 13th centuries. The walls of the apse incorporate parts of a 6th or 7th-century Merovingian church.

Medieval Quarter

Across the much-repaired **Pont Romain**, on the south bank of the Ouvèze, lies the **Haute Ville**, which dates from the 13th and 14th centuries. Narrow, cobblestone alleys lead up the hill past restored houses. At the summit, which affords a nice view, is the 12th-century **Château**, modernised in the 15th century but later abandoned.

Places to Stay

Camping Three-star *Camping Le Moulin de César* (☎ 90.36.00.78) is 500 metres southeast of town along the river at the end of Ave César Geoffray. It charges 11FF a tent and 17FF per adult; for children it's 9FF each.

Hostel The nearest youth hostel is the *Auberge de Jeunesse* (☎ 90.46.93.31) in Séguret, a village 10 km south-west of Vaison that was restored by a community of artists who now sell their works to visitors. The hostel is closed from January to mid-March. To get there from Vaison, take the Lieutaud bus heading to Orange and get off at the Séguret Poste stop.

Hotel Just beside Camping Le Moulin de César is the quiet *Centre International de Séjour* (☎ 90.36.00.78). Singles/doubles cost 111/155FF, including breakfast. It's closed from Christmas to February.

Getting There & Away

The bus station, where Lieutaud buses (☎ 90.36.09.90) has an office, is east of the Roman/modern town on Ave des Choralies. There are services from Vaison to Orange (22.50FF; 45 minutes; three a day), Avignon (30FF, 1½ hours) and Carpentras (45 minutes; one a day).

MONT VENTOUX

The narrow, east-west oriented ridge known as Mont Ventoux is the most prominent geographical feature in northern Provence, thanks to its height – 1909 metres – and its isolation from mountains of similar size. The radar and antenna-studded top, accessible by road, affords spectacular views of Provence, the southern Alps and – when it's especially clear – even the Pyrenees! At night, the towns and cities of the Provence's flatlands sparkle like jewels. Visibility is usually best early in the morning and around sunset.

Mont Ventoux marks the boundary between the fauna and flora of northern France and those of southern France. Some species – including the snake eagle, numerous spiders and a variety of butterflies – are found only here. The mountain's native forests were felled 400 years ago to build ships, but since 1860 some areas have been reafforested with a variety of species, including the majestic cedar of Lebanon. The mix of deciduous trees makes the mountain especially colourful in autumn.

Just west of Mont Ventoux, the sharp pinnacles of the limestone **Dentelles de Montmirail** (*dentelle* means lace, *dentelé* means jagged) rise from an area of great hiking terrain. Near the eastern end of the Mont Ventoux massif is the village of **Sault**, surrounded in summer by a patchwork of purple lavender.

Climate

As the name Ventoux suggests (*vent* means wind), the ridge is frequently very windy. The icy blasts are especially fierce during the mistral. The mountain can also become cloud-covered with little warning. In general, the earlier in the day you begin your outing the better.

Since the summit is considerably cooler than the surrounding plains (up to 20°C less) and receives twice as much precipitation, it's a good idea to bring along warm clothes and even rain gear. Areas above 1300 metres are usually snow-covered from about December to April.

Maps

Didier-Richard's 1:50,000 scale map No 27, entitled *Massif du Ventoux*, includes Mont Ventoux, the Monts du Vaucluse and the Dentelles. It is available at some of the area's larger tourist offices and many bookshops and newsagents.

Hiking

The GR4, coming from the Ardèche to the west, crosses the Dentelles before crawling up Mont Ventoux's northern face. It then joins the GR9, and both trails follow the bare, white ridge before parting ways, with the GR4 winding eastward to the Gorge du Verdon. The GR9, which takes you to most of the area's ranges (including the Monts du Vaucluse and the Lubéron) is perhaps the most spectacular trail in this part of Provence.

Cycling

It is possible for cyclists in excellent shape to ride all the way to the top of Mont Ventoux, and the Tour de France sometimes includes an ascent. On a blazing hot day in the 1960s, the race favourite, Tommy Simpson, died while working his way to the summit.

Skiing

During the winter, there are ski stations at Le Chalet Reynard and Mont Serein.

Getting There & Away

If you've got a car, the summit of Mont Ventoux can be reached from either Malaucène or Saint Estève via the D974 – built in the 1930s – or from Sault via the D164. For information on bus services in the area, see Getting There & Away under Carpentras.

CARPENTRAS

The sleepy, agricultural town of Carpentras (population 28,000), an important trading centre in Greek times and later a Gallo-Roman city, became the capital of the papal territory of the Comtat Venaissin in 1320. It flourished in the 14th century, when it was visited frequently by Pope Clement V (who preferred it to Avignon) and numerous cardinals. During the same period, Jews expelled from territory controlled by the French crown (especially Languedoc and Provence) sought refuge in the Comtat Venaissin, where they could live – subject to certain restrictions – under the protection of the pope. Today, Carpentras's 14th-century synagogue is the oldest such structure in France that's still in use.

Orientation

In the 19th century, the city's fortifications and walls were replaced by a ring of boulevards: Ave Jean Jaurès, Blvd A Rogier, Blvd du Nord, Blvd Maréchal Leclerc, Blvd Gambetta and Blvd Albin-Durand. Inside the boulevards is the partly pedestrianised old city.

If you arrive by bus, walk north-east to Place Aristide Briand, a major traffic intersection at the southernmost point on the ring of boulevards. North-east-bound Ave Jean Jaurès goes to the tourist office, while Rue de la République, which heads due north, takes you straight to the cathedral and the 17th-century Palais de Justice (Law Courts), which is next door. The Hôtel de Ville is a few blocks north-east of the cathedral.

Information

Tourist Office The tourist office (☎ 90.63.00.78) at 170 Ave Jean Jaurès is generally open Monday to Saturday from 9 am to 12.30 pm and 4 to 6.30 pm. In July and August, it's open daily from 9 am to 7 pm. Foreign currency can be exchanged here when the banks are closed.

Post Carpentras's postcode is 84200.

Synagogue

Carpentras's synagogue was founded on this site in 1367, rebuilt in 1741-43 and restored in 1954. For centuries, it served as the focal point of the town's 1000-strong Jewish community. The 1st-floor sanctuary is decorated with wood panelling and liturgical objects from the 18th century. Down below, there's an oven that was used until 1904 to bake *matza (pain azyme* in French; unleavened bread) for Passover.

The synagogue, a discrete building opposite the Hôtel de Ville on Place Juiverie, can be identified by a stone plaque, positioned high on the wall, which is inscribed with Hebrew letters. It can be visited on weekdays

from 10 am to noon and 3 to 5 pm. Just ring the bell to get in.

Arc de Triomphe

Hidden in a corner just off Rue d'Inguimbert – next to the cathedral and behind the Palais de Justice (built 1640) – this triumphal arch (or what's left of it) is the town's only Roman relic. Built under Augustus in the 1st century, it has regrettably become little more than a public urinal. One of the carvings depicts two chained prisoners, their faces worn away by time and the weather.

Cathedral

Carpentras's one-time cathedral, now officially known as Église Saint Siffrein, was built in the Meridional (southern-French) Gothic style between 1405 and 1531. The doorway, whose design is classical, was added in the 17th century. The bell tower is modern. The **trésor** (treasury) displays various precious ritual objects from the 14th to 19th centuries.

Museums

The **Musée Comtadin**, which displays artefacts related to local history, and the **Musée Duplessis**, whose paintings are from the personal collection of Monseigneur d'Inguimbert, are both on the western side of the old city at 234 Blvd Albin-Durand. The same 18th-century building houses the **Bibliothèque Inguimbertine**, a large library with numerous rare books, incunabula and manuscripts.

The **Musée Sobirats**, one block west of the cathedral at 112 Rue du College, is an 18th-century private residence decorated in the Louis XV and Louis XVI styles. The 18th-century **Hôtel Dieu** at Place Aristide Briand has an old-time pharmacy, complete with pharmaceutical ceramics. It's open to the public on Monday, Wednesday and Thursday from 9 to 11.30 am. The hospital's chapel is also of interest.

Markets

Friday is market day in Carpentras. In the morning, Provence's finest produce takes over the old centre and the shady parking area in front of the tourist office. From November to the beginning of March, truffes (truffles) are sold on Place Aristide Briand. In July and August, there's a wine market in front of the tourist office.

Wine Tasting

During July and August, free tastings of Côtes du Ventoux vintages are held around Carpentras. Enquire at the tourist office for details.

Places to Stay

The only time of the year when you're likely to have trouble finding accommodation is from mid-July to early August, when the annual music festival pumps life into the town. Contrary to what the tourist office may tell you, the *Logis des Jeunes*, a youth hostel-type place, does not generally accept people who are passing through.

Camping The riverside *Camping Villemarie* (☎ 90.63.09.55) is on Ave du Camping about two km west of the town centre. It is closed during January and February. To get there from Place Aristide Briand, walk up Blvd Albin-Durand (by car, you'll have to take a tour of the ring road) and turn left onto Ave Petrarque (turn right if you're driving). After crossing the railway tracks, turn right onto Ave du Camping.

Hotels Carpentras's liveliest hotel – there's often live music on summer nights – is the *Hôtel Le Saint Croc* (☎ 90.63.04.89), which is near the Hôtel de Ville at Place Charretier. Singles and doubles start at 140FF; quads with toilet start at 180FF.

At the northern end of town, the *Hôtel La Lavande* (☎ 90.63.13.49) on Blvd A Rogier has decent rooms from 100FF. To get there from the tourist office, follow Blvd Jean Jaurès north-eastward until it becomes Blvd A Rogier; the hotel is on the right just past the intersection of Rue Porte de Mazan.

Le Théâtre (☎ 90.63.02.90) is not far from the bus station on Blvd Albin-Durand, which heads north-westward from Place Aristide

Briand. Basic rooms start at 115FF; hall showers cost 15FF.

Just up the road, *Le Cours* (☎ 90.63. 10.07) has singles/doubles from 85/120FF. Unfortunately, this place is run down and a bit smelly.

Places to Eat

Restaurants Your best bet for a cheap meal is to dine at one of the smaller hotels. The two-star *Hôtel L'Universe* (☎ 90.63.00.05) at Place Aristide Briand has a good three-course *menu* for 55FF. Both *Le Saint Croc* and *La Lavande* (see Hotels) have *menus* from 60FF; the former even throws in a glass of wine.

The closest thing to a vegetarian restaurant is *La Saladine* (☎ 90.60.27.77) at 88 Rue Porte de Mazan, where salads start at 35FF. Pizzas begin at 40FF.

Getting There & Away

The railway station is served by goods trains only, so buses operated by Cars Comtadins and Cars Arnaud provide Carpentras's only intercity public transport. The open-air bus station is on Place Terradou, 150 metres south-west of Place Aristide Briand. Schedules are available from the bus office on the square (open Monday to Saturday from 8 am to noon and 2 to 6 pm) and the tourist office.

There are hourly services daily to Avignon (16.60FF; 45 minutes; about 15 a day) and less frequent runs to Orange (40 minutes; five a day), Cavaillon (45 minutes) and L'Isle-sur-Sorgue (20 minutes). Even less frequent are buses (weekdays only) to Vaison-la-Romaine (45 minutes), Bédoin (at the western foot of Mont Ventoux; 40 minutes) and Sault (on the eastern side of Mont Ventoux; 1½ hours).

FONTAINE DE VAUCLUSE

The mighty spring for which this small town (population 600) is named is actually the spot where the Sorgue River ends its subterranean course and gushes onto the surface. At the end of winter, up to 200 cubic metres of water per second issue forth magnificently from the base of the cliff, forming one of the world's most powerful springs. During dryer periods, the much-reduced flow simply seeps through the rocks at various points downstream from the cliff, and the spring itself becomes little more than a deep, still pond.

One of the most appealing aspects of the Fontaine de Vaucluse is the mysterious depth of its source. Fed by rainwater which seeps through the limestone plateaux to the north, it flows in caverns deep underground before surging up to the surface. So far, all human and robotical attempts to reach the bottom have been unsuccessful. The latest try got to a depth of 315 metres.

Place to Stay
There's a *youth hostel* (☎ 90.20.31.65) on Chemin de la Vignasse, which is uphill from the bus stop in the direction of Lagnes. It's closed from mid-November to mid-February.

Getting There & Away
Fontaine de Vaucluse is 20 km south-east of Carpentras and about seven km east of L'Isle-sur-Sorgue, the nearest real town. From Avignon, Voyages Arnaud runs a bus (one hour; two or three daily) with a stop at the village of Fontaine de Vaucluse, from where it's a short walk to the spring. There are buses from Carpentras to L'Isle-sur-Sorgue (20 minutes).

GORDES
On the white, rocky southern face of the Vaucluse Plateau, the tiered village of Gordes (population 1600) forms an amphitheatre overlooking the Sorgue and Calavon rivers. In summer, this once-typical Provençal village is inundated with tourists, but it's still worth a wander around if you've got the wheels to get you there.

Crowned by a sturdy castle built from the 11th to 16th centuries, Gordes is home to an exhibition of works by Vasarely (see Fondation Vasarely in the Aix-en-Provence listing), which is open daily except Tuesday.

Getting There & Away
Gordes is just east over the ridge from the Fontaine de Vaucluse and about 20 km west of Apt.

ROUSSILLON
Two millennia ago, the Romans used the distinctive ochre earth around Roussillon (population 1300), situated in the valley between the Vaucluse Plateau and the Lubéron range, for producing pottery glazes. These days the whole village is built of reddish local stone, making it a popular place for watercolourists eager to try out the range of their palettes. The red and orange hues are especially striking given the white bareness of nearby areas.

Getting There & Away
Roussillon, which is nine km east of Gordes (towards Apt), is inaccessible unless you've got your own transport.

APT & THE LUBÉRON
The Lubéron hills stretch from Cavaillon in the west to Manosque in the east, and from Apt southward to the Durance River. The area is named after the main range, a compact massif with a gentle, 1100-metre-high summit. Its oak-covered northern face is steep and uneven, while its southern face is dryer and more Mediterranean in both weather and flora and includes expanses of garrigue. Much of the Lubéron is within the boundaries of the Parc Naturel Régional du Lubéron. The area has some great hiking trails.

The landscape of the Lubéron is sprinkled with *bories*, one or two-storey huts with pointy roofs constructed without mortar using thin wedges of limestone. Built between the Iron Age and the 18th century, it is not clear whether the bories were intended as permanent residences or as seasonal shelter for nomadic herders.

The town of Apt is largely unexceptional except for its *fruits confits* (candied or crystallised fruit). However, it is the most central base for exploring the Lubéron.

PROVENCE

Information
Tourist Office As you enter Apt from Cavaillon, the tourist office (☎ 90.74.03.18) is just over the bridge on Place de la Bouquerie. It's open from 8.30 am to noon and 2 to 6 pm (7 pm from May to August). The IGN map of the Vaucluse (35FF) is on sale here.

Regional Park Office Information on the Parc Naturel Régional du Lubéron, including details about the park's 20-odd gîtes d'étape, is available in Apt from the Maison du Parc (☎ 90.74.08.55) at 1 Place Jean Jaurès, which is in the middle of the maze of alleys in the town centre. The office also sells detailed maps and the excellent topoguide *Tour du Lubéron* (78FF), which covers the GR9, GR92 and GR97 trails.

Parc Naturel Régional du Lubéron
The 1200 sq km of the Lubéron Regional Park encompass numerous villages, desolate forests (some of them recently scarred by a huge fire), unexpected gorges and abandoned farm houses, well on the way to falling into ruin – or perhaps restoration by wannabe fans of Peter Mayle, whose purchase and re-outfitting of a house around here formed the basis of his bestselling novel, *A Year in Provence*. The area is ideal for hiking.

Places to Stay
Camping *Camping Les Cèdres* (☎ 90.74.14.61), run by the Apt municipality, is by the river a few hundred metres out of town on Route de Rustrel. It's open all year.

Hostel There's an *Auberge de Jeunesse* (☎ 90.74.39.34) six km south-east of Apt in the village of Saignon. To get there, you have to choose between using your feet or your thumb.

Hotels In Apt, the *Hôtel Le Palais* (☎ 90.04.89.32) at Place Gabriel Péri (behind Place de la Bouquerie) has decent rooms and prices. The *Hôtel L'Aptois* (☎ 90.74.02.02) on Cours Lauze de Perret, a busy road at the eastern edge of the town centre, has rooms starting at 135FF.

Getting There & Away
Bus Buses to Aix-en-Provence (1½ hours; two a day) leave from Apt's Place de la Bouquerie (near the tourist office) at 6.45 am and 5 pm. The trip to Avignon takes 1¼ hours. There is also a service to/from Digne-les-Bains.

There is bus service to Cavaillon from Avignon (35 minutes), Carpentras (45 minutes) and Marseille.

Getting Around
Bicycle Bikes can be hired from Garage Maretto (☎ 90.74.16.43) on Quai Général Leclerc, which is along the river east of Place de la Bouquerie.

Arles & Nîmes Region

ARLES
The attractive city of Arles (population 51,000), which is at the northern tip of the Camargue alluvial plain, is on the Grand Rhône River just south of where the Petit Rhône splits off. It began its ascent to prosperity and political importance in 49-46 BC, when victorious Julius Caesar – to whom the city had given its support – captured and despoiled Marseille, which had backed Caesar's rival Pompey. Arles soon replaced Marseille as the region's major port and became the sort of Roman provincial centre that, by the late 1st century AD, needed a 20,000-seat amphitheatre and a 12,000-seat theatre. These days, the two structures are still used to stage cultural events and bullfights.

Vincent Van Gogh (1853-90), who settled in Arles in 1888, created hundreds of drawings and paintings of the city and nearby rural areas. His swirls and colours may have been more lurid than reality, but the atmosphere he conveyed was far from unreal. On hot days, you can watch the waves of heat rising from the haze of the Camargue, just as van Gogh did a century ago, and olive groves and vineyards still cover the slopes that lead north-east from Arles to the chalky Alpilles hills. Arles's rooftops are still red, and the narrow alleys continue to serve as a cool refuge on hot summer's days.

Orientation

The centre of Arles is enclosed by the Grand Rhône River (to the north-west), Blvd Émile Combes (to the east) and Blvd des Lices and Blvd Georges Clemenceau (to the south). It is shaped somewhat like a foot, with the train station, Place de la Libération and Place Lamartine (where van Gogh once lived) at the ankle, the Arènes at the anklebone and the tourist office squashed under the arch. It's a relatively small area, easily explored on foot.

Information

Arles has a long list of interesting things to see. Several discount combination tickets are available, including one that will get you into everything for 44FF (31FF for students and children). The tourist office has details on other combo ticket options.

Tourist Office Arles's main tourist office (☎ 90.96.29.35) is in a small pavilion on Blvd des Lices. It's open Monday to Saturday from 9 am to 6 pm (7.30 pm from April to September, 8 pm in July and August). Between Easter and 30 September, it's also open on Sunday from 9 am to 1 pm. The tourist office annexe at the train station is generally open similar hours. Both make hotel bookings (4FF), exchange foreign currency and sell maps of the region, including 1:50,000-scale IGN maps.

Money There are several banks at Place de la République. The Caisse d'Épargne (☎ 90.93.52.19) is open Tuesday to Friday from 8.10 to 11.30 am and 1.30 to 5 pm and on Saturday morning.

Post The main post office (☎ 90.96.07.80) on Blvd des Lices is open weekdays from 8.30 am to 7 pm and on Saturday until noon.

Arles's postcode is 13200.

Laundry The small laundrette at Rue Jean Granaud is open daily from 8 am to 7 pm.

Les Arènes

Arles's Roman amphitheatre (☎ 90.49. 36.86), apparently built towards the end of the 1st century AD, measures 136 metres by 107 metres, making it marginally larger than its counterpart (and rival) in Nîmes. Like other such structures around the Roman empire, it was built to stage sporting contests, chariot races and the wildly popular and bloody spectacles so beloved by the Roman public. Wild animals were pitted against other animals or gladiators, and gladiators (usually slaves or criminals) fought each other until one of them was either killed or surrendered (in the latter case his throat was usually slit). Executions were carried out either by the executioner or by pushing the victim into the arena with a wild animal.

In the early medieval period, during the Arab invasions, the Arènes were transformed into a fortress, three of whose four defensive towers can still be seen. The structure was later turned into a residential area that by the 19th century – when it was cleared so restoration work could begin – included over 200 houses and two chapels. These days, the Arènes have a capacity of more than 12,000 and still draw a full house during bullfighting season. (See the aside on bullfighting.)

The Arènes, which are hidden away in the web of narrow streets in the city centre, are open daily – unless there's some kind of a performance going on – from 9 am to 12.30 pm and 2 to 6 pm. In summer, hours are 8.30 am to 7 pm.

Théâtre Antique

The Roman theatre (☎ 90.96.93.30), which dates from the end of the 1st century BC, was used for many hundreds of years as a convenient source of construction materials, so little of the original structure remains except for two imposing columns. Entered through the Jardin d'Été on Blvd des Lices, it hosts open-air dance, film and music festivals in the summer. Without a ticket, you can get a

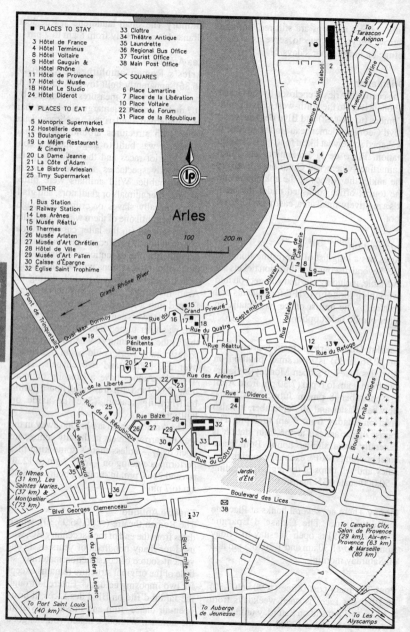

PROVENCE

■ PLACES TO STAY
3 Hôtel de France
4 Hôtel Terminus
8 Hôtel Voltaire
9 Hôtel Gauguin &
   Hôtel Rhône
11 Hôtel de Provence
17 Hôtel du Musée
18 Hôtel Le Studio
24 Hôtel Diderot

▼ PLACES TO EAT
5 Monoprix Supermarket
13 Hostellerie des Arènes
13 Boulangerie
19 Le Méjan Restaurant
   & Cinema
20 La Dame Jeanne
21 La Côte d'Adam
23 Le Bistrot Arlesian
25 Timy Supermarket

OTHER
1 Bus Station
2 Railway Station
14 Les Arènes
15 Musée Réattu
16 Thermes
26 Musée Arlaten
27 Musée d'Art Chrétien
28 Hôtel de Ville
29 Musée d'Art Païen
30 Caisse d'Épargne
32 Église Saint Trophime

33 Cloître
34 Théâtre Antique
35 Laundrette
36 Regional Bus Office
37 Tourist Office
38 Main Post Office

✕ SQUARES
6 Place Lamartine
7 Place de la Libération
10 Place Voltaire
22 Place du Forum
31 Place de la République

Arles

0   100   200 m

To Tarascon
& Avignon

Grand Rhône River

To Nîmes
(31 km), Les
Saintes Maries
(37 km) &
Montpellier
(73 km)

To Camping City,
Salon de Provence
(29 km), Aix-en-
Provence (63 km)
& Marseille
(80 km)

Jardin
d'Été

Boulevard des Lices

To Port Saint Louis
(40 km)

To Auberge
de Jeunesse

To Les
Alyscamps

glimpse of these shows through the trees on Rue du Cloître. The Théâtre Antique is open to visitors the same hours as the Arènes.

Église Saint Trophime

This austere, Provençal Romanesque-style church, once a cathedral (Arles was an archbishopric from the 4th century until 1790), stands on the site of several earlier churches. It was built in the late 11th and 12th centuries – perhaps using stone cut from the Théâtre Antique – and was named after St Trophime, a late 2nd or early 3rd-century bishop of Arles. Unlike the almost-unadorned interior, the main doorway facing Place de la République, carved around 1190, is richly decorated in a manner reminiscent of a Roman triumphal arch. Two lateral chapels were added in the 14th century. The choir and the ambulatory are from the 15th century, when the structure was significantly enlarged.

Just south of the church across the courtyard is the serene **Cloître** (☎ 90.49.36.36), surrounded by superbly sculptured columns. The two Romanesque galleries are from the 1100s, while the two Gothic galleries date from the 1300s. The cloister is open daily from 9.30 am to 12.30 pm and 2 to 7 pm. From June to September, hours are 8.30 am to 7 pm.

Thermes

The 4th-century Roman baths in the Palais Constantin (Palais de la Trouille), which is near the river on Rue du Grand Prieuré, are only partly preserved.

Les Alyscamps

This large burial ground one km south-east of the Arènes was founded by the Romans; it was taken over by local Christians in the 4th century. Because of the reputed presence among the dead of Christian martyrs said to work miracles, Les Alyscamps became a very popular last resting place. According to some sources, coffins were at one time floated down the Rhône to be fished out of the water by Arles gravediggers, whose digging fee was sent in the coffin along with the deceased.

The necropolis was treated very badly during and after the Renaissance, and today the area is but a shadow of its former glory. Some of the original sarcophagi are preserved in the Musée d'Art Chrétien. Van Gogh used to paint Les Alyscamps with great vividness.

Museums

Arles has four principal museums. The **Musée d'Art Païen** (Museum of Pagan Art), housed in a 17th-century former church on Place de la République, displays Roman statues and artefacts (including some from the Théâtre Antique) as well as marble sarcophagi.

The **Musée d'Art Chrétien** on Rue Balze, which occupies a 17th-century Jesuit chapel, has a renowned collection of early Christian sarcophagi, many of them from the 4th century. Through the museum you can visit the **Cryptoporticus**, underground storerooms most of which were carved out in the 1st century BC. Both museums are open daily from 9 am to 12.30 pm and 2 to 6 pm (7 pm from May to September).

The **Musée Arlaten** (☎ 90.96.08.23) on Rue de la République, founded by the Nobel Prize-winning poet Frédéric Mistral (see Language at the beginning of this chapter), is dedicated to preserving and displaying everyday objects related to traditional Provençal life: furniture, crafts, costumes, ceramics, wigs, a model of the Tarasque (a human-eating amphibious monster of Provençal legend), etc. It occupies a 16th-century townhouse constructed around Roman remains and is open from 9 am to noon and 2 to 5 pm (7 pm in July and August).

The **Musée Réattu** (☎ 90.49.37.58) at 10 Rue du Grand Prieuré exhibits works by some of the world's finest photographers, modern and contemporary art, and paintings by 18th and 19th-century Provençal artists. It also has 57 drawings by Picasso. Hours vary according to the time of year, but in general the museum is open daily from 9 am to 12.30 pm and 2 to 7 pm; in winter, it opens at 10 am and closes at either 5 or 6 pm.

PROVENCE

Festivals

Arles has a full calendar of summertime cultural events. From mid-July to mid-August, the International Photography Festival and its exhibits attract photography fans from around the world. The Festival of Arles, which runs through July, brings dance, theatre, music and poetry readings to the city. The bullfighting season begins around Easter with the Feria and runs until September.

Places to Stay

Except during festivals, bullfights and July and August, Arles has plenty of reasonably priced accommodation.

Places to Stay – bottom end

Camping The nearest camping ground is the two-star *Camping City* (☎ 90.93.08.86) at 67 Route de Crau, one km south-east of the city centre on the road to Marseille. It's open from Easter to 31 October and charges 15FF (9FF for a child) plus 15FF for a tent and 8FF to park. To get there, take bus No 2 to the Hermite stop.

Hostel The *Auberge de Jeunesse* (☎ 90.96. 18.25; fax 90.96.31.26), which charges 72FF (including breakfast), is nearly two km from the centre at 20 Ave Maréchal Foch. It is closed during January. To get there, take bus No 3 or 8 to the Fournier stop.

Hotels The *Hôtel Le Studio* (☎ 90.96.33.25), which is right in the city centre at 6 Rue Réattu, has basic but adequate singles and doubles from 80FF and triples from 150FF. Singles and doubles with shower start at 120FF. There is no hall shower. Reception is closed on Sunday except between June and August.

There are three hotels on Place Voltaire. The *Hôtel Voltaire* (☎ 90.96.13.58) at No 1 is a nondescript place with serviceable corner rooms from 120FF. The recently renovated *Hôtel Gauguin* (☎ 90.96.14.35) at No 5 is more modern. Singles/doubles – all equipped with automatic alarm clocks – begin at 130/140FF. The old-fashioned and rather cluttered *Hôtel Rhône* (☎ 90.96. 43.70) at No 11 has singles/doubles from 120/150FF and an efficient watchdog.

Preferable to any of these is the *Hôtel de Provence* (☎ 90.96.03.29) at 12 Rue Chiavary, which is two streets to the west. Comfortable singles/doubles start at 90/130FF.

The hotel nearest the train station is the *Hôtel de France* (☎ 90.96.01.24) at 1 Place

---

Vincent Van Gogh

When Van Gogh (1853-90) arrived in Provence in 1888, the quality of the light and colours were a great revelation to him. He spent an intensely productive year at Arles, during which he painted all sorts of local scenes, among them the **Pont de Langlois**, a little bridge that has been rebuilt three km south of Arles (from town, take bus No 1 to the Pont van Gogh terminus). A famous painting of the bridge entitled *The Bridge at Arles* is on display in the Kröller-Müller National Museum in the Netherlands.

In 1888, Van Gogh's friend and fellow artist Gauguin came to stay with him for several months. But the two men's different temperaments and approaches to art soon led to a quarrel, after which Van Gogh – overcome with despair – chopped off part of his left ear. In May 1889, because of recurrent bouts of madness, he voluntarily retreated to an asylum in Saint Rémy (25 km north-east of Arles over the Alpilles), staying there for a full year during which he continued to be amazingly productive. In 1890, while in Auvers-sur-Oise (just north of Paris), Van Gogh – lonely to the point of desperation and afraid his madness was incurable – shot and killed himself.

There are few tangible remains of Vincent Van Gogh's stay in Arles. All traces of his yellow rented house and the nearby café on Place Lamartine – both of which appear in his paintings – were wiped out in WW II. Rebuilding after the war has replaced them with modern, practical structures. ■

Lamartine, where somewhat crowded but clean singles/doubles/quads start at 100/145/210FF. Hall showers cost 10FF. This place closes from mid-November to mid-February.

Next door at 5 Place Lamartine, the recently renovated *Terminus* hotel (☎ 90.96.12.32), also known locally as the Hôtel Van Gogh, has similar rooms starting at 130FF.

Places to Stay – middle

The *Hôtel du Musée* (☎ 90.93.88.88; fax 90.49.98.15) at 11 Rue du Grand Prieuré, which occupies a 15th-century building, is spacious and calm and has a tropical terrace out back. Singles/doubles with shower and toilet start at 170/210FF. This place is closed in November.

The *Hôtel Diderot* (☎ 90.96.10.30), almost overlooking the Arènes at 5 Rue Diderot, has nice singles/doubles from 150/175FF.

Places to Stay – top end

One of the finest three-star abodes in Arles is *Hôtel Atrium* (☎ 90.49.92.92) at 1 Rue Émile Fassin. Many of its large, comfortable rooms, all of which sport Van Gogh reproductions, have terraces facing the old town centre which at sunset offer superb views of the swallows soaring over the crimson rooftops. Singles/doubles with full facilities start at 400/600FF.

Places to Eat

Blvd Georges Clemenceau and Blvd des Lices are lined with plane trees and brasseries with terraces. The latter are fine for a meal if you don't mind dining à la traffic fumes.

Restaurants – middle Calm, breezy *Le Méjan* (☎ 90.93.37.28), down by the riverfront at 23 Quai Max Dormoy, doesn't provide a view of the water, but it does have an appetizing *menu* for 90FF. It is attached to a cinema of the same name.

Hostellerie des Arènes (☎ 90.96.13.05) at 62 Rue du Refuge has a terrace with an excellent view up towards the amphitheatre. It offers a good selection of pricey salads and a *menu* for 70FF. It's closed on Tuesday.

Restaurants – bottom end Place du Forum, an intimate square shaded by eight large plane trees, turns into one big dining table for lunch and dinner. Most of the restaurants here are mid-range places, though *Le Bistrot Arlesian* on the corner of Rue des Arènes has salads from 30FF and reasonably priced snacks. The popular *La Côte d'Adam* (☎ 90.49.62.29), nearby at 12 Rue de la Liberté, is slightly cheaper than its counterparts on the square. If you're impressed by recommendations plastered on the window, this is the place to come.

La Dame Jeanne (☎ 90.96.37.09) on Rue des Pénitents Bleus is devoid of pretension. It offers a good, three-course *menu* for 65FF. *Le Studio* (☎ 90.96.33.25) at 6 Rue Réattu, affiliated with the hotel of the same name, offers a 50FF lunchtime *menu*. It is closed on Sunday.

Self-Catering The *Timy supermarket* on Rue de la République is open Monday to Saturday from 8.30 am to 12.15 pm and 3.30 to 7.30 pm. The large *Monoprix* on Place Lamartine is open weekdays from 8.30 am to 12.25 pm and 2.30 to 7.25 pm; there's no midday closure on Saturday.

On Wednesday, heaps of *market stalls* are set up on Blvd Émile Combe along the outside of the city walls. The food section is at the northern end. On Saturday, the market moves to Blvd des Lices.

On Rue du Refuge, there's a *boulangerie* that's open from 6 am to 2 pm and 4 to 8 pm (closed Tuesday).

Entertainment

Outside festival time, Arles is rather tame at night.

Cinema *Le Méjan* (☎ 90.93.33.56) at 23 Quai Max Dormoy is a laid-back place dedicated to screening nondubbed films. Tickets for adults/students cost 33/25FF. Everyone pays 25FF on Wednesday.

Pubs The brasseries along Blvd des Lices are the liveliest spots in town for a drink. There are more subdued bars around Place Voltaire.

Getting There & Away

Train Arles's modern train station, which is at the end of Ave Paulin Talabot, is about one km north of the Arènes and a bit more from the main tourist office. The information office is open Monday to Saturday from 9 am to 12.50 pm and 2 to 6.30 pm. The station itself stays open 24 hours. For telephone enquiries, call the SNCF in Avignon on ☎ 90.82.50.50. Minibus No 4 meets all trains and will whisk you into the city centre for 4.50FF.

Major rail destinations include Nîmes (38FF; 30 minutes; six a day), Montpellier (66FF; one hour; six a day), Marseille (64FF; 45 minutes) and Avignon (33FF; 20 to 25 minutes; 14 to 18 a day).

Bus The bus station is on the north side of the city centre next to the train station. The information office (☎ 90.49.38.01) is open daily from 8 am to 12.30 pm and 2.30 to 6 pm. Most intercity buses stop here but, depending on where you're going and which company you use, many also stop at 24 Blvd Georges Clemenceau, where two regional bus companies, Les Cars de Camargue and Ceyte Tourisme Méditerranée, have their offices.

The office of Les Cars de Camargue (☎ 90.96.36.25) is open weekdays and Saturday morning from 8.15 am to noon and 2 to 6 pm. It has service to Nîmes (30FF; one hour; five a day), Aix-en-Provence (60FF; 1¾ hours; two a day) and Marseille (76FF; two hours 20 minutes; two a day). The latter two lines depart from Blvd Georges Clemenceau only.

Les Cars de Camargue buses also link Arles with various parts of the Camargue, including Les Saintes Maries (31.50FF; 55 minutes; four a day), Port Saint Louis (32.50FF; 65 minutes; four a day) and many stops en route such as Pont de Rousty, Pioch Badet and Pont de Gau. If you're under 26 and will be staying in the Camargue for a few days, it might be worthwhile purchasing a Pass Camargue (150FF), which gives you three days of unlimited travel on the three main bus routes.

Ceyte Tourisme Méditerranée (☎ 90.93.74.90) also has buses to Aix-en-Provence and Marseille. Prices are the same but you can get on at the bus station. The company also offers service to Les Baux-de-Provence (24.50FF; 30 minutes; one to four a day).

Car Eurorent (☎ 90.49.60.14, 90.93.50.14) is near the train station at 22 Blvd Victor Hugo.

Getting Around

Bus Local buses are run by STAR (☎ 90.96.87.47). The information office at 16 Blvd Georges Clemenceau, which is just to the west of the tourist office, is open weekdays from 8.30 am to 12.30 pm and 1.30 to 6 pm. This is also the main bus hub, though most buses also stop at Place Lamartine, which is a bit south of the train station. In general, STAR buses run until 7.30 pm (6.30 pm on Sunday). A single ticket costs 4.50FF; a 10-ticket carnet is 38FF.

Bicycle Bikes can be hired from the train station for 55FF a day (44FF a day for three or more days). You have to leave a 1000FF deposit.

AROUND ARLES

The **Alpilles** (Little Alps) is a range of wooded hills whose jagged crests rise from the plains about 20 km north-east of Arles. Because the soil is dry and chalky, the Alpilles have been largely ignored by humans in search of economic opportunities, leaving the area wild and ideal for hikers and cyclists.

Heading north-eastward from Arles, your first sight of the Alpilles will be **Les Baux-de-Provence**, a little village situated on a 900-metre-long mesa once occupied by a huge castle. It is an extremely popular stop for tourists. The view is at its best during the build-up to a thunderstorm. For information on buses to Les Baux, see Getting There & Away under Arles.

NÎMES

Nîmes (population 135,000) is graced by some of the best preserved and most impressive Roman public buildings in all of Europe. Most famous are the Arènes, an amphitheatre reminiscent of the Colosseum in Rome, and a temple known as the Maison Carrée. The ancient city – which became Roman in 121 BC and reached its height during the 2nd century AD – received its water from a Roman aqueduct system that included the Pont du Gard, an awesome arched bridge 27 km north-east of town.

The elegant and typically southern-French atmosphere of Nîmes becomes almost Spanish during the Ferias, the city's bullfighting festivals. The surrounding countryside is covered with vineyards and garrigue; the natural perfumes of the latter are overwhelming, especially in spring. Nîmes is a good base from which to explore nearby limestone hills, the picturesque village of Uzès and the Pont du Gard.

Orientation

Everything, including traffic, revolves around the Arènes. North of the Arènes, the old centre – now largely free of vehicles – is enclosed by Rue Porte de France, Rue de la République, Blvd Amiral Courbet and Blvd Gambetta. East of the amphitheatre is Esplanade Charles de Gaulle, a large open square, from where wide Ave Feuchères leads south-eastward to the train and bus stations.

Information

Tourist Office The main tourist office (☎ 66.67.29.11) is at 6 Rue Auguste. From October to Easter, it is open weekdays from 8 am to 7 pm, on Saturday from 10 am to 5 pm and on Sunday from 10 am to noon. The rest of the year, it's open weekdays from 8 am to 7 pm (8 pm in July and August), on Saturday from 9 am to 7 pm and on Sunday from 10 am to 5 pm. The staff can make hotel reservations and, when the banks are closed, exchange foreign currency.

The tourist office annexe (☎ 66.84.18.13) inside the train station is open Monday to Saturday from 9.30 am to 12.30 pm and 2 to 6 pm. Between Pentecost (Whitsunday, the 7th Sunday after Easter) and 30 September, it's also open on Sunday from 10 am to 3 pm.

For information on the region, the Maison de Tourisme (☎ 66.21.02.51) at Place des Arènes is open weekdays from 8.45 am to 6 pm and on Saturday from 9 am to noon. In July and August, hours are 8 am to 7.30 pm on weekdays and 9 am to 1 pm and 2 to 6 pm on Saturday.

Money Near the train station, the Banque de France (☎ 66.67.87.83) on Square du 11 Novembre 1918 is open weekdays from 8.30 am to 12.15 pm and 1.45 to 3.30 pm.

Blvd Amiral Courbet and Blvd Victor Hugo are lined with banks.

Post The main post office (☎ 66.76.67.06) is on the corner of Ave Feuchères and Blvd de Bruxelles. It's open weekdays from 8 am to 7 pm and on Saturday until noon.

Nîmes's postcode is 30000.

Laundry The laundrette on the corner of Rue du Grand Couvent and Rue de l'Agau is open daily from 7 am to 10 pm.

Emergency Hôpital Gaston Doumergue (☎ 66.27.41.11.) is at 5 Rue Hoche.

Les Arènes

This superb Roman amphitheatre (☎ 66.21.00.36) on Place des Arènes, built around 100 AD to seat 24,000 spectators, is better preserved than any comparable structure in France. The structure even retains its upper storey – unlike its counterpart in Arles. The interior has four tiers of seats and a system of exits and passages designed so that the 'haves' attending the bloody gladiatorial combats so popular with the Roman public never had to rub shoulders with the 'have nots'. From the top, there's a great view of both the amphitheatre – a fine showcase of the Romans' impressive architectural skills – and the city's red rooftops.

In summer, the Arènes is used for theatre and music performances and bullfights. Unless there's something on, it's open daily

---

Denim

During the 18th century, Nîmes' sizeable Protestant middle class – banned from government posts and various other ways of earning a living – turned its energies to trade and manufacture. Among the products made in Protestant-owned factories was a twilled fabric known as *serge de Nîmes*.

When Levi Strauss (1829-1902), a Bavarian-Jewish immigrant to the USA, began producing pants in California during and after the Gold Rush (late 1840s), he discovered that the miners wanted garments that would last. After trying tent canvas, he began importing Nîmes-made serge, a durable material now better known as denim, a contraction of *de Nîmes* ('of Nîmes'). ■

---

from 8.30 am to noon and 2 to 6 pm. From mid-June to mid-September, hours are 8 am to 8 pm. Admission costs 20FF (15FF for students and children). A ticket good for both the Arènes and Tour Magne costs 28FF (20FF for students and children), a savings of a few francs.

Maison Carrée

The rectangular, Greek-style temple known as the Maison Carrée (literally Square House; ☎ 66.3626.76) on Place de la Comédie is one of the most remarkably preserved Roman temples anywhere. Built around 5 AD to honour Augustus' grandson, it survived the centuries as a meeting hall (during the Middle Ages), a private residence, a stable (in the 17th-century), a church and, after the Revolution, as an archive. Until 1995, the interior will be enlivened by three paintings created especially for the temple by American artist Julian Schnabel.

The Maison Carrée, entered through six symmetrical Corinthian columns, sits rather isolated at the end of Rue Auguste. It is open the same hours as the amphitheatre. Admission is free.

Jardin de la Fontaine

The Fountain Garden is home to Nîmes's other important Roman relics: the **Temple de Diane** and the **Tour Magne**, the largest of the many towers that studded the city's seven-km-long Roman ramparts.

Jardin de la Fontaine, laid out around Source de la Fontaine (the site of a spring, temple and baths in Roman times), still has an opulent atmosphere, with statue-adorned

paths running around deep, slimy-green waterways. The Temple de Diane is to the left through the main entrance. A 10-minute walk through the gardens takes you to the crumbly shell of the Tour Magne, the top of which affords a fine view of the countryside around Nîmes. Admission to the tower is 10FF (8FF for students and children). It's open the same hours as the amphitheatre.

The garden is almost one km north-west of the amphitheatre. Bus No 5 or 8 from Ave Feuchères stop near the main entrance at the intersection of Ave Jean Jaurès and Quai de la Fontaine, the city's classiest thoroughfare. The grounds close around sunset; in summer, they stay open until 10 pm.

Museums

The **Musée du Vieux Nîmes** (☎ 66.36.00. 64), housed in the 17th-century episcopal palace on Place aux Herbes, is the city's most appealing museum. Though themes change annually, the emphasis is always on some aspect of Nîmes's history. This museum is open daily from 10 am to 6 pm. Admission is free.

The **Musée d'Archéologie** (☎ 66.67.25. 57) at 13 Blvd Amiral Courbet brings together columns, mosaics, sculptures and personal effects from the Roman and pre-Roman periods that were unearthed around Nîmes. In the same building, the **Musée d'Histoire Naturelle** has a musty collection of stuffed animals and rows of bulls' horns. Both are open daily except Sunday and Monday mornings. From mid-September to mid-June, hours are 9 am to noon and 1.30 to 6 pm; summer hours are 9 am to 7 pm. Admission is free. Next door, the **Musée Taurin** houses temporary exhibitions on bull art. It's open from 9.30 am to 12.30 pm and 2 to 6 pm daily except Sunday and Monday mornings.

The **Musée des Beaux-Arts** (☎ 66.67.38.21) on Rue de la Cité Foulc has an unsurprising collection of Flemish, Italian and French works as well as a Roman mosaic. It's open the same hours as the Musée d'Archéologie. Entry is 20FF (15FF for children).

The ultra-modern **Musée d'Art Moderne** on Place de la Comédie was inaugurated in April 1993. For details, enquire at the tourist office.

Festivals

Ferias & Bullfights The popular and bloody Feria festivals – of which there are three: one in spring, another at Pentecost and yet another around grape-picking time – revolve around a series of *corridas* (bullfights; see the aside on bullfighting), two of which are held each day. Tickets to a corrida cost between 95 and 450FF. Reservations usually have to be made months in advance.

Much less cruel are the nonlethal *courses Camarguaises*, held on the weekend before a Feria and at other times during the bull-fighting season. Tickets cost between 50 and 80FF.

Music L'Été de Nîmes, the city's main cultural festival, is held during July and August in the Arènes and other places around town. It livens up the city with performances of jazz, pop, rock, dance, theatre, etc.

Places to Stay – bottom end

Camping *Domaine de la Bastide* (☎ 66.38.09.21) on Route de Générac is about four km south of town on the D13 to Générac. Tariffs are 30/50/60FF for one/two/three people with a tent. This place is open year round. To get there, take bus No 4 from Ave Feuchères to the Font Dame stop.

For information on camping near the Pont du Gard, see Pont du Gard in the Around Nîmes section.

Hostel The *Auberge de Jeunesse* (☎ 66.23.25.04) is on Chemin de la Cigale about 3.5 km north-west of the train station. It's open all day long. A bed costs 56FF, including breakfast. From the train station, take bus No 20 to the Auberge de Jeunesse stop or, somewhat less conveniently, bus No 8 to the Stade stop.

Hotels Nîmes has plenty of cheap, appealing hotels, most of them superbly situated in the old centre.

The *Hôtel Concorde* (☎ 66.67.91.03) at No 3 on quiet, pedestrianised Rue des Chapeliers has small but adequate singles/doubles from 95/105FF. The management is laid-back and the atmosphere is casual. Slightly up-market, the *Hôtel Carrière* (☎ 66.67.24.89; fax 66.67.28.08) at 6 Rue Grizot has classically styled singles/doubles for 120/130FF (170/190FF with a shower). It has a private garage.

The *Hôtel La Mairie* (☎ 66.67.65.91) at 11 Rue des Greffes has dull décor but clean, quiet rooms from 85/95FF. For an excellent view of the amphitheatre, the *Hôtel La France* (☎ 66.67.23.05; fax 66.76.22.30) at 4 Blvd des Arènes has an assortment of rooms and a pricing policy similar to the one used by the Romans at the Arènes: the higher up you go, the cheaper the bed. Fourth-floor singles/triples start at 90/145FF, 3rd-floor single/doubles begin at 100/110FF, and so on.

Places to Stay – middle

Just up from its namesake, the *Hôtel Amphithéâtre* (☎ 66.67.28.51) at 4 Rue des Arènes is one of the city's loveliest options. Rooms are outfitted with an eclectic array of furnishings, but most have a shower and toilet; prices for singles/doubles/quads start at 135/160/210FF.

The friendly *Maison Carrée* (☎ 66.67.32.89; fax 66.76.22.57) at 14 Rue de la Maison Carrée is popular with travellers. Some of the rooms are a bit poky but most have shower, toilet and TV, and a few at the front have terraces. Prices for singles/doubles start at 115/210FF.

Places to Stay – top end

While the majority of Nîmes's multistar hotels are scattered around the city's periphery, there are a few located centrally. One of the

PROVENCE

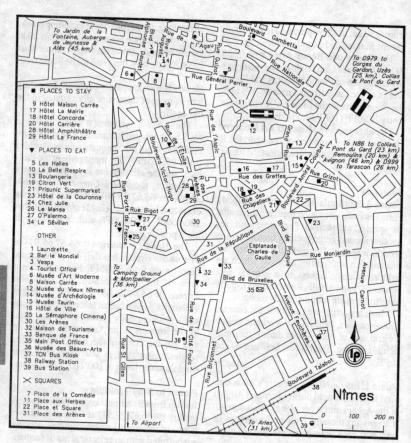

PROVENCE

Map legend:

■ PLACES TO STAY
9 Hôtel Maison Carrée
17 Hôtel La Mairie
18 Hôtel Concorde
20 Hôtel Carrière
28 Hôtel Amphithéâtre
29 Hôtel La France

▼ PLACES TO EAT
5 Les Halles
10 La Belle Respire
13 Boulangerie
19 Citron Vert
21 Prisunic Supermarket
23 Hôtel de la Couronne
24 Chez Julie
26 Le Mansa
27 O'Palermo
34 Le Sévillan

OTHER
1 Laundrette
2 Bar le Mondial
3 Vespa
4 Tourist Office
6 Musée d'Art Moderne
8 Maison Carrée
12 Musée du Vieux Nîmes
14 Musée d'Archéologie
15 Musée Taurin
16 Hôtel de Ville
25 La Sémaphore (Cinema)
30 Les Arènes
32 Maison de Tourisme
33 Banque de France
34 Main Post Office
36 Musée des Beaux-Arts
37 TCN Bus Kiosk
38 Railway Station
39 Bus Station

✕ SQUARES
7 Place de la Comédie
11 Place aux Herbes
22 Place et Square
31 Place des Arènes

Nîmes

0   100   200 m

best is the four-star *Hôtel de la Baume* (☎ 66.
76.28.42) on Rue Nationale just north of the
old centre's winding streets. Singles/doubles
start at 500/600FF and, of course, all rooms
have private facilities plus TV and air-con.

Places to Eat

The slopes of the Jardin de la Fontaine are a
peaceful spot for a picnic.

Restaurants The places to eat along Rue
Porte de France offer a wide choice of cui-
sines from around the world. Relaxed *Chez
Julie* at No 40 offers Polish, American and

Russian dishes; *menus* cost 45FF to 70FF.
Across the road at No 17bis, down the small
impasse (dead-end street), *Le Mansa*
(☎ 66.21.09.18) offers African cuisine
amidst a kaleidoscope of colours. Main
courses average 65FF.

O'Palermo (☎ 66.21.74.99) at 11 Rue Bigot
has Sicilian specialities and pizzas from
about 40FF. There's a small terrace out the
back. *Le Sévillan* on Rue de la Cité Foulc has
a 49FF *menu* that includes a glass of wine.
Similar but heartier is the 50FF *menu* served
at *Hôtel de la Couronne* on Place de la
Couronne.

In the pedestrianised heart of the city, Rue de l'Étoile has an abundance of mostly mid-range restaurants. At No 12, *La Belle Respire* (☎ 66.21.27.21), has designer décor and a fine *menu*. Main dishes start at about 70FF. For some greens, modern but calm *Citron Vert* (☎ 66.36.11.67) at 7 Rue des Chapeliers offers salads from 35FF. From October to February, this places is closed by 7 pm.

Self-Catering *Les Halles*, a large, modern covered food market between Rue Guizot and Rue des Halles, is open daily until midday.

The upstairs food section of the *Prisunic* on Blvd Amiral Courbet is open Monday to Saturday from 8.30 am to 7 pm. If you happen to be looking for bread shaped like a bull's head (or just a traditional baguette), the *boulangerie* on the Grand Rue is open Monday to Saturday until 8 pm.

Entertainment

Music In summer, there are lots of opportunities to hear live music – check the posters to see which names from the worlds of jazz, classical and rock are in town.

Live local rock can be heard some nights at *Bar Le Mondial* on Blvd Gambetta.

Cinema Nondubbed films are screened at *La Sémaphore* (☎ 66.67.83.11), at 25a Rue Porte de France. Tickets cost 30FF but are cheaper on Wednesday and in the middle of the day.

Bars There are late-night bars along Ave Victor Hugo.

Getting There & Away

Air Nîmes-Garons Airport (☎ 66.70.06.88) is halfway between Nîmes and Arles.

Train The train station (☎ 66.23.50.50) is at the south-eastern end of Ave Feuchères. The information office is open Monday to Saturday from 8 am to 6.30 pm. In general, the ticket windows are open from 5.45 am to 10 pm. The station closes for two hours from midnight.

Major rail destinations include Paris's Gare de Lyon (347FF; five hours), Alès (39FF; 40 minutes; five a day), Arles (38FF; 30 minutes; six a day), Avignon (40FF; 30 minutes; 15 a day), Marseille (85FF; 1¼ hours; 12 a day) and Montpellier (45FF; 30 minutes; 20 a day).

Bus The bus station is behind the train station on Rue Sainte Félicité. Several companies have offices here. Regional operators such as STD Gard, Cariane and Les Rapides de Camargue are at one end of the terminal, while long-haul operators like Eurolines and Intercars are at the other. The regional bus information office (☎ 66.29.52.00) is open weekdays from 8 am to noon and 2 to 6 pm.

Destinations served include Pont du Gard (26.50FF; 35 minutes; five a day), Collias (on the Gard River; 30FF; one hour), Uzès (26FF; 40 minutes; eight a day) and Alès (32.50FF). There are also buses to/from Avignon (1¼ hours; five a day) and Arles (30FF; one hour; five a day).

Eurolines and Intercars serve Spain, Portugal and Morocco; Eurolines also covers other European destinations. The Eurolines office (☎ 66.29.49.02) is open Monday to Saturday from 9 am to noon and 2 to 7 pm. A one-way ticket to Barcelona (six hours) costs 255FF (205FF if you're under 26). Intercars (☎ 66.29.84.22) is open the same hours but is closed on Saturday afternoon. The fare to Madrid (18 hours) is 370FF (355FF for people under 26).

Car Citer (☎ 66.29.04.12) is on Rue de Lionceaux at the corner of Blvd Allende. To contact ADA, call ☎ 66.84.25.60.

Motorbike Vespa (☎ 66.67.67.46) at 6 Blvd Alphonse Daudet has a good selection of two-wheeled conveyances. Scooters/motorcycles cost 150/200FF a day and require a 1000/5000FF deposit. This place is open on Monday from noon to 6 pm, Tuesday to Friday from 9 am to noon and 2 to 6 pm and on Saturday morning.

PROVENCE

Getting Around

To/From the Airport Airport buses leave from Blvd de Prague (on Esplanade Charles de Gaulle) about an hour before each flight.

Bus Local buses are run by TCN (☎ 66.38.15.40), whose kiosk on Ave Feuchères can supply route maps (as can the tourist office). There's no single bus hub, but lots of buses stop along Ave Feuchères, on the boulevards surrounding Esplanade Charles du Gaulle and on Blvd Talabot (to the right as you exit the train station). A single ride costs 6FF; a carnet of five tickets is 22FF.

Taxi Taxis can be found around Esplanade Charles de Gaulle. To order a cab, call ☎ 66.29.40.11.

Bicycle Bikes can be hired from the train station luggage room (☎ 66.70.41.87), which is open from 8 am to 8 pm. Tariffs are 33/44FF a half/full day; a 1000FF deposit is required. Vespa at 6 Blvd Alphonse Daudet (see Motorbike under Getting There & Away) also rents bicycles for 60FF a day; a 500FF deposit is required.

AROUND NÎMES
Pont du Gard

The exceptionally well-preserved Roman aqueduct known as the Pont du Gard – photographs of which invariably make an appearance in textbooks of Western history – was once part of a 50-km-long system of canals constructed around 19 BC by Agrippa (the powerful deputy of Augustus Caesar) to bring water from near Uzès to Nîmes. The 35 arches of the 275-metre-long upper tier, which is 49 metres above the Gard (or Gardon) River, carry a 1.2 by 1.75-metre watercourse designed to transport 20,000 cubic metres of water a day. The road bridge on the aqueduct's downstream side was added in 1743.

Measures are being taken to protect the Pont du Gard against pollution and erosion. A project is under way to set up two new entrance points and a museum, **Écomusée de la Garrigue**, as well as a four-km-long path around the site. For the time being, you can walk to and even upon the Pont du Gard from car parks (18FF) on either side. The Pont du Gard is visited by 1½ million people each year.

Places to Stay There are a couple of camping grounds near the Pont du Gard. Two-star *Camping de Valive* (☎ 66.22.81.52) is about 800 metres from the bridge (1.75 km from the bus stop) on the northern side. Tariffs are 30/50/60FF for one/two/three people with a tent. This place is open all year. Bike rental costs 80FF a day.

At the other end of the scale is the hotel *La Bégude Saint-Pierre* (☎ 66.22.96.96), located about two km north-west of the Pont du Gard on the D981 towards Uzès. This ancient mansion with its enclosed courtyard was used as a horse and carriage stop in olden days. Recently converted to a stunning hotel, it has spacious rooms of simple yet flamboyant design and an intimate restaurant which almost calls for tie and tails. Double rooms start at 400FF.

Getting There & Away The Pont du Gard is 27 km north-east of Nîmes, 26 km west of Avignon and four km north-west of Remoulins. Buses from Avignon, Nîmes and Uzès stop one km north of the bridge.

Gard River

The beautiful and wild Gard River – also known as the Gardon – descends from the Cévennes mountains. Known for its unpredictability, torrential rains can raise the water level by two to five metres in a short time. During long dry spells, though, the Gard sometimes dries up completely.

The Gard flows through the hills in a long gorge from Russen to the village of **Collias**. Five km further downstream it passes under the Pont du Gard.

Boating In Collias, Kayak Vert (☎ 66.22.84.83) and Canoë Le Tourbillon, both based under the local bridge, offer excursions by kayak, canoe and mountain bike. You can paddle down to the Pont du Gard (165/100FF for a kayak/canoe) or arrange to be dropped off 25 km upstream, whence there's a great descent back.

Hiking The GR6 follows the river from Collias to the Pont du Gard.

Getting There & Away Bus No 168 from Nîmes's bus station stops in Collias (30FF; one hour) but there's only one a day. It departs just after 6 pm.

Uzès

Uzès (population 7800) is a laid-back but sophisticated little town set among the garrigue-covered hills 25 km north of Nîmes. With its Renaissance façades, **Duché** (Ducal Palace), narrow streets and ancient towers, it's a charming place to wander around. Uzès is also big on festivals and fairs – one of the more animated is the **Foire à l'Ail** (Garlic Fair), held in late June. On Saturdays in winter, there's a truffle market.

Information The tourist office (☎ 66.22. 68.88) is on Ave de la Libération next to the bus station.

Places to Stay Uzès is a pleasant day trip from either Nîmes or Avignon. However, if you decide to stay overnight there is a handful of hotels in town. The least expensive is the *Hostellerie Provençale* (☎ 66.22.11.06) at 1 Rue Grande Bourgade which has ordinary doubles from 130FF.

Getting There & Away Half of the bus services linking Uzès with Nîmes (26FF; 40 minutes; eight a day) stop near the Pont du Gard (15.50FF; 15 minutes), as do buses to/from Avignon (38FF; one hour; five a day). There are three buses a day to Alès (31.50FF; one hour), which is on the border of the Cévennes.

CAMARGUE

The sparsely populated, 780-sq-km delta of the Rhône River, known as the Camargue, is famed for its desolate grandeur and the incredibly varied bird life its wetlands

support. Over 400 species of land and waterbirds inhabit the region, including storks, bee-eaters and some 160 other migratory species. Huge flocks of pink flamingoes come here to nest during the spring and summer, and many set up house near the **Étang du Fangassier**. In 1991, 13,000 pairs of flamingoes spent 2½ months hatching and raising their offspring before heading back to Africa with 9050 young 'uns in tow. Visitors who'd like to do a bit of bird watching will find binoculars a useful item to bring along.

The Camargue has been formed over the ages by sediment deposited by the Rhône River as it flows into the Mediterranean. In the southern Camargue, the areas between the embankments that line past and present water channels are taken up by shallow salt marshes, inland lakes and lagoons whose brackish waters shimmer in the Provençal sun. The northern part of the delta consists of dry land, and in the years following WW II huge tracts were desalinated as part of a costly drainage and irrigation programme designed to make the area suitable for large-scale agriculture, especially the cultivation of rice. Rice production has dropped sharply since the 1960s.

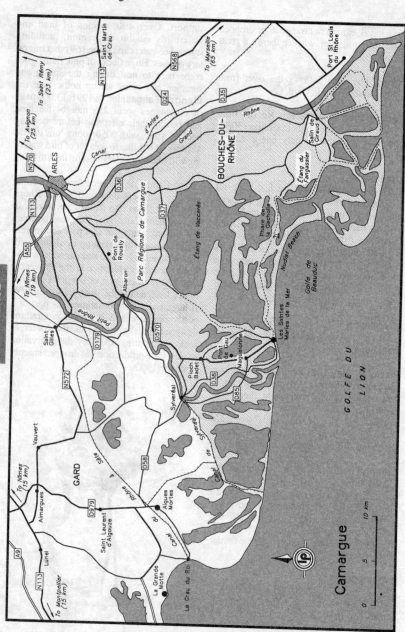

PROVENCE

Camargue

To Marseille (65 km)

Port St Louis du Rhône

Saint Martin de Crau

To Saint Rémy (23 km)

To Avignon (25 km)

Saint Laurent d'Aigouze

BOUCHES-DU-RHÔNE

Rhône

Grand Rhône

d'Arles

Canal

ARLES

Parc Régional de Camargue

D36

D37

Étang de Vaccarès

Pont de Rousty

Albaron

Petit Rhône

Salin de Giraud

Étang du Fangassier

Phare de la Gacholle

Nudist Beach

Golfe de Beauduc

GOLFE DU LION

Saint Gilles

D179

D570

Plan Bade

Pont de Gau

Maguelonne

D38

DB5

Sylvéréal

To Nîmes (19 km)

Canal de Sylvéréal

Vauvert

N572

GARD

D58

Sète

Canal du Rhône à Sète

To Nîmes (15 km)

Aimargues

D979

Aigues Mortes

To Montpellier (15 km)

Lunel

La Grande Motte

Le Grau du Roi

Les Saintes Maries de la Mer

0   5   10 km

At some places along the coast, the delta continues to grow, leaving one-time seaside towns many km from the Mediterranean. Elsewhere, sea currents and storms have, in recent centuries, swept away land that had been around long enough for people to build things on. The course of the Rhône has changed repeatedly over the millennia, but the Grand Rhône (which carries 90% of the river's flow) and the Petit Rhône have followed their present channels for about 500 years.

Most of the Camargue wetlands are within the **Parc Naturel Régional de Camargue**, which was set up in 1970 (some areas had been declared protected in 1928) to preserve the area's fragile ecosystems by maintaining an equilibrium between ecological considerations and the region's economic mainstays: agriculture, salt production, hunting, grazing and tourism.

The Camargue's famous herds of cream-coloured horses and black bulls (raised for bullfighting), roaming free under the watchful eyes of a cowboy-like *gardian* (herdsman), can still be seen in certain areas. But you're much more likely to see bulls grazing in fenced-in fields and horses that are saddled and tethered, waiting in rows under the blazing sun for tourists willing to pay through the nose for a ride. At least one traditional Camargue phenomenon is alive and well: the area's savage mosquitoes are flourishing, feeding on the blood of hapless passers-by just as they have for countless eons.

Orientation

Shaped like a croissant with the **Étang de Vaccarès** (a lake) forming the centre, the 850-sq-km Parc Naturel Régional de Camargue is enclosed by the Petit Rhône and Grand Rhône rivers. The Étang de Vaccarès and nearby peninsulas and islands form the **Réserve Nationale de Camargue**, a 135-sq-km nature reserve.

Rice is cultivated in the northern sections of the delta. There are enormous salt evaporation pools around Salin de Giraud, which is at the Camargue's south-eastern tip.

Information

Tourist Office Les Saintes Maries de la Mer, the Camargue's main town, has a tourist office (☎ 90.47.82.55) at 5 Ave van Gogh.

Regional Park Office The Parc Naturel Régional de Camargue has a Maison du Parc (visitors centre; ☎ 90.97.86.32) at Pont de Gau, which is five km north of Les Saintes Maries. Exhibits focus on environmental issues. From the foyer you can watch birds – often including flamingoes – in the nearby marshes. The centre is open from 9 am to 6 pm (closed Friday). From October to March, hours are 9.30 am to 5 pm. Entry is free.

Musée Camarguais

Housed in a sheep shed built in 1812, the Camargue Museum (☎ 90.97.10.82) at Pont de Rousty (12 km south of Arles on the N570 to Les Saintes Maries) provides a thoughtful and interesting picture of traditional life in the Camargue. From October to March it's open from 10 am to 5 pm (closed Tuesday). The rest of the year, it's open daily from 9 am to 6 pm. Entry costs 20FF (10FF for student and children).

Parc Ornithologique

At Pont de Gau, this bird park (☎ 90.97.82.62) – situated next to the Maison du Parc – is an excellent place to get a look at some of the area's flying fauna. A six-km path through the swamp gives you a sense of the Camargue at its wildest, mosquitoes and all. The park, which also has some caged birds, is open daily from 9 am to sunset. Entry costs 25FF (12FF for children).

Aigues Mortes

On the western edge of the Camargue, 28 km north-west of Les Saintes Maries, is the curiously named Aigues Mortes, a tiny walled town established in the mid-13th century by Louis IX (Saint Louis) so the French crown would have a Mediterranean port under its direct control. (At the time, the area's other ports were controlled by various rival powers, including the counts of Provence.) In 1248; Louis IX's ships – some 1500 of

PROVENCE

them! – gathered here before setting sail to the Holy Land for the Seventh Crusade.

Aigues Mortes' sturdy, rectangular ramparts, the top of which affords great views over the marshlands, can easily be circumambulated. Inside the walls, there's a fair bit of tourist hype.

Les Saintes Maries de la Mer

This coastal resort (population 2000) is known for its fortified Romanesque church (12th to 15th centuries) and the nearby beaches.

Les Saintes Maries is most animated during the annual gypsy pilgrimage (see the The Gypsy Pilgrimage aside below) that takes place on 24-25 May. There's another pilgrimage on the Saturday and Sunday following 22 October.

Beaches

The coast near Les Saintes Maries is lined with a good 15 km of uninterrupted beaches. The area near Phare de la Gacholle, the lighthouse 11 km east of town, is frequented by nudists.

Hiking

The Parc Naturel Régional has numerous walking paths.

Places to Stay

Camping *La Brise* (☎ 90.97.84.67) on Ave du Docteur Cambon is north-east of the centre of Les Saintes Maries. It's open from January to 30 September. The charge for one person with a tent is 45FF.

Hostel There's an *Auberge de Jeunesse* (☎ 90.97.91.72) in the hamlet of Pioch Badet, which is about eight km north of Les Saintes Maries on the N570 to Arles. Turn right at the one-millionth mosquito and left at the two-millionth. A bed costs 41FF; meals are about 40FF. The hostel is closed until 5 pm. Les Cars de Camargue buses from Arles to Les Saintes Maries drop you at the door – see Bus under Getting There & Away in the Arles section for details.

Hotels Heaps of hotels line the roads into Les Saintes Maries, and there are more hotels in town, but few are cheap. The best bets are on Ave Théodore Aubanel, which runs along the port west of the tourist office – *L'Abrivado* (☎ 90.97.84.02) at No 2 and *Les Vagues* (☎ 90.97.84.40) at No 12 both have doubles from 180FF.

Getting There & Away

Bus For details about bus connections to/from Arles (via Pont du Gau and Pont de Rousty) and the three-day Pass Camargue ticket, see Bus under Getting There & Away in the Arles section. During July and August, infrequent buses link Les Saintes Maries with Montpellier via Aigues Mortes.

The Gypsy Pilgrimage

Every year, for three days at the end of May, *gitans* (gypsies) from all over Europe gather at the Camargue fishing village of Les Saintes Maries de la Mer to honour their patron saint, Sarah. According to Provençal legend, Sarah, along with Mary Magdalene, Mary Jacob, Mary Salome and other New Testament figures, fled the Holy Land in a small boat, drifting around for a while before making landfall near the Rhône River.

In 1448, skeletal remains believed to belong to Sarah, Mary Jacob and Mary Salome were found in a crypt in Les Saintes Maries. Gypsies have been coming here on pilgrimage ever since, though these days they make a few concessions to modernity: whereas the pilgrims once arrived by horse or carriage, these days they pull into town by car and camper van. But there's still plenty of dancing, music is performed in the streets and a statue of Sarah is carried through the town accompanied by men and women in traditional dress. Courses Camarguaises (non-lethal bullfights) are also held. ■

Getting Around

Bicycle As long as you can put up with the insects and stiff sea breezes, bicycles are an excellent way to explore the Camargue, which is of course very flat. East of Les Saintes Maries, areas along the seafront and further inland are reserved for hikers and cyclists.

The Auberge de Jeunesse in Pioch Badet rents bikes for 35/60FF for a half/whole day. In Les Saintes Maries, there are several rental shops with similar prices, including Le Vélociste (☎ 90.97.83.26) on Place des Remparts, which can provide route information.

North-Eastern Provence

DIGNE-LES-BAINS

Provence hits the Alps and the land of snow meets the land of olives around Digne-les-Bains (population 18,000), which is 106 km north-east of Aix-en-Provence and 152 km north-west of Nice. The town is named for its thermal springs, visited annually by 11,000 people in search of a water cure for rheumatism, respiratory ailments and other medical conditions. The area is also known for its production of *lavande* (lavender), which is harvested in August. In spring, flowering poppies sprinkle the green fields with blazes of bright red.

Digne itself is unremarkable, though it was the home of a very remarkable woman, Alexandra David-Neel, an adventurer whose travels to Tibet brought her wide acclaim. The shale around Digne is rich in fossils.

Orientation

Digne is built on the eastern bank of the Bléone River. The major roads into town converge at the Point Rond, a roundabout 400 metres north-east of the train station. The main street is plane tree-lined Blvd Gassendi (named after a 17th-century philosopher born near here), which heads north-eastward from the Point Rond and passes Place du Général de Gaulle, the town's main public square.

Information

The tourist office (☎ 92.31.42.73), which is at the Point Rond, is open Monday to Saturday from 9 am to noon and 2 to 6 pm. From mid-June to mid-September, it's open daily from 9 am to 12.30 pm and 2 to 7 pm.

Digne's postcode is 04000.

Fondation Alexandra David-Neel

Paris-born writer and philosopher Alexandra David-Neel, who spent her last years in Digne, is known for her incognito voyage early in this century to Tibet. Her memory – and her interest in Tibet – are kept enthusiastically alive by the Fondation Alexandra David-Neel (☎ 92.31.32.38), which occupies her erstwhile residence at 27 Ave Maréchal Juin. It is just over a km from town on the road to Nice. From October to June, free tours (with headphones for English speakers) start at 10.30 am, 2 pm and 4 pm; from July to September, tours begin at 10.30 am, 2 pm, 3.30 pm and 5 pm.

Cathedral & Museum

In town, the **Cathédral Saint Jérome** dates from around 1500 but was restored in the mid-19th century. The small **Musée Municipal** at 64 Blvd Gassendi has displays of art, archaeology and minerology.

Réserve Naturelle Géologique

Digne is in the middle of the Réserve Naturelle Géologique, whose spectacular fossil deposits include the footprints of prehistoric birds as well as ammonites, spiral shells that look like a ram's horn. You'll need a detailed regional map (sold at the tourist office) and your own transport (or a patient thumb) to get to most of the 18 sites, most of which are around **Barles** (24 km north of Digne) and **Barrême** (28 km south-east of Digne). Three km north of Digne on the road to Barles (and one km north of the Centre de Géologie), there's an impressive limestone slab with some 500 ammonites.

The Réserve Naturelle's headquarters, the **Centre de Géologie** (☎ 92.31.51.31) at Saint Benoît, is two km north of town off the road to Barles. Its exhibitions on matters mineral and geological are open daily (weekdays only from November to March) from 9 am to noon and 2 to 5.30 pm (4.30 pm on Fridays). Entry to the centre costs 13FF (11FF for students, 7FF for children). To get there, take TUD bus No 1, get off over the bridge and take the road to the left. Cars aren't allowed up, so it's a 15-minute walk along the rocky overhang above the river.

Places to Stay

Camping *Camping du Bourg* (☎ 92.31. 04.87), nearly two km east on the Barcelonnette road, is open all year and costs 53FF for two people with a car and tent. To get there take the bus towards Barcelonnette and get off at the Notre Dame du Bourg stop. From there it's a 600 metre walk.

Hostel Hikers can avail themselves of the *gîte d'étape* (☎ 92.31.20.30) on Ave Pompidou, which is nearly two km from the town centre off the road to Sisteron. It's open all year and costs 40FF per person.

The peaceful *Centre de Géologie* (☎ 92. 31.51.31) at Saint Benoît, two km north of town off the road to Barles, has dorm beds for 45FF. Singles/doubles cost 55/100FF.

Hotels The little *Hôtel L'Origan* (☎ 92.31. 62.13) at 6 Rue Pied de Ville has a posh restaurant but affordable singles/doubles from 90/100FF.

Le Coin Fleuri (☎ 92.31.04.51) at 9 Blvd Victor Hugo has functional rooms for 120/150FF and a great garden to relax in.

The *Hôtel Central* (☎ 92.31.31.91) at No 26 on shaded Blvd Gassendi has rooms from 120/140FF.

A bit up-market is *L'Aiglon* (☎ 92.31. 02.70) at 1 Rue de Provence, whose deceptive entrance hides calm, pastel rooms starting from 295FF.

Places to Eat

Restaurants Away from the terraces on Place du Général de Gaulle, *La Braisière* (☎ 92.31.59.63) at 19 Place de l'Évêché has a good lunch *menu* for 66FF and a fine view over the town. *Le Point Chaud* (☎ 92.31.

30.71) at 95 Blvd Gassendi is a dark local haunt offering 58FF *menus* for both lunch and dinner.

Self-Catering The *Casino supermarket* on Blvd Gassendi is open Monday to Saturday from 7 am to 12.30 pm and 2 to 7.30 pm. From July to September, it's open on Sunday until noon. A *food market* takes over Place du Général de Gaulle on Wednesday and Saturday mornings.

Getting There & Away

Train The train station (☎ 92.31.00.67) is a 10-minute walk westward from the tourist office. The ticket windows are open from 8.30 am to 7 pm. There are four trains a day to Marseille (102FF; 2¼ hours).

The government-owned Chemins de Fer de la Provence runs four or five trains a day to Nice's Gare du Sud (97FF; three hours 20 minutes) along a scenic and winding narrow-gauge line. See Train under Getting There & Away in the Nice section of the Côte d'Azur chapter for more information.

To get to town from the train station, follow Ave Pierre Semard to the roundabout, go straight across and continue to the second bridge, across which you'll find the tourist office.

Bus The bus station (☎ 92.31.50.00) is behind the tourist office; the information and ticket office is under it. Regional companies operate buses to Nice (80FF; 2¼ hours; at 1.10 pm) via Castellane (near the Gorges du Verdon; 57FF; 1¼ hours) as well as Marseille (70FF; 2½ hours; four a day) and Apt (55FF; two hours; two a day).

GORGES DU VERDON

The 25-km-long Gorges du Verdon (also known as the Grand Canyon du Verdon), the largest canyon in Europe, slices through the limestone plateau midway between Avignon and Nice. It begins at Rougon (near the confluence of the Verdon and Jabron rivers) and continues westward until the river flows into

Lac de Sainte Croix. The snoozy village of Castellane is east of Rougon.

Carved by the greenish waters of the Verdon River, the gorge is 250 to 700 metres deep. The bottom is eight to 90 metres wide, while the rims are 200 to 1500 metres apart.

The Canyon

The bottom of the gorge can be visited only on foot or by raft, but motorists and cyclists can enjoy spectacular (if dizzying) views from two cliffside roads:

- **La Route des Crêtes** (the D952 and D23), which follows the northern rim and passes the **Point Sublime** overlook at the canyon's entrance, whence the GR4 trail leads to the bottom of the canyon;

- **La Corniche Sublime** (the D71), which goes along the southern rim and takes you to such landmarks as **Balcons de la Mescla** (the Mescla Terraces) and **Pont de l'Artuby** (Artuby Bridge), the highest bridge in Europe.

A complete circuit of the Gorges du Verdon via Moustiers Sainte Marie involves about 100 km of driving. The only real village en route is La Palud, two km north-east of the northern bank of the gorge. In the summer, heavy traffic often slows travel to a crawl.

The bottom of the canyon, first explored in its entirety in 1905 by the father of French speleology, Édouard-Alfred Martel, presents hikers and white-water rafters with an overwhelming series of cliffs and narrows. You can walk most of the gorge along the often difficult GR4, which is covered by Didier-Richard's 1:50,000-scale map No 19, entitled *En Haute Provence*. The full hike takes two days, though short descents into the canyon are possible from a number of points. Bring along a torch (flashlight) and potable water. You can camp rough en route on gravel beaches.

The water level of the river can rise suddenly if the EDF (France's electricity company) opens the hydroelectric dams upstream, making it difficult if not impossible to ford (or reford) the river.

Rafting & Cycling

Verdon Insolite (☎ 92.77.33.57), based in La Palud, runs white-water rafting trips and rents out mountain bikes. At Castellane, contact Aqua Verdon (☎ 92.83.72.75) on Routes des Gorges.

Bungi Cord Jumping

On most weekends from May to early July and from late August until the weather gets too cold or wet, Latitude Challenge (☎ 91.25.64.30; fax 91.25.64.62), based at 5 Blvd Rabatau (8e) in Marseille, offers bungi cord jumping *(benji* or *saut à l'élastique)* from Pont de l'Artuby on La Corniche Sublime. One jump costs around 550FF.

Moustiers Sainte Marie

The small village of Moustiers Sainte Marie, situated a few km north of Lac de Sainte Croix and downriver from the Gorges du Verdon, is famous for its production of faïence, whose heyday lasted from the late 17th century until the mid-19th century. Ceramics production was revived in the 1920s.

Set in a narrow gorge, the village is susceptible to flash flooding by the Rioul. A long chain from which dangles a gold star links the two sides of the gorge. The chain is said to have been placed there by a knight in fulfilment of a vow. Overlooking the village is Église Notre Dame de Beauvoir, the only reminder of the monastery founded here in the 5th century.

Places to Stay

Camping *Camping de Bourbon* at La Palud charges 10.50FF per person and 6FF a tent. Near Castellane, the river is lined with seasonal camping grounds that tend to be crowded and pricey. The *Auberge de Jeunesse* (see Hostels) near La Palud takes campers.

Hostels There's an *Auberge de Jeunesse* (☎ 92.77.38.72) just outside La Palud at the beginning of La Route des Crêtes. It is closed from 30 November to 1 March. Mountain bikes can be hired here.

In Castellane, *La Galoche* (☎ 92.83.63.20) on Chemin des Listes is a gîte d'étape for hikers.

Hotels If you're looking for something inexpensive, it's not a bad idea to head to Castellane. The *Hôtel du Verdon* (☎ 92.83.62.02) on Blvd de la République or the *Hôtel La Forge* (☎ 92.83.62.61) at Place de l'Église are two of the cheapest.

In Aiguines (postcode 83630), the *Hôtel Altitude 823* (☎ 94.70.21.09) – named after the village's elevation – has reasonably priced rooms. It is open from March to November.

About 10 km south-east of the canyon in Comps-sur-Artuby (postcode 83840), the *Grand Hôtel Bain* (☎ 94.76.90.06), which has been run by the same family for eight generations (since 1737), has doubles starting around 160FF. Except from 11 November to Christmas, the hotel restaurant serves meals daily (daily except Thursday from Christmas to March) from noon to 2.30 pm and 7.30 to 9 pm. Menus start at around 70FF.

Getting There & Away

Bus Public transport to, from and around the Gorges du Verdon is limited. Autocars Sumian (☎ 42.67.60.34) runs a bus from Marseille to Castellane and La Palud with a stop at Aix-en-Provence and other places en route. It leaves Marseille at 8.30 am and Aix at 9 am, arriving at La Palud at 11.20 am and Castellane at noon. The return bus leaves Castellane 15 minutes later. Unfortunately, this line runs only on Monday, Wednesday and Saturday from 1 July to 15 September. The rest of the year, it runs on Saturday only.

A daily bus between Grenoble and Nice via Digne-les-Bains and Grasse, run by VFD (☎ 76.87.45.45 in Grenoble, 93.85.24.56 in Nice), stops in Castellane. It leaves Grenoble at 9.30 am and arrives in Castellane five hours later. From Nice, the 1½-hour trip to Castellane begins at 7.30 am.

Côte d'Azur & Monaco

The Côte d'Azur (Azure Coast), part of which is known as the French Riviera, stretches along France's Mediterranean coast from Toulon to the Italian border. Technically part of Provence, it includes most of the *départements* of Alpes-Maritimes and Var. Many of the towns along the coast – Nice, Monaco, Antibes, Cannes, Saint Tropez – have become world-famous thanks to the recreational activities of the rich, famous and tanned, especially as portrayed in films and in the tabloids. The reality is rather less glamorous, but the Côte d'Azur still has a great deal to attract visitors: sun, 40 km of beaches, sea water as warm as 25°C, all sorts of cultural activities and – sometimes – even a bit of glitter.

The capital of the Côte d'Azur is Nice, whose plentiful hotels and excellent rail links make it a good base for exploring the region. As you follow the coast westward from Nice, you come to the attractive town of Antibes, the wealthy resort of Cannes and, just west of the stunning red mountain known as the Massif de l'Esterel, Saint Raphaël and Fréjus. Inland, the hills overlooking the coast are dotted with towns and villages such as Grasse (renowned for its perfume production), Vence, Saint Paul de Vence and Bormes-les-Mimosas.

The forested Massif des Maures stretches from Saint Raphaël to Hyères. West of the fashionable port town of Saint Tropez you'll find the region's most unspoilt coastline – capes and cliffs alternate with creeks and beaches, the latter sheltered from the open sea by the Îles d'Hyères, three large islands (and a couple of tiny ones) some 10 or so km offshore. The middle island, Île de Port Cros, is a national park. Toulon, best known for its role as a naval base, is at the western edge of the Côte d'Azur.

East of Nice, the tail end of the Alps foothills plummets precipitously into the Mediterranean. Three roads known as the Corniches take you from Nice past a number of villages overlooking the sea to Menton and the Italian border. The tiny principality of Monaco, part of which is known as Monte Carlo, is roughly midway between Nice and Menton.

This chapter begins in Nice and follows the coast westward to Toulon. It then covers the stretch of the Côte d'Azur between Nice and the Italian border, including Monaco.

History

Occupied by the Ligurians since the 1st millennium BC, the eastern part of France's Mediterranean coast was colonised around 600 BC by Phocaean Greeks, who settled in Marseille, then known as Massilia. The colony soon expanded to other points along the coast, including Hyères, Saint Tropez, Antibes and Nice. Called in to help Massilia against the threat of Celto-Ligurians from Entremont in 125 BC, the Romans defeated the Celts and Ligurians and created the Provincia Romana – the area between the Alps, the sea and the Rhône – from which the name Provence is derived.

In 1388 Nice and its hinterland, also known as the County of Nice, was incorporated into

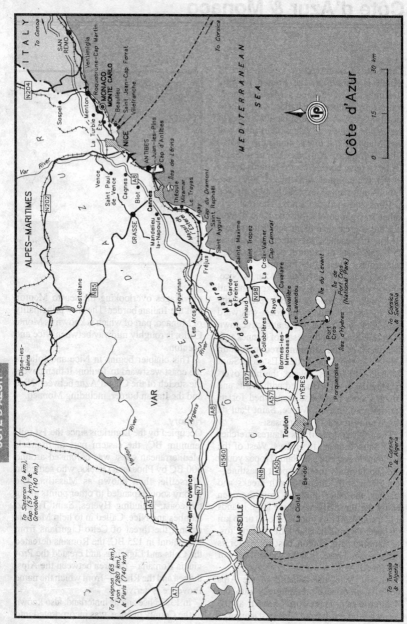

Côte d'Azur

the lands of the House of Savoy. The rest of Provence became part of the kingdom of France in 1482; the centralist policies of the French kings saw the region's autonomy greatly reduced. In 1860, after an agreement between Napoleon III and the House of Savoy helped drive the Austrians from northern Italy, France took possession of Savoy and the area around Nice.

In the 19th century rich French, English, Russian and American tourists discovered the Côte d'Azur. Primarily a winter resort, the area attracted an increasing number of affluent visitors thanks to its beauty and temperate climate. The intensity of the region's colours and light appealed to many artists, including Cézanne, Matisse, Picasso and Van Gogh. Writers and other celebrities were also attracted to the region and contributed to its fame. Little fishing ports became fashionable, exclusive resorts and in no time the most beautiful spots were occupied by private villas looking more like castles. With improved rail and road access, and the advent of paid holidays for all French workers in 1936, even more tourists flocked to the region, leading to its development as a summer resort.

In recent years, the Maures and neighbouring Esterel ranges have suffered from massive forest fires. The charred landscape – the result of blazes thought, for the most part, to have been caused by carelessness – will be visible for many years.

Radio

Monte Carlo-based Riviera Radio, an English-language radio station that's on the air 24 hours a day, can be heard on 106.3 MHz FM in Monaco and 106.5 MHz FM along the rest of the Côte d'Azur. BBC World Service news is broadcast every hour. The commercials and local programming (gardening shows, etc) provide a glimpse of Anglophone expatriate life along the Riviera.

Dangers & Annoyances

Theft – from backpacks, pockets, cars and even laundrettes – is a serious problem along the Côte d'Azur. To avoid becoming a victim, keep a sharp eye on your bags, especially at train and bus stations; on overnight train rides (the Rome-Nice-Barcelona line is notorious for thefts); in tourist offices; in fast-food restaurants; and on the beaches. Use the lockers at train stations if you'll be sleeping outside (for instance, on the beach). In crowded areas, make sure wallets and purses are shielded from passersby. And *never* leave anything in your car.

In the peak summer months, travelling by road along the Côte d'Azur can be very time-consuming because the region attracts far more cars than its roads can handle. Be prepared for long traffic jams, not just within towns but also between them. During this period it's also a good idea to arrange accommodation in advance – the earlier you make a booking the better, but even just phoning ahead in the morning may save you from having to run from hotel to hotel in the afternoon.

In August, the beaches are overcrowded and you may find yourself with only a square metre or two for your towel or mat from early in the morning.

Getting There & Away

For information on ferry services from Nice and Toulon to Corsica, see Getting There & Away in the Corsica chapter.

Getting Around

SNCF trains shuttle back and forth along the coast between Saint Raphaël and the Italian border, making Nice a great base for exploring the eastern half of the Côte d'Azur. The area between Saint Raphaël – where the train line veers inland – and Toulon can be reached by bus. For more information, see Train under Getting There & Away in the Nice section and Bus under Getting There & Away in the Nice, Cannes, Saint Tropez and Toulon sections.

The Côte d'Azur is notorious for its traffic jams, so if you'll be driving along the coast – especially in summer – be prepared for slow going. Around Saint Tropez, for instance, it can sometimes take hours to move just a few km, which is why some of the truly wealthy have taken to reaching their seaside properties by helicopter.

Except for the traffic-plagued high season, the Côte d'Azur is easily accessible by car. The fastest way to get around is the unscenic A8 autoroute, which, travelling west to east, starts near Aix-en-Provence, approaches the coast at Fréjus, skirts the Esterel range and then runs more or less parallel to the coast from Cannes all the way to the Italian border at Ventimiglia (Vintimille in French).

Nice to Toulon

NICE

The fashionable but fairly relaxed city of Nice (population 338,000), considered the capital of the Riviera, is an exceptionally attractive place for a stroll and makes a great base from which to explore the rest of the region. The city has lots of relatively cheap places to stay and is only a short train or bus ride away from Monaco, Cannes and other Riviera hotspots. Nice's beach may not be much to write home about, but the city is blessed with as fine an ensemble of museums as you'll find outside of Paris – and most of them are free!

Less happily, Nice is – along with Marseille – one of the most important bastions of Jean-Marie Le Pen's extreme right-wing National Front party, which gets about 25% of the citywide vote (compared to 12.5% nationally). Racist comments, especially about North Africans, are not uncommon. In part, the city's inter-ethnic tensions are the result of the great difference between rich and poor, and you're likely to pass as many beggars as owners of flashy sports cars.

Nice has also been known for its corrupt, right-wing municipal government. The city's former mayor, Jacques Médicin (son of another former mayor, Jean Médicin) escaped to Uruguay before being convicted (in absentia) in 1992 of misuse of public funds.

History

The area where Nice now stands was occupied some 400,000 years ago by groups of hunters who lived by stalking elephants.

Nice was founded around 350 BC by the Greek seafarers who had founded Marseille. They named the colony Nikaïa, apparently to commemorate a victory (*nike* in Greek) over a nearby town. In 154 BC the Greeks were followed by the Romans, who settled farther uphill around what is now Cimiez, site of a number of Roman ruins.

By the 10th century, Nice was ruled by the counts of Provence. In 1388, the town refused to recognise the new count of Provence, Louis of Anjou, and turned instead to Amadeus VII of the House of Savoy. During the 17th and 18th centuries, Nice was temporarily occupied several times by the French, but did not definitively become part of France until 1860, when Napoleon III struck a deal with the House of Savoy. The agreement (known as the Treaty of Turin) was ratified by a plebiscite.

During the Victorian period, Nice became popular with the English aristocracy who came to enjoy the city's mild winter climate. They were soon followed by royalty from all over Europe.

Orientation

Ave Jean Médecin runs south from near the train station to Place Masséna. The modern city centre, the area north and west of Place Masséna, includes the pedestrianised Rue de France and Rue Masséna. The famous Promenade des Anglais follows the gently curved beachfront from the city centre all the way to the airport, six km to the west. Vieux Nice (Old Nice) is delineated by Blvd Jean Jaurès, Quai des États-Unis and – to the east – the hill known as Le Château. Place Garibaldi is at the northern tip of Vieux Nice.

The wealthy residential neighbourhood of Cimiez, home to several outstanding museums, is north of the city centre.

Information

Tourist Offices The main tourist office (☎ 93. 87.07.07) is next to the train station. It is

Top: Monaco Ville, upon the Rock of Monaco, Côte d'Azur (DR)
Left: The beach at Nice and the Baie des Anges, Côte d'Azur (DR)
Right: Baroque church and Cours Saleya market, Nice, Côte d'Azur (SR)

Top: Coffee, croissants and *Le Monde*; breakfast time in France (LL)
Middle: Frenchman on his moped (LL); Chatting at the market (GC);
Weighing the garlic (LL)
Bottom: Soaking up the sun near Plage des Marquisats, Annecy (DR)

open Monday to Saturday from 8.45 am to 12.30 pm and 2 to 6 pm. From July to September it's open Monday to Saturday from 8.45 am to 7 pm and on Sunday from 8.45 am to 12.30 pm and 2 to 6 pm. Hotel bookings (available only for the night of the day you arrive) cost 12FF per star (ie 24FF for a two-star hotel); partial reimbursement is usually given if you stay somewhere with two or more stars.

The tourist office has an annexe (☎ 93.87. 60.60) near the beach at 5 Ave Gustave V. From February to October it's open on weekdays from 8.45 am to 12.30 pm and 2 to 6 pm. From May to September it's open on Saturday as well. The annexe is closed from October to December. Hotel reservations can be made here as well.

Near the airport, the tourist office branch (☎ 93.83.32.64) on Promenade des Anglais (a bit towards town from the airport terminal) is open Monday to Saturday from 7.30 am to 6.15 pm.

If you'll be going on to Italy, you might want to stop by the Office National Italien du Tourisme (☎ 93.87.75.81) at 14 Ave de Verdun. In the off season, it's open weekdays from 9 am to noon and 2 to 4 pm.

The Centre Information Jeunesse (☎ 93. 80.93.93) at 19 Rue Gioffredo (on the corner of Rue Delille) has information on accommodation, sports, activities and so on. It is open weekdays from 8.45 am to 6.45 pm.

Money The Banque de France (☎ 93.13.54. 00) at 14 Ave Félix Faure, which as usual offers by far the best rate in town, is open from 8.45 am to 12.15 pm and 1.30 to 3.30 pm.

American Express (☎ 93.87.29.82) at 11 Promenade des Anglais is open Monday to Friday from 9 am to noon and 2 to 6 pm. From May to August, it's open weekdays from 9 am to 1 pm and 2 to 6 pm and on Saturday morning from 9 am to 1 pm. The rate is good but not the best.

Opposite the train station, Office Provençal Change (☎ 93.88.56.80) at 17 Ave Thiers (to the right as you exit the terminal building) offers decent rates and is open every day of the year from 7 am to midnight. Office

Provençal Change has another branch (☎ 93.13.45.44), with the same opening hours, at 64 Ave Jean Médecin.

There are lots of places to change money along Ave Jean Médecin near Place Masséna. The Banque Niçoise de Crédit at 17 Ave Jean Médecin has a 24-hour currency exchange machine.

In Vieux Nice, the Banque Populaire de la Côte d'Azur (☎ 93.85.71.04) at 20 Blvd Jean Jaurès is open weekdays from 8.15 to 11.45 am and 1.45 to 4.15 pm.

Post The main post office (☎ 93.88.52.52), which will exchange foreign currency, is at 23 Ave Thiers, a block to the right as you exit the train station. It is open weekdays from 8 am to 7 pm and on Saturday from 8 am to noon. In Vieux Nice, the branch post office (☎ 93.80.71.00) at 2 Rue Louis Gassin is open weekdays from 8 am to 6.30 pm (except between 12.15 and 1.15 pm on Wednesday) and on Saturday from 8 am to noon. Poste restante services are also available at American Express – see Money.

The postcode for areas of central Nice north and west of Blvd Jean Jaurès and Ave Gallieni, including the train station and Promenade des Anglais, is 06000. The postcode for the area south and south-east of that line, including Vieux Nice and the ferry port, is 06300. If writing to a hotel, museum or office that appears on the map, you can figure out the postcode by checking which side of Blvd Jean Jaurès the dot is on.

Foreign Consulates The UK Consulate (☎ 91.53.43.32) is at 2 Rue du Congrès (2nd floor), next to the American Express office. The US Consulate (☎ 93.88.89.55) at 31 Rue du Maréchal Joffre is open weekdays from 9 to 11.30 am and 1.30 to 4.30 pm. For a new US passport, you have to go to Marseille.

Anglican Church The Église Anglicane (☎ 93.87.19.83) at 11 Rue de la Buffa, which has a mixed American and British membership, functions as something of an Anglophone community centre. Mass is held at 11 am on Sunday.

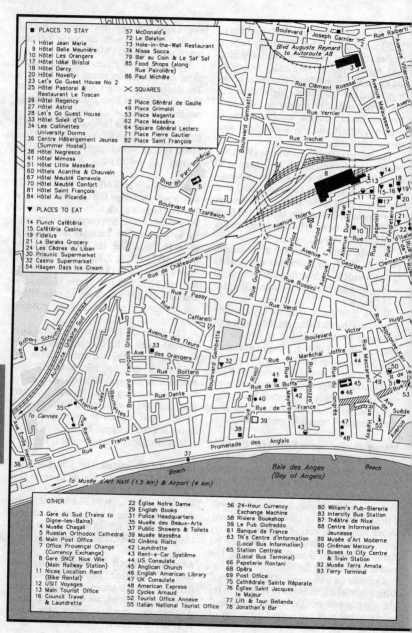

■ PLACES TO STAY

1 Hôtel Jean Marie
9 Hôtel Belle Meunière
10 Hôtel Les Orangers
17 Hôtel Idéal Bristol
18 Hôtel Darcy
20 Hôtel Novelty
23 Let's Go Guest House No 2
25 Hôtel Pastoral & Restaurant Le Toscan
26 Hôtel Regency
27 Hôtel Astrid
28 Let's Go Guest House
33 Hôtel Soleil d'Or
34 Les Collinettes University Dorms
36 Centre Hébergement Jeunes (Summer Hostel)
38 Hôtel Negresco
41 Hôtel Mimosa
51 Hôtel Little Masséna
60 Hôtels Acanthe & Chauvain
67 Hôtel Meublé Genevois
70 Hôtel Meublé Confort
81 Hôtel Saint François
84 Hôtel Au Picardie

▼ PLACES TO EAT

14 Flunch Caféteria
15 Caféteria Casino
19 Fidelius
21 La Baraka Grocery
24 Les Cèdres du Liban
30 Prisunic Supermarket
32 Casino Supermarket
54 Häagen Dazs Ice Cream

57 McDonald's
72 Le Balafon
73 Hole-in-the-Wall Restaurant
74 Nissa Socca
79 Bar au Coin & Le Saf Saf
85 Food Shops (along Rue Pairolière)
86 Paul Michèle

✕ SQUARES

2 Place Général de Gaulle
49 Place Grimaldi
53 Place Magenta
62 Place Masséna
64 Square Général Leclerc
71 Place Pierre Gautier
82 Place Saint François

OTHER

3 Gare du Sud (Trains to Digne-les-Bains)
4 Musée Chagall
5 Russian Orthodox Cathedral
6 Main Post Office
7 Office Provençal Change (Currency Exchange)
8 Gare SNCF Nice Ville (Main Railway Station)
11 Nicea Location Rent (Bike Rental)
12 USIT Voyages
13 Main Tourist Office
16 Council Travel & Laundrette
22 Église Notre Dame
29 English Books
31 Police Headquarters
35 Musée des Beaux-Arts
37 Public Showers & Toilets
39 Musée Masséna
40 Cinéma Rialto
42 Laundrette
43 Rent-a-Car Système
44 US Consulate
45 Anglican Church
46 English American Library
47 UK Consulate
48 American Express
50 Cycles Arnaud
52 Tourist Office Annexe
55 Italian National Tourist Office
56 24-Hour Currency Exchange Machine
58 Riviera Bookshop
59 Le Pub Giofreddo
61 Banque de France
63 TN's Centre d'information (Local Bus Information)
65 Station Centrale (Local Bus Terminal)
66 Papeterie Rontani
68 Opéra
69 Post Office
75 Cathédrale Sainte Réparate
76 Église Saint Jacques le Majeur
77 Lift & Tour Bellanda
78 Jonathan's Bar
80 William's Pub-Biererie
83 Intercity Bus Station
87 Théâtre de Nice
88 Centre Information Jeunesse
89 Musée d'Art Moderne
90 Cinémas Mercury
91 Buses to City Centre & Train Station
92 Musée Terra Amata
93 Ferry Terminal

CÔTE D'AZUR

Boulevard Joseph Garnier
Blvd Auguste Reynard to Autoroute A8
Rue Clément Roassal
Rue Vernier
Rue Trachel
Blvd du Parc Impérial
Boulevard du Tzaréwich
Rue de Châteauneuf
Rue F Passy
Caffarelli
Avenue des Fleurs
Ave des Orangers
Rue Bottero
Rue Dante
Rue de France
To Cannes
To Musée d'Art Naïf (1.5 km) & Airport (4 km)
Beach
Baie des Anges (Bay of Angels)
Beach
Promenade des Anglais
Boulevard Gambetta
Boulevard Victor Hugo
Avenue Thiers
Avenue Georges
Rue Rossini
Rue Verdi
Boulevard du Maréchal Joffre
Rue de la Buffa
Rue de France

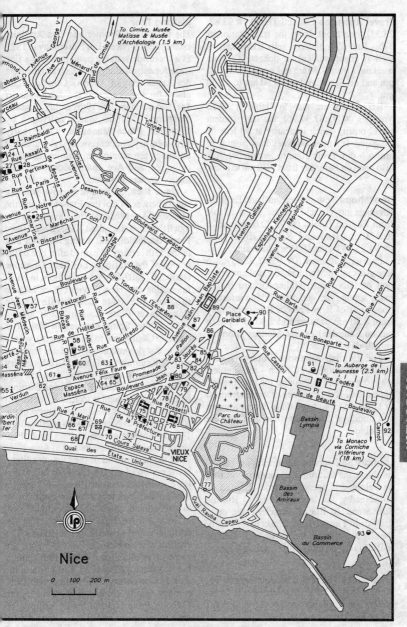

CÔTE D'AZUR

Nice

0   100   200 m

Travel Agencies Council Travel (☎ 93.82.23.33), one block from the train station at 37bis Rue d'Angleterre, sells BIJ tickets as well as cheap student air tickets. It's open weekdays from 9.30 am to 1 pm and 2 to 6.30 pm and on Saturday from 9.30 am to 12.30 pm.

BIJ tickets are also available at USIT Voyages (☎ 93.87.34.96), the Irish student travel outfit, which is nearby at 10 Rue de Belgique. It's open on weekdays from 9.30 am to 6 pm. From June to September, it is also open on Saturday from 9.30 am to noon.

Bookshops New and second-hand English-language novels and guides are available from English Books (☎ 93.80.02.66) at 26 Rue Lamartine and Riviera Bookshop (☎ 93.85.84.61) at 10 Rue Chauvain.

Papeterie Rontani (☎ 93.62.32.43) at 5 Rue Alexandre Mari has an excellent selection of IGN maps, Didier-Richard hiking maps, topoguides and other hiking information, most of it in French. It is open daily from 8.30 am to noon and 2.30 to 7 pm (6 pm on Saturday) except Monday morning and all-day Sunday.

The English-American library is very close to the Anglican Church – the simplest way to get there is through the passageway opposite 17 Rue de France. It's open from 10 to 11 am and 3 to 5 pm daily except Sunday and holidays. Short-term memberships are available.

Laundry Self-service laundrettes are plentiful. Near the station, the laundrette on Rue de Belgique is open daily from 7 am to 11 pm. Nearby, the laundrettes at 14 Rue de Suisse and 16 Rue d'Angleterre are open daily from 7 am to 9 pm. Closer to the beach, the slightly cheaper laundrette at 39 Rue de la Buffa is open daily from 7 am to 9 pm.

Emergency The police headquarters (☎ 93.92.62.22) is at 1 Ave Maréchal Foch. Interpreters are available for people who don't speak French.

Walking Tour

The palm-lined **Promenade des Anglais**, established by Nice's English colony in 1822 as a shoreside walking path, provides a fine stage for a stroll along the beach and the Baie des Anges (Bay of Angels). Other pleasant places for a walk include the **Jardin Albert 1er**, laid out in the late 19th century; **Espace Masséna**, a public square enlivened by fountains; **Place Masséna**, whose early 19th-century, neoclassical-style arcaded buildings are painted in various shades of ochre red; and **Ave Jean Médecin**, Nice's main commercial street.

Vieux Nice, an area of narrow, winding streets between Quai des États-Unis and the Musée d'Art Moderne, has looked pretty much the same since the 1700s. Arcade-lined **Place Garibaldi**, built during the latter half of the 18th century, is named after one of the heroes of the unification of Italy, Giuseppe Garibaldi (1807-82), who was born in Nice. Interesting churches in Vieux Nice include the baroque-style **Cathédrale Sainte Réparate** at Place Rossetti, built around 1650; **Église Saint Jacques le Majeur** at Place du Gésu (close to Rue Rossetti), whose baroque-style ornamentation dates from the mid-17th century; and the mid-18th-century **Chapelle de la Miséricorde**, which is next to Place Pierre Gautier. **Rue Benoît Bunico**, which is perpendicular to Rue Rossetti and was once known as the Giudaria (street of the Jews), served as Nice's Jewish ghetto after a 1430 law restricted where Jews could live. Gates at each end were locked at sunset.

At the eastern end of the Quai des États-Unis, on top of a 92-metre-high hill, is the **Parc du Château** (open 8 am to 7 pm), a shady public park where local families come to walk around, admire the panoramic views of Nice and the Baie des Anges, visit the artificial waterfall and munch on snacks. The chateau after which the hill and park are named was established in the 12th century but was destroyed in 1706. Just north of the park is a **cemetery** filled with ornate 19th-century family tombs; it is divided into Catholic, Protestant and Jewish sections. To get to the top of Le Château, there's a lift

(3FF one way, 4.40FF return) from under the Tour Bellanda, which is near the eastern end of Quai des États-Unis. It runs from 9 am to 6.45 pm (7.30 pm in summer).

Musée d'Art Moderne

The Musée d'Art Moderne et d'Art Contemporain (☎ 93.62.61.62) specialises in startling French and American avant-garde works from the 1960s to the present. The building, which is on the south side of Ave Saint Jean Baptiste one block north-west of Place Garibaldi, was inaugurated in 1990 and is in itself a work of modern art. The museum is open from 11 am to 6 pm (10 pm on Friday) daily except Tuesday. Entrance is free. It is served by bus Nos 3, 5, 7, 16 and 17.

Musée Chagall

The Musée National Message Biblique Marc Chagall (☎ 93.81.75.75), whose main exhibit is a series of incredibly vivid paintings illustrating stories from the Old Testament, is across the street from 4 Ave Docteur Ménard close to Blvd de Cimiez. It is open from 10 am to 12.30 pm and 2 to 5.30 pm (closed Tuesday). From July to September, hours are 10 am to 7 pm. Entrance costs about 30FF (24FF for students) in summer (when there are special exhibits) and 18FF (9FF reduced price) during the rest of the year. You can catch bus No 15 from Place Masséna to get there.

Musée Masséna

The Musée Masséna (☎ 93.88.11.34), also known as the Musée d'Art et d'Histoire, has entrances at 35 Promenade des Anglais and 65 Rue de France. The eclectic collection of paintings, furniture, icons, ceramics and religious art, housed in an early 19th-century Italian-style villa, can be viewed for free from 10 am to noon and 2 to 5 pm (closed Monday). From mid-April or May to September, afternoon hours are 3 to 6 pm.

Musée des Beaux-Arts Jules Chéret

The Fine Arts Museum (☎ 93.44.50.72) at 33 Ave des Baumettes is housed in a late 19th-century villa just off Rue de France. It has the same opening hours as the Musée Masséna. Entrance is free.

Musée Matisse

The newly refurbished Musée Matisse (☎ 93.81.08.08), which has a fine collection of works by Henri Matisse (see the Matisse aside), is 2.5 km north-east of the train station in Cimiez at 164 Ave des Arènes de Cimiez. A restoration job that took six years to complete has increased the gallery's exhibition space twofold. To get there, take bus No 15, 17, 20 or 22 and get off at the Arènes stop. The museum is open from 11 am to 7 pm (closed Tuesday). Entrance is free.

Musée d'Archéologie

The new Archaeology Museum (☎ 93.81.59.57) and the nearby Gallo-Roman Ruins (which include public baths and an amphitheatre) are in Cimiez at 160 Ave des Arènes. The museum (free) and the baths (5FF or 2.50FF) are open from 10 am to noon and 2 to 5 pm daily except Sunday morning and Monday. From June to September they are open from 11 am to 6 pm. The amphitheatre is open daily from 8 am to 7 pm unless there's something on. The museum is closed in November. To get there, follow the directions to the Musée Matisse.

Musée d'Art Naïf

The Musée International d'Art Naïf Anatole Jakovsky (☎ 93.71.78.33), with a collection of naive art from all over the world, is three km west of the city centre on Ave du Val Marie. To get there, take bus No 10, 12 or 24; get off at the Fabron stop, from where you can walk or take bus No 34 to the Musée Art Naïf stop. The museum is open Wednesday to Monday from 10 am to noon and 2 to 5 pm (6 pm from May to September). Admission is free.

Cathédrale Orthodoxe Russe Saint Nicolas

The multicoloured Russian Orthodox Cathedral (☎ 93.96.88.02), crowned by six onion domes, was built between 1903 and 1912 in early 17th-century style. Step inside and you're transported to Imperial Russia, a world of gilded icons and Cyrillic characters. The cathedral, opposite 17 Blvd du Tzaréwich, is open from 9 or 9.30 am to noon and 2.30 to 5 pm (5.30 pm in spring and autumn, 6 pm from May to September). The entry fee is 12FF (10FF for students). Short shorts, miniskirts and sleeveless shirts are forbidden.

Musée Terra Amata

Just east of Bassin Lympia (the port) on Blvd Carnot, this museum displays objects from an encampment on this site that was inhabited some 400,000 years ago by predecessors of *Homo sapiens*. It is closed on Monday.

Activities

Nice's **beach** is great if you hate sand since it's covered with smooth little rocks. From mid-April to mid-October the sections of beach open without charge to the public alternate with private beaches, for which you have to pay 40 to 60FF a day. The private beaches offer all sorts of amenities (mattresses, showers, changing rooms, parasols, a reduced chance of theft, etc), some of which involve further charges.

Along the beach you can hire catamaran paddleboats (80FF an hour), sailboards and jet skis, take a parachute ride (220FF for 10 minutes) and go water skiing (120FF for 10 minutes). There are public indoor showers (12FF) and toilets (2FF) opposite 50 Promenade des Anglais.

Festivals

The colourful Carnaval de Nice, held every spring on Mardi Gras (literally, fat Tuesday), also known as Shrove Tuesday, fills the streets with floats and musicians. Mardi Gras is the day before Ash Wednesday, which is the first day of Lent (the 40 weekdays preceding Easter).

Places to Stay – bottom end

Nice has oodles of reasonably priced places to stay. During the Easter university holidays, lots of US students descend on Nice, making cheap accommodation hard to come by after 10 or 11 am. Nice is crowded with budget travellers during July and August, too.

For most of the year, but especially from Easter to September, the inexpensive places fill up by late morning – come by or call ahead by 10 am. Most overnight trains from major cities such as Paris, Barcelona or Rome and the overnight ferries from Corsica will get you into Nice sometime around 7 or 8 am, the perfect time to start looking for accommodation.

In summer, lots of young people sleep on the beach, some because the hotels are full, others because it's free. This is theoretically illegal, but the Nice police usually look the other way.

Hostels The *Hôtel Belle Meunière* (see Hotels – Train Station Area) has nonbunk dorm beds for 50 to 77FF. The friendly and clean *Let's Go Guest House* (☎ 93.13.97.92), a favourite with backpackers, is on the 3rd floor at 22 Rue Pertinax. One floor below Let's Go is the peculiar *Abadie Guest House* (☎ 93.85.81.21, 93.52.62.87), whose garrulous owner personally selects 'nice, smiling, clean' guests each morning at the train station. Dorm beds in co-ed rooms cost 50FF; a double with shower is 110FF. The hostel is closed – unless it's raining – from noon to 6 pm, but there's no curfew.

The same people run another *guesthouse* (☎ 93.80.98.00) with the same unfortunate name (dubbed Let's Go Guest House No 2 on the map) two blocks away in an unmarked building at 26 Blvd Raimbaldi (1st floor). Both locations may be closed from mid-December to mid-January. The crowded and haphazardly managed *Hôtel Novelty* (☎ 93.87.51.73) at 26 Rue d'Angleterre has dorm beds for 70FF.

Nice's *Auberge de Jeunesse* (☎ 93.89. 23.64) is five km east of the train station on Route Forestière de Mont Alban. It is often full so call ahead before going all the way out there. In summer you will need to arrive by 10 am. Beds cost 57FF. Curfew is at 11 pm (midnight in summer) and rooms are locked from 10 am to 5 pm. To get there, take bus

No 14 (last one at 8.20 pm) from the Station Centrale municipal bus terminal on Ave Félix Faure, which is linked to the train station by bus Nos 5 and 17.

The *Centre Hébergement Jeunes* (☎ 93. 86.28.75) at 31 Rue Louis de Coppet (in the Espace Magnin building), half a block from 173 Rue de France, serves as a hostel from mid-June to mid-September. A bed in a six-person room costs only 55FF, but if you don't have a youth hostel or student card you must buy an MJC card for 25FF. This place has several disadvantages: rooms are locked from 10 am to 6 pm, there's a midnight curfew and bags must be stored in the luggage room during the day.

Les Collinettes University Dorms (☎ 93.97.10.33) at 3 Ave Robert Schuman, 1.5 km west of the train station and 600 metres north of the beach, will put up travellers of all ages during July and August. A single (all they have) costs 90FF. It's a good idea to phone ahead as this place is often full. You can check in 24 hours a day. To get there from Rue de France, walk north on Ave Émile Henriot, which becomes Ave Robert Schuman. From the train station, take bus No 10, 23 or 24.

Hotels – Train Station Area The *Hôtel Idéal Bristol* (☎ 93.88.60.72) at 22 Rue Paganini, a friendly place popular with backpackers, has fairly basic but clean doubles from 134FF (174FF with shower and toilet). Rooms for four/five people with shower and toilet are 328/385FF. There's no charge to use the hall showers. You can lounge around or have a picnic on the rooftop terrace.

The *Hôtel Belle Meunière* (☎ 93.88. 66.15), a clean, welcoming place that attracts lots of young people, is at 21 Ave Durante. Dorm beds cost 50 to 77FF. Large doubles/triples with high ceilings, some with century-old décor, start at 114/171FF (169/251FF with shower and toilet). Rooms with kitchenettes are also available. This place is closed in December and January. Down the block, the *Hôtel Les Orangers* (☎ 93.87. 51.41) charges 80 to 85FF per person in large, plain rooms with shower, hot plate and

fridge. The *Hôtel Darcy* (☎ 93.88.67.06) at 28 Rue d'Angleterre has singles/doubles for 130/160FF (175/210FF with shower and toilet). Triples and quads are also available. Prices are slightly higher from May to September.

The *Hôtel Pastoral* (☎ 93.85.17.22), just off Ave Jean Médecin at 27 Rue Assalit (1st floor), has large, old-fashioned and clean singles/doubles with fridge from 97/104FF; showers cost 10FF. Doubles with shower and toilet are 160FF, and quads with shower are 210FF. Kitchenettes cost 15FF extra per person a day. Reception is open daily from 8 am to 3 pm and 6 to 8 pm. The *Hôtel Astrid* (☎ 93.62.14.64), above the kosher restaurant at 26 Rue Pertinax, has clean, pleasant doubles/triples/quads with refrigerator for 140/210/280FF. Doubles/triples with shower are 180/270FF; hall showers are 10FF. Reception closes at 8 pm.

The *Hôtel Regency* (☎ 93.62.17.44) at 2 Rue Saint Siagre, close to the corner of Rue Pertinax, has tacky but large split-level studios with shower, toilet, kitchenette and fridge for two/three people for 150/180FF (180/260FF from May to September).

Hotels – Vieux Nice The *Hôtel Saint François* (☎ 93.85.88.69, 93.13.40.18) at 3 Rue Saint François, near the *place* of the same name! has small singles from 80FF, doubles with one/two beds for 120/150FF and triples from 210FF. Showers cost 15FF. Reception is open daily from 8.30 am to 10.30 pm. You might also try the *Hôtel Au Picardie* (☎ 93.85.75.51), opposite the bus station at 10 Blvd Jean Jaurès. It has singles/ doubles ranging from 100/120FF to 150/ 180FF; the pricier rooms include toilet and shower. This place also has triples and quads. Showers are 10FF, and an extra bed costs 45FF.

The *Hôtel Meublé Genevois* (☎ 93.85. 00.58), in an unmarked building at 11 Rue Alexandre Mari (3rd floor), has 1950s-style singles/doubles with kitchenette from 90/ 110FF. Huge studios with shower and toilet are 130 to 200FF for three or four people. If no one answers the *sonnerie* (bell), push the little red button. The *Hôtel Meublé Confort*

(☎ 93.85.00.58), which is run by the same people and whose prices are similar, is down the block in an unmarked building at 17 Rue Alexandre Mari (4th floor). Both are near the Station Centrale bus terminal.

Just north of Espace Masséna, the *Hôtel Chauvain* (☎ 93.85.34.01) at 8 Rue Chauvain has big, old-fashioned doubles from 140FF; showers cost 15FF. Reception stays open until 1 am.

Hotels – City Centre The *Hôtel Little Masséna* (☎ 93.87.72.34) is right in the centre at 22 Rue Masséna. Reception, which stays open until 7 pm, is on the 5th floor (yes, there's a lift). Doubles with hot plate and fridge range from 100 to 180FF; hall showers are free.

The relaxed, family-style *Hôtel Mimosa* (☎ 93.88.05.59) is a block north of the Musée Masséna at 26 Rue de la Buffa (2nd floor). Depending on the season, good-sized, utilitarian rooms cost 100 to 130FF for one person and 130 to 160FF for two. There are two fridges in the hall and hot plates can be hired for 10FF a day. Showers cost 10FF. You can check in 24 hours a day.

Hotels – Elsewhere The *Hôtel Soleil d'Or* (☎ 93.96.55.94) is 1.25 km south-west of the train station at 16 Ave des Orangers. Simple singles with high ceilings cost 75FF, doubles start at 104FF and an extra bed is 40FF. Showers are 12FF. Doubles with shower and toilet are 180FF. This place is closed in November.

The *Hôtel Jean Marie* (☎ 93.84.87.23), one km north of the train station at 15-17 Rue André Theuriet, has dim but serviceable shower-equipped doubles (all they have) without/with toilet starting at 140/160FF. The inconvenient location means that this place may have rooms when other hotels are full. To get there from the train station, walk to Ave Jean Médecin and take bus No 2, 4 or 18 (northbound).

Places to Stay – middle
Near the train station, there are lots of two-star hotels along Rue d'Angleterre, Rue d'Alsace-Lorraine, Rue de Suisse, Rue de Russie and Ave Durante.

The *Hôtel Acanthe* (☎ 93.62.22.44) is half a block north of Espace Masséna at 2 Rue Chauvain. Half of their 50 rooms are singles/doubles costing 160/170FF (a bit less in winter); the other half have shower and toilet and cost 250FF. Hall showers are free. Reception is open 24 hours a day.

Places to Stay – top end
The pink-domed *Hôtel Negresco* (☎ 93.88. 39.51; fax 93.88.35.68) at 37 Promenade des Anglais, built in the *belle époque* style at the beginning of the 20th century and recently declared a historic monument, is Nice's fanciest hotel. In the off season, rooms without a sea view start at 1200FF; at other times, singles/doubles start at 1550/2250FF. A continental breakfast costs 100FF. The hotel also has an excellent restaurant (See Restaurants – City Centre). At 1 Promenade des Anglais, there's another very stylish four-star hotel, the *Méridien* (☎ 93.82.25.25; fax 93.16. 08.90), known for its very comfortable rooms and the rooftop pool. Singles/doubles cost 1130/3300FF.

For a touch of class at more reasonable prices, try the *Westminster* (☎ 93.88.29.44; fax 93.82.45.35) at 27 Promenade des Anglais. Rooms go for 700/1200FF.

Places to Eat
Restaurants – Train Station Area *Restaurant Le Toscan* (☎ 93.88.40.54), a family-run Italian place at 1 Rue de Belgique, offers large portions of home-made ravioli, pasta or tripe daily, except Sunday, from noon to 2 pm and 6.45 to 10 pm. Both the 55FF and 90FF *menus* let you choose from among a wide selection of dishes. *Fidelius* (☎ 93.82. 05.92) at 4 Rue de Belgique is small but a popular place with a diverse 54FF *menu*. It is closed on Sunday.

Vietnamese There are over a dozen Vietnamese and Chinese restaurants on Rue Paganini, Rue d'Italie and Rue d'Alsace-Lorraine.

Lebanese On the east side of Ave Jean Médecin at 27 Blvd Raimbaldi, *Les Cèdres du Liban* (☎ 93.80.35.37) serves inexpensive Lebanese food in an informal atmosphere. It is open daily, except all-day Sunday and Friday before 4 pm; hours are 9 am to 10 pm.

Restaurants – City Centre The Rue Masséna pedestrian mall and nearby streets are lined with touristy outdoor cafés and restaurants. Unfortunately, the places in this area do not offer particularly good value. See Cafeterias & Fast Food for details of cheaper places to eat around here.

For traditional French food in a luxurious setting, try the restaurant at the Hôtel Negresco. Known as the *Chantecler* (☎ 93.88.39.51), it offers impeccable service and tantalising cuisine. Specialities include seafood and fish dishes. An à la carte meal will cost around 400 to 600FF.

Restaurants – Vieux Nice Many of the narrow streets of Vieux Nice are lined with restaurants, cafés, pizzerias and so on that draw locals and visitors alike. At night, the area – brightly lit with neon signs and street lights – is a fine place for a stroll.

A perennial favourite with locals is *Nissa Socca* (☎ 93.80.18.35) at 5 Rue Sainte Réparate, which specialises in such delicious Niçois dishes as socca, a thin layer of chickpea flour and olive oil batter baked in a very hot bread oven. Spaghetti and pasta cost 32 to 38FF. Nissa Socca is open daily from Monday (evening only) to Saturday. It is closed during January. Nearby streets such as Rue de l'Abbaye are lined with restaurants.

There are dozens of cafés and restaurants on Cours Saleya and around Place Pierre Gautier. This somewhat touristy pedestrianised area stays open until midnight (later during the summer). Farther north, Place Rossetti at the western end of Rue Rossetti has four competing restaurants offering three or four-course *menus* from about 60FF.

Pizza Up towards Place Saint François, *Bar au Coin* (☎ 93.62.32.59) at 2 Rue Droite is a popular terrace pizzeria. *Maison de la Pizza* (☎ 93.85.45.39) at 12 Rue Mascoïnat (30 metres north of Cathédrale Sainte Réparate) serves pizza, pasta and lasagna Monday to Saturday from noon to 3 pm and 7 to 11 pm. The *menu* costs 60FF.

African *Le Balafon* (☎ 93.62.65.90) at 6 Rue de l'Abbaye offers West African specialities, including many nonmeat dishes; main courses start at about 60FF. The background music is great. There's an inviting Tunisian haunt, *Le Saf Saf*, next to Bar au Coin at 2 Rue Droite.

Cafeterias & Fast Food Cheap, family-style places near the train station include the *Flunch Cafétéria* (☎ 93.88.41.35), to the left as you exit the station building. It is open daily from 11 am to 10 pm. Nearer the beach, there is another *Flunch Cafétéria* (☎ 93.82.17.73) at 7 Rue Halévy. It serves full meals from 11 am to 2.30 pm and 6 to 9.30 pm (10 pm in summer); a limited selection of dishes is available from 2.30 to 6 pm.

The *Cafétéria Casino* (☎ 93.82.44.44i at 7 Ave Thiers, near the train station, serves breakfast from 7 to 11 am, lunch from 11 am to 2.30 pm and dinner from 6 to 10 pm. This place has a *menu* for around 44FF.

The *McDonald's* at 20 Ave Jean Médecin is open daily until midnight. There's another *McDonald's* at 49 Ave Jean Médecin.

Sandwiches For Niçois-style sandwiches (10 to 17FF), pizza (6 to 10FF per piece) and other takeaway dishes, you can't beat *Paul-Michèle* at 1 Rue Pairolière, an enduring favourite with the locals. It is open from 8 am to 9 pm (closed Monday).

Ice Cream The *Häagen Dazs* ice-cream shop (☎ 93.88.64.69) at 2 Place Magenta charges an outrageous 13.50FF for one scoop. It is open daily from 11 am to at least 10 pm.

Self-Catering The *Prisunic supermarket* across the street from 33 Ave Jean Médecin is open Monday to Saturday from 8.30 am to 7.15 pm (9 pm in July and August). On the west side of the city, there's a *Casino super-market* at 27 Blvd Gambetta.

A few blocks from the train station, *La Baraka grocery* at 10 Rue de Suisse has bread, cheese, wine, etc. It is open from 3 pm to midnight (closed Tuesday).

In Vieux Nice, the food shops along Rue Pairolière include a *fromagerie* (closed Sunday and Monday) at No 37, a *boulangerie* (closed Sunday afternoon and Monday) at No 30 and another *boulangerie* (closed Monday) at No 10. For fruit and vegetables, try the shop (closed Sunday afternoon) at No 26. Near the branch post office, the *Express Minimarket* at 2 Rue Louis Gassin is open from 7 am to 12.30 pm and 4 to 7.30 pm daily except Sunday afternoon.

Entertainment

The tourist office has brochures and other information on Nice's abundant cultural activities. Tickets to events of all sorts can be purchased at the ticket office of the FNAC store at 24 Ave Jean Médecin, which is in Nice-Étoile, Nice's main shopping mall.

Bars Nice has lots of bars and terrace-equipped cafés that are perfect for quaffing beer or sipping pastis. For a taste of some excellent Belgian brew, try *Le Pub Gioffredo*, which is two blocks east of Ave Jean Médecin on the corner of Rue Chauvain and Rue Gioffredo. A note for the uninitiated: beware of both alcohol content – especially in the Trappist beers – and the prices.

Live Music *William's Pub-Biererie* (☎ 93. 85.84.66) at 4 Rue Centrale, across the street from the bus station, has live rock music every night except Sunday starting at around 10 pm. The pub itself is open Monday to Saturday from 6 pm to 2.30 am. You can play pool, darts and chess in the basement. A demi on tap costs 15FF. *Jonathan's*, another *bar à musique* just down Rue Centrale from Ave Jean Jaurès, has live music (country, boogie-woogie, Irish folk, etc) every night except Monday. Bottles of beer and soft drinks are 22 to 30FF.

The *Hole-in-the-Wall Restaurant* (☎ 93. 80.40.16) at 3 Rue de l'Abbaye is both a restaurant and a venue for live music. Open nightly except Monday from 8 pm to midnight, this place has main dishes for 35 to 65FF and salade niçoise (made with tomatoes, tuna, hard-boiled eggs, string beans, olives and anchovies) for 38FF. Beer (in bottles) is 22 to 28FF.

Gay Nightclubs There are a couple of gay nightclubs in the city centre. *Gay Zodiac* (☎ 93.87.78.87) is at 6 Passage Émile Négrin, and *Le Blue Boy* (☎ 93.44.68.24) is at 9 Rue Spinetta, off Blvd François Grosso.

Classical Music Operas and orchestra concerts are held at the *Opéra* (☎ 93.80.59.83), built in 1885, whose entrance is in Vieux Nice at 4 Rue Saint François de Paule (around the building from Quai des États-Unis). The ticket office is open Tuesday to Saturday from 11 am to 7 pm. Tickets in the highest balcony start at about 40FF. If you opt to make reservations by phone, you can send payment by post (postcode 06300).

Theatre The *Théâtre de Nice* (☎ 93.80. 52.60), whose entrance faces the Musée d'Art Moderne, is one block west of Place Garibaldi. The two halls host a wide variety of first-rate theatre performances and concerts. Ticket prices begin at around 60FF. The information desk is open Tuesday to Saturday from 1 to 7 pm.

Cinemas Nice has two cinemas offering nondubbed (v.o.) films, many of them in English. The 10-screen *Cinémas Mercury* (☎ 93.55.32.31 for a recorded message in French) occupies contiguous buildings at 12 and 16 Place Garibaldi. Regular tickets cost 37 or 40FF; except on weekends, students pay 25 to 28FF. Everyone gets in for the reduced price on Wednesday. The *Cinéma Rialto* (☎ 93.88.08.41) at 4 Rue de Rivoli, which is slightly more expensive, also has English-language films.

Getting There & Away

Air Nice's international airport, Aéroport International Nice-Côte d'Azur (☎ 93.21.30.30), is six km west of the city centre. It is the second-busiest airport in France, handling 5½ million passengers a year.

Airlines with offices or representatives in Nice include:

Air France
  10 Ave Félix Faure (☎ 93.83.91.00) or at the airport (☎ 93.83.91.00)
British Airways
  At the airport (☎ 93.18.04.06); for reservations, call ☎ 05.12.51.25 (toll-free)
Garuda Indonesia
  6 Ave Suède (☎ 93.82.00.31)
KLM
  At the airport (☎ 93.83.19.83)

Train Nice's main train station, Gare SNCF Nice Ville (☎ 93.87.50.50 for information), is on Ave Thiers, 1.25 km north of the beach. The information office, which is often crowded in summer, is open Monday to Saturday from 8 am to 6.30 pm and on Sunday from 8 am to noon and 2 to 5.30 pm.

There is fast, frequent service (up to 40 trains a day in each direction!) to towns along the coast between Saint Raphaël and the Italian border, including Antibes (20FF; 25 minutes), Cannes (28FF; 40 minutes), Menton (21FF), Monaco (16FF; 20 minutes) and Saint Raphaël (47FF). From June to September there are trains every 20 or 30 minutes from 5 am to 11 or 11.30 pm. The rest of the year, trains run at least once an hour.

The TGVs that link Nice with Paris's Gare de Lyon (465FF; seven hours) are rather infrequent, so you may find it more convenient to go via Marseille. Two of the three overnight trains to Paris (11 hours) have only couchettes, for which a supplement of 86FF must be paid even if you have a Eurail pass. The third night train has both couchettes and seats; an optional seat reservation for the latter costs 16FF. A ticket to Rome costs 250FF and a ticket to Barcelona is 337FF.

The luggage lockers (consigne automatique), which cost 15, 20 or 30FF depending on the size, are open from 6 am to 12 midnight. If you have a problem, go to the left-luggage office (consigne manuelle), which is open from 6 am to 9 pm and charges 30FF per bag a day.

Reimbursements for train tickets are available in an office (☎ 93.82.62.11) in the train station complex that is directly opposite the Office Provençal Change located at 17 Ave Thiers. It is open Monday to Friday from 8.45 am to noon and 1.30 to 5.30 pm.

Two-car diesel trains operated by Chemins de Fer de la Provence (☎ 93.88.28.56 for information) begin the scenic trip to Digne-les-Bains (97FF one way; 3⅓ hours; four or five a day) from Gare du Sud (☎ 99.84.89.71), the railway station at 33 Rue Malaussena. You can stop at a number of small towns en route, and hikers can take the train to the trailhead of their choice.

Bus Lines operated by some two dozen bus companies stop at the intercity bus station, which is opposite 10 Blvd Jean Jaurès. The helpful, but often busy, information counter (☎ 93.85.61.81) is open Monday to Saturday from 6.30 am to 8 pm. There's slow but frequent service daily until about 7.30 pm to Antibes (22FF; 1¼ hours), Cannes (26FF; 1½ hours), Grasse (31FF), Menton (24FF return; 1¼ hours), Monaco (18FF return; 45 minutes) and Saint Raphaël (47FF; two hours). Hourly buses run to Vence (17FF; 50 minutes). To Castellane (near the Gorges du Verdon) there's one bus a day at 7.30 am (88FF; 1½ hours). Student discounts are not applicable for travel within the Alpes-Maritimes département.

For long-haul travel, Intercars (Eurolines; ☎ 93.80.08.70), which has an office at the bus station, can take you to various destinations, including London (700/660FF for adults/students; 16 hours), Madrid (505/455FF; 11 hours) and Lisbon (710FF; 21 hours).

Car Rent-a-Car Système (☎ 93.87.87.37; fax 93.87.95.55) at 25 Promenade des Anglais rents Fiat Pandas for 268FF a day, including insurance and unlimited km. The excess (deductible) is 900FF. Their cheaper rates may involve an excess of up to 8000FF. The office is open daily from 8 am to 12.30 pm and 1.30 to 7 pm.

For information on the three corniches that link Nice with Menton, see the Corniches section later in this chapter.

Motorbike Nicea Location Rent (☎ 93.82.42.71) at 9 Ave Thiers rents mopeds from 150FF a day, 50 cc scooters for 285FF a day and 125 cc motorcycles for 385FF a day. You lose your deposit if the bike is stolen. The office is open daily, except Sunday, (daily from March to October) from 9 am to 6.30 pm. Cycles Arnaud (☎ 93.87.88.55) at 4 Place Grimaldi (see Bicycle under Getting Around) rents 80 cc scooters for 250FF a day.

Boat The fastest and least expensive SNCM ferries from mainland France to Corsica depart from Nice. For details, see Getting There & Away near the beginning of the Corsica chapter.

The SNCM office (☎ 93.13.66.66), which is at the ferry terminal on Quai du Commerce, may be able to issue tickets when the computers at travel agencies say everything is full. It is open daily Monday to Friday from 8 am to noon and 2 to 5.45 pm, and on Saturday morning. From mid-June to September weekday hours are 6 am to 8 pm and Saturday hours are 6 am to noonn On Sunday, the office opens two hours before a scheduled departure. To get to the ferry port from Ave Jean Médecinl take bus No 1 or 2 and get off at Place Île de Beauté.

Getting Around

To/From the Airport TN bus No 23 (9FF), which runs every 20 or 30 minutes from about 6 am to 8 pm, can be picked up at the train station or on Blvd Gambetta, Rue de France or Rue de la Californie. From the intercity bus station on Promenade des Anglais, you can also take the bus (20FF) which has *spécial aéroport* written on it and has as its symbol an aeroplane with its nose pointed upwards. It runs every 20 minutes from 6 am to 9 pm.

Bus Local buses, run by Transports Urbains de Nice (TN), cost 9FF for a single ride; a carnet of five tickets is 27.40FF. After you time-stamp your ticket, it's valid for one hour and can be used for one transfer. The Carte Nice Vacances, valid for one day (20FF), three days (77FF) or seven days (107FF), is available at TN's Centre d'Information (see the next paragraph) and the outlets of Office Provençal Change (see Money under Information).

The Station Centrale, TN's main bus hub, takes up three sides of Square Général Leclerc, which is between Ave Félix Faure and Blvd Jean Jaurès (near Vieux Nice and the intercity bus station). Bus information and route maps are available at TN's Centre d'Information (☎ 93.62.08.08), opposite the Station Centrale at 10 Ave Félix Faure. It is open Monday to Friday from 7.15 am to 7 pm and Saturday from 8 am to 6 pm. The TN kiosk at the Station Centrale (across Ave Félix Faure from the Centre d'Information) is open daily from 6.15 am to 8 pm.

Bus No 12, which runs daily from 6 am to 12.30 am, links the train station with Promenade des Anglais and the beach. To get from the train station to Vieux Nice and the intercity bus station, take bus No 5 (which runs until midnight) or bus No 17.

Taxi There's a taxi stand right outside the train station. To order a taxi, call ☎ 93.80.70.70.

Bicycle If you'd like to get out of Nice by bicycle, your best bet is probably to take the Corniche Inférieure, which follows the coast (see the Corniches section later in this chapter). Monaco (18 km each way) is an eminently enjoyable day trip.

Cycles Arnaud (☎ 93.87.88.55) at 4 Place Grimaldi has bicycles for 90FF a day. The shop is open Monday to Friday from 9 am to 6.30 pm. Several kinds of bicycles are available for 120FF a day from Nicea Location Rent (☎ 93.82.42.71) at 9 Ave Thiers (see Motorbike under Getting There & Away).

Matisse

One of the most famous French artists of this century, Henri Matisse (1869-1954) was renowned for his passion for pure colour. As a leader of the fauvists (who came to prominence starting in 1905), his paintings epitomised their radical use of violent colour, heavy outlines and simplified forms. And though fauvism was short-lived, Matisse continued to employ its method of setting striking complementary colours against one another throughout his career.

Compared to other important painters, Matisse was a relative latecomer, not becoming interested in painting until he was 20. By the time he was 22 he had given up his law career in his home region, Picardy, and had gone to Paris to be a painter.

Matisse studied art for many years under the symbolist painter Gustave Moreau. While visiting Brittany, he met an Australian artist, John Russell, who introduced him to the works of Van Gogh, Monet and other impressionists, prompting (so it is believed) Matisse's change from a rather sombre palette to brighter colours. He also spent time in Corsica, whose rich Mediterranean light was to have a lasting influence on his work. By the early 1900s he was well known in Paris among followers of modern art and his paintings were being exhibited, but he was still struggling financially. It wasn't until the first fauvist exhibition in 1905, which followed a summer of innovative painting in the fishing village of Collioure in Roussillon, that his financial situation improved. By 1913 he had paintings on display in London and New York.

In the 1920s Matisse moved to the Côte d'Azur but still spent much time travelling – to Étretat in Normandy and abroad to Italy and Tahiti. During these years he painted profusely but was less radical, though his work's characteristic sensuality and optimism were always present. The 1930s, however, saw a return to more experimental techniques, and a renewed search for simplicity, in which the subject matter was reduced to essential elements only. In 1948 he began working on a set of stained-glass windows for the Chapelle du Rosaire in Vence, run by Dominican nuns. He ended up designing not only the windows but nearly the entire chapel – a project that took several years. He died in Nice three years later. ■

AROUND NICE

Vence

More serene than it's coastal counterparts, Vence is a beautiful but very touristy little inland town nine km north-west of Nice. Though the area is rather built up with holiday homes and villas, the medieval centre is perfect for a stroll past the many art galleries. The main gate of the 13th-century wall that encircles the old town leads to the pretty little Place du Peyra with its fountain. The Romanesque cathedral in the centre of the old town was originally built in the 11th century but was extensively reworked in the 17th and 18th centuries.

Worth visiting is the nearby **Château-Musée du Parfum et de la Liqueur**, which is on the way to Grasse. This 19th-century museum, built on the site of a medieval abbey, contains antique machinery used in the manufacture of perfume and liqueur.

Also near Vence is the **Chapelle du Rosaire** (☎ 93.58.03.26), 800 metres north of town on the Route de Saint Jeannet, whose interior was designed and decorated by Matisse. It is only open on Tuesday and Thursday from 10 to 11.30 am and 2.30 to 5.30 pm. Entry is free but a contribution is requested by Sister Magdalena, the person in charge.

Information The Vence tourist office (☎ 93.58.06.38) on Place du Jardin is open Monday to Saturday from 9 am to noon and 2 to 6 pm. From July to September it's open on Sunday between 10 am and noon and stays open on other days until 7 pm.

Getting There & Away To get to Vence, you can take bus No 400 or 410 from Nice's intercity bus station (17FF; 50 minutes).

Saint Paul de Vence

This picturesque and very touristy hilltop village south of Vence is home to a great many artists and writers. It is most famous for the nearby **Fondation Maeght** (☎ 93. 32.81.63), one of France's foremost centres for contemporary art. Set on a hill in the

CÔTE D'AZUR

beautiful Provençal countryside amid gardens embellished with sculptures and fountains, the gallery was opened in 1964. Apart from an exceptional permanent collection of 20th-century works featuring such artists as Braque, Bonnard, Matisse and Mirò, it also organises important exhibitions each year, as well as concerts and other performances. It is open from 10 am to 12.30 pm and 3 to 7 pm (to 6 pm in winter). Entry is 40 FF (30 FF students).

If you want to stay in Saint Paul de Vence you will need to book well ahead, particularly if you want to stay in the famous *Colombe d'Or* (☎ 93.32.80.02) in Place du Général de Gaulle. The works of world-renowned artists decorate the walls of this three-star hotel, which has long attracted writers and cinema celebrities. An à la carte meal in the restaurant will cost at least 400FF.

ANTIBES AREA
Cagnes-sur-Mer

Cagnes-sur-Mer is made up of Haut de Cagnes, the old hill town; Le Cros de Cagnes, the old fishing village by the beach; and Cagnes Ville, a fast-growing modern quarter. The old town with its ramparts is dominated by the 14th-century Château Grimaldi, which houses the **Musée de l'Olivier**, a museum of contemporary art that stages a yearly international art festival. Near Cagnes Ville is the **Musée Renoir**, home of the artist Renoir from 1907 to 1919. It has retained its original décor and has several of the artist's works on display.

Biot

This charming village was once an important pottery-manufacturing centre specialising in enormous earthenware oil and wine containers. Metal containers brought an end to this industry but Biot is still active in the production of handicrafts. The village streets are a pleasant place for a stroll, but you will have to get there early to beat the tourist hordes. The attractive **Place des Arcades** dates from the 13th to 14th centuries. At the foot of the village is a **glass factory** where you can watch glass-blowers at work.

Musée Fernand Léger In Biot on Chemin du Val de Pomme, the museum (☎ 93.65. 63.61) dedicated to the artist Fernand Léger (1881-1955), contains 360 of the artist's works, including paintings, mosaics, ceramics and stained-glass windows. A huge, colourful mosaic decorates the museum's façade. It is open daily, except Tuesday, from 10 am to noon and 2 to 6 pm (5 pm from end September to early April).

Antibes

Directly across the Baie des Anges from Nice, Antibes has as many attractions as its neighbour but is not quite as touristy. It has beautiful sandy beaches, 16th-century ramparts that run right along the sea, an attractive pleasure-boat harbour (Port Vauban) and an old city with narrow, winding streets and flower-bedecked houses.

The city was first settled around the 4th century BC by Greeks from Marseille, who named it Antipolis. It was later taken over by the Romans and then by the Grimaldi family, who ruled it from 1384 to 1608. Because of its position on the French-Savoy border, it was fortified in the 17th and 18th centuries, but these fortifications were torn down in 1894 to give the city room to grow. Antibes appealed to many artists, most notably Picasso, Max Ernst and Nicolas de Staël.

Orientation & Information Ave Amiral de Grasse, which runs along the waterfront, is the main road in Antibes. The train station is on Ave Robert Soleau, close to Port Vauban. The old town is just west of Ave Amiral de Grasse. Place Général de Gaulle is in the centre of the city – this is where you'll find the tourist office (☎ 93.33.95.64). The staff are friendly and have a good free map of the city as well as lots of other useful information.

Things to See & Do In the old town, Antibes's cathedral, the church of the Immaculate Conception, has an ochre-coloured Romanesque façade and a tall Romanesque bell tower.

Steps lead up to the Château Grimaldi,

which is set on a spectacular site overlooking the sea and the cathedral. It served as Picasso's workshop during part of 1946 and has since been turned into a museum. Known as the **Musée Picasso** (☎ 93.34.91.91), it contains an excellent collection of paintings, lithographs, drawings and ceramics as well as interesting displays about the artist's life. The museum has also reproduced a number of Picasso's works on embossed paper with titles in Braille. The sculpture-lined terrace looks out over the sea. The museum, which also has a collection of contemporary art, is open daily, except Tuesday and public holidays, from 10 am to noon and 2 to 6 pm in winter (7 pm in summer). It is closed in November. Entry is 20FF (10FF students).

The **Musée Archéologique** (☎ 93.34.48.01) in Bastion Saint André has information about Antibes's history as a Greek city. It is open daily, except Tuesday, from 9 am to noon and 2 to 6 pm in winter (to 7 pm in summer). It is also closed in November. Entry is 10FF (5FF students).

Apart from visiting the museums and the old town, it's very pleasant to walk along the ramparts, go to the beach, or simply watch the locals playing pétanque in the park.

Places to Stay Accommodation in Antibes is fairly expensive. If you're on a tight budget, the best choice is probably the *Relais International de la Jeunesse* (☎ 93.61.34.40), open all year, which is is idyllically set on the Cap d'Antibes on Blvd de la Garoupe. A bet costs 60FF, including breakfast. Rooms are locked from 10 am to 5.30 pm. If you arrive during the day, you can leave your bagsn To get there from Antibes's bus station, take the bus to Cap de la Garoupe.

Close to the bus station, the *Modern Hotel* (☎ 93.34.03.05) at 1 Rue Fourmilière is basic but clean with singles/doubles from 140/200FF.

Very close to the old town at 61 Place Nationale is the small but welcoming *Auberge Provençale* (☎ 93.34.13.24), which charges between 250 and 350FF for a room.

Places to Eat The old town has lots of good, cheap restaurants, especially in Place Nationale and, a bit to the west, Rue James Close. For some delicious, if expensive, seafood and fish dishes, try *L'Oursin* (☎ 93.34.13.46) at 16 Rue de la République. An à la carte meal will cost between 150 and 250FF. The restaurant is open daily except Sunday evening and Monday; it is closed during the last week of July and all of August.

Getting There & Away There are frequent trains to/from Nice and Cannes. Call ☎ 93.33.63.51 for information.

The bus station is just off Rue de la République, close to Place Général de Gaulle. Buses also leave from Place Général de Gaulle for Nice, Cannes and other nearby towns.

Juan-les-Pins

Juan-les-Pins, contiguous to Antibes, is known above all for its beautiful two-km-

Statue in the Musée Picasso

long sandy beach backed by pine trees. A jazz festival is held here each year in the second half of July, attracting musicians and music-lovers from around the world. The tourist office (☎ 93.61.04.98) is at 51 Blvd Guillaumont.

Cap d'Antibes

Luxurious villas are well hidden behind a thick screen of plants and trees on this peninsula, which is slightly south of Antibes and Juan-les-Pins. The **Jardin Thuret**, established in 1856, is home to a wide variety of exotic plants.

CANNES

It's the money of the affluent, spent with fashionable nonchalance, that keeps Cannes's many expensive hotels, fancy restaurants and exorbitant boutiques in business and its ocean-liner-sized yachts afloat. It may be true that the well-heeled are, for the most part, boring (or at least predictable), especially when they are on holiday, but watching people whose lunch hors-d'œuvre cost more than this book has its fascinations. In any case, the harbour, the bay, Le Suquet hill, the beachside promenade, the beaches and the people sunning themselves provide more than enough natural beauty to make at least a day trip well worth the effort.

Cannes is famous for its many festivals and cultural activities, the most renowned of which is the International Film Festival, a 10-day extravaganza held in mid-May. You may be relieved to find out that Cannes has only one museum and, since its speciality is ethnography, the only art you're likely to come across is in the many rather snobbish galleries. People come to Cannes all year long, but the main season runs from May to October.

From Cannes, the Route Napoléon winds northwards passing Grasse, Castellane and Digne-les-Bains on its way to Gap and beyond. It is named after Napoleon I, who, after escaping from Elba in March 1815, passed by here as he headed for Paris, gathering an army en route for his triumphal return to the capital on 20 May.

Orientation

The train station and Rue Jean Jaurès are several blocks north of the huge Palais des Festivals et des Congrès, which is just east of the Vieux Port (old port). Cannes's most famous promenade, the magnificent, hotel-lined Blvd de la Croisette begins at the Palais des Festivals and continues eastward along the Baie de Cannes to Pointe de la Croisette. Place de l'Hôtel de Ville, where the bus station is located, is at the north-west corner of the Vieux Port. The hill west of the port is called Le Suquet.

Information

Tourist Office The main tourist office (☎ 93. 39.24.53), which is on the ground floor of the Palais des Festivals, is open Monday to Saturday from 9 am to 6.30 pm. During festivals and conventions, it's open on Sunday as well. In July and August the office is open daily from 9 am to 8 pm. The staff will reserve accommodation free of charge but will not exchange foreign currency.

The tourist office annexe (☎ 93.99.19.77) at the train station is open Monday to Saturday from 9 am to 12.30 pm and 2 to 6 pm. In July and August it opens half an hour earlier and closes half an hour later. To get there, go left as you exit the terminal building and walk up the stairs next to Frantour Tourisme. Be prepared for long queues in summer.

Money The Banque de France (☎ 93.38. 79.95) at 8 Blvd de la Croisette is open weekdays from 8.40 am to 12.10 pm and 1.35 to 3.35 pm. There are banks along Rue d'Antibes and on Rue Buttura.

American Express (☎ 93.38.15.87) at 8 Rue des Belges is open from 9 am to noon and 2 to 6 pm daily except Saturday afternoon and Sunday.

Post The main post office (☎ 93.39.13.16) at 22 Rue Bivouac Napoléon is open weekdays from 8 am to 7 pm and on Saturday until noon. It offers foreign currency exchange.

Cannes's postcode is 06400.

Laundry The laundrette nearest the train

station is at 9 Rue Hélène Vagliano. It's open daily from 8 am to 8 pm (10 pm in summer).

Bookshop English-language novels are available at the English Bookshop (☎ 93.99. 40.08) at 11 Rue Bivouac Napoléon.

Walking Tour

Since people-watching is the main reason to come to Cannes, and people are best watched while strolling, and strolling is one of the few activities in Cannes that doesn't cost anything, taking a leisurely walk is highly recommended.

The best places to walk are not far from the water. The pine and palm-shaded walkway along **Blvd de la Croisette** is probably the classiest promenade on the whole Riviera. Some of the largest yachts you'll ever see are likely to be bobbing gently in the **Vieux Port**, which was once Cannes's fishing harbour. The nearby streets are particularly pleasant on a summer's night, when the many cafés and restaurants – overflowing with laughing patrons in fashionable clothes – light up the area with coloured neon signs.

The hill just west of the Vieux Port, **Le Suquet**, affords spectacular views of Cannes, especially in the late afternoon and on clear nights. Musée de la Castre is at the summit.

Musée de la Castre

The Musée de la Castre (☎ 93.38.55.26), housed in the chateau atop Le Suquet, has a diverse collection of Mediterranean and Middle Eastern antiquities as well as objects of ethnographic interest from all over the world. It is open daily, except Tuesday and holidays, from 10 am to noon and 2 to 5 pm. In May, June and September, afternoon hours are 2 to 6 pm; in July and August, they're 3 to 7 pm. Admission is only 3FF (free on Sunday).

Beaches

Each of the fancy hotels that line Blvd de la Croisette has its own private section of the beach where the beachside equivalent of room service is available for those willing to pay 60FF to have a serving of fresh melon delivered to their deck chair! Unfortunately, this arrangement leaves only a small strip of sand near the Palais des Festivals for the bathing pleasure of the public. From the promenade, you can catch glimpses of people so bronzed that they would be perfectly camouflaged among the red rocks of the Massif de l'Esterel.

Free public beaches, the **Plages du Midi** and **Plages de la Bocca**, stretch for several km westward from the old port along Blvd Jean Hibert and Blvd du Midi.

Îles de Lérins

The eucalyptus and pine-covered **Île Sainte Marguerite**, where the Man in the Iron Mask – made famous by Alexandre Dumas (1802-70) – was held during the late 17th century, lies one km from the mainland. The island, which measures only 3.25 by one km, is encircled and crisscrossed by trails and paths. Its beaches are less crowded than those on the mainland. The smaller, forested **Île Saint Honorat** (1500 by 400 metres) was once the site of a renowned and powerful monastery founded in the 5th century. Todayl it is home to a Cistercian monastic order that owns the island but welcomes visitors.

The Société Cannoise Maritime (SCM; ☎ 93.99.62.01) runs ferries to Île Saint Honorat (40FF return; 20 minutes) and Île Sainte Marguerite (35FF return; 20 minutes); both islands can be visited for 50FF. The ticket office, which is at the Vieux Port across Jetée Albert Édouard from the Palais des Festivals, is open daily from 8.30 am to 12.15 pm and 2 to 6 pm. From early May to August it's open from 8.30 am to 6 pm. In July and August, when there are *nocturnes* (night cruises, 75FF) three nights a week, it stays open until 9.30 pm.

For part of the year, there are boats to the Îles de Lérins from Juan-les-Pins.

Places to Stay – bottom end

Hotel prices in Cannes fluctuate wildly according to seasonal demand. Tariffs can be

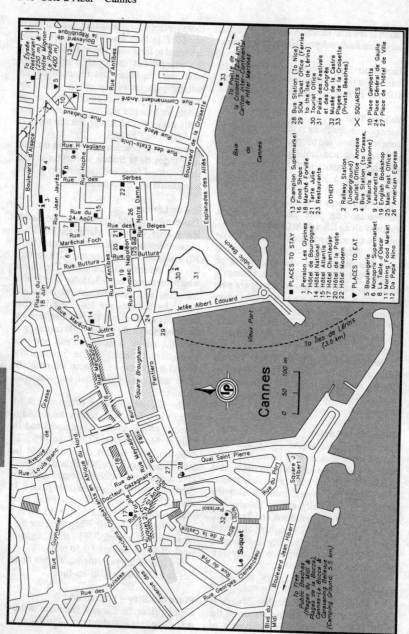

COTE D'AZUR

Cannes

0   50   100 m

PLACES TO STAY
1   Pension Les Glycines
14 Hôtel de Bourgogne
15 Hôtel National
17 Hôtel Atlantis
20 Hôtel Chanteclair
22 Hôtel de la Poste
    Hôtel Modern

PLACES TO EAT
5   Boulangerie
6   Monoprix Supermarket
8   La Table d'Oscar
11 Morning Food Market
12 Da Papa Nino

13 Champion Supermarket
16 Food Shops
18 Marché Forville
21 Tarte Julie
23 Restaurants

OTHER
2   Railway Station
3   Tourist Office
    (Underground) Annexe
4   Bus Station (to Grasse,
    Vallauris & Valbonne)
9   Laundrette
19 English Bookshop
25 Main Post Office
26 American Express

28 Bus Station (To Nice)
29 SCM Tourist Office (Ferries
    to the Iles de Lérins)
30 Tourist Office
31 Palais des Festivals
    et des Congrès
32 Musée de la Castre
33 Plages de la Croisette
    (Private Beaches)

SQUARES
10 Place Gambetta
24 Place Général de Gaulle
27 Place de l'Hôtel de Ville

up to 50% higher in July and August – when you're lucky to find a room at any price – than they are in winter. Don't even think of staying here during the film festival (mid-May) unless you book a room many months in advance (a year in advance at the cheaper places). There are no hostels of any sort in Cannes.

Camping Camping in Cannes is not cheap. *Caravaning Bellevue* (☎ 93.47.28.97) at 67 Ave Maurice Chevalier in Cannes-La Bocca, about 5.5 km west of the centre of town, is open from April to mid-September. This place charges 71FF for two people with a tent, and 7FF for parking. Bus No 9 from the bus station, at Place de l'Hôtel de Ville, stops about 400 metres away. The three-star *Camping Le Grand Saule* (☎ 93.47.07.50), open from April to October, is in Cannes-La Bocca at 24-26 Blvd Jean Moulin (formerly Blvd de la Frayère). Two people with a tent pay 81FF in the low season and 116FF in the high season. Parking costs 17FF. To get there, take bus No 9.

Hotels Cannes should have more places like the 17-room *Hôtel Chanteclair* (☎ 93.39.68.88) at 12 Rue Forville. This friendly hotel, a backpackers' favourite, has simple singles/doubles for between 130/150FF (mid-October to mid-April) and 160/220FF (during peak periods). Hall showers are free. Two-wheeled conveyances can be parked in the courtyard. The *Hôtel National* (☎ 93.39.91.92) at 8 Rue Maréchal Joffre, run by an English proprietor, has singles/doubles from 100/150FF (150/220FF in the high season). Doubles with shower and toilet are 200 to 300FF.

The large *Hôtel Atlantis* (☎ 93.39.18.72) is at 4 Rue du 24 Août. Despite its two-star rating, singles/doubles with TV cost only 150/180FF during the low season. The price of a double shoots up to 265FF during festival periods and in July and August. The *Hôtel de Bourgogne* (☎ 93.38.36.73; fax 93.68.37.65) at 13 Rue du 24 Août has singles/doubles for 154/176FF in the off season and 170/220FF in summer. Showers cost 20FF.

The *Pension Les Glycines* (☎ 93.38.41.28) at 32 Blvd d'Alsace, an old place east of the train station, has singles/doubles from 120/150FF (170/300FF in summer). A huge triple/quad costs 200FF from September to April and 300FF the rest of the year. Showers are 7FF. Further north of the railway tracks, the amiable *Mignon-Le Prado* (☎ 93.38.49.40), in a residential neighbourhood at 7 Rue Marcellin Berthelot, is a two-star hotel with one-star prices. Comfortable doubles start at 120FF (250FF in July and August).

Places to Stay – middle

Although it may not quite live up to its name, the *Hôtel Modern* (☎ 93.39.09.87) at 11 Rue des Serbes has clean and serviceable, though small, rooms – all with TV – from 200/270FF in the off season and 280/350FF at other times. Opposite the main post office, the *Hôtel de la Poste* (☎ 93.39.22.58) at 31 Rue Bivouac Napoléon has decent rooms from 200FF.

Places to Stay – top end

It's not to hard to find Cannes's top hotels – most of them are along Blvd de la Croisette. The ornate and extremely comfortable *Carlton Inter-Continental* (☎ 93.68.91.68; fax 93.38.20.90), 58 Blvd de la Croisette, has singles/doubles from 1400/3200FF. Some of the rooms offer great sea views. At 73 Blvd de la Croisette is the *Martinez* (☎ 93.92.98.73.00; fax 93.39.67.82), complete with pool and tennis courts. It took a long time to renovate this place but the results are impressive. Singles/doubles cost around 1400/3400FF.

Places to Eat

Cheap dining is not Cannes's forte.

Restaurants There are a few inexpensive restaurants around the Marché Forville and lots of little, though not necessarily cheap, restaurants along Rue Saint Antoine.

Near the train station, *La Table d'Oscar* (☎ 93.38.42.46i at 26 Rue Jean Jaurès has a reasonable 60FF *menu*. Nearby, the Sicilian restaurant *Da Papa' Nino* (☎ 93.38.48.08) at

16 Blvd de la République has many varieties of pizza and a good-value three-course *menu* for 58FF. It is closed on Wednesday. *Tarte Julie* (☎ 93.39.67.43) at 33 Rue Bivouac Napoléon has a range of salads from 32FF, but it's the house specialities – sweet/savory tarts from 12/18FF a slice – that really draw the crowds.

North of the train tracks, *L'Élysée* (☎ 93.68.33.88) at 67 Blvd de la République is an unpretentious restaurant serving a hearty three-course *menu* for 59FF and a variety of salads from 34FF.

Self-Catering Square Brougham, next to the old port, is a great place for a picnic.

There's a *food market* at Place Gambetta every morning except Monday (every morning during the summer). Food shops in the vicinity include a *boulangerie* (closed Tuesday) at 9 Rue Jean Jaurès. The *Marché Forville*, a fruit and vegetable market on Rue du Marché Forville, a block north-east of the Hôtel de Ville, is open every morning except Monday.

The *Monoprix supermarket* at 9 Rue Maréchal Foch has an in-house bakery and is open Monday to Saturday from 8.45 am to 7 pm (7.30 pm from June to September). Along the pedestrianised Rue Meynadier, the *Champion supermarket* at No 6 is open Monday to Saturday from 8.30 am to 7.45 pm. Other food shops along Rue Meynadier include *boulangeries* at Nos 18 and 48 and *fromageries* at Nos 22 and 56.

Entertainment

Nondubbed films are screened from time to time at the cinemas along Rue Félix Faure and its continuation, Rue d'Antibes. To see what's on, consult the movie listings posted at the tourist offices and various cafés around town.

Getting There & Away

Train The train station (☎ 93.99.50.50 for information) is on Rue Jean Jaurès. The 1st-floor information office is open daily from 8.30 am to noon and 2 to 6 pm. From mid-July to mid-September hours are 8.30 am to 6.45 pm.

Destinations within easy reach include Saint Raphaël (32FF; 25 minutes; two an hour), from where you can get buses to Saint Tropez, and Toulon (87FF; 1¼ hours; hourly). For other Côte d'Azur connections, see Getting There & Away under Nice.

Bus Buses to Nice (28FF; 1½ hours), Nice airport (65FF for the 40-minute trip via the autoroute, 44FF for the 1½-hour trip via the highway) and other destinations leave from Place de l'Hôtel de Ville. Most are operated by Rapides Côte d'Azur. The information office (☎ 93.39.11.39) is open Monday to Saturday from 6 am to noon and 2 to 6 pm and on Sunday from 8 am to 2 pm. No student discounts are available.

Buses to Grasse (line No 600; 17.50FF; 45 minutes), Vallauris, Valbonne and elsewhere depart from the bus station to the left as you exit the train station. The information counter (☎ 93.39.31.37) is open from 9 am to noon and 2 to 6.30 pm daily except Wednesday, Sunday and holidays.

Getting Around

Bus Bus Azur serves Cannes and destinations up to seven km from town. Their office (☎ 93.39.18.71) at Place de l'Hôtel de Ville (in the same building as Rapides Côte d'Azur) is open daily from 7 am to 7.30 pm. Single tickets cost 6.50FF and a 10-ticket carnet costs 43FF.

Taxi Call ☎ 93.38.30.79 or 93.39.60.80 to order a taxi.

GRASSE

If it weren't for the scents being concocted in Grasse (population 42,000) – just 17 km north of Cannes and the Mediterranean – your nostrils would have a fair chance of noticing the sea breeze. But for centuries, Grasse, with its distinct orange roofs rising up the slopes of the Pre-Alps, has been one of France's three most important centres of perfume production (the other two are Paris and Montpellier).

These days there are five famous master perfumers – or *'nez'* (noses), as they're called – in the world. Combining their natural gift with seven years of study, they are able to identify, from no more than a whiff, about 6000 scents. Somewhere between 200 and 500 of these are used to make just one perfume. Compelling reading associated with Grasse is *Perfume*, a novel by Patrick Süskind about the fantastic life and amazing nose of Jean-Baptiste Grenouille.

Grasse and the surrounding region also produce some of France's most highly prized flowers, including jasmine, Centifolia rose, lavender, mimosa, orange blossom and violets.

History

Founded by the Romans, Grasse became a small republic by the Middle Ages, exporting tanned skins and oil. It was taken over by the Counts of Provence in 1226 and became part of France in the 16th century. Already a strong trading centre, Grasse grew even richer with the advent of perfumed gloves in the 1500s. Once established, the perfumed glove-makers split from the tanners, setting up a separate industry that eventually led to the creation of perfumeries. These in turn flourished in the 18th century, when perfume became fashionable and members of high society saw to it that they never went anywhere without leaving a distinct aura in their wake.

Orientation

While the town of Grasse and its suburbs sprawl over a wide area of the hill and valley, the old town is a tiny area, densely packed into its hillside perch. Its steep cobbled stairways and roads (somewith impossibly tight hairpin bends) are best explored on foot. The N85, better known as the Route Napoléon, which leads north to Castellane and Digne-les-Bains and south to Cannes, runs right through the heart of town, where it serves as Grasse's main (and often congested) thoroughfare under the name of Blvd du Jeu de Ballon.

There's a wide view over the rather built-up valley from Place du 24 Août near the Tour d'Horloge (clock tower).

Information

Tourist Office The main tourist office (☎ 93. 36.03.56) is at Place de la Foux. It's open Monday to Saturday from 9 am to 12.30 pm and 2 to 6.30 pm. In summer, it's open daily from 9 am to 8 pm. The small tourist office annexe in the Palais de Congrès operates during summer.

Money Banks line Blvd du Jeu de Ballon. The Société Générale (☎ 93.36.44.17) at Rue Maximin Isnard is open weekdays from 8.30 am to 12.15 pm and 1.45 to 4.45 pm.

Post The main post office (☎ 93.70.49.07) on Blvd Fragonard is open weekdays from 8 am to 6.30 pm and on Saturday until noon.

Grasse's postcode is 06130.

Laundry The laundrette at 1bis Rue Gazan is open daily from 7 am to 9 pm. There's another laundrette open the same hours on Blvd Fragonard, directly opposite the main post office.

Perfumeries

Follow your nose along Rue Jean Ossola to the archway at the beginning of Rue Tracastel, where several perfumeries have been conjuring up new odours for many years. The air around the alley entrance is saturated with aromas.

While more than 40 perfumeries exist in Grasse, only three are open to the public. They have free tours in English (arranged on the spot), will exchange foreign currency (don't expect good rates), forbid smoking and have parking. It's unlikely that you'll know any of them by name, as their perfumes are sold only from their factories or by mail order. The names the world knows are the big name brands who buy the perfumers' essence and reap considerable profit from it.

During a tour, you'll be taken through every stage of perfume production, from extraction and distillation, to the work of the 'noses'. The guides will explain the differ-

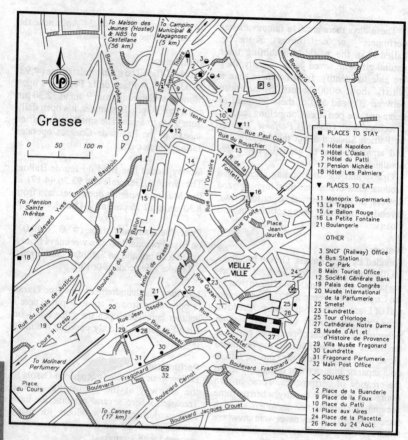

Grasse

0   50   100 m

■ PLACES TO STAY
1 Hôtel Napoléon
5 Hôtel L'Oasis
7 Hôtel du Patti
17 Pension Michèle
18 Hôtel Les Palmiers

▼ PLACES TO EAT
11 Monoprix Supermarket
13 La Trappa
15 Le Ballon Rouge
16 La Petite Fontaine
21 Boulangerie

OTHER
3 SNCF (Railway) Office
4 Bus Station
6 Car Park
8 Main Tourist Office
12 Société Générale Bank
19 Palais des Congrès
20 Musée International
    de la Parfumerie
22 Smells!
23 Laundrette
25 Tour d'Horloge
27 Cathédrale Notre Dame
28 Musée d'Art et
    d'Histoire de Provence
29 Villa Musée Fragonard
30 Laundrette
31 Fragonard Parfumerie
32 Main Post Office

✕ SQUARES
2 Place de la Buanderie
9 Place de la Foux
10 Place du Patti
14 Place aux Aires
24 Place de la Placette
26 Place du 24 Août

ences between perfume, which contains 20% pure essence, and its weaker partners, eau de toilette and eau de Cologne, which contain 2% to 6% concentrate. You'll also hear about the extraordinary number of flowers needed to make one litre of essence. At the end you'll be squirted with a few of the house scents, invited to purchase as many as you'd like, and leave reeking.

Fragonard If you're on foot the most convenient perfumery is Fragonard (☎ 93.36. 44.65) at 20 Blvd Fragonard in the old town. Among Grasse's oldest perfumeries, it is

named after one of the town's original perfume-making families and is housed in a 17th-century former tannery. There is also a perfume museum here. The factory gives a brief introduction to perfume but these days it's more a tourist showcase than a working factory; the real production factory (also open for free visits) is out of town on the N85 to Cannes. From October to February the perfumery in the old town is open from 9 am to 12.30 pm and 2 to 6 pm. The rest of the year it is open daily from 9 am to 6.30 pm.

Molinard Housed in a turreted, Provençal-style villa surrounded by immaculate lawns and a blaze of flowers, Molinard (☎ 93.36.01.62) at 60 Blvd Victor Hugo (the continuation of Cours Honoré Cresp) is a ritzier production than Fragonard. It's open most of the year daily from 9 am to 1.30 pm and 2 to 5 pm; from July to September hours are 9 am to 6 pm.

Galimard The third perfumery, Galimard (☎ 93.09.20.00), is at 73 Route de Cannes (the N85), way out of town near Fragonard's factory. Unless you have wheels it's not a feasible option.

Museums

All of the museums mentioned here are closed in November.

Villa Musée Fragonard Named after the artist Jean-Honoré Fragonard, who was born in Grasse in 1732, this villa (☎ 93.36.01.61) at 23 Blvd Fragonard, now a museum, is where the artist came to live for a year in 1790. The artist's paintings, famous for their licentious scenes, are on display in the museum. It is open Wednesday to Sunday from 10 am to noon and 2 to 5 pm. From June to September it's open daily from 10 am to 1 pm and 2 to 7 pm. Entry is free.

Musée International de la Parfumerie Opened in 1989, the International Perfume Museum (☎ 93.36.80.20) at 8 Place du Cours examines every detail of perfume production, from extraction techniques to sales and publicity – there's even a tacky airport duty-free lounge. One of the most appealing sections of the museum is the rooftop conservatory, where lavender, mint, thyme and jasmine are grown in a heady mix of scents. It is open Wednesday to Sunday from 10 am to noon and 2 to 5 pm. From 1 June to 30 September it's open daily from 10 am to 7 pm. Admission is 12FF for adults (6FF for students and children).

Musée d'Art et d'Histoire de Provence Sandwiched between the other musuems and struggling vainly to compete is the Museum

of Provençal Art & History (☎ 93.36.01.61) at 2 Rue Mirabeau. It's unexceptional apart from a collection of local 18th-century faïence and a few nice old baths and bidets. It has the same opening hours as the Musée Fragonard. Entrance costs 6.60FF for adults (3.30FF for students and children); on Sunday and Wednesday it's free for everyone.

Cathédrale Notre Dame du Puy

Although rather uninteresting in itself, the former cathedral contains a painting by Fragonard entitled *Washing of the Feet* and three early paintings by Rubens.

Places to Stay

Although the number of hotels in Grasse has doubled in the past five years, the choice is still pretty limited.

Camping The two-star *Camping Municipal* (☎ 93.36.28.69) on Blvd Alice de Rothschild (the continuation of Ave Thiers), one km north-east of the tourist office is the nearest camp site. It charges 20FF per person, including tent, and 15FF for a car. It is closed in January. Bus No 8, which is marked 'Piscine', leaves from the bus station and stops at the front of the camping ground. It runs Monday to Saturday, and the last one is at 6.30 pm.

Hostel The only hostel-type place in town is the *Maison des Jeunes et de la Culture* (MJC; ☎ 93.36.35.64) on Ave Honoré Lions, up the hill to the north of the town. It's open all year and charges 40FF for a bed without breakfast. Following the sinuous roads, it's about three km from town. Head up Blvd Eugène Charabot to Blvd Louis Barthou, turn right at the T-intersection and keep going up. For the less energetic, bus No 8 from the bus station stops out front.

Hotels The cheapest option is the *Hôtel Napoléon* (☎ 93.36.05.87), on a busy corner at 6 Ave Thiers. It has ordinary singles/doubles/triples from 103/130/184FF. This place is closed from the end of December to the end of January. Opposite is the small,

CÔTE D'AZUR

two-star *Hôtel L'Oasis* (☎ 93.36.01.00) at Place de la Buanderie, which has comfortable rooms from 160FF.

If you have a car or don't mind an uphill amble, the *Pension Sainte Thérèse* (☎ 93.36.10.29) at 39 Blvd Y E Baudoin, just over one km from the tourist office, is a good choice. From the hotel you get a panoramic view of the valley and the dusty orange township. Singles/doubles start at 135/160FF; private parking is available. The hotel is closed from October to mid-November. Another option on the same road is *Les Palmiers* (☎ 93.36.07.24) at No 17. Prices fluctuate according to the season: in winter they start at 140/160FF for one or two people and in summer they start at 216FF. Lastly, for those planning to stay a few days, there's the *Pension Michèle* (☎ 93.36.06.37) at 6 Rue du Palais de Justice. The owner takes visitors only on a *demi-pension* basis – a good deal at 138FF per person – but you must stay for a minimum of three days. It's closed in November.

For something more up-market, try the modern *Hôtel du Patti* (☎ 93.36.01.00) on Place du Patti, right in the heart of the old town. It has pleasant singles/doubles with private bath and toilet from 320/400FF. Parking is available.

Places to Eat

When the people of Grasse want a night out, they're likely to head for the bright lights of Cannes twinkling in the distance. Fortunately, attempts to enliven the local eating scene are beginning to show some results.

Restaurants *La Petite Fontaine* (☎ 93.36.84.60) at 12 Rue de la Fontette has tables along the narrow cobbled stairs. A traditional *menu* costs 55FF. At 14 Blvd du Jeu de Ballon, *Le Ballon Rouge* (☎ 93.36.38.46) has a large terrace where you can choose from a number of *menus* starting at 65FF. It is pricier on weekends. *La Trappa*, down the little Rue du Rouachier near Place Patti, also has a three-course *menu* from 55FF. The *Hôtel Napoléon* (see Hotels) serves a hearty 65FF *menu*.

Self-Catering The *Monoprix* store on Place du Patti has a basement supermarket; it is open Monday to Saturday from 8.45 am to 12.15 pm and 2.30 to 7 pm. There are several *boulangeries* along Rue Jean Ossola – you'll find at least one of them open every day of the week.

Entertainment

Entertainment-wise Grasse is very tame, offering only bars along Blvd du Jeu de Ballon and on Place aux Aires.

Getting There & Away

Train Although the rail line has yet to reach Grasse, the SNCF has an information office at the bus station which is open Monday to Saturday from 8.30 am to 12.15 pm and 1.30 to 6 pm. For information, call ☎ 93.99.50.50 in Cannes.

Bus The bus station is on Place de la Buanderie. There are luggage lockers inside the main building, which closes at 6 pm.

Several companies operate services from here. Rapides Côte d'Azur (☎ 93.36.08.43) is open from 8 am to noon and 2 to 5 pm and has buses to Nice (31FF) via Cannes (17.50FF; 50 minutes) every half-hour (hourly on Sundays). TACAVL (☎ 93.42.40.79), open from 8 am to noon and 2 to 4 pm, runs less frequent services to Nice (26FF) via Vence (19.50FF; one hour). VFD has a line to Grenoble (238FF; six hours) which stop in Castellane (near the Gorges du Verdon) and Digne-les-Bains.

Getting Around

Local buses are run by STGA (☎ 93.64.88.84), which has an information office at the bus station on Place de la Buanderie. A single ticket costs 5FF.

CANNES TO SAINT TROPEZ
Massif de l'Esterel

The most stunning natural feature of the entire Côte d'Azur is the mountain of red porphyry rock known as the Massif de l'Esterel. Covered by pine, oak and eucalyptus trees until the devastating fires of 1985 and 1986, this range lies between Saint Raphaël and La Napoule, which is inland from Cannes. A drive or walk along the Corniche de l'Esterel (also known as the Corniche d'Or and the N98) – the coastal road that runs along the base of the range – is not to be missed – the views are spectacular. Along the way you'll find many small summer resorts and inlets where you can go swimming. Some of the places worth visiting include: Le Dramont, where the 36th US Division landed on 15 August 1944; Agay, a pretty, sheltered bay with a good beach; the resorts of Le Trayas and Théoule-sur-Mer; and Mandelieu-la-Napoule, a pleasant resort with a large pleasure-boat harbour near the ruins of a 14th-century castle.

There are all sorts of walks you can go on in the Massif de l'Esterel, but for the more difficult trails you will need to come equipped with a good map. Many of the walks, such as those up to the Pic de l'Ours (496 metres) and the Pic du Cap Roux (452 metres), are signposted.

Places to Stay There are camping grounds at various places along the coast, including Le Dramont, Agay, Anthéor, Le Trayas and Mandelieu-la-Napoule.

There is an *Auberge de Jeunesse* (☎ 93.75. 40.23) at Le Trayas, midway between Cannes and Fréjus (about 20 km from each), on a beautiful site overlooking the sea. The hostel, which is closed in January, is on Ave de la Veronese, 1.5 km up the hill from the Trayas Auberge bus stop. The hostel is closed from 10 am to 5 pm and has a midnight curfew. A bed costs 40FF and breakfast (obligatory from June to September) is 15FF. Kitchen facilities are available. You must have an IYHF card. Telephone reservations are not accepted. You can camp for 21FF.

Anthéor, Miramar, Théoule-sur-Mer and Mandelieu-la-Napoule each have hotels, though most are in the middle to top-end range. Miramar and Mandelieu-la-Napoule offer the greatest choice.

Fréjus & Saint Raphaël
Fréjus, initially founded by Massiliots

(Greeks who settled Marseille) and colonised by Julius Caesar around 49 BC as Forum Julii, is known for its Roman remains. Once an important port, the town was sacked by various invaders, including Saracens (Muslims), from the 10th century AD on. Much of the town's commercial activity ceased after its harbour silted up in the 16th century. The collapse of the nearby Malpasset dam in the Reyran Valley in 1959 led to the death of over 400 people and the destruction of the western part of the town.

At the foot of the Massif de l'Esterel is Saint Raphaël, a beachside resort town two km south-east of Fréjus. This was one of the main landing bases of the US and French troops in August 1944.

Orientation & Information Although Saint Raphaël is two km south-east of Fréjus, the suburbs of the two have now become so intertwined that they seem almost to form a single town. Fréjus comprises the hillside Fréjus Ville, 1.5 km from the seafront, and Fréjus Plage, on the Gulf of Fréjus. Of greatest interest is Fréjus Ville, where all the Roman ruins are to be found.

Tourist Offices The Fréjus tourist office (☎ 94.51.54.14) at 325 Rue Jean Jaurès is open Monday to Saturday from 9 am to noon and 2 to 6 pm. From June to mid-September, it's open daily from 9 am to noon and 2.30 to 7 pm. The staff can make hotel reservations and have a good map of the town showing the location of its archaeological treasures. From June to September the tourist office annexe (☎ 94.51.48.52) at the beach (opposite 11 Blvd de la Libération) is open daily from 10 am to noon and 3 to 8 pm.

Saint Raphaël's tourist office (☎ 94.95.16. 87) is on Rue Waldeck Rousseau across the street from the train station. It's open Monday to Saturday from 8.15 am to noon and 1.30 to 6 pm. In July and August it's open Monday to Saturday from 8.15 am to 12.30 pm and 1.30 to 7.30 pm and on Sunday from 8.30 am to noon. The staff will make hotel reservations from mid-July to mid-August only.

Post Fréjus's post office (☎ 94.51.56.39) is on Ave Aristide Briand and is open from 8.30 am to 7 pm (noon on Saturday).

Fréjus's postcode is 83600 and that of St Raphaël is 83700.

Roman Ruins West of Fréjus's old town on Rue Henri Vadon (past the Porte des Gaules) are the 1st and 2nd-century **Arènes** (amphitheatre), once able to seat an audience of 10,000 and now used for rock concerts and bullfights. At the eastern end of town, near Place de la Glacière, is the **Porte Dorée**, the only extant arcade of the thermal baths. Nearby are the remains of a Roman aqueduct and theatre.

Cathédrale Notre Dame et Saint Étienne In the centre of town on Place Formigé, on the site of a Roman temple, is the 11th and 12th-century cathedral, one of the first Gothic buildings in the region, though it retains certain features from the Roman period. The impressive carved-wood doors at the main entrance were added during the Renaissance. The cathedral is open from 9 am to noon and 2 to 5.30 pm, and 9 am to 7 pm in summer. It is closed on Tuesday.

To the left of the cathedral is the octagonal 5th-century baptistry, with a Roman column at each of its eight corners.

Stairs from the narthex lead up to the lovely 12th and 13th-century cloister, whose features include some of the columns of the Roman theatre and painted wooden ceilings from the 14th and 15th centuries. It looks out onto a beautiful courtyard with a well-tended garden and an enourmous well.

Musée Archéologique In the cathedral's cloister is the Archaeological Museum, which has a marble statue of Hermes, a head of Jupiter and a magnificent 3rd-century mosaic depicting a leopard. The museum is open daily from 9 am to noon and 2 to 5.30 pm; in the off season it is closed on Tuesday.

Beaches Both Fréjus Plage and Saint Raphaël have long, sandy beaches. The beachfront at Fréjus, lined with buildings from the 1950s, is less pretentious and more middle class than that at Saint Raphaël.

Places to Stay There are various accommodation options in Fréjus and Saint Raphaël, but they are not particularly cheap.

Camping Fréjus has several camping grounds, but in summer you will want to get in early as they become very crowded. The best of these is the *Holiday Green* (☎ 94.40.88.20), on the road to Bagnols, which is open from the end of March to the end of September. It is six km from the beach, but it is equipped with an enormous pool. The camping ground nearest the beach is the *Parc de Camping de Saint Aygulf* (☎ 94.81.30.53) at 270 Ave Salvareli in Saint Aygulf, south of Fréjus. Open from June to mid-September, this huge camping ground – with room for over 1500 tents – offers well-maintained facilities and lots of shade.

In Saint Raphaël you can pitch a tent at *Camping Beauséjour-Les Tasses* (☎ 94.95.03.67) on Ave Beauséjour. It is open from May to September.

Hostel The *Auberge de Jeunesse* (☎ 94.52.18.75), on Chemin du Counillier near Fréjus Ville, is open all year. Set in a seven-hectare park, this pleasant hostel has dorm beds for 55FF including breakfast. You can also camp here for 26FF a night. If you arrive by train, get off at Saint Raphaël and take the Fréjus-Valescure bus from the bus station to the hostel. This service only runs in summer.

The very comfortable *Centre International du Manoir* (94.95.20.58; fax 94.83.85.06), on Chemin de l'Escale, is five km south-east of St Raphaël in Boulouris. You can choose between a dorm bed or a room with private bathroom; prices range from 105FF for a dorm bed and breakfast, to 200FF for a double. A small membership fee applies the first time you stay here.

Hotels In Fréjus, the *Hôtel Bellevue* (☎ 94.51.42.41) on Place Paul Vernet, close to the cathedral, is reasonably priced at 110FF for singles and 140 to 190FF for doubles. The

Auberge du Vieux Four (☎ 94.51.56.38) at 49 Rue Grisolle has well-kept rooms with bath from 260FF. It also has a very good restaurant.

At Fréjus Plage, the *Hôtel Oasis* (☎ 94.51.50.44) in a quiet location at Impasse Charcot, has comfortable singles/doubles with TV for 260/320FF. Parking is available. The hotel is closed from 1 December to 1 February. Also at Fréjus Plage is the *Hôtel Sable et Soleil* (☎ 94.51.08.70) at 158 Rue P Arène, where singles/doubles cost 280/340FF. There are also facilities for disabled people.

For budget accommodation in Saint Raphaël, try the *Hôtel Les Templiers* (☎ 94.95.38.93) on Place de la République. More up-market is the *Hôtel France* (☎ 94.95.17.03) on Place Gallieni. It is closed in December and, in the off season, on Sunday.

Places to Eat *Les Potiers* (☎ 94.51.33.74) in Fréjus at 135 Rue des Potiers is closed at lunchtime on Wednesday and Saturday and from mid-November to mid-December.

For great fish dishes and seafood don't miss *La Voile d'Or* (☎ 94.95.17.04) at 1 Blvd du Général de Gaulle in Saint Raphaël.

Near Fréjus Plage, there's a *Casino supermarket* at 173 Blvd de la Libération. Close by are lots of inexpensive tourist restaurants.

One block from Saint Raphaël's beach, the *Monoprix* store at 50 Blvd Félix Martin has a supermarket section at the back. It is open Monday to Saturday from 8.30 am to 12.30 pm and 2.30 to 7 pm. In July and August hours are 8.30 am to 7.30 pm.

Getting There & Away Both Fréjus and Saint Raphaël are on the train line from Nice. For information call ☎ 94.51.30.53. There's especially frequent service from Nice to Gare de Saint Raphaël-Valescure, which is 250 metres from Saint Raphaël's beach.

SAINT TROPEZ

In 1956, Saint Tropez (current population 6000) was the setting for the film *Et Dieu créa la femme* (And God Created Woman) starring Brigitte Bardot. Its stunning success brought about the destruction of Saint Tropez – or at least that's what some people say. But one thing is clear: the peaceful little fishing village of Saint Tropez, somewhat isolated from the rest of the Côte d'Azur at the end of its own peninsula, suddenly became the talk of the jet set, who propelled the little port into world fame. Ever since, Saint Tropez has lived on its sexy image, delivered to an adoring public by the media.

Attempts to keep Saint Tropez small and exclusive have created at least one tangible result: you'll probably have to wait in huge traffic queues to drive into town. Yachts, way out of proportion to the size of the old harbour, long ago chased away the simple fishing boats. And while painters jostle each other and their easels along the harbour quay, in summer there's little of the intimate village air that artists such as the neo-impressionist Paul Signac found so alluring. Mercifully, winter is much calmer.

Orientation

Saint Tropez lies at the southern end of the narrow bay of Saint Tropez opposite the Massif des Maures. The old town, with its narrow streets, is packed between Quai Jean Jaurès, the main quay of the Vieux Port; Place des Lices, a shady rectangular 'square' a few blocks inland; and what's left of the 16th-century citadel overlooking the town from the north-east.

Information

Tourist Office The tourist office (☎ 94.97.41.21), which is part of the bus station, is at the south-western edge of town on Ave Général de Gaulle, the one main road out of town. From October to April it is open Monday to Saturday from 9 am to 12.30 pm and 2 to 6.30 pm. In summer it's open from 9 am to 7 or 8 pm and Sunday from 10 am to 1 pm and 3 to 7 pm. There is also a more conveniently placed tourist office branch at Quai Jean Jaurès (☎ 94.97.45.21).

Money At the port, the Crédit Lyonnais (☎ 94.97.48.55) on 21 Quai Suffren is open weekdays from 8 am to noon and 1.30 to 4.45 pm. It has a 24-hour exchange machine.

Thomas Cook (☎ 94.97.88.00) at 10 Rue Allard, one street from the port, is open daily from 9 am to 4.30 pm and from 8.30 am to midnight from 1 June to 30 September. American Express (☎ 94.97.16.56) is at 23 Ave du Général Leclerc.

Post The main post office (☎ 94.97.00.00) at Place Celli, one block from the port, is open weekdays from 9 am to noon and 2 to 5 pm, and Saturday until noon. There is an exchange service.

Saint Tropez's postcode is 83990.

Laundry The laundrette at Ave Général Leclerc, a block from the tourist office, is open from 8 am to 11 pm, but it charges an unbelievable 34FF a load.

Musée de l'Annonciade

If you've had enough of wandering around the old port and the village, you can visit the Musée de l'Annonciade (☎ 94.97.04.01) on Place Grammont at the waterfront of the Vieux Port. It contains an impressive collection of modern art, including works by Matisse, Bonnard, Dufy, Derain and Rouault. Paul Signac, the pointillist artist who set up his home and studio in Saint Tropez, is well represented. The museum is open daily, except Tuesday, from 10 am to noon and 2 to 6 pm. Between June and the end of September, hours are 10 am to noon and 4 to 8 pm. It is closed in November. Entry is 20/10FF for adults/children.

Musée Naval

If you're really hunting for something to do, the Naval Museum (☎ 94.97.06.53) in the citadel at the end of Montée de la Citadelle is open daily, except Tuesday, from 10 am to 5.45 pm (closed mid-November to mid-December). Apart from displays about the town's maritime history, it also has information about the Allied landings that took place here in August 1944.

Beaches

About four km south-east of the town starts a magnificent sandy beach, Plage de Tahiti,

and its continuation, Plage de Pampelonne. It runs for about nine km between Cap du Pinet and the rocky Cap Camarat. To get there on foot, head out of town along Route de la Belle Isnarde. Otherwise, the bus to Ramatuelle, a village south of Saint Tropez, stops at various points along a road that runs about one km inland from the beach.

The coastline east of Toulon, from Le Lavandou to the Saint Tropez peninsula (including spots around the peninsula), is well endowed with *naturiste* (nudist) beaches. It's legal in some places, mostly on secluded beaches or along sheltered creeks farther inland.

On the south side of Cap Camarat is a secluded nudist beach, **Plage de l'Escalet**. Several creeks around here also attract naturists. To get there you can take the bus to Ramatuelle, but you'll have to walk or if lucky, hitch, the four km south-east to the beach. Closer to Saint Tropez is **La Moutte**, a naturist beach 4.5 km east of town – take Route des Salins, which runs between two of the homes of BB (as Brigitte Bardot is still known).

Walks

The Sentier Littoral (Coastal Walk) goes all the way from Saint Tropez south to the beach of Cavalaire along some 40 km of splendid rocky outcrops and hidden bays. In parts the setting is reminiscent of the tropics minus the coconuts. If the distance is too great, you can walk as far as Ramatuelle and take the bus back.

Places to Stay – bottom end & middle

Surprise! Surprise! There's not a cheap hotel, let alone a hostel, to be found. However, the beach is free and, though it's technically illegal to sleep there, sleeping backpackers are tolerated until very early in the morning, when the police might come by to chase them away. To the south-east along Plage de Pampelonne, there are plenty of multistarred camping grounds.

Saint Tropez's cheapest hotel is the *Hôtel Les Chimères* (☎ 94.97.02.90) at the south-western end of Ave Général Leclerc (you'll pass by it as you're coming into town on the N98 from Sainte Maxime or La Croix-Valmer). Singles/doubles start at 180/250FF, including breakfast, but in July and August the rates rise to 250/310FF. The next place on the price ladder is the *Hôtel La Méditerranée* (☎ 94.97.00.44) at 21 Blvd Louis Blanc (which leads to Place des Lices). It has one room for 150FF, and all the rest start at 238/278FF for singles/doubles, including breakfast.

Places to Stay – top end
One of St Tropez's choice offerings is the four-star *Byblos* (☎ 94.97.00.04; fax 94.97.40.52) on Ave Paul Signac, very close to the old town. This luxurious hotel complex has sumptuously furnished rooms from 1600/2700FF for singles/doubles. There is also a good restaurant, known as Les Arcades, and a pool.

Of the same calibre is *Résidence La Pinède* (☎ 94.97.04.21; fax 94.97.73.64) at Plage de la Bouillabaisse, one km south of town. The rates are the same as for Byblos, and you will get superb views over the bay from most rooms.

Not quite as expensive is *Le Yaca* (☎ 94.97.11.79; fax 94.97.58.50) at 1 Blvd d'Aumale in the heart of the old town. This stylish, small hotel has very comfortable rooms from 1100/2000FF.

Places to Eat
Restaurants Quai Jean Jaurès is lined with restaurants, most with *menus* from 100FF and with a strategic view of the dinner plates of those dining on the yachts. Near the quay, *Häagen Dasz* ice-cream cones cost 12/19FF for one/two scoops.

Pizzeria Margherita on Place de la Garonne, between the port and Place des Lices, has pizzas from 50FF. *Cantina El Mexicano* (☎ 94.97.40.96) on 14 Rue des Remparts near the Port des Pêcheurs has enchiladas for 68FF. Next door is *Le Snack*, with sandwiches and drinks. *Café des Arts* on Place des Lices has long been favoured by artists. It has a large terrace from where you can cheer on a game of pétanque.

Self-Catering The *Prisunic supermarket* on Ave Général Leclerc (near the tourist office) is open Monday to Saturday from 8 am to 8 pm. The *market* on Place des Lices is held on Tuesday and Saturday mornings, and the one on Place aux Herbes behind Quai Jean Jaurès is open daily until lunchtime.

Getting There & Away
Saint Tropez makes a great day trip, but note that there may not be anywhere to leave your luggage.

The nearest train station is in Saint Raphaël. Sodetrav (☎ 94.65.21.00 in Hyères) has eight buses a day (none on Sunday) from Saint Raphaël's train station to Saint Tropez's bus station. The buses go via Fréjus and take 1½ hours (41FF one way). Buses from Saint Tropez to Toulon (80FF; two hours) go inland before joining the coast at Cavalaire; they also stop at Le Lavandou and Hyères.

Buses to Ramatuelle (three a day), a village in the middle of the peninsula, leave from the bus station and run parallel to the coastline about one km inland. For more information on buses, ask at the tourist office.

SAINT TROPEZ TO TOULON
Massif des Maures
Stretching from Hyères to Fréjus, the massif is covered with pine, chestnut and cork oak trees. These make it appear almost black and give rise to its name, which comes from the Provençal word 'mauro' (dark pine wood). Tradition, however, ascribes the name to the Moors (Maures in French), who raided this area for 1000 years from the 8th to the 18th centuries.

The massif offers superb walking and cycling opportunities. There are four roads you can take through these hills, the northernmost one being a ridge road, the Route des Crêtes, which runs close to La Sauvette (779 metres), the massif's highest peak. It continues east through the village of **La Garde Freinet**, once a Muslim stronghold and now a perfect getaway from the summer hordes. Within the massif are a number of places worth visiting. If you like chestnuts, the place to go is **Collobrières**, a small town renowned for its chestnut purée and *marrons glacés*, chestnuts cooked in syrup and glazed. Twelve km east of Collobrières are the ruins of a 12th to 13th-century monastery, **La Chartreuse de la Verne**. North-east of the monastery is the village of **Grimaud**, notable for its castle ruins, small Roman church and pretty streets.

While you are in the Massif des Maures, be particularly careful to put out matches or cigarettes as this area is very susceptible to fires.

Bormes-les-Mimosas
Within the Massif des Maures is the 12th-century village of Bormes-les-Mimosas, famous for its great diversity of flora. This beautiful village has attracted lots of artists and craftspeople, many of whom you will see at work as you wander through the tiny streets. With stretches of fine sand and numerous inlets, the seafront offers lots of watersports. Various festivals are held here through the year – if you're around in September, don't miss the Fête des Vendanges (Grape Harvest Festival).

Le Lavandou
Formerly a fishing village, Le Lavandou (five km east of Bormes-les-Mimosas) is becoming a popular destination, thanks mainly to its 12-km-long sandy beach, which is well protected and perfect for swimming, sunbathing and strolling. Although the town itself may not have much to offer, it is a good base for exploring the nearby Massif des Maures, especially if you are interested in doing some cycling. The resort is also close to the idyllic Îles d'Hyères which you can reach easily by boat.

The Compagnie Maritime (☎ 94.71. 01.02), which has an office at the ferry terminal in Le Lavandou, operates boats daily to Île du Levant and Port Cros (both cost 97FF return). To Porquerolles there is a boat three times a week from Le Lavandou; the return fare is 115FF.

Corniche des Maures
This 26-km-long coastal road (part of the D559) stretches from Le Lavandou north-east to La Croix-Valmer. All along here you can enjoy breathtaking views. There are also lots of great beaches for sunbathing, swimming or windsurfing. Some of the towns the road passes include Cavalière, Pramousquier and Le Rayol.

Îles d'Hyères
The oldest and largest nudist colony in the region is on Île du Levant, the easternmost of the three Îles d'Hyères. Indeed, half of this eight-km-long island is reserved for naturists. There are boats directly to the island from Le Lavandou (35 minutes) or Hyères (one hour). For details on buses to these towns, see Getting There & Away under Toulon or Saint Tropez.

Parc National de Port Cros Created in 1963 to protect at least one small part of the Côte d'Azur from overdevelopmentl Port Cros is France's smallest national park, encompassing 700 hectares of land – basically the island of Port Cros – as well as an 1800-hectare zone of water around it. The middle island of the three Îles d'Hyères, Port Cros is mainly a marine reserve but is also known for its rich variety of insects and butterflies. Keeping the water around it 'pure' (compared with the rest of the coast) is one of the reserve's main problems.

The park's head office (☎ 94.65.32.98) is on the mainland at 50 Ave Gambetta in Hyères (postcode 83400). The island can be visited all year but hikers must stick to the marked paths. Fishing, camping and fires are not allowed.

Getting There & Away Boats to the Îles d'Hyères leave from various towns along the coast, including Hyères and Le Lavandou. Boats from Toulon run only from Easter to September and are operated by several companies, one of which is Transmed (☎ 94.92. 95.88). All depart from Quai Stalingrad. The voyage to Porquerolles (40/70FF one way/ return) takes one hour. It's another 40 minutes to Port Cros, from where it's a 20-minute hop to Île du Levant.

TOULON

Toulon (population 170,000) is France's most important naval port, serving as a base for the French navy's Mediterranean fleet. As a result of heavy bombing in WW II, the city's run-down centre seems rather grim when compared to Nice or Cannes, but it is currently being revamped, street by street.

Initially a Roman colony, Toulon only became part of France in 1481. The city grew in importance after Henri IV founded an arsenal there. In the 17th century the port was enlarged by Vauban. The young Napoleon Bonaparte first made a name for himself in 1793 during a siege in which the English, who had taken over Toulon, were expelled.

In November 1942, 73 ships, cruisers, destroyers and submarines – the major part of the French fleet, which was under the command of Admiral Jean-Baptiste Laborde – were scuttled by their crews in order to prevent the Germans from seizing them. The city was liberated by French troops under Général Lattre de Tassigny in August 1944.

As in any large port, there's a lively quarter with heaps of bars where locals and sailors seem to spill out of every door. Women travelling on their own should avoid some of the old town streets at night, particularly around Rue Chevalier Paul.

As far as entertainment goes, it's not the casino but the rugby stadium, very close to the centre, that locals frequent. Toulon's rugby team is one of France's best and is strongly supported. All in all, it's a city like no other on the Côte d'Azur. To the east are the three lovely Îles d'Hyères (see the Îles d'Hyères section).

Orientation

Toulon is built around the *rade*, the marvellously sheltered bay brimming to the quays with yachts. To its west is the naval base and to the east the ferry terminal, from where boats set sail to go to Corsica. The city is at its liveliest along Quai Stalingrad, where ferries depart for the Îles d'Hyères, and in the old town. North of the old town are the train station and tourist office. Separating the old town from the northern section is a multi-lane, multinamed thoroughfare (known as Ave du Maréchal Leclerc and Blvd de Strasbourg as it runs through the town centre), which teems with traffic. It continues west to Marseille and east to the French Riviera.

Quite a few of the streets in the old town are pedestrianised, including Rue d'Alger, Rue de la Glacière, part of Rue Jean Jaurès and nearby streets.

Information

Tourist Office The main tourist office (☎ 94.22.08.22) at 8 Ave Colbert is open Monday to Saturday from 8.30 am to 6.30 pm; in July and August it's open from 8 am to 7 pm and Sunday afternoon. The branch (☎ 94.62.73.87) in the railway station is open Monday to Saturday from 8.30 am to noon and 2 to 6.30 pm; in July and August it's open daily from 7.30 am to 8 pm.

Money The Banque de France (☎ 94.09.54.00) is on Ave Vauban, just two blocks from the station. It's open weekdays from 8.30 am to noon and 1.30 to 3.30 pm. Commercial banks line Blvd de Strasbourg.

There's an exchange bureau (☎ 94.92.60.40) at 15 Quai Stalingrad open daily from 9 am to 7 pm (9 pm in July and August).

Post The main post office (☎ 94.46.47.93) on Rue Bertholet (with another entrance on Rue Ferrero) is open weekdays from 8 am to 7 pm (6 pm on Wednesday) and until noon on Saturday.

Toulon's postcode is 83000.

Laundry There are several laundrettes in the old town, including the one on Rue Baudin that is open daily from 7 am to 9 pm.

Musée de Toulon

The Toulon Museum (☎ 94.93.15.54) at 113 Ave du Maréchal Leclerc is an unexceptional art and natural history museum housed in a Renaissance-style building. It's free and open daily from 1 to 7 pm.

Musée Naval

The Naval Museum (☎ 94.02.02.01) in the old arsenal at Place Monsenergue is open Wednesday to Monday from 10 am to noon and 1.30 to 6 pm. In July and August it is open daily from 10 am to noon and 2.30 to 7 pm. Entry is 22FF for adults (11FF for students and children).

Mont Faron

Overlooking the old city from the north is the 580-metre-high Mont Faron, from which you can get a clearer idea of the size of Toulon's port. Near its summit rises the Tour Beaumont Mémorial, which commemorates the Allied landings that took place along the coast here in August 1944.

A *téléphérique* (☎ 94.92.68.25) climbs the mountain from Ave de Vence. It runs from 9 am to noon and 2.15 to 6.15 pm daily except Monday and costs 20/30FF one-way/return (15/20FF for students and children). Bus No 40 from Place de la Liberté stops at the téléphérique.

Boat Trips

Excursions around the harbour, with a commentary (in French) on the events that took place here during WW II, leave from Quai Stalingrad or its continuation, Quai de la Sinse. Trips cost an average of 35FF for one hour.

Beaches

As parts of the Mediterranean Sea are heavily polluted, it is inadvisable to swim around the main ports. East of Toulon and on the Îles d'Hyères, you will find a beautiful coastline and far better beaches (see the Saint Tropez to Toulon section).

Naturism

For information on nudist spots near Toulon, enquire at Les Amis du Soleil de Toulon (☎ 94.36.23.19) at 570 Blvd Maréchal Joffre, east of the old town, or at Azur et Soleil (☎ 94.93.06.49) at 4 Place de la Cathédrale.

Places to Stay

Camping The closest camping ground is *Le Beauregard* (☎ 94.20.56.35), on the coast seven km east in Quartier Sainte Marguerite. It costs 15FF per person and 13FF for a tent. To get there take bus No 7 or 23 from the train station to the Sainte Marguerite stop.

Hostels The youth hostel is constantly on the move from one empty school building to another. In July and August you're most likely to track it down at a college called La Rode (☎ 94.31.16.35) on Rue Philippe Rameau, south-east of town. Take bus No 7 from the train station to the Émile Olivier stop – but call ahead first to make sure it's there.

Hotels There are plenty of cheap options in the old town, though a few of these (eg those at the western end of Rue Jean Jaurès) also double as brothels.

In a quiet location in the pedestrianised part of town is the not-too-dirty *Hôtel des Trois Dauphins* (☎ 94.92.65.79) at 9 Place des Trois Dauphins. Reasonable singles/doubles start as low as 70/90FF. Parking is possible out the front but *only* from 7.30 pm to 9 am. Opposite the Trois Dauphins is the similar but more pleasant *Little Palace* (☎ 94.92.26.62) at 6 Rue Berthelot, with rooms from 80/100FF.

On Rue Jean Jaurès, the *Hôtel de Provence* (☎ 94.93.19.00) at No 53 is welcoming but often full. Basic rooms start around 100/120FF. On the same street is the slightly snazzier *Le Saint Nicolas* (☎ 94.91.02.28) at No 49, which has similar prices but is also often full. The two-star *Continental Métropole* (☎ 94.22.36.26) at 1 Rue Jean Racine has decent rooms from 120FF.

Places to Eat & Drink

Pricey seafood restaurants, terraces and bars with occasional live music are abundant along the quays. Cheaper fare can be found in the old town's more dilapidated streets around Rue Chevalier Paul. Plenty of prostitutes ply their trade in this area.

PLACES TO STAY

11 Hôtel Continental Métropole
13 Hôtel de Provence
14 Hôtel Le Saint Nicolas
15 Hôtel des Trois Dauphins
17 Hôtel Little Palace

PLACES TO EAT

5 Boulangerie
6 Le Malaga
18 Restaurant de l'Opéra
19 Monoprix Supermarket
21 Covered Market
22 Constantinois
26 Le Chaudron
30 Market
31 Le Jardin d'Any

OTHER

2 Sodetrav (Bus Office)
3 Railway Station
7 Banque de France
8 Musée de Toulon
9 Tourist Office
10 RMT (Bus) Kiosk
12 Main Post Office
20 Laundrette
24 Musée Naval
25 Exchange Bureau
29 Cathédrale Sainte Marie Majeure
33 Rade Boat Trips
34 Ferries to Îles d'Hyères

SQUARES

1 Place de l'Europe
4 Place Albert 1er
16 Place des Trois Dauphins
23 Place Monsenergue
27 Place Gustave Lambert
28 Place de la Cathédrale
32 Place Louis Blanc

Boulevard Louvois
To Mont Faron & Téléphérique
Boulevard P Toesca
Boulevard Commandant Nicolas
Rue Mirabeau
Rue Gimelli
Rue Peiresc
Rue Revel
Rue Gimelli
Boulevard de Tesse
Vauban
Avenue
Rue Dumont d'Urville
Rue de Chabanne
Rue V Clappier
Avenue Colbert
Place de la Liberté
Avenue du Maréchal Leclerc
To Marseille (60 km) & Aix-en-Provence (78 km)
Boulevard de Strasbourg
To Hyères (18 km), Le Lavandou (30 km), Saint Tropez (69 km) & Nice
Ave J Moulin
Rue Dugommier
Rue A Guiol
Rue Bertholet
Rue Jean Jaurès
Rue Ferrero
Rue Racine
Rue Berthelot
Place V Hugo
Avenue Général Magnan
Place d'Armes
Rue de Pomet
Place Louis Blanc
Rue Alézard
Rue Baudin
Vieille Ville
Rue Anatole France
Rue Pierre Sémard
Rue Chevalier Paul
Rue N Laugier
Rue Andrieux
Rue Hoche
Rue de la Glacière
Rue Michelet
Rue d'Alger
Rue Zola
Cours Lafayette
Rue Merle
Ave de Besagne
To La Rode (Hostel) (500 m) & Camping le Beauregard (7 km)
Quai Stalingrad
Avenue de la République
Quai de la Sinse
Petite Rade
Toulon
0 100 200 m
To Îles d'Hyères
To Ferry Terminal (100 m)

CÔTE D'AZUR

Restaurants One of the cosiest places in the city centre is *Le Chaudron* (☎ 94.93.54.22) at 2 Place Gustave Lambert, which serves an appetizing four-course *menu* for 69FF. You can dine either inside or out on the terrace tucked behind the fountain. In Rue Pierre Sémard you can have a hearty meal in the humble Algerian restaurant *Constantinois*. It's mainly frequented by local men but visitors are more than welcome. A generous serving of couscous with salad costs as little as 30FF and the coffee is really thick. Another eatery popular with the locals is *Restaurant de l'Opera* on Rue de Pomet. If you can forgo designer décor, you'll get one of the best value three-course *menus* in town for 46FF. At the southern end of Cours Lafayette, near Place Louis Blanc, is *Le Jardin d'Any* (☎ 94.41.01.22) at No 115, with Armenian dishes as well as a 50FF *menu*. It closes early, usually by 8 pm.

Near the train station, *Le Malaga* (☎ 94. 92.04.21) at 32 Rue Gimelli is a Spanish tapas restaurant. A 50FF *menu* is served at lunchtime only, but not on Sunday.

Self-Catering Cours Lafayette is one long open-air *food market* held, in typical Provençal style, under the plane trees. It is open daily except Monday.

There's a *Monoprix supermarket* on Rue Hoche. Near the train station, the *boulangerie* at 21 Rue Mirabeau is open daily from 5 am to 7 pm (until 1 pm on Sunday).

Getting There & Away

Train The train station (☎ 94.91.50.50 for information) is at Place Albert 1er. The information office is open Monday to Saturday from 8 am to 7 pm. There are frequent connections to cities along the coast, including Marseille (51FF; 50 minutes), Saint Raphaël (66FF; 50 minutes; hourly) and Nice (104FF; 1¾ hours; hourly).

Bus Intercity buses leave from the terminal on Place de l'Europe, to the right as you exit the station. Information and bus tickets for the several companies that service the region can be bought from Sodetrav (☎ 93.92.

26.41) at 4 Blvd Pierre Toesca (opposite the bus terminal), which is open daily from 6 am to 12.30 pm and 2 to 6 pm.

The buses to Hyères (31FF; 40 minutes; seven a day but not on Sunday) continue eastward along the coast, stopping at Le Lavandou (1¼ hours) and other towns, before arriving in Saint Tropez (2¼ hours). To go to Aix-en-Provence (75/120FF one way/return; 1¼ hours) there are four buses a day (only two on Sunday and during July and August).

Boat Ferries to Corsica and Sardinia are run by the SNCM (☎ 94.41.25.76), which has an office at 49 Ave de l'Infanterie de Marine (opposite the ferry terminal). It is open from 9 am to noon and 2 to 5.45 pm daily except Sunday afternoon. For more information, see the introductory Getting There & Away section of the Corsica chapter.

Ferries to Porto Torres (Sardinia) operate between June and August only, leaving on Sunday. For details, refer to the Sea section in the Getting There & Away chapter.

Getting Around

Local buses are run by RMT (☎ 94.27. 20.38), which has an information kiosk at the main local bus hub on Place de la Liberté. Single tickets cost 7FF. Buses generally run until sometime between 7.30 and 8.30 pm. There is only limited service on Sunday.

Nice to Menton

THE CORNICHES

Nice and Menton (and the 30-odd km of towns between them) are linked by three corniches (coastal roads), each one higher up the hill than the last. If you're in a hurry and don't care if you don't see anything of interest before you reach your destination, you can drive a bit farther inland and take the A8.

Corniche Inférieure

The Corniche Inférieure (also known as the Basse Corniche or Lower Corniche) stays pretty close to the villa-lined waterfront and the nearby train line, passing (as it goes from Nice eastward to Menton) through Villefranche-sur-Mer, Saint Jean-Cap Ferrat, Beaulieu-sur-Mer, Èze-sur-Mer, Cap d'Ail and Monaco.

Villefranche-sur-Mer Set in one of the Côte d'Azur's most charming harbours, this little port, also known simply as Villefranche, overlooks the Cap Ferrat peninsula. It has a well-preserved 14th-century old town with a 16th-century citadel and a 17th-century church. Steps break up the tiny streets that weave through the old town, the most interesting of which is the arcaded Rue Obscure. Watch out for occasional glimpses of the sea as you wander through the streets that lead down to the fishing port. Villefranche-sur-Mer was a particular favourite of Jean Cocteau, who decorated the 17th-century **Chapelle Saint Pierre** with frescoes in 1957.

Saint Jean-Cap Ferrat Once a fishing village, the seaside resort of Saint Jean-Cap Ferrat lies on the spectacular wooded peninsula of Cap Ferrat, which conceals numerous millionnaires' villas. On the narrow isthmus of Cap Ferrat is the **Musée Île de France**, a villa built in the style of the great houses of Tuscany for the Baroness Beatrice de Rothschild. It abounds with paintings, tapestries, porcelain and antique furniture and is surrounded by beautiful gardens. From September to the end of June the museum is open from 2 to 6 pm (closed Monday); from July to the end of August, it's open from 3 to 7 pm. It is closed in November.

Beaulieu-sur-Mer Protected by the high cliffs that encircle it, this popular winter and summer resort is right next to Saint Jean-Cap Ferratn The town faces onto the pretty Baie des Fourmis, which is lined with palm trees. At the eastern end of the bay is the **Villa Kerylos**, a reconstruction of an ancient Greek residence. For those after riskier forms of entertainment, there is also a casino.

Moyenne Corniche
The Moyenne (middle) Corniche clings to the hillside, affording great views if you can find somewhere to stop. It takes you from Nice past the Col de Villefranche, Èze and Beausoleil, the French town up the hill from Monte Carlo.

Èze Perched on a rocky peak at an altitude of 427 metres is the picturesque village of Èze, once occupied by Ligurians and Phoenicians. Below it is its coastal counterpart, Èze-sur-Mer. Make your way to the exotic garden for fabulous views over the coast. The German philosopher Friedrich Nietzsche spent some time here, during which he started to write part of *Thus Spake Zarathustra*; the path that links Èze-sur-Mer and Èze is named after him.

Grande Corniche
The Grande Corniche – whose panoramas are by far the most spectacular – leaves Nice as the D2564. It passes the **Col d'Èze**, where there's a great view; **La Turbie**, which is on a promontory directly above Monaco and offers a stunning night-time vista of the principality; **Le Vistaëro**, offering a view of the whole coastline; and **Roquebrune**.

Roquebrune Commanding this appealing hilltop village, which lies just between Monaco and Menton, is a medieval donjon complete with a re-created manor house. Its tortuous little streets, which lead up to the castle, are lined with shops selling handicrafts and souvenirs and are overrun with tourists in the high season. Carved out of the rock is the impressive Rue Moncollet, featuring arcaded passages and stairways.

Roquebrune is also famous for its religious festivals, in particular the procession of the Dead Christ, held on Good Friday, and the procession of the Passion, held annually on 5 August. For more information, contact the tourist office (☎ 93.35.62.87) in nearby **Cap Martin**, an extension of Menton.

The exclusive suburb of Cap Martin is renowned for its sumptuous villas and famous past residents, including Winston Churchill and the architect Le Corbusier.

MENTON

Menton (population 25,000), reputed to be the warmest spot on the Côte d'Azur (especially during the winter), is only a few km from the Italian frontier. In part because of the weather, Menton is popular with older holiday-makers, whose way of life and preferences have made the town a particularly tranquil – some would say boring – and well-heeled corner of the Riviera. The town's main drawcard is that it's quiet – the opposite extreme of Nice.

Menton is renowned for its production of lemons and holds a two-week Fête des Citrons (Lemon Festival) that begins every year on Mardi Gras.

Orientation

Promenade du Soleil runs south-west to north-east along the beach; the train line runs approximately parallel about 500 metres inland. Ave Édouard VII links the train station with the beach. Ave Boyer, where the tourist office is located, is 350 metres east of the train station (turn left out of the station and walk along Ave de la Gare to Ave Boyer). The Vieille Ville is on and around the hill at the eastern end of Promenade du Soleil; the Vieux Port is a bit farther east.

Information

Tourist Office The tourist office (☎ 93.57. 57.00) is in the Palais de l'Europe at 8 Ave Boyer. It is open Monday to Saturday from 8.30 am to 12.30 pm and 2 to 6.30 pm. From mid-June to mid-September it's open Monday to Saturday from 8.30 am to 7.30 pm, and Sunday from 9.30 am to 12.30 pm.

Money There are plenty of banks along Rue Partouneaux: Barclays Bank (☎ 93.28. 60.00) at 39 Ave Félix Faure is open weekdays from 8.30 am to noon and 2 to 4.30 pm.

Post The main post office (☎ 93.35.45.00) on Cours George V is open weekdays from 8 am to 6 pm and until noon on Saturday.

Menton's postcode is 06500.

Laundry The little laundrette in Rue Palmero, a small lane between Rue de la Marne and Rue Trenca, is open weekdays from 9 am to noon and 2.30 to 6.30 pm (on Wednesday in the morning only) and Saturday from 9 to 11 am.

Église Saint Michel

The early 17th-century church of St Michael, the grandest baroque church in this part of France, sits perched in the centre of the Vieille Ville, which has many narrow, winding passageways. The church is open from 10 am to noon and 3 to 6 pm daily except on Saturday mornings. The ornate interior is Italian in inspiration.

Cimetière du Vieux Château

Farther up the hill is the cypress-shaded Cimetière du Vieux Château, open from 7 am to 6 pm (8 pm from May to September). Graves of English, Irish, Americans, New Zealanders and other foreigners who died here during the 19th century can be seen in the cemetery's south-west corner (in the section along the road called Montée du Souvenir). The view alone is worth the climb.

Musée Jean Cocteau

The Jean Cocteau Museum (☎ 93.57.72.30) on Quai de Monléon displays work by the poet, dramatist and film director in a 12th-century seafront bastion near the old city. It contains a good deal of the artist's work, including drawings, tapestries, ceramics and mosaics. It's open daily, except Tuesday, from 10 am to noon and 2 to 6 pm; from mid-June to mid-September afternoon hours are 3 to 7 pm. Admission is free. Don't miss Cocteau's frescoes in the Salle des Mariages in the Hôtel de Ville.

Beach

The beach along Promenade du Soleil is public but, like its counterpart at Nice, is covered with smooth little rocks. There are more beaches directly east of the old city (ie just north of the Vieux Port) and east of Port de Garavan, the main pleasure-boat harbour.

Places to Stay

Camping Two-star *Camping Saint Michel* (☎ 93.35.81.23), open from April to October, is north-east of the train station on Route des Ciappes de Castellar. It costs 12FF per person, 12FF to pitch a tent and 12FF to park. The two-star *Camping Fleur de Mai* (☎ 93.57.22.36) at 67 Vallée de Gorbio, two km west of the train station, is open from late March or early April to September. The charge for two people with a car and small tent is 68FF.

Hostel The *Auberge de Jeunesse* (☎ 93. 35.93.14), one km up Plateau Saint Michel (the hill north-east of the train station), is reached by Route des Ciappes de Castellar. Beds cost 60FF with breakfast. During the day it is closed from 10 am to 5 pm; curfew is at midnight. The hostel is closed from mid-December to around mid-January. From about 7 am to 7 pm, you can get to the hostel from the train station by minibus – this privately run service operates like a shared taxi.

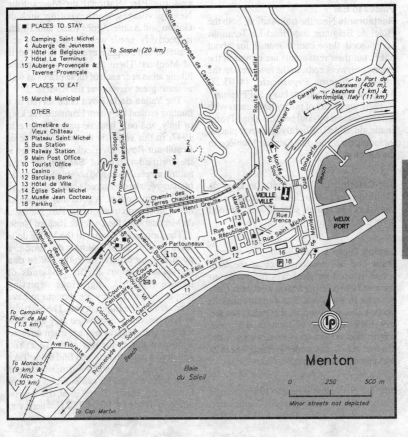

PLACES TO STAY
2 Camping Saint Michel
4 Auberge de Jeunesse
6 Hôtel de Belgique
7 Hôtel Le Terminus
15 Auberge Provençale &
Taverne Provençale

PLACES TO EAT
16 Marché Municipal

OTHER
1 Cimetière du
Vieux Château
3 Plateau Saint Michel
5 Bus Station
8 Railway Station
9 Main Post Office
10 Tourist Office
11 Casino
12 Barclays Bank
13 Hôtel de Ville
14 Église Saint Michel
17 Musée Jean Cocteau
18 Parking

Menton

0   250   500 m

Minor streets not depicted

CÔTE D'AZUR

Hotels The *Hôtel Le Terminus* (☎ 93.35.77.00) at Place de la Gare has a few basic singles and doubles starting at 120 or 130FF. Hall showers are free. Reception is closed after 11 am on Saturday and after 5 pm on Sunday. The entire hotel is closed from mid-October to mid-November. Half a block down the road, the *Hôtel de Belgique* (☎ 93.35.72.66) at 1 Ave de la Gare has singles/doubles from 167/241FF, including the obligatory breakfast. This place is closed in November. Bordering the old city, the *Auberge Provençale* (☎ 93.35.77.29) at 11 Rue Trenca has decent rooms from 150FF.

Places to Eat

Restaurants Near the train station, both the Hôtel de Belgique and Hôtel Le Terminus serve good three-course *menus* for about 65FF, but their restaurants are closed in the evening on weekends. In the town centre, the low-key *Taverne Provençale* (☎ 93.28.45.98) at 1 Rue Palmero has a 55FF *menu*.

There are plenty of pricey restaurants with terraces fanned by cool breezes along Promenade du Soleil. Slightly cheaper places, including pizzerias, line Quai de Monléon in the old city.

Self-Catering In the old city on Quai de Monléon, the *Marché Municipal*, also known as Les Halles, sells all sorts of food daily from 5 am to 1 pm.

Getting There & Away

Train The information office at the train station is open on weekdays from 8 am to noon and 2 to 6.30 pm and on weekends from 8.30 am to noon and 2 to 6 pm. Trains to Ventimiglia, right across the Italian border, cost 10FF and take 10 minutes. For more information on rail services along the Côte d'Azur, see Trains under Getting There & Away in the Nice section.

Bus The bus station is next to 12 Promenade Maréchal Leclerc, the northern continuation of Ave Boyer. The information office

(☎ 93.35.93.60) is open from 8 am to noon and 2 to 6 pm daily except Saturday afternoon and Sunday. There are buses to Nice (24FF return; 1¼ hours), Monaco (12FF return; 30 minutes), Sospel (46FF return; 45 minutes), Sainte Agnès (42FF return; 45 minutes) and Ventimiglia (14FF; 30 minutes).

AROUND MENTON

There are lots of interesting places to visit near Menton, the most notable of which are the Vallée de la Roya (Roya Valley), the Vallée des Merveilles (Valley of Wonders) and the Parc National du Mercantour. Nearby villages worth visiting include Gorbio and Sainte Agnès (nine and 10 km respectively north-west of Menton), and Castellar and Sospel (seven and 19 km north of Menton). There are good walking and hiking areas near each of these places as well as some great views over the Riviera.

The **Vallée de la Roya** once served as a hunting ground for Victor Emmanuel II, king of Italy, and only became part of France in 1947. In this valley is the pretty village of **Breuil-sur-Roya**. Overlooking the valley is the fortified village of **Saorge**, set in a natural amphitheatre and notable for its maze of narrow, stepped streets and its 15th to 17th-century houses. A good map for walks in the area, particularly in the Parc National du Mercantour, is the Didier & Richard No 9.

The Gorges de Bergue in the Vallée de la Roya lead to **Saint Dalmas de Tende**, a good base for excursions to the **Vallée des Merveilles**, famous for its thousands of Bronze Age rock engravings depicting people and bulls. They are thought to have been created by a Ligurian cult. The best time to visit the valley is between July and September, as the engravings are often covered with snow during the rest of the year. You will need a guide to help you find them. Take sturdy walking shoes and warm, waterproof gear. Jeeps and guides can be hired at Saint Dalmas de Tende. There is also a tourist office in Tende (☎ 93.04.73.71) where you can get more information.

Monaco

The Principality of Monaco, which has been under the rule of the Grimaldi family for most of the period since 1297, is a sovereign state whose territory, surrounded by France, covers only 1.95 sq km. It has been ruled since 1949 by Prince Rainier III (born in 1923), whose sweeping constitutional powers make him far from a mere figurehead. For decades, the family has been featured on the front pages of the sensational press, though since the death in 1982 of the much-adored Princess Grace (remembered from her Hollywood days as Grace Kelly), the media has concentrated on the couple's daughters, Caroline and Stephanie.

The citizens of Monaco (known as Monégasques), of whom there are only about 5000 (out of a total population of 30,000), pay no taxes. The official language is French, though efforts are being made to revive the principality's traditional dialect. The official religion is Catholicism. There are no border formalities upon entering Monaco. The principality was admitted to the UN as a full member in 1993.

Despite the things people always complain about – the border-to-border high-rise buildings, the huge number of tourists, the principality's unabashed preference for wealthy visitors – there's still something magical and exhilarating about walking around Monaco and watching it twinkle at night. Given its undeniable charms and the quality of several of its museums, a visit to Monaco makes a perfect day trip from Nice.

Orientation

Monaco consists of four principal areas: Monaco Ville (also known as the old city and the Rocher de Monaco), a 60-metre-high outcrop of rock 800 metres long on the south side of the Port de Monaco; Monte Carlo, famous for its casino and annual Grand Prix motor race which is north of the port; La Condamine, the flat area south-west of the port; and Fontvieille, the industrial area south of Monaco Ville. The French town of Beausoleil is just up the hill from Monte Carlo.

Information

Tourist Office The Office National de Tourisme (☎ 93.50.60.88) is at 2a Blvd des Moulins, across the public gardens from the Casino. It is open Monday to Saturday from 9 am to 7 pm and on Sunday from 10 am to noon. From mid-June to mid-September there are several tourist office kiosks around the principality, including one at the train station, another next to the Jardin Exotique and yet another on Quai des États-Unis (the street that runs along the north side of the port).

Money The currency of Monaco is the French franc. Both French and Monégasque coins are in circulation but the latter are not widely accepted outside the principality.

In Monte Carlo there are lots of banks in the vicinity of the Casino (along Ave Princesse Alice, for instance). In La Condamine, try Blvd Albert 1er. You can also change money at the train station information office.

American Express (☎ 93.25.74.45) is near the tourist office at 35 Blvd Princesse Charlotte. It is open weekdays from 9 am to noon and 2 to 6 pm and Saturday until noon.

Post & Telecommunications Monégasque stamps, one of the principality's few symbols of independence, are valid only within Monaco. Postal rates are the same as those in France. Monaco's public telephones accept either Monégasque or French télécartes.

The main post office (☎ 93.25.11.11) is in Monte Carlo at 1 Ave Henri Dunant (inside Palais de la Scala). It is open weekdays from 8 am to 7 pm and Saturday until noon, but does not exchange foreign currency. There are other post offices in Monaco Ville at Place de la Visitation (near the Musée Océanographique) and near the train station (look for the sign to the Hôtel Terminus).

Monaco's French-style postcode is 98000.

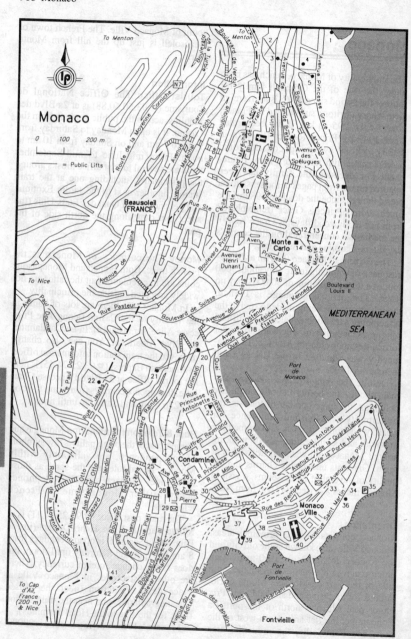

Monaco

0   100   200 m

— = Public Lifts

■ PLACES TO STAY	OTHER	34 Public Lift to Parking
		des Pêcheurs
6 Hôtel Cosmopolite	1 Plage du Larvotto	35 Parking des Pêcheurs
(Beausoleil)	3 Public Lift	36 Musée
9 Hôtel Mirabeau	4 Musée National (Dolls &	Océanographique
14 Hôtel de Paris	Automatons Museum)	37 Palais du Prince
16 Hermitage	5 Public Lift	39 Musée des Souvenirs
25 Youth Hostel	7 Public Lift	Napoléoniens
26 Hôtel Cosmopolite	8 American Express	40 Cathedral
(La Condamine)	11 National Tourist Office	41 Jardin Exotique &
& Hôtel de	13 Casino of Monte Carlo	Musée
France	17 Main Post Office	d'Anthropologie
	18 CAM (Local Bus	Préhistorique
▼ PLACES TO EAT	Company) Office	42 Public Lift
	19 Public Lift	
10 Codec Top	21 Public Lift	✗ SQUARES
Supermarket	22 Laundrette	
23 Monaco Market	24 Fort Antoine	2 Place des Moulins
Supermarket	28 Railway Station	12 Place du Casino
27 Hôtel Helvetia	29 Post Office	15 Square Beaumarchais
Restaurant	31 Rampe Major (Path to	20 Place Sainte Dévote
30 Place d'Armes &	Palais du Prince)	33 Place de la Visitation
Food Market	32 Post Office	38 Place du Palais

Laundry On the Monaco-France border, the laundrette at 1 Rue Jean Jaurès is open daily from 7 am to 9 pm.

Musée Océanographique

If you're planning to see just one aquarium on your whole trip, the world-renowned Musée Océanographique de Monaco (☎ 93.15.36.00) should be it. The fish in the sea-water aquariums (about 90 of them) can only be described in superlatives: the bluest, the spiniest, the frilliest, the pink-and-yellowest, the one you'd least like to meet in a back alley in Chicago at 2 am...Upstairs are all sorts of exhibits on ocean exploration. The museum, on Ave Saint Martin in Monaco Ville, is open daily from 9 or 9.30 am to 7 pm (9 pm in July and August). The entrance fee (brace yourself) is 50FF (30FF for students).

Palais du Prince

The changing of the guard takes place outside the Palace of the Prince (☎ 93.25.18.31), in Monaco Ville at the southern end of Rue des Remparts, daily at precisely 11.55 am. The guards, who carry out their duties of state in spiffy dress uniforms (white in summer, black in winter), are apparently resigned to the comic-opera nature of their circumstance.

From June to October only, about 15 rooms in the palace are open to the public daily from 9.30 am to 6.10 pm (10 am to 5 pm in October). The entry fee is 25FF (15FF for children and students). Thirty-minute guided visits in English leave every 15 or 20 minutes.

Musée des Souvenirs Napoléoniens Situated in the south wing of the palace, this museum displays some of Napoléon's personal effects (handkerchiefs, a sock, etc) and a fascinating collection of the sort of bric-a-brac (medals, coins, swords, uniforms) that princely dynasties collect over the centuries. The museum, which costs 15FF (7FF for children and students), is open daily except Monday. Tickets are on sale from 10.30 am to 12.30 pm and 2 to 4.30 pm. From June to September they're on sale from 9.30 am to 6.30 pm. The museum is closed in November.

Walk around the Rock

The touristy streets and alleys facing the palace are surrounded by beautiful, shady gardens affording great views of the entire principality – and a good bit of France and some of Italy as well.

Jardin Exotique

The steep slopes of the wonderful Jardin Exotique (☎ 93.30.33.65) are home to some 7000 varieties of cacti and succulents from all over the world. The spectacular view alone is worth at least half the entrance fee of 32FF (16FF for students), which also gets you into the on-site **Musée d'Anthropologie Préhistorique** and includes a half-hour guided visit to the **Grottes de l'Observatoire**, a network of stalactite and stalagmite caves located 279 steps down the hillside.

The Jardin is open daily from 9 am until 5 pm (in December), 5.30 pm (in November and January), 6 pm (in October, February and March), 6.30 pm (in September and April) and 7 pm (from May to August). To get there, take bus No 2 to the Jardin Exotique terminus.

Grottes de l'Observatoire

Casino

The drama of watching people risk their money in Monte Carlo's spectacularly ornate Casino (☎ 93.50.69.31), built between 1878 and 1910, makes visiting the gaming rooms almost worth the stiff entry fees: 50FF for the Salon Ordinaire, which has French roulette and trente et quarante, and 100FF for the Salons Privés, which offer baccarat, blackjack, craps, American roulette, etc. You must be 21 to enter. Short shorts (but not short skirts) are forbidden in the Salon Ordinaire. For the Salons Privés, men must wear a tie and jacket after 9 pm. Income from gambling now accounts for 4.3% of Monaco's total state revenues (it used to account for most of the government's budget). The area in front of the Casino is beautifully landscaped.

Musée National

Housed in a villa built by Charles Garnier, the Musée National (☎ 93.30.91.26), also known as the Museum of Dolls & Automatons, contains a fascinating collection of 18th and 19th-century dolls and mechanical toys. The museum is in Monte Carlo at 17 Ave Princesse Grace and is open from 10 am to 12.15 and 2.30 to 6.30 pm (closed on public holidays).

Places to Stay

Cheap accommodation is almost nonexistent. Mid-range rooms are also scarce and often full. Indeed, over three-quarters of Monaco's hotel rooms are classified as 'four-star deluxe'. Fortunately, Nice is not far away.

Places to Stay – bottom end & middle

Hostel The *Centre de la Jeunesse Princesse Stéphanie* (☎ 93.50.83.20; fax 93.25.29.82), Monaco's youth hostel, is at 24 Ave Prince Pierre, 120 metres up the hill from the train station. You must be between 16 and 30 to stay here and, officially, anyone over 26 must also be a student. The cost is 60FF per person, including breakfast and sheets. Stays are usually limited to one night during the summer. Beds are given out each morning on a first-come first-served basis; numbered tickets are distributed from 9 am or even earlier. Registration begins at 10.30 am.

Hotels In La Condamine, the clean and pleasant *Hôtel Cosmopolite* (☎ 93.30.16.95) at 4 Rue de la Turbie has decent doubles/triples/quads from 154/230/305FF. Showers cost 12FF. The *Hôtel de France* (☎ 93.30.24.64) at 6 Rue de la Turbie has singles/doubles/triples with shower, toilet and TV for 255/310/370FF. Breakfast is 30FF.

In Beausoleil, the unrelated *Hôtel Cosmopolite* (☎ 93.78.36.00) at 19 Blvd Maréchal Leclerc – up the hill from the Casino – has singles/doubles with shower and TV for 215/230FF (240/270FF with toilet, too). The even-numbered side of Blvd Maréchal Leclerc is in Monaco and is called Blvd de France. The nearest bus stop is named Crémaillère and is served by bus Nos 2 and 4.

Places to Stay – top end
For the ultimate in luxury, head for the world-famous *Hôtel de Paris* (☎ 92.16.30.00; fax 93.15.90.03) at Place du Casino. Superbly furnished rooms cost from 2600/2900FF for singles/doubles. Another of Monaco's most famous hotels is the four-star *Hermitage* (☎ 92.16.40.00; fax 93.50.47.12) at Square Beaumarchais, near the main post office. Prices reflect the *belle époque* ambience of the hotel: 1700/2700 for singles/doubles. This hotel also has an excellent restaurant.

Slightly less expensive is the *Mirabeau* (☎ 92.16.65.65; fax 93.50.84.85), 1-3 Ave Princesse Grace, which has very comfortable singles/doubles around 1400/2000FF.

Places to Eat
Restaurants There are a few cheap restaurants in La Condamine along Rue de la Turbie. The *Hôtel Helvetia* (☎ 93.30.21.71), nearby at 1bis Rue Grimaldi, has a decent three-course *menu* for 55FF.

On a totally different level is *Le Louis XV* (☎ 92.16.30.01) in the Hôtel de Paris, offering high-quality dishes (with prices to match) prepared by Alain Ducasse, one of France's top chefs. *Menus* start at 650FF; an à la carte meal will cost around 850FF.

The restaurant at the Hôtel Mirabeau, *La Coupole* (☎ 92.16.66.99), is another excel-

lent choice. *Menus* cost around 350FF and à la carte meals range from 400 to 550FF. In summer you can enjoy your meals on the terrace.

Self-Catering In Monte Carlo, the *Codec Top supermarket* opposite 33 Blvd Princesse Charlotte (a block from the main tourist office) is open Monday to Saturday from 8.30 am to 12.15 pm and 3 to 7.15 pm. It has an in-house bakery.

In La Condamine, there's a daily *morning food market* at Place d'Armes and a *Monaco Market supermarket* on Blvd Albert 1er (on the corner of Rue Princesse Antoinette). It's open weekdays from 8.45 am to 12.30 pm and 2.45 to 7.30 pm (nonstop on Friday) and on Saturday from 9 am to 7 pm.

Getting There & Away
Train Rail service to Monaco's train station, which is on Ave Prince Pierre, is run by the SNCF. The information office is open daily from 8 am to noon and 2 to 6 pm. For telephone enquiries, call the SNCF in Nice on ☎ 93.87.50.50.

There are frequent trains eastward to Menton (7FF; 10 minutes) and the first town in Italy, Ventimiglia (16FF; 25 minutes). For trains to Nice and connections to other towns, see Getting There & Away in the Nice section.

Bus There is no single bus station in Monaco – intercity buses leave from various points around the city.

Getting Around
Bus Monaco's urban bus system has six lines. You're most likely to use line No 2, which links Monaco Ville with Monte Carlo and then loops back to the Jardin Exotique; and line No 4, which links the train station with the tourist office. Rides cost 8FF, which is pretty steep given how small the country is. Four/eight-ride magnetic cards are on sale from bus drivers for 17/27FF. The bus system operates daily until 8.45 or 9 pm. Bus maps are available at the tourist office.

The local bus company, Compagnie des

Autobus de Monaco (CAM; ☎ 93.50.62.41), has offices at 3 Ave Président John F Kennedy, which is on the north side of the port.

Lifts Six large public lifts *(ascenseurs publics)* run up and down the hillside. They operate from 6 am to 10 pm.

Taxis Taxis can be ordered by calling ☎ 93.15.01.01 or 93.50.56.28.

Languedoc-Roussillon

The region of Languedoc-Roussillon, created in the 1960s by uniting the historic provinces of Languedoc and Roussillon, comprises the *départements* of Lozère, Gard, Hérault, Aude and Pyrénées-Orientales. The capital of Languedoc-Roussillon is Montpellier. The region stretches in an arc along the coast from Provence to the Pyrenees, and in the north it borders the Massif Central.

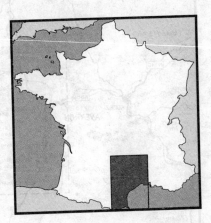

Languedoc

Languedoc is named after the old Provençal language, *langue d'oc*, which was distinct from the forerunner of modern French spoken north of the Loire, the *langue d'oïl* (the words *oc* and *oïl* being their respective words for 'yes'). When France's new regional boundaries were mapped out, Languedoc's historic centre, Toulouse, was excluded from Languedoc-Roussillon.

Along the Mediterranean coast, a number of modern resorts have been built with the aim of attracting visitors from the over-crowded Côte d'Azur. The most famous of these is the futuristic La Grand Motte, near Montpellier. The coast, popular with nudists, has a number of large naturist resorts, such as the one at Cap d'Agde. On the whole, however, tourism has been slow to develop along the monotonous coastline in spite of the good beaches and mild climate.

Rising above the Languedoc plain is Upper Languedoc (Haut-Languedoc), a highland area as varied as it is hard to define. It includes Lozère, France's most thinly populated region, which takes in part of the Cévennes, an impenetrable mountain area long inhabited only by the hardy, seekers of solitude, and exiles in need of a home. The Parc National des Cévennes now covers much of this territory, some of which was crossed by the writer Robert Louis Stevenson and his donkey Modestine in 1878. To the west are the Grands Causses – bare, desolate plateaux fascinating in their solitude, which rise above deep gorges such as the Gorges du Tarn and Gorges de la Jonte.

Upper Languedoc is quite distinct from the sun-soaked lowlands to the south or the Auvergne region of the Massif Central to the north. It has a palpable sense of isolation that is especially appealing to visitors in search of the great outdoors. Vultures circle the skies, there are wolf and bison reserves, and exceptional trails lead you through unpopulated lands and forests filled with blueberries and chestnuts. The main towns of Mende, Florac and Millau are small places separated by wild terrain.

Public transport is almost nonexistent, so if you don't have private transport, getting around will take a very patient thumb.

History

Languedoc was inhabited as early as 450,000 BC. Phoenicians, Greeks, Romans, Visigoths and Moors passed through the region before it came under Frankish rule. The Franks were happy to leave the affairs of the region to local rulers, and around the

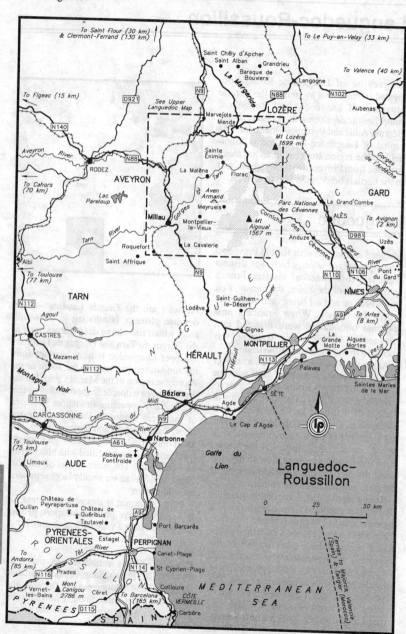

To Saint Flour (30 km) & Clermont-Ferrand (130 km)

To Le Puy-en-Velay (33 km)

Saint Chély d'Apcher
Saint Alban
Grandrieu

La Margeride

Langogne

To Valence (40 km)

D921

N9

N88

N102

See Upper Languedoc Map

Marvejols
Mende

LOZÈRE

Aubenas

To Figeac (15 km)

N140

Aveyron River

N88

RODEZ

AVEYRON

To Cahors (70 km)

Lac Pareloup

Millau

Mt Lozère 1699 m

Sainte Enimie

La Malène

Tarn

Florac

Aven Armand

Meyrueis

Montpellier-le-Vieux

Mt Aigoual 1567 m

Parc National des Cévennes

Gorges de l'Ardèche

GARD

La Grand'Combe

ALÈS

To Avignon (2 km)

D981

Uzès

Pont du Gard

River

N106

N110

Gorges du Tarn

Corniche des Cévennes

Anduze

Cévennes

Gard

Roquefort

La Cavalerie

Saint Affrique

To Toulouse (77 km)

TARN

Agout River

N112

CASTRES

Mazamet

N112

N9

Lodève

Saint Guilhem-le-Désert

HÉRAULT

Hérault River

Gignac

N113

NÎMES

To Arles (8 km)

A9

La Grande Motte

MONTPELLIER

Aigues-Mortes

Palavas

Petit Rhône

Saintes Maries de la Mer

Montagne Noire

D118

CARCASSONNE

Canal du Midi

Aude River

N9

BÉZIERS

Agde

SÈTE

Le Cap d'Agde

To Toulouse (75 km)

A61

Narbonne

Golfe du Lion

LP

Limoux

AUDE

Abbaye de Fontfroide

Quillan

Château de Peyrepertuse

Château de Quéribus

Tautavel

A9

PYRENEES-ORIENTALES

Estagel

Tét River

PERPIGNAN

To Andorra (85 km)

N116

Prades

ROUSSILLON

Canet-Plage

St Cyprien-Plage

N114

Languedoc-Roussillon

0   25   50 km

Vernet-les-Bains

Mont Canigou 2786 m

Céret

Collioure

CÔTE VERMEILLE

To Barcelona (165 km)

D115

PYRENEES

SPAIN

Port Barcarès

MEDITERRANEAN SEA

Cerbère

Ferries to Majorca, Valencia (Spain) & Tanger (Morocco)

12th century the Occitan civilisation (which existed where the langue d'oc was spoken) reached its height; a rich literary tradition was created by the troubadours. Eventually, however, the Albigensian Crusade, launched to suppress the 'heresy' of Catharism, resulted in Languedoc's annexation by the French kingdom, and langue d'oc was suppressed in favour of the langue d'oïl.

Geography

Languedoc has two distinct areas: the hot plains of Lower Languedoc (Bas-Languedoc), and the wild, mountainous lands of Upper Languedoc (Haut-Languedoc) to the north. From the plains rise the region's towns and cities, including Montpellier, a thriving university centre. Bordering Provence are the old Roman town of Nîmes and the nearby Pont du Gard aqueduct (see the Provence chapter). Following the coast south-westward, you come to the port of Sète and, just inland, the cities of Béziers and Narbonne. Further inland, the walled city of Carcassonne hovers over the plain's heat wave like a medieval mirage.

The coastline is broken by a string of lagoons that are separated from the sea by sandy beaches. Here the national and regional governments' attempts to encourage tourism are most in evidence: the lagoons have been cleaned up and cleared of mosquitoes, and modern resorts have been erected.

Away from the coast, the scene is dominated by ruined castles crowning rocky outcrops, and by the countless vineyards which make Languedoc the prime wine-producing area of France, in volume if not always in quality. The département of Hérault around Montpellier has more vineyards than any other in France. Rare is the village without its *cave* (wine cellar) and central square shaded by plane trees, where the men gather to catch up on the latest gossip.

To the north is the high country that's neither part of the plain nor of the Massif Central further north. More or less comprising the sparsely populated département of Lozère and part of the département of Gard, it's wild and isolated, home to the Parc National des Cévennes and the weird and wonderful Grands Causses, limestone plateaux cut by deep canyons such as the Gorges du Tarn. The small towns of Mende, Florac, Alès and Millau dot the area.

Activities

The most popular outdoor pursuit in Upper Languedoc is hiking. There are spectacular walks through the Parc National des Cévennes, on the Grands Causses and in the Margeride range north of Mende. Cross-country cycling also attracts visitors, as does the lure of rock climbing and canyon descents in the gorges. Hang-gliders and parapenters fill the skies above Millau.

Food

As in Provence, food here is cooked and served with liberal amounts of olive oil. Many of Languedoc's olive groves died following a heavy frost in the mid-1950s, but trees were replanted and new oil mills for pressing set up, reviving the industry. In the north, the country's most famous blue cheese, Roquefort, is nurtured, as is another regional favourite, Bleu des Causses.

Wine

Wine has long been the mainstay of Languedoc's economy. Up to 40% of France's wine, mainly cheap red table wine, is produced here. But the last two to three decades have seen tough times. Competition from Italy and Spain, where table wine is produced more cheaply, has caused a market glut. More recently, French attitudes towards wine have been changing, and many people now drink less wine but tend to seek out vintages of better quality.

Following violent protests over Italian imports in the mid-1970s, farmers were subsidised to cut down their vines and encouraged to replant with better quality AOC grapes. Some did and now produce many of the fine Côteaux du Languedoc, Corbières and Minervois wines. Others restarted with orchids while some simply abandoned the fields, leaving the gnarled stumps of the vines protruding from steep, rocky hillsides. There's still plenty of table wine though, and the large wine co-operatives still operate on the edge of villages and towns where you can fill up big plastic tubs for as little as 3.50FF a litre.

Getting There & Away

Ferries sail from the port of Sète to Tangier (Morocco) and, during summer, to the Balearic Islands, with onward service to the Spanish city of Valencia. For details, see Getting There & Away under Montpellier and the Sea section of the Getting There & Away chapter.

Getting Around

City to city travel is no problem thanks to the train network, and most towns and villages on the plain generally have bus services, though perhaps only one or two a day. Getting to remote hilltop castles will pose a challenge for those without their own transport, as will travelling around most of the northern Languedoc area (the Lozère, Grands Causses and Cévennes). With only a small population, this particular region has little need and few resources to establish public transport; trains are sparse and buses almost nonexistent.

MONTPELLIER

The vibrant city of Montpellier (population 220,000), just 12 km from the sea, lures visitors with its reputation for innovation and vitality. But not so long ago, Languedoc's largest city simply slumbered under the Midi sun. Things began changing in the 1960s when many of the *pieds-noirs* repatriated from Algeria settled here. Later a dynamic left-wing local government came to power, promoting the pedestrianisation of the old town, designing an unusual central housing project and enticing high-technology industries. The result is one of France's fastest growing cities.

Nearly a quarter of the city's population are students, and the university is famous for its science, law and literature faculties. But its most prestigious field is medicine; Europe's first medical school was founded here early in the 12th century, attaining university status in 1289. Over the centuries Montpellier became a melting pot of trade and intellect, and its decaying splendour is still evident as you wander through the maze of quiet alleys in the old town. Beside the stone arches and fine *hôtels particuliers* (private mansions), you'll find decaying façades and graffiti-smeared walls.

Orientation

Surrounded by boulevards, the centre of the city is around the huge Place de la Comédie, which is lined with distinguished buildings including the Opéra. Down a flight of stairs at the north-eastern end of this square is the main tourist office. Off to its east is the Polygone, a modern shopping complex,

The Canal du Midi

This beautiful canal, which affords great views over the shimmering Languedoc plain, runs from Agde on the Mediterranean coast to Toulouse, where it connects with another canal leading to the Atlantic Ocean at Bordeaux. Built in the 17th century by 15,000 labourers, this 240-km-long waterway was designed to enable cargo vessels to travel from the Atlantic to the Mediterranean without having to sail all the way around Spain.

The Canal du Midi passes many villages and cities as it follows the curve of the Montagne Noire foothills via aqueducts and 103 locks, sometimes as many as nine in a row (as is the case near Béziers). Along its entire length it is flanked by plane trees that provide shade and control evaporation. Although its significance for trade has greatly diminished, barges still ply the waters of the canal and its connecting waterways. In summer they are joined by canal boats hired by tourists, and queues often develop at the locks. ∎

behind which lies Antigone, a housing project with grand colonnaded façades designed for middle-income rent payers.

North of Place de la Comédie is Esplanade Charles de Gaulle, a tree-lined promenade favoured in daylight by poodle-paraders, after dusk by some unsavoury types. To the west is the city's oldest quarter, a web of pedestrianised lanes which weave between Rue Foch, Rue de la Loge and Grand Rue Jean Moulin. North-west of here is the university's medical faculty next to the twin-turreted Cathédrale Saint Pierre. Outside the main boulevards to the south are the train and bus stations.

Information

Tourist Office The city has four tourist offices, all with efficient staff who will book accommodation and, except at the train station, exchange currency. The main office (☎ 67.58.67.58) is under Place de la Comédie on the Passage du Tourisme. From 1 June to 30 September it's open Monday to Saturday from 9 am to 7 pm; the rest of the year hours are 9 am to noon and 1 to 6 pm. The train station bureau (☎ 67.92.90.03) is open Monday to Saturday from 10 am to 1 pm and 3.30 to 6.45 pm.

The other tourist offices are most useful if you're arriving by car – one is to the east on the road to the airport at Pont Chauliac, the other at the Rond Point des Près d'Arènes at the southern entrance to the A9 autoroute.

Regional Information The Comité Départemental de Tourisme (☎ 67.84.71.70) at 1977 Ave des Moulins has heaps of regional information but it's out of the centre to the west; bus No 9 stops nearby.

Money The Banque de France (☎ 67.20. 83.20) at 6 Blvd Ledru-Rollin is open weekdays from 8.30 am to noon and 1.30 to 3 pm. Next door, the Caisse d'Épargne (☎ 67.92. 68.40) is open Tuesday to Friday from 8.15 am to 12.15 pm and 1.45 to 5.30 pm, and Saturday morning.

Close to the station, there's a BNP (☎ 67.92.65.32) at 8 Rue Maguelone. Other banks can be found on Place de la Comédie. The Midi Point Change bureau (☎ 67.58. 00.55) in the train station, open daily from 8 am to 8 or 9 pm, has low rates. It handles Visa cash advances.

Post The main post office (☎ 67.34.50.00) at 5 Rue Rondelet is open weekdays from 8 am to 7 pm and Saturday until noon. The city-centre branch (☎ 67.60.70.11), in the prefecture on Place des Martyrs de la Résistance, is open the same hours.

Montpellier's postcode is 34000.

Travel Agencies Frantour Tourisme (☎ 67. 92.85.85) at the train station organises BIJ tickets. Council Travel (☎ 67.60.89.29) is at 20 Rue de l'Université.

Bookshops Rue de l'Université is lined with specialist bookshops, including the Bookshop (☎ 67.68.09.08) at No 4 which has English-language novels and travel guides. It's open Tuesday to Saturday from 9.30 am to 1 pm and 2.30 to 7 pm.

At the Polygone's entrance, Sauramps (☎ 67.58.85.15) has a good upstairs guide-book/map section. It's open Monday to Saturday from 10 am to 7 pm.

Emergency The police headquarters (☎ 67. 22.78.22) is at 22 Ave Georges Clemenceau near the main post office. In the city centre, there's an annexe (☎ 67.58.01.77) on Place de la Comédie.

Laundry Near the youth hostel, the laundrette on Rue des Écoles Laïques is open daily from 7.30 am to 9 pm. Close to the station, there's another on Rue Sérane with the same hours.

Hôtels Particuliers

During the 17th and 18th centuries, Montpellier's wealthier merchants built fine, tastefully designed *hôtels* (mansions) with large inner courtyards. Two of the most interesting are the **Hôtel de Varennes** on Place Pétrarque, a harmonious blend of Romanesque and Gothic styles, and the **Hôtel Saint**

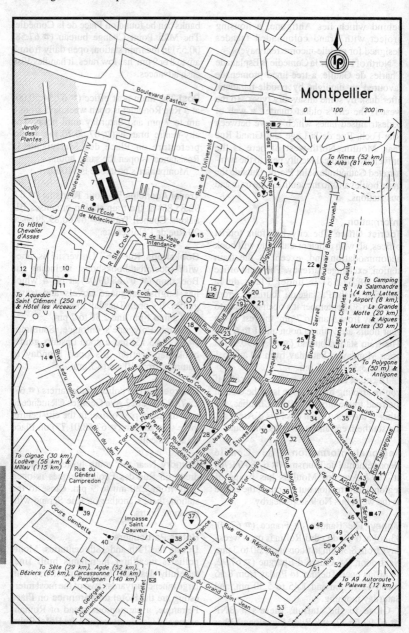

Montpellier

0   100   200 m

Boulevard Pasteur

Jardin
des
Plantes

Boulevard Henri IV

R. de l'École
de Médecine

To Hôtel
Chevalier
d'Assas

R. Ste Croix

R. de la Vieille
Intendance

Rue de l'Université

Rue des Écoles
Laiques

To Nîmes (52 km)
& Alès (81 km)

Boulevard Bonne Nouvelle

Rue d'Aiguillerie

Boulevard Sarrail

Esplanade Charles de Gaulle

To Camping
la Salamandre
(4 km), Lattes,
Airport (8 km),
La Grande
Motte (20 km)
& Aigues
Mortes (30 km)

To Aqueduc
Saint Clément (250 m)
& Hôtel les Arceaux

Rue Foch

Boulevard Blvd Ledru Rollin

Rue Saint Guilhem

Rue de la Loge

Rue de l'Ancien Courrier

Rue Jacques Cœur

To Polygone
(50 m) &
Antigone

Rue Baudin

Rue Boussairolles

Rue du Four des Flammes

R. du Petit St Jean

Rue en Condeau

Rue Jean Moulin

Rue des Étuves

Rue Maguelone

Rue de Verdun

To Gignac (30 km),
Lodève (56 km) &
Millau (115 km)

Rue du Jeu de Paume

Rue du
Général
Campredon

Cours Gambetta

Impasse
Saint
Sauveur

Grand Rue Jean Moulin

Rue Loys

Blvd Victor Hugo

Rue Joffre

R. Aristide Olivier

R. Serane

To Sète (29 km), Agde (52 km),
Béziers (65 km), Carcassonne (148 km)
& Perpignan (140 km)

Rue Anatole France

Rue de la République

Rue Jules Ferry

Ave Georges
Clemenceau

Rue Rondelet

Rue du Grand Saint Jean

To A9 Autoroute
& Palavas (12 km)

LANGUEDOC

■ PLACES TO STAY	33	Épicerie de Nuit	30	Opéra
	37	Halles Laissac	34	Air France Office
2 Auberge de Jeunesse	46	Le Steph	36	BNP (Bank)
29 Hôtel des Étuves			40	Spinella (Bike Hire)
35 Hôtel des Touristes		OTHER	41	Main Post Office
38 Hôtel Littoral			45	Laundrette
39 Hôtel Abysse	4	Laundrette	48	SMTU Bus Office
42 Hôtel Édouard VII	7	Cathédrale Saint Pierre	49	Budget
43 Hôtel de Paris	8	Medical Faculty,	50	Europcar
44 Hôtel Le Mistral		Musée Atger &	52	Railway Station
47 Hôtel Altaï		Musée d'Anatomie	53	Bus Station
	10	Palais de Justice		
▼ PLACES TO EAT	11	Arc de Triomphe	✕	SQUARES
	12	Promenade du Peyrou		
1 Alimentation Générale	13	Caisse d'Épargne	5	Place de la
3 Au Calzone Doré	14	Banque de France		Chapelle Neuve
6 Le Vieil Écu	15	The Bookshop	17	Place des Martyrs
9 Don Peppino	16	Post Office Branch		de la Résistance
18 Halles Castellane	21	Hôtel de Varennes,	19	Place Pétrarque
20 La Diligence		Musée du Vieux	23	Place Jean Jaurès
24 Tripti Kulai		Montpellier &	31	Place de la Comédie
25 Brasserie Prosper		Musée Fougau	51	Place Auguste Gibert
27 Crêperie Les	22	Musée Fabre		
Blés Noirs	26	Main Tourist Office		
32 Monoprix Supermarket	28	Hôtel Saint Côme		

Côme on Grand Rue Jean Moulin. The latter, the city's first anatomy theatre for medical students, now houses the Chamber of Commerce and has a superb stained-glass window visible from the courtyard. There are other such mansions on Rue des Trésoriers de la Bourse and Rue des Trésoriers de France.

Museums

The city's showpiece is the **Musée Fabre** (☎ 67.66.06.34) at 39 Blvd Bonne Nouvelle, home to one of France's richest collections of French, Italian, Flemish and Dutch works from the 16th century on. The 19th-century realist artist Gustave Courbet has a small room; the top floor has more contemporary works. It's open Tuesday to Friday from 9 am to 5.30 pm and weekends from 9.30 am to 5 pm; admission costs 20/10FF for adults/students.

There are four other museums (all free) that individually won't take much time and are worth seeing if your visit coincides with their limited opening hours. Two are upstairs

in the Hôtel de Varennes on Place Pétrarque. The first you come to is the **Musée du Vieux Montpellier** (☎ 67.66.02.94), a storehouse of the city's memorabilia from the Middle Ages to the Revolution. It's open Monday to Saturday from 1.30 to 5 pm. Continue upstairs for the **Musée Fougau**, which deals with traditional Occitan life. It's open on Wednesday and Thursday from 3 to 6.30 pm.

The others are in the university's medical faculty on Rue de l'École de Médecine (closed during university holidays). The **Musée Atger** (☎ 67.66.27.77), housing a striking collection of French, Italian and Flemish drawings, is open weekdays from 1.30 to 4.30 pm. The **Musée d'Anatomie** (☎ 67.60.73.71) is also worth a look if you enjoy anatomy in jars. It's open weekdays from 2.15 to 5 pm.

Promenade du Peyrou

Overlooking the city at the end of Rue Foch, this large, tree-lined square is a wonderfully peaceful spot for a bench picnic or a lazy afternoon. Designed in the 18th century, it's dominated by the **Arc de Triomphe** at one end and an octagonal water tower at the other. Stretching away from the latter is the **Aqueduc Saint Clément**, an aqueduct under which there's a bustling flea market on Saturday and *pétanque* games most afternoons. To the north off Blvd Henri IV is the **Jardin des Plantes**, France's oldest botanical garden, founded by Henry IV in 1593.

Beaches
The closest beach is at **Palavas**, 12 km south of the city and backed by a nasty concrete skyline. However, it's easy to get to by local bus (No 28 or 17) and, in summer, there's a bus/bike deal (see the Getting Around section) which will help you find a patch of sand away from town.

About 20 km east of Montpellier is **La Grande Motte**, a resort famous for its futuristic, loopy architecture. It's not the sort of place to be in during the height of summer or dead of winter, but if you're interested in beach resorts it's worth a look. For bus details, see the Getting There & Away section.

Places to Stay – bottom end
Except for camping grounds and the youth hostel, accommodation is largely clumped in a semicircle north of the train station.

Camping The closest grounds are around the suburb of Lattes, about four km south of the city centre. The only one open all year is the two-star *Camping La Salamandre* (☎ 67.65. 76.26) at Carrefour de Boirargues, off Route de Carnon in the direction of La Grande Motte. It charges 49FF for one or two people with a tent and car. To get there, take bus No 28 from the bus station to the Boirargues stop and walk about 200 metres.

Hostels The *Auberge de Jeunesse* (☎ 67.60. 32.22), 2 Impasse de la Petite Corraterie, on the corner of Rue des Écoles Laïques, is ideally located within the old centre. The mosaic entrance contrasts with the basic dorms above, but there's a large courtyard.

Reception is open until 11 pm or midnight. A bed costs 56FF, including breakfast. To get there from the station, take bus No 2 or 4 to the C Ursulines stop. Le Rabelais night buses also stop here.

Hotels Popular with travellers for its low prices, the *Hôtel des Touristes* (☎ 67.58. 42.37) at 10 Rue Baudin has keen owners and large rooms, all with showers. Singles/doubles start at 90/110FF; the cheapest triples/quads cost 180/300FF. Close by, the *Hôtel de Paris* (☎ 67.58.37.11) at 15 Rue Aristide Olivier is an unpretentious two-star joint with basic but functional doubles from 120FF, or 160FF with shower. A hall shower costs 10FF.

North-west of the station, the *Hôtel des Étuves* (☎ 67.60.78.19) at 24 Rue des Étuves is excellently located on a pedestrian-only street in the old core. Inside, the place creeps up like a vine around a dark spiral staircase but the rooms are nice and the welcome warm. Singles with toilet start at 80FF, or there are doubles with toilet and shower from 140FF.

Near the Laissac market, the *Hôtel Littoral* (☎ 67.92.72.20) at 3 Impasse Saint Sauveur (off Rue Anatole France) is homy and relatively peaceful, though it's down a glum alley and there's no nearby parking. Large, basic singles/doubles start at 90/128FF; there are rooms with shower from 150/160FF. Hall showers cost 15FF.

Three blocks away, the *Hôtel Abysse* (☎ 67. 92.39.05), situated at 13 Rue du Général Campredon, has basic but pleasant singles from 99FF, or singles/doubles with shower from 129/149FF. Street parking is available nearby.

Places to Stay – middle & top end
There are several hotels north-east of the station. The pick of the crop is the recently renovated *Hôtel Altaï* (☎ 67.58.37.99) at 10 Rue Sérane. Fresh rooms in pastel tones start at 125/175FF for a single/double; all have private shower and toilet.

The *Hôtel Le Mistral* (☎ 67.58.45.25; fax 67.58.23.95) at 25 Rue Boussairolles is a rather grand place with basic singles without shower for 110FF (there's no hall shower) and large, classically styled singles/doubles with shower from 165/185FF. Triples go for 235FF and two-bed quads from 260FF. Private parking costs 30FF but there's street parking all around.

Another two-star place is the *Hôtel Édouard VII* (☎ 67.58.42.13; fax 67.58.93.66) at 10 Rue Aristide Olivier. It's more modern in tone, and has basic singles from 100FF and rooms with shower from 130/150FF. There are only a few rooms at these prices – the bulk of the rooms cost 170/190FF.

Next to the Aqueduc Saint Clément, the *Hôtel Les Arceaux* (☎ 67.92.03.03; fax 67.92.05.09), 33 Blvd des Arceaux, has rooms from 230/275FF. For a real splurge in spacious surroundings, the *Chevalier d'Assas* (☎ 67.52.02.02; fax 67.04.18.02), 18 Ave d'Assas, just north of the Promenade du Peyrou, is a pleasant hotel with friendly owners. Rooms start at 440FF.

Places to Eat
The restaurant scene is an appetising one, in both variety and price, but many places close on Sunday.

Restaurants – North of Rue Foch
At the top end of Rue de l'Aiguillerie is Place de la Chapelle Neuve, a shady square lined with little restaurants including *Le Vieil Écu* (☎ 67.66.39.44), 1 Rue des Écoles Laïques. Specialising in regional fare, it has a two-course *menu* for 55FF (lunchtime only). If you order à la carte, main dishes start at 70FF. It's closed Sunday. Nearby at No 10, *Au Calzone Doré* is a takeaway pizza joint open weekdays only until 11 pm. A basic margherita starts at 33FF.

For good dine-in Italian food, try *Don Peppino* (☎ 67.52.89.75) at 13 Rue Sainte Croix. Hidden down a quiet backstreet, it has a terrace with a view of the cathedral, and pizzas from 28FF. Nearby, Rue de l'Université has a few cheap brasseries and snack places.

Restaurants – South of Rue Foch
A good hunting ground is around Rue du Petit Saint Jean. Just off it is *Crêperie Les Blés Noirs* (☎ 67.60.43.03) at 5 Rue Four des Flammes, a cosy spot with buckwheat (sarrasin) pancakes from 20 to 35FF and seafood or vegetarian salads from 33 to 47FF.

Through the stone arch on Rue Jacques Cœur is *Tripti Kulai* (☎ 67.66.30.51) at No 20. A popular vegetarian place, it has salads from 37FF, burgers for 46FF and a *menu* for 60FF. It's open weekdays from noon to 2 pm and 6 to 9 pm, and on Saturday night.

La Diligence (☎ 67.66.12.21) is nearby at 2 Place Pétrarque. The back patio is spanned by one of the Hôtel de Varennes's Gothic-style galleries. The 69FF *menu* includes a glass of wine and is served for lunch and dinner (only until 8 pm); it's not available on Friday and Saturday nights.

Those into poodle-watching could try *Brasserie Prosper* (☎ 67.52.71.17) at 17 Blvd Sarrail, which also sets up a large dining terrace on Esplanade Charles de Gaulle. *Menus* cost 68FF.

Close to the train station, *Le Steph* (☎ 67.92.63.79) at 33 Rue de Verdun is a true local's retreat. The restaurant is hidden at the back of the bar. Although the service does not always come with a smile, the hearty three-course *menu* costs only 49FF.

Self-Catering
Food *markets* operating daily till about noon include one on Place Jean Jaurès and the adjoining Halles Castellane, and another in the corkscrew-shaped Halles Laissac on Place Laissac. The *Polygone* centre is bursting with shops – boulangeries, fromageries, the works – that are generally open Monday to Saturday until 6 or 7 pm.

The *Monoprix* store on Place de la Comédie has a ground-floor grocery section that's open Monday to Saturday from 8.30 am to 7.30 pm. For late-night shoppers, *Épicerie de Nuit* at 4 Rue Boussairolles is open on Sunday from 1.30 pm to 2 am, Monday to Thursday from 6.30 pm to 2 am and Friday and Saturday until 4 am. Near the youth hostel, the little *Alimentation*

Générale at 21 Blvd Pasteur is open daily from 9 am to midnight.

Entertainment

There's generally a fair bit happening in Montpellier. To find out what and where, pick up the free weekly *Sortir* guide from the tourist office. For a drink, a few local haunts flank Rue en-Gondeau. The *London Pub* is on Place Jean Jaurès. Late into summer nights, street entertainers gather on Place de la Comédie. A month-long international dance festival starts in the last week of June.

Getting There & Away

Air Montpellier's airport (☎ 67.20.85.00) is off Route de Carnon, about eight km south-east of the city. Courriers du Midi's bus No 120 will get you there (20FF one way; 20 minutes).

Air France (☎ 67.92.48.28) is at 6 Rue Boussairolles.

Train The double-level train station (☎ 67.58.50.50 for information) is on Place Auguste Gibert, 500 metres south of Place de la Comédie. The train information office is open Monday to Saturday from 8 am to 7 pm, while the station's upper level and the ticket windows are open from 5 am to 10.30 pm. On the ground floor there's a left-luggage room (30FF a day) open from 8 am to 8 pm and plenty of 72-hour lockers.

Major connections from Montpellier include: Paris's Gare de Lyon (365FF plus TGV fee; five hours; five a day), Carcassonne (105FF; 1½ hours; 16 a day), Millau (120FF; three hours; six a day) and Perpignan (102FF; 1½ hours; 16 a day). More locally, there are connections to Nîmes (45FF; 30 minutes; 20 a day), Sète (29FF; 20 minutes) and Agde (25FF; 30 minutes).

Bus The bus station (☎ 67.92.01.43) is at Place du Bicentenaire, to the left as you leave the train station. All the regional companies plus Eurolines have offices here, which are usually open Monday to Saturday from 9 am to noon and 2 to 7 pm. On Sunday you can get information from the duty officer or consult the posted timetables.

Courriers du Midi (☎ 67.92.05.00) operates an hourly bus to La Grande Motte (20.50FF; 40 minutes); in summer, a few of these buses continue on to Aigues Mortes (31FF; 1½ hours; three a day) and Les Saintes Maries de la Mer in the Camargue (two hours). Autocars du Languedoc (☎ 67.92.60.35) has buses to Gignac (40 minutes) and points further inland.

The Eurolines office (☎ 67.58.57.59) is open Monday to Saturday from 9 am to 12.15 pm and 3.30 to 6 pm. It has buses to many European destinations including Barcelona (five hours), which costs 220/175FF one way for those aged over/under 26 years, and London (17 hours), which costs 590/335FF (60FF more in summer). There are also services to Morocco, Prague and Frankfurt.

Car If you arrive by car, finding the city centre can be a headache. By following the 'Centre Historique' signs you'll get as close as is allowed to the pedestrianised core.

For car rental, ADA (☎ 67.58.10.15) has an office at 8 Blvd Berthelot, south-west of the train station. Both Europcar (☎ 67.58.16.17) and Budget (☎ 67.92.69.00) have offices on Rue Jules Ferry, in front of the train station, as well as at the airport.

Hitching Auto Stop (☎ 67.64.28.88), open weekdays from 10 am to 6 pm, arranges paid lifts with drivers.

Boat SNCM and COMNAV ferries to the Moroccan port of Tangier, and summer services run by Transmediterranea (Balear Ferry) to Majorca and Ibiza, leave from the port of Sète, 29 km south-west of Montpellier. Tickets and information for both services are available from the SNCM (☎ 67.74.70.55) at 4 Quai d'Alger in Sète. For information on fares, see the Sea section in the introductory Getting There & Away chapter.

The Compagnie Marocaine de Navigation has a ferry to Tangier on the northern tip of Morocco, once or twice a week, depending on the season. The trip takes 36 hours. One-way adult fares start at 1150FF but for a group of four or more it's 860FF each. The passage costs 800FF for students and those under 26, and 575FF for children. Normal tariffs for cars/motorbikes start at 1400/500FF, though there are discounts if you're a student, under 26 or in a group of at least four people.

Balear Ferry sails to Majorca and Ibiza, two of the Balearic Islands off the east coast of Spain, from late June to early September. The first stop is the town of Palma (15 hours) on Majorca, the next is Ibiza (21 hours) and then Valencia (29 hours) on the Spanish coast. One-way fares start at 507FF per passenger and 914/366FF for cars/motorbikes.

Getting Around

Bus City buses are run by SMTU (☎ 67.22.87.87), whose office at 27 Rue Maguelone is open Monday to Saturday from 7 am to 7 pm. Regular buses run daily until about 8 pm, after which a night-bus service known as Le Rabelais takes over. Le Rabelais does a loop around the old town from the train station, the last bus leaving the station at 12.30 am. Bought separately, bus tickets cost 6FF; a 10-ticket carnet is 42FF. A weekly pass is available for 50FF.

Taxi Taxis wait outside the station or can be ordered by calling TRAM (☎ 67.58.10.10) or Radio Taxi (☎ 67.58.74.82).

Bicycle Vélo Pour Tous (☎ 67.58.56.44) at 24 Blvd du Jeu de Paume has free bikes, given out on Esplanade Charles de Gaulle, between May and August from 9 am to 9 pm (until 5 pm during the rest of the year). All you must do is leave an 800FF deposit. Spinella (☎ 67.92.12.46) at 4 Cours Gambetta hires out mountain bikes for 80FF a day. It's closed on Sunday and Monday.

In summer, STMU (see the previous Bus section) operates a bus/beach/bike package where you buy a ticket (50FF) at the bus station in Montpellier for a return trip (bus No 17 or 28) to Palavas's bus station from where you pick up a bike for the day. There's an 800FF bike deposit and the bike must be returned by 6.45 pm.

SÈTE

Sète (population 41,000) is the largest French fishing port on the Mediterranean, and the country's second-largest commercial port after Marseille. Established by Louis XIV in the 17th century, it prospered as the ports of Aigues Mortes and Narbonne were gradually cut off from the sea by build-ups of sand.

Situated at the base of Mont Saint Clair (from where there is a great view), Sète is a pleasant town with waterways and canals, outdoor cafés and seafood restaurants. Its beaches attract hordes of tourists in summer, but the town's other economic activities help it maintain an identity that doesn't depend on tourism.

Sète was the birthplace of the poet and essayist Paul Valéry (1871-1945), and the childhood abode of the singer Georges Brassens (1921-81). Both these French greats are buried here. Try to visit Sète in the last weekend in August for the *joutes nautiques* – jousting contests that go back 300 years, in which participants try to knock each other into the water from rival boats, spurred on by orchestras.

The Sète tourist office (☎ 67.74.71.71) is at 60 Grand'Rue Mario Roustan, with branch offices at the train station and opposite the ferry terminal. See the Montpellier Getting There & Away section for information about trains and ferries to/from Sète.

AGDE

Originally a Greek settlement at the mouth of the Hérault River, Agde (from the Greek word *agathos*, which means 'good') is a picturesque fishing port with narrow streets. The fortified **Cathédrale Saint Étienne** dates mainly from the 12th century but its foundations are those of a 5th-century Roman church. As with many other buildings in town, it's made of black volcanic stone. The tourist office (☎ 67.94.29.68) is at Espace Molière.

Regular shuttle buses ply the five-km

route to the modern tourist resort of **Cap d'Agde**, famous for its long beaches and large nudist colony, including the self-contained *quartier naturiste* in the resort itself. The money you save on laundry bills won't compensate for what you'll spend on everything else.

BÉZIERS

Béziers (population 79,000) was first settled by the Phoenicians and was an important military post in Roman times. It was almost completely destroyed in 1209 during one of the more notorious episodes of the Albigensian Crusade, involving the slaughter of thousands of Biterrois, as the people of Béziers are known. In happier times, the local tax collector, Paul Riquet (1604-80), moved heaven and earth to fulfill his dream and build the Canal du Midi, which enters the Mediterranean (Golfe du Lion) some 15 km away.

Today the graceful town of Béziers is the wine capital of Languedoc, and wine tasting tops the agenda of most tourists who visit, particularly during the wine-harvest festivals in October. **Cathédrale Saint Nazaire**, on a hill overlooking the town, was destroyed in 1209 but was soon rebuilt. It's a fortified church typical of the region, with massive towers and an interesting façade with a huge rose window.

The locals are keen on rugby and bullfighting, and opponents of the latter activity would be wise to stay away during the *feria* in early August. The classical music and opera festival in mid-July should appeal to more refined tastes.

The tourist office (☎ 67.49.24.19) is at 27 Rue 4 Septembre.

NARBONNE

Once a coastal port but now 13 km inland as a result of siltation, Narbonne (population 45,000) is a quiet provincial town with a long and proud history. As the capital of Gallia Narbonnensis, it was one of the main centres of Roman rule in Gaul. With the collapse of Rome, it became the capital of the Visigoth kingdom before passing to the Moors and then the Franks; it was incorporated into France in 1507.

The town is dominated by the massive **Cathédrale Saint Just** and the adjoining **Archbishop's Palace**. Construction of the cathedral was halted in the early 14th century, but its choir is still one of the highest in France. The cathedral treasury contains a beautiful Flemish tapestry of the Creation. South of the cathedral, on Place de l'Hôtel de Ville, the fortified former archbishop's palace comprises a number of buildings, including the 13th-century Gilles Aycelin tower (worth climbing for the view) and Viollet-le-Duc's 19th-century town hall, which houses an art museum and an interesting archaeology museum.

If you have private transport, the Cistercian **Abbaye de Fontfroide** 15 km south-west of town is worth visiting for its stunning cloister.

Narbonne's tourist office (☎ 68.65.15.60) is on Place Roger Salengro, in the north-western shadow of the cathedral.

CARCASSONNE

From afar, Carcassonne (population 45,000) looks as though a fairy-tale medieval city had been brought to life. Bathed in late-afternoon sunshine and highlighted by dark and menacing clouds, the Cité (as the walled old town is known) is truly breathtaking, which is why it featured in the 1991 film *Robin Hood, Prince of Thieves*.

The Cité's defences are the culmination of many centuries of fortifications built on this spot by the Gauls, Romans, Visigoths, Moors and Franks. In the 13th century, they served as one of the major strongholds of the Cathars.

The ancient ramparts and towers were saved from ruin in the mid-1800s by the architect Viollet-le-Duc. His zealous restoration of the ramparts, keeps, barbicans and machicolations was completed in 1910, and the end result looks almost too good to be true. Indeed, historical accuracy sometimes played second fiddle to the architect's personal preferences. However, the Cité does give visitors a sense of what siege warfare was like in the Middle Ages and the tactics, equipment and architecture used to make a city impregnable. During the summer months, the entire Cité is packed to the gills with tourists.

But there's a 'normal' town as well, the Ville Basse, which was established in the mid-13th century after Carcassonne's inhabitants tried and failed to recapture the Cité, which had fallen to Simon de Montfort during the Albigensian Crusade. They were eventually permitted to return on the condition they rebuild their city on the lowland on the left bank of the Aude River.

Orientation
The Aude River separates the Ville Basse – a perfect grid of one-way streets enclosed by a series of one-way boulevards – from the Cité, which is on a hill half a km to the south-east. The train station is on the northern edge of the Ville Basse, just across the Canal du Midi from the north end of pedestrianised Rue Georges Clemenceau.

The main gate to the Cité is Porte Narbonnaise, from which Rue Cros Mayrevieille leads up the hill. At the top, the entrance to the Château Comtal is to the right and Basilique Saint Nazaire is to the left.

Information
Tourist Office The main tourist office (☎ 68.25.07.04) is at 15 Blvd Camille Pelletan (opposite Square Gambetta), which is about halfway from the train station to the Cité. It's open Monday to Saturday from 9 am to noon and 2 to 6.30 pm. From mid-June to mid-September it's open from 9 am to 7 pm and on Sunday from 10 am to noon. The staff will exchange money on weekends. There's a 5FF commission for hotel reservations.

In the Cité, there's a tourist office annexe (☎ 68.25.68.81) in the Tour Narbonnaise, to the right as you walk through Porte Narbonnaise. It's staffed from Easter to the end of October and is open daily (except Sunday afternoon) from 9 am to noon and 1.30 to 6 pm. In July and August, it's open daily from 9 am to 7 pm.

For information on the Aude département, and reservations for accommodation, you can stop by the Comité Départemental de Tourisme (CDT; ☎ 68.47.09.06) at 39 Blvd Barbès during regular office hours.

Money The Banque de France (☎ 68.25.02.20) at 5 Rue Jean Bringer is open weekdays from 8.30 am to 12.30 pm and 1.50 to 3.50 pm.

Near the main tourist office, the Caisse d'Épargne (☎ 68.25.04.92) at 5 Blvd Camille Pelletan is open Tuesday to Saturday from 8.30 to 11.30 am and 1 to 4 pm. It has a 24-hour exchange machine for foreign banknotes. The rest of Carcassonne's banks are open Monday to Friday.

In the Cité, if you're desperate you might try the exchange bureau 20 metres up Rue Cros Mayrevieille from Porte Narbonnaise. It's open from 1 April to 30 November. The Crédit Agricole has a branch next to 3 Rue Cros Mayrevieille.

Post The main post office (☎ 68.25.03.53) at 43 Rue Jean Bringer is open weekdays from 8 am to 7 pm, Saturday until noon. In the Cité, the branch opposite 17 Rue Porte d'Aude is open Monday to Friday from 9 am to noon and 1.50 to 5 pm, and on Saturday from 8.45 to 11.45 am. Both bureaux exchange foreign currency.

Carcassonne's postcode is 11000.

Laundry The laundrette at 31 Rue Aimé Ramon is open daily from 9 am to noon and 2 to 7.30 pm. Closer to the train station, Lav 2000 at 68 Rue Jean Bringer is open daily from 8 am to 9 pm.

Cité
While the streets in the Ville Basse and the towpaths along the Canal du Midi are pleasant for wandering, the Cité – illuminated at night – is Carcassonne's only major sight. It is enclosed by two walls – the inner one 1.3 km long, the outer one 1.7 km – that constitute one of the longest city fortifications in Europe. The ramparts are studded with 52 stone towers.

LANGUEDOC

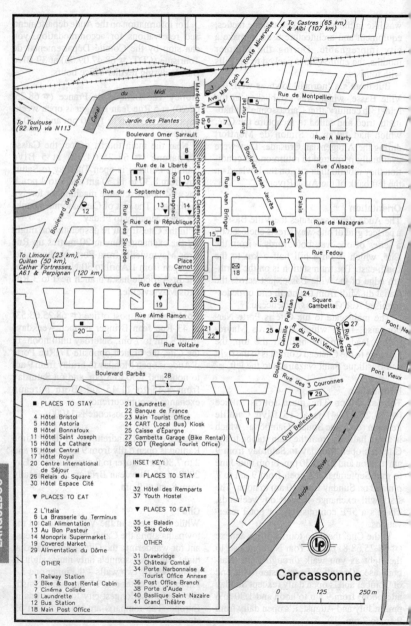

Carcassonne

0   125   250 m

■ PLACES TO STAY
4   Hôtel Bristol
5   Hôtel Astoria
8   Hôtel Bonnafoux
11 Hôtel Saint Joseph
15 Hôtel Le Cathare
16 Hôtel Central
17 Hôtel Royal
20 Centre International
    de Séjour
26 Relais du Square
30 Hôtel Espace Cité

▼ PLACES TO EAT
2   L'Italia
6   La Brasserie du Terminus
10 Cali Alimentation
13 Au Bon Pasteur
14 Monoprix Supermarket
19 Covered Market
29 Alimentation du Dôme

OTHER
1   Railway Station
3   Bike & Boat Rental Cabin
7   Cinéma Colisée
9   Laundrette
12 Bus Station
18 Main Post Office

21 Laundrette
22 Banque de France
23 Main Tourist Office
24 CART (Local Bus) Kiosk
25 Caisse d'Épargne
27 Gambetta Garage (Bike Rental)
28 CDT (Regional Tourist Office)

INSET KEY:

■ PLACES TO STAY
32 Hôtel des Remparts
    Youth Hostel

▼ PLACES TO EAT
35 Le Baladin
39 Sika Coko

OTHER
31 Drawbridge
33 Château Comtal
34 Porte Narbonnaise &
    Tourist Office Annexe
36 Post Office Branch
38 Porte d'Aude
40 Basilique Saint Nazaire
41 Grand Théâtre

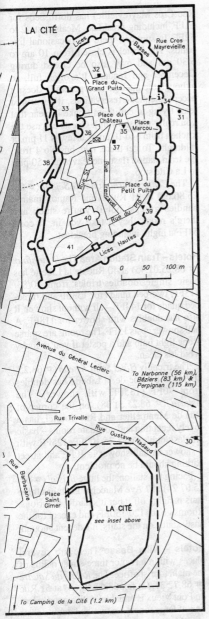

LA CITÉ

Lices Basses

Rue Cros Mayrevieille

32

Place du Grand Puits

33

Place du Château

34

31

35

Place Marcou

36

37

38

Rue St Jean

Rue Trencavel

Place du Petit Puits

Rue du Plo

40

39

41

Lices Hautes

0   50   100 m

Avenue du Général Leclerc

To Narbonne (56 km),
Béziers (83 km) &
Perpignan (115 km)

Rue Trivalle

Rue Gustave Nadaud

30

Rue Barbacane

Place Saint Gimer

LA CITÉ
see inset above

To Camping de la Cité (1.2 km)

Only the lower sections of the walls are original. The rest – including the inauthentic roofs shaped like witches' hats (the originals were flatter and weren't covered with slate) – were added by Viollet-le-Duc, so the Cité's impressive silhouette is mainly a product of the 19th century.

To get to the Cité's main entrance from the train station or Square Gambetta, take bus No 4, which runs every 30 minutes. On foot, the walk from the station takes 35 to 40 minutes – from Square Gambetta, the nicest route is along Rue du Pont Vieux, over the humped Pont Vieux, along Rue Trivalle and up Rue Gustave Nadaud to the main entrance. There's a smaller entrance for those on foot at Porte d'Aude. People with cars/camper vans can park them at the main entrance for 20/30FF, or can look for a rare spot in the nearby streets.

Once across the drawbridge (*pont-levis*) over the dry moat, you're immediately faced with a massive bastion, the **Porte Narbonnaise,** inside which the tourist office has an annexe. There's a dull arts museum above the tourist office; entry is free. You can also wander around the grassy fields (*lices*) between the inner and outer walls; there's no entry fee. Rue Cros Mayrevieille, almost suffocated in kitschy souvenir shops, leads up to **Place du Château**, the heart of the Cité.

Through another archway and across a second dry moat is the **Château Comtal** (Counts' Palace), built in the 12th century. A 40-minute tour of the castle and the ramparts – both of which are accessible only if you join a tour – costs 25/14FF for people aged over/under 25. In July and August (and perhaps June), an excellent English-language version of the tour departs several times a day, usually at 12.30, 2 and 3 pm. There's also a more extensive 1½-hour tour (42FF; 31FF for students and those under 25), but it's conducted only in French.

The chateau is open daily from May to mid-September from 9 am to 6.30 pm (7.30 pm in July and August). From mid-September to April, it's open daily from 9 am to 12.30 pm and 2 to 6.30 pm (5 pm from November to March). Tickets for the last guided tour (in French) are sold half an hour before closing time at both midday and in the afternoon.

South of Place du Château at the end of Rue Saint Louis is **Basilique Saint Nazaire**. The nave with its round arches is Romanesque, while the graceful transept arms and choir – and the curtain of exquisite stained-glass windows in the latter – are Gothic. The rose windows in the transepts are from the 14th to 16th centuries; the organ case was added in the 17th century. The basilica is open daily from 9 am to noon and 2 to 5.30 pm (7 pm in summer).

Next to the basilica is the **Grand Théâtre**, an open-air stage used during the summer.

Festivals

On 14 July, the Cité is illuminated with a mass of fireworks to celebrate National Day. Known as Carcassonne in Flames, it's quite a spectacle.

Throughout July, the Festival de la Cité brings to the walled city a heady programme of music, opera, dance and theatre. Les Médiévals, held during two of the first three weeks of August, includes concerts of medieval music, tournaments and, in the evening, a *spectacle* in the theatre next to the basilica.

Places to Stay

Many of Carcassonne's hotels hide average rooms behind a grand reception area. Once you cross to the Cité side of the river, prices skyrocket. During the festivals, advance bookings are essential.

Camping *Camping de la Cité* (☎ 68.25. 11.77) on Route de Saint Hilaire, about 3.5 km south of the main tourist office, charges 41FF for one person plus a tent or 66FF for two people with a tent and car. It's open between March and 30 October. To get there, take bus No 5 (hourly until 6.40 pm) from Square Gambetta to the Route de Cazilhac stop.

Hostels In the heart of the Cité, the pleasant, 120-bed *Auberge de Jeunesse* (☎ 68.25. 23.16) on Rue Vicomte Trencavel (just off Rue Cros Mayrevieille) has dorm beds for 61FF, including breakfast. Meals cost 42 to 52FF. In summer, there are occasional live bands. The hostel is closed from 10 am to 5.30 pm and may also be closed during December and January. It's often full, so although the management generally doesn't accept telephone reservations, it's worth at least trying to call them (make it clear that you really will show up). Guests can use the kitchen from 6 to 10 pm. Curfew is 11 pm or midnight. To get there, take bus No 4 from the train station (last one leaves at 6.50 pm) to La Cité stop.

The *Centre International de Séjour* (☎ 68. 25.86.68) at 91 Rue Aimé Ramon mainly handles groups, but if you're stuck and there's room, they'll take you in. It costs 54FF a night, including breakfast.

Hotels – Train Station Area The *Bonnafoux* (☎ 68.25.01.45) at 40 Rue de la Liberté has basic singles/doubles/triples from 70/83/ 113FF, two-bed quads for 133FF and three-bed quads for 144FF – all without shower. It also has doubles with shower for 118FF. A hall shower costs 15FF. The rooms are sparse – one light bulb and a poster if you're lucky – but it's clean.

The friendly *Hôtel Saint Joseph* (☎ 68.25. 10.94) at 81 Rue de la Liberté has doubles from 90FF (135FF with shower). The *Astoria* (☎ 68.25.31.38), on the corner of Rue de Montpellier and Rue Tourtel, has a lovely reception and adequate rooms – basic singles/doubles cost 75/100FF, 125FF with a shower. A hall shower is 10FF and street parking should be no problem.

Facing the station, the huge *Bristol* (☎ 68. 25.07.24) at 7 Ave Maréchal Foch has three stars hanging off it but it's hardly luxurious. Rooms go for 120/150FF, and except for the nasty statue on the stairs, it's decent enough.

Hotels – Ville Basse There are several places within a two or three-street radius of the main tourist office. The *Relais du Square* (☎ 68.72.31.72; fax 68.47.49.66) at 51 Rue du Pont Vieux is amiable, with a good selection of large rooms – a two-bed double costs

120FF, a double with shower is 160FF, and a two-bed quad is 220FF. *Le Cathare* (☎ 68.25.65.92) at 53 Rue Jean Bringer has small, ordinary doubles from 100FF, with shower from 125FF, and triples with shower and TV from 175FF. Hall showers cost 18FF.

On busy Blvd Jean Jaurès, the two-star *Central* (☎ 68.25.03.84) at No 27 has sparsely furnished, adequate doubles, all with shower and TV, from 140FF. There's also one room without shower (there's no hall shower) for 120FF. Across the road, the *Hôtel Royal* (☎ 68.25.19.12; fax 68.47.33.01) at No 22 has standard rooms, all with shower, from 130/140FF. At both these places you'd do well to ask for a room at the back.

Hotels – Cité In the vicinity of the Cité, rooms start at 240FF. The cheapest choice outside the walls is the new, salmon-toned *Espace Cité* (☎ 68.25.24.24) at 132 Rue Trivalle. Doubles/triples with full facilities start at 240/290FF and two-bed quads start at 340FF. There's private parking.

Inside the walls, the *Hôtel des Ramparts* (☎ 68.71.27.27) at 3 Place du Grand Puits has a lovely stone façade that hides garishly modern rooms from 270FF; parking costs 20FF. This place is closed in January.

Places to Eat
If you're after value for money, steer clear of the Cité area unless it has been a slow season and prices have been dropped to drum up trade.

Restaurants – Train Station Area *L'Italia* (☎ 68.47.08.64), a little pizzeria at 32 Route Minervoise, is big on atmosphere and the size of its pizzas (from 35FF). The 60FF *menu* includes a glass of wine.

For a hearty meal, a good choice is *La Brasserie du Terminus* (☎ 68.25.25.00) at 2 Ave du Maréchal Joffre. The 58FF *menu* includes an entrée and a dessert which you choose from a buffet.

Near the station, there are a number of restaurants along Blvd Omer Sarrault.

Restaurants – Ville Basse Possibly the cheapest *menu* in town can be found at the *Relais du Square* hotel (see the Places to Stay section). It has two restaurants: the pricey, street-front *Le Gargantua* and the unpretentious, nameless diner out the back, which has a 49FF *menu du jour* and a 70FF *menu* of regional fare.

Au Bon Pasteur (☎ 68.25.46.58) at 29 Rue Armagnac is a cosy seafood place with a range of *menus* from 65FF.

Restaurants – Cité Between noon and 2.30 pm and from 7 pm until late, the Cité comes alive with places to eat. Restaurateurs, in particular those on Place Marcou and Place du Château, pack in so many clients that the hum of voices completely drowns out the clinking of cutlery.

Sika Coko (☎ 68.71.05.83), out of the hubbub at 6 Rue du Plô, offers Caribbean food served in a large garden. *Menus* start at 65FF. It also sometimes has live music. *Le Baladin* (☎ 68.47.91.90) at 6 Place du Château has pizzas from 32FF. There's a dining area out the back.

Self-Catering At Place Carnot, *market* mornings are Tuesday, Thursday and Saturday, but in summer a few enthusiastic market gardeners set up there daily. The *covered market* on Rue de Verdun is open Monday to Saturday.

The *Monoprix supermarket* on Rue de la République is open Monday to Saturday from 8.30 am to 7 pm. One street up, *Cali Alimentation* at 42 Rue Armagnac is open Monday to Saturday from 8 am to 12.30 pm and 3 to 8 pm, and on Sunday morning. Closer to the Cité, tiny *Alimentation du Dôme* at 13 Rue des 3 Couronnes has basic supplies. It's open daily from 8.30 am to 12.30 pm and 4 to 7 pm (closed Monday afternoon).

In the Cité, the *boulangerie* at 11 Rue Cros Mayrevieille is open daily (except Monday from November to March). Across the street at No 10 there's a small, overpriced *grocery*.

Entertainment
Cinéma Colisée (☎ 68.25.08.09) at 10 Blvd Omer Sarrault screens nondubbed films on

Wednesday and Thursday nights (except in July and August). In summer, the youth hostel sporadically has live bands and many restaurants in the Cité have guitarists.

Getting There & Away

Train The train station (☎ 68.47.50.50 for information) is at the end of Rue Georges Clemenceau, about one km north of the main tourist office and two km from the Cité. The train information office is open Monday to Saturday from 9 am to 6.20 pm; the station building closes from 2.30 to 5 am. The luggage room, open between 5.30 am and 8 pm, contains a few lockers. You can also leave things with the attendant for 30FF a day.

Carcassonne is on the important railway line that links Toulouse (66FF; 50 minutes; 15 a day) with Narbonne (46FF; 30 minutes; 14 a day). From Narbonne, trains continue north-east to Montpellier (105FF; 1½ hours) and south to Perpignan (84FF; 1½ hours; 10 a day).

Bus The bus station (☎ 68.25.12.74) is next to 20bis Blvd de Varsovie, about 700 metres south-west of the train station. The information shed is open weekdays from 8 am to noon and 2 to 6 pm. Regional buses are run by Trans Aude, which has services to Narbonne (36FF; 1½ hours) and Montréal (20FF; 35 minutes).

Eurolines, whose buses mainly serve Spain and Portugal, drops off and picks up passengers at the bus station. The company has three buses a week to Barcelona (170/155FF for those aged over/under 26).

Getting Around

Bus Local buses are run by CART, which has an information kiosk on Square Gambetta, the central bus hub. Bus No 4 runs half-hourly between the station, Square Gambetta and the Cité. Single tickets cost 4.80FF. Buses run until about 6.30 or 7 pm. There's no service on Sunday.

Taxi Taxis can usually be found at the station. To order a taxi call ☎ 68.71.50.50.

Bicycle Mountain bikes can be hired from Gambetta Garage (☎ 68.71.55.55), on the corner of Square Gambetta and Rue des Calquières, for 35/70FF for a half/full day. It is open daily from 9 am to 8.30 pm. The company also has a cabin by the canal at the train station, which is open in summer from 10 am to 8.30 pm.

Boat Motor boats and house boats can be hired under the bridge linking the train station with the Ville Basse.

AROUND CARCASSONNE
Cathar Fortresses

Some of the most inaccessible fortresses in which the Cathars sought refuge were built along the boundary between the French and Aragonese spheres of influence a century or more before the Albigensian Crusade. The two most famous of these, Peyrepertuse and Quéribus, are about midway between Carcassonne and Perpignan along the D14.

Peyrepertuse The 2.5-km-long ramparts of this dramatic fortress once enclosed a whole village, a church and two castles. These days all that's left is a shell, breathtakingly set on a rocky perch that affords magnificent views of Quéribus across the valley. Peyrepertuse is open between Easter and 30 September from 9 am to 7 or 8 pm. The rest of the year you can climb up, but there are some steep and potentially dangerous areas that are best avoided in stormy or windy weather.

Quéribus About nine km south-east of Peyrepertuse, this fortress sits at an altitude of 728 metres, overlooking the plain, the Corbières hills and the Pyrenees. Built in the 11th century, it was one of the last islands of Cathar resistance. Opening months are the same as for Peyrepertuse, but the hours are 10 am to 6 or 8 pm.

Getting There & Away

From Carcassonne, the easiest way to get to the castles is to take the train to Quillan (43FF; one hour 20 minutes; three a day) and then bus No 10 towards Perpignan (two a

The Cathars

In Languedoc you'll often come across the term *les Pays Cathars* (the Cathar Lands), which evokes memories of the cruel Albigensian Crusade – the hounding and extermination of a religious sect called the Cathars.

The dualistic doctrine of Catharism (from the Greek word *katharos*, meaning pure or clean) was based on the belief that the 'Good' kingdom of God was locked in battle with the 'Evil' world created by Satan. Good was invisible, spiritual and eternal while Evil was the material, temporal reality. Cathars believed that a pure life, completed by several reincarnations, would free the spirit from its satanical body. Asceticism was practised by the *parfaits* (the perfect), clergy as well as lay people, who had strict vegetarian diets and abstained from sex; in order to become 'perfect' they had to undergo an initiation ceremony.

Catharism expanded in the Toulouse, Albi and Carcassonne regions during the 12th and 13th centuries. Reacting against the materialistic attitude of the church in Rome, and preaching in the local tongue, *langue d'oc*, the sect found many followers among common people as well as the aristocracy. The latter even welcomed the perfects into their castles.

This was a thorn in the eye of Rome, and in 1208 Pope Innocent III preached the crusade against the Cathars, who were also called Albigensians after the town of Albi (the terms 'Albigeois' and 'Cathars' were mainly used by their enemies; the followers themselves simply called each other 'Good People' or 'Friends of God'). The Albigensian Crusade was an occasion for the Capetian kings in the north to expand their territory into Languedoc, supported spiritually by Saint Dominique of Toulouse and in the field by the cruel Simon de Montfort.

After long sieges, the major Cathar centres such as Béziers and Carcassonne, the village of Minerve and the dramatically sited fortresses of Montségur, Quéribus and Peyrepertuse, were conquered. Hundreds of perfects were burnt at the stake as heretics. The final massacre took place at Montségur, when 200 Cathars, refusing to renounce their faith after the castle was taken in 1244, were burnt alive in a mass funerary pyre. In 1321 the burning of the last perfect, Guillaume Bélibaste, in the chateau of Villerouge-Termenès (a village on the D613, which runs between Narbonne and Couiza), marked the end of Catharism in Languedoc. ■

day, at 7.50 am and 4.15 pm) to the village of Maury, which is on the D117. From here it's a four-km uphill walk to Quéribus and about 15 km to Peyrepertuse, though you can hitch. See the Around Perpignan section for information about transport to/from the east.

MENDE

Mende (population 12,000) is the capital of Lozère, France's most underpopulated département. Though a quiet little town, it's no unsophisticated backwater: the narrow streets of the old town sport an ample number of boutiques, brasseries and fine-food shops. If you have a car, Mende makes a good base for exploring the northern part of Upper Languedoc. The hotels are noticeably cheaper than those in the towns nearby.

Orientation & Information

The pedestrianised town centre is enclosed in a one-way ring road. As the road goes uphill, the tourist office (☎ 66.65.02.69) is on your left at 14 Blvd Henri Bourrillon (for directions from the train station, see Getting There & Away). This is the place to go to for information on the town, the region and bus services. Most of the year it's open weekdays from 8.30 am to 12.30 pm and 2 to 6 pm, and Saturday from 9 am to noon. In July and August it's open until 8 pm.

Things to See

You can wander through Mende in a matter of minutes, but if you have time on your hands, the tourist office has a walking-tour brochure in English which points out every façade, nook and cranny of historical interest. The town's most outstanding feature is the 14th-century, twin-towered **Cathédrale Notre Dame** on Place Urbain V. If you arrive from the north, the cathedral is set off strikingly against the high mountains. The highest of its two towers offers a good view of the town.

Places to Stay

July and August are the only busy times, and most hotel owners here are friendly towards visitors from abroad.

Camping The two-star *Tivoli* (☎ 66.65. 00.38), about two km west of town on the N88 to Florac, charges 21.50FF for two people with a tent. There's a Super U supermarket between the camping ground and town. One of Mende's free but infrequent buses stops nearby; it can be picked up at the bus station.

Hotels The *Hôtel du Marché* (☎ 66.65.12. 52) on Place Chaptal has airy and inviting pastel-coloured rooms. There's only one single (95FF); doubles without/with shower start at 125/155FF. The hall shower is 15FF. Opposite the bus station, the *Hôtel du Commerce* (☎ 66.65.13.73) on Blvd Henri Bourrillon is a rustic, labyrinthine place with clean, modern singles/doubles from 120/140FF.

The cheapest option is the *Hôtel du Gévaudan* (☎ 66.65.14.74) on 2 Rue d'Aigues Passes, three blocks to the right as you exit the tourist office. Small, nondescript rooms start at 105FF; the hall shower is free.

Places to Eat

The low-budget hotels are the best bet for a substantial meal. The *Hotel du Gévaudan* has a much-frequented but well-hidden upstairs restaurant where you can get a full *menu* for 54FF during lunch or dinner.

Around Place de la République you'll find plenty of *boulangeries*. There's an *Intermarché supermarket* on Place Théophile Roussel, to the right down the hill as you exit the tourist office. *Street markets* take over the central squares on Wednesday and Saturday.

Getting There & Away

Train The train station (☎ 66.23.50.50 for information) is north of the town centre across the river. The tourist office is about one km away – turn left as you leave the station and then right into Allée Piencourt, which goes straight up to the ring road; from here, either cut through the old town streets or follow Blvd du Soubeyran up and round until you come to the office on your right.

There are infrequent trains in two directions. The principal line goes east to La Bastide Puylaurent (38FF; one hour), which is on the main north-south line between Clermont-Ferrand (143FF; four hours) and Nîmes (102FF; three hours). The other goes west to Le Monastier on a secondary line, from where there are connections to Marvejols (31FF; 40 minutes) and on to Rodez (75FF; three hours with two changes).

Bus Buses leave from either the bus station on Place du Foirail, about 100 metres to the left as you exit the tourist office, or from the train station. One bus a day goes to Rodez (three hours), Marvejols (50 minutes) and Le Puy (two hours). In July and August there's a morning bus to both Florac and Sainte Énimie, but the rest of the time you'll have to rely on your thumb to get to these places.

AROUND MENDE
Wolf Reserve

Wolves used to roam freely through the forests in Lozère, but today they're seen only in the Parc des Loups du Gévaudan (☎ 66.32.09.22) at Sainte Lucie, seven km north of the town of Marvejols (about 25 km west of Mende). The reserve was set up with help from the Brigitte Bardot Foundation by a local man with a love for wolves. Mongolian, Canadian and European wolves live here in 'semi-liberty', though it's still sad to see these animals surrounded by wire and disturbed by noisy school groups. Admission is 20/10FF for adults/children. For details on getting to Marvejols, see Mende's Getting There & Away section. There's no public transport from Marvejols to the reserve.

La Margeride

One of the most desolate areas of Lozère, La Margeride is a granitic range running north-south from the Massif Central towards Mende. This high plateau is covered with pine forests and patches of sunburnt moss.

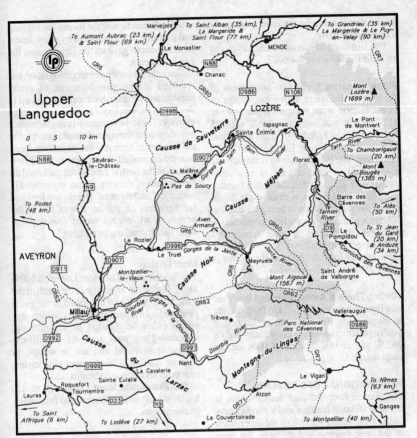

Dotted with occasional old stone villages and without a major town as its base, it's ideal hiking and cross-country cycling terrain. In winter you can ski. The region is also home to a new bison reserve, set up to ensure the survival of Europe's diminishing species.

A good base for exploring La Margeride is **Baraque de Bouviers** (population five; altitude 1418 metres), halfway between the nearest towns worth mentioning, Saint Alban and Grandrieu. *Bouviers* is the name of the local herders who bring their flocks to the high country in summer. Around one of

their old shelters has grown a small centre (☎ 66.47.41.54) open all year to those engaging in outdoor pursuits. It's an excellent base for hiking (the GR4 and GR43 pass by here), mountain biking, rock climbing and cross-country skiing. All the necessary equipment can be hired here.

Places to Stay & Eat The centre has a modern *gîte d'étape* where you can stay for 40FF in a dorm, 60FF per person in single/double/triple rooms. Four-person studios cost 895/1325FF a week in the low/high season (the high season is July and August).

Reservations are wise in case a group is scheduled to arrive.

The laid-back *hotel/restaurant* has rooms for 120FF and *menus* for 60FF.

Bison Reserve Eight km north-west of Baraque de Bouviers above the village of Sainte Eulalie is the Parc des Bisons (☎ 66. 31.57.01). It was set up in 1992 with 25 European bison railed over from a national park in Poland where Europe's last 1000 bison live. The French reserve is intended as a safeguard in case disease or any other catastrophe should befall the Polish bison.

Within the 1.8-sq-km reserve the bison roam freely. A museum is being built at the reserve's entrance from where horse-drawn carriages take visitors on a tour. A protected walking path also allows you to glimpse these mighty animals. Entry to the reserve is about 25FF.

Getting There & Away Trains and buses are nowhere to be seen. The 40 km from Mende to Baraque de Bouviers can be hitched if you're patient and have a good map – IGN's 2637E and 2638E (scale 1:25,000) are the most detailed.

PARC NATIONAL DES CÉVENNES

The diverse Parc National des Cévennes is home to isolated hamlets and a wide variety of flora and fauna – much of the latter, such as red deer, beavers and vultures, has been reintroduced over the last two decades.

It comprises four main areas: Mont Lozère, much of the Causse Méjean, the Cévennes valleys and Mont Aigoual. Though not within the park, the town of Florac, where you'll find the Maison du Parc information centre (see the Florac Information section), is the best base for exploration.

History

The 910-sq-km park was created in 1970 to bring ecological stability to a region which, because of religious and later economic upheavals, has long had a destabilising human presence. Population influxes, which saw the destruction of the forests for logging and pastures, were followed by mass desertions as people gave up the fight against the harsh elements.

Since the mid-19th century emigration has resulted in the abandonment of many hamlets and farms, which were bought up in the 1960s by wealthy Parisians and foreign tourists. These newcomers brought money but they also brought new threats to the environment; tourism has therefore been heavily controlled. It's illegal to build new houses in the central zone of the park, and all renovations of existing places must blend in with local architecture. Hotels are few and far between except in towns along the periphery, while gîtes ruraux (country cottages) are increasing in number.

Mont Lozère

The desolate world of Mont Lozère, a 1699-metre-high lump of granite in the north of the park, is probably best described in the guide produced by the park authorities, which says you'll either be dazzled or see nothing, depending on your state of sensitivity. Shrouded in cloud and ice in winter, in summer it's full of heather and blueberries, peat bogs and flowing streams.

The **Écomusée Mont Lozère** (☎ 66.45. 80.73) at Le Pont de Montvert has full details on this region.

Causse Méjean

For details on the Causse Méjean, see the following Grands Causses section.

Cévennes Valleys

Sweet chestnut trees, first planted back in the Middle Ages, carpet the Cévennes valleys, the park's central region of inaccessible ravines and jagged ridges, along one of which runs the Corniche des Cévennes road (see the following Getting There & Away section). In earlier times chestnuts, a staple of the mountain people's diet, were eaten raw, roasted or dried. These days they feed the *sangliers* (wild boars).

Mont Aigoual

Only 70 km from the coast, Mont Aigoual (1567 metres) and the neighbouring Montagne du Lingas region are known more for searing winds and heavy snowfall than for a Mediterranean climate. Cross-country skiing is popular, and so is summer tourism. The area is thick with beech trees thanks to a successful reafforestation programme that was begun in 1875 by a forward-thinking forester to counteract the years of logging.

The meteorological station on Mont Aigoual offers a stunning 360° **view** over the Cévennes, and on clear winter days you can see all the way from the Alps to the Pyrenees.

Activities

In winter there's cross-country skiing on Mont Aigoual. For hikers, there's a well-developed network of footpaths. The park authorities have added 22 paths to the six GR trails crossing the area, which include the Vosges-Pyrenees track (GR7) and the Aigoual (GR66), Cévennes (GR67) and Mont Lozère (GR68) circuits. Maps and booklets are available at the Maison du Parc in Florac, where you can also pick up the gîtes d'étape brochure which lists 98 places where you can hole up for the night.

Getting There & Away

If you don't have private transport, the region is almost as impenetrable as it was

centuries ago. A limited bus service runs between Florac and Alès (see the Florac and Alès Getting There & Away sections for details). By car, the most spectacular route between the two towns is the wild Corniche des Cévennes, a ridge road offering fantastic views as it winds along the mountain crests of the Cévennes.

FLORAC

Florac (population 2000) is the best base for exploring the Parc National des Cévennes and for indulging in some of the region's outdoor activities. Located at the northern end of the wild Corniche des Cévennes ridge road, Florac is draped along the Tarnon River, one of the tributaries of the Tarn, and is immediately likeable for its intimate atmosphere. It gets pretty busy here in summer. Florac has one main road, Ave Jean Monestier, which runs parallel to the river.

Information

Tourist Office The tourist office (☎ 66.45.01.14) is on Ave Jean Monestier in the town centre. Opening hours vary: between 1 July and 30 September it's open from 8.30 am to 12.30 pm and 2 to 7.30 pm (Sunday from 9 am to noon); between 1 October and 15 April it's open weekdays only from 9 am to noon; between mid-April and 30 June it's open Monday to Saturday from 9 am to noon and 2 to 5 pm.

The Camisard Revolt

Early in the 18th century, the Cévennes were the scene of what some historians describe as the first guerilla war in modern history, which was fought by the Protestants against Louis XIV's army.

The Revocation of the Edict of Nantes in 1685 took away the rights the Huguenots had enjoyed since 1598. Many French Protestants emigrated, while others fled into the wilderness of the Cévennes, from where a local Huguenot leader named Roland led the resistance against the French army sent to crush them in 1702. Poorly equipped but with great motivation and intimate knowledge of the countryside, they held out for two years. They fought in their shirts – *camiso* in langue d'oc, hence their popular name, Camisards. The royal army slowly gained the upper hand, and on the king's orders the local population was either killed or forced to leave. Most of the villages were methodically destroyed. Each September, thousands of French Protestants meet at Roland's birthplace of Le Mas Soubeyran, a hamlet between Saint Jean du Gard and Anduze along the Corniche des Cévennes road. The house where he was born is now a museum detailing the persecution of Protestantism in the Cévennes during the century between 1685 and the re-introduction of religious freedom with Louis XVI's Edict of Tolerance in 1787. ■

Maison du Parc Located in the restored 17th-century chateau in Florac's centre, the Maison du Parc (☎ 66.49.53.01) has information, maps, wildlife books and guides on the Parc National des Cévennes. Most of the detailed guides are in French, but the *Parc National des Cévennes* guidebook (70FF) is available in English.

The region's most detailed map, the IGN 354 (1:100,000), is on sale for 43FF. The information centre is open daily in July and August from 9 am to 7 pm, the rest of the year weekdays only from 9 am to noon and 2 to 7 pm.

Activities

The tourist office has details on all sorts of outdoor activities, including cave exploration and canyon descents. For hiking details, contact the Maison du Parc (see also Activities in the previcus Parc National des Cévennes section).

Glider Flights Gliders take off from Chanet airstrip in the centre of the Causse Méjean, about 17 km west of Florac. It costs about 200FF for an hour. For more information, call the airstrip (☎ 66.45.15.46) from 9 am to noon only.

Donkey Treks If you'd like to follow Robert Louis Stevenson's lead, you can hire a donkeys about 1.5 km north of Florac at Le Pont du Tarn. The charge is 80/150FF for a half/full-day trek. For more details, contact Dominique Serrano on ☎ 66.45.20.89.

Cycling Bikes can be hired from VTT Évasion (☎ 66.45.09.56), which in July and August has an office on Place Boyer in the centre of Florac. At other times the operation is run from Croupillac, a village six km south on the D907 towards the Corniche des Cévennes. If you're unable to get there, just ring and the owner, Richard Taillandier, will bring the bikes into town.

Prices are 70/110FF for a half/full day. If there are at least five participants, he will transport you and the bikes (10FF each) to

the Causse Méjean for some flat cycling before you make the descent back to Florac.

Places to Stay & Eat

The choice is lean between December and March when many hotels close. This in turn makes finding somewhere to eat harder as the hotel restaurants serve the best meals.

Camping The two municipal camping grounds are 1.5 km from the town centre in opposite directions. Both charge 10/3FF for adults/children and 6/10FF for a car/tent. *Le Pont du Tarn* (☎ 66.45.18.26), off the N106 as it heads north towards Mende, is open from mid-April to 30 September. To the south, *La Tière* (☎ 66.45.04.02) on the D907 is open from mid-June to 30 September.

Gîte d'Étape For hikers, there's a *gîte d'étape* (☎ 66.45.14.93) on Rue de l'Église in the centre of town. It's open from April to December.

Hotels The two-star *Grand Hôtel du Parc* (☎ 66.45.03.05) on Ave Jean Monestier, a block from the tourist office, lives up to its name with spacious rooms, a pool and gardens. Singles/doubles start at 95/120FF. It is open from mid-March to mid-December. The restaurant has a hearty *menu* for 75FF.

Les Gorges du Tarn (☎ 66.45.00.63) on Rue du Pêcher, close to the Maison du Parc, has adequate rooms from 150/220FF without/with shower (open from April to 30 September).

The modern *Le Pont Neuf* (☎ 66.45. 01.67) at Quartier Pont Neuf, about 800 metres south of the tourist office, is open all year. The cheapest rooms start at 210FF; all have bath and toilet. The restaurant serves a four-course *menu* for 65FF.

Getting There & Away

This is no easy task. No trains pass by here and buses are sporadic, to say the least, and don't run on Sunday. One bus a day goes to Alès (54FF; 1½ hours), leaving at 9 am (8 am on Saturday). In July and August only there's one bus to Sainte Énimie (50 minutes); it leaves at noon (1 pm on Saturday). Unfortunately, the bus back leaves Sainte Énimie at 2 pm. During summer there's a bus to Mende at 7 am.

All three lines leave from the yellow rectangle painted on Place 19 Mars 1962, behind the tourist office. For more information, ask at the tourist office or Cars Reilhes (☎ 66.45.00.18) at 52 Ave Jean Monestier opposite the tourist office.

ALÈS

Alès, the second-largest town in the Gard département, is a gritty industrial town 44 km north-west of Nîmes and 70 km north-east of Montpellier. Coal mining has long been the town's livelihood, with the result that it has little to offer tourists in the way of sights. From here, however, you can pick up a bus to Florac, 71 km to the north-west, and if nothing else, Alès is a convenient overnight stop if you're heading to/from the Cévennes region.

Information

Alès's main tourist office (☎ 66.78.49.10) is in the Chambre de Commerce building at 49 Rue Michelet in the heart of town. It is open Monday to Thursday from 8.30 am to noon and 1.30 to 5.30 pm, and Friday from 1.30 to 4.30 pm. From May to October there's also a small annexe (☎ 66.78.49.10) on Place Gabriel Péri, on the bank of the Gardon River south of the town centre.

Things to See

If you have time on your hands, it's possible to explore Alès's underground mine museum, the **Mine Témoin** (☎ 66.30.45.15). It's on Chemin de la Cité Sainte Marie, west of the town centre in the neighbouring suburb of Rochebelle. Take a sweater – it's only 13°C down in the mine tunnels.

Those interested in the clandestine way of life of the Camisards (see the Camisard aside) may want to visit the **Musée du Désert** (☎ 66.85.02.72) close to the hamlet of Mialet, about 17 km south-west of Alès; the nearest village of any size is Saint Jean du Gard, eight km south of Mialet. The

museum occupies a house known as the Mas Soubeyran, which was the birthplace of Roland, one of the Camisard leaders. It is open daily from March to November.

Places to Stay

There's an *Auberge de Jeunesse* (☎ 66.34. 27.82) at 8 Rue Jules Guesdes in La Grand'Combe, a town 14 km north of Alès on the Alès-Le Puy-en-Velay train line.

There are two hotels conveniently located opposite the train and bus stations. The two-star *Hôtel Le Riche* (☎ 66.86.00.33) at 42 Place Pierre Sémard has comfortable modern singles/doubles from 180/250FF. In contrast to the rooms, the hotel's restaurant is classically elegant, providing the perfect setting for the sumptuous cuisine created by local chef Jean Chevallier. *Menus* start at 95FF, and for what you get, this is excellent value.

For a cheaper abode try the next-door *Hôtel La Terrasse*, which has basic singles/doubles from 100FF without shower, or 145FF with shower.

Getting There & Away

Alès's train station (☎ 66.23.50.50) and bus station (☎ 66.30.24.86) are both on Place Pierre Sémard to the north of the town centre. The main train destinations south are Nîmes (39FF; 40 minutes; five a day) and Montpellier (70FF; one hour; two a day). There are two trains a day north to Le Puy-en-Velay (145FF; four hours).

If you're heading into the Cévennes, there is one bus a day to Florac (54FF; 1½ hours). On weekdays, the bus leaves at 4.10 pm and on Saturday at 11.30 am. There's no bus on Sunday. Four buses a day go from Alès to Saint Jean du Gard (30FF; one hour).

GRANDS CAUSSES

To the west of the Cévennes, the Grands Causses are harsh limestone plateaux on the southern rim of the Massif Central. Scorched in summer and windswept in winter, their stony surfaces hold little moisture – the water filters through the limestone to form an underground world of caves ideal for spele-

---

Cardabelles

In spring, the ground of the causses is covered with cardabelles (often described as 'suns'), a carline flower with spiky acanthus leaves. The emblem of the causses, you'll see it hanging above many doors, as it is believed to bring luck. The locals also use it as a barometer: the dead flower opens in sunny weather, but closes up when it forecasts rain. In addition, the leaves are served in salads. ■

---

ologists and adventurers. Over the millennia, the Tarn, Jonte and Dourbie rivers have cut deep gorges through the 5000-sq-km plateau, creating four distinct causses: Sauveterre, Méjean, Noir and Larzac. Each is different in its delicate geological forms. One may look like a dark lunar surface and another like a Scottish moor, while the next is gentler and more fertile, but all of them are eerie and empty except for the occasional lonely shepherd wandering with his flock.

Causse de Sauveterre

The northernmost causse is a gentle, hilly plateau, meagrely dotted with lonely farms capable of withstanding the severe climate. Compact and curiously built, these farms resemble fortified villages. Every possible patch of fertile earth on the causse is cultivated, creating irregular, intricately patterned wheat fields.

Causse Méjean

The Causse Méjean, the highest of the causses at an average altitude of 1000 metres, is also the most barren and isolated. Occasional fertile depressions dot the poor pastures, and streams disappear into the limestone through holes and cracks.

Underground, this combination of water and limestone has created some spectacular scenery. One of the most famous caves is **Aven Armand** (☎ 66.45.61.31) on the plateau's south-west. Lying about 75 metres below the surface, the cavern stretches 200 metres and encompasses a subterranean forest of stalagmites. Discovered in 1897 by Louis Armand, a colleague of the 'father of speleology', Edouard-André Martel, it's 17 km south-west of Sainte Énimie and 26 km north-east of Millau. Entry is 35/18FF per

person aged over/under 18 years; it's open from mid-March to the end of September. For details on getting to Aven Armand, see Getting There & Away in the Millau section.

The vultures you see circling above the Causse Méjean were successfully reintroduced to the region after almost disappearing by the 1940s. They can often be observed above the Jonte and Tarn gorges, nesting on the ridges above Le Truel near where the gorges meet. Their numbers have risen to about 100, and the youngsters are now known to visit their relatives in the Pyrenees.

For cycling on the Causse Méjean, see Activities in the Florac section.

Causse Noir

Rising immediately east of Millau, this 'black' causse is encircled by gorges. It's best known for **Montpellier-le-Vieux** (☎ 65.60.66.30), a chaotic area of jagged rocks 18 km north-east of Millau overlooking the Gorges de la Dourbie. Created by water eroding the limestone plateau, the result is 120 hectares of formations with fanciful names such as the Sphinx and the Elephant. Three walks, ranging from 30 minutes to two hours' duration, cover the site, as does a tourist train.

Officially it's open only from April to October, but in other months there's nothing to stop you from going in. If you enter between 9 am and 7 pm during the 'open' months, there's an entrance fee of 20/12FF for adults/children; outside those hours it's free. For details on buses and organised tours to the Causse Noir, see the Millau section.

Causse du Larzac

The Causse du Larzac (elevation 800 to 1000 metres) is the largest of the causses. An endless sweep of faraway horizons and rocky steppes broken by medieval villages, it is known as the 'French Desert'. To the west is the Roquefort region; Millau is to the north.

This area is known in particular for its old, fortified villages such as **La Couvertoirade** and **Sainte Eulalie**, long the capital of the Larzac region. They were built by the Templars, a religious military order that distinguished itself during the Crusades. When the Templars were suppressed early in the 14th century, their possessions passed to their brothers-in-arms, the Hospitallers, who erected most of the fortifications still visible today.

More recently, the region was the scene of strong, and successful, local opposition against the French government's decision to expand the military camp north-east of the main village, La Cavalerie.

GORGES DU TARN

From the village of Ispagnac, between Mende and Florac, the spectacular Gorges du Tarn wind south-west for 50 km, ending north of Millau. En route are two villages, the medieval Sainte Énimie (a good base for canoeing and hiking along the gorges), and further downstream, La Malène.

The gorge, which is 400 to 600 metres deep, marks the boundary between the Causse de Sauveterre to the north and the Causse Méjean to the south. When you look down from these plateaux, the gorge looks like a white, limestone abyss. The green waters deep down below are dotted here and there with colourful spots – canoes. From the river gazing up, you might see vultures circling or nesting on the cliffs. Indeed the best way to appreciate this stunning landscape is either from the water or the ridges high above (see Sainte Énimie for information). The riverside road is often nothing more than a monstrous traffic jam of buses and caravans.

Information

The tourist office (☎ 66.48.53.44) in Sainte Énimie near the bridge is open daily between June and August from 9 am to 12.30 pm and 2 to 6 pm. The rest of the year it is open weekdays from 10 am to noon and 2.30 to 5 pm.

Sainte Énimie

Sainte Énimie (population 700) is named after a Merovingian princess who founded a monastery here after she drank the local water and recovered from an illness. Like an avalanche of grey-brown stone, this village blends perfectly into the steep slope behind it. Long isolated, Sainte Énimie is now a popular destination for day trippers and one of the starting points for descending the Tarn by canoe or kayak.

The tiny **museum** in the middle of the village has one vaulted room full of old local furniture, and a funny lady waiting to lead you in. Admission is 10/4FF for adults/children.

Tarn Descent Riding the Tarn is possible only in summer when the river is (usually) low and the descent a lazy trip over sometimes rapid, but mostly calm, water. You can go as far as the impassable Pas de Soucy, a barrier of boulders about nine km downriver from La Malène.

A handful of companies, based in Sainte Énimie along the river, organise canoe and kayak descents. Their prices are roughly the same. From Sainte Énimie to La Malène (14 km), it costs 180FF for a canoe (two people) or 90FF for a kayak (one person). To the Pas de Soucy, 22 km from Sainte Énimie, it's 240/120FF for a canoe/kayak. If you bivouac for the night on the shore somewhere and continue the next day, the charge is 300/150FF.

Hiking

This is the other ideal way to see the gorges. At Sainte Énimie, the GR60 winds down from the Causse de Sauveterre, crosses the bridge, and then climbs up to the Causse Méjean.

Places to Stay

The camping grounds along the gorge road cost about 55FF for two people with a tent. The hotels in Sainte Énimie and La Malène are overpriced tourist traps and usually full. If possible, you're better off heading for Mende, Florac or Millau.

LANGUEDOC

Getting There & Away

Public transport along the Gorges du Tarn is virtually nonexistent. Only in July and August is there a bus from Millau and another from Florac (see their Getting There & Away sections for details). From Millau there are also infrequent organised tours.

MILLAU

Lying between the Causse Noir and Causse du Larzac at the confluence of the Tarn and Dourbie rivers, Millau (pronounced 'mee-OH'; population 24,000) is a prosperous town enjoying the benefits of being the region's main centre. Convenient places for take-offs and good thermals have combined to make it a thriving hang-gliding and parapente centre. The huge sheep population in the region is evident in the abundance of leather goods (gloves in particular) and the production of some of France's most pungent blue cheeses – those produced in the nearby town of Roquefort are the most famous. The pétanque world series is held in Millau over four days around 15 August, attracting more than 1000 players and even more spectators.

Orientation

The Gorges du Tarn and the Causse Méjean lie to the north-east, the escarpment of the Causse Noir rises to the east, and that of the Causse du Larzac is to the south. Millau's old town (mostly pedestrianised) and the surrounding modern core are easily navigated from the town's hub, Place du Mandarous.

Information

Tourist Office In a garden at 1 Ave Alfred Merle, the tourist office (☎ 65.60.02.42) is open Monday to Saturday from 9 am to noon and 2 to 6 pm. In July and August it's open daily from 9 am to 12.30 pm and 2 to 7 pm.

Money The Banque de France (☎ 65.60.40.53) on Place Bion Marlavagne, near the train station, is open weekdays from 8.45 am to 12.15 pm and 1.30 to 4.30 pm.

Post The main post office on Ave Alfred Merle is open weekdays from 8.30 am to 7 pm and Saturday until noon.

Millau's postcode is 12100.

Laundry The tiny laundrette at 15 Ave Gambetta is open daily from 8 am to 10 pm.

Old Town

The town itself takes very little time to see. The belfry of the old town hall on Rue Droite is the centrepiece of the old town, and the tourist brochures make a big song and dance about the Vieux Moulin (old mill) near Pont Lerouge.

Museum

The museum (☎ 65.59.01.08) on Place du Maréchal Foch has a rich collection of fossils, including mammoth molars and a dinosaur skeleton dug up from the Causse du Larzac. In the cellar is a huge array of plates and vases excavated at La Graufesenque (see the next section). Upstairs the leather displays shouldn't be missed by anyone with a glove fetish.

The museum is open daily from 10 am to noon and 2 to 6 pm, except from 1 October to 31 March, when it's closed on Sunday. Admission costs 20/15FF for adults/children.

La Graufesenque

In Gallo-Roman times, La Graufesenque (☎ 65.60.11.37) was the site of the town's pottery workshops. Hundreds of thousands of pieces of rich-red pottery were made here, some of which are now on display in the town's museum. Only archaeology fans are likely to find the site riveting. It is off the Montpellier road, about one km past the gîte d'étape, and is open daily from 9 am to noon and 2 to 6 pm. Admission, including a French-speaking guide, costs 20/6FF for adults/children.

Hang-Gliding & Parapente

Two companies run introductory courses (about 1400FF for five days) as well as tandem flights (300FF), that take off from Brunas, the tower-topped plateau to the north

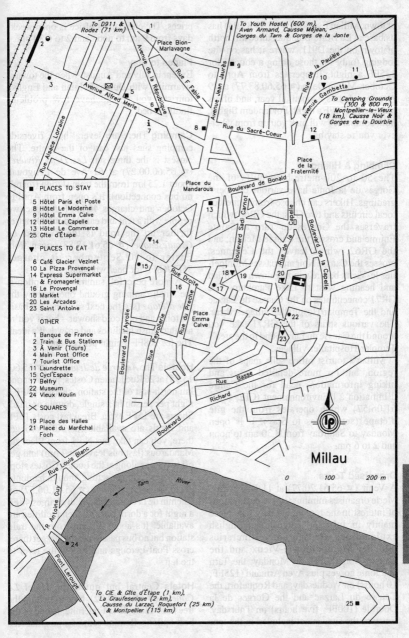

To D911 & Rodez (71 km)

Place Bion-Marlavagne

To Youth Hostel (600 m), Aven Armand, Causse Méjean, Gorges du Tarn & Gorges de la Jonte

Avenue de la République

Rue F Fabié

Rue Jean Jaurès

Avenue Alfred Merle

Rue Alsace Lorraine

Rue de la Paulèle

Avenue Gambetta

To Camping Grounds (300 & 800 m), Montpellier-le-Vieux (18 km), Causse Noir & Gorges de la Dourbie

Rue du Sacré-Cœur

Place de la Fraternité

Place du Mandarous

Boulevard de Bonald

Boulevard Sadi Carnot

Rue de la Capelle

Boulevard de la Capelle

PLACES TO STAY
5 Hôtel Paris et Poste
8 Hôtel Le Moderne
9 Hôtel Emma Calvé
12 Hôtel La Capelle
13 Hôtel Le Commerce
25 Gîte d'Étape

PLACES TO EAT
6 Café Glacier Vezinet
10 La Pizza Provençal
14 Express Supermarket & Fromagerie
16 Le Provençal
18 Market
20 Les Arcades
23 Saint Antoine

OTHER
1 Banque de France
2 Train & Bus Stations
3 À Venir (Tours)
4 Main Post Office
5 Tourist Office
11 Laundrette
15 Cycl'Espace
17 Belfry
22 Museum
24 Vieux Moulin

✕ SQUARES
19 Place des Halles
21 Place du Maréchal Foch

Boulevard de l'Ayrolle

Rue Peyrollerie

Rue Droite

Rue du Prêche

Place Emma Calvé

Rue Basse

Rue Richard

Boulevard

Rue Louis Blanc

R Antoine Guy

Pont Lerouge

Tarn River

Millau

0   100   200 m

To CIE & Gîte d'Étape (1 km), La Graufesenque (2 km), Causse du Larzac, Roquefort (25 km) & Montpellier (115 km)

of town. Millau Évasion (☎ 65.59.83.94) has its base at La Borie Blanque, three km north of town on the D911, where it has on-site lodging (only for those doing a course) for 135FF a night. It operates from April to October. Millau Delta (☎ 65.60.83.77) at 79 Ave Jean Jaurès is open all year, and offers lodging for 50FF a night. For tandem flights, both companies will pick you up from wherever you're staying.

Climbing & Hiking

The 50 to 200-metre-high cliffs of the Gorges de la Jonte have various climbers' gradings. Hikers can choose from numerous local circuits and two GRs: the GR60, which traverses the Gorges du Tarn at Sainte Énimie and crosses the Causse Méjean; and the GR62, which leaves the Cévennes, crosses the Causse Noir and passes Montpellier-le-Vieux before winding down to Millau and heading west to Lake Pareloup. The GR71 concentrates on the Causse du Larzac and the Templar/Hospitaller villages there. The various spurs of the GR71 take you around the Causse du Larzac and to the area's Templar/Hospitaller villages.

Millau's tourist office sells maps of the region, but for more detailed maps and hiking information, head for the Centre d'Initiation à l'Environnement (CIE; ☎ 65. 61.06.57) which operates from the gîte d'étape (see Places to Stay). It is open Monday to Saturday from 8.30 am to noon and 2 to 6 pm.

Organised Tours

À Venir (☎ 65.61.20.77) at 11 Rue Alfred Merle organises minibus trips to destinations of interest in the region, but they take place mainly in July and August and English explanations are sporadic. Itineraries include: Montpellier-le-Vieux and the Causse Noir (80FF) on Monday; the Tarn and Jonte gorges plus Aven Armand (125FF; 10 hours) on Wednesday; and Roquefort, the Causse du Larzac and the Gorges de la Dourbie (100FF; five hours) on Thursday. Entry to the sites is not included in the tour prices. The company's office is open weekdays from 9 am to noon and 2 to 6.30 pm.

Places to Stay

Except in July and August, when the town is swarming with Dutch, Belgian and English tourists, you should have few problems finding a bed.

Camping There are several huge riverside camping sites just east of the centre. The closest is the three-star *Les Deux Rivières* (☎ 65.60.00.27) at 61 Ave de l'Aigoual, about 1.25 km from the train station (there's no bus connection). It's open from April to October and charges 46/62FF for one/two people with a tent and car. About 500 metres further up the road is the two-star *La Graufesenque* (☎ 65.61.18.83), open from Easter to 30 September; it charges 35FF/68FF for one/two people.

A more peaceful, summer-only option is the small camping ground operated by the *gîte d'étape* (see the next section). It's basic – a toilet and one cold shower – but if you're not into plush facilities and crowds it's ideal. The fee is 8FF a night per person.

Hostels The *Auberge de Jeunesse* (☎ 65.60. 15.95) at 26 Rue Lucien Costes, just over one km north-east of the station, charges 43FF a night per person in a single, double or quad. Sheets are 15FF extra. Breakfast costs 16FF and meals are available for 30FF. To get there, you can take bus No 1 from Place du Mandarous (last bus leaves at 7 pm) and get off two stops along at the Lucien Costes stop.

In a much calmer setting, though harder to get to, is the *gîte d'étape* (☎ 65.61.06.57) on Chemin de la Graufesenque. It charges 48FF a night for a dorm bed. Kitchen facilities are available. It's about 2.5 km from the train station but no bus passes nearby. To get there, cross Pont Lerouge and follow the river to the left.

Hotels Central but quiet, the *Hôtel La Capelle* (☎ 65.60.14.72), hidden behind the trees at 7 Place de la Fraternité, is one of the best options. Reminiscent of a hospital (it's actually an old leather factory), the rooms are fine and the large terrace out the front is perfect for breakfast with a view. Basic doubles start at 130FF, or 185FF with shower, and triples/quads are 230/250FF. Private parking is free. It's closed from October to Easter.

Another good choice is the stylish *Emma Calve* (☎ 65.60.13.49) at 28 Ave Jean Jaurès, with rooms, all with bath and toilet, from 150FF. About 300 metres further along at No 56 is *Les Causses* (☎ 65.60.03.19), a two-star Logis de France hotel with pleasant rooms from 120FF.

The *Hôtel Le Moderne* (☎ 65.60.59.23) at 11 Ave Jean Jaurès has adequate singles/doubles from 106FF but it's closed from October to 31 March. On the busy Place du Mandarous, the *Hôtel Le Commerce* (☎ 65.60.00.56) at No 8 has singles/doubles from 95/120FF. Reception is three storeys up (there's a lift) and the (frosty) welcome can match the altitude. Close to the train station, the *Hôtel Paris et Poste* (☎ 65.60.00.52) at 10 Ave Alfred Merle has doubles from 125FF.

Places to Eat

Restaurants Several hotels serve reasonable three-course meals – the *Emma Calve* and *Les Causses* hotels (see the previous section) offer the best value, with *menus* from 45FF and 55FF respectively.

Mightily popular with tourists are the pizzerias and Chinese restaurants along Rue de la Capelle, which runs off Place du Maréchal Foch. *Les Arcades* (☎ 65.60.87.88) at 3 Place du Maréchal Foch has a terrace and *menus* from 55FF. Just off the square and slightly hidden by the archway is little *Saint Antoine*, which has a four-course *menu* for 59FF. Another good place away from the main restaurant area is *Le Provençal* (☎ 65.60.73.95) at 7 Rue Peyrollerie. It's laid-back and has a 49FF regional *menu*, but is closed for lunch on Tuesday.

For snacks, *Café Glacier Vezinet* on Ave de la République is much appreciated for its ice creams. *La Pizza Provençale* (☎ 65.60.89.36) at 9 Ave Gambetta, open daily until 10 pm, has takeaway pizzas baked in wood-fired ovens.

Self-Catering *Market* mornings are Wednesday and Friday on Place du Maréchal Foch and in the covered market on Place des Halles. The small *Express supermarket* on Blvd de l'Ayrolle is open Monday to Saturday from 8.30 am to 12.30 pm and 2.30 to 7.30 pm. Next door at No 17, *Aux Fruits des Pâturages* is a fromagerie with all the local specialities. It's open Monday to Saturday (and on Sunday mornings in summer) from 7.30 am to 12.30 pm and 2.15 to 7.30 pm.

Things to Buy

Leather goods and sheepskins hang everywhere, from the plush showrooms of André Sales to local butcher shops. The tourist office is also in on the act, selling leather postcards for 15FF.

Getting There & Away

Train The train station (☎ 65.60.11.65) is at the end of Ave Alfred Merle, 500 metres from the centre of town. Connections include Paris's Gare de Lyon (324FF; eight hours; three a day via Clermont-Ferrand), Béziers (81FF; 1¾ hours; six a day), Montpellier (121FF; 2¾ hours) and Toulouse (175FF; 3¾ hours). Via Rodez there are trains to Albi (100FF; two hours with the direct morning train). The train station closest to Roquefort is at Tournemire (22FF; 20 minutes; seven a day), a tiny village three km east of town from where you must hitch.

Bus The bus station (☎ 65.60.28.63) is in front of the train station. Its office is open weekdays from 8 am to noon and 2 to 6.30 pm. Buses go to Montpellier (85FF; 2¼ hours; five a day), Rodez (50FF; 1¾ hours; four a day) and Albi (70FF; three a day).

Regional services are very limited. Many operate only during July and August when there's one bus a day at 10.15 am to Le Rozier (20FF; 30 minutes); this is the closest stop (12 km away!) to Montpellier-le-Vieux. A return bus leaves Le Rozier at 3 pm.

To Aven Armand, the closest bus stops at

Meyrueis, again 12 km away (37FF; 1¼ hours). This service is even more limited, running only on Wednesday and Saturday. To Sainte Énimie (50FF; 1¾ hours) on the Gorges du Tarn there's one bus at 10.15 am with a return bus at 2 pm. To Roquefort (20FF) you have to take the Toulouse bus (three a day) and get off at Lauras, from where it's a four-km uphill walk.

Getting Around
Bus The local network is run by TUM (☎ 65.61.05.43). All buses stop at Place du Mandarous. The tourist office has timetables.

Car À Venir (see the earlier Organised Tours section) is an agent for Budget rental cars. It's best to give them two days' warning as cars have to be brought over from Rodez.

Bicycle Mountain bikes can be hired at Cycl'Espace (☎ 65.61.14.29) at 21 Blvd de l'Ayrolle (closed Monday) for 85/110/450FF a day/weekend/week. In summer they organise a one-day cycling tour around one of the causses for about 150FF, including lunch. City bikes are available at the train station for 55FF a day.

AROUND MILLAU
For information about Aven Armand and Montpellier-le-Vieux, see the previous Grands Causses section, and the Organised Tours section under Millau.

Roquefort
About 25 km south of Millau, the village of Roquefort-sur-Soulzon (as it's known in full) is where ewe's milk is turned into France's most famous blue cheese. Clinging to a hillside, its steep, narrow streets are burdened with cheese-laden semitrailers and tourists making their way to the cool natural caves where 13 producers have thousands of cheeses ripening.

If you want to see how they're made, La Société (☎ 65.60.23.05) at Rue de la Cave has tours costing 30/20FF for adults/students. Le Papillon (☎ 65.59.90.03) at Rue de la Fontaine has free tours of its equally pungent caves. Both companies are open daily from about 9.30 am to 6 pm.

The village is hard to get to without a car. For information on trains, buses and organised tours, see the previous Millau section. Buses shuttle cheese workers from Roquefort to their homes in Saint Affrique, leaving Roquefort at about noon and again at 5 pm. If there's a place, you'll be welcome on board.

Roussillon

Roussillon, also known as French Catalonia, lies at the eastern end of the Pyrenees, on the doorstep of Spain. The main city is Perpignan. The area's most famous peak is Mont Canigou (2784 metres).

Roussillon was long a part of Catalonia (the region in the north-east of what is now Spain), and has kept many symbols of Catalan unity. The *sardane*, a dance expressing both peace and revolt, is still performed in towns at festival times, and the Catalan language is widely spoken.

History
Roussillon was inhabited since prehistoric times, and one of the oldest skulls in Europe was unearthed in a cave near Perpignan. After a long series of invasions by the same groups who passed through Languedoc, Roussillon came under the control of Catalonia-Aragon in 1172. In the 13th and 14th centuries, Perpignan was the capital of the kingdom of Majorca, but apart from a brief period of French rule in the 15th century, Roussillon spent much of the late Middle Ages under Aragonese rule.

In 1640, the Catalans revolted against the Castilian kings in Madrid, who had engulfed Aragon. After a two-year siege, Perpignan was relieved with the help of the French king Louis XIII and Cardinal Richelieu. This led in 1659 to the Treaty of the Pyrenees, which defined the border between Spain and France once and for all. The northern section of

Catalonia, Roussillon, was given to the French, much to the resentment of the locals.

Geography
The southern end of the Languedoc plain is dominated by Roussillon's main city, Perpignan, to the west of which rises Mont Canigou. All around is a mosaic of vineyards, orchards and vegetable fields, a varied garden where the eternal cricket song is heard among the fig and olive groves. The flat coastline ends abruptly with the rocky foothills of the Pyrenees at the Côte Vermeille, an area which inspired the most renowned Fauvist artists.

Food & Wine
In Roussillon, Spanish influences are obvious. *Tapas* (the Spanish word for hors d'œuvres and snacks traditionally eaten at the counter of a bar), including flame-grilled mushrooms and seafood, are served in many *bodegas* (wine bars or taverns).

Banyuls and Rivesaltes are two of Roussillon's most delicious sweet white wines. They are drunk cool – but without ice – as an apéritif.

PERPIGNAN
More Catalan than French, Perpignan (population 120,000) was the capital of the kingdom of Majorca from 1278 to 1344, which stretched from here to Montpellier and included the Balearic Islands. Perpignan developed into an important commercial centre in the following centuries, and is still the second-largest Catalan city after Barcelona. It is the centre of Roussillon, an area that the French kings only incorporated after a series protracted campaigns that culminated in the Treaty of the Pyrenees.

Today Perpignan still has a strong Catalan 'feel'. Plane trees rustle alongside palms, and music and conversation reverberate until late. Situated at the edge of the Languedoc plain, at the foothills of the Pyrenees and with the Côte Vermeille to the south-east, it makes a great base for day trips into the mountains or along the coast.

Orientation
The city stretches along the Têt River, but it's the Basse River running through the city centre that you're more likely to encounter. It has immaculate gardens along both banks. The old town, encircled by boulevards and largely pedestrianised, has its heart at Place de la Loge.

Information
Tourist Office The tourist office (☎ 68.66.30.30) in the Palais des Congrès at Place Armand Lanoux (at the north-eastern edge of Promenade des Plantanes) is open Monday to Saturday from 8.30 am to noon and 2 to 6.30 pm. From June to September it's open nonstop from 9 am to 7 pm (Sunday from 9 am to 1 pm and 3 to 7 pm). The staff will reserve a hotel room for no charge.

Copious amounts of information about the Roussillon region can be picked up from the Comité Départemental du Tourisme (CDT; ☎ 68.34.29.94) at 7 Quai de Lattre de Tassigny, open Monday to Saturday from 9 am to noon and 2 to 6.30 pm (9 am to 8 pm daily in July and August).

Money The Banque de France (☎ 68.51.39.33) at 3 Place Jean Payra is open weekdays from 8.45 am to noon and 1.30 to 3.30 pm.

Nearby there are several banks on Blvd Clemenceau. To change money outside of bank hours, try the exchange kiosk in the train station, which is open daily from 8 am to noon and 4.30 to 7 pm. In summer, the exchange bureau outside the tourist office is open weekdays from 10 am to 6 pm (1 pm on Sunday).

Post The main post office (☎ 68.56.00.66) on Rue du Docteur Zamenhoff is open weekdays from 8 am (9 am on Wednesday) to 7 pm, and Saturday until noon.

Perpignan's postcode is 66000.

Laundry The laundrette at 23 Rue du Maréchal Foch is open daily from 7 am to 8 pm. The more chaotic one on Place Jean Payra is open Monday to Saturday from 9 am to 7 pm.

ROUSSILLON

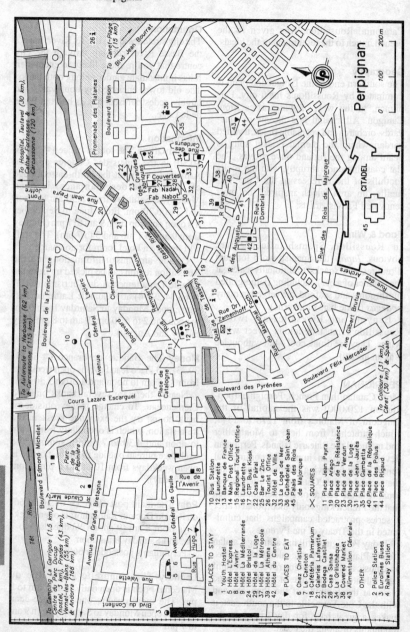

Perpignan

PLACES TO STAY

1 Youth Hostel
5 Hôtel L'Express
8 Hôtel Avenir
9 Hôtel La Méditerranée
24 Hôtel Bristol
29 Hôtel de la Loge
39 Hôtel La Métropole
42 Hôtel Athéna
42 Hôtel du Centre

PLACES TO EAT

6 Chez Christian
7 Le Caneton
18 Cafétéria Palmarium
21 Galeries Lafayette
28 Bodega Castillet
34 Casa Sansa
34 La Grillothèque
38 Covered Market
43 Alimentation Générale.

OTHER

2 Police Station
3 Eurolines Buses
4 Railway Station
10 Bus Station
12 Laundrette
13 Banque de France
14 Main Post Office
15 Regional Tourist Office
16 Laundrette
17 CTP Bus Kiosk
22 Casa Pairal
25 Bar Le Zinc
36 Tourist Office
33 La Loge de Mer
36 Cathédrale Saint Jean
45 Palais des Rois
   de Majorque

✕ SQUARES

11 Place Jean Payra
20 Place Arago
23 Place de la Résistance
23 Place de Verdun
30 Place de la Loge
31 Place Jean Jaurès
35 Place Gambetta
40 Place de la République
41 Place des Poilus
44 Place Rigaud

Place de la Loge

Place de la Loge is home to a few lovely old stone structures, including **La Loge de Mer**, a 14th-century building that housed the exchange and maritime tribunal but is now home to a hamburger joint. Next door, the **Hôtel de Ville**, in typical Roussillon style, has a pebbled façade.

Casa Pairal

This folklore museum (☎ 68.35.42.05) is in the 14th-century, red-brick, fortified town gate known as **Le Castillet** on Place de Verdun. Once a prison, it's the only vestige of Vauban's fortifications, which surrounded the city until the early 1900s, when they were demolished to make room for a growing population. The museum now houses bits and pieces of everything Catalan, including the traditional women's bonnets, a row of cow bells and B&W photos of the Procession de la Sanch (see Festivals).

Casa Pairal is open most of the year from 9 am to noon and 2 to 6 pm. Between 1 June and 15 September, its opening hours are 9.30 am to noon and 2.30 to 7 pm. Admission is free.

Palais des Rois de Majorque

The Palace of the Kings of Majorca (☎ 68.34.48.29) sits on a small hill, entered via Rue des Archers. Built in 1276 for the ruler of the newly founded kingdom, it was once surrounded by extensive fig and olive groves and a hunting reserve. These grounds were lost when the palace was enclosed by the formidable walls of the citadel.

Though it's undergoing renovation, you can wander through most of the palace. There's little to admire except two lovely chapels and the architecture, which has traces of Gothic highlighting the Romanesque courtyard and plenty of pebbled façades. It's open daily between 1 June and 30 September from 10 am to 6 pm. Between 1 October and 31 May hours are 9 am to 5 pm. Admission costs 10/5FF for adults/students.

Cathédrale Saint Jean

Squeezed into Place Gambetta and topped by a curious wrought-iron bell cage, Cathédrale Saint Jean has a flat, red-brick, pebbled façade. Inside, the single nave is illuminated by narrow rays of light coming through the stained glass and little else. This is great for viewing the windows but makes it difficult to see the splendid Catalan altarpieces.

A chapel on the south side of the cathedral contains a realistic wooden crucifix known as the *Devout Christ*, which portrays Jesus' suffering very realistically. To see that you have to drop a coin into the light box. The cathedral is open daily from 7.30 am to noon and 3 to 7 pm.

Festivals

On Good Friday an impressive religious parade of red-hooded people, La Procession de la Sanch, makes its way through the old town's streets. During the midsummer Fête de Saint Jean, a sacred flame is brought down from Mont Canigou amid much singing and dancing.

Places to Stay

Choice is plentiful with many decent hotels right in the centre. Some hotels (the tourist office has a list) offer a weekend package, whereby if you book a room on Friday or Saturday, you'll get the next night free. This is not available in July and August.

Camping *La Garrigole* (☎ 68.54.66.10) on 2 Rue Maurice Lévy, about 1.5 km west of the train station, charges 29/48FF for one/two people with a tent; parking is 4FF. It's closed in December. To get there, take bus No 2 from the station and get off at the Garrigole stop, from where it's a 150-metre stroll.

Hostels Behind the police station in the Parc de la Pépinière, the *Auberge de Jeunesse* (☎ 68.34.63.32) is a villa-like place at the end of Rue Claude Marty. It's near the river but unfortunately is separated from the water by a busy road. Beds in dorms or four-person rooms cost 57FF, including breakfast. If it's full, you can put your tent up in the small garden out the front for the same price. Kitchen facilities are available. The hostel is closed between 10 am and 6 pm and from mid-December to mid-January.

The calm *Centre du Parc Ducup* (☎ 68.54. 48.52), three km west on the Route de Prades, charges 105FF for bed and breakfast plus lunch or dinner for those under 25. It is closed from mid-December to mid-January. The Courriers Catalans bus to Prades stops 200 metres from the door.

Hotels – Train Station Area There's a string of hotels along Ave du Général de Gaulle. The *Hôtel L'Express* (☎ 68.34.89.96) at No 3 has small but functional rooms from 90FF, or 110FF with shower. Two-bed quads go for 180FF. About 400 metres further from the station, the friendly *La Méditerranée* (☎ 68.34.87.48) at No 62bis has nicer but still basic singles/doubles/triples, a few with private terrace, from 90/110/160FF. Use of the hall shower costs 15/25/35FF. Singles/doubles with shower start at 140/160FF.

The quiet *Hôtel Avenir* (☎ 68.34.20.30) at 11 Rue de l'Avenir is in the process of changing owners, but at last notice good-value singles/doubles were 75/110FF.

Hotels – City Centre There are plenty of affordable options here but parking is a problem. For Spanish ambience, head for the *Athena* (☎ 68.34.37.63) at 1 Rue Queya, where guests are greeted by a palm tree and pool. Although the rooms are not as plush as the décor, they are good value, starting at 120FF for basic rooms, 160FF with shower. The hotel has private parking (30FF). Close by, the *Hôtel du Centre* (☎ 68.34.39.69) at 26 Rue des Augustins (it's actually down the alley off here called Rue Dombrial) is a welcoming place with clean, quiet rooms from 100FF, or 130FF with shower. The hall shower is 15FF.

Close to Casa Pairal, the *Hôtel Bristol* (☎ 68.34.32.68) at 5 Rue des Grandes Fabriques is a cavernous place with basic singles/doubles from 105/125FF. Hall showers are 15FF. The *Hôtel La Métropole* (☎ 68.34.43.34) at 3 Rue des Cardeurs is

about the cheapest option in the city centre. It has an attractive foyer but the rooms are not nearly as appealing, though they're still good value at 90FF, including use of the hall shower. Rooms with shower and toilet cost 135FF and two-bed triples cost 175FF.

For a splurge, the *Hôtel de la Loge* (☎ 68. 34.54.84) at 1 Rue des Fabriques d'en Nabot, overlooking the Hôtel de Ville, has rustic rooms with everything you need from 250/300FF.

Places to Eat
Perpignan offers lots of opportunities to try out tapas in a bodega.

Restaurants In the city centre, *Casa Sansa* (☎ 68.34.60.35) on Rue des Fabriques d'en Nadal is a popular Catalan restaurant, but it's often full. *Bodega Castillet* (☎ 68.34.88.98), in the narrow Rue des Fabriques Couvertes one street up, is owned by the same people. The ambience is unmistakably Catalan: you can eat tapas (for around 25FF a plate) at the counter or at a table, and the whole room is occasionally flooded with the aroma of grilled calamares or caramelized desserts.

For substantial fare, *La Grillothèque* (☎ 68.34.06.99) at 7 Rue des Cardeurs has a 60FF *menu* and salads from 36FF. *Cafétéria Palmarium* (☎ 68.34.51.31) on Place Arago is a large self-service place open until 9.30 pm.

The restaurants facing the train station are surprisingly pricey. Better are those a block away along Ave du Général de Gaulle, such as *Chez Christian* (☎ 68.34.60.40) at No 11 which has a good-value *menu* for 48FF. Close by, *Le Caneton* on Rue Victor Hugo must be one of the cheapest 'restaurants' in France. Little more than a room in a private house, it is very simple with absolutely no frills, but the 30FF *menu* will fill you up.

Self-Catering *Food markets* are held every morning on Place des Poilus, and in the covered hall on Place de la République from 7 am to 1 pm and 4 to 7.30 pm daily except Monday. On Saturday mornings, market gardeners bring their produce to Place Rigaud.

The *Galeries Lafayette* on Place de la

Résistance has a basement grocery section that's open Monday to Saturday from 8.30 am to 7.30 pm. On Sunday mornings it's no problem to find shops open around Place de la République. If you're really stuck, the little *Alimentation Générale* on Place Rigaud is open daily (except Monday) from 8 am to 9.30 pm; it's closed between 1 and 7 pm on weekends. Near the station there are a few *épiceries* along Ave Général de Gaulle.

Entertainment

On certain summer evenings (check with the tourist office), a band sets up on Place de Verdun and the sardane is danced until late. The terraces on Place de la Loge are the main nightlife hang-outs. *Bar Le Zinc* on Rue des Grandes Fabriques is a cocktail bar with a variety of beers.

Getting There & Away

Train Perpignan's small train station (☎ 68. 35.50.50 for information) is the last major stop before entering Spain at Cerbère. It's at the end of Ave Général de Gaulle, about two km to the tourist office (take bus No 3 to the Palais des Congrès stop). The train information office is open Monday to Saturday from 8 am to 6.30 pm; the station itself is open from 4 am to 12.30 am.

Major destinations include Paris (389FF; 10 hours; several daily), Montpellier (102FF; two hours; hourly), Carcassonne (80FF; 1½ hours; 12 a day) via Narbonne, and Barcelona, Spain (90FF; 3½ hours; 10 a day). Closer to home are Collioure (24FF; 20 minutes; hourly) and Prades (50FF; 40 minutes; seven a day).

The closest you can get to Andorra by train is Latour de Carol (110FF; 3½ hours; six a day). For information on transport from there to Andorra-la-Vella, see Getting There & Away in the Andorra chapter.

Bus Several companies, including Les Courriers Catalans, are based at the bus station (☎ 68.35.29.02) on Ave du Général Leclerc.

Bus No 35 runs to Céret (28FF; 40 minutes; 14 a day) and No 44 to Collioure

(26FF; 40 minutes; seven a day). No 20 goes to Vernet-les-Bains (43FF; 1½ hours, six a day), though with some services you have to change to a connecting bus in Villefranche.

To get to Andorra, you have to change buses at Latour de Carol (69FF; four hours; leaves at 8 am) – see Getting There & Away in the Andorra chapter.

Eurolines buses leave from the office (☎ 68.34.11.46) to the left as you exit the train station. It's open daily from 7.45 to 11.45 am and 2 to 6 pm (4 pm on Sunday). Major destinations include Barcelona (90FF; three hours; two buses a day) and London (590FF; 20 hours; four a week). People under 26 get a discount.

Car ADA can be contacted on ☎ 68.35. 69.80. Eurorent (☎ 68.56.96.96; fax 68.56. 65.42) is at 2 Blvd des Pyrénées.

Getting Around

Local buses are run by CTP, which has an information kiosk (☎ 68.61.01.13) on Place Arago. Buses leave from several hubs: the train station, Place Arago or along Promenade des Platanes. They run until about 8 pm. Single tickets cost 6FF and a six-ticket carnet is 28FF. For a taxi, call ☎ 68.35.15.15.

AROUND PERPIGNAN
Coastal Beaches

East of Perpignan is the southernmost stretch of the monotonous Languedoc-Roussillon coast. The nearest beach is **Canet-Plage**, 15 km away, connected by bus No 1 from Promenade des Platanes (12FF one way). Nudists are tolerated south of Torreilles (which is north of Canet) and at Saint Cyprien to the south. Two buses a day link the whole coast from Port Barcarès to Cerbère on the Spanish border.

Côte Vermeille

Near the Spanish border is the Côte Vermeille (Vermilion Coast, named after the red colour of its soil), which starts where the Pyrenees foothills reach the sea. Set against a backdrop of vineyards, this coastline is riddled with small, rocky bays and little ports that once lived from sardine fishing but now have economies based on tourism.

One such port is the picturesque **Collioure**, whose small harbour is filled with brightly coloured fishing boats. Known to the Phoenicians and once the port of Perpignan, it found fame early this century when it inspired the Fauvist art of Matisse and Dérain. The port's castle was the summer residence of the kings of Majorca. The tourist office (☎ 68.82.15.47) at Place de la Mairie on the waterfront can give you all the details.

For information on getting to Collioure, see Bus under Perpignan's Getting There & Away section.

Cathar Fortresses

The castles of Quéribus and Peyrepertuse (see Around Carcassonne), 36 km and 47 km respectively north-west of Perpignan, are a worthwhile excursion. From Perpignan's bus station, the No 10 bus towards Quillan (two a day) will drop you off at the village of Maury (30FF). From here it's four km to Quéribus and about 15 km to Peyrepertuse.

Tautavel

Thirty km north-west of Perpignan, the village of Tautavel is home to what seems to be Europe's oldest known skull. Thought to be 450,000 years old, it can be viewed in the **Musée de la Préhistoire** (☎ 68.29.07.76) along with all the other prehistoric items found in the Arago cave, which is a few km north of town. The museum is open daily from 10 am to 12.30 pm and 2 to 6.30 pm (10 am to 10 pm in July and August). Entry is 20/10FF for adults/children.

Unfortunately, no buses pass this village except to pick up school children. To get there, take bus No 10 towards Quillan and get off at the crossroads two km after the village of Estagel (22FF; 30 minutes; five a day). From here, it's a six-km walk or hitch.

Vernet-les-Bains

A thermal town long beloved by elderly Brits, Vernet-les-Bains (altitude 650 metres) is the best base for climbing **Mont Canigou** (2784 metres), the easternmost peak in the Pyrenees. Three tracks wind up from Vernet; if you go up one side and down the other, you're in for a 30-km hike that will take about 12 hours. From Marialles, 10 km further up one of the tracks (accessible by car), it's a seven-hour return hike. The lazy or rich can take a jeep (150FF) from Vernet to Les Cortalets (2175 metres) and walk the rest of the way (three hours return).

On each of the three tracks is a *refuge* where you can stay overnight for free. At Les Cortalets there's a *chalet* (62FF a night) and a *gîte d'étape* (32FF). *Les Cents Randonnées*, a topographical guide of the eastern Pyrenees, gives full details. It's available at the Vernet tourist office or the CDT in Perpignan.

Vernet, 55 km west of Perpignan, is six km off the N116, which goes to the Spanish border and Puigcerdà. To get there by bus from Perpignan, see Getting There & Away in the Perpignan section. You can also take the train from Perpignan to Prades, from where you can pick up the bus for the last 20 minutes of the trip.

Céret

Lovers of cubist art will be attracted to Céret, a town 30 km south-west of Perpignan, which is famous for its **Musée d'Art Moderne** (☎ 68.87.27.76) on Rue Jean Parayre. It specialises in the works of artists who lived and worked in the region at the beginning of this century, including Matisse, Braque and Jacob, and especially Picasso. The museum is open from 10 am to 6 pm daily except Tuesday (daily until 7 pm between July and September). See the Perpignan Getting There & Away section for bus details.

Corsica

Corsica is the most mountainous and geographically varied of all the islands of the Mediterranean. Because of its extraordinarily diverse landscape and its modest size (only 8720 sq km), it in many ways resembles a miniature continent.

Corsica's 1000 km of coastline, lapped by the transluscent, turquoise waters of the Mediterranean, includes vertiginous cliffs, flatland marshes and countless km of fine-sand beaches. Only a few tens of km inland, soaring granite mountains sparkle white with snow until well into summer. In between, the gentle (and not so gentle) hills support a low covering of trees and bushes known as the maquis. This typically Corsican form of vegetation, which provides many of the spices used in traditional island cooking, long sheltered outlaws, bandits, revolutionaries and – during WW II – fighters of the French Resistance, who themselves became known as 'maquis'. Corsica even has an uninhabited desert area, the Désert des Agriates, on the north coast.

For the visitor, Corsica – known as Corse in French and Corsica in both Corsican and Italian – offers wonderful beaches, breathtaking scenery, superb hiking trails and a welcoming ambience suffused with the island's distinctive culture, language, cuisine and way of life.

Facts about the Region

History

Corsica's human habitation goes back at least 8000 years. A number of important prehistoric sites – the most impressive of which is Filitosa – have been excavated and opened to visitors.

The Phocaeans (Greeks from Asia Minor), who arrived in the 6th century BC and introduced olive trees, grapevines and cereal crops, were followed by other seafaring

Mediterranean nations: the Etruscans, the Carthaginians and the Romans. The Roman philosopher, statesman and orator Seneca (4 BC to 65 AD) was banished to Corsica from 41 to 49 AD after Emperor Claudius charged him with committing adultery with a princess who happened to be the emperor's niece.

After six relatively peaceful centuries, during which Corsica's culture and language underwent a slow process of Latinisation, the island was invaded in the 5th and 6th centuries by the Vandals, the Ostrogoths, the Byzantines and then the Lombards, all of whom brought anarchy and impoverishment. In the 8th century the Lombards were thrown out by the Franks, but before long the Frankish king Pepin III (Pepin the Short, the son of Charles Martel) and his son Charlemagne ceded the island to the papacy. Muslim raiders (often referred to as Saracens) from North Africa attacked the Corsican coast repeatedly during the 8th, 9th and 10th centuries and occupied parts of the island for significant periods.

In 1077 Pope Gregory VII gave the island to the bishop of the Italian city-state of Pisa,

Corsica
(Corse)

who had numerous Romanesque churches built by architects and stonemasons brought from Tuscany. But Pisan supremacy was contested – and in 1284 ended – by Pisa's commercial rival, Genoa. In the early 15th century, the Genoese managed to defeat the Aragonese, who had been given Corsica and Sardinia by Pope Boniface VIII in 1297.

In the mid-15th century Genoa handed over governance of Corsica – beset at the time by near anarchy, in part because of Muslim raids on coastal areas – to the Office de Saint Georges (also known as the Banque de Saint Georges), a powerful financial organisation with its own army. To prevent seaborne raids from North Africa, the office built a massive early-warning and defence system that included hilltop watchtowers all along the coast (many of which can be seen to this day) and a number of citadels.

On a number of occasions, Corsican discontent with Genoese rule expressed itself in open revolt. In the 1560s one such uprising was led by Sampiero Corso, a Corsican from Bastelica who sought to free Corsica from Genoese rule by enlisting the help of the French. An especially widespread rebellion, later known as the War of Independence, broke out in 1729.

Around the same time, Westphalian adventurer Baron Theodor von Neuhof (1694-1756) convinced a group of Corsican prisoners in Genoa that if they made him their king he would free their island. He talked some Greek and Jewish traders in Tunis into providing him with funding and supplies and in 1736, after landing on the island, he was in fact crowned Theodore I, King of Corsica. But the new king had only managed to mint some coins and bestow a few titles on friends before the kingdom's military fortunes turned and a civil war broke out, prompting him to flee the island.

In 1755, after 25 years of intermittent warfare, the Corsicans declared their island independent. They were led by the extraordinary Pasquale Paoli (Pascal Paoli in French, 1725-1807), under whose enlightened rule they set up a National Assembly and adopted the most democratic constitution in Europe. The Corsicans chose Corte as their capital, established a navy, set up a system of justice to replace the vendetta, founded a school system and established a university. But in 1768 the Genoese ceded Corsica (over which they had no effective control) to their ally the French king Louis XV, whose troops defeated Paoli's army in 1769. The island then became a province of France.

France has ruled Corsica ever since – except for two brief periods. From 1794 to 1796, Paoli, who had lived in England for 20 years before returning home after the Revolution, joined forces with the British navy to establish a short-lived Corsican kingdom under British auspices. The second period of non-French rule came during WW II, when Corsica was occupied by German and Italian troops – Mussolini had long claimed that Corsica belonged to Italy. Because of the tenacity of the maquis (partisans), the ratio of Axis soldiers to Corsican civilians, children included, was one to two. In late 1943, thanks to the maquis and Free French forces landed by submarine, Corsica became the first French *département* to be liberated.

Corsica's most famous native son is Napoleon Bonaparte, emperor of the French (1805-15) and – around 1810 – ruler of much of Europe. One of the most celebrated personages in all of Western history, his rule had a tremendous effect on French and Western European jurisprudence, government, military organisation and education. But his abiding passion was for military conquest, and his campaign to establish French hegemony over Europe caused almost two decades of constant warfare. Napoleon was born in Ajaccio on 15 August 1769, the year the island became part of France, and left at the age of nine to study on the mainland. He visited Corsica for the last time in 1799, when he stopped off for a week on his way back from defeat in Egypt and Ottoman Palestine.

Vendettas Until the 20th century, and even up until WW II, Corsica was notorious for its bitter vendettas (blood feuds). When a clan felt that one of its number had been wronged, it would – to safeguard its honour and enforce a rough sort of justice – go out and kill a member of the clan held responsible. During the early 19th century, hundreds of people died each year in vendetta attacks.

Geography

Corsica (8720 sq km), the fourth-largest island in the Mediterranean after Sicily, Sardinia and Cyprus, is 183 km long (from north to south) and 83 km across at its widest point. Its coasts are 170 km south-east of France's Côte d'Azur, 360 km east-south-east of Marseille, 83 km from Italy's west coast and 450 km east of northern Spain. On the south, it is separated from the Italian island of Sardinia (Sardaigne in French) by the 12-km-wide Strait of Bonifacio. Because of its position on major maritime trade routes and between competing Mediterranean powers, Corsica has long been of great strategic and commerical importance.

Considering its size, Corsica has an incredibly varied landscape. The island is divided into two distinct geographic regions by the *sillon central*, a lowland area (it has no peaks over 700 metres) running northwest to south-east from l'Île Rousse via Corte to Solenzara. The area south-west of this line – about two-thirds of the island – is dominated by a range of soaring granite mountains, 20 of which have peaks over 2000 metres above sea level. Corsica's highest mountain is the 2706-metre-high Monte Cinto, whose summit is a mere 25 km south-east of the coastal town of Calvi. Since these summits, which are covered with snow for most of the year, are only an hour's drive from the beach, you can easily take refuge in the cool mountains if you tire of the heat along the coast.

The section of Corsica north of the depression, including the Castagniccia region and Cap Corse, is also an upland area, but the schist mountains here are much younger and not as high. The highest point in this part of Corsica is Monte San Petrone, whose summit is 1767 metres above sea level.

Corsica has slightly more than 1000 km of coastline, much of which – especially on the west coast – is a rugged mixture of gulfs, capes, coves and cliffs interspersed with fine- sand beaches. A partly marshy alluvial plain, cleared of malaria by the US Army after WW II, runs along the east coast between Bastia and Solenzara. Since the eradication of malaria (accomplished using the 'wonder pesticide' DDT), much of this area – the only truly flat part of the whole island – has been given over to agriculture. At the extreme southern tip of the island (around Bonifacio), there is a 60-sq-km limestone plateau.

In 1791 the Convention in Paris divided Corsica into two départements with Bastia (the island's long-time Genoese capital) and Ajaccio as prefectures. In 1811 Napoleon – reportedly at his mother's request – personally ordered that Corsica become a single département with his hometown of Ajaccio as its capital. In the mid-1970s, the island was redivided into two départements: Corse-du-Sud (Southern Corsica), with its prefecture at Ajaccio; and Haute-Corse (Upper Corsica), whose prefecture is Bastia. This arrangement has done much to mellow the rivalry between Corsica's two largest towns. The border between the two départements runs along a string of mountain summits about 20 km south-west of a line running from Calvi via Corte to Solenzara.

Climate

Corsica's weather varies widely according to latitude and altitude. Obviously, the higher the elevation, the cooler it is, but unlike anywhere else in Europe, the average temperature gets warmer as you move from south to north. In other words, although Ajaccio gets more hours of sunlight a year than any other place in France (2900 hours per annum), Bastia is, on average, warmer.

Along the coast and in low-lying areas, the warm Mediterranean climate – which can get scorchingly hot and dry in summer – is moderated by the sea and its breezes, especially in spring and autumn. Above 1200 metres, the climate is alpine, with cool temperatures even in summer and enough snow in winter to render many roads periodically impassable.

The island receives an average of 900 mm of precipitation a year, with increasing rainfall as you move from south to north, from west to east (another anomaly) and from coastal areas towards the centre of the island. Most of this generous dose of rain, however, falls from November to April, leaving the rivers practically dry between June and October.

Flora

Corsica's most famous form of vegetation is the maquis, an aromatic undergrowth of arbutus, cistus, lavender, laurel, myrtle, rosemary, thyme and various other shrubs and trees. During the spring, it produces a lovely fragrance that wafts far offshore. During the long dry season, the maquis become highly flammable and pose a serious fire danger.

About one-fifth of Corsica is forested. The island's most majestic tree is the laricio pine (*pin laricio*), which can live for 600 years and reach a height of 60 metres. One of the tallest trees in Europe, its trunk is as straight as a telephone pole and has been used to fashion the masts of ships since Roman times. Cork oaks (*chênes-lièges*), which as their name suggests are where cork comes from, are most numerous around Porto Vecchio. While on the tree, cork (the tree's outer bark, made up of flexible, air-filled cells) protects the inner bark from the ravages of the sun and wind. It can be harvested once every eight to 12 years, the time it takes for a new layer of sufficient thickness to grow back. Despite various synthetic substitutes invented in recent years, cork – which is one-fifth the weight of water – still makes the most effective stopper for wine bottles.

Chestnut trees (*châtaigniers*), once an important source of the island's food, cover several hundred sq km of the island, especially in the Castagniccia region.

Government

Despite having spent only 14 years as a self-governing country, the people of Corsica have retained a fiercely independent streak. Though few Corsicans support the Front de Libération Nationale de la Corse (FLNC) – whose initials are spraypainted all over the island, especially on road signs – or other militant separatist organisations, they remain very proud of their language, culture and traditions. Many islanders are concerned by touristic overdevelopment, which threatens to ruin parts of the coast. In 1982 Corsica became the first region in France to have its own elected Regional Assembly.

Economy

Corsica's economy is based mostly on tourism. Its main exports are wine, cheese, olive oil and citrus fruit.

Population

Corsica's population is about 250,000, only about 50% more than two centuries ago. About 40% of the island's inhabitants live in either Ajaccio or Bastia.

Each year, around 2000 Corsicans, including many of the more dynamic young people, continue a long tradition of emigration and leave the island in search of better opportunities. Corsicans are prominent in the French police and military, as these jobs provide pensions that make it possible for emigrants to return to the island when they retire.

During WW I, Corsica lost an astounding 14,000 men (5% of the total population), more than any other French département. In the 1950s and early 1960s, almost 20,000 Corsicans who had emigrated to French-ruled North Africa and Indochina moved back to Corsica.

Language

Although virtually everyone on the island speaks French, many Corsicans still use their rich and almost exclusively oral language, Corsu (Corsican) – a Romance tongue similar in many ways to Italian – at home, in cafés and in the workplace. There are variations in vocabulary and pronunciation between the south-west and the north-east, in part because the latter was more influenced by Tuscan. Many place names, whose

French or Italian equivalents terminate with an 'o', end with a 'u' in Corsu.

After the arrival of the Romans in the 3rd century BC, the local language slowly became Latinised. Beginning in the 9th century, it absorbed a great deal from Tuscan, which was used for official documents by the Pisans, Genoese and even the French until the mid-19th century. Church business was conducted in Italian until the early 20th century. Today, Corsu constitutes an important component of Corsican identity, and many people – especially at the university in Corte – are working to ensure its survival. Nationalist groups demand that the study of Corsican in school be made mandatory; at present it's optional.

Facts for the Visitor

Costs

Even during the off season, hotels, camping grounds and land transport are perhaps 40% more expensive on Corsica than on the mainland. Restaurant *menus* are also dearer, with almost nothing under 65FF. Prices for accommodation, car rental, etc rise substantially (in some cases by 200%!) from July to mid-September.

When to Go

The best time of year to visit Corsica is during May and June, when the island is generally sunny, the wildflowers are in bloom and there aren't too many tourists around. Earlier in the spring, particularly before Easter, there are almost no tourists, but neither is there much of a tourist infrastructure, since many hotels, camping grounds and restaurants operate only seasonally and stay closed until Easter or even later. September and October are also good months in which to visit, though the countryside is less green than in the spring and the days are short. Despite its southerly latitude, Corsica has several resorts offering cross-country and even downhill skiing when there's enough snow (see Skiing under Activities).

During July and August, and especially between mid-July and mid-August, Corsica is overrun with holidaymakers, mostly Germans and Italians. Indeed, almost half of the more than one million tourists who come to Corsica each year do so during July and August. As a result, hotel rooms, space in camping grounds and even places on the ferries (especially for cars) become extremely expensive – if you can even find a spot. Most people who come during this period make reservations several months in advance.

Business Hours

Most shops, including those that sell food, are closed from noon or 12.30 pm to 2.30 or 3 pm. Many hotels, restaurants and shops that cater to the tourist trade are closed from November until March or April.

Festivals

Corsica's distinctive folk traditions are alive and well, at least as far as religious festivals and processions are concerned. Some of the larger processions – in which hooded penitents re-enact the Passion – are held on Maundy Thursday and Good Friday, the Thursday and Friday of the week before Easter (Holy Week). Corte has processions on both Maundy Thursday and Good Friday, as does Erbalunga, a coastal village 10 km north of Bastia. Calvi has a ceremony on Maundy Thursday, while Sartène has a special commemoration on the eve of Good Friday (see the Sartène section).

Assumption Day is especially lively in Ajaccio, where religious fervour melds with enthusiasm for Napoleon Bonaparte – born in Ajaccio on Assumption Day in 1769 – to make 15 August the biggest celebration of the whole year.

Books

The *Blue Guide to Corsica* by Roland Gant, a slim, paperback volume published in London by A & C Black and in New York by WW Norton, has lots of detailed information about the island. Michelin's Guide Vert (Green Guide) series includes a volume on Corsica but it is available only in French, Italian and German. Guides Bleus (Hachette) also publishes a French-language guide, *Corse*, to Corsica.

Granite Island: A Portrait of Corsica by Dorothy Carrington (Penguin, 1984, paperback), is perhaps the best account of Corsica's history and people. *Corsica – A Traveller's Guide* (London, John Murray, 1988) by John Lowe, also available in paperback, is an eminently readable and informative account of the author's travels around the island in 1963 and 1986.

For details on books of interest to hikers and cyclists, see the following Hiking and Cycling sections under Activities.

Dangers & Annoyances

When Corsica makes the headlines, it's usually because nationalist militants seeking Corsican independence have engaged in some act of violence, such as bombing a public building, robbing a bank or blowing up a vacant holiday villa. But such attacks, many of which are carried out by the largest separatist organisation, the FLNC, are *not* targeted at tourists, and there is no reason for visitors to the island to fear for their safety.

Indirectly, however, visitors will probably be slightly inconvenienced by the activities of the militants. Drivers may get lost (or at least confused) on occasion, since road signs – especially those written in French (rather than Corsican) – are a favourite target of nationalist spraypaint artists. And to get into a bank, you may have to leave all your belongings (including your keys) in a locker before passing through a metal detection chamber.

Note that ferry services between France and Corsica are not infrequently suspended by strikes.

Activities

Parc Naturel Régional de Corse The Corsican Regional Park, established in 1972, covers about 2500 sq km (almost a third of the island) and includes some of Corsica's highest peaks and most beautiful forest areas. For more information, contact the Informations Randonnées office in Ajaccio (see Regional Park Office under Information in the Ajaccio section), whose mailing address is Rue Général Fiorella, Boîte Postale 417, 20184 Ajaccio CEDEX.

Hiking Corsica's superb hiking trails are renowned among serious hikers for their challenging itineraries and spectacular scenery. Because of snow, some routes are open for only a few months a year. Gîtes d'étape and *refuges* provide hikers with places to stay (see Gîtes under Accommodation in this section). Food can be purchased in villages along the way. Didier Richard publishes 1:50,000 scale hiking maps of the island.

The legendary GR20, also known as Fra Li Monti (literally, between the mountains), stretches over 160 km from Calenzana (10 km south-east of Calvi) to Conca (20 km north of Porto Vecchio). Since it follows the island's 'continental divide', much of the route is above 2000 metres. Walking the entire length of the trail, segments of which are very difficult, takes at least two weeks. The GR20 is passable only from mid-June to October. From January to April accomplished cross-country skiers can follow part of the GR20 route.

Three Mare a Mare (Sea to Sea) trails cross the island from west to east. In the south, the Mare a Mare Sud trail, which is passable throughout the year, allows you to walk from Propriano to Porto Vecchio in about five days. In the centre of the island, the seven-day Mare a Mare Centre links La Crociata (about 25 km south of Ajaccio) with Ghisonnaccia; it is open from about May to November. The Mare a Mare Nord, which connects Cargèse with Moriani (40 km south of Bastia), takes seven to 10 days (depending on your route) and is passable only from about May to November. The Mare e Monti (Sea & Mountains) trail from Cargèse to Calenzana, via Évisa, Ota, Girolata and Galéria, takes about 10 days. It is open all year but is at its best in spring and autumn.

CORSICA

In addition to these long-distance trails, certain areas offer *sentiers de pays* (regional footpaths), perfect for day hikes.

Some 600 km of trails, including the GR20, are covered in *Walks in Corsica* (100FF), an invaluable topoguide translated into English by Harry Pretty & Helen McPhail and published in London by Robertson McCarta. It is based on the topoguides to Corsica published by the Fédération Française de la Randonnée Pédestre. *Walks in Corsica* is available in many Corsican bookshops and the Regional Park office in Ajaccio.

Cycling If you're planning on mountain biking (often a strenuous activity on Corsica) and can read French, you may want to pick up *Corse du Nord* and/or *Corse du Sud*, two of the volumes in Didier Richard's Les Guides VTT series. Both are by Charles Pujos and are available at larger Corsican bookshops. Bicycles can be brought to Corsica by ferry for a small fee and can be transported on the trains for 55FF a ride, regardless of distance.

Skiing In good years, downhill skiing is possible in February and March and sometimes earlier or later, depending on the weather. In bad years, there may not be enough snow to ski at all.

Ski stations offering downhill skiing include:

Haut Asco (1450 to 1850 metres; ☎ 95.47.84.12)
Ghisoni (1580 to 1800 metres; ☎ 95.57.61.28)
Vergio (1400 to 1800 metres; ☎ 95.48.00.01)
Bastelica (1600 to 1850 metres; ☎ 95.28.70.71).

Cross-country skiing centres include Vergio, Bastelica, Évisa (☎ 95.26.20.09), Quenza (☎ 95.78.64.79, 95.78.63.39) and Zicavo (☎ 95.24.40.05).

Accommodation

Camping There are lots of camping grounds around Corsica, but almost all of them close during the colder half of the year, and some

are open only from June to September. Charges are quite a bit higher than on the mainland. Camping outside of recognised camping areas *(camping sauvage)* is strictly prohibited, in part because of the danger of fires. However, people have been known to sleep on the beach in summer. In remote areas, hikers are authorised to bivouac around *refuges*.

Hostels Corsica's only youth hostels are in Calvi and Ota (near Porto).

Gîtes Depending on how far away the beach is, *gîtes ruraux* (country cottages) with shower and toilet for two or more people can be rented for 900 to 2000FF a week. From June to September, prices are considerably higher, and they reach 1500 to 3500FF a week in August, when most places are booked up months in advance. *Chambres d'hôte* (B&Bs) are available by the night, starting at about 200FF for two, including breakfast.

Gîtes de France's Corsican bureau at 24 Blvd Dominique Paoli in Ajaccio (postcode 20000) has two sections: Loisirs Accueil (☎ 95.22.70.79; fax 95.20.43.36) and Relais des Gîtes Ruraux (☎ 95.20.51.34). Reservations for gîtes ruraux (one week minimum stay) can be booked by phone or in writing through Loisirs Accueil, which acts as a liaison between owners and renters. Relais des Gîtes Ruraux does not make reservations but does provide information about gîtes d'étape, chambres d'hôte and gîtes ruraux not available through Loisirs Accueil. To make bookings, you have to contact the owner yourself; the relevant details and addresses are available in the booklet *Vacances en Gîtes de France – Corse*, which the Relais can send you for a fee of about 40FF. Both offices are open Monday to Friday from 8 am to noon and 2 to 6 pm (5 pm on Friday).

Hikers can take advantage of an excellent network of gîtes d'étape (which accept reservations) and *refuges* (which don't). In general, both are indicated on hiking maps.

For details, contact the Informations Randonnées office in Ajaccio (see Regional Park Office under Information in the Ajaccio section) or one of the larger tourist offices.

Hotels Hotel rooms in Corsica are considerably more expensive than on the mainland. For one of the rare cheap doubles without shower or toilet, virtually nothing is available for less than 120FF. To make matters worse, hotel standards in Ajaccio and Bastia are generally quite dismal, especially at the three-star places. In terms of price and quality, some of the best deals are in the 150 to 250FF-a-night range. On the brighter side, Corsican hotels do not charge for hall showers.

In July and August, many hotels raise their tariffs considerably (in some cases by over 200%!) and may require that you take at least *demi-pension*, but unless you make reservations months in advance (or arrive early in the morning *and* get lucky) you probably won't have the opportunity to pay them – except, perhaps, at four-star places that were exorbitant to begin with. On the other hand, wintertime visitors will find that outside of Bastia, Ajaccio and Corte, the vast majority of hotels shut down completely between November and Easter. Where possible, the text includes hotels that stay open all year and specifies the months of operation for those that don't.

Food & Drinks

The maquis provide many of the spices, aromatic herbs and berries with which Corsican cuisine – basically simple, solid peasant fare – is flavoured, often with great vigour. Picnickers will find many Corsican foods (meats, cheeses, wines, etc) readily available in grocery stores and supermarkets. Shopkeepers will happily recommend personal favourites.

Because of Corsica's geography, mutton, goat and wild boar have historically been more plentiful than beef. The island is known for its *charcuterie* (pork-based sausages and salamis) and *prissutu* (prosciutto, ie cured ham). Tripe, prepared from the stomach lining of a sheep, is a common dish. Along the coast, fish and shellfish are plentiful and are often made into *aziminu* (bouillabaisse, ie fish soup). Trout, found in mountains streams, is usually served grilled. Traditionally, Corsicans are also fond of blackbird (*merle*), the local specimens of which are said to be particularly tasty because they feed on the fruit of the maquis (olives, juniper berries, etc).

Also popular are pasta and ravioli dishes similar to those found across the sea in Italy. These are sometimes prepared with the most noteworthy of Corsica's cheeses, *brocciu*, which is made from a mixture of either goat or sheep's whey and milk. *Falculella*, a kind of cheesecake, is made with brocciu. Other native cheeses include Niolo, Calenzana and Venaco. Something like one-tenth of the Roquefort produced on the mainland is made from sheep's milk brought all the way from Corsica. Chestnut flour is used to make a number of cakes and pastries, though chestnuts are no longer the staple they once were.

Corsica has long produced honey and olives; the latter are often harvested by suspending nets under the trees to catch the ripe, black olives as they drop. Grape vines grow in many areas, especially on Cap Corse (known for its white wines), along the east coast (the Porto Vecchio area also produces whites), in the vicinity of Ajaccio (known for its reds) and in the area around Sartène and Olmeto (whose speciality is also red wine). Among aperitifs, pastis is the most popular. A favourite locally distilled after-dinner drink is *cédratine*, a sweet, syrupy liqueur made from the *cédrat* (citron), a lemon-like fruit which makes excellent jellies and candied fruit.

Things to Buy

In recent years, effort have been made to revive Corsican handicrafts, such as stoneware, jewellery, dolls and woodcarvings. Food products for which the island is known include honey, olive oil, spices from the maquis, fruit preserves, cheeses, sausages and salami.

CORSICA

Getting There & Away

Air

Corsica's four main airports – at Ajaccio, Bastia, Figari (near Bonifacio) and Calvi – are linked with Paris, Nice and France's other large metropolitan areas as well as cities elsewhere in Europe. Airlines serving Corsica include Air Inter, Air France, Corse Méditerranée, TAT and Kyrnair; to avoid competition *(quelle horreur!)*, the French government has arranged for different routes to be handled by different carriers. Reservations and air tickets for travel to Corsica are available from almost all travel agents in France and many travel agents elsewhere in the world.

Flights to Corsica from Nice cost 393FF, but people under 25 or over 60 may qualify for a 273FF fare. Although the regular one-way fare from Paris is 1195FF, charters and certain discounted tickets cost as little as 500FF one way depending on when you go, whether you are young (or old) enough, if you're buying a return ticket, etc. If you qualify for a heavily discounted fare, flying from Paris to Corsica will probably cost much less, and take much less time, than taking the train and then a ferry. You might also consider flying one way and going by sea and overland in the other.

Boat

During the summer – especially from mid-July to mid-August – reservations for vehicles and couchettes on *all* routes must be made well in advance (several *months* in advance for the most popular sailings). Strikes frequently cut all ferry links between Corsica and the mainland with little or no warning, sometimes for weeks at at time.

To/From Mainland France Car and passenger ferry services between the French mainland (Nice, Marseille and Toulon) and Corsica (Ajaccio, Bastia, Calvi, l'Île Rousse and Propriano) are handled by the state-owned Société Nationale Maritime Corse-Méditerranée (SNCM; ☎ 93.13.66.66 in Nice, 91.56.30.10 in Marseille). SNCM's modern car ferries are not exactly luxury liners, but they are a fairly classy operation, with comfortable sleeping berths, lounges, places to eat and lots of deck space. The trip betweeen Nice and Bastia takes 6½ hours for a daytime crossing and 12 hours at night, when the cruising speed is reduced so passengers have time to sleep and so the boat docks at 7 or 8 am (the perfect time to begin looking for a hotel). To/from Marseille, count on 10½ to 12 hours of sailing time.

In summer there are four or five runs a day between Corsica and the mainland. In winter, service is much less frequent, with about one ferry a day to/from one of the three ports with off-season services: Ajaccio, Bastia and l'Île Rousse. In other words, unless you plan your trip around the ferry schedule, you could find yourself either waiting several days for the next boat or travelling to the other side of the island to catch a ferry that fits in with your plans. Reservations and ticketing can be organised through many French travel agents, who can also supply details on tariffs and schedules.

The basic deck-class fare for one-way passage to the Corsican port of your choice is 230FF from Nice and 255FF from either Marseille or Toulon. This sum entitles you to sit in the kind of *fauteuil* (armchair) you find on trains, not a great place for a good night's sleep. On overnight runs, the cheapest couchette costs only 75FF extra, less than most hotel beds.

People aged 12 to 25 qualify for a discount of about 25%. The basic one-way youth fare is 160FF on all sailings between Corsica and Nice. For travel to/from Marseille and Toulon, the 180FF one-way youth fare is available only during blue periods (approximately November to April) and perhaps white periods (May to September except for parts of July, August and early September). Children under 12 pay the *tarif enfant*, which is about 45% less than the adult fare. People over 60 get 45% off the full fare. Student discounts apply only if you're a resident of Corsica.

Transporting a small car costs at least 200FF during blue periods, 380FF during white periods and 550FF during red periods (parts of July, August and early September). Motorcycles over 100 cc cost about 30% less than small cars, and bicycles cost 78FF.

If you're on one of the ferries whose cabin doors have electronic combination locks, the combination will appear on your boarding card. If you have an upper bunk and it's fastened to the wall, you'll have to find a member of the crew equipped with a special key to unlatch it.

To/From Italy Corsica Ferries (☎ 95.31.18.09, fax 95.32.14.71 in Bastia; ☎ 010-593301/5531000 in Genoa; ☎ 0586-881380/ 886328 in Livorno) has year-round car ferry service to Bastia from Genoa (Gênes in French, Genova in Italian), La Spezia and Livorno (Livourne in French). Except for overnight runs, the crossing takes four to five hours. From mid- May to mid-September the company also runs ferries from Genoa to Ajaccio and Calvi. Depending on which route you take and when you travel, individuals pay 145 to 200FF. Small cars cost between 205 and 565FF each way. Taking your dog along will set you back 55FF. Couchettes are available.

From mid-April to October, Mobylines (☎ 95.31.46.29, fax 95.32.17.94 in Bastia; ☎ 0586-890325/891326 in Livorno), formerly known as Navarma, links Bastia with the Italian ports of La Spezia and Livorno (four to five hours). From early or mid-June to August, Mobylines' car ferries also link Bastia with Genoa (six hours), Piombino and Porto Santo Stefano. Depending on when you travel, the one-way fare between Genoa and Bastia is 150 to 185FF for pedestrians and 180 to 565FF for a small car. Certain sailings between mid-June and August are the most expensive. Couchettes start at 125FF (105FF during some periods), including breakfast.

Monday to Saturday from mid-June to mid-September, Mobylines has passenger *hydroglisseurs* (hydrofoils) from Bastia to Livorno (225FF per person one way; two hours). During the same period on Sunday and holidays, Mobylines has hydrofoils from Bastia to Portoferraio (185FF one way, 270FF same-day return; 1⅓ hours), on the island of Elba.

Between April and September, Corsica Marittima (☎ 95.54.66.66 in Bastia; 0586-897851/898952 in Livorno) runs ferries between Bastia and Livorno. From July to mid-September the company also has limited service from Livorno to Porto Vecchio. On the Livorno-Bastia run, passengers pay 150 to 175FF; cars start at 370FF (450FF from mid-June to early September). Couchettes start at 80FF.

Car ferries between Bonifacio (at Corsica's southern tip) and the Sardinian port of Santa Teresa di Gallura (commonly known as Santa Teresa) are operated by two companies, Saremar (☎ 95.73.00.96 in Bonifacio; 0789-754165 in Santa Teresa) and, from mid-April to early October, Mobylines (☎ 95.73.00.29 in Bonifacio; 0789-755260 in Santa Teresa). See Getting There & Away in the Bonifacio section for details.

Getting Around

Air
Kyrnair (☎ 95.20.52.29) has flights from Ajaccio to both Figari and Calvi.

Train
Chemins de Fer de la Corse, Corsica's metre-gauge, single-track rail system, is operated by the SNCF but has more in common with the Kalka-Simla line through the Himalayan foothills of north-western India than it does with the TGV. The two and four-car trains make their way unhurriedly through the stunning mountain scenery of the interior, stopping at tiny rural stations and, when necessary, for sheep, goats and cows. Sometimes the wind blows sand onto the beachside tracks near Calvi and the conductor has to hop out and shovel the minidunes off the rails. At higher elevations, special

snowploughs keep the tracks passable in winter. Frequently, passengers include Foreign Legionnaires in starched uniforms and white kepis on their way to or from the Légion Étrangère (Foreign Legion) base near Calvi. This is definitely the most romantic way to tour the island.

The 232-km network consists of two lines that meet to exchange passengers at Ponte Leccia. The Ajaccio-Corte-Bastia line is served by four trains a day (two on Sunday from mid-September to mid-June). Two daily trains link Ponte Leccia with l'Île Rousse and Calvi; their schedules are coordinated with the Ajaccio-Bastia service. From late April to October, Calvi, l'Île Rousse and intermediate destinations are served by a seaside tram line known as Tramways de la Balagne.

Corsica's rail system, which takes passengers from sea level to an altitude of 900 metres and back down again, was begun in 1878; the parts now in service were largely completed by 1894. Many of the viaducts, bridges and 38 tunnels (including one at Vizzavona that is four km long) were seriously damaged during WW II. The 130-km line along the east coast, finished in 1935, suffered damage during the war and has never been put back into service.

Tariffs Chemins de Fer de la Corse uses a tariff system that's completely different from the one used by the SNCF on the mainland. It does *not* accept Eurail passes or give any discounts except to holders of the Inter Rail pass, who get 50% off. If you have a bicycle, you can bring it along and hang it up in the front of the carriage for 55FF no matter how far you're going. Or, for the same price, you can send your bike on a goods train and pick it up at the other end. At train stations, backpacks and suitcases can be left at the ticket windows (there is no *consigne*) for 15FF per 24 hours. Remember that they can be retrieved only when the ticket windows are open.

Bus

Bus transport around the island is slow, infrequent, relatively expensive (100FF from Ajaccio to Bastia) and handled by an unfathomably complicated network of independent companies. On the longer routes, most of which are operated by a company called Eurocorse, there are only one or two and at most four runs a day. Except during July and August, only a handful of intercity buses operate on Sunday and holidays. However, buses are a bit faster and cheaper than trains, especially if you qualify for a student discount. That is, they're not faster if you have a student card, just cheaper...

Corsica's bus network covers almost every part of the island, including many tiny mountain villages. When there are two buses a day, one usually leaves in the morning and the other in the afternoon. As a general rule, morning buses begin their runs between 6 and 8.30 am, while afternoon buses depart sometime between 3 and 5 pm.

Car & Motorbike

Travelling by road is a fantastic way to explore Corsica, especially if you take the narrow secondary and tertiary roads that wind their way along the coast or through the mountains from hamlet to hamlet. Unfortunately, hairpin curves are not preceded by any sort of warning, and guardrails – if there are any at all – are usually little more than low stone walls. Shoulders are narrow or nonexistent and bridges are often single-lane. When it rains, little streams cascade down the hillsides and onto the road. Even on the main highways, you have to keep an eye out for cattle, goats, pigs, farmers' dogs and nationalists defacing the road signs. Count on averaging 50 km/h.

The most beautiful roads in Corsica include the D84 from Porto to Vergio Ski Station and the D69 from the N193 to Ghisoni. The fastest road on the island is the N198, which runs along the flat east coast from Bastia to Bonifacio. A good road map (such as Michelin's convenient, yellow-jacketed 1:200,000 map No 90) is indispensible because so many road signs have been graffitied into illegibility.

The best car-rental deals are listed in the

Getting There & Away sections of each town. Except at the height of the summer season, you might try haggling over prices a bit, especially at the smaller agencies. ADA lets you pick up a car at one office and return it at another.

Taking your own car to Corsica by ferry is a fairly expensive proposition, especially in the summer, when some sailings are booked up months in advance. See Boat in the Getting There & Away section for details of fares.

Hitching

Word on the street has it that hitching doesn't work very well on Corsica, in part because most holidaymakers' cars are packed to the gills with family members, dogs, tents, etc. Cars registered in the département of Haute-Corse have number plates that begin with '2B', while those from Corse-du-Sud begin with '2A'.

Ajaccio to Porto

Corsica's wildest, most spectacularly scenic coast runs from Ajaccio northward to Calvi. The entries in this section are listed from south-to-north, so travellers going the other way will have to follow it backwards.

AJACCIO

The port city of Ajaccio (population 55,000), birthplace of Napoleon Bonaparte (1769-1821) and prefecture of the département of Corse- du-Sud, is a great place to begin a visit to Corsica. The city enjoys frequent air and ferry links to mainland France and is connected by train and bus to the rest of the island. Although old-timers complain that Ajaccio has been spoiled by the traffic and the building boom of recent decades, this pastel-shaded, French-Mediterranean city is still a fine place for a stroll, especially along the narrow streets that wind through the older parts of town. Ajaccio is pronounced 'ah-ZHAK-syo'; the city's Corsican name,

spelled 'Aiacciu', is pronounced 'Ah-YATCH-ooh'.

Napoleon may have done little for his native town (or his native isle, for that matter), and he may not have bothered to visit after becoming emperor, but the Little Corporal's military and political exploits seem to have more than covered for him in the eyes of local people. Indeed, every public space in Ajaccio not taken up by a Napoleonic museum seems to be graced by a statue, monument or plaque dedicated to the diminutive emperor. None of the museums is scintillatingly interesting, but they will tell you more than you ever wanted to know, not about Napoleon the megalomaniac (or Napoleon the person), but about how the people of his small, quiet hometown prefer to look back on their local hero and his grandiose (if bloody) ambitions.

Orientation

Ajaccio's main street is Cours Napoléon, which stretches from Place de Gaulle northward past the train station and beyond. Another long avenue, this one running east-to-west, links Place Foch with Place d'Austerlitz, one km to the east. The old city is bounded by Place Foch, Place de Gaulle and the mid-16th-century Citadelle, which is still a military base and is closed to the public.

Information

Tourist Office The syndicat d'initiative (☎ 95.21.40.87, 95.21.53.39) at 1 Place Foch is less than outstandingly helpful. It is open Monday to Friday from 8.30 am to 6 pm and on Saturday from 8.30 am to noon. From mid-June to mid-September it's open daily from 8 am to 8 pm. The staff don't make hotel reservations unless you can't speak French *and* appear upset.

At the airport, the information desk (☎ 95.21.03.64) is open daily from 7 am to 10 pm.

Regional Park Office The Informations Randonnées office (☎ 95.21.56.54) on Rue Général Campi, 1⅓ short blocks up the hill

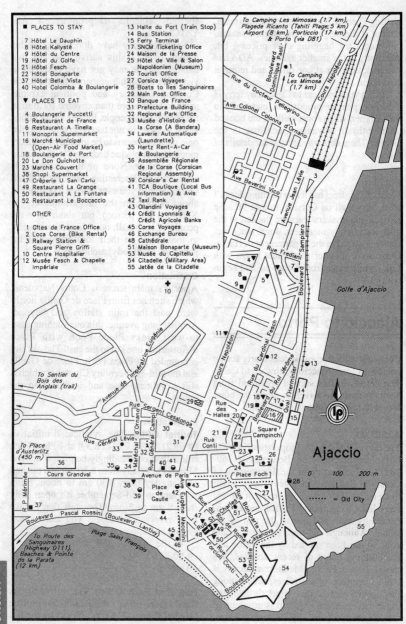

PLACES TO STAY

7 Hôtel Le Dauphin
8 Hôtel Kallysté
9 Hôtel du Centre
19 Hôtel du Golfe
21 Hôtel Fesch
22 Hôtel Bonaparte
37 Hôtel Bella Vista
40 Hôtel Colomba & Boulangerie

PLACES TO EAT

4 Boulangerie Puccetti
5 Restaurant de France
6 Restaurant A Tinella
11 Monoprix Supermarket
16 Marché Municipal
   (Open-Air Food Market)
18 Boulangerie du Port
20 Le Don Quichotte
23 Marché Couvert
38 Shopi Supermarket
47 Crêperie U San Carlu
49 Restaurant La Grange
50 Restaurant A La Funtana
52 Restaurant Le Boccaccio

OTHER

1 Gîtes de France Office
2 Loca Corse (Bike Rental)
3 Railway Station &
   Square Pierre Griffi
10 Centre Hospitalier
12 Musée Fesch & Chapelle
   Impériale

13 Halte du Port (Train Stop)
14 Bus Station
15 Ferry Terminal
17 SNCM Ticketing Office
24 Maison de la Presse
25 Hôtel de Ville & Salon
   Napoléonien (Museum)
26 Tourist Office
27 Corsica Voyages
28 Boats to Îles Sanguinaires
29 Main Post Office
30 Banque de France
31 Prefecture Building
32 Regional Park Office
33 Musée d'Histoire de
   la Corse (A Bandera)
34 Laverie Automatique
   (Laundrette)
35 Hertz Rent-A-Car
   & Boulangerie
36 Assemblée Régionale
   de la Corse (Corsican
   Regional Assembly)
39 Corsicar's Car Rental
41 TCA Boutique (Local Bus
   Information) & Avis
42 Taxi Rank
43 Ollandini Voyages
44 Crédit Lyonnais &
   Crédit Agricole Banks
45 Corse Voyages
46 Exchange Bureau
48 Cathédrale
51 Maison Bonaparte (Museum)
53 Musée du Capitellu
54 Citadelle (Military Area)
55 Jetée de la Citadelle

Top Left: The walls of Carcassonne, Languedoc (DR)
Top Right: Liqueur advertisement, Languedoc (GC)
Bottom Left: Rock pools along the Orbieu River, near Lagrasse, Languedoc (LL)
Bottom Right: Delivering the mail in a small village, Languedoc (GC)

Top: City statue, Paris (GE)
Middle: Fountain of Saturn, Versailles (GE); Jeanne d'Arc, Place des Pyramides,
Paris (DR); Hercules on top of the Palace of Versailles (TW)
Bottom: Fountain of Apollo in the gardens of the Palace of Versailles (TW)

from Place de Gaulle, has lots of information on the Parc Naturel Régional de Corse, its hundreds of km of hiking trails and the island's many gîtes d'étape. It can also provide details on hiking guides, group hikes, horse-riding trips and the like. Throughout the year the office is open on weekdays from 9 am to noon and 3 to 6 pm. Summer hours are slightly longer.

Gîtes Office For details on Gîtes de France's Ajaccio office and renting a gîte rural in Corsica, see Gîtes under Accommodation in the Facts for the Visitor section at the beginning of this chapter.

Money The Banque de France (☎ 95.21.00.05), near the Prefecture building at 8 Rue Sergent Casalonga, is open Monday to Friday from 8.30 am to noon and 1.30 to 3.30 pm.

On the south side of Place de Gaulle, the Crédit Agricole Mutuel de la Corse (☎ 95.21.34.34) has abominable rates and a 30FF commission, while the nearby Crédit Lyonnais (☎ 95.50.99.00) has decent rates but charges 50FF! Both are open Monday to Friday until 4.30 pm.

From June to September the exchange bureau on the corner of Blvd Pascal Rossini (formerly Blvd Lantivy) and Ave Eugène Macchini is open daily from 8 am to 9 pm. The exchange bureau at the airport is open from about mid-April to mid-October. Inside the bus station, the *change* is open around Easter and during summer.

Post The main post office (☎ 95.21.13.60) at 5 Cours Napoléon is open Monday to Friday from 8 am to 6.30 pm and on Saturday from 8 am to noon. Exchange services are available.

Ajaccio's postcode is 20000.

Travel Agencies Ferry and air tickets are available from travel agents all over town. Ollandini Voyages (☎ 95.21.10.12) on the east side of Place de Gaulle at Rue du Roi de Rome is a good place to try, as is Corsica Voyages (☎ 95.21.14.08) at the bottom of

Place Foch (technically 16 Ave Antoine Sérafini). The latter is open from 8 am to noon and 2 to 6.30 pm daily except Saturday afternoon and Sunday.

Down the hill from Place de Gaulle, Corse Voyages (☎ 95.51.17.77), on Blvd Pascal Rossini next to the Salle de Congrès, is open from 9 am to noon and 2.30 to 6.40 pm daily except Saturday afternoon and Sunday. In summer it's also open on Saturday afternoon.

Books & Maps The Maison de la Presse (☎ 95.21.81.18) at 2 Place Foch has a wide selection of guides to Corsica (most of them in French), Michelin and IGN maps, foreign newspapers and *Walks in Corsica*, the English-language topoguide to Corsica's trails. There's a stationery section and a photocopy machine upstairs.

The least expensive place to pick up maps is the IGN office (☎ 95.21.35.35) at 19 Cours Napoléon, Entrance B.

Laundry Near Place de Gaulle, the Laverie Automatique at 1 Rue Maréchal d'Ornano is open daily from 7 am to 9 pm. This place isn't cheap: it costs 30FF to wash a six-kg load or 34FF for seven kg. Automatic dry cleaning is 60FF.

Medical Services The Centre Hospitalier (☎ 95.21.90.90) is about 800 metres north of Place de Gaulle on Ave Napoléon III.

Walking Tour
A good way to get a feel for Ajaccio is to visit some of the town's omnipresent monuments to Napoleon. Beautiful, tree-shaded **Place Foch**, a favourite gathering place for locals and a great spot for a picnic, is graced by a fountain and a statue of the Little Corporal as First Consul. The Salon Napoléonien (see Museums) is down the block. Just up the hill, modern and rather harsh **Place de Gaulle**, once known as Place du Diamant, is enlivened by an equestrian statue of Napoleon in Roman dress. The Emperor is surrounded by his four brothers, whom he made the kings of Spain, Holland and

Westphalia and the Prince of Canino & Musignano.

Place d'Austerlitz, in a residential area at the western end of Ave du Général Leclerc (the western continuation of Cours Grandval), is one km west of Place de Gaulle. The statue of Napoleon in frock coat and bicorn hat, reached via a giant flight of stairs, is a replica of the one in the courtyard of the Invalides in Paris, which once stood atop the column in the middle of Paris's Place Vendôme. Place d'Austerlitz is named after one of Napoleon's greatest victories, in which French forces defeated Russian and Austrian troops in Moravia (now part of the Czech Republic) in 1805.

Museums

The **Maison Bonaparte** (☎ 95.21.43.89) on Rue Saint Charles, the house where Napoleon was born and lived until he was nine, is now a national museum. It was sacked by Pasquale Paoli's nationalists in 1793 and rebuilt (with a grant from the Directoire in Paris) at the end of the 1790s. Sir Hudson Lowe, who later supervised Napoleon's exile on the remote South Atlantic island of St Helena, was billeted here during the brief tenure of the Anglo-Corsican kingdom (1794-96). The less-than-fascinating exhibits include furniture that postdates Napoleon's last visit, assorted memorabilia and a death mask *(masque mortuaire)* made about two days after Napoleon's death in May 1821.

The house is open daily, except Sunday afternoon and Monday morning, from 10 am to noon and 2 to 5 pm; from 2 May to 30 September hours are 9 am to noon and 2 to 6 pm. In July and August it is open from 9 am to 6 pm. The entry fee of 17FF (9FF for people aged 18 to 25 and over 60) includes a guided tour in French. Ask at the counter if they have a brochure in English.

The **Musée Fesch** (☎ 95.21.48.17) at 50-52 Rue du Cardinal Fesch, named after Napoleon's maternal uncle, has an outstanding collection of 14th to 19th-century Italian primitive-style paintings. There's an exhibit of Napoleonia in the basement. This place is

open daily, except Sunday, Monday and holidays, from 9.30 am to noon and 2.30 to 6 pm; from May to September hours are 9.30 am to noon and 3 to 6.30 pm. During July and August it's also open on Friday night from 9 pm to midnight.

Entrance costs 25FF (15FF for students aged 18 to 25 and people over 60). Bags must be left in the lockers at the far end of the room to the right of the ticket counter. There is a separate fee of 10FF (5FF concession) to get into the Renaissance-style **Chapelle Impériale**, which is off the courtyard. It was built in the 1850s as a sepulchre for members of the Bonaparte family. Of course, Napoleon himself is buried in the Invalides in Paris.

The **Salon Napoléonien** (☎ 95.21.90. 15), an exhibit of Napoleonic memorabilia, is on the 1st floor of the Hôtel de Ville at Place Foch. It is usually open Monday to Friday from 9 am to noon and 2 to 5 pm. The fee is only 2FF, but visitors must be properly dressed (no shorts, beachwear or tank tops). Napoleon is serious business around here.

The **Musée d'Histoire de la Corse** (☎ 95. 51.07.34), also known as A Bandera, at 1 Rue Général Lévie, contains exhibits on Corsica's military history. Entrance costs 20FF (10FF for students). The small, privately run **Musée du Capitellu** (☎ 95.21. 50.57) at 18 Blvd Danielle Casanova has four rooms of paintings, engravings, porcelain and other household objects, most of them from the 19th century. From mid-March to October it is open from 10 am to noon and 2 to 6 pm daily except Sunday afternoon and Monday morning. During July and August it's also open Monday to Saturday nights from 9 to 11 pm or midnight. Entrance costs 20FF for everyone over 10.

Cathédrale

Ajaccio's Venetian Renaissance-style cathedral (☎ 95.21.07.67), built during the latter half of the 1500s, is in the old city on the corner of Rue Forcioli Conti and Rue Saint Charles. It is known for Napoleon's marble baptismal font (to the right of the entrance as you walk in) and the painting *Vierge au*

Sacré-Cœur by Eugène Delacroix (1798-1863), which, as you face the altar, is on the wall of the chapel situated in the back corner of the left-hand wall. The cathedral is open daily, except Sunday afternoon, from 7 to 11.30 am and 3 to 6.30 pm (6 pm in winter). Throughout the year masses are held on Saturday at 6.30 pm and on Sunday at 8.30 and 10 am. You can turn the lights on by putting 10FF in the gadget in the wall next to the entrance.

Pointe de la Parata

Pointe de la Parata, a wild, black granite promontory 12 km west of the city on Route des Sanguinaires (the D111), is famed for its sunsets, which can be contemplated from the base of a crenellated, early 17th-century Genoese watchtower reached by a short trail. For information about bus No 5, which links Ajaccio with the Pointe, see Bus under Getting Around.

Visible from the Genoese tower are the **Îles Sanguinaires**, a group of small islands that turn a deep red (hence the name) as the sun sets. From about May to October the islands can be visited on three-hour boat excursions (70FF) that leave from the quay next to Place Foch.

Hike to the Pointe Pointe de la Parata can be reached on foot from Ajaccio by taking a trail known as the Sentier du Bois des Anglais. It begins on Ave Nicolas Piétri, which is slightly north of Place d'Austerlitz and about 1.5 km west of Place de Gaulle. To get to the trailhead by bus, take line No 7, which runs about once an hour, to the Bois des Anglais stop.

As the Sentier du Bois des Anglais wends its way westward through the maquis, its name changes to the Sentier des Crêtes and a number of paths lead down the hill to the coast and its beaches (see the next paragraph). The Sentier des Crêtes itself hits the coast near a bus stop called Terre Sacrée, which is on the coast just over one km east of Pointe de la Parata. After hiking out to the Pointe, you can get back to town on bus No 5.

Beaches

Ajaccio's beaches are nothing to write home about. **Plage Saint François**, which is a block south of Place de Gaulle, is quite dreadful. A much better bet is **Plage de Ricanto**, popularly known as Tahiti Plage, about five km east of town on the way to the airport. Like the airport, it can be reached by taking bus No 1 (see To/From the Airport under Getting Around); get off at the Ricanto stop. The ritzy resort town of **Porticcio**, 17 km south of Ajaccio across the bay, has a great beach.

There are a number of small, segmented bathing spots along Route des Sanguinaires (the D111) between Ajaccio and Pointe de la Parata. To get there take bus No 5 (see Bus under Getting Around) and get off at the Ariadne, Neptune, Palm Beach or Marinella stops.

Organised Tours

Autocars Roger Ceccaldi (☎ 95.21.38.06; fax 95.21.32.47) offers half and full-day bus excursions (90 to 150FF) to Filitosa, Bonifacio, Corsica's west coast, Calvi, a number of mountain villages near Ajaccio and the mountains of the Parc Naturel Régional. There's a different itinerary each day of the week. Reservations can be made through many hotels.

Festivals

The biggest day on Ajaccio's celebratory calendar is 15 August, which is both Assumption Day and Napoleon's birthdayn The traditional religious procession is accompanied by fireworks and other events.

Places to Stay – bottom end

Ajaccio suffers from a serious shortage of cheap hotel rooms. In July and August all but the most expensive rooms are usually booked up weeks and even months in advance, and young people have been known to sleep on the beach.

Camping *Camping Les Mimosas* (☎ 95.20. 99.85), open from April to October, is about three km north of the centre of town on Route d'Alata (postcode 20090). To get there, take bus No 4 from Place de Gaulle or Cours Napoléon to the roundabout *(rond-point)* at the western end of Cours Jean Nicoli and walk up Route d'Alata for about one km. A tent site and a place to park cost 9FF each; the charge for adults is 22FF per person.

Hotels The tiny *Hôtel Colomba* (☎ 95.21. 12.66) at 8 Ave de Paris (3rd floor), which faces Place de Gaulle, is the best deal in town. Clean, pleasant singles and doubles cost 130 to 150FF, while triples cost 200FF. Toilets are down the hall. Adding an additional bed costs only 30FF. This place is open all year. Checkout is at 10 am. The helpful owner doesn't know much English so reservation letters not in French won't do much good.

The two-star *Hôtel Bella Vista* (☎ 95.21. 07.97; fax 95.21.81.88), near the beach at the intersection of Blvd Pascal Rossini and Blvd Sylvestre Marcaggi, has simple but tasteful singles/doubles/two-bed triples with shower and toilet for 180/ 190/200FF (from October to March) and 230/240/310FF (from July to September). Rooms on the seaward side, especially those with balconies, afford great views of the bay.

Places to Stay – middle

The small, friendly and central *Hôtel Kallysté* (☎ 95.51.34.45) at 51 Cours Napoléon is open all year, 24 hours a day. Eminently serviceable singles/doubles with air-con and minibar – more comfortable than some nearby three-star rooms – cost 200/235FF. Prices are about 15% higher during May, June, October and the first half of November and 25% higher from July to September. Studios with kitchenettes for one/two people range from 225/260FF to 300/350FF (plus electricity), depending on the season. It costs 65FF to have an extra bed added to the studios. This place usually has space in the morning, even in summer.

The two-star *Hôtel du Centre* (☎ & fax 95.21.62.02) at 45 Cours Napoléon (1st floor) has singles and doubles with shower and TV for 200FF and triples with bath, toilet

and TV for 350FF. The old-style rooms have high ceilings, some of which are elaborately painted, and almost-antique furniture. This place is open all year.

The two-star *Hôtel Bonaparte* (☎ 95.21. 44.19), 200 metres south-west of the ferry terminal at 1-2 Rue Étienne Conti (2nd floor), has small, ordinary singles/doubles/ triples/quads with shower and toilet for 220/260/360/450FF. Prices are marginally higher during the summer high season, when most rooms are reserved at least a month in advance. This place, which is right behind the Marché Couvert (covered food market), is open from mid-March to mid-November.

Between the ferry terminal and the train station is the older *Hôtel Le Dauphin* (☎ 95.21.12.94, 95.51.29.96; fax 95.21. 88.69) at 11 Blvd Sampiero, open all year. Ordinary singles/doubles/triples with shower and toilet cost 202/238/292FF (214/274/362FF in July and August), including breakfast. Reception is at the bar.

Places to Stay – top end

The three-star *Hôtel du Golfe* (☎ 95.21. 47.64; fax 95.21.71.05) is one block from the ferry terminal at 5 Blvd du Roi Jérôme. Modern, nondescript singles/doubles with cable TV, air-con and soundproofing cost 380/360FF (310/390FF with a sea view) throughout the year. An extra bed costs 130FF.

Also open throughout the year is the three-star *Hôtel Fesch* (☎ 95.21.50.52; fax 95.21. 83.36) at 7 Rue du Cardinal Fesch. It has unsurprising singles/doubles with satellite TV (including CNN and the Super Channel) for 285/305FF (325/345FF from July to mid-September). An extra bed is 105FF.

Places to Eat

Lots of small restaurants are scattered around the old city. There are a number of cafés along Blvd du Roi Jérôme.

Restaurants – expensive In the old city, *A La Funtana* (☎ 95.21.78.04), a French restaurant at 9 Rue Notre Dame, has a *menu* for 120FF, fish dishes for 85 to 100FF and foie gras for 85 to 120FF. It is open all year from noon to 3 pm and 7 pm to midnight; it's closed Saturday at midday and on Sunday. In July and August it's also open on Sunday evening. Across the street, *La Grange* (☎ 95.21.25.32) at 4 Rue Notre Dame specialises in traditional French and Corsican cuisine. There are *menus* for 60, 120 and 200FF. Except from mid-December to mid-February, it is open Tuesday to Sunday from noon to 2 pm and 7 to 11.30 pm.

A Tinella (☎ 95.21.13.68) at 86 Rue du Cardinal Fesch, a favourite with local gourmets, has *menus* for 110 to 220FF. Meat dishes are around 80FF, while fish costs 30 to 35FF per 100 grams.

Restaurants – mid-range *Restaurant de France* (☎ 95.21.11.00) at 59 Rue du Cardinal Fesch has an 'excellent price-quality ratio', as the French are fond of saying. The *menu* costs 89FF, and fish dishes are in the 65 to 80FF range. This place is closed on Sunday.

Le Boccaccio (☎ 95.21.16.77) at 19 Rue du Roi de Rome serves excellent Italian cuisine. Main dishes are 50 to 60FF and the summer *menu* costs about 90FF. Le Boccaccio is open daily throughout the year (except during January) from noon to 2.30 pm and 7 to 9 pm. It closes later at night in the summer.

Restaurants – inexpensive *Crêperie U San Carlu* (☎ 95.21.30.21) at 16 Rue Saint Charles has crepes of all descriptions for 10 to 50FF. From April to September it is open from 11 am to 9.30 or 10 pm (2 am in July and August). There are other restaurants along the same narrow street.

Le Don Quichotte (☎ 95.21.27.30), near the Hôtel Fesch on Rue des Halles, has pizzas from 35 to 48FF and *menus* from 65FF.

Self-Catering Near the ferry terminal, the *Marché Couvert* at 1bis Blvd du Roi Jérôme is open from 6 am to 12.30 pm and 4 to 8 pm daily except Sunday afternoon. In July and August it's open from 6 am to 10 pm daily

except Sunday afternoon. Nearby at Square Campinchi, the *Marché Municipal* (open-air food market) operates every day except Monday (daily from the end of May to mid-October) from 6 am until about 1 pm. *Boulangerie du Port*, down the block on Blvd du Roi Jérôme, is open from 7 am to 12.30 pm and 4 to 7.30 pm daily except Saturday and Sunday afternoon. From mid-July to mid- September it's open daily from 5.30 am to 9 pm.

Near Place de Gaulle, the *Shopi supermarket* opposite 4 Cours Grandval is open Monday to Saturday from 9 am to 12.30 pm and 3.15 to 7.30 pm. The *boulangerie* at 8 Ave de Paris, which is just down the block, is open every day from 7.30 am to 1 pm and 3 to 8 pm. Nearby, the *boulangerie* at 2 Cours Grandval is open daily from 6.30 am to 9 pm.

Along Cours Napoléon, the *Monoprix supermarket* opposite No 40 is open Monday to Saturday from 8.45 am to 12.15 pm and 2 to 7 pm; the food section is on the 1st floor. From July to mid-September there's no midday closure. *Boulangerie Puccetti* at 53 Cours Napoléon has excellent breads shaped like the Mercedes trademark. It is open daily from 7 am to 1 pm and 3 to 8 pm (8.30 pm in summer).

Entertainment

The wealthy resort of Porticcio, 17 km south of Ajaccio across the bay, attracts a wealthy, somewhat snobbish clientele whose preferences have made the village a lively nightspot. The Porticcio tourist office (☎.95.25.07.02) is near the beach. During summer it may be possible to get from Ajaccio's pleasure port to Porticcio by water taxi.

Getting There & Away

Air Aéroport d'Ajaccio-Campo dell'Oro (☎ 95.21.07.07) is eight km east of the city. For more information on flights to/from Corsica, see Air in the Getting There & Away section at the beginning of this chapter.

Train Trains to Corte (56FF; two hours), Bastia (105FF; 3½ to four hours), Calvi (122FF; 3½ to 4½ hours) and intermediate destinations can be caught either at the train station (☎ 95.23.11.03), at Square Pierre Griffi, or at the Halte du Port train stop, which is next to the bus station and ferry terminal. See Train in the Getting Around section at the beginning of the Corsica chapter for more information.

Bus Ajaccio's bus station is on Quai l'Herminier just north of the ferry terminal, to which it is linked by a corridor. About a dozen companies operate buses daily except Sunday and holidays to Bastia (100FF; two a day), Bonifacio (105FF; two a day), Calvi (110FF) via Ponte Leccia, Corte (55FF; two a day), Porto and Ota (55FF; two a day), Sartène (62FF; two a day), Propriano and many other destinations. From mid-May to mid-October there's a bus from Porto to Calvi (60FF) every day except Sunday and holidays, making it possible to go all the way up the island's west coast. Since the Porto-Calvi bus leaves in the morning, you'll have to stay overnight in Porto.

Eurocorse (formerly Ollandini; ☎ 95.21. 06.30, 95.70.13.83), which handles most of the 'long-distance' lines, keeps its kiosk open Monday to Saturday from 8 to 11 am and 2 to 6.30 pm (7 am to 6.30 pm in July and August). Most of the other companies leave their kiosks unstaffed except when one of their buses is about to depart, in which case the driver comes to sell tickets. If a number of people are travelling together, you might try haggling over the price a bit.

The bus station's information booth (☎ 95.21.28.01), which is in the middle of the hall, can provide schedules and tell you which company covers the route you need. It is open Monday to Saturday from 7 am to 6.30 or 7 pm. From mid-June to mid-September it's open daily and may close later than 7 pm.

Car The best car-rental prices in town are offered by Corsicar's (☎ 95.21.87.12), on the ground floor of the building known as Résidence Diamant II at 6 Place de Gaulle. Office hours are Monday to Saturday from 8 am to noon and 2 to 6 pm (7 pm from late April to September). During the warm months, they're often open on Sunday as well. With unlimited km, a Peugeot 106 or a Citroën AX costs 290/1550FF a day/week (340/1700FF from June to September), including insurance. Camping cars for two to four people cost from 950 to 1300FF for three days and 4150 to 5100FF for a week.

Another place with decent prices is ADA (☎ 95.20.95.56; fax 95.20.95.68), whose Ajaccio office is about four km towards the airport from town in the Centre Commercial Saint Joseph (next to the Total petrol station). You can make reservations by phone and have them bring your vehicle to the airport or into town. ADA also allows you to return the car in Bastia if you make arrangements to do so in advance.

About a dozen car-rental companies (including Budget, Europcar, Avis and Hertz) have bureaux at the airport, but the least expensive is probably Aloha (☎ 95.20. 52.00; fax 95.23.17.35). Aloha will arrange for you to pick up the car in town if you reserve by telephone. The company also hires out 4WD vehicles with drivers.

Motorbike Loca Corse (☎ 95.20.71.20; fax 95.20.44.52) at 10 Ave Beverini Vico rents 50/80 cc scooters for 200/250FF a day and 1000/1400FF a week; 125 cc motorcycles are 350/1800FF a day/week. From October to March it's open Monday to Saturday from 9 am to noon and 3 to 6 pm. During the rest of the year, it's open Monday to Saturday from 8.30 am to noon and 2 to 6.30 pm. During July and August, Loca Corse stays open on Sunday as well.

Boat The ferry terminal is on Quai l'Herminier next to the bus station. SNCM's ticketing office (☎ 95.29.66.99), across the street at 3 Quai l'Herminier, is open Monday to Friday from 8 to 11.45 am and 2 to 6 pm and Saturday from 8 to 11.45 am. On days when there's an evening ferry, the SNCM bureau in the ferry terminal sells tickets for pedestrian passengers *only* two or three hours before the scheduled departure time.

If you have a car, motorbike or bicycle,

drive to the *guérite* (sentry's box) next to the *contrôle d'embarquement* (embarkation office) 1½ hours before sailing. If you don't have a ticket, get there two hours earlier (three hours in summer) to see if there's space.

Getting Around

To/From the Airport TCA bus No 1 links the airport with the centre of Ajaccio (Cours Napoléon, Place de Gaulle and Blvd Pascal Rossini) for 15FF. Heading *towards* the airport, this line runs daily from 6.45 am (6 am during summer) to 8.15 pm. From Monday to Saturday there's a bus every 20 minutes; on Sunday and holidays, there's a bus every 40 minutes. The last bus from the airport to Ajaccio leaves at around 10 pm. After 7.30 pm or so, buses into town run about once every half-hour.

A taxi from the airport to the centre of Ajaccio should cost approximately 75 to 80FF during the day and 100FF at night, including a 10FF surcharge for being picked up at the airport. It costs 5FF extra for a fourth passenger and 4FF extra if you have a dog.

To get from the city centre to the airport by car, take Cours Napléon northward and follow its continuations around the bay. Watch out for the incredibly peculiar traffic patterns.

Bus For route maps and timetables on local bus services, contact the TCA Boutique (☎ 95.50.04.30) at 2 Ave de Paris (opposite Place de Gaulle). It is open weekdays from 8 am to noon and 3 to 6 pm and Saturday from 8 to 11.15 am. Bus tickets cost 7FF if bought on board but a carnet of 10 – available at the TCA Boutique and some tabacs (tobacconists) – costs only 49FF.

Bus No 5 follows Route des Sanguinaires (the D111) from Place de Gaulle westward past a number of beaches to Pointe de la Parata. From October to mid-May it runs eight times a day (from 7 am to 6 pm) on weekdays and Saturday and six times a day (from 10 am to 5 pm) on Sunday and holidays. The last bus back to town departs from

the Pointe at 6.30 pm (5.30 pm on Sunday and holidays). From mid-May to September there are at least 13 buses a day between 7 am and 7 pm; the last bus back to town is at 7.30 pm. In July and August line No 5 runs every half-hour or so until 8 pm, and the last bus from the Pointe to Ajaccio leaves at 11.45 pm.

Taxi There's a taxi rank (☎ 95.21.00.87) on the east side of Place de Gaulle. To order a taxi, you can call Radio Taxis (☎ 95.51. 15.67) or Radio Taxis Ajacciens (☎ 95.20. 52.56). If you have a problem with a taxi (eg overcharging), call ☎ 95.21.42.36.

Bicycle Mountain bikes are available for 80/300FF a day/week from Loca Corse (see Motorbike under Getting There & Away).

Boat From about May to October excursions (☎ 95.25.46.27; 70FF) to the Îles Sanguinaires (see Pointe de la Parata) leave from the waterside opposite Place Foch. There may also be water taxis to Porticcio.

CARGÈSE

Perched on a steep promontory at the northern end of the Golfe de Sagone, Cargèse (population 900), founded two centuries ago by Greek settlers, retains the appearance and ambience of a Greek village.

In the 1670s, about 600 Greeks from the southern Peloponnese, fleeing their Ottoman-controlled homeland, were given refuge on Corsica by the Republic of Genoa. Loyal to the Genoese and relatively prosperous, the Greek settlers soon became the object of hostility from their Corsican neighbours. After suffering repeated attacks elsewhere on the island, the descendants of the original settlers founded Cargèse in 1774. Over the last two centuries, the Cargèse Greeks have gradually assimilated: local families' Greek surnames have been Corsicanised and the Greek language, long passed from generation to generation, is no longer spoken by any of the present-day residents.

Orientation

Cargèse's main street, the D81, changes name at the post office (which marks the centre of town): it is known as Ave de la République towards Ajaccio and Rue Colonel Fieschi towards Porto. The square stone thing 250 metres up Rue Colonel Fieschi from the post office was once used for washing clothes.

The semicircular bay north of Cargèse is known as the Golfe de Pero.

Information

The syndicat d'initiative (☎ 95.26.41.31) on Rue du Docteur Dragacci is down the steps across Ave de la République from the post office. Throughout the year, it is open Monday to Saturday from 3 to 5 pm. From June to September it's open daily from 8.30 am to noon and 4 to 7 pm.

The Banque Populaire Provençale et Corse, which exchanges foreign currency, is round the corner from the post office.

Cargèse's postcode is 20130.

Churches

Cargèse is well known for its two Catholic churches – one Eastern (Greek) rite, the other Western (Latin) – which face each other across a patchwork of neatly tended vegetable plots. The squares in front of both structures afford fine views of the town and the sea.

The 19th-century **Latin church** has a square, white bell tower on the side of the structure, while the **Greek church** has stone buttresses and a polygonal bell tower on top of the building. The interior of the Greek church – constructed from 1852 to 1870 by the faithful, who worked on Sunday after mass – is adorned with a number of icons brought from Greece by the original settlers in the 1670s. Masses are held in Greek using prayerbooks that include both a transliteration of the Greek text into Latin characters and a French translation.

Beaches

About one km north of the town centre is **Plage de Pero**, a long, wide stretch of sand

overlooked by the Genoese towers on top of Pointe de Cargèse and Pointe d'Omigna. To get there, take the road leading down the hill from the square stone thing on Rue Colonel Fieschi.

Other beaches in the vicinity of Cargèse include **Plage de Ménasina** (2.5 km south of town), **Plage de Stagnoli** (7.5 km south) and **Plage de Chiuni** (six km north).

Hiking

A trail leads to the Genoese tower on Pointe d'Omigna, the tip of the promontory on the other side of Golfe de Pero from Cargèse.

For information on the Mare e Monti and Mare a Mare Nord trails, both of which have termini at Cargèse, see Hiking under Activities in the Facts for the Visitor section at the beginning of this chapter.

Places to Stay

Open from March to mid-October, the one-star *Hôtel Cyrenos* (☎ 95.26.40.03) is 100 metres from the post office on Ave de la République. Doubles with shower and a view of town cost 165FF except from mid-June to mid-September, when the price goes up to 200FF.

The *Motel Punta e Mare* (☎ 95.26.44.33) on Route de Paomia is at the northern edge of Cargèse just up the hill from the square stone thing on Rue Colonel Fieschi. Open all year, the pleasant, functional doubles with shower and toilet cost 180 to 250FF, depending on the season. Just down Rue Colonel Fieschi from the square stone thing, you might also try the *Hôtel de France* (☎ 96.25. 41.07), open from May to October. Doubles with shower and toilet cost 160 to 180FF.

The *Hôtel Bel' Mare* (☎ 95.26.40.13; fax 95.26.48.24), open from March to 10 November, is on the southern outskirts of town on Rue de la République. Singles/doubles/triples cost 160/180/200FF in March and April and 220/300/380FF the rest of the time. Demi-pension is obligatory in August.

Places to Eat

The homy *Hôtel Cyrenos restaurant*

(☎ 95.26.40.03) on Ave de la Republique has a *menu* for 87FF. The *Hôtel Bel' Mare restaurant* (☎ 95.26.40.13), on the southern outskirts of Cargèse, has *menus* for 88 and 102FF. *Restaurant Le Continental* (☎ 95.26.42.24) has copious portions of excellent family-style Corsican cuisine for about 100FF per person.

There are several food stores and a couple of small supermarkets in the vicinity of the post office.

Getting There & Away

Cargèse is 50 km north of Ajaccio and 32 km south of Porto. The two buses a day to Porto and Ajaccio stop in front of the post office.

PIANA

The hillside village of Piana (population 500), just south of Les Calanche, affords spectacular views of the Golfe de Porto and the soaring mountains of the interior. Its altitude is 435 metres.

Things to See & Do

Beaches in the area include **Plage de Ficajola**, right below Piana and reached by a four-km road, and **Plage d'Arone**, which is about 10 km south-west of town via the scenic D824. From the D824, a hiking trail leads westward to the tower-topped **Capo Rosso**.

Places to Stay

The grand old *Hôtel des Roches Rouges* (☎ 95.27.81.81), built in 1928 and reopened in the mid-1980s after two decades of closure, is furnished and decorated much as it was in the 1930s. It is open from April to October or November. Spacious, simply furnished doubles/triples with high ceilings, showers, toilets and balconies – many with spectacular views of the sea – cost 265/335FF. Two-room suites for up to four people are 450FF. Breakfast costs 40FF in the ground-floor restaurant, which has been declared an historic monument.

The two-star *Hôtel L'Horizon* (☎ 95.27.80.07), on the D81 on the edge of town towards Cargèse, is open from April to October. Attractive one or two-bed doubles with balconies cost 170 to 220FF; triples are 280FF. From June to August, when demi-pension is obligatory, doubles skyrocket to 500FF.

Getting There & Away

Porto-Ajaccio buses stop near the post office.

LES CALANCHE

Corsica's single most famous natural sight is Les Calanche (Les Calanques de Piana in French), a truly spectacular mountain landscape of red and orange granite forms resembling both nightmarish and fairly normal people, animals, buildings and the like. Created by the rock's uneven response to the forces of erosion, these amazing formations have been made even more weird by the dissolving action of water that has seeped into the granite's many fissures and carved out the spherical cavities known as *taffoni*.

Les Calanche, accessible from the D81 between Piana and Porto, plunge 300 metres from their multitoned pinnacles to the deep blue waters of the sea below. When it's clear, there are stunning views of both the Mediterranean and the mountains northward across the Golfe de Porto. Less rocky areas are covered with pine and chestnut forests.

Calanche is the plural of the Corsican word *calanca* and is pronounced 'kah-LAHNK', the same as its French equivalent, *calanques*.

Hiking

About eight km south-west of Porto on the D81 is **Le Chalet des Roches Bleues**, a modern stone and wood building that serves as a useful landmark even if you're not interested in buying any of the proffered souvenirs. Four trails begin in the immediate vicinity:

La Corniche This steep, 40-minute walk, which leads up to a fantastic view of the Calanche as well as a forest of laricio pines, begins on the inland side of the bridge situated 50 metres down the hill (towards Porto) from the chalet. It rejoins the D81 about 500 metres further on towards Porto. The new trail markings are yellow, but some of the old blue markings are still visible.

Chemin du Château-Fort This one-hour trail passes in and among Les Calanche on its way to the Château-Fort, a solid block of rock that looks like a donjon and affords stunning views of the Golfe de Porto. It begins 700 metres down the hill (towards Porto) from the chalet. The trailhead is to the right of the rock on the seaward side of the D81 that everyone says looks like a dog's head and really does. The trail markings are blue.

Chemin des Muletiers The Mule-Drivers' trail begins 400 metres up the hill (towards Piana) from the chalet on the inland side of the D81. The trailhead is 15 metres down the hill from the roadside sanctuary dedicated to the Virgin Mary. This rather steep, one-hour trail, with blue markings, rejoins the D81 about a km towards Piana from where it starts.

La Châtaigneraie This three-hour circuit, which begins 25 metres up the hill and across the road from the chalet, takes you up to a forest of chestnut trees. It rejoins the D81 about two km from the chalet towards Porto.

Getting There & Away
If you'd like to take one of the hikes that begin near Le Chalet des Roches Bleues, hop on an Ajaccio-Porto bus and ask the driver to drop you off at the chalet.

PORTO
The pleasant little seaside town of Porto, nestled among huge outcroppings of red granite, is renowned for its sunsets. It is an excellent base for exploring some of Corsica's most beautiful sights, including Les Calanche, Girolata and the Gorges de Spelunca. The town pretty much shuts down from mid or late October until the week before Easter, though a couple of hotels do stay open.

Orientation
The marina *(marine)* is 1.5 km down the hill from Porto's pharmacy *(pharmacie)* – an important landmark – and the big, new Bravò supermarket, both of which are on highway D81. The part of Porto known as Vaïta is spread out along the road linking the D81 to the marina.

Information
Tourist Office The syndicat d'initiative (☎ 95.26.10.55) is in the Vaïta area 500 metres towards the marina from the D81. It is closed in the off season.

Money The exchange bureaux are open only during the tourist season.

Post Porto's postcode is 20150.

Things to See & Do
The tastefully overdeveloped **marina** is surrounded by hotels and places to eat. A short trail leads to the **Genoese tower**, which looks like it's about to collapse, overlooking the harbour. The estuary of the Porto River is just behind the line of buildings to the left as you face the sea. On the far side of the river, accessible by a bridge, is a modest **beach** of grey gravel and sand and one of Corsica's best known **eucalyptus groves**.

Hiking The trail to Girolata (see the Girolata section) intersects the D81 about 10 km north of Porto near the Col de la Croix. For information on the Gorges de Spelunca, see the Ota section.

Boat Excursions From mid-April to October there are excursions (150FF) by glass-bottomed boat from Porto to Girolata and back to Porto with a sail-by of Les Calanche and the Réserve Naturelle de Scandola (see the Girolata section). Unless it's stormy, there are two daily excursions, at 9.30 am and 2.30 pm. In Porto, boats dock either at the marina or at the mouth of the Porto River. If you take the morning boat, you can catch Revellata's afternoon boat (☎ 95.65.28.16, 95.65.29.65) from Girolata to Calvi; the one-way fare from Porto to Calvi is 185FF.

For tickets and information, contact the Hôtel Monte Rosso (☎ 95.26.17.10, 95.26.11.50; fax 95.26.12.23) at Porto's marina. In July and August it may be necessary to book a day ahead.

Boat Rental & Waterskiing Motorboats (155 horsepower) for up to six people can be rented from mid-April to October for 800/1500FF for a half/full day, not including petrol. Water-skiing equipment is an additional 100FF. For details, call ☎ 95.26.12.31.

Places to Stay – bottom end
Camping The Huge *Camping Sole e Vista* (☎ 95.26.18.03), open from mid-April to late October, is behind the Bravò supermarket near the pharmacy. Charges are 9FF for a tent, 9FF to park and 23FF per person. The three-star *Camping Les Oliviers* (☎ 95.26.14.49), which occupies an olive-shaded hillside, is a few hundred metres down the D81 next to the bridge over the Porto River.

Hostels For information on the gîtes in the nearby village of Ota, see the Ota section.

Hotels On the left-hand side of the marina (as you face the sea), the one-star *Hôtel du Golfe* (☎ 95.26.13.33), open all year, has shower-equipped doubles without/with toilet for 160/200FF (180/220FF from June to September).

Places to Stay – middle
The two-star *Hôtel Monte Rosso* (☎ 95.26.11.50) at the marina, the third building from the Genoese tower, has decent doubles with shower and toilet for 220FF (260FF in July and August). It is open from mid-April to October.

The two-star, pool-equipped *M'Hôtel Cala di Sole* (☎ 95.26.12.44), open all year, is in the Vaïta area overlooking the Porto River. Spacious, spotless doubles/quads with kitchenettes are reasonably priced at 250/400FF (360/560FF during July and August). If no one is at reception, enquire at Le Pub, the bar across the street.

Places to Eat
Many of Porto's hotels, including those at the marina, double as restaurants.

There are two supermarkets, one of which is the new *Supermarché Bravò*, near the pharmacy. The *supermarket* a few buildings up the hill from the tourist office is only open during the tourist season.

You'll find a number of ice-cream places at the marina.

Entertainment There are several bars at the marina.

Getting There & Away
Bus Autocars SAIB (☎ 95.26.13.70) has two buses a day linking Porto with Ajaccio (55FF; three hours). From mid-May to mid-October the company also has a morning bus to Calvi (60FF; three hours) and a mid-afternoon bus from Calvi to Porto. Autocars SAIB's buses, which do not operate on Sunday and holidays, stop at both the pharmacy and the marina.

There are several buses a day to Ota (10 minutes). Unfortunately, neither Porto nor Ota is connected by public transport with Évisa (except, maybe, in summer).

Motorbike & Bicycle From late April to late September, Monsieur Antoine Bartoli (☎ 95.26.10.13) rents motorbikes and bicycles from his home, which is opposite the pharmacy.

Boat For information on boat services from Porto via Girolata to Calvi, see Boat Excursions under Things to See & Do.

OTA
Ota (elevation 310 metres), a tiny village of stone houses perched on the hillside above the Porto River, is not far from the trail up the celebrated Gorges de Spelunca. It has some of the best budget accommodation on the island.

CORSICA

Hiking

The **Pont de Pianella**, an especially graceful Genoese bridge, is just under two km east of Ota along the D124. About 300 metres away, the two single-lane Ponts d'Ota span the Onca and Aïtone rivers, which merge here to form the Porto River.

The trail (once a mule track) up the **Gorges de Spelunca** to Évisa (three hours) via the **Pont de Zaglia** (another Genoese bridge) begins on the left bank of the Aïtone (ie on the far side of the far bridge if you're coming from Ota), whose clear, greenish waters crash and tumble between the canyon's granite walls. The Gorges de Spelunca can also be hiked in the other direction, starting from Évisa. The trail markings are orange. If you'd like to walk one way and ride back, see Getting There & Away for information on taxis.

The Mare e Monti trail from Cargèse to Calenzana passes through Ota a few hundred metres towards Porto from the centre of the village.

Places to Stay

Ota has several excellent year-round options for hostellers. *Gîte d'Étape Les Chasseurs* (☎ 95.26.11.37) charges 50FF for a bed in a dormitory room and 100FF for a double. The large, pleasant kitchen is a good meeting place. Reservations are accepted. Reception is in the Bar des Chasseurs.

Gîte d'Étape Chez Félix (☎ 95.26.12.92) at Place de la Fontaine has beds in four and six-person rooms for 50FF. Doubles and triples cost 150FF and rooms for five people are 300FF. Kitchen facilities are available. In July and August, it's a good idea to call ahead.

The 40-bed *Gîte d'Étape Communal* (☎ 95.26.16.41), above the post office, also functions as a youth hostel, but it's closed for repairs until 1994.

Places to Eat

Restaurant Chez Félix (☎ 95.26.12.92) at Place de la Fontaine offers family-style Corsican cuisine all year, though in the off season there may be only one main dish

(50FF) available. The four-course *menu* costs 90FF. There's a bar below the restaurant.

The *grocery store* opposite the church is open Monday to Saturday from 8 am to noon and 3 to 7 pm. From July to mid-September it's open daily from 7 am to 12.30 pm and 3 to 8.30 pm.

Getting There & Away

Ota, five km east of Porto's pharmacy via the D124, is linked to both Porto (10FF; 10 minutes) and Ajaccio (three hours) by several buses a day except on Sunday and holidays. Buses stop at two places in Ota: at the post office and Place de la Fontaine. There is no public transport from Ota to Évisa, but Gîte d'Etape Chez Félix (☎ 95.26.12.92) can supply a taxi for transport to/from Évisa for 200FF one way.

ÉVISA

The peaceful village of Évisa (population 250; altitude 830 metres) is between the Gorges de Spelunca and the majestic Forêt d'Aïtone. Surrounded by chestnut groves, it is something of a hill station, with fresh, crisp mountain air and a wealth of salutary walking trails nearby.

Information

Évisa's postcode is 20126.

Forêt d'Aïtone

The Aïtone Forest, which surrounds the upper reaches of the Aïtone River at an altitude of 800 to 2000 metres, has some of Corsica's most impressive stands of laricio pines, perfectly straight trees up to 60 metres high and several hundred years old. The forest, whose trees once provided beams and masts for Genoese ships, begins a few km east of Évisa and stretches all the way to the 1477-metre-high **Col de Vergio**. The **Cascades d'Aïtone** (Aïtone Falls) are four km north-east of Évisa via the D84 and a half-km footpath.

Gorges de Spelunca

See Hiking under Ota.

Hiking

There are lots of mountain trails in the vicinity of Évisa, especially in the Forêt d'Aïtone. One circuit goes from near the Maison Forestière de Catagnone in the Forêt d'Aïtone to Col de Salto (1390 metres) and Col de Cocavera (1475 metres). Consult a hiking map for details.

Places to Stay

Hostel To get to the *gîte d'étape* from the post office, go down the stairs; when you get to the road, turn left and walk 100 metres. *Gîte Rural U Mulinu* (☎ 95.26.22.89), open from Easter to September, is across the street from Hôtel L'Aïtone.

Hotels The two-star *Hôtel L'Aïtone* (☎ 95.26.20.04; 95.26.24.18), open all year except in November and December, is on the upper outskirts of town. Pleasant, slightly rustic, shower-equipped rooms without/with toilet cost 180/240FF throughout the year. Deluxe rooms with balconies in the new section cost 300 to 400FF (350 to 450FF from mid-July to mid-September). There's a pool at the back. For cheaper rooms, try the one-star *Hôtel du Centre* (☎ 95.26.20.92), which is across the main road from the church tower. It is open from June to September.

Gîte Rural Le Belvédère (☎ 95.26.20.95) is the unmarked orange building with red shutters to your right as you stand in the parking area above the church. The minimum stay is usually one week, but three or four nights will suffice in the off season. A two/three-room apartment for three/five people costs 1650/1900FF a week in summer and – because of heating costs – in winter, too. The rest of the year, prices are a bit cheaper.

Places to Eat

Bar de la Poste, near the post office, is a favourite with locals. There's a grocery store 50 metres down the hill from the post office.

Getting There & Away

The D84 from Porto to Évisa, which looks out over the Gorges de Spelunca, is one of the most spectacular roads in Corsica.

Apparently there are two buses a day (except Sunday and holidays) from Ajaccio to Évisa via Sagone and Vico. There is no public transport linking Évisa with Ota or Porto except perhaps in the summer. For information on taxis, see Getting There & Away in the Ota section.

VERGIO SKI STATION

Vergio (☎ 95.48.00.01), one of Europe's smallest ski stations, is 14 km up the D84 from Évisa. It is operational whenever there is enough snow, which at this elevation is most likely to be between December and February. Use of the five ski lifts costs 80FF a day; ski rental is 70FF, including boots.

Place to Stay

The 40-room *Hôtel Castel del Vergio* (☎ 95.48.00.01), a rare remnant of the cheap, plasticky modernism popular around 1960, has somewhat gloomy doubles/triples/quads with shower and toilet for 230/280/350FF. It is open all year. The postcode is 20224.

GIROLATA

Girolata, a small fishing village with a few pricey restaurants (specialising in fish and seafood, of course), is about 15 km north of Porto. It is virtually inaccessible by land and maintains contact with the rest of the island by boat.

The fantastic orange rock formations and cliffs of the **Réserve Naturelle de Scandola** (Scandola Nature Reserve), the peninsula west and north of Girolata, are home to many rare (and rarely visible) birds, such as the *balbuzard* (sea eagle, also known as the fish eagle). Birds you're more likely to see include seagulls and cormorants. To protect La Scandola from human encroachment, members of the public are not allowed to go ashore, so the only way to see the area is from a boat.

Place to Stay

To contact Girolata's *refuge*, call ☎ 95.20.16.98.

Getting There & Away

Girolata is accessible either on foot (see Hiking under Porto) or, from mid-April to October, by boat from Porto and Calvi. For information on getting to Girolata by sea, see Boat Excursions in the Calvi and Porto sections.

South of Ajaccio

FILITOSA

Filitosa (☎ 95.74.00.91 for information), which is about 25 km north-west of Propriano along the N196 and then the D57, is Corsica's most important prehistoric site. Inhabited from 6000 BC until the Roman period, its fortifications, buildings, megaliths and anthropomorphous statue-menhirs armed with swords (held vertically) and daggers have been the subject of intense study since their discovery in 1954. Various artefacts discovered here are displayed in the **museum**. The site is open daily from 8 am until sunset.

SARTÈNE

The somewhat sombre and introverted hillside town of Sartène (population 3500), whose unofficial slogan is 'the most Corsican of Corsica's towns', is a delightful place to spend a few hours. Built mostly of grey stone, its old residential quarters have alleys and rough-hewn staircases instead of streets. The people of Sartène have long had a reputation for being politically conservative and unreceptive to newfangled ideas.

Despite its medieval appearance, Sartène was founded by the Genoese in the early 16th century. In 1583, pirates from Algiers raided the town and carried 400 local people off into slavery in North Africa; such raids did not end until the 18th century. The town was long notorious for its banditry and bloody vendettas, and in the early 19th century a violent struggle between rival landowners deteriorated into house-to-house fighting, forcing most of the population to flee.

There are a number of prehistoric sights south and south-west of Sartène along the D48.

Orientation

From Place de la Libération, Sartène's main square, Cours Sœur Amélie leads southward down the hill, while Cours Général de Gaulle heads northward down the hill. After a few blocks, Cours Général de Gaulle makes a sharp turn to the left and changes its name to Ave Jean Jaurès. The old Santa Anna quarter is north of Place de la Libération within the V-shaped area created by Cours Général de Gaulle and Ave Jean Jaurès.

Information

Tourist Office The syndicat d'initiative (☎ 95.77.15.40) is at 6 Rue Médecin-Capitaine Louis Bénédetti, which is 30 metres up the hill from Place de la Libération. It is open only during the warm part of the year.

Money The Crédit Lyonnais at 13 Cours de Gaulle is open Monday to Friday.

Post Sartène's postcode is 20100.

Place de la Libération

Local people often gather in this square to meet friends and discuss the affairs of the day (in Corsican, of course). You may hear an intergenerational conversation in which the older person speaks Corsican and the younger person responds in French. In the middle of the *place* is a memorial to the many young men from the commune of Sartène who died in WW I.

Hôtel de Ville & Other Sights

On the north side of Place de la Libération, the Hôtel de Ville, formerly the Palace of the Genoese Governors, is pierced by an arch that leads to the **Santa Anna quarter**, a residential neighbourhood of austere, grey-granite houses and sombre, almost-medieval alleyways and staircases. Next to the Hôtel de Ville stands the granite **Église Sainte Marie**. Inside, on the wall to the left of the entrance, you can see the 31½-kg oak cross and 14-kg chain which is carried and dragged by the red-robed penitent in the annual Procession du Catenacciu. The baroque-style marble altar was crafted in Italy in the 17th century.

Musée de Préhistoire Corse

The Museum of Corsican Prehistory (☎ 95.77.15.40), housed in a three-storey stone building built as a prison in the 1840s, is open from 10 am to noon and 2 to 4 or 5 pm daily except on weekends and holidays. To get there from Cours Bonaparte (the street across Place de la Libération from the church), turn right at the 'Urgence Hôpital' sign and take the first left.

Festivals

On the eve of Good Friday, the people of Sartène perform an ancient ritual known as the Procession du Catenacciu. In a re-enactment of the Passion, the Catenacciu (literally, the chained one), an anonymous, barefoot penitent covered from head to foot in a red robe and cowl, carries a huge cross through the town while dragging a heavy chain shackled to his ankle. He is followed by a procession of other penitents, members of the clergy and local notables. As the chain clatters by on the cobblestones, local people look on in great (if rather humourless) excitement. Needless to say, everyone is curious to find out the identity of the penitent, who is selected by the parish priest from among applicants seeking to expiate a grave sin.

Places to Stay

The only hotel in central Sartène is the two-star *Hôtel Les Roches* (☎ 95.77.07.61), which is off Ave Jean Jaurès, just below the Santa Anna quarter. From November to March doubles/triples with shower and toilet cost 263/388FF, and, from April to October, 294/414FF. Same-day telephone reservations are not accepted unless business is slow.

The small *Hôtel Fior di Riba* and the larger *Hôtel Villa Piana* (☎ 95.77.07.04) are on the N196 about 1.5 km towards Ajaccio and Propriano from Place de la Libération. Both are open only in the warm season.

Places to Eat

Restaurant La Chaumière (☎ 95.77.07.13) at 39 Rue Médecin-Capitaine Louis Bénédetti (near the tourist office) is open all year except from January to mid-March. An à la carte meal will cost about 100 to 200FF.

Wines from the Sartène area, sold straight from 300-litre barrels for 7FF a litre (if you bring your own container), are available from *La Cave Sartenaise*, an old-time wine shop at Place de la Libération on the ground floor of the Hôtel de Ville. Labelled bottles of local wine start at 15 or 20FF. This place is open daily from 8 am to 8 pm except when the proprietor decides to eat lunch.

There are various grocery stores, wine shops, boulangeries, pizzerias and bars along

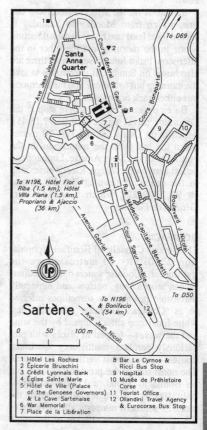

Sartène

```
0      50      100 m
```

1 Hôtel Les Roches
2 Épicerie Bruschini
3 Crédit Lyonnais Bank
4 Église Sainte Marie
5 Hôtel de Ville (Palace of the Genoese Governors) & La Cave Sartenaise
6 War Memorial
7 Place de la Libération
8 Bar Le Cyrnos & Ricci Bus Stop
9 Hospital
10 Musée de Préhistoire Corse
11 Tourist Office
12 Ollandini Travel Agency & Eurocorse Bus Stop

CORSICA

Cours Général de Gaulle and Cours Sœur Amélie. *Épicerie Bruschini*, an old-fashioned, small-town grocery at 12 Cours Général de Gaulle (about 100 metres down the hill from Place de la Libération), is open from 8 am to 12.15 pm and 4.30 to 8 pm daily except Sunday afternoon.

Getting There & Away
Given the dearth of reasonably priced hotels, you might want to stop off here on your way from Ajaccio to Bonifacio, or visit Sartène on a day trip from Ajaccio (the 86-km bus trip costs 62FF) or Bonifacio (53 km southeast).

Sartène is on the Ajaccio-Bonifacio bus line, which from Monday to Saturday is served by at least two buses in each direction – one in the morning and the other in the afternoon. From June to September there are also buses on Sunday. It is possible to take the morning bus to Sartène and the afternoon bus either back or onward.

Buses operated by Eurocorse stop at the Ollandini travel agency (☎ 95.77.18.41), which is on Cours Gabriel Péri 50 metres down the hill from the roundabout at the bottom of Cours Sœur Amélie. Luggage can be left here for no charge. Ricci's buses stop in the centre of town at Bar Le Cyrnos (☎ 95.77.11.22), which is at 14 Cours Général de Gaulle.

BONIFACIO
The famous Citadelle of Bonifacio (population 2700) sits 70 metres above the translucent, turquoise waters of the Mediterranean atop a long, narrow and eminently defensible promontory sometimes referred to as 'Corsica's Gibraltar'. On all sides, white limestone cliffs sculpted by the wind and the waves – topped in places with precariously perched, multistorey apartment houses – drop almost vertically to the sea. The north side of the promontory looks out on Bonifacio Sound, a 1.5-km-long fjord only 100 to 150 metres wide, while the citadel's southern ramparts afford views of the coast of Sardinia, 12 km to the south

across the Strait of Bonifacio (Bouches de Bonifacio).

Some of Bonifacio's residents still speak the local language, a Ligurian (ie Genoese) dialect incomprehensible to other Corsicans.

History
Archaeologists have uncovered evidence of human habitation around Bonifacio as far back as the 7th millennium BC. Given the distinctive geographical details supplied by Homer about Odysseus' encounter with the cannibalistic Laestrygonians, it is possible that this episode of the *Odyssey* was set in Bonifacio Sound. The present city was founded in 828 AD. Late in the 12th century, it was taken from the Pisans by the Genoese, whose colonists established what became an almost-autonomous minirepublic. Bonifacio – even more so than Calvi – was long known for its loyalty to the Republic of Genoa.

From the Middle Ages until the 19th century, Bonifacio Sound sheltered both pirate vessels and, less frequently, fleets of warships. The city endured several cruel sieges, including the terrible and ultimately unsuccessful five-month siege laid by the Aragonese in 1420. In 1554, only 25 years after two-thirds of the population had died of the plague, Bonifacio withstood another bloody siege, this time by a peculiar joint expeditionary force consisting of the soldiers of Henry II of France and the fleet of the Turkish corsair Dragut. They tricked the city into surrendering and then pillaged the town and massacred the garrison. The Genoese took over again in 1559 after the treaty of Cateau-Cambrésis.

Orientation
Bonifacio consists of two main areas: the marina *(marine)*, which is along the southern side of the eastern end of Bonifacio Sound (Goulet de Bonifacio); and the Citadelle, also known as the Vieille Ville (old city) and the Ville Haute (upper city). The latter occupies the middle section of the 250-metre-wide promontory that separates Bonifacio Sound from the Strait of Bonifacio. The area across the water from the marina is known

as Giovasole. The ferry port is on the southern side of Bonifacio Sound below the Citadelle. The road to Porto Vecchio is called Ave Sylvere Bohn as it heads northward from the marina.

Ave Charles de Gaulle links the marina with the Citadelle. The Citadelle has three entrances: Porte de Gênes, passable only to pedestrians; Porte de France, now a one-way exit for cars; and the motorable road that ends up at the Foreign Legion monument after passing under Fort Saint Nicolas.

Information

Tourist Office The syndicat d'initiative (☎ 95.73.11.88) is in the Citadelle on the ground-floor of the Mairie – from Place de l'Europe, go in the entrance on the building's eastern side. It is open from 9 am to noon and 2 to 6 pm daily except Saturday afternoon and Sunday. From mid-June to mid-September, it's open Monday to Saturday from 9 am to 1 pm and 3 to 7 pm.

From mid-June to mid-September the tourist office annexe at the marina is open Monday to Saturday from 10 am to 1 pm and 4 to 7 pm and on Sunday from 10 am to 7 pm.

Money At the marina, the Société Générale (☎ 95.73.02.49) at 7 Rue Saint Érasme has decent rates and a reasonable commission. Throughout the year, it's open Monday to Friday from 8.30 to 11.30 am and 2 to 4.45 pm. From mid-April to mid-October the Office de Change (☎ 95.73.02.76) on the other side of Rue Saint Érasme is open daily from 8 am to 8 pm (10 pm from July to September).

Post In the Citadelle, the post office (☎ 95.73.01.55) at Place Carrega (up the hill from the tourist office) is open Monday to Friday from 9 am to noon and 2 to 5 pm (6 pm from June to August) and Saturday from 9 am to noon. Exchange services are available.

Bonifacio's postcode is 20169.

Travel Agencies Air and ferry tickets to/from all parts of Corsica are available from Ollandini (☎ 95.73.01.28) at 77 Quai Jérôme Comparetti. Throughout the year, it's open from 9 am to noon and 2 to 6 pm daily except Saturday afternoon and all-day Sunday; summer hours may be slightly longer.

Citadelle

Bonifacio Sound is linked to the Citadelle via two sets of stairs. One – known as Montée Rastello and, further up, Montée Saint Roch – links Rue Saint Érasme at the marina with Porte de Gênes. The other one connects the ferry port with Porte de France.

The old city has something of a medieval ambience, in part because of the cramped alleyways, which are lined with tall, narrow stone houses. The flying buttresses overhead carry rainwater to cisterns. Although most of the street-level shops cater to tourists, on the floors above local people continue to live as they have for centuries – or at least since the 19th century, when many of the town's two-storey buildings were extended skyward as the population increased.

Rue des Deux Empereurs is named after Charles V and Napoleon, who once slept in the houses at Nos 22 and 31 repectively. Charles V spent three days in Bonifacio on his way to Algiers in 1541, while Lieutenant Colonel Bonaparte was based here for several months in early 1793 while planning an expedition to Sardinia.

Église Sainte Marie Majeure, a Romanesque structure built in the 14th century but significantly modified since then, is known for its square campanile and its giant porch, under which is a large communal **cistern**, a vital asset in time of siege. It is now used as a conference hall. Inside, the marble altar dates from the early 17th century.

The impressive **Porte de Gênes**, reached by a drawbridge dating from 1598, was the only entrance to the Citadelle until the Porte de France was built in 1854. From nearby **Place du Marché** and **Place Manichella**, there are great views of the old city's southern cliffs, the clear turquoise waters at their base and, in the distance, the hills of Sardinia. At the other end of the old city, the

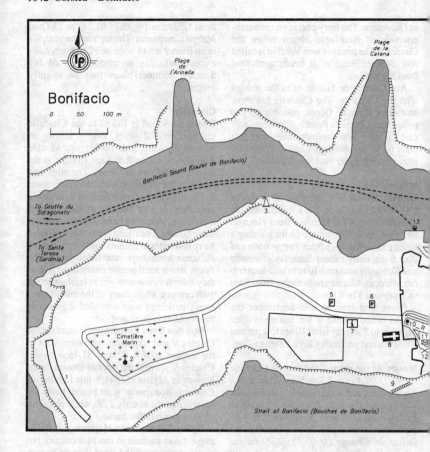

Bonifacio

0   50   100 m

Plage de l'Arinella

Plage de la Catena

Bonifacio Sound (Goulet de Bonifacio)

To Grotte du Sdragonato

To Santa Teresa (Sardinia)

Cimetière Marin

Strait of Bonifacio (Bouches de Bonifacio)

Escalier du Roi d'Aragon (Staircase of the King of Aragon), whose 187 steps were built, according to legend, by Aragonese troops during the siege of 1420, leads down the cliff from the south-western corner of the Citadelle. (Another version says that Bonifacio's inhabitants built the stairs themselves so they would have another opening to the sea, after the Aragonese had blocked the port with their ships.)

The vehicular road up to the Citadelle enters the old city proper right next to the **Monument de la Légion Étrangère** (Foreign Legion Monument), which origi-

nally stood in a remote Algerian village but was relocated to Bonifacio in 1963 when Algeria achieved independence (and part of the Foreign Legion was transferred from Algeria to Bonifacio).

West of the Citadelle

The rather desolate and derelict plateau at the western end of the promontory is worth a wander, if only for the view. The round towers are all that remain of Bonifacio's erstwhile windmills. The simple **Église Saint Dominique**, built by the Dominicans between 1270 and 1343, is one of the only

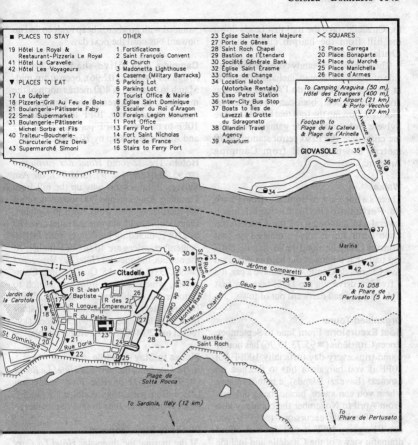

■ PLACES TO STAY	OTHER	23 Église Sainte Marie Majeure	✕ SQUARES
19 Hôtel Le Royal &	1 Fortifications	27 Porte de Gênes	
Restaurant-Pizzeria Le Royal	2 Saint François Convent	28 Saint Roch Chapel	12 Place Carrega
41 Hôtel La Caravelle	& Church	29 Bastion de l'Étendard	20 Place Bonaparte
42 Hôtel Les Voyageurs	3 Madonetta Lighthouse	30 Société Générale Bank	24 Place du Marché
	4 Caserne (Military Barracks)	32 Église Saint Érasme	25 Place Manichella
▼ PLACES TO EAT	5 Parking Lot	33 Office de Change	26 Place d'Armes
	6 Parking Lot	34 Location Moto	
17 Le Guêpier	7 Tourist Office & Mairie	(Motorbike Rentals)	To Camping Araguina (50 m),
18 Pizzeria-Grill Au Feu de Bois	8 Église Saint Dominique	35 Esso Petrol Station	Hôtel des Étrangers (400 m),
21 Boulangerie-Pâtisserie Faby	9 Escalier du Roi d'Aragon	36 Inter-City Bus Stop	Figari Airport (21 km)
22 Small Supermarket	10 Foreign Legion Monument	37 Boats to Îles de	& Porto Vecchio
31 Boulangerie-Pâtisserie	11 Post Office	Lavezzi & Grotte	(27 km)
Michel Sorba et Fils	13 Ferry Port	du Sdragonato	
40 Traiteur-Boucherie-	14 Fort Saint Nicholas	38 Ollandini Travel	Footpath to
Charcuterie Chez Denis	15 Porte de France	Agency	Plage de la Catena
43 Supermarché Simoni	16 Stairs to Ferry Port	39 Aquarium	& Plage de l'Arinella

---

Gothic churches on Corsica. Further west you pass the **caserne** (barracks) which served as a Foreign Legion base after 1963. At the far western tip of the plateau, just before the concrete fortifications, is the walled **Cimetière Marin**, a whole neighbourhood of family crypts in a hotchpotch of architectural styles.

Marina

Quai Jérôme Comparetti, a pleasant, palm-shaded (though touristy) promenade, runs along the marina. The small but attractive **Aquarium** (☎ 95.73.03.69) at 71 Quai Jérôme Comparetti has a dozen tanks of species native to the Strait of Bonifacio, including a giant *murène* (moray eel). It is open from April to October daily from 10 am to 7 pm; in July and August, it stays open until midnight. Entrance costs 20FF (10FF for students). **Église Saint Érasme** on Rue Saint Érasme, dedicated to the patron saint of sailors, has a model of a sailing craft hanging from the ceiling.

Beaches

To get to **Plage de Sotta Rocca**, a small bit of rocky coast below the south-east corner of

CORSICA

the Citadelle, take the trail that heads down the hill from the hairpin curve on Ave Charles de Gaulle.

There are several sandy coves on the north side of Bonifacio Sound, including **Plage de la Catena** and **Plage de l'Arinella**. If you don't have a boat, both can be reached on foot by following the trail that begins on Ave Sylvere Bohn next to the garages built into the cliffs near the Esso petrol station (ie 70 metres down the hill from Camping Araguina).

Walks
There's a fine view of Bonifacio from **Phare de Pertusato** (Pertusato Lighthouse), several km south-east of the Citadelle on Capo Pertusato. It can be reached on foot from the Citadelle along the 45-minute, clifftop path that begins at the hairpin curve on Ave Charles de Gaulle. If you have a car, it's a five-km drive via the D58; take the first right as you head eastward out of town.

Organised Tours
Boat Excursions From June to September, Rocca Croisières (☎ 95.73.13.96) has hourly round trips every day (officially 100FF but 80FF if you bargain a bit) to the **Îles de Lavezzi** (Lavezzi Islands), a nature reserve where you can swim, picnic, hang out, etc. From April to November the company also offers 40-minute excursions (50FF if you don't bargain, 40FF if you do) that afford dramatic views of the Citadelle and include a visit to the **Grotte du Sdragonato**, whose roof is pierced by a hole that is said to resemble a backwards silhouette of Corsica. Several other boat companies offer similar excursions.

Festivals
A procession of penitents is held on Good Friday.

Places to Stay – bottom end
Bonifacio has no really inexpensive hotels and relatively few hotels at all. If you're in town during July or August and can't afford to spend lots of money, it's easy to get stranded with nowhere cheap to sleep and no onward bus until the next day.

Camping The olive-shaded *Camping Araguina* (☎ 95.73.02.96), open from mid-March to October, is 400 metres north of the marina on Ave Sylvere Bohn. Staying here doesn't come cheap: 10FF to pitch a tent, 10FF to park and 24FF per person. In July and August, it fills up by 10 or 10.30 am.

Hotels The 32-room *Hôtel des Étrangers* (☎ 95.73.01.09; fax 95.73.16.97), on Ave Sylvere Bohn a short way up the hill from Camping Araguina and 500 metres north of the marina, is open from April to October. Plain doubles with shower and toilet cost 180 to 210FF, including breakfast; from July to September, prices are 40 or 50FF higher. At the marina, the one-star *Hôtel Les Voyageurs* (☎ 95.73.00.46) at 15 Quai Jérôme Comparetti, which is open from late March to October, has doubles with shower for 150FF. Unfortunately, demi-pension is obligatory from July to September, when prices sky-rocket to 220/440FF for a single/double.

Places to Stay – middle
In the Citadelle, the two-star *Hôtel Le Royal* (☎ 95.73.00.51) on Rue Fred Scamaroni (Place Bonaparte) has doubles for 300FF (500FF from mid-June to mid-September).

Places to Stay – top end
At the marina, the three-star *Hôtel La Caravelle* (☎ 95.73.00.03; fax 95.73.00.41) at 35 Quai Jérôme Comparetti has singles/doubles for 390/490 to 490/590FF. It is open from a week before Easter to 15 November.

Places to Eat
Restaurants In the Citadelle, the best deal for an informal meal is *Restaurant-Pizzeria Le Royal* (☎ 95.73.00.51), a café-style place on Rue Fred Scamaroni at Place Bonaparte. It is open daily from noon to 3 pm and 7 to 10 pm. Pizzas cost 32 to 55FF, *menus* go for 60 or 70FF and the various plats du jour are around 50FF. *Pizzeria-Grill Au Feu de Bois* (☎ 95.73.13.31), nearby at 5 Rue Fred

Scamaroni, has pizza (36 to 44FF) and pasta (42 to 48FF) as well as Italian and Corsican dishes. It is open Monday to Saturday from 11 am to 3 pm and 7 pm to midnight; from April to November it's also open on Sunday. Somewhat more up-market is *Le Guêpier* (☎ 95.73.08.77) at 7 Rue Fred Scamaroni.

There are lots of touristy restaurants around the marina.

Self-Catering In the Citadelle, many of Bonifacio's unique cakes and pastries are available from *Boulangerie-Pâtisserie Faby* at 4 Rue Saint Jean Baptiste. Specialities include a nut-and-raisin bread known as pain des morts (literally, bread of the dead; 14FF), big, flat, sugar-covered biscuits known as fougazi (14FF), aniseed and lemon-flavoured biscuits called canistrelli (14FF a bag), cheese tarts called canistrone (made only in the summer) and bread with big sugar crystals on top called moustachole. This place, which also has pizza, is open daily from 7.30 am to 12.30 pm and 3.30 to 7 pm; there's no midday closure from June to October. Nearby is a *small supermarket* at 16 Rue Doria.

At the marina, Bonifacio's pastry specialities are sold at *Boulangerie-Pâtisserie Michel Sorba et Fils* at 1-3 Rue Saint Érasme. This place may be closed from 12.30 to 4.15 pm. Cheese and prepared meats are sold at *Traiteur-Boucherie-Charcuterie Chez Denis* at 55 Quai Jérôme Comparetti. *Supermarché Simoni* is slightly east on Quai Comparetti.

Getting There & Away

Air Bonifacio's international airport, Aéroport de Figari (☎ 95.71.00.22), is 21 km north of town.

Bus From Monday to Saturday, Rapides Bleus (☎ 95.31.03.765 in Bastia) has buses to Porto Vecchio (three times a day) and Bastia (once a day). Eurocorse (☎ 95.21. 06.30 in Ajaccio) has buses to Ajaccio via Sartène (105FF; twice a day). All buses leave from the parking lot across the street from

the eastern end of the marina. Eurocorse is thinking of opening an office in Bonifacio, but in the meantime tickets are sold on board. Hours are posted at the Ollandini travel agency at 77 Quai Jérôme Comparetti (see Travel Agencies under Information).

Car From about mid-March to mid-October, Aloha Auto Location (☎ 95.71.04.31, 95.20. 52.00; fax 95.23.17.35) has an office at Figari Airport. Ollandini (see Travel Agencies under Information) acts as an agent for Avis.

Bonifacio is 186 km south of Bastia along the fastest highway on the island, the N198, and 137 km south-east of Ajaccio.

Motorbike In Giovasole, Location Moto (☎ 95.73.15.16, 95.73.04.77) has mopeds/motorbikes for 160/320FF a day or 850/1800FF a week.

Boat Up until the 1960s, the only way to get your car across the Strait of Bonifacio to the Italian island of Sardinia was to have it winched aboard a fishing boat. These days, things are much simpler: Saremar (☎ 95.73.00.96 in Bonifacio, 0789-754156 in Santa Teresa) offers year-round car ferry service from Bonifacio to the Sardininan port of Santa Teresa. There are two to four sailings a day, depending on the season. Saremar's office in the ferry port building is open daily from 9 am to noon and 2.30 to 5 pm. From mid-April to early October, Mobylines (☎ 95.73.00.29 in Bonifacio, 0789-755260 in Santa Teresa) also runs ferries from Bonifacio to Santa Teresa.

With Saremar, one-way pedestrian passage costs 49FF (54FF from June to September). Cars start at 135FF (160FF in summer), bicycles are 21FF and dogs and cats cost 28FF each. Mobylines is slightly more expensive. If you want to get a vehicle across at any time of the year, it's a good idea to make reservations at least a week in advance. The crossing takes one to 1½ hours.

Bastia Area

BASTIA

Bastia (population 45,000), Corsica's most important centre of business and commerce, is served by more ferries from France and Italy than any other Corsican port. Thanks to the Genoese, the city's old quarters have an Italian atmosphere found nowhere else on the island. You can easily spend a day wandering around, but there's not all that much to see or do, and most tourists move on pretty quickly. If you have a car, Bastia is a good base for exploring Cap Corse, the 40-km-long peninsula north of Bastia.

Bastia was the seat of the Genoese governors of Corsica from the 15th century – when construction of the *bastiglia* (fortress) from which the city's name derives began – to the 18th century. In 1943, the city was seriously damaged by US bombing and German pre-withdrawal sabotage.

Orientation

The focal point of the modern city centre is 300-metre-long Place Saint Nicolas. Bastia's main thoroughfares are the east-west oriented Ave Maréchal Sebastiani, which links the ferry terminal building with the train station, and the north-south oriented Blvd Paoli, a fashionable shopping street one block west of Place Saint Nicolas. Campinchi (as in Rue César Campinchi) is pronounced 'com-PAN-shee' in French and 'com-PAN-kee' in Corsican.

Along the coast north of Place Saint Nicolas is the Nouveau Port (ferry port) and, further north still, the pleasure-boat harbour, Port de Plaisance Toga, located in the suburb of Toga. South of Place Saint Nicolas are the town's three older neighbourhoods: Terra Vecchia, the Vieux Port (old port) and the Citadelle (Terra Nova). A tunnel under the Vieux Port and the Citadelle links Place Saint Nicolas with Bastia's southern suburbs.

Information

Tourist Office The helpful Office Municipal du Tourisme (☎ 95.31.00.89) is at the northern edge of Place Saint Nicolas. It is open Monday to Saturday from 8 am to 6 pm. During July and August, it's open every day from 7 am to 10 pm. The staff do not make hotel reservations. If you'll be spending a bit of time in Bastia, ask for the English version of their free brochure, *Visite Guidée du Vieux Bastia*.

During summer, tourist information is also available in the ferry terminal building from the syndicat d'initiative, run by Bastia's Chambre de Commerce (Chamber of Commerce).

Money The Banque de France (☎ 95.31.24.09) is half a block south of the southern end of Place Saint Nicolas at 2bis Cours Henri Pierangeli. It's open Monday to Friday from 8.45 am to 12.10 pm and 1.55 to 3.30 pm. From late March or early April to October, the exchange bureau in the ferry terminal building is open daily from 9 am to 6.30 pm (8 pm in July and August). The rate is inferior.

There are quite a few commercial banks in the city centre along Rue César Campinchi and Rue du Conventionnel Saliceti.

Post The main post office is a block west of Place Saint Nicolas on the even-numbered side of Ave Maréchal Sebastiani. It is open Monday to Friday from 8 am to 7 pm and on Saturday from 8 am to noon. Exchange services are available.

Bastia's postcode is 20200.

Travel Agencies Kallistour (☎ 95.31.71.49; fax 95.32.35.73) at 6 Ave Maréchal Sebastiani is open Monday to Friday from 8.30 am to noon and 2 to 6.30 pm and on Saturday from 9 am to noon.

Bookshops Librairie Jean-Patrice Marzocchi (☎ 95.34.02.95) at 2 Rue du Conventionnel Saliceti has topoguides, IGN maps, Didier-Richard hiking maps and (usually) the English topoguide *Walks in Corsica*. It is open from 9.30 am to 12 pm and 2.30 to 7 pm daily except all-day Sunday and Monday morning.

Laundry The laundrette in the parking lot at the northern terminus of Rue du Commandant Luce de Casabianca is open daily from 7 am to 9 pm.

Medical Services The Centre Hospitalier (☎ 95.55.11.11) is several km south-west of Bastia on Route Impériale. It can be reached by bus Nos 1 and 2.

Walking Tour

The parts of Bastia of interest to visitors stetch along the coast south of the tourist office.

Place Saint Nicolas, a palm and plane tree-lined esplanade almost as long as three football pitches, was laid out in the late 19th century. There's usually at least one game of *boules* (bowls) being played somewhere between the war memorial, the bandstand, the statue of Napoleon dressed as a Roman emperor and the trees. The west side of the *place* is lined with shops and cafés.

Just south of Place Saint Nicolas is **Terra Vecchia**, a neighbourhood of old houses (some from the 18th century), towering tenements and narrow streets. It is centred around the shady **Place de l'Hôtel de Ville**, now an open-air marketplace and a parking lot. Nearby is the **Oratoire de l'Immaculée Conception** (Oratory of the Immaculate Conception), construction of which began in the late 1500s, opposite 3 Rue Napoléon. It was given its rich interior decoration during the 18th century. There's a small exhibit of *art sacré* (religious art) in the sacristy, to the left of the altar.

On the southern side of Place de l'Hôtel de Ville is the back of **Église Saint Jean Baptiste**, whose classical façade, graced by two towers, overlooks the picturesque, horseshoe-shaped **Vieux Port** (old port). Built in the mid-1600s and redecorated in the 18th century, this church has become Bastia's most recognisable architectural symbol.

The entrance to the Vieux Port is guarded by two beacons. **Jetée du Dragon**, the jetty that leads to the red beacon, affords great views of the harbour, where pleasure craft mingle with the local fleet of bright blue and white wooden boats.

Further south still is the **Citadelle**, also known as Terra Nova, built by the Genoese between the 15th and 17th centuries. It can be reached by climbing the stairs through **Jardin Romieu**, the hillside park on the south side of the Vieux Port.

Just inside the Citadelle, at Place du Donjon, is the **Ancien Palais des Gouverneurs** (Former Genoese Governors' Palace), which houses a dusty anthropology museum, the **Musée Ethnographique Corse** (☎ 95. 31.09.12). It is open daily from 9 or 10 am to noon and 2 to 5 or 6 pm and costs 10FF (5FF for children). Up the stairs from the courtyard of the Palais des Gouverneurs, the ramparts have been turned into a garden with panoramic views of Bastia and the sea.

The **conning tower** you pass is from the WW II submarine *Casabianca*, which, under the command of Captain l'Herminier (who has a street in Ajaccio named after him), helped Corsica keep contact with Free French forces based in Algeria during 1942-43. The submarine was named after the young Corsican hero of the Battle of Aboukir Bay (Battle of the Nile), which Napoleon's fleet lost to British admiral Horatio Nelson near Alexandria, Egypt in 1798. **Église Sainte Marie**, whose entrance is through the side of the building facing Rue de l'Évêché, was begun in 1495 and served as a cathedral from 1570 to 1801. Its interior ornamentation is in the baroque style, which was in fashion in the 17th and 18th centuries. The alleyways around the church can be explored on foot.

Beaches

At the southern edge of Bastia is the less than lovely **Plage de l'Arinella**, served by bus Nos 5 and 8. A much better bet is **Plage de la Marana**, about 12 km south of Bastia at the southern edge of the Étang de Biguglia (see that section). During summer, it is served by bus No 8, which has a stop opposite the tourist office on the north side of Ave Pietri.

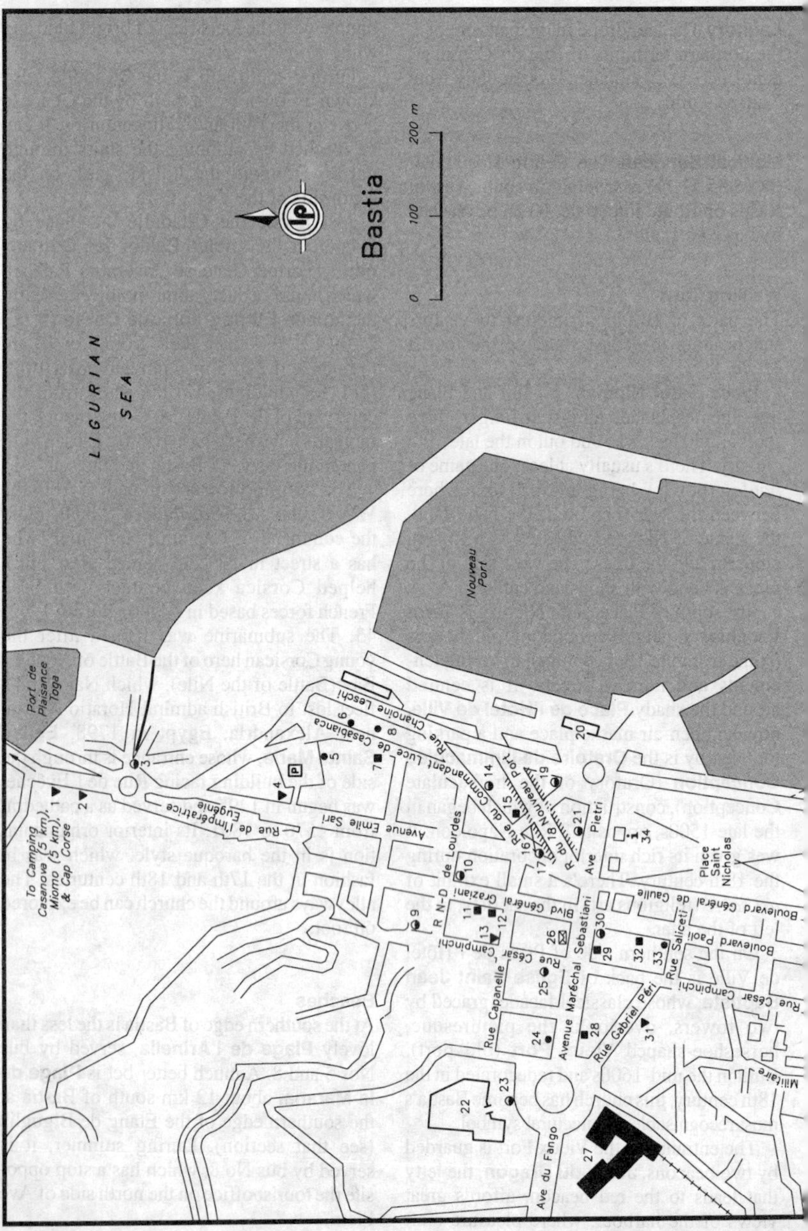

Bastia

LIGURIAN SEA

Port de Plaisance Toga

To Camping
Casanova (5 km),
Miomo (5 km),
& Cap Corse

Nouveau Port

Rue de l'Impératrice Eugénie

Avenue Emile Sari

Rue Chanoine Leschi

Rue de Casablanca

Rue du Commandant Lucce de Casabianca

Rue Napoléon

Rue du Commandant L'Herminier

R N-D de Lourdes

Blvd Général Graziani

Rue César Campinchi

Rue Capanelle

Avenue Maréchal Sébastiani

Rue Gabriel Péri

Rue César Campinchi

Ave Pietri

Place Saint Nicholas

Boulevard Général de Gaulle

Boulevard Paoli

Rue Saliceti

Ave du Fango

Militare

0   100   200 m

CORSICA

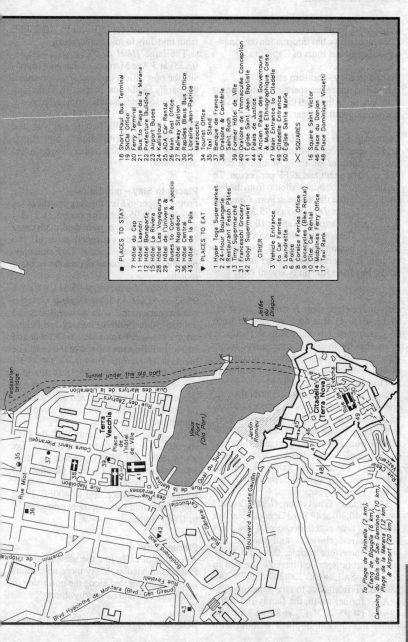

■ PLACES TO STAY
7   Hôtel du Cap
11 Hôtel Leandri
12 Hôtel Bonaparte
15 Hôtel La Riviera
28 Hôtel Les Voyageurs
29 Hôtel de l'Univers &
    Buses to Corte & Ajaccio
32 Hôtel Napoléon
36 Hôtel Central
43 Hôtel de la Paix

▼ PLACES TO EAT
1   Hyper Toga Supermarket
2   24-Hour Boulangerie
4   Restaurant Fesch Pâtes
13 Timy Supermarché
31 Franceschi Grocery
42 Sodyl Supermarket

OTHER
3   Vehicle Entrance
    to Car Ferries
5   Laundrette
6   Police
8   Corsica Ferries Office
9   Locacycles (Bike Rental)
10 Citer Car Rental
14 Mobylines Ferry Office
17 Taxi Rank

18 Short-Haul Bus Terminal
19 SNCM Office
20 Ferry Terminal
21 Bus to Place de la Marana
22 Prefecture Building
23 Airport Buses
24 Kallistour
25 ADA Car Rental
26 Main Post Office
27 Railway Station
30 Rapides Bleus Bus Office
33 Librairie Jean-Patrice
    Marzocchi
34 Tourist Office
35 Taxi Stand
37 Banque de France
38 Oratoire & Confrérie
    Saint Roch
39 Former Hôtel de Ville
40 Oratoire de l'Immaculée Conception
41 Église Saint Jean Baptiste
44 Palais de Justice
45 Ancien Palais des Gouverneurs
    & Musée Ethnographique Corse
47 Main Entrance to Citadelle
49 Citadelle Entrance
50 Église Sainte Marie

✕ SQUARES
16 Square Saint Victor
46 Place du Donjon
48 Place Dominique Vincetti

Organised Tours

The tourist office has information on companies offering bus tours of Cap Corse.

Places to Stay – bottom end

Bastia has more inexpensive hotel rooms than Ajaccio. Almost all the city's hotels stay open throughout the year.

Camping *Camping Casanova* (☎ 95.33. 91.42), open from June to October, is about five km north of Bastia in Miomo. It costs 9FF to pitch a tent and 22FF per person. To get there, take the bus to Miomo from the bus terminal on Rue du Nouveau Port. *Camping du Bois de San Damiano* (☎ 95.33.68.02), open April to October, is about 10 km south of Bastia. Charges are 10FF for a tent site, 22FF per person and 10FF if you have a vehicle. It is served by a rather infrequent public bus from Rue du Nouveau Port.

Hotels The eight-room *Hôtel du Cap* (☎ 95. 31.18.46) at 11 Rue du Commandant Luce de Casabianca has the cheapest rooms in town. Run by an elderly woman who wears only black, this place has small, simply furnished doubles for only 120FF. The shower and toilet are down the hall.

You can't get much more central than the one-star *Hôtel La Riviera* (☎ 95.31.07.16, 95.31.63.04) at 1bis Rue du Nouveau Port. Fairly large rooms with shower cost 150FF (250FF from July to mid-September) for one or two people; singles/doubles with shower, toilet and TV are 230/260FF (420FF for either from July to mid-September). This place is open all year.

The small, family-run *Hôtel Leandri* (☎ 95.31.40.30) at 47 Blvd Général Graziani (1st floor) is an excellent choice if you don't mind shared showers and toilets. For one/two/three/four people, the eight fairly spacious rooms, which haven't changed in decades, cost 130/150/200/200FF (170/200/280/300FF from June to mid-September).

A bit further south, the family-run *Hôtel Central* (☎ 95.31.71.12) at 3 Rue Miot (1st floor) has decent doubles without/with

shower and toilet for 150/200FF (170/250FF from mid-July to mid-September).

The large *Hôtel de l'Univers* (☎ 95.31. 03.38) at 3 Ave Maréchal Sebastiani (opposite the post office) is cheap and convenient but hardly salubrious. In fact, it's something of a dive. Singles/doubles/triples that could be cleaner cost 120/150/180FF with sink and bidet, 180/200/250FF with shower and 220/240/300FF with shower and toilet. Prices are 10% to 20% higher in August and September.

Places to Stay – middle

From October to May the very central *Hôtel Napoléon* (☎ 95.31.60.30; fax 95.31.77.83) at 43 Blvd Paoli is a great deal, with comfortable doubles equipped with all the amenities for only 250FF. Unfortunately, prices rise precipitously during the summer months.

The *Hôtel Bonaparte* (☎ 95.34.07.10; fax 95.32.35.62) at 45 Blvd Général Graziani has ordinary rooms with shower, toilet and TV for 150 to 180FF in January and February, 350 to 480FF from May to October and 250 to 300FF during the rest of the year. The pleasant *Hôtel Les Voyageurs* (☎ 95.31. 61.03, 95.31.08.97; fax 95.31.44.25) at 9 Ave Maréchal Sebastiani (1st floor) has doubles with shower, toilet and one/two beds for 210/240FF (250/270FF from July to mid-September).

Up the hill from the Vieux Port, the two-star *Hôtel de la Paix* (☎ 95.31.06.71; fax 95.33.16.95) at 1 Blvd Hyacinthe de Montera (formerly Blvd Général Giraud) has fairly spacious doubles for 250 to 300FF; triples and quads are 300 to 400FF. From mid-May to mid-October room prices are 50 to 100FF higher.

Places to Eat

A number of cafés line the western side of Place Saint Nicolas. Many more restaurants and cafés are located along the north side of the Vieux Port and on nearby streets.

Self-Catering A food market is held at Place

de l'Hôtel de Ville every morning except Monday.

Near the train station, *Franceschi grocery* at 1-2 Rue Gabriel Péri is open Monday to Saturday from 8 am to noon and 3 to 7 pm. Two blocks north, the *Timy Supermarché* at 2 Rue Capanelle is open Monday to Saturday from 8.30 am to 12.30 pm and 3.30 to 7.30 pm. South of the centre near the Vieux Port, the *Sodyl supermarket* at 6 Blvd Paoli, 20 metres up the hill from the department store of the same name, is open Monday to Saturday from 8.15 am to 12.15 pm and 2 to 7.15 pm. North of the centre of town, opposite Port de Plaisance Toga, the huge *Hyper Toga supermarket* is open Monday to Saturday from 9 am to 8 pm.

Along Rue César Campinchi, there are several boulangeries, all of which are closed on Sunday afternoon. The *boulangerie* at 26 Rue César Campinchi is open Monday to Saturday from 7 am to 1 pm and 3 to 8 pm. North of the town centre near the vehicle entrance to the ferry port, the *boulangerie* near Port de Plaisance Toga is open 24 hours a day, seven days a week. In addition to bread and pastries, it also has pizzas.

Getting There & Away

Air France's fifth-busiest airport, Aéroport de Bastia-Poretta (☎ 95.54.54.54), is 20 km south of the city.

Train The train station (☎ 95.32.60.06) is across the roundabout from the western end of Ave Maréchal Sebastiani. Tickets to Ajaccio (105FF; 3½ to four hours), Calvi (80FF; three hours) and Corte (49FF; one hour 40 minutes) are sold Monday to Saturday from 6.20 am to 7.50 pm and Sunday from 7.45 am to noon and 3 to 7 pm.

Bus Long-haul buses stop at various points along Ave Maréchal Sebastiani. Rapides Bleus (☎ 95.31.03.79), whose office is at 1 Ave Maréchal Sebastiani, handles tickets to Porto Vecchio (100FF one way, or 150FF return fare for students) and Bonifacio (with a change of buses at Porto Vecchio). It is open Monday to Saturday from 8 am to noon

and 2.30 to 6 pm (5.30 pm on Saturday). There are services on Sunday from mid-June to mid-September.

Eurocorse's twice-daily bus to Corte and Ajaccio (100FF) stops in front of the Hôtel de l'Univers at 3 Ave Maréchal Sebastiani. It runs on Sunday and holidays from July to mid-September. Tickets are sold on board. The bus to Calvi leaves from slightly further up the block.

Rue du Nouveau Port has been turned into a bus terminal for short-haul buses serving the Bastia area.

Car The cheapest place in Bastia to rent a car is ADA Location de Véhicules (☎ 95.31.09.02; fax 95.31.17.43) at 35 Rue César Campinchi. It is open Monday to Saturday from 8 am to noon and 2 to 7 pm. Vehicles can be returned on Sunday or at ADA's Ajaccio office if you make arrangements in advance. The ADA agency (☎ 95.54.55.44) at the airport is open daily throughout the year whenever aeroplanes arrive. Citer (☎ 95.31.16.15) is at 44bis Rue Général Graziani.

Motorbike Locacycles (☎ 95.31.02.43) at 40 Rue César Campinchi rents out motorbikes and mopeds during the warm part of the year.

Boat The ferry terminal building is at the quayside terminus of Ave Maréchal Sebastiani.

For travel to mainland France, the office of SNCM (☎ 95.54.66.99), across the roundabout from the ferry terminal, is open from 8 to 11.30 am and 2 to 5.30 pm daily except Saturday afternoon and Sunday. The SNCM counter in the ferry terminal, which sells tickets for same-day travel only, opens two hours (three hours on Sunday) before each sailing.

If you're going to Italy, Mobylines (☎ 95.31.46.29) at 4 Rue du Commandant Luce de Casabianca is open Monday to Saturday from 8 am to noon and 2 to 6 pm. From mid-April to October the company's bureau in the ferry terminal is open daily from 10

CORSICA

am until the boat leaves. Corsica Ferries' office (☎ 95.31.18.09) is on the 1st floor of the building next to the Mobil petrol station at 5 Rue Chanoine Leschi. Corsica Marittima (☎ 95.54.66.66 via SNCM), whose ferries go to Livorno, has a bureau in the ferry terminal building.

For more details on ferry service to/from Corsica, see Boat in the Getting There & Away section at the beginning of this chapter.

Getting Around

To/From the Airport Municipal buses to the airport (32FF) depart from the Préfecture building (across the roundabout from the train station) about an hour before the departure of each flight. Buses from the airport to Bastia are also coordinated with flight schedules. An airport bus timetable is available at the tourist office.

A taxi to the airport should cost about 150FF during the day and 175FF at night or on Sunday.

Bus Local buses, which cost 7.50FF for a single ride, are operated by SAB (☎ 95.31.06.65). The most useful line for visitors is probably No 1, which goes (north to south) from Port de Plaisance Toga via Ave Émile Sari, Blvd Paoli, the Palais de Justice (at the southern terminus of Blvd Paoli) and the Citadelle (Place Dominique Vincetti) to the hospital. From Monday to Saturday it runs every 10 or 15 minutes from 6.15 am to 8.15 pm; on Sunday and holidays, there are two buses an hour.

During the summer period, bus No 8 links Bastia with Plage de la Marana seven times a day, seven days a week (including holidays).

Taxi There is a taxi rank (☎ 95.34.07.00 for 24-hour radio dispatch) at Square Saint Victor, one block north of the tourist office. There's another taxi stand (☎ 95.31.03.02) at the southern end of Place Saint Nicolas on Rue Miot.

Bicycle During summer, bikes can be hired from Locacycles (☎ 95.31.02.43) at 40 Rue César Campinchi.

CAP CORSE

The long, narrow peninsula at Corsica's northern tip, known as Cap Corse, stretches about 40 km northwards from Bastia. This 15-km-wide strip of valleys and mountains up to 1300 metres high affords spectacular views of the sea, particularly along the steep and rocky west coast. Once intensively cultivated, the maquis have now reclaimed areas where grapevines, olive trees and fruit orchards once flourished. Cap Corse can be visited on a car or bus excursion from Bastia.

On the east coast, there are sandy beaches slightly north of **Macinaggio**, a small fishing village near the northern tip of Cap Corse, and at **Marine de Pietracorbara**, midway between Bastia and Macinaggio. The west coast has lots of small, sandy coves.

ÉTANG DE BIGUGLIA

This 12-km-long lagoon, a favourite nesting site of waterbirds, is connected to the sea by a narrow neck of water that's about four km south of Bastia. **Plage de la Marana** (see Beaches in the Bastia section) and **Plage de Pineto** are along the half-km-wide peninsula that separates the lagoon from the Mediterranean.

THE CASTAGNICCIA REGION

La Castagniccia, the mountainous area east of Ponte Leccia and Corte, is known for its forests of chestnut trees, some of which are 20 metres high. The Corsicans began planting and tending chestnut trees in the 16th century, when the island's Genoese rulers started taking all of Corsica's grain crop for use back home. The tree became known as *l'arbre à pain* (the bread tree) because of the many uses the Corsicans found for chestnut flour. Indeed, the region owes its name to the Latin word for chestnut, *castanea* (which, via Spanish, also gave us the English word 'castanets', the Spanish musical instrument). These days, chestnut flour is used to make various Corsican pastries but little else. The meat of pigs raised on chestnuts is famous for its tastiness.

In the 18th century, La Castagniccia was the cradle of the Corsican nationalist rebellion against Genoese rule. Indeed, Pasquale Paoli was born here in the village of Morosaglia in 1725. Once the richest area of the island thanks to the chestnut crop and the objects local artisans made from chestnut wood (such as furniture), the area's hills and mountains – which in the 17th century supported 100 people per sq km – are now dotted with abandoned hamlets, their residents having long since left to seek employment in the lowlands or overseas.

The North Coast

CALVI

The citadel-town of Calvi (population 3600) sits atop a promontory at the western end of a beach-lined, half-moon-shaped bay. For much of the year, seaside sunbathers can either admire the iridescent turquoise waters of the Golfe de Calvi or, if they turn around, ponder Monte Cinto (2706 metres) and its snowy neighbours only 20 km or so inland. The coast between Calvi and l'Île Rousse is dotted with a string of fine-sand beaches. Calvi is the largest settlement in the Balagne region (see Around Calvi).

From the 13th to the 18th centuries, Calvi was a Genoese stronghold. Its citizens' renowned loyalty to Genoa is immortalised in the motto accorded to the town by the Republic of Genoa in 1562 and carved over the gate to the Citadelle: *Civitas Calvi Semper Fidelis* (the city of Calvi, forever faithful). In 1794, a British expeditionary fleet assisting Pasquale Paoli's Corsican nationalist forces, who had fallen out with the island's post-1789 Revolutionary government, besieged and bombarded Calvi. In the course of the battle, a certain Captain Nelson – later known to the world as Admiral Horatio Nelson – was wounded by rock splinters and lost the use of his right eye.

Orientation

The Citadelle, also known as the Haute Ville (Upper City), is on the rocky promontory north-east of the marina *(port de plaisance)*, which runs along the coast of the Basse Ville (Lower City). Calvi's major thoroughfare, which runs through the centre of town, is known as Blvd Wilson between Place Christophe Colomb and the post office and as Ave de la République as it passes the train station. As it heads south-eastward out of town, it becomes Ave Christophe Colomb and then the N197. The roundabout on Ave de la République that is decorated with a statue of a woman carrying a pail of water is aptly called Place de la Porteuse d'Eau.

Information

Tourist Office The municipal tourist office (☎ 95.65.16.67; fax 95.65.14.09) is upstairs from the Capitainerie (harbour master's office). From the train station, cross the tracks and go out the back gate. Don't confuse the tourist office with the syndicat d'initiative booth next to the train station.

The tourist office is open all year on weekdays from 9 am to noon and 2 to 6 pm. From mid-June to mid-September it's open every day from 9 am to 1 pm and 3 to 7.30 pm. If you'd like to explore the Citadelle, you might want to purchase the brochure *Guide of the Fort*, an interesting self-guided tour that follows a route marked by numbered plaques.

Money One of the few places that changes money throughout the year is the Crédit Lyonnais (☎ 95.65.08.27) on Blvd Wilson, which has a good rate but charges a 50FF commission for both travellers' cheques and cash. It is open Monday to Friday from 8.20 am to 12.15 pm and 1.50 to 4.40 pm. From June to September it has slightly shorter hours – until noon in the morning and 4.30 in the afternoon. There are lots of other, mostly seasonal, exchange places along Blvd Wilson.

Post The main post office (☎ 95.65.00.40), at the bottom of Blvd Wilson (right where it

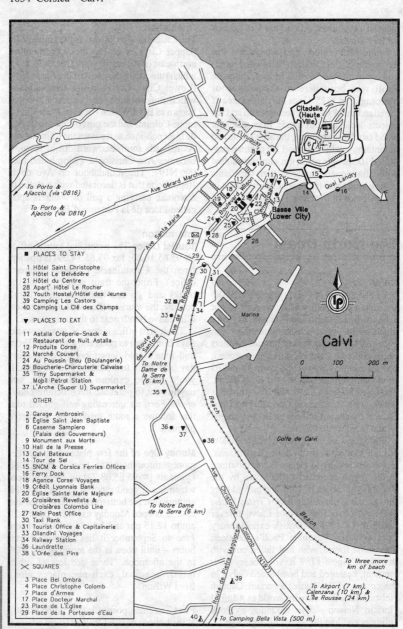

Calvi

Citadelle (Haute Ville)

Basse Ville (Lower City)

Quai Landry

To Porto &
Ajaccio (via D816)

To Porto &
Ajaccio (via D816)

Ave Gérard Marche

Ave Santa Maria

Rue de l'Uruguay

Boulevard Wilson

R Clemenceau

Route de Centre

Route de la République

Marina

Golfe de Calvi

To Notre
Dame de
la Serra
(6 km)

To Notre Dame de
la Serra (6 km)

Ave Christophe Colomb (N197)

Beach

Beach

Route de Pietra Maggiore

To three more
km of beach

To Airport (7 km),
Calenzana (10 km) &
L'île Rousse (24 km)

To Camping Bella Vista (500 m)

0   100   200 m

■ PLACES TO STAY
1 Hôtel Saint Christophe
8 Hôtel Le Belvédère
21 Hôtel du Centre
28 Apart' Hôtel Le Rocher
32 Youth Hostel/Hôtel des Jeunes
39 Camping Les Castors
40 Camping La Clé des Champs

▼ PLACES TO EAT
11 Astalla Crêperie-Snack &
   Restaurant de Nuit Astalla
12 Produits Corse
22 Marché Couvert
24 Au Poussin Bleu (Boulangerie)
25 Boucherie-Charcuterie Calvaise
35 Timy Supermarket &
   Mobil Petrol Station
37 L'Arche (Super U) Supermarket

OTHER
2 Garage Ambrosini
5 Église Saint Jean Baptiste
6 Caserne Sampiero
   (Palais des Gouverneurs)
9 Monument aux Morts
13 Hall de la Presse
14 Calvi Bateaux
15 Tour de Sel
15 SNCM & Corsica Ferries Offices
16 Ferry Dock
18 Agence Corse Voyages
19 Crédit Lyonnais Bank
20 Église Sainte Marie Majeure
26 Croisières Revellata &
   Croisières Colombo Line
27 Main Post Office
30 Taxi Rank
31 Tourist Office & Capitainerie
33 Ollandini Voyages
36 Railway Station
36 Laundrette
38 L'Orée des Pins

✕ SQUARES
3 Place Bel Ombra
4 Place Christophe Colomb
7 Place d'Armes
17 Place Docteur Marchal
23 Place de L'Église
29 Place de la Porteuse d'Eau

becomes Ave de la République), is open Monday to Friday from 8.30 am to 5 pm and Saturday from 8.30 am to noon. During July and August it opens at 8 am and closes at about 7 pm (noon on Saturday). Exchange services are available all year.

Calvi's postcode is 20260.

Travel Agencies Agence Corse Voyages (☎ 95.65.00.47) on Blvd Wilson is open Monday to Friday from 9 am to noon and 2 to 6.30 pm. From May to mid-October it is also open the same hours on Saturday. Ollandini is on Ave de la République next to the youth hostel.

Bookshops The best place for topoguides, hiking maps and foreign-language periodicals is Hall de la Presse (☎ 95.65.05.14) at 13 Blvd Wilson. Throughout the year it's open from 7.30 am to 12.30 pm and 2 to 7.30 pm daily except Sunday afternoon. During July and August opening hours are 7.30 am to about 11 pm.

Laundry About 500 metres south of the train station, there's a laundrette (☎ 95.65.04.22) across the parking lot from L'Arche supermarket on Ave Christophe Colomb.

Citadelle

Set atop an 80-metre high granite promontory surrounded by massive Genoese fortifications, the Citadelle affords great views of the whole Calvi region: the Golfe de Calvi, the Mediterranean, the Balagne region and the mountains, whose summits remain snowcapped until early summer.

Palais des Gouverneurs

The imposing Genoese Governors' Palace at Place du Donjon, built in the 13th century and enlarged in the mid-16th century, is just above the entrance to the Citadelle. Now known as Caserne Sampiero, it serves as a barracks and mess hall for officers of the Foreign Legion. The last tourist who wandered inside was subsequently seen wearing a kepi in a former French colonial town so

remote that no Lonely Planet guide even mentions it...

Église Saint Jean Baptiste

Up the street from Caserne Sampiero is the church of St John the Baptist, built in the 13th century and rebuilt in 1570; the main altar dates from the 17th century. The women of the local elite used to sit in the screened boxes, whose grilles served to shelter them from the inquisitive or lustful gaze of the rabble. To the right of the altar is *Christ des Miracles*, an ebony statue of Jesus that was paraded around town in 1553 shortly before the besieging Turkish forces fell back. Credited with saving Calvi from the Saracens, it has since been the object of great veneration.

A marble plaque marks the site of the house where, according to local tradition, the Genoese navigator Christophe Colomb (Christopher Columbus) was born. After all, in 1441 Calvi *was* part of the Republic of Genoa...

Beaches

Calvi's famous four-km-long beach begins just east of the marina and stretches around the Golfe de Calvi. Tramways de la Balagne (see Train under Getting There & Away) makes several stops along the beach.

Between Calvi and l'Île Rousse is a series of attractive beaches. While some of them are fairly inaccessible, others are served by Tramways de la Balagne. When you see a promising strip of sand, you can just hop off at the next stop to check it out. There are popular beaches at **Algajola** (see the Around Calvi section) and **l'Île Rousse** (see that section).

West of Calvi, the little inlets tend to have more rocks than sand.

Hiking

There are lots of trails in the Balagne region (see Around Calvi). If you're in the mood for a short hike from Calvi, you can walk to **Notre Dame de la Serra**, a 19th-century chapel whose hilltop perch six km southwest of town affords spectacular views of the whole area. To get there, walk up Route de

Santore (which intersects with Ave Christophe Colomb) and follow the signs.

Two of Corsica's most celebrated long-distance trails begin at Calenzana, 10 km south-east of Calvi. For more information on the Mare e Monti trail to Cargèse and the GR20, which goes all the way to Conca, see Hiking under Activities in the Facts for the Visitor section at the beginning of this chapter.

Scuba Diving

Calvi Bateaux (☎ 95.65.02.91), a boat equipment and repair shop on Quai Landry, rents out motorised boats and scuba equipment and can refill diving tanks. Throughout the year, it's open Tuesday to Saturday (daily from June to September) from 8 am to noon and 2 to 6 pm. The tourist office can provide information on other companies with boats for hire.

Organised Tours

From mid-April to October there are 1½-hour guided visits (45FF) of the town in English, French and German. For reservations, call ☎ 95.65.36.74.

For information on the day-long coach tours of Corsica offered by Autocars Mariani (☎ 95.65.00.47, 95.65.02.55), contact Agence Corse Voyages (see Travel Agencies under Information).

Boat Excursions

From late April to September or October, Croisières Revellata, also known as Vedettes Revellata (☎ 95.65. 28.16, 95.65.29.65), and Croisières Colombo Line (☎ 95.65.03.40) offer boat excursions (185FF) from Calvi's marina to the seaside hamlets of Galéria and Girolata via the Réserve de Scandola (see Around Calvi). For more information on Girolata and boats linking it with Porto, see Boat Excursions under Things to See & Do in the Porto section.

Festivals

Calvi has colourful religious processions on Maundy Thursday and Good Friday.

Places to Stay – bottom end

Except for the hostel and some of the bungalows, Calvi suffers from a shortage of inexpensive accommodation, especially in the summer.

Camping & Bungalows *Camping Les Castors* (☎ 95.65.13.30), open from April to October, is 800 metres south-east of the centre of town on Route de Pietra Maggiore. To get there, turn right off Ave Christophe Colomb 400 metres past L'Arche supermarket. Charges are 20FF per adult, 8FF to pitch a tent and 7FF to park. Rustic, two-person bungalows with exterior showers and toilets cost only 80FF a night (160FF a night in July and August). This is by far the cheapest accommodation in town. Two-person studios with shower, toilet and kitchenette cost 185FF (290FF in July and August).

A couple of hundred metres further south along Route de Pietra Maggiore, you come to the two-star *Camping La Clé des Champs* (☎ 95.65.00.86), open from April to October. Campers pay 15FF per person, 8FF for a tent site and 8FF to park. Two-person, kitchenette-equipped bungalows without/with private shower and toilet range from 130/170FF in April, May and October to 220/285FF in August. Three and four-person bungalows are also available. From July to September, you can rent on a weekly basis only.

The three-star *Camping Bella Vista* (☎ 95.65.11.76, 95.60.72.52), open from Easter to October, is 500 metres further south along Route de Pietra Maggiore. It costs 13FF to pitch a tent and 22FF per person.

Hostel The friendly, 136-bed *Youth Hostel/ Hôtel de Jeunes* (☎ 95.65.14.15; fax 95.65.33.72) on Ave de la République, affiliated with the BVJ hostels in Paris, is open from late March to October. Also known as Corsotel, it is one of the best places on the island to meet other travellers. Reception is staffed daily from 8 am to 1 pm and 5 to 10 pm. Beds in rooms of two to eight people cost 105FF per person, including a filling breakfast. Reservations are not accepted

Top: The port from the Citadelle, Calvi, Corsica (DR)
Left: Laneway in Bonifacio, Corsica (DR)
Right: Bastia's Vieux Port and the ferry port from the Citadelle, Corsica (DR)

Top Left: Springtime on Île d'Ouessant, Brittany (GC)
Top Right: A Citroën 2CV rolls past a field of wildflowers (GC)
Bottom Left: Poppies setting the countryside ablaze, Provence (GC)
Bottom Right: A flowerbed in front of Rouen's Cathédrale Notre Dame, Brittany (LL)

from individuals. Guests do not need a hostelling card. There are lots of rules and regulations intended to make things run smoothly, which they do.

Places to Stay – middle

The *Hôtel du Centre* (☎ 95.65.02.01) at 14 Rue Alsace-Lorraine is open from late May or early June to mid-October. Doubles/triples start at 200/250FF (260/300FF in the middle of summer). The *Hôtel Le Belvédère* (☎ 95.65.01.25) at Place Christophe Colomb, open all year, has small, cheaply appointed doubles with shower and toilet for 200 to 250FF (350FF in August).

Apart' Hôtel Le Rocher (☎ 95.65.20.04), across Blvd Wilson from the post office, is a great deal in the off season, when mini-apartments with air-con, kitchenettes, fridges, dishes, etc for two or three people are only 250FF. In July and August, however, the price rises to 800FF! Two-room suites for four or five people range from 400 to 1000FF, depending on the season. Reception is not staffed from November to early April, but they'll be happy to open up if you call ☎ 95.65.15.02 on a weekday at least a day before your arrival.

Places to Stay – top end

The three-star *Hôtel Saint Christophe* (☎ 95.65.05.74) on Rue de l'Uruguay next to Place Bel Ombra is open from April to October. The sea view doesn't come cheap – it's 500FF a night for a double, including breakfast. From mid-July to mid-August a double with obligatory demi-pension is 960FF.

Places to Eat

The marina is lined with restaurants, and there are several places to eat along Rue Clemenceau. You won't find many *menus* for under 70FF.

For sandwiches (14 to 18FF), a good bet is *Au Poussin Bleu* (☎ 95.65.01.58) at 8 Blvd Wilson, open from 5.30 am to 12.30 pm and 3 to 8 pm daily except Monday (daily from mid-April to October). From June to September there's no midday break and it may

close later than 8 pm. *Astalla Crêperie-Snack* (☎ 95.65.06.29) at 11 Rue Clemenceau has some of the cheapest food in Calvi, including crepes (8 to 15FF) and omelettes (15 to 28FF). From May to October, it is open daily from 11 am until at least 11 pm (and often much, much later – until 4 am, sometimes).

Self-Catering The *Marché Couvert*, a small food market opposite Hôtel du Centre, is open Tuesday to Saturday from 7 am to noon throughout the year. From mid-June to mid-September it is also open on Monday and doesn't close until 1 pm. There's a *Timy* supermarket 300 metres south of the train station (next to the Mobil petrol station) and a larger *L'Arche supermarket*, also known as Super U, a few hundred metres further along Ave Christophe Colomb.

Most of the makings of a picnic can be purchased at *Boucherie-Charcuterie Calvaise* at 5 Rue Clemenceau, which sells prepared dishes, local cheeses, Corsican meat products and wines. From April to September it stays open daily; from March to November it is closed on Sunday afternoon and Monday. For bread, you might try *Au Poussin Bleu* at 8 Blvd Wilson (see the preceding section for opening hours).

Entertainment

From mid-June to October, *Restaurant de Nuit Astalla* (☎ 95.65.06.29), at 11 Rue Clemenceau next to Astalla Crêperie-Snack, has dancing and live music (jazz, Corsican, etc) every night until dawn.

Things to Buy

Rue Clemenceau is lined with souvenir shops. For local wines, cheeses, jams and the like, try *Produits Corse* (☎ 95.65.01.36) at 42 Rue Clemenceau. From April to October, it's open daily from 9 am to 7 pm, and from mid-June to mid-September it doesn't close until midnight.

Getting There & Away

Air Aéroport Calvi-Sainte Catherine (☎ 95. 65.03.54) is seven km south-east of Calvi.

CORSICA

There is no bus service from Calvi to the airport; taxis cost 60 to 70FF (85 to 90FF on Sunday, holidays and at night).

Train Calvi's train station (☎ 95.65.00.61) is conveniently linked with l'Île Rousse, Corte (67FF; 2½ hours), Bastia (80FF; three hours) and Ajaccio (122FF; 3½ to 4½ hours).

From late April to October, the one-car diesel *navettes* (shuttle trains) – also known as Michelines – of Tramways de la Balagne make 19 stops along the coast between Calvi and l'Île Rousse. The navettes run every two hours (every hour in July and August) until the early evening. Printed schedules are available at train stations. The line is divided into three sectors – you need one ticket (available on board for 8FF) for each sector you travel in. Carnets of six tickets are sold at stations for 36FF. The 45-minute trip between Calvi and l'Île Rousse requires three tickets one way and six tickets return.

Bus Throughout the year (except on Sunday and holidays), the early morning bus to Bastia leaves from Place de la Porteuse d'Eau. In summer buses to Calenzana also depart from Place de la Porteuse d'Eau. From mid-May to mid-October, Autocars SAIB (☎ 95.26.13.70) has a mid-afternoon bus from Calvi to Porto (60FF; three hours) and a morning bus from Porto to Calvi daily except Sunday and holidays. See Bus under Getting There & Away in the Porto or Ajaccio sections for information on bus services between Porto and Ajaccio.

The tourist office has bus information posted in the window and can supply photo-copied time schedules.

Car Aloha Auto Location (☎ 95.65.28.08, 95.20.52.00; fax 95.23.17.35) is probably the cheapest car rental option in Calvi. Their office at Aéroport Calvi-Sainte Catherine is open from about mid-March to mid-October. Other companies with offices at the airport include Citer (☎ 95.65.16.06), Europcar (☎ 95.65.10.19; fax 95.65.21.09) and Budget (☎ 95.65.23.39).

Motorbike Garage Ambrosini (☎ 95.65.02.13), which is just off Rue de l'Uruguay, rents 50 to 125 cc scooters for 180 to 250FF a day. The longer you rent, the more prices drop. The garage is open throughout the year from 8 am to noon and 2 to 6 pm daily except Saturday morning and Sunday.

Boat For information on getting from Calvi to Porto by sea, see Boat Excursions in the Porto section.

The SNCM runs ferries between Calvi's Quai Landry and both Nice and Marseille, but during winter service is very infrequent; the SNCM also has ferries to/from l'Île Rousse. From mid-May to mid-September, Corsica Ferries links Calvi with Genoa. Both companies have offices at the ferry dock on Quai Landry. Ferry schedules are posted at the tourist office. For more information, see Boat in the Getting There & Away section at the beginning of this chapter.

Getting Around
Taxi There's a taxi rank (☎ 95.65.03.10 to order a taxi 24 hours a day) at Place de la Porteuse d'Eau.

Bicycle Garage Ambrosini (see Motorbike under Getting There & Away) rents 10-speeds/mountain bikes for 50/70FF a half-day and 70/95FF a day.

AROUND CALVI
The Balagne Region
La Balagne is an area of low hills between the Monte Cinto massif and the sea. Its coastline stretches from Galéria north-eastward all the way to the **Désert des Agriates**, the desert area that begins 18 km east of l'Île Rousse.

La Balagne, known as the 'Garden of Corsica', is renowned for the fertility of its soil, whose bounty once made the region among Corsica's wealthiest. Traditional products include olive oil, wine, cheese and fruit. The area has a number of 11th and 12th-century Pisan churches. The main inland town, **Calenzana**, is 10 km south-east of Calvi, to which it is linked by bus during the summer. For information on long-distance hikes from Calenzana, see Hiking under Activities in the Facts for the Visitor section at the beginning of this chapter.

Algajola

Algajola (population 230), 15 km north-east of Calvi and nine km south-west of l'Île Rousse, is known for its long beach of golden sand, part of which is lined with ugly little beach bungalows. Once an important port, it was sacked by Muslim raiders in 1643, an event that prompted the Genoese to build ramparts and fortifications two decades later. Today, parts of the Citadelle can still be seen.

Getting There & Away Algajola is served by Tramways de la Balagne (see Train under Getting There & Away in the Calvi section).

L'ÎLE ROUSSE

The port and beach resort of l'Île Rousse (population 2600), 24 km north-east of Calvi, was founded by the Corsican nationalist leader Pasquale Paoli in 1758 to compete with fiercely pro-Genoese Calvi. Known as Isola Rossa in Corsican, its name is derived from the red granite of Île de la Pietra, a rocky island (now connected to the mainland) whose Genoese watchtower presides over an active commercial and passenger port.

Orientation

The ferry port is on a peninsula about half a km north of the train station. To get from the train station to Place Paoli, l'Île Rousse's main square, follow the railway tracks southeastward (ie away from Calvi) for 400 metres. To orient yourself in Place Paoli, remember that the church is on the west side of the *place* (that is, it's to your left as you face north).

Information

Tourist Office The syndicat d'initiative (☎ 95.60.04.35) on the south side of Place Paoli operates from April to October. During July and August, it's open Monday to Saturday from 9.30 am to noon and 3 to 7 pm. The

rest of the time, it's open Monday to Friday from 10 am to noon and 2.30 to 5.30 or 6 pm.

Walking Tour

The beachfront **Promenade Marinella** runs along the coast between the train tracks and the sand. The area of narrow streets north of Place Paoli is known as the **old city**. On **Île de la Pietra**, the reddish island-turned-peninsula where the ferry port is located, there's a **Genoese tower** and, at the far end, a **lighthouse**, from which there are views of nearby islets.

Beaches

There's a fine-sand beach where Place Paoli comes nearest the seashore and another stretch of sand between the train station and the ferry port. There's more sandy coastline east of town past the rocks.

Musée Océanographique

L'Île Rousse's privately run aquarium (☎ 95.60.27.81) is across the parking lot from the rocky area at the eastern end of the beach. It is open from Easter to October. Entrance costs 39FF (27FF for children aged four to 12 and students) and includes a 1¾-hour guided tour in French, Italian or German. The museum is open daily from 3.30 to 5.30 pm; from July to September it's also open in the morning.

Places to Stay

The *Hôtel Le Grillon* (☎ 95.60.00.49) is at 10 Ave Paul Doumer – from Place Paoli, walk south on Ave Piccioni and take the first left. Unsurprising but decent rooms with shower and toilet cost 180FF except from May to September, when the price rises to 240FF. Although this place is not exactly open from mid-November to February, you're welcome to stay here if you call ahead. The five-room *Villa Les Mimosas* (☎ 95.60.01.72), open all year, is in an unmarked villa with a large garden at 11 Ave Paul Doumer. It has large, spotless doubles/triples with shower but without toilet for 160/210FF to 170/230FF. The one

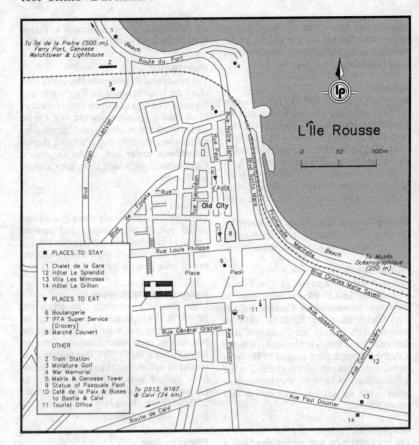

L'Île Rousse

Old City

PLACES TO STAY
■ 1 Chalet de la Gare
■ 12 Hôtel Le Splendid
■ 13 Villa Les Mimosas
■ 14 Hôtel Le Grillon

PLACES TO EAT
▼ 6 Boulangerie
▼ 7 IFFA Super Service (Grocery)
▼ 8 Marché Couvert

OTHER
2 Train Station
3 Miniature Golf
4 War Memorial
5 Mairie & Genoese Tower
9 Statue of Pasquale Paoli
10 Café de la Paix & Buses to Bastia & Calvi
11 Tourist Office

To Île de la Pietra (500 m), Ferry Port, Genoese Watchtower & Lighthouse

Beach
Route du Port

Rue Notre Dame
Rue Paoli
Bld Jean Lançon
Bld de Fogata
Rue Napoléon
Rue d'Agila
Bld Sotto Mare
Promenade Marinella Beach
Rue Louis Philippe
Place Paoli
Rue Général Graziani
Ave Joseph Calizi
Ave Piccioni
Ave Comte Valéry
Bld Charles Marie Savelli
Ave Paul Doumer
Route de Calvi

To Musée Océanographique (250 m)
To D513, N197 & Calvi (24 km)

0   50   100m

CORSICA

showerless double is only 130FF. Overall, this is an excellent deal.

The seven-room, seaside *Chalet de la Gare* (☎ 95.60.00.94), opposite the train station, has very basic rooms for one to three people without shower or toilet for 150 to 200FF. It is open from right before Easter until about mid-October.

The two-star, 60-room *Hôtel Le Splendid* (☎ 95.60.00.24; fax 95.60.04.57), open from March to October, is 50 metres from the beach on Ave Comte Valéry. Except from mid-June to mid-September, huge, airy shower-equipped singles/doubles cost

135/210FF without toilet and 180/270FF with toilet. In summer, doubles without/with toilet cost 135/190FF per person. Prices skyrocket from mid-July to mid-August, when demi-pension is mandatory.

Places to Eat

Self-Catering On the north side of Place Paoli, there are a number of food shops around the *Marché Couvert* (morning food market), the distinctive wooden structure held aloft by columns.

IFFA Super Service, on the west side of the Marché Couvert, is open from 7.30 am to 12.30 pm and 4 to 7.30 pm daily except Sunday afternoon and Monday. From June to mid-September it's open every day for slightly longer hours.

Just north of the Marché Couvert on Rue Paoli, the *boulangerie* on your left (as you walk north) is open from 7 am to 12.30 pm and 3.30 to 7.30 pm (closed Monday). From June to mid-September it's open daily from 6 am to 8 pm.

Getting There & Away

Train It's possible to leave luggage at l'Île Rousse's train station (☎ 95.60.00.50).

Even from November to late April, when Tramways de la Balagne (see Train under Getting There & Away in the Calvi section) doesn't run, you can go on a day trip from Calvi by taking an early morning or early afternoon train towards Ponte Lecchia and then catching the evening train back to Calvi.

Bus Buses on the Calvi-Bastia run stop at Ave Piccioni in front of Café de la Paix, which is around the corner from the tourist office.

Boat SNCM car ferries link l'Île Rousse with Nice at least once a week throughout the year. In summer, there are also ferries to/from Marseille and Toulon.

Corte Area

CORTE

When Pasquale Paoli led Corsica to independence in 1755, one of his first acts was to make Corte (population 5500; altitude 400 metres), a fortified town at the geographical centre of the island, the country's capital. Paoli – whose world-view was steeped in the ideas of the Enlightenment – founded a national university here in 1765, but it was closed in 1769 when the short-lived Corsican republic was taken over by France. To this day, Corte remains a potent symbol of Corsican independence.

The Università di Corsica was reopened in 1981 and now has about 3000 students, making Corte (pronounced 'kor-TEH' and spelled Corti in Corsican) the island's youngest and liveliest town. You can thank the students for the late-night sandwich shops and inexpensive pizzerias. Since its economy is based only partly on tourism, most hotels, restaurants and shops stay open all year. Indeed, in many ways Corte is more animated during the school year – when the students are around – than in summer. Corte is an excellent base for hiking, as some of the island's highest mountains are a bit west of town, while to the east lies the Castagniccia region (see that section).

Orientation

Corte's main street is the shop-lined Cours Paoli. At its southern end is Place Paoli, from where the narrow streets of the Ville Haute (Upper City) wind their way westward up to the Citadelle. The train station is about one km south-east (and down the hill) from Cours Paoli along Ave Jean Nicoli. Allée du Neuf Septembre encircles the southern part of town, leading from the train station around Quartier Porette (the area around the HR Hôtel) to the bridges across the Restonica and Tavignanu rivers (which merge further downstream) and on to Ave du Président Pierucci. The latter leads up the hill to Ave Xavier Luciani and the centre of town.

Information

Tourist Office The Bureau d'Information Touristique (☎ 95.46.24.20, 95.61.01.62) is in the Citadelle – from the gate, go up the vehicle ramp, walk to the far end of the long building to your right and go in the entrance with a '1' above it. It is open Monday to Friday from 9 am to noon and 1.30 to 5 pm. From May to October, when the office moves to the building on the left as you walk through the Citadelle gate, it's open daily from 9 am to noon and 2 to 6 pm (9 am to 8 pm from mid-June to mid-September).

Regional Park Office From June to September the Parc Naturel Régional de Corse has an information office (☎ 95.46.27.44) on the right as you walk through the Citadelle gate. It's open Monday to Saturday from 10 am to 1 pm and 3 to 7 pm.

Money There are several banks along Cours Paoli.

Post The main post office is on Ave du Baron Mariani and is open Monday to Friday from 8 am to noon and 2 to 5 pm and Saturday from 8 am to noon.

Corte's postcode is 20250.

Bookshops The Maison de la Presse (☎ 95. 46.01.38) at 24 Cours Paoli sells maps and topoguides.

Medical Services Hôpital Santos Manfredi (☎ 95.46.05.36) is on Allée du Neuf Septembre in Quartier Porette.

Citadelle
Corte's citadel (☎ 95.46.24.20, 95.61.01.61) towers above the town from a rocky promontory overlooking the alleyways of the Ville Haute (to the east) and the Tavignanu and Restonica rivers (to the south and west). It is the only such fortress in the interior of the island. The **Château** (the highest part) was built in 1419 by a Corsican nobleman allied with the Aragonese and was considerably expanded by the French during the 18th and 19th centuries. A staircase leads from the **Belvédère** (lookout), described in every tourist brochure as resembling a *nid d'aigle* (eagle's nest), down to the river.

Occupied by the Foreign Legion from 1962 (when the unit stationed here pulled out of Algeria) until 1983, the Citadelle is now open to the public. It houses the **Musée de la Corse** (☎ 95.61.00.61), a brand new museum of Corsican folk traditions, crafts and anthropology, and the **Font Régional d'Art Contemporain** (regional modern arts museum; ☎ 95.46.22.18), which puts on temporary exhibitions of contemporary art. The upper section, including the Château and the Belvédère, is open only from May to October.

Palazzu Naziunale
The Genoese-built Palais National (National Palace), down the hill from the Citadelle gate, served as the seat of Corsica's government during the island's short-lived independence. Today, the structure is occupied by a Corsican studies centre affiliated with the university. The basement, which once served as a prison and is now used to house temporary exhibitions, is open Monday to Friday from 2 to 6 pm; from May to October, it is also open from 10 am to 1 pm.

Further down the hill at Place Gaffori is the mid-15th-century **Église de l'Annonciation** (Church of the Annunciation), enlarged during the 17th century.

Università di Corsica Pasquale Paoli
The main campus of Pasquale Paoli University, Corsica's only university, is on Ave Jean Nicoli midway between Cours Paoli and the train station. Established in 1765 by Pasquale Paoli, who had been inspired by universities he'd seen in Italy, and closed only four years later, it was reopened in 1981. It now plays an important role in the revival of the Corsican language and culture. Although the courses are taught in French, students are required to study Corsican for at least one year and the signs around campus are in both Corsican and French.

Festivals
Religious processions are held on Maundy Thursday and Good Friday. The Festival Folklorique International (International Folklore Festival) takes place in late July. A festival of Corsican culture is usually held during the first weekend of August.

Places to Stay
Camping The attractive, olive-shaded *Camping Alivetu* (☎ 95.46.11.09), open from Easter to mid-October, is just south of Pont Restonica on Allée du Neuf Septembre. It costs 10FF to camp, 10FF to park and 22FF per person. You can camp under the trees at *Gîte d'Étape U Tavignanu* (see Hostels) for 9FF plus 15FF per person.

Hostels Quiet – except for the birds and rushing water – and very rural, the *Gîte d'Étape U Tavignanu* (☎ 95.46.16.85), open all year, charges 45FF for a bed, 55FF for dinner and 20FF for breakfast. To get there from Pont Tavignanu, walk westward along Chemin de Baliri and follow the signs. The gîte is about 500 metres past the small bridge and 250 metres from the end of the narrow road.

During July and August, travellers with student cards can stay in the dorms of the *Università di Corsica* on Ave Jean Nicoli. Singles/doubles cost 56/80FF. There's never a shortage of rooms, but to get one you have to go to the CROUS Secrétariat (☎ 95.46.02.61), which is on the university's main campus in Résidence Pasquale Paoli (the building to the right as you walk down the ramp), one floor above the restaurant. It is open Monday to Friday from 9 am to noon and 2 to 5 pm.

Hotels The 135-room *HR Hôtel* (☎ 95.61.01.21; fax 95.61.02.85) at 6 Allée du Neuf Septembre is 300 metres to the left as you exit the train station in a complex of converted apartment blocks. It is open all year. Clean, utilitarian rooms for one or two people cost 135FF (with shower and toilet in the hall) or 155FF (with shower and toilet in the room). Prices are slightly higher from mid-July to mid-September. This place almost always has rooms available, even in summer.

The one-star *Hôtel de la Poste* (☎ 95.46.01.37) is a few blocks north of the centre of town at 2 Place du Duc de Padoue. A spacious, simply furnished double with shower costs 135 to 175FF, depending on how big it is; triples are 200FF. This place is closed in December. Another alternative is the slightly gloomy *Hôtel Colonna* (☎ 95.46.26.21 at reception, 95.46.01.09 at the bar), also known as the Hôtel Cyrnos, which is at 3 Ave Xavier Luciani. Reception is usually at the bar. Decent rooms, many of them recently renovated, cost 140 to 200FF (20 to 30FF more from June to September). This place has an annexe across the street at 4 Ave Xavier Luciani.

Places to Eat

Corsican *Restaurant Le Bip's* (☎ 95.46.06.26 or 95.46.04.48) at 14 Cours Paoli, which is at the bottom of the flight of stairs 20 metres down the hill from Brasserie Le Bip's, specialises in Corsican cuisine. The *menu* costs 70FF and changes each day; main dishes are 60 to 70FF. Food is served daily, except Saturday (daily in summer), from 11.30 am to 3 pm and 6 pm until very late at night.

Fast Food *Point Chaud* at 18 Cours Paoli is a great place to get a cheap, easy meal – a Corsican pastry, a slice of pizza, etc. It's open Monday to Saturday from 9 am to 9 pm. The *Sandwicherie* at 3 Place Paoli sells Italian-style hot and cold sandwiches daily from noon to 2 or 3 am.

University Restaurant Students are welcome to eat at the restaurant on the main campus of the *Università di Corsica* on Ave Jean Nicoli. Located on the ground floor of the building known as Résidence Pasquale Paoli, it is open from October to June on weekdays from 11.30 am to 1.30 pm and 6.30 to 9 pm. Meal tickets (12FF) are sold on weekdays from 11 am to 1 pm next to the restaurant.

Self-Catering Two blocks east of Cours Paoli, the small *Eurospar supermarket* next to 7 Ave Xavier Luciani is open Monday to Saturday from 8 am to noon and 3 to 7.30 pm. The *boulangerie* at 3 Cours Paoli is open Monday to Saturday.

On Allée du Neuf September, the large *Éco Marché supermarket* opposite the hospital is open Monday to Saturday from 9 am to 12.15 pm and 3 to 7.15 pm. In July and August hours change slightly.

Entertainment

In the evening, university students often congregate in the town centre to buy pizza, munch things in sandwich shops or sip a beer with friends. The city is at its liveliest on weeknights as many students go home for the weekend.

Corte

0   100   200 m

Things to Buy

During the tourist season, Corsican products of all sorts (including many edible ones) are sold at U Granaghju, a shop on Cours Paoli right where it hits Place Paoli. There are several pottery and crafts shops in the area between the Citadelle and Place Paoli.

Getting There & Away

Train There are excellent train links to/from Ajaccio (56FF; two hours), Bastia (49FF; one hour 40 minutes) and Calvi (67FF; 2½ hours), making Corte an easy stopover on any cross-island rail journey, or even a

potential day trip from Ajaccio, Bastia or Calvi. The train station (☎ 95.46.00.97), about a km south-east of the city centre, is open Monday to Saturday from 8 am to noon and 2 to 6.30 pm and on Sunday from 9 to 11 am. From mid-June to mid-September, Sunday hours are the same as for other days.

Bus Eurocorse buses to Bastia and Ajaccio stop in front of Bar Colonna at 3 Ave Xavier Luciani, a lively hang-out for older local men where coffee is 5 or 7FF and hot chocolate is 7FF. From Monday to Saturday (daily from July to mid-September), there are two

■ PLACES TO STAY	OTHER	15 Citadelle Entrance, Tourist Office (May to October) & Regional Park Office
2 Hôtel de la Poste	1 Main Post Office	
4 Hôtel du Nord	3 Maison de la Presse	
11 Hôtel Colonna	6 Chapelle Sainte Croix	16 U Granaghju Shop
17 Hôtel Colonna Annexe	8 Tourist Office	19 Palazzu Naziunale
25 HR Hôtel	(November to April)	(Palais National)
	9 Font Régional d'Art Contemporain	20 Église de l'Annonciation
▼ PLACES TO EAT	11 Eurocorse Buses to Ajaccio & Bastia	21 Belvédère
5 Point Chaud	13 Università di Corsica Pasquale Paoli (Arts & Law Faculties) & University Restaurant	22 Railway Station
7 Restaurant Le Bip's		23 Stadium
10 Boulangerie		24 Hôpital Santos Manfredi
12 Eurospar Supermarket		27 Università di Corsica (Science Faculties)
18 Sandwicherie		
26 Éco Marché Supermarket	14 Musée de la Corse	

buses a day in each direction; tickets are sold on board. A schedule is posted outside the bar. Autocars Cortenais (☎ 95.46.02.12, 95.46.22.89) has buses from Place Paoli to Aléria and, three times a week, to Bastia as well.

Car If you'll be driving from Corte to the east coast and are up for a wonderfully scenic detour, you might take the D69 via the forests of the Regional Park to Ghisoni, whence the D344 leads to the coast. The D69 continues southward from Ghisoni all the way to Sartène. This route may be impassable in winter.

HIKING AROUND CORTE

South-west of Corte, the crystal-clear, greenish-blue waters of the Restonica River pass by pine and chestnut groves as they tumble down **Gorges de la Restonica**, a deep valley whose grey-white granite walls are studded with bushes and trees.

Some of the area's choicer trails begin about 16 km from Corte at the Bergeries de Grotelle sheepfolds (altitude 1375 metres), which can be reached by car via the narrow D623. Trails from here lead to a number of glacial lakes, the nearest of which are **Lac de Mello (Melu)** (altitude 1711 metres), a one-hour walk from the Bergeries, and **Lac de Capitello (Capitellu)** (altitude 1930 metres), 40 minutes beyond Lac de Mello. Lac de Mello is ice-covered for about half the year, while the latter, which is very near the GR20, is frozen over for an even longer period.

There are more arduous hiking trails on the **Tavignanu River valley**, including one to **Lac Nino (Ninu)** (altitude 1743 metres), which is 9½ hours' walk from Corte.

Glossary

(m) indicates masculine gender, (f) indicates feminine gender

accueil (m) – reception
alimentation (f) – grocery store
arrondissement (m) – administrative division of large city. Abbreviated on signs as 1er (1st arrondissement), 2e or 2ème (2nd), etc
auberge de jeunesse (f) – youth hostel

baie (f) – bay
billet (m), **billeterie** (f) – ticket, ticket office
billet jumelé (m) – combination ticket, good for more than one site, museum etc
boulangerie (f) – bread shop, bakery
brasserie (f) – restaurant or brewery

capitainerie (f) – harbour master's office
carrefour (m) – crossroad
carte (f) – card
caserne (f) – military barracks
cave (f) – wine cellar
chambre (f) – room
chambre d'hôte – B&B
charcuterie (f) – pork butcher's shop & delicatessen
cimetière (m) – cemetery
col (m) – mountain pass
consigne (f) – left-luggage office
consigne automatique (f) – left-luggage lockers
correspondance (f) – linking tunnel or walkway eg in metro; rail or bus connection
couchette (f) – sleeping berth in a train or ferry
cour (f) – courtyard
crémerie (f) – dairy, cheese shop

dégustation (f) – wine tasting
demi (m) – 33 ml glass of beer
demi-pension (f) – half-board (B&B with either lunch or dinner)
département (m) – administrative division of France
douane (f) – customs

église (f) – church
embarcadère (m) – pier, jetty
épicerie (f) – small grocery store

fauteuil (m) – seat on trains and ferries
fête (f) – festival
forêt (f) – forest
foyer (m) – workers' or students' hostel
fromagerie (f) – cheese shop
funiculaire (m) – funicular railway

galerie (f) – covered shopping centre or arcade
gare, or gare SNCF (f) – railway station
gare maritime (f) – ferry terminal
gare routière (f) – bus station
gendarmerie (f) – police force, police station
gîte d'étape (m) – hiker's accommodation, usually in a village
gîte rural (m) – country cottage
golfe (m) – gulf

halles (f, pl) – covered market/central food market
halte routière (f) – bus stop
horaire (m) – timetable/schedule
hôtel de ville (m) – town hall, city hall
hôte payant – paying guest
hydroglisseur (m) – hydrofoil

laverie (f)/**lavomatique** (m) – laundrette

jardin (m) – garden
jardin botanique (m) – botanical garden

mairie (f) – town (or village) hall
maison de la presse (f) – newsagency
marché (m) – market
marché couvert (m) – covered market
menu (m) – fixed-price meal with two or more courses
mobylette (f) – brand of moped
musée (m) – museum

navette (f) – shuttle bus/train/boat

1066

Palais de Justice (m) – Law Courts
parlement (m) – parliament
pâtisserie (f) – cake and pastry shop
place (f) – square, plaza
plage (f) – beach
plat du jour (m) – daily special (in a restaurant)
pont (m) – bridge
port (m) – harbour, port
port de plaisance (m) – marina/pleasure-boat harbour
porte – gate (in city wall)
poste (f)/**bureau de poste** (m) – post office
poste (m) – telephone extension
préfecture (f) – prefecture (capital of a *département*)
presqu'île (f) – peninsula
pression (f) – draught beer

quai (m) – quay, railway platform
quartier (m) – quarter, district

refuge (m) – mountain hut, basic hikers' shelter
rive (f) – bank of a river
rond-point (m) – roundabout
routier (m) – truckers' restaurant

sentier (m) – trail
sortie (f) – exit
spectacle (m) – performance, play, theatrical show
square (m) – public garden
supplément (m) – supplement
syndicat d'initiative (m) – tourist office run by local businesses

tabac (m) – tobacconist's (for bus tickets, télécartes, etc)
télécarte (f) – phonecard
téléphérique/téléférique (f) – cableway or cable car

télésiège (m) – chairlift
téléski (m) – ski lift/tow
tour (f) – tower
tour d'horloge (f) – clock tower

vallée (f) – valley
vieille ville (f) – old city
ville neuve (f) – new city
v.f. *(version française)* – film dubbed in French
v.o. *(version originale)* – a nondubbed film
voie (f) – train platform

ACRONYMS

The French love acronyms as much as the British or Americans. Many transport companies are known by acronyms whose derivations are entirely unknown by the average passenger.

BP *(boîte postale)* – post office box
le FN – le Front National (National Front)
GR – grande randonnée (long-distance hiking trail)
l'ONU – l'Organisation des Nations Unies (the UN)
le PC – le Parti communiste
le PS – le Parti socialiste
le RPR – le Rassemblement pour la République (right-wing political party)
SNCF – Société Nationale des Chemins de Fer (state-owned railway company)
SNCM – Société Nationale Maritime Corse-Méditerranée (state-owned ferry company linking Corsica and France)
TGV – train à grande vitesse (high-speed train, bullet train)
l'UDF – l'Union pour la démocratie française (right-wing political party)
VTT – mountain bike

Index

MAPS

TEXT

From the Authors

Daniel Robinson The last bit of work on this book was done at Lonely Planet's Melbourne headquarters, where I was able to see first-hand the hard work and dedication of my editors, Adrienne Costanzo and Greg Alford, and project artist Ann Jeffree. I would also like to thank the other artists who worked on the book, and Europe regional editor Rob van Driesum. I am also indebted to Leon & Bette Kustin; Leslee, Gary & Sarah Braun; Allison Kustin; and Gail Morrison.

My research in France would not have been possible without the help of many hundreds of people, including Michelle de Kretser, then at Lonely Planet's Paris office; George Whitman of Shakespeare & Company bookshop; Maurice & Eliane Bebe; Rabbi Pauline Bebe; Antoine Bebe; Mary Guggenheim; Gérard Boulanger; the ever-helpful George Pamphile; Sylvia Star; Natalie Zend; Rebecca Bennet; Cressida Reese; Richard Hallward; Sarinah Kalb; Cathy Karnow; Liza Boyd; Miel de Botton; Thierry di Costanzo; Sylvia & Robert Nathusius; Cherif, Momo & M Sadou; John O'Brien; Julia Wilson; Beth Reisberg; Andrew Singer; Liza Hall; Karl Orend; Allison Bigelow; Angela Rowland; Eva Ludemann; Andras Hamori, professors Avraham Udovitch and André Maman of Princeton University; Liza Levenberg; Micah Robinson; Leah Orbach-Front & Dani Front; Stephen Lenoir of EuroDisney; Mme Prunier, Mme Guillot and M Defferard of the SNCF in Paris; Luigi Cerri of Comerio, Italy; Pierre-Michel Menard; Segen Ravid Avidar; and Zahia Hafs of Lonely Planet's Paris office.

Leanne Logan The hard thing about writing a thank you list is not starting it but having to decide where to finish. Many people, both in France and outside, helped us produce this book – either by providing information and many other forms of assistance or simply by sharing an enthusiasm for our project, and France in general, that never failed to be infectious.

In France, *merci beaucoup* to Madame Bohic for her Breton hospitality and for being a spontaneous guide; the Déloupys for lovingly initiating us to Midi ways; Lucy & Lucien Hebert for sharing their old Norman tales and, of course, their Calvados; Pierre Huart for his untiring devotion as a National Park guide; Micheline & Bernard Normand for such enormous generosity and the best French food anywhere; and Paul for the exhilarating introduction to VTTs.

A few non-French friends to whom we owe gratitude include Roos & Bert Cole for sending the Duvels when they were most needed; Nev & Dee Logan for filling in the Breton question marks; Mark 'Floyd' Douglas for somewhere to bunk down during the frantic Winter Olympics; Sixy and Bluey for keeping their trunks up; and Chris Nestel and Alex in London for putting us up, and putting up with us, towards the final stage of the book.

Tourist organisations all over France were invaluable but in particular we want to thank the following people from the Comité Départemental de Tourisme (CDT) offices for their extra effort: Jean-Louis Badier (Aube); Jacques Bouchet (Haute-Vienne); Gisèle Bourrillon-Sigillo (Alpes-de-Haute-Provence); Brigitte Cavaillé (Marne); Madame Ermel (Ille-et-Vilaine); Isabelle Ferragut (Gard); Jean-Paul Jougla (Tarn); Monsieur Jourdain (Finistère); Armelle Le Goff (Calvados); Monsieur Le Prieur (Manche); Yves Le Sidaner (Côtes-d'Armor); Monsieur Lopez (Pyrénées Orientales); Daniele Micand (Haute-Savoie); Micheline Morissonneau (Dordogne); Madame Mossolin (Corrèze); Philippe Podevin (Morbihan); Monsieur Rabany (Seine-Maritime); Corinne Raih (Savoie); François Raynaud (Aude); Catherine Sciberras (Aveyron); Messieurs Spirito & Garnier (Lozère); André Tibere-Inglesse (Hérault); and the staff of the Bouches-du-Rhône CDT.

Sincere thanks to many Office de Tourisme people including: Bruno Bodard (Vannes); François Dulondel (Le Mont Dore); Madame Giorgetta (Vichy); Yves Meriais (Bourg d'Oisans); Martine Meunier (Digne); Madame Pellat (Gignac); Bernard

Prudhomme (Chamonix); Marie-France Reymond (Nice); and the staff of Aix-en-Provence, Belle Île, Brest and Saint Malo.

Also much appreciated was the help given by Nadine Clerc-Rincoletto from the Comité Régional de Tourisme (CRT) in the Alpes Dauphiné and Geneviève de Faucigny from the Côte d'Azur CRT. Thanks, too, to P&O European Ferries and the people at the Centre Ornithologique on Île d'Ouessant.

Lastly, thank you to all the Lonely Planet staff in Melbourne who worked on the book and also to Michelle de Kretser for being a valuable go-between.

PLANET TALK
Lonely Planet's FREE quarterly newsletter

PLANET TALK

**Slovenia:
River Deep, Mountain High**

We love hearing from you and think you'd like to hear from us.

When...is the right time to see reindeer in Finland?
Where...can you hear the best palm-wine music in Ghana?
How...do you get from Asunción to Areguá by steam train?
What...is the best way to see India?

For the answer to these and many other questions read PLANET TALK.

Every issue is packed with up-to-date travel news and advice including:

- *a letter from Lonely Planet founders Tony and Maureen Wheeler*
- *travel diary from a Lonely Planet author - find out what it's really like out on the road*
- *feature article on an important and topical travel issue*
- *a selection of recent letters from our readers*
- *the latest travel news from all over the world*
- *details on Lonely Planet's new and forthcoming releases*

To join our mailing list contact any Lonely Planet office.

Also available: Lonely Planet T-shirts. 100% heavyweight cotton (S, M, L, XL)

LONELY PLANET PUBLICATIONS
Australia: PO Box 617, Hawthorn 3122, Victoria
tel: (03) 9819 1877 fax: (03) 9819 6459 e-mail: talk2us@lonelyplanet.com.au

USA: Embarcadero West, 155 Filbert St, Suite 251, Oakland, CA 94607
tel: (510) 893 8555 TOLL FREE: 800 275-8555 fax: (510) 893 8563
e-mail: info@lonelyplanet.com

UK: 10 Barley Mow Passage, Chiswick, London W4 4PH
tel: (0181) 742 3161 fax: (0181) 742 2772 e-mail: 100413.3551@compuserve.com

France: 71 bis rue du Cardinal Lemoine – 75005 Paris
tel: 1 44 32 06 20 fax: 1 46 34 72 55 e-mail: 100560.415@compuserve.com

World Wide Web: http://www.lonelyplanet.com/

Guides to Europe

Central Europe on a shoestring
From the snow-capped peaks of the Austrian Alps, the medieval castles of Hungary and the vast forests of Poland to the festivals of Germany, the arty scene in Prague and picturesque lakes of Switzerland, this guide is packed with practical travel advice to help you make the most of your visit. This new shoestring guide covers travel in Austria, Czech Republic, Germany, Hungary, Liechtenstein, Poland, Slovakia and Switzerland.

Eastern Europe on a shoestring
This guide has opened up a whole new world for travellers – Albania, Bulgaria, Czech Republic, eastern Germany, Hungary, Poland, Romania, Slovakia and the former republics of Yugoslavia.
'...a thorough, well-researched book. Only a fool would go East without it.' – *Great Expeditions*

Mediterranean Europe on a shoestring
Details on hundreds of galleries, museums and architectural masterpieces and information on outdoor activities including hiking, sailing and skiing. Information on travelling in Albania, Andorra, Cyprus, France, Greece, Italy, Malta, Morocco, Portugal, Spain, Tunisia, Turkey and the former republics of Yugoslavia.

Scandinavian & Baltic Europe on a shoestring
A comprehensive guide to travelling in this region including details on galleries, festivals and museums, as well as outdoor activities, national parks and wildlife. Countries featured are Denmark, Estonia, the Faroe Islands, Finland, Iceland, Latvia, Lithuania, Norway and Sweden.

Western Europe on a shoestring
This long-awaited guide covers all of Western Europe's well-loved sights and provides routes for cycling and driving tours, plus details on hiking, climbing and skiing. All the travel facts on Andorra, Austria, Belgium, Britain, France, Germany, Greece, Ireland, Italy, Liechtenstein, Luxembourg, Netherlands, Portugal, Spain and Switzerland.

Austria – travel survival kit
This book is an invaluable guide to independent travel in Austria. It covers attractions and activities for every budget, from mountain chalet villages to museums in centuries-old cities. Whether you fancy a wine tour in the Danube Valley, exploring the splendour of Habsburg Vienna or soaking up the magic of Mozart's Salzburg, this guide has the information you need.

Baltic States & Kaliningrad – travel survival kit
The Baltic States burst on to the world scene almost from nowhere in the late 1980s. Now that travellers are free to move around the region they will discover nations with a rich and colourful history and culture, and a welcoming attitude to all travellers.

Britain – travel survival kit
Britain remains one of the most beautiful islands in the world. All the words, paintings and pictures that you have read and seen are not just romantic exaggerations. This comprehensive guide will help you to discover and enjoy this ever-popular destination.

Czech & Slovak Republics – travel survival kit
The Czech and Slovak Republics are two of the most exciting travel destinations in Europe. This guide is the essential resource for independent travellers. It's full of down-to-earth information and reliable advice for every budget – from five stars to five dollars a day.

Dublin – city guide
Where to enjoy a pint of Guinness and a plate of Irish stew, where to see spectacular Georgian architecture or experience Irish hospitality – Dublin city guide will ensure you won't miss out on anything.

Finland – travel survival kit
Finland is an intriguing blend of Swedish and Russian influences. With its medieval stone castles picturesque wooden houses, vast forest and lake district, and interesting wildlife, it is a wonderland to delight any traveller.

Greece – travel survival kit
Famous ruins, secluded beaches, sumptuous food, sun-drenched islands, ancient pathways and much more are covered in this comprehensive guide to this ever-popular destination.

Hungary – travel survival kit
Formerly seen as the gateway to eastern Europe, Hungary is a romantic country of music, wine and folklore. This guide contains detailed background information on Hungary's cultural and historical pas as well as practical advice on the many activities available to travellers.

Iceland, Greenland & the Faroe Islands – travel survival kit
Iceland, Greenland & the Faroe Islands contain some of the most beautiful wilderness areas in the world This practical guidebook will help travellers discover the dramatic beauty of this region, no matter wha their budget.

Ireland – travel survival kit
Ireland is one of Europe's least 'spoilt' countries. Green, relaxed and welcoming, it does not take travellers long before they feel at ease. An entertaining and comprehensive guide to the whole country

Italy – travel survival kit
Italy is art – not just in the galleries and museums. You'll discover its charm on the streets and in the markets, in rustic hill-top villages and in the glamorous city boutiques. A thorough guide to the thousands of attractions of this ever-popular destination.

Poland – travel survival kit
With the collapse of communism, Poland has opened up to travellers, revealing a rich cultural heritage This guide will help you make the most of this safe and friendly country.

Prague – city guide
Since the 'Velvet Revolution' in 1989, Prague and its residents have grasped their freedom with a youthfu exuberance, even frenzy. This thoroughly comprehensive guide will show you the sights and hidden delights of this vivacious city.

Russia, Ukraine & Belarus – travel survival kit
This practical guidebook helps you navigate the surviving red-tape and explore the new found freedom of tourism in post-Soviet Russia. It takes you to all points of this vast region, from the birthplace of the Eastern Orthodox churches and the last resting place of the Soviet Union to the forests and volcanoes o Siberia and the Russian Far East.

Slovenia – travel survival kit
From trekking near Triglav National Park to the sights of Ljubljana, this comprehensive guide reveal the many delights of a country often described as 'Europe' in miniature.

St Petersburg – travel survival kit
Whether you're strolling the alleyways and canals of Dostoevsky's Crime and Punishment, discovering the splendours of the tsars and tsarinas palaces or experiencing the fast-changing face of a city re-emerging with post-Soviet vigour as one of Europe's finest – this is an indispensable guide to histori and contemporary St Petersburg.

Switzerland – travel survival kit
Ski enthusiasts and chocolate addicts know two excellent reasons for heading to Switzerland. This trave survival kit gives travellers many more: jazz, cafés, boating trips...and the Alps of course!

Trekking in Greece
Mountainous landscape, the solitude of ancient pathways and secluded beaches await those who dare to extend their horizons beyond Athens and the antiquities. Covers the main trekking regions and includes contoured maps of trekking routes.

Trekking in Spain
Aimed at both overnight trekkers and day hikers, this guidebook includes useful maps and full details on hikes in some of Spain's most beautiful wilderness areas.

Trekking in Turkey
Few people are aware that Turkey boasts mountains with walks to rival those found in Nepal. This book gives details on treks that are destined to become as popular as those further east.

Turkey – a travel survival kit
This acclaimed guide takes you from Istanbul bazaars to Mediterranean beaches, from historic battlegrounds to the stamping grounds of St Paul, Alexander the Great, Emperor Constantine and King Croesus.

Vienna – city guide
There's so much to see and do in Vienna and this guide is the best way to ensure you enjoy it all.

Also available:
Central Europe phrasebook
Languages in this book cover travel in Austria, the Czech Republic, France, Germany, Hungary, Italy, Liechtenstein, Slovakia and Switzerland.

Eastern Europe phrasebook
Discover the most enjoyable way to get around and make friends in Bulgarian, Czech, Hungarian, Polish, Romanian and Slovak.

Mediterranean Europe phrasebook
Ask for directions to the galleries and museums in Albanian, Greek, Italian, Macedonian, Maltese, Serbian & Croatian and Slovene.

Scandinavian Europe phrasebook
Find your way around the ski trails and enjoy the local festivals in Danish, Finnish, Icelandic, Norwegian and Swedish.

Western Europe phrasebook
Show your appreciation for the great masters in Basque, Catalan, Dutch, French, German, Irish, Portuguese and Spanish (Castilian).

Baltic States phrasebook
Essential words and phrases in Estonian, Latvian and Lithuanian.

Greek phrasebook
Catch a *ferrybot* to the islands, laze the day away on a golden *baralia*, and say *stin iyia sas!* as you raise your glass to the setting sun... you can explore *tin acropoli* another day.

Moroccan Arabic phrasebook
Essential words and phrases for everything from finding a hotel room in Casablanca to asking for a meal of *tajine* in Marrakesh. Includes Arabic script and pronunciation guide.

Russian phrasebook
This indispensable phrasebook will help you get information, read signs and menus, and make friends along the way. Includes phonetic transcriptions and Cyrillic script.

Turkish phrasebook
Practical words and phrases that will help you to communicate effectively with local people in almost every situation. Includes pronunciation guide.

Lonely Planet Guidebooks

Lonely Planet guidebooks cover every accessible part of Asia as well as Australia, the Pacific, South America, Africa, the Middle East, Europe and parts of North America. There are seven series: *travel survival kits*, covering a country for a range of budgets; *shoestring guides* with compact information for low-budget travel in a major region; *walking guides*; *city guides, phrasebooks, audio packs* and *travel atlases*.

EUROPE

Austria • Baltic States & Kaliningrad • Baltics States phrasebook • Britain • Central Europe on a shoestring • Central Europe phrasebook • Czech & Slovak Republics • Dublin city guide • Eastern Europe on a shoestring • Eastern Europe phrasebook • Finland • France • Greece • Greek phrasebook • Hungary • Iceland, Greenland & the Faroe Islands • Ireland • Italy • Mediterranean Europe on a shoestring • Mediterranean Europe phrasebook • Poland • Prague city guide • Russia, Ukraine & Belarus • Russian phrasebook • Scandinavian & Baltic Europe on a shoestring • Scandinavian Europe phrasebook • Slovenia • St Petersburg city guide • Switzerland • Trekking in Greece • Trekking in Spain • Vienna city guide • Western Europe on a shoestring • Western Europe phrasebook

NORTH AMERICA & MEXICO

Alaska • Backpacking in Alaska •

Baja California • Canada • Hawaii • Honolulu city guide • Los Angeles city guide • Mexico • Pacific Northwest USA • Rocky Mountain States • San Francisco city guide •

CENTRAL AMERICA & THE CARIBBEAN

Central America on a shoestring • Costa Rica • Eastern Caribbean • Guatemala, Belize & Yucatán: La Ruta Maya

SOUTH AMERICA

Argentina, Uruguay & Paraguay • Bolivia • Brazil • Brazilian phrasebook • Chile & Easter Island • Colombia • Ecuador & the Galápagos Islands • Latin American Spanish phrasebook • Peru • Quechua phrasebook • Rio de Janeiro city guide • South America on a shoestring • Trekking in the Patagonian Andes • Venezuela

AFRICA

Africa on a shoestring • Cape Town city guide • Central Africa • East Africa • Trekking in East Africa • Kenya • Swahili phrasebook • Morocco • Arabic (Moroccan) phrasebook • North Africa • South Africa, Lesotho & Swaziland • West Africa • Zimbabwe, Botswana & Namibia • Zimbabwe, Botswana & Namibia travel atlas

Mail Order

Lonely Planet guidebooks are distributed worldwide. They are also available by mail order from Lonely Planet, so if you have difficulty finding a title please write to us. US and Canadian residents should write to Embarcadero West, 155 Filbert St, Suite 251, Oakland CA 94607, USA; European residents should write to 10 Barley Mow Passage, Chiswick, London W4 4PH; and residents of other countries to PO Box 617, Hawthorn, Victoria 3122, Australia.

NORTH-EAST ASIA

Beijing city guide • China • Cantonese phrasebook • Mandarin Chinese phrasebook • Hong Kong, Macau & Canton • Japan • Japanese phrasebook • Japanese audio pack • Korea • Korean phrasebook • Mongolia • Mongolian phrasebook • North-East Asia on a shoestring • Seoul city guide • Taiwan • Tibet • Tibet phrasebook • Tokyo city guide

INDIAN SUBCONTINENT

Bengali phrasebook • Bangladesh • Delhi city guide • India • India & Bangladesh travel atlas • Hindi/Urdu phrasebook • Trekking in the Indian Himalaya • Karakoram Highway • Kashmir, Ladakh & Zanskar • Nepal • Trekking in the Nepal Himalaya • Nepali phrasebook • Pakistan • Sri Lanka • Sri Lanka phrasebook

SOUTH-EAST ASIA

Bali & Lombok • Bangkok city guide • Cambodia • Ho Chi Minh city guide • Indonesia • Indonesian phrasebook • Indonesian audio pack • Jakarta city guide • Java • Laos • Lao phrasebook • Malaysia, Singapore & Brunei • Myanmar (Burma) • Burmese phrasebook • Philippines • Pilipino phrasebook • Singapore city guide • South-East Asia on a shoestring • Thailand • Thailand travel atlas • Thai phrasebook • Thai audio pack • Thai Hill Tribes phrasebook • Vietnam • Vietnamese phrasebook • Vietnam travel atlas

MIDDLE EAST

Arab Gulf States • Egypt & the Sudan • Arabic (Egyptian) phrasebook • Iran • Israel • Jordan & Syria • Middle East • Turkey • Turkish phrasebook • Trekking in Turkey • Yemen

ISLANDS OF THE INDIAN OCEAN

Madagascar & Comoros • Maldives & Islands of the East Indian Ocean • Mauritius, Réunion & Seychelles

AUSTRALIA & THE PACIFIC

Australia • Australian phrasebook • Bushwalking in Australia • Islands of Australia's Great Barrier Reef • Outback Australia • Fiji • Fijian phrasebook • Melbourne city guide • Micronesia • New Caledonia • New South Wales & the ACT • New Zealand • Tramping in New Zealand • Papua New Guinea • Bushwalking in Papua New Guinea • Papua New Guinea phrasebook • Queensland • Rarotonga & the Cook Islands • Samoa • Solomon Islands • Sydney city guide • Tahiti & French Polynesia • Tonga • Vanuatu • Victoria • Western Australia

lonely planet travel survival kit

Stylish, diverse, celebrated by romantics and revolutionaries alike, France is a destination that's always in fashion.

Sample a local wine in Bordeaux, ski the Pyrenees, try star-spotting in Cannes, or soak up the ambience on a café terrace in Paris. Whether you're a first-time visitor or seasoned francophile, you'll find this comprehensive guidebook packed with invaluable advice.

- over 140 maps including colour map of regional railway system
- accommodation and restaurant options to suit all budgets
- extensive coverage of museums, churches and art galleries
- details on outdoor activities – cycling, hiking, kayaking and more
- language section and glossary

ISBN 0-86442-192-3

9 780864 421920

Australia RRP $29.95
USA $21.95
UK £13.95
Canada $27.95
Singapore $37.95

1st Edition